The Storyteller's Sourcebook

The Storyteller's Sourcebook:

A Subject, Title, and Motif Index to Folklore Collections for Children

FIRST EDITION

by MARGARET READ MacDONALD

Neal-Schuman Publishers, Inc.
in association with
Gale Research Company
Book Tower
Detroit, Michigan 48226

Copyright © 1982 by
Margaret Read MacDonald

Library of Congress Cataloging in Publication Data

MacDonald, Margaret Read.
    The storyteller's sourcebook.

    A portion of this work is based on part of the
author's thesis (doctoral) -- Indiana University, 1979.
    Bibliography: p.
    1. Folklore--Juvenile literature--Classification.
2. Folk literature--Themes, motives. 3. Tales--
Indexes. 4. Tales--Bibliography. I. Title.
GR74.6.M3   016.3982'088054   82-954
ISBN 0-8103-0471-6   AACR2

To my mother

MILDRED AMICK READ

who first showed me the Squidjicum Squees
under the cabbage leaves.

Contents

Preface

WHEN LEARNING A NEW TALE, storytellers like to examine and compare many variants before deciding on the particular form to use. Yet until now the only access to juvenile folktale collections has been through the outdated Eastman *Index to Fairy Tales, Myths and Legends* and supplements (1926, 1937, 1952) and the Ireland *Index to Fairy Tales, 1949–1972, Including Folklore, Legends, and Myths in Collections* (1973) and *Index to Fairy Tales, 1973–1977, Including Folklore, Legends and Myths in Collections* (1977). These works, published by Faxon, are basically tale title listings. Ireland includes a subject index, though it is less extensive than that in *The Storyteller's Sourcebook*.

    The Storyteller's Sourcebook is the first reference tool to bring together from children's collections variants of each folktale, and to supply descriptions of them. It aims to fill a long-felt need in the school, public, and university library, and is specifically designed for quick and easy access by the teacher or librarian who wants to locate (1) tales about a given subject, (2) the location of a specific tale title in collections, (3) tales from an ethnic or geographical area, (4) variants of a specific tale.

Scope

This work indexes 556 folktale collections and 389 picture books. These are indexed in the Motif Index, the Tale Title Index, the Subject Index, and the Ethnic and Geographic Index. Some of these collections (designated with a "P" in the Bibliography of Collections and Single Editions Indexed) are only partially indexed because part of their material does not fall within the scope of this index. Seventy-two additional collections (designated with a "G" in the Bibliography of Collections and Single Editions Indexed) are indexed in the Ethnic and Geographic Index only.

    The Storytellers Sourcebook includes within its scope all the folktale titles that appeared in *Children's Catalog*, 1961 through 1981. An attempt was made to include all the folktale collections falling within the limits of this index that were reviewed in the American Library Association *Booklist* from 1960 through 1980. In addition, the index includes some 1981 titles and older titles that are still in use in children's libraries. A special attempt was made to include those older titles that are still popular with storytellers and children's librarians.

    It was necessary to limit the scope of this work. Epic, romance, and tall tale hero materials are usually omitted. Collections devoted entirely to historical or supernatural legend are omitted. This index does not include tales that are the invention of an author; thus modern fairy tales by authors such as Eleanor Farjeon are not included.

The Motif Index

Folklorists use two kinds of classification to discuss folktales. A type index, developed by Finnish folklorist Antti Aarne in 1910, assigns type numbers to each entire tale. For example, the tale "Cinderella" is Type 510.

The other scheme assigns each small part of a tale a motif number specific to the particular action, actor, or object of that part. Thus "Cinderella" includes such motifs as Glass slipper—F823.2; Cruel stepmother—S31; Three-fold flight from ball—R221; and many others. This motif index was developed in 1932 by the Indiana University folklorist Stith Thompson and published by Indiana University Press as the *Motif-Index of Folk-Literature*, with a revised edition published 1955–58.

These two classification schemes are internationally accepted and facilitate the discussion of folktales. Though a tale may appear in many languages and under many different titles, it can be identified by its type and motif numbers. Once a type or motif number of a tale is identified, it is possible to trace the tale through scholarly publications and locate other variants.

The Storyteller's Sourcebook follows Stith Thompson's classification but has adapted it to meet the needs of teachers and children's librarians. The *Sourcebook* differs in two important ways from Stith Thompson's *Motif-Index:*

1. The format of the *Sourcebook's* Motif Index has been expanded to include an entire description of many tales at one point within the index. Thus some of the features of a type index are incorporated into the Motif Index. Cross references are made to each tale description from its constituent motifs within the index. This technique was used especially for tale types classified in the Aarne–Thompson *The Types of a Folktale* type index under Section II, Ordinary Folktales (Types 300–1190). A type listing (pages 781–784) gives those motifs under which certain tale types are described here.

2. Since this tool is designed primarily as a finding tool for storytellers, and only secondarily as a reference tool for folktale scholars, the minute type of motif indexing provided in the Stith Thompson index is not attempted. Tales are indexed under their most important action motifs, with cross references to some subsidiary action motifs; very few entries have been made under actor or object motifs. To help the user note relationships between tales, I have devised a "+" notation to indicate that two action motifs occur in conjunction within a tale. This notation is not used for every multi-episodic tale.

These adaptations may be initially disturbing to the folklorist, but they serve to make this a more useful tool for its intended audience. Every effort has been made to create a tool that is folklorically accurate, yet particularly suited to the needs of school and public children's librarians and teachers.

Acknowledgments

This project could not have been completed without the support of the Folklore Institute and the Graduate Library School at Indiana University. The preparation of this motif index of children's folktale collections was encouraged from its inception by Dr. Richard M. Dorson, Director of the Folklore Institute there. Dr. Robert J. Adams and Dr. Mary Ellen Lewis of the Folklore Institute, and Associate Professor Margaret R. Sheviak and Dean Bernard Fry of the Graduate Library School provided guidance and valuable criticism in the dissertation stages of this index. (The motif index was submitted as a portion of the dissertation "An Analysis of Children's Folktale Collections," Indiana University, January 1979. It has since been revised and updated.)

I am grateful to colleagues at the University of Washington School of Librarianship and at King County Library System for giving me courage to continue with this project despite many difficulties.

My gratitude should be expressed as well to Shirley Buckingham for endless typing and proofreading through several drafts.

I must thank my long-suffering family, which has survived amid piles of index cards for over ten years! To Julie, Jenny, and Jim . . . thank you. And to my parents, Mildred, Murray, and Jane Read . . . your apple pies and fried chicken helped!

How To Use This Book

The Storyteller's Sourcebook: A Subject, Title, and Motif Index to Folklore Collections for Children includes the following parts: Motif Index, Tale Title Index, Subject Index, Ethnic and Geographic Index, Key Motifs for Aarne–Thompson Types 300–1199, and Bibliography of Collections and Single Editions Indexed.

Motif Index

The General Synopsis of the Index, which precedes the Motif Index, outlines for the user the Stith Thompson classification (see the Preface for a fuller discussion of Stith Thompson). *The Storyteller's Sourcebook* Motif Index will not, of course, contain entries for each item in the Stith Thompson outline.

The Motif Index entries contain the following information:

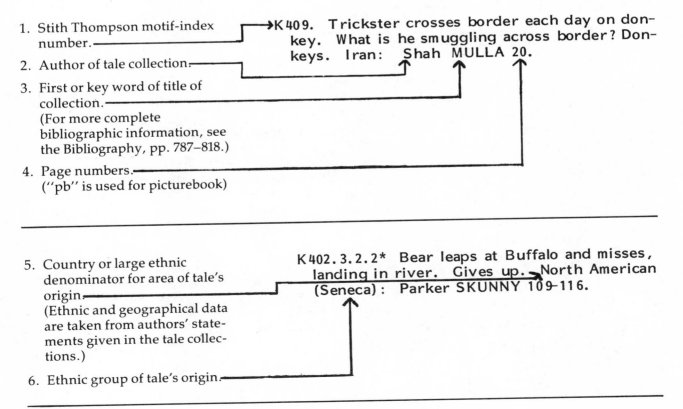

1. Stith Thompson motif-index number.

2. Author of tale collection.

3. First or key word of title of collection.
(For more complete bibliographic information, see the Bibliography, pp. 787–818.)

4. Page numbers.
("pb" is used for picturebook)

→K409. Trickster crosses border each day on don-key. What is he smuggling across border? Don-keys. Iran: Shah MULLA 20.

5. Country or large ethnic denominator for area of tale's origin.
(Ethnic and geographical data are taken from authors' statements given in the tale collections.)

6. Ethnic group of tale's origin.

K402.3.2.2* Bear leaps at Buffalo and misses, landing in river. Gives up. North American (Seneca): Parker SKUNNY 109–116.

7. SEE ALSO refers to a related motif elsewhere in the index.

E451.11* Ghost laid when hidden letter found and burnt. Japan: Buck FAIRY 218-220. SEE ALSO: E415.1.3.

8. A citation enclosed in slashes /.../ has the same text as the preceding entry.

B651.1.1* Fox's daughter gives student a mirror in which he sees her face if studies hard. Passes exams and weds her. China: Carpenter TALES..CHINESE 226-234/Sheehan FOLK 118-126/; Ritchie TREASURE 65-74 /Arbuthnot ANTHOLOGY 331-332/, /Arbuthnot FAIRY 181-183/.

9. Preceding variant differs in this way.

J425.2. Buffalo refuses tiger's invitation to dinner. He sees fire prepared to cook him. Aesop: Aesop AESOP'S (Watts) 119 (lion and bull).

Information is provided for use in pursuing variants of a tale:

1. Motif numbers in parentheses within the description indicate that the segment immediately preceding is also described at the motif number given.

J1051.1* Man to come when Death sends a sign he can see or hear, goes deaf and blind. Never dies. Wastes away to nothing, whiskers still seen as corn ears (A2685.1.0.1). U.S. (Alabama): Courlander TERRAPIN'S 108-111.

2. A motif number preceded by a "+" refers to a motif that often occurs in combination with this motif. (see p. xiii)

K11.9. Obstacle race between deer and hare. Hare accused of removing obstacles from his course. +A2326.1.1.1.1.* (Deer's horns). Native American (Cherokee): Bell JOHN 67-69; Scheer CHEROKEE 55-57.

In addition, technical information is supplied for the folklorist:

1. An asterisk* indicates that this number is an extension, added by Macdonald, of the Thompson motif-index.

J644.2* Monkey sees all tracks going into pond and none coming out. Drinks through straw. India: Ryder PANCHATANTRA 454-461.

2. Motif numbers originating in other indexes are indicated by their index author in parentheses. (Motif numbers were adapted from Clarke, Kirtley, and Baughman.) (see p. xiii)

K499.8.1* (Clarke) Poorly dressed spider on courting expedition persuades well-dressed companion to exchange clothes. Spider gets fine wife. Ghana (Accra): Courlander COW-TAIL 95-102. Nigeria (Yoruba): Courlander OLODE 19-23.

3. The Aarne–Thompson type number is given only when it appears within a Thompson motif entry or in rare cases when a tale collection provided tale type numbers. Likewise Ikeda and O'Suilleabhain (see p. xiii) type numbers are given when collection authors provided this information.

H389.1. Girl to find way around palace without becoming lost. Girl leaves distaff at door and unwinds thread. Type 874*. Rumania: Ure RUMANIAN 19-21.

Tale Title Index

Part 2, Tale Title Index, lists the title of each tale indexed. Entries include the author's last name, the first word of the collection title, the page number on which the tale is found, pb if it is a picturebook, and major motif numbers at which the tale is indexed in the Motif Index. If a tale is a single-tale edition, the title appears in capital letters, and is not repeated following the author's name. Examples of an entry for a tale in a collection and for a single-tale edition follow:

> Aladdin. Manning-Sanders - BOOK..WIZARDS 58-
> 77 (D871.1); Manning-Sanders - CHOICE 108-127.
>
> AKIMBA AND THE MAGIC COW. Rose pb (D861.1G).

Complete bibliographical citations for the collections and the single-tale editions appear in the Bibliography on pages 787–818.

Subject Index

The Subject Index is arranged alphabetically by subject heading (in capital letters). Under each subject heading tale descriptions are alphabetized by underlined key words.

A reference is given to the motif number under which each item is indexed in the Motif Index. In some cases SEE references direct the user to an entire section of the Motif Index. The Subject Index is also cross referenced to other pertinent subject entries. An example with both kinds of cross references follows:

> BAD LUCK: Man misses gold left on path by Bad
> Luck--N141.0.2; foolish imitation of good man
> by bad man—SEE ALL ENTRIES J2415*ff*; bad
> luck put into sack--N112.1. SEE ALSO FOR-
> TUNE; LUCK.

Ethnic and Geographic Index

The Outline of Ethnic and Geographic Index, which precedes the Ethnic and Geographic Index proper, is a guide to the index's organization.

The Index is designed as a quick way to locate tale collections derived from specific ethnic and/or geographic areas. Some individual tales found in general collections are also listed by area here. This index is a finding tool for area only and is not cross referenced to the Motif or Title Indexes.

Key Motifs for Aarne–Thompson Types 300–1199

Aarne–Thompson Types 300–1199 are listed here, with SEE references to the key motif number under which they are described in the Motif Index. (For a fuller discussion of these types, see the Preface, p. viii .)

Bibliography of Collections and Single Editions Indexed

This Bibliography gives complete bibliographical citations for the works indexed throughout the book. The following notations are used to designate certain items in the Bibliography: pb (picturebook); P (collection only partially indexed: not all the items in this collection fall within the scope of this index); N (not indexed: though this collection is not indexed in the Sourcebook, one or more tales found in it are indexed because they were anthologized in other collections); G (included in the Ethnic and Geographic Index only).

*Quick and Easy Guide to Use of the **Sourcebook***

You Know:	You Want To Know:	Do:
TALE TITLE	publication containing the tale	look under the tale title in the Tale Title Index
	tale synopsis and/or tale variants	Step 1: look up the tale title in the Tale Title Index to find the motif number Step 2: look under that number in the Motif Index
SUBJECT OF TALE	publication containing the tale	Step 1: look up the subject in the Subject Index to find the motif number Step 2: look under that motif number in the Motif Index
	tale synopsis and/or tale variants	Step 1: look up the subject in the Subject Index to find the motif number Step 2: look up that motif number in the Motif Index
TALE MOTIF NUMBER	publication containing this motif	look under the motif number in the Motif Index
	tale synopsis and/or tale variants	look under the motif number in the Motif Index
NAME OF ETHNIC GROUP OR GEOGRAPHIC AREA	publication containing tales from this group or area	look under that name in the Ethnic and Geographic Index

Works Consulted in the
Preparation of This Sourcebook

Aarne, Antti, and Thompson, Stith. *The Types of the Folktale*. Folklore Fellows Communications, no. 184. Helsinki: Suomalainen Tiedeakatemia, 1961.

Baughman, Ernest W. *Type and Motif-Index of the Folktales of England and North America*. Indiana University Folklore Series, no. 20. The Hague: Mouton & Co., 1966.

Booklist. 1960–1980. American Library Association.

Children's Catalog. 12th, 13th, & 14th eds. New York: H.W. Wilson, 1971, 1976, 1981.

Clarke, Kenneth Wendell. "A Motif-Index of the Folktales of Culture-Area V, West Africa." Ph.D. dissertation. Indiana University, 1958.

Eastman, Mary Huse. *Index to Fairy Tales, Myths and Legends*. 2nd ed. Boston: F.W. Faxon, 1926. Supplement, 1937. 2nd Supplement, 1952.

Hansen, Terence L. *The Types of the Folktale in Cuba, Puerto Rico, the Dominican Republic, and Spanish South America*. University of California Publications, Folklore Studies, no. 8. Berkeley: University of California Press, 1957.

Ikeda, Hiroko. *A Type and Motif Index of Japanese Folk-Literature*. Folklore Fellows Communications, no. 209. Helsinki: Suomalainen Tiedeakatemia, 1971.

Ireland, Norma Olin. *Index to Fairy Tales, 1949–1972, Including Folklore, Legends and Myths in Collections*. Westwood, Mass.: F.W. Faxon, 1973.

————. *Index to Fairy Tales, 1973–1977, Including Folklore, Legends and Myths in Collections*. 4th supplement. Westwood, Mass.: F.W. Faxon, 1979.

Kirtley, Bacil Fleming. *A Motif-Index of Traditional Polynesian Narratives*. Honolulu: University of Hawaii, 1971.

Kipple, May A. "African Folktales with Foreign Analogues." Ph.D. dissertation. Indiana University, 1938.

O'Suilleabhain, Sean, and Christiansen, Reider Th. *The Types of the Irish Folktale*. Folklore Fellows Communications, no. 188. Helsinki: Suomalainen Tiedeakatemia, 1963.

Roberts, Warren Everett. *The Tale of the Kind and the Unkind Girls: AA-Th 480 and Related Tales*. Berlin: W. de Gruyter, 1958.

Thompson, Stith. *Motif-Index of Folk-Literature*. 6 vols. rev. ed. Bloomington: Indiana University Press, 1955–1958.

Ziegler, Elsie B. *Folklore: An Annotated Bibliography and Index to Single Editions*. Westwood, Mass.: F.W. Faxon, 1975.

1

Motif Index

General Synopsis of the Index

This is a synopsis of the Stith Thompson Motif Index classification. The Storyteller's Sourcebook does not contain entries in all of these categories.

A. MYTHOLOGICAL MOTIFS

A0 – A99.	Creator
A100 – A499.	Gods
A100 – A199.	The gods in general
A200 – A299.	Gods of the upper world
A300 – A399.	Gods of the underworld
A400 – A499.	Gods of the earth
A500 – A599.	Demigods and culture heroes
A600 – A899.	Cosmogony and Cosmology
A600 – A699.	The universe
A700 – A799.	The heavens
A800 – A899.	The earth
A900 – A999.	Topographical features of the earth
A1000 – A1099.	World calamities
A1100 – A1199.	Establishment of natural order
A1200 – A1699.	Creation and Ordering of Human Life
A1200 – A1299.	Creation of man
A1300 – A1399.	Ordering of human life
A1400 – A1499.	Acquisition of culture
A1500 – A1599.	Origin of customs
A1600 – A1699.	Distribution and differentiation of peoples
A1700 – A2199.	Creation of Animal Life
A1700 – A1799.	Creation of animal life – general
A1800 – A1899.	Creation of mammals
A1900 – A1999.	Creation of birds
A2000 – A2099.	Creation of insects
A2100 – A2199.	Creation of fish and other animals
A2200 – A2599.	Animal Characteristics
A2200 – A2299.	Various causes of animal characteristics
A2300 – A2399.	Causes of animal characteristics: body
A2400 – A2499.	Causes of animal characteristics: appearance and habits
A2500 – A2599.	Animal characteristics – miscellaneous
A2600 – A2699.	Origin of trees and plants
A2700 – A2799.	Origin of plant characteristics
A2800 – A2899.	Miscellaneous explanations

B. ANIMALS

B0 – B99.	Mythical animals
B100 – B199.	Magic animals
B200 – B299.	Animals with human traits
B300 – B599.	Friendly Animals
B300 – B349.	Helpful animals – general
B350 – B399.	Grateful animals
B400 – B499.	Kinds of helpful animals
B500 – B599.	Services of helpful animals
B600 – B699.	Marriage of person to animal
B700 – B799.	Fanciful traits of animals
B800 – B899.	Miscellaneous animal motifs

C. TABU

C0 – C99.	Tabu connected with supernatural beings
C100 – C199.	Sex tabu
C200 – C299.	Eating and drinking tabu
C300 – C399.	Looking tabu
C400 – C499.	Speaking tabu
C500 – C549.	Tabu: touching
C550 – C599.	Class tabu
C600 – C699.	Unique prohibitions and compulsions
C700 – C899.	Miscellaneous tabus
C900 – C999.	Punishment for breaking tabu

D. MAGIC

D0 – D699.	Transformation
D10 – D99.	Transformation: man to different man
D100 – D199.	Transformation: man to animal
D200 – D299.	Transformation: man to object
D300 – D399.	Transformation: animal to person
D400 – D499.	Other forms of transformation
D500 – D599.	Means of transformation
D600 – D699.	Miscellaneous transformation incidents
D700 – D799.	Disenchantment
D800 – D1699.	Magic objects
D800 – D899.	Ownership of magic objects
D900 – D1299.	Kinds of magic objects
D1300 – D1599.	Function of magic objects
D1600 – D1699.	Characteristics of magic objects

D1700 – D2199.	Magic Powers and Manifestations
D1710 – D1799.	Possession and employment of magic powers
D1800 – D2199.	Manifestations of magic power

E. THE DEAD

E0 – E199.	Resuscitation
E200 – E599.	Ghosts and Other Revenants
E200 – E299.	Malevolent return from the dead
E300 – E399.	Friendly return from the dead
E400 – E599.	Ghosts and revenants – miscellaneous
E500 – E699.	Reincarnation
E700 – E799.	The Soul

F. MARVELS

F0 – F199.	Otherworld Journeys
F200 – F699.	Marvelous Creatures
F200 – F399.	Fairies and elves
F400 – F499.	Spirits and demons
F500 – F599.	Remarkable persons
F600 – F699.	Persons with extraordinary powers
F700 – F899.	Extraordinary places and things
F900 – F1099.	Extraordinary occurrences

G. OGRES

G10 – G399.	Kinds of Ogres
G10 – G99.	Cannibals and cannibalism
G100 – G199.	Giant ogres
G200 – G299.	Witches
G300 – G399.	Other ogres
G400 – G499.	Falling into ogre's power
G500 – G599.	Ogre defeated
G600 – G699.	Other ogre motifs

H. TESTS

H0 – H199.	Identity tests: recognition
H200 – H299.	Tests of truth
H300 – H499.	Marriage tests
H500 – H899,	Tests of Cleverness
H500 – H529.	Tests of cleverness or ability
H530 – H899.	Riddles
H900 – H1199.	Tests of Prowess: Tasks
H900 – H99.	Assignment and performance of tasks
H1000 – H1199.	Nature of tasks
H1200 – H1399.	Tests of Prowess: Quests
H1200 – H1240.	Attendant circumstances of quests
H1250 – H1399.	Nature of quests
H1400 – H1599.	Other Tests
H1400 – H1449.	Tests of fear
H1450 – H1499.	Tests of vigilance
H1500 – H1549.	Tests of endurance and power of survival
H1550 – H1569.	Tests of character
H1570 – H1599.	Miscellaneous tests

J. THE WISE AND THE FOOLISH

J0 – J199.	Acquisition and possession of wisdom (knowledge)
J200 – J1099.	Wise and Unwise Conduct
J200 – J499.	Choices
J500 – J599.	Prudence and discretion
J600 – J799.	Forethought
J800 – J849.	Adaptability
J850 – J899.	Consolation in Misfortune
J900 – J999.	Humility
J1000 – J1099.	Other aspects of wisdom
J1100 – J1699.	Cleverness
J1110 – J1129.	Clever persons
J1130 – J1199.	Cleverness in the law court
J1200 – J1229.	Clever man puts another out of countenance
J1230 – J1249.	Clever dividing
J1250 – J1499.	Clever verbal retorts (repartee)
J1500 – J1649.	Clever practical retorts
J1650 – J1699.	Miscellaneous clever acts
J1700 – J2749.	Fools (and other unwise persons)
J1700 – J1749.	Fools (general)
J1750 – J1849.	Absurd misunderstandings
J1850 – J1999.	Absurd disregard of facts
J2000 – J2049.	Absurd absent-mindedness
J2050 – J2199.	Absurd short-sightedness
J2200 – J2259.	Absurd lack of logic
J2260 – J2299.	Absurd scientific theories
J2300 – J2349.	Gullible fools
J2350 – J2369.	Talkative fools
J2370 – J2399.	Inquisitive fools
J2400 – J2449.	Foolish imitation
J2450 – J2499.	Literal fools
J2500 – J2549.	Foolish extremes

J2550 – J2599.	Thankful fools
J2600 – J2649.	Cowardly fools
J2650 – J2699.	Bungling fools
J2700 – J2749.	The easy problem made hard
J2750 – J2799.	Other aspects of wisdom or foolishness

K. DECEPTIONS

K0 – K99.	Contests won by deception
K100 – K299.	Deceptive bargains
K300 – K499.	Thefts and cheats
K500 – K699.	Escape by deception
K700 – K799.	Capture by deception
K800 – K999.	Fatal deception
K1000 – K1199.	Deception into self-injury
K1200 – K1299.	Deception into humiliating position
K1300 – K1399.	Seduction or deceptive marriage
K1400 – K1499.	Dupe's property destroyed
K1500 – K1599.	Deceptions connected with adultery
K1600 – K1699.	Deceiver falls into own trap
K1700 – K2099.	Deception Through Shams
K1700 – K1799.	Deception through bluffing
K1800 – K1899.	Deception by disguise or illusion
K1900 – K1999.	Impostures
K2000 – K2099.	Hypocrites
K2100 – K2199.	False accusations
K2200 – K2299.	Villains and traitors
K2300 – K2399.	Other deceptions.

L. REVERSAL OF FORTUNE

L0 – L99.	Victorious youngest child
L100 – L199.	Unpromising hero (heroine)
L200 – L299.	Modesty brings reward
L300 – L399.	Triumph of the weak
L400 – L499.	Pride brought low

M. ORDAINING THE FUTURE

M0 – M99.	Judgments and decrees
M100 – M199.	Vows and oaths
M200 – M299.	Bargains and promises
M300 – M399.	Prophecies
M400 – M499.	Curses

N. CHANCE AND FATE

N0 – N99.	Wagers and gambling
N100 – N299.	The ways of luck and fate
N300 – N399.	Unlucky accidents
N400 – N699.	Lucky Accidents
N410 – N439.	Lucky business ventures
N440 – N499.	Valuable secrets learned
N500 – N599.	Treasure trove
N600 – N699.	Other lucky accidents
N700 – N799.	Accidental encounters
N800 – N899.	Helpers

P. SOCIETY

P0 – P99.	Royalty and nobility
P100 – P199.	Other social orders
P200 – P299.	The family
P300 – P399.	Other social relationships
P400 – P499.	Trades and professions
P500 – P599.	Government
P600 – P699.	Customs
P700 – P799.	Society – miscellaneous motifs

Q. REWARDS AND PUNISHMENTS

Q0 – Q99.	Deeds rewarded
Q100 – Q199.	Nature of rewards
Q200 – Q399.	Deeds punished
Q400 – Q599.	Kinds of punishment

R. CAPTIVES AND FUGITIVES

R0 – R99.	Captivity
R100 – R199.	Rescues
R200 – R299.	Escapes and pursuits
R300 – R399.	Refuges and recapture

S. UNNATURAL CRUELTY

S0 – S99.	Cruel relatives
S100 – S199.	Revolting murders or mutilations
S200 – S299.	Cruel sacrifices
S300 – S399.	Abandoned or murdered children
S400 – S499.	Cruel persecutions

T. SEX

T0 – T99.	Love
T100 – T199.	Marriage
T200 – T299.	Married life
T300 – T399.	Chastity and celibacy
T400 – T499.	Illicit sexual relations

T500 – T599.   Conception and birth
T600 – T699.   Care of children

U. THE NATURE OF LIFE

U0 – U99.   Life's inequalities
U100 – U299.   Nature of life – miscellaneous motifs

V. RELIGION

V0 – V99.   Religious services
V100 – V199.   Religious edifices and objects
V200 – V299.   Sacred persons
V300 – V399.   Religious beliefs
V400 – V449.   Charity
V450 – V499.   Religious orders
V500 – V599.   Religious motifs – miscellaneous

W. TRAITS OF CHARACTER

W0 – W99.   Favorable traits of character
W100 – W199.   Unfavorable traits of character
W200 – W299.   Traits of character – miscellaneous

X. HUMOR

X0 – X99.   Humor of discomfiture
X100 – X199.   Humor of disability – physical
X200 – X599.   Humor of Social Classes
X200 – X299.   Humor dealing with tradesmen
X300 – X499.   Humor dealing with professions
X500 – X599.   Humor concerning other social classes
X600 – X699.   Humor concerning races or nations
X700 – X799.   Humor concerning sex
X800 – X899.   Humor based on drunkenness
X900 – X1899.   Humor of lies and exaggeration

Z. MISCELLANEOUS GROUPS OF MOTIFS

Z0 – Z99.   Formulas
Z100 – Z199.   Symbolism
Z200 – Z299.   Heroes
Z300 – Z399.   Unique exceptions
Z400 – Z499.   Historical, genealogical or biographical motifs
Z500 – Z599.   Horror stories

Motif Index

A0 - A99. Creator.

A0. Creator. SEE: A610 (Creation of universe by creator).

A46. Creation contest. Jupiter creates man, Neptune creates bull, Minerva creates horse. Judge Momus suggests major alterations in each. Jupiter drives the fault finding critic from Olympus. Aesop: Aesop AESOP'S (Grosset) 92-93.

A100 - A499. Gods.

A110. Origin of gods.

A112.2. Male and female creators beget gods. Japan: MacAlpine JAPANESE 10-15.

A112.3. Gods born from various parts of creator's body. Japan: MacAlpine JAPANESE 10-15.

A116. Twin Gods. SEE: A515.1.1. (Twin culture heroes).

A132. God in animal form.

A132.2. Monkey as god. SEE: B241.2.2. (King of monkeys).

A132.15.1* God as tortoise. Kim Qui, golden turtle, gives Emperor An Duong Vuong magic golden nail with which he can build wall to protect Vietnam from China. Vietnam: Robertson FAIRY..VIETNAM 66-74.

A132.16* Elephant-god. Ganesha. India: Reed TALKATIVE 83-88.

A132.17* Cat-goddess. Bast, cat-goddess, has cat lead man to lost girlfriend. He had saved cat's life. Egypt: Carpenter WONDER..DOGS 184-194.

A132.17.1* Cat is holy. Cat sent to heaven on errand is kept as companion of Saras Vati, wife of Brahma. India: Carpenter WONDER..DOGS 81-88.

A160. Mutual relations of the gods.

A162. Conflicts of the gods.

A162.9* Bataru Guru gives rice to man, calf Lembu Gumarong tries to destroy, battle of gods ensues. +A2685.6.1.1. Indonesia: Asia FOLK I 7-12.

A163. Contests among the gods.

A163.1.1. Gods play chess. SEE ALSO: D2011.1.3. (years thought days).

A163.1.1.1* Mortal watches quietly and serves wine to two old men encountered playing chess on mountain top. They reward by changing his death age in Book of Dead to 99 years rather than 19. China: Carpenter TALES..CHINESE 252-261. Vietnam: Sun LAND 120-153.

A180. Gods in relation to mortals. SEE: K1811.1. (Gods [saints] in disguise visit mortals); Q1. (Hospitality rewarded--opposite punished); T111.1. (Marriage of a mortal and a god).

A185.12.1.1* God resuscitates man. Nyame resuscitates dead boy to fulfill Ananse's promise. +K251.1.0.1. West Africa: Appiah ANANSE 1-26.

A189.1.1. Man as helper of thundergod. SEE: K1112.2.

A200. Gods of the upper world.

A220.1. Sun-goddess.

A220.1.1* The goddess of the sun goes into a cave taking her light along when her brother Prince Susano plays a trick on her and ruins her handmaiden's loom. He is banished and she is coaxed out. +K929.1.1. Japan: Uchida DANCING 27-33.

A240. Moon-god.

A240.1.1* Moon-goddess: Childless bamboo cutter finds tiny maiden in bamboo stalk. She grows rapidly. Golden coins are found in bamboo stem each day thereafter. When grown she sets suitor tasks (H355). She requests: a branch from golden tree with white ball on mountain; a stone bowl used by Buddha; a ball of five jewels from the throat of a dragon; a cowrie shell which Horai Mountain swallow has within it; the skin of a tree rat from China. All fail or produce fake items. She returns to the moon people at full moon, leaving the emperor a poem and elixir of eternal youth. He casts these into Mt. Fuji. The smoke carrying these to Princess Kaguya in heaven may still be seen (A2816.1). Japan: MacAlpine JAPANESE 127-187; Ozaki JAPANESE 98-118; Uchida: DANCING 75-85 (-emperor).

A280. Weather-god.

A282.2* Wind-god. Pampero, south wind, bringer of rain, does not come. Carob tree advises man that gods are asleep. Great bird of the Underworld sleeps in tree nightly, men frighten it off. It flees, gods wake, Pampero returns. Argentina: Carpenter SOUTH 11-17.

A284. God of Thunder. SEE ALSO: K1112.2.

A284.2. Thunderbird. A giant bird usually thought of as a thunder-god.

A284.2.1* Origin of Thunderbird. Giant Nasan has feathered wings made and flies to woo Evening Star. Draws magic circle and refuses to return her. Is tempted out to kill white deer for her, captured by Great Spirit and turned to Thunderbird. Voice is thunder, flapping of wings is lightning. Native American (Winnebago): Chafetz THUNDERBIRD 3-13/DeWit TALKING 27-33/.

A284.2.1.1* Origin of Thunderbird. Skinkoots (coyote) and Old-Man are carried to Thunderbird nest. Old-Man manages to kill Thunderbirds. From eyes of one slain Thunderbird come crow size birds. These are present day Thunderbirds. Native American: Field AMERICAN 40-54.

A284.2.2* Thunderbirds leave. Nahnuk, caught by Thunderbird, is asked to burn plumage of dead Thunderbird son and dance to drum which sounds like heartbeat of T's wife. N. seeks just the right material for drum and performs rite. Thunderbird (eagle) flies out of flames and all Thunderbirds fly north, never to return. Eskimo (Bering Strait): Melzack DAY 85-92.

A284.4* Man overhears thunder-spirits come to temple to borrow thunder-cart for attack on his district. He warns the farmers. China: Birch CHINESE 101-110.

A284.5* Thunder gives medicine pipe to be smoked when Thunder returns with rains in spring. T. had stolen man's wife and was forced to return her eyes when Raven aided man. Native American: Field AMERICAN 55-61.

A285.2* Goddess of Lightning, Hiiaka. Sent to deliver message of Pele, H. kills Forest Demon, Lizard Women, Man-eating Shark, Great Mo-o. Pele has meantime destroyed her lehua groves and turned her friend Hopoe to stone. Hawaii: Thompson HAWAIIAN..EARTH 20-27.

A287. Rain-god. SEE: B11.7. (Dragon as rain-spirit).

A289.2* Goddess of snow, Poliahu. Duels with Pele, Goddess of Fire, and vanquishes her. Certain slope of Maunakea left to Poliahu is snow-covered. Hawaii: Thompson HAWAIIAN ..EARTH 28-32.

A289.3* Meeting with Snow King. Man asks Snow King to freeze river so he can walk on it, S. says is too late in the year but promises to visit man next year. Man stores much fuel and manages to save self from Snow King's visit. SEE ALSO: A1158.1.1. Native American (Naskapi): Cunningham TALKING 60-65.

A289.4* Witsduks (snow the wind blows and drifts). Rock squirrel woman traps them but fox opens bag and some witsduks escape, thus they are still at large. Fox is white-haired and suspicious from the encounter. Native American (California): Curry DOWN 90-100.

A300 - A399. Gods of the Underworld.

A310. God of the world of the dead. SEE ALSO: F81 (Descent to lower world of dead).

A310.1.1* Goddess of world of the dead. Maui tries to kill Death, Hinenui. She embraces him. He dies. Polynesia: Berry MAGIC 89-97.

A316. Goddess divides time between upper and lower worlds. Persephone spends six months on earth and six in Hades. SEE: A1150.2.

A400 - A499. Gods of the earth.

A411. Household gods.

A411.1* Door-gods. Shen Shu and Yu Lu, Guardians of the Gate. China: Carpenter TALES..CHINESE 47-55.

A411.2* Kitchen-gods. Emperor wants secret of Chang Kung's happiness. Writes "kindness" 100 times. Becomes Kitchen God. China: Carpenter TALES..CHINESE 39-46; Chang TALES 7-9; Dolch STORIES..OLD CHINA 131-137.

A420. God of water. SEE ALSO: F420 (Water-spirits).

A421. Sea-god. SEE ALSO: F725.

A421.0.2* Tsar of the Blue Sea asks Sadko to play for him undersea. Tells S. to bet merchants of Novogorod that there are fish with golden fins in Lake Ilmen. S. becomes wealthy. At sea Tsar of the Blue Sea produces storm in anger until Sadko leaps from ship with his gusli. Tsar's wife tells S. to break strings of gusli because whenever Tsar dances to gusli, ships are wrecked. S. is told to choose certain daughter as bride. He awakens on shore of lake surrounded by treasure. Russia: Arbuthnot ARBUTHNOT ANTHOLOGY 290-293; Arbuthnot FAIRY 149-153; Dolch OLD RUSSIA 19-35; Downing RUSSIAN 55-63; Ransome OLD 40-53.

A421.1.1* Sea-goddess. Dolphin with fish clinging to tail is released by Chen. Shipwrecked years later he is ordered executed by queen of strange land. Her maid recognizes him as man who saved them. China: Williams-Ellis ROUND 43-52.

A421.1.2* Miss Lin, the Sea Goddess. Girl dreams father and two brothers are being lost in storm. She holds brothers in hands and father's boat in teeth. Mother wakes her and she opens her mouth to answer and loses father's boat. He is lost but brothers are saved. She plunges into sea to seek him. If she appears in storm sailors will reach shore safely. China: Carpenter TALES..CHINESE 235-241.

A430. God of vegetation.

A433.1.1. God of rice-fields. SEE: A2685.6.1.

A460. Gods of abstractions.

A483.1. Goddess of mercy. Kwan Yin. China: Carpenter TALES..CHINESE 29-38.

A489.5* God of Righteousness, Dharma. King Yudhisthera refuses to enter heaven unless dog is admitted. Dog becomes Dharma. India: Turnbull FAIRY 168-170.

A489.6* Krishna the Avenger. Krishna is worshipped by cowherds. Hindu: Courlander TIGER'S 63-71.

A490. Miscellaneous gods of the earth.

A493.1. Goddess of fire. Pele. Hawaii: Colum LEGENDS 25-37; Thompson HAWAIIAN..EARTH 15-19.

A500 - A599. Demigods and culture heroes.

A500. Demigods and culture heroes.

A501.2* Eight Immortals. China: Carpenter TALES..CHINESE 150-158; Wyndham FOLK.. CHINA 44-49 (Chang Kuo); Wyndham FOLK.. CHINA 50-53 (Eight Immortals help build bridge, enabling a mother to fulfill her vow); Wyndham FOLK..CHINA 37-43.

A501.3* Eighteen Lo-Hans. Bandits become saints after meeting white horse bodisatva. Vietnam: Vo-Dinh TOAD 105-113.

A510. Origin of the culture hero (demigod).

A511.1.3.4* Mother of Confucius steps in Unicorn's footprint. It appears and hands her a jade bearing "Thy son shall be a ruler without a throne." She bears Confucius. China: Wyndham TALES..CHINA 34-37.

A511.1.4.5* Chu Mong, founder of Korea, is born when cloud floats inside mother's dress and turns to egg. Thrown to wild boars, dogs, horses--the animals protect him. He calls to the river dragon for aid and fish form a bridge so he may escape over their backs. Korea: Carpenter TALES..KOREAN 27-35.

A511.1.8.4* Tan Kun, culture hero, born of she-bear who has become a woman by remaining in cave for 21 days after eating 21 garlic cloves. Korea: Carpenter TALES..KOREAN 27-35.

A511.1.9. Culture hero born from egg. SEE: B241.2.2.1. (Sun Wu-Kung).

A511.2.2.3* Tepoztan, culture hero, is ordered killed. Abandoned in maguey plant, leaves cover hero and sap nourishes him. Ants feed honey and cover with rose petals. He is set adrift in box on river, rescued by fisherman and raised. Mexico: Brenner BOY 28-33; Frost LEGENDS 190-199.

A515.1.1.4* Twin culture heroes. (A116). Twins Hun-Apu and Xbalanque vanquish god Vukub Cakix and son Zipacna. Mayan (Popul Vuh): Courlander RIDE 243-249; Garner CAV..GOBLINS 4-10; Williams-Ellis ROUND 217-222.

A520. Nature of the culture hero (demigod).

A522.1.3. Coyote as culture hero. See following collections - Native American: Courlander PEOPLE; Curry DOWN; Fisher STORIES; Heady TALES..NIMIPOO; Martin NINE TALES OF COYOTE.

A522.2.2. Raven as culture hero. See following collections - Native American: Martin NINE TALES OF RAVEN; Melzack RAVEN.

A522.3.1. Spider as culture hero. See following collections - W. Africa: Appiah ANANSE; Arkhurst ADVENTURES. W. Indies: Sherlock ANANSI.

A526.1.1.1* Culture hero is invincible. Crazy Horse chews flint to powder before battle and smears self with this, becomes invincible. Ogla-la Sioux: Matson LEGENDS 42-43.

A530. Culture hero establishes law and order.

A531. Culture hero (demigod) overcomes monsters. Eskimo: Melzack RAVEN 83-91 (raven). SEE ALSO: F912.

A541. Culture hero teaches arts and crafts. Korea: Carpenter TALES..KOREAN 27-35 (Tan Kun). China: Birch CHINESE 3-8 (Fu-Hsi). Inca: Carpenter LATIN 115-122 (Manco Capac and Mama Oullo). SEE ALSO: A1404.

A541.0.1* Tiny God appears in sweet potato leaf boat. Scarecrow identifies him as a God. He teaches the prince industries and crafts then swings back into sky from stalk of grain. (A566). Prince Okuminush teaches the people these skills. Japan: Uchida MAGIC 113-121.

A560. Culture hero's (demigod's) departure.

A566. Culture hero returns to upper world. SEE ALSO: A541.0.1; A240.1.1.

A566.3* Eetoi killed after men feel he has become evil. He returns to life thrice. Buzzard (ancient animal) elicits Sun's aid. Sun spits in pool and scalds Eetoi to death. Eetoi then requests sun carry him to Underworld. Pima: Baker AT 33-42.

A568.1* Raven leaves the world after daring to combat serpent without cloak of immortality. Eskimo: Melzack RAVEN 85-91.

A590. Demigods and culture heroes—miscellaneous.

A591.1* Mantis obtains a female mate. Blue

Crane magically turns to girl. Mantis subdues her by rubbing his sweat on her face, she dresses in women's clothes and goes home. Bushmen: Helfman BUSHMEN 68-71.

A600 - A899. COSMOGONY AND COSMOLOGY

A600 - A699. The universe.

A610. Creation of universe by creator. The creator is existing before all things. China: Manton FLYING 9-12 (Pan Ku).

A614. Universe from parts of creator's body. Ymir makes the world from his members--mountains from bones, cliffs from teeth, heavens from skull, etc. China: Birch CHINESE 3-8; Carpenter TALES..CHINESE 14-21.

A614.0.1* Earth Magician scrapes dust from his chest, rolls this into world ball, breathes on magic water and freezes it into sun and moon and stars, makes buzzard from shadow of own left eye. Pima: Baker AT 1-6.

A617.2. Creation of universe from calabash. Top = sky, pieces = sun and moon, seed = stars, rest = earth. Hawaii: Thompson HAWAIIAN.. EARTH 11-14. SEE ALSO: A641.3.

A618.3* Raven catches snowflakes on wing making snowball, alights on ball, finds clay under snow and makes seeds. Sends sparrow to fetch light, ball of gold for sun and ball of iron for moon. Eskimo: Melzack RAVEN 15-24.

A620. Spontaneous creation of universe.

A620.3* In the beginning chaos, lighter parts rise, heavier sink, thus dividing into heaven and earth. Japan: MacAlpine JAPANESE 3-4.

A625.2. Raising of the sky. Originally the sky is near the earth.

A625.2.2.1* Why the sky receded upward: it was struck by a woman's pestle. Woman hangs her comb and necklace on sky while pounding rice, hits sky with pestle and it recedes taking her jewels with it. Origin of moon and stars. (A760; A740). Philippines (Bukidnon): Sechrist ONCE 12-13/Cathon PERHAPS 110-111/.

A625.2.3. Raising the sky: striking with broom. Old woman's hump strikes clouds as she sweeps. She strikes at sky with broom and thus raises it. Haiti: Thoby-Marcelin SINGING 82-83 (strikes clouds because they tickle her ears as she sweeps).

A625.2.5. After sky is lifted, plants and shrubs begin to grow. Leaves remain flat from sky resting on them. Maui pushes sky up. Polynesia: Courlander TIGER'S 132-139. Hawaii: Colum LEGENDS 38-64; Williams SURPRISING 13.

A625.2.6* Dancing warrior pierces sky with spear and wounds angel. God moves sky away. Philippines: Sechrist ONCE 15-16.

A625.2.7* Father tries to poke moon down for son to play with. Moon moves away taking sky with it. +A751.5.2.3. Assam (Ao Nagas): Jablow MAN 22.

A625.2.8* People can break off pieces of sky to eat in the beginning. They break off more than they need. The sky pulls away and man must work for his food (A1346.2). U.S. Black: Lester BLACK 38-41.

A652.2.9* All tribes push together to raise sky. Native American (Snohomish): Matson LEGENDS 90-93.

A625.2.10* Man opens moutain tops letting fire in earth out. Leper with flaming arms emerges and burns sky. Sky raises itself. Upper Volta: Guirma TALES 1-15.

A625.2.11* Tao strikes sky with pestle, raising it. Throws sun, moon, and belt of stars into sky in anger. Philippines: Asian FOLK FOUR 47-53.

A630. Series of creations.

A630.1* Series of creations: Earth Magician, unhappy with created man, pulls sky down and goes through hole in sky into second, third and fourth worlds. Buzzard helper gets Coyote, child of Moon and Sun, and Eetoi, child of Earth and Sky, to help with creation on fourth try. Native American (Papago; Pima): Baker AT 1-6.

A640. Other means of creating the universe.

A641.3* Giant pumpkin, Feegba, chases boy who cuts it. Smashes all in path. Shepherd with horned sheep stops it, splits it in two. Half forms earth, half sky. Seeds = stars, pulp = milky way. SEE ALSO: A617.2. Upper Volta: Guillot TALES 96-97.

A660. Nature of the upper world.

A661.0.1.2. Saint Peter as porter of heaven. SEE: F1037.1.1; Q565.

A665.2.0.1.1* Pillars supporting sky. Empress Jokwa mends broken pillar supporting heaven and torn sky using five colored stones. Japan: Ozaki JAPANESE 283-296.

A700 - A799. The heavens.

A700. Creation of heavenly bodies.

A701. Creation of the sky. SEE: A852.1; A625.2.

A705. Origin and nature of clouds. SEE: A1133.

A710. Creation of the sun. (cf: A1411). SEE

ALSO: A1412.5.

A710.1* Woman wishes for light. Sun, moon and stars appear. Greenland Eskimo: Leach HOW 37-38.

A711. Sun as man who left earth. Man, usually of supernatural birth, ascends to the sky and becomes the sun.

A711.0.1* Sun = Kwaku Tsin, moon = K's father Anansi, stars = other captives who escape dragon by climbing sky on rope ladder made by K. Ghana (Ashanti): Jablow MAN 83-85.

A711.1.1* Sun, Sua, as creator's son. Moon, Chia, is creator himself, Nemequene. Colombia (Chibcha): Courlander RIDE 224-225.

A712. Sun as fire rekindled every morning. Morning star announces coming. Kingfisher (laughing jackass) announces sunrise. +A714.3.1. (cf. A781.1). Australia: Parker AUSTRALIAN. Australia (Euahlayi): Leach HOW 18-19.

A714. Sun from object thrown into sky.

A714.0.1* Sun shines from armpits of Sun-Man. He becomes old and sleeps too much. Old woman instructs children to throw sleeping Sun-Man into Sky where he becomes the Sun. Bushmen: Helfman BUSHMEN 48-50.

A714.3.1* Crane throws emu's egg into sky and it splatters on heap of firewood and wood bursts into flames. Sky spirit decides to kindle fire each day. +A712. Australia: Parker AUSTRALIAN. Australia (Euahlayi): Leach HOW 18-19.

A715.1. Sun and moon born from a woman. SEE: A762.1Bd.

A717.2* Coyote makes sun and moon from balls of tule grass and has hawk carry to sky and light. He uses wet grass for moon, hence too dim. Why Coyote howls at moon, sorry that he made moon so dim (A2427.4). North Wind blows on moon at time and causes it to wane (A755). California (Southern Pomo): Fisher CALIFORNIA 16-23.

A720. Nature and condition of the sun. SEE ALSO: A751.5.2.2.

A720.1.1* Formerly 10 suns. Yi, Heavenly Archer, shoots 9 down, Emperor Yao hides 10th arrow so one sun is saved. SEE ALSO: A751.8.7. China: Birch CHINESE 9-19.

A720.1.2* Formerly 6 suns. Archers fail to shoot them down. Prince Howee aims at reflections in pool and 5 disappear. Sixth hides in cave. Only cock can coax him out. W. China: Hume FAVORITE..CHINA 27-32.

A721.1. Sun kept in box. Theft of sun. The sun, which is kept by a monster, is stolen and brought to earth. SEE ALSO: A728; A758; A1411 (Theft of light); A1415 (Theft of fire).

A721.1.1* Ogre steals sun and keeps in box. Raven takes place of ogre baby and asks to play with sun. Flies out smokehole with it. Has to peck off pieces to get it through smokehole, these become stars (A764.0.1). Native American: Manning-Sanders CHARMS 81-84.

A721.1.2* Theft of dawn (A1179.2). Blue Jay and Ground Squirrel raid village of Dawn People. B.J. gets basket containing dawn and releases it. G.S. carries off acorns, sunflower seeds, and obsidian chips therefore back is striped from sharp obsidian (A2413.2). California: Curry DOWN 38-47.

A721.1.3* Arctic Hare plays kick ball with sun while visiting Ke'let, evil spirits who stole sun. Hare kicks sun into sky and escapes. Ke'let chief asks eagle to carry him after hare. Eagle carries ever higher asking thrice how earth looks. Drops K. (K1041.0.1.1). Ke'let's head sticks into earth on landing and hare pounds K. into ground. Thus Ke'let live underground. Native American (Chuckee): Newell RESCUE 51-62.

A721.1.4* Fox plays ball with sun among peoples owning sun. Steals and relays to deer, magpie, Saynday. Native American: Marriott WINTER 3-12/Haviland NORTH 60-64/.

A721.1.5* Coyote steals sun to bring light. Native American (Yokuts): Curry DOWN 22-37 (deermice chew straps, coyote steals from two old women, trims off pieces for stars, moon); Leach HOW 44.

A721.1.6* Chief Kahoa takes away sun, moon, stars. Niheu and Kana try to retrieve. K. succeeds with aid of blind aunt, Woman-Who-Walks-in-Darkness. Hawaii: Thompson HAWAIIAN..EARTH 33-39.

A721.3.1* Stolen sun restored to sky. Sun is to belong to first person hitting sun with arrow. Brother-in-law wins sun and takes it away. Nephew, aided by totem and mouse, wins it back. Agree to let sun move about and light entire world. Native American (Snohomish): Matson LEGENDS 80-86.

A722.5. Sun at night lowers arm. The sun, a man, lies with arm uplifted. The shining comes from his armpits. When his arm is lowered the shining ceases. Bushmen: Helfman BUSHMEN 48-50.

A727.1. Sun originally so hot that it threatens all life.

A727.2* Sun falls on earth. Mole pushes it back. Blinded and has forepaws bent from effort. Native American (Achomawi): Belting LONG 51-53.

A727.3* Sun withers mulberry trees so that hunter shoots arrow in eye of sun and moon. They refuse to rise for three years. Cow, tiger, call to rise. Cock succeeds. China (Ch'uan Miao): Leach HOW 92-93.

A727.4* Cottontail shoots sun down and pastes thin slices of liver over sun so it does not shine so hotly. Cottontail's back is scorched in act. Native American (California): Curry DOWN 48-50.

A728. Sun caught in snare. SEE ALSO: A721.1.

A728.0.1* Sun caught in Tcakabesh's squirrel snare. Animals try to free. Squirrel jumps backward singeing tail, mouse frees sun but hair is scorched from back (A2311.11;A2378.9.6; A2441.1.13). Canada (Algonkian): Jablow MAN 79-80.

A728.1. Sun-snarer: burnt mantle. A boy is angered because the sun burnt his mantle. He makes a snare and catches the sun and delays him so that everything is burning up. A mouse finally gnaws the snare. Native American: Field AMERICAN 71-73. Native American (Menominee): Cunningham TALKING 66-69 (sun is choking in snare and world becomes dark; mantle is a cloak of snow goose feathers).

A728.2. Sun-snarer: fast sun. The sun goes too fast to dry clothing. The hero snares the sun's legs with a rope as he is climbing up from the underworld. He releases the sun upon the promise to go more slowly. Polynesia: Berry MAGIC 74-80. Hawaii: Colum LEGENDS 38-64; /Cathon PERHAPS 103-109/; Thompson HAWAIIAN..EARTH 60-64; Williams SURPRISING 17. New Zealand (Maori): Courlander RIDE 14-19. Polynesia: Courlander TIGER'S 132-139.

A728.2.1* Sun snarer: sun too far away. Sun is caught in snare. Beaver gnaws sun free. Given broad teeth and two fur coats by He-Who-Made-The-Animals. (A2311.10; A2345.10). Native American (Cree): Belting LONG 79-84.

A735.0.1* Moon flees from sun. Sun weds girl, jealous moon attacks, now flees from sun. Kenya (Kamba): Jablow MAN 64-66.

A736.1. Sun and moon as man and woman. American Black: Courlander TERRAPIN'S 112-114.

A736.1.1.1* Sun sisters and moon brother. Two sisters on moon persuade brother on sun to trade places so people can't stare at them. They stick embroidery needles in your eyes if you look at sun. China: Carpenter TALES 22-28.

A736.1.2.1* Sun-brother and moon-sister. Brother and sister decide to start new lives. He objects to all her suggestions for lives they might try as animals. Agrees to become moon. Each lights a torch and rises into sky, sister puts out his torch for his reluctance. Eskimo: Field ESKIMO 14-16.

A736.1.2.2* Brother and sister run with torches. He falls and torch goes out. Why moon is dim. They have a two room house in the sky. In summer the moon stays inside. In winter sun stays inside. The moon disappears at times as he has other duties too. Eskimo: Caswell SHADOWS 19-23.

A736.1.2.3* Sky brother and sister climb down pine to earth and become sun and moon. Sparks from sun's face become stars (A764.0.1). Native American (Nez Percé): Heady TALES 15-20.

A736.1.3.1* Sun and moon as lovers. Sun King woos Vela Chow, Beautiful Dawn, and fails to return to heavens therefore no night. The stars hide his chariot and he cannot return to the sky. He weeps = gold. She weeps = silver (A978.4). She becomes moon. He kisses her at times = eclipse (A737.0.1). Thai: Carpenter ELEPHANT'S 212-219.

A736.1.4.4* Sun and moon married. Why the sun and moon live in the sky. Water people invited to visit flood house, and sun and moon must go up into sky to live. Nigeria (Ibibio): Jablow MAN 59-61. Nigeria (Efik): Leach HOW 20-21. E. Nigeria (Ibibio): Arnott AFRICAN 133-134. S.W. Nigeria (Efik-Ibibio): Dayrell WHY pb. Nigeria: Luzatto LONG 36-43 (-moon).

A736.1.4.4.1* Man makes love potion to catch moon. Sun forbids her to go to him so moon jumps in cooking pot to kill self. It is cold, she jumps to door sill, roof of hut, betel tree, sky. Papua, New Guinea: McDowell THIRD 129-130.

A736.4.1* Sun, moon and stars are three sisters rescued from Tiger by God of Heaven. +K311.31. Korea: Kim STORY 76-82.

A737. Causes of eclipses (sun or moon). SEE ALSO: A736.1.3.1.

A737.1.1* Fireball, dog of king of the Land of Darkness, tries to bring moon and sun to Land of Darkness. Takes each in turn in mouth but heat of sun and cold of moon force to spit out = eclipse. Korea: Kim STORY 23-30.

A737.9.1* Mink persuades sun to let him carry torch, falls into Milky Way and torch is extinguished = first eclipse. Later eclipses remind earth creatures that they cannot take the place of heavenly bodies. Native American (Puget Sound, Swinomish): Matson LEGENDS 123-127.

A737.12* Two sisters slap slave girl in face with spoon. She prays for vengeance in future life. Sisters are reborn as sun and moon. She is Rahu, the eclipse. She slaps them in face. Thai: Brockett BURMESE 5-7.

A739.6.1* Cock asks sun to come to aid if he calls and sun agrees. Cock calls in false alarm and sun rises (A2489.1.1). Assam (Ao Naga): Jablow MAN 88-90.

A740 – A759. The moon.

A740. Creation of the moon.
SEE ALSO: H621.4.1.; A625.2.2.1.

A740.1* Anansi can't decide which son should get moon. Nyame sets it in the sky. Ashanti: Courlander HAT 59-62.

A741.4* Moon object (person) thrown into sky. Greedy Luno cannot be filled. King of the Sharks throws him into sky. L. becomes the moon. When he lies on back and floats = new moon. Eats and gets fatter. Shiny face is from coconut sauce. Samoa: Holding SKY 11-23.

A741.5* Moon is ostrich feather thrown into sky by Mantis. Bushmen: Helfmen BUSHMEN 92-99.

A744.1* Smith Ilmarinen makes moon and stars of silver covered with gold, by order of Vanaisa. Lithuania: Maas MOON 11-16; Withers PAINTING pb.

A747. Person transformed to moon.
SEE ALSO: A762.1Bd.

A747.1* Bochica bans wife Chia to sky, becomes moon. Columbia (Chibcha): Jagendorf KING 81-83.

A750. Nature and condition of the moon.

A751. Man in the moon.

A751.0.1* Man climbed to moon on liana to escape nagging wife. Ecuador (Jibaro): Jablow MAN 19.

A751.0.2* Hunchbacked old man sitting under banyan tree plaiting bark fishing line. He plans to fish up everything from earth. Rat gnaws line every night. Cat tries to catch rat. Malay: Jablow MAN 21; Leach HOW 31.

A751.0.3* Boy kills game for people with his magical powers. Offended because they don't give best meat to his father, he goes out smoke hole, tearing off pants leg and rises to moon. May be seen with one pant leg missing. Native American, N.W. Canada (Loucheux): Jablow MAN 21.

A751.0.4* Ancestor father falls to earth from moon and returns on ladder taking one man along. Man, Porang, is left there and ancestor descends and removes ladder. Porang may be seen with bow and arrows. He shoots the souls of the dead as his game. Malaya (Besisi): Jablow MAN 22.

A751.1.1. Man in moon has punishment for burning brush (gathering sticks) on Sunday. U.S.: Jablow MAN 3-5.

A751.1.2.1* Man selling wilted vegetables swears "If I am deceiving you may I fly to the moon."

Flies there with his cart. Netherlands: De-Leeuw LEGENDS 112-113.

A751.1.4.1* Man stealing turnips, grabs at thornbush as is pulled up. Bush is seen with him on moon. Luxembourg: Jablow MAN 6.

A751.1.5* Man who eats people is pulled up by moon. Hangs onto hawthorn bush, seen with him on moon. Altai-Tatar: Leach HOW 30.

A751.1.6* Old man pounding paddy and throwing chaff to rabbit wishes for old woman to help. Moon goddess comes to assist him. He wishes to return and live with her. Seen on moon pounding chaff with hare. Burma: Htin Aung KINGDOM 71-73.

A751.1.8* Boy who saves wounded sparrow is given magic pumpkin seed. Gold and silver pour from the pumpkin. Bad boy wounds sparrow, then heals. Given seed and told to climb vine to moon. To chop all branches from cinnamon tree before returning. Still there. SEE ALSO: J2415.13. China: Jablow MAN 11-13; Wyndham FOLKTALES..CHINA 117-121.

A751.1.9* Princess Radha weds Prince Moon. Tiny yellow man carries grandfather off to moon. Radha clings and is carried too. Marries Prince Moon. When dark, little yellow man is angry. When full, can see old grandfather laughing. India: Spellman BEAUTIFUL 94-98.

A751.1.10* Man in moon has monster dog. Greenland (Eskimo): Jablow MAN 44-45.

A751.2. Man in the moon a rabbit (hare, other animal).

A751.2.1* The Buddha as hare offers self as food for hungry old man. Shakes off fleas first so they need not die in fire. Old man has been given food by monkey, otter, fox, jackal, etc. but hare has only self to give.

A751.2.1.1* Hare is taken to live on moon with old man who is Old-Man-of-the-Moon. Japan: Sakade JAPANESE 35-37.

A751.2.1.2* Hare's picture is drawn on moon in honor of sacrifice. The flames of fire were cool and hare was unharmed. India: Turnbull FAIRY 151-157 (God Sakra); Wyatt GOLDEN 112-117. Burma: Keeley CITY 106-109.

A751.2.1.3* Hare's charred remains are put on moon. Japan: Pratt MAGIC #10. Buddhist: Cathon PERHAPS 250-252.

A751.2.2* Hare persuades crane to carry him to moon. +A2320.3.2 (Crane's red head). +2371.2.14 (Crane's legs). Native American (Cree): Belting LONG 67-70.

A751.3. Frog in moon. SEE ALSO: A762.1Bd.

A751.3.1.1* Man in moon is a frog which has

jumped into a person's face and remains there; two frogs at moon's house don't like places given to sit. Sit on moon's face. SEE ALSO: A1131.0.1. Native American, British Columbia (Lillooet): Jablow MAN 24.

A751.3.1.2* Three frog girls washed into moon's house by whirlpool jump into moon's face. Native American, British Columbia (Lillooet): Leach HOW 31-33.

A751.3.1.3* God Bayamey as frog on moon swallows ocean for overflowing onto earth. Animals try to make frog laugh and spit out water. Eels succeed by tying self in knots. When frog sucks in tide recedes. He thinks of eels and laughs and tide goes back. Australia: Carpenter WONDER..SEAS 29-36.

A751.4. Man in the moon: tarring of the moon. Man sets out to tart the moon and remains with his tar-bucket in the moon. Lithuania: Maas MOON 11-16 (Vanapagan); Withers PAINTING pb. (Devil sends assistant).

A751.5. Man in the moon from scratches or paint.

A751.5.1. Man in the moon: moon's face scratched by hare in retaliation for injury to hare (A2342.1). SEE ALSO: A1335.1.0.1. South Africa (Hottentot): Jablow MAN 23.

A751.5.2. Man in moon: dung (ashes) on moon's face smeared there by sun. Philippines (Tinguian): Sechrist ONCE 14 (sand thrown in face).

A751.5.2.2* Sun and moon brawl. Moon has swollen mouth and one eye out. Sun is ashamed and shines so bright no one can look at him (or has red face). (A720). Masai: Jablow MAN 19; Leach HOW 34.

A751.5.2.3* Spots on moon's face are dirt thrown by angry man trying to poke moon down so boy can play with it. +A625.2.7. Assam (Ao Nagas): Jablow MAN 22.

A751.5.2.4* Dirty handprints of boy grabbing at moon. SEE: 758.2.

A751.5.6* Tears on moon. Moon takes mistreated orphan boy up to cry on moon. First tears in world. Boy blessed and returned to earth, tears may be seen on moon. +A1344.1. Algeria (Kabyle): Jablow MAN 10.

A751.5.7* Attempt to secure moon for prince. Tower built (F772.1.2.2). Engineer's shoulder's push against moon but efforts to dislodge it cause moon to break, pouring lava onto country below. Congo: Green FOLKTALES 75-81.

A751.5.8* God Takei plots to ensnare moon and douse her light by throwing salt water on her. His mother replaces the salt water with fresh and moon is only splotched by mud. Fiji: Gittens TALES 28-29.

A751.7. Two children in moon with yoke and bucket. (Taken up by moon who pities their hard work, suggested as origin of Jack and Jill). Old Norse: Leach HOW 33-34.

A751.7.1* Girl with water buckets carried to moon for offending moon by gaping at it. Siberia (Yakut): Jablow MAN 19. SEE ALSO: A751.8.5.

A751.7.2* Girl with water buckets carried to moon, rescued thus from cruel stepmother. Ural Mountains (Votyak): Jablow MAN 21.

A751.8.1.1* Man in the moon is an old woman weaving a head strap. Once a month she lays it down to stir hominy pot by her side and cat unravels it. Native American (Iroquois): Jablow MAN 14.

A751.8.3.1* Goddess in moon with calabash at her side. Hina climbs moon rainbow taking tapa board and calabash of water. Thus escapes her husband. Hawaii: Colum LEGENDS 173-175/ Colum STONE 117-119/; Thompson HAWAIIAN.. EARTH 76-80.

A751.8.5. Girl with tree carried to moon and is seen there.

A751.8.5.1* Girl with yoke of waterskins clinging to willow tree is carried to moon, seen there with tree. (A751.7.1). Siberia (Yakuts): Deutsch MORE 79-84.

A751.8.5.2* Chu Cuoi sees tiger use healing banyan leaves on cubs. He plants tree in his garden and heals and weds princess. (B512). His wife cuts the tree's roots and it flies to the moon with C. clinging to it. Still seen there. Vietnam: Asia FOLK..THREE 55-59; Robertson FAIRY 25-35; Schultz VIETNAMESE 31-33.

A751.8.7* Heng O, the moon lady. Heng O, sister of God of the Waters, Ho Po, weds heavenly archer Hou Ye. She swallows his pill of longevity and flees to moon. Sneezes and pill flies out of mouth and becomes white jade hare. Hou Ye has shot down nine of ten suns (A720.1.1) is put on the sun and given a golden bird to wake him (ancestor of the rooster). China: Carpenter TALES..CHINESE 206-216.

A751.8.8* Woman in the moon is antelope's mother, hidden there when animals ordered to kill mothers. Yoruba: Courlander OLODE 72-76.

A751.12* Owl in moon. Thrown there with his stone club by Buffalo-calf. Native American (Comanche): Jablow MAN 15-17.

A753. Moon as person.

A753.1.0.1* Moon as wooer. Moon comes for girl on sleigh. Reindeer turns her into a lamp and moon fears to touch. He leaves tent and she calls "here I am" then changes back into a lamp.

Repeats this until Moon becomes so exhausted that his bone marrow dries up and she can tie him down. Moon agrees to light the night and measure the year if released (A1485). Siberia (Chuckchee): Jablow MAN 30-34.

A753.1.3.1* Moon (goddess, woman) cohabits with mortal man. Princess Kaguya, moon maiden, is loved by emperor, must return at full of moon. Japan: MacAlpine JAPANESE.

A753.1.4. Moon married to mortal woman. SEE ALSO: A762.1.

A753.1.4.0.1* Moon takes wife to live on moon. Her face is seen laughing there when moon is full. Her father taught the craft of pottery making to man. Indonesian: Deleeuw INDONESIAN 51-55.

A754. Moon kept in box. SEE ALSO: A758; A755.1.

A754.1.1.1* Moon falls into pit but is rescued by man. Moon comes to earth to see if evil things dominate in the dark of the moon. She is trapped in a bog but manages to throw back her hood so that light saves lost man in bog. Men return and free her. Great Britain: Jacobs MORE 110-117/Jacobs BURIED pb./; Wiggin FAIRY 118-119. Wales: Pugh TALES 55-65.

A755. Causes of moon's phases. SEE ALSO: A758.1; A717.2.

A755.1. Moon's phases caused by being put in box. (A754).

A755.1.1* Moon's phases are a silver hare in box. Hare peeps out a little more each night, then goes back and closes lid. Burma (Shan): Jablow MAN 23.

A755.2. Moon's phases caused by watcher's death. Moon is hung in tree and is tended by four men. As one dies it loses a quarter. Later it is united in the lower world. Grimm: Grimm BROTHERS 93- 96.

A755.4.0.1* Moon cut in two by sun: hence waxes and wanes. Sun cuts pieces off moon so he won't shine so brightly. Moon asks Sun to leave at least his backbone. Then Moon goes away to recover. Bushmen: Helfman BUSHMEN 48.

A755.8* Moon is child, youth, then old man (full moon). Man visits moon, sees all of this, and receives gifts. Papua New Guinea: Jablow MAN 41-43.

A758. Theft of moon. Moon is kept by a monster. It is stolen and brought to earth. SEE ALSO: A721.1 (sun); A1411 (light).

A758.1* Raven puts bear to sleep with stories. Fox steals moon from bear's bag and throws into sky. Bear calls "Stop moon. Let there be no moonlight." Fox calls "Sail on moon." For this reason some nights are dark and some light.

(A755). Canada, Native American (Kutchin): Jablow MAN 39-40.

A758.2* Boys release moon from pot in old woman's hut. They try to catch it, climbing tree. One grabs it, leaving dirty handmarks, but moon escapes to sky. Papua New Guinea: Jablow MAN 18.

A759.8* Why moon is cool, beautiful and loved. At feast moon hides food under her long fingernails for mother the Star. Mother curses her other children. Sun is to be hot and hated, Wind is to be hated. She blesses the Moon. S. India: Wiggin TALES 388-389.

A760 - A789. The stars.

A760. Creation and condition of the stars. SEE ALSO: A1412.5; A744.1; A625.2.2.1; A1174.1.1.; E741.2 (Soul in form of star).

A761. Ascend to stars. People or animals ascent to the sky and become stars.

A761.0.1* Man sees dancing stars on river with jewelry of teeth and shells. He startles them and they leap into the sky. New Guinea (Papua): Jablow MAN 99.

A762. Star descends as human being.

A762.1. Star-husband. Star takes mortal maiden as wife. (F56.1).

Aa: The Moon Husband. Girl weds moon, sees little men with one eye looking through hole in ground in sky country. She can see her home on earth through the hole. Moon husband takes her home for a visit. Tabu: letting her parents see husband (C32.1). Mother lights lamp, ash falls on him, he leaves (C916.1). Girl later flies off to sky with dog sled = Pleiades (A773). (cf. H1385.4). Type 425. Eskimo: Maher BLIND 139-158.

Ab: The Moon Husband. Woman weds moon, is homesick and sees home through hole in floor. Husband takes her home on sled. She bears son later. Eskimo: Caswell SHADOWS 19-23.

Ba: Star Husband, Spider-Man. Girl wishes to wed star. Bears son. Breaks tabu by digging up huge turnip and looking through hole to earth (F56.1). Spider-Man lets her down to earth. Son not to touch earth for 14 days, breaks tabu and becomes North Star (A774). The half-circle of stars to east of North Star is lodge of Spider-Man. Native American (Blackfoot): Cunningham TALKING 87-94.

Bb: Star Husband and the Two Ermines. Two sisters wish for star husbands, roll back stone in sky country and see through to home below. Allowed to return, they must not open eyes until hear songs of chickadee, red squirrel and chipmunk. Open eyes too soon and have only descended as far as tree tops. Former husband refuses to rescue. Star husband turns them to ermines so they can descend. Native American (Algonquin): Williams-Ellis ROUND 223-230.

Bc: Star Husband, son born. Two girls wish to wed stars. One climbs tree after porcupine, it carries her to star land. She breaks tabu and digs up plant (F56.1). Lets self down hole on grass ropes, falls and is killed. Son survives. Native American (Cheyenne): Field AMERICAN 13-31.

Bd: Star Husband, son becomes moon. Twin girls wish for star husbands, wed. One digs up forbidden camas root and descends on cedar rope to Skagit country. Rope dropped forms Big Rock Mountain near Mt. Vernon, Washington. Son born is later taken to sky and becomes moon (A747). She is small frog on moon's face (A751.3). Son of sister becomes Sun (A715.1). Native American (Skagit): Matson LEGENDS 63-74.

Be: Girl wishes for star husband. Bears son, Moon. Digs hole in sky and longs for earth. Lets self down by unraveling gown to make rope. Native American (Plains): Mobley STAR pb.

C: Porcupine lures girl up tree to sky-world. Weds as old man. She pulls up turnip and sees through to lower world. Lets self down on sinew rope. Buzzard and Hawk carry her rest of way. Native American (Arapaho-Caddo): Brown TEPEE 39-42.

A762.2. Mortal marries star-girl. SEE ALSO: F302.4.2.4.

A762.2.1* Rairu and the Star Maiden. Man thinks of evil things under roof, thus breaking tabu. Star wife leaves him. Brazil: Finger TALES 87-94/Frost LEGENDS 263-269/Dalgliesh EN-CHANTED 219-225/.

A762.2.2* Youngest of seven star princesses is sent to wed old beggar as reward. Must return to heaven after one year. Rich mandarin wants to swap wives with him. She advises to agree. On arrival at his home she turns house to lake, guests to frogs, she disappears. Frog's still croak, calling for promised feast. China: Carpenter TALES..CHINESE 190-197.

A763.3* Stars from objects thrown into sky. Animals decorating earth leave pile of shiny objects. Coyote thinks they are useless and tosses them into sky = stars. Native American (Hopi): Courlander PEOPLE 25-26.

A763.3.1* Badger carefully sets out stars forming constellations. Coyote impatiently flings rest into sky. Native American: Baker PARTNERS pb.

A764. Stars as pieces of the moon. SEE ALSO: J2271.2.2. (Stars made from old moon). Turkey: Downing HODJA 35. Iran: Shah MULLAH 74.

A764.0.1* Stars as pieces of the sun. SEE: A721.1.1; A736.1.2.3.

A770. Origin of particular stars.

A770.1* Seven Brothers and Sister. Brothers rescue sister from Double Teethed Bull. Moksois shoots arrow into sky and tree appears. They climb to heavens and become stars. Girl is head star. Little one on side is Moksois. Native American (Cheyenne): Haviland NORTH 40-43/Penney, Grace TALES OF THE CHEYENNES /.

A771.0.1* Origin of the Great Bear (Ursa Major). Bear (four stars of dipper) comes out of cave in spring and crosses sky, pursued by Robin, Chickadee with pot (star Alcor), and Moosebird (three stars in handle). These kill bear in fall and blood turns maples red (A2769.2). Hunters, pigeon, bluejay, big owl (Arcturus in Boötes), and the Acadian Owl, Saw-whet, also follow bear. Two give up chase in the fall. Native American (Micmac): Leach HOW 133-134.

A771.0.2* Seven helpers are Big Eater, Fast Runner, etc. (Type 513, F601.2De). They become seven stars of Great Bear. Chinese Mongolia: Jablow MAN 105-112.

A771.0.3* Summer birds are imprisoned to make winter last forever. Fisher stuffs wax in beak of crow sentinel and releases summer. Wendigo (crazed hunter) shoots fleeing fisher, hence bend in tail of big dipper. Fisher becomes Big Dipper. Native American (Chippewa): Leekley WORLD 76-78.

A771.0.4* Hunters chasing elk as sky is raised. Elk jumps onto sky and three hunters and dog follow = Big Dipper. Native American (Snohomish): Matson LEGENDS 90-93.

A772.1* Origin of Orion. Three men hunting bear on sled. Boy falls off and sled rises into sky after bear. Bear is star Betelgeuse in Orion. Three hunters are stars in Orion's belt, sledge is Orion's sword. Central Eskimo: Leach HOW 138-139.

A773. Origin of Pleiades. SEE ALSO: A762.1Aa.

A773.1. Pleiades a princess and six suitors among whom she could not choose. Denmark: Hatch MORE 79-87 (+F660.1Cb).

A773.2. Pleiades six repudiated wives. They have been cast out for apparent infidelity.

A773.2.1* Pleiades six repudiated wives. Cast out for eating onions. They ascend to heaven on ropes of eagledown. One has a daughter = Taurus. Native American (California, Mono): DeWit TALKING 117-121; Fisher CALIFORNIA 54-59.

A773.4 Pleiades seven illegitimate children.

A773.4.1* Seven brothers are not fed enough.

Biggest brother leads little brothers to the sky and they become Pleiades. Brazil (Amazon Indians): Jablow MAN 100-101. Native American (Blackfoot, Assiniboine): Hulpach AMERICAN 43-45.

A773.4.1.1* Boys play wheel and stick game so much that mother cooks the stone wheels of the game and serves with their corn. Indignant, they ask spirits to take them to the sky. Become the Pleiades. Native American (Cherokee): Leach HOW 136-137.

A773.4.1.2* Eight children dance despite warnings. Parents refuse them food and they rise lightheaded from hunger to the sky. One looks back and becomes a falling star. The seven remaining are the Pleiades. Native American (Onondaga): Cunningham TALKING 37-40.

A773.5. Pleiades from hunters marooned in sky after felling world-tree. Mayan (Popul Vuh): Courlander RIDE 243-249; Garner CAV..GOBLINS 4-10.

A773.8* Mother hen killed as feast for Phyain, protector of the Buddha. Her six chicks jump into the water after her. She is reborn with chicks as the Pleiades. Thai: Brockett BURMESE 1-4.

A773.9* Pleiad and the Star of Dawn are wronged brother and son lifted to sky. For tale description see: P253.2.0.1E. Greek: Wilson GREEK 11-20.

A774. Origin of the North Star. SEE: A762.1Ba.

A774.1* Constellation "Hand of the North Star." One finger is short since it was bitten off by a rattlesnake. Native American (Luiseño): Leach HOW 112.

A778. Origin of the Milky Way.

A778.3.1* Spinning maiden Chuc Nu weds shepherd Ngau Lang and they neglect duties. Are set on opposite shores of river (milky way). Once every year in the seventh moon all ravens go to heaven and form a bridge for them to cross and meet. The lovers weep in that month and rain falls. Vietnam: Graham BEGGAR 91-95; Sun LAND 39-41; Vo-Dinh TOAD 35-39. Japan: Sakade JAPANESE 77-83.

A778.3.2* Cowherd steals robes of one of seven bathing fairies. Spinning maid weds him, bears two children, then returns to heaven. His dying carabao tells to wrap self in hide and will ascend to heaven. May see once a year in the seventh moon. They reside on either side of the milky way. The Empress of Heaven drew a line with her silver hairpin between them = milky way. China: Bonnet CHINESE 89-96; Carpenter TALES..CHINESE 182-189 (Magpies form bridge; two lovers are stars, she with her two children); Cheney TALES 97-106; Lin MILKY 24-26 (she crosses river on golden hair-

pin); Manton FLYING 13-17.

A778.8 Milky Way is smoke (ashes). Bushmen: Helfman BUSHMEN 25 (ashes thrown into sky by girl). Africa: McDowell THIRD 23-24.

A778.11* Milky Way as bridal veil of Linou, daughter of God Uko. She awaited suitor, Northern Light, too long and father placed her in sky. She directs the migrations and nesting of the birds. Estonia: Jablow MAN 102-104.

A778.12* Man drives stolen wagon of straw into sky to hide and loses straw = milky way. Persia; Africa: Dobbs ONCE 51-53.

A778.13* Chief of Sharks thrown into sky by strong man Ka-ulu becomes milky way. Hawaii: Thompson HAWAIIAN..EARTH 40-44.

A779.4* Saynday puts hand in sky = five stars seen in summertime. Stories are not to be told when this constellation is visible. Native American: Marriott WINTER 83.

A780. The planets (comets, etc.).

A781.0.1* Origin of Venus (planet). Girl, La Belle Venus, with star on forehead is kept hidden in hut in forest. Mother sings to her to open door. Son of her employer follows and imitates voice. Uses medicine to soften coarse voice. Third try he succeeds (K311.3). They are wed but are sent to live on a mountain top so her star will not blind people. She can be seen walking in her garden in the evening with her husband. Haiti: Johnson HOW 47-54.

A781.1. Origin of the Morning Star. SEE ALSO: A712; A773.9.

A781.1.1* Morning Star's wife, Lynx, is hexed by hyena. Dawn's Heart (morning star) routes hyena. Drives spear into earth as strides across sky each A.M. Bushmen: Helfman BUSHMEN 36-39.

A781.1.2* Hunter pursuing ghost elk is taken to sky. Becomes Morning Star. Native American (Seneca): DeWit TALKING 9-12.

A781.2.1* Origin of Evening Star. Legba, messenger god, finds piece of fire fallen from sky. Agwe, sea god, surrounds it so it can't burn things. Ogoun, god of ironsmiths, forges chain to capture. Shango, god of lightning, fastens it to thunderbolt and hurls to city. Each claims it. Nananbouclou, their mother, hurls the piece of fire into the sky. It becomes Baiacou, the evening star. Haiti: Courlander PIECE 62-63.

A790. The heavenly lights.

A791. Origin of the rainbow.

A791.2.1* Rainbow as snake. During drought, small snake says to throw him into the sky and he will scratch rain and snow from the blue ice sky meadows. He becomes the rainbow. Native American (Shoshone): Hulpach AMERICAN 40-41.

A791.5.1* Man seeking lost love, Daughter of the Mist, turns to rainbow when old and bent. Is set in sky to meet her. Polynesia: Berry MAGIC 45-48.

A791.9.1* Origin of rainbow. Girl, wooed by both windbird and sun, turns to rainbow in mist of her mother's tears. Glows when the sun shines. South Africa (Hottentot): Arbuthnot ARBUTH-NOT ANTHOLOGY 326-327; Gruenberg MORE 121.

A791.11* Old Man Above asked by emissary spiders to give sign to men when rain is over. Spiders make ropes to four cardinal points and he imagines a giant colored fox tail as rainbow sign. Spiders are given their own rainbow in dew drops on their webs as a reward. Native American, California (Achomaloi): Fisher CALIFORNIA 60-73.

A791.12* After wolf and wicked men kill son of Rain and Creator, Rain sends Fire as rainbow around cloud. Fire flashes from rainbow killing wolf and bad people. Bushmen fear rainbow. Bushmen: Helfman BUSHMEN 26-29.

A791.13* Mkunga Mbura (rain being) leaves cloak behind when leaves = rainbow. East Africa: Heady WHEN 77-80.

A791.14* Hina's rainbow tapa hangs over Cave-of-the-Mists near Rainbow Falls on the Wailuku River. Hawaii: Thompson HAWAIIAN..EARTH 65-69.

A795.1* Origin of the Northern Lights (Aurora Borealis). Piece of light trapped in seal gut and given to former owner and daughter who move to north pole. +A1411.2. Eskimo: Maher BLIND 39-54.

A797. Origin of colors at sunrise and sunset. SEE: T554.12.2.; A1179.2 (Origin of dawn); A1128.3.

A800 - A899. The earth.

A800. Creation of the earth. SEE ALSO: A963.12.

A801.2* Raven beats wings until darkness condenses into land. Native American (Northwest): Martin NINE 6-18/ Martin RAVEN 11-15/, /Haviland NORTH 46-43/.

A810. Primeval water. In the beginning everything is covered with water.

A811.1. Earth originates from fish brought from bottom of sea. SEE: A955.8.

A812. Earth Diver. From a raft in the primeval sea, the creator sends down animals to try to bring up earth. After a number of animals have failed, one (often the muskrat) succeeds. The earth is made from the bit brought up.

A812.4* Duck dives from stump in primeval sea, on suggestion of Coyote, who is assistant to Eagle creator. Native American (Yokuts): Leach HOW 44.

A812.5* Crawfish dives for earth in primeval sea. Stirs up mud with tail so owner's of mud can't see. Buzzard stretches earth. Native American (Yuchi-Creek): Leach HOW 15-16.

A812.6* In the beginning nothing exists but a rock mountain. Ducks dive for earth, mudhen returns dead but with beak and ears full of mud. Coyote and eagle cause this to spread and form earth. Native American (California): Curry DOWN 9-21.

A812.7* Apa, Great Father, sends otter, muskrat and beaver to dive for earth. Only muskrat succeeds. Apa breathes on earth and forms world. Native American (Shoshone): Heady SAGE 15-19.

A812.8* Water-beetle dives for mud. It grows into earth. Native American (Cherokee): Bell JOHN 4-7.

A812.9* Manabozo sends beaver to dive for earth, beaver fails. Muskrat dives and brings up ball of earth. Manabozo puts ball on water and sets mouse on it to spin ball. Ball enlarges and more running animals are added. Native American (Chippewa): Leekley WORLD 35-49.

A814.8. Earth from lotus seed placed on water. Rahu descends sprouted lotus stalk and returns with handful of sand. Vishnu rolls sand into ball and places on water to become earth. Vishnu creates first man from earth, a Brahmin. Ceylon: Tooze WONDERFUL 32-35.

A815. Earth from turtle's back. Earth erected on back of a turtle floating in primeval water. California, Native American: Fisher STORIES 10-15 (California created on backs of six turtles).

A815.0.1* Earth rebuilt after flood with magic mold carried on back of tortoise. Dragon makes water course to drain off flood waters with his tail. China: Birch CHINESE 20-23.

A818* Other earth origins from primeval sea.

A818.1* Kite flies between primeval sea and sky. Goes nearer to sky. Jealous sea splashes against sky. Sky drops rocks and earth on sea = Phillippine Islands (A955). Philippines: Sechrist ONCE 3-7.

A818.2* Earth cooled by creator's breath and fire ordered inside. Animals sent to test crust and see if is firm yet. Upper Volta: Guirma TALES 1-15.

A820. Other means of creation of earth.

A822.2* Earth (island) from mud dripping from spear of culture hero, Izanagi = Japan. Through prayer other islands of Japan appear. Japan: MacAlpine JAPANESE 4-15.

A830. Creation of earth by creator. SEE ALSO: A963.12.

A840. Support of the earth.

A842. Atlas. A man supports the earth on his shoulders. SEE ALSO: L114.1A.

A842.3* Nicola Pesce. Ordered to dive and discover underpinnings of Sicily. Nicola Pesce finds three pillars, one almost eaten through by fire. Ordered to bring fire up, he cannot. He remains beneath the sea holding up the pillar until the earth is free from suffering. Sicily: Jagendorf PRICELESS 66-75; Toor GOLDEN 159-165.

A844.1. Earth rests on turtle's back. SEE: A815.

A850. Changes in the earth.

A852.1* Making the earth smaller. Nili makes the earth and Nipu makes the sky (A701). The earth is too big and must be squeezed up to fit. Thus mountains are created. (A960). India (Khowa, Bugun): Leach HOW 17.

A853. Making the earth larger. Gradually extended during the creation. See references to A812 in which this idea is always involved.

A900 - A999. Topographical features
of the earth.

A910 - A949. Water features.

A910. Origin of water features--general. SEE: A1110.

A913. Origin of tides.

A913.5* Giant crab comes out of hole and ocean pours into hole = ebb tide. When he crawls back into hole = full tide. Malay: Leach HOW 27. Philippines: Sechrist ONCE 75-78.

A913.6* Man sits on hole in ocean. Promises to get up twice a day and let tides go into hole = ebb. Native American (Tahltan): Leach HOW 25-27.

A920. Origin of the seas.

A920.1.0.1. Origin of particular lake. SEE: F944.1A.

A920.1.0.1.1* Coyote puts paw into newly formed spreading earth = Coyote Lake. His foot slips into ocean while running up coast = San Francisco Bay. Native American (California): Curry

DOWN 9-21.

A920.1.2. Lakes from digging of primeval ox. Ashanti: Courlander COW-TAIL 113-118 (Lake Bouro).

A920.1.8. Lake bursts forth to drown impious people. SEE: F944.1A.

A920.1.10.1* Lakes as footprints of Ojje Ben Onogh. Ethiopia: Courlander FIRE 103-104.

A920.1.17* Origin: Lake of Balaton. Cruel queen calls down lake on all because of jealousy of fair shepherdess with golden goats. Hungary: Baker TALKING 191-198.

A920.1.18* Origin of Lake Polaman. Man pursued throws fish from basket to stop pursuers (bull, rescues lady from funeral pyre..tigers..bats). Basket opens and spring flows forth to form lake filled with Sacred Fish. Indonesian: De Leeuw INDONESIAN 140-150.

A924.5* Ocean created when Brer Rabbit cuts string holding banks of river together. U.S. Black: Harris COMPLETE; Harris NIGHTS 334-338.

A930. Origin of streams.

A934. Various origins of rivers. SEE: A2433.7.2.

A934.1. Rivers from digging of primeval ox (bull). Ashanti: Courlander COW-TAIL 113-118.

A934.13* Origin of rivers. From pond into which crab's head is thrown. Eastern Nigeria (Ikom): Arnott AFRICAN 35-39.

A934.14* Hot black hill arises from mountainside. Priest says it is the devil's knee and exorcises it. Pool left where knee withdrew. River Cupatizo changes course and flows in two channels now. Mexico: Ross IN 162-174.

A934.15* Origin Columbia River. Struggles of Coyote with monster Ilswetsix. Nez Percé: Matson LEGENDS 64-69.

A934.16* Origin Snake River. Ejupa, Coyote, drops basket of fish in water. Water runs off forming snake river. Native American (Shoshone): Heady SAGE 23-26.

A934.17* Origin River Emajogi. Vanaisa, creator, asks animals to die. Estonia: Maas MOON 44-46.

A934.18* Origin River Bee, River Catoon. Drawn by Sartak-Pai and son Adoochee with forefingers. Altai: Deutsch TALES 17-27.

A935. Origin of falls (cataracts).

A935.1* Origin Idaho Falls, American Falls, Twin Falls, Shoshone Falls. Dams thrown up by Coyote to stop flow of Snake River. Native

American (Shoshone): Heady SAGE 20-23.

A935.2* Pontius Pilate when thrown into Tiber and Thone causes storms. Put in small lake on mountain top causes water to run over into larger lake at bottom. Switzerland (German): Duvoisin THREE 138-145.

A935.3* Origin of Hawili Falls. Hawili, Goddess of the Forest, calls on farmer to vow his love for her. He does so and a falls with seven basins appears on the spot. The water murmurs her voice. Philippines: Robertson FAIRY.. PHILIPPINES 97-105.

A935.4* Origin Tequedama Falls. Columbia (Chibcha): Jagendorf KING 81-83.

A939* Origin of characteristics of streams and waterfalls.

A939.1* Why the river Metsch runs white. Flour of wheat thrown into river by farmers to keep prices up. Switzerland (German): Duvoisin THREE 230-233.

A939.2* Herdsman who cheated others is condemned to churn the waters of the Navigance. Why waters turn white each year. Switzerland (French): Duvoisin THREE 89-93.

A939.3* Father kills daughter eloping with son of enemy. Bamboo shoots grow from spot where cut, blood flows from them and turns river red. Giant black cat chases father into river and flood destroys. Sight of cat now foretells coming flood. Stream in Cotabato runs blood-red since then. Philippines: Robertson FAIRY.. PHILIPPINES 81-90.

A939.4* Volga and Vazouza. Vazouza wakes first in spring and rushes off to sea. Volga wakes more slowly but then roars angrily after her. She lets him take her to the sea. Russia: Ransom OLD 321-323.

A940. Origin of other bodies of water.

A941. Origin of springs. SEE ALSO: A2681.15.

A941.0.2* Origin of the Fountain of Arethusa. Huntress Arethusa flees river god Alpheus. Diana makes tunnel under ocean so Arethusa can escape to Island of Ortygia. Alpheus pursues and their waters mingle in the fountain. Sicily: Toor GOLDEN 123-125.

A941.5.9* (Kirtley) Origin of springs: god steals water container and flies. His victims see him and throw a rock which hits the container. The water which drips out becomes a series of springs. He is sometimes tickled to make him spill the water. Samoa (Apolima, Monono): Holding SKY 111-124.

A941.5.9.1* Water dripping from bowl as Yehl (Raven) flies back after stealing from Kanukh becomes lakes and springs. +A1111.2. Native

American (Tlingit): Hardendorff JUST 121-126; Martin NINE 6-18/Martin RAVEN 11-15/, /Haviland NORTH 40-43/.

A943* Origin of polar ice cap. Raven fixes earth so it won't tip by putting pile of ice across northern end. Native American (Tahltan): Leach HOW 25-27.

A950 - A999. Land features.

A950. Origin of the land.

A955. Origin of islands. SEE ALSO: A817.1.

A955.0.1.1* Islands created by order of deity. Particular island created. Cebu created and peopled by sun god for his son Lupa. Philippines: Sechrist ONCE 107-109.

A955.3.1.1* Origin of an island's shape. Manabozo and companion walk around island and it grows as they walk. Native American (Chippewa): Leekley WORLD 111-117.

A955.3.1.2* Giant Lizard of Nimple cuts Yap into four pieces while thrashing in death throes. Yap: Courlander TIGER'S 140-143.

A955.8. Island fished up by demigod (hero). Maui uses magic fish hook, baited with own blood from nosebleed, to fish up island (New Zealand). Hooks doorway of Tonga Nui, land of sea-god Tangaroa. His four brothers argue over the new land and cut it up = origin of inlets. mountains, valleys, islands. New Zealand: Berry MAGIC 81-88. New Zealand (Maori): Colum LEGENDS 38-64; Williams-Ellis ROUND 242-252. Hawaii: Courlander RIDE 14-19; Thompson HAWAIIAN..TRICKSTER 66-71 (brothers break tabu and look back, island falls back into sea); Williams SURPRISING 21. Polynesia: Courlander TIGER'S 132-139.

A955.8.1* Maui fishes up islands. Pushes up sky with shoulders to let sunlight in. God Tangaloa throws down mountainous islands and plants with vines. Plucks pieces of vine and leaves in sun, from decayed vines comes worm = first animal. Maui in bird form pecks worm in half = first men. Canoe full of wives sent later by Gods. Tonga/Samoa: Gittins TALES 50-51.

A955.10.1* Islands from transformed object or person. God, Bathala, sends storm and three king suitors of Princess Maring are lost during sailing race. Three islands, Tres Reyes, appear. Princess Maring can now wed lover Duque. They rule isle of Marinduque. Philippines: Robertson FAIRY..PHILIPPINES 33-41.

A955.10.2* Origin of island from exploding serpent killed by raven. Eskimo: Melzack RAVEN 15-24.

A955.10.3* Origin of Taiwan. Taiwan is cut off tail of dragon father. Mountain range is little dragon under tail. Father is Himalya mountains. Ragged seacoast of China is where baby dragons nipped sleeping father to waken him. Young dragons still playing in Taiwan Straits cause weather. Taiwan: Cheney TALES 13-16.

A955.13* Origin of island's characteristics. Princess foretold to be carried off by mandril. She is sent to an island to escape. The island is called after her, Sicilia. It takes on her own radiance. Sicily: Toor CARNATION 137-142.

A956. Origin of peninsulas.

A956.1* Origin of irregular coastline from Alaska to Puget Sound. Pathasos harpoons hair seal carved of cedar and filled with evil spirits. It drags him to Alaska. Returning home he hurls harpoon at shore to find way causing landslides and coastal irregularities. Native American (Skagit/Swinomish): Matson LEGENDS 105-111.

A957. Origin of desert.

A957.1* Origin of particular desert spot. He who beats Efu, the hunchback, on hump is to have rain on his farm. Ananse beats until he kills Efu. Nyankopon, the Almighty, allows no rain to fall on Ananse's farm ever again. West Africa: Appiah ANANSE 113-122.

A960. Creation of mountains (hills). SEE ALSO: A852.1.

A961. Mountains from primeval animal. SEE ALSO: A815.

A961.1. Hills from flapping of primeval bird. Hills and valleys are formed from the flapping of a giant turkey-buzzard when the earth is still plastic. Native American (Yuchi/Creek): Leach HOW 15-16. Native American (Cherokee): Bell JOHN 4-7. Native American (Papago/Pima): Baker AT 1-6.

A961.1.1* Impatient Coyote runs up and down earth as it dries, throwing up mountain ranges in his footprints. Origin of Sierra Nevada Mountains and Coastal Range. Khotoi, the Raven, sent to dry earth by flapping wings, flaps too hard and beats Coastal Range down. Native American (California): Curry DOWN 9-21.

A961.2. Mountains from hacked up fish drawn from bottom of primeval water. Earth originates from a fish drawn from the water. It is hacked up and made to form mountains. SEE: A955.8.

A962. Mountains (hills) from ancient activities of god (hero).

A962.0.1.1* Raja Rahit taught pottery craft by Kajangka, ruler of moon. Covers mountain tops with water jars, creating Mt. Merbabu. Indonesia (Dyak): De Leeuw INDONESIAN 51-55.

A962.0.1.2* Dewi Jurangga, giant's daughter, wants to wed rakshasa. He is set task to create sea of sand in one night. Giant crows to make

cock crow before R. is finished. R. throws his batok (coconut shell scraper) upside down = Mt. Batok. Dewi turns into Mt. Kembang (lovely mt.), R. turns into Mt. Segarawedi. Her giant father sits in Mt. Smeru smoking. Indonesia: De Leeuw INDONESIAN 45-50.

A962.0.1.3* Chief of Pillco peoples calls on sun-god Inti to wed his daughter. Inti takes Cari-Huayti to heavens and turns her three suitors to stone = Mt. Rondos, Mt. Maramba and Mt. Paucarbamba. City of Huanuco derives name from Inti's call of "Huanucuy" ("Live no more on earth") as he carried Cari-Huayti off. Inca: Carpenter SOUTH 123-128.

A962.1. Mountains from parts of deity's (hero's) body.

A962.1.1* Ixtlaccihuatl (Sleeping Lady) and Popocatepetl (Smoking Mountain) are banished lovers, a Toltec princess and Chichimec prince, turned into mountains. Mexico: Jagendorf KING 181-186; Ross IN 62-74.

A962.1.2* Daughter of Teutli (mountain) is turned to mountain with her lover by father. She is Malintzin (Sleeping Lady). He is Tepotazlan (Smoking Mountain). Mexico: Brenner BOY 23-26.

A962.1.3* The five daughters of Kintail. Five elder daughters wait forever for suitors which husbands of youngest two girls promised would come for them from Ireland. Turned to mountains watching sea at head of Loch Duich by Isle of Skye. Scotland: Finlay TATTERCOATS 15-23.

A962.5.1* Princess of heaven drops ring to earth. Servant sent to retrieve it rakes fingers in mud searching, thus forming mountains and rivers. Korea: Kim STORY 17-18.

A963. Mountains from stones (soil, sand) dropped or thrown.

A963.10* Hanomat tears open bag of sand in anger and Mt. Karang and Mt. Pulosari are formed. Indonesia: De Leeuw INDONESIAN 104-108.

A963.11* Origin of mountains: pieces of rock tossed when great bull is smashing rock. Ashanti: Courlander COW-TAIL 113-118.

A963.12* Old-Man-Above throws snow through hole in sky to make Mt. Shasta. Creates trees, blows on leaves to make birds, breaks stick and small end = fish, middle = animals, large = grizzly bear (A830). Old-Man-Above runs down mountainside after daughter, melting snow in his speed. Snow never sticks to that place since then. Native American (Shasta): Fisher STORIES 24-35.

A963.13* Thunar smashes Ubbink's oven and U. must take bread to Jolink's house to bake. Gets shoes full of sand en route and dumps out shoes = two hills. Netherlands: Spicer THIRTEEN

MONSTERS 93-100.

A963.14* Giants catch girl. She escapes, causing Ellert to fall and die. His brother, Brammert, blows sand covering the village. Origin of Ellert's field and Brammert's Heap. Netherlands (Drenthe): Spicer THIRTEEN MONSTERS 19-31.

A966. Origin of volcanoes. SEE ALSO: A969.1.

A966.1* Origin of Mount Maron. Gat Malayo, foreign lover, kills wooer, Datu Buhawen. She is killed in turn and maid, Daragang Magayon, kills self. Earth rises into volcano over burial spot = Mount Maron. Philippines: Robertson FAIRY..PHILIPPINES 107-115.

A966.2* Why Mt. Fuji smokes. Smoke is carrying message from emperor to Moon Maiden. Japan: McAlpine JAPANESE 185-187.

A966.3* Hanomat compelled to snip tops off Mt. Karang which reaches to heaven and create group of small volcanoes from the thirds snipped off. Indonesian (Baduwis): De Leeuw INDONESIAN 104-108.

A968. Origin of cliffs.

A968.2. Cliff from lover's leap. Lovers in dispair throw themselves from a high place. This becomes a cliff.

A968.2.1* Edmond is to wed Calixte if can climb cliff carrying her. He succeeds but dies of exhaustion. She leaps from cliff holding his body. Cliff named La Cote des Deux Amants, on River Andelle in Normandy. France: Picard FRENCH 129-137.

A968.2.2* Chinese General's son Trong Thuy weds Ny Chau, daughter of Vietnamese emperor. Betrays father. Emperor flees with daughter. Golden Tortoise, Kim Qui, tells him daughter betrayed. He kills her and leaps into the sea. Trong Thuy, following, finds her body and leaps from the cliff. Vietnam: Robertson FAIRY 66-74.

A968.2.3* Lovers leap into pool at Natset on Chindwin River. Burma: Keeley CITY 147-159.

A968.2.4* Father of girl wed to crocodile man kills son-in-law. Daughter leaps after body. Surinam (Carib): Carpenter SOUTH 18-26.

A969. Creation of mountains and hills--miscelaneous.

A969.1.1* Mountain from buried giant. Oba's lazy son Oloquitur refuses to make mountains needed by Panamanians. Oba throws him into the earth and he sinks under soft ground. His walking about beneath the earth as he tries to find a way out causes mountain ranges. Where he sits down = hills. He still is crawling about = earthquakes (A1145.1). When he roars = volcanoes (A966). Panama (Cuna): Barlow LATIN 97-103.

A969.8.1* Origin of crevasse. Gorge on Oahu, Valley of the Leaky Canoe, place where soldiers drag canoe up cliff in pursuit of Kupua. Hawaii: Thompson HAWAIIAN..EARTH 45-52.

A969.10* Animals sing mountains up. Black and white Hactcins (Holy Ones) have created mountains, animals sing them up. Origin: San Juan Mountains, Colorado. Native American (Jicarilla Apache): Leach HOW 23-24.

A969.11* Origin of characteristics of mountains and hills.

A969.11.1* Why hill in Singapore is called Red Hill. Boy suggested fence of banana trunks to stop attacking swordfish. The swordfish impaled themselves on the fence. King had this wise boy killed. The earth of this hill turned blood red. Singapore: Asian FOLK I 37-40.

A969.11.2* Why Palermo's hills are golden. Sea gods give golden ransom required by King of Tunis to beautiful weaver lass so that she can redeem self. Radiance of the ransom tints hills of Palermo = La Conca D'Oro. Italy (Palermo): Toor GOLDEN 145-150.

A969.11.3* Why the Dolomites are white. Prince of the Dolomites weds Princess of the Moon. The earth is too gloomy for her so dwarfs weave webs of moonlight to cover the peaks. Italy: Toor CARNATION 179-190.

A969.12* Origin of butte. Children pursued by bear pray and ground raises with them forming butte. Bear claws sides. Fleecy, white clouds above butte are their spirits (A1133.6). Thunder is bear growling (A1142.11). Native American (Lakota): Yellow Robe TOKWEYA 24-30.

A969.13* Origin of mountains from friendship between earth and sky. Part of earth wants to stay near to sky = mountains. Tanzania: Luzzatto LONG 8-19.

A970. Origin of rocks and stones.

A972.0.1* Indentations on rocks from prints left by man. Pedro Alvarado leaps after Indian girl fleeing him by leap into stream. She is swept away. His disappointment leaves heavy footprints in the stone as he leaves. El Salvador: Jagendorf KING 119-121.

A974. Rocks from transformation of people to stone.

A974.0.1* Jealous first wife refuses to follow husband and second wife. She turns to stone = Standing Rock at Fort Chase, North Dakota. Native American (Sioux): Matson LEGENDS 55-58.

A974.0.2* Woman refuses all suitors, turns to

stone from legs up. Then calls that she will wed anyone, but men ignore her and she turns completely to stone. Eskimo: Field ESKIMO 64-66.

A974.0.3* Seven brothers leave small brother behind. He is adopted by a giant Lo'lhiliu. Brothers come seeking him and behave rudely. Giant lifts them and their canoe onto cliff and turns them to stone. Native American (Chuckee): Newell RESCUE 107-118.

A974.0.4* Certain stones are Cavillaca and her son, turned to stone by High God as they plunge into the sea. Peru (Andean): Carpenter LATIN 50-56.

A974.0.5* Stone on mountain is Sapa Nusta, poised to protect her shepherd lover. Inca: Carpenter SOUTH 129-136.

A974.0.6* Cruel Knight of Waldenburg gives stone to hungry woman. Cursed to turn to stone. Switzerland (German): Duvoisin THREE 208-213.

A974.0.7* Heart of slain monster Iltswetsix turned to stone. Rock in Northern Idaho. Native American (Nez Percé): Matson LEGENDS 64-69.

A974.0.8* Old Man of the Mountains gives tub of butter as large as church, daily, to man who spares chamois. Chamois is killed. Old Man of the Mountains turns cows to stone, butter tub to rock = Hasellehn Peak. Switzerland (German): Duvoisin THREE 190-195.

A974.0.9* God turns his demon horse to stone in field near Shilin. Horse had ravaged rice fields nightly until young hero killed it. Taiwan: Cheney TALES 107-114.

A975.1.2* Why stones do not grow. God asks what each thing wishes to do. Stones don't want to do anything. God curses them never to grow. Cracks them with his voice. They will be worn away by wind and water. Serbia: Spicer LONG 70-72.

A977. Origin of particular stones or groups of stones.

A977.1.1* Saints throw stones. Saint Keverne throws stones after Saint Just, who has stolen his chalice. Explanation of why stones from Crouza Downs lie scattered at a distance. Cornwall: Manning-Sanders PETER 120-124.

A977.5. Origin of particular rock.

A977.5.0.1* Rock is otter transformed by Itsayaya (Coyote) for molesting Salmon. Family of spotted dogs who chase deer are transformed into the Hoonee rock by Coyote. Native American (Nez Percé): Heady TALES 57-61.

A977.5.0.2* Rock is frog transformed by Coyote for leaving her husband, skunk, to date lizard. Native American (Nez Percé): Heady TALES 95-

100.

A977.5.0.3* Rocks on Koos-koos-ki River are fishnet and bear on either side of river transformed by Coyote. Bear reminded fishing Coyote that he was missing the buffalo hunt and angered him. Native American (Nez Percé): Heady TALES 29-31.

A977.5.0.4* Two stones in Koos-koos-ki River are yellow jackets and ants fighting over picnic spot. Transformed by Coyote. Native American (Nez Percé): Heady TALES 32-34.

A977.5.0.5* Cotopaxi volcano spews out huge rock shaped like head of Atahualpa after this Inca chief has been killed by Pizarro. Ecuador: Jagendorf KING 113-116.

A978. Origin of minerals.

A978.3.1* Origin of emeralds. Animals fleeing man consume forests and Tree Goddess asks God Ches to preserve her forest. He refuses and she turns the crystals of a cave green as her forest. In anger Ches bursts the cave apart, scattering emeralds all over the world. Columbia (Esmeralda Indians): Barlow LATIN 82-88.

A978.4* Origin of gold and silver. Tears of sun and moon. (A736.1.3.1). Thai: Carpenter ELEPHANT'S 212-219.

A978.5* Origin of salt. Peasant sees phoenix on mound of earth and takes earth to king thinking it treasure. He is beheaded but drops of moisture from the basket accidentally fall into the king's soup. Thus salt is discovered. China: Wyndham TALES..CHINA 9-13.

A979.2* Origin of green Amazon stones which heal and bring luck. Received from Goddess of Moon Mirror Lake during men's annual visit to the Amazons (female tribe). Brazil: Carpenter SOUTH 100-107.

A980. Origin of particular places.

A982* Origin of caves.

A982.1* Origin of Wind Cave. Gift of Giant White Buffalo. Native American (Oglala Sioux): Matson LEGENDS 39-42.

A983. Origin of valleys or hollows.

A983.1* Hollow where thrown bull landed near Batooda. Ashanti: Courlander COW 113-118.

A983.2* Pitch lake formed when Great Spirit covers valley with tar. Indians had slaughtered hummingbirds which were the souls of the dead. Bones still rise from tar lake. Trinidad (Chayma): Jagendorf KING 249-251.

A983.3* Origin of Hole of the Burgundians. Place where Burgundians were buried after defeat of Charles the Bold, Duke of Burgundy, by the

Swiss at Morat. Swiss (French): Duvoisin
THREE 122-125.

A999. Origin of place names.

A999.1* How Celebes got its name. Portuguese
ask blacksmith making kris the name of the island. He thinks they ask name of kris and replies "Sele basi." Indonesia: Courlander
KANTCHIL'S 40-41.

A999.2* Origin of street name. Calle de la Mach-
incuepa. Proud girl is forced to turn somersaults in the plaza in order to learn to laugh at
herself. Mexico: Ross IN 50-61.

A1000 - A1099. World calamities
and renewals.

A1000. World catastrophe.

A1002. Doomsday.

A1002.2.5* Disappearance of Big Dipper would indicate end of the world. Native American
(Tahltan): Leach HOW 135.

A1009.4* At end of world Beaver, Keeper of the
World, will be instructed by Old One to gnaw
through pole on which earth spins and which
fastens this world to upper world. Native American (Thompson Indians): Newell RESCUE 81-
84.

A1010. Deluge. Innundation of whole world or
section. SEE ALSO SUBJECT INDEX: FLOOD;
SEE ALSO: A1414.7.2.1; W154.8.5. Philippines
(Igorot): Sechrist ONCE 8-11. Philippines
(Tinguian): Sechrist ONCE 11-12.

A1011.1.1* Flood partially caused by breaking
forth of springs. Man covers springs with basket. Monkey Irrawaka removes it and springs
flood world. Men and animals climb palms on
highest hill, rains for nine days, man drops
coconut each day. Tenth day he hears no
splash. Carib: Sherlock WEST 21-26.

A1011.2.1* Flood caused by rising of river.
Bochica's wife Chia causes Funza River to flood
and destroy all. Columbia (Chibcha): Jagendorf KING 81-83.

A1011.2.2* Niang-Tzu dreams flood comes when
eyes of two stone temple lions turn red. Tricksters paint eyes red. She flees. Flood comes.
Only she and son are saved. China: Wyndham
FOLK..CHINA 73-97; Wyndham TALES..CHINA
52-54 (origin Liang-Ti lake).

A1014* Flood from slain monster. Manabozo slays
Pichou. Flood flows from cave. Manabozo and
animals escape on raft. M. calls to birch tree
to grow taller to save little bear in water. Native American (Chippewa): Leekley WORLD
35-49.

A1015. Flood caused by gods or other superior

beings. SEE ALSO: A1411.2.1.

A1015.0.1* The Yellow Emperor, Ruler of Heaven,
sends Kung-Kung, Spirit of Water, with a flood.
China: Birch CHINESE 20-33.

A1016.1. Flood from animals boring into ground
(turtles, crawfish, etc.). U.S. Black: Harris
COMPLETE 14-17; Harris SONGS 20-23.

A1018.4* Flood as punishment. People sing all
night, children all day. Chief of Heavens,
irate at lose of sleep, sends flood. People escape in canoes to mountain tops. Eagles shed
feathers on waters as sign of peace. Covered
with down, the waters subside. Eskimo: Caswell SHADOW 88-95.

A1020. Escape from deluge.

A1021. Deluge: escape in boat (ark). Bible:
Bollinger NOAH pb; Singer WHY pb; Emberley
ONE pb.

A1021.0.0.1* Tiny fish saved by Manu grows bigger than large vessels. Put in Ocean it tells
Manu to build an ark, taking seven sages and
seeds from all plants. Flood occurs. Giant fish,
now grown, pulls ark to Himalayan peaks. Fish
reveals self as Vishnu, instructs Manu to re-
create animals, men and gods. India: Reed
TALKATIVE 79-82.

A1021.0.7* Deluge: escape in clay jar. Coyote
dreams of flood, tells dream so that it comes
true. Eetoi and animals escape in clay jar. Coyote floats in Eetoi's flute, Earth Magician floats
on his magic stick. Birds wing the waters down
before they reach the sky. Native American
(Pima): Baker AT 8-15.

A1024.1* People waiting in underworld after flood
are led out by Mother-Corn. Badger, mouse,
and mole aid in digging to surface. Kingfisher
pecks down bridge for people to cross, and
wings trees to one side, loon parts waters of
lake. Dog protects people from whirlwind and
vows to guard always. Mother-Corn turns to
cedar tree. Native American (Arikara): Brown
TEPEE 65-70.

A1100 - A1199. Establishment of
natural order.

A1110. Establishment of present order: waters.
SEE ALSO: A910.

A1111. Impounded water. Water is kept by monster so that mankind cannot use it. A hero defeats the monster and releases the water.

A1111.1* Water in chest kept by family. They
fear to open the chest. Stranger releases. A
second chest contains fire (A1414.7.4). Native
American (Thompson River): Newell RESCUE
91-98.

A1111.2* Yehl (raven) steals water from Kanukh's

well. +A941.5.9.1. Native American (Tlingit): Hardendorff JUST 121-126; Martin NINE 6-18/ Martin RAVEN 11-15/, /Haviland NORTH 40-43/.

A1115.2. Why the sea is salt: magic salt mill keeps grinding salt. Type 565. SEE: D1651.3.1 (Magic mill obeys only master).

A1115.2.1* Magic mortar. Old man advises to take rice cakes to shrine and make dwarfs give stone mortar as reward. Magic mortar (D1262) produces anything when turned to right. Stops if turned to left. Younger brother steals mortar in boat. Makes salt, cannot stop, boat sinks. Japan: Uchida MAGIC 32-41.

A1115.4* Salt falls from broken bridge. Sipgnet, Goddess of the Dark, asks Ang-ngalo, first man, who is also a giant, to build white castle for her. He builds bamboo bridges over ocean and has men carry salt bricks over from Salt Kingdom of Asin. The ocean dislikes this commotion and wrecks the bridges. The salt falls into the sea. Philippines (Ilocano): Sechrist ONCE 17-19.

A1116. Origin of sea-waves. SEE ALSO: A913 (Tides).

A1116.2* Mrs. Water and Mrs. Wind fight over children of Wind. Water tries to drown them. Whitecaps are children calling to their mother Wind. U.S. Black: Lester KNEE 21-24.

A1120. Establishment of present order: winds.

A1122.3.1* Wind loses son and refuses to blow for seven years in grief. Cock tells him that he, cock, loses scores of children daily but remains merry. Wind laughs and blows once more. Polish: Borski GOOD 46; Zajdler POLISH 79.

A1122.4.1* Wind comes through holes in sky when gut covering is cut. Little wooden boy carved by old couple comes to life, whistles and cuts holes letting in winds through gut sky cover. Eskimo (Bering Strait): Cothran MAGIC 13-17.

A1122.5* Wind kept in bag in sky (C322.1). Young man snared and kept in bag on earth until promised not to hurt his people, then returned to bag in sky. Native American (Thompson River): Cunningham TALKING 30-32; De-Wit TALKING 161-168.

A1124 (Kirtley). Winds kept in calabash. SEE ALSO: C322.1.

A1124.1* Maui borrows wind from small calabash to fly kite. Next day he calls out winds from large calabash against the order of the Keeper-of-the-Winds. Storm follows. Maui later learns to forecast the weather by flying a kite and noting the wind directions. Hawaii: Thompson HAWAIIAN..EARTH 70-75.

A1128.3* Regulation of winds. Boy traps wind in blanket. Makes it promise to give warning... red sky in morning (A1147.1) when going to

blow. Eskimo (Thompson River): Newell RESCUE 119-124.

A1129.2.1* Origin of monsoon. Spirit of Sea and Spirit of Mountain woo Ni Nuon. Mt. Spirit wins but sea tries again each year = monsoon. Vietnam: Robertson FAIRY 60-65.

A1129.4* Origin of particular wind. Coyote dances and calls up the Chinook, a warm west wind. Native American (Nez Percé): Heady TALES 62-66.

A1130. Establishment of present order: weather phenomena. SEE ALSO: A797 (Rainbow); A2426.4.1.2.1 (Rain for frogs).

A1131.1. Rain from tears. SEE ALSO: A1231.2.

A1131.1.0.1* Courting snake and beaver rejected by frog maidens. Beaver's tears bring rain causing flood. Frog maids are whirled to moon (A751.3.1.1). Native American (Lillooet): Leach HOW 31-33.

A1133. Origin of clouds (cf. A705.1).

A1133.5* Snake attacks spinning spider maiden and sun pulls her to sky by thread to rescue. She now spins fleecy clouds for sun. +B652.2. Japan: Sakade JAPANESE 59-65.

A1133.6* White clouds are children's spirits, chased by bear. +A969.12. Native American (Lakota): Yellow Robe TONWEYA 24-30.

A1134. Origin of mist (fog).

A1134.1* Support of the Sun swims in the Pacific Ocean and dries clothes over fire lit by her brother the Sun as he sets. Steam makes the fog. Native American (Nez Percé): Heady TALES 21-24.

A1134.2* Bear (mountain spirit) takes sleeping man for dead and carries him home. Man kills bear, is pursued by bear's wife. He calls mountains to rise, stream to overflow (D672). She crosses mountains, tries to drink stream dry and bursts (G522.1). Origin fog. Eskimo: Hardendorff JUST 56-57; Caswell SHADOWS 68-71.

A1134.3* Origin of mist. Great Spirit punishes men quarreling while smoking the peace pipe. He drops smoke over mountains as a reminder and turns these quarrelsome offenders into Indian Pipe plants (A2667). Native American (Cherokee): Bell JOHN 78-80/ Cathon PERHAPS 133-134/.

A1135.2.1. Origin of snow. Snow from feathers or clothes of a witch (Frau Holle). SEE: Q2.1.2Aa (Mother Holle).

A1141. Origin of lightning.

A1141.2.1* Thunder borrows Lynx's sword at dance and does not return. Dances, flashing sword and beating drum in sky. India (Khasis): Jablow MAN 93-96.

A1141.8.1* Lightning is sparks from millstone made from old moon. SEE: J2271.1.1.

A1141.8.2* Lightning is ram. Thunder his mother, ewe, who calls after him to behave. E. Nigeria (Ibibio): Arnott AFRICAN 32-34.

A1141.8.3* Mosquito tells thunder he gets blood from tree tops. Thunder shoots at tree tops. Native American (Thompson Indians): Newell RESCUE 69-74.

A1141.8.4* Swen-Naba, King of Warlocks. People must become slaves to get food from warlocks who turn selves to fireballs and burn up rains every year. Old man sheltering in Wend-Waogha's house is treated kindly, causes splinter of kindling to stick in thigh of W's wife, son and daughter born from swelling. When grown, king plans to wed Poko and execute Raogo. They flee with sword given by old man. Old man sits in river bathing and asks them to scrub his back. Poko stops to do so, hole appears in back and magic peanut shell, piece of wood, stone, egg and white cloth are taken out. Peanut shell = canoe to cross river. Thrown behind wood (D672) becomes forest, stone = mountain, egg = lake. Warlocks pursue and R. and P. ascend into sky. Raogo's voice is thunder, after rumble is her gentle scolding. Lightning is R's sword. After rain Poko waves the white cloth and sun colors it = rainbow. Upper Volta: Guirma TALES 85-99.

A1142. Origin of thunder.

A1142.3.1* Thunder is caught in tree in Chaco. He is helped back into sky by a man who builds a green smoke fire under the tree at Thunder's direction. Argentina (Toba): Jablow MAN 97-98.

A1142.3.2* Brother and sister who are deserted consider becoming animals. Decide to become Lightning and Thunder. She strikes flint for lightning. He shakes dried carabou hide = thunder. Eskimo: Field ESKIMO 18-20; Maher BLIND 99-105.

A1142.6.1.1* Hail, Lightning, Rain, Thunder seen when Thunder and his daughters fight. Native American (California): Curry DOWN 68-79.

A1142.9.0.1* Thunder made by giants fighting. Strong man boasting of strength meets baby who can pull him from well. Wife hides him from her giant husband. Man escapes pursued by giant. Men met as he flees who are hoeing, planting, etc. refuse to aid. Another giant fights for him. They are fighting still. Moral: there is always someone stronger than you are. Africa: Arnott AFRICAN 43-55.

A1142.10* Thunder beats drum. SEE: A1142.2.1.

A1142.11* Thunder is bear growling. +A969.12.

Native American (Lakota): Yellow Robe TONWEYA 24-30.

A1145. Cause of earthquakes. SEE ALSO: A1515.5.

A1145.1. Earthquakes from movements of subterranean monster. Panama (Cuna): Barlow LATIN 97-103 (A969.1.1).

A1145.2.1* Earthquakes when six turtles bearing earth on backs move. Native American (California): Fisher STORIES 10-15.

A1145.3* Earthquakes when strong man holding up world shifts positions. Eskimo: Caswell SHADOWS 96-106.

A1145.4* Pillar of red copper holding up corner of Heaven is held by strong man. He shifts weight and earth quakes. Korea: Kim STORY 39-40.

A1147.1. Origin of red sky (blood). SEE:1128.3; A797 (origin of sunsets).

A1150. Determination of seasons.

A1150.2. Winter while Persephone in underworld. Her mother Demeter withdraws. Half of the year Persephone is above ground. Then Demeter comes forth bringing spring and summer (cf. A316; F80). Greece Frost LEGEND 113-119. Sicily: Toor CARNATION 129-133 (Cerere). Zulu: Tracy LION 93-98 (daughter of Chief Above Ground weds Chief Below Ground, spends half of year with him).

A1150.3* Animals decide on equal lengths for the four seasons. Robin convinces them that certain animals prefer each season. Native American (Shoshone): Heady SAGE 35-38.

A1151. Theft of the seasons. Certain seasons are lacking. A culture hero steals the season from a monster and brings it to his people. (cf. 1411. Theft of light).

A1151.1* Skinkoots (coyote) steals with aid of Softest-Walker, Farthest-Thrower, and Strongest One (Grizzly). Softest-Walker stuffs warm pitch in old woman's mouth, Farthest-Thrower flings out bag with Spring in it and Strongest One rips it open. Native American: Field AMERICAN 32-39/ Bleecker BIG 153-160/. Native American (Kootenai): Cothran WITH 76-83; DeWit TALKING 113-117.

A1151.1.1* Coyote sends fox to steal summer. C. pretends to be chasing fox too and befuddles owner. Wolf, Rabbit and Hawk relay. Animals vote to let summer out of bag six months of year. Native American (Great Plains): Jones COYOTE 1-13.

A1153.1* Seasons produced by agreement between Summer and Winter. Glooskap fetches Summer from the South but she agrees to go back south in winter and allow Winter to rule. Native

American (Micmac): Haviland NORTH 58-59 (carried by whale); Toye HOW pb /Macmillan CANADIAN /.

A1158.1* Old man Peboan brags he blows and water freezes. Young Seegwun says "I breathe and flowers spring up." The Sun melts old man Peboan. Spring flowers appear where lodge fire of two men had been. SEE ALSO: A289.3. Native American: Bierhorst FIRE 5-10. Native American (Chippewa): Brown TEPEE 79-80 /Cathon PERHAPS 130-132/.

A1158.1.1* Duel between man and old man Peboan, winter. Native American (Micmac): DeWit TALKING 39-43.

A1159.1* Origin of hazy Indian Summer days. Shadows of dead brother and sister return and cause this haze. Native American (Canada): Littledale GHOST 111-120 /Macmillan CANADI-AN /.

A1160. Determination of the months. SEE ALSO: K688.1.

A1162* Quarrel between the months. March quarrels with February and May, likes only April because she lent him a day once when he wanted to freeze a peasant. Poland: Borski GOOD 18-19.

A1170. Origin of night and day. SEE ALSO: A1412 (origin of light).

A1170.1* Sun and moon separate. Thunder rules that Sun may care for daughter Earth in day and Moon at night. Lithuania: Jablow MAN 62-63.

A1172. Determination of night and day.

A1172.0.1* Sun and moon argue. Agree to share time equally. Native American (Thompson Indians): Newell RESCUE 85-90.

A1172.2* Lad kills seven horned djabbe from within. Opens purse found in djabbe's stomach = day. Closes purse = night. Haiti: Johnson HOW 55-58.

A1172.4* Right to light won in contest (A1412). Owl repeats "night" over and over. Rabbit repeats "light." Owl slips up and says "light" losing the contest. Rabbit allows night to exist part of the time anyway for those animals who hunt in the dark. Native American (Menomoni): Hardendorff JUST 22-23. Eskimo: Field ES-KIMO 10-11 (fox and hare). Native American (Nez Percé): Heady TALES 25-28 (chipmunk and bear +A2217.2; +A2481.1). Native American (Iroquois): Leach HOW 75-76 (chipmunk, bear, A2217.2).

A1172.4.1* Chipmunk sets fire to tree standing over light of world so that tree falls and light comes out. Grizzly throws earth on tree to put out fire. They compromise at last. C's back is

scratched by G. (A2217.2). Native American (Thompson Indians): Newell RESCUE 63-68.

A1172.5* Fearsome throws magic powder and causes darkness. Guards pursuing throw powder and cause light. Nigeria: Courlander OLODE 96-99.

A1172.6* Chipmunk suggests day be divided evenly between night and day, as are stripes on raccoon's tail. Bear scratches back (A2217.2). Native American (Creek): Brown TEPEE 62-63.

A1174. Origin of night.

A1174.1. Night (darkness) in package. Released.

A1174.1.1* Weasel rips open pack of strange Indian Tcoitcak and darkness pours out. Weasel opens second pack = stars (A760), daybreak (A1179.1), etc. Mink cuts a hole in Darkness at the East (Dawn) (A1179.2). Native American (Modoc): Cunningham TALKING 16-18.

A1179.1. Origin of twilight. SEE: A1174.1.1; A797 (origin of sunset).

A1179.2. Origin of dawn. SEE ALSO: A721.1.2; A1174.1.1; A797.

A1179.2.2* Creator sends birds to peck sunrise free. Raven fails, Wagtail makes a tiny hole and frees sunrise but wears out beak and wings. Is given new wings and sharp beak. Native American (Chuckchee): Leach HOW 41-43.

A1195.1* Origin of echo. Sound of Tepozteco's sacred drum is still heard. Mexico: Jagendorf KING 190-193 /Arbuthnot ARBUTHNOT 411-412/.

A1200 - A1699. Creation and Ordering of Human Life.

A1200 - A1299. Creation of man.

A1230. Emergence or descent of first man to earth.

A1231. First man descends from sky.

A1231.2* Warau climb down rope ladder to earth. Old woman "Rainstorm" sticks in hole trying to climb back up. Rains when she cries (A1131.1). Carib: Sherlock WEST 39-44.

A1231.3* Makonaima, brother Pia, and two girls, Mazaruni and Cuyuni, descend on rope ladder through crack in clouds. They propagate. The mountain where they descended is Mt. Roraima (mother's name), smaller mountains are Pakarai-mas (sisters). The land is called Guyana after aunt since river there flows like her talk. Guyana: McDowell THIRD 75-80.

A1236. Mankind emerges from tree. McDowell THIRD 131-132.

A1236.0.1* Men rise up from under willow trees at beginning of earth. Greenland Eskimo: Leach HOW 37-38.

A1240. Man made from mineral substance.

A1241. Man made from clay (earth). Indonesia: De Leeuw INDONESIAN 113-116 (created by Allah).

A1241.3.1* Men and animals made of mud. Sun's warmth brings to life. Columbia (Chibcha): Courlander RIDE 224-225.

A1241.3.2* Coyote makes his image of man and pours water on images attempted by other animals to ruin them. Each wanted man created in their own image. Final product combines features of all with Coyote's cunning. Native American: Frost LEGENDS 161-164.

A1241.3.3* Goddess Nu-Kua creates man of clay image. China: Birch CHINESE 3-8.

A1250. Man made from vegetable substance.

A1255.2.1* Man from ears of corn. Creator tries clay, it melts. Cork, floats away. Ripe corn, teeth are white, hair silky = first Caribs. Honduras: Jagendorf KING 162-163.

A1260. Mankind made from miscellaneous materials.

A1263.1.3* Man created from blood. First people from drop of blood which falls from sun and sinks into earth. Native American (Yuchi-Creek): Leach HOW 15-16.

A1263.7. Man created from animal bone. Native American (Chuckee): Leach HOW 41-43.

A1263.7.1* Man and brother kill possum, eat, and throw bones into river. Bones turn into man. Later large tree is cut open and men and women come out. McDowell THIRD 131-132.

A1270. Primeval human pair. SEE ALSO: W 154.8.5.

A1271.5* First man and woman emerge from bamboo pecked open by kite. Lumawig has caused this bamboo to grow. Philippines: Sechrist ONCE 3-7.

A1275.11* Creation of first man's (woman's) mate. Man creates woman from leaf of palm, petal of lily, head of snake, eye of octopus, heart of dog, leg of ant. Adds parrot's tongue. Is sorry later. New Guinea: McDowell THIRD 119-129.

A1279.2* First human pair caught in fish trap by Chameleon. Mulungu says to put them on earth and they will grow. They make fire, kill animals. Chameleon climbs tree, animals flee, Mulungu has spider spin rope and climbs up to live in the sky. Yao: Leach HOW 39-40.

A1290. Creation of man - other motifs.

A1291.2* Creation of Bushmen. Bee carries Mantis over water at beginning of world. Puts Mantis in heart of water flower, seeds of first humans in Mantis. Bee dies. Mantis comes alive in morning sun. First Bushman born. Bushmen: Helfman BUSHMEN 62-63.

A1300 - 1399. Ordering of human life.

A1310. Arrangement of man's bodily attributes.

A1311.1.1* The lizard hand. Lizard asks that man have five fingers like himself. Coyote agrees on condition that man must die = origin of death (A1335). Native American (Yokuts): Leach HOW 44.

A1316.6.1* Why children's teeth fall out. In memory of fleeing Hadji whose teeth were knocked out by stone thrown into cave where he was hiding. +B523.1. Indonesia: Courlander KANTCHIL'S 76-79.

A1319.15* Why women's elbows are always cold, why man stands with backside to fire. Tried to stop hole in ark with elbows and backside. +A1811.2. Leach LION 6-7.

A1320. Determination of span of life.

A1321. Men and animals readjust span of life. SEE: B592.

A1330. Beginnings of trouble for man.

A1333.2* Confusion of tongues caused when peoples migrating upriver under Godasiyo, woman chief, disagree and each take separate fork in river. Two canoes bearing Godasiyo's litter part and she is drowned. Native American (Seneca): Brown TEPEE 71-74.

A1335. Origin of death. SEE ALSO: A1311.1.1; A2355.1.2.2.

A1335.1.0.1* Origin of death from falsified message. Hare as messenger of moon tells man they will die and not be reborn. Tortoise brings correct message and people split hare's lip in anger. Hare escapes to moon, scratching its face as he lands. (A751.5.1; A2342.1). South Africa (Hottentot): Courlander KING'S 106-108 (grasshopper gives message but hare muddies); Withers MAN 23. Bushmen: Helfman BUSHMEN 46-47 (slow tortoise forgets message also).

A1335.1.0.2* Tortoise arrives first with message from God. Is to report that there is to be no death and no sickness but he is so tired that he can only mutter "death" and "sickness." Dog dawdled along way eating bones and arrives too late to correct T's message. Why dogs must crunch bones and nose at roadside. Nigeria (Ibo): Robinson SINGING 16-23.

A1335.8.1* Origin of death because world is overpopulated. Saynday asks red ant if men should revive again after death. She advises against this, feeling there are too many people. +A2355.1.2.2. Native American: Marriott WINTER 31-35.

A1335.8.2* Raven says some must die or world will run out of food. Later his son dies and he wishes to change law. Native American (Swinomish): Matson LEGENDS 119-123.

A1335.16* Cat wants creatures to die. Dog goes to Creator asking that man live forever. Cat puts bone in dog's path distracting him and reaches God first with request that creatures die. Haiti: Courlander PIECE 34-36; Wolkstein MAGIC 65-70 (dog wants to revive dead).

A1335.17* Woman wishes for light and death. Sun, moon and stars appear. Every dead soul becomes a new star (E741.2). Greenland Eskimo: Leach HOW 37-38.

A1335.18* Coyote rules man shall die. Coyote Itsayaya's daughter wooed by Kilosk, otter who offers l. salmon. I. weds her to the five wolf brothers who offer venison dowry. Kilosk kills wolves and I's daughter. I. follows them to A-Kum-Kinny-Koo, land of spirits. He is allowed to bring them back (F81.1) by wrapping their bones in white buckskin and returning over seven mountains without looking back (C331; C953). On seventh mountain he looks back and bones return to A-Kun-Kinney-Koo. He ordains that man too shall suffer this loss. Native American (Nez Percé): Heady TALES 109-118.

A135.19* Crow sent for waters of immortality by Creator drinks of it. Only enough left to give man life, not immortality. Indonesia: De Leeuw INDONESIAN 113-116.

A1335.20* Old Man throws buffalo chip in river. If it floats people to be reborn after four days; if sinks, to die. Woman wants stone used, it sinks. Native American (Blackfoot): Brown TEPEE 59-62.

A1337. Origin of disease.

A1337.0.5.1* Disease as punishment caused by animals in revenge on man for not asking their pardon when killing animals. Native American (Cherokee): Bell JOHN 7-12.

A1337.0.8* Sweat of Earth Magician's hands turns to disease and sickness. Eetoi grabs hands of Earth Magician disappearing into earth. Native American (Pima): Baker AT 8-15.

A1341. Origin of war among men.
SEE ALSO: A1388.

A1341.4* Origin of unkindness on earth. Bat enters forbidden Valley of Flowers and eats white lily and drinks red juice from roots. Medicine of Evil Spirits in roots sickens Bat and he snaps at red-winged blackbird starting

chain of unkindliness. Bat is punished by Great Spirit to fly only at night (A2491.1). Native American: Chafetz THUNDERBIRD 15-26.

A1342. Origin of quarrelling. SEE ALSO: A1388.

A1342.1* Devil Aghiutsa (Saraila) turns hermits Chirila and Manaila against each other. Pretends to tell each a secret and tells each nothing. Rumania: Ure RUMANIAN 126-130.

A1344.1* Origin of tears and sighs. Orphan taken up by moon to cry on moon. Origin first tears in world +A751.5.6. Algeria (Kabyle): Jablow MAN 10.

A1346.2. Man must labor for a living: at first everything too easy. Full crops produce themselves, trees drop sugar, etc. SEE: A625.2.8.

A1370. Origin of mental and moral characteristics.

A1372.1. Why women are prattlers. Native American (Shasta): Fisher CALIFORNIA 104-110.

A1375.2* Origin of avariciousness. Why everyone looks for "money." Man "Money" weds chief's daughter to a suitor and absconds with brideprice. Upper Volta, Ghana (Gurensi): Courlander KING'S 13-16.

A1378* Origin of debt. Chain tale. Anansi advises man in debt to say "Whoever drinks this palm wine takes debt." Anansi drinks the wine, he plants grain, birds eat the grain, lay eggs, tree breaks egg, tree blossoms and monkey eats blossoms, lion eats monkey. Ashanti kills lion and feeds meat to all Ashanti people. How debt came to the Ashanti. Ghana (Ashanti): Courlander COW-TAIL 103-106; Courlander HAT 77-79. Yoruba: Fuja FOURTEEN 11-21.

A1382.2* Orgin of confusion. Ape directs all animals to do disruptive things. Indonesia: Courlander KANTCHIL'S 52-56.

A1384.3* Origin of evil. Upper Volta: Guirma TALES 1-15. Ghana (Akan): Arnott AFRICAN 5-12 (B216Ac).

A1388. Origin of hatred.
SEE ALSO: A1341; A1342.

A1388.2* Nez Percé girl weds Blackfoot boy. Serpent sinks their canoe. This is taken as a sign that enmity should continue between their tribes. Native American (Nez Percé): Matson LEGENDS 69-75.

A1389* Origin of Ruin. Strong man Ahoro who destroys homes becomes Ruin, father of decay. Wife Elipa becomes small plant that grows amid ruins. Yoruba: Fuja FOURTEEN 152-155.

A1390. Ordaining of human life--miscellaneous.

A1391. Why other members must serve belly.

Result of a debate between members of the body. SEE ALSO: J461.1. Liberia (Mano): Dorliae ANIMALS 16-21. Aesop: Jacobs AESOP'S 57; Aesop: Aesop AESOP'S (Grosset) 46.

A1392.1* Creator sends for news of man. Ptarmigan, Polar Owl, Yellow Fox, Arctic Fox fail. Wolf reports man is afraid to sit down. Creator goes and orders man to sit. Native American (Chuckchee): Leach HOW 41-43.

A1399.2.1.1* Sleep, The-One-You-Don't-See-Coming. Three hunters try to capture him at waterhole but he sneaks up on each. They agree to leave him alone as he always returns their brains after a few hours. Liberia (Jabo): Courlander COW-TAIL 31-40.

A1399.5* Why baby says Goo. Is cry of triumph. Strongest man in village cannot make baby obey --just answers "Goo." Native American (Penobscot): Gruenberg FAVORITE 333-335.

A1400 - A1499. Acquisition of culture.

A1400. Acquisition of human culture. SEE: A541 (Culture hero teaches arts and crafts).

A1404. Gods teach people all they know. Columbia (Chibcha): Jagendorf KING 81-83.

A1410. Acquisition of livable environment.

A1411. Theft of light. Light originally is stolen by culture hero. SEE ALSO: A721.1 (Theft of sun); A758 (Theft of moon); A1151 (Theft of the seasons); A710 (Creation of the Sun).

A1411.1.1* Raven steals fire-ball from owner of light. Disguised as boy, R. steals, breaks off pieces and flings into sky as runs, hence suns appear at erratic distances from each other. Eskimo (Bering Strait, Yukon Valley): Cothran MAGIC 3-7. Eskimo: Melzack DAY 51-59.

A1411.2. Theft of light by being swallowed and reborn. The hero transforms himself to a particle. The daughter of the guardian of light swallows him as she is drinking water. He is reborn. As a child in the house he steals light. (Usually asks to play with ball). Eskimo: Casswell SHADOWS 64-67 (R. bursts ball on beach so people can see to catch oolichans--A2229.7); Cunningham TALKING 19-23 (R. as leaf on girl's dress asks baby to request daylight to play with); Maher BLIND 39-54 (+A795.1); Melzack RAVEN 61-69.

A1411.2.1* Raven is born to daughter of Old-One-at-the-River who owns sun, moon and stars. Cries for each bag and releases each. Men won't give fish to Raven, flee from brightness and become fish and animals (A1715). Old-One twists hat and causes flood (A1015). Raven saves four children by clinging to sky with beak. Native American (Northwest): Martin NINE 6-18 /Martin RAVEN 17-25/,

/Haviland NORTH 44-51/.

A1411.3* Gull keeps light in box. Raven wishes thorn into gull's foot and gull must release light so R. can see to remove it. Native American (Haida): Robinson COYOTE 35-40.

A1412. Origin of light--miscellaneous. SEE ALSO: A1170 (origin of night and day); A1172.4.

A1412.4* Origin of light. Earth under Big Sleep. White Cloud fights Black Cloud. Their sweat washes hole in Earth and animals are released from Big Sleep. White Cloud of North calls Blue Cloud from South and Yellow Cloud from West to shed light. Native American (Navaho): Hulpach AMERICAN 12-16.

A1412.5* Primeval voice asks "Who will make light?" Star tries, moon, not enough light, sun appears. (cf. A760; A710). Native American (Yuchi-Creek): Leach HOW 15-16.

A1412.6* Spider spins web to sky. Mouse, fly and spider go to upper world to seek light. King sets tasks: cut grass on plain--ants come. Eat whole cow--mouse buries. Choose right box. Fly has overheard. Rooster in red box. Crows and light comes. E. Africa (Sukuma): Bernstein FIRST pb.

A1414. Origin of fire.

A1414.1.1. Fire drill invented.

A1414.1.1.1* Coyote sent for fire to cremate Wiyot, first ancestor, returns to find Bluefly has made fire by twirling sticks. Bluefly still rubs hands together (A2479.10). Native American (Luiseño): Leach HOW 108.

A1414.1.1.2* Fire drill given by creator. Later it is left behind and turns into a man, the first Russian. Creator gives Russian responsibility of trading with His people. Native American (Chuckchee): Leach HOW 41-43.

A1414.1.1.3* Carancho teaches use of fire drill with pitaladik and kuwak'a wood. Toba: Leach HOW 52.

A1414.4. Origin of fire--gift from god (superatural person). Greek myth: Gruenberg FAVORITE 411-412 (Prometheus).

A1414.4.1* Maui asks fire of Mafuike in the underworld. She gives him burning fingernail but he extinguishes it and returns, wishing to learn secret of kindling fire. She gives nine nails thus, the tenth she flings after Maui, starting a fire. Maui calls rain to extinguish and hides some fire in trees. It may be released by rubbing. Polynesia: Berry MAGIC 89-97; Courlander TIGER'S 130-139; Courlander RIDE 14-19.

A1414.4.2* Redstart convinces god of Tir-nan-

Og to let him carry fire to man. Must find kind, unselfish person to give it to. All try to kill. Little boy and mother on Isle of Islay are kind. Redstart still has red streak on tail. (A2411.2.1.13). Scotland: Finlay TATTER-COATS 47-52.

A1414.5. Origin of flint and tinder.

A1414.5.1* Troll flies to pieces on seeing sun. Pieces become flint. Denmark: Owen CASTLE 65-74. SEE ALSO: G561.1; G304.2.5.

A1414.5.2* Rabbit causes flint to explode scattering everywhere. Hare's lip is split. +A2342.1.1. Native American (Cherokee): Bell JOHN 41-43; Parker SKUNNY 85-94.

A1414.7.1. Tree as repository of fire. SEE: A1415.2.3. (sycamore struck by lightning); A1414.7.2.1 (bamboo); A1415.2.2.1.1 (stump).

A1414.7.2.1* Rock as repository of fire. During flood fire hides in piece of iron, rocks, and in two bamboo trees. Philippines (Luzon, Tinguian): Leach HOW 22.

A1414.7.4* Fire in chest. Family guard two chests but fear to open. Stranger opens. Water is in one (A111.1). Fire is in the other. This is the origin of fire. Native American (Thompson River): Newell RESCUE 91-98.

A1414.7.5* Star as fire. Spider spins web. Wind blows to sky. Woodpecker pecks hole in sky and stars appear. Man climbs and fetches piece of star = fire. Zaire: Luzzatto LONG pb.

A1414.8* Ant shows how to make fire with flints. Kabyle: Leach HOW 53-54.

A1415. Theft of fire. Mankind is without fire. A culture hero steals it from the owner. (cf. A1411). Greek myth: Gruenberg FAVORITE 411-412 (Prometheus).

A1415.0.2.1* Hare steals fire from buzzards and gives to man. Warms feet at buzzard's fire with pine splinters between toes. Native American (Catawba): Leach HOW 47-48.

A1415.0.2.2* Ostrich keeps fire under wings. Mantis gets him to pick plums and snatches when arm is raised. Since then Ostrich keeps wings close to body and never flies (A2377.4; A2431.4). Bushmen: Helfman BUSHMEN 63-65.

A1415.0.2.3* Cranes possess fire. Ejupa (coyote) visits Koontex and dances setting headdress afire. Passes fire to rock squirrel to hide. Squirrel's breast burnt (A2218). Native American (Shoshone): Heady SAGE 30-34.

A1415.0.2.4* Maui gets secret of fire from mud hens. Puts dummy in boat so they think he is fishing and kindle fire. He catches one and forces to tell secret of fire-making. Pacific Islands: Carpenter ELEPHANT'S 204-211. Hawaii: Colum LEGENDS 38-64; Cothran MAGIC 45-48; Williams SURPRISING 25-29.

A1415.0.2.5* Manabush goes as white rabbit to Dawn People. Two daughters of old man who owns fire take wet hare in to warm self. He steals brand and flees. Ordains that fire be kept always in center of lodge. Native American (Menominee): Cunningham TALKING 33-36. Native American (Chippewa): Leekley WORLD 11-19 (takes spark in fur and runs to Nokomis, A2218).

A1415.0.2.6* Rabbit dances at weasel's fire and sets pine tar on head afire. Thunderbirds, who had given weasels fire by striking sycamore tree on island with lightning, send rain but Rabbit hides fire in hollow tree. Native American (Creek): Brown TEPEE 70-71. Native American (Hitchiti): DeWit TALKING 49-51 (people's fire).

A1415.2.1.1* Theft of fire by bird. Owl steals fire back from men who robbed family. Given name "sparkling fire owl"--Kennreirk. Native American (Hooper Bay Eskimo): Gillham BEYOND 44-50.

A1415.2.2.1* Theft of fire by coyote. Coyote steals fire from two old women. Animals relay fire back. Frog last, loses tail, swallows fire and escapes under water. Frog dies but his ghost spits up coal onto wood. Native American (Karok): Fisher CALIFORNIA 46-53. Native American: Hardendorff JUST 73-77.

A1415.2.2.1.1* Coyote plans relay to steal fire from man. Frog is last. Caught, he drops tail (A2378.2.6) and throws fire into tree stump, where it may be found today (A1414.7.1). Native American (Wintu): Belting LONG 34-36.

A1415.2.2.1.2* Coyote steals fire from three Fire Beings. Touched on tail, his tail turns white (A2411.1.3.2). Squirrel carries, back scorched and tail up (A2378.9.6). Chipmunk carries, clawed = stripes on back (A2413.2). Frog carries, caught he drops tail (A2378.2.6), throws to Wood and Wood swallows (A1414.7.1). Coyote shows man how to get fire out of wood by rubbing sticks. Native American: Haviland NORTH 52-56. Native American (Crow): Robinson COYOTE 79-84.

A1415.2.2.2.* Coyote, dog, deer, and mouse steal fire from Thunder and two daughters. Mouse chews apronstrings of daughters to delay. Coyote speakes and drops his coal. Dog laughs and coal falls from ear. Mouse hides coal in flute and flute is relayed back. Thunder catches frog who loses tail. Flute flies onto skunk's stump and Thunder is routed. Native American (California): Curry DOWN 68-79.

A1415.2.2.3* Fox, Sandpiper, Mole and Weasel steal fire from Wind People and relay home. Coyote begs to carry and drops it. In ensuing brush fire spider hauls animals up in wolf's overturned lodge by tying rope to sky. Coyote makes a hole in lodge to see out and falls through hole. Must dangle there and tail is scorched (A2218). Native American (California): Curry DOWN 51-67.

A1415.2.2.4* Coyote organizes relay of men to steal fire from the Beings. Coyote's sides scorched by fire (A2411.1.3.2). Native American (Paiute): Hodges FIRE pb.

A1415.2.3* Theft of fire by spider. Sycamore tree on island is struck by lightning (A1414.7.1). Animals try to fetch fire. Raven scorched hence black (A2411.2.1.5); screech owl's eyes burnt hence red eyes and cannot see in daytime; hoot owl gets white on wings and around eyes from ashes; black racer snake scorched black (A2411.5.9); bib blacksnake is burned black; water spider makes a bowl of his thread on back and carries coal in bowl--succeeds. He still carries bowl (tusti) on back. Native American (Cherokee): Bell JOHN 15-18; Leach HOW 49-51; Scheer CHEROKEE 25-30.

A1415.2.4* Theft of fire by dog. Dog shelters with boa constrictor who owns fire. Catches tail afire and flees. How Denka people obtained fire. Egypt: Carpenter WONDER..DOGS 89-94.

A1415.5* Maui Kiji-Kiji follow father, Maui Atalonga to spirit-land. Wrestles with grandfather, Maui, and throws him breaking all bones. Maui has lain weak ever since but whenever he turns earth trembles (A1145). Kiji-Kiji smuggles fire back to earth. Tonga: Gittens TALES 52-55.

A1420. Acquisition of food supply for human race. See entries for A2600 - A2699.

A1421. Hoarded game released.

A1421.0.0.1* Coyote disguises as baby and releases fish kept behind dam by witches. Witches turn each other into caddis flies in anger. Native American (Nisqually): Matson LEGENDS 28-31. Native American: Fisher CALIFORNIA 96-102. Native American (Nez Percé): Heady TALES 50-56; Martin NINE.. COYOTE 46-53.

A1423. Acquisition of vegetables and cereals.

A1423.0.1.1* Caribs are sent magic coomacka tree by Kabo Tano. Wild pig and rat find tree but refuse to show to others. They are forced to show tree. Voice instructs to cut down this tree which produces all foods and plant cuttings from it. Hence Caribs have cultivated foods close to their dwellings. Carib: Sherlock WEST 7-12.

A1423.1. Origin of yams (sweet potatoes, taro).

SEE ALSO: A2794.2.2; A2686.4.1.

A1423.1.1* Abu seeks yam from foreign country. Hostage is required as foreigners fear the Ashanti will become overly strong if fed on yams. Abu's sister sends son, hence Ashanti leave inheritance to sister's son. Ashanti: Courlander HAT 96-100.

A1423.1.2* Arrow chain shot into moon (F53). Man in moon tosses down yams for hero. New Hebrides: Gittens TALES 85-87.

A1425. Origin of seed.

A1425.0.1.1* Hoarded seeds. Ground squirrel steals acorns and sunflower seeds from Dawn People and brings back. Native American (California): Curry DOWN 38-47.

A1425.0.1.2* Coyote (Ejupa) and crow steal pine nuts from geese who own them. Crow carries under wings and a few drop in valley of Shoshoni country. Native American (Shoshone): Heady SAGE 46-48.

A1425.0.1.2.1* Red Squirrel steals bag but stops at each stream to eat, thus distributing all over the land. Native American (Shoshone): Heady SAGE 49-50.

A1425.2* Man given first seeds of squash, beans, and corn. Gruenberg MORE 392-395.

A1429.2.1* Man taught to make bread by ant. Kabyle: Leach HOW 53-54.

A1430. Acquisition of other necessities.

A1435.9* Origin of particular buildings.

A1435.9.1* Castle of Vufflens with four towers. Swiss (French): Duvoisin THREE 115-121.

A1437. Acquistion of clothing.

A1437.1* Origin of headdress. Fostedina, early Christian maid, is forced to wear crown of thorns. Later at her wedding she wears a golden helmet to hide the scars. This helmet is adopted by the Frisian women. Netherlands: De Leeuw LEGENDS..HOLLAND 52-56; Frost LEGENDS 177-180.

A1427.2* Origin of fez. King has contest for ideas to make Fez famous. Boy suggests red hat called "Fez." North Africa: Holding KING'S 9-17.

A1437.3* Origin of fox fur hats. China: Chang TALES 56-67.

A1437.4* Origin of sleeping robes. Native American (Thompson Indians): Newell RESCUE 99-106.

A1438. Origin of medicine (healing). SEE ALSO: A2693.

A1438.2* Plants offer selves to man as healing agents, whisper uses to Medicine Man. Native American (Cherokee): Bell JOHN 7-12.

A1438.3* Medicines vomited by Mother Goddess. Japan: McAlpine JAPANESE 10-15.

A1439.5* Origin of steam engines. Water wants to wed fire. Russian carpenter makes this possible in iron boiler. Child is steam. Russia: Carey BABA 81-83.

A1440. Acquisition of crafts.

A1441. Acquisition of agriculture.

A1441.5. Origin of onion growing. SEE ALSO: D551.2.5. Korea: Kim STORY 11-16.

A1447.3.1* Origin of onion shaped iron lanterns of Strozzi Palace in Florence. Florence: Jagendorf PRICELESS 95-101.

A1451.1* Origin of pottery. Kojangka, ruler of the moon, shows man how to make pottery. Indonesia: De Leeuw INDONESIAN 51-55.

A1453.2.1* Origin of weaving. Man copies spider and devises art of weaving. West Africa (Fan): Aardema TALES 18-23. SEE: A1465.2.1.

A1453.5. Origin of bark-cloth. Maikoha turns self to paper mulberry tree to provide for daughters. They learn to make tapa from bark. Maikoha is guardian goddess of tapa making. Hawaii: Thompson HAWAIIAN..EARTH 53-59.

A1455. Origin of cooking.

A1455.2.1* Origin of simnel cake. Green CLEVER 130-133.

A1457.1.1* Origin of the fish hook. Maui invents barbed fish spear. Maori: Courlander RIDE 14-19. Polynesia: Courlander TIGER'S 132-139.

A1457.3.1* Origin of the net for fishing. Man copies spider making webs and makes nets to catch animals. West Africa (Fan): Aardema TALES 18-22. SEE: A1453.2.1; A1465.2.1.

A1457.3.2* Boy sees fairy people using net. He detains them until dawn and obtains their net when they vanish. New Zealand: Sleigh NORTH 139-143.

A1457.5. Origin of fish-traps. Maui invents trap-door for eel pot. Maori: Courlander RIDE 14-19. Polynesia: Courlander TIGER'S 132-139.

A1457.9.1* Origin of the tuna industry. Fisherman dreams the Lord gives him catch of huge fish, awakens to see these fish under boat. Catches them. Tuna industry thus born. Spain: Gunterman CASTLES 241-246.

A1458.2* Origin of rabbit-trap. Man sees rabbit run into tree and kill self. He waits for another rabbit to decease in same way and refuses to work for food (J2215.4). Rabbits fail to drop dead at his feet so he devises rabbit trap. Taiwan: Cheney TALES 115-118.

A1459.1. Acquisition of weapons.

A1459.1.6* Origin of the kris. Son born with golden kris over shoulder. Java: De Leeuw INDONESIAN 9-13.

A1459.1.7* Origin of faery sword Claidheamh Ceann-Ileach. Scotland: Wilson SCOTTISH 107-114.

A1459.2. Acquisition of seamanship (sailing, etc.).

A1459.2.1* Chinese Emperor Kotei invents boats after seeing spider on leaf. Japan: Ozaki JAPANESE 54-59.

A1460. Acquisition of arts.

A1461. Acquisition of music.

A1461.0.1* Four monkeys invent instruments: flute, lute, cymbal, drum. Teach friends of princess to play. Cambodia: Tooze THREE.. MONKEY #1.

A1461.0.2* Shoshone learn their music from the wind and the birds. Hymn to the morning learned from meadowlark. Native American (Shoshone): Heady SAGE 85-88.

A1461.1.1* Origin: horse-headed fiddle. Dead horse instructs how to make fiddle of his bones. Tendons for strings, tail hair for bow. China: CHINESE 34-35; Otsuka SUHO pb.

A1461.8. Origin of flute.

A1461.8.1* Flute from paxiuba palm springing from grave of boy who sang marvelously. Latin America: Eels TALES..AMAZON 225-229.

A1461.8.2* Origin flute. Scornful princess Nima-Cux will wed ragged minstrel when he learns song of every bird in forest. God of the Forest shows how to make a flute. Guatemala (Mayan): Carter ENCHANTED 50-56 /Arbuthnot ANTHOLOGY 409-410/; Jagendorf KING 132-135.

A1461.9* Origin of alphorn. Lad meets three men brewing on mountain, offered choice of red milk (strength), green milk (wealth), or white milk (ability to play magically on alphorn). Chooses latter. Switzerland (German): Duvoisin THREE 218-222.

A1461.10* Origin drums and drummers. Sons asked by dying father "How will you bury me?" Third son, "In drum." He is sent for the drum. Shares food with beggar (really Merisier). M. gives three nuts to throw if pursued. Steals drum of Elephant King. At throw of last nut drum breaks into pieces, each piece = a drum.

Elephant king breaks also into pieces, each piece = a drummer. They disperse throughout the land. Haiti: Courlander PIECE 9-14.

A1464.2.1. Origin of particular song. Wales: Baker TALKING 45-57 (ghostly fiddler, E425.2.5).

A1465. Origin of decorative art.

A1465.2.1* Origin of lace making. Girl finds husband killed in battle has been shrouded in spider web. She weaves a delicate lace shroud imitating the spider's web. This is called ñanduti lace of Itagua, Paraguay. Paraguay: Jangendorf KING 226-229. SEE: A1453.2.1; A1457.3.1.

A1465.2.1.1* Origin of ñanduti lace. Boy saves spider from drowning. Later he competes for hand of girl. Most exquisite gift to win her. The spider spins him a lace mantilla. Paraguay (Guarani): Barlow LATIN 43-49.

A1465.3.3. Origin of metal ornaments.

A1465.3.3.1* Sculpture Lorenzo di Cione Ghiberti of Florence is cursed so can't carve doors. Little people form doors with their bodies and turn to bronze, thus are immortalized. Italy: Belting ELVES 11-14.

A1465.5. Origin of wood carving.

A1465.5.1* Origin of Toromiro carvings of Rapa-Nui. Chief sees two sorcerors asleep with skeleton bodies. Dares not speak of this so carves four figures. Two showing them as men, two as skeletons. People understand and sorcerors leave islands. Easter Island: Courlander RIDE 279-282.

A1465.9* Origin of specific objet d'art.

A1465.9.1* Statue (painting) of peddlar of Swaffham and his dog in Swaffham. Great Britain (Norfolk): Colwell ROUND 61-63; Jacobs MORE 98-100. SEE ALSO: N531.1.

A1480. Acquisition of wisdom and learning.

A1481. Origin of human wisdom.

A1481.1* Anansi collects all wisdom in world in pot and tries to carry it up tree. Son sees him struggling with pot and suggests he tie it on his back. A. hurls pot to ground in a fury and it breaks, scattering wisdom to all corners of the world. Ashanti: Appiah ANANSE 147-152 (pot slips); Courlander HAT 30-31; Leach HOW 45-46. Nigeria: Walker NIGERIAN 35-36 (tortoise). Liberia/Ghana: Arkurst ADVENTURES 50-58 (Nyame gave pot of wisdom to A.). U.S. Black: Courlander TERRAPIN'S 24-27 (terrapin is caretaker for sense collected by animals, falls, t. still crawling looking for spilled sense A2312.1.4; A2441.4.5.1).

A1481.2* Origin of stories.

A1481.2.1* Anansi obtains stories by performing assigned tasks +H961. Ashanti: Courlander HAT 3-8; Haley STORY pb. Jamaica: Sherlock ANANSI 3-12 /Haviland FAIRY 86-91/; Sherlock WEST 45-48. Liberia: Haskett GRAINS 40-42 (hare earns wisdom). Africa: Aardema SKY-GOD pb.

A1481.2.2* Boy gives slain birds to stone. Stone tells legends. Native American (Iroquois): Bruchac TURKEY 15-16. Native American (Seneca): Cunningham TALKING 3-15; DeWit TALKING 5-9.

A1481.3* Ol man N'ba Noangma, storyteller, dies. Black bear found in his hut grows to ceiling. Children climb it and reach sky. Are taught wisdom. Return as old men. Tell tales and disperse wisdom. Upper Volta: Guirma TALES 1-15.

A1482. Origin of language. SEE ALSO: A1333.2.

A1482.2* Origin of Puget Sound languages. Doh-Kwi-Buhch, creator, had odd lot of languages left in basket when he reached Puget Sound. Gave them all out, hence variety of languages spoken in this small area. Native American (Snohomish): Matson LEGENDS 90-93.

A1484.2. Origin of alphabet.

A1484.2.1* King introduces Korean alphabet by writing on leaves with honey so ants will eat out the letters. Says they are a miracle from heaven. Korea: Carpenter TALES..KOREAN 135-139.

A1485. How people learned about calculating time and the seasons. SEE: A753.1.0.1 (Moon measures year).

A1485.1* Scots learn how to calculate Shrove Tide date: Michael Scot to go to Rome to ask Pope when Shrove Tide falls. He forgets and goes quickly by magic horse on last day. Pope reveals that Shrove Tide is first Tuesday of first moon in Spring. Scotland: Wilson SCOTTISH 38-40.

A1500 - A1599. Origin of customs.

A1529* Origin of farming customs.

A1529.1* Why one-fifth of crop is given to those who help harvest. Woman who failed to make sacrifice lost her crop. Kind woman found a golden grain and gave helper Dongso one-fifth of crop. Start of tradition. Village was named Derma after this woman. Java: De Leeuw INDONESIAN 30-35.

A1530. Origin of social ceremonials.

A1533.1* Origin of the peace pipe: chief's daughter dreams of peace pipe. Native American : Chafetz THUNDERBIRD 27-41.

A1533.2* Origin peace pipe: Buffalo challenges coyote, C. cannot hide from him so offers peace pipe. Native American (Kutenai): Arnott ANIMALS 1-5.

A1533.3* Maiden appears with peace pipe to two men seeking food during famine. One wishes she would wed him. Fog rolls in leaving only his bones for this impure thought. Native American (Oglala Sioux): Matson LEGENDS 36-39.

A1539.2* Origin of Spirit Societies. Man sleeping in deserted house see Gafes (evil spirits of the dead) bring medicine bag. He frightens them off by imitation of the cry of a wara (small animal which Gafes fear) and keeps the medicine bag. Forms first spirit society. Liberia: Haskett GRAINS 71-74.

A1539.3* Motzeyouf teaches sacred ceremonies. Origin of Cheyenne Dog Soldiers. Native American (Cheyenne): Brown TEPEE 46-59.

A1540. Origin of religious ceremonials.

A1541.2. Origin of feasts in honor of certain god (goddess).

A1541.2.2* Origin of fast for 64 yoginees by mothers in Maharashtra State on last day of Shravana. India: Spellman BEAUTIFUL 26-27.

A1541.7* Origin of Chinese New Year's celebration. Mother saves son to be sacrificed to dragon by smearing red blood on door and burning loud popping bamboo. Custom of pasting red paper and setting off firecrackers on New Year's evolves to drive dragon away. China: Cheney TALES 17-24.

A1542. Origin of religious dancing.

A1542.1. Origin of particular manner of dancing.

A1542.1.1* Why women dance like sparrows and men like monkeys. Old man steals wine from dancing monkeys. Woman steals wine from dancing sparrows. Each tastes wine of other and man begins sparrow-like dance and woman begins monkey dance. They change wines and dancing styles of men and women originate. Japan: Sakade JAPANESE 25-28.

A1542.2. Origin of particular dance. SEE ALSO: H1284.1 (Sun-dance origin).

A1542.2.2* Eagle mother teaches man to build kagsse, feast hall, to make songs and to dance. Tells to invite other men. Sends animal pairs in human form to feast. Eskimo: Haviland NORTH 101-106.

A1542.2.3* Boy shows spirit monster body of dead son. She rewards with spirit mask and water to revive dead and teaches dance. Native American (Kwakiutl): Curtis GIRL 21-30.

A1542.3* Origin of walking on hot stones. Eel shows skill to man who spares him. Fiji: Gittens TALES 11-13.

A1545.1. Regulations for sacrifices.

A1545.1.1* Origin of Bromo Feast. Sacrifice made to Brahma at Bromo crater each year. Java: De Leeuw INDONESIAN 26-29.

A1545.3. Origin of animal sacrifices.

A1545.3.0.1* Origin of animal sacrifices to Saint Gabre Manfas. Ethiopia (Tigre): Davis LION'S 162-166.

A1545.3.4* Origin of Tortoise sacrifice to Osanyin. Courlander OLODE 73-79.

A1546.0.1. Origin of symbols of worship.

A1546.0.1.1* Origin of Bhuddist ritual object: bamboo pole with black crow at top and white cloth fluttering. Vietnam: Vo-Dinh TOAD 29-34.

A1546.0.4* Man visiting underwater longhouse is given magic Quedelish (two cedar disks representing clean mind and clean body). Native American (Skagit): Matson LEGENDS 114-117.

A1547.1.1* Tzu Heng originates custom of giving paper objects to dead rather than living sacrifices and real objects. China: Manton FLYING 35-39.

A1547.4. Ungrateful son sees lamb kneel to mother and repents, runs to make amends to mother and she flees in terror and leaps into river, wood tablet rises from spot. He carves her name on it and honours tablet in his home. Origin of ancestor tablets. China: Carpenter TALES..CHINESE 66-71.

A1549.2.1* Origin of Sangasang Ceremony for dedicating house before commencement of building. Philippine (Tinguian): Sechrist ONCE 82-86.

A1550. Origin of customs of courtship and marriage.

A1558. Origin of divorce. Japan: McAlpine JAPANESE 16-22 (+F81.1.0.1).

A1570. Origin of regulations within the family.

A1578.1. Origin of family crests.

A1578.1.1* A people who slaughter goats senselessly are invited to feast by goat clan in human guise and are destroyed. One kind boy is saved. He is given goatskin to make way safely down mountain. Takes goat as clan totem. Native American (Tsimshian): DeWit TALKING 137-142; Harris ONCE 5-30; Martin NINE 43-46 /Martin RAVEN 53-60/; Toye MOUNTAIN pb.

A1578.2* Origin of family heirlooms.
SEE: F381.8.1 (Witch's mantle).

A1578.3* Origin of tradition that ancestor was a great harp player. Many harps owned by ancestor are found and give rise to legend. Actually he played poorly. Burma: Courlander TIGER'S 35-37.

A1579. Origin of regulations within the family--miscellaneous.

A1579.2* (Clarke). Origin of crying child's habit of answering "nothing" when asked why they cry. "Nothing's" wife asks children to cry for her dead husband. Ghana, Accra: Courlander COWTAIL 102.

A1590. Origin of other customs.

A1598. Origin of customs of hospitality.

A1598.1* Origin of custom of inviting strangers to share feast. Old man decides to let self be eaten by bears. Changes mind at last minute and gives bears feast instead. Bears befriend him. Thereafter strangers are invited to feasts. Native American (Tlingit, Wrangell): Cothran MAGIC 8-12.

A1599.4.1. Origin of other aspect of female grooming.

A1599.4.1.1* Origin of foot binding. China: Carpenter TALES..CHINESE 81-88.

A1599.5.1.2* Origin of painting eyebrows. China: Carpenter TALES..CHINESE 56-65.

A1599.17* Origin of saying "Whoever falls asleep on highway loses either his hat or his head." Iran: Shah MULLAH 145.

A1600 - A1699. Distribution and differentiation of peoples.

A1610. Origin of various tribes.

A1610.7* Vandai becomes giant eagle and harasses village. Eetoi is hidden by woman in Vandai's cave. She sings Vandai asleep. Eetoi kills V. and sprinkles V's blood on dead with eagle feather. First to revive are warlike = Apaches. Second are unintelligible = Maricopas. Third had been dead too long, are faded, weak, crying = white men. E. sends all away so they won't trouble his own people. Native American (Pima): Baker AT 25-32.

A1610.8* Monster Iltswetsix is killed by Coyote and cut up. Head = Nez Percé, sent to occupy Wallowa Valley. Legs = Blackfoot. Arms = Cayuse. Skin = Flathead. Body = Yakimas. Native American (Nez Percé): Heady TALES 101-108.

A1611.1.2. Origin of Eskimo. Eskimo: Caswell SHADOWS 24-25.

A1611.1.3* Origin of Puget Sound tribes. Twu-Yaletsa is told by crow to make skin robe and wave over fire, people appear. Driven out, his tribe flees on rafts, drift apart = origin various tribes of Puget Sound. Native American (Swinomish, Kikiallus): Matson LONGHOUSE 31-38.

A1611.1.4* Origin Makah people. Wild dogs at Neah Bay turned into Makah by Kwatee, taught ways. Native American (Makah): Matson LEGENDS 106-109.

A1611.1.5* Origin of Yokut people. Created by Eagle and Coyote and given qualities. Courage and sharp eyes from eagle, a fine voice and swift feet and swimming skill from coyote. Native American (Yokut): Fisher STORIES 36-45.

A1611.1.6* Restoration of Eagle clan of Tsimshian. Princess saved from massacre, floats in hollow log to Haida islands. Her four sons and daughter return to kill Bear clan leader and restore Eagle clan. Native American (Tsimshian): Harris ONCE 115-148.

A1611.3.1. Origin of Bushmen. Bushmen: Helfman BUSHMEN 102-108.

A1611.5. Origin of various European peoples.

A1611.5.5* Origin of Magyars and Huns. Baker TALKING 199-203.

A1611.5.6* Origin of Laplanders. Lippo weds Tellervo, daughter of Tapio, God of the Forests. Lippo fails to weave shelter tight enough and starlight strikes wife. She leaves. Son of union wanders north when grown. Laplanders descend from him. Finland: Bowman TALES 65-72.

A1614. Origin of white and colored races.

A1614.2. Races dark-skinned from bathing after white men. All peoples bath in the river, the white man first, then in turn, the Spaniard, the Indian, and the Negro--each becoming darker, because of the condition of the water. SEE ALSO: A2375.11. U.S. Black: Harris COMPLETE 109-110; Harris SONGS 166-167.

A1614.2.1* God Mungu makes three men of black clay, cannot tell them apart. Sends them to wash in white pool. One is covered with white, second finds not much water left, is pale brown. Third wets palms and soles only. M. sends white north, brown east, keeps black as companion. E. Africa: Heady WHEN 91-94 /Arbuthnot ARBUTHNOT 316-317/.

A1614.2.2* First group bathe in moonlight = white. Second bathe at dawn = yellow. Third at noon = red. Last in evening, only puddle left, palms and soles washed, rest remains black. Upper Volta: Guirma TALES 1-15.

A1614.4.3. Origin of different peoples according to choice of bows and arrows. SEE: A1671.2.

A1614.6.1* Makonaima uses white clay from sky to make some Indians white. He rests and clay becomes dirty. Rest are made black. Native American (Warau/Caribe): Eels TALES..AMAZON 141-151.

A1614.9. Origin of white man.

A1614.8.1* White man is set adrift in boot sole by mother who was mated to a dog. Eskimo: Caswell SHADOWS 24-25.

A1650. Origin of different classes--social and professional.

A1650.4* First father chases lazy progeny out of house. From those who hide in house descend leaders, those under house = servants, those in fields = farmers, those far away = traders, those farthest away = other peoples. Philippines: Sechrist ONCE 3-7.

A1670. Characteristics of various people--in industry and warfare.

A1671.1.1* Why the negro works. Great spirit gives black man first choice of boxes, he takes larger box containing hoes, water pots, etc. White man's box contains only pencil and paper but with these he can write down the things he learns while the black man's wisdom dies with him. Congo (Luban): Burton MAGIC 72.

A1700 - A2199. Creation of
Animal Life.

A1700. Creation of animals.

A1714.3.2* All animals are inside mountain. Spider smokes them out. Slower ones are caught as they flee and domesticated. Liberia (Mano): Dorliae ANIMALS 10-15.

A1715. Animals from transformed men. SEE: A1863; A1966; A1411.2.1.

A1716.2* Animals from pieces of monster slain. Native American (Chippewa): Leekley WORLD 92-99.

A1717* Animals from transformed supernatural beings.

A1717.1* Star people select animal tokens brought to sky by hunter, become animal whose token they select. +F302.4.2.4. Native American: Haviland NORTH 97-100.

A1800 - A1899. Creation
of mammals.

A1810. Creation of felidae.

A1811.2. Creation of cat: sneezed from lion's nostrils. Devil as mouse gnaws hole in bottom of ark. Noah asks lion's help. Lion sneezes and cat comes from lion's nostril and eats mouse. Leach LION 6-7.

A1811.4* Rats eat up skyline and man and woman braid earth and sky back together. Natzi (god) sends them to ask tiger for a cat. Tiger gives piece of his liver which turns into a cat. China (Ch'uan Miao): Leach HOW 63-64.

A1820. Creation of mustelidae.

A1825* Creation of mink. SEE: F53.2.

A1830. Creation of canidae and other carnivora.

A1831. Creation of dog. SEE ALSO: A2513.1.

A1831.1.1* Devil creates wolf. God makes dog to protect sheep. Rumania: Leach HOW 59.

A1831.3* In the beginning there are three dogs. Mbwela, jackal, goes west, prefers darkness. Mbwiku, wild dog, goes east, prefers daylight. Mbwa, common dog, looks for a protector. E. Africa: Heady WHEN 42-46.

A1831.4* Brahma creates dog and sends to find master. +A2513.1.1. India: Carpenter ELEPHANT'S 75-81.

A1832.1* Origin of arctic fox. Boy seeks aid of four winds to vanquish Fox the Trickster. North Wind freezes and carries to Northland. Fox turns white from fright. Native American (Lakota): Yellow Robe TONWEYA 42-51.

A1833.4* Evil spirit Kurat creates wolf. Must say "come alive and devour your master" to give life. Flees. Wolf still seeks Kurat. Estonia: Maas MOON 56-59.

A1834.1.1* Creation of coyote. Itsayaya, supernatural ancient coyote, fails to confess sins before climbing rope to A-Kum-Kinny-Koo in sky. Is dropped and becomes ordinary coyote. Present world order begins. Native American (Nez Percé): Heady TALES 119-124.

A1834.3. Creation of hyena. SEE: K1041.0.2.

A1836.1* Origin of certain bear. Old woman raises polar bear cub. It is attacked and old woman sends it away for protection. She dips her hands in black oil and strokes side of its head as it leaves. Bear with black spots on head is still seen. Eskimo: Melzack DAY 77-84.

A1837. Origin of seal. SEE: A2101; A2109.

A1838. Origin of walrus. SEE: A2101; A2109.

A1840. Creation of rodentia.

A1859.2* Creation of chipmunk. Mother turns son to Chipmunk to save from witch. Witch claws him, hence stripes (A2413.2). Native American: Hardendorff JUST 42-43.

A1859.2.1* Old-Man turns Bad Sickness into chipmunk in return for secrets. Native

American: Field AMERICAN 3–12.

A1860. Creation of primata.

A1861. Creation of monkey. SEE ALSO: A1863.

A1861.3.1* Man carves monkeys to clean up after lazy villagers. Villagers go to trees and become real monkeys. Columbia: Newman FOLK 53–60. South America: Finger TALES 170–187.

A1861.3.2* Girls preening in cave mock old woman. Cave closes except for small hole. They turn to monkeys to escape. Africa (Luo): Harman TALES 103–108.

A1861.4* Scaffold to obtain moon breaks hole in moon and lava covers plain. Men turn to gorillas and baboons. Children to monkeys and escape into treetops. Congo: Aardema TALES 62–66.

A1861.5* Dying monkey king sends for three sons. First to arrive is given red tail, white mane and whiskers and is to be new king, Tebe. Second with long black and white fur to be prime minister, Colobus. Last with long nose and gray fur to be lowest, Baboon. Africa: Heady SAFIRI 11–16.

A1863.1* Creation of baboon. Lazy men hang hoes behind and go for walk (or lean on planting sticks to rest). Handles become tails and they turn into baboons (monkeys). Africa (Zulu): Leach HOW 5–8. Philippines (Tinguian): Sechrist ONCE 37–38.

A1870. Creation of ungulata.

A1871.1.1* Origin of wild boar. St. Peter and Christ leave four piglets in cave of woman. On return she says two fattest pigs have died (really are hidden). Christ turns these to wild boars. Portuguese: Lowe LITTLE 38–40.

A1873. Creation of Camel.
SEE ALSO: A2356.2.13.

A1873.1* Horse asks Zeus to give him a longer neck, broader chest, built-in saddle. Zeus creates from this horse the camel. Green BIG 26. Aesop: Aesop AESOP'S (illus. Artzybasheff) 7–72; Hardendorff JUST 54–55.

A1873.2* Camel asks for broad feet to walk on sand, humps to carry food and water. Everyone laughs so he asks to have gifts removed. This cannot be done so he is given a disdainful look so others will feel inferior to him. China: Gruenberg MORE 111–112.

A1875.2* Mantis creates an eland. Bushmen: Helfman BUSHMEN 92–99.

A1878. Creation of bison (buffalo).

A1878.2* White Crow discovered with buffalo meat at dance. Animals try to watch where he flies. Dragonfly sees farthest and discovers

W.C.'s home. Saynday as white puppy is taken in by White Crow's daughter. She reveals rock covering hole in earth where buffalo are kept. Saynday chases them out and escapes as cocklebur on leg of last. Sends buffalo to live on plains. Native American: Marriott WINTER 12–24.

A1878.3* Coyote turns self to dog and son of Humpback adopts. He releases buffalo for people. Native American (Apache/Comanche): Brown TEPEE 63–65.

A1881. Creation of horse.

A1881.2* Nirantali (god) makes horse of wooden pieces, broom reeds for tail, burning coal for eyes, fastened together with beeswax. Blows dust of earth into nostril and it comes to life. He gives it to man. Kond: Leach HOW 66.

A1881.3* Prayer to Great Spirit for bigger dogs to pull travois so can keep up with buffalo. Horse appears. Native American (Sioux): Matson LEGENDS 53–55.

A1881.4* Piegan Blackfoot man told by voice that he may try four times to catch horse from herd which vanishes into lake. Catches colts and mares and stallions follow. Native American (Blackfoot): Brown TEPEE 98–99.

A1881.5* Water Spirit's son leads orphan boy to father, tells to ask for oldest mallard and its young. Not to look back as he leads it home, turn to horses. Native American (Blackfoot): Brown TEPEE 99–101.

A1882. Creation of ass.

A1882.2* Origin of Donkeys on Haiti. Loa (spirit) warns boy his stepmother is really a donkey. At feast he pokes her and guests with stick and they turn to donkeys and flee. One little donkey is left behind. Donkeys of Haiti descend from it. Haiti: Johnson HOW 9–12.

A1884.0.2* Creation of sheep. First true sheep emerge from stomach of All-devourer after he has eaten sheep, bushes, Mantis and Kwammang-a. Young Mantis and Young Kwammang-a cut All-Devourer open and true bushes and sheep emerge. Bushmen: Helfman BUSHMEN 110–118.

A1900 – A1999. Creation of birds.

A1900. Creation of birds.

A1905* Warriors ask for wings to cross river. Great Spirit turns them into birds. Those wearing white widower's headbands have white on heads, others black. Philippines (Tinguian): Sechrist ONCE 20–22.

A1906. Birds from pieces of monster bear. Native American (Chippewa): Leekley WORLD 92–99.

A1907. Glosskap turns dead leaves to birds to please children. Native American, Canada: Frost LEGENDS 287-294.

A1908* Maui calls forth brightly colored singing birds to top visitor's brag about bright flowers in his land. Hawaii: Williams SURPRISING 9.

A1912.3.1* Creation of robin. Boy making his fast in winter cannot be visited by his clan spirit as it is a robin. He paints body red in preparation for death and dies. Returns as robin with red breast. Brings spring each year. Native American (Iroquois): Jones LONGHOUSE #1.

A1937.1* Creation of hawk. Man wed to star maiden becomes white hawk along with wife and son. +F302.4.2.4. Native American: Haviland NORTH 97-100.

A1945.2. Gull a transformed ravished maiden. While he is sleeping, the maiden the hero has stolen is ravished by another man. The hero thereupon turns her into a gull. (Smith Ilmarinen transforms maid.) Finland (Karelia): Deutsch TALES 36-43.

A1947.1.1* Creation of guillemots. Old man curses shouting children and rock closes over them. They turn to guillemots. Curse him to change to frost. Eskimo: Gillham CLAPPING 35-40.

A1948.1* Creation of dove. Child, impatient because food takes long to cook, makes wings of nipa leaves and wishes self a bird. Dove is thus the only bird to understand human language. Philippines (Tinguian): Sechrist ONCE 20-22.

A1957. Creation of woodpecker. SEE: A1958.0.1.

A1958. Creation of owl.

A1958.0.1. The owl is a baker's daughter who objected to the size of the dough put into oven for Jesus when he appeared in her house as a beggar. +A2356.2.14. Type 751A. (cf. Q292.1; K1811.1). England: Williams-Ellis FAIRY.. BRITISH 103-105 (old woman transforms). England (Gloucestershire): Leach HOW 98. Norway: Sperry SCANDINAVIAN 260 (woodpecker; Undset TRUE 147-148 (woodpecker). Lurie CLEVER 30-34 (fairy).

A1958.0.2* Blodeuedd is turned to an owl by Gwydion for betraying husband. Wales: Sheppard-Jones WELSH 63-68.

A1966. Creation of stork.

A1966.1* Judge mocks criminals, turns to stork. North Africa: Holding KING'S 80-86.

A1970. Creation of miscellaneous birds.

A1999.1* Origin of puffin. Man who married a snow goose. Eskimo: Maher BLIND 79-88.

A1999.2* Origin of quetzal bird. Quetzal is told he will never die, uncle steals his amulet and kills. Q. turns to bird. Guatemala (Quiche): Barlow LATIN 126-132.

A1999.3* Origin of tickbird. Boy Indipi befriends exhausted red bird. When I. dies of drought white ghost bird seeks him. Asks cattle where he went. S. Africa (Zulu): Courlander RIDE 112-115.

A1999.4* Lazy person under basket turns to bird.

A1999.4.1* Kakok bird origin: lazy bride curls up under hat, wishes she were bird. Husband lifts hat, bird flies off calling "kakok kakok." Philippines (Tinguian): Sechrist ONCE 22-24.

A1999.4.2* Sigakok bird origin: mother drops basket over lazy boy sitting in sun. Returns to find bird flying off calling "sigakok" (lazy). Philippines (Tinguian): Sechrist ONCE 24-25.

A1999.5* Origin chingala bird. Boy seeking herb for dying mother turns to bird. Calls "che sy asy" (my mother is sick). Calls to warn whenever cold south wind is about to blow. Paraguay (Guarani): Courlander RIDE 213-214.

A1999.6* Origin kakui bird. Brother takes cruel sister into treetop and deserts her there. She turns into kakui and flies at night calling "turay!" (brother). Argentina: Carpenter SOUTH 160-166 (bee tree); Courlander RIDE 202-205.

A2000 - A2099. Creation of insects.

A2000. Creation of insects.

A2001. Insects from body of slain monster. SEE: A2034.2; A2091.3.

A2011.2. Creation of ant: avaricious man transformed. Aesop: Aesop AESOP'S (Watts) 159.

A2011.3* Wise man thrown to heavens to assume place among gods breaks into millions of pieces when falls = ants. He had feigned being able to "smell" what was inside of cupboards, ants really can. China: Wyndham TALES..CHINA 55-62.

A2012.0.1.1* Creation of honeybee. Girl who obeys mother by leaving dough to go to her side immediately when called, becomes golden bee after death. Paws carry yellow dough (pollen). Tatar: Ginsburg KAHA 53-54.

A2034. Origin of mosquitoes.

A2034.3.1* Monster Kloo-teeke caught in pit by carved image and voice thrown through kelp tube. Monster is burned in pit but turns into mosquitoes. Pacific Northwest: Harris ONCE 89-111.

A2034.3.2* Woman Rooted-to-the-Floor gives magic objects to throw behind (D672) when pursued by Cannibal at the North End of the World.

Whetstone = Mountain. Comb = yew forest. Oil = lake. Arrows = tree trunks. Three fleeing brothers call on Raven. R. digs pit of hot rocks and cannibal falls in and burns. Ashes become mosquitoes, gnats, fleas and houseflies. Native American (Northwest Coast): Martin NINE 38-42 /Martin RAVEN 45-52/.

A2034.4* Giant mosquito Moppo shot by coyote's magic arrow. Shrinks to present size. Native American (Shoshone): Heady SAGE 65-69.

A2034.5* God of Medicine lets Ngoc Tam restore wife by letting three drops of blood fall on her body. She leaves him for another man. He asks for the three drops of blood back. She gives them, withers and dies, turns to a mosquito. Still trying to get back those three drops of blood. Vietnam: Schultz VIETNAMESE 56-59.

A2041.1* Creation of butterfly. God snips off bits of flowers to become butterflies. To be companions for flowers. U.S. Black: Lester BLACK 15-20.

A2062.1* Origin of locust. Goddess Kayamanan grants farmer's request for good crops. Later she is turned away in beggar guise (K1811). She turns his rice into locusts. Philippines (Zambal): Sechrist ONCE 34-37.

A2091.2* Origin of spider. Daughter weaving refuses to go to mother when called. Turned to spider. Tatar: Ginsburg KAHA 53-54.

A2091.3* Tarantula steals warrior's costume. Villagers capture him using magic deer and antelope made by grandmother and two war-gods. They burn Tarantula and he explodes, pieces become tarantulas. Native American (Zuñi): Brown TEPEE 115-123.

A2094.1* Creation of fireflies. Firefly given lantern for finding lost jewel of insect king. Philippines: Robertson FAIRY..PHILIPPINES 91-95.

A2100 - A2199. Creation of fish
and other animals.

A2100. Creation of fish.

A2101* Origin of seals, whales, walrus, etc. Sedna flees bird husband with father and brothers. Sea Gods threaten to sink boat for stealing wife of Petrel (loon). Brothers throw Sedna into sea, cut off her hands as she clings to boat. Finger pieces become seal, walrus, whales. She becomes sea goddess. Eskimo: Caswell SHADOWS 26-34 /Haviland NORTH 60-64/; DeWit TALKING 168-174 /Carpenter WONDER..SHIPS 39-46/; Field ESKIMO 46-48 (Nuliajuk, orphan girl, thrown overboard); McDermott SEDNA pb; Melzack DAY 27-34.

A2102* Manabozho kills giant sturgeon. Pieces become fish. Native American (Chippewa): Leekley WORLD 79-91.

A2103* Raven scatters alder leaves on water,

become fish. Native American (Northwest): Martin NINE 6-18 /Martin RAVEN 11-15/, /Haviland NORTH 40-43/. DeWit TALKING 149-154.

A2108. Peopling of particular bodies of water with fish.

A2108.1* Grasshopper plague. Great Spirit sends Coyote to eat grasshoppers. He also digs at spring and Clear Lake forms, remaining grasshoppers plunge into water and turn to fish. Native American (Pomo): Fisher CALIFORNIA 80-86.

A2109* Other fish origins.

A2109.1* Salmon, seals, walrus from chips whittled from stick by old man Qayunqayung. Eskimo: Maher BLIND 79-98.

A2109.2* Raven finds floating house with man who catches fish everytime, scraps thrown back become baby fish. Raven carries him aloft on pretext. Drops stone which changes to island then rolls over four times and drops man into ocean (K1041). Raven takes possession of house but Halibut Man returns and clubs Raven and tosses in water. Raven returns with news that house is dangerously near whirlpool at the edge of the world. Killer whales tow house back near to beach. Raven calls to people to sing house closer to shore. They sing and house pours forth fish to fill all waters of the world. Native American (Northwest Coast): Martin NINE 55-60 /Martin RAVEN 83-88/; Robinson COYOTE 103-112 (Raven causes house to sink by spinning it, -killer whales).

A2116* Origin of moonfish. Moon leaves job to skip on water. Sea creatures tear at her. God cuts off torn parts and throws into sea = phosphorescence. Makes moonfish to populate waters. W. Indies: Carter GREEDY 3-8.

A2121.1* Creation of mackerel. Kauila strikes sea witches kidnapping his father with lightning, splintering them into pieces = mackerel. Hawaii: Cothran MAGIC 49-52.

A2126. Origin of flounder. SEE: A2332.4.4.

A2130.1* Origin of humu-humu-nuku-a-puaa, a grunting fish with piglike snout. Kamapuaa, Pig Man, changed to this fish when he tried to woo Pele. Hawaii: Thompson HAWAIIAN.. EARTH 45-52.

A2130.2* Origin Ikan Leleh fish. Wicked woman, Leleh, teases crocodiles with food eaten before them. They turn her into ikan leleh fish. Crocodiles have loaned their gamelan to villagers for feast. Indonesia: De Leeuw INDONESIAN 94-98.

A2135.1. Origin of narwhal.

A2135.1.1* Blind boy uses sister as hunting bladder. Shoots only small whales so she won't be dragged under water. Cruel mother insists on large whale, she acts as bladder, is pulled out to sea, turns to narwhal, her hair becomes horn. Eskimo: Caswell SHADOWS 41-47.

A2135.1.2* Blind boy throws cruel grandmother into lake wrapped in walrus hide. She becomes white whale with grey hairs in brain. Eskimo: Maher BLIND 17-30.

A2135.3.1* Origin of dolphin. Slaves diving for raja's buckle turn to dolphins (A2275.5.4.1). Indonesia: Courlander KANTCHIL'S 42-44

A2135.4. Vari-ma-te-takere tears off piece of own flesh and creates Vatea, first man, half fish. Vatea tears off piece of own flesh and throws into sea = porpoise. Why porpoise is half man, half fish. Polynesia: Leach HOW 85.

A2140. Creation of reptiles.

A2145.2. Snake preserved in ark: to stop hole with tail. +A1811.2. Leach LION 6-7.

A2145.9.1* Origin of rattlesnake. Evil clan who slay others after dancing contests are turned to rattlesnakes with dancing rattles fixed to tails. Native American (Iroquois): Jones LONGHOUSE #3.

A2146.1* Creation of crocodile. Wife (spirit of magic calf's fat) made to cook melts and runs into river. Becomes alligator. Gold Coast: Carpenter AFRICAN 161-168.

A2147.1* Creation of tortoise (turtle). Girl polishing two brass trays refuses to go to mother when called. Trays stick to her = turtle. Tatar: Ginsburg KAHA 53-54.

A2160. Origin of amphibia.

A2170. Origin of miscellaneous animal forms.

A2171.2. Creation of crab.

A2171.2.1* Origin of fiddler crab. Land crabs lose war with waves and are drowned. Only shrimp, with head bent under, sees waves coming and escapes. Children of land crabs become fiddler crabs constantly running at waves and then retreating. Philippines (Visayan): Sechrist ONCE 31-34. Philippines: Arnott ANIMAL 92-94.

A2171.2.3* Crabs from pieces of slain monster crab's body. Native American (Haida): Harris ONCE 33-58.

A2171.2.4* Da Trang seeks lost magic pearl in sea, spirit is in crabs, still ceaselessly rolling up balls of sand in hopes of filling up ocean and finding pearl. Vietnam: Schultz VIETNAMESE 74-79.

A2171.4* Princess throws lover's paltry gift of prawns into ocean, become red prawns of Vatu-Lele. Leaves they were wrapped in become seaweeds. Fiji: Gittens TALES 30-31.

A2182.6* Creation of sea raven. Raven weds two geese. Is unable to keep up on flight south and they dump him into sea. He breaks into pieces and pieces become sea ravens, small black sea creatures. Eskimo: Caswell SHADOWS 54-56.

A2200 - A2599. Animal Characteristics.

A2210. Animal characteristics: change in ancient animal.

A2211.2. Rabbit laughs: cause of hare-lip. SEE ALSO: A2342.1. Scandinavia: Wiggin TALES 309-310. Netherlands: Cathon PERHAPS 62-63.

A2211.7.1* Why turkey has white tail feathers. Turkeys helping little brother up mountain are last to arrive. Tail feathers hang down into flood. Native American (Tewa): Belting LONG 89-92.

A2213.2.1.1* Bobcat pulls out nose of sleeping coyote. Native American (Shoshone): Heady SAGE 61-64.

A2215.5. Fox struck with churn-dash: hence white tail. SEE ALSO: K934 (Fox as shepherd); A2378.8.1 (Why fox's tail is white on tip). Jacobs EUROPEAN 42-50.

A2216.1. Bear fishes through ice with tail: hence lacks tail. SEE: K1021; K1982.1. Native American: Martin NINE..COYOTE 23-30.

A2217. Appearance of animals from marking or painting. SEE: All A2411 entries.

A2217.2. Chipmunk's back scratched: hence his stripes. As he is trying to escape, bear catches him with his claws and marks him permanently. +A1172.4. (cf. A2413.2). Native American (Iroquois): Leach HOW 75-76. Native American (Nez Percé): Heady TALES 25-28. Native American (Creek): Brown TEPEE 62-63.

A2218. Animal's characteristics from burning or singeing. SEE ALSO: A2412.1.2.1; A1415; A727.1; A728.

A2219.1. Animal has color spilled on him: cause of his color (A2411.1.7.1.3; A2411.2.1.5).

A2220. Animal characteristic as reward.

A2221.1. Animals blessed for honoring infant Jesus. (cf. B250).

A2221.1.1* Nightingale given sweet song for singing babe to sleep (A2426.2.1). Fir tree weaves branches into shelter, made evergreen (A2711.4; A2765). Robin catches sparks on breast to protect child, given red breast (A2353.2; A2411.2.1.18). These things occurred on first birthday of Jesus while Gypsy's sheltered with Holy Family. Gypsy: Sawyer THIS 109-116.

A2221.5. Animals blessed for helping holy fugitive.

A2221.5.1. Ox helps patriarch who in joy kisses him on the lips: hence no hair on ox's lips. Jewish: Dobbs MORE 72–74 (steer carries Joshua to Jericho).

A2221.5.2* Why men do not kill spider. Spider's web hid fleeing Mohammed (B523.1). SEE ALSO: A2231.7.1.2. Indonesia: Courlander KANT-CHIL'S 76–79 (Hadji); De Leeuw INDONESIAN 90–93.

A2221.5.3* Warthog leads moslems to water. Flesh of pigs never eaten by Moslems. Africa (Hausa): Kaula AFRICAN 23–24.

A2229.7* People always share oolichans with raven as reward for bringing light. SEE: A1411.2.

A2230. Animal characteristics as punishment.

A2231.1. Animal's characteristics: punishment for discourteous answer to God (saint).

A2231.1.3. Discourteous answer: why crab has eyes behind (A2232.4.2). Poland: Borski GOOD 47.

A2231.1.3.1* Discourteous answer: why crayfish has eyes at back of head. Estonia: Maas MOON 44–46.

A2231.1.4. Discourteous answer: tortoise's shell. Zeus celebrates a wedding and invites the animals. Tortoise is late. Why? "I like my house." "May you bear your house always." Aesop: Aesop AESOP'S (Watts) 59.

A2231.1.5* Animal's characteristic from discourteous answer: Coyote flattens rattlesnake's head (A2320.1.0.1), pushes up grizzly bear's nose (A2335.2.7), pulls out cougar's tail (A2378.3.6).

A2231.7.1. Animals cursed for betraying holy fugitive.

A2231.7.1.2* Why lizard Tjikjak is killed by man. L. called "tjk" to betray hidden Hadji in cave. SEE ALSO: A2221.5.2; B523.1. Indonesia: Courlander KANTCHIL 76–79.

A2231.7.1.3* Hornbill refused to give water to moslems, may drink only every third day. Africa (Hausa): Kaula AFRICAN 23–24.

A2231.7.1.4* Scorpion wanted to sting hiding Mohammed. Indonesia: De Leeuw INDONESIAN 90–93.

A2231.10. Crab beats deity's forbidden drum: eyes left out of body. (cf. A2332.4.2; A2320.4). Africa (Fjort): Leach HOW 121–122 (Nzambi sentences crab to live without head since he acts as if doesn't have one, can stick eyes out to see).

A2232.1. Camel asks for horns: punishment short ears. SEE: A2325.4. Aesop: Aesop AESOP'S (Viking) 50–53.

A2232.2. Bees pray for sting: punishment, first sting suicidal. SEE ALSO: A2346.1. Aesop: Aesop AESOP'S (Grosset) 74 (punishment by Jupiter). Aesop AESOP'S (Watts) 35.

A2232.8.1* Donkey's ambassador sent to God to complain of being a beast of burden. Donkeys seek news of ambassador: why donkeys sniff each other. Ethiopia: Courlander FIRE 41–44.

A2233.1.1. Animals refuse to help dig well: may not drink from river or spring. Type 55. SEE ALSO: A2435.1.1. Native American (Cherokee): Bell JOHN 54–56; Scheer CHEROKEE 47–50 (+K471, K581.2). Congo: Kirn BEESWAX pb. Africa: Tracey LION 110–113. Africa (Thonga): Aardema BEHIND 48–56. U.S. Black: Courlander TERRAPIN'S 46–49 (pump handle screeches "quit hangin' round" when hare nears well); Faulkner DAYS 122–127. West Virginia: Haviland NORTH 109–114.

A2233.3 Owl as watchman goes to sleep: does not see by day. He is placed as watchman of wren who is imprisoned in a mousehole. +A2491.2.4. Grimm: Green BIG 47–51; Grimm GRIMM'S (Follett) 150–153; Wiggin TALES 172–175.

A2234.2. Animals eat deity's forbidden fruit: punished.

A2234.2.1* Crow sent by Allah for water of immortality drinks of it. There remains only enough to give man life. Crow turned black as punishment (A2411.2.1.6). +A2236.4.1. Indonesia: De Leeuw INDONESIAN 113–116.

A2235. Animal characteristics caused by animal's lateness at distribution of qualities. Congo (Luban): Burton MAGIC 101–102 (Sendji rat lacks tail, A2378.2.9). E. Africa: Heady WHEN 68–71 (Hydrax lacks tail, Mungu distributes, A2378.2.5).

A2235.1. Animal characteristic caused by animal's earliness at distribution of qualities. SEE ALSO: A2335.3.3. Congo (Luban): Burton MAGIC 101–102 (elephant receives longest nose).

A2235.2* Coyote stays up all night so as to be first at distribution of bows. Falls asleep and gets shortest (hence least power). Karok man intercedes with God Chareya on Coyote's behalf and C. is decreed most cunning of all. C. befriends Karoks since then. Native American (Karok): Fisher CALIFORNIA 74–79.

A2236.1. What creature has sweetest blood: gnat's tongue torn out. Assembly to decide who has the sweetest blood so that it may be the food for the serpent. Gnat discovers that man has the sweetest blood. Rather than let him tell his secret, swallow tears out his tongue. Gnat can only buzz (cf. A2344.2.1;

A2426.3.3). Armenian: Tashjian THREE 36-39 (dragon sends horsefly, man cuts out tongue). Siberia (Altai Mts.): Deutsch MORE 15-17 (bee sent by seven headed giant).

A2236.4.1* Magpie tells Allah that crow drank of water of life. Magpie turned half black for telling.+A2234.2.1. (cf. A2411.2.1.10). Indonesia: De Leeuw INDONESIAN 113-116.

A2240. Animal characteristics: obtaining another's qualities.

A2241. Animal characteristics: borrowing and not returning. Animal borrows a member (or quality) from another and refuses to return it.

A2241.12* Cricket arranges exchange of earthworm's eyes for snake's voice. Snake receives eyes but cricket asks to borrow voice from earthworm, telling him to ask for it when he wants it. As earthworm is voiceless, cricket still has voice. (cf. A2426.3.4; A2332.6.4). Japan: Novak FAIRY 81-84.

A2241.13* Wild Turkey borrows whippoorwill's feathers for election of king and keeps. Mayan: Bowes BIRD 15-18.

A2242.1* Wagtail borrows wren's tail to wear to lark's wedding. Keeps it. Rumania: Leach HOW 99.

A2242.2* Dragon borrows cock's golden horns to wear to banquet in heaven. Keeps them. China: Bonnet FOLK 111-114.

A2243.1. Spider hands box to ant and refuses to take it back: hence ants carry huge loads. W. Africa (Ashanti): Leach HOW 107 (Anansi).

A2250. Animal characteristics result of contest.

A2252.4. Flounder complains in race: crooked mouth. In race between fish he cries out in jealousy because herring is winning. He is punished with crooked mouth. German: Wiggin TALES 71 (sole).

A2260. Animal characteristics from transformation.

A2261.7* Transformed hawk seeking lost juju circles fires. (cf. A2442.2.5). +D672J. W. Africa (Ashanti): Courlander HAT 80-85.

A2262.4* Kwatee, the Changer, changes man making tools into animals. Knife = deer's antlers; club = beaver's tail; spear = mink's tail and teeth. Native American (Makah): Matson LEGENDS 106-109.

A2270. Animal characteristics from miscellaneous causes.

A2271.1. Thrus teaches dove to build nest. Type 236. SEE ALSO: A2431.3.11.

A2271.1.1* Magpie teaches nest making. First

make cake of mud. Thrush leaves with only this information = origin of thrush nest. Put twigs around nest, blackbird leaves = origin blackbird nest. Twigs around outside, sparrow leaves = sparrow nest. Line with feathers, starling leaves. Turtle remained throughout but learned nothing. England: Jacobs ENGLISH 200-204; Wiggin TALES 231-232.

A2271.1.2* Magpie is taught to build nest by other birds. Keeps saying "I knew that afore" learns nothing. Why magpie's nest is an untidy bundle of sticks. England: Williams-Ellis FAIRY..BRITISH 179-180.

A2272.1. Animal cries: imitation of sounds.

A2272.1.4* Thunder imitates sound of Vainamoinen's boots, river imitates sound of V's cloak, trees--sound of V's sleeves, birds--sound of V's harp, man--all of these. Finland: Deutsch MORE 1-5.

A2275. Animal habit a reminiscence of former experience.

A2275.5.3. Bat, diver, and thornbush are shipwrecked. Bat brought money, bush put on clothes, and diver brought leather. All shipwrecked. Diver is looking for his leather. Bush looks for his clothes and holds fast to all passers-by. Bat is abroad only at night to escape creditors. SEE ALSO: A2491.1. Aesop: Aesop AESOP'S (Watts) 174 (bat, bramble and seagull, s. is looking for lost shipment).

A2275.5.4.1* Raja loses jeweled buckle in sea and sends slaves to dive for it. They cannot return until it is found. They turn into Dolphins (A2135.3). Indonesia: Courlander KANTCHIL'S 42-44.

A2281.1. Cat loses dog's certificate: Enmity between dogs and cats. Dog is given a certificate of nobility (A2494.1.2). Through cat's carelessness it is lost. SEE: D882.1.1. Ukraine: Deutsch MORE 25-29. Latvia: Carpenter WONDER..DOGS 35-42.

A2281.0.1* Cat excused from work for cleanliness, dog for loyalty. Dog buries their document. Jealous horse, donkey and ox have rat dig it up and destroy. Origin of enmity between dog and cat. Palestine: Dobbs MORE 83-85 (cf. A2494.1.4; A2494.4.3.1; A2493.37).

A2281.0.2* Count gives animals written order for master to feed them. Donkey, dog and cat use. Rat uses last then tears up to make nest. Origin of enmity between the four. Italy: Hardendorff TRICKY 87-91.

A2281.0.3* God gives paper saying dog can eat animals which are down on the ground. Dog misinterprets and eats man's horse. Cat has lost certificate and dog cannot produce it. +A2471.1. Latvia: Carpenter WONDER..DOGS 35-42.

A2284.1. Animal persuaded to amputate limb: therefore lacks it. SEE: J758.1.3.

A2300 - A2399. Causes of animal characteristics: body.

A2300. Origin of animal characteristics: body. SEE ALSO: A2377.2 (flying squirrel).

A2305.1.2. Origin of flounder's flat body. SEE: A2332.4.4.

A2305.2.1* Why cockroach is flat. Too slow in putting tortoise's shell back together. T. squashes. Yoruba: Courlander OLODE 72-76.

A2305.3* Why mantis has flat sides. Slapped sides with hands on seeing destruction caused by a chain of events. +Z43.6.1. Ashanti: Courlander HAT 46-48.

A2305.4* Why horned toad has flat body. Smashed by rolling magic rock. Native American (Shoshone): Heady SAGE 24-26.

A2305.5* Why bedbug is flat. Squashed in drunken fight with louse and flea. Korea: Kim STORY 34-38.

A2305.6* Why crab is flat. Cow stepped on crab. China: Cathon PERHAPS 77.

A2310. Origin of animal characteristics: body covering.

A2311.5.1* Origin of porcupine's quills. Trapped by fox, p. prays to god Nohku and hairs are turned to quills. Honduras (Mayan): Barlow LATIN 113-118.

A2311.5.2* Origin of porcupine's quills. Fox has p. roll in mud, then puts thorns in back to protect from other animals. Native American (Seneca): Parker SKUNNY 117-123.

A2311.9.1* Why lizard has rough skin. Moloch Lizard throws boomerang and hits cockatoo on head knocking out feathers. C. rolls l. in thorny bush whence lizard's prickly, knobbly back. Australia: Arnott ANIMAL 76-78.

A2311.10* Where beaver got his fur. SEE: A728.2.1.

A2311.11* Why mouse has short hair on back. SEE: A728.0.1.

A2311.12* Why bear's coat is dark, coarse, and singed on tips. SEE: K1013.2 (Bowman).

A2312.1. Origin of tortoise's shell.

A2312.1.0.1* Turtle rewarded for bringing Nyame leopard's drum. Hard shell given to protect from jealous animals. +K714.2.5. W. Africa (Ashanti): Courlander HAT 32-37.

A2312.1.0.2* Tailor promises Allah will not steal cloth again, turns to tortoise with colors of all clothes stolen when he steals again. N. Africa: Holding KING'S 48-57.

A2312.1.0.3* Lizard hides from enemies between shields and dives into creek. Turns into turtle. Australia: Frost LEGENDS 295-297.

A2312.1.1. Origin of cracks in tortoise's shell. SEE ALSO: K1041.1.1.1; A2231.1.4; J2671.4.1.1; J657.2.3. Africa (Bemba): Kaula AFRICAN 80-83.

A2312.1.3. Tortoise carried by birds talks and loses hold on stick. Falls, cracking shell. SEE ALSO: J2357. Ceylon: Tooze WONDERFUL 107-110; Tooze THREE..TURTLES 8-21.

A2312.1.3.1* Turtle carried up to monkey's tree by holding onto liana speaks and falls. Cambodia: Tooze THREE..TURTLES 24-43.

A2312.1.4* Terrapin falls from tree spilling pot of wisdom and cracking shell. +A1481.1. U.S. Black: Courlander TERRAPIN'S 24-27.

A2312.1.5* Terrapin teases woman and she throws stone at him cracking shell. He rejoins it with magic words but the cracks still show. Native American (Creek): Belting LONG 54-56.

A2312.1.6* Turtle thrown into pond. Sings medicine song and mends shell back together. It hit a rock when thrown into pond. +K581.1. Native American (Cherokee): Bell JOHN 80-83; Scheer CHEROKEE 65-68.

A2312.1.7* Turtle beaten by man when turtle's war party attacks. Native American (Iroquois): Bruchac TURKEY 26-29.

A2312.1.8* Tortoise possesses first needle. Sews up cracked shell with thread given by Jungies. Native American (Seneca): Parker SKUNNY 132-138.

A2312.1.9* Tortoise being hauled up on rope to dog's mother is dropped. Nigeria: Fuja FOURTEEN 186-195; Walker NIGERIAN 27. Nigeria (Yoruba): Courlander OLODE 70-76 (antelope's mother).

A2312.3.1. Origin of crab's shell. SEE: C432.1.2.1.

A2313.6* Wild turkey's feathers borrowed from whippoorwill. (A2241.13). Mayan: Bowes BIRD 15-18.

A2313.7* Whippoorwill's (puhuy) feathers borrowed by wild turkey and not returned (A2241.13). W. has to clothe self with old feathers found in forest floor. +A2332.5.10; A2426.2.21; A2491.6. Mayan: Bowes BIRD 15-18.

A2313.8* Origin of owl's feathers. Owl lent feathers by other birds for ball. He never returns. (A2411.2.4.2). Puerto Rico: Alegria

Three 64-65.

A2315.2. Why blowfish is covered with spines. Japan: Bang MEN 35-37 (+K544.1).

A2317.2.1* Why beetle is bald. Beetle tries unsuccessfully to glue wig on head, declares all beetles bald henceforth. Native American (Hopi): Courlander PEOPLE 46-49.

A2317.2.2* Why spider is bald. Ananse's head is rubbed with hot oil as punishment for theft. W. Africa: Appiah ANANSE 95-104. SEE ALSO: W125.3.1 (Hat shaking dance).

A2317.3.0.1* Why buzzard is bald. Hare pours hot ashes on buzzard's head. U.S.: Field AMERICAN 154-156.

A2317.3.0.2* Eetoi defeats Buzzard in battle, takes scalp. Native American (Pima): Baker AT 43-49.

A2317.3.1* Why eagle is bald. Coyote pulls out head feathers in revenge. Native American (Nez Percé): Heady TALES 50-56.

A2317.7. Why vulture is bald.

A2317.7.1* In drought only vulture offers to carry sacrifice to heaven for people. His head and neck are burnt by sacrifical fire and his home is ruined by ensuing rains. Still none will take him in. His burnt feathers remind others of their own selfishness. Nigeria (Yoruba): Fuja FOURTEEN 64-68.

A2317.7.2* Vulture refuses to help Arap Sang to reach shade. Cursed. Africa: Harman TALES 109-117.

A2317.7.3* Vulture reveals his pet peeve, wants top knot respected. In ensuing fight it is burnt off. Nigeria (Yoruba): Courlander OLODE 54-57.

A2317.12. Why opossum has bare tail.

A2317.12.1* Bear catches opossum by tail. P. escapes but hair comes off tail. U.S. Black: Harris FAVORITE 178-181/ Harris COMPLETE 87-90/; /Harris SONGS 131-137/.

A2317.12.2* Racoon advises wrapping tail in sycamore bark and putting tail in fire to get stripes like his. Native American (Creek): Belting LONG 46-50.

A2317.12.3* Hare has cricket dress opossum's tail for dance. C. clips hair short. Native American (Cherokee): Bell JOHN 47-51; Hardendorff JUST 85-87; Scheer CHEROKEE 75-79.

A2317.13* Why squid has bald head. Manu Manu took crab, frigate bird and rat for ride in canoe. Canoe sank. Squid gave rat ride to shore but R. nibbled hair off squid's head. Since then Squid chases rats and fish hook is shaped like rat. Ellice Islands: Gittens TALES 82-84.

A2320. Origin of animal characteristics: head.

A2320.1.0.1* Why rattlesnake's head is flat. Native American (Iroquois): Bruchac TURKEY 26-29. SEE ALSO: A2231.1.5.

A2320.1.2* Why spider's head is small. Anansi joins spirits splashing stream dry. They use own skulls to dip water, he imitates. Cannot put head back on (or puts it on his behind). W. Africa (Akan-Ashanti): Leach HOW 82-83; McDowell THIRD 31-34.

A2320.3.1. Origin of mudhen's red head. Hawaii: Cothran MAGIC 45-48. Pacific Islands: Carpenter ELEPHANT'S 204-211.

A2320.3.2* Origin of crane's red head. Reward given by rabbit for carrying him to moon. +A751.2.2. Native American (Cree): Belting LONG 67-70.

A2320.4. Why crab has no head. SEE ALSO: A2231.10.

A2320.4.1* Crab tricks elephant and hawk. They behead him and throw into pond. Prawn puts eyes on shoulders. Eastern Nigeria (Ikom): Arnott AFRICAN 35-39.

A2320.8* Why catfish has flat head. Beaten on head for stealing tadpoles. Vietnam: Vo Dinh TOAD 23-27.

A2321.5.1* Origin of kingfisher's crest. Wenebajo is angry because his nephew was drowned. Puts nephew's white beads around Kingfisher's neck intending to catch him. K. escapes but head is ruffled = crest. White necklace still worn. Must dive for a living henceforth. Native American (Chippewa): Leach HOW 96.

A2321.10. Origin of cock's red crest. SEE ALSO: A720.1.2.

A2321.10.0.1* Origin of cock's red crest. Stolen from hawk which had been feasted to sleep with henbane. Ukraine: Deutsch TALES 1-6.

A2321.10.0.2* Sun gives comb to rooster, he puts it on head teeth up. China (Ch'uan Miao): Leach HOW 92-93.

A2321.12* Origin of cockatoo's crest. Lizard hits c. on head with boomerang causing scraggly crest. +A2311.9.1. Australia: Arnott ANIMALS 76-78.

A2321.13* Origin of crowned crane's head feathers. Cranes help thirsty Arap Sang to shade, are given golden crowns. Africa: Harman TALES 109-117.

A2325. Origin of animal's ears.

A2325.1.1* Why rabbit has long ears. Creator vows to make r. bigger if he brings feather of eagle, tooth of lion, egg of serpent. Clever r. gets. Creator stretches ear. W. Indies: Carter GREEDY 62-67. Nicaragua: Jagendorf KING 211-218 (skin of crocodile, tiger and monkey).

A2325.3.1* Why ass has long ears. When animals are being named, ass keeps forgetting his name. The Lord pulls his ears repeating his name. Sicily: Jagendorf PRICELESS 122-124. Italy: Dobbs MORE 86-89 (Adam).

A2326.1.1.1.1* Why deer has antlers: as reward for not cheating. Beaver carves horns, bear greases, and fox polishes. Horns are prize in race. Hare cheats (K11.9) and horns are awarded to deer. Native American (Cherokee): Bell JOHN 67-69; Belting LONG 57-59; Scheer CHEROKEE 55-57.

A2326.2.3. Originally cock had horns. China: Bonnet CHINESE 111-114.

A2330. Origin of animal characteristics: face.

A2330.5. Why flea's face is red. From too much drink. Korea: Kim STORY 34-38.

A2330.9* Why owl has a flat face. Raven slams owl against wall of igloo after owl violates fox-wife's tabu by mentioning her odor. Eskimo: Melzack RAVEN 53-60.

A2332.1.5.1* Where owl got his eyes. Owl watches as Ra-wen-io creates Hare. Punishment: his head is pushed into shoulders, eyes are made large and fixed, must live in dark. +A2491.2. Native American (Seneca): Parker SKUNNY 72-74.

A2332.1.6* Where snake got his eyes. SEE: A2241.12.

A2332.3.1.1* Why coyote's eyes are large. Native American (Shoshone): Heady SAGE 42-45. +J2423.1.

A2332.3.2.1* Why eel's eyes are narrow. Laughed too much after tricking porgy into fishtrap. Vietnam: Vo-Dinh TOAD 45-49.

A2332.4.2. Why crab lifts eyes out of body or has eye behind. SEE: A2231.10; A2231.1.3.

A2332.4.4* Why flounder has two eyes on same side of face and is flat. Lobster mad at flounder for stirring up water, stamps him flat. F. complains that one eye is in sand, so L. sticks it on top of F.'s head. Polynesia: Leach HOW 117.

A2332.5.7. Why wild duck has red eyes. Dances for trickster. SEE ALSO: K826. Native American (Chippewa): Leekley WORLD 50-54 (grebe warns ducks and Manabozo gives red eyes and pulls out tail, A2378.2.10). Native American (Senceca): Parker SKUNNY

43-51.

A2332.5.9* Why porgy's eyes are red. From crying after eel tricks him into fish trap. Vietnam: Vo-Dinh TOAD 45-49.

A2332.5.10* Why whippoorwill's eyes are red. From crying. +A2313.7. Mayan: Bowes BIRD 15-18.

A2332.5.11* Why crane's eyes are blue. Substitutes blueberries for eyes after Kayak steals eyes. +J2199.1.3. Eskimo: Gillham CLAPPING 76-85.

A2332.5.12* Blackbird late for dance looks over tabu cedar fence and eyes are burnt by coals. Given white shell beads as eyes. Falls in fire and coat is black. Tongue burnt and can only call "Tank, Tank" henceforth. Native American (Navajo): DeWit TALKING 75-79.

A2332.6.4. Why worm is blind. SEE: A2441.12.

A2332.6.5. Why mole is blind. SEE: A727.2.

A2335.2.3* Why raven has nose marked as if it had been broken off. Raven's beak is hooked by fisherman and broken off. R. follows broken beak half to village of Herring People, Shark People, Gull People as it is passed on. All call it the Nose of Konakadet. R. cannot enter village easily as his shaman's hat (beak) is half gone when he assumes man form. He creates a Butterfly to carry him to enter villages in man form. Finally retrieves. Native American (Northwest Coast): DeWit TALKING 142-149; Martin NINE 27-30 /Martin RAVEN 37-43/.

A2335.2.5. Why steer has no hair on his nose. SEE: A2221.5.1.

A2335.2.6* Why dog has cold, wet nose. Dog helps collect animals for the ark and is last one on board. There is not enough room and his nose sticks out. Jewish: Dobbs MORE 68-71.

A2335.2.6.1* Arawidi, sun-spirit turns fish into dogs as companions for man. They are held by noses as are formed, hence nose is still cold. Carib: Sherlock WEST 34-38.

A2335.2.6.2* Dog tries to plug leak in ark with nose. +A1811.2. Leach LION 12.

A2335.2.7* Why grizzly bear's nose is pushed up. SEE: A2231.1.

A2335.3.3* Why elephant has long nose. He was given the first nose. There was not enough material left for long noses for the rest. +A2235.1. W. Africa (Ashanti): Courlander HAT 9-12 (+B841.1.2).

A2335.3.4* Fish with bent noses. Fish stole grain of rice needed by Prince Sotat. Nose turns down in shame. They swim upstream to temple of Buddha on the Mekong each year in rainy season to request forgiveness. Cambodia: Carpenter ELEPHANT'S 22-30.

A2335.4.1.1* Why pig has short snout. Anansi drops pig's money in bamboo tube. Pig gets trunk stuck fishing for it. A. cuts trunk off to free pig. W. Africa: Appiah ANANSE 39-46.

A2341.1. Why flounder's mouth is crooked. SEE: A2252.4.

A2341.4* Why fish have gills. Swallowed girl cuts slits in throat. Rarotonga: Holding SKY 75-86.

A2342.1. Why hare's lip is split. A2216.3; A2211.2; A1335.1.0.1. Scandinavia: Wiggin TALES 309-310 (laughs).

A2342.1.1* Rabbit gets secret of flint from fox, told will die if makes arrows. R. tries to get rid of flint by burning. It explodes. Chip flies and hits in face, splitting lip. +A1414.5.2. Native American (Seneca): Parker SKUNNY 85-94.

A2342.1.2* Hare drives wedge into sleeping flint and f. explodes. Hare's lip split with chip. Native American (Cherokee): Bell JOHN 41-43.

A2342.2. Why ox has no hair on his lips. SEE: A2221.5.1.

A2342.3. Why donkeys have short upper lip. Donkey asked to leave portion of lip at gate when visiting Hyena, then accused of sneering and attacked. Ethiopia: Courlander KING'S 74-77.

A2343.1.5* Where duck got bill. Mallard duck gave horn spoons at wedding feast. Ducks took them home and now wear on noses. Native American (Sahaptian): Belting LONG 74-75.

A2343.1.6* Why crane has long beak. Emu hurls spear at crane which comes out crane's month. Gumaitj: Leach HOW 101.

A2343.3.3* Why parrot's beak is bent. Bent making first hammer. +B841.1.2. W. Africa (Ashanti): Courlander HAT 9-12.

A2343.3.4* Why owl's beak is hooked. Coyote bends it in revenge. Native American (Nez Percé): Heady TALES 50-56.

A2343.3.5* Why frigate bird can't catch fish. He and brown pelican trade beaks. W. Indies: Sherlock IGUANA'S 11-28.

A2344.2. Why animal has no tongue.

A2344.2.1. Why gnat has no tongue. SEE: A2236.1.

A2344.3.1.1* Why horsefly has no tongue. SEE: A2236.1.

A2344.4* Why animal has long tongue.

A2344.4.1* Dog tattles on hunter continuously. Hunter pulls his tongue out long as punishment. Native American (Caddo): Brown TEPEE 26-28.

A2345.3.1* Why deer have short teeth. Saynday tricks them into mud and files off teeth while they are stuck. This is done so they cannot hurt people. Native American (Kiowa): Marriott WINTER 25-31.

A2345.3.2* Hare chews grapevine almost through then pretends to bite it into two pieces with one bite. Deer wants sharp teeth too and lets hare file his teeth. Native American (Cherokee): Bell JOHN 70-73; Scheer CHEROKEE 58-60.

A2345.5.1* Where Rattlesnake got his fangs. Earth Mother gave R. fangs since everyone made fun of him. Native American (Luiseño): Leach HOW 112.

A2345.10* Where Beaver got his teeth. SEE: A728.2.1.

A2350. Origin of animal characteristics: trunk.

A2351.4.4* Origin of giraffe's long neck. Caught by tornado while stretching into tree for leaves. Neck stretched. Africa: Heady SAFIRI 82-86.

A2351.5.1* Why turtle has a long neck. Tries to climb pine tree, falls, and neck sticks in mud. Stretches neck in pulling it out. Sweats so much in effort that others smell him and get the idea of making turtle soup. Native American (Seneca): Parker SKUNNY 146-152.

A2351.8* Origin of turkey's wattle. Turkey steals scalp from terrapin returning from war. +A2371.2.13. Native American (Cherokee): Bell JOHN 61-63; Scheer CHEROKEE 43-46.

A2351.8.1* Scalp of Stone Coat Giant is worn around turkey's neck = wattle. +G511.2. Native American (Seneca): Parker SKUNNY 196-203.

A2351.9* Why buzzard has no neck feathers. Hare hits him over head with guitar when b. tries to drop hare during flight. Nicaragua: Jagendorf KING 205-208.

A2353.2. Why robin has red breast. SEE: A2221.1.1.

A2354.2* Why animal bellies are lighter than backs. SEE: F53.2.

A2355.1.1. Why spider has small waist.

A2355.1.1.1* Ananse's waist is burnt half through. W. Africa: Appiah ANANSE 123-138.

A2355.1.1.2* Ananse's waist pulled thin by rope around waist. Liberia/Ghana: Arkhurst ADVENTURES 5-11. Bantu: Nunn AFRICAN 79-80. Ashanti: Courlander HAT 18-19. Liberia: Courlander RIDE 116-118. (+J2183.1.3). SEE ALSO: Z49.6.

A2355.1.2. Why ant has small waist.

A2355.1.2.1* Ant as go-between for wooing earthworm and centipede laughs at their distaste for each other. Ties string around waist so won't burst. Korea: Carpenter KOREAN 151-154.

A2355.1.2.2* Saynday accepts red ant's advice not to revive dead (A1335.8.1). Her own son dies and she cuts self almost in half as reminder of what she caused world to suffer. Native American (Kiowa): Marriott WINTER 31-35.

A2355.1.2.3* Frog invites ants to feast, dives into pond and never returns. After seven days of waiting they tighten their belts and go home hungry = small waists. Altai: Deutsch TALES 32-35.

A2355.1.3* Why wasp has small waist. Brer wasp laughs so hard he pinches waist small clapping sides in laughter. U.S.: Frost LEGENDS 174-176.

A2356. Origin and nature of animal's back.

A2356.2.1.1* Why toad has warts on back. Ashes burn him when captured and tortured. Friend Peeper saves him. Native American (Seneca): Parker SKUNNY 190-195.

A2356.2.8. Why spider has thread in back of body.

A2356.2.8.1* Spider set to making string by creator swallows string. Told to keep it if he wants it that bad. Native American (Wishosk, Wiyot): Leach HOW 84.

A2356.2.11. Why alligator has rough back. U.S. Black: Faulkner DAYS 128-131; Harris COMPLETE 220-224 /Harris NIGHTS 141-145/.

A2356.2.13. Why camel has humped back. SEE ALSO: A1873.

A2356.2.13.1* Camel asks Lord of Heaven for larger feet and hump. When laughed at he asks also for proud look. China: Ross BURIED 135-138.

A2356.2.14* Hump on owl's back is loaf of bread put there as penance. +A1958.0.1. Gloucestershire: Leach HOW 98.

A2356.2.15* Why shrimp has broken back. Vietnam: Vo-Dinh TOAD 51-55.

A2356.2.16* Why lobster has humped back. SEE: J953.20.

A2362.1.1* Why baboon's buttocks are shiny. Falls on them when hare's mother cuts chain. Sierra Leone (Krio): Robinson SINGING 8-15.

A2362.2* Why elephant's hind part is small. Ananse got elephant stuck between two trees and told he must cut off hind part to get free. Ananse took the meat. E. sent sons to reclaim but A's sons played drums and the elephants had to dance. Three sons and father each tried but gave up. E's live in grasslands now. W. Africa (Ashanti): Courlander HAT 38-45.

A2367.1. Animal characteristics: bones.

A2367.1.2* Why jellyfish has no bones in body. SEE: K544.1.

A2367.1.3* Why octopus has no bones. SEE: K544.1.

A2370. Animal characteristics: extremities.

A2371.1. Origin of animal's legs.

A2371.1.1* Origin of dog's hind leg. Buddha turns lotus blossom into hind leg for dog. +A2473.1. Vietnam: Vo-Dinh TOAD 75-80.

A2371.2.13* Why turkey has small bones in legs. Pursuing terrapin shoots cane splints into legs. +A2351.8. Native American (Cherokee): Bell JOHN 61-63; Scheer CHEROKEE 43-46.

A2371.2.14* Why crane has long legs. Stretched carrying rabbit to the moon. +A751.2. Native American (Cree): Belting LONG 67-70.

A2375.2. Nature of animal's feet.

A2375.2.7. Why mole's "hands" are turned backward. SEE: A727.2.

A2375.2.8.1* Duck's have flat feet since sky fell on duck's feet. Chukchansi Yokut: Belting LONG 39-41.

A2375.2.9.1* Why frog's hands are flat. Frog shakes hands with everyone to thank them for land clearing. God suggests sending a messenger to announce thanks next time. Liberia: Courlander COW-TAIL 129-131.

A2375.2.10.1* Why the guinea fowl has red feet. Put out grass fire when world was new. +B841.1.2. W. Africa (Ashanti): Courlander HAT 9-12.

A2375.11* Why apes, monkeys, gorillas, chimpanzees have face, hands and feet, like men. Any animal washing in pot of oil to become man. God changes mind and breaks pot. Monkeys wash face, hands, and feet in spilled puddles. SEE ALSO: A1614.2. U.S. Black: Lester BLACK 21-37.

A2376. Animal characteristics: claws and hoofs.

A2376.1.0.1* Why carabao has cloven hoof. Kicked turtle in anger after losing race. +K11.1. Tagalog: Sechrist ONCE 56-60.

A2377. Animal characteristics: wings.

A2377.1. Why emu has no wings. +A2486.5. Turkey convinces hen is better to cut them off. Australia: Parker AUSTRALIAN 15-19; Sleigh NORTH 13-18.

A2377.2* Flying squirrel stretched to make wings. SEE ALSO: B261.1.0.2.1. Native American (Creek/Cherokee): Belting LONG 16-25.

A2377.3* Birds cut wings of leather for bat. +B261.1.0.2.1. Native American (Creek/Cherokee): Belting LONG 16-25.

A2377.4* Why ostrich keeps wings close to body and never flies. SEE: A1415.0.2.2.

A2378. Origin and nature of animal's tail.

A2378.1.1. Where baboon got tail. SEE: A1863.

A2378.1.6.1* Where beaver got tail. Beaver sits on tail to slide with otters, flattens tail and wears off hair. Native American (Shoshone): Heady SAGE 39-41.

A2378.1.7.1* How dog got its tail. Dog gambles with hoop and pole and keeps losing hoop. People curl his tail into a permanent hoop = why dog's tail curls. Native American (Lipan Apache): Belting LONG 26-28; Leach HOW 62.

A2378.2.2.1* Why goat's tail is short. Lions invite animals to dance, planning to push goats into fire. Dog and Goat see fire and flee. Dog leaps into creek. Goat hides in haystack. Dog provokes lion into throwing haystack at him. Goat's tail comes off in lion's claws but G. is safe. Puerto Rico: Belpre TIGER 97-103; Belpre DANCE pb ; Jagendorf KING 244-248.

A2378.2.3.1* How frogs lost tails. Punishment for conceit. Frog to guard Nyame's well refuses water to other animals. Nyame takes his tail away. W. Africa (Ashanti): Courlander HAT 93-95. Sukuma: Kaula AFRICAN 63-64. Haiti: Courlander PIECE 15-19 (lizard). SEE ALSO: A1415.2.2.1.

A2378.2.5. Why hydrax has no tail. SEE: A2235.

A2378.2.6.1* How tadpoles lost tails. Told by God to weed cornfield but Devil tempted them to go swimming. God took away their tails, then relented and gave them legs to swim with. N. Carolina Negro: Leach HOW 113-114.

A2378.2.9* Why sendji rat has no tail. SEE: A2235.

A2378.2.10* Grebe's tail pulled out by Manabozo.

SEE: A2332.5.7.

A2378.2.11* Why cormorant has no tail. At banquet given by cormorant, c. cuts off gudgeon's tail. As host he is forced to replace it with his own. Burma: Brockett BURMESE 131-135.

A2378.3.5* Why wagtail has long tail. +A2242.1. Rumania: Leach HOW 99.

A2378.3.6* Why cougar has long tail. Pet cougar hauls boy up on tail when pursuing buck. Tail stretches. Native American (Shoshone): Heady SAGE 80-84. SEE ALSO: A2231.1.5.

A2378.4. Why animal has short tail. SEE ALSO: J429.3.

A2378.4.1. Why hare has short tail.

A2378.4.1.1* Hare loses tail ice fishing. +K1021. U.S. Black: Harris FAVORITE 11-14 / Harris COMPLETE 80-83; Harris SONGS 122-126/. Jamaica: Williams-Ellis ROUND 195-196.

A2378.4.1.2* Hare's tail comes off when bear catches. Native American (Cherokee): Bell JOHN 43-47; Scheer CHEROKEE 69-74.

A2378.4.1.3* Man throws hatchet chopping off tail of hare. Hare puts piece of cotton there. U.S. Black: Harris COMPLETE 252-257 /Harris NIGHTS 185-192/.

A2378.4.1.4* Lynx has hare pull him out of hole with tail. Bites hare's tail off. Native American (Seneca): Parker SKUNNY 75-84.

A2378.4.1.5* Why hare has short tail. +K579.2.2. Japan: Courlander TIGER'S 87-89. Baganda/ Alabama Negro: Leach HOW 69.

A2378.4.2. Why bear has short tail. SEE ALSO: K1021.

A2378.4.2.1* Bear loses tail imitating mud turtle by sliding on rock. U.S. Black: Harris NIGHTS 113-117 /Harris COMPLETE 199-202/.

A2378.4.7.1* Why crow has short tail. Mr. Crow gets tail caught in Clapping Mountains (D1553.1) while showing off. Eskimo: Gillham BEYOND 31-42 /Gruenberg MORE 113-118/.

A2378.4.8* Why wren has short tail. SEE ALSO: A2242.1. Rumania: Leach HOW 99.

A2378.4.9* Why the groundhog has a short tail. Pulled off as he escaped through hole. +K606.2. Native American (Cherokee): Bell JOHN 83-86; Belting LONG 29-33; Scheer CHEROKEE 31-32.

A2378.4.10* Why deer has short tail. S.E. China: Hume FAV..CHINA 109-114 (+J2132.5.1).

A2378.4.11* Why lynx has short tail. Fox lowers rope to pull lynx from pit but drops rock on lynx's tail as l. jumps for rope. Native American (Seneca): Parker SKUNNY 75-84.

A2378.4.12* Why coyote has short tail. Animals cut off sleeping Coyote's tail. Native American (Nez Percé): Heady TALES 50-56.

A2378.4.12.1* Why coyote has short tail. Tail frozen in ice while tail fishing (K1021). Native American (Pueblo): Cothran WITH 44-48.

A2378.4.13* Why wolf has short tail. Told moon's reflection is cheese. Covers with tail until farmer goes to sleep, tail sticks to ice (K1021). Scotland: Montgomerie TWENTY FIVE 30-31.

A2378.4.14* Why bobcat has short tail. Coyote pulls tail off with magic while bobcat sleeps. Native American (Shoshone): Heady SAGE 61-64.

A2378.4.15* Why wildcat has short tail. Wildcat lets fire go out and steals from giant carrying brand in tail. Tail is burnt to a stub. Cougar has food and no fire. Wildcat has fire and no food. They join forces. Native American (Nisqually): Matson LEGENDS 19-24.

A2378.4.16* Why elephant's tail is short and black. Persuaded to tie weeds to tail and set afire to smoke bees. Africa (Luo): Nunn AFRICAN 88-95.

A2378.6. Why animal has bushy tail.

A2378.6.2* Why coyote has bushy tail. Bobcat changes coyote's tail and squeezes his nose while c. sleeps. Native American (Shoshone): Heady SAGE 61-64.

A2378.7.1. Why beaver has flat tail. SEE: A2378.1.6.1.

A2378.8. Origin of color of animal's tail. SEE ALSO: A2211.7.1 (turkey); A1415.2.2.1.2 (coyote); A1414.4.2 (redstart).

A2378.8.1. Why end of fox's tail is white. SEE ALSO: A2215.5.

A2378.8.1.0.1* Mice bit fox's fur off in night. Fox covered self with pitch and rolled in fur but mice had bitten all color out of tip of tail. Native American (Acoma): Belting LONG 93-94.

A2378.9. Nature of animal's tail--miscellaneous. SEE ALSO: A2317.12 (possum).

A2378.9.1.2* Why sculpin (devilfish) has short, pointed tail. He mocks fox and fox rips fat off tail. Eskimo: Gillham CLAPPING 117-120.

A2378.9.5.1* Why Giant Rat's tail is two-colored. Pursuing lion pulls half the skin off tail. Liberia: Haskett GRAINS 51-54.

A2378.9.6* Why squirrel's tail turns up. It was singed in attempt to release snared sun.

+A728.0.1. SEE ALSO: A1415.2.2.1.2. Native American (Karok): Fisher CALIFORNIA 46-53.

A2378.9.7* Why cat's tail has curl at end. Pet Siamese cat keeps tail curled around cup to keep anyone from poisoning king. Thailand: Carpenter WONDER..DOGS 43-51.

A2400 - A2499. Causes of animal characteristics: appearance and habits.

A2410. Animal characteristics: color and smell.

A2411. Origin of color of animal. (cf. A2217).

A2411.1.1.1. Color of leopard.

A2411.1.1.1.1* Leopard rescues tortoise from tree where hyena has tied him. T. makes paint from flower and paints L. in gratitude. Also paints Zebra and Giraffe, but smears Hyena's colors. Africa (Zulu): Heady TEMBA 78-84; Kaula AFRICAN 88-90.

A2411.1.1.1.2* Leopard sings well and is given a fine coat by medicine man, Ngamu. Animals are to pay for their coat with a song. E. Africa: Heady WHEN 53-58.

A2411.1.1.1.3* Why leopard has spots. Trapped and taken to Nyame in a drum, L. falls into fire when breaking out of drum. +K714.2.5. W. Africa (Ashanti): Courlander HAT 32-37.

A2411.1.2.1.2* Why weasel is white. He saved Old-Man from Win-to-coo, Man-Eater, and was given a white coat for winter, brown for summer. Native American: Field AMERICAN 62-70.

A2411.1.2.1.2.1* Why weasel turns white in winter. Mink to walk along shore following shoreline exactly. He cuts across sandpoint and is struck dead. Weasel revives mink but now mink looks like weasel. Weasel turns self white each winter to remind mink of mistake in disobeying Great Spirit. Native American (Puget Sound): Matson LEGENDS 115-121.

A2411.1.2.6* Color of raccoon. Coyote smears with charcoal, origin rings. Native American (Nez Percé): Heady TALES 50-56.

A2411.1.3.1. Color of fox.

A2411.1.3.1.1* Fox turns red in shame when lady mouse escapes by singing. +K606. Eskimo: Gillham BEYOND 99-105 /Cathon PERHAPS 48-52/.

A2411.1.3.1.2* Old Man Autumn is to wipe paint brushes on fox if he can paint reflection of a leaf. He does this by trickery and wipes brushes on fox. Why fox has grey chest, charcoal on red back. Native American (Seneca): Parker SKUNNY 43-51.

A.2411.1.3.2. Color of coyote. SEE: A1415.2.2.2;

A1415.2.2.4.

A2411.1.3.2.1* Coyote imitates bluebird's dip in lake (A2411.2.1.20.1) and turns blue, but falls in dust, hence brown today. Native American (Pima): Brown TEPEE 146.

A2411.1.3.3* Color of wolf. Coyote smears with charcoal, hence is gray. Native American (Nez Percé): Heady TALES 50-56.

A2411.1.3.4* Origin of color of wolf. Grey wolf imitates bluebird's dive into lake for blue coat. He doesn't wait for it to dry and gets covered with grey dust. Native American (Seneca): Parker SKUNNY 139-145.

A2411.1.4.1. Color of squirrel.
SEE ALSO: A1415.0.2.3.

A2411.1.4.1.1* Manabozo paints squirrel with red brown sides and red-white tummy for help in vanquishing monster. Fluffs up tail. Native American (Chippewa): Leekley WORLD 79-91 /Haviland NORTH 19-20/.

A2411.1.4.3. Color of rat.

A2411.1.4.3.1* Rat loses race with beetle for colorful coat. Brazil: Newman FOLK 67-71.

A2411.1.6.8* Color of giraffe. Painted by tortoise. SEE: A2411.1.1.1.

A2411.1.6.9* Color of hartebeest. H. sings poorly, making a sneezing noise only and is rewarded by Ngamu with a plain brown coat. E. Africa: Heady WHEN 53-58.

A2411.1.7.1. Origin of color of hyena.

A2411.1.7.1.1* Tortoise cuts Hyena's hair different lengths and smears with paints mixed together. +A2411.1.1.1. Africa (Zulu): Arnott TEMBA 78-84; Kaula AFRICAN 88-90.

A2411.1.7.1.2* Hyena sings poorly and Ngamu rewards with a poor coat. E. Africa: Heady WHEN 53-58.

A2411.1.7.1.3* Hyena has paint pot thrown at him. Africa: Heady SAFIRI 67-70.

A2411.1.7.2* Origin of color of paca. P. has dull coat because lost race with beetle. SEE: K11.10.

A2411.2. Origin of color of bird.

A2411.2.0.1* Origin of colors of birds. Birds fly through rainbow when leaving ark. North Carolina Negro: Leach HOW 89-90.

A2411.2.0.2* Raven paints birds for war dance against Grizzly Bear. R. eats feast alone as birds leave. Native American (Tahltan): Belting LONG 37-38.

A2411.2.0.3* The Summer Birds of K'yakime.

Maid married to rain god bears supernatural son. He obtains wood for bow and arrows from bear on promising to give bear his mother. Shoots bear with obsidian points which bear thinks are coals. Plants prayer stick in gratitude and bird's feathers turn bright colors. Native American (Zuni): DeWit TALKING 80-87.

A2411.2.1.5. Color of Raven.
SEE ALSO: A1415.2.3.

A2411.2.1.5.1* Raven and Loon decorate each other. Raven won't stand still to be painted so Loon dumps charcoal box on him. In anger R. throws stones at Loon and injures his legs. +A2411.2.6.1; A2441.2.3. Eskimo: Caswell SHADOWS 33-34.

A2411.2.1.5.2* Raven and Owl paint each other. Owl spills lamp black on raven who won't stand still. Central Eskimo: Melzack DAY 21-25; Newell RESCUE 75-80.

A2411.2.1.6. Color of crow.
SEE ALSO: A2234.2.1.

A2411.2.1.6.1* Peacock knocks over paints and only black is left for crow. Hardendorff JUST 37-39. China: Kirn PEACOCK pb.

A2411.2.1.6.2* White crow carrying tokens from monarch of the rains to princess is intercepted and jewels he carries are turned to scorpions. Crow is turned black in punishment and can only crow. Indonesia: De Leeuw INDONESIAN 14-20.

A2411.2.1.8. Color of jay.
SEE: A2426.2.26.1.

A2411.2.1.9.1* Color of red-winged blackbird. Flies too close to fire built to kill ogress Ninambitz. Native American (Shoshone): Heady SAGE 51-53.

A2411.2.1.10. Color of magpie.
SEE: A2236.4.1.

A2411.2.1.13. Color of red-bird.
SEE ALSO: A2411.2.1.19.3; A1414.4.2.

A2411.2.1.13.1* Raccoon plasters sleeping wolf's eyes with mud. Kind redbird pecks dried mud off and grateful wolf shows bird red rock with which to paint self. Native American (Cherokee): Belting LONG 62-66; Scheer CHEROKEE 62-68.

A2411.2.1.18* Color of robin.
SEE ALSO: A2221.1.1.

A2411.2.1.18.1* Robin's red breast from flying too near to fire. Native American (Shoshone): Heady SAGE 51-53.

A2411.2.1.18.2* Robin gets camwood powder from merchant, it dribbles down his breast as he flies home. Why his breast is red and wife is drab. Congo: Leach HOW 95.

A2411.2.18.3* Robin fans fire and saves hunter after bear tries to extinguish fire. Starts fires elsewhere = northern lights. Red breast. Cathon PERHAPS 181-182.

A2411.2.1.19* Origin of color of hummingbird. Hummingbird flew through all colors of rainbow on leaving ark. North Carolina Negro: Leach HOW 89-90.

A2411.2.1.19.1.1* Hummingbirds take colors from snakeskin. Given early choice thus chooses brightest colors. +A2411.2.5.1. Venezuela: Arnott ANIMALS 100-103.

A2411.2.1.19.2* Birds give hummingbird feathers for wedding dress. Great Spirit allows her to keep it. Mayan: Bowes BIRD 72-77.

A2411.2.1.19.3* Hummingbird pecks mud from eyes of panther. P. shows bright colored clays and jewels with which flowers are colored. +A2411.2.1.13. South America: Finger TALES 49-53.

A2411.2.1.20* Origin of bluebird's color. Rawen-io (creator) tells bluebird to dip in lake four mornings. Fourth day not to touch anything but water. Emerges sky-blue, rests on red clay bank a moment, hence red breast. Native American (Seneca): Parker SKUNNY 139-145.

A2411.2.1.20.1* Bluebird bathes in lake four times each morning for four days and sings song. On fifth morning is blue. Coyote imitates but falls into dust afterward. (A2411.3.2.1). Native American (Pima): Brown TEPEE 146.

A2411.2.1.21* Origin of ground dove's color. Ground dove given bright feathers in return for messenger jobs. She dawdles admiring self and power of flight is taken from her. Mayan: Bowes HOW 58-64.

A2411.2.1.21.1* Color of dove. Dove has blue bead because is struck on head by mouse when asks rudely for food. Korea: Kim STORY 19-22.

A2411.2.1.22* Color of kingfisher. Manabozo paints kingfisher after he gives information regarding M's nephew wolf, killed by giant lynx Pichou. Native American (Chippewa): Leekley WORLD 27-34.

A2411.2.2.1* Origin of eagles with red tipped wings. +B317.1. Native American (Lakota): Yellow Robe TONWEYA 102-114.

A2411.2.4.2. Color of owl.
SEE ALSO: A2313.8.

A2411.2.4.2.3* Children throw dry sumach on fire so it flares lighting face of courting owl. He turns back and sparks burn coat. Why owl has spotted coat. Native American (Cherokee): Bell JOHN 18-21.

A2411.2.4.2.4* If owl can leave log of jungie's without touching it he is to become snow white. Weasel kicks rotten log and splatters owl. Native American (Seneca): Parker SKUNNY 204-212.

A2411.2.4.2.5* Owl and Raven paint each other. Central Eskimo: Melzack DAY 21-25; Newell RESCUE 75-80.

A2411.2.5.1.1* Color of cormorant. Cormorant catches water snake and all birds take colors of snakeskin for their feathers. Cormorant takes what is left--black from snake's head and flakes of white from underbelly. (cf. A2411.2.5.2 [Heron]; A2411.2.6.6 [Guinea]; A2411.2.5.3.2 [Stork]; A2411.2.6.13 [Toucan]; A2411.2.1.19.1 [Hummingbird]). Venezuela: Arnott ANIMALS 100-103.

A2411.2.5.2.1* Color of heron. Heron takes white of snake's belly to decorate feathers. +A2411.2.5.1. Venzuela: Arnott ANIMALS 100-103.

A2411.2.5.3.2* Color of stork. Why jabiru stork has red neck. Takes color from snakeskin. +A2411.2.5.1. Venezuela: Arnott ANIMALS 100-103.

A2411.2.6.1. Color of loon.
SEE ALSO: F952.7.1. (Loon's necklace).

A2411.2.6.1.1* Raven decorates loon. +A2411.2.1.5.1. Eskimo: Caswell SHADOWS 33-34.

A2411.2.6.6. Color of guinea-fowl.
SEE ALSO: A2411.2.5.1.1.

A2411.2.6.6.1* Cow rewards Guinea Fowl for help in battling Lion. Gives blue camouflage by sprinkling with milk. American Black: Harris COMPLETE 257-261 /Harris NIGHTS 193-197/.

A2411.2.6.6.2* Guinea-fowl takes olive and brown colors from snakeskin. Venezuela: Arnott ANIMALS 100-103.

A2411.2.6.7. Color of peacock.

A2411.2.6.7.1* Quetzal (peacock) borrows feathers of puhuy (roadrunner) to wear to election of bird king. P. is found naked and given modest covering. El Salvador (Mayan): Barlow LATIN 119-125. Mayan: Bowes BIRD 7-14 (+ why roadrunner runs on road calling "puhuy" "Where is he?").

A2411.2.6.7.2* Crow paints peacock. China: Hardendorff JUST 37-39; Kirn PEACOCK pb.

A2411.2.6.8. Color of partridge. Wiskedjak pushes baby partridge into mud, becomes brown all over. Native American: Leekley WORLD 64-68.

A2411.2.6.9.1* Color of pheasant. Cheeks are red because he asked rudely for food and mouse struck cheeks. Korea: Kim STORY 19-22.

A2411.2.6.10.1* Color of cuckoo. Chaac, God of Fields, directs birds to gather seeds for next crop but Fire God burns fields and birds flee. Only cuckoo stays and saves seeds. Feathers turn gray and eyes red. Other birds agree to guard her young. Mexico (Mayan): Barlow LATIN 134-137 /Kouzel CUCKOO'S pb /.

A2411.2.6.13* Color of toucan. Takes colors from snakeskin. Given first choice thus bright colors. +A2411.2.5.1. Venezuela: Arnott ANIMALS 100-103.

A2411.2.6.14* Why crane is white. Manitou gives golden feathers on condition crane never leave territory. C. flies south and M. tells water in Land of Many Rivers to take away gold. Native American (Shoshone): Hulpac AMERICAN 99-101.

A2411.2.6.14.1* Crane fans fires of Osni (cold) and singes wings and beak. Otter helps defeat cold and crane gives gift of not feeling cold. Native American (Assiniboin): Belting LONG 23-25.

A2411.3.3* Origin of color of beetle. Wins race arranged by parrot between self and rat, prize green and gold coat (K11.10). Brazil: Carpenter SOUTH AMERICAN 108-113 (paca opponent); Cathon PERHAPS 18-22 /Eels FAIRY.. BRAZIL /; Newman FOLK 67-71.

A2411.3.4* Why cockroach is black. SEE: Z32.3.1. Mehdevi.

A2411.5.6. Color of chameleon.

A2411.5.6.2* Chameleon and monitor lizard decorate each other. SEE ALSO: A2411.5.8. Philippines (Bagobo): Sechrist ONCE 49-51.

A2411.5.8* Color of monitor lizard. Chameleon and monitor lizard decorate each other. Hunters approach as M. is being painted and C's hand shakes and he flees before finished. SEE ALSO: A2411.5.6.2. Philippines (Bagobo): Sechrist ONCE 49-51.

A2411.5.9* Color of blacksnake. Black-racer snake scorched black in attempt to fetch fire. Big blacksnake burned black as he climbs burning tree in attempt to fetch fire. SEE: A1415.2.3.

A2411.5.10. Why crayfish is red. Scorched in early times when sun was too low. Native American (Cherokee): Bell JOHN 4-7.

A2412.1. Markings of mammals. SEE ALSO: A2218 (Scorched).

A2412.1.2. Spots on leopard. L. chasing boy who owns magic piece of yam is beaten with dye sticks. Africa: Fuja FOURTEEN 43-47; Heady SAFIRI 67-70 (Painted by hyena).

A2412.1.2.1. Why wildcat has spots. Hare kicks coals on him. Native American (Shawnee):

Belting LONG 71-73.

A2412.1.2.2* Leopard and Kenki (ball of ground, boiled corn) wrestle and L. is thrown into fire and spotted by ashes and charred wood. Africa: (Akan-Ashanti): Aardema MORE 7-11; Aardema HALF pb.

A2412.1.7. Why bobcat has spots. Saynday tells rolling meat ball he is starving and she allows him to take small bite of her. Runs ahead and repeats. She flees and drowns in pond. S. puts hot stone in pond and makes soup. Bobcat eats soup while S. goes for spoon. S. stones B's reflection. Soup splashes on fur. Native American: Marriott WINTER 62-70.

A2412.1.8* Jabuty paints Jaguar. Jaguar paints Jabuty's shell poorly. Brazil (Amazon): Carpenter LATIN AMERICAN 43-49.

A2412.1.9. Why mink has white down on chest. Given by eagle for caring for eaglets. Native American (Seneca): Parker SKUNNY 124-131.

A2412.3.1. Why louse has mark on his back. Bruised in fight with flea and bedbug. Korea: Kim STORY 34-38.

A2412.4.6* Ina seeks ride to Tinirau, lord of all fishes. She strikes fish who refuse to carry her all the way, marking them. Why Avini has stripes, Paora has blue marks, Sole flattened, Shark has bump on forehead. Cook Islands: Gittens TALES 76-78.

A2412.5.2.1. Why frog is spotty all over. SEE: Z49.6.0.5. Withers.

A2413. Origin of animal's stripes.

A2413.1. Stripes of zebra. Painted by tortoise. SEE: A2411.1.1.1.1.

A2413.1.1* Zebra sings and dances well and is rewarded by medicine man Ngamu with fine coat. Zebra still sings his barking song. East Africa: Heady WHEN 53-58.

A2413.2. Stripes of chipmunk. SEE: A721.1.2; A2217.2; A1415.2.2.1.2.

A2413.4. Stripes of tiger. Vietnam: Schultz VIETNAMESE 15-18; Vo-Dinh TOAD 65-73.

A2416. Origin and nature of animal's smell.

A2416.8. Why fox smells bad. Cursed by Coniraya for failure to aid. Peru (Andean): Carpenter LATIN 50-56.

A2420. Animal characteristics: voice and hearing.

A2421.6. Why cocks crow. SEE ALSO: A2426.2.18.

A2422. How animal lost voice or power of speech. SEE ALSO: A2241.12 (Earthworm, snake).

A2422.1. Why dog lost his power of speech.
SEE: N385.1.2. (Dog reveals god's secret).

A2422.11* Why earthworm has no voice.
SEE: A2241.12.

A2422.12* Why snake has no voice.
SEE: A2241.12.

A2422.12.1* Why birds only repeat words man teaches them. Sao bird testifies against master, has testimony discredited (J1151.1.3.1) and life threatened. Escapes and tells all birds to only repeat. Thai: Carpenter ELEPHANT'S 58-65.

A2422.13* Why chilota bird does not sing. Once Apanatl, an Indian maiden led battle with chilota bird on shoulder. She died and bird sang self to death on grave. Never sang since. Ecuador: Jagendorf KING 111-113.

A2422.14* Why fish do not speak. Animals choose voices by imitating sounds. Fish can not hear under water, imitates what he sees-- opening mouths. Finland: Deutsch MORE 1-5.

A2422.15* How porcupine lost voice. Brags of bravery but shrieks in horror at own reflection. Never regains voice. Native American (Shoshone): Heady SAGE 57-60.

A2423.1.2. Peacock's ugly voice. SEE ALSO: W128.4.

A2423.1.2.1* Peacock sent to carry message of baby born to king in France, rehearses until loses voice. Queen chooses p. after testing voices of several animals. Haiti: Johnson HOW 75-82.

A2423.1.2.2* Anansi chooses animals with best voices to talk at court. Prince hidden behind screen chooses voice he wants for self. Chooses peacock's voice. Peacock is given half of Anansi's reward, a room full of clothes. Hence finely clothed but no voice. Trinidad: McNeil DOUBLE 31-35.

A2423.1.4. Why ass brays. West Indies: Sherlock IGUANA'S 43-52. W. Africa: Appiah ANANSE 71-88.

A2423.1.4.1* Why donkey laughs. Remembering how he tricked lion into trying to kill him with eagle feather. Ethiopia: Courlander FIRE 105-110.

A2425. Origin of animal cries.

A2425.2.1* Why bush-fowl cries at dawn. SEE: Z49.6.0.2 (Why 'laughing jackass' laughs at dawn). Australia (Euahlayi): Leach HOW 18-19 /Parker AUSTRALIAN/.

A2426.1. Cries of mammals.

A2426.1.7* Origin of coyote's voice. Native American (Yokut): Fisher STORIES 36-45.

A2426.2. Cries of birds.

A2426.2.0.1. Mockingbird gives call to all birds. Native American (Hopi): Courlander PEOPLE 60-62.

A2426.2.1. Nightingale's song.
SEE ALSO: A2221.1.1.

A2426.2.6. Cawing of crow. Raven talks crow into giving feast, tells animals he, Raven, is giving feast so crow gets no return potlatches. Loses voice in long singing. Native American (Upper Skagit): Matson LEGEND 77-82.

A2426.2.11.1. Why parrot has harsh voice. Cursed by Coniraya for failure to help. Peru (Andean): Carpenter LATIN 50-56.

A2426.2.18. Origin and meaning of cock's cry "cock-a-doodle-do." SEE ALSO: B755.

A2426.2.18.1* Cock crows each morning to remind world that weak have right to justice, reminding of war between animals and birds. Upper Volta: Guirma TALES 29-44.

A2426.2.19* Origin of loon's call. Kuloskap teaches loon cry. Native American (Passamaquoddy): Leach HOW 97.

A2426.2.20* Why catbird makes only small sound. Refuses when mockingbird gives out calls. Native American (Hopi): Courlander PEOPLE 60-62.

A2426.2.21* Why whippoorwill (Puhuy) cries "Puhuy." Means "Where is he?" Seeks turkey who stole his feathers. +A2313.7. Mayan: Bowes BIRD 15-18.

A2426.2.22* Mockingbird's song. M. hides and listens to lessons blackbird is giving cardinal's daughter. At concert cardinal's daughter persuades m. to hide and sing for her. Father discovers and praises mockingbird. Mayan: Bowes KING 32-39.

A2426.2.23* Origin of wren's cry. Says "I am King." Called the Hedge King because lives in hedges. Grimm: Green BIG 47-51; Grimm GRIMM'S (Follett) 150-153; Wiggin TALES 172-175.

A2426.2.24* Bookoo bird calls "Boo koo" (plant rice) at rice planting season. China: Alexander PEBBLES 26.

A2426.2.25* Partridge borrows terrapin's whistle and doesn't return. Native American (Cherokee): Bell JOHN 63-64.

A2426.2.26* Origin of blue jay's cries. Condemned to have coarse cry for addressing moon disrespectfully when sent to awaken moon. Native American (Nisqually): Matson LEGENDS 24-28.

A2426.2.26.1* Jay gives princess Lakshmi his

voice so she can win blind prince Rama. On return she wraps scarf around him and wishes his feathers as lovely as scarf. (A2411.2.18). India: Spellman BEAUTIFUL 3-7.

A2426.2.27* Why Francolin cries at dawn and dusk. To tell men when to begin hunting and when to stop. Great Ground Hornbill has told Hyena he'd arranged for continuous night and raiding party was caught at dawn. Francolin taken as new medicine man. East Africa: Harman TALES 144-152.

A2426.2.28* Blackbirds chatter. Are laughing about tricking coyote. +K711.5. Native American (Pueblo): Dolch PUEBLO 79-85.

A2426.3.3. Fly's buzz. SEE: A2236.1 (Horsefly); Z49.6.0.1.

A2426.3.4. Crickets chirp. (How cricket got voice). SEE: A2241.12.

A2426.3.5. Mosquito's buzz. SEE ALSO: Z49.6.0.3.

A2426.3.5.1* Why the male mosquito does not buzz or sting. Philippines (Pampangan): Sechrist ONCE 64-66.

A2426.4.1. Frog's croak. Croaks in indecision over which wife to visit. +J2183.1.2. Congo (Bakongo): Courlander KING'S 58-59.

A2426.4.0.1* Old man and wife drop staff and melon into water then fall in. Fairy turns to frogs. Still talk of melon (Gwa) and staff (Fuer). Croak "Gwa-fuer." China: Alexander PEBBLE 15; Hume FAVORITE 33-38.

A2426.4.1.2. Why frog croaks in wet weather. Afraid mother's grave by river will wash away. Knowing he always does opposite of what she asks, she asked to be buried there but really wanted to be buried on mountain. Korea: Leach HOW 115.

A2426.4.1.2.1* Toad, wasp, tiger, and cock go to complain to Jade Emperor about lack of rain. Wasp routs soldiers, tiger takes on Heavenly dog, cock fights thunder and lightning. Rain-god agrees to rain whenever toad croaks. SEE ALSO: Z52.1. Vietnam: Schultz VIETNAMESE 101-105 (called 'uncle' of heaven); Vo-Dinh TOAD 15-22.

A2426.4.1.2.2* In drought Rain Spirit responds when frogs dig deep holes and all croak. When frog croaks it will rain. Africa (Chagga): Kaula AFRICAN 57-59.

A2426.4.3* Why lizard says 'tzch.' Dispossessed rich man loses bragging contest, becomes lizard. Vietnam: Vo-Dinh TOAD 81-87.

A2427.1. Why jackal cries in the night. SEE: A2513.1.2.

A2427.4* Why coyote howls at moon. SEE ALSO: A717.2.

A2427.4.1. Ejupa (coyote) gets star Tatsempin to carry him to sky. Taken to moon E. finds it so cold he loses hold and falls. Fall causes him to forget his magic. Why coyotes howl at full moon. Native American (Shoshone): Heady SAGE 70-73.

A2430. Animal characteristics: dwelling and food.

A2431.1. How bird learned to build nest. SEE: A2271.1 (blackbird, owl, sparrow, starling, turtle dove).

A2431.2.1. Why cuckoo has no nest.

A2431.2.1.1* Four sons neglect ill mother. She turns to cuckoo and flies away. Why c. abandons children. Arctic (Samoyeds) Nenetz: Deutsch MORE 69+.

A2431.3.5. Swallow's nest. Swallow as Great Spirit's messenger has no time to build nest. Given leave to build nest he and wife ignore advice of other birds and don't learn how to build nest. Wasp teaches how to build nest of mud. +B362.1. Mayan: Bowes BIRD 51-57.

A2431.3.6.4. Why crow must roost in bare tree without nest in winter. Punished for giving away god's gifts intended for man. Gives to stone (not to feel old) and tree (bear fruit without replanting). China: Chang CHINESE 31-33.

A2431.3.9* Why motmot lives in hole in bank. Toj (motmot) was too vain to help birds with dam which Yum Chac, rain god, demands them to build. Motmot hides in hole but tail of which he is so vain sticks out and is trod upon and ruined by workers. In shame he hides in hole. Mayan: Bowes BIRD 65-71.

A2431.3.10* Quail family nested in treetops. Tells hunters where wild turkey is hiding. Great Spirit, Halach-Vinic, punishes quail: to live henceforth in grasses. Mayan: Bowes BIRD 19-23.

A2431.3.11* Why magpie's nest is poorly made. All birds copy man and build nests except magpie. Great Spirit sends four eagle feathers to leave eggs in all nests. Magpie throws one together in a hurry. SEE ALSO: A2271.1. Native American (Piegan): Hulpach INDIAN 139-141.

A2431.3.12* Hammerhead told by dove not to build near stream, flooded. Now builds near dove in bush. East Africa: Heady SAFIRI 58-61.

A2431.3.13* Marsh wren builds in cat-tail tips in marsh. Crane builds nearby following wren's example. Native American (Shoshone): Heady SAGE 27-29.

A2431.3.14* Why black turnstone builds nest near sea. Man offered hat to turnstone to lay eggs in. Guards her nest. In return he has good luck at fishing. Eskimo: Gillham BEYOND 127-134.

A2431.3.15* Why egas keep building and tearing down nests. Ega parents move to be rid of obnoxious children, young follow and father tears apart new nest. King rules father is responsible for young. Africa (Yoruba): Fuja FOURTEEN 116-119.

A2431.4* Why ostrich leaves egg outside of nest. To remind him of what he is doing as he becomes absent-minded brooding over loss of fire. SEE: A1415.0.2.2. Bushmen: Helfman BUSHMEN 63-65.

A2433. Animal's characteristic haunt.

A2433.3.1.3* Why cat lives with men. Animals make drum, each contributing part of ears. King Eliri is mocked for small contribution. He seeks aid from Ayan, god of drum, in vengeance. Drum will sound only when no one is near--Eliri and Ayan cause this. Cat eats Eliri and says he's eaten drummer and drum will never sound again. He is driven back to town and lives there with man ever since. African (Yoruba): Fuja FOURTEEN 146-151.

A2433.2.2. Animals that inhabit water.

A2433.2.2.1* Why otter lives in water. Coyote calls "The End of the World is Coming," and otters hide in water. Coyote takes their drying crayfish. Native American (Nez Percé): Heady TALES 81-85.

A2433.2.2.2* Hare tells otter to run into river if rains fire in night. Tosses coal into air and otter dives. Hare steals coat. Otter lives in river ever since. Native American (Cherokee): Bell JOHN 43-47; Scheer CHEROKEE 69-74.

A2433.3. Haunts of various animals--mammals.

A2433.3.0.1* Blanket tied by its corners to mountains of North, South, East, and West. Each animal gets onto blanket and lives wherever he falls off. Mountain goat runs from cover to cover to cover. Lives on mountain tops. (cf. A2433.3.22). Native American (Tahltan): Belting LONG 85-88.

A2433.3.1. Cat's characteristic haunt. SEE ALSO: A2513.

A2433.3.1.1. Why cat inhabits chimney corner. Helped man build house. Dog refused to help. Leach LION 25.

A2433.3.3.1.2* Why cat lives in palace. Wrestling match held to decide which animal could live in palace. Cat cannot be thrown as always lands on feet. Nigeria (Hausa): Courlander OLODE 107-109.

A2433.3.4.1. Why hyena hides in rock dens. Fled during war between birds and animals. Ostrich left feathers outside cave and he thinks

she is still on guard. +B261.0.1. Soudan: Carpenter AFRICAN 87-92.

A2433.3.4.2* Why hyena lives apart. Hyena solicits lion and leopard to help him kill ten guests as sacrifices at mother's funeral. Guests flee. Lion and leopard still hunt for sacrifices. H. lives apart. Africa (Yoruba): Fuja FOURTEEN 60-63.

A2433.3.6. Why hog lives in sty. SEE: J2671.4.2.

A2433.3.9. Why squirrel lives in tree. +K2323.0.1. Finland: Bowman TALES..TUPA 249.

A2433.3.12.1. Why beaver lives along rivers. Skunks invite beaver medicine men to cure their sick and then eat them. Last beaver left is told by dog that his relatives are not really dead but live under water. He goes under ice and joins them. Native American (Pawnee): Belting LONG 42-45.

A2433.3.14. Why wolf lives in woods. SEE: R111.1.13.2.

A2433.3.15.1* Why elephant lives in bush. Result of tug of war with whale. +K22. Bahama Negro: Leach HOW 80-81.

A2433.3.16.1* Why lion stays away from settlements. Lion originally was kept as cat, scratched baby and was driven out. Yao: Leach HOW 77.

A2433.3.19.0.1* Why monkey lives in tree. Monkey swings through trees searching for lost grinding stone. Tortoise had daughter pretend to grind meal on his back, then throw him into forest in feigned anger at monkey. Tortoise claims money he owes m. is in that grinding stone. Africa: Nunn AFRICAN 17-20.

A2433.3.20.1* Why mole lives underground. Hiding from medicine men after he stole sleeping girl's heart and carried to lover. If lover swallows heart girl must come to him. Native American (Cherokee): Scheer CHEROKEE 51-54.

A2433.3.20.2. Fox and mole are being carried to moon by Condor. Parrot cuts rope and mole falls. Ashamed mole now lives underground. Peru: Barlow LATIN 62-67.

A2433.3.22* Why mountain goat lives on mountain tops. SEE: A2433.3.0.1.

A2433.3.23* Why raccoon lives in trees. To avoid fox. SEE: K1023.1.0.1.

A2433.3.24. Why hedgehog lives underground. Nigeria (Yoruba): Fuja FOURTEEN 28-31.

A2433.3.25* Why badger lives underground. SEE: R111.1.13.2.

A2433.4.7* Why wren lives in hedges. Calls self "Hedge King." Grimm: Green BIG 47-51;

Grimm GRIMM'S (Follett) 150-153; Wiggin TALES 172-175.

A2433.4.8* Why egret (ricebird, tickbird) rides buffalo's back (lives among cattle). Philippines: Carpenter ELEPHANT'S 91-99. +K82.1.1. East Africa: Heady WHEN 27-30.

A2433.4.8.1* Why blackbird rides buffalo's back. SEE: R111.1.13.2.

A2433.4.9* Why hawk flies high into air. SEE: R111.1.13.2.

A2433.5.2.1* Why flies swarm around Kenki (ball of pounded, boiled corn). Only Kenki agrees to untie fly after leopard ties him up. Africa (Akan-Ashanti): Aardema HALF pb; Aardema MORE 7-11.

A2433.5.3. Haunts of Spider.

A2433.5.3.1. Why spider lives under stones. SEE ALSO: A2211.6.

A2433.5.3.2* Why spider walks in grass. SEE: W125.3.1 (Hat Shaking Dance).

A2433.5.3.3* Why spider lives in ceiling. Ghana/ Liberia: Arkhurst ADVENTURES 12-20, 40-49 (rafters). Northern Nigeria (Hausa): Arnott AFRICAN 16-21. West Africa: Appiah ANANSE 139-146. West Africa (Ashanti): Courlander HAT 20-24 (in rafters). West Indies: Sherlock WEST 59-64 (+K1066.5). Sierra Leone: Green FOLKTALES 9-13. SEE ALSO: F1021.2.1.1 (in thatch).

A2433.5.3.3.1* Man-crow is killed by Soliday, spider claims feat and princess. Soliday produces tongue, spider hides in roof in shame. Jamaica: Carter GREEDY 73-78; Sherlock WEST 65-70.

A2433.5.3.4* Why spider lives in dark corners. Ghana/Liberia: Arkhurst ADVENTURES 40-49. SEE ALSO: A2433.5.3.3.

A2433.5.3.5* Why spiders hide under leaves. +D877.1.1.1. West Indies: Sherlock WEST 125-129.

A2433.5.3.6* Why spiders hide in bananas. Jamaica: Arnott ANIMAL 87-91.

A2433.6.1.3* Haunts of tortoise (turtle). After tug-of-war (K22) both elephant and hippopotamus invite tortoise to live with them. T. goes to live in water with h. and sends brother to live with e. Why there are both land and water tortoises. Africa: Montgomerie MERRY 28-31.

A2433.7* Haunts of fish.

A2433.7.1* Why whale lives in sea. Result of tug of war with elephant. +K22. Bahama Negro: Leach HOW 80-81.

A2433.7.2* Whale brothers tire of lake and dig

river to sea with their noses. SEE ALSO: A934. Native American (Bella Bella): Belting LONG 60-61.

A2433.8* Why octopus lives alone. +K544.1. Japan: Hearn JAPANESE 83-86.

A2433.9* Why crayfish lives in streams under stones. Native American: Bierhorst FIRE 42-46.

A2434.1.4.1* Why black ants are everywhere. Mocked ant king sends worm into King Lion's ear. Ant then is called to fetch worm out. Lion rules ants should live everywhere in world. Burma: Leach HOW 105-106.

A2434.2.2.1* Why foxes (badgers) do not live on a certain island. Japan: Novak FAIRY 16-21; Stamm VERY pb.

A2434.2.4* Why there are no mosquitoes on Kambara and no shellfish on Oneata. Chief of Oneata told buzzing outside curtain is singing of mosquitoes, trades shellfish for them. Polynesia: Gittens TALES 3-10; Williams-Ellis ROUND 233-241.

A2434.2.5* Why there are no more tigers in Haiti. Tiger poses as friend and asks boy for tiger skins, turns them to tigers. He is tiger in disguise as boy. Father returns in time to shoot him, others become skins again. Haiti: Wolkstein MAGIC 183-188.

A2434.4* Why animals live in certain cities.

A2434.4.1* Why there are pigeons in New York but turtle remains in Haiti. Haiti: Wolkstein MAGIC 188-194.

A2435.3. Food of various animals--mammals.

A2435.3.1.1* Food of dog. Why dogs crunch bones. Nigeria (Ibo): Robinson SINGING 16-23.

A2435.3.2.1* Why cats mew when chewing at food. C. frightened off larger animals by ferocious noises made while eating. SEE ALSO: K2324. Russia: Higonnet-Schnopper TALES 82-90.

A2435.3.4.1* Why coyote steals food from camp at night. SEE: R111.1.13.2.

A2435.1.18* Why monkeys eat bananas. SEE: K741.0.1.

A2435.4.8.2* Why cock eats worms. Is revenge on earthworm who advised cock to loan horns to dragon. Dragon never returned them. China: Green CAVALCADE..DRAGONS 157-160 /Bonnet CHINESE 111-114/; Young ROOSTER'S pb.

A2435.4.1.12* Why insects come out when woodpecker knocks. Woodpecker calls back son of Sartak-Pai who is digging river in wrong direction, rewarded. To get food by pecking on on bark and calling "The son of the Khan is celebrating his wedding and you are invited." Insects come out on hearing this. Altai: Deutsch TALES 17-27.

A2436. Why animals lack fire. Sent to steal fire but are lazy and fail. SEE: A2513.1.2. (cf. A1415.2).

A2435.1* Why animals are afraid of fire. Having built fire they are unable to extinguish it until Rain comes to their aid. Karok: Belting LONG 76-78.

A2436.2* Why animals lack fire. Man and animals fight over fire which appear on rock. Jackal as diviner has left signs saying "The gift of god will be found on the big stone" but both animals and man think it is left for them. Animals win but overfeed it. Fire eats everything then dies drinking from lake. Man picks up red bones and keeps them thus domesticating fire. Africa: Guillot GUILLOT'S 33-39.

A2440. Animal characteristics: carriage.

A2441.1.4.1* Cause of hyena's walk. Why hyena limps. Bushmen: Helfman BUSHMEN 36-39. East Africa: Heady JAMBO 91-93 (+K1041.0.5).

A2441.1.10.1* Cause of cat's walk. Why cats always land on feet. Reward for killing snake about to strike sleeping prophet. Arabia: Carpenter WONDER..DOGS 145-152.

A2441.1.11.1* Cause of hare's hopping gait. Hare flees when half finished, back legs long, front still short. Native American (Seneca): Parker SKUNNY 72-74.

A2441.1.13* Why squirrel often hops backward. Singed in attempt to free sun from snare. SEE: A728.0.1.

A2441.1.14* Cause of bear's walk. Bears rear daughter of Old Man Above on Mt. Shasta. Old Man Above is angered and curses them to go on four feet henceforth and speak no more. Native American (Shasta): Fisher STORIES 24-35.

A2441.1.15* Why coyote slinks. Coyote tries to destroy four witches by burning, youngest escapes and pursues. C. slinks away, she curses him to slink always. Native American (Upper Skagit): Matson LEGENDS 41-48.

A2441.2. Cause of bird's walk.

A2441.2.3* Why loon walks awkwardly. Injured by raven throwing stones. +A2411.2.1.5. Eskimo: Caswell SHADOWS 33-34.

A2441.2.4* Why sparrow hops. Sparrow is beaten on legs when flies and he takes case to Hananim. Korea: Anderson BOY 84-91; Carpenter KOREAN 237-241.

A2441.4.5* Why turtle walks slowly and stays close to home. SEE: K1041.1.1.

A2441.4.5.1* Why turtle crawls. Still looking for spilled wisdom. +A1481.1. U.S. Black: Courlander TERRAPIN 24-27.

A2442.2.5.1* Hawk's flight. Hawk soars and dives seeking lost ring. Togo (Ewe): Courlander KING'S 41-44. SEE ALSO: A2261.7.

A2442.3. How birds began to fly.

A2442.3.1* How ptarmigans learned to fly. Family of ptarmigan get so mad at bird trying to carry off baby that they all hop into air and fly. Even the ptarmigan babies can fly. Eskimo (Hooper Bay): Gillham BEYOND 86-98.

A2442.3.2* How seagulls learned to fly. Eskimo (Hooper Bay): Gillham BEYOND 17-30.

A2450. Animal's daily work.

A2455.6. Why dogs steal meat. Hare attempts to cure dog of theiving. Meat is laid out in evening for use in dog's cure in morning. Dog takes meat into bed with him to guard it, onto pillow, onto head, into mouth. Eats. No cure now possible. Dog still steals. Africa (Ashanti): Courlander HAT 49-54; Williams-Ellis ROUND 181-185. Africa (Akan-Ashanti): Aardema MORE 22-25. Liberia (Mano): Dorilae ANIMALS 52-55 (eats instruments of fortune-teller.

A2458.1* Why cockroaches clean up houses. East Africa: Heady SAFIRI 36-39.

A2460. Animal characteristics: attack and defense.

A2466.1. Why opossum plays dead when caught. +T92.11.2. Native American (Cherokee): Bell JOHN 51-53; Scheer CHEROKEE 33-36.

A2466.2.1. Why terrapin draws into shell. Ashamed at loss of whistle. Native American (Cherokee): Bell JOHN 63-64.

A2470. Animal's habitual bodily movements.

A2471.1.1. Why dogs sniff one another. +A2281.1. Latvia: Carpenter WONDER..DOGS 35-42. SEE ALSO: A2232.8.

A2471.1.2* Why dogs bare teeth on meeting. To show they are not the old toothless dog who dropped ring in river. Man sent dog and cat to daughter with ring, lost and never found. (cf. D882.2). SEE ALSO: A2479.1.1.2; A2534.2. Philippines (Visayan): Sechrist ONCE 38-42.

A2472.2. Why grasshopper chews tobacco. Gluskabe steals all of grasshopper's tobacco crop. Grasshopper asks for some back and Gluskabe puts piece in grasshopper's mouth--to last forever. Native American (Penobscot): Leach HOW 109-110.

A2473.1. Why dogs lift their legs. Buddha turned lotus blossom into hind leg for dog (A2371.1.1), thus he lifts it when he urinates. Vietnam: Vo-Dinh TOAD 75-80.

A2474.1.1* Why lizard bobs head up and down: watching for Ananse whose bride he stole. Africa (Ashanti): Appiah ANANSE 47-56.

A2474.1.2* Why lizard bobs head up and down: shakes head in dismay at way man treats companion dog. Northern Rhodesia (Bemba): Courlander KING'S 98-100.

A2476.1. Why rabbit continually moves mouth. SEE: Z49.6 Htin Aung.

A2477.2. Why hen scratches in ground. SEE ALSO: A2494.13.10.3.

A2477.2.1* Rooster refuses meal of corn pone, didn't realize meat and greens were underneath. Always scratches before eating now. U.S. Black: Harris NIGHTS 59-60 /Harris COMPLETE 158-161/.

A2479.1. Why wagtail moves tail up and down. To make sure wren hasn't come back for it. Rumania: Leach HOW 99. SEE ALSO: A2242.1.

A2479.9. Why flies fly around ox's eyes. Fly told to keep watching bull's eyes and he won't forget to give fly portion of elephant he is butchering. Bull neglects fly's portion. Fly still watching. Nigeria (Yoruba): Fuja FOURTEEN 210-213.

A2479.10* Why fly rubs hands together. Outcome of case between fly and sparrow brought before Hananim, fly rubbed hands together begging mercy. Korea: Anderson BOY 84-91; Carpenter KOREAN 237-241. SEE ALSO: A1414.1.1.1.

A2479.12* Why dogs wag tail. To show they are not dog who was to have tail cut off for dropping ring in river. +A2471.1.2; +D882.2. Philippines (Visaya): Sechrist ONCE 38-42.

A2479.13* Why ducks pull up one leg when sleeping. Four ducks with one leg each hear god complaining that incense burner has four legs too many. They ask for the extra legs. Must be protected since are gold so pull up under wings at night. Other ducks see and imitate. Vietnam: Schultz VIETNAMESE 86-89.

A2479.14* Why whale spouts. Given tobacco to smoke by Kuloskap for ferrying him to Nova Scotia. Native American (Passamaquoddy): DeWit TALKING 188-191; Leach HOW 79.

A2480. Periodic habits of animals.

A2481.1. Why bears hibernate. Animals stop up hollow tree to be rid of disliked bear. He sleeps all winter. Origin of habit. Black (North Carolina): Leach HOW 73-74. Native American (Nez Percé): Heady TALES 25-28 (+1172.4).

A2482.4* Why Siberian brown owl does not migrate. Eagle sends brown owl south to scout for warmer land. Owl says he found none,

planning to keep new land for himself. As punishment owl must winter in arctic while eagle takes other birds south. Siberia: Arnott ANIMAL 83-86. Siberia (Yakuts): Deutsch TALES 52-55.

A2486.5. Why turkey has only two young. +A2377.1. Australia: Parker AUSTRALIAN 15-19; Sleigh NORTH 13-18.

A2489.1.1. Why cock crows to greet the sunrise. SEE: A739.6; A2426.2.18; B755.

A2490. Other habits of animals.

A2491.1. Why bat flies by night. Bat changes sides in bird/animal war. To fly alone at night henceforth (B261.1.0.3). Nigeria (Yoruba): Leach HOW 71-72; Walker NIGERIAN 26. Aesop: Aesop AESOP'S (Viking) 45-66. Altai: Deutsch MORE 7-10. SEE ALSO: A1341.4; A2275.5.3.

A2491.1.0.1* Bat tells bush-rat he boils self in pot to make soup, bush-rat tries and dies (J2415). Order for bat's arrest. Why flies at night. Eastern Nigeria (Ibibio): Arnott AFRICAN 150-152.

A2491.1.1. Why bat sleeps by day. Why bat never goes out in daylight. +B261.1.0.1. Aesop: Aesop AESOP'S (Grosset) 214-215.

A2491.2. Why owl avoids daylight. SEE ALSO: A2233.3; A2332.1.5.11; J2332.1.

A2491.2.1* Cuckoo prescribes sitting in water as relief for mud pellet shot into owl. Owl doesn't pay cuckoo's bill. Crow, who guaranteed owl's payment, must watch cuckoo's nest. Owl hides henceforth during day. Burma: Brockett BURMESE 84-86.

A2491.2.2* Owl spills pan of bird's tears meant for ritual drowning of wren. Hides in shame. +K11.2. Wales: Sheppard-Jones WELSH 59-62.

A2491.2.3* Punishment for looking while creator makes hare. Owl to live in dark and not see goings on of world. Native American (Seneca): Parker SKUNNY 72-74.

A2491.2.4* Owl set to guard wren falls asleep (K11.2). +A2233.3. Grimm: Green BIG 47-51; Grimm GRIMM'S (Follett) 150-153; Wiggin TALES 172-175.

A2491.2.5* Owl prefers to read rather than dance at King Kukul's (Quetzal) party. He begins to read story to other birds and sunlight hurts his eyes. Blind during day as punishment of Great Spirit. Mayan: Bowes BIRD 45-50.

A2491.2.6* Owl lent feathers for ball, never returns them. Puerto Rico: Alegria THREE 64-65.

A2491.2.7* Owl suggests covering ugly bird Cu with pitch and giving her a feather from each bird. She fails however in task and owl and bird Cu become night birds to escape anger of others. Mexico: Barlow LATIN 138-144.

A2491.2.8* Owl courts girl but hides eyes and face. Flees at dawn. Friend Rooster wins the girl. Haiti: Wolkstein MAGIC 29-36.

A2491.6* Why whippoorwill is nocturnal. Ashamed of appearance since turkey stole his fine feathers. +A2313.7. Mayan: Bowes BIRD 15-18.

A2491.7* Why certain animals are nocturnal. All plants and animals asked to stay awake seven nights. Only owl, panther, and a few others stay awake. Given power to see in the dark. Native American (Cherokee): Bell JOHN 4-7.

A2493. Friendships between animals.

A2493.4.1* Friendship between man and dog. Man trapped in cave by crocodile is dug out by dog. Men keep dogs as pets henceforth. Yao: Leach HOW 60-61.

A2493.36* Friendship between mousedeer (kant-chil) and elephant. Indonesia: Courlander KANTCHIL'S 46-51.

A2493.37* Why horse, donkey and ox share food and quarters with rat. +A2281.0.1. Palestine: Dobbs MORE 83-85.

A2494. Why certain animals are enemies.

A2494.1.2. Enmity between cat and dog. SEE ALSO: A2281.1; D882.1. +D882.1.1.

A2494.1.2.1* Cat or dog drops ring into sea. +D882.2. Korea: Anderson BOY 19-32; Carpenter KOREAN 47-54 /Gruenberg MORE 125-129/; Jewett WHICH 82-94. Finland: Arnott ANIMAL 112-121.

A2494.1.2.2* Cat runs home with ring ahead of dog and claims reward. Chinese: Green BIG 32-33.

A2494.1.2.3* Dog and cat buy ham, cat climbs tree and eats. U.S. Black: Lester KNEE 9-11.

A2494.1.2.4* Cat asks god for "misery" thinking this is name of syrup, is given dog in bag. Haiti: Courlander PIECE 37-38.

A2494.1.4* Enmity between cat and rat. Palestine: Dobbs MORE 83-85. SEE ALSO: A2281.0.2.

A2494.1.5* Cat takes name "stranger," dog "traveler." Yoruba chief feeds "stranger" not "traveler" by custom. Fight over meat causes enmity. Nigeria (Yoruba): Fuja FOURTEEN 237-242. SEE ALSO: A2494.4.6.

A2494.1.6* Enmity between cat and tiger. Burma: Htin KINGDOM 53-55. SEE ALSO: A2581.

A2494.4.3.1* Enmity between dog and rat.

Palestine: Dobbs MORE 83-85. SEE ALSO: A2281.0.1; A2281.0.2.

A2494.4.4.1* Enmity between dog and rabbit. Brer Rabbit steals dog's new shoes, why dogs chase rabbits. U.S. Black: Harris COMPLETE 369-371 / Harris NIGHTS 349-352/, / Harris FAVORITE 118-120/.

A2494.4.6* Enmity between dog and cat. Dog invites four cats to dinner, one steals dog's avocado-pears. Dog chases cats out, son starts fire while dog is gone and house burns down. Why dogs hate cats. Jamaica: Sherlock WEST 93-96. SEE ALSO: A2494.1.5.

A2494.14* Enmity between dog and porcupine. Porcupine allowed to live with dog destroys sugar cane fields. Case taken to court. P. arranges case in early morning so that dog arrives shivering from walking through wet grass and is judged guilty. Africa: Green ANIMAL 186-188.

A2494.4.15* Enmity between dog and wolf. Russia: Carpenter WONDER..DOGS 213-221. +K231.1.3; +J581.1. SEE ALSO: A2513.1.2.1.

A2494.8.3* Enmity between bear and peasant. +K171.1. Russia/Yiddish: Ginsburg THREE ROLLS 27-29.

A2494.9.3* Enmity between fox and raccoon. Native American (Seneca): Parker SKUNNY 23-30 (+K1023.1.0.1).

A2494.10.4* Enmity between tiger and monkey. Burma: Brockett BURMESE 71-78. Indonesia: Courlander KANTCHIL'S 46-51 (why tiger eats orangutan).

A2494.11.2. Enmity between crocodile and elephant. Crocodile arranges trek of animals to new waterhole. Places elephants in rear and has snake wake man's dogs before elephants are safe. Bushmen: Aardema BEHIND 11-18.

A2494.11.4* Enmity between elephant and tiger. Why elephant doesn't walk with tiger. Indonesia: Courlander KANTCHIL'S 46-51.

A2494.12.4.1* Enmity between coyote and the blackbirds. +K711.5. Native American (Pueblo): Dolch PUEBLO 79-85.

A2494.13.1. Enmity between crow and owl. Crow protests choice of owl for king, turtledove chosen. India: Babbitt JATAKA 90-92.

A2494.12.10.3. Enmity between hawk and hen. (cf. A2477.2.1).

A2494.13.10.3.1* Hen loses hawk's ring, she must hunt for it. He carries off her children until found. Philippines: Arnott ANIMAL 152-154. Africa (Kikuyu): Nunn AFRICAN 36-40 (loses wembe [razor]). Philippines (Tagalog): Sechrist ONCE 25-27 (bracelet). Ukraine: Deutsch TALES 1-6 (pearl necklace stolen, breaks).

A2494.13.10.3.2* Hen promises hawk two chicks of ten for juju. Fails to keep promise. Orisha gives hawk permission to take any can catch. Nigeria (Yoruba): Fuja FOURTEEN 113-115.

A2494.13.10.3.3* Girl pulled into pool by goddess Oluweri. Hawk rescues in exchange for coop of fowls. Takes one at a time. Still taking. Nigeria (Yoruba): Fuja FOURTEEN 203-209.

A2494.13.10.7* Rooster wakes buzzard in time to catch sun and collect debt. Sun finds out who woke him so early and replies he may collect debt in chickens. West Africa (Fula): Jablow MAN 91-92.

A2494.15.1* Why seals flee whales. Raven had tricked them by covering eyes with gum and pretending to lead inside whale so could eat whale. Really led them south until sun melted gum. They think selves inside whale and flee animals of forest, thinking whale has spirits inside. They return to sea and flee from whales in future. Eskimo: Melzack RAVEN 47-52.

A2494.16.1.1* Enmity between frog and stork. Armenian: Tashjian THREE 40-41.

A2494.16.2.1. Enmity between chameleon and monkey. Chameleon blamed by monkey for theft, points out c's half-closed eyes and nodding head. Man beats c. Later c. accuses m. of setting fire. Points out blackened palms. Congo (Bakongo): Courlander KING'S 60-63.

A2495.1. Why cat buries its excrement. To make trail difficult for tiger to follow. +A2581. Burma: Htin KINGDOM 53-55.

A2500 - A2599. Animal Characteristics-- Miscellaneous.

A2510. Utility of animals.

A2511.2* Why hare's flesh is sweet. Because of honey eaten. Africa (Wakamba): Nunn AFRICAN 26-30.

A2513.1. Origin of dog's service. Dog must serve and obey man for meager recompense. SEE: N385.1.2 (dog betrays god's secret); A2545.3.1; A1831.

A2513.1.0.1. Dog as man's companion. Caribbean: Sherlock WEST 24-38. Lapland: Carpenter WONDER..DOGS 15-24.

A2513.1.1. Dog looks for most powerful master. Stays for food in man's service since man fears no one. Siberia (Nenetz Nenei): Deutsch TALES 7-16. India: Carpenter ELEPHANT'S 75-81 (elephant, lion, man). East Africa: Heady WHEN 42-46 (hartebeeste, elephant, lion, man).

A2513.1.2* Dog goes to steal fire for jackal, stays with man. Jackal still calls to dog from bush at night. (cf. A2346). Congo (Bushong): Arnott AFRICAN 1-4. SEE ALSO: A2427.1.

A2513.1.2.1. Dog sent to steal fire by wolf is well-fed and stays with man. Native American (Coeur d'Alene, Idaho): Leach HOW 57. U.S. Black: Harris FAVORITE 272-277 /Harris COMPLETE 292-298/.

A2513.1.3* How dog was domesticated. Two wolves settle in Indian camp. Forest wolf steals meat. Prairie wolf tells Indians, who drive forest wolf out. Prairie wolf stays and becomes dog. Native American: Green BIG 55-56.

A2513.1.5* At feast dog leaps for bone making embarrassing mess. Leaves forest in shame to lodge with man. Liberia: Haskett GRAINS 101-102.

A2513.2. How cat was domesticated. Kazakh: Masey STORIES 84-87. SEE: A2545.2.

A2513.2.1. Cat seeks fearless companion: hare, jackal, hyena, cheetah, man. Man afraid of wife. Cat stays with woman. East Africa: Heady WHEN 85-90.

A2513.2.2. Cat seeks strongest creature as companion. Finds each stronger than the last-- wildcat, leopard, lion, elephant, man, woman. Stays with woman. Africa: Tracy LION 115-117.

A2513.2.3* Cat sent by God Mahadeo to find out if man has fire. Cat stays. India (Kols): Leach LION 11.

A2513.2.4* Creator goddess Nirantali sees cat catch mouse and lets it into house. Lives there since. India (Khonds): Leach LION 10.

A2513.4.1* Why goat gives milk to people. East Africa: Heady WHEN 15-20.

A2513.6.1* Chicken sent for fire stays with man. Mpongwe: Leach HOW 91.

A2513.7* Why donkey serves man. Ethiopia: Courlander KING'S 74-77.

A2513.8* Why honey guide bird leads man to honey. Revenge on bees. Africa: Arnott TEMBA 78-84.

A2520. Disposition of animals.

A2523.2.1. Why rattlesnake is dangerous. Rattlesnake given poison because everyone steps on him. Given rattles so animals can hear him. U.S. Black: Lester BLACK 42-53.

A2523.2.2* Why black snake, the ooyu-bu-lui, is poisonous. Tricked iguana into letting him hold iguana's poison box. Australia: Courlander RIDE 20-24.

A2525.4* Why magpie is known for cunning and shyness. Korea: Kim STORY 19-22.

A2528.2* Why jaguar is strong. Peru (Andean): Carpenter LATIN 50-56.

A2534.1.1. Why crab flees from men. SEE: C432.1.2.

A2534.2* Why cats fear water. Philippines (Visaya): Sechrist ONCE 38-42. Korea: Carpenter KOREAN 47-54 /Gruenberg MORE 125-129/ (+D882.2).

A2538.1* Why monkey mimics. West Indies: Sherlock WEST 135-143.

A2540. Other animal characteristics.

A2541.3. Why killing condor brings bad luck. C. blessed by Coniraya for aid given. Peru (Andean): Carpenter LATIN 50-56.

A2542.3* Why dog must sleep out-of-doors with food on ground. Ghana (Akan-Ashanti): Aardema NA OF WA pb.

A2545.2. Why cat eats first (eats before washing). South Carolina Negro: Leach HOW 65. Netherlands: Dobbs ONCE 67-69; Hardendorff TRICKY 121-122. SEE ALSO: K562.

A2545.2.1* Why cat has first place in household. +D882.1.1.2. Ghana (Akan-Ashanti): Aardema NA OF WA pb.

A2545.3.1* Why dog is given first place among animals in household. SEE ALSO: H621.3. Burma: Carpenter ELEPHANT'S 114-124 (saves master's life).

A2571.2* How Kennreirk (Sparkling Fire) owl got its name. Eskimo (Hooper Bay): Gillham BEYOND 44-50. SEE ALSO: A1415.2.1.1.

A2579* Why or how animal dies.

A2579.1. Why snake turns belly to sky in death. Shows that he was not guilty of eating Anansi's yams. Ashanti: Courlander HAT 55-58.

A2581. Why tiger lacks some qualities of cats. Cat, his teacher, omitted to teach him all he knew (thus T. can't catch cat). Burma: Htin KINGDOM 53-55 (tiger can't move tail soundlessly). Russia/Yiddish: Ginsburg THREE 40 (tiger can't climb trees, A2495.1). China: Chang CHINESE 30. SEE ALSO: J1662.0.1 (cat teaches all tricks except one).

A2581.1* Why goat cannot climb trees. Cat, his teacher, catches goat teaching dog and discontinues lessons. Haitian Creole: Leach HOW 67. Haiti: Thoby-Marcelin SINGING 15-16. SEE ALSO: J1662.0.1.

A2585.2* Why mouse and flea bother man. Originally played practical jokes on each other, scaring each other out of skin. This got out of hand and they teamed up to bother man. Eskimo: Gillham BEYOND 68-75.

A2586* Why sharks do not kill people near Raiatea. Polynesia (Raiatea): Holding SKY 24-28.

A2600- A2699. Origin of trees and plants.

A2600. Origin of plants.

A2600.1* Origin of particular tree. SEE: K741.0.10 Walker.

A2611.0.1. Plants from grave of dead person or animal. SEE: E631.

A2611.3.1* Coconut tree from head. Tattling mischief-maker is beheaded. Head talks and causes death of servant reporting this by refusing to talk again (B210.2.3.1). Head laughs and is buried. Tree of coconuts grows from spot. The coconut still gurgles. Burma: Htin KINGDOM 43-45.

A2611.3.2* Turtle lover sends gift. To behead turtle and bury head. Coconut grows, shell hard like turtle's shell, inside like turtle tears. Polynesia (Magaia): Holding SKY 49-60. Cook Islands: Gittins TALES 72-75 (eel lover, marks of eyes and mouth on coconut).

A2612. Plants from tears.

A2612.4* Hunchback girl meets angel on Christmas Eve and is given three wishes. Uses the wishes on her family, forgetting self. Family gives her no thanks for sudden fortune. Her tears fall on snow and turn blood red. Angel removes her hunchback. Tears become holly. Italy (Umbria): Jagendorf PRICELESS 125-130.

A2650. Origin of flowers.

A2650.1* Origin of camlet flower. Little Caucasian girl saves drowning Indian boy but is herself drowned. Tupa (an Indian god) gives her immortality as the camlet flower; it is the color of her blue eyes. Uruguay: Courlander RIDE 215-216.

A2667. Origin of Indian pipes. Men quarrel even while smoking peace pipe. Great Spirit turns them into Indian pipe plant. Native American (Cherokee): Bell JOHN 78-80 /Cathon PERHAPS 133-134/.

A2668* Origin of blue camas flower. Girls throw eyes into air, blue camas flowers appear when they fall. Native American (Shoshone): Heady SAGE 42-45.

A2681.1.1* Origin of pussy willow. Coyote throws eyes into air, they stick in willow tree. Native American (Shoshone): Heady SAGE 42-45.

A2681.5. Origin of palms. Woman helpful to tribe is changed to palm tree by moon. Boy is instructed in use of tree's parts. Hardendorff FROG'S 25-28 /Duarte LEGEND pb/.

A2681.5.1. Origin of coconut tree. SEE ALSO: A2611.3.

A2681.5.1.1* During flood cat arrives at mountain top floating on coconut. Thus coconut saved from flood. Apayo: Leach HOW 126.

A2681.6.1* Origin of Winter Bamboo. Boy weeps daily in bamboo grove because there are no shoots for ill mother. God of Bamboo takes pity and winter shoots grow. Called Meng Tsung bamboo in his memory. China: Cheney TALES 119-121.

A2681.14* Origin of balsam tree. Lover and his warriors killed in attempt to steal girl. Girl Nabá goes with six attendants to tend the wounded. Her angry father kills them. Seven Nabá trees (balsam) grow from the spot, with power to heal wounds. El Salvador: Courlander RIDE 241-242.

A2681.15* Origin of waringen tree. Second wife of king poisons heir, Jamojaja. He dies but wife beseeches Kama Jaja and he is turned into the waringen tree and wife Dewi Kesumo becomes a spring (A941.1). Raden Samisan refuses the throne and is turned into a bird as he wanders forever crying "Kakapatat" ("I look for my brother"). Java: De Leeuw INDONESIAN 81-89.

A2681.16* Origin of the waru wanggi tree. Kawitjaksana is attacked by other hermits. A snake from Brahma drops at his feet and becomes a waru wanggi tree. A lance shaft is cut from tree and given to K. The head appears magically on shaft. Indonesia: De Leeuw INDONESIAN 61-64.

A2681.17* Origin of wili wili trees. Three sisters Wili wili-oheohe, Wili wili-peapea, Wili wili-kuapuu refuse to help Moho-lani when her husband is stolen. Her son, Kauila, turns them to wili wili trees. Hawaii (Kau district): Cothran MAGIC 49-52.

A2681.18* Origin of certain tree with seed like turtle's back. Man went to tabu place where turtles were called from ocean. Turned to tree. Fiji: Gittins TALES 32-36.

A2683.1* Origin of moss.

A2683.1.1* Origin of spanish moss. Moon answers mother's prayer and hangs moss on trees to warm freezing children. Native American (Choctaw): Arbuthnot ARBUTHNOT ANTHOLOGY 392.

A2683.1.2* Origin of red moss on tundra. Bloody path of four undutiful sons pursuing mother who was turned to a cuckoo. Arctic (Samoyeds) Nenetz: Deutsch MORE 69.

A2684. Origin of cultivated plants. Fox persuades condor to take him to heavenly feast of birds. Fox overeats and uses poor manners. The birds lower him on vine and he abuses passing parrots who then threaten to cut rope. Third time they cut rope--fox falls and bursts, all he had consumed is scattered, origin of seeds. Bolivia: Jagendorf KING 43-48.

A2685.1. Origin of corn.

A2685.1.0.1. Origin of corn silk. Man unwilling to go with Death wastes away among corn, his whiskers still seen on corn ears. +J1051.1. U.S. (Alabama): Courlander TERRAPIN'S 108-111.

A2685.1.0.2* Crow brings first grain of corn in his ear when comes from land of Sun to earth. Therefore, crow has right to first new corn, watches fields, and eats corn-beetle grubs. Native American (Iroquois): Leach HOW 100.

A2685.1.1. Origin of maize. Ma-ix, daughter of creators Bitol and Tzakol, weds Teosinte, son of sunbeam and river. They become two corn stalks with her red hair and his pearly teeth. Her parents take her plant home and cultivate it--origin of maize. His plant is left to grow wild--origin of wild maize. Guatemala: Jagendorf KING 122-126.

A2685.5. Origin of manioc. Chief's daughter to bear white skinned son by stranger. Baby girl Mani, her father was son of Pachacamac and Pacha-Mama. Mani passes to heaven and manioc plant grows from her grave. She and father appear in dreams and instruct in use and care of manioc. South America (Aymara): Carpenter LATIN 57-63.

A2685.5.1* Mandioca is left behind by Sumé god but no seeds are left. Chief's daughter has boy, Mani, who dies when lost mandioca root dies. Mandioca springs from his grave. Brazil: Eels TALES..AMAZON 179-183.

A2685.6* Origin of rice.

A2685.6.1* God turns daughter, Tisna Wati, and human lover into rice stalks. She is the goddess of mountain rice. Indonesia: De Leeuw INDONESIAN 21-23; Kimishima PRINCESS pb.

A2685.6.1.1* Bataru Guru, lord of gods, wants to wed Dewi Sri, girl hatched from egg cared for by cow with calf Lembu Gumarong. Gods poison her and rice grows from grave. Calf Lembu Gumarong tries to destroy rice and battle of gods ensues (A162). Indonesia: Asia FOLK I 7-12.

A2686. Origin of vegetables. One tree has all vegetables. Man tries to chop it down to get seeds. It regrows nightly. Animals are caught replacing chips at night. Tree is felled and seeds scattered. Maya: Gruenberg FAVORITE 377-379.

A2686.4.1. Origin of sweet potato. SEE: A1423.1.

A2686.4.4* Origin of potato plant. Pachacámac appears as white condor and tells Sopalla people to give enemy Karis green fruit on new plant to appear that night. Sopallas to wait until plants wither and take underground fruit. Enemy sickens from eating 'fruit' and is defeated. Bolivia (Aymara): Barlow LATIN 50-56.

A2687.3. Origin of berries.

A2687.3.1. Origin of strawberries. Wife leaves husband in anger and Great Spirit plants berries in her way to detain her so husband can catch up. She ignores all until he invents new berry = strawberries. She stops to pick and is re-united with husband. Native American (Cherokee): Bell JOHN 23-26 /Cathon PERHAPS 19-21/; Hulpac NORTH AMERICAN 131.

A2688.2. Origin of along-along grass. Hermit refused charity by villagers receives magic self-replenishing rice. Villagers now prey off his rice. He stops cutting and lets it die. Villagers rush to raid shed of rice left as offering to gods. Shed turns to stone and rice to along-along grass. Sumatra: De Leeuw INDONESIAN 40-44.

A2689.1* Origin of lichen. Wiskedjak's blood on rocks and willows become lichen. Native American: Leekley WORLD 64-68.

A2691.2. Origin of tobacco. Bird falls from sky, flame from sky burns it up, live coal in ashes turns to little man who gives seeds to plant in ashes. To smoke leaves and receive contentment and pleasant dreams. Canada: Frost LEGENDS 283-286.

A2691.5. Origin of betel. Two brothers love one girl. Elder weds. Younger turns to limestone rock in grief. Brother seeks, turns to areca tree. Wife to betel vine. King Hung Vuong comes to the site of legend and chews three together, resulting in blood red spittle. Vietnam: Asia FOLK..I 47-51; Robertson FAIRY 89-93; Schultz VIETNAMESE 67-71.

A2691.6. Origin of yerba maté. Guarani man saves Cloud Goddess and Moon Goddess from tiger. They give him tree of yerba maté. Paraguay (Guarani): Barlow LATIN 38-42.

A2693* Origin of medicinal plants. SEE ALSO: A1438.

A2693.1* Origin of dittany plant. Gold eagle given to chieftain by Ches is returned by burning at temple when princess is ill. Plant growing from spot cures her. Tea made from leaves cures, blossoms yield perfume. Venezula (Timotean Indians): Barlow LATIN 89-96.

A2700 - A2799. Origin of plant characteristics.

A2700. Origin of plant characteristics.

A2701* Gadong (jungle yam, Dagum (ground vine) and Japong (maize) argue who should replace rice. King Solomon favors maize and plants begin to fight. Maize is speared (why maize is

pierced). Yam is shot with poison arrow (why yam is poison). Dagum vine is pulled out of shape (why twisted). In fight trees' bark is scratched. Melons become pale on bottom from being shoved around. Bamboo stretches tall in order to see. Marsh grass runs off water's edge in fright. Solomon stops the fight and orders Dagum to crawl on ground, yam to set in ground, maize to stay in fields away from jungle. Malaya: Courlander TIGER'S 127-131.

A2710. Plant characteristics as reward.

A2711.3.1* Christ, fleeing from soldiers, hid in kernel of pine cone. His hand left mark on inside. Salerno: Jagendorf PRICELESS 59-60.

A2711.4. Tree protects Jesus from rain; is green all year.

A2720. Plant characteristics as punishment.

A2723.1. Discontented pine tree: cause of needles. Pine tree given silk leaves, glass leaves, etc. Always discontented. Finally has needles again. Dobbs ONCE 3-7.

A2730. Miscellaneous reasons for plant characteristics.

A2741.1. Bean laughs till it splits: cause of black stripe. (cf. A2793.1). Europe: Leach HOW 127-128. Germany (Grimm): Gag MORE 95-98; Grimm GRIMM'S (Grosset) 214-215; Grimm GRIMM'S (World) 280-281. SEE ALSO: F662.3; F1025.1.

A2760. Leaves of plant.

A2760.2* Why trees regain leaves in spring. Wolf-Wind pursuing children kills all deciduous trees but evergreens shelter children. Glooskap promises that dead trees will always revive in spring. Canada: Frost LEGENDS 287-294.

A2761.3. Why plant leaves are flat. SEE: A625.2.5.

A2765. Why leaves are evergreen. SEE ALSO: A2221.1.1.

A2765.1* Coniferous trees and plants are told to stay awake and keep watch for seven nights. Only a few stay awake--these are evergreen, the others sleep all winter. Native American (Cherokee): Bell JOHN 4-7; Leach HOW 125.

A2765.2* Conifers flaunt green needles in winter's face as promise of spring. Oak joins them, but tamarack is envious and failed to drink deep enough of magic oil so loses needles. Native American (Seneca): Parker SKUNNY 153-158.

A2769.2* Why leaves of maples turn red in fall. Blood from Great Bear (constellation) killed in sky. +A771.0.1. Native American (Micmac): Leach HOW 133-134.

A2770. Other plant characteristics.

A2771.4.1. Why rice has ears only at top. Angel of grains sent to strip stalk as punishment to men, is persuaded by birds to leave bit at top of stalk. China: Chang CHINESE 31-33.

A2774.2* Why baobab tree appears to be growing upside down. Baobab thought veld too hot and moved to high plains. Was too cold and asked Mungu (god) to move him to veld again. Mungu plants baobab upside down so he can't complain any more. East Africa: Heady WHEN 59-61.

A2793.8.1* Why millet root tops are flattened. Korea: Kim STORY 76-82.

A2794.2.1* Why yams and cassava hide in ground. Yams and cassava originally marched around singing and were thought devils. Little boy catches one and boils and eats. Thereafter they have to hide underground for protection. Liberia: Haskett GRAINS 47-50.

A2794.2.2* How yams got eyes. Bird sent to Rapu to bring yam. Sticks beak in it. (cf. A1243.1). Easter Island: Leach HOW 129.

A2796.1* Why tinni plant cuts one. Anansi steals magic cutting sword and slays enemy in war. Forgets word to stop sword and it kills his own soldiers too. Finally sticks self into ground. Turned to tinni plant. Still cuts. Africa (Ashanti): Courlander HAT 88-92.

A2800 - A2899. Miscellaneous explanations.

A2811. Origin of silk. China: Carpenter TALES ..CHINESE 98-106 (+B611.3).

A2813. Origin of honey. Bee and wasp given instructions by God in making honey. Bee listens carefully and wasp does not. Bee makes honey, wasp makes only poison. Nigeria (Yoruba): Walker NIGERIAN 43-44.

A2816. Origin of smoke.

A2816.1* Why Mt. Fuji smokes. Japan: McAlpine JAPANESE 127-187; Ozaki JAPANESE 98-118.

A2817. Origin of the will-o'-the-wisp (jack-o'-lantern). SEE: Q565 Smith and Devil.

B. ANIMALS

B0 - B99. Mythical animals.

B10. Mythical beasts and hybrids.

B11. Dragon. SEE ALSO: A2426.2.18; B11.4.1.1; W156.1.

B11.2.1.2.1* Dragon as modified lizard. Monster Mo-o killed by Maui. Hawaii: Thompson HAWAIIAN..EARTH 65-69.

B11.2.1.2.2* Giant lizard lured into swamp by Coyote. Coyote shoots arrow chain into sun and hides sun under water. Lizard comes from cave in ensuing darkness and is blinded when Coyote releases sun. Native American (Chinook): Robinson COYOTE 73-78.

B11.2.1.3* Dragon as modified fish. Carp succeeds in trial. Dives across three divine waves. He is changed into the first dragon. Vietnam: Vo-Dinh TOAD 51-55.

B11.4.1.1* Flying dragon. Dragon Tuparin terrorizes castle of Prince Vladimir. Strong man (supernatural youth) Alyosha Popovich and companion strong man Maryshko Papanov's son wrestle dragon. Alyosha Popovich calls on Holy Mother of God to raise storm and wash off dragon's paper wings. Unable to fly, dragon falls to earth and Alyosha Popovich kills. Russia: Higonnet-Schnopper TALES 129-140.

B11.6.1. Dragon helps hero out of gratitude. SEE ALSO: B389.2.

B11.6.1.1* Dragon and man like brothers. Man is left to guard hoard. He tells man that if egg in casket is broken, dragon will die. Man breaks egg (E711.1). Dragon returns. End of friendship. Green CAVALCADE..DRAGONS 26-27.

B11.6.1.2* King Pindus and dragon are friends. Brothers kill King Pindus. Dragon kills brothers and guards the body of King Pindus until people of Macedon come. Green CAVALCADE.. DRAGONS 16-20.

B11.6.1.3* Samebito (sharkman) is banished from dragon king's underground palace. Man shelters, feeds. Samebito's tears form jewels. Hearn BOY 5-13.

B11.6.1.4* A boy invites the Dragon to his birthday party. The dragon is so overjoyed that he is invited that he sobs a river of tears of happiness. The Dragon turns into a dragon-boat and swims down river with the boy on his back. China: CHINESE 20-21. Japan: Sakade JAPANESE 19-23.

B11.6.1.5* Dr. Ma heals dragon. Taken to heaven and made patron of veterinarians. China: Manton FLYING 24-29.

B11.6.2.4* Woman takes baby and enters Vouivre's lair. Throw stale bread in cave on Palm Sunday eve and may have all treasure crumbs touch. Cave closes with babe inside. Mother camps at entrance and leaves food for babe on ledge. Rescues it next Palm Sunday eve. France: Holman DRAC 73-84.

B11.6.11* Dragons guard dragon gate. If fish passes through it becomes a dragon. Carp tricks dragon into proving he can fly, slips in gate. (K722). China: Cheney TALES 75-80.

B11.7. Dragon as rain-spirit. Man in yellow on white horse with four attendants visits home of Wu. Horse is covered with scales and is of five colors. Grandmother advises this is the Yellow Dragon of the storms and his followers, the four winds. In ensuing storm Wu's home alone is dry. One scale from horse is given him for hospitality. Cures ill with this. Becomes emperor's magician. China: Dolch STORIES..OLD CHINA 121-129; Manning BOOK..DRAGONS 55-61.

B11.7.0.1* Li Ching taken aloft on horse by dragons in charge of rain and allowed to drop rain drops from jar. Seeing village he likes he drops twenty drops = twenty feet of rain. China: Birch CHINESE 101-110.

B11.7.1. Dragon controls water supply. Emperor Chu-Ti as lad is sent to distant province by stepmother. Priest gives three papers to read in need (J21D). First tells to build city in wilderness (Peking). Second tells to dig in spot for water. This digging disrupts cave of dragon couple. They ask permission to leave city taking water from the well, they take all the water. Last paper tells Chu-Ti to pierce the baskets dragon couple are taking away on cart. Water floods forth. Priest hooks one of baskets and drops into ground by temple. Artesian spring forms there. China: Arnott ANIMAL 122-128; Carpenter TALES..CHINESE 166-174; Dolch STORIES..OLD CHINA 93-97; Manning-Sanders BOOK..DRAGONS 95-102.

B11.10. Sacrifice of human being to dragon. SEE: R111.1.3; A1541.7.

B11.11. Fight with dragon. SEE: R111.1.3.

B11.11.2. Hera's dogs (horse) prevent dragon's heads from rejoining body. England: Spicer MONSTERS 109-115 (princess won, church on River Rye on spot, dog carries parts off magic ground so cannot rejoin body).

B11.11.7. Woman as dragon slayer. Martha and servant arrive from Syria in small boat to spread Christianity. Martha tames dragon with sign of cross and holy water. Leads back tied with her braids and villagers kill it. (St. Martha of Bethany). France: Holman DRAC 41-55.

B11.11.7.1* Girl entices Afanc water monster out of water and sings to sleep. Men bind and oxen pull to Llyn Fynnon. Leave it there. Wales: Sheppard-Jones WELSH 43-47.

B11.11.7.2* Maid sent as annual sacrifice kills serpent with aid of dog. China (Ch'in Dynasty): Kendall SWEET 33-38.

B11.11.9* Ivan the peasant's son and the Three Dragons. Three brothers to kill dragon at bridge. Elder two sleep and youngest slays six, nine and twelve-headed dragons named Chudo Yudo. Three wives and mothers of dragons plot revenge but Ivan overhears and saves brothers from well, tree, carpet and sow which would kill them. Russia: Riordan TALES..CENTRAL 96-105.

B11.11.10* Dragon fed sheep stuffed with sulfur drinks Vistula almost dry, bursts. Poland: Domanska KING pb.

B11.12.4.1. Dragon is fed great quantities of milk to keep him pacified.

B11.12.4.1.1* Lambton Worm. Man curses and fishes on Sunday (C631). Catches a worm (dragon). Old man tells him he must keep worm. It terrorizes countryside. Lad of Lambton Hall makes pilgrimage to Holy Land. Worm comes daily to Lambton Hall to be fed milk of nine cows, continues for seven years. Childe of Lambton must kill dragon in battle on rock near River Wear. To kill first thing meets when returning home after battle or no Lambton will die in bed for three times three generations. Dog meant to come to meet him, father comes instead. Curse befalls family. England: Green CAVALCADE.. DRAGONS 109-114; Jacobs MORE 215-221.

B11.12.4.1.2* Deerhurst Worm. England: Spicer MONSTERS 32-40.

B11.12.7.1* Human-dragon marriage. Dragon King's daughter wed to dragon who mistreats her. She asks student Liu to carry message of her plight to her father. To strike girdle against tree thrice and dragon comes from lake and escorts to her father. Her uncle, Chien Tang, chained to pillar for 2,000 years for causing flood. Breaks loose on hearing this and swallows the offending river dragon. Dragon's daughter weds student and he gains dragon's life span (10,000 years). China: Carpenter TALES..CHINESE 72-80 /Hoke DRAGONS 43-50/; Manning-Sanders BOOK..DRAGONS 20-24; Palmer DRAGONS 46-54 /Hoke DRAGONS 223-230/.

B11.12.7.2* Dragon King's daughter pines after music of abandoned flute player. Wed. China:

Lin MILKY 76-86.

B13. Unicorn. SEE: K771.

B16. Devastating animals.

B16.2.8. Giant man-eating mice. SEE: B871.2.7.

B16.5.1.3* Girl offers self as sacrifice to marauding snake. Toad fights for her. Both toad and snake die. Korea: Kim STORY 116-122.

B16..5.1.4* Antelope Carrier kills giant serpent with fourth magic arrow and saves Thunderbird's young. Rewarded with lightning stick. Birds to follow. Native American (Arikara): Brown TEPEE 22-26.

B16.6.5. Devastating centipede. SEE: Q82.3.

B19.1.1* Origin of Red Buffalo of the underworld and White Buffalo of the clouds. Native American (Seneca): Parker SKUNNY 183-189.

B20. Beast-men.

B27. Man-lion. Man with lion's head. Manticore of North Cerney, befriends boy, gives flute. Image carved on church. England: Spicer MONSTERS 116-127.

B29.9.1* Origin of the Sasquatch. Native American (Skagit): Matson LEGENDS 123-125. Native American (Swinomish): Matson LEGENDS 117-119.

B30. Mythical birds.

B31.1. Roc. A giant bird which carries all men in its claws. Arabian Nights: Rackham ARTHUR 71-110; ARABIAN NIGHTS (Jr. Lib.) 79-125. SEE ALSO: H1385.3Fa; K1861.1.

B31.1.3* Kukali is given magic self-replenishing (D1652.1.7.2) banana. Carried off by huge bird with hoods on wings to rock valley where keeps victims. K. feeds victims on banana. Restored to health they feign death and kill bird. Hawaii: Berry MAGIC 13-21.

B31.5. Simorg: giant bird. SEE: B535.0.5.1.

B50. Bird-men.

B51. Sphinx. Has face of woman, body and tail of lion, wings of bird. SEE ALSO: H761 (Riddle).

B51.1* Sphinx promises throne to Thothmes if he clears sand from her. Egypt: Carpenter AFRICAN 63-70.

B56. Garuda-bird. Lower part man, upper part bird. India: Ryder PANCHATANTRA 94.

B80. Fish-men.

B80.1. Seal-men. SEE: B389; B651.8.

B81. Mermaid. SEE: F948.5 (city buried in sand); D1349.2.4. SEE ALL: F420 - F429.

B81.2. Mermaid marries man. SEE ALSO: F420.5.2.2.3 (Nix at pond); F420.6.1.3.1 (Urashima Taro); D1415.2.4.2.

B81.2.1* Sven and Lilli. Lad lost at sea is taken home by whale. Serves mermaid, whale's daughter. Returns home with her, but is rejected by all but great grandmother. Whale sends wave to destroy village. Only great grandmother saved, she rides waves in rocker. Denmark: Manning-Sanders CHOICE 89-94 /Manning-Sanders BOOK..MERMAIDS 9-14/.

B81.2.2* Nefyn the mermaid. Mermaid bears five sets of twins. After father's death, mother returns to sea. Wales: Sheppard-Jones WELSH 109-114.

B81.2.3* Mermaid abducts man. Lad diving for lost ring in lake finds garden tended by lost boys. Ugly, fat mermaid insists he stay to wed her. He escapes. Ireland: Manning-Sanders CHOICE 295-300 /Manning-Sanders BOOK..MERMAIDS 73-78/.

B81.2.4* Lad takes comb of mermaid. She weds for seven years. Then he must come with her. Grandmother brands youngest of her seven children with cross and it cannot be taken back to sea. Orkney: Cutt HOGBOON 108-113.

B81.3.3* Mermaid stranded in pool asks lad to carry her back to sea. Wade in a little farther, etc. Mermaids sing and entice him on. He says prayer and escapes. Cornwall: Manning-Sanders PETER 11-16; Sleigh NORTH 23-30.

B81.13.6. Mermaid sings divinely in church (before enticing man away). Cornwall: Manning-Sanders PETER 178-182.

B81.13.11. Mermaid captured.

B81.13.11.1.1* The Untidy Mermaid. Man tricks mermaid into handing him her magic belt, feigns to feel magic in purse. She lends belt to show real magic. He keeps her captive. Goose-boy returns her treasures (comb, mirror, belt, pouch) and she rewards. Man never able to get boat into sea again. Scotland: Manning-Sanders BOOK..MERMAIDS 79-85.

B81.13.11.1.2* Fisherlad and the Mermaid King. Lad catches mermaid and makes her promise to give him his true love. Magic ring given, to put on true love's finger after one year. Lass shelters with him, after a year he puts ring on her finger. Scotland: Nic Leodhas THISTLE 119-135.

B82.1.1* Merman marries maiden. Margrette caught by merman king. Prince wants to wed. Merman king brings ugly daughter of neighbor merking to wed and Margrette drips candle on her, causing to leave in discomfiture. Prince allowed to wed Margrette. Home on visit she is kissed by dog and forgets merman. Hears sea calling and returns. France (Breton): Manning-Sanders BOOK..MERMAIDS 46-53.

B82.1.3* Princess abducted by son of Great Spirit of the Sea. Weds. Her hair still seen drifting with tide in Deception Pass. Native American (Samish): Matson LEGENDS 19-27.

B82.6* Merman caught by fisherman (released). The Four Abdullahs. Merman (Abdullah of the Sea) caught by Abdullah the Fisherman. Merman offers to exchange basket of jewels for basket of fruit daily. A. shares wealth with Abdullah the Baker who has fed him during lean times. Abdullah the King makes the two Abdullahs his advisors. Arabia: Manning-Sanders BOOK..MERMAIDS 122-128.

B90. Other mythical animals.

B94.1. Mythical crab. Crab tries to catch moon. Princess summons help with conch shell and saves moon. Philippines: Sechrist ONCE 75-78.

B98.1* Mythical frog. Man steals from old woman. She turns to giant man and says he has offended Great Spirit of the Toad. He must go about helping others, carrying toad on shoulders as penance. Japan: Pratt MAGIC #5.

B100 - B199. Magic animals.

B100. Treasure animals.

B102.1. Golden bird. Bird with golden feathers. SEE: H1331.1.3 (quest for golden bird).

B103.0.4.1* Grateful snake gives gold piece daily. India: Ryder PANCHATANTRA 331-332. SEE: D876.2; J15.

B103.1.1. Gold-producing ass. Droppings of gold. SEE: D861.1.; K111.1.

B103.1.5. Gold-making bird (golden dung). India: Ryder PANCHATANTRA 359-360. SEE: D861.1F.

B103.2.1. Treasure-laying bird. Bird lays money or golden eggs or an egg at every step. SEE: D861.1F.

B103.3.2* Prince of the Seven Golden Cows. Black Valet buys farm with master's gold. Is found out and expelled. When master falls on ill times and is deserted by friends, Black Valet takes to farm and cares for him. Prince reveals secret of wealth. Cut reed in marsh at midnight. Cut no matter what form it takes-- serpent, baby, sweetheart. Make into flute and play certain tune on midsummer eve. Seven golden cows emerge from ground and their milk turns to gold--seven sacks full. France: Manning-Sanders JONNIKIN 106-114; Picard FRENCH 148-156.

B113.1. Treasure producing bird heart. SEE: D551.1; R111.1.3AL.

B115.1. Ear-cornucopia. Animal furnishes treasure or supplies from his ears. SEE: R221F (Rushen Coatie); H1385.5B (Black Bull of Norroway); B335.2 (Billy Beg and his Bull et al.).

B130. Truth telling animal.

B133.3. Speaking horse-head. Type 533. The helpful magic horse (B401) is killed (B335). The head is preserved and placed on the wall. It speaks and reveals the treachery practiced against the heroine. The princess has been forced to change places with her maid on way to wedding (K1911.1.1). She has lost handkerchief with three drops of her mother's protecting blood. She serves as goose girl (K1816.0.2) and asks wind to carry off goose boy's hat to distract him from her discovery. King asks her to tell her secret to stove and overhears (H13.2.7). Wed. Grimm: Arbuthnot FAIRY 66-68; De La Mare ANIMAL 213-223; Grimm BROTHERS 158-165; Grimm GOOSE pb (De Angeli); Grimm GRIMM'S (Follett) 127-137; Grimm GRIMM'S (Grosset) 67-75; Grimm GRIMM'S (World) 152-158; Grimm HOUSEHOLD 20-25; Holme TALES 105-108; Lang BLUE 286-294 /Lang FIFTY 81-87/; Rackham GRIMM'S 32-38; Wiggin FAIRY 236-243. SEE ALSO: K1911.1.1.

B143.1.5* Golden cock warns against attack. Cock causes Tzar's sons to be all sent into battle. They slay each other. Tzar refuses to return cock to sorcerer and cock kills him. Russia: Dolch OLD RUSSIA 61-79.

B145.2.1* Prophetic snake. Snake interprets king's dream for man, ungrateful man fails to reward. Second time he attacks snake, third time he shares and apologizes. Snake says man was deceitful, warlike, peaceful according to the tenor of the times (as revealed in king's dream). Snake excuses man. USSR: Courlander RIDE 154-158.

B150. Oracular animals.

B151.1.1.0.4* Lover's horse borrowed for wedding ride to duke's home. In dark, horse takes path to his young master's home by instinct and bride is brought to her lover instead of waiting bridegroom. France: Picard FRENCH 77-83. SEE ALSO: N721.

B165.3* Canadian Geese language learned from two pet geese. Eskimo (Hooper Bay): Gillham BEYOND 1-16.

B170. Magic birds, fish, reptiles, etc.

B171.1. Demi-coq. A cock is cut in two and is made magic. Carries ladder, fox, and stream of water under wings. SEE: Z52.2.

B171.1.1. Demi-coq crows in king's body. SEE: A52.4.2.

B171.1.2* Half chick on way to see king refuses aid to clogged stream, dying fire, wind caught in branches. At Madrid is cooked in pot. Water, wind and fire refuse to aid his pleas for help. Wind carries to steeple where is set as wind-vane. Spain: Dobbs ONCE 8-14; Lang GREEN 29-34 /Arbuthnot FAIRY 131-133/; Haviland SPAIN 36-49; Haviland FAIRY 66-70 /Arbuth-not ANTHOLOGY 264-266/; Martignoni ILLUS-TRATED 246-248; Wiggin FAIRY 337-343 (Rome, St. Peter's, Coquerico).

B175.3. Fish must be eaten from head downward as this turns fish toward land and into nets. Fisherman's daughter eats incorrectly. Father loses luck. She catches fish on quay which says, "Eat me from the head downward; put bones back into sea." Luck restores. (cf. C980). Cornwall: Manning-Sanders PETER 43-47.

B180. Magic quadrupeds.

B182.1. Magic dog. SEE: D1571.1.

B182.1.0.1.2* Tiny magic dog kept hidden in boy's hair, when in trouble dog grows to size of pony and saves life. Native American (Swin-omish): Matson LEGENDS 85-90.

B184.1. Magic horse. SEE: B133.3 (Goose girl).

B184.1.3. Magic horse from water world. SEE: F420.1.3.3.

B184.2.1.1.2. Magic cow gives impossible quan-tity of milk. SEE: G274.1.1.

B184.2.2. Magic ox. SEE: B154; B871.1.1 (Paul Bunyan).

B184.2.2.2. Magic cow from water world. Russia: Manning-Sanders BOOK..OGRES 9-19. SEE: ALSO: F420.6.1.5.1.

B184.2.2.2.1* White fairy cow gives healing milk, causes farmer to prosper. Prepares to butcher cow, fairy calls back to lake. Cow, progeny return to lake. Wales: Belting ELVES 53-54; Sheppard-Jones WELSH 115-118.

B184.2.2.3* Oxen size of peppercorns are given by demon to man about to hang self. They haul enormous loads, perform tasks, then carry count and bailiff to hell and return with wagon full of gold. Hungary: Manning-Sanders BOOK..DEVILS 69-75.

B184.2.3. Magic bull. SEE: B115 (cornucopia); B335.2.

B200 - B299. Animals with human traits.

B210. Speaking animals.

B210.1.1* Person frightened by animals and objects replying to his remarks. Yam (D983.2), dog, palm branch, stone, fish trap, bundle of

cloth, river, stool. Man runs to tell chief. Chief disdains such foolishness. His stool speaks up. Ghana: Courlander COW 25-29 /Gruenberg FAVORITE 354-357/. U.S. (Ala-bama): Courlander TERRAPIN'S 87-90 (horse speaks, master disdains report, master's dog speaks up).

B210.1.2* Goat talks, killed. Meat talks, thrown in river. Skin talks, burnt. Ashes talk tell-ing thieves to put ashes on lips as disguise--shout "Here are the thieves." Ethiopia: Cour-lander FIRE 93-98.

B210.2. Talking animal or object refuses to talk on demand. Discoverer is unable to prove his claims and is beaten.

B210.2.1* Singing tortoise refuses to sing. Own-er driven out of town. Ghana (Accra): Cour-lander COW 65-71 (tortoise plays sansa [thumb piano] and sings, discoverer forbidden (C450) to tell). Haiti: Thoby-Marcelin SINGING 21-29 (tortoise escapes, toad substituted).

B210.2.1.1* Wife lets singing turtle escape. Bragging husband to be shot. Turtle sticks head out of river and sings. Haiti: Courlander PIECE 29-33.

B210.2.1.2* Bad man tries to imitate good man by stealing turtle, he is beaten and kills turtle. Good man buries and tree (F54.2.2.2) grows to sky from grave. Hundreds of turtles come down and each drops a gold piece in his hand. Bad man imitates and they come down and stick out tongues and go back. (cf. J2415). Japan: Sakade JAPANESE 93-100; Scofield HOLD 9-14.

B210.2.2* Hunter tells leopard "Stupidity brought you here." Leopard replies "Cleverness will bring you here." Man stakes reputation on talking leopard. Leopard refuses to talk. Man driven from town. Congo (Bakongo): Cour-lander KING'S 64-66.

B210.2.3* Skull to man: "Talking brought me here." Man claims skull talks. Skull is silent. Man is killed. Man's skull: "Talking brought me here." Africa (Nupe): Frobenius AFRICAN 161-162. U.S. Black: Courlander TERRAPIN'S 74-75. Florida: Leach THING 49-50. Congo: Littledale GHOSTS 67-72 /Savory CONGO/.

B210.2.3.1* Beheaded head tells servant to fetch king. On return head is silent and servant is beheaded. Head laughs. Head is buried and coconut grows from head. Coconut still gur-gles (A2611.3.1). Burma: Htin KINGDOM 43-45.

B211.3.4.1* Talking parrot is unable to say "Cataño." Owner threatens "Say 'Cataño' or I'll kill you!" Bird is thrown into hen yard to be eaten on Sunday. Found threatening chick-ens "Say 'Cataño' or I'll kill you!" Puerto Rico: Jagendorf KING 242-244.

B216. Knowledge of animal language. Person understands them. SEE ALSO: D1415.2.3.5; K1633.1.

A* The animal languages. Type 670.

Aa* Shepherd rescues snake from fire with staff. Snake takes to his father, the King of the Snakes, to ask as reward knowledge of language of animals. To die if he reveals this (C425). Snake kisses are blows on mouth. He hears dogs plotting to share sheep with wolves. Hears his wife's horse complain of her weight and laughs. Forced to tell wife secret. He overhears cock tell how he rules hens and learns thus how to rule own wife (T252.2). Serbia: Spicer LONG 11-28. Yugoslavia: Fillmore LAUGHING 253-266; Lang CRIMSON 42-48. Russia: Ransome OLD 260-268. Albania: Wheeler ALBANIAN 45-64.

Ab* Otwe. Man saves snake, given magic feather that allows him to hear animals' thoughts. Tabu on telling. Wife forces to tell. He confesses and dies. Snake revives him. Africa (Nuer): Aardema OTWE pb.

Ac* Man who learned language of animals. Palm wine tapping pots broken on three nights. Man follows deer to animal kingdom, receives understanding of animal speech from leopard king. Tabu on telling. Second wife forces him to tell. He tells and dies. She is burnt and the ashes scattered. Wherever they fell, jealousy and selfishness took root. The origin of evil in the world (A1384). Ghana (Akan): Arnott AFRICAN 5-12.

Ad* Language of the birds. Magician gives servant language of birds. Tabu on telling. Wife forces to tell. Cock's conversation with hen shows him his folly. North Africa: Gilstrap SULTAN'S 88-95.

Ae* King learns language of animals from hermit. Queen forces to tell. Monkeys mock king and suggest he tell queen anyone hearing secret must receive sixty lashes first. India: Wyatt GOLDEN 50-58.

Af* The Billy Goat and the King. King about to turn to stone for telling wife secret of his knowledge of animal languages sees Billy Goat rule wife by butting. India: Farjeon CAV.. QUEENS 62-68 /Lang OLIVE 85-89/.

B* Da-Trang, the sand crab. Da-Trang saves black snake from enemy snake. Is given pearl (ruby) giving understanding of animal speech. He shoots at blackbird (raven) in anger. In revenge bird uses his arrow to commit a murder. Da-Trang is jailed. In jail he predicts flood and famine and is rewarded. King borrows magic jewel. It drops from his mouth into sea. Da-Trang in the form of a sand crab still searches for the jewel. Vietnam: Robertson FAIRY 81-88; Vo-Dinh TOAD 89-97.

B216.2* Legend of Eilean Donan Castle. If first sip is taken from raven's skull, lad will understand language of animals. Reveals that starlings predict father will serve him. He is exiled (L425). Tells King of France that sparrows are beseiging castle because their nesting grove is being cut. Rewarded. Returns home rich, builds Eilean Donan Castle. Scotland: Wilson SCOTTISH 49-55.

B216.4* Tintinyin knows language of animals, learns secret identity of King of Spirit World from ega bird. Wins contest. Nigeria (Yoruba): Fuja FOURTEEN 180-185.

B216.5* Huathiacuri is taught language of animals by father Paricaca. Learns that lover's father can be cured by killing serpent in storehouse and two-headed frog--really girl's stepmother and her lover. Wins suitor tests (H310) with gift of foxes--replenishing chicha gourd and flute with one hundred pipes. Costume contest between challenging stepbrother and Huathiacuri. H. wears jaguar skin. Housebuilding contest--birds bring feathers, animals aid. Race--H. touches stepbrother on shoulder as passes and stepbrother turns into a deer. Peru (Inca): Carpenter SOUTH 27-35.

B216.6* Jack aids old woman, given stone which advises what to do. Kills giant with stone, gets gold reward. Overhears fox and squirrel tell that city with dried up well will find water in front of clock tower, mayor will regain sight if rubs eyes with leaves of this tree, princess with horns will be restored if eats three apples from tree by fountain. J. rewarded, is rich. (cf. H1273.22). Wales: Hampden GYPSY 139-146.

B217.1.1. Animal languages learned from eating serpent. Type 673. The white snake. Servant tastes of forbidden dish, white snake, understands voices of animals. Hears bird say lost ring of queen is in its throat (N451). +B582.2 (grateful animals). Grimm: Grimm GRIMM'S (Follett) 399-406; Grimm GRIMM'S (Grosset) 80-85; Grimm GRIMM'S (World) 29-33; Grimm HOUSEHOLD 93-97; Lang GREEN 305-310; Rackham GRIMM'S 17-21. Armenia: Tashjian ONCE 57-69. SEE ALSO: H1213.1K.

B217.9* The three languages. Type 671. Lad learns language of dogs, birds, frogs; predicts father will serve him (L425). Father orders him killed. His executioners spare him (K512.2). In tower inhabited by wild dogs he learns treasure must be removed to break dogs' enchantment. At Rome he hears frogs say he'll be made Pope. Two white doves light on his shoulders as he enters church (H171.2). He is named Pope and doves whisper mass to him. Grimm: Gag MORE 89-94; Rackham GRIMM'S 29-31. Switzerland: Müller-Guggenbühl SWISS 177-180. Europe: Jacobs EUROPEAN 66-71 (frogs reveal way to heal sick girl); Lang ROSE 64-71 (sparrows say one of three travelers will be chosen ruler, eagle alights on him).

B217.9.1* Wise Alois: learns language of frogs, dogs, fish at school. Hears frogs say holy wafer frog holds in mouth would cure dying woman, hears dogs say twelve robbers will rob inn --catches them. Hears fish say one of three companions will be elected president of Sion. It is he. Switzerland (German): Duvoisin THREE 234-245.

B220. Animal kingdom.

B221.2. Kingdom of rats. SEE: N777.0.3.

B222.5* Land of sparrows. SEE: Q285.1.1.

B225.1. Kingdom of serpents. SEE: K1931.2V.

B236.0.1. Animal king chosen as result of contest. Type 221. Baganda: Kaula AFRICAN 67-70 (chameleon, +K11.2.1). SEE ALSO: K11 (Race won by deception); K25 (Flying contest won by deception).

B236.1.1* Condor flies highest in contest. Made king of the mountains. Bolivia: Arbuthnot ANTHOLOGY 405-406; Jagendorf KING 503-523.

B240. King of animals.

B240.4. Lion as king of animals. SEE ALSO: K961.1.1; K962; K1632.

B240.9.1* Dog as king of animals. Each animal rejected for kingship because of weaknesses. Dog chosen steals the meat. Since then animals have no king. Haiti: Courlander PIECE 97-100.

B240.16* Jackal as king of animals. J. learns hermit's magic chant and turns self into king of animals, then king of men. Asked by hermit to prove he can make lion roar. Roar frightens elephant carrying lion carrying jackal. His royal steeds panic and j. is trampled. India: Wyatt GOLDEN 6-12.

B241.2.2. King of monkeys. (A132.2).

B241.2.2.1* Sun Wu-Kung, Monkey God. Born of a stone egg (A511.1.9). Causes uproar in heaven. Travels to the west in search of Buddhist scriptures. China: Carpenter TALES.. CHINESE 107-116; Dolch STORIES..OLD CHINA 107-111; Manning-Sanders BOOK..MAGICAL 45-48; Manton FLYING 121-126; Williams-Ellis ROUND 27-42. Waley, Arthur. MONKEY (a translation and abridgement of the Hsi Yu-Chih [Travels to the West] of Wu Cheng-En); Wriggins, Sally Hovey. WHITE MONKEY KING. India: Turnbull FAIRY 1-11.

B241.2.2.2* When monkeys are trapped by men, King of the Monkeys ties branch to waist and leaps stream making living bridge with body. Subjects escape thus. India (Jataka): Gaer FABLES 143-146; Reed TALKATIVE 58-61.

B241.2.3. King of cats. SEE: B342.

B241.2.5.1* King of mice. Shrew mouse Umulumba and vole mouse Mgeva compete for kingship. Mgeva hides food and then reveals

hiding place when all other food is gone. Voted king. Mice still search for his other hiding places. East Africa: Heady SAFIRI 71-74.

B241.2.10. King of deer.

B241.2.10.1* The Banyan Deer. Banyan Deer (Buddha) and Monkey Deer send one of their group each day to king to slay so that he will cease wanton hunting. The lot falls to a doe with young child so the Banyan Deer king offers himself in her place. King orders deer left alone in future. India: Babbitt JATAKA 58-62 /Arbuthnot FAIRY 166-167/, /Gruenberg MORE 109-110/, /Haviland FAVORITE..INDIA 91-95/, /Arbuthnot ANTHOLOGY 349/; Ross BURIED 81-88. SEE ALSO: W28 (self-sacrifice).

B241.2.10.1.1* The Golden Deer. Golden Deer (Buddha) saves man from stream. Queen dreams of stag and wants it. It is captured. Man betrays location of deer to king's men. Deer tells king of betrayal and king orders safety of all deer and other animals in future. India (Jataka): Reed TALKATIVE 52-57.

B241.2.10.1.1.1* The golden stag. Queen dreams of stag, orders it killed. Old hunter sees and tells son. Son snares stag but releases out of compassion on seeing two deer remain by stag in attempt to free it. Stag gives hunters hairs and wisdom. Queen allows young hunter to become hermit. India: Wyatt GOLDEN 1-5.

B241.2.11. King of elephants. India: Ryder PANCHATANTRA 274-276, 308-315.

B242. King of birds.

B242.1.2. Wren king of birds. Wins contest for kingship. SEE ALSO: B236.1.

B245.1. King of frogs. SEE: J643.1.

B250. Religious animals. SEE ALSO: A2221; A2231.

B251.1.2. Animals speak to one another at Christmas.

B251.1.2.4* Ass and goose travel to wishing well Christmas Eve. They are in love and each wishes to be the other. Ass becomes goose, goose becomes ass. Sawyer LONG 99-107.

B259.6* Wild goose is considered bird of the Five Virtues: love, right behavior, good form (in flying), wisdom (goes south), faithfulness (return). Korea: Carpenter KOREAN 75-77.

B260. Animal warfare.

B261. War of birds and quadrupeds. SEE: K2323+. SEE ALSO: G530.2K.

B261.0.1* Birds drop eggs on animals. Bees finish rout. Soudan: Carpenter AFRICAN 87-92. Upper Volta: Guirma TALES 29-44. SEE ALSO: A2433.3.4.1.

B261.1. Bat in war between birds and quadrupeds. Bat joins first one side then another.
He is discredited by both the birds and the
quadrupeds for his double-dealing actions.
Nigeria (Yoruba): Leach HOW 71-72; Walker
NIGERIAN 26. Aesop: Aesop AESOP'S (Viking)
45-46; Aesop AESOP'S (Watts) 133; Aesop FIVE
76; Bulatkin EURASIAN 111-113.

B261.1.0.1* Bat in war of birds and quadrupeds.
Bat refuses to fight with either side; neither
accepts him in peace. Aesop: Aesop AESOP'S
(Jacobs) 47; Aesop AESOP'S (Grosset) 214-215;
Reeves AESOP 55-56. Upper Volta: Guirma
TALES 29-44. SEE ALSO: A2491.1.1.

B261.1.0.2* Bat in ball game of birds and animals
is refused by both sides. Makes winning catch
for animals and is accepted as animal henceforth. Leach HOW 70. Native American (Cree): Brown
TEPEE 147.

B261.1.0.2.1* Bat and flying squirrel not allowed
on animals' side in ball game. Birds make them
wings and they win game for birds (A2377.2,
A2377.3). Native American (Creek/Cherokee):
Belting LONG 16-25. Native American (Cherokee): Bell JOHN 87-91.

B261.1.0.3* Bat refuses to pay taxes as either
bird or animal. Why flies by night--to avoid tax
collectors (A2491.1). Central Asia (Altai):
Deutsch MORE 7-10.

B261.1.0.4* Weasel catches bat, says he never
releases a bird. Bat claims he is animal. Second
weasel catches, says never releases an animal.
Bat claims is bird. Aesop: Aesop AESOP'S
(Watts) 5.

B261.1.0.5* Fruit bat dying, neither animals nor
birds will claim. He dies alone. Burton MAGIC
52-53.

B263.3. War between crows and owls (K2026).
India: Korel LISTEN 13-64; Ryder PANCHA-
TANTRA 291-378.

B263.5. War between frogs and birds.

B263.5.2* Sea birds attack land birds, are routed. Maori: Arnott ANIMALS 38-42.

B263.9* War between insects and animals. Insects
cloud sun and sting animals in dark. Cricket
and lion start feud. Ross BURIED 95-102.

B263.10* Contest between whale and sandpiper.
Each claims his kind is more numerous. All
whales, sharks, tuna called by whale. Sandpiper calls all sandpipers, crows, plovers.
Whales and kind attempt to eat up land so birds
will die. Birds attempt to drink up ocean. Folly
is seen and truce called. Micronesia (Marshall
Islands): Cothran MAGIC 38-44.

B263.11. King of Yorubas declares war on country of the frogs. Frogs, on advice of tortoise,
get Yoruba king's juju from his wife, defeat King
Olusegbe. Leopard helps O. revenge self on
tortoise. Nigeria (Yoruba): Fuja FOURTEEN
214-236.

B264.3. Duel of buffalo and tiger. Buffalo arms
self, covers self with straw and mud. China:
Chang CHINESE 53; Dolch STORIES..OLD
CHINA 17.

B264.3.1* Duel of leopard and lizard. Lizard
cakes self in mud, vanquishes leopard. Sri
Lanka (Ceylon): Asia FOLK..II 47-52.

B264.6* Duel of water buffalo. Karbau calf from
Sumatra is starved. Given steel-tipped horns. It
nuzzles bull of Javanese rajah and kills. Sumatrans' freedom was staked on duel. Sumatrans
shape roofs like horns of karbau and call land
Minangkabau Indonesia: Courlander KANT-
CHIL'S 12-16.

B264.7* Fight between giant bulls. Ashanti:
Courlander COW 113-118. SEE ALSO: B335.2.

B267.5* Alliance of lion and dolphin proves useless as dolphin can't leave water to aid in battle.
Aesop: Aesop AESOP'S (Grosset) 39.

B268.7* Army of snakes. Man Djisdaah kills rattlesnake. Snakes declare war. Truce on condition man treat snakes with respect in future and
never name another man Djisdaah. Bruchac TUR-
KEY 35-37.

B268.12* Army of boars. Carpenter's pet boar
organizes other boars to kill tiger. India (Jataka): Reed TALKATIVE 64-67.

B270. Animals in legal relations.

B271.3. Animals ring bell and demand justice. A
king has a bell which petitioners for justice may
ring and thus summon him. The bell is rung by
an old horse who wishes to complain against
cruel master. Russia: Carey BABA 27-32.

B279.1. Saint makes covenant with wolves.

B279.1.1* Saint Stanislaus gives wolf permission
to eat human flesh, but only blacksmith. B.
clubs wolf. Wolf decides blacksmith's flesh is
bitter. SEE ALSO: K553.1.0.5. Poland: Frost
LEGENDS 44-49; Hardendorff JUST 110-115.

B279.1.2* St. Francis tells wolf to kill no more
men and they will feed it. W. begs from door to
door. Italy: Vittorini OLD 102-105.

B280. Animal weddings.

B281.2.2. Wedding of mouse and cockroach. SEE:
Z32.3.

B281.9.1. The cat as vixen's husband. Frightens
the other wild animals invited by the vixen.
SEE: K2324.

B282.23. The courtship of the stork and crow. SEE: W123.3.

B284.1.1. Wedding of frog and mouse. "Frog went a-courtin'." Jacobs MORE 184-185; Langstaff FROG pb.

B285.4.1* Wedding of bluebottle. Courts princess, horse, cat, woodpecker, weds bluebottle who nurses back to health. England: Wiggin TALES 346-350.

B285.8. Wedding of cockroach to rat. SEE: Z32.3.

B296. Animals go a-journeying. SEE ALSO: K335.1.4, K1161.1.

B296.0.1* Pig goes to build a house, joined by sheep, goose, hare, cock. Each helps. Association TOLD..GREEN 36-39; Richardson GREAT 153-160. SEE ALSO: K1161.2.

B296.2* Two traveling frogs meet at mountain top. Standing up to look at other side of mountain decide destination is identical to home so they return home. They had forgotten their eyes are in the back of the head so each looked back the way he had come. (cf. X583.1). Japan: Lang VIOLET 111-113 /Gruenberg MORE 119-120/; Van Woerkom SEA FROG, CITY FROG pb.

B300 - B349. Helpful animals--general.

B300. Helpful animals--general.

B301.2.1* Faithful animal at master's grave avenges murder. King arranges duel between dog and man he appears to be accusing. France: Carpenter WONDER..DOGS 119-127.

B301.9.2* (Kirtley). Whale fed and tamed. Tintirau's pet whale is killed by jealous sorcerer Kae. T.'s wife and forty women avenge. Tell jokes until enemy laughs so can identify him by his shark teeth. Maori: Berry MAGIC 113-121.

B313. Helpful animal reincarnation of parent. Dead mother appears in form of helpful animal. SEE: R221F (Rushen Coatie).

B313.1.1* Dead mother returns as helpful cow. Feeds daughter. Stepmother kills. Cow tells to toss bones into river. Pillar of fire appears there. Cow emerges and rides off with daughter on back. Daughter weds chief in distant land. Africa: Nunn AFRICAN 104-111.

B314. Helpful animal brothers-in-law. Type 552A. Three Animals as Brothers-in-law.

A* The lion, the tiger and the eagle. Three brothers. Youngest agrees to wed sisters to lion, tiger and eagle. Fairy in crystal chamber to belong to youngest when sisters are wed. Fairy flees and he must seek. Reaches homes of three sisters. Each elicits aid of animal husband and sends on to next. They call all animals, all birds. Last to come is hawk. H. takes him to spring. He has worn out an iron staff and shoes. Weds fairy. Greece: Frost LEGENDS 120-126.

B* Wind demon. Watch at tomb of father. Entering robbers beheaded one at a time. Sisters wed to lion, tiger, Bird Padishah. Brother attacks wind demon. He is cut in pieces. Pieces reach animal brothers-in-law. He is restored. Secret of demon's soul obtained. He obtains dove (demon's soul) under pretense of herding ox on island. Turkey: Buck FAIRY 306-320.

C* The death of Koshchei the Deathless. (Marya Morevna). Sisters wed to falcon, eagle, raven by mother. Hero visits Marya Morevna, the warrior princess. Gives water to chained Koshchei the Deathless, and K. escapes taking M. (G671). Carries off Marya. Prince is forgiven twice because of drink given. Killed third time. Silver spoon token left with sisters darkens and animal brothers-in-law restore him to life. +H1199.12.4B. Russia: Buck FAIRY 35-46; Riordan TALES..CENTRAL 148-160; Whitney IN 107-120. Serbia: Garner CAVALCADE..GOBLINS 63-75 (Bash Tchelik, wed to dragon, eagle, falcon, +E710 heart in egg).

D* Three enchanted princes. Sisters wed to falcon, stag, dolphin. Youngest brother visits, given tokens to summon brothers-in-law. Rescues princes from dragon with aid. Italy: Mincieli OLD 73-83. Naples: Hampden HOUSE 25-32.

E* The beautiful Fiorita. Three sisters wed to first three men to pass at noon--pig-keeper, hunter, gravedigger. Brother given tokens to call them to his aid. He visits princess hidden in harpsichord (K1341.1). Suitor tests: tell from one hundred maidens. She gives him a magic rose to draw itself to her. Eat room full of fruits--pigs aid. Put princess to sleep--birds sing her to sleep. Create a two-year-old baby--throws magic bone given by gravedigger and it appears. Italy: Toor GOLDEN 83-90.

F* The Great Fish (Picking Flowers). Three princesses are carried off by a fish which demands them of their father (or they disappear while picking flowers). Brother takes magic boats, cloak of invisibility and key that opens any lock from boys quarreling over them. He visits sisters wed to King of the Fishes, King of the Birds, and King of the Seals. A princess or third sister is held by ogre whose soul is in egg in dove in casket in sea (E710). Brothers-in-law fetch casket. Portugal: Lang ROSE 25-33; Michael PORTUGUESE 92-104; Rackham FAIRY 77-83.

G* The Little Nobleman. Lad seeks sister sold before his birth. Gets cloak of invisibility, saddle of swiftness from two boys quarreling. Throws huge apple for them to chase. Brother-in-law gives golden feather to call him if in need. He weds brother-in-law's sister. They leave, taking along bush they pass. It is home of demon. Demon kidnaps wife and son. Imprisons in tree. Wife discovers where key to tree is kept. In egg--in duck--in goose--in calf--in cow--in cask--in forest. (E710). Brother-in-law helps find key. Demon can be killed only when putting on boots. Killed. Gypsy: Manning-Sanders RED 118-126.

B316. Abused and pampered horses. Hero is ordered by ogre to feed and care for certain horse and to neglect other horse. Hero disobeys and feeds neglected horse. Latter is enchanted prince and helps hero. Type 314 (The youth transformed to a horse).

A* Scurvyhead. Type 314. Lad in witch's service disobeys and feeds white horse rather than black. Finds tabu spring and hair turns to gold on touching water (C912). He flees on horse. Bridle thrown behind (D672) becomes mountain of bridles. Comb becomes mountain of combs. Bottle becomes mountain of bottles. As king's gardener he hides hair under wig, called Scurvyhead. In armour provided by horse, he routs (R222) enemy thrice. Wounded (H56) and identified by broken spear. Horse is cut in two and becomes a prince. French Canada: Barbeau GOLDEN 73-89.

B* The Widow's Son. Lad not to look in four rooms. Rod in first, pitcher in second, cauldron boiling without fire in third (C912) turns finger gold, fourth contains horse with coals at head and hay at tail. He changes. Horse tells to take oldest armour, bathe in cauldron (becomes handsome), flee with rod, stone, pitcher, and ointment. Throws rod, becomes forest. Stone becomes mountain. Pitcher becomes lake (D672). Trolls burst drinking lake dry. Takes work with wig of moss as gardener. Wins battle thrice in armour given by horse. Recognized by wound. Beheads horse which becomes a king. Norway: Asbjornsen EAST 128-141; Asbjornsen EAST 71-84; Aulaire EAST 58-69.

C* Hookedy-Crookedy. Jack, King of Ireland's son, hired by Giant of the Hundred Hills. Puts hay before horse, meat before bear. Finger sticks to ring in door and he cuts off to escape. Spared twice for service his father did for giant's father. Third time horse and he flee. Throws chestnut which becomes woods. Drop of water becomes lake. Giant drinks. Disguised as hookedy-crookedy fellow Jack works for King of Scotland. Accompanies two sons-in-law on quest for water from Well of the World's End. He wishes for bottle of water. Other two use stream water. They give him golden ball token of their weddings for his water and let him write on their backs. Enters battle thrice in armour given by horse and wins the day. Given magic cloth, purse and comb by king. Produces tokens, shows backs of sons-in-law, weds youngest princess. Helpful horse turns into girl, bear was her brother. Ireland: Wiggin FAIRY 125-145.

B317.1* Helpful birds raised by hero. Tonweya

falls into eagle's nest. Feeds young on his rawhide cord until old enough to fly and carry him to safety. They remain his companions. He paints their wing tips red (A2411.2.2.1) in gratitude. Native American (Lakota): Yellow Robe TONWEYA 102-114.

B331. Helpful animal killed through misunderstanding.

B331.0.1* Severed head of cat leaps onto poisonous snake in rafters. Japan: Pratt MAGIC #3.

B331.2. Llewellyn and his dog. Dog has saved child from serpent. Father sees bloody mouth, thinks dog has eaten child, and kills dog. Wales: De La Mare ANIMAL 111-114; Jacobs CELTIC 209-211; Sheppard-Jones WELSH 134-136 (Hound Gelert).

B331.2.1. Woman slays faithful mongoose which has saved her child. India: Ryder PANCHA-TANTRA 432-434.

B332.1* Too watchful dog killed. The Hobyahs. Hobyahs come nightly and dog barks to frighten away. Old man, irate at barking, cuts off tail, legs, finally head. Hobyahs now eat man and woman and carry off girl. Hunter finds her in bag and substitutes dog (K526). England: Jacobs MORE 127-133 /Fenner GIANTS 174-177/, /Tashjian JUBA 51-54/.

B335. Helpful animal killed by hero's enemy. SEE: B133.3 (goose girl). SEE ALSO: D1571.1.

B335.2. Life of helpful animal demanded as cure for feigned illness.

A* Billy Beg and His Bull. Type 511A, Type 320B. Stepmother feigns illness, needs organs (blood) of bull. Bull with Billy on back knocks stepmother down, killing her, and flees. Food in left ear, stick in right which becomes strength-giving sword (B115.1). Bull fights three bulls, last to kill him (B264.7). Billy to make belt of bull's hide which makes him invincible. Hired to guard cattle from giants, Billy kills giants with three, six and twelve heads. Cattle now give so much milk it forms a lake which is still there. Billy kills dragon. Rescued princess takes his shoe as he flees. Knight claims feat but shoe does not fit. Shoe tried on all men (H36.1). Billy wed. Ireland: MacManus IN CHIMNEY CORNERS /Hutchinson CHIMNEY.. FAIRY 167-183/, /Adam BOOK OF GIANT 1-18/, /Fenner GIANTS 64-78/, /Haviland FAVORITE..IRELAND 39-60/. Curley BILLY (novel).

B* Jack and the Bull. Master's wife sends daughters with one, two, and three eyes to spy on Jack. His black bull gives bread in left horn and milk in right (B115.1). Jack plays fiddle until one-eye and two-eyes sleep. Three-eyes keeps one eye open (D830.1.1). Woman demands spleen of bull for health. Jack has her hold bull and strikes her instead of bull, they flee. Bull fights three bulls--blue, red and white.

Jack to cut strip of hide with horns attached when dead. Say "tie strop tie. Beat horns beat", (D1401.3). Jack herds sheep for woman. As wages she offers "Hard gripes or sharp shins." Jack calls strop to aid and receives new suit, bag of gold, horse and saddle. Hired to watch hogs. Giant woman tries to steal. Strop ties her. Rewarded with sack of money. U.S. (Appalachia): Chase JACK 21-30.

C* Little Bull-Calf. Stepfather plans to kill bull calf so boy flees. Bull fights wild animals. To hide in tree during battle and squeeze cheese saying is stone. This intimidates dangerous monkeys (K62). Dragon kills bull. To blow up bull's bladder and will kill everything it hits. Boy kills dragon and cuts out tongue. Forefinger bitten off by dragon, ring tied in his hair by princess. He shows tokens later and weds. England: Jacobs MORE 186-191 /Green CAVALCADE..DRAGONS 115-119/; Manning-Sanders RED 93-97; Pilkington SHAMROCK 10-15. Gypsy (England): Arnott FOLK 210-219 (heart); Hampden GYPSY 17-23 (horn).

D* Kari Woodenskirt. Blue bull gives food providing cloth from ear. Queen has maid spy on stepdaughter and feigns illness. Says needs blue bull's meat. Bull and Kari flee. Tabu--breaking leaf in copper wood. Kari breaks so bull must fight three-headed troll of forest (F811.1; C513). Silver wood, same routine, a six-headed troll. Golden wood, nine-headed troll. Bull defeats all. Asks Kari to behead him, skin, and wrap copper and silver leaves and golden apple in skin and hide in mountain. To wear woodenskirt and take service at palace. +R221L, threefold flight from church. Norway: Aulaire EAST 123-137; Baker GOLDEN 19-33; LANG RED 192-207.

E* Ox of the Wonderful Horns. Mistreated by father's wives, Mugalo leaves with white ox. Strike right horn three times and wish. Left horn twice, it vanishes. Crossing desert, M. wishes for grass, food. Ox fights head bull of herd and wins. Ox fights bull guarding mountain pass and is killed. Horns to provide food, house, land for M. Has freed village from oppressing bull and herd. Chief exchanges horn in night, M. discovers and re-exchanges. He is turned out at next village for shabby appearance, obtains clothes from horn and is now welcomed. Weds chief's daughter. South Africa (Kaffir): Bryan OX 29-41. South Africa (Xhosa): Arnott AFRICAN 78-84.

F* The Spotted Cow. Turned out by father, boy serves as cowherd. Spotted cow shares magic horn with food producing cloth inside. Farmer's wife has him spied upon, plans to kill cow. They flee. Cow raises boy until grown to full strength. Tests by lifting stone. Third year boy heaves it out of valley. To kill enemy dragon under stone. Sword in left horn. Boy cuts off two of dragon's three heads, lights hollow tree where dragon hides with tinderbox from cow's left horn. Dragon destroyed. Cow turns

into princess. Wed. Hungary: Manning-Sanders GLASS 86-93.

G* The Magic Pony. Pony warns prince stepmother plans to poison. She plans to kill pony saying that she needs the heart to cure herself. Pony flies off with prince. Takes service as gardener at castle. To burn hair of mane--pony appears. In love with princess, pony brings royal regalia and has prince ride in moonlight. Princess sees and weds. Persia: Arnott ANIMAL 14-22.

H* Peppi. Oxherd mistreated. Ox tells him to ask for ox as wages. They travel. Ox fights bull. Defeats. Suitor test: to harrow king's fields in one day. Ox performs. Peppi weds princess. Ox dies telling P. to plant bones in field. Orchard and garden there in morning. His wife's sisters discover secret and their husbands wager they can tell P. how it was done. Win all he owns. He travels. Three old men, each sends to older. Oldest sends to lion with needle to remove thorn from foot. Lion takes P. to serpent, serpent hides P. under wing and takes him to sun. P. accuses sun of telling secret. Sun reveals that wives told but agrees to rise at nine next day. Bets brothers-in-law on this. Wins his own goods back. Sicily: Manning-Sanders CHARM 85-97.

I* Baby born to third wife fed to cow. Piebald calf born. Told to take bowl of food to mother he pushes it to third wife. First and second wives fall ill, demand piebald calf's liver and skin. Another calf's substituted. Years later, neighboring girl tossed ball into courtyard to choose husband. Calf catches it. Turns to youth and weds (B621.9). China: Kendall SWEET 92-97.

B335.6. A small animal (hare, bitch) gives timely warnings to the hero about the trap prepared by his enemy. Animal warning about trap killed.

B335.6.1* Kalulu hare sees leopard grasp horns of hiding bushbuck thinking them tree branches. K. tries to be friend of both--calls to leopard not to let go or will lose dinner, to bushbuck not to move or will be detected. Both dislike him thereafter. Africa (Congo): Burton MAGIC 94-95.

B335.7. Helpful cow to be killed because of refusal to help stepdaughter. SEE: Q2.1.1Eb.

B342. Cat leaves house when report is made of death of one of his companions. His master has been told to say "Robert is dead." As soon as this is said the cat leaves.

B342.1* King of the Cats. Cat exclaims "Then I'm King of the Cats" and leaves. England: Farjeon CAVALCADE..KINGS 56-58; Galdone KING pb; Hoke SPOOKS 175-177; Jacobs MORE 169-171 /Harper GHOSTS 57-59/, /Littledale GHOSTS 121-124/; Sleigh NORTH 31-33; Williams-Ellis FAIRY..BRITISH 106-109.

B342.2* Knurre-Murre is dead. Cat is really a dwarf whose sweetheart was claimed by Knurre-Murre. De La Mare ANIMAL 71-73. Zeeland: Manning-Sanders BOOK OF DWARFS 9-13 /Manning-Sanders CHOICE 49-53/.

B342.3* Molly Dixon's dead. Cat goes to sister's funeral. Was really fairy. De La Mare ANIMAL 71-73.

B350 - B399. Grateful animals.

B350. Grateful animals. SEE ALSO: D817.3

B360. Animals grateful for rescue from peril of death. SEE ALSO: B582.2.

B360.1* Animals grateful for rescue from unkind master. Boy buys mistreated animals. SEE: D882.1B.

B361. Animals grateful for rescue from pit. SEE ALSO: W154.8.

B362.1* Swallow rescues wasp on leaf in the well. Wasp shows swallow how to make a nest of mud. +A2431.3.5. Mayan: Bowes BIRD 51-57.

B362.2* Dove rescues ant in spring. Ant later bites heel of fowler, saving dove. Aesop: Aesop AESOP'S (Grosset) 36; Aesop AESOP'S (Viking) 79; Aesop AESOP'S (Random) 49-50; Aesop AESOP'S (Walck) 85; Green ANIMAL 73. China: Cheney TALES 53-58.

B363.1. Lion is freed from net by mouse. Mouse asks that his son marry lion's daughter. The mouse is trampled to death by his bride. Aesop: Aesop AESOP'S (Viking) 24-25. SEE ALSO: B545.2; B371.1.

B364.4* Bird grateful for being saved from attacking serpent. Rata frees King of the Birds, heron. H. has birds carve canoes and carry to sea for R. Elder brothers attempted and failed, refused to aid heron. Polynesia: Berry MAGIC 30-44. Cook Islands: Gittins TALES 66-71.

B366. Animal grateful for ransom from captivity. SEE: F420.6.1.3.1.

B371.1. Lion spared mouse: mouse grateful. Later releases lion from net. Aesop: Aesop AESOP'S (Golden) 56; Aesop AESOP'S (Grosset) 137-138 (+J411.8); Aesop AESOP'S (Macmillan) 21 (+J411.8); Aesop AESOP'S (Random) 5-8; Aesop AESOP'S (Viking) 23-24; Aesop AESOP'S (Walck) 16-18; Aesop AESOP'S (Watts) 16; Aesop FIVE 42; Aesop (Kent) MORE 32-35; Arbuthnot FAIRY 225; Green ANIMAL 223 (+J411.8); Martignoni ILLUS-TRATED 94-95; Rice ONCE 10-15; Rockwell THREE 14-16; TALL.. NURSERY 108-109. Greece: Wilson GREEK 148-150. La Fontaine: La Fontaine LION pb. SEE ALSO: B545.2; B363.1.

B375.1. Fish returned to water: grateful. The Fisherman and His Wife. Wife wishes for ever increasing wealth. Beginning in hut or vinegar jug, wishes mansion, king, emperor, Pope. When wishes to be God she is returned to original state. Grimm: Arbuthnot ANTHOLOGY 193-196; Arbuthnot FAIRY 56-60; Association TOLD..GREEN 88-100; Carle ERIC 39-48; Grimm (Gag) TALES 149-168 /Martignoni ILLUS-TRATED 237-242/; Grimm BROTHERS 102-111; Grimm FISHERMAN pb (illus. Gekiere); Grimm FISHERMAN pb (illus. Laimgruber); Grimm FISHERMAN pb (illus. Zemach); Grimm GRIMM'S (Grosset) 114-124; Grimm GRIMM'S (World) 237-246; Grimm HOUSEHOLD 100-108; Grimm GRIMM'S (Scribners) 46-52; Grimm GRIMM'S (Follett) 70-81; Grimm JUNIPER 94-112; Hutchinson CHIMNEY CORNER FAIRY 107-116; Lang GREEN 331-341 /Lang FIFTY 295-303/; Rackham GRIMM 104-113; Sleigh NORTH 57-69; Wiggin TALES 102-110. Netherlands: Spicer OWL'S 29-40 (coal scuttle home, fish named Timperte). Russia: Ransome OLD 212-227. England (Family tradition): Godden OLD pb. SEE ALSO: D1651.3.1.1; F420.6.1.3.1; J2071.1; C773.1.2.

B375.1.3* Foolish Emilyan and the Talking Fish. Fish returned to water gives ability to do work magically. Lad weds princess. Tsar throws him into sea in barrel. Pike saves and gives second wish--for wisdom. Has palace built for self and exiled princess. Russia: Riordan TALES.. CENTRAL 165-174 (-wisdom); Wyndham RUSSIAN 12. Poland: Baker TALKING 210-217.

B375.1.4* Fish returned to water, grateful. Fish provides answers to riddles posed by threatening demon, saves benefactor. Armenia: Tashjian ONCE 41-49.

B375.2. Bird released, grateful. SEE: B625.2.

B381. Thorn removed from lion's paw (Androcles and the Lion). In gratitude the lion later rewards the man. Aesop: Aesop AESOP'S (Grosset) 32-33; Aesop AESOP'S (Random) 26-28; Aesop AESOP'S (Macmillan) 44-45; Aesop AESOP'S (Watts) 31-32; Gruenberg FAVORITE 414-416; Jacobs EUROPEAN 107-109. Romulus: Green ANIMAL 11-13 (shepherd spared in arena). Swazi: Kaula AFRICAN 94-95 (lion brings meat to man).

B381.3* Thorn removed from elephant's foot by carpenters. He devotes life to hauling logs for them. India: Babbitt JATAKA 69-73; Gaer FABLES 148-149.

B381.3.1* King removes thorn from elephant's foot. Elephant devotes self to king, asked to defend son on king's death. E. tells elephants of enemy to run amok and this saves city. India: Wyatt GOLDEN 93-97.

B381.4* Ape grateful for removal of thorn from foot. Later returns man's stolen son. West Africa: Aardema TALES 77-85.

B382.1* Tiger grateful for bone removed from throat. Ravages capital and student alone can kill. Teaches to heal wounds with bear paste from temple of Hungryung. Korea: Kim STORY 138-144.

B389.1* Seal grateful for removal of knife from side. The seal catcher and the merman (B80.1). Rider comes for fisherman and turns him to seal and takes to underseas palace where seal's father lies wounded by man's knife. Only his hand can heal. He withdraws knife and binds wound. Promises never to wound seals again. Rewarded with gold. Scotland: Baker TALKING 63-70.

B389.2* Thoas raised wounded baby dragon. Robbers attack and dragon kills (B11.6.1). Green CAV..DRAGONS 11-15.

B389.3* Boy saves injured eaglet. E. rescues from canoe accident. Hardendorff FROG'S 17-24.

B389.4* Prize for capture of four wild bulls. Lad who raised them brings, asks four bulls as reward. +D672. Mexico: NcNeil DOUBLE 24-29.

B392. Hero divides spoil for animals. SEE: D532.

B393.1* Badger grateful for sheltering with priest ten winters. Priest needs three pieces of gold. Badger returns in three years with gold. Had to get gold by honest means for such a purpose so smelted it himself. Japan: Buck FAIRY 91-95.

B394. Cow grateful for being milked. SEE: Q2.1.2Cb.

B400 - B499. Kinds of helpful animals.

B400. Helpful domestic animals.

B401. Helpful horse. SEE: B133.3 (goose girl); B316; H1331.1.3; R222.1; H1199.1.2.3.

B401.2* Helpful horse Marth carries lord to safety before tidal wave, then dies. Lord plans to kill self in grief but maiden stops him and causes horse to grow wings and fly off. They wed and build "The Chapel of the Brave Horse" on the spot. Cornish: Manning-Sanders PETER 26-32.

B411. Helpful cow. SEE: B184.2; B335.2F (The Spotted Cow).

B411.1. Helpful bull. SEE: Magic Bull B184.2.3; B335.2 (Billy Beg and His Bull).

B411.2. Helpful ox. SEE: B184.2.2 (Magic Ox); B335.2E (Ox of the Wonderful Horns).

B413.1* Grateful goat brings gold to butcher who spared. India: Manning-Sanders BOOK..MAGICAL 86-90.

B421. Helpful dog. SEE: T543.3.2 (Momotaro); D1571.1; B548.1.

B422. Helpful cat. SEE: B331.0.1; B548.1.

B430. Helpful wild beasts.

B431.2. Helpful lion. SEE: S12.1; B381.

B431.3. Helpful tiger. (cf. B535).

B431.3.1* Tiger ordered to take place of son eaten. Performs filial duties faithfully. S.W. China: Hume FAV..CHINA 74-78.

B431.3.2* Lao Tzu charms raiding tiger, leaves sleeping kid goat in tiger's den. T. begins to care for kid, is tamed, turns into a man. N. China: Hume FAV..CHINA 85-92.

B437.2.1* Helpful mouse. Faithful lantern bearer Lee-Su stays by horse all night in cold. Freezes stiff but mouse lies on his joints to warm them. Takes golden mouse as family crest. He was to wait while Lord of Han visited hermit Ch'en Chu. China: Ritchie TREASURE 40-64.

B437.2.2* Mouse brings coins to stonecutter asking that he share food with mouse. Cats force mouse to feed them too. Stonecutter makes a crystal ball for mouse to hide in. When cats attack they are cut by the crystal and withdraw. India: Gaer FABLES 149-152; Wyatt GOLDEN 45-49.

B437.2.3* St. Cadog and the mouse. Mouse brings grains of corn to St. Cadog in famine. By tying string to leg and following mouse, hidden store of grain is found. Wales: Sheppard-Jones WELSH 149-151.

B441.1. Helpful monkey. SEE: T543.3.2 (Momotaro).

B441.1.0.1* Temba helps monkeys escape hunters, is shown edible roots and berries. Men decide to kill no more monkeys in future. Africa: Arnott TEMBA 70-77.

B441.1.0.2* The monkey nursemaid. Seven brothers hire monkey nursemaid. Monkey sulks on being scolded so hides seven lads in tree and places knives on trunk of palm tree so Demon wounds self. M. heals in return for outfits and horses for seven lads and hogs for self and Demon to ride. Rides home with lads and is feasted. Quits job and rides off on hog with Demon. India: Manning-Sanders DEVILS 51-55.

B450. Helpful birds. SEE: R221B (Ash-maiden); Q285.1.1; B652.2; B538.1; T543.3.2; K522.4.4.

B451.7. Helpful sparrow. SEE: Q285.1.1.

B455.3.1* Boy gives part of catch to eagles. People desert him. Eagles drop food to boy and brother. Raven carries message of his good luck to girl who aided him. Clan returns, he forgives them, and weds girl. Native American (Northwest Coast): Martin NINE 31-37 /Martin RAVEN 75-82/.

B455.3.2* Navaho spy for eagles is lowered by people of Kintyel to eagle's nest on cliff to steal young. He climbs into nest and stays. He has been warned by eagles that Kintyel people plan to kill him. Eagles carry him to upper world. He aids eagles by defeating their enemies, bumblebees and tumbleweeds. He sends both to earth and warns never to make trouble again. After learning eagle rites, he returns to Kintyel and obtains their giant shell on pretext of curing their sick. Flies to sky with shell. Native American (Navaho): Brown TEPEE 28-39.

B463.3 Helpful crane. SEE: B652.2.

B463.4. Helpful stork. Stork brings pearls to princess, becomes her companion. Neighbor tears down stork's nest and stork leaves. Sultan buys house of nest with two pearls given by stork and restores stork to home. This house still stands in Marrakesh. Morocco (Marrakesh): Heady KING'S 18-27.

B469.4. Helpful duck. SEE ALSO: G412.1 (Hansel and Gretel); B582.2.

B469.4.1* Helpful duck drowns pursuing wolf. Belgium: Frost LEGENDS 309-312 (+G412.1).

B469.9. Helpful parrot. Parrot tells girl which beggar is king in disguise. She had befriended parrot. Nigeria: Walker NIGERIAN 63-64.

B469.10. Helpful pheasant. SEE: T543.3.2 (Momotaro).

B469.11* Helpful peacock. SEE: K522.4.4.

B472. Helpful whale. SEE: D1154.1.

B477. Helpful octopus.

B477.1* Octopus catches shark, forces to promise to eat no more people from Kandavu. Fiji: Gittins TALES 32-36.

B481.1. Helpful ant. SEE: B582.2.

B489.1. Helpful spider. SEE: B523.1.

B491.1. Helpful serpent. SEE: W154.8; B216.

B491.1.1* Helpful snake. Boy loses birch bark message in stream, taken to underwater home of snake chief by two watersnakes. Snake tests his bravery and strength, asks to pull feather from roof of cave, tomahawk from wall of cave. To call snakes when in need, using magic tomahawk and feather. Attacked. Snakes coil round enemies and pin arms so can't shoot. Native American (Southeastern): Arnott ANIMAL 23-30.

B491.1.2* Python doctor agrees to come when children sing to him and carry him down to village on their shoulders. Africa: Tracey LION 10-14 /McDowell THIRD 25-28/.

B491.1.3. Cruel brother inherits all, cuts off

sister's hand to get pumpkin she grew. Sister climbs tree in forest and weeps. Prince weds. Brother accuses her of being witch and she and son are banished. Snake whom she befriends protects her, restores hands. She lives in Snake Kingdom. Returns with magic ring and casket. Builds home near palace and prince comes to visit. Reunited. East Africa (Swahili): Arnott AFRICAN 85-100.

B491.3.1* Helpful crocodile. Bukango elopes with rich man's daughter with aid of crocodiles who cause storm to hinder pursuers. B. can call the crocodiles with special magic call. Kenya (Samia): Harmon TALES 29-56.

B493.1.1* Helpful frog. Frog takes shape of girl and beats clothing in stream so she can escape from condor. Gets star-shaped jewel on forehead where girl kisses her. Peru: Barlow LATIN 57-61.

B500 - B599. Services of helpful animals.

B501. Animal gives part of body as talisman for summoning its aid. SEE: B314.

B505. Magic object received from animal. SEE: D817.3.

B505.1. Magic object received from animal brother-in-law. SEE: B314.

B510. Healing by animals.

B512. Medicine shown by animal. It heals another animal with a medicine (herb, water, etc.) and thus shows the man the remedy. Sometimes the medicine resuscitates the dead. The animal is most frequently the serpent. Type 160, 303, 590, 612. SEE: B522.1; B491; S12.1; A751.8.5.2.

B520. Animals save person's life. SEE: B331.0.1.

B522.1. Serpent shows condemned man how to save prince's life. Bites the prince and then shows the man the proper remedy (B512). SEE: W154.8.

B522.1.1* Cat shows monk spell to save rich man's daughter. She has put spell on her for drowning kittens. +D1641.13.1. Japan: Novak FAIRY 72-80.

B522.1.2* Snake put in Ashoremashika's basket by evil man kills king's bellman. A. is imprisoned. Snake gives a powder to mix with blood of murderer and restore princess he has bitten. Only true murderer's blood is effective (J1140). Nigeria: Walker DANCING 35-41.

B523.1. Spider-web over hole saves fugitive. SEE ALSO: A2221.5.2. Indonesia: Courlander KANTCHIL'S 76-79 (Hadji, +A1316.6.1); De Leeuw INDONESIAN 90-93. Jewish: Ish-Kishor WISE 44-48 (King David).

B524.1.1. Dogs kill attacking cannibal (dragon). SEE: K1853.2.1.1.

B524.1.2. Dogs rescue fleeing master from tree refuge. Type 315A. SEE ALSO: R251; G275.2.

A* The Black Dog of the Wild Forest. Witches give to hero dogs Hear-All, Spring-All and magic rod causing bridge to appear and vanish. To throw ball between horses ears and follow. Weds princess. Is now safe from Black Dog of the Wild Forest, who was to eat him when he came of age. He leaves bridge out by accident and Black Dog comes. Black Dog tells old woman to find his lucky bone if he is killed and drop it in the prince's ear. She ties up dogs but prince calls and they break chains and kill Black Dog. Old woman kills prince with bone put in ear but his dogs remove it and restore him. They ask to be beheaded and become princesses. Gypsy: Manning-Sanders RED 139-145.

B* Little Tailor and the Three Dogs. Three Dogs ask to accompany tailor. At tavern dogs instruct him to walk out without paying leaving knapsack, coat and yardstick, they grab these and flee. Magic gifts from dogs' right ears: ointment that makes persons stick, stick that kills, horn which calls them. Lad pretends to sell dogs to 24 ogres. Smears their chiars and they must remain sitting. Kills them with stick. Ogre king puts him in tree to hang, he calls dogs and they kill ogre. Dog's disenchanted become king, queen, princess. Lad weds. German: Manning-Sanders BOOK..OGRES 101-109.

C* The Three Dogs. Wife tries to get husband's magic secrets. Wife goes to forest with him, ties up dogs with her hairs which turn to chains. Wife turns into heifer. Vows vengeance for wild cattle man has killed. He climbs mango tree, restores it with three magic rice grains as she gouges it with horns. His mother sees vial turn to blood and unleashes dogs. He turns self into a needle (has told her he turns into an egg). Dogs arrive, kill wife before she can discover him. Haiti: Thoby-Marcelin SINGING 57-65.

D* Iron Wolf. Parson gives lad egg for twelve years' service. Do not open until home. Opens and castle comes out. Iron Wolf puts castle back in exchange for lad's pledge to let self be eaten by Iron Wolf on wedding day. Iron Wolf leaps through protective guard on wedding day. Lad flees, shelter in each of three huts, is given three cakes, and three dogs who can hear I.W. from afar. They kill Iron Wolf and save master. Russia: Wiggin FAIRY 253-258.

Db* Iron Head. Old lady gives three napkins and three cakes, throws cakes behind and turn to dogs. Strike wall of fire with napkins to pass. To wed girl. She strikes fire with napkins to test truth of his story. Iron Head gets through and trees lad. He calls dogs and they kill Iron Head. Back home lad's wife has remarried. He wishes on ring girl gave him and she appears. Wed. Hungary: Manning-Sanders BOOK..

DEVILS 56-68.

E* Ojo. Ojo flees ogress with mouths all over body. Sprinkles magic powder to restore trees she gnaws away. Three dogs arrive and kill ogress. Maiden pretends to have been captive of ogress, turns to ogress' sister at night but dogs kill her too. Nigeria (Yoruba): Fuja FOURTEEN 243-251.

F* Bobo. Black Dog and the Cannibal Woman. Dog warns boy of dangers from cannibal woman. Witch gnaws at tree where boy hides, dog holds her and boy drops ax, killing. Made chief. Basutoland: Carpenter WONDER..DOGS 101-110.

G* Sasa and Gogwana the Witch. Brother and sister are separated from family by flood. Brother at witch's home, dog refuses poisoned food and lad avoids. Witch gets dog tied up, trees boy, and begins to gnaw tree down. He calls dogs and they break chain and kill witch. Giant bird called Mapimbiro, son of witch ogress, appears and lad kills. Lad becomes chief of village of women there. Witch had eaten all men and boys. Tshindao: Aardema BEHIND 66-73.

H* Wiley and the Hairy Man. Hairy Man trees Wiley. W. charms chips back onto tree as H. chops, until dogs come. Later W. tricks Hairy Man into turning self to possum and ties in bag (K722.0.2). Treed again, W. tricks H. into dissolving all rope in country, thus tied dogs are freed and rescue. Mother tells H. he may have baby in house, is piglet. H. leaves, having been tricked three times. Alabama: Bang WILEY pb; Haviland NORTH 126-133.

B524.1.4.1. Dog defends master's child against animal assailant. SEE: K231.1.3.

B524.2.1.2* Helpful fly lands on leg of enemy sleeper causing him to move leg, thus freeing King David. Jewish: Ish-Kishor WISE 44-48.

B526.2. Helpful mare cools boiling bath for master. Hero is made to bathe in boiling mare's milk. His mare blows on the milk and cools it. SEE: H1331.1.3C (The Firebird and Princess Vasilisa); H1331.1.3D.

B529.3* Animals revive dead man. Bear hugs dead man to warmth. Crow and white heron fail to find his scalp which enemy has taken. Pigeon hawk retrieves scalp from enemy's lodge. Birds sprinkle with dew and crow vomits on scalp to make stick to head. Native American (Iroquois): Jones LONGHOUSE #4.

B531.5. Birds save man from hunger by pitching themselves to roast in fire he has made. SEE: A751.2.

B531.6* Friendly large animal calling itself Baluba offers to lift waterpots for children. Invites them to feast and gives raspberries to take home. Uganda: Serwadda SONGS 1-5.

B535. Animal nurse. Animal nourishes abandoned child. SEE: D431.3.

B535.0.5.1* Rustem is raised in nest of Simurgh. Persia: Palmer DRAGONS 79-86.

B535.0.8.1* Leopard as nurse for boy. When grown leopard kills princess and gives boy magic juice to revive her. Weds. Nigeria: Walker DANCING 84-93.

B535.0.9.1* She-wolf as nurse for child. Romulus and Remus set adrift in basket are cared for by wolf. They found the city of Rome. Italy (Rome): Toor GOLDEN 169-176.

B535.0.15* Boy raised by bears. Native American (Iroquois): Bruchac TURKEY 51-57.

B535.0.15.1* Twins of dead mother raised by wolf and bear. When grown Throwmount and Oakpull are given magic mile-at-a-step slippers by dwarf and sent to kill dragon and win princess. Poland: Borski GOOD 29-33.

B535.0.16* Child taken by Manstin, rabbit. M. rescues baby from ogre and then turns child into a giant child with long ears and split lip like hare. Keeps child as companion. Palmer DRAGONS 68-74.

B536.2* Helpful wolves carry injured man to lair and nurse him back to health. He hunts game for them thereafter. Returns to his village and gives evil sister-in-law who had tried to murder him to animals as captive. Native American (Lakota): Yellow Robe TONWEYA 66-85.

B538.1. Bird gives shelter with wings. (cf. B450).

B538.1.1* Flamingo shields sleeping man with wings. +J429.2. India (Panchatantra): Green ANIMAL 116.

B538.3* Men live with animals.

B538.3.1* Girl left in cave of muezzin is wooed by him. She flees, gazelles care for her. Her hair grows long and covers her body. King sees her choose salted food and knows she is human. Weds. Wicked vizier steals her baby and woos her. She seeks baby in disguise. At inn father, brother, muezzin, vizier, and king all arrive same evening. She tells tale (H11). Morocco: Carpenter AFRICAN 77-86.

B538.3.2* Maldonada. Girl cares for puma and young for a time. Later abandoned to die by Spanish, puma cares for her. People force cruel captain to relent and take girl back into settlement. Asuncion, Buenos Aires and Maldonado are founded. Argentina: Jagendorf KING 23-27; Newman FOLK LATIN 83-88.

B538.3.3* Boy lives with wild pig people. Follows bacurau bird into forest, is lost. Cannot re-cross stream. Woodpecker offers to carry but boy is too frightened. Alligator offers, boy flees. Heron hides in crop. Boy joins wild pig people. Later finds mother and returns to life among people, but always recalls ways of the wild pig people. Brazil: Jagendorf KING 59-64.

B538.3.4* Man lives with bears. Sees bear he revived after being killed. To retreat seven days before returning to mankind. Wife insists on seeing him after fifth day, bear nature is still with him and he dies soon afterward. Native American (Cherokee): Bell JOHN 33-38; Brown TEPEE 18-22.

B538.3.5* Man lives with porcupines. Man fleeing battle is taken in by porcupine clan. Weds porcupine. Returns home with his children. Origin: porcupine clan. Native American (Iroquois): Bruchac TURKEY 59-61.

B538.3.6* Girl left behind by people is cared for by wolves. She returns to ask people to adopt wolves' custom of caring for those unable to hunt. Native American (Sioux): Matson LEGENDS 51-52.

B538.3.7* Dying father asks son and daughter to care for little brother. They abandon him and he is cared for by wolves. He turns into a wolf. Native American: Bierhorst FIRE 66-76.

B542.1.1. Eagle carries man to safety. SEE: F101.3.

B542.1.3. Measuring worm rescues from a height. SEE: B482.4.1.

B545. Animal rescues from trap (net).

B545.2. Rat (mouse) gnaws net. Ashanti: Appiah ANANSE 89-94 (lion). Mexico: Edmonds TRICKSTER 77-85 (coyote, +J1172.3). SEE ALSO: B371.1; B363.1.

B545.3* Heron caught in coral is freed by turtle. Later fisherman catches T. Heron loosens snares, dances to distract men and sings commands to help T. escape. Solomon Islands: Arnott ANIMAL 49-58.

B548.1. Animals recover lost wishing ring. SEE: D882.1.

B548.2.1. Fish recovers ring from sea. SEE: N211.1; B582.2.

B548.2.3. Fish recovers lost fish hook from sea. SEE: U136.0.1.

B549.2. Dragon makes bridge across stream for holy man. SEE: A511.1.4.5.

B549.4. Animal rescues from cave. SEE: A2493.4.1.

B552. Man carried by bird. SEE: F62; K1861.1.

B555. Animals serve as bridge across stream. SEE: K579.2.

B560. Animals advise men.

B562.1. Animal shows man treasure. SEE: B100 – B119.

B562.1.1. Hogs root up gold (treasure) for saint. Mexico: Brenner BOY 1-11 (silver for pig-herd).

B570. Animals serve men.

B571.2. Animals fight together with their master. SEE: T543.3.2 (Momotaro); R111 (dragon slayer).

B580. Animal helps man to wealth and greatness.

B582. Animal helps person to success in love. SEE: B651.1B.

B582.1.1. Animal wins wife for his master (Puss in Boots). SEE: K1917.3.

B582.2. Animals help hero win princess. SEE ALSO: R111.1.3Cd; H1385.3 F, M.

A* The Queen Bee. Type 554. Two princes molest ants, ducks, bees, youngest prince saves. At castle little gray-haired man lets them in and feeds. Task written on stone table. First: collect 1,000 pearls by sunset. First two brothers fail and are turned to stone. Third succeeds with aid of ants. Second: find key from lake bottom. Ducks bring (B469.4; H1132.1.2). Third: pick youngest of three princesses. Queen bee shows. Wed, stone spell broken. Grimm: De La Mare ANIMAL 180-186; Gag MORE 155-162; Grimm GRIMM'S (Grosset) 98-100; Grimm HOUSEHOLD 262-264; Grimm GRIMM'S (Follett) 268-271; Hutchinson CANDLELIGHT 41-47; Rackham GRIMM'S 63-65; Shubb ABOUT 55-57.

Ab* The Cobbler's reward. Cobbler befriends ants, bees, ducks. Witch holding maid prisoner sets tasks. Sort bag of poppy seeds from sand --ants aid. Fetch key from lake--ducks aid. Identify maid among veiled maids--bee aids. Wed. Poland: Reid COBBLER'S pb.

B* Princess with the Golden Hair. Lad sent to fetch princess for king. Puts fish back in river, kills serpent in nightingale's nest, kills falcon attacking crow. Crow pecks out eyes of two giants guarding princess. Nightingale brings water from Fountain of Dew to disenchant her. Fish brings lost ring from river (H1132.1.1). Majorca: Mehdevi BUNGLING 45-55.

C* The White Snake. Rescues fish, kills horse for young ravens to eat. They help perform suitor tasks: ring from sea bottom (H1132.1.1); sacks of millet gathered; apple from tree of life. +B271.1.1. Grimm: Grimm HOUSEHOLD 93-97; Grimm GRIMM'S (Follett) 399-406. Armenia: Tashjian ONCE 57-69.

D* Benito the Faithful. Lad frees bird, King of Fishes offers ride over sea. Fairy gives sword to kill giants and rescue princess. King of Fishes carries back. She drops ring and refuses to wed until it is found. All fish are called by King of the Fishes. One has swallowed ring. Earring is lost in forest. King of Mice aids, one mouse swallowed. Water from heaven and water from nether world needed. Sparrow hawk fetches but dies. Water of heaven beautifies princess. Water of nether world destroys king. She weds Benito. Tagalog: Sechrist ONCE 156-167.

E* Tall Peter and Short Peter. Short Peter spares mice, bees, eaglets. Tall Peter tells master S.P. can build palace of wax surrounded by earthen wall with twelve-toned bell. Bees and mice build. Eagle takes to realm of Vanapagan for bell. Drops stick, sand, water as V. pursues = forest, mountain, sea. V. drinks sea and bursts (D672). S. tells master Tall Peter bragged could sleep in stove heated with seven cords of wood. End of Tall Peter. Estonia: Maas MOON 47-55.

F* Koi and the Kola Nuts. Youngest son given only kola nuts. Shares with snake, ants, alligator. Task: chop down leaning palm so it falls away from village. Snakes wrap tails around tree and pull. Task: pick up grain, ants aid. Find ring from river, crocodile brings. K. weds chief's daughter. Liberia: Aardema TALES 54-61. SEE ALSO: H1385.3; H1385.1.

B582.6. King Fox. Abandoned lad shares food with fox who invites bear, monkey, jackal, golden eagle to join. These steal caravan foods for lad. Steal princess for his wife. Witch entices princess to look into jar, pushes her in and flies back to palace with her. Eagle brings her back to lad. Animals kill witch, defeat king's army. With aid of rodents who gnaw straps of sleeping army, they are defeated. King has to accept son-in-law. Italy: Manning-Sanders GIANNI 76-102. Serbia: Manning-Sanders BOOK.. MAGICAL BEASTS 164-176. Yugoslavia: Carpenter WONDER..DOGS 245-255.

B583. Animal gives treasure to man. SEE: B562.1.

B587.3. Grateful bull draws one hundred carts for wager for master. India: Babbitt JATAKA 21-24.

B590. Miscellaneous services of helpful animals.

B591. Animal avenges murder. SEE: B301.2.

B592. Animals bequeath characteristics to man. Horse gives him the characteristics of youth (fiery), cow of middle age (avaricious), and the dog of old age (fractious). Aesop: Aesop AESOP'S (Watts) 188-189.

B599.4* Helpful elephant refuses to let wagon pass until full fee is paid his mistress for his work. India: Babbitt JATAKA 77-83 /Arbuthnot FAIRY 163-164/, /Arbuthnot ARBUTHNOT ANTHOLOGY 348/.

B600 – B699. Marriage of person to animal.

B600. Marriage of person to animal.

B601.12.1* Marriage to cat. King told a daughter is born, it is really a white kitten. A prince agrees to wed the grown cat to save the king's wives from punishment should the truth be known. His mother prays to Parvati, wife of Shiva, and Parvati turns the cat into a maiden. India: Carpenter WONDER..DOGS 153–162.

B601.14. Marriage to fox. SEE ALSO: B651.1.

B601.14.1* White fox weds a girl. Showers during sunshine on wedding day occur. Henceforth this phenomenon is called "fox's bride going to her husband's house." Japan: Rackham FAIRY 87–88.

B603.1* Marriage to fish (whale). Girl eats two fish with silver brooches on scales. Father throws brooches into lake and she is pulled under water by Ga-Ye-Was, fish ruler. Weds. Native American: Jones LONGHOUSE #2.

B604.1. Marriage to snake. SEE ALSO: B646.1; B656.2; B654.

B604.1.1* Marriage to naga. Exiled prince weds naga and has two sons. Returned home, sons fear turtle. He throws turtle over waterfall and turtle tells Naga King that prince wants Naga King to wed his sister. Snakes infest city until prince agrees to this. Palmer DRAGONS 89–95.

B605.1* Marriage to dragon. Man lets innkeeper's daughter fall in love with him, then fails to return. She attacks him as dragon. He hides under temple bell and she beats bell with her tail until it is red hot and he perishes. Japan: Pratt MAGIC #9.

B610. Animal paramour.

B610.1. Girl's animal lover slain by spying relatives. SEE: B654; R221Qa.

B610.1.1* Girl's brother as fly spies, fish friend is killed. Girl drowns self, gives birth to many children as she dies = water lilies. Nigeria (Yoruba): Lester BLACK 57–61.

B610.1.1.1* Brother spies, fish lover is killed. Girl sinks alive into earth in hopes of finding him in Land of Dead. He is restored to princely form by this act. Wed. Haiti: Thoby-Marcelin SINGING 104–111.

B610.1.1.2* Girl's ring falls into spring and fish Tayzanne returns it, fills pail for her daily. Brother spies, parents call fish up using her chant and kill. Three drops of blood appear on her breast as sign. She sinks into earth in mourning. Haiti: Wolkstein MAGIC 57–64.

B610.2* Girl leaves caravan rather than wed, lives with lion in cave. Brother finds her and wounds lion. Since then lions mistrust humans. Touareg: Holding KING 69–79.

B611.3. Maid promises to wed horse if he fetches father home from war. Father has horse killed. Skin leaps to surround her, she turns to silkworm on mulberry tree. (A2811). China (Han Dynasty): Kendall SWEET 80–85; Manton FLYING 18–23.

B612.3* Whale paramour. Mermaid loves whale. Gets Ichabod the Whaler to pledge not to harpoon Long John Whale if he'll let mermaid bridle and ride him. Long John spouts and blows her into lake, thus rid of her. Native American: Manning-Sanders BOOK..MERMAIDS 54–58.

B620. Animal suitor.

B620.1. Daughter promised to animal suitor. SEE: D735.1.

B621.9* Cow as suitor. SEE: B335.2H.

B635.1.4* Son of bear and woman tests strength on clubs his human father makes. Goes to live in woods with hare, fox, wolf, and bear. Baba Yaga beats each when try to drink from lake. Ivan Bear's son beats Baba Yaga. Russia: Riordan TALES..CENTRAL 59–62.

B640. Marriage to person in animal form.

B640.1. Marriage to beast by day and man by night. SEE: H1385.4 (East of the Sun); D735.1 (Beauty and the Beast).

B641. Marriage to person in beast form. SEE ALSO: N831.1 (Mysterious housekeeper).

B641.0.1* The Mouse (Cat, Frog, etc.) as bride. Type 402. The youngest of three brothers succeeds best in the quest set by his father. He brings the best cloth, the most beautiful bride, etc. The mouse (cat, etc.) who has helped him changes herself into a beautiful maiden.

A* The Frog. Flax woven, dog trained, shirt sewn by frog (B645.1.2). Three witches laugh so hard at sight of frog in pony cart that they are cured of blindness, hunchback, and thorn in throat. They turn her to a girl with real carriage and money purse. Italy: Lang VIOLET 186–192; Manning-Sanders BOOK..MAGICAL 142–148.

Ab* Frog: thread spun, lad to hang wedding dress in vestry, frog hops under dress and turns to maid. Switzerland (German): Duvoisin THREE 167–177.

Ac* Frog: Handkerchief embroidered, cow cooked and Juan to break off horn at meal. Twelve silver place settings and roast beef appear from horn. To choose middle maid when awakened from hammock. Weds. Philippines (Visayan): Sechrist ONCE 150–156.

Ad* Frog: King blows three feathers and sons seek where they fall. Youngest meets toad (frog). Given carpet, ring, most beautiful woman. Last test..brides must jump through hoop in hall. Frog bride wins. Grimm: Grimm JUNIPER 3-10; Shubb ABOUT 58-61; Wiggin FAIRY 208-212. Great Britain: Finlay TAT-TERCOATS 28-36.

Ae* Frog: Sons follow three arrows (H1226.2). Youngest meets frog. Provides linen so fine can fit in walnut shell, dog so small fits in nutshell, loveliest bride in world. Wed. Italy: Toor GOLDEN 25-27. German: Lang GREEN 207-213 (Puddocky: arrows shot, frog is girl Parsley, taken by witch because mother stole parsley from witch). De La Mare ANIMALS 233-243 (frog is girl Cherry under enchantment).

Af* Frog: arrows shot to choose wife. Frog provides fine clothes, fine cake. Other two wives imitate her method of baking disastrously. She carries bones in right sleeve and wine (soup) in left. Tosses bones and turns to pillar with cat running up and down singing and telling stories. Tosses wine and river appears with swans on water. Other wives imitate and bones hit king. Ivan burns her frog skin (D721.3) and she must leave. Is really Vasilisa the Wise. He seeks her. +H1385.3K. Russia: Whitney IN 37-42. Ukraine: Manning-Sanders CHOICE 26-38 /Manning-Sanders BOOK.. PRINCES 84-96/; Riordan TALES..CENTRAL 129-137; Whitney IN 37-43.

Ag* Cow Maiden: embroiders handkerchief. On being presented to king, mother tells her to look back and she regains true maidenly form. She has worn a cow's head as punishment for jumping from tower to prince (F848). She fills sleeves with bacon, shakes and diamonds and flowers fall. Other bride imitates and all slip on messy floor. Portugal: Lowe LITTLE 106-113.

Ah* Frog: wish for child even if only a frog (T554). Frog takes lunch to father, and prince hears her singing in tree and vows to wed. Loveliest flower to win kingdom for one of three princes. She rides up on cock, clothed in golden sun rays, bringing up spear of wheat. Turns to girl when puts on gown at gates. To wed. Yugoslavia: Fillmore LAUGHING 163-170; Frost LEGEND 240-244.

B* Mouse Bride. Mouse spins fine thread, weaves strong linen. Given ring token, mouse comes riding on cock with ring in mouth. Witch sees and laughs, thus breaking spell (B641.0.1A). Weds. French: Picard FRENCH 205-216 /Arbuthnot FAIRY 124-128/.

Bb* Forest bride. Lad seeks direction tree falls. She bakes bread, spins flax to fit in nutshell. Mouse bride comes in nutshell coach drawn by mice. Is kicked off bridge into river and spell is broken. Finland: Fillmore SHEP-HERD'S 26-39; Bowman TALES 25-33 /Fenner PRINCESSES 103-104/, /Fillmore MIGHTY MIK-KO/, /Provensen PROVENSEN 83-92/.

Bc* Mouse: bakes cake, weaves cloth to fit in

nutshell, is drawn in silver spoon by twelve beetles. Asks that lad cut off handle of spoon with sword = coach. Cut off her head (D711) = princess. She had been under Troll's spell. Sweden: Kaplan FAIRY 209-229.

Bd* Rat: rat provides linen, wool thread. Says to pull saying "short before and long behind" and he finds he has many ells when he reaches home. Rides in frying pan pulled by rats, these turn to carriage and she to maid. Wed. Wiggin FAIRY 35-42.

Be* Doll in the grass: Twelve sons seek wives. Cinderlad is given a tiny shirt of linen spun, woven, and sewn in one day by tiny maid (F535.1.1F). She goes to palace in silver spoon pulled by mice, is dumped into lake, merman brings her up and she is now a full-size girl. Wed. Norway: Asbjornsen EAST (Row) 28-30; Aulaire EAST 222-224; Hutchinson CANDLE-LIGHT 11-15; Wiggin FAIRY 51-53.

C* Monkey. Little Pet Rani: seven sons follow arrows (H1226.2). Monkey says to invite his father to dinner. Is taken into hollow tree and served by lady. He enquires after monkey, it is really the lady. India: Williams-Ellis ROUND 57-66.

Cb* Magic Monkeys: monkey sends letter to king saying has found wife. She turns to princess when taken to court. Her gift of singing birds in box wins crown for her husband. Italy: Manning-Sanders SORCEROR'S 112-121.

Cc* Monkey bride. Uigur: Ginsburg KAHA 72-87.

D* Miller's Apprentice and the Cat: apprentice bringing best horse to inherit mill. Serves cat seven years in cat kingdom. Cat comes as princess bringing horse. Wed. Grimm: De La Mare ANIMAL 134-142; Grimm GRIMM'S (Follett) 262-267; Grimm JUNIPER 178-186.

Db* The White Cat. Youngest son serves cat one year in castle of cats. Is given tiny dog in acorn, cambric so fine fits inside millet grain, inside wheat, inside cherry pit, inside filbert, inside walnut. Asks to have her head and tail cut off = maiden. Comtesse D'Aulnoy: Arbuthnot ARBUTHNOT ANTHOLOGY 224-231; Arbuthnot FAIRY 115-122; Dalgliesh ENCHANTED 162-179; Lang BLUE 172-191 /Farjeon CAVAL-CADE..QUEEN'S 1-22/; LeCain WHITE pb; Lubin WHITE pb; Wiggin FAIRY 312-325.

Db* Lad serves white cat for three years and is given chain of gold stretching thrice around castle and chest of gold. Cuts off cat's head = princess. Denmark: Hatch THIRTEEN 107-121.

Dc* White Fox. Youngest son serves white fox for three years. Receives bottomless purse, longest gold chain, loveliest bride. Cuts off head = princess. Weds. Sweden: Owen CAS-TLE 27-38.

Dd* Palace of the White Cat. Daughter of Moorish governor is turned to white cat for becoming Christian. Knight with cross on armour (St. James of Compostella) slays dragon (R111.1.3) which turns into ten snakes, twenty vultures, forty girls, red hot coals. He scoops coals into shield bearing cross and they turn to maiden. Portugal: Michael PORTUGUESE 164-171.

E* Tortoise: three arrows shot (H1226.2). Youngest son reaches home of Tortoise. He weds her. Sultan is ill, her food heals, that of other two wives spoils. She asks to ride billy goat or goose borrowed from sister-in-law. They refuse and ride these themselves in imitation. She arrives and is princess. Sprinkles rice on her hair and it becomes gems. Other two brides imitate and mess hair. Egypt: Carpenter AFRICAN 205-223.

B641.1. Marriage to person in dog form. Girl is to be green, boy to be greyhound until prince kisses girl and princess offers to spend life with dog. Lost king comes to their castle and his life is spared on condition that his daughter be sent to them for a year. She agrees to stay forever. Dog is thus disenchanted. At wedding feast a prince kisses girl. Wed. Scotland: Wilson SCOTTISH 148-155.

B641.4. Marriage to person in ass form. Barren queen bears donkey. Weds princess. Donkey plays lute, takes off skin at night. Skin is burnt and D. freed. Craig DONKEY pb; De La Mare ANIMAL 203-211.

B641.5. Marriage to person in hedgehog form. Type 441. Wish for child if only a hedgehog. (T554). H. herds pigs. Lost king promises to give his daughter in return for directions out of forest. H. rides to castle on cock. Rejected, he has castle surrounded by hedgehogs. Weds and turns to man. Poland: Baker GOLDEN 119-122; Borski GOOD 13-17; Haviland FAV.. POLAND 3-12. Latvia: Huggins BLUE 43-49 (porcupine, princess burns quills and he suffers but turns to prince after two weeks, D721.3). Grimm: Grimm JUNIPER 11-22; Grimm BROTHERS 151-157; Lang GREEN 298-304 (two lost kings, first ungracious, servant burns skin and H. turns to man, D721.3).

B641.6. Marriage to person in horse form.

B641.6.1* Batim the Horse. Youngest princess agrees to wed horse (enchanted son of ogress). Tabu: telling. He passes palace in man form twice. She tells sisters that he is husband. Must seek him with shoes and staff of iron (H1385.4). She drops ring token into his water. Ogress sets tasks. He aids. They flee. Obstacle Flight (D672). Bulgaria: Hampden GYPSY 89-95.

B641.6.2* The Little Horse. Hans cares for horse, father sells. H. seeks horse and gets princess to buy it back. King's eldest daughter loses ring, horse catches fish with ring. Hans to

wed eldest princess. Youngest princess embraces horse and calls dearest friend. Horse turns to prince. Wed. Denmark: Hatch MORE 150-166.

B642.1* Marriage to person in crow form. Couple wish for son. Crow comes. Wants to wed maid. Turns to man. E. Africa: Heady WHEN 47-52.

B642.6.2* Marriage to god in bird form. Sosondowah, Great Night, woos maid as blackbird in summer, bluebird in spring, night-hawk in autumn. Dawn binds S. and turns maid into star over forehead. Native American (Iroquois): Cunningham TALKING 95-97.

B643.4* Marriage to person in spider form. Lad to wed first woman met. Meets spider, weds. She spins lace and he sells. He goes to visit mother and passes stone where he met her, stone turns to palace, spider to princess, her cock to horse. Italy: Manning-Sanders GIANNI 62-66.

B644.1* Marriage to person in fish form. Muchie Lal. Pet fish of Ranee grows as big as tank. Girl to be sacrificed to fish is given three stones by Naga to throw at fish as he charges at her. Weds fish. Stepsister pushes her into stream Naga keeps her in his cave until fish husband comes for her. India: Wiggin FAIRY 398-406.

B645.1.2. Marriage to person in frog form. SEE: B641.0.1A.

B645.1.2.1* The Frog Jacket. Girl frog calls nobleman "father" and is kept as daughter. Her ring falls out while visiting and hostess proposes marriage of his daughter to her son. Discover she is a frog but wedding takes place anyway. After ten days she becomes a maiden and he burns her jacket. Tooze WONDERFUL 71-73.

B645.1.2.2* A Fortune from a Frog. Man agrees to shelter frog who has eaten all fish in pond. Wants to wed most beautiful girl in land. Wed. Frog has her slit skin and man emerges from frog skin, is son of the King of the Stars. Korea: Carpenter KOREAN 97-105.

B645.1.2.3* Noble Frog. Whoever frees general can wed Emperor's daughter. Frog, general's son, spits poison and paralyzes enemy. Test: choose princess from among handmaidens. Frog dreams of yellow carnation and chooses maiden wearing that. Takes off frog skin. Princess steals skin as frog-prince sleeps and sends it to her father. He puts it on and can't get it off. China: Chang CHINESE 6-8.

B645.1.2.4* Soldier's Return. Frog refuses water to girls unless they wed him, youngest agrees as water is needed for ill father. He takes her to his palace, has a cruel stepmother. She sees him out of his skin and throws it into the fire, both burn hands in struggle. He must leave. She tends sheep. Soldier with burnt hands passes one day. Wed. Nepal: Hitch-cock KING 111-122.

B646.1. Marriage to person in snake form. SEE ALSO: D195.1.1; B604.1. Type 433B.

B646.1.1* Childless couple rear snake son. He sends father to ask hand of princess. Impos-sible tasks assigned: turn fruit in orchard to gold, pave with jewels, turn palace to gold. He achieves and turns into prince. Sweden: Owen CASTLE 91-98. Italy: Mincielli OLD 42-53 (+skin burnt by king, he leaves as dove and she seeks with aid of fox, kills prophesying birds who say their blood will restore prince, kills fox also when learns his blood is needed).

B646.1.2* Tasks: level forest, plant, reap, and make cake in twenty-four hours. Task: build golden bridge to princess in palace with golden fruit trees on sides. Snake son performs these tasks. Turns to prince and weds. Gypsy: Manning-Sanders RED 127-131. Gypsy (Ru-mania): Arnott ANIMAL 166-177; Hampden GYPSY 79-83.

B646.1.4* The Snake Prince. Woman pledges three daughters to snake for figs. Tells stream, cow, boy, not to tell snake she passed. They tell. Youngest d. agrees to wed. Mother burns skin when snake is out of it at night. Jealous sisters swing her and baby and push into sea. Rescued by stork and cared for on island. Prince hears her singing lullaby and rescues. Burma: Brockett BURMESE 13-30.

B647.1.1. Marriage to person in crab form.

B647.1.1.1* Golden crab caught by fisherman leaves plate of gold for dinner. Asks to wed princess. Performs wonders. Wed. Man at night. Tournament to choose more fitting hus-band. Crab sends wife to knock on golden gate with rod, and black man brings out armour and silver apple which he throws to princess in tournament. Second day: golden apple. Moth-er burns crab shell. Old man follows dog to underground palace and sees twelve eagles turn to princes, one toasts princess and curses queen who burnt his shell. Storytellers are in-vited to cheer princess. Old man tells this. She goes to palace and breaks enchantment. Greek: Lang YELLOW 33-44; Manning-Sanders BOOK..MAGICAL 106-113.

B649.1* Marriage to person in egg form. Egg son weds rich man's daughter, builds marvelous house. Comes from shell at night. She crushes shell and he must leave forever. China: Lin MILKY 64-71.

B650. Marriage to animal in human form.

B650.2* Bull as man courts woman. Boy in her service overhears magic words and uses to turn back to bull. Treed, lad throws three eggs at bull-man chopping tree and eggs knock off arms. Bull-man gnaws at tree, third egg

knocks off head (R251). Turns to bull and leaves. Louisiana: Field AMERICAN 147-153.

B651.1. Marriage to fox in human form. S. China: Hume FAV..CHINA 99-100. Eskimo: Melzack RAVEN 53-60. SEE ALSO: N831.1.

B651.1.1* Fox's daughter gives student a mirror in which he sees her face if studies hard. Passes exams and weds her. China: Carpenter TALES..CHINESE 226-234 /Sheehan FOLK 118-126/; Ritchie TREASURE 65-74 /Arbuthnot ANTHOLOGY 331-332/, /Arbuthnot FAIRY 181-183/.

B651.2. Marriage to buffalo in human form.

B651.2.1* Buffalo wife. Husband also assumes buffalo form and must race male buffalo for wife. Tosses magic herb and mud behind (D672). Son is seen turning to buffalo and wife and son leave. Native American (Caddo): Brown TEPEE 123-128.

B651.5. Marriage to deer in human form. Nigeria (Yoruba): Fuja FOURTEEN 126-132; Walker NIGERIAN 11-19.

B651.5.1* Man weds moose-maid. Leaves village and second wife to become moose and live with his "winter wife." Native American (Abenaki): Crompton THE WINTER WIFE pb.

B651.8. Marriage to seal in human form (B80.1). Scotland (Shetland Isles): Arnott ANIMAL 95-99 (wife). Outer Hebrides (N. Uist): Wilson SCOTTISH 1-7 (skin taken, leaves when found, Clan MacCodrum of the Seals origin). Scotland (MacDonald of the Isles, Isle of Skye): Nic Leodhas HEATHER 81-93 (wife to leave if speaks in anger, does so, son goes to her when grown).

B651.9. Marriage to tiger in human form. Man breaks tigress' spell by not looking as she changes forms. She can become woman. Wed. Korea: Child Study Assoc. CASTLE 243-257; Jewett WHICH 29-40.

B651.12* Marriage to donkey in human form. Two donkeys become humans for a season. She mar-ries man. When male donkey calls in spring she breaks all pots in house and returns to life as a donkey. Haiti: Wolkstein MAGIC 23-28.

B652.1. Marriage to swan in human form. SEE ALSO: D361.1; H1385.3F.

B652.1.1* The Golden Slipper, the Magic Ring, and the Twigs. Lad adventuring grabs foot that enters hole in cave, golden slipper comes off. Likewise gets ring from finger of hand ap-pearing from lake, sees spirit make love to dead son of Khan. Touches hoe and shovel which spirit used to unearth body and they turn to twigs and grow to sky palace. He climbs and meets three swan maidens there. They will wed one who has their shoe, ring, and twigs. He weds all three. Kazakh: Masey STORIES 122-131.

B652.1.2* King spares swan. Turns to maid and weds. Witch kills. Willow flute sings of murder (E632). Cornwall: Manning-Sanders PETER 63-70.

B652.2. Man marries crane in human form. Siberia (Yakuts): Ginsberg MASTER 59-80. Type 413A.

B652.2.1* Man saves crane. Maiden appears and weds him or comes as daughter. Weaves marvelous cloth. Asked to weave a second cloth. Tabu: no one may look (C31.1.2). Husband (mother-in-law, parents) peek and see crane weaving with down from own body. Crane-maiden leaves (C932). Japan: Bang MEN 47-53; Bartoli STORY pb; Matsutani CRANE pb; Novak FAIRY 156-164 (not to sell cloth until he has spent first three coins, sells too soon, finds dying crane); Pratt MAGIC #8; Sakade JAPAN-ESE..FAVORITE 59-65 (spider maiden, +A1133.5). Sakade JAPANESE CHILDREN'S 15-18; Uchida MAGIC 133-144; Uchida DANCING 135-144 (clam maiden weaves flax for fisherman, disappears after is sold).

B653.2* Marriage to centipede in human form. Silk merchant wed to widow. Every time he crosses bridge he hears his father's voice call to kill her as she is an evil spirit. She had been changed to a centipede as punishment and tortured by great rooster for 1,000 years. Now a woman again, rooster tried to get husband to kill her by faking his father's voice. Her enchantment is broken by his refusal for fifteen days to harm her. Dead cock is found under bridge. Korea: Carpenter TALES..KOREAN 261-265.

B653.3* Marriage to snail in human form. SEE: N831.1.

B654. Marriage to fish in human form. SEE ALSO: B610.1.

B654.1* The Beautiful Girl and the Fish. Girl sings song and fish-man husband comes from river. Brother learns song and kills (B610.1). They feed fish to girl (G61). She asks river to turn blood red if he is really dead, leaps into river and becomes mermaid. Nigeria (Yoruba): Fuja FOURTEEN 32-38.

B654.2* Mirzhan and the Lord of the Kingdom under the Sea. Serpent (B604.1) sets on girl's clothes and makes pledge to wed him. Year later she returns with two children. Mother learns charm used to call serpent from sea, calls and kills (B610.1). Girl turns to cuckoo, son to nightingale and daughter to swallow in grief. Russia (Tolstoy): Daniels FALCON 29-31; Masey STORIES 38-45.

B654.3* The Sea Snake Bride (B604.1).

Youngest daughter finds snake, King of the Sea, on blouse and has to promise to wed. He comes for bride and family give a goose. Titmouse sings of trick. Given a nanny goat, titmouse sings. Girl taken. Later she visits mother with three children and then returns to husband. Latvia: Huggins BLUE 93-100.

B562.2. Marriage to serpent in human form.

B562.1* The White Snake. Lad rescues snake being tortured by boys. Weds maid who appears. Monk warns of danger and he stays in hilltop temple. She causes flood but monk spreads robe and protects mountain top. She is imprisoned under pagoda but bears son to him. Son is God of Writing and Books. China: Bonnet CHINESE 43-48; Carpenter TALES.. CHINESE 159-165.

B700 - B799. Fanciful traits of animals.

B750. Fanciful habits of animals.

B752.1. Swan song. Swan sings as she dies. She will be hungry and in danger no longer. Aesop: Aesop AESOP'S (Watts) 190 (swan sings only once, when about to die); Aesop FIVE 50.

B755.1* Animal calls the dawn. The sun rises as a result of the animal's call. SEE ALSO: A2426.2.18.1; A739.6.1. China (Ch'uan Miao): Leach HOW 92-93. Native American (Hopi): Courlander PEOPLE 126-128.

B755.2* Golden cock calls dawn. Taiwanese Lin Tachian told by seer to shoot three arrows toward mainland China at cockcrow and will become emperor. Wife wakes cock early and he crows too soon. Arrows strike emperor's throne in China before he arrives. Cock killed and mountain splits in half. Golden bars buried there have never been found. Cocks in Taiwan crow at all hours today. Taiwan: Cheney TALES 150-156.

B755.3* Animals contest in calling the dawn. Mockingbird wins and gets maiden. Native American (Hopi): Brown TEPEE 14-18.

B765.1. Snake takes tail in mouth and rolls like wheel. SEE: X1321.3.1.

B771.0.2* Wild animal will not harm honest and true human. Japan: Novak JAPANESE 174-183 (wolf, girl).

B786. Monkeys alway copy men.

B786.1* Caps for Sale. Monkeys steal cap seller's wares. He throws own cap on ground in anger and they throw down all their caps from tree in imitation. Slobodkina CAPS pb. India: Bulatkin EURASIAN 69-70. England: Williams-Ellis FAIRY..BRITISH 9-10 (nightcaps). Egypt, Soudan: Carpenter AFRICAN 71-76 (fez, tarboosh).

B 800 – B 899. Miscellaneous animal motifs.

B 800. Miscellaneous animal motifs.

B 811.7* Sacred hen. Stone hen in Roman days feeds Christian girl starved by relatives. Lord has given hen the grace to live on in stone and lay eggs for the good. Florence: Jagendorf PRICELESS 131–137.

B 841.1.1* Animals debate as to which is the elder. Elephant recalls banyan when small enough to step over, monkey recalls eating topmost leaves, partridge (bodisat) planted seed. India: Gaer FABLES 159–161. Tibet: Withers WORLD 79.

B 841.1.2* Age debate. Guinea fowl put out grass fire when earth was new (A2375.2.10.1). Parrot made first hammer with beak (A2343.3.3). Elephant had first nose (A2335.3.3). Porcupine recalls earth too soft to walk on. Anansi recalls time before ground existed. He had to bury his dead father in his head. Ashanti: Courlander HAT 9–12.

B 841.1.3* Goat and bull argue over who is elder. Goat, with beard, wins. Haiti: Courlander PIECE 70.

B 841.1.4* Whose family is older? Fox is referred to in Han Dynasty classics. Hare may be seen on moon. Toads were killed accidentally when Pandora was repairing a rent in the heavens and while the first Empress Chiu was building her palace. Central China: Hume FAVORITE.. CHINA 23–26.

B 841.1.5* Eagle wants to wed someone old and wise. Stag, Salmon, Thrush, Toad each claim oldest. Toad has eaten many hills by eating grain of dust daily. Owl is older yet. Wales: Sheppard-Jones WELSH 54–58.

B 841.1.6* Deer helped put stars in sky. Rabbit planted tree to make ladder deer used. Toad's three sons planted trees to make hammer handle to nail stars to sky; spade handle to dig channel for milky way; hammer handle to nail sun and moon to sky. Toad acknowledged as oldest. Korea: Kim STORY 31–33.

B 842. Faithful dog to be killed. SEE: K335.1.4.

B 842.1. Faithful old horse to be abandoned. SEE: K335.1.4.

B 846. Monkeys construct a bridge across the ocean (Ramayana).

B 846.1* Vijaya returns to Ceylon via monkey's bridge. Ceylon: Carpenter ELEPHANT'S 135–140.

B 848. Man unharmed in den of animals. SEE: H328.9.

B 848.1. The musician in the wolf-trap. Meets wolf already trapped and saves himself by playing music. SEE: K551.3.1.

B 848.2.1* Woman removes lion's whisker without harm to self. Does this by patiently gaining lion's confidence with food and attentions. The lion's whisker is required by wise man in order to make her husband love her. He suggests wooing husband with same patience used on lion. Ethiopia (Somali): Davis LION'S 7–9. Amhara: Kaula AFRICAN 142–145.

B 857. Animal avenges injury.

B 857.1* Frog shames man who boasts of bravery in frog hunting. Drops legs around man and carries him off into water. Guiana: Jagendorf KING 129–141.

B 857.2. Yamabushi, priest, blows conch shell in badger's ear to frighten, badger transforms self into ghostly procession to frighten Y. Japan: Scofield FOX 26–32.

B 870. Giant animals.

B 870.1.2. Giant bull. SEE: B264.7; B335.2.

B 871.2.7. Giant mice. SEE: B16.2.8; D435.2.1.

B 873.1. Giant louse. SEE: H522.1.1.

B 873.3. Giant spider. SEE: E423.8.

B 874.3. Giant whale. SEE: B874.9.

B 874.6. Giant clam. SEE: B874.9; B652.2 (clam maiden).

B 874.9. Giant octopus. Ratu defeats giant clam and giant octopus. Rescues parents from inside of giant blue whale. Polynesia: Berry MAGIC 30–44; Colum LEGEND 77–83. Cook Islands: Gittins TALE 66–71.

B 877.1. Giant sea monster. SEE: B874.9.

B 877.1.3* Boy kills giant whale which has dog head by painting magic symbols on hand and kayak. Symbols are crab, hand, star, kayak. Whale is powerless and beaches self. Eskimo: Maher BLIND 31–38.

C. TABU

C0 - C99. Tabu connected with supernatural beings.

C10. Tabu: profanely calling up spirit (devil, etc.).

C11. The Old Man and Death. Weary old man wishes for death. When Death appears at this summons, he asks for help with the load. Aesop: Aesop AESOP'S (Grosset) 180-181; Aesop AESOP'S (Macmillan) 137; Aesop AESOP'S (Viking) 28-29; Aesop AESOP'S (Watts) 207.

C12.2. Oath: "May the devil take me if..." Devil does. Ireland: MacManus HIBERNIAN 10-24 (+Q565 Smith and Devil).

C12.2.1* Younger brother shares food with little red mannikin. R. M. serves brother. Sent to work for elder brother, mannikin hears servants and brother say "The devil take this linen...sow...etc." He takes all. Explains that he is the Devil when younger brother is taken to court for thieving servant. Court rules younger brother may keep goods. Carpathian: Manning-Sanders DEVILS 110-116.

C12.2.2* Oath: "May the devil take me if I marry him" says girl. "May thief steal my horse if I marry her," says man. They wed. Thief and Devil join forces to collect due. Thief to say, "The devil take the bride's soul" each time she sneezes. Devil reveals that he fears certain switch. Thief calls, "God help you" and chases devil off with switch. Given horse as reward. Latvia: Durham TIT 70-74.

C12.2.3* "May the Mischief take me if I ever come here again." Mischief does. Manning-Sanders RED 55-61.

C12.5. Devil's name used in curse. Appears.

C12.5.9* "May the Devil swallow them." Curses when finds horses and weapons missing. Follows trail and finds black goat on wagon. Turns to Devil and wrestles with him. Disappears leaving fiery rod in lad's hand. Lad, who had previously cursed Devil often, reforms. Italy (Firenze): Jagendorf PRICELESS 40-46.

C15.1. Wish for star husband realized. SEE: A762.1.

C15.1.1. Wish for star wife realized. SEE: A762.2.

C17. Tabu: mocking the belief in demons (ghosts). One mocking belief dares to cross marsh (haunted place) alone. Is found in A.M. senseless or dead. Wales: Pugh MORE.. WELSH 95-105. Netherlands: Spicer THIRTEEN GHOSTS 45-52.

C20. Tabu: calling on ogre or destructive animal.

C21. "Ah me!": ogre's name uttered. He appears. Greek: Wilson GREEK 1-8.

C25. "Bear's Food." To urge on his horses a man threatens them with the bear, calling them "bear's food." The bear hears and comes for them. Fox imitates hunter and calls to farmer. Bear pretends to be a log and has farmer tie him and thrust ax into him to prove. Farmer's wife gives fox dog in bag rather than promised hens (K235.1). +J2351.1 (fox scolds his parts). Spain: Sawyer PICTURE 75-76 /Hardendorff TRICKY 63-70/. Ukrainia: Bloch UKRAINIAN 64-67. Russia: Arnott ANIMAL 179-183. Norway: Undset TRUE 176-179. Scandinavia: Wiggin TALES 284-286. Russia: Higonnet-Schnopper TALES 76-81. Berber-Kabyl: Frobenius AFRICAN 89-91 (lion, jackal tricks). Jacobs EUROPEAN 42-50.

C26. Wish for animal husband realized. Girl says she will marry a certain animal. Latter appears and carries her off. Type 552. SEE ALSO: H1385.5B.

C26. Three girls say will wed whale, eagle, sea scorpion--are carried off. Fourth refuses men in kayak, says would rather marry a stone. Turns to stone. Family rescue girl wed to whale. He pursues. They throw back parka, kamik, etc. He stops, thinking each is wife (D672). He has made her a house of his own bones and forgot to put hip bones back when in pursuit. Beaches self and dies. Eskimo: Caswell SHADOWS 76-80.

C30. Tabu: offending supernatural relative.

C31.1.2. Tabu: looking at supernatural wife on certain occasion (Melusine). The husband must not see the wife when she is transformed to an animal. SEE: B652.2.1 (Crane Wife); U136.0.1 (Crocodile); F420.6.1.5.1 (Melusine).

C31.3.1* Tabu: disobeying supernatural wife. Tabu: singing magic song to get bisan (spirits) to show camphor trees. He reveals magic song and bisan wife turns to locust, He follows her into forest. Never more seen. Malaya: Carpenter ELEPHANT'S 40-48.

C31.3.2* Lad weds sun's daughter. Tabu: letting sun strike her. She must leave. He is to follow and not look back. Looks and one-third of reindeer herd disappear. Again--other two-thirds. He must follow herds now as they are wild reindeer. Lapland: Jablow MAN 81-82.

C31.4.2.1* Tabu: scolding supernatural wife. Supernatural wife harvests green wheat, he calls her "bad fairy"--tabu. She leaves, he finds grain ripened magically. Swiss-French: Duvoisin THREE 94-100.

C31.5. Tabu: boasting of supernatural wife. SEE: H1385.3. French: Picard FRENCH 84-92 (vanishes).

C31.8* Man grabs dancing fairy, overhears her

name and is able to keep her as wife. Will leave if struck with iron. He strikes. Descendants called "Pellings" after her name, Penelope. Welsh: Sheppard-Jones WELSH 72-77.

C39.9.1* Tabu: revealing secrets of supernatural wife. Maba, spirit of honey. Husband becomes drunk on Kashiri (honey liquor) and reveals her name. She leaves. The Guianas: Jagendorf KING 148-151. SEE ALSO: T115.1.

C31.10. Tabu: giving garment back to supernatural (divine) wife. SEE: F302.4.2.

C31.13* Tabu: attempts to force supernatural wife to speak. He pretends to throw child into flames. She snatches daughter and disappears. Greece: Haviland FAV..GREECE 83-90.

C32.1. Tabu: looking at supernatural husband. SEE: H1385.4 (East of the Sun); A762.1 (Star-husband); B641.

C35.2* Tabu: spying on animal wife (housekeeper). Snail girl must leave. Chinese: Birch CHINESE 37-42.

C35.3* Tabu: burning skin of animal wife. Husband throws into fire, crane dies. Siberia (Yakut): Ginsberg MASTER 59-80.

C35.4* Tabu: returning skin of animal wife. Siberia (Yakut): Ginsberg MASTER 59-80.

C35.5* Tabu: offending animal wife. Food sent by swan-maiden's father called "goose food" by tribesman. She leaves. Smith Sound Eskimo: Cunningham TALKING 98-104.

C35.6* Tabu: offending animal wife. Guest owl mentions "foxy" smell of wife--tabu. Eskimo: Melzack RAVEN 53-60.

C40. Tabu: offending spirits of water, mountain, etc.

C41.2. Tabu: letting ball fall into water. SEE: D195 (Frog Prince).

C41.5* Devil tempts girl guardian of well away and pig boy dirties water. Well-spirit overflows forming lake. Llyn Glasfryn. Wales: Spicer THIRTEEN GHOSTS 53-64.

C50. Tabu: offending the gods.

C51.4.3. Tabu: spying on secret help of fairies. SEE: F361.3.1; F348.8; F381.10.

C57.1.3. Tabu: eating from offerings made to gods. Ratu Loro Kidul, goddess of bird's nest comes, takes vengeance. Indonesia: De Leeuw INDONESIAN 117-134.

C61.4. Tabu: disbelief in particular supernatural power. SEE: C17.

C69.1* St. Beatus' cloak ceases to be magic after he commits sin of laughing during Mass. Swiss: Müller-Guggenbühl SWISS 213-223.

C91.1. Tabu: stealing garment from a rock. The rock pursues. The offended rolling stone. Native American (Ute): Robinson COYOTE 9-22. Native American (Salish-Blackfoot): Brown TEPEE 109-111.

C100 - C199. Sex tabu.

C120. Tabu: kissing. SEE: H1385.4.

C200 - C299. Eating and drinking tabu.

C211.1. Tabu: eating in fairyland. SEE: F324; F320.4.

C229.7* If porridge spills, wife must eat, man must not. Wife spills on purpose. Kikuyu: Nunn AFRICAN 57-61.

C300 - C399. Looking tabu.

C300. Looking tabu. SEE: C31.1.2; C32.1; C35.2; F420.4.7; F361.3; F348.8.

C311.1.5. Tabu: observing supernatural helpers. Girl insists on seeing goblin who helps her wash. To go to stable at midnight. Sees black pig, crosses self (tabu), sees goblin no more. French: Picard FRENCH 138-142.

C320. Tabu: looking into certain receptacle.

C321. Tabu: looking into box (Pandora). Gruenberg FAVORITE 413-414. SEE ALSO: F420.6.1.3.1 (Urashima Taro).

C321.1. Tabu: opening too much of magic box at a time. A priest gives a prince a sealed packet which he is to open in time of distress. He must open only one portion at a time. SEE: B11.7.1.

C321.2. Tabu: opening gift box prematurely. SEE: G530.2K.

C322.1. Bag of winds. Wind is confined in a bag. Man breaks prohibition against looking into bag and releases wind. Wales: Pugh MORE 67-76 (bottle). SEE ALSO: A1122.5; A1124.

C322.3* Child of Sun God told to request Melaia of moon. He asks for Monuia instead. Warned not to open until on land, he opens at sea. Is red pearl shell which draws fish to him. Their weight sinks his canoe. Tonga: Gittins TALES 60-65.

C331. Tabu: looking back. SEE: F81.1 (Orpheus).

C331.4* Those looking back while being carried to safety by cloud horse will fall into sea and be caught by Rakshas. Ceylon: Carpenter ELEPHANT'S 135-140.

C377. Tabu: looking up chimney. SEE: Q2.1.2Cb.

C400 – C499. Speaking tabu.

C400. Speaking tabu. Scotland: Nic Leodhas HEATHER 95-110 (speaking breaks spell, +D2183.1).

C420. Tabu: uttering secrets.

C420.2.1* Tabu: not to speak about a certain happening. Man enchanted in wolf form to be freed if lad refrains from telling secret for seven years. Girl friend forces to tell. Ireland: Spicer MONSTERS 101-108.

C421. Tabu: revealing secret of supernatural husband. SEE: C31.9; C32.

C423.3.1* Tabu: speaking of extraordinary sight. Shepherd given golden vase of jewels by spirits. Entertained in their palace. Never to tell of this. Wife makes him reveal secret. Jewels and vase vanish. Palace may be entered by human only once in 1,000 years. Argentina, Patagonia (Tehuelche): Barlow LATIN 9-17.

C424.1* Tabu: speaking of good luck. Wife finds piece of money one day, peso, pot of gold next. Voice warns not to tell husband. She tells. He tells. All is stolen. Philippines (Visayan): Sechrist ONCE 125-128.

C425. Tabu: revealing knowledge of animal languages. SEE: B216.

C429.2. The secret of Heather-ale. Type 2412E O'Suilleabhan Scots (Irish) try to get secret of brewing heather-ale from last two Picts (Danes) who know secret. Old man says to kill son, who is weakening under torture and he will tell. They do so. Secret now safe. They must kill him. Scotland: Wilson SCOTTISH 46-48.

C429.3* Abbot threatens Indians with curse on generations if tell hiding place of treasure. Statue of monk points to treasure, but points ten different directions. Venezuela: Jagendorf KING 265-269.

C430. Name tabu: prohibition against uttering the name of a person or thing.

C432.1. Guessing name of supernatural creature gives power over him. SEE: E443.3; D2183 (Tom Tit Tot); C31.8.

C432.1.1* Ogre builds bridge (G303.9.1.1) in return for carpenter's eye unless can guess name. Overhears ogre children singing name-- Oniroku. Japan: Matsui ONIROKU pb; Uchida SEA 72-83.

C432.1.2* Boy captured by witch to be freed if guesses name. Crab tells-- Casi Lampera Lentemué. Witch asks animals to admit which one told secret. Crab admits. She beats, he flees. Why crabs run from people. (A2534.1.1). W. Indies: McDowell THIRD 81-88. Puerto Rico: Belpré TIGER 75-82.

C432.1.2.1* Old woman Crim gives maids no pay unless guess name. Anansi goes as girl and flatters crab into telling. Old woman Crim has calabash full of the tears of 100 girls. Throws calabash at crab and tears make it stick. Origin of crab's shell. SEE: A2312.3.1. W. Indies: Sherlock WEST 86-92.

C432.1.2.2* Maid to guess name of old woman or be given no food. Crab tells. Name is: In The Storm, Coffin On Your Back. She asks who told. Crab admits. She slips on rock and crab eats her up. Haiti: Wolkstein MAGIC 117-122.

C432.1.3. Skunny Wunny and fox in name guessing contest. Fox fails after four tries. Skunny Wunny guesses fox's name, winning all of fox's stories. S. W. saves them in an otter skin bag for people to find later. Native American: Parker SKUNNY 13-22.

C435.1.1. Tabu: uttering name of supernatural wife. Man weds sister of the honeybees, Maba. She makes casseri (honey wine) by dipping finger in calabash. He brags, telling her name. She leaves and bees hide honey from him henceforth. Guiana: Carpenter SOUTH 175-181. SEE ALSO: H1385.3.

C450. Tabu: boasting. SEE ALSO: B210.2.1.

C456. Tabu: boasting of riding giant piggyback. G. has carried hero home from shipwreck after brothers tossed him into sea. He arrives in time to rescue princess from marrying his brother. Boasts of riding giant and g. appears, threatening. Giant is convinced that boasting was result of drink and happiness. Giant forgives. +N411.4. Russia: Colwell SECOND 21-34; Ransome OLD 294-315; Zemach SALT pb.

C460. Laughing tabu.

C460.1* Laughing reveals presence to ogres. SEE: N777.0.1.2 (person hiding from ogre giggles); J2415.23 (old man being carried by monkeys laughs).

C494. Tabu: cursing. SEE: T551.3 (calling a Christian a beast).

C495.1. All questions to be answered "I don't know." A youth is so advised by his horse.

C495.1.1* Girl to answer all questions, "The Gods know" after trading places with Sacred Horse in temple. Horse goes free. She becomes goddess. Thieves try to steal horse. She speaks, "The Gods know" and thieves flee. Horse returns years later and asks her friendship. She embraces and horse turns to prince. China: Frost LEGENDS 55-63.

C495.2.2.2* "We ourselves", "Because we wanted

to," "And rightly so": phrases of foreign language. Three Haitians in Dominican Republic each know one phrase in Spanish. They incriminate themselves. Dominican Republic: Jagendorf KING 106-110.

C495.3. All questions to be answered "Thanks." Youth is so advised by old woman helper. SEE: D1413.17.

C498. Speaking tabu: the one forbidden expression.

C498.2* Anansi discovers "Wheeler" in tree. Puts in hand and is grabbed. "Who's got me?" "Wheeler" "Then let me see you wheel!" Is thrown a mile. A. tricks other animals into doing this. Cat feigns ignorance and tricks A. W. Indies: Carter GREEDY 84-90; Sherlock WEST 144-151.

C498.2.1* Anansi finds mossy stone which makes one fall unconscious when remark made about moss. Tricks others. Spotted deer feigns ignorance and tricks A. N. Africa: Manning-Sanders SORCERER'S 122-125.

C498.2.2* Anansi has witch make spell so that anyone saying "five" falls dead. Tricks others into counting yams. Mrs. Dove gets A. to show her how to count. He falls dead. Jamaica: Williams-Ellis ROUND 204-207.

C500 - C599. Tabu: touching.

C513. Tabu: breaking twig. SEE: B335.2D (Kari Woodenskirt); F811.1.

C523. Tabu: digging. SEE: 56.1.

C600 - C699. Unique prohibitions and compulsions.

C610. The one forbidden place.

C611. Forbidden chamber. Person allowed to enter all chambers of house except one. SEE: S62.1 (Bluebeard); G561 (Sister's rescued); G530.1.1.

C611.0.1* Forbidden chamber. Priest in old woman's house breaks tabu and looks in room. Full of bones and blood. She is a cannibal. He flees. Dawn arrives before she catches him (G273.3). Japan: Ozaki JAPANESE 140-147.

C611.0.2* Trim Tram Turvey. Girl at home of wizard enters forbidden door, sees ox drawing water in garden beyond window. Wizard tells her to say certain chant to ox. Ox falls dead for seven days and prince who owns garden gets a new ox. Same happens. Ox tells prince about girl at window. Prince spies and asks wizard for her hand. This is allowed but she cannot speak to prince until he says "By the head of Trim Tram Turvey." She performs remarkable feats and other brides of prince

imitate and are killed. He spies and hears jug swear "By the head of..." She says she could speak to prince if only he would say that. Italy: Manning-Sanders GIANNI 161-172.

C611.1. Forbidden door. All doors may be entered except one.

C611.1.1* Olode the hunter taken to huge tree by Olvigbo, King of the Bush. Enters tree and becomes Oba of town there. Never to open door in third house. Opens and finds self back in forest with gun and loin cloth. Africa: Courlander OLODE 32-36.

C631. Tabu: breaking the sabbath. SEE: B11.12.4.1.1.

C645. Lazy man to learn self control. To have all desires as long as taps drum with hands intead of sticks. Becomes drunk and beats with sticks, all goods vanish. Returns to Water Spirit to ask again for aid. Given gourds with vermin inside. Africa: Burton MAGIC 24-29.

C700 - C899. Miscellaneous tabus.

C723.1. Tabu: combing hair during certain time. SEE: K217 (Bearskin).

C752.2.1. Tabu: supernatural creatures being abroad after sunrise.

C752.2.1.1* Raven sings ice up and freezes Konkadet monster in ice (D2144.5). K. had been diving for R's reflection (J1791.5). At dawn Raven gives call and all supernatural creatures must return to homes. Caught, Konkadet dies. Raven's companion puts on skin of Konkadet and swims to K's lair. Leaves salmon on beach nightly but mother-in-law claims she is a Shaman and had produced the fish. Brings one whale, tries for two whales and is caught in skin at dawn and dies. Mother-in-law claims this is her Spirit but Raven shows the son-in-law's body inside skin. Raven restores dead Konkadet-son-in-law and he takes wife away to live with him beneath sea. Native American (Northwest Coast): Martin NINE 47-50 /Martin RAVEN 69-74/.

C761.2. Tabu: staying too long at home. SEE: D735.1 (Beauty and the Beast).

C761.3. Tabu: staying too long at ball. Must leave before certain hour. SEE: R221+ (Cinderella).

C761.4. Tabu: staying too long in certain place. Man is shown (discovers) cave of treasures. Must leave by midnight. Second man imitates and stays too long (J2415). Mexico: Brenner BOY 44-50 (Tepoztan shows cave open only on New Year's Eve). Switzerland (German): Duvoisin THREE 185-189. SEE ALSO: N455.3 (Open Sesame).

C771.1. Tabu: building too high a tower. (Tower of Babel).

C771.1.2* Prince wants moon, scaffolding built. Moon breaks, destruction follows. Congo: Aardema TALES 62-66.

C773.1.2* Lord appears to devout Oudette. She wishes for little house, It appears. Asks for cow, dress, rich husband. Insists lord call her Madame Countess. He threatens to send her back to her cave. She decides to be content. Italy: Manning-Sanders GIANNI 103-107. SEE ALSO: B375.1.

C773.1.3* Coconut seed turns to man. Offers three wishes. Greedy man wishes (1) house with cellar full of food, (2) more food, (3) chute into cellar of never ending food. Is buried in food. Calls for fourth wish. Coconut man wishes he reform from gluttonous ways. Chile: Newman FOLK..LATIN 31-37.

C822. Tabu: Solving sphinx's riddle, sphinx perishes. Leach NOODLES 45. Egypt: Carpenter AFRICAN 63-70. SEE ALSO: H761 (Riddles of the Sphinx); B51 (Sphinx).

C824. Tabu: finding name of ghost. SEE: E443.3.

C837. Tabu: losing bridle in selling man transformed to horse. Disenchantment follows. Type 325. SEE: D1711.0.1 (Magician's Apprentice).

C900. Punishment for breaking tabu.

C911. Golden finger as sign of opening forbidden chamber. SEE: B316.

C912. Hair turns to gold as punishment in forbidden chamber. SEE: G671; B316; G530.2.

C913. Bloody key as sign of disobedience. SEE: G561 (Sisters rescued); S62.1 (Bluebeard).

C916. Continuous action started by breaking tabu. SEE: D1711.0.1 (Sorcerer's Apprentice).

C916.1. Trespass betrayed by dripping candle. Type 425. SEE: H1385.4 (East of the Sun); A762.1 (Star-husband).

C916.3. Magic porridge pot (D1601.10.1) keeps cooking. Against command, mother of owner bids pot to cook. It fills house with porridge and will not stop until ordered by mistress. Type 565. Germany (Grimm): De Paolo STREGA NONA pb; Gag MORE 43-46; Grimm GRIMM'S (Follett) 320-321; Rockwell THREE 110-112; TALL..NURSERY 117-119. German: Wiggin TALES 127. SEE ALSO: D1651.3 (magic mill).

C916.3.1. Three sons of Father Frost are given lodging. Two freeze house. Third gives bags of hot and cold. Rich man steals hot bag.. Nearly burns up house. Brother with cold bag has to rescue. Estonia: Maas MOON 17-25.

C920. Death for breaking tabu. SEE: F420.6.1.3.1; H1411.4.2 (Golden Ball).

C931. Building falls because of breaking tabu. Warned not to build by seashore, merman destroys castle. Scotland: Manning-Sanders BOOK..MERMAIDS 108-113.

C932. Loss of wife (husband) for breaking tabu. Type 400, 425. SEE: F81.1.0.1; B652.2.1; U136.0.1.

C939.13* (Kirtley) Great Drum becomes soundless to punish man for breaking his word. Efate: Holding SKY 87-98 (does not say thank you for gift of drum).

C952. Immediate return to other world because of broken tabu. SEE: C31.

C953. Person must remain in other world because of broken tabu. SEE: F81.1 (Orpheus).

C961.2. Transformation to stone for breaking tabu. SEE: S268.

C980. Miscellaneous punishment for breaking tabu. SEE: B175.3.

C984.5. Disastrous lightning for breaking tabu. Jaguar brags of strength to lightning and tears limbs from trees. L. shows his strength pursuing J. until he reforms. Guiana: Jagendorf KING 142-144.

D. MAGIC

D0 – D699. Transformation.

D100 – D199. Transformation: man to animal.

D100. Transformation: man to animal.

D100.1* Enemies throw Avunang through seal hole. He turns to seal. Pursued he turns to fox, etc. Tries all animals and returns home to relate adventures. Eskimo: Caswell SHADOWS 72-75.

D100.2* Boy jealous of two adopted boys wishes he were a snow goose. Becomes snow goose, rabbit, reindeer. Can become boy again if caught by kind hunters. Happy with lot now. Eskimo: Melzack DAY 41-48.

D110. Transformation: man to wild beast (mammal). SEE: D532 (lion); P253.2 (deer).

D112.2.1.3* Transformation: man to tiger. Fanged Raja. Raja demands human blood daily. Kampar the Fighter assumes tiger form, chases Raja off. Malaysia: Asia FOLK..FOUR 34-41.

D113.1.1.1* Transformation: man to wolf. To be wolf always if can't find clothing. Unfaithful wife hides clothing. Wolf becomes companion of king. Attacks wife and new husband. She confesses and returns clothing. France: Picard FRENCH 93-98 /Palmer DRAGONS 55-62/.

D113.2.2* Transformation: man to bear. Snow White and Rose Red. Type 426. Girls give bear shelter in home. Rescue a dwarf with beard caught in cleft of tree, in fishline (K1111.1), and being carried off by eagle. D. is angered by their interference (W154.2). Bear kills dwarf, regains form as prince, and recovers treasure. Grimm: Arbuthnot FAIRY 49-51; Dalgliesh ENCHANTED 57-65; Gag TALES 207-221; Grimm GRIMM'S (Follett) 299-308; Grimm GRIMM'S (Grosset) 298-306; Grimm GRIMM'S (Scribner) 262-269; Grimm HOUSE 125-142; Grimm SNOW (illus. Adams) pb; Grimm SNOW (illus. Cooney) pb; Hutchinson CHIMNEY.. FAIRY 153-163 (guardian angel watches children in wood, V238); Lang BLUE 277-285 /Lang FIFTY 270-276/; Wiggin FAIRY 228-236.

D114.1.1. Transformation: man to deer. SEE: P253.2.

D117.1.1* Transformation: man to mouse. Lord of Dyfed besieged by mice sent to enchanter Llwyd. Lord of Dyfed catches one mouse, realizes is wife of Llwyd. Demands return of own wife and stepson, land, etc. before releasing. Wales: Williams-Ellis FAIRY..BRITISH 312-328.

D130. Transformation: man to domestic beast (mammal). SEE: G263.1.0.2 (horse); D551.1 (ass); P253.2 (goat); P253.2 (sheep).

D131. Transformation: man to horse. SEE: G263.1.0.2.

D134. Transformation: man to goat. SEE: P253.2.

D135. Transformation: man to sheep. SEE: P253.2.

D136.1* Transformation: man to swine. The Castle in the Silver Wood: lad meets three witches who refused silver branches. Pig in silver wood asks lad to kill witches with branches. Does so, thus disenchanting pig (king) and 12 daughters. Weds princess. Denmark: Owen CASTLE 3-9 /Sheehan FOLK 8-13/.

D141. Transformation: man to dog. Grateful dwarf gives girl magic seeds to transform her to dog. Gives her lover, blacksmith's son, seeds to restore her. Thus averts wedding to cousin. Scotland: Nic Leodhas THISTLE 17-38.

D150. Transformation: man to bird. SEE: D771.11.1 (nightingale); P253.2 (raven); D721.5 (dove).

D151.5. Transformation: man to raven. SEE: P253.2.

D153.2. Transformation: man to owl. SEE: A1958.

D153.2.1* Tranformation: man to owl. The Conjure Wives: Conjure wives refuse to open door for threatening voice. Put bit of dough on fire for it. Dough grows and fills house. Wives fly out of windows calling "Who'll cook for you? Who?" Turn to owls. On Halloween turn back to conjure wives. U.S. (Southern): Harper GHOSTS 44-47 /Frances G. Wickes HAPPY HOLIDAYS/, /Sechrist HEIGH-HO 9-12/, /Haviland NORTH 122-125/. Hoke SPOOK 157-160.

D154.1. Tranformation: man to dove. Pin stuck into girl's head turns her to dove. SEE: D721.5 (Three oranges).

D154.1.1* Three sons return home as turtledoves. Mother kills one and serves to father (G61). Other two doves take bones from plate and the three fly off. Alight and turn to sons. Haiti: Wolkstein MAGIC 87-90.

D154.2.1* Transformation: man to pigeon. Girl lost in wood is befriended by pigeon who stores goods in tree. Asks her to bring plain ring from old woman's cottage, sees old woman trying to slip out with bird, ring in bird's beak. She obtains ring and disenchants pigeon. Grimm: Grimm GRIMM'S (Scribner's) 242-244. SEE ALSO: D771.11.1.

D155.1. Transformation: man to stork. SEE ALSO: D624.1.

D155.1.1* Caliph Stork: Caliph buys box with magic word which turns person to animal. If laughs will forget word and remain animal. He and vizier become storks, laugh, find princess in owl form in palace, overhear magician talk of secret word, disenchant selves and princess. Arabia: Buck FAIRY 269-280; Lang GREEN 35-46; Wiggin FAIRY 355-356. Iraq: Courlander

RIDE 66-76.

D157.1* Transformation: man to parrot. Simple Seng and the Parrot. Youth turns to parrot to be by side of love who spurns him. His body lies in trance. She promises to wed him if returns to body, gives shoe as pledge. Wed. China: Carpenter TALES..CHINESE 242-251 /Dalglies ENCHANTED 204-211/.

D161.1. Transformation: man to swan. Ireland: Child CASTLE 259-289 (Deidre); Frost LEGENDS 25-33 (Lir).

D161.2.1* Transformation: man to goose. Three Tailors and the White Goose: Three lads reach castle where gray goose feeds. Task: refusing to eat or drink at hands of girl who comes at midnight. Task: to pass forest without touching leaves. Two tailors take leaves and go home. Third finds giant tied to ground while white geese trample him and maid who brought cake plays harp. Giant asks to be killed. Lad obliges and giant and white goose become prince and princess, other geese all servants. Maid with harp becomes witch and flees. Rewarded with magic tablecloth. Two giants take by force and give "Everyone Out, Everyone In" sack instead. Soldiers in sack retrieve cloth. Tailors steal cloth. Same. (D881). Denmark: Hatch THIRTEEN 58-72.

D180. Transformation: man to insect. SEE: D532 (bee).

D190. Transformation: man to reptiles and miscellaneous animals. SEE: D195A (Manning).

D192. Transformation: man to worm (often = snake). SEE: D732.

D195. Transformation: man to frog. Hutchinson FIRESIDE 143-150.

D195.1* Frog Prince. Type 440. Princess drops ball into well. Frog returns demanding entrance to princess's table and bed. She throws him against wall after repeated demands and he turns to prince (D712.2). Sometimes is disenchanted merely by admittance to bed (D734). Usually accompanied by Faithful Henry motif: servant had three iron bands around heart, these break with joy as he drives carriage home. Germany (Grimm): Arbuthnot FAIRY 43-45; Dalgliesh ENCHANTED 199-203; Darrell ONCE 43-46; Gag TALES 179-188; Grimm BROTHERS 55-60; Grimm GRIMM'S (Follett) 82-88; Grimm GRIMM'S (Grosset) 89-60; Grimm GRIMM'S (Scribner's) 1-6; Grimm GRIMM'S (World) 286-290; Grimm HOUSEHOLD 32-36; Grimm JUNIPER 169-179; Gruenberg FAVORITE 295-298; Haviland FAIRY 114-117; Haviland FAVORITE..GERMANY 3-12; Holme TALES 63-68; Opie CLASSIC 183-187.

D195.1.1* Oda and the Snake. Daughter asks for whatever father finds in wagon on way home. Little snake. Asks to come into house, upstairs, etc. Sleeps in her arms. In morning

is prince. (D734). Austria: Manning-Sanders SORCERER'S 65-68.

D195.1.2* Man kills snake met at spring by Chofi. She promises him reward. He sings at gate and mother orders her to take him into house, into bedroom, into bed, etc. Haiti: Wolkstein MAGIC 37-42.

D195.2* Well of the World's End. Type 440. Stepdaughter sent to fill sieve at well of the world's end. Frog instructs (H1023.2) to daub moss and clay, asks her to obey him for one night. Eats with her, taken to bed, in morning he asks her to behead him. He becomes prince. Wed. England: Jacobs ENGLISH 224-229; Manning-Sanders BOOK..MAGICAL 235-239; Reeves ENGLISH 212-220; Steel ENGLISH 244-248; Williams-Ellis FAIRY..BRITISH 69-75.

D197. Transformation: man to lizard. Son gets holy man to turn him to lizard and creeps through crevices to rescue father, dragging him out in lizard form. Son does not get out of grotto before holy man has to return to his grove. Son must remain as lizard. De Leeuw INDONESIAN 117-126.

D211.1. Transformation: man (woman) to orange. SEE: D721.5 (Three Oranges).

D215.9* Princess enchanted in tree form. The talking tree. One thing missing from palace-- talking tree. King seeks. Tree is enchanted daughter of King of Spain. Ingratiates self with ogre's daughter and obtains magic ax. Cuts heart of girl from tree, cuts witch's head off. Wed. She turns to wood. Grease on ax caused this. He cuts ogre's daughter with ax and steals antidote she uses when grease turns her to wood. Italy: Baker TALKING 9-17.

D300 - D399. Transformation: animal to person.

D300. Transformation: animal to person. SEE: B650 (marriage to animal in human form).

D312.4* Which was witch. Man is attended by two identical wives. Holds to each until dawn. One turns to wild cat. Korea: Jewett WHICH 11-15 /Arbuthnot FAIRY 183-184/, /Hoke WITCHES 172-175/, /Arbuthnot ANTHOLOGY 343/.

D313.1.1. Transformation: fox to person. Fox gives self away. Turns to one-eyed man. Gets blind eye on wrong side. He obeys woman's suggestion to get into rice bag (K711). Lets her tie him up (K713.1) and put on fire shelf to smoke. Japan: Pratt MAGIC #2.

D313.1.2* Son cuts tail of fox fleeing from ill mother's room, follows blood trail to neighboring house. Sees tail under coat of one of men there. He wears fox's tail and pretends to be fox in man guise, too. Serves poison wine. Three dead foxes found in morning. Mother recovers. China: Dolch STORIES..OLD CHINA 65-81.

D313.1.3* Lad throws rock and knocks fox into pond. Shelters with old woman. She polishes her teeth and then leaps and bites him. He falls over and wakes in pond. Japan: Bang MEN 55-59.

D313.1.4* Lad throws bread to wolf, wife curses wolf. Fox in man form gives him a fine cow, also gives box to be opened only by wife. Man opens on way home. Flames shoot out and cause forest fire. Meant for wife. Why plain of Bessans is not forested. France: Picard FRENCH 142-147.

D313.1.5. Transformation: fox to person. Fox uses magic pearl in changing form. Turns to fortune teller. +W154.8.3. Japan: Novak FAIRY 100-107.

D315.1. Transformation: rat to person.

D315.1.1* Rat eats student's nail clippings and assumes identity. Cat let loose attacks rat student. Korea: Kim STORY 166-171.

D315.3. Transformation: badger to person. SEE: D612.1.

D318.1.1* Transformation: monkey to person. Monkey insists on keeping house for lawyer. Friends disenchant with charm. Turns back to man. Italy (Rome): Hampden HOUSE 89-93.

D334.1* Transformation: goat to person. Goatherd knocks goat off cliff with thrown rock. Picks up in remorse and goat turns to maid. Leads to flock of huge goats. King goat butts lad off cliff. Wales: Sheppard-Jones WELSH 146-148.

D361.1. Swan maiden. SEE: B652.1.

D361.1.1. Swan maiden finds her hidden wings and resumes her form. Types 400, 465A. Smithsound Eskimo: Cunningham TALKING 98-104. SEE ALSO: F302.4.2 (animal in maiden form); H1385.3F.

D361.1.2* The Red Swan. Boy sees red swan, follows. Third night reaches lodge where task is assigned. Fetch stolen scalp of wampum. He finds and returns. Given sister-red swan to wed. Native American: Bierhorst FIRE 11.

D364. Transformation: goose to person. SEE: R221Z (Tattercoats, geese turned to pages).

D366. Transformation: tikgi bird to person. Tikgi birds reap and transport rice to granary by magic. Lad gives party to thank and they turn into a maiden. Weds her. Philippines (Tinguian): Sechrist ONCE 86-90.

D400 - D499. Other forms of transformation.

D410. Transformation: one animal to another.

D411.6.1. Transformation: mouse to horse. SEE: R221 (Cinderella).

D421.8. Transformation: badger to object. Changes to floor mat: matmaker spending night in temple starts to mend floor mat. Nun cries in pain and he holds handful of badger fur. Temple vanishes. Follows trail of blood to dead badger in a.m. Novak FAIRY 95-99. SEE ALSO: B587.2; D612.1.1 (mooring pile); D612.1.2 (priest); D1171.3.1; K607.4; D313.1.

D431.1. Transformation: flower to person. SEE: D621.2.2.

D431.1.2.1* Transformation: carnation to person. Type 652. The Pink. Cook steals prince and keeps in tower seven years. Angel doves feed. Prince has power of wishing. Cook has him wish a castle and maiden. Cook asks maid to kill prince and bring tongue and heart. She brings heart of hind. He turns cook to black poodle and maid to pink in pocket. Returns home and reveals self. Weds girl restored from pink form. Germany (Grimm): Grimm GRIMM'S (Grosset) 91-97; Grimm GRIMM'S (World) 93-98.

D435.2.1. Picture comes to life.

D435.2.1.1* Cats drawn on temple wall kill giant rat in night, saving artist. Japan: Gruenberg FAVORITE 373-376; Hearn JAPANESE 29-35 / Hearn JAPANESE (Pauper) 38-44 /, /Hearn BOY 14-20/, /Littledale GHOSTS 27-33/; Carpenter WONDER..DOGS 195-203.

D435.2.1.1.1* Cat descends from scroll and kills rats. China: Manton FLYING 154-160.

D435.2.1.2* Artist's paintings are so lifelike they come to life. Receives magic brush in dreams. Emperor demands even grander paintings, is finally drowned in tempest artist paints. China: Chang CHINESE 26-29; Dolch STORIES.. CHINA 1-15; Mui MAGIC pb; Wyndham TALES ..CHINA 73-82.

D435.2.1.3* Painting falls into stream and fish swim from it. Japan: Hearn BOY 33-42.

D435.2.1.4* God caught by painter. Hands burnt but skill in painting requested is granted. Paintings come to life. Paints dowry for daughter. Mother-in-law sets fire to chest of paintings but daughter pulls out picture of waterfall in time to quench flames. China: Wyndham FOLK..CHINA 13-16.

D435.2.2* Frog-like man begs not to sell woodland as frog's marsh will dry up if trees are cut. Man agrees. Bare screen becomes covered with paintings of frogs in night, wet frogprints led from marsh to screen. Japan: Bang MEN 79-84.

D445. Transformation: image of animal vivified. SEE: D435.

D445.1.2* Mud image of pony comes alive and aids boy. Native American (Pawnee): De Wit TALKING 99–107.

D450 – D499. Transformation: object to object.

D450. Transformation: object to another object.

D451.3.3. Transformation: pumpkin to carriage. SEE: R221 (Cinderella).

D452.1.6.1.1* Widowed father tells children about food they'll eat one day to stifle their hunger. Neighbors bring real food. Portugal: Lowe LITTLE 58–61.

D454.7.2* Transformation: comb to bamboo thicket. Magic boat is woven of bamboos to carry hero to undersea kingdom. +U136.0.1. Japan: Uchida DANCING 61–72.

D475.1.1. Transformation: coals to gold. SEE: F451.5.1.4; F342.1.

D475.1.6. Transformation: rice to gold. Japan: Sakade JAPANESE 87–93.

D480. Size of object transformed.

D482.1. Transformation: stretching tree. A tree magically shoots upward.

D482.1.1* Crow cannot reach pelican babies in nest, in anger calls Tuckonie elves to sing tree up. Thus pelicans' mother cannot reach them either. Woodpecker succeeds. Australia (Aborigine): Arnott ANIMAL 195–201.

D482.1.2* Coyote climbs pine tree for eagle's feather. Tabu: father not to look up. Does so and tree grows to heaven. Two spider grandfathers lower coyote back to earth in web. Native American (Nez Percé): Heady TALES 35–40.

D482.1.3* Jealous companion causes tree on which rain maker sits to grow to sky. No rain for four years. Sisters locate tree. Little black ants and big red ants climb tree and push it into ground. Kahp-too-oo-yoo descends and brings rain again. Native American (Pueblo): Wiggin FAIRY 381–290.

D482.1.4* Boy clings to magically growing bamboo shoot. It falls, leading way to sea. Japan: Matsutani TARO pb.

D482.4.1* Stretching rock: two bluebird brothers sleep on rock. Crow sings rock up. Mother bluebird seeks rescuer. Measuring worm succeeds. Native American (California): Curry DOWN 121–128. Native American (Miwok): Fisher CALIFORNIA 88–95 (origin two rocks in Yosemite Valley).

D483.1.1* Deer challenges rabbit to jump over river, then widens river magically, leaving rabbit on other side. Native American (Cherokee): Bell JOHN 73–75.

D500 – D599. Means of transformation.

D515. Transformation by plucking flower in enchanted garden. SEE: P253.2B (Twelve Brothers).

D531. Transformation by putting on skin. By putting on the skin, feathers, etc. of an animal, a person is transformed to that animal. SEE: B645.1.2.3.

D532. Transformation by putting on claw, feather, etc. of helpful animal.

A* The Ogre's Heart in the Egg. Type 302. Lad divides an ox for lion, ant and eagle. (B314F,G). Given tokens to turn into each. Visits imprisoned princess as eagle. She discovers where giant keeps his life (E710), in egg, in dove, in porcupine's head. As lion he fights porcupine. P. says, "If I were in my mudhole I could win." Lad, "If I had...maiden's kiss I could win." Next day master's daughter gives kiss. He kills giant (K956). Weds princess. Puerto Rico: Alegria THREE 100–106.

Ab* Lad divides for dog, bear, bird and worm. Weds princess only when no sunlight must fall. Sun strikes and troll takes her. She obtains secret of troll's invincibility. Lad kills dragon with hare, dove, egg inside. Sweden: Owen CASTLE 101–119.

Ac* Lad divides for eagle, ant, lion. Aids dogfish, to call if in need. As ant he enters abode of captive girls whose blood witch drinks. Brings food and medicine, girl learns secret of witch's strength is egg in seven-headed tiger. Drops into sea on return, dogfish retrieves. Witch killed. Lad weds. +R111.1.3Aj. Italy: Toor GOLDEN 69–79.

Ad* The Giant Who Had No Heart in His Body. (Helpful animals, no transformation). Six sons seeking wives turned to stones by giant. Boots goes to rescue. Aids raven, salmon, wolf. Wolf is given horse, carries Boots on back to giant's house and advises. Captive princess learns where giant keeps heart––decorates places he claims to keep it. Third night learns truth: In egg in duck in well in church on island in lake. Wolf carries Boots to lake. Raven gets church keys. Salmon gets egg from well. Brothers restored. Giant killed. Norway: Adams BOOK..GIANT 41–52; Asbjornsen EAST 45–46; Asbjornsen EAST (Row) 64–72; De Regniers GIANT 81–93; Fenner GIANT 39–49; Manning-Sanders BOOK..GIANTS 98–106; Mayne BOOK..GIANTS 108–118, Undset TRUE 108–117.

B* Fetching the Sword (Ring). Type 665. Mermaid and the Boy. Lad pledged by father to mermaid. He shares with lion, bear, bee. Given token to transform self to lion, bear, bee. As bee he visits unapproachable princess and woos. Suitor test: fetching king's sword. He turns to lion and fetches. En route he drinks at stream and mermaid takes. Red Knight claims princess. Princess plays violin by sea and mermaid takes him to hear, as bee he escapes. Defeats Red Knight in magic changing contest. Weds. Lapland: Lang VIOLET 219-233.

C* Silver Penny. Type 665. Lad gives to beggar, is Wizard of the Wood, grants wishes--to change to hare, dove, salmon. Suitor test: whoever fetches king's ring to wed princess. He fetches and gives p. tokens. Enemy kills lad in hare form and claims princess. Wizard revives hare, tokens shown. Wed. Hungary: Manning-Sanders BOOK..WIZARDS 86-94.

D* The Strange Adventures of Alcavilo. Alcavilo shares with old nun, given leaf to chew and can understand language of animals and birds. Lion gives hair to turn self into animal and to wish self wherever wants to be. Finds captive girl on volcano. Flees place as bird, is caged by another girl. As ant he escapes, eats her cooking nightly. Caught, tells tale and learns that volcano princess is sister of this girl. As lion he rescues girl at volcano and claims sister as his reward. Chile (Araucanian): Barlow LATIN 28-37.

D535. Transformation to horse (ass, etc.) by putting on bridle (halter). SEE: D1711.0.1.1.

D551.1. Transformation by eating fruit. SEE ALSO: G263.1.0.2 (Carpenter); D881.1.

A* Donkey Lettuce. Hunter gives alms to old woman, to shoot into nine birds fighting over cloak. One will fall dead. Eat its heart and find gold piece under pillow each morning. (B113.1). Cloak is wishing cloak. An old woman has daughter (K2213). Makes him vomit up bird's heart and she swallows. Has him take her to far-off mountain with cloak, steals cloak and returns. He hears giant say clouds higher up mt. would carry him off. Is carried to lettuce (cabbage) garden. Eats of one and turns to donkey (D130). Other restores. Sells to old woman, her maid and daughter. Gives three donkeys to miller to be worked, eventually restores maid and weds daughter. Old woman dies of overwork as donkey. German: Grimm GRIMM'S (Follett) 55-65; Grimm GRIMM'S (Grosset) 135-143; Grimm GRIMM'S (World) 79-86; Lang YELLOW 52-60 /Lang FIFTY 46-52/; Manning-Sanders BOOK..WITCHES 72-82.

Ab* Who eats of bird's head to be king, of heart to find purse of gold under pillow each morning. Sons eat these tidbits while bird is roasting. Grown. One becomes king. Wife of second steals purse every morning. He discovers donkey figs, restoring grass. Wife, aunt and maid turned to donkeys, etc. Spain: Eells TALES..SPAIN 45-56.

Ac* Who eats of head to be emperor, heart to find gold under pillow. Hen laid diamond eggs.

Princess feeds lad who eats heart bitter coffee so vomits up heart. She takes it. He discovers apple to make person ass or restore. Turns her into ass. Case is taken to Emperor who is his brother. She is forced to repent. Hungary: Manning-Sanders RED 16-22.

B* The Three Magic Objects and the Wonderful Fruits. Type 566. (cf. D831). Father gives three sons hat of invisibility, never empty purse (D1541), wishing horn. (D1470.1). Queen steals all from him during card game. (D861.6). He discovers figs which cause nose to grow (D1376.1), cherries which restore. Disguised, he sells to queen then "doctors" her until regains magic objects. Italy: Zemach TOO pb.

Bb* Magic objects given by dwarf: Wishing cloak, never empty purse, soldier producing horn. Dwarf also supplies restorative pear for long nose caused by apple. Grimm GRIMM'S (World) 163-170; Grimm HOUSEHOLD 103-119; Wiggin TALES 111-117; Wiggin FAIRY 220-228.

Bc* Gifts from old lady, princess wins at cards, black figs grow horns, white remove. Weds princess. (D1376.1; D881.1). Jacobs EUROPEAN 72-80.

Bd* Lad with magic purse, cloth, and cap, wishes self beside princess. Wishes them at end of world. She steals objects and leaves. Magic nose-growing apples cause her to restore objects and wed him. Norway: Baker TALKING 118-122.

Be* Four lads find magic oranges which cause hair to grow on faces, peaches which remove. Suitor task: keeping magic objects (tablecloth, cloak of invisibility, inexhaustible purse) for one year. Queen and King steal objects back. They regain with fruit. The four Juans wed the four Juanitas. Bolivia: Newman FOLK.. LATIN 39-52.

Bf* Princess of Tombaso. Princess steals from three princes: purse; troop-producing bugle; wishing belts. They regain with nose-producing apples, nose-producing plums. French Canadian: Barbeau GOLDEN 26-45.

Bg* Shepherd finds ring that makes wearer sneeze. Steals magic cloth, purse and pipe from robber under tree where he spends night. Makes princess laugh with sneezing ring (H341). Imprisoned. Escapes and finds figs causing nose to grow. Regains gifts and weds princess. Sicily: Hampden HOUSE 73-84.

Bh* Father leaves son wealth and magic objects. Warns not to court "Peerless Beauty." She steals all. Horn-producing grapes. Yugoslavia: Fillmore LAUGHING 27-50.

C* The Crow's Pearl. Man whose buffalo has wandered feigns dead and catches crow. Forces to give magic jade (pearl) which grants wishes. Wishes for wife. She steals gem. Golden Turtle (Kim Qui) gives white flowers (smell and nose grows) and red (shortens). Recovers gem. Viet Nam: Robertson FAIRY 36-42; Vo Dinh TOAD 115-122 (Buddha gives roses).

D* Lazy Boy. Yellow fig falls on head. He eats and nose grows. Blue fig = nose shortens. Gives away yellow and tries to sell blue. Is beaten and left with own nose long. Reforms and another blue fig falls to him. South American: Newman FOLK..LATIN 89-93.

E* King refuses daughter to humble officer and expels. In woods lad eats orange and nose grows. Second and shrinks. Sells to princess, cures, wed. Haiti: Thoby-Marcelin SINGING 84-90.

F* Lad obtains magic sword Samosek by shooting arrow for two arguing leshi to chase. Kills Nemal Chelovek and frees princess. Weds. She substitutes sword and he is defeated. Eats berries and horns grow. Others cause to fall. Sells to princess, doctors, regains sword and place. Russia: Downing RUSSIAN 174-188.

G* Mr. Luck bathes in pool and becomes monkey. Second pool restores. Sells to princess. Cures and weds. Burma: Htin Aung KINGDOM 18-23.

H* Toivo shoots arrow. First to reach to be king. T. gives golden flying ship and treasure. Takes princes to isle. Eats of berries and falls asleep. She leaves. He finds berries which produce or remove horns. Sends to princess. Cures and weds. Finland: Bowman TALES..TUPA 42-52 /Arbuthnot FAIRY 139-143/.

I* The Gizzard. Lad eats magic gizzard which rich man has asked mother to cook. Covered with silver nightly. Weds princess. She causes him to vomit up gizzard and she eats. He goes blind. Discovers apple which heals, apple which causes blindness. Sells to royal family. Gives princess purgative to "cure" blindness. She vomits up gizzard and he re-swallows. Haiti: Wolkstein MAGIC 99-112.

D555.1. Transformation to animal by drinking from animal's track or from certain stream. SEE: P253.2.0.1E.

D555.2.5* Transformation by eating onions. Men see each other as cows. Eating onions eliminates this error and they stop eating each other. Korea: Kim STORY 11-16.

D564.2. Transformation by smelling flower. SEE: D551.1C.

D567. Transformation by sunlight. SEE ALSO: G304.2.5 (troll bursts).

D567.1* Demons vanish when setting sun strikes them. Japan: Novak JAPANESE 188-201.

D582. Transformation by sticking magic pin into head. SEE ALSO: D721.5; D765.1.2; K1911Ac.

D582.0.1* Anaise and Bovi. Anaise is killed for loving prince Bovi. Bird sings to Bovi, enchants king. King says B. would wed bird if it were a girl. Bird asks to prick her head with pin and turns to girl. Wed. Haiti: Thoby-Marcelin SINGING 42-45.

D582.2. Transformation by magic needle. Wife Silver-Tree asks trout in well who is most beautiful queen in world. Answer: Gold-Tree. Silver-Tree demands Gold-Tree's heart and liver. G. sent away and goat heart given. Trout reveals truth. S. goes to G.'s new palace and stabs with poison stab. G. is in locked room but S. convinces her to put out little finger at keyhole and stabs. King husband keeps G.'s body in room. New wife removes stab and G. revives. S. returns with poison cup for G. Second wife forces S. to drink and dies. (cf. Z65.1 Snow White). Ireland: Jacobs CELTIC 97-101 /Adams BOOK..PRINCESS 56-60/.

D600 - D699. Miscellaneous transformation incidents.

D612. Protean sale. Man sells youth in successive transformations. Type 325. SEE: D1711.0.1 (Magician's Apprentice).

D612.1. Illusory transformation of animals in order to sell and cheat. SEE ALSO: D421.8.

D612.1.1* Badger turns to mooring pile and swims off with boat moored to him. Boatmen pretend to be fooled a second time, tie up badger pile and beat with paddles. Japan: Pratt MAGIC #6.

D612.1.2* Man going to trap badger in cave passes priest hurrying down mountain. Looking back he sees his house on fire. Hurries home to find wife baking. Climbs mountain, looks back again to see flood. Finds wife washing clothes. The priest had been the badger. He gives up. Japan: Scofield FOX 15-19.

D612.1.3* Sohei beats beggar to death, believing him to be badger in disguise. A priest shaves his head and dresses as a monk to say prayers over body. Friends find him in rags praying over statue with head shaved. Badger's trick after all. Japan: Bang MEN 39-45.

D612.2* Illusory transformation of animals in order to aid benefactor. SEE: D1171.3.1 (badger kettle).

D612.2.1* Fox turns into kettle, then horse, and is sold. Returns in fox form. Turns into maiden and dances to earn for old couple. Japan: Novak FAIRY 131-137.

D615. Transformation combat. Fight between contestants who strive to outdo each other in successive transformations.

D615.0.1* Elephant in guise of man tries to learn hunter's secret transformation. Wife stops him before tells <u>last</u> transformation. Elephant attacks each transformation but cannot find last. Hunter is water insect. Nigeria: Walker DANCING 51-57.

D615.1.1. Transformation contest between magic badgers. Loser must leave island (A2434.2.2.1). Prince's procession thought to be trick of opponent and badger mocks. Soldiers attack him. Japan: Novak FAIRY 16-21 (fox defeated by badger, no foxes on Sado Island); Stamm VERY pb.

D615.1.1.1* Fox challenges badger to contest, hides. Badger thinks is nobleman and cries, "I found you!" Is killed. Japan: Wiggin TALES 429-431.

D615.2. Transformation contest between master and pupil. Type 325. SEE: D1711.0.1.1.

D621.0.2* Periodic transformation. Alive by night, disappears in day. Gypsy finds dead band of gypsies and girl he loved in wood. Carries her off. She is alive only by night. Gypsy: Jagendorf GYPSIES' 93-101.

D621.2.2. Flower by day: girl by night (D431.1). SEE ALSO: N712.

D621.2.2.1* Poet weds peony maiden. Builds wall to protect garden. Appears as peony beside her after death. China: Carpenter TALES..CHINESE 124-133.

D624.1. Storks become men in Egypt in winter. SEE ALSO: D155.1.

D624.1.1* Entire village turned to storks for stoning stranger. Found spring on island which turns them to men, another turns back to storks. They return home as storks yearly. Shipwrecked lad drinks and becomes stork. To carry vial of water home around neck, restore self there. Breaks vial, must remain stork that year. Hides sister's necklace in his nest. Proves truth of tale next year when reappears in human form by fetching necklace from nest. Bulgaria: Pridham GIFT 67-80.

D670. Magic flight.

D671. Transformation flight. Fugitives transform themselves in order to escape detection by pursuer. Types 313, 325, 327. SEE: D721.5C; G530.2.

A* Man Who Ate His Wives. Man fattens wives till can't move. Misána regains strength by licking snow. Leaves dummy to answer for her. Flees (D1611). Turns self to piece of hard wood when pursued. Eskimo: Hardendorff JUST 88-91.

B* Fundevogel. Man raises child found in tree top where bird had carried it. Cook plans to cook F. Man's daughter Lina helps flee. Turns to rosebush, church, pond. Cook tries to drink, duck drowns her. Germany (Grimm): Grimm GRIMM'S (Follett) 28-32; Grimm GRIMM'S (Grosset) 216-218; Grimm GRIMM'S (World) 159-162; Rackham GRIMM'S 71-74.

D672. Obstacle flight. Fugitives throw objects behind them which magically become obstacles in pursuers path. Type 313, 314, 325, 327, 502. SEE: A1134.2 (Origin of Fog); A1141.2.1; A1141.8.4 (origin thunder); A2034.3.2; B316; B389.4; B582.2E; B641.6; B651.2; C26.1; D721.5C; F53.1 (arrow chain); G530.2 (Master Maid); H522.1.1.1; H1331.3; K1611D (Fereyel and Debbo Engyl); Q2.1.2Ceba (Baba Yaga). Japan: McAlpine JAPANESE 16-22 (+F81.1.0.1 comb = grapes; comb = bamboo shoot; urinates = river). Italy: Mincielli OLD 34-41 (+F848.1 three bitternuts = bulldog, lion, wolf).

A* Water-nixie. Brother and sister fall down well, water-nixie makes them work. Flee. Throw hairbrush = hill of spikes. Comb = ridge of teeth. Mirror = mountain of mirrors. Gag MORE 23-25; Rockwell THREE 53-55.

B* Cruel Giant. Lad and giant's daughter flee (G530.2). Throw comb = forest. Razor = ridge. Mirror = lake. Giant drowns. Wales: Sheppard-Jones WELSH 85-88.

C* The Four Sacred Scrolls. Monk's apprentice shelters with witch. Is allowed out with rope tied to waist. He ties scroll to rope and it answers for him (D1611). Flees. Throws scroll behind = river, fire, wall of swords. Witch drinks water, puts out fire with it. He reaches temple sanctuary. Japan: Novak FAIRY 22-30.

D* The Flight. Good fairy as dove gives princess comb, brush, apple, sheet to flee witch. Throws comb = river, brush = forest, apple = mountain, sheet = sea. Witch riding cock drowns (dies of anger). Poland: Baker GOLDEN 131-134; Borski JOLLY 134-139.

E* Motinu and the Monkeys. Girl taken to play for monkey dance. Hunter gives eight wooden images of monkeys to toss as flees. Monkeys stop to investigate, she escapes. Weds hunter. Nigeria (Yoruba): Fuja FOURTEEN 80-87.

F* The Turtle Prince. Youngest son, turtle, insists on wedding youngest of three princesses along with older brothers. Seeks flame-colored cock. Old ladies en route give magic stone, stick, charcoal to throw down. Steals cock from Rakshasa. Throws stone = mountain; bamboo stick = fence; charcoal = fire. Appears as prince at feast and wife burns turtle jacket. Ceylon: Tooze WONDERFUL 64-70.

G* The Hard-Hearted Rich Man. Rich man's wife disappears. Old woman feeds him stew to calm him. Made from caribou which wife gave her. Puts stick on roof which, after two days, points direction he must follow (cf. H1385.3). Reaches smoking Blue Mountain. Wife prisoner of Old Goose in rock igloo on mountain top. Old G. thinks he smells man, wife say is own charms. Flee. Build wall of flames. Old G. swallows. They throw ivory beads, make well to hide in. O.G. sits in river, dams till overflows. They throw another bead to make wall against water, wall crumbles. Wife calls on her father, Winter Spirit at North Pole. He freezes water, O.G. freezes fast. Escape. Eskimo: Maher BLIND 115-131.

H* The Wonderful Hair. Poor man dreams angel tells him he'll find mirror, handkerchief, scarf under pillow in morning. To go to wood and comb hair of bathing maiden. Pulls out her red hair and flees. Drops scarf, handkerchief, mirror. She stops to pick up each, he escapes. Hair sells for 1,000 ducats. Tsar splits and finds scroll with secrets of nature inside. Yugoslavia: Fillmore LAUGHING 219-228.

I* The Beautiful Feathers. Boys shelter in hut. Amazimu, giant ogre, comes. They flee. Temba goes back for headdress left behind. Sets arrow in ground, if it falls he is dead. Old lady gives him lump of fat to rub on stone and delay Amazimus. They stop to fight over stone and T. escapes. East Africa: Arnott TEMBA 85-93.

J* The Elephant's Tail. Koji seeks tail of queen of elephants. To walk firmly over sleeping e's back or they will awaken. Cuts tail. Flees. Throws egg = river. Elephants become crocodiles. Throws egg = mountain. Elephants become herons. Egg = impenetrable forest. Elephants come to home, K. calls to wife to throw him his magic juju, it falls into fire and he says "Turn into a hawk." He becomes hawk but since juju burns he is still hawk (A2261.7). Ashanti: Courlander HAT 80-85.

K* Wind and Wave and Wandering Flame. Smith Liam drops hammer to earth. Arton catches and returns. Given magic rose to throw into sea and call "Darthuil"--maid arises to wed. Stolen by Myrdu, A. calls on L. for aid. Is given wind, wave and wandering flame to help. Must catch M. before he passes White Rocks in North. Wind sent ahead to encourage D. M. throws twigs = trees, fire burns. M. throws knife = chasm. Wave sent to bring A. back and wash M. away. Ireland: Pilkington SHAMROCK 169-177.

D700 - D799. Disenchantment.

D700. Person disenchanted.

D702.1.1. Cat's paw cut off: woman's hand missing. A man spends a night in a haunted mill where he cuts off a cat's paw. In the morning the miller's wife has lost her hand (G211.1.7). (cf. H1411.2). Appalachia: Chase JACK 76-82; Hoke SPOOKS 141-146; Leach THING 95-98.

D702.1.1.1* Fish peddler attacked by cats, gaffs head of cat called Old Woman Kowashi. Finds Kowashi's mother with wounded head, beheads, turns to cat. Japan: Leach THING 91-94.

D711. Disenchantment by decapitation. SEE: B641.0.1; H1199.12.3; H1331.1.3 (Quest for Golden Bird).

D711.2. Disenchantment by cutting person in half. Golden fish released by girl has mate turn self to dervish and help her escape on winged horses to her lover. Dervish then cuts her in half. Serpent emerges in fear of being cut up. Its poison had caused her to be a shrew. Arabia: Arnott ANIMAL 231-240.

D712.2. Disenchantment by slinging against something. Type 440. SEE: D195 (The Frog Prince).

D721.3. Disenchantment by destroying skin (covering). SEE: B641.0.1Ad; B641.5; D861.1J.

D721.5. Disenchantment from fruit (flower) by opening it. Type 408. The Three Oranges. Beautiful woman emerges from the fruit (flower). (cf. D980).

A* Quest for three golden oranges. Sent from Sun to Moon to East Wind. Daughters of Sun, Moon and Wind hide hero and ask father to aid. Hero reaches garden and manages to break oranges without climbing tree (tabu). Opens one en route in thirst and maiden emerges. She asks for bread and when he cannot supply she vanishes. He provides bread and opens second orange. This maid asks for water. Third agrees to wed. Waiting for him to fetch carriage, she hides in tree and gypsy witch sees reflection and breaks pitcher in anger at loveliness (J1791.6.1). Third time her pitcher is metal and will not break. She sticks a pin into the girl's head turning her to a dove (D582). A wise woman removes it later, she wed hero. Spain: Gunterman CASTLES 132-150 (pitcher, pin omitted); Boggs THREE 17-35 /Sheehan FOLK 61-71/. Italy: Mincielli OLD 108-120 (sent on by ogresses).

B* To pick three lemons from glass hill. At Castle of Lead, giant's mother hides, giant gives lead dumplings to take along. Castle of Silver, Castle of Gold same. Glass Hill (F751). Hero throws lead, silver and gold dumplings onto glass mountain to make stairway. Lemons fall into his hands. Opens two on way home, maids appear, loses. Prepares food, drink, clothing to offer third. Weds. Queen in ivory tower by lake. Old woman not invited to wedding dresses her hair. Sticks pin in head, turning queen into dove. Old woman takes queen's place (K1911). King removes pin from dove's head, disenchants. Hungary: Manning-Sanders GLASS 146-158.

C* Prince breaks bottle of old woman and he laughs. Cursed to be unhappy until finds girl of milk and blood. Finds three pomegranates in forest. Breaks one = girl. Has nothing to offer her so she returns to pomegranate. Second = same. Third = offers her his heart. She goes with him. Witch pursues. They throw behind walnut = chapel, self = priest, lad = assistant (D672, D671). Hazelnut = rose garden, gardeners. Almond = river of steel knives. Witch killed. Italy: Toor GOLDEN 49-53.

D722. Disenchantment by taking off bridle, man transformed to horse (ass) thus released. SEE: D1711.0.1 (Magician's Apprentice).

D732. Loathly lady. Man disenchants loathsome woman by embracing her. Type 402A.

D732.0.1* The Laidley Worm of Spindleston Heugh. Girl to be worm (D192) until her brother, Childe Wynd, kisses her three times. Sent to vanquish dragon worm, he obeys its command to kiss it. Sister restored. Step-mother queen turned to toad. England: Green CAVALCADE ..DRAGONS 103-108; Jacobs ENGLISH 190-196; Steel ENGLISH 89-94; Williams-Ellis FAIRY.. BRITISH 306-311. England (Northumberland): Colwell ROUND 34.

D734. Disenchantment of animal by admission to woman's bed. Type 440. SEE: D195 (Frog Prince).

D735. Disenchantment by kiss. Type 410. SEE: D1960.3 (Sleeping Beauty).

D735.1. Beauty and the Beast. Disenchantment of animal by being kissed by woman (man). SEE ALSO: H1385.4 (East of the Sun); D758.1 (disenchantment by enduring in silence).

A* Type 425C. Beauty and the Beast. Flower which daughter requested is picked at expense of daughter. She must join beast in his castle. Returns home for visit and overstays (C761.2). Returns to find beast near death. She kisses and he turns to prince. France (Madame de Villeneuve): Dalgliesh ENCHANTED 130-153; Evans SLEEPING novel pb; Harris BEAUTY pb; Haviland FRENCH 38-59; Holme TALES 35-44; Jacobs EUROPEAN 34-41; Lang BLUE 106-128 /Arbuthnot FAIRY 107-115/; /Arbuthnot ANTHOLOGY 216-223/; Mayer BEAUTY pb; McKinley BEAUTY pb; Opie CLASSIC 137-150; Pearce BEAUTY pb; Perrault PERRAULT'S (Dodd) 115-134; Rackham ARTHUR 49-65 /Provensen PROVENSEN 33-48/; Sekorová EUROPEAN 121-135; Tarrant FAIRY 68-88.

B* Great Bear of Orange. Youngest daughter wishes to wed Great Bear of Orange. He comes for her. She refuses to wed. Is thrown to snakes. Sings to charm them. Sharks same. Lions same. She agrees to wed and he turns to prince. Invisible servants disenchanted also. Ireland: Manning-Sanders BOOK..SORCERER'S 56-64.

C* The Enchanted Castle. Youngest daughter asks for three shoots from tree. Bear claims her. She reads from book in castle describing enchantment and enchantment is broken. Bear becomes prince. Slovenia: Kavcic GOLDEN 78-86.

D* Lily and the Bear. Finds bear wounded on spot where her lily was broken. Bear sprang from ground when lily was pulled. She puts her finger on stem of broken lily and he turns to prince. Wed. Spain: Eels TALES 109-116.

E* The Golden Carnation. Wizard claims daughter for picked carnation. Overstays visit at home, if ring turns its stone to her palm he needs her. Almost dead when returns. Kisses = prince. She had tree whose leaves point up when joy at her home, droop in sadness. Italy:

Toor GOLDEN 15-21.

F* White Cat and the Green Snake. Exiled princess comes to crystal palace of Cubits (men one cubit high). White cat rules palace. She breaks tabu by going near lake and meets Green Snake. Is bathed in boiling milk as punishment. Repeat--boiling oil. Snake comes to her sick bed and begs her to wed him. She refuses repeatedly. Finds him dying by lake and agrees to wed. He becomes prince. Brittany: Manning-Sanders PRINCES 108-117.

G* The Monkey Prince and the Witch. Maid bathes wounds of monkey who comforts her in her sorrow. This kindness breaks enchantment of witch Minggayang and he becomes Prince Ucoy again. Weds maid. Philippines: Robertson PHILIPPINES 23-32.

H* The Dog and the Maiden. Girl weds dog. Turns to prince at night. Her father discovers her and beats, she leaps into river. Meanwhile dog-prince has killed enchanting fairy and broken spell. Returning he causes her body to rise and revives with a kiss. Gypsy: Manning-Sanders RED 154-158.

D735.2. Three Redeeming Kisses. (Die Weisse Frau.) A woman can be disenchanted from animal form if man will kiss her three times, each time she is in the form of a different terrifying animal. SEE: D732.0.1.

D750. Disenchantment by faithfulness of others.

D753.5. Disenchantment by returning key (ball) unbloodied. Ogre turns to man and weds girl. SEE: G561.2B.

D754.1* Disenchantment by guarding sleeping man. SEE ALSO: H1473; K1911.1.4 (False brides finish task); L145.1B (Kate Krackernuts). Two eldest daughters take large cake without mother's blessing. Task: to guard sleeping man. Asked if they are alone, they do not reply. Are turned to flagstones. Youngest daughter takes blessing and small cake, shares with old woman. Is advised to always answer when spoken to, to do what dared, to turn back never. She answers sleeper. Follows him through horrors Quaking Bog, Burning Forest, Cove of Terror, Mountain of Glass. Old lady helps through all. To leap into Dead Sea. Obeys and finds self in his arms. Restores sisters. Weds. Ireland: Manning-Sanders SORCERER'S 24-32.

D754.1.1* The Sleeping Prince. Girl seeks prince at East Wind, West, South, North. Wears out iron shoes. Throws white roses at lions. Enters palace and watches sleeping prince. He wakes on St. John's Eve, sees, weds. Spain: Lurie CLEVER 74-83.

D757. Disenchantment by holding enchanted person during successive transformations. Type 403, 450. SEE: F324.3.

D757.1* Pure girl to kiss enchanted maid on lips

on St. John's Eve and never let go of golden pitcher. Maid turns to ape, demon, etc. Girl who disenchants wakes with golden pitcher still in hand. Gold coins in it when she reaches in. Red ants when aunt tries (Q2.1). Spain: Gunterman CASTLES 13-33 /Fenner GHOSTS 147-165/.

D758.1. Disenchantment by three nights' silence under punishment. (cf. D735.1 Beauty and the Beast). SEE: H1385.3; H1385.4.

D758.1.1* The Crow. Crow to be disenchanted if princess will live with him and keep silent no matter what. Serves thus for two years, works as servant for one year. He becomes prince. Poland: Lang YELLOW 104-106.

D758.2. Disenchantment by maintaining silence for a year or more. SEE: P253.2B+ (Twelve Brothers).

D760. Disenchantment by miscellaneous means.

D762.2. Disenchantment by being wakened from magic sleep by proper agent. SEE: D1960.3 (Sleeping Beauty).

D763. Disenchantment by destroying enchanter. SEE: D113.2 (Snow White and Rose Red).

D765.1.2. Disenchantment by removal of enchanting pin (thorn). SEE: D582; D721.5; K1911Ac.

D765.1.2.1* The Nine Doves. Princess in tower breaks window with bone. Nine doves pass, white dove enters room and she gives tokens. Simpleton has entered door in tree and seen nine doves and her tokens, tells princess. White dove is under enchantment of eight black doves. Princess has special house with iron walls made. White dove flies in and she closes door on black doves. They turn to dragons and burst in fury. She pulls three pins from head of white dove and he turns to prince. Greece: Manning-Sanders CHOICE 63-73 /Manning-Sanders DRAGONS 43-54/.

D771.11.1* Disenchantment by flower. Witch turns brother Joringel to stone, sister Jorinda to nightingale (D150). Later disenchanted, Joringel seeks red flower which he dreams will break enchantment. Touches birds and all turn to girls. Touches witch and she is powerless. Type 405. Grimm: Gag JORINDA pb; Gag MORE 229-239; Grimm BROTHERS 43-46; Grimm GRIMM'S (Follett) 174-178; Grimm GRIMM'S (Grosset) 33-36; Grimm GRIMM'S (World) 191-193; Grimm JORINDA AND JORINGEL pb (illus. Adams); Lang FIFTY 162-165; Lang GREEN 264-268; Rackham GRIMM'S 82-85. SEE ALSO: D154.2.1.

D777.1. Disenchantment by covering with cloth. SEE: G530.2D.

D800 - D1699. Magic Objects.

D800 - D899. Ownership of magic objects.

D810. Magic object a gift.

D812. Magic object received from supernatural being. SEE: N250.5.

D812.7. Magic object received from dragon king. SEE: F420.6.1.3.1; U136.0.1.

D812.15. Swamp maiden asks man to carry letter to her parents in another swamp. He complies and she gives him a magic refilling purse (D1451). Her father feasts him and gives him more gold. Japan: Uchida SEA 42-54.

D815.2. Magic object received from father. D882.1E.

D817.1.2. Magic object received from grateful father of redeemed snake. Warned to accept only wishing ring as reward. Congo (Luban): Burton MAGIC 29-35. India: Jacobs INDIAN 110-112 (ring and food producing pot and spoon). Poland: Lang GREEN 47-52; Zajdler POLISH 1-19.

D817.1.2.1. Magic object received from grateful redeemed snake (dove, mongoose, etc.). Finland: Arnott ANIMAL 112-121 (wishing ring). Nepal: Hitchcock KING 61-75 (jewel from snake's forehead). Ghana (Akan-Ashanti): Aardema NA OF WA (wishing ring from dove). Burma: Brockett BURMESE 51-62 (wishing ring from mongoose); Carpenter ELEPHANT'S 114-124 (wishing ring from weasel). Grimm: Grimm GRIMM'S (World) 367-371 (wishing stone from bear). SEE ALSO: D882.1B.

D817.1.2.2. Magic object received from grateful father of snake saved from flames. Warned to ask for ring only as reward. Man saved maiden from fire by throwing sand on flames, she turned to snake and wound around neck. Russia: Daniels FALCON 92-110.

D830.1. Attempt to learn about magic object by spying.

D830.1.1* One Eye, Two Eyes, Three Eyes. Old Woman gives Two Eyes magic goat (cow). It provides food or spins for her. One Eye spies and she sings her to sleep (D1781). Three Eyes spies and she sings only two of her eyes to sleep. Goat is killed. She buries heart by door and tree of silver leaves and gold fruit grows. Only she can pick fruit. Prince comes. She picks fruit for him. Wed. SEE ALSO: B335.2B (Jack and the Bull). Grimm: Arbuthnot FAIRY 62-66; Grimm GRIMM'S (Follett) 251-261; Hutchinson CHIMNEY 41-52; Lang FIFTY 176-183; Lang GREEN 253-256. Latvia: Durham TIT 24-29. Russia: Carey BABA 109-113; Riordan TALES..CENTRAL 238-240.

D830.1.1.1* Three girls spy on princess. Three Eyes and Two Eyes given sleeping potion. One Eye doesn't drink it and sees magic parrot enter. +H1385.5Ac (Bird lover). Brazil: Baker TALKING 179-183.

D831. Magic object acquired by trick exchange. By means of second magic object hero recovers first. (Cf. D881; N813). SEE ALSO: D551.1.

A* The Knapsack, the Hat and the Horn. Type 569. Youngest brother finds magic cloth, exchanges for knapsack of soldier, sends back for cloth. Gets hat that causes dozen guns to shoot, horn that causes walls to fall. He defeats his elder brothers, forces king to wed him to princess. She gets secret of knapsack, hat. He blows horn, she and king die in rubble. He rules. Grimm: Grimm HOUSEHOLD 222-227.

Ab* Dummling. D. is given golden acorn by oak. Oak gives magic napkin. D. trades for beating rod. Sends rod back for napkin. Trades for belt that creates lake, sends back for napkin; hat that shoots from six corners--same. D. is killed and buried under princess' window. Her tears fall on grove and tree grows. She picks apple, tears touch and apple turns to Dummling. Magic objects run to him. King gives in. D. weds princess. Hungary: Manning-Sanders GLASS 100-114.

B* Blue and Green Wonders. Includes N813 plus: Captain forces Anders to trade Blue and Green Wonders for magic building axe. Blue and Green Wonders regain axe. Trades for magic harp, iron box with soldiers. Defeats king, axe builds new castle. Latvia: Huggins BLUE 101-102.

Bb* Includes N813Fb plus: Bandit forces to trade 'Nothing' for killing club, trades, has club kill bandit. Trades for magic gusly, pluck first string and sea appears, second and ships appear, third and ships' guns fire. Defeats Tsar. Russia: Downing RUSSIAN 100-121; Riordan TALES..CENTRAL 243-261 (D831Bb; N813Fa).

Bc* Includes N813 plus: 'Shmat the Wise' tells lad to trade him for captain's wonders--park in box, ship-building ox, cavalry-producing horn. S. returns. King defeated. Russia: Whitney IN 1-24.

C* King Johnny. Three brothers find castle with gold. Elder two beat youngest and leave. He serves giants. Is given magic table. Trades to hermit for cornet that calls up troops. Sends troops back for table. Second hermit gives sack with castle in it--same. King borrows table and refuses to return. Johnny takes table and princess with army. Slavonia: Manning-Sanders CHOICE 171-182 /Manning-Sanders BOOK..GIANTS 67-78/.

D831.1* Straw coat of invisibility (D1361.12) acquired by trick exchange. Man gets Tengu to give it to him for a look through telescope bamboo tube. His mother (wife) burns coat. He rolls in ashes and becomes invisible. When drinking sake, ashes get wet and face and hands appear.

Jumps in stream and confesses. Japan: McAlpine JAPANESE 121-126.

D832. Magic objects acquired by acting as umpire for fighting heirs. When hero gets object he refuses to return it. Type 400, 518. SEE: F1015.1.1 (Twelve Dancing Princesses); H1385.3 (Quest for vanished husband).

D832.1* Hat that sees all, shoes that fly, stick that dissolves all are taken from goblins by acting as umpire. Hero dissolves goblins and dissolves unseen goblins eating up food at wedding feast. Estonia: Manning-Sanders BOOK.. GHOSTS 90-94.

D833. Magic object acquired by tricking giant. Giant is persuaded to give the objects to the hero. SEE: G512.0.4 (Jack the Giant Killer); K1917.3 (Puss in Boots).

D838. Magic object acquired by stealing. Types 570, 581. SEE: G610 (Pinkel); K1611 (Molly Whuppie).

D839.3. Magic object acquired by trickery. Badger turns self to little girl and gives three tengu children each a bun. Says whoever closes eyes longest may have fourth bun. Takes magic fan. +D1376.1.3. Japan: Sakade JAPANESE 73-77.

D850. Magic object otherwise obtained.

D856. Magic object acquired by gaining love of owner. Type 580. Given wishes. Youngest brother wishes every woman to fall in love with him. Innkeeper's wives give lad magic scissors, tablecloth, barrel top. Exiled to beggar's island. He feeds and clothes all. Sells two objects to princess for right to sleep in her room. Must wed him to get third, now in love, she weds. Norway: Williams-Ellis ROUND 120-129.

D861. Magic object stolen. SEE: S12.1.

D861.1. Magic object stolen by host (at inn). Type 563. SEE: D881; D877.1.1 (magic object washed); J1703.5 (goat in Chelm).

A* Lad who went to the North Wind. North Wind gives lad magic tablecloth (D1472.1.8), ram that gives gold, cudgel (D1401.1). Innkeeper substitutes for all. Cudgel forces return of goods. Norway: Arbuthnot FAIRY 76-77; Asbjornsen EAST 24-29; Asbjornsen EAST (Row) 135-138 /Association TOLD 58/; Haviland FAVORITE..NORWAY 67-74; Hutchinson CHIMNEY..FAIRY 67-74. Scandinavia: Hardendorff TRICKY 111-118 (goat). Poland: Hampden GYPSIES 113-118 (lamb). U.S. Appalachia: Chase JACK 47-57. Rockwell OLD 65-78.

B* Table, Ass, Stick. Three apprentices given magic table, gold-giving ass (B103.1.1), cudgel. Innkeeper steals all. Third brother with cudgel retrieves. +K1151. Grimm: Galdone TABLE pb; Grimm GRIMM'S (Follett)

323-339; Grimm GRIMM'S (Grosset) 228-242; Grimm GRIMM'S (Scribner's) 104-116; Grimm GRIMM'S (World) 130-141; Grimm HOUSE 56-80; Grimm HOUSEHOLD 149-159; Wiggin FAIRY 163-173.

C* Ass, Table, Stick. Apprentice given gold-producing ass, magic table, cudgel. Innkeeper substitutes. Cudgel regains. England: De La Mare ANIMAL 144-148; Jacobs ENGLISH 215-219; Reeves ENGLISH 196-209; Steel ENGLISH 241-244. Lang FIFTY 213-219 (serves ogre, jewels from ass). Italy (Tuscany): Hampden HOUSE 64-71.

D* Grateful Snake. Lad shares food with snake and cares for it. Grows and is put into pool, river. Turns to dragon. Gives gold-producing donkey, magic tablecloth, cudgel. Innkeeper steals, cudgel reclaims. China: Chang TALES 37-45; Dolch STORIES..OLD CHINA 25-41.

E* Bottle Hill. Man forced to trade cow for bottle. Two tiny men come from bottle and serve dinner on gold plates. Landlord borrows and replaces. Second bottle = two big men with sticks. Ireland: Manning-Sanders DWARFS 64-72 /Manning-Sanders CHOICE 54-62/; Pilkington SHAMROCK 89-93. India: Spellman BEAUTIFUL 22-25.

F* Rich farmer tells poor to go to the devil with his pig. He receives magic objects which are stolen by innkeeper and regained. Finland: Bowman TALES 12-24 (Magic mill, Tablecoth, Wallet with men who perform tasks, beat enemies, construct castle. Go to Hiisi). Czechoslovakia: Fillmore SHEPHERD'S 172-184 (tablecloth, gold producing cock [B103.1.5], cudgel). Sweden: Baker GOLDEN 54-57 (silver-laying rooster [B103.2.1], magic mill, hornet's nest).

G* Ass, Table, Stick. Variants.

Ga* Gold-producing ram, hen lays golden eggs, tablecloth, basket of oak and beech switches. Old lady steals. Poland: Borski JOLLY 41-48.

Gb* Genie gives woodsman magic tablecloth for sparing log. Gold-dropping donkey, mill, cudgel, mayor borrows and substitutes. Armenia: Tashjian THREE 22-31.

Gc* Lad threatens little folk and receives blue duck that lays golden eggs, napkin, caubeen, from which men with clubs emerge. Ireland: MacManus HIBERNIAN 240-250.

Gd* Three lads work for tiny lord. Do not enter house where dance music is heard. First disobeys. Fired and given magic tablecloth. Second given donkey-producing gold. Third obeys. Given knapsack with cudgel. Regains prizes from innkeeper. Germany (Grimm): Gag MORE 99-115.

Ge* Lad plants bean. Climbs plant to heaven (F54.2). St. Peter gives magic table. Innkeeper steals. Gold-spitting donkey. Beating cane. Italy: Manning-Sanders GIANNI 119-126.

Gf* Lad given coin-producing handkerchief by mendicant he serves. Exchanged in night lodgings. Given stick. Recovers. E. Pakistan: Siddiqui TOONTOONY 70-81.

Gg* Goddess Durga gives replenishing pot. Innkeeper steals. Pot with demons given. Recovers first. India: Towle MAGIC pb.

Gh* Holy man gives to father of too many children. Magic basket, gold-dropping cock, cudgel. Beats innkeeper and cannot put latter back in bag. Holy man takes back gifts. France: Lang ROSE 72-83.

Gi* Wind takes flour, gives magic food-producing cloth. Rich brother substitutes. Sun takes milk, gives gold-giving goat. Frost takes soup, gives sack with two strong men. Russia: Riordan TALES..CENTRAL 23-30.

Gj* Cow gives gold. Sheep gives silver. Chicken lays eggs. Stick--beats. Africa: Rose AKIMBA pb.

H* The Magic Drum. The king's child eats tortoise's palm nut. T. requests king's magic food-producing drum as retribution. Breaks tabu by stepping over stick and three hundred warriors with sticks emerge from drum and beat. Exchanges drum with king for foo-foo-bearing tree. If picked twice in same day tree will die (D877). His children follow him and pick also from tree. It dies and spot grows over with raffia palm. T's family dwell under palm leaves ever since. Nigeria (Yoruba): Arnott AFRICAN 124-132; Carpenter AFRICAN 31-40.

I* Tabu on magic self-replenishing food broken.

Ia* Anansi finds magic pot "Do what you can" which fills with food. Tabu = touching pot with palm nut kernel. A. breaks tabu and cord comes out and whips A. Finally cord tells A's sons phrase to say to stop it. Appiah ANANSE 51-57. S. Ghana: Sleigh NORTH 83-89.

Ib* Lazy Tito finds magic pot. Always to leave some food in pot. His sons spy, eat all. Guiana (Waurau): Carpenter SOUTH 167-174.

Ic* Aja the dog gets fufu pear tree by calling chant to it. Takes one fufu each time. Ijapa, tortoise, discovers and takes all. Tree falls and kills I. Courlander OLODE 104-106.

J* Brahmin requests aid of rich jackal wed to eldest daughter. Given melon to plant with jewels inside. Neighbor lady discovers and buys them all. Given food-providing pot. Rajah takes pot when next door neighbor tattles. Given stick in pot. Invites Rajah and neighbor. Treasures returned. Jackal's skin is burnt and he becomes prince . (D721.3). India: Baker GOLDEN 58-79.

K* Turnips sown on dovecot stolen. Old man seeks house full of children. They give, in exchange for turnips, a magic tablecloth, gold-sneezing goat. Wife exchanges. Whistle, three whips beat. Wife makes old man carry her in bag up to dovecot, has to hold bag in teeth. She keeps questioning. He answers and bag falls (J2133.5.1). Russia: Ransome OLD 155-183/ Fenner ADVENTURE 82-102/.

D861.2. Magic object stolen by neighbor. Type 564.

D861.2.1. Neighbor's disastrous attempt to procure similar magic object. Ajaji is given food-producing spoon by Olokun, sea god. Tortoise imitates and is given whip (J2415). Nigeria (Yoruba): Fuja FOURTEEN 196-202.

D861.4. Magic object stolen by rival for wife. SEE: D1223.1.1.

D861.5. Magic object stolen by hero's wife. SEE: D551.1., K2213.

D861.6. Magic object stolen in card game. SEE: D551.1.

D871.1. Magic object exchanged for worthless. Foolish brother (wife) exchanges old object for new. Type 561. SEE: D882.1E. Fake uncle sends lad into cave to steal magic lamp with aid of magic ring (D1470.1.15). Is trapped there. Rubs ring and genie appears. Lamp also produces genie by rubbing (D1470.1.16, D1421.1.5). Has princess transported to his home by magic on several nights. Produces marvels required by king. Builds palace (D1131.1). Weds. Magician trades new lamps for old and transports palace (D2136.2). Genie of ring helps him to recover (D881). SEE ALSO: D1421.1.2. Arabia: Arbuthnot ANTHOLOGY 302-309; Arbuthnot FAIRY 167-174; Manning-Sanders CHOICE 108-127 /Manning-Sanders BOOK..WIZARDS 58-77/; Martignoni ILL 268-281; Rackham ARTHUR 153-181. India: Frost LEGEND 147-153. Philippines (Tagalog): Sechrist ONCE 184-188 (magic tabu = coconut cup; -princess and castle episodes.)

D876. Magic treasure animal killed (Goose that laid the golden egg). Aesop: Aesop AESOP'S (Grosset) 25; Aesop AESOP'S Macmillan) 113; Aesop AESOP'S (Viking) 27; Aesop AESOP'S (Watts) 2; Martignoni ILLUSTRATED 398; TALL NURSERY 120; Untermeyer AESOP'S 33-35; White AESOP'S 13-14.

D876.1. Bird gives magic feather each day. Feather fills pot with mush. Wife kills bird for feathers and magic ceases. Congo (Luban): Burton MAGIC 109-111.

D876.2. Brahman's son would kill gold-producing serpent for hoard. Snake kills son. Brahman takes food and reconciliates snake. (cf. B103.0.4.1). SEE ALSO: J15. India: Ryder PANCHATANTRA 331-332.

D876.3* Man kills milk-giving cows and they vanish. Prunes fruit-giving vine and it dies. Tries to pry open food-giving rock and it closes. Africa (Bantu): Aardema BEHIND 42.

D876.4* Man trades magic bluebird for wife. All goods provided by bird vanish. Wife leaves. Spain: Wiggin FAIRY 343-348.

D877. Magic object loses power by overuse. SEE: D861.1H; D861 .1I; D925.0.2.1.

D877.0.1* Widow to pluck feather from golden goose (dead husband) when in need. She plucks all. They turn to real feathers and goose never returns. India: Gaer FABLES 164-166.

D877.0.2* All of replenishing food never to be eaten. Swiss: Müller-Guggenbühl SWISS 125-126 (cheese); Müller-Guggenbühl SWISS 126-128 (peas). SEE ALSO: D861.1H, I.

D877.1.1* Magic object loses power by being cleaned. SEE ALSO: D861.1.

D877.1.1.1* Wind ruins Anansi's tree. Gives him magic cloth. Wife cleans and no longer works. Pot--same. Club--whole family is beaten. Jamaica: Sherlock ANANSI 13-19. West Indies: Sherlock WEST 125-129 (-whip + cloth; Anansi finds pot, whip. A. turned to spider and hides under leaf, A2433.5.3.5).

D877.3* Wife sells baked hen produced by magic mud. It was intended as gift to monks. Husband's pet hen provided magic mud when he spared her life as sacrifice. Every third day the magically produced hen was to be given to monks. Now hen scatters magic mud and vanishes. Husband becomes monk and wife becomes chicken-like. Taiwan: Cheney TALES 143-149.

D881. Magic object recovered by using second magic object. SEE: D871.1.; D831; D161.2.1; H1385.3Cc.

D881.1. Recovery of magic object by use of magic apples. These apples cause horns to grow. SEE: D551.1.

D881.2. Recovery of magic object by use of magic cudgel. SEE: D861.1.

D882. Magic object stolen back.

D882.0.1* Brer Wolf steals Brer Rabbit's lucky rabbit's foot. Brer Rabbit steals it back. U.S. Black: Harris FAVORITE 162-168 /Harris NIGHTS 166-176/, /Harris COMPLETE 239-246/; Brown WORLD 88-97.

D882.1. Stolen magic object stolen back by helpful animals. (cf. B548.1). Type 560. SEE ALSO: H1321.1Ae.

A* The wine seller. Guest repays hospitality with magic stone which causes jug to be always full. Man opens wine shop. Stone disappears and his dog and cat seek. Cat forces rat to gnaw box open and mouse to retrieve ring. Returning across river cat drops ring (D882.2). Fish with ring inside is caught (N211.1). Why dog and cat are enemies (A2494.1.2). Korea: Anderson BOY 19-32; Carpenter TALES..KOREAN 47-54 /Gruenberg MORE 125-129/; Jewett WITCH 82-94; Manning-Sanders CHARMS 21-33, 82-94. China: Green BIG 32-33.

B* The Grateful Beasts. Boy buys dog, cat and snake, rescuing them. Snake gives magic ring (D817.1.2). Ring is stolen by treachery. Dog and cat retrieve with aid of mouse. Returning over river cat drops ring. Found in fish. Nepal: Hitchcock KING 61-75 (Jewel brings magic palace, thief steals, K362.10.1. Rat, also saved, retrieves D882.1.1). Finland: Arnott ANIMAL 112-121 (Weds princess with aid of magic ring, she steals ring). Afghanistan: Asia FOLK..THREE 5-10. Italy: Sheehan FOLK 72-83 (animals given to hero along with ring, princess steals). Iran: Mehdevi PERSIAN SIX (cat, dog, snake). Ceylon: Tooze WONDERFUL 88-93 (cobra, parrot, cat, Ring of Suleiman). Poland: Zajdler POLISH 1-19 (magic crown from snake's father, performs tasks and weds princess, she steals ring). Lang GREEN 47-52 (snake's father gives watch which grants wishes, princess steals).

Ba* Mouse, bear, ass. Put in boat adrift, animals rescue. Bear gives magic stone. Merchants steal. Animals retrieve. Crossing river, ass on bear's back drops. All frogs are asked to bring a stone to build a wall. Stone is found. Grimm: De La Mare ANIMALS 170-178; Grimm GRIMM'S (World) 367-371.

Bb* Leprous wife, dog, hawk, rat and snake rescued. Snake has asked his father for magic ring reward. Heals sick, grants wishes. Caution: Never let a woman in the house. Does and she steals. Hawk and rat retrieve, argue, hawk drops rat with ring. Dog finds. Congo (Luban): Burton MAGIC 29-35.

Bc* Animal grateful for rescue. Lizard rescued from burning woods with shepherd's crook. Brings stone from father's crown, grants wishes. Neighbor steals, transports palace. Cat and duck retrieve. Cat causes thief to sneeze. Duck drops, In fish. Bulgaria: Pridham GIFT 130-137.

Bd* Pemba digs hole and saves python from fire. Python gives gourd. To unstop in need. White cloud makes enemy vanish. In trouble. Grateful rat brings gourd to him. Central Africa: Carpenter AFRICAN 113-120.

Be* Cat, dog, weasel. W. gives ring. Thief steals and palace vanishes. Cat hides necklaces of genie's daughter (F302.4.2.2) and orders path to island (D882.1.1.1). Which of three deserve greatest reward (H621.3). Burma: Brockett BURMESE 51-62 (mongoose); Carpenter ELEPHANT'S 114-124; Carpenter WONDER..

CATS 52-63.

Bf* Snake's father gives magic ring. Princess lets loose golden hair, it floats down river and prince sees and steals her. Ogre's aunt steals ring. Cat holds rat bridegroom and forces rats to reprieve. India: Jacobs INDIAN 110-122.

Bg* Dog, cat, dove. Dove gives magic ring. Wishes self chief of village. Ananse's niece steals. Ghana (Akan-Ashanti): Aardema NA pb; Bryan ADVENTURES pb.

Bh* Fisherman catches carp, son of Dragon King. Taken to undersea palace. To ask for green gem which grants wishes. Old lady steals. Their mansion vanishes. Dog and cat retrieve. Gem falls in river. Fish with gem caught. Dog and cat enemies. Korea: Kim STORY 99-115.

C* Sack of Sand. Boy buys dog and cat, rescuing. Sent away for this. Works three years. Choice of sack of silver or sack of sand. Meets maiden in fire and douses flames with sand. She turns to snake and twines round his neck. Takes to father in underground kingdom and gives ring reward. Weds princess after performing tasks. Princess steals ring. Cat and dog force mouse to retrieve. Drop. Force crab to locate, in fish. Russia (Afanas'ev): Daniels FALCON 92-110; Lang YELLOW 192-206.

D* The Stone in the Cock's Head. Man selling cock hears two wizards say stone in its head is magic. Keeps. Wishes palace. Weds princess. Two wizards give his daughter mechanical doll for ring. Hero seeks, asks mouse kingdom for help. Mice retrieve. Hero turns wizards to donkeys loaded with cheese for mice. Italy: Haviland ITALY 43-53; Hampden HOUSE 57-63; Manning-Sanders CHOICE 95-107; Manning-Sanders BOOK..WIZARDS 9-21; Wiggin TALES 25-29.

Ea* Jack and His Golden Snuffbox. Type 560. Jack takes big cake with mother's curse. Father gives gold snuffbox to use if near death (D815.2). Task: create lake with man-o-war on it firing gun by eight o'clock in morning or be killed. Three little men come from box and perform tasks. Second morning--clear forest. Third-- build castle (D1131.1), soldiers to salute at eight o'clock. Weds king's daughter. Servant finds snuffbox in jacket and transports to castle (D2136.2, D871.1). Jack given a year and a day to return it. King of Mice calls all mice, whereabouts unknown, sends to King of Frogs, sends to King of Birds. Eagle takes Jack there with mouse and frog helpers. M. steals snuffbox. Frog and mouse argue over it and drop into sea. Frog recovers. Castle restored. England: Jacobs ENGLISH 82-95; Reeves ENGLISH 158-175. Gypsy: Manning-Sanders RED 72-83; Steel ENGLISH 27-39. Gypsy (Wales): Hampden GYPSY 25-33. Paul Sébillot: Lang GREEN 139-145 (snuffbox found, builds castle and weds, -tasks, -helpful animals, seeks at moon, sun, wind, steals snuffbox back himself).

Eb* Sir Buzz. Son finds six shillings in dead father's coat pocket, travels. Pulls thorn from tiger's paw. Given box reward. Not to open until goes nine miles. Drops at eight and one-quarter miles. Span high man, Sir Buzz, comes out and serves. Carries off Princess Blossom for master. Prince and Princess Blossom visit Brahman, really vampire. Burn hair to summon Sir Buzz to aid. He and vampire compete in changes contest. Vampire changes to rose in King Indra's lap. B. to musician granted rose. V. to mouse. B. to cat. India: Haviland FAVORITE..INDIA 63-82.

Ec* Son of the Baker of Barra. Baker's son lets three old ladies taste cake for king's daughter. They promise reward. At castle princess chooses him as husband. King sets task: provide castle. Travels to world's end. Three old ladies give iron bar, three lads in box build castle. Spae wife steals and carries off castle and princess. Third old woman turns driftwood into ship and cat in order to rescue box. Cat threatens rat in kingdom of rats and rat fetches box. Scotland (Isle of Barra): Nic Leodhas SEA-SPELL 3-23.

Fa* Three Butterflies. Carpenter's apprentice opens forbidden twelve boxes, three butterflies in inner box do bidding. Bring princess to his rooms. She is trailed, he arrested, then pardoned and wed. Ifan steals butterfly box from carpenter. Carpenter tells his wife he has wrong box and trades. Wishes I. on distant isle. Old lady sends rat to take him to her sister who sends mouse to aid. M. finds box in castle. Ifan repossesses. Wales: Pugh MORE 13-28.

Fb* Lars My Lad. Prince finds nest of boxes. Paper inside says "Lars, my Lad." When read, Lars appears and does bidding. Brings princess. Wed. Lars takes back paper and they wake in hut. Prince to be hung. Lars passes and prince snatches back paper. L. restores palace. Sweden: Haviland FAVORITE..SWEDEN 60-92.

Fc* Weaver's wife finds box he has buried and opens. Thirteen flies come out and ask for work. Do work in a minute and ask for more. To be rid of them she asks them to bring the whole river with sieves. They do this and flood home. France: Manning-Sanders JON-NIKIN 47-53.

Ga* The Kindly Ghost. Man left to die in desert by brothers. He finds axe and arrow in tree and survives. Frees rat and hawk caught. Ghost of hermit (E363.5), who once lived in tree, gives bag holding its finger bones. This grants wishes. Man wishes village. Wed. Brothers steal bag. Rat and hawk recover. Africa: Manning-Sanders BOOK OF GHOSTS 103-110.

Gb* Jirimpimbira. Temba, abandoned in forest by companions, shares food with rat and hawk. Catches tiny old man in trap. Is given two magic bones. Throw on ground and say "Jirim-pimbira" and wishes will be fulfilled. Three companions steal bones, destroy T's village and make own. Rat and hawk recover. Bantu: Arnott TEMBA 52-64.

H* The Bronze Ring. Ill king to revive if certain dogs are burnt and king boiled in water with ashes of dogs thrown on king's rearranged bones. Rejuvenates as twenty year old. Bronze ring given to gardener's son as reward. Old lady whom he befriended has advised this. Weds princess. Wizard gets ring. Cat forces mice to steal back. Tail dipped in pepper and wizard sneezes. Three mice argue over who gets credit and drop ring into sea. Ring found inside fish. Asia Minor: Lang BLUE 1-14.

I* Magic Mirror. Lion asks Braian to help fight demon. The two choose magic mirror as reward from King. Four screws, turn and genies appear and bring food, house, garden, princess. Witch steals mirror and transports castle back to her father's kingdom. He is thrown into rat's cave trying to retrieve mirror but cat kills rats and rats gnaw witch to pieces and bring mirror. Latvia: Huggins BLUE 50-64.

D882.1.1. Stolen magic object stolen back by helpful cat and dog. They steal the ring from thief's mouth. Type 560. SEE ALSO: A2281.1. Nepal: Hitchcock KING 61-75. India: Jacobs INDIAN 110-122. Russia: Daniels FALCON 92-110. Poland: Zajdler POLISH 1-19. Italy: Sheehan FOLK 72-83; Lang YELLOW 192-206.

D882.1.1.1* Stolen magic object stolen back by helpful cat and dog. Mouse bites finger, etc. Italy: Haviland FAVORITE..ITALY 43-53; Hampden HOUSE 57-63; Wiggin TALES 25-29. Grimm: Grimm WORLD 367-371. Finland: Arnott ANIMAL 112-121. Congo (Luban): Burton MAGIC 29-35. Burma: Brockett BURMESE 51-62; Carpenter ELEPHANT'S 114-124; Carpenter WONDER..CATS 52-63 (cat forces fairies to give her dry path to thief's island and recovers ring, +F302.4.2.2).

D882.1.1.2* Stolen magic object stolen back by helpful cat and dog. They force mouse to gnaw through box. SEE: D882.1. China: Green ANIMAL 32-33; Manton FLYING 154-160. Korea: Anderson BOY 19-32; Carpenter KOREAN 47-54; Gruenberg MORE 125-129; Lang GREEN 47-52; Manning-Sanders CHARMS 21-33. Ghana (Akan-Ashanti): Aardema NA pb.

D882.2. Recovered magic articles dropped by rescuing animals into sea. SEE: A2471.1.2; A2494.1.2; D882.1.

D895. Magic object returned in payment for removal of magic horns. SEE: D551.1.

D900 - D1299. Kinds of magic objects.

D925.0.2.1* Wine-seller frees monkey from crab. Grateful monkey shows him pool of wine in mountains (F718.3). He tries to fill jars twice in one day and finds pool dry (D877). Japan: Uchida SEA 22-32.

D931.0.5* Magic jade assures luck. Stone shot at jaguar hits woodpecker. W. carries jade under wing. Mayan: Bowes BIRD 24-31.

D931.0.6* Magic stone is mocked by coyote. It pursues him. Heady SAGE 24-26.

D931.0.7* Stone thrown away grows and blocks path. Turns to ogre and abducts sister. Temba carves canoe which flies through air with him when he chants. Rescues sister from ogre. E. Africa: Arnott TEMBA 44-51.

980. Magic fruits and vegetables. SEE: D721.5.

D981.2. Magic peach. SEE: T543.3.2 (Momotaro); F81.1.0.1.

D981.11.1* Magic pumpkin. Old woman rides in rolling pumpkin. India: Skurzinski MAGIC pb.

D981.13. Magic bananas. SEE: D1652.1.7.2.

D983.2. Magic yam. SEE: B210.2 (Talk).

D983.2.1. Ticky-Picky Boom-Boom. Tiger chops up yams as he digs. They pursue him, stamping along in anger. Dog and duck refuse to hide T. Goat butts yams into river where they break to pieces. W. Indies: Sherlock WEST 76-83.

D1010. Magic bodily members--animal.

D1011.1.1* Magic antlers. Coyote Itsayaya hangs antlers in tree. Anyone hanging something on them will have good luck. Native American (Nez Percé): Heady TALES 86-89.

D1015.5.2* Magic stomach swallows friends to carry along. SEE: K1161.5; Z52.1.

D1030. Magic food.

D1033.2. Magic wheat. The Little Fox. Girl eating kernel of wheat before going to stepmother's house cannot be harmed. Third mornig she does not eat this and is enchanted. Little fox comes out of nut she cracks and calls her mommy. She is abandoned as a witch but little fox brings food to her, reveals truth to king (B137). Hungary: Manning-Sanders RED 98-104.

D1050. Magic Clothes.

D1050.2* Two Feathers and Turkey Brother. Magical clothing, pouch and pipe stolen and Two Feathers left in hollow tree. Spider tries to rescue and web breaks. Black snake pulls out by tail. Imposter in clothing of Two Feathers is rejected by chief's daughter. Magic pouch bites him. Attempts to imitate T.F.'s magical production of wampum produce only worms and lizards. (J2415). Native American

(Iroquois): Bruchac TURKEY 39-48. Native American (Seneca): De Wit TALKING 13-21.

D1052.2* Magic poncho. Lover emerges from under poncho when conditions are propitious. Is not to be seen at other times. Inca: Carpenter SOUTH 129-136.

D1056. Magic shirt. SEE: K2213.

D1065.3.1* Magic snowshoes. Glooscap gives magic snowshoes to imprisoned Micmac in Huron camp. He escapes and returns to rescue mother. Native American (Micmac): De Wit TALKING 192-197.

D1065.5. Magic sandals. SEE: D1521.1.1; D1520.10.1; H1132.1.5.3 (moccasins).

D1065.7.1* Magic slippers. Dwarf turned out by family is taken in by old lady with dog and cats. Dog friend advises to flee with magic flying slippers. He becomes king's messenger because of swiftness. Arabia: Manning-Sanders BOOK ..DWARFS 53-63.

D1067.1. Magic hat. SEE ALSO: D1475.4.

D1067.1.1* Magic sombrero. Boy who's stealing hides under sombrero and it sticks forever to his head. Called El Sombrerón. Guatemala: Jagendorf KING 126-131.

D1067.2.1* Magic cap enables man to understand talk of birds and plants. Japan: Uchida MAGIC 2-10.

D1076. Magic ring. SEE: B548.1; D882.1.1; D817.1.2; D1316.17.

D1076.1* King Solomon's Ring. Makes happy men sad, sad men happy. Benariah ordered to produce such a ring. Brings Solomon ring engraved "This too shall pass." Jewish: Ish-Kishor WISE 19-26.

D1081. Magic sword. SEE: D1651.2.

D1094. Magic cudgel (club). SEE: D861.1.

D1101. Magic armour. Magic armour makes wearer invincible. Christian knight thus routes Moors. Spain: Gunterman CASTLE 251-261.

D1131.1. Castle produced by magic. SEE: D871.1 (Aladdin); D882.1E (magic snuff box).

D1150. Magic furniture.

D1151.2. Magic chair. SEE: D1413.6.

D1153. Magic tables. SEE: D1472.1.7.

D1154.1. Magic bed. Mermaid holds prince captive in cave. Girl taken to rescue on whale's back. Tells him to discover meaning of runes on bed. Learns it is magic. They fly home on it. Whale restrains mermaid. Wed. Iceland: Manning Sanders BOOK..MERMAIDS 15-24.

D1162. Magic light. SEE: G610.

D1162.2.1.1* Hand-of-glory, magic candle made of criminal's hand, points out treasure and causes sleepers to sleep on. Maid sees robber using this, extinguishes by putting pot over hand. Wakens men of the house to rout robbers. England: Lurie CLEVER 53-56; Spicer 13 GHOSTS 16-23 (at Spital House on Stainmoor).

D1162.2.2* Candle of Death. Draws all who glimpse into it and they die. Ogress Grana eats. Regan, youngest of Fianna, goes with magic cap and snuffs candle. She falls in River Shannon in fury. Ireland: Spicer 13 Monsters 52-58.

D1163. Magic mirror. SEE ALSO: Z65.1 (Snow White).

D1163.1* Barber says mirror will show spots on face of any who have sinned. King to wed pure girl. Only peasant girl dares look into mirror. Portugal: Michael PORTUGUESE 28-34.

D1170. Magic utensils and implements.

D1171.1. Magic pot. D1412.2; D1615.6; D1605.1.

D1171.3.1. Magic teakettle (D612.1) is transformed badger (D421.8). When bought by priest and put on stove, head, paws and tail pop out and it cries, "Too hot." Priest returns kettle to junkman for whom grateful kettle usually dances or walks tightrope. Kettle returned in end for preservation of temple. Morinji Temple in Tatebayashi. Japan: Buck FAIRY 89-91; Haviland FAVORITE..JAPAN 23-29; Hearn JAPANESE 69-79; Lang CRIMSON 229-233 (-temple, +D1415); McAlpine JAPANESE 202-210; Manning-Sanders BOOK..MAGICAL 130-137; Novak FAIRY 131-137 (fox, turns into maiden to dance, +D612.2.1); Ross BURIED 161-172; Sakade JAPANESE 17-24; Scofield FOX 40-44 (-dancing); Uchida DANCING 3-12; Wiggin TALES 417-420.

D1172.2. Magic bowl. Magic crock fills with whatever is wished for. SEE: Z52.4.2.

D1174. Magic box. SEE: F420.6.1.3.1.

D1177. Magic spoon. SEE: N777.0.1 (magic rice paddle).

D1181. Magic needle. SEE: Z11.4; H1311.2.

D1181.1* Old woman holds out needle and boy too large to enter igloo door enters through eye of needle. +X1723. Eskimo: Cothran MAGIC 18-21; Leach NOODLES 83.

D1184. Magic thread. SEE: Z11.4.

D1185. Magic shuttle. SEE: H1311.2.

D1186. Magic spindle. SEE: H1311.2.

D1192.1* Magic purse. Fortunatus. Dame Fortune offers gift, he chooses everfull purse (D1451). Lang ROSE 34-43 (Cyprus).

D1208.1* Magic whip helps to build great wall of China. China: Carpenter TALES..CHINESE 134-141.

D1209.3. Magic plow. Given by old woman spirit of the field on condition farmer never curse again. He curses and plow leaps into river. Ireland: Spicer 13 GHOSTS 36-44.

D1210. Magic instruments.

D1211. Magic drum. SEE: D861.1; D1415.2.7; D1611D.

D1223.1. Magic flute. SEE ALSO: D1563.1.4.1.

D1223.1.1* Magic flute. Snake dances to flute playing and gives piece of gold daily. To die. Instructs Yannikas to bury him in garden and tree will bear quinces if plays a sad tune, orange if lively. Y. bets sea captain this is a quince tree..wins. Repeats. Captain gets flute and secret from wife of Y. (D861.4). Y. loses next bet. Sun aids, tells Y. to bet sun will rise in west. Does so. Greek: Wilson GREEK 68-75.

D1233. Magic violin (fiddle). SEE: D1415.2.5.

D1233.0.1* Gypsy fiddle. Gypsy sells fiddle to Devil but takes soul out before selling. D. returns it. G. keeps gold too. Hungary (Gypsy): Hampden GYPSY 155-157; Manning-Sanders GLASS 122-125.

D1233.0.2* Devil turns girl's father into fiddle, mother to bow, brothers to fiddle strings. Playing this, girl can win lover. They are taken by Devil and fiddle left behind, found by gypsies. Gypsy: Jagendorf GYPSIES' 102-106.

D1250. Miscellaneous magic objects.

D1252.3.1* Magic gold. Khang-lo asks for all he can put in bag on visit to China. Takes black gold, the mother of yellow gold. Makes bell of black gold. When struck, the golden buffalo from palace in China flies to its "mother." Viet Nam: Vo-Dinh TOAD 129-135.

D1262. Magic grinding stone. Japan: Uchida MAGIC 32-41 (Mortar, +A1115.2.1). SEE: D1601.21.

D1263. Magic mill. SEE: D1601.21.

D1274.1.1* Magic conjuring bag attacks woodpecker who steals it. He has to return it to Old Rabbit owner. U.S. (Missouri): Haviland NORTH 115-121.

D1275.4.1* Magic poem. Princess composes poem which stops river from flooding. Japan: Ozaki JAPANESE 74-86.

D1282.1. Magic knot. SEE: D2142.0.2.

D1300 - D1599. Function of magic objects.

D1310. Magic object gives supernatural information.

D1310.4. Magic object tells how another fares. SEE: E761 (life token).

D1311.2. Mirror answers questions. SEE: D1163; D1323.1; Z65.1 (Snow White).

D1313.1. Magic ball indicates road. Rolls ahead. SEE: N777; F1015.1.1; K1931.2B.

D1313.1.2.1* Girl in search of brothers follows cake made of own tears. +P253.2E. Finland: Bowman TALES 116-124.

D1313.4. Blinded trickster directed by trees. He asks them their names and by their answers he call tell where he is. He knows where each grows. Native American (Kiowa): Marriott WINTER 39-46 (Saynday with head caught in buffalo skull). Native American (Chippewa): Leekley WORLD 58-63 (Wiskedjak, jay stuck in bear skull).

D1313.17* Magic carriage always points towards the south. Invented by Chinese emperor Kotei to direct army. Japan: Ozaki JAPANESE 54-59.

D1314.1.3. Magic arrow shot to determine where to seek bride. SEE: B641.

D1314.5. Hand-of-glory indicates location of treasure. SEE: D1162.2.1.

D1316.5. Magic speaking reed (tree) betrays secret. King has whispered secret to hole in the ground. Reed growing from this hole tells his secret. SEE ALSO: E632.

D1316.5.0.2* King has servant bring him chaff to eat and warns never to tell. Servant whispers into hollow tree. Tree is made into drum. Drum says "The Great King eats chaff." Burma: Courlander TIGER'S 33-34.

D1316.5.0.3* Emperor's barber whispers to hole in ground "Emperor Trojan has goat's ears." Flutes made from three reeds from hole sing this. (cf. N465). Serbia: Lang VIOLET 46-49. Wales: Sheppard-Jones WELSH 69-71 (King March).

D1316.5.1. Voice comes forth from tree revealing truth. SEE: N271B (The Rose Bush).

D1323. Magic object gives clairvoyance.

D1323.4. Magic clairvoyant sphere. SEE: E632.0.4.

D1323.20* Spin scissors in winnowing sieve

ninety-nine times on Halloween and see man to wed. Orkney: Cutt HOGBOON 56-59.

D1330. Magic object works physical change.

D1337.1.7. Magic needle transforms a room from plainness to beauty. SEE: H1311.2.

D1338.1.1. Fountain of Youth. Water from certain fountain rejuvenates. SEE: H1331.1A (Water of Life).

D1338.1.1.2* Husband drinks at spring and becomes young. Wife imitates, drinking too much, and becomes baby. (cf. J2415). Japan: Hearn BOY 1-4; Hearn JAPANESE (Pauper) 26-36; Sakade JAPANESE CHILDREN'S STORIES 64-68. Crimea: Bulatkin EURASIAN 120-122.

D1346.7.1* Magic pill of immortality eaten by servant. Emperor orders killed but servant points out that he cannot be killed after eating pill, and if he should die then emperor will have been found to have killed over a sugar pill. China (Han Dynasty): Kendall SWEET 89-91.

D1349.2. Magic object produces immunity from old age. SEE ALSO: F420.6.1.3.1.

D1349.2.4* Fisherman's daughter takes bite of caught mermaid's shoulder. Will never age. Mermaid (B81) puts stick into sand. Will return when this takes root. Three generations tend stick. Drowned mermaid is washed up and buried by stick. It blooms into tree. Fisherman's daughter embraces tree, ages, and dies (D1890). Japan: Pratt MAGIC #1.

D1355. Love-producing magic object. SEE ALSO: D1323.20.

D1360. Magic object effects temporary change in person.

D1361.6. Magic flower renders invisible. SEE: F1015.1.1D.

D1361.12. Magic cloak of invisibility. SEE: D831.1; F1015.1.1.

D1361.14. Magic hat renders invisibility. SEE: F1015.1.1Bc.

D1361.14.1* Giant at wedding feast wears hat of invisibility (Dulde Hat) and eats all. Lad fetches Halde Hat, which enables wearer to see giant. Directs guests to stab where he points and giant is slain. Sweden: De Regniers GIANT 106-108.

D1361.15. Magic cap renders invisible. SEE: F1015.1.1Bb.

D1361.15.1. Magic turban renders invisible. SEE: F1015.1.1C.

D1361.15.2* Man knocks magic invisible hood off goblins who are eating up his ancestor offerings. He steals with hood, is caught. Merchant uses, cap is knocked off by threshers and trampled underfoot, destroyed. Korea: Kim STORY 180-185.

D1361.17.1. Magic ring renders invisible. Nanco, youngest brother, finds magic ring in seashell which makes lad invisible. He slays seven-headed beast and one-legged ogre, rescuing captives. Weds chief's daughter. Chile (Araucanian): Carpenter SOUTH 151-159.

D1361.25.2. Magic stick renders invisibility. SEE: F1015.1.1B.

D1364.4.1. Apple causes magic sleep. SEE: Z65.1 (Snow White); S12.1.

D1364.9. Comb causes magic sleep. SEE: Z65.1 (Snow White).

D1364.17. Spindle causes magic sleep. SEE: D1960.3 (Sleeping Beauty).

D1364.23. Song causes magic sleep. SEE: D830.1.1 (One-Eye, Two-Eyes, Three-Eyes).

D1375.1. Magic object causes horns to grow on person. SEE: D551.1.

D1376.1. Magic object makes nose long (restores it). SEE: D551.1.

D1376.1.3* Magic fan makes nose grow long. Badger obtains tengu's magic fan by trickery (D839.3). Makes rich man's daughter's nose long, then restores it, winning her as bride. +D1376.1.3.1. Japan: Sakade JAPANESE 73-77; Uchida SEA 33-41 (+D1376.1.3.1).

D1376.1.3.1* Badger fans self with tengu's magic fan until nose grows to sky. Nose is made into bridge over Milky Way. Workers pull him up by nose. +D1376.1.3. Japan: Sakade JAPANESE 73-77; Uchida SEA 33-41 (+D1376.1.3, fans to shorten and is raised, drops fan and remains dangling).

D1376.1.3.2* Blue-nosed tengu stretches nose into valley and fine cloth is hung on it. Withdraws nose and gathers cloth. Red-nosed tengu imitates and nose is used as swing by little boys. SEE: J2415. Japan: Sakade JAPANESE 29-34.

D1376.1.3.3* Woodcutter finds tengu's fan and uses. Nose grows. Tengu ties nose to tree and friend has to chop him loose. Japan: Pratt MAGIC #7.

D1367.1.4* Dwarf Long Nose, herb disenchants. German (Literary Tale by Wilhelm Hauf): Lang VIOLET 148-173 /Dalgliesh ENCHANTED 80-106/, /Green CLEVER 56-86/.

D1380. Magic object protects.

D1381.10. Magic armour protects from attack. SEE: Q82.3; D1101.

D1385.18.1* Magic thread protects against demons.

Man sent up haunted Louvie alp in winter escapes with life because clothing is sewn with blessed thread. Bagne Valley folk now have thread in clothing blessed on day of the Holy Agethey, Feb. 5, in church of Chables. Switzerland: Duvoisin THREE 126-129.

D1391. Magic object saves person from extinction. SEE: D1421.1.2.

D1401. Magic object overcomes person. SEE ALSO: D861.1.

D1401.1. Magic club (stick) beats person. Italy: Williams-Ellis ROUND 109-116 (given as reward for finishing song of hunchback dwarfs, F344.1).

D1401.3. Magic whip beats person. SEE: B335.2B (Jack and the Bull, magic strap and horns beat); D861.1.

D1410. Magic object renders person helpless.

D1410.4. Possession of mermaid's belt gives power over her. SEE: B18.13.11A.

D1412.1. Magic bag draws person into it. SEE: K213 (Devil in Knapsack).

D1412.2. Magic pot draws person into it. SEE: D1605.1.

D1412.1. Tree from which one cannot descend. SEE: Z111.2.1 (Death Stuck to a Tree); Q565 (Smith and Devil).

D1413.6. Chair to which person sticks. SEE: Q565 (Smith and Devil). SEE ALSO: Z111.2 (Misery's Enchanted Chair).

D1413.17. Magic adhesive stone. Makes all who poke in the fire stick and say "Fiddevav." Old woman gives stone to lad. To say "thanks" to anything asked in house and put stone in fire. Reward for stopping charm. He removes stone and wins daughter of household. Type 593. (cf. C495.3). Denmark: Hatch MORE 138-149; Haviland FAVORITE..DENMARK 15-26.

D1413.17.1* Lad puts paper charm under table leg in inn. All must sing chant "Six plus four makes ten in this robber's den, cheating honest men." Stops and weds innkeeper's daughter. Welsh: Pugh TALES 47-59.

D1415. Magic object compels person to dance. +D1171.3.1. Japan: Lang CRIMSON 229-233 (dancing kettle). SEE ALSO: D2174.

D1415.2. Magic musical instrument causes person to dance. SEE: F348.7.1.3 (fairy harp); Z111.6 (bell).

D1415.2.1. Magic horn causes dancing. Type 592. James the Huntsman. Dwarf gives reward for moving cow from dwarf's hole. To choose plainest horn, gun and horse in palace of dwarf's father, dwarf king. Gun kills all, horn causes all to dance. Bird advises to free a princess and prince. Dwarf king is forced to twirl on nose, dancing until he frees princess. Lad gives horn and gun back in exchange for disenchantment of the horse--really a prince. Hatch THIRTEEN DANISH 3-15.

D1415.2.3.1* Magic flute causes dancing. The Prince and the Sky-Blue Filly. Stepmother turns out prince. Hermit gives magic flute. Makes giant dance until gives back sheep, gives over suit of armour, magic sword and sky-blue filly. Rescues stepsister from dragon. Dragon dances until shrinks away. Weds stepsister. Yugoslavia: Manning-Sanders BOOK..PRINCES 14-27.

D1415.2.3.2* Shepherd's magic flute (pipe). Sheep dance. Cruel mistress (master) must dance, all who come along dance too. Still dancing. Bulgaria: Pridham GIFT 16-20. Spain: Boggs THREE 119-124.

D1415.2.3.3* Boy gives oranges to St. Peter and Christ. Given magic flute. Makes donkeys carrying pottery dance. Break pots. Judge must dance. Judge's old mother dances. He is forgiven. Portugal: Lowe LITTLE 44-46.

D1415.2.3.4* Shepherd plays and sheep dance, master and wives are danced to death, oxen dance over cliff, Cadi and court dance to death. Shepherd takes over houses and sheep of Cadi and master. Rich. Returns flute to Jinn's cave where found. Algeria: Carpenter AFRICAN 145-152.

D1415.2.3.5* Boy understands language of birds and beasts (B216). Taught magic words to make things stick to spot or dance (H341.1). Herds cows thus. Causes Khan and family to stick together. Plays flute and says magic word and they dance out of land. Russia (Altai): Ginsburg LITTLE pb.

D1415.2.4.1* Magic pipe causes dancing. Dead mother gives son reed pipes, blow first and tears vanish, second--laugh, third--dance. Cows dance, passing king dances. Sends to kidnapper of king's daughters. Makes dance until daughters returned. Weds. Latvia: Huggins BLUE 7-14.

D1415.2.4.2* Blind lad pipes and all dance. Creatures of sea join dance. He goes under sea with mermaid who promises him sight. Ireland: Manning-Sanders BOOK..MERMAIDS 59-65.

D1415.2.5. Magic fiddle causes dancing. SEE ALSO: K671.1; N150.4.

D1415.2.5.1* Freddy and His Fiddle. Type 592. Lad underpaid for years of work gives last three pennies to three beggars, really same in disguise, given three wishes. Fiddle that causes dancing. Gun that never misses. Inability to answer "no" to his first question. Sends former master into thorns for magpie he shoots and fiddles so that master dances in thorns. To be hung, asks to play fiddle as last request

(K551.3.1). All must dance. He leaves. Norway: Arbuthnot ANTHOLOGY 249-251; Arbuthnot FAIRY 87-90; Asbjornsen EAST (Row) 85-92; Asbjornsen NORWEGIAN 61-66; Dobbs MORE 49-62 (-dance in thorns); Manning-Sanders BOOK..DWARFS 14-24; Undset TRUE 190-197. Germany: Grimm HOUSE 81-94.

D1415.2.5.2* Viet, unjustly accused of murder, plays violin as last request. All must dance. Accusers dance to death. Origin St. Vitus dance. Luxembourg: Courlander RIDE 169.

D1415.2.6.1. Magic lute causes animals to dance. Psaltry that plays by itself taken as reward. He has to give most precious thing in his house in return and finds father dead when goes home. Pigs dance when plays for swineherd and princess demands a dancing pig. Must show legs to obtain. He tells where her birthmark is (on leg) and wins contest to wed (H525). Russia: Whitney IN 79-82.

D1415.2.7* Magic Drum. Three younger brothers take advantage of older brother who is slow but strong. When head chief threatens them, older brother carves a drum and hides three brothers in it. Plays drum and wild animals met dance. Chief and warriors dance until peaceful. Umpume is rewarded with gun gift. Brothers are grateful. Congo (Luban): Burton MAGIC 19-24.

D1415.2.7.1* Tiger comes from wood and dances to hand drum inheritance of younger brother. King buys. +K335.1.1.4. Korea: Jewett WHICH 136-157; Kim STORY 186-198.

D1415.3* Bird's singing causes people to dance. Uganda: Serwadda SONGS 21-25.

D1420. Magic object draws person.

D1421.1.2. Magic fire-steel summons genie. The Blue Light. Witch sends old soldier into well for blue light. He refuses to hand it up and she leaves him there in anger. He lights pipe with the blue light and little man appears, leads to freedom, shows witch's treasure. He had little man bring princess to his rooms. She is followed, he jailed. Last request (K551) to smoke, sends for his pipe and light, has blue man beat all. King gives kingdom and daughter. SEE ALSO: D871.1 (Aladdin). Grimm: Grimm BROTHERS 133-138; Grimm GRIMM'S (Follett) 33-40; Grimm GRIMM'S (Grosset) 209-213; Grimm GRIMM'S (World) 318-323. Andersen: Lang YELLOW 266-275; Manning-Sanders BOOK ..MAGICAL 49-60; Opie CLASSIC 206-215.

D1421.1.5. Magic lamp summons genie. SEE: D871.1 (Aladdin).

D1421.1.6. Magic ring summons genie. SEE: D871.1 (Aladdin).

D1425.1. Magic spindle brings back prince for heroine. SEE: H1311.2.

D1427.1. Magic pipe compels one to follow. Pied Piper of Hamelin. France: Lang RED 217-224 (Hamel, Germany)/Lang FIFTY 235-240/. England: Jacobs MORE 1-6. Germany: Baumann PIED pb; Holme TALES 120-127.

D1427.1.1* Wicked Banikan is given power to bewitch children one day of each year. B. sings and children must follow dancing into jungle (D1781). Philippines: Sechrist ONCE 28-31.

D1441.1.2. Magic pipe (whistle) calls animals together. Hungary: Harper GHOSTS 212-221 (+H341.1Aa). SEE ALSO: H1045 (Sack of lies); H1112 (herding horses).

D1445.2. Magic spear kills animals. SEE: D1602.6.

D1450. Magic object furnishes treasure. SEE ALSO: B100 (Treasure Animal).

D1451. Inexhaustible purse furnishes money. SEE: D812.15 (Swamp maiden's gift); N250.5 (God of Poverty); D551.1; D1192.

D1451.3* Magic string of cash is self-replacing. Cash from King's treasury fly to string. Korea: Carpenter KOREAN 165-172.

D1454.1.2. Jewels from hair. Type 403. SEE: Q2.1.1A.

D1454.2. Treasure falls from mouth. SEE ALSO: Q2.1.1A.

D1454.2.0.1* Basia, the babbler. Mermaid rescued by fisherman gives his wife reward. Penny drops with every word--too many. Changes to gold coin for every day of silence--too hard. Two gold coins for every sensible sentence-- just right. Poland: Borski GOOD 41-45.

D1454.4.2. Jewels from tears. SEE: Q2.1.1.

D1469.18* Magic nosebag. Seller tells dupe not to annoy magic nosebag or it will stop providing. It stops and dupe thinks it is annoyed and buys donkey for it. He always buys a nosebag for his donkey when it is annoyed. Iran: Shah MULLAH 58-59.

D1470. Magic object as provider. SEE: D1601.21.

D1470.1. Magic wishing object. Object causes wishes to be fulfilled. SEE: D551.1.

D1470.1.9. Magic wishing cloth. SEE: D861.1.

D1470.1.15. Magic wishing ring. SEE: H1385.3; D882.1.1B; D882.2.

D1470.1.16. Magic wishing lamp. SEE: D871.1 (Aladdin).

D1470.1.46. Magic wishing hammer. SEE: N777.0.3 (rice pounder); F535.1.0.1 (Momotaro).

D1470.2.1. Provisions received from magic tree. SEE: R221.

D1472.1.3.3* Magic food-producing twigs. Obtained in town of animals by orphan driven out by men. Yoruba: Fuja FOURTEEN 156-179.

D1472.1.7. Magic table supplies food and drink. SEE: D861.1B.

D1472.1.8. Magic tablecloth supplies food and drink. SEE: D861.1A.

D1472.1.9. Magic pot supplies food and drink. SEE: D1171.1.

D1472.1.24.5* Rice from stroking cat's fur. Three daughters of scholar thus supported in his absence. Korea: Carpenter KOREAN 157-162.

D1472.2.12* Gold knob or spindle rolls away. Man accuses troll Kidmus of taking it, receives cow that never goes dry in return. Asks for more. Given oatmeal to make porridge, makes more than couple can ever eat. Asks troll for ladder to reach heaven so can take porridge to St. Peter. Ladder sways and the couple fall with their porridge. Type 563. Iceland: Manning-Sanders BOOK..OGRES 38-43.

D1473.1. Magic wand furnishes clothes. SEE: R221 (Cinderella).

D1475.1. Magic soldier-producing horn. SEE: D551.1.

D1475.4. Magic soldier-producing hat. SEE: D861.1G MacManus; D1067.1.

D1485.1. Magic shuttle makes carpet. SEE: H1311.2.

D1487.3.1* Kin Kin, smallest forest bird, sings, telling King of Forest to repair ravages of animals trying to build garden. Sings jungle back each night. Cat kills. Yoruba: Fuja FOURTEEN 140-145.

D1500. Magic object controls disease.

D1500.3.1. Charm shifts disease to another person.

D1500.3.1.2* Friend lends her beauty to leprous friend, Lilas, at night. Lilas elopes leaving Seraphine a leper. S. seeks L. and grasps her hand. Their traits are re-exchanged. Lilas is left leprous. Haiti: Thoby-Marcelin SINGING 100-103.

D1505.5. Magic water restores sight. SEE: N452.

D1520. Magic object affords miraculous transportation. SEE ALSO: F1015.1.1 Pridham (frying pan); D551.1 (cloak).

D1520.6. Magic transportation by cloak (cape). SEE: D555.1.

D1520.10.1. Magic transportation by sandals. Inca: Newman FOLK 13-18 (Sun god gives to Hualachi).

D1520.10.2* Magic brogues walk man into lake so water demon can entrap. +G561.C. Finland: Fillmore SHEPHERD 40-52.

D1520.15. Transportation in magic ship. SEE: F601.2; H341.1; F1015.1.1Bc (Magic fast traveling boat carries to Brazil).

D1521.1. Seven-league boots. Boots with miraculous speed. SEE: K1611C (Hop of my Thumb).

D1521.1.1. Sandals with magic speed. God Pachacámac gives magic sandals to Hualachi, Quipu carrier in Cuzco. Peru (Inca): Courlander RIDE 220-223; Newman FOLK 13-18.

D1521.1.2* Magic slippers cause disaster when stolen. Udmurt: Ginsburg STRIDING pb.

D1532.11. Magic journey in flying boat. SEE: D1533.1.1.

D1532.14* Magic frying pan flies. SEE: F1015.1.1 Pridham.

D1533.1.1. Magic land and water ship. SEE: F601.2A; H341.1.

D1543.7. Magic calabash (gourd) controls winds. SEE: A1124.

D1550. Magic object miraculously opens and closes.

D1552.2. Mountain opens to magic formula. SEE: N455.3 (Open Sesame).

D1553. Symplegades. Rocks that clash together at intervals. SEE ALSO: H1385 Ff; F601.2Ea.

D1553.1* Mountains that clap together at intervals and kill birds who must pass between. +A2378.4.7.1. Eskimo (Hooper Bay): Gillham BEYOND 1-16; Gillham BEYOND 31-34 /Gruenberg MORE 113-118/. Eskimo: Caswell SHADOWS 64-67.

D1553.2* Swinging gate at end of world. Native American (Nisqually): Matson LEGENDS 24-28.

D1553.3* Girl enticed between clashing rocks by "la vieja capusa." Father sees her playing outside of rock one day and throws stone between rocks to make them snap shut behind her. Peru: Jagendorf KING 238-241.

D1556.3* Saynday amuses self in tree by calling "open" and "close." Magpie calls "tree close in and hold him tight." Aggravated tree complies. Native American: Marriott WINTER 54-60.

D1560. Magic object performs other services for owner.

D1563.1.4.1* Magic flute (D1223.1) played causes fields to prosper. King has crops destroyed--flute restores. Flute causes palace to rise. King must stand seven years in sun and rain before wed. King forgets injunction and touches girl. She turns into tree. Tries again Third time wins her. Meanwhile his kingdom is lost. The old peasant, in reality a magician, now restores king's youth (Twenty-one years have passed = 3x7) and reconquers kingdom. Italy: Baker GOLDEN 89-100.

D1563.2.1. Magic chain renders orchard barren. SEE: N452B.

D1571.1. Magic ashes revivify trees (J2415.21). Dog (B182.1) shows old man where to dig for treasure. Neighbor borrows dog (J2415) and digs up refuse or bones, kills dog (B335). Old man plants tree over grave, dreams dog says to make mortar of tree. Magic mortar turns rice to gold. Neighbor borrows, rice turns to putrefying refuse. He burns mortar. Old man sprinkles ashes on cherry trees and they blossom. Daimyo is pleased and rewards. Neighbor tries and is punished for throwing ashes at daimyo. Japan: Buck FAIRY 281-285; Carpenter WONDER DOGS 136-149; Lang VIOLET 121-128; McAlpine JAPANESE 95-105; Matsutani HOW pb; Novak FAIRY 184-190 (rice increases for good, diminishes in mortar for bad); Ozaki JAPANESE 177-188; Sakade JAPANESE 87-93; Uchida DANCING 147-156.

D1600 - D1699. Characteristics of magic objects.

D1600. Automatic object.

D1601.5.3* Magic golden apple beats enemy until nothing left but dust. Obtained from werewolf and used on him. Rumania: Ure RUMANIAN 65-68.

D1601.10.1. Self-cooking pot. SEE: C916.3 (obeys only one master); Q82.3.

D1601.14. Self-chopping axe. SEE: H1115.1.

D1601.16. Self-digging spade. SEE: H1115.1.

D1601.21. Self-grinding mill. Grinds whatever owner wishes. SEE: Z52.4.2.

D1601.21.1. Self-grinding salt mill. SEE: A1115.2 (why sea is salt); D1651.3.1 (obeys only master).

D1602.6. Self-returning spear. Jealous wife gives magic potion to chief's favorite son and he becomes constantly hungry. Grown, he meets old woman who cuts him open in sleep and removes tumor, curing him. She gives magic spear. Sprinkle it with cardamon before throwing and will return. He forgets the cardamon and it is carried off by an elephant in side. Following he reaches the sea and meets first white men coming to trade. W. Africa: Aardema MORE 26-31.

D1605. Magic thieving object. Steals for master.

SEE: K301.3.

D1605.1. Magic thieving pot. Boy sells pot to neighbors and when they have put things into it pot returns to the boy. Type 591. Often poor man and rich man. In the end pot carries rich man off. Denmark: Arbuthnot ANTHOLOGY 235-236; Association TOLD..GREEN 81-87; Coombs MAGIC pb; Haviland FAVORITE..DENMARK 3-13; Hatch THIRTEEN 16-24; Hutchinson FIRESIDE 93-103; Manning-Sanders BOOK.. DEVILS 9-14.

D1610. Magic speaking objects. SEE: B210.1.1.

D1610.34.1. Fiddle (flute, drum) made from wood to which secret has been confided. Reveals it. SEE: D1316.5.

D1610.35. Speaking river. SEE: B210.1.1.

D1611. Magic object answers for fugitive. Left behind to impersonate fugitive and delay pursuit. SEE: D671 (Transformation Flight); D672 (Obstacle Flight); F53.1; G530.2 (Master-Maid).

D1612.5.2. Magic harp gives alarm when it is stolen. SEE: F54.2.

D1615.6.1* Pots dance and sing while potter is gone. Has to break pots. Throws away stirring stick. It sings "your magic stick is drowning" and he realizes what bewitched pots. E. Africa: Heady WHEN 36-41.

D1620. Magic automata.

D1620.1.4. Statue of Virgin sews for suppliant. SEE: D1623.2.

D1622.2.1* Hunchback carves crib for Christ Child. Babe smiles, Mary smiles. Brittany: Sawyer LONG 135-150.

D1622.2.2* Clockmaker spends year on clock for Christ Child. Sells to aid sick neighbor. Child reaches down to accept apple offered by clockmaker. Sawyer THIS 51-60.

D1622.2.3* Bernardino saves money for pilgrimage to Bethlehem several times. Each time some pressing need takes his savings. Last Christmas Eve animals lead him to chapel and he finds the Babe in the manger there. B. is found dead surrounded by animals. Hand as if clenched around baby's. Monks carve creche scene in his memory = first creche. Spain (Cantabria): Sawyer WAY 85-96.

D1623.2* Virgin given material for new robes by friar. He repainted her but doesn't know how to sew. She sews own robes. Later also makes wedding gown for poor neighbor girl and lace mantilla of spiderwebs. Spain (Seville): Sawyer WAY 229-236.

D1626.1. Artificial flying horse. Carpenter builds flying machine for son. Prince tries it and falls off. Woos princess there and flies off

with her. SEE: K1346. Ceylon: Tooze WONDERFUL 15-25. China: Chang CHINESE 12-19. Persia: Adams BOOK..ENCHANTMENT 201-230.

D1635. Golem. Automatic statue animated by insertion of written magic formula into opening. Jewish: Serwer LET'S 39-54.

D1640. Other automatic objects.

D1641.2.1.1* Pious man polishes marble block until smooth. Unable to move it to Jerusalem. Elijah the prophet and his five angels appear and help him move it. Is transported in a rush to Temple in Zion. Jewish: Baker TALKING 232-235.

D1641.13.1* Coffin moves itself. Cat causes coffin of rich man's grandmother to rise in air. Only monk who befriended her kittens can say spell to lower it. He is rewarded. +B522.1.1. Japan: Novak FAIRY 72-80.

D1650. Other characteristics of magic objects.

D1651.2.1* Magic sword responds only to magic commands. Mows down friends as well as enemies when Anansi forgets command to stop sword. Ashanti: Courlander HAT 88-92.

D1651.3. Magic cooking pot obeys only master. Pyle WONDER 123-133. SEE ALSO: C916.3.

D1651.3.1* Magic mill (D1601.2.21.1) obeys only master. Rich brother buys, then has to pay poor brother to take it back, as it floods house with herrings and chowder. SEE ALSO: A1115.2 (Why sea is salt); C916.3 (porridge). (cf. J2415). Lang BLUE 148-153; Wiggin TALES 291-295; Williams-Ellis ROUND 130-144. Denmark: Baker TALKING 104-112; Undset TRUE 149-155. Japan: Sakade JAPANESE CHILREN'S STORIES 43-46; Uchida MAGIC 32-41 (mortar).

D1651.3.1.1* Magic mill obeys only master. Poor brother has been told to take his bacon and go to the devil. He is given the mill for the bacon there. Ship captain buys and mill sinks ship. Why sea is salt (A1115.2). Latvia: Huggins BLUE 85-92 (oatmeal). Norway: Arbuthnot ANTHOLOGY 287-288; Asbjornsen EAST (Row) 139-144; Asbjornsen NORWEGIAN 108-111; D'Aulaire EAST 38-44; Gruenberg FAVORITE 418-421; Haviland FAVORITE..NORWAY 30-44.

D1651.3.1.2* Fisherman exchanges King of the Fishes caught for brother's handmill, on advice of wee man. It grinds salt, he prospers. Wife demands ever grander goods (B375.1). Sea captain buys it from servant. Sinks ship as he cannot stop it. Why sea is salt. Great Britain: Finlay TATTERCOATS 9-14.

D1651.4. Inexhaustible pitcher stops pouring only at owner's command. Pyle WONDER 123-133.

D1651.15* Self-hoeing hoe obeys only master. Kotoko, porcupine, chants and hoe works. Anansi steals but doesn't learn the word to stop hoe. Hoe hoes clear across sea to country of white people. They make more like it and bring them and cross the sea to sell to the Ashanti. Ashanti: Courlander HAT 86-87.

D1651.16* Do-all ax clears, plows, plants and cuts in three days. Stolen, it runs amuck as thief doesn't know chant to stop it. U.S.South: Courlander TERRAPIN'S 80-83.

D1652.1. Inexhaustible food. SEE ALSO: D1601.21 (mill).

D1652.1.7.2. Magic banana skin always full of fruit. +B31.1.3. Hawaii: Berry MAGIC 13-21.

D1652.1.7.3* Self-replenishing pear. Obtained by climbing on statue of Buddha to reach. Climbs into nostril and Buddha sneezes. Korea: Jewett WHICH 41-46.

D1652.1.8.3* Badger seeks Glooskap's inexhaustible tallow at direction of Green Giant. Native American (Micmac): De Wit TALKING 197-203.

D1652.5.4. Inexhaustible pitcher. Pyle WONDER 123-133 (blessed by saint).

D1652.5.7. Inexhaustible pot. Pyle WONDER 123-133 (blessed by saint).

D1652.5.7.1* Magic pot duplicates anything put in it including wife, etc. China: Ritchie TREASURE 142-154 /Child Study Association CASTLES 291-299/, /Arbuthnot ANTHOLOGY 333-334/, /Colwell MAGIC 118-123/.

D1652.5.8. Inexhaustible food basket. Wales: Sheppard-Jones WELSH 131-133.

D1652.5.10. Inexhaustible rice-stores. SEE: Q82.3 (inexhaustible rice bag).

D1652.8. Inexhaustible cloth. SEE: Q82.3.

D1653.1.7. Infallible gun. SEE: D1415.2.5A.

D1654.0.1. Magic immovability of saints (or their possessions). SEE: V128.0.1.

D1654.8.1. Sacred image impossible to remove from the spot. SEE: V120.0.1.

D1658.1.5. Apple tree grateful for being shaken. SEE: Q2.1.2Cb.

D1658.2.1. Grateful stone. SEE: Q2.1.2Cb.

D1658.3.4. Grateful objects help fugitive. SEE: Q2.1 (Kind and Unkind Girls); G530.2L (Master Maid).

D1662.4* Magic Meerschaum pipe summons St. Nicholas when stroked on Christmas Eve. U.S.: Arbuthnot FAIRY 191-196.

D1700 - D1799. Possession and means of employment of magic powers.

D1710. Possession of magic powers.

D1711.0.1.1* Magician's Apprentice. Type 325. Lad secretly surpasses magician's skills. Returned home, he has father sell him as animal. The bridle must be retained (D535). The magician buys, keeping the bridle, and boy cannot resume form. Somehow the lad gets the bridle off and a transformation contest ensues (D615.2). Usually bird, fish, gold ring on princess' finger, final transformation lad changes to grains of corn, magician to cock to eat them, lost grain to fox. Africa: Manning-Sanders BOOK..WIZARDS 22-25 (ends with both as snake, draw) /Manning-Sanders CHOICE 276-279/. Argentina: Carpenter SOUTH 71-82. Finland: Bowman TALES 141-146. Germany (Grimm): Gag MORE 197-205 /Gag SORCERER'S pb/, Child Study Association CASTLE 127-133/. Greece: Wilson GREEK 1-8. Norway: Manning-Sanders BOOK..WIZARDS 47-57; Undset TRUE 97-107 (+ father seeks lad taken by Farmer Weathersky). Portugal: Lowe LITTLE 75-80; Pyle WONDER CLOCK 51-61. Serbia: Garner CAVALCADE.. GOBLINS 105-114; Spicer THIRTEEN DEVILS 7-18 (devil). South America: Hardendorff FROG'S 131-140. Spain: Boggs THREE 127-131.

D1711.0.1.1.1* Two friends learn trades. Their families are stolen meanwhile. One who studied magic turns self to ring for friend to sell to thieves. Never let fall into hands of a Setta (magician). Thus money is stolen back from thieves and family of friend redeemed. Friend now sells as horse to Setta. Transformation battle ensues as above. Upper Volta: Guirma TALES 45-56.

D1711.0.1.2* Sorcerer's Apprentice reads forbidden book, calls up Beelzebub. Must set task. "Water the plants." He cannot stop watering. (cf. J2411.4). England: Jacobs ENGLISH 74-77; Williams-Ellis FAIRY..BRITISH 181-185. Westmoreland: Colwell ROUND 27-29. Russia: Littledale GHOSTS 21-25. Cook SORCERER'S pb.; Rostron SORCERER'S pb; Weil SORCERER'S pb.

D1711.0.1.3* Magician's apprentice never to show off skill. Can walk through walls. Brags of this and runs at wall. Knocks self out. China: Wyndham TALES..CHINA 67-72.

D1711.0.1.4* Lame gardener boy, son of wizard, reads forbidden book and causes flowers to sing and birds dance for visiting king. This king is horrified and refuses war alliance sought. Enemy king, however, on hearing of this marvel refuses to attack such a country. Wales: Pugh MORE 29-37.

D1711.1.1. Solomon as master of magicians. (King Solomon legends are listed here but not described.) Jewish: Baker TALKING 218-231; Ish-Kishor CARPET (The Carpet of Solomon);

Serwer LET'S 22-28 ("The Wind and the Ant")'
Serwer LET'S 9-17 ("King of the Demons and
the Worm Shamir"). SEE ALSO: H540.2.1 (bee
shows answer to Sheba's riddle).

D1711.6.3. Taoist priests as magicians. China:
Birch CHINESE 80-88.

D1711.6.4. St. Mary of Trefrew sent in guise of
beggar as wizard in Prince Llewellyn's party so
that Prince has wizard the equal of King John's.
Wales: Sheppard-Jones WELSH 137-141.

D1711.6.5. Friar Bacon (Roger Bacon 1214-1292)
as magician. In collaboration with Friar Bungay
makes head of brass. Must hear it when it
speaks or all is lost. Servant to wake them
fails. Head speaks: "Time Is" "Time Was"
"Time Past." Breaks. Britain: Williams-Ellis
FAIRY..BRITISH 186-195.

D1711.6.6. St. Cadog to send 100 cows for each
of King Arthur's soldiers slain by Ligersawe in
order to redeem latter. Half-way across river
cows turn to bales of hay. Wales: Sheppard-
Jones WELSH 152-155.

D1720. Acquisition of magic powers.

D1720.1. Man given power of wishing.

D1720.1.2* Volkh given six wishes for self, three
for Prince Danilo. They work only when wished
for other person. Russia: Colwell SECOND 46-
56.

D1720.1.3* Fairy offers weaver wish if will stop
cutting tree. Wife says ask for extra head and
hands so can do twice as much work. Is taken
for a demon and killed. India: Ryder PAN-
CHATANTRA 449-452.

D1720.1.4* Lad cuts branches to shade sleeping
maids and fairies reward with wishes granted.
Wishes bundle of sticks would carry him home.
Princess laughs. Wishes she were wed to him.
King has them sealed in a barrel and set adrift.
He wishes barrel were ship, ship a castle, self
handsome. Italy (Naples): Hampden HOUSE
111-118.

D1720.1.5* Day Dreamer. Fish offers lad three
wishes. He absent-mindedly wishes bucket
would carry self home. Climbing pear tree he
wishes could see whole kingdom and tree carries him about. Passes princess's window and
wishes could wed her and have son. She bears
child, king lets child choose father to wed princess. He tosses ball to lad. Wed. Sweden:
Owen CASTLE 147-154.

D1724. Magic power from Death. Death as godfather. Death at head of bed. Death as godmother warns not to cure princess. Godfather
Devil has shown arts of healing. Death shows
candle of princess is nearly out. Hero tries to
light a new one for her and drops it putting
out another candle--his own (E765.1.3). SEE
ALSO: D1825.3.1. Puerto Rico: Alegria

THREE 52-55.

D1760. Means of producing magic power.

D1761. Magic results produced by wishing. SEE:
D1720.1.

D1781. Magic results from singing. SEE: D830.1.1
(One-Eye, Two-Eyes, Three-Eyes); D1427.1.1.
(children follow); F601.2Ga (sleep); T543.3.2
(object drawn to shore by song).

D1782.3. Magic results from loosening knots.
SEE: D2142.1.2.

D1800 - D2199. Manifestations
of magic power.

D1810. Magic knowledge.

D1810.8.5* Feigned knowledge from dream.
Anansi claims "old hag" will trouble any who
brings gifts to her. To leave them in Anansi's
yard. W. Indies: Sherlock ANANSI 20-29.

D1812.3.3.2.1* Fortune-telling dream. Student
sleeping on priest's porcelain pillow crawls inside pillow and finds self in wealthy future
about to be beheaded. Awakes content with
current lot. China: Wyndham TALES..CHINA
14-19. Vietnam: Schultz VIETNAMESE 90-92.

D1812.3.3.5.2* Prophetic dreams allegorical.
Serpent interprets. U.S. (Georgia): Manning-
Sanders BOOK..MAGICAL BEASTS 65-68.

D1820. Magic sight and hearing.

D1821. Means of acquiring magic sight. SEE:
D1331.

D1821.3.11* Magic sight by looking through
wolf's eyelashes. Can see real humans and
those with animal heads. Japan: Novak FAIRY
174-183.

D1825.3.1. Magic power of seeing Death at head
or foot of bed and thus forecasting progress of
sickness. SEE: D1724 (Death as Godfather);
K213 (Devil in Knapsack).

D1825.3.1.1* Man granted power to see death at
head or foot of bed turns bed, thus saving pa-
tient. Wales: Pugh TALES 21-28 (+K717.5).
Poland: Wojciechowska WINTER 8-21
(+E765.1.3). Dominican Republic: Carter
GREEDY 9-13 (+E765.1.3, +K213D). USSR
(Byelorussia): Courlander RIDE 145-153. U.S.
(Appalachia): Chase JACK 172-179.

D1825.3.1.1.1* Godfather Death (D1724). Man
refuses God as godfather. God gives to the
rich and leaves poor hungry--unjust. Refuses
Devil--deceiver. Chooses Death--the equalizer.
As gift godson is shown healing herb to use
when Death stands at head of bed. Bed is
turned. Taken to place of burning candle.
Death drops his candle and extinguishes.

(E765.1.3). Germany (Grimm): Grimm BROTH-ERS 97-101; Grimm JUNIPER V.2 228-235.

D1825.3.1.1.2* Tinker of Tamlacht. God refused as godfather--unfair. Death taken. Rewarded with bottle of loc Slainte (Ointment of Health) to be used if Death stands at foot of bed. Bed turned. +Q565Af. Ireland: MacManus HIBER-NIAN 10-24 /Hoke SPOOKS 97/.

D1825.3.1.1.3* Drinking with Death. Lad with keg of beer refuses to drink with Providence (Lord). Lord treats men unequally. Drinks with death who treats all equally (J486.1). Death causes keg to be always full, gives power to heal sick if death at foot of bed. Turns bed. (K557). Devil takes him. Wait until I say the Lord's Prayer. Never says it (K551.1.0.1). Death hangs written prayer over bed and lad reads it on waking without thinking. Taken by death. Norway: Asbjornsen NORWEGIAN 131-134; Undset TRUE 132-136.

D1840. Magic invulnerability.

D1840.1.4* Asura King, Hitanyaksipù, conquers gods and rules over the three worlds. Brahma has promised neither man, beast nor god will kill him. He will not die at night or day, in-side or outside of palace. At twilight on porch, Vishnu strikes him down. India: Reed TALK-ATIVE 89-99.

D1841.4.3.3* Boy who sleeps all day abandoned on rock in ocean by two sweethearts. Gone-Down-To-The-Sea walks on water to him. Takes to dance at Land of Many Souls, walking there on water. Returns with gifts and wishes girls turned to stone. Native American (Wiyot): Curtis GIRL 35-41.

D1860. Magic beautification. SEE: Q2.1.

D1890. Magic aging. SEE: D1349.2.4 (Bite of mermaid keeps from aging); D2011; F377; F420.6.1.3 (Urashima Taro).

D1898. Morning star vows she will age if taken from her lover Gray Elk. She does so. White deer leads her away to new home by Redfish Lake with Gray Elk. Native American (Sho-shone): Heady SAGE 89-94.

D1899* Magic aging--miscellaneous.

D1899.1* Girl held prisoner in Finfolkaheem is rescued by fisherman. Ages and dies in a day when returned to land. Was imprisoned until "iron floats." Ship had just been launched--iron floated. Orkney: Cutt HOGBOON 152-158.

D1960.1. Seven sleepers. (Rip Van Winkle). Magic sleep extending over many years. Type 673. Washington Irving: Rackham ARTHUR 246-265 (Rip Van Winkle). Field AMERICAN 77-107. Germany (Grimm): Grimm GRIMM'S (Grosset) 220-227 (Karl Katz, sets bowling pins for dwarfs, drinks, twenty years sleep). SEE

ALSO: D2011 (years thought days); F377 (supernatural lapse of time in fairyland).

D1960.1.1* Man disobeys tabu and crosses lake after dark. Thunderbird carries to nest. Falls asleep. Wakes thirty years later. Native Amer-ican (Ojibway): Cunningham TALKING 24-29.

D1960.1.2* Man digs buried hiaqua on top of Mount Tacoma. Twelve otters surround him and tap tails at every thirteenth stroke as he digs. He fails to give hiaqua offering to Elk Spirit Stone and is surrounded by angry spirits. Falls unconscious, wakes to find self aged. Reforms and becomes great Medicine Man. Native Amer-ican (Squallyamish): Cothran WITH 67-75.

D1960.1.3* Taoist magician Ch'en T'uan sleeps for eight hundred years. China: Birch CHIN-ESE 80-88.

D1960.2. Kyffhäuser. King asleep in mountain (Barbarossa, King Marko, Halger Danske, etc). Will awake one day to succor his people. SEE ALSO: E502. Scotland: Nic Leodhas GHOSTS GO 103-112 (old Kings of Dailriadgh-Fergus, Angus, Lorne and six sons).

D1960.2.2* King Arthur. Welshman cuts hazel staff. Man asks where he cut it. Spot is where King Arthur and Knights lie in cave. He may take as much gold as he can carry. Tabu on touching bell. If bell is touched Knights will wake and ask "It it time?", must answer "No. Sleep on." Returns again and makes wrong reply. Is beaten and tossed out. Never finds spot again. Wales: Colwell SECOND 133-138; Frost LEGENDS 19-25; Sheppard-Jones WELSH 19-25. England (Cheshire): Colwell Round 15-18 (man wants to buy horse, takes to cave of sleeping warriors). Sleigh NORTH 207-215.

D1960.2.3* Lad finds cave where Arthur sleeps but fails to complete charm. Draws sword and cuts garter but fails to blow bugle. Great Brit-ain: Finlay TATTERCOATS 100-110.

D1960.3. Sleeping Beauty. Magic sleep for a definite period (e.g. a hundred years). Type 410.

A* Briar Rose variant. Frog tells bathing queen she will bear daughter. One of fourteen fairies not invited to christening as there are only thirteen golden plates. She curses baby to prick finger on spindle at age fifteen and die (F361.1.1). One fairy has not yet bestowed wish. She softens curse. To sleep for one hundred years. Attempts to burn all spinning wheels fail. Briar Rose pricks finger on spin-dle and falls into magic sleep. Entire castle sleeps. Protective hedge allows no one to enter. After one hundred years, hedge opens for hero who wakes her with a kiss, thus disenchanting castle (D735). Germany (Grimm): Dalgliesh Enchanted 226-230; Darrell ONCE 51-54; Gag MORE 31-41; Grimm BROTHERS 39-42; Grimm GRIMM'S (Follett) 186-191; Grimm GRIMM'S (Grossett) 101-106; Grimm GRIMM'S (Scribners)

D. MAGIC

140-143; Grimm GRIMM'S (World) 34-37; Grimm HOUSEHOLD 204-207; Grimm SLEEPING (illus. Hoffman) pb; Grimm SLEEPING (illus. Hutton) pb; Grimm SLEEPING (illus. Schwartz) pb; Grimm THORN pb; Hutchinson CHIMNEY 65-70; Hyman SLEEPING pb; Shubb ABOUT 23-27; Tarrant FAIRY 20-33; Wiggin FAIRY 243-247. De La Mare TALES 181-192 (-frog, -golden plates, Uninvited fairy curses to sleep for one hundred years). Adams BOOK..PRINCESS 84-89 (-frog, Queen returns fish to water, wish for daughter granted).

B* Sleeping Beauty variant. One of seven fairies not invited to christening as there are only six golden place settings. Seventh curses to prick finger on spindle and die. Last fairy softens charm to sleep one hundred years. When finger is pricked dwarf in seven-league boots goes to inform good fairy, who hurries to palace in dragon chariot and puts all to sleep with wand. After one hundred years, prince arrives and she awakes (no kiss). They wed. As the prince's mother is an ogress, he keeps the wedding secret and visits her in the forest. Daughter, Dawn, and son, Day, are born. On becoming king he brings family to palace. Queen-mother orders Dawn, Day, and queen served to her. Steward hides them and serves lamb, kid and hind. Ogress discovers and prepares to throw into pit of serpents. Prince returns. In rage, ogress casts self in pit. France (Perrault): Carey FAIRY 16-26 /Martignoni ILLUSTRATED 248-251/; Haviland FAVORITE.. FRANCE 60-75; Holme TALES 58-62; Lang BLUE 66-67 /Fenner PRINCESS 154-167/, /Arbuthnot FAIRY 99-101/, /Arbuthnot ANTHOLOGY 207-209/; Perrault FAMOUS (Watts) 3-22; Perrault PERRAULT'S (Dodd) 1-15; Perrault PERRAULT'S (Dover) 1-22; Perrault SLEEPING (illus. Chappell) pb; Perrault SLEEPING (illus. Rackham) pb; Opie CLASSIC 81-92; Rackham FAIRY 52-65 /Rackham ARTHUR 182-189/; Sekorová EUROPEAN 83-86. Association TOLD ..GREEN 139-145 (A. only, -dwarf and wand induced sleep).

D1960.5* Holy man, Chyavana, meditates so well ants build mound over him. Later meditates in river bottom. Caught up with fish, he demands to be sold with fish. Refuses all prices except holy cow. A cow is priceless. India: Reed TALKATIVE 18-21.

D1962.1. Magic sleep through curse. SEE: D1960.3 (Sleeping Beauty).

D2000. Magic forgetfulness.

D2003. Forgotten fiancée. Young husband visiting his home breaks tabu and forgets his wife. Later she succeeds in reawakening his memory. SEE: G530.2; H1385.4; H1385.5.

A* Little Horse of Seven Colors. Christian taken prisoner by Moors is to wed King's daughter if can teach something does not know. Teaches religions. Youngest agrees to wed.

Flee on seven-colored horse. He goes ahead to fetch clothing for her, lets nurse embrace him, and forgets. Disguised as groom, she brings horse and chants to him. He remembers. Wed. Portugal: Lowe LITTLE 17-21.

D2006.1.1. Forgotten fiancée reawakens husband's memory by detaining lovers through magic. Heroine takes up residence, etc. SEE: D1413.16; H1385.4B (Three Feathers); G530.2 (Master Maid).

D2006.1.3. Forgotten fiancée reawakens husband's memory by having magic doves converse. Type 313. SEE: G530.2 (Master Maid).

D2006.1.4. Forgotten fiancée buys place in husband's bed and reawakens his memory. SEE: H1385.4 (East of the Sun et al.); H1385.5; G530.2.

D2011. Years thought days. Years spent in the other world or asleep seem as days because of magic forgetfulness. Type 470. SEE: D1960.1 (Rip Van Winkle); D1890 (Magic Aging); F377 (Supernatural lapse of time in fairyland); F420.6.1.3.1 (Urashima Taro); Q1.1C (In Garden of Paradise).

D2011.1. Years seem moments while man listens to song of bird. Wales: Sheppard-Jones WELSH 164. Latvia: Durham TIT 90-91.

D2011.1.3* Years seem moments while man watches two men playing chess. Indonesia: Courlander KANTCHIL'S 110-116 (Chong-Kak). Korea: Carpenter TALES..KOREAN 213-218; Jewett WHICH 74-81. China: Gruenberg MORE 236-241 /Wiggin TALES..WONDER/. SEE ALSO: A163.1.1.1.

D2011.1.3.1* Two cousins see two fairies playing chess before cave. Seasons change as white hare jumps up and down. They enter cave using magic reed to open. Are trapped. Are made Liu Chu'an, God of Good Luck, and Yuan Chao, God of Ill Fortune. China: Bonnet FOLK 175-178.

D2011.1.4* Friends vow to invite each other to wedding even if dead. Groom goes to friend's grave to invite. Stays to drink two cups of wine. Gone three hundred years. Russia: Littledale GHOSTS 97-100.

D2011.1.5* Two young men spend six months with lovely pair of maidens in forest. Return to find village destroyed by earthquake two hundred years ago. China: Manton FLYING 72-76.

D2030. Other temporary magic characteristics.

D2031.0.2.1* When lost, Kuo comes onto groups of men feasting, they magically create path and he follows it home. In morning he returns to find remains of feast but no path. China: Littledale GHOSTS 83-86.

D2060. Death or bodily injury by magic.

119

D2061.2.10* Death by magic packet placed on chair. Friend exchanges packets and murderer dies. Nigeria: Walker DANCING 94-97.

D2064.1. Magic sickness because girl has thrown away her consecrated wafer. SEE: N452B.

D2072.7* Old woman cares for lost boys. Causes hunter sent to kill them to become paralyzed. Repeats thrice. Villagers build large boat to take boys home. Kotzebue Eskimo: Curtis GHOST 99-110

D2100. Magic wealth.

D2100.2.1* Three pennies multiply, were given by beggar in return for tobacco for pipe. Receiver misuses gift. Beggar returns and sells jade for three pennies. It turns to hot coal and burns shop down. Back as tobacco seller. China: Wyndham FOLK..CHINA 98-101.

D2105. Provisions magically furnished. SEE: D1450.

D2120. Magic transportation.

D2121.5.1* Man sells soul to devil (M211). To be saved if hears masses at Church of Nativity in Jerusalem, St. James in Galicia in Spain, and St. Peters in Rome during one night. Gets Devil to carry him about to prove speed. D. suspects and leaves him on dome of St. Peters. Priest delays mass and people rescue him from dome. Saved. Italy: Vittorini OLD ITALIAN 96-101.

D2125.1.0.1* Magic power to walk on water. Fishermen mock girl telling to pray to "Saint Porthole" and will find church. She runs over water to ask them to repeat directions. Italy (Salerno): Jagendorf PRICELESS 89-91.

D2126. Magic underwater journey. SEE: F212 (Fairyland under water).

D2135.0.3.1* People learn magic words so can fly. All slaves fly back to Africa. U.S. Black: Lester BLACK 147-154.

D2136.2. Castle magically transported. SEE: D871.1 (Aladdin); D882.1E.

D2138. Magic travel into another time.

D2138.1* Lad enters deserted castle at midnight and is called on to read history to dying King Hakon Hakonson. King died six hundred and fifty years earlier. Orkney: Cutt HOGBOON 169-173.

D2140. Magic control of the elements.

D2142.1.2. Wind raised by loosening certain knots. Untie first knot = storm, untie second = waves fall. Untie third = winds blow wherever one wishes. Lad saves a kidnapped princess and weds. Latvia: Ginsburg LAZIES 21-25.

D2142.1.6. Wind raised by whistling.

D2142.1.6.1* Befriended frog teaches lad whistle to raise storm. Great Hetman who wishes to eat lad's pet duck vanquished thus and lad named Great Hetman by soldiers. Poland: Turska WOODCUTTER'S pb.

D2144.1.2. Man with power to make everything freeze. Wears cap over ear. Should he wear it straight everything would freeze. SEE: F601.2D.

D2144.5.1. Ice produced by magic. SEE: C752.2.1.1.

D2145.2.2. Fruit magically grows in winter. SEE: H1023.3.

D2150. Miscellaneous magic manifestations.

D2157. Magic control of soil and crops. SEE: D1487.3.

D2157.3.2. Tree regains life and verdure after treasure it hides in its roots is given away. SEE: H1292.2.

D2161.3.5. Deafness magically cured.

D2161.3.5.1* Badger seeks herb to make poultice and restore hearing to man who befriended him. Native American: Hill BADGER 66-74.

D2161.5.7.1* Cure by seventh daughter. King has seventh daughter abandoned. Raised by priest, she becomes mudang (healing woman). Heals ill queen when grown. Becomes guardian spirit of mudangs. Korea: Carpenter KOREAN 205-210.

D2171.1. Object magically attaches itself to a person. SEE: E373.1.1.

D2171.1.0.1* Woodcutter mends three broken branches of pine. Is showered with gold. Bad woodcutter who broke branches goes to tree. Is showered with sap which sticks for three days, one day for each broken branch. (cf. J2415). Japan: Sakade JAPANESE 55-58. SEE ALSO: E373.1.

D2172.1. Magic repetition. Person must keep on doing or saying thing until released. SEE: D1413.17 (Fiddevav).

D2172.2. Magic gift: power to continue all day what one starts. One woman measures linen, another throws water on the pig. Sweden: Wiggin TALES 459-461 (legs break, nose pulled. Fish grants wishes). SEE ALSO: J2073.1; Q3.

D2173. Magic singing. SEE ALSO: D1427.1.1.

D2174. Magic dancing. Enchanted persons dance till released. Type 306. SEE ALSO: D1415; D1427.1.1.

D2174.1* In drought Vodoun priest advises tree lizard, Zandolite, to give a festival. St. John is sent by God to ask them to stop the noise. St. John is given a seat by the drummers and cannot keep from dancing. St. Patrick, St. Peter, God follow. All dance. The drought ends. Haiti: Courlander PIECE 50-54.

D2174.2* Anansi's singing compels Granny to dance, A. robs garden. W. Indies: Bryan DANCING pb.

D2177.1. Demon enclosed in bottle. SEE: K717.

D2183. Magic spinning. Usually performed by a supernatural helper. Girl wedded to prince must fulfill mother's false boast to spin impossible a-mount of yarn or to spin gold (H1021.8). Imp promises to help but she must give her child or self if cannot guess his name. Name is overheard (N475) by her messenger or husband. Imp van-ishes on hearing name (C432.1). Type 500, 501. SEE ALSO: F381.1.1.

A* Rumpelstiltskin. Germany (Grimm): Ar-buthnot FAIRY 60-62 /Arbuthnot ANTHOLOGY 197-198/; De La Mare TALES 171-180; Grimm BROTHERS 139-144; Grimm GRIMM'S (Follett) 279-284; Grimm GRIMM'S (Grosset) 125-129; Grimm GRIMM'S (Scribners) 155-158; Grimm GRIMM'S (World) 38-41; Grimm HOUSEHOLD 228-231; Grimm RUMPELSTILTSKIN pb; Gruen-berg FAVORITE 310-313; Haviland FAVORITE ..GERMANY 41-50; Haviland FAIRY 158-161; Holme TALES 46-48; Lang BLUE 101-105; Mar-tignoni ILLUSTRATED 204-206; Opie CLASSIC 195-198; Rackham GRIMM'S 39-43; Shubb ABOUT 77-79; Sleigh NORTH 70-82.

B* Tom Tit Tot. England: Baker TALKING 33-39; De La Mare ANIMAL 89-96; Jacobs ENG-LISH 1-9 /Arbuthnot FAIRY 21-23/, /Arbuthnot ANTHOLOGY 160-164/, /Jacobs TOM pb/; Hutchinson CHIMNEY 3-15; Reeves ENGLISH 148-155; Steel ENGLISH 18-27; Wiggin TALES 205-210; Williams-Ellis FAIRY..BRITISH 11-19.

C* Ripopet-Barabas. Girl nibbles pancake in lacy pattern. Prince weds as pillow-lace maker. Goblin makes, but she must remember his name in year. She falls ill at year's end. Advised to drink of spring. Sends servant, queen, prince --none return. She goes and sees all watching goblins sing of coming wedding of Ripopet-Barabas. France: Picard FRENCH 168-173.

D* Peerifool. Eldest princess carried off by giant stealing cabbages. Refuses to share food with fairy Peerie Folk and is therefore unable to finish task. Second daughter--same. Youngest shares. Peerie boy spins and weaves for her. To guess his name. Old woman overhears and tells girl. Giant meets Peerie Folk with long lips from wetting wool and decides not to make maid spin anymore. She sends "grass" to mother for cow by giant. Sisters hidden underneath (G561). They pour boiling water from window and kill him. Scotland: Haviland SCOTLAND 25-48.

E* Duffy and the Devil. Devil to do work for bride for three years. Squire hears name when he happens onto a witches' revel. All that Devil knit vanishes when Devil does, clothing on Squire at time, etc. Duffy forbids wife to knit

again. Cornwall: Manning-Sanders PETER 202-212; Zemach DUFFY pb.

F* The White Hen. Hen weaves for weaver, daughter to be given if can't guess name in year. Daughter overhears fairies singing hen's name. Ireland: MacManus BOLD 169-178.

G* Trillevip. Girl muttering pretends to have said can spin twenty spindles in night. Dwarf spins. Hunter sees dwarfs chanting name Trille-vip and girl guesses name. Dwarf then tells her to acknowledge three deformed women who come to wedding. Husband vows she will never spin again lest become deformed too (D2183.1). Den-mark: Baker GOLDEN 41-45.

H* Whuppity Stoorie. Woman releases hare and heals its leg. Old lady in green cures sick sow in exchange for "whatever she wants." Claims baby. Woman has three days to guess name. Hare tells to go listen in glen. Hears lady sing-ing name--"Whuppity Stoorie." Great Britain: Finlay TATTERCOATS 53-59.

D2183.1. Through false boast bride is compelled to perform impossible feat of spinning (H1021.8), sewing, cooking. Three old women help. In re-turn she must invite them to wedding. When groom hears that they became deformed through spinning, etc. he forbids bride to perform task ever again. Denmark: Baker GOLDEN 41-45 (+D2183G). England: Jacobs MORE 195-200 (Aiding woman in cave seen through hole in stone. Told to bring husband to look through stone. Taken into cave with deformed spinning fairies, Habetrot, Scantlie Mab and others). Ger-many (Grimm): Gag MORE 131-137; Grimm GRIMM'S (Grosset) 18-22; Grimm GRIMM'S (World) 326-329; Grimm HOUSEHOLD 82-84. Ireland: Haviland IRELAND 61-84; MacManus HIBERNIAN 233-239. Karelia: Ginsburg LA-ZIES 49-55 (knocks on mountain stone and three come out). Puerto Rico: Carter GREEDY 106-111 /Arbuthnot ANTHOLOGY 403-404/. Scan-dinavia: D'Aulaire EAST 216-222 /Martignoni ILLUSTRATED 243-245/. Spain: Gunterman CASTLES 61-80 (sunbeam fairies [F499.1.2] do task. Tell girl to invite three deformed women to wedding); Eells TALES..SPAIN 37-43 (after three fairies spin, girl eats whole bag of nuts and hides shells under mattress, says shells cracking are bones cracking from overwork, for-bidden to work again). Sweden: Kaplan FAIRY 58-70 (to spin straw into gold, H1021.8).

D2183.1.1* Cat takes girl to two witches who de-mand special items--thistledown, wheatstraw and black thorns. Items set on spinning wheel, loom and garment then spin, weave and sew by selves. Win contest. Spell to break if speaks (C400). King asks to wed, third time says yes. Cat talks no more. Witches are enabled to fly away on special brooms that never touch ground (C242.1), striking with coin from gypsy boys' pocket, wear-ing rings neither mined nor minted (she makes of hair), carrying jugs of water that never saw light). Scotland: Nic Leodhas HEATHER 95-111.

E. THE DEAD

E0 - E199. Resuscitation.

E0. Resuscitation.

E3.1* One feather from slain ostrich falls into water. Grows into another ostrich and returns to wives of dead ostrich. Bushmen: Helfman BUSHMEN 55-56.

E21.1. Resuscitation by removal of poisoned apple. By shaking loose the apple from the throat of the poisoned girl the prince brings her to life. SEE: Z65.1 (Snow White).

E30. Resuscitation by arrangement of members. SEE: H621.4 (skillful companions resuscitate).

E33. Resuscitation with missing member. In reassembling the members one has been inadvertently omitted. The resuscitated person or animal lacks this member. SEE: F243.3.1 (animals eaten by fairies); G530.2.

E38.2* Spirit of Chief killed in battle returns to body and passes through fire surrounding body to re-enter it. He lives again. Native American (Chippewa): Cunningham TALKING 58-59.

E43. Resuscitation by placing bite of oatmeal mixed with victim's blood in victim's mouth. Corpse has killed three boys and ordered girl to mix drop of blood from finger of each with oatmeal and eat it. She hides it with her scarf instead and learns she can resuscitate lads later with this mixture. Ireland: Bang GOBLINS 29-40.

E44. Return to living form by walking around church in opposite direction of widershins. Lad has walked around widershins to prove doesn't believe in superstition and turned to ghost. Scotland: Nic Leodhas GHOSTS 35-42.

E80. Water of life. SEE: H1321.1; H1331.1.3Ah.

E80.5* Sentaro prays to Jofuku for elixir of life. Jofuku gives Sentaro paper crane to ride to land of Perpetual Life. After three hundred years he wants to return home as everyone there wants to die. His crane gets wet, he falls into the sea, and is almost eaten by sharks. He awakens and finds self still praying. Seven days have passed. A messenger from Jofuku gives him a book teaching how to live and tells him to forget his longing for eternal life. Japan: Ozaki JAPANESE 87-97.

E82. Water of life and death. One water kills, the other restores to life.

E82.1* Girl resuscitates sisters with water of life. Fills pitcher with water of death and ogre attempting to heal own wound kills self. +G561C. Finland: Fillmore SHEPHERD'S 40-52.

E121.4. Resuscitation by saint.

E121.4.2* St. Francis is served his favorite fish. He prays and it is restored. Italy: Jagendorf PRICELESS 147-149.

E121.4.3* Good man (Brother Santiago de los Caballeros de Pedro) gives poor Indian tiny lizard. It turns to emerald (gold) and is sold for medicine and food for family. Later poor man is able to redeem lizard and return it to monk. It is set on ground and scampers off. Guatemala: Courlander RIDE 250-252; Jagendorf KING 135-138; Newman FOLK 107-110.

E200 - E599. Ghosts and other revenants.

E200 - E299. Malevolent return from the dead.

E210. Dead lover's malevolent return.

E211.3* Dead sweetheart follows faithless lover in form of pig. Prince Edward Isle: Leach THING 65-67.

E215. The Dead Rider (Lenore). Dead lover returns and takes sweetheart with him on horseback. She is sometimes saved at the grave by the crowing of the cock, though the experience is usually fatal. Type 365.

E215.1* Rejected old lover carries golden hair off. Young lover pursues and cuts her hair by which ghost drags her, freeing her. Corsica: Manning-Sanders BOOK..GHOSTS 21-24.

E221.1.1* Dead wife from India haunts husband who threw her overboard. Black hand appears to frighten his lovers and servants. Orkney: Cutt HOGBOON 60-65.

E221.6* Second husband takes wife's gold and returns from Taiwan to China to first wife. Abandoned woman hangs self and pays fortune teller to transport her over water under umbrella so she can frighten husband to death. Plants Na-Tao trees on corners of his yard as he had done to her fields. These trees are only planted on graves of dead. Taiwan: Cheney TALES 87-92.

E230. Return from dead to inflict punishment. SEE ALSO: N271.

E231.6. Coffin comes out of ground twice, put on cart. Horses race to scene of crime and dump coffin in pit there. Dead men found buried there. Netherlands (Drie, N. Gelderland): Spicer THIRTEEN GHOSTS 65-72.

E231.7. Ghost of slain girl appears to murderer. He commits suicide. She reached his home by having student call to her every time he crossed stream. Rewarded with treasure. China: Birch CHINESE 62-79 (#5) /Mayne GHOSTS 168-183/.

E235. Return from dead to punish theft

of part of corpse. SEE ALSO: Z13.1.

E235.4.1. Return from dead to punish theft of golden arm from grave. Type 366. Husband usually has taken it. English: Jacobs ENGLISH 143-144 /Fenner GHOSTS 185-187/; Leach THING 33-36.

E235.4.2.1* Valet digs up gold leg of lord's wife. She calls from grave. Gravedigger, lord, maid go and voice continues. "Give me my leg of gold." Valet is sent. She drags him underground and eats. France: Manning-Sanders BOOK..GHOSTS 124-127.

E235.4.3. Return from dead to punish theft of bone from grave. Cumulative series ending "Give me my bone." "Take it." Type 366. England: Hutchinson FIRESIDE 3-6; Jacobs ENGLISH 57-58 /Harper GHOSTS 225-227/, /Sechrist HEIGH-HO 47-48/; Rockwell THREE 78-80; Seuling TEENY pb; TALL..NURSERY 49-50; Williams-Ellis FAIRY..BRITISH 30-31; Withers I SAW 59-61.

E235.4.3.1* Chunk o' Meat. Old man, old woman. Little boy finds fat meat in hollow log, takes and cooks. "Where's my chunk o' meat?" Boogie comes down chimney. "What you got such big eyes for?" "Stare you through." etc. Teeth... "Eat you up" (Z18.1). Appalachia: Chase WICKED 231-233.

E235.4.3.2* Man cuts off tail of critter and eats it. Creature returns for tail repeatedly. "You know and I know that I'm here to get my tailypo." U.S. (Appalachia): Galdone TAILYPO pb.

E236.1* Return from dead to demand clothing stolen from grave. Orkney: Cutt HOGBOON 80-86.

E236.1.1. Return from dead to demand ring stolen from grave. "I'm under the window, at door, under bed, etc." Pulls wife by hair toward window, she throws ring out window, ghost leaves. Spain: Manning-Sanders BOOK..GHOSTS 87-89.

E236.5. Return from dead to demand money stolen from corpse. Silver dollars from eyes. Harris NIGHTS 161-165; Harris COMPLETE 235-238.

E250. Blood thirsty revenants.

E251.1.3* Vania and the Vampire. Refuses to return coffin lid until vampire tells how to revive man killed that night. Tinker revives man but locals take him for a swindler. Judge takes them to cemetery and stake is driven through vampire's heart. Russia: Spicer THIRTEEN GHOSTS 92-100.

E256. Ghosts eat corpse.

E256.1* Boy taken up on rider's horse is forced to hold corpse from graveyard. Hag and rider cut up corpse to cook, feed to boy but he gives it to dog under table. Sent back for whip he dropped, boy flees. Cock crows and boy is safe. Danaher FOLKTALES 24-30.

E261.1.2. Speaking skull tells about previous life, reveals future events, etc. SEE: B210.2.3.

E261.2.1. Coffin bursts; dead arises and pursues attendant. SEE: B857.1.

E279.6.1* Ghost punishes man who molests him. Blind man who can see evil spirits drives spirit from bride. Spirit escapes through hole poked in door by spying servant. King tests his prowess. He says king has three mice before him. There is one mouse and king orders him executed. Later discovers mouse is pregnant and orders signal flag leaned to right, signal to spare him. Wind (spirit) blows it to left, taking revenge. Korea: Kim STORY 172-179.

E281. Ghosts haunt house. SEE: Q82; H1411.

E291. Ghosts protect hidden treasure. SEE: Q82; H1411.

E300 - E399. Friendly return from the dead.

E320. Dead relative's friendly return.

E321.6* Dead husband returns to remove written vow sworn on Odin Stone which prevents wife from remarrying. Orkney: Cutt HOGBOON 46-50.

E323.1.1. Dead mother returns to suckle child. SEE ALSO: P253.2E.

E323.1.1.1* Dead mother buys milk for babe in grave. Baby is found alive in grave with empty milk bottles. Alabama (Black): Leach THING 60-62.

E323.1.1.2* Ghost lady milks cow to care for babe in tree until someone finds. Scotland: Nic Leodhas GHOSTS 43-53.

E324.3* Dead child's friendly return to parents. Return of the Land-Otter. Drowned son returns to help parents catch fish in famine. Leaves when they return to people. Native American (Tlingit): Littledale GHOSTS 13-20.

E324.3.1* Land-otter nephews return to help uncle. Move carved canoe to sea and bring devilfish bait. He burns their skins and they become boys again. Native American (Northwest Coast): Martin NINE 19-26 /Martin RAVEN 27-35/.

E328. Dead family's friendly return. Peasant girl wed to king is rejected by populace. She returns home to find parents now in castle. King is allowed to reinstate the now wealthy girl. Parents ask her to remain with them one more night after others return to palace. She wakes in ruins of their old hut. They were ghosts, returned to aid her. Siberia: Manning-Sanders BOOK..GHOSTS 95-100.

E329.1. Dead aunt visits party. They learn she died at that moment. U.S. (Maryland): Leach THING 73-74.

E330. Locations haunted by non-malevolent dead.

E332.3.3.1. The Vanishing Hitchhiker. U.S. (Illinois): Leach THING 71-72 (on bus).

E340. Return from dead to repay obligations.

E341.1. Dead grateful for having corpse ransomed. Corpse is being held unburied because of non-payment of debts. Hero pays debt and secures burial of corpse. Types 505-508. SEE ALSO: G512.

A* The Companion. Lad pays for burial of corpse. Dead man joins on travels. Knocks on mountain and orders troll hag to sit on chair, self sticking chair. She must give magic sword to get free. Second mountain--repeat with ball of golden yarn. Third--hat. Throw ball over fjord = bridge, they escape and bridge rolls up after. Trolls leap for end and drown. Suitor task: keep pair of golden scissors overnight, princess steals back. Grateful dead learns from princess' flying ram that she visits her lover at night. He follows in invisibility hat, steals scissors back. Ball of golden yarn--repeat. Fetch what I'm thinking of (troll's head). Grateful Dead beheads. Tells lad to beat troll hide off princess with nine birch brooms and rub in three tubs of milk. She becomes sweet. Grateful Dead asks one-half of all lad breeds in five years as reward. Claims one-half of child too. Lad agrees and Grateful Dead stops sword and returns to heaven. Norway: Asbjornsen NORWEGIAN 84-96.

B* The King of Greece's Daughter. Dead man unburied. Youngest of three traveling lads buries. Giant digs up. Lad pays debt and buries. Two-headed giant--same. Three-headed. Grateful Dead joins lad as servant. Grateful Dead tells giant King of Ireland is coming and hides giant in cellar. Takes gold. Cloak of Invisibility, Shoes of Swiftness, Sword of Sharpness. King of Greece's daughter enchanted by King of Darkness. Lad follows her and twelve maids who cry "A boat, A boat" and fly over river to King of Darkness. He follows prince, returns rings left there as token by princess, beheads King of Darkness (can be killed only by Sword of Sharpness). Weds princess. Ireland: MacManus WELL 112-137.

C* The True Name of the Princess. Lad pays dead man's debt. Grateful Dead goes thrice as bird and overhears secret name of princess (H323). Lad wins her. Grateful Dead also exchanges his good looks for lad's ugly countenance before returning to grave. Haiti: Thoby-

Marcelin SINGING 75-81.

D* The Turkish Slave. Lad ransoms dead man, buys Turkish slave girl and weds. Father disowns and wife paints pictures to sell. Not to tell who paints them. Turks recognize (H35.3) work of Sultan's daughter and steal her back. Lad and old fisherman are taken slaves by Turks and tend Sultan's garden. He and princess elope, take old man along. Old man was Grateful Dead. Italy (Istria): Hampden HOUSE 99-109.

E* King Stork. Lad carries old man over river, turns to youth called King Stork and aids in following princess to rendezvous with witch. Disenchanted. Pyle WONDER 293-304 /Fenner GIANTS 3-17/.

E345.1. Dead returns to replace boundary marks. Feud over boundary stones. Two keep moving it back and forth, finally they give up. Ghosts of their fathers and grandfathers continue to move it back and forth. Scotland: Nic Leodhas GAELIC 58-67.

E354. Old woman near Aletsch Glacier invites souls of those lost on glacier in to warm selves every night. She forgets to add "without harm to me" and they suffocate her with their number. A procession of lights is seen moving from her house to the glacier as the souls escort her after death. Switzerland (German): Duvoisin THREE 214-217.

E363.2.1* Ghost returns to protect the living. Grateful Old Cailleach. Family are hospitable to old lady. She appears to man on rainy night and insists he drive long way home. Bridge over river fell that night. She died two weeks before. Scotland: Nic Leodhas GAELIC 46-56.

E363.2.2* Ghost temporarily wounds man, causing him to be left behind. Companions are killed, he escapes. Native American (Arapaho): Brown TEPEE 158-159.

E363.5. Dead provide material aid to the living. SEE ALSO: D882.1G.

E363.5.2* Ghosts of Kahlberg. Tenant to be evicted after lord's death. Ghost child sent to invite him to gathering of Langeberg family of ghosts at ruins of Kahlberg castle. Ghosts reward him for his family's years of service to their family--show treasure. France (Alsace-Lorraine): Harper GHOSTS 234-249.

E373. Ghosts bestow gifts on living. SEE: Q82.

E373.1. Money received from ghosts as reward for bravery. A voice says "I am letting it fall." The man: "Let it." Money falls to the ground. SEE ALSO: H1411.1. Gypsy: Jagendorf GYPSIES' 111-117.

E373.1.1* Voice calls "Hold tight or stick tight." Old man answers "Whatever you like." Gold pieces fly and stick to him (D2171.1). Neighbor imitates (J2415) and is covered with tar. Waiting wife drops candle and sets him afire. SEE ALSO: D2171.1. Japan: Scofield HOLD 34-39.

E373.1.2* First brother hears voice in woods "Take me or leave me." Flees. Second brother same. Third says "Jump on my back." Gold sticks to back. Japan: Novak FAIRY 54-60.

E379.6* Three drowned men carry coffin of newly drowned man ashore for burial. Scotland: Nic Leodhas GHOSTS 65-78.

E379.7* Man sees girl in gown of ancient dynasty, who casts no shadow, turns to blue pigeon, leads him to cave and asks in dream that he take place of Buddhist hermit who once lived there. Man descends, saves village when flood is imminent. Korea: Jewett WHICH 124-135.

E400 - E599. Ghosts and revenants-- miscellaneous.

E400. Ghosts and revenants--miscellaneous.

E402.1.3. Invisible ghost plays musical instrument. SEE ALSO: E425.2.5.1.

E402.1.3.2* Newcomers have no bogle in their house. They invite any ghost in the cemetery who has no family to join them. A bagpiper who plays poorly comes. Scotland: Nic Leodhas GAELIC 100-110.

E410. The unquiet grave.

E411.0.2.1.1* Return from dead to do penance. Maria Sat on the Fire. Cook who wasted fire and food returns after death to cook as penance. She sits on the fire at night. Priest blesses her and she disappears. Mexico: Brenner BOY 121-124.

E412.3.0.1* Dead woman's skeleton hanging in tree. She appears as woman and leads to skeleton. Rests when buried properly. Native American (Lakota): Yellow Robe TONWEYA 94-101.

E412.3.3. Dead man asks for shoes (was buried without them). Littledale GHOSTS 153-156.

E414.0.1* Drowned man must guard spot where he drowned until next drowned person takes his place. Forms close friendship with fisherman. China: Manton FLYING 134-140.

E414.2* Gangster killed in car is seen in rearview mirror. Cigar smell is in car, mumbling heard. U.S.: Leach THING 77-79.

E415.1.2. Return from dead to uncover secretly buried treasures.

E415.1.2.1* Hans and His Master. Servant lies in coffin alongside master, feigns dead, and accompanies on nightly haunts to discover cause

of unrest. Hoard of gold must be given to orphanage. Hungary: Manning-Sanders CHOICE 224-230 /Manning-Sanders BOOK..GHOSTS 55-61/.

E415.1.2.2* Old Nanny's Ghost. Old woman's ghost tells lad to dig up treasure, give half to her sister. He keeps all. She haunts. He restores. England (Yorkshire, North Riding): Spicer THIRTEEN GHOSTS 73-82.

E415.1.3* Ghost returns to hunt lost article. Letter from woman's lover hidden in chest. She returns to stare at chest nightly until priest discovers and burns letter. Littledale GHOSTS 73-78. SEE ALSO: E451.11.

E415.2.1. Lady makes husband promise to devote any field she can walk around to bread for the poor. Though ill she walks around large field. He does not keep vow. Her ghost sits on wheat and refuses to allow threshing until vow is kept. Scotland: Nic Leodhas GAELIC 68-74.

E419.6.1* Ghost of girl haunts house until owner discovers diary telling that she wanted to be buried beside lover. He has her remains moved and ghost leaves. Scotland: Nic Leodhas GHOSTS 24-34.

E420. Appearance of revenant.

E421.2.1.1* Ghost leaves no footprints. Visiting chief refuses to dance. Feet do not bruise leaves. Vanishes when puhala fruit is thrown at spirit. Hawaii: Thompson HAWAIIAN.. TRICKSTERS 38-42.

E421.3.8. Luminous ghosts. Lad follows girl with two red lights all night on hills. Is really Osgaert, devil ghost of Hooge Duivel in Gelderland, North Veluwe. Netherlands: Spicer THIRTEEN GHOSTS 45-52.

E422.1.1. Headless revenant. SEE ALSO: E545.19.1.1.

E422.1.1.3.0.1* Headless woman given ride leads to church full of headless revelers with spiked wheel with heads on it. Home again, wife berates man for this tale. He says a headless woman is at least a good woman as has no tongue. Ireland: Manning-Sanders BOOK..GHOSTS 119-123.

E422.1.1.3.2* Headless horseman challenges to race. Is pleased when man dares to accept and helps man's old mare win races thereafter. Ireland: Manning-Sanders BOOK..GHOSTS 80-86.

E422.1.1.3.3* Horseman (not headless) in black lures youths to death over precipice. Lad sets rope trap and De Merci himself plunges over cliff. Never seen on Isle Gonave again. Haiti: Johnson HOW 59-66.

E423.1.8.2* Revenant as cow. Priest returns dead souls to cattle by calling them from graves and feeding them black powder. Boy braves priest, who tries to pretend to be ghost in bell tower. Boy lets bell knock priest from tower and priest goes up in smoke. Animals disenchanted. Mexico: Brenner BOY 100-102 /Frost LEGENDS 199-214/.

E423.2.6.1* Revenant as deer. Ghost of Great White Stag protects animals from timber wolf. Parker SKUNNY 213-224 /Gruenberg MORE 148-153/. Native American (Seneca): De Wit TALKING 9-12 (elk).

E423.3.0.1* Revenant as bird. Dead lover appears daily as bird. Girl pines and dies. Bird is seen no more. Native American: Bierhorst FIRE 47-57.

E423.3.12* Revenant as bat. Five Kauai fishermen, men disappear nightly. Huge batlike spirit seen. Trapped in hut with decoys and burnt. Hawaii: Thompson HAWAIIAN..TRICKSTERS 9-13.

E423.8.1* Revenant as spider. Priest playing samisen offers it to man. It turns to spider web and entraps him. He manages to wound priest-spider. Spider leaves at dawn. Bloody trail followed and spider goblin killed. Japan: Hearn JAPANESE (Pauper) 22-32; Hearn JAPANESE 18-20.

E423.8.2* Maiden in teahouse plays samisen. Everytime she strikes middle string man feels thread around throat. String snaps and encircles him, his sword flies out and pierces samisen. In morning trail of blood is followed to giant dead spider pierced by sword. Japan: Novak FAIRY 138-144; Garner CAVALCADE.. GOBLINS 78-81.

E423.8.3* Spider spectre in pool is ghost of Empress Otawa. Blacksmith feigns sleep and lets her tie his feet, transfers webs to trees and kills with hammer. Mouse turns back to princess. Weds. Japan: Spicer THIRTEEN GHOSTS 24-35.

E423.10* Revenant as cricket. Son releases captured cricket, falls into well and is unconscious. Fighting cricket comes to his father and wins riches for him. Son awakes--dreamed was a cricket. China: Carpenter TALES..CHINESE 217-225; Ziner CRICKET pb.

E425.1.3. Revenant as seductive woman.

E425.1.3.1* The Cegua, lovely dark girl who asks for ride. If taken on horse she turns to a devil with horse's skull. The rider dies of fright if evil, wastes away if survives. Costa Rica: Carter ENCHANTED 97-101.

E425.1.8* Lady of the Moors leads men astray. Man tears off part of her gown--this turns to weed in morning. France: Holman DRAC 57-71.

E425.1.9* Greedy woman demands 4 bags of coins for night's shelter. Pursues man to collect. At

dawn he turns to skeleton and disappears among tombs. She dies of fright. Haiti: Carter GREEDY 99-105.

E425.1.10* Man sleeps by bones of woman unknowingly. Her ghost follows him, attempts to kill entire tribe by trapping in lodge with smoke. His mother offers ghost pipe to smoke in effort to distract her but she is drawn off by ghost and dies. Native American (Blackfoot): Brown TEPEE 160-166; Hardendorff JUST 139-149.

E425.1.11* Malintzin, translator for the Spaniards, dies of sadness at mistreatment of Indian people. The wind carries her to Mt. Texocotepec. Her wailing can be heard in the wind there. During the revolution she appeared to lead the troops. Mexico: Brenner BOY 125-128.

E425.2.5. Revenant as piper. SEE ALSO: E402.1.3.2.

E425.2.5.1* Piper enters cave of little people to challenge their pipers. Never returns. Heard playing underground at times. Scotland: Wilson SCOTTISH 28-32. WALES: Baker TALKING 45-47 (+A1464.2.1); Belting ELVES 22-26 (fiddler, All Hallow's Eve).

E427. Revenant as spirit animal changes shape from that of one animal to another, usually in quick succession.

E427.1* Hedley cow. Old woman's pot of gold gets heavier, turns to huge cow and runs off. England: Jacobs MORE 55-59; Manning-Sanders BOOK..MAGICAL 3-7; Mayne GHOSTS 103-106; Palmer DRAGONS 63-67; Steel ENGLISH 188-190.

E430. Defense against ghosts and the dead.

E434.11. Blind lute player Hoichi is forced to sing of battle for samurai ghosts of Taira clan. Priests protect him by writing scriptures all over his body. They forget his ears and ghost takes these. Japan: Garner CAVALCADE 128-132; Hearn EARLESS pb.

E434.12* Girl refuses to go to feast with parents. Evil spirit disguised as friend comes to spend night. They go frog hunting. Spirit says he's eating them as fast as can catch them. She runs home and upturns all pots, then hides on roof till dawn. Guiana: Jagendorf KING 144-148.

E439.11* Girl cleans house, paints and airs it out. Bogles go back to graveyard. Scotland (Blairgowrie): Nic Leodhas HEATHER 113-128.

E440. Walking ghost "laid." SEE: H1411.

E443. Ghosts exorcized by name. (cf. C824, C432.1).

E443.3.1* Man overhears ghosts tell names (N475) and dispositions, while sheltering in haunted temple. They attack him but he vanquishes each by guessing its name. Next day, searches them out on temple grounds and buries them. Long Frayed One = shoelace; Bare Snapping One = horse skull; Pot-bellied One = broken pot; Thin Toothless One = comb; Bent and Shiny One = Cock's tail. Japan: Novak FAIRY 165-173.

E451.5. Ghost laid when treasure is unearthed. SEE: H1411.

E451.11* Ghost laid when hidden letter found and burnt. Japan: Buck FAIRY 218-220. SEE ALSO: E415.1.3.

E451.12* Goblin in tower released from haunting when full-blown rose is brought in January. Man brings embroidered rose scented with perfume. Italy: Belting ELVES 91-94.

E451.13* Ghost must finish reading holy book before is free. Widow's seven sons hold candle for ghost to read, rewarded with gold. Spain: Manning-Sanders BOOK..GHOSTS 24-29.

E451.14* Skeleton of wooer who killed lady comes each night to take her skull. His head was crushed as a punishment. The skull asks a girl to hold it all night in bed and keep skeleton from taking skull. Spell broken. Tyrolese: Manning-Sanders BOOK..GHOSTS 38-42.

E459.8* Ghost of Treageagle is called up to prove tenant paid rent. T. refuses to go back as demons await him. Saints set him task bailing bottomless pool with holed limpet shell until world ends. Later taken to Land's End to sweep sand. Can be heard howling on stormy nights. Cornwall: Manning-Sanders PETER 48-55.

E460. Revenants in conflict.

E461. Fight of revenants with living person. Girl abducted by revenants with whom she has danced. Kept in Baobab seven weeks until loses flesh. Her lover battles phantoms and demon Naga Singsangrie who guard tree. Kinkingas whom he saved have given powder of death and life in gratitude. He kills demon with this and revives lover. Spider has spun web to keep phantoms from tree where girl is kept. Dwarf advises. Upper Volta: Guirma TALES 16-28.

E461.1.1* Pupu of Kohala regains food plants stolen by evil spirits. Small Barbed Hook, companion, hides in basket and advises. P. defeats spirits in spear throwing contest. Voice of 'God' in basket orders spirits to let P. go. Hawaii: Thompson HAWAIIAN..TRICKSTERS 28-37.

E461.1.2* Sioux wrestles with ghost. Discovers that ghost stengthens when fire dies. Kicks more fuel onto fire and wins. Native American (Sioux): Brown TEPEE 166-167.

E463.1. Man convinces ghost that he too is a ghost, learns that ghosts fear human spittle. Ghost turns to goat, man spits on it preventing it from resuming ghost form, and sells it as a goat. China: Birch CHINESE 62-79 /Mayne GHOSTS 168-183/; Wyndham TALES..CHINA 48-51.

E463.2* Lad pretends is skeleton and gives cane and gourd to feel as arm and head. Carries spirit of girl which spirits steal and releases her when spirits flee at cockcrow. +K335.1.1.4. Korea: Jewett WHICH 136-157; Kim STORY 186-198.

E474. Cohabitation of living person and ghost.

E474.2* Young man woos maiden at her home. Her father discovers this and takes him to spot. Home has vanished and only her tomb is there. He still has souvenirs she gave him. China: Buck FAIRY 51-63.

E474.2.1* Student poet meets lovely maiden wearing robe in ancient style. Finds she died years ago. SEE ALSO: T111.1.5.1. China: Cheney TALES 157-160.

E474.3* Dead wife reborn as young girl weds husband again years later. Japan: Buck FAIRY 125-128.

E474.4* Caro. Girl wishes to wed ghost by spring. He can wed her only if she is dead. She runs into his arms, kisses him and dies. He is never seen again. Haiti: Thoby-Marcelin SINGING 17-20.

E474.5* Man sleeps covered with butterflies, chief's dead daughter weds. Native American (Sioux): Harper GHOSTS 99-102.

E474.6* Marriage to spirit. Man taken to underground spirit world weds. Brings tobacco presents to spirit people from his village. Receives gift of long life and good hunting for his village in return. Native American: Bierhorst FIRE 78-89.

E474.7* Father refuses to marry daughter. Ghost suitor brings rich gifts and takes her to island of ghosts. Native American (Nisquali): Curtis GIRL 5-20.

E480. Abode of the dead.

E481.2.0.1. Island of the dead. SEE: F129.4.4.1. Native American, Canada: Littledale GHOSTS 111-120.

E481.8.1. Account book of men summoned to death kept in heaven. SEE: K975.1.1.

E481.10* Land of dead under water.

E481.10.1* Man refuses to eat or permit final services to be performed for dead wife. Vodoun priest goes beneath water and returns with message from dead wife and token earring, instructing husband to go on living. Haiti: Courlander PIECE 71-75.

E500. Phantom hosts.

E501.5.5.1. The Wild Hunt. Old woman hides hare in basket and wild hunt passes by. Turns to lady, freed from being pursued nightly. Williams -Ellis FAIRY..BRITISH 302-305.

E501.5.5.1.1* Hare leaps to beekeeper for safety from dogs. Gypsy advises to tie hare to arm on All Hallow's Eve and leave house. Ask bees to aid. At midnight hare struggles, turns to girl. Witch is found in house, stung to death by bees. Scotland: Nic Leodhas THISTLE 106-118.

E501.18.4.1* Wild hunt carries person off. Man scoffs at old ways. Told to go to bridge at midnight. Sees water bubbling and hears hounds overhead. Sorcerer explains what he witnessed. His friend drowned self there at midnight and the Hounds of Hell came for him. Wales: Pugh TALES 83-96.

E502. The Sleeping Army. Soldiers killed in battle come forth on occasions from their resting place (hill, grave, grotto) and march about or send their leader to do so. SEE ALSO: D1960.2. Scotland: Nic Leodhas GAELIC 81-90 (Culloden).

E510. Phantom sailors and travelers. SEE ALSO: E535.3.

E511.1.2. Flying Dutchman sails because of pact with devil. Netherlands: Littledale GHOSTS 125-134.

E513* Gaucho neglects wife and cattle to weave poncho for festival. On way horse throws him and poncho becomes hoard of claws tearing and accusing him of neglect. He is doomed to roam the pampas forever. Argentina: Jagendorf KING 18-23 /Littledale GHOSTS 39-44/.

E514* The New-Ice-Runner. Man and son fall through ice in sleigh. Man is kept to be the New-Ice-Runner. Must drive a sleigh with golden runners beneath the ice in Autumn to protect from those who might fall through. The son is sent home in his sleigh. Finds two chunks of ice have turned to silver. When old he learns father must ride until another person falls through the ice. He takes father's place. Estonia: Maas MOON 123-127.

E520. Animal ghosts.

E521.1 Ghost of horse. Orkney: Cutt HOGBOON 51-55.

E521.2.3* Ghost of dog. Sandy MacNeil and His Dog. Ghost dog follows lad, he throws shoe at it telling it to bring whatever luck it has. Dog bounds through wall, revealing hidden treasure. Scotland: Nic Leodhas GAELIC 17-29 /Littledale GHOSTS 139-152/.

E521.2.4* The Old Laird and His Dogs. Dead grandfather and his two dogs guard grandson against scheming nephew. Ghost hounds chase off nephew. Statue of grandfather in cemetery puts hands on dogs' heads and they raise their heads. Still may hear their baying. Scotland: Nic Leodhas GAELIC 91-99.

E521.2.5* Wish-Hound. Man sees wish-hound, eyes big as cartwheels with red, blue and white rings, lays on step and he can't get into house. Cornwall: Manning-Sanders PETER 166-168.

E521.2.6* Ghost dog of South Mountain. Wicked son kills dog of good son. Dog's ghost haunts until he leaves. Shows hidden inheritance to returning good son. U.S. (Pennsylvania): Carpenter WONDER..DOGS 163-172.

E525* Ghost of butterfly. Butterfly maiden seeks vengeance on cruel mandarin who tortures butterflies. China: Carpenter TALES 198-205.

E530. Ghosts of objects.

E530.1.7. Ghost light indicates route funeral will take.

E530.1.7.1* Lad follows corpse candle and hears voice predict his death in a year, a month and a day. He locks self in tower for that time. On the night time is up an adder warmed by fire crawls from bundled faggots and bites. Wales: Pugh TALES 37-45.

E531.1. Ghostly burning house, traveler struck by bolt of fire. In morning discovers is merely site of fire in which evil man Duncan MacBain died. Scotland: Nic Leodhas GHOSTS GO 11-23.

E533.2.1* Ghost of serpent will free man if distant temple bell rings at midnight. Two pheasants whom man had saved from serpent beat selves against bell. Korea: Jewett WHICH 59-64; Kim STORY 123-128.

E535.1. Phantom coach and horses. Wild Driver gives ride from station. Lad falls out just in time. Bag is carried over cliff in ghost cart. Site of accident. Scotland: Nic Leodhas GHOSTS GO 54-64.

E535.3. Ghost ship. SEE ALSO: E511 (Flying Dutchman).

E535.3.3* The Phantom Ship. Pirate kills shipful of missionaries. Ghost ship flies in air around pirate's castle three years. Third time crashes into castle killing pirate. Netherlands (Friesland): Spicer THIRTEEN GHOSTS 7-16.

E540. Miscellaneous actions of revenants.

E545.19.1.1* The dead cannot speak unless spoken to. Man ignores headless ghost (E422.1.1) twice. Third time speaks and ghost tells where to find money. Leach THING 41-43.

E555. Dead man smokes pipe. Saves life of lad

who holds pipe for him. Native American (Iroquois): Garner CAVALCADE..GOBLINS 175-177.

E577.1.1* Dead persons play ball. Soccer game on Dung-Ting Lake. Boatman sees five men rise from lake and play soccer with silver phosphorescent ball. Old man playing is his father, lost at sea years ago. Others turn to monsters. He fights them off and rescues father. Father had been spared by fish-goblins because was good soccer player. China: Bang GOBLINS 41-46.

E577.2.1.1* Playing cards with a dead man (ghost). No one will play with lad, he invites ghosts to gamble. They gamble for his money and clothes, don't allow him to play. Scotland: Nic Leodhas GAELIC 39-45.

E577.2.1.2* Gamblers refuse to play after midnight on Shrove Tuesday (i.e. during Lent). Lad gambles with hare, loses all lands. Found in fountain in morning, loses all money and land and leaves. Nothing but hares left on land. Danaher FOLKTALE 59-62.

E577.3. Dead person's bowl. SEE: H1440A (learning of fear); D1460.1 (Rip Van Winkle).

E581.4. Ghost rides bus. SEE: E332.3.3.1.

E593. Ghost takes things from people.

E593.6* Robber ghost. Robber's ghost continues to hold up people who pass site of his death. Scotland: Nic Leodhas GHOSTS GO 91-102. Netherlands (Drie, N. Gelderland): Spicer THIRTEEN GHOSTS 65-72.

E599.14* Ghost decides not to be a ghost any longer. Becomes a cat, cats have nine lives, no ghosts. Scotland: Nic Leodhas GHOSTS 79-90.

E599.15. Don't ever kick a ghost! Man kicks white thing in road. It grows to size of dog. Kicks again--grows big as cow. Man flees. Leach THING 114.

E600 - E699. Reincarnation.

E600. Reincarnation.

E605.7.2* Ghost can be reborn as baby if is in room when birth occurs. Father sends ghost on repeated errands to keep away. Taiwan: Cheney TALES 93-96.

E607.2. Person transforms self, is swallowed up and reborn in new form. SEE: A1411.2.

E610.1.1. Reincarnation: boy to bird. Boy returns as bird, who later becomes the boy. SEE: N271A (Juniper Tree).

E613.0.1. Reincarnation of murdered child as bird. SEE: N271A (Juniper Tree).

E614.3. Reincarnation as crocodile. South America: Finger TALES 21-30 /Fenner ADVENTURES 39-50/.

E631. Reincarnation in plant (tree) growing from grave. (Usually mother.) (cf. D1316.5+). SEE: R221B+; N271A (Juniper Tree).

E631.6.1* Nurse prays to Fudo-Sama to let her die in place of child. Cherry tree planted in Saihoji temple in her honor blooms on every anniversary of her death. Japan: Buck FAIRY 221-223.

E632. Reincarnation as musical intstruments. The Singing Bone. A musical instrument made from the bones of a murdered person, or from a tree growing from the grave, speaks out. Tells of the crimes. Type 780. SEE ALSO: B652.1.2; N271.

E632.0.1* Harp of breastbones and hair of girl drowned by sister sings truth. England: Jacobs ENGLISH 43-47.

E632.0.2* The Singing Reed. Three sons seek olive blossoms to cure father's blindness (H1321.1). Elder two refuse aid to old woman. Third shares. Told where tree is. Brothers lock in hut and take flowers. Shepherdess hears reeds by door of hut singing. Takes to king. Sings "Father come and set me free." Son in deep coma inside hut. Revives. Venezuela: Courlander RIDE 226-230; Newman FOLK.. LATIN 111-117.

E632.0.3* Willow flute sings of witches' murder of queen. Flute turns to queen when witch flings to ground. Cornwall: Manning-Sanders PETER 63-70.

E632.0.4* The Silver Saucer and the Transparent Apple. Youngest daughter asks father for silver saucer and transparent apple. Twirls apple in saucer and sees world in it. Two sisters kill her for saucer and apple. Reed grows from grave. Shepherd makes whistle--sings truth. She is unearthed--reed sings to fetch water from well of Tzar. Revives. Weds Tzar. Russia: Higonnet-Schnopper TALES 118-128; Ransome OLD 18-39; Riordan TALES..CENTRAL 138-143 (Rosy apple; golden bowl).

E632.0.5* Chili plant grows from girl murdered by stepmother, sings to brother, father. They dig up girl and she is alive, protected by Virgin. Puerto Rico: Alegria THREE 59-63.

E632.1. Speaking bones of murdered person reveal murder. Mother kills girl for returning without pear. Brother digs in potato patch and pulls buried hair. She calls to him. Leach THING 99-101.

E632.2* Stepmother kills son and feeds to father. Bone sings truth. Taken to king as a marvel. The king recognizes the truth. Has stepmother stand by fire where she melts. King greases bone with her fat and son is restored. Haiti:

Wolkstein MAGIC 91-98.

E633.1* Girl falls in love with sound of fisherman's flute. Finds fisherman himself is ugly. He dies of love for her. A crystal is found in his boat from which a goblet is made for the princess. From it comes the sound of his flute. In remorse she too dies. Vietnam: Graham BEGGAR 57-69; Taylor FISHERMAN pb /Arbuthnot ANTHOLOGY 344-346/.

E710. External soul. A person (often a giant or ogre) keeps his soul or life separate from the rest of his body. SEE: K956; D532; B314 (animal brothers-in-law); K975.2.

E711.1. Soul in egg. SEE: B11.6.1.1 (dragon's); D532.

E711.4. Soul in necklace. A maiden's life depends upon her necklace which always must be kept in her possession. She marries a prince. A jealous girl steals the heroine's necklace so that the heroine seemingly dies. She comes to life whenever her rival removes the necklace. The prince finds her body and recovers the necklace. India: Turnbull FAIRY 12-26 /Sheehan FOLK 100-111/.

E711.10.1* Soul in sword. The Boy with the Golden Star. Type 302B. Guest gives apple for couple to divide. Give half to two fillies. One bears foal, one unicorn. Son with gold star on forehead born. Magic sword given. If anyone else draws it he will die. Two red roses that will fade if he dies. Strong, swings horse overhead. Becomes blood brothers with strong black man, gives rose token. Blood brothers with brave drinker, gives rose. Kills robbers and frees princess. Weds. Czar sends witch to kill. Witch gets secret of his strength from wife, draws sword. He is lifeless. Drinker and black man recover sword. Drinker drinks lake where witch threw sword. Czar's soldiers defeated with aid of unicorn. SEE ALSO: R111.1.3A. Bulgaria: Pridham GIFT 143-156.

E713. Soul hidden in a series of coverings. This motif is combined with several others. Usually the soul will be hidden in an egg, in a duck, in a well, in a church, or a similar series. SEE: B3146F; D532.

E725. Soul leaves one body and enters another. SEE: K1175.

E741.2. Soul becomes star after death (A760). +A1335.18. Greenland Eskimo: Leach HOW 37-38.

E756.2. Soul won from devil in card game. +Q565 (Smith and Devil); K1811.6. Jagendorf PRICELESS 138-146.

E760. Life Index. Object or animal has mystic connection with person. Changes in one correspond to changes in other.

E765.1. Life bound up with candle. When the candle goes out, person dies.

E765.1.1.1* Devil builds home for shoemaker (G303.9.1.13) in return for soul (M211). Given choice of waiting ten minutes or until candle burns up. Chooses latter. Puts candle in Bible --can never be burnt up as devil can't touch. Manning-Sanders PETER 169-177.

E765.1.1.2* Juan dreams self in heaven. Cleans his lamp so will burn longer. Costa Rica: Jagendorf KING 89-93.

E765.1.1.3* Man to live as long as candle lasts, blows candle out but candle shrivels up anyway. Dies. Wales: Sheppard-Jones WELSH 29-31.

E765.1.3. Life-lights in lower world. Each light mystically connects with the life of a person. When light is extinguished, person dies. SEE: D1825.3.1 (Death at foot of bed); D1724 (Godfather Death).

E765.3.3. Life bound up with tree. SEE: F441.2.3.1.1.

E765.3.4. Girl lives until her cowslip is pulled. England (Lincolnshire): Garner CAVALADE.. GOBLINS 216-221.

E765.3.6* Life bound up with magic wish fulfilling thread. Italy: Vittorini OLD 79-85.

E780. Vital bodily members.

E781.4. Substituted eyes. Fox hangs coat and tail out to dry, hangs one eye on twig to watch them. Magpies steal eye. Fox substitutes blueberry--world is too dark, cranberry--red, piece of ice--bright. Ice melts and he seems to be crying. Russia: Ginsburg ONE 21-27.

E782.3.2* Kappa reclaims severed arm. Man fails to force Kappa to sign pledge not to molest neighborhood. K. says he can't write. Japan: Pratt MAGIC #11.

E782.3.3* Man cuts off arm of ogre at gate. Keeps arm in box. His old nurse begs to see it, turns to ogre and flees with arm. Japan: Ozaki JAPANESE 262-272.

F. MARVELS

F0 - F199. Other world journeys.

F10. Journey to upper world.

F15. Visit to star world. SEE: A762.1 (Star husband).

F17.1* Sons of Sun seek father. Spider woman gives magic eagle feathers, with these on feet boys pass clapping thorns and clapping rocks. (D1553). Wife of Sun hides. Sun throws them against jeweled spikes on four walls, grinds in grinding stones, gives poison tobacco, has Fire God burn them in sweat bath, still unhurt. He acknowledges. They choose weapons and defend men from roaming monsters. Native American (Navajo): Curtis GIRL 81-95.

F53. Ascent to upper world on arrow chain. Hero shoots arrows which join one another in the air to form chain. SEE ALSO: A1423.1.2; G530.2 (Mastermaid).

F53.1* Boy stolen by moon. Boy is disrespectful to moon and is abducted. Friend shoots arrow chain at star near moon and climbs to sky. Granddaughter takes to sky-woman who gives magic spruce cone, twig of devil's club, rose bush and piece of whetstone (D672). Leaves spruce cone to cry for boy (D1611). When pursued they throw rosebush = bri ; whetstone = cliff. Type 313. Native American (Tlingit): Cunningham TALKING 70-79; Dolch ALASKA 11-25; Jablow MAN 35-38.

F53.1.1* Similar to F53.1. Abducted child is a girl. Grandson of sky-woman leads boy rescuer to grandmother. Thrown fish eye = lake, rose = briars, stone = mountain. Sleator ANGRY pb.

F53.1.2* Star steals boy for disrespect. Father shoots arrow chain. Person met on way advises leaving wooden figure in boy's place. He has brought along tobacco, paints, and stones. He throws these behind as flees and pursuers stop to pick up. Gives tobacco to helpful person who swells so pursuers cannot pass. Type 313. Eskimo: Caswell SHADOWS 83-87.

F53.2* Boy seeks father, the sun. Shoots arrow chain and climbs to sky. Asks father to let him carry torches one day. Lights all at once and scorches animals' backs (A2354.2). Turned to mink by father (A1825). Canada (Bella Coola): Jablow MAN 86-87.

F54.2. Plant grows to sky. (Jack and the Beanstalk). SEE ALSO: Q2.1.5Ab; D861.1G; Z52.4.2; G610.

F54.2.1* Jack and the Bean Stalk. Boy climbs magic bean stalk and is hidden by ogre's wife, steals magic hen that lays golden eggs, golden self-playing harp, and bag of gold, cuts beanstalk and ogre falls to death. (cf. 684).

England: De La Mare TALES84-106; De La Mare JACK pb; Jacobs ENGLISH 59-68 /De Regniers GIANT 18-30/, /Fenner GIANTS 115-125/, /Haviland FAIRY 78-85/, /Haviland FAVORITE ..ENGLAND 3-21/, /Mayne BOOK OF GIANTS 98-107 /; Manning-Sanders CHOICE 39-48 /Manning-Sanders BOOK..GIANTS 9-17/; Rackham ARTHUR 41-48; Reeves ENGLISH 128-146; Steel ENGLISH 97-109 /Martignoni ILLUSTRATED 164-168/; Stobbs JACK pb; Williams-Ellis FAIRY..BRITISH 155-168.

F54.2.1.1* Jack and The Beanstalk. F54.2.1. +Fairy informs Jack that giant stole treasures from his father. Adams BOOK..GIANTS 78-91; Lang RED 128-142; Opie CLASSIC 162-174.

F54.2.1.2* Jack and The Bean Tree. F54.2.1. +Jack steals rifle, knife, coverlet covered with bells. U.S. (Appalachia): Chase JACK 31-39.

F542.2.1.3* The Bean Tree. + Lad climbs beanstalk, given magic objects by St. Peter. SEE: D861.1G. Italy: Manning-Sanders GIANNI 119-126.

F54.2.2* Other magic growing plants. SEE ALSO: Z52.4.2.

F54.2.2.1* Cabbage seed grows to sky. Old man must carry old woman up to sky country in bag in teeth. She keeps asking how far to go and answering he drops her (J2133.5.1). Russia: Dolch OLD RUSSIA 37-43.

F54.2.2.2* Tree from grave of helpful turtle grows to sky, turtles descend with gold. SEE: B210.2.1. Japan: Scofield HOLD 9-14.

F56.1. Sky-window from digging or uprooting plant (tree) in upper world. SEE: A762.1 (Star Husband).

F58. Tower (column) to upper world. SEE: J2133.6.2.1.

F59.1. Man stretches self until he reaches upper world. SEE: D1376.1.3.1.

F62. Bird carries person to or from upper world. SEE: K1931.2.

F75. Ascent to heaven by holding on to elephant's tail. J2133.5.2.

F75.1* Ascent of emperor to heaven by dragon. Empress and retainers hold on and are carried to heaven also, others fall back. Japan: Ozaki JAPANESE 54-59.

F80. Journey to lower world. SEE ALSO: A1150.2; K1931.2.

F81.1. Orpheus. Journey to the land of dead to bring back person from the dead (cf. C331 Tabu = looking back; C953 Return to other world for breaking tabu). Native American (Nez Percé): Heady TALES 109-118 (Itsayaya, Coyote,

A1335.17).

F81.1.0.1* Izanagi descends to bring Izanani back from Land of the Dead. Tabu on looking (C932) while she asks god of the lower world for permission. He lights a tooth of comb in his hair and enters her room. Sees decayed corpse surrounded by eight demons of thunder. She sends female demons to pursue him. He throws down obstacles (D672) comb turns to grapes; comb to bamboo shoots; urinates and turns to river. They stop. Eight thunder demons pursue. He throws peaches, anathema to demons, and they stop. Inami pursues. He rolls stones over entrance to underworld and pronounces their marriage severed. Origin of divorce formula (A1558). She threatens to kill one thousand people a day. He will cause one thousand five hundred to be born. Japan: McAlpine JAPANESE 16-22.

F81.1.0.2* Sun will allow man to live forever if his dead daughter can be brought back from the Darkening Land in the West. Seven men go. Break tabu and lift lid of box her spirit is in before reaching her body. Spirit flies out and enters a redbird. Native American (Cherokee): Cunningham TALKING 41-44.

F81.1.0.3* Kewalu hangs self. Huku seeks her in underworld. Lets self down on liana and pulls her up. Hawaii: Berry MAGIC 98-112.

F81.1.0.4* Brother seeks sister in Land of Shadows. Crosses water in white stone canoe. She has eaten there and cannot return. He returns to become a chief. Native American, Canada: Littledale GHOST 111-120.

F81.1.0.4.1* Man follows dead lover to Land of Shadows. Crosses in white stone canoe. Returns without her to become a chief. Native American: Bierhorst FIRE 29-38.

F81.1.0.5* Coyote and Eagle visit land of dead and bring back dead, carrying in bag over river. Coyote puts them in a trance with magic song, but they must reach shore before daylight. He succeeds but all choose to return to land of dead. Native American (Yakima): Robinson COYOTE 113-124.

F92. Pit entrance to lower world. Entrance through a pit, hole, spring or cavern. SEE: G425.2.5 (revenant piper); K1931.2.

F92.2.1. Girl gathering flowers swallowed up by earth and taken to lower world. SEE: A1150.2.

F92.7. Hole to underworld kingdom of snakes. SEE ALSO: D817.1.2; D817.1.2.2; K1931.2V. Russia: Daniels FALCON 92-110.

F101.3. Return from lower world on eagle. SEE: K1931.2D, E.

F102.1. Hero shoots monster (or animal) and follows it into lower world. SEE: K1931.2.

F103.1. (Baughman). "Green children" visit world of mortals, continue to live with them. England (Suffolk): Colwell ROUND 70-73.

F110. Journey to terrestrial other worlds.

F112.2. City of women. SEE: H1385.4B.

F127.1. Journey to serpent kingdom. SEE: D817.1.2; F92.7.

F129.4.4. Voyage to Isle of the Dead. SEE ALSO: E481.2.0.1.

F129.4.4.1* Trader lands in country of ghosts. Gold given turns to paper money buried at funerals when they return to ship. China: Birch CHINESE 62-79 /Mayne GHOSTS 168-183/.

F133. Submarine other world. SEE: F212 (Fairy land under water); F725 (Submarine world).

F153.2* Otherworld reached by leaping into red wave (spirit canoe). Tui Liku survives six nights of torture by demons on the Isle of Tuvana who toss him in air as game. Lingandua, a one-armed lord of the spirit world takes him to the spirit land. He visits four times, returning with nuts, seeds, and bird. Sandpiper had pecked eye out of his body. Still calls "Tui Liku" in his honor. Fiji: Gittins TALES 14-21.

F173.2.1* Otherworld land of peace. Fisherman enters peach blossom forest and finds land isolated for hundreds of years and in peace. Forest has vanished when he seeks it again. China: Manton FLYING 77-82.

F200 - F699. Marvelous creatures.

F200. Fairies.

F206. Namashepani. Small, long black hair, wear white cobweb-like clothing, fly. If one calls them 'small' becomes one of them. Cobweb cloaks can be seen drying on hills in early morning. E. Africa: Heady WHEN 21-26.

F210. Fairyland.

F212. Fairyland under water. (cf. F133). SEE: F420.6.1.3.1 (Urashima Taro).

F235.4.1. Fairies made visible through use of ointment.

A* (Baughman). Mortal midwife or nurse to fairy child gets some of fairy ointment (F372.1) in her eyes as she anoints eye of child. She is able to see fairies as they are. Later he asks which eye she sees him with; she tells him and he puts out the eye. Wales: Lang FIFTY 73-76 /Lang LILAC 54-61 /; Sheppard-Jones WELSH 142-145. England: Jacobs ENGLISH

220-223. Great Britain: Williams-Ellis FAIRY 140-145. France: Hollman DRAC 1-17 (Drac).

B* Girl sees her fairy master with another woman after rubbing ointment on her eyes, slaps him next time he tries to kiss her, her lovely gown turns to rags and she is sent home (F348.0.1). Cornwall: Colwell ROUNDS 117-121; Manning-Sanders PETER 85-97. SEE ALSO: F361.3

F243.3.1.1* Animals eaten by fairies whole again. Three Cows. Eaten by fairies in night then reassembled by magic. Farmer spies wondering why cows so thin, sees them reassemble third cow. Leave out one bone (E33), limps henceforth. England: Jacobs MORE 89-91.

F244.2. Fairy shows hiding place of treasure in return for freedom. SEE: J1922.3.1.

F271.2.8.1* (Kirtley). Fairies transport large stone to its present location. Villagers place stones on menehunes' fields in land clearing. M's put stone back each night. Lazy Pi, who is half menehune, gives menehunes poi gifts and and asks them to throw stones into sea. Hawaii (Kauai): Berry MAGIC 22-29.

F282.4. (Baughman). Mortal travels with fairies, he drinks too much in wine cellar where they revel. He is being hanged by owner when fairy appears, tells him to use the formula he had used night before. He escapes but is warned not to travel with fairies again. SEE ALSO: G242.7 (witches fly). Manning-Sanders PETER 1-6 (fairies call "Ho and away for Par Beach", fly off).

F282.4.1* Mortal echoes fairies call "My horse and bridle and saddle", flies with them to France. Brings back King of France's daughter. Crosses her to himself, thwarts fairies. They curse her with dumbness. Year later, he discovers herb by door will disenchant her. Ireland: Jacobs CELTIC 6-28; Rackham FAIRY 24-51.

F282.4.2* Wee Red Cap. Man echoes fairies cry "I wish I had my wee red cap" and flies with them. In palace he throws cap at girl and becomes invisible. Sentenced to hang, he asks for cap once more and wishes self home. Ireland: Sawyer THIS 31-41 /Sawyer WAY 111-120/. Scotland: Sleigh NORTH 195-201.

F300. Marriage or liaison with fairy.

F302.1. Man goes to fairyland and marries fairy.

F302.1.3. Connla is given magic replenishing apple by fairy maid. She returns for him and takes away in crystal boat. Jacobs CELTIC 1-4 /Arbuthnot ANTHOLOGY 180/, /Arbuthnot FAIRY 138-139/.

F302.1.4* Youngest son swears to wed a fairy, falls in love with common girl instead and weds. She is actually a fairy. Takes him to magic land inside chest. His brothers, the emperor, general, and minister covet chest. Wave floods land destroying all except fairy and husband inside chest. China: Wyndham FOLK..CHINA 17-21.

F302.1.5* Man goes to fairyland and marries fairy. Einon weds fairy Olwen, bears son Taliesin. Wales: Sheppard-Jones WELSH 48-53.

F302.1.6* The Adventures of Nera. Prize to all who will tie withe around foot of man hung on Halloween. Nera tries. Hanged man asks to be taken on back to fetch drink of water. First house has lake of fire around it, means fire is covered at night. Second house has no water left in tubs overnight. Third house has water. Dead man drinks and sleepers die. When Nera returns to Ailill's hall for reward he finds elves have burnt it. He follows elfin plunderers into elfin Mound of Curachon. He is given a wife and made to fetch wood daily. Wife sends him to warn Ailill that the plundering he 'saw' will not occur until next Halloween. He warns Ailill and the men of Connaught destroy the elves and take elf king's crown. Nera and wife live yet in the mound. Ireland: Garner CAVALCADE.. GOBLINS 92-97.

F302.3.1.5* Yara (Oiarais) entices man away from village. He shoots four arrows at her and follows. Never seen again. Brazil: Carpenter SOUTH AMERICA 137-143.

F302.4.2. Fairy comes into man's power when he steals her wings (clothes). She leaves when she finds them. (cf. C31.10). SEE ALSO: H1385.3Fe (husband seeks lost fairy wife). Philippines: Robertson FAIRY..PHILIPPINES 53-62 (third bathing fairy, bears daughter, daughter cries and looks at bamboo pole where wings are hidden). Visayan: Sechrist ONCE 67-75 (wings hidden in bamboo post of house).

F302.4.2.0.1* Fairies beg wings back and take husband to visit home in sky. Their father plans to kill him, aardvark bores hole in sky for him to escape. Spider lets down cord. Rat warned him. Tshindao: Aardema BEHIND 19-25.

F302.4.2.0.2* Man finds angel's feather robe, returns it. She dances for him. Memory makes happy all life. Japan: Sakade JAPANESE CHILDREN'S STORIES 29-33.

F302.4.2.0.3* Deer advises woodcutter to take feather robe of bathing fairy. Not to return it until she bears four children. He shows robe after she bears three children and she leaves with children. Could not have carried four. Deer advises to ride up to heaven in water bucket. Happy there but returns to earth to see mother. Touches ground and can never return. Keeps calling to heaven. Turned into rooster. Korea: Kim STORY 86-90.

F302.4.2.1. Fairy comes into man's power when he steals her clothes. She leaves when she finds them. Greece: Haviland FAV..GREECE

39-51 (handkerchief from tenth fairy at spring bears daughter. She requests husband to go to dance, vanishes).

F302.4.2.1.1* Fairy comes into man's power when he steals her clothes. She leaves when he breaks tabu. SEE ALSO: C31. Greece: Haviland FAVORITE..GREECE 83-90 (veil of one of three dancing fairies). Smith Sound Eskimo: Cunningham TALKING 98-104 (Seventh bathing swan maiden, finds clothes in cedar tree, leaves when offended, +D361.1.1).

F302.4.2.2* Animal (bird) in maiden form comes into man's power when he hides her skin. She leaves when she finds it or he breaks tabu. SEE ALSO: C35; D361.1.1. Scotland (Shetland Isles): Arnott ANIMAL 95-99 (seal maiden of Selkie folk, daughter tells where skin is hidden). Yoruba: Fuja FOURTEEN 126-132 (deer, bears son, finds skin and leaves); Walker NIGERIAN 11-19; Walker DANCING 27-34 (deer, tabu-telling, second wife gets secret and throws skin at deer maiden, becomes deer, kills second wife and leaves). Eskimo: Melzack RAVEN 53-60 (fox, offended leaves, +N831.1). S. China: Hume FAVORITE..CHINA 99-100 (fox, he shows children skin to prove mother is fox, +N831.1).

F302.4.2.2.1* Cat hides bathing fairies' necklaces or clothing and demands dry path or bridge to island where thief of her master's ring dwells. (D882.1.1.1; D882.1B). Burma: Brockett BURMESE 51-62; Carpenter ELEPHANT'S 114-124.

F302.4.2.3* Golden Duck and Seven Ducklings emerge from lake one day each year. Man throws rosary around them and they change to maiden and seven children. Persuade him to join them in underwater palace where her father took them to escape white men. Golden Duck and eight ducklings emerge each year. Columbia: Jagendorf KING 83-88.

F302.4.2.4* Waupee sees star maidens descend to earth in basket and dance. Changes self to a mouse and catches youngest. Wed. (A762.2). She weaves basket and ascends to sky with son. Star Chief invites Waupee to come to sky bringing tokens of all animals and birds he has killed. Star people choose token each and become animals and birds (A1717.1). W. and wife and son become white hawks. (A1937). Native American: Bierhorst RING pb; Haviland NORTH 97-100.

F305.1.2* Faery Flag of Dunvegan. Left on babe's crib by faery mother who must return to people. To wave, will save clan MacLeod from danger. May be used three times. Scotland (Skye): Wilson SCOTTISH 66-74.

F311.1. Fairy godmother. Attendant good fairy. SEE: R221 (Cinderella).

F316.1. Fairy's curse partially overcome by another fairy's amendment. SEE: D1960.3 (Sleeping Beauty).

F320. Fairies carry people away to fairyland.

F320.1* Wee Meg Barnileg reforms. Ireland: Greene MIDSUMMER 72-86; Sawyer WAY 205-216.

F320.2* Lad to be released if finds lost vase by noon, finds in lake, released. Greece: Haviland FAVORITE..GREECE 61-69.

F320.3* Man to cook for fairies sends them home for bowls, spoons, etc. Says can't work without cat, dog, baby, etc. Raise a din. Fairies send all home. Scotland: Nic Leodhas HEATHER 35-43 /Minard WOMEN 135-145/, /Greene CLEVER 13-24/.

F320.4* Mr. Noy. Girl to be freed if lover will refrain from eating or drinking until all fairy babies are rocked to sleep (C211.1). Fails. Cornwall: Manning-Sanders PETER 183-190.

F321. Fairy steals child from cradle.

F321.0.2* Lazy mother left child dirty, returned on condition she reform. Cornwall: Manning-Sanders PETER 17-21.

F321.1. Changeling. Fairy steals child from its cradle and leaves fairy substitute. Changeling is mature and only seems to be a child.

F321.1.1. Changeling betrays his age when his wonder is excited. Usually pottage is boiled in an eggshell. The changeling: "I shall soon be a hundred years old but I never saw this done before!" Real child is then returned usually. SEE ALSO: K975.1.2. German: Grimm HOUSEHOLD 174; Grimm JUNIPER 150-151; Shubb ABOUT 34. Welsh: Sheppard-Jones WELSH 178-182. Great Britain: Williams-Ellis FAIRY..BRITISH 44-48. France: Picard FRENCH 107-112 (Korrigan's son, a poulpican). Celtic: Jacobs CELTIC 242-244 /Greene CLEVER 28-31/. Scotland: Wilson SCOTTISH 107-114.

F321.1.4.1.1* Changeling plays on bagpipes and causes all to dance. Farmer moves and as they cross river changeling howls "You tricked me" and leaps into water. Ireland: Belting ELVES 55-60.

F321.1.4.1.2* Passing changeling widershins around well every Wednesday at dawn is not efficacious. Changeling's wife calls to him and he answers he enjoys riding the goody's back to well every Wednesday and playing the fool there. Cornwall: Manning-Sanders CHARMS 120-124.

F321.1.4.5. When changeling is threatened with burning, child is returned. Scotland: Nic Leodhas THISTLE 74-81; Wilson SCOTTISH 107-114.

F321.1.4.5.1* When changeling is threatened with drowning, child is returned. Wales: Sheppard-Jones WELSH 178-182. Celtic: Jacobs CELTIC 242-244 /Greene CLEVER 28-31/.

F321.1.4.6. Changeling beaten and left outside; the mortal child is returned. Scandinavia:

D'Aulaire D'AULAIRE'S 44-45.

F321.1.4.10* Changeling left under stones of churchyard stile until midnight. Own baby returned. Cornwall: Manning-Sanders PETER 120-124.

F321.3. Man goes to fairyland and rescues stolen child.

F321.3.0.1* Sticks metal dirk in door of fairyland, fairies can't touch metal so can't close door. Carries bible to protect, cock to crow so they must get door closed. Gets son back and cursed not to talk. Forges a fairy sword as he has seen it forged, thus breaking spell. Scotland: Wilson SCOTTISH 107-114.

F321.3.0.2* Woman buys child back from sidh with extraordinary white cloak of nechtan and golden stringed harp of wrad which she makes. Scotland: Nic Leodhas THISTLE 46-61 /Minard WOMENFOLK 1-13/.

F321.3.2* Boy appears to smith in dream and asks to free from giant Mahon MacMahon. Horse kicks smith in forehead, mark shows dream was real. Must choose correct boy from many. Ireland: Palmer FAIRY 78-84.

F321.9. Fairy child (foundling) raised by mortal. Returns to fairies when grown. Greece: Haviland FAVORITE..GREECE 53-59.

F324. Youth abducted by fairy. Type 312D.

F324.0.1* Childe Rowland. Burd Ellen runs widershins round church and is carried off by fairies. Merlin directs rescue to King of Elfland. Two fail. Youngest succeeds. Not to eat or drink in fairyland (C211.1). To behead everyone who speaks to him there. Kills giant (or King of Elfland) and restores brothers, rescues sister. English: Jacobs ENGLISH 122-129; Steel ENGLISH 193-202; Williams-Ellis FAIRY..BRITISH 196-205.

F324.3.1* Tamlane. Tamlane rides widershins round church and finds self in elfland. Betrothed grabs him when riding with Queen of Elfland on Halloween. She holds through successive transformations (D757) and restores. British Isles: Jacobs MORE 172-176 /Harper GHOSTS 90-94/; Williams-Ellis FAIRY..BRITISH 263-271; Wilson SCOTTISH 41-45.

F324.4* Girl offends fairies by embittering waters of stream with her tears. Is carried off and left immobile in cave. Her lover finds and as daylight's last rays strike her she revives. Greece: Haviland FAVORITE..GREECE 71-81.

F329.1. Fairies carry off youth; he has gift of prophecy when he returns to earth. (Thomas the Rhymer.) Taken by queen of fairyland for three days (seven years). In later life a white hart and hind come to fetch him back to fairyland. Scotland: Baker GOLDEN 148-160; Finlay TATTERCOATS 111-118; Wilson SCOTTISH

8-17.

F329.4.1. Lost fairy child found by mortals. Mortals feed, warm it, keep it until one day it hears voice calling, "Coleman Grey!" It leaves with the remark "Ho! ho! ho! My daddy's come!" Cornwall: Colwell ROUND 122-124; Manning-Sanders PETER (Skillywidden, Mammy comes).

F329.4.2. Fairy child found--cared for, but it pines away. Suffolk: Colwell ROUND 68-69.

F329.4.4* Baby found on shore is raised. She returns to sea when hears sea in shell. Orkney: Cutt HOGBOON 103-106.

F330. Grateful fairies.

F331.1. Mortal wins fairires' gratitude by joining in their dance. SEE: F344.1.

F331.3. Mortal wins fairies' gratitude by joining in their song and completing it by adding the names of the days of the week. SEE: F344.1.

F331.4. Mortal wins fairies' gratitude by playing for their dance. Italy: Manning-Sanders GIANNI 173-178 (given elfin fiddle). Wales: Sheppard-Jones WELSH 123-128 (To have been rewarded but old woman comes out of hut and frightens off fairies).

F336.1* Farmer plows up fairies' field. They vow revenge. He must agree to restore field and they agree not to harm him or his sons. One hundred years later they carry off a son of the house. Wales: Sheppard-Jones WELSH 6-12.

F339.2. Fairies care for tulip bed out of gratitude to owner for not plucking any blossoms. England: Reeves ENGLISH 98-102.

F340. Gifts from fairies.

F341. Fairies given fulfillment of wishes. SEE ALSO: J2075.

F341.3* Brothers aid Goddess of the Forest as hag and are given seven wishes. +Z42.0.2. Japan: Titus TWO pb.

F342.1. Fairy gold. Fairies give coals (wood, earth) that turn to gold. SEE ALSO: F451.5.1.4; F344.1.3. Czechoslovakia: Haviland FAVORITE..CZECHOSLOVAKIA 35-47. Friesland: Spicer OWL'S 86-105 (leaves and dirt sprinkled with holy water turn to gold, +F344.1).

F342.1.1* Cook who fed fishes rewarded. Wakes in night to find ship aground. Explores and brings bucket of sand back to bunk. In morning finds gold in bucket. Japan: Uchida SEA 11-21.

F342.1.2* Girl asks for coal for fire of brownie camp, coals turn to gold. Netherlands (North Gelderland): Spicer THIRTEEN GHOSTS 101-111.

F342.1.3* Sandal seller trades wares with charcoal seller, charcoal turns to gold. New Year's Eve. SEE ALSO: J1873.1. Japan: Sakade JAPANESE CHILDREN'S STORIES 24-28.

F342.3* Lady of the Tylwyth Teg gives ferryman silver coin which replaces self. Wales: Palmer FAIRY 50-54.

F343.10. Fairies give mortals fairy bread. Brittany: Belting ELVES 77-83.

F343.21* Poor servant woman never having home of her own leaves on Christmas Eve in famine time. Finds fairy cabin built for her on mountain. Never seen again, though child saw her and cabin. Ireland: Sawyer LONG 45-60.

F344.1. Fairies remove hunchback's hump (or replace it). Type 503. SEE ALSO: J2415.12; J2415.25.

F344.1.1* Old man joins dance of tengus. They take his wen as pledge he will return. Mean old man next door imitates, dances poorly. Given back first man's wen in addition to own (J2415). Japan: Hearn JAPANESE 53-56; Ozaki JAPANESE 272-282; Sakade JAPANESE CHILDREN'S STORIES 34-36; Uchida DANCING 37-45; Wiggin TALES 415-416. Korea: Asia FOLK..FOUR 24-29.

F344.1.2* Old man told to dance for dwarfs at full moon. They will remove his wen if pleased. He dances poorly, they give second lump. He tries again next month, succeeds. They remove lumps. He sells this secret to neighbor and others. China: Buck FAIRY 232-236; Lang GREEN 215-221.

F344.1.3* Fairies remove hunchback's hump. He supplies suitable conclusion to their song, usually adding day of the week. Another imitates, given hump. Spain: Boggs THREE 49-58 (guitar player). Italy: Williams-Ellis ROUND 109-116 (fairies too lose humps, his completion of their song broke spell. Given stick [D140.1] which beats enemies as reward, stepbrother imitates--given nothing). Ireland: MacManus WELL 21-30 (inside fairy hill). Haiti: Thoby-Marcelin SINGING 3-6 (counts to eight, spoils song of devil, hump taken as punishment, given to twin brother who imitates). Japan: Bang GOBLINS 1-13 (wen taken by goblins to insure return, no imitator). Friesland: Spicer OWL'S 86-105 (given choice of looks or wealth chooses looks, miser imitates asks for "what Sjored rejected"--given hump; S. teaches Little Earth Men last line of song breaking spell so they can stop dance. Given leaves and dirt reward, which turn to gold (F342.1). Wales: Pugh TALES 97-104 (first has nose shortened, second nose to never stop growing).

F344.1.4* Tailor and goldsmith enter circle of dancing fairies. Their beards and hair are cut off, their pockets filled with coals. Hair regrows, coals (F342.1) turn to gold in morning. Greedy goldsmith repeats. His gold of first night turns back to coal, his hair never grows

back. He had been humpbacked, now has hump on chest also. Germany (Grimm): Gag MORE 123-130; Grimm GRIMM'S (Follett) 202-206.

F346.2. Fairies make shoes for shoemaker. Leave when given gift of clothes (F381.3) and watched. Germany (Grimm): Arbuthnot ANTHOLOGY 199; Arbuthnot FAIRY 35-36; Association TOLD.. GREEN 47-51; Gag MORE 251-257; Grimm ELVES (Hewitt) pb; Grimm GRIMM'S (Follett) 66-69; Grimm GRIMM'S (Grosset) 178-180; Grimm GRIMM'S (World) 324-325; Grimm HOUSEHOLD 171-172; Grimm SHOEMAKER (Adams) pb; Haviland FAIRY 118-121; Haviland FAVORITE.. GERMANY 13-20; Hutchinson CHIMNEY 119-124; Manning-Sanders DWARFS 109-111; Martignoni ILLUSTRATED 203-204; Rockwell THREE 71-77; Shubb ABOUT 31-32; Wiggin TALES 170-171.

F348.0.1. Fairy gift disappears or is turned to something worthless when tabu is broken. SEE ALSO: F235.4.1; F460.4.2.

F348.0.1.1* Fairy spins for goat girl. Not to grumble when winding it. It disappears. Czechoslovakia: Haviland FAVORITE..CZECHOSLOVAKIA 35-47.

F348.5.1* Mortal not to betray secret of fairies' gift. Tells. It vanishes. Wales: Spicer THIRTEEN GHOSTS 120-128 (green goblin ghosts). Switzerland: Müller-Guggenbühl SWISS 121-122.

F348.7.0.1* Fairies leave gold for bath water until miller tells. Wales: Sheppard-Jones WELSH 101-105.

F348.7.1. Abuse of fairy gifts brings about their loss. SEE ALSO: B184.2.2.2.

F348.7.1.1* Magic scythe never to be tempered in fire, melts. Iceland: Belting ELVES 84-90.

F348.1.2* Cow holds back half of milk for little people. Wife prepares charm to get rid of them. Cow gives only thin milk thereafter. Cornwall: Manning-Sanders PETER 156-165.

F348.7.1.3* (Baughman). Man who gets magic (D1415.2) harp from fairies makes people dance with it. It disappears. Wales: Sheppard-Jones WELSH 25-28.

F348.7.1.4* Fairy gifts must be taken possession of immediately.

F348.7.1.4.1* Girl given golden chain for industrious knitting; unravels yarn to find way back. Cannot find end of yarn. Wales: Sheppard-Jones WELSH 98-100.

F348.7.5* Man taken to serve three fairies. Shown treasure. Asked what he'll do with it--build castle, hire servants, never work again. Too greedy. They give sip of broth, his magic vision vanishes. Ireland: McNeil DOUBLE 88-94.

F348.8. Tabu: mortal for whom fairy works must not watch him at work. SEE: F381.10; F346.1.

136

F348.10 (Baughman). Tabu: mortal for whom fairy works must not thank fairy. SEE ALSO: F346.1. England: Jacobs MORE 28-36 (Yallery Brown). Wales: Pugh Tales 117-128 (Ruddy-My-Beard). Lincolnshire: Garner CAVALCADE ..GOBLINS 42-51 (Yallery Brown).

F348.11* Tabu: speaking while digging treasure shown by ghostly body. One member of family cries out in concern at weight of coffer being unearthed. It slips back into pit forever. Netherlands: Spicer THIRTEEN GHOSTS 83-91.

F349.5. Flying fairy boat seen by kind lad. He asks it to go into his basket and it shrinks and does so. He is to wed emperor's daughter in exchange for boat. Emperor sends him instead to House of the Red and Green Demons. He shows no fear and is rewarded for his virtue with treasure. Weds princess. Central China: Hume FAVORITE..CHINA 69-73; Ross BURIED 139-146.

F350. Theft from fairies.

F351.2. Theft of money from fairies by frightening them away from it. Cornwall: Manning-Sanders PETER 82-84.

F351.2.1* Woman turns nightgown inside out as charm against spriggans and chases them off to gain their treasure, they had left her one coin nightly heretofore. One touches her nightgown as flees. She is now rich but can never sleep for prickling of nightgown.

F352.1. Theft of cup from fairies when they offer mortal drink at fairy banquet or celebration. Scotland: Haviland FAVORITE..SCOTLAND 3-12 (escapes by running on wave wetted stones by shore where fairies can't touch).

F360. Malevolent or destructive fairies (= pixies).

F361.1.1. Fairy takes revenge for not being invited to feast. SEE: D1960.3 (Sleeping Beauty).

F361.1.2.2* Fairy Drak arrives last and is mocked by man sharing food with fairies, "For those who arrive late, there is nothing but regret." He bedevils the man and causes to arrive too late to be considered as suitor for girl. Cites same slogan. Palmer FAIRY 23-30.

F361.2.3. Fairies bind man fast to ground after he has attempted to capture fairy prince and princess. Cornwall: Manning-Sanders PETER 103-109 (Spriggans, at dawn he finds ropes are merely spiderwebs).

F361.3. Fairies take revenge on person who spies on them. Spy uses magic salve on one eye. Fairies tear out the eye. SEE: F235.4.1A; F420.4.7.1. Cornwall: Manning-Sanders PETER 194-201.

F361.3.0.1* Giant takes sea captain to Isle of Youth, Eilean-h-oige, giant tries to escape with cargo but captain takes case to King Fiorn and giant is caught despite attempts to remain invisible. He asks which eye captain saw him with and pokes it, blinding. Scottish Hebrides: Nic Leodhas SEA 161-177.

F361.4.1* Man builds house in fairy path. Constant trouble, finally burnt down. Ireland: Danaher FOLKTALES 77-80.

F361.14.6. (Baughman). Fairy lames girl who forgets to leave food out for him. Britain: Williams-Ellis FAIRY..BRITISH 284-287 (to be cured if recalls curing herb Bustgusticeridis. Seven years later boy hits her leg with herb and cures, she had forgotten to leave water out for pisgies).

F361.17.8. Fairies chase man who dares them to come chase him. He barely gets home ahead of them; they drive iron javelin (sword) through iron-covered door. England (Durham): Colwell ROUND 40 (Midridge).

F369.7. Fairies lead travelers astray. Yorkshire: Colwell ROUND 51-53 (Tailor did not believe in fairies).

F369.10* Man has died, in grief fairy turns destructive, is banished to Red sea for fourteen generations, Gwarwyn-a-throt. Wales: Sheppard-Jones WELSH 13-18.

F370. Visit to fairyland.

F372.1. Fairies take human midwife to attend fairy women. SEE: F235.4.1A; F451.5.1.4.1.

F372.2.2* Woman stands godmother to fairy child. Short time is really years (F377). Rewarded with gold. Germany (Grimm): Grimm HOUSE-HOLD 173 (elves); Shubb ABOUT 33 (elves). Brittany: Belting ELVES 77-83 (Korrigan's).

F373.1* Arawn. Voice in room arranged for unborn prince calls "Long is the day and long is the night and long tarries Arawn." After eighteen years all eighteen year old boys are to come to castle so king can choose heir. Fairy horse carries Owen there, he answers riddling questions, is escorted to room and vanishes along with horse and fairy maid. Said to have been taken to Land of Enchantment. Wales: Pugh TALES 61-81.

F373.2* Land of Greenies, little men in green, fisherman seeks land again, disappears. England (Lancashire): Colwell ROUND 19-22.

F374. Long in fairyland to visit home. SEE: F420.6.1.3.1 (Urashima Taro); T294.

F377. Supernatural lapse of time in fairyland. Years seem days. SEE ALSO: D2011; F420.6.1.3.1 (Urashima Taro); F372.2.2 (human godparent); D1960.1 (Rip Van Winkle); F378.1; G312.8; D1890 (magic aging).

F377.0.1* Princess of Mount Nam-Nhu. Girl

appears at Flower Festival in temple garden and is fined for plucking peach. Mandarin's son offers own robe in payment for her. Seeks her. Reaches Mount Nam-Nhu, heavenly mountain, and weds Giang Huong. Returns home after one year. One hundred years have passed on earth. Vietnam: Robertson FAIRY..VIET-NAM 44-59.

F377.0.2* (Baughman). Person held enchanted by fairy music for many years. He returns home a stranger, crumbles to death on doorstep. Wales: Sheppard-Jones WELSH 6-12; Sheppard-Jones WELSH 164 (bird sings until sycamore dies of old age--D2011.1).

F378.0.1. Mortal expelled from fairyland for breaking tabu.

F378.0.1.1* Elidorous brings golden ball to mother. Is forbidden to re-enter fairyland. Wales: Sheppard-Jones WELSH 89-92.

F378.1A. (Baughman). Tabu: touching ground before dog riding a horse touches ground. Those who forget are turned to dust. King Herla has gone to wedding of King of Elves, seems gone a short time. Hundreds of years have passed (F377). British Isles: Belting ELVES 41-46.

F378.5. Tabu: Plucking flowers from bed tended by fairies. Wales: Sheppard-Jones WELSH 129-130 (Door to fairyland closed forever).

F379.5A. (Baughman). Person joins dance of fairies and cannot be seen. His companion is suspected of murdering him and is given a certain time (a year and a day) to clear himself. He goes to the spot where his companion has disappeared, contrives to see his friend (by putting his foot inside fairy ring on grass) and pulls him out of ring. Wales: Sheppard-Jones WELSH 159-163; Sheppard-Jones WELSH 119-122 (daughter riding fairy ponies, father rescues). Hebrides (Isle of Arran): Nic Leodhas SEASPELL 53-71.

F380. Defeating or ridding oneself of fairies.

F381.1. Fairy leaves when he is named. Type 500. SEE ALSO: D2183 (Tom Tit Tot).

F381.1.1* Gwarwyn-A-Throt, overheard chanting as spins, leaves house when maid taunts with name. Wales: Sheppard-Jones WELSH 13-18.

F381.3. Fairy leaves when he is given clothes. SEE ALSO: F346.1 (Shoemaker and Elves). Cornwall: Manning-Sanders PETER 56-68. Ireland: Palmer DRAGONS 38-42; Pilkington SHAMROCK 52-54 (Pooka in ass form).

F381.3.1* Cauld Lad of Hilton. England: Jacobs ENGLISH 212-214; Mayne GHOSTS 99-101; Williams-Ellis FAIRY..BRITISH 110-113.

F381.8. Spinning fairies lured away from house by fire alarm. Scotland: Haviland FAVORITE ..SCOTLAND 59-70; Wilson SCOTTISH 115-120.

F381.8.1* The Horned Women. Send housewife to fetch water in sieve. Voice says to dab with clay and moss (H1023.2.0.1) and call out three times "the mountain of the Fennin women is on fire." They rush to Slievemamon. Spirit of the Well tells to sprinkle water in which child's feet were washed on threshold and other wise prepare house. Feetwater, door, cake thus refuse to open to witches when they return. Witch mantle dropped is kept in family (A1578.2). Ireland: Baker TALKING 48-51; Jacobs CELTIC 34-37; Hoke WITCHES 1-4; Littledale GHOSTS 61-66; Manning-Sanders BOOK..WITCHES 123-127 (Blackstairs Mountain).

F381.10. Fairies leave when person watches them at work. (Same as F348.8.) SEE: F346.1.

F381.14* Getting rid of fairies. Man reaches through ceiling with fork and spears one of pixies by coat-tail. All flee and revel there no more. England (Devonshire): Colwell ROUND 114-116.

F381.15* Man tells wife to prepare for fifteen reapers "according to our means." She roasts a sparrow. Fairies leave this impoverished house. Wales: Sheppard-Jones WELSH 106-108.

F381.16* Minister divides parish lands into three parts, named Paradise, Purgatory and Hell. Farmer on Hell orders hogboon (boggart) to go to Paradise where minister lives. Minister orders to go to Hell. Orkney: Cutt HOGBOON 87-99.

F383.4.3.1* Sunlight fatal to fairies. Daughter of the Mist weds man. Cannot stay after sunrise. Husband covers windows and tricks her. Sunlight strikes and she turns to mist. Polynesia: Berry MAGIC 45-48.

F384.5* Jealous girl rubs bowl of milk left for helpful fairies with gentian root. They never return. Swiss (French): Duvoisin THREE 101-110.

F391.4* Woman of Peace (faery woman) borrows kettle and returns full of bones each eve. Husband refuses kettle to faery lady one day. She charms it out chimney and doesn't return. Wife goes after it and barely escapes faery dogs. Never sees Woman of Peace again. Scotland (Sandray Isle, Outer Hebrides): Wilson SCOTTISH 99-102.

F400 - F499. Spirits and demons.

F400. Spirits and demons (general).

F401.3.9* Student spending night in haunted pavilion. Man in black, man in red come and are warned by voice within that student is still awake. He discovers true identity of these evil spirits and kills black pig, red cock and scorpion in pavilion (H1411.4.2). China: Birch CHINESE 95-100.

F403.2.2.4. Spirit in bottle (bag) as helper. SEE: D871.1A (Aladdin).

F405. Means of combatting spirits. SEE: E430; F380.

F405.7. Spirit leaves when report is made of death of one of his kind. SEE: B342.

F405.8. Spirits leave when report is made of fire at their home. SEE: F381.8.

F405.11. House spirit leaves when gift of clothing is left for it. SEE: F348.11.

F420. Water-spirits. SEE ALSO: B81 (mermaids); Q3.1; B11.7.1.

F420.1.2. Water-spirit as woman (water nymph, water nix).

F420.1.3.3. Water-spirit as horse.

F420.1.3.3.1* Cledog and the "Ceffyl-Dur." Man tames water-horse by getting between horse and lake disguised as ox. Horse will work for man until saddle and bridle are returned by a maiden. Man's daughter finds them years later and saddles horse. It carries her into lake. Wales: Pugh MORE..WELSH 115-121 /Green MIDSUMMER 63-68/.

F420.1.3.3.2* Morag and the Water Horse. M. combs hair of handsome man, seaweed in comb. She flees, leaps running water (burn) and is safe. Was the Water Horse. Scotland: Wilson SCOTTISH 103-106.

F420.1.3.3.3* Water horse asks to join church. Priest drives staff into ground and orders to leave. Columba of Iona accepts him into fold. Horse assumes human form. Staff blossoms and turns to wild cherry tree which blossoms every Christmas. Scotland: Finlay TATTERCOATS 70-77.

F420.1.3.4* Water-bull of Benbecula. Girl frees fairy calf of water horse when it is stuck in bog. Water horse as man get her to comb his hair, she sees seaweed and flees. Little bull fights and kills water horse. Scotland (Isle of Benbecula): Nic Leodhas SEA 121-137.

F420.1.4.1. Body of water-spirit is half human and half fish or snake. SEE: B81 (mermaid).

F420.4.6.0.1* Water sprite faints away when kept too long from water. Disappears and returns to pool. Africa: Tracy LION 61-65.

F420.4.7.1* Man paid well for ferrying Fin man home. Sees at fair and Fin man blinds him for recognizing (F361.3). Orkney: Cutt HOGBOON 130-133.

F420.4.9. Water spirit controls water supply. SEE: B11.7.1 (Dragon).

F420.5.1.1. Water-spirits protect and warn sailor agains storm and in tempest. Wales: Sheppard-Jones WELSH 1-5 (mermaid rewards for release from net).

F420.5.1.7.4. Water-spirit returns to the wood-chopper a silver axe in place of the one he has lost. SEE: Q3.1.

F420.5.1.10.1* Seal woman saves three children from rising tide. Their father had saved her young once. Orkney: Cutt HOGBOON 119-123.

F420.5.1.11* Seal who ruined poor fisherman's net appears as human and helps find passage home when in need. Orkney: Cutt HOGBOON 114-118.

F420.5.2.1. Water-spirits lure mortal into water. Zajdler POLISH 52-60.

F420.5.2.2. Water-spirits kidnap mortals and keep them under water. SEE ALSO: R111.1.3Cd. Poland: Zajdler POLISH 52-60.

F420.5.2.2.3* The Nix of the Mill-Pond. Type 316. Nix gives miller 'happiness' in exchange for "that which has just been born" at home. Son grows, weds, is pulled into pond by nix. Wife goes to pond, dreams old woman helps, goes to cottage and is given golden comb. Nix comes and takes. Golden flute--same. Sees husband each time but cannot reach. Golden spinning wheel, husband is pulled free of wave, pursued by wave, old woman changes lovers to frog and toad so that they survive, but they are parted. Years later working as shepherd they meet again. German (Grimm): Grimm GRIMM'S (Abbott) 285-291. German: Lang YELLOW 124-129; Manning-Sanders BOOK..MERMAIDS 66-72.

F420.5.2.2.4* Little girl rescued but Maksil, God of the Gulf, continues to claim one victim each year in whirlpool. Philippines: Asia FOLK..II 40-46.

F420.5.2.2.5* Two princes, Sun Prince and Moon Prince, are kidnapped by water-spirits when fail to answer riddle. Star Prince stays away from water and answers riddle. Redeems brothers. India: Babbitt JATAKA 63-68.

F420.5.2.3. Water-spirit keeps souls of drowned persons in dishes in his house. Poland: Zajdler POLISH 52-60.

F420.5.2.6.6. Water-spirits take revenge on mortals for pollution of water. SEE ALSO: F324.4.

F420.5.2.6.6.1* Water kelpie curses water which girl drinks so that she cannot speak. She has dropped a comb into the well. Later she retrieves comb but fails to dry it before putting it back in her hair. Now talks incessantly. Scotland: Nic Leodhas THISTLE 82-97 /Arbuthnot ANTHOLOGY 166-170/.

F420.5.2.13* Laminak (river gorge dwarfs) to

claim soul if castle completed by cock crow.
+K1886.3.1.1. France (Pays Basque): Spicer
THIRTEEN MONSTERS 41-51.

F420.5.3.2. Water-spirit calls human midwife.
Poland: Zajdler POLISH 52-60.

F420.6.1.1.1* Mortal woman weds Fin man in seal
form. Lives with Fin people. Mortal husband
visits and she gives him charm to win new wife.
Orkney: Cutt HOGBOON 147-151.

F420.6.1.1.2* Girl wed to Fin in seal form. Father and brothers visit. Given talisman knife
which will allow to visit again. Drops knife in
water. Orkney: Cutt HOGBOON 134-139.

F420.6.1.3. Mortal goes to home of water-spirits
and marries.

F420.6.1.3.1* Urashima Taro. Fisherman releases (B375.1) caught turtle or buys torment-
ed turtle from boys. Turtle (or maiden) escorts fisherman to underwater palace of Dragon
King. He weds Dragon Princess and remains
three years. On longing for home he is given
a box which he must not open. Three hundred
years have passed (D2011; F377). He opens
the box and ages immediately to death and dust
(C321; D1349.2). Japan: Asia FOLK..THREE
29; Hearn JAPANESE (Pauper) 30-36 (Kingdom
on island) /Hearn JAPANESE 80-88/, /Hearn
BOY 21-26/; McAlpine JAPANESE 106-120;
Matsutani FISHERMAN pb; Ozaki JAPANESE
26-42; Ross BURIED 173-187; Sakade JAPA-
NESE CHILDREN'S STORIES 9-14; Uchida
DANCING 13-23 /Arbuthnot FAIRY 177-181/,
/Arbuthnot ARBUTHNOT'S ANTHOLOGY 338-
341/; Yashima SEASHORE pb. China: Cheney
TALES 64-74.

F420.6.1.3.1.1* Fisherman releases princess in
fish form. Turtle escorts, stays one day =
three hundred years. Given box with magic
sea stone that grants wishes, tabu on opening.
Does good with box. Governor orders box
opened, he turns to dust, sand flows from box
covering cottage. Man or turtle is seen going
out to sea. Novak FAIRY 85-92.

F420.6.1.3.2* Shipwrecked sailor taken by mermaid. Touches tabu statue and it kicks him out
of the kingdom. Has a few jewels left in pockets. India: Manning-Sanders BOOK..MER-
MAIDS 41-45.

F420.6.1.5. Water-maidens make conditions for
lovers.

F420.6.1.5.1* Water-maid refuses hard baked
bread, unbaked, agrees to wed when offered
soft baked bread. He must pick her from
among three sisters, does so by strap of sandal. Her dowry of cattle emerges (B184.2.2.2)
from lake, as many as she can count in one
breath, so counts by fives to get more. Condition: if he strikes her with iron (or without
just cause) to lose (C31.8). By accident tabu
is broken. She leaves taking dowry but she

but returns to teach sons the art of healing,
famous Physicians of Myddfai. Wales: Jacobs
CELTIC 64-67; Manning-Sanders BOOK..MER-
MAIDS 114-121; Sheppard-Jones WELSH 36-42;
Sleigh NORTH 216-223; Williams-Ellis FAIRY..
BRITISH 255-262.

F420.6.1.5.1.1* Lad traps blue cow from sea by
placing three blue stones between cow and sea.
Maid herding cows comes with Boro and weds
lad. He strikes her thrice and she leaves taking blue herd with her. Son becomes veterinarian, daughter spae-wife. Orkney: Cutt
HOGBOON 140-146.

F420.6.1.5.2* Melusine met at spring asks lad to
ask his cousin for spring and as much land as
skin of deer will cover, cuts deer hide into
strips. Weds lad, never to see her on Saturdays as she is half serpent then. If seen will
never regain woman's form but will become immortal (C31.1.2). He spies on her. She still
wails about Lusignan castle. France: Picard
FRENCH 101-106.

F420.6.1.5.3* Fisherman catches old lady. She
provides herd of cattle. Is mistreated. Returns
to lake with cattle. Luo: Harman TALES 90-
95; Nunn AFRICAN 41-45.

F424.1.1* Man cutting willows finds silver and
gold willows and follows upstream. Finds maid,
born of foam, lives one year unless drinks of
water of well of wisdom. He seeks, finds also
well of riches--stones now turn to gold when he
touches. Saves her. Weds. Gypsy: Manning-
Sanders BOOK..SORCEROR'S 37-44.

F430. Weather spirits.

F433.0.1* Rain spirit courts woman in form of
bull. She rides bull's back away. Rubs bull
with herbs until he sleeps and leaves. Bushmen: Helfman BUSHMEN 23-25.

F433.2* Ice Spirit. People can't put out fire in
huge poplar stump, send for Ice Man. He
causes so much rain and hail that they have to
ask frost spirit to send him home. Native A-
merican (Cherokee): Bell JOHN 92-98; Brown
TEPEE 78-79 (-frost, + lake formed).

F434. Spirit of thunder. SEE ALSO: A284.3;
A1142.

F434.1* Thunder moves to sky after seeing man
roll over in sleep without awakening. T. fears
man and flees. Uganda: Harman TALES 19-28.

F441.2.0.2* Tree-spirit (chestnut) tells girl that
tree is to be made into ship. Ship will not move
until girl touches it. Rewarded by prince.
Japan: Novak FAIRY 61-65.

F441.2.3.1.1. Man marries spirit of willow tree.
She must part from him when tree is cut down
(E765.3.3). He returns to her parents' home
and finds three willow stumps. Japan: Buck
FAIRY 297-305; Garner CAVALCADE..

GOBLINS 36-39; Hearn JAPANESE (Pauper) 13-21; Hearn JAPANESE 89-100.

F450. Underground spirits.

F451.0.1. Luchrupain (Leprechauns). SEE: J1922.2.1 (Marking the pot of gold).

F451.2.3.1. Long bearded dwarf. Type 426. SEE: D113.2 (Snow White and Rose Red); F451.6.1; K1111.1.

F451.3.2.1.2. Dwarf otherwise caught and forced to procure what hero demands. SEE: F451.5.1.6.

F451.3.2.1.3* Lad fishes with menehunes. Delays them until dawn. They flee leaving nets. He learns how to make nets. Hawaii: Belting ELVES 66-69.

F451.3.2.2.1* Dwarfs must harvest all crops between midnight and sunrise on last day of year. Must also spread all gold in sun one hour or turns red. Lad helps, is given pay. Dwarfs dump all gold turned red into hole. He takes. France: Manning-Sanders JONNIKIN 68-73.

F451.3.3.8. Dwarfs made invisible by magic caps. SEE: F282.4.2.

F451.4.4.4* Farmer throws his slops onto invisible house. Wee man asks him to stop and has him put foot on dwarf's so can see house. Farmer cuts a door in back of his house to toss slops out. Wales: Sheppard-Jones WELSH 156-158. Great Britain: Williams-Ellis FAIRY.. BRITISH 76-81.

F451.5.1.2. Dwarfs adopt girl as sister. SEE: Z65.1 (Snow White).

F451.5.1.4. Dwarf's gold. Seemingly worthless gift given by dwarfs turns to gold. Type 503. SEE ALSO: F342.1 (fairies gold).

F451.5.1.4.1* Midwife at birth of dwarf (F372.1) given apronful of coal. She lets coal spill on way. Once home those remaining turn to gold. Switzerland: Müller-Guggenbühl SWISS 120-121.

F451.5.1.4.2* Girl borrows coals to start fire from three men camped in meadow. Returns three times as coals die. Coals are gold in the morning. Switzerland: Müller-Guggenbühl SWISS 135-137.

F451.5.1.4.3* Child overeager for gift is given piece of coal by dwarf. Turns to jewel in morning. Switzerland: Müller-Guggenbühl SWISS 113-114.

F541.5.1.4.4* Skipper transports dwarfs to new local. Sees only rats and mice. Given sack of shavings and sack of coal. Turn to gold and silver. Jutland: Manning-Sanders DWARFS 73-77.

F451.5.1.5. Money or treasure given by dwarfs.

F451.5.1.5.0.1* Two elder brothers refuse stew to little man, stew is knocked over. Youngest feeds and catches. Shown treasure (cf. K1931.2). Northamptonshire: Colwell ROUND 82-84.

F451.5.1.5.0.2* Dwarf King Laurin is given hospitality on Christmas Eve by three lads. He orders them to turn cartwheels and sweets, oranges, and gold and silver fall from their pockets. Austria (Tirol): Sawyer WAY 71-81.

F451.5.1.5.0.3* Shepherd finds dwarf's lost bell. Trades for magic stick which causes sheep to thrive. Rugen: Manning-Sanders DWARFS 89-94.

F451.5.1.6.2* Man helps tiny kayak with five little people lost at sea. They cause successful hunting ever after. Eskimo: Belting ELVES 47-52.

F451.5.1.6.3* Man realizes beetle on cross is dwarf. Cannot leave cross. He releases. Asks wish. Plow small enough to be turned by dog. Dig deep as if drawn by six oxen. Prospers. Island of Rugen: Belting ELVES 35-40.

F451.5.1.6.4* Cook gives food to dwarf as requests three times, entire meal taken each time though "spoonful" asked. Second servant refuses dwarf. First is given wishing box. Turkey: Belting ELVES 61-65; Manning-Sanders BOOK..GHOSTS 30-37 (second gets box with goblin with club inside--J2415). Estonia: Manning-Sanders BOOK..GHOSTS 30-37.

F451.5.1.6.5* Lad seeks aid of little people, refuses to clean old woman's eyes. Takes little people for children and waits in vain for their parents to return. Second boy cleans her eyes, is told to address little people as elders. Is given cattle (J2415). Africa: Belting ELVES 15-21.

F451.5.1.10. Dwarfs heal (give medicine).

F451.5.1.10.1* Woman asked by dwarfs to gather pine cones elsewhere, obliges and finds silver cones, is given healing herb for ill husband by Gubrich, King of Dwarfs. Germany: Manning-Sanders BOOK..DWARFS 125-128.

F451.5.1.10.2* Little people rub back of ill boy and cure. His mother gives them materials for twelve pairs of tiny moccasins. They accept and give boy a pair of moccasins that never wear out. Native American (Onondaga): Belting ELVES 27-34.

F451.5.2. Malevolent dwarf.

F451.5.2.6.1* Bad hunter kidnaps two dwarfs. While eating dried salmon, voice says "Bite down hard." His jaws freeze together. Good hunter releases dwarf. Told to pour water on snow by by hut before sleeping, it freezes to ice. All else on island is blown away in wind storm. Eskimo: Maher BLIND 107-114.

F451.5.2.6.2* Dwarf offered hospitality by only one couple causes avalance killing all others. Switzerland (German): Duvoisin THREE 203-207.

F451.5.2.9.1* Dwarfs scold mortals. Greedy hunters told by dwarf not to kill more game than they can use. Native American (Onondaga): Belting ELVES 27-34.

F451.5.5. Dwarfs have human woman as midwife. SEE: F451.5.1.4.1; F372.1.

F451.5.10.4.1* Dwarfs return what they borrow. Hill man borrows saucepan. Given old one since hill men are good tinkers. He mends but on return pan burns quantity of milk equivalent to prince of tinkering. Ireland: Hutchinson CANDLELIGHT 51-54; Pilkington SHAMROCK 16-18.

F451.5.10.6. Dwarfs pay for being ferried across water. SEE: F451.5.1.4.4.

F451.5.14.1* Spider, Nihancan, tells dwarf he cannot really shoot huge arrow. Dwarf shoots and imbeds spider in ground. Native American (Arapaho): Brown TEPEE 114-115.

F451.5.15.1. Dwarf promises mortal much money if he will guess his name. SEE: C432.1; H521.

F451.5.15.2. Dwarf makes return of child dependent upon guessing of riddle. SEE: H540.1.

F451.5.15.3. Dwarf suitor desists when unwilling maiden guesses his name. SEE: C432.1; F381.1.

F451.5.17. Dwarfs invisibly attend wedding or christening feasts of mortals. Lad taken with dwarf. To serve. At wedding feast he drops powder to make bride sneeze. If sneezes thrice and no one says "God bless us" dwarf can take bride. Lad calls "God bless us." Ireland: Manning-Sanders CHOICE 191-199; Manning-Sanders BOOK..DWARFS 95-103.

F451.6.1. Dwarf caught by beard in cleft of tree. SEE: F451.2.3.1; K111.1; D113.2 (Snow White and Rose Red). Type 426.

F451.6.2.5* Goblin lives with grocer who feeds it jam. Puts grocer's wife's tongue on cask to make it talk after student insults him saying he has no more knowledge of poetry than the cask. Grimm: Grimm HOUSE 36-45.

F451.9. Dwarfs emigrate. SEE: F451.5.1.4.4.

F451.9.5. Emigrating dwarfs are ferried over water. SEE: F451.5.10.6.

F455.8.1. Trolls turn to stone at sunrise. SEE: F531.6.12.2.

F456.2.2.5* Knockers. Miner is saved from rock fall by knocker calling his name. Friend disbe-

lieves, sleeps in mine and finds knockers all around, one lays his hammer on man's knee. It is stiff thereafter. Cornwall: Manning-Sanders PETER 191-193.

F456.2.2.6* Knockers ask two brothers to share their fuggan. One does and is led to diamond cave. Other tries, has ladder broken and is stoned (J2415). Cornwall: Manning-Sanders PETER 64-71.

F456.2.2* Mining spirit: "Blue Cap." Boy shares tart with knocker, Blue Cap, and is shown tin lode daily. Blue Cap is seen as a blue flame. Cornwall: Colwell SECOND 13-20.

F456.4. Miscellaneous mine spirit motifs. Poland: Zajdler POLISH 178-190.

F456.4.2* Trapped miner follows vision of Jesus and escapes. Russia: Sawyer WAY 285-294.

F456.4.3* Lad dreams of Genie of the Silver Mines. Seeks spot dreamed of and meets pilgrim who asks loan of mule. Mule's bags returned full of rocks. They are silver ore. Spain: Gunterman CASTLES 34-45.

F460. Mountain spirits.

F460.4.2.6* Helpful mountain men. Bergmännlein cares for cowherd's cattle through winter, tabu--not to call them before they descend to pasture in spring. He calls to one and it falls from cliff, others safe. Switzerland (German): Duvoisin THREE 152-157.

F460.4.2.8* Dwarf buys poor cowherd's last cow with magic gold piece, multiplies sevenfold each night. Envious neighbor dies of rage. Switzerland (German): Duvoisin THREE 178-184.

F470. Night spirits (Poltergeist).

F473.2.1.1* Cradle found washed up in storm, rocks by self. Visitor sees woman rocking baby. They burn cradle, hear baby crying as it burns. Leach THING 75-76.

F473.6.10* Unseen piskies spin plates on floor. Cornwall: Bleecker BIG 53-63.

F473.6.11* Pint measure dances on dresser as sign to go to bed and let piskies have room. Suitor replaces fallen pint one night. It never taps early again. Great Britain: Palmer FAIRY 31-44.

F480. House spirits.

F481.0.1.1.1* Cobald hatched out. Man carries cock's egg under armpit for three weeks. Hatches a dwarf servant. Causes mischief. Must pull down cobald's house, old barn, to rid. Switzerland (French): Duvoisin THREE 30-37.

F481.0.1.1.2* Woodman brings home six eggs found on Halloween night. Goblin babies hatch and stare transfixed at candle. He leads them

them back to woods with candle. Scotland: Harper GHOSTS 49-56.

F481.1.1* Kobalds help with remodeling of castle, are to receive annual honey feast as reward. Women of house try to break tradition and ill befalls. Alexander Dumas: Palmer FAIRY 59-68.

F481.3.1* Duende friends follow lad when he goes to city. Cause trouble in house where he takes service. He has to return to country. Mexico: Ross IN 191-205.

F482.3.1.1. Brownies live in house. Move when persons move. Farmer is so bothered by brownie that he decides he must move to get rid of the annoyance. He piles his furniture on wagon and starts for new home, meets acquaintance who remarks: "I see you're flitting." Brownie sticks head out of churn on top of load and answers: "Yes, we're flitting." Farmer goes back to former home. England: Harper GHOSTS 222-224; Leach THING 17-19; Littledale GHOSTS 35-38.

F482.3.1.2* Bauchan of MacIntosh family refuses to travel to America on boat with MacLeods and MacDonalds. When MacIntosh arrives in America bauchan is already there, took an earlier boat. Scotland (Isle of Muck): Nic Leodhas SEA 179-200.

F482.5.4.1. Brownie rides for midwife (nurse) when needed. Others fear night ride. Haviland FAVORITE..SCOTLAND 49.

F482.5.4.3* Brownies collect rent for impoverished couple. Scotland: Nic Leodhas HEATHER 45-59.

F482.5.5. (Baughman). The fairy in the sack of the thief or the poacher. A fairy takes place of game in poacher's bag, speaks, scares poacher. Sussex: Colwell ROUND 108-109 (piglet).

F490. Other spirits and demons.

F491. Will-o'-the-Wisp. (Jack o' Lantern.) Light seen over marshy places. SEE: A2817; E742.2.

F499.1.2. Sunbeam sprites will care for child all life if sunbeams fall on cradle when first put into cradle. +D2183.1. Spain: Gunterman CASTLES 61-80.

F499.4* Spirit of string figures. Boy making string figures at night while others sleep is challenged by Totanguok, Spirit of String Figures. Spirit uses own intestines when runs out of string. Eskimo: Field ESKIMO 39-41.

F500 - F599. Remarkable persons.

F510. Monstrous persons.

F511.0.2.1. Two-headed person. SEE: G512A (Jack the Giant Killer).

F511.0.4.2* Beast Mapundu steals princess Tusi. A Lungulebe (half man) takes her to Lungulebe village to fatten and kill. She calls to heavens and lightning kills chief, rain puts out fire to boil her. Frog leads her to his chief. She opens her head and puts her belongings inside. Head becomes large now. Chief refuses to wed huge headed girl. Chief's sister discovers truth. Weds. Zulu: Aardema BEHIND 57-65.

F511.2.2. Person with ass's (horse's) (goat's) ears. SEE: D1316.5.3.

F531. Giant. SEE ALSO: F628.2.3.1.

F531.5.1.5. Holiburn, giant, taps human friend in play and kills. He weeps in sorrow until a stream forms and flows to the sea. Cornwall: Manning-Sanders PETER 125-128.

F531.5.4. Giant thinks hammer blow on head is a nut falling. Man strikes with all his might. SEE: F615.3.1.1.

F531.5.9. The giant on the ark. Noah saves a giant on the ark. SEE: F531.6.12.8.2.

F531.6.6.3.1* Giant digs course for Severn River. Giant plans to dam up Severn and drown Shrewsbury. Cobbler says he wore out all these old shoes coming from there and giant believes it is too far away. He dumps his spadeful of earth where he stands = Wretin hill near Wellington, and scrapes his boots = little hill Ercoll. England (Shropshire): Colwell ROUND 95-96; Williams-Ellis FAIRY..BRITISH 114-116.

F531.6.7. Giant's treasure. SEE: G512A (Jack the Giant Killer); F628.2.3 (Tom Hickathrift).

F531.6.8.3.2.1* Giant of one island steals river from other island. Giant of that Isle catches him and tickles him until he spits some water out, escapes with enough for small river. South Pacific: Mayne BOOK..GIANTS 27-34.

F531.6.9. Giants as warriors (in army).

F531.6.9.1* Giant turns self to small boy and is adopted by twin girls. When village is attacked he resumes true stature and defends. Fiji: Gittins TALES 41-46.

F531.6.12.2. Sunlight turns giant or troll to stone. SEE: G304.2.5 (Troll bursts); D567.1.

F531.6.12.6. Giant slain by man. Bible: Adams BOOK..GIANTS 35-40 (David and Goliath); De Regniers GIANT 39-46 (David and Goliath).

F531.6.12.6.0.1. Hercules slays Antaeus. Pygmy friends of the dead giant drive Hercules off with attempted revenge. Adams BOOK..GIANTS 100-133.

F531.6.12.8.2. Giant drowned in Deluge. All giants drowned trying to stop flood by stomping onto springs and holding hands over heavens.

One giant, Og, escapes riding on roof of Ark. Jewish: De Regniers GIANT 131-134.

F531.6.12.8.3* Marec the Enchanter turns giant to stone for stealing sheep. Tide comes up to giant's nose and recedes before Marec releases spell. England (Cornwall): Manning-Sanders PETER 77-81.

F531.6.13.3* Archaeologist finds giants' bones in cave. They wake up and throw him into the sea. Scotland: Nic Leodhas GAELIC 30-38 / /Mayne BOOK..GIANTS 195-203/.

F531.6.15.1.1* Thor, Loke, and Thiaffe visit giants' hall. Challenged to show skills. Lose eating contest, drinking, running, lifting cat, wrestling. Giants reveal tricks. Were contesting with Fire, Sea, Thought, lifting Midgard, Wrestling Old Age. Norse: De Regniers GIANT 94-105.

F533. Remarkably tall man. SEE: F531.2.1.

F535.1. Thumbling. Person the size of a thumb. Types 327B, 700.

F535.1.1. Adventures of Thumbling. SEE ALSO: K1611 (Hop o' My Thumb); F615.3.1.3.

A* Tom Thumb. Type 700. Parents wish for son even if no bigger than thumb. Merlin the Magician grants wish. Queen of fairies dresses him. He steals marbles from boys, falls into pudding and is thrown out. Is taken into cow's mouth (F911.3.1), but calls out and cow drops. Is carried by raven, dropped in sea and swallowed by fish. King Arthur's cook opens (F913). Becomes court favorite. Rides mouse, needle as sword. England: Reeves ENGLISH 64-70.

Ab* A+ Queen jealous. Hides in snail shell, freed from mouse trap by cat, sometimes killed by spider. Jacobs ENGLISH 145-152 /Martignoni ILLUSTRATED 184-186/, /Haviland FAIRY 72-77/, /Haviland FAVORITE..ENGLAND 30-43/; Steel ENGLISH 144-152; Tarrant FAIRY 34-50; Wiggin FAIRY 103-109; Wilkinson DIVERTING pb.

Ac* A+ Raven carries to giant who swallows T. From stomach T. raises a ruckus and is vomited into sea. Brooke GOLDEN pb; Opie CLASSIC 30-46.

B* Tom Thumb (Grimm's). Wish for son even if no bigger than thumb. Thumbling drives horse for father riding in ear. He is sold to two men, rides on their hat brim, hides in the mouse hole and escapes. Pretends is helping robbers and raises noise so that victim is alerted. Is eaten by cow, calls out from stomach, and cow is slaughtered. Wolf swallows entrails and Tom. He directs wolf to father's storehouse, raises alarm. Rescued (K565). Germany (Grimm): Carle ERIC 49-60; Grimm GRIMM'S (Follett) 349-357; Grimm GRIMM'S (Grosset) 268-275; Grimm GRIMM'S (Scribner's) 117-123; Grimm GRIMM'S (World) 184-190; Grimm HOUSEHOLD 160-166; Jacobs EUROPEAN 194-200 (beans mother strings turn to thumb size boys, all drown but one); Manning-Sanders BOOK.. DWARFS 42-48; Rackham GRIMM 91-98.

C* Tom Thumb variants.

Ca* Tom Thumb's Travels (Grimm). Darning needle as sword, carried up chimney by steam, helps rob King's treasury as robbers' accomplice. Swallowed by cow, cow slaughtered, T. made into black pudding, jumps out when pudding is cut. Fox swallows, lets out of stomach in exchange for hens from Tom's father's henyard (K565). Germany (Grimm): Grimm HOUSEHOLD 181-185.

Cb* Kernel. Old woman with whom couple share lunch gives back the leaf which food was wrapped in. A tiny boy is inside. Kernel is eaten by cow, cow slaughtered, wolf eats entrails and K., vomits K. up. K. accompanies mule drivers, thieves steal mule with money bags and K. shouts and frightens them off--gets mules and money for family. Portugal: Michael PORTUGUESE 112-117.

Cc* Lipunishka. Wish for child. Boy crawls out of cotton fluff. Carries lunch to father and helps plow. Sold to rich man. Escapes and runs home. Russia: Carey BABA 96-98.

D* Other small heroes.

Da* Little Shell. Wish for son if no bigger than seashell. Hides in fishbasket and startles fish woman with shout as leaves fish. Obtains cow's head from man likewise. Chief's daughter agrees to wed but chief banishes Little Shell. The spell is broken by her love and he grows to normal size. Philippine (Visayan): Sechrist ONCE 93-97.

Db* Hazel Nut Child. Wish for son if no bigger than hazelnut. Carried to Africa on stork's back. Given diamond by chief. Returns home with gift. Bukovina: Lang YELLOW 239-241; Manning-Sanders BOOK..DWARFS 84-88.

Dc* Three Inch. Wish for child. Eats magic cucumber too soon, bears three inch man. Father sells self into slavery in his shame. Three Inch asks for father's freedom, needs 10,000 ruples. Frog advises to get axe from tiny blacksmith. Three Inch ties blacksmith's beard to tree and obtains ax for releasing. Chops down tree, freeing frog's wife. Rewarded with medicine to cure blindness of king's daughter. May wed princess if brings bodies of eight thieves. Tells thieves king wishes to choose one of them as groom for princess. Chops off heads as they enter 'to see King' one at a time. Weds princess. Pakistan: Siddiqui TOONTOONY 91-97.

Dd* Master Thumb. Mother abuses Sun for not shining when she needs. Sun curses her with thumb size son. T. defeats ogre (K1161.5). Defeats Sun (Z52.5). Burma: Htin Aung KINGDOM 46-52.

De* Digit the Midget. Woman asks for small son as seven brothers eat too much. Digit brings home bull, steering in ear. Stole it from Cherak (monster) on dare of brothers. Steals mule load of meat from C. likewise. Brothers burn his house. He escapes down rabbit holes. Digit fills mule's bags with ashes. Spends night at rich man's house and claims someone had exchanged his flour for ashes. Given flour. His brothers imitate and are beaten. Digit put in basket to set afloat by brothers. Tells Arab merchant he is Allah's messenger and basket will fill with gold at noon. A. gives Digit horse and money to go buy donkeys to carry off gold. Tells brothers he found horse and to go for more in morning when he whistles. Ties their feet together in sleep and whistles. Ethiopia (Amhara): Ashabraner LION'S 53-61 /Green FOLK 83-95/.

E* Issun-Boshi. Little One-Inch. Parents pray for baby if only as big as thumb. He goes adventuring in rice bowl with chopstick oar, needle sword. Hired as companion of princess, he routs ogre, stabbing in face with needle-sword. Ogre flees leaving magic wishing hammer. Princess strikes hammer and wishes him taller. They wed (or he is promoted). Japan: Brenner LITTLE pb; Haviland FAVORITE.. JAPAN 3-22 /Haviland FAIRY 162-169/; Ishii ISSUN (red, green and black ogres); Manning-Sanders BOOK..DWARFS 104-108 (without princess motif, kills ogre, ogre breathes last breath into thumbling's nostrils and T. grows. Rewarded). Sakade JAPANESE 66-70 (attacked by frog en route); Uchida DANCING 159-169 (swallowed by ogre, stabs in stomach and is brought up, F914).

F* Thumbelina. Thumb size girl. SEE ALSO: B641.0.1Be (doll in the grass). Denmark (Andersen original tale): Holme TALES 13-20; Lang YELLOW 283-296; Manning-Sanders BOOK ..DWARFS 112-124; Opie CLASSIC 219-229.

Fb* Little Finger: wish for child if no bigger than little finger. Four fairy godmothers give gifts of beauty, voice, early speaking, one will come when in need. Prince hears singing and vows to wed. Attends ball thrice (R221). He hits her each time, refusing to let tiny maid go, and she goes as princess with aid of fairy godmother. Says came from "Country of Slop," etc. Prince pines of love. Ring in cake. She reveals self as tall princess. Wed. Italy: Manning-Sanders GIANNI 127-140.

F535.1.1.11. Thumbling as accomplice to robbers. Raises ruckus. Slovenia: Kavcic GOLDEN 87-92.

F540. Remarkable physical organs.

F543.1. Remarkably long nose. SEE: D1376.1.3.2.

F544.3.5.1* Remarkably long teeth. Man meets three men (ghosts, duppys), each with longer teeth. Dutch Guiana (Paramaribo Black): Leach THING 44-45.

F545.1.0.1. Beardless man. SEE: K2275.

F545.2.1. Gold star on forehead. Type 400, 533. SEE: Q2.1.

F556. SEE: K311.3 (Wolf and Seven Kids).

F556.1.1. Voice made smooth by swallowing hot iron. SEE ALSO: K311.3 (Wolf and Seven Kids). West Indies: Sherlock WEST 112-117.

F556.1.2. Voice made smooth by having ant bite tongue. Berber-Kabyl: Frobenius AFRICAN 77-79. Tanganyika (Kamba): Arnott AFRICAN 140-149.

F556.2. Voice changed by work of silversmith (goldsmith). Russia: Carrick STILL 15-22 (voice forged, +K311.3).

F557.0.1* Nose, feet, eyes, hands, etc. can be removed when convenient. For example, can leave lower jaws at home in market to avoid arguments. Congo: Aardema MORE 38-43.

F560. Unusual way of life.

F565.1. Amazons.

F565.1.2. All male children killed by Amazons. Sickly Pahy Tura is hidden by mother. Squeezed in tipity (mesh for squeezing manioc) and crooked body straightened. He is given into keeping of Lake Spirit in fish form. Another Amazon sees this and fishes for lad. He breaks two nets, third is made of Amazon's hair and he cannot break it. Brazil: Carpenter SOUTH AMERICAN 100-107.

F569.3.1. Silent princess. SEE: H343; F954.2.1.

F570. Other extraordinary human beings.

F571.2. Sending to the older. Old person refers inquirer to his father, and so on for several generations. Usually seven. Type 726. Norway: Asbjornsen NORWEGIAN 13-14 (each father weaker than last, seventh, tiny man in powder horn gives permission to spend night. Fine table, bed appear). Allard MAY pb.

F576.1* Ugly princess moves north to land of perpetual darkness. Weds blind minstrel. Portugal: Michael PORTUGUESE 105-111.

F582.1.1* Tale of the Tontlawald. Mistreated stepdaughter is taken in by woman and daughter in Tontlawald (enchanted forest). Old man makes clay figure of girl with piece of bread, drop of blood, and snake inside. Sent to take her place. Snake comes from mouth of figure and kills stepmother. Father eats bread from figure and dies. Girl lives with magical family nine years. She ages, they do not. She turns to eagle and flies. Is shot down by prince. Turns to girl on ground. Weds. Tells this tale when old. Estonia: Lang VIOLET 1-16; Maas

MOON 31-43.

F600 - F699. Persons with extra-ordinary powers.

F600. Persons with extraordinary powers.

F601. Extraordinary companions. A group of men with extraordinary powers travel together. SEE: K1931.2I.

F601. Extraordinary companions help hero in suitor tasks. Type 513. 514. SEE ALSO: H1151.6.2.1; F660.1A,C,D; H1385.3Fe.

A* Flying Ship (D1520.15).

Aa* Youngest of three brothers befriends old man who gives magic ship that goes on sea or land. Takes along Listener, Runner, man with straw which cools, Sharpshooter, Eater, Drinker, man with sticks which can raise army. Task: eat twelve oxen, drink forty barrels of wine, sit in red hot iron bathhouse. Fetch water of life. Runner naps, Listener hears snore, Shooter wakes. Russia: Buck FAIRY 129-137; Frost LEGEND 89-98; Haviland FAVORITE.. RUSSIA 66-86; Lang YELLOW 214-223; Ransome FOOL pb (illus. Shulevitz); Ransome OLD 76-87 /Fenner ADVENTURE 1-15/, /Association TOLD..GREEN 101-112/; Riordan TALES..CENTRAL 78-85 (-water).

Ab* Old man asks lads what they try to build. They lie, "trough," "churn," etc. So be it. Youngest answers truthfully, "Ship that goes on land and sea." So be it. Takes on eater, drinker, listener, sharpshooter, runner, man with summers and fifteen winters inside. They perform tasks. Task: eat storehouse of meat, drink cellar of wine, bring water from end of world. Runner falls asleep. Listener hears, Sharpshooter wakes. Task: sit on burning granary. Norway: Asbjornsen NORWEGIAN 170-177; Aulaire EAST 27-37.

Abb* Ab + Smash-all softens bed of nails--task: sleeping on bed of harrow pins. Task: harvest nineteen sacks of stars, Aim-well shoots down. Task: fetch water from world's end before witch does. She puts magic sleeping pin in Speed-well's head, Know-well knows this, Aim-well shoots it out, Blow-well blows witch out of sight. Ireland: MacManus BOLD 101-119.

Abc* Ab -water fetching, -fire sitting, +strong man sweeps soldiers aside with broom, bellows blow off cavalry. France: Picard FRENCH 159-167.

Abd* Ab -water fetching, -fire sitting, +strong man carries off dowry. Italy: Withers WORLD 9-17.

Ac* Old man hired by youngest brother (older brothers refused to hire the old). Oversees ship that goes on land or sea. Old man taken along. Companions: one who can put fog in bag; strong man; drinker; archer; long legs. Task: carry letter to underworld--hell. Runner falls asleep, archer wakes. Task: drink cellar of wine--drinker performs. Dowry all one man can carry--strong man. Man with fog lets it out and pursuing king is lost. Old man claims one-half of princess as reward and relinquishes all when sees hero really will cut her in two to keep word. Sicily: Lang ROSE 95-105.

Acb* Youngest of three brothers befriends old woman. Given magic whistle to herd horses (H1112), befriends old man, given magic ship, takes on eater, drinker, cooler, runner. Task: herd horses. Task: eat meat. Task: drink all wine in cellars. Task: take sauna bath, is overheated. Task: bring water of life. Wed. Finland: Bowman TALES 1-11.

Ad* Hardy Hardhead. Old man befriended gives Jack tiny folded ship that sails on land. Companions: Hardy Hardhead, Eatwell, Drinkwell, Runwell, Hackwell, Seewell, Shootwell. Tasks: turn somersault onto hackle, HH does. Out-eat witch, out-drink, out-run. Race for eggshell full of sea water. Witch puts Runwell to sleep with charmed horse's jawbone under head. Hackwell hears, Seewell sees, and Shootwell awakes. Jack weds king's daughter freed from witch. U.S. Appalachia: Chase JACK 96-105; Williams-Ellis FAIRY..BRITISH 124-131.

Ae* The Three Ivans. (R111.1.3) Ae + given cudgel to strike oak and ship comes out. Forgets to close and fleet comes by. Companions: Drinker, Eater, Freezer, Astrologer, One-who-turns-into-a-fish. Tasks: eating, drinking, bath house. Princess escapes as star--atrologer fetches. As fish, fish-man brings back. Russia: Manning-Sanders BOOK..SORCERER'S 69-90.

B* Six Servants--The Stolen Princess. Fat, Listener, Tall, Sharp Eyes, Always Cold, Shatter-Eyes. Task: fetch ring from Red Sea. Sharp Eyes sees, Fat drinks sea dry, Tall fetches. Task: drink and eat huge amount--Fat does. Task: guard girl until midnight. Fat bars door, Tall stretches around room, but all magically are put to sleep and girl stolen. Fifteen minutes till midnight. Listener hears her, Sharp Eyes sees, Tall Man goes there, Shatter Eyes shatters rock. Task: sit on bonfire--Cold One does. Shatter Eyes destroys remaining enemy. Wed. Germany (Grimm): Gag TALES 39-61; Grimm GRIMM'S (Grosset) 280-289 (+H465); Grimm GRIMM'S (World) 211-218 (+H465); Wiggin TALES 184-190 (+H465).

C* Long, Broad and Quick Eye. Prince to choose bride from portraits in tower chamber. Chooses twelfth. Is in wizard's power. Long (stretching man), Broad (spreading man) and Quick Eye (shattering eyes) join. To guard princess three nights. They doze and she is stolen. Q. sees as acorn on tree, Long fetches.

Second night as stone in mountain. Third as ring at sea bottom. One iron band on waist of wizard breaks at each success. He turns to bird and flies off. Castle disenchanted and statues come to life. Czechoslovakia: Fillmore SHEPHERD'S 103-118. Russia: Bulatkin EURASIAN 44-56. Bohemia: Manning-Sanders BOOK.. WIZARDS 26-39. Lang FIFTY 184-192; Ness LONG pb.

D* How Six Traveled Through the World. Race for spring water. Companions of discharged soldier, Strong Man, Sharp Shooter, Blower, Runner (with one leg buckled up), Frost Bringer (puts hat straight and frost comes). Task: bring water from spring before princess. Runner dozes, Sharp Shooter wakes. Task: enduring hot iron room. Reward all gold one man can carry--Strong. Pursued, Blower blows troops away. Germany (Grimm): Gag MORE 63-75; Grimm BROTHERS 139-145; Grimm GRIMM'S (Follett) 154-161; Grimm GRIMM'S (Grosset) 322-329; Grimm GRIMM'S (Scribner's) 185-191; Grimm GRIMM'S (World) 142-147; Grimm HOUSEHOLD 3-8; Lang YELLOW 107-114 /Lang FIFTY 137-142/. Italy: Wiggin TALES 14-19 (-frost bringer). Italy (Naples): Hampden HOUSE 41-48 (-frost bringer).

Db* Minus Freezer and Blower. Race with giant. Hero has supernatural strength from biting off end of boa's tail, forces companions to join by besting in wrestling match. Princess to wed one who brings golden carriage, old woman gives. Philippines (Tagalog): Sechrist ONCE 196-204.

Dc* The Pugilist and His Helpers. Man who defeats twenty-four at a time. Companions met. Reward for bringing herb for sick king. Runner goes, Sharpshooter awakens, Strong man carries off, Blower blows back soldiers. Germany: Withers WORLD 35-42.

Dd* The Queen's riddles. Chief to wed queen if guesses her riddles. 1. Where is certain door? Farsighted companion sees. 2. Which of three dogs is hers? Listener hears. 3. Fetching water race. Straight Shooter causes woman to drop calabash, Swift Runner wins. 4. Find man to live in hot and cold spots. Man-Who-Dies-in-the-Cold and Man-Who-Dies-in-the-Fire go. Hawaii: Cothran MAGIC 31-37.

De* The Great Bear. Listener hears Khan is planning to conquer empire. Swallower swallows sea and spits out again after they cross, they are tested by Khan. Sky Shooter, Mountain Lifter and Swift Runner prove selves. In heated iron house Sea Swallower spits out sea, floods city and palace also. Those five plus two brothers they accompany become seven stars of Ursa Major (A771.0.2). Chinese Mongolia: Jablow MAN 105-112.

E* Other.

Ea* Lad joined by Hungryman, Thirstyman, Frostyman, Speedyman, Bangerman. Perform tasks: eating, drinking. Task: bring live water and dead water from where mountains knock together (D1553) before old woman returns. She puts Speedyman to sleep. Bangerman wakes. Frostyman in red hot house of iron. Red King and his daughter killed and hero weds Green King's daughter. +L425Ab. Rumania: Farjeon CAVALCADE..KINGS 33-46; Ure RUMANIAN 45-56.

Eb* Friends Blowo, Porto, Ropo (unbreakable ropes), Listeno. B. blows storm away. P. hurls boulder at wall. L. hears crying. R. makes rope to climb wall. Knight kills demon. Her father had cursed her to "go to the horned one" for bad temper. He cuts off demon's ear. When princess proves too bad tempered to live with, he gives demon ear to take her back. Spain: Gunterman CASTLE 46-60.

F* African variants.

Fa* The chief's daughter is stolen by robber chief. Lad seeks, five companions met. First interprets signs sent by chief's daughter and discovers her. Second foresees future and warns robber is coming. Third digs tunnel and rescues. Fourth builds boat. Fifth as eagle lifts boat out of robber's reach, as crocodile eats robber. West Africa (Hausa): Carpenter AFRICAN WONDER 187-194.

G* Polynesian variants.

Ga* Octopus restores tree Lasa cuts for canoe, thrice. Fourth time Lasa catches octopus. They build canoe together. O. warns L. to take on anyone met. Picks up Hungry Spirit, Thieving Spirit and Octopus. On demon's island tests are set. Eat = Hungry Man performs. Shake Vi tree, if any fruit hits ground to die = octopus catches. Land crab gathering race = Thieving Spirit sings "Tongan wakeful eye, Fijian sleepy bye" until sleeps (D1781) then steals Fijian's crabs. Cook Islands: Gittins TALES 79-81.

H* The Riddle of the Drum. Drum of certain skin. Suitor to guess (H522.1.1). Companions aid. Corrín Corrán (runner), Tirín Tirán (archer), Oyín Oyá (listener), Soplín Soplán (blower), Comín Comán (eater). Listener hears name of skin (flea). Runner races witch for water. Blower blows her back. Archer wakes sleeping runner. Eater eats cartload of food. Mexico: Aardema RIDDLE pb.

I* Boy-Who-Snared-The-Wind and the Shaman's Daughter. Old woman advises to take along in canoe ducks, ants, buffalo, conch shell, antelope, and Ati-Tia bird. He seeks each out. Shaman sets tasks. Dive for copper paddle = ducks execute. Split boulder = buffalo. Leap from craig onto head = ram. Find scattered beads = ants. Hear message from afar = conch. Race daughter = antelope. Make music and love beauty = Ati-Tia bird lends song to flute. Weds shaman's daughter. Native American (Thompson River): DeWit TALKING 161-168. SEE ALSO: H335.7.3.

F601.7. Animals as extraordinary companions. SEE: T543.3.2 (Momotaro).

F610. Remarkably strong man. SEE: K1931.2I.

F610.0.1. Remarkably strong woman. SEE: F617.2.

F610.3. Warrior of special strength.

F610.3.5. Strong son refuses to fight for plunder. In time when his father is attacked he defeats enemy unarmed by sheer strength. Fights only in cause of justice. Morocco (Berber): Holding KING'S 87-97.

F610.3.7* Jan the Eighth Van Arkel chins self on beam holding horse between knees. Revolting burghers are intimidated and rebellion dies out. Netherlands: De Leeuw LEGENDS..HOLLAND 101-102.

F610.3.8* Badang the Strong. Catches demon stealing fish. Offered gift to free. Chooses strength. Singapore: Asia THREE 42-47.

F611.3.2. Hero's precocious strength. Has full strength when very young.

F611.3.2.1* Ku-nan, precocious strength and growth. Kills tiger by swinging by tail. Gains magic tiger skin. China: Dolch STORIES.. OLD CHINA 43-47.

F611.3.2.7* Kintaro. Strong boy has bear, deer, monkey, and hare as friends. Is seen pulling up (F621) tree to use as bridge and is taken in service as a samurai. He kills a cannibal monster. Japan: Ozaki JAPANESE 60-73; Sakade JAPANESE CHILDREN'S STORIES 103-120.

F611.3.3.3. Precocious hero tests bows made by father. Three break, fourth holds. Seeks tail of the Boom Boomy beast. Sings to charm beasts and mother of B. gives son's tail. Escapes by singing. West Africa: Carpenter AFRICAN WONDER 13-20.

F613. Strong man's labor contract. Type 650. SEE ALSO: F628.2.3.1; F601.2.

F613.1.1* Master tries to get rid of servant, sent to dark woods for 'lost' cow, returns with bear. Sent to Devil's Mill to collect rent of devils. He threatens to tie up all devils and they fill his hat (bottomless) with silver. Merchant and wife flee. He hides in sack and goes along. They drown him. He changes place with wife and she is thrown in river. His blow at year's end kills master. Russia: Downing RUSSIAN 202-207. SEE ALSO: K172 (Anger Bargain).

F613.2. Strong man's labor contract: all grain he can carry. Type 650. SEE: F628.2.3.1 (Tom Hickathrift).

F613.2.1. Labor contract: as much money as my companion (strong man) can carry. SEE: F601.2Abd, D (Withers).

F615.3. Strong hero overawes master.

F615.3.1.3* Thumbling the Dwarf and Thumbling the Giant. Giant raises Thumbling (F535.1.1) and teaches strength. Thumbling works for smith. To give two strokes each fortnight to smith as wages--lays smith low. Farmer hires, carries wagon and horse. Giant rolls millstones onto T. to rid self of him, T. wears as necklace, complains of chickens scratching 'gravel' (millstones) onto him. Beats ghosts in haunted mill. Takes wages and leaves. Germany (Grimm): Adams BOOK..GIANTS 134-144; Grimm GRIMM'S (Grosset) 54-61; Grimm GRIMM'S (World) 194-201; Wiggin TALES 129-130.

F615.3.1.4* Lod the Farmer's Son. Breaks three clubs before finding one strong enough. Works for three giants, kills each with club. Wrestles and kills giant's mother and takes treasure. Scotland: Wilson SCOTTISH 18-27.

F615.3.1.5* Son nursed 3 x 7 years uproots tree. Seeks vengeance on Connacht men who mistreated his Donegal father. Hires self to king. Threshes barn half full and destroys barn before breakfast. Sent to bring Wild Bull, beats brains of nineteen bulls out with King Bull. Sent to Dragon Mountain for timber, drags fifty oaks home while riding dragon. Sent to Giant of Five Heads and Five Trunks to ask tribute, brings Giant and goods. To fetch King of Connacht's grandfather from hell, brings half of hell back. Millstone's thrown on him as he digs well, he says crows are scratching dirt down. Wears millstones as hat. Pay is weight in gold to get him to leave. Insists on being weighed with "hats" on. Ireland: MacManus HIBERNIAN 1-9.

F615.9* Remarkable strong man is unable to move when certain feather (straw) falls on him. Ethiopia (Somali): Courlander FIRE 103-104 (Ojje Ben Onogh, slain by Moses). Haiti: Courlander PIECE 23-24 (bird drops kernels on head).

F615.9.1* Kassa Kena Genanina with two strong companions. None can lift feather off K. Woman with child blows it off and gives dead bird from which feather came to child as plaything. +K1931.2Z. Mende: Courlander COW-TAIL 41-45.

F617. Mighty wrestler.

F617.2.1* Sumo wrestler meets girl, her mother, and grandmother, all can out-wrestle him. They train him and he becomes champion wrestler of Japan. Japan: Stamm THREE pb /Minard WOMENFOLK 93-105/.

F617.2.2* Peasant's wife wrestles strong man on bet and wins. In fear peasant hits her over head with ax on way home to rid self of her. She wakes up and reassures him she will always obey. Gypsy: Hampden GYPSIES' FIDDLE 39-46.

F617.2.3* Animals must defeat woman's little girl

in wrestling in order to get fire. All are thrown to sky and harmed in landing. Why leopard has spots, cat says meow, etc. Finally thrown. Her mother and she cry = origin of crying. Sierra Leone: Aardema MORE 62-67.

F617.3* Sumo wrestler wrestles sixty foot serpent. Snake wraps tail around man's legs and head around tree across river. Snake snaps in two and man wins. It later takes one hundred thirty men on rope to budge him. Japan: Courlander TIGER'S 83-86.

F617.4* Fourth son mocked for weakness by his brothers. He wrestles nightly with Strength Giver and bathes in magic pool. Uproots tree to test strength. On hunt he outshines brothers by overpowering three sea lions. They abandon him on rocks. Raven calls down copper canoe from sun to aid. Native American (Northwest Coast): Martin NINE 51-54 /Martin RAVEN 61-68/.

F621. Strong man: tree-puller. Can uproot and carry off trees. SEE ALSO: F611.3.2.7. Nigeria (Hausa): Arnott AFRICAN 40-42 (+F660.1).

F622. Mighty blower. Man turns mill with his blowing. SEE: F601.2.

F624.1. Strong man lifts horse (ox, ass). SEE ALSO: F610.3.7.

F624.1.0.1. Dourble Arend of Meeden picks up wife's family, table, chairs and all and puts outside after wife dies. King seeks taxes payment. D. intimidates by picking up horse and plow. Netherlands: De Leeuw LEGENDS..HOLLAND 33-37.

F628.2.3.1* Strong man kills giant. Tom Hickathrift. Incident 1: Sent for straw, Tom is told to take all he can carry, carries off huge load (F613.2). Incident 2: Tom drives brewer's cart past giant's road. Giant challenges and Tom kills with axletree. He receives giant's treasure (F531). Colwell ROUND 64-67; Jacobs MORE 46-54 (+ fight with tinker); Manning-Sanders PETER 110-119 (-incident 1, + Tom weds girl found in castle, discovers hidden room by throwing hammer through window from outside, then searching inside until finds hammer. Treasure in hidden room) /Mayne BOOK ..GIANTS 138-147/; Williams-Ellis FAIRY.. BRITISH 216-248 (-incident 1, +draw with Jack the Tinkard, Tinkard to wed Tom's daughter Geneva. Tinkard rescues her from enchanter by nailing hand to door with arrow. Horse turns to adder, enchanter vanquished. G. disenchanted by charm, wed.).

F636.6* Remarkable thrower. Strong man drives spear through Baobab Tree, making hole large enough to jump horse through. Nigeria (Hausa): Arnott AFRICAN 40-42 (+F660.1).

F639.2. Mighty diver. Can stay extraordinary time under water. Western Sudan (Mandingo):

Withers I 142 (+F660.1C).

F640. Extraordinary powers of perception.

F641. Person of remarkable hearing. SEE: F601.2 (extraordinary companions). Western Sudan (Mandingo): Withers I 142 (hears grain fall overboard, F660.1C).

F642. Person of remarkable sight. SEE: F601.2 (extraordinary companions).

F642.1. Remarkable star-gazer. Sees birds in nest in distant tree. SEE: F660.1.

F642.9* Person can shatter objects with his gaze. SEE: F601.2B (extraordinary companions).

F647. Marvelous sensitiveness. SEE: H1571 (Test).

F655. Extraordinary perception of blind man. SEE: U170.

F660. Remarkable skill.

F660.1. Brothers acquire extraordinary skill. Return home and are tested. Type 653, 654, 1525. SEE ALSO: H621.4; F601.2; K301.3; H621.2.4.

A* Four Clever Brothers. Astronomer counts number of eggs under chaffinch. Thief steals, Marksman shoots all five in half with one shot. Tailor sews back together and chicks hatch with only red seam on necks. They rescue a princess (R111.1.3). Astronomer sees, Thief steals, Marksman kills dragon, Tailor resews broken ship. King gives each one-fourth kingdom, none gets princess (H621.2). Germany (Grimm): De La Mare TALES 15-24; Grimm FOUR pb; Grimm GRIMM'S (Grosset) 307-312; Grimm GRIMM'S (Scribners) 236-241; Grimm GRIMM'S (World) 125-129; Haviland FAVORITE..SPAIN 18-35 (coppersmith instead of tailor).

B* Three Brothers. One with best trade to get inheritance. First shaves hare on run, second shoes horse on gallop, third flourishes sword so fast keeps dry in rain. Third wins. Germany (Grimm): Gag TALES 171-176 (gnat on wing shod); Grimm GRIMM'S (Follett) 340-343; Wiggin TALES 72-73. Germany: Withers WORLD 55-56.

Bb* Woman leaves pear tree to son with greatest skill. One can skin hare in flight. Second one can shoe horse on gallop, third one can catch all feathers if featherbed opened on windy day. He wins. Germany: Withers WORLD 33.

C* The Seven Simeons.

Ca* Seven brothers, each with remarkable trade, obtain distant princess for king. First builds tall pillar, second sees her from pillar. Third builds ships, seventh steals, fourth dives to ocean bottom with ship. Fifth shoots princess when she escapes as a swan. Sixth catches as she falls. Hungary: Lang CRIMSON 26-41

/Lang FIFTY 304-315/; Manning-Sanders GLASS 10-21/, /Provensen PROVENSEN 57-67/. Russia: Artzbasheff SEVEN pb; McNeil DOUBLE 42-48; Whitney IN 123-129.

Cb* Seven Stars. Troll steals princess. First brother makes ship, second steers, third hears where she is, fifth climbs glass mountain with thief, sixth steals. Troll pursues--fourth, marksman, kills. Bursts into flint pieces. Fairy turns all seven to stars as they cannot decide who she should marry (A773.1). Denmark: Hatch MORE 79-87.

Cc* Ogre's Breath. Ogre sucks princess out window and carries off. First brother carries all to ogre's castle, second hears where she is, third smashes doors, fourth steals, fifth raises iron tower to hide her. Ogre sucks her out. Sixth kills ogre but princess is killed too. Seventh revives. All claim could not have saved her without the others. Sicily: Manning-Sanders BOOK..OGRES 32-37. Bulgaria: Spicer THIRTEEN DEVILS 53-62 (-sucking motif, devil freezes her by seeing finger in tower, was taken beneath sea, one brother drinks sea dry).

D* Seven remarkable brothers defy ruler. Big Strength pushes gate down, Wind blows inner gate, Iron Man cannot be beheaded, Fearless Heat shields all from burning, Long Legs and Big Foot cannot be drowned, Big Mouth drinks sea dry and spits onto court, killing all. SEE ALSO: F601.2. China: Chang CHINESE 64-65. SEE ALSO: Bishop, Claire Hutchet FIVE CHINESE BROTHERS pb.

Db* Six Chinese Brothers need to fetch pearl from king's palace to save ill father. First is clever. Second stretches arm into palace to take pearl. Third cannot be beheaded. Fourth cannot be stabbed because of iron skin. Fifth can withstand heat. Sixth can stretch legs and not drown. Finds jewels on sea bottom and repays king. China: Hou-Tien SIX pb.

E* Which is most skillful? Three skillful brothers, who most skillful? One hears grain fall from boat. Second one dives for it, third one counts rest of grains in sack to verify it is missing. Western Sudan (Mandingo): Withers I 142. Mali: Withers WORLD 60.

Eb* Which son is cleverest? First drove spear through Baobab tree and leapt through hole, thus made. Second jumped over tree. Third pulled up tree and carried off. North Nigeria (Hausa): Arnott AFRICAN 40-42; Courlander KING'S 50.

F* Three sons left magic bow, deer, bird. Youngest, with bird that tells all, becomes the prime minister. Second, with deer that carries wherever wants to go, carries to enemy. Elder, with arrow, kills enemy king. By cooperation they achieve. Mexico: Brenner BOY 90-94.

F660.1.1* Skillful brother and extraordinary swift acts. First brother sees horse tied to cloud. Second shoots cutting rope. Third catches as falls. It bounces out of hands however and lands in village. Old woman there is so quick she has killed, cooked, and eaten horse by time they arrive. Mali: Withers WORLD 62-63.

F660.1.2* Extraordinarily swift acts. First man falls, changes to old clothes before hits ground. Second shoots antelope, runs ahead and kills with knife, skins, packs meat and grabs bullet before can pierce meat packet. Mali: Withers WORLD 61-62. Western Sudan (Mandingo): Withers I 142. Mende: Frobenius AFRICAN 153-154 /Courlander KING'S 17-18/ (man falling weaves mat, man puts forty chicks in baskets and catches hawk as it swoops).

F661. Skillful marksman. SEE: F601.2.

F661.4. Skillful marksman shoots eggs scattered over table. SEE: F660.1.

F661.9. Skillful marksman grazes ear of sleeping person and awakens him. SEE: F601.2.

F661.13* Skillful boy flicks pebbles at leaves cutting intricate patterns in them. He is taken to court to flick mud pellets into mouths of talkative courtiers when they open mouths. Laos: Asia FOLK I 32-36.

F662. Skillful tailor. SEE: F660.1; H621.2 (coppersmith mends).

F662.3. Skillful tailor sews bean together after bean has split from laughing. SEE ALSO: A2741.1 (bean laughs until it splits); F1025.1. Europe: Leach HOW PEOPLE 127-128; TALL.. NURSERY 90-91. Germany (Grimm): Brooks HOUSE 120-123; Gag MORE 95-98; Grimm BROTHERS 21-22; Grimm GRIMM'S (Grosset) 214-215; Grimm GRIMM'S (World) 280-281; Grimm HOUSEHOLD 98-99.

F663. Skillful smith shoes running horse. Type 654. SEE: F660.1. Germany: Withers WORLD 33 (F660.1C).

F663.1.1* Skillful smith shoes gnat on the wing. Gag TALES 171-176 (+F660.1B).

F664.1. Skillful flayer skins running rabbit. Germany: Withers WORLD 33.

F665.1. Skillful barber shaves running hare. SEE: F660.1B.

F667.1. Skillful fencer keeps sword dry in rain. Swings it so fast. Type 654.

F667.1.1* Skillful fencer keeps self dry in rain by swinging sword over head. SEE: F660.1B.

F673. Man can keep feathers together in a great wind. Germany: Withers WORLD 33 (+660.1B).

F676. Skillful thief. SEE: K305.1; K301.

F681. Marvelous runner.

F681.1. Marvelous runner keeps leg tied up. To prevent him from running away. SEE: F601.2.

F684. Marvelous jumper. Nigeria (Hausa): Arnott AFRICAN 40-42 (jumps over Baobab tree +F660.1).

F685.1* Marvelous withstander of heat. SEE: F601.2.

F700 - F899. Extraordinary places and things.

F700. Extraordinary places.

F708.1. Country without cats. SEE ALSO: N411.1; J2101. Italy: Jagendorf PRICELESS CATS 47-58.

F718.3. Well of wines. Task: stirring with staff until spring turns to wine. SEE: D925.0.2.1. Appalachia: Chase JACK 89-95.

F725. Submarine world. SEE ALSO: A420 (Sea God).

F725.3. Submarine castle (palace). SEE: K544.1.

F742. Magic invisibility of otherworld island. SEE ALSO: F420.4.7.1; F420.6.1.1.2; F420.6.1.1.1.

F742.1* Man learns spells enabling to see Fin's island. Performs spells evicting Fins and claims island as Eyn-Hallow, part of Orkneys. Orkney: Cutt HOGBOON 124-129.

F743.5* Island of ogres. SEE: T543.3.2 (Momotaro).

F751. Glass mountain. SEE: H331.1.1; P253.2A (Seven Ravens; are in glass mountain); H1385.5; D721.5.

F772.1.2. Tower reaches moon. SEE ALSO: J2133.6.2.

F772.1.2.1* Vanapagan has ladder built to tar moon. Top rungs are made of prickly kadakas bushes and break. Tar bucket falls on V. Second try V. himself does the tarring. Vanaisa sentences him to stick there. May still be seen (A751.4). Lithuania: Maas MOON 11-16.

F772.1.2.2* Tower built to obtain moon for prince. Moon ruptures spilling lava onto earth. Dark spots still seen on moon (A751.5.6). Congo: Green FOLKTALES 75-81.

F772.1.3* Baboons build tower of their bodies to reach dead king up to God. Ant coming to mourn stings foot of bottom baboon to get his attention. Tower crumbles. Ethiopia (Guragie): Davis LION'S 132-135.

F800. Extraordinary rocks and stones. SEE ALSO: N511.6.1.

F809.5.1* Cock crow stone. Cursed by witch it must turn round thrice each time cock crows. Piskies roll it into sea where it won't have to keep turning. Cornwall: Manning-Sanders PETER 21-23.

F809.5.2* Nine troll stones move when whistle is blown. Orkney: Cutt HOGBOON 15-45.

F809.10* Stone near Krakow bears legend "If you turn me over, I shall tell you something." Turned over at great expense. Finds words underneath "I was so heavy." Poland: Borski GOOD 61.

F810. Extraordinary trees, plants, fruits, etc.

F811.1. Trees of extraordinary material. SEE: B335.2D (Kari Woodenskirt--woods of copper, silver, gold); F1015.1.1.12 (Twelve Dancing Princesses).

F811.19. Tree grows miraculously fast from seed. SEE: D1571.1.

F813.1.1. Golden apple. SEE: H1331.1.3 (quest for golden birch).

F813.3.4. Silk handkerchief concealed in a nut. SEE: F821.2 (dress in nutshell).

F813.8.3* Three Pomegranates. Three princesses. Youngest loves father like salt (H592.1). Wed to poor man as punishment. He joins caravan, meets dragon at well (water sprite). Is civil and receives three pomegranates. Not to cut until home. Sends one to wife. Pomegranate is full of diamonds, she builds palace. He returns home. Opens other two, same. Is generous to poor. King visits. Is served food without salt. Reunited with daughter. Greece: Haviland FAVORITE..GREECE 21-27; Manning-Sanders BOOK..DRAGONS 123-128. Greece (Thrace): Neufeld BEWARE 28-35. Armenia: Lang OLIVE 119-130 /Lang FIFTY 106-114 (-salt motif).

F815. Extraordinary plants. SEE: B210.1.1 (Talk).

F815.1. Vegetables (plants) which mature in miraculously short time. SEE: D2157.2; G263.1.0.2.

F821.1.3. Dress of raw fur. Cat fur, mouse fur or other undressed fur. SEE: R221D (Cat-skin).

F821.1.3.1. Bearskin. Man dressed in bear hide. Type 361. SEE: K217 (Bearskin).

F821.1.3.2. Cloak made from fur of all animals in realm. SEE: F221D.

F821.1.5. Dress of gold, silver, color of sun, moon and stars. SEE: R221D+.

F821.1.6. Dress of feathers. SEE: R221Db.

F820. Extraordinary clothing and ornaments.

F821.2. Dress so fine that it goes in nutshell.

SEE: R221D; K1931.2D.

F822. Extraordinary handkerchief. SEE: F813.3.4.

F823.2. Glass shoes. SEE: R221 (Cinderella et. al.).

F823.5* Conal plays pipes and miserly cobbler's shoes march to homes of needy. Fairies replace shoes so cobbler never misses them but shoes pinch so that he never sells another pair. Ireland: Sawyer WAY 259-270.

F830. Extraordinary weapons.

F833.1. Sword so heavy that hero must take drink of strength before swinging it. SEE: H1385.3.

F840. Other extraordinary objects and places.

F842.1.5. Bridge of straw. SEE: Z32.1; F1025.1.

F848.1. Girl's long hair as ladder into tower. Rapunzel. Wife craves rapunzel (lettuce) in the witch's garden. Husband caught stealing. Third time must pledge unborn child. Girl kept in tower, witch ascends via long hair. As prince ascends, witch cuts off hair letting prince drop. Thorns blind him. Prince wanders in wilderness. Years later meets R. with twins she bore him. Rapunzel's tears fall on eyes and cure blindness. Type 310. Grimm: Arbuthnot ARBUTHNOT..ANTHOLOGY 204-206; Darrell ONCE 47-50; De La Mare TALES 201-207 (prince gives R. knife to cut hair and witch falls to her death); Gag TALES 135-145; Grimm BROTHERS 34-38; Grimm GRIMM'S (Follett) 272-278; Grimm GRIMM'S (Grosset) 130-134 (rampion herb); Grimm GRIMM'S (World) 70-74; Grimm HOUSEHOLD 72-75; Grimm JUNIPER 247-255; Grimm RAPUNZEL pb (-babes, witch left in tower shrivels up and birds feed to young); Grimm RAPUNZEL (Crowell) pb; Haviland FAVORITE.. GERMANY 21-31; Hoke WITCHES 85-89; Lang RED 286-292 /Hope-Simpson CAV..WITCHES 203-209/, /Lang FIFTY 231-234/; Manning-Sanders BOOK..WITCHES 18-26; Martignoni ILL 374-375; Shub ABOUT 39-42.

F848.1.1* Petrosinella or Parsley. Mother steals parsley, ogress overheard to say can't escape without three bitternuts on rafter. Prince and P. make straw ladder, escape, obstacle flight (D672) throw nut = bulldog, ogress feeds. Second nut = lion. Ogress puts on donkey skin and frightens lion away. Third nut = wolf. Wolf eats ogress, taking her for a donkey. Italy: Mincielli OLD 35-41.

F848.1.2* The Little Horse of Seven Colors. Mother keeps daughter in tower, escapes with prince. Mother calls to look back--receives cow's head +(B641A). Portugal: Lowe LITTLE 106-113.

F852.1. Glass coffin. SEE: Z65.1 (Snow White).

F852.1.2* The Glass Coffin. Tailor spends night in tree, sees light, spends night in hut. Sees goat and black beast fight. Goat carries tailor off on horns to stone hole. Stands on stone in middle and it sinks into chamber below with two glass coffins--one has castle, one has maid. He opens maid's coffin and she wakes, enchantment broken. Rise on stone with castle. Goat was her brother. She weds tailor. Germany (Grimm): Grimm GRIMM'S (Scribner's) 270-277; Lang GREEN 281-287.

F861.4.3. Carriage from pumpkin. SEE: R221 (Cinderella).

F875. Iron bands around heart to keep it from breaking. When master is disenchanted bonds around heart of faithful servant snap one by one. SEE: D195 (Frog Prince).

A900 - F1099. Extraordinary occurrences.

F910. Extraordinary swallowings. SEE: A1411.2; F535.1 (Thumbling); K2011 (Red Riding Hood).

F911.2.1. Raven dwells inside a whale. Loves whale-spirit maiden. Tries to escape with her. She withers, whale dies. Eskimo: Melzack RAVEN 42-44.

F911.2.1.1* Raven dwelling inside whale drinks of whale oil and causes whale-spirit lamp to go out. Whale dies and spirit-maiden vanishes. Raven makes villagers think whale meat is poison and gets all for self. Eskimo: Robinson COYOTE 85-94.

F911.4.1* Girl swallowed by fish cuts slits in throat and escapes. Origin gills (A2341.4). Rarotonga: Holding SKY 75-86 /Arbuthnot ANTHOLOGY 357-358/.

F911.4.2. Punia in shark's belly lives off shark meat, begs shark not to take him to beach, shark does so, dies. Hawaii: Thompson HAWAIIAN..TRICKSTERS 23-27.

F911.6.2* Chief's daughter feeds pet worm. It becomes devouring dragon. She sings to get it to open mouth for food and all run out. Hero kills it. Eskimo: Caswell SHADOWS 88-92.

F912. Victim kills swallower from within. SEE ALSO: K952; P361.10; Z33+.

F912.2.1* Elephant eats two children of Unanana. U. takes knife and searches. Elephant eats her. Many people living inside. She cuts off and roasts meat for them. Elephant dies. Unanana cuts hole and all escape. Zulu: Aardema BEHIND 74-80; Arnott AFRICAN MYTHS 68-73 /Minard WOMENFOLK 127-134/.

F912.2.2* Cannibal swallows victims whole. Nkongola cuts self out with razor as cannibal sleeps. Bantu: Holladay BANTU 24-25.

F912.2.3* Man lets giant bear swallow him. Cuts open and rescues all there. Eskimo: Field ESKIMO 31-32.

F912.2.4* Kagwaii, giant whale, eats boy disguised as halibut. Is killed from within with knife. Boy disguises as Naguaii and kills giant crab Kostan. Native American (Haida): Harris ONCE 33-58.

F912.2.5* Weasel leaps down sleeping monster's throat, eats heart and kills, saving old man. Native American: Field AMERICAN 62-70.

F912.2.6* Rabbit disguised as man gets self swallowed by man-eating hill. Stabs heart and rescues all inside. Takes home fat. Native American (Sioux): Garner CAVALCADE..GOBLINS 1-2.

F912.2.7* Manabozho kills giant sturgeon cutting heart from within aided by squirrel. Native American (Chippewa): Leekley WORLD 79-91 /Haviland NORTH 19-20/.

F912.2.8* Djabbe with seven horns killed by cutting from within. Purse found in stomach gives day and night. Haiti: Johnson HOW 55-58.

F912.2.9* Coyote kills monster Iltsweltrix (G332) by letting self be swallowed and cutting out heart. Native American (Nez Percé): DeWit TALKING 122-126; Heady TALES 101-108; Matson LEGENDS 64-69.

F912.2.10* Tepozton swallowed by giant cuts hole in stomach and kills. Mexico: Brenner BOY 34-37 /Frost LEGENDS 190-199/.

F912.2.11* Old woman sucks in all (G332), boy, Falling-Star cuts hole and lets out all. Native American (N. Cheyenne): Field AMERICAN 13-31.

F912.2.12* The Tiger of Kumgang Mountains. Lad seeks tiger who killed his father. Practices until can shoot handle off mother's waterjug on head, eye out of held needle. Old woman met makes him practice twice three years again. Shoot leaf off tree, ant off cliff. Shoots four tigers met in human form. Bullets bounce off teeth of giant white tiger. Eaten, he finds girl in tiger's stomach. They cut hole, killing tiger and escape. Wed. Korea: Kim STORY 199-214.

F912.2.13* Hunter swallowed by giant fish, Dakwa. Cuts way out with mussel shell. Head bald from acids in stomach thereafter. Native American (Cherokee): Brown TEPEE 132-133.

F912.3.1. Swallowed person tickles serpent's throat and is disgorged. SEE: K952.

F912.3.1.1* Anaconda eats daughter. Father tosses hot stone down throat and anaconda regurgitates daughter. Choco: Carpenter SOUTH AMERICAN 144-150.

F912.3.2* Ukko Untamoinen asks Seppo Ilmarinen to dance on his tongue and swallows. S. forges bird of copper which pecks at U's insides until disgorged. Finland: Bowman TALES..TUPA 73-80.

F913. Victims rescued from swallower's belly. Types 123, 333, 450, 700. SEE: F535.1.1 (Thumbling); K311.2 (Wolf and Seven Kids); K891.1.3; K2011; J2133.7.1 (Haviland); Z33+.

F913.2* Monster eats family, servants, cattle and beer pots. Temba escapes and brings help. Monster defeated tells to cut off his big toe. All exit. East Africa: Arnott TALES 65-69.

F913.4* Little girl rescued from gorilla's stomach. His little finger is cut off and she comes out. Baganda: Serwadda SONGS 45-51 (K311.3J).

F913.5* Iya sucks in all people (G332). They live inside monster. Coyote feigns brotherhood and learns his secret fear (K601). Tells men to make huge racket and Iya dies of fear. Cut open and all escape. Native American (Great Plains): Jones COYOTE 41-49. Native American (Nez Percé): Martin NINE..COYOTE 53-60 (builds fire and cuts out heart).

F914.0.1. Person swallowed and disgorged. Tortoise claims to like all of rock python's attentions--embrace, toss into air, swallowing, etc. Rock Python regurgitates him and allows to wed daughter (H310). Congo: Burton MAGIC 98-101.

F915. Victim speaks from swallower's body. SEE: Z49.3.1.

F915.1. Victim pecks on swallower's stomach. Bird eaten by king pecks on his stomach. King vomits and bird escapes. SEE: F912.3.2; Z49.3.1 (Picaro Bird).

F929. Extraordinary swallowings--miscellaneous.

F929.3* Fat cut from inside of cow. Greedy trickster cuts heart (tabu) and cow dies. West Africa: Aardema TALES..THIRD 9-18 (Anansi). American Negro: Harris FAVORITE 291-295; Harris COMPLETE 111-115; Harris UNCLE REMUS: HIS SONGS 168-174 (Brer Rabbit).

F929.4* Mantis rescues springbok from stomach of elephant. Enters through navel and leaves via trunk. Bushmen: Helfman BUSHMEN 74-76.

F940. Extraordinary underground (underwater) disappearance.

F944. City sinks into the sea (or lake).

F944.1. (Baughman). City sinks into water after populace refuses hospitality to holy person, beggar, or witch. SEE ALSO: F993. Dolomites: Sawyer LONG 121-134 (Christ child, +F993). Wales: Sheppard-Jones WELSH 82-84 (Mervyn gives jeweled glove to babe to play with, only babe floating in cradle survives flood, origin Llangose Lake). Yorkshire: Colwell ROUND

43-45 (Origin Semerwater Lake). Luo: Harman TALES 95-103 (old woman beggar).

F944.1.2* City is sunk in lake as punishment. Bird calls vengeance and beckons harper away before inundation. Wales: Sheppard-Jones WELSH 78-81.

F944.5* Dyke keeper leaves dyke open and village is inundated. Sigh of ruler Gwyddno Garanhir is still heard there. Wales: Sheppard-Jones WELSH 131-133.

F944.6* King Gralon's daughter Dahut kills hunchback lad to get keys to dyke, opens gate and sea unundates town. Dead lovers whom she has caused to leap into sea in despair claim her. Bells of Ys still heard on Easter Day. (F993). France: Colum STONE 30-35; Frost LEGEND 215-222.

F944.7* King Corc sends daughter to fetch more water at feast. She falls into well. Until her golden pitcher is brought up water will not stop. They go on dancing in palace at bottom of Lough of Cork. Ireland: Adams BOOK..PRINCESS 116-120; Pilkington SHAMROCK 150-152.

F945.1* Pirate hoards gold. Flood engulfs pirate, house, and gold covered table. Table can still be seen at bottom of pool. Jamaica: Jagendorf KING 176-180.

F948.5. City is buried under sand. Mermaid is caught and mistreated by villagers. In vengeance she or her husband cause village to disappear in sand banks. (cf. B81). Denmark: Manning-Sanders CHOICE 166-170 /Manning-Sanders BOOK..MERMAIDS 36-40/. Netherlands: De Leeuw LEGENDS..HOLLAND 28-32 (Westerschouwen); Frost LEGENDS 186-189 (Westerschowen).

F950. Marvelous cures.

F952.1. Blindness cured by tears. SEE: F848.1 (Rapunzel).

F952.7.1* Loon dives thrice or four times with blind boy on back. Boy's sight is restored. He gives loon white necklace in gratitude (A2411.2.6.1). Eskimo: Caswell SHADOWS 41-47; Maher BLIND 17-30; Toye LOON'S pb.

F953.1. Hunchback cured by having hump severely beaten. SEE: F344.1.

F954.2.1. Dumb princess brought to speech by tale ending with a question to be solved. Type 945. SEE ALSO: H343; H621.2; N141.0.1. Denmark: Hatch THIRTEEN 46-57.

F954.2.1.1* Lad puts bird in chest and has 'chest' tell story ending with riddle (H621). She gives answer. Wed. Greece: Neufield BEWARE 42-51 (repeat three times, +H621, H621.1, H621.2); Wilson GREEK 58-64. Latvia: Huggins BLUE 65-73.

F960. Extraordinary nature phenomena--elements and weather.

F962.5.0.1* Man approaches from east with hail falling on him from clear sky. Woman seeing this takes hail as her spirit medium. Native American (Upper Skagit): Matson LONGHOUSE 100-102.

F962.11.2* Miraculous snow in mid-summer confirms innocence of woman. Netherlands: De Leeuw LEGENDS..HOLLAND 60-65.

F963.1. Wind serves Solomon as horse and carries him everywhere. SEE: D1711.1.1.

F969.8* Extraordinary volcanic eruption. Boqueron volcano destroys San Jorge de Olancho where Spaniards refused gold for virgin's crown. Honduras: Jagendorf KING 167-170.

F971.7.1* Priest refused pear by peddlar buys one, eats, plants seed, waters, it grows, blossoms, bears as they watch. He picks fruit and hands to crowd. Chops down tree and carries it off. Peddler realizes his cart is empty and one handle has been chopped off. China: Carpenter TALES..CHINESE 142-149; Courlander RIDE 38-41.

F981.6. Animal dies of broken heart. SEE: F1041.1.2.2.5.

F983.2. Louse fattened. SEE: H522.1.1.

F990. Inanimate objects act as if living.

F993.1* Sunken bell sounds at certain time. SEE ALSO: F944 (Frost). Sawyer LONG 121-134 (+F944.1).

F993.1.1* Bell of Stavoren not blessed when it is moved. Joost (devil) claims bell, plays toss with it and drops it into the Fluessen. Sounds to warn marines of shoals. Netherlands: Spicer OWL'S 41-55.

F993.2* Pirates steal bells of abbey. Abbot curses them and they swell until sink ship. Still heard. Scotland: Nic Leodhas THISTLE 98-105.

F993.3* Danes steal largest of church bells of Boshom. It causes ship to sink. Attempt to raise it with six white horses later fails, perhaps one horse not pure white. Still heard. Sussex: Colwell ROUND 105-107.

F993.4* Giants Ing and Ir fight causing tidal wave. Plain of Lyenese is covered. Bells of the one hundred and forty churches drowned can still be heard. Cornwall: Manning-Sanders PETER 26-32.

F1010. Other extraordinary events.

F1015.1.1. The danced-out shoes. Every morning girl's shoes are danced to pieces. SEE ALSO: H1411.4.5. Type 306.

A* Twelve Dancing Princesses. Prize to one discovering secret. Old woman gives cloak of invisibility to man (D1361.12). He follows princesses and breaks twigs from enchanted trees of silver, gold, and diamond woods (F811.1). Steals goblet from dance. Produces tokens and proves princesses were dancing in underground kingdom each night. Weds one. Usually twelve princesses dance with twelve enchanted princes. Germany (Grimm): Adams TWELVE pb; Dalgliesh ENCHANTED 124-129; De La Mare TALES 61-73 (old soldier, refuses to wed princess suggesting they wed twelve princes of underground palace) /Colwell SECOND 85-96/; Fenner PRINCESSES 57-63; Grimm BROTHERS 112-116; Grimm GRIMM'S (Follett) 365-372; Grimm GRIMM'S (Grosset) 1-6; Grimm GRIMM'S (Scribner's) 231-235; Grimm GRIMM'S (World) 24-28; Grimm TWELVE (Le Cain) pb; Grimm TWELVE (illus. Shulevitz) pb; Holme TALES 81-88; Lunn TWELVE pb; Opie CLASSIC 188-194; Rackham GRIMM'S 54-59; Sleigh NORTH 44-56.

B. The Twelve Pair of Danced-out Slippers. Lad shares food with old man, given ball to (D1313.1) follow and stick of invisibility (D1361.25.2). Ball rolls to castle of princess who wears out twelve pair of golden slippers nightly. He feigns sleep and keeps golden needle stuck in foot to test, breaks boughs of silver, gold and diamond woods. Takes her gold place setting and twelve pairs of slippers. Reveals 'dream' in morning and produces tokens. Returns and sticks troll's heart with golden needle, catches three drops of blood in golden thimble, troll dies. Puts drop of blood on each wood and trees turn to people of three kingdoms, weds and rules these. Denmark: Baker GOLDEN 34-40; Hatch MORE 88-104.

Bb* Dragon carries princess off nightly. Hero meets two demons arguing over magic frying (D1520) pan that flies when struck with silver stick, and cap of invisibility (D1361.15). He holds these for demands and steals (D832). Gathers tokens = bouquet princess and dragon play with, piece of bridge and tree, golden apple. Produces tokens and weds princess. Bulgaria: Pridham GIFT 21-29.

Bc* Hero meets two fighting over hat of invisibility. Throws oranges and takes hat (D1361.14) (D832). Meets two more men fighting over fast traveling boat (D1520.15). Same. Follows princess to Isle of Brasil where she danced out seven iron-soled slippers with dead pirates raised from deep by sorcerer. Hero steals sorcerer captain's magic book as token. When opened she must dance. Wed. Portugal: McNeil DOUBLE 16-22.

C* Lad finds three quarreling over turban of invisibility (D1361.15), and carpet which flies when whip cracked. He shoots arrow for them and steals (D832). Padisha's daughter disappears nightly. Follows Peri who carries her off on golden shield. Breaks twigs of silver, diamond and jeweled trees. Lad hides her jeweled slippers and silverware, cuts off Peri's head.

Produces token and weds her to his brother. He had been seeking brother and assembles entire town to find brother. Turkey: Buck FAIRY 257-263.

D* Cowherd instructed by lady in thrice repeated dream to go to castle as gardener. Given golden rake and bucket and silken towel to care for cherry, laurel and rose laurel. To wipe with towel until grown and will grant wish. Becomes invisible when wearing flower (D1361.6). Follows princess and breaks sprigs of silver, gold and diamond. Princesses plot to give him potion to enchant with other princes. Youngest stops him from drinking it thus breaking enchantment. Princes all freed, wed princesses. France: Haviland FAVORITE..FRANCE 3-25; Lang RED 1-15.

F1021.2.1. Flight so high that sun melts glue of artificial wings. SEE: K1041.1.

F1023. Creation of a person by cooperation of skillful men. Type 945. SEE: J563.2 (four scholars resuscitate lion); H621.

F1025. Objects go journeying together. SEE: B296 (Animals go a-journeying).

F1025.1. Bean, straw and coal go journeying. Coal burns straw in two and falls into the water. Bean laughs until it splits. Type 295. (cf. A2741.1. Bean laughs until it splits , F662.3 Tailor sews bean together). SEE ALSO: Z32.1. Europe: Leach HOW 127-128; TALL..NURSERY 90-91. Germany (Grimm): Brooks HOUSE 120-123; Gag MORE 95-98; Grimm BROTHERS 21-22; Grimm GRIMM'S (Grosset) 214-215; Grimm GRIMM'S (World) 280-281; Grimm HOUSEHOLD 98-99.

F1025.1.1* Bubble, straw and shoe go journeying. Straw breaks and shoe falls in river, bubble bursts laughing. Russia/Yiddish: Daniels FALCON 90-91; Ginsburg THREE ROLLS 22.

F1025.1.2* Mouse and coal go journeying. Coal burns through straw and drowns in water. Mouse laughs until it burst. +Z41.4.1. Switzerland (French): Duvoisin THREE 44-47.

F1025.2. Turtle's war-party. Turtle recruits war-party of strange objects (knife, brush, awl etc.) and animals. Because of their nature the companions (rattlesnake, porcupine, skunk) get into trouble. Type 297A. Native American: Bruchac TURKEY 26-29; Parker SKUNNY 159-164.

F1034. Person concealed in another's body. SEE: K1175.

F1037.1.1* Footstool thrown from heaven. Tailor allowed into Heaven by St. Peter (A661.0.1.2), sits in Lord's armchair and throws footstool at sinner. He is turned out. Type 800. Germany (Grimm): Gag MORE 117-122.

F1041.1.2.2.5* Death from broken heart. Female

duck stabs breast wih beak and dies before hunter who killed her mate. Hunter becomes priest and kills no more. Japan: Buck FAIRY 223-224.

F1041.1.11.4. Man dies from frog's bite, thinking it snakebite. India: Hardendorff JUST 17-18.

F1041.4.1* Wife (spirit of magic calf's fat) melts and runs into river when forced to cook. Becomes alligator. She had emerged from jar of fat of old woman's pet calf which king's men butchered. Each day she cleaned house (N831.1). Gold Coast: Carpenter AFRICAN 161-168.

F1041.4.2* Fattest-Of-All. Wife melts in sun. Sister, Little-Thin-One, collects fat and resuscitates. Africa: Sleigh NORTH 9-12.

F1068. Realistic dream.

F1068.0.1* Girl seeks stars, receives advice from fairies and pursues them, falls out of bed and wakes up. Jacobs MORE 177-181; Jacobs STARS pb; Reeves ENGLISH 178-181.

F1068.2. Wound received in dream. Still there when person wakes. SEE: F321.3.2.

F1068.3* Painter dreams becomes fish and is caught and to be eaten by friends. Wakes and sends word to friends to stop feast before he is eaten. Japan: Hearn BOY 33-42. China: Birch CHINESE 55-61.

F1068.4* Hunter dreams female dove wants to bring tiger to kill him but mate in bag says to wake him so can flee before hollow floods and he is drowned. He hunts no more. India: Korel LISTEN 49-53.

F1068.5* Fool dreams he hurts foot, bandages it in morning. Is told to wear shoes to bed. Greece: Jagendorf NOODLEHEAD 43-44; Leach NOODLES 28-29.

F1068.5.1* Fool dreams goes bear hunting, takes dog to bed with him next night. Greek: Leach NOODLES 17.

G. OGRES

G10 - G399. Kinds of ogres.

G10. Cannibalism.

G61. Relative's flesh eaten unwittingly. SEE ALSO: B654.1; D154.1; N271 (Juniper Tree).

G61.3* Badger serves soup made of wife to old man. Japan: Ozaki JAPANESE 43-53.

G82.1.2. Boy caught by Mr. Miacca (Sneezy Snatcher). Tells wife he'll go home for pudding for her. Doesn't return. Caught again, hides under sofa. To put out leg, puts out sofa leg. England: Jacobs ENGLISH 171-173 /Ness MR. MIACCA pb /; Manning-Sanders CHOICE 144-147 (Sneezy Snatcher, -leg episode) /Manning-Sanders BOOK..GIANTS 32-35/; Williams-Ellis FAIRY..BRITISH 146-148.

G84. Fee-fi-fo-fum. Cannibal returning home smells flesh and makes exclamation. SEE: F54.2 (Jack and the Beanstalk); G512 (Jack the Giant Killer); N777.0.1 (Oni smells old woman hiding in Jizo); R111.1.3Ah.

G200 - G299. Witches.

G200. Witch.

G201.1. Three witches (hags) deformed from much spinning. SEE: D2183.1.

G204. Girl in service of witch. Type 310, 428. SEE: Q2.1.2Cb.

G205. Witch stepmother. SEE: Q2.1.

G211.1.1.2A* (Baughman). Witch rides man after transforming him to horse with magic bridle. He manages to get bridle on her, rides her all night over rough country, has her shod. The shoes are still on her feet (or wounds from nails) when she changes back to usual form. SEE ALSO: G241.2.1. Scotland: Harper GHOSTS 192-194; Hoke WITCHES 219-220 /Olcott WONDER/.

G211.1.6. Witch in form of hog (G275.12). Witch steals two children and fattens. Father beats pig that runs between his legs and follows it home. Finds sick woman (pig) and children. Witch dies--turns to pig. Haiti: Johnson HOW 31-38.

G211.1.7. Witch in form of cat. SEE: D702.1.1; K1611E; Q2.1.2H.

G211.1.7.1* Man follows wife in night, sees her become a cat and consort with witches. He is discovered and transported to a cliff edge. Squirrel mother feeds him and drops pine seed over ledge. Seed grows to 1,000 foot high ledge in four days. Feeds witch wife pine seeds given by squirrel and she turns into a pine tree. Manning-Sanders RED /Hope-Simpson CAVALCADE..WITCHES 23-34/,/Colwell SECOND 122-

132/.

G211.1.7.2* Witch in form of cat. Ah Tscha The Sleeper (tale contains also non-folk motifs). Chrisman SHEN 159-172 /Hoke WITCHES 5-14/, /Gruenberg FAVORITE 388-393/.

G211.2.7. Witch in form of hare.

G211.2.7.2* Tailor imitates witch who jumps into water and turns to hare. Follows to meeting. Is discovered. She beats him home and is dumping out water as he arrives. He leaps into it but back of neck remains covered with fur thereafter. Danaher FOLK TALES 52-58.

G219.3.1* Witch with long knife-like toenail. Girl cuts toenail, reduces power. Restores sisters wed to witch's sons. Witch has cut out their hearts with toenail and eaten (G262.2.1). Native American (Upper Skagit): Matson LONG-HOUSE 49-59.

G219.9. Witch's back covered with nails and broken glass. SEE: Q2.1.6B; Q2.1.2H.

G220. Characteristics of witches.

G229.1.1. Witch who is out of skin is prevented from reentering it when person salts or peppers skin. Puerto Rico: Alegria THREE 86-89 (rising sun touches her skinless body and she burns to ashes). U.S. Black: Harris COMPLETE 101-105 (brother, black wolf tries to put on) /Harris NIGHTS 154-160/, /Harris COMPLETE 230-235 (skin is shrunk, black wolf tries to enter/.

G240. Habits of witches.

G241.2.1. Witch transforms man to horse and rides him. SEE: G211.1.1.2.

G242.1. Witch flies through air on broomstick. Scotland: Nic Leodhas HEATHER 95-110 (+D2183.1, broom must never have touched ground).

G242.7. Mistakes made by person traveling with witches. Person watches witches preparing to fly through air. He imitates their actions and words and flies with them, usually to house of rich woman where they feast and drink in kitchen or wine cellar. The interloper does something wrong and falls to the ground or is caught in the wine cellar. SEE: F282.4 (flying with fairies).

G242.7.1* (Baughman) Man gets drunk in strange castle while feasting with witches, he is caught by owner, escapes hanging with aid of magic cap. Wilson SCOTTISH 33-37 (to be killed, asks to wear blue cap as last wish, calls "Kintail, Kintail, Back again", returned to hill; witches put on blue caps and called "Carlisle" to fly).

G242.7.2* (Baughman) Person traveling with witches goes to sleep in castle. Owner catches him. Witch returns, saves him from gallows by giving him magic cap. England (Herefordshire):

Colwell ROUND 97-100 (white cap "Here's off" "Here's after").

G242.7.3* (Baughman) Person forgets word charm, falls to ground. +G242.7, +K335.1.1.3. Costa Rica: Hoke WITCHES 186-187; Lupe de Osma WITCHES /Harper GHOSTS 228-233/, /Arbuthnot ANTHOLOGY 407/.

G243.1.2* Witches from Haddam and East Haddam fight over rights to kill cattle. Indian Devil Chief orders them off. They never return. Noises of Devil Chief still issue from Mount Tom. Jagendorf NEW ENGLAND / Hoke WITCHES 187-191/.

G252. Witch in form of cat has hand cut off; recognized next morning by missing hand. SEE: D702.1.1.; G211.1.7; G275.12.

G260. Evil deeds of witches.

G261.2* Witch steals maid. The Hunting. Devil sends witch to steal Starost's daughter. Devil flees, witch comes as beggar lady to hut where she shelters, flees, boy hid her broom so pursues on sieve. Second hut--sieve hidden--pursues on black cock. Hunter shoots witch--turns to ashes. Hunter weds daughter. Poland: Borski JOLLY 29-40.

G262.2.1* Witch removes victims' livers with stone finger as they sleep and eats. SEE ALSO: G219.3.1. Native American (Cherokee): Bell JOHN 27-33; DeWit TALKING 52-56.

G262.6* Witch kills with magic forked stick. Weasel woman Tsihlihla lures victims by feigning distress. Coyote breaks her stick and throws into river. Native American (Nez Percé): Heady TALES 75-80.

G263.1. Witch transforms persons into animals.

G263.1.0.1.1* Witch of Lok Island. Witch turns all lovers into fish. Lad hears them call from frying pan--touches with magic knife, they turn to men and warn. Witch turns him into frog. Girl friend seeks with magic staff when hears magic bell ring warning of his danger. Hobgoblin on cliff advises (is really witch's enchanted husband), has suit of cabbage made for her to wear. She goes as suitor, throws witch's magic steel net over witch, frees all with knife. Brittany: Mason FOLK /Harper GHOSTS 176-191/, /Hoke WITCHES 206-218/, /Sechrist HEIGH-HO 34-46/.

G263.1.0.2* Inn mistress sows grain in fireplace at night. It grows. She reaps it, makes into cakes. In morning guests eat (D551), are turned to horses (D130). Hero seeks remedy for companion. Lets an old man eat his lunch, mountain spirit then tells of magic eggplant with seven pods which will break spell. He returns to inn, substitutes cakes so innkeeper and wife eat own cakes. Japan: Novak FAIRY 110-118. China: Birch CHINESE 89-94; Hume FAVORITE..CHINA 79-84 (-old man's assistance and companion).

G263.1.0.2.1* Man sheltering with couple, they tap with four sticks and turn him to ox. He eats turnips by accident and regains form. He steals four sticks and turns Prime Minister to half-ox and sells remedy for high position. Korea: Carpenter TALES..KOREAN 57-63.

G263.1.0.3* Lazy Hans. Lad hired by witch. To plant stick in cornfield. Plants in leaf pile as sleeps, barn fills with leaves. Witch turns him to pig. Second chance, to put stick in dairy, puts in dump pile--barn fills with garbage. Turned to gander. After year enchanting scarf around neck is torn off in fight and he becomes boy again. Reforms and returns home and works harder. Germany: Manning-Sanders BOOK.. WITCHES 27-37.

G263.1.3.1* The Enchanted Cow. Girl raised by witch is turned to cow when wants to wed. Lover disenchants with crucifix, holy water and verbena, cow to trample witch. Halter put on witch. Turns to cow, stampedes, passing under gate of San Gallo in Florence. St. Anthony's statue falls and strikes cow--earth swallows her up. Italy (Florence): Hoke WITCHES 37-44 /Davis TRUCE/.

G263.2.1. Witch transforms to stone. SEE: R111.1.3A (Blood brothers).

G263.2.1.2* King to be King of England if climbs hill to see Long Compton Church. Witch turns king and his men to stones as approach. Turns self to eldern tree. England (Warwickshire): Colwell ROUND 77-81.

G264.3. Female ogre seduces men with charm (words). SEE ALSO: G369.1.5.

G264.3.2* Witch as maid pretends to be chained to witch in spring. Asks lad to steal mother's savings for her. Ill mother gives it to him. In remorse he throws bag at witch tearing veil and revealing face. Chain keeps her from reaching him. She flees. Sweden: Hoke WITCHES 112-124 /Harper GHOSTS 67-72/.

G265.6.1.2* Witch causes pigs to behave unnaturally. Witch wants to buy sow, owner refuses. Sow pines away, wreaks havoc nightly. Taken to market sow falls into drain. Madgy Figgey, the witch, gives a loaf of bread for the sow. It follows her meekly home. Cornwall: Calhoun WITCH'S pb; Manning-Sanders PETER 144-149.

G266.2* Witches steal eyes when allowed to comb lad's hair. Lad slaps their hands and forces to return old man's eyes. Given owl's eyes-- throws into river. Wolf's eyes--same. Pike's eyes. Threatens to throw witch into river. Given man's eyes. Bohemia: Manning-Sanders BOOK..WITCHES 115-122 /Manning-Sanders CHOICE 81-88/.

G270. Witch overcome or escaped.

G271.2. Witch exorcised by use of religious ceremony, object, or charm. Black Cat of the Witch Dance Place. Witch Waterlinde in form of black cat traps fleeing Christian girl inside magic circle. Girl says Christian prayer and wind dashes witch against rocks and turns to stone. Hoke WITCH 194-196.

G271.4.1.1* Witch burns up when book intended to bind girl's soul to Devil is burned by priest. Orkney: Cutt HOGBOON 66-79.

G273.3. Witch powerless at cockcrow (dawn). Japan: Ozaki JAPANESE 140-147 (+C611.0.1).

G273.8* Witches of Ascalon. Witches powerless when feet off ground. Rabbi Simon takes eighty men with urns over heads to witches' cave in rain. Pretends they came walking between raindrops and are accepted as wizards. Dance with witches, hold witches over heads and carry powerless to mountain top where cannot harm people. Jewish: Hirsh RABBI pb (witches shrink in rain); Serwer LET'S 3-8.

G274.1.1* Magic cow gives endless milk (B184.2.1.1.2). Witch of Pendle causing drought tries to milk it dry. She drowns and dissolves in stream of milk when cow kicks over her bottomless pail. England: Spicer THIRTEEN MONSTERS 59-65.

G275.1. Witch carried off by devil.

G275.1.2* Witch of Fraddam. Witch sells soul to devil in exchange for destruction of Marec the Enchanter. Prepares hell-broth to get Marec's horse to drink and it will throw Marec, throw broth over him and will be helpless. M. suspects, puts witch in tub with hell-broth and sets adrift. Still there. When she stirs sea with her ladle = high seas. Cornwall: Manning-Sanders PETER 72-76; Williams-Ellis FAIRY.. BRITISH 170-178.

G275.2. Witch overcome by helpful dogs of hero.

G275.7.0.1* Witch pinned to log by ear lobes under pretense of piercing her ears. Shining boy is born of tears of lost girl's mother which fell into limpet shells, rescues girls. Evil girl had wished witch to take them, had found her own way home by picking up dropped sea shell trail (R135). Native American (Tsimshian): Harris ONCE 61-85.

G275.12. Witch killed by placing salt or pepper inside skin while it is laid aside. SEE: G229.1.1.

G275.12. Witch in the form of an animal is injured or killed as a result of the injury to the animal. SEE ALSO: G211.1.6; G211.1.1.2A; D702.1.1.

G275.12.1* The Angakok. Man asked to heal ill young man by his tornaks, spirits, who have saved him from capsized canoe. He sees evil spirit and harpoons it in foot. Aunt is found with bleeding foot. Dies. Eskimo: Caswell SHADOWS 57-63.

G275.12.2* (Baughman) Witch as hare injured (or killed) when hare is shot. De La Mare ANIMAL 75-76.

G275.12.3* (Baughman) Injury to witch as bird causes injury or death to witch. Nahual bird with human head is shot, neighbor has bullet in leg. Mexico: Brenner BOY 52-58.

G276.2* Escape from witch. Witch eats peddler's mackerel, horse. He flees, hides in her house. She muses "Shall I have tea or rice cakes?" He whispers "rice cakes", eats them while she goes for soy sauce. She: "Shall I sleep upstairs on quilt or downstairs in kettle?" He" "Kettle", puts on lid, lights fire. She thinks fire noise is bird (G512.3.2.2). Type 333B. Japan: Novak FAIRY 66-71 (thinks voice is Fukurokyin, God of Good Fortune; ate goods in form of boy then turned to witch, lad hides in tree, she sees reflection in water (R351), obeys his suggestion to climb tree with rock on head holding to dry branches); Uchida MAGIC 83-90.

G276.3* Elephant and buffalo hide twelve girls in mouths, tell witch they went other way. Skirt of youngest hangs out of elephant's mouth. He says is drooping lower lip. Witch curses lower lip to hang down thereafter. Laos: Carpenter ELEPHANT'S 176-183.

G300 - G399.   Other ogres.

G302.7.1.   Sexual relationship between man and demons. SEE ALSO: G303.12.5.1 (Devil).

G302.7.1.1* Sorcerer weds girl, keeps in pit, three sons of her nursemaid rescue. Youngest weds. Transylvania: Manning-Sanders SOR-CERER'S 99-111.

G302.7.1.2* Girl refuses all suitors. Aunt creates three handsome suitors by sorcery. She weds each--finds only flower in bed in morning. Aunt makes three flowers into "giglio"--lily for shield of Florence. Italy (Florence): Jagendorf PRICELESS 81-88.

G302.7.1.3* Girl weds handsome stranger. Is really a Marimi, giant two mouthed ogre. Kikuyu: Nunn AFRICAN 96-103.

G302.7.1.4* Three sisters wed to beasts with tails. Servant sees them dancing in moonlight in true form. The girls leave banana trunks in beds, escape. Madagascar: Carpenter AFRICAN 93-102.

G302.7.1.5* Einion weds goblin lady. Puts half of ring under eyelid one day, sees her in real form. Britain: Garner CAVALCADE..GOB-LINS 56-61.

G303.3.3.1.3.1.   Devil as Pancho Villa's horse. Mexico: Jagendorf KING 202-204 /Arbuthnot ANTHOLOGY 413/.

G303.3.1.4.1* Devil in form of cow (bull, ox). Black bull chases boy up onto rock. He later finds pennies there. Bull was Bucca. Mother makes him throw pennies into fire. Cornwall: Manning-Sanders PETER 33-38.

G303.3.3.1.6.1* Devil in form of goat. La Biche, huge white nanny goat, detains all who pass. Will not let church be built on her corner. Channel Islands (Guernsey): Spicer THIRTEEN MONSTERS 77-82.

G303.3.5.3.1* Bird taken on back becomes heavier, turns to Dry-Bone man. Goat, Rabbit, Anansi tricked thus. West Indies: Sherlock WEST 77-85.

G303.9.1.1.   Devil as builder of bridges. SEE: C432.1.1 (Oniroku); G303.16.19.4; M211.2.1.

G303.9.1.6.1* Shoemaker talks Devil into building bridge over river Dibble at Thrope Fell Top to prove can do good if wants. England (Yorkshire): Spicer THIRTEEN DEVILS 19-24.

G303.9.1.13.   Devil builds a building. SEE: E765.1.1.1; M211.2.

G303.9.6.1.3* Devil fights with man. Man wrestles with Devil, wears charm given by parson which burns Devil if he touches. Wins. Cornwall: Manning-Sanders PETER 129-138.

G303.12.5.1.   Girl married to the devil. SEE: G302.7.1.

G303.12.5.8.   Girl gives devil lover three golden ducats her fiance had left her. The crosses on the ducats cause devil to wilt. Netherlands (Friesland): Spicer OWLS 74-85.

G303.12.5.9* Girl who married stranger. Spies and sees him entertaining demons. Flees. Mother had gotten charm so she would wed. Haiti: Johnson HOW 13-22.

G303.12.5.10* Demon Loango. She sticks with pin and he oozes yellow blood. Goes with him anyway. At night he has wolf's head. Mother gets charm to save her. Haiti: Johnson HOW 67-74.

G303.12.5.11* Leave It There. Demon husband's clothes, arms, etc. fall off as leads girl to his home. House full of bones. She sings for brothers to aid. They hear and kill demon. Sierra Leone: Robinson SINGING 50-65.

G303.12.5.12* Young Girl and the Devil. Girl weds suitor with gold teeth, turns to pig, brother hides and learns devil's magic song, sings at wedding and devil turns to pig. Priest throws holy water on pig and protects brother with crucifix. Pig flees. Puerto Rico: Alegria THREE 80-83.

G303.12.5.13* My Beauty. Lolo pricks My Beauty's suitor and puss comes out--is Devil. Hides under nuptial bed and cuts off Devil's arms, legs, head with magic sword. Turns self to prince with magic wand (given by godmother) and weds. Haiti: Thoby-Marcelin SINGING

30-37.

G303.14.1. The devil destroys by night what is built by day. SEE: G303.16.19.4.

G303.14.1.2* Blebvorden (owl's boards) added to barn are repeatedly destroyed until stone is used. Devil has no power over stone. Netherlands (Friesland): Spicer OWL'S 15-28.

G303.16.1. By help of the Virgin Mary the Devil can be escaped. SEE: T251.1.1.3.

G303.16.3.1. Devil is driven away by cross.

G303.16.3.1.1* Pancho Villa sells soul to Devil and Devil acts as his horse (G303.3.3.1.3). Has cross around neck at death and Devil cannot take. Mexico: Jagendorf KING 202-204 /Arbuthnot ANTHOLOGY 413/.

G303.16.3.1.2* Baby found turns into Tiyanak demon. Is helpless at sight of cross woodcutter wears. Gives gold and leaves. Philippines: Robertson FAIRY..PHILIPPINES 117-127.

G303.16.3.1.3* Woman's daughter wed to Devil. They lock him in room with crosses on everything except keyhole. He escapes via that and is trapped in jug. Cross put on stopper and buried. Man finds and makes living with "talking jug." Wife releases when Devil promises riches. U.S.: Credle TALL 122-132.

G303.16.8. Devil leaves at mention of God's name.

G303.16.8.1* Devil in troubador contest cannot answer verse "Jesus, Joseph, Mary." Puerto Rico: Alegria THREE 84-85.

G303.16.8.2* Sidi-Barabah. Ferryman sells soul to devil (M211). Tosses into water, challenges devil to bowl with hand tied behind and leaves. Plays memory game "I go to the fair at Sidi-Barabah?" Each must name all items named before. Devil cannot name "cross." Hardendorff FROG 59-74; Tashjian DEEP 42-55.

G303.16.12.1* Devil attempts to flood Rhone valley, cannot touch churches. Retreats in defeat to mountain peak, causes wind storm--the Vaudaire. Switzerland (French): Duvoisin Three 111-114.

G303.16.19.3. One is freed if he can set a task the devil cannot perform.

G303.16.19.3.4* Task devil can't perform. 1. Catch sneeze. 2. Straighten curly hair. 3. Lick away mole on elbow. Wife offers own soul as well as husband's (M211) if devil can perform. Russia: Carey BABA 75-78.

G303.16.19.3.5* Task Devil can't perform. Michael Scott plagued by demon because he hid the plague in a bag in Glencoe Abbey where Devil couldn't reach it. Scott sets impossible tasks for demon. 1. Build bridge on river. 2. Make three mountains out of one. 3. Make rope of sand (H1021.1). Scotland: Nic Leodhas THISTLE 136-143.

G303.16.19.3.6* Three brothers sell souls to Devil (M211). To be free if can pose tasks he can't perform. Miller asks that he restore flour to original state. Devil cannot reconstruct-- only destruct. Lumberman asks Devil to restore wood to trees. Ship captain asks Devil to run on water holding anchor behind ship and drop it. Ship going so fast when anchor stops it that Devil can't stop that quick and runs into ship. Netherlands (Frisia): Spicer THIRTEEN DEVILS 82-90.

G303.16.19.3.7* Schoolmaster vanquishes Devil in cemetery. 1. Count dewdrops. 2. Count grains of wheat. Devil accomplishes. 3. Make rope of sand and wash it in stream. England: Spicer THIRTEEN DEVILS 63-70.

G303.16.19.4. Devil (Satan) flees when cock is made to crow.

G303.16.19.4.0.1* Railroad bridge destroyed nightly (G303.14.1) will be built by Devil. Payment (G303.9.1.1) one hundred fifty souls if completed by cockcrow. Cock is made to crow. Bridge falls first time train passes over and three hundred are killed. Devil gets his due. Mexico: Brenner BOY 79-83.

G303.16.19.4.0.2* Church to be built by Devil for number of unbaptized babes yearly if done by cockcrow. Honduras (Curaren): Carter ENCHANTED 109-114.

G303.16.19.6.1* Devil fiend sent to raise racket from steeple during church service. When shown twelve babes fiend flees from sight of innocence. Cornwall: Manning-Sanders PETER 139-143.

G303.16.19.10. Devil exorcised at time of Christ's Nativity. Spain: Sawyer WAY 21-31 (defeated by Archangel Michael and Heavenly Hosts, shepherds witness).

G303.16.19.19.1* Lad has shepherds beat Devil. Satan turns to pond. Lad turns shepherds to fish which bite water. Satan to tree, shepherds to birds to peck. Satan takes demons and goes underground. Years later Julian as a hermit is tempted by Devil. Julian reminds Devil of beating and Devil goes up in smoke. Mexico: Brenner BOY 84-89.

G303.19.3* Devil to take last cardplayer to leave room. Last one points to shadow saying it is last. Switzerland: Müller-Guggenbühl SWISS 213-223.

G303.22.11.1* Devil as advocate of falsely condemned man. Type 821. Man fated to die violent death travels and does good work. He orders neglected statue of Devil refurbished. Accused falsely of theft and to hang. Devil forces landlady to confess crime and she hangs in place. Fate thus changed. BRAZIL: Frost

LEGENDS 269-273; Spicer THIRTEEN DEVILS 72-81.

G303.24.1.7.0.1. Devil writes names of those who sleep in church on goat's hide. Tries to stretch hide longer and it splits causing him to bump head on pulpit. At this St. Beatus laughs out loud waking sleepers and thus saving their souls. Switzerland: Müller-Guggenbühl SWISS 213-223.

G303.25.17.2.1* Fiddler engaged to play on Christmas Eve for Devils. Sees monk there, taken for sleeping in church. Drops iron, salt, and bone at monk's feet and plays holy carol-- dancers turn to demons, monk evaporates--soul freed. Isle of Man: Sawyer WAY 35-43 /Fenner GHOSTS 121-130/, /Sawyer LONG 33-44.

G304.2.5. Troll bursts when sun shines on him. Or he may become stone. SEE ALSO: A1414.5.1 (origin of flint); G561 (Hen skips); K1917.3C, D; Q285.1.1.

G304.2.5.1* Demons vanish when struck by setting sun. Japan: McAlpine JAPANESE 188-201.

G310. Ogres with characteristic methods.

G312.8* Cannibal ogre. The Red King and the Witch. Type 315A. Cupboard emptied nightly. Three sons guard. Youngest sees baby sister turn to witch with shovel teeth and eat. He leaves. Meets maid whittling one stick per day, will die when entire forest gone. He passes Plain of Regret and reaches home of the Wind where there is no death or age. Remains there. Nears Plain of Regret and remembers home. Told millions of years have passed. Finds maid whittling last stick. Father's palace gone. Sister witch still waiting by well leaps to devour him. He makes sign of cross and she dies. He meets old man who says all he knew is gone. Digs up treasure he had buried. Death and old age are also in chest. He dies. (F377). Gypsy: Manning-Sanders RED 49-54. Russia: Ransome OLD 136-154.

G332. Sucking monster. Giant (sometimes a giant hall or cave) sucks in victims. SEE: F912.2.9.11; F913.5.

G351.2. Cat as ogre. SEE ALSO: D435.2.1.1 (boy who drew cats); K1853.2.1.1 (Schippeitaro).

G351.2.1* The Cat and the Dream Man. Cat's dream emerges as fox faced man. Man fastens cat in house of three stones. Lad cuts thread. Cat haunts. With aid of grandmother and magic ax cat is vanquished. Withers I 184-207. Bolivia: Finger TALES 184-207.

G361.2. Great head as ogre. Head detached from body pursues or flies about doing damage. Native American (Iroquois): Garner CAVALCADE ..GOBLINS 101-104 (Great Head, brother of Mole Man, defeats witch and regains and restore bones of nine lost elder brothers).

G369.1.5* Rakshasa. Man persecuted by Rakshasa in form of beautiful wench Vijaya sees in light of grass lamp and her true demon form appears. Ceylon: Carpenter ELEPHANT'S 135-140.

G378* Killing pot. Green bird falls into pot. Pot splashes green broth all over village. Coyote and Eetoi kill pot. Old woman and grandson who drink of broth become brown and black. Native American (Pima): Baker AT 16-24.

G400 - G499. Falling into ogre's power.

G400. Person falls into ogre's power.

G401. Children wander into ogre's house. SEE: K1611 (Molly Whuppie et al.); G412.1 (Hansel and Gretel).

G405.1* Ogress (witch) forces man to wed her, plotting his destruction.

G405.1.1* The Groach of the Isle of Lok. Lad discovers fish in frying pan are witch's former husbands. He is turned to a toad by magic net but girlfriend comes and conquers witch, disenchanting fish with magic knife. Lang FIFTY 88-97 /Lang LILAC 310-321. Breton: Manning-Sanders BOOK..MERMAIDS 86-97.

G405.1.2* The Dragon of the North. Witch Maiden to wed, would seal pact with three drops of man's blood. He stalls until obtains King Solomon's Ring, the object of his quest. Vanquishes dragon with this magic ring's aid. Lang YELLOW 12-26 /Green CAVALCADE..DRAGONS 125-132/, /Hoke DRAGONS 179-191/. Estonia: Maas MOON 128-141.

G412.0.1* Children lured into ogre's house. Two girls follow trail of ivory toys and come to witch's stone hut, other children there, to be cooked. Yarayato scrapes stone loose and all flee. Fathers return and one ties her feet on pretense of cutting toenails. She is killed. Eskimo: Melzack DAY 59-67.

G412.1. Ogre's gingerbread house lures children.

G412.1.1* Hansel and Gretel. Type 327A. Abandoned children find way back by trail of pebbles (R135). Crumb trail is eaten by birds. Gingerbread house lures children. Hansel shows witch bone instead of finger in fatness test. Gretel tricks witch into oven (G526, G512.3.2). Usually are carried over lake by duck on way home (B469.4). Germany (Grimm): Arbuthnot FAIRY 45-48; Darrell ONCE 59-65; Gag TALES 3-24; Grimm BROTHERS 124-132; Grimm GRIMM'S (Follett) 139-149; Grimm GRIMM'S (Grosset) 330-340; Grimm GRIMM'S (Scribners) 37-45; Grimm GRIMM'S (World) 15-23; Grimm HANSEL (illus. Lobel) pb; Grimm HANSEL (illus. Crawford) pb; Grimm HOUSEHOLD 85-92; Grimm JUNIPER v. 1 152-168; Grimm NIBBLE (illus. Anglund) pb; Haviland FAVORITE..GERMANY 51-71; Jacobs EUROPEAN

180-187 (+witch drinks stream and bursts, G522); Lang BLUE 267-276 /Lang FIFTY 98-105/, /Fenner GIANTS 126-137/, /Arbuthnot ANTHOLOGY 185-187/; Manning-Sanders BOOK ..WITCHES 83-93; Martignoni ILLUSTRATED 178-183; Opie CLASSIC 236-244; Rackham ARTHUR 269-277; Shubb ABOUT 99-107.

G412.1.2* Brother and sister nibble on candy house of wolf. He pursues. Repeat three times. Third time they ask ducks to carry over river. Wolf asks to be carried also and ducks abandon him in middle--he drowns (B469.4; J2415). Belgium: Frost LEGENDS 309-312.

G422.1.1* Girl in drum. Stranger catches girl going for water. Puts her in drum and forces to sing. Parents hear voice, take her from drum and fill with bees (K526). Bantu: Rockwell WHEN pb.

G422.1.1.1* Girl finds shell, returns for it and ogre puts her into drum and makes sing. In her village mother substitutes snake in drum. Driven from town for failure to sing. On spot where ogre dies giant pumpkin appears. Rolls after three sisters (R261) who pluck it. Rolls into village and men cut up and burn. Swahili: Aardema TALES 86-94. Bantu: Arnott AFRICAN 179-185.

G422.1.1.2* Girl swims in river (tabu) and leaves earrings on rock. Returns for them. Old man puts in sack and makes sing. A relative recognizes voice, substitutes mud and stones for girl. He is driven out of town when mud splatters out as he strikes sack. Puerto Rico: Alegria THREE 107-110; Belpre TIGER 27-31. Kaffir: Carpenter AFRICAN 195-204 (cannibal, snake, spiders, wild dog substituted, other cannibals kill him for fiasco).

G422.1.1.3* Magic tree (ogre) grows in an hour, bends for children to climb on and runs home with them. Prince Maran refuses to get on. Donkey (ogre) stretches to make room for Prince Maran, he refuses. Princess Niassa caught thus is kept in bag and made to sing. Prince Maran recognizes voice and substitutes dog. Africa: Manning-Sanders BOOK..PRINCESS 9-13.

G500 - G599. Ogre defeated.

G500. Ogre defeated. SEE ALSO: T543.3.2 (Momotaro).

G501. Stupid ogre. SEE: K526 (Buttercup and the Witch); K1611 (Molly Whuppie, Hop o' my Thumb). Types 1045-1115. SEE ALSO: K1951.1 (The Valiant Tailor).

A* Small hero intimidates ogre by seeming feats of strength. Squeezes water from stones (cheese, K62). Throws a stone (bird, K18.3). Threatens to bring whole well (K1741.3), fell whole forest (K1741.1). To bring ox prepares

to bring ten (K1741.2.1) or shoot one thousand boars (K1741.2). To bring entire lake (K1744). Throwing contest trick (K18.4). To throw into cloud (moon) (K1746). Troll imitates slitting of stomach in eating contest and dies (K81.1). Puts billet on bed and claims giant's blows in night were little insect bites (K525.1). Shows battle axe already on moon (in clouds) (K18.2; K1746). Trickster binds ogre's eyes and beats --whistling contest (K84.1).

Aa* Ash lad. K62; K1741.3; K81.1. Norway: Asbjornsen NORWEGIAN 81-83.

Ab* Shoemaker intimidates Samson. K62; K18.3; +J2326.5. Slovenia: Kavcic GOLDEN 150-156.

Ac* Dwarf and giant, K62 (flour). Carried by giant, dwarf says is holding on to sky to account for light weight. To bring all wine from cellar. Bread from oven falls on him, says is holding on stomach for stomach-ache. Giant's sneeze blows dwarf to rafter, "Do that again and I'll pull out this beam and break it over your head." Russia (Georgia): Hardendorff JUST 92-97; Manning-Sanders BOOK..GIANTS 18-24 (+K71 riding tree).

Ad* Ghul, K62 (egg, salt); K1741.3; K525.1; +K1715.2 (told fox to bring six Ghuls). Iran: Williams-Ellis ROUND 73-80.

Ae* Giant Devil Monsieur Rapotou to destroy village. Midget intimidates, K62; K18.3; K525.1; K1741.1. France: Cooper FIVE 76-87.

Af* Tailor and Giant. K1741.3. (One thousand wild boar at a shot.) Giant and wife trick tailor onto bent willow and spring him into air. Never returns. German: Wiggin TALES 155-156.

Ag* Gypsy and dragon. K62; K18.4. Gypsy: Arnott ANIMAL 66-70. Russia (Georgia): Papashvily YES 201-210.

Ah* Boy challenges giant to contests, stone squeezing (uses cheese, K62), ax throwing. Work bargain--to lose three strips of skin if works poorly (K172), cuts oxen up and pokes through hole. Churn in bed beaten (K525.1). Eating contest, uses satchel, slits it, giant imitates (K81.1). Sweden: Löfgren BOY 5-24.

B* Hero intimidates devil.

Ba* Takes service with Devil, to bring lake (K1744); forest (K1741.1); throw bear (K18). Beaten billet in night (K525.1). Sent off with saddlebags of donkey full of money. Changes mind and pursues. El Bizarron lies with feet in air saying he kicked donkey into sky and is putting up feet to break donkey's fall. Devil flees. Antilles: Carter GREEDY 23-29.

Bb. Gypsy takes service with devil. Well (K1741.3); forest (K1741.1). Beaten billet (K525.1). Stomping match--water under his stone. Hammer throwing, calls (K18). Whistling contest, puts wool in Devil's ears and blindfolds, then beats (K84.3). Russia: Spicer THIRTEEN DEVILS 43-52

C* Stan Bolovan. Type 1149. Stan Bolovan asks for children, is given a houseful. Takes service to vanquish dragon for one-third shepherd's sheep (trying to feed children). Dragon takes home to serve his mother. Squeezes milk from stone (K62), to throw club into moon (K18) (K1746). Bring well (K1741.3). Bring forest (K1741.1). Pig's trough in bed (K525.1). Dragon carries gold home for him. Children run out with knives and forks yelling "food" and dragon flees. Rumania: Lang FIFTY 281-290 / Lang VIOLET 96-110/, /Green CAVALCADE..DRAGONS 138-147/, /Colwell MAGIC 41-50/; Manning-Sanders CHOICE 307-319 /Manning-Sanders BOOK..DRAGONS 25-37/; Manning-Sanders RED 10-15 (+kills one hundred flies at a blow [K1951.1G]). Blown backwards and forwards by dragon's breath, says is deciding whether or not to kill dragon; sprung into air on bent bough, lands on hare--was killing hare) /Hoke DRAGONS 149-154/; Sleigh NORTH 155-169; Ure RUMANIAN 101-113 (+ shows battle axe already on moon, [K18.2; K1746]; Van Woerkom ALEXANDRA pb (wife, Alexandra, performs feats). Gypsy: Jagendorf GYPSIES' 24-34 (gypsy and giant snake; test of whistling, ties up eyes of snake and beats [K84.1]; to bring all oxen [K1741.2.1]; well, forest, children).

*D Stupid Peiko. Peiko challenges Matti to build bridge not wood, stone, iron. M. leans over river himself to form bridge. To guard door. M. brings it to wedding (K1413). M. feigns drinking lake dry. Paid for roofing Tupa with hatful of silver. M. has hole in hat on hollow stump. To push over birch. M. falls with hidden axe, chops. Lift tree, M. stands on branches, P. can't lift. Squeeze rock--boiled potato (K62). Throw stone--bird (K18.3). Throw hammer (K1746). P. fears snakes. M. says hissing of green twigs on fire is snakes, P. flees. To gild beard in tar--stuck (K1013.1). M. puts huge shoes by mill, P. fears giant, stays away (K1717). P. carries off haystack thinking is reed discarded from M.'s mother's loom (K1718.2). Thinks old boat is mother's shoe, takes. Thinks millstone is mother's spinning wheel, hangs on neck, sinks crossing lake (K1718.2). Finland: Bowman TALES..TUPA 207-219.

E* Jack in the Giant's New Ground. Hired as giant killer. Fills leather apron with milk and food. Squeezes milk out of stone (against apron). (K62). Cuts self open and sews back up. Giant tries and dies (G524). Throws stones and tricks two giants into fighting (K1082). Bringing home the stream (K1744). Throwing crowbar to his uncle in Virginia (18). Giant's wife tries to get Jack on shelf by oven, "Show me how"...he pushes her in (G526). Hides giant from "King's men" and receives reward from giant for saving his life. U.S.(Appalachia): Chase JACK 3-20.

F. Gianni and the Ogre. Gianni fills ogre's bag with stones and flees (K526). Ogre eats before discovering trick. Gianni says he climbed stack of plates to reach church steeple. Ogre tries and falls. Glasses--repeat. Bottles--ogre reaches tower and Gianni kicks bottles over. Ogre killed. Italy: Manning-Sanders GIANNI 7-12.

G* The Blacksmith in the Moon. Cobbler about to hang self tells demon he is making noose to tie up all demons in underworld. Demon bribes him with boat full of money. He cuts hole in boat. Pipe smoking contest. Cobbler shoots gun (K1057) into demon's mouth. Hare catching contest. Cobbler releases two, has a third claimed caught hidden in bag. To throw iron door to brother the blacksmith on the moon (K18). Germany: Jablow MAN 7-9.

H* Donal from Donegal. Challenges giant to toss crowbar, kills giant when he bends over. Takes magic white mare. Two giants seek vengeance, Donal throws stones and gets to fight. One kills other. Donal threatens with crowbar, offers Cloak of Darkness and Sword of Sharpness. Takes also chestnut mare and Mare of Swiftness from stable of these giants. +R111.1.3Cb. Ireland: MacManus Bold 64-82.

G511. Ogre blinded. SEE ALSO: K602, K603.

G511.2. Stone coat giants are invincible except for soles of feet. Buffalo Bird instructs Turkey to peck out their eyes. Moose hides in cave with horns protruding and giants pierce feet on horns and die. +A2351.8.1. Native American: Parker SKUNNY 196-203.

G512. Ogre killed. SEE: G501 (Stupid Ogre).

G512.0.4* Jack the Giant Killer. Type 328. Incident 1: Jack digs a pit and tricks giant Cormoran into it, (K735). Given sword and belt embroidered with deed. Blunderbuss captures Jack but Jack snares Blunderbuss and his brother by necks from above as they enter castle and kills. Rescues maidens, (R111.1.4).

Incident 2, Type 1115. Jack puts billet on his bed and two-headed Welsh giant thinks he beats Jack. Jack claims he felt a rat run across in night (K525.1). Jack pretends to slit self open. Giant imitates (G524, K81.1; Type 1088). Son of King Arthur pays debts of corpse to ransom from crowd (E341.1). Jack offers to serve prince. Tells giant prince arrives with one thousand men and hides giant. Prince and Jack pass night at giant's castle and steal gold. Jack also secures giant's magic coat, cap, sword and slippers (D833).

Incident 3, Type 507A. Prince must show lady her handkerchief in morning to wed (H322.1). Jack follows her using magic shoes, cloak of invisibility and knowing-all cap. She goes to Lucifer and leaves handkerchief. Jack retrieves. Second task: Show the lips I kissed, Jack beheads Lucifer and brings head. Spell is broken and lady weds prince.

Incident 4: Jack kills another giant by wearing invisible coat and releases captives and divides treasure.

Incident 5: Jack saws through drawbridge and revenging giant Thunderdell falls to death. Arrives calling Fee Fi Fo Fum (G84).

Incident 6: Jack passes fiery griffins in invisible cloak and blows trumpet. Whoever blows will overthrow giant Galliganta. Jack kills giant, conjuror is turned to a whirlwind, enchanted populace is restored along with duke's daughter whom Jack weds. De Regniers GIANT 3-15; Jacobs ENGLISH 102-116 /Fenner GIANTS 138-154/, /Steel ENGLISH 54-72/, /Mayne BOOK.. GIANTS 83-87/; Lang BLUE 351-357; Manning-Sanders BOOK..GIANTS 44-66; Opie CLASSIC 47-65; Rackham ARTHUR 111-127; Rackham FAIRY 1-14.

G512.3.2. Ogre burned in his own oven. SEE: G412.1 (Hansel and Gretel); G526.

G512.3.2.0.1* Girls work together and push witch into fire. Native American (Snohomish): Matson LEGENDS 86-90.

G512.3.2.2* Witch burned up in kettle. Muses "Shall I sleep upstairs on quilt or downstairs in kettle?" Trickster whispers "kettle." Puts on lid and lights fire. +G276.2; K891.1.2.6. Japan: Novak FAIRY 66-71; Uchida MAGIC 83-90.

G512.11. Ogre drowned.

G512.11.1* Children forbidden to open door do so. Mother beats and they flee. Meet ten giants. Tenth is a two-headed monster. They comb his heads and he sleeps. Bind him and flee in canoe taking pumice and stones. Boy walks on water using pumice. Giant imitates with rocks and drowns. Rotuma: Gittins TALES 47-49.

G520. Ogre deceived into self injury.

G522. Ogre persuaded to drink pond dry bursts. Jacobs EUROPEAN 180-187 (+G412.1.1). South America (Aymara): Arnott ANIMAL 224-230 (fox drinking Lake Titicaca dry). SEE ALSO: G530.2; A1134.2; K526.2.

G524. Ogre deceived into stabbing himself. He imitates the hero who has stabbed a bag of blood. U.S. (Appalachia): Chase JACK 3-20 (+G501E); G512A (Jack the Giant Killer).

G524.0.1* Ogre made to believe hero has cut out heart cuts out own. Brazil: Carpenter SOUTH AMERICAN 93-99.

G524.0.2* Giant made to believe Coyote has cut off legs and grown new ones. Imitates. Native American (Navaho): Robinson COYOTE 23-24.

G526. Ogre deceived by feigned ignorance of hero. Hero must be shown how to get into oven (or the like). Ogre shows him and permits self to be burned. SEE ALSO: G512.3.2; K715; R251; G610; G412.1 (Hansel and Gretel); K526 (Buttercup); G501E (Jack in the Giant's New Ground). Russia: Downing RUSSIAN 81-99 (+K213 Devil in Knapsack; death shows how to get into coffin, is nailed in).

G526.1* The Kittel-Kittel Car. Type 327D. Ogre's woman hides children, he smells, prepares to hang them. Girl gets him to show them how, ogre left hanging. He offers his Kittel-Kittel car full of gold and silver for freedom. They flee, he pursues. They pay farmers passed to say haven't seen them. Washerwoman hides and ogre drowns trying to cross river in her laundry basket. She has suggested that he do this and he follows suggestion. France (Alsace): Manning-Sanders DEVILS 87-97.

G530. Ogre's relatives aid hero.

G530.2. Help from ogre's daughter or son. (Maid). Type 313C. SEE ALSO: D672 (Obstacle chain); H1385.1E (Sigurd); F53 (Arrow chain); H1331.3 (Helpful horse).

Aa* The Mastermaid. Type 313C. Prince in service of giant enters tabu (C611) rooms with boiling pots which turn locks of hair copper, silver, and gold (C912). Performs tasks with aid of princess 1. cleaning stables, 2. bridling horse, 3. fetching rent from hell. They flee leaving three drops of blood to answer (D1611). They toss behind salt = mountain; flask = sea (D672). He goes ahead to prepare her arrival, forgets (D2003) warning, eats, forgets her. She lodges in pig's hut. She causes suitors to bank fire, shut door, pull calf's tail all night. They suggest use of her shovel, door and calf to repair broken coach en route to wedding. He comes to thank her and sees golden cock and hen conversing to remind him of former bride. Wed. Norway: Lang BLUE 129-147; Lurie CLEVER 35-44; Undset TRUE 37-56. France (Brittany): Wiggin FAIRY 265-290 (she throws copper bullet = bottomless pit; silver bullet = ship; second silver bullet = giant swordfish to rout pursuing giant; golden bullet causes her pig hut to become covered with gold).

Ab* Nix Nought Nothing. Type 313C. Giant promised first thing at home. Gives herd-boy, shepherd. G. detects by questioning and sends back. Tasks: clean stable, cut forest with glass axe; maid aids. Fetch eggs from tree top. Maid to be cut in pieces and bone used as ladder, revive with flask. He forgets little finger (E33). Flee leaving apple pieces to answer (D1611). Throw behind twigs = forest; glass ax = mountain; flask = stream. Giant drinks and bursts. He lets self be kissed at home and forgets her. She buys three nights by his side with dresses. Recognized and wed. Jacobs EUROPEAN 142-158. Ireland: Pilkington SHAMROCK 1-9 (she jogs his memory by conversing with cock). Great Britain: Finlay TATTERCOATS 37-46 (maid hides in tree over well, thought own reflection by gardener's wife and daughter).

Ac* Nix Nought Nothing. Ab + lake draining task. Hen wife puts sleeping enchantment on prince. England: Jacobs ENGLISH 32-38; Steel ENGLISH 127-138.

Ad* Prince Andrea and Princess Meseria. First living thing at home to be given to Sea Queen. Duck, pig thrown in and refused. Prince never to go near sea. At eighteen he goes to shore and is taken to underwater palace. Suitor tasks there. 1. Mow meadow and restore grass. 2. Clean stable. 3. Clean pigsty. Princess aids. Quest to Wood Queen. Princess gives objects to distribute en route and instructions. He is protected and allowed to escape by witch's animals to whom he has given gifts. Sausage he was meant to eat answers witch and reveals his position. He has only hidden sausage in his coat and tosses it away. Princess leaves three drops of blood on bows to answer. They flee. Turn to two mice, horses to two bushes. Turn to two birds in two trees. (D671). He speaks while visiting home and forgets her. Girls sees face of princess reflected in well, thinks self lovely and leaves blind father, princess takes her place. Three suitors are compelled to continue tasks all night. 1. Opening and closing door. 2. Opening and closing oven damper. 3. Holding calf's tail. They recommend use of her magic objects and calf to repair and draw wedding carriage. At wedding she produces three birds who argue over three gold grains. His memory is restored. Kaplan FAIRY 71-107.

Ae* The King's Son and Little Aasa. King promises son to troll who shows him way out of wood. Task: felling forest, cleaning pigsty, taking wild horse to brook. Flees with maid. Two sticks in oven answer. Turn to thornbush, rose and stone; willow, churchyard and old woman; drake, pond and duck. Witch destroyed at pond. Lad is kissed at home and forgets maid. She causes suitors to shovel coals, close gate, pull calf's tail. They are used to mend coach. At feast two doves converse and he remembers. Says he lost old key and found again (Z62.1). Sweden: Owen CASTLE 123-144.

Af* The Forgotten Bride. Type 313C. Stepmother plots to kill girl's lover. They flee. She turns him to lake, self to duck (D671). At his home he is kissed and forgets her (D2003). She raises magic tower next door, is brought before king and sings of their adventures. He remembers. Greek: Wilson GREEK 141-147.

Ag* Lady Featherflight. Type 313C. Tasks: thatch barn with feathers (H1104.1.1); sort seeds (H1091); make one hundred ropes of sand. Giant's maid performs first two, they flee. Throw stick = forest; vial = lake (D672). Giant drinks and bursts (G522). She hides in tree while he goes ahead. Women see reflection and leave husbands. Husbands to kill her as witch. Jack returns and saves. Adams BOOK..GIANT 159-175.

Ah* The Two King's Children. King's son taken by stag at age sixteen. To watch each of three daughters one night. D. tells stone image to answer for him. Tasks: cut forest with glass axe. Youngest performs. Dig ditch with glass spade. Build castle on rocky hill. They flee. She turns to rosebush; church; pond with fish. Queen tries to drink pond and fails. Gives daughter three walnuts to aid since cannot hinder. He goes ahead, kisses and forgets her. She trades dresses from magic nuts for three nights with him. Grimm: Grimm GRIMM'S (Scribner's) 222-230.

Ai* Jack and King Marok. Jack gambles with King Marok and wins one of his daughters. Old Man Freezewell helps J. find girls. Freezes all beer of man who knows secret and gives J. magic rod to thaw beer. J. is rewarded with knowledge of where girls bathe. J. takes cast off greyhound skin of youngest. She aids. Tasks: find ring in thorn thicket. Empty well and find thimble. Build house of rocks. Choose youngest from sisters, she sticks out tongue. They flee on oldest steeds which become handsome. Plant thorn = thicket; water = river; gravel = mountain. J. goes home, dog kisses and he forgets. Shoemaker's daughter and wife see reflection of girl in spring and leave home. She becomes maid for shoemaker. Suitors are stuck to fire shovel, gander. Jack comes and is stuck to calf. Rooster and banty hen talk at wedding and restore J's memory. U.S. (Appalachia): Chase JACK 135-150.

Ba* Jack and the Devil's Daughter. Type 313A (Youth Promised to Devil). Jack loses soul to Devil gambling. To be free if can reach D's house by next day. Jumps on bald eagle as she bathes, feeds bull when e. calls, feeds her his own arm and leg when out of meat. Devil has wife hand him out an arm and leg before he comes in. Tasks: fell one hundred acres of trees; dip water from one hundred foot well; pluck goose on tree top and not lose a feather. Devil's daughter does tasks. Flee. Turn to lake, ducks and hunter. Turns rosebush into three thousandmile thornbush. U.S. Black: Lester BLACK 73-90.

Bb* The Sailor and the Devil's Daughter. Type 313A. Jack is thrown overboard and swims to Devil's Island. Devil's mother instructs to hide clothing of bathing granddaughters. Youngest aids. Tasks: clean stables; recover pulverized diamond ring from river (H1132.1.1). Banana trunk left in bed is struck by Devil. Flee. Turn to pond, duck and fisherman; churchyard, priest, old lady. Throw kernel = river. Devil and horse drink and burst (G522). Virgin Islands (St. Thomas): Cothran MAGIC 75-82.

Bc* Glass Axe. Type 313A. Prince's feet never to touch ground. Do so and fairy takes him. Tasks: cut forest with glass ax; cut wood up; build palace. Maid performs. Flee. Throws rock = palace all around fairy. Turns self to pond, prince to duck; tower and guard. He is to kill every creature he sees. Boar has hare inside, dove inside hare, egg in dove, throws egg at attacking vulture, turns to girl.

Hungary: Lang YELLOW 156-164.

Bd* A Prince and a Dove. Type 313A. Prince loses freedom gambling. Woman at house of master advises to catch bathing dove and make give three things. Dove gives ring, collar, and plume to call when in need. Tasks: sow, reap and bake by a.m., dove performs; find ring from sea, dove has self beheaded (H1132.1.1) and thrown into sea, returns with ring and becomes princess; break colt, horse is her father, saddle is mother, stirrups are sisters, bridle is herself. He beats with a club. Flee. She turns to nun, hermit, chapel; rosebush, ground, gardener; eel, pond, turtle. Cursed to forget princess. Princess and sisters in dove form talk before him and his memory returns. Portugal: Lang VIOLET 193-202.

Be* The Grateful Prince. First thing at home promised to goblin. Peasant's daughter given instead of son. Prince vows to rescue. Takes service with demon. Girl helps perform tasks. Cut hay and clean stable, horse is demon's grandmother, don't let her eat. To milk cow, he threatens it. To stack haystack and herd calf. Flee with red ball from brain of calf. Ball turns her to brook, he to fish; rosebush and rose; breeze and midge. Escape to upper world and follow trail of peas home. Estonia: Lang VIOLET 73-95.

Bf* The Demon's Daughter. "New soul" promised. King meant boot sole. Task set prince. Demon's daughter steals father's iron whip and calls up demons to perform tasks. Third task requires building a church of sand with cross on dome. Demons cannot do this. They flee. Turn to church and priest; tree and bird; cornfield and quail; pond of milk and duck. Demon swallows all in form of goose. Milk boils inside and goose bursts. Safe. Wed. Transylvania: Manning-Sanders BOOK..DEVILS 15-29.

Bg* White Dove. Two brothers promise witch unborn brother. Tasks: dove aids. He kisses and she turns to princess. To tie red thread to her finger and ask her as bride for reward. Recognizes her even in form of old hag. Flee. Blocks of wood left to answer for them. Throw flowerpot = mountain; water = lake. Girl breathes on witch, flock of white doves cover, turn witch to stone. Denmark: Manning-Sanders BOOK..WITCHES 104-115.

Bha* Kalle and the Wood Grouse. K. aims at wood grouse thrice then spares. W. carries K. to seek chest without a key. Asks thrice how sea looks and drops K., then catches. This is to repay for his own terror when aimed at, (K1041). Taken to sisters in copper, silver, golden castles. Third has chest. Spell now broken and grouse can become a man. Castle comes from chest. Magician will take K. home if he gives what was born while he was away. Son grows, seeks magician. M's daughter aids. They flee. She raises mountain, river. Turns to chapel, sexton, and priest. Wed. She has key to chest. Finland: Bowman TALES 129-

140.

Bhb* Ivan the Merchant's Son and Vasilisa the Wise. Bha + encounter with Baba Yaga as son seeks magician. Steals wings of magician's youngest daughter, Vasilisa the Wise. Forgotten bride episode at end. Dove in pie restores memory. Russia (Afanas'ev): Daniels FALCON 32-51.

Bi* Urho and Marja. Sea god requests "whatever born in home." Peasant girl and boy given answer incorrectly. Stool aids real king's children when they are sent. Wolf carries them home. Throw pebbles from ear = mountain. Perch says "I see you" when Sea God puts down tool he used to clear mountain. Sea God has to take tools back home before continuing. Sea God catches Urho and Marja. Sends fish for white flower charm to make Marja love him. Reindeer helps U. and M. escape. They throw a handful of mane = mountain of brush. He catches.. fox helps escape, throw brand of fire = mountain of flames. Marja puts out flames as she loves Sea God now. Sea God turns to needle and leaps into Urho's head. Fox lays near U. and needle jumps at fox. Fox leaps aside and needle lodges in tree. U. revives and all go home. Love spell leaves M. on entering church. Finland: Bowman TALES 147-160.

Bj* The Witch's Daughter. Man gambles his sons, pledging to wed witch's daughters. First two are killed. Hermit advises a third. To throw pearl and wand to lion and tiger, push door with cherry branch. Tasks: plant linseed in hard field full of weeds. Pigs aid. Gather seed, ants aid. To find hidden daughter, she tells him she will be a peach. To bring white jade bed from dragon king's palace, daughter gives magic trident. To fetch gong of King of the Monkeys, daughter advises to roll in mud and pretend to be Monkey King. Throw water = lake; stone = mountain; oil = oily mountain. Task: cut two bamboo canes, ogre lives in them. Wears fiber cloak and bamboos on fingers, ogre grabs but gets only cloak and bamboos. Lad weds witch's daughter. Flee. Witch sends flying knife. They throw cock behind which is killed instead. Repeat and girl is killed. To cover her with lotus blossoms and wait seven times seven days. He uncovers on forty-eighth day and she dies. China: Wyndham CHINA 26-36.

Bk* The Grateful Prince. King promises first thing met at home to Devil. King gives peasant girl instead of son. Prince seeks to save her. Tasks: clean stable for white mare, is really Devil's grandmother; milk black cow; bring in haystack. Girl advises to threaten each. Take white headed calf to pasture. Sow barley, reap, thresh, etc. and make beer for breakfast. Girl gives key to henhouse where spirits are kept and they perform. Flee. Take amber ring from inside head of calf. Ring lights way to flee. Turn to brook and fish; rose and bush; wind and gnat. Open rock with ring and escape to other world. Estonia: Maas MOON 60-81.

Bl* The Giant Okab. Yusaf promises son to Giant Okab on wedding day. Son cries out as talons pierce and father offers self instead. Father cries out and wife offers self. She cries and daughter offers self. She cries and an unknown maid offers self and is taken. Does not cry out. Giant Okab turns to warrior. Enchanted until found one who knew no pain and feared no death. Maid weds lad. Persia: Mehdevi PERSIAN 62-68.

C* The Troll's daughter. Lad serves troll. To feed all animals in mile long barn. Turned to hare for a year and a day. Second--to raven. Third--to herring. As herring he woos troll's daughter in undersea palace. She advises to loan his pay to king to repay debt to troll and accompany him as jester--cause damage there and troll will demand answers to riddles. Riddles reveal secret of daughter. He chooses her from one thousand and one maids (H161) and selects fish containing troll's heart from one thousand and one fish. Destroys fish and troll bursts into flint pieces. Wed. Denmark: Hatch MORE 59-78; Lang FIFTY 327-334 /Lang PINK 247-257/; Manning-Sanders BOOK..TROLLS 110-122.

Da* Sweetheart Roland. Girl changes places with stepsister so stepmother kills her own daughter. Girl flees with Sweetheart Roland leaving three drops of blood to answer. Change selves to lake and duck; rose and fiddler, he plays and witch must dance self to death. She turns to stone while he makes wedding arrangements. He forgets her. She turns to flower, is taken to shepherd's home and housework is magically done. He throws cloth over flower and it turns to girl (D777.1). At Roland's wedding she sings and R's memory returns. Weds. Grimm: Grimm GRIMM'S (Grosset) 62-66; Grimm HOUSEHOLD 232-235; Rackham GRIMM 99-103.

Db* King Kojata. King's beard is grabbed as drinks, forced to promise 'that which he finds at home', it is a son. Prince sets out, hides garment of one of thirty ducks. Youngest duck agrees to wed. Tells to approach father on knees, helps with suitor tasks. They flee. Her breath left on window pane answers. Turns self to river, he to bridge. To woods and paths. Church and monk. King is unable to go beyond a church, turns back. She turns to stone, etc. as in Da. Russia: Buck FAIRY 141-153; Lang GREEN 192-206; Manning-Sanders BOOK..WIZARDS 95-108.

E* Bukola. Type 313G. Cow Bukola lost, moos and lad finds in cave of trolls. Pursued. Hair of B's tail thrown down = river. Troll sends ox to drink. Second hair = fire. Ox spits out water. Third hair = mountain. Troll is stuck boring through. Turns to stone. Iceland: Courlander RIDE 194-196; Manning-Sanders BOOK..OGRES 75-79.

F* Lad as suitor: suitor tasks.

Fa* Three tasks. Suitor tasks: 1. Clean stables. 2. Thatch stables with bird feathers. Fiona does all. 3. Fetch eggs from treetop, she gives bones from foot for ladder, he forgets one (E33). Flee. Apple pieces left to answer. Throw objects from mare's left ears. Chips of wood = woods. Pebble = mountain. Pitch = river of pitch. Ireland: MacManus HIBERNIAN 202-211.

Fb. The Enchanted Knife. Suitor tasks: tame three horses and bring loaded with gold. Daughter gives magic knife which draws horses, tells where to dig up gold. Wed. Serbia: Lang VIOLET 129-132.

Fc* Winning of Kwelanga. Suitor tasks. 1. Retrieve all sowed corn. 2. Chop forest. 3. Pluck thorn from top of tree on cliff. Daughter performs with magic song. Wed. Zulu: Aardema BEHIND 34-41.

Fd* King of Araby's Daughter. Suitor tasks. 1. Empty lake. 2. Make wood into barrel. 3. Herd five square miles of beasts. Choose her from three pigeons..she has black feather under wing. Flee. Apple pieces answer. Turn to spinning wheel, yarn, and old woman; fisherman, rod, boat; captain, wheel, ship. They reach Ireland. Ireland: MacManus BOLD 83-100.

G* Rescuing the Princess.

Ga* Giant of the Brown Beech Wood. To rescue three princesses from giant. Tasks. 1. Stop raven's croaking, she performs, he is to ask hound (sister) as reward. 2. Stop wind in field which blows cows away, she performs, he asks filly (sister). 3. To make seven thousand beds from feathers blown into castle with one hundred open windows, he asks her as reward. She obtains keys to three doors. First calls when opened, second calls louder, third wakes giant. Lad reaches sword in inner room and slays giant. Ireland: MacManus BOLD 138-157 /Mayne BOOK..GIANTS 119-137/.

Gb* Tritil, Litil, and the Birds. Three sons seek stolen princesses. Youngest shares food with little men and birds. They aid when takes service with troll woman. Tasks. 1. Clean stables. 2. Spread pillow feathers in sun, then put back. To ask reward of little chest (jewels), silver ship that goes on land or sea, and three fur slippers under bed (two brothers and princess). Weds. Iceland: Manning-Sanders BOOK.. OGRES 20-31.

H* The Lost Sister. Liels and Laura, the Farmhand's Children. Sister carried off to wed stranger. Brother grows up and seeks in underworld. To pull three hairs from back of demon husband to dull anger and will accept brother. Tasks. 1. Clean stable and feed white mare. Is demon's mother, Laura warns not to feed and he won't dirty stable. 2. Haul firewood with mare. Threatens to beat her and she pulls. 3. Herd calf, ties ball of yarn to leg. To escape they split calf's head, duck comes out, egg in duck rolls up path to sun-light. Pursued. Turn to rose and bush; lake and drake. Throw towel = river; hairbrush = forest. Reach upper world. Latvia: Huggins BLUE 74-84.

I* Jankyn and the Witch. J. takes smock of bathing maid (K1335). Weds. She obtains her smock and leaves. He seeks at witch's house. Tasks. 1. Cut forest. 2. Bail lake with sieve. 3. Restore forest. 4. Restore lake. She per-forms. Flee. Turn to meadow with flower; church with monk; goose with gander; pond with swan. Witch attempts to drink pond, swan kills her. Wife does pilgrimage for three years to expiate mother's sins. Drops ring token in glass on return (H94.4). Hungary: Manning-Sanders RED 31-41.

J* Jack and the Wizard. Tasks assigned as wizard's servant. 1. Find key, he gives up and breaks twig in anger, key is inside. 2. Plant coltsfoot plants, must plant upside down. 3. Find wizard, picks up egg by luck. Reward: one coin with blessing or hatful with curse. Takes one coin. Rubs ring found and wizard's daughter appears. Grants wishes, weds. Wales: Manning-Sanders CHOICE 268-275 /Manning-Sanders BOOK..WIZARDS 78-85/.

K* The Girl as Helper (Type 313B) + The War of the Birds (Type 222) + The Forbidden Box (Type 537). Prince kills serpent in war of birds (B261). Rewarded with package: not to open until reaches place he wishes to live. Opens and castle comes out (C321.2). Giant puts back in return for eldest son. Cook's son, butler's son, returned. Tasks. 1. Clean stable. 2. Thatch stable with bird's down. 3. Fetch eggs from top of tree, uses girl's finger, leaves one bone at top (E33). Chooses wife from three sisters, one lacks little finger. Flee. Apple pieces answer. Throws from filly's ear a twig = thorn wood; stone = rock; bladder of water = loch. Giant drowns. Lad is kissed and for-gets her. Shoemaker's wife and daughter see reflection and think selves beautiful and leave, she takes their place. Three suitors stuck in awkward positions while courting. She brings pigeons to argue at feast. He remembers. Scotland: Jacobs CELTIC 223-241; Rackham FAIRY 15-27; Wilson SCOTTISH 156-172.

L* Witch's son aids maiden. Girl grabbed pick-ing plums and kept in house of plum stones as servant. Benvenuto, witch's son, offers to help with tasks. 1. Grind wheat and make bread in one hour. 2. Bring jewels from sister witch. B. gives oil, bread, rope, broom. She oils gate, feeds dog, cleans hearth, gives rope to woman drawing well. Grateful objects let her escape (D1658.3.4). To tell color of cock crowing = yellow, black, white. B. tells. Thrice. They flee. She has refused to kiss him, now does so. Wed. SEE ALSO: Q2.1.2Ce. Italy: Manning-Sanders BOOK..WITCHES 62-71.

M* A Ride to Hell (H1273.1). Jealous steward

tells king that lad can collect loan from Devil. Lad goes on Billy Goat. Raven met shows mag-ic shattering sword. Tells to greet sister at gate of hell from "brother in the forest." Lad kills twelve-headed monster and rescues twelve maids. Twenty-four headed monster, twenty-four maids. Thirty-six. Ignores attempts of devil's grandmother to lead him astray. Greets serpent at gate from raven, allowed to pass. Devil's grandmother advises D. to give him the money. Serpent asks him to pull off her skin = princess. Flee. Pursued by Devil and Devil's grandmother. Princess spits on road = lake. Throws glass bead = glass mountain. Cries, "light before, dark behind" (R255), Devil lost in darkness. Raven asks to be beheaded = prince. Denmark: Manning-Sanders BOOK.. DEVILS 98-109.

N* The Hungry Old Witch. Witch sees reflec-tion of boy in pond, sends ants up tree to bite so he falls out (R251), catches him in net. Aid-ed by girl at witch's house, they flee with mag-ic stone and powder. Throw powder behind = leaves turn to rabbits and witch stops to eat. Throws again - thornbushes turn to foxes; grass = ants; stones = turtles. Witch drowns. They wed. Uruguay: Finger TALES 135-145 /Hoke WITCHES 90-100/, /Fenner GIANTS 50-63/, /Harper GHOSTS 30-43/, /Davis BAKER'S 1-20/.

P* Musk and Amber. Mother curses Marika--"May the kerchief on your head fly away to the tower of the ogress." M. follows it to ogress. Must clean forty rooms by evening or be eaten. Preparing for wedding of son, Musk and Amber. Musk and Amber tells her to open windows of tower and call twelve winds of heaven. To wash wedding clothes - call all washerwomen of the world. Fill mattresses--call all birds from mountain top. Fetch flutes and fiddle from sis-ter's house. Musk and Amber advises to trim eyelashes of old woman met on way, call thistles soft, exchange lion's chaff for ass's bones. Flees with flute and fiddle - lion, etc. will not stop. Weds Musk and Amber. Ogress banish-ed. Greece: Wilson GREEK 107-119.

G550. Rescue from ogre.

G550.1. Rescue from ogre. Maiden rescued from maiden lover. Has rescuer beaten and mourns lost lover. Numbskull rescuer: "There's no accounting for such tastes." Iran: Shah MUL-LAH 133.

G552.1* Rescue from ogre by helpful animals. Prince and princess hide on pillar from ogre. Falcon carries. Ogre causes flames to singe falcon and he drops on tower. They throw cakes to ogre, he eats and sleeps. Wolf carries over river. Ogre can't cross. Fox and bear live with wolf and children. Ogre changes to prince and gets Olya to throw scarf over river to him. It turns to bridge and he crosses. Has magic bone which jumps into Ivan's head. Wolf puts own head near I's as bone jumps to his head. Bear takes from wolf. Fox acts as if to take then leaps aside and bone flies into ogre's head. Manning-Sanders BOOK..OGRES 44-52.

G555.1.1* Sing or I'll eat you. Ogre threatens. Coyote tells baby Hopi turtle to sing or will eat. Turtle begs not to be thrown in water (K581.1). Native American (Hopi): Jagendorf NOODLE-HEAD 274-277 (fox); Williams-Ellis ROUND 231-232.

G555.1.2* Coyote wants to learn locust's song. Forces locust to sing, stumbles and forgets song. Returns and repeats. Locust puts rock in her shell and flees. Coyote breaks teeth on rock (K525.1.4). Native American (Pueblo): Dolch PUEBLO 67-77. Nicaragua: Courlander RIDE 234-237. Native American (Hopi): Courlander PEOPLE 82-85 (dove and coyote).

G555.1.3* Coyote forces hare to sing song for him, keeps forgetting and returning. Proposes heat endurance contest for property of song. Hare escapes through hole in end of heated cave. Native American: Curry DOWN 104-110.

G555.1.4* The Gunniwolf. Wolf forces little girl to sing for him. Harper GUNNIWOLF pb.

G561. Ogre tricked into carrying his prisoners home in bag on his own back (S62.1). (cf. Q2.1.2Ca); SEE ALSO: D2183D.

G561.1* Girls in ogre's power not to enter forbidden chamber (C611). Two sister trespass getting key (ball) bloody and are killed (C913). Third girl sends sisters home in bag by ogre. Then has self carried home. He thinks he is carrying gift to her mother. When he stops to rest she calls "I see you" and he continues.

A* Hen trips in the mountain. Chasing hen girl falls through trapdoor in mountain. Troll asks to wed and beheads when refuses. Second daughter same. Third daughter agrees to wed. Revives sisters with magic ointment she sees troll use on goat. Puts sisters in bag and sends "gold" to mother. Makes dummy of self and escapes. Gets sharpshooter to fire on troll. Troll sees sun and bursts (G304.2.5). Norway: Aulaire EAST 207-215; Minard WOMENFOLK 156-163; Manning-Sanders BOOK..DEVILS 117-126 (goat butts demon away from girl's hut).

B* Fitcher's Feathered Bird. Beggar causes girl to jump into his basket, to care for egg, soils egg in forbidden room, third sister puts pieces of sisters' bodies together and revives. Sends home as gift to parents. Makes dummy of self and escapes covered with honey and feathers as Fitcher's Feathered Bird (K521.1). Germany (Grimm): Grimm BROTHERS 72-76; Grimm JUNIPER 71-79.

C* Three Chests. demon grabs beard of farmer leaning over lake and demands to wed daughter, takes ring from forbidden room, blood stains hand, beheaded, second--same. Farmer now avoids lake but pair of magic brogues he puts on walk him into lake (D1520.10.2).

Youngest daughter restores sisters with 'Water of Life' pitcher. Sends home as gifts, makes dummy of self and goes in third trunk. Demon falls off roof tugging at dummy and pouring 'Water of Life' on wound kills self, girl has put Water of Death in pitcher (E82.1). Finland: Fillmore SHEPHERD'S 40-52.

Cb* Jurma and the Sea God. Farmer cooling feet has feet caught by Sea God. Daughter demanded. She loves Sea God. Not to enter room. Tar touches hand as she tries on gold ring in room. Thrown into tar pit. Second daughter same. Third--father tries on shoes he finds and they carry him into the water. Third sister finds Water of Life and Water of Death and revives sisters. Puts Water of Death in Water of Life bottle. Sends sisters and self home in chest, leaving dummy of self. He hurts self knocking over dummy on return and drinks 'Water of Life' to cure wounds. Dies. Finland: Bowman TALES..TUPA 81-90.

D* The Princess who lived in a Kailyard. Giant steals cabbages of exiled queen. Three daughters. Eldest daughter guards, taken to serve giant, she refuses food to dwarf who knocks. Giant puts her in hen house. Second daughter same. Youngest feeds stranger and he helps her with spinning. She sends heather to mother by Giant. Sister is hidden inside. Second sister same. Third same. Scotland: Sheehan FOLK 20-21.

E* Lucifer's Wedding. Wed to devil, not to enter twelfth room, drops golden apple there. Second daughter same. Third sends sisters home in basket as gift. Makes dummy and is carried home herself. Calls "I see you" if devil tarries. Slovenia: Kavcic GOLDEN 127-133.

F* Masha and the Bear. Girl serves bear. Sends pies to grandparents, self in basket. Calls "I see you" when bear tarries. Russia: Carey BABA 117-120; Riordan TALES..CENTRAL 190-193.

G* The Pig Troll. Three girls follow pig into woods, turns to troll. Troll explodes in anger, pieces = flint (A1414.5.1). Denmark: Owen CASTLE 65-74.

H* Merman Rosmer takes daughter, three brothers attempt to rescue, third reaches, kept as slave, to be sent home, sister sends chest of gold with him, self in chest. Merman destroys castle of mother in rage. They had been warned not to build by shore (C931). Scotland: Manning-Sanders BOOK..MERMAIDS 108-113.

G561.2* Girl imprisoned by ogre escapes (or weds disenchanted ogre). SEE: R221S.

A* Girl in Chest. Vampire offers money to mother for bride. She refuses to drink with him and he kills. Second same. Third flees. Yugoslavia: Fillmore LAUGHING 201-218.

B* Secret Room. Follows bull in cabbage patch,

black cat offers to tell how to remove blood from key if fed, third sister agrees, touch key with sickle. Bull disenchanted when finds her without bloodstains. They wed (D753.5). Britain: Williams-Ellis FAIRY..BRITISH 149-152.

C* Three Silver Balls. Girl sent for cabbage from goblin's garden, given silver ball and told to look through house but not forbidden room, slimy pit, gets ball dirty, thrown into pit. Second daughter same. Third daughter rescues sisters. Discovers where soul of goblin resides and breaks eggshell containing soul. Italy: Manning-Sanders BOOK..GHOSTS 111-118.

D* The Rabbit's Bride. Daughter sent to shoo cabbage eating rabbit. He carries her off on tail third time. Has her cook for wedding guests. He plans to wed her. She dresses straw figure and escapes. He knocks over figure and thinks killed her. Germany (Grimm): Grimm HOUSEHOLD 1-2; Grimm JUNIPER II 275-277.

Db* The Girl Who Picked Strawberries. Three dwarfs capture girl picking strawberries. To wed her. She makes dummy of straw and escapes. They strike figure and think killed it. Germany: Manning-Sanders CHOICE 291-294; Manning-Sanders BOOK..DWARFS 49-52.

G586* Ogre steals boy but returns him home when boy continues to cry despite riches ogre showers on him. Ogre grieves for riches he can never know--a family. Slovenia: Kavcic GOLDEN 134-140.

G600 - G699. Other ogre motifs.

G610. Theft from ogre. SEE ALSO: F54.2 (Jack and the Beanstalk); K1611 (Molly Whuppie et al.). Type 328.

Aa* Pinkel. Brothers tell King that Pinkel can fetch golden lantern from witch's isle. Pinkel salts (K337) pot, steals light when daughter is sent for water. Sent for goat with bells. Stuffs wool in bells. Robe. Visits witch and pretends is eating self to death, stuffs porridge in bag under clothing and slits and feigns dead, escapes with robe. Weds princess. Sweden: Haviland FAVORITE..SWEDEN 33-49; Wiggin FAIRY 27-35.

Ab* Thirteenth. Thirteenth meows and ogress thinks is cat. Steals coverlet. King rewards. Task: steal horse. Climbs rope ladder and feeds horse cakes. Bring ogre. Goes as monk with chest. Asks ogre if Thirteenth would fit in chest. Ogre gets in to see. Italy: Hampden HOUSE 11-16.

Ac* Cinderlad and the Troll's Silver Ducks. Elder brothers tell king Cinderlad can get troll's seven silver ducks. Rows over lake in kneading trough (only inheritance). Coaxes ducks with rye and wheat. Troll calls, "Is that you who stole my ducks?" "Yes." "Will you come

again?" "Perhaps." Task: steal bedspread with gold and silver squares. Steals while being aired. Task: steal gold harps which gladden one when played. Lets self be caught. Puts out little finger when daughter comes to cut little finger. Second time stick. Third time candle, is ready to eat. He shows daughter how to sharpen knife, beheads. Disguised as daughter plays harp and flees. Calls that troll ate own daughter. Troll bursts in anger. C. takes treasures, weds princess. Norway: Aulaire EAST 100-107; Haviland FAVORITE.. NORWAY 75-88.

Ad* Mother's Pet. Youngest son's inheritance is kneading trough. Sails. Works in king's kitchen. Suitor task: Bring hen that lays golden eggs, golden self-grinding mill, lantern that sheds light and learning on whole kingdom. Sails in kneading trough to troll land. Lets self down trap door in roof and steals hen. Second trip. Hits sleeping troll on toe and fights with wife. Steals mill and lantern. Trolls call after him and he retorts. Trolls try to drink sea and burst. He weds princess. Denmark: Hatch DANISH 25-36.

Ae* Little Ederland. Youngest daughter inherits only broom, apron and wooden bowl. Elder sisters tell lord youngest can bring candlestick which burns without a candle. Broom advises her to make boat of bowl with apron for sail and broom for mast. She sails to troll's island, pours salt down chimney, steals candlestick when troll wife goes for water. Horse with bells growing from legs, stuffs bells with flax. Troll calls and she retorts. Pig from which bacon can repeatedly be cut. Caught. Shows cook how to put head on block (G526). Weds lord. Two sisters set out in bowl never return. Sweden: Owen CASTLE 157-167.

Af* Corvetto. Jealous courtiers say Corvetto can steal ogre's horse, tapestry and coverlet. Steals palace. Helps ogre's wife split wood and kills, tricks ogre into pit. Weds king's daughter. Italy: Mincielli OLD 64-72.

Ag* The Terrible Olli. Troll offers own daughters as brides to three brothers. Youngest brother changes nightcaps with girls and troll beheads own daughters. Youngest steals troll's horse with hairs of gold and silver, waters it for troll's wife and steals. Troll calls--retort. Steals money bags while watching bread for troll's wife. Bores hole in roof and pours water on bed so wife hands coverlet up to dry--steals. Caught. Has troll wife show how to get in oven (G526). Troll calls. He says wife is behind him--troll turns and sees sun rising. Bursts. Finland: Fillmore SHEPHERD'S 53-63 /Gruenberg FAVORITE 380-387/, /Fenner GIANTS 162-173/, /Fillmore MIGHTY/; McNeil DOUBLE 116-121 (all trolls flee, no trolls in Southern Finland since).

Ah* Esben and the Witch. Youngest given no horse so cuts stick horse which then carries him. Changes caps of brother and witch's daughters. So she kills eleven of her own thirteen daughters. Sir Red tells king the eleven older brothers can bring dove with gold and silver feathers. Esben flies over river on horse, entices dove from witch's yard with peas. Witch calls--he retorts. Boar with tusks of gold and silver bristles. Lamp that shines over seven kingdoms--salt in porridge. Coverlet with golden bells--caught. Fattened, shows nail, then piece of fat. Has daughter go back for hat and locks in her room. Flees. Witch explodes in anger. Origin of flint. Denmark: Manning-Sanders CHOICE 128-143 /Manning-Sanders BOOK..WITCHES 46-61/.

Ai* Constantes and the Dragon. Three brothers cut wheat field thinking owner will pay them. Dragon appears and sends Constantes to wife with letter to cook him. He changes letter (K511) instructing her to feed him. Dragon takes them home for dinner. C. steals wife's ring in night and they flee. Envious elder brother tells king that Constantes can get dragon's diamond coverlet. Old woman advises C. to put three reeds full of insects on coverlet. Dragon hangs it out window. Steals horse and bell, stops bell's forty-one holes with wooden plugs so can't ring. Dragon calls after him -- he retorts. Dressed as carpenter pretends to be making casket for C. Dragon gets in to try size. Taken to king. Elder brother asked to open lid. Dragon devours. Greece: Haviland FAVORITE..GREECE 3-19; Manning-Sanders CHOICE 235-245 /Manning-Sanders BOOK.. DRAGONS 9-19/.

Aj* Chilbik and the Greedy Czar. C. substitutes ogress' daughters for his brothers. Sends her to fetch water in sieve. Drops stone down chimney and ogress throws pot out for splattering her. He steals. Pricks her and she throws 'flea' ridden blanket out. Causes goat with golden horns to bleat all night and she drives goat out. Ordered to fetch all by Czar. Crosses bridge of ashes to escape. Pretends to be making trunk to protect ogress' belongings from Chilbik, locks ogress in it and takes to Czar. Ogress gobbles up everyone in sight on being released by Chilbik causes her to fall from tree and burst. Russia (Avar): Titiev HOW 9-26.

Ak* The Lad With the Goatskin. Ash-lad beats giant and gets magic club. Second giant--magic fife that causes dancing. Third giant--healing ointment. Makes princess laugh thrice by defeating all knights. Task: kill wolf. Brings to court and makes dance. Task: fetch flail from hell. Danes flee, flail burns way back to hell. Goat-skin weds princess. Ireland: Jacobs CELTIC 245-255.

G666. Grateful ogres.

G666.1* Lad feeds children of troll wife. She gives magic fish hooks. He shares catch and she gives treasure. Iceland: Manning-Sanders BOOK..OGRES 91-100.

G666.2* Shepherd pulls pitchfork from foot of wounded giant. Is given invisibility belt and taken to giants' feast, steals loaf of bread there. Gold coin falls with each bite taken. Leaves gold by princess' pillow daily. Forgets belt and is caught. Weds. Rumania: Lang YELLOW 86-89; Manning-Sanders BOOK..GIANTS 118-125 /Manning-Sanders CHOICE 216-233/.

G666.3* Simple Durac greets ogre Sibilim, is taken into service. Given three pennies pay. Gives two to poor, buys cat with third. Sells in land of rats (N411.1). Throws gold into sea and it washes back. Buys incense cargo and it burns up. Ogre says needs clever wife to stand in water and catch fish with gold ring around neck. Turns to girl and wed. +B184.2.2.2. Russia: Manning-Sanders BOOK..OGRES 9-19.

G671. Wild man released from captivity aids hero. SEE ALSO: B314C (Koschei the Deathless); H321C (Fairy Helena); H331.1.1D.

A* The Wild Man. Type 502. Iron Hans. Arm in pool pulls all under. Pond drained and wild man caged. Prince loses golden ball in wild man's cage, persuaded to unlock cage in return for ball, taken away by wild man. To let nothing fall into spring, dips fingers--turns gold, hair falls--turns gold (C912). Turned out. Takes service as gardener with cap covering gold hair. Princess sees and loves. He goes to war thrice on nag, receives horse from Iron Hans and distinguishes self. Three times catches golden ball (H316) princess tosses (H331.1.1D, Princess on the Glass Mountain). Wears three disguises given by Iron Hans. Discovered by wound (H56) and three golden apples and hair. Wed. Spell on Iron Hans is broken. Germany (Grimm): Gag MORE 207-288; Grimm GRIMM'S (Follett) 162-173; Grimm GRIMM'S (Grosset) 356-364; Grimm GRIMM'S (Scribner) 245-254; Grimm GRIMM'S (World) 358-366.

B* The Golden Lynx. Son opens door freeing "golden lynx" (wild dog). Exiled. Servant lets down well for water, refuses to draw up unless changes places. Servant tells king his 'servant' can herd wild animals. A. brings back four colts with golden manes and tails, four bullocks with golden horns and hooves, lynx performs. B. herds bears, wolves, doves, dog gives bell to ring and animals dance to his pipe. He now reveals identity and weds princess. Poland: Baker GOLDEN 123-130. Yugoslavia: Carpenter WONDER..DOGS 235-244.

H. TESTS

H0 – H199. Identity tests: recognition.

H0. Identity tests

H10. Recognition through common knowledge.

H11. Recognition through story-telling. Telling of a story known to both persons concerned brings about recognition. SEE: B538.3.1.

H11.1.1. Recognition at an inn where all must tell their life histories. Type 425D.

A* Hans shoots at giants and causes them to quarrel. Drinks of flask and beheads giants with sword as come through door. Takes princess' shoe and half handkerchief as token. Princess sets up inn by road and makes all tell tale for lodging. Jutland: Manning-Sanders BOOK..GIANTS 36-43.

H12.2.0.1* Recognition by verse of song. Girl abandoned by brother is raised by caravan traders, taken by brother as bride when grown. She sings of her plight and parents overhear and recognize. N. Nigeria (Hausa): Arnott AFRICAN 160-166.

H13.2.7. Recognition by overheard conversation with stone. SEE: B133.3 (Goose Girl); K1931.2C.

H30. Recognition through personal peculiarities.

H35.3. Recognition by unique needlework. SEE: E342.1D (painting).

H35.3.3* Recognition by weaving. Shah captured by slave traders weaves rug so fine only queen can afford to buy. Weaves message in ancient Persian letters. Persia: Carpenter ELEPHANT'S 31-39.

H35.3.3.1. Recognition by weaving. Captive weaves rug and send to his father who pays ransom. East African: Heady WHEN 31-35.

H36.1. Slipper test. Identification by fitting of slipper. SEE: R221 (Cinderella); B335.2A (Billy Beg and His Bull).

H36.1.2. Oni, born with boots which grow as he grows. Oni kills giant eagle Anodo, loses boot under bird as it falls. Another claims feat. Boot tried on all. Flies majestically to Oni's foot. Nigeria (Yoruba): Fuja FOURTEEN 48-59.

H36.3. Search for finger which fits ring. SEE: T555.1.1.

H41.1. Princess on the pea. Princess recognized by her inability to sleep on bed which has a pea under its dozen mattresses. Andersen: Adams BOOK..PRINCESS 31-32; Andersen PRINCESS pb /Holme TALES 49/; Hutchinson CANDLELIGHT 71-75/, /Fenner PRINCESSES 29-32/, /Haviland FAIRY 170-172/, /Opie CLASSIC 216-218/; Rackham ARTHUR 140-142 /Martignoni ILLUSTRATED 212/; Wiggin TALES 182-183.

H41.1.1* Princess (Prince) tests. Cannot sleep with straw under sheets on hard bed, etc. Helpful animal warns to complain. SEE: K1917.3C; K1952.0.3.

H50. Recognition by bodily marks or physical attributes.

H56. Recognition by wound. SEE: G671; R222.1; B316.

H71.8.1* Princess weeps pearls. Recognized by sight of type of pearl she weeps. Lad is given emerald book with pearl inside after carrying increasingly heavy witch who clings to his back. Princess had appeared as ugly daughter of witch, lad returns and sees her bathing without mask. Witch has saved all pearls she wept as inheritance. Turns hut into palace and she weds lad. Her father banished her for saying she loved him like gold (H592.1). Witch cared for her until banishment over. Germany (Grimm): Grimm GRIMM'S (Scribner) 292-304.

H80. Identification by tokens.

H87.1* Christian knight wearing almond blossom emblem is thus known by Christian slave girl (his former love) when he comes to free her. He enters Moorish tournaments, carries her off. Spain: Gunterman CASTLE 166-178.

H90. Identification by ornaments.

H94. Recognition by ring. SEE: H36.3; H1411.4.3.1.

H94.1. Identification by ring in food. Lang GREEN 178-182 (girl's ring falls into bread, prince to wed whom it fits). SEE ALSO: R221D; P253.2 (Seven Ravens); G530.2I.

H94.4.1* Black Colin away on crusade for seven years. Returns as wife is about to wed. Drops ring in soup. Scotland: Wilson SCOTTISH 56-65.

H105.1.1. False dragon head proof. Imposter cuts off dragon heads (after tongues have been removed) and attempts to use them as proof of slaying the dragon. SEE: R111.1.3.

H105.5.1.2* Hatan, shipwrecked, weds princess. Three brothers-in-law plan hunt. Hatan kills bear, leopard and jackal and when others claim kill, he produces nose, tail and ear. India: Carpenter ELEPHANT'S 184-194.

H105.5.4.1* Son who brings perfect slain lion to become chief. Abdullah kills and cuts off tip of tail. Mohammad claims prize. Abdullah produces tip. Algeria: Holding KING'S 98-108.

H161. Recognition of transformed person among identical companions. Pre-arranged signals. SEE: B582.2; G530.2N.

H161.0.1.1* Girls dress alike to keep man from carrying off Tipingee. All claim to be the girl stepmother has given him. Haiti: Wolkstein MAGIC 129-134.

H171.2. Bird indicates election of king (pope). Kirghiz: Ginsburg KAHA 90-96 (One on whom white falcon rests to be new khan). SEE ALSO: H1440B; B217.

H171.7* Tsar tosses crown into air to fall on one chosen to wed princess. It falls thrice on shepherd instructed by angel to go as suiter. While building shrine to thank God, the Church of Ochara is unearthed. A scroll in excavated church foretells all this. Serbia: Spicer LONG 116-129.

H171.8. First person to pass gate is to be new judge. Ireland: MacManus HIBERNIAN 160-173 (+L223).

H200 - H299. Tests of truth.

H220. Ordeals. Guilt or innocence thus established.

H221.4.1. Ordeal by boiling water. Suspected thieves to drink hot water. Tortoise arranges to serve others, giving water time to cool when he drinks. Walks about showing everyone what a big gourdful he is taking, cooling it further. Nigeria: Courlander OLODE 90-95.

H221.4.2. Task: drinking boiling water. Trickster declares it's lukewarm and sets cup in sun to heat up. Jamaica: Sherlock ANANSI 95-103; Sherlock WEST 130-134 (Anansi).

H263. Test of sin. SEE ALSO: D1163.1.

H263.1* Poor man jailed for stealing pears gives pear seed to Emperor. Says it will bear golden pears if planted by a man who has never stolen or cheated. No one at court will venture to plant it. Then by what justice is he imprisoned for stealing a pear? Released. China: Wyndham TALES..CHINA 20-24.

H300 - H499. Marriage tests.

H310. Suitor tests. SEE: B216.5; F914.0.1 (Rock python father).

H316. Suitor test. Apple thrown indicates princess's choice. SEE: G671; H331.1.2.2.

H321. Suitor test. Hiding from princess. She has magic sight. Type 329.

A* The Twelve Windows. Three chances to hide from princess. She looks through twelve windows and sees all (D1323.3). Fox turns lad to hare and he hides under her hair behind her. De La Mare TALES 155-165.

B* The Fisherman's Son. Lad saves fish, stag, crane, fox. Saves tokens to call them. They help him hide from princess. Her magic mirror reveals all hiding places. Fox digs passage under her chair and hides him there. Ginsburg FISHERMAN'S pb; Manning-Sanders BOOK.. MAGIC 39-44.

C* The Fairy Helena. Lad releases prisoner who turns into demon (G671). Demon takes lad to palace. He follows demon's daughters as they turn into doves and fly off each evening. They convene with fairy Helena. He courts her. Can wed if hides so she can't find. Demon aids. Turns to pin in cover of her magic book. Hungary: Manning-Sanders GLASS 139-145.

D* Accomplished prince's efforts to hide are to no avail. Magician teacher suggests a blank page in king's magic book. Wins princess. Russia: Manning-Sanders BOOK..PRINCES 40-48.

E* Hides in heart of hare, bear. She finds. Hides in her heart—succeeds. Old man aids. Lad had found princess inside of forbidden twenty-fourth door while serving old man. Finland: Bowman TALES..TUPA 96-104.

F* Dapplegrim: Youngest of twelve sons given twelve mares inheritance. Twelve foals born, dapple-grey foal tells to take other eleven away and let it nurse all twelve mares for three years. Takes service with king. Jealous knights tell king he bragged could rescue princess from troll (H911). Horse needs shoes of twenty pounds iron plus twelve pounds steel. Climbs glass mountain and rescues princess from troll's cave. Task: make sun shine in king's hall. Horse needs new shoes. Stamps rock into the ground. Task: bring horse as fine as Dapplegrim for princess. Needs new shoes, takes twelve sacks rye, barley, twelve beef, twelve spiked cowhides, twelve barrels tar. Distract wild birds, animals, with these en route to hell. Dapplegrim battles giant horse wearing spiked hides, deflects and horse becomes identical twin of Dapplegrim. Task: find the princess. Duck, Dapplegrim says aim gun at her. Loaf of bread, Dapplegrim says cut. Task: hide from princess. Fly in Dapplegrim's nostril. Clod between hoof and shoe of Dapplegrim. Wed. Norway: Aulaire EAST 188-201; Manning-Sanders BOOK MAGICAL BEASTS 70-83; Undset TRUE 83-96; Wiggin FAIRY 59-69.

H321.1* Hiding from the devil. Type 329. Troll will eat lad if finds thrice. Dwarf with whom he shared food hides him—found. Third time in fish. Witch fishes for him in washtub. Dwarf raises storm and drowns her. Denmark: Manning-Sanders BOOK..OGRES 123-127.

H322.1. Suitor test: finding object hidden by princess. Type 507A. SEE: G512 (Jack the Giant Killer, Incident 4). SEE: K1341.1.

H323. Suitor test: learning girl's name (N475). SEE: E341.1C.

A* Tortoise and Babrinsa's Daughters. Tortoise hides in tree and tosses down bundles of flowers. Three girls call to each other and he hears names. They turn to objects rather than wed him = leaf, fern, water in river. He realizes his ambition was unnatural, hides. Why tortoise hides. Nigeria: Walker DANCING 73-79.

B* Chief's (Sky-god's) daughter to be given to whoever guesses name. Ananse hides and hears name. Sends lizard as messenger (or has lizard translate as he plays name on drums). Lizard gets bride. Ghana (Ashanti): Appiah ANANSE 49-56 (+A2474.1); Courlander KING'S 36-40 (drops mangoes from tree and servant hands them to girl--calls name).

C* Chief's daughter to be given to one who guesses name of most useful tree. Swallow overhears and tells friend muskrat who wishes to wed daughter. Tree is the Mwabi. Congo (Luban): Burton MAGIC 56-59.

D* Anansi puts basket of fruit on bed of king's three daughters and hears each call the name of other. Teaches crow, bullfrog, and rat to sing their names and serenades palace. Offered any reward if will only leave and never return. The group take gold and silver. Rat takes from king's eldest daughter and stays. Jamaica: Sherlock ANANSI 59-63.

H328.7* Sun and moon must withstand forest of swords, pond of teeth, rising waters, smoke and fire. Moon flees. Sun stays and weds girl. Kenya (Kamba): Jablow MAN 64-66.

H328.8* Suitor test: standing seven years in sun and rain. Touches before time is up and all turn to tree trunk. Begin again. And again. Youth and kingdom magically restored at end of test. Italy: Baker GOLDEN 89-100.

H328.9* Shepherd refuses to say "to your good health" when king sneezes. Is thrown to bear, stares it down. Thrown to wild boars, plays flute and they dance, etc. Refuses to say this until wed to princess. Now says it. Type 858. Russia: Lang CRIMSON 18-25 /Lang FIFTY 322-326/, /Fenner PRINCESSES 3-10/, /Haviland FAVORITE..RUSSIA 3-19/, /Lang TO YOUR pb/; Sleigh NORTH 170-177.

H328.10* Suitor test: power of endurance. Father of girl sets tests. 1. Sleeping in room full of snakes. 2. Room full of bees and centipedes. Princess gives him scarf that causes creatures to vanish. Third task: must find arrow shot into woods. Father then sets fire to woods. A mouse hides prince in underground nest and finds arrow. Prince returns to tie sleeping father-in-law by hair to chair and table (K635). He rolls boulder over door and escapes with princess. Japan: Uchida MAGIC 53-62.

H328.11* The wooing of Seppo Ilmarinen. Plow field of snakes barefoot, sing up pool of fish, fetch chest from under sea. Finland: Bowman TALES..TUPA 73-80.

H331. Suitor contests: bride offered as prize.

H331.1.1. Suitor contest: riding up glass mountain. Type 530. SEE ALSO: F751; R222.

A* Meadow is cropped every St. John's Eve (H1471). Three sons guard. Youngest catches horse carrying brass armour grazing. He tames by throwing steel from tinderbox over horse's back. Second year - horse with silver armour. Third - golden. Suitor task: carrying off three golden apples from lap of princess on glass mountain. Hero competes thrice on his three horses, winning apples. All men in kingdom to appear before king in search for hero. Hero is rewarded (R222). Norway: Arbuthnot ANTHOLOGY 240-243; Arbuthnot FAIRY 80-84; Asbjornsen EAST (Macmillan) 30-44; Asbjornsen EAST (Row) 101-111; Aulaire EAST 45-57; Colwell SECOND 115-121; Haviland FAVORITE.. NORWAY 80-84; Hutchinson CHIMNEY..FAIRY 89-104; Lang BLUE 340-350 /Lang FIFTY 220-230/, /Association TOLD..GREEN 122-138/, /Fenner PRINCESS 115-127/; Wiggin FAIRY 69-79. Brazil: Frost LEGEND 273-277 (to take carnation from her hair). Slovenia: Kavcic GOLD 113 (to catch ring tossed from windows, in war wound bound with king's scarf, recognized. behead three horses = three kings, R222.1).

B* Three sons to guard father's grave (H1460). Eldest sends youngest to perform task. Father appears and gives token nightly. Silver whistle - blow and silver horse with silver trappings appears. Second night - gold. Third - diamond. He rides up glass hill thrice and removes ring from finger of princess. Token discovered in search for hero. Latvia: Durham TIT 48-55.

C* Suitor task: reaching princess in castle on top of glass mountain. Seven years pass and many knights fall to death. Golden knight almost succeeds but eagle causes to fall. Hero on foot fastens lynx claws to feet. Eagle carries him off. He cuts off eagle's feet when over castle and falls by magic apple tree. Apple peel heals wounds of eagle's claws. Apple thrown to guardian dragon and dragon vanishes. Weds princess. Dead eagle's blood restores dead knights on mountain. Poland: Lang YELLOW 130-135.

D* Little son releases caged dwarf (G671) to retrieve golden ball. He is to be killed, boar's head taken instead. Grows up as herdsman. Princess on glass mountain. Suitor task. Dwarf appears with horse and armour of steel, silver, gold. He competes thrice, gains apple. Princess to chose among assembled men. Recognizes him in shepherd's hood. SEE ALSO: G671A (The Wild Man). Sweden: Baker TALKING 88-103; Kaplan FAIRY 35-37.

E* Suitor Contest. To run up hill without

without stopping. Ragged man reached girl on top. Changes to fine clothes once home. E. Africa: Tracy LION 83-87.

F* Suitor contest: Leaping high enough to kiss princess. Fairy gives youngest brother three horses. Weds (R222.1). Gypsy: Manning-Sanders RED 132-138.

H331.1.2.2* Suitor contest: snatching necklace from princess in high window. Three princes to guard devastated tree. Has red, green and blue branches. Youngest catches red horse. Glues red branch, blue, green. Given three hairs to burn in need. Suitor task: Snatching necklace from high window. Hero succeeds thrice. Puts tripe on head and feigns baldness (K1818.2). Princess to hit with apple her intended, hits him (H316). King disowns. +R222. Arabia: Mittleman BIRD 82-98.

H331.1.2.3* Youngest guards grave of father. Given three steeds. Captures portrait and kerchief of princess from high wall. She gives three balls and identifies by wiping of mouth in handkerchief. Russia: Whitney IN 97-104.

H331.1.2.3.1* Youngest guards grave of father. Given chestnut gray steed. Climbs in one ear and out the other and emerges in finery. Leaps high as princess's tower and she plants seal on forehead. Identified and wed. Russia: Riordan TALES..CENTRAL 184-189.

H331.4.3* Suitor contest: shooting birds. Pikoi takes aim in calabash of water. Hawaii: Cothran MAGIC 27-30.

H331.9.1* Suitor test: catching five pigeons in basket, really are daughters. England: Hampden GYPSY 59-64.

H331.10.1* Suitor contest: carrying bowl of laban on head while climbing palm. Not to spill one drop. Syria (Gypsy): Hampden GYPSIES' 111-112.

H331.18* Suitor contest: Suitor must count to ten before spear he hurls reaches ground. Small antelope counts five, ten, and wins. Liberia: Carpenter AFRICAN 47-52; Tashjian DEEP 56-60.

H335.0.2.2. Suitor task: prince to learn a trade. Rumania: Ure RUMANIAN 117-125.

H335.0.2.2.1* Suitor forced to learn trade. Becomes weaver. Kidnapped he weaves handkerchief by which queen identifies him. Is rescued. North Africa: Gilstrap SULTAN'S 51-60.

H335.7* Suitor tasks: doing the impossible.

H335.7.1* Temba wins a bride. Magic red feather advises Temba to pass dangers by approaching bravely. All vanish. Shares with ants, fish, woodborer. Tasks: ants gather seeds, fish finds necklace, woodborers gnaw tree so Temba can fell in one blow. If pot is cold, parents to know

is dead. East Africa: Arnott TEMBA 124-144.

H335.7.2* Princess Sun and Princess Moon. Tests: cook rice in no pot with no water and no wood burnt = Clay bowl with snow, straw fire. Comes with neither man nor woman, not on steps, ground, in air or water = with child on wall. Mother identification test = To pull on child. Strong, keen of eye, loved by gods, build palace in night. Sakko, king of the sky provides. India: Wyatt GOLDEN 34-44.

H335.7.3* Ducks retrieve copper paddle, Buffalo lends strength to wreck boulder. Mountain goat lends horns so can leap onto head. Ants sort beads. Shell listens to distant chief. Bird makes music. Antelope lends speed in race with fire. Wed. Native American (Thompson Indians): De Wit TALKING 161-168; Newell RESCUE 125-142. SEE ALSO: F601.2.I.

H335.7.4* The Fish with Bent Noses. Suitor Tasks. Small birds, insects, animals sent by Buddha help retrieve grains. Fishes retrieve mice. +A2335.3.4. Cambodia: Carpenter ELEPHANT'S 22-30.

H341. Suitor test: making princess laugh. Sad faced princess has never laughed. SEE ALSO: D551.1Bg; F954.2.1; H343; J2461A,C.

H341.1. Princess brought to laughter by people sticking together. SEE ALSO: D1415.2.3.5.

Aa* The Golden Goose. Youngest brother shares with old man. Shown tree with golden goose. Everyone who touches it sticks, chain is formed. Innkeeper's daughters, parson, sexton, etc. Princess sees and laughs. Weds. Germany (Grimm): Grimm GOLDEN pb (illus. Stubbs). Norway: Asbjornsen EAST (Row) 77-84; Asbjornsen NORWEGIAN 20-24; Haviland FAVORITE..NORWAY 50-64 (Old woman gives goose). Hungary: Harper GHOSTS 212-221 (Magic flute, singing donkey, and lamb with diamond star in forehead to which all stick); Manning-Sanders GLASS 22-26 (gold fleeced ram). Denmark: Hatch MORE 192-213 (Old woman gives magic sled with carved bird).

Ab* The Golden Goose and suitor tests. Bringing a man who can drink a cellarful of wine, eat a mountain of bread. Bringing a ship that sails on land and sea (D1520.15). Old man provides these. Germany (Grimm): Brooke GOLDEN pb; Grimm GRIMM'S (Follett) 122-126; Grimm GRIMM'S (Grosset) 201-207; Grimm GRIMM'S (World) 87-92; Grimm HOUSEHOLD 265-269; Haviland FAIRY 58-65; Lang RED 336-343; Martignoni ILLUSTRATED 303-306; Rackham GRIMM'S 22-28; Shubb ABOUT 47-51; Wiggin TALES 124-128.

H341.2. Princess brought to laughter by small animals. Golden Goose. Lang RED 172-177 (Swan) /Manning-Sanders BOOK..MAGICAL 114-120/.

H341.2.1* The Bee, the Harp, the Mouse and

the Bumclock. Jack trades three coins for the above. Their antics cause the princess to laugh twice. Fenner PRINCESSES 64-74; Hutchinson CHIMNEY..FAIRY 73-86 /MacManus DONEGAL /, /Haviland IRELAND 3-25/; Wiggin FAIRY 146-154.

H341.3.1. Princess brought to laughter by indecent show in quarrel with old woman at well. Italy: Mincielli OLD 3-13.

H341.3.2* Princess brought to laughter by foolish actions of hero. He shakes dog in court demanding payment in meat he "sold" dog. Denmark: Hatch THIRTEEN 37-45; Jagendorf NOODLEHEAD 147-155. Scandinavia: Hardendorff TRICKY 101-108.

H341.4* Lad has magic ring which causes sneezing. He makes king sneeze and princess laugh. Sicily: Hampden HOUSE 72-84.

H341.5* Lad tells tall tale which ends with fox opening paper saying "now princess can eat for she has laughed." SEE ALSO: X905 (Beardless man). Serbia: Fillmore LAUGHING 3-26 /Fenner TIME 85-107/, /Gruenberg MORE 215-225/.

H342. Suitor Test: outwitting princess.

H342.1. Suitor test: forcing princess to say "That is a lie" (H1045). Tells story of tall tales. Usually ends with insult to princess' father which she calls a lie. Type 852. Norway: Asbjornsen NORWEGIAN 17-19; Fenner PRINCESSES 99-102; Undset TRUE 173-175; Williams-Ellis ROUND 117-119; Withers I 86-88. Spain: Boggs THREE 111-116. Slovenia: Kavcic GOLDEN 56-59 (Task: making girl's mother say "that's a lie," +Z51.4). Denmark: Hatch THIRTEEN 139-147; Withers WORLD 90-100.

H342.2* Princess to wed one who knows language she does not know. Shepherd who understands language of animals wins. Finland: Bowman TALES..TUPA 91-95 /Fenner PRINCESSES 148-153/, /Arbuthnot ANTHOLOGY 262-263/.

H342.3* Test: forcing another to say "that's a lie." Tells string of tall tales, usually ending with insult to listener or family (X905.1). Celtic: MacManus HIBERNIAN 36-47; Wiggin TALES 55-61 (King of Munster, Jack knocked three better gentlemen out of a fox). Russia: Higonnet-Schnopper TALES 21-29 (Gentleman's father pulling manure cart in hell).

H342.4* If calls teller liar to become his slave. Fourth man tells tale saying other three are already his slaves. Burma: Courlander RIDE 42-45.

H343. Suitor test: bringing dumb princess to speak. SEE: F954.2.1, H341. East Africa: Heady WHEN 72-76 (Lad hoes up maize, she berates).

H343.3* One who gets girl down from mpafu tree to wed. Lad ignores her, feeds yams to dog and meat to goat. She berates and comes down to show him how. Congo: Burton MAGIC 107-109.

H343.4* Girl to wed lad who makes her speak. Kelfala brings her to laughter through his clowning but his two companions claim part in feat so releases her to try again later, alone. Kenya: Robinson THREE 17-31.

H346. Princess given to man who can heal her. Type 610. Elder brothers tell old woman they have frogs, sticks, etc. in basket. Fruits become thins named. Youngest is truthful, fruits are blessed with curative powers. Denmark: Hatch MORE 105-119; Haviland FAVORITE.. DENMARK 65-76 (En route he puts fish back in water, settles dispute between honey and bees. They help with tasks. Fish recovers wine from lake [H1132.1.1]. Bees build castle of wax. Rower fetches coals from troll's castle. Wed). Annam: Carpenter ELEPHANT'S 166-175 (healing mango). Spain: Sawyer PICTURE 11-24 (pears, +H1045, herding the hares). France: Picard FRENCH 198-204 (oranges, plus given whip to chase off flies, whistle to call hares [H1112], ring to force princess to wed him, performs tasks and wins princess).

H355. Suitor test: finding an extraordinary object. SEE: A240.1.1.

H355.0.1. Who will find the most marvelous thing? Each finds some marvelous thing. It turns out that to save girl's life all the things must be used together. First with telescope sees ill princess; second with flying carpet takes them there; third with healing apple restores. To whom does she belong? Type 653A. Persia: Buck FAIRY 98-124. Puerto Rico: Alegria THREE 15-24. SEE ALSO: H621.

H359. Suitor test: telling tale lasting from dawn to dusk. Nigeria: Walker NIGERIAN 57-58 (+Z11.1).

H359.3. Suitor must be unafraid to pull king's beard. King cries "Boo!" and all jump back. Private La Ramee pulls hard and startles king. Switzerland (French): Duvoisin THREE 61-66.

H359.4* Suitor test. Man who stops rain is to wed princess and become king. Tailor mends hole in sky. Poland: Borski JOLLY 15-28 /Haviland FAVORITE..POLAND 13-27/, /Bleecker BIG 17-28/.

H359.5* Suitor tests (which of the two women courted would he save if she fell into the river. Suitor to fat, rich woman--"Can you swim?"). Iran: Shah MULLAH 84.

H360. Bride test.

H363. Deceased wife marriage test. Man will marry woman meeting certain specifications prescribed by his deceased wife. SEE: R221D (catskins).

H381.1. Bride test: making dress from worsted flax. Suitor hears mistress mock maid for making dress of her leavings. He weds maid. Type 1451. German: Wiggin TALES 165; Grimm MORE..GRIMM 59-60.

H382.1. Bride test: Key in flax reveals laziness. Suitor hides key in flax on spinning wheel. Finds it there the next day. Type 1453. Denmark: Hatch THIRTEEN 73-80. Norway: Asbjornsen NORWEGIAN 128.

H383.2.4* Bride test: Maleyato will wed girl whose needle makes no sound as she sews. Eskimo: Melzack DAY 69-75.

H388. Bride test: wisdom (cleverness). Kirghiz: Ginsburg KAHA 90-96 (test: three riddles).

H389.1. Girl to find way around palace without becoming lost. Girl leaves distaff at door and unwinds thread. Type 874*. Rumania: Ure RUMANIAN 19-21.

H460. Wife test.

H461. Test of wife's patience. Griselda. Children stolen and attendance at wedding to another demanded. Type 887. France: Perrault PERRAULT'S (Dodd, Mead) 100-114.

H465. Test of wife's endurance. Haughty princess married to a beggar and must endure poverty and menial work.

A* King Thrushbeard. Princess scorns all suitors, calls or mocks for dropping seed in beard while eating. Father decrees she will wed first person to pass (T62). King Thrushbeard weds as beggar, forces to do menial labor, sell pots in market, is spurned in palace or at wedding of King Thrushbeard, reveals self (T251.2; T72.2.2). Germany (Grimm): Grimm BROTHERS 118-123; Grimm GRIMM'S (Follett) 179-189; Grimm GRIMM'S (Grosset) 27-32; Grimm GRIMM'S (World) 64-69; Grimm HOUSEHOLD 208-212; Grimm KING THRUSHBEARD (illus. Hoffman) pb; Grimm KING GRISLEY-BEARD (illus. Sendak) pb; Shubb ABOUT 91-95; Wiggin TALES 93-97; Werth KING (illus. Werth) pb. Puerto Rico: Alegria THREE 122-128 (bag of food hidden in skirt falls out and embarrasses when called in by Count; Count Crow). Portugal: Michael PORTUGUESE 146-152 (Count of Extremadura). Ireland: Sawyer WAY 319-333 /Ross BLUE 91-109/. Italy (Bologna): Hampden HOUSE 49-55.

B* Compromised Princess. Princess must compromise self in order to obtain memorable objects of rejected suitor in disguise. Wed and humiliated.

Ba* Two birds saved from hawk give magic ring which tells how to win princess. Weaves marvelous cloth, she weds to possess; hen which lays pearl eggs and hatches gold chicks. Spain:

Gunterman CASTLES 179-201.

Bb* Give kisses for golden ball, golden comb with silver mirror, music box. Made to marry. Pyle WONDER 269-278 /Adams BOOK..PRINCESSES 200-208/, /Fenner PRINCESSES 33-42/.

Bc* Grayfoot. Princess of England spurns Prince of Denmark. In guise of herdsman, he sells her golden spindle, reel, shuttle for three nights outside her door. King forces her to wed him for this. He forces her to sell pots in marketplace, etc. Uses her as model for bride's gown--reveals self. Denmark: Hatch MORE 3-21; Haviland DENMARK 44-63.

C* Queen o' the Tinkers. Princess chooses tinker to wed rather than King of Ireland. Remains true to end. Reveals self as King of Ireland. Ireland: MacManus HIBERNIAN 99-107 /MacManus WELL 83-97/, /Fenner PRINCESS 177-188/.

D* Rags and Tatters. Princess to wed one who catches rose, is water-carrier, she dreams she is in palace with relations and they point at "Rags and Tatters" (husband) on roof watching. Second time she asks relatives not to mention Rags and Tatters. She wishes him there and enchantment breaks. Enchanted until princess brought to poverty by him should love. Really King of Portugal. Sicily: Manning-Sanders BOOK..PRINCESS 118-124. Italy: Baker GOLDEN 111-118.

E* The Six Servants. Princess kept as pigherd's wife for a week before husband's true identity is revealed. +F601.2B (Six Servants). Germany (Grimm): Grimm GRIMM'S (Grosset) 280-289; Grimm GRIMM'S (World) 211-218; Wiggin TALES 184-190.

F* The Fig Tree Beggar. Lazy boy lays under fig tree until fruit drops (W115.8.3). Fig floats downstream to princess. She will wed only one who brings fruit. He is carried to her. The two are set adrift in banishment. Khotan becomes a hard working farmer. Gods reward with magic gong. He strikes and receives fine clothing, fine figure, beauty, servants, musicians, wisdom. Return to rule. Laos: Wolkstein LAZY 30-43.

H466.1.1* Feigned absence to test wife's faithfulness. Squire Robert of Flanders accepts bet with Raoul of Hainaut that wife will be unfaithful during his absence on pilgrimage. Wife accompanies him disguised as a page and serves seven years, proving fidelity. France: Frost LEGEND 230-239.

H495. Mother test.

H495.4* Baby camel cries and mother runs to suckle it. Judge rules it belongs to owner of this mother camel. Russia: Masey STORIES 12-15.

H500 - H899. Tests of cleverness.

H501.4* Test of wisdom. Ananse fulfills task: bring kingdom to Nyame with one grain of corn. West Africa: Appiah ANANSE 1-26.

H501.5* Test of wisdom. Accused asks each of judges to write definition of bread. All give different answer. When they can agree on a simple thing like that, then they may judge him. Iran: Shah MULLAH 50.

H504. Test of skillfulness in handiwork.

H504.1.4* Painter's apprentice scolded for losing fish from bucket, paints fish on stairs, and master thinks is real fish. Italy (Siena): Jagendorf PRICELESS 15-24.

H504.3* Contests in rapid painting. To paint dragon during drum rolls. Dips fingers in ink and makes ten earthworms (earth dragons). Vietnam: Vo-Dinh TOAD 137-141.

H504.4* Skill in painting. King goes to collect painting of cock commissioned one year ago. Artist paints it in five minutes. Practiced one year to become so skilled. China: Chang TALES 45-46.

H506.1. Test of resourcefulness: weighing elephant, man puts him on boat, marks waterline, fills boat with stones until it sinks to same line, weighs stones. China: Alexander PEBBLES 11; Lu CHINESE 11-19.

H506.3. Test of resourcefulness: carrying wolf, goat and cabbage across stream. Leach NOODLES 59.

H506.4. Test of resourcefulness: putting thread through coils of snail shell. Thread tied to ant who pulls it through. Japan: Uchida SEA 61-71 (+J151.1, passing through curved hole in log).

H506.10. Test of resourcefulness: to find relationships among three sticks; they are put in vessel of water; degree of sinking shows what part of tree each comes from. SEE: L425.

H506.11.1* Test of resourcefulness: to discover how old, respectively, three horses are. Fed oats, hay, grass. Oldest eats oats, etc. SEE: L425.

H506.12. Test: bring wind in paper and fire in paper. Daughter-in-law buys fan and paper lantern (H583.4.7). China: Gruenberg FAVORITE 349-352; Lin MILKY 72-75; Tashjian DEEP 64-69; Wiggin TALES 407-411; Wiggin FAIRY 259-264; Wyndham TALES..CHINA 25-33.

H506.13* Maharaja of India sends three golden dolls to Khan of Mongolia. To determine which is worthless, which is precious. Prisoner solves --runs straw into hole in ear of each. One comes out mouth--tells all. Second comes out ear--remembers nothing. Third--into stomach. Guards all knowledge, prized. Mongolia: Bulatkin EURASIAN 71-74.

H507. Wit combat. Test in repartee.

H507.1.0.1. Princess defeated in repartee by means of objects accidentally picked up. Hero: What red lips you have! Princess: There is a fire inside. Hero: Then boil this egg. Boots produces magpie, willow twig, broken saucer, crooked horns, wedge, bootlace, boot sole with witty repartee. Weds. SEE ALSO: Z11.5. Norway: Adams BOOK..PRINCESS 215-223; Arbuthnot ANTHOLOGY 247-248; Asbjornsen EAST (Row) 119-123; Asbjornsen NORWEGIAN 77-80; Dobbs ONCE 110-117; Hutchinson CANDLELIGHT 125-122.

H507.1.0.1.1* Dead crow, old shoe, mud. Ends by flinging mud on princess. So mad can't speak! Lang YELLOW 324-329 /Lang FIFTY 9-13/. Denmark: Hatch MORE 49-57.

H507.1.0.1.2* Egg, crooked stick, nut. Questions answered by means of objects picked up. In ordeal to watch all night (H1473) he dozes, says was fishing and shows fish picked up. England: Jacobs MORE 229-232.

H507.2.1* Test: making the king say "Enough, no more" to storyteller. He tells endless tale (Z11.1). Ethiopia: Courlander FIRE 99-102.

H507.7. The false knight. Boy and knight converse. Lad's comments always get the better of knight. England: Williams-Ellis FAIRY..BRITISH 88.

H509.5. Test: telling skillful lie. SEE: X905 (lying contests).

H509.5.1. Test: telling five lies which so closely resemble the truth that the tester will believe them himself. Ceylon: Tooze WONDERFUL 121-124.

H509.5.2* Suitor test: telling one hundred lies. Tells 99 lies. "I told one hundred lies." Wrong. Right since last statement was one hundredth. Karakalpak: Ginsburg KAHA 151-159.

H509.5.3* Task: telling long string of lies. Lad wins. Portugal: Lowe LITTLE 72-74. Kazakh: Deutsch MORE 55-64.

H509.5.4. Suitor test: telling a story tsar has never heard. Courtiers plot to swear they have heard this before. He tells tall tale ending that tsar owes him trunkful of gold. He receives the gold. Russia: Bulatkin EURASIAN 75-79.

H510. Tests in guessing.

H511.1. Princess offered to correct guesser. Type 621. Three caskets. Princess offered to man who chooses correctly from three caskets.

H522.1.1. Test: guessing nature of certain skin (louse-skin). Louse (flea) is fattened and its

skin made into coat (drum, etc.). Type 621.
SEE ALSO: F601.2H. Puerto Rico: Withers
WORLD 67-68 (louse skin drum, mouse befriend-
ed tells, weds princess).

H522.1.1.0.1* Tambourine of flea skin; boy befriends ant, beetle, and rat en route to palace,
ant identifies skin, rat gnaws hole in pouch so
takes endless gold to fill it. Spain: Sawyer
PICTURE 37-52 /Haviland FAVORITE..SPAIN
5-17/, /Ross BURIED 53-54/, /Bleecker BIG 101-
109/.

H522.1.1.1* Task: guessing material of slippers
made from gigantic pet caterpillar. Demon knows
and claims princess. Billy Goat carries her as
she flees Demon. Throws comb = toad, shoe =
mountain, tinderbox from goat's ear = flowing
river, stick = bridge for them. Demon falls into
river (D672). She kisses demon and he turns to
prince. Manning-Sanders BOOK..PRINCES 28-
39 /Manning-Sanders CHOICE/.

H522.1.1.2* Princess to one who guesses origin of
hide (flea). Devil guesses and takes her. Bulgaria: Spicer THIRTEEN DEVILS 53-62
(+F660.1Cc). Greece: Neufeld BEWARE 42-51
(+F954.2.1.1, mosquito).

H523. Test: guessing nature of devil's possessions. Type 812. SEE: M211.7.1.

H524. Test: guessing person's thoughts.

H524.2* "What am I thinking?" "That you will
trick me." Germany: Edmonds TRICKSTER 45-
50 (Tyl Eulenspigel).

H525. Test: guessing princess's birthmarks.
D1415.2.6.1.

H529. Tests in guessing--miscellaneous.

H529.1* Prize to one who can dance the "Kokioko",
a secret dance the king has made up. Malice
spies on king dancing and teaches to Bouki.
Bouki wins, then Malice has him do new dance.
"If you have no sense put your sack on the
ground." M. steals. Haiti: Wolkstein MAGIC
79-86.

H540. Propounding of riddles.

H540.2.1. Queen of Sheba propounds riddle to
Solomon. (cf. D1711.1.1).

H540.2.1.1. Queen of Sheba proposes riddle to
Solomon. "Which flower is real?" Bee alights on
real. Jewish: Dobbs MORE 19-23; Hardendorff
JUST 150-158. Ancient Israel: Gruenberg
FAVORITE 357-359.

H541. Riddle propounded with penalty for failure.

H541.1.1. Sphinx propounds riddle on pain of
death. SEE: H761.

H541.1.2* Chief kills all who cannot answer riddle.
Lad answers, I found answer in my "head."

They are to feed the chief's "body" to the lions.
"Head" and "body" were answer (N688). Hawaii:
HAWAIIAN..TRICKSTER 72-79.

H541.4* Four sons of woodcutter unable to answer
riddles and turned to stars. Father answers all
four riddles and is rewarded. Pakistan: Courlander RIDE 53-58.

H542. Death sentence escaped by propounding
riddle king (judge) cannot solve. Mexico: Brenner BOY 59-64 /Bleecker BIG 93-98/ (princess
suggests this, he weds her.) U.S. (Ozarks):
Leach NOODLES 47-48 (mother saves seven
sons).

H543. Escape from devil by answering his riddles.
Netherlands (Friesland): Spicer THIRTEEN
DEVILS 25-32. Armenia: Tashjian ONCE 41-49
(demon).

H548. Riddle contests. Hawaii: Thompson HA-
WAIIAN..TRICKSTER 86-99, 54-65.

H551. Princess offered to man who can out-riddle
her. SEE ALSO: H507.1.0.1 (princess defeated
in repartee). Leach NOODLES 50-53.

H551.0.1* Princess offered to man who can out-
riddle her. On way youth sees something which
suggests riddle to him. She visits youth in
night and obtains riddle but leaves token. By
token he weds her. Puerto Rico: Alegria
THREE 115-121 (H802). Germany (Grimm):
Lang GREEN 293-297 /Lang FIFTY 241-244/.
Gypsy: Manning-Sanders RED 62-65.

H561. Man marries girl who guesses his riddle.

H561.1. Clever peasant girl asked riddles by
king. Type 875. Girl replies to king in enigmas,
answers his riddles (H630-H659), and/or performs paradoxical tasks (H1050). Weds king,
never to interfere in his rule. He rules that a
colt is born to a wagon. She tells plaintiff to
fish in road--as likely as...(J1191.1). King
exiles her, may take most precious possession,
takes king (J1545.4). SEE ALSO: H583. Estonia: Maas MOON 116-122 (weds). Kirghiz:
Ginsburg KAHA 90-96. Leach NOODLES 49.
Greek: Wilson GREEK 24-27. Europe: Jacobs
EUROPEAN 188-193. Russia: Lurie CLEVER 9-
16.

H561.1.1. Conflict between peasant and nobleman
decided so that each must answer riddles; peas-
ant's daughter solves them. +H1050. Estonia:
Maas MOON 116-172; McNeil DOUBLE 50-55.
Rumania: Ure RUMANIAN 131-143. Poland:
Wojciechowska WINTER 22-31. Czechoslovakia:
Fillmore SHEPHERD'S 144-152 (weds burgomas-
ter) /Minard WOMENFOLK 146-155/, /Arbuth-
not ANTHOLOGY 280-282/. Egypt: Carpenter
AFRICAN 21-30 (+H1053.2; H1054). Russia:
Lurie CLEVER 9-16.

H561.1.1.2* Clever peasant girl asked riddles by
king. Counter riddles plus tricks. Final formula: he--how many leaves has your plant?

(H7205.3). She--How many stars in heaven (H702.3). He--how many kisses did you give the candy peddler (king in disguise)? She--better to kiss a candy peddler than a donkey's tail (K1288.1). (cf. H1045). Puerto Rico: Belpre TIGER 89-94. Chile: Carpenter SOUTH 83-92.

H561.1.2. Found mortar taken to king reveals peasant girl's wisdom. Peasant finds mortar in field and against his daughter's advice takes to the king who demands the pestle as well. Peasant laments that he has not followed daughter's advice. King summons her. Wales: Pugh TALES 105-115.

H561.2. King and abbot. King propounds three riddles for abbot to answer on pain of death. Herdsman disguises as abbot and answers questions. King asks "What am I thinking?" Herdsman, "that I am an abbot" (H524.2). United Kingdom: Courlander RIDE 189-193. Majorca: Mehdevi BUNGLING 109-117 (gardener, rewarded with weight in gold). Norway: Asbjornsen EAST (Row) 133-134; Asbjornsen NORWEGIAN 15-16; Undset TRUE 233-234. Russia: Daniels FALCON 71-74 (cook, prior). Slovenia: Kavcic GOLDEN 25-31 /Greene CLEVER 101-107/. Netherlands: De Leeuw LEGENDS 15-20 (Charles V). England: Jacobs MORE 159-162 (Abbot of Canterbury, King John). Italy: Vittorini OLD 45-49 (H524.2; miller, Milan).

H561.4. King and clever youth. King asks questions. Youth returns riddling answers. Rewarded. German: Edmonds TRICKSTERS 45-50 (Tyl Eulenspiegel); Grimm MORE 47-49; Hardendorff JUST 40-41; Rockwell OLD 82-87; Wiggin TALES 160-161.

H561.4.1* King asks riddles of nobles. 1. What season best? 2. What time of day is best? 3. What part of hour best? Shepherd answers in return for silver, gold and rings. This season best for he became rich, this hour best for he came face to face with king, this moment best for saved three nobles from beheading. Armenia: Tashjian THREE 8-15.

H561.6.1. King and peasant. The plucked fowl. The king gives riddling questions to a peasant who always interprets them right. The king says that he will send the peasant a fowl which he shall pluck. The king gives the same questions to his courtiers who cannot interpret them. They pay the peasant good money for the answers. Peasant tells king that he has plucked the fowl. SEE ALSO: H585.1 (four coins). Poland: Courlander RIDE 142-144; Ish-Kishor WISE 160-170 (which is more seven or five = summer better than winter; thirty-two better = teeth; house burned down twice = two daughters wed). Rumania: Ure RUMANIAN 147-152 (fleeces rams +H585.2.1; Will harvest the food? If three galleons come full = summer months full of rain). Portugal: Lowe LITTLE 52-59 (snow on the mountains = grey hair; did your house burn down = daughter's wed).

H561.6.2. Peasant forbidden to give solution to enigmatic statements to tsar's advisers unless in tsar's presence. Tells to tsar's adviser's anyway. Says was in tsar's presence--face on rubles. Russia: Hardendorff JUST 159-161. Italy: Dobbs ONCE 34-37 (+J1161.7).

H580. Enigmatic statements. Apparently senseless remarks (or acts) interpreted figuratively prove wise.

H582.1.1. The full moon and the thirtieth of the month. Prince sends servant to clever girl with a round tart, thirty cakes, and a capon and asks her if it is full moon and the thirtieth of the month and the cock has crowed in the evening. She replies that it is not full moon, that it is the fifteenth of the month, and that capon has gone to the mill, but that the prince should spare the pheasant for the partridge's sake. She thus shows him that the servant has stolen half the tart, half of the cakes, and the capon. +H561.1. India: Jacobs INDIAN 225-234; Jacobs EUROPEAN 188-193. Greece: Leach NOODLES 49; Wilson GREEK 24-27.

H583. Clever youth (maiden) answers king's inquiry in riddles. SEE: H561.1.

H583.2.2. King: what is your father doing? Youth: makes many out of few (sows grains). Leach NOODLES 57.

H582.2.3. King: what is your father doing? Youth: makes better from good. (Hedges his field). Estonia: Maas MOON 116-122 (grinding grain).

H583.2.3.1* King: what is your father doing? Youth: makes better from good (grinds grain into flour). Estonia: McNeil DOUBLE 50-55.

H583.2.6* What is your father doing? He is cutting live trees and planting dead ones (cutting bamboo to make fences). Vietnam: Vo-Dinh TOAD 99-104.

H583.3. King: what is your brother doing? Youth: he hunts, he throws away what he catches and what he does not catch, he carries with him (hunts for lice on his body). Estonia: Maas MOON 116-122 (mother, fleas); McNeil DOUBLE 50-55 (mother, fleas on dog).

H583.3.2. King: what is your brother doing? Youth: he sits between heaven and earth (in a tree). Estonia: Maas MOON 116-122; McNeil DOUBLE 50-55.

H583.3.3* What is your brother doing? He ventures one hundred rubles in hopes of gaining five rubles. Chases hare on expensive horse. Russia: Bulatkin EURASIAN 27-38.

H583.4.2. King: what is your mother doing? Youth: she is baking the bread we ate last week (to pay back borrowed bread).

H583.4.2.1* Boy: my parents are gathering yesterday's food in fields. (Taking wool left in briars by sheep to pay for yesterday's meal.) Puerto Rico: Belpre TIGER 63-66.

H583.4.2.2* Parents have gone to exchange their sorrows. To wake others, in time their wake will be held. Russia: Bulatkin EURASIAN 17-38.

H583.4.7. What is your mother doing? She is selling the wind to buy the moon. (Selling fans and buying oil for lamps.) Vietnam: Vo-Dinh TOAD 99-104. SEE ALSO: H506.12.

H583.5.1* King: what is your sister doing? Turning her back to the wind (burning rubbish). Estonia: Maas MOON 116-122.

H583.6. King: what are you doing? Youth: I boil those which come and go. (Beans which keep rising and falling in water.) Type 875, 921. Puerto Rico: Belpre TIGER 63-66 (picking up the ones which have risen and waiting for the ones which are to rise--boy to youth).

H583.8. Maiden (to King): The house has neither eyes nor ears. (No child at window nor dog in yard to announce king's approach: he therefore finds her not dressed to receive him.) Leach NOODLES 55. Russia: Bulatkin EURASIAN 27-38.

H585.1. The four coins (Focus). King: what do you do with the four coins you earn? Peasant: First I eat (feeds self); second I put out at interest (give my children); third I give back (pay debts); fourth throw away (give my wife). (cf. W11.3). SEE: H561.6.1 (plucked fowl). Italy: Dobbs ONCE 34-37 (+H561..6.1)

H585.1.1* Woodcutter to king: first part of savings I invest (give to poor); second give to creditors (parents); third throw away (wine and gambling); fourth give to enemy (wife). King doubts that wife is enemy. Offers gold to solver of riddles. Woodcutter to be imprisoned if he tells answer. His wife extracts answer from him and tells it. He points out that wife is enemy and is freed. Thailand: Brockett BURMESE 31-38. Russia: Hardendorff JUST 159-161 (twenty rubles for tax, twenty for debts = father, twenty loans = son, twenty thrown out window = daughter); Wyndham TALES..RUSSIA 33-37.

H585.2. King: Why did you not do it (marry so that sons could help you?). Peasant: I did, but it was not God's will (I married three times, but it was not God's will to give me sons).

H585.2.1* Why didn't you rise up early? I did but Lord did not allow me (had children but died). Rumania: Ure RUMANIAN 147-152. Poland: Courlander RIDE 142-144.

H585.3. Wife draws picture on board telling tale of injustice, hangs on husband's back and sends to king. Peasant shares lunch with hunter

(king) in wood and explains board. King's twelve ministers are unable to interpret. Poland: Zajdler POLISH 103-108.

H586. Riddling remarks of traveling companion interpreted by girl (man) at end of journey. SEE ALSO: W181.2 (Gobborn Seer). India: Jacobs INDIAN 225-234; Wiggin TALES 263-268.

H586.3. One traveler to another: Let us carry each other and shorten the way. (Let us tell tales and amuse ourselves on the way.) SEE ALSO: W181.2 (Gobborn Seer). India: Jacobs INDIAN 225-234; Wiggin TALES 263-268.

H586.4. One traveler to another: that field (uncut) is already harvested. (Belongs to spendthrift who has already spent the money.) India: Jacobs INDIAN 224-234; Wiggin TALES 263-268.

H586.8.1* Asks companion to take knife and get two horses (walking sticks) with it. India: Jacobs INDIAN 225-234; Wiggin TALES 263-268.

H588.7. Father's counsel: find treasure within a foot of the ground. (Sons dig everywhere and thus loosen soil of vineyard which becomes fruitful.) Aesop: Aesop AESOP'S (Grosset) 120-121; Aesop AESOP'S (Watts) 45; Leach LUCK 69-70; Reeves AESOP'S 108-109.

H588.7.1* Son left bag of 'gold' on condition he bury it. Bag contains rice. Son obeys and prospers. Burma: Courlander TIGER'S 19-32.

H588.7.2* Father-in-law says secret of alchemy demands two pounds of down from banana leaves grown by self. Plantation itself turns to gold. Thailand: Brockett BURMESE 177-185.

H588.7.3* Fox tells lazy boy he has a hidden treasure left by Jungies for boy in field. Boy digs up fields and mother plants corn. Native American (Seneca): Parker SKUNNY 52-59.

H588.7.4* Father left magic formula for "TIM" charm for wealth and happiness. Clear plot of bush 10,000 square feet and keep all sweat in calabash. Now strong and wealthy, he weds princess. Realizes value of work and continues to labor though wed to princess. Upper Volta: Guirma TALES 100-113.

H598.7.5* Instructions: shake dust from magic box on corners of fields each day. Thus overseen farm prospers. Italy: Sawyer WAY 219-225.

H591.4. Extraordinary actions explained. Wise man pours water into bowl with eyes only on top of jar--says he'll look at the bottom when he is interested in it. He wants to see the water reach the top. Interpretation: a pupil must be ready to accept learning before he can be filled with knowledge. Iran: Shah MULLAH 54.

H592.1. "Love like salt." Girl compares her love for her father to salt. Experience teaches him the value of salt. SEE: H71.8.1. Spain: Edmonds TRICKSTER 91-98 (uncle).

H592.1.0.1* Youngest daughter "loves father like salt" is banished. Weds a prince and invites father to feast without revealing her identity. Serves food without salt. Rumania: Ure RUMANIAN 74-83. Sweden: Courlander RIDE 163-165; Lang GREEN 178-182. Greece: Haviland FAVORITE..GREECE 21-27. Greece (Thrace): Neufeld BEWARE 28-35. U.S. (Appalachia): Chase GRANDFATHER 124-129 (banished daughter finds king wandering mad and takes him in).

H599. Other enigmatic statements.

H599.3. Clever flatterer: Sir, you are a full moon, and my sovereign is a new moon (the full moon will decline but the new moon has but started its growth). Iran: Shah MULLAH 43.

H599.7* Teacher mounts ass backward to lead students through village. Why? If they go in front it is disrespectful to him. If he rides in front with his back to them it is disrespectful to them. Iran: Shah MULLAH 82. Turkey: Downing HODJA 65.

H599.8* Sent to study historical wisdom of Eastern mystical teachers, wise man submits one word summary of findings--"Carrots." Explanation: The best part is buried, few except the farmer know about it, if you don't work it will deteriorate, many donkeys are associated with it. Iran: Shah MULLAH 127.

H599.10* Wise man admonishes rich man who has servants throw stones over wall into road. "Don't throw stones from not yours to yours." Later rich man becomes impoverished, bumps feet on stones in road. Israel: Courlander RIDE 99-100.

H599.11* The Mourner Who Sang and the Nun Who Danced. King discovers enigmatical meanings of old man weeping, nun dancing, and mourner singing. Sets exam on this topic so that poor scholar who explained all this to him in chance meeting can pass exam. Korea: Carpenter KOREAN 143-147.

H600. Symbolic Interpretations.

H601. Wise carving of the fowl. Clever person divides it symbolically: head to head of house, neck to wife, wings to daughters, legs to sons, keeps rest for himself. +H601.0.1. Russia (Yiddish): Ginsburg THREE ROLLS 8-11. Russia: Bulatkin EURASIAN 125-128; Daniels FALCON 78-80; Dolch STORIES..OLD RUSSIA 45-51-59; Wyndham TALES..RUSSIA 16-21. Poland: Borski GOOD 1-2. Italy: Toor GOLDEN 41-46 (Prince as host divides; peasant's daughter explains, +J1191, J1545.4). Iran: Kelsey MULLAH 38.

H601.0.1. Rich neighbor attempts H601 with five geese and fails. First peasant called back to divide geese: gives one to lord and lady = "now you are three", one to two sons = three, one to two daughters = three, keeps two for self = three. He is rewarded, rich man punished. (cf. J2415). Russia (Yiddish): Bulatkin EURASIAN 125-128; Daniels FALCON 78-80; Dolch STORIES..OLD RUSSIA 45-51-59; Ginsburg THREE ROLLS 8-11; Wyndham TALES..RUSSIA 16-21. Poland: Borski GOOD 1-2.

H602.3.1* A million men must be buried to ensure invincibility of Great Wall being built. Man named 'Million' is sacrificed. China: Manton FLYING 53-59.

H607.1.1* Discussion by symbols. Sign language. Sufi mystic meets Mulla and points at sky to say "there is one truth which covers all." The Mulla takes out a rope. His companion thinks the Mulla means to tie up the mad Sufi. The Sufi takes it to mean "ordinary humanity tries to find truth by methods as unsuitable as attempting to climb into sky with a rope." Iran: Shah MULLAH 149. SEE ALSO: J1804.1 (Conversation by sign language mutually misunderstood).

H607.2.1. Learned professor from one university examines by signs a professor at another university. (Actually shoemaker or the like.) Ireland: MacManus HIBERNIAN 224-232 (One-eyed fool opponent, one finger meaning one God interpreted as insult to One Eye. Threatened with fist, interpreted as Trinity, etc.). Russia (Georgia): Papashvily YES 61-64 (Feargal the the scholar).

H607.3.1* Princess declares her love through sign language. Three princes, hand turned three times, points at mirror. Lives in third court, come on fifteenth when moon full. He elopes with her, aided by master swordsman, Molo. China: Baker TALKING 251-255.

H620. The unsolved problem: enigmatic ending of tale.

H621. Skillful companions create a woman. To whom does she belong? Woodcarver carves a doll, tailor clothes her, gardener gives her speech (or the like). Greece: Wilson GREECE 58-64 (last prays to God to give her life). (cf. H355.0.1). Russia: Black WOMAN pb. Poland: Borski GOOD (+N141.0.1). Czechoslovakia: Bulatkin EURASIAN (+N141.0.1). Latvia: Huggins BLUE 65-73 (man).

H621.1. Skillful companions resuscitate girl. To whom does she belong? Greece: Neufield BEWARE 42-51 (+F954.2.1, first sees her in magic mirror, second takes her on magic carpet, third revives--apple of life). Ghana (Ashanti): Courlander KING'S 28-31 (magic mirror, hammock, ability to revive dead) /Tashjian DEEP 70-74/.

H621.1.1* Triplets of Tunis, first has crystal box telling news of world, learns she died; second can revive with magic medicine; third has flying carpet. She turns out to be ugly behind veil, so all three settle for a camel as a reward. North Africa: Holding KING'S 28-38.

H621.2. Girl rescued by skillful companions. To whom does she belong? Type 653. SEE ALSO: F954.2.1 (Silent princess speaks); F660.1 (Brothers acquire extraordinary skill); H355.0.1 (most marvelous thing).

H621.2.1* Artist finds baby, tailor dresses, teacher teaches to speak. Denmark: Hatch THIRTEEN 46-57.

H621.2.2* First suitor plays harp, charms crocodile, second shoots, third saves drowning girl. Ethiopia (Somali): Davis LION'S 179-184.

H621.2.3* Brother with far-seeing spectacles sees princess on dragon's isle, thief steals her, marksman shoots dragon, coppersmith mends boat needed in flight. King awards her to coppersmith. Spain: Haviland FAVORITE..SPAIN 18-35.

H621.2.4* Four clever brothers (F660.1A), astronomer sees, thief steals, marksman kills dragon, tailor repairs boat. Germany (Grimm): Grimm FOUR pb; Grimm GRIMM'S (Grosset) 307-312; Grimm GRIMM'S (Scribner's) 236-241; Grimm GRIMM'S (World) 125-129.

H621.2.5* Devil guesses princess's secret of mosquito skin and carries her off. Three rescue. First can run fast--carries. Second can move quietly--claps devil into wine jug. Devil escapes and third, good catcher, shoots devil and catches princess as she falls. Greece: Neufield BEWARE 42-51.

H621.2.6* Wise man discovers where princess is, magician takes to abducting dragon, hero slays. Judge awards her to hero. India: McNeil DOUBLE 57-61.

H621.3* Mongoose (weasel) gives benefactor magic ring. It is stolen and cat retrieves. Another thief appears and threatens master's life, dog chases thief off. Which animal deserves first place in household? Princess Learned-in-Law settles case. Dog is first for he saved master's life. +A2545.3. SEE ALSO: D882.1.1. Burma: Brockett BURMESE 51-63; Carpenter ELEPHANT'S 114-124; Carpenter WONDER.. CATS 52-63.

H621.4. Four skillful brothers (F660.1) resuscitate father. One arranges bones, one covers bones with flesh, one adds blood, one gives power of speech. Which deserves cowtail switch award? Liberia: Courlander COW-TAIL 5-12.

H621.4.1* Six skillful brothers save father Anansi's life. See Trouble, Road Builder, River Drinker, Game Skinner, Stone Thrower, Cushion. Anansi wants to give moon to most deserving. Gives to Nyame to hold while he decides and Nyame puts moon in sky (A740). Ashanti: Courlander HAT 59-62; McDermott ANANSI pb.

H621.4.2* The honey gatherer's three sons. One hears fall, one follows trail and puts back together. Repeat. Argues as to who is most important and all refuse to help on third day. Father dies. Burton MAGIC 39-41 /Arbuthnot ANTHOLOGY 325/.

H630. Riddles of the superlative.

H631.3. What is strongest? Earth. Jacobs EUROPEAN 188-193.

H632.1. What is swiftest? Thought. Czechoslovakia: Fillmore SHEPHERD'S 144-152. Rumania: Ure RUMANIAN 131-143. Leach NOODLES 57.

H633. Riddle: what is sweetest? Poland: Wojciechowska WINTER 22-31 (love).

H633.1. What is sweetest? Sleep. Czechoslovakia: Fillmore SHEPHERD'S 144-152.

H636.1. What is richest? Autumn. Jacobs EUROPEAN 188-193 (Harvest).

H636.2* What is richest? Earth. Czechoslovakia: Fillmore SHEPHERD'S 144-152. Rumania: Ure RUMANIAN 131-143.

H641.1. What is most beautiful? The spring. Jacobs EUROPEAN 188-193.

H643.1. What is deepest? The heart of man. Leach NOODLES 57.

H646.1. What is greenest? The month of May. Leach NOODLES 57.

H648.1. What is best? Food. Rumania: Ure RUMANIAN 131-143 (goodness of food).

H648.3* Riddle: What is most precious thing in the world? Virtue. Poland: Wojciechowska WINTER 22-31.

H653.2. What is the fattest? A good deed. Poland: Wojciechowska WINTER 22-31.

H659.27* What is heard at greatest distance. Thunder and a lie. Serbia: Spicer LONG 145-158.

H659.28* What is the most precious thing in the world? Sorcerer can be vanquished only by buying most precious thing in world. Wanderer brings out salt to eat lunch, and castle with sorcerer vanishes. Wales: Pugh TALES 135-143.

H659.29* Count wanting to wed must tell girl what is "food of all foods", "spice of all spices", "honey of all honeys." Shepherd tells = bread, salt, May honey. Majorca: Mehdevi BUNGLING 7-16.

H660. Riddles of comparison.

H675. Which is most useful--the sun or the moon? The sun shines in daytime when there is already light, therefore the moon is most useful. Turkey: Downing HODJA 65. Turkestan, W. China: Jablow MAN 75.

H680. Riddles of distance.

H681.1.1. How far is it from one end of the earth to the other? A day's journey since the sun makes it daily. Type 922. Norway: Asbjornsen EAST (Row) 133-134; Asbjornsen NORWEGIAN 15-16; Undset TRUE 233-234. United Kingdom: Courlander RIDE 189-193. Kirghiz: Ginsburg KAHA 90-96. England: Jacobs MORE 159-162; Leach NOODLES 50-53.

H681.3.1. Where is the center of the earth? Here; if you don't believe it, measure it yourself (under hoof of donkey). Turkey: Downing HODJA 40-41; Kelsey HODJA 100-107. England: Jacobs MORE 159-162. Majorca: Mehdevi BUNGLING 109-117 (under throne).

H681.4.1. How deep is the sea? A stone's throw. SEE ALSO: H696.1.1. How much water in the sea? Leach NOODLES 50-53; Netherlands: De Leeuw LEGENDS 15-20.

H682.1.1. How far is it from earth to heaven? A day's journey since Christ went to heaven in one day (a half-day's journey, similar reason). Told thief "Today you shall be with me in paradise." Estonia: Maas MOON 116-122; McNeil DOUBLE 50-55. Slovenia: Kavcic GOLDEN 25-21 /Green CLEVER 101-107/.

H682.1.3. How far is it from earth to heaven? So and so high, if you don't believe measure it yourself. Italy: Vittorini OLD 45-49.

H682.1.4.1* Old man asks boy which is farther, sun or Ch'ang An. Sun, since he can see it. Next day old man takes him to town to show off wisdom. Child says Ch'ang An is nearer, changed mind when he saw all the people in town from Ch'ang An. China (Six Dynasties): Kendall SWEET 21-22.

H682.1.7. How far is it to heaven? A cat's (fox's) tail, if it were long enough. Netherlands: De Leeuw LEGENDS 15-20.

H682.1.9. How far is it to Heaven? One step for Jesus, He stands with one foot on the ground and one in Heaven. Leach NOODLES 50-53; Spicer THIRTEEN DEVILS 25-32.

H685.2* How far is it from truth to falsehood? Four fingers distance between eye and ear. Russia (Kirghiz): Ginsburg KAHA 90-96.

H690. Riddles of weight and measure.

H691.1.1. How much does the moon weigh? A pound for it has four quarters. Type 922. Estonia: Maas MOON 116-122 (How long is

moon? Four quarters).

H696.1.1. How much water is in the sea? Stop all the rivers and I will measure it. SEE ALSO: H681.4.1 (How deep is the sea?). German: De La Mare ANIMAL 107-109; Grimm MORE 47-49; Hardendorff JUST 40-41; Rockwell OLD 82-87; Wiggin TALES 100-102.

H696.1.2. Riddle: How much water is in the sea? So and so much and if you don't believe it, go measure it yourself. Italy: Vittorini OLD 45-49.

H697.1* Riddles of size. How big is the moon? Size of penny. Penny held before eye covers moon. Estonia: McNeil DOUBLE 50-55.

H701.1. How many seconds in eternity? A bird carries a grain of sand from a mountain each century. When the whole mountain is gone, the first second of eternity has passed. German: De La Mare ANIMAL 107-109; Grimm MORE 47-49; Hardendorff JUST 40-41; Rockwell OLD 82-87; Wiggin TALES 160-161.

H702. Riddle: How many stars in the heavens? Type 922. SEE ALSO: H705.3.

H702.1. How many stars in the heavens? As many as the grains of sand; if you don't believe it, count them yourself. Slovenia: Kavcic GOLDEN 25-31 (as grains of flour in sack) /Green CLEVER 101-107/.

H702.1.1. How many stars in the heaven? Two million. If you don't believe, count them yourself. Russia: Daniels FALCON 71-74.

H702.2.1. How many stars in the heavens? As many as the hairs in the goatskin (on a donkey). Turkey: Downing HODJA 40-41; Kelsey HODJA 100-107. Germany: Edmonds TRICKSTER 45-50 (bearskin).

H702.3. How many stars in the heavens? As many as the points on paper. If you don't believe me count them yourself. Germany: De La Mare ANIMAL 107-108; Grimm MORE 47-49; Hardendorff JUST 40-41; Rockwell OLD 82-87; Wiggin TALES 160-161. SEE ALSO: H561.1.1.2.

H703.1. How many hairs are there in the head? As many as are in the tail of my ass; if you don't believe it, we will keep pulling out one hair from your beard and one from his tail. Turkey: Downing HODJA 40-41; Kelsey HODJA 100-107. Leach NOODLES 57.

H703.4* How many hairs on my head? Trickster pulls one and "one less than before." Germany: Edmonds TRICKSTER 45-50 (Tyl Eulenspiegel).

H705.3. Riddle: How many leaves on the tree (plant)? Counter-question: How many stars in the sky? Puerto Rico: Belpre TIGER 89-94 (Albahaca plant). SEE ALSO: H561.1.1.2.

H707.2* When will the world end? It will end

twice: first when my wife dies and second when I die. Turkey: Downing HODJA 92.

H710. Riddles of value.

H711.1. How much am I (the king) worth? Twenty-nine pieces of silver, for Christ was sold for thirty. Type 922. Majorca: Mehdevi BUNG-LING 109-117. Norway: Asbjornsen EAST (Row) 133-134; Asbjornsen NORWEGIAN 15-16; Undset TRUE 233-234. Russia: Daniels FALCON 71-74 (fifteen pieces, half that of Lord). Slovenia: Kavcic GOLDEN 25-31 /Greene CLEVER 101-107/. Italy: Vittorini OLD 45-49.

H711.2* How much am I (the king) worth? A sovereign (twenty shillings) plus a crown (five shillings) = twenty-five shillings. United Kingdom: Courlander RIDE 189-193.

H712.2. How much is king's beard worth? A May rain (three rains in summer). Serbia: Spicer LONG 145-158 (in drought = three summers of rain).

H720. Metaphorical riddles.

H734.1* What runs without legs? Water. SEE: J163.7.1 (Pottle of Brains).

H742. Riddle: two legs, three legs, four legs? (Man, three legged stool, dog).

H761. Riddle of the Sphinx: what is it that goes on four legs in the morning, two at mid-day, and on three in the evening? (cf. C822). SEE ALSO: B51. Leach NOODLES 45. Egypt: Carpenter AFRICAN 63-70. Mexico: Brenner BOY 59-64 /Bleecker BIG 93-98 Hawaii: Thompson HAWAIIAN..TRICKSTERS 43-48. U.S. (Louisiana): Haviland NORTH 134-138.

H761.2* What has no legs, then two, then four? SEE: J163.2.1.

H762.1* What is yellow and shining but not gold. Sun. SEE: J163.2.1 (Pottle of Brains).

H770. Riddles of explanation.

H775* What does woman want most? Her own way. England: Garner CAVALCADE..GOBLINS 116-125 (King Arthur, Sir Gawain).

H790. Riddles based on unusual circumstances.

H793. Riddle: seven tongues in a head. (A horse's head in which a bird's nest is found with seven birds in it.) Leach NOODLES 50-53.

H802. Riddle: one killed none and yet killed twelve. Horse is poisoned; raven eats of him and dies; twelve robbers eat raven and die. Germany (Grimm): Lang GREEN 293-297 (H551.0.1) /Lang FIFTY 241-244/.

H802.1* Donkey eats two poison cakes intended for lad and dies. Three vultures eat and die.

Lad shoots at two ravens but hits third he had not seen, drinks coconut water. Riddle: two killed Panda but she killed three; I shot what I saw but killed what I didn't see. I drank water which never sank into earth or fell down from sky. Puerto Rico: Alegria THREE 115-121 (+H551.0.1).

H802.2* Horse eats poisoned cakes and dies. Three buzzards feed on carcass as floats down river. Lad makes riddle king cannot answer. U.S. (Louisiana): Haviland NORTH 134-138.

H808. Lad sells parents and uses money to buy clothing and horse. King sent with Uriah letter but he dips into well to suck water and then reads. Riddle: I wore my mother, I rode my father. I drank water with my death. Gypsy: Manning-Sanders RED 62-65 (+H551.0.1).

H840. Other riddles.

H881.2* Riddles with "none" as answer. Second cow pierces first cow's behind with horns. Which cow can say "I have tail and horns at the same end of my body?" Neither. Cows can't talk. Iran: Kelsey MULLAH 108-112.

H887* How long will men continue to live and die? Until heaven and hell are full. Turkey: Downing HODJA 59.

H900 - H1199. Tests of prowess: tasks.

H950 - H999. Performance of tasks.

H951. Countertasks. When a task is assigned, the hero agrees to perform it as soon as the assigner performs a certain other task. SEE: H561.1 (Clever peasant girl).

H951.1* Clever peasant wife. Husband's sign boasting of her intelligence is seen by magistrate. Task set: weave cloth long as a road, make as much wine as water in sea, raise pig as big as mountain. She asks magistrate to measure road, measure water, weigh pig. China (Han Dynasty): Kendall SWEET 14-17.

H952. Reductio ad absurdum of task. Countertask so absurd as to show the manifest absurdity of the original task. SEE: H1021.12.

H952.1* Jean Sotte ordered to fetch bull's milk. Tells king his father bore twins, possible if bulls give milk. To answer riddle on April 1. Answers riddle of Sphinx (H761). Asks riddle king cannot answer (H802.2). U.S. (Louisiana): Haviland NORTH 134-138.

H961.1. Tasks performed by cleverness. Trickster assigned seemingly impossible tasks to earn thing he requests. By trickery, he succeeds. SEE ALSO: A1481.1.1. West Indies: Carter GREEDY 62-67 (larger, +A2325.1); U.S. (Alabama): Courlander TERRAPIN'S 60-64 (K713.1.9; K711.5, to win princess); Harris COMPLETE 264-268 /Harris NIGHTS 203-207/, /Brown

BRER 127-132/ (To be made smarter by Mammy-Bammy Big Money, +K713.1.9, +K711.7). Harris COMPLETE 261-264 /Harris NIGHTS 198-202/ (for love charm, +K771).

H1000 - H1199. Nature of tasks.

H1021. Task: construction from impossible kind of material.

H1021.1. Task: making a rope of sand. Type 1174. SEE: H1144.2.1 (countertask: bring waves). Scotland: Nic Leodhas THISTLE 136-143 (+G303.16.19.3, tasks for Devil).

H1021.2.1* Task: making one thousand ropes of ashes. Rope is soaked in salt water, then burnt. +J151.1. Japan: Uchida SEA 61-71.

H1021.8. Task: spinning gold. SEE: D2183 (Rumpelstiltskin).

H1021.8.1* Hag makes three daughters spin gold. Youngest talks to prince and thread tarnishes. Prince abducts girl, witch hurls witch bundle after him and girl is thrown into stream. He sickens. Year later he hears waterlily singing and goes to goldspinner's house again. Girls find magic cake and can hear birds talk. They bring message from Finnish Sorcerer to cover self in mud and say "Man into crayfish." As crayfish he digs up lily roots, says "Lily into maid, crayfish into man." Emerges naked as man with lost bride. Coach passes and drives to king and queen (his parents), wed. Returns to poison witch and rescue other girls. Estonia: Maas MOON 86-89.

H1021.12* Task: making a lute of stone. Countertask providing carrying pad of smoke. Bemba, N. Rhodesia: Courlander KING'S 95-97.

H1021.13* Task: making a cape of stone. Countertask: providing thread made of sand. Iraq: Carpenter ELEPHANT'S 195-203.

H1021.14* Task: making man of iron. Countertask: one thousand loads of charcoal from human hair and one hundred pots of tears to forge with. Uganda (Baganda): Arnott AFRICAN 119-123; McDowell THIRD 29-30.

H1022.2.2. Task: weaving a shirt of one piece of thread. Countertask: making a loom from a rod. Russia: Bulatkin EURASIAN 27-38 (stalk of flax--birch twig).

H1022.3. Task: making sails for ship from the bundle of linen. Countertask: making spindle and loom from one stick of wood. Serbia: Spicer LONG 145-158.

H1022.3.1* Task: making bedcurtains of two skeins of silk. Countertask: making loom of two splinters of wood. Wiggin FAIRY 53-58.

H1022.6.0.1* Task: making one hundred dishes of small bird. Countertask: making stove, pan, and knife of needle. Tagalog: Sechrist ONCE 173-177.

H1023.1.1. Task: hatching boiled eggs. Countertask: sowing cooked seeds and harvesting the crop. Serbia: Spicer LONG 145-158 (sends father to sow boiled beans "as easy as...."). Russia: Bulatkin EURASIAN 27-38 (plant millet porridge).

H1023.1.2. Task: hatching eggs immediately. Countertask: sowing seeds and bringing in crop next morning. Czechoslovakia: Fillmore SHEPHERD'S 144-152.

H1023.2. Task: carrying water in a sieve. SEE: Z41.10 (crow cries 'daub'); Q2.1.2Ab.

H1023.2.0.1. Task: carrying water in a sieve; sieve filled with moss (leaves, clay, etc.). Burton MAGIC 43-47 (+K335.0.4.6). SEE ALSO: F381.8.1 (horned woman); K1611B (Mutsmag); D195.2 (Well of the World's End, frog advises).

H1023.2.0.1.1* Brer fox tries to find excuse for eating baby rabbits. Tells to break off sugar cane. Bird sings "Gnaw it." Fetch water in a sieve. Bird sings "Daub with clay and mud." Fetch log. Bird sings "Roll it." U.S. (Black): Brown WORLD 49-53; Harris FAVORITE 258-261; Harris COMPLETE 71-74; Harris UNCLE 108-112.

H1023.2.6* Task: House to go to son who fills it completely. One brings a horse, second--hay, youngest--a candle which fills it with light. Lithuania: Wyndham TALES..RUSSIA 13-15. Russia (Latvia): Ginsburg TWELVE 51.

H1023.6.2* Task: washing elephant white. Countertask: making pot large enough to wash elephant in. Jealous potter suggests that king assign washerman task. Washerman requests pot. Burma: Brockett BURMESE 142-146; Carpenter ELEPHANT'S 13-21.

H1026. Task: changing the course of time. SEE: D2138.1.

H1045. Task: Filling a sack full of lies (truths). Type 570. SEE ALSO: H561.1.1.2 (clever peasant girl); H342.1. (cf. K1288).

H1045.0.1* Herding the hares. Type 570. The brother aids old woman and receives magic whistle which calls hares to it. Suitor tasks: herding (H1112) hares. Chambermaid, princess and king try to get whistle from him, pay with kisses, king must kiss horse's rump (K1288.2). Suitor test: filling a sack with lies. He is stopped when begins to tell of king's kiss. Sack is full. Weds princess. Norway: Aulaire EAST 15-26; Baker GOLDEN 9-18; Undset TRUE 161-172. France: McNeil DOUBLE 82-86. U.S. (Appalachia): Chase JACK 89-95 /Arbuthnot FAIRY 197-198/ (Old man gives magic drill that causes hare to run in circles around it; old man's wife kisses Jack). Scandinavia: Lang VIOLET 133-147 /Lang FIFTY 152-161/ (Queen and king made to act fools). Spain: Sawyer PICTURE 11-24 (+H346 healing fruits).

H1049.5* Task: bringing self-beating drum. Bee is inside. Japan: Uchida SEA 61-71 (+J151.1).

H1050. Paradoxical tasks. SEE: H561.1.

H1051.1* Task: coming neither by road nor by foot-path (lets goat wander there). Estonia: Maas MOON 116-122; McNeil DOUBLE 50-55. Rumania: Ure RUMANIAN 131-143.

H1051.2* Task: coming neither by road nor by footpath. Comes across fields. Wales: Pugh TALES 105-115.

H1052. Task: standing neither inside nor outside of gate (forefeet of horse inside, hind feet out-side). Estonia: Maas MOON 116-122; McNeil DOUBLE 50-55.

H1053.1. Task: coming neither on horse nor on foot (comes on another animal). Estonia: McNeil DOUBLE 50-55.

H1053.3. Task: coming neither on horse nor on foot (comes sitting on animal but with feet reach-ing ground). Estonia: Maas MOON 116-122 (goat). Rumania: Ure RUMANIAN 131-143. Poland: Wojciechowska WINTER 22-31. Egypt: Carpenter AFRICAN 21-30. Russia: Lurie CLEVER 9-16.

H1053.2. Task: coming neither on horse nor on foot (comes with one leg on animal's back, one on ground). Czechoslovakia: Fillmore SHEP-HERD'S 144-152. Ethiopia (Somali): Courlander FIRE 81-88 (Abunawas).

H1053.7* Task: come not driving, not riding, not walking, not sliding. (On ram with feet drag-ging ground in fishnet.) Norway: Asbjornsen NORWEGIAN 137-138.

H1053.8* Task: come neither alone, nor on horse, but led. Has rabbit lead her. Russia: Bulat-kin EURASIAN 27-38.

H1053.9* Task: come neither on horse nor on foot. Crawls. Wales: Pugh TALES 105-115.

H1053.10* Task: come neither walking, driving, nor riding. Ties net to horse and is dragged. Jacobs EUROPEAN 188-193.

H1054.1. Task: coming neither naked nor clad. (Comes wrapped in net or the like.) Estonia: Jacobs EUOPEAN 188-193; Maas MOON 116-122 (net); McNeil DOUBLE 50-55. Czechoslo-vokia: Fillmore SHEPHERD'S 144-152. Russia: Bulatkin EURASIAN 27-38; Lurie CLEVER 9-16. Rumania: Ure RUMANIAN 131-143. Wales: Pugh TALES 105-115. Poland: Wojciechowska WINTER 22-31 (flowers). Ethiopia (Somali): Courlander FIRE 81-88 (Abunawas). Haiti: Courlander PIECE 68-71. Egypt: Courlander AFRICAN 21-30.

H1055. Task: coming neither barefoot nor shod (comes with one shoe on, one off; or in soleless shoes). Type 875. Slovenia: Kavcic GOLDEN 71-77 (+J151.1).

H1056. Task: coming neither with nor without a present (game). (Lets bird fly as she reaches it toward king.) Leach NOODLES 56; Jacobs EUROPEAN 188-193. Poland: Wojciechowska WINTER 22-31. Russia: Bulatkin EURASIAN 27-38; Lurie CLEVER 9-16.

H1057. Task: coming neither by day nor by night. (Comes by twilight.) Czechoslovakia: Fillmore SHEPHERD'S 144-152 (dawn). Wales: Pugh TALES 105-115 (dawn). Poland: Wojciechowska WINTER 22-31 (dawn).

H1057.1* Task: coming neither in shadow nor in sun. Wears sieve over face. Jacobs EUROPEAN 188-193.

H1063. Task: coming neither hungry nor satiated. (Eats a thin soup, a leaf, a single grain, or the like.) Norway: Asbjornsen NORWEGIAN 137-138. Wales: Pugh TALES 195-115 (eats a leek).

H1064. Task: come laughing and crying at the same time. Egypt: Courlander AFRICAN 21-30.

H1078* Task: Birth of horse neither gray nor black nor brown, etc. Countertask: send groom for horse neither on Monday, Tuesday, Wednes-day, etc. U.S. (Georgia): Hardendorff JUST 21.

H1091. Tasks requiring miraculous speed. SEE: G530.2; B582.2C; D2183; H1331.1.3.

H1110. Tedious tasks. SEE: G530.2.

H1112. Task: herding rabbits. SEE: F601.2Acb; H1045 (sack of lies); H346 (Picard).

H1112.0.1* Old woman befriended by youngest brother herds hares for him with magic whistle. He wins princess. Syria: Hampden GYPSY 119-125. Finland: Bowman TALES 1-11 (+F601.2A).

H1115.1. Task: cutting down huge tree which magically regrows. SEE ALSO: D1487.3.1; F601.2Ga.

H1115.1.1* The King's Tasks. Type 577. Espen Cinderlad investigates sound in forest and finds self-chopping axe, spade, walnut with spring flowing from it. Older two brothers fail at suitor tasks. E. cuts oak, digs well and pro-vides water with spade and walnut. Weds prin-cess. Norway: Arbuthnot FAIRY 77-74; Asbjornsen EAST (Row) 112-118; Association TOLD..GREEN 146-155; Aulaire EAST 93-98; Hutchinson CHIMNEY..FAIRY 55-62.

H1129.12* Task: tending olive twig until it sprouts leaves. Sinner kills man who tries to cut down tree. Is pardoned nevertheless for man he killed was a worse sinner than he. Greece (Lemnos): Neufeld BEWARE 36-41.

H1130. Superhuman tasks.

H1132.1.1. Task: recovering lost ring from sea. SEE: B582.2B,C; F601.2B; G530.2Bb; H346A.

H1132.1.2. Task: recovering lost key from sea. SEE: B582.2.

H1132.1.5. Task: recovering lost fish-hook. Done by sea king. SEE ALSO: U136.0.1.

H1132.1.5.1* Task: recovering lost knife. Wakwajima loses chief's knife in river. Ordered to recover. Taken to king of fishes. King returns knife and warns him never to borrow or lend. Gives hunt dog that always gets kill. If used more than once per day will return to king of fishes. Chief borrows and overuses. Never borrow or lend. Congo (Luban): Burton MAGIC 35-39.

H1132.1.5.2* Podhu loses magic spear of brother. It is carried off by elephant. Podhu must recover. Old woman tells where elephant's kraal is and gives magic blue bead. He obtains spear and elephants ask that children sit in fields and beat pans so elephants can tell which crops are cultivated. Son of brother swallows magic bead. Brothers decide to live apart. Luo: Harman TALES 64-88.

H1132.1.5.3* Hakala loses magic arrow of his brother. Bird flies off with arrow in side. Turns to man, Red Plume. Using strike-a-light bag and magic coup stick of brothers and wearing own magic mocassins (D1065.5) he pursues and pulls arrow from side of Red Plume, disguised as medicine man. Native American (Lakota): Pinkney TONWEYA 59-65.

H1141. Task: eating enormous amount. SEE: F601.2; H341.1.

H1143. Task: dipping out the sea with a spoon. Countertask: stop all the rivers. Serbia: Spicer LONG 145-158 (cup, dam streams with bundle of hemp).

H1144.2.1. Task: bringing the waves. Countertask: make rope of sand to catch them (cf. H1021.1). Tagalog: Sechrist ONCE 173-177.

H1149.9. Task: lifting mountain. Countertask: placing it on my shoulders. India (Telugus): Withers WORLD 76-77.

H1150. Tasks: stealing, capturing, or slaying.

H1151.3. Task: stealing sheet from bed on which person is sleeping. SEE: K301 (Master Thief). Japan: Edmonds TRICKSTER 61-67 (tickles with feather till rolls to one side then to other).

H1151.6.2* Task: stealing elephant's tail (tusks). Task: bring enough ivory to build palace. Accomplished by pouring wine in pool where

elephants drink and cutting tusks from drunken elephants. SEE ALSO: H1213.1H.

H1151.6.2.1* Son of hunter. Type 513C. Father asks wife not to let son become hunter. He disobeys. Performs task (H1151.6.2). Second task assigned. Bring sister of seven brothers to king's wife. Companions aid. Eater, Drinker, Always Cold (steam bath). Jumper goes in race to spring. Listener hears sleeping. Quaker shakes earth and wakes (F601.2). Girl turns minister to mouse, king to cat, weds hero. Greece: Courlander RIDE 120-127; Wilson GREEK 40-42.

H1151.6.2.2* The Crow-Peri. Crow in snare offers more precious thing if released. Beautiful bird appears and lad gives to Padishah. Assigned task: Ivory palace to house bird. Also sent for bird's mistress, entices on board and sails. Sent for drug for Peri, crow aids in all. Peri recognizes crow as enchanted maid servant and disenchants. Weds youth. Turkey: Buck FAIRY 29-34.

H1180. Miscellaneous tasks.

H1199.12. Task: unusual pasturing. (cf. H1385.1).

H1199.12.3* Task: following seven foals all day and reporting what they have eaten. The Seven Foals. Type 471. First two sons take drink offered by hag and let her comb hair, sleep. Third follows foals, refuses hag. Youngest foal takes on back. Enters birch tree. To drink from strength giving pitcher, wield sword and behead foals and put heads (D711) at tails, turn back to princes. He follows foals to church and sees them turn to princes and take communion. Shows wafer and wine to king-- what they eat. Beheads and restores. Weds princes. Norway: Arnott ANIMAL 141-151; Lang RED 344-352 /Lang Fifty 245-252/; Manning-Sanders BOOK..MAGICAL 148-157; Undset TRUE 72-82.

H1199.12.4* Task: herding witch's sheep and finding mare.

A* Lad seeking three kidnapped princesses befriends wolf, crow, fish. Given tokens to call each. First day wolf bites largest sheep, it turns back to mare. Second, crow finds in clouds. Third, fish finds in sea. Lad gets choice of colt for task. Chooses poorest. Turns to finest. Rescues princesses from unclean spirit on horse. Gypsy: Manning-Sanders RED 169-173.

B* Koschei the Deathless. B314C + goes to get steed equal to Koschei's from Baba Yaga, to herd mares three days for colt. Befriended bird, bee, lion cub aid. Herd mares home. Mangy colt taken. Steals Marya Moryevna from Koschei with this steed. Russia: Buck FAIRY 15-46; Riordan TALES..CENTRAL 148-160; Whitney IN 107-120.

C* The Nine Peahens and the Golden Apples. H1385.3J + herding of mares to obtain magic steed. Yugoslavia: Fillmore LAUGHING 107-138 (fish, fox, rower aid). Hungary: Manning-Sanders GLASS 27-40. Serbia: Lang VIOLET 50-64; Rackham FAIRY 100-111. Russia: Lang YELLOW 172-191.

H1199.12.5* The Three Sons of Gorla. Mist carries off daughter, eldest son seeks, takes big bannock not blessing, refuses food to Raven. To herd three cows for old man, leaves them to chase gold cock and silver hen and other magic distractions. Milk is thin, he is turned to stone, shares with son. Second son--same. Youngest takes small cake and blessing, shares with raven, follows cows despite all, through fire and flood, milk rich. Three tasks: 1. Bring deer from mountain--Raven sends hound. 2. Bring duck from lock--Raven brings duck. 3. Trout from pool--Raven sends otter. Sister and brothers are restored as reward. Scotland: Wilson SCOTTISH 137-147.

H1199.19* Task: discovering why Gruagach Gaire stopped laughing. Ireland: Jacobs CELTIC 134-143; Pilkington SHAMROCK 161-168.

H1200 - H1399. Tests of prowess: quests.

H1210. Quest assigned.

H1213. Quest for remarkable bird caused by sight of one of its feathers. SEE: H1331.1.3 (quest for golden bird).

H1213.1. Quest for princess caused by sight of one of her hairs dropped by a bird (or floating on a river, or found on path). Type 521.

A* Ferdinand the Faithful--Ferdinand the Unfaithful. Godfather gives key to castle, at age fourteen castle appears and horse. En route picks up writing quill from path, puts fish hook into water. Ferdinand the Unfaithful tells (H1381.3.1) a king that Ferdinand can find maiden. With horse's advice he takes meat to pacify huge birds and bring princess. Drops magic quill but fish fetches it. Queen beheads but his head is restored. King attempts same. Dies. (J2411.1) Horse becomes a prince. Germany (Grimm): Grimm JUNIPER..v.II 298-309.

B* The Haggary Nag. Type 531. Lad treats horse well despite contrary instructions. Picks up shining hair despite horse's advice. King searches for maiden. Magical horses, "White Mare of the Raven-Tree Wood" and other horses seven days journey apart, aid in quest. Princess must grant request one hour each seven years when she combs hair. He asks her to mount horse and flees with her. Returns for three drops from hearts of the Ravens of Life that she requests. Horse orders to kill horse and hide in skin, catch ravens as come to feed. Three drops of raven's blood restores. Princess

orders any who would wed to leap from tower onto spears. King and courtiers die. Hero drinks of raven's blood and succeeds. Wed. Ireland: MacManus WELL 138-155.

C* The Magic Mare. Type 531. Jealous mother tells king that Franco can bring lady of seven veils. Little mare, the Cavallina, assists. Franco returns fish to sea, feeds ants, crow, kills snake pursuing dove. Lady of seven veils is taken on horse for a ride. Crow and fish assist. Task: sort grains. Ants assist. Task: water from heaven and hell. Dove brings. Lady has hero cut into pieces and boiled, revived with water of heaven. King imitates--dies. Italy: Toor GOLDEN 57-66.

D* Tropsyn. Type 531. Lad raises foal. Changes nightcaps on witch's daughters and saves brothers. Picks up golden feather. Count sends for bird. Turns to flea and bites witch, steals bird. To fetch Maiden of Marvelous Beauty from bottom of Danube, takes on horse for ride. Must return for her herd of horses. Groom to bathe in boiling mare's milk. Hero emerges lovelier. Count dies. Gypsy: Manning-Sanders RED 105-111. De La Mare ANIMAL 260-265.

E* Ivan the Fool. Youngest brother catches horse stealing hay. Bears three colts, to keep humpbacked colt. Brothers tell Tsar he can fetch pig with golden bristles (H1331.1.3) and silver tusks. Horse assists. To bring Tsarina from the sea, entices her into tent and captures. Groom to bathe in boiling water. Ivan emerges handsome. Tsar dies. Russia: Dolch OLD RUSSIA 131-167.

F* The Imposter. Lad taken as godson by prince sheltering in hut on night of birth. Sent with locket token when of age. Tabu: must turn back if meets a beardless man. One such abandons youth in well and takes place, making him vow not to reveal truth until has died and restored to life. Lad must serve imposter. Hears birds speak of Princess with Golden Hair (he understands language of birds). Is sent to fetch her. Performs tasks with aid of grateful ants (sorting grains) and queen bee (identifying princess). Imposter kills hero, princess restores with water of life. Can now reveal truth. Greece: Wilson GREEK 200-211.

G* Mons Tro. Beggar stands godfather, gives key. House appears on sixteenth birthday which key unlocks, horse inside. Food in horse's ear. Three golden feathers picked up against horse's advice. Picture of girl appears on them. Paints copies of picture. King orders to fetch. Achieves with horse's aid (horse turns self to poodle). Grateful fish retrieves lost key, grateful whales and giants carry castle. Mother raven fetches water of life and water of death when her babe is killed and adder is put in nest. Hero becomes handsomer, king uses wrong flask and dies. Horse was godfather. Denmark: Manning-Sanders CHOICE 148-165.

H* The Golden Horse. Blessing of dead parents is drawn up from flooded city by grown son in net. It is in form of a golden horse. Traveling prince finds a golden feather and golden girdle. Disobeys horse's orders to sell to first person met. King sends for bird that dropped feather. Greets Lamia ogress civilly and is aided. Fills lake with wine and bird falls asleep (H1151.6.2). Sent for Fair One of the World for whom girdle was made. To climb tower and take flute from under pillow. Play it. Tower will follow. Golden Bird, her brother, has been killed and room made of his feathers and mother-of-pearl bones. She turns king and vizier to hound and hare and weds prince. Greece: Wilson GREEK 167-169.

Ia* The Firebird and Princess Vasilisa. Type 531. Hero finds feather of firebird. Horse warns not to pick it up but he disobeys. King sees and orders to bring firebird. Horse enables to capture. King now orders to bring Princess Vasilisa. Horse has tent set up and invites her and drugs her. She requests dress from under rock in middle of sea at end of the world for wedding dress. Horse forces giant crab to fetch. Vasilisa orders hero thrown into tub of boiling water. Horse charms him and he emerges handsomer. King imitates and is killed. Hero weds Princess Vasilisa. SEE ALSO: H1331.1.3 (Quest for golden bird). Russia: Ransome OLD 242-257 /Dalgliesh ENCHANTED 35-47/, /Arbuthnot FAIRY 153-158/, /Arbuthnot ANTHOLOGY 294-298/; Whitney IN 71-76.

Ib* Humpbacked Horse. Type 531. Three brothers to guard fields. Youngest catches horse doing damage. Given three horses as reward. One is humpbacked. He finds golden hair and keeps despite horse's warning. King demands princess who lost hair. They entice into tent but she escapes. Repeat. Obtain princess. She requires ring from sea which is brought by talking fish and crab; wedding dress from her brother on the moon. She asks hero to bathe in boiling milk, horse cools and he emerges handsome. King imitates and dies. Gypsy: Jagendorf GYPSIES' 52-92.

J* The Golden Castle that Hung in the Air. Ashlad sees picture of maid on tree, keeps it (T11.2). Brothers say he bragged could find princess pictured. Follows ball given by hog. Raven aids--they return troll's lost child and receive reward. Takes little donkey. Donkey asks what sees. "Sparkling like star." Asks again. "Shining like moon"--that is the silver castle. Princess gives drink of flask and beheads troll with three heads. Second castle-- golden, same--six headed troll. Third castle-- golden castle in air which has Water of Life and Death (H1321.1). Fills pitcher. Sees sleeping princess. Takes piece of dress token. Red knight gets oldest princess to put him to sleep with Water of Death once home. Third princess comes. False hero claims her. Ashlad revived. Weds. Donkey beheaded = prince. Norway: Asbjornsen NORWEGIAN 139-149.

K* Zlatovloska the Golden Haired. Cook tastes

of white snake served king and understands language of animals (B217.1.1). Sent to fetch princes from whom golden hair came. Helps ravens, fish, ants. Tasks: find pearls--ants aid, fetch ring from sea--fish aids, fetch Water of Life and Water of Death--ravens aid. Saves fly from spider's web with Water of Life. Test: choose Z. from twelve princesses, fly aids. Beheaded by king, Z. restores with Water of Life and Death. King imitates--dies. Dalgliesh ENCHANTED 21-34 /Fillmore SHOEMAKER'S 23-44/.

H1226.2. Pursuit of magic arrow leads to adventure. SEE: B641C,E (leads to bride); B641.0.1 A (bride).

H1230. Accomplishment of quests.

H1232. Directions on quest given by sun, moon, wind and stars. SEE: H1385.4; P253.2A (Seven Ravens).

H1250 - H1399. Nature of quests.

H1252.1.1* Quest to other world for relative. Maui follows mother to underworld in search of father. Father dips him in river making strong but forgets to make immortal, hence is only a demi-god. Polynesia: Berry MAGIC 65-73. New Zealand (Maori): Williams-Ellis ROUND 242-252.

H1273.1. Quest to devil in hell for return of contract. SEE: G530.2M.

H1273.2. Quest for three hairs from devil's beard. Type 461. SEE ALSO: B216.6.

A* The Giant with Three Golden Hairs. Prophecy that child will wed princess. King offers to rear child, sets adrift on stream, miller raises. King discovers grown child and sends to queen with letter to execute. Friendly robbers in night lodging exchange letter while lad sleeps (K1355). New letter says to wed princess (K511). King sets task: obtain three golden hairs from giant. En route is asked to get answers to questions (H1292). 1. Why fountain of wine in market is dry? 2. Why golden apple tree doesn't bear? 3. How ferryman can be released from service? Grandmother of giant hides him, in ant form, in her gown. Pulls out hairs as giant sleeps and asks questions each time he wakes. Remove toad from fountain, mouse (serpent) from tree root, ferryman to put oar in hand of passenger and leave him in ferry. Lad receives rewards for these answers en route home. King wants similar treasure (J2415), sets out and is handed oar by ferryman. Germany (Grimm): Adams BOOK..GIANTS 149-148; Carle ERIC 25-38; Grimm BROTHERS 170-177; Grimm GRIMM'S (Grosset) 313-321; Grimm GRIMM'S (Scribner's) 78-86; Grimm GRIMM'S (World) 228-229; Grimm JUNIPER v. I 88-93 (devil); Manning-Sanders BOOK..GIANTS 107-117.

Ab* Grandfather Know-It-All (Sun). Old at

Night, Young in Morn. King overhears three fates foretell future + A above. Czechoslovakia: Fillmore SHEPHERD'S 119-133; Haviland FAVOR-ORITE..CZECHOSLOVAKIA 67-90. Russia: Bulatkin EURASIAN 9-21 (Grandad Sol). Gypsy (Transylvania): Hampden GYPSY 35-43 (Sun King, fairy changes letter).

B* Mother of Time. To free brothers transformed to doves (P253.2E), sister seeks Mother of Time. En route whale asks her to ask how he can swim in safety, mouse--how be free of cats, ants--why have such short lives, oak--why men do not eat acorns. These direct her on. Old man advises to take weights from clock and return only if Mother of Time assures her safety. She is hidden and Mother asks Time questions. There is treasure under the oak, cats must wear bells, ants to live one hundred years if abstain from wearing wings; whale to be guided by sea rat; doves to sit on horns of plenty--they light on ox's horns and are restored. She digs up oak treasure, robbers steal, mice gnaw her free, and ants show her robber's treasure. Whale carries her home. Italy: Toor GOLDEN 107-119.

C* Peasant and His Hen. Peasant goes to ask sun where his hen hides eggs. Pear tree--ask why I bear no fruit? Apple tree--why do I have no roots? Woman--why is daughter unwed? Fish--why must swim on top of water? Sun replies: hen lays eggs on ridge of roof, gold under pear tree, girls face sun when carrying out garbage and offend sun, fish must feed on a man. Peasant delivers messages and takes gold. Poland: Borski GOOD 62-65.

D* The Griffin. Three feathers of griffin's tail to cure girl. Jack seeks. Ask also--why farmer's daughter is in bed, where key to money box is, why boatmen cannot leave service. Griffin's wife hides, pulls feather from tail and asks. Girl--put lock of her hair hidden in swallow's nest into her hand; key is in crock in kitchen floor; boatman to hand oar to another. Jack cures girl and weds. Danaher FOLKTALES 81-92.

E* Bird of Seven Colors. Cruel mother sends daughter to find Bird of Seven Colors to mend broken pitcher. Mango tree--ask why does not bear. Sea--why has no fish. King--why his daughters have no children. Mother of bird hides her. Wakes bird when asleep and asks to fix pitcher, answer questions. Treasure under tree, sea must swallow something, king's daughters must stop gazing at moon. Mother seeks equal treasure. Sea swallows her. Puerto Rico: Alegria THREE 25-30.

F* Marko the Rich and Vasily the Luckless. Three old men prophesy that the son of Ivan the Luckless will be heir of Marko the Rich. Marko throws Vasily over cliff, is returned. Set adrift is raised by monks. Sent with letter for execution, three old men breathe on it, it changes (K1355). Wed to daughter of Marko. Sent on quest to receive twelve year's rent of

Tsar Zmy in land of Thrice-Nine in Empire of Thrice-Ten. Also wants news of twelve wrecked ships. En route is asked to find out why rotten oak still stands, why whale must serve as bridge, why ferryman must serve. Maiden asks dragon questions in sleep. Oak must be kicked over, treasure underneath. Ferryman pushes boat off with another in it. Whale must spit up twelve ships of Marko the Rich which he swallowed. Marko the Rich sets out to seek like treasure--is given ferryman's service. Russia: Williams-Ellis ROUND 90-101. Serbia: Lang VIOLET 22-23.

G* Reward for giving last loaf. Old man eats boy's lunch three days. Reveals self as Mountain God and sends lad on quest to Tenjoku temple. There a god answers questions encountered en route. Why is rich man's daughter ill?; Why does tree not bloom? When will ferry woman enter heaven? He weds rich man's daughter. Ikeda Type 460B. Japan: Uchida SEA 121-132.

H* Stupid, lazy man visits Allah to ask relief from poverty. Wolf, apple tree, fish have questions to be asked also. Answers: jewel in fish's throat, gold buried under tree, wolf must devour lazy, stupid man to cure pain. Man is too lazy to remove jewel or gold, wolf eats him. Azerbaijan: Bulatkin EURASIAN 106-110; Ginsburg LAZIES 1-7. Armenia: Tashjian ONCE 3-10 /Arbuthnot ANTHOLOGY 283-284/.

I* Antti and the Wizard's Prophecy. Two wizards pass night in farmer's tupa. Reveal that newborn is to wed daughter of rich merchant sleeping above. He 'adopts' baby and abandons. Discovers years later. Sends to wife with message to kill. Thieves change letter at place where he sleeps. Reads "wed to king's daughter." King sends Antti on quest. Asks Louhi, Mistress of the Northland, what trade brings greatest happiness. Giant wants to know why fruit in orchard molds. Second giant--where is lost key? Third--why can't descend from tree-top? Old lady ferrying--why must stay in boat. Daughter of Louhi hides him, asks questions. Happiest trade--tilling soil. Worm in garden, key in stone by door, spell broken on fruit by striking treeroots, leap from boat and leave passenger there. Given treasure by all. Father-in-law imitates --gets ferrying. Finland: Bowman TALES.. TUPA 53-69 /Fenner ADVENTURES 148-161/.

J* Man goes to Buddha for aid. Woman asks why daughter cannot speak (has red strand in hair); lord--why no grain in granary (cock under); farmer--why cistern goes dry (frog); Snake--why has not become a spirit yet (pearl on head). Lad had been on quest for these four objects. China: Lin MILKY 16-23.

K* Envoy sent to find out why sun stopped shining. Sun's sister hides him, feeds sun honey and asks questions. Poland: Borski GOOD 57-59.

La* Man goes to Oracle of Western Mountain. To ask: why dragon can't enter heaven (remove the magic pearl from head); why tree won't bear (gold and silver buried); why girl won't speak (will when she sees one she loves). Girl speaks to him. Weds. China: Chang CHINESE 9–11.

Lb* Poor man travels to ask Kuan Yin why he is poor. Uses up three questions for others. Why snake is not dragon--must remove six of seven pearls from head; why innkeeper's daughter cannot speak--must meet husband; why tree in garden never blooms--dig up seven jars of gold and give away half. He is given treasure and pearls, weds girl. China: Kendall SWEET 23–29.

M* Lovesick lad is set three impossible tasks. Goes to Buddha's temple for advice. En route dragon asks why is not spirit, turtle--same, lion accompanies. Dreams answers to questions of dragon and turtle. Turtle must let loose of earthly shell, dragon must spit out pearl in mouth. Lad had been sent to find a pear-shaped pearl, a spirit's cast-off house, and a golden-maned lion. Weds. China: Wyndham FOLK..CHINA 108–116.

N* Four hairs from the beard of the Devil. Stepmother sends lad to fetch four hairs from beard of the Devil. King of Spain asks to find out why daughter limps. King John asks to find out why well is dry. Guard asks to find out why no one relieves him of duty. Devil's wife aids. Answers: put sulphur powder from rock on daughter's toe, take guava out of well, give gun to first who passes to hold. Haiti: Wolkstein MAGIC 43–48.

H1280. Quests to other realms.

H1284. Quest to sun for answers to questions. Type 400, 461. SEE ALSO: H1385.3; H1273.2.

H1284.1* Scarface. Lad with scarred face seeks sun to ask removal of scar so can wed maid. Asks directions of bear, badger, wolverine guides. Two swans carry to isle of sun and moon. Moon, Sun's wife, hides. Sun smells man, moon convinces to keep as companion for morning star. Scarface kills birds who attack morning star, rewarded with bride of choosing. Scar removed. Sun Dance instructions given (A1542.2) and medicine lodge plans. Native American (Blackfeet): Cunningham TALKING 80–86; Davis BAKER'S 189–207; Haviland NORTH 83–93; San Souci LEGEND pb.

H1289.3.2. Quest to giant's land. Giant of Bang Beggar's Hall. Bridge torn down every night. Third night Jack watches and sees giant. Giant plays cards with Jack for life and wins. Gives second chance--if can find giant's castle in a year to be redeemed. Jack travels, meets a giant who calls one-third birds of air, none know whereabouts of Bang Beggar's Hall. Loans Jack nine mile boots and sends to brother. Second giant calls one-half birds of air. Third giant--all birds of air. Last to come--eagle knows whereabouts. Carries Jack there. Jack weds giant's daughter. MacManus IN /Adams BOOK..GIANT 176–197/.

H1290. Quests to the other world--miscellaneous.

H1300. Quests for the unique. SEE: B641.

H1305.2.1* King seeking wise man to appoint asks to bring best dish in the world. Applicant brings tongue. Tongue sings, gives orders, etc. Therefore is best. Asked to bring worst dish. Brings tongue. Cuba: Courlander RIDE 257–258. U.S. (Alabama): Courlander TERRAPIN'S 84–86.

H1311.2. Quest for bride richest and poorest. Type 585. Spindle, Shuttle and Needle. Prince will marry the girl who is at once the poorest and richest. She possesses marvelous heirloom: a spindle that brings the prince to her, a needle that transforms the room, a shuttle that makes a magic road. Germany (Grimm): Grimm GRIMM'S (Scribner's) 305–308; Grimm JUNIPER v. I 55–62; Grimm TALES 65–73; Lang GREEN 276–280 /Lang FIFTY 277–280/; Sheehan FOLK 32–36; Vittorini OLD 69–72; Wiggin FAIRY 248–251.

H1312. Quest for the greatest of fools. SEE ALSO: H1273.2H.

H1312.1. Quest for three persons as stupid as his wife (fiancé). Type 1384. +J2063. Leach LUCK 15–18. Italy (Venetian): Haviland FAVORITE..ITALY 55–56; TALL..NURSERY 98–104. England: De La Mare TALES 125–130; Jacobs ENGLISH 10–15; Steel ENGLISH 73–78; Wiggin TALES 218–221; Williams-Ellis FAIRY.. BRITISH 249–254. Ireland: MacManus HIBERNIAN 48–59. Greece: Neufeld BEWARE 52–57. Armenia: Bulatkin EURASIAN 90–94. U.S. (Appalachia): Chase JACK pb; Jacobs THREE pb; Zemach THREE pb.

H1312.2* Quest for persons sillier than own family. Russia: Jagendorf NOODLEHEAD 235–240. Persia: Mehdevi PERSIAN 33–43 (+K1767). Italy: Vittorini OLD 55–61.

H1312.4* Magistrate orders three fools brought. First carries load to save horse (J1874.1). Second tries to take pole crosswise through gate (J2171.6.2). Magistrate suggests he saw pole in two (he is third). China: Kendall SWEET 45–48.

H1320.3* Ivan Young in Years, Old in Wisdom. Thirty-three sons born from eggs found. Youngest guards king's hay, catches Horse with Golden Mane. Sent on quest for Playing Harp, Dancing Goose, and Singing Cat. Baba Yaga aids giving ball of yarn to follow to second Baba Yaga. Third Baba Yaga hides him and talks Dragon son into playing cards with him. He wins the magic objects. Russia: Riordan TALES..CENTRAL 213–221.

H1321.1. Quest for marvelous objects or animals. SEE ALSO: S12.1C.

A* The Water of Life. Type 551. SEE ALSO: H1213.1J; E632.0.2.

Aa* Three sons seek Water of Life for father (D1338.1.1). Elder two shun dwarf, youngest is kind. Given iron wand to open door, loaves for two lions. To leave before clock strikes twelve. Takes rings from enchanted princess, magic sword and loaf, maiden tells to return in year and wed (H81.1). Saves three countries from war and famine with sword and bread. Brothers substitute salt water for Water of Life. King orders him killed, executioner lets escape. Kings he saved send gifts--King forgives. Princess builds gold road to castle, two brothers ride on side of road, he rides straight up on to it--is the one. Wed. Germany (Grimm): Arbuthnot FAIRY 69-72; Grimm GRIMM'S (Follett) 388-398; Grimm GRIMM'S (Grosset) 181-188; Grimm GRIMM'S (Scribner's) 214-221; Grimm GRIMM'S (World) 305-311; Holme TALES 76-80; Shubb ABOUT 65-73; Wiggin FAIRY 213-220.

Ab* The Fountain of Youth. Elder two brothers unkind to old woman, turned to salt. Youngest given advice to aid. Jump on back of bear and say, "Bear, I dare." Bear will carry over bridge of razors. Two giants sleep at noon. Gets water and carries sleeping princess off. Bear refuses to carry giants over bridge. Brothers steal flask and toss him overboard. Princess puts salt water in flask, brothers thrown into sea by king. Youngest returns. French Canadian: Barbeau GOLDEN 90-108.

Ac* The Search for the Magic Lake. Two brothers fail to find water from lake at end of world for ill prince. Substitute ordinary water. It disappears in golden flask. Sister goes. Given feathers to form magic traveling fan by grateful sparrows. It also protects from lake monsters--giant crab, alligator and flying serpent. She marries prince. Ecuador (Inca): Barlow LATIN 68-81.

Ad* Well O' The World's End. Queen feigns ill and puts geasa on stepson to bring water from Well O' The World's End. Geasa on her to watch from tower. House of scarlet logs, half-brothers turn to stone in fright. Old man of house gives copper ball to follow to brother. Sky-blue house. Third brother-- white house. Turns flower to ship to carry to Island of the World's End. Bridle to shake three times and horses come, choose grey nag, leap across the walls, do not dally. He takes water, magic cloth, horn, loaf, jug of nectar, one-half ring of sleeping queen and kisses her. Gives magic goods to three old men helpers. Stepmother dies on his return. Queen wakes and seeks. Wed. Ireland: MacManus HIBERNIAN 251-263; MacManus WELL 1-20; Pilkington SHAMROCK 74-88.

Ae* The Spring of Youth. Three sons send for water of youth. Three roads divide. Leave rings under stone. Youngest frees serpent from burning cave, silver ring to show to brother in silver palace. Puts golden fish back into water, dragon appears and gives diamond to show to maid in jeweled palace. At next palace gives water to golden eagle. Finds sleeping maid. She gives gold ring to wear on left hand and draw water from spring. To grant wishes too. Wishes self and brothers at crossroads. They borrow ring and wish him away. Wish princess there and elder weds. Eagle bites finger so that he removes ring. Eagle carries to younger. SEE ALSO: D882.1. Bulgaria: Pridham GIFT 35-44.

B* The King of England and His Three Sons. Type 551. Ill king needs golden apple. Youngest seeks. Stays with old man in wood. Bitten by frog and snakes, not to move or will become one. Given horse to carry to brother. Throw ball of yarn between horse's ears. Second-- same. Third--calls swans to carry to castle in name of the Griffin of the Green Wood. Exchanges watch, handkerchief and garter with sleeping princess and kisses. Brothers switch apples. To be executed. Bear befriends. Is really man Jubal. Princess comes. Neither brother can walk over handkerchief token. Youngest does. Wed. Three helpful older men rejuvenated by beheading. Are her brothers. Jacobs MORE 142-158. Wales (Gypsy): Hampden GYPSY 69-78. Gypsy: Manning-Sanders RED 159-168.

C* Other Magic Remedies. SEE ALSO: E632 (Singing Reed); H1321.1.

Ca* The Princess of the Garden of Eden. Apple of Life sought. Youngest brother tied to iron gate, millstone, tree--still follows. Three roads, divide. King of Beasts, Birds, Fishes each call subjects and send on to next. Sprat takes. Silver ferry with three swans goes every seven years to isle and returns the same hour. He misses return ferry. Weds princess of the Garden, has son. She throws golden thread over water making bridge for him to visit home. Brothers substitute crab-apple. He is to be killed. Princess comes. Ireland: MacManus WELL 164-189.

Cb* Golden Apples of Loch Erne. Stepmother puts geasa on Conn to bring three golden apples from tree of King of the Firbolgs. Geasa on her to watch from turret. Druid of Slieve Bann gives magic steed, choose poorest nag. Nurse says to tell Druid that the Callymor of the Three Hills commands help. Druid sends on with ring token for blind man on Slieve Mich. Copper ball to follow. Goes to undersea kingdom of Finbolg king. To throw lamb to dragon on bridge. Grease self with ointment from horse's ear and pass fire unharmed. To skin horse, rub skin with ointment and wear hide through second fire. Revive horse with spring water--turns to prince, son of

King of Firbolgs. Three apples obtained. Queen stepmother dies. Ireland: MacManus BOLD 179-192.

Cc* The Magic Mirror. Rejuvenating mirror. Three brothers seek. Youngest sent on by each of three old women to older. They call all animals, birds, third calls two-headed eagle who takes prince on back. Throw feathers to two bears and they sleep. Takes mirror from under princess's pillow, dawdles, takes her ring. Eagle dips into water thrice on return to show how he felt when prince dawdled (K1041). Old women give magic wishing rod, grain full sack, clothes cutting scissors. His brothers take mirror and set him adrift. He creates own city with magic tools. Weds princess who must wed one stealing her ring. Estonia: Maas MOON 104-105.

Cd* A Handful of Hay. Youngest catches devastating white stallion, given hair to burn to summon. King to give princess to one who brings healing jewel from neck of king pelican. Horse advises to give hay to doe. She gives tip of golden horn which purifies poison pool. Grateful animals aid--fox gives drugged wine for plants. Lion gives cakes for guarding lion's cubs. Ram says to eat strength giving apple from dragon's tree and draw sword there. King Pelican fears and gives jewel. Cornwall: Manning-Sanders PETER 71-82.

D* The Lost Children. Stepmother leaves children in woods. Old woman hides them from her brother dragon. Cat flees with them, stealing dragon's flying carpet, mirror and healing flask. Cat and children must live in hut seven years until magic will work. Cat sees ill father in mirror. Boy kisses her and she turns to a girl. They fly to her father's castle on carpet, heal with flask. Hungary: Manning-Sanders GLASS 187-194.

E* The King's Dream. King dreams of golden tree with silver flowers and silver cock. Three sons seek meaning of dream. Youngest kills demon after being advised by old lady. Kills Naga king. Goes to kingdom of dead Naga king and asks riddles of his three daughters. Princesses ask to be beheaded--tree, flower and cock appear. He cuts down tree. Girls reappear. Wed. Ceylon: Tooze WONDERFUL 43-49.

F* Dwarf in dream tells Ko-Ling to fetch water from country of sleep in the South-West to cure ill father. After adventures in strange lands (Feathery people, People of the Flying Carts, plants, pygmies). He reaches country of Sleep, fetches water. Two huge birds carry him home. China: Ritchie TREASURE 102-141.

H1331.1.3. Quest for Golden Bird. Type 550. SEE ALSO: H1385.3J (Nine Peahens); H1213.1 (golden hair).

A* The Firebird. Golden apples disappear from tree nightly. King's three sons guard (H1471), youngest succeeds in catching golden bird (B102.4) at theft. It escapes leaving behind a golden feather. Three sons seek. Three roads divide. Eldest ignores fox's requests, youngest feeds (sometimes fox eats his horse). Fox carries on back and directs on quest. He ignores fox's advice in procuring bird (usually takes golden cage rather than common one) and is caught. Required to bring extraordinary horse in exchange for bird. Disobeys fox (touches golden bridle and is caught). To bring fair maiden. Obeys fox and succeeds (or fox performs task himself). Fox substitutes for maid, horse and bird (or instructs in trickery) so that hero escapes with all three treasures. Hero is warned to "buy no gallows meat." He rescues brothers being hung. They leave him dead and take prizes. Fox restores to life. On arriving in Court, bird begins to sing, maid to smile, and horse to eat. Fox often asks to have head cut off (D711). Turns to prince.

Ab* A + Mermaid required. Wolf turns self to boat and hero entices her ashore. Germany (Grimm): Lang GREEN 316-325.

Ac* A + King ill. Blossoms of life giving plant eaten each midsummer eve; song of golden bird will heal; omit death at hands of brothers motifs. Denmark: Green MIDSUMMER 48-60; Hatch MORE 214-237.

Ad* A + Grey wolf carries to castle of Kostchey the Deathless, caught stealing bird and thrown behind stables, stealing horse and thrown into bear pit. Thinks of grey wolf and he appears. Steals sleeping tsaritza from tower and takes seven golden apples back. Throws apples at Kostchey, seventh kills and sleeping tsaritza awakens. Russia: Wyndham RUSSIAN 70-94.

Ae* A + Bear helper, to strike cliff with hazel twig and will open. Bird, horse inside; sea maiden caught by peddling wares at shore, hold hand and wish self with horses, etc. Yugoslavia (Slovenia): Kavcic GOLDEN 15-24.

Af* A + uses dream grass and break-lock plant to pass guards and enter stables; crow forced to fetch Water of Life; hero gives self-playing pipe that makes all dance and invisible club which reforms brothers. He drops ring in cup to toast princess. Poland: Haviland FAVORITE..POLAND 56-81.

Ag* A + brothers lose all gambling at Parcheesi. Blue horse, red girl; brothers let down in well for water and cut rope, wolf digs tunnel and rescues. Russia (Georgia): Papashivly YES 9-27.

Ah* A + wolf grabs crow feeding on corpse and forces other crow to fly for Water of Life and Death to revive Ivan (E80). Whitney STORY pb. Russia: Downing RUSSIAN 189-201; Fenner ADVENTURES 127-147; Riordan

TALES..CENTRAL 34-44.

Ai* A + bird in golden linden tree, tabu on touching tree, troll owners require horse, girl. Fox in plaited gown of rye straw poses as preacher and says he heard of them passing in grandmother's time, etc. Trolls laugh and go home. Brothers put hero in barrel in sea. Fox rescues. Norway: Asbjornsen NORWEGIAN 49-55; Frost LEGEND 79-88; Wiggin FAIRY 42-51.

Aj* A + to kiss girl as goes to bathhouse and she will follow. Do not let her bid parents farewell. Disobeys, caught. To remove mountain from king's window in eight days. Fox performs task, fox is brother of princess. Germany (Grimm): De La Mare ANIMAL 189-201; Grimm GRIMM'S (Follett) 111-121; Grimm GRIMM'S (Grosset)7-17; Grimm GRIMM'S (Scribner's) 124-133; Grimm GRIMM'S (Viking) 119-127; Grimm GRIMM'S (World) 202-210; Grimm HOUSEHOLD 236-243; Grimm JUNIPER v. II 201-216; Hutchinson CHIMNEY..FAIRY 119-132. Ireland: Adams PRINCESS 186-189 (King of Spain's bird, King of Morocco's horse, King of Greece's daughter) /Jacobs MORE CELTIC 110-124/.

Ak* Golden blackbird. Father to die unless bird is obtained. Hare aids youngest. Touches cage. Porcelain maiden. Takes clothes while bathing in lake and she agrees to follow. Brothers throw him in lake. Hare rescues. Maid and bird sing as arrives. France (Paul Sebillot): Lang GREEN 146-152.

Al* Quest for most marvelous bird in the world. Fox aids. Disobeys and uncovers bird. Giant catches. White glaive of light from Realm of the Big Women. Pretends to be baby and is given glaive to hold. Do not unsheath. Sun Goddess, daughter of the King of the Fionn. Fox takes place of each. Asks to be beheaded, is brother of Sun Goddess. Gypsy (Ireland): Manning-Sanders RED 1-9.

Am* Omit golden apple guard motifs; brother motif. Hero shoots at Blue Falcon and feather falls, stepmother requires him to fetch bird. Fox aids. Bird belongs to giant of five heads, five humps and five throttles. To fetch white sword of light from the Big Women of Dhiurmadh, yellow bay filly of the King of Eirinn, daughter of the King of France. Fox turns to boat to sail to France. Princess comes on board and ship sails. Fox changes to sword, horse, etc. and destroys giant and Big Women. Hero turns sharp edge on sword toward stepmother and her magic is turned back onto self. She becomes a bundle of faggots. Scotland: Wilson SCOTTISH 121-136.

An* Bird of the Golden Feather. Bird plucks hair from king's beard daily. Feather falls. Sons seek. Path divides. Youngest meets jinni, puts sweets in jinni's mouth and combs hair. Takes to older brother, same. Third jinni takes to garden of birds. Touches wrong cage, caught. Steed. Caught. Pomegranate from garden of life. Badia the beautiful, daughter of the king of the Jinn. She gives tokens. Jinni takes tokens of girl, horse, etc. Must be given rosewater to drink and regains own form, left in well by brothers. Bird turns white, pomegranate black, horse to nag, girl weeps. Hero kills dragon pursuing snake. Snake turns to maid and gives three hairs to burn in need and returns him to home. Hero feigns baldness with dried tripe on head and takes place as servant. Baldness thought to be lucky. Badia asks for tokens identical to those given hero. He 'makes' tokens for master, goldsmith. Hero goes to tournament on horse provided by snake maiden. Reveals self. Arabia: Mittleman BIRD 7-29.

B* Firebird with Baba Yaga motif. Youngest son watching apple tree gets feather. Three sons divide at crossroads. Youngest calls to Baba Yaga's hut to turn to him. Baba Yaga smells a Russian. He threatens and subdues her, is given a boot heel on parting, sent to sister, given comb, third sister, brush. Disobeys orders and takes cage, is pursued and tosses heel = mountain. Comb = forest and brush = flaming river. Brothers meet and throw into pit. He digs way out and rescues a maiden being thrown to a six-headed monster. With three bundles of sticks he strikes off serpent's six heads. Weds princess and flies home on backs of two ravens. Firebird has turned to crow, is restored when arrives. Russia: Higonnet-Schnopper TALES 93-108.

C* Descent to other world. SEE ALSO: K1931.2.

Ca* The Golden Phoenix. Type 301A. Youngest catches feather of bird stealing silver apple of wisdom nightly. Three sons and father seek. Youngest enters trap door lowered with basket (K1931.2). Tricks unicorn into running horn into wall. Beheads lion. Runs around seven headed serpent until it gets its heads tangles up then beheads. Suitor task: finding the king. King as fish, rose, pear is caught. Takes cage of Phoenix as dowry. Phoenix always returns to cage at night. Flee. Two beans in frying pan left to answer. Pulled up and stone rolled over door so Sultan can't follow. French Canadian: Barbeau GOLDEN 7-25 /Colwell SECOND 67-69/.

Cb* The Three Brothers. Youngest keeps awake by putting thorns under chin. Shoots hawk which breaks church windows nightly. As hawk falls, abyss opens. Let down on rope. Girl in castle of copper combing hair. Second in home of silver. Third gold. Drinks and swings sword. Kills witch-hawk. Brothers raise princesses and leave brother. Magician agrees to carry to earth if will protect children in golden apple tree from servant. He kills serpent, is carried to upper world on magician's back. Weds. Poland: Lang YELLOW 152-155.

D* The Little Lame Fox. Father's one eye laughs, other weeps. Tells tale to youngest who remains even after knife is thrown at him. Says his magic grapevine that gave him a bucket of wine per hour was stolen. Sons seek. Fox befriended carries. To dig up vine with wooden spade, uses golden, caught. To bring golden apple tree. Fails to use wooden pole. Golden maiden. Fox takes place of each. Brothers leave in well as dead. Fox revives, turns to maiden. Maid, horse, vine, tree weep until Janko arrives. Wed. Jugoslavia: Fillmore LAUGHING 73-106. Serbia: Manning-Sanders BOOK..MAGICAL BEASTS 209-223.

E* Nightingale lacking from mosque.

Ea* Nightingale in the Mosque. SEE ALSO: Type 707. Dervish say mosque lacks nightingale Gisar. Three sons seek. Youngest aids three old women, they each solicit aid of husband, send on to next. Fights three eagles, cuts off beak of one, wing, leg of others. Hidden by old woman. Her three daughters, the eagles, bathe in milk, turn to maidens. Say would tell anything to one who harmed them. He reveals self. They aid in stealing nightingale. Brothers take, leave as dead. Nightingale refuses to sing. Warrior princess who owned nightingale comes, orders one who stole to come out. Elder two brothers sent out, killed as imposters. Youngest freed. Wed. Yugoslavia: Fillmore LAUGHING 171-200.

Eb* Golden Nightingale. Golden nightingale lacking from church built. Three sons seek. Ogress treated well aids youngest, ask her forty sons to treat as brother. Second ogress same--bring maid. Old man advises each time. Lad aims at vulture, vulture gives feather to call in need for sparing; fish, fox--same. Tasks: hide so ogress can't find. Vulture hides in closet, fish in sea, fox under earth. Rides off with all three treasures, returns. Brothers throw into well. Bird won't sing, princess weeps, etc. Old man rescues from well. Tells truth to court. Wed. Greece: Wilson GREEK 129-140.

F* Bird turns to stone. Type 707.

Fa* The White Parrot. Old lady says house lacks fountain of silver water. Brother seeks. Tree with leaves of silver, nuts of gold--same. White parrot. Doesn't wait until head under wing, is turned to stone. Sister seeks. Waits. Seizes parrot. All stones in garden come to life. Spain: Eells TALES..SPAIN 3-13.

Fb* Above + three brothers. To turn to stone if turns around when climbing hill of talking bird. Each hears voices, turns. Sister doesn't turn. Fills pitcher at spring of Water of Life, breaks twig of eternal beauty, puts bird into cage. Spills water on stones and restores all. Spain (Catalan): Lang ROSE 122-130.

Fc* The Aderna Bird. Princess to one bringing Aderna bird. He who touches to turn to stone if heart impure. Elder two brothers turn to stone. Youngest captures, forces fiend to release brothers. They take bird. Bird refuses to sing, tells

truth. Old man gives Juan magic cape. Weds. Tagalog: Sechrist ONCE 131-135.

Fd* Small White Stones. Three sisters seek work. Eldest have refused old woman. First turns around when white stone cries to her as she descends hill, turns to stone. Second same. Youngest ignores cries of stone, reaches old woman in cottage on hilltop. Spell broken. Wales: Hampden GYPSY 127-131.

Fe* The King's True Children. Six jealous queens put stone in place of young wife's babies. Fisherman raises children. Grown boy seeks Yogi seen in dream. Not to look to left or right or behind self as passes gorge. Looks, turns to stone. Milk in post at home changes color. Sister seeks. Fills water pot at source of sacred stream, sprinkles stone pilgrims to revive. Reunited with king father. India: Spellman BEAUTIFUL 49-55.

H1331.3.4* Quest for marvelous cattle. (cf. G530.2). Santiago and The Fighting Bulls. Search for four wild bulls. Santiago cared for them as youth (B389.4). Horse warns not to eat at home of devil. Puts horse's tears in eyes to stay awake. Takes what is on shelf by door and flees. Throw behind needles = cactus. Dish = sea. Mirror = ice and freezes devil (K672). Asks four bulls as reward. Weds princess. Mexico: McNeil DOUBLE 24-29.

H1331.3.5* Quest for calf that makes music. Palace of the Seven Little Hills. Wicked stepmother. Stepmother sets geasa on stepson. May never eat twice from the same table, sleep twice in same bed until fetches calf that makes music from Isle of Loneliness. Maid gives prince magic wand. Touches cow who pursues when calf is stolen, she turns back. Steals self-playing dulcimer from wolf guarded Isle of Calamity--same. Steals Princes Above-All-Measure-Beautiful. Weds. Stepmother falls dead. Ireland: Manning-Sanders BOOK..SORCERER'S 45-55.

H1370. Miscellaneous quests.

H1376.2. Quest: learning what fear is. SEE: H1440.

H1376.10* Quest to learn what poverty is. Dahomey: Courlander KING'S 45-49.

H1376.11* Brer Fox meets "Mr. Trouble." Stand at barn door and holler "Wahoo." Hounds come out. U.S.(Black, South Carolina): Faulkner DAYS 137-138.

H1377. Enigmatical quests.

H1377.1. Quest for glass of all waters (Sea water). Puerto Rico: Belpre TIGER 63-66; Carter GREEDY 119-124.

H1377.2. Quest for bouquet of all flowers. (Beehive). Puerto Rico: Belpre TIGER 63-66 (honey); Carter GREEDY 119-124.

H1377.3. Quest for hazelnuts of ay, ay, ay.

(Brings hazelnuts with thorns so that the king cries "Ay, Ay, Ay" when he takes them). Puerto Rico: Belpre TIGER 63-66 (crabs in nuts); Carter GREEDY 119-124. Haiti: Courlander PIECE 20-22 (food called "whee-ai", cactus).

H1381.3.1.1. Quest for bride for king (prince). SEE: H1213.1.

H1381.3.1.1.1. Quest for bride for king like picture he has seen. SEE: S268; T11.2.

H1385.1. Quest for stolen princess. Types 301. 403, 506. SEE ALSO: K1931.2; H1199.12; R111.1.3.

A* Harp that Harped Without a Harper. Whirlwind carries off tsar's two daughters. Brother born seeks with harp. Takes magic tablecloth, boots, invisibility cap from fighting demons. Baba Yaga obeys his commands and sends Monster of the Forest who has one sister, she hides him and Master claims Russian soul is there. He reveals self and appeases Monster with magic cloth. Sent to Monster of the Sea where second sister lives, plays harp and beguiles monster. Sister sends to Tsar-Maiden. Sturgeon carries him. Twenty white doves by pool change to maids. Tsar-Maiden agrees to wed him. He orders monsters to give up sisters. Proves that harp is as great as sword. Russia: Frost LEGEND 99-113.

B* Alberto and the Monsters. Three princesses carried off by wind. Boy seeks. Takes magic boat from quarreling men; key, hat of invisibility--likewise opens rock with key, drinks monster's water and can swing sword. Cuts off monster's seven heads, second--ten heads, third--twelve heads so strong breaks chair and bed down too. Takes three princesses' hands. Gives handkerchief token to youngest. She will wed one with handkerchief like his--wed. Tagalog: Sechrist ONCE 204-213.

C* The Kingdom Without Day. Turtledove released from trap gives boy three feathers. Magician in city of no sun has star of morning princess imprisoned. Three feathers multiply and become bird which advises. Light of day is hidden in box at foot of money tree in king's garden. To sing certain chant as digs up. King tries to sing counter-chant but bird drops dropping on king's nose and interrupts. Sun rises to sky, lad weds Star of Morning. Haiti: Thoby-Marcelin SINGING 7-14.

D* The Prince with the Golden Hand. Princess abducted by dragon. Two brothers seek, find in silver palace on cock's foot, wind freezes them. Son born to mother with hand of gold, full grown in three months, seeks brothers. Passes poppy field by cutting down poppies so can't put to sleep. Calls to cottage on cock's foot to turn to him. Old crone with two girls there aids, gives pin cushion to lead, cooling drink to protect from dragon's father to hurt wind. Reaches palace on cock's foot and calls to turn bridge to him so can cross chasm.

Drinks from Heroic Well, kills dragon. Revives brothers with water that revives and water that restores. Takes water that makes young to repay old crone and she becomes young princess. He answers her three riddles and weds. Russia (Slav): Manning-Sanders DRAGONS 103-113.

E* Sigurd the King's Son. King weds troll Ingeborg. Son Sigurd stays with her while father hunts. She hides him and tells troll's wife who calls that he's out with father. Troll wife comes twice wading in floor up to ankles, knees, waist. Says he will turn to cock until he finds her if near enough to hear curse. Ingeborg gives ring token and golden ball to follow. Troll wife keeps him seven years and gives strengthening wine until can throw her. Gives stick that brings night or hail. Sigurd finds Princess Helga in power of troll men. Using ring, she turns him to wool bundle at night to deceive troll. They escape on magic carpet. Troll pursues--stick causes hail and kills troll. Ingeborg's dog comes with tears in eyes as sign Ingeborg is in danger. Sigurd arrives in time to save her from stake. Weds Helga. (cf. G530.2). Iceland: Manning-Sanders BOOK..OGRES 53-56.

F* The Big Bird Dam. Twelve princesses disappear, twelve princes seek. After seven years of storm youngest goes ashore to rescue dog and is led to castle. Dog turns to princess and troll prince friend advises on task. Sail seven years more and slay troll king, she gives sword and draught from horn for strength. Twelve princesses scratching twelve heads of troll. Behead. After treasure and twelve princesses are on board he returns for their forgotten crowns. Red Knight sails and leaves prince. Bird Dam asks four barrels rye to eat and carries lad to troll prince with crowns and chest of gold. He waits seven years until ships sail by. He boards and sees that youngest princess sleeps with drawn sword as protection against Red Knight. Troll prince gives magic iron boat to pursue and iron club to cause storm so brothers don't see his ship pass. Arrives first and pretends to be shipwrecked beggar. Shows crown to princesses and is recognized. Weds youngest. Norway: Aulaire EAST 108-122; Undset TRUE 118-131.

G* The Wonderful Tree. Princess stolen. Jack nurses sick pigling. Princes brings seven pairs boots, napkin--to climb tree for seven days and reach dragon's country. Takes service. To give nag only oats and hay, nag asks for red-hot coals. Turns to golden winged horse. Is pigling's brother. Horse advises to find boar in wood, hare in boar, box in hare, nine wasps in box are nine lives of dragon. Horse crushes box. Hungary: Manning-Sanders GLASS 1-9.

H* The Ailpein Bird, The Stolen Princess and the Brave Knight. Princess stolen by enemy king. Harper sees and sings of whereabouts of king. Knights seeks in guise of monk. Ailpein bird flies to her. Takes her to its own castle. They cross land of ice to castle of snowy owl. Land of fire to castle of raven. Mountain of glass to golden castle of Ailpein bird. Old woman servant of princess directs knight on quest and gives three feathers dropped by bird to use in need. First = cloak to protect in ice land. Owl turns to red-haired man and they wrestle. Second feather = plume to carry over fire. Raven turns to blackhaired man and wrestles. She chooses to return home with knight. Ailpein bird carries her back. Ailpein bird is yellow-haired man, king of the birds. Scotland (Argyllshire, Macalpine clan): Nic Leodhas HEATHER 15-33.

H1385.3. Quest for vanished wife (mistress). SEE ALSO: D672G; K1861.1B.

A* Soria Moria Castle. Type 400. Cinderlad goes to sea, goes ashore when becalmed and is left behind when wind rises. Finds three princesses in castles, they give flask of strength giving drink and sword to swing, cuts off heads of three-headed troll, six, nine. Lives with three princesses. Gives wishing ring when gets homesick. Tabu: mentioning their names when (C435.1.1; C31.5) at home, taking off ring. He names and wishes them there. They comb his hair and take back ring and leave. He seeks. Old couple trade twenty mile boots for house, ask moon, west wind, where castle is. Wind is on way to dry wedding clothes. Puts ring in cup. Wed. Norway: Asbjornsen EAST 109-124; Asbjorsen NORWEGIAN 67-76; Aulaire EAST 79-92; Lang RED 37-51; Sleigh NORTH 184-194; Undset TRUE 57-71.

B* Endurance test, ring to wish self home.

Ba* Three Princesses of White Land. Type 400. Water spirit promised "what wife wears under girdle." King rears lad to protect. Grown. Boat bears all to Whiteland. Three princesses buried up to neck. Old man advises to obey third princess. To hear whisper by trolls (D758.1) in castle one night. Flask of ointment to restore and may then kill trolls. Weds youngest princess. Given wishing ring to wish home. Do not do as mother asks. Disobeys. Wishes wife were there. She ties a ring in his hair. Leaves. He seeks. Lord of Beasts calls all beasts, none know whereabouts. Gives magic self-returning snowshoe to carry to brother, Lord of Birds. Same. Lord of Fish. Pike knows. Gets hat, cloak and boots from guardian brother by trick on way (D832). North Wind advises to toss groom out door and North Wind will carry him off. Does so. Reunited with wife. Norway: Asbjornsen EAST (Doubleday) 61-70; Asbjornsen EAST 100-108; Asbjornsen EAST (Row) 20-27; Fenner PRINCESSES 168-176; Lang RED 180-187.

Bb* King of the Golden Mountain. Merchant promises first thing to rub against legs. Son grown draws circle around self and father. Mannikin agrees he may be set adrift instead. Drifts ashore. To bear torments of twelve men at night. If speaks no word for three nights serpent will beome maid and restore with Water of Life. Weds. Gives wishing ring to visit home. Tabu wishing her there. Break tabu,

left. Seeks. Takes sword, mantle of invisibility and boots from three giants arguing (D832). Arrives in time to stop wedding and reveal self to wife. Germany (Grimm): Grimm GRIMM'S (Grosset) 247-254; Grimm GRIMM'S (Viking) 75-81; Grimm GRIMM'S (World) 254-260.

Bc* Lost and Found. First thing he meets at home to go to devil. Son draws circle around father and self. Son must stay there for year and day unless princess carries him off. A princess takes to her castle South of the Sun and East of the Moon. Given wishing ring to go home. Wishes her there (tabu). Seeks. Takes magic boots from quarreling imps. King of fishes, king of birds, king of winds call subjects. North Wind shows way. Wed. Denmark: Hatch MORE 119-137.

C* Disenchantment by waiting.

Ca* The Raven. Queen wishes naughty child were raven. She turns to one. Raven calls to man to disenchant her. Stand on Tanbark heap for three days and await her. Neither eat nor drink. He breaks tabu, takes a sip and sleeps. Third time she leaves a ring and inexhaustible food. To seek her at Golden Castle of Stromberg. Shares food with giant and giant carries. Glass Mountain. Camps there one year. Takes invisible cloak, stick that opens door, and horse that climbs glass mountain, drops ring in cup. Reunited. The enchantment is broken. Wed. Germany (Grimm): Grimm GRIMM'S (Grosset) 148-154; Grimm GRIMM'S (Scribner's) 207-213; Grimm GRIMM'S (World) 295-300; Grimm HOUSEHOLD 26-31.

Cb* The Blue Mountains. Lad to spend three nights in room, beaten by monsters each night (D758.1). She revives with magic flask in the morning. To wait for her. Boy serving him sticks pin in coat and he falls asleep. Second day she leaves sword and goes. To seek in Blue Mountains. Old man sends to brother, second sends to brother. Last calls birds. Eagle carries. Feeds when turns head. Runs out of food and eagle dumps into sea. Swims ashore. Weds. Lang YELLOW 255-265.

Cc* The Little Soldier. Serpent with head of woman (Ludovine, daughter of the king of the Low Countries) asks deliverance. Brings tunic from closet. Eight hands attack (D758.1). She puts on and is maid to waist. Again--skirt, eight arms--maid to knee. Shoes and stockings eight goblins--all maid. To come at nine in morning when she goes in carriage. He is given wine and oversleeps, second day given sleep inducing flower, third scented scarf. Fisher girl lends him magic purse and mantle. He wishes self in Low Countries. She gets purse by deception then ignores him. He wishes she and self at ends of the world. She gets secret of cloak and abandons him there. He recovers with magic horn-producing plums (D881.1). Weds fisher girl. (Charles Devlin): Lang RED 153-171.

D* Cat 'n Mouse. Type 401. Jack fights off varmits three nights in a row and disenchants cat and mouse, sisters (D758.1). Next night witch herself comes, Jack not to let her do anything for him, she tries to turn his meat but he holds her in fire until burnt up. They visit Jack's house and his brothers' wives hide in shame. U.S. (Appalachia): Chase JACK 127-134.

E* The Nine-Headed Giant. Husband seeks wife and maid carried off. Old woman pounding rice sends to next. Old woman washing radishes gives him a ginseng to eat for strength. Lifts stone and enters underground world. Drinks 'general's drink' until can wield giant's sword. After three months giant returns. Hero's wife gives giant nine barrels of wine to drink. Hero beheads. Heads spring back to body. Wife and maid cover head with ashes as they fall to ground to prevent this. Korea: De Regniers GIANT 31-38 /Zong-in Sob FOLK TALES FROM KOREA/.

F* Swan Maiden. SEE ALSO: B652.1.1.

Faa* The Adventures of King Sutan. Hunter hides wing of youngest of seven bathing fairies (F302.4.2). King weds. Wife given wing back and she leaves. King follows past Splitting Rock and bird Roc (B31.1) carries to Ksyangan. Drops wing token in water jug. Suitor tasks. 1. Clear forest--God of Seventh Heaven sends elephants to perform. 2. Burn trees without fire--god sends birds with fiery beaks. 3. Pick up scattered seed--birds come (B582.2). 4. Choose daughter's finger--fly shows. Malaysia: Asia FOLK 1 21-27.

Fab* The Peacock Maidens. See Faa. Splitting Rock, suitor tasks. Choosing hand in dark test. Firefly shows. China: Dolch STORIES..OLD CHINA 139-165.

Fba* The Swan Maidens. Wife finds robe. Leaves. He hunts East of the Sun and West of the Moon. Old man calls beasts, second--birds, third--fish. Dolphin knows where land lies. He gets invisible cap and flying shoes from quarreling men. Flies to land. Suitor test: tell wife from sisters. Forefinger is pricked by needle sewing for children. Jacobs EUROPEAN 98-104.

Fbb* The Palace of Rainbow Fountains. Youngest son catches swan trampling garden. To seek in Land of Rainbow Fountains beyond sun and moon. Takes book, cloak and cannon-noise producing hat from three quarreling giants (D832). Goes to mother of moon, sun, seven winds. Seventh wind has been drying bride's linen there. He pledges her to wed only him. Leaves sword on wall with message. Takes magic loaf and wine and leaves. Gives loaf to country in famine. Wine to country of no laughter. Son born, four years old asks for sword. She sees inscription and goes after husband. Calls for him to be sent out from palace. Two brothers come--rejected. He comes. SEE ALSO: H1331.1C. Poland: Zajdler POLISH 33-51.

Fbc* East of the Sun and North of the Earth. Youngest brother catches three swan maidens trampling meadow and hides feathers. She agrees to wed in three years. Weds, must leave, gives ring, bridesmaids give two golden apples. Seeks. Takes hundred mile boots from quarreling trolls by "dividing so that neither is jealous." He takes boots. Cap of invisibility, magic sword which kills or revives, obtained in same way. Addresses old woman kindly. She calls birds. Phoenix takes. Asks Prince "what do you see?" (K1041). Arrives. Gives tokens. Kills troll captors and restores throne. Weds. Sweden: Kaplan FAIRY 142-161.

Fc* The wife from another world. Grateful stag tells hunter to take fairy's wings. Do not return until fourth child is born. Cannot carry four and will not leave child behind. Gives her wings after three children. She leaves. Stag tells to go to seventh pool and get into bucket lowered from heavens. Never returns. Korea: Jewett WHICH 109-123.

Fd* The Adventures of Magboloto. Magboloto hides wings of goddess, weds, she finds wings and leaves. He seeks, asks North Wind, East, South, West, Eagle takes him there. Grandmother sets tasks: spread ten jars of grain and retrieve again--ants aid. Task: hull hundred bushels of rice--rats aid. Fell all trees on mountain--bear aids. Philippines (Visayan): Sechrist ONCE 67-75.

Fe* The Swan Princess. Cat, sparrow, and dwarf keep house. If witch Baby Yaga Spindle-Shank comes to count spoons, dwarf is to hide. He hears her count his spoon and calls to "leave my spoon alone!" Caught and carried off in mortar. Calls and cat and sparrow come. Second day--same. Third day--cat and sparrow don't hear. Huntsman shoots hole in window and rescues dwarf. Dwarf tells hunter to hide by lake and take feathers of swan maiden (F302.4.2). To wed if he prays for her every Sunday for a year and never mention her beauty. He mentions beauty. To seek a mountain of glass. Reaches mountain. Calls sparrow who had given him a feather to call on in need. Swan turns him to sparrow, to drop feather thrice on way up. To perch on feather to rest. At top voice says do not drink or you cannot set me free. He drinks. Must seek in Kingdom of Everlasting Night. Calls cat and cat changes him to cat. There Swan Princess strokes him and he becomes man. She sends him to her house. To employ three strong men there and take to prince's castle to claim her. Prince orders to eat and drink huge amount (F601.2). Servants Glutton and Soaker do task. Boiling bath prepared, Freezer cools. Prince of Kingdom of Everlasting Night thus defeated. Sun Maiden and he (as sparrow) fly home, wed. Hoke WITCHES 176-186.

Ff* The Man Who Married a Snow Goose. Boy kept imprisoned to escape prediction breaks seal on window and sets out. Follows white snow geese and hides garments of smallest. Weds. Sister-in-law mocks and she finds cloak and leaves. He seeks. Crosses boiling pot by leaping from one chunk of meat to next; passes two bears by tossing one-half salmon to each; passes clapping mountains (D1553) by wearing absurd disguise and walking backwards chanting strange words. He distracts mountains and they fail to clap; old lady directs to her brother; Qayungayung, old man whittling wood from stick, chips become salmon, eels, walrus. Boy snatches Qayungayung's hatchet and forces to aid. Chips off huge king salmon which carries to lost wife. Finds in winter village of birds. He breaks tabu and looks into their meeting-house. They move. Eagle carries him and drops into ocean. Son turns to puffin and nests by sea crying (A1999). Eskimo: Maher BLIND 79-98.

Fg* The Rabbit Prince. R. pulls feather from thieving bird. Turns to princess. Asks for feather back later--throws at rabbit and he turns to prince. They go to sky land, meet her father, magic feather grows to climb to sky, feather protects from father. Mouse and woodpecker companions aid. Africa (Shangani): Berger BLACK 91-105.

Fh* Vaino and the Swan Princess. Vaino burns robe of one of nine swan maidens. She calls "If you are older, you shall be my father; if younger, my brother; if same age, my husband." Her father sets tasks to rid self of Vaino. Task: bring golden chains from clouds. Old woman tells to ride horse she gives with eyes closed, stretch hands up and grab golden chains when feels horse slipping away. Falls to earth in land of death. Settles quarrel between skeletons fighting over debt by telling them debt no longer matters in land of dead. They give him a stone to take back. Settles quarrels over land and rivers same way. Rattles chains and all sea creatures come--cannot carry him from land of dead. Birds--bald eagle comes. He throws stones to make islands for eagle to rest. Weds. Golden chains disenchant other eight princesses. Finland: Bowman TALES..TUPA 34-41.

J* Bird maiden caught, bound demon freed.

Ja* The Nine Peahens and the Golden Apples. Youngest son catches peahen robbing golden apple tree (H1471). Makes love to one nightly. Brothers send witch to spy. She snips lock of maiden's hair and she turns to peafowl and flees. Seeks. Finds lake where peahens bathe but old woman gives serving man bellows to put him to sleep as he waits. Repeat. Peahen comes no more. Seeks. Finds in castle. Do not open twelfth room. Opens and gives water to dragon in cask. Dragon carries off princess. He follows and steals her back. Dragon catches but spares for sake of drink given. He attempts to earn horse as swift as dragon's. Returns and steals princess. SEE: H1199.12.4C; H1331.1.3 (quest for golden bird). Yugoslavia: Fillmore LAUGHING 107-138. Hungary: Manning-Sanders GLASS 27-40. Serbia: Lang VIOLET 50-64; Rackham FAIRY 100-111.

Jb* Witch and Her Servants. Youngest son catches swan stealing fruit. She is in power of witch who once cut off a lock of her hair. Gives ring to lead to her. Will die if goes wrong way. Old man gives crumbs and hare to give wild animals in wood. Dwarf with two lions thanks him for feeding animals and lets pass. Reaches castle of maid. Breaks tabu and opens door. Gives water to man in cauldron of pitch. Castle carried off. Old man suggests he work for witch. Obtains magic horse and defeats magician (H1199.12.4C). Russia: Buck FAIRY 172-180 (freed demon motif); Lang YELLOW 172-191.

Jc* The White Dove. Youngest son catches dove stealing pears. Follows to mountain top, greets little grey man "God bless you." Thus releasing from spell. Finds dove caught in spider's web, turns to princess at sight of him. Weds. Germany (Grimm): Shubb ABOUT 52-53.

K* The Frog Princess.

Ka* SEE: B641A (Frog Bride). Offended frog maid flies off as swan. Must be sought in Land of Koschei the Deathless. Old man gives rolling ball to follow. He spares bear, drake, pike, at Baba Yaga's hut. Baba Yaga tells that Koschei's death lies on point of needle in egg in duck in hare in trunk in oak. Bear, hare, drake, pike help obtain these. Russia: Riordan TALES.. CENTRAL 129-137; Whitney IN 37-43.

Kb* SEE: B641A. Offended frog maid turns to cuckoo and leaves. Must be sought on glass mountain. Old man gives ball to follow, gives advise to pass three giant guards. To throw bones of cock miller eats for supper at mountain to climb. Witch assigns task--empty pond with thimbles. Princess performs, witch turns to rain cloud. He sticks darkest part and kills. Russia (Ukraine): Manning-Sanders CHOICE 26-38 /Manning-Sanders BOOK..PRINCES 84-96/.

L* The Handless Maiden. Evil one buys "what stands behind mill"--is miller's daughter. She washes and draws circles around self and he cannot touch. Devil tells father not to give her water to wash. She bathes in tears. Devil has her hands cut off. She bathes arms in tears. Devil gives up. She wanders. Angel opens path to royal garden. King discovers her stealing his pears--weds. Babe born. Evil one changes letter from king to order to kill her. She flees. King seeks for seven years. Discovers with aid of angel. Germany (Grimm): Grimm GRIMM'S (Scribner's) 87-94.

M* The Sky People. Sky people steal Kunda's wife and cow. Animals he formerly befriended aid him (B582.2). Rain bird tells where went. Python forms rope to sky. Ant bear digs hole in sky. Sky people set task: eat pile of food. Driver ant performs. Split rock and light fire under it--lightning performs. Identify wife-- fly lights on head. Identify cow-- tickbird does. Rewarded and released. Heady WHEN 62-67.

H1385.4. Quest for vanished husband. SEE ALSO: A762.1Aa; B641.6.1 (cf. D735.1 Beauty and the Beast; D2003).

Aa* Type 425. East of the Sun. Girl wed to white bear (B640.1), looks at him when sleeping (C32.1), candle drips on shirt (C916.1). Leaves to wed troll with nose three ells long. She seeks, Is given golden apple by old woman who sends to another, golden spinning wheel, golden carding comb. East, West, North, South winds carry on way (H1232). Buys three nights by prince's bed for golden objects. Third night he refuses sleeping potion and hears her. Test: washing tallow spots from shirt. Troll princess and others fail and explode in rage as she succeeds. Norway: Asbjornsen EAST (Doubleday) 19-34; Asbjornsen EAST (Macmillan) 1-16; Asbjornsen EAST (Row) 7-16; Asbjornsen EAST (Viking) 139-152; Baker TALKING 123-127; Dalgliesh ENCHANTED 66-79; Hutchinson CHIMNEY.. FAIRY 134-150; Minard WOMENFOLK 111-126; Undset TRUE 236-249; Wiggin FAIRY 17-27.

Ab* Brown Bear of Norway. Youngest princess says will wed Brown Bear of Norway. Three children born, carried off by eagle, greyhound and lady. Visits parents, advised to burn his bearskin. Must seek. Visits three huts where three sons are cared for, gives magic scissors, comb, hand-reel. Takes service with woodman. Courting footman has horns put on head by magic gifts. Three nights outside prince's chamber for three gifts. Wed. Ireland: Arbuthnot ANTHOLOGY 252-256; Arbuthnot FAIRY 90-95; Lang FIFTY 37-45 /Lang LILAC/; Lang BLUE 24-37; Lang FIFTY 63-72; Williams-Ellis ROUND 145-160.

Ac* Whitebear Whittington. Father picking flower for daughter must pledge first thing met at home--daughter. White Bear takes daughter. Speaks name and bear leaves. Old women give golden chinquapin, hickory nut, and walnut. To open if in trouble. Washes shirt but other claims performed task and is to wed. She trades wool, wheel, loom from nuts for nights with bear. He asks if should keep old key or new (Z62.1). U.S. (Appalachia): Chase WICKED 52-64 /Ross BLUE 123-137/.

B* Three Feathers. Type 425N. Girl lights candle to see unseen bridegroom, must work as laundress for seven years. Given three magic feathers by bird husband, do all work. Wooers are compelled to perform task all night, closing shutters, pouring brandy, bringing in laundry, etc. Prince arrives after seven years and weds. England: Jacobs MORE 37-42; Steel ENGLISH 43-51. Ireland: MacManus WELL 98-111 (wed to magpie, city of women, three women are compelled to perform task all night) /Provensen PROVENSEN 49-56/.

C* White Bear King Valemon. Youngest daughter pledges self for bear's golden wreath. Eldest daughter's are given. He asks questions and detects and returns. Youngest "have you ever sat softer?" "No, never." Drop of tallow betrays as looks at him. Goes to wed troll. Old woman gives scissors that snip cloth from air, replenishing flask, magic tablecloth. Feeds impoverished family and smith makes her claws to climb steep mountains. Trades magic objects for night with bear. Trolls dropped through trap door in bridge during bridal procession. Norway: Asbjornsen NORWEGIAN 150-157; Manning-Sanders BOOK..MAGICAL 184-195.

D* The Soaring Lark. Pledges to wed lion in return for lark. If ray of light touches lion will turn to dove for seven years. Wife persuades to attend sister's wedding. Turns to dove. Lets fall drop of blood, white feather every seven miles. Sun and moon give casket and egg to open in need. Four winds aid. Lion to fight enchanted princess in caterpillar form. Maid must cut eleventh reed on shore of Red Sea and beat caterpillar to break spell. To leap on griffin's back with lover after battle, disenchanted princess leaps on instead. Trades dress from casket, gold hen with chicks from egg for nights with lion husband. They flee on griffin. She drops nut given by North Wind halfway across Red Sea and tree sprouts for Griffin to rest. Germany (Grimm): Darrell ONCE 38-42; Grimm GRIMM'S (Grosset) 366-373; Grimm GRIMM'S (Scribner's) 199-206.

E* The Disenchanted Husband. Type 425B. The witch's task, the unseen bridegroom. Pulls up bush and finds stairs into underground palace, weds unseen bridegroom. Drops fall from lamp as she looks at him. Old woman gives twig, strike ground if in need, second gives raven feather. To see again she must satisfy his mother. Tasks: separate grains, strikes with twig and ants aid. Fill twelve mattresses with mixed feathers--four geese, four ducks, four stoats. Raven's father brings birds to help. Task: bring gift from Queen of Nether World. Puts copper coin between teeth for ferryman, tabu on speaking, gives dog loaf, tabu on eating or sitting in cave. Tabu on opening gift, opens and can't get dancing dolls back in box. Husband tells to strike ground with golden bough and go back in box. Restored to husband. Jacobs EUROPEAN 129-141.

Eb* The White Dog. Father promises first thing met at home. Tallow drops on heart of husband. Must serve witch. To bring musicians for wedding in box. Advised by dog husband to replace log in bridge, put gate on hinge, roll barrel over for dog to sleep in. Tabu on eating at witch's house. Puts food inside dress and it answers witch's call convincing her girl ate. Guardians refuse to stop her. She opens box. Dog puts musicians back in box. Task: washing tallow from shirt. Her tears remove them. Enchantment broken. Scandinavia: Owen CASTLE 51-62.

F* Prince Hat Beneath the Earth. First thing king meets in return for three singing leaves daughter wants. Spark of light falls on prince. He takes her to his sister's palace. Leave son there. Do not let sister greet him or will see no more. Forgets. Troll wives help on quest when greeted properly. Give self-spinning wheel, gold loom, ever-full purse. Troll witch who has her husband in power sends girl to live in goose house, she adorns it regally with magic gifts' aid. Trades articles for time with husband. They conspire and push witch into kettle as she checks its heat. Sweden: Kaplan FAIRY 162-199.

G* Sprig of Rosemary. Girl pulls rosemary and man asks why she steals his firewood and leads through hole to underground palace. Not to use one key. Sees his snakeskin in chest. Palace vanishes. Sun, moon and wind give nuts to open in need. Trades for chance to see groom. Touches with sprig of rosemary and his memory returns. Spain (Catalan): Lang ROSE 107-113.

H* Lame Dog. Youngest says will wed even lame dog. Weds. Drop of oil reveals her looking at him. Toad offers to help find if will be his friend. Refuses as can love only lame dog. Wolf, chained lion same. Nightingale tells to loosen lion's chains. Turns to prince. Sweden: Baker TALKING 77-87.

I* The Enchanted Pig. Youngest daughter to wed pig from the north. Weds. Man by night. Witch advises to tie thread around ankle to break spell. He leaves. Seek until wear out three pair iron shoes and steel staff. Goes to moon, sun, wind. Given chicken and toad by mother of each to save bones. Hidden by mothers of moon, sun, wind who question their sons. Climbs to top of roof of husband's house by making ladder of chicken bones, uses little finger for one lost. Enchantment broken. Lang RED 98-113.

J* Lion Lover. Lion promised first thing met at home. She visits home. To return by cockcrow, fails. Must wear out iron shoes. Sun and moon help. At castle throws shoes at door and they open. Spell broken. Puerto Rico: Alegria THREE 34-39.

K* The Ruby Prince. Prince emerges from ruby, weds princess. Tabu: asking his origin. He turns into green serpent with ruby in forelock and leaves. Maid tells of seeing little men emerge from smoke hole in wood and dance. Wife hides and sees, dances for king of these men. Granted wish. He grows to full size. Pakistan: Siddiqui TOONTOONY 144-154.

L* Celery. Girl pulls up celery. Plant pulls her underground. Old gentleman keeps her in palace. She dreams of prince nightly. Refuses to wed old man. Finally agrees. He is prince, spell half broken by marrying him. She bears son. Tabu on opening little iron door. She opens. Old women spinning there push her through wall--finds self alone in forest. Remembers nothing. Old gentleman husband visits

nocturnally and kisses her and leaves baby clothes while she sleeps. She is warned and remains awake third night and grabs him. He vanishes leaving only coat with celery in pocket. She burns this and this breaks the spell. Manning-Sanders GIANT 43-53.

H1385.5. Quest for vanished lover.

A. Bird lover. Type 432.

Aa* Finist the Bright Falcon. Type 432. Youngest daughter asks for feather of Finist the Bright Falcon. Turns to prince on striking ground. Comes as falcon nightly. Sisters wound with knives on windowsill. Must wear out three pair of iron shoes, three iron staffs, and eat three stone loaves before sees. Old lady gives silver spinning board and golden spindle, follows ball of thread to second--golden egg and silver fish, third--golden embroidery hoop and needle. Trades for nights with husband. Flee and return home. She goes to church with Finist three times before father sees carriage go to his house and discovers. Russia: Riordan TALES..CENTRAL 63-72; Whitney IN 85-94.

Ab* Golden Wand. Girls to eat salty yeast. Man who gives water in dreams will wed. Youngest dreams of golden wand. Father brings from trip. Turns to prince in form of dove. Washes in cup and becomes man. She leaves knife in cup and he is hurt when sister tries to call him. He leaves. She pursues. Dove tells to heal prince with certain bark and spring water. She disguises as doctor and cures. Tells tale and reveals self. Greece (Epirus): Neufeld BEWARE 3-10.

Ac* Parrot of Limo Verde. Jealous woman sends three daughters to spy on princess. Three eyes, two eyes, one eye (D830.1.1.1). Princess gives sleeping potion to first two. One eye sees all. Parrot bathes in water and becomes youth. They put knives on window ledge. Princess wears out shoes of bronze to seek. She goes to moon and is given pillow for pillow-lace making with gold bobbins. Wind takes her to prince's castle. She acts as lace seller, he sees and they are reunited. Brazil: Baker TALKING 179-183.

Ad* The Blue Bird (Madame d'Aulnoy). Stepmother hangs tree with knives. Girl seeks. Old woman gives four eggs to break. Ivory hill--first egg = gold hooks to climb. Second--chariot to carry. Buys three nights in chamber of echoes under his room. Etc. D'Aulnoy: Lang GREEN 1-28.

Ae* Three Golden Eggs. Stepmother substitutes own daughter as bride of Prince of Greece. She turns him to hawk, hound, linnet as he repeatedly tries to return to Maeve. Witch stepsister turns tree branches to serpents which bite him as he tries to sing to Maeve. At River of Healing he is persuaded by witch to forget Maeve and wed her daughter. Maeve trades contents of three golden eggs (silver spinning wheel and tiny maid, tiny weaver and loom, tiny coach) for three nights with him. Ireland: MacManus HIBERNIAN 25-35 /MacManus WELL 31-48/.

Af* The Pigeon's Bride. Princess has pigeon suitor, bathes in milk and becomes youth. She breaks tabu, tells father. Seeks with three pair iron shoes and three iron staffs. Builds bathhouse and gives free bath to all who tell story. Poor girl sees twelve pigeons in little house bathe in milk and become men. Tells this story. Rooster in wooden shoes crying "I'm late" is followed there. Yugoslavia: Fillmore LAUGHING 51-72.

Ag* The Green Knight. Stepmother puts poison nail in oar and wounds prince visiting girl nocturnally. Bird tells her to make soup of a baby snake and go as maid to serve him. Cured. Wed. Denmark: Lang VIOLET 203-218.

Ah* Earl of Mar's daughter will wed no one but pet dove who becomes man nightly. Bears seven sons whom his mother raises. Dove asks mother to turn twenty-four men to storks, seven sons to swans, self to goshawk, carry her off from bridal party. Scotland: Nic Leodhas BY LOCH 44-52. Britain: Finlay TATTERCOATS 24-27; Jacobs ENGLISH 166-170; Manning-Sanders BOOK..MAGICAL 177-183.

B* Black Bull of Norroway. Type 425. Girl wishes to wed Black Bull of Norroway (C26). He comes for her. To eat from his right ear (B115.1), drink from left. Stops at castle of his three brothers, given apple, pear, plum to open when in danger. To fight Old Bull, if all turn blue, he won; if red, he lost. Not to move or will be lost to him. She moves, must seek. Reaches hill of glass (F751). Serves smith seven years for iron shoes. Climbs hill. Whoever washes blood from knight's clothes may wed. She washes but witch substitutes own daughter. Trades gold jewelry in apple for night with knight. Pear, plum same. Chants "Seven long years I served for thee" etc. He is awake third night. Weds. Regained human form by defeating Old Bull. England: De La Mare ANIMAL 225-231; Frost LEGENDS 13-19; Jacobs MORE 20-27; Lang BLUE 358-363; Williams-Ellis FAIRY..BRITISH 89-95.

Bb* Three magic nuts given by old woman to crack in need. Little women carding, spinning, reeling come out. At three castles visited with bull she asks that he be put in field at first castle, stable second, with her third. She pulls a thorn from his foot and disenchants. To be bull only by day now. Arbuthnot FAIRY 24-27; Arbuthnot ANTHOLOGY 162-165; Steel ENGLISH 110-117.

C* Pinto Smalto. Father asked to bring quantities of sugar and almonds from fair. Girl makes a marzipan prince. Wicked queen steals. She seeks. Old woman tells to say three magic

phrases in need. A jeweled coach, a singing bird, gold cage, and bolts of embroidered cloth appear. She exchanges for three nights outside prince's door. Sleeping potion. Reunited. Italy (Il Pentamarone, Basile): Green CLEVER 90-97; Mincielli OLD 98-107.

D* The Iron Stove. Lost princess reaches iron stove with enchanted prince inside. Will wed if she returns and scrapes hole in stove with knife. Her father sends miller's daughter. Prince asks "Is it dawn?" "Yes, I can hear my father's mill." Swineherd's daughter "Hear my father's horn." Princess sent. Wishes to bid father farewell. Tabu--saying more than three words. Breaks tabu and prince vanishes. Seeks. Stays with toads in hut, given three needles to climb mountain of glass, ploughwheel to cross three swords, given three nuts with dresses to buy three nights by prince. Return to toads, are sons of king. Nut becomes castle. Germany (Grimm): Grimm GRIMM'S (Scribner's) 255-261. Lang YELLOW 41-47 /Lang FIFTY 146-151/.

H1385.6. Quest for lost sister. SEE ALSO: H1385.1.

H1385.6.1* Lass who went out at the cry of dawn. Elder sister goes out at dawn to wash in dew for beauty and never returns. Younger sister seeks. Parents give blessing and father gives purse and goldpiece, mother gives bobbin of yarn, paper of pins, golden needle, silver thimble and wee knife in white towel. Gives gold in purse to tinker to buy horse for cart. Given advise "Things are not what they seem." Gives ragged man pins. "Gold and silver are a match for evil." Reaches wizard who holds sister captive. Hears sister calling but recalls advice and ties her arm to a chair with the yarn so she cannot go toward sound. To choose sister from seven statues, puts thimble on each, turns black on all but one. Flee--throws gold needle at pursuing wolf and kills. Wizard pursues--knife with blessings of mother and father kills. Ragged man becomes prince and weds sister. Tinker becomes prince and weds younger sister. Scotland: Nic Leodhas THISTLE 62-73 /Minard WOMENFOLK 83-92/.

H1400 - H1599. Other tests.

H1400. Fear test.

H1409.1* Princess Finola and the Dwarf. Dwarf can rescue princess if is willing to "pay the price." Is asked for each eye as price by fairy and cormorants met en route. Gives. Turns to prince. Rescues princess. Ireland: Sheehan FOLK 37-50.

H1410. Fear test: staying in frightful place.

H1411. Fear test: staying in a haunted house. SEE: Q82; E440 (walking ghost 'laid').

H1411.1. Fear test: staying in haunted house where corpse drops piecemeal down the chimney. Dead man's members call out to hero "Shall we fall or shall we not?" Ghost laid by fearlessness. Rewarded with treasure. SEE ALSO: E373.1; H1440 (learning fear). Spain: Boggs THREE 99-108. Mallorca: Manning-Sanders BOOK.. GHOSTS 9-13 (had to box ghost's ears to free soul). Leach THING 46-48. Wales: Sheppard-Jones WELSH 167-172.

H1411.2. Fear test. Staying in haunted house infested by cats. Type 326. SEE: D702.1.1 (cat's paw cut off, woman's hand missing); H1440 (learning fear).

H1411.2.0.1. Hero whacks each of thirteen cats as they leave, visits thirteen sick women in village that morn and takes their catskins and gold bribe to keep secret. Mill thus rid of annual haunting (D702.1.1). Denmark: Owen CASTLE 41-48.

H1411.4. Fear test. Spending night in house (hall) haunted by demon (monster).

H1411.4.1* Cobbler to resole shoe at night in haunted chalet on Guggialp. Giant boar's head appears at window, pushes cobbling tools about, cobbler slaps paw. Cobbler melts cheese on toast. Boar roasts paw over fire and cuts pieces and eats, cobbler refuses to eat. Boar leaves in rage. Vanquished. Switzerland (German): Duvoisin THREE 196-202.

H1411.4.2* Objects or animals in haunted building are identified as evil spirits and destroyed. China: Birch CHINESE 95-100 (pig, cock, scorpion).

H1411.4.2.1* Lad challenged by demon after winning archery contest. Frost LEGENDS 69-75 (Paper bag, mud, seven-headed and seven-armed demon).

H1411.4.2.2* Harp, shoes, sticks, kettle and sieve are playthings of ghosts. Two brothers attempt to destroy objects but third brother rescues and lives on in house in friendship with ghosts. Korea: Jewett WHICH 16-28 /Littledale GHOSTS 45-59/.

H1411.4.3* Endurance test in haunted room to free princess.

H1411.4.3.1* The Invisible Hands. Lad sleeps in haunted castle--invisible hands serve food. Voice says is Moorish girl under spell. Will give three bags of replenishing gold if stays three nights. Beaten by invisible hands each night. Ointment heals. He succeeds. Travels to land of Moors. Viceroy's daughter to be wed. He shows ring token (H94). She asks guests if should use old or new key (Z62.1). Wed. Portugal: Michael PORTUGUESE 20-27.

H1411.4.3.2* Lad to spend night in haunted rooms. After each endurance princess gives him the objects of inheritance quest. Curse of

vampire uncle broken. He weds princess. Wins inheritance from father. Spicer LONG 73-91.

H1411.4.3.3* Simon. To rid castle of ghost and wed princess. Tells ghost to open door himself. This releases ghost. Asks head cut off, white bird flies off. Wed. He goes home, is robbed en route and parents disbelieve his tale. Princess arrives and reveals. Poland: Zajdler POLISH 148-169.

H1411.4.4* The death watch. Boy sees princess remove head and knows her to be a witch. Princess dies and asks that he read Psalter over her body for three nights. He draws circle around self with knife and does not look behind. Witch comes from coffin first night, creepy thing second, denizens of hell third. He reads on. Stake is driven through witch's heart and body buried on third morning. Russia: Downing RUSSIAN 152-155.

H1411.4.5* Enchanted Prince. Maid who watches in room all night will break spell. Two older sisters fail. Youngest follows ghost to underground kingdom. Breaks gold and silver branches in morning and hides in apron. He sees branches in morning and throws out window. They turn to gold and silver palaces. Wed. SEE ALSO: F 1015.1.1 (Twelve Dancing Princesses). Hungary: Manning-Sanders CHOICE 183-190 /Manning-Sanders BOOK..PRINCES 49-56/.

H1411.4.6* Lady's ghost appears in library and terrorizes by removing head and making faces. Lad is unimpressed. Second night she finds him there she leaves in disgust. China: Birch CHINESE 62-79 /Mayne GHOSTS 168-183/.

H1411.4.7* Old woman sleeping in haunted room sees ghost counting hidden gold. Money found. Ghost laid. Netherlands: De Leeuw LEGENDS ..HOLLAND 81-88 /Littledale GHOSTS 87-96/.

H1411.4.8* Cracks nuts with ghost who comes in on first night, knocks skeleton apart second night and has to reassemble, dead man with slit throat on third night shows buried gold. To reveal murderer to magistrate. Wales: Hampden GYPSY 53-58.

H1411.4.9* Lad spends night in haunted castle. Two men bring coffin in. He must divide coins in bag equally or die. Cuts last one in half. Given treasure. Poland: Borski GOOD 34-40.

H1411.4.10* Lad sheltered in haunted castle. Seven women bring chest with ghost of old man inside. Lad sets ghost by fire and gives pipe and glass of whiskey, ghost drops them. Lad forces ghost to pay for breakage. Ghost gives gold to pay off his debts so soul may rest. Gypsy: Manning-Sanders RED 55-61.

H1411.4.11* Golden Ball. Type 326A. Young man gives two girls each a golden ball. If lost, loser will hang. Youngest loses ball. Her sweetheart seeks. Must spend three nights in house of bogles. Giant looks out window and lad cuts in two, bogles clamor for second half. Second night--front cut in two and halves go up chimney. Third night bogles play with ball under bed, he cuts off arms and legs and they flee leaving ball. On gallows she calls for mother, father, lover. He arrives with ball and saves her. England: Jacobs MORE 12-15; Manning-Sanders BOOK..GHOSTS 62-67; Steel ENGLISH 79-83.

H1412. Fear test: spending night in church.

H1412.2. Tailor to sew pair of trousers in church at night. Ghostly head rises from floor. "Do you see this head?" "I see that but I'll sew this!" Neck, chest, etc. Finishes and flees into MacDonald castle. Ghost hits gate. Handprint still there. Scotland: Jacobs CELTIC 68-71; Manning-Sanders BOOK..GHOSTS 43-46. Scotland (Isle of Man): Spicer THIRTEEN GHOSTS 112-119.

H1419. Other tests of fear.

H1419.1* Man dares to cross Seoul during storm and drive three nails in roof of East gate. Rescues girl hanging by hair in tower en route and is to wed her. Her parents set him studying to be a scholar. He flees. Fears only one thing--learning. Korea: Jewett WHICH 65-73.

H1419.2* Fearless girl needs no husband. Girl grinds in mill at night, throws goblin into hopper and grinds him until he promises to leave off haunting mill. Sees mouse later and screams in terror. Consents to wed. Scotland: Nic Leodhas HEATHER 69-79.

H1419.3* Man eats garlic, wrestles ghost who blows freezing wind in face. He blows garlic back and keeps ghost from winning until dawn when ghost turns to a coffin plank. China: Birch CHINESE 62-69 /Mayne GHOSTS 168-183/.

H1419.4* Fiddler goes through bog repeatedly despite boggles. Fights boggles off once, second time he starts to fall into river but belt catches on branch and saves him. Found in morning with shred of ghost's shroud cloth in hands. Scotland: Spicer THIRTEEN MONSTERS 9-18.

H1440. The learning of fear. Type 326. SEE ALSO: H1411.1.

A* The Youth Who Could Not Shudder. Sexton to teach him fear appears as ghost in bell tower, is tossed downstairs. Questing for fear youth takes seven corpses from gallows and warms them by fire. In castle cats ask to play cards, he feigns cutting their nails and screws paws to bench (H1411.2). Bed flies about room with him. Second night body falls piecemeal down chimney (H1411.1) and he must play skittles with bones. He turns skulls on his lathe to round so will roll better (H1433). Third night six men bear in a coffin. He takes corpse into bed to warm it and it tries to strangle him. A

huge bearded man tests his strength at the anvil and youth splits anvil catching beard of old man in it (K1111.1). He asks mercy and gives three chests of gold, one for poor, one for king and one for self. Spell on castle broken. To wed king's daughter. Her maid pours cold water with fish on him in bed--he shudders. Germany (Grimm): Bang GOBLINS 15; Carle ERIC 75-88; Grimm GRIMM'S (Scribner's) 7-18; Grimm GRIMM'S (World) 261-272; Grimm JUNIPER 23-41; Lang BLUE 88-100.

B* Lad taught fear. Boy falls.

Ba* Corpse on Bell Rope. Voice "I'm going to fall." "Go ahead." Devil falls in piecemeal (H1411.1). Lad continues to eat calmly amidst devils. Rewarded. To wed girl if she can show him fear. She sends for sieve with crow under it, bird flies up as he lifts sieve and frightens by startling. Slovenia: Kavcic GOLDEN 60-70.

Bb* Boy doomed to roam until frightened. Body falls piecemeal in haunted house (H1411.1). Is ghost of owner, shows treasure. Instructs how to lay ghost. Girl must make him afraid or cannot cease wandering to wed her. Gives two doves in basket, they fly out, startling him and he shudders. Portugal: Michael PORTUGUESE 133-138.

C* The Boy Who Was Never Afraid. No indication that he ever learns. Deacon as ghost in bell tower is pushed down, squire as ghost in barn is knocked over. Lad plays cards with trolls and pursues them underground to collect debt, is given healing wax by old man, heals ill troll and is shown gold in haunted mill under guard of troll and four cats. One-third for self, one-third to poor, one-third to miller. With wax, he also cures ill king and weds princess. Denmark: Hatch MORE 182-198.

D* Lad seeks fear, camps with robbers, sent to cook in graveyard. He whacks hand which reaches from grave for his cake. Sent to pool, girl asks him to lift her up to reach crying child in high swing over pool. She tries to press him into water when lifted, he manages to toss her off and bracelet falls from her arm. Man in next town claims bracelet is his. Cadi keeps bracelet until mate is produced by one of claimants. Lad sees ship sinking offshore, swims to it, dives beneath and subdues maiden beneath waves who is pulling ship down. Later sees three doves dive into pool and turn to maidens. They drink to the health of the lad who knows no fear. They are the hand from the grave, girl with the swing, and sea maiden. He reveals himself and asks for the mate to the bracelet. They take him to an underground chamber and give it. Later he comes to country where a pigeon is to be let loose to choose new king (H171.2). He feels a cold shiver and realizes this responsibility will cause him to never be free of fear again. Turkey: Lang FIFTY 14-20 /Lang OLIVE 213-221/.

H1450. Vigilance Test. SEE ALSO: D754.1 (Vigil

by sleeping prince).

H1460. Test: vigil at tomb. SEE: H331.1.1B.

H1471. Watch for devastating monster. Youngest alone successful. Types 301, 514, 550. SEE: H1331.1.3 (Quest for Golden Bird); H331.1.1 (Princess on the Glass Mountain); H1385.3J (nine peahens); H1213.1; K1931.2.

H1471.0.1* The Horse of Seven Colors. Wheat field trampled nightly. Youngest catches horse with coat of seven colors, is given seven hairs, rub and horse appears. Suitor task: bring perfect olive blossom. Horse takes to enchanted castle where white hand serves and gives blossom. To say "Hail white hand" when presenting it. Weds. Puerto Rico: Cothran MAGIC 60-65.

H1473. Vigilance test. To guard sleeping princess without dozing. SEE ALSO: H507.1.0.1 (Jacobs); F601.2C.

H1540. Contests in endurance.

H1546. Two men vie for job as Grand Vizier. Hodja sets them task of surviving on mountain top, gives each only one-half of supplies. They must cooperate to survive. Assigns the scholar to head the army and puts the soldier in charge of records--they must still cooperate. Turkey: Edmonds TRICKSTER 36-49.

H1550. Tests of character.

H1554.1. Test of curiosity. Mouse in jug. The new Eve. A woman has boasted of a lack of curiosity and blamed Mother Eve. The King entertains her in his castle. She may see everything but must not look into a certain silver jug. She does so and finds a mouse in it. Type 1416. England: Jacobs MORE 118-119 (Man complains his sorry lot of hard work is fault of Adam. After test "don't blame Adam."). Wiggin TALES 244-245. France: Lang ROSE 131-137. Nigeria: Walker DANCING 65-71. Italy (Rome): Hampden HOUSE OF CATS 33-38 (bird). Leach NOODLES 73.

H1554.1.1* Couple criticizing curiosity of Adam and Eve are given a chance at 'Paradise'--life of luxury at court. Do not uncover one dish--bird flies out. Italy: Jagendorf PRICELESS 102-108.

H1556.1.1. Cock feigns death to see what hens will say about him. Each praises him in different way. "There are as many ways to love a rooster as there are hens who love him." India: Reed TALKATIVE 15.

H1558. Tests of friendship. SEE ALSO: S268.

H1558.1.0.1* Rich brother's wife produces fake corpse to prove importance of brother. Poor brother helps bury, rich friends betray to mandarin. Vietnam: Graham BEGGAR 11-21; Schultz VIETNAMESE 136-142.

H1558.4. The hare with many friends. In the final test none help and only her legs save her. Aesop: Jacobs AESOP'S 138-139 /Arbuthnot FAIRY 224/; Rice ONCE 34-39.

H1558.4.1* Wolf asks cat who kindest men are in village. He needs shelter from pursuing dogs. It turns out that he has harmed all she names so can expect no mercy. Russia: Carey BABA 18-19; Wyndham TALES..RUSSIA 68-71.

H1561.1* Spirit of the Stone. Man kills pig. Door in rock opens and he is taken for seven days by Master of the Stone whose pig he killed. En route home, seven men attack. He kills all. Goes to giant's home and challenges and kills. Voice says Spirit of Stone wanted to kill him so could not wed girl Spirit wanted. Now may wed her. Philippines (Subanum): Sechrist ONCE 98-101.

H1562.9.1* Test of strength through wrestling. King's nephew throws king winning his case against king. Sierra Leone: Robinson THREE 33-47.

H1574.3. King chosen by test. SEE: H171.2.

H1574.4* Prime minister chosen by test. King asks three ministers what object in stream is. Two give opinion. Third swims out to fetch it. Burma: Brockett BURMESE 147-149.

H1574.4.1* King sends servant to ascertain cause of noise. Takes four trips to observe all king needs to know. Sends minister. Returns having observed all. That is why he is minister and other is servant. Laos: Asia FOLK..FOUR 33.

H1578. Test of sex: to discover person masking as other sex.

H1578.1.7* Mizilca disguises as knight sent by father to Sultan's court. Father's three daughters each offer to go but father changes to boar and lion and each flees. Mizilca attacks dragon form, so sent. Sultan lays out clothing and weapons. M. chooses weapons. Puts pearls in kasha, she ignores them. Calls to her as she leaves, asking to reveal true identity. She opens shirt revealing true sex. European: Lurie CLEVER 23-29.

H1594. Foot racing contest.

H1594.3* Girl racer of Payupki wins all goods and wives from Tikuvi men. Spider grandmother aids. Native American (Hopi): Courlander PEOPLE 101-104; De Wit TALKING 63-75.

H1591.1.1* Two men going to sow millet. First: "It is sweet." Next year. Second: "What is sweet?" Third year. First: "Honey." Mali: Withers WORLD 59.

H1596.4* Test: One with most beautiful voice to be chosen. SEE ALSO: K934. Haiti: Johnson HOW 75-82 (to carry message). Trinidad: McNeil DOUBLE 31-35 (how would talk if at court, prince secretly plans to steal voice).

J. THE WISE AND THE FOOLISH

J0 - J99. Acquisition and possession of wisdom (knowledge).

J10. Wisdom (knowledge) acquired from experience.

J11. Shipwrecked shepherd distrusts the sea. He had formerly envied sailors. Aesop: Aesop AESOP'S (Grosset) 221.

J13. Young sparrows have learned to avoid men. Sparrow quizzes his four young as to how to avoid men. Their year of experience has taught them enough. (cf. J1122). Hardendorff JUST 15-16.

J13.1* Magpie, if smart enough to ask, "What if stone already in hand of man?" smart enough to fend for selves. England: Wiggin TALES 338.

J14. Old racehorse in mill laments vanity of youth. Aesop: Aesop AESOP'S (Watts) 123 (longs for the old days).

J15. Serpent (bird) having injured man refuses reconciliation. He knows that neither can forget their injuries. SEE: B103.0.4.1; D876.2.

J15.0.1* Serpent kills farmer's son, farmer cuts off serpent's tail, serpent bites cattle, farmer takes food to reconciliate, serpent refuses. Aesop: Aesop FABLES (Macmillan) 11; Aesop AESOP'S (Watts) 149 (snake bites son, father cuts off serpent's tail).

J15.1* Snake gives gold piece daily and is given bowl of milk. Son tries to kill serpent to get all gold at once (D876.2). He is bitten and dies. Father tries to reconciliate snake in vain. India: Jacobs INDIAN 136-138.

J21. Counsels proven wise by experience. Type 910. SEE ALSO: J163.4.

Aa* Three pieces of advice taken as wages. 1. Never take new road over old. 2. Do not go where old man has young wife. 3. Honesty is the best policy. Given cake to take to wife--coins are inside. He avoids thieves and disaster by following advice taken as wages. Ireland: Jacobs CELTIC 212-216.

Ab* 1. Never ask about something not your concern. 2. Never leave a path once taken. 3. Suppress your anger until morning. Aliki THREE pb.

Ac* Advice bought. 1. Don't try your courage when the waters are at the flood. 2. Suppress anger until morning. Rumania: Ure RUMANIAN 69-71.

Ad* Cake with gold inside also given. Dog with whom farmer shared food recommended this employment. England (Cornwall): Manning-Sanders PETER 150-155

Ae* Three counsels bought with purses wife embroiders for sale. She leaves, he travels, hole in ship. 1. Have courage and jump right in --saves ship, rewarded. Kingdom in drought. 2. Where willows are there is water--rewarded. 3. When you draw it, hold it back. Latvia: Durham TIT 107-116.

Af* Gold in bread. Wales: Pugh MORE 107-114.

B* Advice given student, Maung Pauk Kyaing, ends in adventure. 1. Keep on and will reach goal. 2. Ask and will find out what you need to know. 3. Keep alert and stay alive. Goes to Tagaung (1), asks and finds queen needs husband. (2) all killed on wedding night. Puts banana trunk in bed and keeps alive. (3) Kills Naga. She stuffs Naga and has bones made into hairpins. Set riddle about this. His parents share food with crows on way to visit and crows tell answer. Burma: Brockett BURMESE 39-50; Keeley CITY 13-32.

C* Student given three packets to open when in need. Destitute, he opens first. Go sit at gate of Bodhi Temple, monk there has money left unbeknownst to him by dead uncle. Failing exams --second--go sit at certain restaurant, overhears professors discussing exam and learns questions. Third--opens when very ill. "Make your will." China: Birch CHINESE 48-54.

D* Three packets to open in time of need given Prince Chu-Ti. First gives plans for building Peking. Second tells how to get water supply. Third tells how to stop flood. SEE: B11.7.1.

E* Cartmen given three pieces of advice as wages. Village council asks him to cart body away for cremation. 1. Never disobey or refuse village council--finds gold on body. 2. Never tell a secret to a woman--lies to wife saying he drank certain poisonous juice and hair turned to gold. Villagers hear rumor, try and die. Taken to court. 3. Never tell a falsehood in a law court. Tells truth and is acquitted. India: Spellman BEAUTIFUL 59-63 /Arbuthnot ANTHOLOGY 351/.

F* Prince buys three pieces of advice. "Do not close eye when passing night in strange place" --saves self from murderer. "If man has a married sister and visits her in pomp, received well; if in poverty disowned"--proves true. Third piece of advice, "Do work yourself with might and without fear." Changes places with man to wed princess, sees husbands die on wedding night, he watches and kills two Shamans which came from her nostrils. Weds princess. India: Jacobs INDIAN 126-135.

J21.1.1* Poet's son recites verse composed to an ox while barber shaves king. Barber takes words "I know what you're trying to do" literally and confesses plot to kill king. SEE: N611.1. Pakistan: Siddiqui TOONTOONY 50-54.

J21.2.1* "Do not act when angry." Wife shows son her own shadow on wall nightly, saying it is his father. When returned father is told by son that his father comes each night, he thinks wife unfaithful. Later discovers truth. Vietnam: Graham BEGGAR 71-77.

J21.12.1* "Sorrow not over what is lost forever." Advice of released bird. +K604. Aesop: Aesop FABLES (Macmillan) 115; Aesop AESOP'S (Grosset) 69-70.

J21.13.1* "Never believe a captive's promise." Advice of released bird. +K604. Aesop: Aesop FABLES (Macmillan) 115; Aesop AESOP'S (Grosset) 69-70.

J21.14.1* "Keep what you have" advice of released bird. +K604. Aesop: Aesop FABLES (Macmillan) 115; Aesop AESOP'S (Grosset) 69-70.

J21.15. "If you wish to hang yourself, do so by the stone which I point out." Counsel proved wise by experience. Father has left money which will fall out when the spendthrift son goes to hang himself in despair. Ireland: MacManus HIBERNIAN 148-159.

J21.37. "Do not take a woman's advice." Counsel proved wise by experience. Pyle TWILIGHT /Hardendorff FROG'S 142-154/, /Child Study Association CASTLE 197-209/.

J21.53* Advice of camel to child proves true. Dying mother advises child not to sleep on mounds, to stay in center of caravan, etc. He finds disobeying brings discomfort. China: Chang CHINESE 68-69.

J30. Wisdom (knowledge) acquired from inference.

J31.0.1* Encounter with clever child dissuades man from visit. Storyteller of Tashkent journeys to small village to challenge rural tale-teller. Tells little daughter who greets him at door that he brought Turkmen rug so long other end is still on ship. She says that will be just right size to mend the spot a spark burnt in her father's rug. He leaves without meeting her father. Russia: Wyndham TALES ..RUSSIA 62-67.

J31.1.1* Cleverness of man disguised as peasant dissuades rival from dispute. Philosopher in farmer's clothing working in field is questioned by traveling theologian and answers so well that theologian passes this village by. If common farmers are so wise, the town's philosopher would only make a fool of him. Turkey: Downing HODJA 35-36.

J32. Arrow as man's message shows lion how terrible man himself must be. Aesop: Aesop AESOP'S (Watts) 139.

J33. Blind man who feels young wolf recognizes his savage nature. Aesop: Aesop AESOP'S (Grosset) 78.

J34. Odor of the wine lost. How fine wine must have been to leave so good an odor. Aesop: Aesop FABLES (Macmillan) 161.

J50. Wisdom (knowledge) acquired from observation.

J52. King observes retaliation among animals: becomes just. Dog breaks fox's foot; man breaks dog's; horse breaks man's leg; horse steps in hole and breaks his. India: Arbuthnot FAIRY 231.

J100. Wisdom (knowledge) taught by necessity.

J101. Crow drops pebble into waterjug so as to be able to drink. Aesop: Aesop AESOP'S (Golden) 67-69; Aesop AESOP'S (Grosset) 58-59; Aesop AESOP'S (Viking) 19; Aesop AESOP'S (Walck) 95-100; Aesop AESOP'S (Watts) 17; Aesop FABLES (Macmillan) 180, 213; Aesop FIVE 60; Arbuthnot FAIRY 229; Green ANIMAL 21; Kent MORE 24-25; Rice ONCE 46-51.

J101.1. Boy loses ball in hollow tree. Fill with with water until ball rises. China: Alexander PEBBLES 14; Dolch STORIES..CHINA 49-55 (fills with dirt and stirs with stick so keeps rising to top).

J103. Father says 'necessity' will teach son how to fix cart if it breaks. This proves true. Rumania: Ure RUMANIAN 62-64.

J120. Wisdom learned from children.

J121. Ungrateful son reproved by naive action of his own son: preparing for old age. Man gives old father half a carpet to keep him warm. Child keeps the other half and tells his father he is keeping it for him when he grows old. Rumania: Ure RUMANIAN 35-37 (saddlecloth).

J121.1. Ungrateful son reproved by naive action of his own son preparing for old age (wooden drinking cup or bowl). Italy: Vittorini OLD 86-91.

J121.3. Ungrateful son reproved by naive action of his own son. Man taking father to wood on sled to abandon him is reminded by son to bring back sled as he'll need it to take him to wood one day. +J151.1. Lettish: Deutsch TALES 63-68. Nepal: Asia FOLK..FOUR 42-46 (Doko basket).

J123. Wisdom of child decides lawsuit. King in disguise sees child's game which represents case. N. Africa: Gilstrap SULTAN'S 40-50.

J123.0.1. Wisdom of child decides lawsuit. Child tricks moneylender into revealing presence at scene of crime. Vietnam: Vo-Dinh TOAD 99-104.

J130. Wisdom (knowledge) acquired from animals. SEE ALSO: B216A.

J132.1* Donkey thinks Karbau is making the row. Second donkey explains that small dog is the noisemaker. Often is the smaller who makes the most noise. Indonesia: Courlander KANT-CHIL'S 105-108.

J140. Wisdom (knowledge) through education.

J144. Well-trained kid does not open door to wolf. SEE: K815.15 (Budulinek); K311.3 (Wolf and seven kids).

J146.1. King prefers educated men as company. Ethiopia: Davis LION'S 26-28 (King can make courtiers but only God can make a wise man).

J150. Other means of acquiring wisdom (knowledge).

J151.1. Wisdom of hidden old man saves kingdom. In famine all old men are ordered killed. One man hides his father. When all goes wrong in the hands of the young rulers, the old man comes forth, performs assigned tasks and aids with his wisdom. SEE: K311.3.1 (Old ordered killed, mother kept in tree).

J151.1.1* Old woman hidden by son tells how to perform impossible tasks and saves kingdom. Ruler relents on edict of banishment for the aged. +H1021.2.1; +H506.4; +H1049.5. Japan: Uchida SEA OF GOLD 61-71.

H151.1.2* Old person advises threshing thatch again, old no longer abandoned. +J121.3. Lettish: Deutsch TALES 63-68.

J151.1.3* Snake coils round king, old couple advise throwing a frog to snake. Congo: Burton MAGIC 73-74.

J151.1.4* Father solves riddles (K52.1). +H1055. Slovenia: Kavcic GOLDEN 71-77.

J151.1.5* Task: diving for pitcher, old father advises is reflection, climbs tree and fetches. Mongolia: Bulatkin EURASIAN 22-26. Mongolia (Buryat): Ginsburg KAHA 13-20.

J151.1.6* Famine. Old advise to plough up land. seeds dropped from carts sprout. Rumania: Ure RUMANIAN 169-171.

J163.2.1. Fool is told to get a pottle of brains. He tries to buy them. He finally learns that advice was to marry a clever girl. Riddles are asked. What runs without feet = water (J734.1). What is yellow and shining and not gold = Sun (H762.1). What has no legs, two legs, then four legs = tadpole (H761.2). England: Jacobs MORE 134-141; Reeves ENGLISH 104-113. Wales: Pugh TALES 29-36.

J163.2.2* Fool told will remain fool until he gets a coat of clay. He rolls in mud. She meant until buried. England: Jacobs MORE 82-88.

J163.4. Good counsel bought. SEE ALSO: J21.

J163.4.1* Dwarf buys freedom with a piece of advice. Says merely "Take your jacket when the sky is blue, when it's wet, it won't matter what you do." Switzerland: Müller-Guggenbühl SWISS 134.

J163.4.2* Porter given true piece of insulting advice as wages. Porter adds own advice, "And don't believe anyone who tells you the china in this crate isn't broken." Drops the crate. China: Chang TALES 30-33.

J200 - J1099. Wise and Unwise Conduct

J200 - J499. Choices.

J210. Choices between evils.

J211. Choice: free poverty or enslaved wealth. SEE: L450.

J211.2. Town mouse and country mouse. Latter prefers poverty with safety. Aesop: Aesop AESOP'S (Golden) 57-59; Aesop AESOP'S (Grosset) 146-148; Aesop AESOP'S (Random) 10-11; Aesop AESOP'S (Watts) 112-113; Aesop FABLES (Macmillan) 12-13; Aesop FABLES (Walck) 40-42; Aesop FIVE 56; Association TOLD..GREEN 74-77; Galdone TOWN pb; Martignoni FAIRY 227; TALL..NURSERY 12-15; Wiggin TALES 274-277. Greece: Wilson GREEK 28-30; Nigeria: Walker NIGERIAN 49. Norway: Asbjornsen NORWEGIAN 116-119.

J212.1. Ass envies horse in fine trappings. Horse killed in battle, ass content. Aesop: Aesop FABLES (Macmillan) 155. SEE ALSO: L452.1.

J212.2* Ox envies pig's diet. But pig is fattened to be killed. India: Babbitt JATAKA 74-76.

J212.3* Fat capons mock lean. Fat are eaten. Aesop: Aesop AESOP'S (Viking) 14-15.

J212.4* Bramble tells fir it will wish it was lowly bramble when woodsmen come with axes. Aesop: Aesop AESOP'S (Grosset) 189; Aesop AESOP'S (Watts) 28.

J214. Choice: suffering in youth or old age.

J214.1* Clarinha. Eagle gives choice of hard work in youth or age. Chooses youth. Eagle causes trouble so she loses every job. Prince she is betrothed to thinks her a duck girl. Brings servants gifts. She asks for stone. Asks it to open sharp edges so she can lie on them after telling it her sufferings. Stone splits. Prince has overheard. Weds. Portugal: Lowe LITTLE 90-94.

J214.2* Catherine. Fate gives choice. Enjoy life in youth or age, chooses to suffer in youth. Fate causes her to lose all jobs. She ends as a servant who carries bread up mountain to the Fate of Baker's wife daily. Asks this Fate to intercede with her own Fate. Is given a tiny piece of silk. Prince needs one small piece to complete robe. Weight of silk in gold. Scales will not tip. Prince's crown added--tips. Weds. McNeil DOUBLE 74-80.

J215. Present evil preferred to change for the worse. Don't drive away flies. Wounded animal (man) refuses to have the flies driven away since they are now sated and their places will be taken by fierce and hungry flies. Aesop: Aesop AESOP'S (Grosset) 26-27; Aesop AESOP'S (Watts) 205-206; Aesop FABLE (Macmillan) 127 (fox, mosquitoes).

J215.2. Oxen decide not to kill butchers, since inexpert killers might replace them. Aesop: Aesop AESOP'S (Watts) 96.

J215.2.1. Old woman prays for safety of cruel tyrant for fear a worse one will succeed him. Italy: Cimino DISOBEDIENT #7 (Nero).

J216.2. Lamb prefers to be sacrificed in temple rather than be eaten by a wolf. Aesop: Aesop AESOP'S (Watts) 139.

J217.0.1.1. Unsatisfactory life preferred to death. Trickster overhears man praying for death to take him; the trickster appears at man's house, usually in disguise, says he is Lord (or the devil). The man tells him to take his wife (or he runs away). Haiti: Courlander PIECE 91-92.

J217.0.1.2 Man seeks death. Death's agent gives man money to live comfortably until Death gets here. He is sorry to see Death come. Nigeria (Yoruba): Courlander OLODE 15-18.

J217.3* Horse leaves master but finds lack of food and drink and danger of wolves worse than servitude. Yeman: Courlander RIDE 95-98.

J218.1. Lion and wild boar make peace rather than slay each other for benefit of vulture. Aesop: Aesop AESOP'S (Grosset) 56 (lion and goat); Aesop AESOP'S (Golden) 26; Aesop AESOP'S (Viking) 30 (goat); Aesop AESOP'S (Watts) 65; Aesop FABLES (Walck) 74-75 (lion and goat). Greece: Wilson GREEK 198-199.

J218.1.1* Lion and bear fight over carcass to exhaustion. Fox takes kill. Aesop: Aesop AESOP'S (Grosset) 110; Aesop AESOP'S (Viking) 80-81 (lion, tiger); Aesop AESOP'S (Watts) 83-84.

J219.1* Enemies lose lives to a third party rather than make peace. Clam (oyster) catches beak of crane (heron) trying to eat him. Clam warns crane he'll die of starvation thus. Crane warns clam he'll die of thirst. Fishermen take both. CHINA: Chang TALES 46-47; Hardendorff TRICKY 41-43 (oyster, heron).

J225.0.1. Angel and hermit. Angel takes hermit with him and does many seemingly unjust things. Later shows why each of these was just. Jewish: Ish-Kishor WISE 62-67; Serwer LET'S 9-17 (Benaiah travels with King of Demons Ashmodai). Russia: Downing RUSSIAN 171-173 (angel sent to live on earth explains his seemingly strange actions).

J229.3.1* Choice money or three walnuts given 'from the heart.' When opened walnuts are found to contain sheep, bullock and plow, maid. Bulgaria: Pridham HEART 11-15.

J231.2* Two merchants robbed. One with no merchandise but with knowledge in head makes way to wealth easily in new city. Jewish: Serwer LET'S 19-21.

J234* Characteristics of others seem more desirous than one's own. Youngest guest and oldest guest at Shah's banquet accuse the other of eating up all food. Young says old bolts food without taking time to chew. Old says young eats more easily since old lacks teeth. Russia (Georgia): Hardendorff JUST 133-134.

J240. Choice between useful and ornamental.

J241.2. Peasant leaves honey tree standing. Sparrows and crickets ask peasant to leave tree standing. He refuses, but when he finds honey in the tree he consents. Aesop: Aesop AESOP'S (Watts) 58.

J242.1. Contest between rose and amaranth; worth lies not in beauty. Aesop: Aesop AESOP'S (Watts) 188.

J242.3. Fox and panther contest in beauty. Fox's spirit worth more than pather's skin (leopard). Aesop: Aesop AESOP'S (Viking) 7-8; Aesop AESOP'S (Watts) 205 (wits); Martignoni ILLUSTRATED 399.

J242.3.1. Fox thinks his brains are more valuable than leopard's fine spots. Aesop: Aesop FABLES (Walck) 34-35.

J242.4. Peacock proved to be bad king. Chosen because of beauty, too weak to defend flock. Aesop: Aesop AESOP'S (Viking) 4-5.

J242.5. Peacock and Crane in beauty contest. Better to be able to soar like a crane than to strut like a peacock. Aesop: Aesop AESOP'S (Viking) 76; Aesop AESOP'S (Watts) 9.

J243.1. Dog and hog dispute over other's children: worth lies not in speed. Aesop: Aesop AESOP'S (Watts) 5 (sow says hers can see at birth but dog's are born blind).

J244.1. Father with handsome son and hideous daughter. Advises both to look in mirror daily lest son exchange handsome face for bad character; daughter to triumph over face by good manners. Aesop: Aesop AESOP'S (Watts) 143.

J253* Mechanic works hours trying to open chest by secret method. Never thinks to just lift lid. Russia: Wyndham TALES..RUSSIA 71-73.

J260. Choice between worth and appearance.

J262.1. Fox and noisy but empty drum. India: Gaer FABLES 37-38; Ryder PANCHATANTRA 41-42 (jackal).

J267.1. Raven drowns his young who promise to aid him when he becomes old. He saves one who admits he will not help because will have to carry own young. Tolstoy: Green BIG 92-93.

J267.1.1* Guinea hen asks eggs what will do for her when hatched. Sixth egg, Fo-Fo, replies "Nothing." Mother abandons him. He gets out of shell anyway and follows. Is insufferable to everyone he meets. She sets snare for him. Liberia (Mano): Dorliae ANIMALS 56-62.

J281.1. "Only one, but a lion." Lioness thus answers fox (hog) who twits her that she has only one cub. Aesop: Aesop AESOP'S (Golden) 13-15; Aesop AESOP'S (Grosset) 117; Aesop AESOP'S (Watts) 91; Aesop FIVE 52; Green ANIMAL 71; Martignoni ILLUSTRATED 152.

J290. Choice: between real and apparent values--miscellaneous.

J291* Choice large or small. Horse and bull advise knee-high man to grow large and strong so can win fights. Owl advises staying small--then no one will challenge to fight--better yet. U.S. Black: Lester KNEE 27-28.

J292. Manabozo wishes to learn to hunt with the wolves. Changes himself to a large wolf with big tail like one of the wolves he admires. Discovers it is a small, quiet wolf who actually is the best hunter. Learns not to judge a hunter by his tail. Native American (Chippewa): Leekley WORLD 20-26.

J310. The present preferred.

J313. Palm wine tapper gives wine to "Whence we come" not to "Where we go." Judge advises of error. Past can give nothing more. Attend to the future. Angola (Mbaka): Courlander KING'S 67.

J321.1.1. Today's catch of fish traded for prospective larger catch tomorrow. Ghana: Courlander COWTAIL 47-57. Akan-Ashanti: Bryan OX 3-10. Liberia/Ghana: Arkurst ADVENTURES 32-38. Haiti: Courlander PIECE 64-69.

J321.2. Little fish in the net kept rather than wait for uncertainty of greater catch. Aesop: Aesop AESOP'S (Grosset) 8; Aesop AESOP'S (Watts) 43; Aesop FABLES (Macmillan) 105.

J321.2.1* Nightingale asks hawk to let him go and wait for bigger bird. No. Aesop: Aesop AESOP'S (Watts) 187-188.

J321.3. Lion leaves sleeping hare to follow the shepherd. Loses both victims. Aesop: Aesop AESOP'S (Watts) 146 (chases stag).

J321.5* Heron waits for larger fish worthy of him and ends up with none. Aesop: Aesop AESOP'S (Random) 68-70.

J340. Choices gain and loss.

J344.1. The monkey and the last lentil (pea). Lets all others he has in his hand fall in order to search for it. India: Gaer FABLES 153-154; Reed TALKATIVE 68-69.

J345.1. Herdsman neglects his she-goats in favor of wild goats. She-goats die; wild goats run off. Aesop: Aesop AESOP'S (Grosset) 31; Aesop AESOP'S (Watts) 222-223.

J347.4. Rich merchant is poorer in happiness than poor man. SEE ALSO: J1085.1.

J347.4.1* Farmer follows beggar who sheltered at house and sees him take gold dust from under stone over fountain trough. Farmer takes some gold dust to city. Rich merchant is same man as beggar. Shows farmer that he will be happier without gold's worry. Tyrolean: Manning-Sanders BOOK..WIZARDS 40-46.

J352.2. Snake is willing to suffer indignity of serving frog king as mount because frog king gives him frogs to eat. India: Ryder PANCHATANTRA 368-372.

J370. Choices: important and unimportant work.

J371.1. Bull refuses to fight goat. Bull being pursued by lion tries to go into cave, goat refuses to let him in. Bull must go on, for with lion pursuing him he has no time to fight goat. Aesop: Aesop AESOP'S (Grosset) 129 (bull lets goat butt him while hiding in cave).

J390. Choices: kind strangers, unkind relatives.

J391.2* Baby crows chase hawk who raised them as mother rather than crow who abandoned. Native American (Cochiti): Brown TEPEE 148-150.

J400. Choice of associates. SEE: J951+.

J401.2* Old friends are best. Japan: Sakade JAPANESE CHILDREN'S STORIES 53-57 (elf cries over one lost friend though has many new).

J411.6. Dolphin and whale scorn crab (sprat) as peacemaker. Aesop: Aesop AESOP'S (Watts) 26.

J411.8. Mouse on lion's mane. Lion angry at impudence of mouse. SEE ALSO: B371.1. Aesop: Aesop AESOP'S (Grosset) 137-138; Aesop AESOP'S (Watts) 105; Aesop FABLES (Macmillan) 21; Green ANIMAL 223.

J414. Marriage with equal or with unequal (different habits).

J414.3.1* Catfish wants to marry lizard. Neither can stand other's habitat. Liberia: Haskett GRAINS 82-83.

J414.3.2* Squirrel weds porcupine. Too quickly. Keeps asking porcupine to move over until porcupine falls from tree. Squirrel weds squirrel. Poland: Kavcic GOLDEN 114-117.

J414.3.3* Golden mallard to wed peacock. Prefers another mallard once she sees peacock strut and brag and hears ugly voice. India (Jataka): Gaer FABLES 146-147.

J414.3.4* Dog wishes to live with coyote in woods but finds each must stick to his own place. SEE ALSO: L451.3. Mexico: Ross IN 15-34.

J416. One's own kind preferred to strangers. SEE ALSO: T211.6.

J416.2* Sungura's fiancée refuses lion, elephant and other grand suitors. Prefers hare like herself. East Africa: Heady JAMBO 78-84.

J416.3* Mrs. Longspur refuses suitors swan, crane, crow, etc. after her husband's death. Weds another longspur. Eskimo: Gillham BEYOND 106-116 /Bleecker BIG 81-89 /.

J425.1. Earthen and brazen pots in river. Brazen pot thinks that they should stay together for company. Earthen pot, however, fears approach of brazen pot. Aesop: Aesop AESOP'S (Grosset) 149; Aesop AESOP'S (Watts) 100; Aesop FABLES (Macmillan) 101.

J425.2. Buffalo refuses tiger's invitation to dinner. He sees fire prepared to cook him. Aesop: Aesop AESOP'S (Watts) 119 (lion and bull).

J425.2.1* Brer Rabbit, invited for dinner, sees butcher knife on table. Flees. U.S. (Black): Harris COMPLETE 1-6; Harris SONGS 3-7.

J425.3* Kitten and rat play together until parents tell them that they are prey and predator. Surinam (Paramaribo): Leach LION 21-22.

J426. Association of rat with cat ends as soon as mutual danger has passed. The rat, threatened by the mongoose and the owl, allies himself with a cat caught in a net. Saved by the cat, he rescues the cat with precaution, then prudently renounces further relations with her. India: Reed TALKATIVE 25-27.

J426.2. Friendship of snake and frog ceases when snake wants to eat frog. India: Ryder PANCHATANTRA 388-394.

J429.2.1* Associating with a bad friend is fatal. Flamingo shields sleeping man with wings (B538.1), but being awakened by crow dropping twigs in mouth he shoots flamingo. India (Panchatantra): Green ANIMAL 116.

J429.2.2* Association with a bad friend is fatal: swan and owl. Owl hoots at caravan and swan is killed by arrow aimed at sound. India: Ryder PANCHATANTRA 129-131.

J429.3* Short-tailed (A2378.4) animals organize protest meeting but larger, long-tailed animals take over. U.S. (Black, South Carolina): Faulkner DAYS 115-121.

J450. Association of the good and the evil.

J451.1. Ass buyer returns ass which has associated with lazy companions. Aesop: Aesop AESOP'S (Watts) 150.

J451.2. Stork killed along with cranes. Ill-advised association ends fatally. Aesop: Aesop AESOP'S (Grosset) 151-152; Aesop AESOP'S (Viking) 8; Aesop AESOP'S (Watts) 123.

J451.2.1* Animals refuse to help stop fight between dog and cat. They are killed in chain of events which follows. Upper Volta: Guirma TALES 70-84.

J451.3. God of wealth in bad company. Hercules on his arrival in heaven fails to greet Plutus, the god of wealth. He has seen him in such bad company. Aesop: Aesop AESOP'S (Watts) 204.

J451.5* Elephant kept near thieves hears talk of killing and becomes dangerous. Wise man advises having good men talk of gentleness in his presence. He reforms. India: Babbitt JATAKA 52-57.

J451.6* Twin parrots. One raised by bandit calls "kill him", when king approaches. One raised by brahmin calls "Feed him." India (Panchatantra): Gaer FABLES 28-30.

J460. Unnecessary choices.

J461.1. The belly and the members. Debate as to their usefulness. All mutually useful. SEE ALSO: A1391. Aesop: Aesop AESOP'S (Viking) 6; Aesop AESOP'S (Watts) 128.

J461.9* House poles, floor, roof argue as to most useful. Philippines (Tinguian): Sechrist ONCE 80-82.

J462.3.1.1. Unnecessary choice of religion. Father gives son three wives. Only one is good although all look the same. Same with religions. Italy: Vittorini OLD 92-95.

J463. Unnecessary choice: to go uphill or downhill. Camel prefers the level. Aesop: Aesop AESOP'S (Grosset) 96; Aesop AESOP'S (Viking) 18. Hardendorff JUST 28.

J466.1. Pomegranate and apple tree dispute as to which is worth most. Blackberry reproves them for useless jangling. Aesop: Aesop AESOP'S (Watts) 83.

J486.1* Death given drink. God refused. Death treats all equally. SEE ALSO: D1825.3.1ff. Haiti: Wolkenstein MAGIC 75-78.

J500-J599. Prudence and discretion.

J510. Prudence in ambition.

J511.1.1* Master tries to scrub Ethiopian slave white, not realizing it is skin color. Aesop: Aesop AESOP'S (Watts) 84.

J512.1. Crab comes ashore. Killed by fox. Aesop: Aesop AESOP'S (Watts) 160.

J512.3. Camel tries in vain to dance (imitating monkey). Aesop: Aesop AESOP'S (Grosset) 114-115; Aesop AESOP'S (Viking) 58; Aesop AESOP'S (Watts) 131.

J512.6. Crow tries to imitate partridge's walk. Only spoils his own. Arbuthnot FAIRY 231.

J512.7. Mouse, bird and sausage keep house together. When they exchange duties, all goes wrong. Type 85. Germany (Grimm): De La Mare ANIMAL 11-14; Gag MORE 27-30; Grimm GRIMM'S (Grosset) 48-49; Grimm HOUSEHOD 126-127; Rackham GRIMM'S 60-62. France: Wiggin TALES 6 (mouse and sausage) /Hardendorff FROG'S 155-157/. Latvia: Ginsburg LAZIES 46-48.

J512.7.2* Flowerpot, mud cake, cabbage, flea, feather and needle keep house. Mud cake brings water--melts. Cabbage watches cow-- eaten. Flea watches ox--killed. Feather threshes grain--blown away. Needle sweeps floor--lost. Flowerpot jumps off shelf to see what happened to everyone--smashed. China: Chang TALES 51-54.

J512.8. Ass tries to get a cricket's voice. Asks crickets what they eat to get such a voice. They answer "dew." He tries it and starves. Aesop: Aesop AESOP'S (Grosset) 64.

J512.13. Jackal accidentally made king but joins other jackals in howling at night. Killed. SEE: J2131.5.6. Asia: Green BIG 61 (imitates lion but roar is only jackal's howl).

J513.3* Big fish feels too good for this pool, swims downstream and is attacked by bigger fish. Returns. Senegal (Fulani): Arnott AFRICAN 156-159.

J514.2. Wolf tries to eat bowstring. Finds hunter, gazelle and wild boar dead. Tries to eat the bowstring and is mortally wounded. India: Gaer FABLES 90-91 (Jackal); Ryder PANCHATANTRA 235-237 (Jackal).

J514.7* Mother Luck will fill beggar's sack but he must stop before it breaks or all will be lost. All is lost. Latvia: Durham TIT 93-95.

J516* Don't meddle with things you don't understand. Monkey tries to fish and nearly drowns in net. Aesop: Aesop FABLES (Walck) 40-42.

J550. Zeal--temperate and intemperate.

J552.3. Serpent (weasel) tries to bite on file. Aesop: Aesop AESOP'S (Macmillan) 51; Aesop AESOP'S (Watts) 91 (viper asks tools for something to eat, file says he will not feed viper who always takes and never gives); Aesop FIVE 54.

J552.5.1* Man from town with patron Saint Agata tries to buy figurine of this saint and figurine of other town's patron, Saint Venere. Vendor is resident of Saint Venere's town. He charges two cents for Venere, one cent for Agata. Buyer pays two cents for Agata, one cent for Venere. Vendor will not accept the three cents on these terms. Italy: Cimino DISOBEDIENT 12.

J561.2. Cow-herd looking for cattle thief recognizes him in the lion. Aesop: Aesop AESOP'S (Watts) 153 (promises Jupiter calf if finds stolen bull, finds lion, promises Jupiter bull if he escapes).

J563.1* Ooka agrees to bring stone lion to life for grandson, reminding him it will eat them all. Japan: Edmonds OOKA 22-26.

J563.2* Four Brahmins restore dead lion. First arranges skeleton, second puts on flesh, third breathes life into body. Fourth (sometimes a watching farmer) climbs tree. Lion eats first three wise men. Ethiopia (Amhara): Davis LION'S 70-72. India: Courlander TIGER'S 72-75; Dobbs ONCE 24-26; Ryder PANCHATANTRA 442-443.

J580. Wisdom of caution.

J581.1. Wolf as dog's guest sings. He has drunk too much and sings in spite of the dog's warnings. SEE ALSO: J2137.6. Type 100. Russia: Carpenter WONDER..DOGS 213-221 (+A2494.15; K231.1.3; dog chases wolf out). Russia (Ukraine): Bloch UKRAINIAN 44-48 (+K231.1.3). Finland: Bowman TALES 260.

J581.3. Monk's (Brahmin's) enemies quarrel and thus save him. Robber who wants to steal cow and devil (ghost) who wants to steal soul quarrel as to which shall begin first. They thus awaken him. India: Ryder PANCHATANTRA 343-345.

J581.4. Drones dispute possession of honey. Ordered to make honey. Dispossessed. Phaedrus: Green BIG 178-179.

J582.2. Hidden stag discovered when he begins to eat grapevine too soon after hunters have passed. Aesop: Aesop AESOP'S (Grosset) 233; Aesop AESOP'S (Watts) 138.

J611.1* Bard makes up derisive song about king. King demands it retracted. Blows given bard by king cannot be retracted now, neither can a song once it has spread. Mali (Gindo): Courlander KING'S 9-12.

J613.1. Frogs fear increase of sun's power which will dry up all their puddles. Object to Sun's wedding and possibility of offspring. Aesop: Aesop AESOP'S (Viking) 67; Aesop AESOP'S (Watts) 29.

J613.1.1. Frogs see roofs afire and begin to cry as they fear man will come and dip up their pond water to throw on fire. Ethiopia (Shoa): Courlander FIRE 111-112.

J620. Forethought in prevention of other's plans.

J621.1. The swallow and the hemp-seeds. Swallow in vain urges other birds to eat seed as fast as it is sown. Ridiculed he builds his nest among the dwellings of man. Later, birds are caught in nets made from the hemp. SEE ALSO: U160. Aesop: Aesop AESOP'S (Grosset) 182-183; Aesop AESOP'S (Viking) 25-26; Aesop FABLES (Macmillan) 23.

J621.2* Owl advisor warns birds to kill oap saplings, birdlime made of mistletoe on oaks. Says archer will feather his arrows with their feathers (U161). Aesop: Aesop AESOP'S (Watts) 50; Aesop FIVE 78.

J623.1. Snake complains to Zeus that people step on him. Zeus: "If you had bitten the first foot that stepped on you it would not be done now." Aesop: Aesop AESOP'S (Watts) 190.

J624.1.1* Jackal licking spilt blood caught between clashing rams and killed. India: Ryder PANCHATANTRA 61-62.

J625.1* Wolf orders sheep to pay bushel of corn to hart. Sheep agrees but refuses to keep bargain when hart comes to collect alone. Aesop: Aesop FIVE 16.

J640. Avoidance of other's power.

J641.2* What will cranberries do if wolves come? Green--climb Shingoub Tree. White--hide in hominy. Red--hide under snow. Wolves eat hominy, trample snow. Only green escapes. Native American: Bierhorst FIRE 41-42.

J642.1. Lion suitor allows his teeth to be pulled and his claws to be cut. He is then killed (or mocked). Aesop: Aesop AESOP'S (Grosset) 94-95; Aesop AESOP'S (Viking) 48; Aesop AESOP'S (Watts) 172-173; Aesop FABLES (Macmillan) 141; Aesop FIVE 88; Dobbs MORE 81-82.

J642.1.1* Lion convinces bull to have 'ugly' horns cut off. Aesop: Aesop AESOP'S (Watts) 193.

J643.1. Frogs demand a live king, King Log. Zeus has given them a log as King, but they find him too quiet. He then gives them a stork who eats them. Aesop: Aesop AESOP'S (Golden) 42; Aesop AESOP'S (Grosset) 47-48 (Jupiter); Aesop AESOP'S (Viking) 58-59; Aesop AESOP'S (Watts) 62; Aesop FABLES (Macmillan) 24-25 (Jove); Aesop FIVE 20 (heron, Jupiter). Kenya: Harman TALES 57-63.

J644.1. Fox sees all tracks going into lion's den but none coming out. He saves himself. Usually being taken to see sick lion. Aesop: Aesop AESOP'S (Golden) 80-81; Aesop AESOP'S (Grosset) 161; Aesop AESOP'S (Random) 19-20; Aesop AESOP'S (Viking) 67; Aesop AESOP'S (Watts) 54; Aesop FABLES (Macmil-lan) 145; Aesop FABLES (Walck) 105-107; Green ANIMAL 129; Rice ONCE 40-45. Greece: Wilson GREEK 222-223.

J644.1.1* Sick wolf gets fox to bring deer to dance for him, kills. Mountain sheep, antelope, same. Native American (California): Curry DOWN 111-120.

J644.2* Monkey sees all tracks going into pond and none coming out. Drinks through straw. India: Ryder PANCHATANTRA 454-461.

J646.2. Bird hears voices from within unhatched eggs and flies away. Voices plot to dine on their bird mother when they are born. SEE: J267.1.

J652.1. Frog persists in living in puddle in road Disregards advice of another frog and is run over. Aesop: Aesop AESOP'S (Watts) 126.

J652.4.3* Rev Hillel does not admire Roman culture. Worm does not admire song of bluebird-- he is to be its dinner. Jewish: Serwer LET'S 30-37.

J652.5* Hen disobeys cock and jumps out of henyard. Hawk grabs her. Cock calls men who rescue. Cock "I told you so." Sweden: Wiggin TALES 457-458.

J656.1. Thornbush blamed by fox for wounding him. He should have known better then to lay hold of something whose nature is to lay hold of others. Aesop: Aesop AESOP'S (Grosset) 206-207; Aesop AESOP'S (Watts) 212.

J656.2* Boy stung by nettles. If he had grasped them lightly they would not have stung. Aesop AESOP'S (Grosset) 139; Aesop AESOP'S (Watts) 57; Aesop FABLES (Walck) 19.

J657.2. Tortoise lets self be carried by eagle. Dropped and eaten. SEE ALSO: A2312.1.1; K1041; J2357.

J657.2.1* Tortoise persuades eagle to teach him to fly. Dropped and eaten. Aesop AESOP'S (Golden) 41-42; Aesop AESOP'S (Grosset) 170-171.

J657.2.2* Tortoise persuades eagle to carry to new home. Crow advises dropping tortoise on rocks to crack shell. Dropped and eaten. Aesop: Aesop FABLES (Macmillan) 93.

J657.2.3* Tortoise wishing to return visits of eagle hides in bundle (gourd) and is carried to eyrie. Eagle tries to throw him out but turtle hangs onto eagle's leg until replaced on ground. Congo (Luban): Burton MAGIC DRUM 116-119. Bemba: Kaula AFRICAN 80-83 (Vulture, tortoise cries out before reaching nest and surprised vulture drops bundle, J2357.1; +A2312.1.1).

J670. Forethought in defence against others.

J671.1. Belling the cat. Mice decide that a bell

should be put on the cat but can find no one to tie it on her. La Fontaine: Green ANIMAL 148-149 (rats). Aesop: Aesop AESOP'S (Golden) 27-29; Aesop AESOP'S (Grosset) 13; Aesop AESOP'S (Random) 50-51; Aesop AESOP'S (Watts) 4; Aesop FABLES (Macmillan) 133; Aesop FABLES (Walck) 81-84; Aesop FIVE 72; Arbuthnot FAIRY 228; Kent MORE 52-53; Leach LION 23-24; Rice ONCE 22-27; Wiggin TALES 336-337.

J671.1.1* Brer Rabbit proposes sewing dog's mouth shut. U.S.(Georgia): Harris COMPLETE 331-343 /Harris NIGHTS 311-313/.

J674.1. Wild boar sharpens tusks when no enemy is in sight. Tells fox that when enemy comes there are other things to do. Aesop: Aesop AESOP'S (Grosset) 200; Aesop AESOP'S (Watts) 70; Aesop FABLES (Walck) 76.

J680. Forethought in alliances.

J681.1. Rat and frog tie feet together to cross marsh. Carried off by falcon. Aesop: Aesop AESOP'S (Grosset) 177-178; Aesop AESOP'S (Random) 45-46; Aesop AESOP'S (Watts)57; Aesop FIVE 24. Martin Luther: Green BIG 74 (buzzard).

J681.1.1. Jackal and leopard tie tails together for mutual protection. Frightened, they run apart and injure each other. SEE: K1715.2.

J683.1. Ass turns on his driver who would save him from falling over precipice. Aesop: Aesop AESOP'S (Grosset) 227-228; Aesop AESOP'S (Watts) 146.

J684.1. Fox with lion protection goes hunting alone and is killed. Aesop: Aesop AESOP'S (Watts) 202.

J684.1.1* Fox precedes lion (tiger), shows how all flee from his approach. In reality, they flee lion. China: Courlander TIGER'S 46-48; Hume FAVORITE..CHINA 67-68. Russia: Ginsburg ONE 9.

J1684.1.1.1* Lion flees noisy rooster astride donkey's back fearing will rouse farmer. Donkey, thinking he frightened lion, goes out without rooster and is attacked. Ethiopia (Danakil): Ashabranner LION'S 80-85.

J701. Provision for future.

J701.1. Planting for the next generation. Man who is planting tree told it will never mature in his day. He is planting for the next generation. +J2425.1. Jewish: Gross FABLE pb.

J701.3* Caravan driver thinks journey almost over and discards water. Nearly dies of thirst. Babbit JATAKA 25-29; Babbit JATAKA 44-51.

J702. Necessity of work.

J702.3* Dying father insists son earn at least one rupee before he dies or be disinherited. Mother gives one rupee but father throws it into fire. Third time son actually works for it. Grapples

in fire to retrieve coin. "Someone else's rupee is not worth an anna but one's own is valued." Armenia: Bulatkin EURASIAN 39-43.

J703. Planning for the greater office.

J703.3* Wears net on shoulders to remind self of humble origins until modesty impresses king and he is made judge. Now he no longer wears the net. "No need of a net once the fish has been caught." Iran: Shah MULLA 88.

J710. Forethought in provision for food.

J711. Ant and lazy cricket (grasshopper). Lazy bird is put to shame by thought of industrious bird. In winter he is in distress. Type 249. Aesop: Aesop AESOP'S (Golden) 13-15; Aesop AESOP'S (Grosset) 12; Aesop AESOP'S (Random) 32-33; Aesop AESOP'S (Viking) 20; Aesop AESOP'S (Watts) 125; Aesop FABLES (Macmillan) 71; Aesop FABLES (Walck) 44-45; Aesop FIVE 19; Arbuthnot FAIRY 224; Kent MORE 28-31; La Fontaine: Arbuthnot FAIRY 232-233; Greece: Wilson GREEK 9-10 (beetle).

J711.3. King for a year provides for the future. Knowing that the custom is that he is to be deposed in a year, he sends provisions to a safe place out of the kingdom. Jewish: Ish-Kishor WISE 32-38 (to be abandoned on a desert isle, sends articles to make it liveable).

J730. Forethought in provision for clothing.

J731.1. More than one swallow to make a summer. Spendthrift youth seeing swallow concludes summer has come and sells clothes. There is frost the next day and he is cold. Aesop: Aesop AESOP'S (Grosset) 150; Aesop AESOP'S (Viking) 11; Aesop AESOP'S (Watts) 10.

J740. Forethought in provision for shelter.

J741.1. Bear (hare) builds house of wood; fox of ice. Fox's house fails him in summer. Fox appropriates Hare's house. Wolf and bear fail to drive fox out. Cock brags of two sharp scythes and fox flees. Type 43. (cf. K1711.2). Russia: Brown NEIGHBORS pb; Carey BABA 45-48; Carrick STILL 1-14; Ginsburg FOX pb; Riordan TALES..CENTRAL 112-114.

J752. In planning future, profit by the past.

J752.1. Frogs decide not to jump into the well. Their spring having dried up, they consider jumping into a well. They decide that the well may also dry up. Aesop: Aesop AESOP'S (Grosset) 210; Aesop AESOP'S (Watts) 160.

J758.1. Tailless fox tries in vain to induce foxes to cut off tails. Aesop: Aesop AESOP'S (Grosset) 97-98; Aesop AESOP'S (Random) 36-38; Aesop AESOP'S (Viking) 75-76; Aesop AESOP'S (Watts) 68; Aesop FABLES (Macmillan) 128; Aesop FIVE 64.

J758.1.0.1* Tailless fox takes foxes to vineyard,

ties tails of each to bush he is to eat from. A-
rouses farmer, foxes flee leaving tails. Palestine:
Arnott ANIMAL 6-13. Syria: Hampden GYPSIES'
105-109 (has others tie tails under bellies and
takes to vineyard, enemy cannot identify). Persia: Mehdevi PERSIAN 22-32 (jackal).

J758.1.3* Tailless hare persuades other hares to
cut off tails: escapes detection. Africa (Tugen):
Nunn AFRICAN 62-67; Tracy LION 26-29.

J758.1.4* Tailless monkey tells others men are
hunting them for tails. All cut off tails. King
catches all monkeys, starves them. On third
day he tosses food to monkeys in tree. All reach
with both hands, trying to hold on with tail,
and fall. Only monkey who is accustomed to being tailless holds on with hand. Thus detected.
Ethiopia (Amhara): Davis LION'S 32-44.

J758.1.5* Tailless fox persuades other foxes to
fish in ice with tails (K1021.0.3). Lose tails
also. Russia: Ginsburg ONE 17-20.

J758.3. Fish refuse fox's invitation to live on dry
land and thus escape danger of fishermen (and
waterfall). China: Chang TALES 3. Jewish
(Talmud): Dobbs MORE 66-67.

J762.2* Asked to breathe on foot and cure it of
mange, holy man does so but recommends a lib-
eral dosage of the usual medicine also. Turkey:
Downing HODJA 61.

J800 - J849. Adaptabilitiy.

J810. Policy in dealing with the great.

J811.1. The Lion's Share. Ass divides booty equally between himself, fox and lion. Lion eats ass.
Fox then divides: gives lion meat and he takes
bones. Type 51. Aesop: Aesop AESOP'S (Grosset) 107; Aesop AESOP'S (Viking) 62; Aesop
AESOP'S (Watts) 196-197. Somalia: Courlander
KING'S 78-79 (wolf slapped in eyes by lion,
jackal divides). Russia: Ginsburg ONE 29-30
(bear, wolf, vixen--wolf displeases and is
struck by bear, vixen divides--gives all to bear
--learned to divide from wolf).

J811.1.1. Lion divides the booty. Best part goes
to himself as king of beasts; second as strongest; third as most patient; fourth "touch it if
you dare." Aesop: Aesop AESOP'S (Golden) 20-
21; Aesop AESOP'S (Grosset) 160; Aesop
AESOP'S (Random) 60-61; Aesop AESOP'S (Viking) 82; Aesop AESOP'S (Watts) 85; Aesop
FABLES (Macmillan) 2.

J811.1.2* Nine hyenas hunt with lion, find ten
guinea hens. Lion takes nine, gives one to hyenas. Their father goes to complain, sees lion
in strength and offers tenth as present. Ethiopia (Danakil): Ashabranner LION'S 77-80.

J811.2.1* Lion asks for judgment of his breath.
Sheep tells truth, wolf flatters--both killed.
Fox has a cold can't smell. Aesop: Aesop

Aesop'S (Grosset) 154-155. Burma (Shan): Courlander TIGER'S 20-23 (hare has cold, tiger eats
boar and monkey).

J811.7. Judge settles quarrel saying "You are
right to both sides." Wife: "They can't both be
right." Judge: "You are right." Turkey: Downing HODJA 22.

J815.1. Liar rewarded by apes. King of apes asks
visitors how they like his children (courtiers).
Truthful visitor says they are very ugly, is
punished. Liar praises their beauty and receives
reward. Types 48, 68. Aesop: Aesop AESOP'S
(Watts) 39.

J829.1.1* Man wears magnificent turban to court,
lies that it cost a fantastically high price. Says
he paid this high price because he knew only
one king in the world would buy it. The king
buys. Iran: Shah MULLA 116.

J830. Adaptability to overpowering force.

J832. Reeds bend before wind (flood). Save themselves. White oak is uprooted. Aesop: Aesop
AESOP'S (Golden) 62; Aesop AESOP'S (Grosset)
179; Aesop AESOP'S (Viking) 36-37; Aesop
AESOP'S (Watts) 36; Aesop FABLES (Macmillan)
73; Aesop FABLES (Walck) 27; Montgomerie
TWENTY-FIVE 60.

J832.1* The olive brags of never losing her leaves.
A heavy snow breaks her. The barren fig survives. Aesop: Aesop AESOP'S (Watts) 65.

J836. Man starts to strike a dog rummaging in a
grave but the dog snarls at him. "Never mind,
carry on!" Turkey: Downing HODJA 68.

J840. Adaptability to miscellaneous situations.

J841* Man who has never seen a hare captures
one, fetches the doctor and judge to view it. His
wife meanwhile lets it escape and puts a measure
of corn in the bag instead. When the man drops
the corn out before the judge and doctor he is
surprised but covers with "32 of these make a
bushel." Turkey: Downing HODJA 18.

J842* Friend insists on ordering a dish which his
companion hates. The friend falls ill and his
companion rushes off. "To get a doctor?" "No,
to change the order." Iran: Shah MULLA 128.

J860. Consolation of a trifle.

J861.2. Man on sinking ship eats salt. Otherwise
he will not enjoy the large amount of water that
he must drink. Italy: Cimino DISOBEDIENT #16.

J861.3. Mouse (fly) dying in meat tub is happy
that he has eaten to satisfaction. Aesop: Aesop
FIVE 34.

J870. Consolation by pretending one does not
want the thing he cannot have.

J871. The fox and the sour grapes. La Fontaine:

Green ANIMAL 15; Aesop: Aesop AESOP'S (Golden) 23-25; Aesop AESOP'S (Grosset) 14; Aesop AESOP'S (Random) 20-21; Aesop AESOP'S (Viking) 12; Aesop AESOP'S (Watts) 208-209; Aesop FABLES (Macmillan) 61; Aesop FABLES (Walck) 57-58; Aesop FIVE 12; Arbuthnot FAIRY 229; Galdone THREE #1; Gruenberg MORE 406-407; Martignoni ILLUSTRATED 156.

J873. Fox in swollen river claims to be swimming to distant town. Aesop: Aesop AESOP'S (Watts) 208-209.

J874. Dog driven out of dining room claims to be drunk. Says that he has drunk so much that he does not know how to get out of the house. Aesop: Aesop AESOP'S (Grosset) 172-173; Aesop AESOP'S (Viking) 68-70; Aesop AESOP'S (Watts) 45.

J880. Consolation by thought of others worse placed.

J881.1. More timid than the hares. Hares take heart when they see that frogs are more timid than they. Refrain from planned mass suicide. Type 70. Aesop: Aesop AESOP'S (Grosset) 79; Aesop AESOP (Viking) 16; Aesop AESOP'S (Watts) 22; Aesop FABLES (Macmillan) 29; Aesop FIVE 38. Russia: Carrick STILL 88-94. Poland: Borski GOOD 60. Finland: Bowman TALES 266 (thinks acorn falling into water fears him). Estonia: Deutsch MORE 19-23. Netherlands: Cathon PERHAPS 62-63 (+A2211.2).

J881.2. Lion comforted for his fear of the cock. Finds that elephant is afraid of the gnat. Aesop: Aesop AESOP'S (Watts) 170.

J890. Consolation in misfortune--miscellaneous.

J892* Partridge mistreated by game cocks in hen-yard notices that they mistreat each other also. Aesop: Aesop AESOP'S (Viking) 32.

J894* When misfortune befalls, man waits for luck to change. Runaway horse returns with stallion. He now waits for good luck to change to bad. Is thrown, injured but spared from war because of injury. China: (Han Dynasty): Kendall SWEET 39-41.

J900 - J999. Humility.

J950. Presumption of the lowly.

J951. Lowly masks as great. SEE: J2131.5.6.

J951.1. Ass in lion's skin unmasked when he raises his voice. India: Gaer FABLES 157-159; Hardendorff TRICKY 109-110; Jacobs INDIAN 182-183; Montgomerie TWENTY-FIVE 34-35. Aesop: Aesop AESOP'S (Golden) 32; Aesop AESOP'S (Grosset) 113; Aesop AESOP'S (Viking) 40-41; Aesop AESOP'S (Watts) 53; Aesop FABLES (Macmillan) 47; Aesop FABLES (Walck) 24-26.

J951.2. Jay (jackdaw) in peacock's (pigeon's) skin (feathers) unmasked. Type 244. Aesop: Aesop AESOP'S (Golden) 47-49; Aesop AESOP'S (Grosset) 190-191; Aesop AESOP'S (Random) 40-41; Aesop AESOP'S (Watts) 58-59 (paints white as pigeon); Aesop AESOP'S 68-69 (discarded feathers); Aesop FABLES (Macmillan) 41 (peacock's plumes on tail); Aesop FIVE 86.

J951.3. Crow tries to prophesy like raven: detected by his voice. Aesop: Aesop AESOP'S (Watts) 206.

J951.6. Jackal puts old shoes on ears and calls self Rajah. Lizard refuses to pay tribute and outsmarts. India: Turnbull FAIRY 84-90.

J951.7. Polecat appointed king of the barnyard. Turkmen: Carey BABA 17.

J952.1. Presumptuous wolf (jackal) among lions. Large wolf called by his comrades "Lion." Presumes to mix with lion but is only a wolf. Ceylon: Tooze WONDERFUL 94-95 (jackal).

J952.1.1. Wolf raised by lioness thinks self equal of cubs until learns they could kill him. Flees. India: Korel LISTEN 44-48.

J952.2. Ass follows after lion and is punished. Ass and cock are surprised by lion. Cock crows and scares lion who runs. Ass thinks that he has scared lion and pursues. Aesop: Aesop AESOP'S (Grosset) 53; Aesop AESOP'S (Viking) 29; Aesop FABLES (Walck) 120.

J952.3. Dog follows lion. Flees at lion's roar. Aesop: Aesop AESOP'S (Watts) 155.

J952.4. Ass who has worked with ox thinks himself equal to ox. Aesop: Aesop AESOP'S (Watts) 183 (after work asks who shall carry master home. You, of course).

J953.1. Dog proud of his clog. Thinks that the clog on his neck is a decoration. Aesop AESOP'S (Grosset) 77; Aesop AESOP'S (Viking) 10. Aesop AESOP'S (Watts) 3.

J953.4. Ass who carried divine image thinks people bow before him. Aesop: Aesop AESOP'S (Watts) 165.

J953.5. Disdain of wolf for the dog. Is fleeing from dog's master, not from him. Aesop: Aesop AESOP'S (Watts) 219.

J953.10. Gnats apologize for lighting on bull's horns. He had not felt their weight. Aesop: Aesop AESOP'S (Golden) 10-11; Aesop AESOP'S (Grosset) 18; Aesop AESOP'S (Viking) 42; Aesop AESOP'S (Watts) 30.

J953.10.2. Fly on coach wheel "What a dust I raise!" Fly on horse's buttocks "At what a rate I drive." Aesop: Aesop AESOP'S (Viking) 15; Kent MORE 54-55.

J953.13.1. Wolf thinks self great from size of

shadow and ceases to fear lion. Eaten. Aesop: Aesop AESOP'S (Watts) 191.

J953.19* Tlacuache (small raccoon) nominated to be saint in rainmaking procession becomes so vain he forgets to perform his part of the ritual. Clouds laugh so hard at spectacle that they spill rain anyway. Mexico: Ross IN 121-133.

J953.20* Eagle thinks he is biggest creature in world, lights on two sticks = antennae of lobster. Lobster thinks self largest, lights on mountain = whale. Whale sneezes, lobster back is broken (A2356.2.16). China: Chang CHINESE 4-5. Japan: Sakade JAPANESE 47-50.

J953.21* Ox criticizes axletrees for groaning. It is oxen who do the work. Aesop: Aesop AESOP'S (Grosset) 91; Aesop AESOP'S (Watts) 61.

J954.1.1. Mule brags mother was a racehorse. Master tries to hurry him, reminds master that his father was only a jackass. Aesop: Aesop AESOP'S (Grosset) 162-163; Aesop AESOP'S (Viking) 66.

J954.1.2. Mule says father was high spirited horse, later when tired says father must have been an ass after all. Aesop: Aesop AESOP'S (Watts) 154.

J955.1. Frog tries in vain to be big as an ox. Bursts. Aesop: Aesop AESOP'S (Golden) 70; Aesop AESOP'S (Grosset) 108-109; Aesop AESOP'S (Random) 14-16; Aesop AESOP'S (Viking) 28; Aesop AESOP'S (Watts) 81; Aesop FABLES (Macmillan) 42; Aesop FIVE 26; Arbuthnot FAIRY 227; Green BIG 200; Rice ONCE 52-57; Rockwell OLD 79-81. Evans BUNDLE pb.

J972. One cock takes glory of another's valor. Victor in cock fight crows over his victory. He is taken off by eagle. A second cock then comes out of hiding and struts among the hens. Aesop AESOP'S (Grosset) 212-213; Aesop AESOP'S (Watts) 114.

J974. Kid perched on house jeers at wolf. Wolf fears kid might fall, kid thinks wolf is concerned for own health. Aesop: Aesop AESOP'S (Grosset) 88; Aesop AESOP'S (Random) 72-73; Aesop AESOP'S (Watts) 67; Aesop FABLES (Macmillan) 31; Aesop FABLES (Walck) 114; Martignoni ILLUSTRATED 400.

J975. Hare demands equal rights for all animals. Reprimanded for presumption by lions. Aesop: Aesop AESOP'S (Golden) 71-73; Aesop AESOP'S (Watts) 145.

J981. Presumptious smith chants *The Divine Comedy*. Dante throws his tools in the street. Blacksmith: "You ruin my work!" Dante: "You ruin mine!" Spain: Gunterman CASTLE 247-250 (Bootmaker sings ballads, French minstrel botches up boots in revenge, takes to judge. "He spoils my songs!".)

J1000 - J1099. Other aspects of wisdom.

J1020. Strength in unity.

J1021. The quarreling sons and the bundle of twigs. Peasant puts twigs together and cannot break them. Separated, they are easily broken. His sons apply the lesson. Aesop: Aesop AESOP'S (Golden) 52; Aesop AESOP'S (Grosset) 122; Aesop AESOP'S (Random) 62-63; Aesop AESOP'S (Viking) 62-63; Aesop AESOP'S (Watts) 49; Aesop FABLES (Macmillan) 143 (dying father); Evans Bundle pb. Czechosolovakia: Courlander RIDE 128-130 (King Svatoplok of greater Moravia).

J1022. Fight of lions and bulls. Lion succeeds only when bulls separate. Aesop: Aesop AESOP'S (Grosset) 30; Aesop AESOP'S (Viking) 34; Aesop AESOP'S (Watts) 98; Aesop FABLES (Macmillan) 103. Bavenda: Kaula AFRICAN 100 (Waterbuck).

J1024. Quails (dove) caught in net rise up in a body with net and escape. As soon as they quarrel they are caught. SEE ALSO: K581.4.1. India: Babbit JATAKA 30-33; Ryder PANCHATANTRA 213-288 (doves).

J1025.3* Ooka hires bully to beat up quarreling grandsons. Gives them each a stick and suggests they join forces in future. They do. Japan: Edmonds OOKA 75-80.

J1030. Self-dependence.

J1031. Grain will be cut when the farmer attends to it himself. Lark leaves her young in the cornfield. They hear farmer tell sons to go to neighbors for help in harvesting. Lark tells young not to worry. Farmer decides to harvest it himself. Larks move for they know it will be done. Aesop: Aesop AESOP'S (Grosset) 103-105; Aesop AESOP'S (Random) 30-31; Aesop AESOP'S (Viking) 39-40; Aesop AESOP'S (Watts) 102; Green ANIMAL 38-39.

J1032. Stag found by master when overlooked by servants. Hides under hay and escapes until master himself comes. Type 162. Aesop: Aesop AESOP'S (Grosset) 156-157; Aesop AESOP'S (Watts) 24; Aesop FABLES (Macmillan) 53.

J1034. God helps those who help themselves. Ox driver must put shoulder to the wheel before Hercules will help him. Aesop: Aesop AESOP'S (Grosset) 100; Aesop AESOP'S (Viking) 73; Aesop AESOP'S (Watts) 82-83; Aesop FABLES (Macmillan) 121; Arbuthnot FAIRY 226.

J1040. Decisiveness of conduct. SEE ALSO: J2183; W123.

J1041.2. The miller, his son and the ass: trying to please everyone. Miller blamed when he follows his son on foot; when he takes the son's place on the ass; when he takes the son behind him; and when he puts the son in front of him. Usually ends by carrying the donkey, which sometimes kicks loose crossing stream and drowns. Aesop: Aesop AESOP'S (Golden) 87; Aesop AESOP'S (Grosset) 50-52; Aesop AESOP'S (Random) 22-26; Aesop AESOP'S (Viking) 21-22; Aesop AESOP'S (Watts) 136; Aesop FABLES (Macmillan) 124-125;

Aesop FABLES (Walck) 51–52; Gruenberg MORE 388–389; Haviland FAIRY 102–103. La Fontaine: La Fontaine MILLER pb; Wildsmith MILLER (carrying donkey so as not to get it dirty). Dobbs ONCE 38–41. McGovern HEE HAW (donkey turned loose and flees, trader thought him ill since carried). Showalter DONKEY pb. Turkey: Downing HODJA 21. Taiwan: Cheney TALES 133–136.

J1041.2.1* Ologbon-Ori and son on camel seek wisdom, find wisdom of one town is stupidity of another. Yoruba: Courlander OLODE 65–68.

J1041.3. Man builds oven facing east and his neighbor advises it should face west. Rebuilds facing west and other neighbor advises it should face east. Rebuilds oven on cart. Iran: Kelsey MULLAH 20–23.

J1050. Attention to warnings.

J1051.1* Man to come when Death sends a sign he can see or hear, goes deaf and blind. Never dies. Wastes away to nothing, whiskers still seen as corn ears (A2685.1.0.1). U.S. (Alabama): Courlander TERRAPIN'S 108–111.

J1060. Miscellaneous aspects of wisdom.

J1060.1* Seeing parrots for sale for high price, he offers his hen for same price. She has wonderful thoughts and annoys no one with her chatter. Iran: Shah MULLA 81.

J1060.2* Claiming to be able to play the lute, he strums one note over and over. Others are searching for the perfect note, he has found it. Turkey: Downing HODJA 93. Iran: Kelsey MULLA 128–131.

J1060.3* How can one attain wisdom? "Listen to what those who know tell you and if someone is listening to you, listen carefully to what you are saying." Turkey: Downing HODJA 32.

J1060.4* Object which no one can identify is brought to philosopher. He laughs and cries at the same time. "I am laughing because none of you is wise enough to know what this is; I am crying because I don't know either." Iran: Courlander RIDE 63–65 (compass); Kelsey MULLAH 79–82.

J1061.1. The cock and the pearl: prefers a single corn to a peck of pearls. Aesop: Aesop AESOP'S (Golden) 16; Aesop AESOP'S (Grosset) 73; Aesop AESOP (Viking) 3–4; Aesop AESOP'S (Watts) 120; Aesop FABLES (Macmillan) 5; Aesop FIVE 90.

J1061.1.1* Ass prefers thistles to the delicacies on his back. Aesop: Aesop AESOP'S (Grosset) 42–43; Aesop AESOP'S (Viking) 12.

J1061.2. Baldheaded man finds the comb: it is useless. Tigre: Davis LION'S 158–160 (two bald men fight over it).

J1061.4. Miser's treasure stolen. Advised to im-

agine that his treasure is still there: he will be as well off as before. Aesop: Aesop AESOP'S (Grosset) 86–87; Aesop AESOP'S (Random) 16–17; Aesop AESOP'S (Watts) 208; Aesop FABLES (Macmillan) 123.

J1061.5. Poor man with no money but sense offers to multiply money for rich man with no sense. Does so by causing mollusks to produce pearls. Rich man with no sense puts pearls into hollow brick to avoid paying duty. Poland: Borski GOOD 51–54.

J1062.1. Frog as beauty doctor unable to cure own ugliness. Aesop: Aesop AESOP'S (Grosset) 224–225; Aesop AESOP'S (Watts) 56.

J1062.3. Prophet foretelling future is advised his home has been robbed. Aesop: Aesop AESOP's (Watts) 103.

J1062.3.1* Witch professes to be able to avert anger of the Gods. Is condemned to death––can't avert anger of men. Aesop: Aesop AESOP's (Watts) 207.

J1063.1. Mother crab blames her children for not walking straight. SEE ALSO: U121.1. Aesop: Aesop AESOP'S (Grosset) 192; Aesop AESOP'S (Viking) 33–34; Aesop FABLES (Macmillan) 95; Aesop FIVE 40.

J1064.1. Raven killed by apes who will not receive his teaching that shining stone (firefly) is not fire. SEE ALSO: J1761.3. India: Ryder PANCHATANTRA 183.

J1064.2* Sparrow's nest destroyed by monkey who is angered by her repeated suggestions that he build a house. India: Ryder PANCHATANTRA 415–416.

J1082.1. Horn will tell the tale. Thus answers goat to herdsman who begs her not to tell master that he has broken off her horn. Aesop: Aesop AESOP'S (Watts) 166; Aesop FABLES (Walck) 118.

J1085.1.1* Shoemaker given wealth by rich man, returns it. La Fontaine RICH MAN pb; Lowe LITTLE 47–48.

J1085.5* Happiest couple in land have only one shirt. King gives them riches. They become miserable. SEE ALSO: N135.3. Armenia: Tashjian: THREE 62–77.

J1087.1* Keep secrets to yourself. You cannot expect others to act as one's own storehouse. Turkey: Downing HODJA 57.

J1100 – J1699. Cleverness.

J1100 – J1249. Clever persons and acts.

J1110. Clever persons.

J1111. Clever girl. SEE: H586; H561.1.

J1111.4.1. Peasant girl puts leaves on water so passing general can only sip slowly so will not become ill. Wed. After death she is buried where kite with her name falls. Place called Village of the Pure Queen. Korea: Carpenter KOREAN 175-180.

J1122. Clever younger generation. SEE ALSO: J13.1.

J1122.2* Vixen tells cub she's warming paws at fire far below. Cub says spark from fire burned her nose. Mother thinks she'll be a fine cunning fox. Russia: Ginsburg ONE 39.

J1122.3* Young groundhogs see traces of spring root on mother's teeth. Disbelieve her warnings that spring has not yet come and leave burrow. Native American: Bierhorst FIRE 39-41.

J1130. Cleverness in law court—general. SEE ALSO: B271.3.

J1130.1* Judge is asked what the ruling would be on a certain case and then told defendant is really himself. "If your cow killed ours, what is the law?" "The cow is not responsible for its actions." "Good, it was our cow that killed yours." "That's more complicated. Hand me that black book." Turkey: Downing HODJA 45; Kelsey HODJA 123-129.

J1140. Cleverness in detection of truth. SEE ALSO: B522.1.2.

J1141.1. Guilty person deceived into gesture (act) which admits guilt.

J1141.1.0.1* Suspects are to pull donkey's tail believing it will bray when thief pulls. Judge has rubbed spearmint on tail. By having each suspect touch his nose and beard, he detects the thief, who was afraid to touch the donkey's tail. Iran: Kelsey MULLA 83-88.

J1141.1.2.1* Money taken from pickle barrel, judge says hands of thief will smell. Cetain suspects sniff hands. Japan: Edmonds OOKA 87-91.

J1141.1.3.2* Tree as witness. Plaintiff sent to summon tree. Defendant claims never to have been at tree yet accurately answers when asked if plaintiff has had time to reach tree yet. Russia: (Steppes of S.W. Asia): Deutsch TALES 28-31 /Arbuthnot FAIRY 158-159/, /Arbuthnot ANTHOLOGY 299/. Japan: Edmonds OOKA 45-50 (willow).

J1141.1.3.3* Fly as witness. Boy: "The fly was on the moneylender's nose." Moneylender: "No, it was on the housepole." Thus admitting he was present. Vietnam: Vo Dinh TOAD 99-104.

J1141.1.2.4* Jizo statue brought to court. As fine for laughing everyone must bring a three inch square of cloth. One is from the stolen silk. Japan: Edmonds OOKA 61-64.

J1141.1.3.4.1* Stone tried and lashed for stealing. Everyone fined a penny for laughing and poor boy's lost money thus returned. Burma (Shan): Courlander TIGER'S 24-28.

J1141.1.3.4.2* Money from fritter basket stolen. Stone beaten. Each of laughing crowd must drop 20 cash fine into bowl of water. Grease on coins betrays thief. China: Alexander PEBBLES 19; Lu Mar CHINESE 71-85.

J1141.1.3.4.3* Rock called as witness. Everyone who laughs when judge has rock beaten must drop ten coins into large jar of water. As stolen coins had been wrapped in oily paper, the thief's coins leave oil on water. China: Lu Mar CHINESE 41-95.

J1141.1.4. "Guilty man's stick will grow during the night." Guilty man chops end off stick. Nigeria (Hausa): Sturton ZOMO 3-13 (Hyena cuts off stick to escape detection as thief).

J1141.9.1. Laziest person to carry drum. Monkey says he won't carry it. No one had asked him thus admits it was he who didn't do part in work. Ghana (Ashanti): Courlander KING'S 32-35.

J1141.10.1* Suspects to vow to innocence on head of roadside Jizo. Only one returns without dusty hand, afraid to touch dusty head of statue. Japan: Edmonds OOKA 87-91.

J1141.10.2* Suspect to place hands on temple bell believing it will peal when thief touches. Only one suspect returns with clean hand from soot covered bell. Thief was afraid to touch. China: Kendall SWEET 30-32; Lu Mar CHINESE 29-41.

J1141.10.3* Blackened pot to crow when guilty touches. One has no black thumb. Wales: Sheppard-Jones WELSH 32-35.

J1141.17* Thief claims horse. Owner asks which eye is blind. Thief tries to guess. Neither. Russia: Ginsburg THREE 12.

J1144.3* Eaters of stolen food detected. Children asked at school to write about what they ate last week. Thief of hare detected. Japan: Edmonds TRICKSTER 61-67.

J1149.13* Moonlight to strike thief first. Nigeria (Fulani): Arnott AFRICAN 101-104.

J1150. Cleverness connected with the giving of evidence.

J1151.1. Testimony discredited by inducing witness to talk foolishly.

J1151.0.1* Man finds gold nugget. Takes it to Khan but wife substitutes rock in bag. He acts the fool. Is sent home. Russia: Masey STORIES 132-139.

J1151.1.1. Talkative wife discredited. Husband tells talkative wife about treasure he has discovered. To discredit her report he tells her also of impossible things (woodcock in the fishnet, fish in the bird trap, etc.). Usually shows her these accompanied by pancake rain, etc. She repeats it all. The whole story is disbelieved. Husband my keep his treasure. Type 1381. SEE ALSO: J1151.1.3. Finland: Jagendorf NOODLEHEAD 202-206; Lang VIOLET 114-120. Russia: Daniels FALCON 24-28 (rain of pancakes); Dolch OLD RUSSIA 1-9; Riordan TALES..CENTRAL 233-237. Russia (Ukraine): Yaroslava TUSYA (steward being beaten with sausages he stole). Poland: Zajdler POLISH 80-81 (+sheep bleating in mourning because master carried off by devil, fence of sausages, rains blood). Denmark: Hatch MORE 22-32. Scandinavia: Ross BURIED 65-74 (rains bread, landlord beaten by devil, enemy attacked).

J1151.1.3. The sausage rain (or rain of figs, fishes or milk). A mother in order to discredit testimony of her foolish son who has killed a man or discovered treasure, makes him believe it has rained sausages. When he says this occurred on the night it rained sausages, his tale is discredited. SEE: J1151.1.1. Italy: Baker TALKING 18-24; Manning-Sanders GIANNI 31-42; Mincielli OLD 14-23.

J1151.1.2.1* Master simulates rainstorm to confuse talking Sao bird and discredit testimony. Thailand: Carpenter ELEPHANT'S 58-65.

J1151.1.3.1.1* Lorikeet tells neighbors that farmer stole buffalo. Farmer puts brass pot over lorikeet, drips water to simulate rainy night. Testimony discredited. Lorikeet turned out of house. Lorikeet advises parrot to only mimic men's words. Thailand: Courlander RIDE 34-37.

J1151.1.3.2* Husband hides wife in potato pit, simulates noises of "Silly Goose War", tells her bagel he tosses into her lap fell from heaven, dog howling is devil torturing baron. Testimony of finding pot of money is discredited. Latvia: Durham TIT 37-40.

J1151.1.4. Fool tells of treasure found, kills man on road. Brother replaces buried body with dead goat. Fool's tale is discredited. Russia: Downing RUSSIAN 156-159.

J1152.2. Witness claims borrowed coat: discredited. Trickster summoned to court on Jew's complaint, refuses to go unless he has a new coat. Jew lends him his. In court the trickster says that the Jew is a liar. "He will claim I am wearing his coat." The Jew does so and no one believes him. Turkey: Downing HODJA 37-39; Kelsey HODJA 139-150. Arabia: Courlander TIGER'S 90-99 (Abunuwas borrows cloak, donkey).

J1155.2. Man tells tall tale, imprisoned for lying. Tells second tale showing first must be true. France: Jagendorf NOODLEHEAD 142-146.

J1159. Excellent witnesses. Witnesses lie marvelously, win case. "How could you believe such scoundrels?" Judge: "They may be no good morally but they are excellent witnesses when it comes to a quarrel about a lute." Turkey: Downing HODJA 71.

J1160. Clever pleading.

J1161. Literal pleading: letter of the law has been met.

J1161.3.1* Trespasser's defense: standing on his own land. Type 1590. Ordered never to set foot on king's ground again. Trickster passes standing on cartload of own ground. Philippines (Tagalog): Sechrist ONCE 173-177.

J1161.3.2* Trickster never to show face again, shows backside. Never to set foot on Haitian soil again. Fills boots with soil from Barbados. Haiti: Courlander PIECE 58-61. Somali: Courlander FIRE 81-88 (Ethiopian puts Egyptian soil in shoes).

J1161.7. Ruler forbids blacksmith to reveal solution of riddle unless he has seen him one hundred times. Smith reveals solution on receipt of one hundred crowns bearing the ruler's likeness. SEE: H561.6.2.

J1161.12* Letter of the law: Finder of lost object must shout fact three times in market place. He refuses to tell roused villagers what he was shouting. Might be breaking the law to repeat it a fourth time. Iran: Shah MULLA 76.

J1169.1. The woman with the bad eyes. Physician called to doctor woman's eyes bandages them and then steals things each day. She refuses to pay fee and is hauled to court. She says that her sight is worse than ever for whereas she used to see many things in her house, she now sees very little. Theft is thus revealed. Aesop: Aesop AESOP'S (Grosset) 184-185; Aesop AESOP'S (Watts) 13.

J1169.7. Suit about the ass's shadow. Man hires ass and driver for trip. In the heat, the traveler sits down in the ass's shadow. Driver contends he didn't hire the ass's shadow. SEE ALSO: J1172.2.3. Cambodia: Carpenter ELEPHANT'S 100-107. Aesop: Aesop AESOP'S (Grosset) 41; Aesop AESOP'S (Watts) 44 (ass flees); Aesop FABLES (Walck) 64.

J1169.7.1* Peddler buys shade of cypress tree in rich man's yard. Follows shade into house when it falls there. China: Chang TALES 34-47.

J1170. Clever judicial decisions.

J1171.1. Solomon's judgment: the divided child. Two women claim a child. Judge offers to cut it in two. Real mother refuses.

J1171.1.2* Solomon's judgment fails. Judge has fortune of child told. Twenty years hence he will be invalid, supported by mother. False mother drops case. Japan: Edmonds OOKA 57-60.

J1171.1.3* Motherhood test. One to fill pot with tears is mother. Raven claiming egret chicks loses. East Africa: Heady SAFIRI 46-50.

J1171.5* Judgment over true owner of a slain elephant to be made in morning. One man wails all night over elephant, second leaves. Elephant awarded to first. Angola (Mbaka): Courlander KING'S 68-70.

J1172.2. Payment with the clink of money. Man sued for payment for enjoyment of the flavor of meat when roasting. Japan: Edmonds OOKA 7-11 (Student over tempura shop flavors rice with smell). SEE ALSO: K231.14.2. Mexico: Balet FENCE pb. Italy: Vittorini OLD 24-27. Peru: Hardendorff FROG'S 29-39. Turkey: Downing HODJA 44; Kelsey MULLA 122-127 (steam absorbed by bread).

J1172.2.0.1. Payment for smell of food with smell of money (rice hung over pot to absorb flavor). Cambodia: Carpenter ELEPHANT'S 100-107.

J1172.2.0.2* Payment for smell of fish with shadow of money. Burma: Htin KINGDOM 15-17.

J1172.2.0.3* Payment for smell of bakery with feel of money. Peru: Newman FOLK 19-26.

J1172.2.1* Payment with the clink of money. Laborer claims payment for grunting while his companion worked. Turkey: Downing HODJA 108-115; Walker WATERMELONS 35-36.

J1172.2.2* Punishment for 'stealing' smell--beating shadow. Rich man who makes accusation forced to beat shadow of sloogeh dog until exhausted. Congo: Aardema TALES FROM THE STORY HAT 24-31 /Arbuthnot ANTHOLOGY 323-324/. Bulgaria: Pridham GIFT 63-66.

J1172.2.3* Payment for shadow of buffalo with shadow of money (or sound). SEE ALSO: J1169.7 (suit about the ass's shadow). Cambodia: Carpenter ELEPHANT 100-107.

J1172.3. Ungrateful animal returned to captivity. A man rescues a serpent (bear) who in return seeks to kill his rescuer. Fox as judge advises the man to put the serpent back into captivity. +J1172.3.2. SEE ALSO: W154.8; W154.2.1.1.

Bushman rescues adder. Fox reenacts. India: Gaer FABLES 30-33. Greece: Wilson GREEK 53-57.

Brahman frees tiger, jackal re-enacts. India: Arbuthnot FAIRY 164-166; Baker TALKING 236-241; Buck FAIRY 168-171; Haviland FAVORITE..INDIA 83-90; Jacobs INDIAN 81-85. Pakistan: Siddiqui TOONTOONY 104-108. Punjab: Bleecker BIG 135-138. Arbuthnot ARBUTHNOT 350; Steel TIGER pb; Wiggin FAIRY 391-394.

Farmer entraps bear, releases. Fox re-enacts. Finland: Bowman TALES..TUPA 264-265.

Goat rescues lion--man re-enacts. Nigeria: Walker NIGERIAN 40-42.

Hare frees rattlesnake, coyote re-enacts.

Mexico: Ross BURIED 89-94.

Hare held wolf, terrapin re-enacts. U.S. (Georgia, Black): Harris FAVORITE 182-186; Harris COMPLETE 315-320; Harris NIGHTS 274-279.

Jackal tells snake to get down from man's head to plead case or will look silly. Judge Elephant steps on snake. Shankilla: Davis LION'S 143-149.

Man frees bear, fox re-enacts, broke tabu on showing reward for pot of honey. Bulgaria: Pridham GIFT 95-99.

Man frees dragon, fox reenacts. Poland: Zajdler POLISH 20-27. Norway: Undset TRUE 250-253. Green CAVALCADE..DRAGONS 23-25.

Man frees snake, fox re-enacts. Jacobs EUROPEAN 165-169.

Man ferries snake over river, snake to bite, wife tricks into cook pot. Africa: Tracy LION 6-9.

Man rescues snake from under rock--fox re-enacts. Italy (Piedmont): Hampden HOUSE 85-87; Vittorini OLD 34-37.

Man releases snake from jar. Fox re-enacts. Bulgaria: Pridham GIFT 55-62.

Man rescues snake, squirrel judge has scene re-enacted. Indonesia: De Leeuw INDONESIAN 36-39.

Man saves wolf from hunter. Old man re-enacts. China (Ming Dynasty): Kendall SWEET 49-59.

Master Kho frees tiger, rabbit re-enacts. Burma: Brockett BURMESE 120-125.

Monk sucks poison from snake bitten tiger, hare re-enacts. Vietnam: Carpenter ELEPHANT'S 151-158.

Mouse frees lion by chewing rope, Anansi re-enacts. Ashanti: Appiah ANANSE 89-94.

Mouse frees rattlesnake, coyote re-enacts. Mexico: Edmonds TRICKSTER 77-85.

Opossum frees snake, hare re-enacts. U.S. Black (South Carolina): Faulkner DAY 99-105.

Peasant saves wolf, fox re-enacts. Russia: Carrick STILL 105-116; Ginsburg ONE 10-13.

Rat rescues panther from pit, spider re-enacts. Africa: Green ANIMAL 141-142.

Traveler releases tiger. Fox re-enacts. India: Korel LISTEN 89-97.

Warthog rescues lion, warthog re-enacts. East Africa: Heady WHEN 81-84.

J1172.3.0.1* Karbau (carabao) rescues crocodile from under log and is threatened by crocodile. Kantchil re-enacts scene and advises Karbau to leave crocodile under log. Indonesia: Courlander KANTCHIL'S 87-94.

J1172.3.0.2* Karbau rescues crocodile from under log and is threatened. Kantchil advises tossing crocodile into river. Indonesia: Bro HOW 39-48.

J1172.3.0.3* Carter carries stranded crocodile back to river. Crocodile asks to be taken in deeper and grabs bullock's leg. Hare advises whacking crocodile on nose. Burma: Brockett BURMESE 126-130. Dobbs ONCE 54-59 (grabs man's foot, hare re-enacts).

J1172.3.0.4* Man frees monkey with tail caught in tree. Monkeys capture man anyway. Man lures them to his trap and captures. Monkeys planned to club man with fruit of sausage tree. Sudan: Aardema TALES 38-43.

J1172.3.0.5* Man frees lion stuck in mud. Cat challenges to race to mudhole--leaves lion stuck. +J1172.3.2. Philippines (Bagobo): Sechrist ONCE 46-49.

J1172.3.0.6* Tortoise as barber ties hair of leopard to the tree. Snail frees leopard. Lion plans to eat snail. Appeal to God of the Sun, Oloja. Oloja sends eclipse and snail escapes. Yoruba: Fuja FOURTEEN 69-72.

J1172.3.2. Animals render unjust descision against man since man has always been unjust to them. +J1172.3.

Ass and horse judge against man. Greece: Wilson GREEK 53-57.

Banyan tree, camel, bullock, eagle, alligator favor tiger not man. Baker TALKING 236-241; Wiggin FAIRY 391-394.

Carabaos, cows, dogs favor lion not man. Philippines (Bagobo): Sechrist ONCE 46-49.

Cow, tree favor adder instead of man. India: Gaer FABLES 30-33.

Fig tree and plum tree judge against man. Africa: Tracy LION 6-9.

Greyhound and horse judge against man. Italy: Vittorini OLD 34-37.

Horse, dog against man. Russia: Carrick STILL 105-116.

Horse and dog judge against man. Bulgaria: Pridham GIFT 55-62; Undset TRUE 250-253. Poland: Zajdler POLISH 20-27.

Horse, mulberry tree favor snake not man. Italy (Piedmont): Hampden HOUSE 85-87.

Monkey, nat (dislikes man), vulture (wants pickings of man). Favor tiger over monk. Vietnam: Carpenter ELEPHANT'S 151-158.

Palm tree, brook favor snake instead of man. Indonesia: De Leeuw INDONESIAN 36-39.

Pipal tree, buffalo turning waterwheel, road judge against man (brahman) in favor of tiger. India: Bleecker BIG 135-138; Buck FAIRY 168-171; Jacobs INDIAN 81-85 /Haviland FAVORITE..FAIRY 83-90/; Korel LISTEN 89-97. Pakistan: Siddiqui TOONTOONY 104-108 (oak). Arbuthnot FAIRY 164-166; Arbuthnot ANTHOLOGY 350.

Skull of ox, banyan tree favor tiger instead of man. Burma: Brockett BURMESE 120-125.

Tree, cow judge against man. China: Kendall SWEET 49-59.

J1172.3.2.1* Cooking pot rules in favor of crocodile seeking to eat rescuer Carabao since pot has received bad for good. Indonesia: Bro HOW 39-48.

J1172.3.2.2* Animals render unjust decision against man in fear of strong animal.

Hare, hound favor snake. Jacobs EURASIAN 165-169.

Water buffalo, jackal fear tiger, judge against monk. Vietnam: Courlander ELEPHANT'S 151-158.

J1172.3.2.3* Ungrateful snake threatens to eat owner who can no longer feed it. Crane rules in favor of man, turtle in favor of snake. Crow eats snake. Vietnam: Vo-Dinh TOAD 29-34.

J1172.3.2.4* Ungrateful snake would eat farmer who hid it from enemies. Sycamore tree, river, and grass judge in favor of snake. Wind tells each to act according to his nature and to sing thanks that things are thus he gives drum to each. As they drum the wind sings to snake "as your nature is to eat man, eat man." To man, "As your nature is not to be eaten, do not be eaten." Man flees. Ethiopia: Courlander FIRE 51-56.

J1173. Series of clever decisions. Plaintiff voluntarily withdraws. 1. Man pulls off borrowed horse's tail: he shall keep horse till tail grows on. 2. Man falls out of bed and kills a baby (or causes a miscarriage): he shall beget new baby for the mother. 3. Man falls from a bridge and kills boatman's son: shall allow boatman to fall from bridge and kill him. Philippines (Tagalog): Sechrist ONCE 177-184 (Carabao, +K251.2.1). Russia: Daniels FALCON 67-70; Riordan TALES..TARTARY 195-198. Italy: Vittorini OLD 14-18. Iran: Edmonds TRICKSTER 51-60 (+moneylender given poor man's family, nagging wife, invalid son, etc. to keep till debt is paid). Hardendorff JUST 116-120 (Yukpachen--to have hands cut off for throwing stone at runaway pony, pony's owner to have tongue pulled for calling out, etc.).

J1173.1. Novel settlement: snake's wife must wait to kill prince till princess bears as many sons as snake has. India: Turnbull FAIRY 117-126.

J1173.1.2* Novel settlement: woman to be killed as soon as broken vase is paid for. To pay one mon per year for one hundred years. Japan: Edmonds OOKA 92-96.

J1175.1. The cat in the warehouse. Each companion owns one leg of cat. Owner of broken leg left to guard cat in warehouse. Cat sets fire to warehouse--owner of other three legs must pay since broken leg couldn't walk. Ceylon: Tooze WONDERFUL 118-120.

J1177. Story told to discover thief. Judge tells story of lady, her husband, her lover, and the robbers. Which was most generous? Witness says that the robber was. This shows he has the robber's point of view. Type 976.

J1177.2* Suspects tell story of cleverest man they've heard of. Thief tells of thief. Japan: Edmonds TRICKSTER 61-67.

J1179. Clever judicial decisions--miscellaneous.

J1179.5. Servants would not have left the coats. Merchants complain to nobleman that his servants have robbed them of money. Nobleman asks whether merchant had on those good coats when robbery took place. When told yes, he said that the robbers were not his servants, for they would never have left good coats. Iran: Shah MULLA 53 (thieves could not be from this town for they do things thoroughly here).

J1179.15* Miser boards up all doors but one to avoid paying door tax. Judge orders him to pay no tax and boards up remaining door. Then orders him to take in twelve orphans thus becoming tax exempt. Japan: Edmonds OOKA 39-44.

J1179.17* Judge declares apprentice is entitled to keep any objects given (i.e. thrown) to him. Japan: Edmonds OOKA 33-38.

J1179.18* Dog who tears robe of neighbor who kicks him to be rewarded with pat in future for trying to stop 'thief.' Japan: Edmonds OOKA 12-16.

J1179.19* Shopkeeper offers to let boy have three porcelain dogs if he'll carry one home alone. Judge advises boy to break one and carry in pieces, will still have two. Japan: Edmonds OOKA 17-21.

J1179.20* Judge lets reformed thief go free on condition thief sneak stolen rice back nightly until debt repaid. Japan: Edmonds OOKA 27-32.

J1179.21* Judge charges ten shilling fine which Geordie asks as lawyer for the five men. Tells to agree to go to jail, once in city they agree to pay fine. Thus got ride to market (worth nineteen shillings for ten shilling fine). Scotland: Edmonds TRICKSTER 30-35.

J1179.22* Tiger claims goat stepped on her tail. To eat anyone who treads on tail. Goat, however, is facing her in cleft in hill where met. India: Wyatt GOLDEN 81-84.

J1179.23* Rich woman accused of crime forces servant to change clothes with her. Judge rules servant should pay for crime since this woman had always put blame on servants in past. Korea: Edmonds TRICKSTER 138-143.

J1179.24* Old woman kills cat loaned to bride next door and demands two hundred ounces of silver as reimbursement. Bride in court finds her father-in-law once loaned a wooden ladle to woman, claims this was magic and asks three thousand ounces for its loss. China: Wiggin TALES 404-406.

J1179.25* Monkey frees jackal from snare, later taken to jackal as judge. Judge recalls favor and rules monkey must climb tree as punishment. West Africa: Carpenter AFRICAN 153-160.

J1179.26* Farmer claims merchant owes him debt. Governor tells farmer he may cut off man's ear in payment. He declines. Governor offers merchant chance to cut off farmer's ear and he begins. Judge rules for farmer. Man who would cut off an ear over money is not to be trusted. Kashmir: Courlander TIGER'S 78-79.

J1179.27* Merchant gets Ikkyu to promise to carry money home "as he directs"--directs not to cross bridge. Ikkyu sets out to walk around river-- six months journey--with merchant's money bags. Merchant finally carries Ikkyu over river to retrieve money bags. Japan: Edmonds TRICKSTER 14-20.

J1180. Clever means of avoiding legal punishment.

J1185.1. Sheherezade: story with indefinite sequels told to stave off execution.

J1185.2* Tengu forces kidnapped man to tell stories nightly. Allows to return home during day. Man's grandmother tells him new tales and by the time tales are exhausted he and Tengu are friends so he is not eaten. Palmer DRAGONS 30-37.

J1189.4* Anyone who breaks Sesshu's painted vase to die. Ikkyu breaks it so Daimyo Kii will not have to keep word, otherwise some servant would certainly have died. Japan: Edmonds POSSIBLE 105-114.

J1189.5* Punishment escaped since crime and punishment contradict each other. Edict: who does not tell truth will be hanged. Lie: "I am going to be hanged." If he is hanged he will have told the truth. Iran: Shah MULLA 21.

J1190. Cleverness in the law court--miscellaneous.

J1191. *Reductio ad absurdum* of judgment. SEE ALSO: J1530.

J1191.1. *Reductio ad absurdum:* the decision about the colt. A man ties his mare to a second man's wagon. The mare bears a colt which the wagon-owner claims saying that the wagon has borne a colt. Real owner of the colt shows the absurdity by fishing in the street or by telling that his wife is shooting fish in the garden. Neither of these are so absurd as the decision. Czechoslovakia: Fillmore SHEPHERD'S 144-152 /Arbuthnot FAIRY 147-149/. Estonia: Maas MOON 116-122 (goat follows stallion home and is claimed, clever daughter has father sift sand for fish); McNeil DOUBLE 50-55. Poland: Wojchiechowska WINTER 22-31. Wales: Pugh TALES 105-115. Rumania: Ure RUMANIAN 131-143 (says frogs are eating flour lake). Russia: Bulatkin EURASIAN 27-38; Lurie CLEVER 9-16. Italy: Jacobs EUROPEAN 188; Toor GOLDEN 41-46.

J1191.1.1. "The sea is on fire." Not more absurd than the decision about the colt. Colt exchanged for calf and horse sold to have born latter. Judge Hare arrives later--busy putting out a burning sandbank in river. Burma: Brockett BURMESE 87-91; Htin Aung KINGDOM 62-65.

J1191.1.2* Leopard claims jackal's calf was born to his goat. Judge Baboon makes them wait while he plays 'music' on a stone. Possible if goat can bear calf. Ethiopia: Courlander FIRE 29-34.

J1191.1.3* Hyena claims jackal's calf was born to his bull. Judge Rabbit is late as earth opened up and he had to walk around "In what country does earth open?" "Where bulls bear calves." Amhara: Davis LION'S 61-67.

J1191.1.4* King claims kitten was born of his cat because it goes to his. He rubbed catnip on his cat. Wife points out that his is a male. Chile: Carpenter SOUTH 83-92.

J1191.2. Suit for chickens produced from boiled eggs. Countertask: harvesting crop produced from cooked seeds. Turkey: Downing HODJA 53; Walker WATERMELONS 68-72; Walker TALES 236 (witness arrives late at court, says he was planting boiled seeds, no more foolish than to sue for chicks that might have hatched from boiled eggs). Greece: Aliki EGGS (sea-captain ate eggs in restaurant). China: Chang TALES 25-30 (eats chicken). Rumania: Ure RUMANIAN 38-41 (boils corn). Poland: Borski GOOD 75-77 (boils peas). Japan: Edmonds POSSIBLE 51-59 (to pay with future fruit of plum pit). Portugal: Lowe LITTLE 32-35 (roasted chestnuts, lawyer is the Devil); Michael PORTUGUESE 118-120 (chestnuts).

J1191.2.1* Woman given three eggs to eat puts them to hatch instead. Later sued for share of all goods gained from chain thus started.

Beggar suggests sowing cooked beans to court. Case dismissed. Haiti: Wolkenstein MAGIC 49-56.

J1191.7. Rice pot on pole, fire far away. As easy to cook rice thus as to warm a man at a distance from a lamp on a balcony. SEE: K231.14.1.

J1193.1. Killing the fly on the judge's nose. The judge has told boy that he should kill a fly wherever he sees one. SEE ALSO: J2102.3; N333. Italy: Cimino DISOBEDIENT #13 (Giufa); Jagendorf NOODLEHEAD 173-174 (Giufa). Majorca: Mehdevi BUNGLING 17-35. Iran: Bulatkin EURASIAN 103-105 (if hits fly it is guilty, misses and hits judge). Puerto Rico: Carter GREEDY 112-118. Portugal: Lowe LITTLE 36. Slovenia: Kavcic GOLDEN 118-126.

J1193.1.0.1. Abunuwas accuses flies of stealing rice and caliph Haroun-al-Rashid warrants him to kill flies. Wreaks havoc in marketplace and strikes fly on caliph. Arabia: Courlander TIGER'S 90-99.

J1193.1.1* Fool should have done what master always does on seeing fly. "There's one on my head now." "I always hit it." "Then do so." Knocks sense into head with blow. Fenner TIME TO LAUGH 3-16 /Gruenberg MORE 255-260/.

J1193.2. The value of a blow. A judge awards damages of a penny against a friend of his for giving a blow. The defendant goes to get the money and is gone long. Meanwhile the plaintiff gives the judge a blow and tells him to use the penny as damages. Turkey: Downing HODJA 10.

J1199.1* How to get rid of beggars--have two pillars of cliff carved into statues. This takes all wealth. Beggars no longer bother. Korea: Carpenter KOREAN 191-196.

J1199.2* Asked value of golden plow, Solomon-the-Wise replies: "If it doesn't rain in May--nothing." Rumania: Ure RUMANIAN 158-159.

J1199.3* King of Naxos obtains squash seeds from Attica for his people in famine. They refuse to eat them. He places seeds under guard and all are stolen. Greece (Naxos): Neufeld BEWARE 22-27.

J1199.4* Youngest son and mother left only small inheritance and scroll. Scroll is to be shown to wise judge when son reaches maturity. Message on scroll tells of hidden treasure, judge interprets. China: Mar CHINESE 89-96.

J1199.5* Emperor stops fighting by ruling that all must wear two inch clay hats with heavy fine for breaking one. Plotting thus stopped also as they cannot lean close enough to whisper. Korea: Carpenter TALES..KOREAN 39-44.

J1210. Clever man puts another out of countenance.

J1211.2. Clever thief may keep booty. He has

seen his victim in a disgraceful position and is allowed to keep the booty as a price for his silence. Turkey: Downing HODJA 26-27 (took cloak from judge lying drunk).

J1211.4* Jester to win portion of kingdom if finds crime for which excuse is worse than crime. Sneaks into Sultan's room at night--kisses him. Excuse: he thought it was the king's wife. North Africa: Gilstrap SULTAN'S 75-80.

J1225.1* Farmer puts visitor out of countenance. Soldier lays sword on table ostentatiously. Farmer brings in manure shovel and puts beside it. If you have a big knife, you'll need a big spoon to go with it. Rumania: Ure RUMANIAN 144.

J1229.1* Local philosopher appears on platform with "cultural delegation" sent by king to answer questions of the masses. He says he'll answer any questions they can't answer. Iran: Shah MULLA 68.

J1229.2* After receiving no alms in villages, the hodja is asked to decide fate of a chicken stealing fox. He puts his cloak and scholar's turban on fox. Now people will take it for a scholar, it will starve to death within a week. Turkey: Downing TALES 32.

J1229.3* At bath he is given poor robe and towel, no service--he leaves large tip. Next time he receives excellent attention, leaves small tip. This tip is for the last time, the tip last time was for this time. Turkey: Downing HODJA 63.

J1229.4* Pedagogue asks ferryman if he has never studied grammar. "Then half your life has been wasted." Boat begins to sink. Ferryman asks pedagogue if he ever learned to swim. "Then all your life is lost." Iran: Shah MULLA 17. Jewish: Dobbs MORE 39-42.

J1230. Clever dividing. SEE ALSO: K171.1.

J1241.6* Fox lends viscachas needles, thread to sew blanket. Claims middle is his. Argentina: Jagendorf KING 15-18.

J1241.7* Anansi gives one of four plantains to each family member, keeps none for self. To reward his sacrifice, each gives him one-half of their share. He ends up with two. West Indies: Sherlock ANANSI 64-69.

J1249.2* Clever dividing. Judge lets one of the disputants make division. Then lets other make first choice of his half. Japan: Edmonds OOKA 65-69. Russia: Lurie CLEVER 9-16

J1249.3* Judge bets other judge his horse that he can solve dispute of two men each claiming half of thirteen horses. Adds his horse and gives each seven horses. Takes judge's horse for self. Japan: Edmonds OOKA 81-86.

J1249.4* Big boy tells small boy his moon cake should be half moon. Eats part to transform. Decides crescent moon better--eats more.

Asked to restore he eats all--moon wanes before waxing. China: Wiggin TALES 403.

J1249.5* Three men buy 17 donkeys. One pays half price; one--one-third, one--one ninth. Cannot divide. Mulla adds his donkey, making 18. Give first man one-half = 9; second, one-third = 6; third, one-ninth = 2. Rides off on his. Persia: Bulatkin EURASIAN 64-68.

J1249.6* Otter, jackal are unable to share fish as each wants head, belly. Hare solves by cutting fish lengthwise. Burma: Htin KINGDOM 39-41.

J1249.7* One partner does work, other takes "tiredness." West Africa: Arkhurst ANANSI 32; Courlander COW-TAIL 47.

J1250 -J1499. Clever verbal retorts (repartee).

J1250. Clever verbal retorts--general.

J1250.1* He is throwing crumbs around. Why? To keep the tigers away. But there are no tigers around here. Effective, isn't it? Iran: Shah MULLA 18.

J1250.2* Sitting on camel trying to eat finely ground corn. It blows away before reaching his lips. What are you eating? If it goes on like this, nothing! Turkey: Downing HODJA 56.

J1250.3* Asked how old he is. Forty. Asked ten years later. Still forty. He cannot go back on his word. Turkey: Downing HODJA 11.

J1250.4* He tells a Yogi that a fish saved his life once and is accepted as being one who communes with nature. Later explains. He was on verge of starvation when he caught it. Iran: Shah MULLA 64-65.

J1250.5* He visits old temple and is afraid roof will fall in. But this place proclaims the glory of God! Yes, but I'm afraid it'll be carried away by religious fervor and come crashing down around our ears. Turkey: Downing HODJA 96.

J1250.6* Asked by villagers to move away from town. Why don't they all move away from him? It would be easier for them to set up housekeeping than for an old man to move out alone. Turkey: Downing HODJA 9.

J1250.7* Dipping bread in a lake full of ducks. What are you eating? Duck soup. Turkey: Downing HODJA 93.

J1250.8* He once invented the idea of eating bread and snow together but even he didn't like it. Turkey: Downing HODJA 69.

J1250.9* He once caused an entire tribe of bedouins to run. He ran and they ran after him. Iran: Shah MULLA 36.

J1250.10* Wife when unveiled after wedding proves

ugly. She asks to whom he wishes her to show her face. "Anyone but me." Iran: Shah MULLA 99.

J1250.11* Crash. It was his cloak hitting the floor. But he was in it at the time. Turkey: Downing HODJA 92. Iran: Shah MULLA 94.

J1250.12* He never made halva for never had flour and butter in the house at the same time. Never? Well, they were both there, he was not at home. Turkey: Downing HODJA 53.

J1250.13* Asked what part he had in prank, schoolboy replies "Nothing. All I did was to watch and laugh." Iran: Kelsey MULLAH vii.

J1250.14* Arguing with wife in bed, she brings up her first husband and he brings up his first wife. Explaining to the judge, he says a friend of his wife got in bed with them and then a friend of his got in bed with them and then his wife fell out. Turkey: Walker TALES 234.

J1260. Repartee based on church or clergy.

K1261.1.1.1* God as father-in-law. Man asks lodging saying he is God's son-in-law. Taken to mosque. Stay in your father-in-law's house. Turkey: Walker WATERMELONS 45-48; Walker TALES 234.

J1280. Repartee with ruler (judge, etc.).

J1286.1* Peasant addresses man carrying grapes with high titles hoping to be given grapes. Man refuses to answer to these titles--"I am not a sheik," "I am not a highness," etc. Peasant, "Soon we'll find that these are not grapes." Iran: Shah MULLA 148.

J1289.4.1* The needy philosopher. Wealthy man says he is as learned as philosopher so why should he give donation to his equal. "When you have walked thirty miles and returned humiliated and empty-handed then you'll be my equal." Turkey: Downing HODJA 66.

J1289.21* King threatens mystic with death if he doesn't prove his mystical powers. Mystic at once sees demons and spirits. How? "Fear is all you need!" Iran: Shah MULLA 37.

J1289.22* Cruel ruler tells of enjoyable journey through countryside on which calamities befell all on his route. Peasant: Thank God you returned. Had you stayed longer there would not have been one stone left upon another. Turkey: Downing HODJA 48.

J1289.23* Fraudulent tax-collector made to swallow his records. Clever successor prints all records on bread (yufka) and tells ruler either of them can "swallow" these records. Turkey: Walker WATERMELONS 29-32.

J1289.24* Peasant accused of being bad omen for ruler to see is beaten (or sentenced to be hung). Peasant: "Who is a bad omen for who?" Iran:

Shah MULLA 140. Turkey: Walker TALES 229-232.

J1289.25* Ruler: "Am I a tyrant or a learned man?" "Neither. We have been such tyrants that God sent you to scourge us." Turkey: Walker TALES 229-232.

J1289.26* Disguised tyrant listens to sermon attacking himself, then reveals identity. Preacher to congregation: "Brethern, we have performed a congregational prayer. New we shall start a congregational funeral." Iran: Shah MULLA 144.

J1289.27* Unrecognized tsar tells peasant he will know Tsar when they enter field as all will remove their hats except Tsar. They enter field. Tsar: "Well, you and I are the only ones with our hats on. One of us must be the Tsar." Russia: Wyndham TALES..RUSSIA 33-37.

J1289.28.1* Repartee with God. Man asks God for money. No answer. Says that God might as well kill him then. An axe falls from tree barely missing him. "Why do you listen now?" Ethiopia (Guragie): Ashabranner LION'S 130-131.

J1289.29* King has donkey led in with name of boy's father painted on it. Boy, nonplussed, changes sign to read Chu Kuo Tze Yu's donkey. China: Mar CHINESE 23-27.

J1289.30* Lad praises king, is beaten. Tries insulting king, is rewarded. Italy: Vittorini OLD 19-23.

J1289.31* Prince of Chu asks why such a poor ambassador is sent from Chi. Ambassador retorts that poor ambassador is sent to poor country. China: Courlander TIGER'S 53-54.

J1289.32* Mirali insists there are flies only where there are people. Sultan rides into desert with M. to prove otherwise and finds a fly. Mirali points out that there are people where the fly was found, the two of them. Turkmen: Ginsburg KAHA 140-141.

J1289.33* Grandpa curses Lord for underpaying him for mowing. Let the grass rise back in its place in the meadow." Russia (Chuvash): Ginsburg TALES 22-23.

J1300. Officiousness or foolish questions rebuked.

J1309.1. Man asks naked Indian if he is not cold. Indian asks if man's face is cold. Man replies that it is not. Indian replies: "Me all face!" (Jew responds to Polish landlord, all nose.) Jewish: Ish-Kishor WISE 160-170.

J1310. Repartee concerning wine.

J1319.2* Old woman smells empty wine jar. Must have been fine wine to leave behind such a smell. Aesop: Aesop AESOP'S (Watts) 90; Aesop FABLES (Macmillan) 161.

J1319.3* King's daughter asks Joshua why God keeps wisdom in such a plain container. Joshua points out that fine wines keep best in earthenware vessels, spoil when put in gold and silver. Jewish: Dobbs MORE 34-38.

J1319.4* Thief made hole at bottom of wine barrel but is not accused since wine is missing from top. Spain: De La Iglesia CAT #12.

J1330. Repartee concerning beggars.

J1331. Persistent beggar invited upstairs. A beggar will not come in but insists on the man coming down to the door. When he asks alms the man bids him come upstairs. Then he says he has nothing for him. "You made me come down for nothing; I make you come up for nothing." Turkey: Downing HODJA 75. Iran: Kelsey Mullah 24-31 (minaret); Shah MULLA 93 (on roof).

J1340. Retorts from hungry persons. SEE ALSO: J1286.1.

J1340.1* Stranger enters bakery and begins eating pie. Shopkeeper, thinking he will not pay, begins to beat him. "What kind of town is this, where they beat a man as soon as he starts eating?" Iran: Shah MULLA 134.

J1340.2* Hungry man eyes baked goods and is not offered any. To baker: "Are these yours? Then eat them!" Turkey: Downing HODJA 43.

J1340.3* Boys beg for some grapes and one boy is given three. "They all taste the same. It makes no difference if you taste one hundred or a quarter of one." Turkey: Downing HODJA 55.

J1341.2. Asking the large fish, parents serve boy a small fish and keep back a large one for themselves. Knowing this, the boy puts the fish to his ear. He says that he has asked the fish a question. Says the fish cannot answer but tells him to ask the large fish under the bed. England: Jagendorf MERRY 69-76.

J1341.7. Stingy innkeeper cured of serving weak beer. She always gives the servants a pitcher of weak beer before meals so as to fill them up. One of them: "I wash out my insides so as to have more room for food." She changes her practice. Type 1566. Latvia: Durham TIT 41-42 (water--stretches stomach).

J1341.7.1* Stingy man throws fish out. They 'steal' rice by causing family to eat more rice when having such a fine meal. Japan: Bang MEN 4-5.

J1341.7.2* Baron gives beggar soup, roast, porridge. He replies is full after each course -- yet eats it. Explains: box full of stones is full, can add a pail of sand--full. Can add a pail of water. Latvia: Durham TIT 46-47.

J1344. Unwelcome guest tells about the hidden food. Having seen his hostess hide it, he tells about it in the form of a tale. SEE ALSO: K842.

J1344.1* Fool with raven wrapped in cowhide shelters at mill and overhears miller's wife entertaining priest. On miller's arrival, raven prophesies where food is hidden. Says devil is in linen chest--priest flees. Germany (Grimm): Grimm GRIMM'S (World) 107-113.

J1344.2* Rusty Jack: crow caught by hiding under oxhide feigned prophet. Tells where he hid food and young girl guest. Sells crow-catching oxhide, weds young girl. New York: (Schoharie Hills): Cothran WITH 9-17.

J1347* Etiquette requires eating with two fingers and thumb. "Why are you eating with five fingers?" "Because I haven't got six." Turkey: Downing HODJA 26.

J1350. Rude retorts.

J1352.3* King tells fool "You are not far removed from a donkey." Fool, sitting near king: "Only a couple of yards." Turkey: Downing HODJA 82.

J1353. Whom it concerns. There is someone carrying a goose. "How does that concern me?" "He is carrying it to your house." "How does that concern you?" Turkey: Downing HODJA 63.

J1369.6* Finding appointment has been forgotten, caller writes: "Stupid Oaf" (ass) on gate and leaves. His friend arrives at his home later. "I remembered our appointment as soon as I saw your name on my gate." Iran: Shah MULLA 26. Uygur: Ginsburg KAHA 88-89.

J1380. Retorts concerning debts.

J1381. Where you got it last year. Person tells borrower to get the corn at the same place as he got it last year. There is none there. "Then you didn't return it as you said you would and there is none to lend you this year." Iran: Kelsey MULLA 32-37 (money).

J1382.3* Man asks friend to buy him a guitar. Friend keeps forgetting. Finally, he gives money to buy guitar. "Ah, I see you really intend to play the guitar." Italy: Cimino DISOBEDIENT #15.

J1383. Unstable security. Stag tries to borrow grain from the sheep using the wolf as security. Sheep says that they are both so swift that he does not know where they will be on the day of payment. Aesop: Aesop AESOP'S (Watts) 97.

J1390. Retorts concerning thefts.

J1391.1. Thief's excuse: the big wind. Vegetable thief is caught in a garden. Owner: "How did you get into the garden?" "A wind blew me in." "How were the vegetables uprooted?" "If the wind is strong enough to blow me in, it can uproot them." "How did they get into your bag?" "This is what I was wondering." Turkey: Downing HODJA 80.

J1391.2. The ladder market. A thief climbs over a wall by means of his ladder. When caught in the garden he says that he is a seller of ladders. Owner: "Is this a ladder market?" "Can't one sell ladders everywhere?" Turkey: Downing HODJA 79.

J1391.9* Lame excuse. Caught stealing fruit in tree, thief claims to be a songbird. Asked to sing, he warbles badly. "I'm a nightingale from a foreign land where birds sing like this." (or "I'm a young bird still learning to sing " or "I'm from a family of birds famous for their voices.") Turkey: Downing HODJA 70. Iran: Kelsey MULLAH 61-64; Shah MULLA 70.

J1391.10* Lame excuse. He nibbles up honey left in his care. "Where is my honey?" "How nice if you hadn't asked that and I didn't have to reply." Turkey: Downing HODJA 54-55.

J1392. Owner assists thief.

J1392.1* Owner helps thief fill sack. Thief questions him. "I thought we were moving." Turkey: Downing HODJA 43.

J1392.1.2* Owner found hiding in cupboard. "Hiding from shame there is nothing in this house worthy of your attention." Iran: Shah MULLA 34. Uygur: Ginsburg KAHA 88-89. SEE ALSO: J2223 (the thief as discoverer).

J1392.6* Sees thieves breaking into a house but he does not want to get involved. Tells his pupil they are playing the rebāb. "We shall hear the music tomorrow." Turkey: Downing HODJA 28.

J1392.7* Issy-Ben-Aran helps a 'wounded' man. Thief steals horse. Issy pursues to present bill of sale so thief won't be killed as a horse thief. Makes thief promise not to tell of this lest men fear to help the wounded. Spain: Gunterman CASTLES 81-83.

J1393. The double fool. A numskull caught changing meal from other's sacks into his own. Miller asks him what he is doing. "I am a fool." "Why then don't you put your meal into their sacks?" "I am only a simple fool. If I did that I should be a double fool." Turkey: Downing HODJA 49.

J1395. Was going to give it to him anyway. Thus a hunter answers a thief who steals his hare. Aesop: Aesop AESOP'S (Watts) 222.

J1410. Repartee concerning fatness.

J1411. The hay wagon and the gate. A parson arriving late at a city gate asks if he can get in. Guard sees that he is fat and in fun says he doesn't know. The parson: "Why not, doesn't the hay wagon get in?" Italy: Cimino DISOBEDIENT #2.

J1420. Animals retort concerning their dangers.

J1421. Peace among the animals. (Peace Fable.) The fox tries to beguile the cock by reporting a new law establishing peace among the animals. Dogs appear: the fox flees. "The dogs have not heard of the new law?" Type 62. Aesop: Aesop FABLES (Macmillan) 117; Aesop AESOP'S (Grosset) 82-83. Uruguay: Jagendorf KING 256-259 /Arbuthnot ANTHOLOGY 408/. Kijima LITTLE WHITE HEN pb. Jewish: Ginsburg THREE ROLLS 48 (thrush). Spain: De La Iglesia CAT #4 (flees wolf). Russia: Carey BABA 61-62 (grouse); Carrick STILL 117-119 (law says woodcocks cannot perch in trees); Masey STORIES 113-115.

J1423. Roast falcon. A falcon reproaches a cock for fleeing from the master who has fed him. The cock: "I have never seen a falcon roasted." India: Gaer FABLES 36-37.

J1430. Repartee concerning doctors and patients.

J1432. No physician at all. A bad physician having predicted the immediate death of a patient meets him recovered. "How go things below?" "They put you at the head of the list of bad physicians but I maintained that you were no physician at all." Aesop: Aesop AESOP'S (Watts) 202-203.

J1435* Sick man sweats. Doctor calls that a good sign. He shivers, has fever--more good signs. "I am dying of good signs." Aesop: Aesop AESOP'S (Watts) 131.

J1440. Repartee--miscellaneous.

J1454. The lion and the statue. A man points out the statue to show the supremacy of man. The lion: "If it had been a lion sculptor, the lion would have been standing over the man." Statue of Hercules overcoming lion. Aesop: Aesop AESOP'S (Grosset) 153; Aesop AESOP'S (Viking) 66; Aesop AESOP'S (Watts) 66; Aesop FABLES (Macmillan) 69.

J1465. Trumpeter's false defense. A trumpeter, captured, pleads that he did not fight. Answered: "You may not fight but you encourage your men to do so." Aesop: Aesop AESOP'S (Grosset) 218; Aesop AESOP'S (Viking) 70; Aesop AESOP'S (Watts) 105; Aesop FABLES (Macmillan) 157.

J1473. The greedy dreamer. He dreams that he receives nine coins. He demands ten. He wakes and finds that he has dreamed. He is willing to accept the nine. Turkey: Downing HODJA 11. Iran: Shah MULLA 96.

J1473.1. The 999 gold pieces. A man prays for a thousand gold pieces and says that he will not accept one less. A joker sends him 999. He says that he will trust God for the other coin. Arabia: Courlander TIGER'S 90-99. Turkey: Kelsey HODJA 139-150.

J1475. Is ready to go. A peddler scolds his dog

who is waiting and tells him to get ready to go with him. The dog replies that he has nothing to carry, that it is the peddler who is late. Aesop: Aesop AESOP'S (Watts) 69.

J1477. Demonstrate here. A man boasts of his jump on Rhodes and says that if he were in Rhodes he could prove his boast. Reply: "No need to go to Rhodes. Show us your jump here." Aesop: Aesop AESOP'S (Grosset) 60; Aesop AESOP'S (Watts) 43.

J1478. Husband and wife burn their mouths. A wife served overhot soup, forgets and burns herself so that tears come to her eyes. She says that her departed mother liked soup so much that she weeps when she eats it. The husband is also burned and weeps: "I am weeping because your accursed mother didn't take you with her when she died." Iran: Shah MULLA 101. Turkey: Downing HODJA 69.

J1482. 1. Disciple asks for a "secret" to help him advance faster. "Can you keep a secret?" Disciple: "I'd never tell anyone." Master: "Then I can keep it as well as you." Iran: Shah MULLA 104.

J1483.2. Where his mule will. A man on a runaway mule is asked "Where are you going?" "Wherever my mule wants to." Aesop: Aesop AESOP'S (Watts) 98 (horse).

J1488. What the bear whispered in his ear. Paid guide climbs tree and leaves traveler to mercy of bear. Traveler feigns death and the bear sniffs at him and leaves. The guide: "What did the bear say to you?" "He said, never trust a coward like you." Aesop: Aesop AESOP'S (Golden) 30-31; Aesop AESOP'S (Grosset) 166-168; Aesop AESOP'S (Random) 42-44; Aesop AESOP'S (Viking) 71; Aesop AESOP'S (Watts) 30-31; Aesop FABLES (Macmillan) 99; Aesop FABLES (Walck) 103-104; Kent MORE 42-45. Yiddish: Ginsburg THREE ROLLS 20. China: Alexander PEBBLES 23. Greek (Babrius): Green BIG 34. Montgomerie TWENTY-FIVE 53.

J1495.1. Man runs from actual or supposed ghost. The ghost runs beside him. The man stops to rest. The ghost stops, says, "That was a good run we had!" The man says, "Yes and as soon as I get my breath, I'm going to run some more." U.S. (Alabama): Leach THING 21-22 (Ghost catches running man, "You're running fast." Man: "I'll run faster!").

J1495.2. When Caleb (Martin) comes. Man in haunted house. Cats enter saying "Wait till Caleb comes." "When Caleb comes, tell him I was here and left." Man flees. U.S. (West Virginia): Leach THING 23-26. U.S. (South): Harper GHOSTS 195-198.

J1495.3* (Baughman) Man attempts to stay in haunted house all night. Ghost tells him "There ain't nobody here but you and me." Man says, "And I ain't going to be here long."

U.S (Alabama): Leach THING 21-22.

J1495.4* Man runs from ghost who tries to return guitar. "Keep it!" Surinam (Paramaribo): Leach THING 20-21.

J1499.1* Donkey brays when Mullah calls pomegranates for sale. "Who is selling these, me or you?" Iran: Kelsey MULLAH 15-19.

J1500 - J1649. Clever practical retorts.

J1510. The cheater cheated.

J1511.6.1* Potter and farmer going to market. Camel eats farmer's vegetables and potter laughs. Camel lies down to rest and smashes pots. Farmer laughs. "There's no telling on which side a camel will lie down." India: Reed TALKATIVE 78.

J1511.7. No clothes needed for Day of Judgment. Friends tell a man that the next day is the Day of Judgment and urge him to kill a lamb and give a feast. He apparently consents. He then burns up their clothes. They will not need clothes on the Day of Judgment. Turkey: Jagendorf NOODLEHEAD 105-110 (Hodja); Kelsey HODJA 71-78. Iran: Shah MULLA 95.

J1511.14.1* Lizard claims tortoise's bundle. "Found along road." Tortoise was dragging it on a string. Court rules lizard gets one-half. Tortoise finds lizard on road. Takes him to court, is given one-half of lizard. Bantu: Arnott AFRICAN 13-15. Kikuyu: Nunn AFRICAN 21-25.

J1511.17. Ox bought: buyer also claims load of wood attached (or vice versa). Later deceived man disguises and sells another ox for "handful of coppers." He is allowed by court the hand as well. Russia: Masey STORIES 73-83 (woodcutter's daughter tricks rich man).

J1511.17.1* Barber buys all wood ox is pulling in exchange for shaving woodcutter and helper. Demands wood and cart. Judge rules he must then shave 'helper'--the ox. Japan: Edmonds OOKA 70-74. Iran (Isfahan): Hardendorff JUST 44-48 (donkey).

J1516. Rogues exchange objects and cheat each other. Pakala and Tandala: trade bag of nutshells for bag of weeds, dung, etc. Join forces and take service--each claims his work easy and they trade--both hard. Usually one steals earnings of both and feigns dead when other comes for his share. Rumania: Jagendorf NOODLEHEAD 222-226; Ure RUMANIAN 9-15. Kalmuk: Bulatkin EURASIAN 98-102. Russia (Georgia): Papashavily YES 181-187. Arabia: Mittleman BIRD 58-66 (Syrian from Damascus and Egyptian from Cairo). Madagascar: Carpenter AFRICAN 103-112 (Koto and Maha).

J1516.1* Guno and Koyo find kris. Guno hides

it under water but Koyo finds. Koyo hides it in haystack but Guno finds. They share. Java: Courlander TIGER'S 118-121.

J1521.1. The shoes carried into the tree. Tricksters induce a numskull to climb a tree, planning to steal his shoes. He takes them in his belt with him. "Perhaps I shall find a nearer road home up there and shall need my shoes." Turkey: Downing HODJA 74; Walker WATERMELONS 23-24.

J1521.5. Catching by words.

J1521.5.2* He agreed to work for "nothing" and now demands "nothing." Told to look under carpet..what do you see? "Nothing." "There is your payment." Turkey: Downing HODJA 23-24. SEE ALSO: J2496.1.

J1521.5.3* Friend to "give me back whatever you want" of three hundred ducats left in care. Gives back ten. Judge rules he must give back two hundred and ninety--"what he wanted." Italy: Cimino DISOBEDIENT #3; Vittorini OLD 50-54.

J1521.6* Merchant pretends bowl is worthless, planning to return and buy it cheaply. Second merchant buys it meantime. India: Babbitt JATAKA 13-17.

J1521.6.1* First accomplice persuades diamond merchant to try to sell large diamond (really glass) for eight hundred coins. Second accomplice offers to buy it for prince, leaves four hundred down payment. Merchant pays eight hundred to first accomplice to acquire diamond. Thailand: Brockett BURMESE 156-162.

J1529. Cheater cheated--miscellaneous.

J1529.1* When teacher's donkey dies, students hide behind stable and moan. Teacher says for all to hear: "That must be the brothers of the donkey." Iran: Kelsey MULLAH 105-107.

J1530. One absurdity rebukes another. SEE: J1191.

J1530.0.1* Boyar insists peasant work till sun's little brother, the moon, sets too. Peasant takes two sacks of maize as pay. One is little brother of the other. Rumania: Ure RUMANIAN 87-88.

J1531.2. The iron-eating mice. Trustee claims that mice have eaten the iron scale (balance beam) confided to him. The host abducts the trustee's son and says a falcon (hawk) carried him off. India:Ryder PANCHATANTRA 192-195 (hawk). Spain: De La Iglesia CAT #14 (jewels). Evans MICE pb.

J1531.2.0.1* Gold dust entrusted turns to sand. Friend's son turns to parrot. Tibet: Montgomerie TWENTY-FIVE 58-59.

J1531.2.1. The dog-eating bugs. Man keeps dog

for boy, tells him when he comes for it that the chinch bugs have eaten it. The boy borrows a mule from the man, tells him a buzzard has carried it away. United States: Arbuthnot ANTHOLOGY 370-372 (buzzards carry off mule); Credle TALL 43-42.

J1531.3. The pot has a child and dies. A borrower returns a pot along with a small one saying that the pot has had a young one. The pots are accepted. He borrows the pot a second time and keeps it. He sends word that the pot has died. Turkey: Downing HODJA 9 (pot is returned to Hodja with "baby" as joke and he accepts, later Hodja borrows pot and keeps). Iran: Shah MULLA 19. Arabia: Courlander TIGER'S 90-99 (Abunuwas). China: Chang TALES 31-33. Saudi Arabia: Courlander RIDE 85-91 (Abunuwas). Jewish: Dobbs MORE 22-25; Serwer LET'S 55-58 (silversmith borrows spoon, goblet, gold watch--latter dies); Singer WHEN 3-13 (silver spoons give birth, eight silver candlesticks die).

J1545.4. The exiled wife's dearest possession. A wife driven from home by her husband is allowed to take her dearest possession. She takes her husband. +H561.1, J1191.1. Serbia: Spicer LONG 145-148. Kirghiz: Ginsburg KAHA 90-96. Estonia: Maas MOON 116-122; McNeil DOUBLE 50-55. Czechoslovakia: Fillmore SHEPHERD'S 144-152 /Arbuthnot FAIRY 147-149/. Wales: Pugh TALES 105-115 (Queen Marged). Rumania: Ure RUMANIAN 131-143. Poland: Wojciechowska WINTER 22-31. Russia: Bulatkin EURASIAN 27-38. Netherlands: De Leeuw LEGENDS 71-74 (Emma of Haarlem). Italy: Toor GOLDEN 41-46.

J1545.4.2* Wife is promised a last request before dying. Requests that husband (king) die when she does. Chile: Carpenter SOUTH AMERICAN 83-92.

J1545.4.3* The queen as gusli player. Wife of captured king plays gusli for enemy king and chooses husband as her boon. She does not reveal identity and he berates wife for failing to rescue him. Disguised again as gusli player she performs for him and chooses him as boon. Identity revealed. Russia: Higonnet-Schnopper ATOP 141-160; Lang VIOLET 65-72.

J1547* Merchant has sign over shop "Man's guile triumphs over woman's." Blacksmith's daughter makes him think she is cadi's daughter. He weds--discovers a disfigured bride. She mocks his 'guile', advises pretending is relative of gypsies. Cadi annuls wedding. He weds smith's daughter. Arabia: Mittleman BIRD 117-125.

J1550. Practical retorts: borrowers and lenders.

J1551. Imaginary debt and payment. SEE: J1172.1.

J1551.6. The hare at third remove. A man receives a present of a hare. Later a crowd comes to him for entertainment saying that they are friends of the man who presented the hare. This happens a second time. He serves them clear water. "It is the soup from the soup of the hare." Turkey: Downing HODJA 76; Kelsey HODJA 157-164. Iran: Shah MULLA 156. Bulgaria: Pridham GIFT 45-47.

J1551.6.1* Man invited for duck soup is given radish broth. He invites host to hunt 'green-heads' shows him radish tops. Japan: Bang MEN 9-12.

J1551.9. Half of money thrown into tank. The monkey to the grocer: "You sold half water and half milk." India: Spellman BLUE 28-30.

J1552.1.1. Loans refused. The ass is not at home. A man wants to borrow an ass. The owner says that the ass is not at home. The ass brays and the borrower protests. "Will you believe an ass and not a graybeard like me?" Turkey: Downing HODJA 11. Spain: De La Iglesia CAT #15. Saudi Arabia: Courlander RIDE 85-91 (if you want a bray, here's one. Abunuwas brays). Arabia: Courlander TIGER'S 90-99.

J1552.1.1.2* Told master of house is not at home visitors declare they saw him enter and not leave. Master sticks his head out of the window. "I could have gone out the back door, couldn't I?" Iran: Shah MULLA 13.

J1552.2.1* Thirty reasons for not loaning one hundred lire. "First, I don't have one hundred lire." "Second." "First is adequate." Italy: Cimino DISOBEDIENT #8.

J1552.5. Asked to give a piece of chicken. "It belongs to my wife." Then why are you eating it. "She told me to." Turkey: Downing HODJA 49.

J1552.6. Asked to lend forty year old vinegar. "Cannot lend it on principle." "What principle?" "The principle that if I'd give it to everyone who asks I'd never have any forty year old vinegar." Turkey: Downing HODJA 65.

J1552.7. Asked to lend clothesline. "My wife has hung flour on it." "Whoever heard of that?" "Those to whom one does not wish to lend it." Turkey: Downing HODJA 79.

J1552.8* Man asks to borrow large sum. King cannot loan so much. Small sum—not worthy of a king. Spain: De La Iglesia CAT #16.

J1552.9* Rider asks to share capon. Introduces self as Juan Mendoza Gonzáles de Gautan y Guevera. Declined on grounds that there are too many of him. Spain: De La Iglesia CAT #3.

J1552.10* Lad claims he dreamed the good Lord told Don Alfonso would loan him money. Don Alfonso dreamed the good Lord told him not to lend him a penny. Spain: De La Iglesia Cat #6.

J1560. Practical retorts: hosts and guests.

J1561.3. Welcome to the clothes. A man at a banquet is neglected because of his poor clothes. He changes clothes, returns and is honored. "Feed my clothes," he says, "for it is they that are welcomed." Sometimes stuffs food into clothes. Turkey: Downing HODJA 90; Kelsey HODJA 29-33; Walker WATERMELONS 51-54. Iran: Shah MULLA 40. Italy: Jagendorf PRICELESS 31-34(Giufa) /Arbuthnot ANTHOLOGY 272/. Rumania: Ure RUMANIAN 72-73 (guest is God). Mexico: Jagendorf KING 190-193 (Tepozteco) /Arbuthnot ANTHOLOGY 411-412/.

J1561.3.1* Man says coat is hungry and "feeds" it equal portions. Near East: Van Woerkom ABU pb.

J1562.1.1* Porridge with pool of butter in middle. A. "One should travel a straight road." Draws line letting butter run to his side. B. "It could go this way." To his side. C. "Soon things will be mixed up like this." Mixes butter into porridge. Tartar: Bulatkin EURASIAN 123-124.

J1562.1.2* Plum pudding. Captain has plums put on his side. Mate turns pudding admiring bowl. Captain does same, etc. Dobbs MORE 18-21.

J1565. Inappropriate entertainment repaid.

J1565.1. Fox and crane (stork) invite each other. Fox serves the food on a flat dish so that the crane cannot eat. Crane serves its food in a bottle. Type 60. Iran: Mehdevi PERSIAN 44-50 (stork). Russia: Carrick STILL MORE 37-42. Aesop: Aesop AESOP'S (Golden) 86; Aesop AESOP'S (Grosset) 66-68; Aesop AESOP'S (Random) 3-5; Aesop AESOP'S (Viking) 74-75; Aesop AESOP'S (Watts) 23; Aesop FABLES (Walck) 95-96; Aesop FIVE 49; Galdone THREE 2; Kent MORE 22-23; Montgomerie TWENTY-FIVE 36; Rice ONCE 28-33.

J1565.1.1* Spider (Anansi) and turtle invite each other. Spider insists turtle wash repeatedly. Turtle serves under water and insists spider remove jacket weighted with rocks. Spider pops to surface. (cf. W158). SEE ALSO: K278. Ashanti: Courlander FIRE 107-112 /Gruenberg MORE 130-132/; Kaula AFRICAN 26-31.

J1565.1.2* tortoise and Baboon invite each other. Tortoise gives food in bowls in tree. Baboon forced to cross charred field and return to wash repeatedly. SEE ALSO: K278. Nyansa, Nyasaland: Arnott AFRICAN 22-24. East Africa: Heady SAFIRI 40-45. Bantu: Holladay BANTU 78-79 (frog insists black-handed monkey wash until hands are white, return feast in tree, frog falls). Colwell MAGIC 107-110 (baboon-hare).

J1565.1.3* Host winds self around bowl. Tortoise makes long-tail of grass (rope) and wraps around bowl at return feast. Nigeria: Courlander OLODE 37-39 (boa); Walker NIGERIAN 47-48 (snake); Walker NIGERIAN 46-47 (boar).

J1565.1.3.1* Guest bullsnake fills kiva with tail forcing host out. Coyote makes cedar-bark tail and returns visit. Native American (Hopi): Courlander PEOPLE 47-100.

J1565.1.4* Jackal invites tiger then leaves and does not return. Tiger invites jackal and feeds sticks and bones. Pakistan: Siddiqui TOONTOONY 32-36.

J1565.1.5* Coyote finds hummingbird in garbage pile covered except for beak. Coyote picks up beak, says "I thought it was a needle." Invites hummingbird to his kiva. Coyote covers self with dirt except for nose. Hummingbird picks up nose, "I thought it was a jug." Native American (Hopi): Courlander PEOPLE 143-144.

J1566.1. Luxury of host rebuked. Philosopher spits in king's beard. It is the only place he can find at the royal table not covered with gold and jewels. Spain: De La Iglesia CAT #13.

J1600. Practical retorts--miscellaneous.

J1606.2* Montieri folk are tired of eating polenta. Ask guest to make them like polenta again. He takes them on long hike and they become hungry for polenta. Italy: Jagendorf PRICELESS 76-80.

J1611. The stolen meat and the weighed cat. A man buys three pounds of meat. His wife eats it and says that the cat ate it. The man weighs the cat and finds that it does not weigh three pounds. Turkey: Downing HODJA 10. Iran: Kelsey MULLAH 8-14; Shah MULLA 23. Type 1373.

J1612. The lazy ass was repaid in kind. Loaded with salt, he falls down in the river and lightens his burden. His master then loads him with sponges so that the next time the ass tries the trick he increases his load. Iran: Shah MULLA 30. Type 211. Aesop: Aesop AESOP'S (Grosset) 16-17; Aesop AESOP'S (Watts) 40-41; Aesop FABLES (Walck) 40-41; Wilson GREEK 88-89. Central Asia: Ginsburg LAZIES 56-58 (blankets).

J1612.0.1* Mule drivers rub chili peppers on legs of mule and they move faster, tie sponges to legs and they get fluffier, rub salt on legs and lose the salt cargo. Mexico: Brenner BOY 21-22.

J1612.1. Aesop calls to fellow slaves to take smallest loads. He takes largest--is bread for noon meal. He has no load in the afternoon. Greece: Edmonds TRICKSTER 68-76.

J1612.1.1* Horseman refuses ride to Indian. Indian eats lunch and now has lighter burden and more strength. Horseman offers ride now in

hopes of sharing load, but Indian no longer needs lift. Costa Rica: Courlander RIDE 238-240.

J1615. That which was promised him. A tenant promises his daughter to his master against her will. The master sends for "that which was promised him." The daughter sends the horse, and it is taken into the master's chamber. Type 1440. Norway: Asbjornsen EAST (Row) 124-128; Asbjornsen NORWEGIAN 56-60; Asbjornsen THE SQUIRE'S BRIDE pb; Frost LEGENDS 76-78; Undset TRUE 209-212.

J1650 - J1699. Miscellaneous clever acts.

J1650. Miscellaneous clever acts.

J1650.1* Sent to buy grapes for a friend, he haggles price down. Keeps the grapes since he did all the work of bargaining for them. Turkey: Downing HODJA 86.

J1650.2* Asked to give change for a gold coin, he doesn't want to admit he has no change. Says the coin is underweight. "Then give me its value whatever it is." "This coin is so underweight that if I changed it for you, you would owe me a shilling." Turkey: Downing HODJA 87.

J1650.3* Tells a sanctimonious man not to run from God's rain. Later he is seen running in a downpour. "I thought you told me not to run from God's rain." "Oh, I am running so as not to defile it with my feet." Iran: Shah MULLA 58.

J1653.1* Cock given passage to Cadiz free if can please captain with his coplas. Sings telling passengers to pay their fares--captain likes. Spain: Sawyer PICTURE 87-96.

J1661. Clever deductions.

J1661.1.1. Deduction: the one-eyed camel. A she-camel has passed, blind in one eye; on one side she carries wine and on the other, vinegar. Deduced because she grazed on only one side of the road, droppings from her loads observed, etc. Hardendorff JUST 52-53. Kazakh: Deutsch MORE 65-68.

J1662. The cat's only trick. She saves herself on a tree. The fox, who knows a hundred tricks, is captured. Type 105. Green ANIMAL 192-193. Aesop: Aesop AESOP'S (Grosset) 111; Aesop AESOP'S (Random) 65-66; Aesop AESOP'S (Viking) 43-44; Aesop FABLES 75. Germany (Grimm): Gag MORE 61-62; Grimm GRIMM'S (World) 330-331. Germany: Wiggin TALES 81. Poland: Borski GOOD 55-56 (tells fox that dogs on leash are calves, fox is killed). Leach LION 18-19.

J1662.0.1* Cat teaches all tricks except one. SEE: A2581 (why tiger lacks some qualities of cats); A2581.1 (why goat cannot climb trees).

J1662.0.1.1* Cat teaches tortoise all of his wrestling jujus except one, later wins match with that one. Yoruba: Fuja FOURTEEN 22-27.

J1662.1. One basket of wit better than twelve carloads of it. Female jackal saves herself and husband by quick thinking. +K622.1. East Pakistan: Arnott ANIMAL 136-140 (foxes escape tiger).

J1662.2* Fox and crane in pit. Fox with a thousand thoughts is killed. Crane with one thought feigns dead and escapes (K522.4). Russia (Yiddish): Ginsburg THREE 34-36. Russia: Carey BABA 21. Russia (Ukraine): Bloch UKRAINIAN 36-38. Bulgaria: Rudolph MAGIC 62-71 (fox and hedgehog).

J1662.3* Fish with one hundred wit and one thousand wit rely on intelligence to save selves from fishermen. Frog with one wit flees and saves self. India: Ryder PANCHATANTRA 444-446.

J1662.4* Hedgehog with threefold understanding has fox throw him out of pit. Fox with seventy-sevenfold understanding cannot get self out. Russia: Wiggin TALES 41-42.

J1664.1.1* People never satisfied with seasons. People complain in winter that it is too cold and in summer that it is too hot, they are never content. "Yes but have you noticed they seldom complain in the spring?" Turkey: Downing HODJA 57.

J1675.2.1. Tidings to the king: You said it, not I. The messenger announces it so that the king says the words in form of a question. Rumania: Ure RUMANIAN 167-168 (Whoever tells Turk his horse is dead must pay for it).

J1675.5.1. Farmer told organ in the city is made of pigs in boxes who squeal when tails are pulled. He constructs one. Switzerland (French): Duvoisin THREE 20-23.

J1685* Yasohichi tells innkeeper that pharmacist is paying for fleas. On next visit, beds are flea-free. Japan: Bang MEN 7-9.

J1686* Sage Wang Shen challenges pupils to get him out of cave. They cannot. But one says he can get him back into cave if he comes out. He comes out to see. China: Alexander PEBBLES 25.

J1687* Girl falls into water jar. Boy throws stone breaking jar and saves her. China: Alexander PEBBLES 16.

J1688* Old man on mountain top sees impending tidal wave. Sets fire to own rice fields. Villagers race up mountain to aid him. Are saved. Japan: Bryant BURNING pb; Hodges WAVE pb /Lafcadio Hearn GLEANINGS IN BUDDHA FIELDS /.

J1689* Miscellaneous clever actions.

J1689.1* Volcano put out with long hose made of bark stretching to sea. Boy considered a coward invents. Ecuador: Newman FOLK 27-30.

J1689.2* College educated son has father put frogs in churn to churn butter, invents self-kicking machine. U.S.: Credle TALL 89-95.

J1689.3* Gypsy and wife carry pots over river by floating them across in giant cauldron. Gypsy: Jagendorf GYPSIES' 170-176.

J1700 - J2799. Fools (and Other Unwise Persons).

J1700 - J1729. Fools (general).

J1703. Town (country) of fools. SEE ALSO: SUBJECT INDEX--Fools, Town of. Netherlands: De Leeuw LEGENDS..HOLLAND 46-51 (Kampen); Jewish: Simon WISE (Helm); Simon MORE (Helm); England: Jagendorf MERRY (Gotham).

J1703.1* Mayor to wear leather shoes over gold ones to protect. Jewish: Jagendorf NOODLE-HEAD 48-52; Serwer LET'S 74-79; Simon MORE 44-49.

J1703.2* Fool hired to keep thieves from Chelm has series of mishaps letting thieves escape. Jewish: Simon MORE 102-110; Simon WISE 55-61.

J1703.3* Villagers lie down in future cemetery plot to assess size of cemetery that will be needed. Jewish: Simon MORE 50-53.

J1703.4* In time of sour cream shortage water is called "sour cream" to remedy shortage. Jewish: Singer WHEN 45-51.

J1703.5* Trickster repeatedly substitutes billy goat for nanny on way to Chelm. Town council decides climate there is bad for nanny goats. It turns all to billy goats (D861.1). Jewish: Simon MORE 80-101; Singer WHEN 55-69.

J1703.6* Town of fools tries to buy wisdom. Are given bag of wasps, mouse, etc. Switzerland (French): Duvoisin THREE 24-29 (wasps). Yugoslavia: Jagendorf NOODLEHEAD 244-248 (mouse). Jewish: Simon WISE 67-76 (rotten fish).

J1703.7* Town of fools buys trumpet, thinking it puts out fires. Jewish: Singer WHEN 55-69.

J1710. Association with fools.

J1712. Numskulls quarrel over a greeting. Three men greeted by a stranger. Quarrel as to whom he greeted. "I greeted the biggest fool among you." A contest is held in which tales are told to decide which is the biggest fool. Iraq: Carpenter ELEPHANT'S 125-134.

J1712.1* Wind, Sun and Frost quarrel over greeting. Sun: "I'll roast you." Wind: "I'll keep you cool." Frost: "I'll freeze you." But Frost is powerless without wind. Russia: Downing RUSSIAN 169-170; Riordan TALES..CENTRAL 106. Jewish (Slavonic): Dobbs MORE 43-44.

J1730 - J1749. Absurd ignorance.

J1730. Absurd ignorance.

J1733. Why do pigs shriek? The sheep does not understand why the pig being carried to its slaughter shrieks. Aesop: Aesop AESOP'S (Watts) 171.

J1735. Fool cannot tell his right hand in the dark. Turkey: Downing HODJA 66 (Told a candle is by his right hand fool cannot find it). Iran: Shah MULLA 96.

J1736.1.1* Fools accuse lobster of eating ten barrels of salted herring they had placed in river to 'reproduce.' Punish lobster by drowning. Yiddish: Simon WISE 29-34.

J1742. The countryman in the great world. SEE ALSO: J1795.2.

J1742.3.2* At epicure's banquet, peasant wonders why all just admire food. "It does look strange but it's probably food. Let's eat it before it eats us." Iran: Shah MULLA 138. SEE ALSO: J1340.

J1746.2. Bouki buys glasses. They are no good --he still can't read. Haiti: Courlander PIECE 89-90.

J1749.3* Welshman threatens to knock out all thirty-two of Irishman's teeth. Irishman runs home and counts, wonders how Welshman knew how many teeth he had. Hardendorff JUST 19.

J1750 - J1849. Absurd misunderstandings.

J1750. One animal mistaken for another.

J1758.1. Tiger mistaken for goat. Fool trying to steal goat in dark catches thieving tiger. SEE: N392.1.1.1.

J1758.5. Lion thought to be a donkey: drunkard rides it. SEE ALSO: K1951.1 (seven at a blow, chase); N392.1.1. Egypt: Courlander KING'S 39-47 (panther). Hungary: Jagendorf NOODLEHEAD 212-215 (grabs wolf's tail, is pulled home).

J1761.3. Glowworm (firefly) thought to be a fire. The bird who tries to keep the monkeys from this error is killed for her pains. SEE ALSO: J1064.1. India: Ryder PANCHATANTRA 183.

J1761.6.0.1. Snake thought to be a belt. Snake squeezes tiger who wraps it around waist. SEE

ALSO: K1023.1.1. Indonesia: De Leeuw INDONESIAN 68-74.

J1761.8. Man mistakes dragon for log. Sits on it. Chops in two. England (Somerset): Colwell ROUND 110-113.

J1761.10. Blind men and elephant. Four blind men feel an elephant's leg, tail, ear and body respectively, and conclude it is like a log, a rope, a fan, and something without beginning or end. India: Leach NOODLES 54; Quigley BLIND pb; Saxe BLIND pb.

J1762.2.2* Bear in coach. Fur coat is admired. England: Williams-Ellis FAIRY..BRITISH 169.

J1762.2.3* Bear trapped in hollow tree by man escapes pushing head into man's hat plugged over hole. Bear in hat is taken for man by wife and landlord. He cuffs both. Man is treated with respect from then on. U.S. (Applachia): Credle TALL 55-63.

J1762.2.3.1* Bear aids henpecked man. Enters house and cuffs wife. She reforms. Eskimo: Field ESKIMO 52-54; Melzack DAY 35-40.

J1762.2.3.2* Dog trades places with master. Puts wife in place. She treats husband and dog well thereafter. Native American (Kwakiutl): Arnott ANIMAL 71-75.

J1762.4. Deer thought to be man with basket on head. Leach NOODLES 15-16 (chair).

J1762.10* Old woman tells buzzard how he reminds her of husband. Flies off to heaven, just like husband. El Salvador: Jagendorf KING 117-119.

J1770. Objects with mistaken identity.

J1772.1. Pumpkin thought to be an ass's egg. Numskull thinks he has hatched out an ass's egg. He thinks the rabbit which runs is the colt. Type 1319. Turkey: Kelsey HODJA 151-156. India: Jagendorf NOODLEHEAD 19-23 (pupils drop horse egg [watermelon] brought for guru. He wouldn't want such a swift beast anyway). France: Hardendorff TRICKY 119-120; Withers WORLD 18 (pumpkin as donkey's egg). Danaher FOLKTALES 34-41 (turnip as horse's egg); Varga MARE'S pb.

J1772.15* Fox thinks icicle is bone. Hears self gnawing--feels bone but can't taste a thing. Hardendorff JUST 20.

J1780. Things thought to be devils, ghosts, etc.

J1782.5. Animal with lighted candle thought to be ghost. SEE: K301A.

J1782.8. Person in haunted house shoots off all his toes thinking they are ghosts. Nova Scotia: Leach THING 15-16.

J1782.8.1* Shoeless orphan boy pursued by

Qalutaligssuag monster sticks bare foot in face and wiggles toes. "Watch out for my big toe. It eats men!" Qalutaligssuag flees. Eskimo: Caswell SHADOWS 81-82.

J1785.1. Grasshopper thought to be devil. Jagendorf MERRY 119-123.

J1785.8* Goose shot as ghost. U.S. (Louisiana): Jagendorf NOODLEHEAD 284-286.

J1790. Shadow mistaken for substance.

J1790.1 Numskull thinks his shadow is a man pursuing him. Iceland: Withers WORLD 69.

J1791. Reflection in water thought to be original of the thing reflected. SEE: K1715.1.

J1791.1. Drinking the moon. The numskull sees a cow drink from a pool where the moon is reflected. The moon goes under a cloud. He thinks the cow has eaten the moon and slaughters her to recover it. Spain: Jagendorf NOODLEHEAD 249-252 (donkey).

J1791.2. Rescuing the moon. A numbskull sees the moon in the water and throws a rope in to rescue it, but falls in himself. He sees the moon in the sky. At least the moon was saved! Turkey: Downing HODJA 73; Jablow MAN 50; Kelsey HODJA 41-45; Leach NOODLES 39.

J1791.2.1* Man thinks stars reflected in water will drown. Sees own reflection and thinks he's fallen in too. Germany: Jablow MAN 76.

J1791.2.2* Numskulls try to capture the moon. Tie up reflection in barrel of water (borsht). Think it melted. Jewish: Serwer LET'S 80-85; Simon WISE 35-42 (borsht). Jewish (Poland): Jablow MAN 51.

J1791.3. Diving for cheese. Man (animal) sees moon reflected in water and, thinking it a cheese, dives for it. Type 34. SEE ALSO: J1791.3.3.

J1791.3.0.1* Dupe let down in well in bucket. +K651. Wolf tricked by fox. Jewish/Spanish: Dobbs MORE 93-96.

J1791.3.0.2* Rake it up. England: De La Mare TALES 128-130; Front THREE pb; Jacobs ENGLISH 10-15; Jagendorf MERRY 45-50; Leach NOODLES 36; Montgomerie TWENTY-FIVE 14-15; Steel ENGLISH 73-78; Wiggin TALES 218-221; Williams-Ellis FAIRY..BRITISH 249-254; U.S. (Applachia): Chase JACK pb; Zemach THREE pb.

J1791.3.0.3* Hyena drops bone and dives for moon; another hyena takes bone. South Africa (Zulu): Jablow MAN 48-49.

J1791.3.0.4* Coyote tricked by fox; rocks tied on to help dive. Native American (Pueblo): Dolch PUEBLO 105-117. Native American (Southern Plains): Robinson COYOTE 41-42.

J1791.3.0.5* Tiger tricked by hare, rocks on foot. Puerto Rico: Alegria THREE 44-51.

J1791.3.0.6* Fox tricked by coyote, stone to tail. Native American: Gruenberg FAVORITE 338-340.

J1791.3.2. Dogs by river try to get food in river by drinking river dry. Aesop: Aesop AESOP'S (Watts) 145 (trying to get at hides, bursts).

J1791.3.2.2* Oni try to drink river dry to catch fleeing old lady. She makes such funny faces that they laugh and spit out water. +N777.0.1. Japan: Hearn JAPANESE (Pauper) 53-60; Hearn JAPANESE 21-28; Mosel FUNNY LITTLE WOMAN pb.

J1791.3.3. Moon's reflection thought to be gold in water. Fools dive for it or haymakers rake for it. SEE ALSO: J1791.3. England (Wiltshire): Jablow MAN 51 (rake). U.S. (Black, Georgia): Harris FAVORITE 125-129 (Brer Rabbit tells Brer Fox, B'ar and Wolf that pot of gold is with moon in pond. They sieve for it); Harris NIGHTS 100-107; Harris COMPLETE 183-194.

J1791.3.3.1* Sunbeam in water thought to be pearl ornament. Fools of Masi tie stones to selves and dive for it. Solomon Islands: Gittins TALES 88-89.

J1791.3.5* Coyote (Itsayaya) dives repeatedly for reflected chokeberries in river. Native American (Nez Percé): Heady TALES 41-44.

J1791.4. Dog drops his meat for the reflection. Crossing a stream with meat in his mouth, he sees his reflection; thinking it another dog with meat, he dives for it and loses his meat. Aesop: Aesop AESOP'S (Golden) 37; Aesop AESOP'S (Grosset) 176; Aesop AESOP'S (Random) 58-60; Aesop AESOP'S (Viking) 46; Aesop AESOP'S (Watts) 75; Aesop FABLES (Macmillan) 6; Aesop FABLES (Walck) 36-37; Aesop FIVE 18; Arbuthnot FAIRY 228; Martignoni ILLUSTRATED 158; Rockwell THREE 100-101; Wilson GREEK 120-121.

J1791.5. Diving for reflected enemy. SEE: C752.2.1.1.

J1791.5.3* Chick attacks own reflection in well. Nigeria: Walker NIGERIAN 39-40.

J1791.6.1. Ugly woman sees beautiful woman reflected in water and thinks it herself. Prides herself on her beauty. Type 408. England: Jacobs ENGLISH 32-38. SEE: D721.5 (Three Oranges).

J1791.7. Man does not recognize his own reflection in the water. Iran: Kelsey MULLAH 100-104.

J1791.7.2* Man sees reflection in well and thinks it a thief. Wife sees her reflection and thinks thief has brought his wife along. Iran: Kelsey

Mullah 100-104.

J1791.8. Goose dives for star, thinking it a fish and is mocked. The next day when she sees fish, she lets it escape, fearing to err again. Tolstoy: Green ANIMAL 177 (duck-moon).

J1791.9. Fools see bee's nest reflected in water; try to carry off the well. Ceylon: Jagendorf NOODLEHEAD 72-73 (Tumpane).

J1791.12. Elephant frightened at agitated reflection of moon in water. SEE: K1716.

J1793. Mask mistaken for face. Aesop: Aesop AESOP'S FABLES (Macmillan) 39 (fox sees theatrical mask).

J1793.1* Carved head--it's a fine head but has no brains. Aesop: Aesop AESOP'S (Golden) 82; Aesop FIVE 48.

J1795. Image in mirror mistaken. SEE ALSO: K1715.1.2.

J1795.1.1* Lutin is shown 'picture' of guest soon to arrive--mirror. Lutin flees before horrid creature arrives. French Canadian: Carlson SASHES 80-91 /Littledale GHOSTS 101-110/.

J1795.1.2* Demon so ugly killed by looking on him. He is shown mirror and dies. Poland: Wojiechowska WINTER 61-65.

J1795.2. The Matsuyama mirror. Image in mirror mistaken for mother. Daughter thus is consoled after mother's death (J1742). Japan: Hearn JAPANESE (Pauper) 46-52; Hearn JAPANESE 102-108; Ozaki JAPANESE 119-139 (wicked stepmother is jealous but reforms on discovering truth); Ross BLUE 149-161; Wiggin FAIRY 374-379.

J1795.3* Image in mirror mistaken for another. Man buys mirror thinking his father is in it; wife thinks he has brought another woman. Nun tells her the woman has repented and become a nun. Japan: Bang MEN 67-69; Hearn JAPANESE 110-125.

J1795.3.1* Wife thinks mirror is husband's lover, he thinks is her lover; judge thinks is new judge. Korea: Carpenter KOREAN 255-258. China: Abisch MAI pb (+mother and father).

J1795.3.2* Man thinks mirror is picture of his father. Wife thinks is picture of herself and is flattered that he cares for her, becomes a better wife. Wales: Pugh TALES 129-133.

J1795.3.3* Wife thinks husband has brought another woman from town. Mother-in-law thinks he should have chosen a younger one. China: Kendall SWEET 86-88.

J1795.3.3.1* Husband sent for comb shaped like moon buys mirror. Wife thinks he has brought home another woman, mother sees old woman, boy sees boy, grandfather sees old man, drops mirror and breaks. Korea: Kim STORY 44-50.

J1795.4. Man finds box of jewels with mirror in lid. Thinks man in box is owner and begs pardon. China: Withers WORLD 75.

J1800. One thing mistaken for another--miscellaneous.

J1801.1* Man blows on soup to cool it, blows on hands to warm them. Satyr shuns company of one who blows hot and cold in same breath. Aesop: Aesop AESOP'S (Viking) 42-43; Aesop AESOP'S (Watts) 86-87; Aesop FABLES (Macmillan) 111; Kent MORE 12-15. Rumania: Ure RUMANIAN 24-25.

J1802.1. "I don't understand." Foreigner asks who owns property, clothing, servants, whose wife an attractive woman is, whose funeral is in progress. Answer to each question is "I don't understand" which foreigner takes to be a person's name. SEE ALSO: J2496.1. Ghana: Courlander COW-TAIL 59-64; Green FOLK 53-55.

J1803.1.1. Dolphin saves monkey from shipwreck believing him to be an Athenian. Asks if monkey knows Piraeus. "Yes, I know him well." Piraeus is a city. Dolphin dives abandoning the pretender. Aesop: Aesop AESOP'S (Grosset) 198-199; Aesop AESOP'S (Watts) 184; Aesop FIVE 66.

J1804.1* Conversation by sign language misunderstood by bystander. Iran: Shah MULLA 149. SEE ALSO: H1607.1.1 (Sufi mystic meets Mulla).

J1805.1.2* Man who calls wife liar to be rewarded. Ol' Guinea man asks her to teach him the names of the year. Mispronounces "July"--"You lie." Virgin Island: Cothran MAGIC 71-72.

J1805.2* Monkey thinks syrup is called "Misery." Demands that God give him some. God gives him a sackful of dogs. Haiti: Wolkstein MAGIC 113-116.

J1806. Setting sun mistaken for fire. Brer Rabbit tells Brer Wolf to go warm self at fire (setting sun). U.S. (Georgia): Harris COMPLETE 284-289 /Harris NIGHTS 230/.

J1819. Physical phenomena misunderstood--miscellaneous.

J1819.3.1* Fools wake with shutters closed and think it is still night. Italy: Jagendorf PRICELESS 61-65 (also open cupboard instead of window).

J1819.3.2* Fool waking in night in room without windows thinks self blind and offers innkeeper ten cows to restore sight. He brings a light. Ethiopia (Amhara): Davis LION'S 68-69.

J1819.4* Countryman thinks city is strange. Stones are tied up (cobblestones) and dogs run loose. England: Withers WORLD 47.

J1820. Inappropriate action from misunderstandings.

J1826.1* Trained parrot given as gift. How did you like the parrot? It was delicious. Spain: De La Iglesia CAT #5.

J1849.5* Juan Bobo thinks pig wants to go to mass with his mother. Dresses her in clothes and sends to church. Puerto Rico: Alegria THREE 31-37; Belpre TIGER 49-54; Jagendorf NOODLES 260-262. Greece: Haviland FAVORITE..GREECE 29-37 (sow dressed for wedding).

J1849.6* Fool asks where is new moon, looks at pointer's finger. India: Jablow MAN 52.

J1849.7* Man thinks of soup and boy knocks on door begging for soup. "Not even my thoughts are my own. I dream of soup and my neighbors smell it." Turkey: Downing HODJA 49-50.

J1849.8* Boy thinks muzzein calling from minaret is stuck in tower. "If you were stuck in a tree I'd help but I can't climb this tower." Turkey: Downing HODJA 33.

J1850 - J1999. Absurd disregard
of facts.

J1850. Gift or sale to animal (or object).

J1851.1.3. Numbskull throws money to frogs to repay them. They have frightened his fleeing ass from the water. Iran: Shah MULLA 31.

J1851.1.5* Sent to buy #7 needles, frogs call "8, 8, 8." Fool throws needles to them to prove are #7. They keep needles. Louisiana (French): Leach NOODLES 26-27.

J1852.1.3* Numskull sells meat to dogs, takes them to court for payment. Denmark: Jagendorf NOODLEHEAD 147-155; Hatch THIRTEEN 37-45. Scandinavia: Hardendorff TRICKY 101-108. Majorca: Mehdevi BUNGLING 17-35.

J1852.1.4* Numskull sells honey to flies, takes case to court. +J1193.1. Majorca: Mehdevi BUNGLING 17-35. Puerto Rico: Carter GREEDY 112-118 (syrup); Newman FOLK 95-99 (omit court).

J1853.1.0.1* Fool sells (gives) clothing to a stick. Majorca: Mehdevi BUNGLING 17-35 (naked statue of St. Sebastian). Ireland: MacManus WELL 156-163 (knocks over trying to button and finds gold). Slovenia: Kavcic GOLDEN 118-126.

J1853.1.1. Money from the broken statue. Fool sells goods to a statue and when it will not repay him, knocks it to pieces. He finds treasure inside. Italy: Baker TALKING 18-24;

Manning-Sanders GIANNI 31-32; Mincielli OLD 14-23.

J1853.2* Fools sell butter to stove, it eats butter (butter melts) and when it does not pay, fool knocks stove over. Finds treasure beneath. SEE ALSO: J1871. Denmark: Hatch THIRTEEN 37-45; Jagendorf NOODLEHEAD 147-155. Scandinavia: Hardendorff TRICKY 101-108.

J1853.3* Fool gives ox to wild rosebush to farm with, will split profits. Returns in fall and finds only skull of ox, tears up bush and finds pot of gold. Russia (Georgia): Papashvily YES 201-210. Russia: Downing RUSSIAN 156-159 (birch tree); Ginsburg TWELVE 27-31.

J1853.4* Fool sells hen to tree. Knocks it down and finds bag of gold. Pyle WONDER 219-228.

J1856.1. Meat fed to cabbages. Type 1386. Slovenia: Kavcic GOLDEN 118-126.

J1860. Animal or object absurdly punished.

J1861. Thief punishes the escaped ox. An ox strays on the rascal's land but escapes from him. The next week he sees the ox yoked up and gives him a beating. The master is astonished. The rascal: "Let me alone; he knows well enough what he has done." Turkey: Downing HODJA 77. Iran: Shah MULLA 97.

J1862. The ass deprived of his saddle. A man's coat is stolen when he leaves his ass for a moment. He takes the saddle off the ass and says that he will give it back if the ass will return the coat. Turkey: Downing HODJA 72. Iran: Kelsey MULLA 48-53.

J1863. Cow punished for calf's misdeeds. Blamed for not teaching calf better. Iran: Shah MULLA 69.

J1865. Sickle punished by drowning. In a land where the sickle is not known, the new sickle cuts off the head of a man. It is drowned. SEE ALSO: J1909.8. Finland: Bowman TALES ..TUPA 220-223 (sickle catches on boat and tips it over and is drowned).

J1870. Absurd sympathy for animals or objects. SEE ALSO: J1973.

J1871. Filling cracks with butter. Numskull sees cracks in the ground and feels so sorry for them, he greases them with butter he is taking home. SEE ALSO: J1853.2. Africa: Jagendorf NOODLEHEAD 85-88. Germany (Grimm): Grimm GRIMM'S (Grosset) 290-297; Grimm HOUSEHOLD 248-255; Grimm JUNIPER v.2 187-200.

J1873.1* Old man gives hats he was selling to six Jizo statues on cold day, sometimes gives his own hat to last statue. The six Jizo's bring food (or a giant rice cake) to his door on New Year's Eve. SEE ALSO: F342.1.3. Japan:

Bang MEN 21-25; Sakade JAPANESE 106-110; Uchida SEA 84-90.

J1874.1. Rider takes the meal-sack on his shoulder to relieve the ass of his burden. Iran: Kelsey MULLA 132-134 /Gruenberg FAVORITE 353-354/. Turkey: Downing HODJA 63. Russia (Yiddish): Ginsburg THREE ROLLS 6 (horse). England: Jagendorf MERRY 40-44; Leach NOODLES 37 (Gotham). Ireland: Leach NOODLES 37 (keg of rum on shoulder to lighten boat). Japan: Bang MEN 6-7 (mortar). China: Kendall SWEET 45-48.

J1874.3* Man sits on load so as to take weight off donkey. Iran: Shah MULLA 51.

J1874.2.1* Soldier lends Knucklehead John his knapsack to balance Knucklehead's own. England: Jagendorf NOODLEHEAD 122-124.

J1879.2* Man apologizes to donkey for hard work. Doesn't matter if donkey understands or not--he did what a human being should. Turkey: Walker TALES 235.

J1880. Animals or objects treated as if human--miscellaneous.

J1881.1. Object sent to go by itself. SEE ALSO: J2461.

J1881.1.1. Cheeses thrown down to find their way home. England: Hutchinson CANDLE-LIGHT 103-104; Jacobs MORE 202-228 (Gotham); Jagendorf MERRY 43-48; Steel ENGLISH 203-208; Wiggin TALES 236-240. England (Nottinghamshire): Colwell ROUND 85-86.

J1881.1.2. One cheese sent after another. Numskull lets one roll down the hill, sends the other to bring it back. Danaher FOLK TALES 34-41 (butter). Germany (Grimm): Grimm GRIMM'S (Grosset) 290-297; Grimm HOUSEHOLD 248-255; Grimm JUNIPER v.2 187-200.

J1881.1.3. Three legged pot sent to walk home. England: Hutchinson FIRESIDE 9-14; Jagendorf MERRY 51-63 (trivet). Puerto Rico: Alegria THREE 74-75; Carter GREEDY 112-118.

J1881.1.5. Spinning wheel is sent home by itself. The man asks his wife if it has arrived before him; finds it has not. "I thought not. I came a shorter way." Scotland: Jagendorf NOODLE-HEAD 127-129 (spins in the wind as he lets it go by itself).

J1881.1.8* Flour sent home by wind since wind wants to carry it. +J2461C. Majorca: Mehdevi BUNGLING 57-67.

J1881.1.8* Helmites invest in tons of feathers and send home with the wind. Send more feathers out from Helm to show them the way. None return and the Helmites take this as a sign to leave Helm and disperse into the world themselves. Yiddish: Simon WISE 127-135.

J1881.2. Animal sent to go by itself.

J1881.2.2. Fools send money by rabbit. Since he is a swift animal, they expect it to reach the landlord in time. England: Jacobs MORE 222-228; Jagendorf MERRY 105-112; Steel ENGLISH 203-208; Wiggin TALES 236-240.

J1881.2.3.1* Eels sent to cross stream by themselves since ferryman charges too much. Italy: Cimino DISOBEDIENT #1.

J1881.2.4* Hens turned loose to walk ahead to market run in every direction. To Rooster: "You can tell day is coming when it's still dark but can't tell the way to town in broad daylight." Turkey: Downing HODJA 94.

J1885. Singing snails rebuked. A boy roasts some snails and they make noise in cooking. He says "Wretches, your house burns and yet you sing." Aesop: Aesop AESOP'S (Watts) 39.

J1889.1* Donkey brays every time vegetable seller calls his wares. "Who's selling these, me or you?" Turkey: Downing HODJA 47. Iran: Kelsey MULLAH 15-19.

J1891.3. Sea foolishly accused of cruelty. Sea says that it is calm itself but the wind blew it up and broke the ship. Aesop: Aesop AESOP'S (Watts) 70.

J1891.4* Donkey flogged publicly for breaking olive oil jars. All other donkeys made to watch punishment as a lesson. Greece: Jagendorf NOODLEHEAD 40-41.

J1900. Absurd disregard or ignorance of animal's nature or habits.

J1901.1. The overfed hen. A woman wants her hen to lay many eggs. Overfeeds her and she stops laying altogether. Aesop: Aesop AESOP'S (Grosset) 232; Aesop FABLES (Walck) 54.

J1901.2. Numskull feeds hens hot water so they will lay hard boiled eggs. Ireland: Jagendorf NOODLEHEAD 130-132.

J1902.1.1* Numskull throws hen in well to get a drink. Tells her to call when finished. Sits on eggs for her in the meantime. Majorca: Mehdevi BUNGLING 57-67.

J1903.5* Woman drives cows into river to drink, drowns. Pushes pig's head into trough, chokes. England: Jacobs HEREAFTER THIS pb; Jacobs MORE 7-11; Wiggin TALES 224-227.

J1903.6. Horse with tail in feed box. Leach NOODLES 70-71.

J1904.1. Cow (hog) taken to roof to graze. Type 1210. SEE ALSO: J2132.2 (ties rope to leg as cow grazes on roof); J2063. Ireland: MacManus HIBERNIAN 48-59 (mule). Netherlands: Frost LEGENDS 181-182 (cow strangles). England:

Jagendorf MERRY 77-86 (cow put on roof as ruse to knock down hidden money). Front THREE pb; Rockwell OLD 10-22; Zemach THREE pb.

J1904.2. The pent cuckoo. Fools build an enclosure to keep in the cuckoo. She flies over the hedge. They say that they have not built the hedge high enough. England (Gotham): Jacobs MORE 222-228; Jagendorf MERRY 19-24; Jagendorf NOODLEHEAD 117-118; Leach NOODLES 30-34; Steel ENGLISH 203-204; Wiggin TALES 236-240. England (Cornwall): Manning-Sanders PETER 213-215. England (Cumberland): Colwell ROUND 30-33.

J1904.4.1. Fish will climb trees like buffaloes. Numskull considers what will happen if river burns. Uygur: Ginsburg KAHA 88-89. India: Withers WORLD 50.

J1908.1. The cat and the candle. A man has a cat trained to hold up lighted candles in its paws or on its head. A mouse is let loose. The cat drops the candle and chases the mouse. Italy: Jagendorf PRICELESS CATS 92-94.

J1908.2. Cat transformed to maiden runs after mouse. Aesop: Aesop AESOP'S (Golden) 46; Aesop AESOP'S (Grosset) 229 (Venus turns cat to maiden to wed love, returns to cat when nature is revealed); Aesop AESOP'S (Watts) 118; Aesop FABLES (Macmillan) 151 (Jupiter turns cat to maiden, Venus tests); Aesop FABLES (Walck) 61; Kent MORE 36-41; Leach LION 26-27.

J1908.4* Wolf cub raised with sheep to act as watch dog. Russia (Assyria): Ginsburg TWELVE 71.

J1909.1. Fisherman fails to make fish dance to his flute. Later in his net they jump about without the aid of his flute. Aesop: Aesop AESOP'S (Grosset) 194-195 (bagpipes); Aesop AESOP'S (Watts) 180. Aesop FABLES (Macmillan) 83 (bagpipes).

J1909.3. Numskull tries to shake birds from tree like fruit. Greece: Jagendorf NOODLEHEAD 37-39.

J1909.5.1* Wolf criticizes shepherds greedily devouring mutton. What would they say if they saw me partaking of a similar supper? Aesop: Aesop AESOP'S (Grosset) 230.

J1909.8* Attempt to drown sea creature. (cf. J1865).

J1909.8.1* Salt fish thrown into pond to breed. Eel drowned for eating them (K581). England: Jacobs MORE 222-228 (Gotham); Jagendorf MERRY 99-104; Leach NOODLES 35; Leach NOODLES 30-34; Steel ENGLISH 203-208. England (Cornwall): Manning-Sanders PETER 213-215 (fools drown fish); Wiggin TALES 236-240.

J1909.8.2* Sea creature to be drowned by fool.

Ireland: MacManus HIBERNIAN 48-59 (Loch monster).

J1909.8.3* Lobster taken for tailor with shears. His 'directions' are followed and cloth is cut in wrong places. Sentenced to death and thrown into sea by citizens of Holmola. Finland: Jagendorf NOODLEHEAD 192-193.

J1909.9* Farmer refuses to say what he is planting for fear pigeons will hear. Japan: Jagendorf NOODLEHEAD 100-101.

J1910. Fatal disregard of anatomy.

J1914. Horse taught to live without food. Dies. Type 1682. SEE ALSO: K491. Turkey: Downing HODJA 56 (ass). Iran: Shah MULLA 114 (donkey). Leach NOODLES 28-29.

J1914.1. The underfed warhorse. Fails in the war. Aesop: Aesop AESOP'S (Watts) 95.

J1919.1. The remodelled stork. A trickster cuts off the bill and legs of a stork to make him look more like a real bird. Iran: Shah MULLA 98 (falcon).

J1919.2. Where the ducks ford. A fool is asked where the river is fordable. He says, "Everywhere." The man tries to ride across and is almost drowned. The fool, "Those little ducks were able to cross here; why couldn't a fellow like you?" Rumania: Ure RUMANIAN 33-34.

J1919.2.1* Man crossing river hears frog call "knee deep" and wades in. Frog was just talking to hear himself. U.S. (Georgia/Black): Courlander TERRAPIN'S 91-92; Harris COMPLETE 45-48 /Harris SONGS 69-72/.

J1920. Absurd searches for the lost.

J1922.1. Marking the place on the boat. An object falls into the sea from a boat. Numskulls mark the place on the boat rail to indicate where it fell. Sudan: Courlander KING'S 87-89 (necklace). Switzerland (German): Duvoisin THREE 146-151 (Meiringen). Leach NOODLES 28-29. Scandinavia: Ross BURIED 55-64. China: Wyndham TALES..CHINA 66. Denmark: Bascom THOSE 9-26 (Molboes hide bell).

J1922.1.1* Clever boatman feigns above numskull act--marking place on boat, then bets crooked boatmaster he can find lost object--dives and produces exact duplicate--wins bet. Burma: Brockett BURMESE 136-141.

J1922.2. Marking the place under the cloud. Numskulls leave a knife in the field marking the place by putting it under a heavy cloud. Next day the cloud is gone and the knife is lost. England: Jagendorf NOODLEHEAD 119-121 (Austwick).

J1922.2.1* Marking the place. Having forced caught leprechaun to tell where gold is, he marks with a kerchief (or red garter) and goes for a shovel. Returns to find every bush so marked. Ireland: Boden FIELD pb; Haviland FAVORITE..IRELAND 85-91; Jacobs CELTIC 29-33; Manning-Sanders BOOK..DWARFS 38-41; Pilkington SHAMROCK 71-73; Sleigh NORTH 111-115; Williams-Ellis FAIRY..BRITISH 135-139.

J1925* Hunting the lost object outside. Too dark to search for object in house where it was lost. Turkey: Downing HODJA 71. Iran: Kelsey MULLA 119-121; Shah MULLA 24.

J1930. Absurd disregard of natural laws.

J1932.5. Sowing needles (like seed). France: Jagendorf NOODLEHEAD 133 (barefoot fools of Sainte-Dodo feel needles sticking out of ground and think they're sprouting).

J1934. A hole to throw the earth in. Numskull plans to dig a hole so as to have a place to throw the earth from his excavation. Turkey: Downing HODJA 15. Mexico: Jagendorf KING 193-198 (Lagos). Java: Courlander TIGER'S 115-117 (Guno and Koyo, well). Scandinavia: Ross BURIED 55-64 (town of Mols).

J1936. How he looks in his sleep. A man stands before mirror with his eyes shut to see how he looks in his sleep. Greece: Jagendorf NOODLEHEAD 39.

J1936.1. Man takes mirror to bed to see whether he sleeps with his mouth open. Greece: Leach NOODLES 17.

J1936.2* Man peeks in own window to see if he sleepwalks. Iran: Shah MULLA 86.

J1938. Porridge in the ice hole. They put meal in the boiling current of the ice hole and then, one after another, they jump in to taste the porridge. Africa: Jagendorf NOODLEHEAD 85-88 (throw flour in lake, wife jumps in to stir, husband thinks she's eating all the soup and jumps in after her). Finland: Bowman TALES 220-230 (Holmola). England: Jagendorf MERRY 64-68.

J1941. How far his voice will reach. A numskull cries from a tower and then runs away to see how far his voice will reach. Iran: Kelsey MULLAH 71-74.

J1942. Holding in the heat. A numskull ties yarn around the stove to keep the heat from escaping.

J1942.1* Fools wrap stove in rabbit net to keep heat from escaping. Germany: Jagendorf NOODLEHEAD 189-191 (Schilda).

J1946. As tired as if he had walked. So says the numskull after riding to town on his stickhorse. Nova Scotia: Leach NOODLES 24.

J1959.3* Woman thinks tide recedes because she dipped out water. Returns it. Tide comes back in. Melansia (Fiji): Berry MAGIC 50-55.

J1959.4* Fool thinks sleeping anteater is dead, finds it 'stolen' when he returns to carry it home. Tells friends he knows the meat was fresh because it was still warm and blowing up and down. Guianas: Jagendorf KING 151-154.

J1961.2. Trying to catch night in the basket trap. Man finally finds dark under basket and thinks he has caught night. SEE ALSO: J2123 (carrying light into house). Congo: Burton MAGIC 61-63.

J1964.0.1* Tree trunks laid cross-ways of the sledge. Chelmites cannot decide if right or left end of log should enter Synagogue courtyard first. Try to cut off right end but two ends remain so carry in sideways. Houses along route are torn down to let log pass. SEE ALSO: J2171.6.2. Yiddish: Simon WISE 43-54.

J1964.1. Trying to stretch the beam. Type 1244. Russia: Jagendorf NOODLEHEAD 235-240.

J1968.0.1* Foolish fight with the sea. Plover attacks ocean for stealing his eggs. Birds unite to empty ocean with their beaks. Failing, they enlist Garuda's aid. He persuades Vishnu to dry up ocean with fire-arrow unless ocean returns plover's eggs. India: Ryder PANCHATANTRA 145-162.

J1968.0.2* Foolish criticism of the sea. "To think that something with such pretensions is not worth drinking." Iran: Shah MULLA 109.

J1968.0.3* Foolish criticism of the sea. Man pours fresh water into sea. "You make a lot of noise for nothing. See what real water tastes like." Turkey: Downing HODJA 28-29.

J1972.1* Fools swim in dry river bed. Indonesia: Courlander KANTCHIL'S 58-62.

J1973. Tree pulled down in order to give it water to drink. Type 1241. Switzerland (German): Duvoisin THREE 146-151 (went to lake, +J2133.5).

J1973.1* Saplings pulled up by monkeys to see length of roots in order to judge amount of water to give each. (cf. J2126). India (Hitopadesa): Gaer FABLES 120-122; Green ANIMAL FABLES 18-20.

J1973.2* Impatient farmer pulls rice daily to make it taller--kills it. China: Courlander TIGER'S 38-39.

J1978* Quilt too short, feet stick out--wife cuts strip off top to sew to bottom. Finland: Jagendorf NOODLEHEAD 196-201 (Holmola).

J2010. Uncertainty about own identity.

J2012.1.1* Scholar, bald man and barber travel. Barber shaves scholar's head as sleeps. Then awakens scholar to keep watch. Scholar feels head and tells barber he has awakened the wrong man. Greece: Leach NOODLES 25.

J2012.1.2* Layman made to believe he is a monk. Head shaven and monk prisoner escapes. He wakes to find monk with shaven head there,"But where am I?" (cf. J2314). China: Kendall SWEET 106-107.

J2012.2. Woman's garments cut off: does not know herself. Usually asks husband if she is at house and, receiving affirmative answer, she is convinced is not self. Wanders off. Has cut own garments reaping, Clever Else. +J2063. Germany (Grimm): Gag TALES 123-132 /Dobbs ONCE 96-104/; Grimm HOUSEHOLD 248-255. U.S.: Chase WICKED 150-155. England: Jacobs MORE 65-66; Steel ENGLISH 231. Germany: Withers WORLD 43-44.

J2012.2.1. Husband hangs fowlers net over sleeping wife. She doesn't know self on waking. Germany (Grimm): Arbuthnot FAIRY 51-53 (Clever Else) /Arbuthnot ANTHOLOGY/; Grimm GRIMM'S (Scribner's) 99-103; Grimm GRIMM'S (World) 343-347; Grimm HOUSEHOLD 145-148; Rackham GRIMM'S 86-90.

J2012.2.3. Wife tarred and feathered. Doesn't know self. Norway: Undset TRUE 202-208.

J2012.4. Fool in new clothes does not know self. Jewish: Serwer LET'S 68-73 (put's on Rabbi's robes in morning by mistake). Russia (Moldavia): Ginsburg TWELVE 54-55.

J2012.5. Man does not know himself from another identically clad. Turkey: Downing HODJA 95.

J2012.6. Fool at baths believes he is someone else. Sees everybody naked. Puts straw on his shoulder to identify. Straw floats to another bather. "You are me and I am you!" Jewish: Serwer LET'S 68-73.

J2013.3. Pumpkin tied to another's leg. A numskull ties a pumpkin to his leg at night so that he shall know himself in the morning. Someone ties the pumpkin to another's leg and the numskull is not sure of his identity next morning. Turkey: Downing HODJA 29 (aubergine). Iran: Shah MULLA 151 (bladder). Persia: Jagendorf NOODLEHEAD 93-96 (wrestler from Hums); Withers WORLD 80-81.

J2014. Fool does not recognize his own house and family. U.S. (Ohio): Jagendorf NOODLEHEAD 278-280 (Sam'l Dany).

J2014.2* Fool sets shoes (staff) pointing toward destination at night. A prankster turns them around and returning home he thinks himself in the foreign town. Korea: Courlander TIGER'S 11-15 (staff, scholar travels from Kosei to Pyongyang). Jewish: Jagendorf NOODLEHEAD 53-58 (Helm). Yiddish: Simon WISE 89-102 (Helmite convinces entire village they are in Warsaw instead of Helm); Singer WHEN 99-116. Russia (Veps): Ginsburg TWELVE

12-19 (sleds).

J2020. Inability to find own members, etc.

J2021. Numskulls cannot find their own legs. A stranger helps them with a switch. (Usually get them mixed up when they sit down to bathe their feet). Type 1288. SEE ALSO: J2311.12. Yiddish: Simon WISE MEN 102-108 (Chelm); Singer ZLATEH 39-50. Ireland: MacManus HIBERNIAN 48-59 (throws water on). Russia (Veps): Ginsburg TWELVE 85-89.

J2021.0.1* Boys tease teacher saying they cannot find their own legs. He helps them with a switch! Turkey: Kelsey HODJA; Walker WATERMELONS 42-44.

J2022. Numskull cannot find ass he is sitting on. Turkey: Kelsey HODJA 1-6. Type 1288A. SEE ALSO: J2031.2 (there are ten horses).

J2022.1* Numskull cannot find camel he is sitting on. Attempts to count by matching string of beads with camels and not coming out even, discards first bead then camel until all are gone. N. Africa: Gilstrap SULTAN'S 9-17.

J2024. Numskull rides backward. "I didn't get on backward but the horse seems to be left-handed." Turkey: Downing HODJA 68.

J2024.1* Numskull rides backward having never seen a horse before. Native American (Apache): Jagendorf NOODLEHEAD 271-273.

J2024.2* Noodle saddles horse backward. Says to turn it around to ride it. England: Jagendorf NOODLEHEAD 122-124.

J2030. Absurd inability to count.

J2031. Counting wrong by not counting oneself. Numskulls conclude that one of their number is drowned. Type 1287. England: Jacobs MORE 222-228; Jagendorf MERRY 124-130; Leach NOODLES 30-34; Steel ENGLISH 203-208; Wiggin TALES 236-240. Ireland: MacManus HIBERNIAN 48-59 (reapers, one lost). Jewish: Simon MORE 111-119 (man whips each and counts yells). Denmark: Bascom THOSE 27-35 (one lost, stick noses in mud to count).

J2031.0.1* Numskulls believe one eaten by tiger. Boy counts their flour sacks and discovers all are there. They rejoice over brave companion who fought off tiger and returned. Ethiopia: Courlander FIRE 45-50.

J2031.0.2* Twelve men of Kadawbawa count themselves and bundles of fence posts and find one man missing. Passerby suggests that each pick up a bundle and they find all are there. Ceylon: Tooze WONDERFUL 125-126.

J2031.0.3* Six fishermen lose one member. Boy squeezes hands as they count and all are there. England: Elkin SIX. Philippines (Luzon): Sechrist ONCE 141-143 (old man counts as they dive into river).

J2031.2. There are ten horses (donkeys): then when he is mounted there are only nine. Why? SEE ALSO: J2022 (numskull cannot find ass he is sitting on). Syria: Jagendorf NOODLE-HEAD 63-67. Turkey: Dobbs ONCE 91-95; Kelsey HODJA 1-6 /Arbuthnot FAIRY 185-186/, /Arbuthnot ANTHOLOGY 300-301/. Middle East: Kirn NINE IN A LINE (camels); Van Woerkom ABU pb. Russia (Armenian): Gins-burg TWELVE 33-35.

J2035.1. Interrupted calculation. Customer thinks mathematician's figuring is statement of ever higher prices. Agrees to pay exorbi-tant price then shopkeeper becomes aware of his question and quotes price of one ducat. Jewish: Simon MORE 11-15.

J2050 - J2199. Absurd short-sightedness.

J2060. Absurd plans. Air castles. Type 1430.

J2060.1. Quarrel and fight over details of air-castle. Germany (Grimm): Grimm BROTHERS 87-92.

J2060.1.1* Bouki is angry at son for pretending to ride burro he dreams of buying with profits accrued after sale of yam. Haiti: Courlander PIECE 55-57.

J2060.1.2* Wife refuses to let husband drink milk of future cow as it's for future calf. Argue. Germany (Grimm): Gag TALES 201-203.

J2060.2.1* Moneylender told he'll be paid with fleece caught on thornbush. Moneylender laughs and man says he sees he is happy to have money in such good hands. Turkey: Downing HODJA 22-23.

J2061. Air-castle shattered by lack of fore-thought.

J2061.1. Air-castle: the jar of honey to be sold. In his excitement, he breaks the jar. Germany (Grimm): Gag TALES 191-197 (strikes future child tending geese); Grimm BROTHERS 87-92. Lebanon: Skurzynski TWO pb (butter pot, sons tending sheep).

J2061.1.1. Air-castle: basket of glassware to be sold. In his excitement he breaks the glass-ware. Jacobs EUROPEAN 110-114.

J2061.1.2. Air-castle: basket of eggs to be sold, In her excitement she breaks all the eggs. Ser-bia: Spicer LONG 92-97 (one egg--slaps chest bragging of riches). Andersen WOMAN pb; D'Aulaire DON'T COUNT pb.

J2061.1.2.1* Brahman kicks future wife and breaks jar of barley meal. India: Gaer FABLES 110-111 (in potter's shop); Ryder PANCHA-tantra 453-454; Turnbull INDIAN FAIRY TALES

49-50. Laos: Withers I SAW 119.

J2061.2. Air-castle: pail of milk to be sold. Proud milkmaid tosses her head (or kicks the pail in her sleep) and spills the milk. Aesop: Aesop AESOP'S (Golden) 53-55; Aesop AESOP'S (Grosset) 10-11; Aesop AESOP'S (Random) 8-10; Aesop AESOP'S (Viking) 63-64; Aesop AESOP'S (Watts) 25; Aesop FABLES (Macmillan) 153; Aesop FABLES (Walck) 97-98; Aesop MILKMAID pb; Arbuthnot FAIRY 229; Gruen-berg FAVORITE 407-408; Rockwell OLD 34-36; TALL..NURSERY 23-24. Ireland: Danaher FOLKTALES 31-32. Mexico: Brenner BOY 12-13.

J2061.3. Air-castle:, to sell hide of sleeping deer. In his excitement he wakes the deer who runs off. Indonesia: Courlander KANTCHIL'S 28-32; De Leeuw INDONESIAN 109-112 (with his tobacco pouch on antlers).

J2061.3.1* Air-castle: to sell tail of sleeping fox. Sweden: Haviland FAVORITE..SWEDEN 30-32; Wiggin TALES 462; Withers I SAW 89. France: Edmonds TRICKSTER 99-102.

J2061.3.2* Air-castle: to sell hare. Russia (Yid-dish): Ginsburg THREE ROLLS 31. Russia: Carrick STILL MORE 43-46; Withers WORLD 23.

J2061.5* Man weaving palm baskets in tree top daydreams of profits, kicks 'servant' and falls from tree. Cambodia (Khmer): Asia FOLK 18-20.

J2061.6* Liesl dreams of cow she'd buy if she had four coins. Lenz wants to drink milk. Ar-gument ensues. Germany (Grimm): Gag TALES 201-203.

J2061.7* Tadpole foretold to be new king of frogs gives feast, gets drunk and breaks leg; lame, cannot be king. Nigeria (Yoruba): Fuja FOURTEEN 39-42.

J2062.1. Which way the sheep shall return. One man plans to buy sheep; another says that he shall not drive them across bridge. They quar-rel over the sheep, which have not yet been ac-quired. A third numskull, to convince them of their foolishness, pours all his meal out in the water so as to show them the empty sack. "How much meal is in the sack?" he asks. "None." "There is just that much wit in your heads." England: Jacobs MORE 222-228; Jagendorf NOODLEHEAD 115-117 (Gotham); Jagendorf MERRY 25-30; Steel ENGLISH 203-208; Wiggin TALES 236-240.

J2062.4* Two hunters argue over how to prepare geese they are aiming at. Geese fly away. China: Kendall SWEET 98-99.

J2063. Distress over imagined troubles of unborn child. (Clever Else) Girl sent to cellar to get wine to serve the suitor begins weeping over the troubles of the child she might have if she married the suitor (J2176). Her parents join her. Meanwhile the suitor leaves (or is impressed and weds). +H1312.1 (quest for three greater fools), +J2012.2; +J1904.1, J1791.3, J2161.1. Italy (Venetian): Haviland FAVORITE..ITALY 55-66; TALL..NURSERY 98-104 (pickaxe). Germany (Grimm): Arbuthnot FAIRY 51-53 /Arbuthnot ANTHOLOGY/; Dobbs ONCE 96-104; Front THREE pb; Gag TALES 122-132; Grimm GRIMM'S (Scribner's) 99-103; Grimm GRIMM'S (Viking) 86-90; Grimm GRIMM'S (World) 343-347; Grimm BROTHERS 82-86; Grimm HOUSEHOLD 145-148; Rockwell OLD 10-22. England: De La Mare TALES 125-130; Jacobs ENGLISH 10-15; Steel ENGLISH 73-78; Wiggin TALES 218-221; Williams-Ellis FAIRY..BRITISH 249-254. Scotland: MacManus HIBERNIAN 48-59. Greece (Kos): Haviland FAVORITE..GREECE 29-37; Lang RED 188-191; Leach LUCK 15-18; Neufeld BEWARE 52-57. Zemach THREE pb.

J2063.2* Woman drops log on foot and imagines it might have been dropped on her unborn grandson. Husband joins her. Son, still single and childless, leaves in search of a sillier family. Russia: Jagendorf NOODLEHEAD 235-240.

J2063.3* Girl sent for wine begins planning wedding dress. Mother and father join her. Suitor leaves. Denmark: Hatch THIRTEEN 73-80.

J2063.4* Girl sent for water fears unborn son may fall into spring. Armenia: Bulatkin EURASIAN 90-94.

J2063.5* Girl wails for unborn son who might cry out at Bar Mitzvah and be struck dead. Whole village joins. Jewish: Simon MORE 54-62.

J2066.5. Wolf waits in vain for the nurse to throw away child. She has threatened to throw the child to the wolf. Leo Tolstoy: Green ANIMAL 212. Aesop: Aesop AESOP'S (Golden) 66; Aesop AESOP'S (Grosset) 164-165; Aesop AESOP'S (Watts) 89; Aesop FABLES (Macmillan) 91.

J2066.7. Dupe waits for rear wheels of wagon to overtake front wheels. Is told that money is thus made. U.S. (Georgia, Black): Harris FAVORITE 24-29; Harris COMPLETE 540-545 (Brer Fox [dupe] and Brer Rabbit).

J2070. Absurd wishes.

J2071. Three foolish wishes. Three wishes will be granted: used up foolishly. SEE ALSO: J2075.

J2071.1* Fish grants wish. Old woman wishes buckets to come and go by themselves; whatever she hits will break off--laughs at buckets and slaps at knees; whatever she pulls will get long--cries and pulls nose. SEE ALSO: B375.1; J2073.1. Sweden: Haviland FAVORITE..SWEDEN 50-59.

J2071.2* Tailor hiding Napoleon from soldiers is given three wishes. Asks for roof, dress for wife, wants to know how N. felt when soldiers drove spear through quilts where he was hiding. N. sentences tailor to death for impudence. At last second frees. "Now you know how I felt" (K1041). Jewish: Serwer LET'S 59-67.

J2072.1. Short-sighted wish: Midas's touch. Everything to turn to gold. Farjeon CAVALCADE..KINGS 113-132; Gruenberg FAVORITE 408-410.

J2073.1. Wise and foolish wish: Keep doing all day what you begin. One begins pulling linen out of a box; other in anger begins throwing water on the pig and must do so all day. Type 750A. SEE ALSO: Q1.1. Estonia: Maas MOON 26-30 (second sneezes); Arbuthnot ANTHOLOGY 285-286. Sweden: Wiggin TALES 495-461 (legs break, nose pulled, fish grants wishes). Finland: Bowman TALES..TUPA 126-128 (pine cone to bring luck, second woman sneezes).

J2073.1.1* St. Christopher and St. Nicholas grant wishes, poor couple fold linen and count money, rich wife waters pigs and husband beats her. Pyle WONDER 123-133.

J2073.1.2* St. Peter, second lady cuts up cloth. Netherlands: De Leeuw LEGENDS..HOLLAND 152-157. Flanders: Manning-Sanders BOOK..WIZARDS 109-117.

J2074. Twice the wish to the enemy (the covetous and the envious). A can have a wish, but B will get twice the wish. A wishes that he may lose an eye so that B will be blind. Aesop: Aesop FABLES (Macmillan) 107 (Jupiter grants wishes); India: Jacobs INDIAN 184-187; Wiggin TALES 385-387.

J2075. The transferred wish. A husband, given three wishes, transfers one to his wife who wastes it on a trifle; in his anger, he wishes the article in her body and must use third to get it out. Type 150A.

J2075.1* Fairy gives wish for sparing tree, sausage on nose. Dobbs ONCE 86-90; Galdone THREE pb. Jacobs MORE 107-109; Opie CLASSIC 151-155; Perrault FAMOUS 127-134; Perrault PERRAULT'S 89-91 (Jupiter); TALL..NURSERY 85-89; Wiggin TALES 7-9. Sweden: Gruenberg FAVORITE 344-346.

J2075.2* Old man, gives wife three wishes, asks for ladle. Husband arrives and wishes it on her back. Puerto Rico: Belpré TIGER 119-121.

J2075.3* Damsel from Heavenly Isles gives couple three wishes. She wishes a string of sausages. He wishes it on her nose. They laugh at selves and are rewarded with a baby on doorstep. Korea: Jewett WHICH 104-108.

J2075.4* Saint gives three wishes, wishes husband were there. He wishes donkey's ears on her, then off. Later son born as gift for lesson learned. Puerto Rico: Alegria THREE 76-79.

J2075.5* Lake spirit gives three wishes. Wife--broom. Husband--on her head. Son restores. U.S. (Penobscot, Maine): Leach LUCK 93-94.

J2075.5* Four wishes for four horns. He wishes wolves would take stumbling horse; he wishes he were home. He wishes horns on her head. She wishes them off. SEE ALSO: Q1.1B. Denmark: Haviland DENMARK 77-90.

J2080. Foolish bargains.

J2081.1. Foolish bargain: horse for cow, cow for hog, etc. Finally nothing left. +N11 (wager on wife's complacency). Andersen: Bleecker BIG 113-121 /Andersen FAIRY (World) 77/, /Andersen ANDERSEN'S (Grosset) 304; Rackham AR-THUR 278-279. Norway (Asbjornsen): Arbuthnot FAIRY 84-86; Asbjornsen EAST (Row) 35-40; Asbjornsen NORWEGIAN 178-181; Aulaire EAST 202-206; Fenner TIME 162-174; Undset TRUE 184-189. England: Arbuthnot FAIRY 17-19; Colwell YOUNGEST 121-126; Hutchinson CHIMNEY 111-116; Jacobs ENGLISH 27-31; Leach LUCK 71-75; Steel ENGLISH 138-144; Wiesner HAPPY pb; Williams-Ellis FAIRY.. BRITISH 96-102. Poland: Borski GOOD 78-81. Austria: Jagendorf NOODLEHEAD 216-221. Russia: Ginsburg TWELVE 75-81; Riordan TALES..CENTRAL 181-183.

J2081.1.1* Foolish bargain: horse for cow, cow for hog, etc. Fool thinks each bargain lucky, ends with heavy stone. When it falls in well and is lost he is delighted to be relieved of the burden. Germany (Grimm): Carle ERIC 11-24; Grimm GRIMM'S (World) 45-51; Grimm HANS (illus. Hoffman) pb; Grimm HANS (illus. McKee) pb; Grimm HOUSEHOLD 14-19; Hutchinson FIRESIDE 129-139; Wiggin TALES 62-67. U.S. (Appalachia): Chase JACK pb.

J2083.7. Wife's silver bracelet sold with thread to make thread weigh more on scale. Arabia: Jagendorf NOODLEHEAD 68-71.

J2085.1. Lost ass, saddle, and bridle offered as reward to the finder. Turkey: Downing HODJA 14.

J2087. The persuasive auctioneer. The auctioneer praises the man's worthless cow so much in his speech that the man takes her back himself. Turkey: Downing HODJA 62 (donkey); Kelsey HODJA 63-70 (donkey). Arabia: Jagendorf NOODLEHEAD 68-71 (cow).

J2091. Thief warned what not to steal. The numskull tells the thief where his doorkey, his cakes and his roasts are and warns him not to steal them. Iran: Bulatkin EURASIAN 103-105.

J2092.1. Man asks porter to carry his bag to his house but refuses to tell porter where he lives. Porter might be a thief. Iran: Shah MULLA 85.

J2092.2* Porter disappears with man's bag. Seeing porter in street a week later man hides--porter might demand pay for carrying bag seven days. Turkey: Downing HODJA 60.

J2093.3* Man steals robber's jacket as he is robbing house. China (Ch'ing Dynasty): Kendall SWEET 78-79.

J2093.7* Ignorant peasant given job as King's evaluator. Values five hundred horses as worth one measure of rice. Asked value of rice = an entire city. India: Babbitt JATAKA 34-38.

J2099.2. Seller cuts off donkey's dirty tail and takes in a bag. Buyer: "What good is a donkey without a tail?" Seller: "Let us first decide on a price for the donkey. The tail is not a thousand miles away." Turkey: Downing HODJA 90.

J2099.3* Two order wine (price one copper per catty) and are given vinegar (price two coppers). They are afraid to complain for fear they will be charged added price for vinegar. China (Ch'ing Dynasty): Kendall SWEET 13.

J2100. Remedies worse than the disease.

J2101* Getting rid of the cat. In a land in which cats are not known, one is bought at a great price. It eats many mice. By misunderstanding, they think the cat is a monster. In order to get rid of it they set the house on fire. Type 1281. SEE: N411.1 (Whittington); F708.1. Germany (Grimm): Gag MORE GRIMM 189-196; Grimm GRIMM'S (Grosset) 23-26; Grimm GRIMM'S (World) 99-102. Germany: Leach LION 15-17 (Schildburg). Jewish: Simon WISE 119-126 (Helm).

J2101.0.1* Cat, having rid country of mice, is thought to be a monster. When soldiers are sent to kill it, cat leaps on horse's back and all flee to palace. Shah dies of fright on cat's approach and courtiers flee. Karakalpak: Ginsburg KAHA 142-150.

J2101.1. Lighting the cat's tail. Woman wishing to punish a cat fastens cotten to its tail and lights it. The whole village is burnt. Aesop: Aesop AESOP'S (Watts) 117 (fox).

J2101.2* House burnt down to rid it of cat, cat runs to next house, etc. Entire village burnt down. Jewish: Simon WISE 119-126.

J2102.2. Snake rids himself of wasps: he lets himself be run over by a cartwheel along with them. Aesop: Aesop AESOP'S (Watts) 178.

J2102.3. Bald man aims at a fly: hurts his head. SEE ALSO: J1193.1. Aesop: Aesop AESOP'S (Watts) 129; Aesop FABLES (Macmillan) 35. Philippines: Withers I SAW 131-132 (King as judge kills mosquito with gavel).

J2102.5. Burning the wasp nest. The house catches fire and burns. Great Britain:

Jagendorf MERRY 87-92 (Jack of Dover, blacksmith burns down smithy).

J2112.1. Young wife pulls out his grey hairs; old wife his black. Soon all are gone. Aesop: Aesop AESOP'S (Grosset) 196; Aesop AESOP'S (Viking) 78-79; Aesop AESOP'S (Watts) 134; Aesop FABLES (Macmillan) 89.

J2112.2* Two wives take turns pulling out hairs until husband is bald. India: Jagendorf NOODLEHEAD 24-29.

J2113. Getting the calf's head out of the pot. A calf gets its head caught in a pot. A fool cuts off the calf's head and then breaks the pot to get it out. India: Reed TALKATIVE 76 (buffalo, waterjar).

J2120. Disregard of danger to objects (or animals).

J2123. Sunlight carried into windowless house in baskets. When this plan does not succeed they gradually pull down the house to get the light. Type 1245. SEE: J1962.2. England: Jagendorf MERRY 6-16 (Gotham); Leach NOODLES 30-34 (Gotham). Switzerland (German): Duvoisin THREE 146-151 (Meiringen). Yiddish: Simon WISE 7-16 (Chelm). Finland: Bowman TALES 220-230. Norway: Undset TRUE 202-208.

J2123.1. Roof removed from windowless town hall to let in light. Put back when it rains. One day torches go out and they see light shining through crack and conceive idea of windows. Germany: Jagendorf NOODLEHEAD 184-188 (Schilda).

J2123.2. Tupas built on sunny day to trap sunlight inside. Finland: Bowman TALES 220-230.

J2123.3* No sunlight in house. Is there sunlight in your garden? Then put your house in the garden. Turkey: Downing HODJA 83.

J2126. Numskull to water roots of tree. Digs up tree to find roots. SEE: J1973.

J2126.1. Trees cut down to gather the fruit. India: Montgomerie TWENTY-FIVE 22-23.

J2130. Foolish disregard of personal danger.

J2131.2.2* Coyote insists on looking into mole's bag. It is full of fleas. Native American (California): Curry DOWN 101-103.

J2131.4.1. Looking through the gun barrel. The numskull (stupid ogre) is shot. Types 1158, 1228. Gypsy: Jagendorf GYPSIES' 122-128.

J2131.5.2.1* Ansige Karamba gets head stuck in mortar. West Africa: Courlander COW-TAIL 119-127.

J2131.5.4. Numskull sticks his head into the hole of a millstone. It rolls into the lake. Type 1247. Jewish: Simon WISE 23-28 (first millstone rolls into river and is drowned. Fool puts head in second so he can tell Chelmites where it went. When he doesn't reappear from river they think he's stolen it).

J2131.5.6. Jackal's head caught in pot of blue dye. Animals make him king but detect him from his cry and turn him out. (cf. J512.13; J951). India: Gaer FABLES 69-71 (other jackals trick him into howling); Gobhai BLUE pb; Ryder PANCHATANTRA 122-124. India (Panchatantra): Green ANIMAL 216-219. China: Brown BLUE pb; Chang CHINESE 66-67 (fox tricked into howling by foxes).

J2131.5.6.1* King offers one-half kingdom and daughter for blue cat. Dyed cat is given, falls in tub and loses color. Daughter convinces father that prosperity (supposedly brought by blue cat) is state of mind. Her husband is spared. Indonesia: Carpenter ELEPHANT'S 159-165.

J2132.2. Numskull ties the rope to his leg as the cow grazes on the roof. The cow falls off and the man is pulled up the chimney. Type 1408. +J2431. SEE ALSO: J1904.1. TALL..NURSERY 98-104 (woman, three greater sillies). England: De La Mare TALES 125-130; Jacobs ENGLISH 10-15; Steel ENGLISH 73-78; Wiggin TALES 218-221; Williams-Ellis FAIRY..BRITISH 249-254.

J2132.2.0.1* J2132.2 + wife cuts rope, he falls into soup. Russia: Daniels FALCON 75-77; Hutchinson CANDLELIGHT 85-89. Bohemia: Gag GONE pb. Norway: Arbuthnot FAIRY 86-87; Asbjornsen EAST (Macmillan) 20-23; Asbjornsen EAST (Row) 73-76; Martignoni ILLUSTRATED 161-162. Lurie CLEVER 92-96.

J2132.5. Animal allows himself to be tied to another's tail and is dragged to death. SEE ALSO: K713.1.2.

J2132.5.1. Other animal's tail tied to tiger's (leopard's): killed when tiger flees. SEE ALSO: K1715.2.1. India: Spellman BLUE 75-78 (fox tied to tiger). Burma: Brockett BURMESE 71-78 (monkey tied to tiger's tail). Ceylon: Tooze WONDERFUL 111-114 (jackal and leopard tied together). S.W. China: Hume FAVORITE.. CHINA 9-14 (fox and tiger). Tibet: Hume FAVORITE..CHINA 93-98 (baboon and tiger). S.E. China: Hume FAVORITE..CHINA 109-114 (deer's tail pulled off +A2378.4.10). Ethiopia: Courlander FIRE 65-72. China: Kendall SWEET 73-77 (fox, tiger , +K1715.12.2).

J2132.5.2* Animal persuaded to be tied by promise of food. Fox tied to horse's tail to catch horse. China: Chang CHINESE 41.

J2132.5.2.1* Animal allows himself to be tied to another's tail and is dragged to death. Told he can catch horse by tying his tail to horse's tail. Japan: Uchida MAGIC 103-111 (bear dupes fox).

J2132.5.3* Jackal ties lion to tail of sham-dead horse so lion can drag it home. Horse takes lion to farmer and is thus reprieved despite old age. Pakistan: Siddiqui TOONTOONY 65-69.

J2132.5.4* Foxes tie sham-dead burro to their tails to drag home. Burro drags them to village. Bolivia: Jagendorf KING 49-51.

J2133.4. Numskull cuts off tree-limb on which he sits. Type 1240. +J2311.1. Turkey: Downing HODJA 41; Kelsey HODJA 93-99; Walker WATERMELONS 13-23. Switzerland: Duvoisin THREE 3-7. Haiti: Courlander PIECE 76-80. Turkmenian: Ginsburg KAHA 131-137. Uruguay: Jagendorf KING 252-256. Ethiopia: Courlander FIRE 19-24.

J2133.5. Men hang down in a chain until top man spits on his hands. Type 1250. SEE ALSO: J2516.3.2. Switzerland (German): Duvoisin THREE (+J1973 Meiringen). England: Jagendorf MERRY 45-50.

J2133.5.0.1. Elephant driver grabs legs of man dangling from tree to rescue, elephant walks out from under.

J2133.5.0.1.1* Elephant driver sings to attract help and man holding to tree claps hands. India: Montgomerie TWENTY-FIVE 46-47; Withers WORLD 89.

J2133.5.0.1.2* Four men hold cloth for two to jump. Their weight cracks heads of four together. Burma: Htin KINGDOM 66-70. Khmer: Asia BOOK..1 18-20.

J2133.5.1. Wife carried up tree to sky in bag in husband's teeth. She asks question and he drops her when he answers. +D861.1K. Russia: Dolch OLD RUSSIA 37-42 (+F54.2.2.1); Ransome OLD 155-158 /Fenner ADVENTURE 82-102/.

J2133.5.2. Numskull going to heaven holding on tail of divine elephant loses his hold to make gesture. He and all holding fall. India: Asia FOLK..FOUR 13-23; Gruenberg FAVORITE 394-395.

J2133.6.0.1* Wolf given tailor to eat. Tailor pretends to measure wolf first and harms. Wolves form ladder to reach him but flee at his sneeze. Estonia: Maas MOON 99-103. Ukraine: Bloch UKRANIAN 28-35.

J2133.6.0.2* Tigers climb on backs to reach man in tree. Man threatens baby tiger at top and mother on bottom screams and all fall. Man repeats claim "Papa God first, Man next, Tiger last." Haiti: Wolkstein MAGIC 177-182.

J2133.6.2* Building tower to the moon (F772.1.2). King on top has bottom box sent up. Dominican Republic: Courlander RIDE 265-267; Newman FOLK 101-105.

J2133.6.2.1* Tower built to heaven by Lepchas of Sekkim. One guard on each tier. Call is passed down to "send up hooks" becomes "cut us down" by the time it reaches bottom. Tibet (Sekkim): Hume FAVORITE..CHINA 62-66.

J2133.8. Stargazer falls into well looking at stars. Spain: De La Iglesia CAT #11. Aesop: Aesop AESOP'S (Watts) 148.

J2137.1. The louse invites the flea. The flea bites the man and jumps away. The bed is searched and the louse killed. India: Ryder PANCHATANTRA 119-122.

J2137.6. Camel and ass together captured because of ass's singing. SEE ALSO: J581.1. India: Ryder PANCHATANTRA 446-449.

J2137.6.1* Camel swims river to cane field with jackal on back. After eating jackal howls and camel is beaten. Returning across river jackal explains "It is my custom to sing after dinner." Camel rolls over drowning jackal. "It's my custom to roll after dinner." Gaer FABLES 26-28; Hutchinson CANDLELIGHT STORIES 79-82; Wiggin FAIRY 396-397.

J2137.6.2* Fish carries snake on back and snake bites. "That's my way." Fish dives, drowning snake. "That's my way." Yiddish: Ginsburg THREE 49.

J2137.8* Crow dives for seals by tying rock around neck. Drowns. Eskimo (Hooper Bay): Gillham BEYOND 51-67.

J2137.9* Passenger refuses to pray in storm. Safety of the ship is concern of the crew not the passengers. Iran: Shah MULLA 112.

J2160. Other short-sighted acts.

J2161.1. Jumping into the breeches. Trying to draw both legs on at once. Type 1286. Italy: Jagendorf NOODLEHEAD 164-172 (socks). Italy (Venetian): Haviland FAVORITE..ITALY 55-66. England: De La Mare TALES 125-130; Jacobs ENGLISH 10-15; Steel ENGLISH 73-78; Wiggin TALES 218-221; Williams-Ellis FAIRY ..BRITISH 249-254. Front THREE pb. Lang RED 188-191. Rockwell OLD 10-22. TALL..NURSERY 98-104. Zemach THREE pb.

J2161.2. Putting on the shirt. The shirt is sewn together at the neck. The man's head is cut off so that the shirt can be put on him. Type 1265. U.S. (Appalachia): Chase JACK 6 (wife beats husband over head trying to pound hole into shirt). Norway: Undset TRUE 206-208.

J2163.3* Four Chelmites to carry Berel the Beadle on his rounds so he will not track up snow. Jewish: Dobbs MORE 45-48; Simon WISE 119-126; Singer ZLATEH 29-34.

J2163.4* Stork is tramping down wheat. Eight men carry the one elected to chase off so he won't tramp field down. Scandinavia: Ross BURIED 55-64 (Moles).

J2165. Carrying load up hill to roll it down. Fools carry log (millstone) down hill. They realize that they might have rolled it down. They therefore carry it back uphill to roll it down. Jewish: Dobbs MORE 45-48 (stones, Chelm); Simon WISE 43-54.

J2171.1.3. Dupe makes boat of mud. It melts. Japan: Buck FAIRY 96-97; Ozaki FAIRY 43-53 (+K2345.0.1, hare tricks badger).

J2171.1.3.0.1* Maki in wooden barrel, landlord in earthen vessel, Maki smashes and landlord sinks. +K1051.0.1.' China: Chang TALES 11-24.

J2171.2.1. Does not need roof when it is fair; cannot put it on when it rains. Brazil: Jagendorf KING 52-55 (monkeys to build house tomorrow).

J2171.6. Man on camel has doorway broken down so he can ride in. It does not occur to him to dismount. India: Reed TALKATIVE 76.

J2171.6.1. Mounted bride and groom cannot pass through gate. Consider cutting off heads, donkey's feet, tearing down gate. Stranger slaps on top of head to bend. Kicks horse—passing bride through. (Priest asks them to dismount as other courses are work and it is Sunday.) Portugal: Jagendorf NOODLEHEAD 253-255. Italy (Venetian): Haviland FAVORITE ..ITALY 55-66. Leach LUCK 15-18 (bride too tall on foot). Greece: Haviland FAVORITE ..GREECE 29-37.

J2171.6.2* Potter cannot get pole through gate. It is suggested that he go sideways. SEE ALSO: J1964.0.1 (tree trunk crosswise of sledge). China: Kendall SWEET 45-48 (+H1312.4); Wyndham TALES..CHINA 64.

J2172.1. The shepherd who cried "wolf" too often. When the wolf really comes no one believes him. SEE ALSO: J2199.1. Aesop: Aesop AESOP'S (Golden) 17-19; Aesop AESOP'S (Grosset) 132; Aesop AESOP'S (Random) 54-56; Aesop AESOP'S (Viking) 74; Aesop AESOP'S (Watts) 41; Aesop FABLES (Macmillan) 85; Aesop FABLES (Walck) 59-60; Arbuthnot FAIRY 227; Gruenburg FAVORITE 416-417; Martignoni ILLUSTRATED; TALL..NURSERY 74-76.

J2172.2.2.1* Wolf locked up with the sheep. Trickster sews wolf into sheepskin and sells to each of three brothers as spirited sheep. Their folds are decimated. France: Cooper FIVE 49-57.

J2175.1.2* Anticipatory whipping. Father beats daughter before she fetches water to prevent her from breaking the pitcher. Turkey: Downing HODJA 86.

J2175.2. Scolding the drowning child instead of helping him. Aesop: Aesop AESOP'S (Grosset) 234; Aesop AESOP'S (Watts) 55; Aesop

FABLES (Walck) 78-79.

J2175.2.1. Wolf pities fox fallen in well. Save pity and fetch a rope. Aesop: Aesop AESOP'S (Viking) 82.

J2176. Fool lets wine run in the cellar. Fool falls into a study (or chases a dog) while the spigot is open. +J2063; J2431. Germany (Grimm): Grimm GRIMM'S (Grosset) 290-297 (wife); Grimm HOUSEHOLD 248-255 (wife); Grimm JUNIPER v. 2 187-200 (wife).

J2183.1.1* Disastrous hesitation. He keeps alternating until the meals are over. Man invited to feasts upstream and downstream. Keeps changing direction and misses both. Indonesia: Courlander KANTCHIL'S 34-38.

J2813.1.2* Frog's two wives invite him at the same time. He doesn't want to offend either by refusal. Goes to neither. +A2426.4.1. Congo (Bakongo): Courlander KING'S 58-60. Angola: Bryan OX 11-14.

J2183.1.2.1* Monk invited to two feasts. Both men pull him in their direction. He refuses both at last. Laos: Courlander TIGER'S 113-114.

J2183.1.3* Spider invited to two feasts. Ties rope around waist and sons are to pull when feast begins. Both begin at same time. SEE ALSO: A2355.1.1.1.2 (why spider has thin waist). Liberia/Ghana: Arkhurst ADVENTURES 5-11. Bantu: Nunn AFRICAN 75-80. Ashanti: Courlander HAT-SHAKING 18-19 (Anansi). Liberia: Courlander RIDE 116-118.

J2183.1.4* Man can't decide whether to eat red or yellow mangoes first. Fruit falls from tree and rots. Bantu: Holladay BANTU 30-32.

J2186.1* Raven creates a bird companion with one hummingbird wing, one heron wing. Bird cannot fly well, fuddles all Raven's directions and soars up when told to land, never seen again. Native American (Pacific Northwest): Robinson COYOTE 63-72.

J2192.0.1* Messenger without message. Presents empty envelope at house and joins in feast. Says he left so fast sender didn't have time to write anything. Turkey: Downing HODJA 48.

J2199.1. Alarm sounded foolishly. SEE ALSO: J2172.1.

J2199.1.3* Crane's eyes left on bank call to him that kayak is coming. Is only sticks on river first two times. Third time kayak comes and eyes are stolen. +A2232.5.11 (Why crane's eyes are blue). Eskimo: Gillham BEYOND 76-85.

J2199.1.4* Ruler raises alarm, calling out troops simply to amuse his wife. Third time enemy really attacks but soldiers refuse to respond.

China: Manton FLYING 40-45.

J2199.4.1. Numskull is glad to hurt his feet instead of new shoes. Leach LUCK 62.

J2199.5* Fools (usually animals) invite all comers to join them in abode until house ruptures. Russia (Ukraine): Tresselt MITTEN pb (mitten bursts). Scotland: Nic Leodhas ROOM pb (people, house bursts).

J2199.5.1* Animals invite all comers to join them living in horse's skull. Bear squashes all. Russia: Ransome OLD 228-230; Riordan TALES ..CENTRAL 76-77.

J2200 - J2259. Absurd lack of logic.

J2200. Absurd lack of logic--general.

J2201.1* Beautiful lakeland scene. If only they had not put water in it. Iran: Shah MULLA 154.

J2201.2* Numskull digging cellar pokes a hole into neighbor's cowshed. Tells wife he's found a cave full of cows dating from the time of Diocletian. Turkey: Downing HODJA 33.

J2210. Logical absurdity based upon certain false assumptions.

J2211.3. The murderous master. Dogs flee from their master because in time of famine he has killed his cattle. If he kills his cattle, he will surely kill the dogs. Aesop: Aesop AESOP'S (Grosset) 223 (oxen); Aesop AESOP'S (Watts) 199.

J2211.5* Black crow steals soap. "Never mind, he needs it worse than I do." Iran: Kelsey MULLAH 75-78; Shah MULLA 87.

J2212.2. Buried in old grave to deceive angel. Fool thinks that the angel who comes to question him will pass him by since he has apparently been dead a long time. Turkey: Downing HODJA 77.

J2212.2.1* Burial upside down so as to be right side up when all are cast headlong on Judgment Day. Turkey: Downing HODJA 60.

J2212.5. Swift when only a calf. A numskull who rides an ox to a tournament is ridiculed. He says, "He is swifter than a horse. You should have seen him run when he was only a calf." Turkey: Downing HODJA 67. Iran: Shah MULLA 51.

J2212.6.1* Born under the sign of the donkey. "Never heard of that sign." "You're too old. We've had some new ones since your time." Iran: Shah MULLA 69.

J2212.7* Boat expected to grow into a ship. Denmark: Bascom THOSE 30-47.

J2212.10* Who is older, you or your brother? Same age now. He was one year older last year. Turkey: Downing HODJA 79.

J2213.3. The seventh cake satisfies. Fool regrets that he had not eaten number seven first since that was the one that brought satisfaction. Indonesia: Courlander KANTCHIL 72-74 (Guno -six rice cakes). Russian/Yiddish: Ginsburg THREE ROLLS 7 (three rolls and one doughnut).

J2213.6. Selling his half of the house. A man owns half a house. He wants to sell his half so as to get money to buy the other half and thus have a whole house. Turkey: Downing HODJA 44.

J2213.6.1* Abunawas sells top floor of house. No buyer for bottom so sends workmen to tear down bottom. Owner of top half buys it. Saudi Arabia: Courlander RIDE 85-91.

J2213.9. Numskull finds that one feather makes a hard pillow. Thinks a sackful would be unbearable. Canada: Jagendorf NOODLEHEAD 263-267 (Pat the Irishman). Ireland: Danaher FOLKTALES 59-51.

J2213.10* Arithmetic problem: If you have four pennies in your pocket and they fall out, what's left? Fool: A hole in my pocket. Russia: Ginsburg THREE 23.

J2214.1.1* Fool eats hot soup. "Run for your lives. My belly's on fire!" Turkey: Downing HODJA 94.

J2214.2. Conclusion: youth and old age are alike. Reason: he tried in vain as a youth to lift a certain stone; he has also tried in vain as an old man. Iran: Kelsey MULLAH 89-94.

J2214.3.2. Waiting for thief to return for the bolster. After the cover is stolen, the numskulls conclude that the thief will certainly return for the bolster. Greece: Leach NOODLES 20.

J2214.3.4* Ax hidden from cat. Cat stole meat and might steal something worth more next time. Turkey: Downing HODJA 46. Iran: Shah MULLA 113.

J2215.4. Fool waits for God to provide. Nearly starves. SEE ALSO: A1458.2.

J2215.4.0.1* Brer Buzzard waits for the lord to feed him. Brer Hawk mocks, dives after Brer Rabbit and is killed hitting stump (or railing). Brer Buzzard eats. U.S. (Georgia/Black): Courlander TERRAPIN'S 11-14; Harris COMPLETE 378-380; Harris NIGHTS 362-365.

J2215.4.0.1.1* Buzzard waits for above to repeat itself. Nearly starves. Haiti: Courlander PIECE 111-112.

J2215.4.0.2* Three students reject fish cat

catches saying "God will provide" their food. Later they decide the hand of God was on the cat and they eat the fish. Ireland (15th Century): Leach LION 8-9.

J2215.7* Roasted quail stolen and live one left in place. Cook returns. "Allah, that was a miracle! But what have you done with my firewood, salt, butter and spices, and my work?" Turkey: Downing HODJA 45.

J2215.8* Man prays for wife's cow to die and finds his own donkey dead next morning. "Allah, can't you tell the difference between a cow and a donkey?" Turkey: Walker WATERMELONS 55-57.

J2215.9* Is the will of Allah always done? "If it were not surely my will would stand a chance once in a while." Turkey: Downing HODJA 92.

J2220.   Other logical absurdities.

J2223.   The thief is discoverer. The fool lies still as the thief enters the house, hoping that the thief may find something so that he can take it back from the thief (J1392). Turkey: Downing HODJA 11.

J2224.   Taking the seed out at night. Numskull plants seed in daytime and takes it out at night. "Man must guard his treasures" (or "Growing in daytime is enough"). Turkey: Downing HODJA 56 (saplings).

J2231.   Why can't we have holidays the year round? Turkey: Downing HODJA 90.

J2232.   Imitation and the real pig. Imitator of pig's cries applauded. Fool brings real pig but fails. Aesop: Aesop AESOP'S (Grosset) 174-175; Aesop AESOP'S (Watts) 101-102; Aesop FABLES (Macmillan) 159.

J2233.   Logically absurd defenses. Thief brought to judgment for breaking into house blames mason for building poor house. Etc. SEE ALSO: Z49.11.2. Ceylon: Courlander TIGER'S 49-51 (goldsmith can't be spared so stranger hung).

J2233.2.   Innocent man executed because guilty is too tall for gallows. Ethiopia (Galla): Davis LION'S 112-115. Egypt: Courlander RIDE 101-104.

J2233.3*   Thief upheld. Victim berated for leaving door unlocked, not being awake, etc. "Isn't the thief to blame too?" Turkey: Downing HODJA 36.

J2233.4*   Thief upheld. Passerby criticizes victim who has subdued thief and is sitting on him. "Let that little man up and give him a chance!" Victim: "You ignore the trouble I had getting him down." Iran: Shah MULLA 135.

J2235.   Would have shot himself. Fool shoots full

of holes a garment left out at night to dry. "It was a good thing I did not have it on or I would have shot myself." Turkey: Downing HODJA 14; Kelsey HODJA 34-40; Leach THING 30; Leach LUCK 62; Shah MULLA 89.

J2235.1*   Man shoots deer through sheet and explains holes by saying he was shot to cover illegal hunting. U.S. (New England): Jagendorf NOODLEHEAD 287-289.

J2235.2*   Coat falling makes loud noise. He was in it. Turkmenian: Ginsburg KAHA 139.

J2237.   The bathroom in the minaret. The fool can sing in the small bathroom but cannot be heard from the minaret. He wants a bathroom built on the minaret so that his voice will carry. Turkey: Downing HODJA 80.

J2238.1*   Book gives wisdom. Scholar displays book as evidence of wisdom. "And I wrote it myself." Wit displays brick as evidence of house for sale "And I built it myself." Iran: Shah MULLA 121.

J2241.   The doctor no longer needed. As the fool starts for the doctor the wife changes her mind. He continues to the doctor so as to tell him about it and to say that now he need not come. Turkey: Downing HODJA 62.

J2241.1.1*   Man sent to wise man for child's name falls down and loses name. Passerby says, "It's ridiculous." Ridiculous taken as name. SEE: J2671. Ethiopia (Gondar): Courlander FIRE 113-118.

J2242.0.1*   Fool thinks self dead. As no one comes past he goes home to tell wife, then returns and lies down dead again. Turkey: Downing HODJA 70.

J2242.1.   Scribe cannot write a letter because he has bad leg. Must carry letter in person since no one else can read it. Iran: Shah MULLA 73.

J2242.1.1*   Scribe cannot write letter because he has no time to make a trip to interpret it just now. No one can read his writing. Turkey: Downing HODJA 64.

J2242.2.1*   Scribe writes in large letters to deaf man. Jewish: Simon WISE 119-126.

J2242.3.   Scholar cannot read letter because of bad handwriting. "You wear a scholar's turban and can't even read a letter?" "Here, you wear the turban and see if you can read it." Turkey: Downing HODJA 25.

J2243.1*   Sleeping is not doing anything. Fox told to observe what everyone does and thus guard shop, ignores "sleeping" thief. Iran: Shah MULLA 79.

J2259.1*   Thief stealing bronze bell tries to break it up for the bronze, stuffs ears with cotton fearing din will raise authorities. China: Wyndham TALES..CHINA 63.

J2259.2* If fool found a purse with 50,000 rubles he would ask a reward if it belonged to a rich man, would ask none if it belonged to a poor man. Jewish: Simon MORE 63-64.

J2259.3* Beardless man must take after mother's side of the family as she is beardless too. Jewish: Simon WISE 1-10.

J2259.4* Asked the time of day. He can't tell, he's a stranger in this town himself. Turkey: Downing HODJA 57. Iran: Shah MULLA 129.

J2260. Absurd scientific theories.

J2261. Disciple shakes self in middle of each meal. At length master asks why. He can eat more this way. Master beats him for not telling this sooner. "I knew the limits of eating must be farther ahead than I can attain." Iran: Shah MULLA 123.

J2270. Absurd astronomical theories.

J2271. Absurd theories concerning the moon. SEE ALSO: J1791.3.

J2271.2.1. Lightning made from the old moon. Turkey: Downing HODJA 75. SEE ALSO: A1141.

J2271.2.1.1* Millstone made from old moon. Lightning is sparks from millstone. Turkey: Downing HODJA 75. SEE ALSO: A1141.

J2271.2.2. Stars made from the old moon. Turkey: Downing HODJA 35. Iran: Shah MULLA 74. SEE ALSO: A764. Ugyur: Ginsburg KAHA 88-89. Western China (Turkestan): Jablow MAN 75 (Allah).

J2271.5* Fear moon will burn crops when low in sky. Villagers throw rocks to scare it away. Ceylon: Jagendorf NOODLEHEAD 73-74 (Rayigam Korle--town of fools).

J2271.6* Simba Islanders want moon to shine only on them, failing to catch it, they throw mud to dim it so won't shine on anyone. Solomon Islands (Simba): Holding SKY 99-110.

J2273.1. Bird thinks that the sky will fall if he does not support it. SEE: Z93.3.

J2273.1.1* Hummingbird lies on back with feet in air. He has heard sky is going to fall and must do his bit to help. SEE: Z43.3.1.

J2274.1.1* Why people go in opposite directions each morning. The world would tip over if all went the same way. Turkey: Downing HODJA 70.

J2275.2* Youth tries to knock down star with bamboo pole. Monk calls him a fool, says to try from the roof. Japan: Jablow MAN 76.

J2287.1* Fools pull island nearer to their town with ropes. Jugoslavia: Jagendorf NOODLEHEAD 241-243 (Prach).

J2289.1* Telegraph thought to work because other end of wire turns when he turns this one. Jewish: Simon MORE 63-68.

J2289.2* Numskull advises sailors to tie up bottom of boat, not topsail, to steady it. Turkey: Downing HODJA 53.

J2300 - J2349. Gullible fools.

J2300. Gullible fools.

J2311. Person made to believe that he is dead.

J2311.0.1.1* Three women bet landlord can make fools of husbands. Convince three that one is dead, one a devil, one mad. Type 1406. U.S. (Appalachia): Chase WICKED 156-161 (one convinced is dead, second persuaded to wear suit of virgin sheep's wool, which he can't see because of telling lies, K445). Ireland: MacManus HIBERNIAN 174-184.

J2311.1. Numskull is told that he will die when his horse breaks wind (or donkey brays) three times. When this happens he lies down for dead. Turkey: Downing HODJA 41 (donkey brays); Kelsey HODJA 93-99 (donkey brays). Turkmenian: Ginsburg KAHA 131-137 (stumbles, +J2311.12). Italy: Manning-Sanders GIANNI 141-144 (sneezes).

J2311.1.1* Since prediction that numskull would fall from tree (J2133.4) came true he accepts this one. Switzerland: Duvoisin THREE 3-7 (donkey sneezes). Haiti: Courlander PIECE 46-80. Slovenia: Kavcic GOLDEN 118-126 (he sneezes). Jewish: Simon MORE 24-30.

J2311.1.3.2* Numskull thinks self dead when frightened by bird. Turkey: Downing HODJA 20.

J2311.1.6* Person made to believe that he is dead. Told will fall off tree limb and die. He falls off and believes self dead, or told he'll fall off tree limb he does so and believes one who warned him can predict the future. +J2133.4. SEE ALSO: J2311.1. Turkey: Downing HODJA 41; Kelsey HODJA 95-99; Walker WATERMELONS 13-23. Ethiopia: Courlander FIRE 19. Uruguay: Jagendorf KING 252-256.

J2311.2. The "poisoned" pot. The wife tells the husband that a certain pot of preserves is poison. He decides to kill himself and eat the preserves. He believes that he is poisoned and lies down for dead. +J2431. Jewish: Singer ZLATEH 55-65 (undertaking wife's work).

J2311.2.1* Boy left to mind house. All goes wrong and he commits suicide by eating the "poison"--a pot of pickled walnuts (or preserves). Italy: Baker TALKING 18-24: Manning-Sanders GIANNI 21-42; Mincielli OLD 14-23. Slovenia: Kavcic GOLDEN 18-126. China: Kendall SWEET 42-44 (wine).

J2311.2.2* Acolyte eats honey which master says is poison. Claims to have been attempting suicide. Japan: Edmonds POSSIBLE 13-23 (Ikkyu).

J2311.2.3* Lad eats off duck crust thinking it can roast a second. Commits suicide with "poison" jam. Russia: Wiggin TALES 45-46.

J2311.2.4* Cakes said to be poisoned so boys will not touch. Boy eats and says he was trying to commit suicide. Turkey: Downing HODJA 87.

J2311.3. Sham revenant. A man takes refuge from robbers in an open grave. Robbers see him and ask what he is doing. "It is my grave. I went out to get a breath of air." Turkey: Downing HODJA 81.

J2311.3.1* Sham revenant. A man takes refuge from believed robbers in an open grave. They come to investigate. "I am here because of you and you are here because of me." Turkey: Shah MULLA 14.

J2311.4. The dead man speaks up. A numskull who has lain down thinking he is dead is carried off in a bier. The carriers lose their way. He speaks up. "I always went that way when I was alive." Turkey: Downing HODJA 41; Kelsey HODJA 93-99; Walker WATERMELONS 13-23. Haiti: Courlander PIECE 76-80. Jewish: Simon MORE 24-30. Italy: Manning-Sanders GIANNI 141-144.

J2311.6. Sham-dead man punished. A numskull lies in an old grave to see the Day of Judgment. He hears bells and thinks that the Last Day has come. He is beaten by mule drivers when he tells them that he is a dead man. He returns home, tells his wife that he returns from the dead. "How goes it in heaven?" "For one thing, avoid mule drivers." Turkey: Downing HODJA 33-35 (he frightens mules and is beaten); Shah MULLA 105; Walker WATERMELONS 13-23; Walker TALES 228-229.

J2311.7. Cold hands and feet for the dead man. His wife has told him that one tells a dead person by his cold hands and feet. He freezes his feet and hands and lies down for dead. Wolves eat his ass. "Lucky for you that his master is dead." Iran: Shah MULLA 153. Turkey: Walker WATERMELONS 13-23.

J2311.7.1* Cold hands and feet are signs of dead person. Man with cold hands and feet believes self dead. Turkey: Walker WATERMELONS 13-23.

J2311.12. Supposed dead man roused with whip. +K113. Turkmenian: Ginsburg KAHA 131-137. Slovenia: Kavcic GOLDEN 118-126.

J2311.13* Supposed dead man speaks up. Clubbed to death as a ghost. +J2133.4; J2311.1.6. Uruguay: Jagendorf KING 252-256.

J2311.14* Gravedigger thinks self dead, disturbed by boy stamping on grave. He had enjoyed the peace and quiet. Mexico: Brenner BOY 96-99.

J2311.15* Ogre (Old Stupid Head) told he has died runs home to see if it is true. Prince escapes. Kashmir: Manning-Sanders BOOK.. PRINCES 125-128.

J2311.16* Fool who thinks self dead feels hungry on seeing donkey nosing avocado. Chases off and eats himself, then goes home to eat. Hungry even if he is dead. Haiti: Courlander PIECE 76-78.

J2311.20* Fool misunderstands identity of the dead. SEE ALSO: P262.2.

J2311.20.1* Woman at wake of daughter's father-in-law thinks her own husband has died. Korea: STORY 41-43.

J2314. Layman made to believe he is a monk. SEE: J2012.1.2.

J2315.2. Gullible husband made to believe he has cut off his wife's nose. She is in another house, has had her nose cut off by mistake. She makes him believe he has done it by making him angry enough to throw a razor at her. When he throws the razor she claims it has cut off her nose. +K1512. India: Ryder PANCHATANTRA 62-71.

J2321.1. Parson made to believe that he will bear a calf. In having his urine examined by a doctor, a cow's is substituted by mistake. (Or he dreams that he has borne a calf.) When a calf comes into house he thinks he has borne it. Type 1739. Russia: Riordan TALES..CENTRAL 211-212.

J2326. The student from paradise. A student tells a woman that he comes from Paris. She understands him to say from paradise and gives him money and goods to take her to her husband. Type 1540. SEE ALSO: K362.1. Jacobs EUROPEAN 159-164.

J2326.1. Foolish woman gives swindler money for her parents (husband, son) in heaven. +K341.4.1.1; K346.1. SEE ALSO: K362.1. Indonesia: Courlander KANTCHIL 64-70 (Thief claims to come from Gunung Agung - home of the dead). S. India: Courlander TIGER'S 58-52 (thief from Kailasa--heaven). Latvia: Durham TIT 75-80. Russia: Daniels FALCON 15-20 (told son herds birds in heaven and tears cloth--sends forty yards of cloth). England: Jacobs ENGLISH (+K341.9); Reeves ENGLISH 2-9. Greece: Neufeld BEWARE 52-57. Norway: Undset TRUE 202-208 (+K341.9). Ireland: MacManus HIBERNIAN 48-59. Persia: Mehdevi PERSIAN 51-61.

J2326.2.1* Boar dreams he is to eat antelope. King rules he may. Ape dreams he is to wed king's daughter. King reverses decision. Indonesia: De Leeuw INDONESIAN 65-67.

J2326.5* Trickster pretends to be trying to jump back into heaven. Was thrown out while wrestling. Lady sends goods to her dead son. Czechoslovakia: Fillmore SHEPHERD'S 153-159. Slovenia: Kavcic GOLDEN 150-156 (thrown into yard by giant, explains arrival by air thus).

J2328. The moving church tower. To see whether the church is moving someone lays down his coat in front of it. It is stolen. They think the church has passed over it.

J2328.1* The moving church. Fools lay their jackets in a line as attempt to push the church to that line. Someone steals the jackets and they believe the church has been pushed over them. Switzerland: Jagendorf NOODLEHEAD 229-232 (Belmont). Jewish: Simon WISE 17-22 (watermill).

J2332. Fool locked in dark room made to believe it is continuous night.

J2332.1* Roosters revenge on owls for dancing nightly with hens. Pedro Animal gives a party for owls and seals cracks in windows so daylight cannot get in. Ties rooster's beak so cannot crow. When hens see owls in daylight they are ashamed. Owls stay in dark thereafter and rooster remains king of barnyard. Cuba: Jagendorf KING 94-101.

J2332.1.1* Old Woman Crim has party to keep owls until after daylight so they will become helpless and unable to leave. She wants to keep them for companions. Owls bring roosters to crow at dawn and thus escape. West Indies: Sherlock IGUANA'S 29-42.

J2346.1* Fool's errand. Fox tricks woodchuck. Tells to climb "you-find-it" tree on certain day and eat eight bugs together and will obtain secret of fox's cleverness. Fox has gambled with magic dice which are really tobacco beetles transformed. Native American (Seneca): Par-Parker SKUNNY 60-67.

J2350 - J2369. Talkative fools.

J2351. Animal betrays himself to his enemies by talking. SEE: W141.

J2351.1. Fox holds conversation with his members, attracts attention and is caught. He scolds in turn his feet, his eyes, ears and tail. In his excitement he sticks his tail out from his hiding place. Type 154. Bulgaria: Rudolph MAGIC 51-61. Spain: Sawyer PICTURE 75-76 /Hardendorff TRICKY 63-70/. Jacobs EUROPEAN 42-50. Russia: Ginsburg ONE 31-37 Higonnet-Schnopper TALES 76-81. Mexico:

Courlander RIDE 253-256; Hardendorff TRICKY 55-61 (Puts tail out for waving dogs on). SEE ALSO: C25.

J2351.1.1* Man puts legs on pillow to reward for carrying him. Head is put on ground for doing nothing. Gypsy: Jagendorf NOODLEHEAD 156-158.

J2351.1.2* Manabozho tells feet to watch baking ducks as he sleeps. Indians steal birds and Manabozho roasts feet until they hurt, to punish. Native American (Chippewa): Leekley WORLD 55-57.

J2353. The wife multiplies the secret. To prove that a woman cannot keep a secret the man tells his wife that a crow has flown out of his belly (or that he has laid an egg). She tells her neighbors that two crows have flown. Soon he hears from his neighbors that there were fifty crows. Rumania: Ure RUMANIAN 153-157.

J2356.1* Foolish farmer calls to wife that he has hidden hoe. She says thief may have heard. He investigates and returns to whisper "It's stolen." China: Hardendorff TRICKY 51-53; Withers WORLD 73-79.

J2357. Tortoise speaks and loses his hold on the stick. He is being carried through the air by a bird. +A2312.1.1 (why shell is cracked). SEE ALSO: J657.2 (lets self be carried by eagle). India: Babbitt JATAKA 18-20 (geese); Jacobs INDIAN 123-125; Gaer FABLES 162-164 (wild ducks); Green ANIMAL 196 (geese); Korel LISTEN 76-81 (cranes); Montgomerie TWENTY-FIVE 48-49; Ross BURIED 75-80; Ryder PANCHATANTRA 147-149 (two geese); Turnbull FAIRY 45-47 (geese). Somali: Davis LION'S 189-191 (eagles). China: Chang CHINESE 42-43 (herons); Chang TALES 49-51 (cranes, herons); Lin MILKY 11-15 (egrets). Ceylon: Tooze THREE 8-21; Tooze WONDERFUL 107-110 (storks, falls to mocking jackal). Russia: Carey BABA 33-38 (frog); Garshin TRAVELING FROG (ducks). Nicaragua (Nicarao Indians): Barlow LATIN 104-112. Haiti: Wolkstein MAGIC 189-194. Domanska LOOK pb.

J2357.1* Tortoise speaks and frightens bird carrying him into dropping him. +A2312.1.1. (cf. J657.2.3). Bemba: Kaula AFRICAN 80-83.

J2368* Panditji addresses guava trees, "May I pluck four or five of your fruit?" Guava answers, "Why not forty or fifty?" Caught by gardener, he is put into well basket. Gardener calls to well, "Shall I give Panditji a plunge?" Panditji answers absentmindedly, "Why not forty or fifty?" India: Spellman BEAUTIFUL 90-97.

J2370. Inquisitive fools.

J2376. Testing the evidence by experiment: biting the ear off. The accused pleads that the plaintiff bit his own ear off. The judge takes time for consideration, tries to bite his own ear, but falls down and breaks his head. Turkey: Downing HODJA 41.

J2376.1. The accused pleads that the plaintiff bit his own ear off. "Are you a camel that you can bite your own ear?" Turkey: Downing HODJA 49.

J2377. The philosophical watchman. A master sets his servant to watch over his horse at night. He soon asks the servant if he is a-sleep. "No, I was thinking of who created so many stars in the sky." The second time the servant answers, "No, I was thinking of who dug the sea. Where did he put the soil?" The third time: "I was wondering who would carry the saddle now that the horse is stolen." Leach NOODLES 38.

J2381. Question: did the man ever have a head? A man's head is snatched off by accident and his companions do not see what has happened. Debate: did he ever have a head? Type 1225. Turkey: Downing HODJA 74. Gypsy: Jagendorf GYPSIES' 122-128. Finland: Bowman TALE 220-230 (bear bites off).

J2400 - J2449. Foolish imitation.

J2400. Foolish imitation. SEE ALSO: K635.2.

J2411.1. Imitation of magic rejuvenation unsuccessful. SEE ALSO: K113 (pseudo-magic object sold); H1213.1A. Germany (Grimm): Grimm JUNIPER v. 1 129-149 (resuscitation by reassembling pieces of body; +K213 Devil in knapsack). Norway: Undset TRUE 137-146 (+Q565 Smith and Devil).

J2411.1.0.1* Lord pounds St. Peter on anvil to rejuvenate. Blacksmith tries this with his old father. Italy: Jagendorf PRICELESS 109-113.

J2411.1.0.2* Devil as smith's apprentice rejuvenates boyar's wife by throwing in fire then bathing in milk. She forces smith to do same for her husband. He is to hang for murder. Devil offers to save for soul. Smith's father had sold soul to Devil (M211) and sign of Devil hangs over forge door. Smith tosses Devil and sign into fire as reply. Boyar revives and wife ages again. Russia: Spicer THIRTEEN DEVILS 91-100.

J2411.1.0.3* Lad imitates doctor by cutting open princess and blowing on face--fails. Doctor performs for him and revives queen. Lad has eaten hare's kidney and claimed had none. Doctor divides money. "One for me, one for you, one for who ate the hare's kidneys." Armenia: Tashjian THREE 48-61.

J2411.2. Imitation of miraculous horse-shoeing unsuccessful. Christ takes off horse's foot to shoe it and then successfully replaces it. Norway: Undset TRUE 137-146 (+Q565 Smith and Devil).

J2411.2.1* Wee Red Man: cuts off horse's legs and puts into fire to reshoe. Donal imitates with King of Ireland's horse. Wee Red Man puts two hags in fire and maidens emerge (J2411.1). Donal tries with wife and mother-in-law. Wee Red Man shows Donal how to cut off King of France's head and boil to cure. Donal refuses part of reward to Wee Red Man. Donal tries same with King of Spain and fails. Wee Red Man appears and aids. Given reward this time. Donal's wife, mother-in-law and King of Ireland's horse are restored and he may return home. Ireland: MacManus HIBERNIAN 85-98 /MacManus DONEGAL /, /Fenner TIME 217-240/.

J2411.3. Unsuccessful imitation of magic production of food. Type 552 B. SEE ALSO: J2425.

J2411.3.1* Father visits daughter's troll husbands. They produce food by banging head on wall and throwing broken pieces into pot, diving for fish, lighting fingers as candles. Father imitates on return home. Dies. Type 552B. Denmark: Baker TALKING 113-117.

J2411.3.1.1* Father tries unsuccessfully to imitate actions of supernatural son-in-law. Sun bakes pancakes on head, moon lights cellar with finger, wind floats wife on fur coat on river to cool off. Lithuania: Jablow MAN 67-70.

J2411.6.2* Brer Rabbit supposedly burnt in hollow log says honey dripped over him and preserved from heat. Brer Wolf has self burnt thus. U.S. (Georgia, Black): Harris COMPLETE 335-338; Harris NIGHTS 302-305.

J2412.2. Foolish imitation of healing. Pulling out the eye so that the pain will cease. He has had a tooth pulled and the pain ceased. Turkey: Downing HODJA 70.

J2412.4. Imitation of diagnosis by observation: ass's flesh. A doctor tells his patient that he has eaten too much chicken. This the patient confesses. The doctor's son wants to know how the diagnosis was made. The doctor says that as he rode up he observed chicken feathers and made his conclusions. The son imitates. He sees an ass's saddle. Diagnosis: you have eaten too much ass's flesh. Iran: Shah MULLA 115 (doctor saw green apple cores under bed, imitator sees saddles and bridles).

J2413.1. Foolish imitation by an animal. Tries to go beyond his powers. Ass tries to caress master like the dog. He is driven off. Aesop: Aesop AESOP'S (Grosset) 71-72; Aesop AESOP'S (Viking) 56; Aesop AESOP'S (Watts) 27-28; Aesop FABLES (Macmillan) 19; Green ANIMAL 84-85; Montgomerie TWENTY-FIVE 28-29.

J2413.3. Daw tries to carry off lamb like eagle. Is caught in lamb's fleece. Aesop: Aesop

AESOP'S (Grosset) 123-124 (crow); Aesop AESOP'S (Random) 66-68; Aesop AESOP'S (Watts) 134-135; Aesop FABLES (Walck) 22-23; Green ANIMAL 144-145.

J2413.4.2.1* Craney crow thinks all birds have taken off their heads to sleep. Wants to imitate. Brer Rabbit fetches 'Doc' Wolf to perform the operation. U.S. (Georgia, Black): Harris FAVORITE 296-300; Harris COMPLETE 640-647.

J2413.4.5* Brer Fox and wife convinced sleeping with heads off is the fashion. Wife cuts off Brer Fox's head. Dead in morning. "Better dead than out of fashion," says she. U.S. (Georgia, Black): Harris FAVORITE 301-309; Harris COMPLETE 647-653.

J2413.6. Monkey sneezes in King's presence like rabbit. Killed. India: Gaer FABLES 14-18.

J2413.10* Raven persuades fox to imitiate his sliding game. Raven flies over mud puddle at bottom but fox lands in mud. Alaska: Dolch ALASKA 119-123.

J2413.11* Hunters examine green grass snake on path and pass on. Cobra thinks it must be safe spot and sleeps there. Is killed. Congo (Mongo): Arnott AFRICAN 105-107.

J2415. Foolish imitation of lucky man. Because one man has good luck a numskull imitates and thinks he will have equal luck. He is disappointed. SEE ALSO: A1115.2 (magic object works only for master); A2491.1.0.1 (bush bat boils self in imitation of bat); B210.2.1 (singing tortoise refuses to sing); C761.4 (tabu: staying too long in treasure cave); C916.3 (magic object works only for master); D861.2.1 (man given magic spoon and tortoise whip); D1050.2 (imitation of magic wampum production); D1338.1.1 (fountain of youth); D1376.1.3.2 (tengus stretch noses); D1571.1 (old man who made cherry trees blossom); D1651.3.1 (magic works only for master); D2171.1.0.1 (pine sap); E373.1.1 (good man covered with gold); F344.1 (fairies remove wens); F451.5.1.6.5 (brother respectful to little people); F451.5.1.6.4 (dwarf given food by cook); F451.5.2.6.1 (dwarfs cause bad hunter's jaws to freeze); F456.2.2.6 (one miner shares with Knocker); G412.1.1.2 (wolf is carried by ducks); H601.0.1 (carving the fowl); H1273.2 (quest for Three Golden Hairs, king handed oar becomes ferryman); J2073.1 (doing all day what started); K32.1 (mean farmer puts roots in net, turns to magic dog); K710.1.1 (camel imitates hare in tricking cobra); N182.2.1 (treasure turns to vermin for bad man); N250.4 (bad luck buried by poor brother); N452 (attempts to overhear secrets of animals); N455.3 (forgets 'open sesame' formula); N777 (dropped ball leads to adventure); Q1.1 (hospitality rewarded); Q2.1 (modest request rewarded); Q2.1.2 ff. (kind and unkind girls); Q285.1.1 (tongue-cut sparrow); W48.1 (demons overheard); Z33.6 (bear imitates squirrel's jump); Z52.4.1 (cock swallows gold, hen swallows wasps).

J2415.1. The two presents to the king: the beet and the horse. A farmer takes extraordinary beet as present to the king and receives a large reward. His companion is eager for a reward and leads a handsome steed to the palace. Imitation: the king rewards him with the beet. Germany (Grimm): Grimm GRIMM'S (Follett) 358-364; Grimm GRIMM'S (Grosset) 260-263; Grimm GRIMM'S (World) 148-151. Ethiopia (Falasha): Davis LION'S 172-177 (apple, horse). De La Mare TALES 107-118 (turnip). Puerto Rico: Belpré TIGER 123-127 (one perfect fig reward, imitator with cart of figs has them thrown at him). Jewish: Gross FABLE pb (+J701.1); Jagendorf NOODLEHEAD 59-62 (old man to bring figs to emperor if lives to see them ripen--rewarded, imitator has figs thrown at him. +J2563).

J2415.1.0.1* Merchant gives king of rat-infested island two cats and is rewarded (N411.1C). Another greedy merchant presents load of riches to king and is given two cats. Italy: Arbuthnot FAIRY 130-131; Jagendorf PRICELESS 47-58; Vittorini OLD 28-33.

J2415.8* The magic geta. Priest in dream gives magic geta to man sleeping in shrine. Coin falls at each step. Tabu on overuse or will grow shorter at each step. Greedy neighbor borrows and runs until only inches high. Japan: Scofield HOLD 15-20.

J2415.9* Journey to land of cats. Orphan journeys to Cat Hill in Inaba Mountains to visit his friend cat. Is entertained, given gifts to open once home, and package to hold over head to ward off other cat's attacks. Gift is picture of dog with bared teeth. Gold coins fall from teeth and boy buys freedom. Mistress imitates and is torn to pieces by cat. Japan: Novak FAIRY 44-53.

J2415.10* The Doll. Poor girl buys doll. It sneezes gold. Bad neighbor steals. Doll sneezes soot. Throws doll and it fastens onto king's back. He offers to wed whomever removes it. Girl does so. Italy: Manning-Sanders GIANNI 67-75. SEE ALSO: Q2.1 (kind and unkind girls).

J2415.11* Kind man takes rock python to river on request. Is given lovely wife. Bad man imitates. Gets shrew. Central Africa: Burton MAGIC 75-77.

J2415.12* Drunkard--to opium eater. Drunkard in cemetery passes as ghost, learns of buried treasure. Opium eater imitates. Falls asleep and ghosts stretch his nose. Drunkard returns and learns remedy to shrink nose (F344.1). Burma: Htin Aung KINGDOM 74-79. S. China: Hume FAVORITE..CHINA 47-54.

J2415.13* Poor brother heals wounded bird. Given magic treasure producing seed. Rich brother imitates. Given destruction producing seed. Korea: Carpenter KOREAN 221-228; Kim STORY 145-153 (swallow, pumpkin);

Williams-Ellis ROUND 1-15. China: Bonnet FOLKTALES..CHINA 117 (second climbs vine to moon, vine strands him there, A751.1.8); Jablow MAN 11-13.

J2415.14* Kind brother loses ax in sea, dives after it and reaches palace of Rajah of Fishes, is polite and receives treasure. Unkind brother imitates. Is torn to bits by fish for rudeness. Sarawak: Arnott ANIMAL 59-66.

J2415.15* Good brother's silkworms prosper, bad brother cuts in half; both halves grow. Bad brother tries, loses crop. Good brother finds wishing mallet in dream of children. Bad brother imitates, children pull nose off. Japan: Wiggin TALES 421-429.

J2415.16* Poor brother given gold by stone lion who vomits gold into bucket. Must stop him before bucket overflows. Rich brother imitates, lets overflow. Lion closes mouth on arm, turns to stone. Wife must feed him thus for months until all money gone. On hearing this lion laughs and man is released. Manning-Sanders BOOK..MAGIC 127-128.

J2415.17. Three orphan girls rescue bird. It lays rice and fish for them. Uncle borrows, eats bird, they bury bones, tree grows with leaves of silk and blossoms of jewelry. Indonesia: De Leeuw INDONESIAN 151-156.

J2415.18* Bird brings flocks to eat bugs off corn of good brother, bad brother's crop consumed. Show treasure to good brother, bad brother imitates, never returns. Argentina: Newman FOLK 73-81.

J2415.19* Girl given magic cloth by beggar, makes her lovely, pain leaves. Mistress, master use it. Become monkeys. China: Lin MILKY 33-40; Wyndham FOLK..CHINA 102-107.

J2415.20* Girl, mother turn selves to snakes, enter crack in cave, bring back gold coins. Unkind relatives steal magical tools and try. Don't know word to restore selves to human. Left as snakes. Abaluya: Harman TALES 163-185.

J2415.21* Little Liang's dog plows for him. Big Liang kills. Bamboo grows from grave, sheds nuggets. B.L. tries, mosquitoes attack. Cuts down tree. L.L. makes chicken coop, pheasants lay eggs. B.L. tries, pheasants drop droppings on head. Burn coop. L.L. fertilizes pumpkin patch with ashes=giant pumpkins (D1571.1). Monkeys steal pumpkins, L.L. hides, scares them off. They leave their golden candle holder. B.L. tries, sleeps, wakes, cries out. They drop pumpkins off cliff. China: Chang CHINESE 54-57.

J2415.22* Man slips, gets syrup all over self. Goblins think him candyman, carry off. He steals magic drum. Neighbor tries, to be boiled in pot, flees, nose pulled long. First returns, leaves remedy: beat drum, say "shrink." Wife of second beats too much, nose falls off. China: Chang CHINESE 36-37.

J2415.23* Farmer disguised as scarecrow taken for Jizo statue by monkeys. They carry him to cave. He takes their offerings to Jizo, leaves. Neighbor tries same. As monkeys carry him over river he laughs (C460.1) at their chant, they drop him. Japan: Novak FAIRY 145-150 (Buddha); Scofield HOLD 27-33.

J2415.24* The Devil's Granny: brother told to "go to hell with your sausages." Devil's grandmother gives one of her hairs, turns to gold once home. Mean brother tries. Seven devils eat him. Germany: Spicer THIRTEEN DEVILS 102-110.

J2415.25* Chin-Chin of the Long Nose. Good brother spends night in pagoda, hears immortals tell how to purify spring (remove toad), complete bridge (remove treasure). Also finds magic wand they left behind. Mean brother imitates. Immortals pull his nose long. Older brother goes to immortals to learn remedy for nose, strike with wand, call thief fourteen times. SEE ALSO: F344.1 (old man and the wens). China: Wyndham FOLK..CHINA 54-60.

J2417.2. To imitate leader. He slips and falls to floor. Netherlands: De Leeuw LEGENDS 57-59 (falls into rice pudding). Japan: Edmonds TRICKSTER 129-137 (hits self with rice ball).

J2417.3* Worshippers all fall on floor imitating priest who slips. Russia: Riordan TALES.. CENTRAL 146-147.

J2423.1* The eye-juggler. Ejapa, coyote, sees two girls throwing eyes into air. Become blue camas flowers when fall. Coyote tries but does not learn magic word so eyes stick in willow tree = pussywillow. Coyote stumbles over dead buffalo calf. Takes its eyes (A2332.3.1.1). Native American (Shoshone): Heady SAGE 42-45.

J2425. The bungling host. A trickster (animal) visits various animals who display their peculiar powers in obtaining food (often magic). He returns the invitation and tries to provide food in similar ways. He fails and usually has a narrow escape from death. SEE ALSO: J2411.3.1. Native American (Caddo): Brown TEPEE 150-153 (coyote); Martin NINE 19-22 (coyote).

J2431. A man undertakes to do his wife's work. All goes wrong. Type 1408. +J2132.2 (cow on roof); +J2176 (wine running in cellar); +J2311.2 (poison eaten). Hutchinson CANDLELIGHT 85-89. Russia: Daniels FALCON 75-77. Majorca: Mehdevi BUNGLING 57-67 (doing chores for wife). Bohemia: Gag GONE IS GONE pb. Norway: Arbuthnot ARBUTHNOT 246; Arbuthnot ANTHOLOGY 244-245; McKee MAN pb; Minard WOMENFOLK 106-110; Undset TRUE 198-201; Wiesner TURNABOUT pb. Scandinavia: Haviland FAIRY (Briggs) 48-55; Wiggin TALES 296-300. Lurie CLEVER 92-96.

J2434. Man saved from well by rope. Disastrous attempt to save him from tree in same way. Iran: Kelsey MULLAH 113-118.

J2449.1* Coyote insists on learning secret of sapsucker's hairdo. Refuses to believe true recipe so sapsucker tells to use pitch. Coyote approaches too near flame and catches on fire. Native American (California): Curry DOWN 88-89.

J2450 - J2499. Literal fools.

J2450. Literal fool.

J2461. What should I have done (said)? The mother teaches the boy (the man his wife) what he should say (do) in this or that circumstance. He uses the words in the most impossible cases and is always punished. Type 1696.

A* Lazy Jack. Boy loses penny. Put in pocket next time. Milk--carry on head. Cream cheese--in hands. Tom cat--on string. Meat--on shoulder. Donkey. Rich girl laughs. Wed. +H341.1. England: Galdone OBEDIENT pb; Hutchinson CHIMNEY CORNER STORIES 101-106; Jacobs ENGLISH 159-161; Jacobs LAZY pb; Martignoni ILLUSTRATED 163-164; Rockwell THREE 92-99; Steel ENGLISH 51-54; Werth LAZY JACK pb. Maitland IDLE pb. TALL.. NURSERY 71-73.

Aa* Jack and the King's Girl. To make King's daughter laugh (H341.2). Jack carries needle behind. "Stick in shirt." Sword. "Carry on shoulder." Colt. "Ride." Heifer. Princess laughs. Wed. Type 371. U. S. (Appalachia): Chase JACK 83-88.

B* Epaminondas. Boy brings cake in hands--carry in hat. Butter--wrap in leaves and cool in stream. Puppy--on string. Ham. Kept home. Be careful how you step in pies. Steps carefully in each. Bryant EPAMINONDOUS pb /Colwell SECOND 35-38/. Merriam EPAMINON-DOUS pb.

C* Tony Di-Moany. Lets wind carry flour home (J1881.1.8). To tie to donkey's back next time. Pig. To lead on rope. Copper kettle. Wrap in straw. Needle. +J2176, J1902.1.1, J2431. Majorca: Mehdevi BUNGLING 57-67.

D* How Pat Got Sense. Take dog to gather sheep. He drags it on rope. "Remember four legs travel faster than two." He sends table to go by self. "Take in cart." Matches. "In pocket." Honey. "In jar." Puppy. "Tie on string." Leg of beef. Fenner TIME 3-16 /Gruenberg MORE 255-260/.

E* Silly Saburo. Told to dig potatoes and spread in sun--finds pot of gold. To wrap up what you find dead--dead cat. Throw in river --tree stump. Break into pieces--teapot. Japan: Sakade JAPANESE..FAVORITES 45-48.

F* Discreet Hans. Carries needle in hay. Knife in sleeve, kid in pocket, bacon on rope, calf on head, girl puts in stall. Weds. Germany (Grimm): Grimm GRIMM'S (Scribner's) 95-98; Grimm GRIMM'S (World) 312-317

(+J2462.2, casts sheep's eyes at her); Grimm HOUSEHOLD 140-144 (+J2462.2); Wiggin TALES 90-92.

G* Jack the Fool. Needle in hay, butter in coat, milk on leaf, puppy in can, mutton on string. Ireland: MacManus WELL 156-157.

H* Pedro de Malas Artes. Pig on back. Jug on string. Needle in hay. Portugal: Lowe LITTLE 84-89.

I* The Suitor is Given Gifts. Penknife in hay, chickenfat in pocket. Silver coin in hay, eggs in purse, duck in basket covered with straw, goldfish in cage. Fools decide road is dangerous since all gifts meet disaster. Jewish: Singer ZLATEH 39-50.

J* Ah Po thinks mussels are clicking and sighing at him, throws into river, dives after them and clothes are stolen, takes red funeral cloth for covering, is beaten. Mother says he should have expressed sympathy--wedding passes--give congratulations--house burns--throw water --blacksmith--offer help--boys smearing paint on walls--stop them--painter, etc. China: Wyndham FOLK..CHINA 22-25.

K* The Fool. Old man brings home needle in bundle of twigs. "Stick in robe." Wheel axle. "Drag on rope." Puppy. "Call and it will follow." Hare. "Say: Stop like a stone." Stranger. "Say: A happy day and many more like it to you." Funeral. "What a misfortune." Wedding. Turkmenian: Ginsburg KAHA 131-137.

J2461.1.9* Told to hitch horses two before and two behind, numskull hitches two behind the wagon. Hungary: Jagendorf NOODLEHEAD 207-211.

J2461.2. Literal following of instructions about greetings. Numskull gives wrong greeting and is told how to give correct one. When he tries it, however, the conditions are wrong. SEE ALSO: J2671.2.1. Turkmenian: Ginsburg KAHA 131-137 (+J2461K).

A* Boy and the Cloth: Told to salaam, salaams to donkeys--say "Fri Fri," says to birds--say "Lag, Lag," says to thieves--say "Let go of this one and take another," funeral. Kashmir: Courlander TIGER'S 80-82.

B* Soap, Soap, Soap. Boy sent to buy soap. Repeats the phrase. He slips in mud and forgets phrase. Man says, "It's slick as soap." Boy repeats and is thought to be mocking man. Say, "Sorry I done it, won't do it again." Etc. Old woman in ditch. Man with wagon stuck. One-eyed man. Woman with child fallen in creek. Sends him home to get soap and wash. Boy remembers his mission and buys the soap. His mother washes him and hangs him by shirttail on the line to dry. +J2671.2.1. U.S.: Chase WICKED 130-136.

C* Just say hic. Boy repeats "hic" meaning

'salt' and 'nothing', fishermen say "May there be five or ten", funeral--"God bless his soul", dead fish--"oh what a smell", ladies--"oh how lovely", fighting man--"please sir stop fighting sir", stops fighting--"out dog", shoemaker says nothing, i.e. "hic", repeats hic and remembers to buy salt. +J2671.2.1. Turkey: Walker JUST SAY HIC pb.

D* Silly Jean. Takes wheat to mill. To answer if anyone asks way to Cassoway. Tells farmer with runaway goat how to go to Cassoway. Should have said "So you're leading your goat to the fair." Meets bridal procession. Say "going for a promenade." Meets firemen. Throw water on fire--farmer's wife's oven. Say "So you're working"--tramp asleep. "So you're taking a rest." Miller. Switzerland (French): Duvoisin THREE 38-43.

E* Boy to ask someone when his tripe is washed enough, calls in sailors on sea. Should have said "May you have a strong wind." Says this to reapers. Say "Let nothing make them fall." Bird catcher. "May there be much blood." Men fighting. "May God separate them." Bride and groom. "May there be many days like this one." Funeral. "May our Lord take him straight to Heaven." Baptism. Portugal: Lowe LITTLE 84-89.

F* Told to rub elbows with people. Does so literally with threshers. Should say "May there be no end to your carting." Funeral. "Oh the pity of it." Wedding. Dance and pipe. Burning barn. Throw water. Hog being singed. Russia: Deutsch MORE 85-93.

G* Literal following of instructions about greetings--The Suitor. Mother instructs him what to say. "How are you and why are you always at home?" Meets her on street. "Let's go dancing"--at father's wake, "May he go to heaven"--butchering pigs, "May you have many more like this one, big and fat"--going to have wart removed, "may it dry up and disappear"--planting rose, "May it grow deep roots and last a thousand years"--thorn in palm. He is thrown out. Majorca: Mehdevi BUNGLING 93-98.

J2461.4.1* Boy sent for honey told to take what he needs from storehouse. Eats up provisions. Fenner TIME 3-16 /Gruenberg MORE 255-260/.

J2461.7. To sell some cloth for four rupees. Fool refuses to take six rupees for it. Kashmir: Courlander TIGER'S 80-82.

J2461.10* Kampuaa, hog-boy, told to provide taro for family, digs up neighbor's patch. Told never to steal from neighbor, he steals from chief. Never to steal chief's hens again, steals rooster. Captured by chief. Chief says, "May I never be troubled by your trickery again." Kamapuaa kills chief so that this may be so. Hawaii: Thompson HAWAIIAN..TRICKSTERS 49-53.

J2462.2. Foolish bridegroom follows instructions literally. Type 1685. Casting sheep's eyes at bride. The foolish bridegroom is told to cast sheep's eyes at the bride. He buys some at the butcher shop. Throws them at her. Germany (Grimm): Grimm HOUSEHOLD 140-144 (+J2461).

J2463.3. Three foolish brides sent home. First knocked ashes of pipe onto father-in-law's bald head. Second carried embers in a horsehair sifter. Third let neighbor put hands in her bosom to warm. Korea: Kim STORY 56-57.

J2465.4* Disastrous following of instructions. Washing the child. Fool uses boiling water. Kills it. Mexico: Brenner BOY 14-18 (mother washed).

J2466.2. The reckoning of the pot. A man counts the days of the fast month by throwing a pebble each day into the pot. His daughter throws a handful of pebbles in. Asked the day of the month, he says that it is the 125th. Turkey: Downing HODJA 78.

J2469.3. Dividing all they have. So advised, they cut their beds, houses, etc. in two. Russia (Assyrian): Ginsburg TWELVE 62-63 (still waiting for soaking axe to soften so can be divided).

J2470. Metaphors literally interpreted. SEE: J163.2.2 (coat of clay); K1413 (guarding the door).

J2478. The numskull buys water at market. He looks at bread. The merchant: "It is as good as butter." The merchant: "It is as sweet as oil." He decides on oil. The merchant: "It is as clear as water." He decides on water. Pakistan: Siddiqui TOONTOONY 61-64 (miser). Jewish: Simon WISE 77-78 (hens rich as schmaltz--oil--water); Suhl SIMON pb.

J2495.1.1* Prayer in tiny mosque is more efficacious than prayer in large mosque. "You should be ashamed. Your little son did what you could not." Turkey: Downing HODJA 29; Kelsey MULLAH 95-99.

J2496.1. Boy who worked for "nothing at all" goes to town and demands "nothing at all." SEE ALSO: J1521.5.2; J1802.1. Turkey: Downing HODJA 23-24.

J2496.3* Three travelers know each one phrase of a foreign language. They incriminate themselves. Three Haitians in Dominican Republic. Dominican Republic: Jagendorf KING 106-110. SEE ALSO: J1802.1.

J2499.8* Told to dress the chicken for dinner, clothes it. Louisiana French: Leach NOODLES 26-27.

J2499.9* Told to put out the light. Puts it outdoors. Louisiana French: Leach NOODLES 26-27.

J2499.10* Timekeeper for church rings bells by clockmaker's clock. Clockmaker sets his clocks by church bells. China: Lum TALES 4.

J2500 - J2549. Foolish extreme.

J2500. Foolish extremes.

J2511. The silence wager. A man and his wife make a wager as to who shall speak first (close the door). The man (woman) becomes jealous and scolds: loses the wager. Turkey: Downing HODJA 30-31. SEE ALSO: T255.8 (silent wife); T255.4.

J2511.0.1* The silence wager. Thief robs couple and rubs soot on their faces. In morning wife cries "your face is black!" India: Jagendorf NOODLEHEAD 34-36.

J2511.0.2* First to speak must water calf in future. Beggar takes food from silent husband, barber shaves him and receiving no pay shaves off beard and ruins hair, passing woman takes him for a female and puts wig and make-up on him, thief robs house, returning wife sees "woman" and speaks. Persia: Mehdevi PERSIAN 93-103. Jewish: Simon MORE 16-23 (-thief and woman's wig).

J2511.0.3* First to speak must close door. Cat and dog eat sugar, thief eats pie and steals silver, wife talks when he takes teapot. Husband: "close the door." Dobbs ONCE 105-109. Netherlands: De Leeuw HOLLAND 97-100 (must return paffertjes pan, Burgomaster takes possessions away as fine for silence, husband talks when pipe is taken). Bulgaria: Pridham GIFT 30-34. Russia: Ginsburg LAZIES 8-10; Higonnet-Schnopper TALES 30-33 (to wash pot, both in bed all day, neighbor told to care for them and take coat as wages, wife speaks).

J2511.0.3.1* First to speak must do dishes rest of life. Husband is put into coffin silent but wife speaks. Why women wash the dishes. Philippines: Robertson PHILIPPINES 71-80.

J2511.1.2.1* Abu Nowas and wife feign dead to receive money in aid from king and queen. King told by Abu Nowas that his wife died. Queen told by wife that Abu Nowas died. They each give gifts. Later go to solve argument as to which is dead and find both arrayed as corpses. King: "I'd give one thousand gold pieces to know the truth about this." Abu Nowas sits up. "Give them to me." Tunis: Lang CRIMSON 158-167. Poland: Frost LEGENDS 49-54 (jester); Haviland FAVORITE..POLAND 82-90 (Matenko, jester).

J2512.1* Mustn't mention the robe. Visiting with friend who is wearing his robe, man says "This is my robe." He is rebuked so at next house they visit he says "This is his robe." Rebuked again. At next house he says "The robe...we mustn't say anything about it, must we?" Iran: Shah MULLA 63.

J2516. Directions followed literally.

J2516.3.2. The polite rescuers. Pupils are taught to clap their hands and say "God bless you" when one sneezes. As they are rescuing a drowning man by a rope he sneezes. They all clap their hands and he falls back into the water. SEE ALSO: J2133.5. Carpenter ELEPHANT'S 125-134.

J2516.9. "Forsee the possible event." Asked to call a doctor when his master falls ill, the fool also calls the undertaker. Iran: Shah MULLA 119.

J2517. Couldn't wait to dress. The overzealous visitor rides naked to see his friends. Turkey: Downing HODJA 66.

J2549. Other foolish extremes.

J2549.1* He wakes wife in the middle of the night and makes her fetch a candle so he can write down inspired poem. When completed it consists of two absurd lines. Turkey: Downing HODJA 96.

J2549.2* Numskull runs after wedding procession to tell daughter that he forgot important advice: always tie a knot in the end of thread before trying to thread a needle. Turkey: Downing HODJA 86.

J2549.3* He refuses to read prayers over dead friend. They have had a quarrel and he knows friend wouldn't listen. Turkey: Downing HODJA 19.

J2550 - J2599. Thankful fools.

J2561. Fool thanks God that he was not sitting on the ass when it was stolen. Turkey: Downing HODJA 14. Leach LUCK 62.

J2562. Thankful that the recipe is left. A hawk (buzzard) steals the fool's meat. He is grateful that the recipe remains. Turkey: Downing HODJA 94; Walker WATERMELONS 67 (it won't do you any good--I've got the recipe; crow). Iran: Shah MULLA 35.

J2563. "Thank God they weren't peaches!" A man plans to take peaches as a present to the king. He is persuaded rather to take figs. They are green and the king has them thrown in his face. He is thankful that they weren't peaches. +J2415.1. Turkey: Downing HODJA 82 (figs not beets); Kelsey HODJA 46-53 (figs not beets); Walker TALES 229-232. Type 1689. Iran: Shah MULLA 141 (figs not turnips). Jewish: Jagendorf NOODLEHEAD 59-62 (neighbor took figs and was rewarded--he has them thrown at him, lucky they weren't peaches).

J2564. "Thank God that camels have no wings." They might fly about and kill people. Turkey: Downing HODJA 16.

J2566. One fewer to pay for. A man carries blind men over a stream at a certain price per head. One falls down and drowns. He comforts the others that there is one fewer to pay for. Turkey: Downing HODJA 84.

J2571. "Thank Fortune it wasn't a melon." Man contends that melons should not grow on slender vines but on tall trees. He is hit on the nose by a falling nut. Is thankful it wasn't a melon. Turkey: Downing HODJA 54 (walnuts--eggplants); Jagendorf NOODLEHEAD 102-104 (Hodja -- walnuts, watermelons); Kelsey HODJA 79-85 (pumpkin, walnuts) /Cathon PERHAPS 201-204/; Walker WATERMELONS 27-28 (walnuts, watermelons). Indonesia: Bro MOUSE DEER 49-54 (pumpkins, dates: Kantjil sees date fall on man's head and praises wisdom of Allah). Kashmir: Courlander TIGER'S 76.

J2600 - J2649. Cowardly fool.

J2600. Cowardly fool.

J2612. The attack on the hare (crayfish). Seven men make strenuous plans for the attack on the fierce animal. One screams with fright and the animal runs away. SEE ALSO: J1736.1.1. Germany (Grimm): Carle ERIC 89-93; Gag MORE 1-7 (Seven Swabians); Wiggin TALES 162-164.

J2613. Surrender to the rake. Fool steps on a rake and falls down crying, "I surrender." Germany (Grimm): Gag MORE 1-7.

J2632.1* Asked to frighten quail, teacher scares boy's mother and self as well. Iran: Shah MULLA 29.

J2633. Tiger frightened of leak in house. Overhears householder say he fears leak. SEE ALSO: N392.1.1. India: Courlander RIDE 46-52 ("perpetual dripping"); Price VALIANT; Wiggin FAIRY 406-414. Southeast China: Hume FAVORITE..CHINA 109-114 (Luo).

J2650 - J2699. Bungling fool.

J2650. Bungling fool.

J2661.0.1. Being rescued from under tree fool is set on sharp splintered stump, dropped from stretcher, etc. Liberia (Gio): Dorliae ANIMALS 26-31.

J2663. Bungling fool carries milk in hat. Turns it inside out and puts eggs in other side. Turns back to show where milk was put. Russia (Moldavia): Ginsburg TWELVE 57-59.

J2671.2.1. Fool's talking to himself thought to be inappropriate greeting. He keeps repeating a word to remember it but changes it so that it seems to refer unfavorably to people whom he meets. SEE ALSO: J2461.2. U.S. (Appalachia): Chase WICKED 130-136. Jacobs MORE 211-214 (stupid's cries, lad sent to market).

Turkey: Walker JUST pb.

J2671.4. Foolish messenger muddles message.

J2671.4.1. The Bojabi Tree. Animals must get name of tree from old woman to make fruit fall. Several animals try, all forget name on return by stumbling. Tortoise succeeds. West Africa: Williams-Ellis ROUND 186-191. East Africa: Heady JAMBO 46-53; Rickert THE BOJABI TREE pb.

J2671.4.1.1* Animals who are sent to Mavera, High God, for name of tree forget. Tortoise returns with name but animals trample him in effort to pick fruit. Ants fasten his shell back together (A2312.1.1). Tortoise uproots tree, killing animals. Domanska TORTOISE pb.

J2671.4.2* Pig told by judge he may have "corn and peas and silken bed." Pig chants to remember. Fox chants "scraps and slops and a bed of mud" confuses pig who tells farmer he was awarded the latter (A2433.3.6). Norway: Sperry HEN 39-46 /Sperry SCANDINAVIAN 44-48/.

J2671.5* Silly Matt. Forgets wife's name and looks for it on ground. Digs for it. Man tells him name. He runs to return spade, drops it and forgets again. Chants "Solvy, Solvy is my darling" when trying to remember. Norway: Jagendorf NOODLEHEAD 180-183.

J2672. The stolen bedcover. A man hears a noise outside the house at night. He wraps a bed cover about him and goes to investigate. The robbers take the bed cover and flee. The wife asks what the debate was about. "About the bed cover. When they got it, the quarrel was over." Turkey: Downing HODJA 15; Kelsey HODJA 45-47. Iran: Shah MULLA 33.

J2689.1* Master puts on mismatched pair of shoes. Sends servant back for other pair. Servant returns empty-handed. Second pair is same as first. China: Jagendorf NOODLEHEAD 75-77; Leach NOODLES 22.

J2700 - J2749. The easy problem made hard.

J2700. The easy problem made hard.

J2711.1* How the tower was built. Asked to judge among three answers: A. It fell from heaven. B. It was built in a well. C. It grew like cacti. None are correct. Answer: It was built by a giant with a longer reach than ours. Iran: Shah MULLA 130.

J2712.1. Guess what I have in my hand and I will give it to you to make egg-cake with. What does it look like? White outside and yellow inside. It is a hollowed turnip filled with carrots. Turkey: Downing HODJA 78.

J2712.2. Guess how many eggs I have and you

shall get all seven. Leach NOODLES 11.

J2712.3* Man coming out of vineyard. "Guess what I have in my basket?" Italy: Cimino DISOBEDIENT #11.

J2712.4* We have a new baby! A boy? No. A girl? What a good guesser! Italy: Cimino DISOBEDIENT #5.

J2722. Telling their horses apart. One fool docks the tail of his horse. The horse of the second gets tail caught in gate, is docked too. One notches the ear of his horse; the second notches its ear on the fence. Finally they measure height of their horses. The black horse is taller than the white. Leach NOODLES 21.

J2723. The sombreros of the men of Lagos: Six men sit on bench with their sombreros beside them. Arriving, six more men have no place to sit. All rise, don sombreros to pull bench to stretch it. Now they fit. Mexico: Jagendorf NOODLEHEAD 268-270.

J2724* Coyote insists recipe for sour acorn cakes must be more difficult than women say. They finally reveal their "secret" to get rid of him. He is given a long, painful set of directions. Native American (Yorok): Robinson COYOTE 95-105.

J2750. Other aspects of wisdom or foolishness.

J2752. Traveler asks how long it will take to reach the next town and receives no reply. He starts walking away and is answered. "Why didn't you answer when I first asked you?" I had to see how fast you were walking." Turkey: Walker TALES 232; Walker WATERMELONS 60-61.

K. DECEPTIONS

K0 - K99. Contests won by deception.

K0. Contest won by deception--general.

K2.1. Fortune to go to direction cat jumps. King will give wealth to person toward whom the cat jumps. Clever warrior has brought mouse along and thus entices the cat.

K2.1.1* Bag of gold to carver whose mouse cat pounces. One carves of dried fish. Japan: Sakade JAPANESE CHILDREN'S STORIES 74-76.

K2.1.2* King rubs catnip on his cat to make kitten come to it. Wife points out that his cat is a male and couldn't be cat's mother. Chile: Carpenter SOUTH AMERICAN 83-42.

K5. Contest with magician won by deception. SEE: D1711.0.1.

K10. Athletic contest won by deception.

K11.1. Race won by deception: relative helpers. One of the contestants places his relatives (or others that resemble him) in the line of the race. The opponent always thinks the trickster is just ahead of him. (Told of animals or men; often of the hare and the turtle.)

K11.1.0.1* Ants defeat elephant. India: Reed TALKATIVE 28-29.

K11.1.0.2* Chameleon defeats elephant. Africa: Green ANIMAL 16.

K11.1.0.3* Hedgehog and wife defeat hare. England: De La Mare ANIMALS 3-8 /De La Mare TALES 9-14/; Hutchinson FIRESIDE 67-73; Wiggin TALES 340-343 /Association TOLD.. GREEN 30-35/. Germany (Grimm): Gag MORE 163-170; Grimm HEDGEHOG AND THE HARE pb; Gruenberg MORE 114-147.

K11.1.0.3.1* Hedgehog tricks fox. Poland: Domanska BEST pb.

K11.1.0.4* Jabuty tricks jaguar. Brazil: Carpenter LATIN 43-49.

K11.1.0.5* Terrapin defeats hare. U.S. (Black): Courlander Terrapin's 28-30; Harris FAVORITE 86-90 /Harris COMPLETE 57-60/, /Harris SONGS 87-93/, /Brown WORLD 117-121/. Native American (Cherokee): Bell JOHN 58-60; Scheer CHEROKEE 37-42.

K11.1.0.6* Toad tricks donkey. W. Indies: Sherlock IGUANA'S 43-52.

K11.1.0.6.1* Toad tricks horse. Haiti: Wolkstein MAGIC 143-150.

K11.1.0.7* Tortoise defeats reedbuck. Congo (Luban): Burton MAGIC 95-98.

K11.1.0.7.1* Tortoise jumps over elephant, wife lands on other side. E. Africa: Heady SAFIRI 62-65.

K11.1.0.8* Turtle defeats Brer Rabbit. U.S. (Black, South Carolina): Faulkner DAYS 132-136.

K11.1.0.8.1* Turtle defeats lion in swimming contest. Turtle holds hibiscus in mouth as identifier, maid on opposite bank holds same. Ceylon: Arnott ANIMAL 190-194; Tooze THREE..TURTLE 45-61.

K11.1.0.8.2* Turtle defeats carabao. +A2376.1.0.1. Philippines (Tagalog): Sechrist ONCE 56-60.

K11.1.0.8.3* Turtle defeats Anansi. Jamaica: Sherlock ANANSI 47-57 /Arbuthnot ANTHOLOGY 396-398/.

K11.1.0.8.4* Turtle defeats bear, he races under ice. Native American (Seneca): Parker SKUNNY 171-186. Native American (Iroquois): Bruchac TURKEY 23-25.

K11.1.0.9* Snail defeats monkey. Liberia (Mano): Dorliae ANIMALS 22-25.

K11.1.0.9.1* Snail defeats Kantchil (mousedeer). Indonesia: Asia FOLK..THREE 18-22.

K11.1.1* Relative helpers. Miscellaneous.

K11.1.1.1* Race for chief's daughter. Chief's daughter to one who returns with packet of salt from ocean first. Tortoise has relatives along way. E. Africa: Heady SAFIRI 87-92.

K11.1.1.2* Calling contest. Coucal and Elephant call to wives to prepare dinner. Coucal's call is soft but other coucal's pass message on. He wins bet. E. Africa: Heady SAFIRI 27-30.

K11.2. Race won by deception: riding on the back. One contestant rides on the other's back. SEE ALSO: K25.1.

K11.2.0.1* Chameleon clings to Cheetah's tail (B236.0.1). Baganda: Kaula AFRICAN 67-70.

K11.2.0.1.1* Chameleon clings to elephant's tail. Wins race. Green ANIMAL 16.

K11.2.0.2* Crab rides Fox's tail. Virgin Islands: Cothran MAGIC 73-74.

K11.2.0.3* Cricket rides Fox. U.S. (Black): Harris FAVORITE 30-34; Harris COMPLETE 772-779.

K11.2.0.4* Frog on tiger's tail, jumping contest. S.W. China: Hume FAVORITE..CHINA 9-14.

K11.2.0.5* Horsefly on fox's tail. Chile: Jagendorf KING 69-71.

K11.2.0.6* Lobster hangs on to fox's tail. Russia: Carrick STILL MORE 61-63.

K11.2.0.7* Turtle on beaver's tail, nips tail at end of race and is thrown over his head by tail jerk. Native American (Seneca): Bruchac

TURKEY 20-22; Parker SKUNNY 165-170.

K11.2.1. The lame boy frees the tall boy on condition he carry him along in race. Tall boy rests near finish line and lame boy goes ahead and wins race. N. Africa (Biskra): Holding KING'S 117-125.

K11.3. Hare and Tortoise Race: sleeping hare. In a race between the fast and the slow animal, the fast animal sleeps on the road and allows the slow animal to pass him. Aesop: Aesop AESOP'S (Golden) 83-85; Aesop AESOP'S (Grosset) 34-35; Aesop AESOP'S (Random) 33-36; Aesop AESOP'S (Viking) 30-31; Aesop AESOP'S (Watts) 92; Aesop FABLES (Macmillan) 135; Aesop FABLES (Walck) 68-73; Aesop FIVE 70; Aesop HARE (illus. Galdone) pb; Arbuthnot FAIRY 230; Du Bois HARE AND THE TURTLE pb; Kent AESOP'S 16-19; Martignoni ILLUSTRATED 157; Rockwell OLD 48-51; TALL..NURSERY 105-107. La Fontaine: La Fontaine HARE (illus. Wildsmith) pb. Nigeria: Walker NIGERIAN 45-46.

K11.5. Race won by deception: Sham-sick trickster. The trickster feigns lameness and receives a handicap in the race. He then returns and eats up the food which is the prize. Native American: Marriott WINTER 45-54 (coyote tricks Saynday). Native American (Great Plains): Jones COYOTE 15-22 (fox tricks coyote).

K11.6. Race won by deception: rabbit is 'little son' substitute. A man challenged by an ogre to a running race persuades the ogre to race with his little son instead. By this he means a rabbit. Type 1072. SEE ALSO: K1781.

A* The Boy and the Necken: Youngest brother left only ropes as inheritance. Snares squirrel, hare, bear. Little water-sprite (necken) is sent from lake by father to see what boy is doing. Says he is going to tie up lake. Necken challenges to tree-climbing match--sends squirrel. Race--hare. Wrestling match--bear's grandfather. Necken gives hat full of gold to go away. Digs hole under hat. Sweden: Haviland FAVORITE..SWEDEN 2-13; Kaplan FAIRY 200-208.

B* How the Devil was outsmarted by a man. Man meets Devil, says he is looking for something to make rope to catch devils--given gold to desist. Devil wrestles with grandfather (bear). Races son (hare). Whistling contest. Man blindfolds Devil first, hits over head as whistles (K84.1). Devil flees. Hardendorff JUST 127-132.

K11.9. Obstacle race between deer and hare. Hare accused of removing obstacles from his course. +A2326.1.1.1.1.* (Deer's horns). Native American (Cherokee): Bell JOHN 67-69; Scheer CHEROKEE 55-57.

K11.10* Race won by deception. Beetle wins green and gold coat given by parrot (A2411.3.3). Brazil: Carpenter SOUTH

AMERICAN 108-113 (Paca dawdles); Newman FOLK 67-71 (rat).

K11.11* Race won by deception. Snail rides downstream on piece of wood. Indonesia: Bro MOUSE DEER 107-117.

K11.12* Race downhill. Porcupine rolls down. Russia: Dolch OLD RUSSIA 11-17.

K15.2* Climbing match. Monkey reaches top of the tree first. Tortoise bets double he can reach ground first. Jumps. Panama: Carter ENCHANTED 83-86.

K16.2. Diving match: trickster eats food while dupe is under water.

K16.2.0.1* Anansi tricks land turtle, takes money. Jamaica: Sherlock ANANSI 47-57 /Arbuthnot ANTHOLOGY 396-398/.

K16.2.0.2* Terrapin tricks mink. Harris FAVOR-ITE 113-117 /Harris COMPLETE 386-389/, /Harris NIGHTS 373-376/.

K16.2.0.3* Hare tricks elephant. Burton MAGIC 81-84.

K17.1. Contest: Jumping into the ground. A hole is already dug and covered with boughs. Type 1086. E. Africa: Heady SAFIRI 31-33 (chameleon challenges elephant to stomping contest).

K17.1.1. Contest: Who can go deepest into the earth? Wren goes into mouse hole. Type 278. Germany (Grimm): Green BIG 47-51; Grimm GRIMM'S (Follett) 150-153; Wiggin TALES 172-175.

K17.5* Jumping contest won by deception. Hare calls "Go" when fox's attention is distracted. Finland: Bowman TALES..TUPA 253.

K17.6* Deceptive stomping contest. To stomp on other's foot, Kantchil digs sharp hoof into Elephant's foot and wins. Indonesia: Bro HOW 88-95.

K18. Throwing contest won by deception. SEE ALSO: G501 (Stupid ogre); K1781; K1746.

K18.2. Throwing contest: golden club on the cloud. Trickster shows the ogre the club he has thrown (really only a bright spot on the cloud; K1746). SEE ALSO: G501. Rumania: Ure RUMANIAN 101-113 (Battle axe on moon).

K18.3. Throwing contest: bird substituted for stone. The ogre throws a stone; the hero a bird which flies out of sight. SEE: G501 (Stupid ogre); K1951.1 (Seven at a blow).

K18.4* Throwing contest: trickster has a stick, drops behind him and pretends to have thrown it out of sight. Dragon gives iron rod to throw. Gypsy: Arnott ANIMAL 66-70.

K18.5* Throwing the stone into the cliff. A mud clod is thrown. Ireland: MacManus BOLD 120-137 (+K1951.1K).

K22. Deceptive tug-of-war. Small animal challenges two large animals to a tug-of-war. Arranges it so that they unwittingly pull against each other (on one end of rope that is tied to a tree).

K22.0.1* Hare arranges tug between elephant and hippo. E. Africa: Heady JAMBO SUNGURA 18-22. Bantu: Arnott AFRICAN 153-155. Nigeria: Schatz EXTRAORDINARY pb.

K22.0.2* Porcupine arranges tug between elephant and hippo. Africa (Baluba): Kaula AFRICAN 72-76.

K22.0.3* Tortoise (Jabuty) arranges tug with whale and tapir. Brazil (Amazon): Carpenter LATIN 36-42. South America: Maestro TORTOISE'S pb.

K22.0.4* Tortoise arranges tug between elephant and hippo. +A2433.6.1.3. Nigeria: Walker NIGERIAN 59-60. Africa: Montgomerie MERRY 28-31.

K22.0.5* Hare (B'Rabby) arranges tug between elephant and whale. +A2433.3.15.1; +A2433.7.1. Bahama Negro: Leach HOW 80-81. Louisiana: Cothran WITH 34-39. Africa: Tracy LION 26-29.

K22.1* Trickster sells fictitious horse to elephants for one hundred baskets of corn and to hippopotamus for one hundred baskets of fish. Changes tug so that each family thinks it is pulling in horse. N. Nigeria (Hausa): Aardema MORE 32-37 (Golden); Arnott ANIMAL 202-209 (spider). Nigeria (Hausa): Sturton ZOMO 114-125 /Arbuthnot ANTHOLOGY 318-320/ (hare).

K22.2* Deceptive tug-of-war. Large animal's tail tied to tree root.

K22.2.0.1* Wattle weasel tricked by Brer Rabbit. U.S. (Georgia, Black): Harris COMPLETE 347-351; Harris NIGHTS 319-324.

K22.2.0.2* Terrapin tricks Brer Rabbit. U.S. (Georgia, Black): Brown WORLD 122-126; Harris FAVORITE 95-99; Harris COMPLETE 83-87; Harris UNCLE REMUS 126-131.

K23. Deceptive shinny match. Mih-kit-tee prairie falcon defeats crow by magic. Crow had won other animal's parts (tongue, leg, etc.) in previous games. Must now repay. North American (California, Yokut): Cothran WITH 56-64.

K25.1. Flying contest won by deception: riding on the other. Wren hides in eagle's wings. Type 221. (cf. K11.2). Scotland: Montgomerie TWENTY-FIVE 54-55. Wales: Sheppard-Jones WELSH 59-62. Germany (Grimm): Green BIG 47-51; Grimm GRIMM'S (Follett) 150-153; Wiggin TALES 172-175.

K25.1.1* Flying to Tonga: butterfly challenges crane to fly to Tonga. Rides back. Crane fails to make distance and drowns. Butterfly too is lost. Fiji: Arnott ANIMAL 161-165.

K31. Shooting contest won by deception.

K31.1. Contest: shooting an unheard of bird. The man sends his wife on all fours in tar and feathers. The ogre has never heard of such a bird. To lose soul to devil if he can't produce animal he's never seen before. (cf. K216.2; K1691). Netherlands (Friesland): Spicer THIRTEEN DEVILS 25-32. France: Cooper FIVE 58-75. Poland: Borski GOOD 72-74 (hog offers to save him if he'll wed her, after washing off honey and feathers she turns to lovely maid, enchantment broken). European: Lurie CLEVER 1-8.

K31.4* Skill proven by deception: hit on back as he shoots, arrow hits bird in neck. Claims he is so humiliated for having missed bird's eye that he'll never shoot again. Indonesia: Courlander KANTCHIL'S 122-128.

K32. Trapping contest won by deception.

K32.1* Mean farmer takes fish from neighbor's net and puts sticks from his net into neighbor's net. Willow root turns to magic helpful dog. +D1571.1. Japan: Novak: FAIRY 184-190.

K42.1. Threshing contest. Type 1089. Ireland: MacManus BOLD 120-137 (+K1951.1K, he paralyzes grain so no chaff flies).

K42.2. Mowing contest won by trickery. The man takes the center of the field. The one is given a dull sickle and mows around the outside of the field. SEE ALSO: K171.1. Ireland: MacManus BOLD 120-127. +K1951.1K. England (Northamptonshire): Conger TOPS pb.

K46. Tree-pulling contest.

K46.1. Strong man pushes over trees previously weakened to intimidate opponent. Opponent gives up contest. Haiti: Courlander PIECE 105-110. U.S. (Alabama): Courlander TERRAPIN'S 69-73.

K47.1* Sewing contest won by deception: the long thread. The ogre sews with the whole length of the thread. When he has returned from first stitch, the tailor has finished his task. Type 1096. SEE ALSO: K1781.1.

K50. Endurance contest won by deception.

K51. Waking contest won by deception. England: Wiggin TALES 339 (cock, cuckoo and blackcock).

K52.1. Contest in seeing sunrise first: sun on the trees. The fox places himself on a hill facing east; the hog in a lower place facing high trees to the west. The sun shines on the top of the trees and the hog wins (sometimes told

with human actors). Slovenia: Kavcic GOLDEN 71-77 (man sees sun on mountain +J151.1).

K52.3* Mouse climbs onto camel's hump and wins. Why first year in Chinese year is Year of the Mouse. Steppes: Masey STORIES 118-121.

K54* Contest in sitting still on branch. Heron yells at monkey and he falls off in fright. Hardendorff JUST 98-104.

K60. Absurd contest won by deception.

K61. Contest in pushing hole in tree. Hole prepared beforehand. Hero and ogre to vie in pushing a hole in tree with their heads. Ceylon: Tooze WONDERFUL 55-58 (pushes hole in wall).

K62. Contest in squeezing water from a stone. The ogre squeezes a stone; the trickster a cheese or egg. Types 1060, 1640. SEE: G501 (stupid ogre); K1951.1 (seven at a blow); B335.2 (Little Bull Calf). Russia: Downing RUSSIAN 81-99. +K213 (Devil in knapsack).

K62.1* Contest in beating dust from flint with sledge hammer. Brer Rabbit has ashes in slippers, cracks heels together each time he swings. U.S. (Black): Faulkner DAY 141-145; Harris FAVORITE 108-112; Harris COMPLETE 98-101; Harris SONGS 149-153.

K63. Contest in biting a stone. The ogre bites a stone. The man a nut. Types 1061, 1640. Russia: Downing RUSSIAN 81-99. +K213 (Devil in knapsack).

K70. Contest in strength won by deception.

K71. Deceptive contest in carrying a tree: riding, the trickster has the dupe carry the branches of a tree while he carries the trunk. He rides on the trunk. U.S. (Georgia): Manning-Sanders BOOK..GIANTS 18-24. +G501. SEE ALSO: K1915.1 (Seven at a blow). Also occurs in some variants of G501.

K75* Deceptive biting contest. Anansi to pay snake postman by allowing him to take a bite of Anansi's head. Puts pot on head and snake calls off bargain. Jamaica: Carter GREEDY 79-83; Sherlock WEST 71-76.

K80. Contests in other physical accomplishments won by deception.

K81.1. Deceptive eating contest: hole in bag. The hero slips his food into a bag and makes the ogre believe that he is the greater eater. In many versions the hero cuts open the bag; the ogre imitates and kills himself (J2401). SEE: G501 (Stupid Ogre); G512 (Jack the Giant Killer); K1951.1 (Seven at a blow). Norway: Asbjornsen NORWEGIAN 81-83 (G501).

K82.1.1. Deceptive drinking contest: rising and falling tide. Buffalo and heron wager as to which can drink the sea until the water falls. The buffalo drinks as the tide is coming in; the heron drinks in the falling tide and wins. Philippines: Carpenter ELEPHANT'S 91-99 (Egret, ricebird, tickbird contest to decide if he may ride buffalo's back or not, A2433.4.8). Philippines (Tagalog): Sechrist ONCE 43-46 (hummingbird and carabao).

K84.1. Contest in shrieking or whistling. Trickster covers ogre's eyes then beats. Ogre thinks whistling causes pain. Type 1084. Gypsy: Jagendorf GYPSIES' 24-34 (G501). Russia: Hardendorff JUST 127-132 (K11.6B); Spicer THIRTEEN DEVILS (G501).

K84.2* Roaring contest between elephant and tiger (lion). Winner to eat other. +K1715.2.1. Indonesia: Courlander KANTCHIL'S 46-51. Burma: Brockett BURMESE 71-78. Vietnam: Vo-Dinh TOAD 57-64.

K92.4* Gambling contest won by deception. Peasant bets merchant he doesn't have what he needs--eyeglasses for ox. Merchant sends to a friend and telephones ahead. Second merchant bets with peasant and peasant changes request --asks for gaiters for his canary this time. Poland: Borski GOOD 26-28.

K100 - K299. Deceptive bargains.

K100. Deceptive bargains.

K110. Sale of pseudo-magic objects.

K110.1* Rogues cause person to lose in sale of cow. Convince is a donkey (K451.2) or convince to crop tail and ears. In retaliation trickster sells them bill paying hat (K111.1), message carrying hare (K131.1.1), etc. Bulgaria: Pridham GIFT 84-94 (+K842). Finland: Bowman TALES 231-236. Netherlands: Ross BURIED 127-134. Afghanistan: Carpenter ELEPHANT'S 82-90 (+K111.1., K113). Pyle WONDER 163-174 (goat is messenger).

K111.1. Alleged gold-dropping animal sold. Type 1539. Afghanistan: Carpenter ELEPHANT'S 82-90. Ireland: Danaher FOLK TALES 9-18 (hid gold in oats and horse ate--droppings). Greece (Cyclades): Neufeld BEWARE 11-21 (donkey).

K111.1.1* Alleged gold dropping ass sold. Secret of gold dropping from mouth (put gold in mouth) sold for one hundred more coins. Fools are still delighted with purchase. (Merchant shuts self in house and dies in despair at world full of such fools.) Ethiopia (Amhara): Davis LION'S 45-53.

K111.2. Alleged bill-paying hat sold. Previous arrangement with restauranteur. Type 1539. SEE: K110.1. Haiti: Courlander PIECE 39-49. Russia: Higonnet-Schnopper TALES 43-44. Puerto Rico: Alegria THREE 66-73. Finland: Bowman TALES 231-236. Netherlands: Ross Buried 127-134. Puerto Rico: Cothran MAGIC 55-59.

K111.5* Goat producing well sold. Throw pair of horns down in evening and get goat in morning. Ethiopia (Amhur, Eritrea): Courlander FIRE 57-64 /Colwell SECOND 97-103/.

K112.1. Alleged self cooking kettle sold. Type 1534. SEE ALSO: K842. Switzerland (French): Duvoisin THREE 8-15 (beats with stick). Japan: Jagendorf NOODLEHEAD 97-99. Ireland: Danaher FOLKTALES 9-18. Haiti: Courlander PIECE 39-49. Scandinavia: Hardendorff TRICKY 11-22.

K112.1.1* Alleged self-cooking kettle sold. Said to have been rendered useless by buyer by polishing off all magic. Japan: Jagendorf NOODLEHEAD 97-99.

K112.1.2* Alleged self cooking kettle returned. Dupe sold self heating stump it had been sitting on. Scandinavia: Hardendorff TRICKY 11-22.

K112.2. "Soup stone" wins hospitality. Tramp (soldier) makes stone soup (nail, hatchet) for hostess. Says soup would be even better with vegetables, meat added--she produces these. Type 1548. Russia/Yiddish: Ginsburg THREE 25-26 (hatchet). Sweden: Green CLEVER 142-152; Haviland FAVORITE..SWEDEN 14-29; Wiggin TALES 463-467; Zemach NAIL SOUP. Russia: Carey BABA 73-74; Higonnet-Schnopper TALES 45-48; Riordan TALES..CENTRAL 56-58; Wyndham TALES..RUSSIA 38-42 (hatchet). Belgium: Courlander RIDE 186-188. England: Edmonds TRICKSTER 113-119. France: Brown STONE pb.

K113. Pseudo-magic resuscitative object sold. Dupe kills his wife (mother) and is unable to resuscitate her. Bladder of blood under blouse of wife of trickster (K1875.1). Types 1535, 1539. SEE ALSO: K842C; J2411.1. Switzerland (French); Duvoisin THREE 8-15 (whistle). Russia (Georgia): Papashvily YES 67-75 (guitar [chianouri]). Afghanistan: Carpenter ELEPHANT'S 82-90 (green rod, six brothers kill housekeeper). Scandinavia: Hardendorff TRICKY 11-12 (ram's horn). Ireland: Danaher FOLKTALES 9-18 (innkeeper flees at sight of trickster killing wife, no object sold). Turkmenian: Ginsburg KAHA 131-137 (fool believing self dead is revived with whip; J2311.12+). Pyle WONDER 163-174 (horn). Greece (Cyclades): Neufeld BEWARE 11-21 (pipe). Lang GREEN 182-191.

K114.1. Alleged oracular cowhide sold. SEE: K842A. Wales: Pugh TALES 13-19 (+K1051.0.1).

K119.3* Self warming undershirt sold. Trickster tied to millstone carries it around all night to keep warm and is perspiring in morning though left to freeze. China: Chang TALES 11-24.

K119.4* Soldier pretends to be too hot in 'magic' tattered coat. Couple persuade him to trade for fur coat. Russia: Higonnet-Schnopper TALES 15-20.

K119.5* Sale of magic gun. Shoots in air three times and when he gets home birds have fallen in yard and wife is plucking. If anone touches it, it won't work. Haiti: Courlander PIECE 34-49.

K130. Sale of worthless animals.

K130.1* False claim: Man claims ox that travels one thousand li in a day, cock that crows every hour, dog that reads. One comes to verify this. Wife says husband has gone to Peking on ox, cock crows, does so whenever visitor arrives. Dog is teaching in the city, so can't be seen. China: Withers WORLD 70-72.

K131.1.1. Alleged speaking hare sold as messenger. Usually one hare released and accomplice produces second saying it delivered message. SEE ALSO: J2311.0.1.1; K110.1; K842. Afghanistan: Carpenter ELEPHANT'S 82-90. Russia (Georgia): Papashvily YES 67-75. China: Dolch STORIES 83-91 (fox). Pyle WONDER 163-174 (goat). Bulgaria: Pridham GIFT 84-94. Russia: Galdone STRANGE pb; Jameson TALES 43-63.

K131.1.2* Fox alleged to have taken chickens home. One fox released with hens and runs off. Second fox kept at home and chicken dinner served to dupe. China: Chang TALES 11-24.

K131.1.3* Alleged message carrying goat sent home to order dinner. Sold. Lang GREEN 183-191.

K131.2. Bird sold as messenger. Second crow at home, wife accomplice to trick. Russia: Higonnet-Schnopper TALES 34-44.

K134. Deceptive horse sale.

K134.2. The horse swifter than the rain. Caught in the rain, a trickster finds that his horse will not budge. He undresses, puts his clothes under the horse's belly and keeps them dry. When he reaches the king, he reports that his horse has run so fast that he had not time to get wet. The king buys the horse. Turkey: Downing HODJA 67 (king borrows horse and gets wet).

K134.9* Donkey bites and kicks prospective buyers. Returned to seller who didn't plan to sell donkey anyway. "I just wanted everyone to see what I put up with." Turkey: Downing HODJA 92.

K134.10* Woman buys back legs of donkey so driver can't beat, ears, sides, etc. until has all donkey. Next day he beats donkey again--has a new donkey. She buys legs. Haiti: Courlander PIECE 81-83.

K140. Sale of worthless objects.

K144.3.1* Honey eaten by monkey and replaced with mud. Queen passes it around, not aware of exchange, and all agree with her that it is excellent honey. Ethiopia (Amhara): Davis

LION'S 32-44.

K170. Deception through pseudo-simple bargain.

K171. Deceptive division of profits.

K171.0.2.1* Lion uses Anansi and hare on hunt for brains. Claims all meat for self, plans to kill Anansi. Anansi poisons meat and lion dies, accomplice hare sickens. W. Africa: Appiah ANANSE 27-38.

K171.0.2.2* Nansii and hare kill huge bird. Bury it. Nansi returns and takes it to wife to cook. Nansi ties rope to leg and tells wife when soup is done. Hare cuts rope and ties to own leg. Hare is pulled to house by Nansi's wife and fed. Liberia: Aardema TALES 44-48.

K171.1. Deceptive crop division: above the ground, below the ground, of root crops the ogre (stupid animal) chooses the tops; of other crops the roots. (cf. J1230). +K42.2 (Deceptive mowing contests). Type 1030.

K171.1.0.1* Bear and fox: bear gets grain bottoms, turnip tops. Norway: Asbjornsen EAST (Row) 31. Scandinavia: Wiggin TALES 311.

K171.1.0.2* Bear and fox. Bear gets tops of carrots, bottoms of strawberries. Japan: Uchida MAGIC 103-111.

K171.1.0.3* Bear and man. Bear gets wheat bottoms, turnip tops. Bear refuses to farm more, eats meat since. Holland: De Leeuw LEGENDS 109-111.

K171.1.0.4* Bear: bear and peasant, bear gets tops of turnips, bottoms of wheat. +A2494.8.3. Russia/Yiddish: Ginsburg THREE 27-39.

K171.1.0.5* Bear and peasant, turnip tops, rye roots. Why bear and peasant are enemies. Russia: Carey BABA 84-85.

K171.1.0.6* Bear and peasant--bear to get turnip tops, wheat roots. Russia: Higonnet-Schnopper TALES 76-81.

K171.1.0.7* Coyote and badger, coyote gets potato tops, melon bottoms. Native American: Baker PARTNERS pb.

K171.1.0.8* Coyote and bear, coyote gets bottoms of corn, potato tops. Native American (Pueblo): Dolch PUEBLO 17-25.

K171.1.0.9* Coyote and bear, coyote gets potato tops, wheat roots. Native American (Pueblo): Dolch PUEBLO 17-25.

K171.1.0.10* Devil: God and devil, devil gets top of potatoes, bottom of wheat. Latvia: Durham TIT 34-36.

K171.1.0.11* Devil gets potato tops and corn bottoms. U.S. (Appalachia): Chase WICKED 88-99.

K171.1.0.12* Priest and devil, devil gets turnip tops, wheat bottoms, all goats which cross stream without raising tails, devil loses another bargain and leaves forever (K172). Serbia: Spicer THIRTEEN DEVILS 111–117.

K171.1.0.13* Devil gets bottoms of barley, tops of carrots, tops and bottoms of beans. France: Cooper FIVE 58–75.

K171.1.0.14* Devil gets bottoms of barley. Netherland (Friesland): Spicer THIRTEEN DEVILS 25–32.

K171.1.0.15* Fox and armadillo. Fox gets wheat bottoms and potato tops, tops and bottom of corn. Argentina: Barlow LATIN 23–27.

K171.1.0.16* Fox and hedgehog. Potatoes; wheat. +K11.1. Poland: Domanska BEST pb.

K171.1.0.17* Fox: Brer Fox and Brer Rabbit. Fox gets tops and bottoms of corn. U.S. Black (South Carolina): Faulkner DAYS 110–114.

K171.1.0.18* Goblin: Goblin gets bottoms of corn, tops of carrots. England (Northamptonshire): Conger TOPS pb.

K171.1.0.19* Brownie and farmer, brownie gets wheat bottoms, turnip tops, mowing match in corn with iron rods in brownie's half. England (Northamptonshire): Garner CAVALCADE.. GOBLINS 11–12.

K171.1.0.20* Boggart and man, boggart gets wheat bottoms, potato tops, iron rods in boggart's wheat half. Britain: Williams-Ellis FAIRY..BRITISH 82–87. England (Lincolnshire): Colwell ROUND 57–60.

K171.1.0.21* Boggart gets carrot tops, rye bottoms, rowan rods in reaping half. England: Spicer THIRTEEN GOBLINS 35–44.

K171.1.0.22* Jackal and hedgehog, jackal gets bottoms of wheat, tops of onions. Tunisia: Berson WHY pb.

K171.1.0.23* Sharecropper and plantation owner, owner gets tops of potatoes, bottoms of oats, and top and bottom of corn—sharecropper gets middle. U.S. (Black): Courlander TERRAPIN'S 104–107.

K171.1.0.24* Troll and farmer, troll gets carrot tops, corn bottoms. This is troll's recompense for plowing up road. He is content. Wiggin TALES 322.

K171.1.0.25* Wolf: Brer Wolf and Brer Rabbit. Brer Wolf gets tops of peanuts. U.S. Black (South Carolina): Faulkner DAY 106–109.

K171.1.1* Woman and the Devil. Devil gets grain bottoms, root crop tops. They fight. He with clothes prop, she with rolling pin. He cannot wield prop indoors. They go outside and trade weapons. She still has best of deal. They trade curses and part. She sticks carding combs into Devil's back—her curses. Rumania: Ure RUMANIAN 57–61.

K171.2. Deceptive grain division: the corn and the chaff. The bear chooses the chaff because of its greater bulk. At the mill the fox's grain makes a different sound from the bears. Type 9B. Finland: Bowman TALES..TUPA 247–248.

K171.4. Deceptive division of pigs: curly and straight tails. All with curly tails belong to trickster, others to dupe. Type 1036. U.S. (Applalachia): Chase WICKED 88–99 (man and devil throw pigs over fence to divide, he puts corn in his pen and all devil's come over, claims he put a curl in tail of each as he threw it over).

K171.7.1* Two brothers divide. Elder gets bed from sunset to sunrise, bottom half of cows, top of apple tree. Younger brother gives mattress a bath in the afternoon, beats cow on head while it is being milked, chops down tree while brother is in top picking apples. India: Korel LISTEN 37–41.

K171.9. Monkey cheats fox of his share of bananas. Climbs on a tree and tosses peelings down upon fox. SEE ALSO: K1161.6 (monkey tosses green persimmons at crab).

K171.9.1* Turtle finds tree, monkeys help carry for half. Takes top half which withers, picks fruit of turtle's from tree and throws down skins, etc. SEE ALSO: K1161.6. Philippines: Courlander RIDE 25–27.

K171.10* Deceptive division. All cattle who go back into barn belong to dupe—it is a fine day. Russia (Georgia): Papashvily YES 201–210.

K172. Anger bargain. The trickster makes a bargain with his master that the first to become angry must submit to punishment (usually a strip off back). He thereupon heaps abuse on master or feigns stupidity till the latter breaks out in anger and must take his punishment. Types 650A, 1000. +K1691. SEE ALSO: F613.1.1; G501A. Denmark: Hatch THIRTEEN 148–169 (+K1691, K404.1). Puerto Rico: Belpre TIGER 37–41 (+K1691). Armenia: Bulatkin EURASIAN 57–63 (+K1691). Deutsch MORE 45–54; Tashjian ONCE 29–39 (+K1691). Jacobs EUROPEAN 115–120 (claims pulled off pigs' tails, K404.1); cleans horses and stables inside and out, kills horse and cleans insides; shoots master's wife claiming thought was wolf in bush). U.S. (Appalachia): Chase JACK 67–75 (K362.10). Slovenia: Kavcic GOLDEN 141–149 (to put oxen into pen without opening gate, cuts up; to light way at night, set fire to house; trades places with wife and helps master toss 'himself' into water). Serbia: Spicer THIRTEEN DEVILS 111–117 (Devil returns to hell forever, +K171.1). Ireland: Fenner TIME 17–35 / Fillmore MIGHTY/; Jacobs CELTIC 198–208. Berson HOW pb.

K172.0.1* Pact with devil, enough skin for pair

of boots. Cuts wagon and oxen up to put through hedge (K1411). Paints home red--burns (K1412). Billet in bed, struck instead of lad hiding. Boots of Devils hide will never wear out--still in use. Finland: Spicer THIRTEEN DEVILS 33-42.

K172.0.2* Lad not to leave until told "Be off with you." Rides too close to chief and is ordered off. Leaves on stallion. Caucasus (Ossete): Deutsch TALES 44-52.

K176.1. First to greet the other in the morning will lose (beauty) contest. Dispute to be settled thus. Majorca: Mehdevi BUNGLING 17-35 (curate loses head to trickster, +K366.1.1).

K182. Deceptive bargain: an ox for five pennies. A woman who has been left the ox on condition that she give the proceeds to the poor offers it for five pennies, but it must be bought along with a cock at twelve florins. She gives the five pennies to the poor and keeps the twelve florin. Norway: Undset TRUE 202-208.

K182.0.1* Tricked into saying he'll sell the donkey for one dinar, man ties donkey to cat and sells two together asking one hundred dinar for the cat. Iran: Kelsey MULLAH 54-60.

K182.2. Beard sold. New owner makes such a nuisance that high price is paid to regain it. Gypsy: Jagendorf GYPSIES' 17-23.

K182.3* House sold except for peg. Lad claims right to come in and hang hat on peg whenever he wishes. Rumania: Ure RUMANIAN 42-44.

K185.3.1* Deceptive land purchase: as much land as goose can fly over without lighting. St. Kavin rejuvenates King O'Toole's pet goose with this bargain. Gains large tract of land. Jacobs CELTIC 102-108 /Arbuthnot FAIRY 136-138/, /Arbuthnot ANTHOLOGY 177-179/; Williams-Ellis FAIRY..BRITISH 24-29.

K187. Strokes shared. The boy promises the soldier what the king has promised to give him. The soldier receives a beating in place of the boy. Type 1610. Denmark: Hatch THIRTEEN 37-45; Jagendorf NOODLEHEAD 147-155. Scandinavia: Hardendorff TRICKY 101-108. Pyle WONDER 219-228. Italy: Vittorini OLD 38-44. Russia: Wyndham TALES..RUSSIA 57-61. Japan: Edmonds POSSIBLE 85-93 (doorman half, chamberlain half, Ikkyu). China: Chang CHINESE 48-49.

K187.1* Strokes shared. Doorman demands half reward from fisherman carrying huge fish to king. Fisherman requests lashes. Doorman given his half and fisherman given position at court. Burma: Brockett BURMESE 171-176; Htin KINGDOM 34-38. Italy (Puglia): Jagendorf PRICELESS 114-121 (servants ask for half, each given half of remains, six lashes left over, he sells these in market place). China: Cheney TALES 59-63.

K188. Stealing only a small amount. Steals a rope with a mare on end of it. China: Withers WORLD 73; Wyndham TALES 38-39 (ox).

K191. Peace between sheep and wolves. As hostages the dogs are handed over to the wolves, the young wolves to the sheep. The wolves then attack and kill the sheep. Aesop: Aesop FIVE 58.

K192. The man helps the horse against the stag. The horse must agree to be saddled and bridled. The man then refuses to release him. Aesop: Aesop AESOP'S (Grosset) 28-29; Aesop AESOP'S (Viking) 36 (boar); Aesop AESOP'S (Watts) 211; Aesop FABLES (Macmillan) 64.

K196.2. The tall hog. Man boasts of hog so big that a man could not reach its back if he holds his hand as high as possible. The hog's back is much below his hand when he holds it as high as possible. Leach NOODLES 65.

K200. Deception in payment of debt.

K210. Devil cheated of his promised soul. SEE ALSO: M210; G303.16.19.3; S241.1.

K213. Devil pounded in knapsack until he releases man. Type 330B. SEE ALSO: Q565 (Smith + Devil); Z111.2+; J2411.1.

A* The Wonderful Knapsack: Soldier given three pennies salary, gives them to three beggars (K1811). He is given three wishes--1) a long life, 2) knapsack will never wear out, 3) anything he wishes to go into knapsack and anything he wishes to come out. In haunted inn he wishes trolls into knapsack and gets secret of treasure. Has knapsack beaten until only dust remains of trolls. Denmark: Hatch THIR-TEEN 81-93 /Child Study Association CASTLE'S 97-107/; Haviland FAVORITE..DENMARK 26-42; Owen CASTLE 13-24 (first wish--courage never to fail).

B* Death and the Soldier: Soldier shares food with beggar. In haunted house he intimidates devils by 1) squeezing water from a stone (beet; K62), 2) chewing walnuts (lead bullets; K63), 3) asking "can you get into my knapsack?" (K717). Has devils beaten at smithy. They give a wishing bag (wishing anything into bag) in return for freedom. He traps Death in bag--lets out on promise to take no one for thirty years. Has death show how to lie in coffin (G526) and nails shut and tosses into river. Death is intimidated by shaking sack at him third time and flees. Soldier still lives. Russia: Downing RUSSIAN 81-99; Riordan TALES ..CENTRAL 115-126.

C* "Brother Gaily." Soldier shares thrice with beggar (St. Peter). Taken as companion. Sees saint resuscitate (J2411.1) dead by cutting in pieces and reassembling. St. Peter arrives in time to undo damage. Gives him a magic knapsack to remove temptation of reviving dead for

for wealth. Nine devils caught in knapsack and beaten at smithy. One survives and warns of him in hell, he is turned away (Q565). Returns knapsack to St. Peter in heaven, then wishes self into it--thus enters heaven (K2371.1.1). Germany (Grimm): Grimm JUNIPER v.1 129-149.

D. Soldier Jack. Incident 1: Retired soldier gives last three loaves of bread to beggar. Given magic cards (never lose) and knapsack--whatever is wished into knapsack stays. In haunted palace wins treasure from demons, then has beaten in sack, released on condition one comes whenever he calls.
Incident 2: becomes renowned for ability to predict death as demon assistant gives glass of water to look into, if see Death at feet man will recover, if at head will die (D1825.3.1). Trades life spans with Prince about to die.
Incident 3: Gets Death into knapsack and ties in treetop. Years later he heeds plight of the very old in need of Death and releases. Death refuses to take him now. Devil also refuses and gives ransom of two hundred and fifty souls to get him to leave (Q565). Unable to buy his way into heaven with these he has last soul carry his knapsack in (K2371.1.1). To call him into it once inside. The soul forgets and the soldier wanders forever on earth. U.S.S.R. (Byelorussia): Courlander RIDE 145-153. U.S. (Appalachia): Chase JACK 172-179 (-knapsack into heaven, refused in hell motifs). Russia: Downing RUSSIAN 81-99 (incident three only).

E* Death a Prisoner: Man with cask of wine refuses to drink with Lord because of bad year. Meets Death and tricks into bung hole of cask (K717). No one dies for years, he forgets and opens bung--all die and spot becomes a desserted stony moutainside. Switzerland: Müller-Guggenbühl SWISS 52-56.

K216.2. Bringing the devil an unknown animal. The man sends his naked wife on all fours in tar and feathers. The devil has never seen such an animal. Type 1091. SEE: K31.1.

K217. Devil gets another soul instead of one bargained for. The devil bargains with a man for his soul but the man fulfills his contract and escapes. In envy two persons commit suicide. The devil rejoices that though he lost one he has gained two. Type 361.

A* Soldier Who Did Not Wash. Devil (M211) will give man anything he wants if does not wash, groom self or change clothes for fifteen years (C723.1). Tsar in debt agrees to wed youngest daughter to him in exchange for gold. Two oldest daughters said they would "marry the Devil before wedding him." Devil gets their souls. Russia: Downing RUSSIAN 138-142.

B* Bearskin: K217A + wears bearskin. Redeems indebted man and is offered daughter. Gives her half ring token. Later, as handsome man, he drops his half token in cup. Two elder daughters drown selves in jealousy. Devil gets. Germany (Grimm): Grimm BEARSKINNER pb; Grimm JUNIPER v.2 217-237.

C* Devil's Little Brother-In-Law. Lad serves Devil seven years. Everyone told him to "go to the Devil." Is given magic purse but is unkempt and blackened from service. Claims is Devil's brother-in-law. Lends money to prince in exchange for youngest daughter. Two eldest refused him. Devil takes them. He is now Devil's brother-in-law. Frost LEGENDS 127-141.

K219.5. Man cheats devil by giving him sole instead of soul. Man pledges Devil soul. Witch Bertraude extorts money in pretense of winning soul back from Devil. Peasant girl friend tricks Bertraude into calling up Devil to prove she can. Offers her own soul for lover's. Writes "sole" in pact and gives Devil her shoe. France: Cooper FIVE 7-25.

K220. Payment precluded by terms of bargain.

K221.1* Devil wants crops. Almond blossoms first, he waits for fruit. It ripens last. He misses other crops. Portugal: Lowe LITTLE 50.

K230. Other deceptions in the payment of debt.

K231.1.3. The dog refuses to help the wolf. A farmer plans to kill a faithful old dog. The wolf makes a plan to save the dog. The latter is to rescue the farmer's child from the wolf. The plan succeeds and the dog is rewarded. The wolf in return wants to steal the farmer's sheep. The dog refuses his assistance. Type 101. Germany (Grimm): Grimm HOUSEHOLD 195-197 (+K2323; K2324.0.1) /Wiggin TALES 149-151/. Russia: Carpenter WONDER..DOGS 213-221 (+J581.1). Ukraine: Bloch UKRAINIAN 44-48 (+J581.1). Van Woerkom MEAT pb.

K231.1.3.1* Dog arranges for coyote to feign stealing turkey and let dog rout him. Coyote changes mind and keeps turkey. Mexico: Ross IN 134-149.

K231.1.3.2* Monkey to be killed for age asks boar to help. Boar "steals" child and lets monkey "rescue." Japan: Ozaki JAPANESE 148-152.

K231.1.3.3* Fox steals sausages letting old dog bark to prove worth as watchdog. Also provides mice to old cat to redeem worth as mouser. This in return for aid in animal's war (K2323). Germany (Grimm): Lang GREEN 326-330.

K231.6.1.1. Order to put a small vessel of milk into a huge container. Shrewd group each by himself pours water thinking this will not be detected if the others pour milk. Bamum, Cameroun: Courlander KING'S 56-57 (wine). China: Kendall SWEET 18-20 (wine).

K231.14.1* Wagering that he can stay all night without a fire, he watches distant candle (or reads by candlelight). Said to have lost wager because of heat of candle, he must provide feast for winners. He places cooking pot over candle (cf. J1191.7). Turkey: Downing HOD-JA 18-19; Kelsey HODJA 12-20; Walker WATER-MELONS 37-41. Haiti: Courlander PIECE 101-104 (pot across room from fire, cook had contradicted emperor that fortress on mountain was cold). Near East: Van Woerkum ABU pb. Iran: Shah MULLA 27.

K231.14.2* Man who warms self with sight of fire on distant mountain loses bet to stand all night with fire. He feasts winners with smell of food. SEE ALSO: J1172.2.1. Ethiopia: Courlander FIRE 7-14 /Courlander RIDE 106-111/, /Arbuthnot ANTHOLOGY 312-313/; McNeil DOUBLE 63-66.

K233.4.1* Man has trousers wrapped to purchase, then exchanges them for a coat. He refuses to pay for the coat since he traded the trousers for it and refuses to pay for the trousers since he didn't take them. Turkey: Downing HODJA 91.

K235.1. Fox is promised chickens. Is driven off by dog. Type 154. Greece: Wilson GREEK 53-57. SEE ALSO: C25.

K235.1.0.1* Fox is beaten when he comes for promised chickens. Poland: Zajdler POLISH 20-27. Norway: Undset TRUE 250-253.

K236.1.1* Gods promised one hundred coins for recovery. Pays with little tallow oxen. Gods make him dream of finding one hundred crowns on seashore. He goes there and is captured by robbers and sold for one hundred crowns. Aesop: Aesop AESOP'S (Watts) 194-195.

K251.1. The eaten grain and the cock as damages. A trickster has only a grain of corn; this is eaten by a cock, which he demands and receives as damages. Likewise when a hog eats the cock and the ox eats the hog. Type 1655. (cf. N421). SEE ALSO: Z47; K2138.

K251.1.0.1* Ananse brings an entire kingdom to Nyame with one grain of corn (H501.4). Chicken , goat, cow, dead boy--claims he is Nyame's son and host's children killed him, thus king brings all people to beg leniency of Nyame (A185.12.1). W. Africa: Appiah ANANSE 1-26.

K251.1.0.2* Travels of a fox. Fox leaves bag with bee in it, cock eats bee and fox claims cock, pig, ox, boy. Boy is rescued and dog put in his place--dog eats fox. Hutchinson CHIMNEY 91-98. U.S.: Arbuthnot FAIRY 15-16; Association TOLD..GREEN 40-46; Richardson GREAT 16-26; Rockwell OLD 23-33; Withers I SAW 18-21.

K251.1.0.2.1* Fox finds rolling pin, chicken, goose, daughter--given dog. Asks parts how they helped. Tail put out. Russia: Carey BABA 39-41; Montgomerie MERRY 8-13.

K251.1.0.2.3* Stick, hen, goose, lamb, boy--dog. Russia (Jewish): Ginsburg ONE 3-7.

K251.1.0.2.4* Sliver removed from foot, hen, ducks, goose, lamb, daughter-in-law--dog. Tail put out. Ukraine: Bloch UKRAINIAN 49-59.

K251.1.0.2.5* Lazy man given pea as wages. Chick, sow, mare, girl--dog. European: Jacobs EUROPEAN 13-18.

K251.1.0.3* Duck eats boy's worm. Fox eats duck. Wolf eats fox. Boy makes drum of wolf-skin, broken, demands chief's daughter. Wed. Native American (Abenaki): De Wit TALKING 183-187.

K251.1.1* Boy with bean, cat eats bean, dog, pig, horse. Goes to castle and tells king tale--hired as jester. Italy: Hardendorff TRICKY 75-80.

K251.1.2* One bargain too many. Rat gives stick to fireless man and receives lump of dough. Dough to potter--receives pot. Pot to buffalo milker--now demands buffalo. Wedding party eats buffalo--demands bride. Bride's mother prepares a warm room for him--oven. He vows never to bargain again. (cf. N421.1). W. Pakistan: Siddiqui TOONTOONY 23-31.

K251.1.3* Boy with gebetta board. Somalis burn board--give knife. Man borrows knife and breaks--repays spear. Spear--horse, horse--axe. Axe--limb. Limb--gebetta board. Returns home and father says "What better than a gebetta board to keep a small boy out of trouble?" (Z41.5). Ethiopia: Courlander FIRE 77-80.

K251.1.4* Mother eats boy's yams--gives calabash. Children break--give spear. Spear--axe. Axe--cloth. Cloth--ox-hide shield. Shield--assegai. Possession of assegai makes boy a warrior. Bantu: Arnott TALES 116-123.

K251.1.4.1* Grandmother eats boy's honey--gives corn, hens--egg, shepherds use as ball and give staff, elephant's tusk--give knife, ox skinners--oxtail, puts tail in ground and tells people they broke it off--gets one hundred oxen more from each person (K404.1.1). Tanganyika (Sukumu): Withers I SAW 139-140.

K251.1.4.2* Mother eats boy's bird and gives corn, termites--earthen pots, cataract--fish, hawk--feather, wind--fruit, Baboon--nothing to give so boy takes him. Sierre Leone; Liberia (Temne): Withers I SAW 135-138.

K251.1.5* Juan weds princess. Gambler finds centavo. Chick eats dog. Iron gate. Stream. Princess (bathing in stream). Weds. Philippines (Bicol): Sechrist ONCE 135-140.

K251.6* Hare eats berry cache and blames ostrich. Claims feather. Man loses feather--gives meat. Woman eats meat, gives milk. Ants eat--takes bowl of ants. Trades to lion for water from well. He was forbidden water for not helping dig. Thonga: Aardema BEHIND 48-56.

K251.1.7* Goats horn lost in river, gives fish. Fire scorches--gives ax. Woodcutter gives wood. Woman gives skirt. Cothran MAGIC 66-68.

K251.2.1* Judge rules defendant must return house post but plaintiff must return rice eaten. (cf. J1173). Philippines (Tagalog): Sechrist ONCE 177-184.

K254.1. Dog as wolf's shoemaker eats up the materials. Devours the cow, hog, etc. furnished him. Type 102. Poland: Zajdler POLISH 28-32 (Fox has wolf walk through lime wash and receive boots "light as air." Wolf has been cursed by Saint Nicholas to go crookshanks).

K254.1.1* Fox as leopard's tailor consumes nine sheep but produces no sheepskin jacket. Palestine: Arnott ANIMAL 6-13. Syria: Hampden GYPSIES' 105-109 (panther).

K263. Agreements not to scratch. In talking the trickster makes gestures and scratches without detection. U.S. (Black): Brown BRER 22-28 /Bleecker BIG 143-150/; Gruenberg MORE 105-108; Harris FAVORITE 19-23 (kills mosquitoes) /Harris NIGHTS 214-222/, /Harris COMPLETE 272-278/.

K263.1* Breaking the bad habit: Monkey agrees not to scratch. Rabbit agrees not to twitch. Each does so via gestures in storytelling. W. Africa: Carpenter AFRICAN 41-45.

K263.2* Friar wanting to loosen belt after meal removes it to illustrate tale of lengthy serpent "this long." Reties it loosely. Portugal: Lowe LITTLE 30.

K263.3* Suitor tasks. 1) To stay in room full of mosquitoes without driving them off. Tells story and slaps body to show where spots were on horse. 2) To eat red pepper without grimacing; calls to chicks as he eats pepper "zoo, zoo." Nigeria: Walker NIGERIAN 57-58.

K275. Counting out pay. Hole in the hat and hat over a pit. Type 1130.

K275.1* Ananse to fill hole with yams to buy lizard's cloak of flies, a hidden pit is under the hole. Ashanti: Courlander HAT 70-76.

K278. Dupe denied food until hands are clean. Grass burned around food makes continued washup unavailing. SEE: J1565.1.2; Z41.2.1.

K278.0.1* Baboon forced to cross charred field by tortoise. Nyansa: Arnott AFRICAN 22-24; Colwell MAGIC 107-110 (baboon-hare).

K278.0.2* Spider (Anansi) sends turtle repeatedly to wash before feast. Ashanti: Courlander COW-TAIL 107-112 /Gruenberg MORE 130-132/;

Kaula AFRICAN 26-31.

K285. To keep first thing touched. Wealth (or woman) is on platform. First thing touched is ladder leading up. Russia (Chechen): Titiev HOW 1-8 (Moolah).

K289* Deceptive bargains--miscellaneous.

K289.1* Peasant outwits baron, convinces him that peasant's horse is better or easier to guard at night and disadvantageous trade is made. Each to carry the other, one to be carried as long as he keeps singing. Peasant never stops. Russia: Bulatkin EURASIAN 95-97; Downing RUSSIAN 135-137 (Russian and Tatar).

K289.2* Man pretends to be going to buy five dozen eggs, counts them into farmer's arms and then walks off. U.S.: Leach NOODLES 69.

K300. Thefts and cheats--general.

K301. Master thief. Man undertakes to steal various closely guarded things. Succeeds by cleverness. Type 1525. SEE ALSO: F660.1 (skillfull brothers); K341.7.

A* Theft of Dog, Horse, Sheet, or Ring. Type 1525A. Lad learns skills as thief. Theft assigned. He steals horses by getting stablehands drunk. Gets sheet and ring from count's wife (H1151.3) while count shoots and buries a corpse (K362.2). Gets parson and sexton into sacks, convincing day of judgment is at hand. Candles placed on crabs' backs move in churchyard and appear to be ghosts. Germany (Grimm): Grimm JUNIPER 113-128.

Ab* Feigns hung twice and farmers leave cattle to go back to see first corpse again (K341.6); to steal horse from under lord, takes lord's horse to go catch thief with finger in bung-hole of cask (K341.9.1). Type 1525D. European: Jacobs EUROPEAN 121-128.

Ac* A thief steals lord's daughter in dressmaker disguise, steals lord with doomsday routine. Scotland (Isle of Skye): Nic Leodhas SEA-SPELL 25-50.

Ad* A thief lad joins noble's band, feigns hung, drops shoes, etc. (K314.6); steals poison; twelve horses from under twelve grooms; horse from under squire (K341.9.1), sheet and nightgown. Norway: Undset TRUE 213-232.

Ae* A thief steals oxen from plowing man, the king's horse, queen's ring. Germany: McNeil DOUBLE 123-128.

Af* A thief steals king's boots, horse, cow. Latvia: Ginsburg LAZIES 28-32.

Ag* A thief joins robbers, feigns hung (K341.6), drops shoes, moos like lost cow (K341.7), steals twelve horses, rabbit for pet, sheet. U.S. (Appalachia): Chase JACK 114-126.

Ah* A thief feigns hanging, steals cashbox, horse. Russia: Daniels FALCON 56-60.

Ai* A thief bleats and steals goat (K341.7), sultan's nugget, Khan's goatskin with bells--as Devil frightens Khan away; steals gold on road with tarred shoes (K378.1); steals gold bag with white horse colored black on one side (K419.5). Russia: Masey STORIES 88-103.

Aj* Drops boots, steals sheep by bleating. Fenner ADVENTURES 109-115 /MacManus IN CHIMNEY/.

B* Iwa the Crafty One. Iwa steals red cowry from Chief's fishing line. 1) Ordered to steal sacred axe of chief. It is on rope tied to necks of two old women. He takes crier's place and announces curfew and all go to bed. Tells old woman to feel axe to make sure is safe. Pulls rope and cracks their heads together. 2) To steal more in one night than six thieves. Robs the thieves after they go to sleep. Made guardian of king's treasure house. Hawaii: Thompson HAWAIIAN..TRICKSTER'S 80-85.

C* The Thief in the King's Treasury. Thief tests three nephews. 1) Each in room with cake on twig from rafters--to get cake. Third throws sponge until softens and falls. 2) Rob king's treasury square which is littered with gold coins. Glue on shoe soles (K378.1). 3) Camel loaded with jewels. Guards made drunk. Thief and aunt melt down camel for grease. King sends servants to beg for grease--mark doors. 4) To confess crimes to king's daughter. Places fake hand in hers. She holds tight and calls for help. He escapes. He weds her and becomes heir. Cyprus: Neufield BEWARE 58-67.

D* The Sly Thief of Valenciennes. Thief steals half king's treasury. Attempts to catch him 1) gold coins on floor at ball (K378.1), he smears tar on soles. 2) To enter princess's room, she marks X on forehead, he marks everyone. 3) Trap door in princess's room. He falls in, she screams, and all run and fall. King offers her to thief. Forty claim to be thief. She recognizes his voice. Wed. French Canada: Barbeau GOLDEN 121-138.

E* Clever Sim who would "Squeeze." Yun sent to spy on Sim. Sim fastens tiger skin to colt of Yun's mare and mare flees with Yun. Sun sent to spy, hidden in chest while visiting lover. Chest to be tossed in river. Kum sent to spy. Is convinced has slept on hill for two hundred years and appears to be deranged. Sim put in charge of treasury--too clever to catch. Korea: Carpenter KOREAN 245-252.

F* The Master Thief. Son wants to become thief. Steals goat by leaving boot in road (K341.7), bleats and steals second. Shops for whee-ai, pops peppery seeds into master's mouth. Father wants to learn trade but touches electric wire while bank robbing and dies. Son cuts off head to prevent identification of corpse. Haiti: Wolkstein MAGIC 135-142.

K301.3* Three brothers set out to learn skills (F660.1). One receives cracked bowl from old woman he worked for. Throws it away but it follows. Bowl tells him to say he has become master their, have uncle agree may keep gold if not caught. Bowl steals (D1605), replaces servants' rods with flutes. Uncle calls to enquire after money box. Stablehand thinks he wants it put on horse. Trickster leads off horse. Confesses next day, allowed to keep gold. Japan: Uchida SEA 99-111.

K305.1. Thieving contest: first steals eggs from under bird. Second meantime steals first's breeches. Often apprentice thief. +K301 (Master Thief). Russia: Daniels FALCON 56-60; Masey STORIES 88-103.

K306.5* Zomo and Biri to share well full of treasures. Biri (monkey) plans to leave Zomo (hare) in well. Zomo hides in last bale and is hauled out. Zomo carries off goods and fills bales with trash. SEE ALSO: J1516. N. Nigeria (Hausa): Sturton ZOMO 89-99.

K310. Means of entering house or treasury.

K311.3. Thief disguises voice and is allowed access to goods (children). (cf. G413). SEE ALSO: A781.0.1 (suitor); K815.15.

A* The Wolf and the Seven Little Kids. Type 123. Wolf poses as mother (K2011.1), eats chalk to disguise voice (F556). Puts dough, flour on paws to disguise. Kids open door on third try. All but one are eaten. Mother goat cuts open sleeping wolf (F913, fills with stones (K256; Q426). He falls into well, drowns. Germany: (Grimm): Arbuthnot FAIRY 34-35; Gag MORE 241-249; Grimm GRIMM'S (Follett) 407-412; Grimm GRIMM'S (Grosset) 50-53; Grimm GRIMM'S (World) 180-183; Grimm HOUSEHOLD 40-42; Grimm WOLF (illus. Hoffman) pb; Grimm WOLF (illus. Svend) pb; Haviland FAIRY 16-21; Martignoni ILLUSTRATED 74-76; Shubb ABOUT 17-19; TALL..NURSERY 62-69; Wiggin TALES 166-169. Russia: Carrick STILL 15-22 (F556.2, kids not rescued).

B* The Terrible Carlanco. Three kids to open only when hear mother's knock. Carlanco (ogre) imitates, is let in. Kids flee to roof, mother fetches Abbess wasp whom she once rescued. Wasp routes Carlanco. Spain: Haviland FAVORITE..SPAIN 50-57; Sawyer PICTURE 63-64.

C* The Cunning Snake. Snake vows vengeance on woman who eats its egg. She hides own child, to open only when hears chant. Snake rehearses and is let in. Mother rescues daughter from sleeping snake's belly. U.S. (Georgia, Black): Harris COMPLETE 302-309 /Harris - NIGHTS 255-259/.

D* The Jackal and the Lambs. Jackal imitates ewe's call, lets ants (F556.1.2) bite throat so will sound like sheep. Is let in, eats two lambs. Ewe revenges self by tossing her hay bundles onto jackal and laying on it until shepherd comes to kill jackal. Berber-Kabyl: Frobenius AFRICAN 77-79.

E* Father keeps three children in treehouse. Let down ladder when hear chant (K1622). Witch tries. Lets brown ants, black ants, scorpions bite tongue on advise of wizard. Voice changes. Is let in (F556.1.2). Tanganyika (Kamba): Arnott AFRICAN 140-149.

F* Brer Rabbit's children open door when Brer Wolf imitates Brer Rabbit's chant. Succeeds on third try after practice. Eats. At trial guilty one will fall when trying to jump over fire. Brer Wolf falls into fire. U.S. (Georgia, Black): Harris NIGHTS 248-254; Harris COMPLETE 297-302.

G* Girl hidden in woods from suitors. Tiger has smith put hot iron down throat (F556.1.1), sings song in mother's voice, eats, ruins voice, repeats. Eats. Parents die of sorrow. SEE: A781.0.1. Jamaica: Sherlock WEST 112-117.

H* Witch pretends to be girls' aunt, is allowed into house. One suspects when witch begins crunching bones in bed, says is eating peanuts. Runs for priest, tricks witch out with food on doorstep. Witch returns feigning mother's voice, Is let in. Ah-Lee climbs tree (R251), requests boiling peanut oil to bathe in before jumping into witch's mouth. Pours oil on witch, turns to tiger ghost. Taiwan: Cheney TALES 122-132.

I* The Three Little Girls. Tiger fakes mother's voice saying is hoarse, eyes red from pepper, hands yellow from plaster. Girls escape up tree. Tell to oil tree before climbing. God of Heaven pulls them up in golden bucket. Tiger pulled up with rotted rope and falls into millet field. Why millet root tops are matted (A2793.8.1). Three girls made sun, moon and stars (A736.4.1). Korea: Kim STORY 76-82.

J* Nsangi. Gorilla practices until can imitate mother's song. Eats girl. Ten gorillas questioned and guilty has finger cut off to rescue girl. Uganda: Serwadda SONGS 45-52.

K* Devil learns mother's song. Has voice tightened at plumber. Carries off three girls. Third, unfavorite daughter, who was not called in mother's song does not come and is not taken. Mother goes mad. Philamondré weds King. Later takes in wandering madwoman mother. Haiti: Wolkstein MAGIC 165-170.

K311.3.1* All mothers are to be killed or eaten (J151.1). One animal hides his in tree. Other spies and learns song to sing for her to lower rope. He is discovered before reaches top and dropped. SEE ALSO: K944.

K311.3.1.0.1* Dog's mother, tortoise dropped. Nigeria: Walker NIGERIAN 27.

K311.3.1.0.2* Antelope's mother, tortoise dropped. Yoruba: Courlander OLODE 72-76.

K311.3.1.0.3* Dog's mother, tortoise and several other animals dropped. Nigeria: Fuja FOURTEEN 186-195.

K311.3.1.0.4* Hare's mother, baboon dropped. Sierre Leone (Krio): Robinson SINGING 8-15.

K311.3.1.0.5* Cutta Cord-la. Wolf has blacksmith burn throat. Imitates Brer Rabbit's chant. Brer Rabbit calls to her to cut rope, wolf falls. U.S. (Georgia, Black): Harris NIGHTS 236-240; Harris COMPLETE 289-292.

K311.3.1.1* Anansi hides mother in tree. Sends Sister Hen up tree on rope. Calls to mother to whack her when reaches top. Monkey sees, feigns innocent victim. Sends Anasi up rope first then mocks. West Indies: Sherlock WEST 135-143.

K330. Means of hoodwinking the guardian or owner.

K331.6.1* Hermit keeps money in staff. Servant attempts to steal, serpent engulfs him. India: Korel LISTEN 103-107.

K333.1. Blind dupe. A blind man's arrow is aimed for him by his mother (or wife) who deceives into thinking that he has missed his aim. She eats the slain game herself. Eskimo: Caswell SHADOWS 41-47; Maher BLIND 17-30.

K333.2. Theft from three old women who have but a single eye among them. The hero seizes the eye. Type 581. Norway: Asbjornsen NORWEGIAN 9-12 (single eye of three trolls taken by two boys, demand two pails of silver and gold and two steel bows before will return).

K334.1. The raven (crow) with cheese in his mouth. The fox flatters him into singing so that he drops cheese. Type 57. SEE ALSO: K721 (persuaded to crow with eyes closed). Aesop: Aesop AESOP'S (Golden) 60-61; Aesop AESOP'S (Grosset) 5-6; Aesop AESOP'S (Random) 51-54; Aesop AESOP'S (Viking) 59-60; Aesop AESOP'S (Watts) 6; Aesop FABLES (Macmillan) 1; Aesop FABLES (Walck) 66-67; Aesop FIVE 84; Arbuthnot FAIRY 225; Galdone THREE FOX #3; Martignoni ILLUSTRATED 160; Rice ONCE 5-9; Rockwell OLD 62-64; TALL..NURSERY 76-77. Greece: Wilson GREEK 126-128. India: Gaer FABLES..INDIA 156-157. La Fontaine: Arbuthnot FAIRY 232; Green ANIMAL 195. Nigeria: Walker NIGERIAN 48-49. Phillippines (Pampangan): Sechrist ONCE 54-56 (wildcat flatters heron).

K334.3* Monkey flatters cat into pulling chestnuts from fire. She burns paw. Monkey eats chestnuts. Aesop AESOP'S (Random) 38-40.

K335. Thief frightens owner from goods. Type 1166.

K335.0.1. Owner frightened from goods by report of approaching enemy.

K335.0.1.1* Two hunt or steal together, trickster reports approaching enemy and partner flees leaving game. West Indies: Sherlock WEST 118-124 (Anansi, tiger).

K375.0.1.2* Hare tricks tortoise but she crawls into bag with yams and eats as he runs. South Africa: Bryan OX 22-28.

K375.0.1.3* Hare tricks other animals into fleeing after tricking them into killing Mugassa's cow. Uganda: Green FOLKTALES 29-35.

K335.0.1.4* Sly Peter tricks Hodja. Bulgaria: Pridham GIFT 124-129.

K335.0.1.5* Dog tricks leopard. Uganda: Aardema TALES 49-53.

K335.0.1.6* Brer Rabbit tricks Brer Fox. U.S. (Georgia, Black): Harris NIGHTS 128-131 /Harris COMPLETE 209-212/.

K335.0.1.7* Brer Rabbit tricks Brer Fox. U.S. (Georgia, Black): Harris NIGHTS 280-285 /Harris COMPLETE 320-324/.

K335.0.4. Owner frightened away by a bluff.

K335.0.4.1. Dupe made to believe that trickster becomes a wolf when he yawns three times, flees and leaves his clothes behind him. Aesop: Aesop AESOP'S (Watts) 156.

K335.0.4.3* Hyena disguises self with leaves as green monster and hare flees, leaving food. E. Africa: Heady JAMBO 34-38 (by third day hare recognizes trick and eats beans before "monster" can appear). SEE ALSO: K1991.

K335.0.4.3.1* Hyena takes off skin to disguise self as monster and hare flees leaving food. Bantu: Arnott AFRICAN 108-111 (third day hare makes bow and shoots "monster").

K335.0.4.4* Kantjil terrifies elephant and water buffalo and panther in disguise as raksha. Indonesia: Bro HOW 29-38.

K335.0.4.5* Crow pretends to be ghost and Mrs. Mink throws delicacies for him in fear. She sees his peck marks on bowl later and throws stick, hitting 'ghost' next time. Eskimo (Hooper Bay): Gilham BEYOND 51-67.

K335.0.4.6* Leopard hides spring, sends Bushbuck away with basket for water, cooks and eats porridge using spring water before Bushbuck returns. Tortoise advises Bushbuck to plaster basket with clay (H1023.2.0.1). Gives advice in exchange for white beans from Bushbuck's sides. Tortoise then hangs moon around Bushbuck's neck, sun on head, stars on chest. Tells to impersonate Vidye Mubi, the Evil Spirit. Terrified, Leopard is forced to stir porridge with paws and tail by "Vidye Mubi." Africa: Burton MAGIC 43-47.

K335.0.4.7* Brer Rabbit rolls in honey and leaves. Scares everyone off as will-er-de-wust. U.S. (Georgia, Black): Arbuthnot FAIRY 219-220; Brown WORLD 42-48; Harris COMPLETE 133-136 /Harris NIGHTS 21-25/; Harris COMPLETE 389-391 /Harris NIGHTS 377-380/ (Hold in water and

leaves come off, is exposed).

K335.0.4.8* Brer Rabbit hears sapsucker singing of ambush ahead. He ties tin plates and coffee-pot on self, attacks as old man Spewter-Splutter. They flee. U.S. (Georgia, Black): Harris COMPLETE 202-206 /Harris NIGHTS 122/.

K335.0.4.9* Brer Rabbit sings into drum making scary noise and frightens animals at Brer Fox's party away. Gets the food. U.S. (Georgia, Black): Harris COMPLETE 161-166 /Harris NIGHTS 61-67/.

K335.0.12.1* Owner frightened away by thief disguised as devil. Poor man refuses burial for wife, finds pot of gold while digging grave. Priest in goatskin guise imitates devil and convinces that gold is devil's. Gets the gold but goatskin grows to his back. Russia: Downing RUSSIAN 143-147.

K335.1.1.1. Door falls on robbers from tree. They flee and leave money. Type 1650, 1653. SEE ALSO: K1913; K362.1; N696.1.1. U.S. (Louisiana, Cajun and Creole): Leach LUCK 59 (Jean Sot). Mexico: Brenner BOY 14-18. Gypsy: Manning-Sanders RED 112-117.

K335.1.1.1.1* Mr. Vinegar. England: Arbuthnot FAIRY 17-19; Colwell YOUNGEST 121-126; Hutchinson CHIMNEY 111-116 (fools sleeping in tree with door); Jacobs ENGLISH 27-31; Steel ENGLISH 138-144; Williams-Ellis FAIRY..BRITISH 96-102.

K335.1.1.1.2* Hereafter this. U.S. (Appalachia): Chase WICKED 14-149 (thief returns and she fastens clothespin to his tongue--all flee).

K335.1.1.1.3* Frederick and Katelizabeth. Nuts and vinegar also dropped, thought hail and dew (J2176; J1881.1.2; J1871). Germany (Grimm): Grimm GRIMM'S (Grosset) 290-297; Grimm HOUSEHOLD 247+255; Grimm JUNIPER v. 2 187-200.

K335.1.1.2.1* Person falls on robber. Man flying with witches forgets charm and falls (G242.7.3), cries "Make way for this poor devil"--robbers think him the Devil and flee. Costa Rica: Hoke WITCHES 186-187 /Lupe de Osma WITCHES/, /Harper GHOSTS 228-233/, /Arbuthnot ANTHOLOGY 407/.

K335.1.1.3.2* Person falls on demons. They flee. India: Baker GOLDEN 80-88.

K335.1.1.4* Three Who Found Their Hearts' Desire: First brother inherits hand-mill (desires fortune); second--bamboo walking stick and gourd bowl (desires wife like mother); third--drum (desires fame). First sleeps in tree, grinds mill and noise frightens off robbers--riches left. Third meets tiger which responds to drum beat (D1415.2.7.1), becomes famous as trainer. Second sleeps in graveyard and convinces Tokgabbi that he is skeleton by showing bowl for skull, stick arm (E463.2). Is taken to ill girl's room to catch her soul in bag. He procrastinates until dawn, weds her. Korea: Jewett WHICH 136-

137; Kim STORY 186-198.

K335.1.4. Animals climb on one another's backs and cry out; frighten soldiers. Type 130. +K1161.1. Belgium: Frost LEGENDS 302-309 (en route to become choristers at Saint Gudule in Brussels). Pakistan: Siddiqui TOONTOONY 136-129. Puerto Rico: Alegria THREE 9-14. Scotland: Wilson SCOTTISH 81-87. Yugoslavia (Slovenia): Kavcic GOLDEN 93-99.

K335.1.4.1* Bremen Musicians (donkey, dog, cat, cock [hen]). Germany (Grimm): Arbuthnot FAIRY 37-39; Arbuthnot ANTHOLOGY 200-201; Association TOLD..GREEN 67-73; De La Mare ANIMAL 151-158; De La Mare TALES 25-32; Fenner ADVENTURE 103-108; Grimm BREMEN (illus. Galdone) pb; Grimm BROTHERS 23-27; Grimm GRIMM'S (Follett) 41-46; Grimm GRIMM'S (Grosset) 144-147; Grimm GRIMM'S (World) 301-304; Grimm (Gag) TALES 87-97; Grimm HOUSEHOLD 46-55; Grimm HOUSEHOLD 136-139; Grimm TRAVELING pb; Haviland FAVORITE..GERMANY 72-85; Haviland FAIRY 110-113; Martignoni ILLUSTRATED 219-220; Rackham GRIMM'S 114-118; Richardson GREAT 104-112; Rockwell OLD 52-61; Shubb ABOUT 111-115; Wiggin TALES 77-80.

K335.1.4.2* Jack and the Animals. England: Hutchinson CANDLELIGHT 107-113; Jacobs ENGLISH 24-26; Manning-Sanders BOOK..MAGIC BEASTS 199-208; Steel ENGLISH 185-188. Ireland: Jacobs CELTIC 124-133; MacManus HIBERNIAN 212-223 (Jack, three sequences) /MacManus BOLD 3-18/; Pilkington SHAMROCK 46-51.

K337. Oversalting food of giant so that he must go outside for water. SEE: G610.

K337.0.1* Solomon feeds Sheba spicy food. She has promised to wed him if she takes anything from palace he does not personally give her. She must get up in the night and take a drink of water. Ethiopia (Falasha): Davis LION'S 168-171.

K341. Owner's interest distracted while goods are stolen. Type 15. SEE ALSO: D882.1.1.

K341.1.1* Raven claims to have left whale on beach. His grandchildren go to fetch it, he eats their cooking seal. Eskimo: Maher BLIND 133-137.

K341.2. Thief shams death and steals. Type 1. SEE ALSO: K607.3; K751. Spider feigns death, comes from 'grave' to rob garden nightly. Liberia/Ghana: Arkhurst ADVENTURES 40-49. Ashanti: Courlander HAT 20-24.

K341.2.0.1* Trickster shams death to avoid debt. Goat feigns death to avoid payment of deat to Hare. Hare warns of grave robber Hyena, comes in night and frightens Goat from grave. N. Nigeria (Hausa): Sturton ZOMO 48-57.

K341.2.0.1.1* Man feigns dead to avoid debts. Robbers in church flee leaving money when corpse rises. Majorca: Mehdevi BUNGLING

99-107. Russia: Daniels FALCON 81-83.

K341.2.0.2* Man feigns death rather than share. Greedy is almost buried before gives in and agrees to share rice with Watch-Pot. W. Africa: Aardema MORE 56-61.

K341.2.0.3* Man feigns death rather than reap wheat. Discovers dead must work in heaven too so revives. Armenia: Tashjian THREE 2-7.

K341.2.0.4* Spider shams death thinking dead must be well fed since dead elephant is swollen. Liberia (Mano): Dorliae ANIMALS 32-39.

K341.2.1. Animal feigns death repeatedly and then entices owner from goods. Dupe leaves goods in road to go back and pick up dead rabbit (etc.). SEE ALSO: K341.6 (shoes dropped); K371.1.

K341.2.1.0.1* Brer Rabbit tricks. U.S. (Black, Georgia): Harris FAVORITE 223-225. Harris COMPLETE 48-50; Harris SONGS 73-76.

K341.2.1.0.2* Zomo Rabbit entices farmer from goods. Nigeria (Hausa): Sturton ZOMO 77-88.

K341.2.1.0.3* Rabbit entices jackal from goods. North Africa: Gilstrap SULTAN'S 61-66.

K341.2.1.0.4* Hare lures man from bananas. India: Gaer FABLES 14-18.

K341.2.1.0.5* Rabbit tricks tiger. Puerto Rico: Alegria THREE 44-51.

K341.2.1.0.6* Fox gets hare to feign dead so girl will put down rolls. Germany: Wiggin TALES 191-192. Ludwig Bechstein: Green ANIMAL 24-25.

K341.2.1.0.7* Shepherds coming on shepherd hanging a second time go back to inspect first, leaving ram. Russia: Daniels FALCON 56-60.

K341.2.1.1* Animal tries to imitate trickster's stunt (K341.2.1) unsuccessfully. U.S. (Black, Georgia): Harris FAVORITE 226-228; Harris COMPLETE 130-133; Harris NIGHTS 17-20.

K341.2.2.2* Thief shams sickness and steals. Brer Rabbit feigns to be poisoned by meat. Wolf goes for doctor. Rabbit takes the meant. U.S. (Black, Georgia): Harris NIGHTS 297-301; Harris COMPLETE 331-335.

K341.3. Thief distracts attention by apparently hanging (stabbing) himself. Type 1525D. SEE ALSO: K301A. Russia: Daniels FALCON 56-60.

K341.4.1.1. Owner of house climbs tree after thief, who drops down and rides off on owner's horse. +J2326. SEE ALSO: K341.9; K346.1. Indonesia: Courlander KANTCHIL'S 64-70. S. India: Courlander TIGER'S 58-62.

K341.5.2. Partridge pretending to be wounded entices woman from food while jackal (fox) eats it. Russia: Ginsburg ONE 31-37. Poland: Haviland FAVORITE..POLAND 39-54.

K341.5.2.1* Shrike leads fish merchant on chase while fox eats fish. Fox leaves none for shrike. Shrike suggests fox turn into stick before merchant returns. Shrike perches on stick, merchant grabs stick and misses shrike, hitting tree. Stick turns to fox and flees. Japan: Scofield FOX 20-25.

K341.5.3* Onsongo blows horn from thorntree top and Masai leave cattle to investigate strange bird. Onsongo releases crane with horn tied to leg and Masai chase it. Onsongo's brothers have stolen cattle meanwhile. Thus artist manages bride price in stolen cattle. Africa (Kisii): Harman TALES 118-143.

K341.6. Shoes dropped to distract owner's attention. The thief drops two shoes in different places and steals a ram while the shepherd goes after the shoes. Type 1525D. SEE ALSO: K341.2.1 (feigns dead), K301. Majorca: Mehdevi BUNGLING 69-83 (sheath and sword). U.S. (Black): Courlander TERRAPIN'S 37-40 (hare tricks bear). Nicaragua: Jagendorf KING 218-221 (hare). Bulgaria: Pridham GIFT 124-129.

K341.6.1* Unsuccessful imitation of K341.6. Fox attempts hare's trick next day. Bear picks up both shoes and fox tries to reclaim them and is beaten. Says found ten dollars in them. U.S. (Black): Courlander TERRAPIN'S 37-40. U.S. (Black, Georgia): Harris UNCLE 130-136; Harris COMPLETE 560-562.

K341.7. Animal's cry imitated to distract owner's attention from his goods. Meantime rascal steals an animal. Type 1525D. SEE: K301. Majorca: Mehdevi BUNGLING 69-83 (sheep).

K341.7.0.2* Sound of animals fighting imitated to distract owner from sleep. Claps corks together to simulate rams fighting. Majorca: Mehdevi BUNGLING 69-83.

K341.8.1. Trickster pretends to ride home for tools to perform tricks. Rides away on horse. Scandinavia: Hardendorff TRICKY 11-22. Native American: Marriott WINTER 82 (Saynday). Turkey: Downing HODJA 28. Russia (Tatar): Ginsburg TWELVE 46-47.

K341.8.1.0.1* Farmer to go home for "intelligence" which Tiger came to see. Ties Tiger up first so he can be trusted alone with buffalo. Sets fire to tree. Vietnam: Robertson FAIRY.. VIETNAM 76-80; Schultz VIETNAMESE 15-18 (+A2413.4); Vo Dinh TOAD 65-73.

K341.8.1.0.2* Shy Peter leaves Hodja holding up fence (K1251) while he goes home for bag of lies. Bulgaria: Pridham GIFT 124-129.

K341.9. Thief tells his pursuer that the thief has gone to heaven by way of a tree. While the man lies on the ground and looks up, the thief steals his horse. Type 1540. SEE ALSO: K341.4.1.1.

England: Jacobs ENGLISH 39-42 (+J2376.1); Reeves ENGLISH 2-9 (+J2326.1). Norway: Undset TRUE 202-208 (+J2326.1).

K341.9.1. Thief persuades owner to take his place so he can go and catch thief: really steals owners horse. SEE ALSO: K346.1; K301. Russia: Daniels FALCON 15-20.

K341.16. Stone thrown to attract attention of shark guardians. Man then slips in cove and steals lobsters. (cf. K1080). Hawaii: Colum LEGENDS 92-96; Colum STONE 44-99; Mohan PUNIA pb; Thompson HAWAIIAN ..TRICKSTERS 23-27.

K341.19.1* Student teaches inn mistress Pira Pira game. Gives her end of ball of yarn to hold and backs out door calling "Pira Pira Pira." Flees. Portugal: Lowe LITTLE 62-63.

K344. Owner persuaded that his goods are spoiled. Drags meat at distance on string, trickster steals. U.S. (Black, Georgia): Harris NIGHTS 123-127; Harris COMPLETE 206-209; Harris FAVORITE 238-242. West Indies: Carter GREEDY 30-34.

K344.1.5* Crow makes animals believe beached whale is poison. He gets it all. Eskimo (Hooper Bay): Gillham BEYOND 51-64.

K344.1.6* Aldar-Kas throws shoes in pot with food. Eats in night. Russia (Steppes): Masey STORIES 65-72.

K345.2. Thief sent into well by trickster. A weeping boy tells a passing thief that he lost a silver cup in a well. The thief takes off his clothes and goes after the cup, intending to keep it. He find nothing. When he comes up, his clothes have been stolen. Aesop: Aesop AESOP'S (Grosset) 187-188.

K346.1. Thief guards his pursuer's horse while the latter follow a false trail. Type 1540. SEE ALSO: K341.9.1. Latvia: Durham TIT 75-80. Armenia: Tashjian ONCE 51-55. Persia: Mehdevi PERSIAN 51-61.

K352. Theft by posing as doctor. Trickster advises wife to slaughter pig and have the trickster eat it all. Jamaica: Williams-Ellis ROUND 197-203 (Anansi).

K352.1* Anansi as doctor to old lady fish has frying pan and oil brought. Eats patient. Jamaica: Sherlock ANANSI 70-75.

K354.1. Crow asks hospitality of sparrow and gradually takes possession of nest and kills young. Crow's nest, poorly made, had washed away. Sparrow had left crow out in rain some time before letting her in. India: Spellman BEAUTIFUL 12-14; Wiggin TALES 269-270.

K355. Trickster pollutes house so that he is left in possession. He is in upper room and throws filth on those below. SEE ALSO: K344. U.S.

(Black, Georgia): Brown BRER 1-5; Harris FAVORITE 610; Harris COMPLETE 137-141; Harris NIGHTS 26-32.

K355.2* Raccoon pretends roast geese were poisoned. Sells fox remedy. Native American (Seneca): Parker SKUNNY 31-42.

K359.2. Thief beguiles guardian of goods by assuming equivocal name. SEE ALSO: K602.

K359.2.2* Sungura claims name is "visitor" takes all food set out for the visitors. Africa: Heady SAFIRI 22.

K359.2.3* Fox says 'nothing at all' would be enough as payment, gives 'nothing at all.' England: Montgomerie TWENTY-FIVE 37.

K359.4. Crow makes friends with pigeon so as to be able to steal food in household to which he belongs. Cook catches crow and pigeon must leave because of association. Ceylon: Tooze WONDERFUL 100-102 (parrot). India (Jataka): Gaer FABLES168-171; Jacobs INDIAN 270-272.

K360. Other means of theft.

K361.1. Jackal ordered to take meat to lion's family takes it to his own. India: Montgomerie MERRY 38-41.

K362.1. For the long winter. The muskrat has been told to keep the sausage "for the long winter." When the trickster hears this, he claims to be Long Winter and receives the sausage. TYPE 1541. SEE ALSO: J2326. Italy: Dobbs MORE 15-17 (wife to prepare things for "the holidays", give everything to two women who call themselves The Holidays. Armenia: Tashjian ONCE 51-55 (Shrovetide, +K346.1). Great Britain: Jacobs MORE 7-11 (+K335.1.1.1; Hereafter This); Jacobs HEREAFTER THIS pb; Wiggin TALES 224-227 (Hereafter This). Netherlands: Ross BURIED 121-126 (Jan., Feb., March, twelve pieces, tramps come in twelve disguises).

K362.1.1* Husband divides butchered hog for Present Need, By and By, and Hereafter. Wife takes Mr. Presnell Sneed for Present Need and gives him one-third of hog and tells to send "By and By if he sees him." Trickster changes clothes and returns twice more to collect whole hog. U.S. (Appalachia): Chase WICKED 140-149.

K362.2. Ring to put on corpse's finger. A thief holds a corpse up to a lord's window. The lord shoots the corpse and leaves to bury it. The thief goes to the lady and gets a sheet to bury the corpse in and a ring to put on his finger. Type 1525A. SEE: K301.

K362.10. Give him what he wants. Thief sent to man's house for water, demands money. Man's wife refuses and thief shouts to husband who replies, "Give him what he wants." U.S. (Appalachia): Chase JACK 67-75 (Kiss, +K172). U.S. (Black, Georgia): Harris COMPLETE 709-714.

K362.10.1* Man sent to house for rupee, demands jewels. He calls to husband who replies, "Give it to him." India: Spellman BEAUTIFUL 61-75. Russia (Steppes): Masey STORIES 65-72 (says came for 'Biz', husband meant 'awl' called 'biz', trickster obtains daughter 'Biz' from wife). SEE ALSO: D882.1B Hitchcock.

K362.10.2* Lad takes precious rugs and feast and gold service for 'masters' picnic. Russia: Jameson TALES 17-29.

K364. Partner misappropriates common goods. SEE ALSO: K641.1.

K364.1* Elephant and Giraffe farm with hare. Each thinks hare does half work. Africa (Hausa): Arnott ANIMAL 241-252.

K364.2* Brer Rabbit advises Brer Wolf to roast peanuts before planting. Brer R. eats as they plant, claims moles ate. U.S. (Black, South Carolina): Faulkner DAYS 102-105.

K365. Theft by confederate.

K365.4* One thief waves arms at end of field. When farmer goes to see what is wrong he says "I can't believe it." Farmer is plowing with only one mule. By this time, confederate has stolen one of farmer's mules. Farmer can't believe it either. Armenia: Tashjian THREE 32-35 /Arbuthnot ANTHOLOGY 285/.

K366.1.1. Cow makes a hundred-fold return. The trickster has a cow that leads the parson's cow to him. He thus tests the parson's text "He who gives in God's name shall have it back a hundredfold." Type 1735. Majorca: Mehdevi BUNGLING 17-35 (+K176.1). England: Jagendorf MERRY 31-39 (Jack of Dover).

K366.1.2.1* Old Nag is substituted by thief for fine horse. Salt is fed to nag and it returns to former owner's stable in need of water. Thief thus discovered. Korea: Carpenter TALES.. KOREAN 231-234.

K366.1.3.1. Animal shams death and is sold. Returns to master. (cf. K1860). Japan: Wiggin TALES 429-431 (badger).

K371. Trickster hides in food and eats it. Nigeria (Hausa): Sturton ZOMO 2-13 (jackal). Nigeria (Fulani): Arnott AFRICAN 101-104 (hares go to "Sittincawnbin").

K371.1. Trickster throws fish off the wagon. The fox plays dead; a man throws him on the wagon of fish. The fox throws the fish off and carries them away. Type 1. SEE ALSO: K341.2.1; K1860. Lapland: Arnott ANIMAL 79-82 (feigns dead four times--fourth sleigh has fish, gnaws rope and drops sleigh off); Deutsch MORE 11. European: Jacobs EUROPEAN 42-50. Russia: Carey BABA 67-70; Carrick STILL 90-94; Daniels FALCON 84-89; Ginsburg ONE 17-20;

Riordan TALES..CENTRAL 20-22. Finland: Bowman TALES..TUPA 205-206. Scotland: Montgomerie TWENTY-FIVE 11-13. France: Edmonds TRICKSTER 99-102. U.S. (Black, Georgia): Harris COMPLETE 338-342; Harris NIGHTS 306-310 (wagon full of money, hare given ride). Van Woerkom MEAT pb.

K371.2* Hare feigns dead and is thrown on woman's basket of bananas on her head. Eats. Cambodia: Asia FOLK..FOUR 12-16.

K372. Playing godfather. By pretending that he has been invited to be godfather, the trickster makes an opportunity to steal the provisions stored by him and the dupe for the winter. When he returns on successive occasions he reports the name of the child as "Just Begun" "Half Done", etc. Type 15.

K372.0.1* Cat and Mouse. Germany (Grimm): Gag TALES 27-35 /Bleecker BIG 43-50/; Grimm GRIMM'S (Follett) 47-51; Grimm GRIMM'S (Grosset) 76-79; Grimm GRIMM'S (World) 291-294; Grimm HOUSEHOLD 37-39; Haviland FAVORITE ..GERMANY 32-40; Hurlimann CAT pb; Wiggin TALES 146-148. De La Mare ANIMAL 59-69. Lang YELLOW 1-4.

K372.0.2* Fox. Fox goes to christening. Partner suggests guilty party will ooze butter (honey). Scotland: Baker TALKING 71-76. Jacobs EUROPEAN 42-50. Pyle WONDER 281-290 (oozing butter).

K372.0.3* Brer Rabbit hears wife calling. Is ill, sinkin', all gone. +K401.1. U.S. (Black, Georgia): Harris FAVORITE 252-257; Harris SONGS 81-87; Harris COMPLETE 53-57.

K372.0.4* During morning fox has invitations to christening, wedding and anniversary, goes off to funeral when wolf comes to open lunch box. Switzerland (French): Duvoisin THREE 48-52.

K372.0.5* Other variants. Russia (Georgia): Papashvily YES 31-37 (fox tricks bear. Puerto Rico: Belpré TIGER 43-47 (fox tricks wolf, +K401.1).

K372.0.6* Fox tells wolf he is midwife. Eats honey. Russia: TALES..CENTRAL 179-180.

K372.2* Flea and louse steal milk and rice for pudding. Flea suggests a wood chopping contest--winner take all. Flea slips back and eats pudding during contest. Nepal: Hitchcock KING 76-79.

K378.1* Trickster walks back and forth over gold coins in street--with tar on his shoe soles. Cyprus: Neufeld BEWARE 58-67 (+K301C). French Canada: Barbeau GOLDEN 121-138 (+K301D).

K378.1.1* Gizo, Spider, coats stomach with wax and crawls over crow's fig pile, figs stick to stomach. Hausa: Aardema TALES 31-40.

K400. Thief escapes detection.

K401.1. Dupe's food eaten and then blame fastened on him. Trickster eats the common food supply and then, by smearing the mouth of the sleeping dupe with the food, escapes the blame. Type 15. U.S. (Black, Georgia): Harris FAVORITE 252-257, Harris COMPLETE 53-57, Harris SONGS 81-87. Puerto Rico: Belpré TIGER 43-47 (+K372; fox tricks wolf). Scotland: Baker TALKING 71-76 (butter to ooze from skin of guilty, fox tricks wolf). Jewish: Dobbs MORE 90-92 (monkey dupes goat). E. Africa: Heady SAFIRI 75-81 (leopard dupes genet). Native American: Gruenberg FAVORITE 338-340 (coyote dupes fox). Nigeria: Walker DANCING 59-64 (tortoise dupes bat, tortoise brushes teeth).

K401.1.2* Trail of stolen goods made to lead to dupe. Fox steals chickens from table and runs to barn where bear is stealing. Bear is caught. Netherlands: Green ANIMAL 97-115.

K401.2.2. Necklace dropped by crow into snake's hole on advice of fox leads men to kill snake which had eaten the crow's fledglings. India: Gaer FABLES 34-36; Korel LISTEN 107-114; Ryder PANCHATANTRA 74-81. Spain: Sawyer PICTURE 25-36.

K401.2.3. Surreptitious transfer of stolen article to innocent person's possession brings condemnation.

K401.2.3.1* (Clarke) Hare eats up future mother-in-law's stored benniseed while courting in sky world. Rubs seed on spider and blame is placed on spider. Spider returns to earth taking web along and animals have no way to return to earth (had climbed up web). Must jump and all are killed except hare, who rides elephant's back to break fall. Central Nigeria (Tiv): Arnott AFRICAN 74-77.

K402.1. The goose without a leg. Accused of eating the goose's leg, the thief maintains that it had no leg, and cleverly enforces his point by showing geese standing on one leg. (Usually the master confounds the rascal by frightening the geese so that they use both legs). Turkey: Kelsey HODJA 86-92 (Hodja takes one-legged goose to Tamarlane, camel roars and frightens nearby geese into putting down legs). Italy: Vittorini: OLD 2-13 /Greene CLEVER 117-123/. Portugal: Michael PORTUGUESE 130-132. Rumania: Ure RUMANIAN 16-18 (You should have yelled like that when I served the goose, yell has caused geese to put down second leg, gypsy cook).

K402.3.1* The ass without a brain. Lion tells ass of truce then kills. Fox eats brains--tells lion ass had none or would not have been tricked. Aesop: Aesop AESOP'S (Macmillan) 147.

K402.3.2* Dupe led to lion by trickster. Lion leaps at dupe and misses. Trickster persuades dupe to return a second time and lion kills.

Trickster steals brains and insists animal had none or would not have returned. Aesop: Aesop AESOP'S (Watts) 212-214 (fox dupes stag). Greece: Wilson GREEK 103-106.

K402.3.2.1* Lion leaps at donkey and misses. Fox convinces donkey he saw a female donkey and he returns. India: Korel LISTEN 31-36.

K402.3.2.2* Bear leaps at Buffalo and misses, landing in river. Gives up. North American (Seneca): Parker SKUNNY 109-116.

K403. Thief claims to have been transformed into an ass. While the owner sleeps the thief steals his horse, hitches himself to the wagon, and claims that he is the horse transformed into a man. Type 1529. Switzerland (French): Duvoisin THREE 16-19 (thief takes donkey's place under absent-minded farmer). England: Withers WORLD 45-46. Spain: Boggs THREE 39-46. Morocco: Holding KING'S 109-116.

K403.1* Boy substitutes self for donkey on rope and says he was transformed into a donkey for disobeying his mother. He is released and dupe returns to market and sees his stolen donkey there. "What? You disobeyed your mother again!" Turkey: Downing HODJA 74; Kelsey MULLAH 1-7; Walker WATERMELONS 62-64. Lebanon: Skurzynski THREE 17-27.

K404.1. Tails in ground. Thief steals animals and sticks severed tails into the ground, claiming that animals have escaped underground. Type 1004. Denmark: Hatch THIRTEEN 148-169 (pigs). U.S. (Black, Georgia): Harris FAVORITE 219-222; Harris COMPLETE 65-68; Harris SONGS 99-104; Harris NIGHTS 241-247; Harris COMPLETE 293-297. U.S. (Black, South Carolina): Faulkner DAY 152-157.

K404.1.1* Tails in ground. Trickster asks aid in pulling ox from mud and accuses dupe of pulling tail off. Tanganyika (Sukumu): Withers I SAW 139-140. U.S. (Black, Georgia): Harris NIGHTS 230-235; Harris COMPLETE 284-289. W. Africa: Aardema TALES 9-18 (head). Nepal: Hitchcock KING 47-52 (jackal tricks bear).

K409. Trickster crosses border each day on donkey. What is he smuggling across border? Donkeys. Iran: Shah MULLA 20.

K415. Marked culprit marks everyone else and escapes detection. Type 950. SEE: N455.3 (Ali Baba, trickster finds door marked, marks all doors). SEE: J758.1 (tail cut off).

K415.0.1* Fire to burn Anansi's house. Tells Anansi to leave out laundry to identify house. Anansi gets Tiger dupe to hang out laundry and Tiger's house is burned. West Indies: Carter GREEDY 68-72.

K415.0.2* Aldar-Kas smears dung over white spot on own horse and makes chalk mark on enemy's mare. Enemy kills own horse in night. Russia (Steppes): Masey STORIES 65-72.

K419.5. Thief paints horse black on one side and leaves other side white. Hoodwinked guardians make conflicting report of theft. SEE ALSO: K301Ai (Masey).

K419.5.1* Two friends never quarrel. Neighbor wears hat half red and half green to provoke quarrel. Nigeria: Walker DANCING 80-83.

K419.11* Anansi and Moos-Moos (mouse) are caught in tree while stealing Kisander's (cat) pudding from dokanoo tree. Moos-Moos calls to Anansi in disguised voice calling him "Ceiling Thomas" and Kisander doesn't catch them. West Indies: Sherlock ANANSI 35-40.

K420. Thief loses his goods or is detected.

K439.7.1. Tortoise asks greedy man to give him back first ruby it has given him to be sure second one will be perfect match; disappears into water with it. India: Hardendorff JUST 71-72.

K440. Other cheats.

K441.5* Otter and Badger exchange honey and fish. Hare tells each that goods make other's family ill so both make a present of goods to hare. E. Africa: Heady JAMBO 66-71. Nyakyusa: Kaula AFRICAN 46-48.

K443.14* Trickster steals robes and turban of drunken judge. Says stole them from a drunk. Judge cannot claim without revealing his drunkenness. Russia: Jameson TALES 9-16.

K444. Dream bread. The most wonderful dream. Three pilgrims agree that the one who has the most wonderful dream shall eat the last loaf. One eats it and declares that he dreamed that the others were dead and would not need it. Russia: Dolch OLD RUSSIA 11-17 (porcupine dreams ate ham, did); Downing RUSSIAN 135-137; Ginsburg ONE 14-16 (bear dreams eats honey, fox has same dream so eats honey since bear won't be hungry). Tatar: Bulatkin EURASIAN 123-124 (one dreamed went to mosque, second that became swan and flew off, third saw them leave so ate goose). French Canada: Leach NOODLES 17-18 (dreamed he ate partridge, must be true as it's gone).

K445. The emperor's new clothes. An imposter feigns to make clothes for the emperor and says they are visible only to those of legitimate birth. The emperor and courtiers are all afraid to admit that they cannot see the clothes. Finally, a child seeing the naked emperor reveals the imposture. Type 1620. SEE ALSO: J2311.0.1.1. Andersen: Haviland FAIRY 174-179 /Gruenberg FAVORITE 317-321 /; Lang YELLOW 27-32; Martignoni ILLUSTRATED 229-232; Rackham ARTHUR 240-245. Ceylon: Tooze WONDERFUL 26-31.

K445.1* Lord demands suit from tailor that will be noticed. Tailor uses cowhide and burlap sacks. Lord is pleased. Russia (Latvia): Ginsburg TWELVE 66-67.

K451.2. The wager that sheep are hogs. A trickster wagers with a sheep driver that the sheep he is driving are hogs. The next man to overtake them will act as umpire. The trickster's confederate now arrives and declares that they are hogs. Type 1551. SEE ALSO: K110.1.

K451.2.1* Three ogres meeting brahman claim his goat is dog, cow, donkey. He thinks it is a demon and drops it. India: Korel LISTEN 27-31; Ryder PANCHATANTRA 324-326.

K451.2.2* Priest, provost, and mayor convince dupe his pig is a dog and he leaves it behind. Pyle WONDER 163-174.

K451.3. Concealed confederate as unjust witness. A rascal who has hidden with a simple man a treasure found by them carries it away secretly, trying to have his associate condemned on the witness of a tree in which his father is concealed. India: Ryder PANCHATANTRA 184-190.

K452. Unjust umpire misappropriates disputed goods.

K452.1.1* Fox divides fish for two otters. Head to one, tail to other, middle for fox. SEE ALSO: K815.7. India (Jataka): Gaer FABLES 139-141; Reed TALKATIVE 62-63.

K452.1.2* Monkey divides rice cakes for two cats. Nibbles on each cake until both even = gone. Japan: Uchida SEA 55-60. Hungary: Ginsburg TWO pb (fox, bears).

K453. Cheating through knowledge of the law.

K453.1. (Clark) Trickster beats trail into guinea fowl's farm. Then claims farm on evidence of trail. Africa: Arnott AFRICAN 64-67 (spider tricks squirrel). Egypt: Kaula AFRICAN (monkey tricks stork). Ashanti: Courlander HAT 70-76 (Anansi tricks lizard). Togo: Courlander COW-TAIL 87-93.

K473. Sham blood and brains. Fox covers his head with milk and says that his brains have been knocked out. Frightens bear. Bear carries 'injured' fox who sings "the sick carries the sound" or some such ditty. Changes song when questioned. Type 3. SEE ALSO: K1241; K1875. Jacobs EUROPEAN 42-50. Finland: Bowman TALES..TUPA 258-260. Russia: Carey BABA 67-70; Riordan TALES..CENTRAL 20-22.

K473.1* Fox smears bread dough on face and tells woman she beat his brains out. She lets 'wounded' fox ride on her back. Russia: Daniels FALCON 84-89.

K473.2* Badger says he can only be killed by being beaten with bulrush. Medoc (Moutain Lion) beats him with cattail and takes fuzz for brains. (cf. K580). Native American (Micmac/Wabanaki): Hill BADGER 56-61.

K474.1* Man says is going to climb to heaven. Crowd which gathers tramples down clods and

field is prepared for crop thus. Japan: Bang MEN 2-4.

K475.1. The stolen meat is handed about. The thief hands it to his confederate. He says, "I haven't it." The confederate says, "I didn't steal it." Aesop: Aesop AESOP'S (Watts) 200-201.

K475.1.1. Ijapa carries wife on shoulders to Bamideleo's storehouse and she fills basket with yams. At shrine he swears he never picked up yams. She swears she never walked to Bamideleo's storehouse. Yoruba: Courlander OLODE 69-71.

K484.4* Hare tells animals that cow belongs to Great Mugassa. They kill and prepare feast under H's directions. H. warns that Mugassa will be furious if liver is stolen. Cries "Here comes Mugassa, Run." and all stampede leaving cooked cow. Africa (Waganda): Aardema TALES 9-17.

K491.0.1* Trickster paid to educate an ass. Puts grain between pages and teaches ass to turn pages saying "Eee," "Aah"--learning vowels already. SEE ALSO: K551.11; K1914. Flemish: Jagendorf NOODLEHEAD 175-179 (Tyll Ulenspiegel). India: Carpenter WONDER-DOGS 204-212 (dog).

K491.3* Trickster paid to educate calf tells woman he is rich man now. Man throws her out. Russia: Riordan TALES..CENTRAL 262-263.

K499.3.1* Giant cheated because of ignorance of agriculture. Farmer says thistles are only picked in Moon of Gobbages. Giant had required a bagful of thistledown. Scotland (Isle of Man): Mayne BOOK..GIANTS 170-176.

K499.8.1* (Clarke) Poorly dressed spider on courting expedition persuades well-dressed companion to exchange clothes. Spider gets fine wife. Ghana (Accra): Courlander COW-TAIL 95-102. Nigeria (Yoruba): Courlander OLODE 19-23.

K499.11* Nakim promised any reward for healing wife and baby. When asked one hundred riyals is given twenty and told he spilled medicines ruining priceless oriental rug. Arabia: Courlander TIGER'S 100-105.

K500 - K699. Escape by deception.

K500. Escape from death or danger by deception.

K510. Death order evaded.

K511. Uriah letter changed. Falsified order of execution. A messenger is sent with a letter ordering the recipient to kill the bearer. On the way the letter is changed so that the bearer is honored. India: Spellman BEAUTIFUL 82-85 (Prince sent by cruel stepmother to her mother (witch) with letter. SEE: H1273.2 (Three

Golden Hairs); K1355 (Robbers change letter); Z215 (Son of Seven Queens); G610Ai (Constantes and the Dragon).

K511.0.1* Mamadi who never lies is sent with message that chief will arrive soon. Chief deliberately stays away to prove Mamadi a liar. Mamadi garbles the message so much that he cannot be said to have lied. W. Africa (Soninke): Courlander COW-TAIL 79-86.

K511.0.2* King's fool sent by advisor with letter of execution saying "Execute this man." Advisor's son offers to deliver it for him. India: Reed TALKATIVE 22-24.

K511.1. Death evaded by persuading executioner that another victim was ordered (e.g. boy was ordered to kill hare. Hare persuades the boy that the father said, "Kill the rooster for the hare."). Africa (Swahili): Heady JAMBO 13-17 (Sungura hare tricks boy).

K512. Compassionate executioner. A servant charged with killing the hero (heroine) arranges the escape of the latter. SEE ALSO: B217.9; R111.1.3; Z65.1 (Snow White). Japan: Ozaki JAPANESE 74-86. Pyle WONDER 3-14 (bearskin).

K514. Disguised as girl to avoid execution.

K514.0.1. The Brave Man of Gola: Brave man is captured along with woman. Woman named 'Ladi' is treated well as that is a name in captor's tribe. Brave braggart also claims to be named 'Ladi.' Nigeria (Hausa): Courlander KING'S 51-55.

K520. Death escaped through disguise, shamming or substitution.

K521.1. Escape by dressing in animal (bird, human) skin. Types 311, 510B, 1137. SEE: R221D. (Catskin, Bearskin, Donkey skin, etc.); G561.1B. Grimm (girl escapes covered with honey and feathers).

K521.1.1. Man sewed in animal's hide carried off by birds. SEE: K1861.1.

K521.4.1.5* Finn McCoul is described as babe in cradle when (K1839.12) giant Cucullin calls. Wife Oona feeds Cucullin cakes with griddles baked inside, asks him to turn house 'as Finn does', 'baby' Finn bites off Cucullin's magical finger. Cucullin decides not to stay and meet Finn. Ireland: Adams BOOK..GIANTS 92-99; De Regniers GIANT 109-124; Jacobs CELTIC 171-183; Manning-Sanders BOOK..GIANTS 25-31; Williams-Ellis FAIRY..BRITISH 56-58 /Mayne BOOK..GIANTS 148-160/, /Greene CLEVER 41-54/; Sleigh NORTH 103-110.

K521.10. Hare escapes lion by being bundled in brushwood. East Africa: Heady JAMBO 24-33 (hare throws bundle of grass out of tree--is inside bundle).

K522. Escape by shamming death. Type 33. U.S. (Georgia, Black): Harris FAVORITE 247-251; Harris COMPLETE 9-12; Harris UNCLE 11-16 (Brer Possum).

K522.4. Captive parrots in net play dead and are thrown out: escape. SEE: J1662.2.

K522.4.0.1* Parrot has parson ask lawyer how to escape from cage. Lawyer faints. Parrot takes hint and feigns dead, owner tosses out. Hardendorff JUST 49-51. Tatar: Bulatkin EURASIAN 85-89.

K522.4.0.2* Cock in treasury eats gold then feigns dead. Thrown out. +Z52.4.1. Hungary: Manning-Sanders GLASS 83-85.

K522.4.1. Trout pretends to be dead. Fisherman ignores him. India: Montgomerie TWENTY-FIVE 18-19.

K522.4.2* Fox in pit feigns dead. Man throws him out. +K652.0.1. Finland: Bowman TALES 261-262.

K522.4.4* The Golden Peacock: Trapped peacock feigns dead and escapes. Recaptured he tells King how to conquer enemy by wearing precious peacock's golden tail feather. King shares kingdom with peacock and they rule together. Ceylon: Tooze WONDERFUL 36-42.

K522.9.1* Brer Wolf holes Brer Fox up in tree. Brer Buzzard set to guard. Fox stops singing and feigns dead. Escapes when hole unstopped. U.S. (Black, Georgia): Harris COMPLETE 185-189; Harris NIGHTS 95-99.

K523.1. Escape by shamming madness. Jewish: Ish-Kishor WISE 44-48 (King David is not imprisoned by enemy).

K525.1. Substituted object left in bed while intended victim escapes. Attempted murder with hatchet. Butter chest (or the like) in the hero's bed so that the ogre coming to murder him stabs the object. Type 115. SEE: G501 (Stupid Ogre); G512A (Jack the Giant Killer); K1951.1 (Seven at a Blow).

K525.1.0.1* Miss Goose leaves clothes bundle on bed. Brer Fox steals that. U.S. (Black, Georgia): Harris NIGHTS 3-7; Harris COMPLETE 119-123; Harris FAVORITE 35-38.

K525.1.4* Cicada (locust) leaves skin with rock inside. Coyote attacks and breaks teeth on rock. Nicaragua: Courlander RIDE 234-237. Native American (Pueblo): Dolch PUEBLO 67-77. Native American (Hopi): Courlander PEOPLE 82-85.

K526. Captive's bag filled with animals or objects while captive escapes (G501). Type 327C. SEE ALSO: B332 (Hobyahs); G422.1 (girl in drum); G501F (Gianni and the Ogre); K1611B (Mutsmag); K311.3 (Wolf and Seven Kids).

A* Buttercup. Witch with head under arm entices Buttercup from hiding with silver knife, spoon, fork on three visits. Naps on way home and he cuts self from bag and replaces with stones. Third time taken to witch's house. Witch's daughter to kill and make soup, doesn't know how to behead Buttercup. He shows her, makes soup of her (G526). Calls down chimney and drops stone on witch and her husband, killing them. Takes treasure home. Norway: Abjorsen NORWEGIAN 97-101; Fenner GIANTS 108-114; Undset TRUE 156-160 /Hoke Witches 32-36/.

B* Jack Buttermilk. Jack refuses buttermilk to witch, put into bag. Fills bag with thistles and escapes. Second time--stones. Third--taken to her house Jack fills bag with her dishes, climbs out chimney and escapes, she dumps out 'Jack' breaking all her dishes. England (Nottinghamshire): Colwell ROUND 87-89.

C* The Boy in the Bag. Little Jip: Witch One-Eye entices Jip (a little goblin) into bag of cherries--he gets out and fills with thorns. Second--bag of pears--he replaces with stone. Third time she disguises as peddler, has Jip hide in churn on pretence fox is coming to get him. Jip escapes at witch's house and calls down chimney, throws stone down killing witch. England: Manning-Sanders BOOK..GHOSTS 74-79.

D* Aram and the Dervish: Dervish puts Aram in bag. Aram escapes. Second time fills bag with rocks. Third time Dervish's wife to behead Aram. Aram tests knife for sharpness and kills her and cock. Calls down from loft. Dervish tries to climb to lift on rifle and shoots self. Aram inherits house. Armenia: Tashjian THREE 16-21.

K526.1* The Little Red Hen. Fox runs in circles to make her fall dizzy from perch. She cuts way out of bag and fills with rock and sews up. When he dumps into kettle the water splashes and scalds him. TALL..NURSERY 51-53. Kijima LITTLE pb.

K526.2* Mother Gull fills fox's sack with thorns and frees her chicks. In revenge fox tries to drink Lake Titicaca dry. He bursts (G522). Bolivia, Peru (Aymara): Arnott ANIMAL 224-230.

K526.3* Sungura Hare, eats honey from bag while being carried by Temba. Substitutes stones. E. Africa: Heady JAMBO 40-45.

K526.4* Brer Rabbit put hornet's nest in fox's bag, frees terrapin. U.S. (Black, Georgia): Harris FAVORITE 187-192; Harris NIGHTS 386-395; Harris COMPLETE 395-401.

K527. Escape by substituting another person in place of the intended victim. SEE ALSO: K842; R153.3.3.

K527.1* Trickster's children are being taken in

bag by enemy to be eaten. He substitutes enemy's own children. Congo: Burton MAGIC 41-43 (bushbuck tricks leopard). East Africa: Heady JAMBO 54-59 (bees substituted; hare tricks baboon).

K540. Escape by overawing captor.

K543. Biting the foot. Fox to bear, who is biting his foot: "You are biting the tree root." Bear lets loose. Type 5. Ceylon: Tooze THREE 8-21; Tooze WONDERFUL 107-110 (turtle to jackal). Jacobs EUROPEAN 42-50. Colwell YOUNGEST 236-239 (jackal to crocodile). India: Haviland FAVORITE..INDIA 53-62 (jackal to alligator); Montgomerie MERRY 38-41 (jackal to lion); Wiggin TALES 258-262 (jackal to crocodile). Scandinavia: Wiggin TALES 314 (fox to bear). U.S. (Black): Harris FAVORITE 110-113; Harris COMPLETE 39-41; Harris SONGS 59-63 (Terrapin to fox); Harris COMPLETE 757-760 (Hare to Bear). Brown WORLD 98-102. Yoruba: Fuja FOURTEEN 214-236. U.S. (Black, South Carolina): Faulkner DAYS 80-84 (hare to wolf).

K543.0.1* Kantchil (or jackal) to crocodile who is biting on his foot. "You are biting a tree root" (or stick of wood). Crocodile lets loose. Indonesia: Asia FOLK..THREE 18-22; De Leeuw INDONESIAN 77-80. N. Pakistan: Siddiqui TOONTOONY 55-60 (jackal). Malaysia: Arnott ANIMAL 155-160. Bangladesh: Asia FOLK 5-10. Hutchinson FIRESIDE 107-115.

K543.0.2* Kantchil to crocodile who is biting the root: "You are biting my leg." Crocodile pulls back into water and he escapes. Indonesia: Courlander KANTCHIL'S LIME PIT 87-94. Jacobs EUROPEAN 42-50 (fox to bear).

K544. Escape by alleged possession of external soul. Monkey caught for his heart (liver, etc.) as remedy makes his captor believe he has left his heart at home. (cf. K961.1).

K544.0.1* Shark needs heart for ill king. Swahili: Arnott AFRICAN MYTHS 135-139 /Sheehan FOLK 93-99/; Kaula AFRICAN 130-132.

K544.0.2* Crocodile needs heart for wife. India: Gaer FABLES 126-129; Galdone MONKEY pb; Korel LISTEN 14-20; Ryder PANCHATANTRA 381-423.

K544.0.3* Crocodile needs heart for mother. India: Babbitt JATAKA 3-9.

K544.0.4* Dragon needs heart for wife. Dobbs ONCE 15-18.

K544.0.5* Turtle needs hare's liver for queen. Dubois HARE pb.

K544.0.6* Turtle needs hare's liver for dragon king's daughter. Korea: Carpenter KOREAN 127-132.

K544.0.7* Turtle needs monkey's heart for ill

wife. Monkey offers to fetch more monkeys. +K553.1. China: Hume FAVORITE..China 39-46.

K544.0.8* Alligator needs Brer Rabbit's gizzard. U.S. (Black, Georgia): Harris FAVORITE 193-202; Harris COMPLETE 698-708.

K544.1. Jellyfish sent to fetch monkey to Dragon Queen's palace. Jellyfish tells monkey queen plans to eat his liver and monkey claims he left it at home. Jellyfish is beaten to a pulp for failure (A2367.1.2). (cf. K961.1). Japan: Bang MEN 27-35 (why octopus has no bones, A2367.1.3; why blowfish has spines, A2315.2); Farjeon CAVALCADE..GOBLINS 158-162; Hearn JAPANESE 36-41 (+A2433.8); Hoke DRAGONS 63-75; Leach HOW 118-120; Ozaki JAPANESE 189-202; Pratt MAGIC #4 (sea-turtle sent for monkey, jellyfish as gatekeeper tells of liver); Sakade JAPANESE 83-86 (res-cues drowning monkey on condition he gives liver, princess recovers without liver and octo-pus who masterminded downfall of jellyfish is banned and jellyfish made favorite); Wiggin TALES 432-434. Philippines: Robertson FAIRY 43-52. Swahili: Montgomerie TWENTY-FIVE 26-27 (shark). E. Africa: Heady SAFIRI 93-96 (shark).

K547.15* Carved ice bear causes polar bear to stop transfixed. Man kills it. Eskimo: De Wit TALKING 174-177; Melzack DAY 13-20.

K551. Respite from death granted until particu-lar act is performed. SEE ALSO: D1421.1.2 (pipe smoked).

K551.1. Respite from death until prayer is fin-ished. It lasts until rescue comes. SEE: S62.1 (Bluebeard); K555.1.0.1.

K551.1.0.1* Respite from death until Lord's Prayer is said. It is never said. +D1825.3.1. Norway: Asbjornsen NORWEGIAN 131-134; Undset TRUE 132-136.

K551.1.0.2* Respite until prayer is finished. Captive prays so loudly help is summoned. Poland: Zajdler POLISH 119-126.

K551.3.1. Respite from death while one plays the fiddle. Rescue arrives. SEE: D1415.2.5; B848.1. Germany (Grimm): Grimm HOUSE-HOLD 52-55; Grimm GRIMM'S (World) 372-375.

K551.11. Ten (five) year respite is given cap-tive while he undertakes to teach elephant (ass) to speak. Captive explains to friend that in that time, the captor, the elephant (ass), or himself is likely to die. SEE ALSO: K491. Flemish: Jagendorf NOODLEHEAD 175-179 (Tyll Ulenspiegel tells rector of Erfurt Univer-sity he can teach any creature to read and write, is given an ass and five years, K491.0.1). Italy: Cimino DISOBEDIENT #14 (elephant).

K551.25.1* Brer rabbit wants to show treasure

before being eaten by Hawk. U.S. (Black, Georgia): Harris COMPLETE 381-385; Harris NIGHTS 366-369.

K551.29* Respite from death until prince who wid-owed snake bears as many sons as she now has. Hardendorff JUST 64-70.

K551.30* Escape by pretending to know secret. Cottontail tricks coyote. Native American (Sia): De Wit TALKING 127-130.

K553. "Wait till I get fat." Captured person (ani-mal) persuades his captor to wait and fatten him before eating him. U.S. (Black, Georgia): Harris COMPLETE 381-384; Harris NIGHTS 366-369 (Brer Rabbit tricks Hawk).

K553.0.2. Calf: "Wait till I grow up." Latvia: Durham TIT 43-45 (lamb).

K553.0.3* "I'll be fatter when I return." Lamb-kin en route to grandmother's house thus passes jackal, vulture, tiger. Returns rolling inside a drum. India: Hutchinson CANDLELIGHT 3-8; Jacobs INDIAN 23-26; Richardson GREAT 113-121; Rockwell OLD 37-47; Wiggin TALES 271-273.

K553.0.3.1* Hare tricks jaguar, lion, fox, returns in barrel rolling. Panama: Carter ENCHANTED 87-90.

K553.0.3.2* Old woman visiting daughter tricks fox, tiger, king of monkeys, returns in gourd. Nepal: Asia FOLK 28-33.

K553.0.3.3* Old woman tricks tiger, jackal, bear, returns in pumpkin. India (Bengali): Bang OLD pb. India: Skurzynski MAGIC (illus. Rocco Negri) pb.

K553.1. "Let me catch you better game." Cap-tured animal pretends to help captor bring more desirable victim. Escapes. Ethiopia: Cour-lander FIRE 105-110 (lion and hare). China: Hume FAVORITE..CHINA 39-46 (+K544). Phil-ippines (Zambal): Sechrist ONCE 60-63 (mon-key crosses river on crocodile's back, taking to more monkeys).

K553.1.0.1* Lion falls in buffalo's trap. Offers to kill game for buffalo if freed. Buffalo asks ever increasing amount of meat. Finally asks for one of every kind of animal in forest. Lion begins by killing buffalo. Congo (Luban): Burton MAGIC 59-61.

K553.1.0.2* Partridge offers to decoy others into net if released. Falconer says traitor deserves to die and kills partridge. Aesop: Aesop AE-SOP'S (Grosset) 90; Aesop AESOP'S (Viking) 5; Aesop AESOP'S (Watts) 215; Aesop FABLES (Walck) 50.

K553.1.0.3* Trapped mother offers to give bear her children. Once home locks door. Russia: Wiggin TALES 43-44.

K553.1.0.4* Let me catch some better game. Brer Rabbit tricks hawk. U.S. (Black, Georgia): Harris COMPLETE 381-384; Harris NIGHTS 366-369.

K553.1.0.5* Brer Rabbit offers to catch bigger game for Brer Bar if released. Shows him man with gun. SEE ALSO: B279.1.1. U.S. (Black, South Carolina): Faulkner DAYS 85-88. Indonesia: Asia FOLK..THREE 18-22 (Kantchil).

K553.1.0.6* Tiger to sit with mouth open while Rabbit beats brush to send sparrows his way. Rabbit sets fire to brush. Korea: Kim STORY 58-65.

K553.1.0.7* Fox persuades coyote to climb tree while he catches prairie chickens. Fox flees. Native American (Southern Plains): Robinson COYOTE 41-52.

K553.2. Wait for the fat goat. Troll lets the first two goats pass on the bridge so that he may eat the biggest one. He is thrown into the water. Type 123. SEE ALSO: Z33.6 (Sody Sallyrytus). Scandinavia: Asbjornsen EAST (Row) 17-18; Asbjornsen THREE (illus. Brown) pb; Asbjornsen THREE (illus. Galdone) pb; Asbjornsen THREE (illus. Stobbs) pb; Arbuthnot ANTHOLOGY 237; Arbuthnot FAIRY 72-73; Association TOLD..GREEN 21-23; Aulaire EAST 175-178; Haviland FAIRY 56-57; Haviland FAVORITE..NORWAY 45-49; Hutchinson FIRESIDE 35-39; Richardson GREAT 122-128; Rockwell THREE 56-62; TALL..NURSERY 46-48. Germany: Wiggin TALES 442-443 (elf under bridge). Sweden: Löfgren BOY 29-31.

K553.3. Ram promises to jump into wolf's belly. Gives him a hard knock. The stunned wolf thinks he has swallowed the ram. SEE ALSO: K579.5.1. Latvia: Durham TIT 43-45. Lithuania: Deutsch TALES 56-62. Slavonic: Dobbs MORE 75-80. Russia: Riordan TALES ..CENTRAL 207-210.

K553.3.1* Ram promises to jump into wolf's belly. Gives him a hard knock. SEE ALSO: Z33.7. Russia: Hutchinson FIRESIDE 37-40. Russia (Ukraine): Bloch UKRAINIAN 28-35. Poland: Zajdler POLISH 119-126.

K553.4. Wolf is requested by horse to start eating from the rear: kicked to death. SEE ALSO: K566 (pull thorn from coat before eating); K1121 (wolf as sham doctor). Russia: Hutchinson FIRESIDE 37-40 (tail). Russia (Ukraine): Bloch UKRAINIAN 28-35. Russia (Steppes): Masey STORIES 116-117.

K553.5. "Soak me in the pond so that I will be juicy" (K581.1). Ceylon: Tooze WONDERFUL 107-110 (turtle to jackal).

K553.5.1* Tortoise says shell will come off if rubbed with mud at river--slips from grasp of captor. East Africa: Heady JAMBO 24-33 (lion). U.S. (Black, Georgia): Harris FAVORITE 140-146 (fox); Harris COMPLETE 563-568.

K553.5.2* Goose persuades wolf to wash him first. Dives. Poland: Zajdler POLISH 119-126.

K553.5.3* Turtle persuades tiger's cook to put his tail in river and will sing more sweetly. Escapes. West Indies: Sherlock ANANSI 31-34 /McDowell THIRD 72-74/. Haiti: Courlander PIECE 29-33; Thoby-Marcelin SINGING 21-29.

K555.1.0.1* Respite from death while gander prays. Endless tale (Z11). SEE ALSO: K551.1. De La Mare ANIMAL 78-79.

K561.1. Animal captor persuaded to talk and release victim from his mouth.

K561.1.0.1* Rabbit causes crocodile to laugh and escapes from his mouth. Burma: Brockett BURMESE 126-130.

K561.1.0.2* Boy caught by clam persuades clam that he feels pearl in it. Clam opens to see and boy escapes, his chickens crowing encouragement. Why chickens call "Tautavaya-o." Fiji: Heading SKY 39-48.

K561.1.0.3* Fox persuaded to talk, usually to taunt pursuers. Latvia: Durham TIT 91-92. Chaucer: Chaucer CHANTICLEER pb; Green BIG 158-164. Scotland: Wilson SCOTTISH 91-92. Aesop: Aesop FABLES (Walck) 115-117.

K561.1.0.4* Wolf agrees to call owl's children "I ate owl." Portugal: Lowe LITTLE 103-105.

K561.1.0.5* Fox asks Bear with Seagull in mouth which way wind blows. "North"--Gull dropped and Fox takes. Should have said "East." Finland: Bowman TALES 257; Fillmore SHEPHERD'S 69-71 (grouse).

K561.1.0.6* Cock persuades wolf to hold by tail. Feathers cause to sneeze. Poland: Zajdler POLISH 119-126.

K561.1.1. Cat fails to be beguiled into releasing mouse. The mouse tells the cat a tale. The cat answers at last, "Even so, I eat you up." England: Jacobs ENGLISH 48-50.

K561.2. Sheep persuade the wolf to sing. Dogs are summoned. Russia (Georgia): Papashvily YES 41-45 (calf). Aesop: Aesop AESOP'S (Watts) 151-152 (kid persuades wolf to play for him to dance, gods guarding flock hear and come).

K561.3. Crocodile persuaded to open his mouth. When he does, he shuts his eyes automatically and monkey escapes. SEE ALSO: K607.2.3.

K562. Rat persuades cat to wash face before eating. Escapes. Type 122B. SEE ALSO: A2545.2; K1121.2.1. U.S. (South Carolina Negro): Leach HOW PEOPLE 65 (mouse). Netherlands: Hardendorff TRICKY 121-122 (sparrow). Dobbs ONCE 67-69 (bird). Hardendorff JUST

78-81 (sparrow). Leach LION 13 (mouse).

K562.1. Captive trickster persuades captor to pray before eating. Escapes.

K562.1.0.1* Cock tricks fox. Norway: Asbjornsen (Row) EAST 32-33; Asbjornsen NORWEGIAN 135-136. Scandinavia: Hardendorff TRICKY 71-74; Wiggin TALES 287-288.

K562.1.0.2* Goose tricks fox. Scotland: Montgomerie TWENTY-FIVE 20-21.

K562.1.0.3* Squirrel tricks fox. German (Medieval): Green BIG 132-133.

K562.1.0.4* Old woman escapes animals. Nepal: Asia FOLK 28-33.

K562.1.0.5* Hare tricks wolf. U.S. (Black, Georgia): Harris FAVORITE 282-285; Harris NIGHTS 146-153; Harris COMPLETE 224-230.

K565. Thumbling in animal's belly persuades latter to go to his father's house for plunder: rescued. SEE: F535.1.1.

K566. Ass begs wolf to pull thorn out of foot before eating him. Kicks wolf in mouth. SEE ALSO: K553.4 (start eating from rear); K1121 (wolf as sham doctor). Majorca: Mehdevi BUNGLING 85-91 (horse and giant). Slavonic: Dobbs MORE 75-80. Aesop: Aesop AESOP'S (Watts) 130. Greece: Wilson GREEK 40-41.

K566.1* Ass asks wolf to take off his shoes before eating. Russia (Georgia): Papashvily YES 41-45. Byelorussian: Ginsburg LAZIES 12-17.

K567.2. Mother meadowlark sends chick to borrow kettle so she can prepare meal for snake. She flies off. Native American: Firethunder MOTHER pb.

K571. Escape by pretending to dance so as to be untied.

K571.0.1* Little girl unties Brer Rabbit. U.S. (Black, Georgia): Brown WORLD 102-108; Harris NIGHTS 12-17; Harris COMPLETE 126-129.

K571.0.2* Turtle playing flute and dancing untied by children. Brazil: Jagendorf KING 55-59.

K579.2.1* Kantchil (mouse deer) takes census of crocodiles, crossing stream on their backs. Usually says this is by order of Allah. Malaysia: Arnott ANIMAL 155-160. Indonesia: Bro HOW 22-28; Courlander KANTCHIL'S 87-94; De Leeuw INDONESIAN 77-80.

K579.2.2* Hare crosses to mainland by counting crocodiles. Usually white hare of Oki isle. Tail bitten off or fur pulled in revenge. (cf. A2378.4.1). Japan: Courlander TIGER'S 87-89 (+A2378.4.1.5, hare); Gruenberg FAVORITE

347-348; Haviland FAVORITE..JAPAN 73-89; Hearn JAPANESE 42-46; Ozaki JAPANESE 214-223; Sakade JAPANESE 103-105 (sharks); Uchida DANCING 49-57. Baganda/Alabama Negro: Leach HOW 69 (A2378.4.1, counts alligators to cross swamp).

K579.2.3* Fox jumps on log which rolls and dumps him into sea. He asks paws to paddle and tail to steer. Tail steers out to sea. He calls sea animals to surface so he can count them and crosses to shore on their backs. Russia (Yiddish): Ginsburg ONE 21-27.

K579.5.1. Wolf acts as judge before eating the rams. They are to go to the end of the field and run to him. They run at him and kill him. SEE ALSO: K553.3. Majorca: Mehdevi BUNGLING 85-91 (giant). Russia (Georgia): Papashvily YES 41-45 (choose fattest tail).

K579.8. A plea for a larger audience. Fox asks cock to come down from a tree and to sing for him. Cock asks fox to awake his companion, a dog, first. Dog kills fox. Colwell YOUNGEST 82-84. Aesop: Aesop AESOP'S (Watts) 29; Rice ONCE 58-64.

K579.9* Escape by promising false reward.

K579.9.1* Mussel releases crow on promise of uncle's kayak and goods. Crow has no uncle. Eskimo: Gillham BEYOND 121-126.

K580. Captor persuaded into illusory punishment. SEE: K473.2; K1611.

K581. Animal "punished" by being placed in favorite environment. SEE ALSO: J1909.8.1; K1611.

K581.1. Drowning punishment for turtle (eel, crab). By expressing horror of drowning, he induces his captor to throw him into the water-- his home. +A2312.1.6. SEE ALSO: J1860 (fools drown eel); K553.5; G555.1.1. India: Babbit JATAKA 10-12. Cherokee: Bell JOHN 80-83; Scheer CHEROKEE 65-68. Angola: Roche CLEVER pb. Philippines: Courlander RIDE 25-27.

K581.2. Briar Patch punishment for rabbit. By expressing horror of being thrown into briar patch he induces his captor to do so. He runs off. +K741 (tar baby); +A2233.1.1. Africa (Shona): Tracey LION 110-112 (hare thrown into sand). Native American (Cherokee): Scheer CHEROKEE 47-50. U.S. (Black): Arbuthnot FAIRY 215-216; Arbuthnot FAIRY 216-218; Courlander TERRAPIN'S 41-45; Faulkner DAYS 122-127; Harris COMPLETE 12-14; Harris FAVORITE 51-54; Harris SONGS 16-19. U.S. (W. Virginia): Haviland NORTH 109-114 (+K581.10).

K581.4.1. Birds caught in net fly away with it. SEE ALSO: J1024; K687.

K581.4.1.1* Birds in snare fly to king of mice

who gnaws them free. India: Gaer FABLES
191-196.

K581.7* Bullfrog persuades Bear to set him on
rock in millpond and kill with axe. Jumps away.
U.S. (Black, Georgia): Harris FAVORITE 233-
237; Harris COMPLETE 77-80; Harris SONGS
117-122.

K581.8. Turtle suggests being put in older bag.
Gnaws self free. Africa: Fournier COCONUT
THIEVES pb.

K581.9. Ijapa the Tortoise suggests that he be
killed by covering with grain. W. Africa (Yoruba); Courlander OLODE 86-89.

K581.10* Rabbit convinces others to feed him good
things to eat in cupboard until fat and then
throw in air and let burst--runs off.
+K741.0.3.2. U.S. (W. Virginia): Haviland
NORTH 109-114.

K600. Murderer or captor otherwise beguiled.

K601. Escape by posing as member of murderer's
family or tribe. SEE ALSO: F913.5.

K601.3* Escape by posing as member of murderer's family or tribe. Hen tells crocodile he can't
eat her as he is her brother. Both came from
eggs. Fjort: Leach HOW 111. E. Africa:
Heady SAFIRI 17-21. Bakongo/Fjort: Lexau
CROCODILE pb.

K602. "Noman." Escape by assuming an equivocal name. SEE ALSO: J1082.1; K359.2;
K1013.1.

K602.0.1* Odysseus tells Cyclops Polyphemus, he
is "Noman." Polyphemus tells other Cyclops
that "Noman" is slaying him. Odysseus then escapes under ram's belly (K603). De Regniers
GIANT 70-78. Greece: Wilson GREEK 97-102.

K602.1. Fairy child injured by man who says his
name is "Self." Child tells mother "Self did it."
Scotland: Wilson SCOTTISH 95-98 ('Ainsel',
brownie). England: Jacobs MORE 16-19.

K602.3* Mr. Badger inadvertently entering cave
with giant Black Snake of the Mountains, gives
his name as "Badger" and is thought to be a
badger in human form. Each tells what he fears
most (K975.1). Snake--hot tar; man--says he
fears gold. Man sends villagers to pour tar on
snake, he escapes and pours baskets of gold
(N182) into Mr. Badger's home in revenge.
Snake leaves area in embarrassment on learning
truth. Japan: Bang MEN 15-19; Uchida SEA
112-120.

K602.4* Peasant tells gatekeeper he is called "Me-
Myself," tells lord he is named "Hold-Me-Back",
cook--"The Cat." Cook tells master "The Cat"
wants to stay in the kitchen all night. Trickster takes supplies. Lord calls "Stop Hold-Me-
Back", servants do so, etc. France: Hardendorff TRICKY 81-85.

K603. Escape under ram's belly. +K602. SEE
ALSO: R153.3.3.

K603.1* Conal Yellow Claw: Giant throws ring to
escaped Conal which sticks to finger and answers Giant's call. Conal cuts off finger, casts
into sea and Giant is drowned. Ireland:
Manning-Sanders BOOK..GIANTS 85-89.

K603.2* Giant keeps Jack in slavery seven years.
Jack puts out Giant's one eye and escapes in
dog skin. England: Jacobs MORE 92-93.

K603.3* Lads seek to know what evil is. Tailor
is eaten by one-eyed Likho (Evil). Blacksmith
blinds her and escapes under sheep, touches
gold handled axe in tree and sticks to it. He
cuts off hand to escape. Knows what evil is.
Russia: Downing RUSSIAN 148-151.

K604. The three teachings of the bird (fox). In
return for release from captivity the bird (fox)
gives man three teachings. These usually mock
the man for his foolishness in releasing what he
has. Type 150. +J21.12.1; +J21.13.1; +J21.14.1.
Aesop: Aesop AESOP'S (Grosset) 69-70 (nightingale); Aesop FABLES (Macmillan) 115. Wilson
SCOTTISH 93-94.

K606. Escape by singing song. Captive gradual-
ly moves away and at last escapes. Eskimo:
Gillham BEYOND 99-105 (mouse tricks fox,
+A2411.1.3.1.1). Russia (Steppes): Masey
STORIES 116-117 (sheep dance and escape).

K606.0.4. Ten cloth merchants captured are ordered to dance. The leader sings in code instructing them to attack the three robbers.
They succeed. India: Jacobs INDIAN 160-163.

K606.1. Escape by playing music.

K606.1.2. Musician in hell playing for the devils,
purposely breaks fiddle strings. Must return to
earth to repair strings. Once home Devil who
accompanies him sleeps in bread trough and maid
kneads him in the morning. Devil escapes.
Later tries to take Fiddler John back. John
cries that maid is coming again and Devil flees
(T251.1.1). Latvia: Durham TIT 96-106.

K606.1.5* Giant's wife warns man to play song
poorly on balangi. He is thrown out. If had
played well Giant would have considered him a
rival and beaten him. Sierra Leone (Krio):
Robinson SINGING 34-43.

K606.2. Escape by persuading captors to dance.

K606.2.0.1* Raven tricks marmot. Eskimo (Bering Strait): Cothran MAGIC 22-24.

K606.2.0.2* Weasel tricks raven. Eskimo: Melzack RAVEN 71-78.

K606.2.0.3* Geese persuade wolf to sing. Byelorussian: Ginsburg LAZIES 12-17.

K606.2.1* Groundhog teaches wolves song and

dance. Edges nearer hole and escapes. +A2378.4.9. Native American (Cherokee): Bell JOHN 83-86; Belting LONG 29-33; Scheer CHEROKEE 31-32. Colwell MAGIC 70 (hare) /Manning-Sanders TORTOISE/.

K606.2.3* Kwatee persuades wolves to dance in search of 'real' killer of wolf and escapes. Native American (Makah): Matson LEGENDS 103-106.

K607. Enemy in ambush (or disguise) deceived into declaring himself. SEE: S211.

K607.1. The cave call. ("Hello, house!") An animal suspecting the presence of an enemy in his cave (house) calls and receives no answer. He then says, "Don't you know, oh cave, that we have agreed that I must call you when I come home from abroad and that you in turn must answer me?" The hiding animal answers and the other flees.

K607.1.0.1* Leopard in spider's house. Liberia/ Ghana: Arkhurst ADVENTURE 12-20.

K607.1.0.2* Lion in jackal's cave. India: Korel LISTEN 60-63 (goat's cave); Ryder PANCHA-TANTRA 361-362.

K607.1.0.3* Alligator in jackal's house. S. India: Wiggin TALES 258-262. India: Haviland FAVORITE..INDIA 53-62; Spellman BEAUTIFUL 37-39. W. Pakistan: Siddiqui TOONTOONY 55-60.

K607.1.0.4* Tiger in Rabbit's house. Puerto Rico: Alegria THREE 44-51.

K607.1.0.5* Brer Wolf in Brer Rabbit's house. U.S. (Black, Georgia): Harris FAVORITE 159-161; Harris COMPLETE 551-554 /Arbuthnot FAIRY 218-219/.

K607.1.0.6* Lion in Hare's house. E. Africa: Heady JAMBO 72-77.

K607.1.0.7* Turtle tricks tiger. West Indies: Sherlock IGUANA 76-95.

K607.1.0.8* Tortoise in monkey's cave. China: Hume FAVORITE..CHINA 39-46.

K607.2. Crocodile masking as log obeys suggestion that he move upstream (sink). He thus betrays himself.

K607.2.0.1* Kantchil tricks crocodile. Indonesia: Courlander KANTCHIL'S 87-94; De Leeuw IN-DONESIAN 77-80.

K607.2.0.2* Jackal tricks crocodile. India: Spellman BEAUTIFUL 33-39.

K607.2.1* Crocodile in ambush betrays self by talking. Crocodile masking as rock. Monkey calls to rock "Why don't you answer as usual?" India: Babbitt JATAKA 3-9; Gaer FABLES 126-129; Wyatt GOLDEN 98-100.

K607.2.2* Crocodile in ambush in berry patch obeys suggestion (by jackal) that patch should roll about. India: Haviland FAVORITE.. INDIA 53-62 (pile of figs); Spellman BEAUTI-FUL 37-39. S. India: Wiggin TALES 258-262 (pile of figs). Bangladesh: Asia FOLK..FOUR 5-10. Hutchinson FIRESIDE 107-115 (pile of figs).

K607.2.3* Crocodile masking as rock obeys suggestion to open mouth. Does so closing eyes and trickster (monkey) jumps on head to opposite shore. India: Babbitt JATAKA 3-9; Wyatt GOLDEN 98-100.

K607.2.4* Crocodile in ambush obeys suggestion-- "I always see little crabs peeping up through mud"--pokes up snout. "Crabs always blow bubbles." Blows bubbles. Hutchinson FIRE-SIDE 107-115. S. India: Wiggin TALES 258-262. India: Haviland FAVORITE..INDIA 53-62. Colwell YOUNGEST 236-239.

K607.3. Sham dead man deceived into making gesture. Obeys suggestion as to how dead man should act and betrays himself. SEE ALSO: K571.

K607.3.0.1* Fox yells 'Wahoo.' U.S. (Black, Georgia): Brown WORLD 112-116; Harris FAVORITE 136-139; Harris COMPLETE 36-39; Harris SONGS 54-58.

K607.3.0.2* Jackal gets crocodile to wag tail. W. Pakistan: Siddiqui TOONTOONY 55-60. India: Turnbull FAIRY 27-32 (crab as crocodile's accomplice).

K607.3.0.3* Tiger plays dead to help Anansi lure Kling-Kling bird, Kling-Kling says all dead laugh. Jamaica: Sherlock ANANSI 41-46.

K607.3.0.4* Wolf, dead always grin. U.S. (Black, Georgia): Harris COMPLETE 372-374; Harris NIGHTS 353-356.

K607.3.0.5* Jaguar rolls over. Brazil: Eels TALE..AMAZON 164-169.

K607.3.4* Sham-dead animal comes to life when pinched (tickled). Liberia (Mano): Dorliae ANIMALS 2-9 (leopard). Native American (Seneca): Parker SKUNNY 68-81 (raccoon, crabs pinch lizard, he eats all).

K607.4* Fox disguised as Buddha obeys suggestion of monk who says "The real Buddha always sticks out his tongue when I say my prayers." Thrown in boiling pot (cf. D421.8). Japan: Schofield FOX 33-39.

K607.4.1* Witch as old lady is carried by man. Once in home she turns to statue of Kannon (Kwan Yin). He says real Kannon always smiles and reaches for food when he offers. Throws into boiling pot. Japan: Bang MEN 61-65.

K607.5* Witch masking as donkey lengthens self when trickster says there is not room for him on back. SEE: K1611D (Fereyl and Debbo Engyl).

K611.5* Boy crunches dry bread to arouse dying father. Gives Death some to crunch too and Death misses moment to reap. Gypsy: Jagendorf GYPSIES" 129-133.

K619.4* Murderer or captor beguiled--miscellaneous. Man falls into hole in tree (well). Monkey pursuer puts tail in hole and man pulls it off. +N392.1.1. Japan: Pratt MAGIC #12; Uchida MAGIC 12-21.

K620. Escape by deceiving the guard.

K622.1. Escape by pretended debate as to which must be judged. Jackals thus induce leopard to permit them to enter their cave, while he waits in vain. E. Pakistan: Arnott ANIMAL 136-140 (foxes escape tiger).

K629.2.3* Captured Anansi is thrown in itchy cowitch plants. He calls that queen's coming and captors run off to see. Jamaica: Jagendorf KING 171-176.

K629.2.4* Brer Rabbit is trapped in hollow tree. Pretends to think Turkey Buzzard is Brer Fox, knowing that Brer Fox has left Turkey Buzzard to guard hole. Brer R. says he'll chase squirrel out other side of tree, T. runs around to catch it and R. escapes. U.S. (Black): Brown WORLD 63-66; Harris COMPLETE 21-25; Harris UNCLE REMUS 30-36; Harris FAVORITE 61-65.

K629.2.5* Brer Buzzard pretends Brer Rabbit is still captive in tree and lets returning Brer Fox chop away trying to get Brer Rabbit out. Brer Fox finally captures Brer Buzzard instead but Brer Buzzard's tail feathers come out and he flies off. U.S. (Black): Brown WORLD 67-71; Harris COMPLETE 25-28; Harris FAVORITE 66-70; Harris UNCLE REMUS 36-41.

K630. Escape by disarming (making pursuit difficult).

K632. Mice gnaw enemies' bow strings and prevent pursuit. Tibet: Hume FAVORITE..CHINA 102-108 (in return King builds levees to keep river from flooding mice's nest and banishes cats).

K635. Sleeping enemies--hair tied to an object prevents pursuit. Japan: Uchida MAGIC 53-62 (+H328.10).

K635.2* Two-headed hermit captures brother and sister. They comb his hair and tie down so can escape. They tie pumice to arms and legs and escape by sea. Ogre ties real stones on self and drowns (J2400). Tongatabu: Holding SKY 61-74.

K635.3* Double Face ogre takes place of lover eloping with girl. She ties his hair to tipi poles as he sleeps. Beaver pet gnaws tree to make bridge for her escape. Native American (Lakota): Yellow Robe TONWEYA 52-58.

K636.2* Brother Fox cannot catch Brother Rabbit even though is rowing. B. Rabbit, poling boat, just pushes rowboat away with pole. U.S (Georgia, Black): Harris COMPLETE 391-395; Harris NIGHTS 381-385.

K639.1* Crane removes bone from lion's throat but props mouth open with stick first as precaution. India: Jacobs INDIAN 1-5.

K640. Escape by help of confederate.

K641. One animal saves another by frightening enemy away.

K641.1* Fox and goose farm together. Fox leaves all work to goose then claims crop. Greyhound friend of goose kills fox. SEE ALSO: K364.1. Spain: Wiggin TALES 10-11.

K641.2* Fox brings wolf to help exact taxes of ram. Ram buys Camel. Fox leaves. Russia: Carrick STILL 66-72.

K641.3* Brown chameleon threatens to eat lion in loud voice and lion flees. Chicken thus rescued lays eggs and saves life of starving lizard in turn. Africa (Gogo); Kaula AFRICAN 51-54.

K641.4* Sheep promises to aid turtle if in need. Turtle invites female turtle to dinner. She brings friends. Too many come and he calls on sheep for aid. Sheep tramples turtles and they leave. Haiti: Johnson HOW 83-87.

K641.5* Hornets route Brer Wolf and Brer Fox who are chasing Brer Rabbit. U.S. (Black, South Carolina): Faulkner DAY 164-167.

K642.2* Turtle gnaws deer free from snare while crow distracts hunter (or brings water to soften cords). Turtle caught. Released deer leads hunter away then circles back to release turtle from bag. Burma: Brockett BURMESE 191-194. India: Gaer FABLES 136-139 (woodpecker); Korel LISTEN 83-89 (mouse helps gnaw turtle free); Wiggin TALES 193-196; Wyatt GOLDEN 22-26.

K642.3* Jackal lures deer into snare. Crow advises deer to feign dead, once taken out of snare, crow distracts farmer's attention and deer flees. Farmer throws cudgel at fleeing deer which hits and kills jackal. India: Gaer FABLES 74-77.

K642.3.1* Jackal refuses to help free deer. Crow and woodpecker distract man while turtle gnaws deer free. Man throws axe at crow, killing jackal instead. Ceylon: Tooze WONDERFUL 96-99.

K644. Monkey (trickster) attracts attention of mowers until young birds can fly away from the harvest field. SEE ALSO: J1031.

K644.1* Kantchil distracts mowers for six days until ground-owl eggs hatch and fledglings can escape. Indonesia: Bro HOW 96-106.

K648.1* Hare distracts dog so that crow can escape. Russia: Ginsburg THREE 51.

K649.5.1* White Rabbit warns Bear of pendulum rock trap set by red fox. Korea: Anderson BOY 39-47.

K649.9. Confederate causes confusion so that prisoner can escape.

K649.9.1* Lion steals ostrich chicks and council members fear to disput his word that they are his. Mongoose has ostrich dig tunnel under anthill. He calls out that ostrich chicks have feathers so belong to ostrich, then he escapes via anthill tunnel. Ostrich chicks and other animals escape as lion chases mongoose. Masai: Aardema TALES 70-76. E. Africa: Heady JAMBO 85-90.

K649.9.2* Little animals dig pit in cave and Brer Tiger and Brer Bear, who are forcing Brer Rabbit to lead to Brer Gilyard's treasure, fall in. U.S. (Black, South Carolina): Faulkner DAYS 178-185.

K649.13* Confederate leads pursuer away by getting pursuer to chase self. Sungura hare saves hunter from lion. E. Africa: Heady JAMBO 24-28.

K650. Other means of escape.

K651. Wolf descends into well in one bucket and rescues fox (rabbit) in the other. Type 32.

K651.0.1* Fox and Rabbit. U.S. (Black Georgia): Arbuthnot ANTHOLOGY 385; Brown BRER 12-15; Harris FAVORITE 1-5; Harris COMPLETE 50-53; Harris SONGS 76-81.

K651.0.2* Wolf and Fox. Gerhard von Minden (13th century): Green ANIMAL 155-156. Spanish/Jewish: Dobbs MORE 93-96 (+J1791.3).

K652. Fox climbs from pit on wolf's back. Type 31.

K652.0.1. Fox asks wolf to stand on hind legs and see if sun is rising--leaps out on wolf's shoulders. Wolf asks fox to sit down and tell him when sun rises, pulls back into pit by dangling tail. Fox feigns dead and man throws out and wolf leaps out on man's shoulders (K522.4.2). Finland: Bowman TALES..TUPA 261-262.

K652.1. Kantchil persuades animals to come down in pit for safety at end of the world (or sky is falling). Says any who sneeze must be thrown out of holy pit--he sneezes. (Sometimes climbs on backs of animals.) Indonesia: Courlander KANTCHIL'S 6-10 (elephant, bear, tiger) /Courlander RIDE 28-31/; De Leeuw INDONESIAN 77-80 (climbs on elephant).

K652.1.0.1* Giant Gergasi tricked into hole lined with rubber latex on pretext world is coming to an end. Gergasi promises to leave area and

Kantchil has birds bring berry juice to dissolve latex and free Gergasi (K741.2). Indonesia: Bro HOW 72-78.

K652.2* Vixen in well invites goat in to bathe. Escapes on goat's horns. Bulgaria: Pridham GIFT 81-83. Greece: Wilson GREEK 65-67. Aesop: Aesop AESOP'S (Random) 73; Aesop AESOP'S (Viking) 53-54; Aesop AESOP'S (Watts) 42; Aesop FABLES (Macmillan) 163; Aesop FABLES (Walck) 14-15; Rice ONCE 16-21.

K652.3* Hedgehog asks fox to throw him out of pit. Tells fox to help self with his seventy-seven-fold understanding. Russia: Wiggin TALES 41-42.

K661.3. Insect in nose of murdered person simulates snoring and allays suspicion. Masai: Aardema TALES 41-50 (hare puts hornets in dead lion cub's nostrils).

K671.1* Anansi and son Kwaku Tsin captured by dragon escape up sky ladder. Throw bones to dragon who must go back down ladder to eat them. On second try magic fiddle is played and dragon must back down ladder to dance (D1415.2.5). Third time rope is cut. Kwaku Tsin made sun, Anansi moon, other captives = stars. Ghana (Ashanti): Jablow MAN 83-85.

K687. Birds escape death by flying away with net (K581). SEE: K581.4.1; J1024.

K687.1* Greedy man tries to trap one hundred ducks at once. Birds carry off trap and hunter with it. He falls, turns into duck, falls into snare, tears dissolve ropes and restore to human form. He never eats flesh again. Japan: Sakade JAPANESE 37-40; Uchida SEA 91-98.

K687.2. King of pigeons is caught in net. Fellow pigeons carry net with king in it to mouse who gnaws pigeon free. Crow seeing this wishes to make friends with the helpful mouse also. India: Montgomerie TWENTY-FIVE 38-40.

K688* Trickster tells villain that he plans to go to one area, then goes elsewhere. Escapes villain's ambush.

K688.1* March asks where sheperd is taking the sheep and rains there. Shepherd goes elsewhere. At end of month Shepherd tells truth about where he plans to go on morrow. March borrows a day from April and snows on him. Never returned day to April, why March has thirty-one days. Italy (Tuscany): Vittorini OLD 2-6 /Arbuthnot FAIRY 129-130/, /Arbuthnot ANTHOLOGY 269-270/.

K688.2* Leopard asks Tota monkey where he will pasture next day. T. says valley but goes to hills, etc. Ethiopia (Guragé): Courlander FIRE 65-72.

K688.3* Bouki asks Ti Malice's son Malisso where calf sleeps at night. M. tells, then changes place each night. Finally tells that calf sleeps in cave, B. grabs hold of tiger in cave, tells family to beware of that calf Ti Bef. Haiti: Courlander PIECE 94-96.

K688.5* Jackal asks bulbul bird where he plans to go each day, b. lies and escapes. Jackal finally goes to opposite of place b. said and does catch b. Nepal: Hitchcock KING 97-100.

K688.6* King's son is exiled to Lanai for uprooting breadfruit plants, mother smuggles cuttings to him. Spirits on Lanai ask where he sleeps but he outwits by lying to them and sleeping elsewhere. He forces spirits to work, saying only those who share the work can share the food. They flee to Koolawe to escape work. Having successfully grown a new crop and freed island of spirits he can return home again. Hawaii: Thompson HAWAIIAN..TRICKSTERS 14-22.

K688.7* Beetle calls to Long Nosed Mice to get out of way of his throwing stick and then throws it at place where they have fled. Mantis sends Striped Mouse to vanquish B. S. does not go where B. points, catches stick and throws back killing B. Revives dead mice. Bushmen: Helfman BUSHMEN 80-84.

K689. Other means of escape.

K689.1* Earthworm on hook tells fish not to bite—is thrown away by fishermen. Vietnam: Vo-Dinh TOAD 41-44.

K700 - K799. Capture by deception.

K700. Capture by deception.

K710. Victim enticed into voluntary captivity or helplessness.

K710.1* Attempts to entice victim into voluntary captivity fail.

K710.1.1* Camel, imitating hare's tricks, tries to trick Black Cobra into satchel by arguing with self that cobra won't fit. Cobra chases camel off. N. Nigeria (Hausa): Sturton ZOMO 77-88.

K711. Deception into entering bag. SEE ALSO: D313.1.1; K717.2; K842.

K711.5* Blackbirds tie coyote in bag so 'hail' won't hurt him. They stone sack and he thinks is hail. Native American (Pueblo): Dolch PUEBLO 79-85. Native American (Central Plains): Robinson COYOTE 53-62 (mice).

K711.6* Blackbirds enter bag to be weighed. U.S. (Black, Alabama): Courlander TERRAPIN'S 60-64.

K711.7* Squirrels get in bag to help crack nuts. Captured. U.S. (Black, Georgia): Brown BRER 127-132; Harris COMPLETE 264-268; Harris NIGHTS 203-207.

K713.1. Deception into allowing self to be tied. SEE ALSO: D313.1.1; J2132.5.1.

K713.1.1. Animal allows himself to be tied so as to avoid being carried off by storm. Puerto Rico: Alegria THREE 44-51; Belpre TIGER 11-18 (hare-tiger). West Indies: Sherlock IGUANA 76-95 (turtle tricks tiger). U.S. (Black, Georgia): Faulkner DAYS 89-94 (tiger); Harris COMPLETE 351-355 (lion); Harris NIGHTS 325-329.

K713.1.2. Animal allows himself to be tied to another for safety. Carried to his death. SEE: J2132.5.

K713.1.3. Animal persuaded to be tied by promise of food. Switzerland (French): Duvoisin THREE 61-66 (fox tied to pole and lifted into cherry tree).

K713.1.3.1* Brer Fox lets self be tied when Brer Rabbit promises Rooster to eat. Brer R. calls hounds. U.S. (Black, South Carolina): Faulkner DAYS 95-98.

K713.1.9* Snake allows self to be tied to pole to measure length. Anansi ties Python. Ashanti: Aardema SKY-GOD pb; Courlander HAT 3-8. Liberia: Haskett GRAINS 40-42. Jamaica: Sherlock ANANSI 3-12 /Haviland FAIRY 86-91/. U.S. (Black, Georgia): Brown BRER 127-132; Harris COMPLETE 264-268; Harris NIGHTS 203-207. U.S. (Black, Alabama): Courlander TERRAPIN'S 60-64 (to have back straightened).

K713.1.10* Animal allows self to be tied as part of game. Leopard tricked by Anansi. W. Africa: Haley A STORY pb (tiger). Switzerland (French): Duvoisin THREE 61-66 (lion).

K713.1.11* Animal ties tail to tree to effect rescue from pit. Leopard tricked by Anansi. Ashanti: Courlander HAT 3-8.

K713.1.12* Monkeys pull out feathers of adjutant bird. A. convinces monkeys to tie tails together to keep boat from rolling. A. has accomplice tortoise act as plug, then lets boat sink. Borneo: Williams-Ellis ROUND 274-278.

K713.3. Hare persuades wolf and fox to put their heads in loop or rope to strangle tiger and are dragged to death. Tibet: Hume FAVORITE.. CHINA 55-60.

K713.4* Fox allows partridge to sew his mouth shut so he can learn to whistle. Argentina: Barlow LATIN 18-22.

K714.2.3* Victim tricked into entering bag.

K714.2.3.1* Tortoise tricks lion into hiding in bag to catch prey. Puts bag into boiling pot. Nigeria: Walker NIGERIAN 66-67.

K714.2.3.2* Kantchil claims to have magic bag

that will make two tigers out of one. SEE ALSO: N228. Indonesia: Courlander KANTCHIL'S 118-121.

K774.2.4* Victim tricked into entering cage.

K714.2.4.1* Hare plays balafon for dancing guinea fowl. To run into cage if it rains, sprinkles them with wet broom. Africa: Guillot AFRICAN 84-87.

K714.2.4.1.1* Hare tells birds that cage will protect from snake. Liberia: Haskett GRAINS 40-42.

K714.2.4.2* Hare builds 'house' (cage) for crocodile. Fire is built quite near and crocodile promises to steal no more sugar cane. N. Nigeria (Hausa): Sturton ZOMO 100-112.

K714.2.4.3* Farmer constructs trap looking like palanquin for jackal. Jackal invites tiger to go to wedding in palanquin. Pakistan: Siddiqui TOONTOONY 32-36.

K714.2.5* Victim tricked into entering drum. Turtle tells Osebo (leopard) that his drum is smaller than Nyame's (Sky-God) because Osebo can get into Nyame's drum. Osebo enters drum and is trapped. +A2312.1.0.1; A2411.1.1.1.3. West Africa (Ashanti): Courlander HAT 32-37.

K714.2.6* Dupe tricked into entering gourd. Anansi pours water on hornet's nest to invite them to shelter from rain in his gourd. West Africa (Ashanti): Aardema SKY-GOD pb; Courlander HAT 3-8; Haley A STORY pb.

K714.3. Dupe tricked into entering hollow tree. U.S. (Black, Georgia): Harris NIGHTS 74. U.S. (Black, South Carolina): Faulkner DAYS 139-140 (Brer Rabbit tricks Brer Wolf).

K715.1. Deception into allowing oneself to be trapped. "Show me how." (cf. G526).

K715.1.1* Hyena shows guinea fowl how to enter cage. Unsuccessfully imitating hare's trick. +K714.2.4.1. Africa: Guillot AFRICAN 84-87.

K717. Deception into a bottle (vessel). Insects (or a spirit) having escaped from a bottle are told that they cannot return. They accept the challenge and go back into the bottle. Type 331. SEE ALSO: K722 (Deception to small size); K213 (Devil into Knapsack). Germany (Grimm): Grimm GRIMM'S (Follett) 309-316.

K717.1* Deception into pot. Fox masquerading as Bhudda obeys suggestion that Bhudda always bathes in rice pot before dinner. Japan: Scofield FOX 33-39.

K717.2* Animal proves it can fit into basket. Trapped. Bahamas: Jagendorf KING 28-30 (Jack tricks snake into noose, birds into basket). Africa: Burton MAGIC 89-94 (Hare tricks antelope, birds into bag to see if k. can lift them).

K717.3* 'Sorrow' tricked into making self small enough to get into hub of cart wheel. Trapped. +N250.4. Russia: Downing RUSSIAN 122-128.

K717.3.1* 'Trouble' tricked into making self small enough to fit into crack in log. Trapped. Pyle WONDER 29-38.

K717.4* Children captured by ogre challenge him to prove he was one who captured them. He shows cloak of invisibility. They put it on and escape. China: Lin MILKY 57-67.

K717.5* Knapsack. Devil bet he can't fit into knapsack. Wales: Pugh TALES 21-28 (+D1825.3.1.1). Russia: Downing RUSSIAN 81-89 (+K213).

K717.6* Wine cask. Devil tricked into entering bung hole. Switzerland: Müller-Guggenbühl SWISS 52-56 (+K213, Devil in Knapsack).

K717.7* Ghost who claims to have entered through keyhole taunted into bottle. England: Littledale GHOSTS 79-82.

K718.1.2.1* Tails of adjutant birds in boat tied together on pretense of keeping boat from rolling. Boat sinks and they nearly drown. Borneo: Williams-Ellis ROUND 274-278.

K721. Cock persuaded to crow with closed eyes. Seized. Type 62. SEE ALSO: K334.1 (persuaded to sing). Scandinavia: Hardendorff TRICKY 71-74; Wiggin TALES 287-288. Norway: Asbjornsen EAST (Row) 32-33; Asbjornsen NORWEGIAN 135-136. Chaucer: Green BIG 158-163; Chaucer CHANTICLEER pb. Aesop: Aesop FABLES (Macmillan) 115-117.

K721.2* Leopard persuaded to open mouth wide and display five teeth. Hare knocks two out. Liberia: Haskett GRAINS 40-42.

K722. Giant tricked into becoming mouse, cat eats him up. Types 545A, 545B. SEE ALSO: K1917.3 (Puss in Boots); K717 (deception into bottle). De Regniers GIANT 79-80.

K722.0.1* Fox tricked into becoming dumpling. Boy eats him. Japan: Scofield FOX 9-14.

K722.0.2* Wiley tricks Hairy Man into becoming opossum. Puts in bag. +B524.1.2H. U.S. (Alabama): Bang WILEY pb; Haviland NORTH 126-133.

K729.1* Brer Rabbit helps Brer Fox roof house. Nails Brer Fox's tail down. U.S. (Black, Georgia): Harris COMPLETE 361-364; Harris NIGHTS 339-343; Harris FAVORITE 15-18.

K730. Victim trapped.

K735. Capture in pitfall. SEE: G512 (Jack the Giant Killer).

K735.0.1* Fox, wolf and bear in pit. Old woman jeers at them and falls in too. Man kills animals rescues old woman. Norway: Asbjornsen EAST (Row) 54-56. Scandinavia: Wiggin TALES 289-290.

K735.1.1* Ananse digs pit outside door of his house and covers. All sent to arrest him fall in. Thus Ananse conquers entire kingdom of leopard. Divides it with cohort rats (he was living in rat kingdom). W. Africa: Appiah ANANSE 105-112.

K735.5. Dupe tricked into well: left there. SEE ALSO: K651.

K735.5.1* Kantchil guards Emperor Singa's well. Harimau (tiger) given permission to drink. Pushed into well. Indonesia: Bro HOW 13-21.

K741. Capture by tar baby. An image covered with tar (or other adhesive substance) captures the intruder who addresses it and finally strikes it so that he sticks to it. +K581.2 (briar patch punishment). SEE ALSO: K1917.3E (Sechrist).

K741.0.1* Why Bananas belong to monkeys. Old woman catches monkeys with wax doll. Monkeys call to sun to melt wax and sun obeys. Old woman flees. Latin America: Newman FOLK.. LATIN 61-66.

K741.0.2* Frog sings juju chant in market and causes everyone to leave, leaving goods. Sticky carved figure with pot of groundnuts captures him. W. Africa (Yoruba): Fuja FOURTEEN 252-256.

K741.0.3* Brer Rabbit caught by tar man set by Brer Fox. +K581.2 (Briar patch). U. S. (Black, Georgia): Brown BRER 6-11; Harris SONGS 7-11 /Arbuthnot ANTHOLOGY 383-384/, /Arbuthnot FAIRY 214-215/, /Arbuthnot FAIRY 216-218/, /Martignoni ILLUSTRATED 331-352/, /Gruenberg FAVORITE 336-338/, /Harris COMPLETE 6-8/, /Harris FAVORITE 47-59/. U.S. (Black, South Carolina): Faulkner DAYS 122-127 (tar girl, +A2233.1.1).

K741.0.3.1* Buh Possum catches Buh Rabbit with tar man in corn patch, throws into briar patch (K581.2). U.S.: Courlander TERRAPIN'S 41-45.

K741.0.3.2* Animals set tar figure trap for thieving rabbit who steals from well (A2233.1.1). Native American (Cherokee): Bell JOHN 54-56 (tar wolf); Scheer CHEROKEE 47-50. U.S. (W. Virginia): Haviland NORTH 109-114 (+K581.10).

K741.0.4* Farmer sets scarecrow covered with mud and sap and captures thieving hare (Sungura). E. Africa (Swahili): Heady JAMBO 13-17.

K741.0.5* Hare caught by tortoise with sap in back (K582.2). Rhodesia: Tracy LION 110-113.

K741.0.5.1* Beeswax on tortoise shell catches jackal. Congo: Kirn BEESWAX pb.

K741.0.6* Elephant catches hare with clay man. +K581.2. W. Africa: Davis WAKAIMA /Haviland FAIRY 104-109/, /Green FOLK..AFRICA 57-63/.

K741.0.7* Anansi (spider) caught stealing food by tar doll. Liberia/Ghana: Arkhurst ADVENTURES 40-49 (Straw man with beeswax, set by wife for Anansi). W. Africa (Ashanti): Courlander HAT 20-24. Nigeria (Hausa): Arnott AFRICAN 16-21 (rubber man).

K741.0.8* Thieving squirrel caught by sticky figure. Mayagoli: Nunn AFRICAN 112-118.

K741.0.9* Gum doll set by spider (Anansi) captures fairy. W. Africa: Aardema SKY pb; Haley A STORY pb.

K741.0.10* Tortoise stealing food by means of magic dancing palm tree. Is caught by tarred clay man. Tree is still where he left it (A2600.1). Nigeria: Walker DANCING 15-26.

K741.0.11* Thieving ape caught by tar man becomes helper. Philippines (Visayan): Sechrist ONCE 110-118.

K741.0.12* Monkey picking bananas for old woman gives her only poor half. She catches with wax boy. Monkeys make tower to sky and plead to sun to melt wax figure. It does and monkeys gain control of bananas. Brazil: Dobbs ONCE 60-66.

K741.0.13* Man catches thieving skunk with pine gum doll. Skunk persuades passing fox that he is being fed by man and fox takes captive's place (K842.0.11). Fox escapes after singing and sends coyote to man saying his fur fell off because he was fed so much corn. +K1251. Native American: Haviland NORTH 71-75.

K741.2* Capture in tarred pit. Giant Gergasi tricked into hole with rubber latex on pretext world is coming to an end (K652.1). Gergasi promises to leave area and Kantchil has birds bring berry juice to dissolve latex and free. Indonesia: Bro HOW 72-78.

K741.3* The Bodhisattva as a prince is stuck in hair of demon he attacks. Stuck at five points, feet, hands and head. Demon is torn asunder by thunderbolt of knowledge in his stomach. Converts. India: Courlander TIGER'S 52-57; Jacobs INDIAN 235-242.

K741.4* Captive lured into pit by image (not sticky) and voice thrown with kelp tube. Native American (Northwest Coast): Harris ONCE 89-111.

K741.5* Straw ox smeared with pitch captures animals. SEE: Z32.4.1.

K741.6* Coyote in exuberant mood hits old alder stump. Arms, legs, head stick. Woodcock pecks him out. Native American (Wintu, California, Sacramento Valley): Cothran WITH 65-66.

K750. Capture by decoy.

K751. Capture by feigning death. Types 47A, 56A. SEE ALSO: K757; K1867. (cf. K607.3).

K751.0.1* Hare promises to help wildcat catch turkeys, if released. Hare has wildcat feign dead and calls turkeys to celebrate. Native American (Mississippi): Arnott ANIMAL 220-223. U.S. (Black, Georgia): Harris NIGHTS 286-290; Harris COMPLETE 324-328.

K751.0.2. Hare has coon feign dead, frogs to dig hole to bury coon, when too deep for them to jump out, coon revives, frogs trapped. U.S. (Black, Georgia): Harris FAVORITE 104-107.

K751.0.3* Great Hunter Oniyeye to wed king's daughter if brings back beast with 152 tails. He feigns dead and all animals come. Beast comes orders him carried back on back. Oniyeye revives. Africa: Carpenter AFRICAN 133-139.

K751.0.4. Raccoon feigns dead, covering self with grubs and catches crayfish who come to feed. Native American: Bierhorst FIRE 42-46.

K752.1* Tortoise rolls in mud and hides under log, grabs fox's foot and tortoise recovers stolen quills. U.S. (Black, Georgia): Harris COMPLETE 173-177; Harris NIGHTS 79-82.

K753. Hare caught by tortoise hiding in pot of of beans. Hare had been stealing beans of elephant and catching pursuer in snare each day. Africa: Burton MAGIC 78-81.

K754. Capture by hiding in artificial animal. SEE ALSO: K1341 (entrance to woman's room in hollow artificial animal).

K754.2.1* Capture by artificial elephant. Prince is lured through forest in attempt to tame white elephant with his lute playing. He is thus brought to princess. Ceylon: Tooze WONDERFUL 74-76.

K757. Capture by feigning illness. Type 50. SEE: K751. U.S. (Black, Georgia): Harris SONGS 3.

K770. Other deceptive captures.

K771. Unicorn (bull, cow) tricked into running horn into tree. SEE ALSO: K1951.1 (Seven at a Blow).

K771.0.1* Cow tricked by Brer Rabbit. Hen then milks her. U.S. (Black, Georgia): Brown WORLD 72-77; Harris FAVORITE 71-76 /Harris COMPLETE 28-32/, /Harris SONGS 41-47/.

K771.0.2* Elephant tricked by Brer Rabbit. U.S. (Black, Georgia): Harris COMPLETE 261-264; Harris NIGHTS 198-202.

K771.0.3* Bush cow tricked by Zomo rabbit, Zomo milks her. Nigeria (Hausa): Sturton ZOMO 77-88.

K800 - K999. Killing or maiming by deception.

K815. Victim lured by kind words approaches trickster and is killed. Type 242.

K815.1.2* Fox poses as confessor for cock. Russia: Riordan TALES..CENTRAL 127-128.

K815.7. Cat acts as judge between sparrow and hare; eats them both. India: Korel LISTEN 21-25 (partridge and hare); Ryder PANCHATANTRA 315-321.

K815.8. Hawk persuades doves to elect him their king. Kills them. Aesop: Aesop AESOP'S (Grosset) 44-45 (pigeons); Aesop AESOP'S (Viking) 32-33 (Kite and pigeon); Aesop AESOP'S (Watts) 220 (Kite and pigeon).

K815.11. Wounded wolf persuades lamb to bring him a drink, adding that he will get his own food. (cf. K2061.5). Aesop: Aesop AESOP'S (Watts) 109.

K815.13.2. Cat holds party. Eats guests. SEE: K815.16.1. Aesop: Aesop AESOP'S (Golden) 74-75.

K815.14. Fish tricked by crane into letting selves be carried from one pond to another. The crane eats them when they are in his power. +K1815.14. India: Babbitt JATAKA 84-89; Gaer FABLES 84-86; Jacobs INDIAN 57-61; Ryder PANCHATANTRA 76-80 (heron); Williams-Ellis ROUND 53-56. Spain: Sawyer PICTURE 53-62. Burma: Brockett BURMESE 195-198 (Heron).

K815.14.0.1* Cormorant. Crayfish is intermediary. La Fontaine: Green ANIMAL 66-67.

K815.14.0.2* Frog spys on slaughter and warns fish. +A2494.16.1.1. Armenia: Tashjian THREE 40-47.

K815.14.0.3* Arabe duck claims to be astrologer. Spain: Hardendorff TRICKY 45-50.

K815.14.2* Crab asks king to carry to another pool saying may repay one day. Tells story of four friends. Crow tells serpent to bite man, crow looks into knapsack and crab there pinches neck, crow agrees to suck poison from man, does so then crab kills crow anyway. India: Korel LISTEN 81.

K815.14.3* Crow leads crocodile to better river. Plans to eat exhausted crocodile. Burma: Brockett BURMESE 126-130.

K815.15. Cat lures young foxes from den with music. Kills them (cf. K311.3).

A* Budalinek. Warned not to open door by grandmother. Boy lets fox in on third day. Lishka gives boy a ride on her tail, then carries off to her hole. An organ grinder lures foxes from den one at a time with music. Rescues Boy.

Czechoslovakia: Fillmore SHEPHERD'S 94-102,
/Arbuthnot ANTHOLOGY 274-275/, /Haviland
FAIRY 92-98/, /Arbuthnot FAIRY 143-146/,
/Fenner ADVENTURES 51-59/, /Fillmore SHOE-
MAKER'S/.

B* Cock warned by cat not to open door. He
opens to fox, is rescued by cat. Third time
cat is too far away to hear call. Cat fiddles before fox's den and catches little foxes and mother as they emerge one at a time. Rescues cock.
Cossack: Wiggin TALES 36-38. Russia:
Montgomerie MERRY 32-37 (fiddling, cock is
eaten by fox). Russia (Ukraine): Bloch U-
krainian (plays bandura).

C* This tale lacks the lure from den with music
motif, but is otherwise similar to the above.
Smolicheck disobeys Stag Golden Antlers and
opens door to wood maidens. Golden Antlers
rescues. Second time Golden Antlers is too far
away and Smolicheck is carried off to cave.
Golden Antlers rescues. Smolicheck reforms.
Czechoslovakia: Fillmore SHEPHERD'S 87-93.

K815.16.1* Cat as monk. Mice worshippers dis-
appear daily. Type 113B. China: Hardendorff
TRICKY 27-32. Russia: Carey BABA 55-57.
Tibet: Carpenter WONDER..CATS 111-118.
Montgomerie MERRY 42-46.

K815.16.2* Fox feigns holiness but seizes praying
guinea hens (K826). India (Jatakas): Gaer
FABLES 129-132.

K815.19.1* Hare takes lion hunting for honey.
Stakes lion out in place to 'catch' honey. Rolls
boulder onto him. Africa: Tracy LION 30-33.

K815.20* Elephant told he has been chosen king,
comes to be crowned. Is killed. Nigeria: Walker NIGERIA 61-63. India: Gaer FABLES 71-
74.

K826. Hoodwinked dancers. A trickster induces
ducks to dance with closed eyes. Kills them. SEE
ALSO: K815.16.2. Native American (Chippewa):
Leekly WORLD 50-54 (Manabozo tricks ducks and
geese, grebe warns, A2332.5.7). Native Amer-
ican (Sioux): Matson LEGENDS 48-50. Native
American: Marriott WINTER 47-54. Native
American (Seneca): Parker SKUNNY 43-51.
Native American (Lakota): Yellow Robe TON-
WEYA 86-93. Native American (Great Plains):
Jones COYOTE 15-22 (coyote). Native Ameri-
can (Dakota): DeWit TALKING 93-98.

K826.1* Coyote tricks prarie dogs into dancing
with eyes closed. Races skunk for them and
skunk retraces steps and eats. Native American
(Comanche): Brown TEPEE 111-113.

K827.4.1* Cat in mouse country shams death.
Eats mouse pallbearers. SEE ALSO: K2061.9.
Puerto Rico: Belpre TIGER 21-25.

K828.1. Fox (wolf) in sheepskin gains admission
to fold and kills sheep. Aesop: Aesop AESOP'S
(Watts) 24 (wolf); Aesop FABLES (Macmillan)

77 (wolf); Arbuthnot FAIRY 230 (wolf).

K828.1.1* Fox in sheepskin caught. Greece:
Wilson GREEK 180-191. Aesop: Aesop AE-
SOP'S (Golden) 70; Aesop AESOP'S (Grosset)
2 (shepherd reaches in fold and kills wolf by
mistake); Aesop FABLES (Walck) 20-21.

K828.1.2* Fox disguised as shepherd, cannot run
in smock, caught. La Fontaine: Green ANIMAL
224-225. Aesop: Aesop FIVE 74.

K828.1.3* Fox in sheepskin caught and hung in
tree. Aesop: Aesop AESOP'S (Viking) 26.

K842. Dupe persuaded to take prisoner's place in
a sack: killed. The trickster is to be thrown
into the sea. The trickster keeps shouting that
he does not want to go to heaven (or marry the
princess); the dupe gladly substitutes for him.
+K1051. Russia (Georgia): Papashvily YES 67-
75. Scandinavia: Hardendorff TRICKY 11-22.
Bulgaria: Pridham GIFT 84-94 (+K110.1).

Aa* Hudden, Dudden and Donald O'Neary.
Type 1535. Hudden and Dudden kill Donald's
cow. He puts coins in hide which fall when he
beats it. Sells. Brothers kill their cows to sell
hides. Tied in sack Dudden trades places with
farmer and takes farmer's sheep. Says sheep
came from lake bottom and brothers dive (K1051).
Celtic: Jacobs CELTIC 54-63 /Jacobs HUDDEN
pb/, /Bleecker BIG 67-77/, /Fenner ADVEN-
TURES 16-25/, /Wiggin TALE 47-53/.

Ab* Aa + Magpie in cowhide (K114.1), his
mother put in Donal's bed and Nidden and Didden murder her. Donal sets up mother by well
so servants knock her in by accident. They
bribe him not to reveal murder. Says 'old mother' sold for weight in gold so Nidden and Didden murder theirs to sell. Ireland: MacManus
HIBERNIAN 141-147. France: Cooper FIVE
47-57; Duvoisin THREE 8-15; Lang GREEN 183-
191.

Ba* The Little Peasant. Pretends raven wrapped in cowhide prophesies. Tells returned husband where wife has hidden food and lover
(J1344.1). Gets paid for information. Says he
got money by selling cowhide and others kill
their cows to sell hides. He is to be thrown into
water in cask. Changes places with shepherd.
Others dive after 'sheep' (J1344.1). Germany
(Grimm): Grimm HOUSEHOLD 256-261; Grimm
WORLD 107-113.

Bb* The Heifer Hide. Heifer is Jack's inheritance. He travels wrapped in hide, feigns is
prophetic hide and tells of wife's hidden food,
trades hide for one hundred guineas and chest
(with lover inside) (J1344.1). Paid one hundred
to throw chest in well. Brothers kill their
horses and wear hides. Put Jack in sack,
trades places with man, brothers dive for sheep.
U.S. (Appalachia): Chase JACK 161-171.

Bc* High John the Conqueror. Master kills
high John's mule. Feigns it tells fortune and

tells white man his wife is with another man. Gets one hundred dollars. Master kills own mule to sell skin. To be thrown in river, friends let Jack out and put stone in bag. Jack returns with money. Master wants to be thrown in river. U.S. (Black): Lester BLACK 93–112.

Bd* Drum full of bees. Drummer puts bee swarm in drum. Says can prophesy, tells husband of hidden food and demon (lover) in chest. Sells 'oracle' drum for one hundred crowns. Tells to smear honey on wife's face, uncover drum and will discover meaning of oracle. Trades places with laborer and offers to chase drummer for farmer--steals horse. Belgium: Frost LEGENDS 312–323.

C* Jack and the Lord High Mayor. Jack sends hare for mother in Galway (K131.1.1). Has two hares--sells. Sells whistle no bird can resist (trained birds). Kills mother and revives with horn (bladder of blood under her dress, K113). In sack to be killed--trades places. SEE ALSO: K113; K131.1.1 (sale of pseudo-magic objects). Ireland: MacManus HIBERNIAN 126–140.

D* The Miller and the Ogre: Ogre kills miller's cow. He takes hide to sell, drops on robbers from tree and gains gold. Ogre kills cows for hides. Miller sells self-cooking pot (K112.1), resuscitating bellows (K113), trades places in sacks. Found donkey and wares at river bottom. Ogre leaps into river. French: Picard FRENCH 183–197.

E* Seventh son, fool, given calf inheritance, brothers kill it. He spends night in tree and frightens robbers off with skin. Brothers believe he sold skin, imitate. Travel with bag half gold and half ashes. Says gold will turn to ashes if touched. Accuses wedding party he helps over river of touching bag. They provide gold for ashes. Brothers to throw into river. Changes places with prince. Brothers have selves thrown in. India: Spellman BEAUTIFUL 86–89.

K842.0.1* Dupe persuaded to take prisoner's place in sack to see marvels prisoner declares he sees there. India: Spellman BLUE 86–89. SEE: K1611 Molly Whuppie.

K842.0.1.1* Dupe takes place to become wise in sack of wisdom. Germany (Grimm): Grimm GRIMM'S (Follett) 358–364; Grimm GRIMM'S (Grosset) 260–263; Grimm GRIMM'S (World) 148–151.

K842.0.2* Dupe persuaded stocks is a hunchback cure, trades places. China: Chang TALES 11–24. Ethiopia: Courlander FIRE 81–88 (buried up to neck, having back straightened) /Green FOLK 65–73/.

K842.0.3* Hyena tied to tree by lion and beaten persuades dupe hyena he is being forced to eat meat. Trade places. Africa: Nunn AFRICAN 46–50.

K842.0.4* Hare tricks fox, going to wedding party. U.S. (Black, Georgia): Harris COMPLETE 94–97; Harris SONGS 143–148.

K842.0.5* Hare tricks fox, forced to eat mutton in box trap. U.S. (Black, Georgia): Harris FAVORITE 213–218 /Harris COMPLETE 216–225/, /Harris NIGHTS 177–184/.

K842.0.6* Hare tells possum can hear singing in clouds from bag. U.S. (Black, Georgia): Harris COMPLETE 252–257 /Harris NIGHTS 185–192/.

K842.0.7* Hare tells bear he is hanging in snare to scare off crows at one dollar per minute. U.S. (Black, Georgia): Brown WORLD 78–81; Harris FAVORITE 229–232 / Harris COMPLETE 74–77/, /Harris SONGS 113–117/.

K842.0.8* Hare tells bear he is resting, hanging from tree. U.S. (Black): Lester KNEE 12–20.

K842.0.9* Hyena says he is being forced to drink palm oil. Masai: Aardema TALES 41–50.

K842.0.10* Bug-a-Bug Hill befriends fleeing prince. Aids in tasks. Bug-a-Bug Hill tells ants to pick fruit of tree set amid poison ants. Sends butterfly to designate certain cows in herd. Tied up to be thrown into river--fills sack with stones. Tells king he obtained crown underwater. Says underwater people want Dagbah (evil advisor) to be crowned next--is thrown into river. W. Africa: Aardema MORE 50–55.

K842.0.11* Skunk persuades fox that he is being fed corn by man, fox trades places, is scalded. +K741.0.13. Native American: Haviland NORTH 71–75.

K843.1* Dupe persuaded to be killed in order to go to heaven. Minister hung as reward, then king hangs self. Anyone hung at this hour to see heaven. India: Asia FOLK I 13–18.

K846.1* Brer Rabbit tells Brer Fox, Wolf, Coon, Bear, that hounds are trying to drive him to barbecue. They take his place. U.S. (Black, Georgia): Harris COMPLETE 729–732.

K850. Fatal deceptive game.

K851. Deceptive game: burning (boiling) each other. Dupe burned (boiled) to death. Native American (Blackfoot): Hardendorff JUST 82–84 (Old man tricks rabbits).

K851.1* Who can stay longest in smokey hole. Deer children trick bear cubs in revenge. Native American (Shoshone): Heady SAGE 74–79.

K869.5* Fatal deceptive game: doing without food or drink. One bird eats grubs in tree. Other bird by creek dies. U.S. (Black, Georgia): Harris COMPLETE 384–386; Harris NIGHTS 370–372.

K870. Fatal deception by narcotic (intoxication).

K872.0.1. Dancing girl leaps from cliff with Japanese general, killing him and self. Korea: Carpenter KOREAN 269-275.

K890. Dupe tricked into killing himself.

K891.1. Intruding wolf tricked into jumping down chimney and killing self. Type 124, 333. SEE ALSO: K2011 (Red Riding Hood B, D).

K891.1.1* Three Little Pigs. Houses built of straw, sticks and bricks. Wolf blows houses of straw and sticks. Invites third pig to pick apples, turnips, pig goes early and returns. To go to fair, pig rolls home in churn frightening wolf. Wolf comes down chimney into pot of boiling waters. England: Brooke GOLDEN pb /Brooke STORY..PIGS pb/, /Association TOLD.. GREEN 5-9/; De La Mare ANIMAL 16-19; Hutchinson CHIMNEY 53-60; Jacobs ENGLISH 69-73 /Arbuthnot FAIRY 10-11/, Haviland FAIRY 22-27/, /Martignoni ILLUSTRATED 80-82/, /Arbuthnot ANTHOLOGY 152-153/; Richardson GREAT 59-65 (apples, fair); Rockwell THREE 81-91; Steel ENGLISH 122-127; TALL..NURSERY 110-116; Wiggin TALES 215-217; Williams-Ellis FAIRY..BRITISH 39-43. Dubois THREE pb. Halliwell STORY pb. Sekorvá EUROPEAN 94-97.

K891.1.1.1* Houses are of mud, cabbage and brick. Wolf scrapes mud, eats into cabbage house, third pig rolls home in kettle. Brother pigs are rescued from fox's den after fox's demise. Germany (Grimm): Lang GREEN 106-110; Wiggin TALES 177-181.

K891.1.1.2* Pigs build of chips, cornstalks, bricks. Wolf asks third pig to let put nose in, paws, shoulders, etc. Pig pretends he hears hounds coming and hides fox in churn, pours boiling water in. U.S. (Applachia): Chase WICKED 81-87.

K891.1.1.3* Goslings, third gosling offers to make macaroni with wolf--pours scalding water on wolf from balcony and kills, cuts open and rescues sisters (F913). Italy: Haviland FAVORITE..ITALY 67-77.

K891.1.1.4* Five little pigs build houses of brush, sticks, mud, plants, rocks. Wolf gets all to open door and eats. Last tricks wolf down chimney and roasts. U.S. (Black, Georgia): Harris COMPLETE 145-148; Harris NIGHTS 38-43.

K891.1.2* Fox tricked into jumping into boiling pot. U.S. (Black, Georgia): Harris COMPLETE 343-347; Harris NIGHTS 314-318 (grandmother, wolf).

K891.1.3* Wolf tricked into hiding in chest. Boiling water poured in. U.S. (Black, Georgia): Harris FAVORITE 286-290 /Harris COMPLETE 42-45/, /Harris SONGS 63-69/.

K891.1.4* One little pig and ten wolves. Wolf begs to be let in--back into sack--scalded. Ten wolves climb on backs to reach pig on roof. He threatens to scald. Bottom wolf flees, dropping ladder. Hungary: Arnott ANIMAL 129-135.

K891.1.5* Told Buddha on altar always bathes in rice pot, fox pretending to be real Buddha climbs in. Japan: Scofield FOX 33-39.

K891.1.6* Witch tricked into pot. Fire lit. SEE: G512.3.2.2.

K910. Murder by strategy.

K911.5. Feigning deafness to lure enemy close and to kill him. SEE: Z33.1.7.

K911.5.1. Brer Fox asks Jack Sparrow to get on my tail, back, head, tooth, feigning deafness. Eats. SEE ALSO: Z33.1 (Gingerbread Man). U.S. (Black, Georgia): Brown WORLD 54-57; Harris FAVORITE 83-85 /Harris COMPLETE 61-65/, /Harris SONGS 93-99/.

K912. Robbers' (giants') heads cut off one by one as they enter house. Type 304. SEE: S62.1.

K912.0.3* Maid beheads robbers as enter. Master has head carved over doorway. In Amsterdam. Holland: De Leeuw LEGENDS..HOLLAND 114-118.

K916. Dancer stabs spectator. Uses one of the figures of the dance as a ruse. SEE: N455.3 (Ali Baba).

K929.1. Murder by leaving poisoned wine. SEE ALSO: K1685.

K929.1.1* Prince Susano sees chopsticks floating downstream, he goes upstream and finds maiden to be eaten by eight headed dragon. He sits on her rock with eight jugs of drugged wine beneath. Dragon sees her face reflected in the eight jugs and drinks all. Prince slays the drugged (R111.1.3) dragon. Finds jeweled sword in dragon's tail which he gives to ruler. He weds the maiden. +A220.1.1. Japan: Uchida DANCING 27-33.

K929.2. One-eyed doe outwitted by approaching from blind side. Accustomed to feed on a cliff with her sound eye next to land. Aesop: Aesop AESOP'S (Grosset) 37; Aesop AESOP'S (Watts) 119; Aesop FABLES (Macmillan) 130.

K930. Treacherous murder of enemy's children or charges.

K933. Trickster eats of tiger's cubs except one. Counts that one many times and deceives tiger. S. Africa: Arnott ANIMAL 104-111. India: Turnbull FAIRY 110-116.

K933.0.1* Spider, Gizo, counts one hundred and one crocodile eggs. Hausa: Arnott TALES 31-40.

K933.0.2* Anansi Spider helps alligator wash twelve eggs. West Indies: Sherlock ANANSI 84-93.

K933.0.3* Bear nurses alligator's young. U.S. (Black, Georgia): Harris COMPLETE 265-269 /Harris NIGHTS 344-348/.

K933.0.4* Jackal teaches crocodiles. Bangladesh: Asis FOLK..FOUR 5-10.

K934. Fox as shepherd. A woman in search of a shepherd tries the voices of applicants. The wolf, the bear are rejected, the fox accepted. Norway: Asbjornsen NORWEGIAN 106-107 (+A2215.5, woman throws cream at fox, tail tip white); Undset TRUE 182-183; Wiggin TALES 444-445.

K940. Deception into killing own family or animals. SEE: K842A.

K941.2. Dupe burns house because trickster reports high price paid for ashes. Pakistan: Siddiqui TOONTOONY 37-43.

K944. Deceptive agreement to kill wives (children). Trickster shams the murder; dupe kills his. SEE ALSO: K311.3.1 (mother in tree).

K944.0.1* Brer Rabbit tricks Brer Fox. U.S. (Black, Georgia): Harris NIGHTS 241-247 /Harris COMPLETE 293-297/.

K944.0.2* Hare hides mother, elephant kills his. Luo: Nunn AFRICAN 88-95.

K950. Various kinds of treacherous murder.

K952. Animal (monster) killed from within. SEE: F912; P361.10.

K952.1. Ungrateful river passenger kills carrier from within. Crawls inside during the passage (porcupine and buffalo). Native American (Nez Percé): Heady TALES 90-94.

K953.3. Crab carried off by crane, clings round his neck and cuts off his head with pincers. +K815.14. India: Babbitt JATAKA 84-89; Gaer FABLES 84-86; Jacobs INDIAN 57-61; Williams-Ellis ROUND 53-56. Spain: Sawyer PICTURE 53-62.

K953.3.0.1* Heron carries crab. Burma: Brockett BURMESE 195-198. India: Ryder PAN-CHATANTRA 76-80.

K953.3.0.2* Arabe duck carries crab. Spain: Hardendorff TRICKY 45-50.

K956. Murder by destroying external soul. SEE: D532; E710; G561.1; K975.2.

K956.0.1* "The Dragon's Strength." Type 302. Eldest two sons follow hare to mill, disappear. Youngest meets old woman who tells that hare is dragon. She obtains secret of Dragon's strength by feigning interest. He tells her it lies under

hearth, she kisses hearth, etc. Lies in sparrow, in pigeon, in hare, in boar, in dragon in distant lake. Lad defeats dragon with aid of two boar-hounds and falcon. Dragon, "If I could dip my head in water I could win..." Lad, "If Tsar's daughter would kiss me..." Third day princess kisses and he wins, boarhounds catch boar, hare. Falcon catches pigeon, elicits secret of brothers' disappearance from sparrow, then kills. Three willow saplings behind mill, cut them, strike the root, door of dungeon opens. Weds princess. Yugoslavia: Fillmore LAUGHING 141-160. Serbia: Manning-Sanders BOOK..PRINCES 66-75.

K960. Other fatal deceits.

K961.1. Disease to be cured by heart of monkey. SEE: K544.

K961.1.1. Tit for tat. Wolf tells sick lion that fox does not esteem him. Fox overhears it. Later fox tells lion that his only cure lies in wrapping himself in the wolf's skin. Wolf is killed. Aesop: Aesop AESOP'S (Watts) 203-204.

K961.1.2. Sick lion plots to eat warthog. Baby warthog hides in pot taken to lion's home and overhears plot--saves father. Africa: Burton MAGIC 68-71.

K962. Camel induced to offer himself as sacrifice. Other animals feign to offer themselves to lion as food. The lion eats the camel. India: Gaer FABLES 77-80; Ryder PANCHATANTRA 134-141.

K962.1. Camel persuaded to offer body to lion at "interest" in return for two bodies. India: Ryder PANCHATANTRA 164-167.

K975. Secret of strength treacherously discovered. Type 590. SEE: K2213; S12.1.

K975.1. Pretended exchanged confidences as to the one thing that can kill (or is feared). SEE: K602.3.

K975.1.2* Man overlooked by Death when pages in Book of Life (N115) stick together. Messenger is sent for him. He avoids, is tricked into revealing self when messenger washes charcoal, says "I've lived nine hundred years and never seen anything so foolish" (F321.1). Messenger and man exchange confidences as to fears. Man makes charm using this knowledge and Death's messenger cannot touch. Says he fears roast pig and beer. Messenger throws this at him. Korea: Carpenter KOREAN 89-94.

K975.2. Secret of external soul learned by deception. SEE ALSO: D532; E710; K956. Italy: Manning-Sanders BOOK..GHOSTS 111-118 (girl breaks eggshell containing goblin's soul, G561.1).

K975.2.1* Girl goes to free prince held by troll woman. Advises him to learn secret of their life. He breaks troll's golden egg and they vanish. Iceland: McGovern HALF pb.

K1000 - K1199. Deception into self-injury.

K1000. Deception into self-injury. SEE ALSO: C25.

K1010. Deception through false doctoring.

K1013. False beauty doctor. The trickster pretends to make the dupe beautiful. Injures him.

K1013.0.1* Fox makes cat's fur fluffy. Gives her bag to open. She is chased up tree and perspiration fluffs her. Puerto Rico: Belpre TIGER 113-117.

K1013.1. Making the beard golden. "Such a one." A man named "Such a one" persuades an ogre to have his beard gilded. He covers it with tar and leaves the ape caught to the tar-kettle. The ape with his tar-kettle wanders about and asks everyone, "Have you seen such a one?" (K359.2; K602). Type 1138. Finland: Bowman TALES 207-219 (+G501D, -K602).

K1013.2. "Painting" on the haycock. The fox persuades the wolf to lie on the hay in order to be painted. He sets fire to it. Finland: Bowman TALES..TUPA 250 (Bear).

K1014. Pepper given as ointment for burns (salt).

K1014.0.1* Hare gives pepper to badger as ointment for burns. Japan: Buck FAIRY 96-97; Ozaki JAPANESE 43-53.

K1014.3. White hare of Inaba. Cruel princes tell injured hare to bathe in salt water and sit in mud. Kind prince tells him to bathe in fresh water and roll in cat-tail pollen. Hare predicts he will wed princess and it is so (N331). +K579.2.2. Japan: Gruenberg FAVORITE 347-348; Haviland JAPANESE 73-89 (Prince Okuni-Mushi-No-Mikoto); Hearn JAPANESE 42-46; Ozaki JAPANESE 214-223; Sakade JAPANESE 103-105 (salt motif); Uchida DANCING 49-57.

K1020. Deception into disastrous attempts to procure food.

K1021. The Tail Fisher. The bear is persuaded (by fox) to fish with his tail through a hole in the ice. He loses his tail. SEE ALSO: A2216.1 (Why bear has short tail); A2378.4.13; K1982.1.

Fox tricks bear. Norway: Arbuthnot FAIRY 75-76; Asbjornsen EAST (Row) 34; Aulaire EAST 138; Haviland FAVORITE..NORWAY 65-66; Martignoni ILLUSTRATED 89-90; Sperry HEN 35-38 (fish bite off tail) /Sperry SCANDI-NAVIAN 27-28/; Undset TRUE 180-181. Germany: Wiggin TALES 176. Europe: Jacobs EUROPEAN 42-50. Finland: Bowman TALES 263. Lapland: Arnott ANIMAL 79-82; Deutsch MORE 11; Hutchinson FIRESIDE 25-26.

Fox tricked by hare. Ludwig Bechstein: Green ANIMAL 24-25.

Fox tricks wolf. Netherlands: Green ANIMAL 97-115 (Reynard). Poland: FAVORITE..PO-LAND 39-54. Russia: Daniels FALCON 84-89; Riordan TALES..CENTRAL 20-22.

Hare tricks fox, stuck until lake thaws. Germany: Wiggin TALES 191-192.

Coyote tricks bear. Native American (Iroquois): Bruchac TURKEY 31-33.

Fox tricks bear. Native American (Cheyenne, Choctaw, Micmac): Hulpach AMERICAN 192-197. Native American (Seneca): Parker SKUNNY 102-108. Native American (Loucheux): Belting LONG 13-15.

Fox tricks hare. +A2378.4.1.1. U.S. (Black, Georgia): Harris FAVORITE 11-14; Harris COMPLETE 80-83; Harris SONGS 122-126.

Bear tricks coyote, coyote waits until thaw to get free (A2378.4.12.1). Native American (Pueblo): Cothran WITH 44-48.

Hare tricks tiger. Korea: Kim STORY 58-65.

K1021.0.1* Fox tells wolf moon's reflection in ice is cheese. To lay tail over it until farmer is asleep. Tail sticks to ice. Fox wakes farmer and fleeing wolf loses tail. Scotland: Montgomerie TWENTY-FIVE 30-31.

K1021.0.2* Fox has wolf fish with tail in ice. Sings "Let Wolf's tail be frozen fast." Says sang "Come and get caught fishes." Calls villagers to chase wolf. Russia: Carey BABA 67-70; Carrick STILL 95-104.

K1021.0.3* Tailless fox convinces other foxes to fish with tails in ice. Now all tailless. +J758.1.5. Russia (Yiddish): Ginsburg ONE 17-20.

K1021.0.4* Anansi tells hare to dip tail in rum and put into sea. Fish bite it off. Jamaica: Williams-Ellis ROUND 195-196.

K1021.1. Tail buried (hair tied). Dupe bound fast and then attacked. U.S. (Black, Georgia): Harris NIGHTS 339.

K1021.3. Bear persuaded to slide down rock. Wears off tail. U.S. (Black, Georgia): Harris NIGHTS 113.

K1022. Dupe overeats and cannot escape.

K1022.0.1* Mouse in corn basket overeats and cannot escape. Weasel advises dieting. Aesop: Aesop AESOP'S (Grosset) 202-203.

K1022.0.2* Fox in hollow tree eats elephant's cache and can't escape. Must diet. Aesop: Aesop AESOP'S (Watts) 56.

K1022.3* Parable of snake who drank contents of

milk bottle and had to spit out milk to escape bottle is told to treasurer who stole. Must spit out all to be released. Ethiopia: Davis LION'S 23-26.

K1022.1. Wolf overeats in the cellar (smokehouse). Cannot escape through entrance hole. Type 41. German: De La Mare TALES 119-124 /De La Mare ANIMAL 31-36/; Gag MORE 9-13; Richardson GREAT 140-146; Wiggin TALES 88-89. Jewish: Jagendorf NOODLEHEAD 45-47 (fox in garden). Netherlands: Green ANIMAL 97-115 (bear). Van Woerkom MEAT pb.

K1023. Getting honey from the wasp-nest. The dupe is stung. Type 49. Norway: Asbjornsen NORWEGIAN 120-121 (fox tricks bear); Wiggin TALES 312-313.

K1023.0.1* Pygmies capture man's wife, demand that man bring them honey. He puts angry bees in comb, flees with wife. Central Africa: Carpenter AFRICAN 53-62.

K1023.0.2* Hare tells fox wasp's nest is clump of grapes. U.S. (Black, Georgia): Harris FAVORITE 130-135; Harris NIGHTS 83-89; Harris COMPLETE 177-182.

K1023.1. Dupe allowed to guard (play) "king's drum": it is a wasp's nest. Indonesia: De Leeuw INDONESIAN 68-74 (Kantchil tricks tiger). Sleigh NORTH 19-22 (gong--red ant's nest).

K1023.1.0.1* Fox trades "hum-house" (hornet's nest) for raccoon's magic paw-paw (fireball root of Jack in the Pulpit), both are injured. +A2433.3.23; +A2494.9.3. Native American (Seneca): Parker SKUNNY 23-30.

K1023.1.0.2* Hare tells coyote hornet's nest is bell to call little hares from school. Coyote rings it. Mexico: Jagendorf KING 187-189.

K1023.1.0.3* Kantchil buries beehive, covers self with ashes and tells monkeys he is spirit and knows where Kantchil's soul is kept. They dig up 'soul' and are stung. Indonesia: Bro HOW 79-87.

K1023.1.1. Dupe allowed to guard (wear) 'king's girdle.' It is a snake, which bites him (or squeezes him). Indonesia: De Leeuw INDONESIAN 68-74 (Kantchil tricks tiger); Sleigh NORTH 19-22 (King's turban).

K1023.1.2* Dupe allowed to eat "king's food" = rotten leaves. Indonesia: De Leeuw INDONESIAN 68-74; Sleigh NORTH 19-22 (pudding = mud).

K1023.1.3* Dupe allowed to play "king's trumpet" = bamboo stalks. Puts tongue between and waits for wind to blow. SEE ALSO: K1111.0.1.1. Indonesia: De Leeuw INDONESIAN 68-74 (Kantchil tricks tiger); Sleigh NORTH 19-22 (harp--bamboo shoot hits on nose).

K1023.1.4* Dupe (crocodile) allowed to eat king's peppers which monkey guards. Are hot peppers. Philippines (Zambal): Sechrist ONCE 60-63.

K1023.5.1* Dupe induced to strike at bee's nest: badly bitten. Fox allowed to run through hare's "laughing place" hits head on hornet's nest. Hare laughs. U.S. (Black, Georgia): Harris FAVORITE 39-46; Harris COMPLETE 604-613.

K1023.5.2* Hare convinces leopard to knock over bee tree. W. Kenya: Nunn AFRICAN 127-133.

K1023.6* Dupe trapped with head in bee-gum. Hare stirs up bees and stung head of bear swells so can't remove it from hole. U.S. (Black, Georgia): Harris FAVORITE 278-281 /Harris COMPLETE 90-94/, /Harris SONGS 137-143/.

K1023.6.1* Brer Rabbit chants riddle--shows answer to fox by getting fox's head stuck in bee-gum and sending Brer B'ar to catch bee-gum robber. U.S. (Black, Georgia): Brown WORLD 34-41; Harris COMPLETE 154-158 /Harris NIGHTS 51-55/.

K1024.1* All animals confess sins. Large animals are absolved by frightened jury. Mouse blamed. U.S. (Alabama): Courlander TERRAPIN'S 53-56.

K1034.1* Brer Rabbit's wife spills boiling water on wolf being pulled up on rope. U.S. (Black, Georgia): Harris NIGHTS 268-274; Harris COMPLETE 311-315.

K1035.1* The Pimmerly Plum. Fox tricked by terrapin into sitting under tree with mouth open waiting for plums to fall. Terrapin escapes. U.S. (Black, Georgia): Brown BRER 16-21; Harris COMPLETE 278-284 /Harris NIGHTS 230-235/.

K1035.2* Grizzly bear is made to respect coyote and Yaka, little brown bear, when they trick him with hard fruit in mouth. Native American (Nez Percé): Heady TALES 67-74.

K1039.1* Brer Rabbit convinces Brer Fox to attack wildcat since its tracks show no claws. U.S. (Black, Georgia): Harris FAVORITE 147-152 /Harris COMPLETE 440-442/, /Harris NIGHTS 260-267/.

K1040. Dupe otherwise persuaded to voluntary self-injury.

K1041. Borrowed feathers. Dupe lets himself be carried aloft by bird and dropped. Type 225. SEE ALSO: A2109.2; A2351.9; G530.2BhL; H1321.1Cc; H1385.3Fbc; J657.2; J2071.2.

K1040.0.1* Eagle carries higher and higher. Eagle punishes jackal who is eating hen's chicks. Offers jackal a ride, asks what jackal sees (three times) and rises higher until jackal replies "nothing" (Too high to see trees, etc.). Eagle then drops passenger. Berber-Kabyl:

Frobenius AFRICAN 83-85. Iran: Mehdevi PERSIAN 44-50 (stork revenges fox for eating young). Hottentot: Aardema BEHIND 26-33 (blue crane drops jackal; thrice carried). Ukraine: Bloch UKRAINE 36-38 (revenge motif). Palestine: Arnott ANIMAL 6-13 (eagle drops fox).

K1041.0.1.1* Eagle carries Ke'let, evil spirit, high and higher. Thrice asks what he sees. Earth as big as lake, forest cover, cannot be seen. Dropped. +A721.1.3. Native American (Chuckee): Newell RESCUE 51-62.

K1041.0.2* Hyenas beg hawk to carry them. Each holds tail of other, hanging in chain from Hawk's tail feather. Hawk sings to Mungu to let tail feather fall out. Hyena's are destroyed. Today's Hyena is descended from old, ugly, lame hyena who was left behind. Africa (Swahili): Nunn AFRICAN 31-35.

K1041.0.3* Turtle begs eagle to teach him to fly. Dropped to death. Aesop: Aesop AESOP'S (Watts) 67.

K1041.0.3.1* Turtle taught by buzzard. Wasn't taught how to land. U.S. (Black, Georgia): Harris COMPLETE 435-437 /Harris FAVORITE 91-94/.

K1041.0.4* Fox takes flying lessons from crane. Russia: Carrick STILL 47-56.

K1041.0.5* Hungry Hyena carried by Kinuru sees goats and lets go. +A2441.1.4.1. E. Africa: Heady JAMBO 91-93.

K1041.1. Flight by putting on bird feathers. Dupe falls. SEE ALSO: K1982.1 (coyote flies with geese by magic).

K1041.1.1* Oldman God tells birds to give turtle a feather so he can fly up and eat cork seeds. Turtle eats all the seeds and Oldman God lets birds take back feathers. Turtle falls to earth, walks slowly, stays close to home since then. (cf. A2441.4.5). Liberia (Mano): Dorliae ANIMALS 46-51.

K1041.1.1.1* Winged creatures given feast in heaven. Turtle borrows feathers and goes. Brags and birds take back feathers. Spider lets turtle down on silk. Turtle sings song mocking her and she drops him. Why shell is cracked (A2312.1.1). Antilles: Carter GREEDY 46-61.

K1041.1.2* Ricebird lends catfish feathers to fly to farmer's tapping bowl at top of palm wine tree. Farmer catches them and ricebird takes back feathers and escapes leaving drunken catfish in treetop. Liberia: Haskett GRAINS 24-25.

K1041.1.3* Anansi borrows feathers to fly to dokanoo tree. Is too greedy and birds take back feathers. Jamaica: Sherlock ANANSI 84-93. W. Indies: Sherlock IGUANA'S 53-67

(A2312.1.1).

K1041.1.4* Turtle borrows pigeons' feathers and flies with them to cornfield. They take back feathers and leave turtle when watchman arrives. Jamaica: Sherlock ANANSI 31-34 /McDowell THIRD 72-74/. Haiti: Courlander PIECE 29-33; Thoby-Marcelin SINGING 21-29.

K1041.1.5* Anansi flies with blackbird to island to feed. Refuses to leave when it is ready so Blackbird takes back his feathers and leaves Anansi. West Indies: Sherlock WEST 130-134. Hausa: Aardema TALES 31-40 (gizo spider and crows in fig tree).

K1041.2* Raven makes a clay egg, hatches a goose (Anana). Tries to go south with geese. Anana and another goose support Raven when exhausted but he falls into sea. Eskimo: Melzack RAVEN 25-31.

K1041.2.1* Raven makes a clay egg, hatches a keewak bird. It cannot learn to fly. Goes up into the air and is never seen again. Eskimo: Melzack RAVEN 25-31.

K1041.3* Tio Conejo (hare) taken to 'feast' in heaven by Tio Buzzard. Buzzard tries to drop Conejo but Conejo hits Buzzard over head with guitar and holds Buzzard's wings outstretched so unconscious Buzzard can glide to earth. Nicaragua: Jagendorf KING 205-208.

K1041.4* Wabassi sticks feathers in belt and tries to fly. South America: Jagendorf NOODLEHEAD 111-114.

K1043. Dupe induced to eat sharp (stinging, bitter) fruit. U.S. (Black, Georgia): Harris COMPLETE 375-378 /Harris NIGHTS 357-361/.

K1043.2. Dupe persuaded to eat stones. Tiger told by Rabbit not to touch any of the ten cakes (hot stones), he counts eleven so eats one. Korea: Kim STORY 58-65.

K1044. Dupe induced to eat filth (dung). SEE: K1023.1.2.

K1047. The bear bites the seemingly dead horse's tail. Is dragged off by the horse. Type 47A. Scandinavia: Wiggin TALES 309-310 (fox).

K1047.0.1* Mammy-Bammy Big Money feigns dead and wolf is tied to her to eat. She runs into river dragging him. U.S. (Black, Georgia): Harris COMPLETE 268-272 /Harris NIGHTS 208-213/.

K1047.0.2* Fox tied to horse's tail. U.S. (Black, Georgia): Harris FAVORITE 243-246 /Harris NIGHTS 8-11/, /Harris COMPLETE 123-126/. Native American (Creek): Brown TEPEE 106-109.

K1047.0.3* Old horse must bring home lion to save position, fox tells lion to tie self to tail of sham-dead horse. Germany: Wiggin TALES

153-154.

K1051. Diving for sheep. A dupe persuaded that sheep have been lost in river. Type 1535. SEE: K842.

K1051.0.1* Dupe persuaded sheep were acquired in underwater land and dives. Usually were given by dupe when changing places with trickster. SEE: K842. China: Chang TALES 11-24 (tells of visiting Sea King's palace and returns with geese, landlord sets out in earthen vessel, +J2171.1.3). Scandinavia: Hardendorff TRICKY 11-22 (riches and livestock). Russia (Georgia): Papashvily YES 67-75. Bulgaria: Pridham GIFT 84-94. Wales: Pugh TALES 13-19 (obtains sheep by sale of oracular oxhide, K114.1). Puerto Rico: Alegria THREE 111-114; Belpre TIGER 11-18 (hare tricks tiger, claims got cheeses). Pakistan: Siddiqui TOONTOONY 37-42 (+K941.2, burning house for ashes).

K1052. Dragon attacks own image in mirror. SEE: R111.1.3Ab.

K1054. Robber persuaded to climb down moonbeam. A man hearing a robber enter tells his wife aloud that he always makes a prayer and then enters the house by climbing down a moonbeam. The thief tries it and falls. Turkey: Downing HODJA 64-65. Medieval Europe: Jablow MAN 53-55. Latin: Berson THIEF pb.

K1055. Dupe persuaded to get into grass in order to learn new dance. Grass set on fire. U.S.: Courlander TERRAPIN'S 33-36 (Hare tricks alligator).

K1055.2* Dupe gets into grass to meet 'trouble.'

K1055.2.0.1* Hare tricks bear. U.S. (Black): Lester KNEE 5-8.

K1055.2.0.2* Alligator is burnt by hare. +A2356.2.11. U.S. (Black, Georgia): Harris COMPLETE 220-224 /Harris NIGHTS 141-145/. U.S. (Black, South Carolina): Faulkner DAYS 128-131.

K1055.2.0.3* Fox tells terrapin he can see 'ole boy' if sits in broomsage. Hare hides terrapin and lures fox onto scorched field. U.S. (Black, Georgia): Harris COMPLETE 182-185; Harris NIGHTS 90-94.

K1055.3* Dupe (buzzard) crawls into bee nest. It is set afire by hare and buzzard perishes. Heat said to be stinging of bees. U.S. (Black, Georgia): Harris COMPLETE 170-173 /Harris NIGHTS 74-78/.

K1057. Gun thought tobacco pipe. The trickster gives the ogre the gun to smoke. Germany: Jablow MAN 7-9.

K1066. Dupe induced to incriminate self. Taught incriminating song or persuaded to wear incriminating clothes.

K1066.1* Monkey dons stolen necklace when tricked into showing off. Thus theft is found out. Ceylon: Tooze THREE..MONKEY #2. Rockwell STOLEN pb.

K1066.2* Ti Malice steals king's sheep "My Joy" (Mon Plaisir). Tells Bouqui to wear sheepskin and sing song "I ate My Joy" and will win costume ball prize. Haiti: Carter GREEDY 91-98; Jagendorff KING 155-161.

K1066.3* Hare as nurse eats lion cubs (K933). Teaches baboons to sing "We're not afraid, we don't care, we killed the cubs when their mother wasn't there." S. Africa: Arnott ANIMAL 104-111.

K1066.4* Hare teaches fox to play on quills and sing. U.S. (Black, Georgia): Harris NIGHTS 68-73.

K1066.5* Anansi eats tiger's food, teaches little monkeys incriminating song. Anansi lives in housetop web now (A2433.5.3.3). West Indies: Sherlock WEST 59-64.

K1066.6* Monkey loaned blanket by hare, hare has gotten it from lion without paying, lion takes monkey for thief. Africa: Colwell SECOND 80-84.

K1066.7* Brer Wolf, Fox, Bear teach Brer Rabbit song to sing at Brer Gilyard's party. "Who stole Brer Gilyard's sheep?" "Yes, yes, yes I did." U.S. (Black, South Carolina): Faulkner DAYS 158-163.

K1066.8* Sis Mockingbird teaches crude courting song to Brer Bar, fine song to Brer Rabbit. U.S. (Black, South Carolina): Faulkner DAYS 75-79.

K1079* Dupe persuaded to voluntary self-injury--miscellaneous.

K1079.1* Bird calls causing women to look up and their waterpots fall from heads and break. Uganda: Serwadda SONGS 11-15.

K1079.2* Lizard climbs tree to mock legless snake while playing snake's drum. Termites aid snake by gnawing tree and lizard's bounces cause it to fall into river. Uganda: Serwadda SONGS 61-69.

K1080. Persons duped into injuring each other. SEE: K341.16.

K1081.3. Blind men duped into fighting: strings leading to water removed. Native American: Leekley WORLD 69-75.

K1082. Ogres (large animals, sharp-elbowed woman) duped into fighting each other. Trickster strikes one so that he thinks the other has done it. Type 1640. SEE ALSO: K1951.1 (Seven at a Blow). U.S. (Appalachia): Chase JACK 3-20 (+G501E).

K1082.0.2* Brer Rabbit poisons meat and leaves by Brer Lion and Brer Gilyard. Pokes and they fight over meat, eat and die. Brer Spider gave thread to follow into cave, Brer Bear gave meat, Brer Snake gave venom, Brer Lightning Bug gives light. U.S. (Black, South Carolina): Faulkner DAYS 168-177.

K1082.3. Bird lighting on the heads of group of men causes them to kill one another with blows on the head. (cf. N333).

K1082.3.1* Quail flies onto old woman, old man strikes wife, wife retaliates. Russia: Ginsburg ONE 31-37.

K1082.3.2* Ape brings one thousand apes with clubs to attack firefly. Firefly flies on nose of one, second strikes and kills first ape, etc. Philippines (Visayan): Sechrist ONCE 51-54.

K1082.3.3* Bug buzzes bear and makes hit self trying to hit bug, friend hare escapes meanwhile (cf. N333). Rumania: Rudolph MAGIC 42-50.

K1084.1.1. Jackal tells tales so as to get buffalo and tiger to kill each other; feeds on the meat. (cf. K2131.2). India: Wyatt GOLDEN 107-111 (lion and bull discover truth and drive out jackal). Gypsy (Syria): Hampden GYPSIES' 105-109 (fox tricks ox and panther).

K1084.1.2* Jackal arranges friendship between bull and lion by making each afraid of other and owing truce to him. Later tells lion if bull approaches timidly he means to attack, tells bull if lion is watchful he means to attack. Lion kills bull. India: Gaer FABLES 60-69; Ryder PANCHATANTRA 19-21.

K1084.1.2.1* Above fails as lion and bull overhear and turn on plotting foxes. India: Korel LISTEN 69-122.

K1084.1.3* Trickster incriminates others. Temba cooks for animals who have been preying on village. Warns they must not look as he cooks or dish will be ruined; leaves out salt and blames hyenas for looking. Lion king orders them killed. Leopards, lions same. Until only king left. E. Africa: Arnott TEMBA 107-115.

K1084.3.1* Boy pretends to know magic word that can kill. Two men come to kill them. He says will tell magic word only to stronger of the two. They fight and kill each other. Eskimo: Edmonds TRICKSTER 21-29.

K1110. Deception into self-injury--miscellaneous.

K1111. Dupe puts hand (paws) into cleft of tree (wedge, vise). Type 38. SEE ALSO: K1023.1. India: Ryder PANCHATANTRA 25 (monkey - private parts). Steppes: Masey STORIES 84-87 (tiger helps man cut wood). Switzerland (French): Duvoisin THREE 61-66. Netherlands: Green ANIMAL 97-115. Native American (Lakota): Yellow Robe TONWEYA 86-93 (+K826).

K1111.0.1* Dupe wishing to learn to play fiddle has finger caught in cleft of tree. Type 151, 1159.

Wolf tricked by fiddler. Germany (Grimm): Grimm BROTHERS 77-81 (bear caught in vise, +K1755); Grimm HOUSEHOLD 52-55; Grimm WORLD 372-375; Lang GREEN 311-315 (bear).

K1111.0.1.1. Dupe wishing to learn to play flute puts tongue in split bamboo. Kantchil tells tiger he may play "king's trumpet", puts tongue between bamboos and waits for wind to blow. Indonesia: De Leeuw INDONESIA 68-74.

K1111.0.1.2* Bear puts paw in split tree so can learn to play the kantele. Karelia: Deutsch MORE 31.

K1111.0.2* Lion wants to meet man, asks steer, horse, etc. All say he is superior. Man tells lion to put paw in split log for him and hold while he goes to fetch "Man." U.S. (Black, Georgia): Harris NIGHTS 33-37 /Harris COMPLETE 141-144/.

K1111.1. Ogre's (dwarf's) beard caught fast. Types 426, 1160. SEE: D113.2 (Snow White and Rose Red); H1440A (learning of fear).

K1111.4* Brer Fox caught when Brer Rabbit drops rail fence on neck. To show pretty girls from Tuscaloosa. U.S. (Black, Alabama): Courlander TERRAPIN'S 18-20.

K1112.2* Bending the stave. Barrel stave snaps and springs tubmaker to sky. He helps Thunder God (A284) pour sacks of rain on earth (A189.1.1). Falls off, lands on tree top, and jumps into blanket held by priests. Japan: Uchida MAGIC 43-50.

K1113. Abandonment on stretching tree. A man is induced to get into a tree which magically shoots upward. SEE: D482.1.

K1113.1. Dupe persuaded to climb tall tree. Falls. U.S. (Black, Georgia): Harris COMPLETE 375-378 /Harris NIGHTS 357-361/.

K1121. Wolf (lion) approaches too near to horse. Kicked in face. Type 47B. SEE: K553.4; K566. Lithuania: Deutsch TALES 56-62 (mare kicks wolf away from colt). Russia (Ukraine): Bloch UKRAINIAN 68-72 (dog).

K1121.0.1. Wolf reads mule's name on hoof. Showing off reading skill to fox. Italy: Green BIG 208. Poland: Zajdler POLISH 119-126.

K1121.1. Wolf (lion) as sham doctor looks at horse's foot; kicked in face. Aesop: Aesop AESOP'S (Grosset) 208-209; Aesop AESOP'S (Viking) 49-50; Aesop FIVE 21; Martignoni ILLUSTRATED 347.

K1121.2. Sow kicks wolf into stream when he comes close to baptize her pigs. Thus she saves them from him.

K1121.2.1* Sow persuades wolf (giant) to wash pigs before eating. Pushes him into stream. (cf. K562). Slavonic: Dobbs MORE 75-80 (squealing attracts dogs). Majorca: Mehdevi BUNGLING 85-91 (bites ankle of giant). Poland: Zajdler POLISH 119-126. Finland: Bowman TALES..TUPA 251-252. Russia: Riordan TALES ..CENTRAL 207-210.

K1121.3* Scorpion asks Hyena to help him hold his bow. Hyena puts nose on Scorpion's tail. N. Nigeria (Hausa): Sturton ZOMO 58-66.

K1151. The lying goat. A father sends his sons one after the other to pasture the goat. The goat always declares that he has had nothing to eat. The father angrily sends his sons from home and learns when he himself tries to pasture the goat that he has been deceived. Type 212. +D861.1B. Germany (Grimm): Grimm GRIMM'S (Follett) 323-339; Grimm GRIMM'S (Grosset) 228-242; Grimm GRIMM'S (Scribner's) 104-116; Grimm GRIMM'S (World) 130-141; Grimm HOUSE 56-80; Grimm HOUSEHOLD 149-159; Wiggin FAIRY 163-173. Poland: Zajdler POLISH 141-147. Ukraine: Bloch Ukrainian 39-43. Russia: Carrick STILL MORE 73-87.

K1161. Animals hidden in various parts of a house attack owner with their characteristic powers and kill him when he enters.

K1161.1* The Bremen Musicians: Animals in various parts of house frighten off thief when he enters. Thief believes cat is witch, dog--man with knife, donkey--ogre, cock--judge. +K335.1.4. Belgium: Frost LEGENDS 203-209 (en route to become choristers at Saint Guoule in Brussels). England: Hutchinson CANDLE-LIGHT 107-113 (cat, dog, goat, bull, cock); Jacobs ENGLISH 24-26 (Jack); Manning-Sanders MAGIC BEASTS 199-208 (Jack); Steel ENGLISH 185-188. Germany (Grimm): Arbuthnot ANTHOLOGY 200-201; Arbuthnot FAIRY 37-39; Fenner ADVENTURE 103-108; Grimm BREMEN pb (illus. Galdone); Grimm GRIMM'S (Grosset) 144-147; Grimm GRIMM'S (World) 301-304; Grimm HOUSEHOLD 136-139; Grimm TALES 87-97; Grimm TRAVELING pb; Haviland FAVOR-ITE..GERMANY 72-85; Haviland FAIRY 110-113; Hutchinson CHIMNEY 127-134; Martignoni ILLUSTRATED 219-220; Rackham GRIMM'S 114-118; Rockwell OLD 52-61; Shubb ABOUT 111-115. Ireland: Danaher FOLK 93-102 (dog, cat, cock, gander and goat); MacManus HIBERNIAN 212-223 (Jack, three squirrels) /MacManus BOLD 3-18/; Pilkington SHAMROCK 46-51 (Jack). New England: Haviland NORTH 141-143 (cat, dog, goat, bull, cock, Jack). Puerto Rico: Alegria THREE 9-14. Scotland: Wilson SCOT-TISH 81-87. U.S. (Appalachia): Chase JACK 40-46 (also ox) /Arbuthnot FAIRY 194-196/, /Arbuthnot ANTHOLOGY 307-309/. Yugoslavia (Slovene): Kavcic GOLDEN 93-99. Richardson GREAT 104-112.

K1161.2* Sheep, pig, goose, hare and cock build house in woods. Wolf neighbors come to visit and are routed believing house full of people. Shoemaker beat with last (sheep), smiths pinched with tongs (pig and goose), hunter looking for gun (hare), "Drag him hither" (cock). Norway: Asbjornsen EAST (Row) 129-132; Asbjornsen NORWEGIAN 102-105. Russia: Riordan TALES ..CENTRAL 222-226 (ox, goat, cock, goose, pig).

K1161.2.1* Donkey, ram, fox and cockerel take possession of cave belonging to wolves and bears. Intimidate with wolfskin (K1715.3). Ter-rorize when bear and wolf think they are looking for knife and rope to hang them--really are running about in panic. Bulgaria: Pridham GIFT 107-115.

K1161.3* Old woman protected by objects.

K1161.3.1* Monkeys destroy garden. Helpful salesmen give lady 1. strawmats for staircase, 2. eggs for stove, 3. pins for mosquito net. Monkeys trip on mats, eggs explode in faces, pins stick--are routed. China: Lin MILKY 87-92.

K1161.3.2* Ogre (Nung-guama) threatens. Help-ful peddlers give 1. needles for door, 2. dung for door, 3. poisonous snakes for waterpot, 4. round fish (poisonous) for cooking pot, 5. eggs for ashes, 6. millstone for bed, 7. iron bar. Ogre killed. She sells carcass. China: Bonnet FOLK 97-102 /Bonnet TERRIBLE pb/.

K1161.3.3* Objects ask woman to take them along. Coconut on hearth, beehive on hook by door, knife on floor, cat by fire. Thief comes. Pakistan: Siddiqui TOONTOONY 141-143.

K1161.3.4* Boar makes demands of old lady and threatens to eat granddaughter. Passers give her needle--stick in door, crabs--in water jar, ox--tied to bedstead, open well dug in yard with sheet of paper over it. Wiggin TALES 412-414.

K1161.3.5* Wolf demands magic coin found by old woman which causes rice urn to be self-replen-ishing. Wolf slips on grass, egg explodes in face, crab in waterjar, door bar beats, frog chases, spinning wheel whines "Hold him", sledge hammer over door falls, old woman kills with sickle. China: Chang CHINESE 50-52.

K1161.3.6* Old woman takes home scorpion fish, wood apple, razor, cowpat, alligator. They attack intruder and rout. India (Bengali): Bang OLD pb.

K1161.3.7* Tiger routed by old woman who puts pepper in water jug, needle in towel, dung by door, mat in yard, backpack by fence. Korea: Kim STORY 51-55.

K1161.4* Couple seek fortune. Objects and ani-mals ask to go along. Enter deserted house in wood, when goblin comes home they invite him to sit--on needle, lobster in water bucket, a-corns in fire for pig explode, ox in barn tosses, horse kicks, duck cries "Smack him well", cock "Chuck him out", Goblin tells friends in Underworld house was full of people--cook with skewer, tinker with pincers, etc. Poland: Baker TALKING 204-209; Haviland FAVORITE..POLAND 28-37.

K1161.5* Thumbling takes bamboo thorn, moss, and rotten egg along in stomach. Enter ogre's house. Thorn in bed, egg in fireplace, moss near water jar. Going for water slips on moss and breaks neck. +F535.1.10. Burma: Htin Aung KINGDOM 46-52.

K1161.6* Crab and monkey. Monkey trades fruit seed for crab's rice. Crab's seed grows into fruit tree, monkey helps pick fruit but throws only green down (sometimes wounding crab). +K171.9.1. Friends, wasp, mortar and egg agree to help. Mortar over door, egg (chestnut) in hearth, wasp (hornet) in water bucket. Japan: Lang CRIMSON 187-190 (kaki fruit); Ozaki JAPANESE 203-213 (crab stoned to death by green persimmons, son revenges); Sakade JAPANESE 94-96; Wiggin TALES 427-428.

K1161.7* Mr. Korbes. Cock, hen go in carriage to visit Mr. Korbes the Fox. Cat, needle, pin, millstone, duck hitch a ride. Hide in various parts of room and rout Mr. Korbes and take over house. England: Williams-Ellis ROUND 166-171. Germany (Grimm): Grimm HOUSEHOLD 179-180; Wiggin TALES 118-123.

K1161.7.1* Fox as innkeeper, only needle taken on. Egg explodes and needle sticks, fox flees. Hen, who insisted on being drawn in carriage, now runs. Bulgaria: Rudolph MAGIC 14-29.

K1161.7.2. The good for nothings. Cock and hen go nutting. Duck made to pull cart. Needle and pin taken on. Innkeeper given hen's egg as pay. In morning they eat egg and leave shells in fire, pin in handkerchief, needle in chair. Landlord is pricked, sits on pin and eggshells explode in face. Germany (Grimm): Gag MORE 77-83; Grimm GOOD pb; Grimm HOUSEHOLD 62-64; Grimm HOUSE 95-102.

K1161.8* Animals hide in tree, fall out and frighten wolves from cave. Wolves return and are attacked by hidden cat, cock and lamb, flee. U.S. (New Mexico): Cothran WITH 49-54.

K1161.9* Rolling egg. Egg rolls off, meets lobster, mouse, cat, rooster, goat who join. At house of twelve robbers they hide and rout foxes. Take home stores for old man and woman. Bulgaria: Rudolph MAGIC 3-13.

K1161.10* Young man and tiger. Man on horse takes along May beetle, egg, crab, rice ladle, awl, mortar, straw mat, pack carrier. Meet girl who lost family to tiger. Tiger returns and is routed. Conclusion: Mortar falls and kills, mat wraps up, pack carrier dumps in river, man weds girl. Korea: UNICEF Asia FOLK #1 26-31.

K1161.11* Brer Rabbit and Brer Terrapin at Miss Meadows place. Terrapin falls from shelf onto Brer Fox as he enters. Rabbit hides in chimney calls out that there is money up chimney and spits tobacco juice in Brer Fox's eyes. U.S. (Black, Georgia): Brown WORLD 82-87; Harris FAVORITE 77-82; Harris COMPLETE 32-36; Harris SONGS 47-53.

K1161.12* Old Verlooka. Old Verlooka gets little girl, little boy, grandma. Grandpa escapes Verlooka and seeks Verlooka with axe. Bob-tail drake, piece of string, mallet, and acorn accompany grandpa. All hide in Verlooka's hut and attack. Grandma and grandchildren rescued and Verlooka killed. Russia: Manning-Sanders CHOICE 301-306.

K1161.13* Juan Bobo sets out to kill tiger. Onion and vine ask to go along. Onion in stew sings "We've come to kill Tiger" and flies in Tiger's eye, vine trips him, and Juan kills. Venezuela: Jagendorf KING 269-273.

K1175. Minister dupes raja into entering body of dead parrot. Then enters rajah's body. Type 678. India: Reed TALKATIVE 30-33 (Queen tricks minister to enter hare's body to show off skill and rajah repossesses own body).

K1181.1* Hot peppers fed cows so they flee tax collector. Burr put under tax collector's horse's tail and he rushes off too. U.S. (Appalachia): Credle TALL 181-182.

K1200 - K1299. Deception into humiliating position.

K1236. Disguises as man to escape importunate lover.

K1236.1* The Twelve Huntsmen: prince must promise dying father to wed girl of his choice, lover comes disguised as man with eleven maids also disguised and takes service with prince. His pet lion warns of the deception. The girls pass tests of manliness, ignoring spinning wheel, etc. But his love faints on hearing prince plans to wed another. Revealed. Wed. Germany (Grimm): Grimm GRIMM'S (Grosset) 341-344; Grimm GRIMM'S (World) 75-78; Grimm JUNIPER v. 1 63-70; Lang GREEN 282-285 /Lang FIFTY 341-344/.

J1236.2* The Green Sergeant. Princess dreams her father will kiss her hand. He orders her killed. She flees and dons man's clothing. Princess falls in love and angry at rejection, says 'he' boasted could perform feats. With aid of magic horse she succeeds. Third task: fetch jewel from sea serpent. Throws behind oil = glassy path. Salt = cloud. Pins = ledge. Once home horse turns to prince. "Green Sergeant" weds king. Princess weds former horse. Five kings come to kiss new bride, one is her father. Brazil: Baker TALKING 184-190.

K1240. Deception into humiliating position--miscellaneous.

K1241. Trickster rides dupe horseback. Usually by feigning sickness he induces the dupe to carry him and then boasts that the dupe always acts as his horse. SEE ALSO: K473 (Sham blood and brains).

K1241.0.1* Hare (Zomo) rides hyena horseback until Zomo returns pilgrim's stolen horse. Nigeria (Hausa): Sturton ZOMO 67-76.

K1241.0.2* Hare rides tiger. Puerto Rico: Alegria THREE 44-51; Belpré TIGER 11-18; Carter GREEDY 41-45.

K1241.0.3* Frog rides elephant. Hardendorff FROG'S 15-16. Angola: Bryan OX 15-21.

K1241.0.4* Anansi carried by tiger. West Indies: Sherlock WEST 105-111.

K1241.0.5* Hare rides deer. U.S. (Black, Gulf Coast): Cothran WITH 40-43.

K1241.0.6* Turtle rides leopard. W. Africa (Temne): Aardema MORE 12-15.

K1241.1. Trickster rides dupe a-courting. Feigns sickness and persuades dupe to carry him. Thus wins the girl.

K1241.1.0.1* Brer Rabbit rides Brer Fox a-courting. U.S. (Black, Georgia): Brown WORLD 58-62; Harris FAVORITE 55-60 /Harris COMPLETE 17-20/, /Harris SONGS 24-30/.

K1241.1.0.2* Hare rides leopard a'courting. Liberia: Haskett GRAINS 51-54.

K1241.1.0.3* Anansi rides donkey a'courting. Tells donkey this will prove his strength to girlfriend. Ashanti: Appiah ANANSE 71-88.

K1241.1.0.4* Brer Rabbit rides Brer Wolf courting. U.S. (Black, South Carolina): Faulkner DAYS 146-151. Native American (Creek): Brown TEPEE 106-109.

K1241.2* Hare feigns ill--rides lion's back, eats honey in sack en route. Tugen: Nunn AFRICAN 62-67.

K1251. Holding up the rock. Trickster makes dupe believe that he is holding up a great rock and induces him to hold it for a while. Type 1530. Puerto Rico: Alegria THREE 44-51. E. Africa: Arnott TALES..TEMBA 36-43.

K1251.0.1* Coyote tricks fox. Native American: Gruenberg FAVORITE 338-340; Haviland NORTH 71-75 (+K741.0.13).

K1251.0.2* Leopard tricked by hare into holding up cave. Liberia: Haskett GRAINS 51-54.

K1251.0.3* Fox tricks coyote. Native American (Pueblo): Dolch PUEBLO 105-117. Native American (Southern Plains): Robinson COYOTE 41-52.

K1251.0.4* Sungura (hare) hears case of lion vs. hunter and wife, has lion hold up cave and sends hunter and wife for sticks--they escape. E. Africa: Heady SAFIRI 51-57.

K1251.0.5* Hare tricks holding up rock. U.S. (Black, Georgia): Harris COMPLETE 757-760.

K1251.0.6* Hare tricks wolf with tree. U.S. (Black, Georgia): Harris COMPLETE 343-347 /Harris NIGHTS 314-318/. Native American (Creek): Brown TEPEE 106-108.

K1251.0.7* Holding up fence. Bulgaria: Pridham GIFT 124-129.

K1251.0.8* Holding up tree, peasant tricks lord. Russia (Tatar): Ginsburg TWELVE 46-47.

K1251.2* Holding up the apple tree. Peasant thinks it about to fall with weight of fruit and enlists passersby to hold it up while he goes for props. They find it stands alone and leave. Gypsy: Jagendorf GYPSIES' 146-147.

K1252. Holding down the hat. Dupe persuaded to guard hat supposed to cover something valuable. It covers a pile of dung (or nothing). Dupe's goods are sometimes stolen. Type 1528. Leach NOODLES 66-68. Czechoslovakia: Fillmore SHEPHERD'S 153-159. Solvenia: Kavcic GOLDEN 150-156. Russia: Daniels FALCON 15-20 (falcon).

K1288. King induced to kiss horse's rump. Trickster then threatens to tell. Type 570. SEE ALSO: H1045.

K1288.1* Fake doctor (girl) has king kiss ass's tail. Later she bests king in riddling by revealing this. +K2389.1. Puerto Rico: Belpré TIGER 89-94. Chile: Carpenter SOUTH 83-92.

K1289. Queen (disguised as peasant) induced to cluck and walk like hen. Trickster later reveals. Scandinavia: Lang VIOLET 133-147.

K1300 - K1399. Seduction or deceptive marriage.

K1310. Seduction by disguise or substitution.

K1321.3. Man disguised as woman courted (married) by another man.

K1321.3.0.1* Barber denied marriage to princess. The lovers flee. She takes his clothing and goes as barber to neighboring king. He is forced to wear her clothing left. King falls in love with him. They reveal ruse and King weds them and sends home. Portugal: Michael PORTUGUESE 139-145.

K1340. Entrance into girl's (man's) room by trick.

K1341.1. Entrance to woman's room in golden lion. Princess's curiosity is aroused and the golden lion carried into room. The youth is concealed inside.

K1341.1.0.1* Golden lion, suitor test--finding the princess (H322). Sicily: Haviland FAV..ITALY 79-90; Lang ROSE 114-121 /Lang PINK 223-229/.

K1341.1.0.2* Golden parrot, suitor test--finding the princess. Spain: Boggs THREE 83-96 /Dagliesh ENCHANTED 180-181/.

K1341.1.0.3* Hidden in harpsichord. Italy: Toor GOLDEN 83-90 (+B314F).

K1341.1.0.4* White bearskin hides. Norway: Asbjornsen EAST 57-75 (+S12.1, Blue Belt).

K1341.1.0.5* Golden candelabras. Persia: Mehdevi PERSIAN 69-80.

K1341.1.0.6* Music box in gilt carriage. Philippines (Visayan): Sechrist ONCE 168-173.

K1346. Hero goes to maiden's room. Enters her tower by means of artificial wings or flying horse. SEE ALSO: D1626.1.

K1346.0.1. The Clever Parrot. Type 546. Parrot tells fowler to sell to king for high price. Becomes advisor to king. Jealous stepmother of king and ladies trap parrot Hiram. To tell which is ugliest. Says all together do not compare to little toe of princess beyond seven oceans. King demands her. He breeds magic horse feeding hot coals and honey until grows wings. Whip horse once and starts, if whip twice will fall. King flees with princess but whips horse twice and falls into forest, Princess captured, scatters crumbs to lure birds, hoping to attract Hiram. He has her feed pony hot coals and honey once more. They escape on pony's back. India: Manning-Sanders CHOICE 200-215. Pakistan: Siddiqui TOONTOONY 114-123.

K1350. Woman persuaded (or wooed) by trick.

K1354.1. "Both?" The youth is sent to the house to get two articles. SEE: K362.10.

K1355. Altered letter of execution gives princess to hero. On his way robbers steal the letter and change so that instead of being killed he is married to the princess. Type 930. SEE ALSO: H1273.2 (Quest for Three Golden Hairs); K511.

A* The Fish and The Ring. Baron sees in Book of Fate that son will wed daughter of poor family. He sets her adrift on river (S331). Fisherman raises. Sent with letter to execute, robbers change and she is wedded to son. Baron throws ring into sea, don't show face until have ring, as cook for lord she finds ring in fish (N211.1) on day Baron comes to dinner. Baron accepts fate. England: Jacobs ENGLISH 199-203; Reeves ENGLISH 36-48. England (Yorkshire): Colwell ROUND 46-50; Steel ENGLISH 226-230. Greece: Wilson GREEK 214-221 (overhears three fates forecast).

B* The Luck Child. To wed king's daughter. King throws him into river, miller raises. Sent with letter for own execution. Robbers in overnight lodging change letter. Wed and made king. Germany (Grimm): Chapman LUCK pb.

K1400 - K1499. Dupe's property destroyed.

K1410. Dupe's goods destroyed.

K1411. Plowing the field: horse and harness destroyed. The youth is told to come home from plowing when the dog does. He beats the dog so that it runs home, then he destroys the horse and harness and goes home. Types 650, 1003. SEE: K172. Finland: Spicer THIRTEEN DEVILS 33-42.

K1412. Lighting the road (or painting the house red). The house is set afire. Type 1008. Finland: Spicer THIRTEEN DEVILS 33-42.

K1413. Guarding the door. It is lifted off and carried away. SEE ALSO: G501D (Stupid Peiko); K335.1.1.1. Ethiopa: Courlander FIRE 81-88 /Green FOLK 65-73/. India: Hardendorff TRICKY 97-99. England: Jagendorf MERRY 6-16. Turkey: Walker WATERMELON 58-59.

K1459.1* Black cobra, Kurmurchi, kills all chickens that stray onto field between his home and Zomo hare's. Zomo loses Kurmurchi's chickens and he kills his own. N. Nigeria (Hausa): Sturton ZOMO 39-47.

K1500 - K1599. Deceptions connected with adultery.

K1512. The cut-off nose (Lai of the Tresses). A woman leaves her husband's bed and has another woman take her place. The husband addresses her, gets no answer and cuts off her nose (hair). In the morning the wife still has her nose (hair). The husband is made to believe that it has grown back by a miracle or that he was dreaming. Type 1417. +J2315.2. India: Ryder PANCHATANTRA 62-71.

K1550. Husband outwits adultress and paramour.

K1556. Old Hildebrand. Hidden cuckold reveals his presence by rhymes. He responds to the rhymes made by the wife and paramour concerning their entertainments. Type 1360C. French-Canadian: Barbeau GOLDEN 109-120 (husband in basket brought by accomplice peddler).

K1561.2. Husband feigns wife's voice, has lover put fingers through hole in wall and cuts off. Tricks wife likewise. Kikuyu: Nunn AFRICAN 81-87.

K1600 - K1699. Deceiver falls into own trap.

K1601. Deceiver falls into his own trap (literally). India (Panchatantra): Gaer FABLES 18-20.

K1611. Substituted caps cause ogre to·kill his own children. The hero and heroine change places in bed with the ogre's children and put on them their caps so the ogre is deceived (G501). Type 327B.

A* Molly Whuppie, sleeping in Giant's house (G401). Molly changes straw necklaces put on self and sisters for gold chain on Giant's girls. He kills own children while Molly and sisters escape. Molly returns to steal Giant's sword, he cannot follow her over bridge of one hair. Steals Giant's purse--same (G610). In return king weds her sisters to his sons. Molly steals ring from Giant's finger, caught and put in bag. She pretends to see wonders and Giant's wife changes places (K842.0.1) with her; is beaten by Giant. Molly has suggested being put in bag with dog, cat, needle, thread and shears and beaten (K581). England: De La Mare TALES 193-200 /Minard WOMENFOLK 20-29/, /Colwell MAGIC 19-25/; Jacobs ENGLISH 130-135 /Adams BOOK..GIANT 53-59/, /Fenner GIANTS 32-38/, /Haviland FAVORITE..ENGLAND 44-55/, /Haviland FAIRY 152-157/; Lurie CLEVER 45-52; Reeves ENGLISH 184-194; Steel ENGLISH 234-241.

B* The Rejected Youngest Sister.

Ba* The Mop Servant. Two sisters take large cake without blessing, forced to take sister along. She takes small cake with blessing. Elder sisters tie her to a tree and leave behind. Her mother's blessing unties. Tied to peat stack, rock, sand. At spring little green man muddies water and won't let them drink. Maol throws him into spring. At giant's house she changes necklaces with giant's daughters and flees carrying sisters across bridge of two-hairs. Earl will wed elder sister to son if Maol brings treasure chest giant sleeps on. She puts cold stones on back of neck till giant rolls over off chest. Second sister to wed for white flame of light (sword). Maol salts porridge from rafters until servant is sent to spring for water with sword as light. Takes. To fetch stag, Maol is caught and put in bag, changes places with giant's wife. Giant pursues over bridge and falls to death. Maol weds youngest son. Ireland: Pilkington SHAMROCK 61-70.

Bb* Mutsmag. Youngest sister must make own journey cake of water brought in sieve. Bluebird tells her daub with moss and clay (H1023.2.0.1). Sisters tie her to a laurel, she cuts loose, locked in sheep house, fox releases. At giant's house she changes nightcaps with giant's daughters. Sisters claim feat and king sends back to kill giant and witch. They flee. Mutsmag puts salt down chimney into soup. Witch throws out lightball to light way to spring. Mutsmag catches on knife and puts in spring. Witch falls and breaks neck. Returns for horse with bells and is caught. "Don't feed me honey and butter" (K581). Does. "Don't put me in sack and beat." Does, she escapes, flees (K526). She says she crossed river by tying rock around neck and throwing it over. Giant tries with millstone and drowns. U.S. (Appalachia): Chase GRANDFATHER 40-52.

Bc* Little Bear. Little Bear follows two sisters. Tied to doorpost she follows with it on back. Rock--same. At home of ogre she sees women sharpening knife and flees. Witch hides sun in her wigwam in anger. Chief sickens. Little Bear puts sugar down smoke hole into kettle and steals sun when witch goes for water. Chief gives eldest son to the eldest sister. North star --same. Little Bear to wed. Further task: bring horse with collar of bells, caught. Put in bag, escapes. Wed. Asks husband to throw her into fire--turns to woman. Native American (Ojibwa): Cothran WITH 84-89.

C* Hop O' My Thumb (F535.1.1) strews pebbles to find (R135) way back home and saves brothers from parent's abandonment. At ogre's house (G401; N776) Tom Thumb changes caps of sleeping brothers for crowns of ogre's daughters. Ogre follows in seven league boots. Ogre naps and Tom Thumb steals boots and returns to tell ogre's wife ogre is captured by thieves and must send ransom. Later he makes fame carrying messages for king. France: Lang BLUE 258-266; Opie CLASSIC 128-136; Perrault PERRAULT'S (Dodd) 26-41; Perrault PERRAULT'S (Dover) 91-116; Perrault FAMOUS 61-80; Rackham ARTHUR 15-29.

D* Thumbling variants.

Da* Bundar Bahadur Poon. Monkey nephew follows uncles. Repeatedly sent home. At ogre's house he changes white blankets of witch's daughters for red blankets of uncles. They flee and hide in tree, witch fells tree on self. They take riches, Bundar gets magic drum which drops gold coins when beaten. Uncles refuse to let Bundar go along to buy seed rice so Bundar plants gourds. Forces rat to harvest all rice and put it into his gourds. Nepal: Hitchcock KING 37-46.

Db* Fereyel and Debbo Engal. Thumbling Fereyel follows ten brothers. Repeatedly sent home. Fereyel changes white robes of boys and blue of girls. Fereyel throws objects to stop witch-- hen's egg = river, stone = mountain (D672). Witch turns self to log, plum bush--Fereyel warns. Turns to donkey and brothers mount. Feyerel says there is no room for him and donkey lengthens (K607.5). Is witch. Girl asks Feyerel to walk with her--changes to python. Fereyel changes to fire and destroys her. Gambia: Arnott AFRICAN 200-211 /Hope-Simpson CAVALCADE..WITCHES 156-167/.

Dc* Moi and the Red Bull. Ten boys shelter in empty house, red bull turns to giant and eats all but youngest, Moi. Moi returns with nine more boys and burns hut and bull. Africa (Nandi): Harman TALES 153-162.

Dd* The boy who wanted to see the world. Ti Pierre sleeps with four children in demon's house, wears one of their nightcaps and demon kills own child. Returns four times thus. Flees and gets home safely. Haiti: Johnson HOW 39-46.

E* The children abed in the ogre's house. Other varieties.

Ea* The Two Lost Babes: This variant lacks the exchanged cap motif but is otherwise similar. Abandoned by parents, Buck drops stones (R135). Second night corn is eaten by birds. At witch's house the boy Cocklepea helps Buck and Bess escape from loft while witch whets knife. Witch pursues in mile-a-clip boots. They hide in crevice in cliff, she waits for them to come out and falls asleep. They push her off cliff and Cocklepea leads the sheriff to a meeting of witches at witch's house. Cats run out and are trapped, turn to witch (G211.1.7). She is tried and burned. Cocklepea weds Bess. U.S. (Appalachia): Chase WICKED 162-179.

F* The Three Brother's and the Giant. Three brothers lost in wood shelter in giant's house. Change crowns with three daughters of giant, three may need friends if bring back treasures of giant. Eldest fetches Gold beard of giant. Second fetches sword. Youngest brings giant self in cage. France: De Regniers GIANT 49-59.

G* Nippy and Yankee Doodle. Mother sends N. for water to bake cake for travel. Bird sings to daub sieve with clay (H1023.2.0.1). Task: Wed daughter if can bring three gold lockets and gold staff from Old Man Across River. N. puts necklaces of three daughters on self and brothers. Old Man kills daughters. Task: bring half moon. N. pours salt in fire, wife comes with half moon light to see. N. takes. Task: fetch Yankee Doodle (whistle). N. plays and is caught. Suggests being fed eggs and butter until fat (K581). Pushes old woman in oven. U.S. (S. Appalachia): Haviland NORTH 155-159.

K1613.3. Poisoner's own son takes the beverage intended for stepbrother. Japan: Ozaki JAPANESE 74-76 (stepdaughter).

K1622. Thief climbing rope discovered and rope cut. He has tricked the guardian of the food-supply in the tree (by imitation of the owner's voice, or he discovered password) to let down the rope. Tanganyika (Kamba): Arnott AFRICAN 140-149 (+K311.3E, not dropped).

K1625 Monkey instead of girl in floating basket: hermit made laughingstock. He has persuaded girl's foolish father to place her in the basket. Prince takes girl and leaves monkey in her place. India: Turnbull FAIRY 91-102.

K1632. Fox leads ass to lion's den but is himself eaten. When he gets there the ass kicks him so that he falls on the lion's bed. Aesop: Aesop

AESOP'S (Watts) 15-16.

K1633.1* Donkey tells ox to feign ill and escape work. Donkey is made to work in ox's stead. Donkey now tells ox he is apt to be killed if doesn't work. Farmer overhears this (B216). Russia: Ginsburg LAZIES 32-35; Green BIG.. ANIMAL 40-42. Russia (Kazakh): Masey STORIES 46-49.

K1636. Maids must rise even earlier. They have killed the cock for waking them too early but their mistress punishes them. Aesop: Aesop AESOP'S (Grosset) 197; Aesop AESOP'S (Viking) 14; Aesop AESOP'S (Watts) 18; Aesop FABLES (Walck) 62-63.

K1655. The lawyer's mad client (Pathelin). On the advice of a lawyer, the client feigns insanity when arraigned in court. When the fee is demanded, he still feigns insanity. Type 1585. France: Cooper FIVE 26-40; Jagendorf NOODLEHEAD 136-141 (shepherd to say "Baah" to all questions). Nigeria: Walker NIGERIAN 55-56 (just say "Rhee").

K1667.1.1. Retrieving buried treasure. Buried money is stolen. Blind owner pretends he is going to bury more. Thief returns the money hoping to get all. Blind man recovers original treasure. Egypt: Edmonds TRICKSTER 120-128.

K1667.2* Man refuses to return money entrusted to his safekeeping. Woman accomplice of wronged man brings large coffer to entrust, he returns first man small sum as proof of trustworthy nature. Russia: Jameson TALES 30-42.

K1673.1* Sage's advice followed: human sacrifice to stop leak in tank. He is thrown in. His garments lodge in tank's crack and stop leak. India: Korel LISTEN 71-75.

K1682. Disguised trickster beaten by man he is trying to frighten. Disguised as ghost. Eskimo (Hooper Bay): Gillham BEYOND 51-67 (crow).

K1682.1. "Big 'Fraid and Little 'Fraid." Man decides to frighten another (or his son or servant). He dresses in a sheet; his pet monkey puts on a sheet and follows him. The person who is doing the scaring hears the victim say, "Run, Big Fraid, run, Little Fraid'll get you." The scarer sees the monkey in the sheet, runs home. U.S. (South): Credle BIG pb; Leach THING 27-28.

K1682.2* Bucca Dhu and Bucca Gwidden. Son tries to scare mother in chest. She pretends to think he is Bucca Gwidden (the good goblin) and tells him to run as Bucca Dhu (bad goblin) is behind him. England (Cornwall): Manning-Sanders PETER 98-102.

K1685. The treasure finders who murder one another. Two (three) men find a treasure. One of them secretly puts poison in the other's wine (food) but the other kills him, then drinks and dies. Type 763. Liberia: Haskett GRAINS 98-100 (found at shrine of Sande-Nyame). Congo (Luban): Burton MAGIC 104-105. Nigeria: Walker NIGERIAN 44-45. SEE ALSO: Chaucer's "Pardoner's Tale."

K1691. The woman as cuckoo on tree shot down. The anger bargain is to cease when the cuckoo crows. The ogre's wife climbs the tree and imitates the cuckoo. She is shot down. Type 1029. +K172. SEE ALSO: K31.1.

K1700 - K2099. Deception Through Shams.

K1700 -K1799. Deception through bluffing.

K1710. Ogre (large animal) overawed. SEE: K18; K60+; K641.3.

K1711.1. Tiger made to believe porcupine bristle is his enemy's hair; overawed. (cf. K1715.12). Indonesia: Courlander KANTCHIL'S 22-27; De Leeuw INDONESIAN 99-103.

K1711.1.0.1* Lion sent cock's tailfeather, bluffed. Bantu: Jagendorf NOODLEHEAD 89-92.

K1711.1.0.2* Lion shows mane, blind man shows porcupine quill. Congo (Luban): Burton MAGIC 119-121.

K1711.2* Small trickster in house of larger animal intimidates with loud boasts and latter fears to attempt repossession of home. SEE ALSO: J741.1 (house of ice); K1715.2 . Tibet: Hume FAVORITE.. CHINA 93-98 (Jackal, tiger). India: Korel LISTEN 115-118 (Goat, lion); Spellman BEAUTIFUL 75-78 (kid, fox). Ceylon: Tooze WONDERFUL 111-119 (mouse deer, leopard). Pakistan: Siddiqui TOONTOONY 109-113 (jackal, tiger).

K1711.2.1* Caterpillar in hare's house frightens off all larger animals, frog roars back and routs. E. Africa: Heady JAMBO 60-65 /Arbuthnot ARBUTHNOT 314-315/. Masai: Aardema TALES 19-30; Aardema WHO'S pb; Kaula AFRICAN 122-125.

K1711.2.2* Squirrel in leopard's house intimidates larger animals. Feeds them meat with nuts in it, they break teeth, he eats with care. Says is leopard meat (K1715.3.2). Congo: Burton MAGIC 47-51.

K1711.2.3* Old woman is adopted by animals and lightning. Giant bird attacks and makes her work for him, calls self "The Merciless One." Buffalo, leopard, lion and elephant try successively to defend her but are routed. Lightning destroys "The Merciless One" and saves her. Congo: Burton MAGIC 63-68.

K1711.3* Blind man, deaf man and the donkey: find chattee, donkey, snuffbox full of ants en route. Lodge in Rakshasa's house. Blind man says is a Bakshas--shows donkey's nose as face, big chattee as body, puts ants in donkey's ears and Donkey screams--voice. Rakshasa flees. The three companions leave. Climb tree when Rakshasa and six other Rakshasas pursue. Fall into Rakshasa and they flee. Quarreling over treasure deaf and blind hit each other and faculties are restored. SEE ALSO: K1715.12. India: Baker GOLDEN 80-88; Haviland FAVORITE.. INDIA 35-52; Palmer FAIRY 45-49; Wiggin TALES 250-257.

K1711.4* Prince sheltering in hut with old lady intimidates demon--shows ropes as topknot, uses tongs in pinching contest, uses millstone in tooth grinding contest, leaps on demon from roof and subdues. India: Spellman BEAUTIFUL 19-21.

K1712. Small animal placed in difficult situation by ogre makes plausible bluff.

K1712.1* Fox weds Tiger wife. Tossed by bull he says was taking a nap, can't get over rock--says is examining it, falls in ravine--was weaving vines for rope, etc. Nepal: Hitchcock KING 23-32.

K1715. Weak animal (man) makes large one (ogre) believe that he has eaten many of the large one's companions. The latter is frightened. Type 126. SEE: K1715.3.

K1715.1. Weak animal shows strong his own reflection and frightens him. Usually hare and lion. It is hare's turn to provide self for lion's daily meal. Arrives late saying lion in well detained him. Lion attacks reflection and is drowned. India: Gaer FABLES 82-84; Jagendorf NOODLEHEAD 30-33 (fox and tiger); Korel LISTEN 108-111; Ryder PANCHATANTRA 81-88 (K1715.0.2, says lion in well ate other four hares sent). S. India: Wiggin TALES 390-392 (jackal). Punjab: Haviland FAVORITE.. INDIA 21-26 (jackal); Montgomerie TWENTY-FIVE 50-52. Nigeria (Hausa): Sturton ZOMO 26-38 (hare's turn to take food to leopard, says leopard in well ate all, collects five thousand cowrie for getting rid of leopard). Burma: Brockett BURMESE 67-70. S. China: Chang CHINESE 44; Hume FAVORITE..CHINA 115-119. Afghanistan: Bulatkin EURASIAN 80-81.

K1715.1.0.1* Hare flees from reflection in well, starting flight of animals. Lion goes to investigate, attacks, and is drowned. Russia: Ginsburg THREE 45-46.

K1715.1.0.2* Animal hears echo of roar in well and attacks. India: Ryder PANCHATANTRA 81-88 (hare and lion).

K1715.1.2. Man shows ghost its own reflection and and frightens it. Bengal: Hardendorff JUST 105-109. SEE ALSO: J1795.1.1.

K1715.2. Bluff: only one tiger; you promised ten. Child or shepherd calls out to the small hero (ape, hare) and makes the tiger (ogre) think that he is lucky to escape alive. Type 1149. (cf. J681.1.1). SEE ALSO: J2132.5.1.

K1715.2.0.1* Kid to fox with tiger tied to tail. India: Spellman BEAUTIFUL 75-78.

K1715.2.0.1.1* Goat calls to fox to bring a younger lion. India: Korel LISTEN 115-118.

K1715.2.0.2* Mouse deer in lion's cave (K1711.2) to jackal tied to leopard. Ceylon: Tooze WONDERFUL 111-114.

K1715.2.0.3* Jackal with tail tied to tiger, wife dressed as man feigns great hunger. Pakistan: Asia FOLK..I 34-39 /Colwell MAGIC 79-82/.

K1715.2.0.3.1* Mother jackal in tiger's cave (K1711.2) to father jackal on arrival of monkey tied to tiger's tail. "Here's the tiger. Shoot him." Sets off firecrackers. Pakistan: Siddiqui TOONTOONY 109-113.

K1715.2.0.4* Fox and tiger approach frogs. S.W. China: Hume FAVORITE..CHINA 9-14.

K1715.2.0.5* Baboon and tiger approach jackal. Tibet: Hume FAVORITE..CHINA 93-98.

K1715.2.0.6* Leopard tied to tiger's whiskers flees frog. Hardendorff JUST 58-63.

K1715.2.0.7* Man tells fox bringing ghul. Iran: Williams-Ellis ROUND 73-80.

K1715.2.0.7.1* Man thanks fox for bringing giant. +K1951.1M. Russia (Steppes): Masey STORIES 1-11.

K1715.2.0.8* Ram to fox bringing wolf. U.S. (Black, Georgia): Harris FAVORITE 153-158; Harris COMPLETE 328-331.

K1715.2.0.9* Donkey thanks jackal for bringing lion. Iran: Mehdevi PERSIAN 104-111.

K1715.2.1* Small hero calls bluff of tiger by riding elephant's back and pretending to be eating elephant. Calls to accomplice monkey who brings tiger (usually tied to his tail, J2132.5.2). "I told you to bring two tigers" or "thanks for the tiger." Tiger flees. Tiger was to have eaten elephant due to winning a roaring contest. Vietnam: Vo-Dinh TOAD 57-64 (hare). U.S. (Black): Courlander TERRAPINS 50-52 (hare bluffs wolf).

K1715.2.1.0.1* Kantchil smears betel juice on elephant's back--blood. Orangutan brings it. Indonesia: Courlander KANTCHIL'S 46-51.

K1715.2.1.0.2* Rabbit eating bananas, feigns brains. Burma: Brockett BURMESE 71-78.

K1715.3. The wolf flees from the wolf-head. The sheep have found a sack and a wolf-head. They make the wolf believe that they have killed a wolf, and he flees in terror.

K1715.3.0.1* Goats frighten jackal with jackal's tail. N. Africa: Gilstrap SULTAN'S 18-25. Jagendorf NOODLEHEAD 256-259.

K1715.3.0.2* Goat butts dead puma, jaguar thinks he killed it. S. America: Hardendorff FROG'S 75-82.

K1715.3.0.3* Sheep and goat, they then climb tree and sheep falls out onto wolf. Goat calls "hand up the wolf" and wolves flee. Russia (Ukraine): Bloch UKRAINIAN 14-23. Russia: Riordan TALES..CENTRAL 161-164 (goats, wolf, bear).

K1715.3.0.4* Donkey, man, fox, cock intimidate wolf. +K1161.1. Bulgaria: Pridham GIFT 107-115.

K1715.3.1* Brer Rabbit offers Brer Wolf taste from jug of fox's blood (molasses). Wolf and Fox accomplice leave. U.S. (Black, Georgia): Harris FAVORITE 262-264; Harris COMPLETE 499-504.

K1715.3.2* Goat begins to build a house. Tiger finds foundation and adds to it. Each thinks god is helping with the work. Discovering their 'partner' they agree to live together. Goat brings in dead tiger and tiger flees. Haiti: Carter GREEDY 35; Thoby-Marcelin SINGING 66-74. Brazil: Courlander RIDE 198-201 (deer and jaguar). Africa (Galla): Kaula AFRICAN 136-138 (monkey and hyena--intimidation, each flees the other). Congo: Burton MAGIC 47-51 (squirrel and leopard, +K1711.2.2); Burton MAGIC 121-124 (bushbuck tricks leopard).

K1715.3.3* Terrapin makes hominy spoon of wolf's ear. Wolves attack. Native American (Cherokee): Bell JOHN 80-83; Scheer CHEROKEE 65-68.

K1715.4. Enemies frightened away by making them think they will be eaten.

K1715.4.0.1* Sweetheart returns with lad, says "I have eaten nine dragons for breakfast and will eat this one." Dragon flees. Macedonia: Manning-Sanders BOOK..DRAGONS 76-78.

K1715.4.0.2* Trickster asks wife if she has eaten seven giants he left her yet. Russia (Steppes): Masey STORIES 1-11 (+K1951.1M).

K1715.4.2* Cock challenges elephant to strength contest. Elephant lays waste to forest, dislodged insects perch on him and weigh him down. While he sleeps, cock eats insects. Elephant awakens and feeling lighter thinks cock is eating him. Flees. Yoruba: Fuja FOURTEEN 120-125.

K1715.12.1* Blind man shows lion porcupine quill for mane (K1711.1), tortoise for tick, elephant tusk for tooth, shoots gun in lion's ear for roar, killing lion. +U174; N642.2. SEE ALSO: K1711.3. Congo (Luban): Burton MAGIC 119-121.

K1715.12.2* Frog challenges tiger to spitting contest and spits out hairs he bit off tiger's tail. S.W. China: Hardendorff JUST 58-63; Hume FAVORITE..CHINA 9-14; Kendall SWEET 73-77 (+J2132.5.1).

K1715.15. Hare tell lion he's killed alligator and bear and shows 'graves.' Lion flees. U.S.: Courlander TERRAPIN'S 57-59.

K1715.16* Kantchil has goats eat red flowers feigning bloody mouths and call out for more tigers to eat. Tigers flee. Kantchil has told feigned dream of world in which goats prey on tigers, tigers think dream came true. Indonesia: Bro HOW 55-71.

K1715.17* Goat trapped in lion's house sings of ten thousand lions he killed yesterday. Lion and his family flee. Trinidad: Williams-Ellis ROUND 192-194.

K1716. Hare as ambassador of the moon. Hare claiming to be ambassador of moon shows elephant the moon, irritated, in a spring. Elephant is persuaded that moon is angry. (cf. J1791.12). India: Gaer FABLES 86-89; Jablow MAN 27; Ryder PANCHATANTRA 308-315.

K1717. Big shoes in front of the barn. Man makes giant shoes and places them so that ogre thinks a giant lives there. Type 1151. Finland: Bowman TALES..TUPA 207-219 (+G501D).

K1718.2. Bluff: millstones said to be pearls of hero's mother. Ogre overawed. Type 1146.

K1718.2.1* Millstone thought to be spinning wheel. G. steals and is drowned. Finland: Bowman TALES 207-219 (+G501D, haystack taken for reed from mother's loom, boat for mother's shoe).

K1722. Monkey (trickster) pretends that his house always answers him. SEE: K607.1 (the cave calls).

K1725.1.1. Man leaves jug set so wind hums over mouth. Fox thinks is dog growling. Discovers jug and drowns it. It gurgles "help" as drowns. Russia (Ukraine): Bloch UKRAINIAN 64-67. Russia: Riordan TALES..CENTRAL 194 (fox drowned also).

K1725.2. Tiger thinks sound of water dropping is sound of dreadful monster. SEE: N392.1.1.

K1728. The bear trainer and his bear. Ogre is driven out by hero's bear. The next year the ogre asks "Is the big cat still living?" Hero says that it now has many kittens. Ogre is overawed. Type 1161. Estonia: Maas MOON 82-84.

K1728.1* Trolls come every Christmas Eve, guest's bear routs. Scandinavia: Asbjornsen EAST 125-127; Dasent CAT pb; Mayne GHOSTS 87-97; Sperry HEN 25-34 /Sperry SCANDIN-AVIAN 29-37/.

K1736. Troll bluffed away from christening. He is invited but told that guests will include the Virgin Mary, Thor the Thunderer, etc. He stays away but sends the finest present. Type 1165. Palmer FAIRY 85-91 (loud band coming).

K1741. Bluff: hero professes to be able to perform much larger task than that assigned.

K1741.1. Felling the whole forest. Told to bring in a tree, the hero asks, "Why not the whole forest?" The ogre is frightened. Type 1049. SEE: G501 (Stupid Ogre); K1951.1 (Seven at a Blow).

K1741.2. A thousand at one shot. Told to shoot one or two wild boars, hero asks, "Why not a thousand at one shot?" The ogre is frightened. Type 1053. Germany: Wiggin TALES 155-156.

K1741.2.1. Bluff: told to bring home an ox, hero prepares to bring home ten. Gypsy: Jagendorf GYPSIES' 24-34 (G501, ties all tails together, snake brings). Germany: Wiggin TALES 155-156. Danaher FOLKTALES 63-76 (+K1951.1D).

K1741.3. Bringing the whole well. Told to get water, hero demands bucket large enough to bring in the whole well. The ogre is frightened. Type 1049. SEE: G501 (Stupid Ogre); K1951.1 (Seven at a Blow).

K1741.3.2* Sent for water prepares to dip up brook. Rumania: Lang VIOLET 96-110 (dragon +G501). Ireland: MacManus WELL 49-64 (+K1951.1C).

K1744. Hero threatens to pull lake together with a rope. The ogre is intimidated. SEE: G501 (Stupid Ogre).

K1746. Trickster threatens to throw weight into a cloud: ogre intimidated. SEE ALSO: G501D; K18.2.

K1746.0.1* Club into moon, dragon. Rumania: Lang VIOLET 96-110.

K1746.0.2* Devil stops man from throwing hammer into heaven. U.S.: Chase WICKED 88-99.

K1755. Ogre terrified by woman's legs..thinks are vise. Germany (Grimm): Grimm BROTHERS 77-81; Lang GREEN 311-315 (bear).

K1760. Other bluffs.

K1761. Bluff: provisions for the swimming match. In a swimming match from a ship the hero takes a knapsack of provisions on his back. His rival is afraid and gives up. Type 1612. SEE ALSO: K46.1. Haiti: Courlander PIECE 105-110 (dressed in white suit and hat with bundle to drop off at Haiti en route from Martinique to Cuba).

K1765. Bluff in court: the stone in the purse. A poor man has a stone in his purse to throw at the judge if he is sentenced. The judge thinks he has money to use as a bribe and acquits him. Type 1660. Russia: Daniels FALCON 67-70.

K1767. Goat singing a threatening song bought off with food and jewels. +H1312.2. Armenia: Bulatkin EURASIAN 90-94. Iran: Mehdevi PERSIAN 33-43.

K1771. Bluffing threat.

K1771.2. Sham threat: either..or. "Either you give me the road or I (will give it to you, or the like)."

K1771.2.1* Bag stolen. "Either return my bag or else!" Bag returned. "Or else what?" "Or else I'd have had to make a new bag." Turkey: Downing HODJA 95; Walker WATERMELONS 49-50.

K1771.2.2* Beggar to woman: "A penny for the poor or else!" Husband appears. "Or else what?" "Or else I'll go away." Italy: Cimino DISOBEDIENT #9.

K1775. Bluff: Insult repeated as harmless remark. The trickster makes an insulting remark, but when called on to repeat what he said he changes it so as to turn aside wrath. Russia: Daniels FALCON 84-89 (fox).

K1775.1* Turtle makes flute of jackal's thighbone, sings of this. Jackal's brother asks what he sings. Says "the bone of a cow makes me a flute." Liberia: Haskett GRAINS 64-67.

K1781.1* Jack at Hell's Gate. Father says would rather be a firestoker in hell than stay here (after twelve sons are born on the same day from an inadvertent wish). Devil takes youngest son, Jack, seeks, threatens to build church over hell's gate. Challenges Devil to race "little brother" hare (K11.6). Sewing contests--gives Jack short piece of thread (K47.1) but Devil has to hop out window and back on every stitch for thread too long. Jack threatens to throw club to brother on earth--club throwing contest, K18). Hungary: Manning-Sanders DEVIL'S 39-50.

K1785.1* Miracle must wait until all agree on when want rain. Priest need not perform miracle. France: Hardendorff TRICKY 93-96.

K1788. Fox threatens to catch bird who feeds him her young as appeasement. He threatens to push down tree or to fly. Type 56A. Russia: Wiggin TALES 39-40 (goose advises dove that fox can't climb, fox asks goose what does when wind blows--puts head under wing and is eaten). Finland: Bowman TALES..TUPA 255-256 (Hawk warns crow, fox feigns dead, eats hawk).

K1797. Uncle Bouki rents a horse, then discovers he doesn't need it. Recovers down payment by making owner think he plans to put entire family on horse's back. Haiti: Courlander RIDE 259-264 /Courlander PIECE 25-28/. U.S.: Credle TALL 64-66.

K1800 - K2899. Deception by disguise or illusion.

K1810. Deception by disguise.

K1811.1. Gods (spirits) disguised as beggars. Test hospitality. SEE: A1958.0.1 (origin owl); A2062.1 (origin locust); K213 (Devil in Knapsack); Q1.1 (hospitality rewarded); Q565 (Smith and Devil).

K1811.6* Where one is fed a hundred can dine. Christ and Twelve Apostles visit peasant hut. Food multiplies as each apostle arrives. Peasant granted wish--to win any game played. Plays Devil for lost man's soul (E756.2), takes to heaven. Reminds St. Peter of dining at his hut. Allowed to take lost soul in. Spain: Sawyer WAY 251-255.

K1812.1. Incognito king helped by humble man. Gives reward. Russia: Lowrie SOLDIER pb.

K1812.1.0.1* Incognito king rescued from robbers by man who enchants them by toasting them. Type 952. Germany (Grimm): Grimm BROTHERS 166-169.

K1814.5* Woman in disguise wooed by her husband. Ignored wife of Caliph camps near him in desert and has affair, bears three sons, receives three tokens. Reveals self. Sons accepted as heirs. Iraq: Carpenter ELEPHANT'S 195-203.

K1815.0.2* Girl's dying mother fastens pot over her head. It cannot be removed. Her master's son wishes to marry her. In a dream her mother gives permission. At wedding the bowl falls from head scattering jewels. Japan: Buck FAIRY 47-50 (man sees her face reflected in stream and vows to wed, T11.5); Hearn JAPANESE 60-68.

K1816.0.2. Girl in menial disguise at lover's court. Type 511, 879. SEE ALSO: B133.3; H151.5; R221.

K1816.0.2.1* Maid Maleen. Type 870. Maid Maleen confined in tower for refusal to wed any other than her love. Digs way out after seven years. Serves as maid in kitchen of lover's castle. Asked to take ugly bride's place. Speaks to nettle, footbridge, church door. Given necklace token. Wife cannot produce token or recall conversations with objects. Maid Maleen is sent for. Recognized. Wed. Germany (Grimm): Grimm GRIMM'S (Follett) 235-245; Lurie CLEVER 57-65.

K1816.0.2.2* Boy to wed girl whose cornmeal sticks to abalone shell. Ugly, dirty girl. Weds. Is beautiful at night. Native American (Hopi): Curtis GIRL 73-80.

K1816.6. Disguise as herdsman (shepherd, swineherd, etc.). Andersen: Holme TALES 99-103; Lang FIFTY 316-321; Opie CLASSIC 230-235.

K1818.2. Scald-head disguise. To avoid having

his gold hair seen, the hero covers his head with a cloth and says that he has the scaldhead. Types 314, 502. SEE: H331.1.2.2 (baldhead); H1331.1.3B (bald head). SEE ALSO: B316.

K1836.5. Disguise of man in woman's dress. Lato, the Stupid One: given old buffalo instead of wife, father thief steals even that. Disguised as a woman, Lato woos father, learns location of gold, ties him down while rubbing back. Takes back buffalo and takes gold. Tempts pursuers into stream where they are drowned. He is a Pisces and swims well. Nepal: Hitchcock KING 101-110.

K1837.6.1* Mulan disguises as soldier and takes father's place in enlistment. Honored as captain. China: Manton FLYING 102-108.

K1837.9* Woman feigns death (K1862) and accompanies lover disguised as man. Recognized and killed. Lover abducts Blackfoot girl and gives to wronged husband. Native American (Cree): Curtis GIRL 61-69.

K1839.12. Disguised as child (in cradle). SEE ALSO: K521.4.1.5 (Cucullin).

K1839.12.1* Kalulu and his money farm. Hare takes money from chief on pretence of planting crop. Warthog, lion sent to collect. Kalulu goes home for forgotten pillow or hoe each time, blows horn to make them think hunter is near and they flee. Tortoise brings along pillow, hoe, refuses to let hare leave sight. H. flees, has wife disguise as baby. Baby is taken as hostage, feigns dead. Hare's wife is given bag of money as recompense for lost child. Mashona: Burton MAGIC 84-89; Kaula AFRICAN 35-42.

K1840. Deception by substitution.

K1853.2.1. Hero substitutes for princess as gift to monster. Kills him.

K1853.2.1.1* Boy sleeping in deserted temple hears goblin cats chanting "Tell it not to Schippetaro." He discovers that Schippetaro is a dog. He and Schippetaro are left at temple in place of maiden to be offered to temple spirit. He and dog rout (B524.1.1) giant golden cat and cohorts. Japan: Carpenter WONDER.. DOGS 128-135; Harper GHOSTS 205-209; Wiggin FAIRY 371-374 /Sheehan FOLK 112-117/.

K1853.2.1.2* Girl offers self instead of maiden as sacrifice to white Sea-Serpent. She kills sea-serpent, finds statue of Mikado in cave, and swims back with both. Statue has been thrown into sea by Mikado's enemy, hence his illness. She is rewarded and her banished father restored. Japan: Arnott ANIMAL 184-189.

K1853.3* Substitute sacrifice. Pigeon will restore eyesight if saved from hawk, hawk will restore virility if given pigeon. Man gets a second pigeon and regains both. U.S. (Black): Lester BLACK 139-146.

K1860. Deception by feigned death (sleep). SEE ALSO: K366.1.3.1 (animal shams death and is sold); K371.1 (trickster throws fish off wagon); K751 (capture by feigning death); K2061.9 (cat hangs on wall feigning dead). SUBJECT INDEX: DEATH, feigned.

K1861.1. Hero sewed up in animal hide so as to be carried to height of bird. Type 936. (cf. B31.1 Roc).

A* The Golden Mountain. Lad takes service. Taken to isle and sewed in skin of animal to be carried up onto mountain by birds. There to throw down treasure. Man's daughter has given him flint and steel to strike if in trouble. Abandoned on mountain top. Strike and two servants appear to take down from mountain. Rehires self to man, drugs and sews him into skin. Abandons on mountain top. Weds daughter. Russia: Downing RUSSIAN 129-134; Wyndham TALES 16-32.

Ba* The Dove Maiden. Lad takes service. Carried to mountain top in skins, abandoned. Finds stairs, home of blind ogre. Enters forbidden fortieth room and finds dove maiden. Steals her feathers as she bathes. Weds. Takes home and mother reveals where feathers are hidden. To seek with shoes of iron and staff. Takes service again and is carried to Ogre mountain. Doesn't throw down jewels. Ogre sends to seek lost wife (H1385.3). Throws staff to two fighting over magic sword, carpet and hat of invisibility--they fight over staff and he takes objects. Flies to Dove Maiden's castle, kills her giant father. They return with eyes for Ogre of Jewel Mountain, formerly stolen by her father. Greece: Wilson GREEK 76-97.

Bb* Peppito. Dragon on the mountain possesses treasure. Dragon gives invisible hat and magic sword to seek lost wife. Her father sets task which she performs for him. Dragoness is brought back as wife for dragon. Greece: Manning-Sanders DRAGONS 62-75.

C* Castle in the Sea. Service. To enter castle and fill sacks with treasure. Raised into doorless castle by magic. Abandonment. Follows rat and finds door and old cook. Told of princess guarded by two lions, revolving millstone and serpent. Follows rat and finds. Throws jacket to lions, shirt to clog millstones, shoe to serpent. Princess gives him handkerchief. He finds self on shores of Spain. Seeks her. Finds her about to wed. Produces handkerchief. Wed. Spain: Eels TALES..SPAIN 57-68.

D* Castle in the Sea. Takes service. To throw jewels from doorless castle. Abandoned. Kept as servant by magician owning castle. To be freed if kills creature behind three doors. With aid of three hundred year old fellow slave he succeeds. They find selves back on plain. Three hundred year old man is now youth. Their pockets full of jewels, they are rich. Spain: Gunterman CASTLES 84-105.

K1862. Death feigned to meet lover. Scotland: Nic Leodhas HEATHER 61-67 (carried to chapel where lover waits). SEE ALSO: K1837.9.

K1867. Trickster shams death to get food. SEE ALSO: K751 (capture by sham death). Liberia (Mano): Dorliae ANIMALS 40-45 (spider cheats boy of eggs, boy feigns death and spider returns eggs fearing death).

K1869.1* Feigned death in embarrassment. Hemp smoker sends sons to take daughters to hemp grower as wives. Late in life hemp smoker visits hemp grower. Hemp grower has arranged marriages badly for girls and feigns death in embarrassment. Hemp smoker, also embarrassed, feigns death as well. The two are put in common grave, sit up at last minute. Fathers to arrange own daughters' weddings in future. S. Rhodesia and Mozambique (Mashona): Courlander KING'S 101-105.

K1869.2* Feigned death to elope with master's wife. Lad warns cruel master will haunt if dies of homesickness. Found dead. Irish friends carry off before doctor arrives. Haunts master. Master gives ghost full pay and leaves country. Master's young wife and "dead" lad later seen in Ireland. Scotland: Nic Leodhas GHOSTS 113-124.

K1870. Illusions.

K1875. Deception by sham blood. By stabbing bag of blood (or otherwise) trickster makes dupe think he is bleeding. Types 2, 1535, 1539. SEE ALSO: K473; K842C.

K1875.1. Trickster makes dupe think he has killed wife by hitting bag of blood. SEE: K113, K842C.

K1875.2. Pretended soothsayer causes blood to pour from rye stack, bag of pig's blood pierced. Meanwhile accomplice steals horse. Latvia: Durham TIT 75-80.

K1886.3.1.1* Mock sunrise: person causes cock to crow (simulates cock crow). Demon thus loses bargain to fulfill tasks by cock crow. (cf. M211.2). SEE ALSO: G303.16.19.4.1; M211.8.1.

K1886.3.1.1.0.1* Stone stairway, ogre puts bag over cock's head but good fairy removes it. Japan: Sakade JAPANESE 97-100.

K1886.3.1.1.0.2* Laminak builds castle, hero lights torch in hen coop causing cock to crow, thus saves soul. France (Pays Basque): Spicer THIRTEEN MONSTERS 41-51.

K1886.3.1.1.0.3* Barn built by Joost, farmer's wife crows in her coop waking cock and saving husband's soul, owl's boards (Bleb vorden) left unfinished. +G303.14.1. Dutch (Friesland): Spicer OWL'S 15-28.

K1886.3.1.1.0.4* St. Thedule, Bishop of Sion carried home by devil. France: Serraillier

BISHOP pb.

K1886.3.1.1.0.5* Bishop Joder asks devil to carry him to Pope and back before cockcrow. Sets cock on steeple so it crows early. Switzerland: Müller-Guggenbühl SWISS 213-223.

K1887.4* Illusory sound. Fox rubs tail on door sounding "Zui", knocks head on door "ten." Zuiten thinks he hears his name called. After repeatedly finding no one there, Zuiten hides and opens door on "ten." Fox tumbles into room. +K607.4. Japan: Scofield FOX 33-39.

K1889.7* Rejected suitor revenges self by tying rope to house pole and shaking, simulating earthquake. Philippines (Visayan): Sechrist ONCE 91-93.

K1890. Other deceptions by disguise or illusion.

K1892.3* Mantis hides in bag to enter lion's house. Winks at baby lion who sees eye peeping out. Flies to sky when discovered. Bushman: Helfman BUSHMEN 86-90.

K1911. The false bride (substituted bride).

A* The Black and White Bride. Type 403. Often found in combination with other types. SEE: D721.5B; P253.2.0.1; Q2.1.1B; Q2.1.5B (kind and unkind girls); R221Bd (Cinderella); R221H.

Aa* Soonimaya. Stepmother sends Soonimaya to bring fodder, gives no knife. Snakes cut limbs for her and make selves into rope to pull home for her. Sent to fetch water in sieve, ants sit in holes. To bring tiger's milk, tiger kittens give it. To bring champa flower from crag, vulture carries her there. Falls on seeing father coming. Golden pillar appears on grave, is taken to king, turns back to girl and weds. Sister pushes Soonimaya into pool and takes place. Two water snakes spare Soonimaya for three days to nurse son. Third night prince sees and rescues. False bride is carried off by snake next morning. Nepal: Hitchcock KING 11-22.

Ab* Witch in stone boat. Witch comes up in stone boat and changes places with queen on deck. Overheard saying "When I yawn I'm a troll." Floor opens and troll brother brings her food. Mother queen comes from floor thrice to nurse babe. Nurse calls king who cuts chain and rescues. Iceland: Lang YELLOW 276-282 /Hoke WITCHES 197-207.

Ac* Bola Bola. Witch gives coriander to put in sister's soup. They turn to cows. Youngest weds king, bears son. Witch sticks pins in temple and turns her to dove. Takes place. Dove asks Bola Bola, talking dog, daily about son. King pulls out pins and restores (D765.1.2). Portugal: Lowe LITTLE 41-43.

K1911.1. The false bride takes true bride's place on way to the wedding. SEE: B133.3 (Goose

Girl).

A* Girl sent away to live with elder sister for killing brother's pet leopard accidentally. Servant Dog Tail, changes clothing while bathing. Little Hen Eagle chases birds from garden with magic song, calls forth parents and possessions from earth with magic iron rod and returns them. This is seen and reported. Usurper is ousted. Zulu: Aardema BEHIND 3-10.

K1911.1.4. False bride finishes true bride's task and supplants her. The true bride must perform a certain task to win her husband, and being exhausted, commits the task to a slave. Type 437. SEE ALSO: D754.1.

A* The Stone of Patience. Bird warns girl of her fate. She is magically transported to palace where prince lies as if dead. To watch by side for forty days. Fourth day she leaves slave girl alone with prince for a few moments. He wakes and weds slave girl. She becomes slave. He is to buy gift from trip. She asks Stone of Patience. His ship will not move until he fetches it. He spies and sees her telling tale to stone. Stone bursts. Weds. Turkey: Buck FAIRY 225-231; Ekrem TURKISH 103-111.

B* Pitcher of tears: girl fills pitcher within two inches of top, sleeps, servant fills rest of way and weds prince. Sells false wife gold hen and chicks, little mannikin and gold doll from nuts given her by fairy. False wife asks to hear stories told and ten tellers are chosen. Zora is last, tells tale--restored. Italy: Mincielli OLD 3-13.

K1911.3.3.1. False bride's mutilated feet. In order to wear the shoes with which the husband is testing the identity of his bride, the false bride cuts her feet. She is detected. SEE: R221B+.

K1916. Robber Bridegroom. Robber marries girl under picture of being a fine gentleman. Type 955. SEE: S62.1C.

K1917.3. Penniless wooer: helpful animal reports master wealthy and thus wins girl for him. Type 545. SEE ALSO: K1952.0.3 (sham prince); N222.3. (cf. B582.1.1).

A* Puss in Boots. Cat as inheritance (N411.1.1) takes game to king from 'Count.' Tells king arriving count has lost clothing in accident. Threatens field hands who say fields belong to 'count.' Tricks ogre into turning into mouse (K722). Takes ogre's castle. France: Arbuthnot ANTHOLOGY 213-215; Arbuthnot FAIRY 104-107 /Lang BLUE 154-160/; De La Mare ANIMAL 52-57; Haviland FAVORITE..FRENCH 26-37; Haviland FAIRY 122-126; Holme TALES 21-28; Martignoni ILLUSTRATED 285-288; Perrault FAMOUS 23-40; Perrault PERRAULT'S (Dodd) 16-25; Perrault PERRAULT'S (Dover) 45-58; Perrault PUSS pb (illus. Fischer, Harcourt); Perrault PUSS pb (illus. Brown, Scribner's); Perrault PUSS pb

(illus. Wilkinson); Opie CLASSIC 110-116; Rackham ARTHUR 233-239; Sekorova EUROPEAN 20-24; Tarrant FAIRY 51-67; Williams-Ellis ROUND 172-180.

B* Earl of Cattenborg. K1917.3A + cat borrows measure and leaves coin in it. Cat warns not to sleep on lowly bed in test. Jacobs EUROPEAN 90-97.

C* Cattenborg. Girl given cat. K1917.3A + girl heroine. Told to say all was different at home. Princess tests--cat teaches manners, warns to claim couldn't sleep when straw under sheet (H41.1.1). Cat tells long story to detain troll castle owner until sun rises. Troll sees sun and bursts (G304.2.5). Take castle. Sweden: Kaplan FAIRY 1-16.

D* Lord Per. K1917.3A + . Exceptions: cat provides rich clothing for Per (no drowning incident). Cat detains troll with long story until sun rises. Troll explodes. Lad takes castle (G304.2.5). Norway: Asbjornsen NORWEGIAN 122-127; Asbjornsen EAST (Row) 57-63; Aulaire EAST 70-78; Manning-Sanders BOOK.. MAGIC 29-37; Sperry HEN 9-24 /Sperry SCANDINAVIAN 48-59/.

E* Thieving fox offers to make rich if released. Gold piece in measure. Jewels. Clothes lost. Says has better things at home. Tells shah that king is attacking. He flees. Lad takes castle. Fox is often thrown on dung heap when dies. The lad repents. Armenia: Tashjian ONCE 13-26. China: Chang TALES 56-67 (king of underworld hidden in fireplace and burnt; D833). Russia (Georgia): Papashvily YES 149-157 (hides nine devi in haystack and burns; D833). Russia: Wyndham RUSSIAN 44-59 (he brings 40 x 40 grey wolves, bears, ermines by telling them there is a feast at palace); Masey STORIES 28-37 (hides dragon in haystack and burns). Philippines (Visayan): Sechrist ONCE 110-119 (witch's house taken, ape helper caught by tar-baby, K741). Sicily: Lang CRIMSON 138-146 (ogre hides in oven, burnt, D833). Slovenia: Kavcic GOLDEN 38-45 (rooster helper, tells halibut and swine is going to golden stream and fifty of each follow to king; robber's castle taken). Finland: Fillmore SHEPHERD'S 11-25 (Mighty Mikko; worm hides and is burnt, D833) /Fenner PRINCESSES 43-56/, /Davis BAKER'S 169-188/.

F* Kind Mouse. Poor man shares with mouse. She measures gold, no clothing ruse, weds king's daughter. Mouse gives castle. Forgotten, mouse is tossed on trash heap. Repenting, mouse is sought out. She ascends to heaven and becomes family's guardian angel (V238). Chile: Jagendorf KING 72-78.

G* The Monkey and Mr. Janel Sinna. Prince gives one thousand gold coins for monkey, banished. Monkey borrows king's measure, asks for clothes saying master's were burnt. Weds king's daughter for large dowry. Says cities are master's as they pass. Magic woman creates palace for them. S.E. Asia: Tooze THREE.. MONKEY #3.

H* The Poor Weaver and the Princess. Jackal eats expensive betel and princess agrees to wed wealthy master. Jackal brings one thousand crows, one thousand jackals, and one thousand cranes and king, hearing chattering, asks master to come alone. Bride smears flour paste on husband and it turns to gold when falls off. Pakistan: Siddiqui TOONTOONY 82-90.

I* Hamdani. Beggar buys gazelle. Gazelle gives diamond. Tells Sultan master was robbed of clothes. Weds daughter. Gazelle kills seven headed serpent and gets house. Hamdani forgets gazelle and he dies. Wife dreams is back in court, Hamdani dreams is poor--both dreams are true. Tanzania: Green FOLK..AFRICA 37-51.

J* The Devil and the Pit. Cat drives devil out of baron's home, tells Devil a monster is coming and D. hides in snuffbox. Cat's master offered wealth but refuses. Latvia: Durham TIT 63-66.

K1930. Treacherous imposters.

K1931.2. Imposters abandon hero in lower world. (cf. F80). Usually let rope drop on which he is to be raised. Type 301. SEE ALSO: F451.5.1.5.0.1; H1331.1.3; H1385.1; W154.8.4.

A* Old Fire Dragaman. Tom, Will, Jack take turns cooking. Dwarf asks each for food. First two brothers refuse and are beaten. Youngest feeds, follows down hole to underworld (F92). Brothers let youngest down in basket. He finds girl and sends up. Second house--second girl. Third house--prettiest girl-gives Jack wishing ring. Brothers leave Jack down home. He wishes self home and ring brings him. Wed. U.S. (Appalachia): Chase JACK 106-113 /Haviland NORTH 160-166/; Cothran WITH 26-33 (Old Bluebeard). Williams-Ellis FAIRY..BRITISH 209-215 (Old Bluebeard).

B* Little Red Hairy Man. Elder brothers refuse to feed dwarf. Youngest, Jack, feeds--is let down in mine by dwarf, given armour to fight giant in copper castle and save princess. To follow copper ball (D1313). Silver castle repeat. Golden castle. He weds third princess and gains treasure. His two brothers try their luck, jump in basket and rope breaks. England (Derbyshire): Colwell ROUND 90-94.

C* The Earth Gnome. Anyone picking apple from king's tree will sink one hundred fathoms into ground. Youngest daughter picks and all three taste, sink. Three brothers seek. Castle with food on table. Gnome asks for bread, beats lad keeping house that day. Second--same. Youngest beats gnome, learns that princesses are in well. Youngest lowered. Beheads three headed, seven headed, nine headed dragons while princesses comb their hair. Abandoned by brothers after sending princesses up in basket. Plays magic flute, the birds and gnome

appear and carry him to earth. Princesses have had to vow not to tell tale that he was rescuer. King has them tell secret to a stone (H13.2.7). Germany (Grimm): Gag MORE 171-187.

D* Three Walnuts. Three princes to discover thief of apples (H1471). Youngest follows ogre to well. Brothers let down rope. Three princesses rescued, youngest gives three walnuts containing dresses and advises that white sheep will carry to upper world, black to lower world. Brothers abandon. He misses the white sheep but catches onto a black and is carried to lower world. Kills serpent there rescuing eagle's eggs. Mother eagle carries him to upper world. As tailor's apprentice sends token dresses 1. with stars and sky, 2. flowers of earth, 3. fishes and sea. Wed. Greece: Wilson GREEK 157-165.

E* Emerald Crested Phoenix. Seven headed monster steals three apples each year. Three princes await. Youngest succeeds in shooting (reads Koran and invokes Allah's aid). Follow wounded monster to well. Eldest two cry out from 'burning' and 'freezing' in well and are pulled up. Youngest succeeds. Kills monster and sends up three princesses. Third gives three hairs from her head. Abandoned. Rubs hair together and white and black sheep appear (SEE: K1931.2D). Emerald crested phoenix carries to upper world, must be fed when turns head. As jeweler's apprentice he provides marvelous items princess requests with aid of genie induced by rubbing three hairs together. Weds. Turkey: Ekrem TURKISH 32-45.

F* Three Men of Power--Evening, Midnight and Sunrise. Three princesses carried off by whirlwind when allowed out of protective chambers. Three princes seek. Dwarf with long beard beats each of six brothers as they take turns at cooking. Sunrise beats dwarf, follows trail to pit. Let down. Copper palace--given flask of strength. Kills three headed serpent. Silver palace--six, gold--twelve. Princesses put palaces into golden, silver and copper eggs. All are drawn up, wed and live in palaces. Russia: Ransome OLD 269-293; Riordan TALES ..CENTRAL 227-232.

G* Peppino. Princess carried off by black cloud at age seven. Well on seashore appears ten years later. Peppino let down on rope, given magic coin producing ring by princess and asked to return at exactly midnight in one month. He is late, all are dead when he arrives. Old lady advises to kill ogre. Horse warns not to get down for ogre's dropped glove, beheads ogre when ogre dismounts. Obtains keys and feather from dead ogre, finds ointment to revive dead in locked cupboard and applies with feather. Revives princess and her twelve maids. She sends him up first. Sentry had planned to abandon him. Italy: Manning-Sanders GIANNI 179-182.

H* Three Princesses in the Blue Mountain.

Three daughters not to be let under open sky until fifteen or snowflake will carry off. Are carried off. Captain, lieutenant, and soldier seek. Soldier throws down meat to bear and lion on bridge. Turns taken cooking, old bearded man with crutch beats second. Soldier catches beard in cleft of log and forces to tell location of princesses. Let down through fire and water (two turn back). Copper castle, troll with seven heads, drink for hour and can swing sword. Troll smells Christian blood, princess claims raven dropped bone down chimney, scratches head of troll to put to sleep. Silver castle, six headed troll. Golden nine-headed. Youngest princess ties gold ring in lad's hair. He is abandoned. Finds gold key, silver whistle in box. Blows and birds appear, mother eagle carries to upper world, puts meat in mouth when turns head. Eldest princess demands gold checkers like those in Blue Mountain before will wed. As goldsmith's apprentice soldier sends eagle for them. Reveals tokens and weds. Norway: Asbjornsen EAST (Macmillan) 76-79; Asbjornsen NORWEGIAN 31-48; Asbjornsen EAST (Doubleday) 85-108; Aulaire EAST 153-174.

I* Shepherd Paul. Strong foundling meets tree climber (F601), iron kneader, stone crusher, each says desire of life is to wrestle Shepherd Paul. He throws each. They take turns cooking. Dwarf throws each. Paul ties dwarf to tree, follows to hole, is let down, kills six-twelve-, and eighteen-headed dragons. Princesses give shirt of strength and drink from flask. Three castles are turned to golden apples and taken along. Paul abandoned. Saves griffin young from rain of fire. Father griffin carries to earth, feeds when turns head. Weds youngest princess. Hungary: Lang CRIMSON 178-186 /Lang FIFTY 253-260/. Switzerland (French): Duvoisin THREE 67-88 (Jean the Bear takes on two strong companions; two lions guard a sleeping princess. Kills seven headed dragon; lions befriend in abandonment, forces old witch to show way out, lions eat two usurping companions).

J* Bensurdatu. Three princesses carried off by cloud. Two knights and Bensurdatu seek, Bensurdatu kills two giants, seven-headed serpent. Abandoned Bensurdatu finds magic wishing purse and wishes self back in world. Weds. Sicily: Haviland ITALY 20-41; Lang ROSE 44-45 /Lang GREY/.

K* The Three Princesses of Connaught. One-eyed giant has three princesses captive. Three brothers lower selves by rope. Youngest succeeds. Wee Red Man aids. To feed brass filings to three chestnut mares. Princesses to ride mares, he to ride hazel rod. Sound ram's horn thrice and flee. Wee Red Man throws ball of yarn at Giant and turns to stone. Princesses hauled up and youngest abandoned. Finds wishing cup and wishes self home. As smith he produces crowns identical to those of princesses. Weds. Ireland: Fenner PRINCESSES 11-28 /MacManus DONEGAL/.

L* Sylvester. Dragon carries off empress. Son seeks, let down by brothers. Rescues three princesses and mother, brothers pull them up, abandon him. Rubs ring found and little man appears and carries home. Fixes magic water to change face and restore, gives marvelous clothes. With changed visage he goes to court as wondrous tailor. Is allowed to wed youngest princess if will be court tailor. Suggests that he and two brothers toss swords into air, sword will fall on heads if unfair. Two brothers are killed. Hungary: Manning-Sanders RED 42-48.

M* The Three Musicians. Three musicians enter haunted castle one at a time. Unseen hands feed. Dwarf beats. Third beats dwarf and tears out beard. Dwarf's strength is in beard. He leads to underground castle and allows to free princess in return for beard. Germany (Grimm): Lang GREEN 342-349.

N* The Three Princesses. Eagle carries off three princesses. Hero let down to Land-Below-the-Earth in basket. Drinks mandrake juice daily until can lift iron pestle. Slays ogre, princess throws ashes on neck stump to keep head from rejoining. Returns in basket and weds youngest princess. Korea: Kim STORY 154-165.

P* Three sons each try to move stone at dragon's behest, youngest succeeds. Goes down hole to encounter princesses in copper, silver, and gold kingdoms. Brothers pull up princesses and abandon lad. Dwarf sends to giant who sends to Baba Yaga. Her eagle carries home, fed en route, eats bite of leg but replaces. Russia: Riordan TALES..CENTRAL 264-268.

V* Varieties without princess rescued motif.

Va* Two Brothers. Younger brother turns over row of clay pots discovered and old lady comes out of last pot. Tells to fell tree, at each stroke livestock emerges. Returning home with this herd, his brother lets him down rope into valley to drink and abandons. Honey bird leads villagers to him later. S. Africa (Zulu): Arnott AFRICAN 195-199.

Vb* The Snake King. Temba abandoned in pit where he and other boys were filling calabashes with honey. Follows scorpion and finds turned to snake kingdom (F92.7). Snake king shows Temba river between kingdoms and he reaches home. Later chief falls ill and Temba is forced to show way to Snake kingdom for heart of Snake King. Snake King has Temba throw him into river and he revives. E. Africa: Arnott TEMBA 94-106.

Z* Three Companions take turns housekeeping (cooking, guarding). Ogre terrorizes each and eats cache. Third subdues ogre.

Za* Kantchil, tortoise, ape, shepherd, giant Gergassi is subdued by Kantchil. Borneo: De Leeuw INDONESIAN 74-77.

Zb* Kassa Kena Genanina kills terrorizing giant bird. +F615.9. Mende: Courlander COW-TAIL 41-45.

K1931.2.1* Imposters abandon hero in upper world. Refuse to lower cord. Type 301.

A* Juanillo. Three princesses in magic castle, elder two brothers fail to reach, youngest scales walls. Princesses instruct to take hair from tail of each of three fire-breathing stallions. Spell thus broken. Princesses lowered from castle by cord, youngest gives necklace token. Brothers leave Juanillo in castle, claim princesses. He leaps to ground holding the three horses, takes service at castle as simpleton. Wed. Still as simpleton. King sets son-in-law tasks. He performs with aid of three magic horses but requires tokens of two brothers to let them claim feats. Shows tokens including brands of brothers, claims real place of honor. Spain: Gunterman CASTLES 106-131.

K1951.1. Sham warrior. Boastful fly-killer. "Seven at a blow." A tailor who has killed seven flies writes on a placard "Seven at a Blow." He is received as a great warrior. Type 1640. SEE ALSO: N392.1.1 (Valiant Chattee Maker).

A* The Gallant Tailor. Kills, makes belt reading "Seven at a blow." Squeezes stone (cheese, K62), throws stone (bird) to intimidate ogre (K18.3). Helps carry (rides) tree (K71). Tailors billet on bed beaten (K525.1) while hero hides, claims fleas bit. To fight giant. Throws stone, giants attack each other (K1082). Tricks unicorn into running horn into tree (K771). Wild boar trapped in chapel when chasing him. Weds princess. She suspects he's tailor as he talks in sleep. Being forewarned he adds in 'sleep' that he'll soon kill soldiers outside door--is feared (K1951.3). Denmark: Hatch THIRTEEN 122-138 (stupid ogre incidents, wedding to princess). Germany (Grimm): Adams BOOK..GIANTS 19-34; Carle ERIC 61-74; Fenner ADVENTURE 26-38; Grimm GRIMM'S (Follett) 89-101; Grimm GRIMM'S (Grosset) 189-200; Grimm GRIMM'S (Watts) 44-53; Grimm GRIMM'S (World) 348-357; Grimm HOUSE 15-35; Grimm HOUSEHOLD 109-117; Jacobs EUROPEAN 81-89; Lang BLUE 330-339 /Lang FIFTY 21-29/, /Wiggin TALES 138-145/; Manning-Sanders BOOK..GIANTS 90-97 (stupid ogre episodes); Martignoni ILLUSTRATED 213-218; Werth VALIANT pb. U.S. (Appalachia): Chase JACK 58-66 (stupid ogre wedding to princess; Jack falls on lion's back, rides into town; cf. J1758.5; N691.1.2).

B* Johnny Gloke. Kills fifty flies. Sets out to slay giants. Throws stone, two giants fight each other. Leads army. Horse runs away. He gets old gallows stuck on horse's neck. Enemies think he comes to hang them--flee (K1591.2). England: Jacobs MORE 78-81; Reeves ENGLISH 24-34.

C* Jack the Ashypet. Kills thirty-three flies. Throws stone, causes giants to fight. Threatens to throw sledge hammer to Donegal (K18.1). To bring river home (K1741.3). Billet in bed (K525.1).

Given all gold giant can carry to go home. Ireland: MacManus WELL 49-64 /Fenner GIANT 18-31/.

D* Tailor of Rathkele. Kills seventy flies, inscribes on sword. Throws stone. Giants fight. Threatens to take whole herd of cattle home (K1741.2.1). To bring whole forest (K1741.1). To throw anvil home to his mother (K18.1). Rips stomach (bag under shirt). Giant imitates, killing self (K81.1). Danaher FOLKTALES 63-76.

E* Ivan the Fool. Kills forty flies. Goes adventuring with sign inviting two famous warriors to join him. They do so and together win king's daughter as wife for Ivan. By luck, Ivan beheads giant in battle. Russia: Daniels FOMA pb (+horse runs off dragging trees, K1951.2); Higonnet-Schnopper TALES 58-75; Whitney IN 59-63.

F* Ergosa Battyr. Mouse advises Ergosa Battyr to have hatchet made inscribed "with this hatchet Ergosa Battyr slew 370 foes." Men approach sleeping Ergosa and flee in terror after reading inscription, leaving herds behind. Dying mouse advises Ergosa to always be generous to musicians so that his fame will be sung everywhere. Russia (Steppes): Masey STORIES 109-112.

G* Yellow Dragon. Old man kills one hundred flies. Dragon reads inscription on table and fears. Man threatens to bring well (K1791.3). Says runs forward and back because breath annoys (really blows back and forth). To bring whole forest (K1741.1). Billet on bed struck (K525.1). Dragon carries gold home for him. Gypsy (Bukovina): Hampden GYPSY 45-50. Hungary: Manning-Sanders RED 10-15.

H* Boy kills forty flies, inscribes sword. Seen while asleep and taken to kill monster, falls on monster's back and rides into palace (N691.1.2). Has self tied to nag, it runs away snaring tree, enemy flees (K1951.2). Turkey: Walker COURAGE pb.

I* Nazan. Kills one thousand flies, makes banner. Giants take him home. Falls on tiger's back and rides into village (N691.1.2). Routs enemy riding runaway horse and snaring tree (K1951.2). Armenia: Tashjian ONCE 71-84.

J* Kara Mustafa. Kills sixty flies, carves on knife. Giant takes him home. Threatens to bring well (K1741B), forest (K1741.1). Billet in bed (K525.2). Giant squeezes until eyes pop--looking to see how far to throw you (K18.1). Giant carries gold home for him. To kill bear--falls on back and rides (N691.1.2). Turkey: Price SIXTY pb.

K* Donal O'Ciaran from Connaught. Inscribes sword after killing 70 flies. King of France's men see sword and take into service. In mowing contest he mows inner circle (K42.2). Throws stone (mud clod) into cliff (K18.5). Russian army surrenders at sight of sword. Ireland: MacManus BOLD 120-137.

L* Sigiris Sinno. Kills twenty flies and in-scribes placard. Hired to kill giant. Intimidates by calling for huge amount of food, ordering crowd to "stand back." Digs hole in wall and seemingly bashes it open with one blow. Ceylon: Tooze WONDERFUL 55-58.

M* Old Man Kurai. Kills one hundred mosqui-toes. Challenges giant to bring up core of earth, pulls up egg yolk. Wants whole well (K1741.3). Billet on bed (K525.1). Asks wife if seven giants he left are eaten up yet (K1715.4). Giant flees and fox brings him. "Thanks for bringing giant" (K1715.2). Russia: Masey STORIES 1-11.

K1951.2. Runaway cavalry hero. When the sham hero goes to war his horse runs away with him. To save himself he grasps a cross from the graveyard and moves it from side to side, put-ting enemy to flight. Type 1640. SEE ALSO: K1951.1B, E, H, I. Ethiopia: Courlander FIRE 121-128 (Eghal Shillet, never reaches battle, calls how lucky enemy didn't have to face him).

K1951.2.1. Runaway cavalry hero tears out limbs of dead tree (or uproots saplings). Wife has tied him to horse, so he cannot ride. He routs enemy. SEE: N392.1.1 (Valiant Chatee Maker); N691.1.2. U.S.: Credle TALL 100-114.

K1951.2.1.1* Man saddles bear in dark (N691.1.2) and rides to job interview. Hired as sheriff. Wife ties to horse and he uproots trees as horse runs away. Is given peace pipe by Indians which he carries home in mouth since can't let loose reins. He retires. U.S.: Credle TALL 100-114.

K1951.6* Little bowman has Big Bima, a washer-man, pose as bowman. Small hero performs deeds, accompanying Bima as servant. He had been refused entry to army because of small size. India: Wyatt GOLDEN 85-92.

K1952.0.3* Sham prince (nobleman). Student with pocket full of peas thought to have pocket full of money. Passes all prince tests despite protestations and weds princess. Eats small portions, can't sleep on hard bed (H41.1.1), etc. En route home woman tells to go to copper castle and give seven headed dragon bread she gives him--it is stone and breaks dragon's teeth. They kill and take castle. SEE ALSO: K1917.3 (Puss in Boots). Hungary: McNeill DOUBLE 68-72.

K1954. Sham rich man.

K1954.3* Slave bets a price of freedom that he will be invited to eat at master's table. Asks master what price of gold lump is. Master thinks he's found treasure and invites to dinner. Cuba: Carter GREEDY 125-131.

K1955.1. Sham physician cures people by threat-ening them with death.

K1955.1.0.1* Fat man comes to be cured. Tells

fat man he'll die in forty days. Worry causes man to lose the weight. Russia: Bulatkin EUR-ASIAN 124-125.

K1956. Sham wise man. SEE ALSO: N611; N612; N688.

K1956.2. Sham wise man hides something and is rewarded for finding it. Russia: Sheehan FOLK 51-60. Burma: Brockett BURMESE 96-105. Rumania: Ure RUMANIAN 26-32. India: Jacobs INDIAN 104-109; Wiggin TALES 393-396; Williams-Ellis ROUND 67-72. Korea: Kim STORY 215-229.

K1956.8. Sham wise man burns house where he pretends to keep his marvelous books, and is free from being called again. Burma: Brockett BURMESE 96-105. Rumania: Ure RUMANIAN 26-32.

K1958.1* Sham teacher sets older students to teach younger. He cannot read. Pretends to read letter and says woman's husband is dead. Found out and expelled from town. Lebanon: Skurzynski TWO 29-39.

K1961.1.3. Sham parson, the sawed pulpit. He has sawed pulpit almost through. He predicts a miracle. The pulpit falls down. Type 1825C. Norway: Asbjornsen NORWEGIAN 25-30.

K1961.1.6* Anansi as sham holy man eats crabs as he baptizes them. Jamaica: Sherlock WEST 95-103.

K1970. Sham miracles.

K1971.6.2* Lad hidden in boat pretends to be angel and commands him to wed daughter to lad. Italy: Cimino DISOBEDIENT #6.

K1977. Spaniard tells Indians that donkey speaks Spanish. Interprets its bray as request for gold. Panama: Jagendorf KING 222-225.

K1980. Other impostures.

K1982.1* Ubiquitous beggar. Coyote and old woman. Coyote changes form and goes ahead to beg for more food. Fifth time old woman gives him fleas. He knocks her off cliff and she turns into grease spot. All meat given earl-ier disappears also. In form of man he now goes to hut of lonely woman. He flees with her five wild geese brothers. Tabu--talking while in air. He speaks and sees all fall (K1041). He turns self to arrow and sticks into ice when lands. Turns self to bear with tail in ice. Pulls free but loses tail (A2216.1). Native American (Nez Percé): Martin NINE..COYOTE 23-30.

K1984.1. The lisping sisters. The lisping girls have been warned against speaking but forget and are found out. Denmark: Hatch THIR-TEEN 73-80.

K1987.1* Devil goes to church. Little Devil sits in back and tries to corrupt folks after service but none know him. Devil tells to get up front and shout and holler next time. U.S.: Courlander TERRAPIN'S 95-97.

K1991. Hare (jackal) makes horns of wax and poses as horned animal. Horns melt by fire. SEE ALSO: K335.0.4.2. Tanzania (Bantu): Arnott ANIMAL 31-37 (hyena--dances in sun).

K1991.1* Hare forbidden drink disguises self in leaves and honey and calls self "King of the Leaves." Drinks. Nicaragua: Jagendorf KING 218-221.

K1995. Trickster disguises as leperous (ill) animal and says trickster is putting a hex on enemies to cause this disease to overtake them. Enemies fear trickster. N. Nigeria (Hausa): Arnott AFRICAN 25-31 (spider disguises as gazelle). Hausa: Aardema MORE 32-37 (spider as gazelle). West Indies: Sherlock IGUANA 76-95 (turtle in goatskin). Louisiana: Cothran WITH 34-39 (hare in deerskin).

K1996* Hidden prince sneezes loudly as princess is exorcised and guards think sound is demon exiting and flee. Prince escapes with princess. Sword tester with wax nose tip advised this sneeze. He had lost nose when sneezed while smelling sword. India: Wyatt GOLDEN 27-33.

K2000 - K2099. Hypocrites.

K2010. Hypocrite pretends friendship but attacks.

K2011. Wolf poses as "grandmother" and kills child (Red Riding Hood). Type 333. (cf. Z18.1; K891.1). SEE ALSO: K311.3.

A* Grandmother and Red Riding Hood eaten. Perrault: Haviland FAIRY 146-150; Lang BLUE 62-65; Opie CLASSIC 93-97; Perrault FAMOUS 105-116; Perrault LITTLE pb; Perrault PERRAULT'S (Dodd) 71-77; Perrault PERRAULT'S (Dover) 23-30; Rackham ARTHUR 266-268. England: Steel ENGLISH 191-193. Germany (Grimm): Grimm GRIMM'S (Scribner's) 73-77 (+woodsman shoots wolf).

B* Wolf cut open (F913) and Red Riding Hood and Grandmother rescued. Stones put in wolf's belly and resewn (Q426). Germany (Grimm): Darrell ONCE 55-58; Galdone LITTLE pb; Grimm GRIMM'S (Follett) 215-221; Grimm GRIMM'S (Grosset) 243-246; Grimm GRIMM'S (World) 60-63; Grimm HOUSEHOLD 132-135 (+ second wolf on roof falls into trough of sausage water and drowns); Grimm LITTLE (illus. Bernadette) pb; Grimm LITTLE (illus. Pincus) pb; Martignoni ILLUSTRATED 175-177; Stobbs LITTLE pb.

C* Wolf cut open and grandmother and Red Riding Hood rescued. De La Mare TALES 74-83; Rockwell THREE 102-109; TALL..NURSERY 7-11 (Red Riding ran for help).

D* Red cap tells grandmother of wolf in woods.

Grandmother fills trough with boiling sausage water. Wolf falls in trying to smell and drowns. Germany (Grimm): Grimm GRIMM'S (Scribner's) 73-77.

E* Little Golden Hood. Wolf swallows hood which magically burns throat. Grandmother holds sack over door and catches wolf, throws into well. France: Lang RED 225-229.

K2011.0.1* Wolf disguises voice (K311.3) and three little girls think is grandmother and let in. He blows out light. "What is that funny thing?" (tail). "A brush for the flies." etc. Eldest offers to pick gingko nuts for wolf and takes sisters into tree. Offer to pull wolf up in basket. Drop three times. Third time wolf is killed (K1034.1). China: Chang CHINESE 22-25 /Minard WOMENFOLK 14-19/.

K2026. Crow accepts owl's hospitality then burns owls to death. SEE: B263.3.

K2028* Fox advises bear to throw dead brother in river. Fox fishes out corpse and eats. Feigns mourning when bear comes. Native American (Commanche): Curtis GIRL 54-57.

K2030. Double dealers.

K2031. Dog alternately bites and caresses hares. Is he friend or enemy? Aesop: Aesop AESOP'S (Watts) 104.

K2060. Detection of hypocrisy.

K2061.1. Wolf offers to act as shepherd: plan detected. Aesop: Aesop AESOP'S (Watts) 120; Aesop AESOP'S (Watts) 169-170.

K2061.1.1. Wolf proposes abolition of dog guards for sheep; plan detected. Aesop: Aesop AESOP'S (Watts) 189.

K2061.4. Wolf tries to entice goat down from high places: plan detected. Aesop: Aesop AESOP'S (Grosset) 134-135; Aesop AESOP'S (Watts) 140; Martignoni ILLUSTRATED 153.

K2061.5. Famished wolf asks sheep to bring him water: plan detected. SEE: K815.11.

K2061.7. Cat offers to act as doctor for cock and hen: plan detected. Aesop: Aesop AESOP'S (Grosset) 54-55; Martignoni ILLUSTRATED 156-157 (fox and hen).

K2061.7.1* Cat offers condolences to sick hen. Hen will feel better if cat just leaves. Aesop: Aesop AESOP'S (Grosset) 133; Aesop AESOP'S (Viking) 73; Aesop AESOP'S (Watts) 10 (aviary); Dobbs MORE 63-65.

K2061.9. Cat hangs on wall pretending to be dead: mice detect plan. SEE ALSO: K827.4.1. Aesop: Aesop AESOP'S (Golden) 22; Aesop AESOP'S (Grosset) 49; Aesop AESOP'S (Viking) 51-52; Aesop AESOP'S (Watts) 2; Martignoni ILLUSTRATED 54.

K2061.10. Fox's plan detected by crickets: cricket wing in his excrement. Aesop: Aesop AESOP'S (Watts) 163.

K2062. Thief tries to feed watchdog and stop his mouth: dog detects plan. Aesop: Aesop AESOP'S (Grosset) 217.

K2090. Other hypocritical acts.

K2100 - K2199. False accusations.

K2130. Trouble-makers.

K2131.1. Cat brings suspicions between eagle and sow. Eagle lives in the top branches, cat in the middle and sow at bottom. Cat tells eagle that sow is trying to root down the tree: eagle is frightened and dares not leave tree. Cat tells sow that eagle plans to carry off pig: sow dares not leave. They starve and fall victim to the cat. Aesop: Aesop AESOP'S (Grosset) 61-63 (wildcat dies and eagle and sow become friends caring for kittens): Aesop AESOP'S (Watts) 106-109.

K2131.2. Envious jackal makes lion suspicious of his friend, the bull. The lion kills the bull. SEE: K1084.1.1.

K2131.6* Brer Rabbit causes trouble between Brer Fox and wife with conflicting tales. U.S. (Black, Georgia): Harris FAVORITE 169-177; Harris COMPLETE 823-833.

K2131.7* Ol-Ambu leaps on giraffe's neck and stabs. Companion Pambito (Lumbwa) laughs and doesn't aid. Ol-Ambu refuses to share with Pambito. Pambito tells Ol's wife Ol is angry and she leaves home. Pambito hides in house and answering for wife receives meat handed in by Ol-Ambu. Kenya/Tanganyka (Masai): Aardema TALES 59-69; Courlander KING'S 90-94.

K2131.8* Mouse deer tries to break up friendship between hare and parrot. Ceylon: Tooze WONDERFUL 103-106.

K2131.9* Brer Rabbit. Tells Brer B'ar that wolf and fox are chasing him, gets Brer Wolf and Brer Fox to help him hunt Brer B'ar. Wolf and Fox are knocked over by Bear according to Rabbit's plan. U.S. (Black, Georgia): Harris FAVORITE 203-212; Harris COMPLETE 783-792.

K2137. The priest's guests and the eaten chickens. The servant who has eaten the chickens tells the guest to flee because the priest is going to cut off his ears, and he tells the priest the guest has stolen two chickens. The priest runs after him calling, "Give them to me." Type 1741. Germany (Grimm): De La Mare TALES 166-170 /Bleecker BIG 125-131/, /Minard WOMENFOLK 71-76/, /Greene CLEVER 109-114/, /Ross BLUE 35-40/; Grimm GRIMM'S (Grosset) 276-279; Grimm GRIMM'S (World) 42-44; Grimm HOUSEHOLD 9-11.

K2137.1* Holy man gives woman two chickens to eat after Ramadan. Husband orders her to feed guest. She tells guest husband plans to cut off ears, tells husband guest stole chicken. He pursues, "Just one." N. Africa: Gilstrap SULTAN'S 67-74.

K2138. Galla farmer visits Amhara farmer. Farmer's bull eaten by 'lions', given goat, goat 'stolen'--given butter, butter used by host's wife--given coffee. Child drinks coffee and becomes ill. Galla gives last two dollars for doctor bill since host lost so much on his account. Galla: Ashabranner LION'S 102-107. SEE ALSO: K251.1.

K2143* Truth, falsehood, fire and water find cattle and are to divide. Falsehood tells water to destroy fire. Tells truth water killed fire. Falsehood and truth then fight. Wind as judge says they are destined to struggle always. Ethiopia (Amhara, Shoa): Courlander FIRE 119-120.

K2144* Raja Adj Saka orders Javanese to give Kris up only to him personally. Then sends servant for kris. The two men kill each other. Indonesia: Courlander KANTCHIL'S 85-87.

K2150. Innocent made to appear guilty. SEE ALSO: K401; K1066.

K2151. The corpse handed around. The thrice-killed corpse. Dupes are accused of murder when the corpse is left with them. Type 1537. U.S. (Appalachia): Chase WICKED 100-105 (finally tied to wild horse and sent off as horse thief).

K2151.2* Makomwa-Meso demands portion of all meat young boy catches. Hyena kills chief's child and puts in lad's basket, lad leaves basket of meat at Makomwa's hut. Makomwa is executed for murder. Congo: Burton MAGIC 105-107.

K2200 - K2299. Villains and traitors.

K2210. Treacherous relatives.

K2212.0.2. Treacherous sister as mistress of robber (giant) plots against brother. SEE: S12.1.0.1.

K2213. Treacherous wife. SEE ALSO: D551.1.

K2213.0.1* The Wonderful Shirt. Type 590A. Dragon hires soldier to tend pot for three years. At end of time looks in pot and sees field marshal who wronged him earlier in pot. Type 475. Is given heroic shirt and heroic horse as wages by dragon. Weds princess. Wife steals shirt and gives to enemy who kills (D861.5; K975). Heroic horse takes body to dragon for water of life. Hero returns and regains shirt with aid of maid. Weds maid. Russia: Manning-Sanders CHOICE 13-25.

K2213.5.1* The faithless resuscitated wife. Three Snake Leaves. Type 612. Pledge to be entombed with wife. In tomb sees snake restore mate with three leaves. He revives wife with leaves. Gives leaves to faithful servant for safekeeping. Wife and paramour ship captain toss him into sea. Servant retrieves body (P361) and revives. King has wife and captain set adrift for this infidelity. Germany (Grimm): Lang GREEN 288-292.

K2270. Deformed villains.

K2275.1* Beardless villain. Tabu: greeting beardless man. Lad disobeys and is cheated. Greece (Cyclades): Neufeld BEWARE 11-21.

K2310. Deception by equivocation.

K2315. Peasant betrays fox by pointing. The peasant has hidden the fox in a basket and promised not to tell. When the hunters come, he says "The fox just went over the hill," but points to the basket. Aesop: Aesop AESOP'S (Grosset) 158-159; Aesop AESOP'S (Viking) 18-19; Green ANIMAL 165.

K2320. Deception by frightening. SEE ALSO: K335 (thief frightens owner from goods).

K2323. The cowardly duellers. In the war between the wild and the domestic animals the cat raises her tail: the wild animals think it is a gun salvo and flee. Type 104. Germany (Grimm): Grimm HOUSEHOLD 195-197; Lang GREEN 226-230 (+K2324.0.1); Wiggin TALES 149-151 (wolf-dog died, cat as dog's second). Van Woerkom MEAT pb.

K2323.0.1* In war between wild and domestic animals cat grabs bear by throat and wild animals flee on seeing bear on his back calling for help. +A2433.3.9. Finland: Bowman TALES ..TUPA 249.

K2323.1. Fox's tail drops and frightens animals. In war between birds and quadrupeds the fox's lifted tail is to be the signal for the attack. Gnats sting the fox under the tail. He drops it and the quadrupeds flee. Type 222. (cf. B261). Bushman: Kaula AFRICAN 105-109 (jackel, bee).

K2323.1.1* Bear has insulted young of wren, King of Birds, wren declares war. Germany (Grimm): Farjeon CAVALCADE..KINGS 47-54; Green ANIMAL 226-229 (hornets); Grimm BEAR pb; Grimm GRIMM'S (Grosset) 37-40; Grimm GRIMM'S (World) 121-124 (Tom-Tit). Germany: Wiggin TALES 74-76.

K2324. Hiding from strange animal. A cat shrieks and the frightened bear falls out of the tree and hurts himself. Cat as husband of she-fox has been invited to feast by animals, they hide and cat pounces on boar's ear, wolf's nose, etc. thinking it is mouse. In ensuing ruckus bear falls and hiding animals flee. Types 103, 103A. Russia: Higonnet-Schnopper TALES 82-90

(+A2435.3.2.1); Jameson KATORY pb; Montgomerie MERRY 47-55; Ransome OLD 106-119 /Gruenberg MORE 127-143/; Riordan TALES.. CENTRAL 91-95; Ross BURIED 19-26; Sleigh NORTH 178-183. Ukraine: Bloch UKRAINIAN 24-27 (Pan Kotsky). Cossack: Wiggin TALES 30-31. Latvia: Carpenter WONDER..DOGS 74-80. Poland: Borski JOLLY 49-62 (+Z39.1). Finland: Bowman TALES..TUPA 245-246.

K2324.0.1* In war or duel cat takes boar's ear for mouse and pounces, boar flees and animals are routed. +K2323. Germany (Grimm): Grimm HOUSEHOLD 195-197; Lang GREEN 326-330; Wiggin TALES 149-151.

K2324.1.1* Ass frightens goats from cave for lion to kill. Lion would have been afraid himself if hadn't known it was an ass. Aesop: Aesop AESOP'S (Grosset) 204-205; Aesop AESOP'S (Viking) 54-55; Aesop AESOP'S (Watts) 103.

K2324.2* Lion hears man's gun go off and flees in fear. Russia: Ginsburg THREE 37-39. Chile (Araucanian): Jagendorf KING 65-69.

K2324.2.1* Lion fears partridge for sound it makes and suddenness of flight. Quiet man shoots and harms. Fear the quiet one not the one who makes a fuss. U.S. (Black, Georgia): Harris NIGHTS 330-333; Harris COMPLETE 358.

K2327. Wolf captor scared by fiddle playing of captive ram who escapes. U.S. (Black, Georgia): Harris COMPLETE 149-154; Harris NIGHTS 44-50.

K2345.0.1* Rabbit sets fire to brush on badger's back. Says sound is name of mountain Katchi-Katchi. +G61.3, +J2171.1.3, +K1014. Japan: Buck FAIRY 96-97; Ozaki FAIRY 43-53.

K2347* Brer Buzzard abandons Brer Rabbit on top of tree. Rabbit remembers now where he hid their gold. U.S. (Black, Georgia): Brown WORLD 109-111 /Arbuthnot FAIRY 221/; Harris SONGS 105-108 /Harris COMPLETE 69-71/, /Harris FAVORITE 121-124/.

K2348* Rabbit bets he can frighten animals a dozen times bigger than self. Jumps off fence into flock of sheep, startling them. Wins bet. Finland: Bowman TALES 254.

K2349* Deception by frightening--miscellaneous.

K2349.1* Tiger comes onto sleeping father and son and thinks is one creature. Crocodile tells to throw one to him and call "Here he comes." Man sneezes and tiger leaps into river calling "Here he comes!" Is eaten by crocodile. Indonesia: Courlander KANTCHIL'S 80-83.

K2349.2* Wife and son convince husband that site where he wants to construct castle is haunted. They fake a monster, using bearskin. Great Britain: Finlay TATTERCOATS 60-69.

K2350. Military strategy.

K2357.16* Disguise to enter enemy's camp. Lad feigns simplemindedness and is taken as cook by robbers. Spies out camp and brings about capture. Switzerland (German): Duvoisin THREE 223-229.

K2365. Enemy induced to give up siege.

K2366.2* City gates are flung open and ruler Chuko Kung Ming plays lute on city walls. Enemy general suspects a trick and retreats. The trick was to make him retreat in suspicion. China: Lu Mar CHINESE 97-110.

K2368.4.1* Enemy induced to give up siege by making it look as if the besieged have received reinforcements. Soldiers change uniform and keep marching past--thought to be many. China: Chrisman SHEN 100-114 (women don soldiers clothing); Fenner ADVENTURES 60-71 /Chrisman SHEN 79-99/.

K2368.6* Fiddler on walls plays such melancholy music that enemy becomes homesick and desert. China: Chrisman SHEN 78-99 /Fenner ADVENTURES 60-71/.

K2368.7* Shepherd lets sheep loose, starving enemy chasing them is scattered and routed. China: Chrisman SHEN 70-99 /Fenner ADVENTURES 60-71/.

K2369.14. Borrowed arrows: Dummys made of straw are fired on by enemy. Arrows thus collected replenish besieged army's store.

K2369.14.0.1* K2319.14 told of Chinese ruler, Chuko Kung (Chuko Liang; Three Kingdoms, 181-234 A.D.). China: Alexander PEBBLES 28; Lu Mar CHINESE TALES 111-128; Wyndham TALES..CHINESE 40-47.

K2369.14.0.2* K2319.14 told of Chinese ruler Chang Shuen (618-905 A.D., Tang). China: Lu Mar CHINESE TALES 43-52.

K2369.15* Kite flown terrorizes enemies who flee. They have never seen a kite and think it comes from the heavens. China: Chrisman SHEN 189-205.

K2369.15.1* General has kite with lantern in it sent aloft. Troops think is new star, good omen. Take heart and rout enemy. Korea: Carpenter TALES..KOREAN 109-116.

K2369.16* Lawsuits to be settled by archery skill tests. All men practice to become expert. Enemy now fears to attack kingdom. China: Chrisman SHEN 79-99 /Fenner ADVENTURES 60-71/.

K2369.17* Clever thief sent to steal items from opposing general's tent nightly. Feeling himself vulnerable, the enemy general grows frightened and flees. China: Alexander PEBBLES 29.

K2370. Miscellaneous deceptions.

K2371.1.1. Heaven entered by trick: permission to pick up cap. Trickster throws cap or leather apron inside gate. SEE: Q565 (Smith and Devil); K213.

K2371.1.1.1* Rabbi Joshua Ben Levi asks for glimpse of paradise while alive. Holds sword of Angel of Death as assurance he will not be harmed. Jumps into heaven with sword and refuses to return it unless allowed to stay there-- alive. Jewish: Ish-Kishor WISE 27-31.

K2371.2.1* Weaver blessed by Krishna to weave wondrous cloth. Cursed by Bramah to lose all gained. Attracts thieves to city. Ordered killed. He outsmarts fates by throwing gold earned to beggars as soon as received. Beggars supply his wants in return. Pakistan: Edmonds TRICKSTER 104-112.

L. REVERSAL OF FORTUNE

L100 – L199. Unpromising hero (heroine).

L110. Types of unpromising heroes (heroines).

L114.1. Lazy hero. Type 675. Ka-ha-si, youngest of chief's three nephews sleeps by fire all day. Loon, messenger from grandfather, "Old Man Who Held Up the Earth" instructs in strength gaining rites. On sea lion hunt two elder brothers fail to leap ashore on sea lion rocks. Ka-ha-si succeeds. Later defeats giant, forest, mountains. Becomes one who holds up world (A842). Eskimo: Caswell SHADOWS 96-106.

L144.2. Farmer surpasses astronomer and doctor in predicting weather and choosing good (curing upset stomach). They return to city. Poland: Borski GOOD 68-71.

L145.1. Ugly sister helps pretty one. Related to type 711.

A* Tatterhood. Queen bears ugly daughter riding a billy goat and carrying a wooden spoon along with lovely daughter because she misused magic rite and ate both child-producing flowers. (T548.2). Tatterhood drives out trolls on Christmas Eve. Sister disobeys warning and pokes head in door and witch replaces it with calf's head. Tatterhood takes her to witch's land in sailing ship and recaptures sister's head. Norway: Aulaire EAST 179-187; Manning-Sanders CHOICE 246-255 /Manning-Sanders BOOK..WITCHES 94-103/.

B* Kate Crackernuts. Queen sends stepdaughter to hen wife. To eat nothing before coming. Third time she obeys and sheep's head jumps from pot onto her shoulders. Her stepsister Kate takes Ann in search of aid. Kate guards sleeping prince and follows when he rides out to fairy ball. She takes nuts from bushes and rolls them to fairy babies who drop silver wand which she realizes will cure her sister. On the second night she likewise gets magic bird to cure prince. She and sister wed prince and his brother. SEE ALSO: D754.1. England: Jacobs ENGLISH 207-211 /Minard WOMENFOLK 65-70/; Lurie CLEVER 66-73; Reeves ENGLISH 50-62; Williams-Ellis FAIRY..BRITISH 49-54.

L200 – L299. Modesty brings new aid.

L223. Modest inheritance best. Oldest left all that's green and isn't green on the woodlands. Second all that's crooked and straight. Third all that moves or stands still. Youngest rest. Judges can't settle. First person to enter gate to be made Chief Judge (H171.8), is Dark Patrick. Rules that older brothers own trees, game--must remove these so youngest, who owns land, can mine his gold. Ireland: Mac-Manus HIBERNIAN 160-173.

L300 – L399. Triumph of the weak.

L310. Weak overcomes strong in conflict.

L311.0.1* Master plans wrestling match between his golden Buddha and servant's wooden Buddha. Loser to be servant of other for life. The wooden Buddha wins. Japan: Uchida MAGIC 21-31.

L315.2. Mouse torments bull who cannot catch him. Aesop: Aesop AESOP'S (Watts) 111.

L315.2.1* Puppy torments tiger who cannot catch him. Tiger leaps back and forth while puppy runs through dog-hole until tiger dies of exhaustion. Korea: Carpenter KOREAN 67-72.

L315.3. Fox burns tree in which eagle has nest. Revenges theft of cub. Aesop: Aesop AESOP'S (Grosset) 80-81 (eagle returns cub when fox threatens with fire); Aesop AESOP'S (Watts) 199-200 (eagle carries burning goat from altar to nest and nest catches fire, fox eats burnt young who fall to ground. Aesop FIVE 32.

L315.6. Insects harry large animal to despair or death.

L315.6.1* Sparrows revenge. Gnat buzzes in elephant's ear and puts him to sleep. Woodpecker pecks out eyes. Frog croaks from pit and elephant follows sound seeking pond and falls to death. India: Gaer FABLES 41-43; Ryder PANCHATANTRA 153-156.

L315.7. Dungbeetle keeps destroying eagle's eggs. Eagle at last goes to the sky and lays eggs in Zeus' lap. The dungbeetle causes Zeus to shake his apron and break the eggs. Beetle is taking revenge for destruction of hare's nest which he had been guarding. Aesop: Aesop AESOP'S (Grosset) 142-143; Aesop AESOP'S (Watts) 178.

L330. Easy escape of weak (small). SEE ALSO: J1662.

L331. Little fishes escape from the net. The large are caught. Aesop: Aesop AESOP'S (Golden) 77-79.

L331.1* Little fish leave deep waters. Big pike remains to starve and be caught. Russia: Ransome OLD 206-211.

L332.1* Mice generals put horns on heads as symbol of authority, cannot escape into holes and are caught by weasels. Aesop: Aesop AESOP'S (Golden) 36; Aesop AESOP'S (Watts) 76-77; Aesop FABLES (Walck) 30-31.

L350. Mildness triumphs over violence.

L351. Contest of wind and sun. Sun by warmth causes traveler to remove coat, while wind by violent blowing causes him to pull it closer around him. Aesop: Aesop AESOP'S (Golden) 63-65; Aesop AESOP'S (Grosset) 130-131;

Aesop AESOP'S (Random) 47-49; Aesop AESOP'S (Viking) 17-18; Aesop AESOP'S (Watts) 18; Aesop FABLES (Macmillan) 119; Aesop FABLES (Walck) 88-91; Arbuthnot FAIRY 228; Gruenberg FAVORITE 405-406; Haviland FAIRY 100; Kent MORE 46-51. La Fontaine NORTH pb.

L351.2. Sun cursed by man for its burning rays, wind for its hot breath, but moon is blessed for its soft, cool and beautiful light. India: Jacobs INDIAN 265-267 (moon hid tidbits under fingernails for mother when visiting aunts Thunder and Lightning, thus blessed).

L351.2.1* Puppy runs in and out of hole in gate. Tiger leaps back and forth over gate after him until dies of exhaustion. Korea: Carpenter KOREAN 67-72.

L390. Triumph of the weak--miscellaneous.

L392. Mouse stronger than wall, wind, moutain. SEE ALSO: Z42.

L392.0.1. Mouse Bride. Mouse dropped by hawk into hand of hermit. He turns mouse into maiden. She seeks strongest husband sun, cloud, wind, mountain, mouse. India: Gobhai USHA pb; Montgomerie TWENTY-FIVE 54-55; Ryder PANCHATANTRA 353-357; Turnbull FAIRY (male mouse dropped to childless couple--seeks wife, moon, cloud, etc). Russia: Masey STORIES 62-64.

L392.0.1.1* Rat daughter of king and queen turned to princess by fairy to wed--sun, cloud, wind, mountain, rat. Turned back to rat to wed. France (15th-16th century): Schiller WHITE pb.

L392.0.2* Mouse Bride. Mouse seeks strongest husband (bride). Sun, clouds, wind, etc. Japan: Bulatkin EURASIAN 82-84; Uchida Dancing 89-94 (sun, cloud, wind, wall, mouse). Burma: Brockett BURMESE 153-155 (sun, rain, wind, mound, bull, rope, mouse). Ethiopia: Courlander FIRE 89-92 (bride sought, god, wind, mountain, mouse). Nepal: Hitchcock KING 53-60 (rat, sun, clouds, wind, mountain, tree, rat). Marie de France: Green ANIMAL 88-89 (asks daughter of sun, cloud, wind, stone tower, mouse). Korea: Carpenter KOREAN 199-202 (mole to wed sky, sun, cloud, wind, stone miryek, mole). Lang FIFTY 143-145 (stone, cloud, wind, wall) /Manning-Sanders BOOK..MAGICAL BEASTS 143-160/; France: Wiggin TALES 3-5 (stone, cloud, wind, wall).

L392.0.3* Maiden's mother seeks strongest husband. Wishes her to marry sun, clouds, wind, mountain, rats, ratcatcher. India: Korel LISTEN 53-59.

L392.0.4* Name of strongest creature sought for cat. Heaven, cloud, wind, wall, mouse, cat. Vietnam: Vo Dinh TOAD 123-128.

L392.0.5* Hare falling on ice asks ice, "Are you strong?" Goes to sun, cloud, wind, stone wall, mouse, cat, housewife, God. Asks God three times and God refuses to answer. Strikes hare with thunderbolt and housewife makes dumplings of him. Siberia (Cheremis): Withers I SAW 100-101. Russia (Nanai): Deutsch MORE 39-43 (boy falls, ice, sun, cloud, wind, mountain, tree, woodsman. Man is strongest. Omit God motif.). Russia: Ginsburg STRONGEST pb (lamb).

L392.0.6* King executes thief. Thief kills chicken, chick eats worm, worm gnaws foot of king and king falls. Vietnam: Withers I SAW 122.

L393.1. Princess asks for "moon snow", says soot offered by chimney sweep is it. Weds. Wales: Pugh MORE..WELSH 89-94.

L395. Frog, tortoise, fish each tell of how long they expect to live. Frog alone does not expect to live a hundred and ten years and alone escapes fisherman's net. India: Spellman BLUE 56-58.

L396* Fly, mosquito, wasp, and horsefly in empty basket argue over who is best. Spider spins basket shut while they argue. Russia: Carey BABA 63-66.

L400 - L499. Pride brought low.

L410.8* Manabozo cannot put toe in mouth as baby does, baby mocks. Native American: Wiggin TALES 400.

L410.8.1* Glooskap cannot subdue Baby who replies "goo" to all threats. Baby still says "goo" recalling this victory. Native American (Algonquin): Garner CAVALCADE..GOBLINS 210-212.

L411. Proud king displaced by angel (King in bath). While the king is in the bath (or hunting) an angel in his form takes his place. The king is repulsed on all sides until he repents of his haughtiness. Type 757. Poland: Borski GOOD 48-50.

L411.1* King follows bird across river and returns to find clothing gone. Dressed as beggar he attends feast given by kind new king for beggars, repents, is restored. Latvia: Durham TIT 67-69.

L417. God finds that his statue sells at low price. He prices it in a statue shop and finds that his price is lower than other gods. Aesop: Aesop AESOP'S (Grosset) 118-119 (Mercury); Aesop AESOP'S (Watts) 71; Aesop FABLES (Walck) 32-33.

L420. Overwhelming ambition punished.

A* The Dream. Type 725.

Aa* The Secret-keeping Boy. Lad given scabbard which grows as he grows. Dreams he will become King of Hungary, refuses to tell dream--

imprisoned. Gives answer to riddles sent by enemy, Sultan of Turkey. 1. Which of three bamboo pieces from top, bottom and middle of cane, put in water, heaviest is from bottom (H506.10). 2. Which of three foals born first, second, third. Feeds oats, hay. Eldest eats oats, etc. (H506.11.1). Witch tries to kill lad but he survives with magic sword and four look alike lads and defeats her and Sultan of Turkey. Weds princess, becomes King of Hungary. Hungary: Manning-Sanders GLASS 50-62.

Ab* Red King and Green King. Lad refuses to tell dream, imprisoned, answers riddles one and two above saving Green King from Red King enemy. +F601.2E. Rumania: Farjeon CAVALCADE..KINGS 33-46; Ure RUMANIA 45-56.

B* The Three Rowers. Types 517, 725. Lord hears birds say parents will serve him. Father throws him overboard. He discovers cause of ravens' molestation of king (they wish king to settle disput). He weds princess and gets half of kingdom as reward. Italy: Manning-Sanders GIANNI 54-61.

L430. Arrogance repaid.

L435.5* Minstrel sings, "Dog is great among dogs, yet he serves men." King refuses to extend to include kings. Minstrel hands king harp while he gives beggar food from king's bowl. Now sings, "King is great among men yet he serves his people." Senegal (Wolof): Courlander KING'S 19-21.

L450. Proud animal less fortunate than humble. SEE ALSO: J211.

L451.2. Wild ass envies tame until he sees his burdens. Aesop: Aesop AESOP'S (Watts) 157.

L451.2.1* Wild ass derides pack-ass's servitude. Lion eats wild ass but pack-ass's master drives it off. Aesop: Aesop AESOP'S (Watts) 158-159.

L451.3. Wolf prefers liberty and hunger to dog's servitude and plenty. Type 201. Aesop: Aesop AESOP'S (Grosset) 22-24; Aesop AESOP'S (Random) 75-77; Aesop AESOP'S (Viking) 9-10; Aesop FABLES (Macmillan) 55; Aesop

FABLES (Walck) 110-111; Green ANIMAL 90-91. SEE ALSO: K414.3.4.

L542.1. Ass jealous of horse, but sees horse later working in mill (or as draft horse). SEE ALSO: J212.1. Aesop: Aesop AESOP'S (Viking) 60-61; Aesop AESOP'S (Watts) 218.

L452.2. Ass jealous of war-horse until he sees him wounded. SEE ALSO: J212.1. Aesop: Aesop AESOP'S (Viking) 60-61.

L456. Calf pities draft ox: is taken to slaughter, ox spared. Aesop: Aesop AESOP'S (Grosset) 65 (calf sacrificed); Aesop AESOP'S (Watts) 144.

L457* Water buffalo envies well-fed pig. Pig is butchered. India (Jataka): Gaer FABLES 132-133. Mexico: Ross IN MEXICO 35-49 (burro).

L458* Lizards envy stag. He is killed by hounds. Aesop: Green ANIMAL 82.

L460. Pride brought low--miscellaneous.

L461. Stag scorns his legs but is proud of his horns. Caught by his horns in trees. Type 77. Aesop: Aesop AESOP'S (Grosset) 125-126; Aesop AESOP'S (Random) 28-30; Aesop AESOP'S (Viking) 83; Aesop AESOP'S (Watts) 74; Aesop FABLES (Macmillan) 49; Aesop FABLES (Walck) 20; Aesop FIVE 62.

L461.1* Elephant, lion, fox, and peacock brag of risks, bravery, courage and feathers. Frog says these are very traits that get them killed by men. India: Reed TALKATIVE 13.

L471.1* Currassow tells jaguar cautionary tale of Kikushie, who kills men. Yet men poison arrows and kill Kikushie. Carib: Sherlock WEST 27-33.

L475. Oil lamps blown out: had thought that it outshone stars. Aesop: Aesop AESOP'S (Grosset) 136; Aesop AESOP'S (Watts) 49.

L478. Gnats having overcome lion are in turn killed by spider. Aesop: Aesop AESOP'S (Watts) 198-199; Green ANIMAL 43. Greece: Wilson GREEK 212-213.

M. ORDAINING THE FUTURE

M200 - M299. Bargains and promises.

M211. Man sells soul to devil. Type 330, 360, 361, 756B, 810, 812, 1170-1199. SEE ALSO: Q565 (Smith outwits Devil); D2121.5; E765.1.1.1; G303.16.19.3 (freed if task set Devil cannot perform); G303.16.8.2; J2411.0.2; K217 (Bearskin).

M211.2. Man sells soul to devil in return for devil's building house (barn, etc.). SEE ALSO: G303.9.1.13 (the devil as a builder); K1886.3.1.1. Netherlands (Friesland): Spicer OWL'S 15-28 (sells soul to Joost for barn).

M211.2.1* Devil builds bridge in one night in return for first soul to cross bridge. Goat is driven across. SEE ALSO: G303.9.1.1; S241.1. Switzerland: Müller-Guggenbühl SWISS 213-223.

M211.2.1.1* Devil builds bridge in return for first soul to cross bridge. Is tricked into crossing first himself. France: Scribner DEVIL'S pb.

M211.7.1* The Dragon and His Grandmother. Three soldiers hide in field from enemy. Dragon helps them escape. Gives whips to crack making coins fall. In seven years must guess riddle or be his forever. Old lady directs to dragon's grandmother who hides them and asks son answers to riddle (H523). Their meat to be dead monkey from North Sea, spoon--rib of whale, cup--hoof of horses. Type 812. Germany (Grimm): Gag TALES 225-234; Hoke DRAGONS 192-198; Lang YELLOW 48-51 /Green CAVALCADE..DRAGONS 120-124/, /Fenner GIANTS 155-161/, /Lang FIFTY 53-56/; Manning-Sanders BOOK..DRAGONS 79-86.

M211.8. Man sells soul to devil for devil's doing one specific job.

M211.8.1* Devil to carry to Pope and back. +K1886.3.1.1. Switzerland: Müller-Guggenbühl SWISS 213-233.

M211.10* Man sells soul to Devil. Allowed one wish before being taken--wishes Devil would ride away and never come back. Williams-Ellis FAIRY..BRITISH 288-291.

M211.11* Farmer given magic stone which makes invisible, in return he and family are to become demon's slaves in five years. Lives well. Keeps appointment but arrives invisible and beats Devil. Is released from promise. Philippines (Pampangan): Sechrist ONCE 119-125.

M211.12* Devil's Field. Man buys field from Devil, to give half gold found there rest of life to Devil. Keep half for soul. Hoards gold rest of life to buy back soul, hiding it under tree. Devil refuses--there is gold under every tree on field. France: Holman DRAC 19-37.

M215. With his whole heart: devil carries off judge. The devil refuses to take anything not offered him with the whole heart. He hears the judge (advocate) cursed for fraud with such sincerity, that he carries him off. Type 1186. Norway: Asbjornsen NORWEGIAN 168-169 (bailiff).

M220. Other bargains.

M221. Beheading bargain. Giant allows hero to cut off his head; he will cut off hero's later. Giant's head can be replaced. Ireland: Fenner ADVENTURES 162-163 (Cuchulain).

M231. Guest must tell tale to receive hospitality.

M231.1. Free keep in an inn exchanged for good story.

A* The Man Who Had No Story. Type 2412B (O'Suilleabhain). Man in night-lodgings has no tale to share. He is cast out and experiences fantastic adventures. Returns with a tale to tell. Ireland: Danaher FOLKTALES 1-8 (forced to help carry coffin, open it, get in); Jacobs CELTIC 217-222 (set to roasting drowned friend on spit); MacManus BOLD 158-168 (at fairy ball sent out for failing to tell tale, has to carry coffin, he is corpse); Manning-Sanders BOOK..GHOSTS 68-73.

B* Man with no tale sees story spirits.

Ba* Traveler can't tell tale, turned out. Visits three houses and sees 1. Man and wife with snake on beams dripping poison on mouths; 2. man sleeping with axe in back; 3. three tongues of flame surrounding house. He returns and tells this tale. Master of house explains. Snake was belt hung on beam instead of put away. Axe was not left in chopping block where belonged. Flames were stories told by three men sleeping there. They protect the house. Rumania: Ure RUMANIAN 172-177.

Bb* Bridegroom says he knows no stories, really just wants all to go to bed so he can be alone with bride. Little sister overhears Spirit of the Story of the Bug plot to turn self to stream on morrow. If he drinks he'll turn to bug. Story of the Knife to be golden knife on road, he'll pick up and be cut and turn to knife. Little sister rides ahead and averts these calamities. Explains. Russia (Steppe): Masey STORIES 104-108.

Bc* Boy told stories by servant never shares with other children. Stories' spirits go into leather bag on wall. Servant hears them plot to harm him on way to wedding. Servant leads horse and refuses to stop for stream, strawberries, removes bag with hot poker, rushes into wedding chamber and kills snake. Tells tale. Korea: Kim STORY 3-10; Williams-Ellis ROUND 279-288.

Bd* Storyteller to lose life if doesn't tell new

tale each night. Gambles with old beggar and loses all including self. Is turned to hare and has fantastic adventures. Tale impresses king so that nightly new tale rule is lifted. Ireland: Jacobs CELTIC 144-157.

M231.2* Wife demands tale of each guest. Guest agrees to tell only if no one interrupts. Tells repetitive endless tale (Z11). Wife interrupts. Russia: Downing RUSSIAN 211-213.

M231.3* Guests' storytelling impresses inhospitable man. He vows to allow guests in future. Wife has allowed three peddlers to stay since all were named Donal, the host's own name. Each tells a wondrous tale. Ireland: MacManus HIBERNIAN 185-201.

M300 - M399. Prophecies.

M300. Prophecies. SEE ALSO: SUBJECT INDEX "Prophecies."

M383* Vain attempts to escape prophesied marriage (H1273.2; K1355).

M383.1* Kabadaluk. Sultan seeks husband for daughter. Wizard throws pebbles into water with names of those to wed. Princess to wed beggar Kabadaluk. King sends him to fetch pebbles from dragon's lake, intending his death. Returns with jewels. Weds princess. Italy: Manning-Sanders GIANNI 13-33.

M383.2* Wei Ku prophesied to wed three-year-old daughter of peasants. Orders her killed. She is spared, later adopted by governor. Wed to Wei Ku at age of seventeen. Recognized by scar over eyes. China: Birch CHINESE 43-47.

M383.3* To avoid prophecy of wedding of daughter to son of slave girl, king has her beheaded and son abandoned. Grown, he is discovered and sent with letter to be beheaded. Princess reads message as he sleeps and changes to "wed princess." India: Buck FAIRY 68-80.

M400 - M499. Curses.

M400. Curses. SEE: Subject Index "Curses."

M405. Curse takes effect too soon. Cursed to break his leg in forty days, the man breaks it immediately. "That's from someone else's curse. When mine takes effect you'll have to crawl." Turkey: Downing HODJA 89.

N. CHANCE AND FATE

N0 - N99. Wagers and Gambling.

N2.6. Wife as wager.

N2.6.0.1* Oseedah, hare, loses both wives to Sayno, skunk, gambling. Native American (Seneca): Parker SKUNNY 95-101.

N10. Wagers on wives, husbands, or servants. SEE: J2311.0.1.1.

N11. Wager on wife's complacency. Though man has foolishly bargained everything away, she praises him and he wins the wager. Type 1415. +J2081.1. Norway (Asbjornsen): Arbuthnot FAIRY 84-86; Asbjornsen NORWEGIAN 178-181; Aulaire EAST 202-206; Fenner TIME.. LAUGH 162-174.

N11.1* Wife is delighted with husband's bargain for cow manure as neighbor just chided her that she'd go borrowing for manure--now she need not borrow any. He wins wager. Austria: Jagendorf NOODLEHEAD 216-221.

N12. Wager as to most obedient wife. The husband tames his shrewish wife so that he wins the wager. Type 901. SEE: T251.2 (Taming of the Shrew). Denmark: Arbuthnot FAIRY 95-98.

N50. Other wagers.

N51. Wager: Who can call three tree names first. The bear names different varieties of the same tree, so that the fox wins the wager. Type 7. Norway: Asbjornsen NORWEGIAN 120-121; Wiggin TALES 312-313.

N66.1. Poor man bets rich he can make woodcutter richer than rich man can. Rich gives much money to woodcutter, all is stolen. Gives magic wishing ring. It is lost in shipwreck. Poor man gives five centavos to buy fish. Fish has ring inside (N211.1). Woodcutter exclaims, "I've found you at last" and thieves overhearing think selves discovered and return stolen gold (N611.1). Philippines (Tagalog): Sechrist ONCE 143-149.

N100 - N299. The ways of

luck and fate.

N111.4.2* Fortune wakes traveler nodding by well, if he'd fallen would have blamed her. Aesop: Aesop AESOP'S (Watts) 224; Leach LUCK 22-23.

N111.4.3* Farmer thanks Goddess of Earth for finding pot of gold. If he lost it he'd blame Fortune. Aesop: AESOP'S (Watts) 48.

N112.1. Bad luck put into sack. Leach LUCK 37-40 (+N250.4).

N115. Book of fate. SEE: K975.1.2. Man hides in bundle and is carried to heaven. Is given better fate from Book of Destiny, but must give it back to rightful owner "Tchapogui" when he claims it. Man becomes wealthy but fears arrival of Tchapogui. Long for child. Baby found under cart with name "Tchapogui." Korea: Jewett WHICH 95-103.

N120. Determination of Luck or Fate.

N129* Lucky time of day. Lucky to get up early? Boy finds bag of gold on road early in morning but man who lost it must have been up earlier than he and was unlucky. Iran: Shah MULLA 108.

N130. Changing of luck or fate.

N135.3. The luck bringing shirt. The king is to become lucky when he puts on the shirt of a lucky man. Only man who says that he is lucky has no shirt. (cf. N135.3). Type 844. North Africa: Gilstrap SULTAN'S 26-31 (shirt of happy man). Dobbs ONCE 27-33 (happy). Denmark: Courlander RIDE 166-168 (prince to have happy marriage if finds linen undergarment of truly happy couple). Leach LUCK 86-87.

N135.3.2* Cure for all troubles: burn a mustard seed from house which has no troubles. Cambodia: Edmonds TRICKSTER 86-90.

N138. Luck depends on what stool Fate sits on when one is born--copper, silver, gold. Merchant's son advises to wed water girl. Fate sat on silver stool when she was born. She buys coals which turn to gold. Russia: Downing RUSSIAN 208-210.

N140. Nature of luck and fate--miscellaneous motifs.

N141. Luck or intelligence? Dispute as to which is the more powerful. Man with intelligence remains poor (is brought into court). Saved by mere luck. Type 945.

N141.0.1* Youth blessed by Dame-know-it-all succeeds in making princess talk (H621), but without luck no one believes him and he is to be hung. Dame-know-it-all concedes and mistress good-luck rescues lad. +F954.2.1. Denmark: Hatch THIRTEEN 46-57. Czechoslovakia:

Bulatkin EURASIAN 114-119. Poland: Borski GOOD 3-12.

N141.0.2* Good Luck and Bad Luck dispute. Man misses gold left in path by Bad Luck (N351.2). Three groats left by Good Luck start chain ending with curing of princess. Latvia: Durham TIT 81-84.

N141.0.3* Wit greater than luck. By luck to wed Boyar's daughter yet so senseless that he is to be hung instead. Wit returns and he convinces by clever talking to let wed after all. Rumania: Ure RUMANIAN 90-98.

N141.0.4* Good luck vs. common sense. Peasant think jewels arranged by good luck are rocks. Common sense returns when one is left. He sells and becomes rich. Greece: Wilson GREEK 21-27.

N141.0.5* Good Luck vs. Great Riches. Riches are lost, hawk carries off purse, horseload of gold, horse runs away, etc. Good Luck gives one coin. To buy first thing sees for sale (N222). Stick to knock olives from tree. Purse falls out. Portugal: Lowe LITTLE 67-71.

N141.0.6* Mazel and Shlimazel. Good Luck causes hero to be taken to palace. Performs task bringing milk of a lioness for ill king. Good Luck's year up. He says he brought "milk of a dog" to be hung. Shlimazel (Bad Luck) wins bet. Lad saved and wed. Jewish: Singer MAZEL pb.

N141.0.7* Rich man brags he got all by cleverness. His ships sink and house burns. Which is better--luck or cleverness? Leach LUCK 48.

N177. Beggar escapes from fire. Refused hospitality, he must sleep outdoors. The house burns down. Leach LUCK 30-31.

N182. Snake turns to gold in answer to dream. Woman tells dream of pot of gold. Robbers overhear but finding only snake in pot turns it loose on woman's bed. It turns to gold. SEE ALSO: K602.3.

N182.1* Man dreams gold falls on head, refuses discovered pot of gold in garden. Greedy neighbor digs it up and finds full of snakes. Pours through hole in roof onto head of dreamer. Snakes turn to gold. Japan: Scofield HOLD 21-26. Vietnam: Schultz VIETNAMESE 80-83 (robbers).

N182.1.1* Man dreams coins fall on hearth, leaves pot of silver in field. Wife tells neighbor but he finds snakes in pot and pours down chimney in anger. Snakes turn to coins on hearth. Afghanistan: Courlander RIDE 60-62.

N182.2* Poor brother finds golden gourd on rich brother's land. Rich claims it but finds only wasp nest. Lets wasps loose in poor brother's house. They turn to gold pieces. Brazil: Carpenter SOUTH 64-70.

N182.3* Man sees snake stare at bird until it falls in terror at his feet. Man decides to wait on Allah to provide. His wife discovers a pot of gold but he makes her dig it up, pour over his head before will accept. N. Africa: Gilstrap SULTAN'S 81-87 /Arbuthnot ANTHOLOGY 310-311/.

N182.4* Man finds treasure. Storekeeper to help fetch it decides to steal, finds filth. Dumps it on man's doorstep. He finds piles of silver on step in morning. Mexico: Wolkstein LAZY pb.

N200. The good gifts of fortune.

N211.1. Lost ring found in fish. (Polycrates). SEE: D882.1; K882.2.1 (grateful animals recover ring); K1355A (The Fish and the Ring); N66.1; (cf. B548.2.1).

A* Rich lady of Stavoren asks captain to bring most precious thing in world--he brings grain. She has it dumped into sea. Tosses ring into sea--as sure she'll never see ring again as she will never be poor. Ring found in fish served her. She is impoverished. Wheat grows into weeds and clogs harbor, sandbank forms and Stavoren languishes. Courlander RIDE 178-185. Netherlands (Friesland): De Leeuw LEGENDS.. HOLLAND 133-138; Spicer OWL'S 56-73.

B* No-king-is-as-great-as-God. Man named No-king-is-as-great-as-God is given ring. King sends to man's wife to buy so king may make a second like it. He then demands man to produce it. They trust in God. Fish served has ring inside. King has to forfeit life. "No-king-is.." is made king. Nigeria: Walker DANCING 43-51.

N211.2. Unavailing attempt to get rid of slippers: they always return. Iraq: Carpenter ELEPHANT'S 66-74. Arabia: Berson KASSIM'S pb; Green ABU KASSIM'S pb.

N222. First objects picked up bring fortune. SEE ALSO: N141.0.5; N421.1.

N222.1* Kannon-Sama grants wish--first object touched on leaving temple will buy luck, falls and grabs piece of straw. Japan: Uchida DANCING 109-119.

N222.2* First object bought to buy fortune, is stick, knocks purse from tree. +N141. Portugal: Lowe LITTLE 67-77.

N222.3* Two wise men predict if poor man with pity picks up dead rat, he'll become rich, poor potter picks up. Cat tells to fill pots with water and honey (K1917.3). Reapers give grass for water, kings gives gold for grass, etc. India: Wyatt GOLDEN 101-106.

N222.4* Supplicant directed by goddess to pick up first thing he touches on leaving temple. Piece of straw. Ties horsefly with it. Boy's mother gives three oranges for fly. Dying lady saved by orange gives three rolls of silk. Buys dead horse and two nights lodging for silk.

Goddess brings horse to life and he trades for three rice fields and house. (cf. N421.1). Japan: Sakade JAPANESE 78-80 (gives oranges to thirsty peddler, cloth to princess, she gives money); Uchida DANCING 109-118.

N228. Leopard tied in bag in water floats to shore and finds a mate. Grateful to trickster who has tied him up. SEE ALSO: K714.2.3.2. Indonesia: Courlander KANTCHIL'S 118-121 (Kantchil and tiger).

N250. Persistent bad luck.

N250.4. Bad luck banished and freed. The poor man in some way banishes his bad luck and becomes prosperous. Out of envy his rich brother sets it free; it then follows him. +K717.3. Latvia: Durham TIT 30-33 (hears fiddlers behind stone [Bad Luck], stuffs in bag and buries +D1415.2.5). Russia: Dolch OLD RUSSIA 81-85-97; Downing RUSSIAN 122-128; Leach LUCK 37-40; Pyle WONDER 29-30; Ransome OLD 184-205; Rudolph I AM pb.

N250.5* Bad luck escaped. Things become so poor man begins to burn floorboards. God of Poverty comes from under floor saying it is too poor for him now. He directs man to wait at Temple of the Four Heavenly Kings just at midnight New Year's Eve and catch the bridle of one passing horseman. He misses yellow=gold, white=silver, and black=copper. Catches grey horse's--God of Poverty. God of Poverty tells him to try again when riders return at midnight on New Year's Day. He manages to catch God of Copper's bridle, bridle turns to a never emptied bag of copper coins (D812; D1451). Japan: Novak FAIRY 39-43.

N255. Escape from one misfortune into worse.

N255.1. Stag escapes from hunter to be eaten by lion. Aesop: Aesop AESOP'S (Watts) 194.

N255.2. Ass gets progressively worse masters. Finally the farmer beats him living and will not spare his hide when he is dead. Aesop: Aesop AESOP'S (Grosset) 38; Aesop AESOP'S (Watts) 158 (Jupiter grants requests for changes; ends at tanners).

N255.4. Fugitive slave takes refuge in mill house, where he must work harder than ever. Aesop: Aesop AESOP'S (Watts) 215.

N255.5. Daw fleeing from captivity caught in trees by thread around foot. Starves. Aesop: Aesop AESOP'S (Watts) 117.

N255.7* Gentleman marries cook to keep her from leaving. She now refuses to cook as is lady of the house. China: Lum TALES 55-57.

N255.8* Merchant living between noisy blacksmith and coppersmith pays each to move. They move into each other's shops. China: Jagendorf NOODLEHEAD 78-83. Haiti: Courlander PIECE 84-88.

N261. Train of troubles from sparrow's vengeance. A man runs over the dog, friend of the sparrow. Through the sparrow's vengeance, the man loses his horse, his property, and finally his life. Type 248. SEE ALSO: Z40+. Germany (Grimm): De La Mare ANIMAL 160-168; Grimm HOUSEHOLD 244-247.

N270. Crime inevitably comes to light.

N271. Murder will out. SEE ALSO: E231.6; E632; Q551.33.

Aa* The Juniper (Almond) Tree. Wish for child red as blood and white as snow (Z65.1). Mother buried under tree. Stepmother slams chest lid on brother, decapitating. Ties head on and makes sister think she knocked head off. Feeds to father in soup (G61). Sister lays bones under juniper tree, bird rises from tree and bones disappear (E631; E613.0.1). Bird sings his tale to goldsmith and is given chain; cobbler --shoes; miller--millstone. He drops chain for father, shoes for sister, millstone onto stepmother. Returns resuscitated under tree. Germany (Grimm): De La Mare ANIMAL 267-278; Grimm BROTHERS 178-186; Grimm GRIMM'S (World) 171-179; Grimm HOUSEHOLD 186-199; Grimm JUNIPER v. 2 314-332.

Ab* The Rose Tree. Stepmother combs girl's hair on chopping block and beheads. Feeds heart and liver to father and brother. Brother buries under rose tree, tears fall onto coffin box, rose tree flowers and white bird appears in tree. Sings tale to cobbler and receives shoes, etc., same as Juniper Tree. England: Jacobs ENGLISH 16-20; Steel ENGLISH 148-153.

B* The Rose Bush. Girl charged with guarding fig tree turned to rose bush by stepmother. Her cousin breaks rose and it sings tale. Only a fig colored pearl hung on branches will disenchant. Her father returns from sea with gifts for her--hangs black pearl on tree and she is restored. Portugal: Michael PORTUGUESE 9-19.

C* Honey-Guide Bird, second wife killed by husband who disbelieves her tale that honey-guide bird led her to bee tree and first wife stole honey. She reappears as honey guide bird and flies over his head singing tale. He kills bird and puts it in tobacco pouch. Asks for bride price back from her father. Father asks for tobacco to smoke and bird flies out and sings. S. Africa (Kaffir): Carpenter AFRICAN 179-186.

N275.0.1* Criminal believes clouds will tell of murder. Burma: Brockett BURMESE 92-95.

N300 - N399. Unlucky accidents.

N300. Accidental killing or death.

N333. Aiming at fly has fatal results. SEE ALSO: J1193.1; J2102.3; K1082+.

N333.0.1* Gnat challenges lion to duel. Lion harms self slapping at gnat. Aesop: Aesop AESOP'S (Watts) 198-199.

N333.0.2* Bear harms self slapping at bees. They revenge theft of honey. Aesop: Aesop AESOP'S (Viking) 78.

N333.0.3* Husband smashes up furniture after fly, has wife hit it on his nose--broken nose. Iceland: Jagendorf NOODLEHEAD 161-163.

N333.2. Man accidentally killed by bear trying to chase away flies. India: Gaer FABLES 39-41 (kills fly on forehead with rock); Ryder PANCHATANTRA 203-205 (monkey).

N350. Accidental loss of property.

N351. Money (treasure) unwittingly given away. Unlucky man given a loaf which is filled with gold exchanges it for another loaf. Type 841. Mexico: Brenner BOY 76-78. Greece: Lowe LITTLE 22-26; Wilson GREEK 151-156.

N351.0.1* Beggar who prays for king given duck stuffed with coins, sells for a shilling to beggar who is praising God, repeat, king discovers, "Clearly shows is better to praise God than king." Palestine: Dobbs MORE 26-30.

N351.2. Beggar accidentally overlooks money put into his way. Type 842, 947A. Latvia: Durham TIT 81-84 (man closes eyes and misses gold put in path by Bad Luck + N141).

N352. Bird carries off ring which lover has taken from sleeping mistress's finger. He searches for the ring and becomes separated from his mistress.

N352.0.1* Pierre of Provence. Opens casket of sleeping lover, a raven carries off ring, Pierre pursues, is lost at sea. Sold as slave in Alexandria. Magdalena opens hospice for sailors in Provence, his homeland. Fish with ring is found. Pierre as shipwrecked sailor appears. Wed. King of Naples, her father, recognizes marriage. Provence and Naples thus united. France: Picard FRENCH 120-128.

N380. Other unlucky accidents.

N381. Drop of honey causes chain of accidents. Hunter drops honey in a grocery: eats honey; cat chases weasel; dog chases cat; grocer kills dog; all the cause of a bloody feud between villagers. (cf. Z20 (cumulative tales). Thai: Brockett BURMESE 150-152 (gecko, cat, dog, owners of cat and dog quarrel, feud between villagers).

N381.0.1* King drops honey but is beneath his dignity to wipe it up--fly, spider, lizard, cat, dog, owners, villagers, kingdom falls in ensuing war. Burma: Htin KINGDOM 28-30.

N384. Death from fright.

N384.0.2* Soldier in deserted house hears screams in ear, hits at something brushing face and hand is covered with blood. He faints of fright. Companion finds dead mosquito on forehead. U.S. (Ozarks): Littledale GHOSTS 135-138.

N384.2. Death in the graveyard: person's clothing is caught. The person thinks something awful is holding him. He dies of fright. Leach THING 37-39 (dared to stick knife in grave, sticks through own clothing).

N385.1. Person has successive misfortunes while making plans because he forgets to say "If God wills." (cf. J5151.4).

N385.1.1* "Si Dios Quiere." Man to go whether God wills it or no. Turned to frog. Three years later another passerby is asked question, frog pipes up and adds "If heaven wills it." Is restored. Spain: Wiggin TALES 12-13.

N385.1.1.1* Man meets stranger, refuses to say "Si Dios quiere." Turned to frog. Hops toward home. Meets stranger. Still won't say it. Finds self back under bridge. Starts again. Says it. Spain: Sawyer PICTURE 1-10 /Ross BURIED 35-42 /.

N385.1.1.2* After seven years restored as man. Pressed to say "If God wills." Still stubborn. "If God wills it good, if not I am quite able to go into the swamp on my own." Italy: Cimino DISOBEDIENT #10.

N385.1.2* God asks workers each day when they plan to finish. They fail to add "If God wills it" and work is undone each night. God's dog tells them the secret. Dog punished, to serve man (A2513.1) unable to talk, only barks (A2422.1). Haiti: Carter GREEDY 14-17; Thoby-Marcelin SINGING 38-41.

N385.1.3* Man refuses to say "Inshallah" (If God wills it). Disasters befall and he returns home. Wife: "Who is it?" "It is I...if God wills it." Turkey: Downing HODJA 12; Kelsey HODJA 130-138.

N392.1.1. Thief fell by accident on tiger's back and is carried away. Each thinks other is a terrible "leak" which they overheard householder say he feared. SEE ALSO: K1725.2; N691.1.2. Japan: Pratt MAGIC #12 (horse thief takes tiger for horse, tiger fears he is "leak"; +K619.4); Uchida MAGIC 12-21 (wolf; +K619.4). S.E. China: Hume FAVORITE.. CHINA 109-114 (flee in opposite directions).

N392.1.1.1* Valiant chatee maker: thief falls on tiger's back. Tiger thinks this is the terrible "leak" he heard old woman complaining about (J2633). Fool rides tiger home and ties it up to donkey (N691.1.2, J1758.1). Fool then taken as hero for army. Set on horse which runs off, he grabs tree and brandishes. Enemy flees (K1951.2.1). SEE ALSO: K195.1.1 (The Valiant Tailor); K1951.2.1; N691.1.2). India: Baker

TALKING 242-250; Courlander RIDE 46-52; Haviland FAVORITE..INDIA 5-20; Lexau IT pb; Price VALIANT pb; Wiggin FAIRY 406-414.

N392.1.2* Thief steals horse (really demon). Demon thinks thief is "Twilight" mentioned by girl he is trying to abduct, and flees. Thief jumps off in tree and monkey calls demon to return. Man bites monkey's tail and demon flees seeing monkey's agonized expression. India: Ryder PANCHATANTRA 462-464.

N392.1.3* Coward falls on hyena's back and is carried home uttering "war-cry." Ethiopia (Galla): Davis LION'S 93-102.

N399. Additional unlucky accidents.

N399.4* Taking a short cut through the wood a man falls into a pit. Obviously this is an unlucky day...think what might have happened had he taken that dangerous highway! Iran: Shah MULLA 146.

N400 - N699. Lucky Accidents.

N410 - N439. Lucky business ventures.

N411.1. Whittington's cat. A cat in a mouse-infected land without cats sold for a fortune. SEE ALSO: G666.3; J2101 (getting rid of cat).

A* Dick Whittington: As he leaves London the bells call to "Turn again thrice Lord Mayor of London town." England: Brown DICK pb; De La Mare ANIMAL 116-126; De La Mare TALES 33-43; Frost LEGENDS 1-13; Jacobs ENGLISH 174-185 /Arbuthnot FAIRY 27-31 /, /Haviland FAVORITE..ENGLAND 56-75/; Lang BLUE 230-239 /Lang FIFTY 115-121/; Lines DICK pb; Martignoni ILLUSTRATED 223-228; Rackham ARTHUR 30-40; Reeves ENGLISH 222-234; Steel ENGLISH 169-178.

B* Three Lucky Brothers. Inherit a cock, scythe, cat. Sell in land of no cocks, no sickles and no cats. Palace is burned down in fear of cat (J2101). De La Mare ANIMAL 128-132; Kavcic GOLDEN 32-37; Wiggin TALES 98-100. Germany (Grimm): Gag MORE 189-196; Grimm GRIMM'S (Follett) 344-348; Grimm GRIMM'S (Grosset) 23-26; Grimm GRIMM'S (World) 99-102.

C* Cats given to country beset by rats. Man rewarded. Another imitates (J2415.1.0.1). Takes riches to the kingdom. He is given the cat. Italy: Jagendorf PRICELESS 47-58; Vittorini OLD 28-33 /Arbuthnot FAIRY 130-131/, /Arbuthnot ANTHOLOGY 270-271/.

D* Kingdom without a cat. King gives half kingdom and princess to miller's youngest son to stay there with cat. France: Carpenter WONDER..DOGS 25-34.

E* Tsap-Tsarap. Aldar Kase receives one coin for year's wages, buys cat, Tsap-Tsarap. Sold to Shah for six camel loads of gold. Tsap-Tsarap terrifies Shah, returns to Aldar Kase. Karakalpak: Ginsburg KAHA 142-150.

N411.1.1. Cat as sole inheritance. SEE: K1917.3 (Puss in Boots); N411.1.

N411.4.1* Salt in saltless land sold for fortune. Ivan the Fool, youngest brother, attains cargo of salt, sells in saltless land for fortune. Weds princess. +C456. Russia: Ransome OLD 294-315 /Colwell SECOND 21-34/; Zemach SALT pb.

N411.6. Lucky fool sells warming pans in West Indies--used there to boil molasses. Sells coal in Newcastle--miners on strike. U.S. (Massachusetts): Jagendorf NOODLEHEAD 281-283.

N421.1. Progressive lucky bargains. Type 1415. SEE ALSO: Z41.4.3 (lending and repaying); K251.1 + (eaten grain and the cock as damages); N222 (object picked up brings lucky exchange); J2081 (progressively worse bargains); Z47.

N421.1.1* Mistreated orphan given chick. Woman raising him orders to sell it for 1000 cowries, by luck he does so. Order to scatter cowries in cornfield, calabash plants grow, she orders him to smash them, 1000 cowries in each. Given only old nag and sent on journey, horse turns to fine stallion, carries to new city. Hearing of locust devastation in his old village he wants to send for family which had mistreated him and care for them. He is made king of new city, has passed test for a truly virtuous and forgiving man. Upper Volta: Guirma TALES 57-69.

N427* Lucky man tries to incur small loss to guard luck. Takes dates to Cairo to trade. While there he finds a ring lost by King of Egypt and is rewarded. Greece: Wilson GREEK 122-125.

N440 - N499. Valuable secrets learned.

N450. Secrets overheard.

N451. Secrets overheard from animal (demon) conversation. Type 516. SEE: B217.1.1; S268.

N452. Secret remedy overheard in conversation of animals (witches).

A* The Two Travelers. Type 613. Shoemaker has bread for seven days. Tailor for two. Shoemaker shares bread on condition he put out eyes of second (S165). Blinded man hears dead men say that dew on their bodies would restore sight. His sight restored, catches and releases foal, stork, duck, bee. Appointed court tailor. Shoemaker spreads rumors Tailor boasted could recover king's lost crow. Ordered to do so. Duck aids. Task: reproduce palace in wax. Bee provides. Task: create fountain in courtyard. Foal creates. To bring son to King through air. Stork brings. Wed to princess. Shoemaker rests

on gallows and two crows pick out his eyes. Germany (Grimm): Grimm GRIMM'S (Follett) 373-387; Grimm JUNIPER v.2 278-297.

Ab* Three brothers--ravens tell of healing water, blinded brother heals wolf, mouse and queen bee with healing water. Tasks. Build palace = three bees build of flowers. Collect all coins in kingdom = mice. Drive all wolves onto hill = wolf brings all and they eat king, older brothers. Youngest weds princess. Hungary: Lang YELLOW 74-85.

B* True and Untrue. Type 613. Untrue eats up True's provisions, then blinds and leaves. True shelters in tree and hears bear, wolf, fox, and hare talk under tree. Dew from lime tree restores sight. King of England's deaf and dumb daughter could be cured if she ate root of this flower (or toad swallowed crumb that fell from the mouth at communion, must find and retrieve crumb). Spring could be found under stone in palace. Gold chain is buried around orchard and keeps from bearing. True restores sight of self and king. Restores princess's speech. Produces well. Digs up gold chain (D1563.2.1). Is now rich. Weds princess. Brother Untrue is now a beggar. Imitates waiting in tree on Midsummer's Eve. Animals hold tongues as someone overheard them the previous year. Norway: Asbjornsen EAST (Row) 93-100; Undset TRUE 28-36.

C* Elder brother wagers that God is stronger than Devil. Meet Devil in disguise who judges "Devil" stronger. Young brother loses money, horse, eyes. Hears vilas bathing in pool say water will cure. Restores sight, cures princess of leprosy and weds. Cruel brother imitates (J2415). Vilas tear him to pieces. Yugoslavia: Fillmore LAUGHING 241-252. Serbia: Spicer LONG 120-144. Russia: Riordan TALES..CENTRAL 45-52 (restores water to village, sight to princess, overhears evil spirits).

D* Foe shares Friend's food, refuses to share own. They part. Friend hears animal tell how to obtain gold, palace, cure princess and wed. Foe imitates (J2415) and is drowned. Iran: Asia FOLK I 19-25.

E* Poor man sleeping under orange tree hears voice in dream tell to make tea with tree's leaf and cure princess. Weds. Friend imitates. Voice warns to "Go away!" Man ignores. Demons eat. Haiti: Wolkstein MAGIC 71-74.

N452.1.2* Reason for dying man is withering tree in garden. Remedy overheard from conversation of birds and plants. Japan: Uchida MAGIC 2-10.

N455.3. Secret formula for opening treasure mountain is overheard from robbers (Open Sesame). Second man imitates opening of cave, forgets formula and is trapped (J2415). First has body of unfortunate sewn together by tailor for burial. Robbers mark his door, he marks all doors (K415). Robbers hiding in jars of oil are overheard. Disguised dancer stabs robber chief (K916). Type 676. (cf. C761.4, staying too long). Arabian Nights: Lang BLUE /Minard WOMENFOLK 51-64/, /Gruenberg MORE 207-214/; Rackham AR-THUR 206-222. Tagalog: Sechrist ONCE 189-196. Arabia: Mittleman BIRD 43-57.

N455.3.1* Hare shows hyena secret cave of lion-ess. Say "Stone open," "Stone close" to enter and close cave. Hyena forgets phrase and is caught by lioness. Masai: Aardema TALES 41-50.

N455.3.2* Brer Rabbit learns magic word to open Brer Wolf's garden gate. Forgets and cannot escape. U.S. (Black, South Carolina): Faulkner DAYS 80-84.

N455.4. King overhears girl's boast as to what she would do as queen.

A* Type 707. Three Golden Sons.

Aa* Dancing Water, Singing Apple, Speaking Bird. King overhears three sisters say what would do if wed to butler (give whole court to drink from one glass), keeper of wardrobe (clothe all with one piece of cloth), King (bear son with sun on forehead, daughter with moon). King weds, children born, sisters put dog in their place and children exposed. Wife put into treadmill. Fairies give children deer to nurse, purse always full, ring that changes color if other is in danger. Grown. Girl is made to believe by emissary of cruel sisters that she needs Dancing Water to make home perfect. Brother seeks. Three hermits, each older, direct on way. To enter when guardian giants and lion have eyes open. Water leaps from basin to basin. Sent back for Singing Apple, enter when shears are open. Sent for Singing bird. Do not answer when bird speaks, answers and turns to stone. Ring turns color and sister goes to rescue. She does not answer bird, obtains feather from bird and anoints all statues, restoring. They invite king to dinner and bird reveals all. Jacobs EUROPEAN 51-65.

Aaa* Twins as 'lovely as flowers,' queen mother substitutes lion cub and crocodile, fisherman raises children. No quests. Prince climbs tree for apple for sister and bird tells not to eat. This is the dancing apple and will show wicked one who tried to drown them and bird will tell truth. King hears story. Apple settles on head of his stepmother. France: Picard FRENCH 174-182.

Ab* "The Talking Nightingale." Checking on blackout. Night lights forbidden. King checking on blackout overhears three girls, youngest to bear sons and daughter with hair half gold, half silver, sunshine when laughs, rain when cries. Weds. Sisters replace children with dog, cat, stone. Gardener finds exposed and raises. Grown. Sisters persuade girl she needs the Tree of Golden Stars. Elder

brother grooms ogre mother, she turns him to onion to hide and intercedes with her sons. He is taken as brother. Ogre son helps carry tree home. Dancing Water, second brother tries--same. Talking Nightingale, both brothers try. Must not turn round at sound of voices as climb hill for bird. Turned to stone. Sister disguises as boy and goes to try luck, ogress hides in rose, she stops ears with cotton and reaches bird. Sprinkles water and revives stone brothers. Nightingale has them invite king to dine and serves carrots and pearls to nightingale. King feeds bird and bird says cannot eat this just as a worm cannot hear a dog, cat or stone. Tells truth. Life restored. Arabia: Mittleman BIRD 67-81.

Ac* The Sun, the Moon and the Star of Morning. Night Lights forbidden (variation of above). Youngest to bear children like Sun, Moon and Star of Morning. Queen substitutes dog, cat, snake. Children set adrift. Hermit raises. Catches one fish each day for self. One day finds he catches two, asks God why. Child washes up. Catches three, four fish, etc. Grown. Sent into world, to burn hair of hermit's beard if in need. Queen disguised tells sisters she needs the Golden Apple guarded by forty ogres. Brothers have purchased an ivory box "whoever buys will wish he hadn't, whoever doesn't buy will wish he had." Winged horse comes from box, came to fetch apple. Need Golden Bough on which apple grew and all birds of world will come to sing. Second brother fetches. Seek the bird Tsitsinena from the farthest mountain who knows the speech of birds and can teach loveliest songs in world. Two brothers go. Tsitsinena chants "stone stone." They turn to stone to knees, thighs, waist. Burn hermit's hair. He tells Tsitsinena to restore them. She brings water of life, returns with them and tells truth to king. Greece: Wilson GREEK 182-197.

Ad* The Golden-Haired Children. Night lights forbidden. To bear two children with golden hair, boy with half moon on forehead, girl with star. Abandoned. Goat nurses, couple owning goat find and raise. Brother sent for branch from garden of Queen of the Peris. Greets Mother of Devils and kisses. She advises. Drop birds into well and call for key, key comes out of well, open cavern doors, reach in and take whatever touch, return key and do not look to see what you have until home. Is branch with singing bird on each leaf. Seeks mirror of Queen of the Peris. Mother of Devils advises. He opens closed door, closes opened. Gives grass by lion to sheep, meat to lion. Puts out flaming furnace and stokes up smoldering one. Takes mirror and flees. Voice orders furnace to stop him. "I cannot, he put me out." Other furnace is grateful and will not. Etc. Seeks Queen of the Peris. To go through stones, call her name loudly. Legs turn to stone, call again, stone to navel, etc. She then sprinkles him and restores. Returns with him. Peri restores his murdered mother, creates a palace, reveals truth to king, etc. Turkey: Buck FAIRY 237-250.

B* Boy who had a moon on his forehead. King hears gardener's daughter say she'll bear son with moon on his forehead and star on chin. Weds. To beat drum when in labour, other queens persuade her to raise false alarm twice. He doesn't come when she is really in labour. Stone said to have been born. Baby buried in box, dog digs up and swallows to nurture in stomach. Spits up every six months to see how is growing. Dog's keeper sees and four queens have dog killled. He gives prince to cow who swallows. Cow killed. Horse takes. Horse to be killed. Tells prince to dress and ride horse past those assembled to kill it. Twists ears of self and horse and they turn to ugly man and donkey. Works for grain merchant. Princess hears him singing and falls in love. To choose husband, she thrice hangs necklace on him. Wed. To bring in game like brother-in-law. He and horse resume own form, he kills much game, brands brother-in-law in return for food. Reveals true self to wife, degrades brother-in-law. Returns home and restores mother to king. Four queens killed. India: Jacobs INDIAN 188-216; Turnbull FAIRY 50-83 (brother-in-law, horse is Aswa, celestial horse).

C* Silver leaves and Golden Blossoms. Three sisters overheard, youngest to bear two sons with golden hair and silver teeth. Wed. Babies killed. Trees with silver leaves and golden blossoms from grave. Trees caress father and lash new wife. Cut down and burnt. Basil plant with golden tips grows from ashes. Ewe eats and bears lambs with silver wool and golden horns. Thrown in river in basket. Duck girl nurses lambs and they turn to boys. Cat tells truth to king. Wife restored. Bulgaria: Pridham GIFT 116-123. Serbia: Spicer LONG 29-46 (Two sparks become lambs, lambs killed, fleece in box washed away, miller finds two boys, grown he disguises as minstrel and sings tale to king). Gypsy: Manning-Sanders RED 66-71 (lamb eaten, two pieces turn to doves, then boys). Rumania: Lang VIOLET 174-185 (Two ashes become golden fish in river, fisherman finds, turns to babies, magically rapid growth. Sing tale for emperor and twelve cushions supporting empress fall away as they sing).

D* Sky God takes fourth wife who says will bear child of gold and child of silver. Other wives put frogs in place, hunter finds and raises. Wife exiled, wanders and finds. Restored. Sky God, Gala, sends three wives to live on earth: Kwo, barn fowl, must raise head before each drink and ask permission. Dopai, deer, to be hunted by men. Si, spider, to spin only fragile webs. One twin becomes Sun, one Moon. Once a year their mother washes them and this shining dust falls on earth, those men on whom it falls become wealthy. Liberia (Loma): Jablow MAN 71-74.

E* Twelve Young Boys with Golden Hair. Listening king to wed girl providing twelve boys with gold hair. Sisters change letter announcing birth and alter reply, ordering her exiled. Crossing a river she drops all but one of children. Resides in palace of twelve towers. Brothers come from river and play with her remaining son nightly. He gets them to count selves and they forget to re-enter water before cockcrow (forget to count selves and keep getting wrong count). Reveal selves to king, restored. Rumania (N. Moldavia): Ure RUMANIAN 114-116.

N455.4.Z. Fragments. Listening king weds second girl. Girl overheard wishing to wed king (no promise). Sisters wed to baker and cook as wished. Portugal: Lowe LITTLE 95-96.

N475. Secret name overheard by eavesdropper. Type 500. SEE: D2183; E443.3; H323.

N500 - N599. Treasure trove.

N500. Treasure trove. SEE: J1853+.

N511.6.1* Stones of Plouhinec. Stones go to river to drink on New Year's Eve and leave treasure uncovered, must carry crowfoot, trefoil, and make human sacrifice to obtain treasure. Innocent lad carving cross on one of stones that evening is meant as sacrifice, stone with cross shelters him and crushes schemer. France: Picard FRENCH 113-119.

N530. Discovery of treasure.

N531.1. Dreams of treasure on bridge. A man dreams that if he goes to a distant city he will find treasure on a certain bridge. Finding no treasure, he tells his dream to a man who says that he too has dreamed of treasure at a certain place. He describes the place which is the first man's home. The latter returns home and finds the treasure. Type 1645. Child Study Association CASTLES 69-77 (Stone dog has seven gold dogs inside). Italy (Verona): Jagendorf PRICELESS 35-39.

N531.1.1* Papenburg bridge in Amsterdam, pot of money in garden in Oosterlitens in Frisia. Visiting Dominie later interprets inscription on pot "under me lies a bigger pot." (N535.0.1). Netherlands: Hardendorff TRICKY 33-39.

N531.1.2* Suitor and bride with same dream, treasure under floor of his chalet on Trichlegg Alp. Switzerland (German): Duvoisin THREE 162-166.

N531.1.3* Peddler of Swaffham, London Bridge, +A1465. England: Jacobs CROCK pb; Jacobs MORE 98-110; Reeves ENGLISH 72-79. England (Norfolk): Colwell ROUND 61-63; Williams-Ellis ROUND 161-165. Crossley-Holland PEDLAR pb. Ireland: Sawyer WAY 239-247

/Arbuthnot ANTHOLOGY 181-183/ (Peddler of Ballaghadereen). Netherlands: De Leeuw LEGENDS..HOLLAND 21-27.

N531.3. Dream of treasure bought. Treasure has been seen by man's soul absent in sleep in form of a fly. The purchaser of the dream finds the treasure. Japan: Novak FAIRY 153-155 (wasp circles pine saying dig here, thief overhears dream and digs first, dream buyer finds empty pot with inscription "First of seven" and digs remaining six, N535.0.1); Uchida MAGIC 93-100 (bee tells in dream of white camelia tree with gold underneath--buyer works as gardener for two years before finding tree).

N534.9* Ferryman agrees to carry ill man upstream on New Year. Man dies en route. Looking for coffin, a cache of money is discovered. Dead was a thief meeting others here to divide loot. China: Kendall SWEET 108-112.

N535.0.1* Inscription on treasure pot "The first of seven" or "Under me lies a bigger pot." Netherlands: De Leeuw LEGENDS..HOLLAND 21-27; Hardendorff TRICKY 33-39 (N531.1). Japan: Novak FAIRY 153-155 (N531.3).

N600 - N699. Other lucky accidents.

N611.1. Criminal accidentally detected. "That is the first" sham wise man. The sham wise man employed to detect theft is feasted. As the servants enter with food he remarks to his wife, "That is the first" (course). The servants, thinking they are detected, confess. Type 1641. SEE ALSO: N66.1; +N688. Denmark: Hatch THIRTEEN 94-106. Germany (Grimm): Gag TALES 77-84; Grimm GRIMM'S (Follett) 52-54; Wiggin TALES 83-85. France: Ross BURIED 113-120. Italy: Manning-Sanders GIANNI 145-160. Leach LUCK 60-61.

N611.1.1. Name of criminal accidentally spoken out (identical with ordinary word in speech). India: Jacobs INDIAN 104-109; Williams-Ellis ROUND 67-72 ("Oh tongue what have you done?" Thief named Tongue, Jihya, +N688). Burma: Brockett BURMESE 96-105 (It was luck). China: Wyndham TALES..CHINA 55-62.

N611.2. Criminal accidentally detected. "That is the first"--sleepy woman counting her yawns. Robber hearing her flees. U.S. (Appalachia): Chase WICKED 205-214.

N611.5* Each of forty thieves eavesdrops under window of sham wise man and they think he is counting them. Actually he is counting off the forty days he was given to discover stolen chest. Thieves confess. Norway: Asbjornsen EAST 25-30. Arabia: Carpenter ELEPHANT'S 49-57. Persia: Hardendorff FROG'S 46-58. Rumania: Ure RUMANIAN 26-32; Walker

STARGAZER pb. Russia: Sheehan FOLK 51-60. Spain: Haviland FAVORITE..SPAIN 58-69 /Gruenberg MORE 261-264/.

N612. Numskull talks to himself and frightens robbers away.

N612.2* Doctor 'Know-it-all' looks for picture in book. "I know you're in there!" Thief in oven thinks he has been detected. Germany (Grimm): Gag TALES 77-78; Grimm GRIMM'S (Follett) 52-54; Wiggin TALES 83-85.

N612.3* Opium eater spends night in haunted house. Talks about supper and unwittingly names four ogres. They flee. "Master Whiskers (lobster), I'll enjoy eating you!" etc. Burma: Brockett BURMESE 63-66.

N612.4* Couple send servant to 'buy' a story. Ignorant farmer sells one--makes up story by describing movements of crane in field. Thief hears old man repeat story and thinks he describes self. "He comes." "He creeps." Robbers flee. Korea: Anderson BOY 53-58; Carpenter KOREAN 183-188.

N620. Accidental success in hunting or fishing.

N621.2* Man shoots and misses mark: "That is how the captain shoots." Misses again: "That is how the general shoots." Hits mark: "That is how I shoot." Turkey: Downing HODJA 84; Kelsey HODJA 7-14; Shah MULLA 56-57; Walker WATERMELONS 46-48.

N624. Man falls into well and accidentally kills cobra. Rewarded. Thai: Brockett BURMESE 111-118.

N640. Accidental healing.

N642.2* Blind man cured by blow on head. He has outwitted lion but companion makes attempt on his life. Sight restored, he kills companion and claims lion's wife. +K1715.12.1. Congo (Luban): Burton MAGIC 119-121.

N650. Life saved by accident.

N659.3* Bear climbing pear tree in dark swipes treed numskull with fruit and he cries, "No, thank you!" Bear falls in terror and is killed. Turkey: Kelsey HODJA 54-62.

N680. Lucky accidents--miscellaneous.

N683.1* Stranger accidentally chosen Mayor. First man to cross bridge to be Mayor, Is a broommaker. Ireland: Danaher FOLKTALES 42-48 (Limerick, Mayor of).

N685.1* Fool repeats rhymes learned at auspicious moments, is thought wise. Wed to daughter of rich man. China: Kendall SWEET 100-105.

N688. What is in the dish: "Poor crab." Type 1614. A sham wise man named Crab is to tell what is in a covered dish (crabs). In despair he says "poor crab" and is given credit for knowing. SEE ALSO: H541.1.2; K1956; +N611.1. Germany (Grimm): Gag TALES 77-84 (fish, +N612.2); Grimm GRIMM'S (Follett) 52-54; Wiggin TALES 83-85. Arabia: Carpenter ELEPHANT'S 49-57 (What in hand--locust). India: Jacobs INDIAN 104-109; Wiggin TALES 393-396; Williams-Ellis ROUND 67-72 (frog, +N611.1). Turkey: Walker STARGAZER pb (grasshopper). Wales: Sheppard-Jones WELSH 32-35. Russia: Sheehan FOLK 51-60 (beetle). Spain: Haviland FAVORITE..SPAIN 58-69 (What did I have in my mind? Took out of my mouth? Put in my pocket? Answer, "cigar", "Poor Juan Cigarron") /Fenner TIME 200-208/, /Gruenberg MORE 261-264/. Norway: Asbjornsen NORWEGIAN 25-30. France: Ross BURIED 113-120. China: Wyndham TALES..CHINA 55-62 (cat in the bag). Leach LUCK 60-61.

N688.1. Doctor-know-all accidentally saves raja. Roof caves in after he has dragged raja out with the intention of killing him and putting an end to all of his questions. Arabia: Carpenter ELEPHANT'S 49-57 (is feigning madness to excuse self from duties as diviner).

N688.2* Sham wise man to guess contents of box, overhears answer but forgets, on seeing fireflies he recalls--fireflies. Thailand: Brockett BURMESE 111-118.

N691.1.2. Stupid man pushes tiger in the dark, ties it up and saddles it believing it to be a horse. It happens to be the tiger for whose capture a reward has been offered. SEE: J1758.5; K1951.1A (Chase), J, H, I; K1951.2.1; N392.1.1 (Valiant Chatee Maker).

N691.1.2.1* Princess gets cowardly husband drunk and sends on horse loaded with liquor. Jar breaks, lion drinks and becomes intoxicated and drunken coward rides the lion home thinking it is his horse. Ethiopia (Galla): Davis LION'S 93-102.

N696.1.1* Man falls out of tree and frightens enemy away. SEE ALSO: K335.1.1.1. Thailand: Brockett BURMESE 111-118.

N700 - N799. Accidental encounters.

N710. Accidental meeting of hero and heroine.

N711.1. King (prince) finds maiden in woods (tree) and marries her. Type 450, 706, 710. SEE: P253.2B (Twelve Brothers et. al.).

N711.1.1. The Lassie and her Godmother. Raised by godmother. Girl opens forbidden door and star, moon and sun fly out. To become ugly or dumb, chooses latter. Prince sees in tree and weds. Foster mother steals children and wife is accused of eating them. To be burned at stake. Foster mother returns with children. Type 710. Norway: Asbjornsen EAST (Doubleday) 54-60.

N712.2* Prince first sees heroine as she comes forth from her hiding. Daughter sells self as sacrifice to river dragon for money to restore father's eyesight. Dragon sends her back in huge lotus. Lotus is taken to king. She emerges only at night. King sees and weds. Father's sight is restored. Korea: Carpenter KOREAN 81-86; Child Study Association CASTLE 135-139.

N721. Runaway horse carries bride to her lover. Bridegroom unwittingly hires a horse belonging to his rival for his bride to ride to the wedding. A storm arises and the horse carries her to his master. France: Arbuthnot FAIRY 122-124 (takes path home in dark). SEE ALSO: B151.1.1.0.4.

N731.2.1* Father-son combat. Neither knows who the other is. The Blind King and the Magic Bird: son prophesied to kill father thrown into stream and raised by miller. Kills father in self-defense when father thinks he is queen's lover. Daybreak reveals identity after deed. Blinded at coronation. Eyesight retored by feather of magic bird fetched by girl of noble birth. Moorish slave girl brings bird. Wed. Portugal: Michael PORTUGUESE 179-185.

N770. Experiences leading to adventure.

N773. Adventure from following animal to cave (lower world). Type 301.

N773.0.1* Marvelous cave with tree bearing agate gems is found when deer is followed into cave. Never found again. Property of Spirit Kaboniyan. Cave named for man who found--Ganoway. Philippines (Tinguian): Sechrist ONCE 78-80.

N776. Light seen from tree lodging place at night leads to adventures. Type 130, 327. SEE: K1611C (Hop o' My Thumb).

N777. Dropped ball (basket) leads to adventure when recovery is attempted. (cf. D1313.1.1, magic ball of thread).

N777.0.1* Dumpling (rice ball) falls down hole in kitchen floor and old woman falls after into another country. She meets three jizos who warn of oni. Third hides her behind his sleeve. Oni smells human (G84). She giggles and is caught (C460.1). Must cook for the oni. Steals their magic rice paddle and flees. +J1791.3.2.2. Japan: Bang GOBLINS 47-57; Hearn JAPANESE 21-28; Hearn BOY 27-32 /Minard WOMENFOLK 44-50/, /Greene CLEVER 32-39/; Wiggin TALES 438-441.

N777.0.2* Dumpling rolls down hole and old man follows. Leads to Jizo, whom old man offers half of dumpling. Jizo tells man to climb onto his head and crow when ogres come and begin gambling (G303.16.19.4.1). Ogres flee leaving gold. Greedy old man next door tries (J2415), laughs when smallest ogre catches nose in

tree branch, is caught and beaten (C460.1).
Japan: Stamm DUMPLINGS pb; Uchida MAGIC
123-131.

N777.0.3* Dumpling rolls down hole. Voice calls
"Roll right in." Man rolls other objects down
hole then falls in himself. In mouse country
(B221.2), they entertain him and give magic
golden hammer and room fills with food. Greedy
old man next door imitates (J2415), jumps at
mice calling "Meow" and is attacked and driven
out. Japan: Sakade JAPANESE 60-73; Scofield
HOLD 40-46; Yoda ROLLING pb.

N777.2. Bucket dropped into well leads to adventures. SEE: Q2.1.1Da.

N777.4. Spindle dropped into well leads to adventures. SEE: Q2.1.1Eb; Q2.1.2A.

N800 - N899. Helpers.

N810. Supernatural helpers.

N813. Helpful genie. Types 561, 562.

A* "Something wonderful": Prince seeks
"something wonderful." Catches little blue
demon, is given magic food providing satchel
for freedom. Catches again--given magic
sword and wish granting whistle. He wishes a
castle, beheads king's army with sword then
wishes heads back on again. Finland:
Manning-Sanders DEVILS 30-38.

B* "The Magic Belt": Shipwrecked prince
found by "My Name is My Name" who provides
food, boat, magically. Lad lives with "My"
seven years then goes into world. Given
magic wishing belt. Pirates put him in a cask.
He uses belt and denounces pirates. He rescues king's daughter from demon's rock with
aid of belt. Weds. Brittany: Manning-Sanders
PRINCES 57-65.

C* The Swan Princess coveted. Onni took
robe of one of three ducks. Weds. Prince
covets. Sets Onni task: 1. bring tablecloth
woven with moon and stars--wife makes. 2.
bring "no-so-what" from "no-so-where."
Wife gives handkerchief token. Aunt of wife
recognizes and calls her birds. Sends to sis-
ter--repeat. Third calls toads, oldest toad
leads. He asks "No-so-what" to follow him
(D1831). Trades magic table for ship captain's
magic soldier producing anvil, defeats kings.
Finland: Bowman TALES..TUPA 105-115.

D* Blue and Green Wonders. Takes wrap of
one of three geese, wed, king covets. Tasks:
Fetch silver apple tree with golden apples from
fortieth kingdom. Wife weaves shawl to provide food and strength. Sister recognizes
needlework and aids--throw shawl over tree
and it shrinks to carry home. Task: diamond
lion in fiftieth kingdom--same, second sister.
Task: bring Blue and Green wonders. Third
sister can't locate. Asks Earth Mother, his

tears wake her from winter sleep. She calls
Air-Flyers, Earth Runners, crawlers and creep-
ers. Frog from slumbering Marsh takes. Blue
and Green joins lad since he feeds Blue and
Green. Giant owners never feed him. Trades
for magical objects, defeats king. +D831.
Latvia: Huggins BLUE 101-102.

E* Go "I Know Not Whither" and fetch "I Know
Not What." Archer shoots dove, turns to girl,
weds. Her magical servants weave tapestry,
king hears of her and sends archer on first.
Follows silver ball, wipes face with napkin--
three maids and mother recognize. Mother calls
fish, frog knows. Leads over fiery river.
Shows kindness to "I Know Not What", sharing
food. "I Know Not What" joins him, carries
off king. Archer and wife named king and
queen. Crown token falls onto their hands
from fate. Russia: Manning-Sanders SOR-
CERORS 9-23.

Fa* "I-Know-Not-What-Of-I-Know-Now-Where":
Archer wounds dove which turns to maid.
Weds. Wife weaves wondrous rug. Tsar hears
of her, sets tasks to rid of husband. 1. See
Tsar's father in other world. Takes counselor
of Tsar along and has taken father's place
pulling cart while he talks with him. 2. Bring
Kot Bayvn the talking cat from Thrice-Ninth
kingdom. Wife gives three hats, pair of pincers and three rods. Grabs cat's leg with pincers and beats till iron and brass rods break,
tin rod bends. Cat agrees to come down from
pole and tell all stories it knows. 3. Task:
go I know not where and buy I know not what.
Wife calls birds, fish, none know. Gives husband ball of wool to follow and towel to dry self.
Call to Baba Yaga's hut to turn on chicken leg
to him. She sees towel and says her daughter
made it. She asks frog of Green Marsh to
lead him. Finds "nothing" and orders to follow. +D831Bb. Russia: Downing RUSSIAN
100-121; Riordan TALES..CENTRAL 243-261.

Fb* Above + Baba Yaga sets task. Bring
deer with golden horns from thrice nine lands.
Three maidens in palace recognize kerchief of
sister. Their mother calls birds, beasts, frog
leads to "Shmat the Wise." +D831. Russia:
Whitney IN 1-24.

N816. Santa Claus as bringer of Christmas gifts.
Sawyer THIS 68-75; Sawyer THIS 119-138.

N816.0.1* Bishop Nicholas of Myra visits Holland
as St. Nicholas. Netherlands: De Leeuw LEG-
ENDS 66-77.

N816.0.2* Man in New Amsterdam rubs meerschaum pipe (D1622.4) and St. Nicholas appears and provides food, fine house, unseen
hands beat burgomaster out of town. Arbuthnot FAIRY 191-196.

N816.1* The Magi as bringers of Christmas gifts
(January 6). Sawyer THIS 86-98; Sawyer WAY
151-170. Puerto Rico: Belpre TIGER 105-

11 (jealous horse get fireflies to fake star and misguide Magi).

N816.2* Baboushka as bringer of Christmas gifts. Russia: Colwell YOUNGEST 249–252; Robbins BABOUSHKA pb.

N820. Human helper.

N831.1. Mysterious housekeeper. Men find their house mysteriously put in order. Discover that it is done by a girl (frequently an animal transformed into a girl). (cf. B653.3). SEE: B651.1 (fox bride); B652.2 (crane maiden); F1041.4.1; G530.2Da; Z65.1 (Snow White). SEE ALSO: D318.1.1.

Clam maiden allowed to stay ten years if husband does not break tabu. He does not. China: Cheney TALES 81–86 (N831.1).

Fox bride of Raven. +F302.4.2.2. Eskimo: Melzack RAVEN 53–60.

Fox, +F302.4.2.2. S. China: Hume FAVORITE ..CHINA 99–100.

Lame duck taken in by old couple keep house as girl in their absence. Neighbors spy and burn her nest. She leaves (B651.2). Hutchinson CANDLELIGHT 117–122.

Maid from shell sent as a reward for filial piety. China: Carpenter TALES..CHINESE 117–123.

Prince to wed princess is given incense box-- mouse emerges and cooks for him, he burns mousely jacket. Ceylon: Tooze WONDERFUL 59–63.

Snail, leaves when seen. China: Birch CHINESE 37–42.

Snail leaves when husband tells of her and tries to salt her. China: Kendall SWEET 66– 72.

Snail leaves when man tries to touch. China: Wolkstein WHITE pb.

N831.1.0.1. Mysterious housekeeper is coveted by lord. Exorbitant requests are made on peasant but with her magical aid all are met. Type 765. Italy: Manning-Sanders GIANNI 108–118 (maid in box). Russia: Titiev HOW 36–53 (dog becomes wife, hides husband from Khan's son, tells hare to find him). Thailand: Brockett BURMESE 8–17 (maid from elephant tusk). Nepal: Hitchcock KING 80–96 (dog, her sister, aid in tasks, third task-- bring tiger's milk, he rides tiger, sprays king with milk). Greece: Wilson GREEK 31– 39 (tortoise). China: Chang CHINESE 58–63 (golden carp).

N831.1.2* Mysterious house intruder. Men find their house mysteriously disturbed. Discover that it is done by a girl (old woman). She leaves in fright.

A* Goldilocks and the Three Bears. Brooke GOLDEN; Colwell YOUNGEST 44–50; Galdone THREE pb; Gruenberg FAVORITE 372–375; Hutchinson FIRESIDE 27–32; Richardson GREAT 27–35; Rockwell THREE 1–13; Stobbs STORY pb; TALL..NURSERY 37–45; Tarrant FAIRY 9–19.

B* Little Old Woman and Three Bears. England: De La Mare ANIMAL 23–28; Haviland FAIRY 36–43; Jacobs ENGLISH 96–101 /Arbuthnot ANTHOLOGY 150–151/; Lang GREEN 222– 226; Rackham ARTHUR 200–205; Steel ENGLISH 13–17 /Arbuthnot FAIRY 89–91/, /Martignoni ILLUSTRATED 69–73/.

C* Scrapefoot: Fox enters house, same as above. Jacobs MORE 94–97 /Association TOLD ..GREEN 24–29/; Wiggin TALES 233–235.

N884.1. Robber helps king. U.S. (Appalachia): Chase GRANDFATHER 65–74 (Robin Hood).

P. SOCIETY

P230. Parents and children.

P231.3.1* Mother love. Poor woman with twelve children drinks rice water left from their meal. Wishes she had another child so would have one more pot of rice water. India: Spellman BEAUTIFUL 31–32.

P236.2. Supposed chest of gold induces children to care for aged father. They think that the chest contains the inheritance. India: Jacobs INDIAN 268–269.

P236.2.1* Father sent to school, friend suggests box of stones ruse. Russia: Wyndham TALES.. RUSSIA 47–56. Russia (Ukraine): Courlander RIDE 137–141.

P242. Children punished for father's sins. Leopard and antelope make peace pact, violator's sin to rest upon children's children. Ethiopia (Shankilla): Davis LION'S 140–143.

P250. Brothers and sisters.

P250.2* Family solidarity. One falcon breaks wing. Three brothers stay to care for it until spring. Native American: Bierhorst FIRE 58–65.

P253.2. Sister faithful to transformed brothers. Type 451.

A* The Seven Ravens. At daughter's birth seven sons sent for water drop pitcher, father curses them and they turn to ravens (D150). Sister seeks at sun, moon, stars (H1232). She is given a bone to open the Glass Mountain, loses it and uses her own little finger (F751). She eats from their plates and cups and puts ring token in one cup (H94.1). They identify ring and are re-united, regaining human form. Germany (Grimm): Diamond SEVEN pb; Grimm BROTHERS 30–33; Grimm GRIMM'S (Follett) 285–289; Grimm GRIMM'S (Grosset) 264–267; Grimm GRIMM'S (World) 282–285; Grimm SEVEN pb. Poland: Wojciechowski WINTER 49–54 (+ burns their cast off feathers).

B* Twelve Brothers. Father vows to kill twelve sons if wife bears daughter. Red flag as signal. Sister with star on forehead seeks. Keeps house for them. Breaks twelve lilies in garden; they turn to ravens. Disenchanted if she refrains from speaking or laughing for seven years (D758.2). She spins in tree top and king sees and weds (N711.1). To be killed for silence. Twelve ravens arrive and turn to brothers. Seven years up. Germany (Grimm): Grimm GRIMM'S (Grosset) 41–47; Grimm GRIMM'S (World) 247–253); Grimm HOUSEHOLD 56–61; Lang RED 279–285 /Lang FIFTY 335–340/; Minard WOMENFOLK 36–43.

C* Twelve Wild Ducks. Wish for girl red as blood and white as snow (Z65.1). Troll grants wish but claims twelve brothers. Turn to wild ducks. Sister keeps house for them. Task to disenchant: weaving twelve caps, twelve shirts, twelve scarves of thistledown without speaking or laughing. King sees her gathering thistledown and takes to wed. Queen mother throws children into snakepit and smears mouth of heroine with blood accusing her of eating young. At execution princes arrive. Sweaters all finished except for sleeve of youngest. Norway: Asbjornsen NORWEGIAN 182–189; Asbjornsen EAST (Row) 46–53 /Sheehan FOLK 14–21/. Andersen: Dalgliesh ENCHANTED 1–20; Wiggin FAIRY 80–96.

D* The Six Swans. Lost king must agree to wed hag's daughter. Hides his six sons and daughter from her. She finds and throws shirts over boys turning to ravens. Sisters seek. Rest same as P253.2C. Germany (Grimm): De La Mare ANIMAL 304–318; Gag MORE 139–154; Grimm GRIMM'S (Follett) 290–298; Grimm GRIMM'S (Grosset) 107–113; Grimm GRIMM'S (Scribner's) 134–139; Grimm GRIMM'S (World) 114–120; Grimm HOUSEHOLD 198–203; Holme TALES 109–112; Lang YELLOW 5–11; Shubb ABOUT 83–87.

Ea* Girl, Ogress and Nine Brothers. Spindle to be set by door if girl, ax if boy. Brothers vow to leave home if a boy is born. Ogress changes sign. Sister seeks with faithful dog. Follows rolling cake made of her own tears (D1313.1.2). Ogress tries to get her to cool feet in pool, dog warns. Ogress kicks dog breaking hind leg. Repeat—front leg. Repeat—destroys dog with charm. Vieno now bathes and ogress splashes water on her face chanting "Your body to me, mine to you." She goes to live with brothers as sister. Sister must tend cattle. Brother overhears her sing of plight. Plots for her to ask water of ogress to bathe sore eyes. Repeats charm in reverse and ogress is driven out. Finland: Bowman TALES 116–125.

Eb* Seven brothers, wrong sign, boys serve ogre, girl hides, forgets to share with cat and is betrayed, boys push ogre into pit, tabu—picking anything from grave (pit), picks rosemary—brothers turn to doves must find Mother-of-Time to disenchant + Grandfather-Know-It-All (H1273.2B). Italy: Toor GOLDEN 107–119.

F* Katrina and the Seven Werewolves. Mother gives seven sons as werewolves for daughter. Sister sews seven shirts, seven towels, seven sheets and seeks. They are men at night. Task to disenchant. Sit seven years on oak stump in forest without speaking, laughing or sleeping. Kings finds and weds. Queen Mother accuses her of eating child, has been abandoned to wolves. On way to execution seven birds ask king to wait. Seven brothers arrive with baby. One misses an eye for she shed one tear when king took her from stump. Latvia: Huggins BLUE 32–42.

G* The Three Ravens. Father curses brothers.

They turn to ravens, sister seeks, fox tells can disenchant by not speaking for three years, wed to count, his mother accuses her of killing children. At execution, three brothers arrive with children whom fairy has saved. Switzerland: Müller-Guggenbühl SWISS 166-170.

P253.2.0.1* Sister faithful to transformed brother.

A* Little Brother and Little Sister. Type 450. Brother and sister flee stepmother, who enchants brooks. If he drinks of first to become tiger, second--wolf, third--fawn. He becomes a fawn (D110). They live in house in woods, he entices hunters on, leads king to her door. Wed. Stepmother has her killed after childbirth and puts her own daughter in place (K1911). Her ghost returns nightly to nurse baby for three nights (E323.1.1). King catches her on third visit after nursemaid overhears her telling fawn she'll come but once more. Stepmother is burnt and fawn brothers restored. Germany (Grimm): Darrell ONCE 66-70; Grimm BROTHERS 47-54; Grimm GRIMM'S (Follett) 192-201; Grimm GRIMM'S (Scribner's) 29-36; Grimm GRIMM'S (World) 376-382; Grimm HOUSEHOLD 65-71; Grimm JUNIPER v. 1 42-54; Lang RED 68-71 /Lang FIFTY 30-36/; Wiggin FAIRY 174-180.

B* Bona and Nello. Type 450. Stepmother has father abandon children in woods. They scatter lupine pods to find way home. Third time scatter bran and it blows away (S300). Stream warns Bona not to let Nello drink. He turns to sheep with golden horns (D130) and she is beautified as he drinks. They live in cave, king sees and weds. Stepmother throws in sea and substitutes own daughter, shark swallows Bona (K1911). Sheep calls to sister in shark, sentry overhears and summons king and she is rescued, sheep restored. Italy: Baker GOLDEN 101-110.

C* Sister Alionushka and Brother Ivanuska. Alionushka warns Ivanushka not to drink from hoofprints of cow, horse, he drinks from goat's (D130) hoofprint--turns to goat. Merchant weds Alionushka. Witch throws her into river with stone on neck and takes place. Goat calls to her in river each day, overheard, she is thrown up, goat turns three somersaults and becomes brother. Russia (Tolstoy): Daniels FALCON 61-66; Ransome OLD 231-241; Riordan TALES.. CENTRAL 107-111.

D* The Stag Prince. Drinks from puddles, turns to stag, keeps sister in tree. Padishah sees reflected in spring. Try to cut tree but stag licks each night and restores tree. Witch disguised as old woman cooks foolishly under tree and third day sister cannot keep silent and comes down to show her how--caught, wed. Jealous slave girl pushes into pool and takes place, fish swallows. Slave girl feigns ill, needs stag's heart. Stag overheard talking to fish and she is rescued, stag restored. Turkey: Buck FAIRY 81-88.

E* Pleiad and the Star of Dawn. Pleiad and her son, Star of Dawn, flee stepmother. Comb = wood, ribbon = plain, salt = lake. Stepmother drowned. Star of Dawn drinks of lamb's footprint (D555.1), turns to lamb. Prince sees her reflection in tree and weds. Queen Mother drowns her in pool, kills lamb--Pleiad buries bones of lamb. Orange tree grows with one orange, no one can pick but Pleiad. It grows to heaven with her and they become Pleiad and the Star of Dawn (A773.9). Greece: Wilson GREEK 11-20.

F* The House in the Woods. Abandoned twins Juan and Maria. Enter house where food appears, voice bids welcome. Grow up there. Prince sees Maria, weds. Juan weds prince's sister. Philippines (Tagalog): Sechrist ONCE 128-131.

P260. Relations by law (in-laws).

P262.2. Imagined death of mothers-in-law causes mutual mistaken mourning by husband and wife. Thailand: Brockett BURMESE 106-110.

P265.2. Glib son-in-law, Mr. Ripe, has answer for everything. Reticent son-in-law, Mr. Raw, replies, "It's only natural" to each question but later shows wisdom behind his comment. Thailand: Asia FOLK..FOUR 54-51.

P300 - P399. Other social relationships.

P320. Hospitality.

P327.1* Barmecide feast. Host places imaginary feast before guest. Guest gets 'drunk' and strikes host. Gruenberg MORE 385-387; Rackham ARTHUR 190-195.

P332. Selfish guest expels host. Porcupine asks rabbit (snakes) for hospitality. When rabbit complains of being pricked, porcupine tells him to leave if he doesn't like it. Aesop: Aesop AESOP'S (Grosset) 89; Aesop AESOP'S (Viking) 55.

P360. Master and servant.

P361. Faithful servant. Type 516. SEE: K2213.5.1; S268.

P361.10* The Inseparable Friends. Chief has eye of slave put out in attempt to stop friendship with son. Son puts out own eye in sympathy. Slave's arm broken--son breaks his own. Son walks into mouth of marauding serpent. Slave follows. They cut liver and kill serpent, rescue villagers inside (F912, K952). Congo: Burton MAGIC 112-116.

P700 - P799. Society-- miscellaneous motifs.

P710. Nations.

P711.10* Megu sends messengers to scrape earth

from boots of foreigners leaving Ethiopia. Soil is most precious thing they own. Ethiopia (Tigrai): Davis FIRE 127-130.

Q. REWARDS AND PUNISHMENTS.

Q0. Rewards and punishments.

Q1.1. Gods (saints)in disguise reward hospitality and punish inhospitality. Usually the hospitable person is poor, the inhospitable rich. SEE ALSO: J2073.1 (do all day what begun in morning); K1811.1. Denmark: Haviland DENMARK 77-90.

A* Type 750D. Three brothers each granted a wish by an angel visitor (for sharing pears). They choose 1. plenty of wine, 2. sheep, 3. a good wife. River is turned to wine, pigeons to sheep. Later as beggar angel is refused hospitality by the two elder and he takes their wine and sheep away. The youngest and his wife are rewarded for hospitality. Yugoslavia: Courlander RIDE 131-136; Fillmore LAUGHING 229-240; Frost LEGEND 245-249. Serbia: Spicer LONG 98-115. Rumania: Ure RUMANIAN 160-166.

B* Ox with four horns. On Christmas Eve man is visited by travelers, serves kid, given wish for each horn. Neighbor imitates (J2415) next year. Says ox had four horns. Misuses wishes. Horns wished on and off wife's head (J2075). Association TOLD..GREEN 165-174.

C* The Silver Tracks. Christ as beggar leaves behind two silver bolts and four golden horseshoes and tells to follow silver tracks and come visit him. Older brother turns back, bolts turn to wood. Second brother same. Poor man inquires after sights seen on way. Returns home from visit and finds years have passed (D2011). Goes back to beggar's house--really Christ's Garden of Paradise. Yugoslavia: Fillmore LAUGHING 267-286; Frost LEGEND 250-262.

D* Poor couple welcome traveling magician on Passover. He produces feast. He is prophet Elijah. Jewish: Shulevitz MAGICIAN pb.

Q2. Kind and unkind. Churlish person disregards requests of old person (animal) and is punished. courteous person (often youngest brother or sister) complies and is rewarded. SEE ALSO: D757.1; J2400 (foolish imitation); Q285.1.1 (tongue-cut sparrow).

A* Goggle Eyes. Eldest son refuses water to Goggle Eyes in tower. Is beaten by all sticks

in forest. Youngest gives drink. Dwarf appears and gives wishing ring. Wales: Hampden GYPSY 133-138.

Q2.1. Kind and unkind girls. Type 480. (cf. J2415). (After Roberts.) SEE ALSO: D757.1; J2415.10; R221.

Q2.1.1* Following the River subtype.

A* The Drink of Water Group.

Aa* Toads and Diamonds. A girl gives an old lady at the spring a drink. She is blessed with beauty and jewels (flowers) fall from her mouth at each word (D1554.2). Her stepsister imitates and is unkind. Snakes and toads fall from her mouth and she becomes ugly. A king sees the first girl and weds her. Perrault: Hutchinson CANDLELIGHT 93-100; Lang BLUE 295-298; Perrault FAMOUS 117-126; Perrault PERRAULT'S (Dodd) 42-46; Perrault PERRAULT'S (Dover) 59-64; Rackham ARTHUR 196-198.

B* The Heads in the Well Group.

Ba* The Three Heads in the Well. Girl leaving cruel stepmother shares food with old man. He gives a wand to cause hedge to part, advises to obey three heads at the well. She washes and combs them on request. They wish her to be lovely, have sweet voice and wed prince, etc. Stepsister imitates, is unkind, given leprosy, harsh voice and cobbler husband. Cobbler has ointment to cure leprosy and harsh voice after wedding. Queen dies of rage and stepdaughter and cobbler stepdaughter and cobbler sent far away. England: Finlay TATTERCOATS 78-86; Jacobs ENGLISH 232-237; Opie CLASSIC 156-161; Reeves ENGLISH 116-126; Sheehan FOLK 1-7; Steel ENGLISH 156-163.

Bb* Bushy Bride. Good sister brushes three heads in well and kisses them. Given gifts of beauty, gold from hair and mouth to drop. Stepsister is rude and is given nose four ells long, jaw three ells long, and fir bush in forehead, ashes to drop from mouth. Brother with picture of sister. King sees and sends for her. Stepmother casues her to go overboard en route. King weds ugly stepsister. Throws brother into snakepit. Maid comes thrice and talks to dog who accompanies to kitchen. Third night king watches and catches. Norway: Lang RED 316-323.

C* The House of Cats Group.

Ca* The House of Cats. A girl takes service as maid in house of cats. She may choose as reward to be dipped in gold or oil. She chooses oil, is dipped in gold. To look at cock when it crows. Does so and star grows on forehead. Unkind sister tries. Chooses gold, is dipped in oil. To look at donkey when it brays--donkey tail grows on forehead. Unkind sister sent to wed prince with veil over face--cats call out and warn that he has wrong girl. Italy (Tuscany): Hampden HOUSE 3-8. Italy: Lang CRIMSON 219-228; Leach LION 43-51. Sleigh NORTH 116-129.

Cb* The Three Mermaids. Sea monster entices girl down cliff to retrieve dropped buckets. There she combs hair of three mermaids. Asked what she sees in their hair--sunbeams, moonbeams and starlight--given buckets of pearls. Chooses to leave by wooden door, sent out front, to look up--golden star falls on forehead. Stepsister imitates--sees seaweed in hair, receives bucket of pebbles and donkey's tail on forehead. Prince given stepsister disguised to wed. Cat calls telling where kind girl is hidden. Italy: Manning-Sanders CHOICE 280-290 /Manning-Sanders BOOK..MERMAIDS 25-35/.

D* The Italian Group.

Da* The Little Bucket. Unkind girl chants "Stub toes" and kind girl trips and drops bucket into well (N777.2). Climbs after it and fish orders her to knock on door, lady invites her to clean and cook there. Rewarded with kiss on forehead and bucket, not to look until home. Finds bucket full of jewels and diamond on forehead. Unkind sister imitates = bucket of scorpions and toads, stone on forehead. Italy: Ross BURIED 103-108.

E* Following the River Subtype. The Lousing Group.

Ea* The Bad Old Woman. Girl must tend cow and spin flax by eve or stepmother will behead. She combs old lady's hair and is advised to put flax in cow's mouth and pull out nose. Cow spins. Jewels fall from old lady's hair as she combs. To turn when cock crows, does so--star falls on forehead. Stepmother sends own daughter. Cow tears up flax, old man comes to have hair combed, snakes fall out. Look when donkey brays, snake twines around neck and bites nose pulling it long. Crow calls and star falls on end of long nose and becomes a wart. Switzerland (Ticino): Duvoisin THREE 130-137.

Eb* The Enchanted Cow. Old man warns girl not to drop distaff (N777.4). Maura drops hers and mother turns to a cow. Task: spinning wool by night fall assigned by father's sister (stepmother). Cow chews and it comes out of ear spun. Third day stepmother's daughter spies. She tries to get cow to spin and is kicked. Cow is killed (B335.7). Maura buries bones + R221Bc (Cinderella). Serbia: Spicer LONG

47-64.

F* Following the River Subtype: Indian Variants.

Fa* A Girl and Her Stepmother. Stepmother sends girl to clean cotton. It blows away and stepmother sends her into forest to ask shebear for golden spindle, bow and spinning wheel and to take these to castle of the seven-mouthed prince to work. She cooks huge amounts for him and one mouth disappears each day. Seventh day she comes out of hiding and reveals self. They wed and father, stepmother and her daughter come to live with them. Ceylon: Tooze WONDERFUL 50-54.

Q2.1.2* The Encounters en route subtype.

A. The Fall Into the Well form.

Aa* Mother Holle. Girl sent to wash spindle drops (N777.4) it into well. Follows to fetch it and finds country at well bottom. Kind girl takes bread from oven and shakes apple tree at their request. Her task, shaking Mother Holle's featherbed, causes snow to fly on earth (A1135.2.1). Shower of gold falls on her as she passes door en route home. Unkind sister imitates. Refuses to aid oven and tree, works poorly. Pitch falls on her as she exits. Germany (Grimm): Arbuthnot ANTHOLOGY 202-203; Arbuthnot FAIRY 39-40; Gag MORE 15-22; Grimm GRIMM'S (Follett) 246-250; Grimm GRIMM'S (World) 103-106; Grimm HOUSEHOLD 128-131; Hutchinson FIRESIDE STORIES 119-125; Lang RED 293-297 /Lang FIFTY 199-202/; Lurie CLEVER 97-103.

Ab* The Maiden in the Country Underground. Stepmother pushes girl into well. She obeys requests to trim hedge, take loaves from oven, feed old woman, shake apple tree, shear ram, milk cow. Serves old woman and daughter. Task: 1. milk wild cow--sparrows calm it; 2. wash black wool white and white black. Woman she fed performs (dip against and with stream). 3. sieve full of water--sparrows advise (H1023.2). Chooses smallest of three caskets as reward. It is lead but is full of jewels. She flees and cow, ram, tree and hedge help escape. Stepsister imitates. Chooses large gold casket--frog and snake fill the house and drive out stepmother and daughter. Weds king. Ireland: Pilkington SHAMROCK 94-101.

Ac* Girl shakes apple tree, milks cow, carries old woman's basket. Given basket of jewels. Stepmother imitates, given basket of snakes and toads. +Z65.1. S. Appalachia: Haviland NORTH 147-154.

B* The Rolling Cake Form. SEE: N777 (Rolling Dumpling).

C* The Pursuit Form.

Ca* The Gold from the Forbidden Room Group. SEE: G561.

Cb* The Long leather Bag Group. Girl seeking work complies with requests and takes bread from oven, milks cow, shakes apple tree. Working for witch she breaks tabu and looks up chimney. Bag of money falls and she flees with it. Tree, cow and oven hide her (D1658.3.4). Sister imitates. Is unkind. Tree reveals her hiding place.

Cba* The Old Witch. England: Jacobs MORE 101-106 /Harper GHOSTS 83-89/, /Hoke WITCHES 80-84/; Manning-Sanders BOOK.. WITCHES 11-17; Steel ENGLISH 83-88.

Cbb* Gallymanders. U.S. (Appalachia): Chase WICKED 18-28; Field AMERICAN 295-302; Hoke WITCHES 15-18.

Cbc* With a Wig, With a Wag. Three girls, meeting house, field, well, first not unkind, third succeeds. U.S. (New England): Cothran WITH 1-8; Tashjian DEEP 89-62.

Cbd* Long Leather Bag. Hag steals money bag, three sisters must seek fortune, eldest two take whole bannock without mother's blessing. Are unkind to horse, sheep, goat, mill. Youngest aids these and escapes with bag found up chimney. Mill grinds witch up and tells daughter to release enchantment on her sisters with magic rod. Witch had turned them to stone. Ireland: Haviland FAVORITE..IRELAND 26-38; Wiggin FAIRY 154-162.

Ce* The Stolen Brother group.

CeA* Baba Yaga's geese steal little brother. Marya seeks. Refuses to eat rye flour pies in oven, wild apples on tree, milk pudding by milk river. Claims she is accustomed to finer foods. Hedgehog shows her Baba Yaga's chicken leg house. Flees with brother. Baba pursues in mortar. She must eat of pudding, apple, pie before they will hide her. Reaches home safely. Russia: Carey BABA 92-95; Riordan TALES.. CENTRAL 175-178 (mouse aids). Lurie CLEVER 17-22; Whitney IN 65-68.

CeBa* Baba Yaga and the kind girl (-unkind girl motif but closely related to Type 480). Stepmother sends girl to Baba Yaga for needle and thread. She has been kind to mouse, he warns that stepmother is Baba Yaga's sister, advises to pick up whatever she finds en route-- handkerchief, bottle of oil, meat scraps, ribbon, loaf of bread are found. She oils gate, gives handkerchief to weeping servant, loaf to dog, Baba Yaga sets girl weaving at loom and sends servant for water to bathe girl so she can be cooked. Girl asks servant to bring water in a sieve so it takes longer. Gives meat to cat, cat weaves for her and answers for her (D1658.3.4). Advises to throw towel behind = river, comb = forest (D672). Dog and gate let her pass. Birch beats her until she ties it with ribbon, then lets her pass. SEE ALSO: G530.2L. Russia: Ransome OLD 88-105 /Hoke WITCHES 19-30/, /Hope-Simpson CAVALCADE..WITCHES 62-74/, /Fenner GIANTS 79-92/; Williams-Ellis ROUND

81-89 (-mouse); Wyndham TALES..RUSSIA 76-87 (mouse, real aunt advises).

CeBab* Brother and sister, grandmother advises, mouse helps spin, cat shows way out of forest, wrens show how to plug sieve when sent to fetch water. Russia: Buck FAIRY 162-167; Lang YELLOW 233-238; Manning-Sanders BOOK ..WITCHES 38-45.

CeBb* Vasilisa the Beautiful. Dying mother gives Vasilisa little wooden doll, feed it and tell it troubles. It does tasks for Vasilisa. Stepmother sends to Baba Yaga for fire. Doll does task for girl. Girl asks who riders were on horses. White horse = day, red = sun, black = night (Z65.3). Sent home with skull of fire on stick. It burns up stepmother and stepsisters. Spins with doll's help and Tsar hears of her and weds. Russia: Dolch RUSSIA 99-129; Downing RUSSIAN 160-168; Riordan TALES..CENTRAL 11-19; Whitney VASILISA THE BEAUTIFUL pb /Whitney IN 43-57/. Russia (Afanasev): Haviland FAVORITE..RUSSIA 20-42.

D* Encounter en route subtype. Indian variants.

Da* Two Sisters. Girl goes to visit ill grandfather. En route she agrees to straighten plum tree branches, clear ashes from fire, bind up broken pipal tree, unclog stream. Grandfather gives her a golden bracelet. Unkind sister imitates and is stung by scorpions and is given no gift. On second visit kind girl is given gifts by stream, tree, fire and grandfather. Unkind girl goes and is accused by other relatives of stealing treasures grandfather gave away. She is beaten and washed downstream and drowned. India: Turnbull FAIRY 33-44.

E* Encounters en route subtype: African and Afro-American tradition. SEE ALSO: Q2.1.6Ba.

Ea* The Snake Chief. Unkind girl snubs mouse, frog, goatherd. Disobeys old lady's advice not to laugh at trees, drink curdled milk, drink water given by man with head under arm. Enters village from wrong side, prepares food poorly for chief's meal. Five headed snake eats the meal then kills her. Kind girl (youngest daughter) obeys advice of mouse, old woman and coney. Ogress to wed snake. Transforms to man. S. Africa (Xhosa): Arnott AFRICAN 186-194.

Eb* Tiwa and the Magic Eggs. Stepmother sends Tiwa to take rice stick to wizard to wash after she drops it. She is questioned by bundle of hoe handles, man with one eye, asked to comb hair of wizard with many eyes. Reward--four eggs, takes small one. To break last where wants to live. From eggs come: 1. servants, clothes, hammocks; 2. soldiers, guards; 3. gold and jewels; 4. house, goat and cow. She beats rice stick on mother's grave and mother comes back to life. Stepmother's daughter is sent. Is unkind to those met. Takes large eggs. Bees, snake, man with whip emerge. Fire from last egg destroys stepmother and self. West Africa: Aardema MORE 44-49.

F* Encounters en route subtype: Japanese tradition.

Roberts cites "The Tongue-cut Sparrow" (Q285.1.1) as related to Type 480.

Fa* Picking Mountain Pears. Eldest two daughters sent to bring mountain pears for sick mother. Refuse advice of old woman and are killed by monster. Youngest obeys directions of old woman, leaves, crow, ground vine. Takes along straw doll, broken bowl found. Breeze in leaves of pear tree warns to climb south side so shadow doesn't warn monster. Throws straw doll in throat and chokes monster. Scoops water in broken bowl to revive dead brothers. Mother is cured. Japan: Bang MEN 71-77.

G* Girl in the Basket. Jealous maids say Margaretina boasted could do all palace laundry in one morning. Can fetch king's instruments that play by selves. Prince advises taking along three quarts of oil, three pounds beef, three brooms, three brushes, three oven cloths. She flatters slimy river and it lets her pass. Gives brooms, brushes and cloths to women cleaning oven with hair, gives meat to three dogs. Steals instruments and flees. Door, dogs, women and river refuse to catch her. She opens box prematurely and instruments come out and she can not get back into box. Prince aids, advises to choose coal chest in cellar as reward. Prince is in chest. Wed. Italy: Manning-Sanders BOOK ..OGRES 66-74.

H* Servant girl sent to find teaspoon washed away by stream. To wash old woman's back, covered with thistles, cuts her hands (G219.9). To cook for woman, makes magic meal with one grain of rice, one bean and one bone. Not to feed cat. She feeds cat. To take small egg at crossroad and break at next crossroad. Silverware comes out. Daughter of mistress sent. Is surly. Hits cat as instructed, cat is really old woman (G211.1.7). Takes large egg. Demons eat her up. Haiti: Wolkstein MAGIC 151-156.

Q2.1.3* The ogre kept at bay subtype.

A* The Piecemeal Request Form.

Aa* The Envious Stepmother. Two demons in haunted house ask girl to dance, she asks for items of clothing one at a time, sends for water to wash giving sieve. Procrastinates thus until cockcrow. Stepmother sends own daughter. She requests all clothing at once, gives bucket with hole to fetch water. They stop holes. She must dance. They take her soul at dawn and leave head in window (Q2.1.4D). Mother calls, "I see you smiling." Bird mocks. Poland: Zajdler POLISH 109-118.

Ab* Goblins at Bathhouse. Goblins to carry off girl at bathhouse, mouse advises her to request certain clothes before going with them.

They send for the clothing items, she thus procrastinates until cock crows. Estonia: Manning-Sanders CHOICE 74-80 /Manning-Sanders BOOK..GHOSTS 14-20.

B* The Blindman's Buff form.

Girl abandoned in hut on order of stepmother shares food with mouse. Bear enters at midnight and orders her to play blindman's buff. Mouse hides her in oven and carries bell to lead bear on all night. She is rewarded in morning with riches. Dog barks saying father is bringing her home rich. Stepmother sends over daughter who is unkind to mouse, beaten or killed by bear. Latvia: Higonnet-Schnopper BLUE 109-117. Russia: Carey BABA 99-102.

C* The House in the Wood form. Type 431.

Girl following millet trail laid by father is lost when birds eat. Comes to house in woods where old man lives with hen, cock and cow. She is unkind to animals and unmindful of his needs. Is put into cellar. Second daughter same, third daughter feeds animals first and cares for old man. House changes to palace at night, he to prince, animals to servants. Sisters are sent to serve charcoal burner until they reform. Germany (Grimm): Arbuthnot FAIRY 40-43; Dagliesh ENCHANTED 116-123; Grimm GRIMM'S (Follett) 207-214; Grimm GRIMM'S (Scribner's) 278-284; Grimm HOUSE 1-14; Lang FIFTY 122-127 /Lang PINK 18-24 /.

Q2.1.4* The Strawberries in the Snow subtype.

A* The Twelve Months form.

Aa* The Twelve Months of the Year. Girl meets twelve old woman in cave. Asked her opinion of months she praises all. Told to fill her apron with coals--turns to gold at home. Unkind sister imitates--turns to snakes. Greece: Wilson GREEK 224-229.

Ab* Grandmother Marta. Girl praises all months, gold coins fall when talks, flowers when smiles. Unkind sister gets snakes, lizards and nettles. Handsome lad weds first girl. Bulgaria: Pridham GIFT 100-106.

Ac* Twelve months. Girl sent for violets in winter meets twelve months around fire. They pass wand from month to month and violets, strawberries, apples, etc. flow. She may take two of each. Stepsister imitates, is unkind. January destroys her and her mother in storm. Czechoslovakia: De Regniers LITTLE pb; Haviland FAVORITE..CZECHOSLOVAKIA 3-20 /Fillmore SHOEMAKER'S APRON pb/, /Dagliesh ENCHANTED 154-161/. Sleigh NORTH 144-154.

Ad* The Months. Twelve youths at inn ask lad what he thinks of months. He speaks well of all. Given a wish-granting casket by March. Brother imitates, curses March, given a whip which beats him when says, "Whip, give me a hundred." Italy: Wiggin TALES 20-24; Wiggin

FAIRY 367-370.

Ae* Woman seeking food for children meets twelve men in tent. She praises all seasons of year and is given jar of gold. Unkind wealthy neighbor imitates but curses months. Given jar of snakes. Greece: Aliki TWELVE pb.

B* The Three Dwarfs form. Type 403B.

Father hangs up boot with hole in sole. If holds water he will wed. It holds water. Stepmother promises to give his daughter milk to bathe in and wine to drink. Will give own daughter water. By third day this is reversed. Daughter sent in paper dress to fetch strawberries in winter. At house of three dwarfs she shares food and sweeps snow from door, strawberries under snow. They make wishes for her: 1. gold drops from mouth when speaks, 2. prettier daily, 3. wed king. Stepmother's daughter goes. 1. Toads when speaks, 2. uglier daily, 3. die horrid death. Stepmother throws queen into river and puts own daughter in place. Queen as duck comes thrice to nurse baby (K1911). Third night king disenchants. Stepmother and daughter killed. Germany (Grimm): Grimm GRIMM'S (World) 273-279; Grimm HOUSEHOLD 76-81; Lang RED 252-259; Manning-Sanders BOOK.. DWARFS 78-83.

Bb* Mother Luck. Sent by stepmother to gather strawberries in winter, girl comes to house of Mother Luck. To sweep snow aside, finds berries. Given box of luck, not to open for three days. Stepmother's daughter imitates. King's son passes and is served ripe strawberries by first daughter, green by second. Kind girl finds jewels in box, weds prince. Fire from unkind girl's box destroys self and stepmother. Latvia: Durham TIT 17-23.

C* The Jack Frost form.

Stepmother sends girl to wed King Frost. She speaks kindly and says is warm despite his attempts to freeze her. She is rewarded with furs and gifts. Stepmother's daughter is sent in nude, frozen. Russia: Buck FAIRY 64-67; Lang YELLOW 224-228 (dog barks as returns prophesying will wed king); Rackham FAIRY 92-99; Ransome OLD 54-69; Riordan TALES.. CENTRAL 86-90; Whitney IN 27-34.

D* Rattle-Rattle-Rattle and Chink-Chink-Chink, (not given in Roberts).

Stepsister takes girl's spindle while she crosses stream, then refuses to return it--claims she spun it. Father is forced to abandon girl. Builds her a hut and leaves mallet hanging so wind will bang it and she'll think he is nearby. Old beggar asks her to wash him and feed. At midnight a dwarf (beggar) brings a bag of gold to her door. Dog calls telling of her wealth as father returns with her. Stepmother flees, daughter sent. Is killed and skull put in window (Q2.1.3Aa). Dog says here comes "Rattle-Rattle." Czechoslovakia: Fillmore SHEPHERD'S

134-143.

Q2.1.5* Other Subtypes and Groups.

A* The Heating the Bath group.

Aa* Mother Sunday. Stepmother sends girl to work for Mother Sunday. Task: wash and feed her children. They are monsters and wild animals. She washes them. Offered box reward, chooses small. To open it at home--cattle emerge. Unkind daughter sent, chooses large trunk. Serpents inside. Italy: Manning-Sanders GIANNI 24-30.

Ab* The Giant Beanstalk. Girl sorting beans leaves one, giant beanstalk grows (F54.2). She climbs and meets old man in hut. He asks her to heat bathhouse, using bones of old carcass for wood, pig pond water, horsetail to scrub with. She fetches proper materials. Reward. Take scarf from storeroom, not from chest cat sits on. It fills with riches once home. Stepmother sends own daughter, she prepares bath as man directs, takes cat's scarf, fire emerges and burns her up. Latvia: Durham TIT 56-62.

B* The Birds on the Axe group. SEE ALSO: K1911 (False Bride).

Ba* Little Rosa and Long Leda. Stepmother sends girl back for axe, she feeds two doves resting on axe handle. They wish her 1. Twice as beautiful, 2. Hair golden, 3. Gold ring falls from lips when smiles. Sister imitates = ugly, thornbush hair, frog when smiles. + Type 403. She is thrown overboard, ashore she buries a dead deer and puts the head on a stick for birds. This turns to a nightingale and lime tree. A king sees her and weds. Her stepmother gives her a gown which turns her into a goose. Thrice she comes to ask after husband and son. King catches second time and disenchants with former gown. Stepmother and her daughter turned to geese. Sweden: Kaplan FAIRY 17-34.

Bba* The Little Duck. Girl sent back for father's mittens finds three birds nesting there. Makes them a nest of moss. They wish her 1. Jewels when she speaks, 2. Gold when combs hair, 3. Beautiful. Stepsister goes = ugly, toads, hair pulls out when brushed. + Type 403A. Her brother offers to bring her to king. She is thrown overboard by stepmother and turns to duck. The brother is imprisoned. Thrice comes to kitchen door, shakes coin from feathers, third time the king sees and disenchants. Sweden: Owen CASTLE 171-181. Denmark: Hatch MORE 33-48.

Bbb* Gives flowers from her hair to hand from well, gifts = loveliness, gold falls from lips, roses in footprints; stepdaughter = foxtails in footsteps, toad from mouth, ugly; as duck is captive of mermaid who pulls back on invisible gold chain after each visit, king holds her third night, she turns to dragon, wolf, self. Sweden: McNeil DOUBLE 106-114.

Bbc* The Geese and the Golden Chain. Girl shares cake with old women, given comb, pearls fall from hair. King to wed if brother's tale is true. Neighbor throws overboard and substitutes own daughter--combs thistles from hair. Brother made gooseherd. Merman has taken charge of girl, allows her to visit brother as he sleeps, his geese tell of visit. She is bound with golden chain to sea. King files it loose. Portugal: Manning-Sanders BOOK..MERMAIDS 98-107.

Q2.1.6* Related variants. (Not outlined in Roberts.)

A* The Wishing Well. Girl seeks wishing well on Hallowe'en Eve. Bird says share cake with me and I'll advise. Advise: Make wish for best beloved, for one who needs it most, for self. First girl wishes all three wishes for self. Receives so much gold she cannot lift it and it falls back into well. Second girl obeys bird. For self asks only for slippers to wear to prince's wedding. Fairies carry gold home for her. She meets prince en route. Weds. England: Harper GHOSTS 166-172.

B* Latin American variant: "Poor Little Girl, Rich Little Girl." Poor girl prays to Virgin for protection from fighting bulls, help crossing stream. At the castle she washes pots for the Señora and scratches her back which is covered with broken glass. She chooses the smallest barrel as reward. It contains gold. A rich girl imitates, is unkind. Receives barrel of snakes and insects. Venezuela: Jagendorf KING 260-264.

C* The Sisters and the Dogs. Three girls seek father. Three dogs scare off Loup Garou met on way. Elder two daughters come home from dance early to feed dogs, are protected on way home by dogs. Youngest forgets to come home on sixth night and dogs fail to protect her on way home. Loup Garou gets. Haiti: Johnson HOW 23-30.

Da* Stepchild and the Fruit Trees. Stepdaughter plants odala seeds, sings and they grow. Stepmother claims fruit. She sings and they die. People come to buy fruit. She sings and fruit becomes full again, thus her ownership established. She sells and becomes rich. Sierra Leone: Arbuthnot ANTHOLOGY 329-330; Robinson SINGING 24-33.

Db* The Magic Orange Tree. Grows for stepdaughter as she chants and bears. Stepmother climbs tree to pick and girl causes it to grow and break. Haiti: Wolkstein MAGIC 13-22.

E* Golden Crow. Girl offered gift by golden crow chooses modest. Brass ladder, small box, contains treasure. Unkind girl chooses gold ladder, large box, gets snake. Burma: Htin Aung KINGDOM 57-61.

Q3. Moderate request rewarded, immoderate punished. SEE: J2400 (foolish imitation); Q272;

Q285.1.1.

Q3.1. Woodsman and the gold axe. A woodsman lets his axe fall into water. Hermes (or goddess) comes to his rescue. Takes out a gold axe but woodsman says that it is not his. Given his own axe and rewarded for his modest choice. His companion tries this plan and loses axe. Japan: Uchida MAGIC 73-81. Aesop: Aesop AESOP'S (Grosset) 3-4 (Mercury); Aesop AESOP'S (Watts) 14-15. Russia: Spicer THIRTEEN GOBLINS 28-34; Wyndham TALES 43-46.

Q3.3* Hermit offers one coin earned honsetly or one hundred dishonestly. Poor man takes the one. Good luck follows. Portugal: Wiggin FAIRY 349-353.

Q10 - Q99. Deeds rewarded.

Q20. Piety rewarded.

Q22.1* Farm girl stands in sun waiting to grow wings. All girls in China imitate. Spirit in charge of wings gives them to her alone. China: Lin MILKY 41-46.

Q42.3. Generosity to saint (God) in disguise rewarded. SEE ALSO: K1811.1; Q1.1.

Q45.1.4* Poor shoemaker gives last pair of shoes to beggar sheltering with him. Beggar is maharajah. India: Spellman BEAUTIFUL 8-11.

Q80. Rwards for other causes.

Q81.2* Reward for perseverance. Two frogs in crock of cream. One drowns. Second kicks until cream turns to butter. Escapes. Russia: Carey BABA 58-60; Ginsberg LAZIES 26-27; Riordan TALES..CENTRAL 241-242. Aesop: Aesop AESOP'S (Random) 21-22.

Q82. Reward for fearlessness. Reward given by devil or ghost. SEE ALSO: H1411.

Q82.0.1* Couple to receive haunted house if can exorcise ghosts. Ghost monks appear to bride and exhort her not to mention them. She obeys and they show her treasure (E373). They were the spirits of the treasure. Yellow monk--gold; white--silver; black--copper. Japan: Novak FAIRY 125-130.

Q82.3. Reward for fearlessness. My Lord Bag of Rice. Type 738. Man steps over serpent on bridge. It is dragon king (or dwarf). Asks him to kill marauding centipede. Shoots three arrows. Spits on third and kills centipede (Z312). Rewarded with magic objects: never-ending roll of silk, fireless cooking pot (D1601.10.1), impenetrable armor, never-ending bag of rice (D1652.5.10), etc. Japan: Hearn JAPANESE 47-52; Manning-Sanders BOOK.. DRAGONS 38-42; Ozaki JAPANESE 1-11.

Q100 - Q199. Nature of rewards.

Q113.3. High position as reward for piety.

Q113.3.1* Fata Morgana offers to make Count Roger King of Sicily. He replies that Christ will give him Sicily, not a fairy. She has made Sicily seem very near mirrored in water. Parts of Sicily can still be seen mirrored in water at Reggio in Calabria. Sicily: Toor GOLDEN 153-156.

Q150. Immunity from disaster as reward.

Q151.4. Faithful old dog threatened with death proves his worth and is spared. SEE: K231.1.3.

Q161.1. Sight restored as reward.

Q161.1.1* Blind prince turned out by father with only pekinese (lion dog) as companion. Sight regained by doing good deeds. China: Carpenter WONDER..DOGS 173-183.

Q200 - Q399. Deeds punished.

Q223.14.1* Chief promises feast to village god, One-Arm, if survives storm at sea. Forgets. God takes voice from giant drum. Fiji: Gittins TALES 22-25.

Q270. Avarice punished. SEE ALSO: D877; Q3.

Q272.1.2* Miller gives paltry five silver marks for crusade. Devil grinds them in mill at night, carries miller off. Netherlands: De Leeuw LEGENDS..HOLLAND 92-96.

Q272.5* Anansi persuades candlefly to show him place where gathers eggs. Anansi takes all. Candlefly leaves Anansi without a light to return home. Anansi stumbles into Tiger's house in dark and tiger eats all eggs. West Indies: Sherlock WEST 97-104.

Q280. Unkindness punished.

Q285.1.1. Punishment for cutting off bird's tongue. The Tongue-cut Sparrow. Wife cuts off tongue of husband's pet sparrow when it eats her starch. Husband seeks pet in Land of Sparrows (B222.5) and is feasted and entertained. Given choice of heavy or light trunk (Q3) as parting gift, chooses light, contains jewels. Wife imitates (J2415), heavy trunk contains toads and snakes (demons), wife is destroyed (or reforms). Ikeda Type 480D. (cf. Q2.1.2F). Japan: Buck FAIRY 181-183 (wife hits sparrow); Hearn JAPANESE 57-59 (old lady next door cuts off Sparrow's tongue, kind old woman and husband visit sparrow); McAlpine JAPANESE 188-201 (wife asks Buddha to rescue from demons, setting sun strikes them and they vanish, G304.2.5); Ozaki JAPANESE 12-25 /Haviland FAVORITE..JAPANESE 31-46/; Rackham FAIRY 89-91; Sakade JAPANESE 38-44; Sleigh NORTH 130-138; Uchida DANCING 123-131; Wiggin TALES 425-426.

Q292.1. Inhospitality to saint (god) punished.

SEE ALSO: A1958.0.1 (owl); Q1.1.

Q292.1.1* Gypsy woman told lord is coming to visit turns away three beggars. They were he. Why Gypsies always take in beggars. Gypsy: Hampden GYPSY 107-110.

Q321. Laziness punished. (cf. W111).

Q321.2.1* Lazy gardener gives magic seed to make rich. Little man in red comes out of flower and forces gardener to work. India: Spellman BEAUTIFUL 15-18.

Q321.2.2* Lazy wife given ten helpers, they enter her fingers and force her to work. Scandinavia: Belting ELVES 70-76 (tomte gives). Portugal: Lowe LITTLE 27-29.

Q321.2.3* Duendes keep putting cleaning equipment in hands of lazy wife. Mexico: Ross IN 175-190.

Q321.3* Laziness punished. Wife hides toothpicks in cracks of tatami rather than dispose of properly. They become tiny samurai and keep her awake dancing at night and chanting "Chin-chin kobakana." Her husband (or parent) hides and strikes at them. They turn to toothpicks. Japan: Hearn JAPANESE (Pauper) 5-12; Hearn JAPANESE 9-17 (also girl who hid plumstones beset by dancing woman in red robes); Palmer FAIRY 69-74; Sakade JAPANESE 49-54; Wiggin TALES 435-437; Wolkstein LAZY 11-18.

Q400 - Q599. Kinds of punishment.

Q426. Wolf cut open and filled with stones as punishment. Types 123, 333. SEE: K311.3 (Wolf and Seven Kids); K2011B.

Q501.4. Punishment of Prometheus. Chained to a mountain with eagles preying on his vitals, which are restored nightly (punishment for theft of fire, A1415). Gruenberg FAVORITE 411-412.

Q551.3.3. Punishment: calf's head in murderer's hand turns to corpse's head (N271). Puerto Rico: Leach THING 63-64.

Q565. Man admitted to neither heaven nor hell. Type 330. SEE: K213 (Devil in Knapsack). (cf. M211, Sells soul to Devil).

A* The Smith and the Devil. Type 330A.

Aa* A saint (Saint Peter) in disguise is fed (K1811) by the smith. He grants three wishes. The smith asks that anyone sitting in his chair stick, that anyone holding his hammer stick, that anyone touching his thornbush be pulled into bush and held. Two little devils and Satan are thus vanquished. The smith is refused entrance to heaven by St. Peter (A661.0.1.2). At hell's gate he is given a coal to go make his own place (A2817). U.S. (Appalachia): Chase GRANDFATHER 29-39; Chase WICKED pb.

Celtic (reset in New England): Barth JACK-O-LANTERN pb (+ coal in pumpkin origin of Jack-o-Lantern, A2817.1). U.S. (Black, Georgia): Harris UNCLE 160-165 /Harris COMPLETE 105-109/ (Jacky-my-lantern).

Ab* Smith sells soul to devil (M211). Old man gives wishes--hammer, chair, purse--whatever enters stays (K213). Devil twice agrees to longer term and gives more money. Third time he agrees to leave Smith alone rest of life. Devil driven from Wales. Wales: MORE..WELSH 77-87.

Ac* Same. Chair, tree, purse. Devil beaten on anvil (K213). France (Gascony): Manning-Sanders DEVILS 76-86.

Ad* Same. Chair, tree, purse, devil beaten (K213) on anvil. Refused in hell, tosses hammer into heaven and gets in (K2371.1.1). Wishes were given after Smith unsuccessfully tried to imitate Lord's shoeing of horse (J2411.2) by cutting off legs and rejuvenating of old mother by putting into fire (J2411.1). Norway: Undset TRUE 137-146.

Ae* Smith sells soul to devil (M211), given three wishes by St. Peter, tree, stool, bag (K213). Twice receives extensions from devil. Tird time has devil carried back to hell in bag. Refused admission in hell, throws jerkin into (K2371.1.1) Heaven and enters. So bored he throws it back out. Still wanders. Is seen in moon at times. Slovenia: Kavcic GOLDEN 46-55.

Af* Tinker of Tamlacht. Three beggars (angels) befriended give wishes. 1. Meal chest filled. 2. Anything into budget stays (K213). 3. Anyone touching apple tree sticks. "May the Devil take me if I ever come this way again" (C12.2). Devil appears. Beaten on anvil in budget. +Grandfather Death (D1825.1.2). Refused in heaven and hell. Turns to Salmon in River Erne. Ireland: MacManus HIBERNIAN 10-24 /Hoke SPOOKS 97/.

Ag* Shoemaker's apron. Shoemaker sells soul to Devil (M211). Christ and St. Peter visit and give three wishes. 1. Whoeversits on cobbler's stool to stick. 2. Whoever looks in window unable to move. 3. Whoever shakes pear tree to stick. Receives reprieve twice from devil, third time devil vows never to return. Refused in heaven and hell, he tosses shoemakers apron in Gate of Heaven and sits on "his own property." Czechoslovakia: Fillmore SHEPHERD'S 185-192.

Ah* Man saves guardian angel in test. Given three wishes. 1. Chair sticks. 2. Shoe mending box sticks. 3. Sycamore tree sticks. Two demons and Devil vanquished thus. Guardian angel gives Jack lantern to carry until Judgment Day, origin "Jack o' Lantern." Ireland: Spicer THIRTEEN MONSTERS 83-92.

Ai* Padre Ulivo: offers hospitality to twelve strangers (twelve disciples). Food appears miraculously. He is given three wishes. 1. Chair to stick. 2. Tree to stick. 3. To always win at cards. Death vanquished twice. Plays cards with Devil and wins souls (E756.2). St. Peter refuses to allow them in. "Tell the Lord I let all of his friends in when he came to my house." All are admitted. Italy: Jagendorf PRICELESS CATS 138-146.

Q580. Punishment fitted to crime.

Q584.2.1* Baron makes men wait on holy days, old man puts bundle on baron's head and turns into horse. Peasant is given horse to use for year. Restored baron reforms. Latvia: Durham TIT 85-89.

Q586. Son on gallows bites his mother's (father's) nose off: punishment for neglect in youth. Types 756B, 838. Aesop: Aesop AESOP'S (Grosset) 140-141 (ear); Aesop FABLES (Macmillan) 87 (ear).

Q589.4. Lad who cuts everything up into pieces with his ax is sent to Piece Land. Everything is in pieces--people, animals, etc. He reforms. Congo: Burton MAGIC 35-55.

R. CAPTIVES AND FUGITIVES

R0 - R99. Captivity.

R10. Abduction.

R49.4* Girl kept in glass case to prevent lovers from reaching her. Type 870A. Newman: FOLK..LATIN 119-123.

R100 - R199. Rescues.

R100. Rescues.

R111.1.3. Rescue of princess (maiden) from dragon. SEE ALSO: B11.11; E711.10; F660.1; K929.1.1; K1853.2.1.1. (cf. H1385.1).

A* Type 303. The Twins or Blood-Brothers. Usually including Type 300--The Dragon Slayer.

Aa* The double Knight. Fisherman's wife to eat piece of fish, feed part to mare, dog, bury part under two olive trees. She, mare, and dog bear twins. Sword appears on tree. One brother slays dragon, weds Infanta Isabella of Madrid. King of Moors captures other brother. First brother rescues, blinding witch jailor with diamond which shines in hand of brave. She explodes. Second brother weds sister of Infanta. Spain: McNeil DOUBLE 7-15.

Ab* Knights of the Fish. Fish instructs to feed to wife and bury part in garden. Two sons born. Two plants grow with shields on top. Part at crossroads. One save princess from dragon by holding up mirror (K1052). Dragon thinks it is another dragon. Hero weds princess. Investigates castle seen in distance. Witch kills. His brother comes and wounds witch. She begs him to restore her and gives formula. He restores brother also and other swine. Witch dies of rage. Spain: Lang ROSE 74-84.

Ac* The King of the Fishes. Fish spared twice gives favor. Throw bones under mare, bitch, rose tree, eat. Twins born with stars on forehead, twin colts, rose bushes with one rose each--withers if lad ill. First brother kills dragon and rescues princess. Takes tongue token. Reveals self and exposes imposter. Wed. Visits witches and is turned to stone. Brother seeks. Forces witch to release. Jacobs EUROPEAN 19-30.

Ad* Castle of No Return. Fish orders to feed to wife, horse, dog. Plant scales. Bears three sons, pups, three swords grow from scales. First brother rescues princess from dragon, weds. Goes to castle, binds the dog and horse with witch's hairs. All turn to stone. Second brother same. Third kills witch. Restores brothers and others. Puerto Rico: Alegria THREE 90-99.

Ae* The Three Ivans. Queen to eat certain fish. Gives leftovers to wives of cook and gardener, three identical boys born. Test--lift stove. Only Ivan Gardener's Son can perform. Witch (Baba Yaga) in land under stone. Refuses to be intimidated by her. Ivan Gardener's Son three times fights giants of three, nine, twelve heads. Basin to overflow if in peril. Two brother Ivans sleep. He hurls his iron glove and his hat at hut and wakes them. They aid and third giant is killed. Witch Boneleg (Baba Yaga) warns them of revenge plotted by giant's mother and widows. They turn selves into apple tree, well and desert--whoever eats or touches to be destroyed. Ivan Gardener's Son kills with sword. + Six Servants, F601.2. Russia: Manning-Sanders SORCERER'S 69-90.

Af* Once In, Never Out Again. Three brothers bury knives at crossroads, if rusty in trouble. Lion given eldest by innkeeper. Kills dragon with lion's aid saving princess. Weds. Enters valley of "Once In, Never Out Again." Witch asks permission to touch lion and lad with stick. Turned to stone. Second brother repeats. Third brother forces witch to release statue. Austria: Hope-Simpson CAVALCADE..WITCHES 95-105.

Ag* The Old Hag of the Forest. Oldest brother with hound, hornet and filly given by mother. Water in hoof marks to turn bloody if dead. Rescues princess from giant, going twice to battle incognito. Shoe pulled off. Slipper test. Wed to princess. At wedding feast a hare steals from kitchen and cook denigrates hero who lets a hare steal. He pursues hare. Witch asks to warm self in hut where he shelters, gives him three hairs to tie up animals who "frighten" her. Turns all to stone. Second brother same. Third brother forces her to restore. Ireland: MacManus IN CHIMNEY CORNERS /Harper GHOSTS 150-165/, /Hoke WITCHES 65-79/.

Ah* The Red Ettin. Whole cake with curse or half with blessing. Eldest takes half. Knife to rust if in danger. Attempts to free princess from Red Ettin. "I smell an earthly man" (G84). Ettin asks riddles and turns to stone when fails to answer. Brother goes. Half cake. Shares with old lady, given wand to beat Red Ettin. Answers riddles. Thing without an end? Bowl. Smaller one most dangerous? Bridge. Dead carries the living? Ship. Kills Red Ettin. Restores brother, weds princess. British Isles: Finlay TATTERCOATS 87-95; Jacobs ENGLISH 136-142; Steel ENGLISH 221-226; Williams-Ellis FAIRY..BRITISH 292-301. Ireland: Pilkington SHAMROCK 55-60. Scotland: Baker GOLDEN 135-147; Lang BLUE 364-372 (Riddle: Ireland or Scotland first inhabited? Man made for woman or woman for man? Men or brutes first?).

Ai* The Twins: African variant.

Fish caught with two knives, two swords inside. Twins born, cat, dog, hawk bear twins also. Uncle gives two leopard cubs as gift. Knives in tree, if rusty in danger. One brother kills six-headed sea monster with aid of animals and

God of Thunder, rescuing princess being sacrificed to Olokun, God of the Sea. Keeps ears as token, princess gives half necklace to dog and cat. Imposter to wed princess. Twin identified by tokens, weds. He pursues large cock out of city, at hut witch gives palm wine to animals and twin and turns to stone. Twin comes and forces witch to restore by revealing magic liquid. Returns home and pours liquid on mother's grave--great rock "Olumo" emerges. Pours at spot father drowned, waters spread out and form Osa Lagoon at Lagos. One twin and pets go to heaven and become Moon. Second is succeeded by son, first king of Oyo. Nigeria (Yoruba): Fuja FOURTEEN 88-112.

Aj* Youth Who Could Become an Ant, a Lion or an Eagle. First says give half to king, piece to wife, mare, dog. Hang smallest bone from kitchen rafters and will sweat blood if in danger. Triplets born to all. +D532Ac (Lad who could become lion, ant, eagle). First enters castle and plays chess with two lonely women, turned to stone. Sisters of witch killed. Second--repeat. Third meets old man who gives two magic pawns. He wins at chess and asks statues returned to life. Dogs kill witches. Italy: Toor GOLDEN 69-79.

Ak* The Gold Children. Goldfish caught gives castle with ever full cupboard. Tabu telling. Wife forces to tell secret. Castle vanishes. Repeat. Third time caught fish instructs to feed two pieces to wife, two to house, bury two. Two golden lilies grow, wither if ill, die if dead. Two golden foals born, two golden children. One travels disguised in bearskin, weds. Chases stag leading to witch's house. Turned to stone. Second brother forces to restore. Germany (Grimm): Grimm GRIMM'S (Follett) 102-110.

Al* The Two Brothers. Types 303, 567. Magic bird head and liver eaten by (B113.1) nephews. Find gold under pillows each morning. Abandoned. Woodsman raises. Grown seek fortune, given dog, rifle and gold. Knife to rust if in danger. They spare hare, fox, wolf, bear, and lion and are given two of young by each. One drinks of magic cups, pulls magic sword from threshold, slays dragon. Princess divides necklace and fine handkerchief among animals. He keeps dragon's tongue (H105.1). Princess to wed. Imposter, lad slain. Hare fetches healing root and restores. Sends animals for food from wedding feast. Wed. Chases white bird into forest, witch asks to touch animals with stick, turns to stone. Brother goes. Threatens to shoot witch with silver coat buttons. She restores statues. On return princess identifies real husband by necklaces on animals. Reveals 'husband' had put sword in bed on first two nights (T351). Brother had been faithful. Germany (Grimm): Grimm GRIMM'S (Scribner's) 159-184. Latvia: Huggins BLUE 15-31 (Old man, Zuema the Cold, turns to stone. Second brother's dog kills Zuema).

Am* Cesarino and the Dragon. Cesarino makes friends with lion, bear and owl young. Kills dragon with aid of animals, rescuing princess and keeping tongue. Imposter to wed. Hermit reveals truth. Weds princess. Envious sisters and mother of Cesarino put poisoned bone in his bed. He dies. They seal animals' ears with wax so can't hear news, animals burst seals, bear has lion reach down throat and pull up bear grease to anoint body, revive with herb. Wound spurts blood when mother and sisters appear revealing truth. Italy: Rackham FAIRY 66-76.

An* Three Princes and Their Beasts. +S12.1.0.1D. Unfaithful stepsister betrays brother to robbers. Faithful animals save. Eldest brother rescues princess from dragon with aid of animals, given tokens, killed by imposter. Wolf kills ox and sets fox to guard carcass and catch bird coming to feed, crow forced to bring water from wells. Weds princess. Old lady who asks to share his fire touches animals. Turned to stone. Youngest brother--same. Second brother forces restoration. Lithuania: Lang VIOLET 34-45.

Ao* Silvervit and Lillvacker. Widowed queen given apple to eat and son will be hero. Shares with friend. Identical boys born. Dagger which shows rusty if in danger, bloody if dead is given. They adventure. Spare bear and she gives two cubs to serve them. Likewise wolf and fox cubs. Part. Lillvacker serves witch. Is careful not to step on ducks. Duck king promises aid when in need. Ants likewise; bees. Tasks: find key to castle--duck king finds in moat. Task: sort grain--ants. Task: choose real princess from seven images. Bee tells. Spell broken. Weds. Meanwhile Silvervit's dagger is bloody. Has won princess from dragon but another claims feat. Silvervit sends his animals for food from wedding feast. Claims princess. Goes to home in wood. Ties dog with witch's hair and they turn to stone (G263.2.1). Lillvacker threatens her and she gives water to restore dead. Also bottle to make anyone stick forever. Restores animals and brothers. Sticks witch to rock. Sweden: Kaplan FAIRY 108-141.

Ap* Bearskin. King overhears fate of miller's son predicted, to wed princess. He has forester execute (K512), a hare's heart is shown king, babe set adrift. She-bear raises. Wearing bearskin he works as swineherd. Blows horn and bear gives horse and armor to kill dragon. Takes tongue and tokens from princess saved. Steward claims princess. Bearskin sends other swineherd with tokens to fetch parts of wedding feast. Appears and produces tongue. Wed. Holme TALES 50-57; Pyle WONDER 3-14.

Aq* Hag-of-the-Mist: princess stolen, three sons seek. Eldest two bring the water for mother to make loaf. Pitcher leaks, hence small loaf and they refuse to share with old lady met. Fail to answer three riddles of hag and are turned to stone. Youngest mends pitcher with clay, shares with old lady, is given magic stick--turns to sword and kills hag's beasts. Answers riddles. Points stick at witch and she sinks into ground. Touches rock and restores to forty lads and forty girls. He weds the princess. All forty girls wed forty boys. Wales: Pugh MORE 39-54.

B* Type 314A. The Shepherd and Three Giants.

Ba* The Good Sword. Type 314A. Shepherd inherits invincible sword. Kills three trolls and takes their dog, horse, armor--three outfits (red, yellow and white). Thrice kills dragons, rescuing three princesses and sowing tongues. Imposters to wed. Sends three dogs for tidbits from wedding feast. Discovered, produces tongues, wed to youngest. Sweden: Owen CASTLE 77-88 /Child Study Association DRAGON 181-195/.

Bb* Thirteenth Son of the King of Erin. Type 314A. Last son given to Fate. Sets out with horse of fleetness and sword of sharpness. Kills three giants and takes their castles. Thrice attacks dragon in garb of black, blue, red, rescuing one princess. Giant's housekeeper gives dried apple to throw into Dragon's mouth, Dragon collapses. Princess grabs one of hero's blue glass boots as flees. Slipper test. Refuses to go. Finally wed. Ireland: Manning-Sanders BOOK..DRAGONS 87-94.

C* Type 300. The Dragon Slayer.

Ca* Renard of Normandy slays Dragon of Jersey. His squire kills him and weds wife. Channel Isles (Jersey): Spicer THIRTEEN MONSTERS 66-67.

Cb* Donal from Donegal. Donal slays giant rescuing princess, she cuts lock from his hair, imposter claims feat. Donal is recognized by missing lock and wed. Ireland: MacManus BOLD 64-82.

Cc* Lad rescues princess from three headed giant. She binds his wound with skirt. Cook claims feat. Lad recognized by wound, wed. Scotland: Wilson SCOTTISH 18-27.

Cd* The Sea-Maiden. Father makes sword strong for son. Third does not break. Son pledged to sea-maiden at age twenty. Meets dog, falcon, otter and settles disput among them. They will aid. Kills three giants as king's cowherd. Kills Laidly Beast in loch and rescues princess. General claims feat. Produces tokens and weds. Sea-maid takes him. Wife plays harp and sea-maid brings him up (F420.5.2.2). He escapes as falcon. Wife is taken. He kills sea-maid by fetching hind on isle, hoodie in hind, trout in hoodie, egg in trout. Dog, falcon and otter aid (B585.2). Ireland: Jacobs CELTIC 158-170.

D* Other rescues of princesses from dragons.

Da* Bride for the Sea God. Fisherman rescues princess sent as sacrifice to Sea God. Returns with her after famine necessitating sacrifice is

over. Ceylon: Carpenter ELEPHANT'S 141-150.

Db* Sorcerer sends girl to be drowned as bride of dragon. Magistrate rules girl chosen is too ugly and sends sorcerer herself to advise dragon--drowned. With sorcerer's wealth magistrate constructs a dam, thus future flood preventing sacrifices unnecessary. China: Lu Mar CHINESE 53-70.

E* Brother with three dogs and unfaithful sister. SEE ALSO: S12.1.0.1.

Ea* Iron, Steel and Strongest of All. Dogs save lad from unfaithful sister. +S12.1.0.1. Lad kills seven headed sea serpent, saving princess and taking tongues. Imposter claims princess. Dogs sent to knock over dishes at wedding feast. Tongue shown. Wed. Dogs are really enchanted king and emperor now disenchanted. Italy: Toor GOLDEN 93-107.

Eb* Three Dogs. Three sheep traded for three dogs. Kill dragon and rescue princess. Imposter claims. Dog sent for food to princess. Dragon's teeth produced. Wed. Sends for sister. Dogs waited to see if would remember sister (kind hare). Turn to birds--fly off. Germany (Grimm): Lang GREEN 350-355. Germany: Manning-Sanders BOOK..DRAGONS 114-122.

F* Christian knights slay dragons.

Fa* St. George of Merrie England. Kill dragon in Egypt saving Princess Sabia, daughter of King Ptolemy. England: Hoke DRAGONS 57-62; Steel ENGLISH 1-13.

R111.1.4. Rescue of princess (maiden) from giant (monster). SEE: G512 (Jack the Giantkiller); R111.1.3 Cb; R111.1.3Cc.

A* Ashipattle and the Giant Sea Serpent. Youngest of seven sons overhears parents talk of secret--to make horse Swift-Go go fast as wind blows through windpipe. He steals pipe and flees. Tricks boatman ashore. Gets seamonster to swallow him and pot of coals, fans fire and Sea Serpent dies, coughing him up. Strikes earth with tongue in death throes cutting passage between Denmark and Sweden. Teeth knocked out = Orkney and Shetland Isles. Dies = Iceland, fire still burning. Ashipattle weds princess. Scotland: Haviland FAVORITE ..SCOTLAND 71-92.

B* Bomba the Brave. Bomba kills lion which controls city's water supply and demands female sacrifices. Bomba leads army against neighboring tribe to capture white cattle but refuses to allow looting and slave taking. King has him abandoned in desert. All women of tribe go with king in show of support. King relents. Carpenter AFRICAN 169-178.

R111.1.13.2* Rescue of girl from buffalo. Coyote swings girl too high and buffalo carry her off. Brothers force coyote to rescue her. She has turned to a ring and buffalo are playing stick and ring game. Coyote grabs ring and relays back via badger, wolf, hawk, and rusty-black-bird. As a result badger decides to live underground henceforth (A2433.3.25), wolf becomes a loner (A2433.3.14), hawk flies far up into sky (A2433.9), rusty-blackbird decides to live with buffalo, riding their backs (A2433.4.8.1) and coyote enters camp only to steal at night (A2435.3.4.1). Native American (Great Plains): Jones COYOTE 23-39.

R121.4.1* Wife of vizier ties thread to beetle's waist, puts drop of honey on nose, and points up tower. He carries thread to top where vizier is imprisoned. Silk thread is tied to cotton thread to stout twine to strong rope. Vizier escapes. India: Turnbull FAIRY 136-150.

R131. Exposed or abandoned child rescued.

R131.21. Children lost while picking flowers are rescued by mothers who hear them singing song. Ghana: Robinson SINGING 44-59.

R135. Abandoned children (wife, etc.) find way back by clue (breadcrumb, grain, pebble, etc.) they have dropped while being led away. SEE: G275.7.0.1; G412.1 (Hansel and Gretel); K1611C (Hop o' My Thumb); S62.1C (Robber Bridegroom).

R153.3.3. Old robber frees his three sons, relates frightful adventures. In order to free them he must relate his adventures, each more frightful than the last. The tales: 1. An adventure with ghostlike cats; 2. Odysseus and Polyphemus (K603); 3. An ogre fooled by the substitute of a corpse for a child who is to be cooked for him (K527) and later by the robber substituting himself in order to save the child. The rescued child in the last tale is the man's present captor. The robber is rewarded. Type 953. Ireland: Jacobs CELTIC 38-53 (Conal Yellowclaw); MacManus HIBERNIAN 74-84; Manning-Sanders BOOK..GIANTS 79-84.

R161.5* Lover hides girl in cave reached by swimming underwater. Her people on isle of Vavau are killed but the lovers flee to Fiji until cruel king of Tonga dies. Tonga: Gittins TALES 56-58.

R220. Flight.

R221. Heroine's threefold flight from ball. Cinderella (Cap O'Rushes) after meeting prince at a ball (church) flees before identification is possible. Repeated three times. Type 510. SEE ALSO: F535.1.1Fb (Little Finger).

A* Cinderella. Stepmother requires girl to clean for two daughters. Lives by hearth. Her godmother turns a pumpkin into a coach, mice into horses, a rat to coachman, and six lizards to footmen. Provides gown and glass slippers for Cinderella. The prince dances with Cinderella at the ball. She must leave by midnight (C761.3). Thrice she attends ball and flees at

twelve. Her slipper is lost. Slipper is tried on all maids of kingdom. It fits her (H36.1). She weds the prince. France (Perrault): Galdone CINDERELLA pb; Gruenberg FAVORITE 281-286; Haviland FAIRY 138-144; Holme TALES 90-98; Hutchinson CHIMNEY..STORIES 137-149 /Association TOLD..GREEN 113-121/; Lang BLUE 78-87 /Arbuthnot ANTHOLOGY 210-212/, /Arbuthnot FAIRY 101-104/; Opie CLASSIC 117-127; Perrault CINDERELLA pb (illus. Brown); Perrault CINDERELLA pb (illus. Beckett); Perrault CINDERELLA pb (illus. Le Cain); Perrault FAMOUS 135-160; Perrault PERRAULT'S (Dover) 65-78; Perrault PERRAULT'S (Dodd) 58-70; Rackham ARTHUR 223-232 /Martignoni ILLUSTRATED 232-236/; Sheehan FOLK 84-92. England: Baker TALKING 25-32; De La Mare TALES 44-60 (sisters trim feet).

Ba* Aschenputtel. Father to bring daughters gifts. Aschenputtel asks for first hazel twig to brush his hat. She plants on mother's grave (E631) and it grows into tree with nesting dove. Aschenputtel must pick up pan of peas before going to ball. Dove calls birds to help. Aschenputtel asks tree to clothe her. She must return by midnight (C761.3). Third night prince puts pitch on steps and slipper is left. Stepsisters cut off toe and heel to fit slipper (K1911.3.3.1). Bird points out truth. Aschenputtel weds prince. Germany (Grimm): De La Mare ANIMAL 285-289; Gag TALES 101-120; Grimm CINDERELLA pb (illus. Svend); Grimm GRIMM'S (Follett) 17-27; Grimm GRIMM'S (Grosset) 155-165; Grimm GRIMM'S (Scribner's) 64-72; Grimm GRIMM'S (World) 52-59; Grimm HOUSEHOLD 118-125 (+ pigeons peck out one eye of each sister on way to wedding, other eye on way back).

Bb* Cinder-Maid. Tree over mother's grave gives clothing in nut. Bird warns to return by midnight. She calls "Mist behind and light before" (R255) and escapes. Third time tar on step catches her shoe. Sisters cut off toe and heel but bird betrays truth. Weds prince. European: Jacobs EUROPEAN 1-12.

Bc* The Enchanted Cow. Mother is turned into cow which spins for girl (Q2.1.1Eb). Cow is killed and buried. Girl to pick up scattered basket of millet when stepmother and daughter go to church. Finds two doves and chest of clothing on grave. Attends church thrice, loses shoe. Slipper test. Cock crows to tell where girl has been hidden. Serbia: Spicer LONG 47-69.

Bd* The Wonderful Birch. Witch takes wife's place, turns wife to sheep and has sheep killed. Daughter told by sheep to bury bones. Task: picking barleycorns from ashes while stepmother attends feast. Tree on grave gives magic branch to perform task, provides clothing and horses. Ring lost in tarred door post at feast. Returns thrice, head circlet, slippers lost. Witch's daughter under table is kicked each evening by prince and wounded during feast. Slipper test. Witch's daughter now has wooden foot, arm, and stone eye because of injuries at feast. She carves these parts to fit slipper, ring, and circlet. Prince recognizes real love and forces witch's daughter to form bridge en route to castle for him to pass over. Takes heroine and leaves witch's daughter as bridge. A golden hemlock grows from her body and warns witch mother. The witch restores her own daughter and turns the new queen to a reindeer placing her daughter in the queen's place (Type 402; K1911). Deer nurses son thrice. Third time king disenchants by destroying skin while old lady combs her hair. Russia (Karelia): Lang RED 114-127.

C* Cenerentola. Stepmother and six daughters mistreat. Cenerentola asks father to bring gift from dove of the fairies of Sardinia. His ship will not move until he fetches fairies' gift. He is given a date tree, golden hoe, golden bucket, and silver napkin. Cenerentola cares for the plant and a fairy emerges. Tree gives clothing for feast. King has her followed and she throws coins to distract followers. Returns thrice, throws pearls behind, loses slipper. Slipper test. Weds prince. Italy: Haviland FAVORITE ..ITALY 3-18; Mincielli OLD 24-34; Toor GOLDEN 31-37 (Zezolla); Vittorini OLD 63-68 (asks father for bird Verelio. Bird dresses her for ball).

Da* Cat-Skin (Allerleirauh). Dying queen asks king to wed only one as fair as she. He decides to wed daughter (H363). She asks for three dresses, one gold as the sun, one silver as the moon, one shining as the stars. She asks for a cloak of one thousand pieces of the fur of every beast in the kingdom (K521.1). She carries the three desses in nutshells and covers self with cloak. A king finds her sleeping in tree and takes as maid. She goes thrice to the ball in her three dresses. Drops tokens in king's soup thrice (H94), ring, brooch, necklace (or ring, golden reel, golden spinning wheel). During third ball king slips ring on her finger. She is thus identified when questioned about soup. Wed. Germany (Grimm): De La Mare ANIMAL 297-306 /Dalgliesh ENCHANTED 48-56/; Grimm GRIMM'S (Scribner's) 192-198; Grimm JUNIPER v. 2 236-244; Lang GREEN 269-275 /Lang FIFTY 193-198/.

Db* Cat-Skin (English). Father who wanted a son decides to wed daughter to first man who asks. An old man requests her hand. Henwife advises her to ask for a coat of silver, one of gold and one of the feathers of all birds of the air, and a catskin coat. She flees and takes service as maid in catskin coat. Attends ball thrice and says she lives at the sign of the "Basin of water," "Broken ladle," "Broken skimmer." Prince has insulted her with these objects as he left to attend ball. Prince discovers her identity and is allowed to wed her. England: Jacobs MORE 204-210; Reeves ENGLISH 82-95; Sleigh NORTH 34-43; Steel ENGLISH 117-122.

Dc* Catskins (Appalachian). Wife of master

dies and he wishes to wed maid. She asks for dress the color of all fish in the sea; all birds in the air; all flowers in the world, and a flying box. She flies off in the box, has it sink under the ground and in a dress patched with catskins is maid to the king. Attends three balls. Identified by ring baked in cake. Wed. U.S. (Appalchia): Chase GRANDMOTHER 106-114.

Dd* Horseskin. King locks three daughters in tower after his remarriage. Two die, youngest rescued. Wears dress made of old horsekin, takes service as maid. Attends ball thrice, king sickens, ring token in soup. Wed. Portugal: Michael PORTUGUESE 62-73.

De* Gulaida. King to wed one who fits anklet. His daughter fits. She leaves in cloak of leather and takes service as maid, claiming self blind and deaf. Thrice attends party. Throws coins behind to escape. Says came from land of "scoops and ladles." Prince seeks this land. She sends loaf with ring token inside along as provisions for his journey. He discovers token and returns to wed. Arabia: Mittleman BIRD 10-12.

Df* Prezioza, the She-Bear. Man to wed one as lovely as wife, chooses daughter. She turns self to bear by putting magic piece of wood in mouth. Prince takes bear home. Sees her in womanly form and sickens of love. Bear cares for him. He kisses bear and wood falls from her mouth. Wed. Italy: Manning-Sanders PRINCESS 76-83; Mincielli OLD 54-63.

Dg* Bearskin. Daughter of king wears bearskin and travels in magic wheelbarrow. Hunting prince takes bear home. She attends ball thrice in dresses of moonbeam, sunlight, starlight. Ring token in soup. Wed. Lang ROSE 56-63.

Dh* Donkey skin. King wed to one as lovely as wife. Daughter flees with dress the color of sky, moonbeams, sunshine. Donkey skin covering. Magic chest holds dresses and follows her underground. Prince spies on her in dress, falls lovesick. Ring in cake. To wed whom it fits. France (Cabinet des Fées): Lang ROSE 1-14. France (Perrault): Perrault PERRAULT'S (Dodd) 92-99.

Di* The Grateful Toad. Man offers daughter in return for rain. Youngest to wed serpent. She asks dowry of one thousand needles, one thousand gourds, one thousand strips of wadding. Floats the gourds with wadding pinned to them in rice fields. Says will wed whoever can sink them. Serpent pierces skin on needles attempting to sink them and dies. Wart-toad woman of the mountain thanks girl for destroying serpent by giving her a skin to wear. She takes service at the mayor's house. His son will get well if marries woman from whose tray he eats. He has seen her without her cloak and is lovesick. Eats from her tray, weds. Japan: Bang MEN 27-31.

E* Cap O' Rushes. Youngest daughter loves father like salt. Banished, she wears a cloak of rushes and works as maid. Thrice attends ball, master's son falls lovesick. Ring token in gruel. Wed. Father served meat without salt (H592.1). Reconciliation. England: Jacobs ENGLISH 51–56 /Haviland FAVORITE..ENGLAND 76–88/, /Minard WOMENFOLK 77–82/; Lurie CLEVER 84–91; Steel ENGLISH 209–216; Wiggin FAIRY 119–123; Williams-Ellis FAIRY..BRITISH 117–123.

F* Rushen Coatie. Stepmother and three ugly daughters. Rushen Coatie is given a coat of rushes and made to sit in ashes. Dying mother told her a little red calf would aid. Bread in his left ear, cheese in right (B115.1). Calf is killed and buried bones grant wishes. Reincarnated calf has shank bone missing. Calf teaches charm to make dinner cook self so she can attend church at Christmas (B313.1). Slipper lost, sisters cut off toes and heels to fit. Raven sings of treachery. Wed. England: Jacobs MORE 163–168.

G* Little Scar Face. Two elder daughters force youngest to sweep hot coals and burn self. Bride test for Great Chief Invisible, she who sees him may wed. His sister conducts tests. The girl who describes properly his shoulder straps and bow string will wed. Elder sisters fail. Youngest asks birch tree in which her mother's spirit may reside for bark to make white dress. She sees the Great Chief Invisible descending with a Rainbow as his shoulder strap, the Milky Way as his bow string. Her face is bathed in dew and the scars caused by ashes disappear. Wed. Native American (Micmac): Arbuthnot FAIRY 109–201 /Arbuthnot ANTHOLOGY 392–393/. Native American: Association TOLD..GREEN 156–161; Cunningham TALKING 105–112 /Child Study CASTLES 59–67/, /Sheehan FOLK 141–148/; Haviland NORTH 94–96 /Macmillan CANADIAN WONDER TALES/. Native American (Algonquin): DeWit TALKING 34–38.

H* Fair, Brown and Trembling. Youngest daughter attends church in dress magically provided by henwife. Honeybird on right shoulder, honey-finer on left, milk-white mare with golden trappings. Second Sunday appears in black, third in red, white and green. Shoe lost. Slipper test. Prince defeats four other princes to win her. Eldest sister pushes into sea when son born (K1911). Whale swallows, spits up thrice. Husband must shoot with silver bullet. Restored. Ireland: Jacobs CELTIC 184–187; Pilkington SHAMROCK 19–39.

I* Korean variant.

Ia* Stepdaughter must husk sack of rice and fill cracked jar with water before attending festival. Tokgabi mends jar with clay, birds husk rice. To weed fields before attending picnic. Black ox eats weeds, leads her to rare fruits. Two stepsisters imitate and are led into thorns. Korea: Carpenter KOREAN 119–124.

Ib* Tokgabbi shells walnuts so girl may go to dance; mend coat so may attend boating party; tell to jump into briars before attending archery contest. She emerges from briars in lovely clothing. Tokgabbi gives magic bow and arrow and she wins contest and becomes attendant in palace. Sisters imitate and are scratched. Korea: Anderson BOY 60–76.

J* Chinese variant. Stepmother lures Shih Chieh's pet fish to shore and kills. Shih Chieh plants fish's bones and they grant wishes. She attends festival clothed by fish and drops shoe. Slipper test. She weds king. He overuses the wishing power of the fish bones and they cease to answer requests. He buries them along with one hundred bushels of pearls on seashore and later finds all have been washed away by sea. Western China: Hume FAVORITE..CHINA 15–22.

K* Ashpet. Two daughters sent to fetch fire from witch refuse to comb her hair. Hired girl Ashpet obliges witch and is given fire and enabled to attend church. Witch causes dishes to wash selves, turns mouse and piece of rawhide to saddled horse, produces dress and shoes from scraps. Ashpet drops shoes to distract prince riding home with her. Bird warns of sister's mutilated feet in slipper test. Ashpet is found hidden under washtub. Wed. U.S. (Appalachia): Chase GRANDFATHER 115–123.

L* Kari Woodenskirt. SEE: B335.2D (Helpful Bull) for tale beginning. In wooden skirt, Kari serves in castle, attends church in copper dress. Knocks on wall and man brings out dress for her (SEE: B335.2D for motivation). Attends church thrice, saying is from "Washingland." She flees chanting "Light in front, dark behind" (R255). Her shoe is caught in prepared pitch. Slipper test. Stepsister cuts foot to fit. Bird calls warning. Wed. Scandinavia: Aulaire EAST 122–137; Baker GOLDEN 19–33; Lang RED 192–207.

M* Ring in the Porridge Bowl. Stepdaughter ordered killed, spared. As maid, attends church in hidden finery. Drops ring in porridge bowl. Weds young lord of the house. Netherlands (Friesland): Spicer OWL'S 106–124.

N* Liisa and the Prince. Ogress spits in face and calls "my body to you, yours to me." Takes body of girl's mother. Mother turns to birch tree spirit. Stepmother makes Liisa gather scattered seeds before she can attend feast. Tree gives magic brush, clothing, horse. Prince given rings seeks one it fits. Earring test. Slipper test. Ogress makes own daughter fit by magic but king suspects, kills witch and daughter and weds Liisa. Finland: Bowman TALES..TUPA 187–198.

O* The Enchanted Black Cat. Stepsister given to prince in place of Marie. Shoes do not fit and black cat calls "She's giving you the wrong one." Cat and Marie set adrift, reach prince's castle. Cat returns to battle witch with water, wind and fire, destroying witch. Cat becomes a man. France: Carpenter WONDER..DOGS 222-234.

Pa* Dress the color of the sea. Girl asks father for chest with wooden wings and dress with stars and sky, sea and fishes, earth and flowers. She flies off in box, escaping old suitor. Prince takes box to palace. She emerges and attends church thrice at Easter. He seeks her. Ring token is in biscuits she bakes as provisions. Wed. Greece: Wilson GREEK 90-96.

Pb* Girl with sea serpent playmate. To wed old king. Asks dresses color of all flowers, color of all sea fishes, color of sky and stars. Sea serpent helps her escape in ship to prince on isle. To call to sea-serpent (enchanted princess) on happiest day of life and release from spell. Forgets. Sea still calls—why sea moans. Brazil: Sheehan FOLK 127-137 /Cathon PERHAPS 217-227/, /Eels BRAZIL/.

Qa* The Jeweled Slipper. Unkind sister steals fish from net of sister and claims reward for biggest catch. Genie tells Cam to keep blue fish. Tam kills it and buries under areca tree. Cock shows Cam place in return for grain. Buries bones under bed and digs up in one hundred days. Have turned to jeweled slippers. Crow drops them in prince's yard. He seeks foot, to wed Cam. Tam leaves her unconscious in wood, old woman cares for her. Her memory is lost. Prince hunting finds her and weds. Tam asks how she got soft skin. Cam says bathing in boiling water. Tam jumps into vat and is killed. Vietnam: Clark IN pb (ends with wedding); Graham BEGGAR 45-55.

R* The Blue Lotus Flower. Elder sister pushes younger into river. White turtle follows younger daughter, is spirit of her mother. Aunt kills it. Daughter throws bone in yard—mango tree grows. Only she can pick fruit. Aunt burns it. Cucumber vine grows from splinters. Only she can pick. Aunt cuts plant up. Root thrown into river = blue lotus. Only she can touch. Plucks it for king. Weds. Ceylon: Tooze WONDERFUL 77-82.

S* The girl in the chest. Vampire weds each of three girls, kills eldest two, youngest flees (G561.1). Prays to God for chest she can lock from inside. Sleeps in chest at night. King sees her, takes chest to castle. She comes out and eats his supper each night. Caught. Chamberlain has her kidnapped, thrown aside as dead when faints, old woman cares for her. King ill and will not eat. She sends dish with curl of her hair on side thrice. He comes for her. Wed. Yugoslavia: Fillmore LAUGHING 201-218.

W* Turkey Girl. Girl tends turkeys. Given lovely clothing and sent to dance by turkeys. Not to stay too long. Overstays and turkeys leave her. Clothing turns back to rags. Native American (Zuñi): Haviland NORTH 76-82.

Y* Disguised heroine weds prince. (The threefold flight motif is missing from these variants, but other motifs seem to relate these tales to this tale group.)

Ya* Polo the Snake-Girl. Girl clothed in water bola skin to hide. Masilo sees her without skin. Weds and burns skin. Basutoland: Carpenter AFRICAN 121-126.

Z* Tattercoats. (This tale lacks the threefold flight motif but is included here because of other similarities to the Type 510 tales.) Aged lord vows never to look on granddaughter's face after his daughter dies in childbirth (S42). She wears rags. The king visits the region and the old man has to cease weeping, cut his overgrown hair, and present himself at court. The gooseherd arranged for Tattercoats to meet the prince on the road and the gooseherd plays on his flute a tune causing the prince to fall in love. Tattercoats promises to bring her geese to the ball at midnight. The gooseherd pipes and her rags turn to robes, the geese to pages bearing her train. She weds the prince. England: Finlay TATTERCOATS 1-8; Jacobs MORE 76-82 /Arbuthnot ANTHOLOGY 158-159/, /Arbuthnot FAIRY 19-21/; Reeves ENGLISH 12-22; Steel ENGLISH 39-43; Wiggin FAIRY 109-113.

R222. Unknown knight (three days' tournament). For three days in succession an unknown knight in different armor wins a tournament and escapes without recognition. Finally identified by tokens. SEE: B316; H331.1.1 (Princess on Glass Mountain).

R222.1* Unknown warrior. Warrior thrice saves battle. Is identified third time by wound received (H56).

A* Disowned princess wed to lonely hero. He wins battle thrice using marvelous horse and armor. King binds wound with handkerchief third time and hero is revealed. Arabia: Mittleman BIRD 82-98 (+H331.1.2.2). Slovenia: Kavcic GOLDEN 113 (H331.1.1A). Gypsy: Manning-Sanders RED 132-138 (+H331.1.1F).

B* Queen Crane. Crane will aid if spared. Hero wins battle thrice using horses and armor provided by Queen Crane. King binds wound with handkerchief third day. Sweden: Baker GOLDEN 46-53.

C* Shepherd's Nosegay. In return for kindness to beggar hero receives magic whip, wallet, axe—sheep will graze near it, pipe—sheep will dance. He kills two giants, finds magic chest with two servants. Forces princess to say "please" to get nosegay each day. Goes thrice as suitor on steeds given by servants of the chest. Wounded and leg tied with handkerchief. Czechoslovakia: Fillmore SHEPHERD'S 72-81 /Haviland FAVORITE..CZECHOSLOVAKIA 49-66/, /Fenner PRINCESSES 128-136/.

R245. Whale boat. A man is carried across water on a whale (fish). Native American (Micmac, Passamaquoddy): Williams-Ellis ROUND 208-216.

R246. Crane-bridge. Fugitives are helped across stream by a crane who lets them cross on his leg. The pursuers are either refused assistance or drowned by the crane. Native American (Comanche): Jablow MAN 15-17 (owl dropped). Native American (Shoshone): Heady SAGE 54-56 (crane drops coyote); Heady SAGE 74-79 (bear dropped).

R251. Flight on a tree which ogre tries to cut down. SEE ALSO: B524.1.2; B650.2; K311.3H.

A* Ivanko and the Witch (Dragon). Father makes dugout boat. Ivanko chants and boat moves. Mother chants and he comes ashore. Witch imitates, has voice changed to sound like mother. Ivanko has witch's daughter show how to get on oven shovel (G526). Ivanko escapes and climbs tree. Witch gnaws it down. Ivanko helps swans to carry him home, they fly off with him and set on roof of house. SEE ALSO: G530.2N. Russia: Bloch IVANKO pb (dragon); Damjan IVAN pb; Wyndham RUSSIAN 32-41.

B* Vengeful enemy trees hunter. Hunter throws down magic pellets three times, pellets vanquish enemies' three dogs. Sierre Leone (Krio): Robinson THREE.

R255. Formula for girl fleeing: behind me night, etc. "Behind me night and before me day that no one shall see where I go." SEE: G530.2M; R221Bb (Cinder-maid); R221L (Kari Woodencoat).

R260. Pursuits.

R261. Pursuit by rolling object. SEE ALSO: G422.1.1.1.

R261.1. Pursuit by rolling head. SEE: G361.2.

R261.2* Pursuit by rolling gourd. Old woman pursued by green gourd she cuts. Groundhog, fox, wildcat, panther, shelter her to no avail. Bear sits on gourd and squashes. U.S. (Appalachia): Chase WICKED 213-221.

R300 - R399. Refuges and recapture.

R310. Refuges.

R311. Tree refuge. Type 162. SEE: F1045 (night spent in tree); R251 (flight on a tree, ogre tries to cut down).

R351. Fugitive discovered by reflection in water. SEE: G276.2 (by watch); U136.0.1 (by maiden).

S. UNNATURAL CRUELTY

S0 - S99. Cruel relatives.

S10. Cruel parents.

S11.3.3.1.1* Father kills son for eating forbidden apple. Test to jump over hole until guilty admit crime. Sisters plead innocent. Brother admits. Haiti: Wolkstein MAGIC 171-176.

S12.1. Treacherous mother, marries ogre and plots against son. Type 590.

A* The Blue Belt. Son finds blue belt (scarf) which gives strength. He intimidates giant (troll). Mother weds giant and plots to rid self of son. At quarry giant throws rock down on lad; mother feigns ill and lad is sent for lion's blood, he kills one and eleven others obey him; sent to brother trolls' castle for apple of sleep. He falls asleep but lions guard and kill trolls. He weds their captive, the King of Arabia's daughter. Mother discovers secret of strength and takes blue belt (D861; K975). He is blinded and set adrift. Lion sees blind hare recover sight from spring (B512), restores his sight. He meets wife, cracks open giant egg on rocky isle and huge bird emerges. Reaching Arabia he buries sailors up to eyes in sand as bait and kills giant bird as it alights. Princess of Arabia to be given to one who finds her. In white bearskin he is taken to her chamber (K1341.1). Norway: Asbjornsen EAST 57-75; Asbjornsen EAST (Row) 35-52.

B* Mother feigns ill and needs strip of hide of Black Bull of the Forest, lad kills; needs nail from toe of tenth Black Cat on Isle of the Ten Black Cats. He must kill each cat ten times, tenth time each turns to a maid, he weds the tenth. Apple from Island of Nine

Black Dogs, wife gives magic boat to take and magic ball of yarn, throw and becomes bridge to return over. Kill each of nine dogs nine times = nine men, wed the nine women of Isle of Cats. Mother discovers source of strength and steals. He is blinded and left in cave, a slave shares food and keeps him alive. Wife seeks and tends, lad falls into well-of-all-healing and sight is restored. Slave steals scarf back for Jack. He kills giants. Ireland: MacManus WELL 65-82.

C* The Bad Mother. Prince in empty house takes sabre from wall and beheads eleven dragons as enter. Captures last, smallest, and keeps in jar. Weds maid. Fetches mother of dragon against maid's warning. Mother enters forbidden room, gives dragon drink of water. Agrees she loves dragons and plots to get rid of son. Mother feigns ill, she needs porker of the sow in the other world. Maid gives horse with twelve wings to carry there. Sow bites off half of horse's tail, maid substitutes ordinary pig and keeps magical. Mother needs golden apple (H1321.1). Water from fresh mountains. Maid aids. Mother plays cards, winner to get wish. She binds him and kills. Maid reassembles parts and resuscitates using magic porker, water and mouth. Lad kills dragon and mother. Gypsy: De La Mare ANIMAL 252-258; Manning-Sanders RED 146-153 /Hoke DRAGONS 22-28/.

S12.1.0.1. Treacherous sister marries ogre and plots against brother. Types 315, 590. SEE ALSO: R111.1.3E (Dragon slayer).

A* Kind Brother, Cruel Sister (K2212.0.2). In den of thieves lad beheads twelve thieves. Their mother revives them and his sister joins in plot to get rid of lad. She sends him for milk of a hare. Hare gives this and becomes servant. Fox, wolf, dragon same. Trapped in haunted mill--pets free him. Sister discovers secret of his strength (magic sword). He is captured by thieves while bathing. He asks to play last hymn on pipe--calls animals who kill thieves. Sister to be released when has cried jar full of tears. Lad weds princess. Animals ask to be beheaded and cremated. From ashes spring trees. To burn these. Twelve new stars appear in heavens. Poland: Zajdler POLISH 61-78.

Ba* Three Fat Ewes for Three Fine Hounds. Lad trades three ewes for three hounds. 1. wise, 2. fast, 3. strong. Sister goes to live with giant, knife over door to kill brother. Wise hound warns. Fleet runs through door to prove. Strong pushes house down on giant and sister killing them. Scotland (Isle of Mull): Nic Leodhas SEA 73-85.

Bb* Finlay the Hunter. Finlay warns sister not to let fire go out or open window. She disobeys. Giant's son comes and woos her. She plots against Finlay. Old woman warns and Finlay defeats with aid of his dogs. Second giant killed, third same. Mother has

Finlay bind dogs with three hairs. He only feigns doing so, defeats her. Sister and giant husband flee. Weds daughter of helping old woman. Takes giant's treasure and magic rod. Scotland: NcNeil DOUBLE 96-104; Williams-Ellis FAIRY..BRITISH 272-283.

C* Iron, Steel and Strongest of All. Lad trades sheep for three dogs. Finding castle where food appears magically he brings sister to live with him. Old man advises her to poison brother. Dogs overturn food. Wine, same. Sent for lemon, dogs locked up. Old man beats but dogs break free and defend. He and dogs leave her in castle. +R111.1.3Ea. Italy: Toor GOLDEN 93-103.

D* Three Princes and Their Beasts. Wolf offers cub to each prince if spared. Lion, fox, boar, hare, bear, same. Arrow taken, blood to flow if dead, milk if alive. Elder kills all but one of robbers in castle, brings stepsister to live there. Stepsister breaks tabu and enters cellar with dead robbers, gives to drink to wounded robber of magic healing bottle he requests. To wed him. Ties brother's thumb behind back to test strength. Third night he cannot break it. Robbers take him. Asks to blow horn thrice, animals come and kill robbers. Stepsister to weep bowl of tears before release. +R111.1.3An. Lithuania: Lang VIOLET 34-45.

S31. Cruel Stepmother. Types 403, 425, 432, 450, 451, 480, 502, 510, 511, 516, 590, 592, 700, 708, 709, 720. SEE: N271; P253.2; Q2.1; R221.

S31.6* Second wife seals sons of first wife in hole to starve. Father rescues and banishes wife. Rescued lad is actually abandoned twin of second wife whom lad had revived. East Africa: Nunn AFRICAN 134-141.

S42. Cruel grandfather. SEE: R221Z. Tattercoats.

S62.1. Bluebeard. Girl marries murderous husband. SEE ALSO: G561.

A* Bluebeard. Type 312. Bride opens forbidden door (C611) and drops key in blood (C913). She asks respite to say prayers (K551.1) until brothers come and kill Bluebeard. France (Perrault): De La Mare TALES 131-141; Lang BLUE 313-319; Opie CLASSIC 103-109; Perrault PERRAULT'S (Dodd) 78-88; Perrault PERRAULT'S (Dover) 31-34; Perrault PERRAULT'S FAMOUS 41-60; Rackham ARTHUR 143-152.

B* Mr. Fox. Type 955. Lady Mary visits suitor's castle and sees murdered victims, chopped hand flies into her lap as she hides. At wedding feast she produces hand with ring to prove story. England: Jacobs ENGLISH 153-158 /De La Mare ANIMAL 245-248/, /Minard WOMENFOLK 130-135/, /Steel ENGLISH 164-168/.

C* Robber Bridegroom. Type 955. (K1916) Bride visits bridegroom's house. Strews peas to find way home (R135). Old woman hides her. Hand of victim falls near her. Produces at wedding feast. Germany (Grimm): Grimm GRIMM'S (Grosset) 255-259; Grimm HOUSE-HOLD 176-179; Rackham GRIMM'S 66-70.

Cb* Robber Bridegroom. Variant. Girl cuts off heads of robber's as they climb in (K912). Chief vows revenge, weds. Old woman advises to make dummy of self and flee. Escapes following trail of white stones she has dropped. Hungary: Manning-Sanders RED 84-92.

S71. The Cruel Uncle. SEE ALSO: S143.2 (Babes in Wood).

S71.2. The Cruel Uncle: Kills both sons of brother. Third child is disguised as girl. Uncle discovers. Lad takes dead brother's trap, knife blade, eagle down, and sour berry along. Uncle catches boy's hand in crack in log by removing wedge and leaves. Boy puts sour berry in crack and it opens. Uncle pushes boy off cliff--eagle down helps float down. Giant clam swallows, cuts with knife. Uncle sets adrift in wooden box. Eagle people find. He weds daughter of eagle chief. As eagle he drops whale on beach for village. Uncle claims he killed. Boy, as eagle, carries uncle up and drops into sea. Takes parents to land of eagle to live. Eskimo: Maher BLIND 53-71.

S100 - S199. Revolting murders or mutilations.

S140. Cruel abandonments and exposures.

S143. Abandoned in forest. Types 327, 450, 708, 872. SEE ALSO: P253.2.

S143.2* Babes in the Wood: two children abandoned to die by cruel uncle. England: Jacobs MORE 120-126; Steel ENGLISH 216-221; Tarrant FAIRY 89-96.

S200 - S299. Cruel sacrifice.

S215.1* Child promised to animals. The Hyena's Egg. Mother flings hyena's egg brought home by daughter into fire. Hyena claims next born. Son, Temba, speaks at birth. Hyena hides in grass bundle. Temba tells bundle to walk--it does (K607). Hyena hides in trap. Temba tells trap to drop stone--it does. Temba says hyena's mouth is not big enough to swallow. Hyena opens mouth. Temba throws knife in and shoots arrow into heart. East Africa: Arnott TEMBA 9-19.

S241.1. Unwitting bargain with devil evaded by driving dog over the bridge first. The first thing that goes over the bridge has been promised as payment for building the bridge. SEE ALSO: K210; M211.2.1. Wales: Sheppard-

Jones WELSH 173-177. England (Westmoreland): Colwell ROUND 23-26. France: Courlander RIDE 173-177 (cat; Bridge at St. Cloud).

S260. Sacrifices.

S261.0.2* Virgin's blood necessary to cast perfect bell. Daughter casts herself into molten metal to save father's life. He will be beheaded if does not cast perfect bell on third try. Her shoe is caught as she leaps. Bell tolls her name "Ko-Ai" and trails off "Hsieh" (word for shoe). China: Buck FAIRY 264-268; Carpenter TALES..CHINESE 175-181; Wyndham FOLK 66-72.

S268. Child sacrificed to provide blood for cure of friend.

A* Faithful John. Type 516 (H1381.3.1.1.1; P361). Love at sight of portrait (T11.2). King abducts by enticing her onto ship to examine goods. Faithful John hears rowers foretell doom of king and princess, if anyone prevents will turn to stone if tells (N451). Faithful John kills deadly horse, burns poison shirt, takes three drops of blood from queen's breast to save her, etc. Condemned, John tells secret and turns to stone (C961.2). Can be revived if smeared with blood of king's two children. King slays children, both Faithful John and children revive. Germany (Grimm): Grimm GRIMM'S (Grosset) 345-355; Grimm GRIMM'S (Scribner's) 19-28; Grimm GRIMM'S (World) 219-228; Lang BLUE 320-329. Italy: Mincielli OLD 84-87 (wants wife white as marble and red as mother's blood, hair black as raven). Jacobs EUROPEAN 170-179 (kills dragon in wedding chamber). Gypsy: Manning-Sanders RED 23-30. Gypsy (Turkey): Hampden GYPSY 147-154 (bald-headed servant, revived by prince scattering earth from native village on grave).

B* Hasan and Husain. Sultan's wife and fisherman's wife to share fish (fish instructs). Bear sons. Husain wins princess for Hasan by stealing three tokens from her (horses tell him how). En route home Hasan opens casket, bird snatches necklace, following it becomes lost. Wife disguises self and Cadi and she and Husain seek Hasan. Dispute over the necklace is brought to her court and Hasan discovered. Husain overhears horses say Jinni is coming to kill Hasan, whoever tells will turn to stone. Son must be killed to restore. Both revive. Arabia: Mittleman BIRD 99-116.

C* Amis and Amile. Two friends. Amis wins bride for Amile by defeating knight. Amis contracts leprosy and becomes beggar. Amile recognizes cup and tends. Will be cured if bathed in blood of two children. All revive. France: Picard FRENCH 69-76.

D* Princess Felicity. Love through sight of portrait (T11.2). Servant hears Spanish wind and wind from France tell how to rescue princess from enchanted castle. Rescues her.

Builds bower so winds can't harm. They are angered that someone overheard. They curse that princess will die if touches grapes of vendor or tries to rescue drowning man. Servant strikes grapes out of hand and cuts off hands of drowning man. Prince kills servant. Princess dreams truth. Prince hears wind say could revive with water of certain well. Does so. France: Manning-Sanders BOOK.. PRINCES 97-107.

E* Pappa Greatnose. Soldier in tree hears old goblin, Pappa Greatnose, tell that twig will become bridge if laid over water. Whoever tells turns to stone. He saves king's troops. Learns that the dust from hollow will rout enemy. To wed princess. She forces him to tell. He turns to stone. She tells. She turns to stone. Soldier's uncle sprinkles stones with certain water after going to tree to overhear remedy. Fearing he will turn to stone he returns to tree. Learns must whisper secret into trunk of certain tree by river. Free. France: Manning-Sanders BOOK..GHOSTS 17-54.

S300 - S399. Abandoned or murdered children.

S300. Abandoned or murdered children. SEE ALSO: P253.2.

S331. Exposure of child in boat (floating chest). SEE: H1273.2 (Three Golden Hairs); K1355 (alter letter of execution); S12.1A.

S352.2* Animal aids abandoned child. The Stork's Daughter. Type 709A. Abandoned girl is raised by stork. Storks leave her to fetch golden bracelet and anklets for her. She lets fire go out and goes to demon's house in search. Leaves trail of ashes on return. Demons follow trail and call "Here are your golden bracelets." Parrot calls "No bracelets, do not open door." Dog, cat warn same. Demon kills each but drinks so much he dies. Storks return with bracelets, wed her to nobleman. Ceylon: Tooze WONDERFUL 83-87.

S366.1. Abandoned children. Sister tells brother to look at elk, buffalo and they drop dead. She wishes them skinned, tepee sewn, etc. and it is so. Sends Raven to drop meat at campfire of people and lure them back. Tells brother to look at them and all drop dead. She revives a few, reformed, to procreate tribe. Native American (Gros Ventre): Curtis GIRL 45-51.

T. SEX

T0 - T99. Love.

T10. Falling in love.

T11.2. Love through sight of picture (H1213.1J; S268).

T11.2.1.1* Love through sight of statue. Ugly prince has golden image made of girl--will wed only one as lovely. Servant mistakes image for her mistress. She is not to see him until after first child is born. He passes her in disguise and stares at her. She leaves in offense. Refuses all his attempts to woo. Sakka, king of the sky, settles the matter by sending seven kings to demand her in marriage. She returns to King Kusa. India: Wyatt GOLDEN 59-80.

T11.2.2* Wife gives husband portrait to take to fields. Lord sees and takes her. Husband serves as pine tree seller at New Year's and wife smiles at him. Lord changes clothes with him so she will smile at him. They lock the gate and take his place. Japan: Asia FOLK I 13-17.

T11.2.3* The Beautiful Princess. Prince sends for girl in portrait. He weds veiled. Servant tells him she is the ugly one and he vows never to look on her face. Visits her only by night. She disguises self as peasant and cuts foot in his presence. He discovers wounded foot belongs to wife that night. Portugal: Michael PORTUGUESE 172-178.

T11.4.8* Love through sight of finger. Type 877. King marries woman whose finger he has seen and whose voice he has heard. She turns out to be another woman. He throws her out. She hangs in a tree. Fairies change into beautiful girl. King takes as wife. Her sister tries to imitate by having self skinned. Sicily: Hampden HOUSE 17-22. Majorca: Mehdevi BUNGLING 37-43 (-sister).

T11.5* Falling in love with reflection in water. Princess first sees prince. SEE: K1815.0.2.

T35.5.1* Hine-Moa tries to cross water to reach flute-playing Tutaneksi. She swims

using gourds as life preservers. And weds.
Maori: Berry MAGIC 56-64.

T53.0.2* Matchmakers arrange affairs. Old woman entices girl to meet Moor who plans to seduce. Bird saves girl by telling her tale to detain her. Spain: Sawyer WAY 297-304.

T53.6* Frog is matchmaker. Hides in pitcher of sun's maid and carries messages from earthly lover. Steals her eyes and father allows her to wed to regain. U.S. (Black): Lester BLACK 62-72.

T53.7* Wali Dad the Simple-Hearted as matchmaker. He saves to buy gift for princess. She returns gift and he sends it to Prince he admires. Prince returns gift, which he sends on to princess. This continues until she wishes to meet gift-giver. Wali sends the prince. India: Buck FAIRY 19-28; Lang FIFTY 345-353; Sleigh NORTH 90-162. China: Ritchie TREASURE 3-39 (Li-Po).

T55.2* Princess declares her love for court jester. Is king in disguise. Poland: Borski JOLLY 63-73 (King Bartek) /Arbuthnot FAIRY 159-162/, /Arbuthnot ANTHOLOGY 274-275/. Samoyed: Titiev HOW 27-35 (disfigured man chosen over handsome groom is real hero).

T62. Princess to marry first man who asks her. SEE: H465 (King Thrushbeard).

T72.2.1. Prince marries scornful girl and punishes. Cannetella. Girl will wed only one with gold head and gold teeth. Wizard, Sciorovante, had one made and claims her. Keeps in stable for seven years. To eat horse's leavings. She escapes and father makes room with seven iron doors. She sends old woman with gift who slips paper charm under pillow which causes all to sleep. Piece of paper falls off as he tries to carry her off. Guards awake and he is killed. She weds a prince and becomes good-natured. SEE ALSO: H465 (King Thrushbeard). Italy: Manning-Sanders BOOK..WIZARDS 118-127.

T75.2.1.1* Rejected suitor's revenge. Girl refuses all suitors, father hangs her by feet over cliff. She calls to former suitors but is rejected. Rope breaks and she falls into sea--becomes sea otter. Upsets canoes of suitors. Sea-otters still upset canoes. Eskimo: Maher BLIND 73-78.

T75.2.1.2* Girl says would rather marry a stone than suitors. Turns to stone. Eskimo: Caswell SHADOWS 76-80.

T75.2.1.3* Foni rejects sorcerer's advances. He turns her goats to stone. Turns her to bear and lover to lion. As bear she cares for lost baby prince. King brings to palace and defeats sorcerer with aid of own court magician. Bonfire is built for twenty days and nights. Sorcerer attempts to put it out--is vanquished. Couple regain form. Sudan: Manning-Sanders BOOK..SORCERERS 91-98.

T81.6.1* Girl kills herself after lover's death. Wife agrees to wed Emperor if he will honor her dead husband. After funeral she leaps to death in river. China: Chang CHINESE 45-47.

T91.4.1.2* Unequals in love. Old lady tells condemned lad she will free if he weds her. She turns to young girl after wedding, reveals that he is really prince. Portugal: Lang ROSE 138-148.

T91.6.4.4* Princess loves man so poor has no clothing. Father and he had only one pair of pants between them so he buried father in the pants. Her father banishes them. A hermit gives magic walking stick and palm hat which turns to palace. King attacks. Whirlwind takes the lovers to heaven. A lake left on the spot. Vietnam: Graham BEGGAR 79-89.

T92.0.1.1* Rivals in love. Girl promised to three men. Judge agrees she shall belong to one in whose yurt she is at that moment. Lover has already abducted her. Mongolia: Masey STORIES 16-27.

T92.11.2. Rivals go courting together. Hare and possum. Hare goes ahead and creates trouble for late arriving possum. +A2466.1. Native American (Cherokee): Bell JOHN 51-53; Scheer CHEROKEE 33-36.

T92.11.3* Bat, spider, and beetle court together. Other two discomfit companion wooer at each attempt. They vow to court alone in future. Burton MAGIC 102-104.

T92.11.4* Leopard and Rabbit court. Kalulu catches suitor's required catch of antelope and birds by tricking into bag. Baboons are too smart to be caught and vow to revenge selves on Kalulu that night. Kalulu lends his house to rival leopard and baboons kill it. Congo: Burton MAGIC 89-94.

T92.15* Old ugly suitor claims rejecting girl has hexed him and she is to drink poison cup. Her lover forces the poison down old suitor's throat and weds girl. Gold Coast: Carpenter AFRICAN 137-144.

T93.6* Hard-hearted lady sends lover on repeated quests, last of which kills him. France: Manning-Sanders BOOK..GHOSTS 101-102.

T100 - T199. Marriage.

T100. Marriage.

T102.1* Master Tobacco. Type 611. Beggar lad sold to ship's captain by Lord Mayor's wife when caught kissing her daughter. Old hag on island calls and he rows over to her. Sent to sister for magic tablecloth, to second sister for magic sword, third for magic healing hymnal. Heals leprous princess, kills enemy soldiers and revives again with sword. Weds daughter of Lord Mayor back home. Wiggin FAIRY 96-102.

T105. Enemy tribes united in marriage. Peace effected. Native American (Crow): Brown TEPEE 135-141.

T110. Unusual marriage.

T111. Marriage of mortal and supernatural being. Type 425. SEE ALSO: D361.1; F302.4.2; H1385.4+.

T111.1.1.1* Maiden chooses disguised god as husband. Asin in disguise as bald, ugly stranger is seen bathing without disguise. She chooses to wed him. Bolivia, Chaco (Pilaga): Courlander RIDE 206-212.

T111.1.3* Marriage to goddess Tchi-Nui. Weds man who has sold self into servitude to get money for father's funeral. She weaves fabulous cloth and buys his freedom. China: Buck FAIRY 154-161.

T111.1.4* Marriage to princess from undersea kingdom. Returning years later sends ring around dog's neck as token to king. (cf. B81.2). N. Nigeria (Fulani): Arnott AFRICAN 167-178.

T111.1.5* Marriage to heavenly maid emerging from painting. China: Wyndham FOLK 61-65.

T111.1.5.1* Jiang Kieu emerges from painting and encourages student in exam. Weds. Tu-Vyen temple in Hanoi origin. Vietnam: Schultz VIETNAMESE 60-66.

T111.5.1* Marriage of mortal and dwarf. Girl serves span-high man. He turns to handsome man, gives her his beard to spin--to become gold. Germany: Manning-Sanders SORCERER'S 33-36.

T115.1* Marriage to ogress. Woman of the Snow freezes companion but spares young man provided he never tell of seeing her. He weds, has ten children, tells wife she looks like Woman of the Snow (C31.9). It is she. She leaves. Japan: Buck FAIRY 251-256; Littledale GHOSTS 157-164.

T117.5. Marriage with a tree. SEE: F441.2.3.1.1.

T117.12* Girl weds man of snow (Moowis). In spring he melts. Native American (Algonquin): Garner CAVALCADE..GOBLINS 52-54.

T173.3. Murderous bride. Black princess asks soldier to guard tomb each night. Emerges as demoness at midnight and kills. Old man gives corporal advice as to how to escape her. Third night to get into coffin while she seeks him and refuse to answer. Spell is broken. She turns white. Wed. Poland: Zajdler POLISH 89-102.

T220 - T299. Married life.

T210. Faithfulness in marriage.

T210.1.1* Faithful wife cutting hair thought to have murderous intent, turned out. She enters a monastery as monk, mothers an abandoned child. Is discovered and turned out. Begs for self and child, is reunited with her husband. King names her Quan-Am Tong-Tu, the Compassionate Protector of Children. Vietnam: Graham BEGGAR 23-31.

T210.2* Queen Cora. King Gedeon has wife thrown into sea in glass coffin for suspected infidelity. She is rescued and lives disguised as man in city-without-women. Passes tests as man but has to flee when nude swimming is proposed. Meets deranged husband in sorrow over dead--restored. Haiti: Thoby-Marcelin SINGING 91-99.

T211.2.1.1* Wife throws herself on husband's funeral pyre. Genii of the Hearth. Wife thinking husband dead remarries. He returns and is accidently set afire in straw pile. She throws herself onto pyre, her second husband throws himself after her. They are appointed Genii of the Hearth: Pham Lang, Trong Cao, Thi Nhi. Vietnam: Graham BEGGAR 33-44.

T211.6. Widowed she-fox neglects suitors who do not resemble her deceased husband. (cf. J416.2). Type 65. Germany (Grimm): De La Mare ANIMAL 81-85; Grimm HOUSEHOLD 166-168 (husband only feigned dead); Grimm HOUSEHOLD 169-170. Norway: Sperry SCANDINAVIAN 38-43. Corrin MRS. FOX'S pb.

T250. Characteristics of wives and husbands.

T251. The shrewish wife. SEE ALSO: K606.1.2.

T251.1.1. Belfagor. The devil frightened by the shrewish wife. A man persuades his shrewish wife to let herself be lowered into a well. When he comes to pull her out he raises a genie (devil) who is glad to escape from the woman. Later he frightens the devil by telling him that his wife has escaped. Type 1164. Latvia: Durham TIT 11-16 (given stick to heal baron, uses thrice, receives wealth. When devil comes for half, a ruckus is raised and he says wife is coming). Hungary: Manning-Sanders GLASS 182-186 (demon turns self into apple to sicken women, lad cures, devil stays in one girl. Lad says wife Kate Contrary is coming. Demon flees). Russia: Daniels FALCON 52-55.

T251.1.1.2* Girl on Devil's Back. Type 1164D. Girl says would dance with anyone--even the devil. She is carried off by devil, refuses to let go of his back. Shepherd helps devil by inviting her onto his back--then tosses coat into ring. As reward devil gives tip that two dukes thinking they are to be taken by devil have been spared. Lad is to feign saving them from the devil. Third duke to be really taken. Lad says girl is coming to jump on devil's back. Devil flees. Czechoslovakia: Fillmore SHEPHERD'S 160-171 /Ross BLUE 110-122/; Spicer THIRTEEN DEVILS 118-127.

T251.1.1.3* Devil demands soul from household--

given wife. He soon begs man to take her back. U.S. (Appalachia): Chase WICKED 95-96. Lapland: Stalder EVEN THE DEVIL pb.

T251.1.1.4* Wife sold to devil prays to Virgin and is blessed. Burns devil if he touches her. Returned (G303.16.1). Gypsy: Jagendorf GYPSIES' 152-163.

T251.2. Taming the Shrew. By outdoing his wife in shrewishness, the husband renders her obedient. Types 900, 901. SEE ALSO: H465 (King Thrushbeard).

T251.2.0.1. Tamed shrew on her way to visit her parents corrects her husband when he calls black birds white. He decides it may rain and turns back home. Repeat. Third day she agrees that swans are storks and he proceeds. +N12. Denmark: Arbuthnot FAIRY 95-98.

T251.2.3.0.1* "I never say a thing twice"--shoots dog, then horse for disobeying. Wife obeys. Denmark: Arbuthnot FAIRY 95-98; Arbuthnot ANTHOLOGY 232-234.

T251.2.6. Lazy wife is not fed until she works. Bulgaira: Pridham GIFT 48-59. Armenia: Ginsburg LAZIES 36-41.

T252.2. Cock shows browbeaten husband how to rule wife. Type 670. SEE: B216A (Animal languages).

T252.4.2* Bet: who rules the roost. To give cow to each woman who rules, horse to each man. All ten cows are given away, no horses. Judge declared he was the ruler but had to get wife's advice before choosing which horse to take. Dominican Republic: Jagendorf KING 102-106 /Arbuthnot ANTHOLOGY 401/.

T255. The obstinate wife or husband. SEE ALSO: J2511.

T255.1. The obstinate wife. Cutting with knife or scissors. At the end of the argument the man throws his wife (or she falls) into the water. As she sinks she makes the motion with her fingers for shearing with the scissors. Type 1365B. Norway: Asbjornsen NORWEGIAN 112-114; Courlander RIDE 159-162; Jacobs EUROPEAN 31-33.

T255.2. The obstinate wife sought for up-stream. When she falls into the stream, the husband concludes that she would be too obstinate to go with the current. Iran: Shah MULLA 102 (mother-in-law). Ethiopia: Courlander FIRE 35-40. Norway: Asbjornsen NORWEGIAN 112-114; Courlander RIDE 159-162. Finland: Bowman TALES..TUPA 201-204 /Arbuthnot ANTHOLOGY 261/; Fillmore SHEPHERD'S 64-65.

T255.4. The obstinate wife: the third egg. The husband and the wife dispute as to who shall eat the third egg. She pretends to die. At the grave she asks him, "Do I eat two of the three eggs?" He gives his consent. She jumps out and cries, "I eat two" and everyone flees except a lone man

who exclaims, "Poor me and the other one. Ecuador: Courlander RIDE 217-219.

T255.8* The Silent Wife. Never speaks. Husband feigns dead and she bemoans loss. Didn't talk for fear he would discover her stammer. Italy: Cimino DISOBEDIENT #4.

T500 - T599. Conception and birth.

T510. Miraculous conception.

T521. Conception from sunlight.

T521.0.1* Uletka. Type 898*. Woman asks sun for daughter if only for twelve years. Kept in closed house but ray of light carries off through keyhole. Sun sees her sadness and sends back to mother. They escape witch who trees them. Tree makes self tough as witch gnaws. People passed in flight misdirect witch. Hungary: Manning-Sanders GLASS 94-99.

T540. Miraculous birth. SEE ALSO: F535.1 (Thumbling).

T542.2* Birth of tiny half girl-half dragon from egg left by pet ducklings. Little Thing insists on going to lantern festival with parents. Turns to real baby inside father's lantern. Taiwan: Cheney TALES 25-36.

T543.3.2. Birth from peach (Momotaro). Old woman sings (D1781) giant peach to her and takes it from stream. Baby boy springs from halved peach. Grows rapidly (T615). Asks parents for millet dumplings which he shares with animals to enlist their companionship on his campaign against Oni Island. Dog, monkey (B441.1), and pheasant help him conquer Oni (G500) and take home treasure. Japan: Arbuthnot ANTHOLOGY 336-337; Buck FAIRY 138-140; Haviland FAVOR-ITE..JAPANESE 47-71 (sings); Hearn JAPANESE 126-132 (M. eats peach halves, gains strength); MacAlpine JAPANESE 81-94; Novak FAIRY 6-15 (+T615.0.1, parents had been driven from island by demons; lower selves by rope into hole under rock leading to open island); Ozaki JAPANESE 244-261; Rackham FAIRY 84-86; Ross BURIED 147-160; Sakade JAPANESE 9-16; Tabrah MOMO-TARO pb; Uchida DANCING 96-106 (sings to make peach float nearer, D1781) /Arbuthnot FAIRY 174-177/.

T546.3* Birth from snow. Snow girl made by old couple comes to life. Melts in spring. Russia: Gruenberg FAVORITE 366-369; Haviland FA-VORITE..RUSSIA 43-52; Ransome OLD 122-135 (+ lost in the woods she refuses to let bear, wolf bring her home--afraid they would eat her. Lets red fox bring but fox is given dog in bag rather than hen as reward. She melts in disgust); Riordan TALES..CENTRAL 53-55; Ross BURIED 27-30.

T548.2. Magic rites for obtaining a child. SEE: L145.1 (Tatterhood).

T551.3.5* Child born with animal head. Woman refuses beggar calling her sow and her children sow's litter. Tabu: referring to a Christian as a beast. She bears a pig-headed daughter. Ireland: Danaher FOLKTALES 20-22.

T553.1* Childless couple treat ox as son. Pay squire to teach to talk. He says sent ox home to them, must have gone somewhere. They see lad named Peter Ox has come to town--adopt him. Denmark: Hatch MORE 167-181.

T554. Woman gives birth to animal. Type 441. SEE ALSO: B641.0.1Ae; B641.5.

T554.8.2* Lizard children. Barren woman finds two green plants in river where twin babies were killed. Cooks but finds too bitter to eat. In morning finds two lizards in pot. Raises. Turn to boy and girl. Africa (Abaluhya): Nunn AFRICAN 68-74.

T554.12.1* Mother's tears fall on clamshell and tiny boy appears. Clamshell boy makes witch think she can become lovely and takes to sea to see reflection. Pushes over and rescues children captured. Native American (Makah): Matson LEGENDS 97-102.

T554.12.2* Clamshell boy makes bow of mother's copper bracelet. Face glows with light reflected. Weather is calm when he sits on beach. If he appears at sunset sky is red and fair weather promised for morrow (A797). Canada: Frost LEGENDS 278-282.

T555. Woman gives birth to a plant or finds plant child.

T555.1.1. Woman gives birth to pumpkin. Wife wants daughter even if looks like pumpkin. A daughter born who turns to pumpkin. Merchant sees girl emerge from pumpkin. Grabs her and ring comes off. He searches for one who fits ring (H36.3). She puts hand out of pumpkin. He weds. Iran: Mehdevi PERSIAN 112-117.

T555.1.1.1* Childless couple. Squash with baby inside. Bath water turns to gold as hits child. They bring ever more water. Child leaves in anger at greed. Philippines: Robertson PHILIPPINES 63-69.

T555.2.1* Old woman prays for help with farm-work. Large gourd turns to boy, smaller gourds to children. They work in day, become gourds in evening. She spies and keeps as children. Trips over boy gourd, Kitete, one day and curses him. He and others turn back to gourds. Tanganyika (Chaga): Arnott AFRICAN 112-118.

T555.3* Temba finds yam shaped liked boy which comes to life. He hides boy in tree and feeds daily. Temba's mother spies and repeats chant to get yam boy out and hide it. Temba cries and is sent outside and allowed to sit in father's camel stool. He aids people there in work and shows how to cook, is given presents and sent home over flooded river on bull's back. E. Africa: Arnott TEMBA 20-35.

T600 - T699. Care of children.

T615. Supernatural growth. SEE: T543.3.2 (Momotaro).

T615.0.1* Boy eats from dish--grows as large as dish, eats from pan--large as pan, etc. Japan: Novak FAIRY 6-15 (+T543.3.2).

T615.1. Precocious speech.

T615.1.1* Asked to define difficult word, son promptly fabricates a fantastic false answer. Father is delighted--"Just like his father!" Iran: Shah MULLA 91.

T677. Substitute for a child. Aged childless couple carve themselves a child from wood, or make one from snow, clay and the like. SEE ALSO: C423.4 (Leppa Polky); T546.3 (snow girl).

T681. Each likes his own children best. Snipe asked sportsman to spare the small ones, easily recognized as being the prettiest in the forest. To be on the safe side he shoots only the ugliest he can find. They are snipes. Type 247. Scandinavia: Wiggin TALES 323 (woodchuck). Mayan: Bowes KING (chick-bul, ani asks hawk to spare). Italy: Ross BURIED 109-112 (owl's young, eagle eats).

T681.2* Jupiter offers prize to prettiest child. Monkey comes to claim prize for her child. Aesop: Aesop AESOP'S (Viking) 64; Aesop - AESOP'S (Watts) 18.

U. THE NATURE OF LIFE

U0 - U99. Life's inequalities.

U10. Justice and injustice.

U11.1.1.1. Animals confess sins to lion holding court. All the powerful animals forgiven. Ass and lamb are punished. Ethiopia: Courlander FIRE 15-18 (donkey).

U21.3. Man complains of injustice of God's wrecking ship because of one man's sin. He then kills whole swarm of ants because one has stung him. Aesop: Aesop AESOP'S (Watts) 192.

U21.4. Wolf objects to lion stealing sheep from him, although he has himself stolen it. Aesop: Aesop AESOP'S (Watts) 96; Kent MORE 8-11.

U31. Wolf unjustly accuses lamb and eats him. When all the lamb's defenses are good the wolf asserts the right of the strong over the weak. (Usually accused of stirring up water from lower in stream). Aesop: Aesop AESOP'S (Golden) 50-51; Aesop AESOP'S (Grosset) 127-128; Aesop AESOP'S (Random) 56-58; Aesop AESOP'S (Viking) 15-16; Aesop AESOP'S (Watts) 9; Aesop FABLES (Macmillan) 15; Aesop FIVE 30.

U31.1* Baby leopard killed accidentally by elephant. Lion avenges self on goats. Ethiopia (Eritrea): Courlander FIRE 25-28.

U32.1* Hawk was only chasing a pigeon over farmer's field when caught. To be killed anyway unless can show what harm pigeon had done him. Aesop: Aesop AESOP'S (Grosset) 116.

U33.1* Cock killed because it crows and wakes man. Aesop: Aesop AESOP'S (Watts) 47.

U33.2* Cat uses crowing as excuse to kill cock. Aesop: Aesop AESOP'S (Watts) 92.

U33.3* Partridge spared as decoy, cock killed despite usefulness, have to eat something. Aesop: Aesop AESOP'S (Watts) 197.

U60. Wealth and poverty.

U69* Unhappy traveler cheered. Man steals his knapsack and leaves it on the road farther on. Traveler finds his knapsack and is overjoyed. Iran: Shah MULLA 107.

U85* Price of object depends on who is the buyer. Shah charged fantastic price for omelet. Not eggs that are rare but the visits of kings. Iran: Shah MULLA 124.

U100 - U299. The nature of life - miscellaneous.

U110. Appearances deceive.

U112. Beard on she-goats do not make a male.

Aesop: Aesop AESOP'S (Watts) 54 (Jupiter reassures male goats).

U114. Mountain in labor brings forth a mouse. Aesop: Aesop AESOP'S (Grosset) 27; Aesop FABLES (Macmillan) 27.

U119.2.1* Ostler wishes to trade places with archbishop's mule. Each is soon glad to change back. Portugal: Michael PORTUGUESE 84-91. Spain: Haviland FAVORITE..SPAIN 70-87.

U119.5.1* Eagle confers title of nightingale on cuckoo. Song remains the same. Russia (Kryvlov): Carey BABA 17.

U120. Nature will show itself.

U121.1. Crab walks backwards: learned from his parents. Asked to demonstrate, he goes sideways. SEE ALSO: J1063.1. Congo (Luban): Burton MAGIC 71.

U121.2.1* Doe and fawn discuss deer's superior speed and horns. When dogs arrive she flees anyway. Aesop: Aesop AESOP'S (Grosset) 9; Aesop AESOP'S (Viking) 54; Aesop AESOP'S (Watts) 71 (hind and fawn).

U125. Wolf loses interest in the sermon when he sees a flock of sheep. A dervish preaches to him. Green ANIMAL 171.

U129.4* Cats at baptism can only meow and turn service into a melee. Haiti: Wolkstein MAGIC 123-128.

U130. The power of habit.

U131.1. Fox finally converses with lion whom he had feared at first. Aesop: Aesop AESOP'S (Grosset) 57; Aesop AESOP'S (Viking) 44; Aesop AESOP'S 72; Aesop FABLES (Macmillan) 67.

U131.2. Men at first frightened by camel take him into their service. Aesop FIVE 82.

U131.2.1* Goat intimidates lions with his horns. Lion's son suggests testing goat's teeth, finding he cannot eat meat they kill him. Congo: Burton MAGIC 125-126.

U133. Man soon learns to stand the smells of the tannery. Aesop: Aesop AESOP'S (Watts) 89.

U136.0.1. Fisher and hunter exchange places for one day. Archer loses brother's magic fish hook. He forges five hundred new hooks from his sword but his brother is unforgiving. Old man advises to seek hook at King of the Sea. He hides in tree by well and daughter of Sea God sees his face reflected (R351). He asks drink and drops jewel into cup and is sent for. King helps him and hook is found in fish's throat (B548.2.3). Stays three years. Given Jewel of Ebbing Tide and Jewel of Flowing Tide to take home. Still unforgiving, his brother attacks him. He uses first jewel to cause waves to rise, then uses second to save brother's life as brother repents. Ikeda Type 470C. SEE ALSO: H1132.1.5. Japan: MacAlpine JAPANESE 23-34 (weds sea princess, after return to home she comes to give birth to child, tabu on looking, C31.1.2. He looks and sees giant crocodile giving birth. She must leave, C932); Ozaki JAPANESE 153-179 (this is the fourth Mikado, descendant of Amaterasu, Sun Goddess); Sakade JAPANESE CHILDREN'S STORIES 58-63 (-magic jewels and flood); Uchida DANCING 61-72 (Lord of the Tides, Shihotsuchi, helps hunter. Throws black comb on ground. Bamboo grove springs up. Basket woven of these will carry to bottom of sea, +D454.7.2); Williams-Ellis ROUND 16-26.

U140. One man's food is another man's poison.

U142. Ox likes loving strokes of man: flea fears them. Aesop: Aesop AESOP'S (Watts) 133.

U143. Collier and fuller cannot live together. One makes things clean, the other soils them. Aesop: Aesop AESOP'S (Watts) 4.

U148.1* Good weather for one is foul for another. Daughter wed to potter wants sun, daughter wed to gardener needs rain. Aesop: Aesop AESOP'S (Grosset) 169; Aesop AESOP'S (Watts) 155.

U150. Indifference of the miserable.

U151. Ass indifferent to enemy's approach: he

could be no more miserable than now. Aesop: Aesop AESOP'S (Watts) 78.

U160. Misfortune with oneself to blame. SEE: J621.1.

U161. Eagle killed with arrow made with his own feather. Aesop: Aesop AESOP'S (Grosset) 186; Aesop AESOP'S (Watts) 50; Aesop AESOP'S (Watts) 88; Aesop FABLES (Macmillan) 149.

U162. Tree cut down with axe for which it has furnished a handle. Aesop: Aesop AESOP'S (Grosset) 201; Aesop AESOP'S (Random) 112-113; Aesop AESOP'S (Watts) 148; Aesop FABLES (Macmillan) 53; Aesop FABLES (Walck) 112-113.

U174* Blind man discovers objects which sighted man does not see, porcupine quills, tortoise shell, etc. Saves them and later uses to overcome lion (K1715.12.1). Congo (Luban): Burton MAGIC 119-121.

U236.2* Animals all have ideas for others to reform. Buh Coon, "You got to begin charity next door. But if you want to reform, it's got to begin at home." U.S. (Alabama): Courlander TERRAPIN'S 15-17.

U242. Hares (hare) fearing death outrun pursuing dog (dogs). Dog, "I was running for my supper. He was running for his life." Aesop: Aesop AESOP'S (Grosset) 21; Aesop AESOP'S (Watts) 111; Kent MORE 20-21.

V. RELIGION

V11.7.1.1* Sacrifice to Serpent. Man shoots Serpent God after leaving offering. Snakes appear in food, bed until he makes amends. Fiji: Gittins TALES 37-40.

V20. Confessions of sins.

V21.7. Matthew's Bed. Merchant promises "that which he doesn't know he has" for aid. Grown son goes to demon. Old man advises to follow first thing at sunset--mouse. Leads to cave of outlaw Matthew. Mother of Matthew hides, Matthew smells, ogress to free if will find out Matthew's fate from demon. Lad enters demon's lair, takes contract and sees Matthew's fate--bed of spikes. Helpful mouse killed by owl. He returns and advises Matthew to plant his

applewood cudgel and bring spring water in mouth until tree bears fruit. Years later he finds Matthew, overgrown with moss beside bearing tree. Stanislaus hears Matthew's confession, an apple falls for each sin--at end Matthew turns to dust and white bird flies to heaven. Poland: Zajdler POLISH 127-140.

V80. Religious services--miscellaneous.

V92. "Our Lady's Tumbler." A tumbler, turned monk, dances while others chant psalms. He is praising God in the only way he knows. (Virgin smiles). Sawyer WAY 273-281. France: Todd JUGGLER pb.

V92.0.1* Juggler causes statue of baby Jesus held on Virgin's lap to smile. Juggler dies. France: De Paola CLOWN pb.

V92.1* The Feast of Fools. King orders celebration of Christmas as a Holiday of Fools, makes a mockery. Only court jester takes no part. Saint Augustine appears on Candlemas and all repent. England: Sawyer WAY 189-200.

V100 - V199. Religious edifices and objects.

V115.5* Church bells cannot be raised to tall steeple. Tepozton performs test. Mexico: Brenner BOY 38-43.

V116.1* Golden altar covered with earth to hide from pirate Henry Morgan. City is burned but altar survives. Panama: Courlander RIDE 231-233.

V120. Images.

V121.0.1* Picture of Christ appears miraculously on painter's easel abandoned in church. It grows each time they try to move so that cannot be taken out of doorway (U128.0.1). Columbia (Cartagena): Jagendorf KING 79-80.

V121.1* Miraculous image of Virgin Mary appears painted on shawl in which Indian gathers roses given by Virgin. Our Lady of Guadalupe. Mexico: Jagendorf KING 198-202.

V123.2. Supplicant angry with wooden idol smashes it, finds coins inside. SEE ALSO: J1853.1.1. Aesop: Aesop FABLES (Macmillan) 81.

V128.0.1* Image cannot be moved from spot.

V128.0.1.1* Buddha's begging bowl in Peshawar miraculously fills when good place donations. Captured, elephants cannot move bowl. Temple built on spot. India: Carpenter ELEPHANT'S 108-113.

V128.0.1.2* Caacupé villagers steal Blue Virgin from Asuncion. Donkey stops on certain spot on return. Will not move. They build church there. In Chaco war Virgin of Caacupé leads soldiers in battle. Paraguay: Jagendorf KING 229-232.

V128.0.1.3* Painting grows so cannot be taken out church door. Columbia (Cartagena): Jagendorf KING 79-80.

V128.0.2* Image keeps returning to spot. Image of Santo Domingo de Guzman taken to Managua each year for two weeks. They attempt to keep it overlong but it miraculously reappears in Santo Domingo de Guzman. Nicaragua: Jagendorf KING 208-211.

V128.0.3* Two boys find lump under blanket in field, throw it away, it returns. Is Statue of Virgin Mary. Church built on spot. Virgin of Suyapa, Honduras. Honduras: Jagendorf KING 164-167.

V128.3* Wooden image of Christ Child walks in fields and rebukes clouds for not bringing rain. Shoes are found muddy the next day. Mexico: Ross IN 104-120.

V128.4* Saint "Quien Sabe" and Saint "Que Pasa." Put over church door one image continually calls to other "Que pasa." He replies, "Quien sabe." Gradually first achieves position with hands to mouth calling, second with shoulders shrugged, hands spaced in gesture. Mexico: Ross IN 75-76.

V128.5* Daughter-in-law ordered to grind wheat with one hand and ring bell with other so can't steal any. Rings bell with toes and stuffs flour under sari. Goes to temple and makes chappatis with flour and butter offering left there. Eats them. Deity puts two fingers in mouth in shock. Reward offered to anyone who restores deity to former pose. She threatens to thrash it with a slipper if it doesn't take fingers from mouth. It is a cobbler's deity. It obeys. India: Spellman BEAUTIFUL 79-81.

V140. Sacred relics.

V143.2. Relics (images) carried away return to their original church. SEE ALSO: V128.0.2.

V143.2.1* Image of Virgin appears beside little tree and man of Tecolutla carves image in tree. Image was meant for Papantla where tree wanted to stop idol worship. Image walks there each night = Virgin of Papantla. Mexico: Ross IN 150-161.

V143.2.2* Holy Relic of Bannockburn. King Robert Bruce sends monk to fetch hand of St. Fillian to battlefield. Monk brings empty silver case. King and Angus of the Isles pray before the case. It flies open and light shines forth from hand in case. Scotland: Nic Leodhas GAELIC 76-80.

V200 - V299. Sacred persons.

V211. Christ.

V211.1.2.2* Stars discuss birth of baby Jesus. Orion, King of the stars, declares him to be the prophesied King. Finland (Gypsy): Sawyer LONG 61-68.

V211.1.8.1. Christ in form of an infant nursed by saint. Sawyer THIS 149-157 (St. Bridhe, St. Bridget).

V211.1.8.4* Christ Child rings bell over unconscious Brother Johnnick on Christmas Eve so that woodcutter can find way to cabin in fog and rescue. Men of Pludihen henceforth wear sheepskin coats and sailcloth kilts on Christmas Eve in memory of Pere Suliac, woodcutter. France (Brittany): Colwell SECOND 39-45.

V220. Saints. SEE: Subject Index "SAINTS."

V221. Miraculous healing by saints.

V221.12.1* St. Genevieve's mother blinded for striking her. Genevieve's tears fall in water mother washes in and sight is restored. France: Frost LEGEND 223-229.

V226. Saints as hermits.

V226.1* Student cares for beggar who is holy Chang Tonyong in disguise. Student is later admitted to spirit world for banquet as thanks. Korea: Jewett WHICH 47-58.

V229.7.2* Invaders miraculously defeated by saints. St. Genevieve persuades Parisians not to desert city by blowing open city gate (miracle). Huns ordered by Attila to pass Paris by unless empty. Paris thus spared. France: Frost LEGEND 223-229.

V229.7.3* St. Magnus appears on battlefield and routs Scots from Orkney. Orkney: Cutt HOG-BOON 161-168.

V229.26* Anecdotes about saints.

V229.26.1.1* Saint Peter feels he is wiser than the Lord. Lord hangs trombone on St. Peter's back as they near wedding and guests beg St. Peter to play, beat him for refusal. If had been wise, should have known how to play. Gypsy: Jagendorf GYPSIES' 47-51.

V229.26.1.2* St. Peter finds people on earth are happy and pay no attention to the Lord. Returns in times of poverty and finds all call on the Lord constantly. Italy: Vittorini OLD 106-110.

V229.27* Saint Neot. Saint Neot stands in well to say prayers. Angel shows fish in water. To eat one every day of life. Servant cooks two. Neot throws both back, prays they return to life. England (Cornwall): Manning-Sanders PETER 59-63.

V229.28* Saint Neot. Saint Neot calls wild animals to help when oxen are stolen. Seeing stag draw plows, thieves repent and return oxen. Stags bear white ring on necks as mark of yoke. England (Cornwall): Manning-Sanders PETER 59-63.

V229.29* Infallible Dr. Ma named patron of veterinarians for curing dragon. China: Manton FLYING 24-29.

V230. Angels.

V238. Guardian angel. Hutchinson CHIMNEY.. FAIRY 153-163 (watches over sleeping children near precipice, +D113.2.2). SEE: K1917.3F (mouse as family's guardian angel).

V400 - V449. Religious virtues.

V400. Charity.

V400.1* Mancio Serra de Languicano gambles away golden sun from Cuzco temple. Reforms and helps Indians henceforth. Peru: Jagendorf KING 233-236.

V400.2* Actress with bad name gives her carriage to priest and walks home. Peru: Jagendorf KING 236-238.

V411. Miraculous reward for charities.

V411.10. Star money. Poor girl gives last food and clothing away. Stars fall from heavens, turn to silver, a linen shift appears for her. Germany (Grimm): Gag MORE 85-86; Grimm GRIMM'S (Follett) 317-318; Rockwell THREE 113-117.

V411.12* Saint Margery Daw gives all food away, sells bed and gives that money away. Lets birds heave the straw off her palette. Piskies carry her off in sheet to her reward. England (Cornwall): Manning-Sanders PETER 39-42.

V412.3* Lady Paula's husband locks up food and forbids her to give to poor, locks open and bread replenishes self miraculously. Caught with apron full of bread, they turn to roses. Husband puts one on his hat. Later all turn back to bread. Italy: Jagendorf PRICELESS 25-30. Medieval: Sawyer WAY 307-315 (Saint Elizabeth).

V420. Reward of the uncharitable.

V429.1* Old woman refuses charity to the poor. St. Cuddy (St. Cuthbert of Melrose Abbey) who is saint of birds, turns woman and her twelve geese to stone. Still on road to Melrose. Scotland: Nic Leodhas THISTLE 39-45.

V429.2* Sister turns own sister away saying has no bread. Loaves in oven speak when cuts them, reminding her of sister. Italy: Vittorini OLD 75-78.

V429.2.1* Sister refuses bread to impoverished sister. Says, "If I have bread may it turn to stone." All bread she buys turns to stone henceforth. Netherlands: De Leeuw LEGENDS ..HOLLAND 119-126.

V429.3* Lady Machtelt refuses charity saying beggar lady's children probably came from the devil. Is cursed. "If my children are from the Lord, may he send you 365 children." She has 365 children. Netherlands: Frost LEGENDS 183-185.

V429.4* Baker won't give 13 in dozen. On St. Nicholas' Day his patron saint appears and warns to be more generous. He reforms. Old lady customer makes him swear on gingerbread St. Nicholas. Baker's dozen is thirteen henceforth. New York (Dutch): Cothran WITH 18-22.

W. TRAITS OF CHARACTER

W0 - W99. Favorable traits of character.

W10. Kindness.

W10.3* Kasiagsak refuses to kill seals, walrus. Lies that he has done so and is exposed. Paddles out to sea and never returns. Eskimo: Caswell SHADOWS 48-53.

W11.3. Generosity. Man divides money into three parts: 1. for the poor, 2. for pilgrims, 3. for himself and family. SEE ALSO: H585.1.

W11.3.1* Brahman will accept only money king earns himself. King earns four anna. Brahman insists king give one anna to his wife, one to son, keep one for self, give one to Brahman as alms. Wife flings the anna (two pice) out window in anger, two trees grow and shower pearls. India: Spellman BEAUTIFUL 33-36.

W11.5.13* Boys set dog adrift in canoe but dog saves him when he falls in. Boy reforms. Congo: Carpenter WONDER..DOGS 95-100.

W11.14.1* Two friends leave China to make way in Bangkok. Vow to eat no meat until well established (too expensive). One succumbs to temptation, soon is indebted. Second teaches lesson by giving small tamarind tree for seasoning, soon leaves are all gone. If wait until tree grows it will be able to supply leaves, always replenish. Thailand: Brockett BURMESE 163-170.

W11.17* Two generous friends. First gives land to second. Gold found there. Both insist belongs to other. Wise man suggests planting garden for poor with money. En route to buy seeds men buy freedom of birds instead. Bird plants garden--it is magic. Fruit kills rich. Replenishes poor. Russia (Kazakh): Masey STORIES 50-61.

W11.18* Tailor makes clothing from scraps for brother and sister so they can enter singing contest. They win, share reward with tailor. India: Spellman BEAUTIFUL 40-43.

W28.5* Self-sacrifice. Wu Feng arranges peace with headhunters of Taiwan by persuading them to consider the forty-five heads taken in a raid as adequate for the two heads per year sacrifice they require for years to come. At the end of this treaty period they demand sacrifices again. He offers only one more--they behead the hooded sacrificial victim and discover it has been Wu Feng himself. They cease head taking in terror of his spirit. China: Cheney TALES 137-142; Lu Mar CHINESE 127-146.

W45.2* Honor. Fire, Water, Honor travel together. If honor lost can never be found again. Fire burns, water evaporates because honor is lost. Indonesia: De Leeuw INDONESIAN 58-60.

W46.1* Filial piety. Sindhu: cares for blind parents in a jungle. Killed in error by hunting king, king promises to care for parents and spare weak animals of forest from hunt. India: Turnbull FAIRY 158-167.

W46.2* Bad girl sees baby mouse lead blind mother to food. She reforms at sight. Korea: Kim STORY 83-85.

W47.1* Cooperation. Everyone in hell has to use yard-long chopsticks. They starve. In heaven same chopsticks are used and all help each other. China: Chang TALE 47-49.

W48.1* Industry. Mother tells son to work for any price but keep working. Second mother advises her son to hold out for job worthy of him. First proves best advice. Later hiding under boat lad hears demons talk of future and is able to save princess--reward. Second lad imitates. Demons throw him into sea (J2415). Greece (Karpathos): Neufield BEWARE 68-75.

W48.2* Industry. Gypsy fishes old copper pots from pond where count has thrown used pots. Mends them and sells them back to count. Gypsy: Jagendorf GYPSIES' 134-145.

W48.3* Industry. Orphan allowed to keep single cowrie dropped by king. Buys lettuce seeds with cowrie--all that stick to one finger (licks finger first). Raises lettuce and presents to king. Given palace position. Later weds princess and rules Mon. Thailand: Asia FOLK..1 41.

W100 - W199. Unfavorable traits of character.

W110. Unfavorable traits of character--personal.

W111. Laziness. SEE: Q321 (laziness punished).

W111.1. Contest in laziness. Each cites instance of his laziness. Type 1950. Gag MORE 51-58; Wiggin TALES 101.

W111.2.4. Boy to see whether it is raining; calls dog (cat) in and feels of his paws. In error--someone had just thrown water on cat. Iran: Shah MULLA 77.

W111.2.6. The Boy eats breakfast, dinner and supper one immediately after the other! Then lies down to sleep. Type 2561. Bahamas: Jagendorf KING 31-33.

W111.3.2. Cat beaten for not working. Lazy wife must hold cat and is scratched. Poland: Borski GOOD 20-25 (back beaten). Greece: Neufeld BEWARE 52-57 (sheep).

W111.5.8. Man with stolen fig in his mouth submits to having cheek lanced rather than open mouth. Iraq: Carpenter ELEPHANT'S 125-134 (two eggs).

W111.5.8.2* Man too lazy to turn around string of doughnuts on his neck. Starves when those in front are gone. China: Lin MILKY 47-50.

W111.5.8.3* Boy so lazy lays under tree waiting for figs to drop. +H465F. Laos: Wolkstein LAZY 40-43.

W111.5.10.1.1* Lazy man taken to be drowned. Rich woman offers to let live in her barn full of toast. Refuses unless she provides someone to spread honey on it. Too lazy to swim, he drowns. Moldavia: Ginsburg LAZIES 92-95.

W111.5.10.1.2* Lazy man has self buried. Man passing procession offers corn to help him get started in life again. He refuses unless it is ground. Trickster disguised as devil makes 'dead' man work all night. He leaps from grave and goes back home to work. Bulgaria: Pridham GIFT 138-142.

W111.6* The Little Red Hen and the Grain of Wheat. Hen preparing bread asks who will help. Mouse and cat answer "Not I." Hen refuses to let them eat when bread is done. Haviland FAIRY 32-34; Holdsworth LITTLE pb; Hutchinson CHIMNEY 63-65; Montgomerie MERRY 14-18; Palazzo LITTLE pb; Pilkington SHAMROCK 102-103 (+Z33.1); Richardson GREAT 9-15; TALL..NURSERY 79-83.

W111.6.1* The Cock, the Mouse and the Little Red Hen. Little Red Hen must do all work of house. Fox carries three off. Hen cuts hole in bag with scissors and they escape putting stones in bag. Cock and mouse reform. Arbuthnot ANTHOLOGY 155-156; Arbuthnot TIME 13-15; Hutchinson CHIMNEY 79-88; Lefevre COCK pb; Richardson GREAT 92-103; Rockwell THREE 17-32.

W111.7* Ready to eat. "Pete, go thresh some wheat." "I can't, I have a stomachache." "Pete, come and eat." "Where's my big spoon?" Russia: Ginsburg THREE 19.

W111.7.1* "Tortoise come to sweep?" "I have no head, I have not feet," etc. "Tortoise, come to eat." "Here is my head, here are my feet." Panama: Carter ENCHANTED 83-86.

W111.7.2* Squire: "Who's going to eat?" Gypsy: "I shall." Squire: "Who's going to drink?" Gypsy: "I shall." Squire: "Who's going to work tomorrow?" Gypsy: "Speak up, man, why should I always be the first to answer?" Poland: Borski GOOD 66-67.

W111.8* Lazy hunter rubs soles of boots on stone to wear out so looks as if walked far. Eskimo: Field ESKIMO 29-30.

W111.9* Lazy Mammo lies down and prays for God to get him up mountain without walking. Another overhears and disguised demon chases Mammo up mountain with sword. Says God sent him to help. Ethiopia (Tigre): Davis LION'S 153-158.

W111.10* Those on whom sun shines while in bed will be short lived, reply of sun to man asking length of life. Native American (Thompson):

Newell RESCUE 23-28.

W111.11* A week of Sundays. Fairy given hospitality grants wish. Wishes for a week of Sundays. By week's end, boredom has set in. Ireland: Gruenberg FAVORITE 359-363.

W116.9* Vanity. Golden oriole proud of golden color eats jackfruit because it matches his color. Perches in coconut tree for same reason and is caught by eagle. Admits sin of pride brought downfall. Eagle eats him anyway. Ceylon: Tooze WONDERFUL 115-117.

W121.1. Cowardice. Hunter wants to be shown lion tracks, not lion himself. Aesop: Aesop AESOP'S (Watts) 216.

W121.2.1. Ass insults dying lion. Aesop: Aesop FABLES (Macmillan) 17.

W121.2.4. Dogs tear up lionskin: fear living lion. Aesop: Aesop AESOP'S (Watts) 187.

W121.2.5. Coward gloats over robber slain by another person. Aesop: Aesop AESOP'S (Watts) 84-85.

W123. Indecision. SEE ALSO: J1040; J2183.

W123.2. Crane courts heron. She refuses and courts him. He refuses, etc. Ad infinitum. Russia: Carey BABA 42-43; Ransome OLD PETER'S 331-334; Riordan TALES..CENTRAL 144-145. Russia (Afanas'ev): Daniels FALCON 21-23. Scotland: Montgomerie TWENTY-FIVE 16-17.

W123.3* Worker set to cutting seed potatoes can't decide which are good and which are bad. Sits in stupor. U.S. (Alabama): Courlander TERRAPIN'S 93-94.

W123.4* Yes-no spirit (Samik) always equivocates in predictions--thus is never proved wrong. Eskimo: Melzack RAVEN 79-84.

W123.5* Manabush can't decide how to eat moose. If start at head then they'll say I ate it head-first, etc. Wolves come and eat. Native American (Menomine): Hardendorff JUST 24-25.

W125.2. Gluttony. Gluttonous wife eats all the meal while cooking it. SEE: Clever Gretel (K2137). Puerto Rico: Belpré TIGER 85-86 (husband spies and reproaches her).

W125.3.1* Anansi at mother-in-law's house (funeral) stuffs hat with hot beans (groundnuts, bananas) and caught puts hat onto head. Jumps about shaking hot hat and claims to be doing the hat shaking dance. His head is burned bald (A2317.2.2). In shame he hides in the grass henceforth (A2433.5.3.2). Ashanti: Courlander HAT 13-17 /Arbuthnot ANTHOLOGY 321-322/. Liberia/Ghana: Arkhurst ADVENTURES 21-31. Sierra Leone: Green FOLKTALES 9-13; Robinson SINGING 66-75.

W125.3.1.1* Monkey agrees to build house for Pretty Girl in return for fifty cents a day and all he can eat. Hides food in hat, is discovered and driven out. Barbados: Jagendorf KING 34-39.

W125.3.2* Ansige Karamba at in-law's home eats everything in sight. Wife covers up for his gluttony until he gets head stuck licking out mortar (J2131.5). Courlander COW-TAIL 119-127.

W125.6* Three gluttons with pot of beans. Each takes one at a time, quarrel over last. A hunter cuts this in three pieces for them and then licks his sword. Which is the greater glutton? Africa (Mali): Withers WORLD 65-66.

W125.7* Three travelers pretend have no food. To share chicken. 'Thin neck' grabs largest piece and chokes to death. 'Narrow chest' strikes chest in delight and dies. 'Wooden leg' dances in glee and falls and dies. Jackal eats chicken. Nepal: Hitchcock KING 33-36.

W128.3. Dissatisfaction. Dissatisfied rivers complain against sea. Say that it makes their water unusable. Aesop: Aesop AESOP'S (Watts) 172.

W128.4. Peacock dissatisfied with his name. SEE ALSO: A2423.1.2. Aesop: Aesop AESOP'S (Viking) 47-48; Aesop AESOP'S (Watts) 77; Aesop FABLES (Macmillan) 63 (Juno refuses peacock lovely voice).

W141. Talkativeness. (cf. J2351).

W141.1* All animals confess weaknesses after revival meeting. Brer Rabbit confesses last. His weakness--he is a gossiper, can't wait to tell all this. Recognition of weakness is good for salvation but if you make it a subject of conversation, you've only yourself to blame. U.S. (Alabama): Courlander TERRAPIN'S 31-32.

W141.1.1* Lion, tortoise and boar pledge peace and each reveals his pet peeve. Each then offends the other and leaves in enmity. To state one's dislike is to initiate one's annoyance. Nigeria: Walker NIGERIAN 42-43. Nigerian (Yoruba); Courlander OLODE 54-57 (lion, hyena, vulture).

W150. Unfavorable traits of character--social.

W151.2.1. Greed. Visitors of sick stag eat up all his provisions so that he starves. Aesop: Aesop AESOP'S (Watts) 140; Aesop FIVE 68.

W151.9.1. Boy with hand stuck in filbert jar told to let some loose from grasp and will be able to pull hand out. Aesop: Aesop AESOP'S (Grosset) 10; Aesop AESOP'S (Random) 63-65; Aesop AESOP'S (Watts) 61; Aesop FABLES (Walck) 119; Kent MORE 26-27.

W151.11* Greedy rich man wants longer summer day so laborers can work more. Climbs tree and tries to hold sun back with pitchfork while wearing heavy clothing of seventy-seven warm garments. Ural Mountains (Udmurt/Votyaks): Deutsch MORE 73-78.

W151.12. Friend was compensated by king for damages caused by a flood. Numskull wants to know how to cause a flood. Iran: Shah MULLA 139.

W151.13* One of Eight Immortals seeks non-greedy man. Points finger at rock and turns to gold. Every man met wants bigger rock. Finally finds man who does not want even biggest gold rock. Thinks he has found non-greedy man at last. This man wants the Immortal's magic finger. China (Ming Dynasty): Kendall SWEET 60-62.

W152.13.2* Stinginess. The Horse and the Groom. Groom steals horse's corn but grooms well. Horse says to give more corn and less currying and he'll look better. Aesop: Aesop AESOP'S (Grosset) 75-76; Aesop AESOP'S (Viking) 67; Aesop AESOP'S (Watts) 6.

W152.18* Frugal man sends son to most frugal man in world for lessons. Takes drawing of pig's head as offering. Son of most frugal man responds with gift of four imaginary oranges. When father returns and he shows how he handed over the oranges father rebukes him for presenting such big ones--fingers too far apart. China: Wiggin TALES 401-402 /Hardendorff JUST 34-36/.

W153. Miserliness.

W153.5.1* Miserliness. Tax Collector. Drowning tax collector refuses to comply when told "give me your hand." Reverses and succeeds by saying, "Take my hand." Turkey: Downing HODJA 26 (imam, holy man); Walker WATERMELONS 65-66.

W153.16* Miser builds wall of flour around house. Falls on hard times and eats even seed corn given by neighboring child. Thus people of his kingdom of Seno are poor to this day. Togo: Courlander COW-TAIL 13-23.

W153.17* Miser dreams is refused entrance to heaven for stinginess. Wakes to find self poor, mends ways. Mexico: Brenner BOY 71-75.

W153.18* Miser, fearing tailor will steal cloth, asks for increasing numbers of caps from piece of cloth. Ends up with ten hats finger size. Spellman BEAUTIFUL 69-70.

W153.19* Stingy Kichiyamu wants to borrow hammer so he won't wear his own down by pounding. Japan: Bang MEN 12-13.

W154.2. Ingratitude. Monster ungrateful for rescue. Type 426. SEE: D113.2 (Snow White and Rose Red).

W154.2.1. Rescued animal threatens rescuer. Type 155. SEE ALSO: J1172.3.

W154.2.1.1* Hermit saves mouse from crow. Turns it to cat, dog, tiger. Tiger plans to kill hermit. Returned to mouse form. India (Hitopadesa): Brown ONCE pb; Gaer FABLES 56-57; Turnbull FAIRY 127-135.

W154.2.2.1* Five colored deer saves man from drowning. Man promises never to tell of deer but soon tells lord for reward. Deer reproaches man before lord and lord bans deer hunting. Japan: Uchida MAGIC 65-71.

W154.3. Crane pulls bone from wolf's throat. Wolf refuses payment. "That you were allowed to take your head from my throat is payment enough." Type 76. Aesop: Aesop AESOP'S (Grosset) 144-145; Aesop AESOP'S (Random) 70-72; Aesop AESOP'S (Viking) 22; Aesop AESOP'S (Watts) 106; Aesop FABLES (Macmillan) 9; Aesop FABLES (Walck) 48-49; Aesop FIVE 80; Martignoni ILLUSTRATED 155. India: Gaer FABLES 166-168 (lion, woodpecker); Jacobs INDIAN 1-5.

W154.4. Hunter beats dog which has grown old in his service. Aesop: Aesop AESOP'S (Watts) 100.

W154.5. Dog tries to bite man rescuing him from well. Aesop: Aesop AESOP'S (Grosset) 7; Aesop AESOP'S (Watts) 171-172.

W154.6. Ungrateful wanderer pulls nut tree to pieces to get the nuts. Aesop: Aesop AESOP'S (Viking) 66.

W154.7. Wanderers in shade of plane tree blame it for not bearing fruit. Aesop: Aesop AESOP'S (Watts) 132.

W154.8. Grateful animals; ungrateful man. A traveler saves a monkey, a snake, a tiger, and a jeweler (goldsmith) from a pit. The monkey gives him fruit; the tiger a necklace of a princess (prince) he has killed. The jeweler accuses him before the king. The serpent saves him by biting the prince and then showing the man the proper remedy (B522.1). Type 160. India: Gaer FABLES 43-49; Ryder PANCHATANTRA 112-117. Ghana: Green FOLK..AFRICA 15-19 (rat, snake, leopard, man, antidote to snake's venom must be mixed with blood of traitor--man rescued). Egypt: Holding KING'S 58-68 (boy, rat and scorpion).

W154.8.1* Man rescues monkey, lion, snake, and Venetian. Monkey gives five years supply of wood; lion--game, snake--diamond. Venetian offers a palace but turns him out when he appears. Jewel merchant claims diamond is stolen. In court Venetian claims he never knew him, animals appear and testify. Palace of Venetian given to man. Picture of animals on wall of palace is still there. Italy: Werth MONKEY pb.

W154.8.2* Man rescues ape, snake and rich man from pit. Ape gives wood, serpent magic jewel which replaces self whenever sold, rich man promises half wealth but fails to do so. Emperor Justinian orders rich man to fulfill promise. Medieval: Green ANIMAL 201-205.

W154.8.3* Man on door in flood saves cooper, fox and snake. Cooper later accuses rescuer of black magic and he is imprisoned. Snake bites mayor and fox in form of fortune teller advises calling man who heals with a touch. (cf. B522.1). Japan: Novak FAIRY 100-107.

W154.8.3.1* Man in flood saves boy, deer, snake. Deer shows treasure cave. Boy betrays man. Snake shows snakebite remedy in prison (B522.1). Lord's wife cured. Korea: Kim STORY 129-137.

W154.8.4* Woman told flood will come when eyes of two stone temple lions turn red. Tricksters paint them red. She and son prepare boat. Flood comes, they rescue ants, sparrows, snakes, wolf and man. Wolf kills the mother. Man rescued (taken as brother) lets lad down tunnel to rescue girl from evil spirit. Pulls her up and leaves lad (K1931.2). Lad frees a tiny dragon and licks stone dragon shows daily to satisfy hunger and thirst. After three years dragon carries lad to upper world. Tasks: sort beans--sparrows perform; sort wheat--ants perform. Carry two gold pillars to tower--snakes move them. Produces brooch token. Weds princess. China: Wyndham FOLK..CHINA 73-97.

W154.8.4.1* Man told flood will come when stone lions' mouths drip blood. Children paint lions with blood. Takan flees and flood destroys all else. Man told to rescue only animals from flood. Rescues boy also. Later he is lowered into pit to rescue maid from monster snake. Soldiers drop rock and abandon. Young dragon carries him to safety through tunnel. Rats dig tunnel to palace and T. enters but is imprisoned. Task: sort salt and sugar--ants perform. Choose Precious Jade from one hundred girls. Butterfly shows. Wed and imposter (lad he saved from flood) is banished. Taiwan: Cheney TALES 37-52.

W154.8.5* Tall Tree is son of heavenly mother and tree. In flood (A1010) father tree falls and saves son who floats on tree. Son rescues ants, mosquitoes, and boy. Old woman raises boy and Tall Tree. Boy says Tall Tree can sort millet from sand. Task assigned. Ants aid. Old woman puts own daughter and stepdaughter each in a room. Boys to choose room. Mosquitoes tell Tall Tree where beautiful daughter is. He weds her. Boy weds stepdaughter. These two couples re-people the world (A1270). Korea: Kim STORY 66-75.

W155.1. Hardness of heart. Hardhearted horse allows ass to be overburdened until it is crushed. Horse must then assume the load. Aesop: Aesop AESOP'S (Grosset) 84-85; Aesop AESOP'S (Watts) 143.

W156. The dog in the manger. Has no use for the manger but refuses to give it up to the horse. Aesop: Aesop AESOP'S (Golden) 43-45;

Aesop AESOP'S (Grosset) 1; Aesop AESOP'S (Random) 3; Aesop AESOP'S (Viking) 20; Aesop AESOP'S (Watts) 60; Aesop FABLES (Macmillan) 79; Aesop FIVE 46; Arbuthnot FAIRY 226.

W156.1* Dragon sitting on hoard like miser (B11) is unable to enjoy hoard or let others use it. Green CAVALCADE..DRAGONS 21-22.

W158. Inhospitality. SEE: J1565.1; K278.

W158.1* Figs promised for dessert are never produced. Guest reads a passage from the Koran after dinner. "By the figs and olives of Mt. Sinai" and omits word "figs." Host, "You forgot 'the figs.'" Guest: "No, you did." Turkey: Downing HODJA 46.

W158.2* Shown new house and dining room at length but offered no food, guest is asked "would you build one like this?" Guest replies that he'll think about it. What ruins a man nowadays is the price of food and in this whole house there's no sign of that. Turkey: Downing HODJA 83.

W165.2.1* False pride. Mother goat sees lamb playing with her son and believes it to be one of her own children. By deduction she decides she must be a sheep. Hardendorff JUST 30-33.

W165.3* Wolf traps goat, goat sees self in pool and decides he need not fear a wolf. Doesn't bother to escape. Wolf returns and eats. Aesop: Montgomerie TWENTY-FIVE 32-33.

W165.3.1* Goat sees reflection and thinks self formidable. Goes into forest fearlessly and is captured by fox and wolf. Bulgaria: Rudolph MAGIC 30-41.

W165.4* False pride. Officious nobleman calls "Case substance to be produced for the quadrupeds." Trickster asks if he'd buy two dozen "quadruped" for very low price and he agrees readily. Trickster then produces two dozen rabbits. They are quadrupeds if you follow the letter of the law. Iran: Shah MULLA 67.

W167. Stubbornness. SEE ALSO: J2511 (The Silence Wager); T255.2 (The obstinate wife sought for upstream).

W167.1. Two stubborn goats meet each other on a bridge. Neither will step aside; both fall into the water. Type 202. Russia (Yiddish): Ginsburg THREE 42.

W167.1.1* Two kings on road. Neither will give way. King of Kosala tells virtues...overthrows strength with strength. King of Benares tells his--anger conquered by calmness, etc. King of Kosala makes way. India: Jacob INDIAN 135-139.

W167.3. Three women go fishing with old man. Each takes turn rowing and though they have not reached destination each refuses to take a second turn. They float back downstream to the village. Russia (Evenk): Ginsburg LAZIES 18-20.

W167.4* Stubborn son does opposite of father's commands. Father seeks to outsmart him and tells him not to raise the flour sacks on donkey crossing the stream. Son says he is reforming now and will obey this command. Turkey: Downing HODJA 50.

W175. Changeableness.

W175.2* Man leaves lame friend who is unable to catch seals, later returns to his hunting partner when he becomes a good hunter. Lame man's friends ask why he didn't want a partner when he was the one catching seals. Eskimo: Field ESKIMO 80-82.

W181.1. Jealousy. Sheep jealous of dog because he does nothing. Do not consider that he guards the flock. Aesop: Aesop AESOP'S (Watts) 169.

W181.1.1* Heir has hedges cut down around vineyards. Vineyards are destroyed by man and beast. "They also serve who only stand and wait." Aesop: Aesop AESOP'S (Grosset) 231.

W181.1.2* Dog (Bureaucracy) thinks itself more important than horse as he guards all. Horse (peasantry) says there'd be nothing to guard if it didn't plow. Russia: Carey BABA 20.

W181.2. King kills architect after completion of great building so that he may never again build one so great.

W181.2.0.1* Gobborn Seer: father sends son to sell sheepskin and get price of it and skin back too (H586). Girl shears it, pays price and returns skin. Wed. Takes son along to help build castle for king. Asked to shorten journey, wife advises to tell a story (H586.3). King plans to kill Gobborn and son after castle is finished. Gobborn sends home for 'tools', message by king's son to Jack's wife to "give him crooked and straight." She locks him in a trunk. King must let Gobborn and Jack go to "ransom son." England: Jacobs MORE 60-64. Ireland: Pilkington SHAMROCK 104-106.

W181.3. Raven wants to be as white as a swan. (Washes in streams constantly and perishes from lack of usual food.) Aesop: Aesop AESOP'S (Grosset) 99; Aesop AESOP'S (Watts) 118.

W185.7. Violence of temper. Maid will wed knight when he overcomes his temper. He arrives late at church and kills priest for not repeating mass. Devil on goat leads him home. Castle and knight are swallowed into earth. Netherlands: De Leeuw LEGENDS..HOLLAND 104-108.

W197. Self-centeredness.

W197.1* Self-centeredness. Animals speculate

about why elephant is praised at court. Donkey thinks it is because of his lovely big ears, ox thinks they have mistaken tusks for horns, etc. In praising others, we praise ourselves. Russia: Wyndham TALES..RUSSIA 73-75.

W197.2* Bricklayer wants to make city walls of brick, carpenter of wood, tanner of leather. Hard to see beyond one's nose. Aesop: Aesop AESOP'S (Grosset) 219-220; Aesop AESOP'S (Watts) 10.

W197.3* Traveler finds hatchet. "Look what I found." Companion, "Look what we found." Meet hatchet's owner. First traveler, "Looks like we are in trouble." Second, "You mean you are in trouble." Aesop: Aesop AESOP'S (Grosset) 21; Aesop AESOP'S (Random) 44-45 (purse).

W197.4* Father hyena and two sons kill cow together but father eats. When attacked sons refuse to help father. "Eat alone, die alone." Ethiopia (Guragie): Davis LION'S 127-129.

W197.5* Ir gets one of everything, Bir gets two, Dau gets three, I get a little one. Eat mangoes. Owner of tree comes. Ir gets one stripe, Bir gets two, Dau gets three. I get off scot-free! India: Withers I 112-114.

W198* Unkindness. Father-in-law's remark is construed as insult and son-in-law returns insulting remark. Chief finds them wrong in insulting each other. "When a thing is bought do not refer to it." Angola (Loanda): Courlander KING'S 71-73.

W200 - W299. Traits of character--

miscellaneous.

W200. Traits of character--miscellaneous.

W211. Active imagination. SEE ALSO: J2632.1.

W211.1.1* Boy loses penny, Is given another. Cries: If I hadn't lost mine, I'd have two now. Russia: Ginsburg THREE 16.

W211.1.1.1* Ijapa, tortoise, bewails death of his horse. Oba gives him another. He wails, "If only my old horse had lived, I'd have two now." Courlander OLODE 40-44.

W211.4* Man frightens self and takes refuge in cave with dervish. Sends dervish to fetch him drink and borrows d's knife to protect self while d. is gone. On d's return he fears d. is a demon and threatens him with knife. D. has to find another cave. Iran: Shah MULLA 60-62.

W211.5* Plants patch of melons for self and one for God. Steals from God's patch and villagers sneak up behind and take his bag. "He caught me!" Turkey: Walker TALES 235.

W211.6* Told he'll need sword to defend self from robbers. Numskull rushes up to first traveler he meets on road and surrenders sword. "Here you take the sword and let me keep the donkey." Iran: Shah MULLA 118.

W211.7* Scimitar is offered for fantastic price--it stretches to five times length in battles. He brings his firetongs to offer at same price. They seem to stretch ten times length when wife chases him with them. Turkey: Downing HODJA 59.

X. HUMOR

X0 - X99. Humor of discomfiture.

X0. Humor of discomfiture.

X12. Man interrupted each time he tries to eat something. North Africa: Gilstrap SULTAN'S 32-39.

X52.2. Wind carries off hunter's wig. He laughs. How could expect wig to stay when his own hair wouldn't. Aesop: Aesop AESOP'S (Grosset) 226; Aesop AESOP'S (Watts) 153; Aesop

FABLES (Walck) 86-87.

X100 - X199. Humor of disability.

X110. Humor of deafness.

X111.1. Deaf persons: search for the lost animal. A. inquires for his lost animal. B. talks about his work and makes a gesture. A. follows the direction of the gesture and happens to find the animals. He returns and offers an injured animal to B. in thanks. B. thinks he is blamed for injuring the animals. Dispute. Taken to a deaf judge. Type 1698A.

X111.1.1* Woman loses sheep (goat), deaf man points, offers lamb (kid) with broken leg as thanks. He thinks he's being blamed and case comes before deaf judge. Judge tells them to marry and make a good home for the 'baby' (goat). Ethiopia: Courlander FIRE 73-76; Davis LION'S 108-112; Green FOLK..AFRICA 21-27.

X111.1.2* Deaf herdsman asks deaf toddy-climber about cattle, is directed and finds. T. thinks he's being accused and case goes to deaf headman. Headman's wife has just left him and he thinks they come from her--tells them to go away. Burma: Htin KINGDOM 31-33.

X111.1.3* Second deaf man thinks first found his lost goat. Tries to give goat with broken horn as thanks. First claims he didn't beat it. Third as judge thinks they want his horse. Rumania: Ure RUMANIAN 145-146.

X111.9. Deaf man visits the sick. He plans the conversation with the expected answers. The answers turn out otherwise. A. How are you? B. I am dead. Thank God! What have you eaten? Poison I think. I hope it agrees with you. Type 1698I. Leach NOODLES 87.

X111.10. "Good day." "A woodchopper." The workman answers the traveler's courtesies with remarks about his work. Leach NOODLES 86.

X111.10.1* Bill collector confronts deaf man making axe handle--final remark "Go to the Devil." "Up the hill and you're there in no time." Norway: Asbjornsen EAST 158-160.

X120. Humor of bad eyesight. SEE: J1761.10 (Blind men and elephant). SEE ALSO: Subject Index "BLIND."

X130. Other physical disabilities.

X131. The wry-mouthed family. Each member has mouth turned in a different way. Unavailing attempts to blow out the light. Colwell SECOND 104-106; Haviland NORTH 144-146; Tashjian JUBA 47-50.

X300 - X499. Humor dealing with professions.

X410. Jokes on parsons.

X452. The parson has no need to preach. Those who know may teach those who do not know. Type 1826. Turkey: Courlander RIDE 82-84; Dobbs MORE 31-33; Downing HODJA 17; Kelsey HODJA 21-28. Iran: Shah MULLA 42. U.S. Black: Courlander TERRAPIN'S 102-103.

X452.2* The parson cannot preach. Dips letter of appointment in broth instead of bread and then throws to dog. "Words you should have heard have gone to the dogs." Norway: Asbjornsen NORWEGIAN 25-30.

X459.2* Farmer grabs tiger by tail before it can pounce. Monk refuses to kill tiger because of religious belief. Monk holds tail so that farmer can kill tiger. Farmer says he has reformed and cannot kill either. Indonesia: Courlander KANTCHIL'S 18-21 /Gruenberg FAVORITE 396-397/.

X459.3* Parson, deacon and bishop all agree to bury dead goat when learn he left inheritance to church. Russia: Riordan TALES..CENTRAL 73-75.

X583.1* Jokes on travelers. Travelers from N. China and S. China meet en route and describe marvels back home. Bridge in south so big one fell off a year ago and hasn't reached water yet. Carrots in north so big there is no need to go north to see them. They will reach the south soon. SEE ALSO: B296.2. China: Withers WORLD 31.

X700 - X799. Humor concerning sex.

X770. Jokes about married life.

X771. Wife dies and man does not grieve but donkey dies and he grieves. Why? Friends told him they'd find him a better wife but no one made such a promise for the donkey. Turkey: Downing HODJA 57.

X772* "Come quick, your wife has lost her reason!" "Impossible, she never had any." Turkey: Downing HODJA 72.

X773* On his deathbed he tells wife to dress up in her finery. Maybe the Angel of Death will take her instead of him. Turkey: Downing HODJA 97.

X900 - X1899. Humor of lies and exaggerations.

X900. Humor of lies and exaggerations. Types 1875-1999. SEE ALSO: Subject Index "LIES."

X900.1* Exaggeration. Munchausen tales. Type 1889. SEE ALSO: Z19.2 (tales of contradictions). England: Hampden GYPSY 101-104. Russia: Ginsburg THREE 52. Syria: Courlander RIDE 77-81.

X902. Liar comes to believe his own lie. He tells a lie so often he believes it himself.

X902.1* Liar believes own tale. Hyena lies that there are many dead asses in next village. He wants to keep one he has found. All rush off and he decides must be true and follows them Africa: Guillot GUILLOT'S 88-89.

X902.2* Man invents vicious dog to frighten off chicken thief. Neighbors believe tale and hold him responsible for acts attributed to his dog. He shoots the dog. French Canada: Carlson

TALKING 30-42 /Courlander RIDE 272-278/, /Colwell SECOND 107-114/.

X902.3* Fool believes own tall tale. Tells tale of bread being given away at other side of town to get rid of crowd at bakery. Then he follows crowd. Iran: Kelsey MULLA 65-70.

X904. The teller reduces the size of his lie.

X904.2.1* Farmer's son saw rabbit as big as ox. Doubted, reduces size until as big a fly. "Now I know you're fibbing." France: Withers I 76.

X904.3* "Soon we're coming to the bridge that breaks down under liars." Twenty pound hare gets smaller as they get nearer. Bridge doesn't appear. "It melted away like the fat on your rabbit." Russia: Ginsburg THREE 3-5.

X904.4* Priest offers to shorten his exaggerations. Doubter to say "ahem" when exaggerates too much. He tells of the tail of St. George's dragon. "It stretched from here to Egypt." "From here to Gaza." "From here to Beirut." Etc. "Without a tail." Lebanon: Courlander RIDE 92-94.

X904.4.1* Devil advises preacher to make story of David and Goliath bigger, sits in first row and shakes head when tale not big enough. Goliath grows until he stretches from Shochoh to Mobile when falls. "And if we don't adjourn this meeting right now we are going to have him laying right on top of us!" U.S. (Alabama): Courlander TERRAPIN'S 98-101.

X904.5* First liar caught fish three feet long. Second caught a burning lanter. First: "How possible?" Second: "If you cut two feet off your fish, I'll blow out my lantern." U.S. Withers WORLD 29.

X904.6* Liar reduces size of lie. Tells of prowess in breaking horse. "What then?" "And then he threw me." Iran: Shah MULLA 142; Turkey: Downing HODJA 22.

X904.6.1* Liar reduces the size of lie. Sprang onto horse which no one would ride. "I couldn't ride him either." Iran: Shah MULLA 142.

X904.7* Liar reduces the size of his lie when one who knows the truth enters. Tells of a hospital which is 10,000 feet long and 100 feet wide. Why so out of proportion? Would have been wider if that fellow had not come in. Turkey: Downing HODJA 83.

X905. Lying contests. British West Indies (Grenada): Withers WORLD 72.

X905.0.1* Three sons, strange old man will reward one who can outlie him. Third begins "Before we begin, let me tell you something true." Chain of lies. Wins. Algeria: Carpenter AFRICAN 129-136.

X905.0.2* Beardless man suggests contest. Lad tells chain of lies ending with kicking fox who dropped parchment reading "The cake is mine, and the beardless one goes empty handed." SEE ALSO: H341.5 (Fillmore). Serbia: Lang VIOLET 3-21 /Lang FIFTY 77-80/. De La Mare 100-105.

X905.1. Master forced to say, "You lie!" SEE ALSO: H342.3 (princess forced to say "that a lie").

X905.1.1* Lie: King owes shepherd a pot of gold. That's a lie. Russia: Ginsburg THREE 13.

X905.1.2* Lie: Shah's father borrowed two jars of gold from Hodja. That's impossible. Wins reward. Hardendorff JUST 135-138.

X905.1.3* Moth, mosquito, fly, anansi spider. Anyone who says "you lie" gets eaten. Anansi tells last tale. He opened three coconuts from his tree and moth, mosquito and fly came out, been trying to catch them to eat ever since. Ashanti: Courlander HAT 25-29.

X905.1.4* Man who calls tale untrue to become slave of others. One says other three were produced by fruits of his cottontree and are his slaves. Burma: Brockett BURMESE 79-83.

X905.1.5* Dragon eats two brothers for not telling story. Third tells on condition he rip dragon open if interrupts. Tells tall tale. Dragon cries "It's a lie!" Rips open and rescues brothers. Russia (Avar): Ginsburg LAZIES 64-70.

X905.1.6* Girl tells tall tale saying rich man murdered her brother. He must call her a liar or lose bet. Russia (Steppes): Masey STORIES 73-83.

X907.1. The second liar corroborates the lie of the first. SEE ALSO: X909.4. Rumania: Ure RUMANIAN 22-23 (Pakala and Tandala, huge cabbage, huge pot. Russia (Chuvash): Ginsburg TWELVE 38-43.

X907.1.1* First liar: saw mill in tree top. Second: saw rat climbing down with flour on whiskers. First: saw horse seven leagues across. Second: saw huge saddle, etc. France: Withers WORLD 7-8.

X909. Other stories about liars.

X909.4* Second liar's tale must be accepted by first liar as it complements his own lie.

X909.4.1* First liar: The huge cabbage. Second: Pot big enough to boil it. Rumania: Ure RUMANIAN 22-23. England: Withers I SAW 71. U.S.: Withers WORLD 28 (pumpkin).

X909.4.2* First liar: huge bird. Second: huge tree for bird to perch in. Liberia (Vai): Withers I SAW 141.

X909.4.3* First: huge ship. Second: tall tree-- necessary as mast for huge ship. Vietnam: Schultz VIETNAMESE 46-57.

X909.4.4* First liar: huge drum. Second: huge ox--necessary for skin to cover drum. China: Withers WORLD 30.

X909.4.5* First liar: lie about child with seven arms. Second: saw shirt with seven sleeves. Must be his. First: heard river caught fire. Second: I saw a lot of burnt fish. Portugal: Withers WORLD 51-53.

X909.5* Liar's tales contradict each other.

X909.5.1* Weapons maker has spear that can pierce any skull. Shield no spear can pierce. China: Courlander TIGER'S 40-42; Kendall SWEET 63-65.

X909.6* Lie with trick ending.

X909.6.1* Giant so big upper lip touches sky and lower lip ground. "Where is his body?" "I don't know, I've only seen him with his mouth open." China: Withers I 128.

X909.7* Ikpoom tells tall tale and beats all those who disbelieve. Anansi invites to eat and gives hot pepper soup. Then says top layer of water is his wife's so he can't give to Ikpoom. Ikpoom calls him a liar and Anansi beats Ikpoom. West Africa: Aardema TALES 51-58.

X909.8* Lying in court for a friend in case about wheat, liar goes on and on about barley. Makes no difference when lying whether one lies about wheat or barley. Turkey: Downing HODJA 59.

X910. Lie: the remarkable man.

X912. Lie concerning babyhood and boyhood of hero.

X912.1* Boy grows so fast shadow can't keep up, has to stand on chair to button collar, head grows out of tip of hat. Eats lard for shortening. U.S.: Leach NOODLES 80.

X930. Lie: remarkable person's physical powers and habits.

X938.1* Lie: person with remarkable sight. Sees a mosquito on cliff a mile away. Second man can't see but can hear it tramping. U.S.: Withers WORLD 28.

X938.2* Dog hears noise, cat sees cause. Hair fell out of horse's tail. India: Leach LION 12.

X941.2.1* Fight on old woman's hand. Wrestler throws elephant into other wrestler's house, daughter of second wrestler calls it a mouse and throws it back out. Old woman has them wrestle on her hand. Her daughter wraps one hundred camels, trees, house, town in blanket as runs from mother. Eats watermelon and stuffs blanket and all into shell. Flood washes it away and breaks it--all come out and settle on spot. Type 2962A. India (Punjab); Withers WORLD 2-6.

X941.4.1* Old woman drinks up huge amount which was wage of strong man pulling tree for her and runs off with his two hundred pound bun. He pursues with tree. She leaps into farmer's eye, four men playing cards there. China: Lin MILKY 51-56.

X1100. Lie: the remarkable hunter.

X1114.3. Wildcat and bear both attracted by steak in saddlebag leap on it from opposite sides, wildcat rams down bear's throat and chokes bear. U.S.: Credle TALL 27-28.

X1120. Lie: the great marksman.

X1122.0.1* Hits flea 365 miles away in right eye. British West Indies (Grenada): Withers WORLD 32.

X1122.3. Lie: ingenious person lends gun barrel to make spectacular shot. U.S. (Appalachia): Chase GRANDFATHER 180-185 (two flocks at once, pants full of birds, etc., ties ducks' feet together and they carry him, X1258.1).

X1124.3. Accidental discharge of gun kills much game, gun kills a bird which falls on loose limb of tree, which falls on bear, etc. Type 1890. Eel pulled up hits boar who dies, weed turns out to be pheasant. Japan: Sakade JAPANESE CHILDREN'S STORIES 84-90.

X1124.3.1. Gunshot splits limb and catches feet of birds. U.S. (Appalachia): Chase JACK 151-160 (+X1133.1.1); Withers WORLD 85-86 (+ button off coat kills hare, gets boots full of fish, etc.).

X1130. Lies: hunter's unusual explanations.

X1130.2. Fruit tree grows from head of deer shot with fruit pits. U.S. (Applachia): Chase JACK 151-160.

X1130.2.1. Tree grows out of horse and gives rider shade. U.S. (Appalachia): Chase WICKED 186-194 (oak and dogwood, saddle carved out of oak, dogwood shades).

X1130.2.2* Old Roaney. Overloaded horse because of so much game shot, back breaks so he skins her and carries game home in skin. Puts back on her later but got sheep hide on in dark by mistake and tied with blackberry vines. They shear her thereafter and pick blackberries off her. U.S. (Appalachia): Chase WICKED 195-204.

X1130.2.3* Basket maker's donkey is cut in two, fastened together with willow vines. They take root. Cuts withers from donkey henceforth. Gypsy (England): Hampden GYPSY 97-99.

X1132.2* Ingenious skinning of animal. (Baughman) Man cuts forehead, hocks of horse, sneaks up behind with switch. The horse jumps out of its skin. U.S. (Appalachia): Chase

WICKED 195-204.

X1133.1.1* (Baughman) Boy who is being carried off by wild geese he has caught in a trap (X1258.1) falls into hollow stump with bear cubs. Mother bear returns, starts coming out of stump backwards. The boy grabs bear's tail, jams knife point into bear. She pulls him out, he shoves her off stump. She breaks neck. U.S. (Appalachia): Chase JACK 151-160.

X1133.3. Man in barrel grabs wolf by the tail and is drawn out of danger.

X1133.8* Gypsy lad buys some cows cheaply but can't get them back across sea, throws them back. Hangs onto tail of last and is carried over himself. Gypsy: Jagendorf GYPSIES' 164-169.

X1200. Lie: remarkable animals.

X1203.1* Horse in snowstorm eats charcoal. Heat from dung keeps gypsy and wife warm next day and heats soldering irons. Gypsy: Jagendorf GYPSY 148-151.

X1204.2. (Baughman) Snakes eat each other up. U.S.: Chase GRANDFATHER 186-194 (three inches left, one was longer than other); Withers WORLD 82.

X1204.3* Two rams fight till nothing left but tails. U.S. (Appalachia): Credle TALL 82-88.

X1210. Lies about mammals.

X1215.7.1* Lie: fast dog. Dog runs beside train. Tightens bolts with teeth (cools off the hot boxes). U.S.: Arbuthnot FAIRY 212-214; Bontemps FAST pb; Weiss SOONER HOUND pb.

X1215.11.1* Dog cut in half catches both rabbits. Happy Boz'll. Gypsy: Hampden GYPSY 67-68; Manning-Sanders RED 174-175; Williams-Ellis FAIRY 32-33.

X1221.1.1. Large bear. Old Wall Eyes. Bear is thrown wagon load of meat, left mules, man escapes only because bear can't climb trees. U.S. Withers WORLD 25-27.

X1233.2.1. Lie: tough hog. Hog finds dynamite supply, eats it. Walks behind the mule. The mule kicks the hog; the explosion kills the mule, blows down the barn, breaks windows out of house. Leach NOODLES 82.

X1235.2.2* Lie: remarkable cow. Cows give ponds of milk. Skim cream from boats. Switzerland: Müller-Guggenbühl SWISS 181 /De Regniers GIANT 174-175/.

X1235.2.3* Cow falls into sinkhole, drowns in her own milk but churns one hundred pounds of butter in the process. U.S. (Appalachia): Chase GRANDFATHER 186-194.

X1236.1.1* Lies about bulls. Bull runs around

fodder stack so fast butts self in rear and knocks brains out. U.S. (Appalachia): Chase GRANDFATHER 186-199.

X1258.1. Lies about geese. Lie: ram carried through air by geese. U.S. (Appalachia): Chase GRANDFATHER 180-185 (+X1122.3); Chase JACK 151-160 (+X1133.1.1).

X1258.2.1* Lie: the tough bird. How to cook a coot. Boil twice, put brick inside bird and bake until brick is done. Throw away the coot and eat the brick. Nova Scotia: Leach NOODLES 74.

X1258.3* Geese sing as fly, one shot continues to sing as is prepared and cooked. Flock flies in and each gives a feath to roasted goose on dinner table. All fly off singing. U.S.(Maryland): Cothran WITH 23-25.

X1265* (Baughman) Lies about turkeys.

X1265.6* Turkey so clever they spare it at turkey shoot. Winner hitches turkey to boat and is pulled home. U.S. (Appalachia): Credle TALL 34-39.

X1280. Lies about insects.

X1286.1.4. Lie: the large mosquito. Large mosquitoes fly off with kettle. They have drilled through kettle. Their bills are clinched inside like nails. U.S.: Withers WORLD 84.

X1286.1.5.1* (Baughman) Mosquitoes confer about eating man where they find him or taking him home. Mosquitoes decide to eat man where they find him to keep the big mosquitoes from taking their prey. U.S.: Withers WORLD 86.

X1306.3* (Baughman) Lies about fish. Tragic end of tame fish. Tame fish falls into river while crossing footbridge and drowns. Withers WORLD 87.

X1320. Lies about reptiles.

X1321.4.11 (Baughman) Frozen, hibernating snake is used for stick or piece of rope.

X1321.4.11.1* Brer Rabbit uses frozen blacksnake as necktie. He warms up and begins to squeeze. U.S. (Alabama): Courlander TERRAPIN'S 21-23.

X1321.4.11.2* Man warms frozen snake, it bites him. That is snake's nature. U.S. (Black): Lester KNEE 24-26. Aesop: Aesop AESOP'S (Grosset) 216; Aesop AESOP'S (Watts) 126; Aesop FABLES (Macmillan) 33.

X1400. Lies about plants, fruits, vegetables, and trees.

X1401.1.2* (Baughman) Lie: the great vegetable. Animals eat into large vegetable, live there for some time. U.S.: Credle TALL (sheep in turnip).

X1402. Lies about the fast-growing plants. Germany: Wiggin TALES 69-80 (turnips).

X1402.1. Lie: fast-growing vine. Withers WORLD 19-22 (pea-vine).

X1402.3.1. The fast-growing cornstalk. U.S. (Appalachia): Chase GRANDFATHER 186-189.

X1410. Lies about fruit.

X1411.2.1* Lies about large pumpkin. Woman crawls into huge pumpkin for pie filling. It breaks loose and rolls off with her. U.S.: Credle TALL 16-20 /Green CLEVER 137-142/.

X1411.4. Lie: the great pear. Switzerland: Müller-Guggenbühl SWISS 181 /De Regniers GIANT 174-175/.

X1420. Lies about vegetables.

X1423.1. Lie: the great cabbage. SEE: X907.1; X909.4.1.

X1439.1. Lies about hot peppers. Family made father so mad so would plant really hot peppers. Have to use fire tongs to pick. U.S.: Credle TALL 67-81.

X1500. Lies about geography and topography.

X1503. Schlaraffenland (Land of Cockaigne). Land in which impossible things happen. Germany: Gag MORE 87-89.

X1506. The extraordinary names. A place where animals and things are designated by senseless names.

X1506.1* Master tells girl silly names for cat, fire, pants, etc. The house catches on fire and she attempts to inform him of this. England: Hutchinson CANDLELIGHT 19-21; Jacobs ENGLISH 230-231 /Arbuthnot FAIRY 17/, /Arbuthnot ANTHOLOGY 157-158/; Rockwell MASTER pb; Steel ENGLISH 232-233; Wiggin TALES 235; Williams-Ellis FAIRY..BRITISH 153-154. Spain: Boggs THREE 77-79 (shepherd given silly names as joke, landlord thinks his fire alarm is nonsense, ignores).

X1506.2* Woman gives peasant only bread and water. Taunts by asking if he knows 'Roast Goose' who lives in 'Pan Village', etc. He puts goose in knapsack, leaves telling her "goose has moved to knapsack village." Russia: Carey BABA 79-80.

X1600. Lies about weather and climate.

X1606.2.4.1. (Baughman) Geese or ducks are frozen into lake; something scares them the next morning and they fly off with the whole lake. U.S.: Credle TALL 96-99.

X1611.1.10.1* (Baughman) Wind blows Louisiana line forty miles east. Why Texas is so big. U.S. (Alabama): Courlander TERRAPIN'S 65-66.

X1620. Lies about cold weather.

X1623.2.1. Lie: words freeze. Frozen words thaw out in spring. U.S.: Credle TALL 40-42.

X1623.2.4* (Baughman) Men put frozen words into baskets and put them by fire to thaw. U.S.: Withers WORLD 30 (thaw out in frying pan).

X1623.7.2* (Baughman) Frozen horn notes. Horn on carriage won't blow in woods, later in inn it begins to blow. Germany: Withers WORLD 48-49.

X1630. Lies about hot weather.

X1632* (Baughman) Extraordinary effect of heat. U.S. (Alabama): Courlander TERRAPIN'S 67-68.

X1633.1. Lies: meadow so hot that corn pops in fields. Animals freeze to death thinking it has snowed. U.S.: Credle TALL 53-54; Withers WORLD 83.

X1650. Lies about precipitation and dampness.

X1651.1. Lie: shingling the fog. Man shingling building during thick fog shingles several feet of fog when he gets beyond the edge. U.S.: Withers WORLD 85.

X1653.3.3* (Baughman) Lies about snow. Men or animals step into chimney during big snow. Gypsy: Jagendorf GYPSIES' 118-121.

X1653.4.2* Snow in summer. Lad sent to hammer tent poles deeper is snowed under as he hammers. Found in morning. Gypsy: Jagendorf GYPSIES' 33-38.

X1655.2* (Baughman) Deep mud. U.S.: Credle TALL 9-15.

X1720. Absurd disregard of anatomy.

X1723.4. Lies about swallowing. A whale of a tale: boy eats cod, seal, ooglook, white whale, pond. Too big for door, window, smokehole, enters eye of needle (D1181.1). Knocks over lamp and explodes. Pond and eaten fish left. Eskimo (Seward Peninsula): Cothran MAGIC 18-21.

X1731.2.1. Lies about falling. Man falls and is buried in earth; feels for spade and digs self out with it. Leach NOODLES 19.

X1760. Absurd disregard of the nature of non-material things.

X1761.3* Fool burned a hole in his coat. Hard to mend. Nothing left but the collar. Russia: Ginsburg THREE 16.

X1761.4* Bagels eaten by dog and holes are lost. Jewish: Simon MORE 36-45.

X1790. Other logical absurdities.

X1791. Lies: deaf, dumb, blind and lame men catch hare. Germany (Grimm): Grimm BROTHERS 15-16.

X1791.1* Lie: deaf and dumb men answer, blind man tells time looking at no watch, naked takes out tobacco pouch, legless chases, etc. England: Hampden GYPSY 63-65.

X1791.1.1* Deaf man hears scream, blind man sees them, crippled man wants to run for help, ragged fears they'll steal our clothes. Ethiopia (Galla): Ashabranner LION'S 92-93.

X1791.2* Two naked, one with no clothes, two guns not loaded, one empty, etc. Man with no clothes puts hands in pocket, asks for pot to cook hare that got away, etc. France: Withers I SAW 77.

X1791.3* Three ponds on point of thorn, two dry and one with no water. Three potters, two with no hands and one handless; last made three pots, two broken, one with no bottom, cook rice in latter, etc. India: Withers WORLD 1.

X1850. Other tall tales.

X1851.1* Man unwittingly hangs powder horn on moon. Is gone in morning, fetches it down next night as moon passes. U.S.: Jablow MAN 46-47.

X1863. Why gypsies have no church. They ate up their churches made of cheese and bacon. Rumania: Ure RUMANIAN 99-100.

Z. MISCELLANEOUS GROUPS OF MOTIFS

Z0 - Z99. Formulas.

Z0. Formulas.

Z11. Endless tales. Hundreds of sheep to be carried over stream one at a time, etc. The wording of the tale so arranged as to continue indefinitely. Type 2300. SEE ALSO: K555.1.0.1; M231.2.

Z11.0.1* Ants cross river in walnut shell two at a time. Sicily: Hampden HOUSE 94-96. Italy: Cimino DISOBEDIENT #17.

Z11.0.2* Ducks cross bridge one at a time. Puerto Rico: Withers I SAW 52.

Z11.1. Endless tale: corn carried away a grain at a time. Canada: Withers I SAW 48 (locusts carrying oats from granary). Ethiopia: Courlander FIRE 99-102. Nigeria: Walker NIGERIAN 57-58.

Z11.2. Endless tale: hundreds of birds in snare fly away one at a time. Pakistan: Siddiqui TOONTOONY 155-157. India: Withers WORLD 101-103 (golden-winged swans).

Z11.3* Endless tale. Rats of Nagasaki meet rats of Satsuma on way to each other's cities and learning there is no food in other port they jump overboard, one at a time. Japan: Withers I SAW 129.

Z11.4* Endless tale with catch. The teller has been allowed in the house on condition he tell tales all night long. He agrees on condition he is not interrupted. A crow flew over a tree, another flew over a tree, etc. "And then?" "And then you interrupted me." He goes to sleep. Jewish: Ginsburg THREE 15.

Z11.5* Old man sells story to lad which can win princess. Oak on Sado Island so big top was in next world. A man climbed down the trunk to measure it and acorns fell as he went. Tells where each of 333,000 acorns fell. +H507.1.0.1. Princess asks: How did you count the acorns? He: By stringing them on a thread. She: What needle and thread can do that? He: I'll string blossoms in your garden and show you. He throws his needle out the window and it kills a thief in the treetop. The needle which can pierce anything and thread which never grows shorter (D1184) had been given him by two beggars to whom he showed kindness in his travels. He weds the princess. Japan: Novak FAIRY 31-36.

Z11.6* Endless tale: monk has tiny bell, he is content hearing it tinkle. Apothecary borrows and does not return. Servant sent for bell finds A. dancing and cannot resist joining him. Etc. If we send someone to find out how story ends they'll stay too... Japan: Novak FAIRY 193-196.

Z12. Unfinished tales. Just as the interest is aroused the narrator quits. "If the bowl had been stronger, my tale had been longer." Types 2250, 2260.

Z12.1* Shepherd pulling on tail of sheep stuck in bog. Takes off coat, spits on hands, etc. Tail breaks, or tale would have been longer. Scotland: Withers I SAW 71. Celtic: Wiggin TALES 54 /Hardendorff JUST 29/.

Z12.1.1* Boy finds box, key, opens, cow's tail inside. If tail had been longer my tale had been longer. Scandinavia: Wiggin TALES 321 /Hardendorff JUST 26-27/.

Z12.2* Boy finds box, key, what's inside? Wait awhile until he opens it and we'll see. Russia (Jewish): Ginsburg THREE 17. Germany (Grimm): Gag MORE ix-x; Grimm BROTHERS 187. Germany: Wiggin TALES 82.

Z13. Catch tales. The manner of the teller forces the hearer to ask a particular question to which the teller returns a ridiculous answer. Type 2200.

Z13.1. Tale-teller frightens listener: yells "boo" at exciting point. Type 366. SEE ALSO: E235.4.1+ (Golden Arm, Teeny Tiny).

Z13.1.1* The Strange Viistor. Body assembles self piece by piece. "Where did you get such big, big feet?" etc. What did you come for? "You!" to old woman. England: Jacobs ENGLISH 186-189 /Sechrist HEIGH-HO 48-51/; Williams-Ellis FAIRY..BRITISH 132-134.

Z13.1.2* The Old Woman and the Bear. Old woman on porch sings "Who'll spend the night with me?" Bear: "Me, by the corral." Etc. "Me by the brush pile." "Me by the chimney corner." Jumps out and eats her up. U.S. (California): Cothran WITH 55.

Z13.1.3* Ghost gets nearer and nearer. "I'm in the room." "I'm in the bed", etc. "I got you!" Leach THING 40.

Z13.1.4* Person enters dark, dark house, down dark, dark hall, etc. Ghost jumps out. Leach THING 51. England: Withers I SAW 67.

Z13.4.4* (Baughman) Startle sell. Unexpected ending horrifies or startles listener.

Z13.4.4.1* The Yellow Ribbon. Girl wears yellow ribbon around her neck all life and refuses to tell her lover-husband why. Dying she allows him to untie it--her head falls off. U.S.: Leach RAINBOW 203-204; Sheehan FOLK 138-140; Tashjian JUBA 44-46.

Z13.5* Fish calls "take me home", "cook me", "eat me." Eaten. "I got you now, Peter." Peter is never seen again. U.S.: Withers I SAW 34.

Z16. Tales ending with a question. SEE: F660.1; H621.2.

Z16.1. Four brothers construct a woman. Where is she? SEE: H621.2.

Z16.2* Which of brothers is most skillful? SEE: F660.1.

Z17. Rounds. Stories which begin over and over again and repeat. Type 2350.

Z17.1* It was a dark and stormy night...the sailors begin telling stories..."it was a dark and stormy night." U.S.: Withers I SAW 35.

Z17.2* Once there was a girl who asked her father "What's a silly question?" and he replied "Once there was a girl who asked her father..." U.S.: Withers I SAW 35.

Z17.3* Shall I tell you the story of Johnny McGory and the Red Stocking? "Yes." "Not yes but shall I tell you..." U.S.: Withers I SAW 45.

Z17.4* A man has a singing bird. A man wants to buy it but he won't sell. Another man wants to buy it, etc. Chile: Withers I SAW 56.

Z17.5* A boy entered a dog in a shaggy dog contest. Won. Wanted to be sure he was shaggiest dog in world so entered in another contest, etc. U.S.: Withers I SAW 36.

Z18. Formulistic conversations.

Z18.1. What makes your ears so big? To hear the better, my child, etc. Type 333. SEE: E235.4.3.1; K2011; Z13.1.1. Ethiopia: Courlander FIRE 65-72 (monkey quizzes baboon).

Z18.2. Series of excuses: Mother "Bring water." Girl (Ayoga) "I'll fall in the lake." Mother "Hold to a bush." Girl "It might break" etc. Neighbor girl performs task. Ayoga falls in water and turns into a goose. Russia (Nanay): Ginsburg LAZIES 59-62.

Z19.2. Tales filled with contradictions.

Z19.2.1* Skoonkin Huntin'. U.S. (Appalachia): Chase GRANDFATHER 137-139.

Z19.2.2* Sir Gammer Vans. England: Jacobs MORE 43-45; Wiggin TALES 203-204; Williams-Ellis FAIRY..BRITISH 206-208.

Z19.2.3* Contradictions. Three hunters--two not dressed, lie. No clothes on, etc. France: Hardendorff PICTURE 23-25.

Z20. Cumulative Tales. SEE: J2461 (what should I have said); J2478 (fool buys water clear as oil, etc.); N381 (drop of honey); X1124.3 (Accidental shot kills much game).

Z21.1. Origin of chess. Inventor asks one wheat grain for first square, two for the second, four the third, eight for the fourth, etc. The king cannot pay. India: Edmonds TRICKSTER 5-13.

Z22.1. The Twelve Days (Gifts) of Christmas. Karasz TWELVE pb; Martignoni ILLUSTRATED 92; Wildsmith TWELVE pb.

Z30. Chains involving a single scene or without interdependence among the individual actors.

Z31.1. Pif Paf Poltrie. The suitor (a broom binder) sent from one relation to other for consent to the wedding. Type 2019. Germany: Wiggin TALES 86-87.

Z32.1. The funeral procession of the hen. Animals one by one join the procession. The funeral carriage breaks down or the procession drowns. Type 2021. Germany (Grimm): Grimm HOUSEHOLD 12-13 (straw, coal and stove try to make bridge, F1025.1); Wiggin TALES 118-123.

Z32.1.1. The Death of the Cock. The cock chokes and the hen seeks aid.

Z32.1.1.1* Willow gives wreath, bride gives silk, well gives water. Too late. +Z32.1. Germany (Grimm): Grimm HOUSEHOLD 12-13 (hen dies); Wiggin TALES 118-123.

Z32.1.1.2* Little Tuppens coughs. Dwarfs give iron, blacksmith plow, etc. Boy shakes oak. Oak gives hen acorn cup for water. Tuppen stops coughing. Richardson GREAT 129-139; Wiggin TALES 358-360.

Z32.1.1.3* Blacksmith gives scythe, etc. Cow gives butter to grease rooster's throat. He recovers. Russia: Carey BABA 15-16.

Z32.1.1.4* Cock dying of heat in sauna. Hen goes for water. Chain. Too late. Finland: Bowman TALES..TUPA 242.

Z32.2.2* Titty Mouse falls in pot and dies. Tatty Mouse weeps, stools hop, broom sweeps, door jars, window creaks, form runs around house, walnut tree sheds leaves, bird moults, girl spills milk, old man thatching rick falls off ladder and breaks neck. Tree falls on form, house, window, door, etc. Tatty Mouse buried in ruins. Hutchinson FIRESIDE 17-22. England: Jacobs ENGLISH 78-81; Richardson GREAT 66-73; Steel ENGLISH 94-96; Wiggin TALES 228-230; Withers I SAW 62-66.

Z32.2.3* Cock drowns in brew vat. Hen mourns, hand mill grinds, chair creaks, door rattles, etc. Farmer's wife smears house with porridge. Norway: Sperry HEN 47-56 /Sperry SCANDINAVIAN 15-20/. Scandinavia: Wiggin TALES 305-308.

Z32.2.3.1* Spider falls in brew vat, flea mourns, door creaks, etc....stream overflows and drowns all. Germany: Wiggin TALES 157-159.

Z32.2.4* Louse falls in soup. Mrs. Louse mourns, dog barks, cart rolls into tree, tree shrinks, bird plucks feathers, boy breaks water jars. Father spanks. Reverse. Boy throws stone at bird, bird pecks tree. Tree shoves cart. Cart runs over dog's foot. Dog bites Mrs. Louse in two. Mr. Louse revives. Belgium: Withers I SAW 79-80.

Z32.2.4.1* Louse falls in brewing beer. Flea weeps, door creaks, broom sweeps, truck squeaks, muck-heap smokes, tree shakes, spring floods and drowns all. Germany (Grimm): Grimm BROTHERS 17-20.

Z32.3. Little ant finds a penny, buys new clothes with it, and sits in her doorway. Various animals pass by and propose marriage. She asks what they do at night. Each one replies with its characteristic sound and none pleases her but the quiet little mouse whom she marries. She leaves him to tend the stew and he falls in and drowns. She weeps and, on learning the reason, bird cuts off its beak, dove cuts off its tail, etc. Type 2023. Portugal: Lowe LITTLE 114-122. Puerto Rico: Alegria THREE 56-58 (cockroach, mourners); Belpré PEREZ pb (-chain of mourners). Mexico: Brenner BOY 19-20 (-death of mouse). Spain: Sawyer PICTURE..SPAIN 111-120; Sleigh NORTH 202-206 (ant, mosquito).

Z32.3.1* Cockroach seeks husband. Asks how wooers would beat her. Grocer--with broom, Butcher--leg of lamb, etc. Mouse--with soft tail. Wed. She falls into river. Refuses rescue until golden ladder fetched. He gnaws one from carrot. Preparing soup for ill cockroach, mouse falls in. In mourning she wears black henceforth. Why cockroach is black (A2411.3.4). Persia: Mehdevi PERSIAN 81-92.

Z32.3.2* Mouse asks wooers how will beat her. Woodsman--with axe, tailor--yardstick, cock--soft feathers. Wed. She is scalded cooking, he fans and revives, he faints--she revives. Turkey: Ekram TURKISH 61-65.

Z32.4.1* The straw ox. Animals are caught on a tarred straw ox (K741.4). Man goes to kill each and is offered reward to desist. Each brings food in gratitude. Russia (Cossack): Association TOLD..GREEN 59-66; Haviland FAVORITE ..RUSSIA 53-65; Hutchinson FIRESIDE 77-89; Manning-Sanders BOOK..MAGICAL 8-13; Richardson GREAT 36-47; Wiggin TALES 32-35.

Z32.6* Animals decide to prepare a feast. Ant gets stuck to gum on bark of breadfruit tree and dies. Grasshopper breaks teeth on stem of ivi nut and dies. Spider slaps thighs in laughter and breaks legs. Frog puffs up laughing and bursts. Crab breaks claws on stones. Sandpiper returns with fish to find self only survivor. Fiji: Gittins TALES 26-27.

Z33. Chains involving the eating of an object.

Z33.1. The fleeing pancake. A woman makes a pancake, which flees. Various animals try in vain to stop it. Finally the fox eats it up. Type 2025.

Z33.1.1* Pig offers ride over river to fleeing pancake, eats. Often with animal names (Z53) Henny-Penny, Goosey-Loosey, etc. Hutchinson CHIMNEY 19-24. Norway: Asbjornsen EAST (Row) 41-45 /Association TOLD..GREEN 10-15/, /Arbuthnot FAIRY 73-74/, /Arbuthnot

ANTHOLOGY 238-239/.

Z33.1.2* Gingerbread Man. Rides on fox's tail, back, head, eaten. Galdone GINGERBREAD pb; Haviland FAIRY 7-11; Holdsworth GINGER-BREAD pb; Rockwell THREE 33-44; TALL.. NURSERY 16-22. U.S.: Arbuthnot FAIRY 190-191.

Z33.1.3* Johnny Cake. Fox feigns deaf till john-nycake comes closer (K911.5). England: Col-well YOUNGEST 72-77; Jacobs ENGLISH 162-165 /Martignoni ILLUSTRATED 77-79/, /Havi-land FAVORITE..ENGLAND 22-29/, /Jacobs JOHNNY (Brock) pb/, /Jacobs JOHNNY (Stobbs) pb/; Wiggin TALES 197-199; Williams-Ellis FAIRY..BRITISH 34-38. U.S.: Withers I SAW 26-31.

Z33.1.4* Wee Bannock. Rolls away and in and out of houses causing havoc, down fox's hole in end--eaten. Scotland: Jacobs MORE 73-77 /Haviland FAVORITE..SCOTLAND 13-24/; Steel ENGLISH 180-184; Wilson SCOTTISH 88-89.

Z33.1.5* Little red hen (W111.6) plus cake rolls off. Ditch digger, washers, fox carries, eats. Ireland: Pilkington SHAMROCK 102-103.

Z33.1.6* Hare, wolf, bear, fox threaten bun. Russia: Hutchinson CANDLELIGHT 25-32; Ri-ordan TALES..CENTRAL 31-33; Ross BURIED 13-18.

Z33.1.7* Hare, fox, pig threaten pancake. Pig feigns deaf till pig comes close (K911.5), eats one-half. Why pigs root, still seek other half. Netherland: De Leeuw LEGENDS..HOLLAND 89-91.

Z33.1.8* Journey cake rolls away from all, leads animals home again thus helping old man and woman. Sawyer JOURNEY CAKE pb. U.S.: Arbuthnot ANTHOLOGY 365-366.

Z33.2. The fat cat. While the mistress is away, the cat eats the porridge, the bowl and the ladle. When the mistress returns she says, "How fat you are!" The cat: "I ate the por-ridge, the bowl, and the ladle and I will eat you." The cat meets other animals and eats them after the same conversation. Finally eats too many. Norway: Asbjornsen NORWEGIAN 161-167. Scandinavia: Wiggin TALES 278-283 (end Billy Goat butts off bridge, cat bursts and all come out). Kent FAT pb.

Z33.2.1* The cat and the parrot. Cat invites parrot to dinner--meager. Return feast huge. Cat eats all. Eats parrot too. Old woman, man and cart, wedding procession, two crabs. Crabs cut hole inside and all emerge (F912). Cat sews up hole. India: Hardendorff SLIP pb; Havi-land FAVORITE..INDIA 27-28.

Z33.4.1. Louse and crow make covenant of friend-ship: louse eats crow despite crow saying, "If I strike you once with my beak you will disappear;

how then can you talk of eating me?" Likewise louse eats loaf of bread, she-goat, cow, buffalo, five sepoys, wedding procession with one lakh of people, elephant, tank of water. A sepoy cuts louse in two with his sword and rescues all. India: Withers I SAW 108-111.

Z33.5* Kuratko, the huge chicken, eats grand-father, grandmother, washerwoman, Kotsor the cat. Kotsor cuts a hole in Kuratko's stomach and all come out (F912). Czechoslovakia: Fill-more SHEPHERD'S 82-86 /Davis BAKER'S 127/, /Fillmore SHOEMAKER'S APRON/; Haviland FAVORITE..CZECHOSLOVAKIA 21-33.

Z33.6* Sody Sallyratus. As they cross bridge (K553.2) bear eats boy, girl, grandfather, grandmother. He chases squirrel up tree. Tries to imitate jump (J2415) and falls. Bursts open (F913). All come out. U.S. (Appalachia): Chase WICKED 75-80; Tashjian JUBA 55-58.

Z33.6.1* Greedy old fat man. Ate a pot of mush, barrel of milk. Boy, girl, dog, etc. Chases squirrel up tree and imitates jump. Falls and bursts (F913). All come out. U.S.: Withers I SAW 24-26.

Z33.7* Clay pot boy made by childless couple eats all in house, old woman, old man, bull, wood-chopper, farmer and wife, rooster, hen and egg, barn, billy goat. Goat runs to jump in mouth and breaks (K553.3). Russia: Jameson CLAY pb.

Z39. Chains involving other events without inter-relations of members.

Z39.1. The goat who would not go home. One animal after another tries in vain to persuade the goat to go home. Finally a wolf (bee) bites goat and drives him home.

Goat in fox's hole, all fear, bee routs. Germany (Grimm): Grimm GRIMM'S (Follett) 323-339; Grimm GRIMM'S (Grosset) 228-242; Grimm GRIMM'S (Scribner's) 104; Grimm GRIMM'S (World) 130-141; Grimm HOUSE 56-80; Grimm HOUSEHOLD 149-159. Poland: Zajdler POLISH 141-147.

Boy cannot get goat out of garden. Association TOLD..GREEN 78-80; Richardson GREAT 74-80.

Goat in hare's house, bee routs, bee and hare live together. Portuguese: Montgomerie MER-RY 56-61.

Goat in fox's house routed by cock. Russia: Carrick STILL 73-87. Russia (Ukraine): Bloch UKRANIAN 34-43.

Goat in fox's hole, crab and hedgehog rout. +K2324. Poland: Borski JOLLY 49-62.

Z39.1.0.1* Goat eats up garden. Old man, old woman try to drive him off. Ant stings him and he flees. Puerto Rico: Belpré TIGER 69-72.

Z39.1.0.2* Lad cannot get goat to go home. Final formula: gives milk to cat, mouse, rope hangs smith, axe splits yoke, ox, water, fire, fir crushes Finn, shoots bear, slays wolf, bites fox, bites goat. SEE ALSO: Z41 (pig over stile). Hutchinson CANDLELIGHT 57-68. Scandinavia: Wiggin TALES 315-320.

Z39.1.0.3* The crested curassow. Quiet powis bird is given crest and mane as leader becomes crested curassow. Finds snake on eggs. Asks cow, pig to help. They fear they will crush eggs if try. Owl suggests ants. They bite snake and it leaves. Carib: Sherlock WEST 13-20.

Z39.2. There was a wee wee woman (wee wee mannie) who had a wee wee cow, won't give milk. Tree won't give stick, etc. Tell cow that laddie with sword is going to cut off head of the "big, big coo." Cow gives milk. Great Britain: Jacobs MORE 192-194; Sewell WEE pb; Williams-Ellis FAIRY..BRITISH 20-23. Scotland: Wiggin TALES 200-202.

Z39.4.3* Crow asks sparrow: "What if you choke on food?" "Scratch it out." If bleeds, drink water; if catch cold, make fire; if fire spreads, flop wings and put out; if wings burn, go to doctor; if no doctor, get well without a doctor. Russia (Yiddish): Ginsburg THREE 43-44.

Z39.5.1. The hen lays an egg. It falls off shelf and breaks. Stove smokes, windows break, geese scatter, fenceposts clatter, granddaughter spills water, milking mother falls off stool, father stands on head until hen lays another egg. Still there. Russia: Zemach SPECKLED pb.

Z39.5.2* Marilka is lost. In sorrow, river dries up, cherry sheds blossoms, etc. Domanska MARILKA pb.

Z40. Chains with interdependent members. SEE ALSO: N261.

Z41. The old woman and her pig. Her pig will not jump over stile. SEE ALSO: Z39.1.0.2 (goat). England: Colwell YOUNGEST 199-202; Galdone OLD pb; Haviland FAIRY 28-31; Hutchinson CHIMNEY 11-16; Jacobs ENGLISH 21-23 /Arbuthnot TIME FOR FAIRY 7-8/, /Association TOLD..GREEN 16-20/; Richardson GREAT 48-58; Rockwell OLD 1-9; Steel ENGLISH 178-180; TALL..NURSERY 92-97; Wiggin TALES 211-214.

Z41.1.1* Cap lost, firefly finds. Won't return unless given bread, chain, end--fetches wind from sea, oak now gives acorn, etc. Italy: Withers I SAW 90-91.

Z41.2.1* Crow must wash beak to eat sparrow's eggs. Well needs pot, potter needs antler to dig clay, deer needs dog to kill him, dog needs buffalo milk, buffalo--grass, field--sickle, blacksmith pities sparrow and kills crow. (cf. K278). N. India (Mahakoshal): Arnott ANIMAL 174-178.

Z41.2.2* Crow must wash beak before eating baby wren. Stream needs pot, potter--mud, mud--buffalo to wallow, buffalo--grass, grass--land, land--trees cleared, fire to clear trees, crow seizes fire and is burnt up. Burma: Brockett BURMESE 186-190.

Z41.2.2.1* Crow cheats sparrow in red pepper eating contest. Hides his and claims right to eat sparrow as prize. First must wash beak, river, pot, potter needs clay, spade, blacksmith, fire, farmer's wife gives fire. Crow has it put on his back to carry and is burnt up. Pakistan: Siddiqui TOONTOONY 44-49. Bangladesh: UNICEF Asia FOLK I 1-12 (Siddiqui).

Z41.2.3* Rooster must clean bill on grass, crow eats grass, stick, river rots, sun dry-up. Sun does. Rooster goes to heron's ball. Cuba: Withers I SAW 53-54.

Z41.4. The mouse regains its tail. The cat bites off the mouse's tail and will return it in exchange for milk, the farmer for hay, the butcher for meat, the baker for bread. SEE ALSO: Z47.3. De La Mare ANIMAL 40-41; Hutchinson FIRE-SIDE 31-33. England: Jacobs ENGLISH 197-198; Richardson GREAT 147-152; Wiggin TALES 222-227.

Z41.4.1. Mouse bursts open when crossing stream. Series of helpers similar to Z41.4. +F1025.1.2. Switzerland (French): Duvoisin THREE 44-47 (shoemaker, needle; sow, thread; miller, bran; field, wheat; ox, manure; meadow, grass; river gives water but by time chain reverses mouse is already dead).

Z41.5. Lending and repaying: progressively worse (or better) bargain. SEE: A1378 (origin of debt); J2081.1 (foolish bargain: horse for cow); K251.1.3 (fox travels); N421.1. Progressively lucky bargains.

Z41.6. Bird's pea gets stuck in mill handle. She goes to carpenter, king, queen, who refuses to help. She asks snake to bite queen, stick to beat snake, fire to burn stick, etc. Final formula: cat eats mouse, mouse cuts plant creeper, creeper snares elephant, elephant drinks up sea, sea quenches fire, fire burns stick, stick beats snake, snake bites queen, queen speaks to king, king chides carpenter, carpenter cuts mill handle and pea is extracted. Questions in rhyme. India: Withers I SAW 102-107.

Z41.6.2* Bird drops grain in post. Mouse threatens net, net snares elephant, elephant drinks water. Fire, stick (lathi), serpent, queen, king, carpenter saws post. India: Spellman BEAUTIFUL 44-48.

Z41.6.3* Crow steals grain and falls in tree. Farmer's wife will chop off his head if not returned. Cat eats mouse, gnaws rope, ties ox, drinks water, fire, stick, snake, queen, king, woodman cuts tree. West Pakistan: Siddiqui

TOONTOONY 124-129.

Z41.6.4* Monkey drops pomegranate seed. Asks owner to cut down olive tree so seed can grow. Judge. King, queen, horse, cat, dog, stick, fire, water, ox, butcher, death. Reverse. Portugal: Lowe LITTLE 97-102.

Z41.7. The wormwood (grass) does not want to rock the sparrow. Final formula: the worms begin to gnaw the rods, the rods to beat the oxen, the oxen to drink the water, the water to quench the fire, the fire to burn the hunters, the hunters to shoot the wolves, the wolves to kill the goats, the goats to gnaw the wormwood, the wormwood to rock me--it rocked me and rocked me to sleep. Russia (Ukraine): Bloch UKRAIN-IAN 60-63. Russia: Carrick STILL MORE 23-31.

Z41.8.1* Toontoony and the Barber. Toontoony bird has thorn stuck in throat. Mosquitoes bite elephant--drinks river--fire--stick--cat--mouse --claws king's stomach--punishes barber--barber removes thorn. E. Pakistan: Bang TUN-TUNI pb; Siddiqui TOONTOONY 98-103.

Z41.10* Munachar and Manachar. Munachar seeks reed to make rope to hang Manachar for eating all raspberries. Rod--axe--flag to whet--water --deer to swim in--hound--butter for claw--cat to scrape churn--etc. Sieve for water. Crow cries "Daub." Does so. Ireland: Jacobs MUN-ACHAR pb; Jacobs CELTIC 92-96.

Z41.11* Dog won't catch turtles. Stick beat dog. Hog--oak--sun--wind. Obey when man begins cursing. U.S.: Withers I SAW 22-23.

Z42. Stronger and Strongest. SEE: L392 (mouse stronger than wall).

Z42.0.1* Ooka gives son three wishes. He wishes to be a daimyo's son, then a higher lord's son. Then self again. Japan: Edmonds OOKA 51-56.

Z42.0.2* Stonecutter wishes he were Raja (prince), sun, cloud, wind, mountain (stone) each stronger than predecessor--stonecutter stronger than mountain. Indonesia: Courlander KANTCHIL 96-100 (Mt. Marati). Japan: Lang CRIMSON 101-105 (wishes given by mountain spirit, F341) /Lang FIFTY 291-294/; Mc-Dermott STONE-CUTTER pb; McNeil DOUBLE 37-40; Titus TWO STONECUTTERS pb (stonecutter uses six wishes thus: rich, prince, wind, sun, cloud, stone. Brother uses his one wish to return him to stonecutter. Goddess of the forest was treated well by brother and gave him seven wishes, F341.3). China: Chang CHINESE 73.

Z42.0.3. Chandala maid wants to wed most powerful person in world. King--priest--shiva--dog urinates on shiva's offerings--dog walks before men of her village--wed. India (Chandala): Montgomerie TWENTY-FIVE 41-43.

Z42.0.4. Who is greatest? Boyar, prince, chancellor, priest, lad, woman each strong in own way. Baby is strongest as none can control it. Rumania: Ure RUMANIAN 84-86.

Z42.0.5* Strong and strongest. The frostbitten foot. Ant's foot freezes and pulls off. Snow give me back my leg. Sun is stronger. Cloud. Wind. Wall. Rat. Cat. Dog. Stick. Fire. Water. Ox. Knife. Man. Death. God. Type 2031. Puerto Rico: Alegria THREE 40-43; Belpré TIGER 57-61.

Z42.0.6* Gazelle throws calabash, killing teacher. Children seek cause. Beat wind. Wall, rat, cat, rope, knife, fire, water, ox, tick. Gazelle (eats tick). Zanzibar: Withers I SAW 143-146.

Z42.4* Grass stalk wants to be herb, tubered plant, mouse, owl, man, still discontented. Eskimo (Bering Strait): Cunningham TALKING 46-57.

Z43.2. The cock strikes out the hen's eye with a nut. The cock blames the hazel bush for tearing its knickers, the hazel bush the goats for gnawing at it, the goat the shepherd boy for not tending it, the boy his mistress for not baking him a bun, the mistress the pig for eating up the dough, the pig the wolf for killing its young. Russia: Withers I SAW 95-96 (Wolf--God com-commanded me to eat).

Z43.3. Nut hits cock in head: he thinks sky is falling. He sends the hen to tell the duck, the duck to tell the goose, etc. Final formula: Fox, who told you? Hare. Hare, who told you? Goose, etc. Sometimes the animals have queer names (Z53). Germany: Withers I SAW 81-84 (boy--duck, goose, dog, colt, calf, beaver investigates).

Z43.3.0.1* Chicken Licken. Fox takes to den. Eats all. Richardson GREAT 81-91; TALL.. NURSERY 55-61; Wiggin TALES 358-360.

Z43.3.0.2* Henny Penny. Fox eats all except hen (Z53). England: Colwell YOUNGEST 169-173; Haviland FAIRY 12-15 /Arbuthnot ANTHOLOGY 154-155/; Hutchinson CHIMNEY 3-8; Jacobs ENGLISH 118-121 /De La Mare ANIMAL 47-50/, /Arbuthnot FAIRY 12-13/; Martignoni ILLUS-TRATED 66-68; Montgomerie TWENTY-FIVE 24-25; Rackham ARTHUR 66-70; Rockwell THREE; Steel ENGLISH 152-156; Wiggin TALES 241-243. Norway: Sperry HEN 57-64 (Henny-Penny dreams must go to top of Dovre Mt. or world will end, she and cock escape when fox eats companions) /Sperry SCANDINAVIAN 21-26/. Galdone HENNY pb; Stobbs HENNY pb.

Z43.3.1. Coconut falls and hare thinks world is falling apart. Starts chain of fleeing animals. Lion retraces rumor to hare and returns to site to investigate. SEE ALSO: K1715.1.0.1 (hare flees reflection). India: Arbuthnot ANTHOL-OGY 347; Arbuthnot FAIRY 163; Babbitt JATA-KA 39-43; Davis BAKER'S 21-28; Gaer

FABLES 123-126; Gruenberg FAVORITE 341-343 (monkey drops coconut). China: Chang CHINESE 38-40. Tibet: Withers I SAW 123-125.

Z43.3.2* Hare flees from falling tree. Coon flees from hare, etc., fox, wolf, bear flee--terrapin retraces steps to hare who explains it was only a tree falling. U.S. (Georgia, Black): Brown WORLD 29-33; Harris COMPLETE 194-198; Harris NIGHTS 108-112.

Z43.3.3* Acorn falls on hen, pig, cow, dog, cock, fox, wolf, bear. Larger animals eat smaller then begin to eat selves, gnawing on own tails. Fox flees such fools. Finland: Bowman TALES..TUPA 239-241.

Z43.4. Fly frightens snake; snake frightens rats; rats frighten monkey, etc. SEE: Z49.6.

Z43.5. Boy changes self to nut; fowl eats nut; bush cat eats fowl; dog eats cat; dog swallowed by python; etc. Found, Boy never tries to hide from father again. Africa: Withers WORLD 57-58.

Z43.5.1* Anansi asks grain of corn to hide him. Cock eats corn. Alligator eats cock. Jamaica: Sherlock ANANSI 105-112.

Z43.6.1* Hare to pay four helpers. He has eaten all crops. Invites all to come on same day. Tells cockroach rooster is arriving and cockroach hides. Betrays hiding place and rooster eats cockroach. Coyote eats rooster, hunter kills coyote. Hare flees. Mexico: Brenner BOY 65-70.

Z43.6.2* Beetle and lion as team. Beetle invites animals to help thatch roof. Hides each as other arrives, then betrays hiding place...cock, hyena, leopard, lion. Lion and beetle share meat. Hausa: Aardema MORE 16-21.

Z43.6.3* Tailor hides rat in trunk, betrays to cat. Dog, tiger, lion. Hunter kills lion. Tailor gets all meat. Haiti: Thoby-Marcelin SINGING 46-52.

Z43.6.4* Zomo invites debtors at same time. Dung beetle flees cock, cock flees arriving cat, dog, hyena, leopard, etc. All must pay Zomo one thousand dollars as he says hedgehog neighbor charges him that much to cross backyard. He thus gains enough to repay last debtor to come --lion. Hausa: Sturton ZOMO 14-25.

Z43.6.5* Madame Giraffe promises leopard to bring game, brings lion, brings elephant to lion. Elephant tramples lion. W. Africa: Aardema TALES 32-37.

Z43.6.6* Man invites animals to planting party. Corn seed says "don't ask termite." Termite "don't ask chicken." Snake, stick, fire, water, sun. Man invites all and they destroy each other. +A2305.3. Ashanti: Courlander HAT 46-48.

Z43.7. Ape creates confusion among animals (A1382.2) by telling bees to drive off buffalo, boy to steal honey, crows to attack unguarded horses, monkeys to eat crow's eggs, etc. Indonesia: Courlander KANTCHIL'S 52-56.

Z44. The House That Jack Built. Galdone HOUSE pb; Rockwell THREE 45-52.

Z45. The Horseshoe Nail. For want of a nail the shoe was lost, for want of a shoe the rider was lost. Germany: Wiggin TALES 152.

Z46. The climax of horrors. The magpie is dead. Overate on horseflesh. Horses dead? Overworked at fire. House burned down? etc. SEE ALSO: Z49.5.1.1. England: Jacobs MORE ENGLISH 182-183. Russia: Higonnet-Schnopper TALES 49-57 (why mother didn't write--no paper--burned in fire, etc.). U.S. (Alabama): Courlander TERRAPIN'S 76-89 (hunting dog ran off, was chasing the ox, snake from fire frightened oxen, etc.).

Z47. Series of trick exchanges. SEE: K251.1 (fox travels).

Z47.2* Series of trick exchanges. Monkey asks barber to cut thorn from tail. Monkey jumps and tail is cut off. Monkey claims razor. Loans to old woman to cut wood--claims wood. Gives to woman to bake cookies--claims cookies. Trades for gong. Climbs tree and sings of exploits. Falls onto thorn bush. Monkeys call him Bobtail Bang-Bang. (cf. K251.1; N421). Japan: Sakade JAPANESE 113-120.

Z47.3* Cat at barbershop has tail cut off, demands razor. Lends to fishwife, demands fish, gives to miller--takes flour, gives to teacher--takes girl, gives to washlady--takes shirt, gives to violinist--takes violin. Plays and sings of conquests. (cf. K251; Z41.4). Portugal: Lowe LITTLE 81-83; Michael PORTUGUESE 15-19; Montgomerie MERRY 19-23; Withers I SAW 72-74.

Z47.4. Jackal has barber remove thorn from nose, nose cut, demands nail cutter used. Lends to potter--takes pitcher. Firecrackers from passing wedding procession break--takes bride. Asks drummer's wife to care for bride, bride falls in fire--takes drum. Climbs tree and sings tale. East Pakistan: Siddiqui TOONTOONY 130-135.

Z47.5. Blackbird pierces claw with pine needle. Gives it to old woman. She burns it trying to pry up candle wick--takes candle. Cow breaks --takes cow. Woman kills--claims bride. Gives to shepherd--takes flute. Sings of events. Turkey: Ekram TURKISH 113-116.

Z49.3.1* The Picaro Bird. Bird has suit, shoes, hat made, doesn't pay. Sings he is grander than king. Is caught, cooked, eaten, causes king to vomit. Gets many new feathers from other birds. Spain: Sawyer PICTURE..SPAIN

121-132.

Z49.3.2* Toontoony Pie. Bird steals from king's treasure and mocks, caught, to be cooked, escapes and frog pie is served to king instead, mocks, etc., swallowed, flies out of king's nostril--guards cut king's nose. E. Pakistan: Bang TUNTUNI pb; Siddiqui TOONTOONY 15-22. India: Spellman BEAUTIFUL 71-74.

Z49.3.3* Impudent mouse. Intimidates tailor, dyer, etc. to make clothes. Sings is grander than king. Put in jail, mocks, let free, mocks, etc. India: Spellman BEAUTIFUL 64-68.

Z49.3.4* Bird caught and cooked flies off singing taunting song to wife who pursues. Uganda: Serwadda SONGS 33-39.

Z49.4. There was once a woman: The woman had a son; the son had red breeches, etc. At last: "Shall I tell it again?"

Z49.4.1* Man took a walk. Man took a walk with his friend one day, etc. End: the dog wore a red jacket with polka dots. The dog was so hungry he bit his master. The master got angry and bit him back. U.S.: Withers I SAW 33.

Z49.5.1.1* Wife goes on a visit. Food left on shelf. Dogs ate. Ran into wood. Wood burned. Water put out fire, etc. SEE ALSO: Z46. Russia: Withers I SAW 97.

Z49.5.2. The wolf who wanted to make bread. The farmer explained to him how bread is made. He keeps on asking: "Shall I then be able to eat?" Decides he will not have enough patience to make bread. SEE ALSO: K555.1.2. Lithuania: Deutsch TALES 56-62. Byelorussia: Ginsburg LAZIES 12-17.

Z49.6. Trial among the animals. SEE ALSO: Z43.4.

Z49.6.0.1* Frog croaks because turtle (snail) carries his house on his head; turtle (snail) carries house because firefly is bringing fire; firefly brings fire because mosquito tried to bite him. Philippines: Withers I SAW 131-132 (King kills mosquito with gavel on forehead and kills self.) Philippines (Pampangan): Secrist ONCE 64-66 (Sinukuan, hermit on Mt. Arayat, is judge, mosquito sentenced to three days in jail loses voice and never sings again = male mosquito, A2426.3.5.1).

Z49.6.0.2* Fly lights on tree and it falls. He claims responsibility. Fly buzzes two boys, they strike at it--hit branch, cause three squirrels to fall on four sticks, frighten five elephants, trample six eggs. Bird refuses to sing to wake sun. Great Spirit investigates. Fly answers only Buzz. To say this henceforth (A2426.3.3). Africa: Elkin WHY pb. Nigeria (Ekoi): Arnott AFRICAN 56-63 (bushfowl, A2425.2.1).

Z49.6.0.3* Squirrel aroused by the queen of mosquitoes. Vanity alarms snake who frightens hare who runs into crab and agouti, agouti jumps onto crow's nest. Mother crow retraces to mosquito who only replies "Ysss" to questioning. Why mosquitoes say "Ysss" (A2426.3.5). West Indies: Sherlock IGUANA 67-75.

Z49.6.0.4* Phoenix, queen of birds, retraces chain of catastrophes. Field mouse stole sparrow's eggs, sparrow stabbed mouse, mouse ran into lion's nostril, lion leaped into water, dragon leaped out of water and knocked over Phoenix's nest. China: Chang CHINESE 70-72.

Z49.6.0.5* Ant bites frog, frog jumps on ladder, squirrel falls, bites stem of gourd in two, falls boar, uproots plantain, bird flies into elephant's ear, elephant uproots rock, kills Raja's son. Ant and frog held guilty. Hair tied round ant hence small waist (A2355.1.1), frog beaten with stinging nettles hence spotty (A2412.5.2.1). Central Assam: Withers I SAW 115-118.

Z49.6.0.6* Lizard say Tjik, deer startled frightens pheasant, flees into hornet's nest, etc. Indonesia: Courlander KANTCHIL'S 102-104.

Z49.6.0.7* Frog frightens hare, hare knocks over pumpkin, seeds in pheasant's eyes, breaks bamboo, falls on snake, bumps wild pig, drags cucumber into pool, awakens Naga. Reverse chain. Naga to kill hare. Hare's nose twitches and Naga laughs and releases. Hare's nose still twitches (A2476.1). Burma: Htin-Aung KINGDOM 24-27.

Z49.6.0.8* Bird catcher sets fire to bush of partridges--snake comes out and bites archer--archer lets loose arrow and hits hawk, cloudburst puts out fire. "Neither fire, arrows, nor the hunter's aim, can harm a feather in the God's domain." India: Reed TALKATIVE 16.

Z49.9. Pulling up the turnip. Final formula: The mouse holds onto the cat, the cat holds onto Mary, Mary holds onto Annie, Annie holds onto grandmother, grandmother holds onto grandfather, grandfather holds onto the turnip--they all pull and pull it out. Tolstoy: Domanska TURNIP pb; Haviland FAIRY 44-47; Tolstoy GREAT pb. Russia: Withers I SAW 98-99.

Z49.11.1. Wall in construction collapses. SEE: J2233.

Z49.11.2. Thief breaks foot climbing wall to rob. Suit against owner for dangerous wall.

Thief prosecutes owner--carpenter--mason--mortar manufacturer--latter too tall for gallows so passing farmer who fits is hung (J2233.2). Ethiopia (Galla): Davis LION'S 112-115.

Thief prosecutes--carpenter--mason--laborer who mixed mortar--potter who sold cracked pot to mix mortar in--woman who distracted potter--goldsmith whose shop she was visiting--latter cannot be spared so first stranger to town is hung (J2233). Ceylon: Courlander TIGER'S

49-51.

Thief prosecutes owner--carpenter--lady in red dress--dyer--dyer too tall for gallows--hang a shorter dyer (J2233.2, rules Kara Koush). Egypt: Courlander RIDE 101-104.

Z49.14. The little old lady who swallowed a fly. She swallows a spider to eat up the fly, a bird to eat up the spider, a dog to eat the bird, a cow to eat the dog. "The little old lady swallowed a horse--she died, of course." U.S.: Colwell MAGIC 89-90; Tashjian JUBA 36-38; Withers I SAW 39-41.

Z49.14.1* Draper swallows a fly in his sake. Doctor advises swallowing frog, snake, boar, hunter. Hunter shoots boar but is too tired to come out. Still in there. Japan: Novak FAIRY 119-122.

Z49.15* Chain of attackers each unaware he is about to be attacked. Locust, mantis, goldfinch, prince. Prince slips missing aim and all escape each other. China: Withers I SAW 126-127.

Z49.16* Man complaining of too much noise procures additional animals as remedy. Each adds more noise. In end he gets rid of animals and original noises seem tranquil. Dobbs NO pb; Hirsh COULD pb; McGovern TOO MUCH NOISE pb; Zemach IT pb. Russia (Ukraine): Bloch UKRAINIAN 73-76.

Z49.17* Little boy under bed given animals to comfort because bed squeaking makes him cry. Puerto Rico: Belpré TIGER 33-35.

Z49.18* Why heron is lean, shrimp won't come upstream, grass too thick, karbao doesn't eat, stake doesn't let go, herdboy neglects work, stomach empty, rice uncooked, firewood wet, rain never stops falling, frog scratches back, because ancestors did so. S. Annam (Shan): Withers I SAW 120-121.

Z49.19* Chain of excuses: Why frogs cry--"hungry"--till field--"dirty work"--"wash"--"it's cold," etc. Japan: Withers I SAW 130.

Z49.20* Origin of debt. Stranger says "whoever drinks my palm wine takes debt." Anansi drinks, gives debt to corn, crow eats, gives to eggs, tree, fruit, monkey, boar, hunter, feeds boar to villagers, hence debt comes to all. Ashanti: Courlander HAT 77-79; Fuja FOURTEEN 11-21 (cricket starts chain).

Z49.22. White ant neglects to watch behind self. Frog is following. Snake. Club, ants, fowl, etc. Each begins to attack the other. Burton MAGIC 126-127 /Arbuthnot ANTHOLOGY 326/.

Z49.23* Monkey forsees chain. Goat will disturb cook and be set afire. Stables will be set afire by goat, elephants will be burned and monkey get sought as remedy. He suggests monkeys flee. India: Wyatt GOLDEN 13-21.

Z49.23.1* Above chain but monkeys are all killed. Monkey king in forest takes necklace of demon from forest pool to king and says anyone bathing in pool gets a necklace. All are eaten by demon. Monkey thus avenges monkeys. India: Frost LEGENDS 142-146.

Z49.24* Cat catches mouse and orders a suit of clothes made or will eat. Each time cat calls for finished product mouse says there was not enough leather for item ordered so will make a smaller item. Coats, pants, vest, cap, gloves, purse. Sign posted--mouse has moved to China. Finland: Bowman TALES..TUPA 243-244.

Z49.24.1* Tailor to make coat of cloth, not enough cloth. Will make pants--not enough cloth. Vest. Gloves. Nothing at all. Sweden: Löfgren BOY 25-28.

Z49.24.1.1* Tailor makes coat. Wears it out so makes jacket, vest, cap. Just enough left to make this story. Schimmel JUST 1.

Z50. Cumulative tales--miscellaneous.

Z51. Chains involving contradictions or extremes. Type 2014.

Z51.2* The airplane crashed. Haystack there, missed the haystack, etc. U.S.: Withers I SAW 22.

Z51.3* Hare tells fox of his marriage. Good. No, that's bad. A real devil. Bad. Dowry and house--good--house burned down. Bad--she with it. Norway: Asbjornsen NORWEGIAN 115.

Z51.4* Task, making girl's mother say "that's a lie" (H342.1). Harvested nine tubs of cabbage. That's good. Rotted. That's bad. Oak trees from compost. Good. Hollow. Bad. Full of honey. Good. Bear ate. That's bad. Squeezed nine tubs of honey from bear. "That's a lie!" Weds girl. Slovenia: Kavcic GOLDEN 56-59.

Z52. Bird avenges mate. Arms self and proclaims war with king. Collects cat, ants, stick and river (all jump into his ear). He is put by king into fowl house, cat eats up fowls. In stable stick beats up horses. In elephant house, ants kill them all. Tied to king's bed, river floods king in his bed. King gives bird back his mate. India: Duff RUN pb.

Z52.1* Drakestail demands king return money. Swallows friend fox, ladder, river and wasp's nest en route. Put in poultry yard and releases fox; well--ladder; furnace--river; taken to court--wasp's nest. King routed and Drakestail crowned. (cf. B171.1). SEE ALSO: A2426.4.1.2.1 (toad, wasp, tiger and cock force rain-god to rain). France: Haviland FAVORITE..FRANCE 76-91; Hutchinson FIRESIDE 51-64; Lang RED 208-216 /Lang FIFTY 57-62/, /Martignoni ILLUSTRATED 83-88/; Manning-Sanders BOOK..MAGICAL 226-234; Wahl DRAKESTAIL pb; Wiggin FAIRY 304-312. U.S.

(Black): Harris COMPLETE 760-771 (Teenchy-tiny duck takes all into satchel).

Z52.2* Half chick (Medio Pollito, B171.1). Half chick trades found bag of coins to miller for sack of meal. Red Hen sends him back to re-exchange. He swallows those who bar way promising a better meal at mill, fox, wolf, river, fire. Put in poultry house--fox eats hens. In mule's stall--wolf aids. In mill--left to choke in chaff--fire burns. Miller returns money if hen puts out fire--river aids. Hen weds Red Hen. Spain: Montgomerie MERRY 24-27; Sawyer PIC-TURE 97-110.

Z52.2.1* Red-chicken goes to collect debt from farmer. Takes fox, wolf and pond in bill. Put in chicken house--fox; barn with cows--wolf; oven--pond. Switzerland (French): Duvoisin THREE 53-60.

Z52.3* Little white hen takes piece of paper to king thinking it a letter. Fox, river and fire go along in basket. Put in poultry yard--fox helps; pursued--river; pursued--fire. Ashes from fire leave hen speckled. Hewett LITTLE WHITE HEN pb. Brazil: Gruenberg MORE 133-136.

Z52.4* Little Rooster demands Turkish Sultan return diamond button. Put in well, magic stomach swallows water. Fire--stomach lets out water. Put in beehive--swallows. Put in Sultan's trousers so Sultan can sit on him--let's out bees. Hungary: Seredy THE GOOD MASTER /Gruenberg FAVORITE 369-373/. Ambrus LITTLE pb; Hardendorff LITTLE pb.

Z52.4.1* Old man's cock taken as pet for king's treasury, eats up gold then feigns dead. Thrown out (K522.4.0.2). Spits out gold for master. Old woman next door tries (J2415). Cock instructs hen to swallow wasps from nest in king's garden. Old woman stung, leaves. Hen goes to live with cock and old man. Hungary: Manning-Sanders GLASS 83-85.

Z52.4.2* Old lady given handful of peas to sow. One grows to sky (F54.2). She climbs and receives a magic self-filling crock with an egg inside. She carries egg under her arm and a cock hatches. Crock stolen by landowner. Cock reclaims. Thrown in well--drinks. Fire--puts out. Chest of gold to suffocate--swallows. Cooked and eaten, calls from landowner's stomach (B171.1.1). Vomited. Goes home and spits out coins. Poland: Zajdler POLISH 170-177.

Z52.4.2.1* Poor couple. Acorn grows to sky (F54.2). Old man climbs, finds cock and sky-blue handmill (D1601.21) that grinds pancakes and pirogs. Merchant steals. Cock recovers. Thrown in well--drinks. Fire--puts out. Takes mill and leaves. Russia: Manning-Sanders CHARMS 62-66; Wyndham RUSSIAN 62-67.

Z52.5* Angry Thumbling attacks sun, rains help Thumbling win battle but flood results. Thumbling lets boat out of stomach and he and party return safely home. +K1161.5, F535.1.1Dd. Burma: Htin Aung KINGDOM 46-52.

Z52.6* The Tipsy Rooster takes purse to king. River refuses to let him pass so he eats it, fox, pine tree, wolf, owl. Put in chicken coop--fox eats hens, cupboard--pine breaks glass vase, stable--wolf eats horses, jar of oil--owl drinks, oven river cools, floods castle. King returns purse. Portugal: Lowe LITTLE 55-57.

Z53. The animals with queer names: as hen (henny-penny), cock (cocky-locky), goose (goosey-loosey). SEE ALSO: Z33.1.1; Z43.3. Hutchinson CHIMNEY 3-8 (Z43.3); Martignoni ILLUSTRATED 66-68.

Z54. Cumulative nonsense. Each repeats the other. I go to Walpe, you go to Walpe. So. so. Together we go. Germany: Wiggin TALES 68.

Z55. Wee Robin's Yule Song. Robin meets and avoids cat, hawk, fox, boy on way to sing for king on Yule morn. Is given wren as wife. Association TOLD..GREEN 162-164; Colwell YOUNGEST; Finlay TATTERCOATS 96-99; Montgomerie TWENTY-FIVE 44-45; Wiggin TALES 380-381.

Z62. Proverbial simile.

Z62.1. The old and new keys. Hero marries his first sweetheart according to the proverb that the old key is better than the new. SEE: G530.2Ae; H1385.4; H1411.4.3.1.

Z65.1. Red as blood, white as snow. Often from blood on snow as suggestion. A wish is made for a child (wife) with skin like snow and cheeks like blood, etc. Type 709. SEE ALSO: N271 (Juniper Tree); P253.2C (Twelve Wild Ducks).

Aa* Snow White and the Seven Dwarfs. Magic mirror tells stepmother queen that Snow White is lovelier than she. Hunter ordered to kill spares (K512). She keeps house for seven dwarfs (N831.1). Sometimes dwarfs use formula "who has been sitting in my chair?" etc. Stepmother in disguise sells girl poison lace, comb, apple. Snow White is placed in glass coffin (F852.1), prince has carried to castle and apple is dislodged from throat by jolt. Wed. Queen has to dance in red hot shoes till dead or dies of rage. Germany (Grimm): Arbuthnot ANTHOLOGY 190-192; Arbuthnot FAIRY 53-56; De La Mare TALES 142-154; Farjeon CAVALCADE.. QUEENS 110-120; Gag SNOW pb; Grimm BROTH-ERS 61-71; Grimm GRIMM'S (Grosset) 166-177; Grimm GRIMM'S (Scribner's) 144-154; Grimm GRIMM'S (World) 332-342; Grimm HOUSEHOLD 213-221; Grimm JUNIPER v. 2 256-274; Grimm SNOW WHITE (ills. Burkert) pb; Grimm SNOW WHITE (illus. Hyman) pb; Gruenberg FAVOR-ITE 286-294; Haviland FAIRY 128-137; Holme TALES 69-75; Hutchinson CHIMNEY..FAIRY 27-38; Jacobs EUROPEAN 201-211; Lang RED 324-335 /Lang FIFTY 261-270/; Manning-Sanders BOOK..DWARFS 25-37 (splinter of looking glass pierces queen's heart as she breaks it);

Martignoni ILLUSTRATED 265-267; Opie CLASSIC 175-182; Rackham GRIMM'S 7-16. U.S. (Appalachia): Haviland NORTH 147-154 (+Q2.1.2Ac).

Ab* The Sleeping Tsarevna and The Seven Giants: Aa + giants. Betrothed breaks glass coffin and she awakens. He asks sun, moon and wind directions. Russia: Dalgliesh ENCHANTED 231-246.

Ac* Landlady's daughter kept locked away for beauty. Men to kill her, spare. Keeps house for robbers. Poison slippers. Prince removes slippers in glass coffin. Wed. Mother turns ugly from anger. Portugal: Michael PORTUGUESE 121-129.

Z65.3* Series: girl at witch's house sees riders in white, red, black. Are explained as day, sun and night. SEE: Q2.1.2Bb; Q2.1.2Ce.

Z65.3.1* Girl at witch's house sees men on stairs, black, green, red. Explained as collier, hunter and butcher. Germany (Grimm): Grimm JUNIPER v. 2 310-313.

Z71.3.3* Five children shelter with raven in blizzard. He sees five fingers on each hand and feels five is a magic number. Goes to live with raven. Eskimo: Melzack RAVEN 71-78.

Z100 - Z199. Symbolism.

Z110. Personification.

Z111.2.1.1* Death personified. Aunt Misery granted a wish by sheltered pilgrim. Pear tree from which one may not descend until she wishes. Death is caught, promises her exemption for his release from tree. Why misery is always in this world. Portugal: Lowe LITTLE 64-66. Puerto Rico: Carter GREEDY 18-24.

Z111.2.2.1* Lord stuck to Misery's maple chair grants one hundred years of life. Death--same. Death's general Verette (Smallpox) carries Misery to heaven but Misery is disruptive. Sent to Purgatory, Hell (Q565). Same. Back to earth until Judgment Day. Haiti: Thoby-Marcelin SINGING 53-56.

Z111.7* Cholera, Death and Fear visit Mecca. Cholera and Death take many. Rest die of fear on hearing this. Indonesia: De Leeuw INDONESIAN 56-57.

Z115.2* Wind personified. Saynday woos whirlwind. Offended, she whirls him away. Native American: Marriott WINTER 70-74.

Z122.0.1* Time personified. Rich man named Time, becomes poor, tell them "Time isn't what it used to be." Eastern Liberia: Courlander COW-TAIL 73-77.

Z122.3. Twelve months as youths seated about fire. SEE: Q2.1.4A.

Z200 - Z299. Heroes.

Z200. Heroes.

Z200.1* Prince Yamato Take. Japan: Ozaki JAPANESE 224-243.

Z215.1* Hero "son of seven mothers." The outcast Queens and the Ogress Queen. Type 462. Seven queens are blinded and thrown into pit at command of ogress queen. Son of youngest provides food for seven mothers. Set tasks by ogress he succeeds with aid of princess who changes all messages given him (K511). India: Jacobs INDIAN 139-154.

Z300 - Z399. Unique exceptions.

Z310. Unique vulnerability.

Z312. Unique deadly weapon. Only one thing will kill a certain man. SEE: Q82.3.

Z312.3* Wabun (West Wind) can be harmed only by oldest thing in earth, certain black rock. Manabozho attacks wind with rock. Wind sends Manabozho to name animals and prepare world for mankind. Native American (Chippewa): Leekley WORLD 100-110.

Z312.4* Wife Blodevedd made of flowers discovers secret vulnerability of husband Llew Llaw Gyffes and has him slain. Wales: Sheppard-Jones WELSH 63-68.

2

Tale Title Index

A-Thishoo. Manning-Sanders - GIANNI 141-144 (J2311.1; J2311.4).

About a Fisherman and His Wife. Shub - ABOUT 5-14 (B375.1).

About Jan the Prince. Haviland - FAVORITE.. POLAND 56-81 (H1331.1.3).

About the Hedgehog. Haviland - FAVORITE.. POLAND 3-12 (B641.5).

The Absent-Minded Farmer. Duvoisin - THREE 16-19 (K403.1).

The Absent-Minded King. Robertson - FAIRY.. PHILIPPINES 91-95 (A2094.1).

ABU ALI: THREE TALES OF THE MIDDLE EAST. Van Woerkom. pb (K231.14.1; J2031.2; J1561.3).

ABU KASSIM'S SLIPPERS. Green. pb (N211.2).

Abu Nowas. Lang - CRIMSON 158-167 (J2511.1.2.1).

Abunuwas the Trickster. Courlander - TIGER'S 90-99 (J1151.2; J1193.1.0.1; J1473.1; J1531.3; J1552.1.1).

Abunuwas, the Wit. Courlander - RIDE 85-91 (J1531.3; J1552.1.1).

The Accomplished and Strange Teakettle. Buck - FAIRY TALES..ORIENT (D1171.3.1).

The Adder and Fox. Gaer - FABLES..INDIA 30-33 (J1172.3; J1172.3.2).

The Aderna Bird. Sechrist - ONCE 131-135 (H1331.1.3Fc).

Adjutant Bird. Williams-Ellis - ROUND 274-278 (K713.1.1.2).

Adrian and Bardus. Green - BIG 201-205 (W154.8.2).

Adventure in the Desert. Shah - MULLAH 36 (J1250.9).

Adventure of Little Peachling. Rackham - FAIRY 84-86 (T543.3.2).

THE ADVENTURES OF AKU. Bryan. pb (D882.1B).

The Adventures of Billy McDaniel. Manning-Sanders - CHOICE 191-199; Manning-Sanders - DWARFS 95-103 (F451.5.17).

The Adventures of Bona and Nello. Baker - GOLDEN 101-110 (P253.2.0.1B).

The Adventures of Chanticleer. Wiggin - TALES 118-123 (K1161.7; Z32.1).

The Adventures of Iain Direach. Wilson - SCOT-TISH 121-136 (H1331.1.3Am).

The Adventures of Kahukura. Belting - ELVES 66-69 (F451.3.2.1.3).

The Adventures of King Suton. Asia - FOLK.. BOOK 1 21-27 (H1385.3Fa).

The Adventures of Kintaro. Ozaki - JAPANESE 60-73 (F611.3.2.7).

The Adventures of Little Peachling. Buck - FAIRY..ORIENT 138-140 (T543.3.2).

The Adventures of Magboloto. Sechrist - ONCE 67-75 (H1385.3Fd).

The Adventures of Nera. Garner - CAVALCADE ..GOBLINS 92-97 (F302.1.6).

The Adventures of Silvervit. Kaplan - FAIRY 108-141 (R111.1.3Ao).

The Adventurous Winnower. Vittorini - OLD 19-23 (J1289.30).

Advices. Chang - TALES..OLD CHINA 30-33 (J163.4.2).

Agayk and the Sharpest Spear. Edmonds - TRICKSTER 21-29 (K1084.3.1).

The Age of the Animals. Withers - WORLD (B841.1.1).

Age of the Partridge. Gaer - FABLES 159-161 (B841.1.1).

Agin' the Law. Harris - FAVORITE 182-186 (J1172.3); Harris - COMPLETE 315-320; Harris - NIGHTS 274-279.

Ah Po, the Simple. Bonnet - FOLK..CHINA 22-25 (J2461J).

Ah Tcha the Sleeper. Gruenberg - FAVORITE 368-393 (G211.1.7.2); Chrisman - SHEN OF THE SEA 159-172; Harper - GHOST 141-149; Hoke - WITCHES 5-14.

Ahoro and His Wife Etipa. Fuja - FOURTEEN 152-155 (A1389.1).

Aili's Quilt. Jagendorf - NOODLEHEAD 196-201 (J1978).

The Ailp King's Children. Wilson - SCOTTISH 148-155 (B641.1).

The Ailpein Bird, the Stolen Princess and the Brave Knight. Leodhas - HEATHER 15-33 (H1385.1H).

Aiming Too High. Green - BIG 144-145 (J2413.3).

Ainsel. Wilson - SCOTTISH 95-98 (K602.1).

AKIMBA AND THE MAGIC COW. Rose pb (D861.1G).

Aladdin. Manning-Sanders - BOOK..WIZARDS 58-77 (D871.1); Manning-Sanders - CHOICE 108-127.

Aladdin and the Wonderful Lamp. Arbuthnot - FAIRY 167-174 (D871.1); Arbuthnot - ANTHOLOGY 302-309.

The Albahaca Plant. Belpré - TIGER 89-94 (H561.1.1.2; H705.3; K1288.1).

Alberto and the Monsters. Sechrist - ONCE 204-213 (H1385.1B).

Aldar-Kas and the Greedy Rich Man. Masey - STORIES 65-72 (K344.1.6; K362.10.1; K415.0.2).

Alenoushka and Her Brother. Ransome - OLD PETER'S 231-241 (P253.2.0.1C).

Alexandra The Rock-Eater. Van Woerkom. pb (G501C).

Ali and the Camels. Gilstrap - SULTAN'S (J2022.1).

Ali Baba. Rackham - ARTHUR 206-222 (N455.3).

All Because of a Pair of Shoes. Simon - WISE MEN 89-102 (J2014.2).

All Change. Jacobs - EUROPEAN 13-18 (K251.1.0.2.5).

The All-Devourer. Helfman - BUSHMEN 110-118 (A1884.0.2).

All Gone. De La Mare - ANIMAL 56-69 (K372).

All Her Faults. Shah - MULLAH 114 (J1914).

All I Needed Was Time. Shah - MULLAH 114 (J1914).

All Light Comes From The Sun. Withers - MAN 83-85 (A711.0.1; K671.1).

All Stories Are Anansi's. Courlander - HAT-SHAKING 3-8 (A1481.2.1; K713.1.9; K713.1.11; K714.2.6).

All the Grapes in the Neighborhood. Harris - FAVORITE 130-135 (K1023.0.2); Harris - NIGHTS 83-89; Harris - COMPLETE 177-182.

All You Need. Shah - MULLAH 137 (J1289.2.1).

Allah Will Provide. Gilstrap - SULTAN'S 81-87 (N182.3); Arbuthnot - ANTHOLOGY 310-311.

Allerleirauh. Grimm - GRIMM'S (Scribner's) 192-198 (R221Da).

The Alligator and the Jackal. Haviland - FAVORITE..INDIA 53-62; Wiggin - TALES 258-262 (K543; K607.1; K607.2.2; K607.2.4).

The Almond Tree. Grimm - HOUSEHOLD 186-194 (N271); Grimm - GRIMM'S (World) 171-179.

Alone in the Desert. Shah - MULLAH 130 (J2711.1).

The Alphorn. Duvoisin - THREE SNEEZES 218-222 (A1461.9).

The Alternative. Shah - MULLAH 13 (J1552.1.1.2).

ALWAYS ROOM FOR ONE MORE. Leodhas. pb (J2199.5).

Alyosha Popovich. Higonnet-Schnopper - TALES 129-140 (B11.4.1.1).

The Ambassador from Chi. Courlander - TIGER'S 43-45 (J1289.31).

The Ambitious Maiden. Montgomerie - TWENTY-FIVE 41-43 (Z42.0.3).

Amin and the Ghul. Williams-Ellis - ROUND 73-80 (G501; K1715.2).

Amis and Amile. Picard - FRENCH 69-76 (S268C).

Anaïse and Bovi. Thoby-Marcelin - SINGING 42-45 (D582.0.1).

Ananse and His Visitor, Turtle. Kaula - AFRICAN (J1565.1.1; K278).

Ananse and the King's Cow. Aardema - TALES 9-18 (F929.3).

Ananse the Spider in Search of a Fool. Bryan OX 3-10 (J321.1.1).

Anansi and Bicycle. Williams-Ellis - ROUND 197-203 (K352.1).

Anansi and Candlefly. Sherlock - WEST 97-104 (Q272.5).

Anansi and Fish Country. Sherlock - ANANSI 70-75 (K352.1).

Anansi and Five. Williams-Ellis - ROUND 204-207 (C498.2.2).

Anansi and Nothing Go Hunting for Wives. Courlander - COW-TAIL SWITCH 95-102 (A1579+; K499.8.1).

Anansi and Snake the Postman. Sherlock - WEST 71-76 (K75).

Anansi and the Alligator Eggs. Sherlock - ANANSI 84-93 (K933; K1041.1.3).

Anansi and the Crabs. Sherlock - ANANSI 95-103 (K1961.1.6).

Anansi and the Elephant Exchange Knocks. Courlander - HAT 63-69 (K869.5).

Anansi and the Elephant Go Hunting. Courlander HAT 38-45 (A2362.2).

Anansi and the Old Hag. Sherlock - ANANSI 20-29 (D1810.8.5).

Anansi and the Plantains. Sherlock – ANANSI 64–69 (J1241.7).

Anansi and Turtle and Pigeon. McDowell – THIRD 72–74 (K1041.1.4); Sherlock – ANANSI 31–34 (K553.5.3).

Anansi Borrows Money. Courlander – HAT 55–58 (A2579.1).

Anansi Hunts With Tiger. Sherlock – WEST 118–124 (K335.0.1).

Anansi Plays Dead. Courlander – HAT 20–24 (K341.2; K741.0.7).

Anansi Plays With Fire, Anansi Gets Burned. Jagendorf – KING 171–176 (K629.2.3).

Anansi Steals the Palm Wine. Courlander – HAT 77–79 (A1378; Z49.20).

Anansi, the Oldest of Animals. Courlander – HAT 9–12 (A2335.3.3; A2343.3.3; A2375.2.10.1; B841.1.2).

Anansi the Spider. McDermott. pb (A740; H621.4.1).

Anansi's Fishing Expedition. Courlander – COW-TAIL 47–57 (J321.1.1; J1249.7).

Anansi's Hat-Shaking Dance. Arbuthnot – AN-THOLOGY 321–322; Courlander – HAT 13–17 (W125.3.1).

Anansi's Old Riding Horse. Sherlock – WEST 105–111 (K1241).

Anansi's Rescue from the River. Courlander – HAT 59–62 (A740.1; H621.4.1).

Andrew Coffey. Jacobs – CELTIC 217–222 (M231.1).

Androcles. Aesop – AESOP'S (Grosset) 32–33 (B381); Jacobs – FABLES 44–45.

Androcles and the Lion. Aesop – AESOP'S (Random) 26–28; Gruenberg – FAVORITE 414–416; Jacobs – EUROPEAN 107–109 (B381).

Anfy and His Landlord. Higonnet-Schnopper – TALES 34–44 (K111.2; K131.2).

The Angakok. Caswell – SHADOWS 57–63 (G275.12.1).

The Angakòk and the Mother of the Seals. DeWit – TALKING 168–174 (A2101); Carpenter – WONDER..SHIPS 39–46.

The Angel. Downing – RUSSIAN 171–173 (J225.0.1).

Angelique and Myrtil. Thoby-Marcelin – SING-ING 84–90 (D551.1E).

The Anger of Sande-Nyana. Haskett – GRAINS

98–100 (K1685).

The Angry Baron. Durham – TIT 85–89 (Q584.2.1).

THE ANGRY MOON. Sleator. pb (F53.1.1).

Ani, The Mother Was Too Proud. Bowes – KING 40–44 (T681).

Aniello. Manning-Sanders – BOOK..WIZARDS 9–21 (D882.1D); Manning-Sanders – CHOICE 95–107.

Animal Friendship. Ginsburg – ONE 29–30 (J811.1).

The Animal Musicians. Alegría – THREE 9–14 (K335.1.4; K1161.1).

The Animal Princes. Hampden – HOUSE 25–32 (B314D).

The Animal's Farm. Sturton – ZOMO 3–13 (J1141.1.4; K371).

The Animals Go On Trial. Sechrist – ONCE 64–66 (A2426.3.5.1; Z49.6.0.1).

The Animals in Winter. Riordan – TALES..CEN-TRAL 222–226 (K1161.2).

Animals Mourn for Da Leopard. Dorliae – ANI-MALS 2–9 (K607.3.4).

The Animals Quarrel. Masey – STORIES 118–121 (K52.1).

Annie Norn and the Fin Folk. Cutt – HOGBOON 147–151 (F420.6.1.1.1).

Another Good Guesser. Cimino – DISOBEDIENT 11 (J2712.3).

Ansige Karamba, the Glutton. Courlander – COW-TAIL 119–127 (J2131.5; W125.3.2).

Ansongo and the Masai Cattle. Harmon – TALES 118–143 (K341.5.3).

The Ant. Aesop – AESOP'S (Watts) 159 (A2011.2).

Ant and Dove. Aesop – FABLES (Walck) 85 (B362.2).

The Ant and the Dove. Aesop – AESOP'S (Gros-set) 36 (B362.2); Aesop – AESOP'S (Random) 49–50.

The Ant and the Frog. Withers – I SAW 115–118 (Z49.6.0.5).

The Ant and the Grasshopper. Aesop – AESOP'S (Grosset) 12; Aesop – AESOP'S (Viking) 20 (J711.1); Aesop – FABLES (Walck) 44–45; Aesop – FIVE 14; Arbuthnot – FAIRY 224; Jacobs – FABLES 71.

The Ant and the Tower to God. Davis - LION'S 132-135 (F772.1.3).

The Ant and the Yellow Jacket. Heady - TALES 32-34 (A977.5.0.4).

The Ant in Search of Her Leg. Alegría - THREE 40-43 (Z42.0.5).

The Ant That Laughed Too Much. Carpenter - KOREAN 151-154 (A2355.1.2.1).

The Ant, The Lamb, The Cricket, and The Mouse. Brenner - BOY 19-20 (Z32.3).

Antelope's Mother: The Woman in the Moon. Courlander - OLODE 72-76 (A2305.2.1; K311.3.1).

The Ants That Pushed on the Sky. Wiggin - FAIRY 381-390 (D482.1.3).

Antti and the Wizard's Prophecy. Bowman - TALES..TUPA 53-64 (H1273.21); Fenner - ADVENTURES 148-161.

The Ape and the Dolphin. Aesop - FIVE 66 (J1803.1.1).

The Ape and the Firefly. Sechrist - ONCE 51-54 (K1082.3.2).

The Apes and the Two Travellers. Aesop - AESOP'S (Watts) 39 (J815.1).

Aplomp. Shah - MULLAH 128 (J84.2).

The Arab and the Camel. Aesop - AESOP'S (Grosset) 96 (J463); Aesop - AESOP'S (Viking) 18; Hardendorff - JUST 28.

The Arabe Duck. Hardendorff - TRICKY 45-50 (K815.14; K953.3); Sawyer - PICTURE 53-62.

Aram and the Dervish. Tashjian - THREE APPLES 16-21 (K526D).

Arap Sang and the Cranes. Harmon - TALES 109 117 (A2317.7.2; A2321.13).

Arawn. Pugh - TALES 61-81 (F373.1).

The Archbishop's Mule. Michael - PORTUGUESE 84-91 (U119.2.1).

The Archer and the Lion. Aesop - AESOP'S (Watts) 139 (J32).

The Archer Who Went I Know Not Where to Fetch I Know Not What. Riordan - TALES..CENTRAL 243-261 (D831B; N813Fa).

Archery by Moonlight. Kelsey - HODJA 34-40 (J2235).

Are Fish Buffaloes? Withers - WORLD (J1904.4.1).

Are There Such Women? Borski - GOOD 78-81 (J2081.1).

Aren't We All Human Beings? Asian - FOLK.. FOUR 30-73 (H1574.4.1).

Armadillo's Story. Sherlock - IGUANA'S 76-95 (K607.1; K713.1.1; K1995).

The Arrow Chain. Withers - MAN 35-38 (F53.1).

Arrows and the Sun. Matson - LEGENDS 80-86 (A721.3.1).

The Art of Reading. Green - BIG 208 (K1121.0.1).

Arthur in the Cave. Frost - LEGENDS 19-25 (D1960.2.2).

The Artificial Earthquake. Sechrist - ONCE 91-93 (K1889.7).

The Artist. Chang - TALES..OLD CHINA 45-46 (H504.4).

As Long As This? Leach - THING 44-45 (F544.3.5).

As Many As.... Leach - NOODLES 57 (H583.2.2; H632.1; H643.1; H646.1; H703.1).

As Pretty as a Pigeon. Sleigh - NORTH 90-102 (T53.7).

As The World Pays. Zajdler - POLISH 20-27 (J1172.3).

Aschenputtel. Grimm - HOUSEHOLD 118-125 (R221B).

The Ash Lad and the Good Helpers. Asbjørnsen - NORWEGIAN 170-177 (F601.2Ab).

The Ash Lad Who Had an Eating Match with the Trolls. Asbjørnsen - NORWEGIAN 81-83 (G501).

Ash Maiden. Grimm - GRIMM'S (Follett) 17-27 (R221B).

The Ashes of the Milky Way. Helfman - BUSHMEN 35 (A778.8).

The Ashlad Who Made the Princess Say "You Lie." Undset - TRUE 173-175 (H342.1); Asbjørnsen - NORWEGIAN 17-19.

Ashormoshika. Walker - DANCING 35-41 (B522.1.2).

Ashpet. Chase - WICKED 115-123 (R221K).

Ashputtel. Child Study Association - CASTLES 109-125 (R221B); De La Mare - ANIMAL 285-295.

Ashypelt. Hampden - GYPSY 53-58 (H1411.4.8).

Ask a Foolish Question. Serwer - LET'S STEAL 30-37 (J652.4.3).

Asleep by the Stream. Curtis - GIRL 35-41 (D1841.4.3.3).

The Ass and His Burdens. Aesop - AESOP'S (Watts) 40-41 (J1612).

The Ass and His Driver. Aesop - AESOP'S (Grosset) 227-228 (J683.1); Aesop - AESOP'S (Watts) 146.

The Ass and His Masters. Aesop - AESOP'S (Grosset) 38 (N255.2); Aesop - AESOP'S (Watts) 158.

The Ass and His Purchaser. Aesop - AESOP'S (Watts) 150 (J451.1).

The Ass and His Shadow. Aesop - AESOP'S (Watts) 44 (J1169.7).

The Ass and the Bear. Aesop - FIVE 28 (J411.1).

The Ass and the Grasshopper. Aesop - AESOP'S (Grosset) 64 (J512.8).

The Ass and the Lap-Dog. Aesop - AESOP'S (Grosset) 71-72 (J2413.1); Aesop - AESOP'S (Watts) 27-28; Jacobs - FABLES 19.

The Ass and the Little Dog. Aesop - AESOP'S (Viking) 56 (J2413.1); Montgomerie - TWENTY-FIVE 28-29.

The Ass and the Mule. Aesop - AESOP'S (Watts) 143.

The Ass and the Old Peasant. Aesop - AESOP'S (Watts) 78 (U151).

The Ass and the Wolf. Aesop - AESOP'S (Watts) 130 (K566).

The Ass Carrying Salt. Aesop - AESOP'S (Grosset) 16-17 (J1612).

The Ass Carrying the Image. Aesop - AESOP'S (Watts) 165 (J953.4).

The Ass Eating Thistles. Aesop - AESOP'S (Grosset) 42-43 (J1061.1.1); Aesop - AESOP'S (Viking) 12.

The Ass Gets the Better of the Wolf. Wilson - GREEK 40-41 (K566).

The Ass in the Lion's Skin. Aesop - AESOP'S (Golden) 32 (J951.1); Aesop - AESOP'S (Grosset) 113; Aesop - AESOP'S (Viking) 40-41; Aesop - AESOP'S (Watts) 53; Gaer - FABLES 157-159; Jacobs - FABLES 97; Jacobs - INDIAN 182-183.

The Ass in the Tiger Skin. Montgomerie - TWENTY-FIVE 34-35.

The Ass, the Cock and the Lion. Aesop - AESOP'S (Grosset) 53 (J952.2); Aesop - AESOP'S (Viking) 29; Aesop - AESOP'S (Watts) 127.

The Ass, the Fox and the Lion. Aesop - AESOP'S (Watts) 15-16 (K1632).

The Ass, the Table and the Stick. De La Mare - ANIMAL 144-148 (D861.1C); Jacobs - ENGLISH 215-219; Steel - ENGLISH 241-244.

The Ass's Brains. Jacobs - FABLES 147 (K402.3.1).

The Ass's Shadow. Aesop - AESOP'S (Grosset) 41 (J1169.7).

Assipattle and the Giant Sea Serpent. Haviland - FAVORITE..SCOTLAND 71-72 (R111.1.4).

The Astrologer. De La Iglesia - CAT 11 (J2133.8).

The Astrologer and the Physician. Borski - GOOD 68-71 (L144.2).

The Astronomer. Aesop - AESOP'S (Watts) 148 (J2133.8).

At Court. Shah - MULLAH 116 (J829.1.1).

At the Lion's Cave. Green - BIG 129 (J644.1).

Augustine the Thief. Mehdevi - BUNGLING 69-83 (K341.6).

Aunt Misery. Lowe - LITTLE 64-66 (Z111.2.1.1).

Aunt Tempy's Story. Harris - NIGHTS 241-247 (K404.1; K944); Harris - COMPLETE 293-297.

Aunt Tilly. Leach - THING 73-74 (E329.1).

Avaricious and Envious. Jacobs - FABLES 107 (J2074).

Avunang. Caswell - SHADOWS 72-75 (D100.1).

Awake or Asleep. Shah - MULLAH 145 (A1599.17).

The Awful Fate of Brer Wolf. Harris - FAVORITE 286-290 (K891.1.3).

The Awful Fate of Mr. Wolf. Harris - COMPLETE 42-45; Harris - UNCLE 63-69.

Axe Porridge. Riordan - TALES..CENTRAL 56-58 (K112.2).

Ayele and the Flowers. Robinson - SINGING 44-59 (R131.21).

Ayoga. Ginsburg - LAZIES 59-62 (Z18.2).

Baba Yaga. Fenner - GIANTS 79-92 (Q2.1.2CeB); Williams-Ellis - ROUND 81-89; Wyndham - TALES ..RUSSIA 76-77.

Baba Yaga and the Little Girl with the Kind Heart. Hoke - WITCHES 19-30 (Q2.1.2CeB); Hope-Simpson - CAVALCADE..WITCHES 62-74; Ransome - OLD PETER'S 88-100.

Baba Yaga's Geese. Carey - BABA 92-95 (Q2.1.2.Ce).

The Babes in the Wood. Steel – ENGLISH 216-221 (S143); Tarrant – FAIRY 89-96.

The Baboon and the Hare. Heady – JAMBO 54-59 (K527.1).

Baboushka. Colwell – YOUNGEST 249-252 (N816.2).

BABOUSHKA AND THE THREE KINGS. Robbins pb (N816.2).

Baby Camel. Masey – STORIES 12-15 (H495.4).

The Baby Mosque. Kelsey – MULLAH 95-99 (J2495.1.1).

The Baby Water Buffalo. Cheney – TALES 133-136 (J1041.2).

The Bachelors and the Python. Burton – MAGIC 75-77 (J2415.11).

Back to Front. Shah – MULLA 82 (H599.7).

The Bad Boy and the Good Dog. Carpenter – WONDER..DOGS 95-100 (W11.5.13).

The Bad Joke That Ended Well. Duvoisin – THREE 24-29 (J1703.6).

Bad Luck Put Into the Bag. Leach – LUCK 37-40 (N112.1; N250.4).

The Bad Mother. De La Mare – ANIMAL 252-258 (S12.1C).

The Bad Old Woman. Duvoisin – THREE 130-137 (Q2.1.1Ea).

The Bad-Tempered Wife. Durham – TIT 11-16 (T251.1.1).

The Bad Tiger. Kim – STORY 51-55 (K1161.3.7).

Badang the Strong. Asia – FOLK..THREE 42-47 (F610.3.8).

The Badger and the Boatmen. Pratt – MAGIC (D612.1.1).

The Badger and the Fox. Novak – FAIRY 16-21 (A2434.2.2.1).

Badger and the Green Giant. DeWit – TALKING 197-203 (D1652.1.9.3).

The Badger and the Magic Fan. Sakade – FAVORITE..JAPANESE 73-77 (D839.3).

Badger on the Run. Hill – BADGER 56-61 (K473.2).

The Badger Priest. Scofield – FOX 15-19 (D612.1.2).

The Badger's Gratitude. Buck – FAIRY 91-95 (B393.1).

The Bag in the Corner. Harris – COMPLETE 395-401 (K526.4); Harris – FAVORITE 187-192; Harris – NIGHTS 386-395.

The Bag of Lies. Pridham – GIFT 124-129 (K335.0.1; K341.6; K1251).

The Bag of Winds. Cunningham – TALKING 30-32 (A1122.5).

Bagged Wolf. Kendall – SWEET 49-59 (J1172.3).

Bahhh! Jagendorf – NOODLEHEAD 136-141 (K1655).

Bahmoo Rides the Wrong Frog. Jagendorf – KING 139-141 (B857.1).

Bahram and the Snake Prince. Mehdevi – PERSIAN 6 (D882.1Ba).

Bajan Budiman, the Sharpshooter. Courlander – KANTCHIL'S 122-128 (K31.4).

The Baker's Daughter. Lurie – CLEVER 30-34 (A1958,0.1); Williams-Ellis – FAIRY 103-105.

The Baker's Neighbor. Hardendorff – FROG'S 29-39 (J1172.2).

The Bald Huntsman. Aesop – AESOP'S (Watts) 153 (X52.2).

The Bald Knight. Aesop – AESOP'S (Grosset) 226 (X52.2); Aesop – FABLES (Walck) 86-87.

The Bald Man and the Fly. Aesop – AESOP'S (Watts) 129 (J2102.3); Aesop – FABLES (Macmillan) 35.

Bald Pate. Manning-Sanders – RED 23-30 (S268A).

Baldpate. Hampden – GYPSY 147-154 (S268A).

The Ball Game of the Birds and Animals. Bell – JOHN 87-91 (B261.1.0.2.1).

The Ballad of Mulan. Manton – FLYING 102-108 (K1837.6.1).

Ballads and Boots. Gunterman – CASTLE 247-250 (J981).

Baltzi. Duvoisin. THREE 158-161 (F460.4.2.6).

The Bamboo-cutter and the Moon-child. Ozaki – JAPANESE 96-118 (A240.1.1).

Bandalee. Arbuthnot – ANTHOLOGY 396-398 (K11.1; K16.2); Sherlock – ANANSI 47-57.

The Banyan Deer. Arbuthnot – ANTHOLOGY 349 (B241.2.10.1); Arbuthnot – FAIRY 166-167; Babbitt – JATAKA 58-62; Gruenberg – MORE 109-110; Haviland – FAVORITE..INDIA 91-95; Ross – BURIED 81-88.

The Baobab Tree. Heady – WHEN 59-61 (A2774.2).

Bardiello. Manning-Sanders – GIANNI 31-42 (J2311.2.1).

Barefoot in Bed. Jagendorf – NOODLEHEAD 43-44 (F1068.5).

Barker's Knee. Manning-Sanders - PETER 191-193 (F456.2.2.5).

The Barmecide Feast. Gruenberg - MORE 385-387 (P327).

The Barmecide's Feast. Rackham - ARTHUR 190-195 (P327).

Barney's Tale of the Wee Red Cap. Sawyer - THIS WAY 31-41 (F282.4.2).

The Barren Stones. Spicer - LONG..SERBIA 70-72 (A975.1.2).

Bartek the Doctor. Wojciechowska - WINTER 8-21 (D1825.3.1.1).

Barter. Ginsburg - TWELVE 75-81 (J2081.1).

Bash Tchelik. Garner - CAVALCADE..GOBLINS 63-75 (B314C).

The Bashful Prince. Michael - PORTUGUESE 105-111 (F576.1).

Basia, the Babbler. Borski - GOOD 41-45 (D1454.2.0.1).

The Basket Makers' Donkey. Hampden - GYPSY 97-99 (X1130.2.3).

Baskets in a Little Cart. Manning-Sanders - DRAGONS 95-102 (B11.7.1).

Bastianelo. Haviland - FAVORITE..ITALY 55-66 (J2063; J2161.1).

The Bat. Deutsch - MORE 7-10 (A2491.1; B261.1.0.3).

The Bat and the Weasels. Aesop - AESOP'S (Watts) 5 (B261.1.0.4).

The Bat, the Birds and the Beasts. Aesop - AESOP'S (Grosset) 214-215 (A2491.1.1); Jacobs - FABLES 47 (B261.1.0.1).

The Bat, the Bramble and the Seagull. Aesop - AESOP'S (Watts) 174 (A2275.5.3).

The Bat Who Belonged to No One. Burton - MAGIC 52-53 (B261.1.0.5).

Batim the Horse. Hampden - GYPSY 89-95 (B641.6.1).

The Bat's Choice. Bulatkin - EURASIAN 111-113 (B261.1).

The Battle between the Birds and the Beasts. Carpenter - AFRICAN 87-92 (A2433.3.4.1; B261.0.1).

A Battle Nobody Won. Thompson - HAWAIIAN.. EARTH 15-19 (A493.1).

The Battle of Eghal Shillet. Courlander - FIRE 121-128 (K1951.2).

The Battle of the Animals. Kaula - AFRICAN 105-109 (K2323.1).

The Battle of the Birds. Arnott - ANIMALS 38-42 (B263.5.2).

The Battle of the Birds. Jacobs - Celtic 223-241 (G530.2K); Rackham - FAIRY 15-27.

The Battle of the Buffaloes. De Leeuw - INDONE-SIAN 135-139 (B264.6).

Battle of the Monkey and the Crab. Wiggin - TALES 427-428 (K1161.6).

The Battle That Tilted the Sea. Holding - THE SKY-EATER 24-38 (A2586).

Battle with the Snakes. Bruchac - TURKEY 35-37 (B268.7).

A Bauchan in the Family. Leodhas - SEA 179-200 (F482.3.1.2).

Be Careful! Leach - LUCK 93-94 (J2075).

Be Prepared. Cimino - DISOBEDIENT #16 (J861.2).

The Bean Pot. Heady - JAMBO 34-38 (K335.0.4.3).

Bean Tree. Manning-Sanders - GIANNI 119-126 (D861.1G).

The Bear. Lang - ROSE 56-63 (R221Dg).

The Bear and the Beehives. Aesop - AESOP'S (Viking) 78 (N333.0.2).

The Bear and the Deer. Heady - SAGE 74-79 (K851.1; R246).

The Bear and the Fox Who Made a Bet. Asbjørn-sen - NORWEGIAN 120-121 (N51).

THE BEAR AND THE KINGBIRD. Grimm. pb (K2323.1.1).

The Bear and the Skrattel. Mayne - GHOSTS 87-97 (K1728).

The Bear and the Travellers. Aesop - AESOP'S (Watts) 30-31 (J1488).

The Bear and the Two Travellers. Kent - MORE 42-45 (J1488).

The Bear and the Wildcat. Credle - TALL 27-29 (X1114.3).

The Bear Goes Fishing. Bowman - TALES..TUPA 263 (K1021).

The Bear Hunt. Harris - COMPLETE 783-792 (K2131.9); Harris - FAVORITE 203-212.

The Bear in the Black Hat. Credle - TALL 55-63 (J1762.2.3).

The Bear in the Coach. Williams-Ellis - FAIRY.. BRITISH 169 (J1762.2.2).

The Bear in the Pear Tree. Kelsey - HODJA 54-62 (N659.3).

The Bear Man. Bell - JOHN 33-38 (B538.3.4); Brown - TEPEE 18-22.

The Bear Says North. Fillmore - SHEPHERD'S 69-71 (K561.1).

The Beard of Mon Plaisir. Thoby-Marcelin - SINGING 66-74 (K1715.3.2).

The Bears. Heady - TALES 67-74 (K1035.2).

The Bear's Head. Leekley - WORLD 58-63 (D1313.4).

Bearskin. Grimm - JUNIPER v.2 217-237 (K217).

Bearskin. Holme - TALES 50-57 (R111.1.3Ap); Pyle - WONDER 3-14.

THE BEARSKINNER. Grimm. pb (K217B).

The Beautiful Blue Jay. Spellman - BEAUTIFUL 3-7 (A2426.2.26.1).

The Beautiful Feathers. Arnott - TEMBA 85-93 (D672i).

The Beautiful Girl and the Fish. Fuja - FOUR-TEEN 32-38 (B654.1).

The Beautiful Princess. Michael - PORTUGUESE 172-178 (T11.2.3).

The Beautiful Weaver and the Golden Shell. Toor - GOLDEN 145-150 (A969.11.2).

The Beauty and Her Gallant. Manning-Sanders - BOOK..GHOSTS 101-102 (T93.6).

Beauty and the Beast. Arbuthnot - ANTHOLOGY 216-223 (D735.1); Arbuthnot - FAIRY 107-115; Dalglish - ENCHANTED 130-153; Harris BEAU-TY pb; Haviland - FRENCH 38-59; Holme - TALES 35-44; Jacobs - EUROPEAN 34-41; Lang - BLUE 106-128; Mayer - BEAUTY pb; McKinley - BEAUTY pb; Opie - CLASSIC 137-150; Pearce - BEAUTY pb; Perrault - PERRAULT'S (Dodd) 115-134; Provensen - PROVENSEN 33-48; Rack-ham - ARTHUR 49-65; Tarrant - FAIRY 68-88.

Beauty and the Horns. Fillmore - LAUGHING 27-50 (D551.1B).

The Beaver's Tail. Heady - SAGE 39-41 (A2378.1.6.1).

Bech, The Ambitious Quail. Bowes - BIRD 19-23 (A2431.3.10).

The Beckoning Cat. Pratt - MAGIC #3 (B331.0.1).

The Bed. Belpré - TIGER 33-35 (Z49.17).

The Bee. Hardendorff - JUST 150-158 (H540.2.1).

The Bee and Jupiter. Aesop - AESOP'S (Watts) 35 (A2232.2).

The Bee Hunter and the Oozie. Htin - KINGDOM 66-70 (J2133.5.0.1).

The Bee, the Harp, the Mouse, and the Bum-Clock. Fenner - PRINCESSES 64-74 (H341.2); Haviland - FAVORITE..IRELAND 3-25; Hutch-inson - CHIMNEY 73-86; Wiggin - FAIRY 146-154.

The Bee Tree. Heady - JAMBO 29-33 (K521.10; K553.5.1).

The Beef Tongue of Orula. Courlander - RIDE 257-258 (H1305.2.1).

The Beekeeper and the Beautiful Hare. Leodhas - THISTLE 106-118 (E501.5.5.1.1).

The Bees and the Drones. Green - BIG 178-179 (J581.4).

The Bees in the Well. Jagendorf - NOODLEHEAD 72-73 (J1791.9).

BEESWAX CATCHES A THIEF! Kirn pb (A2233.1.1; K741).

Beetle. Sheehan - FOLK 51-60 (K1956.2; N688).

The Beetle and a Drop of Honey. Turnbull - FAIRY 136-150 (R121.4.1).

Beetle and the Lion. Aardema - MORE 16-21 (Z43.6.2).

The Beetle and the Paca. Carpenter - SOUTH 108-113 (A2411.3.3; K11.10).

The Beetle's Hairpiece. Courlander - PEOPLE 46-49 (A2317.2.1).

The Beggar Boy and the Fox. Lang - CRIMSON 138-146 (K1917.3).

The Beggar in the Blanket. Graham - BEGGAR 11-21 (H1558.1.0.1).

The Beggar's Friend. Carpenter - KOREAN 165-172 (D1451.3).

The Beggar's Prophecy. Spicer - OWL'S 56-73 (N211.1).

The Beginning of Spirit Societies. Haskett - GRAINS 71-74 (A1539.2).

The Beginning of the World and The Making of California. Curry - DOWN 9-21 (A812.6; A961.1.1; A9201.0.1).

Beinush, the Alert Policeman. Simon - MORE 102-110 (J1703.2).

La Belle Venus. Johnson – HOW 47-54 (A781).

The Bellicose Chicken. Walker – NIGERIAN 39-40 (J1791.5.3).

Belling the Cat. Aesop – AESOP'S (Grosset) 13 (J671.1); Arbuthnot – FAIRY 228; Jacobs – FABLES 133; Kent – MORE 52-53; Leach – LION 23-24; Rice – ONCE 22-27; Wiggin – TALES 336-337.

The Belly and the Members. Aesop – AESOP'S (Grosset) 46 (J461.1); Aesop – AESOP'S (Viking) 6; Aesop – AESOP'S (Watts) 128; Jacobs – FABLES 57.

Belmont Antics. Jagendorf – NOODLEHEAD 229-232 (J2328.1).

Benito the Faithful. Sechrist – ONCE 156-157 (B582.2D).

The Best Liar. Ginsburg – THREE 13 (X905.1.1).

The Best of the Bargain. Domanska – BEST pb (K11.1; K171.1); Hardendorff – JUST 44-48 (J1511.17.1).

The Best Wish. Courlander – RIDE 131-136 (Q1.1A); Fillmore – LAUGHING 229-240; Frost – LEGEND 245-249; Williams-Ellis – ROUND 120-129 (D856).

The Bet Between Matjan and Gadja. Courlander – KANTCHIL'S 46-51 (K84.2; K1715.2.1).

The Betel and the Areca Tree. Schultz – VIET-NAMESE 67-71 (A2691.5).

Beth Gellert. Jacobs – CELTIC 209-211 (B331.2).

The Betrothal. Kendall – SWEET 80-85 (B611.3).

Betty Stogs' Baby. Manning-Sanders – PETER 17-21 (F321.0.2).

Beware the Man Without a Beard. Neufeld – BE-WARE 11-21 (K111.1; K2275.1).

The Bewitched Cat. Sperry – HEN 9-24 (K1917.3D); Sperry – SCANDINAVIAN 49-59.

Big, Big Lies. Withers – A WORLD 90-100 (H342.1).

The Big, Big Rabbit. Withers – I SAW 76 (X904.2.1).

The Big Bird Dam. Aulaire – EAST 108-122 (H1385.1); Undset – TRUE 118-131.

The Big Cabbage and the Big Kettle. Withers – I SAW 71 (X909.4.1).

The Big Chinese Drum. Withers – WORLD 30 (X909.4.4).

The Big Feet of the Empress Tu Chin. Carpenter – TALES..CHINA 81-88 (A1599.4.1.1).

The Big Fire. Heady – SAGE 51-53 (A2411.2.1.18.1).

Big Fox and Little Fox. Montgomerie – TWENTY-FIVE 11-13 (K371.1).

Big Fraid and Little Fraid. Credle – BIG pb (K1682.1); Leach – THING 27-28.

Big Jack and Little Jack. Chase – JACK 67-75 (K172; K362.10).

Big Liang and Little Liang. Chang – CHINESE 54-57 (J2415.21).

Big Liar. Asia – FOLK..THREE 55-59 (A751.8.5.2).

Big Long Man's Corn Patch. Haviland – NORTH 71-75 (K741.0.13; K842.0.11; K1251).

Big Mosquitoes. Withers – A WORLD 86 (X1286.1.5.1).

The Big Mudhole. Credle – TALL 9-15 (X1655.2).

The Big Pumpkin and the Big Kettle. Withers – WORLD 28 (X909.4.1).

The Big Tree and the Big Bird. Withers – I SAW 141 (X909.4.2).

The Biggest and the Best. Chang – CHINESE 4-5 (J953.20).

The Biggest in the World. Sakade – JAPANESE CHILDREN'S STORIES 47-50 (J953.20).

Billy Beg and His Bull. Hutchinson – CHIMNEY.. FAIRY TALES 167-183 (B335.2).

Billy Beg and the Bull. Adams – BOOK..GIANTS 1-8 (B335.2); Curley – BILLY pb; Fenner – GIANTS 64-78; Haviland – FAVORITE..IRELAND 39-60.

The Billy Goat and the Sheep. Bloch – UKRAIN-IAN 19-23 (K1715.3).

Billy Malone. Harris – COMPLETE 246-250 (K842.0.5); Harris – FAVORITE 213-218; Harris – NIGHTS 177-184.

Binnorie. Jacobs – ENGLISH 43-47 (E632.0.1).

The Bird and the Buffalo. Carpenter – ELE-PHANT'S 91-99 (K82.1.1).

The Bird and the Man. Durham – TIT 90-91 (D2011.1).

The Bird Cagemaker. Wiggin – FAIRY 343-348 (D876.4).

Bird Cu. Barlow – LATIN 138-144 (A2491.2.7).

Bird Found. Grimm – GRIMM'S (Follett) 28-32 (D671).

The Bird of Seven Colors. Alegría - THREE 25-30 (H1273.2E).

The Bird of the Five Virtues. Carpenter - KOREAN 75-77 (B259.6).

The Bird of the Golden Feather. Mittleman - BIRD 7-29 (H1331.1.3An).

The Bird on the Roof. Alexander - PEBBLE 26 (A2426.2.24).

The Bird That Told Tales. Carpenter - ELEPHANT'S 58-65 (A2422.12; J1151.1.3.1).

The Bird That Would Not Stay Dead. Carpenter - AFRICAN 179-186 (N271C).

The Bird, the Mouse, and the Sausage. Ginsburg - LAZIES 46-48 (J512.7).

The Bird Which Laid Diamonds. Eells - TALES.. SPAIN 45-46 (D551.1A).

The Bird Who Spoke Three Times. Sawyer - WAY 297-304 (T53.0.2).

The Bird With the Gift of Fire. Finlay - TATTERCOATS 47-52 (A1414.4.2).

Birdcatcher and Partridge. Aesop - FABLES (Walck) 50 (K553.1.0.2).

The Birds, the Beasts, and the Bat. Aesop - AESOP'S (Viking) 45-46 (A2491.1; B261.1); Aesop - AESOP'S (Watts) 133; Aesop - FABLES (Walck) 55-56; Aesop - FIVE 76.

The Birth of Japan. MacAlpine - JAPANESE (I. Takamagahana) 3-4 (A620.3); MacAlpine - JAPANESE (II. Izanagi and Izanami) 4-6 (A822.2); MacAlpine - JAPANESE (III. The Bridge of Heaven) 7-10 (A822.2); MacAlpine - JAPANESE (IV. The Birth of the Islands) 10-15 (A112.2; A112.3; A1438.3); MacAlpine - Japanese (V. Izanagi's Descent to Hades) 16-22 (A1558).

The Birth of Simnel Cake. Green - CLEVER 130-133 (A1455.2.1).

The Birth of the River Emajõgi. Maas - MOON 44-46 (A934.17).

THE BISHOP AND THE DEVIL. Serraillier. pb (K1886.3.1).

The Biter Bit. Lang - GREEN 183-191 (K113; K131.1.3; K842).

Blabbermouth. Daniels - FALCON 24-28 (J1151.1.1).

The Black Bearded Brownies of Bombay. Spicer - THIRTEEN 101-111 (F342.1.2).

The Black Bull of Norroway. Arbuthnot - ANTHOLOGY 162-165 (H1385.5B); Arbuthnot - FAIRY 24-27; De La Mare - ANIMAL 225-231; Frost - LEGENDS 13-19; Jacobs - MORE 20-27; Lang - BLUE 358-363; Steel - ENGLISH 110-117; Williams-Ellis - FAIRY 89-95.

The Black Cat of Cotabato. Robertson - FAIRY.. PHILIPPINES 81-90 (A939.3).

The Black Cat of the Witch-Dance-Place. Hoke - WITCH 194-196 (G271.2).

The Black Charger. Gunterman - CASTLE 251-261 (D1101).

Black Colin of Loch Awe. Wilson - SCOTTISH 56-65 (H94.4.1).

The Black Cow. Nunn - AFRICAN 104-111 (B313.1.1).

The Black Dog of the Wild Forest. Manning-Sanders - RED 139-145 (B524.1.2A).

The Black Geese. Lurie - CLEVER 17-22 (Q2.1.2Ce).

The Black-Handed Monkey. Holladay - BANTU 78-79 (J1565.1.2).

The Black Horseman. Johnson - HOW 59-66 (E422.1.1.3.3).

Black Magic. Boggs - THREE 127-131 (D1711.0.1.1).

The Black Wife of Scar. Cutt - HOGBOON 60-65 (E221.1.1).

The Blackamoor. Aesop - AESOP'S (Watts) 84 (J511.1.1).

The Blackbird and the Pine Needle. Ekram - TURKISH 113-116 (Z47.5).

The Blacksmith and the Devil. Manning-Sanders - DEVILS 76-86 (Q565Ac).

The Blacksmith in the Moon. Withers - MAN 7-9 (G501G).

The Blacksmith Lion and the Conceited Goat. Burton - MAGIC 125-126 (U131.2).

The Blacksmith They Were Afraid to Receive in Hell. Undset - TRUE 137-146 (Q565Ad).

The Blacksmiths. Courlander - PIECE 84-88 (N255.8).

Blacksmith's Dilemma. Arnott - AFRICAN 119-123 (H1021.14).

The Blackstairs Mountain. Manning-Sanders - BOOK..WITCHES 123-127 (F381.8.1).

Blanket Boy and the Shaman. Newell - RESCUE 125-142 (H335.7.3).

The Blessed Gift of Joy. Haviland - NORTH 101-106 (A1542.2.2).

The Blind Boy and the Loon. Maher – BLIND 17-30 (A2135.1.1; F952.7.1; K333.1).

The Blind King and the Magic Bird. Michael – PORTUGUESE 179-185 (N731.2.1).

The Blind Man and the Deaf Man. Baker – GOLDEN 80-88 (K335.1.1.3.2; K1711.3).

The Blind Man and the Whelp. Aesop – AESOP'S (Grosset) 78 (J33).

The Blind Man, the Deaf Man, and the Donkey. Haviland – FAVORITE..INDIA 35-52 (K1711.3); Palmer – FAIRY 45-49; Wiggin – TALES 250-257.

The Blind Man's Daughter. Carpenter – KOREAN 81-86 (N712.2).

The Blind Men and the Elephant. Leach – NOODLES 54 (J1761.10); Quiqley – BLIND pb; Saxe – BLIND pb.

The Blind Mouse. Kim – STORY 83-85 (W46.2).

The Blinded Giant. Jacobs – MORE 92-93 (K603.2).

The Blizzard of '98. Credle – TALL 40-42 (X1623.2.1).

Blockhead Hans. Lang – FIFTY 9-13 (H507.1.0.1); Lang – YELLOW 324-329.

Blodevedd and the Slaying of Llew. Sheppard-Jones – WELSH 63-68 (A1958.0.2; Z312.4).

Blood On His Forehead. Littledale – GHOSTS 135-138 (N384.0.2).

Blue and Green Wonders. Huggins – BLUE 101-122 (D831B).

Blue Beard. Lang – BLUE 313-319 (S62.1); Perrault – FAMOUS 41-60; Perrault – PERRAULT'S (Dodd) 78-88; Perrault – PERRAULT'S (Dover) 31-44; Rackham – ARTHUR 143-152.

The Blue Belt. Asbjørnsen – EAST (Macmillan) 57-75 (K1341.1; S12.1A); Asbjørnsen – EAST (Doubleday) 35-52.

The Blue Bird. Lang – GREEN 1-28 (H1385.5Ad).

The Blue Cap. Wilson – SCOTTISH 33-37 (G242.7.1).

The Blue Cat. Carpenter – ELEPHANT'S 159-165 (J2131.5.6.1).

The Blue Cow from the Sea. Cutt – HOGBOON 140-146 (F420.6.1.5.1.1).

Blue Crane's Story. Helfman – BUSHMEN 68-71 (A591.1).

The Blue Jackal. Brown – BLUE pb (J2131.5.6); Gaer – FABLES..INDIA 69-71; Gobhai – BLUE pb; Green – BIG 216-219.

Blue Jan and the Moon Legend. Matson – LEGENDS 24-28 (A2426.2.26; D1553.2).

The Blue Light. Grimm – BROTHERS 133-138 (D1421.1.2); Grimm – GRIMM'S (Follett) 33-40; Grimm – GRIMM'S (Grosset) 208-213; Grimm – GRIMM'S (World) 318-323.

The Blue Lotus Flower. Tooze – WONDERFUL 77-82 (R221R).

The Blue Mountains. Lang – YELLOW 255-265 (H1385.3Cb).

The Blue Scarf of Strength. MacManus – WELL 65-82 (S12.1B).

The Blue Virgin. Jagendorf – KING 229-232 (V128.0.1.2).

Bluebeard. De La Mare – TALES 131-141 (S62.1); Opie – CLASSIC 103-109.

The Bluebird and the Coyote. Brown – TEPEE 146 (A2411.1.3.2.1; A2411.2.1.20.1).

The Bluebottle Who Went Courting. Wiggin – TALES 346-350 (B285.4.1).

Boar and Fox. Reeves – FABLES 76 (J674.1).

The Boastful Alaskans. Withers – WORLD 30 (X1623.2.4).

The Boastful Bullfrog and the Bull. Aesop – AESOP'S (Golden) 70 (J955.1).

The Boastful Gnat. Wilson – GREEK 212-213 (L478).

The Boastful Tortoise. Lin – MILKY 11-15 (J2357).

The Boasting Traveler. Aesop – AESOP'S (Grosset) 60 (J1477); Aesop – AESOP'S (Watts) 43.

The Boatman from the Hills. Brockett – BURMESE 136-141 (J1922.1.1).

Bob o' the Carn. Colwell – ROUND 117-121 (F235.4.1).

The Bob-Tailed Monkey and the King's Honey. Davis – LION'S 32-44 (K144.3.1).

Bobino. Lang – ROSE 64-71 (B217.9).

Bobo, Black Dog, and the Cannibal Woman. Carpenter – WONDER..DOGS 101-110 (B524.1.2F).

The Bobtail Monkey. Sakade – JAPANESE..FAVORITE 113-120 (Z47.2).

The Bogey Beast. Steel – ENGLISH 188-190 (E427).

The Boggart. Littledale – GHOSTS 35-38 (F482.3.1.1).

The Boggart and the Farmer. Colwell – ROUND

57-60 (K171.1).

The Bogle Ghost of Barra Bog. Spicer - THIR-
TEEN MONSTERS 9-18 (H1419).

The Bogles from the Howff. Leodhas - HEATHER
113-128 (E439.11).

Boiled Axe. Carey - BABA 73-74 (K112.2).

Boiled Wheat for a Bountiful Harvest. Walker -
WATERMELON 68-72 (J1191.2).

THE BOJABI TREE. Rickert pb (J2571.4.1).

Bola Bola. Lowe - LITTLE 41-43 (K1911Ac).

The Bold Heroes of Hungry Hill. MacManus -
HIBERNIAN 212-223 (K335.1.4; K1161.1); Mac-
Manus - BOLD 3-18.

The Bold Little Bowman. Wyatt - GOLDEN 85-92
(K1951.6).

Bomba, the Brave. Carpenter - AFRICAN 169-
178 (R111.1.4B).

The Booby. Wiggin - TALES 14-19 (F601.2D).

The Book of Magic. Littledale - GHOSTS 21-25
(D1711.0.1.2).

Bookay. Harris - FAVORITE 291-295 (F929.3);
Harris - COMPLETE 111-115; Harris - UNCLE
168-174.

The Boom-Boom-Y Beast. Carpenter - AFRICAN
13-20 (F611.3.3.3).

The Boomer Fireman's Fast Sooner Hound. Arbuthnot - FAIRY 212-214 (X1215.7.1).

Boots and His Brothers. Arbuthnot - FAIRY 77-
79 (H1115.1.1); Association - TOLD..GREEN
146-155; Hutchinson - CHIMNEY..FAIRY TALES
55-62.

Boots and the Troll. Haviland - NORWAY 75-88
(G610Ac).

Boots of Buffalo Leather. Grimm - BROTHERS
166-169 (K1812.1.0.1).

The Boots That Never Wore Out. Spicer - THIR-
TEEN DEVILS 33-42 (K172).

Boots Who Made the Princess Say, "That's a
Story." Fenner - PRINCESSES 99-102 (H342.1).

The Bored Tengu. Palmer - DRAGONS 30-37
(J1185.2).

Born a Monkey, Live a Monkey. Sherlock - WEST
135-143 (A2538.1).

Born to be Rich. Lowe - LITTLE 22-26 (N351).

Borrowed Arrows. Lu Mar - CHINESE 111-126
(K2369.14).

The Borrowed Donkey. De La Iglesia - CAT 15
(J1552.1.1).

The Borrower. Serwer - LET'S 55-58 (J1531.3).

The Borrowing of 100,000 Arrows. Wyndham -
TALES..CHINA 40-47 (K2369.14).

Bottle Hill. Manning-Sanders - BOOK..DWARFS
64-72 (D861.1E); Manning-Sanders - CHOICE
54-62.

Bouki and Ti Bef. Courlander - PIECE 94-96
(K646; K688.3).

Bouki Buys a Burro. Courlander - PIECE 55-57
(J2060.1.1).

Bouki Cuts Wood. Courlander - PIECE 76-80
(J2133.4; J2311.1; J2311.4).

Bouki Dances the Kokioko. Wolkstein - MAGIC
79-86 (H529.1).

Bouki Gets Whee-ai. Courlander - PIECE 20-22
(H1377.3).

Bouki Rents a Horse. Courlander - PIECE 25-28
(K1797).

Bouki's Glasses. Courlander - PIECE 89-90
(J1746.2).

The Bow, the Deer and the Talking Bird. Brenner - BOY 90-94 (F660.1F).

A Box on the Ear. Manning-Sanders - BOOK..
GHOSTS 9-13 (H1411.1).

The Box Tortoise's Shell. Parker - SKUNNY 132-
138 (A2312.1.8).

The Box with Something Pretty in It. Hardendorff - JUST 26-27 (Z12.1.1); Wiggin - TALES
321.

The Box with Wings. Wilson - GREEK 90-96
(R221Pa).

A Boy and a Beggar. Jewett - WHICH 47-58
(V226.1).

The Boy and His Magic Robe. Matson - LONG-
HOUSE 31-38 (A1611.1.3).

The Boy and His Sister. Field - AMERICAN 71-
73 (A728.1).

The Boy and Necken. Kaplan - FAIRY 200-208
(K11.6A).

The Boy and the Bull. Manning-Sanders - PETER
33-38 (G303.3.3.1.4).

The Boy and the Cloth. Courlander - TIGER'S
80-82 (J2461.2A; J2461.7).

The Boy and the Dragon. Green - CAVALCADE..
DRAGONS 11-15 (B389.2).

The Boy and the Filberts. Aesop – AESOP'S (Grosset) 106 (W151.9); Aesop – AESOP'S (Watts) 61; Kent – MORE 26–27.

The Boy and the Fox. Withers – I SAW 89 (J2061.3.1).

The Boy and the Leopard. Walker – DANCING 84–93 (B535.0.8.1).

The Boy and the Nettle. Aesop – AESOP'S (Grosset) 139 (J656.2).

The Boy and the Nettles. Aesop – AESOP'S (Watts) 57 (J656.2).

The Boy and the Nuts. Aesop – AESOP'S (Random) 63–65 (W151.9.1).

The Boy and the Piece of Yarn. Fuja – FOURTEEN 43–47 (A2412.1.2).

The Boy and the Sea Monsters. Harris – ONCE 33–58 (A2171.2.3; F912.2.4).

The Boy and the Snails. Aesop – AESOP'S (Watts) 39 (J1885).

The Boy and the Water Sprite. Haviland – FAVORITE..SWEDEN 2–13 (K11.6).

The Boy and the Wolf. Aesop – AESOP'S (Golden) 17–19 (J2172.1).

The Boy Bathing. Aesop – AESOP'S (Grosset) 234 (J2175.2); Aesop – AESOP'S (Watts) 55.

The Boy in the Land of Shadows. Littledale – GHOST 111–120 (A1159.1; E481.2.0.1; F81.1.0.4).

The Boy in the Moon. Withers – MAN 21 (A751.0.3).

The Boy of the Red Twilight Sky. Frost – LEGENDS 278–282 (T554.12.2).

The Boy Pu-nia and the King of the Sharks. Colum – LEGENDS 92–96 (K341.16); Colum – STONE 44–49.

The Boy Who Ate More Than the Giant. Löfgren BOY 5–24 (G501A).

The Boy Who Beat the Devil. Brenner – BOY 84–89 (G303.16.19.19.1).

The Boy Who Became a Reindeer. Melzack – DAY 41–48 (D100.2).

The Boy Who Caught the Wind. Newell – RESCUE 119–124 (A1128.3).

The Boy Who Cut Everything to Pieces. Burton – MAGIC 53–55 (Q589.4).

The Boy Who Drew Cats. Gruenberg – FAVORITE 373–376 (D435.2.1.1); Hearn – BOY 14–20; Hearn – JAPANESE 29–35; Hearn – JAPANESE

(Pauper) 38–44; Littledale – GHOSTS 27–33.

The Boy Who Fished for the Moon. Holding – SKY-EATER 99–110 (J2271.6).

The Boy Who Found Fear at Last. Lang – FIFTY 14–20 (H1440D).

The Boy Who Had a Moon on His Forehead and a Star on His Chin. Jacobs – INDIAN 188–216 (N455.4B).

The Boy Who Had No Story. Danaher – FOLK-TALES 1–8 (M231.1).

The Boy Who Had to Draw Cats. Carpenter – WONDER..DOGS 195–203 (D435.2.1.1).

The Boy Who Lived With the Bears. Bruchac – TURKEY 51–57 (B535.0.15).

The Boy Who Met the Trolls in the Hedal Woods. Asbjørnsen 9–12 (K333.2).

The Boy Who Never Was Afraid. Hatch – MORE 133–138 (H1440C).

The Boy Who Out-Fibbed a Princess. Withers – I SAW 86–88 (H342.1).

The Boy Who Played the Flute. Lin – MILKY 76–86 (B11.12.7.2).

The Boy Who Searched for Fear. Kavcic – GOLDEN 60–70 (H1440Ba).

The Boy Who Snared the Wind and the Shaman's Daughter. DeWit – TALKING 161–168 (A1122.5; F601.2l).

The Boy Who Took Care of the Pigs. Brenner-BOY 1–11 (B562.1.1).

The Boy Who Turned Himself Into a Peanut. Withers – WORLD 57–78 (Z43.5).

The Boy Who Wanted to Learn to Shudder. Bang – GOBLINS 15 (H1440A).

The Boy Who Wanted to See the World. Johnson – HOW 39–46 (K1611Dd).

The Boy Who Was Called Thickhead. DeWit – TALKING 183–187 (K251.1.0.3).

The Boy Who Was Caught by a Clam. Holding – SKY 39–48 (K561.1.0.2).

The Boy Who Was Lost. Jagendorf – KING 59–64 (B538.3.3).

The Boy Who Was Never Afraid. Michael – POR-TUGUESE 133–128 (H1440Bb).

The Boy Who Wore Turtle Shell Moccasins. Yellow Robe – TONWEYA 59–65 (H1132.1.5.3).

The Boy With the Ale Keg. Undset – TRUE 132–136 (D1825.3.1).

The Boy With the Beer Keg. Asbjørnsen - NOR-WEGIAN 121-134 (D1825.3.1).

The Boy With the Golden Star. Pridham - GIFT 143-156 (E711.10).

The Boy With the Long Hair. Matson - LONG-HOUSE 85-90 (B182.1.0.1.2).

The Boy With the Moon on His Forehead. Turnbull - FAIRY..INDIA 50-83 (N455.4B).

The Boy Without a Name. Holding - KING'S 87-97 (F610.3.6).

The Boyar and the Gipsy. Ure - RUMANIAN 33-34 (J1919.2).

Boys With Golden Stars. Lang - VIOLET 174-185 (N455.4C).

The Braggart. Ginsburg - THREE 51 (K648.1).

The Bragging Beasts. Reed - TALKATIVE 13 (L461.1).

The Brahman and the Potter's Shop. Gaer - FABLES..INDIA 110-111 (J2061.1.2.1).

The Brahman, the Tiger and the Seven Judges. Baker - TALKING 236-241 (J1172.3).

The Brahman, the Tiger and the Six Judges. Wiggin - FAIRY 391-394 (J1172.3; J1172.3.2).

The Brahman and the Villain. Gaer - FABLES.. INDIA 43-49 (W154.8).

The Brainy Rabbit. Gilstrap - SULTAN'S 61-66 (K341.2.1).

The Branch of Almond Blossom. Gunterman - CASTLES 166-178 (H87.1).

The Brave Bear-Killer. Brockett - BURMESE 111-118 (N624; N688.2).

Brave In Spite of Himself. Hatch - THIRTEEN 122-138 (K1951.1A).

The Brave Little Prince. Spellman - BEAUTIFUL 82-85 (K511).

The Brave Little Tailor. Grimm - HOUSE 15-35 (K1951.1); Lang - BLUE 330-339; Lang - FIFTY 21-29; Manning-Sanders - BOOK..GIANTS 90-97; Martignoni - ILLUSTRATED 213-218.

The Brave Man of Gola. Courlander - KING'S 51-55 (K514.0.1).

The Brave Men of Austwick. Jagendorf - NOO-DLEHEAD 119-121 (J1922.2).

Brave Porcupine. Heady - SAGE 57-60 (A2422.15).

The Brave Prince. Davis - LION'S 93-102 (N392.1.3).

Brave Rabbit and Bug With the Golden Wings.

Rudolph - MAGIC 42-50 (K1082.3.3).

The Brave Shepherd. Sleigh - NORTH 170-177 (H328.9).

The Brawl Between Sun and Moon. Withers - MAN 19 (A751.5.2.2).

Bread-Free. Kelsey - MULLAH 65-70 (J1849.0.1).

Break Mountains. Courlander - PIECE 23-24 (F615.9).

The Bremen Town Musicians. Fenner - ADVEN-TURES 103-108 (K335.1.4; K1161.1); Grimm - BREMEN pb; Grimm - BROTHERS 23-27; Grimm - GRIMM'S (Follett) 41-46; Grimm - GRIMM'S (Grosset) 144-147; Grimm - GRIMM'S (Viking) 114-118; Grimm - GRIMM'S (World) 301-304; Grimm - HOUSE 46-55; Grimm - HOUSEHOLD 136-139; Haviland - FAIRY 110-113; Haviland - FAVORITE..GERMANY 72-85; Hutchinson - CHIMNEY 127-134; Martignoni - ILLUSTRATED 219-220; Richardson - GREAT 104-112; Rockwell - OLD 52-61; Sherlock - ABOUT 111-115.

The Brenggen Field. Duvoisin - THREE 220-223 (A939.1).

Brer Bear Gets a Taste of Man. Faulkner - DAYS 85-88 (K553.1.0.5).

Brer Buzzard and the Tombstone. Harris - COM-PLETE 185-189 (K522.9.1); Harris - FAVORITE 268-271; Harris - NIGHTS 95-99.

Brer Buzzard's Gold Mine. Harris - COMPLETE 69-71 (K2347); Harris - FAVORITE 121-124; Harris - UNCLE 105-108.

Brer Coon and the Frogs. Harris - FAVORITE 104-107 (K751.0.2).

Brer Fox Follows the Fashion. Harris - FAVOR-ITE 301-309 (J2413.4.5); Harris - COMPLETE 647-653.

Brer Fox Holds The Horse. Harris- FAVORITE 243-246 (K1047); Harris - NIGHTS 8-11; Harris - COMPLETE 123-126.

Brer Fox Meets Mister Trouble. Faulkner - DAYS 137-138 (H1376.11).

Brer Fox Shingles His Roof. Harris - FAVORITE 15-18 (K729.1).

Brer Fox Tries Farming Too. Faulkner - DAYS 110-114 (K171.1).

Brer Goat and Brer Lion. Williams-Ellis - ROUND 192-194 (K1715.17).

Brer Mink Holds His Breath. Harris - COMPLETE 386-389 (K16.2); Harris - FAVORITE 113-117; Harris - NIGHTS 373-376.

Brer Possum and Brer Snake. Faulkner - DAYS 99-105 (J1172.3).

The Brothers of the Donkey. Kelsey – MULLAH 105–107 (J1529.1).

The Brown Bear of Norway. Lang – FIFTY 37–45 (H1385.4Ab).

Brown Owl's Story. Sherlock – IGUANA'S 43–52 (A2423.1.4; K11.1).

The Brownie o' Ferne-Den. Haviland – FAVORITE ..SCOTLAND 49 (F482.5.4.1).

Bruin and Reynard Partners. Asbjørnsen EAST (Row) 31 (K171.1); Wiggin – TALES 311.

The Bubble, and the Straw and the Shoe. Daniels – FALCON 90–91 (F1025.1.11); Ginsburg – THREE 22 (F1025.1.1).

Bucca Dhu and Bucca Gwidden. Manning-Sanders – PETER 98–102 (K1682.2).

Budulinek. Arbuthnot – ANTHOLOGY 274–275 (K815.15); Arbuthnot – FAIRY 143–146; Fenner – ADVENTURES 51–59; Fillmore – SHEPHERD'S 94–102; Haviland – FAIRY 92–98.

The Buffalo and the Mean Old Bear. Parker – SKUNNY 109–116 (K402.3.2.2).

The Buffalo and the Porcupine. Heady – TALES 90–94 (K952.1).

The Buffalo Boy and the Banyan Tree. Schultz – VIETNAMESE 31–33 (A751.8.5.2).

The Buffalo, the Coyote and the Peace Pipe. Arnott – ANIMALS 1–5 (A1533.2).

The Buffalo Who Made Undue Demands. Burton – MAGIC 59–61 (K553.1.0.1).

Buffalo Woman, A Story of Magic. Brown – TEPEE 123–128 (B651.2.1).

The Buffalo's Hump and the Brown Birds. Parker – SKUNNY 183–189 (B19.1.1).

The Buffoon and the Countryman. Aesop – AESOP'S (Grosset) 174–175 (J2232); Jacobs – FABLES 159.

Buh Fox's Number Nine Shoes. Courlander – TERRAPIN'S 37–40 (K341.6; K341.6.1).

Buh Mouse Testifies. Courlander – TERRAPIN'S 53–56 (K1024.1).

Buh Rabbit and the King. Courlander – TERRAPIN'S 60–64 (H961; K713.9).

Buh Rabbit's Big Eat. Courlander – TERRAPIN'S 33–36 (K1055).

Buh Rabbit's Graveyard. Courlander – TERRAPIN'S 57–59 (K1715.15).

Buh Rabbit's Human Weakness. Courlander – TERRAPIN'S 31–32 (W141.1).

Buh Rabbit's Tail. Courlander – TERRAPIN'S 41–45 (K581.2; K741.0.3.1).

Buh Rabbit's Tight Necktie. Courlander – TERRAPIN'S 21–23 (X1321.4.11.1).

Bukano and the Crocodiles. Harmon – TALES 29–56 (B491.3.1).

Bukolla. Courlander – RIDE 194–196 (G530.2E).

The Bull and the Fly. Fuja – FOURTEEN 210–213 (A2479.9).

The Bull and the Goat. Aesop – AESOP'S (Grosset) 129 (J371.1).

A Bull Calf Goes to School. Riordan – TALES.. CENTRAL 262–263 (K491.3).

The Bun. Hutchinson – CANDLELIGHT 25–32 (Z33.1.6); Riordan – TALES..CENTRAL 31–33; Ross – BURIED 13–18.

Bundar Bahadur Poon. Hitchcock – KING 37–46 (K1611D).

A Bundle of Sticks. Aesop – AESOP'S (Grosset) 122 (J1021); Aesop – AESOP'S (Random) 62–63; Aesop – FABLES (Macmillan) 143; Evans BUNDLE pb.

The Bungled Message. Withers MAN 23 (A751.5.1; A1335.1.0.1).

The Bungling Host. Martin – NINE..COYOTES 19–22 (J2425).

Bungling Pedro. Mehdevi – BUNGLING 17–35 (J1193.1; J1852.1.3; J1852.1.4; J1853.1.0.1; K366.1.1).

Bunsuru's Grave. Sturton – ZOMO 48–57 (K341.2.0.1).

The Burglars. Shah – MULLAH 34 (J1392.1.2).

The Buried Moon. Jacobs – BURIED pb (A754.1.1.1); Jacobs – MORE 110–117; Pugh – TALES..WELSH 55–65; Wiggin – FAIRY 113–119.

The Buried Treasure. Hampden – HOUSE 94–96 (Z11.0.1); Ross – BURIED 65–74 (J1151.1.1).

THE BURNING RICE FIELDS. Bryant – pb (J1688).

Burnt Foot. Shah – MULLAH 73 (J2242.1).

Bushy Bride. Lang – RED 316–323 (Q2.1.1Bb).

But for the Grace. Shah – MULLAH 89 (J2235).

The Butcher and His Customers. Aesop – AESOP'S (Watts) 200–201 (K475.1).

Butterball. Asbjørnsen – NORWEGIAN 97–101 (K526A).

Buttercup. Fenner – GIANT 108–114 (K526); Hoke – WITCHES 32–36; Undset – TRUE 156–160.

The Butterfly's Wager. Arnott - ANIMAL 161-165 (K25.1.1).

Buya Marries the Tortoise. Burton - MAGIC 98-101 (F914.0.1).

By Scissors and Sieve. Cutt - HOGBOON 56-59 (D1323.20).

Bye-Bye. Wolkstein - MAGIC 189-194 (A2434.4.1; J2357).

The Cabbage. Dolch - OLD RUSSIA 37-43 (F54.2.2.1).

Cadwalader and His Goat. Sheppard-Jones - WELSH 146-148 (D334.1).

The Calabash Children. Arnott - AFRICAN 112-118 (T555.2.1).

The Calabash Man. Finger - TALES 21-30 (E614.3).

Calabash of the Winds. Thompson - HAWAIIAN.. EARTH 70-75 (A1124).

Caliph Stork. Lang - GREEN 35-46 (D155.1.1).

Callaly Castle. Finlay - TATTERCOATS 60-69 (K2349.2).

Calling the Chinook. Heady - TALES 62-66 (A1129.4).

The Calm Brahman. Spellman - BEAUTIFUL 33-36 (W11.3.1).

The Camel and His Neighbor. Gaer - FABLES.. INDIA 26-28 (J2137.6.1).

The Camel and the Driftwood. Aesop - FIVE 82 (U131.2).

The Camel and the Ram. Carrick - STILL MORE 66-72 (K641.2).

The Camel in the Lion's Court. Gaer - FABLES.. INDIA 77-80 (K962).

Can Good Turns Be Accidental. Shah - MULLAH 31 (J1851.1.3).

The Canary That Liked Apricots. Kelsey - MULLAH 61-64 (J1391.9).

The Candle of Death. Spicer - THIRTEEN MONSTERS 52-58 (D1162.2.2).

Candles, Radishes and Garlic. Simon - WISE 103-108 (J2021).

Candy Man. Chang - CHINESE 36-37 (J2415.22).

Cannetella. Manning-Sanders - BOOK..WIZARDS 118-127 (T72.2.1).

Cannibal. Martin - NINE 38-42 (A2034.3.2); Martin - RAVEN 45-52.

The Cannibal and His Sweet Singing Bird. Carpenter - AFRICAN 195-204 (G422.1.1.2).

The Cannibal Who Ate Too Fast. Holladay - BANTU 24-25 (F912.2.2).

The Canoe of Laka or Rata and Those Who Sailed in It. Colum - LEGENDS 77-83 (B874.9).

Cap O' Rushes. Haviland - FAVORITE..ENGLAND 76-78 (R221E); Jacobs - ENGLISH 51-56; Lurie CLEVER 84-91; Minard - WOMENFOLK 77-82; Wiggin - FAIRY 119-123; Williams-Ellis - FAIRY 117-123.

Capons Fat and Lean. Aesop - AESOP'S (Viking) 14-15 (J212.3).

Caporushes. Steel - ENGLISH 209-216 (R221E).

Capturing the Moon. Withers - MAN 51 (J1791.2.1).

Cardiff Town. Pugh - TALES 97-104 (F344.1.3).

The Cardinal's Concert. Bowes - KING 32-39 (A2426.2.22).

The Carlanco. Haviland - FAVORITE..SPAIN 50-57 (K311.3B).

Caro. Thoby-Marcelin - SINGING 17-20 (E474.4).

The Carp That Became a Dragon. Vo-Dinh - TOAD 51-55 (B11.2.1.3).

The Carpenter's Boar. Reed - TALKATIVE 64-67 (B268.12).

The Carpenter's Son. Asia - THREE 5-10 (D882.1B).

THE CARPET OF SOLOMON. Ish-Kishor pb (D1711.1.1).

Carroll the Carman. Danaher - FOLKTALES 9-18 (K113; R111.1).

The Cartman's Stories. Arbuthnot - ANTHOLOGY 251 (J21E); Spellman - BEAUTIFUL 59-63.

The Case Against the Flies. Cimino - DISOBEDIENT 13 (J1193.1).

The Case of the Calf and the Colt. Htin - KINGDOM 62-65 (J1191.1.1).

Casi Lampu'e Lentemue. Belpré - TIGER 75-82 (C432.1.2).

The Castle. Riordan - TALES..CENTRAL 76-77 (J2199.5.1).

The Castle in the Silver Wood. Owen - CASTLE 3-9 (D136.1); Sheehan - FOLK 8-13.

The Castle of No Return. Alegría - THREE 90-99

(R111.1.3Ad).

Cat and Dog. Sherlock - WEST 93-94 (A2494.4.6).

Cat and Dog and the Return of the Dead. Wolkstein - MAGIC 65-70 (A1335.16).

The Cat and Mahadeo. Leach - LION 11 (A2513.2.1).

Cat and Mouse in Partnership. Grimm - GRIMM'S (Follett) 47-51 (K372); Grimm - GRIMM'S (Grosset) 76-79; Grimm - GRIMM 'S (World) 291-294; Grimm - HOUSEHOLD 37-39; Haviland - FAVORITE..GERMANY 32-40; Wiggin - TALES 146-148.

Cat and Mouse Keep House. Bleecker - BIG 43-50 (K372); Gag - TALES..GRIMM 27-35.

THE CAT AND MOUSE WHO SHARED A HOUSE. Hurlimann pb (K372).

The Cat and Nirantali. Leach - LION 10 (A2513.2.4).

The Cat and the Birds. Aesop - AESOP'S (Watts) 10 (K2061.7.1).

The Cat and the Chanticleer. Bloch - UKRAINIAN 11-18 (K815.15).

The Cat and the Cock. Aesop - AESOP'S (Watts) 92 (U33.2).

The Cat and the Dream Man. Finger - TALES 184-207 (G351.2.1); Withers - I SAW 184-207.

The Cat and the Fox. Aesop - AESOP'S (Random) 65-66 (J1662); Aesop - AESOP'S (Viking) 43-44; Borski - GOOD 55-56; Gag - MORE..GRIMM 61-62.

The Cat and the Fox. Montgomerie - MERRY 47-55 (K2324); Sleigh - NORTH 178-183.

The Cat and the Hen. Dobbs - MORE 63-65 (K2061.7.1).

The Cat and the Meat. Shah - MULLAH 23 (J1611).

The Cat and the Mice. Aesop - AESOP'S (Golden) 27-29 (K2061.9); Aesop - AESOP'S (Grosset) 49; Aesop - AESOP'S (Viking) 51-52; Aesop - AESOP'A (Watts) 2.

The Cat and the Mice. Hardendorff - TRICKY 27-32 (K815.16.1).

The Cat and the Mice. Martignoni - ILLUSTRATED 54 (K2061.9).

The Cat and the Mouse. De La Mare - ANIMAL 40-41 (Z41.4); Hutchinson - FIRESIDE 31-33; Jacobs - ENGLISH 197-198; Richardson - GREAT 147-152; Wiggin - TALES 222-223.

The Cat and the Mouse. Lang - YELLOW 1-4 (K372A).

The Cat and the Parrot. Haviland - FAVORITE.. INDIA 27-34 (Z33.2.1).

The Cat and the Prophet. Carpenter - WONDER 145-152 (A2441.1.10.1).

The Cat and the She-Fox. Higonnet-Schnopper - TALES 82-90 (A2435.3.2.1).

The Cat and the Sparrow. Hardendorff - JUST 78-81 (K562).

The Cat and the Tiger. Ginsburg - THREE 40 (A2581).

The Cat and Venus. Kent - MORE 36-41 (J1908.2).

The Cat Bride. Carpenter - WONDER 153-162 (B601.12).

The Cat Chalice of Vlaardingen. De Leeuw - LEGENDS..HOLLAND 75-80.

A Cat Comes to Helm. Simon - WISE 119-126 (J2101.2; J2163.3; J2242.2.1).

Cat Into Maiden. Leach - LION 26-27 (J1908.2).

A Cat is a Cat is a Cat. Vo-Dinh - TOAD 123-128 (L392.0.4).

The Cat is Wet. Shah - MULLAH 77 (W111.2.4).

The Cat Maiden. Aesop - AESOP'S (Grosset) 229 (J1908.2); Jacobs - FABLES 151.

Cat 'n Mouse! Chase - JACK 127-134 (H1385.3D).

The Cat on the Dovrefell. Asbjørnsen - EAST 125-127 (K1728; Dasent - CAT pb.

The Cat of Bubastis. Carpenter - WONDER 184-194 (A132.17).

Cat-Skin. Dagliesh - ENCHANTED 48-56 (R221D); De La Mare - ANIMALS 297-306.

The Cat That Went to Heaven. Carpenter - WONDER 81-88 (A132.17.1).

The Cat, the Cock, and the Fox. Montgomerie - MERRY 32-37 (K815.15); Wiggin - TALES 36-38 (K815.15B).

The Cat, the Cock and the Lamb. Cothran - WITH 49-54 (K1161.8).

The Cat, the Dog, and Death. Courlander - PIECE 34-36 (A1335.16).

The Cat, the Dog, and the Mongoose. Carpenter - WONDER 52-62 (D882.1.1.1).

The Cat, the Mountain Goat, and the Fox. Belpré - TIGER 113-118 (K1013.0.1).

The Cat, the Tiger and the Man. Masey - STORIES 84-87 (A2513.2).

The Cat Who Became Head-Forester. Gruenberg – MORE 127-143 (K2324).

The Cat Who Came Indoors. Tracy – LION 115-117 (A2513.2.1).

The Cat With the Crooked Tail. Carpenter – WONDER 43-51 (A2378.9.7); Ransome – OLD 106-119.

Catch the Wind. Carey – BABA 27-32 (B271.3).

Catching the Thief. Leach – NOODLES 20 (J2214.3.2).

Catfish and His Terrible End. Haskett – GRAINS 24-25 (K1041.1.2).

Catherine and the Fates. McNeil – DOUBLE 74-80 (J214B).

CATOFY THE CLEVER. Jameson – pb (K2324).

Cat's Baptism. Wolkstein – MAGIC 123-128 (U129.4).

Cat's Only Trick. Leach – LION 18-19 (J1662).

The Cat's Tail. Montgomerie – MERRY 19-23 (Z47.3); Withers – I SAW 72-74.

Catskin. Jacobs – MORE 204-210 (R221Db); Reeves – ENGLISH 82-95; Sleigh – NORTH 34-43; Steel – ENGLISH 117-122.

Catskins. Chase – GRANDFATHER 106-114 (R221Dc).

Cattenborg. Kaplan – FAIRY 1-16 (K1917.3C).

The Cattle Egret. Heady – WHEN 27-30 (A2433.4.8).

Caught. Shah – MULLAH 88 (J703.3).

The Cauld Lad of Hilton. Jacobs – ENGLISH 212-214 (F381.3.1); Mayne – GHOSTS 99-100; Williams-Ellis – FAIRY 110-113.

The Cave That Talked. Korel – LISTEN 60-63 (K607.1).

The Cegua. Carter – ENCHANTED 97-101 (E425.1.3.1).

Celery. Manning-Sanders – GIANNI 43-53 (H1385.4L).

Cenerentola. Haviland – FAVORITE..ITALY 3-18 (R221C).

Cenerentola or Cinderella. Mincielli – OLD 24-34 (R221C).

Cerentala. Vittorini – OLD 63-68 (R221C).

Cesarino and the Dragon. Rackham – FAIRY 66-76 (R111.1.3Am).

Chameleon Finds. Leach – HOW 39-40 (A1279.2).

The Champion. Courlander – TERRAPIN'S 69-73 (K46.1).

Chung Kuo's Adventure with the Immortals. Wyndham – FOLK..CHINA 44-49 (A501.2).

Change the Subject. Shah – MULLAH 148 (J1286.1).

The Changeling. Williams-Ellis – FAIRY..BRITISH 44-48 (F321.1.1).

The Changeling and the Fond Young Mother. Leodhas – THISTLE 74-81 (F321.1.4.5).

The Changelings. Sheppard-Jones – WELSH 178-812 (F321.1.1; F321.1.4.5).

Changing Luck. Leach – LUCK 15-18 (H1312.1).

Chanina and the Angels. Baker – TALKING 232-235 (D1641.2.1.1).

CHANTICLEER AND THE FOX. Chaucer – pb (K561.1.0.3; K721).

A Chapter of Fish. Ransome – OLD 206-211 (L331.1).

The Charcoal Burner. Asbjørnsen – NORWEGIAN 25-30 (K1961.1.3; N688; X452.2).

The Charcoal Burner and the Fuller. Aesop – AESOP'S (Watts) 4 (U143).

The Charger and the Miller. Aesop – AESOP'S (Watts) 123 (J14).

Charles Lejour and His Friend. Courlander – PIECE 91-92 (J217.0.1.1).

The Charmed Ring. Jacobs – INDIAN 110-122 (D817.1.2; D882.1Ba).

Cheng's Fighting Cricket. Carpenter – TALES.. CHINESE 217-225 (E423.10).

Cherry. Manning-Sanders – PETER 85-87 (F235.4.1).

Cherry, or the Frog-Bride. De La Mare – ANIMALS 233-243 (B641A).

Chestnut Gray. Riordan – TALES..CENTRAL184-189 (H331.1.2.3.1).

The Chestnut Tree. Novak – FAIRY 61-65 (F441.2.0.2).

Chestnuts. Leach – NOODLES 28-29 (F1068.5; J1914).

The Cheyenne Prophet. Brown – TEPEE 46-59 (A1539.3).

Chi and Yi. Alexander – PEBBLES 23 (J1488).

Chick, Chick, Halfchick. Sawyer - PICTURE 97-110 (Z52.2).

Chicken Licken. Richardson - GREAT 81-91 (Z43.3); TALL..NURSERY TALES 55-61.

Chief Above and Chief Below. Tracy - LION 93-98 (A1150.2).

The Chief of the Gurensi. Courlander - KING'S 13-16 (A1375.2).

The Chief of the Water Snakes. Arnott -ANIMAL 23-30 (B491.1.1).

The Chief of the Well. Courlander - PIECE 15-19 (A2378.2.3.1).

Chief Spider's Problem. Nunn - AFRICAN 75-80 (J2183.1.3).

A Chiefess and a Riddle. Thompson - HAWAIIAN ..TRICKSTERS 54-65 (H548).

Chien Tang. Manning-Sanders - DRAGONS 20-24 (B11.12.7.1).

Chilbik and the Greedy Czar. Titiev - HOW 9-26 (G610Aj).

The Child and the Fig. Michael - PORTUGUESE 9-14 (N271B).

The Child Is Father to the Man. Shah - MULLAH 51 (J2212.5).

Child of the Sun. Withers - MAN 86-87 (F53.2).

Childe Rowland. Jacobs - ENGLISH 122-129 (F324.0.1); Steel - ENGLISH 193-202; Williams-Ellis - FAIRY..BRITISH 196-205.

The Children in the Wood. Jacobs - MORE 120-126 (S143.2).

The Children of Lir. Frost - LEGENDS 25-53 (D161.1).

The Children of Rain. Helfman - BUSHMEN 26-29 (A791.12).

Children of the Sun. Carpenter - SOUTH 115-121 (A541).

The Children on the Pillar. Manning-Sanders - BOOK..OGRES 44-52 (G552.1).

The Children Who Could Do Without Their Elders. Burton - MAGIC 73-74 (J151.1).

The Children Who Lived in a Tree House. Arnott - AFRICAN 140-149 (F556.1.2; K311.3E).

The Children's Sea. De Leeuw - INDONESIAN 117-126 (D197).

The Chili Plant. Alegría - THREE 59-63 (E632.0.5).

Chimpanzee's Story. Sherlock - IGUANA'S 53-67 (K1041.1.3).

Chin-Chin Kobakama. Hearn - JAPANESE 9-17 (Q321.3); Hearn - JAPANESE (Pauper) 5-12; Palmer - FAIRY 69-74; Wiggin - TALES 435-437.

Chin-Chin of the Long Nose. Wyndham - FOLK.. CHINA 54-60 (J2415.24).

A Chinese Cinderella. Hume - FAVORITE.. CHINA 15-22 (R221J).

The Chinese Red Riding Hoods. Chang - CHINESE 22-25 (K2011.0.1); Minard - WOMENFOLK 14-19.

Chinese Rival Storytellers. Withers - I SAW 128 (X909.6.1).

Chirola and the Black Old Man. Jagendorf - PRICELESS 40-46 (C12.5.9).

Chirry Chee. Sleigh - NORTH 130-138 (Q285.1.1).

The Choristers of Saint Gudule. Frost - LEGENDS 302-304 (K335.1.4).

The Christmas Bear. Sperry - HEN 25-34 (K1728); Sperry - SCANDINAVIAN 29-37.

The Christmas That Was Nearly Lost. Sawyer - THIS 119-138 (N816).

Chu Cuoi's Trip to the Moon. Robertson - FAIRY 25-35 (A751.8.5.2).

Chubbune. Hill - BADGER 66-74 (D2161.3.5).

Chucho, Who's Afraid? Brenner - BOY 113-120 (E423.1.8.2).

Chunk o' Meat. Chase - WICKED 233-231 (E235.4.3.1).

The Cinder-Maid. Jacobs - EUROPEAN 1-12 (R221Rb).

Cinderella. Association - TOLD..GREEN 113-121 (R221A); Baker - TALKING 25-32; Gag - TALES..GRIMM 101-120 (R221B); Galdone - CINDERELLA pb; Grimm - CINDERELLA (Svend) pb; Grimm - GRIMM'S (Grosset) 155-165 (R221B); Grimm - GRIMM'S (Scribner's) 64-72; Grimm - GRIMM'S (World) 52-59; Gruenberg - FAVORITE 281-286; Haviland - FAIRY 138-144; Holme - TALES 90-98; Hutchinson - CHIMNEY 137-149; Martignoni - ILLUSTRATED 232-236; Opie - CLASSIC 117-127; Perrault - CINDERELLA pb; Perrault - FAMOUS 125-160; Perrault - PERRAULT'S (Dodd) 58-70; Rackham - ARTHUR 223-232; Sheehan - FOLK 84-92.

Cinderella and the Glass Slipper. De La Mare - TALES 44-60 (R221A).

The Clever Soldier and the Singing Woman. Higonnet-Schnopper - TALES 45-48 (K112.2).

The Clever Squirrel. De Leeuw - INDONESIAN 36-39 (J1172.3; J1172.3.2).

The Clever Student and the Master of Black Arts. Pyle - WONDER 51-61 (D1711.0.1.1).

The Clever Tailor. Lang - GREEN 311-315 (K1111.0.1; K1755).

The Clever Thief. Ginsburg - LAZIES 28-32 (K301Af).

The Clever Thieves. Arbuthnot - ANTHOLOGY 285 (K365.4); Tashjian - THREE 32-35.

THE CLEVER TURTLE. Roche - pb (K581.1).

The Clever Wife. Ginsburg - KAHA 90-96 (H171.2; H388; H561.1; H681.1.1; H682.1.4.1; H685.2; J1545.4).

The Clever Wife. Kendall - SWEET 14-17 (H951.1).

Cleverer Than the Devil. Ure - RUMANIAN 57-61 (K171.1.1).

The Cliff of the Two Lovers. Picard - FRENCH 129-137 (A968.2.1).

The Cloak of Tiger Skin. Dolch - STORIES.. CHINA 43-47 (F611.3.2.1).

The Clockmaker and the Timekeeper. Lum - TALES 4 (J2499.10).

Clod's Comb. Kendall - SWEET 86-88 (J1795.3.3).

A Close Tongue Keeps a Safe Head. Cutt- HOGBOON 130-133 (F420.4.7.1).

The Cloud Horse. Carpenter - ELEPHANT'S 135-140 (B846.1; C331; G369.1.5).

The Clouds That Carried the News. Brockett - BURMESE 92-95 (N275.0.1).

The Clown and the Countryman. Aesop - AESOP'S (Watts) 101-102 (J2232).

THE CLOWN OF GOD. De Paola - pb (V92.0.1).

Clowns With Sad Faces. Nunn - AFRICAN 31-35 (K1041.0.2).

Coat o' Clay. Jacobs - MORE 82-88 (J163.2.2; J2470).

The Coat of a Thousand Feathers. Bang - MEN 47-53 (B652.2.1).

The Cobbler Astrologer and the Forty Thieves. Hardendorff - FROG'S 46-58 (N611.5).

The Cobbler's Deity. Spellman - BEAUTIFUL 79-81 (V128.5).

THE COBBLER'S REWARD. Reid - pb (B582.2Ab).

Cock and the Fox. Aesop - FABLES (Walck) 115-117 (K561.1.0.3; K721).

The Cock and His Loving Wives. Reed - TALKATIVE 15 (H1556.1.1).

The Cock and the Crested Hen. Wiggin - TALES 457-458 (J652.5).

The Cock and the Dragon. Green - CAVALCADE ..DRAGONS 157-160 (A2435.4.8.2).

The Cock and the Fox. Asbjørnsen - NORWEGIAN 135-136 (K562.1; K721).

The Cock and the Fox. Wilson - SCOTTISH 91-92 (K561.1).

The Cock and the Hen. Manning-Sanders - GLASS 83-85 (Z52.4.1).

The Cock and the Hen. Withers - I SAW 95-96 (Z43.2).

The Cock and the Jewel. Aesop - AESOP'S (Viking) 3-4 (J1061.1); Aesop - AESOP'S (Watts) 120.

The Cock and the Mouse and the Little Red Hen. Rockwell - THREE 17-32 (W111.6.1).

The Cock and the Pearl. Aesop - AESOP'S (Grosset) 73 (J1061.1); Aesop - FIVE 90; Jacobs - FABLES 5.

The Cock and the Sparrow Hawk. Sechrist - ONCE 25-27 (A2494.13.10.3.1).

The Cock and the Wind. Zajdler - POLISH 79 (A1122.3.1).

The Cock, the Cuckoo, and the Black-cock. Wiggin - TALES 339 (K51).

The Cock, the Dog, and the Fox. Rice - ONCE 58-64 (K579.8).

The Cock, the Mouse and the Little Red Hen. Arbuthnot - ANTHOLOGY 155-156 (W111.6.1); Arbuthnot - FAIRY 13-15; Hutchinson - CHIMNEY 79-88; Lefevre - COCK pb; Richardson - GREAT 92-103.

The Cockroach and the Mouse. Lowe - LITTLE 114-122 (Z32.3).

The Cockrow Stone. Manning-Sanders - PETER 21-23 (F809.5.1).

THE COCONUT THIEVES. Fournier - pb (K581.8).

The Coconut Tree. Gittins - TALES 72-75 (A2681.5.1).

Coffin Cash. Kendall - SWEET 108-112 (N534.9).

The Coffin That Moved Itself. Spicer -

THIRTEEN 65-72 (E231.6; E593.0.6).

The Colony of Cats. Lang - CRIMSON 219-228 (Q2.1.1Ca).

Colored Coats. Heady - WHEN 53-58 (A2411.1.1.1.2; A2411.1.7.1.2; A2413.1.1).

Columba and the Water-horse. Finlay - TATTER-COATS 70-77 (F420.1.3.3.1).

The Comb, the Flute and the Spinning Wheel. Manning-Sanders - BOOK..MERMAIDS 66-72 (F420.5.2.3).

The Coming of Asin. Courlander - RIDE 206-212 (T111.1.1.1).

The Coming of Day and Night. Johnson - HOW 55-58 (A1172.2; F912.2.8).

The Coming of Legends. Bruchac - TURKEY 15-16 (A1481.2.2).

The Coming of the Spaniards. Sechrist - ONCE 107-109 (A955.0.1.1).

The Coming of the Yams. Courlander - HAT 96-100 (A1423.1.1).

Compae Rabbit's Ride. Carter - GREEDY 41-45 (K1241).

Compair Lapin and Madame Carencro. Field - AMERICAN 154-156 (A2317.3.0.1).

Compair Taureau and Jean Molin. Field - AMERICAN 147-153 (B650.2).

The Companion. Asbjørnsen - NORWEGIAN 84-86 (E341.1A).

Conaleen and Donaleen. MacManus - WELL 21-30 (F344.1.3).

Conall Yellowclaw. Jacobs - CELTIC 38-53 (R153.3.3); Manning-Sanders - BOOK..GIANTS 79-84.

Concerning the Egas and Their Young. Fuja - FOURTEEN 116-119 (A2431.3.15).

Concerning the Leopard and the Hedgehog. Fuja - FOURTEEN 28-31 (A2433.3.24).

The Conjure Wives. Harper - GHOSTS 44-47 (D153.2); Haviland - NORTH 122-125; Hoke - SPOOKS 157-160; Sechrist - HEIGH-HO 9-12.

Connla and the Fairy Maiden. Arbuthnot - AN-THOLOGY 180 (F302.1.3); Arbuthnot - FAIRY 138-139; Jacobs - CELTIC 1-4.

Constantes and the Dragon. Haviland - FAVOR-ITE..GREECE 3-19 (G610Ai); Manning-Sanders - BOOK..DRAGONS 9-19; Manning-Sanders - CHOICE 235-245.

A Contest with Skillful Spirits. Thompson -

HAWAIIAN..TRICKSTERS 28-37 (E461.1.1).

The Contrary Wife. Courlander - RIDE 159-162 (T255.1; T255.2).

The Contrary Woman. Courlander - FIRE 35-40 (T255.2).

The Cook and the House Goblin. Manning-Sanders - BOOK..GHOSTS 30-37 (F451.5.1.6.4).

Cooking By Candle. Shah - MULLAH 27 (K231.14.1).

The Coomacka Tree. Sherlock - WEST 7-12 (A1423.0.1.1).

Coral Sea Contest. Cothran - MAGIC 38-44 (B263.10).

The Cormorant and the Fishes. Green - BIG 66-67 (K815.14).

Corvetto. Mincielli - OLD 64-72 (G610Af).

The Costly Feast. Jagendorf - NOODLEHEAD 105-110 (J1511.7).

Cottontail and the Sun. Curry - DOWN 48-50 (A727.4).

Cottontail Plays a Trick on Coyote. DeWit - TALKING 127-130 (K551.30).

Cottontail's Song. Curry - DOWN 104-110 (G555.1.3).

The Coucal's Voice. Heady - SAFIRI 27-30 (K11.1.1.2).

Cougar, Wildcat, and the Giant. Matson - LEGENDS 19-24 (A2378.4.15).

COULD ANYTHING BE WORSE. Hirsh - pb (Z49.16).

The Count and the Little Shepherd. Mehdevi - BUNGLING 7-16 (H659.29).

Count Crow and the Princess. Alegría - THREE 122-128 (H465).

The Count of Estremadura. Michael - PORTU-GUESE 146-152 (H465).

Count Roger and the Fata Morgana. Toor - GOLDEN 153-156 (Q113.3.1).

The Counting of the Crocodiles. Courlander - TIGER'S 87-89 (K579.2.2).

The Country Maid and Her Milk Can. Aesop - AESOP'S (Viking) 63-64 (J2061.2).

The Country Maid and Her Milk Pail. Aesop - AESOP'S (Golden) 53-55 (J2061.2); Gruenberg - FAVORITE 407-408.

The Country Mouse and the City Mouse. Aesop

AESOP'S (Random) 10-11 (J211.2); Aesop - AESOP'S (Viking) 37-39; Martignoni - ILLUSTRATED 159; Walker - NIGERIAN 49.

The Country of the Mice. Hume - FAVORITE.. CHINA 102-108 (K632).

The Country Swain. Mehdevi - BUNGLING 93-98 (J2461.2).

THE COURAGE OF KAZAN. Walker pb (K1951.1H).

The Courting of the Bat, the Spider and the Beetle. Burton - MAGIC 102-104 (T92.11.3).

Cousin! Cousin! Harris - FAVORITE 19-23 (K263); Harris - NIGHTS 214-222; Harris - COMPLETE 272-278.

The Cow and the Thread. Jagendorf - NOODLEHEAD 68-71 (J2083.7; J2087).

Cow Bu-cola. Manning-Sanders - BOOK..OGRES 75-79 (G530.2E).

Cow or Donkey. Walker - WATERMELON 55-57 (J2715.8).

The Cow-Tail Switch. Courlander - COW-TAIL 5-12 (H621.4).

The Cow That Cried. Brenner - BOY 100-105 (E423.1.8.2); Frost - LEGENDS 199-214.

The Cow That Never Went Dry. Spicer - THIRTEEN MONSTERS 59-65 (G274.1.1).

Coyote and Little Blue Fox. Robinson - COYOTE 41-52 (K553.1.0.5).

Coyote and Mole. Curry - DOWN 101-103 (J2131.2.2).

Coyote and the Acorns. Robinson - COYOTE 95-102 (J2724).

Coyote and the Alder Stump. Cothran - WITH 65-66 (K741.6).

The Coyote and the Bear. Cothran - WITH 44-48 (A2378.4.12.1; K1021).

The Coyote and the Bear. Dolch - PUEBLO 17-25 (K171.1).

The Coyote and the Blackbirds. Dolch - PUEBLO 79-88 (A2494.12.4.1; K711.5).

The Coyote and the Bobcat. Heady - SAGE 61-64 (A2213.2.1.1; A2378.4.14; A2378.6.2).

Coyote and the Brown Giant. Robinson - COYOTE 23-34 (G524.0.2).

Coyote and the Crying Song. Courlander - PEOPLE 82-85 (G555.1.2; K525.1.4).

The Coyote and the Evil Witches. Matson - LONGHOUSE 41-48 (A2441.1.15).

The Coyote and the Fox. Dolch - PUEBLO 105-117 (J1791.3; K1251); Gruenberg - FAVORITE 338-340.

Coyote and the Giant Lizard. Robinson - COYOTE 73-78 (B11.2.1.2.2).

Coyote and the Mice. Robinson - COYOTE 53-62 (K711.5).

Coyote and the Monster. Matson - LEGENDS 64-69 (A974.0.7; F912.2.9).

Coyote and the Rolling Rock. Brown - TEPEE 109-111 (C91.1).

Coyote and the Swallowing Monster. DeWit - TALKING 122-126 (F912.2.9).

The Coyote and the Two Dogs. Hardendorff - TRICKY 55-61 (J2351.1).

Coyote and the Witches. Matson - LEGENDS 28-31 (A1421.0.0.1).

Coyote Conquers the Iya. Jones - COYOTE 41-49 (F913.5).

Coyote Drowns the World. Baker - AT 8-15 (A1021.0.7; A1337.0.8).

Coyote Eyes. Heady - SAGE 42-45 (A2332.3.1.1; A2668; A2681.1.1; J2423.1).

Coyote Helps Decorate the Night. Courlander - PEOPLE 25-26 (A763.3).

Coyote in the Land of the Dead. Robinson - COYOTE 113-124 (F81.1.0.5).

Coyote Loses His Dinner. Jones - COYOTE 15-22 (K11.5; K826).

Coyote Rescues the Ring Girl. Jones - COYOTE 23-39 (R111.1.13.2).

Coyote Rings the Wrong Bell. Jagendorf - KING 187-189 (K1023.1.0.2).

Coyote Steals a Blanket. Robinson - COYOTE 9-22 (C91.1).

Coyote Steals the Summer. Jones - COYOTE 1-13 (A1151.1.1).

Coyote's Needle. Courlander - PEOPLE 143-144 (J1565.1.5).

Coyote's New Hairdo. Curry - DOWN 80-89 (J2449.1).

The Crab. Borski - GOOD 47 (A2231.1.3).

The Crab and the Crane. Babbitt - JATAKA 84-89 (K815.14; K953.3).

The Crab and the Fox. Aesop - AESOP'S (Watts) 160 (J512.1).

The Crab and the Monkey. Lang - CRIMSON 187-190 (K1161.6); Sakade - JAPANESE..FAVOR—ITES 94-96.

The Crab, the Crocodile and the Jackal. Turnbull - FAIRY..INDIA 27-32 (K607.3).

The Crackling Mountain. Buck - FAIRY 96-97 (K1014).

The Cradle That Rocked by Itself. Leach - THING 75-76 (F473.2.1.1).

Cradoc and the Lake Maidens. Sleigh - NORTH 216-223 (F420.6.1.5.1).

Crafty Crab. Cothran - MAGIC 73-74 (K11.2).

The Crafty Servant. Hardendorff - TRICKY 81-85 (K602.4).

Crafty Yasohachi and the Flea Medicine. Bang - MEN 7-9 (J1685).

Crafty Yasohachi Climbing to Heaven. Bang - MEN 2-4 (K474.1).

The Cranberry Feast. Cothran - MAGIC 8-12 (A1598.1).

The Crane and the Crab. Gaer - FABLES..INDIA 84-86 (K815.14; K953.3).

The Crane and the Fox. Bloch - UKRAINIAN 36-38 (J1662.2).

The Crane and the Heron. Daniels - FALCON 21-23 (W123.2); Ransome - OLD 331-334.

THE CRANE MAIDEN. Matsutani pb (B652.2.1).

The Crane, the Fish and the Crab. Williams-Ellis - ROUND 53-56 (K815.14; K953.3).

The Crane Wife. Pratt - MAGIC (B652.2.1).

The Crane Woos the Heron. Riordan - TALES..CENTRAL 144-145 (W123.2).

The Creaking Wheels. Aesop - AESOP'S (Grosset) 91 (J953.2(.

The Creation of Man (Indian). Frost - LEGENDS 161-164 (A1241.3).

The Creation of the Wolf. Maas - MOON 56-59 (A1833.4).

Creator Makes. Leach - HOW 41-43 (A1179.2.2; A1263.7; A1392.1; A1414.1.1.2).

Creeping Up On Himself. Shah - MULLAH 86 (J1936.2).

The Creetur with No Claws. Harris - FAVORITE 147-152 (K1039.1); Harris - COMPLETE 440-442.

The Creeturs Go to de Barbecue. Harris - COMPLETE 729-732 (K846.1).

The Crested Curassow. Sherlock - WEST 13-20 (Z39.1.0.3).

The Crib of Bo' Bossu. Sawyer - LONG 135-150 (D1622.2.1).

The Cricket and the Ant. Arbuthnot - FAIRY 232 (J711.1).

CRICKET BOY. Ziner pb (E423.10).

The Cricket Fight. Hume - FAVORITE..CHINA 33-38 (A2426.4.1).

The Crock of Gold. Downing - RUSSIAN 143-147 (K335.0.12.1).

THE CROCK OF GOLD. Jacobs pb (N531.1).

CROCODILE AND HEN . Lexau pb (K601.3).

The Crocodile and the Jackal. Asian - FOLK..FOUR 5-10 (K543.0.1; K607.2.2; K933).

The Crocodile's Cousin. Heady - SAFIRI 17-21 (K601.3).

The Crocodile's Daughter. Carpenter - SOUTH 18-26 (A968.2.4).

Crocodile's Share. Courlander - KANTCHIL'S 80-83 (K2349).

The Crooked Pine. Ginsburg - TWELVE 46-47 (K341.8.1; K1251).

Crookshanks. Zajdler - POLISH 28-32 (K254.1).

Crossing the River. Courlander - TERRAPIN'S 91-92 (J1919.2.1).

The Crow. Lang - YELLOW 104-106 (D758.1.1).

Crow and Hawk. Brown - TEPEE 148-150 (J391.2).

Crow and Pitcher. Aesop - Aesop FABLES (Walck) 99-100 (J101).

The Crow and the Flamingo. Green - ANIMAL 116 (B538.1.1; J429.2.1).

The Crow and the Fox. Green - BIG 195 (K334.1).

The Crow and the Grain of Corn. Siddiqui - TOONTOONY 124-129 (Z41.6.3).

The Crow and the Peacock. Hardendorff - JUST 37-39 (A2411.2.1.6; A2411.2.6.7.2).

The Crow and the Pitcher. Aesop - AESOP'S (Golden) 67-69 (J101); Aesop - AESOP'S (Grosset) 58-59; Aesop - AESOP'S (Viking) 19 Aesop - AESOP'S (Watts) 17; Aesop - FABLES 108; Aesop - FIVE 60; Arbuthnot - FAIRY 229; Kent - MORE 24-25.

The Crow and the Raven. Aesop - AESOP'S (Watts) 206 (J951.3).

The Crow and the Serpent. Korel – LISTEN 107–114 (K401.2.2).

The Crow and the Soap. Kelsey – MULLAH 75–78 (J2211.5).

The Crow and the Sparrow. Asia – FOLK 1 1–12 (Z41.2.2.1); Siddiqui – TOONTOONY 44–49; Spellman – BEAUTIFUL 12–14 (K354.1).

The Crow and the Sparrow's Eggs. Arnott – ANIMAL 174–178 (Z41.2.1).

The Crow and the Swan. Aesop – AESOP'S (Watts) 118 (W181.3).

The Crow and the Water Jug. Green – BIG 21 (J101); Rice – ONCE 46–51.

The Crow and the Whale. Gillham – BEYOND 51–67 (K335.0.4.5; K344.1.5; K1682; J2137.8).

The Crow in the Banyan Tree. Gaer – FABLE.. INDIA 34–36 (K401.2.2).

The Crow in the Rose-Apple Tree. Gaer –FABLE ..INDIA 156–157 (K334.1).

The Crow-Peri. Buck – FAIRY 29–34 (H1151.6.2.2).

The Crow, the Cuckoo and the Owl. Brockett – BURMESE 84–86 (A2491.2).

The Crows and the Owls. Korel – LISTEN 13–64 (B263.3).

Crow's Nest. Sawyer – PICTURE 25–36 (K401.2.2).

The Crow's Pearl. Vo-Dinh – TOAD 115–122 (D551.1C).

The Crowza Stones. Manning-Sanders – PETER 120–124 (A977.1.1).

The Cruel Crane Outwitted. Jacobs – INDIAN 57–61 (K815.14; K953.3).

The Cruel Giant. Sheppard-Jones – WELSH 85–88 (D672B).

The Cruel Uncle. Maher – BLIND 53–71 (S71.2).

A Crumb in His Beard. Hampden – HOUSE 49–55 (H465A).

The Crusty Old Badger. Bang – MEN 39–45 (D612.1.3).

The Crystal Coffin. Lang – GREEN 281–287 (F852.1.2).

The Cub's Triumph. Wiggin – TALES 429–431 (D615.1.1.1; K366.1.3.1).

The Cuckoo. Deutsch – MORE 69 (A2431.2.1.1).

The Cuckoo and the Eagle. Carey – BABA 17 (U119.5.1).

Cuckoo in the Hedge. Jagendorf – MERRY 19–24 (J1904.2).

The Cuckoo of Borrowdale. Colwell – ROUND 30–33 (J1904.2).

The Cuckoo's Reward. Barlow – LATIN 134–137 (A2411.2.6.10.1); Kouzel – CUCKOO'S pb.

The Cunning Cat and His Company. Aesop – AESOP'S (Golden) 74–75 (K815.13.2).

The Cunning Snake. Harris – NIGHTS 255–259 (K311.3C); Harris – COMPLETE 302–306.

Curiosity Punished. Borski – GOOD 61 (F809.10).

The Curious Wife. Masey – STORIES 46–49 (K1633.1).

Cut Down On Your Harness Intake. Shah – MULLAH 115 (J2412.4).

Cutta Cord-La. Harris – NIGHTS 236–240 (K311.3.1); Harris – COMPLETE 289–292.

Da Trang's Crabs. Schultz – VIETNAMESE 74–79 (A2171.2.4).

DANCE OF THE ANIMALS. Belpré pb (A2378.2.2.1); Belpré – TIGER 97–103.

The Dance of the Spirit Monster. Curtis – GIRL 21–30 (A1542.2.2).

Dance, Raven, Dance. Cothran – MAGIC 22–24 (K606.2).

THE DANCING GRANNY. Bryan pb (D2174.2).

The Dancing Kettle. Uchida – DANCE 3–12 (D1171.3.1).

The Dancing Palm Tree. Walker – DANCING 15–26 (A2600.1; K741.0.10).

The Dancing Princesses. Colwell – SECOND 85–96 (F1015.1.1); De La Mare – TALES 61–72.

The Dancing Stars. Withers ,MAN 99 (A761.0.1).

The Dancing Water, Singing Apple and Speaking Bird. Jacobs – EUROPEAN 51–65 (N455.4Aa).

Danger Has No Favorites. Shah – MULLAH 29 (J2632.1).

The Dappled Deer and the Intelligent Crow. Gaer – FABLES..INDIA 74–77 (K642.3).

Dapplegrim. Aulaire – EAST 188–201 (H321F); Manning-Sanders – BOOK..MAGICAL 70–83; Undset – TRUE 83–96; Wiggin – FAIRY 59–64.

The Dare. Leach - THING 37-39 (N384.2).

The Dark and Stormy Night. Withers - I SAW 35 (Z17.1).

Dark, Dark, Dark. Leach - THING 51 (Z13.1.4).

The Date Gatherers. Montgomerie - TWENTY-FIVE 22-23 (J2126.1).

Dates to Cairo. Wilson - GREEK 122-125 (N427).

Datu Omar and the Fairy. Robertson - FAIRY.. PHILIPPINES 53-62 (F302.4.2).

Daughter and Stepdaughter. Higonnet-Schnopper - TALES 109-117 (Q2.1.3B).

The Daughter of the Dragon King. Carpenter - TALES..CHINESE 72-80 (B11.12.7.1); Hoke - DRAGONS 43-50.

The Daughter of the Dwarf. Manning-Sanders - GIANNI 108-118 (N831.1.0.1).

The Daughter of the King Ron. Leodhas - HEATHER - 81-93 (B651.8).

David and Goliath. Adams - BOOK..GIANTS 35-40 (F531.6.12.6); De Regniers - GIANT 39-46.

Dawn's Heart. Helfman - BUSHMEN 36-39 (A781.1.1; A2441.1.4.1).

Day and Night: How They Came To Be. Field - ESKIMO 10-11 (A1172.4).

Day-Dreaming. Jacobs - EUROPEAN 110-114 (J2061.1.1).

The Day of the Scholars. MacManus - HIBERNIAN 224-232 (H607.2.1).

The Day the Sky Fell. Withers - I SAW 81-84 (Z43.3).

The Day Tuk Became a Hunter. DeWit - TALKING 174-177 (K547.15); Melzack - DAY 13-20.

The Dead Hand. Pugh - MORE..WELSH 95-105 (C17).

A Dead Man Who Talks. Simon - MORE 24-30 (J2311.1; J2311.4).

The Dead Man Who Was Alive. Brenner - BOY 96-99 (J2311.14).

A Dead Secret. Buck - FAIRY 218-220 (E451.11); Littledale - GHOSTS 73-78.

The Dead Warrior. Cunningham - TALKING 58-59 (E38.2).

Deaf—#2 Bedside Visit. Leach - NOODLES 87 (X111.9).

Deaf Men and Their Answers #1 Fence Post. Leach - NOODLES 86 (X111.10).

Death a Prisoner. Müller-Guggenbühl - SWISS 52-56 (K213E; K717.3).

Death and the Old Man. Courlander - TERRA-PIN'S 108-111 (J1051.1).

Death and the Soldier. Downing - RUSSIAN 81-99 (K213B); Riordan - TALES..CENTRAL 115-126.

The Death of Chanticleer. Wiggin - TALES 305-308 (Z32.2.3).

The Death of Koschei the Deathless. Buck - FAIRY 35-46 (B314C; H1199.12.4B).

The Death of the Hen. Grimm - HOUSEHOLD 12-13 (Z32.1; Z32.1.1.1).

The Death Watch. Downing - RUSSIAN 152-155 (H1411.4.4).

Death's Godchild. Alegría - THREE 52-55 (D1724).

The Debt. Courlander - TIGER'S 78-79 (J1179.26).

The Deceitful Heron. Brockett - BURMESE 195-198 (K815.14; K953.3).

The Deceitful Leopard. Heady - SAFIRI (K401.1).

The Decision. De Leeuw - INDONESIAN 65-67 (J2326.2.1).

The Dedication of the Cemetery. Simon - MORE 50-53 (J1703.3).

The Deeds and Prophecies of Old Man. Brown - TEPEE 59-62 (A1335.20).

The Deer and Its Friends. Tooze - WONDERFUL 96-99 (K642.3.1).

The Deer and the Jaguar Share a House. Cour-lander - RIDE 198-201 (K1715.3.2).

The Deer and the Woodcutter. Kim - STORY 86-98 (F302.4.2.0.3).

The Deer of Five Colors. Uchida - MAGIC 65-71 (W154.2.2.1).

The Deer, the Rabbit, and the Toad. Kim - STORY 31-33 (B841.1.6).

The Deerhurst Worm. Spicer - THIRTEEN 32-40 (B11.12.4.1).

The Deluded Dragon. Hoke - DRAGONS 149-154 (G501C); Manning-Sanders - RED 10-15.

Demeter and Persephone. Frost - LEGEND 114-119 (A1150.2).

Demon Loango. Johnson - HOW 67-74 (G303.12.5.9).

The Demon Mason. Manning-Sanders - PETER

169-177 (E765.1.1.1).

The Demon With the Matted Hair. Jacobs - INDI-AN 235-242 (K741.3).

The Demon's Daughter. Manning-Sanders - BOOK ..DEVILS 15-29 (G530.2Bf).

The Dervish and the Wolf. Green - BIG 171 (U125).

The Desert Island. Ish-Kishor - WISE 32-38 (J711.3).

The Deserted Children. Curtis - GIRL 45-51 (S366.1).

The Deserted Mine. Sawyer - WAY 285-294 (F456.4.2).

The Destiny of Princess Tien Dung. Graham - BEGGAR 79-89 (T91.6.4.4).

The Devil and His Three Golden Hairs. Grimm - JUNIPER TREE 1 80-93 (H1273.2A).

The Devil and the Baliff. Asbjørnsen - NORWE-GIAN 168-169 (M215).

The Devil and the Farmer's Wife. Chase - WICKED 95-96 (T251.1.1.3).

The Devil and the Pit. Durham - TIT 63-66 (K1917.3J).

The Devil and the Railroad. Brenner - BOY 79-83 (G303.16.19.4.0.1).

The Devil and the Tailor. Williams-Ellis - FAIRY ..BRITISH 288-291 (M211.10).

Devil in Church. Courlander - TERRAPIN'S 95-97 (K1987.1).

The Devil in the Wheat. Jagendorf - MERRY 119-123 (J1785.1).

The Devil's Apprentice. Spicer - THIRTEEN 7-18 (D1711.0.1.1).

The Devil's Bride. Arbuthnot - ANTHOLOGY 289-290 (C12.2.2); Durham - TIT 70-74.

The Devil's Bridge. Colwell - ROUND 23-26 (S241.1); Scribner - DEVIL'S pb (M211.2.1.1); Sheppard-Jones - WELSH 173-177.

The Devil's Field: The Carpenter's Drac. Holman - ONCE 19-37 (M211.12).

The Devil's Gifts. Fillmore - SHEPHERD'S 172-184 (D861.1F).

The Devil's Granny. Spicer - THIRTEEN 102-110 (J2415.24).

The Devil's Little Brother-in-Law. Frost - LEGENDS 127-141 (K217).

The Devil's Partnership. Durham - TIT 34-36 (K171.1).

Dewi and the Devil. Pugh - MORE..WELSH 77-87 (Q565Ab).

Dewi Dal. Sheppard-Jones - WELSH 106-108 (F381+).

The Diamond Merchant and the Piece of Glass. Brockett - BURMESE 156-162 (J1521.6.1).

Diamonds and Toads. Opie - CLASSIC 98-102 (Q2.1.1Aa); Perrault - FAMOUS 117-126.

Dick Whittington. De La Mare - TALES 33-43 (N411.1A); Lines - DICK pb; Martignoni - ILLUSTRATED 223-228; Rackham - ARTHUR 30-40.

Dick Whittington and His Cat. Brown - DICK pb (N411.1A); Frost - LEGENDS 1-13; Haviland - FAVORITE..ENGLISH 56-75; Reeves - ENGLISH 222-234; Steel - ENGLISH 169-178.

Did the Tailor Have a Nightmare? Serwer - LET'S 59-67 (J2071.2).

Digit the Midget. Davis - LION'S 53-61 (F535.1.1De); Green - FOLK..AFRICA 83-95.

A Dinar For a Donkey. Kelsey - MULLAH 54-60 (K182.0.1).

Dinewan and Goomblegubbon. Sleigh - NORTH 13-18 (A2377.1; A2486.5).

Dinewan the Emu and Gommlegubbon the Turkey. Parker - AUSTRALIAN 15-19 (A2377.1; A2486.5).

Dinner for the Monk. Courlander - TIGER'S 111-114 (J2183.1.2.1).

The Dinner That Cooked Itself. Birch - CHINESE 37-42 (C35.2; N831.1).

Dinner with the Tota. Courlander - FIRE 65-72 (J2132.5.1; K688.2; Z18.1).

The Dirty Bride. Curtis - GIRL 73-80 (K1816.0.2.2).

Dirty Hands. Heady - SAFIRI 40-45 (J1565.1.2).

The Disappearance of Dan Gruffydd's Daughter. Sheppard-Jones - WELSH 119-122 (F379.5a).

The Disappearance of Rhys. Sheppard-Jones - WELSH 159-163 (F379.5a).

The Disappearing Mill. Holding - KING'S 109-116 (K403).

The Disappointed Bear. Wiggin - TALES 43-44 (K553.1.0.3).

The Discontented Fish. Arnott - AFRICAN 156-159 (J513.3).

The Discontented Grass Plant. Cunningham – TALKING 46-57 (Z42.4).

The Discontented Mason. Chang – CHINESE 73 (Z42.0.2).

Discovery of Salt. Wyndham – TALES 9-13 (A978.5).

The Discreet Hans. Grimm – GRIMM'S (Scribner's) 95-98 (J2461.2); Wiggin – TALES 90-92 (J2461.1F).

A Dish of Laban. Hampden – GYPSIES' 111-112 (H331.10.1).

The Disobedient Eels. Cimino – DISOBEDIENT #1 (J1881.2.3.1).

The Disobedient Giant. Barlow – LATIN 97-103 (A969.1.1; A1145.1).

The Disowned Student. Kim – STORY 166-171 (D315.1.1).

THE DIVERTING ADVENTURES OF TOM THUMB. Wilkinson pb (F535.1.1).

Dividing the Axe. Ginsburg – TWELVE 62-63 (J2469.3).

Division of Labor. Shah – MULLAH 112 (J2137.8).

The Do-all Ax. Courlander – TERRAPIN'S 80-83 (D1651.15).

Do It Yourself. Leach – NOODLES 19 (X1731.2.1).

Do Not Disturb the Camels. Shah – MULLAH 105 (J2311.6).

Do You Know? Jagendorf – NOODLEHEAD 37-39 (J1909.3; J1936).

Doctor and Detective, Too. Hatch – THIRTEEN 94-106 (N611.1).

Doctor Know-all. Gag – TALES 77-84 (N611.1; N612.2; N688); Grimm – GRIMM'S (Follett) 52-54; Wiggin – TALES 83-85.

The Doctor's Servant. Heady – SAFIRI 36-39 (A2458.1).

The Doe and the Lionness. Green – BIG 71 (J281.1).

Dog and Dog's Reflection. Aesop – FABLES (Walck) 36-37 (J1791.4).

The Dog and His Shadow. Aesop – AESOP'S (Random) 58-60 (J1791.4); Aesop – FIVE 18.

The Dog and the Bone. Rockwell – THREE 100-101 (J1791.4).

The Dog and the Cock. Colwell – YOUNGEST 82-84 (K579.8).

The Dog and the Cook. Aesop – AESOP'S (Watts) 45 (J874).

The Dog and the Fox. Aesop – AESOP'S (Watts) 187 (W121.2.4).

The Dog and the Hides. Aesop – AESOP'S (Watts) 195 (J1791.3.2).

The Dog and the Horse. Carey – BABA 20 (W181.1.2).

The Dog and the Karbau. Courlander – KANTCHIL'S 105-108 (J132.1).

The Dog and the Maiden. Manning-Sanders – RED 154-158 (D735.1H)

The Dog and the Ox. Aesop – FIVE 46 (W156).

The Dog and the Shadow. Aesop – AESOP'S (Golden) 37-40 (J1791.4); Aesop – AESOP'S (Grosset) 176; Aesop – AESOP'S (Viking) 46; Aesop – AESOP'S (Watts) 75; Arbuthnot – FAIRY 228; Jacobs – FABLES 6; Martignoni – ILLUSTRATED 158.

The Dog and the Sow. Aesop – AESOP'S (Watts) 5 (J243.1).

The Dog and the Sparrow. De La Mare – ANIMAL 160-168 (N261); Grimm – HOUSEHOLD 244-247.

The Dog and the Wolf. Aesop – AESOP'S (Grosset) 22-24 (L451.3); Aesop – AESOP'S (Viking) 9-10; Jacobs – FABLES 55.

The Dog Chasing a Wolf. Aesop – AESOP'S (Watts) 219 (J953.5).

Dog Couldn't Be Cured. Williams-Ellis – ROUND 181-185 (A2455.6).

The Dog in the Manger. Aesop – AESOP'S (Golden) 43-45 (W156); Aesop – AESOP'S (Grosset) 1; Aesop – AESOP'S (Random) 3; Aesop – AESOP'S (Viking) 20; Aesop – AESOP'S (Watts) 60; Arbuthnot – FAIRY 226; Jacobs – FABLES 79.

The Dog Invited to Supper. Aesop – AESOP'S (Grosset) 172-173 (J874); Aesop – AESOP'S (Viking) 68-70.

Dog Luck. Carpenter – WONDER..DOGS 15-24 (A2513.1.0.1).

A Dog Named Fireball. Kim – STORY 23-30 (A737.1.1).

The Dog That Fought a Duel. Carpenter – WONDER..DOGS 119-127 (B301.2.1).

The Dog That Learned to Read. Carpenter – WONDER..DOGS 204-212.

The Dog, the Cock and the Fox. Aesop – AESOP'S (Watts) 29 (K579.8).

Dog's Hoop. Leach - HOW 62 (A2378.1.7.1).

The Dog's Nose Is Cold. Sherlock - WEST 34-38 (A2335.2.6.1).

The Doko. Asia - FOLK..FOUR 42-46 (J121.3).

The Doll. Manning-Sanders - GIANNI 67-75 (J2415.10).

Doll in the Grass. Asbjørnsen - EAST (Row) 28-30 (B641Be); Aulaire - EAST 222-227; Hutchinson - CANDLELIGHT 11-15; Wiggin - FAIRY 51-53.

Dollar a Minute. Harris - FAVORITE 229-232 (K842.0.7); Harris - COMPLETE 74-77; Harris - UNCLE 113-117.

The Dolphins of Celebes. Courlander - KANT-CHIL'S 42-44 (A2135.3.1; A2275.5.4.1).

The Dolphins, the Whales and the Sprat. Aesop - AESOP'S (Watts) 26 (J411.6).

Don Demonio's Mother-in-law. Boggs - THREE 61-73 (C12.4.1).

Don Fernan and the Orange Princess. Gunterman - CASTLES 132-150 (D721.5A).

Donal from Donegal. MacManus - BOLD 64-82 (R111.1.3Cb).

Donal O'Ciaran from Connaught. MacManus - BOLD 120-137 (K1951.1K).

Donal O'Donnel's Standing Army. Macmanus - HIBERNIAN 240-250 (D861.1G).

The Donkey. De La Mare - ANIMAL 203-211 (B641.4).

Donkey and Scholars. Jagendorf - NOODLEHEAD 175-179 (K491.0.1; K551.11).

The Donkey and the Boar. Green - BIG 146-147 (J411.1).

The Donkey Cabbage. Grimm - GRIMM'S (Follett) 55-65 (D551.1A); Lang - FIFTY 46-52; Lang - YELLOW 52-60.

Donkey Carrying Salt. Aesop - FABLES (Walck) 92-94 (J1612).

Donkey, Cock, and Lion. Aesop - FABLES (Walck) 120 (J952.2).

The Donkey Driver. Courlander - PIECE 81-83 (K134.10).

The Donkey Egg. Kelsey - HODJA 151-156 (J1772.1).

The Donkey Goes to Market. Kelsey - HODJA 63-70 (J2087).

The Donkey In the Lion-Skin. Aesop - FABLES (Walck) 24-28 (J951.1); Hardendorff - TRICKY 109-110.

The Donkey Lettuce. Manning-Sanders - BOOK.. WITCHES 72-82 (D551.1A).

Donkey Mind Your Mother! Kelsey - MULLAH 1-7 (K403.1).

The Donkey of Abdera. Jagendorf - NOODLE-HEAD 40-41 (J1891.4).

THE DONKEY PRINCE. Craig pb (B641.4).

The DONKEY RIDE. Showalter pb (J1041.2).

Donkey Skin. Lang - ROSE 1-14 (R221Dh); Perrault - PERRAULT'S (Dodd) 92-99.

The Donkey, the Ox and the Farmer. Green - BIG 40-42 (K1633.1).

The Donkey, the Table and the Stick. Reeves - ENGLISH 196-209 (D861.1C).

A Donkey Transformed. Walker - WATERMELON 62-64 (K403.1).

The Donkey Which Made Gold. Hampden - HOUSE 64-71 (D861.1C).

The Donkey Who Hit His Mother. Skurzynski - TWO 17-27 (K403.1).

The Donkey Who Sinned. Courlander - FIRE 15-18 (U11.1.1.1).

The Donkey Who Was an Ass. Korel - LISTEN 31-36 (K402.3.2.1).

Donkeys All. Jagendorf - NOODLEHEAD 63-67 (J2031.2).

The Donkeys Ask for Justice. Courlander - KING'S 74-77 (A2342.3; A2513.7).

Donkeys! Dogs! Cats! Rats! Hardendorff - TRICKY 87-91 (A2281.0.2).

Donkey's Eggs. Hardendorff - TRICKY 119-120 (J1772.1); Withers - WORLD 18.

The Donkey's Shadow. Aesop - FABLES (Walck) 64 (J1169.7).

The Donkey's Tail. Kelsey - MULLAH 83-88 (J1141.3).

Don't Beat Your Children Before They're Born. Skurzynski - TWO (J2061.1).

Don't Beat Your Dog. Carpenter - WONDER.. DOGS 89-94 (A1415.2.4).

DON'T COUNT YOUR CHICKS. D'Aulaire pb (J2061.1.2).

Don't Ever Kick a Ghost. Leach - THING 114 (E599.15).

Don't Foul the Well—You May Need Its Waters. Carey - BABA 99-102 (Q2.1.3B).

Don't Make a Bargain With a Fox. Jagendorf - KING 15-18 (J1241.6).

Don't Marry Two Wives. Jagendorf - NOODLE-HEAD 24-29 (J2112.2).

Don't Shake Hands With Everybody. Courlander - COW-TAIL 129-131 (A2375.2.9).

Don't Tease the Tengu! Pratt - MAGIC (D1376.1.3.3).

Don't Throw Stones from Not Yours to Yours. Courlander - RIDE 99-100 (H599.10).

Double Arend of Meeden. De Leeuw - LEGENDS ..HOLLAND 33-37 (F624.1).

The Double Knights. McNeil - DOUBLE 7-15 (R111.1.3Aa).

Double or Quits. Sturton - ZOMO 77-88 (K710.1.1; K771).

The Dove and the Ant. Aesop - AESOP'S (Viking) 79 (B362.2).

The Dove Maiden. Wilson - GREEK 76-87 (K1861.1B).

Down the Well. Duvoisin - THREE 67-88 (K1931.2I).

A Dozen At a Blow - Jacobs - EUROPEAN 81-89 (K1951.1A).

A Dozen Is Thirteen. Cothran - WITH 18-22 (V429.4).

The Drac: The Invisible Demon. Holman - DRAC 1-17 (F235.4.1).

The Dragon. Caswell - SHADOWS 88-92 (F911.6.2).

The Dragon and His Doctor. Manton - FLYING 24-29 (B11.6.1.5; V229.29).

The Dragon and His Grandmother. Fenner - GIANTS 155-161 (M211.7.1); Gag - TALES 225-234; Green - CAVALCADE..DRAGONS 120-124; Lang - FIFTY 53-56; Lang - YELLOW 48-51; Manning-Sanders - DRAGONS 79-86.

The Dragon and the Peasant. Green - CAVAL-CADE ..DRAGONS 23-25 (J1172.3).

The Dragon and the Stepmother. Hoke - DRAG-ONS 22-28 (S12.1C); Manning-Sanders RED 146-153.

The Dragon King and the Lost Fish-Hook. Williams-Ellis - ROUND 16-26 (U136.0.1).

The Dragon of Macedon. Green - CAVALCADE.. DRAGONS 16-20 (B11.6.1.2).

The Dragon of Shervage Wood. Colwell - ROUND 110-113 (J1761.8).

The Dragon of the North. Green - CAVALCADE.. DRAGONS 125-132 (G405.1.2); Hoke - DRAGONS 179-191; Lang - YELLOW 12-26.

The Dragon of the Well. Manning-Sanders - DRAGONS 123-128 (F813.8.3).

Dragons? Vo-Dinh - TOAD 137-141 (H504.3).

The Dragon's Egg. Green - CAVALCADE.. DRAGONS 26-27 (B11.6.1.1).

The Dragon's Grandmother. Hoke - DRAGONS 192-198 (M211.7.1).

The Dragons of Peking. Arnott - ANIMAL 122-128 (B11.7.1).

The Dragon's Revenge. Pratt - MAGIC (B605.1).

The Dragon's Strength. Fillmore - LAUGHING 141-160 (K956).

The Dragon's Tears. Sakade - JAPANESE 19-23 (B11.6.1.4).

Drak, the Fairy. Palmer - FAIRY 23-30 (F361.1.2.2).

Drakesbill and His Friends. Wiggin - FAIRY 304-312 (Z52.1).

Drakestail. Haviland - FAVORITE..FRENCH 76-91 (Z52.1); Hutchinson - FIRESIDE 51-64; Lang FIFTY 57-62; Lang - RED 208-216; Manning-Sanders - BOOK..BEASTS 226-234; Martignoni - ILLUSTRATED 83-88; Wahl - DRAKESTAIL pb.

The Draper Who Swallowed a Fly. Novak - FAIRY 119-122 (Z49.19.1).

Drat the Wind! Withers - I SEE 22-23 (Z41.11).

A Dreadful Boar. Wiggin - TALES 412-414 (K1161.3).

A Dream and a Story. Harris - COMPLETE 185-189 (K522.9.1); Harris - NIGHTS 95-99.

A Dream of the Sphinx. Carpenter - AFRICAN 63-70 (C822; H761).

The Dreamer. Association - CASTLES 69-77 (N531.1).

The Dreamer. Owen - CASTLE 147-154 (D1720.1.5).

Dreams. Leach - NOODLES 17 (F1068.5.1; J1936.1).

Dreams. Leach - NOODLES 17-18 (K444).

The Drop of Honey. Brockett - BURMESE 150-152 (N381).

East of the Sun and North of the Earth. Kaplan – FAIRY 142-161 (H1385.3Fbc).

Easy Bread. Ginsburg – LAZIES 12-17 (K566.1; K606.2; Z49.5.2).

Eat and Like It. Jagendorf – PRICELESS 76-80 (J606.2).

Eat My Fine Coat! Walker – WATERMELONS 51-54 (J1561.3).

Eating Matter and Reading Matter. Shah – MULLAH 35 (J2562).

The Education of a Goat. Thoby-Marcelin – SINGING 15-16 (A2581.1).

Ee-aw! Ee-aw! Haviland – FAVORITE..DENMARK 15-26 (D1413.17).

The Eel and the Porgy. Vo-Dinh – TOAD 45-49 (A2332.3.2.1; A2332.5.9).

The Egg. Lin – MILKY 64-71 (B649.1).

The Egg of Fortune. Spicer – LONG..SERBIA 92-97 (J2061.1.2).

THE EGGS. Aliki pb (J1191.2).

Ei-Nun-Mita or No-So-What. Bowman – TALES.. TUPA 105-115 (N813C).

Eight Donkeys. Ginsburg – TWELVE 33-35 (J2031.2).

The Eight-headed Dragon. Uchida – DANCING 27-33 (K929.1.1).

The Eight Immortals. Wyndham – FOLK..CHINA 37-43 (A501.2).

Eighteen Rabbits. Hampden – GYPSY 119-125 (H1112.0.1).

Einion and the Fair Family. Sheppard-Jones – WELSH 48-53 (F302.1.5).

Ekun and Opolo Go Looking for Wives. Courlander – OLODE 19-23 (K499.8+).

The Elders of Chelm and Genendel's Key. Singer – WHEN 45-51 (J1703.4).

Elephant and Frog Go Courting. Bryan – OX 15-21 (K1241).

Elephant and Giraffe Go Farming. Arnott – ANIMAL 241-252 (K364.1).

The Elephant and the Carpenters. Gaer – FABLES..INDIA 148-149 (B381.3).

The Elephant and the Cock. Fuja – FOURTEEN 120-125 (K1715.4.2).

The Elephant and the Gnat. Gaer – FABLES.. INDIA 41-43 (L315.6.1).

The Elephant and the Tortoise. Walker – NIGERIAN 61-63 (K815.20).

The Elephant at Court. Wyndham – TALES.. RUSSIA 73-75 (W197.1).

The Elephant Girly-Face. Babbitt – JATAKA 52-57 (J451.5).

The Elephant Hunters. Courlander – KING'S 68-70 (J1171.5).

The Elephant's Bathtub. Carpenter – ELEPHANTS 13-21 (H1023.6.2).

The Elephant's Lip. Carpenter – ELEPHANT'S 176-187 (G276.3).

The Elephant's Tail. Courlander – HAT 80-85 (D672J).

Eleven More Licks. Brown – WORLD 67-71 (K629.2.5); Harris Favorite 66-70; Harris – COMPLETE 25-28; Harris – UNCLE 36-41.

Elidorous in Fairyland. Sheppard-Jones – WELSH 89-92 (F378.0.1.1).

Ellert's Field and Brammert's Heap. Spicer – THIRTEEN MONSTERS 19-31 (A963.14).

The Elves. Grimm – HOUSEHOLD 171-172 (F346.1), 173 (F372.2.2.), 174 (F321.1.1).

The Elves and the Shoemaker. Arbuthnot – ANTHOLOGY 199 (F346.1); Arbuthnot – FAIRY 35-36; Association TOLD..GREEN 47-51; Grimm – ELVES (Brandt) pb; Grimm – ELVES (Hewitt) pb; Grimm – GRIMM'S (Follett) 66-69; Grimm – GRIMM'S (Grosset) 178-180; Grimm – GRIMM'S (World) 324-325; Haviland – FAVORITE ..GERMANY 13-20; Haviland – FAIRY 118-121; Hutchinson – CHIMNEY 119-124; Martignoni – ILLUSTRATED 203-204; Shub – ABOUT 31-32; Wiggin – TALES 170-171.

The Elves Ask a Servant Girl to Be Godmother. Shub – ABOUT 33 (F372.2).

The Emerald-Crested Phoenix. Ekram – TURKISH 32-34 (K1931.2E).

The Emerald Lizard. Courlander – RIDE 250-252 (E121.4.3); Newman – FOLK..LATIN 107-110.

Emma of Haarlem. De Leeuw – LEGENDS..HOLLAND 71-74 (J1545.4).

The Emperor's Magic Bow. Robertson – FAIRY.. VIETNAM 66-74 (A132.15.1).

The Emperor's New Clothes. Gruenberg – FAVORITE 317-321 (K445); Haviland – FAIRY (Briggs) 174-179; Lang – YELLOW 27-32; Martignoni – ILLUSTRATED 229-232; Rackham – ARTHUR 240-245.

The Emperor's Questions. De Leeuw – LEGENDS ..HOLLAND 15-20 (H561.2; H681.4.1;

H682.1.7).

The Enchanted Black Cat. Carpenter – WONDER 222–234 (R2210).

The Enchanted Castle. Kavcic – GOLDEN 78–86 (D735.1C).

The Enchanted Castle in the Sea. Eells – TALES ..SPAIN 57–68 (K1861.1C).

The Enchanted Cave. Bonnet – FOLK..CHINA 122–126 (D2011.1.3).

The Enchanted Cow. Hoke – WITCHES 37–44 (G263.1.3.1).

The Enchanted Cow. Spicer. LONG..SERBIA 47–69 (Q2.1.1Eb; R221Bc).

The Enchanted Fisherman. Colwell – ROUND 19–22 (F373.2).

The Enchanted Goat. Simon – MORE 80–101 (J1703.5).

The Enchanted Hedgehog. Borski – GOOD 13–17 (B641.5).

The Enchanted Knife. Lang – VIOLET 129–132 (G530.2Fb).

The Enchanted Mule. Haviland – FAVORITE.. SPAIN 70–87 (U119.2.1).

The Enchanted Palace. Barlow – LATIN 9–17 (C423.3.1).

The Enchanted Peafowl. Fillmore – LAUGHING 107–138 (H1385.3Ja).

The Enchanted Pig. Lang – RED 98–113 (H1385.4I).

The Enchanted Prince. Manning-Sanders – CHOICE 183–190 (H1411.4.5); Manning-Sanders – PRINCES 49–56.

The Enchanted Princess. Colwell – ROUND 34 (D732).

The Enchanted Tortoise. Carpenter – AFRICAN 205–223 (B641E).

The Enchanted Watch. Lang – GREEN 47–52 (D882.1Ba).

The Enchanted Winejug. Manning-Sanders – CHARMS 21–33 (D882.1A).

The Enchanted Wolf. Spicer – MONSTERS 101–108 (C420.2.1).

The End of Brer B'ar. Harris – FAVORITE 278–281 (K1023.6); Harris – UNCLE 137–143.

The End of Mr. Bear. Harris – COMPLETE 90–94 (K1023.6).

The End of Saynday. Marriott – WINTER 93 (A779.4).

The End of the World. Bowman – TALES..TUPA 239–241 (Z43.3.3).

The End of the World. Heady – TALES 81–85 (A2433.2.2.1).

The Enormous Genie. Tashjian – THREE 22–31 (D861.1G).

The Envious Buffalo. Gaer – FABLES..INDIA 132–133 (L457).

The Envious Neighbor. Buck – FAIRY 281–285 (D1571.1); Lang – VIOLET 121–128.

The Envious Stepmother. Zajdler – POLISH 109–118 (Q2.1.3Aa).

Epaminondas. Bryant – EPAMINONDAS pb (J2461); Merriam – EPAMINONDAS pb.

Ergosa-Batyr. Masey – STORIES 109–112 (K1951.1F).

Esben and the Little White Fox. Owen – CASTLE 27–28 (B641Dc).

Esben and the Witch. Manning-Sanders – CHOICE 128–143 (G610Ah); Manning-Sanders – BOOK.. WITCHES 46–61.

Esben Ashblower. Hatch – MORE DANISH 49–57 (H507.1.0.1).

The Escape of the Animals. Pridham – GIFT 107–115 (K1161.2.1; K1715.3).

The Escaped Jackdaw. Aesop – AESOP'S (Watts) 117 (N255.5).

The Eternal Wanderer of the Pampas. Jagendorf – KING 18–23 (E513); Littledale – GHOSTS 39–44.

Evan's Problem. Pugh – TALES 129–133 (J1795.3.2).

EVEN THE DEVIL IS AFRAID OF A SHREW. Stalder pb (T251.1.1.3).

The Everlasting House. Martin – NINE 55–60; (A2109.3); Martin – RAVEN 83–88.

Every Little Helps. Shah – MULLAH 51 (J1874).

Everything Happens to Pablo. Newman – FOLK.. LATIN 95–99 (J1852.1.4).

Evil Rocks and the Evil Spirit of Peru. Jagendorf – KING 238–241 (D1553.3).

The Evil Weed: The Lady of the Moon. Holman – DRAC 57–71 (E425.1.8).

Exchange. Riordan – TALES..CENTRAL 181–183 (J2081.1).

The False Schoolmaster. Skurzynski – TWO 29–39 (K1958.1).

The Family Servants. Wiggin – TALES 68 (Z54).

The Fanged Raja. Asia – FOLK..FOUR 34–41 (D112.2.1.3).

The Farm Cat and the Mice. Montgomerie – MERRY 42–46 (K815.16.1).

The Farmer and Fortune. Aesop – AESOP'S (Watts) 48 (N111.4.3).

The Farmer and His Dogs. Aesop – AESOP'S (Grosset) 223 (J2211.3); Aesop – AESOP'S (Watts) 199.

The Farmer and His Sons. Aesop – AESOP'S (Grosset) 120–121 (H588.7); Aesop – AESOP'S (Watts) 45; Aesop – FABLES (Walck) 108–109.

The Farmer and the Badger. Ozaki – JAPANESE 43–53 (G61.3; J2171.1.3; K1014; K2345.0.1).

The Farmer and the Cheeses. Colwell – ROUND 85–86 (J1881.1.1).

The Farmer and the Demon. Sechrist – ONCE 119–125 (M211.11).

The Farmer and the Fairy Cow. Sheppard-Jones – WELSH 115–118 (B184.2.2.2.1).

The Farmer and the Fox. Aesop – AESOP'S (Watts) 117 (J2101.1).

The Farmer and the Hoe. Hardendorff – TRICKY 51–53 (J2356.1).

The Farmer and the Money-Lender. Jacobs – INDIAN 184–187 (J2074); Wiggin – TALES 385–387.

The Farmer and the Snake. Lester – KNEE 24–26 (X1321.4.11.2).

The Farmer and the Stork. Aesop – AESOP'S (Grosset) 151–152 (J451.2); Aesop – AESOP'S (Watts) 123.

The Farmer and the Troll. Wiggin – TALES 322 (K171.1).

The Farmer and the Viper. Aesop – AESOP'S (Watts) 126 (X1321.4.11).

The Farmer of Babbia. Courlander – FIRE 112–118 (J2241.1.1).

The Farmer, the Bear and the Fox – Bloch – UKRAINIAN 64–67 (K1725.1.1).

The Farmer, the Buffalo and the Tiger. Robertson – FAIRY..VIET-NAM 76–80 (K341.8.1.0.1).

Farmer Weathersky. Manning-Sanders – BOOK.. WIZARDS 47–57 (D1711.0.1); Undset – TRUE 97–107.

Farmer Zia, the Hard-Luck Man. Dorliae – ANIMALS 26–31 (J266.1.0.1).

The Farmer's Clever Daughter. McNeil – DOUBLE (H561.1.1; H583.2.2; H583.2.3.1; H583.3; H682.1.1; H697.1; H1052; H1053; H1054.1; J1191.1; J1545.4).

The Farmer's Old Horse. Siddiqui – TOONTOONY 65–69 (J2132.5.3).

The Farmer's Secret. Jagendorf – NOODLEHEAD 100–101 (J1909.9).

Farmers Three. Bowman – TALES..TUPA 247–248 (K171.2).

The Farmer's Wife and the Tiger. Asia – FOLK 34–39 (K1715.2); Colwell – MAGIC 79–82.

The Farmyard. Block – UKRAINIAN 73–76 (Z49.16).

The Farthing Rushlight. Aesop – AESOP'S (Grosset) 136 (L475).

THE FAST SOONER HOUND. Bontemps pb (X1215.7.1).

THE FAT CAT. Kent pb (Z33.2).

The Fat Man. Cimino – DISOBEDIENT #2 (J1411).

The Fatal Marriage. Aesop – AESOP'S (Viking) 24–25 (B363.1).

Fate and the Faggot Gatherer. Jewett – WHICH 95–103 (N115).

The Fate of Mr. Jack Sparrow. Brown – WORLD 54–57 (K911.5.1); Harris – COMPLETE 61–65; Harris – UNCLE 93–99.

The Fate of Six. Chang – TALES..OLD 51–54 (J512.7.2).

The Father and His Daughter. Aesop – AESOP'S (Watts) 155 (U148.1).

The Father and His Two Daughters. Aesop – AESOP'S (Grosset) 169 (U148.1).

Father and Sons. Aesop – AESOP'S (Watts) 49 (J1021).

Father Bruin. Asbjørnsen – EAST 54–56 (K735.0.1).

Father Bruin in the Corner. Wiggin – TALES 289–290 (K735.0.1).

Father Catfish. Vo-Dinh – TOAD 23–27 (A2320.8).

Father Gatto. Sleigh – NORTH 116–129 (Q2.1.1Ca).

Father Grumbler. Lang – ROSE 72–83 (D861.1G).

A Father-in-law and His Son-in-law. Courlander KING'S 71-73 (W198).

The Father's Legacy. Kim - STORY 186-198 (D1415.2.7.1; E463.2; K335.1.1.4).

Fattest-of-All and Little-Thin-One. Sleigh - NORTH 9-12 (F1041.4.2).

The Fawn and Her Mother. Aesop - AESOP'S (Grosset) 9 (U121.2.1); Aesop - AESOP'S (Viking) 54; Aesop - AESOP'S (Watts) 71.

Fear. Shah - MULLA 60-62 (W211.4).

Fear, the Greatest Enemy. Alexander - PEBBLES 29 (K2369.17).

The Fearless Fisherman and the Dishonest Door-keeper. Brockett - BURMESE 171-176 (K187.1).

The Feast. Bowman - TALES..TUPA 245-246 (K2324).

The Feast. Courlander - KING'S 56-57 (K231.6.1.1).

The Feast for the Fox. Gaer - FABLES..INDIA 18-20 (K1601).

The Feast of Fools. Sawyer - WAY 189-200 (V92.1).

The Feast of the Lanterns. Gruenberg - MORE 236-241 (D2011.1.3).

The Feast of the Mountain Goats. DeWit - TALK-ING 137-142 (A1578.1.1).

Feather o' My Wing. MacManus - WELL 98-111 (H1385.4B); Provensen - PROVENSEN 49-56.

A Feather of Finist the Bright Falcon. Whitney - IN 85-94 (H1385.5Aa).

The Feathered Fiend. Manning-Sanders - PETER 139-143 (G303.16.19.6.1).

Feet For All. Kelsey - HODJA 116-122 (J2021).

THE FENCE: A MEXICAN TALE. Balet pb (J1172.2).

Fenist the Bright-Eyed Falcon. Riordan - TALES ..CENTRAL 63-72 (H1385.5Aa).

Ferdinand Faithful and Ferdinand Unfaithful. Grimm - JUNIPER v.2 298-309 (H1213.1A).

Fereyel and Debbo Engel the Witch. Arnott - AFRICAN 200-211 (K1611Db); Hope-Simpson - CAVALCADE..WITCHES 156-167.

The Ferryman. Tashjian - DEEP 42-55 (G303.16.8.2); Hardendorff - FROG 59-74.

Fickle Miss Frog. Heady - TALES 95-100 (A977.5.0.2).

Fiddivaw. Hatch - MORE 138-149 (D1413.17).

The Fiddle. Manning-Sanders - GLASS 122-125 (D1233.0.1).

The Fiddler Going Home. Manning-Sanders - GIANNI 173-178 (F331.4).

Fiddler John and the Devil. Durham - TIT 96-106 (K606.1.3; T251.1.1).

The Fiddler of Echternach. Courlander - RIDE 169 (D1415.2.5.2).

Fiddler, Play Fast, Play Faster. Fenner - GHOSTS 121-130 (G303.25.17.2.1); Sawyer - WAY 35-43.

Field Mouse and House Mouse. Wilson - GREEK 28-30 (J211.2).

The Field of Boliauns. Jacobs - Celtic 29-33 (J1922.2.1); Williams-Ellis - FAIRY..BRITAIN 135-139.

THE FIELD OF BUTTERCUPS. Boden pb (J1922.2.1).

The Field of Ragwort. Manning-Sanders - DWARFS 38-41 (J1922.2.1).

The Fifty-one Thieves. Sechrist - ONCE 189-196 (N455.3).

Fifty Red Night Caps. Williams-Ellis - FAIRY.. BRITISH 9-10 (B786.1).

The Fig Tree. Cothran - MAGIC 66-68 (K251.1.7).

The Fig Tree Beggar and the Willful Princess. Wolkstein - LAZY (H465F; W115.8.3).

The Fight with Wabun. Leekley - WORLD 100-110 (Z312.3).

The Fight with the Wendigo. Leekley WORLD 92-99 (A1716.2; A1906).

The Fighting Cocks and the Eagle. Aesop - AE-SOP'S (Grosset) 212-213 (J972).

The Fighting Rams. Credle - TALL 82-88 (X1204.3).

Figs for Gold, Figs for Folly. Jagendorf - NOO-DLEHEAD 59-62 (J2415.1).

A Fijian Fable. Gittins - TALES 26-27 (Z32.6).

Fill, Bowl, Fill! Arbuthnot - FAIRY 197-198 (H1045.0.1); Chase - JACK 89-95 (F718.3).

Fill-to-the-Brim-and-Eat. Sleigh - NORTH 83-89 (D861.1la).

Fin M'Coul and Cucullin. Manning-Sanders - BOOK..GIANTS 25-31 (K521.4.1.5).

Find the Thief. Nunn - AFRICAN 62-67

(J758.1.3; K1241.2).

A Fine Cheese. Leach – NOODLES 36 (J1791.3).

The Finest Lion in the World. Lang – FIFTY 77–80 (X905.0.2); Lang – VIOLET 17–21.

Finland's Greatest Fisherman. Bowman – TALES.. TUPA 205–206 (K371.1).

Finlay the Giant Killer. McNeil – DOUBLE 96–104 (S12.1.0.1Bb).

Finlay the Hunter. Williams-Ellis – FAIRY..BRITAIN 272–283 (S12.1.0.1Bb).

Finn McCoul. Adams – BOOK..GIANTS 92–99 (K521.4.1.5).

Finn McCoul and the Giant Cucullin. Sleigh – NORTH 103–110 (K521.4.1.5).

Fior Usga. Pilkington – SHAMROCK 150–152 (F944.7).

Fir Cones. Manning-Sanders – DWARFS 125–128 (F451.5.1.10.1).

The Fir Tree and the Bramble. Aesop – AESOP'S (Grosset) 189 (J212.4); Aesop – AESOP'S (Watts) 28.

Fire and the Moon. Withers – MAN 18 (A758.2).

Fire and Water, Truth and Falsehood. Courlander – FIRE 119–120 (K2143).

The Fire Bird, the Horse and the Princess Vasilissa. Arbuthnot – ANTHOLOGY 294–298 (H1213.1I).

The Fire-bird, the Horse of Power and the Princess Vasilissa. Arbuthnot – FAIRY 153–158 (H1213.1IA); Dalglish – ENCHANTED 35–47; Ransome – OLD 242–259.

THE FIRE BRINGER – Hodges pb (A1415.2.2.4).

The Fire-Goddess. Colum – LEGENDS 25–37 (A493.1).

Fire Magic and the Mud Hen. Carpenter – ELEPHANT'S 204–211 (A1415.0.2.4; A2320.3.1).

The Fire on the Mountain. Arbuthnot – ANTHOLOGY 312–313 (K231.14.2); Courlander – FIRE 7–14; Courlander – RIDE 106–111 (J1172.2).

The Fire Plume. Bierhorst – FIRE 78–79 (E474.6).

The Fire Test. Harris – NIGHTS 248–254 (K311.3F); Harris – COMPLETE 297–302.

Fire, Water, and Honor. De Leeuw – INDONESIAN 58–60 (W45.2).

The Firebird. Downing – RUSSIAN 189–201 (H1331.1.3); Higonnet-Schnopper – TALES 93–108; Riordan – TALES..CENTRAL 34–44

(H1331.1.3Ah); Wyndham – RUSSIAN 70–94.

The Firebird and Princess Vasilissa. Whitney – IN 71–76 (H1213.1IA).

The Firefly. Withers – I SAW 90–91 (Z41.1.1).

Firefly's Story. Sherlock – IGUANA'S 67–75 (Z49.6.0.3).

The Firemakers. Cothran – MAGIC 45–48 (A1415.0.2.4; A2320.3.1).

The Firewalkers. Gittins – TALES 11–13 (A1542.3).

The First Corn. Gruenberg – MORE 392–395 (A1425.2).

The First Eclipse. Brockett – BURMESE 5–7 (A737.12).

The First Emperor's Magic Whip. Carpenter – TALES..CHINESE 134–141 (D1208.1).

The First Fire. Bell – JOHN 15–18 (A1415.2.3); Scheer – CHEROKEE 25–30.

The First Flute. Arbuthnot – ANTHOLOGY 409–410 (A1461.8.2); Carter – ENCHANTED 50–56.

The First Horse-Headed Fiddle. Chang – CHINESE 34–35 (A1461.1.1).

The First Light. Hulpach – AMERICAN 12–16 (A1412.4).

THE FIRST MORNING. Bernstein pb (A1412.6).

The First Narwhale. Caswell – SHADOWS 41–47 (F952.7.1; K333.1).

The First of May. Haviland – FAVORITE.. GREECE 71–81 (F324.4).

The First Quedelish. Matson – LEGENDS 114–117 (A1546.0.4).

The First Shlemiel. Singer – ZLATEH 55–65 (J2311.2).

The First Strawberries. Bell – JOHN 23–26 (A2687.3.1); Cathon – PERHAPS 19–21.

The First Tears. Withers – MAN 10 (A751.5.6; A1344.1).

First Things First. Shah – MULLAH 54 (H591.4).

The First War. Baker – AT 43–49 (A2317.3.0.2).

The First White Man. Caswell – SHADOWS 24–25 (A1611.1.2; A1614.9.1).

The First Woman. McDowell – THIRD 119–129 (A1275.11).

Fish Alive. Jagendorf – PRICELESS 15–24 (H504.1.4).

The Fish and the Ring. Colwell - ROUND 46-50 (K1355A); Jacobs - ENGLISH 199-203; Reeves - ENGLISH 36-48; Steel - ENGLISH 226-230.

Fish in the Forest. Dolch - OLD RUSSIAN 1-9 (J1151.1.1).

Fish Story. Withers - WORLD 29 (X904.5).

The Fish With Bent Noses. Carpenter - ELEPHANT'S 22-30 (A2335.3.4).

Fish With the Rolls. Green - BIG 24-25 (K341.2.1; K1021).

The Fisher. Aesop - AESOP'S (Grosset) 194-195 (J1909.1); Jacobs - FABLES 83.

The Fisher and the Little Fish. Aesop - AESOP'S (Grosset) 8 (J321.2); Jacobs - FABLES 105.

The Fisherlad and the Mermaid's Ring. Leodhas - THISTLE 119-135 (B81.13.11B).

The Fisherman. Courlander - KING'S 22-24 (J2753).

The Fisherman. Courlander - PIECE 64-69 (J321.1.1).

The Fisherman and His Wife. Arbuthnot - ANTHOLOGY 193-196 (B375.1); Arbuthnot - FAIRY 56-60; Association - TOLD..GREEN 88-100; Carle - ERIC 39-48; Gag - TALES..GRIMM 149-168; Grimm - BROTHERS 102-111; Grimm - FISHERMAN pb (illus. Gekiere); Grimm - FISHERMAN pb (illus. Laimgruber); Grimm - FISHERMAN pb (illus. Zemach); Grimm - GRIMM'S (Follett) 70-81; Grimm - GRIMM'S (Grosset) 114-124; Grimm - GRIMM'S (Scribner's) 46-52; Grimm - GRIMM'S (Viking) 104-113; Grimm - GRIMM'S (World) 237-246; Grimm - HOUSEHOLD 100-108; Grimm - JUNIPER 94-112; Hutchinson - CHIMNEY 107-116; Lang - GREEN 331-341; Martignoni - ILLUSTRATED 237-242; Sleigh - NORTH 57-69; Wiggin - TALES 102-110; Zemach - FISHERMAN pb.

THE FISHERMAN AND THE GOBLET. Taylor pb (E633).

The Fisherman and the King's Chamberlain. Htin - KINGDOM 34-38 (K187.1).

The Fisherman and the Mermaid. Sheppard-Jones - WELSH 1-5 (F420.5.1.1).

The Fisherman and the Sea King's Daughter. Novak - FAIRY 85-92 (F420.6.1.3.1).

The Fisherman and the Sprat. Aesop - AESOP'S (Watts) 43 (J321.2).

The Fisherman Piping. Aesop - AESOP'S (Watts) 180 (J1909.1).

THE FISHERMAN UNDER THE SEA. Matsutani pb (F420.6.1.3.1).

The Fisherman's Daughter. Asia - FOLK ..BOOK II 40-46 (F420.5.2.2.4).

The Fisherman's Son. Ginsburg - FISHERMAN'S pb (H321B); Manning-Sanders - BOOK..MAGICAL 39-44.

The Fishes and the Wolf. Dobbs - MORE 66-67 (J758.3).

Fishing for Pots in the Pond. Jagendorf - GYPSIES' 134-135 (W48.2).

The Fishnet and the Bear. Heady - TALES 29-31 (A977.5.0.3).

Fitcher's Bird. Grimm - BROTHERS 72-76 (G561B; K521.1).

Fitcher's Feathered Bird. Grimm - JUNIPER v. 1 71-79 (G561B; K521.1).

FIVE CHINESE BROTHERS. Bishop pb (F660.1Da).

Five Dozen Eggs. Leach - NOODLES 69 (K289.1).

The Five Eggs. Courlander - RIDE 217-219 (T255.4).

Five Improbable Stories, #1. Frobenius - AFRICAN 153-154 (F660.1.2).

Five Lies That Could Be True. Tooze - WONDERFUL 121-124 (H509.5.1).

The Five Little Foxes and the Tiger. Arnott - ANIMAL 136-140 (J1662.1).

Five Musicians. Kavcic - GOLDEN 93-99 (K335.1.4; K1161.1).

The Five Servants. Wiggin - TALES 184-190 (F601.2B; H465E).

The Five Sisters of Kintail. Finlay - TATTERCOATS 15-23 (A962.13).

The Five Strange Ghosts. Novak - FAIRY 165-173 (E443.3.1).

The Five Swallow Sisters. Martin - NINE..COYOTE 46-53 (A1421.0.0.1).

Flail Which Came From the Clouds. Wiggin - TALES 69-70 (X1402).

Flaming Tales. Jagendorf - GYPSIES' 148-151 (X1203.1).

The Flaxen Thread. Duvoisin - THREE 167-177 (B641.0.1Ab).

The Flea. Bleecker - BIG 101-109 (H522.1.1); Haviland - FAVORITE..SPAIN 5-17; Ross - BURIED 43-54; Sawyer - PICTURE 37-52.

The Flea and the Ox. Aesop - AESOP'S (Watts) 133 (U142).

Flies. Ginsburg – KAHA 140-141 (J1289.32).

The Flight. Baker – GOLDEN 131-134 (D672D);
Borski – JOLLY 134-139.

The Flight of the Animals. Gaer – FABLES..INDIA
123-126 (Z43.3.1).

Flint Visits Rabbit. Bell – JOHN 41-43 (A1414.5.2;
A2342.1.2).

The Flood. Caswell – SHADOWS 93-95 (A1018.4).

The Flood. Leekley – WORLD 35-49 (A812.9;
A1014).

The Flood. Shah – MULLA 139 (W151.12).

The Flood. Reed – TALKATIVE 79-82
(A1021.0.0.1).

The Flood. Wyndham – FOLK..CHINA 73-97
(A1011.2.2; K1931.2; W154.8.4).

The Flooding of the Lower Hundred. Sheppard-
Jones – WELSH 131-133 (D1652.5.8; F944.1).

A Flower for a Husband. Jagendorf – PRICELESS
81-88 (G302.7.1.2).

A Flower to Catch a Thief. Robertson – FAIRY..
VIETNAM 36-43 (D551.1C).

The Fly. Aesop – FIVE 34 (J861.3); Vo-Dinh –
TOAD 99-104 (H583.2.6; J123.0.1; J1141.1.3.3).

Fly Again, My Proud Eagle. Harris – ONCE 15-18
(A1611.1.6).

The Fly on the Wagon. Kent – MORE 54-55
(J953.10).

A Fly Upon a Wheel. Aesop – AESOP'S (Viking)
15-18 (J953.10).

The Flying Farmer. Sakade – JAPANESE 37-40
(K687.1).

The Flying Fowl. Jagendorf – NOODLEHEAD 111-
114 (K1041.4).

The Flying Kettle. Withers – WORLD 84
(X1286.1.4).

The Flying Ship. Association – TOLD..GREEN
101-112 (F601.2A); Buck – FAIRY 129-137;
Frost – LEGEND 89-98; Haviland – FAVORITE..
RUSSIA 66-86; Lang – YELLOW 214-223; Riordan – TALES..CENTRAL 78-85.

The Flying Spirits of Niihau. Thompson – HA-
WAIIAN..TRICKSTERS 9-13 (E423.3.12).

The Flying Turtle. Green – BIG 196 (J2357).

The Foam Maiden. Manning-Sanders – SORCER-
OR'S 37-44 (F424.1).

The Fog. Heady – TALES 21-24 (A1134.1).

FOMA THE TERRIBLE: A RUSSIAN FOLKTALE.
Daniels pb (K1951.1).

Foni and Fotia. Manning-Sanders – SORCEROR'S
91-98 (T75.2.1.3).

The Food of the Cloak. Shah – MULLA 40
(J1561.3).

The Fool. Ginsburg – KAHA 131-137 (J2133.4;
J2311.1; J2461K; K113).

The Fool. Masey – STORIES 132-139 (J1151.1.0.1).

The Fool. Shah – MULLA 26 (J1369.6).

The Fool and the Birch Tree. Downing – RUSSIAN
156-159 (J1151.1.4; J1853.3); Ginsburg –
TWELVE 27-31.

The Fool and the Feather Mattress. Danaher –
FOLKTALES 49-51 (J2213.9).

The Fool and the Magic Fish. Riordan – TALES..
CENTRAL 165-174 (B375.1.3).

The Fool of the World and the Flying Ship. Fenner – ADVENTURE 1-15 (F601.2); Ransome –
OLD 70-87; Ransome – FOOL pb.

Foolers Fooled. Papashvily – YES 181-187 (J1516).

The Foolish Ass. Wilson – GREEK 88-89 (J1612).

The Foolish Dog. Bloch – UKRAINIAN 68-72
(K1121).

The Foolish Dragon. Dobbs – ONCE 15-18 (K544).

Foolish Emilyan and The Talking Fish. Wyndham
– RUSSIAN 12 (B375.1.3).

The Foolish Father-in-law. Withers – MAN 67-70
(J2411.3.1).

Foolish Folks. Duvoisin – THREE 146-151
(J1922.1; J1973; J2123; J2133.5).

The Foolish Lad. Hatch – THIRTEEN 37-45
(H341.3.2; J1852.1.3; J1853.2; K187).

The Foolish Lad and the Flies. Lowe – LITTLE 36
(J1193.1).

The Foolish Lion and the Silly Rooster. Jagendorf – NOODLEHEAD 89-92 (K1711.1).

The Foolish Man. Arbuthnot – ANTHOLOGY 283-
284 (H1273.2H); Tashjian – ONCE 3-10.

The Foolish Milkmaid. TALL..NURSERY 23-24
(J2061.2).

Foolish Mother Goat. Hardendorff – JUST 30-33
(W165.2.1).

The Foolish People. Jagendorf – NOODLEHEAD
271-273 (J2024.2).

The Foolish, Timid Little Hare. Babbitt - JATA-
KA 39-43 (Z43.3.1); Gruenberg - FAVORITE
341-343.

The Foolish, Timid Rabbit. Hutchinson - FIRE-
SIDE 43-47 (Z43.3.1).

The Foolish Wife and Her Three Foolish Daughters.
Haviland - FAVORITE..GREECE 29-37 (J1849.5;
J2063; J2171.6.1).

The Foolish Wolf. Dobbs - MORE 75-80 (K566;
K553.3; K1121.2); Riordan - TALES..CENTRAL
207-210.

The Foolish Women. Neufeld - BEWARE 52-57
(H1312.1; J2063; J2326.1; W111.3.2).

The Foolishness of Cochinito. Ross - IN 35-39
(L457).

Fool's Bells Ring in Every Town. Jagendorf -
NOODLEHEAD 164-172 (H1312.3).

Foot Racers of Payupki. Courlander - PEOPLE
101-114 (H1594.3); DeWit - TALKING 63-75.

For an Oven Full of Bread. Duvoisin - THREE
126-129 (D1385.18.1).

For a Lack of Thread. Duvoisin - THREE 44-47
(F1025.1.2; Z41.4.1).

The Forbidden Apple. Wolkstein - MAGIC 171-
176 (S11.3.3.1.1).

Fording the River in a Copper Cauldron. Jagendorf - GYPSIES' 170-176 (J1689.3).

The Forest Bride. Fenner - PRINCESSES 103-114
(B641.0.1Bb); Fillmore - SHEPHERD'S 26-39;
Provensen - PROVENSEN 83-92.

A Forest Mansion. Carey - BABA 63-66 (L396).

The Forest Wolf and the Prairie Wolf. Green -
BIG 55-56 (A2513.1.3).

The Forgotten Bride. Wilson - GREEK 141-147
(G530.2Af).

The Fortunate Maiden. Downing - RUSSIAN 208-
210 (N138).

The Fortunate Shoemaker. Hardendorff -
TRICKY 33-39 (N531.1; N535.0.1).

Fortunatus and His Purse. Lang - ROSE 34-43
(D1192.1).

A Fortune from a Frog. Carpenter - KOREAN 97-
105 (B645.1.2).

The Fortune of the Poet's Son. Siddiqui -
TOONTOONY 50-54 (J21.1.1).

The Forty Thieves. Gruenberg - MORE 207-214
(N455.3); Minard - WOMENFOLK 51-64.

The Forty Whoppers. Deutsch - MORE 55-64
(H509.5.3).

The Fountain of Arethusa. Toor - GOLDEN 123-
125 (A941.0.2).

The Fountain of Youth. Barbeau - GOLDEN 90-
108 (H1321.1Ab).

The Fountain of Youth. Hearn - JAPANESE (Pauper) 26-36 (D1338.1.1.2); Hearn - BOY 1-4.

The Four Abdallahs. Manning-Sanders - BOOK..
MERMAIDS 122-128 (B82.6).

The Four Accomplished Brothers. Grimm -
GRIMM'S (Grosset) 307-312 (F660.1); Grimm -
GRIMM'S (Scribner's) 236-241; Grimm -
GRIMM'S (World) 125-129.

Four Arrows. Kelsey - HODJA 7-14 (N621.2).

The Four Bald Men. Asia - FOLK 18-20 (J2061.5;
J2133.5.0.1).

Four Brays of a Donkey. Kelsey - HODJA 93-99
(J2311.1.1; J2133.4).

The Four Brothers. De La Mare - TALES 15-24
(F660.1).

Four Brothers Who Were Both Wise and Foolish.
Haviland - FAVORITE..SPAIN 18-35 (F660.1A).

THE FOUR CLEVER BROTHERS. Grimm pb
(F660.1).

The Four Deaf Men. Htin - KINGDOM 31-33
(X111.1.2).

The Four Friends. Korel - LISTEN 83-89
(K642.2).

Four Friends. Siddiqui - TOONTOONY 136-139
(K335.1.4).

Four Generals. Fenner - ADVENTURE 60-71
(K2368.4; K2368.6; K2368.7; K2369.16).

Four Good Men. Davis - LION'S 92-93
(X1791.1.1).

Four Hairs from the Beard of the Devil. Wolkstein - MAGIC 43-48 (H1273.2N).

The Four Juans. Newman - FOLK..LATIN 39-42
(D551.1Be).

Four-Legged. Shah - MULLA 67 (W165.4).

The Four Musicians. Arbuthnot - ANTHOLOGY
200-201 (K335.1.4; K1161.1); Arbuthnot -
FAIRY 37-39.

The Four Oxen and the Lion. Aesop - AESOP'S
(Grosset) 30 (J1022); Jacobs - FABLES 103.

The Four Red Caps. Sleigh - NORTH 195-201
(F282.4.2).

Four Riddles. Courlander - RIDE 53-58 (H541.4).

The Four Sacred Scrolls. Novak - FAIRY 22-30 (D672C).

Four Tales of How the Devil Was Outwitted. Müller-Guggenbühl - SWISS #1 213-223 (G303.24.1.7.0.1); #2 213-223 (G303.19.3); #3 213-223 (M211.8.1); #4 213-223 (M211.2.1).

The Four Towers of Vufflens. Duvoisin - THREE 115-121 (A1435.9.1).

Four Very Skillful People. Withers - WORLD 62-63 (F660.1.1).

The Four Young Men. Courlander - RIDE 42-45 (H342.4).

Fourteen Hundred Cowries. Fuja - FOURTEEN 11-21 (A1378; Z49.20).

The Fowler, The Partridge and The Cock. Aesop - AESOP'S (Watts) 197 (U33.3).

Fox and Goat. Aesop - FABLES (Walck) 14-15 (K652.2).

Fox and Grapes. Aesop - FABLES (Walck) 57-58 (J871).

Fox and Raven Steal the Moon. Withers - MAN 39-40 (A758.1).

Fox and Stork. Aesop - FABLES (Walck) 95-96 (J1565.1).

The Fox and the Badger. Ginsburg - ONE 14-16 (K444).

The Fox and the Bear. Uchida - MAGIC 103-111 (K171.1).

Fox and the Bears. Curtis - GIRL 54-57 (K2028).

The Fox and the Bird. Wilson - SCOTTISH 93-94 (K604).

The Fox and the Bramble. Aesop - AESOP'S (Grosset) 206-207 (J656.1); Aesop - AESOP'S (Watts) 212.

The Fox and the Carved Head. Aesop - FIVE 48 (J1793).

The Fox and the Cat. Aesop - AESOP'S (Grosset) 111-112 (J1662); Green - ANIMAL 192-193; Grimm - GRIMM'S (World) 330-331; Jacobs - FABLES 75.

The Fox and the Cat. Wiggin - TALES 81 (J1662.2).

The Fox and the Cat. Wiggin - TALES 30-31 (K2324).

The Fox and the Cock. Durham - TIT 91-92 (K561.1.0.3).

The Fox and the Cock. Hardendorff - TRICKY 71-74 (K721).

The Fox and the Crane. Aesop - FIVE 44 (J1565.1); Carrick - STILL MORE 37-42; Kent - MORE 22-23.

The Fox and the Crow. Aesop - AESOP'S (Golden) 60-61 (K334.1); Aesop - AESOP'S (Grosset) 5-6; Aesop - AESOP'S (Random) 51-54; Aesop - AESOP'S (Viking) 59-60; Aesop - AESOP'S (Watts) 6; Aesop - FABLES (Walck) 66-67; Aesop - FIVE 84; Arbuthnot - FAIRY 232; Arbuthnot - FAIRY 225; Galdone - THREE #3; Jacobs - FABLES 1; Martignoni - ILLUSTRATED 160; Rice - ONCE 5-9; Rockwell - OLD 62-64; TALL..NURSERY 76-77; Wilson - GREEK 126-128.

The Fox and the Dove. Wiggin - TALES 39-40 (K1788).

The Fox and the Dragon. Green - CAVALCADE ..DRAGONS 21-22 (W156.1).

The Fox and the Fish. Chang - TALES..OLD CHINA 3 (J758.3).

The Fox and the Geese. De La Mare - ANIMAL 78-79 (K555.1.0.1).

The Fox and the Goat. Aesop - AESOP'S (Grosset) 15 (K652); Aesop - AESOP'S (Random) 73; Aesop - AESOP'S (Viking) 53-54; Aesop - AESOP'S (Watts) 42; Aesop - FIVE 36; Jacobs - FABLES 163; Rice - ONCE 16-21.

The Fox and the Goose. Wiggin - TALES 10-11 (H641.1).

The Fox and the Grapes. Aesop - AESOP'S (Golden) 23-25 (J871); Aesop - AESOP'S (Grosset) 14; Aesop - AESOP'S (Random) 20-21; Aesop - AESOP'S (Viking) 12; Aesop - AESOP'S (Watts) 1; Aesop - FIVE 12; Arbuthnot - FAIRY 229; Galdone - THREE #1; Green - BIG 15; Gruenberg - FAVORITE 406-407; Jacobs - FABLES 61; Martignoni - ILLUSTRATED 156.

The Fox and the Grasshopper. Aesop - AESOP'S (Watts) 163 (K2061.10).

The Fox and the Gulls. Arnott - ANIMALS 224-230 (K526.2).

The Fox and the Hare. Carrick - STILL 1-14 (J741.1); Ginsburg - FOX pb.

The Fox and the Hedgehog. Aesop - AESOP'S (Watts) 205-206 (J215).

The Fox and the Hedgehog. Wiggin - TALES 41-42 (K652.3).

The Fox and the Horse. Wiggin - TALES 153-154 (K1047).

The Fox and the Icicle. Hardendorff - JUST 20 (J1772.15).

The Fox and the Leopard. Aesop - AESOP'S (Watts) 205 (J242.3).

The Fox and the Lobster. Carrick - STILL 61-63 (K11.2).

The Fox and the Lion. Aesop - AESOP'S (Grosset) 57 (U131.1); Aesop - AESOP'S (Viking) 44; Aesop - AESOP'S (Watts) 72; Jacobs - FABLES 67.

The Fox and the Lion. Ginsburg - ONE 9 (J684.1.1).

The Fox and the Lion in Partnership. Wilson - GREEK 103-106 (K402.3.2).

The Fox and the Little Bannock. Wilson - SCOTTISH 88-90 (Z33.1.4).

The Fox and the Mask. Aesop - AESOP'S (Golden) 82 (J1793); Jacobs - FABLES 39.

The Fox and the Mole. Barlow - LATIN 62-64 (A2433.3.20).

The Fox and the Mosquitoes. Aesop - AESOP'S (Grosset) 26-27 (J215.1); Jacobs - FABLES 127.

The Fox and the Peasant. Carrick - STILL 90-94 (K371.1).

The Fox and the Pitcher. Riordan - TALES.. CENTRAL 194 (K1725.1.1).

The Fox and the Quail. Ginsburg - ONE 31-37 (K341.5.2; K1082.3.1).

The Fox and the Quail. Masey - STORIES 113-115 (J1421).

The Fox and the Rabbit. Bowman - TALES.. TUPA 254 (K2348).

The Fox and the Rolling Pin. Carey - BABA 39-41 (K251.1.0.2.1).

The Fox and the Sheepskin Jacket. Arnott - ANIMAL 6-13 (J758.1.0.1; K254.1.1; K1041.0.1).

The Fox and the Shrike. Scofield - FOX 20-25 (K341.5.2.1).

The Fox and the Stork. Aesop - AESOP'S (Grosset) 66-68 (J1565.1); Aesop - AESOP'S (Random) 3-5; Aesop - AESOP'S (Viking) 74-75; Aesop - AESOP'S (Watts) 23; Galdone - THREE #2; Jacobs - FABLES 37; Montgomerie - TWENTY-FIVE 36; Rice - ONCE - 28-33.

The Fox and the Thrush. Ginsburg - THREE 48 (J1421).

The Fox and the Wolf. Baker - TALKING 71-76

(K372; K401.1).

The Fox and the Wolf. Daniels - FALCON 84-89 (K371.1; K473.1; K1021; K1775).

The Fox and the Woodcock. Carrick - STILL 117-119 (J1421).

The Fox and the Woodman. Aesop - AESOP'S (Grosset) 158-159 (K2315); Aesop - AESOP'S (Viking) 18-19.

The Fox as a Judge. Bowman - TALES..TUPA 264-265 (J1172.3).

The Fox as Herdsman. Undset - TRUE 182-183 (K934).

The Fox as Shepherd. Asbjørnsen - NORWE-GIAN 106-107 (K934).

Fox Atter 'Im, Buzzard Atter 'Im. Harris - COMPLETE 21-25 (K629.2.4); Harris - FAVOR-ITE 61-65; Harris - UNCLE 30-36.

A Fox in Hiding. Green - ANIMAL 165 (K2315).

A Fox in One Bite. Scofield - FOX 9-14 (K722.0.1).

The Fox in Saint's Clothing. Gaer - FABLES.. INDIA 129-132 (K815.16.2).

The Fox in the Hole. Jagendorf - NOODLEHEAD 45-47 (K1022.1).

The Fox in the Well. Aesop - AESOP'S (Viking) 52 (J2175.2.1).

The Fox Outwits the Lion. Wilson - GREEK 222-223 (J644.1).

The Fox Outwits the Tiger. Hume - FAVORITE ..CHINA 67-68 (J684.1.1).

The Fox, the Cock and the Crane. Carrick - STILL 47-56 (K1041.0.4).

The Fox, the Cock and the Dog. Aesop - AE-SOP'S (Grosset) 82-83 (J1421); Jacobs - FABLES 117.

The Fox, the Fish and the Bear. Arnott - ANI-MAL 79-82 (K371.1; K1021).

The Fox, the Hare and the Toad Have an Argu-ment. Hume - FAVORITE..CHINA 23-26 (B841.1.4).

The Fox, the Rabbit, and the Rooster. Carey - BABA 45-48 (J741.1).

The Fox Turned Shepherd. Wiggin - TALES 444-445 (K934).

The Fox Turns a Somersault. Hume - FAVOR-ITE..CHINA 99-100 (B651.1; F302.4.2.2; N831.1).

The Fox Who Served a Lion. Aesop - AESOP'S (Watts) 202 (J684.1).

The Fox Who Wanted to Whistle. Barlow - LATIN 18-22 (K713.4).

The Fox Who Was Not So Smart. Jagendorf - KING 69-71 (K11.2).

A Fox Who Was Too Sly. Pratt - MAGIC (D313.1.1).

The Fox Without a Tail. Aesop - AESOP'S (Grosset) 97-98 (J758.1); Aesop - AESOP'S (Random) 36-38; Aesop - AESOP'S (Viking) 75-76; Aesop - AESOP'S (Watts) 68; Aesop - FIVE 64; Jacobs - FABLES 128.

The Foxes and the River. Aesop - AESOP'S (Watts) 208-209 (J873).

The Fox's Daughter. Arbuthnot - ANTHOLOGY 331-332 (B651.1.1); Arbuthnot - FAIRY 181-183; Ritchie - TREASURE 65-74.

The Fox's Wedding. Rackham - FAIRY 87-88 (B601.14.1).

Fred and Kate. Grimm - HOUSEHOLD 248-255 (J1871; J1881.1.2; J2012.2; J2176; K335.1.1.1C).

Freddy and His Fiddle. Manning-Sanders - DWARFS 14-24 (D1415.2.5.1).

Frederick and Catherine. Grimm - GRIMM'S (Grosset) 290-297 (J1871; J1881.1.2; J2176; K335.1.1.1C).

Frederick and His Katelizabeth. Grimm - JUNIPER v. 2 187-200 (K335.1.1.1C).

The Fresher the Better. Harris - FAVORITE 262-267 (K1715.3.1); Harris - COMPLETE 499-504.

The Friendly Animals. Manning-Sanders - BOOK ..MAGICAL 164-176 (B582.6).

The Friendly Mouse. Montgomerie - TWENTY-FIVE 38-40 (K687.1).

The Friendship of the Hare to the Parrot. Tooze - WONDERFUL 103-106 (K2131.8).

The Friendship of the Tortoise and the Eagle. Burton - MAGIC 116-119 (J657.2.3).

The Frightened Wolves. Riordan - TALES.. CENTRAL 161-164 (K1715.3).

Fritz and Franz. Duvoisin - THREE 178-184 (F460.4.2.8).

The Frog. Lang - VIOLET 186-192 (B641.0.1A).

The Frog. Manning-Sanders - BOOK..MAGICAL 142 (B641A); Manning-Sanders - CHOICE 26-38 (B641.0.1A; H1385.3K); Manning-Sanders

- PRINCES 84-96 (B641.0.1Af; H1385.3K).

The Frog. Ross - BURIED 35-42 (N385.1.1.1); Sawyer - PICTURE 1-10.

Frog and His Two Wives. Bryan - OX 11-14 (J2183.1.2).

The Frog and the Mouse. Aesop - AESOP'S (Random) 45-46 (J681).

The Frog and the Ox. Aesop - AESOP'S (Grosset) 108-109 (J955.1); Aesop - AESOP'S (Random) 14-16; Aesop - AESOP'S (Viking) 28; Aesop - FIVE 26; Arbuthnot - FAIRY 227; Jacobs - FABLES 42; Rice - ONCE 52-57; Rockwell OLD 79-81.

The Frog and the Snake. Hardendorff - JUST 17-18 (F1041.1.11.4).

The Frog and the Stork. Tashjian - THREE 40-47 (A2494.16.1.1.1; K815.14).

The Frog and the Well. Aesop - AESOP'S (Watts) 160 (J752.1).

The Frog Bride. Toor - GOLDEN 25-27 (B641Ae).

The Frog Jacket. Tooze - WONDERFUL 71-73 (B645.1.2.1).

The Frog King. Arbuthnot - FAIRY 43-45 (D195.1); Grimm - GRIMM'S (Follett) 82-88.

The Frog King or Iron Henry. Grimm - BROTHERS 55-60 (D195.1); Grimm - JUNIPER v. 2 169-177.

The Frog Prince. Dalgliesh - ENCHANTED 199-203 (D195.1); Darrell - ONCE 43-46; Gag - TALES..GRIMM 179-188; Grimm - GRIMM'S (Scribner's) 1-6; Grimm - GRIMM'S (Grosset) 86-90; Grimm - GRIMM'S (World) 286-290; Grimm - HOUSEHOLD 32-36; Gruenberg - FAVORITE 295-298; Haviland - FAIRY 114-117; Haviland - FAVORITE..GERMANY 3-12; Holme TALES 63-68; Hutchinson - FIRESIDE 143-150; Opie - CLASSIC 183-187.

The Frog Princess. Riordan - TALES..CEN-TRAL 129-137 (B641Af; H1385.3K); Whitney - IN 37-43.

The Frog That Swallowed an Ocean. Carpenter - WONDER..SEAS 29-36 (A751.3.1.3).

FROG WENT A'COURTIN'. Langstaff pb (B284.1.1).

The Frogs Asking For a King. Aesop - AE-SOP'S (Watts) 29 (J613.1).

The Frogs Desired a King. Aesop - AESOP'S (Viking) 58-59 (J643.1).

The Frogs Desiring a King. Aesop - AESOP'S (Grosset) 47-48 (J643.1); Jacobs - FABLES

24-25.

Frogs in the Moon. Leach - HOW 31-33
(A1131.1.0.1); Withers - MAN 24 (A751.3.1.1).

The Frogs of Yonder Mountain Cry. Withers -
I SAW 130 (Z49.19).

The Frog's Saddle Horse. Hardendorff - FROG'S
15-16 (K1241).

The Frogs Who Asked For a King. Aesop -
AESOP'S (Golden) 42 (J643.1).

The Frogs Who Wanted a King. Aesop - FIVE
20 (J643.1).

Frog's Wives Make Ndiba Pudding. Courlander -
KING'S 58-59 (J2183.1.2).

From Bad to Good to Bad to Good. Kendall -
SWEET 39-41 (J894).

From the Head Downward. Manning-Sanders -
PETER 43-47 (B175.3).

From Tiger to Anansi. Haviland - FAIRY 86-91
(A1481.2.1; K713.1.9); Sherlock - ANANSI 3-
12.

Frost. Rackham - FAIRY 92-99 (Q2.1.4C); Ransome - OLD 54-69; Whitney - IN 27-34.

The Frost, the Sun , and the Wind. Downing -
RUSSIAN 169-170 (J1712.1); Riordan - TALES
..CENTRAL 106.

Frozen Music. Withers - WORLD 48-49
(X1623.7.2).

The Fruits of Health. Hatch - MORE 105-118
(H346).

Fulfilled. Association - TOLD..GREEN 165-174
(Q1.1B).

The Full Moon. Leach - NOODLES 49 (H561.1;
H582.1.1).

Fundevögel. Grimm - GRIMM'S (Grosset) 216-
219 (D671B); Grimm - GRIMM'S (Viking) 71-
74; Grimm - GRIMM'S (World) 159-162.

The Funeral of the Forest King. Fuja - FOUR-
TEEN 146-151 (A2433.1.3).

The Funeral of the Hyena's Mother. Fuja -
FOURTEEN 60-63 (A2433.3.4.2).

Funny, Funny. Brenner - BOY 52-58
(G275.12.3).

The Gallant Tailor. Adams - BOOK..GIANTS
19-34 (K1951.1); Grimm - GRIMM'S (Follett)
89-101; Grimm - GRIMM'S (Grosset) 189-200;
Grimm - GRIMM'S (World) 348-357; Grimm -
HOUSEHOLD 109-117.

Gallymanders! Gallymanders! Chase - WICKED
18-28 (Q2.1.2Cb).

The Gambler and the Hare. Danaher - FOLK-
TALES 59-62 (E577.2.1.2).

The Gambling Ghosts. Leodhas - GAELIC 39-45
(E577.2.1.1).

The Game Board. Courlander - FIRE 77-80
(K251.1.3).

The Game of Chess in the Mountains. Sun -
LAND 120-123 (A163.1.1.1).

The Game of Tlachtli. Williams-Ellis - ROUND
217-222 (A515.1.1.4).

The Gangster in the Back Seat. Leach - THING
77-79 (E414.2).

The Garden of Magic. Pugh - MORE..WELSH 29-
37 (D1711.0.1.4).

The Gardener and His Dog. Aesop - AESOP'S
(Grosset) 7 (W154.5); Aesop - AESOP'S
(Watts) 171-172.

The Gardener and the Bear. Gaer - FABLES..
INDIA 39-41 (N333.2).

The Gardener, the Abbot and the King. Mehdevi - BUNGLING 109-117 (H561.2; H681.3.1;
H711.1).

Gathering Salt. Heady - SAFIRI 87-92
(K11.1.1.1).

The Gay Goss-Hawk. Leodhas - HEATHER
(K1862).

The Geese and the Golden Chain. Manning-
Sanders - BOOK..MERMAIDS 98-107
(Q2.1.5Bbc).

General Chang's Strategy. Lu Mar - CHINESE
43-52 (K2369.14).

"General" Dog and His Army. Carpenter - WON-
DER 245-255 (B582.6).

Genevieve! The Huns are Coming! Frost -
LEGEND 223-229 (V221.12.1; V229.7.2).

The Genii of the Hearth. Graham - BEGGAR 33-
44 (T211.2.1.1).

Gentle Kwan Yin. Carpenter - TALES..CHINESE
29-38 (A483.1).

A Gentleman and His Cook. Lum - TALES..OLD
CHINA 55-67 (N255.7).

Geordie and the Ten Shilling Jock. Edmonds -
TRICKSTER 30-35 (J1179.21).

Gertrude's Bird. Undset - TRUE 147-148
(A1958.0.1).

Get Ready, Get Set, Go. Reed - TALKATIVE 28-29 (K11.1).

Getting Along Together. Newell - RESCUE 23-28 (W111.10).

Getting the Moon Back Into the Sky. Withers - MAN 50 (J1791.2.2).

A Ghost at the Door. Littledale - GHOSTS 153-156 (E412.3.3).

The Ghost Bird. Courlander - RIDE 112-115 (A1999.3).

The Ghost Dog of South Mountain. Carpenter - WONDER 163-172 (E521.2.6).

The Ghost Goblin's Gold. Spicer - THIRTEEN 120-128 (F348.5.1).

The Ghost of the Great White Stag. Gruenberg - MORE 148-153 (E423.2.6.1); Parker - SKUNNY 213-224.

The Ghost That Didn't Want To Be a Ghost. Leodhas - GHOSTS 79-90 (E599.14).

A Ghost Story. Harris - COMPLETE 235-278 (E236.5); Harris - NIGHTS 161-165.

The Ghost Who Was Afraid of Being Bagged. Hardendorff - JUST 105-109 (K1715.1.2).

The Ghost Wife. Harper - GHOSTS 99-102 (E474.5).

The Ghostly Hand of Spital House. Spicer - GHOSTS 16-23 (D1162.2.1.1).

The Ghostly Hitchhiker. Leach - THING 71-72 (E332.3.3.1).

The Ghosts of Kahlberg. Harper - GHOSTS 234-249 (E363.5.2).

Giacco and His Bean. Hardendorff - TRICKY 75-80 (K251.1.1).

Gianni and the Ogre. Manning-Sanders - GIANNI 7-12 (G501F).

The Giant and His Royal Servants. Pilkington - SHAMROCK 1-9 (G530.2Ab).

The Giant and the Dwarf. Hardendorff - JUST 92-97 (G501A); Manning-Sanders - BOOK.. GIANTS 18-24.

The Giant and the Rumanian. Ure - RUMANIAN 24-25 (J1801.1).

The Giant and the Tailor. Wiggin - TALES 155-156 (G501).

The Giant and the Wreton. Colwell - ROUND 95-96 (F531.6.6.3.1).

The Giant Beanstalk. Durham - TIT 56-62

(Q2.1.5Ab).

The Giant Bear. Field - ESKIMO 31-32 (F912.2.3).

The Giant Bones. Leodhas - GAELIC 30-38 (F531.6.13.3); Mayne - BOOK..GIANTS 195-203.

The Giant Elephant. Gaer - FABLES..INDIA 71-74 (K815.20).

The Giant Holiburn. Manning-Sanders - PETER 125-128 (F531.5.1.5).

The Giant in the Cave. Manning-Sanders - BOOK ..GIANTS 85-89 (K603.1).

The Giant Mosquito. Heady - SAGE 65-69 (A2034.4).

The Giant of the Bang Beggars' Hall. Adams - BOOK..GIANTS 176-197 (H1289.3.2); MacManus - CHIMNEY pb.

The Giant of the Brown Beechwood. MacManus - BOLD 138-157 (G530.2Ga); Mayne - BOOK.. GIANTS 119-137.

The Giant of the Fens. Colwell - ROUND 64-67 (F628.2.3.1).

The Giant of the Mount. Manning-Sanders - PETER 77-81 (F531.6.12.8.3).

The Giant Ogre, Kloo-Teekl. Harris - ONCE 89-111 (K741.4).

The Giant Okab. Mehdevi - PERSIAN 62-68 (G530.2.BI).

Giant Pear and Giant Cow. De Regniers - GIANT 174-175 (X1235.2.2; X1411.4); Müller-Guggen-bühl - SWISS 181.

The Giant Snake That Swallowed a Girl. Carpenter - SOUTH 144-150 (F912.3.1.1).

The Giant Sturgeon. Haviland - NORTH 19-20 (A2411.1.4.1.1; F912.2.7); Leekley - WORLD 79-91.

The Giant Who Ate People. Nunn - AFRICAN 96-103 (G302.7.1.3).

The Giant Who Had No Heart in His Body. Adams - BOOK..GIANTS 41-52 (D532Ad); Asbjørnsen - EAST (Macmillan) 45-56; Asbjørnsen - EAST (Row) 64-72; De Regniers - GIANT 81-83; Fen-ner - GIANTS 39-49; Manning-Sanders - BOOK ..GIANTS 98-106; Mayne - BOOK..GIANTS 108-118; Undset - TRUE 108-117.

The Giant Who Overslept. Spicer - THIRTEEN 93-100 (A963.13).

The Giant Who Rode on the Ark. De Regniers - GIANT 131-134 (F531.6.12.8.2).

The Giant Who Stole a River. Mayne - BOOK.. GIANTS 27-34 (F531.6.8.3.2.1).

The Giant With the Three Golden Hairs. Adams - BOOK..GIANTS 149-158 (H1273.2A); Grimm - GRIMM'S (Grosset) 313-321; Grimm - GRIMM'S (Scribner's) 78-86; Grimm - GRIMM'S (World) 226-229.

The Giants and the Herdboy. Lang - YELLOW 86-89 (G666.2).

The Giants of Towednack. Mayne - BOOK..GIANTS 138-147 (F628.2.3.1); Williams-Ellis - FAIRY..BRITISH 216-248.

The Giant's Stairs. Palmer - FAIRY 78-84 (F321.3.2).

The Gift. Keeley - CITY 106-109 (A751.2).

The Gift and the Giver. Davis - LION'S 172-177 (J2415.1).

Gift for the Lazy. Davis - LION'S 130-131 (J1289.28.1).

Gift from a Star. Luzzatto - LONG pb (A1414.7.5).

A Gift from the Heart. Pridham - GIFT 11-15 (J229.3.1).

The Gift of Father Frost. Maas - MOON 17-25 (C916.3.1).

The Gift of Fire. Guillot - GUILLOT'S 33-39 (A2436.2).

The Gift of Fishes. Gunterman - CASTLES 241-246 (A1457.9.1).

The Gift of Gold. Tashjian - THREE 62-77 (J1085.5).

The Gift of Manioc. Carpenter - SOUTH 57-63 (A2685.5).

The Gift of Saint Nicholas. Arbuthnot - FAIRY 191-196 (D1662.4; N816.0.2).

The Gift of the Hairy One. Thompson - HAWAIIAN 53-59 (A1453.5).

The Gift of the Holy Man. Siddiqui - TOON-TOONY 70-81 (D861.1G).

The Gift of the Moon Goddess. Barlow - LATIN 38-42 (A2691.6).

Gift of the Unicorn. Wyndham - TALES..CHINA 34-37 (A511.1.3.4).

A Gift That Came Back. Kelsey - HODJA 46-53 (J2563).

The Gift to the Hummingbird. Bowes - BIRD 72-77 (A2411.2.1.19.2).

Gigi and the Magic Ring. Sheehan - FOLK 72-83 (D882.1.1).

Gimpel's Golden Broth. Simon - WISE 77-88 (J2478).

The Gingerbread Boy. Arbuthnot - TIME 190-191 (Z33.1.2); Galdone - GINGERBREAD pb; Haviland - FAIRY 7-11; Holdsworth - GINGERBREAD pb; TALL..NURSERY 16-22.

The Gingerbread Man. Rockwell - THREE 33-44 (Z33.1.2).

The Gipsies' Church. Ure - RUMANIAN 99-100 (X1863).

The Gipsy and the Goose. Ure - RUMANIAN 16-18 (K402.1).

The Giraffe Hunters. Courlander - KING'S 90-94 (K2131.7).

The Giraffe's Neck. Heady - SAFIRI 82-86 (A2351.4.4).

A Girl and a Stepmother. Tooze - WONDERFUL 50-54 (Q2.1.1Fa).

The Girl and Her Water Buckets. Withers - MAN 19 (A751.7.1).

The Girl and the Golden Chair. Sheppard-Jones - WELSH 98-100 (F348.7.1.4.1).

The Girl and the Puma. Jagendorf - KING 23-27 (B538.3.2); Newman - FOLK..LATIN 83-88.

The Girl in the Basket. Manning-Sanders - BOOK..OGRES 66-74 (Q2.1.2G).

The Girl in the Chest. Fillmore - LAUGHING 201-218 (G561.2A; R221S).

The Girl in the Moon. Deutsch - MORE 79-84 (A751.8.5.1).

The Girl on the Hill. Tracy - LION 83-87 (H331.1.1E).

The Girl Who Climbed to the Sky. Brown - TEPEE 39-42 (A762.1C).

The Girl Who Clung to the Devil's Back. Spicer - THIRTEEN 118-127 (T251.1.1.2).

The Girl Who Could Spin Clay and Straw into Gold. Kaplan - FAIRY 58-70 (D2183.1).

The Girl Who Could Think. Gruenberg - FAVORITE 349-352 (H506.12).

The Girl Who Didn't Know How to Spin. Belting - ELVES 70-76 (Q321.2.2).

The Girl Who Knew the King. Walker - NIGERIAN 63-64 (B469.9).

The Girl Who Lived With a Lion. Holding - KING'S 69-79 (B610.2).

The Girl Who Lived With the Gazelles. Carpenter

-AFRICAN 77-86 (B538.3.1).

The Girl Who Married a Ghost. Curtis - GIRL 5-20 (E474.7).

The Girl Who Married the Stranger. Johnson - HOW 13-22 (G303.12.5.9).

The Girl Who Overpowered the Moon. Withers - MAN 30-34 (A753.1.0.1).

The Girl Who Picked Strawberries. Manning-Sanders - BOOK..DWARFS 49-52 (G561.2Db); Manning-Sanders - CHOICE 291-294.

The Girl Who Played a Trick on the Devil. Cooper - FIVE 7-25 (K219.5).

The Girl Who Sought Her Nine Brothers. Bowman - TALES..TUPA 116-125 (P253.2E).

The Girl Who Used Her Wits. Tashjian - DEEP 64-69 (H506.12).

The Girl Whom the Moon Pitied. Withers - MAN 21 (A751.7.2).

The Girl With the Large Eyes. Lester - BLACK 57-61 (B610.1.1).

The Girl With the Silver Voice. Titiev - HOW 27-35 (T55.2).

The Girls Who Chose Strange Husbands. Caswell - SHADOWS 76-80 (C26.1).

Giufa and the Judge. Jagendorf - NOODLEHEAD 173-174 (J1193.1).

Gizo and the Great Horse. Aardema - MORE 32-37 (K22.1; K1995).

Gizo's Courting Trick. Aardema - TALES 31-40 (K378.1.1; K1041.1.5).

The Gizzard-Eater. Harris - COMPLETE 698-708 (K544); Harris - FAVORITE 193-202.

The Glass Axe. Lang - YELLOW 156-164 (G530.2Bc).

The Glass Coffin. Grimm - GRIMM'S (Scribner's) 270-277 (F852.1.2).

The Glass House. Wyatt - GOLDEN 45-49 (B437.2.2).

The Glass Mountain. Lang - YELLOW 130-135 (H331.1.1C).

Glooskap. Garner - GOBLINS 210-212 (L410.8.1).

Glooskap, the Whale and the Sorcerer. Williams-Ellis - ROUND 208-216 (R245).

The Gluttonous Wife. Belpré - TIGER 85-86 (W125.2).

The Gnat and the Bull. Aesop - AESOP'S (Grosset) 18 (J953.10); Aesop - AESOP'S (Viking) 42; Aesop - AESOP'S (Watts) 30.

The Gnat and the Lion. Aesop - AESOP'S (Watts) 198-199 (N333.0.1); Green - ANIMAL 43 (L478).

A Gnat on the Bull's Horn. Aesop - AESOP'S (Golden) 10-11 (J953.10).

Go, Close the Door! Simon - MORE 16-23 (J2511.0.2).

Go, I Don't Know Where and Bring Back I Don't Know What. Whitney - IN 1-24 (N831Fb).

Go I Know Not Whither and Fetch I Know Not What. Manning-Sanders - SORCEROR'S 9-23 (N831E).

The Goat. Bulatakin - EURASIAN 90-94 (H1312.1; J2063; K1767).

Goat and Goatherd. Aesop - FABLES (Walck) 118 (J1082.1).

The Goat and the Tiger. Carter - GREEDY 35 (K1715.3.2).

The Goat and the Wolf. Montgomerie - TWENTY-FIVE 32-33 (W165.3).

The Goat in the Well. Green - BIG 52-53 (K652).

The Goat Well. Colwell - SECOND 97-102 (K111.5); Courlander FIRE 57-64.

The Goatherd and the Goat. Aesop - AESOP'S (Watts) 166 (J1082.1).

The Goatherd and the Goats. Aesop - AESOP'S (Grosset) 31 (J345.1).

The Goatherd and the Wild Goats. Aesop - AESOP'S (Watts) 222-223 (J345.1).

The Goatherd Who Won a Princess. Boggs - THREE 111-116 (H342.1).

Goat's Ears. Lang - VIOLET 46-49 (D1316.5.0.3).

The Goat's Funeral. Riordan - TALES..CENTRAL 73-75 (X459.3).

The Goat's Who Killed the Leopard. Courlander - FIRE 25-28 (U31.1).

Gobbleknoll. Garner - CAVALCADE..GOBLINS 1-2 (F912.2.6).

Gobborn Seer. Jacobs - MORE 60-64 (W181.2.0.1); Pilkington - SHAMROCK 104-106.

The Goblin and the Grocer. Grimm - HOUSEHOLD 36-45 (F451.6.2.5).

The Goblin of Adachipahara. Ozaki - JAPANESE 140-147 (C273.3; C611.0.1).

The Goblin Spider. Garner - CAVALCADE..GOBLINS 78-81 (E423.8.2).

The Goblin-Spider. Hearn - JAPANESE 18-20 (E423.8.1); Hearn - JAPANESE (Pauper) 22-24.

The Goblins. Grimm - JUNIPER 150-151 (F321.1.1).

The Goblins at the Bathhouse. Manning-Sanders - BOOK..GHOSTS 14-20 (Q2.1.3Ab); Manning-Sanders - CHOICE 74-80.

The Goblins Giggle. Bang - GOBLINS 47-57 (N777.0.1).

God of the Kitchen. Chang - TALES..OLD CHINA 7-9 (A411.2).

The God That Lived in the Kitchen. Carpenter - TALES..CHINESE 39-46 (A411.2).

Godasiyo the Woman Chief. Brown - TEPEE 71-74 (A1333.2).

Godfather Death. Grimm - BROTHERS 97-101 (D1825.3.1); Grimm- JUNIPER v.2 228-235.

The Gods Know. Frost - LEGENDS 55-63 (C495.1.1).

Goggle-Eyes. Hampden - GYPSY 133-138 (Q2A).

Gohei and the God of Poverty. Novak - FAIRY 39-43 (N250.5).

Going Fishing. Carey - BABA 67-70 (K371.1; K473; K1021).

Gold. Manning-Sanders - BOOK..WIZARDS 40-46 (J347.4.1).

The Gold Children. Grimm - GRIMM'S (Follett) 102-110 (R111.1.3Ak).

The Gold Dust That Turned to Sand. Montgomerie - TWENTY-FIVE 58-59 (J1531.2.0.1).

The Gold Giving Serpent. Jacobs - INDIAN 136-138 (J15.1).

The Gold Knob. Manning-Sanders - BOOK.. OGRES 38-43 (D1472.2.12).

The Gold-Lined Donkey. Davis - LION'S 45-53 (K111.1.1).

The Gold of Bernardino. Sawyer - WAY 85-96 (D1622.2.3).

The Gold Table. Jagendorf - KING 176-180 (F945.1).

Gold-Tree and Silver-Tree. Adams - BOOK.. PRINCESS 56-60 (D582.2); Jacobs - CELTIC 97-101.

The Golden Altar of the Church of St. Joseph. Courlander - RIDE 231-233 (V116.1).

The Golden Apple-Tree and the Nine Peahens. Rackham - FAIRY 100-111 (H1385.3J).

The Golden Apples of Loch Erne. MacManus - BOLD 179-192 (H1331.1Cb).

The Golden Arm. Fenner - GHOSTS 185-187 (E235.4.1); Jacobs - ENGLISH 143-144; Leach - THING 33-36.

The Golden Ax. Spicer - THIRTEEN GOBLINS 28-34 (Q3.1); Uchida - MAGIC 73-81.

The Golden Ball. Jacobs - MORE 12-15 (H1411.4.11); Manning-Sanders - BOOK.. GHOSTS 62-67; Steel - ENGLISH 79-83.

The Golden Bird. Asbjørnsen - NORWEGIAN 49-55 (H1331.1.3); De La Mare - ANIMAL 189-201; Frost - LEGEND 79-88; Green - MIDSUMMER 48-60; Grimm - GRIMM'S (Follett) 111-121; Grimm - GRIMM'S (Grosset) 7-17; Grimm - GRIMM'S (Rackham) 119-127; Grimm - GRIMM'S (Scribner's) 124-133; Grimm - GRIMM'S (World) 202-210; Grimm - HOUSEHOLD 236-243; Grimm - JUNIPER v.2 201-216; Hatch - MORE 214-237; Hutchinson - CHIMNEY 119-132; Kavcic - GOLDEN 15-24; Wiggin - FAIRY 42-51.

The Golden Bird. Huggins - BLUE 15-31 (R111.1.3Al).

The Golden Blackbird. Lang - GREEN 146-152 (H1331.1.3Ak).

The Golden Boat. Ross - BURIED 139-146 (F349.5).

The Golden Box. Hampden - GYPSY 25-33 (D882.1Ea).

The Golden Bowl. Ginsburg - KAHA 13-20 (J151.1).

Golden Bracelets, Golden Anklets. Tooze - WONDERFUL 83-87 (S352.2).

The Golden Buffalo. Vo-Dinh - TOAD 129-135 (D1252.3.1).

The Golden Butterfly. De Leeuw - INDONESIAN 14-20 (A2411.2.1.6.2).

The Golden Calf. Lin - MILKY 72-75 (H506.12).

The Golden Candelabra. Mehdevi - PERSIAN 69-80 (K1341.1).

The Golden Carnation. Toor - GOLDEN 15-21 (D735.1E).

The Golden Castle That Hung in the Air. Asbjørnsen - NORWEGIAN 139-149 (H1213.1J).

The Golden Coal. Müller-Guggenbühl - SWISS 135-137 (F451.5.1.4.2).

The Golden Cock. Dolch - OLD RUSSIA 61-65-79 (B143.1.5).

The Golden Crab. Lang - YELLOW 33-40 (B647.1.1.1); Manning-Sanders - BOOK..

MAGICAL 106–113.

The Golden Cranes. Hulpac – AMERICAN 99–101 (A2411.2.6.14).

The Golden Crow. Htin – KINGDOM 57–61 (Q2.1.6E).

The Golden Deer. Reed – TALKATIVE 52–57 (B241.2.10.1.1).

The Golden Dolls. Bulatkin – EURASIAN 71–74 (H506.13).

The Golden Earth. Courlander – FIRE 127–130 (P711.10).

The Golden Fish. Arnott – ANIMAL 231–240 (D711.2).

The Golden Fish. Ransome – OLD PETER'S 212–227 (B375.1).

Golden Flower and the Three Warriors. Carpenter – SOUTH 123–128 (A962.0.1.3).

Golden Goodness. Jagendorf – KING 135–138 (E121.4.3).

The Golden Goose. Brooke – GOLDEN pb (H341.1); Grimm – GOLDEN (illus. Stobbs) pb; Grimm GRIMM'S (Follett) 122–126; Grimm – GRIMM'S (Grosset) 201–207; Grimm – GRIMM'S (Viking) 22–28; Grimm – GRIMM'S (World) 87–92; Grimm – HOUSEHOLD 265–269; Haviland – FAIRY 58–65; Lang – RED 236–243; Martignoni – ILLUSTRATED 303–306; Shub – ABOUT 47–51; Wiggin – TALES 124–128.

The Golden Goose. Gaer – FABLES..INDIA 164–166 (D877.0.1).

The Golden Gourd. Carpenter – SOUTH 64–70 (N182.2).

Golden Hair. Manning-Sanders – BOOK..GHOSTS 21–24 (E215.1); Manning-Sanders – CHOICE 230–234.

The Golden-Haired Children. Buck – FAIRY 237–250 (N455.4Ad).

The Golden Helmet. De Leeuw – LEGENDS 52–56 (A1437.1).

The Golden Horse. Wilson – GREEK 167–179 (H1213.1H).

The Golden Key. Gag – MORE..GRIMM ix–x (Z12.2); Ginsburg – THREE 17; Grimm – BROTHERS 187; Wiggin – TALES 82.

The Golden Lantern, Golden Goat, and Golden Cloak. Wiggin – FAIRY 27–35 (G610Aa).

Golden Life. Kendall – SWEET 89–91 (D1346.7.1).

The Golden Lion. Haviland – FAVORITE..ITALY 79–90 (K1341.1); Lang – ROSE 114–121.

The Golden Lynx. Baker – GOLDEN 123–130 (G671B).

The Golden Mermaid. Lang – GREEN 316–325 (H1331.1.3Ab).

The Golden Mountain. Wyndham – TALES 22–32 (K1861.1).

The Golden Nightingale. Wilson – GREEK 129–140 (H1331.1.3Eb).

The Golden Oriole. Tooze – WONDERFUL 115–117 (W116.9).

The Golden Parrot. Boggs – THREE 83–96 (K1341.1); Dalgliesh – ENCHANTED 180–184.

The Golden Peacock. Tooze – WONDERFUL 36–42 (K522.4.4).

The Golden Phoenix. Barbeau – GOLDEN 7–25 (H1331.1.3Ca); Colwell – SECOND 67–69.

The Golden Pitcher. Bulatkin – EURASIAN 22–26 (J151.1).

The Golden Pitcher. Fenner – GHOSTS 147–165 (D757.1); Gunterman – CASTLES 13–33.

The Golden Shoes. Jagendorf – NOODLEHEAD 48–52 (J1703.1); Serwer – LET'S 74–79.

The Golden Skins. Spellman – BEAUTIFUL 86–89 (K842E).

The Golden Slipper, the Magic Ring, and the Twigs. Masey – STORIES 122–131 (B652.1.1).

The Golden Snuff-box. Reeves – ENGLISH 158–175 (D882.1Ea); Steel – ENGLISH 27–39.

The Golden Stag. Wyatt – GOLDEN 1–5 (B241.2.10.1.1.1).

The Golden Touch. Farjeon – CAVALCADE.. KINGS 113–132 (J2072.1).

The Golden Twins. Spicer – LONG 29–46 (N455.4C).

Golden Wand. Neufeld – BEWARE 3–10 (H1385.5Ab).

The Goldspinners. Maas – MOON 86–98 (H1021.8.1).

Gombei and the Wild Ducks. Uchida – SEA 91–98 (K687.1).

GONE IS GONE. Gag pb (J2132.2; J2176; J2431); Haviland – FAIRY 48–55; Lurie – CLEVER 92–96.

Good Advice. Durham – TIT 107–116 (J21A).

Good Advice. Green – ANIMAL 34 (J1488).

Good Advice, a Guinea a Piece. Ure – RUMANIAN 69–71 (J21A).

Good and Evil. Riordan - TALES..CENTRAL 45-52 (N452C).

The Good Brother's Reward. Carpenter - KOREAN 221-228 (J2415.13).

The Good Child and the Bad Child, and Gattomammone, and What the Kittens Said. Leach - LION 43-51 (Q2.1.1Cb).

Good Day, Fellow! Asbjørnsen - NORWEGIAN 158-160 (X111.10.1).

The Good-For-Nothings. Gag - MORE 77-83 (K1161.7.2); Grimm - THE GOOD FOR pb.

The Good Fortune Kettle. Haviland - FAVORITE ..JAPAN 23-29 (D1171.3.1).

A Good Guesser. Cimino - DISOBEDIENT #5 (J2712.4).

The Good Housewife and Her Night Helpers. Wilson - SCOTTISH 115-120 (F381.8).

The Good Housewife and Her Night Labors. Haviland - SCOTLAND 59-70 (F381.8).

Good Luck and Bad Luck. Durham - TIT 81-84 (N141.0.1; N351.2).

Good Luck and Common Sense. Wilson - GREEK 21-23 (N141.0.4).

Good Luck and Great Riches. Lowe - LITTLE 67-71 (N22.2; N141.0.5).

The Good-Luck Teakettle. Ross - BURIED 161-172 (D1171.3.1).

The Good-Luck Tree. Heady - TALES 86-89 (D1011.1.1).

The Good Man and the Kind Mouse. Jagendorf - KING 72-78 (K1817.3F).

The Good-natured Blacksmith. Kavcic - GOLDEN 46-55 (Q565Ae).

Good Neighbors Come in All Sizes. Cheney - TALES 53-58 (B362.2).

The Good Night. Sawyer - LONG 61-63 (V211.1.2.2).

The Good Ogre. Manning-Sanders - BOOK.. OGRES 9-19 (G666.3).

The Good Old Man. Williams-Ellis - FAIRY 76-81 (F451.4.4.4).

Good or Bad? Withers - I SAW 32 (Z51.2).

Good Sense and Good Fortune. Borski - GOOD 3-12 (H621; N141.0.1).

Good Speed and the Elephant King. Gaer - FABLES..INDIA 86-89 (K1716).

The Good Sword. Association - DRAGON 181-195 (R111.1.3Ba); Owen - CASTLE 77-88.

Good Uncle Crane. Heady - SAGE 54-56 (R246).

The Good Woman. Manning-Sanders - BOOK.. GHOSTS 119-123 (E422.1.1.3.2).

The Goose and the Golden Eggs. Aesop - AESOP'S (Golden) 33-35; Aesop - AESOP'S (Viking) 27.

Goose Dance. Leekley - WORLD 50-54 (A2332.5.7; K826).

The Goose Girl. Arbuthnot - FAIRY 62-66 (B133.3); De La Mare - ANIMAL 213-223; Grimm - BROTHERS 158-165; Grimm - GOOSE (illus. DeAngeli) pb; Grimm - GRIMM'S (Follett) 127-137; Grimm - GRIMM'S (Grosset) 67-75 ; Grimm - GRIMM'S (Viking) 32-38; Grimm - GRIMM'S (World) 152-158; Grimm - HOUSEHOLD 20-25; Holme - TALES 105-108; Lang - BLUE 286-294; Lang - FIFTY 81-87; Wiggin - FAIRY 236-243.

The Goose Girl at the Well. Grimm - GRIMM'S (Scribner's) 292-304 (H71.8.1).

The Goose That Laid the Golden Eggs. Aesop - AESOP'S (Random) 13-14 (D876); Aesop - AESOP'S (Watts) 2; TALL..NURSERY 120.

The Goose With the Golden Eggs. Aesop - AESOP'S (Grosset) 25 (D876); Jacobs - FABLES 113; Martignoni - ILLUSTRATED 398.

Goro, the Wonderful Wrestler. Aardema - MORE 62-67 (F617.2.3).

Goso the Teacher. Withers - I SAW 143-146 (Z42.0.6).

Gotham Way of Counting. Jagendorf - MERRY 124-120 (J2031).

Goto, King of the Land and the Water. Arnott - AFRICAN 167-168 (T111.1.4).

Grace at Meals. Green - BIG 132-133 (K562.1).

Gramarye, Fog and Fire. Cutt - HOGBOON 66-79 (G271.4.1.1).

Grandfather Frost. Riordan - TALES..CENTRAL 86-90 (Q2.1.4C).

Grandfather Tells Some Tales. Arnott - TEMBA 78-84 (A2411.1.7.1.1; A2513.8).

Grandfather's Advice. Deutsch - TALES 63-68 (J121.3; J151.1).

Grandmother Marta. Pridham - GIFT 100-106 (Q2.1.4Ab).

Granny Shelock. Mehdevi - BUNGLING 37-43 (T11.4.8).

Granny's Blackie. Arbuthnot - FAIRY 163-164 (B599.4); Arbuthnot - ANTHOLOGY 348; Babbitt - JATAKA 77-83.

The Grasshopper and the Ant. Aesop – AESOP'S (Golden) 13-15 (J711.1); Aesop – AESOP'S (Random) 32-33; Aesop – AESOP'S (Watts) 125; Arbuthnot – FAIRY 233; Kent – MORE 28-31.

The Grateful Ant. Green – ANIMAL 73 (B362.2).

The Grateful Beasts. Carpenter – ELEPHANT'S 114-124 (D817.1.2.1; D882.1.1.1); De La Mare – ANIMALS 170-178; Grimm – GRIMM'S (World) 367-371.

The Grateful Beasts. Lang – YELLOW 74-75 (N452Ab).

The Grateful Bergmännlein. Duvoisin – THREE 152-157 (F460.4.2.7).

The Grateful Devil. Spicer – THIRTEEN 72-81 (G303.22.11.1).

The Grateful Fox Fairy. Carpenter – TALES.. CHINESE 89-97 (B651.1.2).

The Grateful Goat. Manning-Sanders – BOOK.. MAGICAL 86-90 (B413.1).

The Grateful Lion. Green – ANIMAL 11-13 (B381).

The Grateful Monkey's Secret. Uchida – SEA 22-32 (D925.0.2.1).

The Grateful Mouse. Gaer – FABLES..INDIA 149-152 (B437.2.2).

The Grateful Old Cailleach. Leodhas – GAELIC 46-56 (E363.2.1).

The Grateful Prince. Lang – VIOLET 73-95 (G530.2Be); Maas – MOON 60-81 (G530.2Bk).

The Grateful Rooster. Kavcic – GOLDEN 38-45 (K1917.3E).

The Grateful Statues. Sakade – JAPANESE 106-110 (J1873.1).

The Grateful Stork. Uchida – MAGIC LISTENING 133-144 (B652.2.1).

The Grateful Tiger. Kim – STORY 138-144 (B382.1).

The Grateful Toad. Bang – MEN 27-31 (R221Di).

Gratitude. Novak – FAIRY 100-107 (W154.8.3).

The Gratitude of the Samebito. Hearn – BOY 5-13 (B11.6.1.3).

Grayfoot. Haviland – DANISH 44-63 (H465).

Graylegs. Hatch – MORE DANISH 3-21 (H465Bc).

Graymoss on Green Tree. Arbuthnot – ANTHOLOGY 392 (A2683.1.1).

Grazing on the Roof. Jagendorf – MERRY 77-86 (J1904.1).

The Great and Little Fishes. Aesop – AESOP'S (Golden) 77-79 (L331).

The Great Bear. Withers – MAN 105-112 (F601.2De).

The Great Bear. Leach – HOW 133-134 (A771.0.1; A2769.2).

The Great Bear of Orange. Manning-Sanders – SORCEROR'S 56-64 (D735.1).

The Great Bell. Buck – FAIRY 264-268 (S261.0.2).

The Great Bell of Bosham. Colwell – ROUND 105-107 (F993).

The Great Bell of Peking. Wyndham – FOLK.. CHINA 66-72 (S261.0.2).

THE GREAT BIG ENORMOUS TURNIP. Tolstoy pb (Z49.9).

The Great Bird in the Carob Tree. Carpenter – SOUTH 11-17 (A282.2).

The Great Blessing of the Land. Jagendorf – KING 122-126 (A2685.1.1).

The Great Calamity and If. Simon – MORE 54-62 (J2063.5).

The Great Fifteenth Day. Carpenter – KOREAN 109-116 (K2369.15.1).

The Great Fish. Michael – PORTUGUESE 92-104 (B314F).

The Great Flood. Jagendorf – KING 81-83 (A747.1; A935.4; A1011.2; A1404).

The Great Flood. Kim – STORY 66-75 (W154.8.5); Sechrist – ONCE 8-11 (A1010).

Great Head and Ten Brothers. Garner – CAVALCADE..GOBLINS 101-104 (G361.2).

Great Hunting. Withers – WORLD 85-86 (X1124.3.1).

The Great Lizard of Nimple. Courlander – TIGER'S 140-143 (A955.3.1.2).

The Great Shell of Kintyel. Brown – TEPEE 28-39 (B455.3.2).

The Great Spirit of the Toad. Pratt – MAGIC #5 (B98.1).

The Great Traveler of Chelm. Jagendorf – NOODLEHEAD 53-58 (J2014.2).

The Great Tug of War. Arbuthnot – ANTHOLOGY 318-320 (K22.1); Sturton – ZOMO 114-125.

The Great White Condor. Barlow – LATIN 50-56 (A2686.4.4).

The Greater Sinner. Neufeld – BEWARE 36-41

Guinea Fowl and Rabbit Get Justice. Courlander – COWTAIL 87-93 (K453.1).

Guinea Hen's Children. Dorliae – ANIMALS 56-61 (E66; J267.1.1).

The Guitar Player. Leach – THING 20-21 (J1495.1).

Gulaida. Mittleman – BIRD 30-42 (R221De).

Guleesh. Jacobs – CELTIC 6-28 (F282.4.1); Rackham – FAIRY 34-51.

The Gull. Deutsch – TALES..FARAWAY 36-43 (A1945.2).

A Gullible World. Fillmore – SHEPHERD'S 153-159 (J2326.5; K1252).

The Gun, the Pot and the Hat. Courlander – PIECE 39-49 (K111.2; K119.5).

Guno and Koyo. Courlander – KANTCHIL'S 58-62 (J1972.1).

Guno and Koyo and the Kris. Courlander – TIGER'S 118-121 (J1516.1).

Guno's Hunger. Courlander – KANTCHIL'S 72-74 (J2213.3).

Gwarwyn-a-Throt. Sheppard-Jones – WELSH 13-18 (F369.10; F381.1.1).

The Gypsies' Fiddle. Jagendorf – GYPSIES' 102-106 (D1233.0.2).

The Gypsy and the Snake. Jagendorf – GYPSIES' 24-34 (G501C; K1741.2.1).

The Gypsy Fiddle. Hampden – GYPSY 155-157 (D1233.0.1).

The Gypsy in the Guest House. Jagendorf – GYPSIES' 111-117 (E373.1).

Ha! Tio Rabbit is Bigger. Jagendorf – KING 211-218 (A2325.1.1).

Habetrot and Scantlie Mab. Jacobs – MORE 195-200 (D2183.1).

The Haddam Witches. Hoke – WITCHES 187-191 (G243.1.2).

Hag-of-the-Mist. Pugh – MORE..WELSH 39-54 (R111.1.3Aq).

The Haggary Nag. MacManus – WELL 138-155 (H1213.1B).

The Hairbrained Monkey. Gaer – FABLES..INDIA 153-154 (J344.1).

The Hairy Boggart. Williams-Ellis – FAIRY 82-87 (K171.1).

The Hairy Boggart's Field. Spicer – THIRTEEN 35-44 (K171.1).

The Hairy Man from the Forest. Carpenter – SOUTH 93-99 (G524.0.1).

The Haitians in the Dominican Republic. Jagendorf – KING 106-110 (C495.2.2.2; J2496.3).

Haku's Power. McNeil – DOUBLE 37-40 (Z42.0.2).

Halde Hat and Dulde Hat. De Regniers – GIANT 106-108 (D1361.14.1).

Half-a-Ball-of-Kenki. Aardema –MORE 7-11 (A2412.1.2.2; A2433.5.2.1); Aardema HALF pb.

HALF A KINGDOM. McGovern pb (K975.2.1).

The Half-Chick. Arbuthnot – ANTHOLOGY 264-266 (B171.1.2); Arbuthnot – FAIRY 131-132; Dobbs – ONCE 8-14; Haviland – FAIRY 66-70; Haviland – FAVORITE..SPAIN 36-49; Lang – GREEN 29-34; Martignoni – ILLUSTRATED 246-248; Montgomerie – MERRY 24-27 (Z52.2).

Halibut Man and the House on the Waves. DeWit TALKING 149-154 (A2109.2).

Hallabu's Jealousy. Arnott – AFRICAN 160-166 (H12.2.0.1).

Hamdani. Green – FOLK..AFRICA 37-51 (K1917.3l).

The Hand of Glory. Lurie – CLEVER 53-56 (D1162.2.1.1).

A Handful of Hay. Manning-Sanders – PETER 71-82 (H1321.1Cd).

A Handful of Peas. Reed – TALKATIVE 68-69 (J344.1).

The Hand of the Lord. Jagendorf – PRICELESS 59-60 (A2711.3.1).

The Handkerchief. Gilstrap – SULTAN'S 51-60 (H335.0.2.2.1).

The Handless Maiden. Grimm – GRIMM'S (Scribner's) 87-94 (H1385.3L).

Hans and His Master. Manning-Sanders – BOOK.. GHOSTS 55-61 (E415.1.2); Manning-Sanders – CHOICE 224-250.

Hans Hansen's Hired Girl. Withers – WORLD 43-44 (J2012.2).

Hans Humdrum. Hatch – THIRTEEN 148-149 (K172; K404.1).

Hans in Luck. Carle – ERIC 11-24 (J2081.1; J2081.1.1); Grimm – GRIMM'S (World) 45-51; Grimm – HANS (illus. Hoffmann) pb; Grimm – HANS (illus. McKee) pb; Grimm – HOUSEHOLD 14-19; Hutchinson – FIRESIDE 129-139; Wiggins – TALES 62-67.

Hans Kuhschwanz. Duvoisin - THREE 162-166 (N531.1).

Hans My Hedgehog. Grimm - BROTHERS 151-157 (B641.5); Grimm - JUNIPER v. 1 11-22.

Hans, the Horn, and the Magic Sword. Manning-Sanders - BOOK..GIANTS 36-43 (H11.1.1).

Hansel and Gretel. Arbuthnot - FAIRY 45-48 (G412.1); Darrell - ONCE 59-65; Fenner - GIANTS 126-137; Gag - TALES 3-24; Grimm - BROTHERS 124-132; Grimm - GRIMM'S (Follett) 138-139; Grimm - GRIMM'S (Scribner's) 37-45; Grimm - GRIMM'S (World) 15-23; Grimm - HANSEL (Delacorte) pb; Grimm - HANSEL (Morrow) pb; Haviland - FAVORITE..GERMANY 51-71; Lang - BLUE 267-276; Lang - FIFTY 98-105; Manning-Sanders - BOOK..WITCHES 83-93; Martignoni - ILLUSTRATED 178-183; Opie - CLASSIC 236-244; Rackham - ARTHUR 269-277; Shub - ABOUT 99-107.

Hansel and Grethel. Grimm - HOUSEHOLD 85-92 (G412.1).

Hansel and Grettel. Arbuthnot - ANTHOLOGY 185-187 (G412.1).

Hanstje and the Remarkable Beast. Spicer - THIRTEEN 25-32 (H682.1.9; K31.1; K171.1).

Happiness Is Not Where You Seek It. Shah - MULLA 107 (U69).

Happy Boz'll. Manning-Sanders - RED 174-175 (X1215.11.1); Williams-Ellis - FAIRY..BRITAIN 32-33.

The Happy Cure. Dobbs - ONCE 27-33 (N135.3).

The Happy Ghost. Cheney - TALES 93-96 (E605.7.2).

HAPPY GO LUCKY. Wiesner pb (J2081.1).

The Happy Hunter and the Skillful Fisher. Ozaki - JAPANESE 153-179 (U136.0.1).

The Happy Man. Gilstrap - SULTAN'S 26-31 (N135.3).

The Happy Milkmaid. Brenner - BOY 12-13 (J2061).

The Hardhearted Rich Man. Maher - BLIND 115-131 (D672G).

Hardy Hardback. Williams-Ellis - FAIRY..BRITAIN 124-131 (F601.2Ad).

Hardy Hardhead. Chase - JACK 96-105 (F601.2Ad).

The Hare. Borski - GOOD 60 (J881.1).

The Hare and the Baboons. Colwell - MAGIC 107-110 (J1565.1; K278).

Hare and the Corn Bins. Arnott - AFRICAN 101-104 (J1149.13; K371).

The Hare and the Fox. Wiggin - TALES 191-192 (K341.2.1; K1021).

The Hare and the Frog. Carrick - STILL MORE 88-94 (J881.1).

The Hare and the Hedgehog. De La Mare - ANIMAL 3-8 (K11.1); De La Mare - TALES 9-14; Gruenberg - MORE 144-147; Hutchinson - FIRESIDE 67-73.

The Hare and the Hound. Aesop - AESOP'S (Grosset) 21 (U242); Aesop - AESOP'S (Watts) 111; Kent - MORE 20-21.

Hare and the Hyena. Arnott - AFRICAN 108-111 (K335.0.4.3.1).

The Hare and the Lioness. Arnott - ANIMAL 104-111 (K933; K1066.3).

The Hare and the Lord. Jagendorf - MERRY 105-112 (J1881.2.2).

The Hare and the Tiger. Bulatkin - EURASIAN 80-81 (K1715.1); Vo-Dinh - TOAD 57-64 (K84.2; K1715.2.1).

The Hare and the Tortoise. Aesop - AESOP'S (Golden) 83-85 (K11.3); Aesop - AESOP'S (Grosset) 34-35; Aesop - AESOP'S (Random) 33-36; Aesop - AESOP'S (Viking) 30-31; Aesop - AESOP'S (Watts) 92; Aesop - FABLES 135; Aesop - FIVE 70; Aesop - HARE (Whittlesey) pb; Arbuthnot - FAIRY 230; Kent - MORE 16-19; La Fontaine - HARE (Watts) pb; Martignoni - ILLUSTRATED 157.

THE HARE AND THE TORTOISE AND THE TORTOISE AND THE HARE. Dubois (Doubleday) pb (K544).

The Hare and the Widow. Nunn - AFRICAN 26-30 (A2511.2).

Hare and Tortoise. Aesop - FABLES (Walck) 68-73 (K11.3).

The Hare in the Moon. Cathon - PERHAPS 250-252 (A751.2); Turnbull - FAIRY 151-157; Wyatt - GOLDEN 112-117.

Hare Makes a Fool of Leopard. Haskett - GRAINS 51-54 (A2378.9.5.1; K1241.1; K1251).

The Hare of Inaba. Hearn - JAPANESE 42-46 (K579.2.2; K1014.3).

The Hare That Ran Away. Arbuthnot - ANTHOLOGY 347 (Z43.3.1); Arbuthnot - FAIRY 163; Davis - BAKER 21-28.

The Hare, the Hyena and the Guinea Fowl. Guillot - GUILLOT'S 84-87 (K714.2.4.1; K715.1.1).

The Hare, the Lions, the Monkey and Hare's

Spotted Blanket. Colwell - SECOND 80-84 (K1066.6).

The Hare Who Had Been Married. Asbjørnsen - NORWEGIAN 115 (Z51.3).

The Hare with Many Friends. Arbuthnot - FAIRY 224 (H1558.4); Aesop - AESOP'S (Grosset) 19-20; Jacobs - FABLES 138-139; Rice - ONCE 34-39.

The Hares and the Frogs. Aesop - AESOP'S (Grosset) 79 (J881.1); Aesop - AESOP'S (Viking) 16 ; Aesop - AESOP'S (Watts) 22; Aesop - FIVE 38; Jacobs - FABLES 29.

The Hare's Kidneys. Tashjian - THREE 48-61 (J2411.1.0.3).

The Hare's Lip. Cathon - PERHAPS 62-63 (A2211.2; J881.1).

Harisarman. Jacobs - INDIAN 104-109 (K1956.2; N688); Wiggin - TALES 393-396.

The Harp That Harped Without a Harper. Frost - LEGEND 99-113 (H1385.1A).

The Hart and the Hunter. Aesop - AESOP'S (Grosset) 125-126 (L461); Jacobs - FABLES 49.

The Hart in the Ox-Stall. Aesop - AESOP'S (Grosset) 156-157 (J1032): Jacobs - FABLES 58.

The Hart, the Sheep, and the Wolf. Aesop - FIVE 16 (J625.1).

Hasan and Husain. Mittleman - BIRD 99-116 (S268B).

Hasty Porridge In the Boiling Water. Jagendorf - MERRY 64-68 (J1938).

Hatchet Gruel. Ginsburg - THREE 25-26 (K112.2).

Hatchet Kasha. Wyndham - TALES..RUSSIA 38-42 (K112.2).

The Hated Dog Gban. Dorliae - ANIMALS 52-55 (A2455.6).

The Haunted Alp. Duvoisin - THREE 196-202 (H1411.4.1).

The Haunted House. De Leeuw - LEGEND.. HOLLAND 81-88 (H1411.4.7).

The Haunted Palace. Novak - FAIRY 125-130 (Q82.0.1).

The Hawk and the Farmer. Aesop - AESOP'S (Grosset) 116 (U32.1).

The Hawk and the Heir. Deutsch - TALES 1-6 (A2321.10.0.1).

The Hawk and the Pigeons. Aesop - AESOP'S (Grosset) 44-45 (K815.8).

The Hawk and the Wildcat. Sechrist - ONCE 54-56 (K334.1).

The Hawk, the Kite and the Pigeons. Aesop - AESOP'S (Watts) 220 (K815.8).

The Hazelnut Child. Lang - YELLOW 239-241 (F535.1.1Db); Manning-Sanders - DWARFS 84-88.

He Knows the Answer. Shah - MULLA 97 (J1861).

He Who Is Feared by All. Burton - MAGIC 47-51 (K1711.2.2; K1715.3.2).

He Wins Who Waits. Lang - FIFTY 106-114 (F813.8.3).

The Head. Leach - THING 63-64 (Q551.3.3).

The Head of Brass. Williams-Ellis - FAIRY.. BRITAIN 186-195 (D1711.6.5).

The Head of the Family. Kelsey - MULLAH 38 (H601).

The Head of the Inca. Jagendorf - KING 113-116 (A977.5.0.5).

The Headhunters. Lu Mar - CHINESE 127-146 (W28.5).

The Headless Horseman. Manning-Sanders - BOOK..GHOSTS 80-86 (E422.1.1.3.1.1).

Heartless Beauty. Manton - FLYING 40-45 (J2199.1.4).

Heaven and Earth and Man. Birch - CHINESE 3-8 (A541; A614; A1241.3.3).

Heaven and Hell. Chang - TALES..OLD CHINA 47-49 (W47.1).

The Heavenly Lovers. Carpenter - ELEPHANT'S 212-219 (A736.1.3.1; A978.4).

The Heavenly Spinning Maid. Bonnet - CHINESE 89-96 (A778.3.2).

Heavenly Treasure, Earthly Treasure. Scofield - HOLD 21-26 (N182.1).

Heavy Collar and the Ghost Woman. Brown - TEPEE 160-166 (E425.1.10); Hardendorff - JUST 139-149.

The Hedge and the Vineyard. Aesop - AESOP'S (Grosset) 231 (W181.1.1).

The Hedge King. Grimm - GRIMM'S (Follett) 150-153 (A2426.2.23; A2433.4.7; A2491.2.4; K17.1.1).

THE HEDGEHOG AND THE HARE. Grimm (World) pb (K11.1).

The Hedgehog and the Rabbit. Gag - MORE.. GRIMM 163-170 (K11.1).

The Hedgehog Who Became a Prince. Baker - GOLDEN 119-122 (B641.5).

The Hedley Kow. Jacobs - MORE 55-59 (E427); Manning-Sanders - BOOK..MAGICAL 3-7; Mayne - GHOSTS 103-106; Palmer - DRAGONS 63-67.

HEE HAW. McGovern (Houghton) pb (J1041.2).

The Heifer and the Ox. Aesop - AESOP'S (Grosset) 65 (L456); Aesop - AESOP'S (Watts) 144.

The Heifer Hide. Chase - JACK 161-171 (K842Bb).

The Helmites Capture the Moon. Simon - WISE 35-42 (J1791.2.2).

Help, Thieves in Helm! Simon - WISE 55-66 (J1703.2).

The Hemp Smoker and the Hemp Grower. Courlander - KING'S 101-105 (K1869.1).

The Hen and the Cat. Aesop - AESOP'S (Grosset) 133 (K2061.7); Aesop - AESOP'S (Viking) 73.

The Hen and the Fox. Aeosp - AESOP'S (Grosset) 54-55 (K2061.7); Martignoni - ILLUSTRATED 156-157.

The Hen and the Hawk. Fuja - FOURTEEN 113-115 (A2494.13.10.3.2).

The Hen That Laid Diamond Eggs. Manning-Sanders - RED 16-22 (D551.1Ac).

The Hen That Saved the World. Sperry - HEN 57-64 (Z43.3); Sperry - SCANDINAVIAN 21-26.

The Hen Trips in the Mountain. Aulaire - EAST 207-215 (G561.1A).

Heng O, the Moon Lady. Carpenter - TALES.. CHINESE 206-216 (A751.8.7).

Henny-Penny. Arbuthnot - ANTHOLOGY 154-155 (Z43.3); Arbuthnot - FAIRY 12-13; Colwell - YOUNGEST 169-173; De La Mare - ANIMAL 47-59; Galdone - HENNY pb; Haviland - FAIRY 12-15; Hutchinson - CHIMNEY 3-8 (Z53); Jacobs - ENGLISH 118-121; Martignoni - ILLUSTRATED 66-68; Montgomerie - TWENTY-FIVE 24-25; Rackham - ARTHUR 66-70; Rockwell - THREE 63-70; Steel - ENGLISH 152-156; Stobbs - HENNY pb; Wiggin - TALES 241-243.

Hercules and Plutus. Aesop - AESOP'S (Watts) 204 (J451.3).

Hercules and the Wagoner. Aesop - AESOP'S (Grosset) 100 (J1034); Aesop - AESOP'S (Viking) 73; Aesop - AESOP'S (Watts) 82-83; Arbuthnot - FAIRY 226; Jacobs - FABLES 121.

Herding the King's Hares. Aulaire - EAST 15-26 (H1045.0.1); Undset - TRUE 161-172.

The Herdsman and the Lost Bull. Aesop - AESOP'S (Watts) 153 (J561.2).

The Herdsman of Lona. Duvoisin - THREE 89-93 (A939.2).

The Herdsman's Choice. Duvoisin - THREE 101-110 (F384.5).

Here We Go! Harper - GHOSTS 222-224 (F482.3.1.1); Leach - THING 17-19.

Hereafterthis. Jacobs - HEREAFTERTHIS pb (J1903.5; K362.1); Jacobs - MORE 7-11; Wiggin - TALES 224-227.

The Hermit and the Mouse. Gaer - FABLES.. INDIA 56-57 (W154.2.1.1).

The Hermit and the Sea of Man. Korel - LISTEN 71-75 (K1673.1).

The Hermit Cat. Korel - LISTEN 21-27 (K815.7).

The Hermit with Two Heads. Holding - SKY-EATER 61-74 (K635.2).

The Hero. Jagendorf - NOODLEHEAD 212-215 (J1758.5).

The Hero in the Village. Jagendorf - KING 49-51 (J2132.5.4).

The Hero of Adi Nifas. Courlander - FIRE 45-50 (J2031.0.1).

The Heron. Aesop - AESOP'S (Random) 68-70 (J321.5).

The Heron and the Crane. Carey - BABA 42-43 (W123.2).

The Heron and the Turtle. Arnott - ANIMAL 49-58 (B545.3).

The Heron's Ball. Withers - I SAW 53-54 (Z41.2.3).

Heyo, House. Arbuthnot - FAIRY 218-219 (K607.1); Harris - COMPLETE 551-554; Harris - FAVORITE 159-161.

Hidden Depths. Shah - MULLA 81 (J1060.1).

The Hidden Hoe. Withers - WORLD 73-74 (J2356.1).

Hidden Laiva or the Golden Ship. Arbuthnot - FAIRY 139-143 (D551.1H); Bowman - TALES.. TUPA 42-52.

The Hidden Treasure of Khin. Courlander - TIGER'S 29-32 (H588.7.1).

La Hormiguita. Belpré - TIGER 57-61 (Z42.0.5).

La Hormiguita and Perez the Mouse. Sawyer - PICTURE..SPAIN 111-120 (Z32.3).

A Horned Goat. Borski - JOLLY 49-62 (K2324; Z39.1); Zajdler - POLISH 141 -147 (K1151).

The Horned Woman. Baker - TALKING 48-51 (F381.8); Hoke - WITCHES 1-4; Jacobs - CELTIC 34-37; Littledale - GHOSTS 61-66.

The Horse. Cutt - HOGBOON 51-55 (E521.1).

The Horse and His Rider. Aesop - AESOP'S (Watts) 98 (J1483.2).

The Horse and the Ass. Aesop - AESOP'S (Viking) 60-61 (L452.1; L452.2); Aesop - AESOP'S (Watts) 218; Jacobs - FABLES 155 (J212.1).

The Horse and the Eighteen Bandits. Vo-Dinh - TOAD 105-113 (A501.3).

The Horse and the Groom. Aesop - AESOP'S (Grosset) 75-76 (W152.13.2); Aesop - AESOP'S (Viking) 67; Aesop - AESOP'S (Watts) 6.

The Horse and the Laden Ass. Aesop - AESOP'S (Grosset) 84-85 (W155.1).

The Horse and the Lion. Aesop - AESOP'S (Grosset) 208-209 (K1121.1); Aesop - AESOP'S (Viking) 49-50; Martignoni - ILLUSTRATED 397.

The Horse and the Stag. Aesop - AESOP'S (Watts) 211 (K192).

The Horse and the Wild Boar. Aesop - AESOP'S (Viking 36 (K192).

Horse and Toad. Wolkstein - MAGIC 143-150 (K11.1).

The Horse Egg. Jagendorf - NOODLEHEAD 19-23 (J1772.1).

The Horse, Hunter and Stag. Aesop - AESOP'S (Grosset) 28-29 (K192); Jacobs - FABLES 64.

The Horse of Seven Colors. Cothran - MAGIC 60-65 (H1471.0.1).

The Horse with His Head Where His Tail Ought to Be. Leach - NOODLES 70-71 (J1903.6).

The Horse without a Master. Courlander - RIDE 95-98 (J217.3).

The Horsefly. Tashjian - THREE 36-39 (A2236.1).

Hot Times. Courlander - TERRAPIN'S 67-68 (X1632).

The Hound and the Fox. Aesop -AESOP'S (Watts) 155 (J952.3).

The Hound and the Hare. Aesop - AESOP'S (Watts) 104 (K2031).

The Hound Gelert. Sheppard-Jones - WELSH 134-136 (B331.2).

A House for the Crocodile. Sturton - ZOMO 100-112 (K714.2.4.2).

The House in the Middle of the Road. Aardema - BEHIND 74-80 (F912.2.1).

The House in the Wood. Dalgliesh - ENCHANTED 116-123 (Q2.1.3C); Grimm - GRIMM'S (Scribner's) 278-284; Grimm - HOUSE 1-14; Lang - FIFTY 122-127.

The House in the Woods. Sechrist - ONCE 128-131 (P253.2.0.1F).

The House Mouse and the Country Mouse. Asbjørnsen - NORWEGIAN 116-119 (J211.2).

The House of Cats. Hampden - HOUSE 3-8 (Q2.1.1Ca).

The House of Chang Kung. Dolch - STORIES.. OLD CHINA 131-137 (A411.2).

The House on the Hill. Richardson - GREAT 153-160 (B296.0.1).

The House That Jack Built. Galdone - HOUSE pb (Z44); Rockwell - THREE 45-52.

The House That Lacked a Bogle. Leodhas - GAELIC 100-110 (E402.1.3.2).

The House That Strong Boy Built. Jagendorf - KING 34-39 (W125.3.1.1).

The House with the Grand Door at the Back. Sheppard-Jones - WELSH 156-158 (F541.4.4.4).

The House with the Heads. De Leeuw - LEGENDS ..HOLLAND 114-118 (K912.0.3).

The House without Eyes or Ears. Leach - NOODLES 55 (H583.8).

How a Boy Got a Baboon. Withers - I SAW 135-138 (K251.1.4.2).

How a Fish Swam in the Air. Lang - VIOLET 114-120 (J1151.1.1).

How a Peasant Cured His Wife of Telling Tales. Riordan - TALES..CENTRAL 233-237 (J1151.1.1).

How a Peasant Outwitted Two Merchants. Borski - GOOD 26-28 (K92.4).

How a Piegan Warrior Found the Finest Horses. Brown - TEPEE 98-99 (A1881.4).

How a Young Man Became a Chief. Withers - I SAW 139-140 (K251.1.4.1).

How Abunawas Was Exiled. Courlander - FIRE 81-88 (J1161.3.2; K842.0.2); Green - FOLK.. AFRICA 65-73 (K1413).

How an Old Man Lost His Wen. Ozaki – JAPAN-ESE 273-282 (F344.1.1).

How Animals Brought Fire to Man. Fisher – CALIFORNIA 46-53 (A1415.2.2.1; A2378.9.6).

How Animals Got Their Beautiful Coats. Kaula – AFRICAN 88-90 (A2411.1.1.1; A2411.1.7.1.1).

How Antelope Carrior Saved the Thunderbirds and Became Chief of the Winged Creatures. Brown – TEPEE 22-26 (B16.5.1.4).

How Baboons Came Into the World. Leach – HOW 58 (A1863).

How Baby Wart Hog Saved His Father's Life. Burton – MAGIC 68-71 (K961.1.2).

How Bat Won the Ball Game. Leach – HOW 70 (B261.0.2).

How Bear Got His Stripe. Leach – HOW 127-128 (A2741.1; F662.3; F1025.1).

How Bear Lost His Tail. Bruchac – TURKEY 31-33 (K1021).

How Beaver Got His Fine Fur. Belting – LONG 79-84 (A728.2.1).

How Beetles Got Their Beautiful Coats. Newman – FOLK..LATIN 67-71 (A2411.1.4.3.1; A2411.3.3; K11.10).

How Blanca the Haughty Became Gentle. Gun-terman – CASTLES 179-201 (H465Ba).

How Blue Crane Taught Jackal to Fly. Aardema – BEHIND 26-33 (K1041.0.1).

How Bobtail Beat the Devil. Chase – WICKED 88-99 (K171.1; K171.4; K1746).

How Brer Rabbit Saved Brer B'ar's Life. Harris – COMPLETE 757-760 (K543; K1251).

How Br'er Wasp Got His Small Waist. Frost – LEGENDS 174-176 (A2355.1.3).

How Brother Fox Failed To Get His Grapes. Harris – COMPLETE 177-182 (K1023).

How Brother Fox Was Too Smart. Harris – NIGHTS 260-267, 17-20 (K1039.1); Harris – COMPLETE 306-311, 130-133.

How Brother Rabbit Brought Family Trouble on Brother Fox. Harris – COMPLETE 823-833 (

How Brother Rabbit Frightened His Neighbors. Harris – NIGHTS 118-122 (K335.0.4.8); Harris – COMPLETE 202-206.

How Brother Rabbit Got the Meat. Harris – COMPLETE 209-212 (K335.0.1); Harris – NIGHTS 128-131.

How Buffalo Were Released On Earth. Brown – TEPEE 63-65 (A1878.3).

How California Was Made. Fisher – STORIES 10-15 (A815; A1145.2.1).

How Celebes Got Its Name. Courlander – KANT-CHIL'S 40-51 (A999.1).

How Chameleon Became King of the Animals. Kaula – AFRICAN 67-70 (K11.2).

How Chief Bear Lost His Tail. Parker – SKUN-NY 102-108 (K1021).

How Chipmunk Got His Stripes. Leach – HOW 75-76 (A1172; A2217.2); Newell – RESCUE 63-68 (A1172.4.1).

How Confusion Came Among the Animals. Cour-lander – KANTCHIL'S 52-56 (A1382.2; Z43.7).

How Corn Came to Earth. Brown – TEPEE 65-70 (A1024.1).

How Coyote Became a Friend to Man. Fisher – CALIFORNIA 74-79 (A2235.2).

How Coyote Got His Voice. Fisher – STORIES (A1611.1.5; A2426.1.7).

How Coyote Helped to Light the World. Fisher – CALIFORNIA 16-23 (A717.2).

How Coyote Put Fish in Clear Lake. Fisher – CALIFORNIA 80-86 (A2108.1).

How Coyote Put Salmon in the Klamath River. Fisher – CALIFORNIA 96-102 (A1421.0.0.1).

How Coyote Stole Fire. Haviland – NORTH 52-56 (A1415.2.2.1.2); Robinson – COYOTE 79-84.

How Crab Got a Hard Back. Sherlock – WEST 86-92 (C432.1).

How Crane Got His Long Beak. Leach – HOW 101 (A2343.1.6).

How Crane Got His Long Legs. Belting – LONG 67-70 (A751.2.2; A2371.2.13).

How Death Came. Heady – TALES 109-118 (A1335.18; F81.1).

How Deer Got His Antlers. Bell – JOHN 67-69 (A2326.1.1.1).

How the Deer Got His Horns. Belting – LONG 57-59 (A2326.1.1.1).

How Dog Came to Live With Man. Haskett – GRAINS 101-102 (A2513.1.5).

How Dog Outwitted Leopard. Aardema – TALES 49-53 (K335.0.1).

How Duck Got His Bill. Belting – LONG 74-75 (A2343.1.5).

How El Bizarrón Fooled the Devil. Carter –
GREEDY 23-29 (G501B).

How Fire Came to Tonga. Gittins – TALES 52-
55 (A1415.5).

How Fire Took Water to Wife. Carey – BABA
81-83 (A1439.5).

How Flint-Face Lost His Name. Brenner – BOY
71-75 (W153.17).

How Fox and Raccoon Tricked One Another.
Parker – SKUNNY 23-30 (A2494.9.3).

How Frog Lost His Tail. Kaula – AFRICAN 63-
64 (A2378.2.3.1).

How Frogs Lost Their Tails. Belting – LONG
34-36 (A1415.2.2.1.1).

How God Helped Mammo. Davis – LION'S 153-
158 (W111.9).

How God Made the Butterflies. Lester – BLACK
15-20 (A2041.1).

How Glooskap Found the Summer. Haviland –
NORTH 57-59 (A1153.1).

How Glooskap Made the Birds. Frost – LEGENDS
287-294 (A2760.2).

How Grandpa Moved the Lord's Meadow. Ginsburg – TWELVE 22-23 (J1289.33).

How Grigori Petrovitch Divided the Geese.
Wyndham – TALES..RUSSIA 16-21 (H601).

How Hare Asked for Wisdom. Haskett – GRAINS
40-42 (A1481.2.1; K714.2.4.1.1; K721.2).

How Ijapa, Who Was Short, Became Long. Courlander – OLODE 37-39 (J1565.1.3).

How Ina Tatooed the Fish. Gittins – TALES 76-
78 (A2412.4.6).

How Jack Went to Seek His Fortune. Haviland –
NORTH 141-143 (K335.1.4; K1161.1); Hutchin-
son – CANDLELIGHT 107-113; Jacobs – ENG-
LISH 24-26; Steel – ENGLISH 185-188.

How Joeagah, the Raccoon, Ate the Crabs.
Parker – SKUNNY 68-71 (K607.3.4).

How Juan Married a Princess. Sechrist – ONCE
135-140 (K251.1.5).

How King Yudhisthera Came to the Gates of
Heaven with His Dog. Turnbull – FAIRY 168-
170 (A489.5).

How Kingfisher Got His Necklace. Leach – HOW
96 (A2321.5.1).

How Kwaku Ananse Became Bald. Appiah –
ANANSE 95-104 (A2317.2.2).

How Kwaku Ananse Destroyed a Kingdom. Appiah – ANANSE 105-112 (K735.1.1).

How Kwaku Ananse Won a Kingdom With a Grain
of Corn. Appiah – ANANSE 1-26 (A185.12.1.1;
H501.4; K251.1.0.1).

How Life and Light Came Into the World. Courlander – RIDE 224-225 (A711.1.1).

How Lizard Lost and Regained His Farm. Courlander – HAT 70-76 (K275.1; K453.1).

How Locusts Came to Be. Sechrist – ONCE 34-
37 (A2062.1).

How Long Will It Take? Walker – TALES 232
(J2752); Walker – WATERMELON 60-61.

How Loon Learned His Call. Leach – HOW 97
(A2426.2.19).

How Man Began. McDowell – THIRD 131-132
(A1236; A1263.7.1).

How Man Learned to Make Time. Leach – HOW
52 (A1414.1.1.3).

How Mankind Learned to Make Bread. Leach –
HOW 53-54 (A1414.8).

How Many Donkeys? Arbuthnot – ANTHOLOGY
300-301 (J2031.2); Arbuthnot – FAIRY 185-186;
Dobbs – ONCE 91-95; Kelsey – HODJA 1-6.

How Marriages Are Made. Birch – CHINESE 43-
47 (M383.2).

How Master Thumb Defeated the Sun. Htin –
KINGDOM 46-52 (F535.1.1Dd; K1161.5).

How Maui Fished Up New Zealand. Williams-Ellis
– ROUND 242-252 (A955.8).

How Maui Fished Up the Island. Berry – MAGIC
81-88 (A955.8).

How Maui Snared the Sun. Cathon – PERHAPS
103-109 (A728.2); Colum – LEGENDS 47-52.

How Men Became Enemies. Ure – RUMANIAN
126-130 (A1342.1).

How Michael Scot Went to Rome. Wilson – SCOT-
TISH 38-40 (A1485.1).

How Mr. Crane's Eyes Became Blue. Gillham –
BEYOND 76-85 (J2199.1.3).

How Mr. Rabbit Lost His Fine Bushy Tail. Harris – COMPLETE 80-83 (K1021); Harris –
UNCLE 122-126.

How Mr. Rabbit Succeeded in Raising a Dust.
Harris – COMPLETE 98-101 (K62.1).

How Mr. Rabbit Was Too Sharp for Mr. Fox.
Arbuthnot – FAIRY 215-216 (K581.2); Harris

COMPLETE 12-14 ; Harris - UNCLE 16-19.

How Mr. Rooster Lost His Dinner. Harris - COMPLETE 158-161 (A2477.2.1); Harris - NIGHTS 59-60.

How Mrs. Fox Married Again. Grimm - HOUSEHOLD 167-168, 169-170 (T211.6).

How Molo Stole the Lovely Rose Red. Baker - TALKING 251-255 (H607.3.1).

How Moose and Turkey Scalped the Giants. Parker - SKUNNY 196-203 (A2351.8.1; G511.2).

How Much for a Shadow? Carpenter - ELEPHANT'S 100-107 (J1169.7; J1172.2.0.1; J1172.2.3).

How Much You Remind Me of My Husband. Jagendorf - KING 117-119 (J1762.10).

How Music Began. Tooze - THREE..MONKEY #1 (A1461.0.1).

How Nasrudim Created Truth. Shah - MULLA 21 (J1189.5).

How Nasrudim Spoke Up. Shah - MULLA 142 (X904.6.1).

How Night and Day Were Divided. Brown - TEPEE 62-63 (A1172.6; A2217.2).

How Old Craney-Crow Lost His Head. Harris - COMPLETE 640-647

How Ole Woodpecker Got Ole Rabbit's Conjure Bag. Haviland - NORTH 115-121 (D1274.1.1).

How Ologbon-Oni Sought Wisdom. Courlander - OLODE 65-68 (J1041.2).

How One Turned His Trouble to Some Account. Pyle - WONDER 29-38 (N250.4).

How Owl Got His Spotted Coat. Bell - JOHN 18-21 (A2411.2.4.2.3).

How Pa Learned to Grow Hot Peppers. Credle - TALL 67-81 (X1439.1).

How Pakayana the Spider Got His Small Waist. Courlander - RIDE 116-118 (A2355.1.1.2; J2183.1.3).

How Pan Ku Made the World. Carpenter - TALES..CHINESE 14-21 (A614).

How Papantla Got Its Patron Saint. Ross - IN 150-161 (V143.2.1).

How Partridge Got His Whistle. Bell - JOHN 63-64 (A2426.2.25; A2466.2.1).

How Pat Got Good Sense. Fenner - TIME 3-16 (J1193.1.1; J2461D); Gruenberg - MORE 255-260.

How People Got the First Cat. Leach - HOW 63-64 (A1811.4).

How Possum Got His Tail. Belting - LONG 46-50 (A2317.12.2).

How Poverty Was Revealed to the King of Adja. Courlander - KING (H1376.10).

How Rabbit Brought Fire to the People. Brown - TEPEE 70-71 (A1415.0.2.6).

How Rabbit Fooled Wolf. Brown - TEPEE 106-109 (K1047; K1241.1; K1251).

How Rabbit Stole Fire from the Buzzards. Leach - HOW 47-48 (A1415.0.2.1).

How Rabbit Stole Otter's Coat. Bell - JOHN 43-47 (A2378.4.1; A2433.2.2.2).

How Rattlesnake Got His Fangs. Leach - HOW 112 (A2345.5.1).

How Raven Brought Light to the World. Melzack - DAY TUK 51-58 (A1411).

How Raven Created the World. Melzack - RAVEN 15-24 (A618.3).

How Raven Found the Daylight. Maher - BLIND 39-51 (A795.1; A1411.2).

How Reynard Outwitted Bruin. Wiggin - TALES 314 (K543).

How Robin's Breast Became Red. Cathon - PERHAPS 181-182 (A2411.2.1.18.3).

How Rooster Got His Comb. Leach - HOW 92-93 (A727.3; B755.1).

How Saynday Brought the Buffalo. Marriott - WINTER 12-24 (A1878.2).

How Saynday Got Caught in a Buffalo Skull. Marriott - WINTER 39-46 (D1313.4).

How Saynday Got Caught in a Tree. Marriott - WINTER 54-60 (D1556.3).

How Saynday Got the Sun. Haviland - NORTH 60-64 (A721.1.4); Marriott - WINTER 3-12.

How Saynday Ran a Foot Race with Coyote. Marriott - WINTER 47-54 (K11.5; K826).

How Saynday Tried to Marry the Whirlwind. Marriott - WINTER 70-74 (Z115.2).

How Six Men Got On in the World. Grimm - GRIMM'S (Follett) 154-161 (F601.2D).

How Six Men Travelled through the Wide World. Lang - FIFTY 137-142 (F601.2D).

How Six Travelled through the World. Grimm - GRIMM'S (Grosset) 322-329 (F601.2D); Grimm - GRIMM'S (Scribner's) 185-191.

How Six Travelled the Wide World. Lang – YEL-LOW 107-114 (F601.2D).

How Soko Brought Debt to Ashanti. Courlander – COW-TAIL 103-106 (A1378).

How Some Animals Became As They Are. Chang – CHINESE 41 (J2132.5.2).

How Spider Got a Bald Head. Arkhurst – ADVENTURES 21-31 (W125.3.1).

How Spider Got a Thin Waist. Arkhurst – ADVENTURES 5-11 (A2355.1.1.2; J2183.1.3).

How Spider Got His Thread. Leach HOW 84 (A2356.2.8.1).

How Spider Helped a Fisherman. Arkhurst – ADVENTURES 32-38 (J321.1.1).

HOW SUMMER CAME TO CANADA. Toye pb (A1153.1).

How Sun, Moon, and Wind Went Out to Dinner. Jacobs – INDIAN 265-267 (L351.2).

How Swan Became Rich. Sechrist – ONCE 177-184 (J1173; K251.2.1).

How Tadpoles Lost Their Tails. Leach – HOW 113-114 (A2378.2.6.1).

How Tammas Macivar Macmurdo Macleman Met His Match. Leodhas GHOSTS 103-112 (D1960.2).

How Tepozton Hung the Bells. Brenner – BOY 38-43 (V115.5).

How Tepozton Killed the Giant. Brenner – BOY 34-37 (F912.2.10).

How Terrapin Beat Rabbit. Bell – JOHN 58-60 (K11.1).

How Terrapin's Shell Was Cracked. Belting – LONG 54-56 (A2312.1.5).

How the Animals Made Wings for Bat and Flying Squirrel. Belting – LONG 16-25 (A2377.2; A2377.3; B261.1.0.2.1).

How the Bear Nursed the Little Alligator. Harris – COMPLETE 365-369 (K933); Harris – NIGHTS 344-348.

How the Beaver Came to Build Their Homes in the Water. Belting – LONG 42-45 (A2433.3.12.1).

How the Bee Got His Bumble. Deutsch – MORE 15-17 (A2236.1).

How the Birds Came to Have Their Many Colors. Belting – LONG 37-38 (A2411.2.0.2).

How the Birds Got Their Coloured Feathers. Arnott – ANIMALS 100-103 (A2411.2.1.19.1; A2411.2.5.1.1; A2411.2.5.2.1; A2411.2.5.3.2;

A2411.2.6.6.2; A2411.2.6.13).

How the Black Turnstone Came to Nest Near the Sea. Gillham – BEYOND 127-134 (A2431.3.14).

How the Bluebird Gained the Color of the Sky and the Gray Wolf Gained and Lost It. Parker – SKUNNY 139-145 (A2411.1.3.4; A2411.2.1.20).

How the Bobcat Got His Spots. Marriott – WINTER 62-70 (A2412.1.7).

How the Brazilian Beetles Got Their Gorgeous Coats. Cathon – PERHAPS 22-28 (A2411.3.3).

How the Camel Got His Proud Look. Gruenberg – MORE 111-112 (A1873.2).

How the Camel Got His Proud Look. Ross – BURIED 135-138 (A2356.2.13.1).

How the Cardinal Got His Red Feathers. Belting – LONG 62-66 (A2411.2.1.13).

How the Caribs First Came to Honduras. Jagendorf – KING 162-163 (A1255.2.1).

How the Chipmunk Came to Be. Hardendorff – JUST 42-43 (A1859.2).

How the Church Bell Was Saved. Bascom – THOSE 9-26 (J1923.1).

How the Clever Doctor Tricked Death. Carter – GREEDY 9-13 (D1825.3.1.1).

How the Cock Got His Red Crown. Hume – FAVORITE..CHINA 27-32 (A720.1.2).

How the Coconut Tree Was Saved. Leach – HOW 126 (A2681.5.1.1).

How the Conifers Flaunt the Promise of Spring. Parker – SKUNNY 153-158 (A2765.2).

How the Coyote Stole Fire. Heady – SAGE 30-34 (A1415.0.2.3).

How the Coyote Stole Fire for the Klamaths. Hardendorff – JUST 73-77 (A1415.2.2.1).

How the Cow Flew Across the Sea. Jagendorf – GYPSIES' 164-169 (X1133.8).

How the Cow Went under the Ground. Faulkner – DAYS 152-157 (K404.1).

How the Deer Got His Horns. Scheer – CHEROKEE 55-57 (A2326.1.1.1; K11.9).

How the Deer Lost His Tail. Hume – FAVORITE ..CHINA 109-114 (A2378.4.10; J2132.5.1; J2633; N392.1.1).

How the Devil Constructed a Church. Carter – ENCHANTED 109-114 (G303.6.19.4.0.2).

HOW THE DEVIL GOT HIS DUE. Berson pb

(K172).

How the Devil Was Outsmarted by the Man. Hardendorff - JUST 127-132 (K11.6B).

How the Dog Chose Its Master. Carpenter - ELEPHANT'S 75-81 (A1831.3; A2513.1.1).

How the Donkeys Came to Haiti. Johnson - HOW 9-12 (A1882.2).

How the Dragon Lost His Tail. Cheney - TALES 13-16 (A955.10.3).

How the Earth Was Made to Fit the Sky. Leach - HOW 17 (A852.1).

How the Earth's Fire Was Saved. Leach - HOW 22 (A1414.7.2.1).

How the Eight Old Ones Crossed the Sea. Carpenter - TALES..CHINA 150-158 (A501.2).

How the Fiddler Crabs Came to Be. Sechrist - ONCE 31-34 (A2171.2.1).

How the First Horse Was Made. Leach - HOW 66 (A1881.2).

How the First Rainbow Was Made. Fisher - CALIFORNIA 60-78 (A791.11).

How the Fog Came. Caswell - SHADOWS 68-71 (A1134.2); Hardendorff - JUST 56-57.

How the Fox and the Hedgehog Became Friends. Rudolph - MAGIC 62-71 (J1662.2).

How the Fox Saved the Horse's Life. Arnott - ANIMAL 179-183 (C25).

How the Fox Used His Wits. Eells - TALES.. AMAZON 164-169 (K607.3).

How the Foxes Became Red. Cathon - PERHAPS 48-52 (A2411.1.3.1.1; K606); Gillham - BEYOND 99-105.

How the Indians Got Their Music. Heady - SAGE 85-88 (A1461.0.2).

How the Ghost Got In. Littledale - GHOSTS 79-82 (K717.7).

How the Good Gifts Were Used by Two. Pyle - WONDER 123-133 (D1652.5.7; J2073.1).

How the Great Rocks Grew. Fisher - CALIFORNIA 88-95 (D482.4.1).

How the Great Wall Was Built. Manton - FLYING 53-59 (H602.3.1).

How the Groundhog Lost His Tail. Scheer - CHEROKEE 31-32 (A2378.4.9; K606.2.11).

How the Guillemots Came. Gillham - BEYOND 35-40 (A1947.1.1).

How the Gypsy Boy Outsmarted Death. Jagendorf - GYPSIES' 129-133 (K611.5).

How the Hare Learned to Swim. Heady - JAMBO 40-45 (K526.3).

How the Helmites Bought a Barrel of Justice. Simon - WISE 67-76 (J1703.1).

How the Hodja Outwits the Shah Ali. Hardendorff - JUST 135-138 (X905.1.2).

How the Kadawbawa Men Counted Themselves. Tooze - WONDERFUL 125-126 (J2031).

How the Kakok Bird Came to Be. Sechrist - ONCE 22-24 (A1999.4.1).

How the King Chose a Daughter-in-law. Ure - RUMANIAN 19-21 (H389.1).

How the King Chose His Prime Minister. Brockett - BURMESE 147-149 (H1578.4).

How the King of the Birds Was Chosen. Bowes - BIRD 7-14 (A2411.2.6.7.1).

How the Light Came. Caswell - SHADOWS 64-67 (A1411.2; D1553.1).

How the Lion Rewarded the Mouse's Kindness. Appiah - ANANSE 89-94 (J1172.3).

How the Little Fox Went After Chaff. Bloch - UKRAINIAN 49-59 (K251.1.0.2.4).

How the Little Owl's Name Was Changed. Arbuthnot - ANTHOLOGY 394-395 (A1415.2.1.1); Gillham - BEYOND 44-50.

How the Lizard Fought the Leopard. Asia - FOLK..BOOK 2 47-52 (B264.3.1).

How the Lizards Got Their Markings. Sechrist - ONCE 49-51 (A2411.5.8).

How the Long-Tailed Bear Lost His Tail. Belting - LONG 13-15 (K1021).

How the Masi Dived for a Sunbeam. Gittins - TALES 88-89 (J1791.3.3.1).

How the Milky Way Began. Dobbs - ONCE 33-51 (A778.12).

How the Milky Way Came to Be. McDowell - THIRD 23-24 (A778.8).

How the Millstones Drowned. Simon - WISE 23-28 (J2131.5.4).

How the Miser Turned into a Monkey. Lin - MILKY 33-40 (J2415.19).

How Mr. Rabbit Saved His Meat. Harris - COMPLETE 65-68 (K404.1); Harris - UNCLE 99-104).

How the Monkey Came to Be. Sechrist - ONCE

37-38 (A1863.1).

How the Moolah Was Taught a Lesson. Titiev - HOW 1-8 (K285).

How the Moon and Stars Came to Be. Cathon- PERHAPS 110-111 (A625.2.2.1); Sechrist - ONCE 12-13.

How the Moonfish Came to Be. Carter - GREEDY 3-8 (A2116).

How the Mosquitoes Came to Oneota. Gittins - TALES 3-10 (A2434.2.4); Williams-Ellis - ROUND 233-241.

How the Peacock Lost His Voice. Johnson - HOW 75-82 (A2423.1.2.1).

How the Peasant Divided the Geese. Daniels - FALCON 78-80 (H601); Ginsburg - THREE 8-11.

How the Peasant Helped His Horse. Ginsburg - THREE 6 (J1874.1).

How the Peasant Kept House. Daniels - FALCON 75-77 (J2132.2; J2431).

How the Pelican Babies Were Saved. Arnott - ANIMALS 195-201 (D482.1.1).

How the People Began. Leach - HOW 37-38 (A710.1; A1236; E741.2).

How the People Got Fire. Leach - HOW 49-51 (A1415.2.0.1).

How the People Sang the Mountains Up. Leach - HOW 23-24 (A969.10).

How the Pig Got His Snout. Appiah - ANANSE 39-46 (A2335.4.1.1).

How the Pine Nuts Came. Heady - SAGE 46-48 (A1425.0.1.2).

How the Porcupine Outwitted the Fox. Barlow - LATIN 113-118 (A2311.5.1).

How the Princess' Pride Was Broken. Adams - BOOK..PRINCESS 200-208 (H465Bb); Fenner - PRINCESSES 33-42; Pyle - WONDER 269-278.

How the Ptarmigans Learned to Fly. Gillham - BEYOND 86-89 (A2442.3.1).

How the Rabbit Came to Be Called 'Wise' Rabbit. Brockett - BURMESE 67-70 (K1715.1).

How the Rabbit Fooled the Elephant. Withers - MAN 27 (K1716).

How the Rabbit Made Enemies by Trying to Be Friendly. Burton - MAGIC 94-95 (B335.6.1).

How the Rabbit Showed His Wisdom. Brockett - BURMESE 87-91 (J1191.1.1).

How the Rabbit Stole the Otter's Coat. Scheer -

CHEROKEE 69-74 (A2378.4.1.2; A2433.2.2.2).

How the Rabbit's Lip Was Split. Parker - SKUN-NY 85-94 (A1414.5.2; A2342.1.1).

How the Races Obtained Their Colors. Eells - TALES..AMAZON 141-151 (A1614.6.1).

How the Redbird Got His Color. Scheer - CHER-OKEE 62-68 (A2411.2.1.13.1).

How the Robber Band Was Tricked. Duvoisin - THREE 220-223 (K2357.16).

How the Sea Gull Learned to Fly. Gillham - BE-YOND 17-30 (A2442.3.2).

How the Sea Ravens Came to Be. Caswell - SHADOWS 54-56 (A2182.6).

How the Seven Brothers Saved Their Sister. Haviland - NORTH 33-34 (A770.1).

How the Snake Got His Rattles. Lester - BLACK 42-53 (A2523.2.1).

How the Snake Lost His Voice. Novak - FAIRY 81-84 (A2241.12).

How the Sons Filled the Hut. Wyndham - TALES ..RUSSIA 13-15 (H1023.2.6).

How the Speckled Hen Got Her Speckles. Gruen-berg - MORE 133-136 (Z52.3).

How the Squirrel Got Married. Kavcic - GOLD-EN 114-117 (J414.3.2).

How the Sun, the Moon and the Wind Went Out to Dinner. Wiggin - TALES 388-389 (A759.8).

How the Sun Was Made. Leach - HOW 18-19 (A712; A714.3.1).

How the Terrapin Beat the Rabbit. Scheer - CHEROKEE 37-42 (K11.1).

How the Terrapin Was Taught to Fly. Harris - COMPLETE 435-437 (K1041.0.3).

How the Tiger Got His Stripes. Schultz - VIET-NAMESE 15-18 (A2413.4; K341.8.1.0.1).

How the Travelers Shared Their Meal. Hitch-cock - KING 33-36 (W125.7).

How the Trivet Came Home. Jagendorf - MERRY 51-63 (J1881.1.3).

How the Turkey Got His Beard. Scheer - CHER-OKEE 43-46 (A2351.8; A2371.2.13).

How the Turtle Saved His Own Life. Babbitt - JATAKA 10-12 (K581.1).

How the Twelve Clever Brothers Got Their Feet Mixed Up. Ginsburg - TWELVE 85-89 (J2021).

How the Whales Reached the Sea. Belting -

LONG 71-73 (A2412.1.2.1).

HOW THE WITHERED TREE BLOSSOMED. Matsutani pb (D1571.1).

How the Wolf Lost His Tail. Montgomerie - TWEN-
TY-FIVE 30-31 (A2378.4.13; K1021.0.1).

How the Wood Duck Got His Red Eyes and Sojy
Had His Coat Spoiled. Parker - SKUNNY 43-51
(A2332.5.7; A2411.1.3.2; K826).

How the World Got Wisdom. Arkhurst - ADVEN-
TURES 50-58 (A1481.1).

How the World Was Made. Bell - JOHN 4-7
(A812.8; A961.1).

How the World Was Made. Heady - SAGE 15-19
(A812.7).

How the World Was Made. Manton - FLYING 9-12
(A610).

How the World Was Saved. Curtis - GIRL 81-95
(F17.1).

How the World Will End. Newell - RESCUE 81-84
(A1009.4).

How the Yam Came to New Hebrides. Gittins -
TALES 85-87 (A1423.1.2).

How These Tales Came to be Told. Mincielli -
OLD 3-13 (H391.3.1; K1191.1.4B).

How Thunder and Lightning Came to Be. Maher -
BLIND 99-105 (A1142.3.2).

How Thunder Got Back Into the Sky. Withers -
MAN 97-98 (A1142.3.1).

How Thunder Makes the Lightning. Withers -
MAN 93-96 (A1141.2.1).

How to Become a Dragon. Cheney - TALES 75-80
(B11.6.11).

How to Behave in Heaven. Walker - TALES 228-
229 (J2311.6).

How to Catch a Fish. Reed - TALKATIVE 62-63
(K452.1.1).

How to Cook a Coot. Leach - NOODLES 79
(X1258.2.1).

How to Fool a Cat. Sakade - JAPANESE 74-76
(K2.1.1).

How to Tell a Real Princess. Fenner - PRIN-
CESSES 29-32 (H41.1).

How to Tell a True Princess. Wiggin - TALES
182-183 (H41.1).

How to Weigh an Elephant. Alexander - PEBBLES
11 (H506.1).

How Turkey Got His Beard. Bell - JOHN 61-63
(A2351.8; A2371.2.13).

How Turkey Got His White Tail Feathers. Belting
- LONG 89-92 (A2211.7.1).

How Turtle Won the Race With Beaver. Parker -
SKUNNY 165-170 (K11.2).

How Two Brothers Improved Their Luck. Ginsburg - TWELVE 38-43 (X907.1).

How Two Went Into Partnership. Pyle - WONDERS
281-290 (K372).

How Vanity Made the Dove Sad. Bowes - HOW 58-
61 (A2411.2.1.21).

How Wattle Weasel Was Caught. Harris - COM-
PLETE 347-351 (K22.2); Harris - NIGHTS 319-
324.

How Whale Happens to Smoke a Pipe. Leach -
HOW 79 (A2479.14).

How Wisdom Came to Man. Leach - HOW 45-46
(A1481.1).

How Wisdom Was Spread Throughout the World.
Appiah - ANANSE 147-152 (A1481.1).

How Yams Got Their Eyes. Leach - HOW 129
(A2794.2.2).

Hudden and Dudden and Donald O'Neary. Bleeck-
er - BIG 67-77 (K842Aa); Fenner - ADVEN-
TURES 16-25; Jacobs - CELTIC 54-63; Jacobs -
HUDEN pb; Wiggin - TALES 47-53.

The Hummingbird and the Carabao. Sechrist -
ONCE 43-46 (K82.1.1).

The Hummingbird and the Flower. Finger -
TALES 49-53 (A2411.2.1.19.3).

The Hunchback and the Miser. Spicer - OWL'S
86-105 (F344.1.1.3).

The Hundred Cherries. Sleigh - NORTH 155-168
(G501C).

A Hundred Lies. Ginsburg - KAHA 151-159
(H509.5.2).

The Hunger Time. Martin - NINE..COYOTE 23-
30 (K1982.1).

Hungry for Battle. Higonnet-Schnopper - TALES
58-75 (K1951.1E).

The Hungry Giant. Mehdevi - BUNGLING 85-91
(J1791.3; K566; K579.5.1).

Hungry Hog. Leach - NOODLES 82 (X1233.2.1).

The Hungry Old Lion and the Wise Fox. Aesop -
AESOP'S (Golden) 80-81 (J644.1).

The Hungry Old Witch. Davis - BAKER'S 1-20

(G530.2N); Fenner – GIANTS 50-63; Finger – TALES 135-145; Harper – GHOSTS 30-43; Hoke – WITCHES 90-100.

The Hungry Rider. De La Iglesia – CAT (J1552.9).

Hungry Spider and the Turtle. Courlander – COW-TAIL 107-112 (K278); Gruenberg – MORE 130-132.

A Hungry Wolf. Hume – FAVORITE..CHINA 55-60 (K713.3).

The Hungry Wolf. Hutchinson – FIRESIDE 37-40 (K553.3.1; K553.4).

The Hungry Wolf and the Lamb. Aesop – AESOP'S (Golden) 50-51 (W31).

The Hunter and His Magic Flute. Fuja – FOURTEEN 243-251 (B524.1.2E).

The Hunter and His Talking Leopard. Courlander – KING'S 64-66 (B210.2.2).

The Hunter and His Wife. Ransome – OLD 260-268 (B216A).

The Hunter and the Dakwa. Brown – TEPEE 132-133 (F912.2.13).

The Hunter and the Deer. Walker – NIGERIAN 11-19 (B651.5; F302.4.2.2).

The Hunter and the Dove. Korel – LISTEN 49-53 (F1068.4).

The Hunter and the Hind. Fuja – FOURTEEN 126-132 (B651.5); Walker – DANCING 27-34 (F302.4.2.2).

The Hunter and the Horseman. Aesop – AESOP'S (Watts) 222 (J1395).

The Hunter and the Woodman. Aesop – AESOP'S (Watts) 216 (W121.1).

The Hunter of Perak. Courlander – KANTCHIL'S 28-32 (J2061.3).

The Hunter on the Moon. Withers – MAN 22 (A751.0.4).

The Hunters. Van Woerkom MEAT pb (K2323).

The Hunters and the Antelope. Withers – I SAW 142 (F660.1.2).

The Hunter's Bargain. Heady – SAFIRI 51-57 (K1251).

The Hunter's Dilemma. Robinson – THREE (R251B).

The Hunting. Borski – JOLLY 29-40 (G261.2).

The Hunting Cat. Carpenter. TALES..DOGS 74-80 (K2324).

Hunting in the Light. Kelsey – MULLAH 119-121 (J1925).

The Hurt Sparrow. Buck – FAIRY 181-183 (Q285.1.1).

The Husband and the Stork. Aesop – AESOP'S (Viking) 8 (J451.2).

A Husband for the Chief's Daughter. Burton – MAGIC 107-109 (H343.3).

The Husband of the Rat's Daughter. Lang – FIFTY 143-145 (L392); Manning-Sanders – BOOK.. MAGICAL 160-163.

The Husband, the Wife and the Devil. Jagendorf – Gypsies' 152-163 (T251.1.1.4).

The Husband Who Was Left to Mind the House – Hutchinson – CANDLELIGHT (J2132.2; J2176; J2431).

The Husband Who Was to Mind the House. Arbuthnot – FAIRY 86-87 (J2132.2; J2176; J2431); Arbuthnot – ANTHOLOGY 246; Asbjørnsen – EAST (Macmillan) 20-23; Asbjørnsen – EAST (Row) 73-76; Martignoni – ILLUSTRATED 161-162; Minard – WOMENFOLK 106-110; Undset – TRUE 198-201.

The Hut in the Forest. Arbuthnot – FAIRY 40-43 (Q2.1.3C).

Hwan and Dang. Williams-Ellis – ROUND 1-15 (J2415.13).

The Hyena and the Dead Ass. Guillot – GUILLOT'S 88-89 (X902.1).

The Hyena and the Moon. Withers – MAN 48-49 (J1791.3).

Hyena and the Oil with the Flies in It. Aardema – TALES..THIRD 41-50 (K661.3).

The Hyena's Egg. Arnott – TEMBA 9-19 (S215.1).

The Hyena's Horns. Arnott – ANIMAL 31-37 (K1991).

The Hyena's Medicine Man. Harman – TALES 144-152 (A2426.2.27).

I AM YOUR MISFORTUNE. Rudolph pb (N250.4)

I Know Her Best. Shah – MULLA 102 (T255.2).

I-Know-Not-What-of I-Know-Not-Where. Downing – RUSSIAN 100-121 (D831Bb).

I Know What I'll Do. Walker – WATERMELON 49-50 (K1771.2.1).

I Was Going Along the Road. Hampden – GYPSY 63-65 (X1791.1).

I Was In It. Ginsburg - KAHA 139 (J2235.2).

I Was Traveling Those Parts. Hampden - GYPSY 101-104 (X900.1).

I Was Wondering. Leach - NOODLES 38 (J2377).

The Ice Man. Bell - JOHN 92-98 (F433.2).

The Ice Man and the Messenger of Springtime. Brown - TEPEE 79-80 (A1158.1).

I'd Have Shown You. Shah - MULLA 153 (J2311.7).

If God Wills. Thoby-Marcelin - SINGING 38-41 (N385.1).

If a Pot Can Multiply. Shah - MULLA 19 (J1531.3).

If Heaven Will It. Wiggin - TALES 12-13 (N385.1.1).

If You Don't Like It, Don't Listen. Higonnet-Schnopper - TALES 21-29 (H342.3).

If You Know a Story, Don't Keep It to Yourself. Masey - STORIES 104-108 (M231.1Bb).

Ifor the Scoffer. Pugh -TALES 83-96 (E501.18.4.1).

The Iguana's Poison Bag. Courlander - RIDE 20-24 (A2523.2.2).

Ijapa and the Hot-Water Test. Courlander - OLODE 90-95 (H221.4.1).

Ijapa and Yanrinbo Swear an Oath. Courlander - OLODE 69-71 (K475.1.1).

Ijapa Cries for His Horse. Courlander - OLODE 40-44 (W211.1.1.1).

Ijapa Demands Corn Fufu. Courlander - OLODE 104-106 (D861.1Ic).

Ijapa Goes to the Osanjin Shrine. Courlander - OLODE 86-89 (K581.9).

Ikkyu and the Merchant's Moneybags. Edmonds - TRICKSTER 14-20 (J1179.27).

Ikpoom. Aardema - TALES..THIRD 51-58 (X909.7).

Iktomi and the Ducks. DeWit - TALKING 93-98 (K826); Matson - LEGENDS 48-50.

Iktomi and the Red-Eyed Ducks. Yellow Robe - TONWEYA 86-93 (K826; K1111).

I'll Take the Nine. Shah - MULLA 96 (J1473).

The Ill-Tempered Princess. Gunterman - CAS-TLE 46-60 (F601.2Eb).

I'm In the Room. Leach - THING 40 (Z13.1.3).

I'm Tipingee, She's Tipingee, We're Tipingee, Too. Wolkstein - MAGIC 129-134 (H161.0.1.1).

An Impossible Penance. Vittorini - OLD 96-101 (D2121.5.1).

Impossible Tales. Courlander - RIDE 77-81 (X900.1).

The Imposter. Aesop - AESOP'S (Watts) 194-195 (K236.1.1).

The Imposter. Wilson - GREEK 200-211 (H1213.1F).

The Impudent Little Mouse. Spellman - BEAUTI-FUL 64-68 (Z49.3.3).

In a Dark Wood. Withers - I SAW 67 (Z13.1.4).

In Some Lady's Garden. Harris - COMPLETE 246-250 (K842.0.5); Harris - NIGHTS 177-184.

In the Beginning. Martin - RAVEN 11-15 (A801.2; A941.5.9.1; A1111.2; A2103); Haviland - NORTH 46-53.

In the Beginning. Simon - WISE 1 (J1703).

In the Far South-West. Ritchie - TREASURE 102-141 (H1321.1F).

In the First Times. Sechrist - ONCE 11-12 (A1010).

IN THE LAND OF SMALL DRAGON. Clark pb (R221Qa).

In the Midst of Life. Shah - MULLA 144 (J1289.26).

In the Old Kingdom of Kathomo. Nunn - AFRI-CAN 88-95 (A2378.4.16; K944).

In Unity Is Strength. Kaula - AFRICAN 100 (J1022).

The Indian Cinderella. Haviland - NORTH 94-96 (R221G).

Indian Saynday and White Man Saynday. Marriott - WINTER 74-82 (K341.8.1).

The Indian Shinny Game. Cothran - WITH 56-64 (K23).

Ingle-Go-Jang. Harris - FAVORITE 233-237 (K581.7); Harris - COMPLETE 77-80; Harris - UNCLE 117-122.

The Injured Lion. Kaula - AFRICAN 94-95 (B381).

The Inn of Donkeys. Birch - CHINESE 89-94 (G263.1.0.2).

The Innkeeper's Daughter. Michael - PORTU-GUESE 121-129 (Z65.1Ac).

The Insatiable Beggar. Durham – TIT 93–95
(J514.7).

The Inseparable Friends. Burton – MAGIC 112–
116 (P361.10).

Insha'allah. Kelsey – HODJA 130–138 (N385.1.3).

Inside Again. Jacobs – EUROPEAN 165–169
(J1172.3; J1172.3.2.2).

The Invisible Hands. Michael – PORTUGUESE 20–
27 (H1411.4.3.1).

The Invisible Silk Robe. Tooze – WONDERFUL 26–
31 (K445).

The Invisible Thief. Masey – STORIES 88–103
(K301Ai).

Iron Hans. Gag – MORE..GRIMM 207–208 (G671);
Grimm – GRIMM'S (Grosset) 356–365; Grimm –
GRIMM'S (World) 358–366.

Iron John. Grimm – GRIMM'S (Follett) 162–173
(G671).

Iron, Steel and Strongest-of-all. Toor – GOLDEN
93–103 (R111.1.3Ea; S12.1.0.1C).

The Iron Stone. Grimm – GRIMM'S (Scribner's)
255–261 (H1385.5D); Lang – YELLOW 41–47;
Lang – FIFTY 146–151.

The Iron Wolf. Wiggin – FAIRY 253–258 (B524.1.2D).

Ironhead. Manning-Sanders – DEVILS 56–58
(B524.1.2D).

Irraweka, Mischief-Maker. Sherlock – WEST 21–
26 (A1011.1.1).

Ishcus and the Clamshell Boy. Matson – LEGENDS
97–102 (T554.12.1).

ISSUN BOSHI, THE INCHLING. Ishii pb (F535.1.1E).

Issun Boshi, The One-Inch Lad. Uchida – DANC-
ING 159–169(F535.1.1E).

Issy-Ben-Aran. Gunterman – CASTLE 81–83
(J1392.7).

IT ALL BEGAN WITH A DRIP. Lexau pb (N392.1.1).

It All Came Out of an Egg. Duvoisin. THREE 30–
37 (F481.0.1.1.1).

It All Comes to Light. Manning-Sanders – RED
66–71 (N455.4C).

It Brings the Day. Cunningham – TALKING 95–
97 (B642.6.2).

IT COULD ALWAYS BE WORSE. Zemach pb
(Z49.16).

It, Him, or Me. Cimino – DISOBEDIENT #14
(K551.11).

It Won't Do You Any Good. Walker – WATER-
MELONS 67 (J2562).

It's All In Knowing How. Walker – WATERMELONS
65–66 (W153.5.1).

It's All the Fault of Adam. Walker – DANCING 65–
71 (H1554.1).

It's Better to Be Smart Than Strong. Jagendorf –
KING 244–248 (A2378.2.2.1).

Itsayaya and the Chokecherries. Heady – TALES
41–44 (J1791.3.5).

Itsayaya and the Otter. Heady – TALES 57–61
(A977.5.0.1).

Itsayaya Frees the Salmon. Heady – TALES 45–49
(A1421.0.0.1).

Itsayaya's Revenge. Heady – TALES 50–56
(A2317.3.1; A2343.3.4; A2378.4.12;
A2411.1.2.6; A2411.1.3.3).

IVAN AND THE WITCH. Damjan pb (R251).

Ivan Bear's Ear. Riordan – TALES..CENTRAL
59–62 (B635.1.4).

Ivan the Fool. Dolch – OLD RUSSIA 131–139
(H1213.1E).

Ivan the Fool. Whitney – IN A 59–63 (K1951.1E).

Ivan the Merchant's Son and Vasilisa the Wise.
Daniels – FALCON 32–51 (G530.2Bh).

Ivan the Peasant's Son and the Three Dragons.
Riordan – TALES..CENTRAL 96–105 (B11.11.9).

Ivan the Rich and Ivan the Poor. Riordan –
TALES..CENTRAL 23–30 (D861.1G).

Ivan Young in Years, Old in Wisdom. Riordan –
TALES..CENTRAL 213–221 (H1320.3).

IVANKO AND THE DRAGON. Bloch pb (R251).

Ivashko and the Witch. Wyndham – RUSSIAN 32–
41 (R251).

Ivenga and the Ivory. Aardema – MORE 26–31
(D1602.6).

Iwa the Crafty One. Thompson – HAWAIIAN..
TRICKSTERS 80–85 (K301B).

Iwanich and the Magic Ring. Buck – FAIRY 172–
180 (H1385.3Jb).

The Jabuty and the Jaguar. Carpenter – LATIN
43–49 (A2412.1.8).

Jabuty, the Strong. Carpenter – LATIN 36–42
(K22).

Jack and His Comrades. Jacobs – CELTIC 124–133 (K335.1.4); Manning-Sanders – BOOK..MAGICAL 199–209.

Jack and His Golden Snuff-box. Jacobs – ENGLISH 82–85 (D882.1Ea); Manning-Sanders – RED 72–73.

Jack and His Friends. Pilkington – SHAMROCK 46–51 (K335.1.4; K1161.1).

Jack and His Master. Jacobs – CELTIC 198–208 (K172).

Jack and King Marock. Chase – JACK 135–150 (G530.2Ai).

Jack and the Bean-stalk. Adams – BOOK..GIANTS 78–91 (F54.2); Chase – JACK 31–39; De La Mare – JACK pb; De La Mare – TALES 84–106; De Regniers – GIANT 18–30; Fenner – GIANTS 115–125; Haviland – FAIRY 78–85; Haviland – FAVORITE..ENGLAND 3–21; Jacobs – ENGLISH 59–68; Lang – RED 128–142; Manning-Sanders – BOOK..GIANTS 9–17; Manning-Sanders – CHOICE 39–48; Martignoni – ILLUSTRATED 164–171; Mayne – BOOK..GIANTS 98–107; Opie – CLASSIC 162–174; Rackham – ARTHUR 41–48; Reeves – ENGLISH 128–146; Steele – ENGLISH 97–109; Stobbs – JACK pb; Williams-Ellis – FAIRY..BRITISH 155–168.

Jack and the Bull. Chase – JACK 21–30 (B335.2B).

Jack and the Devil's Daughter. Lester – BLACK 73–90 (G350.2Ba).

Jack and the Doctor's Girl. Chase – JACK 114–126 (K301Ag).

Jack and the Friendly Animals. Danaher – FOLKTALES 93–102 (K1161.1).

Jack and the Giant Galligantua, and the Enchanter. Manning-Sanders – BOOK..GIANTS 60–66 (G512).

Jack and the Giant Tantarem. Manning-Sanders – BOOK..GIANTS 47–49 (G512).

Jack and the Giant Thunderdell. Manning-Sanders – BOOK..GIANTS 57–59 (G512).

Jack and the King of England's Son, and the Giant With Three Heads. Manning-Sanders – BOOK..GIANTS 53–56 (G512).

Jack and the King Who Was a Gentleman. Wiggin – TALES 55–61 (H342.3).

Jack and the King's Girl. Chase – JACK 83–88 (J2461Aa).

Jack and the Lord High Mayor. MacManus – HIBERNIAN 126–140 (K842Ca).

Jack and the North West Wind. Chase – JACK 47–57 (D861.1A).

Jack and the Robbers. Arbuthnot – ANTHOLOGY 367–369 (K1161.1); Arbuthnot – FAIRY 194–196; Chase – JACK 40–46.

Jack and the Three Demons. Spicer – THIRTEEN MONSTERS 83–92 (Q565Ah).

JACK AND THE THREE SILLIES. Chase pb (H1312.1; J2081.1.1; J2161.2).

Jack and the Varmints. Chase – JACK 58–66 (K1951.1A).

Jack and the Welsh Giant. Manning-Sanders – BOOK..GIANTS 50–52 (G512).

Jack and the White Cap. Colwell – ROUND 97–101 (G242.7.2).

Jack and the Wizard. Manning-Sanders – BOOK..WIZARDS 78–85 (G530.2J); Manning-Sanders – CHOICE 268–275.

Jack at Hell Gate. Manning-Sanders – DEVILS 39–50 (K11.6; K1781.1).

Jack Buttermilk. Colwell – ROUND 87–89 (K526B).

Jack Hannaford. Jacobs – ENGLISH 39–42 (J2326.1; K341.9); Reeves – ENGLISH 2–9.

Jack in the Giant's New Ground. Chase – JACK 3–20 (G501E; K1082).

Jack My Hedgehog. Lang – GREEN 298–304 (B641.5).

JACK-O-LANTERN. Barth pb (Q565Aa).

Jack O'Leary's Plow. Spicer – THIRTEEN GHOSTS 36–44 (D1209.3).

Jack Sparrow. Harris – FAVORITE 83–95 (K911.5.1); Harris – COMPLETE 61–65; Harris – UNCLE 93–99.

Jack the Ashypet. Fenner – GIANT 18–31 (K1951.1C); MacManus – WELL 49–64.

Jack the Fool. MacManus – WELL 156–163 (J1853.1.0.1).

Jack the Giant Killer. De Regniers – GIANT 3–15 (G512.0.4); Fenner – GIANTS 138–154; Jacobs – ENGLISH 102–116; Lang – BLUE 351–357; Manning-Sanders – BOOK..GIANTS 44–56; Mayne – BOOK..GIANTS 83–97; Opie – CLASSIC 47–65; Rackham – ARTHUR 111–127; Rackham – FAIRY 1–14; Steel – ENGLISH 54–72.

Jack Who Could Do Anything. Jagendorf – KING 28–30 (K717.2).

The Jackal and the Alligator. Hutchinson – FIRESIDE 107–115 (K543.0.1; K607.2.2; K607.2.4).

The Jackal and the Bear. Hitchcock – KING 47–52 (K404.1.1).

284-286 (J1785.8).

John Shea and the Fairy Treasure. McNeil - DOUBLE 88-94 (F384.7.5).

John the Blacksmith Destroys the Wasps in the Straw. Jagendorf - MERRY 87-92 (J2102.5).

John the Painter. Sheppard-Jones - WELSH 123-128 (F331.4).

John the True. Jacobs - EUROPEAN 170-179 (S268A).

Johnie Croy of Volyar and the Mermaid. Cutt-HOGBOON 108-113 (B81.2.4).

Johnnie and Grizzle. Jacobs - EUROPEAN 180-187 (G412.1.1).

Johnny and the Three Goats. Richardson - GREAT 74-80 (Z39.1).

Johnny and the Witch-Maidens. Manning-Sanders - BOOK..WITCHES 115-122 (G266.2); Manning-Sanders - CHOICE 81-88.

Johnny-Cake. Colwell - YOUNGEST 72-77 (Z33.1.3); Haviland - FAVORITE..ENGLAND 22-29; Jacobs - ENGLISH 162-165; Jacobs - JOHNNY-CAKE (Brock) pb; Jacobs - JOHNNY-CAKE (Stobbs) pb; Martignoni - ILLUSTRATED 77-79; Wiggin - TALES 197-199; Williams-Ellis FAIRY..BRITAIN 34-38; Withers - I SAW 26-31.

Johnny Gloke. Jacobs - MORE 78-81 (K1951.1B); Reeves - ENGLISH 24-34.

Johnny McGorry and the Red Stocking. Withers - I SAW 45 (Z17.3).

The Jolly Sparrow. Ginsburg - THREE 43-44 (Z39.4.3).

The Jolly Tailor Who Became King. Haviland - FAVORITE..POLAND 13-27 (H359.4); Bleecker - BIG 17-28; Borski - JOLLY 15-28.

Jon and the Troll Wife. Manning-Sanders - BOOK ..OGRES 91-100 (G666.1).

Jorinda and Joringel. Gag - JORINDA pb (D771.11.1); Gag - MORE..GRIMM 229-239; Grimm - GRIMM'S (Follett) 174-178; Grimm - GRIMM'S (Grosset) 33-36; Grimm - GRIMM'S (Watts) 82-95; Grimm - GRIMM'S (World) 191-193; Grimm - JORINDA pb; Lang - GREEN 264-268; Lang - FIFTY 162-165.

Jorinde and Joringel. Grimm - BROTHERS 43-46 (D771.11.1).

Joshua and the Princess. Dobbs - MORE 34-38 (J1319.3).

Journey Cake, Ho! Arbuthnot - ANTHOLOGY 365-366 (Z33.1.8); Sawyer - JOURNEY pb.

Journey in a Well. Green - BIG 155-156 (K651).

Juan and the Helpful Frog. Sechrist - ONCE 150-156 (B641Ac).

Juan Bobo. Belpré - TIGER 49-54 (J1849.5); Carter - GREEDY 112-118 (J1193.1; J1852.1.4; J1881.1.3); Jagendorf - NOODLEHEAD 260-262 (J1849.5).

Juan Bobo and the Cauldron. Alegría - THREE 74-75 (J1881.1.3).

Juan Bobo and Old Tiger. Jagendorf - KING 269-273 (K1161.6).

Juan Bobo and the Princess Who Answered Riddles. Alegría - THREE (H551.0.1; H802.1).

Juan Bobo, the Sow and the Chicks. Alegría - THREE 31-33 (J1849.5).

Juan Cigarron. Fenner - TIME 200-208 (N611.5; N688); Gruenberg - MORE 261-264; Haviland - FAVORITE..SPAIN 58-69.

Juan in Heaven. Jagendorf - KING 89-93 (E765.1.1.2).

Juanillo. Gunterman - CASTLES 106-131 (K1931.2.1).

Juanito and the Princess. Alegría - THREE 100-106 (D532).

Judge True. Riordan - TALES..TARTARY 195-198 (J1173).

Judgement. Shah - MULLA 53 (J1179.5).

The Judgement of Hailu. McNeil - DOUBLE 63-66 (K231.14.2).

The Judgement of the Shepherd. Turnbull - FAIRY 117-127 (J1173.1.3).

The Judge's Robe and Turban. Jameson - TALES 9-16 (K443.14).

The Judgment of Karakoush. Courlander - RIDE 101-104 (J2233.2; Z49.11.2).

The Judgment of the Wind. Courlander - FIRE 51-56 (J1172.3.2.4).

The Juggler of Notre Dame. Sawyer - WAY 273-281 (V92); Todd - JUGGLER pb.

The Jumper. Heady - SAFIRI 62-65 (K11.1).

The Juniper Tree. De La Mare - ANIMAL 267-278 (N271); Grimm - BROTHERS 178-186; Grimm - JUNIPER v.2 314-332.

Jupiter and the Bee. Aesop - AESOP'S (Grosset) 74 (A2232.2).

Jupiter and the Camel. Aesop - AESOP'S (Viking) 50-51 (A2232.1).

Jupiter and the Horse. Aesop - AESOP'S (Viking)

71-72 (A1873.1); Hardendorff - JUST 54-55.

Jupiter and the Monkey. Aesop - AESOP'S (Viking) 64 (T681.2); Aesop - AESOP'S (Watts) 48.

Jupiter and the Tortoise. Aesop - AESOP'S (Watts) 59 (A2231.1.4).

Jupiter, Neptune, Minerva, and Monius. Aesop - AESOP'S (Grosset) 92-93 (A46).

The Jurga. Belpré - TIGER 37-41 (K172).

Jurma and the Sea God. Bowman - TALES..TUPA 81-90 (G561Cb).

The Just and the Unjust Brothers. Spicer - LONG 130-144 (N452C).

Just His Luck. Leach - LUCK 22-23 (N111.4.2).

The Just Judgment. Edmonds - TRICKSTER 51-60 (J1173).

Just One 'Simmon More. Harris - FAVORITE 178-181 (A2317.12.1); Harris - COMPLETE 87-90; Harris - UNCLE 131-137.

The Just Reward. Wyndham - TALES..RUSSIA 57-61 (K187).

JUST SAY HIC! Walker pb (J2461.2; J2671.2.1).

Just Say Rhee. Walker - NIGERIAN 55-56 (K1655).

Justice. Courlander - FIRE 73-76 (X111.1.1).

Kabadaluk. Manning-Sanders - GIANNI 13-23 (M383.1).

Kaddo's Wall. Courlander - COW 13-23 (W153.16).

Kahukura. Sleigh - NORTH 139-143 (A1457.3.2).

Kakui, Bird of the Night. Courlander - RIDE 202-205 (A1999.6).

Kaleeba. Serwadda - SONGS 11-15 (K1079.1).

Kalle and the Wood Grouse. Bowman - TALES.. TUPA 129-140 (G530.2Bh).

Kalulu and His Money Farm. Kaula - AFRICAN 35-42 (K1839.12.1).

Kamau, the Gay Bachelor. Nunn - AFRICAN 81-87 (K1561.2).

The Kamiah Monster. Martin - NINE 53-60 (F913.5).

Kantchil's Lime Pit. Courlander - KANTCHIL'S 6-10 (K652.1); Courlander - RIDE 28-31.

Kantjil and the Monkey Business - Bro - HOW 79-87 (K1023.1.0.3).

Kantjil Becomes a Raksha. Bro - HOW 29-38 (K335.0.4.4).

Kantjil Brings the Elephant to Hell. Bro - HOW 88-95 (K17.6).

Kantjil Discovers the Wisdom of Allah. Bro - HOW 49-54 (J2571).

Kantjil Grows Strong at the Welling-Well. Bro - HOW 13-21 (K735.5.1).

Kantjil Holds a Festival. Bro - HOW 107-117 (K11.11).

Kantjil Interprets a Dream. Bro - HOW 55-71 (K1715.16).

Kantjil to the Rescue. Bro - HOW 96-106 (K644.1).

The Kappa's Arm. Pratt - MAGIC 11 (E782.3.2).

Kari Woodencoat. Baker - GOLDEN 19-33 (B335.2D; R221L).

Kari Woodengown. Lang - RED 192-207 (B335.2D; R221L).

Kari Woodenskirt. Aulaire - EAST 123-137 (B335.2D; R221L).

Karl Katz. Grimm - GRIMM'S (Grosset) 220-227 (D1960.1).

Kashalki-Opalki or How a Simpleton Became King. Borski - JOLLY 41-48 (D861.1G).

Kashi and His Wicked Brothers. Siddiqui - TOONTOONY 37-43 (K941.2; K1051.0.1).

Kasiagsak Who Lied. Caswell - SHADOWS 48-53 (W10.3).

Kassa, the Strong One. Courlander - COW 41-45 (F615.9.1; K1931.2Z).

KASSIM'S SHOES. Berson pb (N211.2).

Katcha and the Devil. Fillmore - SHEPHERD'S 160-171 (T251.1.1.2); Ross - BLUE 110-122.

Kate Contrary. Manning-Sanders - GLASS 182-186 (T251.1.1).

Kate Crackernuts. Jacobs - ENGLISH 207-211 (L145.1); Lurie - CLEVER 66-73; Minard - WOMENFOLK 65-70; Williams-Ellis - FAIRY.. BRITISH 49-55.

Katrina and the Seven Werewolves. Huggins - BLUE 32-42 (P253.2F).

Keel-Wee, A Korean Rip Van Winkle. Jewett - WHICH 74-81 (D2011.1.3).

Keenene. Serwadda - SONGS 1-5 (B531.6).

Keep Cool. Jacobs - EUROPEAN 115-120 (K172).

Kefala's Secret Something. Robinson - THREE 17-31 (H343.4).

Kernel. Michael - PORTUGUESE 112-117 (F535.1.1Cb).

Kertong. Kendall - SWEET 66-72 (N831.1).

The Kettle That Would Not Walk. Hutchinson - FIRESIDE 9-14 (J1881.1.5).

The Key in the Distaff. Asbjørnsen - NORWE-GIAN 128 (H382.1).

Khavroshechka. Carey - BABA 109-113 (D830.1.1).

Kibbe's Shirt. Jagendorf - NOODLEHEAD 287-289 (J2235.1).

The Kid and the Tiger. Spellman - BEAUTIFUL 75-78 (K1711.2).

The Kid and the Wolf. Aesop - AESOP'S (Watts) 151-152 (K561.2).

The Kid and the Wolf. Martignoni - ILLUS-TRATED 400 (J974).

The Kid on the Housetop. Aesop - AESOP'S (Watts) 67 (J974).

The Kids and the Wolf. Carrick - STILL MORE 15-22 (F556.2; K311.3A).

Kija's Pottery Hats. Carpenter - KOREAN 39-44 (J1199.4).

The Kildare Pooka. Palmer - DRAGONS 38-42 (F381.3); Pilkington - SHAMROCK 52-54.

The Killing of Eetoi. Baker - AT 33-42 (A566.3).

The Killing Pot. Baker - AT 16-24 (G378).

Kin Kin and the Cat. Fuja - FOURTEEN 140-145 (D1487.3.1).

Kind Brother, Cruel Sister. Zajdler - POLISH 61-78 (S12.1.0.1A).

The Kind Dragon. Dolch - STORIES..OLD CHINA 25-41 (D861.1D).

The Kind-hearted Carter and the Crafty Croco-dile. Brockett - BURMESE 126-130 (K815.14.3).

Kindai and the Ape. Aardema - TALES 77-85 (B381.4).

The Kindly Ghost. Manning-Sanders - BOOK..GHOSTS 103-110 (D882.1Ga).

The Kindly Ghost. Manton - FLYING 134-140 (E414.0.1).

Kinds of Day. Shah - MULLA 129 (J2259.1).

King All-Tusk. Wyatt - GOLDEN 6-12 (B240.16).

The King and Kuffie. Courlander - TERRAPIN'S 84-86 (H1305.2.1).

The King and His Friend. De La Iglesia - #16 (J1552.8).

The King and the Barber. Michael - PORTU-GUESE 139-145 (K1321.3.0.1).

The King and the Monkey. Gaer - FABLES..IN-DIA 143-146 (B241.2.2.2).

The King and the Nagas. Palmer - DRAGONS 89-95 (B604.1.1).

The King and the Peasant. Courlander - RIDE 142-144 (H585.2.1).

The King and the Ring. Walker - DANCING 43-50 (N211.1B).

The King and the Shepherd. Tashjian - THREE 8-15 (H561.4.1).

The King and the Shoemaker. Spellman - BEAU-TIFUL 8-11 (Q45.1.4).

The King and the Wise Man. De La Iglesia - CAT 13 (J1566.1).

The King and the Witch. Colwell - ROUND 77-81 (G263.2.1.2).

The King and the Wrestler. Withers - WORLD 76-77 (H1149.9).

King Arthur and the Shepherd Laddie. Finlay - TATTERCOATS 100-110 (D1960.2).

King Bartek. Arbuthnot - ANTHOLOGY 274-275 (T55.2); Arbuthnot - FAIRY 159-162; Borski - JOLLY 63-73.

King Clothes. Arbuthnot - ANTHOLOGY 272 (J1561.3); Jagendorf - PRICELESS 31-34.

King David's Peril. Ish-Kishor - WISE 44-48 (B523.1; B524.2.1.2).

King Firdy the Just. Davis - LION'S (Z49.11.2).

King Fox. Manning-Sanders - GIANNI 76-102 (B582.6).

KING GRISLEY-BEARD. Grimm pb (H465).

King Herla. Belting - ELVES 41-46 (F378.1).

King John and the Abbot of Canterbury. Cour-lander RIDE (H561.2; H681.1.1).

King John and the Abbot of Canterbury. Jacobs - MORE 159-162 (H561.2).

King Johnny. Manning-Sanders - CHOICE 171-182 (D831C); Manning-Sanders - BOOK..GI-ANTS 67-78.

King Kantjil's Freedom Expands. Bro - HOW 72-

78 (K652.1; K741.2).

King Kojata. Buck - FAIRY 141-153 (G530.2Db);
Lang - GREEN 192-206.

KING KRAKUS AND THE DRAGON. Domanska pb
(B11.11.10).

King Lion Is Ill. Aesop - FABLES (Walck) 105-
107 (J644.1).

King Midas and the Golden Touch. Gruenberg -
FAVORITE 408-410 (J2072.1).

The King o' the Cats. Harper - GHOSTS 57-59
(B342A); Hoke - SPOOKS 175-177; Jacobs -
MORE 169-171; Littledale - GHOSTS 121-124.

The King of Araby's Daughter. MacManus -
BOLD 83-100 (G530.2Fd).

The King of England and His Three Sons. Jacobs
- MORE 142-158 (H1321.1B).

The King of Greece's Daughter. MacManus -
WELL 112-137 (E341.1B).

The King of Sedo. Courlander - KING'S 19-21
(L435.5).

The King of the Animals. Courlander - PIECE
90-100 (B240.9.1).

The King of the Birds. Sheppard-Jones - WELSH
59-62 (A2491.2.2).

The King of the Cats. Farjeon - CAVALCADE..
KINGS 56-58 (B342.1); Galdone - KING pb;
Sleigh - NORTH 31-33; Williams-Ellis - FAIRY..
BRITISH 106-109.

The King of the Demons and the Worm Shamir.
Serwer - LET'S 9-17 (D1711.1.1).

The King of the Fishes. Jacobs - EUROPEAN 19-
20 (R111.1.3Ac).

The King of the Forest. Courlander - TIGER'S
46-48 (J684.1.1).

The King of the Frogs. Harmon - TALES 57-63
(J643.1).

The King of the Golden Mountain. Grimm -
GRIMM'S (Grosset) 247-254 (H1385.3Bb);
Grimm - GRIMM'S (Viking) 75-81; Grimm -
GRIMM'S (World) 254-260.

The King of the Leaves. Jagendorf - KING 218-
221 (K1991.1).

The King of the Mice. Heady - SAFIRI 71-74
(B241.2.5.1).

The King of the Monkeys. Carpenter - TALES..
CHINESE 107-116 (B241.2.2.1); Dolch -
STORIES..OLD CHINA 107-111; Manton - FLY-
ING 121-126.

The King of the Mountain. Hume - FAVORITE..
CHINA 85-92 (B413.3.2).

The King of the Mountains. Arbuthnot - AN-
THOLOGY 405-406 (B236.1.1); Jagendorf -
KING 40-43.

The King of the Noise. Papashvily - YES AND NO
149-157 (K1917.3E).

King of the Restless Sea. Thompson - HAWIIAN..
TRICKSTERS 23-27 (K341.16).

The King On Trial. Durham - TIT 67-69 (L411.1).

King O'Toole and His Goose. Arbuthnot - AN-
THOLOGY 177-179 (K185.3.1); Arbuthnot -
FAIRY 136-138; Jacobs - CELTIC 102-108.

King Solomon and the Queen of Sheba. Davis -
LION'S 168-171 (K337.0.1).

King Solomon's Carpet. Baker - TALKING 218-
231 (D1711.1.1).

King Solomon's Ring. Ish-Kishor - WISE 19-26
(D1076.1).

King Stork. Fenner - GIANTS 3-17 (E341.1E);
Pyle - WONDER 293-304.

King Svatopluk and the Three Sticks. Courlander
- RIDE 128-130 (J1021).

The King, the Saint, and the Goose. Williams-
Ellis - FAIRY..BRITISH 24-29 (K185.3.1).

King Throslebeard. Grimm - BROTHERS 118-123
(H465).

King Thrush-beard. Wiggin - TALES 93-97
(H465).

King Thrushbeard. Grimm - GRIMM'S (Follett)
179-185 (H465); Grimm - GRIMM'S (Grosset) 27-
32; Grimm - GRIMM'S (World) 64-69; Grimm -
HOUSEHOLD 208-212; Grimm - KING (Harcourt)
pb; Shub - ABOUT 91-95; Werth - KING pb.

The King Who Ate Chaff. Courlander - TIGER'S
33-34 (D1316.5.0.2).

The King Who Loved Women. Brockett - BUR-
MESE 31-38 (H585.1.1).

The King Who Rides a Tiger. Hitchcock - KING
80-96 (N831.1.0.1).

The King Who Wanted a Beautiful Wife. Hampden
- HOUSE 17-22 (T11.4.8).

The King Who Wanted a White Elephant. Brockett
- BURMESE 142-146 (H1023.6.2).

The King Who Was a Gentleman. MacManus - HI-
BERNIAN 36-47 (H342.3).

King Wren. Wiggin - TALES 172-175 (A2233.3;
K17.1.1).

132 (H1273.2G).

Kojata. Manning-Sanders - BOOK..WIZARDS 95-108 (G530.2Db).

Koki's Cure for Thieving. Aardema - MORE 22-25 (A2455.6).

A Korean Cinderella. Carpenter - KOREAN 119-124 (R221I).

Koroika and the Serpent. Gittins - TALES 37-40 (V11.7.1.1).

The Korrigan. Picard - FRENCH 107-112 (F321.1.1).

Krencipal and Krencipalka. Baker - TALKING 204-209 (K1161.4); Haviland - FAVORITE.. POLAND 28-37 (K1161.3).

The Kris of Adji Saka. Courlander - KANTCHIL'S 85-87 (K2144).

Krishna the Cowherd: A Hindu Epic. Courlander - TIGER'S 63-71 (A489.6).

Kultani, the Noodle Gossip. Jagendorf - NOODLE-HEAD 202-206 (J1151.1.1).

Kuluilé, the Dancing Girl. Guirma - TALES 16-28 (E461).

Kumurchi's Poultry Farm. Sturton - ZOMO 39-47 (K1459.1).

A Kupua Plays Tricks. Thompson - HAWAIIAN.. EARTH 45-52 (A2130.1).

Kurage. Hoke - DRAGONS 63-75 (K544.1).

Kuratko the Terrible. Davis - BAKER'S 127 (Z33.5); Fillmore - SHEPHERD'S 82-86; Haviland - FAVORITE..CZECHOSLOVAKIA 21-33.

Kuzenko Sudden Wealthy. Wyndham - RUSSIAN 44-59 (K1917.3E).

Kwaku Ananse and the Donkey. Appiah - ANANSE 71-88 (K1241.1).

Kwaku Ananse and the Greedy Lion. Appiah - ANANSE 27-38 (K171.0.2.1).

Kwaku Ananse and the Rain Maker. Appiah - ANANSE 113-122 (A957.1).

Kwaku Ananse and the Whipping Cord. Appiah - ANANSE 57-70 (D861.1Ia).

Kwatee and the Wolf. Matson - LEGENDS 103-106 (K606.2.3).

The Labourer and the Nightingale. Jacobs - FABLES 115 (K604).

The Labourer and the Snake. Aesop - AESOP'S

(Watts) 149 (J15).

A Lac of Rupees for a Bit of Advice. Jacobs - INDIAN 126-135 (J21F).

The Lad and the Fox. Haviland - FAVORITE.. SWEDEN 30-32 (J2061.3.1); Wiggin - TALES 462.

The Lad and the North Wind. Haviland - NORWAY 67-74 (D861.1A).

The Lad Who Went to the North Wind. Arbuthnot - FAIRY 76-77 (D861.1A); Asbjørnsen - EAST (Macmillan) 24-29; Asbjørnsen - EAST (Row) 135-138; Association - TOLD..GREEN 52-58; Hutchinson - CHIMNEY 19-24; Rockwell - OLD 65-78.

The Lad With the Goat-skin. Jacobs - CELTIC 245-255 (G610Ak).

The Ladder of Arrows. Cunningham - TALKING 70-79 (F53.1).

The Ladle That Fell from the Moon. Wiggin - TALES 404-406 (J1179.24).

The Lads Who Met the Highwayman. Leodhas - GHOSTS 91-102 (E593.0.1).

The Lady and the Lion. Darrell - ONCE 38-42 (H1385.4D); Grimm - GRIMM'S (Grosset) 366-372.

Lady Featherflight. Adams - BOOK..GIANT 159-175 (G530.2Ag).

The Lady in the Picture. Bonnet - FOLK..CHINA 61-65 (T111.1.5).

Lady into Silkworm. Manton - FLYING 18-23 (B611.3).

The Lady of Stavoren. Courlander - RIDE 178-185 (N211.1A).

The Lady of the Wood. Garner - CAVALCADE.. GOBLINS 56-61 (G302.7.1.5).

The Lady of Tylwyth Teg. Palmer - FAIRY 50-54 (F342.3).

Lady With the Horse's Head. Carpenter - TALES ..CHINESE 98-106 (A2811).

The Lady's Loaf-Field. Leodhas - GAELIC 68-74 (E415.2.1).

The Laidly Worm. Green - CAVALCADE..DRAG-ONS 103-108 (D732.0.1); Steel - ENGLISH 89-94.

The Laidly Worm of Spindleston Heugh. Jacobs - ENGLISH 190-196 (D732.0.1); Williams-Ellis - FAIRY..BRITISH 306-311.

The Lairdie With the Heart of Gold. Leodhas - HEATHER 45-49 (F485.5.4.3).

The Laird's Lass and the Gobha's Son. Leodhas - THISTLE 17-38 (D141).

The Lake Lady. Williams-Ellis - FAIRY..BRITISH 255-262 (F420.6.1.5.1).

The Lake Maiden. Manning-Sanders - BOOK.. MERMAIDS 114-121 (F420.6.1.5.1).

The Lake That Flew. Credle - TALL 96-99 (X1606.2.4.1).

The Lakota Woman. Yellow Robe - TONWEYA 94-101 (E412.3.0.1).

The Lamb Chased by a Wolf. Aesop - AESOP'S (Watts) 139 (J216.2).

The Lambikin. Jacobs - INDIAN 23-26 (K553.0.3); Hutchinson - CANDLELIGHT 3-8; Richardson - GREAT 113-121; Rockwell - OLD 37-47; Wiggin - TALE 271-273.

The Lambton Worm. Green - CAVALADE..DRAG-ONS 109-114 (B11.12.4.1.1); Jacobs - MORE 215-221.

The Lame Cat and the Potter. Wyatt - GOLDEN 101-106 (N222.3).

The Lame Dog. Baker - TALKING 77-87 (H1385.4H).

The Lame Duck. Hutchinson - CANDLELIGHT 117-122 (N831.1).

The Lame Vixen. Manning-Sanders - BOOK.. MAGICAL 209-223 (H1331.1.3D).

The Lame Warrior and the Skeleton. Brown - TEPEE 158-159 (E363.2.2).

The Lamp. Aesop - AESOP'S (Watts) 49 (L475).

Land of Morning Brightness. Carpenter - TALES ..KOREAN 27-35 (A511.1.8.4; A541).

The Land Where There Were No Old Men. Ure - RUMANIAN 169-171 (J151.1).

The Language of Animals. Jacobs - EUROPEAN 66-71 (B217.9).

The Language of Beasts. Lang - CRIMSON 42-48 (B216A).

The Language of the Birds. Gilstrap - SULTAN'S 88-95 (B216Ad).

The Lantern Baby. Cheney - TALES 25-36 (T542.2).

The Lark and Her Young Ones. Aesop - AESOP'S (Grosset) 103-105 (J1031); Aesop - AESOP'S (Random) 30-31; Aesop - AESOP'S (Viking) 39-40; Green - BIG 38-39.

The Lark and the Farmer. Aesop - AESOP'S (Watts) 102 (J1031).

The Lark, the Wolf and the Fox. Haviland - FAVORITE..POLAND 39-54 (K341.5.2).

Lars, My Lad. Haviland - FAVORITE..SWEDEN 60-92 (D882.1Fb).

Lasa and the Three Friendly Spirits. Gittins - TALES 79-81 (F601.2Ga).

The Lass That Couldn't Be Frightened - Leodhas HEATHER 69-79 (H1419.2).

The Lass That Lost the Laird's Daughter. Leod-has - SEA-SPELL 53-71 (F379.5A).

The Lass Who Went Out at the Cry of Dawn. Minard - WOMENFOLK 83-92 (H1385.6.1); Leodhas - THISTLE 62-73.

The Lassie and Her Godmother. Asbjørnsen - EAST (Doubleday) 54-60 (N711.1A).

The Last Day. Shah - MULLA 95 (J1511.7).

The Last of the Thunderbirds. Melzack - DAY 85-92 (A284.2.2).

The Last Tiger in Haiti. Wolkstein - MAGIC 183-188 (A2434.2.5).

The Laughing Judge. Holding - KING'S 80-86 (A1966.1).

The Laughing Place. Harris - FAVORITE 39-46 (K1023.5); Harris - COMPLETE 604-613.

The Laughing Prince. Fenner - TIME 85-107 (H341.5); Fillmore - LAUGHING 3-26; Gruen-berg - MORE 215-225.

Law of the Jungle. Nunn - AFRICAN 46-50 (K842.0.3).

Lawkamercyme. Jacobs - MORE 65-66 (J2012.2); Steel - ENGLISH 231.

The Laziest Man in the World. Lin - MILKY 47-50 (W111.5.8.2).

Lazy 'Arry, Sunny Jim and Skinny Lizzie: Three Stories. Grimm - Brothers 87-92 (J2060.1; J2061.1).

The Lazy Daughter. Ginsburg - LAZIES 49-55 (D2183.1).

The Lazy Farmer. Gruenberg - FAVORITE 394-395 (J2133.5.2).

The Lazy Fox. Barlow - LATIN 23-27 (K171.1).

The Lazy Gardener and the Little Red Men. Spellman - BEAUTIFUL 15-18 (Q321.2.1).

Lazy Hans. Manning-Sanders - BOOK..WITCHES 27-37 (G263.1.0.3).

Lazy Heinz. Gag - TALES 191-197 (J2061.1).

Lazy Jack. Hutchinson - CHIMNEY 101-106 (J2416A); Jacobs - ENGLISH 159-161; Jacobs-LAZY pb; Maitland - IDLE pb; Martignoni - ILLUSTRATED 163-164; Rockwell - THREE 92-99; Steel - ENGLISH 51-54; TALL..NURSERY 71-73; Werth - LAZY pb.

The Lazy Maiden. Borski - GOOD 20-25 (W111.3.2).

The Lazy Man. Tashjian - THREE 2-7 (K341.2.0.3).

The Lazy Man and the Water Spirit. Burton - MAGIC 24-29 (C645).

The Lazy Man Who Married the Sun's Daughter. Withers - MAN 81-82 (C31.3.2).

The Lazy One. Pridham - GIFT 138-142 (W111.5.10.1.2).

The Lazy People. Newman - FOLK..LATIN 53-60 (A1861.3.1).

Lazy Peter and His Three-Cornered Hat. Alegría - THREE 66-73 (K111.2).

Lazy Peter and the King. Alegria - THREE 111-114 (K1051).

The Lazy Squirrel. Nunn - AFRICAN 112-118 (K741.0.8).

The Lazy Tunrit. Field - ESKIMO 29-30 (W111.8).

A Leak in an Old House. Pratt - MAGIC 12 (N392.1.1).

Lean Liesl and Lanky Lenz. Gag - TALES.. GRIMM 201-203 (J2060.1.2).

The Learned Young Professor. Dobbs - MORE 39-42 (J1229.4).

Learning the Hard Way. Shah - MULLA 93 (J1331).

Leave It There! Robinson - SINGING 50-65 (G303.12.5.11).

Leave Well Enough Alone. Dobbs - MORE 15-17 (K362.1).

Leealura and Maleyato. Melzack - DAY 69-75 (H383.2.4).

A Leg for the Lion. Arnott - TEMBA 36-43 (K1251).

The Leg of Gold. Manning-Sanders - BOOK.. GHOSTS 124-127 (E235.4.2.1).

The Legend of Bala Lake. Sheppard-Jones - WELSH 78-81 (F944.1.2).

A Legend of Christmas Eve. Haviland - DENMARK 77-90 (J2075.5).

Legend of Crazy Horse. Matson - LEGENDS 42-43 (A526.1.1.1).

Legend of Doh-Kwi-Buhch. Matson - LEGENDS 90-93 (A625.2.9; A771.0.4; A1482.2).

The Legend of Eilean Donan Castle. Wilson - SCOTTISH 49-55 (B216.2).

Legend of How Ants Came to Earth. Wyndham - TALES..CHINA 55-62 (A2011.3; N611.1; N688).

A Legend of Knockmany. De Regniers - GIANT 109-124 (K521.4.1.5); Jacobs - CELTIC 171-183.

Legend of Kwatee. Matson - LEGENDS 106-109 (A1611.1.4; A2262.4).

The Legend of Llangose Lake. Sheppard-Jones 82-84 (F944.1a).

The Legend of Pasopati. De Leeuw - INDONESIAN 9-13 (A1459.1.6).

The Legend of Pathasos. Matson - LONGHOUSE 105-111 (A956.1).

The Legend of Pitch Lake. Jagendorf - KING 249-251 (A983.2).

The Legend of Saint Elizabeth. Sawyer - WAY 307-315 (V412.3).

A Legend of Saint Nicholas. De Leeuw - LEGENDS ..HOLLAND 66-70 (N816.0.1).

The Legend of Scarface. Davis - BAKER'S 189-207 (H1284.1); San Souci - LEGEND pb.

Legend of Standing Rock. Matson - LEGENDS 55-58 (A974.0.1).

Legend of Sway-Vock. Matson - LEGENDS 86-90 (G512.3.2.0.1).

The Legend of Tchi-Niu. Buck - FAIRY 154-161 (T111.1.3).

The Legend of the Almond Tree. Lowe - LITTLE 50 (K221.1).

Legend of the Arbutus. Cathon - PERHAPS 130-132 (A1158.1).

The Legend of the Chingolo Bird. Courlander - RIDE 213-214 (A1999.5).

Legend of the First Filipinas. Sechrist - ONCE 3-7 (A817.1; A1271.5; A1650.4).

The Legend of the Golden Helmet. Frost - LEGENDS 177-180 (A1437.1).

The Legend of the Hail. Matson - LONGHOUSE 100-102 (F962.5).

Legend of the Horse. Matson - LEGENDS 53-55 (A1881.3).

The Legend of the Karang. De Leeuw - INDONE-SIAN 104-108 (A963.10).

The Legend of the Mayon Volcano. Robertson - FAIRY..PHILIPPINES 107-115 (A966.1).

The Legend of the Palm Tree. Duarte - LEGEND pb (J2681.5); Hardendorff - FROG'S 25-28.

The Legend of the Peace Pipe. Matson - LEGENDS 36-39 (A1533.3).

Legend of the Sasquatch. Matson - LEGENDS 123-125 (B29.9.1).

The Legend of the Star Children. Matson - LONG-HOUSE 63-74 (A762.1Bd).

Legend of the Wind Cave. Matson - LEGENDS 39-42 (A982.1).

The Legs. Leach - THING 46-48 (H1411.1).

The Length of Life. Spellman - BEAUTIFUL 56-58 (L395).

Leopard and Fox. Aesop - FABLES (Walck) 34-35 (J242.3.1).

The Leopard and the Bushbuck Bury a Drum. Burton - MAGIC 41-43 (K527.1).

The Leopard and the Bushbuck Go Hunting. Burton MAGIC 43-47 (K335.0.4.6).

The Leopard and the Fox. Aesop - AESOP'S (Viking) 7-8 (J242.3); Martignoni - ILLUSTRATED 399.

The Leopard and the Mouse Deer. Tooze - WON-DERFUL 111-114 (J2132.5.1; K1711.2; K1715.2).

The Leopard and the Rabbit Go Courting. Burton - MAGIC 89-94 (K717.2; T92.11.4).

The Leopard Builds a House for the Bushbuck. Burton - MAGIC 121-124 (K1715.3.2).

The Leopard's Daughter. Tashjian - DEEP 56-60 (H331.18).

A Lesson for Kings. Jacobs - INDIAN 155-159 (W167.1.1).

A Lesson for the Bat. Walker - DANCING 59-64 (K401.1).

A Lesson in Sharing. Field - ESKIMO 80-82 (W175.2).

A Lesson Well Learned. Jagendorf - PRICELESS 109-113 (J2411.1.0.1).

Lets' Steal the Moon. Serwer - LET'S 80-85 (J1791.2.1).

Letter of the Law. Shah - MULLA 76 (J1161.12).

Letters from Heaven. Carpenter - KOREAN 135-139 (A1484.2.1).

The Liar's Contest. Courlander - HAT 25-29 (X905.1.3).

Lie-A-Stove. Baker - TALKING 210-217 (B375.1.3).

A Lie and a Half. Schultz - VIETNAMESE 46-47 (X909.4.3).

Liels and Laura, the Farmhand's Children. Huggins - BLUE 74-84 (G530.2H).

Lies. Ginsburg - THREE 52 (X900.1).

The Life Saver. Edmonds - POSSIBLE 105-114 (J1189.4).

Light-a-Leap and the Fowler. Gaer - FABLES..INDIA 91-96 (K581.4.1.1).

Light the Candle. Shah - MULLA 92 (J1735).

Lightening the Load. Leach - NOODLES 37 (J1874.1).

The Lights in the House. Kaula - AFRICAN 136-138 (K1715.3.2).

Liisa and the Prince. Bowman - TALES..TUPA 187-198 (R221N).

Like Master, Like Servant. Jagendorf - NOODLE-HEAD 75-77 (J2689.1).

Like Meat Loves Salt. Chase - WICKED 124-129 (H592.1.0.1).

The Lily and the Bear. Eells - TALES..SPAIN 109-116 (D735.1).

Lin Tachian. Cheney - TALES 150-156 (B755.2).

The Lion and His Three Counselors. Aesop - AESOP'S (Grosset) 154-155 (J811.2.1).

Lion and Honey Badger. Kaula - AFRICAN 46-48 (K441.5).

Lion and Mouse. Aesop - FABLES (Walck) 16-18 (B371.1).

The Lion and Other Beasts. Aesop - AESOP'S (Viking) 82 (J811.1.1).

The Lion and the Ass. Aesop - AESOP'S (Watts) 103 (K2324.1.1).

The Lion and the Ass Go Hunting. Aesop - AESOP'S (Grosset) 204-205 (K2324.1.1).

The Lion and the Ass Hunting. Aesop - AESOP'S (Viking) 54-55 (K2324.1.1).

The Lion and the Boar. Aesop - AESOP'S (Watts) 65 (J218.1).

The Lion and the Bull. Aesop - AESOP'S (Watts) 113 (J425.2).

The Lion and the Crane. Jacobs - INDIAN 1-5

(W154.3).

The Lion and the Dolphin. Aesop – AESOP'S (Grosset) 39 (B267.5).

The Lion and the Fox. Rice – ONCE 40–45 (J644.1).

The Lion and the Goat. Aesop – AESOP'S (Grosset) 56 (J218.1); Aesop – AESOP'S (Viking) 30.

The Lion and the Goat. Korel – LISTEN 115–118 (K1711.2; K1715.2).

The Lion and the Goat. Walker – NIGERIAN 40–42 (J1172.3).

The Lion and the Hare. Aesop – AESOP'S (Watts) 146 (J321.3).

The Lion and the Hare. Korel – LISTEN 108–111 (K1715.1); Montgomerie – TWENTY-FIVE 50–52.

The Lion and the Hare Go Hunting. Courlander – FIRE 105–110 (A2423.1.4.1; K553.1).

The Lion and the Horse. Aesop – FIVE 21 (K1121.1).

The Lion and the Little Jackal. Montgomerie – MERRY 38–41 (K543).

Lion and the Man. Jagendorf – KING 65–69 (K2324.2).

The Lion and the Mouse. Aesop – AESOP'S (Golden) 56 (B371.1); Aesop – AESOP'S (Grosset) 137–138; Aesop – AESOP'S (Viking) 23–24; Aesop – AESOP'S (Watts) 16; Aesop – FIVE 42; Arbuthnot – FAIRY 225; Jacobs – FABLES 21 (J411.8); Kent – MORE 32–35; Martignoni – ILLUSTRATED 94–95; Rice – ONCE 10–15; Rockwell – THREE 14–16; TALL..NURSERY 108–109.

THE LION AND THE RAT. La Fontaine pb (B371.1).

The Lion and the Statue. Aesop – AESOP'S (Grosset) 153 (J1454); Jacobs – FABLES 69.

The Lion and the Three Bulls. Aesop – AESOP'S (Watts) 98 (J1022).

The Lion and the Turtle. Arnott – ANIMAL 190–194 (K11.1).

The Lion and the Wild Ass. Aesop – AESOP'S (Watts) 85 (J811.1.1).

The Lion and the Wily Rabbit. Gaer – FABLES.. INDIA 82–84 (K1715.1).

Lion and the Woman. Kaula – AFRICAN 142–145 (B848.2.1).

The Lion and the Woodcutter. Dobbs – MORE 81–82 (J642.1).

Lion Bones and the Gardula Magicians. Davis –

LION'S 70–72 (J563.2).

Lion, Chameleon, and Chicken. Kaula – AFRICAN 51–54 (K641.3).

Lion, Goat, Vulture. Aesop – FABLES (Walck) 74–75 (J218.1).

The Lion in Love. Aesop – AESOP'S (Grosset) 94–95 (J642.1); Aesop – AESOP'S (Viking) 48; Aesop – AESOP'S (Watts) 172–173; Aesop – FIVE 88; Jacobs – FABLES 141.

The Lion, Jupiter, and the Elephant. Aesop – AESOP'S (Watts) 170 (J881.2).

The Lion-Makers. Dobbs – ONCE 24–26 (J563.2); Ryder – PANCHATANTRA 442–443.

The Lion of Hard-to-Pass Forest. Gaer – FABLES ..INDIA 60–69 (K1084.1.2).

The Lion Sneezed. Leach – LION 6–7 (A1319.15; A1811.2; A2145.2; A2335.2.6.2).

The Lion, the Ass and Fox Hunting. Aesop – AESOP'S (Viking) 62 (J811.1).

The Lion, the Ass, and the Fox. Aesop – AESOP'S (Grosset) 107 (J811.1).

The Lion, the Bear and the Fox. Aesop – AESOP'S (Grosset) 110 (J218.1.1); Aesop – AESOP'S (Watts) 83–84.

The Lion, the Boar, and the Vultures. Aesop – AESOP'S (Golden) 26 (J2181.1).

The Lion, the Fish and the Man. Ginsburg – THREE 37–39 (K2324.2).

The Lion, the Fox and the Ass. Aesop – AESOP'S (Watts) 196–197 (J811.1).

The Lion, the Fox and the Beasts. Aesop – AESOP'S (Watts) 161 (J644.1); Jacobs – FABLES 145.

The Lion, the Fox and the Stag. Aesop – AESOP'S (Watts) 212–214 (K402.3.2).

The Lion, the Mouse and the Fox. Aesop – AESOP'S (Watts) 105 (J411.8).

The Lion, the Tiger, and the Eagle. Frost – LEGENDS 120–126 (B314A).

The Lion, the Tiger and the Fox. Aesop – AESOP'S (Viking) 80–81 (J218.1.1).

The Lion, the Tortoise and the Boar. Walker – NIGERIAN 42–43 (W141.1.1).

The Lion, the Wolf and the Fox. Aesop – AESOP'S (Watts) 203–204 (K961.1.1).

The Lion Wolf. Korel – LISTEN 41–48 (J952.1.1).

The Lioness. Aesop – AESOP'S (Grosset) 117

(J281.1); Martignoni - ILLUSTRATED 152.

The Lioness and the Fox. Aesop - FIVE 52 (J281.1).

The Lioness and the Vixen. Aesop - AESOP'S (Golden) 13-15 (J281.1); Aesop - AESOP'S (Watts) 91.

The Lion's Share. Aesop - AESOP'S (Golden) 20-21 (J811.1); Aesop - AESOP'S (Grosset) 160; Aesop - AESOP'S (Random) 60-61; Courlander - KING'S 78-79; Davis - LION'S 77-80; Jacobs - FABLES - 2.

The Lion's Tail. Holding - KING'S 98-108 (H105.5.4.1).

The Lion's Threats. Heady - JAMBO 24-28 (K649.13).

The Lion's Whiskers. Davis - LION'S 7-9 (B848.2.1).

Lippo and Tapio. Bowman - TALES..TUPA 65-72 (A1611.5.6).

Lipuniushka. Carey - BABA 96-98 (F535.1.1C.

Lisa the Fox and Catafay the Cat. Riordan - TALES..CENTRAL 41-45 (K2324).

The Listening King. Lowe - LITTLE 95-96 (N455.4Z).

Little Bear. Cothran - WITH 84-89 (K1611Bc).

The Little Bird. De La Mare - ANIMAL 107-109 (H696.1.1; H701.1; H702.3).

A Little Bird. Hampden - HOUSE OF CATS 33-38 (H1554.1).

The Little Bird That Found the Pea. Withers - I SAW 102-107 (Z41.6).

The Little Bird's Rice. Spellman - BEAUTIFUL 44-48 (Z41.6.2).

The Little Black Book of Magic. Carpenter - SOUTH 71-82 (D1711.0.1).

The Little Black Men and the Honeybees. Carpenter - AFRICAN 53-62 (K1023.0.1).

The Little Boat. Bascom - THOSE 36-47 (J2212.7).

Little Briar Rose. Grimm - GRIMM'S (Follett) 186-191 (D1960.3).

Little Brother and Little Sister. Grimm - BROTHERS 47-54 (P253.2.0.1); Grimm - GRIMM'S (Follett) 192-201; Grimm - GRIMM'S (Scribner's) 29-36.

The Little Brother and Sister. Grimm - GRIMM'S (World) 376-382 (P253.2.0.1); Wiggin - FAIRY 174-180.

The Little Brother of the Sun. Ure - RUMANIAN 87-88 (J1530.0.1).

The Little Bucket. Ross - BURIED 103-108 (Q2.1.1Da).

The Little Bull Calf. Arnott - ANIMAL 210-219 (B335.2C); Green - CAVALCADE..DRAGONS 115-119.

A Little Bull Calf. Hampden - GYPSY 17-23 (B335.2C).

The Little Bull-Calf. Jacobs - MORE 186-191 (B335.2C); Manning-Sanders - RED 93-97; Pilkington - SHAMROCK 10-15.

Little Burnt-Face. Arbuthnot - ANTHOLOGY 392-393 (R221G); Arbuthnot - FAIRY 199-201; DeWit - TALKING 34-38.

Little Capuchin Monkey's Story. Sherlock - IGUANA'S 29-42 (J2332.1.1).

THE LITTLE COCK. Hardendorff pb (Z52.4).

The Little Cock Who Sang Coplas. Sawyer - PICTURE 87-96 (J1653.1).

THE LITTLE COCKEREL. Ambrus pb (Z52.4).

Little Cricket. Ross - BURIED 113-120 (N611.1; N688).

The Little Crow. Heady - WHEN 47-52 (B642.1).

The Little Daughter of the Snow. Ransome - OLD 122-135 (T546.3).

The Little Duck. Hatch - MORE 33-48 (Q2.1.5Bba); Owen - CASTLE 171-181.

Little Ederland. Owen - CASTLE 157-167 (G601Ae).

The Little Fish and the Big Fish. Jagendorf - MERRY 69-76 (J1341.2).

The Little Farmer. Grimm - HOUSEHOLD 256-261 (K842Ba).

Little Finger. Manning-Sanders - GIANNI 127-140 (F535.1.1Fb).

The Little Folks' Presents. Grimm - GRIMM'S (Follett) 202-206 (F344.1.4).

The Little Fox. Manning-Sanders - RED 98-104 (D1033.2).

The Little Fox. Novak - FAIRY 131-137 (D612.2.1; D1171.3.1).

Little Freddie and His Fiddle. Asbjørnsen - EAST (Row) 85-92 (D1415.2.5.1); Asbjørnsen - NORWEGIAN 61-66.

Little Freddy with His Fiddle. Arbuthnot - ANTHOLOGY 249-251 (D1415.2.5.1); Arbuthnot -

FAIRY 87-90.

Little Frikk with His Fiddle. Undset - TRUE 190-197 (D1415.2.5.1).

The Little Frog of the Stream. Barlow - LATIN 57-61 (B493.1.1).

Little Golden Hood. Lang - RED 225-229 (K2011E).

The Little Gray Mouse and the Handsome Cock. Ekram - TURKISH 61-65 (Z32.3.2).

The Little Gray Goose. Montgomerie - TWENTY-FIVE 20-21 (K562.1).

Little Han Hsin. Dolch - STORIES..OLD CHINA 49-55 (J101).

The Little Hare's Clever Trick. Hume - FAVOR-ITE..CHINA 115-119 (K1715.1).

Little Head, Big Medicine. Jagendorf - NOODLE-HEAD 274-277 (G555.1.1).

Little Hen Eagle. Aardema - BEHIND 3-10 (K1911.1A).

Little Hiram. Manning-Sanders - CHOICE 200-215 (K1346.0.1).

The Little Horse. Hatch - MORE 150-166 (B641.6.2).

The Little Horse of Seven Colors. Lowe - LITTLE 17-21 (D2003A).

The Little House. Ross - BURIED 31-34 (J2199.5).

The Little House in the Wood. Grimm - GRIMM'S (Follett) 207-214 (Q2.1.3C).

The Little Jackals and the Lion. Haviland - FAVORITE..INDIA 21-26 (K1715.1).

Little Jip. Manning-Sanders - BOOK..GHOSTS 74-79 (K526C).

The Little Lame Fox. Fillmore - LAUGHING 73-106 (H1331.1.3D).

The Little Lion Dog and the Blue Prince. Carpenter - WONDER..DOGS 173-183 (Q161.1.1).

The Little, Little Fellow With the Big, Big Hat. Jagendorf - KING 126-131 (D1067.1.1).

The Little Lizard's Sorrow. Vo-Dinh - TOAD 81-87 (A2426.4.3).

The Louse and Little Flea. Grimm - BROTHERS 17-20 (Z32.2.4.1).

The Little Man in Green. Colwell - ROUND 82-84 (F451.5.1.5.0.1).

Little Masha and Misha the Bear. Riordan - TALES..CENTRAL 190-193 (G561.1F).

Little Master Misery. Ransome - OLD 184-205 (N250.4).

The Little Menehunes. Berry - MAGIC 22-29 (F271.2.8.1).

Little Mr. Cricket. Harris - FAVORITE 30-34 (K11.2); Harris - COMPLETE 772-779.

The Little Mouse. Kaplan - FAIRY 209-229 (B641Bc).

Little Mukra. Manning-Sanders - DWARFS 53-63 (D1065.7.1).

The Little Nobleman. Manning-Sanders - RED 118-126 (B314G).

The Little Old Woman and Her Pigs. TALL..NUR-SERY 92-97 (Z41).

Little One-eye, Little Two-eyes, and Little Three-eyes. Lang - GREEN 253-263 (D830.1.1); Lang - FIFTY 176-183.

Little One-eye, Two-eyes, and Three-eyes. Hutchinson - CHIMNEY 41-52 (D830.1.1).

Little One-inch. Brenner LITTLE pb (F535.1.1E); Sakade - JAPANESE 66-70.

The Little Peasant. Grimm - GRIMM'S (World) 107-113 (J1344.1; K842Ba).

The Little Pet Rani. Williams-Ellis - ROUND 57-66 (B641C).

The Little Pot. Rockwell - THREE 110-112 (C916.3).

The Little Rabbit. Harris - FAVORITE 258-261 (H1023.2.0.1.1); Harris - COMPLETE 71-74; Harris - UNCLE 108-112.

The Little Red Bogie-Man. Sheppard-Jones - WELSH 167-172 (H1411.1).

Little Red Cap. Grimm - GRIMM'S (Follett) 215-221 (K2011); Grimm - GRIMM'S (Scribner's) 73-77; Grimm - HOUSEHOLD 132-135.

The Little Red Hairy Man. Colwell - ROUND 90-94 (K1931.2B).

The Little Red Hen. Holdsworth - LITTLE pb (W111.6); Montgomerie - MERRY 14-18; Palazzo - LITTLE pb; Richardson - GREAT 9-15; TALL..NURSERY 79-83.

The Little Red Hen and the Fox. TALL..NUR-SERY 51-53 (K526.1).

The Little Red Hen and the Grain of Wheat. Haviland - FAIRY 32-34 (W111.6); Hutchinson - CHIMNEY 63-65.

The Little Red Mannikin. Manning-Sanders - DEVIL'S 110-116 (C12.2.1).

Little Red Riding Hood. De La Mare - TALES 74-83 (K2011); Galdone - LITTLE pb; Grimm - LITTLE (Harcourt) pb; Grimm - LITTLE (World) pb; Haviland - FAIRY 146-160; Lang - BLUE 62-65; Opie - CLASSIC 93-97; Perrault - FAMOUS 105-116; Perrault - LITTLE pb; Perrault - PERRAULT'S (Dodd) 71-77; Perrault - PERRAULT'S (Dover) 23-30; Rackham - ARTHUR 266-268; Rockwell - THREE 102-109; Steel - ENGLISH 191-193; Stobbs - LITTLE pb; TALL.. NURSERY 7-11.

The Little Rooster and the Turkish Sultan. Gruenberg - FAVORITE 369-373 (Z52.4).

Little Rosa and Long Leda. Kaplan - FAIRY 17-34 (Q2.1.5Ba).

LITTLE RYSTU. Ginsburg pb (D1415.2.3.5).

The Little Sawah. De Leeuw - INDONESIAN 30-35 (A1529.1).

Little Scar Face. Association - TOLD..GREEN 156-161 (R221G).

The Little Scarred One. Cunningham - TALKING 105-112 (R221G); Sheehan - FOLK 141-148.

Little Shell. Sechrist - ONCE 93-97 (F535.1.1Da).

The Little Shepherd Boy. Gag - MORE..GRIMM 47-49 (H561.4; H701.1); Wiggin - TALES 160-161.

The Little Singing Frog. Fillmore - LAUGHING 163-170 (B641Ah); Frost - LEGEND 240-244.

LITTLE SISTER AND THE MONTH BROTHERS. De Regniers pb (Q2.1.4.Ac).

Little Sister and the Zimwi. Aardema - TALES 86-94 (G422.1.1.1).

Little Sister Fox and Brother Wolf. Riordan - TALES..CENTRAL 20-22 (K371.1; K473; K1021).

The Little Slave Girl. Wyndham - FOLK..CHINA 102-107 (J2415.19).

The Little Snake. Hampden - GYPSY 79-83 (B646.1.2).

Little Snow-White. Grimm - BROTHERS 61-71 (Z65.1); Grimm - GRIMM'S (Follett) 222-234; Grimm - GRIMM'S (Scribner's) 144-154.

The Little Soldier. Lang - RED 153-157 (H1385.3Cc).

The Little Springbok. Helfman - BUSHMEN 74-76 (F929.4).

The Little Tailor and the Three Dogs. Manning-Sanders - BOOK..OGRES 101-109 (B524.1.2B).

Little Thumb. Lang - BLUE 258-266 (K1611C).

Little Tom Thumb. Perrault - PERRAULT'S

(Dodd) 26-41 (K1611C); Perrault - PERRAULT'S (Dover) 91-116.

Little Tuppen. Wiggin - TALES 358-360 (Z32.1.1).

Little Tuppens. Richardson - GREAT 129-139 (Z32.1.1.2).

The Little White Cat. Hardendorff - FROG'S 83-107.

THE LITTLE WHITE HEN. Hewitt pb (Z52.3).

LITTLE WHITE HEN. Kijima pb (J1421; K526.1).

The Little White Rabbit. Montgomerie - MERRY 56-61 (Z39.1).

Live Alone, Die Alone. Davis - LION'S 127-129 (W197.4).

The Living Kuan-Yin. Kendall - SWEET 23-29 (H1273.2Lb).

The Lizard and the Catfish. Haskett - GRAINS 82-83 (J414.3.1).

The Lizard and the Cockatoo. Arnott - ANIMAL 76-78 (A2311.9.1; A2321.12).

The Lizard-hand. Leach - HOW (A1311.1.1).

The Lizards and the Stag. Green - ANIMAL 82 (L45.8).

The Lizard's Big Dance. Courlander - PIECE 50-54 (D2174.1).

The Lizard's Tail. Turnbull - FAIRY..INDIA 84-90 (J915.6).

The Loafer. De La Iglesia - CAT #6 (J1552.10).

The Locust and the Coyote. Dolch - PUEBLO 67-77 (G555.1.2).

The Locust and the Oats. Withers - I SAW 48 (Z11.1).

Lod, the Farmer's Son. Wilson - SCOTTISH 18-27 (F615.3.1.4).

The Lodge of the Bear. Yellow Bear - TONWEYA 24-30 (A969.12).

Logic. Kendall - SWEET 21-22 (H682.1.4.1).

The Lonely Lioness and the Ostrich Chicks. Aardema - TALES 70-76 (K649.9.1).

Long Ago When the Earth Was Flat. Luzzato - LONG 8-19 (A969.13).

LONG, BROAD AND QUICKEYE. Ness pb (F601.2C); Lang - FIFTY 184-192.

Long, Broad and Sharpsight. Manning-Sanders - BOOK..WIZARDS 26-39 (F601.2C.

The Long-Howling Jackal. Gaer - FABLES..IN-DIA 90-91 (J514.2).

Long John and the Mermaid. Manning-Sanders - BOOK..MERMAIDS 54-58 (B612.3).

The Long Leather Bag. Wiggin - FAIRY 154-162 (Q2.1.2Cb).

A Long, Long Night. Jagendorf - PRICELESS 61-65 (J1819.3.1).

Long Memories. Withers - WORLD 59 (H1595.1.1).

The Long-Nosed Giant. Lu Mar - CHINESE 11-19 (H506.1).

The Long-Nosed Goblins. Sakade - JAPANESE 29-34 (D1376.1.3.2).

The Long One. Aardema - TALES 19-30 (K1711.2.1).

Long Shanks, Girth and Keen. Fillmore - SHEP-HERD'S 103-118 (F601.2C).

The Longest Story in the World. Novak - FAIRY 31-36 (Z11.4).

Look Behind as Well as Before. Arbuthnot - AN-THOLOGY 326 (Z49.22); Burton - MAGIC 126-127.

Look Here. Withers - MAN 52 (J1849.6).

LOOK THERE IS A TURTLE FLYING. Domanska pb (J2357).

THE LOON'S NECKLACE. Toye pb (F952.7.1).

Lord and Master. Fillmore - LAUGHING 253-266 (B216A).

Lord Per. Aulaire - EAST 70-78 (K1917.3D).

Lord Peter. Asbjørnsen - EAST (Row) 57-63 (K1917.3); Manning-Sanders - BOOK..MAGI-CAL 29-37.

The Lord Said, This Is My House. Jagendorf - KING 79-80 (V128.0.1.2).

Lost and Found. Hatch - MORE 119-137 (H1385.3Bb).

The Lost Boys. Curtis - GHOST 99-110 (D2072.7).

The Lost Camel. Hardendorff - JUST 52-53 (J1661.1.1).

The Lost Children. Hulpach - AMERICAN 43-45 (A773.4.1).

The Lost Children. Manning-Sanders - GLASS 187-194 (H1321.1D).

The Lost City of Ys. Colum - STONE 30-35 (F944.6).

The Lost Paradise. Jagendorf - PRICELESS 102-108 (H1554); Lang - ROSE 131-137.

The Lost Penny. Ginsburg - THREE 16 (W211.1.1).

The Lost Prince. Manning-Sanders - BOOK.. MERMAIDS 15-24 (D1154.1).

The Lost Star Princess. Carpenter - TALES.. CHINESE 190-197 (A762.2.2).

The Lost Stone. Spicer - THIRTEEN MONSTERS 41-51 (F420.5.2B; K1886.3.1).

The Lost Sun, Moon and Stars. Thompson - HA-WAIIAN..EARTH 33-39 (A721.1.6).

A Lot of Silence Makes a Great Noise. Kaula - AFRICAN 130-132 (K544).

Lounging 'Round and Suffering. Harris - FAVOR-ITE 100-103 (K543); Harris - COMPLETE 39-41; Harris - UNCLE 59-63.

The Louse and the Crow. Withers - I SAW 108-111 (Z33.4.1).

The Louse Skin Drum. Withers - WORLD 67-68 (H522.1.1).

The Love Crystal. Arbuthnot - ANTHOLOGY 344-346 (E633.1).

Love Like Salt. Neufeld - BEWARE 28-35 (F813.8.3).

The Love of a Mexican Prince and Princess. Jag-endorf - KING 181-186 (A962.1.1).

The Love of Saint Francis. Jagendorf - PRICE-LESS 147-149 (E121.4.2).

The Lovelorn Pig. Leach - THING 65-67 (E211.3).

Lox and the Two Ermines. Williams-Ellis - ROUND 223-230 (A762.1Bb).

Lu Sinh's Dream. Schultz - VIETNAMESE 90-92 (D1812.3.3.2.1).

Luc, the King's Woodsman. Pugh - TALES 21-28 (D1825.3.1.1).

Lucas the Strong. Sechrist - ONCE 196-204 (F601.2Db).

Lucifer's Wedding. Kavcic - GOLDEN 127-133 (G561.1E).

Luck and Wit. Ure - RUMANIAN 90-98 (N141.0.3).

THE LUCK CHILD. Chapman pb (K1355B).

The Luck Fairies. Eels - TALES..SPAIN 37-43 (D2183.1).

Luck for Fools. Jagendorf - NOODLEHEAD 216-221 (J2081.1; N11.1).

The Luck of the Sea and the Luck of the Mountain. MacAlpine - JAPANESE 23-24 (U136.0.1).

Luckier and Luckier. Leach - LUCK 71-75 (J2081.1).

The Lucky Beggar. Leach - LUCK 30-31 (N177).

The Lucky Cat. Kavcic - GOLDEN 32-37 (N411.1B).

The Lucky Coin. Wiggin - FAIRY 349-353 (Q3.3).

The Lucky Dog. Jagendorf - PRICELESS 35-39 (N531.1).

The Lucky Hunter. Borski - GOOD 72-74 (K31.1).

The Lucky Man. Leach - THING 30 (J2235); Leach - LUCK 62.

Lucky Owen. Sleigh - NORTH 207-215 (D1960.2).

Lucky Scraps. Gag - MORE..GRIMM 59-60 (H381.1).

The Lucky Shirt. Leach - LUCK 86-87 (N135.3).

The Lucky Tea-Kettle. MacAlpine - JAPANESE 202-210 (D1171.3.1).

The Lute Player. Lang - VIOLET 65-72 (J1545.4.3).

Lutey and the Mermaid. Manning-Sanders - PETER 11-16 (B81.3.3); Sleigh - NORTH 23-30.

The Lutin in the Barn. Carlson - SASHES 80-91 (J1795.1.1); Littledale - GHOSTS 101-110.

Lutonya. Jagendorf - NOODLEHEAD 235-240 (J2063.2).

Lyonese. Manning-Sanders - PETER 26-32 (B401.2; F993.4).

Ma Ki. Chang - TALES 11-24 (J2171.1.3.0.1; K119.3; K131.1.2; K842.0.2; K1051).

Ma Liang and His Magic Brush. Wyndham - TALES..CHINA 73-82 (D435.2.1.2).

Ma Tsai and the Landlord. Dolch - STORIES.. CHINA 83-91 (K131.1.1).

MacCodrum of the Seals. Wilson - SCOTTISH 1-7 (B651.8).

The Mad Man, the Dead Man and the Devil. Mac-Manus - HIBERNIAN 174-184 (J2311.0.1.1).

Madam Crab Loses Her Head. McDowell - THIRD 81-87 (C432.1.2).

Madame Giraffe. Aardema - TALES 32-37 (Z43.6.5).

Madgy Figgey and the Sow. Manning-Sanders -

PETER 144-149 (G265.6.1.2).

The Magic Acorn. Wyndham - RUSSIAN 62-67 (Z52.4.2.1).

The Magic Amber. Jewett - WHICH 82-94 (D882.1A).

Magic and Friendship. Guirma - TALES 45-46 (D1711.0.1.1.1).

The Magic Apples. Baker - TALKING 118-122 (H1321B).

The Magic Baby Shoes. Ross - IN MEXICO 104-120 (V128.3).

The Magic Bag. Shah - MULLA 58-59 (D1469.18).

The Magic Banana. Berry - MAGIC 13-21 (B31.1.3; D1652.1.7.2).

The Magic Bell. Lu Mar - CHINESE 29-41 (J1141.10.2).

The Magic Belt. Manning-Sanders - PRINCES 57-65 (N813B).

The Magic Berries. Downing - RUSSIAN 174-188 (D551.1F).

The Magic Bottles. Spellman - BEAUTIFUL 22-25 (D861.1E).

The Magic Box. Sawyer - WAY 219-225 (H588.7; H588.7.5).

The Magic Brush. Dolch - STORIES..OLD CHINA 1-7 (D435.2.1.2); Mui - MAGIC pb.

The Magic Calabash. Cothran - MAGIC 27-30 (H331.4.3).

The Magic Cap. Ross - BURIED 127-134 (K110.1; K111.2).

The Magic Chest. Wyndham - FOLK..CHINA 17-21 (F302.1.4).

THE MAGIC COOKING POT: A FOLKTALE OF IN-DIA. Towle pb (D861.1G).

The Magic Crystal. Graham - BEGGAR 57-69 (E633.1).

The Magic Drum. Arnott - AFRICAN 124-132 (D861.1H).

The Magic Drum. Burton - MAGIC 19-24 (D1415.2.7).

The Magic Eagle. Barlow - LATIN 89-96 (A2693.1).

The Magic Egg. Rudolph - MAGIC 3-13 (K1161.9).

The Magic Fiddle. Dobbs - MORE 49-62 (D1415.2.5.1).

The Magic Garden. Masey - STORIES 50-61 (W11.17).

The Magic Gem. Kim - STORY 99-115 (D882.1Bbc).

The Magic Geta. Scofield - HOLD 15-20 (J2415ff).

The Magic Grocery Store. Brenner - BOY 44-47 (C761.4).

The Magic Hood. Kim - STORY 180-185 (D1361.15.2).

The Magic Horns. Arnott - AFRICAN 78-84 (B335.2E).

Magic in the Carved Chests. Newell - RESCUE 91-98 (A1414.7.4).

The Magic Kettle. Lang- CRIMSON 229-233 (D1171.3.1; D1415; D1610.13.1; D1646.3).

The Magic Lake. Manning-Sanders - CHOICE 295-300 (B81.2.3); Manning-Sanders - BOOK..MERMAIDS 73-78.

The Magic Lamp. Frost - LEGEND 147-153 (D871.1A).

The Magic Listening Cap. Uchida - MAGIC 2-10 (D1067.2.2; N452.1.2).

The Magic Lute Player. Tooze - WONDERFUL 74-76 (K754.2.1).

The Magic Mango. Carpenter - ELEPHANT 166-175 (H346).

The Magic Mare. Toor - GOLDEN 57-66 (H1213.1C).

The Magic Mill. Arbuthnot - ANTHOLOGY 287-288 (D1651.3.1); Huggins - BLUE 85-92.

The Magic Mirror. Huggins - BLUE 50-64 (D882.1I).

The Magic Mirror. Maas - MOON 104-115 (H1321.1Cc).

The Magic Mirror. Michael - PORTUGUESE 28-34 (D1163.1).

The Magic Monkeys. Manning-Sanders - SORCERORS 112-121 (B641C).

The Magic Mortar. Sakade - JAPANESE 43-46 (D1651.3.1); Uchida - MAGIC 32-41 (A1115.2.1; D1262).

The Magic Orange Tree. Wolkstein - MAGIC 13-22 (Q2.1.6Db).

The Magic Oysters. De Leeuw - INDONESIAN 127-134 (C57.1.3).

The Magic Pancakes at the Footbridge Tavern. Hume - FAVORITE..CHINA 79-84 (G263.1.0.2)

The Magic Pipe. Pridham - GIFT 16-20 (D1415.2.3.2).

The Magic Poncho. Carpenter - SOUTH 129-136 (D1952.2).

The Magic Pony. Arnott - ANIMAL 14-22 (B335.2G).

The MAGIC POT. Coombs pb (D1605.1).

MAGIC PUMPKIN. Skurzynski pb (K553.0.3).

The Magic Purse of the Swamp Maiden. Uchida - SEA 42-54 (D812).

The Magic Ring. Daniels - FALCON 92-110 (D882.1.1); Lang - YELLOW 192-206.

The Magic Rock. Heady - SAGE 24-26 (D931.0.6).

The Magic Ruby. Robertson - FAIRY..VIETNAM 81-88 (B216B).

The Magic Sandals. Newman - FOLK..LATIN 13-18 (D152.1.1.1).

The Magic Sandals of Hualachi. Courlander - RIDE 220-223 (D1521.1.1).

The Magic Scythe. Belting - ELVES 84-90 (F348.7.1.1).

Magic! Silly Magic. Jagendorf - NOODLEHEAD 97-99 (K112.1.1).

The Magic Snowshoes. DeWit - TALKING 192-197 (D1065.3.1).

The Magic Spring. Sakade - JAPANESE 64-68 (D1338.1.1.2).

The Magic Stallion. Chang - CHINESE 12-19 (D1626.1).

The Magic Swan. Lang - RED 172-177 (H341.2); Manning-Sanders - BOOK..MAGICAL 114-120.

The Magic Tabo. Sechrist - ONCE 184-188 (D871.1).

The Magic Teakettle. Sakade - JAPANESE 17-24 (D1171.3.1).

The Magic Turban, the Magic Whip, and the Magic Carpet. Buck - FAIRY 257-263 (F1015.1.1C).

The Magical Crock. Zajdler - POLISH 170-177 (F54.2; Z52.4.2).

The Magical Tune. Manning-Sanders - BOOK.. MERMAIDS 59-65 (D1415.2.4.2).

THE MAGICIAN. Shulevitz pb (Q1.1D).

The Magician and His Pupil. Williams-Ellis - FAIRY..BRITISH 181-185 (D1711.0.1.2).

Magicians of the Way. Birch – CHINESE 80–88 (D1711.6.3; D1960.1.3).

The Magician's Castle in the Sea. Gunterman – CASTLES 84–105 (K1861.1D).

The Magpie and Her Children. Hardendorff – JUST 15–16 (J13); Wiggin – TALES 338 (J13.1).

The Magpie's Nest. Hulpach – AMERICAN 139–141 (A2431.3.11).

The Magpie's Nest. Jacobs – ENGLISH 200–204 (A2271.1.1); Wiggin – TALES 231–232.

MAI LING AND THE MIRROR. Abisch pb (J1795.2).

The Maid in the Mirror. Carpenter – TALES.. CHINESE 226–234 (B651.1.1); Sheehan – FOLK 118–126.

Maid Maleen. Grimm – GRIMM'S (Follett) 235–245 (K1816.0.2.1); Lurie – CLEVER 57–65.

The Maid in the Glass Mountain. Aulaire – EAST 45–57 (H331.1.1).

The Maiden and the Rat Catcher. Korel – LISTEN 53–59 (L392.0.3).

Maiden in Distress. Shah – MULLA 133 (G550.1).

The Maiden in the Country Underground. Pilk- ington – SHAMROCK 94–101 (Q2.1.2Ab).

The Maiden of Deception Pass. Matson – LONG- HOUSE 19–27 (B82.1.3).

The Maiden of the Mist. Berry – MAGIC 45–48 (F383.4.3.1).

The Maiden Suvarna. Manning-Sanders – BOOK.. GHOSTS 95–100 (E328).

The Maiden Who Lived With the Wolves. Matson – LEGENDS 51–52 (B538.3.6).

The Maiden With the Wooden Helmet. Buck – FAIRY 47–50 (K1815.0.2).

The Majesty of the Sea. Shah – MULLA 109 (J1968.0.2).

Makato and the Cowrie Shell. Asia – FOLK.. BOOK 1 41 (W48.3).

The Making of the Earth. Tooze – WONDERFUL 32–35 (A814.8).

Making Your Own. Leach – LUCK 69–70 (H588.7).

Makonaima Returns. McDowell – THIRD 75–80 (A1231.3).

Malice, Bouki and Monplaisir. Carter – GREEDY 91–98 (K1066.2).

Malintzin. Brenner – BOY 125–128 (E425.1.11).

A Man, a Snake and a Fox. Pridham – GIFT 55– 62 (J1172.3).

The Man and His Boots. Harris – Complete 560– 562 (K341.6.1); Harris – UNCLE 130–136.

The Man and His Two Sweethearts. Aesop – AE- SOP'S (Watts) 134 (J2112.1).

The Man and His Two Wives. Aesop – AESOP'S (Grosset) 196 (J2112.1); Aesop – AESOP'S (Vik- ing) 78–79; Jacobs – FABLES 89.

The Man and the Lion. Aesop – AESOP'S (Viking) 66 (J1454); Aesop – AESOP'S (Watts) 66.

The Man and the Mango Trees. Holladay – BANTU 30–32 (J2183.1.4).

The Man and the Satyr. Aesop – AESOP'S (Vik- ing) 42–43 (J1801.1); Aesop – AESOP'S (Watts) 86–87; Jacobs – FABLES 111; Kent – MORE 12– 15.

The Man and the Serpent. Jacobs – FABLES 11 (J15).

The Man and the Star. Caswell – SHADOWS 83–87 (F53.1.2).

The Man and the Wood. Aesop – AESOP'S (Gros- set) 201 (U162); Jacobs – FABLES 53.

The Man and the Wooden God. Jacobs – FABLES 81 (V123.2).

Man-Crow. Carter – GREEDY 73–78 (A2433.5.3.3.1).

The Man from Kailasa. Courlander – TIGER'S 58– 62 (J2326.1).

The Man in the Mirror. Withers – WORLD 75 (J1795.4).

The Man in the Moon. De Leeuw – LEGEND..HOL- LAND 112–113 (A751.1.2.1).

The Man Misery. Thoby-Marcelin – SINGING 53– 56 (Z111.2.2.1).

The Man O' the Clan. Leodhas – GAELIC 81–90 (E502).

The Man of Iron. Grimm – GRIMM'S (Scribner's) 245–254 (G671).

The Man, the Boy and the Donkey. Aesop – AE- SOP'S (Grosset) 50–52 (J1041.2); Jacobs – FABLES 124–125.

The Man, the Horse, the Ox and the Dog. Aesop – AESOP'S (Watts) 188–189 (B592).

The Man, the Serpent, and the Fox. Vittorini – OLD 34–37 (J1172.3).

The Man, the Woman, and the Fly. Jagendorf – NOODLEHEAD 161–163 (J1193.1; N333.0.3).

The Man Who Always Helped the Needy. Burton - MAGIC 29-35 (D882.1.1B).

The Man Who Ate His Wives. Hardendorff - JUST 88-91 (D671A).

The Man Who Bought a Dream. Uchida - MAGIC 93-100 (N531.3).

The Man Who Climbed Down a Moonbeam. Withers - MAN 53-55 (K1054).

The Man Who Couldn't Pay His Debts. Mehdevi - BUNGLING 99-107 (K341.2.0.1.1).

The Man Who Cuts the Cinnamon Tree. Bonnet - FOLKTALES..CHINA 117-121 (A751.1.8; J2415.13).

The Man Who Didn't Believe in Ghosts. Leodhas - GHOSTS 24-34 (E419.6.1).

The Man Who Didn't Die. Ish-Kishor - WISE 27-31 (K2371.1.1.1).

The Man Who Feared Nothing. Jewett - WHICH 65-73 (H1419.1).

The Man Who Fled a Nagging Wife. Withers - MAN 19 (A751.0.1).

The Man Who Helped Carry the Coffin. Leodhas - GHOSTS 45-78 (E379.6).

The Man Who Hung His Powder Horn on the Moon. Withers - MAN 46-47 (X1851.1).

The Man Who Killed the Sea Monster. Maher - BLIND 31-38 (B877.1.3).

The Man Who Learned the Language of the Animals. Arnott - AFRICAN 5-12 (A1384; B216Ac).

The Man Who Learned to Think. Grimm - GRIMM'S (Scribner's) 7-18 (H1440A).

The Man Who Lived a Thousand Years. Carpenter - KOREAN 89-94 (K975.1.2).

The Man Who Looked For Death. Courlander - OLODE 15-18 (J217.0.1.1).

The Man Who Lost His Way. Montgomerie - TWENTY-FIVE 46-47 (J2133.5.0.1).

The Man Who Loved Tiny Creatures. Cheney - TALES 37-52 (W154.8.4.1).

The Man Who Married a Snow Goose. Maher - BLIND 79-98 (A1999.1; A2109.1; H1385.3Ff).

The Man Who Nearly Became Fishpaste. Birch - CHINESE 55-61 (F1068.3).

The Man Who Paddled to the Moon's House. Withers - MAN 41-43 (A755.8).

The Man Who Planted Onions. Kim - STORY 11-16 (D551.2.5).

The Man Who Rode the Bear. Credle - TALL 100-114 (K1951.2.1.1).

The Man Who Sold a Ghost. Wyndham - TALES.. CHINA 48-51 (E463.1).

The Man Who Sold the Winds. Pugh - MORE.. WELSH 67-76 (C322.1).

The Man Who Stayed Too Long. Brenner - BOY 48-50 (C761.4).

The Man Who Stole a Rope. Wyndham - TALES.. CHINA 38-39 (K188).

The Man Who Tried to Catch The Night. Burton - MAGIC 61-63 (J1961.2).

The Man Who Walked Widdershins Round the Kirk. Leodhas - GHOSTS 35-42 (E44).

The Man Who Was Always Borrowing and Lending. Burton - MAGIC 35-39 (H1132.1.5.1).

The Man Who Was Full of Fun. Papashvily - YES 67-75 (K113; K131.1.1; K842).

THE MAN WHO WAS GOING TO MIND THE HOUSE. McKee pb (J2431).

The Man Who Was Only Three Inches Tall. Siddiqui - TOONTOONY 91-97 (F535.1.1Dc).

The Man Who Would Know Magic. Wyndham - TALES..CHINA 67-72 (D1711.0.1.3).

The Man With the Best of Spells. Ure - RUMANIAN 26-32 (K1956.2; K1956.8; N611.5).

The Man With the Chair on His Head. Leach - NOODLES 15-16 (J1762.4).

Manabozho and His Toe. Wiggin - TALES 400 (L410.8).

Manabozo's Nephew. Leekley - WORLD 27-34 (A2411.2.1.22).

Manabush and the Moose. Hardendorff - JUST 24-25 (W123.5).

Mancrow, Bird of Darkness. Sherlock - WEST 65-70 (A2433.5.3.3.1).

The Mandarin and the Butterflies. Carpenter - TALES..CHINESE 198-205 (E525).

Manka and the Judge. Lurie - CLEVER 9-16 (H561.1; H1053.2; H1054.1; H1056; J1191.1; J1249.2).

Mannikin Spanalong. Manning-Sanders - SORCEROR'S 33-36 (T111.5.1).

Manny MacGillian's Story. MacManus - BOLD 158-168 (M231A).

The Manitcore of North Cerney. Spicer - MONSTER 116-127 (B27).

Manstin, the Rabbit. Palmer - DRAGONS 68-74 (B535.0.16).

Mantis and the Ostrich. Helfman - BUSHMEN 63-65 (A1415.0.2.2; A2377.2; A2431.4).

Mantis and the Sheep. Helfman - BUSHMEN 102-108 (A1611.3.1).

Mantis Comes Alive. Helfman - BUSHMEN 62-63 (A1291.2).

Mantis Makes an Eland. Helfman - BUSHMEN 92-99 (A741.5; A1875.2).

Many-Fur. Grimm - JUNIPER v.2 236-244 (R221D).

The Many-Furred Creature. Lang - FIFTY 193-198 (R221Da); Lang - GREEN 269-275.

March and the Shepherd. Arbuthnot - ANTHOLOGY 269-270 (K688.1); Arbuthnot - FAIRY 129-130; Vittorini - OLD 2-6.

March's Ears. Sheppard-Jones - WELSH 69-71 (D1316.5.3.0.3).

THE MARE'S EGG. Varga pb (J1772.1).

Margrette. Manning-Sanders - BOOK..MERMAIDS 46-53 (B82.1.1).

Maria Sat on the Fire. Brenner - BOY 121-124 (E411.0.2.1.1).

MARILKA. Domanska pb (Z39.5.2).

Mario and the Yara. Carpenter - SOUTH 137-143 (F302.3.1.5).

Marking the Boat to Locate the Sword. Wyndham - TALES..CHINA (J1922.1).

Marko the Rich and Vasily the Luckless. Williams -Ellis - ROUND 90-91 (H1273.2F).

The Marriage of the Mouse. Courlander - FIRE 89-92 (L392.0.2).

The Marriage of the Robin and the Wren. Colwell - YOUNGEST (Z55); Montgomerie - TWENTY-FIVE 44-45.

The Marriage of the Sun. Aesop - AESOP'S (Viking) 67 (J613.1).

The Marvelous Cow of Llyn Barfog. Belting - ELVES 53-54 (B184.2.2.2.1).

The Marvelous Doors. Belting - ELVES 11-14 (A1465.3.3.1).

The Marvelous Pear Seed. Wyndham - TALES.. CHINA 20-24 (H263.1).

Mary Culhane and the Dead Man. Bang - GOBLIN'S 29-40 (E43).

Mary, Mary So Contrary. Fillmore - SHEPHERD'S 64-68 (T255.2).

Marya Marevna. Riordan - TALES..CENTRAL 148-160 (B314C; H1199.12.4B); Whitney - IN 107-120.

Masha and the Bear. Carey - BABA 117-120 (G561F).

The Mason's Luck. Wyndham - FOLK..CHINA 108-116 (H1273.2M).

The Mason's Marriage. Lin - MILKY 16-23 (H1273.2J).

Masoy and the Ape. Sechrist - ONCE 110-118 (K741.0.11; K1917.3E).

The Master and His Pupil. Jacobs - ENGLISH 74-77 (D1711.0.1.2).

Master and Man. Deutsch - MORE 45-54 (K172).

The Master and the Servant. Tashjian - ONCE 29-38 (K172).

The Master Cat. Arbuthnot - FAIRY 104-107 (K1971.3); Lang - BLUE 154-160.

The Master Cat or Puss in Boots. Arbuthnot - ANTHOLOGY 213-215 (K1917.3); Perrault - PERRAULT'S (Dover) 45-58.

The Master Clockmaker. Huggins - BLUE 65-73 (F954.2.1.1).

Master Jacob. Pyle - WONDER 163-174 (K110.1; K113; K131.1.1; K451.2.2).

Master Kho and the Tiger. Brockett - BURMESE 120-125 (J1172.3.2).

The Master Maid. Jacobs - EUROPEAN 142-148 (G530.2Ab); Lang - BLUE 129-147 (G530.2Aa).

Master of All Masters. Arbuthnot - ANTHOLOGY 157-158 (X1506.1); Arbuthnot - FAIRY 17; Hutchinson - CANDLELIGHT 19-21; Jacobs - ENGLISH 230-231; Rockwell - MASTER pb; Steel - ENGLISH 232-233; Wiggin - TALES 335.

The Master of Magic and Spells. Lowe - LITTLE 75-80 (D1711.0.1.1).

The Master Tailor. Löfgren - BOY 25-28 (Z49.24.1).

The Master Thief. Grimm - JUNIPER 113-128 (K301A); Jacobs - EUROPEAN 121-128 (K301Ab); Undset - TRUE 213-232 (K301Ac); Wolkstein - MAGIC 135-142 (K301F).

Master Tobacco. Wiggin - FAIRY 96-102 (T102.1).

The Mastermaid. Lurie - CLEVER 35-44 (G530.2Aa); Undset - TRUE 37-56.

The Mat-Maker's Adventure. Novak - FAIRY 95-

99 (D421.8; V514).

The Match-Making of a Mouse. Bulatkin - EUR-ASIAN 82-84 (L392).

The Matsuyama Mirror. Hearn - JAPANESE 102-108 (J1795.2); Wiggin - FAIRY 374-379.

A Matter of Brogues. Sawyer - WAY 259-270 (F823.5).

A Matter of Importance. Dobbs - MORE 43-44 (J1712.1).

Matthew's Bed. Zajdler - POLISH 127-140 (V21.7).

Maui and the Fire Goddess. Berry - MAGIC 89-97 (A310.1.1; A1414.4.1).

Maui Catches the Sun. Berry - MAGIC 74-80 (A728.2).

Maui, the Demi-God. Berry - MAGIC 65-73 (H1252.1.1).

Maui, the Fire Bringer. Courlander - RIDE 14-19 (A728.2; A955.8; A1414.4.1; A1457.1.1; A1457.5).

Maui, the Fisherman. Gittins - TALES 50-51 (A955.8.1).

Maui, the Great. Courlander - TIGER'S 132-139 (A625.2.5; A728.2; A955.8; A1414.4.1; A1457.1.1; A1457.5).

Maui-the-Trickster. Thompson - HAWAIIAN..TRICKSTERS 66-71 (A955.8).

Maui Traps Sun. Thompson - HAWAIIAN..EARTH 60-64 (A728.2).

May It Not Happen. Courlander - FIRE 111-112 (J613.1.1).

Mayer Gimpel's Golden Shoes. Simon - MORE 44-49 (J1703.1).

MAZEL AND SHLIMAZEL. Singer pb (N141.0.6).

The Measure of Rice. Babbitt - JATAKA 34-38 (J2093.7).

Meat or Cat? Kelsey - MULLAH 8-14 (J1611).

Meat Pies. Van Woerkom - MEAT (K371.1; K1022.1).

The Mechanical Man of Prague. Serwer - LET'S 39-54 (D1635).

The Melancholy Prince and the Girl of Milk and Blood. Toor - GOLDEN 49-53 (D721.5C).

Mélusine. Picard - FRENCH 101-106 (F420.6.1.5.2).

Men of Different Colors. Arbuthnot -ANTHOL-OGY 316-317 (A1614.2.1); Heady - WHEN 91-94.

The Men of the Wallet. Bowman - TALES..TUPA 12-24 (D861.1F).

The Merchant of Seri. Babbitt - JATAKA 13-17 (J1521.6).

The Merchant's Son. Dolch - STORIES..OLD CHINA 65-81 (D313.1.2).

The Merchant's Son Who Never Smiled. Novak - FAIRY 108-118 (G263.1.0.2).

The Merchant with Nothing to Sell. Serwer - LET'S 19-21 (J231.2).

Mercury and the Man Bitten by an Ant. Aesop - AESOP'S (Watts) 192 (U21.3).

Mercury and the Sculptor. Aesop - AESOP'S (Grosset) 118-119 (L417); Aesop - AESOP'S (Watts) 71.

Mercury and the Woodman. Aesop - AESOP'S (Grosset) 3-4 (Q3.1); Aesop - AESOP'S (Watts) 14-15.

Merisier, Stronger than Elephants. Courlander - PIECE 9-14 (A1461.10).

Merlin, the Magician. Chang - CHINESE 26-29 (D435.2.1.2).

The Mermaid and the Boy. Lang - VIOLET 219-233 (D532B).

The Mermaid in Church. Manning-Sanders - PETER 178-182 (B81.13.6).

The Mermaid of the Moving Sands. Frost - LEG-ENDS 186-189 (F948.5).

Merman Rosner. Manning-Sanders - BOOK..MER-MAIDS 108-113 (C931; G561.1H).

The Merman's Revenge. De Leeuw - LEGENDS..HOLLAND 28-32 (F948.5).

The Merry Little Fox. Montgomerie - MERRY 8-13 (K251.1.0.2.1).

The Merry Tale of the Clever Little Tailor. Grimm - BROTHERS 77-81 (K1111.0.1; K1755).

The Message from the Moon. Courlander - KING'S 106-108 (A1335.1.0.1).

The Messenger. Courlander - KANTCHIL'S 64-70 (J2326; K341.4.1.1).

The Messenger Donkey. Courlander - FIRE 41-44 (A2232.8.1).

The Messenger to Maftam. Courlander - COW 79-86 (K511.0.1).

Mice and Cat. Aesop - FABLES (Walck) 81-84 (J671.1).

The Mice and Cat on the Wall. Aesop - AESOP'S

(Golden) 22 (K2061.9).

The Mice and the Precious Stones. De La Iglesia – CAT 14 (J1531.2).

Mice and Weasels. Aesop – FABLES (Walck) 30–31 (L332.1).

The Mice and the Weasels. Aesop – AESOP'S (Golden) 36 (L322.1); Aesop – AESOP'S (Watts) 76–77.

The Mice in Council. Aesop – AESOP'S (Watts) 4 (J671.1); Aesop – FIVE 72.

The Mice in Trouble. Aesop – AESOP'S (Random) 50–51 (J671.1).

THE MICE THAT ATE IRON. Evans pb (J1531.2).

Michael Scott and the Demon. Leodhas – THISTLE 136–143 (G303.16.19.3.5).

The Midget and the Giant. Cooper – FIVE 76–87 (G501A).

Midnight Fox. Riordan – TALES..CENTRAL 179–180 (K372F).

The Midnight Hunt. Williams-Ellis – FAIRY.. BRITISH 302–305 (E501.5.5.1).

The Mighty Hunter. De Leeuw – INDONESIAN 109–112 (J2061.3).

Mighty Mikko. Davis – BAKER'S 169–188 (K1917.3E); Fenner – PRINCESSES 43–56; Fillmore – SHEPHERD'S 11–25.

The Mighty Warrior in Hare's House. Kaula – AFRICAN 122–125 (K1711.2.1).

The Mighty Wrestlers. Withers – WORLD 2–6 (X941.2.1).

Miguel and the Baker. Newman – FOLK..LATIN 19–26 (J1172.2.0.3).

Milk Bottles. Leach – THING 60–62 (E323.1.1.1).

The Milkmaid and Her Pail. Aesop – AESOP'S (Grosset) 10–11 (J2061.2); Aesop – AESOP'S (Random) 8–10; Aesop – AESOP'S (Watts) 25; Aesop – MILKMAID pb; Arbuthnot – FAIRY 229; Jacobs – FABLES 153; Rockwell – OLD 34–36.

The Milkman and the Monkey. Spellman – BEAU-TIFUL 28–30 (J1551.9).

The Milky Way. Withers – MAN 102–104 (A778.11).

The Milky Way. Lin – MILKY 24–32 (A778.3.2).

The Mill at the Bottom of the Sea. Baker – TALK-ING 104–112 (D1651.3.1).

The Mill That Grinds at the Bottom of the Sea. Asbjørnsen – NORWEGIAN 108–111 (D1651.3.1).

The Miller and the Fairies. Sheppard-Jones – WELSH 101–105 (F348.7.0.1).

The Miller and the Ogre. Picard – FRENCH 183–197 (K842D).

The Miller, His Cook and the King. Green – CLEVER 101–107 (H561.2; H682.1.1; H711.1); Kavcic – GOLDEN 25–31.

The Miller, His Son and Their Ass. Aesop – AESOP'S (Viking) 21–22 (J1041.2); Aesop – AESOP'S (Watts) 136.

The Miller, His Son and Their Donkey. Aesop – AESOP'S (Random) 22–26 (J1041.2); Duvoisin – MILLER pb; Haviland – FAIRY 102–103.

The Miller King. Tashjian – ONCE 13–26 (K1917.3E).

THE MILLER, THE BOY AND THE DONKEY. La Fontaine pb (J1041.2); Wildsmith – THE MILLER pb.

The Miller, the Boy and the Donkey. Aesop – FABLES 51–53 (J1041.2).

The Miller, the Son and the Donkey. Aesop – AESOP'S (Golden) 87 (J1041.2).

The Miller's Sons. Ginsburg – LAZIES 64–70 (X905.1.5).

The Million-Dollar Somersaults. Ross – IN MEXI-CO 50–61 (A999.2).

The Mink and the Eagle. Parker – SKUNNY 124–131 (A2412.1.9).

The Mink and the Sun. Matson – LEGENDS 123–127 (A737.9.1).

The Mink and the Weasel. Matson – LEGENDS 115–121 (A2411.1.2.1.2).

Minu. Green – FOLK..AFRICAN 53–55 (J1802.1).

The Miracle. Nunn – AFRICAN 68–74 (T554.8.2).

A Miracle of a Saint. Jagendorf – PRICELESS 89–91 (D2125.1.0.1).

The Miracle of Our Lady of Guadelupe. Jagendorf – KING 198–202 (V121.1).

The Miracle of the Begging Bowl. Carpenter – ELEPHANT'S 108–113 (V128.0.1.1).

The Miracle of the Rose. Jagendorf – PRICELESS 25–30 (V412.3).

The Miraculous Flute. Lowe – LITTLE 44–46 (D1415.2.3.3).

The Miraculous Stag. Baker – TALKING 199–203 (A1611.5.5).

The Mirror. Bang – MEN 67–69 (J1795.3).

The Mirror of Matsuyama. Ozaki - JAPANESE 119-139 (J1795.2).

Mirzhan and the Lord of the Kingdom Under the Sea. Masey - STORIES 38-45 (B654.2).

The Mischievous Dog. Aesop - AESOP'S (Grosset) 77 (J953.1); Aesop - AESOP'S (Viking) 10; Aesop - AESOP'S (Watts) 3.

The Miser. Aesop - AESOP'S (Random) 16-17 (J1061.4); Aesop - AESOP'S (Watts) 208.

The Miser. Daniels - FALCON 81-83 (K341.2.0.1.1).

The Miser. Dobbs - MORE 22-25 (J1531.3).

The Miser and His Gold. Aesop - AESOP'S (Grosset) 86-87 (J1061.4); Jacobs - FABLES 123.

The Miserly Frog. Deutsch - TALES 32-35 (A2355.1.2.3).

The Miserly Miller. De Leeuw - LEGENDS..HOLLAND 92-96 (Q272.1.2).

The Miser Who Received His Due. Carter - GREEDY 125-131 (K1954.3).

The Miser's Wife. Gilstrap - SULTAN'S 67-74 (K2137).

Misfortune Comes to the House. Sechrist - ONCE 82-86 (A1549.2.1).

Miss Cow and the Persimmon Tree. Harris - FAVORITE 71-76 (K771).

Miss Cow Falls a Victim to Mr. Rabbit. Brown - WORLD 72-77 (K771); Harris - COMPLETE 28-32; Harris - UNCLE 41-47.

Miss Goat. Wyatt - GOLDEN 81-84 (J1179.22).

Miss Lin, the Sea Goddess. Carpenter - TALES.. CHINESE 235-241 (A421.1.2).

Miss Mouse Finds a Bridegroom. Brockett - BURMESE 153-155 (L392.0.2).

Mr. and Mrs. Vinegar. Hutchinson - CHIMNEY 111-116 (J2081.1; K335.1.1.1); Steel - ENGLISH 138-144; Williams-Ellis - FAIRY..BRITISH 96-102.

Mr. Bedbug's Feast. Kim - STORY 34-38 (A2305.2; A2330.5; A2412.3.1).

Mr. Benjamin Ram. Harris - COMPLETE 328-331 (K1715.2); Harris - FAVORITE 153-158.

Mr. Benjamin Ram and His Wonderful Fiddle. Harris - COMPLETE 149-159 (K335.0.4.4); Harris - NIGHTS 44-50.

Mr. Crow and the Mussel. Gillham - BEYOND 121-126 (K579.9.1).

Mr. Crow Takes a Wife. Gillham - BEYOND 31-43 (A2378.4.7.1; D1553.1); Gruenberg - MORE 113-118.

Mister Deer's My Riding Horse. Cothran - WITH 40-43 (K1241).

Mr. Dog's New Shoes. Harris - FAVORITE 118-120 (A2494.4.4.1).

Mr. Fox. De La Mare - ANIMAL 245-248 (S62.1B); Jacobs - ENGLISH 153-158; Minard - WOMENFOLK 130-135; Steel - ENGLISH 164-168.

Mr. Fox and Miss Goose. Harris - COMPLETE 119-123 (K525.1); Harris - NIGHTS 3-7.

Mr. Fox and the Deceitful Frog. Harris - COMPLETE 45-48 (J1919.2.1); Harris - UNCLE 64-72.

Mr. Fox Figures as an Incendiary. Harris - COMPLETE 182-185 (K1055.2); Harris - NIGHTS 90-94.

Mr. Fox Gets Into Serious Business. Harris - COMPLETE 94-97 (K842.0.4); Harris - UNCLE 143-148.

Mr. Fox Goes A-Hunting, but Mr. Rabbit Bags the Game. Harris - COMPLETE 48-50 (K341.2.1); Harris - UNCLE 73-76.

Mr. Fox Is Again Victimized. Harris - COMPLETE 30-36 (K629.2.4); Harris - UNCLE 21-25.

Mr. Fox is "Outdone" by Mr. Buzzard. Brown - WORLD 67-71 (K629.2.5); Harris - COMPLETE 25-28; Harris - UNCLE 36-41.

Mr. Fox Tackles Old Man Tarrypin. Brown - WORLD 98-102 (K543); Harris - COMPLETE 39-41; Harris - UNCLE 59-63.

Mr. Friend and Mr. Foe. Asia - FOLK..BOOK 1 19-25 (N452D).

Mister Frog's Dream. Barlow - LATIN 104-112 (J2357).

Mr. Hawk and Brother Buzzard. Harris - COMPLETE 378-380 (J2215.4.0.1); Harris - NIGHTS 362-365.

Mr. Hawk and Brother Rabbit. Harris - COMPLETE 381-384 (K551.25.1; K553; K553.1.0.4); Harris - NIGHTS 366-369.

Mister Honey Mouth. Cothran - WITH 34-39 (K1995; K22).

Mr. Korbes. Grimm - HOUSEHOLD 179-180 (K1161.7).

Mr. Korbes The Fox. Williams-Ellis - ROUND 166-171 (K1161.7).

Mr. Lion Hunts for Mr. Man. Harris - COMPLETE 141-144 (K1111.0.2); Harris - NIGHTS 33-37.

Mr. Lion's Sad Predicament. Harris - COMPLETE 355-358 (K2324.2.1); Harris - NIGHTS 330-333.

Mr. Louse and Mrs. Louse. Withers - I SAW 79-80 (Z32.2.4).

Mister Luck and Mister Industry. Htin - KING 18-23 (D551.1G).

Mr. Lucky Straw. Sakade - JAPANESE 78-80 (N221.1).

Mr. Man Has Some Meat. Harris - COMPLETE 206-209 (K344); Harris - NIGHTS 123-127.

Mr. Miacca. Jacobs - ENGLISH 171-173 (G82.1.2); Ness - MR. MIACCA pb; Williams-Ellis - FAIRY ..BRITISH 146-148.

Mr. Noy. Manning-Sanders - PETER 183-190 (F320.4).

Mr. Rabbit and Mr. Bear. Brown - WORLD 78-81 (K842.0.7); Harris - COMPLETE 74-77; Harris - FAVORITE 229-232; Harris - UNCLE 112-117; Lester - KNEE 12-20.

Mr. Rabbit Finds His Match Again. Arbuthnot - FAIRY 221 (K2347); Brown - WORLD 117-121.

Mr. Rabbit Finds His Match at Last. Harris - COMPLETE 57-60 (K2347); Harris - UNCLE 87-93.

Mr. Ripe and Mr. Raw. Asia - FOLK..FOUR 54-59 (P265.2).

Mr. Samson Cat. Ross - BURIED 19-26 (K2324).

Mr. Smart. Harris - COMPLETE 130-133 (K341.2.1.1); Harris - FAVORITE 226-228; Harris - NIGHTS 17-20.

Mr. Spider and the Death Eggs. Dorliae - ANIMALS 40-45 (K1867).

Mr. Spider Smokes Out the World's Hole. Dorliae - ANIMALS 10-15 (A1714.3.2).

Mr. Tarrypin Appears Upon the Scene. Brown - WORLD 82-87 (K1161.11); Harris - COMPLETE 32-36; Harris - UNCLE 47-53.

Mr. Tarrypin Shows His Strength. Brown - WORLD 122-126 (K22.2).

Mr. Vinegar. Arbuthnot - FAIRY 17-19 (J2081.1; K335.1.1.1); Colwell - YOUNGEST 121-126; Jacobs - ENGLISH 27-31.

Mr. Wheeler: The Story of How Anansi Acquired His Limp. Sherlock - WEST 141-144 (C498.2).

Mr. Wolf Makes a Failure. Brown - WORLD 112-116 (K607.3); Harris - COMPLETE 36-39; Harris - UNCLE 54-58.

The Mistress and Her Servants. Aesop - AESOP'S (Watts) 18 (K1636).

Mistress Cockroach. Mehdevi - PERSIAN 81-92 (Z32.3).

Mrs. Fox. De La Mare - ANIMAL 81-85 (T211.6).

MRS. FOX'S WEDDING. Corrin pb (T211.6).

Mrs. Gertrude. Grimm - JUNIPER v.2 310-313 (Z65.3.1).

Mistress Good Luck and Dame Know It All. Hatch - THIRTEEN 46-57 (N141.0.1).

Mrs. Longspur's Second Marriage. Bleecker - BIG 81-89 (J416.2); Gillham - BEYOND 106-116.

Mrs. Mag and Her Nest. Williams-Ellis - FAIRY.. BRITISH 179-180 (A2271.1.2).

THE MITTEN: AN OLD UKRAINIAN FOLKTALE. Tresselt pb (J2199.5).

The Mixed-up Feet and the Silly Bridegroom. Singer - ZLATAH 39-50 (J2021).

Mizilca. Lurie - CLEVER 23-29 (H1578.1.7).

Mockingbird Gives Out the Calls. Courlander - PEOPLE 60-62 (A2426.2.0.1).

Mohammed and the Spider. De Leeuw - INDONE-SIAN 90-93 (A2221.5.2; B523.1).

Moi and the Red Bull. Harmon - TALES 153-162 (K1611Dc).

The Mole and the Miryek. Carpenter - KOREAN 199-202 (L392.0.2).

Molla Nasreddin and His Donkey. Bulatkin - EUR-ASIAN 64-68 (J1249.5).

Molly Whipple. Reeves - ENGLISH 184-194 (K1611A).

Molly Whuppie. Adams - BOOK..GIANTS 53-59 (K1611A); Colwell - MAGIC 19-25; De La Mare - TALES 193-200; Fenner - GIANTS 32-38; Havi-land - FAIRY 152-157; Haviland - FAVORITE.. ENGLAND 44-55; Jacobs - ENGLISH 130-135; Lurie - CLEVER 45-52; Minard - WOMENFOLK 20-29; Steel - ENGLISH 234-241.

Momotaro. Hearn - JAPANESE 126-132 (T543.3.2).

Momotaro: Boy-of-the-Peach. Arbuthnot - AN-THOLOGY 336-337 (T543.3.2); Arbuthnot - FAIRY 174-177; Uchida - DANCING 97-106.

Momotaro or the Story of the Son of a Peach. Haviland - FAVORITE..JAPAN 47-71 (T543.3.2); Novak - FAIRY 6-15; Ozaki - JAPANESE 244-261.

MOMOTARO: PEACH BOY. Tabrah pb (T543.3.2).

The Monastery of No Cares. Daniels - FALCON 71-74 (H702.1.1; H711.1).

Money From the Sky. Kelsey - HODJA 139-150
(J1151.2; J1473.1).

The Money Mint. Harris - COMPLETE 540-545
(J2066.7); Harris - FAVORITE 24-29.

Money Talks. Cimino - DISOBEDIENT #15
(J1382.3).

The Monk and the Drunk. Kendall - SWEET 106-
107 (J2012.1.2).

Monkey. Williams-Ellis - ROUND 106-107
(B241.2.2.1).

Monkey and Fisherman. Aesop - FABLES (Walck)
40-42 (J516).

The Monkey and Mr. Janel Sinna. Tooze - THREE
..MONKEY #3 (K1917.3G).

The Monkey and the Camel. Aesop - AESOP'S
(Grosset) 114-115 (J512.3); Aesop - AESOP'S
(Viking) 58; Aesop - AESOP'S (Watts) 131.

The Monkey and the Cat. Aesop - AESOP'S
(Random) 38-40 (K334.3).

The Monkey and the Crocodile. Babbitt - JATA-
KA 2-9 (K607.2.1; K607.2.3); Galdone - MON-
KEY pb; Korel - LISTEN 14-20 (K544); Sechrist
- ONCE 60-63 (K553.1; K1023.1.4).

The Monkey and the Dolphin. Aesop - AESOP'S
(Grosset) 198-199 (J1803.1.1); Aesop - AESOP'S
(Watts) 184.

The Monkey and the Heron. Hardendorff - JUST
98-104 (K54).

The Monkey and the Shark. Montgomerie -
TWENTY-FIVE 26-27 (K544.1).

The Monkey and the Snail. Dorliae - ANIMAL 22-
25 (K11.1).

Monkey-Dance and Sparrow-Dance. Sakade -
JAPANESE 25-28 (A1542.1.1).

Monkey Fat. Wyatt - GOLDEN 13-21 (Z49.23).

The Monkey Gardeners. Gaer - FABLES..INDIA
120-122 (J1973.1); Green - BIG 18-20.

A Monkey in the House. Hampden - HOUSE 89-93
(D318.1.1).

Monkey in the Sausage Tree. Aardema - TALES
(J1172.3.0.4).

The Monkey King's Bridge. Reed - TALKATIVE
58-61 (B241.2.2.2).

Monkey-Lord and Crocodile. Wyatt - GOLDEN 98-
100 (K607.2.3).

The Monkey Nursemaid. Manning-Sanders -
DEVILS 51-55 (B441.0.2).

The Monkey Prince and the Witch. Robertson -
FAIRY..PHILIPPINES 23-32 (D735.1).

The Monkey Princes. Heady - SAFIRI 11-16
(A1861.5).

THE MONKEY, THE LION AND THE SNAKE.
Werth pb (W154.8.1).

The Monkey, the Tiger and the Jackal Family.
Siddiqui - TOONTOONY 109-113 (J2132.5.1;
K1711.2; K1715.2).

The Monkey Who Asked for Misery. Wolkstein -
MAGIC 113-116 (J1805.2).

The Monkeys and the Jizo. Scofield - HOLD 27-33
(J2415.0.1).

The Monkeys and the Little Red Hats. Carpenter
- AFRICAN 71-76 (B786.1).

The Monkey's Buddha. Novak - FAIRY 145-150
(J2415.23).

The Monkey's Heart. Arnott - AFRICAN 135-139
(K544); Gaer - FABLES..INDIA 126-129
(K607.2.1); Heady - SAFIRI 93-96; Sheehan -
FOLK 93-99.

The Monkey's Liver. Pratt - MAGIC (K544).

The Monkey's Pomegranate. Lowe - LITTLE 97-
102 (Z41.6.4).

Mons Tro. Manning-Sanders - CHOICE 148-165
(H1213.1G).

The Monster. Heady - TALES 101-108 (A1610.8;
A2231.1; F912.2.9).

The Monster Eagle. Baker - AT THE CENTER 25-
32 (A1610.7)

The Monster Mo-o. Thompson - HAWAIIAN..
EARTH 65-69 (A791.14; B11.2.1.2.1).

The Months. Wiggin - FAIRY 367-370 (Q2.1.4Ad);
Wiggin - TALES 20-24.

The Moon. Grimm - BROTHERS 93-96 (A755.2).

The Moon and Her Mother. Aesop - AESOP'S
(Viking) 47 (A759.8); Aesop - AESOP'S (Watts)
14.

The Moon and the Hare. Helfman - BUSHMEN 46-
47 (A1335.1.0.1).

The Moon and the Stars. Withers - MAN 75
(J2271.2.2).

The Moon-Cake. Wiggin - TALES 403 (J1249.4).

The Moon Husband. Maher - BLIND 139-158
(A762.1Aa).

The Moon In the Donkey. Jagendorf - NOODLE-
HEAD 249-252 (J1791.1).

The Moon In the Mill Pond. Harris – COMPLETE 189–194 (J1791.3.3); Harris – FAVORITE 125–129.

The Moon In the Pond. Montgomerie – TWENTY-FIVE 14–15 (J1791.3).

A Moon of Gobbages. Mayne – BOOK..GIANTS 170–176 (K499.3.1).

The Moon On the Ground. Jagendorf – NOODLE-HEAD 73–74 (J2271.5).

The Moon Painters. Maas – MOON 11–16 (A751.4; F772.1.2.1).

The Moon Princess. Spellman – BEAUTIFUL 94–98 (A751.1.9).

The Moon Raised the Sky. Withers – MAN 22 (A751.5.2.3).

The Moonrakers. Withers – MAN 51 (J1791.3.3).

Moon Show. Pugh – MORE..WELSH 89–94 (L393.1).

The Moon's a Woman. Courlander – TERRAPIN'S 112–114 (A736.1).

The Moon's Escape. Sechrist – ONCE 75–78 (A913.5; B94.1).

The Moon's Face. Leach – HOW 34 (A751.5.2.2).

Moowis. Garner – CAVALCADE..GOBLINS 52–54 (T117.12).

The Mop Servant. Pilkington – SHAMROCK 61–70 (K1611Ba).

Morag and the Water Horse. Wilson – SCOTTISH 103–106 (F420.1.3.3.2).

More Beautiful Than the Spider's Web. Jagendorf – KING 226–229 (A1465.2.1).

More Trouble for Brother Wolf. Harris – COMPLETE 335–338 (J2411.6.2); Harris – NIGHTS 302–305.

Morgan and the Pot of Brains. Pugh – TALES 29–36 (J163.2.1).

Morgan and the Three Fairies. Sheppard-Jones – WELSH 25–28 (F348.7.1.3).

The Mosquito. Schultz – VIETNAMESE 56–59 (A2034.5).

The Mossy Rock. Manning-Sanders – SORCERORS 122–125 (C498.2.1).

The Most Frugal of Men. Hardendorff – JUST 34–36 (W152.18); Wiggin – TALES 401–402.

A Most Generous Host. Davis – LION'S 102–107 (K2138).

The Most Obedient Wife. Arbuthnot – ANTHOLOGY 232–234 (T251.2.3.0.1); Arbuthnot – FAIRY 95–98.

The Most Precious Gift. Pugh – TALES 135–143 (H659.28).

The Most Precious Possession. Arbuthnot – ANTHOLOGY 270–271 (J2415.1.0.1; N411.1C); Arbuthnot – FAIRY 130–131; Vittorini – OLD 28–33.

The Most Ticklish Chap. Harris – FAVORITE 247–251 (K522.1).

The Most Useful Tree in the World. Burton – MAGIC 56–59 (H323C).

The Mother and the Mother-in-law. Brockett – BURMESE 106–110 (P262.2).

Mother Confessor Fox. Riordan – TALES..CENTRAL 127–128 (K815.1.2).

Mother Holle. Arbuthnot – ANTHOLOGY 202–203 (Q2.1.2Aa); Arbuthnot – FAIRY 39–40; Grimm – GRIMM'S (Follett) 246–250; Grimm – GRIMM'S (World) 103–106; Grimm – MORE..GRIMM 15–22; Lang – FIFTY 199–202; Lang – RED 293–297; Lurie – CLEVER 97–103.

Mother Hulda. Grimm – HOUSEHOLD 128–131 (Q2.1.2Aa); Hutchinson – FIRESIDE 119–125.

Mother-in-law, Today Is Shake-head Day. Robinson – SINGING 66–75 (W125.3.1).

Mother In the Mirror. Hearn – JAPANESE (Pauper) 46–42 (J1795.2).

Mother Luck. Durham – TIT 17–23 (Q2.1.4Bb).

MOTHER MEADOWLARK AND BROTHER SNAKE. Firethunder pb (K567.2).

Mother of the Forest. Burton – MAGIC 63–68 (K1711.2.3).

Mother of the Waters. Wolkstein – MAGIC 151–156 (Q2.1.2H).

The Mother of Time and the Enchanted Brothers. Toor – GOLDEN 107–119 (H1273.2B; P253.2E).

Mother Roundabout's Daughter. Wiggin – FAIRY 35–42 (B641Be).

Mother Sunday. Manning-Sanders – GIANNI 24–30 (Q2.1.5Aa).

Mother's Day. Spellman – BEAUTIFUL 26–27 (A1541.2.2).

Mother's Pet. Hatch – DANISH 25–36 (G610Ad).

Motinu and the Monkeys. Fuja – FOURTEEN 80–87 (D672E).

The Mountain Goats. Martin – NINE 43–46 (A1578.1.1); Martin – RAVEN 53–60.

THE MOUNTAIN GOATS OF TEMLAHAM. Toye pb (A1578.1.1).

The Mountain Lad and the Forest Witch. Novak – FAIRY 66-71 (G276.2; G512.3.2.2).

Mountain-Lucky, Sea-Lucky. Sakade – JAPANESE 58-63 (U136.0.1).

The Mountain of Gold. Downey – RUSSIAN 129-134 (K1861.1A).

The Mountain Witch and the Peddler. Uchida – MAGIC 83-90 (G276.2; G512.3.2.2).

Mountains and Rivers. Kim – STORY 17-18 (A962.5.1).

The Mountains in Labor. Aesop – AESOP'S (Grosset) 27 (U114); Jacobs – FABLES 27.

The Mountains That Clapped Together. Gillham – BEYOND 1-16 (B165.3; D1553.1).

The Mourner Who Sang and the Nun Who Danced. Carpenter – KOREAN 143-147 (H599.11).

Mouse and Mouser. Jacobs – ENGLISH 48-50 (K561.1.1).

The Mouse and the Bull. Aesop – AESOP'S (Watts) 111 (L315.2).

The Mouse and the Flea. Gillham – BEYOND 68-75 (A2585.2).

The Mouse and the Frog. Aesop – AESOP'S (Grosset) 177-178 (J681.1); Green – BIG 74.

The Mouse and the Magician. Montgomerie – TWENTY-FIVE 54-55 (L392.0.1).

The Mouse and the Sausage. Hardendorff – FROG'S 155-157 (J512.7); Wiggin – TALES 6.

The Mouse and the Weasel. Aesop – AESOP'S (Grosset) 202-203 (K1022.0.1).

The Mouse and the Wizard. Turnbull – FAIRY 127-135 (W154.2.1.1).

The Mouse Bride. Bowman – TALES..TUPA 25-33 (B641Bb).

The Mouse-Deer and the Crocodiles. Arnott – ANIMAL 155-160 (K543.0.1; K579.2.1).

Mouse Deer and the Tiger. Sleigh – NORTH 19-22 (K1023.1.1; K1023.1.2; K1023.1.3).

A Mouse from the Mabinogian. Williams-Ellis – FAIRY..BRITISH 312-328 (D117.1.1).

A Mouse In Search of a Wife. Green – ANIMAL 88-89 (L392.0.1).

The Mouse Keeps Her Promise. Wilson – GREEK 148-150 (B371.1).

The Mouse-Princess. Arbuthnot – FAIRY 124-128 (B641.0.1B); Picard – FRENCH 205-216.

The Mouse Surrounded. Reed – TALKATIVE 25-27 (J426).

The Mouse That Turned Tailor. Bowman – TALES ..TUPA 243-244 (Z49.24).

The Mouse, the Bird and the Sausage. De La Mare – ANIMAL 11-14 (J512.7); Gag – MORE.. GRIMM 27-30; Grimm – GRIMM'S (Grosset) 48-49; Grimm – HOUSEHOLD 126-127; Grimm – GRIMM'S (Watts) 60-62.

The Mouse, the Frog and the Hawk. Aesop – AESOP'S (Watts) 57 (J681.1).

The Mouseling. Tooze – WONDERFUL 59-63 (N831.1).

The Mouser. Leach – LION 15-17 (J2101).

The Mouse's Bride. Turnbull – FAIRY..INDIA 103-109 (L392.0.1).

Muchie Lal. Wiggin – FAIRY 398-406 (B644.1).

Mud and Water Do the Work. Harris – COMPLETE 563-568 (K553.5.1); Harris – FAVORITE 140-146.

The Mud-baked Hen. Cheney – TALES 143-149 (D877.3).

Mugassa's Feast. Green – FOLK..AFRICA 29-35 (K335.0.1).

The Mule. Aesop – AESOP'S (Grosset) 162-163 (J954.1.1); Aesop – AESOP'S (Viking) 66; Aesop – AESOP'S (Watts) 154.

The Mullah's Oven. Kelsey – MULLAH 20-23 (J1041.3).

Munachar and Manachar. Jacobs – CELTIC 92-96 (Z41.10); Jacobs – MUNACHAR AND MANACHAR pb.

Musakalala, the Talking Skull. Littledale – GHOSTS 67-72 (B210.2.3).

The Musician of Tagaung. Courlander – TIGER'S 35-37 (A1578.3).

The Musicians. De La Mare – TALES 25-32 (K335.1.4).

The Musicians of Bremen. Gag – TALES..GRIMM 87-97 (K335.1.4; K1161.1); Wiggin – TALES 77-80.

Musk and Amber. Wilson – GREECE 107-119 (G530.2P).

Mutsmag. Chase – WICKED 40-52 (K1611Ea).

My Beauty. Thoby-Marcelin –SINGING 30-37

(G303.12.5.13).

My Lord Bag of Rice.   Hearn – JAPANESE 47-52 (Q82.3); Manning-Sanders – DRAGONS 38-42; Ozaki – JAPANESE 1-11.

My Own Self.   Jacobs – MORE 16-19 (K602.1).

The Mysterious Lake.   Jagendorf – KING 83-88 (F302.4.2.3).

The Mysterious Path.   Littledale – GHOSTS 83-86 (D2031.0.2.1).

The Mysterious Traveller.   Colwell – ROUND 43-45 (F944.1).

The Mystery of the Scroll.   Lu Mar – CHINESE 89-96 (J1199.4).

THE NA OF WA.   Aardema pb (D882.1.1.2).

Naba Zid-Wendé.   Guirma – TALES 1-15 (A625.2.10; A817.2; A1384.3; A1481.3; A1614.2.2).

Nabookin.   Bulatkin – EURASIAN 103-105 (J1193.1; J2091).

The Nail.   Wiggin – TALES 152 (Z45).

NAIL SOUP.   Zemach pb (K112.2).

Namashepani.   Heady – WHEN 21-26 (F206).

The Name.   Wolkstein – MAGIC 117-122 (C432.1.2).

Nananbouclou and the Piece of Fire.   Courlander – PIECE 62-63 (A781.2).

Nangato.   Belpré – TIGER 21-25 (K827.4.1).

Nanny and Conn.   MacManus – HIBERNIAN 48-59 (H1312.1; J1904.1; J2021; J2031; J2326.1).

The Nanny Goat's Corner.   Spicer – THIRTEEN MONSTERS 77-82 (G303.3.3.1.6.1).

Nanny Who Wouldn't Go Home to Supper.   Hutchinson – CANDLELIGHT 57-68 (Z39.1.0.2); Wiggin – TALES 315-320.

Nansi and the Eagle.   Aardema – TALES 44-48 (K171.0.2.2).

Nasreddin Hoca and the Third Shot.   Walker – WATERMELONS 46-48 (N621.2).

Nasreddin Khoja and God's Son-in-law.   Walker – TALES 234 (J1261.1.1.1).

Nasreddin Khoja and Tamerlane.   Walker – TALES 229-232 (J1289.24; J1289.25; J2563).

Nasreddin Khoja and the Overcrowded Bed.   Walker – TALES 234 (J1250.14).

Nasreddin Khoja As Witness in Court.   Walker – TALES 236 (J1191.2).

Nasreddin Khoja Does What a Human Being Should.   Walker – TALES 235 (J1879.2).

Nasreddin Khoja in God's Watermelon Patch.   Walker – TALES 235 (W211.5).

Nasreddin Minds the Door.   Walker – WATERMELONS 58-59 (K1413).

Nasrudin and the Wise Men.   Shah – MULLA 50 (H501.5).

Nazar the Brave.   Tashjian – ONCE 71-84 (K1951.1I).

Necessity.   Ure – RUMANIAN 62-64 (J103).

Ned Purvis' Farewell.   Baker – TALKING 45-57 (A1464.2.1; E425.2.5.1).

The Needle Crop of Sainte-Dodo.   Jagendorf – NOODLEHEAD 133 (J1932.5).

Nefyn the Mermaid.   Sheppard-Jones – WELSH 109-114 (B81.2.2).

THE NEIGHBORS.   Brown pb (J741.1).

Nero and the Old Woman.   Cimino – DISOBEDIENT #7 (J215.2.1).

Netchillik and the Bear.   Melzack – DAY 35-40 (J1762.2.3.1).

Netsersuitsuarksuk.   Field – ESKIMO 52-54 (J1762.2.3.1).

Never Know When It Might Come In Useful.   Shah – MULLA 17 (J1229.4).

Never Mind Them Watermelons.   Leach – THING 21-22 (J1495.1).

Never Trust an Eel.   Jagendorf – MERRY 99-104 (J1909.8.1).

The New Law.   Carey – BABA 61-62 (J1421).

The New Preacher.   Dobbs – MORE 31-33 (X452).

A New Santa Claus.   Sawyer – THIS 68-75 (N816).

A New Way to Boil Eggs.   Jagendorf – NOODLEHEAD 130-132 (J1901.2).

New Year's Hats for the Statues.   Uchida – SEA 84-90 (J1873.1).

A New Year's Story.   Cheney – TALES 17-24 (A1541.7).

News.   Jacobs – MORE 182-183 (Z46).

Niassa and the Ogre.   Manning-Sanders – PRINCES 9-13 (G422.1.1.3).

Nicht Nought Nothing. Finlay - TATTERCOATS 37-46 (G530.2Ab).

Nicola Pesce. Jagendorf - PRICELESS 66-75 (A842.3); Toor - GOLDEN 159-165.

Nidden and Didden and Donal Beg O'Neary. Mac-Manus - HIBERNIAN 141-147 (K842Aa).

A Night at a Tavern in Trondheim. Cutt - HOG-BOON 114-118 (F420.5.1.11).

The Nightingale and the Hawk. Aesop - AESOP'S (Watts) 187-188 (J321.2.1).

The Nightingale and the Khan. Bulatkin - EUR-ASIAN 85-89 (K522.4.0.1).

The Nightingale in the Mosque. Fillmore - LAUGHING 171-200 (H1331.1.3E).

Nihancan and the Dwarf's Arrow. Brown - TEPEE 114-115 (F451.5.14.1).

Niilo and the Wizard. Bowman - TALES..TUPA 141-146 (D1711.0.1.1).

Nils in the Forest. Manning-Sanders - BOOK.. OGRES 123-127 (H321.1).

The Nine Doves. Manning-Sanders - CHOICE 63-73 (D765.1.2.1); Manning-Sanders - DRAGONS 43-54.

The Nine-Headed Giant. De Regniers - GIANT 31-38 (H1385.3E).

NINE IN A LINE. Kirn pb (J2031.2).

The Nine Peahens and the Golden Apples. Man-ning-Sanders - GLASS 27-40 (H1385.3J).

Nine Stones Wake. Cutt - HOGBOON 15-45 (F809.5.2).

Nippy and the Yankee Doodle. Haviland - NORTH 155-159 (K1611G).

The Nix in the Pond. Grimm - GRIMM'S (Scrib-ner's) 285-291 (F420.5.2.2.3).

Nix Naught Nothing. Steel - ENGLISH 127-138 (G530.2Ac).

Nix Nought Nothing. Jacobs - ENGLISH 32-38 (G530.2Ac).

The Nixy. Lang - YELLOW 124-129 (F420.5.2.2.3).

No-Beard. De La Mare - ANIMAL 100-105 (X905.0.2).

No Deal. Cimino - DISOBEDIENT #12 (J552.5.1).

No Head. Leach - THING 41-43 (E545.19.1.1).

No Man and the Cyclops. Wilson - GREEK 97-102 (K602).

No One Can Fool a Helmite. Simon - WISE 17-22 (J2328.1).

NO ROOM. Dobbs pb (Z49.16).

No Supper. Lowe - LITTLE 58-61 (D452.1.6.1.1).

NOAH AND THE RAINBOW. Bolliger pb (A1021).

The Noble Frog. Chang - CHINESE 6-8 (B645.1.2.3).

The Noodle. Kendall - SWEET 100-105 (N685.1).

Noodlehead and the Flying Horse. Jagendorf - GYPSIES' 52-92 (H1213.1lb).

Noodlehead Luck. Jagendorf - NOODLEHEAD 281-283 (N411.6).

Noodlehead Pat. Jagendorf - NOODLEHEAD 263-267 (J2213.9).

The Noodlehead Tiger. Jagendorf - NOODLEHEAD 30-33 (K1715.1).

The North Wind and the Sun. Aesop - AESOP'S (Watts) 18 (L351); Kent - MORE 46-51; La Fon-taine - NORTH pb .

The Northern Frog. Maas - MOON 128-141 (G405.1.2).

The Nose. Grimm - GRIMM'S (World) 163-170 (D551.1B).

Noses. Bascom - THOSE 27-35 (J2031).

The Nose-Tree. Wiggin - FAIRY 220-228 (D551.1B); Wiggin - TALES 111-117.

Not a Pin to Choose Between Them. Undset - TRUE 202-208 (J2012.2.3; J2123; J2161.2; J2326.1; K182; K341.9).

Not Bad— But It Could Be Better. Higonnet-Schnopper - TALES 49-57 (Z46).

Not Driving and Not Riding. Asbjørnsen - NOR-WEGIAN 137-138 (H1053.7; H1063).

Not on the Lord's Day. Jagendorf - NOODLE-HEAD 253-255 (J2171.6.1).

Nothing-At-All. Montgomerie - TWENTY-FIVE 37 (K359.2.3).

Nsangi. Serwadda - SONGS (F913.4; K311.3J).

Number Three Son. Chang - CHINESE 58-63 (N831.1.0.1).

The Nung-guama. Bonnet - FOLK 97-102 (K1161.3.2).

The Nurse and the Wolf. Aesop - AESOP'S (Gold-en) 66 (J2066.5); Aesop - AESOP'S (Grosset) 164-165; Jacobs - FABLES 91.

Nyame's Well. Courlander - HAT 93-95 (A2378.2.3.1).

Nyangara, the Python. McDowell - THIRD 25-28 (B491.1.2); Tracy - LION 10-14.

Nyangondhu, the Fisherman. Nunn - AFRICAN 41-45 (F420.6.1.5.3).

The Oak and the Reed. Aesop - AESOP'S (Golden) 62 (J832); Aesop - AESOP'S (Viking) 36-37; Aesop - AESOP'S (Watts) 36; Aesop - FABLES (Walck) 27; Montgomerie - TWENTY-FIVE 60.

OBEDIENT JACK. Galdone (Watts) pb (J2461A).

The Obedient Servant. Jagendorf - NOODLE-HEAD 207-211 (J2461.1.9).

Oda and the Snake. Manning-Sanders - SOR-CEROR'S 65-68 (D195.1.1).

Odysseus in the Land of the Giants. De Regniers - GIANT 70-78 (K602).

The Ogre. Lang - FIFTY 213-219 (D861.1C).

The Ogre and the Cock. Sakade - JAPANESE 97-100 (K1886.3.1).

The Ogre of Rashomon. Ozaki - JAPANESE 262-272 (E782.3.3).

The Ogre, the Sun and the Raven. Manning-Sanders - CHARMS 81-84 (A721.1.1).

The Ogre Who Built a Bridge. Uchida - SEA 72-83 (C432.1.1).

The Ogre's Breath. Manning-Sanders - BOOK.. OGRES 32-37 (F660.1Cc).

Ogungbemi and the Battle in the Bush. Courlander - OLODE 96-99 (A1172.5).

Oh and Alas. Wilson - GREEK 1-8 (D1711.0.1.1).

Ojeeg, the Hunter, and the Ice Man. DeWit - TALKING 39-43 (A1158.1).

Ojje Ben Onogh. Courlander - FIRE 103-104 (A920.1.10.1; F615.9).

Ojumiri and the Giant. Robinson - SINGING 24-43 (K606.1.5).

Okramon's Medicine. Courlander - HAT 49-54 (A2455.6).

Ol-Ambu and He-of-the-Song-Sleeping-Place. Aardema - TALES 59-69 (K2131.7).

Ol' Guinea Man. Cothran - MAGIC 71-72 (J1805.1.2).

Old Acquaintance Is Soon Forgot. Carrick -

STILL MORE 105-116 (J1172.3).

Old Bass and George. Courlander - TERRAPIN'S 93-94 (W123.3).

Old Bass, John and the Mule. Courlander - TER-RAPIN'S 87-90 (B210.1.1).

Old Bluebeard. Cothran - WITH 26-33 (K1931.2A); Williams-Ellis - FAIRY..BRITAIN 209-215.

Old Brer Rabbit's Hiding House. Brown - WORLD 58-62 (K1241.1).

Old Brother Terrapin Gets Some Fish. Harris - COMPLETE 386-389 (K16.2); Harris - NIGHTS 373-376.

An Old Crab and a Young One. Aesop - AESOP'S (Viking) 33-34 (J1063.1).

The Old Dog and the Gray Wolf. Carpenter - WONDER 213-221 (A2494.4.15; J581.1; K231.1.3).

Old Dry Frye. Chase - ~~WICKED~~ GRANDFATHER TALES 100-105 (K2151).

The Old Father Who Went to School. Courlander - RIDE 137-141 (P236.2).

Old Fire Dragaman. Chase - JACK 106-113 (K1931.2A); Haviland - NORTH 160-166.

Old Fuddlement. Kendall - SWEET 45-48 (H1312.4).

Old Gallymander. Field - AMERICAN 295-302 (Q2.1.2Cb); Hoke - WITCHES 15-18.

Old Grinny Granny Wolf. Harris - COMPLETE 343-347 (K891.1.2; K1251); Harris - NIGHTS 314-318.

The Old Gypsy Woman and the Good Lord. Hampden - GYPSIES' 107-110 (Q292.1.1).

The Old Hag of the Forest. Harper - GHOSTS 150-165 (R111.1.3Ag); Hoke - WITCHES 65-79.

The Old Hag's Long Leather Bag. Haviland - IRELAND 26-38 (Q2.1.2Cb).

The Old Handmill. Finlay - TATTERCOATS 9-14 (D1651.3.1.1).

Old Hardshell. Harris - COMPLETE 57-60 (K11.1); Harris - FAVORITE 86-90; Harris - UNCLE 87-93.

The Old Hound. Aesop - AESOP'S (Watts) 100 (W154.5).

The Old Humpback. Leach - HOW 31 (A751.0.2).

An Old King and His Three Sons of England. Manning-Sanders - RED 159-168 (H1331.1D).

The Old Lady and Her Maids. Aesop - FABLES (Walck) 62-63 (K1636).

The Old Lady and the Monkeys. Lin - MILKY 87-92 (K1161.3.1).

The Old Lady Who Swallowed a Fly. Withers - I SAW 39-41 (Z49.14).

The Old Laird and His Dogs. Leodhas - GAELIC 91-99 (E521.2.3).

The Old Lion. Aesop - AESOP'S (Watts) 54 (J644.1).

The Old Man and Death. Aesop - AESOP'S (Grosset) 180-181 (C11); Aesop - AESOP'S (Viking) 28-29; Aesop - AESOP'S (Watts) 207; Jacobs - FABLES 137.

The Old Man and His Bush. Leach - HOW 30 (A751.1.5).

The Old Man and His Dog. Carpenter - WONDER 136-148 (D1571.1).

The Old Man and His Fishing Line. Withers - MAN 21 (A751.0.2).

The Old Man and His Sons. Aesop - AESOP'S (Viking) 62-63 (J1021).

The Old Man and the Devils. Hearn - JAPANESE 53-56 (F344.1.1); Wiggin - TALES 415-416.

The Old Man and the Fox. Aesop - AESOP'S (Random) 19-20 (J644.1).

Old-man and the Thunder-Birds. Field - AMERICAN 40-54 (A284.2.1.1).

Old Man Hunter from Huntsville. Harris - COMPLETE 48-50 (K341.2.1); Harris - FAVORITE 223-225; Harris - UNCLE 73-76.

The Old Man in the Bramble Bush. Grimm - HOUSE 81-94 (D1415.2.5.1).

The Old Man in the Moon. Htin - KINGDOM 71-73 (A751.1.6).

Old Man Kurai and the One-Eyed Giant. Masey - STORIES 1-11 (K1951.1M).

The Old Man of the Flowers. Uchida - DANCING 147-156 (D1571.1).

The Old Man of the Mountains. Duvoisin - THREE 190-195 (A974.0.8).

The Old Man, the Wolf, and the Vixen. Ginsburg - ONE 10-13 (J1172.3).

The Old Man Who Made the Trees Bloom. MacAlpine - JAPANESE 95-105 (D1571.1).

The Old Man Who Made Trees Blossom. Novak - FAIRY 184-190 (D1571.1; K32.1).

The Old Man Who Made Trees Blossom. Sakade - JAPANESE 87-93 (D475.1.6).

The Old Man Who Wouldn't Take Advice. Lester - BLACK 139-146 (K1853.3).

The Old Man With a Wen. Asia - FOLK..FOUR 24-29 (F344.1.1); Sakade - JAPANESE 34-36.

The Old Man With a Bump. Uchida - DANCING 37-45 (F344.1.1).

The Old Man's Tale of Prince Stephen. Ure - RUMANIAN 147-152 (H561.6.1; H585.2.1).

The Old Man's Wen. Bang FOOLING 1-13 (F344.1.1).

Old Master and Okra. Courlander - TERRAPIN'S 76-89 (Z46).

Old Mr. Rabbit, He's a Good Fisherman. Arbuthnot - ANTHOLOGY 385 (K651); Brown - BRER 12-15 ; Harris - COMPLETE 50-52; Harris - UNCLE 76-81.

Old Moons. Shah - MULLA 74 (A764; J2271.2.2).

Old Nanny's Ghost. Spicer - THIRTEEN GHOSTS 73-82 (E415.1.2.2).

Old Nick's Bridge. Spicer - THIRTEEN DEVILS 19-24 (G303.9.1.6.1).

The Old Old One's Birthday. Carpenter - TALES ..CHINESE 252-261 (A163.1.1.1).

The Old, Old Teakettle. Schofield - FOX 40-44 (D1171.3.1).

Old One-Eye. Chase - WICKED 205-214 (N611.2).

Old Platt. Credle - TALES 43-52 (J1531.2.1).

Old Roaney. Chase - WICKED 195-204 (X1130.2.2; X1132.2).

The Old Soldier and the Mischief. Manning-Sanders - RED 55-61 (C12.2.3; H1411.4.10).

The Old Sow and the Three Shoats. Chase - WICKED 81-87 (K891.1.1.2).

Old Sultan. Grimm - HOUSEHOLD 195-197 (K231.1.3; K2323; K2324.0.1); Wiggin - TALES 149-151.

An Old Sumatran Legend. De Leeuw - INDONESIAN 40-44 (A2688.2).

The Old Traveler. Arbuthnot - ANTHOLOGY 285-286 (J2073.1); Maas - MOON 26-30.

Old Verlooka. Manning-Sanders - CHOICE 301-306 (K1161.12).

Old Wall Eyes. Withers - WORLD 25-27 (X1221.1.1).

The Old Witch. Jacobs - MORE 101-106 (Q2.1.2Cb); Harper - GHOSTS 83-89; Hoke - WITCHES 80-84; Manning-Sanders - BOOK

..WITCHES 11-17.

The Old Woman Against the Stream. Abjørnsen - NORWEGIAN 112-114 (T255.1; T255.2).

The Old Woman and Her Dumpling. Hearn - JAPANESE (Pauper) 53-60 (J1791.3.2.2); Minard - WOMENFOLK 44-50 (N777.0.1).

The Old Woman and Her Hominy Pot. Withers - MAN 14 (A751.8.1.1).

The Old Woman and Her Maids. Aesop - AESOP'S (Grosset) 197 (K1636); Aesop - AESOP'S (Viking) 14.

The Old Woman and Her Pig. Arbuthnot - TIME 7-8 (Z41); Association - TOLD..GREEN 16-20; Colwell - YOUNGEST 199-202; Galdone - OLD pb; Haviland - FAIRY 28-31; Hutchinson - CHIMNEY 11-16; Jacobs - ENGLISH 21-23; Richardson - GREAT 48-58; Rockwell - OLD 1-9; Steel - ENGLISH 178-180; Wiggin - TALES 211-214.

The Old Woman and the Bear. Cothran - WITH 55 (Z13.1.2).

The Old Woman and the Doctor. Aesop - AESOP'S (Watts) 13 (J1169.1).

The Old Woman and the Fish. Haviland - FAVORITE..SWEDEN 50-59 (J2071.1); Wiggin - TALES 459-461.

The Old Woman and the Hare. Asia - FOLK.. FOUR 12-16 (K371.1).

The Old Woman and the Physician. Aesop - AESOP'S (Grosset) 184-185 (J1169.1).

THE OLD WOMAN AND THE RED PUMPKIN. Bang pb (K553.0.3).

THE OLD WOMAN AND THE RICE THIEF. Bang pb (K1161.3.6).

The Old Woman and the Thief. Siddiqui - TOON-TOONY 140-143 (K1161.3.3).

The Old Woman and the Tramp. Green - CLEVER 145-152 (K112.2); Haviland - FAVORITE.. SWEDEN 14-29; Wiggin - TALES 463-467).

The Old Woman and the Wine-Jar. Aesop - AESOP'S (Watts) 90 (J1319.2); Jacobs - FABLES 161.

The Old Woman in the Cottage. Bang - MEN 55-59 (D313.1.3).

The Old Woman in the Gourd. Asia - FOLK.. BOOK 1 28-33 (K553.0.3).

The Old Woman in the Wood. Grimm - GRIMM'S (Scribner's) 242-244 (D154.2.1).

THE OLD WOMAN WHO LIVED IN A VINEGAR BOTTLE. Godden pb (B375.1).

The Old Woman Who Lost the Dumplings. Greene - CLEVER 32-39 (N777.0.1); Hearn - BOY 27-32; Hearn - JAPANESE 21-28; Wiggin - TALES 438-441.

Olga and the Brown Cow. Riordan - TALES.. CENTRAL 238-240 (D830.1.1).

The Olive Tree and the Fig Tree. Aesop - AESOP'S (Watts) 65 (J832.1).

Olli and the Rich Troll. McNeil - DOUBLE 116-121 (G610Ag).

Olobun's Sacrifice. Fuja - FOURTEEN 252-256 (K741.0.2).

Olode the Hunter Becomes an Oba. Courlander - OLODE 32-36 (C611.1.1).

Olusegbe. Fuja - FOURTEEN 214-236 (B263.11; K543).

Omar's Big Lie. Carpenter - AFRICAN 129-136 (X905.0.1).

The Omen. Shah - MULLA 140 (J1289.24).

Omganda and the Gold. Harmon - TALES 163-185 (J2415.20).

ONCE A MOUSE. Brown pb (W154.2.1.1).

Once In, Never Out Again. Hope-Simpson - CAVALCADE..WITCHES 95-105 (R111.1.3Af).

Once There Was and Once There Was Not. Wyndham - TALES..RUSSIA 62-67 (J31.0.1).

One Against a Hundred. Bro - HOW 22-28 (K579.2.1).

One Candle Power. Kelsey - HODJA 15-20 (K231.14.1).

One Day, One Night. Heady - TALES 25-28 (A1172.4; A2217.2; A2428.1).

One Eye, Two Eyes and Three Eyes. Arbuthnot - FAIRY 62-66 (D830.1.1); Durham - TIT 24-29; Grimm - GRIMM'S (Follett) 251-261.

The One-Eyed Doe. Aesop - AESOP'S (Grosset) 37 (K929.2); Jacobs - FABLES 130.

One-Eyed Likho. Downing - RUSSIAN 148-151 (K603.3).

One Good Turn Deserves Another. Green - ANIMAL 223 (B371.1; J411.8).

One Grain More Than the Devil. Hardendorff - DROP 131-140 (D1711.0.1.1).

One Hairball. Kendall - SWEET 73-77 (J2132.5.1; K1715.12.2).

The One Horned Mountain Goat. Harris - ONCE 5-30 (A1578.1.1).

One Hundred Thousand Arrows. Alexander - PEB-BLES 28 (K2369.14).

One-Inch Fellow. Haviland - FAVORITE..JAPAN 3-22 (F535.1.1.1E); Haviland - FAIRY 162-169.

One Last Picnic. Kelsey - HODJA 71-78 (J1511.7).

The One-Legged Chicken. Michael - PORTU-GUESE 130-132 (K402.1).

The One-Legged Crane. Green - CLEVER 117-123 (K402.1); Vittorini - OLD 117-123.

One Little Pig and Ten Wolves. Arnott - ANIMAL 129-135 (K891.1.4).

One Mean Trick Deserves Another. Carpenter - ELEPHANT'S 82-90 (K110.1; K111.1; K113; K131.1.1).

One More Child. Spellman - BEAUTIFUL 31-32 (P231.3.1).

One, My Darling, Come to Mama. Wolkstein - MAGIC 165-170 (K311.3K).

One Roll of Bread. Brenner - BOY 76-78 (N351).

One Spared to the Sea. Cutt - HOGBOON 119-123 (F420.5.1.10.1).

One Trick Too Many. Ginsburg - ONE 17-20 (J758.1.5; K371.1; K1021.0.3).

One! Two! Three! Kelsey - MULLAH 113-118 (J2434).

The One Who Said Tjik. Courlander - KANT-CHIL'S 102-104 (Z49.6.0.6).

The One Who Wasn't Afraid. Deutsch - TALES 7-16 (A2513.1.1).

The One Who Would Not Listen To His Own Dream. Wolkstein - MAGIC 71-74 (N452E).

The One You Don't See Coming. Courlander - COW-TAIL 31-40 (A1399.2.1.1).

One's Own Children Always Prettiest. Wiggin - TALES 323 (T681).

Oni and the Great Bird. Fuja - FOURTEEN 48-59 (H36.1.2).

The Onion and the Rose. Edmunds - TRICKSTER 138-143 (J1179.23).

ONIROKU AND THE CARPENTER. Matsui pb (C432.1.1).

Oniyeye and King Olu Dotun's Daughter. Fuja - FOURTEEN 133-139 (K751.0.3).

Only a Fair Day's Huntin'. Chase - GRANDFATH-ER 180-185 (X1122.3).

Only One Thing Wrong With It. Shah - MULLA 154 (J2200.1).

Ooka and Tasuke's Tax. Edmonds - OOKA 39-44 (J1179.15).

Ooka and the Barbered Beast. Edmonds - OOKA 70-74 (J1511.17.1).

Ooka and the Cleanest Case. Edmonds - OOKA 87-91 (J1141.10.1).

Ooka and the Death Decree. Edmonds - OOKA 92-96 (J1173.1.2).

Ooka and the Halved Horse. Edmonds - OOKA 81-86 (J1249.3).

Ooka and the Honest Thief. Edmonds - OOKA 27-32 (J1179.20).

Ooka and the Marble Monster. Edmonds - OOKA 22-26 (J563.1).

Ooka and the Pup's Punishment. Edmonds - OOKA 12-16 (J1179.18).

Ooka and the Shattering Solution. Edmonds - OOKA 17-21 (J1179.19).

Ooka and the Stolen Smell. Edmonds - OOKA 7-11 (J1172.2).

Ooka and the Stronger Stick. Edmonds - OOKA 75-80 (J1025.3).

Ooka and the Suspect Statue. Edmonds - OOKA 61-64 (J1141.1.3.4).

Ooka and the Telltale Tale. Edmonds - TRICK-STER 61-67 (H1151.3; J1144.3; J1177.2).

Ooka and the Terrible Tempered Tradesman. Ed-monds - OOKA 33-38 (J1179.17).

Ooka and the Two First Sons. Edmonds - OOKA 65-69 (J1249.2).

Ooka and the Wasted Wisdom. Edmonds - OOKA 57-60 (J1171.1.2).

Ooka and the Willow Witness. Edmonds - OOKA 45-50 (J1141.1.3.2).

Ooka and the Wonderful Wishes. Edmonds - OOKA 51-56 (Z42.0.1).

The Opium-eater and the Four Ogres. Brockett - BURMESE 63-66 (N612.3).

Or Else... Cimino - DISOBEDIENT #9 (K1771.2.2).

The Oracle. Chang - CHINESE 9-11 (H1273.2L).

The Orange Tree King. Chang - TALES..OLD CHINA 56-67 (A1437.3; K1917.3E).

Origin of Day and Night. Hardendorff - JUST

22-23 (A1172.4).

The Origin of Disease and Medicine. Bell - JOHN 7-12 (A1337.0.5.1; A1438.2).

The Origin of Indian Pipes. Bell - JOHN 78-80 (A1134.3; A2667); Cathon - PERHAPS 133-134.

The Origin of Lamps. Thoby- Marcelin - SINGING 82-83 (A625.2.3).

The Origin of the Balsam Tree. Courlander - RIDE 241-242 (A2681.14).

The Origin of the Bromo Feast. De Leeuw - INDONESIAN 26-29 (A1545.1.1).

The Origin of the Camlet Flower. Courlander - RIDE 215-216 (A2650.1).

The Origin of the Coconut. Htin - KINGDOM 43-45 (A2611.3.1).

Origin of the Medicine Pipe. Field - AMERICAN 55-61 (A284.5).

The Origin of the Ocean. Harris - COMPLETE 358-361 (A924.5); Harris - NIGHTS 334-338.

The Origin of the Pleiades. Cunningham - TALKING 37-40 (A773.4.1.2).

The Origin of the Water Jars. De Leeuw - INDONESIAN 51-55 (A753.1.4.0.1; A962.0.1.1; A1451.1).

The Orphan Boy and the Magic Twigs. Fuja - FOURTEEN 156-174 (D1472.1.3.3).

Osebo's Drum. Courlander - HAT 32-37 (A2312.0.1; A2411.1.1.1.3; K714.2.5).

Oseedah, the Rabbit Gambler. Parker - SKUNNY 95-101 (N2.6.0.1).

Oshidori. Buck - FAIRY 223-224 (F1041.1.2.2.5).

The Ostrich Chicks. Heady - JAMBO 85-90 (K649.9.1).

The Ostrich Feather. Helfman - BUSHMEN 55-56 (E3.1).

Other People's Mail. Shah - MULLA 122 (J2242.1).

The Otters and the Fox. Gaer - FABLES..INDIA 139-141 (K452.1.1).

OTWE. Aardema pb (B216Ab).

Oudelette. Manning-Sanders - GIANNI 103-107 (C773.1.2).

The Out-foxed Fox. Curry - DOWN 111-120 (J644.1.1).

The Outlaw Boy. Chase - GRANDFATHER 65-74

(N884.1).

To Outleap a Rabbit. Davis - LION'S 61-67 (J1191.1.3).

Outriddling the Princess. Leach - NOODLES 50-52 (H551; H681.1.1; H681.4.1; H793).

The Outwitted Hunter. Gaer - FABLES..INDIA 136-139 (K642.2).

Oversmart Is Bad Luck. Arbuthnot - ANTHOLOGY 408 (J1421); Jagendorf - KING 256-259.

Owl. Leach - HOW 98 (A1958.0.1; A2356.2.14); Wolkstein - MAGIC 29-36 (A2491.2.8).

The Owl and the Birds. Aesop - AESOP'S (Watts) 50 (J621.1); Aesop - FIVE 78.

The Owl and the Raven. Melzack - DAY 21-25 (A2411.2.1.2; A2411.2.4.2.5).

The Owl and the Wolf. Lowe - LITTLE 103-105 (K561.1.0.4).

The Owl in the Moon. Withers - MAN 15-17 (A751.12; R246).

The Owl's Big Eyes. Parker - SKUNNY 72-74 (A2332.1.5; A2441.1.11.1; A2491.2).

The Owl's Punishment. Deutsch - TALES 52-55 (A2482.4).

The Ox and the Ass. Ginsburg - LAZIES 33-35 (K1633.1).

The Ox and the Frog. Aesop - AESOP'S (Watts) 81 (J955.1).

The Ox of the Wonderful Horns. Bryan - OX 29-41 (B335.2E).

The Ox Who Envied the Pig. Babbitt - JATAKA 74-76 (J212.2).

The Ox Who Won the Forfeit. Babbitt - JATAKA 21-24 (B587.3).

The Oxen and the Afanc. Sheppard-Jones - WELSH 43-47 (B11.11.7.1).

The Oxen and the Butchers. Aesop - AESOP'S (Watts) 96 (J215.2).

The Oyster and the Heron. Hardendorff - TRICKY 41-43 (J219.1).

Pacala and Tandala. Ure - RUMANIAN 9-15 (J1516).

Pacala the Lawyer. Ure - RUMANIAN 38-41 (J1191.2).

Pacala Saves Tandala. Ure - RUMANIAN 22-23 (X907.1; X909.4.1).

The Pace of Life. Shah - MULLA 119 (J2516.9).

The Pack-Ass and the Wild Ass. Aesop - AESOP'S (Watts) 157 (L451.2).

The Pack-Ass, the Wild Ass, and the Lion. Aesop - AESOP'S (Watts) 158-159 (L451.2.1).

Paddy and the Leprechaun. Pilkington - SHAMROCK 71-73 (J1922.2.1).

The Page Boy and the Silver Goblet. Haviland - FAVORITE..SCOTLAND 3-12 (F352.1).

The Painted Eyebrow. Carpenter - TALES.. CHINESE 56-65 (A1599.4.1.2).

PAINTING THE MOON. Withers pb (A744.1; A751.4).

Pakpai and Boto. Haskett - GRAINS 64-67 (K1775.1).

The Palace of Rainbow Fountains. Zajdler - POLISH 33-51 (H1385.3Fbb).

The Palace of the Seven Little Hills. Manning-Sanders - SORCEROR'S 45-55 (H1331.3.4).

The Palace of the White Cat. Michael - PORTUGUESE 164-171 (B641Dd).

Pamudjo's Feast. Courlander - KANTCHIL'S 34-38 (J2183.1.1).

Pan Kotsky. Bloch - UKRAINIAN 24-27 (K2324).

The Pancake. Arbuthnot - ANTHOLOGY 238-239 (Z33.1.1); Arbuthnot - FAIRY 73-74; Asbjørnsen - EAST (Row) 41-45; Association - TOLD..GREEN 10-15; Hutchinson - CHIMNEY 19-24; Wiggin - TALES 301-304.

Pancakes and Pies. Manning-Sanders - CHARMS 62-66 (Z52.4.2.1).

Pancho and the Duendes. Ross - IN 191-205 (F481.3.1).

Pancho Villa and the Devil. Arbuthnot - ANTHOLOGY 413 (G303.3.3.1.3; G303.16.3.1.1); Jagendorf - KING 202-204.

The Panditji and the Guavas. Spellman - BEAUTIFUL 90-93 (J2368).

Pandora's Box. Gruenberg - FAVORITE 413-414 (C321).

The Pansu and the Stableboy. Carpenter - KOREAN 231-234 (K366.1.2.1).

The Panther in the Pit. Green - ANIMAL 141-142 (J1172.3).

Papa God and General Death. Wolkstein - MAGIC 75-78 (J486.1).

Papa God First, Man Next, Tiger Last. Wolkstein - MAGIC 177-182 (J2133.6.0.2).

Papa God Sends Turtle Dove. Wolkstein - MAGIC 87-90 (D154.1).

Pappa Greatnose. Manning-Sanders - BOOK.. GHOSTS 47-54 (S268E).

The Parrot. De La Iglesia - CAT (J1826.1).

The Parrot and the Crow. Tooze - WONDERFUL 100-102 (K359.4).

The Parrot and the Parson. Hardendorff - JUST 49-51 (K522.4.0.1).

The Parrot of Limo Verde. Baker - TALKING (D830.1.1.1; H1385.5Ac).

The Parson and the Sexton. Asbjørnsen - NORWEGIAN 15-16 (H561.2; H681.1.1; H711.1); Asbjørnsen - EAST (Row) 133-134; Undset - TRUE 233-234.

Parson Wood and the Devil. Manning-Sanders - PETER 128-129 (G303.9.6.1.3).

PARTNERS. Baker pb (A763.3.1; K171.1).

Partnership. Htin - KING 39-41 (J1249.6).

Partridge and Rock Tripe. Leekley - WORLD 64-68 (A2411.2.6.8; A2689.1).

The Partridge and the Cocks. Aesop - AESOP'S (Viking) 32 (J892).

The Partridge and the Crow. Arbuthnot - FAIRY 231 (J512.6).

The Partridge and the Fowler. Aesop - AESOP'S (Watts) 215 (K552.1.0.2).

The Partridge, the Fox and the Hound. Rudolph - MAGIC 51-61 (J2351.1).

The Past and the Future. Courlander - KINGS 67 (J310; J313).

Patches. Bang - MEN 15-19 (K602.3).

Patient Griselda. Perrault - PERRAULT'S (Dodd) 100-114 (H461).

Patrick O'Donnell and the Leprechaun. Haviland - FAVORITE..IRELAND 85-91 (J1922.2.1).

The Pattern on Tortoise's Back. Kaula - AFRICAN 80-83 (A2312.1.1; J657.2.3; J2357.1).

The Pavilion of Peril. Birch - CHINESE 95-100 (H1411.4.2).

The Payment in Kind. Edmonds - POSSIBLE 51-59 (J1191.2).

The Peace Between the Leopard and the Antelope. Davis - LION'S 140-143 (P242).

The Peace Pipe. Chafetz - THUNDERBIRD 27-41 (A1533.1).

The Peach Blossom Forest. Manton - FLYING 77-82 (F173.2.1).

The Peach Boy. McAlpine - JAPANESE 81-94 (T543.3.2); Ross - BURIED 147-160; Sakade - JAPANESE 9-16.

The Peacock and Juno. Aesop - AESOP'S (Watts) 77 (W128.4); Jacobs - FABLES 63.

The Peacock and the Crane. Aesop - AESOP'S (Viking) 76 (J242.5); Aesop - AESOP'S (Watts) 9.

THE PEACOCK AND THE CROW. Kirn pb (A2411.2.1.6.1; A2411.2.6.7.2).

The Peacock and the Magpie. Aesop - AESOP'S (Viking) 4-5 (J242.4).

The Peacock and the Puhuy. Barlow - LATIN 119-125 (A2411.2.6.7.1).

The Peacock Maidens. Dolch - STORIES..OLD CHINA 139-145 (H1385.3Fab).

The Peacock's Complaint. Aesop - AESOP'S (Viking) 47-48 (W128.4).

The Peacock's Mistake. Gaer - FABLES 146-147 (J1414.3.3).

Peahens and Golden Apples. Lang - VIOLET 50-64 (H1385.3Ja).

The Pearl Necklace. Tooze - THREE..MONKEY #2 (K1066.1).

The Peasant and His Hen. Borski - GOOD 62-65 (H1273.2C).

The Peasant and the Apple-Tree. Aesop - AESOP'S (Watts) 58 (J241.2).

The Peasant and the Baron. Bulatkin - EUR-ASIAN 95-97 (K289.1).

The Peasant and the Bear. Carey - BABA 84-85 (K171.1); Ginsburg - THREE 27-29 (A2494.8.2).

The Peasant and the Hare. Carrick - STILL MORE 43-46 (J2061.3.2).

The Peasant and the Horseman. Courlander - RIDE 238-240 (J1612.1.1).

The Peasant and the King. Zajdler - POLISH 103-104 (H585.3).

The Peasant and the Tsar. Bulatkin - EURASIAN 75-79 (H509.5.4).

The Peasant and the Wolf. Picard - FRENCH 142-147 (D313.1.4).

The Peasant Priest. Riordan - TALES..CENTRAL 146-147 (J2417.3).

The Peasant, the Bear and the Fox. Higonnet-Schnopper - TALES 76-81 (C25; J2351.1; K171.1).

The Peasant's Strong Wife. Jagendorf - GYPSIE'S 34-46 (F617.2.2).

Peboan and Seegwum. Bierhorst - FIRE 5-10 (A1158.1).

The Peddler and the Monkeys. Bulatkin - EUR-ASIAN 69-70 (B786.1).

The Peddler of Ballaghadereen. Arbuthnot - AN-THOLOGY 181-183 (N531.1); Sawyer - WAY 239-247.

The Pedlar of Swaffham. Colwell - ROUND 61-63 (A1465.9.1; N531.1); Jacobs - MORE 98-100; Williams-Ellis - ROUND 161-165.

The Pedlar's Dream. Crossley-Holland - PEDLAR pb (N531.1); Reeves - ENGLISH 72-79.

Pedro. Newman - FOLK..LATIN 31-37 (C773.1.3).

Pedro Alvarado and the Indian Girl. Jagendorf - KING 119-121 (A972.0.1).

Pedro de Malas Artes, or Clumsy Pedro. Lowe - LITTLE 84-89 (J2461.2E).

Peepan Pee. Manning-Sanders - PETER 194-201 (F361.3).

Peerifool. Haviland - FAVORITE..SCOTLAND 25-48 (D2183D).

Pekka and the Rogues. Bowman - TALES..TUPA 231-236 (K111.2).

Pemba and the Python and the Friendly Rat. Carpenter - AFRICAN 113-120 (D882.1Bbb).

Pengersee and the Witch of Fraddom. Williams-Ellis - FAIRY..BRITAIN 170-178 (G275.1.2).

People Can't Be Made from Iron. McDowell - THIRD 29-30 (H1021.14).

The People of Mols. Ross - BURIED 55-64 (J1934; J2163.4)

The People of Redfish Lake. Heady - SAGE 89-94 (D898).

People Who Could Fly. Lester - BLACK 147-154 (D2135.0.3.1).

The People Who Were Afraid to Sleep. Newell - RESCUE 99-106 (A1437.4).

Pepe and the Figs. Newman - FOLK..LATIN 89-93 (D551.1D).

Pepelea's Peg. Ure - RUMANIAN 42-44 (K182.3).

The Peppercorn Oxen. Manning-Sanders -

DEVILS 69-75 (B184.2.2.3).

Peppi. Manning-Sanders - CHARM 85-87 (B335.2H).

Peppino. Manning-Sanders - GIANNI 179-192 (K1931.2G).

Peppito. Manning-Sanders - DRAGONS 62-75 (K1861.1Bb).

Per and the North Wind. Hardendorff - TRICKY 111-118 (D861.1A).

Per, Paal, and Espen Cinderlad. Aulaire - EAST 93-98 (H1115.1.1).

The Perambulatin' Pumpkin. Credle - TALL 16-20 (X1411.2.1); Green - CLEVER 137-142.

Perez and Martina. Allegría - THREE 56-58 (Z32.3).

PEREZ Y MARTINA. Belpré pb (Z32.3).

The Perfect Husband. Hitchcock - KING 23-32 (K1712.1).

The Pet Catfish. Withers - WORLD 87 (X1306.3).

Pete. Ginsburg - THREE 19 (W111.7).

Peter and the Fire-Breathing Dragon. Spicer - MONSTER 109-115 (B11.11.2).

Peter and the Piskies. Manning-Sanders - PETER 1-6 (F282.4).

Peter and the Witch of the Wood. Harper - GHOSTS 67-82 (G264.3.2); Hoke - WITCHES 112-124.

Peter Humbug and the White Cat. Hatch - THIRTEEN 107-121 (B641.0.1Dba).

Peter Ox. Hatch - MORE 167-181 (T553.1).

Peter, Paul and Espen Cinderlad. Asbjørnsen - EAST (Row) 112-118 (H1115.1.1).

Peter Went Fishing on Sunday. Withers - I SAW 34 (Z13.5).

Peter's Adventures. Jagendorf - NOODLEHEAD 147-155 (H341.3.2; J1852.1.3; J1853.2; K187).

Petrosinella or Parsley. Mincielli - OLD 35-41 (F848.1).

The Phantom Ship. Spicer - THIRTEEN GHOSTS 7-16 (E535.3.3).

The Pheasant, the Dove and the Magpie. Kim - STORY 19-22 (A2411.2.1.21.1; A2411.2.6.9.1; A2525.4).

The Pheasant's Bell. Kim - STORY 123-128 (E533.2.1).

The Picaro Bird. Sawyer - PICTURE..SPAIN 121-132 (Z49.3.1).

Picking Mountain Pears. Bang - MEN 71-77 (Q2.1.2Fa).

The Picture Wife. Asia - FOLK..BOOK 2 13-17 (T11.2.2).

The Piebald Calf. Kendall - SWEET 92-97 (B335.2H).

The Piece of Straw. Uchida - DANCING 109-114 (N222.1).

The Pied Piper. Baumann - PIED pb (D1427.1); Holme - TALES 120-127; Jacobs - MORE 1-6; Lang - RED 217-224.

Pierre Jean's Tortoise. Courlander - PIECE 29-33 (B210.2.1.1; K1041.1.4).

Pierre of Provence. Picard - FRENCH 120-128 (N352.0.1).

The Pig and the Sheep. Aesop - AESOP'S (Watts) 171 (J1733).

The Pig-Headed Child. Danaher - FOLKTALES 20-22 (T551.3.5).

The Pig-Headed Wife. Arbuthnot - ANTHOLOGY 261 (T255.2); Bowman - TALES..TUPA 201-204.

Pig Music. Duvoisin - THREE 20-23 (J1675.5.1).

The Pig That Was Really a Troll. Owen - CASTLES 65-74 (A1414.5.1; G561G).

The Pig That Went to Court. Sperry - HEN 39-46 (J2671.4.2); Sperry - SCANDINAVIAN 44-48.

The Pig Woman. Johnson - HOW 31-38 (G211.1.6).

The Pigeon and the Crow. Jacobs - INDIAN 270-272 (K359.4).

The Pigeon's Bride. Fillmore - LAUGHING 51-72 (H1385.5Af).

The Piglet and the Fairy. Colwell - ROUND 108-109 (F482.5.5).

The Pilgrim and the Crab. Korel - LISTEN 81 (K815.14.2).

The Pimmerly Plum. Brown - BRER 16-21 (K1035.1); Harris - COMPLETE 278-284; Harris - NIGHTS 230-235.

The Pine Tree. Dobbs - ONCE 3-7 (A2723.1; J242.9).

The Pink. Grimm - GRIMM'S (Grosset) 91-97 (D431.1.2.1); Grimm - GRIMM'S (World) 93-98.

Pinkel. Haviland - FAVORITE..SWEDEN 33-49 (G610Aa).

Pinto Smalto. Greene - CLEVER 90-97 (H1385.5C); Mincielli - OLD 98-197.

The Piper of Keil. Wilson – SCOTTISH 28–32 (E425.2.5.1).

The Pira Game. Lowe – LITTLE 62–63 (K341.19.1).

The Piskey Revelers. Palmer – FAIRY 31–44 (F473.6.11).

The Piskie Thresher. Manning-Sanders – PETER 56–58 (F381.3).

The Pitch Princess. Zajdler – POLISH 89–102 (T173.3).

The Pixy Visitors. Colwell – ROUND 114–116 (F381.14).

Plans. Ginsburg – THREE 31 (J2061.3.2).

A Plantation Witch. Harris – COMPLETE 101–105 (G229.1.1); Harris – SONGS 153–159.

The Planting Party. Courlander – HAT 46–48 (A2305.3; Z43.6.6).

Please All—Please None. Dobbs – ONCE 38–41 (J1041.2).

Pleiad and Star of Dawn. Wilson – GREEK 11–20 (A773.9; P253.2.0.1).

The Pleiades. Withers – MAN 100–101 (A773.4.1).

Pleiades. Leach – HOW 136–137 (A773.4.1.1; R321).

Plop! Withers – I SAW 123–125 (Z43.3.1).

The Ploughman, the Ass and the Ox. Aesop – AESOP'S (Watts) 183 (J952.4).

Plucking the Rooster. Ish-Kishor – WISE 160–170 (H561.6.1; J1309.1).

Plum Pudding. Dobbs – MORE 18–21 (J1562.1.2).

The Plumage of the Owl. Alegría – THREE 64–65 (A2313.5.8; A2491.2.6).

Podhu and Aruwa. Harmon – TALES 64–88 (H1132.1.5.2).

The Poet and the Peony Princess. Carpenter – TALES..CHINESE 124–133 (D621.2.2.1).

The Poffertjes Pan. De Leeuw – HOLLAND 97–100 (J2511.0.3).

The Pointing Finger. Kendall – SWEET 60–62 (W151.13).

Polo, the Snake Girl. Carpenter – AFRICAN 121–128 (R221Ya).

The Pomegranate, the Apple Tree and the Bramble. Aesop – AESOP'S (Watts) 83 (J466.1).

Pomegranates For Sale. Kelsey – MULLAH 15–19 (J1800).

Pontius Pilate. Duvoisin – THREE 138–145 (A935.2).

The Pool. Keeley – CITY 147–159 (A968.2.3).

The Poor Boy and the Princess. Sechrist – ONCE 168–173 (K134.1.1).

The Poor Brother and the Rich Brother. Dolch – OLD RUSSIAN 81–97 (N250.4).

The Poor Brother's Bad Luck. Durham – TIT 30–33 (N250.4).

The Poor Herdsman and His Sons. Belting – ELVES 15–21 (F451.5.1.6.5).

Poor Little Girl, Rich Little Girl. Jagendorf – KING 260–264 (Q2.1.6Ba).

The Poor Man's Clever Daughter. Ure – RUMANIAN 131–143 (H561.1.1; H632.1; H636.2; H648.1; H1051.1; H1053.2; H1054.1; J1191.1; J1545.4).

A Poor Man's Servant. Ure – RUMANIAN 65–68 (D1601.5.3).

The Poor Miller's Boy and the Cat. De La Mare – ANIMAL 134–142 (B641.0.1D); Grimm – GRIMM'S (Follett) 262–267.

The Poor Miller's Boy and the Little Cat. Grimm – JUNIPER v.2 178–186 (B641.0.1D).

Poor Old Cricket – Leach – LUCK 60–61 (N611.1; N688).

Poor Old Lady, She Swallowed a Fly. Colwell – MAGIC 73–89 (Z49.14).

Poor Old Lady Swallowed a Fly. Tashjian – JUBA 36–38 (Z49.14).

A Poor Peasant and Two Nobles. Bulatkin – EURASIAN 123–124 (J1562.1.1).

The Poor Ploughman and the Rich Nobleman. Jagendorf – MERRY 31–39 (K366.1.1).

Poor Turkey Girl. Haviland – NORTH 76–82 (R221W).

The Poor Weaver and the Princess. Siddiqui – TOONTOONY 82–90 (K1917.3H).

The Poor Widow Bullfighter. Brenner – BOY 106 112 (E423.1.8.2).

The Poor Wolf. Bloch – UKRAINIAN 28–35 (K553.2.1; K553.4).

The Popcorn Frost. Withers – WORLD 83 (X1633.1).

The Popcorn Patch. Credle – TALL 53–54 (X1633.1).

Popo and the Coyote. Ross – IN 134–149 (K231.1.3.1).

The Porcupine and the Dog. Green - ANIMAL 186-188 (A2494.4.14).

The Porcupine and the Snakes. Aesop - AESOP'S (Grosset) 89 (P332); Aesop - AESOP'S (Viking) 55.

The Porcupine Clan. Bruchac - TURKEY 59-61 (B538.3.5).

The Porcupine's Hoe. Courlander - HAT 86-87 (D1651.15).

The Porcupine's Little Quill Coat. Huggins - BLUE 43-49 (B641.5).

The Porcupine's Quills. Parker - SKUNNY 117-123 (A2311.5.2).

Pork and Honey. Wiggin - TALES 312-313 (K1023; N51).

The Pot. Chang - TALES..OLD CHINA 31-33 (J1531.3).

The Pot That Cooked By Itself. Carpenter - SOUTH 167-174 (D861.1lb).

The Pot That Would Not Stop Boiling. TALL.. NURSERY TALES 117-119 (C916.3).

The Pots That Sang. Heady - WHEN 36-41 (D1615.6.1).

The Potter and the Gate. Wyndham - TALES.. CHINA 64 (J2171.6.2).

A Pottle o' Brains. Jacobs - MORE 134-141 (J163.2.1).

Practical Chinese Cats. Manton - FLYING 154-160 (D435.2.1.1.1; D882.1.1.2).

Prahlada. Reed - TALKATIVE 89-94 (D1840.1.4).

Preacher and the Devil. Courlander - TERRA-PIN'S 98-101 (X904.4.1).

The Precious Stone. Pridham - GIFT 130-137 (D882.1Bba).

The Pregnant Priest. Riordan - TALES..CEN-TRAL 211-212 (J2321.1).

Presentneed, Bymeby and Hereafter. Chase - WICKED 140-149 (K335.1.1.1B; K362.1.1).

Presents of the Little Folk. Gag - MORE..GRIMM 123-130 (F344.1.4).

The Pretender. Chang - CHINESE 66-67 (J2131.5.6).

The Pretty Bird. Withers - I SAW 56 (Z17.4).

Pretty Marushka. Sleigh - NORTH 144-154 (Q2.1.4Ad).

Preziosa, the She-Bear. Mincielli - OLD 54-63 (R221Df).

The Price of a Pullet. Chang - TALES 25-30 (J1191.2).

The Price of Eggs. Lowe - LITTLE 32-35 (J1191.2).

The Priceless Cats. Jagendorf - PRICELESS 47-58 (F708.1; J2415.1.0.1; N411.1c).

Pride Goeth Before a Fall. Jacobs - INDIAN 160-163 (K606.0.4).

The Priest and the Pear Tree. Courlander - RIDE 38-41 (F971.7.1).

Prince Ahmed and the Fairy Peribanou. Buck - FAIRY 98-124 (H355.0.1).

Prince Alun and the "Cannwyl Corph." Pugh - TALES 37-45 (E530.1.7).

A Prince and a Dove. Lang - VIOLET 193-202 (G530.2Bd).

The Prince and the Demon. Spellman - BEAUTI-FUL 19-21 (K1711.4).

The Prince and the Dragons. Manning-Sanders - PRINCES 66-75 (K956.0.1).

The Prince and the Giant's Daughter. Wilson - SCOTTISH 156-172 (G530.2K).

The Prince and the Sky-Blue Filly. Manning-Sanders - PRINCES 14-27 (D1415.2.3.1).

Prince Andrea and Princess Meseria. Kaplan - FAIRY 71-107 (G530.2Ad).

Prince Chu Ti's City. Carpenter - TALES.. CHINESE 166-174 (B11.7.1).

Prince Hat Beneath the Earth. Kaplan - FAIRY 162-199 (H1385.4F).

Prince Ivan, the Witch Baby and the Little Sister of the Sun. Ransome - OLD 136-154 (G312.8).

Prince Llewellyn and the Red Haired Man. Sheppard-Jones - WELSH 137-141 (D1711.6.4).

Prince Loaf. Manning-Sanders - BOOK..GIANTS 118-125 (G666.2); Manning-Sanders - CHOICE 216-223.

The Prince of Peking. Dolch - STORIES..OLD CHINA 93-97 (B11.7.1).

The Prince of the Dolomites and the Princess of the Moon. Toor - CARNATION 179-190 (A969.11.1.3).

The Prince of the Seven Golden Cows. Manning-Sanders - JONNIKIN 106-114 (B103.3.2); Picard - FRENCH 148-156.

The Prince of the Six Weapons. Courlander -

TIGER'S 52-57 (K741.3).

Prince Sun and Princess Moon. Wyatt – GOLDEN 34-44 (H335.7.2).

A Prince Went Hunting. Withers – I SAW 126-127 (Z49.15).

The Prince Who Wanted the Moon. Aardema – TALES 62-66 (A1861.4; C771.1).

The Prince Who Wanted the Moon. Green – FOLK ..AFRICA 75-81 (A751.5.6; F772.1.2.2).

The Prince With the Golden Hand. Manning-Sanders – BOOK..DRAGONS 103-113 (H1385.1).

The Princess and Jose. Bleecker – BIG 93-98 (H542; H761); Brenner – BOY 59-64.

The Princess and the Fisherman. Uchida – DANC-ING 135-144 (B652.2.1).

The Princess and the Glass Mountain. Baker – TALKING 88-103 (H331.1.1D).

The Princess and the Herdboy. Sakade – JAPAN-ESE 77-83 (A778.3.1).

The Princess and the Pea. Andersen – PRINCESS pb (H41.1); Holme – TALES 49; Martignoni – ILLUSTRATED 212 (H41.1); Rackham – ARTHUR 140-142.

The Princess and the Scarf. Williams-Ellis – ROUND 43-52 (A421.1.1).

The Princess and the Shepherd. McNeil – DOUBLE 82-86 (H1045.0.1).

The Princess and the Stork. Holding – KING'S 18-27 (B463.4).

The Princess and the String of Lies. Williams-Ellis – ROUND 117-119 (H342.1).

The Princess and the Vagabone. Ross – BLUE 91-109 (H465); Sawyer – WAY 319-333.

The Princess and the Water-Sprite. Babbitt – JATAKA 63-68 (F420.5.2.2.5).

Princess Felicity. Manning-Sanders – PRINCES 97-107 (S268D).

Princess Finola and the Dwarf. Sheehan – FOLK 37-50 (H1409.1).

Princess Fior Vaga. Adams – BOOK..PRINCESS 116-120 (F944.7).

The Princess in the Camphor Tree. Carpenter – ELEPHANT'S 40-48 (C31.3.1).

The Princess in the Tower. Michael – PORTU-GUESE 62-73 (R221Dd).

Princess Maring, the Huntress. Robertson – FAIRY..PHILIPPINES 33-41 (A955.10.1).

Princess of Canterbury. Jacobs – MORE 229-232 (H507.1.0.1).

The Princess of Light. Uchida – DANCING 75-85 (A240.1.1).

The Princess of Mount Nam-Nhu. Robertson – FAIRY..VIET-NAM 44-59 (F377.0.1).

The Princess of the Garden of Eden. MacManus – WELL 164-189 (H1321.1Ca).

The Princess of the Mountain. Sheehan – FOLK 100-111 (E711.4); Turnbull – FAIRY..INDIA 12-26.

THE PRINCESS OF THE RICE FIELDS. Kimishima pb (A2685.6.1).

The Princess of Tomboso. Barbeau – GOLDEN 26-45 (D551.1Bf).

Princess on the Glass Hill. Arbuthnot – ANTHOL-OGY 240-243 (H331.1.1A); Arbuthnot – FAIRY 80-84; Asbjørnsen – EAST (Macmillan) 30-44; Asbjørnsen – EAST (Row) 101-111; Association – TOLD..GREEN 122-138; Colwell – SECOND 115-121; Fenner – PRINCESS 115-127; Haviland – NORWAY 3-29; Hutchinson – CHIMNEY 89-104; Lang – FIFTY 220-230; Lang – BLUE 340-350; Wiggin – FAIRY 69-79.

The Princess on the Pea. Adams – BOOK..PRIN-CESS 31-32 (H41.1); Opie – CLASSIC 216-218.

Princess Sicilia and the Shepherd. Toor – CAR-NATION 137-142 (A955.13).

The Princess Who Always Believed What She Heard. Hatch – THIRTEEN 139-147 (H507.1.0.1).

The Princess Who Always Had To Have the Last Word. Asbjørnsen – NORWEGIAN 77-80 (H507.1.0.1).

The Princess Who Could Not Be Silenced. Arbuth-not – ANTHOLOGY 247-248 (H507.1.0.1); As-bjørnsen – EAST (Row) 119-123.

The Princess Who Couldn't Laugh. Hampden – HOUSE 73-84 (D551.1B; H341.4).

The Princess Who Learned to Work. Ginsburg – LAZIES 36-41 (T251.2.6).

The Princess Who Lived in a Kailyard. Sheehan – FOLK 22-21 (G561.1).

The Princess Who Loved Her Father Like Salt. Haviland – FAVORITE..GREECE 21-27 (F813.8.3; H592.1.0.1).

The Princess Whom Nobody Could Silence. Adams – BOOK..PRINCESS 215-223 (H507.1.0.1); Dobbs – ONCE 110-117; Hutchinson – CANDLE-LIGHT 125-133; Wiggin – TALES 324-327.

The Princess With the Golden Hair. Mehdevi –

The Quack Frog. Aesop – AESOP'S (Grosset) 224-225 (J1062.1); Aesop – AESOP'S (Watts) 56.

The Quarrel. Sherlock – ANANSI 105-112 (Z43.5.1).

The Quarrel. Wilson – GREEK 198-199 (J218.1).

The Quarrel Between the Months. Borski – GOOD 18-19 (A1162).

The Quarrel of the Monkey and the Crab. Ozaki – JAPANESE 203-213 (K1161.6).

The Quarrel of the Quails. Babbitt – JATAKA 30-33 (J1024).

The Quarrelsome Goat. Carrick – STILL MORE 73-87 (J741.1; K1151; Z39.1).

The Quellers of the Flood. Birch – CHINESE 20-33 (A815.0.1; A1015).

The Queen Bee. De La Mare – ANIMAL 180-186 (B582.2); Gag – MORE..GRIMM 155-162; Grimm – GRIMM'S (Follett) 268-271; Grimm – GRIMM'S (Grosset) 98-100; Grimm – GRIMM'S (Viking) 63-65; Grimm – HOUSEHOLD 262-264; Hutchinson – CANDLELIGHT 41-47; Shub – ABOUT 55-57.

Queen Cora. Thoby-Marcelin – SINGING 91-99 (T210.2).

Queen Crane. Baker – GOLDEN 46-53 (R222.1B).

Queen o' the Tinkers. Fenner – PRINCESSES 177-188 (H465C); MacManus – HIBERNIAN 99-107; MacManus – WELL 83-97.

The Queen's Riddles. Cothran – MAGIC 31-37 (F601.2Dd).

A Quest for Halil. Kelsey – HODJA 29-33 (J1561.3).

The Quilt. Kelsey – MULLAH 45-47 (J2672).

Quinces and Oranges. Wilson – GREEK 68-75 (D1223.1.1).

The Quivering Needle. Courlander – RIDE 63-65 (J1060.4); Kelsey – MULLAH 79-82.

Quiz. Shah – MULLA 68 (J1229.1).

THE RABBI AND THE TWENTY-NINE WITCHES. Hirsh pb (G273.8).

Rabbit and Lion. Tracy – LION 30-33 (K815.19.1).

Rabbit and Possum in Search for Wives. Bell – JOHN 51-53 (A2466.1; T92.11.2).

The Rabbit and the Clay Man. Green – FOLK.. AFRICA 57-63 (K741.0.6).

The Rabbit and the Crocodile. Uchida – DANCING 49-57 (K579.2.2; K1014.3).

The Rabbit and the Possum Seek a Wife. Scheer – CHEROKEE 33-36 (A2466.1; T92.11.2).

The Rabbit and the Tar Wolf. Bell – JOHN 54-56 (A2233.1.1; K581.2; K741.0.3.2); Scheer – CHEROKEE 47-50.

The Rabbit and the Tiger. Alegría – THREE 44-51 (J1791.3; K341.2.1; K607.1; K713.1.1; K1241; K1251; K1791.3).

Rabbit and the Wolves. Colwell – MAGIC 70-73 (K606.2).

Rabbit at the Waterhole. Tracy – LION 110-113 (A2233.1.1; K581.2; K741.0.5).

Rabbit, Elephant and Hippopotamus. Tracy – LION 26-29 (J758.1.3; K22).

Rabbit Fat. Ginsburg – THREE 3-5 (X904.3).

Rabbit, Fox and the Rail Fence. Courlander – TERRAPIN'S 18-20 (K1111.4).

The Rabbit Grows a Crop of Money. Burton – MAGIC 84-89 (K1839.12.1).

The Rabbit in the Moon. Pratt – MAGIC #10 (A751.2.1C); Sakade – JAPANESE..FAVORITE 35-37 (A751.2.1A).

The Rabbit Prince. Berger – BLACK 91-105 (H1385.3Fg).

Rabbit Scratches Buh Elephant's Back. Courlander – TERRAPIN'S 50-52 (K1715.2.1).

The Rabbit Servant. Jameson – TALES 43-63 (K131.1.1).

The Rabbit Steals the Elephant's Dinner. Burton – MAGIC 70-81 (K753).

The Rabbit Takes His Revenge On the Elephant. Burton – MAGIC 81-84 (K16.2).

The Rabbit That Rode On a Tortoise. Carpenter – KOREAN 127-132 (K544).

The Rabbit Who Crossed the Sea. Sakade – JAPANESE..FAVORITE 103-105 (K579.2.2; K1014.3).

The Rabbit Who Wanted to Be a Man. Brenner – BOY 65-70 (Z43.6.1).

The Rabbit's Bride. Grimm – GRIMM'S (McGraw) 1-2 (G561.2D); Grimm – HOUSEHOLD 1-2; Grimm – JUNIPER v.2 275-277.

Rabbit's Long Ears. Carter – GREEDY 62-67 (A2325.1.1; H961.1).

The Rabbit's Self-Respect. Bowman – TALES.. TUPA 266 (J881.1).

77-82 (A2426.2.6).

Raven and the Fisherman. Robinson - COYOTE 103-112 (A2109.2).

Raven and the Fox. Melzack - RAVEN 53-60 (A2330.9; C35.6; F302.4.2.2; N831.1).

Raven and the Goose. Melzack - RAVEN 25-31 (K1041.2).

Raven and the Nose of the Gonaqadet. DeWit - TALKING 142-149 (A2335.2.3).

Raven and the Pheasant. Matson - LEGENDS 119-123 (A1335.8.2).

Raven and the Seals. Melzack - RAVEN 47-52 (A2494.15.1).

Raven and the Spirit. Melzack - RAVEN 79-84 (W123.4).

Raven and the Sun. Martin - NINE (A801.2; A941.5.9.1; A1111.2; A1411.2.1; A2103).

The Raven and the Swan. Aesop - AESOP'S (Grosset) 99 (W181.3).

Raven and the Whale. Melzack - RAVEN 42-44 (F911.2.1); Robinson - COYOTE 85-94.

Raven Fools His Grandchildren. Maher - BLIND 133-137 (K341.1.1).

Raven Leaves the World. Melzack - RAVEN 85-91 (A568.1).

Raven Lets Out Daylight. Haviland - NORTH 44-51 (A1411.2.1); Martin - RAVEN 17-25.

Raven Recovers Light for His People. Melzack - RAVEN 61-69 (A1411.2).

The Ravens Build a Bridge. Vo-Dinh - TOAD 35-39 (A778.3).

Raven's Companion. Robinson - COYOTE 63-72 (J2186.1).

Raw Monkey Liver. Bang - MEN 35-37 (K544.1).

The Real Princess. Haviland - FAIRY 170-172 (H41.1); Hutchinson - CANDLELIGHT 71-75.

The Red Bird. Newman - FOLK..LATIN 73-81 (J2415.18).

Red Chicken. Duvoisin - THREE 53-60 (Z52.2.1).

The Red-Etin. Baker - GOLDEN 135-147 (R111.1.3Ah); Lang - BLUE 364-372; Pilkington - SHAMROCK 55-60.

The Red Ettin. Finlay - TATTERCOATS 87-95 (R111.1.3Ah); Jacobs - ENGLISH 136-142; Steel - ENGLISH 221-226; Williams-Ellis - FAIRY ..BRITAIN 292-301.

Red Flowers in White Snow. Jagendorf - PRICE-LESS 125-130 (A2612.4).

The Red Fox and the Walking Stick. Ginsburg - ONE 3-7 (K251.1.0.2.1).

Red Jacket, or, the Rose Tree. Grimm - HOUSE 103-119 (D551.1B).

Red King and Green King. Farjeon - CAVALCADE ..KINGS 33-46 (F601.2E; L425Ab); Ure - RU-MANIAN 45-56.

The Red King and the Witch. Manning-Sanders - RED 49-54 (G312.8).

The Red Prawns of Vatu-Lele. Gittins - TALES 30-31 (A2171.4).

Red Riding Hood. Darrell - ONCE 55-58 (K2011); Grimm - GRIMM'S (Grosset) 243-246; Grimm - GRIMM'S (World) 60-63; Martignoni - ILLUS-TRATED 175-177.

A Red, Ripe Apple, A Golden Saucer. Higonnet-Schnopper - TALES 118-128 (E632.0.4).

Red Shield and Running Wolf. Brown - TEPEE 135-141 (T105).

The Red Swan. Bierhorst - FIRE 11 (D361.1.2).

The Redbird. Cunningham - TALKING 41-44 (F81.1.0.2).

Reflections. Hearn - JAPANESE 110-125 (J1795.2); Ross - BLUE 149-161.

Reform Meeting. Courlander - TERRAPIN'S 15-17 (U236.2).

The Rehepapp and Vanapagan. Maas - MOON 82-84 (K1728).

The Remarkable Ox, Rooster and Dog. Withers - WORLD 70-72 (K130.1).

The Rescue. Kelsey - HODJA 41-45 (J1791.2).

The Rescue of Fire. Curry - DOWN 68-79 (A1142.6.1.1; A1415.2.2.3).

The Rescue of the Sun. Newell - RESCUE 51-62 (A721.1.3).

Rescuing the Moon. Leach - NOODLES 39 (J1791.2).

Rest in Peace. Cutt - HOGBOON 152-158 (D1899.1).

Return of the Ice Man. Brown - TEPEE 78-79 (F433.2).

The Return of the Land-Otter. Littledale - GHOSTS 13-20 (E324.3).

The Return of the Spring. Toor - CARNATION 129-133 (A1150.2).

The Revenge of the Rabbit. Chang – CHINESE 44 (K1715.1).

The Revenge of the Serpent. Jewett – WHICH 59–64 (E533.2.1).

The Reward. Cheney – TALES 59–63 (K187.1).

The Reward for Greed. Edmonds – POSSIBLE 85–93 (K187).

The Reward of the World. Undset – TRUE 250–253 (J1172.3).

The Reward of Treachery. Walker – DANCING ˜ 94–97 (D2061.2.10).

Reynard and Bruin. Jacobs – EUROPEAN 42–50 (A2215.5; C25; J2351.1; K371.1; K372B; K543; K543.0.2; K1473).

Reynard and Chanticleer. Wiggin – TALES 287–288 (K562.1; K721).

Reynard and the Cock. Asbjørnsen – EAST (Row) 22–33 (K562.1; K721).

Reynard and the Fisherman's Dream. Edmonds – TRICKSTER 99–102 (J2061.3.1; K371.1).

Reynard the Fox. Green – ANIMAL 97–115 (K401.1.2).

Reynard Wants to Taste Horse-flesh. Wiggin – TALES 309–310 (K1047).

The Rice Cake That Rolled Away. Uchida – MAGIC 123–131 (N777.0.2).

Rice From a Cat's Fur. Carpenter – KOREAN 157–162 (D1472.1.24.5).

The Rice Puller of Chaohwa. Courlander – TIGER'S 38–39 (J1973.2).

The Rich Landowner and His Worker. Bulatkin – EURASIAN 57–63 (K172).

The Rich Man and the Poor Man. Sechrist – ONCE 143–149 (N66.1).

THE RICH MAN AND THE SHOEMAKER. La Fontaine pb (J1085.1.1).

The Rich Man and the Tailor. Spellman – BEAUTIFUL 69–70 (W153.18).

The Rich Man and the Tanner. Aesop – AESOP'S (Watts) 89 (U133).

The Rich Man's Dinner Party. Ure – RUMANIAN 72–73 (J1561.3).

The Rich Widow of Stavoren. De Leeuw – LEGENDS..HOLLAND 133–138 (N211.1).

Rich Woman, Poor Woman. Manning-Sanders – BOOK..WIZARDS 109–117 (J2073.1).

The Riddle. Lang – FIFTY 241–244 (H551.0.1; H802); Lang – GREEN 293–297; Manning-Sanders – RED 62–65.

THE RIDDLE OF THE DRUM. Aardema pb (F601.2H).

The Riddle of the Sphinx. Leach – NOODLES 45 (C822; H761).

Riddler on the Hill. Thompson – HAWAIIAN.. TRICKSTERS 43–48 (H761).

Riddles. Hardendorff – JUST 159–161 (H561.6.2; H585.1.1).

The Riddling Chief of Puna. Thompson – HAWIIAN..TRICKSTERS 72–79 (H541.1.2).

The Riddling Youngster. Thompson – HAWIIAN.. TRICKSTERS 86–99 (H548).

A Ride to Hell. Manning-Sanders – BOOK.. DEVILS 98–109 (G530.2M).

The Ridiculous Donkey. Green – ANIMAL 84–85 (J2413.1).

The Ridiculous Wishes. Perrault – PERRAULT'S (Dodd) 89–91 (J2075).

The Right Recompense. Walker – NIGERIAN 66–67 (K714.2.3.1).

The Ring. Manning-Sanders – GHOSTS 87–89 (E236.1.1).

The Ring in the Porridge Bowl. Spicer – OWL'S 106–124 (R221M).

THE RING IN THE PRAIRIE. Bierhorst pb (F302.4.2.4).

The Ring in the Seashell. Carpenter – SOUTH 151–159 (D1361.17.1).

Rip Van Winkle. Field – AMERICAN 77–107 (D1960.1); Rackham – ARTHUR 246–265.

Ripopet-Barabas. Picard – FRENCH 168–173 (D2183C).

The Rivalry of Sun and Moon. Helfman – BUSHMEN 43 (A755.4.0.1).

The River. Heady – SAFE 23–26 (A934.16; A935.1).

The River of Stars. Manton – FLYING 13–17 (A778.3.2).

The River Shore Club. Simon – MORE 111–119 (J2031).

The River That Was Stolen. Ross – IN MEXICO 162–174 (A934.14).

The Rivers and the Sea. Aesop – AESOP'S (Watts) 172 (W128.3).

The Robber Bridegroom. Grimm - GRIMM'S (Grosset) 255-259 (S62.1C); Grimm - GRIMM'S (Viking) 66-70; Grimm - HOUSEHOLD 176-178.

The Robe. Shah - MULLA 63 (J2512.1).

The Robe of Feathers. Sakade - JAPANESE 29-33 (F302.4.2.0.2).

The Robin and the Wren. Montgomerie - TWENTY-FIVE 16-17 (W123.2).

Robin Dhu. Sheppard-Jones - WELSH 32-35 (J1141.10.3; N688).

The Rock of the Falling Flower. Carpenter - KOREAN 269-275 (K872.0.1).

The Rogue from Cairo and the Rogue from Damascus. Mittleman - BIRD 58-66 (J1516).

Rolling Cheese Gathers No Moss. Jagendorf - MERRY 93-98 (J1881.1.1).

THE ROLLING RICE BALL. Yoda pb (N777.0.3).

The Rolling Rice-Cakes. Sakade - JAPANESE 69-73 (N777.0.3).

Roland. Grimm - HOUSEHOLD 232-235 (G530.2D).

The Roly-Poly Dumpling. Scofield - HOLD 40-46 (N777.0.3).

The Rope. Heady - TALES 119-124 (A1834.1).

The Rope and the Sky. Shah - MULLA 149 (J1804.1).

The Rooster and the Bean. Carey - BABA 15-16 (Z32.1.1.3).

The Rooster and the Centipede. Carpenter - KOREAN 261-265 (B653.2).

The Rooster and the Hen. Bowman - TALES.. TUPA 242 (Z32.1.1.4).

The Rooster and the Jewel. Aesop - AESOP'S (Golden) 16 (J1061.1).

The Rooster and the Sun. Withers - MAN 88-90 (A739.6.1).

The Rooster and the Wind. Borski - GOOD 46 (A1122.3.1).

The Rooster That Fell in the Brew Vat. Sperry - HEN 47-56 (Z32.2.3); Sperry - SCANDINAVIAN 15-20.

The Rooster, the Hand Mill and the Swarm of Hornets. Baker - GOLDEN 54-57 (D861.1F).

The Rooster, the Mockingbird, and the Maiden. Brown - TEPEE 14-18 (B755.3).

THE ROOSTER'S HORNS. Young pb (A2435.4.8.2).

Rory the Robber. Fenner - ADVENTURES 109-115 (K301Aj).

The Rose and the Amaranth. Aesop - AESOP'S (Watts) 188 (J242.1).

The Rose of Midwinter. Belting - ELVES 91-94 (E451.12).

The Rose Tree. Jacobs - ENGLISH 16-20 (N271Ab); Steel - ENGLISH 248-253.

The Rosy Apple and the Golden Bowl. Riordan - TALES..CENTRAL 138-143 (E632.0.4).

The Royal Journey to Heaven. Asia - FOLK BOOK 1 13-18 (K843.1).

Ruba and the Stork. Mehdevi - PERSIAN 44-50 (K1041.0.1).

The Rubber Man. Arnott - AFRICAN 16-21 (A2433.5.3.3; K741.0.7).

The Ruby Prince. Siddiqui - TOONTOONY 144-154 (H1385.4K).

Ruda, the Quick Thinker. Courlander - KING'S 87-89 (J1922.1).

Ruddy-My-Beard. Pugh - TALES 117-128 (F348.10).

The Rug Maker. Heady - WHEN 31-35 (H35.3.3.1).

RUM PUM PUM. Duff pb (Z52).

Rumpelstiltskin. Arbuthnot - ANTHOLOGY 197-198 (D2183); Arbuthnot - FAIRY 60-62; De La Mare - TALES 171-180; Grimm - BROTHERS 139-144; Grimm - GRIMM'S (Follett) 279-284; Grimm - GRIMM'S (Grosset) 125-129; Grimm - GRIMM'S (Scribner's) 155-158; Grimm - GRIMM'S (Viking) 39-43; Grimm - GRIMM'S (World) 38-41; Grimm - HOUSEHOLD 228-231; Grimm - RUMPELSTILT-SKIN pb; Gruenberg - FAVORITE 310-313; Haviland - FAIRY 158-161; Haviland - FAVORITE.. GERMANY 41-50; Holme - TALES 46-48; Lang - BLUE 101-105; Martignoni - ILLUSTRATED 204-206; Opie - CLASSIC 195-198; Shub - ABOUT 77-79; Sleigh - NORTH 70-82.

Run, Brer Gator, Run! Faulkner - DAY 128-131 (K1055.2).

The Runaway Slave. Aesop - AESOP'S (Watts) 215 (N255.4).

A Rupee Earned. Bulatkin - EURASIAN 39-43 (J702.3).

Rushen Coatie. Jacobs - MORE 163-168 (R221F).

The Russian and the Tatar. Downing - RUSSIAN 135-147 (K289.1; K444).

Rusty Jack. Cothran - WITH 9-17 (J1344.2).

Saburo the Eel-Catcher. Sakade – JAPANESE 84–90 (X1124.3).

The Sack of Truth. Sawyer– PICTURES 11–24 (H346; H1045.0.1).

The Sacred Amulet. Barlow – LATIN 126–132 (A1999.2).

The Sacred Drum of Tepozteco. Arbuthnot – ANTHOLOGY 411–412 (A1195.1; J1561.3); Jagendorf – KING 190–193.

The Sacred Fish of Palaman. De Leeuw – INDONESIAN 140–150 (A920.1.18).

A Sacred Pledge Should Not Be Broken. Jagendorf – KING 208–211 (V128.0.2).

The Sad Fate of Mr. Fox. Harris – COMPLETE 111–115 (F929.3); Harris – UNCLE 163–174.

The Sad, Sorry Sister. Carpenter – SOUTH 160–166 (A1999.6).

The Sad Story of the Tadpole. Fuja – FOURTEEN 39–42 (J2061.7).

A Sad Tale of a Silly Fellow. Jagendorf – KING 252–256 (J2311.1.6; J2311.13; J2133.4).

The Sad Tale of Clever Elsie. Grimm – BROTHERS 82–86 (J2063).

The Sad Tale of the Ant and the Mosquito. Sleigh – NORTH 202–206 (Z32.3).

The Sad Tale of the Crabs. Arnott – ANIMAL 92–94 (A2171.2.1).

The Sad Victory. Jagendorf – NOODLEHEAD 78–83 (N255.8).

The Saddle. Kelsey – MULLAH 48–53 (J1862).

Saddle and Bridle. Harris – COMPLETE 17–70 (K1241.1); Harris – FAVORITE 55–60; Harris – UNCLE 24–30.

Saddle and Spurs. Sturton – ZOMO 67–76 (K1241).

Sadko. Arbuthnot – ANTHOLOGY 290–293 (A421.0.2); Arbuthnot – FAIRY 149–153; Ransome – OLD 40–53.

Sadko the Minstrel. Downing – RUSSIAN 55–63 (A421.0.2).

Sadko the Singer. Dolch – OLD 19–35 (A421.0.2).

A Safe Home. Heady – SAFIRI 58–61 (A2431.3.12).

The Saga of the Waru Wanggi. De Leeuw – INDONESIAN 61–64 (A2681.16).

The Sagacious Monkey and the Bear. Ozaki – JAPANESE 148–152 (K231.1.3.2).

The Sage and the Servant. Korel – LISTEN 103–107 (K331.6.1).

The Sage in the Cave. Alexander – PEBBLES 25 (J1686).

The Sages of Helm. Simon – MORE 1–10 (J2259.3).

The Sailor and the Devil's Daughter. Cothran – MAGIC 45–82 (G530.2Bb).

St. Bridget. Sawyer – THIS 149–157 (V211.1.8.1).

St. Cadog and King Arthur. Sheppard-Jones – WELSH 152–155 (D1711.6.6).

St. Cadog and the Mouse. Sheppard-Jones – WELSH 149–151 (B437.2.3).

St. Cuddy and the Gray Geese. Leodhas – THISTLE 39–45 (V429.1).

St. Francis and the Wolf. Vittorini – OLD 102–105 (B279.1.2).

Saint Gabre Manfas and His Animals. Davis – LION'S 162–166 (A1545.3.0.1).

St. George of Merrie England. Steel – ENGLISH 1–13 (R111.1.3Fa).

St. Magnus for Orkney. Cutt – HOGBOON 161–168 (V229.7.3).

Saint Margery Daw. Manning-Sanders – PETER 39–42 (V411.12).

Saint Neot. Manning-Sanders – PETER 59–63 (V229.28; V229.27).

Saint Peter and His Trombone. Jagendorf – GYPSIES' 47–51 (V229.26.1.1).

Saint Quien Sabe. Ross – IN 75–86 (V128.4).

Saint Sana and the Devil. Spicer – THIRTEEN DEVILS 111–117 (K171.1; K172).

Saint Stanislaw and the Wolf. Frost – LEGENDS 44–49 (B279.1.1).

The Salad. Grimm – GRIMM'S (Grosset) 135–143 (D551.1A); Grimm – GRIMM'S (World) 79–86.

Salakhbai and the Fox. Masey – STORIES 28–37 (K1917.3E).

The Salesman Who Sold His Dream. Novak – FAIRY 153–155 (N531.3).

Salt. Colwell – SECOND 21–34 (C456; N411.4.1); Ransome OLD 294–315; Zemach SALT pb.

Salt and Bread. Courlander – RIDE 163–165 (H592.1.0.1).

The Salt at Dinner. Ure – RUMANIAN 74–83

Salt Is Not Wool. Shah – MULLA 30 (J1612).

The Secret. Shah – MULLA 104 (J1482.1).

The Secret Keeping Boy. Manning-Sanders – GLASS 50-62 (L425Aa).

The Secret of Heather-ale. Wilson – SCOTTISH 46-48 (C429.2).

The Secret of Kaboniyan. Sechrist – ONCE 78-80 (N773.0.1).

The Secret of the Hidden Treasure. Jagendorf – KING 265-269 (C429.3).

The Secret of the Rock. Duvoisin – THREE 185-189 (C761.4).

The Secret Room. Williams-Ellis – FAIRY..BRITISH 149-152 (G561.2B).

A Secret Told to a Stranger. Walker – DANCING 51-57 (D615.0.1).

The Secret Valley. Manton – FLYING 72-76 (D2011.1.5).

The Securing of Light. Curry – DOWN 22-37 (A721.1.5).

The Sedna Legend. Melzack – DAY 27-34 (A2101).

Sedna, the Sea Goddess. Melzack – DAY 26-34 (A2101); Haviland – NORTH 60-64; McDermott – SEDNA pb.

See What I Mean? Shah – MULLA 18 (J1250.1).

The Seed of Happiness. Edmonds – TRICKSTER 86-90 (N135.3).

Seeing Far and Hearing Far. Withers – WORLD 28 (X938.1).

Seerko. Bloch – UKRAINIAN 44-48 (J581.1; K231.1.3).

Segizbai and the Little Mouse-Girl. Masey – STORIES 62-64 (L392.0.1).

The Self-Kicking Machine. Credle – TALL 89-95 (J1689.2).

The Selfish Sparrow and the Houseless Crows. Wiggin – TALES 269-270 (K354.1).

Señor Billy Goat. Belpré – TIGER 69-72 (Z39.1.0.1).

Señor Coyote and the Dogs. Courlander – RIDE 253-256 (J2351.1).

Señor Coyote and the Tricked Trickster. Edmonds – TRICKSTERS 77-85 (B545.2; J1172.3).

Señor Coyote Settles a Quarrel. Ross – BURIED 89-94 (J1172.3).

Señora Will You Snip? Señora Will You Sew?

Sawyer – WHY 229-236 (D1623.2).

Sense and Money. Borski – GOOD 51-54 (J1061.5).

Seraphine and Lilas. Thoby-Marcelin – SINGING 100-103 (D1500.3.1.2).

The Sermon of Nasrudin. Shah – MULLA 42 (X452).

The Serpent. Mincielli – OLD 42-53 (B646.1.1).

The Serpent and the File. Jacobs – FABLES 51 (J552.3).

The Serpent and the Peasant. Manning-Sanders – BOOK..MAGICAL 65-68 (D1812.3.3.5.2).

The Serpent of Wallowa Lake. Matson – LEGENDS 69-75 (A1388.2).

The Serpent Slayer. Kendall – SWEET 33-38 (B11.11.7.2).

The Servant and the Door. Hardendorff – TRICKY 97-99 (K1413).

Seven At a Blow. Fenner – ADVENTURES 26-38 (K1951.1A); Wiggin – TALES 138-145.

Seven Black Crows. Wojciechowska – WINTER 49 (P253.2A).

Seven Brothers. Chang – CHINESE 64-65 (F660.1D).

The Seven Crazy Fellows. Sechrist – ONCE 141-143 (J2031.0.3).

The Seven Foals. Arnott – ANIMAL 141-151 (H1199.12.3); Lang – FIFTY 245-252; Lang – RED 344-352; Manning-Sanders – BOOK..MAGICAL 148-157; Undset – TRUE 72-82.

The Seven Great Deeds of Ma-ui. Colum – LEGENDS 58-64 (A625.2.5; A728.2; A955.8; A1415.0.2.4).

Seven Iron-soled Slippers. McNeil – DOUBLE 16-22 (F1015.1.1Bc).

Seven Lies. Kavcic – GOLDEN 56-59 (H342.1; Z51.4).

The Seven Ravens. Darrell – ONCE 66-70 (P253.2A); Diamond – SEVEN pb; Grimm – BROTHERS 30-33; Grimm – GRIMM'S (Follett) 285-289; Grimm – GRIMM'S (Grosset) 264-267; Grimm – GRIMM'S (World) 282-285.

The Seven Simeons. Riordan – TALES..CENTRAL 199-206 (F660.1Ca).

SEVEN SIMEONS: A RUSSIAN TALE. Artzybasheff pb (F660.1Ca).

The Seven Simeons and the Trained Siberian Cat. Whitney – IN 123-129 (F660.1C).

The Seven Simeons Simeonovich. McNeil - DOU-BLE 42-48 (F660.1C).

The Seven Simons. Lang - CRIMSON 26-41 (F660.1C); Manning-Sanders - GLASS 10-21; Provensen - PROVENSEN 57-67.

Seven Sons. Leach - NOODLES 47-48 (H542).

The Seven Stars. Hatch - MORE 79-87 (A773.1; F660.1Cb).

The Seven Swabians. Carle - ERIC 89-93 (J2612; J2613); Gag - MORE..GRIMM 1-7; Wiggin - TALES 162-164.

The Seven Who Helped. Lang - ROSE 95-106 (F601.2Ac).

The Seven Wishes. Spicer - OWL'S 29-40 (B375.1).

Seven With One Blow. Carle - ERIC 61-74 (K1951.1A).

The Seventh Father of the House. Asbjørnsen - NORWEGIAN 13-14 (F571.2).

Severi and Xappu. Bowman - TALES..TUPA 96-104 (H321E).

The Shadow. Withers - WORLD 69 (J1790.1).

The Shadow on the Wall. Graham - BEGGAR 71-77 (J21.2.1).

The Shady Tree. Lum - TALES..OLD CHINA 34-37 (J1169.7.1).

The Shaggy Dog. Withers - I SAW 36 (Z17.5).

The Shah Weaves a Rug. Carpenter - ELE-PHANT'S 31-39 (H35.3.3).

Shamus O'Connell and the Leprechaun. Sleigh - NORTH 111-115 (J1922.2.1).

Sharing the Crops. Courlander - TERRAPIN'S 104-107 (K171.1).

The Shark in the Milky Way. Thompson - HAWI-IAN..EARTH 40-44 (A778.13).

Shaydoola. Bulatkin - EURASIAN 106-110 (H1273.2H).

The She Bear. Manning-Sanders - PRINCES 76-83 (R221Df).

The She-Goats and Their Beards. Aesop - AE-SOP'S (Watts) 54 (U112).

The Shee an Gannon and the Gruagach Gaire. Jacobs - CELTIC 134-143 (H1199.19); Pilkington - SHAMROCK 161-168.

Sheem. Bierhorst - FIRE 66-76 (B538.3.7).

The Sheep and the Dog. Aesop - AESOP'S (Watts) 169 (W181.1).

The Sheep and the Pig That Built the House. Association - TOLD..GREEN 36-39 (B296).

The Sheep and the Pig Who Set Up Housekeeping. Asbjørnsen - EAST (Row) 129-132 (K1161.2).

A Sheep Can Only Bleat. Jagendorf - NOODLE-HEAD 127-129 (J1881.1.5).

The Sheep, the Wolf, and the Stag. Aesop - AESOP'S (Watts) 97 (J1383).

Sheidulla. Ginsburg - LAZIES 1-7 (H1273.2H).

Shemyaka the Judge. Daniels - FALCON 67-70 (J1173; K1765).

The Shepherd and the Princess. Belpré - TIGER 63-66 (H583.4.2.1; H583.6).

The Shepherd and the Princess. Carter - GREEDY 119-124 (H1377.1; H1377.2; H1377.3).

The Shepherd and the Sea. Aesop - AESOP'S (Grosset) 221 (J11).

The Shepherd and the Wolf. Aesop - AESOP'S (Watts) 169-170 (K2061.1).

The Shepherd Boy. Aesop - AESOP'S (Grosset) 132 (J2172.1); Jacobs - FABLES 85.

The Shepherd Boy and the Wolf. Aesop - AESOP'S (Viking) 74 (J2172.1); Gruenberg - FAVORITE 116-117; Martignoni - ILLUSTRATED 94.

The Shepherd Boy Who Was Wiser Than the King. Hardendorff - JUST 40-41 (H561.4; H696.1.1; H701.1; H702.3); Rockwell - OLD 82-87.

The Shepherd of Myddvai. Jacobs - CELTIC 64-67 (F420.6.1.5.1).

Shepherd Paul. Lang - CRIMSON 178-186 (K1931.2I); Lang - FIFTY 253-260.

The Shepherd Who Laughed Last. Boggs - THREE 77-79 (X1506.1).

The Shepherd With the Curious Wife. Spicer - LONG AGO 11-28 (B216Aa).

The Shepherdess. Lang - GREEN 178-182 (H94.1; H592.1.0.1).

The Shepherds. Sawyer - WAY 21-31 (G303.16.19.10).

The Shepherd's Boy. Aesop - AESOP'S (Random) 54-56 (J2172.1); Arbuthnot - FAIRY 277.

The Shepherd's Boy and the Wolf. Aesop - AE-SOP'S (Watts) 41 (J2172.1).

The Shepherd's Crown. Spicer - LONG 116-129 (H171.7).

The Shepherd's Nosegay. Fenner - PRINCESSES 128-136 (R222.1C); Fillmore - SHEPHERD'S

72-81; Haviland - FAVORITE..CZECHOSLO-
VAKIA 49-66.

A Sherlock Holmes of the Steppes. Deutsch -
MORE 65-68 (J1661.1.1).

A Shilling for a Lie. Withers - WORLD 32 (X905;
X1122.0.1).

The Shinansha, or the South Pointing Carriage.
Ozaki - JAPANESE 54-59 (A1459.2.1; D1313.17;
F75.1).

Shinga-Mambo. Burton - MAGIC 105-107
(K2151.2).

Shingling the Fog. Withers - WORLD 85
(X1651.1).

The Shining Lodge. Cunningham - TALKING 87-
94 (A762.1Ba).

The Ship That Sailed By Land and Sea. Bowman
- TALES..TUPA 1-11 (F601.2Acb).

The Ship That Sailed on Land. Picard - FRENCH
159-167 (F601.2Abc).

The Ship That Sailed on Water and on Land.
Withers - WORLD 9-17 (F601.2.Abd).

The Ship That Went as Well By Land As By Sea.
Aulaire - EAST 27-37 (F601.2Ab).

Shippei Taro and the Monster Cat. Carpenter -
WONDER..DOGS 128-135 (K1853.2.1.1).

The Shipwrecked Man and the Sea. Aesop - AE-
SOP'S (Watts) 70 (J1891.3).

The Shipwrecked Prince. Carpenter - ELE-
PHANT'S 184-194 (H105.5.1.2).

Shish and the Innkeeper. Carey - BABA 79-80
(X1506.2).

A Shiver of Ghosts. Birch - CHINESE 62-79
(E231.7; E463.1; F129.4.4; H1411.4.6); Mayne
- GHOSTS 168-183.

Shlemiel, the Businessman. Singer - WHEN 55-69
(J1703.7).

Shloime, the Mathematician. Simon - MORE 11-15
(J2035.1).

The Shoemaker. Lowe - LITTLE 47-49
(J1085.1.1).

The Shoemaker and the Elves. Gag - MORE..
GRIMM 251-257 (F346.1); Grimm - SHOEMAKER
(Scribner's) pb; Rockwell - THREE 71-77.

The Shoemaker's Apron. Fillmore - SHEPHERD'S
185-192 (Q565).

The Shoemaker's Dream. De Leeuw - LEGENDS..
HOLLAND 21-27 (N531.1; N535.0.1).

Shoes Don't Match. Leach - NOODLES 22
(J2689.1).

Shoes For a Journey. Walker - WATERMELON 23-
24 (J1521.1).

The Shoes Which Were Danced to Pieces. Grimm -
GRIMM'S (Scribner's) 231-235 (F1015.1.1).

Shon Shenkin. Sheppard-Jones - WELSH 164
(D2011.1; F377d).

The Short Cut. Shah - MULLA 146 (N399.4).

The Short Horse. Credle - TALL 64-66 (K1797).

Shorty-the-Bow. Sturton - ZOMO 58-66
(K1121.3).

The Shreds. Wiggin - TALES 165 (H381.1).

The Shrewd Peasant. Bulatkin - EURASIAN 125-
128 (H601.0.1).

Shrewd Todie and Lyzer the Miser. Singer -
WHEN 3-13 (J1531.3).

A Shrewd Woman. Carey - BABA 75-78
(G303.16.19.3.4).

The Shrewish Wife. Daniels - FALCON 52-55
(T251.1.1).

Shrovetide. Tashjian - ONCE 51-55 (K346.1;
K362.1).

The Sick Boy, the Greedy Hunters, and the
Dwarfs. Belting - ELVES 27-34 (F451.5.1.10.2;
F451.5.2.9).

The Sick Lion. Aesop - AESOP'S (Viking) 67
(J644.1).

The Sick Lion. Jacobs - FABLES 17 (W121.2.1).

The Sick Man and the Doctor. Aesop - AESOP'S
(Watts) 131 (J1435).

The Sick Stag. Aesop - AESOP'S (Watts) 140
(W151.2.1); Aesop - FIVE 68.

The Sigakok Bird. Sechrist - ONCE 24-25
(A1999.4.2).

Sigiris Zinno, the Mighty One. Tooze - WONDER-
FUL 55-58 (K1951.1L).

The Sign. Shah - MULLA 69 (J2212.6.1).

The Sign at the Smithy Door. Spicer - THIR
TEEN DEVILS 91-100 (J2411.1.0.2).

The Signal Flag. Kim - STORY 172-179
(E279.6.1).

Sigurd the King's Son. Manning-Sanders BOOK

182 (N455.4A).

The Singing Tortoise. Courlander – COW-TAIL
65-71 (B210.2.1).

The Singing Turtle. Sakade – JAPANESE 93-100
(B210.2.1); Scofield – HOLD 9-14; Thoby-
Marcelin – SINGING 21-29 (K553.5.3; K1041.1.4).

Sinko's Luck. Hampden – GYPSIES' 113-118
(D861.1A).

Sir Buzz. Haviland – FAVORITE..INDIA 63-82
(D882.1Eb).

Sir Gammer Vans. Jacobs – MORE 43-45 (Z19.2.2);
Wiggin – TALES 203-204; Williams-Ellis – FAIRY
..BRITISH 206-208.

Sir Goldenhair. Barbeau – GOLDEN 73-89 (B316A).

Sir Lanval. Picard – FRENCH 84-92 (C31.5).

Sissa and the Troublesome Trifles. Edmonds –
TRICKSTER 5-13 (Z21.1).

Sister Alionushka and Brother Ivanushka. Daniels – FALCON 61-66 (P253.2.0.1C); Riordan –
TALES..CENTRAL 107-111.

Sister Na-Tao. Cheney – TALES 87-92 (E221.6).

The Sisters and the Dogs. Johnson – HOW 23-30
(Q2.1.6C).

The Sisters in the Sun. Carpenter – TALES..
CHINESE 22-28 (A736.1.1.1).

Six and Four. Pugh – TALES 47-59 (D1413.17.1).

SIX CHINESE BROTHERS. Hou-Tien pb
(F660.1Db).

The Six Companions. Wilson – GREEK 42-52
(H1151.6.2.1).

SIX FOOLISH FISHERMEN. Elkin pb (J2031.0.3).

The Six Horsemen. Carpenter – AFRICAN 187-
184 (F601.2Ec).

Six Men Go Far Together in the Wide World.
Grimm – BROTHERS 139-145 (F601.2D).

Six Servants. Gag – TALES..GRIMM 39-61
(F601.2B); Grimm – GRIMM'S (Grosset) 280-
289; Grimm – GRIMM'S (World) 211-218.

The Six Sillies. Lang – RED 188-191 (J2063;
J2161.1).

Six Soldiers of Fortune. Grimm – GRIMM'S
(World) 142-147 (F601.2D); Grimm – HOUSE-
HOLD 3-8.

The Six Swans. De La Mare – ANIMAL 309-318
(P253.2D); Gag – MORE..GRIMM 139-154;
Grimm – GRIMM'S (Follett) 290-298; Grimm –
GRIMM'S (Grosset) 107-113; Grimm – GRIMM'S

(Scribner's) 134-139; Grimm – GRIMM'S (World)
114-120; Grimm – HOUSEHOLD 198-203; Holme –
TALES 100-112; Lang – YELLOW 5-11; Shub –
ABOUT 83-87.

SIXTY AT A BLOW: A TALL TALE FROM TURKEY.
Price pb (K1951.1J).

Skillywidden. Colwell – ROUND 122-124
(F329.4.1); Manning-Sanders – PETER 7-10.

Skinkoots Steals the Springtime. DeWit – TALK-
ING 113-117 (A1151.1).

The Skipper and the Dwarfs. Manning-Sanders –
DWARFS 73-77 (F451.5.1.4.4).

The Skoonkin Huntin'. Chase – GRANDFATHER
137-139 (Z19.2.1).

The Skull. Courlander – TERRAPIN'S 74-75
(B210.2.3); Manning-Sanders – BOOK..GHOSTS
38-42 (E451.14).

Skunk Outwits Coyote. Brown – TEPEE 111-113
(K826.1).

Skunny Wundy Tricks Old Fox. Parker – SKUN-
NY 3-22 (C432.1.3).

The Sky-Eater. Holding – SKY 11-23 (A741.4).

Sky Elk, the Ghost of Whiteface Mountain. DeWit
– TALKING 4-12 (A781.1.2; E423.2.6.1).

THE SKY-GOD STORIES. Aardema pb (A1481.2.1;
K713.1.9; K714.2.6; K741.0.9).

The Sky God's Daughter. Courlander – KING'S
36-40 (H323B).

The Sky People. Heady – WHEN 62-67 (H1385.3M).

The Slave and the Lion. Aesop – AESOP'S
(Watts) 31-32 (B381).

The Slaying of the Sea-Serpent. Arnott – ANI-
MAL 184-189 (K1853.2.1.2).

Sleep is An Activity. Shah – MULLA 79 (J2243.1).

The Sleeper. Manning-Sanders – SORCEROR'S
24-32 (D754.1).

The Sleeping Beauty. Adams – BOOK..PRINCESS
84-89 (D1960.3); Association – TOLD..GREEN
139-145; Carey – FAIRY 16-26; De La Mare –
TALES 181-192; Evans – SLEEPING pb; Grimm –
GRIMM'S (World) 34-37; Grimm – HOUSEHOLD
204-207; Grimm – SLEEPING (illus. Hoffman) pb;
Grimm – SLEEPING (illus. Hutton) pb; Grimm –
SLEEPING (illus. Schwartz) pb; Hyman –
SLEEPING pb; Martignoni – ILLUSTRATED 248-
251; Opie – CLASSIC 81-92; Perrault – FAMOUS
(Watts) 3-22; Rackham – ARTHUR 182-189;
Rackham – FAIRY 52-65; Tarrant – FAIRY 20-33.

The Sleeping Beauty in the Woods. Arbuthnot –
ANTHOLOGY 207-209 (D1960.3); Arbuthnot –

FAIRY 99-101; Fenner - PRINCESSES 154-167; Haviland - FAVORITE..FRANCE 60-75; Holme - TALES 58-62; Lang - BLUE 66-77; Perrault - PERRAULT'S (Dodd) 1-15; Perrault - PERRAULT'S (Dover) 1-22; Perrault - SLEEPING (illus. Chappell) pb; Perrault - SLEEPING (illus. Rackham) pb.

The Sleeping Prince. Lurie - CLEVER 74-83 (D754.1.1).

The Sleeping Tsarevna and the Seven Giants. Dalgliesh - ENCHANTED 231-246 (Z65.1Ab).

Sleepy Feet. Leekley - WORLD 55-57 (J2351.1.2).

The Sleigh Ride. Hatch - MORE 199-213 (H341.1).

SLIP! SLOP! GOBBLE! Hardendorff pb (Z33.2.1).

The Sloogeh Dog and the Stolen Aroma. Aardema - TALES 24-31 (J1172.2.2); Arbuthnot - ANTHOLOGY 323-324.

Slow Train to Arkansas. Courlander - TERRAPIN'S 28-30 (K11.1).

The Sly Fox. Ginsburg - ONE 21-27 (E781.4; K579.2.3).

The Sly Gypsy. Borski - GOOD 66-67 (W111.7.2).

The Sly Gypsy and the Stupid Devil. Spicer - THIRTEEN DEVILS 43-52 (G501B).

Sly Peter at the Fair. Pridham - GIFT 63-66 (J1172.2.2).

Sly Peter's Revenge. Pridham - GIFT 84-94 (K110.1; K131.1.1; K842; K1051.0.1).

The Sly Thief of Valenciennes. Barbeau - GOLDEN 121-138 (K301D).

Small Brother and the Giants. Newell - RESCUE 107-118 (A974.0.3).

The Small Men and the Weaver. Manning-Sanders - JONNIKIN 68-43 (F451.3.2.2.2.1).

The Small People's Cow. Manning-Sanders - PETER 156-165 (F348.7.1.2).

The Small Red Feather. Burton - MAGIC 109-111 (D876.1).

Small Star and the Mud Pony. DeWit - TALKING 99-107 (D445.1.2).

Small White Stones. Hampden - GYPSY 127-131 (H1331.1.3Fd).

Smart Dai-adalla. Jagendorf - KING 144-148 (E434.12).

The Smart Daughter. Pugh - TALES 105-115 (H561.1.2; H1051; H1053.9; H1054.1; H1057; H1063; J1191.1; J1545.4).

Smart Working Man, Foolish Boss Man. Jagendorf - KING 31-33 (W111.2.6).

Smartness for Sale. Jagendorf - NOODLEHEAD 244-248 (J1703.1).

The Smiling Innkeeper. Davis - LION'S 68-69 (J1819.3.2).

The Smith and the Faeries. Wilson - SCOTTISH 107-114 (A1459.1.7; F321.1.1; F321.1.4.5).

The Smoker. Garner - CAVALCADE..GOBLINS 175-177 (E555).

The Smoking Mountain. Ross - IN 62-74 (A962.1.1).

Smolicheck. Fillmore - SHEPHERD'S 87-93 (K815.15C).

The Smuggler. Shah - MULLA 20 (K409).

The Snail and the Leopard. Fuja - FOURTEEN 69-72 (J1172.3.0.6).

The Snake. Daniels - FALCON 29-31 (B654.2).

The Snake. Manning-Sanders - RED 127-131 (B646.1.2).

The Snake and Its Benefactor. Vo-Dinh - TOAD 29-34 (A1546.0.1.1; J1172.3.2.3).

The Snake and Jupiter. Aesop - AESOP'S (Watts) 190 (J623.1).

The Snake and the Dreams. Courlander - RIDE 154-158 (B145.2).

The Snake and the Fish. Ginsburg - THREE 49 (J2137.6.2).

The Snake and the Toad. Kim - STORY 116-122 (B16.5.1.3).

The Snake Chief. Arnott - AFRICAN 186-194 (Q2.1.2Ea).

The Snake in the Bottle. Davis - LION'S 23-26 (K1022.0.3).

The Snake King. Arnott - TEMBA 94-106 (K1931.2Vb).

The Snake King's Crown. Zajdler - POLISH 1-19 (D882.1.1).

Snake Magic. Arnott - AFRICAN 85-100 (B491.1.3).

The Snake Prince. Arnott - ANIMAL 166-173 (B646.1.2); Brockett - BURMESE 18-30 (B646.1.4).

The Snake Son. Owen - CASTLE 91-98 (B646.1).

Snake Story. Withers - WORLD 82 (X1204.2).

Snake the Postman. Carter - GREEDY 78-83 (K75).

The Snake Under the Stone. Hampden - HOUSE 85-87 (J1172.3; J1172.3.2).

The Snake Who Bit a Girl. Tracey - LION 6-9 (J1172.3).

The Snaring of the Sun. Cunningham - TALKING 66-69 (A728.1).

The Sneeze That Won a Wife. Wyatt - GOLDEN 27-33 (K1996).

Sneezy Snatcher and Sammy Small. Manning-Sanders - BOOK..GIANTS 32-35 (G82.1.2); Manning-Sanders - CHOICE 144-147.

Snegourka, the Snow Maiden. Haviland - FAVOR-ITE..RUSSIA 43-52 (T546.3).

The Snooks Family. Colwell - SECOND 104-106 (X131); Tashjian - JUBA 97-50.

Snow-drop. Farjeon - CAVALCADE..QUEENS 110-120 (Z65.1).

The Snow in Chelm. Singer - ZLATEH 29-34 (J2163.3).

Snow in the Mountains. Lowe - LITTLE 52-54 (A561.6.1).

The Snow King. Cunningham - TALKING 60-65 (A289.3).

The Snow Maiden. Gruenberg - FAVORITE 366-369 (T546.3); Riordan - TALES..CENTRAL 53-55.

Snow White. De La Mare - TALES 142-154 (Z65.1); Grimm - HOUSEHOLD 213-221; Grimm - SNOW (Little) pb; Gruenberg - FAVORITE 286-294; Haviland - FAIRY 128-137; Jacobs - EURO-PEAN 201-211.

Snow White and Rose Red. Arbuthnot - FAIRY 49-51 (D113.2.2); Dalgliesh - ENCHANTED 57-65; Gag - TALES..GRIMM 207-221; Grimm - GRIMM'S (Follett) 299-308; Grimm - GRIMM'S (Grosset) 298-306; Grimm - GRIMM'S (Scrib-ner's) 262-269; Grimm - HOUSEHOLD 125-142; Grimm - SNOW (Delacourt) pb; Grimm - SNOW (Scribner's) pb; Hutchinson - CHIMNEY 153-163; Lang - BLUE 277-285; Lang - FIFTY 270-276; Wiggin - FAIRY 228-236.

Snow White and the Seven Dwarfs. Arbuthnot - ANTHOLOGY 190-192 (Z65.1); Arbuthnot - FAIRY 53-56; Gag - SNOW pb; Grimm - GRIMM'S (Grosset) 166-177; Grimm - GRIMM'S (World) 332-342; Grimm - JUNIPER v.2 256-274; Grimm - SNOW (Farrar) pb; Manning-Sanders - DWARFS 25-37; Martignoni - ILLUSTRATED 265-267; Opie - CLASSIC 175-182.

Snowdrop. Grimm - GRIMM'S (Watts) 716 (Z65.1); Holme - TALES 69-75; Lang - FIFTY 261-270;

Lang - RED 324-335.

Snowdrop and the Seven Little Dwarfs. Hutchin-son - CHIMNEY 27-38 (Z65.1).

Snowflake. Ross - BURIED 27-30 (T546.3).

The Snuffbox. Lang - GREEN 139-145 (D882.1E).

So Say the Little Monkeys. Jagendorf - KING 52-55 (J2171.2.1).

Soap, Soap, Soap! Chase - WICKED 130-136 (J2671.2.1).

The Soaring Lark. Grimm - GRIMM'S (Scribner's) 199-206 (H1385.4D).

Soccer Game on Dung-Ting Lake. Bang - GOB-LINS 41-46 (E577.1.1).

Sody Saleratus. Tashjian - JUBA 55-58 (Z33.6).

Sody Sallyraytus. Chase - WICKED 75-80 (Z33.6).

The Soldier and His Horse. Aesop - AESOP'S (Watts) 95 (J1914.1).

The Soldier and His Magic Helpers. Gag - MORE ..GRIMM 63-75 (F601.2D).

The Soldier and the Knapsack. Courlander - RIDE 145-153 (K213).

SOLDIER AND TSAR IN THE FOREST. Lowrie pb (K1812.1).

Soldier Jack. Chase - JACK 172-179 (K213).

The Soldier Who Did Not Wash. Downing - RUS-SIAN 138-142 (K217).

The Soldier's Fur Coat. Higonnet-Schnopper - TALES 15-20 (K119.4).

The Soldier's Return. Hitchcock - KING 111-122 (B645.1.2.4).

The Sole's Mouth. Wiggin - TALES 71 (A2252.4).

Solomon-the-Wise and the Golden Plough. Ure - RUMANIAN 158-159 (J1199.2).

The Sombreros of the Men of Lagos. Jagendorf - NOODLEHEAD 268-270 (J2723).

Some Goes Up and Some Goes Down. Harris - COMPLETE 50-53 (K651); Harris - FAVORITE 1-5; Harris - UNCLE 76-81.

Some Impatient Mule-Drivers. Brenner - BOY 21-22 (J1612.0.1).

Something Fell. Shah - MULLA 94 (J1250.11).

Something Wonderful. Manning-Sanders - DEVILS 30-38 (N813A).

A Son of Adam. Jacobs - MORE 118-119

(H1554.1); Wiggin - TALES 244-245.

The Son of Kim-ana-u-eje and the Daughter of the Sun and the Moon. Lester - BLACK 62-72 (T53.6).

The Son of Seven Queens. Jacobs - INDIAN 139-154 (Z215.1).

The Son of Strength. MacManus - HIBERNIAN 1-9 (F615.3.1.5).

The Son of the Baker of Barra. Leodhas - SEA 3-23 (D882.1Ec).

The Son of the Hunter. Courlander - RIDE 120-127 (H1151.6.2.1).

Son of the Long One. Arbuthnot - ANTHOLOGY 314-315 (K1711.2.1); Heady - JAMBO 60-65.

The Song of Gimmile. Courlander - KING'S 9-12 (J611.1).

The Song of the Fox. Bowman - TALES..TUPA 258-260 (K473).

The Song of the Wolf. Bowman - TALES..TUPA 260 (J581.1).

Soo Tan the Tiger and the Little Green Frog. Hume - FAVORITE..CHINA 9-14 (J2132.5.1; K11.2; K1715.2; K1715.12.2).

THE SOONER HOUND. Weiss pb (X1215.7.1).

Soonimaya. Hitchcock - KING 11-22 (K1911Aa).

The Soothsayer's Son. Jacobs - INDIAN 86-103.

Sop Doll! Chase - JACK 76-82 (D702.1.1); Hoke - SPOOKS 141-146; Leach - THING 95-98.

Sorceror Kaldoon. Manning-Sanders - SORCEROR'S 99-111 (G302.7.1.1).

The Sorceror's Apprentice. Association - CASTLE 127-133 (D1711.0.1.1); Gag - MORE.. GRIMM 197-205; Gag - SORCEROR'S pb.

Soria Moria Castle. Aulaire - EAST 79-92 (H1385.3A); Asbjørnsen - EAST 109-124; Asbjørnsen - NORWEGIAN 67-76; Lang - RED 37-51; Sleigh - NORTH 184-194; Undset - TRUE 51-57.

Sorrow. Downing - RUSSIAN 122-128 (K717.3; N250.4).

The Soul in the Mountain Rice. De Leeuw - INDONESIAN 21-25 (A2685.6.1).

The Sound Is Yours. Walker - WATERMELONS 35-36 (J1172.2.1).

Soup of the Soup. Kelsey - HODJA 157-164 (J1551.6).

The Soup Stone. Courlander - RIDE 186-188

(K112.2).

A Spadeful of Earth. Williams-Ellis - FAIRY.. BRITISH 114-116 (F531.6.6.3.1).

The Spanish Donkey and the Indians. Jagendorf - KING 222-225 (K1977).

The Sparrow and the Blade of Grass. Carrick - STILL MORE 23-31 (Z41.7).

The Sparrow and the Phoenix. Chang - CHINA 70-72 (Z49.6.0.4).

The Sparrow and the Stalk of Grass. Bloch - UKRAINIAN 60-63 (Z41.7).

The Sparrows and the Flies. Carpenter - KOREAN 237-241 (A2479.10).

The Spear and Shield of Huan-Tan. Courlander - TIGER'S 40-42 (X909.5.1).

Spearfinger. Bell - JOHN 27-33 (G262.2.1).

Spearfinger the Witch. DeWit - TALKING 52-56 (G262.2.1).

The Spears of Lightning. Thompson - HAWAIIAN ..EARTH 20-27 (A285.2).

The Specialist. Kelsey - MULLAH 128-131 (J1060.2).

THE SPECKLED HEN. Zemach pb (Z39.5.1).

The Speech of Beasts. Wyatt - GOLDEN 50-58 (B216Ae).

The Spell of the Mermaid. Pratt - MAGIC #1 (D1349.2.4).

The Spendthrift and the Swallow. Aesop - AESOP'S (Watts) 10 (J731.1).

The Spider. Manning-Sanders - GIANNI 62-66 (B643.4).

Spider and Squirrel. Arnott - AFRICAN 64-67 (K453.1).

The Spider and the Flea. Wiggin - TALES 157-159 (Z32.2.3.1).

Spider and the Lion. Arnott - AFRICAN 25-31 (K1995).

Spider Feeds His Family. Arnott - ANIMAL 202-209 (K22.1).

The Spider Specter of the Pool. Spicer - THIRTEEN GHOSTS 24-35 (E423.8.3).

The Spider Weaver. Sakade - JAPANESE 59-65 (A1133.5; B652.2.1).

Spider's Web. Arnott - AFRICAN 74-77 (K401.2.3.1).

Spin, Weave, Wear. Leodhas – HEATHER 95–111
(D2183.1).

Spindle, Shuttle and Needle. Gag – TALES..
GRIMM 65–73 (H1311.2); Grimm – JUNIPER v.1
55–62; Lang – FIFTY 277–280; Lang – GREEN
276–280; Sheehan – FOLK 32–36; Wiggin –
FAIRY 248–251.

The Spindle, the Shuttle and the Needle. Grimm
– GRIMM'S (Scribner's) 305–308 (H1311.2);
Vittorini – OLD 69–72.

The Spinning Maid and the Cowherd. Carpenter
– TALES..CHINESE 182–189 (A778.3.2).

The Spinning Plate. Bleecker – BIG 53–63
(F473.6.10).

The Spirit in the Bottle. Grimm – GRIMM'S (Follett) 309–316 (K717).

The Spirit of Chimborazo. Newman – FOLK..
LATIN 27–30 (J1689.1).

The Spirit of the Moon. Caswell – SHADOWS 19–
23 (A736.1.2.2; A762.1Ab).

The Spirit of the Stone. Sechrist – ONCE 98–104
(H1561.1).

The Spirit Who Dances. Thompson – HAWAIIAN..
TRICKSTER 38–42 (E421.2.1.1).

Spirits Seen and Unseen. Harris – COMPLETE
230–235 (G229.1.1); Harris – NIGHTS 154–156.

The Spiteful Nanny Goat. Bloch – UKRAINIAN
39–43 (Z39.1).

The Spoiled Daughter. Pridham – GIFT 48–54
(T251.2.6).

Spots. Heady – SAFIRI 67–70 (A2411.1.7.1.3;
A2412.1.2).

The Spotted Cow. Manning-Sanders – GLASS 86–
93 (B335.2F).

The Spotted Rug. Courlander – TIGER'S 100–105
(K499.11).

The Sprig of Rosemary. Lang – ROSE 107–113
(H1385.4G).

The Spriggan's Treasure. Manning-Sanders –
PETER 82–84 (F351.2).

The Sprightly Tailor. Jacobs – CELTIC 68–71
(H1412.2).

The Spring By Ah-Petri. Bulatkin – EURASIAN
120–122 (D1338.1.1.2).

The Spring of Youth. Pridham – GIFT 35–44
(H1331.1Ae).

Squire Per. Asbjørnsen – NORWEGIAN 122–127
(K1917.3D).

The Squire's Bride. Asbjørnsen – EAST (Row)
124–128 (J1615); Asbjørnsen – NORWEGIAN 56–
60; Asbjørnsen – SQUIRE'S pb; Frost – LEG-
ENDS 76–78; Undset – TRUE 209–212.

Squirrel and Fox. Hampden – GYPSY 139–146
(B216.6).

Squirrel and the Pine Nuts. Heady – SAGE 49–50
(A1425.0.1.2).

The Stag and His Antlers. Aesop – FIVE 62
(L461).

The Stag and His Reflection. White – AESOP
28–30 (L461).

The Stag and the Lion. Aesop – AESOP'S (Watts)
198 (N255.1).

The Stag and the Vine. Aesop – AESOP'S (Grosset) 233 (J582.2); Aesop – AESOP'S (Watts) 138.

The Stag At the Pool. Aesop – AESOP'S (Watts)
74 (L461); Aesop – FABLES (Walck) 29.

The Stag In the Ox-stall. Aesop – AESOP'S
(Watts) 24 (J1032).

The Stag Looking Into the Water. Aesop – AE-
SOP'S (Viking) 83 (L461).

The Stag Prince. Buck – FAIRY 81–88
(P253.2.0.1D).

The Stag With One Eye. Aesop – AESOP'S (Watts)
119 (K929.2).

Stan Bolovan. Colwell – MAGIC 41–50 (G501C);
Lang – FIFTY 281–290; Lang – VIOLET 96–110;
Manning-Sanders – CHOICE 307–309; Manning-
Sanders – DRAGONS 25–38.

Stan Bolovan and the Dragon. Green – CAVAL-
CADE..DRAGONS 138–147 (G501C).

Star Catching. Withers – MAN 76 (J2275.2).

The Star Dollars. Gag – MORE..GRIMM 85–86
(V411.10).

THE STAR HUSBAND. Mobley pb (A762.1Be).

Star Maiden. Haviland – NORTH 97–100
(A1717.1; A1937; F302.4.2.4).

The Star Money. Grimm – GRIMM'S (Follett) 317–
318 (V411.10); Rockwell – THREE 113–117.

STARGAZER TO THE SULTAN. Walker pb
(N611.5; N688).

The Stars in the Sky. Jacobs – MORE 177–181
(F1068.0.1); Jacobs – STARS pb; Reeves –
ENGLISH 178–181.

Stars in the Water. Withers – MAN 76
(J1791.2.1).

The Statue That Sneezed. Jewitt - WHICH 41-46 (D1652.1.7.3).

Stealing the Bell. Wyndham - TALES..CHINA 63 (J2259.1).

Stealing the Springtime. Bleecker - BIG 153-160 (A1151.1); Cothran - WITH 76-83; Field - AMERICAN 32-39.

Steam - How Much? Kelsey - MULLAH 122-127 (J1172.2).

Stepan Divides a Goose. Dolch - STORIES..OLD RUSSIA 45-51-59 (H601; H601.0.1).

The Stepchild and the Fruit Trees. Arbuthnot - ANTHOLOGY 329-330 (Q2.1.6D); Robinson - SINGING 24-33.

A Stepchild That Was Treated Mighty Bad. Haviland - NORTH 147-154 (Q2.1.2Ac; Z65.1Aa).

Stewed, Roasted or Live? Kendall - SWEET 98-99 (J2062.4).

Sticks and Turnips! Sticks and Turnips! Carpenter - KOREAN 57-63 (G263.1.0.2).

The Sticky-Sticky Pine. Sakade - JAPANESE 55-58 (D2171.1.0.1).

Stingy Kichiyanu and the Iron Hammer. Bang - MEN 12-13 (W153.19).

Stingy Kichiyanu and the Rice Thieves. Bang - MEN 4-5 (J1341.7.1).

Stinkin' Jim. Harris - COMPLETE 32-36 (K1161.11); Harris - FAVORITE 77-82; Harris - UNCLE 47-53.

The Stolen Brain and the Sidh. Minard - WOMEN-FOLK 1-13 (F321.3.0.2).

The Stolen Jewel. Hitchcock - KING 61-75 (D817.1.2.1; D882.1.1).

THE STOLEN NECKLACE. Rockwell pb (K1066.1).

The Stolen Rope. Withers - World 73 (K188).

The Stolen Turnips, the Magic Tablecloth, the Sneezing Goat, and the Wooden Whistle. Fenner - ADVENTURES 82-102 (D861.1K); Ransome - OLD PETER'S 155-183.

The Stolen Winding Sheet. Cutt - HOGBOON 80-86 (E236.1).

The Stolen Wine. De La Iglesia - CAT #12 (J1319.4).

The Stone Crusher of Banjang. Courlander - KANTCHIL'S 96-100 (Z42.0.2).

The Stone Cutter. Lang - FIFTY 291-294; (Z42.0.2); McDermott STONE pb.

The Stone in the Cock's Head. Haviland - FAVOR-ITE..ITALY 43-53 (D882.1.1.1); Wiggin - TALES 25-29.

The Stone in the Garden. Kelsey - MULLAH 89-94 (J2214.2).

The Stone Lute. Courlander - KING'S 95-97 (H1021.12)

The Stone Monkey. Manning-Sanders - MAGICAL 45-48 (B241.2.2.1); Turnbull - FAIRY., INDIA 1-11.

The Stone of Patience. Ekrom - TURKISH 103-111 (K1911.1.4A).

The Stone Owl's Nest. Spicer - OWL'S 15-28 (G303.14.1.2; K1886.3.1; M211.2).

Stone Patience and Knife Patience. Buck- FAIRY 225-231 (K1911.1.4A).

STONE SOUP. Brown pb (K112.2).

The Stone Statue and the Grass Hat. Bang - MEN 21-25 (J1873.1).

The Stone Stew. Edmonds - TRICKSTER 113-119 (112.2).

The Stonecutter. Lang - CRIMSON 101-105 (Z42.0.2).

The Stones of Five Colours and the Empress Jokua. Ozaki - JAPANESE 283-296 (A665.2.0.1.1).

The Stones of Plouhinec. Picard - FRENCH 113-119 (N511.6.1).

Stories about Kampen. De Leeuw - LEGENDS.. HOLLAND 46-51 (J1703).

Stories of a Silly Boy. Kavcic - GOLDEN 118-126 (J1193.1; J1853.1.0.1; J1856.1; J2311.1; J2311.2.1; J2311.12).

The Stork Caliph. Courlander - RIDE 66-76 (D155.1.1).

The Storks and the Night Owl. Wiggin - FAIRY 355-366 (D155.1.1).

The Storm Child. Cutt - HOGBOON 103-106 (F329.4.4).

A STORY A STORY - AN AFRICAN TALE. Haley pb (A1481.2.1; K713.1.10; K714.2.6; K741.0.9).

A Story about the Little Rabbits. Brown - WORLD 49-53 (H1023.2.0.1.1); Harris - COM-PLETE 71-74; Harris - UNCLE 108-112.

The Story Bag. Kim - STORY 3-10 (M231.1Bc).

A Story for Sale. Carpenter - KOREAN 183-188 (N612.4).

Story from Tibet. Chang - CHINESE 48-39 (K187).

The Story of a Pumpkin. Guillot - GUILLOT'S 95-97 (A641.3).

The Story of the Old Man Who Made Withered Trees to Flower. Ozaki – JAPANESE 177–188 (D1571.1).

The Story of the Pigs. Harris – COMPLETE 145–148 (K891.11.4); Harris – NIGHTS 38–43.

The Story of the Seven Simons. Lang – FIFTY 304–315 (F660.1C).

The Story of the Seven Stars. Brockett – BURMESE 1–4 (A773.8).

The Story of the Smart Parrot. Jagendorf – KING 242–244 (B211.3.4.1).

The Story of the Stone Hen. Jagendorf – PRICELESS 131–137 (B811.7).

The Story of the Stone Lion. Manning-Sanders – BOOK..MAGICAL 122–129 (J2415.16).

The Story of the Sun Child. Gittins – TALES 60–65 (C322.3).

The Story of the Three Bears. Arbuthnot – ANTHOLOGY 150–151 (N831.1.2); Arbuthnot – FAIRY 8–9; De La Mare – ANIMAL 23–28; Haviland – FAIRY 36–43; Jacobs – ENGLISH 96–101; Martignoni – ILLUSTRATED 69–73; Steel – ENGLISH 13–17; Stobbs – THREE pb.

The Story of the Three Little Pigs. Arbuthnot – ANTHOLOGY 152–153 (K891.1.1); Arbuthnot – FAIRY 10–11; Brooke – STORY..PIGS pb; De La Mare – ANIMAL 16–19; Halliwell – STORY pb; Haviland – FAIRY 22–27; Jacobs – ENGLISH 69–73; Martignoni – ILLUSTRATED 80–82; Wiggin – TALES 215–217.

The Story of the Tortoise and the Monkey. Hume – FAVORITE..CHINA 39–46 (K544; K553.1; K607.1).

The Story of the Weaving Maid. Cheney – TALES 97–106 (A778.3.2).

A Story of Three Brothers. Ure – RUMANIAN 160–166 (Q1.1A).

The Story of Tom Thumb. Reeves – ENGLISH 64–70 (F535.1.1).

The Story of Urashima Taro, the Fisher Lad. Asia – FOLK..THREE 29 (F420.6.1.3.1); Ozaki – JAPANESE 26–42.

The Story of Wali Dad the Simple-Hearted. Buck – FAIRY 19–28 (T53.7).

The Story of Yukpachen. Hardendorff – JUST 116–120 (J1173).

The Story of Zal. Palmer – DRAGONS 79–86 (B535.0.5.1).

The Story of Zirac. Wiggin – TALES 193–196 (K642.2).

The Story Spirits. Williams-Ellis – ROUND 279–288 (M231.1Bc).

The Story-Teller at Fault. Jacobs – CELTIC 144–157 (M231.1Bd).

A Story to Begin With. Grimm – BROTHERS 15–16 (X1791).

The Story Without an End. Withers – WORLD 101–103 (Z11.2).

The Storyteller. Courlander – FIRE 99–102 (H507.2.1; Z11.1); Siddiqui – TOONTOONY 155–157 (Z11.2).

The Stove and the Town Hall. Jagendorf – NOODLEHEAD 189–191 (J1942.1).

The Straight and Narrow Way. Reed – TALKATIVE 22–24 (K511.0.2).

The Strange Adventure of Paddy O'Toole. Manning-Sanders – BOOK..GHOSTS 68–73 (M231A).

The Strange Adventures of Alcavilu. Barlow – LATIN 28–37 (D532D).

The Strange Feathery Beast. Cooper – FIVE 58–75 (K31.1; K171.1).

The Strange Folding Screen. Bang – MEN 79–84 (D435.2.2).

The Strange Indian and His Pack. Cunningham – TALKING 16–18 (A1174.1.1).

Strange Men with Tails. Carpenter – AFRICAN 93–102 (G302.7.1.4).

A Strange Reward. Vittorini – OLD 38–44 (K187).

A STRANGE SERVANT. Galdone pb (K131.1.1).

The Strange Ship of Captain Fokke. Littledale – GHOSTS 125–134 (E511.1.2).

A Strange Sled Race. Thompson – HAWAIIAN.. EARTH 28–32 (A289.2).

The Strange Visitor. Jacobs – ENGLISH 186–189 (Z13.1); Sechrist – HEIGH HO 48–51; Williams-Ellis – FAIRY..BRITISH 132–134.

The Straw Ox. Association – TOLD..GREEN 59–66 (Z32.4.1); Haviland – FAVORITE..RUSSIA 53–65; Hutchinson – FIRESIDE 77–89; Manning-Sanders – BOOK..MAGICAL 8–13; Richardson – GREAT 36–47; Wiggin – TALES 32–35.

The Straw, the Coal and the Bean. Gag – MORE ..TALES 95–98 (A2741.1; F662.3; F1025.1); Grimm – GRIMM'S (Grosset) 214–215; Grimm – GRIMM'S (World) 280–281; Grimm – HOUSE 120–123; Grimm – HOUSEHOLD 98–99; TALL..NURSERY TALES 90–91.

The Strawberries. Hulpac – AMERICAN 131

(A2687.3.1).

The Street Musicians. Association - TOLD..
GREEN 67-73 (K335.1.4).

STREGA NONA. De Paola pb (C916.3).

The Strength of Wind and Sun. Aesop - AESOP'S
(Golden) 63-65 (L351).

Stretch, Puff and Blazer. Bulatkin - EURASIAN
44-56 (F601.2C).

STRIDING SLIPPERS. Ginsburg pb (D1521.1.2).

The String of Lies. Lowe - LITTLE 72-74
(H509.5.3).

The Striped Mouse and the Beetle. Helfman -
BUSHMEN 80-84 (K88.7).

The Strong Bundle of Sticks. Aesop - AESOP'S
(Golden) 52 (J1021).

The Strong Chameleon. Heady - SAFIRI 31-35
(K17.1).

The Strong Man. Caswell - SHADOWS 96-106
(A1145.3; L114.1).

Strong-Man. Martin - NINE 51-54 (F617.4); Martin - RAVEN 61-68.

The Strongest. Deutsch - MORE 39-43 (L392.0.5).

STRONGEST ONE OF ALL. Ginsburg pb
(L392.0.5).

The Stubborn Farmer. Cimino - DISOBEDIENT
#10 (N385.11.2).

Stubborn Husband, Stubborn Wife. Mehdevi -
PERSIAN 93-103 (J2511.0.2).

A Stubborn Man. Duvoisin - THREE 94-100
(C31.4.2.1).

The Stubborn Sillies. Dobbs - ONCE 105-109
(J2511.0.3).

The Student Who Became a Prince. McNeil -
DOUBLE 68-72 (K1952.0.3).

The Stupid Bear. Bowman - TALES..TUPA 257
(K561.0.5).

The Stupid Fellow. Hardendorff - TRICKY 101-
108 (J1852.1.3; J1853.2; K187).

Stupid Head. Manning-Sanders - PRINCES 125-
128 (J2311.15).

The Stupid Nobleman. Kim - STORY 41-43
(J2311.2.0.1).

Stupid Peikko. Bowman - TALES..TUPA 207-219
(G501D).

The Stupid Wolf. Bowman - TALES..TUPA 251-

252 (K1121.2.1).

Stupid's Cries. Jacobs - MORE 211-214
(J2671.2.1).

Sugar-candy House. Frost - LEGENDS 309-312
(B469.4.1; G412.1.2).

SUHO AND THE WHITE HORSE. Otsuka pb
(A1461.1.1).

The Suitor. Hatch - THIRTEEN 73-80 (K1984.1).

The Sultan's Fool. Gilstrap - SULTAN'S 32-39
(X12).

The Summer Birds. Leekley - WORLD 76-78
(A771.0.3).

The Summer Birds of K'yakime. DeWit - TALKING
80-87 (A2411.2.0.3).

The Summer of the Big Snow. Jagendorf - GYP-
SIES' 35-38 (X1653.4.2).

Summer Snow. De Leeuw - LEGENDS..HOLLAND
60-65 (F962.11.2).

Sun and Moon. Field - ESKIMO 14-16 (A736.1.2.1).

Sun and Moon and the Pretty Girl. Withers - MAN
64-66 (H328.7).

The Sun and the Wind. Haviland - FAIRY 100
(L351).

The Sun Callers. Courlander - PEOPLE 126-128
(B755.1).

The Sun-King's Hair. Hampden - GYPSY 35-43
(H1273.2A).

The Sun Man. Helfman - BUSHMEN 48-50
(A714.0.1; A722.5).

The Sun, the Moon and the Star of Morning.
Wilson - GREEK 182-187 (N455.4Ac).

The Sun, the Moon and the Stars. Heady -
TALES 15-20 (A736.1.2.3).

The Sun Will Always Shine. Jagendorf - PRICE-
LESS 92-94 (J1908.1).

The Sunbeam Sprites. Gunterman - CASTLES 61-
80 (D2183.1).

Supply and Demand. Shah - MULLA 124 (U85).

Surprise for the Black Bull. Credle - TALL 115-
121 (K1181.1).

THE SURPRISING THINGS MAUI DID. Williams pb
(A625.2.5; A728.2; A955.8; A1415.0.2.4;
A1908).

Sven and Lilli. Manning-Sanders - BOOK..MER-
MAIDS 9-14 (B81.2.1); Manning-Sanders -
CHOICE 89-94.

The Swallow and Other Birds. Aesop – AESOP'S
(Grosset) 182-183 (J621.1); Aesop – AESOP'S
(Viking) 25-26; Aesop – FABLES (Macmillan) 23.

The Swallowing Monster. Arnott – TEMBA 65-69
(F913.3).

The Swan. Aesop – AESOP'S (Watts) 190
(B752.1).

The Swan and the Stork. Aesop – FIVE 50
(B752.1).

The Swan Geese. Riordan – TALES..CENTRAL
175-178 (Q2.1.2CeA).

The Swan Goose. Whitney – IN A 65-68
(Q2.1.2CeA).

The Swan Maidens. Cunningham – TALKING 98-
104 (D361.1.1; F302.4.2.1.1); Jacobs – EURO-
PEAN 98-104 (H1385.3Fba).

The Swan Princess. Hoke – WITCHES 176-186
(H1385.3F).

Swan White and Fox Tail. McNeil – DOUBLE 106-
114 (Q2.1.5Bbb).

The Swans of Ballycastle. Association – CASTLE
259-289 (D161.1).

Sweet Misery. Courlander – PIECE 37-38
(A2494.1.2.4).

The Sweet Porridge. Gag – MORE..GRIMM 43-46
(C916.3); Grimm – GRIMM'S (Follett) 320-321.

The Sweet Punishment. Edmonds – POSSIBLE 13-
23 (J2311.2.2).

The Sweet Soup. Wiggin – TALES 137 (C916.3).

Sweetheart Roland. Grimm – GRIMM'S (Grosset)
62-66 (G530.2Da); Grimm – GRIMM'S (Watts) 99-
103.

The Sweetest Song in the Woods. Jagendorf –
KING 132-135 (A1461.8.2).

Swen-Naba, King of the Warlocks. Guirma –
TALES 85-99 (A1141.8.4).

Swift-Runner and Trickster Tarantula. Brown –
TEPEE 115-123 (A2091.3).

The Swineherd. Holme – TALES 99-103 (K1816.6);
Lang – FIFTY 316-321; Opie – CLASSIC 230-
235.

The Swollen Fox. Aesop – AESOP'S (Watts) 56
(K1022.0.2).

The Sword That Fought By Itself. Courlander –
HAT 88-92 (A2796.1; D1651.2.1).

Sworn on the Odin Stone. Cutt – HOGBOON 46-
50 (E321.6).

Sylvester. Manning-Sanders – RED 42-48
(K1931.2L).

Sze-Ma Gwang, the Quick One. Alexander –
PEBBLES 16 (J1687).

The Tabby Who Was Such a Glutton. Asbjørnsen
– NORWEGIAN 161-167 (Z33.2).

The Table, the Ass and the Cudgel. Grimm –
HOUSE 56-80 (D861.1; K1151; Z39.1).

The Table, the Ass and the Stick. Grimm –
GRIMM'S (Grosset) 228-242 (D861.1; K1151;
Z39.1); Grimm – GRIMM'S (Scribner's) 104-116;
Grimm – GRIMM'S (World) 130-141; Grimm –
HOUSEHOLD 149-159; Wiggin – FAIRY 163-173.

The Table, the Donkey and the Cudgel. Grimm –
GRIMM'S (Follett) 323-329 (D861.1; K1151;
Z39.1).

THE TABLE, THE DONKEY AND THE STICK. Galdone pb (D861.1).

The Tail. Hardendorff – JUST 29 (Z12.1); Wiggin
– TALES 54; Withers – I SAW 71.

The Tail of St. George's Dragon. Courlander –
RIDE 92-94 (X904.4).

The Tail of the Cat. Lowe – LITTLE 81-83
(Z47.3).

The Tailless Jackal. Mehdevi – PERSIAN 22-32
(J758.1.0.1).

The Tailor and the Fairies. Colwell – ROUND 51-
53 (F369.7).

The Tailor and the Hare Woman. Danaher – FOLK-
TALES 52-58 (G211.2.7.2).

The Tailor From the Sea. Jagendorf – NOODLE-
HEAD 192-195 (J1909.8.3).

The Tailor in the Church. Manning-Sanders –
BOOK..GHOSTS 43-46 (H1412.2).

The Tailor of Rathkeale. Danaher – FOLKTALES
63-76 (K1951.1D).

The Tailor Who Went to Heaven. Gag – MORE..
GRIMM 117-122 (F1037.1.1).

The Tailor's Bright Daughter. Carpenter – ELE-
PHANT'S 195-203 (H1021.13; K1814.5).

THE TAILYPO. Galdone pb (E235.4.3.2).

Take Along the Little Cat. Leach – LION 8-9
(J2215.4.0.2).

Take Four from Four. Ginsburg – THREE 23-
(J2213.10).

Take Up the Slack. Harris – COMPLETE 83-87

(K22.2); Harris – FAVORITE 95–99; Harris – UNCLE – 126–131.

Takes After His Father. Shah – MULLA 91 (T615.1.1).

Taking a Sacrifice to Heaven. Fuja – FOURTEEN 64–68 (A2317.7.1).

The Tale of a Foolish Brother and of a Wonderful Bush. Manning-Sanders – RED 132–138 (H331.1.1F; R222.1A).

The Tale of a Frog. Withers – I SAW 120–121 (Z49.18).

The Tale of a Pakistan Parrot. Siddiqui – TOON-TOONY 114–123 (K1346.0.1).

The Tale of Bat. Chafetz – THUNDERBIRD 15–26 (A1341.4).

The Tale of Chanticleer. Green – BIG 158–164 (K561.1.0.3; K721).

The Tale of Ivan. Jacobs – CELTIC 212–216 (J21Aa).

A Tale of Naxos. Neufeld – BEWARE 22–27 (J1199.3).

The Tale of Princess Kaguya. MacAlpine – JA-PANESE 127–187 (A240.1.1; A753.1.3; A966.2).

The Tale of Tao. Asia – FOLK..FOUR 47–53 (A625.2.11).

The Tale of the Balaton. Baker – TALKING 191–198 (A920.1.17).

The Tale of the Dog's Skin. Arnott – ANIMAL 71–75 (J1762.2.3.2).

The Tale of the Earl of Mar's Daughter. Leodhas – BY LOCH 44–52 (H1385.5Af).

Tale of the Good, Gay Lady. Jagendorf – KING 236–238 (V400.2).

The Tale of the Gypsy and His Strange Love. Jagendorf – GYPSIES' 93–101 (D621.0.2).

The Tale of the Lazy People. Finger – TALES 159–173 (A1861.3.1).

The Tale of the Men of Prach. Jagendorf – NOO-DLEHEAD 241–243 (J2287.1).

The Tale of the Silver Saucer and the Transpar-ent Apple. Ransome – OLD PETER'S 18–39 (E632.0.4).

The Tale of the Superman. Arnott – AFRICAN 43–55 (A1142.9.0.1).

A Tale of the Tontlawald. Lang – VIOLET 1–16 (F582.1.1).

A Tale of Two Frogs. Carey – BABA 58–60

(Q81.2).

A Tale of Two Rascals. Brockett – BURMESE 96–105 (K1956.2; N611.1.1).

The Tale the Crofter Told. Leodhas – GHOSTS 43–53 (E323.1.1.2).

Tales from Tartari-Barbari. Jagendorf – NOODLE-HEAD 142–146 (J1155.2).

The Talisman. Courlander – RIDE 166–168 (N135.3).

The Talisman Knife. Cutt – HOGBOON 134–139 (F420.6.1.1.2).

Talk. Courlander – COW-TAIL 25–29 (B210.1.1); Gruenberg – FAVORITE 354–357; Leach – THING 49–50 (B210.2.3).

The Talkative King. Ross – BURIED 75–80 (J2357).

The Talkative Tortoise. Gaer – FABLES..INDIA 162–164 (J2357); Jacobs – INDIAN 123–125.

The Talkative Turtle. Davis – LION'S 189–191 (J2357).

The Talking Boat. Cimino – DISOBEDIENT #6 (K1971.6.2).

The Talking Fish. Tashjian – ONCE 41–99 (B375.1.4; H543).

The Talking House. Heady – JAMBO 72–77 (K607.1).

The Talking Nightingale. Mittleman – BIRD 67–81 (N455.4Ab).

The Talking Pot. Arbuthnot – ANTHOLOGY 235–236 (D1605.1); Hatch – THIRTEEN 16–24.

The Talking Skull. Frobenius – AFRICAN 161–162 (B210.2.3).

The Talking Stone. Cunningham – TALKING 3–15 (A1481.2.2); DeWit – TALKING 5–9.

The Talking Tree. Baker – TALKING 9–17 (D215.9).

The Tall Cornstalk. Chase – GRANDFATHER 186–194 (X1204.2; X1235.2.3; A1236.1.1; X1402.3.1).

Tall Hog. Leach – NOODLES 65 (K196.2).

Tall Peter and Short Peter. Maas – MOON 47–55 (B582.2E).

A Tall Turnip. Credle – TALL 30–33 (X1401.1.2).

Tam Lin. Wilson – SCOTTISH 91–95 (F324.3.1).

Tamlane. Harper – GHOSTS 90–94 (F324.3.1); Jacobs – MORE 172–176; Williams-Ellis – FAIRY..BRITAIN 263–271.

Tandala and Pakala. Jagendorf - NOODLEHEAD 222-226 (J1516).

Taper Tom. Asbjørnsen - EAST (Row) 77-84 (H341.1Aa); Haviland - NORWAY 50-64.

Taper Tom Who Made the Princess Laugh. Asbjørnsen - NORWEGIAN 20-24 (H341.1Aa).

The Tar Baby. Haviland - NORTH 109-114 (A2233.1.1; K581.10; K741.0.3.2).

The Tar Baby Tricks Brer Rabbit. Faulkner - DAY 122-127 (A2233.1.1; K581.2; K741.0.3).

The Tarasque: The Terror of Nerluc. Holman - DRAC 41-55 (B11.11.7).

Tarn Wethelan. Garner - CAVALCADE..GOBLINS 116-125 (H775).

The Tatema. Wolkstein - LAZY pb (N182.4).

Tattercoats. Arbuthnot - ANTHOLOGY 158-159 (R221Z); Arbuthnot - FAIRY 19-21; Finlay - TATTERCOATS 1-8; Jacobs - MORE 67-72; Reeves - ENGLISH 12-22; Steel - ENGLISH 39-43; Wiggin - FAIRY 109-113.

Tatterhood. Aulaire - EAST 179-187 (L145.1); Manning-Sanders - BOOK..WITCHES 94-103; Manning-Sanders - CHOICE 246-255.

Tayzanne. Wolkstein - MAGIC 57-64 (B610.1.1.2).

Tcakabesh Snares the Sun. Withers - MAN 79-80 (A728.0.1).

The Tea House in the Forest. Novak - FAIRY 138-144 (E423.8.2).

The Tea-Kettle. Hearn - JAPANESE 69-79 (D1171.3.1); Manning-Sanders - MAGICAL 130-137.

Teaching Baby Crab to Walk. Burton - MAGIC 71 (U121.1).

Teardrop Dragon. Chang - CHINESE 20-21 (B11.6.1.4).

Tecle's Goat. Courlander - FIRE 93-98 (B210.1.2).

Teeny-Tiny. Harper - Ghosts 225-227 (E235.4.3); Hutchinson - FIRESIDE 3-6; Jacobs - ENGLISH 57-58; Rockwell - THREE 78-80; Sechrist - HEIGH-HO 46-47; Williams-Ellis - FAIRY..BRITAIN 30-31; Withers - I SAW 59-61.

THE TEENY TINY WOMAN. Seuling pb (E235.4.3).

Teeth and No-Teeth. Hardendorff - JUST 133-134 (J234).

Tell Me, When Will I Die? Walker - WATERMELONS 13-23 (J2133.4; J2311.4; J2311.6; J2311.7).

Telling the Horses Apart - Leach - NOODLES 21 (J2722).

Temba Becomes a Warrior. Arnott - TEMBA 116-123 (K251.1.4).

Temba Wins a Bride. Arnott - TEMBA 124-144 (H335.7.1).

Temba's Bag of Salt. Arnott - TEMBA 107-115 (K1084.1.3).

Temba's Magic Boat. Arnott - TALES..TEMBA 44-51 (D931.0.7).

Temba's Monkey Friends. Arnott - TEMBA 70-77 (B441.1.0.1).

The Ten Dwarfs of Aunt Greenwater. Lowe - LITTLE 27-29 (Q321.2.2).

Ten Jugs of Wine. Kendall - SWEET 18-20 (K231.6.1.1).

The Tengu's Magic Nose Fan. Uchida - SEA 33-41 (D1376.1.3).

Tepozton. Brenner - BOY 28-33 (A511.2.2.3); Frost - LEGENDS 190-199.

Terrapin Escapes from the Wolves. Bell - JOHN 80-83 (A2312.1.6; K581.1; K1715.3.3).

Terrapin's Pot of Sense. Courlander - TERRAPIN'S 24-27 (A1481.1; A2312.1.4; A2441.4.5.1).

The Terrible Black Snake's Revenge. Uchida - SEA 112-120 (K602.3).

The Terrible Carlanco. Sawyer - PICTURE 63-74 (K311.3B).

The Terrible Leak. Uchida - MAGIC 12-21 (K619.4; N392.1.1).

THE TERRIBLE NUNG GUAMA. Young pb (K1161.3.2).

The Terrible Olli. Fenner - GIANTS 162-173 (G610Ag); Fillmore - SHEPHERD'S 53-63; Gruenberg - FAVORITE 380-387.

The Terrible Stranger. Fenner - ADVENTURES 162-178 (M221).

The Terrible Tempered Dragon. Hoke - DRAGONS 223-230 (B11.12.7.1); Palmer - DRAGONS 46-54.

The Terror of the Ogres. Ure - RUMANIAN 101-113 (G501C).

Tésin, My Good Friend. Thoby-Marcelin - SINGING 104-111 (B610.1.1.1).

The Test. Wojciechowska - WINTER 22-31 (H633; H653.3; H1053.2; H1054.1; H1056; H1057; J1191.1; J1545.4).

Test of a Friendship. Walker - DANCING 80-83 (K419.5.1).

A Test of Skill. Arnott - AFRICAN 40-42 (F621;

F636+; F660.1Eb; F684).

Teutli, the Mountain That Is Alive. Brenner –
BOY 23-26 (A962.1.2).

The Texas Sandstorm. Courlander – TERRAPIN'S
65-66 (X1611.1.10.1).

Thao Kham the Pebble-shooter. Asia – FOLK..1
32-36 (F661.13).

That Fourth Leg of the Dog. Vo-Dinh – TOAD 75-
80 (A2473.1).

That Other Leg. Kelsey – HODJA 86-92 (K402.1).

The Theft of Dawn. Curry – DOWN 38-47
(A721.1.2; A1425.0.1.1).

The Theft of Fire. Cunningham – TALKING 33-
36 (A1415.0.2.5); Curry – DOWN 51-67
(A1415.2.2.2); DeWit – TALKING 49-51
(A1415.2.0.2.6); Leekley – WORLD 11-19
(A1415.0.2.5).

Theoretical Instances. Shah – MULLA 118
(W211.4).

There Are Such People. Jagendorf – NOODLE-
HEAD 34-36 (J2511.0.1).

There Is More Light Here. Shah – MULLA 24
(J1925).

There's Always a Left and a Right. Simon – WISE
43-54 (J1964.0.1).

There's No Telling On Which Side a Camel Will Lie
Down. Reed – TALKATIVE 78 (J1511.6.1).

Thi Kinh. Graham – BEGGAR 23-31 (T210.1.1).

The Thief. Daniels – FALCON 56-60 (K301Ah;
K305.1; K341.3).

The Thief and the Boy. Aesop – AESOP'S (Grosset) 187-188 (K345.2).

The Thief and the Dog. Aesop – AESOP'S (Grosset) 217 (K2062).

The Thief and the Innkeeper. Aesop – AESOP'S
(Watts) 156 (K335.0.4.1).

The Thief in the King's Treasury. Neufeld –
BEWARE 58-67 (K301C).

THE THIEF WHO HUGGED A MOONBEAM. Berson
pb (K1054).

The Thief Who Kept His Hands Clean. Kendall –
SWEET 30-32 (J1141.10.2).

The Thief's Goat. Korel – LISTEN 27-31
(K451.2.1).

Thievery. Kendall – SWEET 78-79 (J2092.3).

The Thieves and the Cock. Aesop – AESOP'S
(Watts) 47 (U33.1).

The Thieving Dragon. Arnott – ANIMAL 66-70
(G501A).

The Thing at the Foot of the Bed. Leach – THING
15-16 (J1782.8).

The Thirteen Flies. Manning-Sanders – JONNIKIN
47-53 (D882.1Fc).

Thirteenth. Hampden – HOUSE 11-16 (G610Ab).

The Thirteenth Son of the King of Erin. Manning-
Sanders – DRAGONS 87-94 (R111.1.3Bb).

Thirty Reasons. Cimino – DISOBEDIENT
(J1552.2.1).

Thirty-two Teeth. Hardendorff – JUST 19
(J1749.3).

This For That. Aardema – BEHIND 48-56
(A2233.1.1; K251.1.6).

This Is How It Began. Jagendorf – MERRY 6-16
(J2123; K1413).

Thomas the Rhymer. Baker – GOLDEN 148-160
(F329.1); Wilson – SCOTTISH 8-17.

Thor and the Giants. De Regniers – GIANT 94-
105 (F531.6.15.1.1).

Thorn Rose, the Sleeping Beauty. Gag – MORE..
GRIMM 31-41 (D1960.3); Grimm – THORN pb.

The Thoroughbred. Deutsch – TALES 44-51
(K172.0.2).

Those Who Quarreled. Sechrist – ONCE 80-82
(J461.9).

A Thousand Pieces of Gold. Gilstrap – SULTAN'S
40-50 (J123).

A Thousand Thoughts. Ginsburg – THREE 34-36
(J1662.2).

Thousands and Thousands of Ducks. Withers – I
SAW 52 (Z11.0.2).

Thousands of Ideas. Carey – BABA (J1662.2).

The Thread of Life. Vittorini – OLD 79-88
(E765.3.6).

The Three Animal Servants. Arnott – ANIMAL
112-121 (A2494.1.2.1; D882.1B).

The Three Animals Who Went to the Law. Brockett – BURMESE 51-63 (D882.1.1.1; H621.3).

The Three Aunts. Aulaire – EAST 216-221
(D2183.1); Martignoni – ILLUSTRATED 243-245.

The Three Bears. Brooke – GOLDEN (N831.1.2);
Colwell – YOUNGEST 44-50; Galdone – THREE
pb; Gruenberg – FAVORITE 273-275;

Hutchinson - FIRESIDE 27-32; Lang - GREEN 222-226; Rackham - ARTHUR 200-205; Richardson - GREAT 27-35; Rockwell - THREE 1-13; TALL..NURSERY TALES 37-45; Tarrant - FAIRY 9-19.

The Three Big Sillies. TALL..NURSERY TALES 98-104 (H1312.1; J2063; J2132.2; J2161.1).

The Three Billy Goats Bruse. Löfgren - BOY 29-31 (K553.2).

The Three Billy-Goats Gruff. Arbuthnot - ANTHOLOGY 237 (K553.2); Arbuthnot - FAIRY 72-73; Asbjørnsen - EAST (Macmillan) 17-19; Asbjørnsen - EAST (Row) 17-19; Asbjørnsen - THREE (Harcourt) pb; Asbjørnsen - THREE (McGraw) pb; Asbjørnsen - THREE (Seabury) pb; Association - TOLD..GREEN 21-23; Haviland - FAIRY 56-57; Haviland - FAVORITE.. NORWAY 45-49; Hutchinson - FIRESIDE 35-39; Richardson - GREAT 122-128; Rockwell - THREE 56-62; TALL..NURSERY TALES 46-48.

Three Bits of Advice. Pugh - MORE..WELSH 107-114 (J21Af).

Three Bridegrooms For One Bride. Masey - STORIES 16-27 (T92.0.1.1).

The Three Brothers. Gag - TALES..GRIMM 171-176 (F660.1); Grimm - GRIMM'S (Follett) 340-343; Wiggin - TALES 72-73; Withers - WORLD 55-56 (F660.1B).

The Three Brothers. Lang - YELLOW 152-155 (H1331.1.3Cb).

The Three Brothers. Novak - FAIRY 54-60 (E373.1.2).

The Three Brothers and the Giant. De Regniers - GIANT 49-59 (K1611F).

The Three Brothers and the Marvelous Things. Alegría - THREE 15-24 (H355.0.1).

The Three Bushy Billy Goats. Aulaire - EAST 175-178 (K553.2).

The Three Butchers from Reims. Cooper - FIVE 26-40 (K1655).

The Three Butterflies. Pugh - MORE..WELSH 13-28 (D882.1Fa).

The Three Chests. Fillmore - SHEPHERD'S 40-52 (D1520.10.2; E82.1; G561.1C).

The Three Children of Fortune. De La Mare - ANIMAL 128-132 (N411.1); Grimm - GRIMM'S (Grosset) 23-26 (J2101); Grimm - GRIMM'S (World) 99-102.

The Three Citrons. Mincielli - OLD 108-120 (D721.5).

The Three Clever Brothers. Spicer - THIRTEEN DEVILS 82-90 (G303.16.19.3.6).

The Three Companions. De Leeuw - INDONESIAN 56-57 (Z111.7).

The Three-Cornered Hat. Cothran - MAGIC 55-59 (K111.2).

The Three Cows. Jacobs - MORE 89-91 (F243.3.1.1).

The Three Cranberries. Bierhorst - FIRE 41-42 (J641.2).

The Three Cups of Water. Durham - TIT 41-42 (J1341.7).

Three Daughters. Ginsburg - KAHA 53-54 (A2012.0.1.1).

The Three Deaf Men. Ure - RUMANIAN 145-146 (X111.1.3).

The Three Dogs. Lang - GREEN 350-355 (R111.1.3Eb); Manning-Sanders - DRAGONS 114-122.

The Three Dogs. Thoby-Marcelin - SINGING 57-65 (B524.1.2C).

The Three Dwarfs. Lang - RED 252-259 (Q2.1.4B).

The Three Enchanted Princes. Mincielli - OLD 73-83 (B314D).

Three Fables: The Little Chest. Wyndham - TALES..RUSSIA 71-73 (J253).

The Three Fairies. Arbuthnot - ANTHOLOGY 403-407 (D2183.1); Carter - GREEDY 106-111.

Three Fast Men. Courlander - KING'S 17-18 (F660.1.2).

Three Fat Ewes for Three Fine Hounds. Leodhas - SEA SPELL 73-85 (S12.1.0.1Ba).

The Three Fates. Wilson - GREEK 214-221 (K1355).

The Three Feathers. Grimm - JUNIPER v.1 3-10 (B641.0.1Ad); Finlay TATTERCOATS 28-36; Jacobs - MORE 37-42 (H1385.4B); Shub - ABOUT 58-61; Steel - ENGLISH 43-51; Wiggin - FAIRY 208-212.

The Three Figs. Belpré - TIGER 123-127 (J2415.1).

The Three Fish and the Fishermen. Montgomerie - TWENTY-FIVE 18-19 (K522.4.1).

The Three Foolish Brides. Kim - STORY 56-57 (J2463.3).

The Three Fools. Vittorini - OLD 55-61 (H1312.2).

Three Fridays. Kelsey - HODJA 21-28 (X452).

The Three Friends. Brockett - BURMESE 191-194

(K642.2); Dolch - OLD RUSSIA (K11.12; K444); Wyatt - GOLDEN 22-26.

Three Friends and a Treasure. Walker - NIGERIAN 44-45 (K1685).

The Three Gifts. Chang - TALES..OLD CHINA 37-45 (D861.1D).

The Three Gluttons and the Hunter. Withers - WORLD 65-66 (W125.6).

The Three Goats. Association - TOLD..GREEN 78-80 (Z39.1); Wiggin - TALES 442-443 (K553.2).

THREE GOLD PIECES: A GREEK FOLKTALE. Aliki pb (J21Ab).

The Three Golden Ducats. Spicer - OWL'S 74-85 (G303.12.5.8).

The Three Golden Eggs. MacManus - HIBERNIAN 25-35 (H1385.5Ae); MacManus - WELL 31-48.

The Three Golden Hairs. Carle - ERIC 25-38 (H1273.2A); Fillmore - SHEPHERD'S 119-133.

The Three Golden Hairs of Grandad Sol. Bulatkin - EURASIAN 9-21 (H1273.2A).

The Three Golden Hairs of Grandfather Know All. Haviland - FAVORITE..CZECHOSLOVAKIA 67-90 (H1273.2A).

The Three Golden Hairs of the Devil. Grimm - BROTHERS 170-177 (H1273.2A).

The Three Golden Hairs of the King of the Cave Giants. Manning-Sanders - BOOK..GIANTS 107-117 (H1273.2A).

The Three Golden Heads. Finlay - TATTERCOATS 78-86 (Q2.1.1Ba).

Three Golden Oranges. Boggs - THREE 17-35 (D721.5); Sheehan - FOLK 61-71.

The Three Goslings. Haviland - FAVORITE.. ITALY 67-77 (K891.1.1.3).

The Three Heads in the Well. Jacobs - ENGLISH 232-237 (Q2.1.1Ba); Opie - CLASSIC 156-161; Sheehan - FOLK 1-7; Steel - ENGLISH 156-163.

The Three Horses. Frost - LEGEND 273-277 (H331.1.1A).

Three Hundred and Sixty-Five Children. Frost - LEGENDS 183-185 (V429.3).

The Three Hunters. Hardendorff - TRICKY 23-25 (Z19.2.3); Withers - I SAW 77 (X1791.2).

The Three Ivans. Manning-Sanders - SORCEROR'S 69-90 (R111.1.3Ae).

The Three Kings Ride. Sawyer - WAY 151-170 (N816.1).

Three Knots. Ginsburg - LAZIES 21-45 (D2142.1.2).

The Three Languages. Gag - MORE..GRIMM 89-94 (B217.9); Müller-Guggenbühl - SWISS 177-180; Grimm - GRIMM'S (Watts) 29-31.

The Three Lemons. Manning-Sanders - GLASS 146-158 (D721.5B).

The Three Little Girls. Kim - STORY 76-82 (A736.4.1; A2793.8.1; K311.3I).

The Three Little Men in the Wood. Grimm - GRIMM'S (World) 273-279 (Q2.1.4B); Grimm - HOUSEHOLD 76-81; Manning-Sanders - DWARFS 78-83.

The Three Little Pigs. Association - TOLD.. GREEN 5-9 (K891.1.1); Brooke - GOLDEN pb; DuBois - THREE pb; Galdone - THREE pb; Lang - GREEN 106-110; Richardson - GREAT 59-65; Rockwell - THREE 89-91; Steel - ENGLISH 122-127; TALL..NURSERY TALES 110-116; Williams-Ellis - FAIRY 39-43.

The Three Luck Children. Grimm - GRIMM'S (Follett) 344-348 (N411.1); Wiggin - TALES 98-100.

The Three Lucky Ones. Gag - MORE..GRIMM 189-196 (N411.1B; J2101).

The Three Magi. Belpré - TIGER 105-111 (N816.1).

The Three Men of Power—Evening, Midnight and Sunrise. Ransome - OLD PETER 269-293 (K1931.2F).

Three Men on the Bridge. Jagendorf - MERRY 25-30 (J2062.1).

The Three Mermaids. Manning-Sanders - BOOK.. MERMAIDS 25-35 (Q2.1.1Cb); Manning-Sanders - CHOICE 280-290.

The Three Monsters of the Sea. Berry - MAGIC 30-44 (B364.4J).

The Three Musicians. Lang - GREEN 342-349 (K1931.2M).

The Three Oranges. Picard - FRENCH 198-204 (H112; H346).

The Three Pennies. Wyndham - FOLK 98-101 (D2100.2.1).

The Three Petitions. Belpré - TIGER 119-121 (J2075).

The Three Pigs. Hutchinson - CHIMNEY 53-60 (K891.1.1).

The Three Precious Packets. Birch - CHINESE 48-54 (J21C).

The Three Princes and Their Beasts. Lang - VIOLET 34-45 (R111.1.3An; S12.1.0.1D).

The Three Princesses. Kim – STORY 154-165 (K1931.2N).

The Three Princesses and the Unclean Spirit. Manning-Sanders – RED 169-173 (H1199.12.4A).

The Three Princesses In the Blue Mountain . Asbjørnsen – EAST (Macmillan) 76-99 (K1931.2H).

The Three Princesses in the Mountain So Blue. Asbjørnsen – EAST (Doubleday) 85-108 (K1931.2H); Asbjørnsen – NORWEGIAN 31-48; Aulaire – EAST 153-174.

The Three Princesses of Connaught. Fenner – PRINCESSES 11-28 (K1931.2K).

The Three Princesses of Whiteland. Asbjørnsen – EAST (Doubleday) 61-70 (H1385.3B) ; Asbjørnsen – EAST (Macmillan) 100-108 ; Asbjørnsen – EAST (Row) 20-27; Fenner – PRINCESSES 168-176; Lang – RED 180-187.

Three Questions. Kelsey – HODJA 100-107 (H681.3.1; H702.2.1; H703.1).

The Three Ravens. Manning-Sanders – GIANNI 54-61 (L425B); Müller-Guggenbühl – SWISS 166-170 (P253.2G).

The Three Rings. Vittorini – OLD 92-95 (J462.3.1.1).

Three Rolls and One Doughnut. Ginsburg – THREE 7 (J2213.3).

The Three Sillies. De La Mare – TALES 125-130 (H1312.1; J1791.3; J1904.1; J2063; J2161.1); Front – THREE pb; Jacobs – ENGLISH 10-15; Jacobs – THREE pb; Rockwell – OLD 10-22; Steel – ENGLISH 43-78; Wiggin – TALES 218-221; Williams-Ellis – FAIRY 249-254; Zemach – THREE pb.

Three Silly Schoolmasters. Carpenter – ELEPHANT'S 125-134 (J1712; J2516.3.2; W111.5.8).

The Three Silver Balls. Manning-Sanders – BOOK..GHOSTS 111-118 (G561.2C).

The Three Sisters Who Were Entrapped Into a Mountain. Minard – WOMENFOLK 156-163 (G561.1A).

Three Skillful Men. Withers – WORLD 60 (F660.1.1).

The Three Sluggards. Wiggin – TALES 101 (W111.1).

Three Snake Leaves. Lang – GREEN 288-292 (K2213.5.1).

The Three Sneezes. Duvoisin – THREE 3-7 (J2133.4; J2311.1).

The Three Soldiers. Jacobs – EUROPEAN 72-80 (D551.1Bc).

Three Sons of a Chief. Courlander – KING'S 50 (F660.1.1Eb).

Three Sons of Gorla. Wilson – SCOTTISH 137-147 (H1199.12.5).

The Three Spinners. Gag – MORE..GRIMM 131-137 (D2183.1).

The Three Spinning Fairies. Grimm – GRIMM'S (Grosset) 18-22 (D2183.1); Grimm – GRIMM'S (World) 326-329.

The Three Spinsters. Grimm – HOUSEHOLD 82-84 (D2183.1).

Three Strong Women. Minard – WOMENFOLK 93-105 (F617.2.1); Stamm – THREE pb.

The Three Suitors. Davis – LION'S 179 (H621.2.2); McNeil – DOUBLE 57-61 (H621.2.6).

The Three Tailors and the White Goose. Hatch – THIRTEEN 58-72 (D161.2.1).

Three Tales of the Mouse-Deer. De Leeuw – INDONESIAN #1, 68-74 (K1023.1; K1023.1.1; K1023.1.2; K1023.1.3); #2, 74-77 (K1931.2I); #3, 77-80 (K543.0.1; K579.2.1; K607.2; K652.1).

The Three Tasks. MacManus – HIBERNIAN 202-211 (G530.2Fa).

The Three Tasks. Walker – NIGERIAN 57-58 (H369; K263.3; Z11.1).

The Three Tests. Kavcic – GOLDEN 71-77 (H1055; J151.1; K52.1).

Three Tests for the Prince. Uchida – MAGIC 53-62 (H328.10).

The Three Tradesmen. Aesop – AESOP'S (Grosset) 219-220 (W197.2); Aesop – AESOP'S (Watts) 110.

Three Unscrupulous Men. Burton – MAGIC 104-105 (K1685).

The Three Walnuts. Wilson – GREEK 157-165 (K1931.2D).

The Three Wasted Wishes. Perrault – FAMOUS (Watts) 127-134 (J2075).

Three Ways to Build a House. Wiggin – TALES 177-181 (K891.1.1.1).

Three Who Couldn't Be Parted. Robertson – FAIRY..VIETNAM 89-92 (A2691.5).

Three Who Found Their Hearts' Desire. Jewett – WHICH 136-157 (K335.1.1.4).

The Three Wishes. Alegría – THREE 76-79 (J2075); Dobbs – ONCE 86-90; Galdone – THREE pb; Gruenberg – FAVORITE 344-346; Jacobs – MORE 107-109; Jewett – WHICH 104-108; Opie – CLASSIC 151-155; TALL..NURSERY TALES 85-

89; Wiggin – TALES 7-9.

The Three Wishes. Spicer – LONG 98-115 (Q1.1A).

Three Wonderful Beggars. Lang – VIOLET 22-33 (H1273.2F).

The Three Young Men Who Told Tall Stories. Brockett – BURMESE 79-83 (X905.1.4).

The Thrifty Soldier. Owen – CASTLE 13-24 (K213A).

The Throne of Tagaung. Keeley – CITY 13-32 (J21B).

Through the Eyes. Lin – MILKY 51-56 (X941.4.1).

Through the Needle's Eye. Leach – NOODLES 83 (D1181.1).

Throw Mountains. Courlander – COW-TAIL 113-118 (A920.1.2; A934.1; A963.11; A983.1; B264.7).

Throwmount and Oakpull. Borski – GOOD 29-33 (B535.0.15.1).

Thud. Chang – CHINESE 38-40 (Z43.3.1).

Thumb-sized Thomas. Kavcic – GOLDEN 87-92 (F535.1.1.11).

Thumbelina. Holme – TALES 13-20 (F535.1.1F); Lang – YELLOW 283-296; Opie – CLASSIC 219-229.

Thumbkin. Jacobs – EUROPEAN 194-200 (F535.1.1B); Manning-Sanders – DWARFS 42-48.

Thumbling. Grimm – GRIMM'S (Scribner's) 117-123 (F535.1.1B).

Thumbling the Dwarf and Thumbling the Giant. Adams – BOOK..GIANTS 134-144 (F615.3A); Grimm – GRIMM'S (Grosset) 54-61 (F615.3.1.3); Grimm – GRIMM'S (World) 194-201.

Thunder and Lightning. Arnott – AFRICAN 32-34 (A1141.8.2).

Thunder and Lightning. Field – ESKIMO 18-20 (A1142.3.2).

Thunder and Mosquito. Newell – RESCUE 69-74 (A1141.8.2).

Thunder, Elephant and Dorobo. Harman – TALES 19-28 (F434.1).

Thunderbird. Chafetz – THUNDERBIRD 3-13 (A284.2.1); DeWit – TALKING 27-33.

Thunderbird. Cunningham – TALKING 24-29 (D1960.1.1).

Ti-Tiriti-Ti. Baker – GOLDEN 89-100 (D1563.1.4.1; H328.8).

The Ticklish Thief. Holding – THE SKY-EATER 111-124 (A941.5.9).

Ticky Picky Boom-Boom. Sherlock – ANANSI 76-83 (D983.2.1).

Ticoumba and the President. Courlander – PIECE 58-61 (J1161.3.2).

The Tiger and the Bulls. Aesop – AESOP'S (Viking) 34 (J102.2).

The Tiger and the Frog. Hardendorff – JUST 58-63 (K1715.12.2).

The Tiger and the Puppy. Carpenter – KOREAN 67-72 (L351.2.1).

The Tiger and the Rabbit. Belpré – TIGER 11-18 (K713.1.1; K1051.0.1; K1241); Kim – STORY 58-65 (K553.1.0.6; K1021; K1043.2).

The Tiger Hunter and the Mirror. Carpenter – KOREAN 255-258 (J1795.3.1).

The Tiger in Court. Hume – FAVORITE..CHINA 74-78 (B431.3.1).

Tiger in the Forest, Anansi in the Web. Sherlock – WEST 59-64 (A2433.5.3.3; K1066.5).

The Tiger in the Palanquin. Siddiqui – TOON-TOONY 32-36 (J1565.1.4; K714.2.4.3).

The Tiger of Kumgang Mountains. Kim – STORY 199-214 (F912.2.12).

Tiger Story, Anansi Story. Sherlock – WEST 45-58 (H1481.2.1).

The Tiger, the Brahman and the Jackal. Arbuthnot – ANTHOLOGY 350 (J1172.3; J1172.3.2); Arbuthnot – FAIRY 164-166; Bleecker – BIG 135-138; Buck – FAIRY 168-177; Haviland – FAVORITE..INDIA 83-90; Jacobs – INDIAN 81-85; Steel – TIGER pb.

The Tiger Witch. Cheney – TALES 122-132 (K311.3H).

Tiger Woman. Association – CASTLE 243-257 (B651.9); Jewett – WHICH 29-40.

The Tiger's Minister of State. Courlander – TIGER'S 20-27 (J811.2.1).

The Tiger's Stripes. Vo-Dinh – TOAD 65-73 (A2413.4; K341.8.1.0.1).

The Tiger's Tail. Courlander – KANTCHIL'S 18-21 (X459.2); Gruenberg – FAVORITE 396-397.

The Tiger's Teacher. Chang – CHINESE 30 (A2581).

The Tiger's War against Borneo. Courlander – KANTCHIL'S 22-27 (K1711.1).

The Tiger's Whisker. Courlander – TIGER'S 16-

19 (B848.2.1).

The Tikgi Birds. Sechrist – ONCE 86-90 (D366).

Tim for Wealth and Happiness. Guirma – TALES 100-113 (H588.7.4).

Time. Courlander – COW-TAIL 73-77 (Z122.0.1).

Time for Everything. Deutsch – MORE 85-93 (J2461.2F).

A Time of Deep Darkness. Thompson – HAWAIIAN ..EARTH 11-14 (A617.2).

The Time of the Ugly. Wojieckowska – WINTER 61-65 (J1795.1.2).

Timimoto. Manning-Sanders – DWARFS 104-108 (F535.1.1E).

Timo and the Princess Vendla. Arbuthnot – AN-THOLOGY 262-263 (H342.2); Bowman – TALES.. TUPA 91-95; Fenner – PRINCESSES 148-153.

Timothy and the Buggane Ghost. Spicer – THIR-TEEN..GHOSTS 112-119 (H1412.2).

Timothy and the Nettle. Aesop – FABLES (Walck) 19 (J656.2).

The Tinderbox. Lang – YELLOW 266-275 (D1421.1.2); Manning-Sanders – BOOK..MAGI-CAL 49-60; Opie – CLASSIC 206-215.

Ting Lan and the Lamb. Carpenter – TALES.. CHINESE 66-71 (A1547.4).

The Tinker and His Wife. Manning-Sanders – RED 112-117 (K335.1.1.1D).

The Tinker and the Ghost. Boggs – THREE 99-108 (H1411.1).

The Tinker of Tamlacht. Hoke – SPOOKS 97 (D1825.3.11.2; Q565Af); MacManus – HIBERNI-AN 10-24.

The Tinner, the Dog, the Jew, and the Cake. Manning-Sanders – PETER 150-155 (J21Ad).

Tintinyin and the Unknown King of the Spirit World. Fuja – FOURTEEN 180-185 (B216.4).

The Tiny Bird and the King. Spellman – BEAUTI-FUL 71-74 (Z49.3.2).

The Tiny God. Uchida – MAGIC 113-121 (A541.0.1).

Tio Paco and His Wonderful Donkey. Boggs – THREE 39-46 (K403).

Tio Rabbit and the Barrel. Carter – ENCHANTED 87-90 (K553.0.3).

The Tipsy Rooster. Lowe – LITTLE 55-57 (Z52.6).

Tit For Tat. Durham – TIT 46-57 (J1341.7.2);

Hutchinson – CANDLELIGHT 79-82 (J2137.6.1); Wiggin – FAIRY 396-397.

Titty Mouse and Tatty-Mouse. Hutchinson – FIRESIDE 17-22 (Z32.2.2); Jacobs – ENGLISH 78-81; Richardson – GREAT 66-73; Steel – ENGLISH 94-96; Wiggin – TALES 228-230; Withers – I SAW 62-66.

Tiwa and the Magic Eggs. Aardema – MORE 44-49 (Q2.1.2Eb).

The Tiyanak. Robertson – FAIRY..PHILIPPINES 117-127 (G303.16.3.1.2).

Tlacuache the Saint. Ross – IN 121-133 (J953.19).

To the Devil With the Money! Baker – TALKING 113-117 (J2411.3.1).

To Tutula. Aardema – MORE 38-43 (F557.0.1).

To Your Good Health. Fenner – PRINCESSES 3-10 (H328.9); Haviland – FAVORITE..RUSSIA 3-19; Lang – CRIMSON 18-25; Lang – FIFTY 322-326; Lang – TO YOUR pb.

Toads and Diamonds. Hutchinson – CANDLELIGHT 93-100 (Q2.1.1Aa); Lang – BLUE 295-298; Rack-ham – ARTHUR 196-198.

Toad Brothers' Warts and the Peeper's Peep. Parker – SKUNNY 190-195 (A2356.2.1.1).

The Toad Is Heaven's Uncle. Schultz – VIETNAM-ESE 101-105 (A2426.4.1.2.1).

The Toad Is the Emperor's Uncle. Vo-Dinh – TOAD (A2426.4.1.2.1).

Toast and Honey. Ginsburg – LAZIES 42-45 (W111.5.10.1.1).

The Tobacco Fairy From the Blue Hills. Frost – LEGENDS 283-286 (A2691.2).

Today Me, Tomorrow Thee. Nunn – AFRICAN 21-25 (J1511.14.1).

Tom and Giant Blunderbuss. Manning-Sanders – PETER 110-119 (F628.2.3.1).

Tom and the Pitcher. Aesop – FABLES (Walck) 119 (W151.9.1).

Tom Hickathrift. Jacobs – MORE 46-54 (F628.2.3.1).

Tom In the River. Aesop – FABLES (Walck) 78-79 (J2175.2).

Tom Thumb. Brooke – GOLDEN pb (F535.1.1A); Carle – ERIC 49-60; Grimm – GRIMM'S (Follett) 349-357; Grimm – GRIMM'S (Grosset) 268-275; Grimm – GRIMM'S (Viking) 91-98; Grimm – GRIMM'S (World) 184-190; Grimm – HOUSEHOLD 160-166; Haviland – ENGLAND 30-43; Tarrant – FAIRY 34-50.

The Transformed Donkey. Withers – WORLD 45-46 (K403).

Transportation Problem. Leach – NOODLES 59 (H506.3).

The Trap. Chang – TALES..OLD CHINA 46-47 (J219.1); Heady – WHEN 81-84 (J1172.3).

The Traveling Frog. Carey – BABA 33-38 (J2357); Garshin – TRAVELING pb.

The Traveling Musicians. De La Mare – ANIMAL 151-158 (K335.1.4; K1161.1); Grimm – TRAVEL-ING pb.

Traveling Through the Chimney. Jagendorf – GYPSIES' 118-121 (X1653.3.3).

Traveling to See Wonders. Withers – WORLD 31 (X583.1).

Traveling With Elijah. Ish-Kishor – WISE 62-67 (J225.0.1).

The Traveller and Fortune. Aesop – AESOP'S (Watts) 224 (N111.4.2).

The Traveller and His Dog. Aesop – AESOP'S (Watts) 69 (J1475).

The Traveller and the Nut Tree. Courlander – TIGER'S 76 (J2571).

The Traveller and the Tiger. Korel – LISTEN 89-97 (J1172.3).

The Travellers and the Bear. Aesop – AESOP'S (Golden) 30-31 (J1488); Aesop – AESOP'S (Viking) 71; Montgomerie – TWENTY-FIVE 53.

The Travellers and the Hatchet. Aesop – AESOP'S (Grosset) 21 (W197.3).

The Travellers and the Plane-Tree. Aesop – AESOP'S (Watts) 132 (W154.7).

The Travellers and the Purse. Aesop – AESOP'S (Random) 44-45 (W197.3).

The Traveller's Tale. Ginsburg – THREE 15 (Z11.4).

The Travels of a Fox. Arbuthnot – FAIRY 15-16 (K251.1.0.2); Association – TOLD..GREEN 40-46; Hutchinson – CHIMNEY 91-98; Richardson – GREAT 16-26; Rockwell – OLD 22-23; Withers – I SAW 18-21.

The Treasure. Hatch – MORE 22-32 (J1151.1.1).

Treasure in the Basket. Kelsey – MULLAH 32-37 (J1381).

The Treasure of Li-Po. Ritchie – TREASURE 3-39 (T53.7).

The Treasure of Tacoma. Cothran – WITH 67-75 (D1960.1.2).

Treasure Trove. Sturton – ZOMO 89-99 (K306.5).

The Treasurers. Zajdler – POLISH 178-190 (F456.4).

Tredril. Manning-Sanders – CHARMS 120-124 (F321.1.4.1.2).

The Tree and the Reed. Aesop – AESOP'S (Grosset) 179 (J832); Aesop – FABLES (Macmillan) 73.

The Tree Goddess. Barlow – LATIN 82-88 (A978.3.1).

The Tree of Health. Haviland – FAVORITE.. DENMARK 65-76 (H346).

The Tree of the Three Branches. Mittleman – BIRD 82-89 (H331.1.2.2; R222.1A).

The Tree With the Difficult Name. Williams-Ellis – ROUND 186-191 (J2471.4.1).

The Trees and the Axe. Aesop – AESOP'S (Watts) 148 (U162).

Tregeagle. Manning-Sanders – PETER 48-55 (E459.8).

The Trial at Avichára-pura. Courlander – TIGER'S 49-51 (J2233; Z49.11.2).

The Trial of the Stone. Courlander – TIGER'S 24-28 (J1141.1.3.4.1).

The Trial of the Stone. Lu Mar – CHINESE 71-85 (J1142.5).

A Trick on the Trek. Aardema – BEHIND 11-18 (A2494.11.2).

A Trick That Failed. Carpenter – LATIN 50-56 (A974; A2426.2.11.1; A2528.2; A2541.3).

The Tricky Fox and the Stork. Aesop – AESOP'S (Golden) 86 (J1565.1).

Tricksy Rabbit. Aardema – TALES 9-17 (K484.4).

Tricky Peik. Hardendorff – TRICKY 11-12 (J1813.4; K112.1.2; K113; K341.8.1; K842; K1051).

The Tricky Tailor. Thoby-Marcelin – SINGING 46-52 (Z43.6.3).

Trillevip. Baker – GOLDEN 41-45 (D2183G; D2183.1).

Trim Tram Turvey. Manning-Sanders – GIANNI 161-172 (C611).

A Trip to Schlaraffenland. Gag – MORE..GRIMM 87-89 (X1503).

Trip to Town. Leach – NOODLES 24 (J1946).

A Trip to the Sky. Withers – WORLD 19-22 (X1402.1).

The Triplets of Tunis. Holding - KING'S 28-38 (H621.1.1).

Tripple-Trapple. Manning-Sanders - BOOK.. DEVILS 9-14 (D1605.1).

Tritil, Litil and the Birds. Manning-Sanders - BOOK..OGRES 20-31 (G530.2Gb).

The Troll's Daughter. Hatch - MORE 59-78 (G530.2C); Lang - FIFTY 327-334.

The Troll's Invitation. Palmer - FAIRY 85-91 (K1736).

The Troll's Little Daughter. Manning-Sanders - BOOK..TROLLS 110-122 (G530.2C).

Tropysin. De La Mare - ANIMAL 260-265 (H1213.1D); Manning-Sanders - RED 105-111,

Trorky the Turtle. Aardema - MORE 12-15 (K1241).

The Troubadour and the Devil. Alegría - THREE 84-85 (G303.16.8.1).

Trouble. Dolch - OLD RUSSIA 87-97 (N250.4).

Trouble in the Fox Family. Harris - COMPLETE 823-833 (K2131.6); Harris - FAVORITE 169-177.

True and Untrue. Asbjørnsen - EAST (Row) 93-100 (N452B); Undset - TRUE 28-36.

The True History of Sir Thomas Thumb. Steel - ENGLISH 144-152 (F535.1.1A).

A True Love Story of Tonga. Gittins - TALES 56-58 (R161.5).

The True Name of the Princess. Thoby-Marcelin - SINGING 75-81 (E341.1C).

True Tears. Heady - SAFIRI 46-50 (J1171.1.3).

True Thomas. Finlay - TATTERCOATS 111-118 (F329.1).

The Trumpeter Taken Prisoner. Aesop - AESOP'S (Grosset) 218 (J1465); Aesop - AESOP'S (Viking) 70; Aesop - AESOP'S (Watts) 105; Jacobs - FABLES 157.

Trust Your Friends. Heady - JAMBO 66-71 (K441.5).

Trusty John. Lang - BLUE 320-329 (S268A).

Truth or Lies. Neufeld - BEWARE 68-75 (W48.1)

Tsap-Tsarap. Ginsburg - KAHA 142-150 (J2101.0.1; N411.1E).

Tsar Boris and the Devil King. Spicer - THIR-TEEN 53-62 (F660.1Cc; H522.1.1.2).

Tsar Peter the Great and the Peasant. Wyndham - TALES..RUSSIA 33-37 (H585.1.1; J1289.27).

The Tsarina's Greatest Treasure. Spicer - LONG 145-148 (H659.27; H712.2; H1022.3; H1023.1.1; H1143; J1545.4).

Tshinyama's Heavenly Maidens. Aardema - BE-HIND 19-25 (F302.4.2.0.1).

Ttimba. Serwadda - SONGS 61-69 (K1079.2).

The Tubmaker Who Flew to the Sky. Uchida - MAGIC 43-50 (K1112.2).

The Tufty Hen. Rudolph - MAGIC 14-29 (K1161.7.1).

Tug of War. Arnott - AFRICAN 153-155 (K22); Heady - JAMBO 18-22; Kaula - AFRICAN 72-76.

Tui Liku and the Demons. Gittins - TALES 14-20 (F153.2).

The Tulip Bed. Reeves - ENGLISH 92-102 (F339.2).

The Tune of Iola Ap Hugh. Belting - ELVES 22-26 (E425.2.5.1).

TUNTUNI, THE TAILOR BIRD. Bang pb (Z41.8.1; Z49.3.2).

Tuppence and Thruppence. Danaher - FOLK-TALES 24-30 (E256.1).

Turkey Brother and the Magic Panther Suit. De-Wit - TALKING 13-21 (D1050.2).

The Turkish Slave. Hampden - HOUSE 99-109 (E341.1D).

TURNABOUT. Wiesner pb (J2431).

The Turnip. De La Mare - TALES 107-118 (J2415.1); Grimm - GRIMM'S (Follett) 358-364; Grimm - GRIMM'S (Grosset) 260-263 (K842.0.1.1); Grimm - GRIMM'S (World) 148-151).

The Turnip. Domanska (Macmillan) pb (Z49.9); Haviland - FAIRY 44-47; Withers - I SAW 98-99.

Turnip Thief! Withers - MAN 6 (A751.1.4.1).

Turnips Are Harder. Shah - MULLA 141 (J2563).

The Turtle and the Herons. Chang - TALES.. OLD CHINA 49-51 (J2357).

The Turtle and the Monkey Share a Tree. Cour-lander - RIDE 25-27 (K171.9.1; K581.1).

The Turtle and the Sheep. Johnson - HOW 83-87 (K641.4).

The Turtle and the Storks and the Jackal. Tooze - THREE (A2312.1.3; J2357; K543).

Turtle Gains a Long Neck and Reveals That He Is Good for Soup. Parker - SKUNNY 146-152 (A2351.5.1).

Turtle Makes War On Men. Bruchac – TURKEY 26–29 (A2312.1.7; A2320.1.0.1; F1025.2).

The Turtle of Tamarua. Holding – THE SKY-EATER 49–60 (A2611.3.2).

The Turtle Outwits the Lion. Tooze – THREE 46–61 (K11.1).

The Turtle Prince. Tooze – WONDERFUL 64–70 (D672F).

Turtle Runs a Race With Bear. Parker – SKUNNY 171–176 (K11.1).

The Turtle, the Storks and the Jackal. Tooze – WONDERFUL 107–110 (J2357; K543; K553.5).

The Turtle Who Couldn't Stop Talking. Babbitt – JATAKA 18–20 (J2357).

The Turtle Who Loved a Monkey. Tooze – THREE 24–43 (A2312.1.3.1).

Turtle's Race With Bear. Bruchac – TURKEY 23–25 (K11.1).

Turtle's Race With Beaver. Bruchac – TURKEY 20–22 (K11.2).

The Turtle's War Party. Parker – SKUNNY 159–164 (F1025.2).

Tusi and the Great Beast. Aardema – BEHIND 57–65 (F511.0.4.2).

TUSYA AND THE POT OF GOLD. Yaroslava pb (J1151.1.1).

The Twelve Brothers. Grimm – GRIMM'S (Grosset) 41–47 (P253.2B); Grimm – GRIMM'S (World) 247–253; Grimm – HOUSEHOLD 56–61; Lang – FIFTY 335–340; Lang – RED 279–285; Minard – WOMENFOLK 36–43.

The Twelve Clever Brothers Go To Town. Ginsburg – TWELVE 12–19 (J2014.2).

The Twelve Dancing Princesses. Adams – Twelve pb (F1015.1.1); Dalgliesh – ENCHANTED 124–129; Fenner – PRINCESSES 57–63; Grimm – BORTHERS 112–116; Grimm – GRIMM'S (Follett) 365–372; Grimm – GRIMM'S (Grosset) 1–6; Grimm – GRIMM'S (Watts) 54–59; Grimm – GRIMM'S (World) 24–28; Grimm – TWELVE pb; Haviland – FRANCE 3–25; Holme – TALES 81–88; Lang – RED 1–15; Lunn – TWELVE pb; Opie – CLASSIC 188–194; Shub – TWELVE pb; Sleigh – NORTH 44–56.

The Twelve Days of Christmas. Karasz – TWELVE pb (Z22.1); Martignoni – ILLUSTRATED 92; Wildsmith – TWELVE pb.

The Twelve Huntsmen. Grimm – GRIMM'S (Grosset) 341–344 (K1236); Grimm – GRIMM'S (World) 75–78; Grimm – JUNIPER v.1 63–70; Lang – FIFTY 331–334.

The Twelve Lazy Servants. Gag – MORE..GRIMM 51–58 (W111.1).

The Twelve Months. Aliki – TWELVE pb (Q2.1.4Ac); Dalgliesh – ENCHANTED 154–161; Haviland – FAVORITE..CZECHOSLOVAKIA 3–20.

The Twelve Months of the Year. Wilson – GREEK 224–229 (Q2.1.4Aa).

The Twelve Wild Ducks. Asbjørnsen – EAST (Row) 46–53 (P253.2C); Asbjørnsen – NORWEGIAN 182–189; Sheehan – FOLK 14–21.

The Twelve Windows. De La Mare – TALES 155–165 (H321A).

The Twelve Young Boys with Golden Hair. Ure – RUMANIAN 114–116 (N455.4E).

Tweriire. Serwadda – SONGS 21–25 (D1415.3).

Twilight, Midnight and Dawn. Riordan – TALES.. CENTRAL 227–232 (K1931.2F).

The Twin Parrots. Gaer – FABLES..INDIA 28–30 (J451.6).

The Twins. Fuja – FOURTEEN 88–112 (R111.1.3Ai).

The Twins and the Snarling Witch. Manning-Sanders – BOOK..WITCHES 38–45 (Q2.1.2CeBa).

Twins of Gold and Silver. Withers – MAN 71–74 (N455.4D).

The Twins of the God Mars. Toor – GOLDEN 169–176 (B535.0.9.1).

Twist-mouth Family. Haviland – NORTH 144–146 (X131).

The Two Beggars. Dobbs – MORE 26–30 (N351.0.1).

The Two Bottles. Pilkington – SHAMROCK 89–93 (D861.1E).

The Two Boxes. Burton – MAGIC 72 (A1671.1.1).

The Two Brothers. Arnott – AFRICAN 195–199 (K1931.2Va).

The Two Brothers. Grimm – GRIMM'S (Scribner's) 159–184 (R111.1.3Ai).

The Two Brothers. Korel – LISTEN 37–41 (K171.7.1).

The Two Brothers. Mittleman – BIRD 43–57 (N455.3).

The Two Chinamen. Brockett – BURMESE 163–170 (W11.14.1).

Two Cows. Kelsey – MULLAH 108–112 (H881.2).

The Two Crabs. Aesop – AESOP'S (Grosset) 192 (J1063.1); Aesop – FIVE 40; Jacobs – FABLES 95.

Two Different Interpretations of the Same Fact. Vittorini - OLD 50-54 (J1521.5.3).

The Two Donkeys. Wolkstein - MAGIC 23-28 (B651.12).

Two Dutiful Sons. Carpenter - TALES..CHINESE 117-123 (N831.1).

Two Feasts for Anansi. Courlander - HAT 18-19 (A2355.1.1.2; J2183.1.3).

Two Feathers and Turky Brother. Bruchac - TURKEY 39-48 (D1050.2).

The Two Fellows and the Bear. Aesop - AESOP'S (Grosset) 166-168 (J1488); Aesop - AESOP'S (Random) 42-44; Jacobs - FABLES 99.

The Two Foolish Cats. Uchida - SEA 55-60 (K452.1.2).

The Two Foxes. Korel - LISTEN 69-122 (K1084.1.2.1).

The Two Friends. Dolch - ALASKA 11-17-25 (F53.1).

Two Friends. Ginsburg - THREE 20 (J1488).

The Two Friends. Littledale - GHOSTS 97-100 (D2011.1.4).

Two Friends, Coyote and Bull Snake Exchange Visits. Courlander - PEOPLE 47-100 (J1565.1.3.1).

Two Friends: How They Parted. Courlander - KING'S 60-63 (A2494.16.2.1).

The Two Frogs. Aesop - AESOP'S (Grosset) 210 (J752.1); Aesop - AESOP'S (Watts) 126 (J652.1).

Two Frogs. Aesop - AESOP'S (Random) 21-22 (Q81.2); Ginsburg - LAZIES 26-27.

The Two Frogs. Gruenberg - MORE 119-120 (B296.2); Lang - VIOLET 111-113.

TWO GREEDY BEARS. Ginsburg pb (K452.1.2).

The Two Headed Giant of Rotuma. Gittins - TALES 47-49 (G512.11.1).

Two Hunters. Burton - MAGIC 119-121 (K1711.1; K1715.12.1; N642.2; U174).

The Two Journeymen. Grimm - JUNIPER v.2 278-297 (N452A).

The Two Kings' Children. Grimm - GRIMM'S (Scribner's) 220-230 (G530.2Ah).

The Two Lost Babes. Chase - WICKED 162-179 (K1611E).

The Two Men and the Two Dwarfs. Maher - BLIND 107-114 (F451.5.2.6.1).

The Two Misers. Siddiqui - TOONTOONY 61-64 (J2478).

Two of Everything. Arbuthnot - ANTHOLOGY 333-334 (D1652.5.7.1); Association - CASTLES 291-299; Colwell - MAGIC 118-123; Ritchie - TREASURE 142-154.

The Two Old Women's Bet. Chase - WICKED 156-161 (J2311.0.1.1).

Two Out of One. Courlander - KANTCHIL'S 118-121 (K714.2.3.2; N228).

The Two Pine Cones. Bowman - TALES..TUPA 126-128 (J2073.1).

The Two Pots. Aesop - AESOP'S (Grosset) 149 (J425.1); Aesop - AESOP'S (Watts) 100; Jacobs - FABLES 101.

The Two Princesses. Reeves - ENGLISH 50-62 (L145.1B).

Two Rascals. Bulatkin - EURASIAN 98-102 (J1516); Carpenter - AFRICAN 103-112 (K421.2).

The Two Sillies. Manning-Sanders - PETER 213-215 (J1904.2; J1909.8.1).

The Two Sisters. Steel - ENGLISH 83-88 (Q2.1.2Cb).

The Two Sisters. Turnbull - FAIRY..INDIA 33-44 (Q2.1.2Da).

The Two Sisters. Vittorini - OLD 75-78 (V429.2).

The Two Soldiers and the Robber. Aesop - AESOP'S (Watts) 84-85 (W121.2.5).

Two Speedy People. Withers - WORLD 61-62 (F660.1.2).

The Two Statues of Kannon. Bang - MEN 61-65 (K607.4.1).

The Two Stone Giants. Carpenter - KOREAN 191-196 (J1199.1).

TWO STONECUTTERS. Titus pb (F341.3; Z42.0.2).

Two Stubborn Goats. Ginsburg - THREE 42 (W167.1).

The Two Travelers. Grimm - GRIMM'S (Follett) 373-387 (N452A).

The Two Travellers. Aesop - FABLES (Walck) 103-104 (J1488).

Two Ways to Count to Ten. Carpenter - AFRICAN 47-52 (H331.18).

The Two Wishes. De Leeuw - LEGENDS..HOLLAND 152-157 (J2073.1).

The Two Wizards. Manning-Sanders - BOOK..

..WIZARDS 22-25 (D1711.0.1.1); Manning-Sanders - CHOICE 276-279.

Tying Up the Stones. Withers - WORLD 47 (J1819.4).

Tyl's Task. Edmonds - TRICKSTER 45-50 (H524.2; H561.4; H703.4).

Tyndal and the Priest. Ginsburg - TWELVE 54-55 (J2012.4).

Tyndal Goes to Market. Ginsburg - TWELVE 57-59 (J2663).

The Tyrannical King. Withers - I SAW 131-132 (Z49.6.0.1).

The Tyrant and the Miller. Vittorini - OLD 45-49 (H561.2; H682.1.7; H696.1.2; H711.1).

The Tyrant Who Became a Just Ruler. Arbuthnot - FAIRY 231 (J52).

Tzarevich Ivan, the Glowing Bird and the Gray Wolf. Fenner - ADVENTURES 127-147 (H1331.1.3Ah).

Tzu Chu's Cheerful Funeral. Manton - FLYING 35-39 (A1547.1.1).

Ubazakura. Buck - FAIRY 221-223 (E631.6.1).

Udleqdjun in the Sky. Leach - HOW 138-139 (A772.1).

The Ugly King. Wyatt - GOLDEN 59-80 (T11.2.1.1).

Uletka. Manning-Sanders - GLASS 94-99 (T521.0.1).

Unanana and the Elephant. Arnott - AFRICAN 68-73 (F912.2.1); Minard - WOMENFOLK 127-134.

The Unanswerable. Kendall - SWEET 63-65 (X909.5.1).

Uncle Boqui and Little Malice. Jagendorf - KING 153-161 (K1066.2).

Uncle Bouki Rents a Horse. Courlander - RIDE 259-264 (K1797).

Uncle Coyote's Last Mischief. Courlander - RIDE 234-237 (G555.1.2; K525.1.4).

Uncle Rabbit Flies to Heaven. Jagendorf - KING 205-208 (A2351.9; K1041.3).

Uncle Remus Initiates the Little Boy. Harris - COMPLETE 106 (J425.2.1).

Unfair. Shah - MULLA 134 (J1340.1).

The Unforgiving Monkey. Frost - LEGENDS 142-146 (Z49.23.1).

The Ungrateful Bear. Pridham - GIFT 95-99 (J1172.3).

The Ungrateful Children. Wyndham - TALES.. RUSSIA 47-56 (P236.2).

The Ungrateful Crocodile. Bro - HOW 39-48 (J1172.3.0.2).

The Ungrateful Lion. Gaer - FABLES..INDIA 166-168 (W154.3).

The Ungrateful Man. Green - FOLK..AFRICA 15-19 (W154.8).

The Ungrateful Snake. Davis - LION'S 143-149 (J1172.3); Wilson - GREEK 53-57 (K235.1).

The Ungrateful Tiger. Carpenter - ELEPHANT'S 151-158 (J1172.3; J1172.3.2; J1172.3.2.2).

The Uninvited Guest. Pridham - GIFT 45-47 (J1551.6).

Universal Story of the Sasquatch. Matson - LEGENDS 117-119 (B29.9.1).

The Unlucky Fisherman. Martin - NINE 19-26 (E324.3.1); Martin - RAVEN 27-35.

The Unlucky Goat. Wilson - GREEK 65-67 (K652.2).

The Unlucky Man. Wilson - GREEK 151-156 (N351).

The Unlucky Shoes of Ali Abou. Carpenter - ELEPHANT'S 66-74 (N211.2).

The Unseen Bridegroom. Jacobs - EUROPEAN 129-141 (H1385.4E).

The Unsuspected Element. Shah - MULLA 33 (J2672).

The Untidy Mermaid. Manning-Sanders - BOOK.. MERMAIDS 79-85 (B18.13.11A).

The Unusual Excuse. Gilstrap - SULTAN'S 75-80 (J1211.4).

The Unwashed Pot. Pridham - GIFT 30-34 (J2511.0.3).

Up and Down the Minaret. Kelsey - MULLAH 24-31 (J1331).

Urashima. Hearn - BOY 21-26 (F420.6.1.3.1); Hearn - JAPANESE (Pauper) 30-36; Hearn - JAPANESE 80-88; Ross - BURIED 173-187.

Urashima Taro. Sakade - JAPANESE 9-14 (F420.6.1.3.1).

Urashima Taro and the Princess of the Sea. Arbuthnot - ANTHOLOGY 338-341 (F420.6.1.3.1); Arbuthnot - FAIRY 177-181; Uchida - DANCING 13-23.

Urho and Marja. Bowman – TALES..TUPA 147-160 (G530.2Bi).

Use a Thorn to Draw a Thorn. Brockett – BURMESE 177-185 (H588.7.2).

USHA THE MOUSE-MAIDEN. Gobhai pb (L392.0.1).

The Vagabond. Grimm – HOUSE 95-102 (K1161.7.1.2); Grimm – HOUSEHOLD 62-64.

The Vain Bear. Bowman – TALES..TUPA 250 (K1013.2).

The Vain Jackal. Tooze – WONDERFUL 94-95 (J952.1).

The Vain Jackdaw. Aesop – AESOP'S (Watts) 68-69 (J951.2).

The Vain Lord. Ginsburg – TWELVE 66-67 (K445.1).

Vaino and the Swan Princess. Bowman – TALES..TUPA 34-41 (H1385.3Fh).

The Valiant Chattee-Maker. Baker – TALKING 242-250 (N392.1.1.1); Haviland – FAVORITE..INDIA 5-20; Price – VALIANT pb; Wiggin – FAIRY 406-414.

The Valiant Lion. Ginsburg – THREE 45-46 (K1715.1.0.1).

The Valiant Little Tailor. Grimm – GRIMM'S (Scribner's) 53-63 (K1951.1A).

The Valiant Potter. Courlander – RIDE 46-52 (J2633; N392.1.1.1).

The Valiant Tailor. Grimm – GRIMM'S (Watts) 44-53 (K1951.1A); Werth – VALIANT pb.

The Valley of Ten Thousand Waterfalls. Jewett – WHICH 124-135 (E379.7).

The Value of the Past. Shah – MULLA 127 (H599.8).

Vania and the Vampire. Spicer – THIRTEEN 92-100 (E251.1.3).

The Vanishing Rice-Straw Coat. McAlpine – JAPANESE 121-126 (D831.1).

Vardiello. Baker – TALKING 18-24 (J1853.1.1; J2311.2.1); Mincielli – OLD 14-23.

Vasilisa and Prince Vladimir. Higonnet-Schnopper –TALES 141-160 (J1545.4.3).

Vasilisa the Beautiful. Dolch – RUSSIA 99-129 (Q2.1.2CeBb); Haviland – FAVORITE..RUSSIA 20-42; Whitney – IN 43-57; Whitney – VASILISA pb.

Vaudai. Duvoisin – THREE 111-114 (G303.16.12.1).

The Vazouza and the Volga. Ransome – OLD

PETER'S 321-323 (A939.4).

The Vegetable Tree. Gruenberg – FAVORITE 377-379 (A2686).

The Veil. Shah – MULLA 99 (J1250.10).

The Vengeance of the Dwarf. Duvoisin – THREE 203-207 (F541.5.2.6.2).

Venus and the Cat. Aesop – AESOP'S (Watts) 118 (J1908.2); Aesop – FABLES (Walck) 61.

Venus and the Lovesick Cat. Aesop – AESOP'S (Golden) 46 (J1908.2).

A Very Happy Donkey. Wolkstein – MAGIC 157-164 (B651.13).

The Very Obstinate Man. Withers – MAN 44-45 (A751.1.10).

THE VERY SPECIAL BADGERS. Stamm pb (A2434.2.2.1; D615.1.1).

The Victorious Lute. Lu Mar – CHINESE 97-110 (K2366.2).

The Victory of the Buffalo. Courlander – KANTCHIL'S 12-16 (B264.6).

The Village of the Pure Queen. Carpenter – KOREAN 175-180 (J1111.4).

The Villas' Spring. Fillmore – LAUGHING 241-252 (N452C).

The Viper and the File. Aesop – AESOP'S (Watts) 91 (J552.3); Aesop – FIVE 54.

The Viper and the Friar's Rope. Lowe – LITTLE 30 (K263.2).

The Virgin of Honduras. Jagendorf – KING 164-167 (V128.0.2).

The Visit. Withers – I SAW 97 (Z49.5.1.1).

A Visit from Mister Sea. Luzzato – LONG 36-43 (A736.1.4.4).

A Visit to the Lions. Helfman – BUSHMEN 86-90 (K1892.3).

Visitor. Heady – SAFIRI 22 (K359.2.2).

A Visitor from Paradise. Jacobs – EUROPEAN 159-164 (J2326).

The Visits of St. Peter to His People. Vittorini – OLD 106-110 (V229.26.1.2).

The Vixen and Her Cub. Ginsburg – ONE 39 (J1122.2).

The Vixen and the Rooster. De La Iglesia – CAT #4 (J1421).

The Voice from the Minaret. Kelsey – MULLAH

71-74 (J1941).

The Voice in the Jug. Credle - TALL 122-132 (G303.16.3.1.3).

Volkh's Journey to the East. Colwell - SECOND 46-56 (D1720.1.2).

The Vouivre: The Flying Serpent. Holman - DRAC 73-84 (B11.6.2.4).

The Voyage Below the Water. Courlander - PIECE 71-75 (E481.10.1).

The Voyage of the Wee Red Cap. Sawyer - WAY 111-120 (F282.4.2).

Vukub-Cakix. Garner - CAVALCADE..GOBLINS 4-10 (A515.1.1.4; A773.5).

The Wagers. Carter - ENCHANTED 83-86 (K15.2).

Wahoo. Harris - COMPLETE 36-39 (K607.3); Harris - FAVORITE 136-139; Harris - UNCLE 54-58.

Wait for the Sheep. Cimino - DISOBEDIENT #17 (Z11).

Wait till Martin Comes. Harper - GHOSTS 195-198 (J1495.2); Leach - THING 23-26.

Waiting for a Turkey. Courlander - PIECE 111-112 (J2215.4.0.1).

Waiting for Rabbits. Cheney - TALES 115-118 (A1458.2).

Waiting On Salvation. Courlander - TERRAPIN'S 11-14 (J2215.4).

Wakaima and the Clay Man. Haviland - FAIRY 104-109 (K741.0.6).

Wali Dad the Simple-Hearted. Lang - FIFTY 345-353 (T53.7).

The Walk. Withers - I SAW 33 (Z49.4.1).

The Walk around the Island. Leekley - WORLD 111-117 (A955.3.1.1).

The Walking Boundary Stones. Leodhas - GAELIC 58-67 (E345.1).

The Walnut Tree. Aesop - AESOP'S (Watts) 66 (W154.6).

The Wandering Cobbler. Borski - GOOD 34-40 (H1411.4.9).

The Wandering Monk and the Tabby Cat. Novak - FAIRY 72-80 (B522.1.1).

Wanja's Choice. Heady - JAMBO 78-84 (J416.2).

War Between the Crocodiles and Kantchil. Courlander - KANTCHIL'S 87-94 (J1172.3.0.1;

K543.0.2; K579.2.1; K607.2).

The War between the Lion and the Cricket. Ross - BURIED 95-102 (B263.9).

War-Horse and Donkey. Aesop - FABLES (Walck) 38-39 (J411.12).

The War of the Animals against the Birds. Guirma - TALES 29-44 (A2426.2.18.1; B261.0.1; B261.1.0.1).

The War of the Plants. Courlander - TIGER'S 127-131 (A2701).

The Warau People Discover the Earth. Sherlock - WEST 39-44 (A1231.2).

A Warning from the Gods. Wyndham - TALES.. CHINA 52-54 (A1011.2.2).

Warthog and Hornbill. Kaula - AFRICAN 23-24 (A2221.5.3; A2231.7.1.3).

The Wasp and the Bee. Walker - NIGERIAN 43-44 (A2813).

The Wasp and the Snake. Aesop - AESOP'S (Watts) 178 (J2102.1).

Wastewin and the Beaver. Yellow Robe - TON-WEYA 52-58 (K635.3).

Watch-Pot and Greedy. Aardema - MORE 56-61 (K341.2.0.2).

The Water Buffalo and the Tiger. Dolch - STORIES..OLD CHINA 17 (B264.3).

The Water-Bull of Benbecula. Leodhas - SEA 121-137 (F420.1.3.4).

Water Drops. Manning-Sanders - BOOK..GHOSTS 90-94 (D832.1).

The Water Dwellers. Maas - MOON 123-127 (E514).

Water for Peking. Dolch - STORIES..OLD CHINA 99-105 (B11.7.1).

The Water Nixie. Gag - MORE..GRIMM 23-25 (D672A); Rockwell - THREE 53-55.

The Water of Life. Arbuthnot - FAIRY 69-72 (H1321.1Aa); Grimm - GRIMM'S (Follett) 388-399; Grimm - GRIMM'S (Grosset) 181-188; Grimm - GRIMM'S (Scribner's) 214-221; Grimm - GRIMM'S (World) 305-311; Holme - TALES 76-80; Shub - ABOUT 65-73; Wiggin - FAIRY 213-220.

The Water of Life. Lang - ROSE 122-130 (H1331.1.3Fb).

The Water Ogre. Kavcic - GOLDEN 134-140 (G586).

Water Spirit's Gift of Horses. Brown - TEPEE 99-101 (A1881.5).

The Water Sprite. Tracy – LION 61-65 (F420.4.6.0.1).

Watermelons, Walnuts and the Wisdom of Allah. Walker – WATERMELONS 27-28 (J2215.6; J2571).

The Watermill That Wouldn't Work. Simon – WISE 7-16 (J2123).

Water's Locked. Williams-Ellis – FAIRY..BRITISH 284-287 (F361.14.6).

Waukewa's Eagle. Hardendorff – FROG'S 17-24 (B389.3).

THE WAVE. Hodges pb (J1688).

Wawanosh. Bierhorst – FIRE 47-57 (E423.3.0.1).

The Way of the Master. Edmonds – TRICKSTER 129-137 (J2417.2).

Wayambeh, the Turtle. Frost – LEGENDS 295-297 (A2312.1.0.3).

The Ways of Foreigners. Shah – MULLA 70 (J1391.9).

We Oppose President Stomach! Dorliae – ANIMALS 16-21 (A1391).

The Weary Spirits of Lanai. Thompson – HAWIIAN ..TRICKSTERS 14-22 (K688.6).

The Weasel. Heady – TALES 75-80 (G262.6).

Weasel and Old Snowy Owl. Parker – SKUNNY 204-212 (A2411.1.2.1; A2411.2.4.2).

The Weaver's Worry. Edmonds – TRICKSTER 104-112 (K2371.2.1).

The Wedding of the Dragon-God. Lu Mar – CHINESE 53-70 (R111.1.3Db).

The Wedding of the Hawk. Courlander – KING'S 41-44 (A2442.2.5).

The Wedding of the Mouse. Uchida – DANCING 89-94 (L392.0.2).

The Wee Bannock. Haviland – FAVORITE..SCOT-LAND 13-24 (Z33.1.4); Jacobs – MORE 73-77; Steel – ENGLISH 180-184.

Wee Camel. Chang – CHINESE 68-69 (J21.53).

The Wee Christmas Cabin of Carn-na-ween. Saw-yer – LONG 45-60 (F343.21).

The Wee Little Woman. TALL..NURSERY 49-50 (E235.4.3).

Wee Meg Barnileg and the Fairies. Green – MID-SUMMER 72-86 (F320.1); Sawyer – WAY 205-216.

The Wee Red Man. Fenner – TIME 217-240 (J2411.2.1); MacManus – DONEGAL 119-143; MacManus – HIBERNIAN 85-98.

Wee Robin Redbreast. Finlay – TATTERCOATS 96-99 (Z55).

Wee Robin's Christmas Day. Association – TOLD.. GREEN 162-164 (Z55).

Wee Robin's Yule Soup. Wiggin – TALES 380-381 (Z55).

The Wee, Wee Mannie. Jacobs – MORE 192-194 (Z39.2); Sewell – WEE pb; Wiggin – TALES 200-202; Williams-Ellis – FAIRY..BRITISH 20-23.

A Week of Sundays. Gruenberg – FAVORITE 359-363 (W111.11).

The Weeping Lady of Llyn Glasfryn. Spicer – THIRTEEN GHOSTS 53-64 (C41.5).

The Well. Courlander – TERRAPIN'S 46-49 (A2233.1.1).

The Well. Sturton – ZOMO 26-38 (K1715.1).

The Well Diggers. Courlander – TIGER'S 115-117 (J1934).

Well Done and Ill Paid. Undset – TRUE 176-179 (C25); Wiggin – TALES 284-286.

The Well of D'yerree-in-Dowan. Pilkington – SHAMROCK 74-88 (H1321.1Ad).

The Well of the Three Heads. Reeves – ENGLISH 116-126 (Q2.1.1Ba).

The Well o' the World's End. MacManus – HIBER-NIAN 251-263 (H1321.1Ad); MacManus – WELL 1-20.

The Well of the World's End. Jacobs – ENGLISH 224-229 (D195.2); Manning-Sanders – BOOK.. MAGICAL 235-239; Reeves – ENGLISH 212-220; Steel – ENGLISH 244-248; Williams-Ellis – FAIRY ..BRITISH 69-75.

The Welshman and the Hazel Staff. Sheppard-Jones – WELSH 19-24 (D1960.2.2).

Wen Yen-Poh, the Thinker. Alexander – PEBBLES 14 (J101).

Wend' Yamba. Guirma – TALES 57-69 (N421.1.1).

The Werewolf. Palmer – DRAGONS 55-62 (D113.1.1.1); Picard – FRENCH 93-98.

The Whale and the Sorceror. Berry – MAGIC 113-121 (B301.9.2).

Whale of a Tale. Cothran – MAGIC 18-21 (D1181.1; X1723.4).

The Whalers and the Dwarfs. Belting – ELVES 47-52 (F451.5.1.6).

What a Bird Should Look Like. Shah – MULLA 98 (J1919.1).

What a Clever Child Can Do. Ure - RUMANIAN 35-37 (J121).

What Became of Rabbit. Bell - JOHN 73-75 (D483.1.1).

What Came of Picking Flowers. Lang - ROSE 25-33 (B314F); Rackham - FAIRY 77-83.

What Happened to Six Wives Who Ate Onions. DeWit - TALKING 117-121 (A773.2.1); Fisher - CALIFORNIA 54-59.

What Has Gone Before... Shah - MULLA 135 (J2233.4).

What Is Trouble. Lester - KNEE 5-8 (K1055.2).

What News? News Enough! Withers - WORLD 7-8 (X907.1.1).

What Should I Do, What Shouldn't I Do? Mehdevi - PERSIAN 104-111 (K1715.2).

What the Good Man Does Is Sure to be Right. Bleecker - BIG 113-121 (J2081.1).

What the Old Man Does Is Right. Rackham - ARTHUR 278-287 (J2081.1).

What the Preacher's Talking About. Courlander - TERRAPIN'S 102-103 (X452).

What the Squirrel Saw. Arnott - AFRICAN 105-107 (J2413.11).

What's a Silly Question? Withers - I SAW 35 (Z17.2).

What's That? Leach - LION 12 (X938.2).

The Wheel of Fate. Reed - TALKATIVE 16 (Z49.6.0.8).

Wheeler. Carter - GREEDY 84-90 (C498.2).

When a Man Is Foolish. Jagendorf - KING 151-154 (J1959.4).

When Boquerón Spoke. Jagendorf - KING 167-170 (F969.8).

When Noodlehead Marries Noodlehead. Jagendorf - NOODLEHEAD 85-88 (J1871; J1938).

When Shlemiel Went to Warsaw. Singer - WHEN 99-116 (J2014.2).

When the Devils Amuse Themselves. Thoby-Marcelin - SINGING 3-6 (F344.1.3).

WHEN THE DRUMS SANG. Rockwell pb (G422.1.1).

Whence Came the Birds? Sechrist - ONCE 20-22 (A1905; A1948.1).

Where Arthur Sleeps. Colwell - SECOND 133-138 (D1960.2).

Where One is Fed a Hundred Can Dine. Sawyer - WAY 251-255 (K1811.6).

Where Sun and Moon Were Jealous. Newell - RESCUE 85-90 (A1172.0.1).

Where the Birds Build. Heady - SAGE 27-29 (A2431.3.13).

Where to Lay the Blame. Association - CASTLE 197-209 (J21.37); Hardendorff - FROG'S 142-145.

Which? Leach - LUCK 48 (N141.0.7).

Which Eye Is Blind? Ginsburg - THREE 12 (J1141.17).

Which Is Better, the Sun or the Moon? Withers - MAN 75 (H675).

Which Is the Greatest? Ure - RUMANIAN 84-86 (Z42.0.4).

Which Was Witch? Arbuthnot - ANTHOLOGY 343 (D312.4); Arbuthnot - FAIRY 183-184; Hoke - WITCHES 172-175; Jewett - WHICH 11-15.

Whippety Stourie. Arbuthnot - FAIRY 31-33 (D2183.1); Wilson - SCOTTISH 75-80.

Whisp of Straw, Lump of Coal, and Little Broad Bean. Grimm - BROTHERS 21-22 (F662.3; F1025.1).

Whistle the Winds. Cothran - MAGIC 13-17 (A1122.4.1).

The White Bear. Manning-Sanders - BOOK..MAGICAL 184-195 (H1385.4C).

White-Bear-King-Valemon. Asbjørnsen - NORWEGIAN 150-157.

Whitebear Whittington. Chase - WICKED 52-64 (H1385.4Ac); Ross - BLUE 123-137.

The White Cat. Arbuthnot - ANTHOLOGY 224-231 (B641Db); Arbuthnot - FAIRY 115-122; Dalgliesh - ENCHANTED 162-173; Farjeon - CAVALCADE..QUEENS 1-22; Lang - BLUE 172-191; LeCain - WHITE pb; Lubin - WHITE pb; Wiggin - FAIRY 312-325.

The White Cat and the Green Snake. Manning-Sanders - PRINCES 108-117 (D735.1F).

The White Crane. Novak - FAIRY 156-164 (B652.2.1).

The White Dog. Owen - CASTLE 51-62 (H1385.4Eb).

The White Dove. Manning-Sanders - BOOK.. WITCHES 104-114 (G530.2Bg).

The White Dove. Shub - ABOUT 52-53 (H1385.3Jc).

The White Elephant. Asia - FOLK..FOUR 17-23 (J2133.5.2).

White-faced Simminy. Williams-Ellis - FAIRY.. BRITISH 153-154 (X1506.1).

The White Fox. Yellow Robe - TONWEYA 42-51 (A1832.1).

The White Hare and the Crocodiles. Haviland - FAVORITE..JAPANESE 73-89 (K579.2.2; K1014.3); Ozaki - JAPANESE..FAIRY 214-233.

The White Hare of Inabi. Gruenberg - FAVORITE 347-348 (K579.2.2; K1014.3).

The White Hen. MacManus - BOLD 169-178 (D2183F).

The White Lady of Pumphul. Spicer - THIRTEEN GHOSTS 83-91 (F348.11).

The White Parrot. Eells - TALES..SPAIN 3-13 (H1331.1.3Fa).

The White Pet. Wilson - SCOTTISH 81-87 (K335.1.4; K1161.1).

THE WHITE RAT'S TALE. Schiller pb (L392.0.1.1).

The White Snake. Carpenter - TALES..CHINA 159-165 (B656.2.1).

The White Snake. Grimm - GRIMM'S (Follett) 399-406 (B217.1.1; B582.2C); Grimm - GRIMM'S (Grosset) 80-85; Grimm - GRIMM'S (Viking) 17-21; Grimm - GRIMM'S (World) 29-33; Grimm - HOUSEHOLD 93-97 (B582.2); Lang - GREEN 305-310 (B217.1.1); Tashjian - ONCE 57-69.

The White Snake Lady. Bonnet - CHINESE 43-48 (B656.2.1).

The White Spider's Gift. Barlow - LATIN 43-49 (A1465.2.1.1).

White Squash Boy. Robertson - FAIRY..PHILIP-PINES 63-69 (T555.1.1.1).

The White Stone Canoe. Bierhorst - FIRE 29-38 (F81.1.0.4.1).

WHITE WAVE. Wolkstein pb (N831.1).

Whittington and His Cat. Arbuthnot - FAIRY 27-31 (N411.1); De La Mare - ANIMAL 116-126; Jacobs - ENGLISH 174-185.

Who? Leach - HOW 15-16 (A812.5; A961.1; A1263.1.3).

Who Am I? Serwer - LET'S STEAL 68-73 (J2012.6).

Who Am I? Shah - MULLA 151 (J2013.3); Withers - WORLD 80-81.

Who Can Break a Bad Habit? Carpenter -

AFRICAN 41-45 (K263.1).

Who Got Brer Gilyard's Treasure? Faulkner - DAYS 178-185 (K649.9.2).

Who Is Older? Courlander - PIECE 70 (B841.1.3).

Who Is Responsible? Tooze - WONDERFUL 118-120 (J1175.1).

Who Is Strongest? Withers - I SAW 100-101 (L392.0.5).

Who Is the Mightiest? Withers - I SAW 122 (L392.0.6).

Who Is Who? Jagendorf - NOODLEHEAD 93-96 (J2013.3).

Who Knows, Maybe You're a Helmite Too! Simon - WISE 127-135 (J1881.1.8).

Who Lived in the Skull? Ransome - OLD PETER'S 228-230 (J2199.5.1).

Who Nibbled Up the Butter? Harris - COMPLETE 53-57 (K372C; K401.1); Harris - FAVORITE 252-257; Harris - UNCLE 81-87.

Who Rules the Roost? Arbuthnot - ANTHOLOGY 401 (T252.4.2); Jagendorf - KING 102-106.

Who Stole Brer Gilyard's Sheep? Faulkner - DAY 158-163 (K1066.7).

Who Was Most Skillful? Withers - I SAW 142 (F660.1C).

Who Will Row Next? Ginsburg - LAZIES 18-20 (W167.3).

Who Will Wash the Porridge Pot? Higonnet-Schnopper - TALES 30-33 (J2511.0.3).

Who Will Wash the Pot? Ginsburg - LAZIES 8-10 (J2511.0.3).

WHO'S IN RABBIT'S HOUSE? Aardema pb (K1711.2.1).

Who's Strong? Jagendorf - KING 142-144 (C984.5).

Who's Shot Was That? Shah - MULLA 56-57 (N621.2).

Whuppity Stoorie. Finlay - TATTERCOATS 53-59 (D2183H).

Why Animals Are Afraid of Fire. Belting - LONG 76-78 (A2436.1).

Why Ants Carry Large Bundles. Leach - HOW 107 (A2243.1).

Why Ants Live Everywhere. Leach - HOW 105-106 (A2434.1.4).

Why Apes Look Like People. Lester - BLACK 21-

37 (A2375.11).

Why Are We Waiting? Shah – MULLA 138 (J1742.3.2).

Why Bananas Belong to Monkeys. Newman – FOLK ..LATIN 61-66 (K741.0.1).

Why Bat Flies Alone. Leach – HOW 71-72 (A2491.1; B261.1).

Why Bear Eats Meat. De Leeuw – LEGENDS 109-111 (K171.1).

Why Bear Sleeps All Winter. Leach – HOW 73-74 (A2481.1).

Why Blackbird Has White Eyes. DeWit – TALKING 75-79 (A2332.5.12).

Why Brer Rabbit Is Bob-Tailed. Harris – COMPLETE 80-83 (A2378.4.1); Harris – FAVORITE 11-14; Harris – UNCLE 122-126.

Why Brother Bear Has No Tale. Harris – COMPLETE 199-202 (A2378.4.2.1); Harris – NIGHTS 113-117.

Why Brother Wolf Didn't Eat the Little Rabbits. Harris – COMPLETE 499-501 (K1715.3.1).

Why Cat Eats First. Leach – HOW 65 (A2545.2; K562).

Why Cat Eats First and Washes Afterward. Leach – LION 13 (K562).

Why Cat Sleeps By the Fire or Keeps the Chimney Corner. Leach – LION 25 (A2433.3.1.1).

Why Cats Always Wash after Eating. Dobbs – ONCE 67-69 (A2545.2; K562); Hardendorff – TRICKY 121-122.

Why Cats and Dogs Are Enemies. Dobbs – MORE 83-85 (A2281.0.1; A2493.37; A2494.1.4; A2494.4.3.1).

Why Cats Live With Women. Heady – WHEN 85-90 (A2513.2.1).

Why Chicken Lives With Man. Leach – HOW 91 (A2513.6.1).

Why Coyote Stopped Imitating His Friends. Brown – TEPEE 150-153 (J2425).

Why Coyotes Howl. Heady – SAGE 70-73 (A2427.4.1).

Why Crabs Are Flat. Cathon – PERHAPS 77 (A2305.6).

Why Crab's Eyes Stick Out. Leach – HOW 121-122 (A2231.10).

Why Crane's Feathers Are Brown and Otter Doesn't Feel the Cold. Belting – LONG 23-25 (A2411.2.6.14.1).

Why Craney-crow Flies Fast. Harris – COMPLETE 640-647 (J2413.4.2.1); Harris – FAVORITE 296-300.

Why Crocodile Does Not Eat Hen. Leach – HOW 111 (K601.3).

Why Crow Has a Right to the First Corn. Leach – HOW 100 (A2685.1.0.2).

Why Crows Are Black. De Leeuw – INDONESIAN 113-116 (A1241; A2234.2.1; A2236.4.1).

Why Deer's Teeth Are Blunt. Bell – JOHN 70-73 (A2345.3.2).

Why Didn't You Tell Me Before? Shah – MULLA 123 (J2260).

Why Do Waves Have White Caps? Lester – KNEE 21-24 (A116.2).

Why Dog Is the Friend of Man. Arnott – AFRICAN 1-4 (A2513.1.2).

Why Dog Lost His Voice. Carter – GREEDY 14-17 (A2422.1; N385.1.2).

Why Dogs and Cats Are Not Friends. Carpenter – WONDER..DOGS 35-42 (A2281.1; A2471.1.1).

Why Dogs Carry Their Tails Over Their Backs. Belting – LONG 26-28 (A2378.1.7.1).

Why Dogs Hate Cats. Lester – KNEE 9-11 (A2494.1.2.3).

Why Dogs Have Long Tongues. Brown – TEPEE 26-28 (A2344.4.1).

Why Dogs Live With Men. Heady – WHEN 42-46 (A1831.3; A2513.1.1).

Why Dogs Wag Their Tails. Sechrist – ONCE 38-42 (A2471.1.2; A2479.12; A2534.2).

Why Donkeys Have Long Ears. Dobbs – MORE 86-89 (A2325.3.1); Jagendorf – PRICELESS 122-124.

Why Ducks Have Flat Feet. Belting – LONG 39-41 (A2375.2.8.1).

Why Ducks Sleep Standing On One Leg. Schultz – VIETNAMESE 86-89 (A2479.13).

Why Elephant and Whale Live Where They Do. Leach – HOW 80-81 (A2433.3.15.1; A2433.7.1; K22).

Why Flounder's Two Eyes Are on the Same Side of His Face. Leach – HOW 117 (A2332.4.4).

Why Fly Rubs His Hands Together. Leach – HOW 108 (A1414.1.1.1).

Why Frogs Croak in Wet Weather. Leach – HOW 115 (A2426.4.1.2).

Why Frogs Speak Chinese. Alexander - PEBBLES 15 (A2426.4.1).

Why Goat Cannot Climb a Tree. Leach - HOW 67 (A2581.1); Leach - LION 20.

Why God Made the Dog. Leach - HOW 59 (A1831.1.1).

Why Grasshopper Spits Tobacco Juice. Leach - HOW 109-110 (A2472.2).

Why Grizzly Bears Walk on All Fours. Fisher - STORIES 24-35 (A963.12; A2441.1.14).

Why Groundhog's Tail Is Short. Belting - LONG 29-33 (K606.2.1).

Why Hawks Feed on Chickens. Nunn - AFRICAN 36-40 (A2494.13.10.3.1).

Why Jellyfish Has No Shell. Leach - HOW 118-120 (K544).

Why Kwaku Ananse Stays on the Ceiling. Appiah - ANANSE 139-146 (A2433.5.3.3).

Why Lion Lives in the Forest. Leach - HOW 77 (A2433.3.16).

Why Men Have to Work. Lester - BLACK 38-41 (A625.2.8).

Why Misery Remains in the World. Carter - GREEDY 18-24 (Z111.2.1.1).

Why Miss Goose Roosts High. Harris - FAVORITE 35-38 (K525.1.0.1).

Why Mr. Dog Is Tame. Harris - COMPLETE 692-698 (A2513.1.2.1); Harris - FAVORITE 272-277.

Why Mr. Dog Runs Brother Rabbit. Harris - COMPLETE 369-371 (A2494.4.4.1); Harris - NIGHTS 349-352.

Why Mr. Possum Has No Hair on His Tail. Harris - COMPLETE 87-90 (A2317.12); Harris - UNCLE 131-137.

Why Mole's Front Paws Are Bent. Belting - LONG 51-53 (A727.2).

Why Monkeys Live in Trees. Nunn - AFRICAN 17-20 (A2433.3.19.0.1).

Why No One Ever Carries the Alligator Down to the Water. Dobbs - ONCE 54-59 (J1172.3.0.3).

WHY NOAH CHOSE THE DOVE. Singer pb (A1021).

Why Owls See Only at Night. Bowes - BIRD 45-50 (A2491.2.5).

Why People Keep Dogs. Leach - HOW 60-61 (A2493.4.1).

Why People Tell Stories. Ure - RUMANIAN 172-

177 (M231.1Ba).

Why People Watch the Dipper. Leach - HOW 135 (A1002.2.5).

Why Porpoise Is Not a Fish. Leach - HOW 85 (A2135.4).

Why Possums Tail Is Bare. Bell - JOHN 47-51 (A2317.12.3).

Why Rabbit Has a Short Tail. Leach - HOW 69 (A2378.4.1.5; K579.2.2).

Why Rabbits Have Short Tails. Arnott - ANIMAL 220-223 (K751.0.1).

Why Rabbits Have Short Tails. Williams-Ellis - ROUND 195-196 (A2378.4.1.1).

Why Robin Has a Red Breast. Leach - HOW 95 (A2411.2.1.18.2).

Why Siberian Birds Migrate in Winter. Arnott - ANIMAL 83-86 (A2482.4).

Why Some Trees Are Evergreen. Leach - HOW 125 (A2765.1).

Why Spider Has a Little Head and a Big Behind. Leach - HOW 82-83 (A2320.1.2).

Why Spider Lives in Ceilings. Arkhurst - ADVENTURES 12-20 (A2433.5.3.3; K607.1).

Why Spiders Hide in Corners. Green - FOLKTALES 9-13 (W125.3.1).

Why Spiders Live in Dark Corners. Arkhurst - ADVENTURES 40-49 (A2433.5.3.3; A2433.5.3.4; K741.0.7).

Why Sun and Moon Live in the Sky. Leach - HOW 20-21 (A736.1.4.4).

Why Ted-oh, the Woodchuck, Climbs a Tree. Parker - SKUNNY 60-67 (J2346.1).

Why the Alligator's Back Is Rough. Harris - COMPLETE 220-224 (A2356.2.11; K1055.2); Harris - NIGHTS 141-145.

Why the Animals Have Fire. Leach - HOW 57 (A2513.1.2.1).

Why the Animals Live Where They Do. Belting - LONG 85-88 (A2433.3.0.1).

Why the Ant Is Almost Cut in Two. Marriott - WINTER 31-35 (A1335.8.1; A2355.1.2.2).

Why the Baboon Has a Shining Seat. Robinson - SINGING 8-15 (A2362.1.1; K311.3.1).

Why the Baby Says "Goo." Gruenberg - FAVORITE 333-335 (A1399.5).

Why the Bagobo Like the Cat. Sechrist - ONCE 40-49 (J1172.3; J1172.3.2).

Why the Bananas Belong to the Monkey. Dobbs –
ONCE 60-66 (K741.0.12).

Why the Bat Comes Out Only at Night. Walker –
NIGERIAN 26 (A2491.1; B261.1).

Why the Bat Flies at Night. Arnott – AFRICAN
150-152 (A2491.1; A2491.1.0.1).

Why the Bear Cannot Play the Kantele. Deutsch –
MORE 31 (K1111.0.1.2).

Why the Bear Has a Stumpy Tail. Wiggin – TALES
176 (K1021).

Why the Bear Is Stumpy Tailed. Arbuthnot –
FAIRY 75-76 (K1021); Asbjørnsen – EAST (Row)
34; Aulaire – EAST 138; Haviland – NORWAY 65-
66; Hutchinson – FIRESIDE 25-26; Martignoni –
ILLUSTRATED 89-90; Undset – TRUE 180-181.

Why the Bear's Tail Is Short. Deutsch – MORE 11
(K371.1; K1021).

Why the Bear's Tail Is So Short. Sperry – HEN
35-38 (K1021); Sperry – SCANDINAVIAN 27-28.

Why the Birds Are Different Colors. Leach – HOW
89-90 (A2411.2.1.19; A2911.2.0.1).

Why the Bush-Fowl Calls at Dawn and Why Flies
Buzz. Arnott – AFRICAN 56-63 (Z49.6.0.2).

Why the Buzzard Eats the Rooster's Children.
Withers – MAN 91-92 (A2494.13.10.7).

Why the Carabao's Hoof Is Split. Sechrist – ONCE
56-60 (A2376.1.0.1; K11.1).

Why the Cat and the Dog Cannot Live at Peace.
Deutsch – MORE 25-29 (A2281.1).

Why the Chameleon Shakes His Head. Courlander
– KING'S 98-100 (A2474.1.2).

Why the Chipmunk's Back Is Striped. Field –
AMERICAN 3-12 (A1859.2.1).

Why the Cock Eats Worms. Bonnet – CHINESE
111-114 (A2242.2).

Why the Cormorant Has No Tail. Brockett – BUR-
MESE 131-135 (A2378.2.11).

Why the Cougar Has a Long Tail. Heady – SAGE
80-84 (A2378.3.5).

Why the Crab Has No Head or How the First River
Was Made. Arnott –AFRICAN 35-39 (A934.13;
A2320.4).

Why the Crocodile Hates Man. De Leeuw – INDO-
NESIAN 94-98 (A2130.2).

Why the Dog and the Cat Are Enemies. Green –
BIG 32-33 (A2494.1.2.2; D882.1A).

Why the Dog and the Cat Are Not Friends. Carpenter – KOREAN 47-54 (A2534.2; D882.1A).

Why the Dog and the Cat Are Not Friends.
Gruenberg – MORE 125-129 (A2494.1.2; A2534.2;
D882.1A).

Why the Dog Has a Cold Wet Nose. Dobbs – MORE
68-71 (A2335.2.6).

Why the Deer Have Short Teeth. Marriott – WIN-
TER 25-31 (A2345.3.1).

Why the Deer's Teeth Are Blunt. Scheer – CHER-
OKEE 58-60 (A2345.3.2).

Why the Fish Do Not Speak. Deutsch – MORE 1-5
(A2272.1.4; A2422.14).

Why the Fish Laughed. Jacobs – INDIAN 225-234
(H582.1.1; H586; H586.3; H586.4; H586.8);
Wiggin – TALES 263-268.

Why the Flea Hops. Hitchcock – KING 76-79
(K372.2).

Why the Guinea-Fowls Are Speckled. Harris –
COMPLETE 257-261 (A2411.2.6.6.1); Harris –
NIGHTS 193-197.

Why the Hare's Lip Is Split. Deutsch – MORE 19-
23 (J881.1).

Why the Hawk Is the Hen's Enemy. Arnott –
AFRICAN 152-154 (A2494.13.10.3.1).

Why the Hawk Never Steals. Fuja – FOURTEEN
203-209 (A2494.13.10.3.3).

Why the Hill is Red. Asia – FOLK..1 37-40
(A969.11.1).

Why the Hyrax Has No Tail. Heady – WHEN 68-71
(A2235).

Why the Jackal Howls. Hitchcock – KING 97-100
(K688.5).

WHY THE JACKAL WON'T SPEAK TO THE HEDGE-
HOG. Berson pb (K171.1).

Why the Jellyfish Has No Bones. Sakade – JA-
PANESE 83-86 (K544.1).

Why the Lion, the Vulture and the Hyena Do Not
Live Together. Courlander – OLODE
(A2317.7.3; W141.1.1).

Why the Lizard Stretches His Neck. Appiah –
ANANSE 47-56 (A2474.1.1).

Why the Mole Lives Underground. Scheer –
CHEROKEE 51-54 (A2433.3.20.1).

Why the Monsoon Comes Each Year. Robertson –
FAIRY..VIETNAM 60-65 (A1129.2.1).

Why the Moon Has Shadows on Her Face. Gittins
– TALES 28-29 (A751.5.8).

Why the Moon Wanes. Reed – TALKATIVE 83-88
(A132.16).

Why the Motmot Lives in a Hole. Bowes - BIRD 65-71 (A2431.3.9).

Why the Negro Is Black. Harris - COMPLETE 109-110 (A1614.2).

Why the Ocean Is Salty. Sechrist - ONCE 17-19 (A1115.4).

Why the Owl Is Not King of the Birds. Babbitt - JATAKA 90-92 (A2494.13.1).

Why the Parrot Repeats a Man's Words. Courlander - RIDE 34-37 (J1151.1.3.3).

Why Pigs Root. De Leeuw - LEGENDS..HOLLAND 89-91 (Z33.1.7).

Why the Possum's Tail Is Bare. Hardendorff - JUST 85-87 (A2317.12.3); Scheer - CHEROKEE 75-79.

Why the Rabbit's Nose Twitches. Htin - KINGDOM 24-27 (Z49.6.0.7).

Why the Raven Is Black. Caswell - SHADOWS 33-34 (A2411.2.1.5.1; A2411.2.6.1.1; A2441.2.3).

Why the Red Elf Cried. Sakade - JAPANESE 53-57 (J401.2).

Why the Sea Is Salt. Asbjørnsen - EAST (Row) 139-144 (D1651.3.1); Gruenberg - FAVORITE 418-421; Haviland - NORWAY 30-44; Lang - BLUE 148-153; Leach - HOW 28-29; Undset - TRUE 149-155; Wiggin - TALES 291-295; Williams-Ellis - ROUND 130-144.

Why the Sea Moans. Cathon - PERHAPS 217-227 (R221Pb); Eells - BRAZIL 177-200; Sheehan - FOLK 127-137.

Why the Sendji Rat Has No Tail. Burton - MAGIC 101-102 (A2235).

Why the Sky Is High. Sechrist - ONCE 15-16 (A625.2.6).

Why the Spider Has a Narrow Waist. Appiah - ANANSE 123-128 (A2355.1.1.1).

Why the Spider Has a Small Head. McDowell - THIRD 31-34 (A2320.1.2).

Why the Squirrel Lives in Trees. Bowman - TALES..TUPA 249 (A2433.3.9; K2323.0.1).

Why the Sun and Moon Are in the Sky. McDowell - THIRD 129-130 (A736.1.4.4.1).

Why the Sun and Moon Live in the Sky. Arnott - JAPANESE 133-134 (A736.1.4.4); Dayrell - WHY pb; Withers - MAN 59-61.

Why the Sun Shines in the Daytime and the Moon Shines at Night. Withers - MAN 62-63 (A1170.1).

Why the Sun Stopped Shining. Borski - GOOD

57-59 (H1273.2K).

WHY THE SUN WAS LATE. Elkin pb (Z49.6.0.2).

Why the Steer Has a Smooth Nose. Dobbs - MORE 72-74 (A2221.5.1).

Why the Terrapin's Shell Is Scarred. Scheer - CHEROKEE 65-68 (K1715.3.3).

Why the Tides Ebb and Flow. Leach - HOW 25-27 (A913.6; A943).

Why the Tides Ebb and Flow. Leach - HOW 27 (A913.5).

Why the Tiger and the Monkey Are Not Friends. Brockett - BURMESE 71-78 (J2132.5.1; K84.2; K1715.2.1).

Why the Tiger Is So Angry at the Cat. Htin - KINGDOM 53-55 (A2494.1.6; A2495.1; A2581).

Why the Tip of the Fox's Tail Is White. Belting - LONG 93-94 (A2378.8.1.0.1).

Why the Tortoise's Shell Is Cracked and Crooked. Walker - NIGERIAN 27 (A2312.1.9; K311.3.1).

Why the Waringen Tree Is Holy. De Leeuw - INDONESIAN 81-89 (A2681.15).

Why the Weasel Is White. Field - AMERICAN 62-70 (A2411.1.2.1.2; F912.2.5).

Why the Whippoorwill Weeps and Wails. Bowes - BIRD 15-18 (A2241.13; A2313.6; A2313.7; A2426.2.21; A2491.6).

Why There Are No Tigers in Borneo. De Leeuw - INDONESIAN 99-103 (K1711.1).

Why There Are Shadows on the Moon. Sechrist - ONCE 14 (A751.5.2).

Why There Is a Man in the Moon. Withers - MAN 3-5 (A751.1.1).

Why There Is Death in the World. Robinson - SINGING 16-23 (A2435.3.1).

Why Tortoises Are Sacrificed. Courlander - OLODE 73-79 (A1545.3.4).

Why Wagtail Wags Her Tail. Leach - HOW 99 (A2242.1; A2378.3.5; A2378.4.8; A2479.1).

Why We Are Here. Shah - MULLA 14 (J2311.3.1).

Why We Have Earthquakes. Kim - STORY 39-40 (A1145.4).

Why Wisdom Is Found Everywhere. Courlander - HAT 30-31 (A1481.1).

Why Women Always Wash the Dishes. Robertson - FAIRY..PHILIPPINES 71-80 (J2511.1.3).

Why Women Talk More Than Men. Fisher -

CALIFORNIA 104-110 (A1372.1).

Why Women Won't Listen. Sherlock - WEST 112-117 (K311.3G).

Why Yams and Cassava Hide in the Ground. Haskett - GRAINS 47-50 (A2794.2.1).

Why You Find Spiders in Banana Bunches. Arnott - ANIMAL 87-91 (A2433.5.3.6).

The Wicked Bankiva. Sechrist - ONCE 28-31 (D1427.1.1).

A Wicked Fox. Hampden - GYPSIES' 105-109 (J758.1.0.1; K1084.1.1; K1254.1.1).

The Wicked House of Duncan MacBain. Leodhas - GHOSTS 11-23 (E531.1).

WICKED JOHN AND THE DEVIL. Chase pb (Q565Aa); Chase - WICKED 29-39.

The Wicked Sister-in-law. Yellow Robe - TONWEYA 66-85 (B536.2).

The Wicked Squire. Spicer - THIRTEEN MONSTERS 66-76 (R111.1.3Ca).

The Wicked Stone Horse of Shilin. Cheney - TALES 107-114 (A974.0.9).

The Widow and the Hen. Aesop - AESOP'S (Grosset) 232 (J1901.1).

The Widow and the Korrigans. Belting - ELVES 77-83 (F343.19; F372.2.2).

Widow Martin and Her Hen. Aesop - AESOP'S (Walck) 54 (J1901.1).

The Widow's Daughter. MacManus - HIBERNIAN 233-239 (D2183.1).

The Widow's Lazy Daughter. Haviland - FAVORITE..IRELAND 61-84 (D2183.1).

The Widow's Son. Asbjørnsen - EAST 128-141 (B316B); Asbjørnsen - EAST (Doubleday) 71-84; Aulaire - EAST 58-69.

The Wife from Another World. Jewett - WHICH 109-123 (H1385.3Fc).

The Wife Who Liked Fairy Tales. Downing - RUSSIAN 211-213 (M231.2).

Wikki, the Weaver. Aardema - TALES 18-23 (A1453.2.1; A1457.3.1).

The Wild Boar and the Fox. Aesop - AESOP'S (Grosset) 200 (J674.1); Aesop - AESOP'S (Watts) 70.

The Wild Dog and the King's Son. Carpenter - WONDER..DOGS 235-244 (G671B).

The Wild Geese and the Tortoise. Turnbull - FAIRY..INDIA 45-49 (J2357).

The Wild Ride in the Tilt Cart. Leodhas - GHOSTS 54-64 (E535.1).

The Wild Swans. Dalgliesh - ENCHANTED 1-20 (P253.2C); Wiggin - FAIRY 80-96.

The Wild Woman of the Woods. Harris - ONCE.. TOTEM 61-85 (G275.7.0.1).

Wiley and the Hairy Man. Haviland - NORTH 126-133 (B524.1.2H; K722.0.2); Bang - WILEY pb.

The Wiliwili Trees. Cothran - MAGIC 49-52 (A2121.1; A2681.7).

The Will of the Wise Man. MacManus - HIBERNIAN 160-173 (H171.8).

Willow. Garner - CAVALCADE..GOBLINS 36-39 (F441.2.3.1.1).

The Wily Fox. Bowman - TALES..TUPA 255-256 (K1788).

The Wily Lion. Aesop - AESOP'S (Watts) 193 (J642.1.1).

The Wily Tortoise. Hardendorff - JUST 71-72 (K439.7.1).

Wind and Sun. Aesop - FABLES (Walck) 88-91 (L351).

The Wind and the Ant. Serwer - LET'S 22-28 (D1711.1.1).

The Wind and the Sun. Aesop's - AESOP'S (Grosset) 130-131 (L351); Aesop - AESOP'S (Random) 47-49; Aesop - AESOP'S (Viking) 17-18; Aesop - FABLES (Macmillan) 119; Arbuthnot - FAIRY 228; Gruenberg - FAVORITE 405-406.

Wind and Wave and Wandering Flame. Pilkington - SHAMROCK 169-177 (D672K).

The Wind Demon. Buck - FAIRY 306-320 (B314B).

Windbird and the Sun. Arbuthnot - ANTHOLOGY 326-327 (A791.9.1); Gruenberg - MORE 121.

The Wine Bibber. Kendall - SWEET 42-44 (J2311.2.1).

Wink, the Lazy Bird, and the Red Fox. Parker - SKUNNY 52-59 (H588.7.3).

The Winning of Kwelanga. Aardema - BEHIND 34-41 (G530.2Fc).

Winter Bamboo. Cheney - TALES 119-121 (A2681.6.1).

Winter Rose. Lin - MILKY 57-63 (K717.4).

THE WINTER WIFE. Compton pb (B651.5.1).

The Wisdom of Cecchino. Jagendorf - PRICELESS 114-121 (K187.1).

The Wisdom of Solomon. Gruenberg - FAVORITE 357-359 (H540.2.1).

The Wisdom of the Lord. Jagendorf - NOODLE-HEAD 102-104 (J2571).

The Wisdom of the Rabbit. Bowman - TALES.. TUPA 253 (K17.5).

The Wisdom of the Water Buffalo. Chang - CHINESE 53 (B264.3).

Wise Alois. Duvoisin - THREE 234-245 (B217.9.1).

The Wise and the Foolish Merchant. Babbitt - JATAKA 44-51 (J701.3Ff).

The Wise Ant. Wilson - GREEK 9-10 (J711.1).

The Wise Bird and the Foolish Bird. Harris - COMPLETE 384-386 (K869.6); Harris - NIGHTS 370-372.

The Wise Doctor. Bulatkin - EURASIAN 124-125 (K1955.1.0.1).

The Wise Dog. Fuja - FOURTEEN 186-195 (K311.3.1).

The Wise Frog and the Foolish Frog. Riordan - TALES..CENTRAL 241-242 (Q81.2).

The Wise Goat. Gilstrap - SULTAN'S 18-25 (K1715.3).

The Wise Judge. Alexander - PEBBLES 19 (J1141.1.3.4.2).

The Wise Judge. Cimino - DISOBEDIENT #3 (J1521.5).

The Wise Judge. Davis - LION'S 108-112 (X111.1.1).

The Wise Judge. Vittorini - ITALIAN TALES 14-18 (J1173).

The Wise Judge. Green - FOLK..AFRICAN 21-27 (X111.1.1).

The Wise King and the Little Bee. Dobbs - MORE 19-33 (H540.2.1.1).

The Wise Man of Gotham. Hutchinson - CANDLE-LIGHT 103-104 (J1881.1.1).

A Wise Man on a Camel. Reed - TALKATIVE 76 (J2113; J2171.6).

The Wise Man's Pillow. Wyndham - TALES.. CHINA 14-19 (D1812.3.3.2.1).

The Wise Men of Chelm. Dobbs - MORE 45-48 (J2163.3; J2165).

The Wise Men of Gotham. Jacobs - MORE 222-228 (J1881.1.1; J1881.2.2; J1904.2; J1909.8.1; J2062.1; J2031).

The Wise Men of Gotham. Jagendorf - NOODLE-HEAD 115-117 (J2062.1).

The Wise Men of Gotham. Jagendorf - NOODLE-HEAD 117-118 (J1904.2).

The Wise Men of Gotham. Leach - NOODLES 30-34 (J1904.2; J1909ff; J2031; J2123).

The Wise Men of Gotham. Steel - ENGLISH 203-208 (J1881.1.1; J1881.2.2; J1904.2; J1909ff; J2031; J2062.1).

The Wise Men of Holmola. Bowman - TALES.. TUPA 220-230 (J1865; J1938; J2123; J2123.2; J2301; J2381).

The Wise Men of Muing An Chait. Danaher - FOLKTALES 34-41 (J1772.1; J1881.1.2).

The Wise Nasreddin. Ginsburg - KAHA 88-89 (J1392.1.2; J1396.6; J1904.4.1).

The Wise Old Camel. Kaula - AFRICAN 150-154 (K453.1).

The Wise Old Shepherd. Hardendorf - JUST 64-70 (K551.29).

The Wise Old Woman. Uchida - SEA 61-71 (H1021.2.1; H1049.5; J151.1).

Wise Padre Ulivo. Jagendorf - PRICELESS 138-146 (Q565Ai).

The Wise Priest. Hardendorff - TRICKY 93-96 (K1785.1).

A Wise Sentence. Vittorini - OLD 24-27 (J1172.2).

The Wise Wife. Bulatkin - EURASIAN 27-38 (H583.3.3; H583.4.2.2; H583.8; J1191.1; J1545.4).

The Wise Witness. Borski - GOOD 75-77 (J1191.2).

The Wise Woodland Maid. Toor - GOLDEN 41-46 (H601; J1191.1).

Wise Words with Golden Profit. Jagendorf - PRICELESS 95-101 (A1447.3.1).

Wiser Than All Kings. Aardema - MORE 50-55 (K842.0.10).

Wisehead the Giant. Gittins - TALES 41-46 (F531.6.9.1).

The Wish-hound. Manning-Sanders - PETER 166-168 (E521.2.5).

The Wishing Cup. Hume - FAVORITE..CHINA 47-54 (J2415.12).

The Wishing Table, the Gold Donkey and the Cudgel-in-the-sack. Gag - MORE..GRIMM 99-115 (D861.1G).

The Wishing Well. Harper - GHOSTS 166-172

(Q2.1.6A).

The Wishing Well. Sawyer – LONG 99–107
(B251.1.2.4).

The Witch. Aesop – AESOP'S (Watts) 207
(J1062.3.1).

The Witch. Buck – FAIRY 162–167 (Q2.1.2CeBa);
Lang – YELLOW 223–238.

The Witch. Melzack – DAY 59–67 (G412.0.1).

The Witch and Her Four Sons. Matson – LONG-
HOUSE 49–59 (G219.3.1).

A Witch and Her Servants. Lang – YELLOW 172–
191 (H1385.3Jb).

The Witch and the Swan Maidens. Manning-
Sanders – PETER 63–70 (B652.1.2).

Witch Cat. Leach – THING 91–94 (D702.1.1.1).

The Witch Hare. De La Mare – ANIMAL 75–76
(G275.12.2).

The Witch in the Stone Boat. Hoke – WITCH 197–
204 (K1911Ab); Lang – YELLOW 276–282.

The Witch of Fraddam. Manning-Sanders – PETER
72–76 (G275.1.2).

The Witch of Lok Island. Harper – GHOSTS 176–
191 (G263.1.0.1.1); Hoke – WITCHES 206–208;
Sechrist – HEIGH-HO 34–46.

The Witches of Ascalon. Serwer – LET'S 3–8
(G273.8).

The Witches Ride. Arbuthnot – ANTHOLOGY 407
(G242.7.3); Harper – GHOSTS 228–233
(K335.1.1.3.1); Hoke – WITCHES 186–187.

The Witch's Daughter. Wyndham – FOLK 26–36
(G530.2Bj).

THE WITCH'S PIG. Calhoun pb (G265.0.1.2).

The Witch's Shoes. Harper – GHOSTS 192–194
(G211.1.1.2A); Hoke – WITCHES 219–220.

The Witch's Skin. Alegria – THREE 86–89
(G229.1.1).

With a Wig, With a Wag. Cothran – WITH 1–8
(Q2.1.2Cb); Tashjian – DEEP 86–92.

With and Without. Leach – NOODLES 56 (H1056).

The Witsduks. Curry – DOWN 90–100 (A289.4).

A Witty Answer. Hardendorff – JUST 21 (H1078).

The Wizard King. Manning-Sanders – PRINCES
40–48 (H321D).

The Wizard of Alderly Edge. Colwell – ROUND
15–18 (D1960.2.2).

The Wizard of Long Sleddale. Colwell – ROUND
27–29 (D1711.0.1.2).

The Woeful Tale of Long Tail Rabbit and Long Tail
Lynx. Parker – SKUNNY 75–84 (A2378.4.1.4;
A2378.4.11).

The Wolf. Deutsch – TALES 56–62 (Z49.5.2).

Wolf and Goat. Aesop – FABLES (Walck) 114
(K2061.4).

The Wolf and His Shadow. Aesop – AESOP'S
(Watts) 191 (J953.13.1).

Wolf and House-Dog. Aesop – FABLES (Walck)
110–111 (L451.3).

The Wolf and the Blacksmith. Hardendorff – JUST
110–115 (B279.1.1).

The Wolf and the Cat. Carey – BABA 18–19
(H1558.4.1); Wyndham – TALES..RUSSIA 68–71.

The Wolf and the Crane. Aesop – AESOP'S (Gros-
set) 144–145 (W154.3); Aesop – AESOP'S (Ran-
dom) 70–72; Aesop – AESOP'S (Viking) 22;
Aesop – AESOP'S (Watts) 106; Aesop – FABLES
(Macmillan) 9; Aesop – FABLES (Walck) 48–49;
Aesop – FIVE 80; Martignoni – ILLUSTRATED 155.

The Wolf and the Fox. Bowman – TALES..TUPA
261–262 (K522.4.2; K652.0.1).

The Wolf and the Fox. De La Mare – ANIMAL 31–
36 (K1022.1); De La Mare – TALES 119–124.

The Wolf and the Fox. Duvoisin – THREE 48–52
(K372D).

The Wolf and the Fox. Gag – MORE..GRIMM 9–13
(K1022.1).

The Wolf and the Fox. Lang – GREEN 326–330
(K2323).

The Wolf and the Fox. Richardson – GREAT 140–
146 (K1022.1); Wiggin – TALES 88–89.

The Wolf and the Goat. Aesop – AESOP'S (Grosset) 134–135 (K2061.4); Aesop – AESOP'S (Random) 72–73; Aesop – AESOP'S (Watts) 140;
Martignoni – ILLUSTRATED 153.

The Wolf and the House Dog. Aesop – AESOP'S
(Random) 75–77 (L451.3).

The Wolf and the Kid. Aesop – AESOP'S (Grosset)
88 (J974) : Aesop – FABLES (Macmillan) 31.

The Wolf and the Kids. TALL..NURSERY 62–69
(K311.3A).

The Wolf and the Lamb. Aesop – AESOP'S (Grosset) 127–128 (U31); Aesop – AESOP'S (Random)
56–58; Aesop – AESOP'S (Viking) 15–16; Aesop
– AESOP'S (Watts) 9; Aesop – FABLES (Macmillan) 15; Aesop – FIVE 30.

The Wolf and the Lion. Aesop - AESOP'S (Watts) 96 (U21.4); Kent - MORE 8-11.

The Wolf and the Old Woman. Green - BIG 212 (J2066.5).

The Wolf and the Ram. Durham - TIT 43-45 (K553.3).

The Wolf and the Seven Goats. Grimm - GRIMM'S (Grosset) 50-53 (K311.3); Grimm - GRIMM'S (World) 180-183.

The Wolf and the Seven Kids. Martignoni - IL-LUSTRATED 74-76 (K311.3); Shub - ABOUT 17-19; Wiggin - TALES 166-169.

The Wolf and the Seven Little Goats. Grimm - HOUSEHOLD 40-42 (K311.3).

The Wolf and the Seven Little Kids. Arbuthnot - FAIRY 34-35 (K311.3); Gag - MORE..GRIMM 241-249; Grimm - GRIMM'S (Follett) 407-412; Grimm - WOLF (Harcourt) pb; Grimm - WOLF (Larousse) pb; Haviland - FAIRY 16-21.

The Wolf and the Sheep. Aesop - AESOP'S (Watts) 109 (K815.11); Aesop - FIVE 58 (K191).

The Wolf and the Shepherd. Aesop - AESOP'S (Watts) 120 (K2061.1).

The Wolf and the Shepherds. Aesop - AESOP'S (Grosset) 230 (J1909.5.1).

The Wolf and the Watch Dog. Green - ANIMAL 90-91 (L451.3).

The Wolf Cub. Ginsburg - TWELVE 71 (J1908.4).

The Wolf in Sheep's Clothing. Aesop - AESOP'S (Golden) 76 (K828.1); Aesop - AESOP'S (Grosset) 2; Aesop - AESOP'S (Viking) 26; Aesop - AESOP'S (Watts) 24; Aesop - FABLES (Macmillan) 77; Aesop - FABLES (Walck) 20-21; Arbuthnot - FAIRY 230.

The Wolf in Shepherd's Clothing. Aesop - FIVE 74 (K828.1.2).

The Wolf in the Ram's Skin. Cooper - FIVE 47-57 (J2172.2.2.1; K842Ab).

The Wolf in the Sack. Jagendorf - NOODLEHEAD 256-259 (K1715.3).

The Wolf That Went Fishing. Carrick - STILL MORE 95-104 (K1021.0.2).

The Wolf, the Fox and the Jug of Honey. Belpré - TIGER 43-47 (K372E; K401.1).

The Wolf, the Mother and Her Child. Aesop - AESOP'S (Watts) 89 (J2066.5).

The Wolf, the Sheep and the Ram. Aesop - AE-SOP'S (Watts) 189 (K2061.1.1).

The Wolf Turned Shepherd. Green - ANIMAL

224-225 (K828.1.2).

The Wolf Wears a Sheepskin. Wilson - GREEK 180-181 (K828.1.1).

The Wolf Who Knew How to Be a Friend. Papashvily - YES 9-27 (H1331.1.3Ag).

The Wolf Who Went to Jerusalem. Papashvily - YES 41-45 (K579.5.1).

Wolf Wisdom. Leekley - WORLD 20-26 (J292).

Wolf! Wolf! Aesop - FABLES (Walck) 59-60 (J2172.1); TALL..NURSERY 74-76.

The Wolf's Breakfast. Zajdler - POLISH 119-126 (K551.1.0.2; K553.5.2; K561.1.0.6; K1121.0.1).

The Wolf's Eyelashes. Novak - FAIRY 174-183 (B771.0.2).

The Wolf's Food. Maas - MOON 99-103 (J1233.6.1).

The Woman and the Changeling Elf. Shub - ABOUT 34 (F321.1.1).

The Woman and the Wolf. Chang - CHINESE 50-52 (K1161.3.5).

The Woman Dressed Like a Man. Curtis - GIRL 61-69 (K1837.9).

The Woman in the Moon. Thompson - HAWAIIAN ..EARTH 76-80 (A751.8.3.1).

The Woman of the Snow. Littledale - GHOST 157-164 (T115.1).

THE WOMAN OF THE WOOD: A TALE FROM OLD RUSSIA. Black pb (H621).

The Woman Tribe. Carpenter - SOUTH 100-107 (A979.2; F565.1.2).

The Woman Who Flummoxed the Fairies. Greene - CLEVER 13-24 (F320.3); Leodhas - HEATHER 35-43; Minard - WOMENFOLK 135-145.

The Woman Who Raised a Bear As Her Son. Melzack - DAY 77-84 (A1836.1).

The Woman Who Turned to Stone. Field - ESKIMO 64-66 (A974.0.2).

The Woman Who Wanted to Cook with Salt Water. Berry - MAGIC 50-55 (J1959.3).

THE WOMAN WITH THE EGGS. Andersen pb (J2061.1.2).

Woman's Guile Triumphs Over Man's. Mittleman - BIRD 117-125 (J1547).

The Wonder of Skoupa. Haviland - FAVORITE.. GREECE 53-59 (F321.9).

The Wonder Ship and Ship's Crew. MacManus - BOLD 101-109 (F601.2Abb).

The Wonder-Tree. De Leeuw - INDONESIAN 151-156 (J2415.17).

The Wonder-working Steeds. Whitney - IN A 97-104 (H331.1.2.3).

The Wonderful Birch. Lang - RED 114-127 (R221Bd).

The Wonderful Bridge. Wyndham - FOLK..CHINA 50-53 (A501.2).

The Wonderful Cake. Pilkington - SHAMROCK 102-103 (W111.6; Z33.1.5).

The Wonderful Hair. Fillmore - LAUGHING 219-228 (D672H).

The Wonderful Knapsack. Association - CASTLES 97-107 (K213A); Hatch - THIRTEEN 81-93.

The Wonderful Lamb. Harper - GHOSTS 213-221 (H341.1Aa).

The Wonderful Mallet. Wiggin - TALES 421-429 (J2415.15).

The Wonderful Musician. Grimm - GRIMM'S (World) 372-375 (K1111.0.1); Grimm - HOUSE-HOLD 52-55.

The Wonderful Pear Tree. Carpenter - TALES.. CHINESE 142-149 (F971.7.1).

The Wonderful Pictures. Wyndham - FOLK.. CHINA 13-16 (D435.2.1.4).

The Wonderful Pipes. Huggins - BLUE 7-14 (D1415.2.4.1).

The Wonderful Plow. Belting - ELVES 35-40 (F451.5.1.6.3).

The Wonderful Pot. Association - TOLD..GREEN 81-87 (D1605.1); Haviland - DENMARK 3-13; Hutchinson - FIRESIDE 93-103.

The Wonderful Shirt. Manning-Sanders - CHOICE 13-25 (K2213).

The Wonderful Stone. Hampden - HOUSE 57-63 (D882.1D).

The Wonderful Talking Bowl. Uchida - SEA 99-111 (K301.3).

The Wonderful Tar-Baby Story. Arbuthnot - FAIRY 214-215 (K741); Arbuthnot - FAIRY 216-218 (K581.2); Arbuthnot - ANTHOLOGY 383-384; Brown - BRER 6-11; Gruenberg - FAVOR-ITE 336-338; Harris - COMPLETE 6-8; Harris - FAVORITE 47-50; Harris - UNCLE 7-11; Mar-tignoni - ILLUSTRATED 331-352.

The Wonderful Tea-Kettle. Wiggin - TALES 417-420 (D1171.3.1).

The Wonderful Tree. Heady - JAMBO 46-53 (J2671.4.1).

The Wonderful Tree. Manning-Sanders - GLASS 1-9 (H1385.1G).

The Wonderful Wooden Peacock Flying Machine. Tooze - WONDERFUL 15-25 (D1626.1).

The Wonders of the Three Donals. MacManus - HIBERNIAN 185-210 (M231.3).

The Wood Carver of Ruteng. Courlander - KANT-CHIL'S 110-116 (D2011.1.3).

The Wood Fairy. Haviland - FAVORITE.. CZECH-OSLOVAKIA 35-37 (F342.1; F348.0.1.1).

The Wood of Tontla. Maas - MOON 31-43 (F582.1.1).

The Woodcutter and the Old Men of the Mountains. Carpenter - KOREAN 213-218 (K2011.1.3).

The Woodcutter and the Trees. Aesop - FABLES (Walck) 112-113 (U162).

The Woodcutter and the Water Demon. Wyndham - TALES..RUSSIA 43-46 (Q3.1).

The Woodcutter of Gura. Courlander - FIRE 19-24 (J2133.4; J2311.1.6).

The Woodcutter's Daughter. Masey - STORIES 73-83 (J1511.17; X905.1.6).

THE WOODCUTTER'S DUCK. Turska pb (D2142.1.6.1).

The Woodcutter's Helper. Kelsey - HODJA 108-115 (J1172.2.1).

The Wooden Bowl. Hearn - JAPANESE 60-68 (K1815.0.2).

The Wooden Bowl. Vittorini - OLD 86-91 (J121).

The Wooden Spoon and the Whip. Fuja - FOUR-TEEN 196-202 (D861.2.1).

The Woodman and the Goblins. Harper - GHOSTS 49-56 (F481.0.1.1.2).

The Woodman and the Serpent. Aesop - AESOP'S (Grosset) 216 (X1321.4.11.1); Aesop - FABLES (Macmillan) 33.

The Woodman's Daughter and the Lion. Alegría - THREE 34-39 (H1385.4J).

The Woodpecker. Sperry - SCANDINAVIAN 260 (A1958.0.1).

The Woodpecker and the Jade Stone. Bowes - BIRD 25-31 (D931.0.5).

The Wooing of Seppo Ilmarine. Bowman - TALES ..TUPA 73-80 (H328.11).

Work-Let-Me-See. Sherlock - WEST 125-129 (A2433.5.3.5; D877.1.1.1).

A World of Nonsense. Withers - WORLD 1 (X17.91.3).

A World's Work. Chang - TALES..OLD CHINA 9-10 (Z43.3.1).

The Would-be Wizard. Carpenter - ELEPHANT'S 49-57 (N611.5).

The Wren. Green - BIG 47-51 (A2426.2.23; A2433.4.7; A2491.2.4; K11.2; K17.1.1).

The Wren and the Bear. Green - BIG 226-229 (K2323.1); Grimm - GRIMM'S (Grosset) 37-40; Wiggin - TALES 74-76.

The Wrestler of Kyushu. Courlander - TIGER'S 83-86 (F617.3).

The Wrestlers. Courlander - OLODE 107-109 (A2433.3.1.2).

The Wrestling Contest between the Cat and the Tortoise. Fuja - FOURTEEN 22-27 (J1662.0.1.1).

The Wrestling Match of the Two Buddhas. Uchida - MAGIC 22-31 (L311.0.1).

The Wrong Man. Leach - NOODLES 25 (J2012.1.1).

Wu Feng. Cheney - TALES 137-142 (W28.5).

Yallery Brown. Garner - CAVALCADE..GOBLINS 42-51 (F348.10); Jacobs - MORE 28-36.

The Yam Child. Arnott - TEMBA 20-35 (T555.3).

The Yamabushi and the Badger. Scofield - FOX 26-32 (B857.2).

Yanni. Manning-Sanders - DRAGONS 76-78 (K1715.4.0.1).

The Year of Nyangondhu's Cattle. Harmon - TALES 90-95 (F420.6.1.5.3).

The Year of the Feast at Simbi. Harmon - TALES 95-103 (F944.1).

The Year of the Monkeys of Ramogi. Harmon - TALES 103-108 (A1861.3.1).

Yehl Outwits Kanukh. Hardendorff - JUST 121-126 (A941.5.9.1; A1111.2).

The Yellow Dragon. Dolch - STORIES..OLD CHINA 121-129 (B11.7).

The Yellow Dragon. Hampden - GYPSY 45-50 (K1951.1G).

The Yellow Dragon. Manning-Sander - DRAGONS 55-61 (B11.7).

The Yellow Ribbon. Sheehan - FOLK 138-140

(Z13.4.4.1); Tashjian - JUBA 44-46.

Yi Chang and the Haunted House. Jewett - WHICH 16-28 (H1411.4.2); Littledale - GHOSTS 45-59.

Yossel-Zissel the Melamed. Simon - MORE 63-68 (J2259.2; J2289.1).

You Can't Be Too Careful. Shah - MULLA 113 (J2214.3.4).

You Can't Please Everybody. Gruenberg - MORE 388-389 (J1041.2).

You Must Pay For the Horse, Aga. Ure - RUMANIAN 167-168 (J1675.2.1).

Younde Goes To Town. Courlander - COW-TAIL 59-64 (J1802.1).

The Young Coyote's Visit. Heady - TALES 35-40 (D482.1.2).

The Young Giant. Wiggin - TALES 129-130 (F615.3.1.3).

The Young Girl and the Devil. Alegría - THREE 80-83 (G303.12.5.12).

Young Happy. Hampden - GYPSY 67-68 (X1215.11.1).

The Young Head of the Cheng Family. Wiggin - FAIRY 259-264 (H506.12); Wiggin - TALES 407-411; Wyndham - TALES..CHINA 25-33.

The Young Hunter and the JuJu Man. Carpenter - AFRICAN 137-144 (T92.15).

The Young Irish Lad from the Hiring Fair. Leodhas - GHOSTS 113-124 (K1860).

The Young Man and the Swallow. Aesop - AESOP'S (Grosset) 150 (J731.1); Aesop - AESOP'S (Viking) 11.

The Young Man and the Tiger. Asia - FOLK 1 26-31 (K1161.10).

The Young Man Who Married a Fairy. Sheppard-Jones - WELSH 72-77 (C31.8).

Young Melvin. Arbuthnot - ANTHOLOGY 370-372 (J1531.2.1).

Young Neverfull. Wiggin - TALES 45-46 (J2311.2.3).

The Young Piper. Belting - ELVES 55-60 (F321.1.4.1.1).

The Young Thief and His Mother. Aesop - AESOP'S (Grosset) 140-141 (Q586); Aesop - FABLES (Macmillan) 87.

The Young Urashima. McAlpine - JAPANESE 106-120 (F420.6.1.3.1).

Your Poor Old Mother. Shah - MULLA 101 (J1478).

The Youth Who Could Become an Ant, a Lion, or an Eagle. Toor - GOLDEN 69-79 (D532Ac; R111.1.3Aj).

The Youth Who Could Not Shudder. Grimm - GRIMM'S (World) 261-272 (H1440A).

The Youth Who Learned What Fear Was. Lang - BLUE 88-100 (H1440A).

The Youth Who Made Friends with the Beasts and the Birds. Carpenter - SOUTH 27-35 (B216.5).

The Youth Who Ploughed with Cats. Kavcic - GOLDEN 100-113 (H331.1.1A); R222.1A).

The Youth Who Trusted in God. Spicer - LONG 73-115 (H1411.4.3.2).

The Youth Who Wanted to Shiver. Carle - ERIC 75-88 (H1440A).

Ys and Her Bells. Frost - LEGEND 215-222 (F944).

Yu-Kong and the Demon. Frost - LEGENDS 69-75 (H1411.4.2).

Yuki-Onna. Buck - FAIRY 251-256 (T115.1).

Yukiko and the Little Black Cat. Novak - FAIRY 44-53 (J2415).

Yung-Kyung-Pyung. Sherlock - ANANSI 59-63 (N475.0.3).

Yvon and Finette. Wiggin - FAIRY 265-290 (G530.2Aa).

Zab. Mehdevi - PERSIAN 51-61 (J2326.1;;K346.1).

Zarian the Star-Gazer. Aesop - FABLES (Walck) 101-102 (J2133.8).

Zeus and the Horse. Green - BIG 26 (A1873.1).

Zezolla and the Date-Palm Tree. Toor - GOLDEN 31-37 (R221C).

Zini and the Witches. Colwell - SECOND 122-132 (G211.1.7.1); Hope-Simpson - CAVALCADE.. WITCHES 23-24.

Zomo Pays His Debts. Sturton - ZOMO 14-25 (Z43.6.4).

Zuiten and the Fox. Scofield - FOX 33-39 (K717.1; K891.1.5; K1887.4).

3

Subject Index

ABANDONMENT: Abandoned child in wood--S143; abandoned man in desert finds axe and arrows in tree, survives--D882.1Ga; abandonment of hero in lower world--K1931.2; abandonment on stretching tree--K1113. SEE Abandoned children--S300ff; Abandonments and exposures--S140-S159.

ABBESS WASP: K311.3B.

ABBEY: Pirates steal bells of abbey. Abbot curses them and they swell until sink ship. Still heard--F993.2.

ABBOT: Herdsman disguises as abbot and answers questions. King asks "What am I thinking?" Herdsman "That I am an abbot."--H561.2.

ABDUCTION: Dwarf makes return of child dependent on guessing riddle--D2183; girl abducted by fairy--F324; princess stolen from rescuer by imposters--K1935.

ABDULLAH: Four Abdullahs--B82.6.

ABOMINABLE SNOWMAN: Origin of Sasquatch--B29.9.1.

ABSENT-MINDEDNESS: Absent-minded person daydreams--J2060ff; thief substituted for ass while absent-minded farmer is riding--K403.1. SEE J2000-J2049.

ABSURDITIES: One absurdity rebukes another--J1530; reductio ad absurdum of judgment--J1191. SEE Absurdities based on false assumptions--J2210ff; lies, logical absurdities--X1790; absurd tasks--K1010-H1049ff.

ABUNUWAS: A. claims ass is not home despite bray-J1552.1.1; A. discredits witness with borrowed cloak--J1151.2; A. and wife feign dead--J2511.1.2.1; A. kills fly on Harun-Al-Raschid--J1193.1; A. claims borrowed pot died --J1531.3.

ACCIDENT: Accident compounded--being rescued from under tree, fool is set on sharp splintered stump, etc.--J2661.0.1; accidental discharge of gun kills much game--X1124.3. SEE Chain of accidents--Z43.4, Z49.6, Z51.1; foolish accidents--J2130-J2199; lucky accidents--N400; unlucky accidents--N300-N399.

ACORNS: Oak on Sado Island so big top was in next world--Z11.5; coyote given false recipe for acorn cake--J2724; acorn cup, oak gives her acorn cup for water--Z32.1.1.2; Dummling is given golden acorn by oak--D831A; acorns in hearth explode and injure intruder--K1161.4; fool thinks acorn falling into water fears him--J881.1; Ground Squirrel carries off acorns, sunflower seeds, obsidian chips, back is striped from sharp obsidian--A721.1.2; acorn grows to sky--Z52.4.2.

ACTRESS: Actress with bad name gives her carriage to priest and walks home--V400.2.

ADAM: Couple criticizing curiosity of Adam and Eve are given a chance at "paradise"--life of luxury at court. They must not uncover one dish--H1554.1.1; Adam pulls donkey's ears long--A2325.1.1.

ADAPTABILITY: SEE J800-J849.

ADERNA BIRD: Aderna bird sought--H1331.1.3Fc.

ADIFOFU RIVER: Origin of Adifofu River, furrow of great bull's horns--A934.1.

ADJUTANT BIRD: Tails of adjutant birds in boat are tied together--K713.1.12.

ADOPTED: Boy, jealous of two adopted boys, wishes he were a snow-goose, becomes one--D100.2.

ADVICE: Good counsel bought--J163.4; counsel proved wise by experience--J21ff; three pieces of advice--J163.4.2; proverbial wisdom--J171ff.

ADVISOR: SEE Prime Minister.

AESOP: Aesop calls to fellow slaves to take smallest loads while he takes largest which is bread for noon meal. He has no load in afternoon--J1612.1.

AFANC: Oxen pull Afanc to Llyn Fynnan--B11.11.7.1.

AGATE: Cave with tree bearing agate gems found by following deer--N773.

AGE: Characteristics of youth, middle, and old age are given man by animals--B592; animals debate which is the elder--B841.1.1; asked ten years later...is still forty, cannot go back on word--J1250; magic aging--D1890; youth and old age alike--J2214.2; old to be killed, wisdom of hidden old person saves community--J151.1; Thor, Loke, and Thraffe visit giant's hall and contest with Fire, Sea, Thought. Try to lift Midgard, wrestle with Old Age--J214. SEE OLD, YOUTH.

AGETHEY: Bagne Valley folk have thread in clothing blessed on February 5, Day of Holy Agethey, in Church of Chables--D1385.18.1.

AGHIUTSA: Devil Aghiutsa (Sarsaila) turns hermits Chirila and Manaila against each other. Pretends to tell each a secret and tells each nothing--A1342.1.

AGRICULTURE: Acquisition of food supply for human race--A1420-A1429.

AGWE: Sea-god surrounds fallen piece of fire--A781.2.

'AH ME': Ogre's name--C21.

AILPEIN BIRD: Ailpein bird carries princess to its castle--H1385.1H.

AIM: Suitor contest in shooting birds, Pikoi takes aim in calabash of water--H331.4.3.

'AINSEL': Brownie gives name as 'Ainsel', boy says "Ainsel did it."--K602.1.

AIR-CASTLE: Shattered by lack of foresight--J2060ff.

AIRPLANE: Airplane crashed, that's bad, no that's good--Z51.2. SEE FLIGHT.

ALADDIN: D871.1.

ALARM: False alarm sounded--J2172.1.

ALBAHACA PLANT: Riddle concerning number of leaves--H705.3.

ALCHEMY: Two pounds of banana-leaf down required to produce gold; plantation itself produces when thus worked--H588.7.2. SEE CHEMISTRY, GOLD

ALDAR KASE: Cat sold in land of no cats--N411.1E.

ALL-DEVOURER: Young Mantis and Young Kwammang-a cut All-Devourer open and true bushes and sheep emerge--A1884.0.2.

ALLAH: Man decides to wait on Allah to decide--N182.3; lazy man visits Allah to ask relief from poverty, wolf must devour lazy stupid man to cure pain--H1273.2H; man says he is God's son-in-law and asks for lodging, sent to mosque--J1261.1.1.1; is the will of Allah always done?--J2215.9. SEE MOHAMMED, MOSLEM, MOSQUE.

ALLERLEIRAUH: R221Da.

ALLIGATOR: SEE CROCODILE.

ALMOND: Christian knight wearing almond blossom emblem is thus known by Christian slave girl when he comes to rescue her from Moors--H87.1.

ALONG-ALONG GRASS: Rice left as offering to gods turns to along-along grass when villagers raid--A2688.2.

ALP: SEE MOUNTAINS.

ALPHABET: King introduces Korean alphabet by writing on leaves in honey so ants will eat out the letters. Says they are a miracle from heaven--A1484.2.1.

ALPHORN: Origin of alphorn, three dwarfs offer lad choice of red milk (strength), green milk (wealth), or white milk (ability to play on alphorn)--A1461.9.

AMAZIMUS: Boy detains giant ogres Amazimus by rubbing fat on stone--D672I.

AMAZONS: All male children killed by Amazons--F565.1.2.

AMBASSADOR: Dog's ambassador to Zeus--A2232.8; ambassador from Chi says poor ambassador is sent to poor country--J1289.23.

AMERICAN FALLS: Origin of American Falls. Dams thrown up by Coyote to stop flow of Snake River--A935.1.

AN DUONG VUONG: Kim Qui, golden turtle, gives Emperor An Duong Vuong magic golden nail with which he can build wall to protect Vietnam from China--A132.15.

ANACONDA: Anaconda eats daughter. Father tosses hot stone down throat and anaconda regurgitates girl--F912.3.1.1.

ANANSI: SEE SPIDER.

ANCESTOR: Origin of family tradition that ancestor was a great harp player--A1578.3.

ANCESTORS: Mule as descendant of war-horse--J954.1.1; origin of ancestor tablets--A1547.4.

ANDROCLES: Androcles and the lion--B381.

ANGAKOK: Evil spirit--G275.12.1.

ANGEL: Rabbi Joshua Ben Levi given glimpse of heaven before death, holds sword of Angel of Death while he jumps into heaven--K2371.1.1; Archangel Michael and heavenly hosts defeat Devil--G303.16.19.10; guardian angel--V238; mouse as family's guardian angel--K1917.3F; lad hidden in boat pretends to be angel--K1971.6.2; angel explains seeming unjust actions--J225.0.1; angel grants wishes to hunchback girl--A2612.4; angel given pears by three brothers gives wishes--Q1.1A.

ANGER: Anger bargain, first to lose temper to punish other--K172; knight with temper kills priest--W185.7. SEE ALSO TEMPER.

ANGUS: Angus asleep in mountain--D1960.2.

ANIMAL: SEE A1700-A2199 Creation of Animal Life; A2200-A2599 Animal Characteristics; B. ANIMALS (entire B classification is devoted to animals); D100-D199 Transformation: man to animal; D300-D399 Transformation: animal to person. SEE NAMES OF SPECIFIC ANIMALS IN SUBJECT INDEX.

ANIMAL, HELPFUL: SEE B300-B590; helpful animals ask to be beheaded--S12.1.0.1A; grateful animals and ungrateful man--W154.8; poor boy aided to princely state by helpful animal--K1952.1.1.

ANIMALS, MAGIC: SEE B100-B199.

ANIMALS, WAR: War of birds and quadrupeds--B261; in war between wild and domestic animals cat grabs bear by throat--K2323.0.1.

ANSIGE KARAMBA: A. gets head stuck licking mortar--W125.3.2.

ANSWER: Ant aids kind hero in task—R111.1.3Ao; finding answer to certain question—H1273.2, girl warned always to answer when spoken to—D754.1; king and peasant vie in riddling questions and answers—H561.6; magic object answers for fugitive—D1611; riddling answers—H583ff; clever verbal retorts—J1250-J1499.

ANT: King introduces Korean alphabet by writing on leaves with honey so ants will eat outline —A1484.2.1; ant bite drives off goat—Z39.1.0.1; witch lets brown ants, black ants, and scorpions bite tongue to change voice—K311.3E; ants bite snake and it leaves nest of curassow —Z39.1.0.3; ant bites frog, begins chain—Z49.6; creation of ant, is transformed avaricious man —A2011.2; creation, ant is transformed man who feigned extraordinary sense of smell—A2011.3; ants cross river in walnut shell, two at a time—Z11.0.1; Saynday asks red ant if men should revive again after death, she advises against this—A1334.8.1; ant rescued from drowning by dove—B362.2; why ants are everywhere—A2434.1.4; ant dies preparing feast—Z32.6; ant's foot freezes, chain—Z42.0.5; ant as go-between for earthworm and centipede—A2355.1.2.1; helpful ant—B481.1; helpful ant eats pile of food—H1385.3M; helpful ant, guesses nature of certain skin—H522.1.1; helpful ant, gathers seeds—H335.7.1; helpful ant, sorts beads—H335.7.3; helpful ant, sorts grain—B582.2C, W154.8.5; Holyman Chyavana meditates so well that ants build mound over him—D1960.5; industrious ant and lazy grasshopper—J711.1; ants killed because one stings—U21.3; tiger told that ant nest is gong—K1023.1; ants challenge elephant to race—K11.1; spider hands box to ant and refuses to take it back—A2243.1; yellow jackets and ants fighting over picnic spot are turned to two stones in Koos-Koos-Ki River—A977.5.0.4; ant teaches use of flint—A1414.8; ant teaches bread making—A1429.2.1; Tepoztan abandoned on ant hill, ants feed honey and cover with rose petals—A511.2.2.3; tree on which Rain-maker sits grows to sky, little black ants and big red ants climb tree and push it into ground—D482.1.3; why ant has small waist—A2355.1.2; youth who could become an ant, lion or eagle—R111.1.3Aj.

ANTAEUS: Hercules slays Antaeus. Pygmy friends of dead giant drive Hercules off—F531.6.12.6.0.1.

ANTEATER: Fool thinks sleeping anteater is dead, finds it stolen when he returns—J1959.4.

ANTELOPE: Counting by fives—H331.18; hare tricks antelope—K717.2; mother to be killed, hidden—K311.3.1; woman on moon is antelope's mother—A751.8.8; a. lends speed in race with girl—F601.2I, H335.7.3; tall tale, hunter shoots a., runs ahead and kills with knife, skins, packs meat and grabs bullet before can pierce meat packet—F660.1.2.

ANTLERS: Good luck to hang things on antlers —D1011.1.1; stag proud of antlers is caught on tree—L461.

ANVIL: Ogre's beard caught in split anvil—K1111.1; Devil beaten on anvil—Q565Ab.

APA: Great father, Apa, sends Muskrat to dive for earth—A812.7.

APACHES: Eetoi kills Vandai and sprinkles blood on dead with eagle feather to revive—A1610.7.

APE: SEE MONKEY.

APPETITE: SEE HUNGER.

APPLE: dried apple to throw into Dragon's mouth, D. collapses—R111.1.3Bb; father kills son for eating apple—S11.3.3.1.1; magic golden apple beats enemy, obtained from werewolf—D1601.5.3; youngest son catches peahens robbing golden apple tree—H1385.3Ja; quest for golden apple—H1321.1B; girl spins rosy apple in golden bowl—E632.0.4; apple peel heals wounds—H331.1.1C; farmer takes huge apple as present to the king—J2415.1; Apple of Life, skillful companions resuscitate a girl —H621.1; Connla is given magic replenishing apple—F302.1.3; fruit causes nose to grow—D551.1B; girl must eat of apple pie before it will hide her—Q2.1.2Cea; poison apple kills Snow White—Z65.1; apple and pomegranate dispute—J466.1; quest for singing apple—N455.4Aa; suitor task snatching apple from lap of princess on glass mountain—H331.1.1; the silver saucer and the transparent apple—E632.0.4; holding up the apple tree—K1251.2; girl aids apple tree—Q2.1.2; wolf invites pig to pick apples—K891.1.1.

APPRENTICE: Judge rules apprentice may keep all given (thrown) to him—J1179.17; magician's apprentice—D1711.0.1.1.

APRIL: March received day from April—K688.1; riddle to be answered on April Fool's Day—H952.1.

APRON: Shoemaker tosses apron into heaven and hops in on "his own property"—Q565Ag.

ARABE: The Arabe duck—K953.3, K815.14.

ARABIA: Lad kills trolls, weds their captive, King of Arabia's daughter—S12.1A; King of Araby's daughter—G530.2Fd.

ARAP SANG: Cranes help thirsty Arap Sang to shade, are given golden crowns—A2321.13.

ARAWIDI: Sun spirit turns fish into dogs as companions for man—A2335.2.6.1.

ARAWN: Owen answers riddles and becomes heir, taken to fairyland—F373.1.

ARBUTUS: Sign of spring—A1158.1.

ARCHAEOLOGIST: Archaeologist finds giant's bones in cave. They wake and throw him into sea—F531.6.13.3.

ARCHBISHOP: Ostler wishes to trade places with archbishop's mule—U119.2.1.

ARCHER: Startled archer loses arrow and starts a chain—Z30; lad challenged by demon after winning archery contest--H1411.4.2; lawsuits to be settled by archery skill contests, all men practice to become expert—K2369.16; skill proven by deception—K31; archer loses fishhook of brother—U136.0.1; Little Bowman has Big Bima pose as bowman while he performs deeds—K1951.6; archer takes aim by looking at reflection in water—A720.1.2, H331.4.3; archer shoots down all suns in sky but one—A720.1ff, A751.8.7; girl given bow and arrows by tokgabbis, wins contest—R221Ib. SEE ALSO ARROW.

ARCHITECT: Architect to be killed so building cannot be duplicated--W181.2.

ARCTIC FOX: Origin—A1832.1.

ARCTIC HARE: Steals sun—A721.1.3.

ARCTURUS: Arcturus, star in Büotes, is big owl following bear across sky with hunter--A771.0.1.

ARECA: Legend explaining origin of chewing areca, lime, and betel together—A2691.5.

ARENA: Lion in arena spares former benefactor--B381.

ARGUMENT: Animals argue over who is the elder—B841; honey-gatherer's sons argue as to who is most important, refuse to aid father when he again needs aid, he dies—H621.4.1; spider spins basket shut while insects within argue—L396.

ARGUS OF THE ISLES: King Robert Bruce sends monk to fetch hand of St. Filian to battlefield—V143.2.2.

ARITHMETIC: If you have four pennies in your pocket and they fall out, what is left? A hole in my pocket—J2213.10. SEE ALSO MATH.

ARK: Birds fly through rainbow when leaving ark and are colored brightly--A2411.2.0.1, A2411.2.1.19 (hummingbird); dog's nose sticks out of ark—A2335.2.6; escape from flood in ark—A1021; giant, Og, rides on roof of Ark--F531.6.12.8.2; hole in ark, lion sneezes cat, snake plugs hole—A1811.2, A2145.2.

ARM: Demon husband's arms fall off on way home—G303.12.5.11; golden arm stolen from grave—E235.4.1; arm of ogre severed, ogre reclaims--E782.3.3; one-armed god—F153.2; Q223.14.1.

ARMADILLO: Armadillo wins in crop division--K171.1.

ARMOR: Magic armor makes wearer invincible--D1101.

ARMPIT: The sun shines from the armpits of the sun man—A722.5.

ARROW: Arrow accidentally makes shot—N621.1; supernatural boy makes obsidian arrows to kill bear--A2411.2.0.3; arrows shot to locate bride--B641A, B641C, B641E, H1226.2; ascent to upper world on arrow chain—F53ff; arrow chain shot into sun—B11.2.1.2.2; eagle killed with arrow made from own feather--U161; arrow as man's message to lion—J32; brother's magic arrow carried off in bird's side—H1132.1.5.3; suitor contest: shooting birds. Pikoi takes aim at reflection in calabash—H331.4.3; one hitting sun with first arrow to own--A721.3.1; task, find arrow shot into woods—H328.10; task, follow three arrows—B641A. SEE ALSO ARCHER.

ART: Culture hero teaches art—A541.

ARTHUR, KING: SEE KING ARTHUR.

ARTIST: Artist obtains bride dowry of stolen cattle by trickery rather than force—K341.5.3; apprentice paints fish on stairs so real master scolds for dropping--H504.1.4; artist's paintings come to life—D435.3.1ff. SEE ALSO PAINTING; SESSHU.

ASCHENPUTTEL: R221Ba.

ASCOLON: Rabbi Simon and eighty men hold witches over heads in dance and carry them away powerless--G273.8.

ASHANTI: How debt came to the Ashanti—A1378; how the Ashanti got hoe—D1651.15; custom of leaving inheritance to sister's son--A1423.1.1; foreigner's fear Ashanti will become overly strong if fed on yams—A1423.1.1. SEE ALSO ETHNIC AND GEOGRAPHIC INDEX.

ASHES: Magic ashes make trees blossom—D1571.1; dupe burns house to sell ashes--K941.2; ashes of coat of invisibility wash off and body parts appear—D831.1; unkind wife's ashes are scattered, wherever they fall jealousy and selfishness take root—B216Ac; maiden sits in ashes—R221; ashes thrown in sky become Milky Way--A778.8; task, making rope of ashes—H1021.2.1; ashes in shoes simulate dust beaten from stone—K62.1; meat talks, is burnt, ashes talk—B210.1.2; thief fills dupe's bag with ashes and cuts hole in bag, follows trail of ashes to hidden food supply--K321; demons follow trail of ashes left by girl who came to borrow fire—S352.2.

ASHMODAI: J225.0.1.

ASHPET: R221K.

ASIN: Asin in disguise as bald, ugly stranger is seen bathing without disguise—T111.1.1.1; Asin as god--A1115.4.

ASS: SEE DONKEY.

ASSEGAI: Chain ends boy's acquisition of assegai—K251.1.4.

ASSOCIATIONS: Folly of associating with bad company—J451ff; choice of associates—J400ff; association of equals and unequals—J1410ff.

ASTROLOGER: SEE ASTRONOMER

ASTRONOMER: Arabe duck claims to read stars —K815.14; astronomer counts number of eggs under chaffinch—F660.1; farmer surpasses astronomer, he returns to city—L144.2; astronomer sees princess, thief steals, marksman kills dragon, tailor repairs boat—H621.2.4; stargazer falls into well—J2133.8.

ASTRONOMY: Absurd astronomical theories— J2270ff. SEE ALSO MOON; SUN; STARS; PLANETS.

ASCUNCION: Founding of Ascuncion—B538.3.2.

ASURA: Vishnu strikes down Asura king— D1840.1.4.

ASWA: Aswa, celestial horse escapes with prince —N455.4B.

ATAHUALPA: Volcano emits rock shaped like head of Inca chief Atahualpa—A977.5.0.5.

ATHENIAN: Shipwrecked monkey pretends to be Athenian—J1803.1.1.

ATLAS: Nicola Pesce holds up Sicily—A842.3.

AUBERGINE: Aubergine tied to leg for identifcation—J2013.3.

AUCTION: Auctioneer praises worthless donkey so much man buys her back himself—J2087.

AUNT: Aunt visits party, later learned to have died at that moment—E329.1; three deformed aunts from spinning—D2183.1.

AURORA BOREALIS: Aurora borealis is piece of light trapped in seal gut and given to former owner and daughter who move to north pole— A795. SEE ALSO NORTHERN LIGHTS.

AUSTWICK: Fools of Austwick—J1922.2.

AUTUMN: Old Man Autumn to wipe paint brushes on fox if can paint reflection of leaf— A2411.1.3.2; what is richest? Autumn—H636.1; why leaves of maple turn red in the fall— A771.0.1, A2769.2.

AVALANCHE: Dwarf offered hospitality by only one couple in village causes avalanche— F451.5.2.6.2.

AVARICE: Avaricious man is transformed to ant —A2011.2.

AVUNANG: Enemies throw Avunang through seal hole and he turns to seal—D100.1.

AWANG DURAHMAN: A. loses deer through daydream—J2061.3.

AWL: Trickster obtains daughter named "Biz" when he asks for awl called a "biz"—K362.10.1.

AX: Man abandoned in desert finds ax and arrows in tree—D882.1Ga; doves on ax handle reward kind girl—Q2.1.5B; kind brother loses ax in sea, goes to palace of Rajah of Fishes and receives treasure—J2415.14; fool hides ax from cat—J2214.3.4; woodcutter loses ax in stream and goddess returns a golden ax—Q3.1; magic building ax—D831B; lad who cuts everything to pieces with ax is sent to Pieceland—Q589.4; to steal sacred ax from chief—K301B; self-chopping ax—H1115.1.1; tree gives handle for ax, then is cut down—U162; girl fears ax might fall on unborn child—J2063.

AXLE: Ox criticizes axletrees for groaning— J953.21; Tom Hickathrift kills giant with axletree—F628.2.3.1.

AYAN: Ayan, god of drum—A2433.1.3.

BAA: SEE BLEATING.

BABA YAGA: Bear's son defeats Baba Yaga— B635.1.4; doll aids girl sent to Baba Yaga— Q2.1.2CeBb; B. counts spoons and dwarf calls out—H1385.3Fe; Baba Yaga's eagle carries lad to upper world—K1931.2P; Baba Yaga helps in search for firebird—H1331.1.3B; Baba Yaga's geese steal little brother—Q2.1.2CeA; girls sent to Baba Yaga for fire (needle)—Q2.1.2Ce; lad gets steed equal to Koschei's from Baba Yaga— H1199.12.4B; Baba Yaga in land under stone— R111.1.3Ae.

BABE: SEE BABY.

BABES: The two lost babes—K1611E; babes in the woods—S143.2.

BABOON: Bees substituted for hare's children in baboon's bag—K527.1; why baboon's buttocks are shiny—A2362.1.1; baboon acquired through chain events—K251.1.4.2; creation of baboon— A1863.1; baboon gives tortoise (hare) inappropriate feast, must wash before eating— J1565.1.2, K278; hare as nurse eats lion cubs, teaches baboons to sing "we killed the cubs"— K1066.3; judge baboon 'plays' rock—J1191.1.2; origin of baboon—A1861.5; pegs driven into backs of baboons become tails—A1863.1; baboons build tower to heaven—F772.1.3.

BABOUSKA: Bringer of Christmas gifts—N816.2.

BABY: Abandoned baby found in boat, basket— B535.0.9, S141; abandoned baby raised by animals—B535.0.5ff; baby trapped in magically opening treasure cave—B11.6.2.4; babe buried with dead mother is fed by her until found— E323.1.1; girl to be freed if lover refrains from eating until all fairy babies are rocked to sleep —F320.4; Finn poses as baby—K521.4.1.5; man falls out of bed onto baby—J1173; over-drinking at fountain of youth, turns into baby —D1338.1.1.2; ghost reborn as baby—E605.7.2; ghostly baby is washed up in cradle—F473.2.1.1; Mervyn gives glove to baby in cradle to play with, only babe floats above flood —F944.1; Glosskap cannot subdue baby, who replies "goo" to all—L410.8.1; why baby says "goo" none can subdue—A1399.5; who is greatest: baby, none can control—Z42.0.4; guess what new baby is?—J2712.4; hairy man promised baby given piglet—B524.1.2H; baby taken hostage feigns dead, hare's wife given money recompense—K1839.12.1; dragon-girl turns to baby in lantern—T542.2; nurse baby—Q2.14B; task: create a two year old baby, throws magic bone given by gravedigger and baby appears—B314E; man must return fate to baby Tchapogui —N115; Manabozho cannot put toe in mouth as baby can—L410.8. SEE ALSO CHANGELING; CHILD.

BACK: earth on turtle's back—A815; tabu: looking back—C331; origin of animal's back—A2356ff; anger bargain, strip from loser's back —K172; animals climb on one another's backs and cry out, frighten robbers—K335.1.4; why man turns back to fire—A1319.15; scratching witches back—Q2.1.2H.

BACKWARDS: Numskull rides horse backwards—J2024.

BACON: Poor brother told to take his bacon to the devil—D1651.3.1; fool drags bacon on rope —J2461F.

BACON, ROGER: Friar Bacon makes head of brass—D1711.6.5.

BAD: "That's bad, no that's good", chain of events—Z51ff; association with bad friend is fatal—J429.2ff; bad luck—N250; breaking bad news to king—J1675.2.1; parrot reared in bad company is bad—J451.6.

BAD LUCK: Man misses gold left on path by Bad Luck—N141.0.2; foolish imitation of good man by bad man—SEE ALL ENTRIES J2415ff; bad luck put into sack—N112.1. SEE ALSO FORTUNE; LUCK.

BADGER: Badger makes mud boat—J2171.1.3; badger helps rescue girl from buffalo, badger decides to live underground—R111.1.13.2; badger 'brained' with cattail—K473.2; badger and coyote farm together—K171.1; deafness magically cured by badger—D2161.3.5; badger shams death and is sold—K366.1.3.1; hare sets fire to wood on badger's back—K2345.0.1; hare gives badger pepper poultice—K1014; hare tricks otter and badger out of goods—K441.5; why badgers do not live on certain island—A2434.2.2.1; magic kettle is transformed badger —D1171.3.1; badger smelts gold to reward priest—B393.1; badger in disguise as priest shaves dupe's head—D612.1.3; snake thinks man is badger, reveals secrets—K602.3; badger sets stars in sky—A763.9.1; badger seeks inexhaustible tallow—D1652.1.9.3; badger steals fan

from tengu children—D839.3; badger obtains tengu's magic fan by trickery—D1376.1.3; transformation duel between two badgers—D615.1.1.; badger transforms to object—D421.8+; badger transforms to mooring pile—D612.1.1; badger transforms to priest—D612.1.2; badger helps dig to upper world—A1024.1; badger cooks old woman and serves—G61.3.

BADIA THE BEAUTIFUL: Hero must steal Badia—H1331.1.3An.

BAG (SACK): trickster stabs bag of blood, ogre imitates—G524; coyote tricked into bag to avoid 'hail'—K711.5; devil tricked into magic bag—Q565Ae; dupe trades places with victim in bag —K842; food stuffed in bag, deceptive eating contest—K81.1; fairy takes place of piglet in thief's bag—F482.5.5; bag filled with objects and captive escapes—K526; giant's wife trades places with girl in bag—K1611; heaven entered by trick, wishing sack thrown in—K213; Hodja's bag stolen, return it "or else"—K1771.2.1; filling a sack with lies—H1045.0.1; bad luck put into sack—N112.1, N250.4; Mother Luck will fill sack but must stop her before it breaks—J514.7; Mantis hides in bag to enter lion's house—K1892.3; girl takes old woman's moneybag—Q2.1.2Cb; ogre tricked into carrying prisoners home in bag—G561; bringing sackful of sunlight into house—J2123; tiger afloat in bag found by female tiger—N228; victim tricked into entering sack—K714.2.3; wife makes old man carry her in bag up to dovecot—D861.1K; J2133.5.1; bag of winds—C322.1; dupe to become wise in sack of wisdom—K842.0.1; witch's bag filled with animals or objects while captive escapes—K526.

BAGEL: Holes in bagels lost—X1761.4; wife made to believe bagel fell from heaven—J1151.1.3.2.

BAGNE VALLEY: Inhabitants of Bagne Valley have thread in clothing blessed—D1385.18.1.

BAGPIPES: Changeling plays on bagpipes and causes all to dance—F321.4.1.1; fisherman tries to make fish dance to bagpipes—J1909.1; ghost plays bagpipes—E402.1.3.2; piper plays underground in fairyland—E425.2.5.

BAIACOU: Origin of Baiacou, evening star—A781.2.1.

BAKER: Magic box given to baker's son by old woman—D882.1Ec; the four abdallahs—B82.6.

BAKERY: Origin baker's dozen—V429.4; retorts from hungry persons at bakery—J1340; payment for smell of food—J1172.2.0.3.

BAKING: Mother is baking the bread we ate last week—H583.4.2; woman turned to owl for objecting to size of dough put into oven for Jesus beggar—A1958.0.1; sister lies that she is not baking—V429.2; woman flummoxes fairies by sending for baking tools—F320. SEE ALSO BREAD; CAKE; DOUGH.

BALAFON: Hare plays balafon—K714.2.4.1.

BALANCE: Task: carrying bowl of laban on head while climbing palm tree—H331.10.1.

BALANGI: Giant's wife warns man to play poorly on balangi—K606.1.5.

BALATON: Jealous queen causes lake of Balaton to form—A920.1.17.

BALDNESS: Why beetle is bald—A2317.2.1; why buzzard is bald—A2317.3; baldheaded man finds the comb—J1061.2; why eagle is bald—A2317.3.1; hero feigns baldness, baldness thought lucky—H1331.1.2An; hero feigns baldness, disgrace—H1331.1.2.2; bald man aims at fly and hurts head—J2102.3; scald-head disguise—K1818.2; man's head is shaved and he thinks self another—J2012.1.1; why spider is bald—A2317.2.2; wig carried off by wind—X52.2; two wives take turns pulling out hairs of husband—J2112.2.

BALL: Bogles play with ball under bed—H1411.4.11; boy loses ball in hollow tree, fills with water until ball rises—J101.1; demons and dead play ball—E577.1; ball must be retrieved or girl dies—H1411.4.11; frog demands visit to princess in return for ball—D195.1; golden ball returned when dwarf is released—H331.1.1D; golden ball rolls into cage of wild man—G671A; magic ball rolls ahead to show road—D1313.1; rolling ball (dumpling) leads to adventures—N777; silver ball stained in forbidden room—G561.1; hare steals sun by playing ball with it—A721.1.3; thrown ball (apple) caught by successful suitor— H331.1.1.

BALL, DANCE: Staying too long at ball—R221.

BALL GAMES: Bat in ball game—B261.1.0.1. SEE ALSO BOWLING; TLACHTLI.

BALLADS: Ballads ruined by bootmaker—J981.

BALLAGHADEREEN: Peddler dreams of treasure—N531.1.

BALSAM: Origin of balsam tree—A2681.14.

BAMBOO: Blood from cut bamboo turns stream red—A939.3; comb thrown turns to bamboo thicket—D672; boat woven of bamboos from thrown comb—D454.7.2; fire hides in bamboo during flood—A1414.7.2.1; first man and woman emerge from bamboo—A1271.5; bamboo grows from grave and sheds nuggets—J2415.21; childless bamboo cutter finds tiny maiden in bamboo stalk—A240.1.1; riddle: cutting live trees (bamboo) and planting dead ones (making fences)—H583.2.6; youth tries to knock down stars with bamboo pole—J2275.2; why bamboo is tall—A2701; task: cut two bamboo canes, ogre lives in them—G530.2Bj; bamboo tube claimed to be telescope—D831.1; test: find relationship between three bamboo sticks: they are put in water, degree of sinking shows part of plant each comes from—H506.10; dupe tricked into believing bamboo stalks are trumpet—K1023.1.3; origin of winter bamboo—A2681.6.1.

BANANAS: Alchemy requires two pounds of banana-leaf down, in raising it plantation prospers—H588.7.2; hare riding elephant eats bananas and says is eating brains—K1715.2.1; magic banana skin always full of fruit—D1652.1.7.2; why bananas belong to monkeys—K741.0.1; K741.0.12; why spiders hide in bananas—A2433.5.3.6.

BAND: Iron band around heart to keep from breaking—D195.

BANDITS: SEE THIEVES.

BANDURA: Cat plays bandura before fox's den—K815.15B.

BANISHMENT: Dream of future greatness causes banishment—L425; girl who loves father like salt is banished—H592.1.0.1.

BANNOCK: Fox feigns dead till Johnny Cake comes closer—Z331.3.

BANNOCKBURN: King Robert Bruce sends monk to fetch hand of St. Fillian to battlefield—V143.2.2.

BANYAN: Banyan tree judges against man—J1172.3.2; old man on moon under banyan tree—A751.0.2.

BAPTISM: Anansi as sham holy man eats crabs as he baptizes them—K1961.1.6; cats create melee at baptism—U129.4. SEE ALSO CHRISTENING.

BAPTISTRY: Baptistry doors decorated with little people—A1465.3.3.1.

BAOBAB: Strong man drives spear through baobab tree and leaps through hole—F660.1Eb; why baobab tree is upside down—A2774.2.

BAR MITZVAH: Foolish girl wails for unborn son who might be harmed on Bar Mitzvah day—J2063.5.

BARBARY: Cat in a mouse-infested land sold—N411.1.

BARBECUE: Brer Rabbit tells Brer Fox that hounds are trying to drive him to barbecue—K846.1.

BARBER: Barber confesses plot to kill king when hears poet—J21.1.1; barber discovers king's goat ears—D1316.5.3; barber shaves silent husband—J2511.0.2; barber made to believe thrown razor cut off wife's nose—J2315.2; judge rules barber must shave ox—J1511.17.1; princess and barber lover exchange places—K1321.3.0.1; barber shaves man's head, man thinks self another—J2012.1.1; skillful barber shaves running hare—F660.2; barber cuts off tail of cat (monkey), cat claims razor—Z47.2; Toontoony bird has thorn stuck in throat, barber aids—Z41.8.1.

BAREFOOT: Coming neither barefoot nor shod—H1055.

BARGAINS: Anger bargain, he who loses his temper loses—K172; beheading bargain, each to behead other—M221; cock claimed as damages for eaten grain—K251.1; foolish bargains, horse for cow, etc.—J2081.1; sent to buy grapes for friend, he haggles price down, then keeps grapes since he did the work of bargaining—J1650.1; progressive lucky bargain—N421.1; lending and repaying, progressively worse (or better) bargain—Z41.5; series of trick exchanges—Z47; man sells soul to devil—M211; trick sale, trickster agrees to sell donkey for one dinar, sold with 100 dinar cat—K182.0.1; wager on wife's complacency—N11. SEE ALL ENTRIES Bargains and promises—M200-M299; Deceptive bargains—K100-K299; Foolish bargains—J2080ff. SEE ALSO SHOPPING.

BARK: Why trees' barks are scratched—A2701.

BARK-CLOTH: SEE TAPA.

BARLEY: Daydreaming brahman breaks pot of barley—J2061.2.1. SEE ALSO MEAL, BARLEY.

BARMECIDE FEAST: Imaginary feast—P327.

BARN: Soul sold to devil to build barn—M211.2.

BARNFOWL: SEE BIRD, BARNFOWL.

BARON: Baron is turned to horse, reforms—Q584.2.1; peasant outwits baron in guarding horses, baron carries peasant on back—K289.1. SEE ALSO LANDLORD.

BARRA: Son of the Baker of Barra—D882.1Ec.

BARREL: King has lovers sealed in barrel and set adrift—D1720.1.4; moon captured in barrel—J1791.2.2; hare escapes in rolling barrel—K553.0.3; barrel stave snaps in springing tubmaker to sky—K1112.2.

BARREN: Barren stones—A975.1.2.

BARTEK, KING: Princess declares her love for court jester—T55.2.

BASH TCHELIK: Sister abducted—B314C.

BASIL: Basil plant with golden tips grows from ashes of dead babies—N455.4C.

BASIN: Basin to overflow if hero in peril—R111.1.3Ae.

BASKET: Cuckold hidden in peddler's basket hears all—K1556; father carrying his father to abandon reminded by son to bring basket back for use on him later—J121.3; prince takes girl from floating basket, leaves monkey in her place—K1625; inexhaustible food basket—D1652.5.8; magic replenishing basket—D861.1G; star maidens descend in basket—F302.4.2.4; sunlight carried into windowless house in basket—J2123.

BAST: Bast, cat goddess—A132.17.

BAT: Bat in ball game of birds and animals—B261.1.0.2ff; bat claims is animal, then claims is bird—B261.1.0.4; bat tells bush rat he boils self in pot to make soup—A2491.1.0.1; bat, spider and beetle court together—T92.11.3; bat enters forbidden Valley of Flowers and eats lily, becomes unkind through Evil Spirit's medicine—A1341.4; why bat flies at night—A2491.1; bat abroad at night to escape creditors—A2275.5.3; fisherman on Niihau abducted by bat-like spirit—E423.3.12; bat refuses to pay taxes as either bird or animal—B261.1.0.3; bat in war of birds and quadrupeds—B261.1ff; why bat has wings—A2377.3.

BAT, FRUIT: Fruit bat dying, neither animals nor birds will claim—B261.1.0.5.

BATARU GURU: Calf Lembu Gumarong tries to destroy rice and battle of gods ensues—A2685.6.1.1; Bataru Guru gives rice to man—A162.9.

BATH: Task: heating bathhouse—Q2.1.5Ab; girl seeking lost lover builds bathhouse and gives free bath to all who tell story—H1385.5Af; fairies leave gold for bath—F348.7.0.1; fool at bath believes self someone else—J2012.6; fox masquerading as Buddha tricked into bath in boiling pot—K891.1.2; goblins at the bathhouse—C311.1.5; bath in boiling milk—B526.2; task: to build bathroom on minaret so voice will sound as good from there as when in bath—J2237; task: washing monster children of Mother Sunday—Q2.1.5Aa; baby from squash, water turns gold as he is washed—T555.1.1.1; man leaves large tip for no service, get service next time—J1229.3. SEE ALSO BOILING.

BATTLE: Hero in disguise wins thrice—R222.1; saint appears on battlefield and routs—V229.7.3. SEE ALSO SIEGE; WAR.

BATTLE-AXE: Throwing contest: battle-ax thrown to moon—K18.2.

BAUCHAN: Bauchan of MacIntosh family refuses to travel to America on boat with MacLeods and MacDonalds—F482.3.1.2.

BAY: Origin of bay—A920.1.0.1.1.

BEAD: Old woman shows way to elephant's kraal and gives magic blue bead—H1132.1.5.2.

BEADLE: SEE BEREL.

BEAK: Crow must wash beak before eats—Z41.2.1ff; origin of crane's beak—A2343.1.6; origin of duck's beak—A2343.1.5; origin of frigate bird and brown pelican beak—A2343.3.4; origin of owl's beak—A2343.3.4; origin of parrot's beak—A2343.3.3; raven loses half beak—A2335.2.3. SEE ALSO BILL.

BEAN: Riddle: I boil those which come and go (beans)—H583.6; sowing boiled beans—H1023.1.1; cat as damages for eaten bean—K251.1.1; three gluttons argue over one bean—W125.6; Anansi hides beans in hat—W125.3.1; bean, straw and coal go journeying—F1025.1; bean laughs till it splits—A2741.1; beans woman is stringing turn into tiny lads—F535.1.1B Jacobs; riddle: pick up those that rise (boiling beans)—H583.6; man given first seeds of squash, beans and corn—A1425.2; why bean has black stripe—A2741.1, F662.3; skillful tailor sews bean together after bean has split sides laughing—F662.3.

BEANPASTE: Tiger shows healing beanpaste—B382.1.

BEANSTALK: Jack and the Beanstalk—F54.2.1; girl climbs beanstalk to land where old man dwells—Q2.1.5Ab; lad climbs beanstalk, meets St. Peter—D861.1G. SEE ALL ENTRIES F54.2ff Plant grows to sky.

BEAR: Trickster eats alligator's cubs, counts remaining one over and over to fool mother—K933; ass on bear's back drops magic stone crossing river—D882.1Ba; bear harms self slapping at bees—N333.0.2; girl forced to play blindman's buff with bear—Q2.1.3B; magic bone jumps into animal's head—G552.1; Brer Rabbit tells Brer B'ar that wolf and fox are chasing him—K2131.9; bear eats all who cross bridge—Z33.6; bug causes bear to hit self—K1082.3.3; bear leaps at buffalo and misses—K402.3.2.2; bull-frog persuades bear to sit him on rock in millpond and kill with ax—K581.7; bear burnt in grass, trying to see 'trouble'—K1055.2; origin of butte called Bear's Lodge—A969.12; bear falls from tree in terror of cat—K2324; bear scratches chipmunk's back—A2217.2; bear in coach taken for passenger in fur coat—J1762.2.2; bear hunt as origin of constellation—A771.0.1; A772.1; constellation, Great Bear—A771ff; blood of constellation Great Bear turns maples red—A2769.2; crop division, bear deceived—K171.1, K171.2; crop division, bear beats coyote—K171.1; bear hugs dead man to warmth—B529.3; fox divides cake for cubs—K452.1.2; bear dreams he eats honey—K444; enchanted bear befriended by Snow White and Rose Red—D113.2.2; bear asks farmer to tie up as if is log—C25; dupe wishing to play fiddle has finger caught in cleft of tree—K1111.0.1; lion and bear fight over carcass to exhaustion, fox takes kill—J218.1.1; bear helps hero obtain firebird—H1331.1.3Ae; bear kills fly on man's head—N333.2; bear tries to drink stream dry and bursts, origin fog—A1134.1; fool mistakes bear for person—J1762.2; fool grabs bear in dark—K1951.2.1.1; man frees bear, fox reenacts—J1172.3; fox steals chicken from table and runs to barn where bear is stealing, bear is caught—K401.1.2; fox eats bear's dead brother—K2028; giant bear swallows man, cut open—F912.2.3; girl serves bear, escapes by sending pies to grandparent and hiding in basket—G561.1F; girl turned to bear by sorcerer cares for baby prince—T75.2.1.3; bear tricked

by fox as godfather—K372; bear squashes gourd—R261.2; bear has lion reach down throat and pull up bear grease to anoint dead hero, revives—R111.1.3Am; bear in hat taken for husband—J1762.2.3; bear lies on haystack, set fire—K1013.2; bear bites off man's head, did he ever have one?—J2381; why bears hibernate—A2481.1; animals invite all comers to enter until house ruptures—J2199.5; fool dreams he is bear hunting, takes dog to bed—F1068.5.1; bear husband leaves when seen—H1385.4; bear builds house of wood, fox of ice—J741.1; bear fishes with tail through ice—K1021; man lives with bears, bear nature is still with him—B538.3.4; bear gives meat to help Brer Rabbit kill Brer Gilyard—K1082.0.2; moon stolen from bear—A758.1; fox asks bear with seagull in mouth which way wind blows—K561.1.0.5; trapped mother offers to give bear her children—K553.1.0.3; bear climbing tree in dark swipes numskull and he cries out, bear falls in terror—N659.3; youngest daughter wishes to wed Great Bear of Orange—D735.1B; origin of certain bear—A1836.1; origin of custom of inviting strangers to share feast—A1598.1; bear overeats and is stuck in storehouse—K1022.1; why bear and peasant are enemies—A2494.8.3; bear beast turns to prince when beauty loves—D735.1; bear defeated by turtle in race—K11.1; boy raised by bears—B535.0.15; bear to carry hero over bridge of razors—H1321.1Ab; rocks on Koos-Koos-Ki River are fishnet and bear—A977.5.0.3; wildcat and bear attack steak in saddlebag, leap from opposite sides and kill each other—X1114.3; man saddles bear in dark and rides—K1951.2.1.1; girl to ask she-bear for golden spindle—Q2.1.1Fa; she-bear eats twenty-one garlic cloves and turns to woman, bears Tankun—A511.1.8.4; little bear rescues sisters—K1611Bc; staying longest in smoky hole—K1066.8; son of bear, woman defeats Baba Yaga—B635.1.4; Brer Bar's courting song—K1066.8; bear is star Betelgeuse—A772.1; man thrown to bear stares it down—H328.9; storyteller dies, black bear found in his hut grows to sky—A1481.3; hare buries cow's tail, convinces bear that cow sank under ground—K404.1; bear makes fox believe he can catch horse by tying fox's tail to horse's tail—J2132.5.2; why bear has short tail—A2378.4.2; bear fishes through ice with tail, lacks tail—A2216.1, K1021; boy grabs bear's tail as she backs into hollow stump, she pulls him out—X1133.1.1; bear persuaded to slide down rock, wears off tail—K1021.3; deceptive tug-of-war, bear's tail tied to tree root—K22.2; three bears—N831.1.2; thunder is bear growling—A1142.11; bear names varieties of same tree and loses bet—N51; bear is thrown wagon load of meat and mules, man escapes because bear can't climb trees—X1221.1.1; bear frightens trolls—K1728; bear, wolf and fox serve twins—R111.1.3Ao; in war between wild and domestic animals cat grabs bear by throat—K2323.0.1; what the bear whispered in his ear—J1488; bear cuffs wife of henpecked man—J1762.2.3.1; bear eats up old woman—Z13.1.2; bear terrified by woman's legs, thinks are vise—K1755; boy tricks necken into wrestling match with bear—K11.6.

BEAR, GREAT (URSA MAJOR): SEE BIG DIPPER.

BEAR, GRIZZLY: Helps steal springtime—A1151.1; stone (hard fruit) thrown into mouth—K1035.1; cause of grizzly's walk—A2441.1.14.

BEAR, POLAR: Ice bear carved causes polar bear to stop transfixed—K547.15.

BEARD: Beardless man must take after mother's side of family as she is beardless too—J2259.3; tabu: greeting beardless man—K2275; beardless man loses lying contest—X905; dwarf with beard in cleft of tree—D113.2.2; beard of she-goats doesn't make male—U112; goats make jackal believe killed jackals with beards—K1715.3; king snaps at servant combing beard—H1561.4; how much is king's beard worth?—H712.2; suitor must be unafraid to pull king's beard—H359.3; ogre grabs king's beard as drinks--G530.2Db; man spits in king's beard—J1566.1; quest for three hairs from devil's beard—H1273.2; must not cut beard for seven years—K217; beard sold—K182.2; princess taunts suitor for seed dropped in beard—H465A; ogre tricked into gilding beard in tar--K1013.1; King Thrushbeard—H465A.

BEARSKIN: Girl in bearskin cloak--R221Dc; she-bear raises prince, in bearskin he kills dragon—R111.1.3Ap; Princess of Arabia to be given to one who finds her, hero in white bearskin disguise is taken to her chamber—S12.1A; man in bearskin cloak not to cut hair for seven years--K217.

BEAST: Beauty and the beast—D735.1.

BEATING: Doorman asks half reward, beating asked as reward—K187.1; self-beating stick--D882.1.

BEAUTY: Beauty and the beast--D735.1; handsome son and homely daughter to watch character--J244.1; friend lends beauty to leprous friend—D1500.3.1.2; fox and panther contest beauty—J242.3; peacock chosen king for beauty--J242.5; quest for most beautiful bride--B641.0.1; rose and amaranth contest beauty—J242.1; Silver Tree asks trout in well who is most beautiful queen--D582.2; Sleeping Beauty--D1960.3; most beautiful thing? Spring—H641.1; task: showing love of beauty--F601.2I; trickster pretends to make dupe beautiful, injures—K1013; useful wins contest over beautiful--J242ff.

BEAVER: Beaver's tears bring rain causing flood—A1131.1.0.1; turtle rides beaver's tail and wins race—K11.2; beaver investigates rumor that sky is falling—Z43.3; beaver gnaws rope releasing sun from snare—A728.2.1; turtle holds beaver's tail in swimming match—K11.2; why beaver has flat tail--A2378.7.1; where beaver got tail—A2378.1.6.1; Kwatee changes tools to animals, club becomes beaver's tail—A2262.4; beaver fells tree making bridge for girl to escape—K635.5; why beaver lives in water--A2433.3.12.1; at end of world, Beaver will gnaw

through pole on which earth spins—A1009.4.

BED: Substituted object left in bed receives blows--K525.1; little boy under bed given animals to comfort because squeaking bed makes him cry—Z49.17; two brothers share bed, elder gets bed from sunset to sunrise—K171.7.1; power to see death at head of bed--D1825.3.1; man falls out of bed and kills baby--J1173; haunted bed flies about--H1440A; magic bed--D1154.1; mother instructs girl to take man to bed—D195.1.2; task: shaking Mother Holle's feather bed--Q2.1.2Aa; disenchantment of animal by admission to woman's bed--D195.1. SEE ALSO FEATHERBED.

BEDBUGS: The dog-eating bugs—J1531.2.1; why bedbug is flat--A2305.2.

BEDOUINS: Once caused whole tribe of Bedouins to run. He ran, they ran after him—J1250.9.

BEE: Bee aids hero in task—R111.1.3Ao; bear harms self slapping at bees—N333.0.2; where bee got buzz--A2236.1; buzzard trapped in bee nest and burnt—K1055.2; bee, harp, mouse and bum-clock dance--H341.2.1; bee dies when stings—A2232.2; oracle drum (bees inside)--K842Bd; self-beating drum (bees inside)—H1049.5; dupe stung, strikes nest, puts head in bee gum, etc.—K1023ff; K1023.5.1ff; bees fight eagles—B455.3.2; elephant persuaded to tie weeds to tail and set afire to smoke bees—A2378.4.16; a bee helps the hero to identify the real flowers among many artificial flowers in a suitor contest--H540.2.1; fools try to carry off well with reflected bee's nest--J1791.9; bee bites goat and drives him home--Z39.1; girl who obeys mother becomes golden bee after death--A2012.0.1.1; hare convinces leopard to knock over bee tree—K1023.5.2; bees substituted for hare's children in baboon's bag—K527.1; drones fail to make honey, bees win hive--J581.4; why honey guide bird leads man to honey--A2513.8; origin of honey--A2813; Kantchil claims soul is in jar, really bees--K1023.1.0.3; at beginning of world bee carries Mantis over water and puts in heart of water flower--A1291.2; bee picks disguised princess for hero—B582.2, H162, H1213.1F; queen bee identifies princess for hero—B582.2A, H1213.1F; origin River Bee--A934.18; rooster swallows bees--Z52.4; test: surviving in room full of bees and centipedes--H328.10; bee flies into man's ear and tells of treasure--N531.3; bees rout animals in war of birds and beasts--B261.0.1; bees sting jackal's tail as battle flag in war--K2323.1; bees build castle of wax--H346; task: build palace of wax, bees aid--B582.2E; witch stung to death by bees—E501.5.5.1.1.

BEECH: Giant of the Brown Beech Wood—G530Ga.

BEEHIVE: Old woman is protected by objects which attack intruding ogre, beehive helps—K1161.3.3. SEE ALSO HORNET'S NETS; WASP'S NEST.

BEE HUNTER: Bee hunter left dangling in tree—J2133.5.0.1.

BEEKEEPER: Hare leaps to beekeeper for safety, bees sting pursuing witch to death—E501.5.5.1.1.

BEELZEBUB: Sorcerer's apprentice reads forbidden magic book and calls up Beelzebub—D1711.0.1.2.

BEER: Baboon invites hare to drink beer in tree top—J1565.1; lad with keg of beer refuses to drink with Providence or Devil, drinks with Death who treats all men equally—D1825.3.1; foolish girl lets beer run in cellar—J2176; man and son die rather than reveal secret of brewing heather beer—C429.2; stingy innkeeper gives weak beer before meal to fill guests—J1341.7; beer thrown at trickster—K975.1.2; beer wagon driven over giant's road angers giant—F628.2.3.1.

BEESWAX: Beeswax on tortoise shell catches jackal—K741.

BEETLE: Why beetle is bald—A2317.2.1; origin of color of beetle—A2411.3.3; bat, spider, and beetle court together—T92.11.3; beetle on cross is dwarf—F451.5.1.6.3; beetle betrays hidden guests—Z43.6.2; industrious and lazy insects—J711.1; prisoner escapes by rope tied to thread carried up tower by beetle—R121.4.1; beetle wins race by flying—K11.10; beetle hits Long Nosed Mice with throwing stick—K688.7.

BEETLE, DUNG BEETLE: causes Zeus to shake eagle's eggs from lap—L315.7.

BEETLE, TOBACCO BEETLE: Fox gambles with magic dice which are really transformed tobacco beetles—J2346.1.

BEETLE, WATER BEETLE: Dives for mud to create earth—A812.8.

BEETS: Farmer takes extraordinary beet to king—J2415.1; man takes figs to king, they are thrown at him, "Thank God they weren't beets"—J2563.

BEGGAR: King forced to clothe as beggar—L411; poor shoemaker gives last pair of shoes to beggar, is Maharajah—Q45.1.4; beggar calls man down from roof to ask alms, he takes beggar up on roof to say "no"—J1331; gods or saints in disguise reward hospitality and punish inhospitality—Q1.1; to get rid of beggars carve two huge statues from cliff, this takes all wealth—J1199.1; beggar in disguise obtains alms three times from same person—K1982.1; unlucky beggar given fowl stuffed with gold sells it to lucky beggar—N351; beggar weds haughty princess (prince in disguise)—H465.

BEGGING BOWL: Buddha's miraculous begging bowl—V128.0.1.1.

BEHEAD: Beheading bargain: giant allows hero to cut off his head, he will cut off hero's later—M221; prince beheads eleven dragons as enter—S12.1C; behead foals and put heads at tails to turn them back into princes—H1199.12.3; girl beheads robbers as enter—K912. SEE ALSO HEAD.

BELL: Pirates steal bells of abbey, they swell and sink ship—F993.2; if bell is touched King Arthur wakes—D1960.2; church bell hidden at sea, place marked on side of boat—J1922.1; dragon beats temple bell with tail until it is red hot and suitor hiding beneath perishes—B605.1; shepherd returns dwarf's bell—F451.5.1.5.0.3; bell made of black gold draws yellow gold to it—K1023.1.0.2; task, steal horse with bells, horse with bells on legs, stuff bells with flax—G610Ae; horse rings bell to demand justice—B271.3; pheasants beat against bell to ring—E533.2.1; Bell of Stavoren not blessed, Joost claims, drops into Fluessen—F993.1.1; sunken bell sounds—F993ff; thief stealing bronze bell stuffs ears with cotton so din will not raise authorities—J2259.1; suspects to place hands on temple bell believing it will peal when thief touches—J1141.10.2; eagle takes hero to realm of Vanapagan for twelve-toned bell—B582.2E; virgin's blood necessary to cast perfect bell, daughter casts herself in—S261.0.2; as Dick Whittington leaves London the bells call to "Turn again"—N411.1A.

BELLING: Belling the cat—J671.1.

BELLTOWER: 'Ghost' in belltower knocked down stairs—H1440A.

BELLY: SEE STOMACH.

BELMONT: Fools of Belmont push church over jackets—J2328.1.

BELT: Son finds blue belt (scarf) which gives strength—S12.1; belt creates lake—D831Ab; belt inscribed "Seven at a blow"—K1951.1; tiger duped into thinking snake is belt—J1761.6.0.1, K1023.1.1; story told as excuse to remove too tight belt after meal—K263.2.

BENBECULA: Water-bull of Benbecula—F420.1.3.4.

BENCH: Stretching the bench—J2723.

BENDING: Reed bends before wind—J832.

BENSURDATU: Three princesses carried off by cloud—K1931.2J.

BENVENUTO: Witch's son offers to help with task—G530.2L.

BEREL THE BEADLE: Berel carried on rounds by men so as not to track up snow—J2163.3.

BERGMÄNNLEIN: Bergmännlein gives self-replenishing cheese to cowherd—F460.4.2.6.

BERRIES: Crocodile in ambush obeys suggestion that he should roll about in berry patch in which he hides—K607.2.2; fox substitutes berries for lost eyes—E781.4; berries cause horns to grow on person—D551.1H; origin strawberries—A2687.3.1; task: bringing berries in winter—Q2.1.4. SEE ALSO BLACKBERRIES; BLUEBERRIES; STRAWBERRIES; ETC.

BESSANS: Why Plain of Bessans is not forested—D313.1.4.

BEST: Riddle: which is best?—H648.1.

BET: SEE WAGER.

BETEL: Jackal eats expensive betel and impresses princess—K1917.3H; Kantchil smears betel juice on elephant to simulate blood—K1715.2.1; origin of betel chewing—A2691.5.

BETELGEUSE: Star is bear—A772.1.

BETRAYAL: Betrayal of fox by pointing peasant—K2315; animal curse for betraying holy fugitive—A2231.7.1; magpie half-black for betraying crow—A2236.4.1; mother betrays son—S12.1; sister betrays brother—S12.1.0.1; wife betrays husband—D551.1; K2213. SEE ALSO SECRET.

BIBLE: Person to live until candle burns up, candle put inside Bible where Devil can't touch it—E765.1.1.1.

LA BICHE: Devil in form of goat—G303.3.3.1.6.1.

BICYCLE: Anansi steals a bicycle and poses as doctor—K352.1.

BIG: Frog tries in vain to be big as ox—J955.1.

BIG DIPPER: Origin of constellation—A771.

BIG ROCK MOUNTAIN: Wife of star husband descends via cedar rope to Big Rock Mountain—A762.1Bd.

BIGFOOT: Origin of the Sasquatch—B29.9.1.

BIL: Boy on moon—A751.7.

BILL: Fox, wolf and pond carried in duck's bill—Z52.1. SEE ALSO BEAK.

BILL: Bill paying hat sold—K111.2.

BILLY BEG: Billy Beg and his bull—B335.2A.

BILLY GOAT: Three billy goats gruff—K553.2. SEE ALSO GOATS.

BINDING: SEE TYING.

BIRCH: Foals living inside birch tree must be beheaded to restore to princes—H1199.12.3; birch tree on grave gives magic branch to perform tasks—R221Bd; tree gives magic clothing and horse—R221N; mother turns to birch tree spirit—R221N; birch beats girl until she ties it

with ribbon—Q2.1.2CeBa.

BIRD: Advice of released bird—J21.12.1+; ball game of birds and animals—B261.1.0.2+; origin of bird's beak—A2343+; birds from pieces of monster bear—A1906; bird brings flock to eat bugs off crop of good brother—J2415.18; brother turned to bird—P253.2; lad sewn in skin to be carried up onto mountain by birds—K1861.1; man carried by bird from lower world—K1931.2; bird persuades cat to wash—K562; bird catcher sets fire to bush, starts chain—Z49.6.0.8; murdered child returns as bird in tree—N271; man raises child found in treetop where bird had carried it—D671B; bird has new clothes made, flies away without paying—Z49.3.1; origin birds' colors—A2411.2; birds painted present colors—A2411.2.0.2; origin bird colors, fly through rainbow—A2411.2.0.1; cooked bird flies off—Z49.3.1; swallowed Seppo Ilmarinen forges copper bird. Pecks at Ukko Untamoinen's insides, disgorges—F912.3.2; origin bird crest—A2321+; cries of birds—A2426.2+; lame gardener boy causes flowers to sing and birds to dance for visiting king—D1711.0.1.4; bird's song causes dancing—D1415.3; task: make one hundred dishes of small bird—H1022.6.0.1; bird taken on back becomes heavier and heavier, turns into Dry-Bone man—G303.3.5.3.1; bird with golden dung—B103.1.5; nature of bird's eggs—A2391+; nature of bird's feathers—A2313+; how birds learned to fly—A2442.3; fox persuades condor to take him to heavenly feast of birds, abuses parrots as is being lowered on rope and is dropped—A2684; birds plant magic garden, fruit kills rich, replenishes poor—W11.17; lad kills giant bird—B524.1.2G; Kassa Kena Genanina kills terrorizing giant bird—F615.9.1, K1931.2Z; hero buries sailors up to eyes in sand as bait and kills giant bird as it alights—S12.1A; giant bird, "The Merciless One" attacks old woman—K1711.2.3; Kukali is carried off by giant bird—B31.1.3; quest for golden bird—H1331.1.3; green bird causes pot to froth—G378, X909.4.2; bird loses grain and starts chain—Z41.6.2+; gunshot splits limb and catches bird by feet—X1124.3.1; hare tricks bird into cage—K714.2.4.1.1; eat bird heart and find gold piece under pillow each morning—D551.1A; mouse, bird and sausage keep house together—J512.7; Jorinda and Joringel, child turned to bird—D771.11; Kin Kin bird sings jungle back each night, animals are trying to clear—D1487.3.1; king of birds as brother-in-law—B314F; Alpein bird king carries prince to its castle—H1385.1H; bird indicates new king—H171.2; Glooskap turns dead leaves to birds to please children—A1907; bird lover—H1385.5A+; dead lover appears daily as bird—E423.3.0.1; magic bird that tells all—F660.1F; magic bird lays rice and fish for orphan girls—J2415.17; quest for most marvelous bird in the world—H1331.1.3; bird sold as messenger—K131.2; bird migrations directed by Linou, goddess of Milky Way—A778.11; monkeys kill bird who tells them firefly is not fire—J1761.3; Shoshone learn their music from the wind and the birds—A1461.0.2; birds fly off with net—K581.4.1; how birds build nests—A2431.1;

numskull believes self dead when frightened by bird—J2311.1.3.2; numskull tries to shake birds from tree like fruit--J1909.3; origin of white and black-headed birds—A1905; Bird Padishah brother-in-law--B314B; prick bird's head with pin, turns to girl--D582.0.1; quest to Bird of Seven Colors who answers questions—H1273.2E; Raden Samisan refuses the throne and is turned into a bird as he wanders forever--A2681.15; bird created by Raven cannot fly--J2186.1; saint of birds (St. Cuddy)—V429.1; birds attempt to drink up sea—B263.10; birds try to empty sea--J1968.0.1; sea birds attack land birds--B263.5.2; bird startles lad and makes him shudder—H1440B; birds sing waters down before reach sky—A1021.0.7; repeating tale, won't sell singing bird—Z17.4; birds in snare escape one at a time, endless tale—Z11.2; king of mice gnaws birds in snare free—K581.4.1.1; man listens to bird song and years pass—D2011.1; princess will wed minstrel when has learned song of all birds in forest—A1461.8.2; caught stealing fruit, theif claims is songbird--J1391.9; quest for speaking bird--N455.4; bird in chest tells story—F945.2.1.1; summer birds imprisoned make winter last—A771.0.3; talking bird believes it rained—J1151.1.3.1; released bird gives captor three teachings--K604; birds tricked into trap--K717.2; treasure-laying bird—B103.2.1; birds ask man to spare tree--J241.2; sound of Vainamoinen's harp is bird song—A2272.1.4; war of birds—G530.2K; war of birds and animals--B261.1+; bird calls causing woman with waterpots to look up and drop pots--K1079.1; bird makes wings for bat and flying squirrel--B261.1.0.2.1; bird shelters with wings--B538.1; poor brother who heals wounded bird is given treasure-producing seed --J2415.13.

BIRD, ADERNA: Quest for aderna bird—H1331.1.3Fc.

BIRD, ADJUTANT: Monkeys pull out feathers of adjutant birds. Adjutant birds convince monkeys to tie tails together to keep boat from rocking. Boat sinks and monkeys drown--K713.1.12.

BIRD, ATI-TIA: Ati-Tia lends song to flute--F601.2I.

BIRD, BARNFOWL: Barnfowl to raise head before drinking--N455.4D.

BIRD, BLACKBIRD: Anansi flies with blackbird to island to feed. The blackbird takes back his feathers and leaves Anansi stranded on the island--K1041.1.5; why the blackbird rids the buffalo's back--R111.1.13.2; orgin of the blackbird's chatter--A2426.2.28; origin of the color of the blackbird--A2332.5.12, A2411.2.1.9.1; blackbird tricks the coyote into a bag—K711.5; why the blackbird has white eyes--A2332.5.12; blackbird pierces his claw with a pine needle, then takes a flute and sings of events—Z47.5; quest for golden blackbird--H1331.1.3Ak; blackbird carries ants, water, etc. in ear and forces the king to return to wife--Z52; origin of the blackbird's nest--A2271.1.1; Sosondowah,

Great Night, woos maid as blackbird in summer, bluebird in spring, nighthawk in autumn—B641.6.2.

BIRD, BLUEBIRD: Bluebird dips in lake, origin color—A2411.2.1.20; wolf imitates bluebird's dive for blue color—A2411.1.3.4; bluebird lover —H1385.5Ad; man trades magic bluebird for wife —D876.4; Sosondowah, Great Night, woos maid as bluebird—B641.6.2; two bluebird brothers sleep on stretching rock—D482.4.1; worm does not admire song of bluebird, is about to be its dinner--J652.4.3.

BIRD, BLUE CRANE: Blue Crane magically turns to girl, Mantis subdues her by rubbing his sweat on her face--A591.1.

BIRD, BLUEJAY: Bluejay's colors—A2426.2.26.1; hunters, pigeon, bluejay, owls follow bear in constellation—A771.0.1; bluejay's cries—A2426.2.26.

BIRD, BOOKOO: Why bookoo bird calls "Boo Koo" at rice planting season--A2426.2.24.

BIRD, BULBUL: Jackal asks bulbul where he goes —K688.5.

BIRD, BUSH FOWL: Refuses to wake sun—Z49.6.0.1.

BIRD, BUZZARD: Why buzzard is bald—A2317.3; buzzard burnt in bee's nest—K1055; buzzard stretches earth—A812.5; Earth Magician makes buzzard from shadow of left eye—A614.0.1; hare steals fire from buzzard—A1415.0.2.1; hare flies on buzzard's back, hits over head with guitar and holds wings outstretched to glide to earth—K1041.3; hills from flapping of buzzard's wings—A961.1; buzzard waits for lord to provide food--J2215.4.0.1; why buzzard has no neck feathers--A2351.9; buzzards carry off mule--J1531.2.1; Brer Buzzard abandons Brer Rabbit on top of tree until Rabbit remembers where he hid gold—K2347; Brer Buzzard guards Brer Rabbit trapped in hollow tree—K629.2.4; sun rules buzzard may collect debt in chickens—A2494.13.10.7; turtle taught by buzzard to fly, not taught how to land—K1041.0.3; old woman tells buzzard how he reminds her of husband—J1762.10.

BIRD, CANADIAN GEESE: Language of geese learned—B165.3.

BIRD, CANARY: Peasant asks merchant for gaiters for canary—K92.4.

BIRD, CARDINAL: Color of cardinal--A2411.2.1.13; cardinal's daughter takes singing lessons—A2426.2.22.

BIRD, CATBIRD: Catbird's call—A2426.2.20.

BIRD, CHICKADEE: Chickadee as star—A771.0.1.

BIRD, CHICKEN: SEE CHICKEN.

BIRD, CHILOTA: Why chilota does not sing—A2422.13.

BIRD, CHINGOLO: Legend of origin—A1999.5.

BIRD, COCKATOO: Origin of cockatoo's crest—A2321.12.

BIRD, CONDOR: Condor blessed by Coniraya, killing brings bad luck—A2541.3; condor flies highest in contest, made King of the Mountains—B236.1.1; condor carries fox to moon—A2433.3.20.2; Pachacamac as white condor gives potato—A2686.4.4.

BIRD, CONEY: Advises girl—Q2.1.2Ea.

BIRD, COOT: How to cook a coot—X1258.2.1.

BIRD, CORMORANT: At banquet given by cormorant gudgeon's tail is cut off. Host cormorant must replace with own—A2378.2.11; cormorant carries fish to new pond, eats—K815.14; cormorant catches snake from which birds take their colors—A2411.2.5.1.1.

BIRD, COUCAL: Coucal wins calling contest—K11.1.1.2.

BIRD, CRANE: Why crane has long beak—A2343.1.6; crane plucks bone from wolf's throat—W154.3; crane's leg as bridge for fugitives—R246; butterfly challenges crane to fly to Tonga—K11.2.1; clam (oyster) catches beak of crane trying to eat him—J219.1; crane courts heron—W123.2; crab cuts off crane's neck—K953.3; cranes help thirsty Arap Sang to shade, are given golden crowns—A2321.13; dupe lets self be carried aloft by bird and dropped—K1041; why crane has blue eyes—A2232.5.11; crane's eyes call false alarm—J2199.1.3.; coyote steals fire from cranes with rock squirrel's aid—A1415.0.2.3; fish tricked by crane into letting selves be carried to new pond—K815.14; crane says ability to fly is better than peacock's finery—J242.5; crane and fox invite each other—J1565.1; origin of crane's red head—A2320.3.2; Craney Crow thinks all birds have taken off their heads to sleep—J2413.4.2.1; crane judges for man not snake—J1172.3.2.3; why crane has long legs—A2371.2.14; crane removes bone from lion's throat but props mouth open with stick first—K639.1; crane maiden spins for benefactor—B652.2; paper crane given to ride to Land of Perpetual Life—E80.5; queen crane aids hero—R222.1B; crane throws emu's egg into sky = sun—A714.3.1; thief hears invented story about crane's motions and thinks self described, flees—N612.4; crane with one thought feigns dead and escapes—J1662.2; tortoise carried by cranes—J2357; war between cranes and peacocks—B263.3; man weds crane in human form—B652.2; why crane is white—A2411.2.6.14; marsh wren builds in cattail tops in marsh, crane builds nearby following example—A2431.3.13. SEE ALSO: BLUE CRANE.

BIRD, CROW: Crow's caw—A2426.2.6; fox flatters crow into singing and dropping cheese—K334.1; crab pinches neck of crow—K815.14.2; color of crow—A2411.2.1.6; crow leads crocodile to better river—K815.14.3; crow must guard cuckoo's nest—A2491.2; man whose buffalo has wandered feigns dead and catches crow, forces to give magic jade which grants wishes—D551.1C; crow advises deer to feign dead, once out of snare flee—K642.3; crow to be disenchanted if princess will live with him and keep silent no matter what—D758.1.1; crow advises eagle to drop tortoise—J657.2.2; crow tries to imitate eagle in carrying off lamb—J2413.3; enmity between owl and crow—A2494.13.1; crow brings first grain of corn in his ear when comes from Land of Sun to earth—A2685.1.0.2; crow drops filth on man, flamingo is shot—J429.2.1; crow pretends to be ghost and steals—K335.0.4.5; golden crow offers gift to kind girl—Q2.1.6E; crow loses grain starting chain—Z41.6.3; hare distracts dog so that crow can escape—K648.1; crow advised by hawk that intimidating fox cannot fly—K1788; crow asks hospitality of sparrow and gradually takes possession of nest and kills young—K354.1; louse and crow make covenant of friendship, louse eats crow—Z33.4.1; mussel releases crow on promise of uncle's kayak and goods, crow has no uncle—K578.9.1; crow drops necklace in snake's hole and men kill snake—K401.2.2; crow drops pebbles into water jug so as to be able to drink—J101; Crow-Peri in snare offers most precious thing if released—H1151.6.2; crow makes friends with pigeon so as to be able to steal food in household—K359.4; coyote and crow steal pine nuts from geese, drop in valleys—A1425.0.1.1; crow tries to prophesy like raven—J951.3; fake prophesying crow—J1344.1; secret remedy overheard in conversation of animals—N452; why crow must roost on bare tree in winter—A2431.3.6.4; crow dives for seeds by tying rock around neck—J2137.8; prairie falcon defeats crow in shinny match—K23; crow eats snake threatening benefactor—J1172.3.2.3; black crow steals soap—J2211.5; couple wish for son, crow comes—B642.1; crow asks sparrow pessimistic questions—Z39.4.3; Gizo, spider, coats stomach with wax and crawls over crow's fig pile, figs stick to stomach—K378.1.1; Gizo, spider, flies with crow to island to feed—K1041.1.5; why crow has short tail—A2378.4.7; crow and turtle free deer—K642.2; crow cannot reach pelican babies in nest, in anger calls Tuckonie Elves to sing tree up—D482.1.1; crow imitates partridge's walk—J512.6; war between crows and owls—B263.3; crow must wash beak before eating—Z41.2.1; crow feeding on corpse caught and sent for water of life—H1331.1.3Af; crow drinks water of immortality—A1335.16; crow forced to bring water from wells with healing, strength, swiftness—R111.1.3An; crow makes animals believe beached whale is poison—K344.1.5; white crow discovered with buffalo meat at dance—A1878.2.

BIRD, CU: Owl suggests covering ugly bird Cu with pitch and giving her a feather from each bird—A2491.2.7.

BIRD, CUCKOO: Color of cuckoo—
A2411.2.6.10.1; crow ordered to watch cuckoo's
nest—A2491.2.1; girl turns to cuckoo when
family kill lover—B654.2; cuckoo flies over
hedge built to contain her—J1904.2; origin of
red moss, bloody path of four sons pursuing
mother who has turned to cuckoo—A2683.1.2;
why mother cuckoo abandons children—
A2431.2.1.1; eagle confers title of nightingale
on cuckoo but song remains the same—U119.5.1;
cuckoo and cocks in waking contest—K51;
woman as cuckoo on tree shot—K1691.

BIRD, CURASSOW: Ants bite snake and it leaves
nest of curassow—Z39.1.0.3; curassow tells
jaguar cautionary tale of Kikushie—L471.1.

BIRD, DAW: Daw fleeing caught in trees by
thread around foot—N255.5.

BIRD, DOVE: Dove rescues ant in spring—
B362.2; doves on ax handle reward kind girl—
Q2.1.5Ba; black doves turn to dragons and
burst in fury—D765.1.2.1; dove warns prince
of false bride with mutilated feet in slippers—
R221B; brothers turned to doves—P253.2E;
good fairy as dove gives princess comb, brush,
sheet, apple to flee witch—D672D; forgotten
fiancee reawakens husband's memory by having
magic doves converse—D1413.16, G530.2,
H1385.4; H1385.5; dove advised by goose that
intimidating fox cannot climb tree—K1788;
hammerhead told by dove not to build near
stream—A2431.3.12; why dove has blue head—
A2411.2.1.21.1; hunter wakened from dream by
dove and saved from flood—F1068.4; dove as
lover—H1385.5Af; dove maid stealing pears—
H1385.3Jc; origin nest of dove—A2271.1; doves
caught in net rise up—J1024; origin of dove,
why doves understand human speech—A1948.1;
pin in head of dove, transformed girl—D721.5;
witch sticks pins in temple and turns girl to
dove—K1911Ac; princess pulls three pins from
head of white dove and he turns to prince—
D765.1.2.1; two white doves light on shoulder
as enters church, lad named Pope and doves
whisper mass to him—B217.9; dove aids, is
kissed and turns to princess—G530.2Bd; dove
gives magic ring—D882.1B; dove flies out of
basket making lad shudder—H1440Bb; sons return as doves—D154.1; coyote wants to learn
dove's song—G555.1.2.

BIRD, DOVE—GROUND DOVE: Ground dove
given bright feathers in return for messenger
jobs—A2411.2.1.21.

BIRD, DUCK: Where duck got bill—A2343.1.5;
ducks cross bridge one at a time—Z11; brothers
transformed to ducks—P253.2C; duck carries
children over lake—G412.1.1; crab pinches
duck's neck—K953.3; ducks tricked, dance with
eyes shut—K826; duck dives in primeval sea—
A812.4; pet duck becomes dragon-girl—T542.2;
duck's flat feet—A2375.2.8.1; duck carries fish
to 'new pond,' eats—K815.14; golden duck,
seven ducklings emerge from lake. Become
maid, children—F302.4.2.3; helpful duck—
B469.4; female duck stabs breast with beak and

dies before hunter who killed her husband,
hunter becomes priest—F1041.1.2.2.5; lame
duck taken in by old couple keeps house as girl
—N831.1; why ducks pull up one leg when
sleeping—A2479.13; magic duck stolen by host
at inn—D861.1G; intruder thinks duck is man
calling "Smack him"—K1161.4; girl as duck is
captive of mermaid who pulls back to lake with
invisible gold chain—Q2.1.5Bba; duck dives
for moon's reflection—J1791.8; ducks retrieve
copper paddle—F601.2I, H335.7.3; mallard to
wed peacock—J414.3.3; queen as duck comes
thrice to nurse baby—Q2.1.4B; crossing river
where ducks cross—J1919.2; lad eats off crust
of roast duck thinking it can roast a second—
J2311.2.3; roast duck reward is stuffed with
coins, unlucky man gives it away—N351.0.1;
Cinderlad sent to steal troll's seven silver ducks
—G610Ac; cat and duck retrieve magic stone
—D882.1Bba; lad raises magic storm to protect
pet duck—D2142.1.6.1; duck aids kind hero in
task—R111.1.3Ao; tortoise carried by wild
ducks—J2357; one hundred ducks carry off
trap and hunter—K687.1; duck drops wolf in
lake—G412.1.2.

BIRD, EAGLE: Eagle killed with arrow made of
own feather—U161; why eagle is bald—A2317.3.1;
helpful eagle brother-in-law—B314; eagle
carries dupe higher and higher—K1041.0.1;
eagle carries hero from lower world—K1931.2;
tortoise carried by eagle—J657.2ff, J2357; eagle
carries Ke'let over river and drops—
K1041.0.1.1; hero offers own flesh to eagle
carrying him—K1931.2; contest for highest fly
er, wren rides eagle—K11.2; coyote pulls out
eagle's head feathers in revenge—A2317.3.1;
eagle creator—A812.4; eagle confers title of
"Nightingale" on cuckoo, song remains the same
—U119.5.1; eagle teaches dance—A1542.2.2; lad
weds daughter of eagle chief, in eagle form he
drops cruel uncle into sea—S71.2; eagle brings
wife back from land of dead—F81.1.0.5; eagle's
eggs destroyed by dungbeetle—L315.7; fox
burns eagle's tree—L315.3; giant eagle killed by
Oni—H36.1.2; eagle killed by hero climbing
Glass Mountain—H331.1.1C; eagle judges for
tiger, not man—J1172.3.2; eagle thinks self
largest animal in world—J953.20; magic eagle
feather servants of Great Spirit—A2431.3.11;
why mink has white down on chest, for caring
for eaglets—A2412.1.9; hero stealing eaglets
abandoned in nest—B455.3.2; eagle wants to
wed someone old and wise, owl—B841.1.5; helpful eagle, ogre's heart in the egg—D532A;
origin of eagles with red-tipped wings—
A2411.2.2.1; eagles shed feathers on water as
sign of peace, covered with down they subside
—A1018.4; twelve eagles turn into princes—
B647.1.1; eagle alights on traveler to be named
ruler—B217.9; hero steals Great Shell of
Kintyel for eagles—B455.3.2; eagle takes to
realm of Vanapagan for twelve-toned bell—
B582.2E; eagle gives choice of suffering in
youth or age—J214; youth who could become an
ant, lion or eagle—R111.1.3Aj.

BIRD, EAGLE CLAN: Restoration of Eagle Clan
of Tsimshian—A1611.1.6.

BIRD, EAGLET: Boy saves injured eaglet, eaglet rescues boy from canoe accident—B389.3; boy falls into nest, nurtures eaglets to maturity, they carry him to ground--A2411.2.2.1.

BIRD, EGA: Why egas keep building and tearing down nests, parents move to be rid of children—A2431.3.15; hero learns secret identity of King of Spirit World from ega bird—B216.4.

BIRD, EGRET: Why egret rides buffalo—A2433.4.8; egret defeats buffalo in drinking contest—K82.1.1; tortoise carried by egrets—J2537.

BIRD, EMU: Emu's eggs thrown in sky = sun--A714.3.1; emu hurls spear at crane—A2343.1.6; emu convinces turkey to kill chicks—A2486.5; why emu has no wings—A2377.1.

BIRD, FALCON: Dog, falcon, otter aid hero—R111.1.3Cd; blue falcon sought by hero in quest—H1331.1.3Am; one falcon breaks wing, three brothers stay to care for it until spring—P250.2; falcon reproaches hen for fleeing master—J1423; falcon lover, Finist the Bright Falcon—H1385Aa; falcon remodeled to look more like regular bird—J1919.1.

BIRD, FALCON--PRAIRIE: Prairie falcon defeats crow in shinny game—K23.

BIRD, FIREBIRD: Quest for firebird--H1213.1la, H1331.1.3.

BIRD, FISHER: Fisher helps release summer, becomes big dipper—A771.0.3.

BIRD, FLAMINGO: Crow drops filth on man, flamingo is shot—J429.2; flamingo shields man with wings—B538.1.1.

BIRD, FRANCOLIN: Why francolin cries at dawn and dusk—A2426.2.27.

BIRD, FRIGATE: Why frigate bird can't catch fish, trades beaks with brown pelican—A2343.3.5; frigate bird rides in canoe—A2317.13.

BIRD, GOOSE: Baba-Yaga's geese steal little brother—Q2.1.2CeA; saw someone carrying a goose to your house—J1353; Mrs. Goose leaves clothes bundle on bed, Brer Fox steals—K525.1.0.1; cooked goose sings on table, others fly in and give it feathers and all fly off—X1258.3; fox leaves all work to goose then claims crop—K641.1; geese tricked into dancing with eyes closed—K826; escape by persuading captor to dance—K606.2; dividing the goose--H601; goose advises dove that intimidating fox cannot climb tree—K1788; geese with feet frozen to lake fly off with lake—X1606.2.4.1; goose shot as ghost--J1785.8; goose that laid the golden egg killed---D876; golden goose to which everyone sticks—H341.1; goose that laid the golden eggs—D876; hunters argue over how to cook geese, geese fly off—J2062.4; deceptive land purchase, as much land as goose can fly over—K185.3.1; lazy girl turns to goose—Z18.2; having eaten leg trickster claims geese are one-legged—K402.1; geese turned to pages by magic flute music of gooseherd—R221Z; Raven makes a clay egg, hatches a goose—K1041.2; visitor being fed poorly and asked if he knows "Roast Goose" who lives in the "Pan Village"—X1506.2; geese persuade wolf to sing, escape—K606.2.1; old woman and twelve geese turned to stone--V429.1; goose feather mantle burned by sun—A728.1; thief thinks goose is man with pincers—K1161.2; transformation, man to goose—D161.2.1; two geese carry turtle on stick—J2357; goose persuades wolf to wash him before eating—K553.5.3; wife is prisoner of old goose in rock igloos on mountain top—D672G; horse Swift-Go goes fast as wind when hero blows through goose's windpipe—R111.1.4A; goose and ass visit wishing well at Christmas—B251.1.2.4;

BIRD, GOOSE -CANADIAN: Language of Canadian Geese learned—B165.3.

BIRD, GOOSE--GANDER: Witch turns lad into gander--G263.1.0.3; respite from death while gander prays—K555.1.0.1.

BIRD, GOOSE GIRL: Goose girl has handkerchief with three drops of mother's protecting blood—B133.3.

BIRD, GOOSE--GOLDEN: Willow plucks feathers of golden goose—D877.0.1.

BIRD, GOOSE--GOSLING: Goslings build houses and meet wolf—K891.1.1.3.

BIRD, GOOSE--SNOW: Jealous boy wishes he were a snow goose—D100.2; man takes cloak of snow goose and weds—H1385.3ff.

BIRD, GOOSE--WILD: Wild geese caught carry boy—X1133.1.1; wild goose is considered bird of the five virtues—B259.6.

BIRD, GOOSEHERD: Causes prince to fall in love with magic flute—R221Z; brother of mermaid queen made gooseherd—Q2.1.5Bbc.

BIRD, GREBE: Grebe given red eyes for warning ducks of Manabozo's plan—A2332.5.7.

BIRD, GROUND OWL: SEE BIRD, OWL--GROUND.

BIRD, GUINEA: Guinea in age debate—B841.1.2; color of Guinea--A2411.2.6.6; Guinea asks eggs what will do for her when hatching--J267.1.1; why guinea fowl has red feet—A2375.2.10.1; hare claims guinea's garden on basis of path—K453.1; hare tricks guineas into cage—K714.2.4.1; guinea hens eaten by fox as holy man—K815.16.2; guineas trick hyena into cage—K715.1.1.

BIRD, GULL: SEE BIRD, SEA GULL.

BIRD, HAMMERHEAD: Told by dove not to build near stream—A2431.3.12.

BIRD, HAWK: Rat and hawk rescue stolen magic bag—D882.1Ga; hawk helps rescue girl from buffalo—R111.1.13.2; hawk was only chasing a pigeon over farmer's field when caught—U32.1; hawk's comb stolen by cock—A2321.10.0.1; hawk advises crow that fox cannot climb—K1788; let me catch you better game—K553.1.0.4; hawk rescues girl being pulled into pool by goddess —A2494.13.10.3.3; hen loses hawk's ring (or fails to keep promise), hawk may carry off hen's children—A2494.13.10.3.1ff; hawk drops mouse into hand of hermit—L392.0.1; hawk carries hyena aloft and drops—K1041.0.2; hawk elected king of pigeons—K815.8; nightingale asks hawk to let him go and wait for bigger bird—J321.2.1; Brer Rabbit wants to show treasure before being eaten by hawk—K551.25.1; hawk soars and dives seeking lost ring—A2442.2.5; hawk and rat retrieve magic ring—D882.1B; man and star wife become white hawks—F302.4.2.4; hawk carries sun and moon to sky—A717.2; hawk to restore virility if given pigeon—K1853.3. SEE ALSO SPARROW HAWK.

BIRD, HERON: Rooster must clean bill on grass at heron's ball—Z41.2.3; clam catches beak of heron—J219.1; heron caught in coral is freed by turtle—B545.3; color of heron—A2411.2.5.2.1; heron and monkey contest in sitting still on branch—K54; heron rejects courting crane— W123.2; crab pinches off neck of deceitful heron—K953.3; heron waits for larger fish and ends with none—J321.5; fish tricked by heron into letting selves be carried to another pond— K815.14; King of birds, heron has birds carve canoe for Rata who rescued him—B364.4; why heron is lean—Z49.18; tortoise carried by herons—J2357; wildcat flatters heron into singing—K334.1.

BIRD, HONEYBIRD: Leads villagers to abandoned lad—K1931.2Va; on maid's shoulder—R221H.

BIRD, HONEY-GUIDE BIRD: Why honey-guide bird leads man to honey, revenge on bees— A2513.8; wronged wife reappears as honey guide bird and sings truth—N271C.

BIRD, HORNBILL: Why hornbill drinks every third day—A2231.7.1.3.

BIRD, HORNBILL--GREAT GROUND HORNBILL: Told hyena he has arranged for continuous night, raiding party caught at dawn— A2426.2.27.

BIRD, HUMMINGBIRD: Color of hummingbird— A2411.2.1.19; coyote returns feast—J1565.1.5; Great Spirit covers valley with tar, Indians had slaughtered hummingbirds, souls of the dead— A983.2.

BIRD, JACKDAW: Jackdaw in pigeon's skin unmasked—J951.2.

BIRD, JAY: Jay in peacock's feathers—J951.2. SEE ALSO BIRD, BLUEJAY.

BIRD, KAKOK: Origin—A1999.4.1.

BIRD, KAKUI: Origin of kakui bird—A1999.6.

BIRD, KENNREIRK: How Kennreirk owl got name —A2571.2.

BIRD, KINGFISHER: Kingfisher pecks bridge for people—A1034.1; color of kingfisher— A2411.2.1.22; origin of crest, white necklace, must dive for living henceforth—A2321.5.1; kingfisher announces sunrise—A712.

BIRD, KINURU: Kinuru carries hyena aloft— K1041.0.5.

BIRD, KITE: Flies too near sky and drops earth on sea = Philippine Islands—A818.1; first man and woman emerge from bamboo pecked open by kite—A1271.5.

BIRD, KLING KLING: Kling Kling causes sham dead tiger to laugh—K607.3.

BIRD, LARK: Lark moves nest when farmer says he will reap field himself—J1031. SEE ALSO MEADOWLARK.

BIRD, LAUGHING JACKASS: Why laughs at dawn —A2425.2.1.

BIRD, LONGSPUR: Widowed longspur weds another longspur—J416.3.

BIRD, LOON: loon restores blind boy's sight, given necklace—F952.7.1; origin loon's call— A2426.2.19; origin color of loon—A2411.2.1.5.1, A2411.2.6.1; loon opens path through water— A1024.1; why loon walks awkwardly—A2441.2.3.

BIRD, LORIKEET: Testimony in court discredited —J1151.1.3.1.1.

BIRD, MAGPIE: Magpie's children ask clever questions—J13; magpie's color—A2236.4.1, A2411.2.1.10; magpie in cowhide, oracular— K842; why magpie is cunning—A2525.4; why magpie's nest is poorly made—A2271.1; A2431.3.11; magpie teaches nest building— A2271.1.

BIRD, MARSH WREN: SEE WREN, MARSH.

BIRD, MEADOWLARK: Hymn to the morning learned from meadowlark—A1461.0.2; mother meadowlark outwits snake—K567.2.

BIRD, MOCKINGBIRD: Gives out calls to birds— A2426.2.0.1; mockingbird calls dawn—B755.3; where mockingbird learned song—A2426.2.22; Sis Mockingbird teaches courting song to Brer Rabbit—K1066.8.

BIRD, MOOSEBIRD: Moosebird is three stars in handle of dipper—A771.0.1.

BIRD, MOTMOT: Why motmot lives in hole in bark—A2431.3.9.

BIRD, MUDHEN: Maui gets secret of fire from mudhens—A1415.0.2.4; origin of mudhen's red head--A2320.3.1; mudhen dives for earth, returns dead with mud in beak--A812.6.

BIRD, NIGHTHAWK: Sosondawah, Great Night, woos maid as nighthawk--B641.6.2.

BIRD, NIGHTINGALE: Eagle confers title of "nightingale" on cuckoo but song remains the same--U119.5.1; nightingale asks hawk to let him go and wait for bigger bird--J321.2.1; bird gives man three teachings in return for release --K604; quest for nightingale for mosque--H1331.1.3Ea; nightingale brings water from Fountain of Dew to disenchant princess--B582.2B.

BIRD, ORIOLE: Proud oriole--W116.9.

BIRD, OSTRICH: Why ostrich leaves egg outside of nest--A2431.4; feather from killed ostrich grows into another ostrich--E3.1; ostrich keeps fire under wings--A1415.0.2.2; why ostrich never flies--A1415.0.2.1; A2377.4; hare eats berry cache, blames ostrich--K251.1.6; lion claims ostrich's chicks, mongoose saves--K649.9.1; moon is ostrich feather--A741.5.

BIRD, OWL: Owl advises killing saplings of oak--J621.1; owl aids kind hero--R111.1.3Am; owl is transformed baker's daughter--A1958.0.1; owl lent feathers for ball, never returns--A2491.2.6; why owl's beak is hooked--A2343.3.4; owl blinded for reading at Quetzal's party--A2491.2.5; Blodevedd turned to an owl for betraying husband--A1958.0.2; devil completes barn except for owl's boards for nest--G303.14.1; K1886.3.1.1; each likes his own children best--T681; color of owl--A2411.2.4.2; conjure wives turn to owls--D153.2; constellation, owl as star --A771.0.1; courting owl burnt--A2411.2.4.2.3; courting owl at dance flees at daylight--A2491.2.8; owl dropped by crane leg bridge--R246; owl suggests covering ugly bird Cu with pitch and giving feathers, fails and both become night birds to escape anger--A2491.2.7; owl to live in dark, punishment for looking while creator made hare--A2491.2.3; why owls avoid daylight--A2491.2; enmity between owl and crow--A2494.13.1; origin owl's eyes--A2332.1.5.1; why owl has flat face--A2330.9; origin owl's feathers--A2313.8; owl steals fire for man--A1415.2.1; guest owl mentions smell of fox wife, tabu--C35.6; owl hoots at caravan and companion swan is killed by arrow aimed at sound--J429.2.1; hump on back of owl--A2356.2.14; if owl can leave log of jungies without touching it he will be snow white--A2411.2.4.2.4; owl in moon--A751.12; origin owl's nest--A2271.1; right to light won in contest, owl repeats 'night' over and over--A1172.4; eagle wants to wed someone old and wise, owl--B841.1.5; Old Woman Crim has party to keep owls past dawn--J2332.1.1; owl and raven paint each other--A2411.2.4.2; owl spills lampblack on Raven--A2411.2.1.5.2; roosters revenge on owls for dancing with hens --J2332.1; animal captor persuaded to talk and release captive from mouth--K561.1; owl beats trees down for people to pass--A1024.1; war

between crows and owls--B263.3; owl as watchman goes to sleep--A2233.3; owl set to guard wren falls asleep--A2491.2.4; owl spills pan of bird's tears meant for ritual drowning of wren, hides in shame--A2491.2.2.

BIRD, OWL--ACADIAN: As star in constellation--A771.0.1.

BIRD, OWL--GROUND OWL: Young saved by Kantchil--K644.1.

BIRD, OWL--HOOT: Why has grey on wings and around eyes--A1415.2.3.

BIRD, OWL--HORNED: Why has grey on wings and around eyes--A1415.2.3.

BIRD, OWL--KENNREIRK: How kennreirk owl got name--A1415.2.1.1, A2571.2.

BIRD, OWL--SCREECH: Why has red eyes--A1415.2.3.

BIRD, OWL--SIBERIAN BROWN OWL: Why does not migrate--A2482.4.

BIRD, PARROT: Parrot in age debate--B841.1.2; parrot aids girl, tells which beggar is disguised king--B469.9; why parrot's beak is bent--A2343.3.3; parrot cannot say cataño--B211.3.4.1; parrot invites cat to dinner--Z33.2.1; trained parrot given as gift is eaten--J1826.1; on advice of lawyer parrot feigns dead and is thrown out, escapes--K522.4.0.1; entrance to woman's room in golden parrot statue --K1341.1; parrot becomes advisor to king--K1346.0.1; Parrot of Limo Verde, parrot lover--H1385.5Ac; parrot cuts rope letting mole being carried to moon fall--A2433.3.20.1; parrot arranges race between beetle and rat--A2411.3.3, K11.10; minister dupes rajah into entering body of dead parrot, then enters rajah's body--K1175; why birds only repeat--A2422.12; friend's son said to have turned to parrot--J1531.2.0.1; testimony in court discredited--J1151.1.3; hen offered for sale at price of parrot, has wonderful thoughts--J1060.1; twin parrots raised by bandit and brahmin--J451.6; parrot's voice--A2426.2.11.1; quest for white parrot--H1331.1.3Fa; youth turns to parrot to be by side of love--D157.1.

BIRD, PARTRIDGE: Partridge in age debate--B841.1.1; cat acts as judge between partridge and hare--K815.7; color of partridge--A2411.2.6.8; crow imitates partridge's walk--J512.6; fox allows partridge to sew his mouth shut so he can learn to whistle--K713.4; partridge notices that game cocks mistreat even each other--J892; partridge offers to lure others into net if released--K553.1.0.2; partridge borrows terrapin's whistle and doesn't return--A2426.2.25; partridge pretending to be wounded entices woman from food while jackal eats it--K341.5.2.

BIRD, PEACOCK: Crane says ability to fly is better than finery of peacock--J242.5; mallard duck to wed peacock—J414.3.3; peacock's feathers—A2411.2.6.7; trapped peacock feigns dead and escapes—K522.4.4; jay in peacock's feathers—J951.2; peacock is bad king, too weak to defend—J242.4; wed to peacock maid—H1385.3Fab; peacock's ugly voice—A2423.1.2; peacock dissatisfied with voice, Juno refuses—W128.4; peacock sent with message to King of France rehearses until loses voice—A2423.1.2.1; Anansi chooses animals with best voices to talk at court, prince hidden chooses voice for self, chooses peacock's voice—A2423.1.2.2; war between cranes and peacocks—B263.3.

BIRD, PELICAN: Crow cannot reach pelican babies in nest, calls Tuckonie elves to sing tree up, now mother cannot reach them—D482.1.1; frigate bird and pelican trade beaks—A2343.3.5; princess to be given to one who brings healing jewel from neck of King Pelican—H1321.1Cd.

BIRD, PHEASANT: Pheasants beat bell to warn—E533.2.1; why pheasant has red head—A2411.2.6.9.1; pheasant as companion for Momotaro—T543.3.2.

BIRD, PHOENIX: Chain ends with Phoenix's nest knocked over—Z49.6.0.4; phoenix on mound of earth indicates salt—A978.5; quest for golden phoenix—H1331.1.3Ca; emerald crested phoenix carries lad to upper world—K1931.2E.

BIRD, PICARO BIRD: Bird has suit, shoes, hat made and doesn't pay—Z49.3.1.

BIRD, PIGEON: Ant saves pigeon's life—B363.2; pigeon restores sight to blind man—K1853.3; crow makes friends with pigeon so as to be able to steal food in household—K359.4; constellation, pigeon as star—A771.0.1; girl lost in wood is befriended by pigeon—D154.2.1; hawk elected king of pigeons—K815.8; pigeon to light on one to be chosen new king—H1440D; king of pigeons is caught in net, fellow pigeons carry net with king in it to mouse who gnaws free—K687; why so many pigeons in New York—A2434.4.1, J2357; pigeon suitor bathes in milk and becomes youth—H1385.5Af; suitor test, catch five pigeons—H331.9.1; pigeons take back feathers and strand turtle—K1041.1.4.

BIRD, POWIS BIRD: Quiet powis bird is given crest and mane as leader and becomes crested curassow—Z39.1.0.3.

BIRD, PTARMIGAN: How ptarmigan learned to fly—A2442.3.1.

BIRD, PUHUY: Origin of puhuy's feathers—A2411.2.6.7; why puhuy cries "puhuy"—A2426.2.21.

BIRD, PUFFIN: Origin of puffin—A1999.1.

BIRD, QUAIL: Fox tries to beguile the quail by reporting a new law establishing peace—J1421; why quail lives in grass—A2431.3.10; quails rise together in net—J1024; roasted quail stolen

and live one left in place—J2215.7; quail causes couple to strike each other—K1082.3.1.

BIRD, QUETZAL: Origin of quetzal—A1999.2; origin of quetzal's feathers—A2411.2.6.7.1; at quetzal's party owl blinded for reading—A2491.2.5.

BIRD, RAVEN: Raven loses half beak—A2335.2.3; brothers transformed to ravens—P253.2; raven kills cannibal at the North End of the World—A2034.3.2; queen wishes naughty child were raven, turns to one—H1385.3Ca; raven saves child who says will not save parent later—J267.1; origin raven's color—A2411.2.1.5; raven creates a companion—J2186.1; motherhood contest, one to fill pot with tears is mother—J1171.1.3; raven calls down copper canoe from sun—F617.4; escape by persuading captors to dance—K606.2; raven calls at dawn and supernatural creatures must retire—C752.2.1.1; raven says some must die or world will run out of food—A1335.8.2; raven beats darkness into earth—A801.2; raven creates earth from snow—A618.3; Khotoi, the raven, sent to dry earth by flapping wings, flaps too hard and beats coastal range down—A961.1.1; raven makes a clay egg, hatches a goose—K1041.2; raven creates fish—A2103; raven brings floating house of fish from Halibut Man—A2109.2; raven persuades fox to imitate his sliding game—J2413.10; raven weds two geese, unable to keep up on flight south he falls into sea, pieces become sea ravens—A2182.6; raven sings up ice and Kon-Kadet is trapped—C752.2.1.1; raven and fox steal moon—A758.1; why people share oolichans with raven—A2229.7; raven flattens owl's face for violating fox wife's tabu—A2330.9; raven paints birds—A2411.2.0.2; twelve robbers eat poisoned raven and die—H802; origin of Polar Ice Cap, raven puts there so earth won't tip—A943; raven asks to be beheaded, becomes prince—G530.2M; raven wrapped in cowhide prophesies—K842B; trickster claims raven prophesies—J1344.1; crow tries to prophesy like raven—J951.3; quest for three drops from hearts of the Ravens of Life—H1213.1B; secret remedy overheard in conversation of animals—N452; raven rescues light from seagull—A1411.3; why seals flee whales, raven tricked—A2494.15.1; origin of island from exploding serpent killed by raven—A955.10.2; raven leaves world after daring to combat serpent without cloak of immortality—A568.1; raven flattered into singing and drops cheese—K334.1; sun stolen by raven—A721.1.1, A1411.2; raven breaks off pieces of sun as flees, hence suns appear sometimes close together, sometimes far apart during year—A1411; raven warns prince of false bride's mutilated feet—R221F; raven steals water from impounding monster—A1111.2; water dripping from bowl as Yehl, raven, flies back after stealing from Kanukh become lake and springs—A941.5.9.1; raven claims to have left whale on beach, eats cooking food when others run off—K341.1.1; raven dwells inside a whale, loves whale-spirit maiden—F911.2.1; raven wants to be white as swan—W181.3.

BIRD, RAVEN'S SKULL: Sip taken from raven's skull gives understanding of animal languages—B216.2.

BIRD, REDBIRD: Spirit flies out of box and enters a redbird—F81.0.2; how the redbird got his color—A2411.2.1.13.1.

BIRD, REDSTART: Redstart brings fire to man—A1414.4.2.

BIRD, RICEBIRD: Why ricebird rides on buffalo's back—A2233.4.8; ricebird defeats buffalo in drinking contest—K82.1.1; ricebird loans catfish feathers—K1041.1.2.

BIRD, ROADRUNNER: Origin of feathers—A2411.2.6.7.1.

BIRD, ROBIN: Color of robin—A2411.2.1.18; robin rejects courting wren—W123.2; creation of Robin—A1912.3.1; animals decide on equal length for seasons, convinced by robin—A1150.3; robin brings spring each year—A1912.3.1; star in dipper—A771.0.4; robin on way to sing for king on Yule morn—Z55.

BIRD, SANDPIPER: Contest between whale and sandpiper—B263.10; sandpiper only survivor of feast—Z32.6; fox, sandpiper, mole, weasel steal fire—A1415.2.2.3; sandpiper calls "Tui Liku," had pecked out his eye—F153.2.

BIRD, SAPSUCKER: Coyote insists on having secret of sapsucker's hairdo, uses pitch and is burnt—J2449.1.

BIRD, SAW-WHET: Star in constellation—A771.0.1.

BIRD, SEAGULL: How seagull learned to fly—A2442.3.2; gull hoards light—A1411.3; gull a transformed maiden—A1945.2; raven steals beak from seagull people—A2335.2.3; gull is looking for lost cargo, bat, bramble and seagull shipwrecked—A2275.5.3; seagull asks land birds about tide—J2753; mother gull fills fox's sack with thorns and frees her chicks, in revenge fox tries to drink Lake Titicaca dry—K526.2.

BIRD, SIGAKOK: Origin of bird, lazy boy—A1999.4.2.

BIRD, SPARROW: Sparrow aids kind girl—Q2.1.2Ab; sparrows besiege castle because nesting grove cut—B216.2; sparrow persuades cat to wash before eating—K562; judge cat eats sparrow—K815.7; crow asks hospitality of sparrow and takes possession of nest—K354.1; why women dance like sparrows—A1542.1.1; sparrow's vengeance on elephants—L315.6.1; wife roasts sparrow for fifteen men and fairies leave in disgust—F381.15; Brer Fox asks Jack Sparrow to get on his tail, back, etc. feigning deafness—K911.5.1; why sparrow hops—A2441.2.4; Land of Sparrows—B222.5; origin of sparrow's nest—A2271.1; sparrow's nest destroyed by monkey—J1064.2; optimistic sparrow—Z39.4.3; sparrow sent to fetch sun and moon

—A618.3; tongue-cut sparrow—Q285.1.1; sparrows ask man to leave tree—J241.2; train of troubles from sparrow's vengeance—N261; sparrow sends crow to wash before eating—Z41.2.1ff; wormwood does not want to rock the sparrow—Z41.7; boy who wounds sparrow told to climb to moon—A751.1.8; boy who saves wounded sparrow given magic pumpkin seed—A751.1.8.

BIRD, SPARROW HAWK: Water from heaven and nether world fetched by sparrow hawk—B582.2D.

BIRD, STARLING: Origin of starling's nest—A2271.1.

BIRD, STORK: Caliph turns to stork, forgets disenchanting word—D155.1.1; stork carries hazelnut child to Africa—F535.1.1Db; color of stork—A2411.2.5.3.2; stork killed along with cranes—J451.2; enmity between frog and stork—A2494.16.1.1; stork carries fish to new pond—K815.14; stork and fox give return feasts—J1565.1; stork drops fox from height—K1041.0.1; abandoned girl raised by storks—S352.2; judge mocks criminals, turns to stork—A1966.1; frogs given stork as king—J643.1; lad carries old man over river, he turns to youth King Stork, helps win princess—E341.1E; sultan buys house with helpful stork's nest and preserves—B463.4; stork remodeled to look like regular bird—J1919.1; tortoise carried by storks—J2357; village turned to storks—D624.1.1; stork tramping down wheat, fools carry man across field to carry stork off—J2163.4.

BIRD, STORK--JABIRU: Jabiru stork—A2411.2.5.3.2.

BIRD, SWALLOW: Swallow sisters dam up salmon, coyote releases—A1421.0.0.1; swallow learns to build nest from wasp—A2431.3.5; swallow gives magpie seed to brother who heals—J2415.13; swallow urges other birds to eat seed as fast as it is sown—J621.1; swallow rescues wasp in well—B362.1; youth seeing swallow sells winter clothes—J731.1.

BIRD, SWAN: Brothers transformed to swans—P253.2; swans tricked into dancing with eyes closed—K826; youngest son catches swan tramping garden—H1385.3Fbb; lad calls swans to carry to castle in name of the Griffin of the Greenwood—H1321.1B; swan maiden—D361.1, F302.4.2ff; marriage to swan maiden—B652.1; swan maiden's clothes hidden—D361.1, F302.4.2.1ff; red swan maiden—D361.1.2; king spares swan who turns to maiden and weds—B652.1.2; food sent by swan maiden's father is called "goose food" by tribesman, she leaves—C35.5; swan maiden finds robe and leaves—H1385.3Fba; three swan maidens will wed one who has their shoe, ring, twigs—B652.1.1; owl hoots at caravan and companion swan is killed—J429.2.2; raven wants to be white as swan—W181.3; swan sings at death—B752.1; transformation, man to swan—D161.1.

BIRD, THRUSH: fox tries to beguile the thrush by reporting a new law establishing peace—J1421; origin nest of thrush—A2271.1.

BIRD, THUNDERBIRD: Thunderbirds killed and crow-size birds fly from eyes, are present thunderbirds—A284.2.1; thunderbird (eagle) flies out of flames and all thunderbirds fly north, never to return—A284.2.2.

BIRD, TICKBIRD: Tickbird defeats buffalo in drinking contest—K82.1.1; why tickbird rides buffalo's back—A2233.4.8; tickbird identifies cow—H1385.3M; origin of tickbird—A1999.3.

BIRD, TIKPI-TIKPI: Tikpi-Tikpi birds reap and transport to granary—D366.

BIRD, TOJ: SEE BIRD, MOTMOT.

BIRD, TOM-TIT: Tom-tit in war of birds and animals—K2323.1.

BIRD, TOUCAN: Color of toucan—A2411.2.6.13.

BIRD, TURKEY: Turkey pecks out eyes of giant—G511.2; why turkey has small bones in legs—A2371.2.13; why turkey has white tail—A2211.7.1; turkey so clever they spare it at turkey shoot—X1265.6; origin of turkey's wattle—A2351.8; hare has wildcat feign dead and calls turkeys to celebrate—K751.0.1.

BIRD, TURKEY--WILD: Wild turkey's feathers borrowed from whippoorwill—A2241.13; quail betrays wild turkey to hunters—A2431.3.10.

BIRD, TURNSTONE: Why Black Turnstone builds nest near sea—A2431.3.14.

BIRD, TURTLEDOVE: Aids hero in quest for daylight—H1385.1C.

BIRD, VULTURE: Lion and boar make peace rather than slay each other for vulture—J218.1; vultures carry off mule—J1531.2.1; animals pledge peace and each reveals his pet peeve—W141.1.1; vulture eats poisoned donkey and dies—H802.1.

BIRD, WAGTAIL: Pecks Dawn free—A1179.2.2; has long tail—A2378.3.5.

BIRD, WHIPPOORWILL: Why whippoorwill's eyes are red—A2332.5.10; whippoorwill's feathers borrowed by turkey—A2313.7; why whippoorwill is nocturnal—A2491.6; why whippoorwill (puhuy) cries "puhuy"—A2426.2.21.

BIRD, WINDBIRD: Girl wooed by both windbird and sun turns to rainbow—A791.9.1.

BIRD, WOODCOCK: Fox tries to beguile the woodcock by reporting new law establishing peace among the animals—J1421.

BIRD, WOODGROUSE: Kalle aims at woodgrouse prince then spares—G530.2Bha.

BIRD, WOODPECKER: The woodpecker is a baker's daughter who is inhospitable to Jesus—A1958.0.1; woodpecker helps save deer from hunter—K642.2; woodpecker pecks out elephant's eyes—L315.6.1; wookpecker steals hare's conjure bag—D1274.1.1; magic jade carried under woodpecker's wing—D931.0.5; woodpecker removes bone from lion's throat—W154.3; to get food by pecking on bark and calling invitation to insects—A2435.4.12; woodpecker rescues stranded pelican babies when crow sings their tree up—D482.1.1; woodpecker aids rabbit prince—H1385.3Fg; woodpecker calls back son of Sartak Pai who is digging river in wrong direction—A2435.4.12.

BIRD, WREN: Contest, wren rides on eagle's back, highest flyer to be king—K25.1; wren goes into mousehole, contest in going deepest into earth—K17.1.1; wren rejects courting robin—W123.2; origin wren's cry—A2426.2.23; why wren lives in hedges—A2433.4.7; wren king declares war on bear and animals—K2323.1; wagtail borrows wren's tail—A2242.1; why wren has short tail—A2378.4.8; wren sends crow to wash before eating—Z41.2.1.

BIRD, WREN—MARSH WREN: Marsh wren builds nest in cattail tops in marsh, crane imitates—A2431.3.13.

BIRTH: SEE ALL ENTRIES T500-T599 Conception and birth; birth of Gods—A112ff; luck depends on what stool fate sits on when one is born—N138; woman gives birth to plant or animal child—T540-T555; pot bears a child—J1531.2ff; raven swallowed and reborn—A1411.2. SEE ALSO CHANGELING; CHILDREN; MIDWIFE; TWINS.

BIRTHDAY: Dragon invited to boy's birthday party—B11.6.1.4.

BISCUITS: Sody sallyrytus needed to make biscuits—Z33.6.

BISON: SEE BUFFALO, BISON.

BITING: Bite causes chain of accidents—Z49.6.0.5; Anansi to pay snake postman by allowing him to take a bite of Anansi's head—K75; contest, a trickster bites a nut, ogre a stone—K63; snake bites a file—J552.3; son on gallows bites off mother's nose—Q586. SEE ALSO FLEA; MOSQUITO; SNAKE.

BITOL: Creator—A2685.1.1.

BITTER: Dupe eats bitter fruit—K1043.

BITTERNUTS: Bitternuts thrown down to bulldog, lion, and wolf—F848.1 Mincielli.

"BIZ": Name both of girl and awl, trickster gets girl—K362.10.1.

BLACK: Black Bull of Norroway—H1385.5; why bird is black—A2411.2.1.5.6; Black Colin, returning crusader—H94.4.1; Black Dog of the Wild Forest--B524.1.2; telling the horses apart, the black one is taller than the white--J2722; girl at witch's house sees riders in white, red, black--Z65.3; washing the black wool white --H1023.6.2. SEE ALSO RACES OF MAN.

BLACK-HANDED MONKEY: SEE MONKEY, BLACK-HANDED.

BLACKBERRY: Blackberry reproves pomegranate and apple for arguing--J466.1.

BLACKBIRD: SEE BIRD, BLACKBIRD.

BLACKFEET: Origin of enmity between Blackfeet and Nez Percé--A1388.2; origin of Blackfeet tribe--A1610.8.

BLACKMAIL: Doorman requires half of reward--K187.1; king induced to kiss horse's rump—K1288; thief may keep cloak taken from victim when drunk--J1211.2.

BLACKOUT: King checking on blackout overhears three telling of sons they will bear—N455.4A.

BLACKSMITH: Ilmarinen forges copper bird to peck Ukko Untamoinen's stomach--F912.3.2; smith defeats Devil--Q565; smith as jack-o-lantern--Q565; Lord beats St. Peter on anvil to rejuvenate, blacksmith imitates--Q565; task: forging living man of iron--H1021.14; Ilmarinen makes moon--A744.1; man living between noisy blacksmith and coppersmith pays each to move --N255.8; smith ruins poet's song–J981.

BLADDER: Bladder tied to leg to identify self—J2013.3; death-dealing bladder of helpful calf--B335.2C; bladder of blood hidden inside confederate's clothing, he is stabbed, feigns death —K1875; blind boy uses sister as hunting bladder, shoot only small whales--A2135.1.1.

BLAME: All animals confess sins, small one blamed—K1024.1; blame for theft fastened on dupe—K401.1.

BLANKETS: Ancestor animals fall off blanket, live where land--A2433.3.0.1; coyote steals blanket from rock--C91.1; child divides blanket for father's old age--J121; fox claims middle of viscacha's blanket--J1241.6; monkey loaned blanket by hare, did not belong to hare--K1066.6; hero changes blankets from brothers' beds with those of witch's daughters--K1611Da. SEE ALSO COVERLET; QUILT; SHEET.

BLEATING: Shepherd to say "Baa" to all questions in court--K1655.

BLESSING: Blessing of dead parents is drawn up from flooded city by grown son in net--H1213.1H; blessing for helping saint--A2221.5.

BLIND: Blind man's arrow aimed by mother—K333.1; blinded at coronation--N731.2.1; blindness cured by blow on head--N642.2; cured by feather of magic bird--N731.2.1; daughter sells

self as sacrifice to dragon for money to restore father's eyesight--N712.2; deaf hears scream, blind sees them, crippled want to run for help--X1781.1.1; blind man cannot see death's signs, does not die--J1051.1; wager that God is stronger than devil, loses money, horses, eyes—N452C; blind discover objects sighted miss--U174; one-eyed doe captured on blind side--K929.2; one of blind men drown while crossing stream, ferryman comforts that there is one less fare to pay--J2566; blind man and elephant--J1761.10; fighting fox transforms to one-eyed man, gets eye on wrong side--D313.1.1; hero puts out giant's eye and escapes in skin or under sheep--K603ff; boy's sight restored by doing good deeds, dog guides--Q161.1.1; blind boy throws cruel grandmother into lake--A2135.1.2; ownership test: thief cannot tell which eye of stolen horse is blind, neither—J1141.17; blind man overawes lion--K1715.12.1; loon dives with blind boy on back, restores sight--F952.7.1; blind minstrel--E434.11; why mole is blind--A2332.6.5; man closes eyes to see how blind feel, misses money in path--N351.2; owl blinded for reading at Quetzal's party—A2491.2; Sindhu cares for blind parents in jungle—W46.1; sight restored by pigeon--K1853.3; prince falls from tower into thorns and is blinded--F848.1; seven queens blinded--Z215.1; secret remedy for blindness overheard in conversation of animals--N452; robbed blind man pretends to have more money to stash, thief puts stolen back in hopes of getting more —K1667.1.1; Saint Genevieve's tears fall in water, mother washes face with water and sight is restored—V221.12.1; blind man can see evil spirits--E279.6.1; lion sees blind hare recover sight from spring, restores lad--S12.1A; blind men duped into fighting, trickster removes guide strings leading to water--K1081.3; Kona steals back sun, moon, and stars with aid of blind aunt, Woman-Who-Walks-In-Darkness--A721.1.6; tears cure blindness (Rapunzel)—F848.1; blinded trickster directed by trees--D1313.4; enemy to have twice the wish, A wishes to lose an eys so that B will be blind--J2074; blind weds ugly--F576.1; Untrue eats up True's provisions, than blinds and leaves--N452B; blind boy uses sister as hunting bladder, shoots only small whales--A2135.1.1; six wives of raja blinded—Z215.1; blind man to identify young wolf--J33; why worm is blind—A2332.6.4. SEE ALSO EYE.

BLINDMAN'S BUFF: Girl forced to play with bear --Q2.1.3B.

BLIZZARD: SEE SNOW.

BLODEVEDD: Owl is a baker's daughter—A1958.0.1; wife discovers secret vulnerability of husband—Z312.4.

BLOOD: Origin blood-red spittle of betel chewing --A2691.5; trickster smears mouth of dupe with blood and escapes blame—K401.1; trickster stabs bag of blood, ogre imitates, stabs self—G524; insect discovers man's blood is sweetest—A2236.1; blood on key betrays entrance to forbidden chamber—G561.1, S62.1; maple leaves turn red from blood of Great Bear—A2769.2; blood on hand believed to be ghost—really mosquito—N384.0.2; mosquito is transformed man trying to recover three drops of blood stolen—A2034.5; handkerchief with three drops of mother's protecting blood—B133.3; girl resuscitates by placing bite of oatmeal mixed with victim's blood in victim's mouth—E43; blood flows from cut bamboo, turning river red—A939.3; sham blood and brains, trickster feigns injury —K473; sham blood, trickster makes dupe think he is bleeding by stabbing bag of blood—K1875; origin of man from drop of sun's blood—A1263.1.3; three drops of troll's blood disenchant people from tree form—F1015.1.1B. SEE ALSO VAMPIRE.

BLOSSOM: Cherry trees magically blossom—D1571.1. SEE ALSO FLOWER.

BLOW: Penny awarded as damages for blow, plaintiff strikes judge and awards him the penny—J1193.2; each to give other three blows, Anansi has hammer made—K869.5; seven at a blow—K1951.1.

BLOWFISH: SEE FISH, BLOWFISH.

BLOWING: Blowing the house in—Z81; man blows on soup to cool it, blows on hands to warm—J1801.1.

BLUE: King offers half kingdom for blue cat—J2131.5.6.1; coyote tries to become blue—A2411.1.3.2.1; blue cow from the sea—F420.6.1.5.1.1; jackal falls in vat of blue dye—J2131.5.6; magic blue light—D1421.1.2; son finds blue belt which gives strength—S12.1A; Blue and Green Wonders aid—D831B.

BLUEBEARD: Impostors abandon hero in lower world—K1931.2; Bluebeard as husband—S62.1.

BLUEBERRIES: Blueberries used as crane's eyes—A2332.5.11.

BLUEBIRD: SEE BIRD, BLUEBIRD.

BLUEBOTTLE: Wedding of bluebottle—B285.4.1.

BLUE FALCON: SEE BIRD, FALCON.

BLUE JAY: SEE BIRD, BLUEJAY.

BLUE MOUNTAINS: Three princesses in the Blue Mountains—H1385.3Cb, K1931.2.

BLUE VIRGIN OF CAACUPÉ: V128.0.1.2.

BLUFF: SEE K1700-1799. SEE ALSO WISE MAN.

BOAR: Boar curls self around bowl—J1565.1.3; stealing boar with tusks of gold and silver bristles—G610Ah; carpenter's pet boar organizes boars—B268.12; boar feigns theft of child so monkey can rescue—K231.1.3.2; Christ turns lying woman's pigs to wild boars—A1871.1.1; boar captured in church—K731;

demon boar terrorizes cobbler in chalet—H1411.4.1; boar's ear pounced on, thought to be mouse—K2324+; boar refuses to fight ass—J411.1; thrown to wild boars, plays flute and they dance—H328.9; man helps the horse against the boar—K192; boar tricked into pit by Kantchil—K652.1; lion and wild boar make peace rather than slay each other for benefit of vulture—J218.1; animals pledge peace and each reveals pet peeve—W141.1.1; wild boar sharpens tusks—J674.1; old woman protected by objects which attack intruding ogre boar—K1161.3.4.

BOARD: Peasant with enigmatic board on back—H585.3.

BOAST: Tabu: bragging that giant carried—C456; jaguar brags of strength to Lightning—C984.5; why lizard says 'Tzch,' rich man loses bragging contest—A2426.4.3; task assigned because of mother's foolish boasting—H914; king overhears girl boast of what she would do as queen—N455.4; man brags of jump on Rhodes—J1477; seven at a blow—K1951.1; tabu: boasting of supernatural wife—C31.5.

BOAT: Tails of adjutant birds in boat tied together—K713.1.12; boat moored to badger transformed as piling—D612.1.1; magic boat made of bamboos—D454.7.2; magic fast traveling boat carries to Brasil—F1015.1.1Bc; dragon boat—B11.6.1.4; flying fairy boat goes into basket of lad—F349.5; flying boat—D1532.11; fox turns into boat to help hero abduct maid—H1331.1.3Aa; boat to grow to ship—J2212.7; boat invented from observing spider on leaf—A1459.2.1; Ivanko and the witch, Ivanko chants and boat moves—R251; transportation in magic ship—D1520.15; dupe makes boat of mud—J2171.1.3; numskull advises sailors to tie up bottom of boat, not topsail, to steady it—J2289.2; numskull marks place on boat where object fell overboard—J1922.1; Brer Rabbit, poling boat, has advantage over paddling Brer Fox—K636.2; boat thought to be huge shoe—K1718.2.1; witch comes up in stone boat and changes places with queen on deck—K1911Ab. SEE ALSO CANOE; CAPTAIN; FERRY; ROWING; SHIP.

BOATMAN: Clever boatman pretends to be numskull, bets can recover lost object by marking place on boat, produces duplicate and wins bet—J1922.2.1; boatman and bookman—J1229.4; why boatman is not minister—H1574.4.1.

BOBCAT: Why bobcat has spots—A2412.1.7; why bobcat has short tail—A2378.4.14.

BOCHICA: A747, A1011.2.

BODHISATTVA: The Bodhisattva as a prince is stuck in demon's hair—K741.3; partridge as Bodhisat in age debate—B841.1.1. SEE ALSO ALL JATAKA TALES. SEE ALSO BUDDHA.

BODY: Origin of animal's body—A2300ff; body enters one piece at a time—Z13.1.1; bodily parts can be removed at will—F557.0.1. SEE ALSO

CORPSE; HAND; HEART; STOMACH; ETC.

BOGGART: Boggart leaves when he is given clothing—F381.3; boggart and man in deceptive crop division—K171.1; family leaves to be rid of boggart, boggart follows—F482.3.1.1.

BOGLE: Bagpiping ghost—E402.1.3.2; bogles in haunted house have lost ball—H1411.4.2; fiddler encounters bogles in bog—H1419.4; bogles leave home when house is aired out—E439.11.

BOILED: Groom to bathe in boiling mare's milk—H1213.1D; fox tricked into boiling pot to bathe—K891.1.2; fool washing child uses boiling water—J2465.4; deceptive game, burning or boiling each other—K851; test: drinking boiling water—H221.4; fox falls down chimney into boiling pot or boiling water poured over fox—K891.1.1; boiled grain (beans, etc.) planted, as easy to grow grain thus as to hatch chick from boiled egg—J1191.2; green boiling pot as ogre—G378; hens fed boiling water to hatch boiled eggs—J1901.2; boiling pot on floor thought to be self-cooking—K112.1. SEE ALSO EGGS, BOILED.

BOJABI: Animals must get name of tree—J2671.4.1.

BOLA BOLA: Dove asks Bola Bola, talking dog, daily about son—K1911Ac.

BOLIANUS: Leprechaun tricks man in field of bolianus—J1922.2.1.

BOLSTER: Bedcover stolen, fool waits for thief to return for the bolster—J2214.3.2.

BONE: Bone to sweat blood if hero in danger—R111.1.3Aj; bowling with bones—H1440A; bones of calf buried grant wishes—R221F; crane pulls bone from wolf's throat—W154.3; dog leaps for bone at feast making mess—A2513.1.1.5; why dogs crunch bones—A2435.3.1; captive sticks out bone instead of finger when cannibal tries to test fatness—G412.1; fish's bones grant wishes—R221J; turtle makes flute of jackal's thighbone—K1775.1; archaelogist finds giant's bones in cave. Bones wake up and they toss him into the sea—F531.6.13.3; bones stolen from grave—E235.4.3; instrument made of bone sings truth—E632; why jellyfish has no bones—A2367.1.2; magic bone dropped in ear, kills—B524.1.2A; magic bone jumps into Ivan's head, kills—G552.1; man created from animal bone—A1263.7; tossed bone turns to pillar with cat running up and down singing and telling stories—B641Af; poisoned bone—R111.1.3Am; bone left out when resuscitating animal, thus a. limps—F243.3.1.1; singing bone reveals crime—E632ff; tiger grateful for removal of bone—B382.1; ghost of hermit gives wishing bones—D882.1Ga; witch crunches pocketful of bones—K311.3H.

"BOO": Tale teller frightens listener by yelling "boo" at exciting point—Z13.1.

BOOGIE: Boogie comes down chimney—E235.4.3.1.

BOOK: When magic book is opened princess is compelled to dance—F1015.1.1Bc; God of Writing and Books—B656.2.1; sorceror's apprentice reads forbidden magic book—D1711.0.1.2; hiding as page in king's magic book—H321D; hiding as pin in cover of magic book—H321; scholar displays book as evidence of wisdom—J2238.1.

BOOK, PICTURE BOOK: Dr. 'Know-it-all' looks for pictures in book—N612.2.

BOOK OF DESTINY: Man given a better fate from Book of Destiny on condition he return it when rightful owner claims it—N115.

BOOK OF LIFE: Pages in Book of Life stick together—K975.1.2.

BOOKMAN: Bookman and boatman, practical knowledge more vital than theoretical—J1229.4. SEE ALSO READING.

BOOKOO: SEE BIRD, BOOKOO.

BOOMER: Boomer's dog runs beside train—X1215.7.1.

BOOMERANG: Boomerang hits cockatoo on head—A2311.9.1, A2321.12.

BOÖTES: Origin of Arcturus star in Boötes—A771.0.1.

BOOT: Fox has wolf walk through lime wash and receive boots "light as air"—K254.1; princess grabs hero's blue glass boot as he flees—R111.1.3Bb; oni born with boots which grow as he grows—H36.1.2; lazy hunter rubs soles of boots on stone to wear out—W111.8; origin of white men, set adrift in boot sole by mother mated to dog—A1614.9; boot full of money as reward, hole cut in bottom—G501G; Puss in boots—K1917.3; seven league boots—K1611C; man standing on own ground, soil in boots—J1161.3.1; father hangs up boot with hole in sole, if holds water he will wed—Q2.1.4B.

BOOTMAKER: Bootmaker ruins songs of ballad maker—J981.

BOQUERON: Boqueron volcano destroys San Jorge de Olancho where Spaniards refused gold for Virgin's crown—F969.8.

BOREDOM: Wish for a week of Sundays, bored by week's end—W111.11.

BORNEO: Tiger made to believe porcupine quill is whisker of Rajah of Borneo—K1711.1.

BORROWING: Animal characteristics - borrowed—A2241ff; "Loan ass? It's not home," ass brays. "Would you believe an ass and not me?"—J1552.1.1; King of Fishes returns knife and warns never to borrow or lend—H1132.1.5.1; borrowed pot returned with 'baby'—J1531.3; refusal for absurd reason—J1552.1.1;

refusal to lend forty-year-old vinegar—J1552.1.6; stag tries to borrow from sheep, using wolf as security—J1383. SEE ALSO LENDING; LOAN.

BORSHT: Numskulls tie up moon's reflection in barrel of borsht—J1701.2.2.

BOTTLE: Ghost tricked into bottle—K717.7; magic self-replenishing bottle—F348.5.1; Mr. Vinegar lives in vinegar bottle—K335.1.1.1; spirit deceived back into bottle—K717; two tiny men from bottle serve dinner—D861.1E.

BOUKI: Bouki tries to discover where calf pastures —K688.3; Bouki learns king's secret dance—H529.1; Bouki is angry at son for action in Bouki's dream—J2060.1.1; Bouki buys glasses, still can't read—J1746.2; Bouki sells alleged magic gun—K119.5; Bouki rents a horse —K1797; Ti Malice steals king's sheep, lays blame on Bouki—K1066.2. SEE Courlander, Harold, PIECE OF FIRE.

BOUNDARY STONES: Ghosts move boundary stones—E345.1.

BOURO, LAKE: Origin of lake from pawing of great bull—A920.1.2.

BOW: Jackal gnaws bow string and bow snaps and kills—J514.2; coyote stays up all night to be first at distribution of bows—A2235.2; hare makes bow and shoots hyena—K335.0.4.3.1; mice gnaw enemy's bow strings and prevent pursuit —K632; man in moon with bow and arrow—A751.0.4; invisible warrior's bow strap is rainbow—R221G; precocious hero tests bows made by father, three break, fourth holds—F611.3.3.3. SEE ALSO ARCHERY; ARROW.

BOWL: Buddha's begging bowl cannot be moved—V128.0.1.1; man gives father wooden bowl, son saves one to use for father when old—J121; thing without an end? Bowl—R111.1.3Ah; bowl over girl's head until wed—K1815.0.2; girl spins apple in golden bowl—E632.0.4; test: carrying bowl of laban on head while climbing palm—H331.10.1; magic bowl steals for master thief—K301.3; merchant pretends bowl is worthless, planning to return and buy it cheaply—J1521.6.

BOWLING: With dead person's bones—H1440A; dwarfs bowling, twenty year's sleep for man observing—D1960.1.

BOWMAN: Little Bowman has Big Bima, a washerman, pose as bowman while he performs tasks—K1951.6.

BOX: Box with three magic butterflies—D882.1F; shake dust from box on corners of field daily to make prosper—H588.7.5; old father treated well by heirs after box of 'treasure' is left in his possession—P236.2; flying box with special dresses for girl—R221Dc; catskins; forbidden box—G530.2K; boy finds box and key, what's inside?—Z12.2; tabu: opening gift box prematurely—G530.2K; tabu: looking into box

(Pandora)—C321; span-high man Sir Buzz comes from box and serves—D882.1Eb.

BOY: Little boy under bed given animals to comfort because bed squeaking makes him cry—Z49.17; foolish boy—J2461ff; boy's glance kills—S366.1; bad boy sent to moon—A751.1.8; boy with hand in pitcher of nuts cannot pull out hand unless lets some loose—W151.9.1; boy changes self to nut—Z43.5; old woman paralyzes would be murderer of lost boys—D2072.7; tiger assumes form of boy—A2434.2.5; boy who cried wolf—J2172.1. SEE ALSO SON.

BOYAR: Devil as smith's apprentice rejuvenates boyar's wife by throwing in fire then bathing in milk—J2411.0.2; boyar insists peasant work till sun's little brother, the moon, sets too—J1530.0.1.

BRACELET: Bracelet from demon maid—H1440D; grandfather gives kind girl bracelet—Q2.12Da; storks bring golden bracelet to girl—S352.2.

BRAG: SEE BOAST.

BRAHMA: Origin of Bromo Feast Sacrifice made to Brahma—A1545.1.1; cat sent on errand by Brahma becomes companion to Saras Vati—A132.17.1; Brahma creates dog—A1831.3; weaver cursed by Brahma to lose all gained, outsmarts—K2371.2.1.

BRAHMIN: Brahmin made to believe goat is demon —K451.2.1; rich jackal aids Brahmin father-in-law—D861.1J; brahmin will accept only money king earns himself—W11.3.1; brahmin with gold-producing serpent—D876.2; ghost and thief argue over who to steal brahmin first—J581.3; brahmin attacked by ungrateful tiger—J1172.3; prince and princess visit brahmin who is really vampire—D882.1Eb.

BRAINS: Fool told to get a pottle of brains—J163.2.1; fox claims dead ass had no brains—K402.3.1; sham blood and brains, trickster pretends harm—K473.

BRAMBLE: Proud fir will wish was bramble when woodsman comes—J212.4. SEE ALSO BRIAR; THORN.

BRANCHES: Girl follows ghost to underground and breaks gold and silver branches, thrown out window they become palaces—H1411.4.5; lad following dancing princesses breaks gold and silver branches—F1015.1.1.

BRASS: Task: find brass fittings for three chestnut mares—K1931.2K; Friar Bacon makes head of brass—D1711.6.5; girl polishing two brass trays refuses to go when mother calls, becomes tortoise—A2147.1.

BRAVERY: Once caused an entire tribe of Bedouins to run, he ran and they ran after—J1250.9; reward for slaying giant Centipede—Q82.3; danger passed by approaching bravely, vanishes—H335.7.1; gallant tailor kills seven flies at once, makes belt boasting of bravery—K1951.1A; frog carries off frog hunter who boasts of bravery—B857.1; porcupine brags of bravery, shrieks at own reflection—A2422.15; dupe falls on tiger's back and rides—N392.1.1; "brave" man claims woman's name when captured —K514.0.1. SEE ALSO DARE.

BRAY: Owner says ass is not home, despite bray —J1552.1.1; numskull believes he will die when donkey brays three times—J2311.1; animal frightened by ass's bray—K2324.1.1.

BRAZIL: Princess carried to Brazil nightly to dance with dead pirates—F1015.1.1Bc.

BREAD: Aesop calls to fellow slaves to take the smallest loads, he takes huge packet of bread, carries nothing after lunch—J1612.1; ant teaches breadmaking—A1429.2.1; bread in charitable woman's apron turns to roses—V412.3; boy gives Death dry bread to crunch—K611.5; maid kneads devil in bread trough—K606.1.2; fairy bread—F343.19; bread is food of all foods— H659.29; hen preparing bread asks who will help—W111.6; judges cannot agree on definition of bread—H501.5; bread loaves in oven reproach uncharitable sister—V420; unlucky beggar sells loaf with gold hidden inside to lucky beggar—N351; ring in bread token—H94.1, R221Dc; fraudulent tax-collector made to eat records, successor writes his on bread— J1289.23; hard baked and unbaked bread refused, soft wins water sprite—F420.6.1.5.1; wolf asks how to make bread, first plant, etc.— Z49.5.2. SEE ALSO LOAF.

BREADFRUIT: King's son exiled to Lanai for uprooting breadfruit plants—K688.6.

BREATH: Lions asks judgment of his bad breath —J811.2.1; man blows hot and cold in same breath—J1801.1.

BREMEN TOWN MUSICIANS: K335.1.4, K1161.1.

BRER RABBIT: SEE HARE. SEE ENTIRE COLLECTIONS HARRIS, JOEL CHANDLER.

BREWING: Brewing beer in eggshells—F321.1.1; cock drowns in brew vat—Z32.2.3.

BRIARS: Briarpatch punishment for rabbit— K581.2; Briar Rose—D1960.3. SEE ALSO BRAMBLE; THORN.

BRIBERY: Dog suspects thief who bribes—K2062; boy to give guard half of what king gives him, asks for blows—K187.

BRICK: Cook a coot with a brick inside, eat the brick—X1258.2.1; house of brick resists wolf— K891.1.1.

BRICKLAYER: Bricklayer wants to make city walls of brick—W197.2. SEE ALSO MASON.

BRIDE: False bride takes true bride's place— K1911.1; foolish brides—J2463.3; white fox weds girl, showers during sunshine on wedding day— B601.14.1; forgotten fiancée—G530.2; runaway horse carries bride to lover—N721; lion bride steps on mouse husband—B363.1; mouse bride seeks strongest spouse—L392.0.1; mounted bride cannot pass through doorway—J2171.6.1; rat demands bride as damages for buffalo— K251.1.2; quest for bride for king—H1381.3.1.1; fool casts sheep's eyes at bride—J2462.2; if bride sneezes thrice and no one says "God bless us" dwarf can take her—F451.5.17; squire's bride, horse is sent in bridal dress—J1615; bride tests—H360-H389; wife proves ugly when unveiled—J1250. SEE ALSO MARRIAGE; WEDDING.

BRIDEGROOM: Robber bridegroom—S62.1C; bridegroom says he knows no stories, really just wants all to go to bed—M231.1Bb.

BRIDGE: Bear eats all crossing bridge—Z33.6; cat forces fairies to produce bridge to island— F302.4.2.2; crane makes bridge of leg for fugitives—R246; bridge of crocodiles—K579.2; devil as builder of bridges—G303.9.1.1; devil builds bridge in one night—M211.2.1; devil to get first thing to cross bridge—S241.1; dream of treasure on bridge—N531.1; elf threatens goats on bridge —K553.2; ghost causes man to bypass fallen bridge—E363.2.1; three billy goats gruff cross bridge—K553.2; man jumps off bridge and kills man below—J1173; girl escapes over bridge of one hair—K1611A; bridge that breaks under liars—X904.3; first person crossing bridge to be new mayor—N683.1; monkeys to construct bridge—B846.1; bridge built by oni Roku— C432.1.1; railroad bridge to be built by Devil for 150 souls—G303.16.19.4.0.1; bridge broken by sea and salt lost—A1115.4; argument whether sheep may be driven over bridge on return from market—J2062.1; smaller bridge most dangerous —R111.1.3Ah; bridge of straw—F1025.1, Z32.1; Tengu's nose fanned with magic fan lengthens and becomes bridge over Milky Way— D1376.1.3.1.

BRIDLE: Bridle thrown on baron turns him to horse—Q584.2.1; man to grab bridle of passing horse, fails twice, third time catches, turns to bag of copper—N250.5; dupe lets self be saddled and bridled and ridden—K1241; fairies call for "horse, bridle, and saddle", fly off—F282.4; husband loses fairy wife for striking with bridle (iron)—F420.6.1.5.1; lad sold as horse must have bridle removed or will remain horse— D1711.0.1.1; lad stealing horse must not touch golden bridle—H1331.1.3Aa; lad transforms witch with magic bridle—G211.1.1.2A. SEE ALSO SADDLE.

BROGUES: Magic brogues walk man into lake— D1520.10.2, G561 Fillmore.

BROKEN LEG: SEE LEG, BROKEN.

BROMO: Origin of Bromo Feast—A1545.1.1.

BROOK: Brook judges against man—J1172.3.2; bluff: bringing the whole brook—K1741.3.2.

SEE ALSO STREAM.

BROOM: Broom advises younger sister to make boat of bowl, with broomstick for mast--G610Ae; woman uses three wishes, wishes broom on her head--J2075; old woman's hump strikes clouds as she sweeps, she hits sky with broom--A625.2.3; witch flies on broomstick--G242.1. SEE ALSO SWEEPING.

BROOM MAKER: Broom maker as new mayor--N683.1; broom maker as suitor--Z31.1.

BROTHER: Baba Yaga's geese steal little brother--Q2.1.2CeA; brother to help bury murdered man--H1558.1; cruel brother blinds brother--N452B; brother decapitated by stepmother with chest lid--N271Aa; fairy turns seven brothers to stars as they can't decide who she should wed--F660.1Cb; girl rescued by skillful brothers. To whom does she belong?--H621.2; boyar makes peasant work until sun's little brother moon sets too. Peasant takes small sack of grain with large one as pay. Second is brother of his salary--J1530.0.1; brothers abandon hero in lower world, let down rope--K1931.2; rich brother buys magic mill then has to pay poor brother to take it back--D1651.3.1; brother and sister as moon and sun--A736.1.2.1; rich brother imitates poor brother--J2415; riddle, what is your brother doing?--H583.3.3; riddle, who is older, you or your brother?--J2212.10; brothers abandon brother on sea lion rocks--F617.4; brother seeks sister in Land of Shadows--F81.1.0.4; brother rescues sister from witch--D771.11.1; brother and sister caught by witch--G412.1.1; brother drinks from hoofprints, becomes deer. Sister cares for him --P253.2.0.1; brothers swing sister and buffalo come to carry her off--R111.1.13.2; treacherous sister betrays brother--S12.1.0.1; sister seeks brothers who are transformed to birds--P253.2; sister frees brothers transformed to stones in quest--N455.4; Podhu loses magic spear of brother--H1132.1.5.2; brothers acquire extraordinary skill--F660.1; rich brother steals poor brother's magic gifts--D861.1.G; youngest brother saves older brothers in home of ogre--K1611. SEE ALSO TWINS.

BROTHER-IN-LAW: Helpful animal brothers-in-law--B314; lowly hero degrades brothers-in-law--N455.4B; hero discomfits brothers-in-law --B316C.

BROWNIES: Girl asks for coal from fire of brownies' camp, coals turn gold--F342.1.2; brownies and farmer in deceptive crop division --K171.1; farmer moves to get rid of brownies, they move too--F482.3.1.1; brownie rides for midwife--F482.5.4.1; brownies collect rent for impoverished couple--F482.5.4.3; child playing with brownie gives name as "Own Self"--K602.1.

BRUCE, ROBERT: King Robert Bruce sends monk to fetch hand of St. Fillian to battlefield --V143.2.2.

BRUSH: Magic brush, paintings come to life--D435.2.1.2.

BUBBLE: Hidden crocodile tricked into blowing bubbles--K605.2.4; bubble, straw and shoe go journeying--F1025.1.1.

BUCCA: Bucca in form of bull chases boy--G303.3.1.4.

BUCCA DHU: Mother makes boy think she is Bucca--K1682.2.

BUCKET: Children with waterbuckets on moon --A751.7; rabbit descends into well in one bucket and fox in other--K651; sea monster entices girl down from cliff to retrieve dropped bucket--Q2.1.1Cb; wish buckets to come and go by selves--J2071.1.

BUDDHA: Buddha's begging bowl--V128.0.1; Buddha creates dog's hind leg from lotus blossom--A2371.1.1; Buddha as Banyan Deer--B241.2.10.1; fish who stole grain of rice needed by Prince Sotat swim to temple of Buddha each year to ask forgiveness--A2335.3.4; fox disguised as Buddha bathes in rice-pot--K717.1; fox Buddha sticks out tongue--K607.4; fox Buddha climbs into pot--K891.1.5; Buddha as hare offers self in fire for beggar--A751.2.1; wooden Buddha defeats golden Buddha in wrestling match--L311.0.1; Buddha gives roses, smell white and nose grows, red and shortens--D551.1C. SEE ALSO BODISATVA.

BUDDHIST: Ghostly girl asks man to take place of ancient hermit--E379.7; origin of Buddhist ritual object--A1546.0.1.1.

BUDGET: Anything put into budget stays, Devil tricked--Q565Ad.

BUDULINEK: K815.15A.

BUENAS AIRES: Founding of Buenas Aires--B538.3.2.

BUFFALO, BISON: Bear leaps at buffalo and misses--K402.3.2.2; Buffalo of the Clouds--B19.1.1; white crow discovered with buffalo meat at dance, followed--A1878.2; Giant White Buffalo gives Wind Cave--A982.1; origin of bison--A1878.2ff; porcupine kills buffalo from within--K952.1; origin of Red Buffalo of the Underworld--B19.1.1; buffalo smashes rock for hero--F601.2I; seven brothers rescue sister from Double Teethed Bull--A770.1; man reveals bison's magic song and bison wife turns to locust--C31.3.1; bison wife must be won in race against bison--B651.2.1.

BUFFALO, CARABAO (KARBAU, WATER-BUFFALO): Why bird rides buffalo's back--A2433.4.8; bride as damages for buffalo eaten by wedding party--K251.1.2; buffalo defeated in drinking contest by heron--K82.1.1; carabao rescues crocodile from under log--J1172.3.0.1, J1172.3.0.2; elephant and water buffalo hide twelve girls in mouths—G276.3; golden buffalo flies to 'mother' black gold bell —D1252.3.1; water buffalo with head stuck in pot--J2113; why carabao has cloven hoof— A2376.1.0.1; water buffalo judges against man in dispute—J1172.3.2; buffalo demands that lion kill one of every species—K533.1.0.1; buffalo and tiger (lion) made enemies by jackal —K1084.1.1; owl tossed into moon by buffalo calf--A751.12; water buffalo envies pig—L457; turtle defeats carabao in race—K11.1; payment for shadow of buffalo--J1172.2.3, J1196.7; buffalo lends strength to break boulder-- H335.7.3; water buffalo from Sumatra is starved and given steel tipped horns, nuzzles Javanese bull and kills—B264.6; duel of buffalo and tiger, buffalo covers self with straw and mud--B264.3. SEE ALSO COW, BULL.

BUG: Bug-a-Bug befriends fleeing prince— K842.0.10. SEE INSECT.

BUILDING: Devil as builder—G303.9.1.1ff; building destroyed because built in tabu place —C931; origin of Sangasang Ceremony for dedicating house before commencement of building—A1549.2.1. SEE ALSO BRIDGE; CHURCH; HOUSE; ETC.; BRICKLAYERS; CARPENTERS; ETC.

BUKOLA: Cow, Bukola, moos when lost-- G530.2E.

BULBUL: SEE BIRD, BULBUL.

BULL: SEE COW, BULL.

BUMCLOCK: Bee, harp, mouse, and bumclock dance--H341.2.1.

BUN: Hare, wolf, bear, fox threaten rolling bun—Z33.1.6.

BUNDLE: Lizard sits on turtle's bundle on road and claims it—J1511.14.1; bundle of twigs strong—J1021.

BUNG: Death tricked into bunghole—K213; Devil tricked into bung-hole—K717.6.

BUNGLING: Bungling fools—J2650-J2699.

BURD ELLEN: Carried off by fairies—F324.0.1.

BUREAUCRACY: Dog (Bureaucracy) thinks self more important than horse as he guards all— W181.1.2.

BURG HILL: Burg Hill is on fire--F381.8.

BURIAL: Ghost haunts until remains are buried beside lover--E419.6.1; ghost leads to unburied skeleton--E412.3.0.1. SEE ALSO: DEAD; FUNERALS; GRAVES.

BURNING: Animal characteristic from burning or singeing—A2218; deceptive game: burning and boiling each other—K851; old man sets fire to rice to draw villagers to mountain top

away from tidal wave—J1688; animal burnt while trying to gnaw sun free—A727ff, A728. SEE ALSO FIRE.

BUS: Ghost rides a bus—E332.3.3.1.

BUSH: Bush taken along is really home of demon—B314G; man in moon with bush— A751.1.4.1; Young Mantis and Young Kwammang-a cut All-Devourer open and true bushes and sheep emerge--A1884.0.2. SEE ALSO THORN (THORNBUSH).

BUSH RAT: Bush rat tricked into boiling self in pot—A2491.1.0.1.

BUSHBUCK: Kalulu hare tries to warn both bushbuck and leopard, loses both friends, leopard has grabbed bushbuck's horns thinking them tree branches—B335.6.1; bushbuck tricks leopard with whom he has built house— K1715.3.2; bushbuck impersonates evil spirit and terrifies leopard—K335.0.4.6.

BUSHMAN: Origin of Bushmen—A1291.2, A1611.3.1.

BUSTGUSTICERIDIS: Fairy lames girl, to be cured if recalls name of herb Bustgusticeridis —F361.14.6.

BUTCHERS: Grateful goat brings gold to butcher who spared—B413.1; stolen meat handed about, thief who holds it "didn't take it"-- K475.1; oxen fear new inexperienced butchers —J215.2.

BUTTE: Origin of butte—A969.12.

BUTTER: Brer Rabbit eats butter supply, blames it on Possum—K401.1; literal fool carries butter on head, melts—J2461.1.5.1; fool spreads butter on cracked ground—J1871; pool of butter in porridge, each tries to get— J1562.1.1; fool sells butter to stone--J1853.2. SEE ALSO CHURN.

BUTTERCUP: Witch captures Little Buttercup— K526A; lad marks buttercup by spot where leprechaun shows treasure—J1922.2.1.

BUTTERFLY: Butterfly challenges crane to fly to Tonga—K25.1.1; butterfly maiden seeks vengeance on cruel mandarin who tortures butterflies—E525; origin of butterflies—A2041; raven creates butterfly-man to aid—A2335.2.3; man sleeps covered with butterflies, chief's dead daughter weds—E474.5; three butterflies perform feats for lad—D882.1F.

BUTTERMILK: Jack refuses buttermilk to witch put into bag—K526B.

BUTTON: Little Rooster and diamond button— Z52.4; story made from worn out button— Z49.24.1.1.

BUZZ: Why fly buzzes--A2426.3.3; why horsefly buzzes—A2236.1; span high man, Sir Buzz comes from box and serves—D882.1Eb.

BUZZARD: SEE BIRD, BUZZARD.

CAACUPÉ: Virgin of Caacupé—V128.0.1.2.

CABBAGE: Giant steals cabbages of exiled queen—G561.1D; giant growing cabbage—F54.2.2.1; girl picking cabbage in goblin's garden caught—G561.2C; house of cabbage eaten into by wolf—K891.1.1 Wiggin; flower-pot, mud cake, cabbage, pea, feather and needle keep house—J512.7.2; lie - huge cabbage, huge pot—X907; lie - huge cabbage—X909.4.1; meat fed to cabbages—J1856.1; cabbage eating rabbit carries girl off—G561.2D; suit of cabbage made for girl on quest—G263.1.0.1.1.

CABEZA DEL INCA: Origin rock—A977.5.0.5.

CABIN: Poor servant woman turned out on Christmas Eve finds fairy cabin—F343.21.

CACTUS: Search for "whee-ai"—H1377.3.

CADI: Cadi and court dance to death—D1415.2.3.4; wife disguises as Cadi and seeks lost lover—S268B.

CAGE: Tabu -- touching bird's cage—H1331.1.3; dupe tricked into entering cage—K714.2.5+; K715.1.1.

CAIRO: Lucky man succeeds even when selling dates in Cairo—N427.

CAKE: Large cake with curse or small with blessing—J229.3; magic cake rolls ahead to show road—D1313.1.2; suicide by eating 'poison' cake—J2311.2.1; ring token in cake—R221Dc+; cake rolls off, people follow—Z33.1.5; origin of Simnel Cake—A1455.2.1; task: getting cake down from twig on rafters, throws wet sponge and softens—K301C. SEE ALSO MOON-CAKE.

CALABASH: Calabash of tears thrown on crab becomes shell—C432.1.2.1; creatures of universe from calabash—A617.2; goddess in moon with calabash at her side—A751.8.3; suitor contest -- shooting birds, Pikoi takes aim in calabash of water—H331.4; charm for wealth requires a calabash of sweat—H588.7.4; Maui uses calabash of winds to fly kite—A1124.1.

CALABRIA: Parts of Sicily seen mirrored in water at Reggio in Calabria—Q113.3.1.

CALENDAR: Origin -- calculation of certain dates—A1485; origin of the year of the mouse—K52.3.

CALF: SEE COW, CALF.

CALIFORNIA: California created on six turtles—A815.

CALIPH: Caliph turns to stork—D155.1.1; ignored wife of Caliph camps near him in desert and has affair—K1814.5.

CALLING: Calling contest, coucal and elephant call to wives—K11.1.1.2.

CAMAS: Girls throw eyes into air, blue camas flowers appear when they fall—A2668; J2423.1.

CAMEL: Advice of camel to child proves true—J21.53; judge rules baby camel belongs to owner of mother who runs to suckle it when it cries—H495.4; camel fails to trick Black Cobra—K710.1.1; numskull forgets to count camel he is riding—J2022.1; camel tries to dance—J512.3; clever deductions about camel which passed—J1661.1.1; man on camel has door broken down so he can enter—J2171.6; men at first frightened at camel, take him into their service—U131.2; thief and aunt melt down stolen camel for grease—K301C; camel asks for horns, given short ears—A2232.1; origin of camel—A1873; camel lies down and smashes pots—J1511.6.1; why camel has proud look—A1873.2, A2356.2.13.1; fox brings wolf to help exact taxes of ram, ram brings camel—K641.2; man, son, camel -- who should ride?—J1041.2; camel prefers level road—J463; camel rolls after eating—J2137.6.1; camel favors tiger over man in dispute—J1172.3.2; camel induced to offer self as sacrifice—K962; "Thank God camels have no wings"—J2564.

CAMELLIA: Treasure under camellia tree—N531.3.

CAMLET: Origin of camlet flower—A2650.

CAMPHOR: The princess in the camphor tree—C31.3.1.

CANARY: SEE BIRD, CANARY.

CANARY ISLAND: Cat in mouse infested land sold—N411.1.

CANDLE: Family trying to blow out candle—X131; cat trained to hold candle—J1908.1; meal cooked over one candle—K231.14.1; candles on backs of crabs wandering in graveyard—K335.0.5.1; candle of death draws all who glimpse—D1162.2.2; Death shows that candle of princess is nearly out—D1724; trespasser betrayed by dripping candle—C916.1; ghostly candle follows path of future funeral procession—E530.1.7; goblin babies hatch from eggs and stare transfixed into candle—F481.0.1.1.2; animal with lighted candle thought to be ghost—J1782.5; hand of glory points out treasure, causes sleepers to sleep on—D1162.2.1.1; life bound up with candle—E765.1+; candle drops tallow on sleeping husband—H1385.4Aa.

CANDLEFLY: Anansi takes all candlefly's eggs in cache—Q272.5.

CANDLEMAS: Christmas celebrated as holiday of fools, St. Augustine appears on Candlemas and all repent—V92.1.

CANDLESTICK: Quest for candlestick which burns without a candle—G610Ae.

CANDY: Goblins think man who fell into syrup is candy man—J2415.22.

CANNETELLA: Girl will wed only one with gold head and gold teeth—T72.2.1.

CANNIBAL: Cannibal baby—G312.8; dog warns boy of cannibal woman—B524.1.2F; cannibal sharpens knife—G83; man in moon pulled up for eating people—A751.1.5; priest shelters with old woman cannibal—C611.0.1; raven kills cannibal at North End of the World—A2034.3.2; relatives' flesh eaten unwittingly—G61. SEE ALL G60-G68. SEE ALSO GIANT.

CANOE: Copper canoe descends from sun—F617.4; eaglet rescues boy from canoe accident—B389.3; octopus helps build canoe—F601.2Ga; birds carve canoe and carry to sea for Rata—B364.4; canoe and seven brothers turned to stone—A974; magic symbols carved on canoe—B877.1.3; Temba carves canoe which flies to stone ogre—D931.0.7; red wave is spirit canoe—F153.2; brother crosses water to Land of Shadows in white stone canoe—F81.1.0.4.

CANTE FABLE: SEE UNDER SONG.

CAP: Firefly won't return cap, chain—Z41.1.1; cap of invisibility—D1361.15; magic cap—D1067.2; magic cap enables to understand talk of birds and plants—D1067.2.1; magic cap enables mortal to fly with witches—F282.4.2, G242.7; substituted cap causes ogre to kill own children—K1611. SEE ALSO HAT.

CAP O' RUSHES: R221E.

CAPE: Task: making a cape of stone—H1021.13.

CAPS: Monkeys imitate peddler selling caps—B786.1.

CAPTAIN: Cock given passage to Cadiz if he can please captain with coplas—J1633.1; suit over chicks from eaten eggs—J1191.2; skipper transports dwarfs to new locale—F451.5.1.4.4.

CAPTIVE: "Never believe a captive's promise," advice of released bird—J21.13.1; in return for release from captivity the bird (fox) gives man three teachings—K604.

CAPTIVES: Mortals captive in fairyland—F324; escape helped by ogre's daughter—G530.2; ungrateful animal returned to captivity—J1172.3; wild man released from captivity aids hero—G671. SEE ALSO: ENTIRE CHAPTER R. CAPTIVES AND FUGITIVES, K500-K699. Captor beguiled.

CAR: Dead gangster haunts car—E414.2.

CARABAO: SEE BUFFALO, CARABAO.

CARANCHO: Teaches use of fire drill—A1414.1.1.

CARAVAN: Caravan driver thinks journey almost over and discards water—J701.3.

CARDAMON: Sprinkle magic spear with cardamon before throwing and will return—D1602.6.

CARDINAL: SEE BIRD, CARDINAL.

CARDING: Woman sticks carding combs into devil's back—K171.1.1.

CARDS: Playing cards with demon cats—H1440A; devil to take last cardplayer—G303.19.3; men playing cards in person's eye—X941.4.1; giant plays cards with Jack, life at stake—H1289.3.2; Padre Ulivo offers hospitality to twelve strangers. SEE ALSO GAMBLING.

CARIBS: Caribs created from corn—A1255.2; magic vegetable tree cut down, origin vegetables—A1423.0.1.1.

CARLANCO: Wasp routes Carlanco—K311.3B.

CARLISLE: Witches cry—G242.7.1.

CARNATION: Girl turned to pink in pocket—D431.1.2.1; carnation picked, daughter demanded in return—D735.1.

CAROB: Great bird in the Carob tree—A282.2.

CARP: SEE FISH, CARP.

CARPENTER: Carpenter's boar—B268.12; carpenter pulls thorn from elephant's foot—B381.3; carpenter to be executed so cannot duplicate building—W181.2; oniroku builds bridge for carpenter—C432.1.1; carpenter saws post for bird—Z41.6.2; carpenter blamed for weak house by thief—Z49.11.2. SEE ALSO BUILDING.

CARPET: Flying carpet carries after Padisha's abducted daughter—F1015.1.1C; skillful companion saves girl on magic carpet—H621.1; Shah recognized by weaving in carpet—H35.3.3. SEE ALSO RUG.

CARRIAGE: Ghostly carriage—E535.1; carriage from pumpkin—F861.4.3; magic carriage always points south—D1313.17. SEE ALSO CART.

CARROTS: Bear to get tops of carrots—K171.1; big lie: giant carrots in North China will reach south soon—X583.1; one word of wisdom, "carrots"—H599.8.

CARRYING: Aesop gets fellow slaves to carry smallest loads, he has bread for noon meal—J1612.1; fool carries things inappropriately—J2461A.

CART: Grateful bull draws one hundred carts—

B587.3; ghostly cart--E535.1; oven built on cart--J1041.3. SEE ALSO CARRIAGE.

CARTAGENA: Cartagena, Columbia--V128.0.1.2.

CARTWHEELS: Dwarf turns cartwheels for boys and sweets fall from pockets--F451.5.1.5.0.2.

CARVING: Clever carving of the fowl--H601; bag of gold to carver on whose mouse cat pounces, one is of dried fish--K2.1.1; origin Toromiro carvings of Rapa-Nui--A1465.5.1.

CASH: Magic string of cash is self-replacing-- D1451.3.

CASI LEMPUA LENTEMÚE: C432.1.2.

CASKET: Trickster gets dragon into casket to try size, nails down lid--G610Ai.

CASSAVA: Why cassava lives in ground-- A2794.2.1.

CASTLE: Castle disenchanted--D705.1; Eilean Donan Castle--B216.2; glass coffin with castle inside--F852.1.2; castle destroyed by merman --C931, G561.1H; origin of handprint on castle gate--H1412.2; wife convinces husband castle site is haunted--K2349.2; castle in the sea-- K1861.1C; castle in which inhabitants sleep-- D1960.3A; castle built in return for soul-- K1886.3.1; castle magically transported-- D882.1E, D2136.2; castle of Vufflens with four towers--A1435.9.1.

CAT: ax hidden from cat since cat stole meat-- J2214.3.4; cat aids girl at Baba Yaga's house-- Q2.1.2CeBa; cat's baptism--U129.4; Bast, cat goddess--A132.17; cat as damages for eaten bean--K251.1.1; belling the cat--J671.1; re-ward for blue cat, dyed cat given--J2131.5.6.1; cat pounces on boar's ear, taking it for mouse --K2324+; cat as bride--B641D; burning the house to get rid of the cat--J2101+; cat trained to hold candle--J1908.1; mouse carved of dried fish attracts cat--K2.1.1; cat rescues cock from fox--K815.15; cat cuts way out of cock's stomach--Z33.5; cat causes coffin to rise and only monk can make descend--D1641.13.1; sight of cat foretells coming flood, stream in Cotobato runs blood red since--A939.3; country without cats--F708.1, N411.1; country, cat on rat infested isle--J2415.1.0.1; creation of cat-- A1811+; cat feigns dead--K2061.9; cat feigns dead and eats mouse pallbearers--K827.4.1; told "Robert is dead," cat leaves at once-- B342; cat asks God to let creatures die-- A1335.16; demon cat's paws screwed down-- H1440A; cat tricks devil into snuffbox-- K1917.3J; cat and dog - SEE CAT AND DOG BELOW; cat helps children flee dragon-- H1321.1D; cat's dream emerges as fox-faced man--G351.2.1; drawn cats come to life and kill rat demon--D435.2.1.1; cat eats drummer, driven back to town to live with man-- A2433.3.1.3; cat is really dwarf, leaves when hears that rival Knurre Murre is dead--B342B; cat eats guests--K815.13.2; enmity between cat

and rat--A2494.1.4; enmity between cat and tiger--A2494.1.6; why cat buries its excrement --A2495.1; cat hides bathing fairies' necklaces --F302.4.2.2.1; cat is really fairy, goes to funeral when hears Molly Dixon's dead--B342C; house set on fire to get rid of cat--J2101; cat with broken leg sets fire to warehouse-- J1175.1; why cat has first place in household --A2545.2.2; fish peddler gaffs cat, finds woman wounded--D702.1.1.1; cat floats atop coconut in flood--A2681.5.1.1; literal fool wraps dead cat up--J2461.2; cat weds fox-- K2324; cat lures foxes from den with music-- K815.15; cat's fur made more fluffy by being chased--K1013.0.1; rice from stroking cat's fur --D1472.1.24.5; ghost decides to become cat-- E599.14; girls as cat and mouse disenchanted-- H1385.3D; cat refuses to teach goat to climb trees--A2581.1; goblin cats in temple-- K1853.2.1.1; students refuse cat's gift of fish, saying God will provide--J2215.4.0.2; cat as godfather eats stores--K372; cats in haunted house--H1411.2, J1495.2; cat offers condolences to sick hen--K2061.7.1; girl serves in home of cats--Q2.1.1C; cat helps man build house, can sleep in chimney corner--A2433.3.1.1; why cat lives in house--A2513.2.4; cat as sole inherit-ance--N411.1.1; cat as judge eats both--K815.7; cat shows girl how to remove telltale blood from key--G561.2 Williams-Ellis; journey to Land of Cats--J2415.9; cat tricks lion back into mud hole--J1172.3.0.5; lion sneezes forth cat--A1811.2; old woman kills cat loaned to bride next door and demands exorbitant re-turn--J1179.24; cat transformed to maiden runs after mouse--J1908.2; why cat says meow-- F617.2.3; why cat meows when chewing-- A2435.2.1; cat as monk eats worshipping mice --K815.16.1; cat shows monk spell to save life of girl--B522.1.1; monkey flatters cat into pulling chestnuts from fire--K334.3; monkey evens out cakes for cat--K452.1.2; cat on moon unravels weaving--A751.8.1.1; cat on moon chases rat--A751.0.2; mouse tells cat a tale, "Even so I eat you up"--K561.1.1; cat orders mouse to make suit of clothes--Z49.24; old cat's worth as mouser redeemed-- K231.1.3.3; cat as ogre--G351.2; cat and par-rot exchange feast--Z33.2.1; Parvati turns cat into maiden--B601.12; cat's paw cut off, wom-an's hand missing--D702.1.1; Siamese cat keeps tail curled around cup to prevent poisoning of king--A2378.9.7; cats always land on feet, re-ward for aiding prophet--A2441.1.10.1; cat wins princess for master, Puss in Boots-- K1917.3; cat called in to feel if it is raining out--W111.2.4; association of cat and rat ends as soon as mutual danger has passed--J426; kitten and young rat end friendship when learn are natural enemies--J425.3; cat becomes companion of Saras Vati--A132.17.1; cat de-scends from scroll--D435.2.1.1; cat sees hair fall from horse's tail, remarkable sight--X938.2; cat's shriek causes bear to fall from the tree-- K2324; cat's severed head kills snake--B331.0.1; donkey sold for one dinar with one hundred dinar cat tied to it--K182.0.1; cat seeks name of strongest thing--L392.0.4; cat swallows all it meets--Z33.2; why cat's tail has curl at end—A2378.9.7; cat has tail cut off by barber, demands razor—Z47.3; cat's tail thought to be sabre—K2323; quest for nail from toe of tenth black cat on Isle of Ten Black Cats—S12.1B; theft of three pounds of meat blamed on cat, cat itself weighs three pounds—J1611; cat didn't teach tiger all his tricks—A2581; cat teaches all tricks except one—J1662.0.1; cat causes troll to burst—K1917.3; in war between wild and domestic animals cat grabs bear by throat—K2323.0.1; rat persuades cat to wash before eating—K562; why cat eats first and washes later—A2545.2; why cats fear water—A2534.2; princess weds snake prince in palace of cubits with White Cat ruler—D735.1F; white cat maiden—B641D; intruder thinks cat is witch with awl—K1161.1; witch cat traps Christian girl—G271.2; witch in form of cat—G211.1.7; witch in form of cat has hand cut off—D702.1.1; cat beaten for not working, lazy wife must hold .at and is scratched—W111.3.2; cat aids girl, .attles witch, turns to man—R221; cat take. girl to witches who help with spinning—D2183.1 Nic Leodhas; maid kind to witch's cat rewarded—Q2.1.2H; why cat lives with woman—A2513.2.1; wrestling match, cat cannot be thrown—A2433.3.1.2.

CAT AND DOG: Dog invites four cats to dinner, one steals dog's avocado pears—A2494.4.6; cat loses dog's certificate, enmity—A2281.1; enmity between dog and cat—A2494.1.2; animals refuse to help stop fight between dog and cat, they are killed in chain of events—J451.2.1; cat finds goat teaching dog to climb—A2581.1; cat reaches God first with request that man die—A1335.16; dog and cat retrieve lost magic object (ring)—D882.1+; mongoose gives magic ring, cat retrieves when lost, dog chases off thief, who deserves first place?—H621.3; cat takes name "Stranger," dog "Traveler," Yoruba chief feeds "Stranger" by custom—A2494.1.5; quarrel between cat and dog causes war—N381+.

CATCH TALES: Z13+.

CATERPILLAR: Caterpillar in hare's house frightens off animals—K1711.2.1; lion to fight enchanted princess in caterpillar form—H1385.4D; guessing material of slippers, made from gigantic caterpillar—H522.1, H1385.4D.

CATFISH: SEE FISH, CATFISH.

CATNIP: King claims kitten was born of his cat because it goes to his, he rubbed catnip on cat, it is a male—J1191.1.4.

CATOON: Origin River Catoon—A934.18.

CATSKIN: Girl in catskin dress—R221D+.

CATTAIL: Badger 'brained' by cattail—K473.2; cattail pollen as remedy for furless hare—K579.2.2.

CATTENBORG: Earl of Cattenborg—K1917.3B.

CAT'S CRADLE: Spirit of string figures uses own intestines when runs out of string—F499.4.

CATTLE: Why birds live among cattle—A2433.4.8; magic old woman emerges from clay pot, gives cattle—K1931.2V; cattle thief recognized in lion—J561.2. SEE ALSO COW.

CAUBEEN: Magic caubeen stolen by host at inn—D861.1G.

CAULD LAD OF HILTON: Fairy leaves when he is given clothes—F381.3.

CAULDRON: Gypsy and wife carry pots over river by floating them across in giant cauldron—J1689.3.

CAVALLINA: Mare, Cavallina, aids lad—H1213.1.

CAVE: Numskull digging cellar pokes hole into neighbor's cowshed and thinks has found ancient cave—J2201.2; hidden enemy tricked into answering when owner calls to cave—K607.1; baby trapped in treasure cave—B11.6.2.4; deer leads way into treasure cave—N773; boys trapped in cave become gods of Good Luck and Bad Luck—D2011.1.3.1; hyena forgets phrase and is caught in magic cave—N455.3.1; King Arthur sleeps in cave—D1960.2; lover hides girl in cave with underwater entrance—R161.5; cave as refuge—R315; animal rescues from cave—A2493.4.1; holding up roof of cave—K1251; sage Wang Shen challenges pupils to get him out of cave—J1686; spider web over cave saves fugitive—B523.1; Tepoztlan shows cave opening on New Year's Eve—C761.4; secret formula for opening treasure cave—N455.3.

CAVE, BIRD'S NEST: Offering of Goddess of Caves eaten—C57.1.3.

CAYUSE: Origin of cayuse according to Nez Percé—A1610.8.

CEBU: Cebu created—A955.0.1.1.

CEGUA: Lovely dark girl who asks for ride—E425.1.3.1.

CEILING: Why spider lives on ceiling—A2433.5.3.3.

CELERY: Girl pulls up celery, is pulled underground—H1385.4L.

CELLAR: Numskull digging cellar pokes hole into neighbor's cowshed and thinks has found ancient cave—J2201.2; fool lets wine run in cellar—J2176; glutton wants cellar full of food—C773.1.3; wolf overeats in cellar—K1022.2.

CEMETERY: Candles on backs of crabs wandering in graveyard—K301; villagers lie down in future cemetery plot to assess size of cemetery needed—J1703.3; statue of old laird and hounds moves—E521.2.4. SEE ALSO DEAD; FUNERAL; GRAVE.

CENERONTOLA: R221C.

CENSUS: Kantchil takes census of crocodiles—K579.2.1.

CENTAVO: Gambler finds centavo, chick eats, etc.—K251.1.5.

CENTER: Where is center of earth?—H681.3.

CENTIPEDE: Devastating centipede—Q82.3; earthworm woos centipede—A2355.1.3; reward for slaying giant centipede—Q82.3; marriage to centipede in human form—B653.2.

CEREMONY: Origin of Sangasong ceremony for dedicating house before building—A1549.2.1; religious ceremonies—V80+.

CERTIFICATE: Cat loses dog's certificate—A2281.1.

CHABLES: Clothing blessed on day of Holy Agethey in Church of Chables—D1385.18.1.

CHACO: Thunder caught in tree in Chaco—A1142.3.1; Chaco war—V128.0.1.2.

CHAFF: Bear gets chaff, fox grain—K171.2; drum whispers secret that king eats chaff—D1316.5.0.2.

CHAIN: Ascent to upper world on arrow chain—F53+; drop of honey causes chain of accidents—N381; human chain, men hang in chain until top man spits on hands—J2133.5; chains around neck exchanged with sleeping ogre's children—K1611; quest for longest chain—B641.0.1Dba, B641.0.1Dc; chain tales—Z20-Z55; chain resulting in wealth—N222.

CHAIR: Magic sticking chair routs Devil—Q565A; troll hag sits on sticking chair—E341.1A.

CHALET: Cobbler dares to cobble in haunted chalet—H1411.4.1.

CHAMELEON: Chameleon blamed by monkey for thefts, points out half-closed eyes and nodding head—A2494.16.2.1; color of chameleon—A2411.5.6, A2411.5.6.2; first human pair caught in fish trap by chameleon—A1279.2; chameleon's relatives answer in race—K11.1; chameleon clings to tail of cheetah (elephant) in race—K11.2; chameleon frightens off lion with loud voice—K641.3.

CHAMPA FLOWER: Vulture carries girl to fetch flower—K1911Aa.

CHANDALA: Chandala maid wants to wed most powerful person in world—Z42.0.3.

CH'ANG AN: Which is nearer, Ch'ang An or sun?—H682.1.4.1.

CHANG KUNG: Secret of happiness is "kindness"—A411.2.

CHANG-TO-RYONG: Disguised as beggar—V266.1.

CHANGE: Coin is so underweight that if I changed it for you, you would owe me a shilling—J1650.2.

CHANGELING: SEE F321.1+.

CHANT: Dog gets fufu from tree by calling chant—D861Ic; Ivanko chants and boat moves—R251A; old woman chants and peach floats ashore—T543.3.2.

CHAOS: In the beginning chaos—A620.3.

CHAPEL: "The Chapel of the Brave Horse" built—B401.2. SEE ALSO CHURCH.

CHAPPATI: Girl makes chappatis with offerings left to Deity and eats them—V128.5.

CHARACTER: Homely daughter to overcome face with character—J244.1; tests of character—H1550+; traits of character— SEE ENTIRE CHAPTER W.

CHARCOAL: Task, making charcoal from human hair; countertask, one hundred pounds of charcoal from human hair—H1021.14; horse in snowstorm eats charcoal, heat from tail keeps gypsy and wife warm—X1203.1; charcoal dumped on raven causes color—A2411.2.1.5.

CHARCOAL BURNER: Charcoal burner and fuller cannot live together—U143.

CHARITY: Issy Ben Aran helps a wounded man. Thief steals horse when well. Issy pursues to give bill of sale, makes thief promise not to tell of event so others won't fear to help the wounded—J1392.7. SEE ALSO ALL ENTRIES V400-V429.4.

CHARLES V: The herdsman disguises as abbot, fools king—H561.2.

CHARM: Love charm given Brer Rabbit—H961.1; charm makes all stick in fire—D1413.17; charm for wealth and happiness requires a calabash of sweat—H588.7.4.

CHATTEE MAKER: Valiant chattee maker rides tiger—N392.1.1.1.

CHEAT: Merchant pretends bowl is worthless in order to buy it cheaply—J1521.6; cheater cheated—J1510+; deer's antlers reward for not cheating—A2326.1.1.1; Devil cheated of promised soul—K210+; rogues cheat each other—J1516; illusory transformation of animals in order to sell and cheat—D612.1. SEE ALL OF K. DECEPTIONS.

CHEEKS: Fool with full cheeks allows them to be cut open rather than open mouth—W111.5.8.

CHEESE: Fox flatters crow into singing and dropping cheese--K334.1; church made of cheese and bacon—X1863; cheese thrown down to find way home—J1881.1.1; fox tells wolf that moon's reflection in ice is cheese—K1021.0.1; diving for cheese (moon)--J1791.3; Bergmännlein gives replenishing cheese—F460.4.2; cheese sent to bring others back—J1881.1.2; contest in squeezing water from a stone, cheese is used—K62.

CHEETAH: Chameleon clings to cheetah's tail in race--K11.2.

CHELM: SEE HELM.

CHERAK: Digit steals bull from Cherak monster—F535.1.1De.

CHERRY: Frog is girl Cherry under enchantment--B641Ae.

CHERRY TREE: Cherry trees made to blossom by old man--D1571.1; cherry tree blooms on anniversary of nurse's death—E631.6; Marilka is lost, cherry tree sheds blossoms in sorrow—Z39.5.2.

CHES: God Ches—A978.3.1.

CHESS: Gods play chess—A163.1.1; invention of chess—Z21.1; supernatural passage of time while watching chess game—D2011.1.3.

CHEST: Flood from magic land in chests—F302.1.4.1; chest lid dropped to behead child—N271Aa; magic chest carries dresses underground--R221Dc; mechanic works hours trying to open chest--J253; paramour in chest betrayed—J1344.1; lad puts bird in chest and has chest tell story—F954.2.1.1; family guard two chests, water in one, fire in other—A1414.7.4.

CHESTNUT: Monkey flatters cat into pulling chestnuts from fire—K334.3; chestnuts on hearth explode--K1161.6.1; suit for eating roasted chestnuts, Devil as lawyer—J1191.2; chestnut tree spirit made into ship which refuses to move unless girl touches—F441.2.0.2.

CHEWING: Youngest at banquet says old eats more rapidly since has no teeth and can't chew—J234; Crazy Horse chews flint to powder—A526.1.1.1.

CHIA: Chia causes river to flood—A1011.2.1; Chia becomes moon—A747.1.

CHIANOURI: Pseudo-magic resuscitating object sold—K113.

CHICHA: Replenishing chicha gourd—B216.5.

CHICHIMAC: Chichimac prince turned into mountain—A962.1.1.

CHICKEN: Chicken rescued lays eggs and saves life of rescuer lizard—K641.3; Red-Chicken

collects debt--Z52.2.1; Chicken Little says sky is falling—Z43.3; why chicken calls "Tautavaya-o" when tide is rising—K561.1.0.2. SEE ALSO EGG.

CHICKEN, CAPON: Fat capons mock lean, fat are eaten—J212.3.

CHICKEN, CHICK: Eagle revenges theft of hen's chicks by jackal--K1041.0.1; don't count chicks before hatched--J2061.1.2; suit over chicks that might have hatched from eaten chicken or egg—J1191.2; half-chick—B171.1, Z52.2; chick attacks reflection in well—J1791.5.3.

CHICKEN, COCK: cock given passage to Cadiz free for coplas—J1653.1; cock eats corn, alligator eats cock—Z43.5.1; cock prefers single corn to peck of pearls—J1061.1; origin of cock's red crest--A2321.10.0.1; why cocks crow--A2421.6; cocks crow each morning to remind world that weak have right to justice—A2426.2.18.1; cock made to crow early to outwit in bargain—K1886.3.1; cock persuaded to crow with eyes closed—K721; why cocks crow at sunrise—A2489.1.1; origin and meaning of cock's cry--A2426.2.18; cock feigns death to hear what hens say—H1556.1.1; demi-coq collects money by means of magic animals—B171.1; devil flees when cock is made to crow—G303.16.19.4; cock drowns in brew vat—Z32.2.3; victorious cock caught by eagle and loser reigns—J972; cock eats all met—Z33.5; elephant thinks cock is eating him—K1715.4.2; falcon reproaches cock for fleeing master—J1423; cock opens door to fox—K815.15; cock persuades fox to pray before eating—K562.1; cock eats king's gold—Z52.4.1; Anansi asks grain of corn to hide him—Z43.5.1; cock as damages for eaten grain of corn—K251.1; haunted object, cock--H411.4.2; old woman carries egg under arm and a cock hatches—Z52.4.2; originally cock had horns—A2326.2.3; lad inherits a cock, sells in land of no cocks—N411.1B; fox tries to beguile the cock by reporting a new law—J1421; cock crows to bring light—A1412.6; lion fears cock—J881.2; cock frightens lion and ass gives chase---J952.2; magic cock stolen by host—D861.1; maids kill cock to sleep later—K1636; why cock lives with man—A2513.6; cock makes king think master is wealthy—K1917.3E Kavcic; cock courting with owl wins the girl—A2491.2.8; ox sold for five pennies tied to twelve florin cock—K182; partridge notices that game cocks mistreat even each other—J892; picture of cock painted in five minutes—H504.4; intruder thinks cock is man on roof—K1161.1; cock agrees to sing for fox if dog invited too—K579.8; cock sold in land without cocks—N411.1B; magic stone in cock's head—D882.1D; only cock can coax sun up—A739.6, B755.1; cock in treasury eats gold then feigns dead, thrown out—K522.4.0.2; cock causes Tsar's sons to be sent into battle—B143.1.5; cock persuades captor to talk and release from mouth—K561.1; cock, cuckoo and black-cock in waking contest—K51; cock shows man how to rule wife—B216Aa; why cock eats worms—A2435.4.8.2. SEE ALSO CHICKEN,

ROOSTER.

CHICKEN, COCKCROW: Brothers forget to enter water before cockcrow, enchantment is broken—N455.4E; Laminak to claim soul if castle completed by cockcrow—F420.5.2.13; cockcrow stone must turn round each time cock crows—F809.5.1; Taiwanese Lin Tachian loses chance at throne of emperor of China because golden cock crows before dawn—B755.2. SEE ALSO CHICKEN; COCK; CROWING.

CHICKEN, HEN: Cat offers condolences to sick hen—K2061.7.1; hen and crocodile—K601.3; 'dressing' the hen in clothes—J2499.8; hen that lays golden eggs—D876; father stands on head until hen lays another egg—Z39.5.1; worshipping hens eaten by fox holy man—K815.16.2; fox is promised a hen, given dog—K235.1; fox offers to doctor sick hen—K2061.7; funeral procession of the hen—Z32.1; hen entices girls to ogres' den—G561A; hen loses hawk's ring—A2494.13.10.3; hens sent home by themselves—J1881.2.4; overfed hen stops laying—J1901.1; hen takes letter to king—Z52.3; hen gives magic mud which produces baked chicken—D877.3; offers hen for sale at same price as parrot, she has wonderful thoughts and annoys no one with her chatter—J1060.1; six chicks become Pleiades, jump in pot after mother—A773.8; little red hen cuts way out of fox's bag—K526.1; little red hen must do all work—W111.6.1; why hen scratches in ground—A2477.2; why hen is speckled—Z52.3; stone hen lays eggs for pious girl—B811.7; quest to discover where hen lays eggs—H1273.2C; hen weaves for weaver—D2183F; fool throws hen in well to get a drink—J1902.1.1.

CHICKEN, HEN AND COCK: Cock chokes and hen seeks aid—Z32.1.1; hen disobeys cock and is caught, "I told you so"—J652.5; cock strikes out hen's eye, chain results—Z43.2; cock and hen go in carriage to visit Mr. Korbes—K1161.7; cock and hen go nutting—K1161.7.2.

CHICKEN, ROOSTER: Rooster's ancestor—A751.8.7; rooster must clean bill on grass—Z41.2.3; sun gives comb to rooster—A2321.10.0.2; rooster criticized, can tell when day is coming in the dark but can't find way home in broad daylight—J1881.2.4; rooster loses dawn calling contest—B755.3; little rooster demands diamond button returned—Z52.4; crowing cock on donkey's back frightens lion. Donkey returns without cock and is attacked—J684.1.1.1; girl follows rooster who cries "I'm late!"—H1385.5Af; lion believes rooster's tail feather is hair—K1711.1; magic rooster stolen by host—D861.1; rooster's revenge on owls for dancing with hens—J2332.1; owls bring roosters to party to crow so can escape before dawn—J2332.1.1; rooster must scratch before eating—J2477.2.1; silver laying rooster—D861.1F; rooster wakes buzzard in time to watch sun and collect debt, sun rules buzzard may collect debt in chickens—A2494.13.10.7;

the tipsy rooster takes purse to king—Z52.6; woodcutter calling after lost fairy wife turned to rooster—F302.4.2.0.3; You Ye set on sun with golden bird to wake him, ancestor of the rooster—A751.8.7. SEE ALSO CHICKEN, COCK.

CHIEF'S DAUGHTER: Given to one returning with packet of salt first—K11.1.1.1.

CHILBIK: Chilbik ordered to fetch treasure of ogress for Czar—G610Aj.

CHILDBIRTH: Woman persuaded to raise alarm, lacks husband when real labor occurs—N455.4B; uncharitable woman cursed by beggar to bear 365 children—V429.3. SEE ALSO BIRTH.

CHILDE ROWLAND—F324.

CHILDREN: Abandoned children kill tribe—S366.1; children abandoned in wood—S143; animal nourishes abandoned child—B535+; boy raised by bears—B535.0.15; friend can be revived if smeared with blood of king's two children—S268A; boy tells old man sun is nearer than Ch'ang An—H682.1.4.1; child tricks moneylender into revealing presence at scene of crime—J123.0.1; why cuckoo abandons children—A2431.2.1; four sons pursue mother turned to cuckoo—A2683.1.2; dog feigns rescue of child—K231.1.3; ega parents move to be rid of obnoxious children—A2431.3.9.15; king lets child choose father, one to wed his mother the princess—D1720.1.5; Banikan sings and children must follow dancing into jungle—D1427.1.1; children escape in invisible cloak—K717.4; judge overhears children's games and learns solution to case—J123; leopard as nurse for boy—B535.0.8.1; barren woman finds two green plants which turn to lizards, then to children—T554.8.2; lost children find way back by crumb trail—R135; children lost picking flowers sing—R131.21; house full of children give magic object to old man—D861.1K; miraculous child—T500-T599; hawk drops mouse to childless couple—L392.0.1; children pull nose of bad brother long—J2415.15; origin of crying children's habit of answering "nothing" when asked why they cry—A1579.2; father (mother) of one hundred children outwits ogre (dragon)—G501C; each likes his own children best—T681; Pied Piper of Hamelin entices children—D1427.1; Guan-am Tong-Tu, the Compassionate Protector of Children—T210.1.1; python doctor agrees to come when children sing to him—B491.1.2; Manstin, rabbit, turns child into giant child with long ears like hare—B535.0.16; children punished for father's sins P242; trickster substitutes enemy's own children in bag—K527.1; ogre fooled by substitution of a corpse for child who is to be cooked—R153.3.3; turtle playing flute is untied by children—K571; wolf waits in vain for the nurse to throw away the child—J2066.5. SEE ALSO BABY; BOY; CHANGELING; DAUGHTER; GIRL; PARENTS; SON; SUPERNATURAL CHILD.

CHILI: Mule drivers rub chili peppers on legs of mules and they move faster—J1612.0.1; chili plant grows from grave of girl murdered, sings—E632.0.5; riddle, number of leaves on chili plant—E632.0.5. SEE ALSO PEPPERS.

CHIMNEY: Bag of money up chimney—Q2.1.2Cb; body falls piecemeal down chimney—H1411.1; Brer Rabbit hides in chimney, spits tobacco juice in Brer Fox's eyes—K1161.11; man steps into chimney during big storm—X1653.3; wolf tricked into jumping down chimney—K891.1.

CHIN CHIN KOBAKAMA: Q321.3.

CHINA: Prince of Chu asks why such a poor ambassador is sent from Chi—J1289.31; travelers from North and South China meet and exchange tall tales—X583.1; magic whip to build Great Wall of China—D1208.1; magic golden nail to build wall to protect Vietnam from China—A132.15; farm girl waits for wings to grow, spirits oblige—Q22.1. SEE ALSO ENTRIES IN ETHNIC AND GEOGRAPHICAL INDEX.

CHINAWARE: Porter given advice as payment, drops crate of china—J163.4.2.

CHINGOLA BIRD: Origin—A1999.5.

CHINOOK: Origin of Chinook wind—A1129.4.

CHIPMUNK: Creation of chipmunk—A1859; seeds stolen from Dawn People by chipmunk—A1425.0.1.1; Old-Man turns Bad Sickness into chipmunk—A1859.2; why chipmunk has stripes—A2217.2.

CHOICES: SEE ALL J200-J499.

CHOKECHERRIES: Coyote dives for reflected chokecherries—J1791.3.5.

CHOLERA: Cholera, Death and Fear visit Mecca—Z111.7.

CHONG-KAK: Watching men play chong-kak, years pass—D2011.1.3.

CHOPSTICKS: Chopsticks float downstream, prince goes upstream and finds maiden—K929.1.1; yard long chopsticks in hell—W47.1; Issun Boshi uses chopsticks as oars—F535.1.1E.

CHRIST: Woman says fattest pigs have died, Christ turns them to wild boars—A1871.1.1; Christ gives magic flute—D1415.2.3.3; baker's daughter refuses bread to Christ, turned to owl—A1958.0.1; picture of Christ appears miraculously on painter's easel—V121.0.1; Christ fleeing from soldiers is hidden in pine cone—A2711.3.1; Fata Morgana offers to make Count Roger King of Sicily, he answers that Christ will give him Sicily—Q113.3.1; Christ as beggar tells to follow silver tracks—Q1.1C; Devil in troubador contest cannot answer verse "Jesus, Joseph, Mary"—G303.16.8.1.

CHRIST AND ST. PETER: St. Peter finds people on earth are happy and pay no attention to the Lord. Returns in time of Poverty and finds all call upon the Lord—V229.26.1.2; Lord hangs trombone on St. Peter's back, guests beat him because won't play—V229.26.1.1; Christ and St. Peter visit and give wishes—K1811.6, Q565. SEE ALSO LORD, ST. PETER.

CHRIST CHILD: Christ Child rings bell over unconscious Brother Johannick until rescue—V211.1.8.4; city sinks into water after populace refuses hospitality to Christ Child—F944.1; clockmaker spends years on clock for Christ Child—D1622.2.2; hunchback carves crib for Christ Child—D1622.2.1; Christ Child smiles at juggler—V92.0.1; monk dead on Christmas with hand in babe's—D1622.2.3; wooden image of Christ Child walks in fields and calls down rain—V128.3.

CHRISTENING: One of fairies is not invited to Christening—D1960.3B; trickster stands godfather and eats up stores—K372; troll told Virgin is coming to christening—K1736. SEE ALSO BAPTISM.

CHRISTIANITY: Fostedina, early Christian, forced to wear crown of thorns—A1437.1; daughter of Moorish governor turned to white cat for becoming Christian—B641Dd; Christian prisoner teaches Moors Christianity—D2003; Christian knight rescues girl from Moors—D87.1; girl says Christian prayer and wind dashes witch against rocks and turns to stone—G271.2. SEE PORTIONS OF V. RELIGION. SEE ALSO CHURCH; CROSS; MONK; PRAYER; PRIEST; SAINTS; VIRGIN; ETC.

CHRISTMAS: Animals blessed for honoring infant—A2221.1; animals speak at Christmas—B251.1.2; ash-maid attends church at Christmas—R221F; devil defeated at time of nativity—G303.26.19.10; Dwarf King Laurin given hospitality on Christmas Eve rewards boys—F451.5.1.5.0.2; poor servant woman driven out on Christmas Eve finds fairy cabin—F343.21; fiddler plays for devils on Christmas Eve—G303.25.17.2.1; origin of holly—A2612.4; visitors on Christmas Eve give wish for each horn on animal—Q1.1B; monk found dead on Christmas Eve with hand in Christ Child's—D1622.2.3; robin on way to sing for King on Yule morn—Z55; St. Bridget nurses baby—V211.1.8.1; staff blooms every Christmas to remind of water-horse admitted to church—F420.1.3.3.1; stars discuss birth of Christ Child—V211.1.2.2; bear frightens trolls on Christmas Eve—K1728; twelve days of Christmas—Z22.1; ass and goose at wishing well on Christmas Eve—B251.1.2.4. SEE ALSO ST. NICHOLAS. FOR ENTIRE COLLECTIONS OF CHRISTMAS TALES SEE: Sawyer, Ruth. JOY TO THE WORLD; THE LONG CHRISTMAS; THIS WAY TO CHRISTMAS.

CHU MONG: Founder of Korea—K511.1.4.5.

CHU-TI: Emperor of China, dragons steal water supply--B11.7.1.

CHUC NU: Heavenly spinning maid—A778.3.1.

CHUKO KUNG MING: Ruler plays lute on city walls and fools besieging army—K2366.2.

CHURCH: Devil in church—K1987; devil writes names of those who sleep in church—G303.24.1.7.0.1; foals in church turn to princes and take communion--H1199.12.3; gypsies' church of cheese and bacon---X1863; threat to build church in hell—K1781; fools attempt to push church to line marked by jackets--J2328.1; knight in temper kills priest--W185.7; king to be King of England if see Long Compton Church—G263.2.1.2; maid attends church in hidden finery—R221M; mermaid sings divinely in church—B81.13.6; church of Ochara unearthed—H171.7; painting cannot be taken out of church--V128.0.1; animals confess weaknesses after revival meeting—W141.1; tailor in church meets ghost—H1412.2; church built on spot where statue of Virgin appears—V128.0.1.2; wild boar captured in church—K1951.1; return to living form by walking around church opposite of widershins—E44. SEE ALSO CHRIST; CHRISTIANITY; MONK; MOSQUE; PRIEST; ETC.

CHURCH BELLS: Church bells cannot be raised to tall steeple—V115.5. SEE ALSO BELL.

CHURN: Cow falls into sinkhole, drowns in milk, churns into butter—X1235.2.3; fox stuck with churn dash, hence white tail—A2215.5; two frogs in crock of cream, one drowns, one kicks until churns to butter—Q81.2; frogs in churn to churn butter, invention--J1689.2.

CHYAVANA: Holy man meditates—D1960.5.

CICADA: Cicada leaves skin with rock inside—K525.1.1.4. SEE ALSO LOCUST.

CIDER: Fool leaves cider spigot open—J2176.

CINDERELLA: R221.

CINDERLAD: Elder brothers tell king Cinderlad can get troll's seven silver ducks—G610Ac.

CINNAMON: Bad boy sent to wood to chop branches from cinnamon tree—A751.1.8.

CITY: City besieged—K2365ff; city sinks into lake—F944; bricklayer wants to make city walls of brick, carpenter of wood, tanner of leather—W197.2. SEE ALSO COUNTRY.

CLAM: Clamshell Boy—T554.12; giant clam swallows boy—S71.2; Ratu defeats giant clam—B874.9; clam catches beak of heron (crane)—J219.1; clam maiden spins cloth—B652.2.1; boy caught persuades clam that he feels pearl, clam opens—K561.1.0.2; clam maiden weds--

N831.1.

CLAN: Origin Porcupine clan—B538.3.5.

CLAP: Rescuing a drowning man by rope, rescuers clap—J2516.3.2; men hanging from tree clap hands—J2133.5.0.1.

CLAPPING MOUNTAINS: Mountains periodically clap together—D1553.1.

CLASSES: Origin of different classes--A1650ff.

CLAY: Clay man as tar baby—K741.0.6; fool to be wise when gets 'coat of clay'--J163.2.2; man made from clay—A1241; plotters forced to wear wide clay hats, cannot lean close enough to whisper--J1199.5; childless couple make clay pot boy—Z33.7. SEE ALSO DIRT; EARTH; MUD.

CLEAN: Food denied until hands are clean—K278.

CLEANING: Bogles leave when house is cleaned—E439.11; why cockroaches clean houses—A2458.1.; magic object loses power if cleaned--D877.1; self-cooking kettle said to have been rendered useless by polishing—K112.1. SEE ALSO WASHING.

CLEAR LAKE: Formation of Clear Lake—A2108.1.

CLEVERNESS: Bride test, wisdom—H388; deduction, the one-eyed camel—J1661.1.1; Clever Elsa—J2063; clever peasant girl—H561.1; tasks performed by cleverness--H961; secret of fox's cleverness—H961; clever persons and acts—J1110-J1699; retorts—J1250-J1649; tests of cleverness—H500-H899. SEE ALL J1100-J1699 Cleverness. SEE ALSO RIDDLES.

CLIFF: Dancing girl leaps from cliff with general--K972.0.1; cliff from lover's leap—A968+.

CLIMBING: Cat saves self with trick of climbing J1662; cat doesn't teach tiger to climb—A2581; task, climbing glass mountain--D721.5B, H331.1.1, H1385.5B; why goat cannot climb trees—A2581.1; climbing match won by trickery—K15.2; wolves climb on top of each other—J2133.6.

CLINK: Payment with clink of money—J1172.2H.

CLOAK: Goose feather cloak burned by sun—A728.1. SEE ALSO CLOTHING; COAT.

CLOCK: Clockmaker spends years on clock for Christ Child—D1622.2.2; clockmaker sets time by church clock, sexton rings bells by clockmaker's clock—J2499.10; youth creating marvelous clock has intelligence, lacks luck—N141.0.1. SEE ALSO TIME.

CLOTH: Girl given magic cloth by beggar which makes her lovely—J2415.19; doing all day what begun, measuring cloth—J2073.1; ten cloth merchants captured—K606.0.4; task, bring cloth long as road—H951.1.   SEE ALSO: SPINNING; TAILOR.

CLOTHES: Bird has suit, shoes, hat made, doesn't pay—Z49.3.1; clothes of bird maiden hidden—H1385.3F; girl dancing with demons sends them articles of clothing to procrastinate —Q2.1.3Aa; emperor's new clothes—K445; man persuaded to roast sheep to feed tricksters who say end of world is coming tomorrow, he burns their clothing—J1511.7; fairy leaves when given clothing—F381.3; fairy comes into man's power if he steals clothes—F302.4.2.1; man gives food to clothes—J1561.3; fool sells clothes to statue—J1853.1.1; Mrs. Goose leaves clothes bundle on bed, fox steals—L525.1.0.1; king's clothing taken, must go as beggar—L411; mouse intimidates tailor, etc. to make clothes— Z49.3.3; task, coming neither naked nor clad— H1054.1; overzealous visitor can't wait to dress, goes naked—J2517; magic pouch bites imposter in clothing of Two Feathers—D1050.2; woman's clothes cut up, does not know self—J2012.2. SEE ALSO CAP; CLOAK; COAT; DRESS; HAT; PANTS; PONCHO; ROBE; SHIRT; SHOES, ETC.

CLOTHESPIN: Clothespin fastened to thief's tongue, flees—K335.1.1.1.

CLOUD: Task, bring golden chains from clouds —H1385.3Fh; clouds as spirits of children— A1133.6; Christ Child calls on clouds to rain— V128.3; fool leaves knife in shadow of cloud to mark spot—J1922.2; old woman's hump strikes cloud as she sweeps—A625.2.3; first brother sees horse tied to cloud—F660.1.1; criminals believe clouds will tell of murder—N275.0.1; origin of clouds—A1133; three princesses carried off by cloud—K1931.2J; clouds spun by spider to thank sun—A1133.5; cloud stronger than sun—L392, Z42.0.1+; White Clouds fight Black Cloud—A1412.4; White Cloud of North calls Blue Cloud from South and Yellow Cloud from West to shed light—A1412.4; Cloud goddess gives Yerba Maté—A2691.6.

CLOUD HORSE: SEE HORSE, CLOUD.

CLUB: Magic club beats person—D1401.1; throwing club into moon—K1746.

COAL: Bean, straw and coal go journeying— F1025.1; dwarf's gift of coal turns to gold— F451.5.1.4+; girl asks for coal for fire from Brownie's camp, turns to gold—F342.1.2; coals turn to gold—F342.1; mouse and coal go journeying—F1025.1.2; coal is sold in Newcastle —N411.6.

COAL CHEST: Reward of coal chest has prince inside—Q2.1.2G.

COAL SCUTTLE: Fisherman and wife live in coal scuttle—B375.1A.

COAT: Witness claims borrowed coat, discredited—J1151.2; man exchanges trousers for coat, pays for neither—K233.4.1; coat falling makes

loud noise, he was in it—J2235.2; feeding the coat—J1561.3; soldier trades 'magic' tattered coat for fur coat—K119.4; hole burnt, nothing left but collar—X1761.3; thieves take coats— J1179.5. SEE ALSO CLOAK; CLOTHING.

COBALD: F481.0.1.1.1. SEE ALSO KOBALDS.

COBRA: SEE SNAKE, COBRA.

COBWEBS: Namashepani fairies wear white cobweblike clothing and fly—F206.

COCK: SEE CHICKEN, COCK.

COCKATOO: SEE BIRD, COCKATOO.

COCKLEPEA: Two lost babes—K1611Ea.

COCKROACH: Why cockroach is black— A2411.3.4; why cockroaches clean up houses— A2458.1; why cockroach is flat—A2305.2.1; cockroach and her suitors—Z32.3.1.

COCONUT: Coconut seed turns to greedy man —C773.1.3; coconut grows from head of tattling man—A2611.3.1; insects born from coconuts belong to Anansi—X905.1.3; moon's shiny face is from coconut sauce—A741.4; origin of coconut tree—A2681.5.1; turtle (eel) lover beheaded, coconut grows with shell like turtle's— A2611.3 2; water which never sank onto earth or fell from sky—H802.1; old woman protected by objects which attack intruding ogre— K1161.3.2.

CODES: Shah weaves message in rug with ancient Persian script—H35.3.3.

COFFIN: Cat causes coffin to rise into air— D1641.13.1; Death trapped in coffin—K213B; glass coffin—F852.1, Z65.1; coffin leaves ground, leads way to scene of murder—E231.6; servant lies in coffin alongside master, feigns death and accompanies him on nightly haunts— E415.1.2.1; man who fails to tell tale sent out, has to carry coffin—M231.1A; to read psalter over witch in coffin three nights—H1411.4.4; witch's secret name is "Coffin on your back" —C432.1.2.

COIN: Lady of the Tylwyth Teg gives ferryman silver coin which replaces self—F342.2.3; wolf demands magic coin which causes rice urn to be self-replenishing—K1161.3.5; tar on trickster's shoes picks up gold coins strewn on street—K378.1. SEE ALSO CHANGE.

COLD, DISEASE: Fox to judge lion's breath feigns a cold—J811.2.1.

COLD: Polish landlord asks ragged tenant if he is not cold, tenant, "Is your nose cold?" "No." "I'm all nose."—J1309.1; crane fans fires of Osni (cold), gives gift of not feeling cold— A2411.2.6.14.1; man blows on soup to cool it— J1801.1; cold water down back makes lad shiver—H1440. SEE ALSO FREEZE; FROST; ICE; SNOW; WINTER; ETC.

COLLARD: Hare convinces wolf he is biting collard stalk—K543.

COLLEGE: College-educated son has father put frogs in butter to churn butter—J1689.2.

COLLIER: Collier and fuller cannot live together —U143.

COLOR: Animal colors—A2410+. SEE BLACK; BLUE; GREEN; RED; WHITE; ETC.

COLT: SEE HORSE, COLT.

COLTSFOOT: Task, plant coltsfoot plants upside down--G530.2J.

COLUMBA: Monk Columba admits water-horse to church--F420.1.3.3.1.

COLUMBIA: Origin Columbia River—A934.15.

COMB: Comb thrown turns to bamboo thicket--D454.7.2, D672; comb as ghost--E443.3.1; kind girl combs head—Q2.1.1Ba; lad steals comb from mermaid—B81.2.4; girl combs hair of three mermaids—Q2.1.1Cb; poison comb bewitches Snow White—Z65.1; sun gives comb to rooster, he puts it on head—A2321.10; girl asked to comb hair of wizard with many eyes--Q2.1.2Eb; good maid combs witch's hair--R221K.

COMMON SENSE: Mechanic works hours trying to open chest, never thinks to just lift lid-- J253. SEE ALSO SCHOLAR.

COMPANIONS: Extraordinary companions—F601; Raven creates a companion—J2186.1; skillful companions resuscitate girl--H621.1; creation of person by cooperation of skillful men— F1023.

COMPASS: Compass is unknown--J1060.4.

COMPASSIONATE: Compassionate executioner— K512; Kasiapsak refuses to kill seals, walrus— W10.3.

COMPLAINING: Fairy spins, girl not to grumble when winding or it will disappear—F348.0.1.1.

CONAL YELLOWCLAW: Conal Yellowclaw escapes blinded ogre under ram—K603.1.

CONCH: Conch hears from afar, aids hero— F601.2I.

CONDOR: SEE BIRD, CONDOR.

CONFESSION: Man discredits confession— J1155.2; confession obtained by a ruse— J1141.1; animals confess sins, weakest blamed —U11.1.1.1. SEE ALSO COURT; GUILT; JUDGE.

CONFUCIUS: Mother of Confucius steps in Unicorn's footprints--A511.1.3.4.

CONFUSION: Origin of confusion--A1382.2.

CONIFERS: Conifers flaunt green needles— A2765.2.

CONIRAYA: Condor blessed by Coniraya— A2541.3.

CONJURE BAG: Rabbit's conjure bag stolen by woodpecker—D1274.1.1.

CONJURE WIVES: D153.2.1.

CONJURER: SEE MAGICIAN.

CONNACHT: Son seeks vengeance on Connacht men--F615.3.1.5.

CONNAUGHT: Donal O'Cearan from Connaught— K1951.1K; men of Connaught destroy elves-- F302.1.6; Three Princesses of Connaught— K1931.2K.

CONNLA: Connla given magic replenishing apple --F302.1.3.

CONQUISTADORES: A972+.

CONSCIENCE: Mirror will show spots on face of any who have sinned—D1163.1.

CONSTANTES: Dragon sends Constantes to wife with letter to cook him—G610Aj.

CONSTELLATIONS: Origin—A770ff. SEE ALSO STARS.

CONTENTMENT: Student sleeping on priest's porcelain pillow finds self in wealthy future— D1812.3.3.2.1.

CONTESTS: Animal characteristics as a result of contest—A2250+; animal king chosen by contest —B236.0.1; contest in beauty—J242.1+; won by deception--K0-K99; contests in endurance --H1546; contests in lying--X905; contests in riddling--H548; roaring contest—K1715.2.1; transformation contest between magicians— D615ff. SEE ALSO GUESSING; RACE; TESTS; WISHING.

CONTRACT: First to lose temper loses contract —K172. SEE ALSO BARGAIN.

CONTRADICTIONS: "That's bad. No, that's good..."--Z51ff; chains with contradictions or extremes--Z53ff; contradictory lies--Z1791ff; tales filled with contradictions--Z19.2.

CONTRARY: Contrary wife sought for upstream --T255.2.

COOK: Crow makes friends with cook's pet pigeon so as to be able to steal food—K359.4; cook feeds dwarf, rewarded--F451.5.1.6.4; cook places pot far from fire--K231.14.1; cook who feeds fishes, given gold—F342.1.1; to cook for fairies sends them home for person's bowl, spoons, etc.—F320.3; ghost of cook sits on fire—E411.0.2.1.1; herdsman disguises as cook and answers king's questions—H561.2;

magic cooking from one bean—Q2.1.2H; gentle-man marries cook to keep her from leaving—N255.7; turtle persuades tiger's cook to put his tail in river—K553.5.3.

COOKED: Suit for chicks from boiled eggs—J1191.2; sowing cooked seeds--J1191.2; cooked bird flies away--X1258.3. SEE ALSO GLUT-TON; RECIPE; TONGUE, BOILED.

COOKING: Task, making one hundred dishes of small bird--H1022.6.0.1; dwarf asks food of each of three lads who take turns cooking—K1931.2A; glutton eats meal while cooking—K2137, W125.2; hunters argue over how to cook geese, geese fly off—J2062.4; magic wife made to cook melts—A2146.1; origin of cooking --A1455; magic cooking pot—C916.3, D1651.3; test, cooking rice with water and no wood burnt--H335.7.2; trickster says dish will be ruined if anyone looks as cooks—K1084.1.3; quest for best dish in world—H1305.2.1.

COOMACKA: Magic vegetable tree cut down, origin vegetables—A1423.0.1.1.

COON: SEE RACCOON.

COOPERATION: Skillful brothers cooperated to achieve end—F660.1; cougar has food and no fire, wildcat has fire and no food—A2378.4.15; creation by cooperation of skillful men—H621, J563.2; race won with relative helper—K11.1; all tribes push together to raise sky—A625.2.9; task, surviving on mountain top, each given half supplies needed to survive—H1546; girls work together and push witch into fire—G512.3.2.0.1.

COOT: SEE BIRD, COOT.

COPLAS: Cock given passage to Cadiz free if can please captain with coplas--J1653.1.

COPPER: Copper canoe descends from sun—F617.4; Clam Shell Boy makes bow of mother's copper bracelet, if he appears at sunset sky is red--T554.12.2; gypsy fishes old copper pots from pond—W48.2.

COPPER BIRD: SEE BIRD, COPPER.

COQUERICO: Half-chick—B171.1.2.

CORIANDER: Witch gives coriander to put in sister's soup, turns them to cows—K1911Ac.

CORK: Dancing in palace at bottom of Lough of Cork—F944.7.

CORMORANT: SEE BIRD, CORMORANT.

CORN: Bird brings flock to eat bugs off corn of good brother--J2415.18; Caribs created from corn—A1255.2; crow brings first grain of corn when comes from Land of Sun to earth—A2685.1.0.2; chicken demanded for eaten grain of corn—K251.1; man given first seeds of corn

—A1425.2; Corn Smut girl wed--K1816.0.2.2; leopard and Kenki (ball of ground corn) wres-tle—A2412.1.2.2; why flies swarm around Ken-ki—A2433.5.2.1; lies - fast growing cornstalk —X1402.3.1; Mother-Corn leads people from underworld after flood—A1024.1; test, bringing a kingdom to Nyame with only one grain—K251.1.0.1; origin of corn silk—A2685.1.0.1; silk, whiskers of man wasted away—K741.0.13; skunk stealing corn caught by gumdoll—K741.0.13; corn eaten by termite, snake eats termite, etc.--Z43.5. SEE ALSO MAIZE.

CORNET: Cornet that calls up troops—D831C.

CORPSE: Only brother will help bury murdered man--H1558.1.0.1; lad pays for burial of corpse, grateful dead man aids—E341.1A; corpse drops piecemeal down chimney--H1441.1; corpse eaten by ghosts—E256; soldier to guard corpse of princess--T173.3; corpse passed around, each thinks he killed it—K2151; corpse redeemed by payment of debts—E341.1; corpse warmed by fire or taken into bed—H1440A. SEE ALSO BODY.

CORVETTO: Jealous courtiers say Corvetto can steal ogre's horse—G601Af.

COSTUME: Ti Malice steals king's sheep "My Joy" and tells Boqui to wear sheepskin and sing "I ate my joy" at costume ball--K1066. SEE ALSO DISGUISE.

COTABATO: Stream in Cotabato runs blood red —A939.2.

COTOPAXI: Volcano—A977.5.0.5.

COTTON: Man claims others were born from his cotton tree, trick lie--X905.1.4.

COTTONTAIL: Cottontail tricks coyote by claim-ing secret—K551.30; cottontail shoots down sun —A727.4. SEE ALSO HARE.

COUCAL: Coucal wins calling contest—K11.1.1.2.

COUGAR: Cougar and wildcat cooperate—A2378.4.15.

COUNSEL: SEE ADVICE.

COUNT: Count of Estremadura—H465A; count in disguise weds haughty princess—H465; Count Roger and the Fata Morgana—Q113.3.1.

COUNTERTASKS: H1021ff, H1023.1ff, J1530.

COUNTING: Failure to count ass one is sitting on—J2031.2; counting camels by matching camels to beads on string—J2022.1; trickster crosses stream on backs of crocodiles by counting them—K579.2ff; brother saves en-chanted brothers by getting them to count selves when they emerge from river, this counting keeps them out of water until cockcrow and they are disenchanted—N455.4E; man counts up to eight and spoils song of devils—F344.1.3; girl can keep as many cattle as counts in one breath, counts by fives—F420.6.1.5.1; counting by fives—H331.18; trickster counts eggs or cubs by showing same one over and over to mother—K933; counting money, doing all day what begun—J2073.1; failure to count self—J2031ff; remarkable counter counts rest of grains in sack to verify one is missing—F660.1.1E; thieves think man counting days is counting them, confess—N611.5.

COUNTRY: At epicure's banquet peasant says of food "Let's eat it before it eats us!"—J1742.3.2; triumph of country over city—L144.2; countryman thinks city strange as cobblestones are tied up and dogs run loose—J1819.4.

COURT: Accused pleads that plaintiff bit his own ear off—J2376; lawsuit over chicks hatched from eaten egg—J1191.2; cleverness in law court—J1120-J1199; deaf litigants and deaf judge—X111.1ff; donkey to bray when thief pulls tail, guilty fears to pull—J1141.1.0.1; defendant must return house post and plaintiff must return rice eaten—K251.2.1; thief defends self by accusing mason of weak wall—J2233; thief sues owner for injuring while breaking into house—Z49.11.2; porcupine arranges trial in early morn so dog arrives shivering and appears guilty—A2494.4.14; Princess Learned-In-Law decides which of three animals did most for master—H621.3; plaintiff has stone in purse, judge thinks is bribe and favors—K1765; series of clever, unjust decisions—J1173. SEE ALSO JUDGE; LAW; LAWYER.

COURTING: Bat, spider and beetle court together and discomfit each other—T92.11.3; crane rejected by heron—W123.2; hare and possum court together, hare causes trouble—T92.11.2; leopard and rabbit court—T92.11.4; trickster rides dupe courting—K1241.1; rivals go courting together—T92.11.2ff; one who makes dust rise from stone to wed—K62.1; suitor tests—H310ff. SEE ALSO SUITOR.

COUSIN: Hen and crocodile as cousins—K601.3.

COVERLET: Coverlet with bells stolen—F54.2; trickster meows and ogress thinks is cat, steals coverlet—G610Ab. SEE ALSO BLANKET; QUILT; SHEET.

COW: Woman drives cows into river to drink and drowns—J1903.5; dupe convinced cow is goat (donkey)—K110.1; cattle going back into barn to be dupe's—K171.10; dwarf cares for man's cows all winter—F460.4.2; cows eaten by fairies and made whole again—F243.3.1.1; fat from inside of cow cut out—F929.3; wife refuses to let husband drink milk of future cow—J2060.1.2; gypsy lad throws cows over sea, hangs onto tail of last—X1133.8; Hedley

cow—E427; helpful cow with food in ears—B335.2F; cow tricked into running horn into tree—K771; girl wears cow's head as punishment—B641Ag; cow judges in favor of adder, not man—J1172.3.2; cow judges in favor of lion, not man—J1172.3.2; cow holds back half milk for little people—F348.7.1.2; magic cow from water world—B184.2.2.2; magic cows give gold milk—B103.3.2; cows give ponds of milk—X1235; cow drowns in milk—X1235.2a; man kills milk giving cows—D876.3; kind girl milks cow—Q2.1.2Ab, Q2.1.2Cb; dead mother's return as helpful cow—B313.1.1; people see each other as cows, onions eaten remedy—D551.2.5; trickster gives cow which leads parson's one hundred back to him—K366.1.1; hot peppers fed cows, so they flee tax collector—K1181.1; Prince of Seven Golden Cows—B103.3.2; cow grazed on roof—J1904.1; cow grazed on roof, numskull ties rope to leg—J2132.2; Saint Cadog to send one hundred cows for each of King Arthur's soldiers chosen—D1711.6.6; magic cow spins flax—D830.1.1; magic cow spins, flax put in cow's mouth and pulled out nose—Q2.1.1E; mother turned into cow which spins for girl—R221Bc; "which cow can say I have tail and horns at same end of body?" Neither, cows can't talk—K881.2; Tom Thumb eaten by cow—F535.1.1B; girl turned to cow by witch, later witch in cow form killed by St. Anthony's statue—G263.1.3.1; Witch of Pendle drowns in streams of milk—G274.1.1. SEE ALSO BUFFALO.

COW, BULL: Bucca as bull chases boy—G303.3.1.4.1; girl wed to Black Bull of Norroway—H1385.5B; bull runs around stack so fast butts self—X1236; bull as man courts woman—B650.2; priest turns dead souls to cattle—E423.1.8.2; fight between giant bulls—B264.7; gnat apologizes for lighting on bull's horns—J953.10; bull pursued by lion has no time to fight goat—J371.1; grateful bull draws one hundred carts on wager for master—B587.3; helpful bull with food in horns—B335.2; lion convinces bull to have horns cut off—J642.1.1; bull promised to Jupiter if man escapes lion—J561.2; lion succeeds when bull's separate—J1022; bull and lion made enemies by jackal—K1084.1.2; bull invited by lion sees cooking preparations and flees—J425.2; magic bull—B184.2.3; Jean Sotte sent for bull's milk—H952.1; mother feigns ill and needs strip of hide of Black Bull of the Forest—S12.1B; mouse torments bull—L315.2; origin of lake, pawing of great bull—A920.1.2; origin of river, furrow by great bull—A934.1; origin of mountains, rock tossed by great bull—A934.11; origin of valleys, where bull landed—A983.1; Rain Spirit as bull courts woman—F433.0.1; Red Bull becomes giant, eats all but youngest—K1611Dc; fairy calf rescues girl from waterhorse—F420.1.3.4; prize for capture of wild wild bulls. Lad raised them—B389.4, H1331.3.

COW, CALF: Baby fed to cow reborn as calf, woos girl—B335.2H; Bouki asks where calf sleeps at night—K688.3; calf of the bull—J1191.1.3; cow punished for calf's misdeeds—J1863; little bull calf gives provisions from ears, killed and bones clothe ash-maid—R221F; calf of the goat —J1191.1.2; calf's head in murderer's hand turns to corpse's head—Q551.3.3; calf of the horse—J1191.1.1; calf Lembu Gumarong tries to destroy rice, battle of the gods ensues— A162, A2685.6.1.1; quest for calf that makes music—H1331.3.4; amber ring from inside head of calf—G530.2Bk; calf pities ox, calf slaughtered—L456; calf from Sumatra kills Javanese bull—B264.6; calf persuades wolf to sing—K561.2.

COW, COWHERD: Cowherd disenchants dancing princesses—F1015.1.1D; heavenly cowherd and spinning maid—A778.3.1; Krishna the Avenger worshipped by cowherds—A489.6.

COW, COWHIDE: Magpie in cowhide—K842; oracular cowhide sold—K114.1; raven in cowhide feigned to prophecy—J1344.1; dupes kill cows to sell hides—K842.

COW, COWSHED: Numskull pokes hole into neighbor's cowshed and thinks has found treasure cave—J2201.2.

COW, HEIFER: Fool rides heifer—J2461.1Aa.

COW, HOLY: Holyman says holy cow is priceless —D1960.5.

COW, OX: Ox bequeaths man middle age—B592; ox aids mistreated stepdaughter—R2211; ass thinks self equal of ox—J952; ox criticizes axletrees for groaning—J953.21; ox to be shaved by cheating barber—J1511.17.1; ox beaten for misdeed committed a week ago—J1861; bluff - bringing ten oxen—K1741.2.1; ox builds house, others intrude—K1161.2; oxen fear inexperienced butchers—J215.2; jealous calf slaughtered—L456; chain, oxen received—K251.1.4.1; oxen killed, dogs flee—J2211.3; why fly watches ox's eyes——A2479.9; eyeglasses for ox—K92.4; ox loves men's strokes, flea fears—U142; ox sold for handful of coppers, court allows to claim hand as well—J1511.17; helpful ox with food in horns—B335.2E, B335.2H; donkey tells ox to feign ill and escape work—K1633.1; intruder thinks ox is man with pitchfork—K1161.1; why ox has no hair on lips—A2221.5.1; magic ox —B184.2.2; Saint Neot calls wild animals to plow when oxen are stolen—V229.28; oxen size of peppercorn—B184.2.2.3; ox envies pig's diet, pig killed—J212.2; why ox shares food and quarters with rat—A2493.37; stolen rope has ox on end—K188; fool loans ox to rosebush—J1853.3; should have seen ox run when just a calf—J2212.5; ox skull judges in favor of tiger—J1172.3.2; ox sold for five pennies tied to twelve florin cock—K182; childless couple treat ox as son—T553.1; animals caught on tarred straw ox—Z32.4.1; tails of cows are buried in ground and trickster tells dupe that cows have sunken out of sight in the mud—K404.1ff; oxen made of tallow are given to gods as an offering —K236.1.1.

COWARD: Coward climbs tree, bear sniffs comrade—J1488; cowardly duelers—K2323; cowardly fools—J2600-J2649; coward falls on hyena's back —N392.1.3; coward falls on tiger's back—N392.1.1.1; lion becomes intoxicated and drunken coward rides—N691.1.2.1; coward gloats over robber slain by another—W121.2.5; numskull rushes up to first traveler met and surrenders sword—W211.6; 'brave' man claims woman's name when captured—K514.0.1.

COWARDICE: SEE W121.

COWRIE SHELL: Good luck charm, cowries reproduce—N421.1; Iwa steals red cowrie—K301B.

COWSLIP: Girl lives until her cowslip is pulled—E765.3.4.

COYOTE: Coyote given false recipe for acorns—J2724; coyote stuck in alder stump—K741; coyote and badger farm—K171.1; coyote as beggar is tricked by old woman—K1982.1; coyote releases bison for men—A1878.3; enmity between blackbirds and coyote—A2494.12.4.1, K711.5; coyote gets shortest bow at distribution, hence least power—A2235.2; coyote swings girl too high and buffalo carry her off—R111.1.13.2; coyote dives for reflected chokecherries—J1791.3.5; cicada (locust) leaves skin with rock inside—K525.1.4; origin Columbia River, coyote struggles with monster—A934.15; cottontail tricks coyote by claiming secret—K551.30; crop division, bear and coyote—K171.1; coyote tricks prairie dogs into dancing with eyes closed—K826.1; coyote brings dead back—F81.1.0.5; Coyote (Itsayaya) rules that man shall die—A1335.18; dog tries to live life of coyote—K414.3.4; coyote sends duck diving for first earth—A812.4; why coyote's eyes are large—A2332.3.1.1; coyote throws eyes into air—J2423.1; return feast, each insults other—J1565.1.4; coyote plans relay to steal fire—A1415.2.2ff; coyote breaks witch's dam and releases fish—A1421.0.0.1; coyote tricked by fox into holding rock (K1251), diving for moon (J179.1.3), climbing tree—K553.1.0.5; coyote tricks giant into cutting off legs—G524.0.2; Great Spirit sends coyote to eat grasshoppers—A2108.1; coyote tricked into bag to escape 'hail' —K711.5; coyote believes hornet's nest is bell—K1023.1.0.2; Coyote kills monster Iltswetrix—F912.2.9; coyote imitates food procuring activities—J2425; coyote befriends Karoks—A2235.2; coyote lures giant lizard into swamp—B11.2.1.2.2; coyote as creator gives man lizard hand—A1311.1.1; coyote makes image of man, creator—A1241.3.2; mice trick coyote into bag—K711.5; coyote opens mole's bag of fleas—J2131.2.2; why coyote howls at moon—A717.2; taken to moon, Coyote (Ejupa) loses hold, falls. Why howls at moon—A2427.4.1; coyote dives for moon—J1791.3; coyote's muzzle pulled long—A2213.2.1.1; coyote tricks otter into water—A2433.2.2.1; Coyote (Ejupa), crow steal pine nuts, drop in valleys—A1425.0.1.2; coyote feigns ill, wins race—K11.5; hare frees rattlesnake, coyote reenacts—J1172.3; coyote tricked, holds up rock—K1251; rolling rock pursues coyote—C91.1; coyote gets secret of sapsucker's hairdo—J2449.1; coyote drops basket of fish, water runs off forming Snake River—A934.16; coyote wants to learn locust's song—G555.1.2; coyote forces hare to sing song—G555.1.3; coyote steals springtime--A1151.1; coyote throws stars into sky--A763.3; why coyote steals food—R111.1.13.2; magic stone is mocked by coyote—D931.0.6; coyote conquers sucking monster—F913.5; coyote steals summer--A1151.1.1; coyote steals sun—A721.1.5; coyote shoots arrow chain into sun—B11.2.1.2.2; coyote makes sun and moon of tule grass—A717.2; supernatural coyote sins, becomes ordinary--A1834.1; why coyote has bushy tail--A2378.6.2; coyote makes cedar-bark tail to visit bullsnake—J1565.1.3.1; why coyote has short tail--A2378.4.12; why coyote has white tail tip--A1415.2.2.1.2; tail in ice, coyote tricks bear--K1021; tail in ice, bear tricks coyote--K1021; coyote climbs pine tree, it grows to heaven—D482.1.2; dog arranges for coyote to feign stealing turkey, coyote really steals—K231.1.3.1; coyote tells baby Hopi Turtle to sing or will eat--G555.1.1; coyote's voice—A2426.1.7; coyote vanquishes Weasel Woman Tsihlihla—G262.6; coyote tries to destroy four witches--A2441.1.15.

COYOTE LAKE: Origin—A920.1.0.1.1.

CRAB: Anansi eats crabs as he baptizes them--K1961.1.6; land-crabs ride in canoe--A2317.13; crab cuts ways out of cat's stomach--Z33.2.1; crab helps crocodile sham death--K607.3; crab pinches neck of crow--K815.14.2; Da-Trang in form of sand crab searches for jewels—B216B; why crab's eyes are out of head—A2231.10; crab breaks claws preparing for feast—Z32.6; origin of fiddler crab—A2171.2.1; why crab is flat—A2305.6; crab flees men—C432.1.2; crab rides fox's tail—K11.2; golden crab asks to wed princess—B647.1.1.1; crab pinches off deceitful heron's neck—J631, K953.3; crab comes ashore, killed--J512.1; crab tries to catch moon--B94.1; crabs in basket of nuts—H1377.3; old woman protected by objects which attack intruding ogre—K1161.3.5; crab scorned as peacemaker—J411.6; what's in the dish, "Poor Crab"—N688; river from pond into which crab's head is thrown—A934.13; crab trades fruit for seed—K1161.6; origin crab's shell—C432.1.2.1; whale killed by painting magic symbols of crab, hand, star and kayak on left hand and on kayak—B877.1; giant crab causes tides—A913.5; father tries to teach child to walk straight--U121.1; crab criticizes child for not walking straight—J1063.1; crab walks backwards—U121.1; why crabs chase waves--A2171.2.1; crab betrays witch's name—C432.1.2.

CRADLE: Ghostly cradle rocks by self—F473.2.1.1.

CRAFT: Culture hero teaches arts and crafts—A541; crafts taught by tiny god—A541.0.1.

CRANBERRIES: What will cranberries do if wolves come?--J641.2.

CRANE: SEE BIRD, CRANE.

CRAWDAD: SEE CRAYFISH.

CRAYFISH: Color of crayfish—A2411.5.10; crayfish dives for earth in primeval sea—A812.5; crayfish has eyes at back of head--A2231.1.3.1; crayfish summons fish for cormorant who carries them off—K815.14; raccoon feigns dead and catches crayfish—K751.0.4; seven men attack crayfish—J2612; why crayfish lives in streams under stones—A2433.9.

CRAZY HORSE: Chews flint to powder, becomes invincible—A526.1.1.1.

CREATION: Creation contest, Jupiter, Neptune, Minerva—A46; distribution of qualities at creation—A2235+; owl punished for watching creation of hare—A2332.1.5; Panku creates world—A610. SEE ALL A600ff Creation of the universe; A700-A799 Creation of heavenly bodies; A800-A899 Creation of earth; A1200-A1299 Creation of man; A1700-A2199 Creation of animal life.

CREATOR: punishment for looking while creator makes hare--A2491.2.3; creator driven off, Mulungu climbs spider web rope back to sky—A1279.2. SEE ALL A0-A99 Creator.

CRECHE: Origin first creche--D1622.2.3.

CREST: Origin of bird's crest--A231ff; origin crest of Florence—G302.7.1.2; origin golden mouse as family crest—B437.2.1.

CRIB: Hunchback carves crib for Christ Child—D1622.2.1.

CRICKET: Origin cricket's chirp—A2426.3.4; lad dreams is cricket, fights—E423.10; grateful cricket spirit aids lad—E423.10; hare has cricket dress opossum's tail for dance—A2317.12; ass wants voice of cricket—J512.8; cricket borrows earthworm's voice—A2241.12; war between insects and animals started by lion and crickets—B263.9; cricket sees cricket wings in fox's excrement and avoids fox—K2061.10.

CRIM: Old Woman Crim tries to keep owls until after daylight--J233.2.1.1.

CRIME: Accidental discovery—N611ff; crime comes to light—N270ff.

CRIPPLED: Deaf hears scream, blind sees, crippled runs for help—X1791.1.

CRITICISM: Momus driven from Olympus for fault finding—A46.

CROCODILE: Why crocodile's back is rough—A2356.2.11; crocodile hiding in berry patch deceived into rolling--K607.2.2; bridge of crocodiles crossed by small trickster—K579.2.1; crocodile tricked into blowing bubbles—K607.2.4; crocodile grabs leg of bullock when carter complies with request to put crocodile back into water—J1172.3.0.3; hare builds 'house' (cage) for crocodile—K714.2.4.2; man who can call crocodiles—B491.3; man trapped in cave by crocodiles—A2493.4.1; Kantchil takes census of crocodiles—K579.2.1; trickster eats all alligator's cubs, counts last cub over many times to deceive—K933; crow leads crocodile to "better" river, strands—K815.14.2; sham dead crocodile obeys suggestion to wag tail—K607.3; crocodiles have loaned their gamelan to villagers for feast—A2130.2; alligator burnt in grass—K1055.2; first suitor plays harp and charms crocodiles, second shoots crocodiles, third saves drowning girl—H621.2.2; hare causes crocodile to laugh and escapes from mouth—K561.1.0.1; hen and crocodile are cousins—K601.3; animal calls to house , and hiding crocodile answers—K607.1; crocodile freed from fallen tree by Karbau threatens to eat—J1172.3.0.1; Kantchil tricks crocodile biting his foot—K543.0.1; crocodile masks as log—K607.2; crocodile wants heart of monkey—K544; crocodile opens mouth and closes eyes—K561.3; crocodile allowed to eat King's peppers—K1023.1.4; cooking pot rules in favor of crocodile—J1172.3.2.1; alligator needs Brer Rabbit's gizzard—K544; reincarnation as crocodile—E614.3; crocodile brings ring from river—B582.2F; crocodile masking as rock betrays self—K607.2.1, K607.2.3; crocodiles cause storm to hinder pursuers—B491.3; alligator favors tiger over man in dispute—J1172.3.2; crocodile arranges trek of animals to new water hole, puts elephants in rear and raises alarm—A2494.11.2; magic wife melts when cooking, runs into river and becomes alligator—A2146.1.

CRONE: Three deformed crones help with spinning—D2183.1.

CROOKED: Crooked mouth family—X131.

CROOKSHANKS: Wolf cursed by Saint Nicholas to go crookshanks—K254.1.

CROPS: Deceptive division of crops—K171.1; crops destroyed by king restored by magic flute—D1563.1.4.1; origin of farming custom—A1529.1.

CROSS: Baby branded with cross so mermaid mother cannot claim—B81.2.4; devil cannot name "cross"—G303.16.8.2; devil driven away by cross—G303.16.3.1; crosses on ducats thwart devil—G303.12.5.8; dwarf cannot leave cross once touched—F451.5.1.6.3; baby found turns into Tiyanak demon, helpless at sight of cross—G303.16.3.1.

CROW: SEE BIRD, CROW.

CROWBAR: Crowbar tossed to uncle—G501E.

CROWING: Why cocks crow—A2421.6; devil deceived by man's crowing—G303.16.19.4.1; crowing scares off oni—N777.0.2. SEE ALSO CHICKEN, COCKCROW.

CROWN: Magic crown from snake's father—D882.1Ba; crowns exchanged from ogre's children—K1611C; Tsar tosses crown into air, to fall on one to wed princess—H171.7.

CRUSADER: Returning Crusader drops ring in

cup—H94.4.1.

CRUELTY: Tribe cruel to mountain goats is destroyed—A1587.1.1. SEE ENTIRE CHAPTER S.

CRYING: Origin of crying child's habit of answering "nothing" when asked why they cry—A1579.2; girl will bear sons which cause sunshine when they laugh, rain when cry—N455.4Ab. SEE ALSO GRIEF; WEEPING.

CRYSTAL: Silver saucer and transparent apple—E632.0.4; stonecutter makes crystal ball for mouse to hide in—B437.2.2; crystal box tells news of world—H621.1.1; crystal coffin—F852.1, Z65.1; crystal flute sounds from crystal—E633.1.

CU: SEE BIRD, CU.

CUBIT: Princess weds snake prince in palace of Cubits—D735.1F.

CUCHULAIN: Giant allows hero to cut off his head, will cut off hero's next—M221; Finn McCoul's wife frightens off Cuchulain—K521.4.1.

CUCKOLD: Husband feigning wife's voice has lover put finger through hole in wall and cuts it off—K1561.2; cuckold reveals presence by rhyme—K1556.

CUCKOO: SEE BIRD, CUCKOO.

CUCULLIN: SEE CUCHULAIN.

CUDDY: SEE SAINT CUTHBERT.

CUDGEL: Magic object stolen by host—D861.1.

CULLODEN: Ghostly battle reenacted—E502.

CULTIVATION: Origin of vegetables—A1423.0.1.1.

CUP: Fairy cup stolen—F352.1; flute sounds from crystal cup—E633.1.

CUPATIZO: River Cupatizo changes course—A934.14.

CURACHON: Elfin hound of Curachon—F302.1.6.

CURASSOW: SEE BIRD, CURASSOW.

CURE: Grateful animal shows man how to save life—B522.1. SEE ALSO DOCTOR; HEALING; MEDICINE.

CURIOSITY: Test of curiosity—H1554.

CURSE: "May the Devil swallow the horses"—C12.5.9; a woman sticks carding combs into Devil's back, her curses—K171.1.1; devil refuses to take anything not offered with whole heart—M215; dog won't catch turtles, obeys when man begins cursing—Z41.11; fairy lays curse on child—D1960.3; curse to break leg in forty days—M405; magic plow to leave if man curses—D1209.3; woman curses beggar as swine, bears pig-headed child—T551.3; transformation through curse—D525; curse on treasure—N591; enraged old woman prophesies for youth who knocked her over—N301.2.1.

CURTAINS: Task, making bed curtains of two skeins of silk—H1022.3.1.

CUSTOMS: SEE ALL ENTRIES A1500-A1599.

CUTHBERT: SEE SAINT CUTHBERT.

CUZCO: Golden sun from Cuzco temple gambled away—V400.1; God Pachacamac gives magic sandals to quipu carrier in Cuzco—D1521.1.1.

CYCLOPS: Odysseus and Cyclops—K602.0.1.

CYMBAL: Monkeys invent instruments—A1461.0.1.

CYPRESS: Dame Fortune offers gift, man chooses ever full purse—D1192.1.

CZAR: Chilbik ordered to fetch ogress's treasure for Czar—G610Aj. SEE ALSO TSAR.

DAILRIARDGH: King of Dailriardgh asleep in mountain—D1960.2.

DAKWA: Giant fish eats man—F912.2.13.

DAM: Dams thrown up by coyote form falls—A935.1; dam constructed prevents future floods and makes sacrifices to dragon unnecessary—R111.1.3Db; birds commanded to build dam by Rain God—A2431.3.9; coyote breaks witch's dam and releases fish—A1421.0.0.1.

DAM, BIG BIRD DAM: Aids lad in quest for stolen princess—H1385.1F.

DAMAGES: Bull eaten by lions, given goat, goat stolen, given butter, etc.—K2138; eaten grain and the cock as damages—K251.1.

DANCE: Hero thrown to wild boars plays flute and they dance—H328.9; Bouki learns king's secret dance—H529.1; girl dancing with demons sends them for articles of clothing, thus procrastinates until cock crows—Q2.1.3A; magic drum causes dancing—D1415.2.7; saints have to dance when hear drums—D2174.1; trickster persuades ducks (prairie dogs) to dance with eyes closed—K826; dwarfs remove wen when man dances—F344.1.2; persuades captors to dance, escapes—K606.2; mortal wins fairies' gratitude, plays for dance—F331.4; magic fiddle causes dancing—D1415.2.5ff; magic flute causes dancing—D1415.2.3ff; fox transformed to maiden dances for benefactors—D612.2.1; visiting chief (ghost) refuses to dance, feet do not bruise leaves—E421.2.1.1; dupe to dance in grass, grass set afire—K1055; hare plays balafon for dancing guinea fowl—K714.2.4.1; magic harp makes people dance—F348.7.1.3; spider dances "hat shaking dance"—W125.3.1; dancing caused by

magic kettle—D1415; kid persuades wolf to play for him to dance, Gods guarding flock hear and come—K561.2; lions invite animal to dance planning to push goats into fire—A2378.2.2.1; origin of male and female dance styles—A1542.1.1; origin of dance—A1542; eight children dance despite warning, are Pleiades—A773.4.1.2; escape by pretending to dance so as to be untied—K551.3.2, K571; Rabbi Simon and eighty men dance with witches of Ascalon holding them helpless over heads—G273.8; evil clan who slay others after dancing contest are turned to rattlesnakes with dancing rattles fixed to tails—A2145.9.1; sheep dance and sing—K606; shoes found danced to pieces—F1015.1.1; Anansi's singing compels Granny to dance—D2174.2; sun dance taught to Scarface—H1284.1; dancing teakettle—D1171.3.1; old man joins dance of tengus, they take his wen—F344.1.1.

DANCER: Dancer stabs spectator using dance routine as ruse—N455.3.

DANES: Danes steal largest of church bells of Boshom, ship sinks—F993.3; task, fetch flail from hell, Danes flee, flail burns way back to hell—G610Ak.

DANUBE: Task, fetch maiden of marvelous beauty from bottom of Danube—H1213.1D.

DAPPLEGRIM: Foal aids—H321F.

DARE: Cobbler dared to cobble in haunted chalet—H1411.4.1; tailor dared to sew in haunted church—H1412.2. SEE ALSO BRAVERY.

DARK PATRICK: L223.

DARKNESS: Chant—dark behind, light before—R221Bb; person enters dark, dark house, down dark, dark hall, etc.—Z13.1.4; fool cannot find right hand in dark—J1735; fool wakes with shutters closed and thinks it still night—J1819.3.1; fools hunt object outside since it is too dark to search inside—J1925; King of Greece's daughter enchanted by King of Darkness—E341.1B. SEE ALSO NIGHT.

DATE: Man counts days of month by putting pebbles in pot, daughter throws in handful—J2466.2.

DATES: Lucky man succeeds even when selling dates in Cairo—N427; magic date tree provides clothing for maid—R221C; thankful dates grow on trees and pumpkins on vine—J2571.

DA-TRANG: Da-Trang still searches for lost jewel in form of sand crab—B216B.

DAUGHTER: Baker's daughter becomes owl—A1958.0.1; girl who obeys mother becomes golden bee—A2012.0.1.1; angry father gives daughter to beggar—H465; virgin daughter casts self into molten metal to make perfect bell for father—S261.0.2; homely daughter to overcome face with character—J244.1; daughter makes series of excuses—Z18.2; father beats daughter before she fetches water to prevent her breaking pitcher—J2175.1; girl dreams father, brothers are drowning—A421.1.2; daughter sent by father as Knight to Sultan—H1578.1.7; moon brings food under her long nails for mother the star—A759.8; daughter promised to ogre as bride—D735.1, H1385.4; daughter loves father like "salt"—H592.1; king has seventh daughter abandoned, she becomes guardian spirit of mudangs—D2161.5.7.1; daughter turned to spider for disobeying mother—A2091.2; tall tale teller's daughter vanquishes visiting storyteller—J31.0.1; girl turned to turtle for refusing to obey mother—A2147.1; daughter-in-law tests, bring wind and fire wrapped in paper—H506.12; youngest daughter banished by father—H592.1. SEE ALSO MOTHER.

DAUGHTER, SUPERNATURAL: Fox daughter—D612.2.1. SEE ALSO SELECTED ITEMS B600-B699 Marriage of person to animal.

DAVID, KING: Escapes by shamming madness—K523.1.

DAW: SEE BIRD, DAW.

DAWN: Blue Jay and Ground Squirrel get basket containing Dawn and release it—A721.1.2; bush fowl refuses to wake the sun—Z49.6.0.2; contest animal calls the dawn—B755.3; contest, first to greet the other in morning wins—K176.1; Dawn People hoard seeds—A1425.0.1.1; Raven calls at dawn and supernatural creatures must retire—C752.2.1.1; elder sister goes out at dawn to wash in dew—H1385.6.1; Dawn binds Night and turns maid into star over forehead—B642.6.2; sun rises as result of animal's call—B755.1; task, come neither by day nor by night, comes at dawn—H1057; wagtail sent to peck sunrise free—A1179.2.2; witch powerless at cockcrow—G273.3. SEE ALSO COCKCROW; DAYLIGHT; MORNING; SUNRISE.

DAY OF WEEK: Countertask, send groom for horse neither on Monday, Tuesday, Wednesday, etc.—H1078; fairies remove hump from man who finishes their song, adding day of week to it—F344.1.3.

DAYDREAM: SEE ALL ENTRIES J2060-J2063ff for disasters caused by daydreaming.

DAYLIGHT: Chipmunk sings up daylight—A2217.2; lad digs up hidden light of day and releases—H1385.1C. SEE ALSO DAWN; LIGHT.

DAYTIME: Djabbe with seven horns killed by cutting from within, purse found in stomach gives day and night—F912.2.8. SEE ALSO NIGHT.

DEAD: SEE DEATH.

DEAF: Deaf persons misunderstand each other, go to court over lost animal—X111.1ff; deaf man visits the sick, plans conversation ahead of time and gives set answers—X111.9; feigning deafness to lure enemy close to kill him—K911.5; fox (pig) feigns deaf to lure pancake closer—K911.5, Z33.1.7; deaf man hears scream, blind sees, crippled runs for help—X1791.1; deaf man gives inappropriate remarks—X111.10ff; deafness magically cured by badger—D2161.3.5.1; scribe uses large letters writing to deaf—J2242.2.1.

DEATH: SEE ENTIRE CHAPTER E. Death's agent gives man money to live well until Death arrives—J217.0.1.1.1; Ananse claims children killed dead boy and demands tribute for Nyame—K251.1.0.1; man on deathbed tells wife to dress up in her finery and maybe Angel of Death will take her instead—X773; red ant advises Saynday not to revive dead—A1335.8.1, A2355.1.2.2; man granted power to see Death at head or foot of bed, turns bed—D1825.3.1ff; Death overlooks man when pages in Book of Life stick together—K975.1.2; Death magically bound to tree—K213, Q565, Z111.2ff; Death given dry bread to crunch—K611.5; Death tricked into bunghole—K213; Death shows that candle of princess is nearly out—D1724; cat wants creatures to die, distracts dog sent to ask creator to let man live forever—A1335.16; Death trapped in coffin—K213; man unwilling to go with Death wastes away among corn, whiskers still seen on corn ears—A2685.1.0.1; Death treats all equally, preferred to God—D1825.3.1, J486.1; feigned death—SEE DEATH, FEIGNED below; fool thinks self dead—J2311.1ff; fool mistakes identity of dead—J2311.2.0.1; fool goes home to tell wife he is dead—J2242.0.1; fool refuses to read prayers over dead friend since they had a quarrel and friend wouldn't listen anyway—J2549.3; fool thinks sleeping anteater is dead—J1959.4; boy's glance kills—S366.1; Godfather Death—D1825.3.1; grateful dead aid hero—E341.1; man takes refuge from robbers in open grave—J2311.3ff; Itsayaya loses daughter to death, vows men too shall die—A1335.18; death imprisoned in knapsack—K213; journey to land of dead to bring back person—F81.1ff; giant makes love to dead son of Khan, hoe and shovel which spirit used to unearth body turn to twigs and grow to sky palace—B652.1.1; Maui tries to kill Death, Hine Nui—A310.1.1; Cholera, Death and Fear visit Mecca—Z111.7; Death's three messengers—J1051.1; in country of ghosts gold given turns to paper money buried at funerals—F129.4.4; man in moon shoots souls of dead—A751.0.4; imagined death of mother-in-law causes mutual mistaken mourning by husband and wife—P262.2; origin of death—A1311.1.1, A1335ff; death penalty to be carried out after payment of one hundred mon fine at rate of one mon per year—J1173.1.2; Raven says some must die or world will run out of food—A1335.8.2; Nyame resuscitates boy—A185.12.1; animals revive dead man—B529.3; dog wants God to revive dead—A1335.16; death sentence escaped by propounding riddle—H542; riddle, "I drank with my death"—H808; riddle, "When will the world end? First, when my wife dies, second when I die"—H707.2; riddle, "How long will man continue to live and die? Until heaven and hell are full."—H887; origin custom of giving paper

objects to dead instead of living <u>sacrifices</u>—
A1547.1.1; Death to send <u>signs</u> before coming—
J1051.1; hero in Land of Dead settles quarrels
between <u>skeletons</u>—H1385.3Fh; woman wishes
for light and death, every dead <u>soul</u> becomes a
new star—A1335.17; <u>sun</u> will allow man to live
forever if his dead daughter can be brought
back from the dead—F81.1.0.2; <u>swan</u> sings song
at death—B752.1; man dying because of with-
ing <u>tree</u> in garden—N452.1.2; <u>trickster</u> overhears man praying for death to take him, trickster appears in disguise and says he is Devil—
J217.0.1.1; <u>Vishnu</u> strikes down Asura king—
D1840.1.4; to cover dead girl with lotus blossoms and <u>wait</u>, opens flowers too soon—
G530.2Bj; <u>Water</u> of Death substituted for Water
of Life and ogre kills self—G561.1 Fillmore; obstinate <u>wife</u> dies for third egg—T255.4; <u>wife</u>
given last request asks that husband die when
she does—J1545.4.2; <u>wife</u> dies and man does not
grieve, donkey dies and grieves—X771; old man
<u>wishes</u> for death, changes mind when death ap-
pears—C11. SEE ALSO ENTIRE CHAPTER E.
DEATH. SEE ALSO GHOSTS; GRAVE; HELL;
SOULS; ETC.

DEATH, FEIGNED: Sham dead animal tricked into
<u>betraying</u> self—K607.3; <u>bird</u> feigns dead and es-
capes hunter—K522.4ff; <u>boy</u> feigns death and
Spider returns stolen eggs, fearing Death—
K1867; <u>capture</u> by feigning death—K751ff; <u>cat</u>
feigns death, eats mouse pallbearers—K827.4.1;
<u>crane</u> with one thought feigns death and is
thrown out of trap—J1662.2; <u>cock</u> feigns death
to hear what hens say about <u>him</u>—H1556.1.1;
man feigns death to consort with <u>dead</u>—E463.2;
death feigned to avoid <u>debt</u>—K341.2.0.1; <u>deer</u>
feigns death and is thrown out of snare, crow
distracts farmer and deer flees—K642.3; <u>escape</u>
by shamming death—K522ff; the fox plays <u>dead</u>
and is thrown on a wagon of <u>fish</u>. He throws
the fish off—K371.1; the <u>hare</u> pretends to be
dead. He is thrown on a <u>basket</u> of bananas—
—K371.1; embarassed <u>hemp</u> smoker and hemp
grower feign death and are put in grave—
K1869.1; lion tied to tail of sham dead <u>horse</u>—
J2132.5.3; animal tied to sham dead <u>horse's</u> tail
—K1047; <u>husband</u> feigns dead and forces wife
to talk—T255.8; death feigned to meet <u>lover</u>—
K1837.9, K1862; <u>man and wife</u> feign dead—
J2511.1.2.1; why <u>oppossum</u> plays dead when
caught—A2466.1; <u>parrot</u> feigns dead and is
thrown out of cage—K522.4.0.1; dead man believes himself dead because wise man <u>predicted</u>
his death—J2311.1.6; <u>raccoon</u> feigns death to
catch crayfish—K751.0.4; animal feigns dead on
<u>road</u> repeatedly and entices owner from goods—
K341.2.1; <u>spider</u> feigns dead and asks to be
buried near garden—K341.2; death feigned to
<u>steal</u>, avoid debt, work, etc.—K341.2ff.

DEBT: Death feigned to <u>avoid</u> debt—K341.2.0.1;
parson tells borrower to get <u>corn</u> in same place
he got it last year, he has not returned it yet—
J1381; <u>origin</u> of debt—Z49.20; Anansi advises
man in debt to say "whoever drinks this <u>palm</u>
oil takes debt", how debt came to the Ashanti—
A1378; <u>tortoise</u> claims debt money is in lost
grinding stone—A2433.3.19.0.1.

DEBTORS: Zomo invites debtors at same time,
dung-beetle flees cock, etc.—Z43.6.4.

DECEPTION PASS: Hair of maiden still seen drifting in waters of Deception Pass—B82.1.3.

DECIDUOUS: Glooskap promises that dead trees
will always revive in spring—A2760.2. SEE
ALSO TREES.

DEEP: "What is deepest?"—H643.1.

DEER: Deer in <u>age</u> debate—B841.1.6; why deer
has <u>antlers</u>—A2326.1.1.1; deer children trick
<u>bear cubs</u> in smoky hole—K851.1; lady deer
<u>courted</u> by hare and leopard—K1241.1; deer
<u>feigns dead</u> in snare—K642.3; <u>dreaming</u> of sell-
ing hide of sleeping deer—J2061.3; <u>golden deer</u>
saves man but is betrayed—B241.2.10.1.1; deer
<u>head</u> on stick turns to nightingale and lime tree
—Q2.1.5Ba; brother transformed when drinks
from animal's <u>hoofprints</u>—P253.2.0.1; deer to be
<u>hunted</u>—N455.4D; <u>Kwatee the Changer</u> changes
man making tools into animals, knife becomes
deer's antlers—A2262.4; three sons left magic
bow, <u>magic deer</u>, magic bird—F660.1F; animal
in maiden form—F302.4.2.2; deer thought to be
<u>man</u> with chair on head—J1762.4; <u>marriage</u> to
deer in human form—B651.5; deer challenges
<u>rabbit</u> to jump river, then widens it magically—
D483.1.1; deer <u>saves</u> man, man betrays deer—
W154.2.2.1; man shoots deer through his <u>shirt</u>
—J2235.1; why deer has short <u>tail</u>—A2378.4.10;
why deer has short <u>teeth</u>—A2345.3.1; tree grows
from deer's head—X1130.2; deer freed by turtle, crow—K642.2; sick <u>wolf</u> gets fox to bring
deer to dance for him, kills—J644.1.1; hide
fairy's feather robe, deer advises woodcutter—
F302.4.2.0.3. SEE ALSO ELK, REEDBUCK.

DEER, BANYAN: Banyan deer king offers self in
place of victim—B241.2.10.1.

DEER, DOE: One-eyed doe outwitted by approaching from <u>blind</u> side—K929.2.

DEER, FAWN: Fawn flees in spite of horns—
U121.2.1.

DEER, HART: Hart hidden in hay noticed by
master—J1032.

DEER, STAG: Stag tries to <u>borrow</u> grain from
sheep using wolf as security—J1383; stag eating
vine <u>discovered</u>—J582.2; <u>ghost</u> of Great White
Stag protects animals from timber wolf—
E423.2.6.1; stag Golden Antlers as Smolicheck's
guardian—K815.15C; <u>golden stag</u> gives compassionate hunter wisdom—B241.2.10.1.1.1;
stag caught by <u>horns</u>—L461; <u>horse</u> has man
saddle him to catch stag—K192; stag escapes
<u>hunter</u>, is eaten by lion—N255.1; grateful stag
tells <u>hunter</u> to take fairies' wings—H1385.3Fc;
<u>lion</u> leaves hare to chase stag—J321.3; <u>lion</u> leaps
at stag and misses, persuaded to return a sec-
ond time—K402.3.2; stag envied by <u>lizards</u> is
killed—L458; <u>Saint Noet</u> calls wild animals to
help when oxen are stolen, stag draws plows—
V229.28; visitors of <u>sick</u> stag eat up all

provisions—W151.2.1; White Stag, origin of Magyars and Huns—A1611.5.5.

DE MERCI: Horseman in black chases youth to death over precipice—E422.1.1.3.3.

DEMON: Brahman made to believe goat is demon—K451.2.1; bush is home of demon, fleeing couple pick it up—B314G; cobbler about to hang self tells demon he is making noose to tie up all demons in underworld—G501G; girl dancing with demons sends them for articles of clothing to procrastinate until cockcrow—Q2.1.3ff; person falls on demons, they flee—K335.1.1.3.1; marriage to demon—G302,7.1, G303.12.5.9; demon shown self in mirror dies—J1795.1.2; monkey king in forest takes necklace of demon from forest pool and says anyone bathing in pool receives such a necklace, all are eaten—Z49.23.1; demons vanish when sunlight strikes—D567.1; demons toss man into air—F153.2. SEE ALSO DEVIL.

DENKA: How Denka people obtained fire—A1415.2.4.

DENMARK: Monster strikes earth with tongue in death throes cutting passage between Denmark and Sweden—R111.1.4A; prince of Denmark in disguise weds haughty princess—H465Bb.

DERMA: Village named Derma after woman who originates custom of giving one-fifth crop to helpers—A1529.1.

DERVISH: Dervish puts boy in bag—K526D; man frightens self and take refuge in cave of dervish—W211.4; golden fish released by girl has mate turn self to dervish and help her escape on winged horse to her lover—D711.2.

DESERT: Origin of desert spot—A957.1; man abandoned in desert finds ax and arrows in tree and survives—D882.1Ga.

DETECTIVE: SEE JUDGE.

DESTINY: SEE FATE; FORTUNE.

DEVI: Devi hidden from soldiers in haystack and burnt—K1917.3E Papashvily.

DEVIL: Devil Aghiutsa turns hermits against each other by pretending to tell each secret—A1342.1; Ashmodai, King of Demons—J225.0.1; St. Thedule, Bishop of Sion, carried home by Devil—K1886.3.1.1; witch gives book of instructions to bind soul to Devil—G271.4.1.1; unwitting bargain with devil avoided by driving dog over bridge first—S241.1; Devil to work for bride for three years—D2183E; Devil tricked into entering bunghole—K717.6; when candle goes out person dies—E765.1ff; woman sticks carding combs into Devil's back, her curses—K171.1.1; cat tricks Devil into snuffbox—K1917.35; Devil falls piecemeal down chimney—H1440B; Devil in church—K1987, X904.4.1; threat to build church in hell—K1781; person causes cock to crow (simulates cockcrow) thus defeating devil

—K1886.3.1.1; Devil and God divide crops—K171.1; Devil to get crops, since almond blossoms first he wants that fruit first—K221.1; Devil driven off by cross—G303.16.3.1.3; curse, "The Devil take it", Devil does—C12.2.1; curse, "May the Devil swallow the horses"—C12.5; gypsy sells fiddle to Devil, with soul taken out—D1233.0.1; Devil turns girl's father into fiddle, mother to bow, brothers to strings—D1233.0.2; man buys field for Devil—M211.12; Devil tempts girl guardian of well away—C41.5; girl on Devil's back refuses to let go—T251.1.1.2; goatskin grows to back of priest imitating Devil—K335.0.12.1; Devil grinds miser's donation in mill—Q272.1.2; quest to find four hairs from beard of Devil—H1273.2N; Devil refuses to take anything not offered to him with whole heart—M215; man admitted neither to heaven nor hell—Q565; princess to one who guesses origin of hide, Devil guesses—H522.1.1.2; husband made to believe he is devil—J2311.0.1.1; Devil intimidated by clever trickster—G501B; Devil pounded in knapsack—K213; Devil bet he can't fit into knapsack—K717.5; maid kneads Devil in bread trough—K606.1.2; Devil's Knee (lava hill) exorcized—A934.14; suit for eating roasted chestnuts, lawyer is Devil—J1191.2; man told to "Go to the Devil" with his gift goes there, receives magic object—D861.1F, D1651.3.1; Devil has hands of maid cut off—H1385.3L; to be saved if hears masses in Jerusalem, Spain and Rome in one night, gets Devil to carry—D2121.5.1; Devil orders moon tarred—A751.4; Devil frightened by threatening to bring mother-in-law—T251.1.1; mowing contest, iron stakes in Devil's field—K178.1; dupe to see Ol' Boy in broom sage, it is set afire—K1055.2; Padre Ulivo offers hospitality to twelve disciples—Q565Ai; paramour in chest thought to be devil—J1344.1; Devil carries man to Pope and back before cockcrow—K1886.3.1.1, M211.8.1; Devil advises preacher to make story of David and Goliath bigger—X904.4.1; quest to Devil for four wild bulls—H1331.3; sent to collect rent from Devil—F613.1.1; Devil rejuvenates, smith imitates—J2411.1; escape from Devil by answering his riddle—H543; robber thinks man falling from sky is Devil and flees—K335.1.1.3; man spoils song of devils, has hump taken away—F344.1.3; man sells soul to Devil—M211ff; soul won from Devil in card game—E756.2, K1811.6; Devil gets soul other than that he bargained for, jealous sisters commit suicide and Devil takes—K217; Devil tempts tadpoles to swim—A2378.2.6.1; devil changes voice to carry off girls—K311.3K; wager that God is stronger than Devil—N452C; Lucifer's wedding, wed to Devil—G561.1E; Devil frightened by shrewish wife—T251.1.1ff; wife made to believe dog howling is man being beaten by Devil—J1151.1.1; wife in tar and feathers is animal Devil cannot identify—K31.1; Devil sends witch to steal Starost's daughter—G261.2; Devil creates wolf—A1833.1.1. SEE ALL ENTRIES G303ff.

DEVILFISH: SEE SCULPIN.

DEVIL'S CLUB: Sky woman gives magic Devil's Club—F53.1.

DEVIL'S GRANDMOTHER: Devil's grandmother aids—G530.2M; Devil's grandmother gives hair, turns gold once home—J2415.24.

DEVIL'S MOTHER: Devil's mother aids—G530.2Bb; boy on quest kisses Mother of Devils, she advises—N455.4Ad.

DEVIL'S TOWER: Motzeyouf leaves earth near Devil's Tower—A1539.3.

DEVOUT: Lord appears to devout Oudette—C773.1.2. SEE ALSO PIOUS.

DEW: Ass eats dew to get voice of cricket—J512.8; dew washes scar from maid's face—R221G.

DEWI KESUMO: A2681.15.

DEWI SRI: Gods poison Dewi Sri and rice grows from grave—A2685.6.1.1.

DHARMA: Origin God of Righteousness, Dharma—A489.5.

DIAMOND: Little rooster and his diamond button—Z52.4; diamond given to Hazelnut Child by African chief—F535.1.1Db; merchant swindled into paying exorbitant price for worthless piece of glass—J1521.6.1; diamonds fall from mouth of kind girl—Q2.1.1; diamond blinds witch, shines in hands of the brave—R111.1.3Aa; twelve dancing princesses pass diamond wood—F1015.1.1.

DIBBLE RIVER: Devil builds bridge over River Dibble—G303.9.1.6.1.

DICE: Fox has magic dice which are transformed tobacco beetles—J2346.1.

DIG: lie - man goes for spade to dig self out—X1731.2.1; digging up field to find treasure, field prospers—H588.7. SEE ALSO TREASURE.

DIGIT: Digit the Midgit—F535.1.1De.

DIKE: Dikekeeper lets in sea—F944; King Gralon's daughter opens gates and sea inundates town—F944.6. SEE ALSO DAM.

DINNER: SEE FEAST.

DIRT: SEE SOIL.

DIRTY: Dirty child stolen by fairies—F321.0.2; Corn Smut girl as dirty bride—K1816.0.2.2.

DISASTER: Climax of disasters—Z46.

DISCONTENT: Discontented ass get progressively worse masters—N255.2; discontented pine tree ends up with needles—A2723.1.

DISEASE: Disease as punishment for not asking pardon of animals when killing them—A1337.0.5.1; trickster disguises as ill animal and tells others that the trickster is putting a

hex on his enemies with this disease—K1995. SEE ALSO DOCTOR; LEPROSY; MEDICINE; SICKNESS.

DISENCHANTMENT: SEE D700-D799 Disenchantment.

DISGUISE: Uncle kills nephews, third escapes in girl disguise—S71.2; disguised hyena tricks hare into leaving food—K335.0.4.3; disguise as man to flee lover—K1236.1; disguise as man to escape with lover—K1837.9; disguise as man to perform feats—K1236.2; princess, barber to change places—K1321.3.0.1; generosity to disguised saint rewarded—Q42.3; woman disguised in city without women—T210.2. SEE ALSO K1800-K1899 Deception by disguise or illusion.

DISH: Why wife washes dishes—J2511.1.3; quest for best dish in the world—H1305.2.1.

DISSENSION: Ape creates confusion among animals—A1382.2, Z43.7.

DISSOLVE: Stick that dissolves all—D832.1.

DITTANY PLANT: Magic plant cures princess, grows from spot where gold eagle given by Ches is buried at temple—A978.3.1.

DIVIDING: SEE DIVISION.

DIVING: Trickster eats food while dupe is under water in diving contest—K16.2; diving for first earth—A812ff; loon dives with blind boy to restore sight—F952.7.1; diving for reflection—J1791.3.5ff. SEE ALSO SWIMMING.

DIVISION: dividing household, divide axe—J2469.3; monkey (trickster) evens out rice cakes, eats both—K452.1.2; wise carving of the fowl—H601; cattle going back to barn belong to dupe—K171.10; peasant takes whole chicken—H601; clever dividing—J1230; clever dividing, first person divides, second person choses his half first—J1249.2; clever dividing, judge divides thirteen horses among two men successfully—J1249.3; deceptive crop division—K171.1; fish head and tail to otters, middle to fox—K452.1.1; lion's share—J811.1ff; dividing the porridge and butter—J1562.1.1; Solomon's judgment, the divided child—J1171.1. SEE ALSO SHARING; UNITY.

DIVORCE: Origin of divorce—A1558, F81.1.0.1.

DJABBE: Djabbe with seven horns killed by cutting from within, purse in stomach gives night and day—F912.2.8.

DOCTOR: Anansi as doctor eats patient—K352.1; man granted power to see death at head or foot of bed—D1825.3.1; farmer surpasses doctor and doctor returns to city—L144.2; doctor tells fat man he will die in forty days, he loses weight—K1955.1.0.1; fool goes to doctor to tell him that wife doesn't need a doctor—J2241; fool calls undertaker as well as doctor—J2516.9; frog doctor asked to cure self—J1062.1; lad imitates doctor, fails—J2411.0.3; Dr. Know-It-All , sham wise man—N612.2, N688; lion (wolf) as doctor looks at horse's foot—K1121.1; doctor cheated of fee on pretense that he spilled medicines and spoiled precious rug—K499.11; fairy wife teaches sons art of healing, famous Physicians of Myddfai—F420.6.1.5.1; doctor asks recovered patient for news of hell, he had predicted death —J1432; sham doctor steals from patient with bad eyes—J1169.1; sham doctor hides something and is rewarded for finding it—K1956.2; sham doctor, holy man breathes on foot to cure but also recommends the usual medicines—J762.2; sick man sweating, shivering, fever, good signs —J1435; theft by posing as doctor—K352. SEE ALSO HEALING; MEDICINE.

DOG: Dog, falcon, otter aid—R111.1.3Cd; resuscitation by throwing ashes of burnt dogs on bones of boiled king—D882.1H; dog digs up baby buried in box—N455.4B; dog bites rescuing hand—W154.5; at feast dog leaps for bone making embarassing mess, leaves feast in shame and lodges with man—A2513.1.5; why dogs must crunch bones and nose at roadside—A1335.1.0.2; why dogs crunch bones—A2435.3.1; dog created by Brahma—A1831.3; chinch bugs said to have eaten dog—J1531.2.1; dog (Bureaucracy) thinks self more important than horse (peasantry)—W181.1.2; dog feigns rescue of child—K231.1.3; dog falsely thought to have killed child—B331.2; dog and hog dispute over their children —J243.1; dog proud of clog—J953.1; dog as man's companion—A2513ff; countryman thinks city strange because stones are tied up and dogs run loose—J1819.4; dog tries to live life of coyote—K414.3.4; boy arranges for coyote to feign stealing turkey, coyote really steals—K231.1.3.1; dog wants God to revive dead—A1335.16; Yudhisthera's dog becomes Dharma—A489.5; servant Dog-tail takes place of bride—K1911.1; how dog was domesticated—A2513.1ff; three dogs help kill dragon and rescue princess, sent to princess for food later reveal hero—R111.1.3E; dogs kill attacking dragon—B524.1.1; hero's dogs prevent dragon's heads from rejoining body—B11.11.2; dogs try to drink river dry—J1791.3.2; dog driven out of dining room claims to be drunk—J874; dog takes sun and moon in mouth causing eclipse—A737.1.1; enmity, dog and rat—A2494.4.3.1; enmity, dog and wolf—A2494.4.15; faithful dog has legs broken by ogress—P253.2E; dog helps steal fire—A1415.2.2.2ff; dog sent to steal fire stays—A2513.1.2ff; Arawidi turns fish into dogs, why dogs have cold noses—A2335.2.6.1; why dog has first place in household—A2545.3.1; literal fool dips dog in river—J2461E; literal fool carries puppy in jar—J2461D; fool sells meat to dogs, takes them to court—J1852.1.3; cock has fox invite dog—K579.8; dog in bag given fox—K235.1; dog chants to get fufu from tree—D861.1IC; ghost dog reveals treasure—E521.2.3; ghost dog haunts killer—E521.2.6; Finlay defeats three giants aided by dog—S12.1.0.1Bb; grateful dwarf gives girl magic seeds to transform her to dog—D141; dog reveals God's secret to man—N385.1; hare outruns dog—U242; dog bites then caresses hare—K2031; dog's re-

markable hearing—X938.2; helpful dog—B421; dog eats up hobyahs—B332; dog refuses to help man build house, must live outdoors—A2433.3.1.1; hunter beats dog grown old in service—W154.5; hunting dog that always gets kill—H132.1.5; imaginary dog has to be shot—X902.2; dog judges against man in dispute—J1172.3.2; dog arrives at court shivering from walk in wet grass and is judged guilty—A2494.4.14; mother to be killed is hidden—K311.3.1; youngest girl says will wed even lame dog, weds—H1385.4H; why dogs lift their legs—A2473.1; origin of dog's hind leg—A2473.1.1; dog following lion flees at roar—J952.3; dogs tear up lion skin—W121.2.4; dogs protect kind sisters from Loup Garou—Q2.1.6C; magic dog—B182.1; willow root turns to magic helpful dog—K32.1; faithful dog produces magic objects after death—D1571.1; tiny magic dog kept hidden in boy's hair, in trouble grows to size of pony and saves life—B182.1.0.1.2; friendship between man and dog—A2493.4; dog in the manger—W156; dogs flee when master kills oxen—J2211.3; cumulative tale ending, master bit him back—Z49.4.1; dog looks for most powerful master, chooses man since man fears no one—A2513.1.1; dog trades places with master, puts wife in her place—J1762.2.3.2; dog takes meat into bed with him to guard, eats—A2455.6; dog steals meat, loses kingship—B240.9; dog as companion of Momotaro—T543.3.2; man in moon has monster dog—A751.1.10; Brer Rabbit proposes sewing dog's mouth—J671.1; dog avenges master's murder—B301.2.1; Island of Nine Black Dogs, kill each of nine dogs nine times become nine men—S12.1B; why dog has wet nose—A2335.2.6; dog bequeaths man old age—B592; origin of dog—A1831ff; Little Liang's dog plows for him—J2415.21; why dog and porcupine are enemies—A2494.4.14; dog prince revives drowned lover—D735.1H; princess brought to laughter by foolish actions of hero—H341.3.2; dog cut in half catches both rabbits—X1215.11; dog taught to read—K491.0.1; dog drops meat for reflection in water—J1791.4; dogs rescue fleeing master from tree refuge—B524.1.2; man rescued from cave by dog—A2493.4.1; boy sets dog adrift in canoe but dog saves him when he falls in—W11.5.13; why dog serves man—N385.1.2; dog's shadow beaten—J1172.2.2; shaggiest dog in world—Z17.5; sheep jealous of dog—W181.1; Shippeitaro kills giant rats—K1853.2.1.1; dog's shoes stolen by Brer Rabbit—A2494.4.4; skull put in window, dog calls here comes "Rattle Rattle"—Q2.1.4D; why dog must sleep out-of-doors—A2542.3; task, bringing smallest dog—H1307; why dogs sniff under each leg—A2232.8; why dogs sniff at one another—A2471.1.1; origin Dog Soldier's Society—A1539.3; why dog lost ability to speak—N385.1.2; statue of grandfather and dogs in cemetery—E521.2.4; stone treasure dog with seven gold dogs inside—N531.1; why dogs wag tail—A2479.12; dog's tail from hoop and pole—A2378.1.7; talking dog—B210.1.1; dove asks Bolo Bolo, talking dog, daily about son—K1911Ac; why dogs bare teeth on meeting—A2471.1.2; dog suspects bribing thief—K2062; thief thinks dog is man with knife

--K1161.1*ff*; task, bringing tiger's milk--
N831.1.0.1; dog's tongue stretched for tattling
--A2344.4.1; dog runs beside train and cools
off hot boxes—X1215.7; waiting dog scolded,
says is ready—J1475; dog restores reputation as
watchdog--K231.1.3*ff*; vicious watchdog rewarded with kindness—J1179.18; dog created as
watchdog--A1831.1.1; girl wed to white dog--
H1385.4Eb; dogs to knock over dishes at wedding feast--R111.1.3Eb; dog protects from
whirlwind--A1024.1; wolf flees master, not dog
--J953.5; wolf prefers liberty, hunger to dog's
servitude, plenty--L451.3; wolf urges abolition
of dog guards--K2061.1.1. SEE ALSO HOUNDS.

DOG, GREYHOUND: Greyhound and horse judge
against man in dispute—J1172.3.2; hero takes
greyhound skin of princes, she aids--
G530.2Ai; girl to be green, son to be greyhound
until prince kisses girl and princess offers to
spend life with dog—B641.1; statue of laird and
hounds—E521.2.4.

DOG, PEKINESE: Dog guides blind prince--
Q161.1.1.

DOG, PORCELAIN: Boy may have all three if
carries one porcelain dog home alone—J1179.19.

DOG, WILD: Son opens door freeing wild dog—
G671B; origin of wild dog--A1831.3.

DOKANOO: Anansi steals pudding from cat's
Dokanoo tree—K419.11.

DOKO: Doko basket used to carry grandfather to
abandon—J121.3.

DOLL: Maharaja of India sends three golden dolls
to Khan of Mongolia--H506.13; doll in the grass,
lad wed to wee maid--B641Be; doll sneezes gold
for poor girl, soot for wicked neighbor--
J2415.10; straw dolls thrown into monster's
throat to choke him—Q2.1.2F; doll does tasks
for girl at Baba Yaga's—Q2.1.2CeBb.

DOLPHIN: Alliance of lion and dolphin--B267.5;
dolphin maid released, saves later—A421.1.1;
dolphin saves shipwrecked monkey claiming to
be Athenian--J1803.1.1; origin of dolphins--
A2135.3; slaves seeking Raja's buckle turn into
dolphins—A2275.4.1; dolphin and whale scorn
sprat as peacemaker—J411.6.

DOMESTICATED: All animals are inside mountain,
spider smokes them out and slower ones are
caught as flee and domesticated--A1714.3.2.
SEE ALSO DOG.

DONAL: Donal O'Ciaran from Connaught—K1951.1K;
Donal from Donegal—G501H; wife allows three
peddlers to stay since all are named Donal, each
tells wondrous tale—M231.3.

DONEGAL: Donegal son seeks vengeance on
Connacht man--F615.3.1.5;

DONKEY: Man apologizes to donkey for hard
work--J1879.2; person calls another an ass--

J1352.3; donkey bites and kicks prospective
buyers, owner doesn't expect to sell, just wanted others to see what he puts up with--K134.9;
boar refuses to fight with ass--J411.1; why ass
brays--A2423.1.4.1; donkey brays everytime
vegetable seller calls—J1889.1; owners says ass
not at home, ass brays--J1552.1.1; eating lettuce (cabbage) turns one to donkey—D551.1;
ass could be no worse off if captured by enemy
—U151; fool fails to count ass he is sitting on—
J2022, J2031.2; numskull believes self dead and
watches wolves eat his ass--J2311.7; numskull
believes will die when donkey brays three times
--J2311.1; numskull doctoring sees bridles under
bed and says patient has eaten too many don-
keys--J2412.4; ass imitates lap dog--J2413.1;
why donkey's ears are long--A2325.3; center of
earth under donkey's hoof—H681.3.1; pumpkin
thought to be ass's egg—J1772.1; mule says
father was high-spirited horse, later when tired
says father might have been an ass after all—
J954.1.2; ass taught to live without food dies—
J1914; fool takes sack on shoulder or sits on
sack to relieve donkey of burden—J1874.1*ff*;
fool cannot find ass he is sitting on--J2022; literal fool carries donkey on shoulder--J2461A;
fox claims ass had no brains—K402.3.1; alleged
gold dropping ass sold—B103.1.1*ff*, K111.1; as
many hairs in head as in ass's tail—H703.1; as
many stars in heaven as hairs on ass—H702.2.1;
origin donkeys of Haiti--A1882.2; ass jealous of
horse--J212.1, L452.1; horse refuses aid and
overburdened ass dies—W155.1; war horse
spurns donkey, later when he is cart horse,
donkey refuses to aid--J411.12; donkey weds
human in winter but returns to donkey mate in
spring--B651.13; ass carrying image thinks
people bow to him—J953.4; ass and horse judge
against man in dispute--J1172.3.2; donkey
thinks Karbau is making row, is dog--J132.1;
why donkey laughs--A2423.1.4.1; ass returned
because of lazy companions—J451.1; ass frightens goats from cave for lion to kill--K2324.1.1;
donkey thanks jackal for bringing lion--K1715.2;
ass chasing lion frightened by cock--J952.2; ass
insults dying lion--W121.2.1; lion leaps at donkey and misses, donkey convinced to return--
K402.3.2.1; fox leads ass to lion's den but is
himself eaten--K1632; ass in lion's skin unmasked when he raises his voice—J951.1; why donkey's have short upper lips- A2342.3; lost ass,
saddle and bridle offered as reward for finder--
J2085.1; magic donkey stolen by host at inn—
D861.1; crossing river on bear's back ass drops
magic stone--D882Ba; complaining ass gets progressively worse masters--N255.2; Mulla divides
seventeen donkeys satisfactorily between three
men--J1249.5; king has name of boy's father
painted on side of donkey as taunt, boy adds
"'s"--J1289.29; ass thinks self equal to ox--
J952.4; donkey tells ox to feign ill and escape
work—K1633.1; vultures eat poisoned donkey
and die--H802; mullah selling pomegranates asks
braying donkey who is selling—J1499.1; ass as
pooka--F381.3; ass pulls away from master trying to save from precipice--J683.1; donkey
prince—B641.4; helpful donkey becomes prince
--H1213.1J; donkey flogged publicly and other
donkeys made to watch punishment as lesson--

J1891.4; why donkey shares food and lodging with rat—A2493.37; task, teaching ass to read —K491.0.1, K551.11; ass killed for drinking moon's reflection—J1791.1; miller, his son, and the ass, who would ride—J1041.2; donkey duped by Ananse into letting Ananse ride him courting —K1241.1; man thinks ass stole his coat so takes ass's saddle—J1862; ass loaded with salt lies in river to lighten load, later tries same with sponges—J1612; why donkey serves man— A2513.7; does man hiring ass hire shadow?— J1169.7; foxes tie sham dead burro to their tails to drag home—J2132.5.4; camel and ass captured because of ass's singing—J581.1, J2137.6; animals confess sins, ass blamed—U11.1.1.1; why donkey's sniff each other—A2232.8.1; donkey sold for one dinar but tied to one hundred dinar cat—K182.0.1; Indians told that donkey speaks Spanish—K1977; ten year respite while teaching ass to speak—K551.11; fool thanks God he wasn't on ass when it was stolen—J2561; donkey (ogre) stretches to make room for prince— G422.1.1.3, K607.5; seller cuts off donkey's dirty tail and brings along in bag—J2099.2; dokey tail on forehead of unkind girl—Q2.1.1C; donkey to bray when thief pulls tail— J1141.1.0.1; king kisses ass's tail—K1288.1; when teacher's donkey dies students hide behind stable and moan, teacher says that must be donkey's brothers—J1529.1; thief steals ass, pretends he is transformed ass—K403; ass prefers thistles to delicacies on his back—J1061.1.1; toad tricks donkey in race—K11.1; ass eats dew to get voice of crickets—J512.8; donkey as girl weds, returns to donkey mate in spring— B651.12; wild ass envies tame—L451.2ff; wild ass eaten by lion, tame saved—L451.2.1; ass and goose visit wishing well at Christmas— B251.1.2.4; saint gives three wishes, donkey's ears wished on wife—J2075; witch as donkey lengthens self to let trickster on—K607.5; witness claims borrowed ass and is discredited— J1151.2; ass asks wolf to pull thorn from foot— K566.

DONKEYSKIN: Girl in donkeyskin cloak—R221Dc.

DOOMSDAY: Kantchil claims doomsday has arrived to get animals into pit—K652.1; rumor started when nut falls—Z43.3ff. SEE JUDGMENT DAY.

DOOR: Baptistry doors decorated with little people—A1465.3.3.1; metal dirk stuck in door of fairyland keeps door open—F321.3.0.1; fox rubs tail on door to make "Zui" sound—K1887.4; forbidden door—C611.1; fool left to guard door lifts it off and takes with him—K1413; Shen Shu and Yu Lu, Guardians of the Gate—A411.1; doorway broken down to permit mounted person to enter—J2171.6ff; door falls on robber from tree—K335.1.1.1; stubborn couple, first to speak must get up and bar the door—J2511; tabu, never to open door—K815.15; miser boards up doors to avoid paying door tax—J1179.15; hunter finds land behind door in tree—C611.1.1.

DOORMAN: Doorman demands half of reward, trickster requests lashes—K187ff.

DOUBLE AREND OF MEEDEN: Strong man— F624.1.

DOUGH: Girl who obeys mother becomes golden bee after death, paws carry yellow dough (pollen)—A2012.0.1.1; conjure wives put dough in pan, it swells—D153.2; fox claims dough is brains beaten out—K473.1; dough fills house— D153.2. SEE ALSO BAKER; BREAD; ETC.

DOUGHNUT: Doughnut satisfies hunger, eaten after three rolls—J2213.3; man too lazy to turn string of doughnuts around on neck— W111.5.8.2. SEE ALSO BAGEL.

DOVE: SEE BIRD, DOVE.

DOVECOT: Wife makes old man carry her in bag up to dovecot—D861.1K.

DOVREFEL: Bear frightens trolls—K1728.

DOWRY: Dowry of cattle emerge from lake, as many as she can count—F420.6.1.5.1.

DOZEN: Baker's dozen, origin—V429.4.

DRAGON: Anansi and son escape dragon to sky— K671.1; lad raises wounded baby dragon— B389.2; dragons in underworld beheaded by hero—K1931.2ff; prince beheads eleven dragons as enter—S12.1C; dragon beats bell with tail until red hot, man hiding underneath perishes— B605.1; dragon sends horsefly to discover creature with sweetest blood—A2236.1; dragon bluffed—K18.4, K1741.1ff, K1746; dragon bluffed by woman with one hundred children—G501C; lad captures smallest dragon and keeps in jar— S12.1C; carp slips through dragon gate— B11.6.11; carp, son of Dragon King, gives magic gem—D882.1Bbc; dragon carries lad to safety—W154.8.4.1; dragon tricked into casket to try size—G610Ai; cat helps children flee dragon—H1321.1D; dragon borrows cock's horns —A2435.4.8.2; knight with cross on armor slays dragon—B641Dd; magic flute causes dragon to dance until shrinks away—D1415.2.3; daughter sells self as sacrifice to river dragon for money to restore father's eyesight—N712.2; fox tricks dragon into haystack, burns—K1917.3E; man frees dragon, fox re-enacts—J1172.3; tiny dragon-girl born to childless couple—T542.2; the dragon and his grandmother—M211.7.1; sons follow hare to mill, turns to dragon—K956.0.1; dragon wants heart of monkey for wife—K544, K961.1; ascent to heaven holding dragon—F75.1; dragon can't enter heaven for must remove pearl from head—H1273.2L; Himalayas are dragon— A955.10.3; imposter claims killed dragon— H105.1.1; dragon intimidated by claim of eating nine dragons—K1715.4.0.1; dragon intimidated by "seven at a blow" inscription—K1951.1; dragon intimidated by one hundred children with knives and forks—G501C; quest for white jade from dragon king's palace—G530.2Bj; dragon king in undersea palace—F420.6.1.3.1; Laidly worm is transformed girl—D732.0.1; man mistakes dragon for log—J1761.8; firecrackers set off at New Year to frighten dragons—

A1541.7; test, rapidly painting dragon--H504.3; dragon must spit out pearl in mouth--H1273.2M; princess abducted by dragon--H1385.1ff; dragon carries off princess nightly--F1015.1.1. Pridham; princess saved from dragon with aid of helpful bull--B335.2A, B335.2Cff; princess rescued by dragon--R111.1.3; astronomer, thief, marksman, tailor rescue princess from dragon--H621.2.4; dragon answers questions on quest--H1273.2F; quest for pebbles from dragon's lake M383.1; dragon vanquished with King's ring--G405.1.2; dragon gives heroic shirt--K2213.0.1; snake grows into dragon--D861.1D; dragon tests lads with stone to move--K1931.2P; dragon fed stone loaf, breaks teeth--K1952.0.3; dragon eats two brothers for not telling story--X905.1.5; dragon fed sheep stuffed with sulphur--B11.11.10; origin of Taiwan is dragon tail--A955.10.3; lad steals dragon's treasure--K1861.1Bb; dragon sitting on treasure hoard is unable to enjoy it--W156.1; man healing dragon named patron saint of veterinarians--B11.6.1.5, V229.29; dragons cause weather in Taiwan Straits--A955.10.3; wed to dragon--B605.1; mother weds dragon and betrays son--S12.1C; dragon drinks drugged wine--K929.1.1; chief's daughter feeds pet worm which becomes devouring dragon--F911.6.2. SEE ALL ENTRIES B11 Dragon; R111 Rescue of maiden from dragon. SEE ALSO SAMEBITO.

DRAGONFLY: Dragonfly sees farthest--A1878.2.

DRAKE: Drakestail--Z52.1. SEE ALSO DUCK.

DRAWBRIDGE: Sawed in two, ogre falls--G512A.

DRAWING: Drawing straws--J1141.1.4. SEE ALSO ARTIST; PAINTING.

DREAM: Boat dreams he is to eat antelope, king rules he may, ape dreams he is to wed king's daughter--J2326.2.1; cat's dream emerges as fox faced man--G351.2.1; dreams he receives nine coins, demands ten, wakes and says he'll settle for nine--J1473; hunter dreams dove saves life, wakes to find true--F1068.4; farmer carried into sky when ducks fly off with trap, falls and wakens--K687.1; painter dreams becomes fish and is caught and to be eaten--F1068.3; fool dreams he hurts foot, plans to wear shoes to bed in future--F1068.5; fool dreams goes bear hunting, takes dog to bed next night--F1068.5.1; dream of future greatness causes punishment--L425; Juan dreams self in heaven, cleans lamp there so will burn longer--E765.1.1.2; feigned knowledge from dream--D1810.8.5; Genie of Silver Mine gives lad silver ore seen in dream--F456.4.3; student sleeping on porcelain pillow has fantastic dream--D1812.3.3.2.1; snake interrupts king's dream--B145.2.1; boy knocks on door begging for soup just as man thinks of soup, "I dream of soup and my neighbors smell it."--J1849.7; girl seeks stars in dream--F1068.0.1; tabu, telling dream, lad punished for refusing to tell dream of future greatness--L425; tigers think Kantchil's feigned dream of world in which goats eat tigers has come true--K1715.16; dream of treasure on bridge--N531.1;

dream of treasure bought--N531.3; one with most wonderful dream to eat food--K444; girl to eat salty yeast, man who gives water in dreams will wed--H1385.5Ab. SEE ALSO DAYDREAM.

DRESS: Dress of catskin, bearskin, etc.--R221Dff; dress color of sun, moon, stars, etc.--R221Dff; dress that fits in a nutshell--R221Dff. SEE ALSO CLOTHING.

DRESSING: Told to dress chicken, fool puts clothes on it--J2499.8.

DRINKING: Ogre persuaded to drink pond dry bursts--G522; deceptive drinking contest, rising and falling tide--K82.1.1; brother transforms when drinks from animal's hoofprints--P253.2.0.1; mighty drinker--F601.2, F660.1D; peasant girl puts leaves on water so general can only sip slowly and will not become ill--J1111.4.1; lad refuses to drink with Providence (Lord) and Devil, drinks with Death--D1825.3.1.1.3; dogs try to drink river dry--J1791.3.2; Oni tries to recover object from river by drinking it dry--J1791.3.2.2; man enchants robbers by drinking to their health--K1812.1.0.1. SEE ALSO SWALLOWER.

DROUGHT: Saints have to dance when hear drums, drought ends--D2174.1.

DROWNING: Dove rescues ant--B362.2; drowning boy saved by little girl--A2650.1; three drowned men carry coffin of newly drowned man ashore for burial--E379.6; drowning child scolded--J2175.2; woman drives cows into river to drink, drown--J1903.5; drowning the eel--J1909.8.1; ghost of drowned befriends fisherman--E414.0.1; numskull throws hen in well to get a drink--J1902.1.1; girl falls into water jar, boy throws stone breaking jar and saving her--J1687; drowned son returns as land otter--E324.3; man to drown eats salt so will enjoy water--J861.2; drowning the sickle--J1865; spider saved from drowning weaves mantilla--A1465.2.1.1; drowning tax collector refuses to "give" a hand--W153.5.1; drowning punishment for turtle--K581.1; swallow rescues drowning wasp--B362.1; water-spirit keeps souls of drowned persons in dishes in his home--F420.5.2.3; drowning wife makes scissors motions as she sinks--T255.1; drowned wife looked for upstream--T255.

DRUM: Animals contribute each part of ear to make drum, Eliri mocked for small contribution seeks aid of Ayan, God of Drum, for vengeance--A2433.1.3; elephant king's drum stolen, breaks into pieces, each becomes a drum, elephant king breaks into pieces, each becomes a drummer--A1461.10; jackal and empty drum--J262.1; crab beats forbidden drum--A2231.10; girl put into drum and forced to sing--G422.1.1; trickster returns rolling inside drum and escapes--K553.0.3; jackal has barber remove thorn from nose, takes drum--Z47.4; leopard tricked into drum--K714.2.5; lizard steals python's drum--K1079.2; louse skin drum--H522.1.1; man steals magic drum, nose pulled long--J2415.22;

magic drum causes dancing, enemies become peaceful—D1415.2.7; four monkeys invent instrument—A1461.0.1; 'oracle' drum sold (bees inside)—K842Bd; huge ox necessary for skin to cover huge drum—X909.4.4; Brer Rabbit sings into drum making scary noises and frightens animals--K335.0.4.9; saints have to dance when hear drums, drought ends—D2174.1; drum made of tree tells secret—D1316.5.0.2; self-beating drum (bee inside)—H1049.5; Great Drum becomes soundless to punish man for breaking word—C939.13; tabu, playing drums with sticks —C645; talking drum used to reveal secret name of chief's daughter—H323B; drum of Tepozteco heard—A1195.1; tiger dances to magic drum—D1415.2.7.1; god takes away voice of drum--Q223.14.1; wasp's nest mistaken for drum—K1023.1.

DRUNKARD: Drunkard in cemetery passes as ghost, learns of buried treasure—J2415.12.

DRUNKEN: Elephants made drunk and tusks stolen--H1151.6.2; thief allowed to keep cloak stolen from drunken judge—J1211.2; lion drinks and becomes intoxicated and drunken coward rides lion thinking it his horse—N691.1.2.1; louse, bedbug and flea in drunken brawl—A2330.5; tipsy rooster takes purse to king—Z52.6.

DRY-BONE: Bird taken on back becomes heavier and heavier, turns to Dry-Bone man—G303.3.5.3.1.

DUCK: SEE BIRD, DUCK.

DUEL: Dog and wolf duel, cat as second, cat's tail thought to be sabre--K2323; duel between dog and master's murderer—B301.2.

DUENDE: Duende friends follow lad when he goes to city--F481.3.1; duendes keep putting cleaning equipment in hands of lazy wife—Q321.2.3.

DUMPLING: Dumplings of lead, silver and gold aid in quest—D721.5B; fox turns self into dumpling—K722.0.1. SEE ALSO RICE BALL.

DUNG: Why cat covers it's dung--A2495.1; bird with golden dung—B103.1.5; ass with golden dung—K111.1; old woman protected by objects which attack intruding ogre, dung aids—K1161.3.2.

DUNGBEETLE: SEE BEETLE, DUNG BEETLE.

DUNVEGAN CASTLE: Fairy flag of Dunvegan—F305.1.2.

DUPE: Trickster eats common food supply and then by smearing the mouth of the sleeping dupe with food escapes the blame--K401.1; property of dupe destroyed--K1400-K1499. SEE ALL OF CHAPTER K. Deceptions. These usually involve a trick played on a dupe. SEE ALSO FOOL.

DUPLICATING: Magic pot duplicates anything put into it—D1652.5.7.1.

DURAK: Simple Durak sells cat in land of rats—G666.3.

DURGA: Goddess Durga gives replenishing pot—D861.1G.

DWARF: Dwarf gives useless advice—J163.4.1; Baba Yaga counts spoons and dwarf calls out revealing hiding—H1385.3Fe; dwarf's long beard caught in split log--D113.2, K1111.1; lad lights pipe with blue light and little man appears—D1421.1.2; Karl Katz sets bowling pins for dwarfs—D1960.1; dwarf released from cage aids hero—H331.1.1D; dwarf asks each of three lads cooking for food—K1931.2ff; dwarf gives up eyes to wed princess—H1409.1; dwarf in haunted castle beats--K1931.2M; Dwarf King forced to twirl on nose dancing until he frees princess—D1415.2.1; Knurre-Murre is dead, cat is really dwarf who lost sweetheart to Knurre-Murre—B342B; dwarf turned out by family is taken in by old lady with dogs and cats--D1065.7.1; Dwarf Long Nose, herb disenchants—D1367.1.4; marriage of mortal and dwarf—T111.5.1; dwarf defeats stupid ogre—G501A Hardendorff; woman asked by dwarfs to gather pine cones elsewhere, finds silver cones—F451.5.1.10.1; dwarf gives ring to kind lad--Q2A; grateful dwarf gives magic seeds to transform girl to dog—D141; span high man, Sir Buzz, comes from box and serves--D882.1Eb; Snow White and the seven dwarfs—Z65.1; girl sweeps snow from door of dwarfs' home and finds strawberries underneath—Q2.1.4B; three dwarfs capture girl picking strawberries--G561.2Db; little man and birds aid in service to troll--G530.2Gb; old man told to dance for dwarfs and they will remove his wen—F344.1.2. SEE ALL F451-F460ff. SEE ALSO LAMINAK; MENHUNES; THUMBLING.

DYE: Jackal falls in vat of blue dye—J2131.5.6.

DYNAMITE: Hog eats dynamite and blows up—X1233.2.1.

EAGLE: SEE BIRD, EAGLE.

EAR: Accused pleads that plaintiff bit his own ear off--J2376.1; king with goat's ears--D1316.5.0.3; in dispute court rules that merchants may cut off farmer's ear, he begins to do so and judge reverses decision--J1179.2.6; thief on gallows bites mother's ear—Q586; blind lute player protected by priest's painting scriptures all over body, ear is missed and ghosts take that—E434.11; animal produces treasure or supplies from ear—B115.1; witch pinned to log by ear lobes under pretense of piercing her ears—G275.7.0.1.

EARL OF MAR: Earl of Mar's daughter—H1385.5Ah.

EARLY: Lucky to get up early, bag of gold found

on road--N129; servant girls kill cock so won't have to rise so early--K1636.

EARTH: Butter given to cracked earth--J1871; center of earth is under donkey's hoof--H618.3.1; distance, how far from one end of earth to other?--H681.1.1; Goddess of Earth thanked for finding treasure--N111.4.3; earth opens up, as logical as bull bearing calf--J1191.1.3; what is richest? Earth--H636.2; what is strongest-- Earth--H631.3; earth would become unbalanced if everyone lived in same place--J2774.1+. SEE A620ff AND ALL A800-A899 FOR CREATION MOTIFS. SEE ALSO MUD; SOIL; WORLD.

EARTH MAGICIAN: Sweat of Earth Magician's hands turns to disease and sickness--A1337.0.8; Earth Magician scrapes dust from his chest and rolls this into world--A614.0.1.

EARTHQUAKE: Rejected suitor fakes earthquakes by shaking houseposts--K1889.7; men stay six months with fairy maids, return to find home destroyed by earthquake two hundred years ago --D2011.1.5; earthquake when Maui moves-- A1415.5; earthquake from movement of subterranean monster--A969.1.1, A1145.1; earthquake when strong man shifts positions--A1145.3, A1145.4; earthquakes caused by movement of turtle on whose back earth rests--A1145.2.1.

EARTHWORM: Why earthworm is blind--A2241.12; why cock eats worms--A2435.4.8.2; ten earthworms painted rapidly using ten fingers-- H504.3; earthworm warns fish not to bite-- K689.1. SEE ALSO WORM.

EAST: How far from east to west--H681.1.1.

EASTER: Bells of Ys still heard on Easter Day-- F944.6.

EASTER ISLAND: Origin of Toromiro carvings of Rapa-Nui--A1465.5.1.

EATING: Trying to eat finely ground corn on camel's back, it blows away--J1250.2; eating contest, food put in bag--K81.1; deceptive game, doing without food or drink--K869.6; epicure's banquet, peasant wonders why all just admire food--J1742.3.2; etiquette requires eating with two fingers, "Why are you eating with five fingers?" "Because I haven't got six."-- J1347; eaten fish calls "I got you now!"--Z13.5; girl must eat of pudding, apple, pie before they will hide her--Q2.1.2CeA; lazy refuses to help until food is brought out--W111.7.2; mighty eater--F601.2, H341.1; disciple shakes self in middle of each meal, can eat more this way-- J2260; can eat more if drinks much first--J1341.7; animal overeats and cannot escape through entrance--K1022.2; tabu, eating in other world-- F320.4; F324; tabu, eating from offerings made to gods--C57.1.3; boy eats all three meals at once then goes to sleep--W111.2.6; wolf thinks he has swallowed the ram--K553.3; wolf requested to start eating horse from the rear--K553.4. SEE ALSO COOK; FEAST; FOOD; GLUTTON; GREED; SWALLOW; ETC.

EATING, EATER: Mighty eater--F601.3.

ECHO: The cave call--K607.1; lion hears echo of roar in well and attacks--K1715.1.

ECLIPSE: Origin of eclipse--A736.1.3.1; A737ff.

ECOLOGY: Why River Metsch runs white, wheat thrown into river--A939.1; farmer throws his slops onto invisible house--F451.4.4.4; Tree Goddess asks preservation of her forests-- A978.3.1; trees cut will dry up marsh, frogs ask that it be saved--D435.2.2; water kelpie curses water girl drinks so she cannot speak, she has dropped a comb into their well-- F420.5.2.6.6.1; girl offends fairies by embittering waters of stream with her tears--F324.4; rabbit muddies waters of well--A2233.1.1.

EEL: SEE FISH, EEL.

EETOI: Eetoi grabs hands of Earth Magician as disappear into earth, sweat from Earth Magician's hands turn to disease--A1337.0.8; Eetoi killed after men feel he has become evil--A566.3; Eetoi kills Vandai and sprinkles blood on dead eagle to revive--A1610.7.

EGA: SEE BIRD, EGA.

EGG: Pumpkin thought to be ass's egg--J1772.1; hen fed hot water to produce boiled eggs-- J1901.2; suit over chickens that might have been produced from boiled eggs--J1191.2; task, hatching boiled eggs--H1023.1.1; lancing his cheeks to remove the two eggs--W111.5.8; old woman carries egg under her arm and cock egg hatches--Z52.4.2; cock's eggs under armpit hatches cobald--F481.0.1.1; trickster counts same egg over and over making mother think all eggs are still there--K933; both hen and crocodile born from eggs--K601.3; culture hero born from egg--A511.1.9; daydreaming of profits from eggs, person breaks all--J2061.1.2; guess what's in my hand and I'll give it to you to make an egg cake with--J2712.1; eggshells explode in ogre's face--K1161.7.2; boiling water in eggshell--F321.1.1; eggshell contains goblin's soul --K975.2; emu's egg thrown into sky = sun-- A714.3.1; eggs explode and injure intruder-- K1161.3.1; man pretends to be buying five dozen eggs, counts them into farmer's arms and walks off--K289.1; fool throws hen in well to get a drink, sits on eggs until she is finished-- J1902.1.1; six eggs found on Halloween night hatch goblin babies--F481.0.1.1.2; contents of three golden eggs traded for three nights with lover--H1385.5Ad; bird lays golden eggs-- B103.2.1, D876; eggs sent to birds by Great Spirit--A2431.3.11; guinea fowl asks what eggs will do for her when hatched--J267.1.1; father stands on head until hen lays another egg-- Z39.5.1; husband tells wife he has laid an egg, rumor multiplies--J2353; kills hen to get eggs-- J2129.3; rescued chicken lays eggs and saves starving lizard--K641.3; ogre's heart in egg-- B314Fb, D532A; why ostrich leaves eggs outside of nest--A2431.4; overfed hen stops laying

--J1901.1; Raven makes a clay egg, hatches a goose—K1041.2; eggs chosen as reward by kind girl contain riches--Q2.1.2Eb; egg rolls off meets other animals who join--K1161.9; egg soiled reveals entrance to forbidden room—G561B; 33 sons born from eggs--H1320.3; soul in egg--D532, E710, G561.1, K956, K975.2.1; task, stealing eggs from under bird--H1151.12; why turkey has only two eggs—A2486.5; eggs dropped in war of birds and animals—B261.0.1; egg son weds rich man's daughter--B649.1; obstinate wife dies for third egg—T255.4.

EGGPLANT: Magic eggplant breaks spell and turns horses back to men—G263.1.0.2; man contends eggplants should grow on trees until nut hits him on head—J2571.

EGHAL: Eghal Shillet—K1951.2.

EGRET: SEE BIRD, EGRET.

EGYPT: St. George kills dragon in Egypt freeing King Ptolemy's daughter—R111.1.3Fa; Syrian and Egyptian exchange objects and cheat each other--J1516; trickster never to set foot on Ethiopian soil again comes with shoes full of Egyptian soil—J1161.3.2. SEE ALSO CAIRO.

EIGHT: Eight Immortals—A501.2.

EIGHTEEN: Eighteen Lo-Hans--A501.3.

EILEAN-N-OIGE: Isle of Youth—F361.3.0.1.

EILEAN DONAN: Building of Eilean Donan Castle —B216.2.

EINON: G302.7.1.5.

EJUPA: SEE COYOTE.

ELBOWS: Why woman's elbows are cold—A1319.15.

ELEPHANT: Elephant in age debate—B841.1.1; elephant protects prince by causing elephants to run amok--B381.3.1; blind men and the elephants—J1761.10; Podhu loses brother's spear, carried off by elephant—H1132.1.5.2; elephant aids carpenter who removes thorn from foot—B381.3; chameleon races elephants—K11.1, K11.2; elephant thinks cock is eating him—K1715.4.2; elephant and coucal in calling contest--K11.1.1.2; crocodile arranges trek of animals to new waterhole with elephants in rear, raises alarm with men—A2494.11.2; drum of elephant king breaks into pieces, each becomes a drum...elephant king breaks into pieces, each becomes a drummer—A1461.10; elephant god, Ganesha— A132.16; elephant and giraffe farm with hare, each thinks hare does half the work —K364.1; elephant catches hare with clay man— K741.0.6; numskull going to heaven on tail of celestial elephant loses hold--J2133.5.2; why elephant's hind parts are small—A2362.2; mysterious housekeeper from elephant tusk— N831.1.0.1; elephant tries to learn hunter's secret transformation—D615.0.1; task, enough ivory to build palace, elephant's made drunk—

H1151.6.1; judgment over true owner of dead elephant, one man weeps all night over dead body, other leaves—J1171.5; Kantchil rides elephant's back to frighten tiger—K1715.2.1; Kantchil escapes from pit on back of elephant—K652.1; friendship between elephant and Kantchil—A2493.36; elephant told has been chosen king, killed—K815.20; why elephant lives in bush—A2433.3.15.1; Mantis rescues springbok from stomach of elephant—F929.4; elephant fears moon's angry reflection in lake--J1791.12, K1716; elephant and buffalo hide twelve girls in mouth, witch curses elephant's lower lip to hang down—G276.3; why elephant has long nose—A2235.1, A2335.3.3; animals speculate about why elephant is praised--W197.1; elephant fears agitated reflection of moon in water—J1791.12, K1716; roaring contest between elephant and tiger—K84.2; elephant tricked into running into tree—K771; ten year respite given captive while he teaches elephant to speak—K551.11; deceptive stamping contest--K17.6; elephant swallows family—F912.2; lad seeks tail of Queen of Elephants--D672J; why elephant's tail is short and black—A2378.4.16; elephant near thieves hears talk of killing and becomes dangerous—J451.5; tug of war between elephant and hippo—K22, K22.1; elephant detains wagons until mistress is paid—B599.4; weighing the elephant—H506.1; washing elephant white--H1023.6.2; white elephant chosen by king—B381.3.1; prince lured through forest in attempt to tame white elephant with his lute playing, thus led to princess—K754.2.1.

ELEPHANT DRIVER: Elephant driver grabs onto legs of man dangling from tree, elephant walks out from under them--J2133.5.0.1.

ELF: Men of Connaught destroy elves and take elf king's crown—F302.1.6; elf cries over lost friend, though has many new--J401.2; elf threatens goats on bridge—K553.2; elfin hound of Curachon—F302.1.6; King of Elfland abducts Burd Ellen—F324. SEE ALSO DWARFS; FAIRIES.

ELIDOROUS: Brings golden ball to mother and is forbidden to re-enter fairyland—F378.0.1.1.

ELIJAH: Pious man polishes marble block but is unable to move it to Jerusalem, Elijah moves--D1641.2.1.1; Elijah shown hospitality by poor couple—Q1.10.

ELIRI: King Eliri mocked for small contribution to drum when each animal contributes part of ears —A2433.3.13.

ELK: Ghost elk—E423.2.6.1.

EMAJOGI RIVER: Origin—A934.17.

EMBRACE: Disenchantment by holding person during successive transformations—D757.

EMBROIDERY: Task, bringing finest embroidery —H1306.1; goblin in tower released from haunting when full-blown rose is brought in January, man brings embroidered <u>rose</u>—E451.12; sun sisters stick embroidery <u>needles</u> in your eyes if you look at sun—A736.<u>1.1.1.</u>

EMERALD: <u>Lizard</u> turned to emerald—E121.4.3; emeralds <u>originate</u> in explosion of Tree Goddess's cave—A9<u>78.</u>3.1.

EMPEROR: Emperor's new clothes—K445.

EMPRESS: Spider spectre in pool is ghost of Empress Otawa—E423.8.3.

EMPRESS JOKWA: Mends broken pillar supporting heavens—A665.2.0.1.1.

ENCHANTER: Marec the enchanter—G275.1.2. SEE ALSO MAGICIAN.

ENDLESS TALES: Z11ff.

ENDURANCE: Lad to endure three nights of <u>beatings</u> to free Moorish girl—H1411.4.3; pure <u>girl</u> to kiss enchanted maid on lips on St. John's Eve and never let go of golden pitcher—D757.1; <u>standing</u> seven years in sun and rain—H328.8; to bear <u>torments</u> of twelve men for three nights —H1385.<u>3Bb.</u> SEE ALSO EMBRACE.

ENEMY: Enemy routed by <u>deception</u>; twice the wish to the enemy—J2074. SEE ALL K2368ff, K2369ff.

ENGINE: Origin of steam engine—A1439.5.

ENMITY: Enmity between <u>animals</u>—A2494ff; origin of enmity between <u>Nez Percé</u> and Blackfoot— A1288.2.

ENVIRONMENT: SEE ECOLOGY.

ENVY: Error of <u>envying</u> others—J212+; water buffalo envies <u>pig</u>—L457. SEE ALSO JEALOUSY.

EPAMINONDOUS: J2461B.

EQUIVOCAL NAMES: Name such as "No man" or "I don't know" given, trickster escapes trouble --J1521.5.2, J1802.1, J2496+, X1506.1.

EQUIVOCATION: Yes-no spirit always equivocates—W123.4.

ERFURT UNIVERSITY: Elephant to be taught to speak--K551.11.

ERGOSA-BATYR: K1951.1F.

ERMINE: Star husband turns wives to ermines so can descend to earth--A762.1Bb.

ERNE RIVER: Tinker of Tamlacht turns to salmon in River Erne—Q565Af.

ESBEN: Esben steals from witch--G610Ah. SEE ALSO ESPEN CINDERLAD.

ESKIMO: Boy eats cod, seal, ooglook, whale, <u>explodes</u>--X1723.4; <u>origin</u> of Eskimo—A1611.1.2.

ESPEN CINDERLAD: H1115.1.1. SEE ALSO ESBEN.

ETERNAL LIFE: Jofuku gives Sentaro paper crane to ride to Land of Perpetual Life—E80.5. SEE ALSO IMMORTALITY.

ETERNITY: How many seconds in eternity?— H701.1.

ETHIOPIA: Forbidden to set foot on Ethiopian soil, trickster fills boots with Egyptian <u>soil</u>— J1161.3.2; <u>soil</u> scraped from boots of leaving foreigners, soil is most precious thing in country—P711.10.

EVENING STAR: <u>Giant Nasan</u> woos Evening Star —A284.2.1; <u>origin</u>--A781.2. SEE ALSO STARS.

EVERGREENS: SEE TREES, EVERGREEN.

EVIL: Lad seeks to <u>know</u> what evil is--K603.3; <u>moon</u> investigates evil things in bog—A754.1.1.1; <u>origin</u> of evil—A1341, A1384; man <u>thinks</u> of evil things under roof, breaks tabu and star wife leaves—A762.2.1.

EXAGGERATION: Doubter to say "ahem" when exaggerates too much--X904.4.

EXCUSES: <u>Crime</u> for which excuse is worse than crime—J1211.4; <u>daughter</u> makes series of excuses—Z18.2; chain of excuses, why <u>frogs</u> cry-- Z49.19; why <u>heron</u> is lean, excuses—Z49.18.

EXECUTION: Execution <u>evaded</u>--J1181; man's own son offers to carry <u>letter</u> to enemy saying "execute this man"—K511.0.2.

EXILE: Exiled wife allowed to take dearest possession, takes husband—J1545.4.

EXTORTION: Doorman demands half reward-- K187.1; the eaten grain and the cock as damages —K251.1.

EYE: <u>Birds</u> peck out eyes of wicked stepsisters --R221B; why <u>blackbird</u> has white eyes— A2332.5.12; why <u>crabs</u> eyes pop out--A2231.10; <u>cranes</u> eyes call false alarm--J2199.1.3; why <u>crane's</u> eyes are blue--A2332.5.11; <u>contest</u> in seeing—K85; woman with bad eyes sees less after <u>doctor</u> leaves, he steals—J1169.1; <u>dwarf</u> gives up eyes to wed princess—H1409; why <u>earthworm</u> has no eyes—A2241.12; <u>fool</u> suggests pulling out eye to stop pain since that worked with teeth—J2412.2; <u>fox</u> substitutes berries for lost eye—E781.4; <u>frog</u> steals eye of sun-maid— T53.6; <u>giant</u> asks which eye captain saw him with and pokes it out—F361.3.0.1; <u>girls</u> throw eyes into air, blue camas flowers appear when fall--A2668; <u>hummingbird</u> pecks mud from eyes of panther--A2411.2.1.19.3; mortal <u>midwife</u> of fairy child gets fairy ointment in eyes and is able to see fairies—F235.4.1A; eyes as payment to <u>ogre</u> for building bridge—C432.1.1; <u>one-eye</u>, two-eyes, three-eyes wicked stepsisters— D830.1.1; Raven covers <u>seal's</u> eyes with gum and leads inside whale—A2494.15.1; casting sheep's eyes at the bride—J2462.2; where snake got eyes—A2241.12; single eye of three trolls taken by lads—K333.2; wind blows group of persons into person's eye—X941.4; witches steal eyes when allowed to comb lad's hair—G266.2; blinded six wives of raja—K961.2.2; raccoon plasters sleeping wolf's eyes with mud—A2411.2.1.13.

EYEBROWS: Origin of custom of painting eyebrows—A1599.4.1.2.

EYELASHES: Wolf's eyelashes give magic sight—D1821.3.11. SEE ALSO BLIND.

EYN-HALLOW: Fin island stolen—F742.1.

FACE: Ragged peasant asked if is cold, "Is your face cold?" "No, I'm all face."—J1309.1; daughter with homely face to watch character—J244.1.

FAIR: Wolf invites pig to fair—K891.1.1.

FAIRIES: Girl rolls nuts to fairy babies and gets magic object—L145.1B; cat is really fairy—B342C; fairy bodies for decorations on baptistry doors—A1465.3.3.1; fairy godmother—R221; good fairy as dove aids princess—D672D; gum doll set by Anansi captures fairy—K741.0.9; hiding from fairy Helena, lad turns to pin in cover of her magic book—H321C; fairies of Sardinia give magic date tree—R221C; fairies spin for girl—D2183.1; girl seeks stars, receives advice from fairies—F1068.0.1; supernatural lapse of time in fairyland—D1960.1, D2011, F377, F378.1, F420.6.1.3.1, G312.8; ogre with two faces—K635.3. SEE ALL ENTRIES F200-F499. SEE ALSO DWARF; ELF; HILLMAN; PISGIES; PISKEY; PLUM; PLUMSTONE FAIRIES; TOKGABBIES; WOOD MAIDENS; ETC.

FAITHFUL: Faithful Henry—D195.1. SEE ALSO PRINCE OF THE SEVEN GOLDEN COWS.

FALCON: SEE BIRD, FALCON.

FALL: SEE AUTUMN.

FALSE ALARM: False alarm sounded—J2172.1.

FALSEHOOD: Dispute among Truth, Falsehood, Fire and Water—K2143; distance from truth to falsehood—H685.2.

FAME: SEE NOTORIETY.

FAMILIARITY: Familiarity breeds contempt—U131.1.

FAMILY: One falcon wounded, brothers stay to care for it until spring—P250.2; ogre grieves for riches he can never know, a family—G586; origin of family heirlooms—A1578.2. SEE ALL ENTRIES P200-P299. SEE ALSO BROTHER; FATHER; MOTHER; SISTER; ETC.

FAMINE: trickster fails to carry out agreement to kill family in famine—K311.3.1; mouse brings grains of corn to St. Cadog, followed and store found—B437.2.3; plough up road, seeds dropped from carts sprout—J151.1; in sour cream shortage water called "sour cream" to remedy shortage—J1703.4; King of Naxos obtains squash seeds, people refuse to eat, puts them under guard and all are stolen—J1199.3.

FAN: magic fan makes nose grow longer—D1376.1.3; sparrows give maid feather to make magic fan—H1321.1Ac; riddle, selling wind to buy moon—H583.4.7; bring wind in paper—H506.12.

FARM: Farm claimed on basis of trail beaten to it from trickster's home—K453.1.

FARMER: Farmer surpasses astronomer, doctor. They return to city—L144.2; camel eats farmer's vegetables and potter laughs, camel lies down on pots—J1511.6.1; farmer's son plants 'gold' = rice—H588.7.1; farmer refuses to mention crop he is planting out loud for fear pigeon will hear—J1909.9; lark to move nest when farmer decides to reap himself—J1031; man to sprinkle magic dust on corners of field daily, under this supervision farm prospers—H588.7.5; origin of farmer class—A1650.4; philosopher in farmer's clothing is questioned by traveling theologian and answers so well that theologian passes that town by—J31.1.1; soldier lays sword on table ostentatiously, farmer brings in manure shovel, big spoon to go with big knife—J1225.1; farmer calls to wife that he has hidden hoe, thief hears—J2356.1; farmer's sons dig for treasure and vineyard flourishes—H588.7; trickster farmer invites animals who destroy each other—Z43.6.1; farm girl waits to grow wings, spirit gives them—Q22.1. SEE ALSO PEASANT.

FARMING: Deceptive crop division—K171.1; fox leaves all work to goose then claims crop—K641.1; what trade brings greatest happiness? Tilling soil—H1273.21; elephant and giraffe farm with hare, each thinks hare does half work—K364.1; hare eats peanuts as plants—K364.2; origin of farming custom—A1529.1. SEE ALSO CROPS; FIELD.

FASHION: Brer Fox and wife convinced that sleeping with heads off is the fashion—J2413.4.5.

FAT, ANIMAL FAT: Wife is spirit of magic calf's fat, she melts when made to cook—A2146.1, F1041.4.1; fat cut from inside of cow—F929.3; cruel stepmother melts when stood by fire—E632.2.

FAT, WEIGHT: Fat companion can broaden self—F601.2C; fat cat, cock, etc. eats all met—Z33ff; fat man can fit through gate if hay wagon can—J1411; animal overeats cannot escape through hole—K1022.2; which woman would suitor save if both fell into river, he asks fat woman if she can swim—H359.5; "wait till I get fat"—K553; fat man told will die, loses weight—K1955.1.0.1; fat wife melts—F1041.4.2.

FATA MORGANA: Fata Morgana offers to make Count Roger King of Sicily—Q113.3.1.

FATE: Fate gives choice of suffering in youth or age—J214; Book of Fate shows baron's son to wed peasant—K1355A; given better fate from Book of Destiny but must give it back when rightful owner comes, "Tchapogui"—N115; last son given to Fate—R111.1.3Bb; luck depends on what stool Fate sits on when born—N138. SEE ENTIRE CHAPTER N. CHANCE AND FATE. SEE ALSO BAD LUCK; FORTUNE.

FATHER: Father ega responsible for young—A2431.3.8.1.16; father leaves bag of 'gold' on condition son bury it= rice—H5887.1; son prophesied to kill father—N731.2.1; girl loves father like salt—H592.1; person sent to ever older man, each sends on to his father—F571.2; four skillful brother's resuscitate father—H621.4; father kills son for eating apple—S11.3.3.1.1; son plans to treat his father as he is treating old father—J121; father leaves treasure in vineyard, sons dig it up and vineyard flourishes—H588.7; old father feigns treasure, treated well—P236.2; father to wed daughter to first man passing—H465. SEE ALSO DAUGHTER; FILIAL PIETY; INHERITANCE; SON; SUITOR.

FATHER-IN-LAW: Wicked father-in-law imitates hero and is left as ferryman—H1273.2|; father tries unsuccessfully to imitate supernatural sons-in-law—J2411.3.1; father-in-law requires two pounds of banana leaf down for alchemy, in producing this, plantation itself produces gold—H588.7.2.

FEAR: Animal feared at first, later treated familiarly—U131.1; man dies from frog's bite, thinking it snakebite—F1041.1.11.4; widow and sons hold candle for ghost to read by—E451.13; hare fearing death outruns dog—U242; lad trying to learn what fear is—H1440; lad fears only one thing - learning—H1419.1; Cholera, Death and Fear visit Mecca—Z111.7; fearless girl needs no husband, grinds goblin in hopper, but screams when sees mouse—H1419.2; king threatens mystic with death if doesn't prove powers, at once sees spirits. "How?" "Fear is all you need."—J1289.21; trickster says he fears most pigs and beer, these are thrown at him—K975.1.2; snake fears hot tar, man says he fears gold, this is poured on him—K602.3; suitor must be unafraid to pull king's beard—H359.3; Napoleon shows tailor meaning of fear—J2071.2; asked to frighten pupil, teacher frightens mother and self as well—J2632.1; fear tests—H1400. SEE ALSO BRAVERY; FRIGHT.

FEARGAL: Learned professor examines another by signs—H607.2.1.

FEAST: Origin of Bromo Feast—A1545.1.1; feast warmed over one candle—K231.14.1; cat holds feast, eats guests—K815.13.2; man rejected for poor clothing puts on fine garments and then gives food to clothes since welcome is for them—J1561.3; origin of custom of inviting strangers to share feast—A1598.1; animals meet disaster preparing for feast—Z32.6; dupe denied food until hands are clean—K278; imaginary feast, guest pretends to eat—P327; coyote imitates food procuring—J2425; inappropriate feast repaid—J1565.1ff; indecision as to which feast to attend—J2183.1ff; origin of dance feast—A1542; guests fed with smell of food—K231.14.2; animals send to steal food from wedding feast for true lover—R111.1.3Ai; origin of feast for sixty-four Yoginees—A1541.2.2.

FEATHER: Borrowed feathers taken back—K1041.1.3; borrowed feathers not returned—A2313.6; lion believes cock's tail feather is hair K1711.1; dress of feathers—R221Db; donkey tricks lion into trying to kill him with eagle feather—A2423.1.4.1; girl covers self with feathers and honey as disguise—G561.1B; sight of golden feather starts quest—H1331.1.3; picture of girl appears on three golden feathers picked up, quest—H1213.1G; widow plucks feather from golden goose—D877.0.1; flowerpot, mud cake, cabbage, feather, etc. keep house—J512.7.2; Kassa Kena Genannina, strong man weighted down by feather—F615.9.1; magic feathers on feet help pass hazards—K17.1; bird killed for magic food giving feathers—D876.1; magic feather that allows one to hear animal's thought—B216; moon is ostrich feather—A741.5; finding one feather makes a hard pillow fool thinks a sackful would be unbearable—J2213.9; feather turns to prince—H1385.5Aa; bird prince gives feather to aid love—H1385.4B; sons to seek where three feathers fell—B641Ad; to pull feather from roof of underwater home of snake chief—B491.1.1; magic feather stretches to sky—H1385.3Fg; wife in honey and feathers is costume Devil cannot identify—K31.1; fool sends feathers to go by wind—F660.1Bb. SEE ALSO TAR AND FEATHERS.

FEATHERBED: Fast man can gather feathers of featherbed in wind—F660.1Bb; task, shaking Mother Holle's featherbed, causes snow to fly on earth—Q2.12Aa.

FEBRUARY: Thread in clothing blessed in church on February 5—D1385.18.1.

FEE-FI-FO-FUM: G84.

FEET: Bride test, size of feet—H36.1; cold hands and feet sign of dead person, man believes self dead—J2311.7; fools cannot find own feet—J2021; Manabozho tells feet to watch baking duck as he sleeps—J2351.1.2; origin of nature of animal's feet—A2375.2ff; stepsister mutilates foot to fit slipper—R221. SEE ALSO FOOTBINDING; LEG.

FEIGNED: SEE DEATH, FEIGNED; ILLNESS, FEIGNED.

FENCE: Brer Fox drops rail fence on Brer Rabbit's neck—K1111.4; riddle—cutting live trees and planting dead (making fences)—H583.2.6.

FENNIN: "Mountain of the Fennin Woman is on fire"—F381.8.1.

FERDINAND: Ferdinand the Faithful and Ferdinand the Unfaithful—H1213.1A.

FERGUS: Asleep in the mountain—D1960.2.

FERRY: Man carries blind men over stream and one drowns, he comforts that there is one less to pay for—J2566; dwarfs ferried across water—F451.1.4.4; eels sent to cross stream by selves since ferryman charges too much—J1881.2.3.1; Lady of the Tylwyth Teg gives ferryman silver coin which replaces itself—F342.3; ferryman to hand oar to another and be relieved of duty—H1273.2; ferryman giving robber ride finds treasure cache—N534.9; pedagogue asks ferryman if he has studied grammar "Then half your life has been wasted." Boat begins to sink and ferryman asks scholar if he can swim "Then all your life is lost"—J1229.4.

FESTIVAL: SEE CEREMONY; FEAST.

FEUD: Drop of honey causes chain of accidents—N381.

FEZ: Origin of red hat called "Fez", originated in city of Fez—A1437.2.

FIANCÉE: Forgotten fiancée reawakens lover's memory—D2003+; slovenly fiancée, key in flax reveals laziness—H382.1; quest for three persons as stupid as fiancée—H1312.1. SEE ALSO BRIDE; SUITOR.

FIANNA: Youngest of Fianna vanquishes ogress—D1162.2.2.

"FIDDEVAW": All who poke fire must say this—D1413.17.

FIDDLE: Devil turns girl's father into fiddle, mother to bow, brothers to strings—D1233.0.1; elfin fiddle given—F331.4; horse-headed fiddle—A1461.1.1; magic fiddle—D1233; magic fiddle causes dancing—D1415.2.3; musician in hell playing for the devils purposely breaks fiddle strings—K606.1.2.

FIDDLER: Cat fiddles to lure foxes from den—K815.15; musician in hell playing for devils on Christmas Eve plays carol—G303.25.17.2.1; dupe wishing to learn to play fiddle has finger caught in cleft of tree—K1111.0.1; fiddler on walls of besieged city plays music so melancholy that enemy become homesick and desert—K2368.6; fiddler in underground fairyland—E425.2.5.1; bad luck as fiddler—N250.4; wolf captor scared by fiddle playing of captive ram—K2327. SEE ALSO VIOLIN.

FIDELITY: Blodevedd turned to owl for betraying husband—A1958.0.2; only brother will help bury 'murdered' man—H1558.1.0.1; bet that wife will be unfaithful to him during pilgrimage—H466.1.1. SEE ALSO FAITHFUL.

FIELD: Man carried over field to chase off stork trampling down field—J2163.4; man says he is going to climb to heaven, crowd gathered tramples down field—K474.1; fairy field plowed up—F336.1; field sprinkled with 'magic' dust daily prospers—H588.7.5; wife pledges husband to give field to poor—E415.2.1; field dug up in search of treasure prospers—H588.7. SEE ALSO FARMING.

FIFE: Trickster steals fife—K1611G.

FIG: Man takes figs to ruler instead of beets, they are thrown at him "Thank God they weren't beets"—J2563; crocodile masking as fig pile—K607.2.2; who eats figs turns to donkey—D551.1A; figs promised for dessert are never produced, guest reads a passage from the Koran after dinner and omits word "figs". Host, "You forgot the figs." Guest, "No, you did."—W158.1; fruit causes nose to grow—D551.1B; olive brags of never losing her leaves, heavy snow breaks her but barren fig survives—J832.1; pearl color of fig will disenchant rosebush—N271B; old man planting fig tree for future generations—J701.1; one fig rewarded, imitator has figs thrown at him—J2415.1; spider crawls over fig pile with wax on stomach and steals—K378.1.1.

FIGHT: Fighting boys join forces against attacking bully—J1025.3; all required to wear two foot wide clay hats and fine imposed for breaking, this stops fighting—J1199.5; animals refuse to help stop fight between dog and cat, they are killed in chain of events—J451.2; owl advises knee-high man to stay small so no one will challenge to fight—J291; trickster dupes ogres into fighting each other—K1082.

FILBERTS: Boy with hand stuck in filbert jar—W151.9.1.

FILE: Serpent attacks file—J552.3.

FILIAL PIETY: Bamboo grows from ground wet with son's tears—A2681.6.1; lad cares for blind parents in jungle—W46.1; Goddess weaves for poor man who sacrificed for father's funeral—T111.1.3; maid from shell sent as reward for filial piety—N831.1; origin of ancestor tablets—A1547.4. SEE ALSO DAUGHTER; SON.

FILL: House to go to son who fills it completely, youngest fills house with light—H1023.2.6;.

FIN: Fin folk aid—F420.5.1.11, F420.7.1; Fin folk injure—F420.4.7.1; woman held captive on Fin Island—D1899.1; Fin's Island taken—F742.1; wed to Fin—F420.6.1.1.1.

FINDER: Finder of lost object must shout fact three times in marketplace, does so at three a.m.—J1161.12.

FINE: Lawyer advises men to go to jail, once there agree to pay fine, thus have gotten trip to city free—J1179.21; to be killed as soon as pays fine of one mon per year for one hundred years—J1173.1.2.

FINGER: Captive sticks out bone instead of finger—G412.1; girl child size of little finger—F535.1.1F; Finn bites off Cucullin's magic finger—K521.4.1.5; "Why are you eating with five fingers?" "Because I haven't got six."—J1347; immortal's magic finger turns all to gold—W151.13; cauldron in forbidden room turns finger gold—B316B; little girl rescued from gorilla's little finger—F913.4; love through sight of finger—T11.4.8; husband feigns wife's voice and has lover put finger through hole in wall, cuts off—K1561.2; witch removes victims' livers with stone finger as they sleep—G262.2.1; four fingers distance from Truth to Falsehood—H685.2; lazy wife given ten helpers, they enter her fingers and force to work—Q321.2.2.

FINGERNAIL: Maui receives burning fingernail of Mafuite when asks for fire—A1414.4; moon hides tidbits under her fingernails for mother—L351.2; rat eats student's nail clippings and turns to student—D315.1.1.

FINLAND: Message of Finnish sorcerer to cover self in mud and say "man into crayfish"—H1021.8.1.

FINN MCCOUL: K521.4.1.5.

FIR: SEE TREE, FIR.

FIRE: Fire goes to burn Anansi's house—K415.0.1; why animals lack fire—A2436.1; ant teaches how to make fire—A1414.8; house on fire illusion created by badger—D612.1.2; brush on badger's back set afire—K2345.0.1; dupe in bees nest told fire is stinging of bees—K1055.3; lucky beggar refused room, house burns—N177; black snake scorched fetching fire—A2411.5.9; house burnt down to get rid of cat—J2101; cock sent for fire stays—A2513.6; Thor, Loke and Thiaffe contest with Fire, Sea and Thought—F531.6.15.1.1; cooking over one candle fire as easy as warming self on moutain watching candle in village below—K231.14.1; cougar has food and no fire, wildcat has fire and no food—A2378.4.15; house has lake of fire around it, means fire is covered at night—F302.1.6; dog sent to steal fire stays—A2513.1.2ff; man domesticated fire's red bones—A2436.1; origin fire drill—A1414.1.2; dupe in grass burnt—K1055; fire carried in basket attacks enemies—Z52.3; fire alarm lures fairies away—F381.8; monkeys believe fireflies are fire—J1761.3; fool throws water on fire in oven—J2461.1.2D; fox punished by setting fire to tail, fields set afire—J2101.1; Fire God to steam sun god's sons in steam bath—F17.1; Goddess of Fire, Pele—A493.1; ghostly burning house—E531.1; ghostly cook sits on fire—E411.0.2.1.1; Fire, Water, Honor travel together—W45.2; iceman called to put out fire in tree—F433.2; lizard rescued from burning brush with shepherd's crook—D882.1Bba; magpie is dead, chain of horrors including fire—Z46; maid given silly names for

objects tries to raise fire alarm—X1506ff; Maui brings fire to Tonga—A1415.5; monkey forsees chain of disasters including fire—Z49.23; tabu, letting the fire go out, girl disobeys and leaves trail leading ogres to door—S12.1.0.1Bb, S352.2; owl scorched fetching fire—A2411.2.4.2ff; task, bringing fire in paper = lantern—H506.12; all who poke fire stick there—D1413.17; man rescues snake from flames—D817.1.2.2; snake maiden saved from fire rewards—D882.1C; animal who steals fire scorched, cause of color—A1415; origin of steam engine—A1439.5; setting sun mistaken for fire—J1806; sun from fire flung into sky—A714.3.1; sun as fire rekindled daily—A712; dispute among Truth, Falsehood, Fire, Water—K2143; vixen tells cub she's warming paws at fire far below, cub says spark burnt her nose—J1122.2; origin of walking on fire—A1542.3; man to spend night on cold mountain warms self by sight of fire below—K231.14.1+; fire put out by water which trickster has swallowed—Z52.1, Z52.4; girls work together and push witch into fire—G512.3.2.0.1; animals must defeat woman's little girl in wrestling to get fire—F617.2.3. SEE ALL A1414 Origin of Fire, A1415.2 Theft of Fire. SEE ALSO FLAME.

FIRE, FIREFIGHTING: Town of fools buys trumpet thinking it puts out fires—J1703.7.

FIREBIRD: Quest for firebird—H1213.1la, H1331.1.3.

FIRECRACKERS: Set off by jackals to frighten tiger—K1715.2.

FIREFLY: Apes attacking firefly hit each other—K1082.3.2; firefly won't return cap, chain—Z41.1.1; sham wise man to guess contents of box—N688.2; firefly carries fire so mosquitoes won't bite—Z49.6.0.1; firefly given lantern for finding last jewel of insect king—A2094.1; monkeys believe firefly is fire—J1064.1, J1761.3.

FIREPLACE: SEE HEARTH.

FIRETONGS: Stretch to ten times length when wife chases him with them—W211.7.

FIRST: First thing touched to be picked up—N222.

FISH: Fish aids lad—B582.2D; Lad turned to fish to escape Amazons—F565.1.2; big fish thinks self too big for pool, swims downstream and is driven back by bigger fish—J513.3; fish brags of long life, is soon caught—L395; today's catch of fish traded for prospective larger catch tomorrow—J321.1.1; fish reward cook with gold—F342.1.1; coyote breaks witch's dam and releases fish—A1421.0.0.1; fish pretends to be dead and fisherman ignores him—K522.4.1; Arawidi turns fish into dogs as companions for man—A2335.2.6.1; tame fish falls off bridge and drowns—X1306.3; earthworm warns fish not to bite—K689.1; eaten fish calls "I got you now"—Z13.5; fish divided by fox--K452.1.1; fish refuses fox's invitation to live on dry land--J758.3; giant fish, Da Kwa, eats--F912.2.13; why fish have gills--A2341.4; to stand in water and watch fish with gold ring around neck, it turns to girl--G666.3; golden fish released by girl helps her escape--D711.2; grasshoppers plunge into water and turn to fish--A2108.1; fish tricked by heron into letting selves be carried to another pond--K815.14; meditating holy man caught with fish --D1960.5; floating house from which fish flow --A2109.2; King of Fishes returns knife and warns never to lend--H1132.1.5; King of Fishes as brother-in-law--B314F; boy says little fish served him is asking about the large one in the kitchen--J1341.2; fish lover is killed by girl's family--B610.1.1, B654, R221Qa; luck lost due to failure to eat fish from head downward--B175.3; twin sons, colts, dogs, olive trees from eating magic fish--R111.1.3Aa; magic fish returned to water gives ability to do work magically--B375.1.3; Manabozho kills Giant Sturgeon and cut up pieces become fish --A2102; girl puts markings on fish--A2412.4.6; marriage to person in fish form--B644.1; monkey tries to fish and nearly drowns in net--J516; fish with bent noses--A2335.3.4; fish to climb trees if river burns, says numskull--J1904.4.1; painted fish comes to life--D435.2.1.3; fish painted on stairs seems real--H504.1.4; painter dreams becomes fish and is about to be eaten by friends--F1068.3; fish peddler attacked by cats gaffs head of cat, finds woman with wounded head--D702.1.1.1; pet fish killed by stepmother, bones grant wishes--R221J, R221Qa; pet fish Muchie Lal grows big as tank--B644.1; three princesses are carried off by fish--B314F; Rajah of Fishes returns lost ax to kind brother-- J2415.14; Raven creates fish from alder leaves-- A2013; Raven turns men to fish--A1411.2.1; fish 'steal' rice by causing family to eat more when having such a fine meal--J1341.7.1; fish provides answer to riddle posed by demon-- B375.1.4; fish recovers ring from sea--B548.2.1; lost ring found in fish--N211.1A; fried fish restored by saint--E121.4.2; Saint Neot eats one fish every day, when cook prepares two, Saint Neot throws them back and they return to life-- V229.27; salted fish thrown into pond to breed-- J1909.8.1; fish saved his life one time, he was on verge of starvation--J1250.4; magic shell draws fish--C322.3; fish down back teaches lad to shudder--H1440; small fish escape through net--L331; small fish kept--J321.2; fish with snake on back dives--J2137.6.2; why fish do not speak--A2422.14; girl swallowed by fish cuts slits in throat and escapes--F911.4.1; girl pulled under water, weds fish ruler--B603.1; fish grants wishes--B375.1; fish with one hundred wit--J1662.3; Witch of Lok Island turns all lovers into fish--G263.1.0.1.1.

FISH, AVINI: Origin markings--A2412.4.6.

FISH, BLOWFISH: Why blowfish has spines-- A2315.2.

FISH, CARP: Carp changed into first dragon-- B11.2.1.3; carp sneaks through dragon gate and becomes dragon--B11.6.11; carp as mysterious housekeeper--N831.1.0.1.

FISH, CATFISH: Catfish borrows feathers to fly --K1041.1.2; why catfish has flat head--A2320.8; catfish wants to marry lizard, neither can stand other's habitat--J414.3.1.

FISH, EEL: Why eel's eyes are narrow-- A2332.3.2.1; man catches much game, eel pulled from stream hits boat and kills, etc.--X1124.3; eel shows man how to walk on hot stones-- A1542.3; eels tie selves in knots, make man on moon laugh--A751.3.1.3; eel lover, coconut grows from cut off head--A2681.5.1; eel drowned for eating salt fish put in pond to breed-- J1909.8.1; eels sent to cross stream by selves-- J1881.2.3.1.

FISH, FLOUNDER: Origin of flounder's body-- A2305.1.2; why flounder has two eyes on same side of face--A2332.4.4; flounder complains in race, is punished with crooked mouth--A2252.4; flounder befriends fisherman and his wife-- B375.1.

FISH, GOLDFISH: Magic goldfish caught gives castle with ever full cupboard--R111.1.3Ak.

FISH, GUDGEON: Cormorant cuts off gudgeon's tail, has to replace with own--A2378.2.11.

FISH, HALIBUT: Halibut man with floating house of fishes--A2109.2.

FISH, HUMU-HUMU-NUKU-NUKU-A-PUAA: A2130.1.

FISH, IKAN LELEH: Origin--A2130.2.

FISH, MACKEREL: Origin--A2121.1.

FISH, MOONFISH: Origin--A2116.

FISH, PAURA: Origin markings--A2412.4.6.

FISH, PORGY: Why porgy's eyes are red-- A2332.5.9.

FISH, SALMON: Tinker of Tamlacht turned to salmon--Q565Af; whittled from stick by old man --A2109.1.

FISH, SCULPIN: Why sculpin has pointed tail-- A2378.9.1.2.

FISH, SHARK: Girl refuses to wed, thrown to sharks, sings to charm--D735.1B; shark takes monkey for heart--K544; octopus forces shark to leave men alone--B477; Punia steals lobsters from sharks--K341.16; Punia in shark's belly lives off shark meat--F911.4.2; why sharks do not kill people near Raiatea--A2586; Chief of Sharks thrown into sky = Milky Way--A778.13; why shark has bump on head--A2412.4.6. SEE ALSO SAMEBITO.

FISH, SOLE: Why has crooked mouth--A2252.4; why flat--A2412.4.6.

FISH, SPRAT: Dolphin and whale scorn sprat as peacemaker—J411.6.

FISH, STURGEON: Manabozo kills Giant Sturgeon, cut up in pieces, become fish—A2102, F912.2.7.

FISH, SUCKERS: Brer Rabbit trapped in well tells Brer Fox he is fishing for "suckers"—K651.

FISH, TROUT: Trout pretends to be dead and fisherman ignores—K522.4.1; silver tree asks trout in well who is most beautiful queen in world—D582.2.

FISH, TUNA: Origin of tuna industry—A1457.9.1; SEE ALSO CRAYFISH; CRAB; WHALE; ETC.

FISH BASKET: Spring from fishbasket forms lake of sacred fish—A920.1.18.

FISH HOOKS: Lad feeds children of Troll wife and she gives magic fish hooks—G666.1; fish hook lost by archer, seeks beneath sea—U136.0.1.

FISH SPEAR: Origin of barbed fish spear—A1457.1.1.

FISH TRAPS: First human pair caught in fish trap by chameleon—A1279.2; origin of fish trap—A1457.5; eel tricks porgy into fishbasket—A2332.5.9; tiny son hids in fishbasket, startles fishwife—F535.1.1Da.

FISHER: SEE BIRD, FISHER.

FISHERMAN: Fisherman weds clam maiden—N831.1; fishermen fail to count selves—J2031.0.3; fisherman fails to make fish dance for bagpipes—J1909.1; doorkeeper demands half of fisherman's reward—K187.1; fisherman given magic gem by carp—D882.1Bbc; ghost of drowned person befriends fisherman—E414.0.1; archer loses fisherman's hook—U136.0.1; fisherman dies of love, flute plays on crystal—E633.1; fisherman returns caught mermaid, she warns of storms—F420.5.1.1; fisherman rescues princess sent as sacrifice to Sea God—R111.1.3.Da; seal repays fisherman for torn net—F420.5.1.11; fisherman weds maiden under the sea—F420.6.1.3.1; wishes given to fisherman and wife—B375.1.

FISHING: With tail through ice—K1021.

FISHING LINE: Fishing line of bark plaited by man on moon—A751.0.2.

FITCHER'S FEATHERED BIRD: G561.1B.

FIVE: Anansi has spell so that anyone saying "five" falls dead—C498.2.2; counting by fives to get more cattle in short time—F420.6.1.5.1; counting by fives to win tossing contest—H331.18; raven thinks five magic number because five fingers on children's hands—Z71.3.3.

FLAG: Faery Flag of Dunvegan given to Clan MacLeod—F305.1.2; spirit blows signal flag to left, sign for death—E279.6.1.

FLAIL: Task, fetch flail from hell—G610Ak.

FLAMES: Flames were stories told by three men sleeping in house. They protect house—M231.1Ba; wind, wave and wandering flame aid—D672K. SEE ALSO FIRE.

FLAMINGO: SEE BIRD, FLAMINGO.

FLATHEAD: Origin of tribe according to Nez Percé—A1610.8.

FLATTERY: Cock crows with closed eyes—K721; elephant chosen king, killed—K815.20; fox flatters raving into singing, drops cheese—K334.1; you are a full moon and my sovereign is a new moon—H599.3.

FLAX: SEE SPINNING.

FLAYING: Skillful flayer skins running hare—F660.1Bb.

FLEA: Flea suggests wood chopping contest, slips back, eats pudding—K372.2; coyote opens mole's bag of fleas—J2131.2.2; flea skin drum, guess what it's made of—H522.1.1; flea's face red from drink—A2330.5; trickster claims giant's blow was like flea bite—K525.1; flowerpot, cabbage, flea, etc. keep house—J512.7.2; innkeeper told that pharmacist is paying for fleas—J1685; louse invites the flea, flea bites man and louse is killed—J2137.1; louse drowns in beer, flea weeps—Z32.2.4.1; flea fears strokes of man—U142; why mouse and flea bother man—A2585.2; riddle, throws away what he catches and carries home those not caught—H583.3; spider falls in brew vat, flea mourns—Z32.2.3. SEE ALSO LOUSE.

FLEDGELINGS: Trickster attracts attention of mowers until young birds can escape—K644.

FLEECE: Moneylender told he'll be paid with fleece caught on thornbush—J2060.2.1. SEE ALSO SHEEP.

FLIGHT: SEE FUGITIVES.

FLING: Ant teaches use of flints—A1414.8; contest, beating dust from fling with sledge hammer—K62.1; Crazy Horse chews flint to powder before battle, becomes invincible—A526.1.1.1; origin of flint—A1414.5.1; rabbit gets secret of flint arrow making. Tries to burn flint and it explodes—A2342.1.1.

FLITTING: Boggart flits too when farmer leaves to get away from him—F482.3.1.1.

FLOOD: Giant Og rides on roof of Ark—F531.6.12.8.2; flood is illusion created by badger—D612.1.2; cat arrives at mountain top floating on coconut—A2681.5.1.1; flood from magic land in chest—F302.1.4; dam prevents future floods—R111.1.2Dd; fire hides in iron, rock, bamboo during flood—A1414.7.2; fox in swollen river claims is swimming—J873; hermit saves villagers from flood—E379.7; flood tide caused by magic jewel—U136.0.1; louse falls in beer, chain, spring floods—Z32.2.4.1; man rescues cooper, fox and snake in flood—W154.8.3; earth rebuilt after flood with magic mold from tortoise's back—A815.0.1; magical poem stops flood—D1275.4.1; white snake lady causes flood —B656.2.1; flood to come when stone temple lions turn red—W154.8.4; Tall Tree re-peoples earth after flood—W154.8.5; thumbling and rain battle sun, flood results—Z52.5; turkey's tail washed white—A2211.7.1; SEE ALL A1010 Deluge. Innundation of whole world or section.

FLORENCE: Origin crest of Florence—G302.7.1.2; origin baptistry doors in Florence—A1465.3.3.1; origin of onion shaped iron lanterns of Strozzi Palace in Florence—A1447.3.1.

FLOUNDER: SEE FISH, FLOUNDER.

FLOUR: Bride pastes flour on husband, turns to gold when falls off—K1917.3H; fools think one is lost, boy counts the flour sacks each carry and find all there—J2031.0.1; man dumps sacks of flour into water to demonstrate emptiness of others; heads—J2062.1; wall of flour built by miser—W153.16; flour sent to go home with wind —J1881.1.8; wolf puts flour on paws to disguise self—K311.3. SEE ALSO MEAL.

FLOWER: Bee shows real flowers—H540.2.1.1; bouquet of all flowers—H1377.2; God snips off bits of flowers to become butterflies—A2041.1; children lost picking flowers—R131.21; flower secured for daughter at expense of first thing met at home—H1385.4, T35.1; girl dies when her flower dies—E765.3.4; flower picked in fairyland, tabu broken—F378.5; bat enters forbidden Valley of Flowers—A1341.4; loveliest flower is wheat—B641Ah; magic flower disenchants sister —D771.11.1; origin of flowers—A2650; two princesses disappear while picking flowers— B314F; gardener boy reads forbidden books and causes flowers to sing—D1711.0.1.4; old man causes snow, young makes flowers bloom— A1158.1; Golden Turtle gives white flowers that cause nose to grow—D551.1C. SEE ALSO ARBUTUS; CAMAS; CARNATION; CHAMPA; COWSLIP; HIBISCUS; LILY; ROSE; ETC.

FLOWERPOT: Flowerpot, mud cake, etc. keep house—J512.7.2.

FLUESSEN: Bell dropped into Fluessen River— F993.1.1.

FLUTE: Bird lends voice to flute—F601.2I; blackbird pierces claw, takes flute and sings of events—Z47.5; hero thrown to wild boars plays flute and they dance—H328.9; fisherman's flute sounds from crystal after his death—E633.1; Dragon King's daughter pines after music of abandoned flute player—B11.12.7.2; fire hidden in flute and relayed home—A1415.2.2.2; gooseherd plays on flute and enchants prince—R221Z; flute springs from grave—A1461.8.1; girl swims to reach flute playing lover—T35.5.1; magic flute causes field to prosper—D1563.1.4.1;

magic flute causes dancing—D1415.2.3ff; Manticore of North Cerney befriends boy and gives flute—B27; four monkeys invent instruments— A1461.0.1; origin of flute, suitor to learn songs of birds—A1461.8.2; flute with one hundred pipes—B216.5; flute reveals secret—D1316.5.0.3; E632ff; to climb tower and take flute from under pillow, play it and tower will follow—H1213.1H; tree to bear quinces if plays sad tunes, oranges if lively—D1223.1.1; turtle playing flute and dancing untied by children—K571; turtle makes flute of jackal's thighbone—K1775.1; willow flute sings of witch's murder—E632.0.3.

FLY: Bald man aims at fly and hurts head— J2102.3; bear kills fly on man's head—N333.2; bear strikes at fly and hits self—K1082.3.3; origin fly's buzz—A2426.3.3; doctor advises swallowing frog to eat fly swallowed—Z49.14.1; fool sells syrup to flies—J1852.1.4; why fly rubs hands together—A2479.10; husband smashes up furniture chasing fly—N333.0.3; identifying wife, fly lights on head—H1385.3M; why flies swarm around Kenki—A2433.5.2.1; boastful fly killer makes belt saying "seven at a blow"— K1951.1; helpful fly causes sleeper to move leg freeing King David—B524.2.1.2; fly helps fetch light from heaven—A1412.6; fly loses lying contest—X905.1.3; fly dying in meat tub—J861.3; lad hits fly on judge's nose—J1193ff: why fly watches ox's eyes—A2479.9; Mirali insists flies only where are people—J1289.32; chain, fly frightens snake—Z43.4; spider spins basket shut —L396; old lady who swallowed a fly—Z49.14; thirteen flies come from box and do work— D882.1Fc; fly on coach wheel, "What a dust I raise"—J953.10.2; fly as witness—J1141.1.3.3.

FLY, BLUEBOTTLE: Makes first fire— A1414.1.1.1.

FLY, HORSEFLY: Why buzzes—A2236.1; clings to fox's tail in race—K11.2. SEE ALSO DRAGONFLY; FIREFLY.

FLYING: Anansi flies with blackbird to island to feed—K1041.1.5; dupe lets self be carried aloft by bird—K1041; man carried by bird—K1861.1; flying box—R221Dc Catskins; man rescues princess on flying carpet—H355.0.1; flying contest won by deception—K25.1; man echoes fairies' cry, flies after them—F282.4.2; flying fairy boat seen—F349.5; flight by putting on bird feathers, dupe falls—K1041.1; Flying Dutchman—E511.1.2; wren rides on eagle's back, highest flyer to be king—K11.2; artificial flying horse made—D1626.1; how ptarmigan learned to fly—A2442.3.1; bird created by Raven cannot fly—J2186.1; flying ship goes on land or sea— F601.2, H341.1Ab; people learn magic word so can fly, slaves fly back to Africa—D2135.0.3.1; turtle carried by eagle—J657.2; turtle carried by geese, talks—J2357; Wabassi sticks feathers in belt and tries to fly—K1041.4; mortal flies with witches—G242.7ff. SEE ALSO WINGS.

FLYING SQUIRREL: Body made larger—A2377.2; birds make wings for flying squirrel—A2377.2, B261.1.0.2.1.

FOAM: Maid born of foam lives one year—
F424.1.1.

FOE: Foe imitates Friend and loses life—N452D.

FOG: Man can put fog in bag—F601.2Ac; origin
of fog—A1134.1; shingling the fog—X1651.1.

FOO-FOO: Magic foo-foo bearing tree—D861.1H.

FOOD: Monkey shows edible foods to man—
B441.1.0.1; lad ignores girl in tree, feeds yams
to dog and meat to goat, she berates and comes
down—H343.3; ignorance of certain food—
J1742.3.2; inexhaustible food—D1652.1ff; guest
reveals hiding places of paramour's feast—
J1344; all of replenishing food never to be eaten
—D877.0.2; riddle, gathering yesterday's food
(paying for it)—H583.4.2.1; spirits to release
Pupu who has been reclaiming stolen food plants
—E461.1.1; trickster demands return of food
just eaten—K251.2.1; trickster makes others
think food is spoiled—K344.1ff; trickster hides
in food and eats—K371; trickster eats food and
blames on dupe—K401.1. SEE ALSO APPLE;
BAKER; BREAD; CABBAGE; CARROTS;
CHEESE; COOK; CROPS; FEAST; FIG; FOO-
FOO; FRUIT; GRAPES; HELVA; MILK; PEARS;
POTATOES; PUDDING; RICE; SOUP; ETC.

FOOLS: Fool to bring pottle of brains—J163.2.1;
fool to be wise when gets 'coat of clay'—
J163.2.2; town of fools—J1703ff; quest for three
persons as stupid as this—H1312.1+; talkative
wife discredited—J1151.1.1ff. SEE ALL EN-
TRIES J1700-J2799. SEE ALSO SPECIFIC
FOOLS GIUFA; GUNO AND KOYO; HODJA;
MULLA. SEE ALSO TOWNS OF FOOLS BEL-
MONT; GOTHAM; HELM; HOLMOLA; HUMS;
LAGOS; MASI; MEIRINGEN; MONTIERI; SAINTE
DODO; SCHILDA; SCHILDBURG.

FOOT: SEE FEET.

FOOTBINDING: Origin footbinding—A1599.4.1.1.

FOOTPRINTS: Lakes are footprints—A920.1.10.1;
transformation of brother by drinking from
hoofprints—P253.2.01.

FOOTSTOOL: Footstool thrown from heaven—
F1037.1.1.

FORBIDDEN: Bat enters forbidden Valley of
Flowers—A1341.4. SEE ALSO ENTIRE CHAPTER
C TABUS.

FORDING: Fording a stream 'where the ducks
cross'—J1919.2.

FOREIGN LANGUAGE: Fool thinks "I don't understand" is man's name—J1802.1, J1803, J2496.1;
three travelers know one phrase each of foreign
language, incriminate themselves—J2496.3.

FOREIGNER: First Father chases progeny out of
house, those farthest away become foreigners—
A1650.4.

FORESIGHT, LACK OF: Ant and lazy grasshopper—J711.1; youth seeing swallow sells winter
clothes—J731.1.

FOREST: Bluff, trickster threatens to bring
whole forest when sent for tree—K1741.1; Kin-
Kin sings telling King of Forest to repair ravages of animals trying to clear for garden, sings
jungle back each night—D1487.3.1. SEE ALSO
TREE; WOOD.

FOREST FIRE: Caused by magic fox's gift to
mean woman—D313.1.4.

FORGETFULNESS: Forgotten fiance—D2003+,
D2006.1+, G530.2. SEE D2000+ Magic forgetfulness. SEE ALL ENTRIES J2671ff Forgetful
fools.

FORGIVENESS: Orphan who forgives stepmother
all cruelties made king—N421.1.

FORK: Pixy's coattail speared with fork—
F381.14.

FORTUNE: Fortune thanked for good luck, blam-
ed for bad—N111.4.2ff; Dame Fortune offers
gift, man chooses ever full purse—D1192.1.
SEE ENTIRE CHAPTER L REVERSAL OF FOR-
TUNE; SEE N100-N299 Ways of Fortune. SEE
ALSO BAD LUCK; FATE; LUCK.

FORTUNE TELLER: SEE WISEMAN, SHAM.

FORTY THIEVES: Eavesdrop under window of
sham wise man and think they hear him counting them—N611.5.

FOSTEDINA: Early Christian martyr—A1437.1.

FOUNDLING: Fairy child raised by mortal—
F321.9.

FOWL: Clever carving of the fowl—H601; plucking
the fowl, king sends peasant to pluck his courtiers—H561.6.1; unlucky man sells fowl filled
with gold coins—N351. SEE ALSO CHICKEN;
TURKEY; ETC.

FOX: Fox aids abandoned lad, enlists help of
other animals, steals princess, etc.—B582.6;
air-castle, selling sleeping fox's tail—J2061.3.1;
fox to guard dead ass, claims it had no brains—
K402.3.1; fox tricks bear into fishing with tail—
K1021; fox steals chicken from table and runs to
barn where bear is stealing, bear is caught—
K401.1.2; fox eats bear's dead brother—K2028;
fox carried in bill, stomach or basket—Z52.1;
dupe lets himself be carried aloft by bird and
dropped—K1041.0.4; Brer Rabbit offers Brer
Wolf taste from jug of fox's blood (molasses)—
K1715.3.1; fox bride—B641.0.1Dc; B651.1ff;
fox transformed to Buddha bathes in rice pot—
K717.1, K891.1.5; fox transformed to Buddha
tricked into sticking out tongue—K607.4; foxes
tie sham dead burro to tails and drag home—
J2132.5.4; Miss Goose leaves clothes bundle on
bed and Brer Fox steals—K525.1.0.1; cock
agrees to sing for fox if dog is invited too—

K579.8; fox persuades cock to open door—K815.15; color of fox—A2411.1.3.2; fox counts sea animals and reaches shore on their backs—K579.2.3; fox tricks coyote into climbing tree—K553.1.0.5, holding up rock--K1251, diving for moon--J1791.3; fox feigns lame and beats coyote in race--K11.5; crab killed by fox--J512.1; cricket sees wings near fox's door and flees—K2061.10; deceptive crop division--K171.1; fox leaves all work to goose then claims crop—K641.1; fox advises crow to drop necklace into snake's den—K401.2.2; fox flatters crow into singing and dropping cheese--K334.1; fox's daughter gives student magic mirror—B651.1.1; fox in pit feigns dead, man throws out—K522.4.2; fox feigns dead, is thrown on wagon with fish--K371.1; Brer Fox imitates Brer Rabbit's trick of shamming dead on road--K341.2.1.1; sham dead Brer Fox tricked into saying "Wahoo"--K607.3; fox divides cake for bear cubs--K452.1.2; fox divides fish, keeps middle--K452.1; fox claims dough is brains—K473.1; bear dreams eats honey, fox has same dream and eats real honey since bear already ate--K444; fox tricked into turning into dumpling--K722.0.1; fox burns eagle's tree--L315.3; fox substitutes berries for lost eye--E781.4; fox imitates hunter, saves farmer from bear--C25; fox, crane exchange inappropriate feast--J1565.1; fox steals fire--A1415.2.2.5; fox helps hero steal firebird--H1331.1.3; shrike leads fishseller on chase, fox eats fish--K341.5.2.1; fox in flood claims is swimming to town--J873; fox grateful for rescue from flood--W154.8.3; fox as godfather eats stores--K372; fox and sour grapes--J871; mother gull fills fox's sack with thorns and frees chicks, fox tries to drink Lake Titicaca dry--K526.2; whose family is older? Fox is referred to in Han Dynasty classics--B841.1.4; hare persuades wolf and fox to put their heads in loops on rope to strangle tiger and are dragged to death--K713.3; origin fox fur hats--A1437.3; hawk advises crow that fox cannot climb--K1788; Brer Fox and wife convinced that sleeping with heads off is fashionable--J2413.4.5; hen substitutes rock for self in fox's bag--K526; fox offers to doctor hen--K2061.7; fox promised hens is given dog in bag--K235.1; alleged courier fox to have taken hens home--K131.1.2; fox in hollow tree eats elephant's cache and can't escape—K1022.0.2; fox as holy man eats hen worshippers--K815.16.2; fox tells baby hopi turtle to sing or will eat--G555.1.1; fox tied to horse's tail to catch horse--J2132.5.2; horsefly clings to fox's tail in race--K11.2; fox trades hornet's nest for "magic paw paw" (jack in the pulpit root) which burns mouth--K1023.1.0.1; mysterious housekeeper—N831.1; fox in human guise--D313.1.2; fox's husband cat feared by animals--K2324; bear builds house of wood, fox of ice--J741.1; fox thinks icicle is bone--J1772.15; fox repeats insult as harmless remark—K1775; small trickster in house of larger animal intimidates with loud boasts--K1711.2; Jack knocked three better kings out of a fox--H342.3; man leaves jug so wind hums over mouth--K1725.1.1; hare defeats fox in jumping contest—K17.5; fox frightened by kid--K1715.2.1; fox thinks animals flee from him, flee from lion

following him--J684.1.1; fox ceases to fear lion--U131.1; fox goes hunting without lion, killed—J684.1; fox tells lion cure lies in wrapping himself in wolf skin--K961.1.1; lion and bear fight over carcass to exhaustion, fox takes kill—J218.1.1; fox sees tracks going into lion's cave only--J644.1; fox to judge lion's breath feigns a cold--J811.2.1; fox leads ass to lion's den but is himself eaten--K1632; magic fox comes from nut and aids--D1033.2; fox maiden comes under power when skin hidden--F302.4.2.2; marriage to fox in human form—B651.1ff; marriage to fox--B601.14; fox mistakes mask for face--J1793; fox makes Shah think his master is wealthy--K1917.3E; Mr. Fox as murdering suitor--S62.1B; fox believes money is minted when rear wheels of wagon catch front wheels--J2066.7; fox and raven steal moon--A758.1; fox prefers sated mosquitoes--J215; foxes lured from den with music--K815.15; Skunny-Wunny and fox in name guessing contest--C432.1.3; Sea-God turns to needle, leaps into head--G530.2Bi; origin of Arctic fox--A1832.1; fox overeats and can't get out of garden--K1022.2; fox and panther contest, fox's spirit worth more--J242.3; fox tricks ox and panther to kill each other—K1084.1.1; kicked fox drops parchment saying teller of this lie gets the prize--X905; fox tells birds peace has been established between animals--J1421; peasant betrays fox by pointing—K2315; fox blows down pig's house--K891.1.1; fox climbs down pit on dupe's back--K652; fox sits under tree waiting for plums to fall into mouth--K1035.1; fox persuaded to pray before eating--K562.1; fox in plaited gown of rye straw poses as preacher--H1331.1.3Ai; fox originates porcupine's quills--A2311.5.2; hare teaches fox to play on quills and sing--K1066; Brer Fox tries to find excuse for eating baby rabbit--H1023.2.0.1.1; enmity between fox and raccoon--A2494.9.3; Raven persuades fox to imitate his sliding game--J2413.10; fox turns red--A2411.1.3.1.1, K606; fox re-enacts rescue—J1172.3; fox shows reflection in well--K1715.1; fox tells wolf moon's reflection in ice is cheese — J1791.3; Brer Rabbit helps Brer Fox roof house, nails Brer Fox's tail down--K729.1; Brer Fox is saddled and bridled by Brer Rabbit--K1241.1; fox Scrapefoot in house of three bears--N831.1.2C; fox strips tail of Sculpin--J2378.9.1.2; fox taken to heavenly feast by birds falls and breaks, scattering seeds--A2684; fox disguised as shepherd cannot run in smock--K828.1.1; fox in sheepshin--K828.1; fox pretends to make sheepskin jacket--K524.1.1; fox sings mocking song, changes words when caught--K473; skunk tricks fox into taking his place as man's captive--K842.0.11; fox's smell--A2416.8; Brer Fox asks Jack Sparrow to get on his tail--K911.5.1; alleged speaking hare sold as messenger--K131.1.1; fox dropped by stork--K1041.0.1; tail seen under coat of fox man--D313.1.2; fox gives boy ride on tail--K815.15; fox's tail steers him to sea--K579.2.3; fox tied to sham dead horse's tail--K1047; fox ties tail to horse's tail to catch it--J2132.5.2; fox struck with churn dash hence white tail--A2215.5; why end of fox's tail is white—A2378.8.1.0.1; fox fishes through ice with tail—K1021; fox's tail banner of advance, hornets sting—K2323.1; fox puts tail out when hiding—J2351.1; fox's tail set afire—J2101.1; tailless fox tries to convince others to cut off tails—J758.1; tailless fox convinces others to fish through ice with tails—K1021.0.3; animal captor persuaded to talk and release victim from mouth—K561.1; Brer Fox sets tar baby—K741; fox brings wolf to help exact taxes of ram—K641.2; magic fox as teakettle—D1171.3.1; fox blames thornbush—J656.1; fox with a thousand thoughts is caught—J1662.2; Brer Fox allows self to be tied by Brer Rabbit—K713.1.3.1; escape by pretended debate, fox escapes tiger—K622.1; kid calls "you promised me ten" to fox bringing tiger—K1715.2; fox tied to tiger dragged—J2132.5.1; fox transforms self to person—D313.1.1ff, D612.2ff; travels of a fox—K251.1; fox pretends to hide treasure, boy digs—H588.7.3; fox wins tree naming wager—N51; cat with one trick climbs tree—J1662; fox meets Mr. Trouble—H1376.11; fox serves twins—R111.1.3An; fox with seventy-sevenfold understanding caught in pit—K652.3; fox claims middle of viscacha's blanket—J1241.6; vixen tells cub she's warming paws at fire far below, cub says spark burnt nose—J1122.2; fox chosen as shepherd for fine voice—K934; white fox weds girl, showers during sunshine on wedding day—B601.14.1; fox weds tiger wife—K1712.1; fox tricks wolf into well—J1791.3, K651; Brer Fox descends into well in one bucket and rescues Brer Rabbit in other—K651; fox allows partridge to sew his mouth shut so can learn to whistle—K713.4; fox's widow chooses fox husband—T211.6; guest owl mentions fox smell of wife, tabu—C35.6; fox's wife's tabu violated—A2330.9; Brer Rabbit convinces Brer Fox to attack wildcat since its tracks show no claws—K1039.1; fox with one basket of wit defeats tiger—J1662.1; fox is white haired and suspicious from encounter with witsduk—A289.4; sick wolf gets fox to bring deer to dance for him, kills—J644.1.1; fox has wolf walk through lime and receive boots 'light as air'—K254.1; injured fox turns to old woman and bites lad—D313.1.3; fox rubs tail on door making sound of boy's name, "Zuiten"—K1887.4.

FOX, VIXEN: Vixen in well invites goat in to bathe—K652.2.

FRACTIONS: SEE DIVIDING; MATH.

FRAID: Big Fraid and Little Fraid—K1682.1.

FRANCE: Peacock sent to carry message of baby born to King in France—A2423.1.2.1; King of France's daughter abducted by hero—H1331.1.3Am; King of France's daughter stolen by fairies—F282.4.1.

FRANCIS: SEE SAINT, FRANCIS.

FRANCOLIN: SEE BIRD, FRANCOLIN.

FREEDOM: Wolf prefers liberty and hunger to

dog's servitude and plenty—L451.3.

FREEZE: Freezer, hero's companion—F601.2; Old Man Freezewell helps Jack find girls—G530.2Ai; mouse lies on joints and keeps man from freezing to death—B437.2.1; Woman of the Snow freezes companion—T115.1. SEE ALSO COLD; FROZEN; ICE; SNOW; WINTER.

FRIENDSHIP: Friend can be revived if smeared with blood of king's two children—S268A; only brother will help bury murdered man—H1558.1.0.1; friends vow to invite each other to wedding even if dead—D2011.1.4; elf cries over lost friend even though has many new—J401.2; Foe imitates Friend and is drowned—N452D; Kalulu hare sees leopard grab bushbuck's horns thinking them branches, tries to warn both, loses both friends—B335.6.1; man leaves lame friend unable to catch seals, later returns when man becomes good hunter—W175.2; friend lends her beauty to leprous friend—D1500.3.1.2; two friends never quarrel, neighbor wears hat half red and half green to provoke quarrel—K419.5.1.

FRIGATE BIRD: SEE BIRD, FRIGATE.

FRIGHT: Tale teller yells "boo"—Z13.1; bear meeting numskull in tree falls in fright—N659.3; deception by frightening—K2320ff; man frightens self and takes refuge in cave with dervish—W211.4; person dies of fright—N384ff; greedy woman pursues man to collect, at dawn he turns to skeleton and she dies of fright—E425.1.9. SEE ALSO FEAR.

FRISIA: N531.1.

FRISIAN: A1437.1.

FROG: Man dies from frog bite thinking it snakebite—F1041.1.11.4; frog insists black-handed monkey wash until hands are white—J1565.1.2; frog bursts laughing—Z32.6; frog's call "knee deep"—J1919.2.1; caterpillar in hare's house intimidates larger animals, frog routs—K1711.2.1; frog starts chain of fright—Z49.6.0.1; frogs put in butter churn to churn butter—J1689.2; two frogs in cream, one drowns, second churns butter—Q81.2; frogs croak, chain—Z49.6.0.1, Z49.19; frog's croak leads elephant to death—L315.6.1; why frogs croak in wet weather—A2426.4.1.2; why frog croaks—A2426.4.1; frog doctor asked to heal self—J1062.1; frog carries fire, throws into stump—A1415.2.2; frog carries off frog hunter who boasts of bravery—B857.1; frog takes shape of girl and beats clothing in stream so girl can escape from Condor, gets star shaped jewel on forehead where girl kisses her—B493.1.1; man turned to frog for refusing to say "If God wills it"—N385.1.1; why frog's hands are flat—A2375.2.9.1; hares find frogs more timid than they—J881.1; frog sings juju chant causing everyone to leave market, is caught with sticky figure—K741.0.2; frog rides on tiger's tail in jumping contest—K11.2; frogs demand a live king, given heron—J643.1;

frog bursts laughing--Z32.6; frog, hearing friends brag of long life, makes no boast, he alone escapes--L395; frog maid sought in land of Koschei the Deathless--H1385.3Ka; frog as matchmaker hides in sun maid's pitcher, steals her eyes--T53.6; marriage to frog maid--B641.0.1A; marriage to person in frog form--B645.1.2; frog's ask marsh saved--D435.2.2; helpful frog gives medicine to win princess--F535.1.1Dc; man and wife are turned into frogs when drop melon into well, still call for melon "Gua"--A2426.4.1; fool throws money to frogs to repay them--J1851.1.3; frog in moon --A751.3ff; two frogs on mountain decide other side of mountain is same and return home--B296.2; frog and mouse tie legs together for safety--J681.1; needles thrown to frogs--J1851.1.5; frog swallows ocean--A751.3.1.3; frog tries to be big as ox, bursts--J955.1; frogs turn to paintings on screen--D435.2.2; frogs see fire and fear men will dip up pond--J613.1.1; at Rome man hears frogs say he will be made Pope--B217.9; frog prince disenchanted by princess--D195.1; when frog croaks it will rain--A2426.4.1.2.2; frog refuses to move from road, is run over--J652.1; why frog's skin is splotchy--Z49.6.0.5; snake serves frog king as mount and eats plebian frogs--J352.2; friendship of snake and frog ceases when snake wants to eat frog--J426.2; evil spirit disguised as a friend comes to go frog hunting, spirit says he is eating them as fast as can catch them--E434.12; frog and tiger in spitting contest--K1712.1; frog's spots--A2412.5.2.1; Star princess turns house to lake and guests to frogs, frogs still call for feast--A762.2.2; why frog and stork are enemies--A2494.16.1.1; frog discovers stork eating fish and warns--K815.14; frogs fear sun will dry up puddles--J613.1; how frog lost tail--A2378.2.3.1, A2378.2.6.1; frogs besiege unkind girl--Q2.1.2Ab; wedding of frog and mouse--B284.1.1; frog to guard Nyame's well refuses water to other animals--A2378.2.3.1; frog set to guard well jumps in--A2233.1.1; frogs decide well may be trap in drought--J752.1; frog teaches magic whistle to call up storm--D2142.1.6.1; frog with one hundred wit--J1662.3; two wives invite frog at same time--J2183.1.2; frogs defeat Yorubas in war--B263.11.

FROG, BULLFROG: Persuades bear to sit him on rock in millpond and kill with ax--K581.7.

FROG, TADPOLE: Catfish steals tadpoles--A2320.8; tadpole foretold to be new king of frogs gives feast, gets drunk and breaks leg--J2061.7; riddle, what has no legs, two, four? Tadpole.--H761.2; how tadpole lost tail--A2378.2.6.1. SEE ALSO TOAD.

FROST: Man with frost in body--F601.2; three sons of Father Frost given lodging--C916.3.1; old man curses shouting children and they turn to guillimots, curse him to change to frost--A1947.1.1; stepmother sends girl to wed King Frost--Q2.1.4C; Wind, Sun and Frost quarrel--J1712.1.

FROZEN: Ant's foot frozen to lake--Z42.0.5; frozen horn, notes thaw--X1623.7.2; frozen words thaw--X1623.2.1. SEE ALSO COLD; FREEZE; ICE; ETC.

FRUIT: Birds plant garden, fruit kills rich, replenishes poor--W11.17; dupe eats bitter fruit --K1043; fruit of youngest brother is blessed by old woman and given curative powers to cure princess--H346; animals cannot eat fruit until learn name of tree--J2671.4.1; girl sings and fruit grows--Q2.1.6D; task, catching shaken fruit, octopus performs--F601.2Ga. SEE ALSO APPLE; FIGS; GRAPE; ORANGE; PEACH; PEAR; PLUM; QUINCE; ETC.

FRYING PAN: Flying frying pan--F1015.1.1 Pridham; witch turns man to fish and fries in pan--G263.1.0.1.1.

FU FU: Dog gets fu fu from tree by calling chant to it--D861.1Ic.

FUDO SAMA: E631.6.1.

FUGITIVES: Animal blessed for helping holy fugitive--A2221.5; grateful objects help fugitive --D1658.3.4; magic objects as decoy for pursuer--D672; fugitives throw objects behind which magically become obstacles--D672; objects thrown behind detain pursuers--R221; fugitives transform selves to escape detection--D671. SEE ENTIRE CHAPTER R CAPTIVES AND FUGITIVES.

FU-HSI: Culture hero teaches arts and crafts--A541.

MT. FUJI: Smoke carries message to Princess Kaguya on moon--A240.1.1.

FULL: Box full of stones can still take pail of sand, pail of water--J1341.7.1.

FULLER: Fuller and charcoal burner cannot live together--U143.

FUNDEVÖGEL: Man raises child found in treetop where bird carried it--D671.

FUNERAL: Sham dead cat eats mice at funeral--K827.4.1; funeral procession of the hen--Z32.1; inappropriate comment as funeral passes--J2461.2C; origin of custom of giving paper objects to dead--A1547.1.1.

FUR: Where beaver got his fur--A728.0.1; A2311.10; cat's fur made fluffy by being chased--K1013.0.1; dress of all furs in kingdom--R221D.

FUR COAT: Bear taken for man in fur coat--J1762.2.2.

FURZE: House of furze blown in--K891.1.1.

FUTURE: Palm wine tapper gives wine to "where we came" not to "where we go", judge advises of error, past can given nothing more--J313;

student sleeping on priest's porcelain pillow finds self in wealthy future--D1812.3.3.2.1; prophet foretelling future is advised his home has been robbed—J1062.3. SEE ENTIRE CHAPTER M ORDAINING THE FUTURE. SEE ALSO PAST; PROPHECY.

GABRE MANFAS, SAINT: Origin of animal sacrifices to Saint Gabre Manfas--A1545.3.0.1.

GAIN: Weaver cursed to lose all gained—K2371.2.1.

GAITORS: Peasant outsmarts merchant who bets he will have anything peasant asks for, asks for gaitors for canary—K92.4.

GALLA: Galla traveler and Amhara farmer—K2138.

GALLOWS: Blind man hears hung men say that dew from their bodies will restore sight—N452; lad takes corpse from gallows to warm by fire--H1440A; fool on runaway horse gets gallows caught on horse's neck--K1951.1B. SEE ALSO HANGING.

GALLYMANDERS: Girl takes old woman's money-bag--Q2.1.2Cb.

GAMBLING: Gambler finds centavos, chick eats, etc., chain--K251.1.5; soul won from devil in card game--E756.2, K1811.6; gambling with ghosts—E577.2.1; youth gambles all away including winter clothes on seeing first swallow of spring—J731.1; wagers and gambling--N0-N99. SEE ALSO CARDS.

GAME, ANIMAL: Trickster tells captor "let me catch you better game"—K553.1.0.4; trickster reports approaching enemy and partner flees leaving game--K335.0.1. SEE ALSO HUNTING.

GAME, SPORT OR PASTIME: Ballgame between birds and animals--B261.1.0.2; Devil cannot name "cross" in game--G303.16.8.2; king in disguise sees children playing game which represents lawsuit wisely, decides case—J123; student steals via "pira pira" game--K341.19.1; prairie falcon defeats crow by magic in shinny match--K23; boys play wheel and stick game so much that mother cooks stone wheels and serves them--A773.4.1.1. SEE ALSO CARDS; CHESS; CHONG-KAK; GAMBLING; GEBETA; HOOP; ETC.

GAMELAN: Crocodiles have loaned gamelan to villages for feast—A2130.2.

GAMMER: Sir Gammer Vans, tale of contradictions--Z19.2.2.

GANESHA: Elephant God Ganesha--A132.16.

GANGSTER: Gangster haunts car--E414.2

GARANGKANG (SPIDER): Spins web over cave to hide Mohammed--A2221.5.2.

GARBAGE: Farmer throws his slops onto invisible house--F451.4.4.4.

GARDEN: Birds plant garden, fruit kills rich, replenishes for poor--W11.17; Kin Kin sings telling King of Forest to repair ravages of animals trying to clear for garden, sings jungle back each night--D1487.3.1; little man in red comes out of flower and forces gardener to work--Q321.2.1; monkeys pull up trees to water roots--J1973.1; gardener needs rain—U148.1; gardener boy reads forbidden book, causes flowers to sing and birds to dance--D1711.0.1.4; bat enters forbidden Valley of Flowers and eats lily, evil spirit's medicine causes bat to become unkind starting chain of unkindness--A1341.4; hare learns magic word to open wolf's garden--N455.3.2. SEE ALSO FARM.

GARLIC: Man blows garlic in ghost's face--H1419.3.

GARMENT: Tabu, giving garment back to supernatural wife—C31.10. SEE DRESS; CLOTHING.

GARTER: Red garter marks pot of gold--J1922.2.1.

GARUDA: B56; Garuda aids birds in war with sea--J1968.0.1.

GATE: Mounted bride cannot pass through gate—J2171.6.1; fat man can fit through gate if haywagon can—J1411; Shen Shu and Yu Lu, guardians of the gate—A411.1; swinging gate at end of world--D1553.2; task, standing neither inside nor outside of gate--H1052; magic word to open gate--N455.3.2.

GAUCHO: Neglects wife and cattle to weave poncho for festival, doomed to roam pampas forever—E513.

GAYUNCAYUNG: Old man chips wood pieces which become seals, sea animals--H1385.3Ff.

GAZELLE: Gazelle cares for girl--B538.3.1; gazelle throws calabash killing teacher, chain—Z42.0.6; gazelle wins bride for master—K1917.3I.

GEASA: Stepmother puts geasa on Conn to bring three golden apples--H1321.1Cb; stepmother sets geasa on stepson—H1331.3.4.

GEBETA BOARD: Progressively lucky borrowing and lending gebeta board--K251.1.3.

GECKO: Drop of honey causes chain of accidents—N381.

GELERT: Hound Gelert--B331.2.

GEMS: Gems fall from mouth--Q2.1.1. SEE ALSO JEWELS.

GENERAL: Mice generals wear horns--L332.1; peasant girl puts leaves on water so general will sip slowly--J1111.4.1.

GENEROSITY: Brahman will accept only money king earns himself. Give one anna to wife, one to son, keep one for self, give one to Brahman--W11.3.1; poor girl gives last food and clothing away, stars fall from heaven and turn to silver--V411.10; man gives land to another, gold found there, both insist gold belongs to the other--W11.17. SEE ALSO HOSPITALITY.

GENIE: Genie appears when lamp is rubbed--D871.1; genie from magic mirror--D882.1I. SEE JINN; PERI; SPIRIT.

GENTIAN: Jealous girl rubs bowl of milk left for helpful fairies with gentian root--F384.5.

GERGASSI: Giant Gergassi subdued by Kantchil--K1931.2Z; Giant Gergassi caught in pit--K741.2.

GETA: Magic geta, coin falls at each step--J2415.8.

GHOSTS: Ghost reborn as baby--E605.7.2; family invites ghost to be their bogle, get bagpiper--E402.1.3.2; bat ghost--E423.3.12; when boy dies of drought white ghost bird seeks--A1999.3; bogles leave house cleaned--E439.11; ghost who claims to have entered through keyhole tricked into bottle--K717.7; ghosts continue to move boundary markers--E345.1; ghostly burning house--E531.1; dead woman's skeleton wants burying--E412.3.0.1; butterfly ghost--E525; dead child returns to parents--E324.3; ghost terrorizes tailor in church--H1412.2; return to living form by walking around church opposite of widershins--E44; ghostly coach and horses--E535.1; coffin points out scene of crime--E231.6; ghost of cook sits on fire--E411.0.2.1.1; dead grateful for having corpse ransomed--E341.1; return of dead to punish theft of part of corpse (golden arm, bone,etc.)--E235.4.1; in country of ghosts, gold given turns to paper money burned at funerals--F129.4.4; Hedley cow--E427; cow ghost--E423.1.8.2; ghost carries off girl with whom he dances--E461; gypsy carries off girl from dead band of gypsies--D621.0.2; disguise as ghost, "Big Fraid and Little Fraid"--K1682.1; dog ghost--E521.2.3; drowned men carry coffin ashore--E379.6; drowned must guard spot where drowned--E414.0.1; drunkard in cemetery passes as ghost, learns of treasure--J2415.12; Flying Dutchman--E511.1.2; student discovers true identity of evil spirits, black pig, red cock, scorpion--H1411.4.2; fake ghost in belltower knocked down--H1440; dead family to visit girl wed to king--E328; fearless traffic with ghosts--H1440; servant feigns dead and joins ghost--E415.1.2.1; man feigns ghost--E463.1+; man feigns being ghost and joins ghost--F463.2; feigned ghost scares--K1860ff; man flees ghost "You run fast." "I'll run faster", etc.--J1495.1; ghost leaves no footprints--E421.2.1.1; frog hunting with ghost--E434.12; gambling with ghosts--E577.2.1.1+; gangster haunts car--E414.2; man blows garlic in ghost's face--H1419.3; ghostly gaucho--E513; souls of dead lost on glacier--E354; greedy woman follows ghost to collect--E425.1.9; green goblin ghosts--F348.5.1; headless ghost--E422.1.1; ghost of hermit gives wishing bones--D882.1Ga; vanishing hitchhiker--E332.3.3.1; horse ghost--E521.1; dead husband returns to remove written vow--E321.6; ghost demands husband fulfill vow to give to poor--E415.2.1; ghost gets nearer and nearer, "I got you"--Z13.1.3; island of the dead--E381.2.0.1; kicked ghost grows--E599.15; lad learning fear--H1440; ghost leaves when letter burnt--E415.1.3; E451.11; dead lover as bird--E423.3.0.1; dead lover returns--E210; ghost lover--E474; ghost reburied by lover--E419.6.1; ghost of Malintzin--E425.1.11; ghost visits party at exact moment of death--E329.1; dead mother returns to suckle child--E323.1.1; ghost of slain girl appears to murderer--E231.7; ghosts exorcised by calling name--E443.3.1; girl with two red lights is really Osgaert--E421.3.8; holding pipe for ghost to smoke--E555; piper ghost--E402.0.3.2; E425.2.5.1; sons hold candle for ghost to read--E451.13; ghost can be reborn as baby--E605.7.2; man shows ghost it's own reflection and frightens it--K1715.1.2; riding with ghosts--E256.1; robber ghost--E593.6; samurai ghosts--E434.11; ghost saves man by wounding so companions leave behind--E363.2.2; ghost saves man from falling bridge--E363.2.1; ghost serpent--E533.2.1; ghost ship--E535.3.3; dead man asks for shoes--E412.3.3; skeleton comes for lady's skull--E451.14; sleeping army--E502; man's mother smokes pipe with ghost in effort to appease--E425.1.10; dead play soccer--E577.1.1; spider ghost--E423.8.1+; Ghost of Great White Stag--E423.2.6.1; tabu, mocking at belief in demons--C17; loyal tenant rewarded by ghost family--E363.5.2; return from dead to punish theft from grave--E235.1+, E235.4.1; thief and ghost argue over who is to rob man first--J581.3; ghost of Treageagle set endless task--E459.8; ghost shows treasure--E415.1.2.2; disguised trickster beaten by man--K1682; girl wed to ghost--E747.7; dead wife haunts--E221.1.1, E221.6; ghost as seductive woman--E425.1.3+; Sioux wrestles with ghost--E461.1.2. SEE ALL ENTRIES E200-E599 Ghosts and other revenants. SEE ALSO H1411+ Fear test: staying in haunted house.

GIANG HUONG: Princess of Mount Nam-Nhu fined for plucking peach, mandarin's son redeems--F377.0.1.

GIANTS: Archaeologist finds giant's bones in cave--F531.6.13.3; giant's wife warns man to play song on balangi poorly--K606.1.5; Giant of Bang Beggar's Hall, quest for castle--H1289.3.2; giant allows hero to behead, he will behead hero later--M221; man beheads giant, wife covers head with ashes so can't rejoin body--H1385.3E; boy tricks giant into slitting stomach in eating contest--G501A; giant takes form of small boy--F531.6.9.1; Giant of the

Brown Beech Wood to rescue three princesses from giant—G530.2Ga; giant steals cabbages of exiled queen and three daughters--G561.1D; giant plans to eat children in night—K1611; giant person breaks three clubs before finding one strong enough—F615.3.1.4; Giant Cormoran, Blunderbus, Thunderdell, Galliganta—G512.0.4; coyote tricks giant into cutting off legs--G524.0.2; Jack puts out giant's one eye and escapes in dog skin—K603.2; fee-fi-fo-fum, giant's roar—G84; three identical lads fight giants--R111.1.3Ae; Finlay's sister lets fire go out and giants abduct her. Finlay defeats with aid of dogs--S12.1.0.1Bb; Giant Gergassi subdued by Kantchil—K1931.2Za; Glooskap as Green Giant—D1652.1.9.3; grateful dead tells giant that King of Ireland is coming and hides giant in cellar, takes gold—E341.1B; quest for three golden hairs of giant—H1273.2; giant hidden while king's men come, gives objects to hero--D833; Jack, King of Ireland's son, hired by Giant of the Hundred Hills—B316C; Jack the Giant Killer—G512.0.4; Tom Hickathrift kills giant with cart shaft—F628.2.3.1; hero kills three giants and takes their castles—R111.1.3Bb; lie, giant so big upper lip touches sky and lowerlip ground--X909.6.1; giant goes into well for cheese (moon)—J1791.3; giant's mother and widow turn selves to apple tree, well, desert, whoever touches to be destroyed—R111.1.3Ae; Yusal promises son to Giant Okab on wedding day—G530.2Bl; giant washes pigs before eating—K1121.2.1; giant to walk on water using pumice given heavy rocks —G512.11.1; giant judges ram—K579.5.1; giant swallows river—F531.6.8.3.2.1; boy appears to smith in dream and asks to free from giant Mahon MacMahon—F321.3.2; lad given invisibility belt steals giant's loaf of bread—G666.2; golden bird stolen from Giant of Five Heads, Five Humps, and Five Throttles—H1331.1.3Am; stone coat giants—G511.2; Marec the Enchanter turns giant to stone for stealing sheep—F531.6.12.8.3; tabu, telling that giant carried on shoulder--C456; Tepozton swallowed by Giant—F912.2.10; giant tricked, thistles only picked on Moon of Gobbages—K499.3.1; Thor, Loke, and Thiaffe visit giant's hall, contest--F531.6.15.1.1; giant raises Thumbling, teaches strength—F615.3.1.3; trickster asks wife if she has eaten seven giants he left her yet—K1715.4.0.2; giant as stupid ogre defeated by trickster--G501; Tsarevna and the seven giants—Z65.1 Dalgliesh; giant at wedding feast wears hat of invisibility—D1361.14.1; sister weds giant and betrays brother--S12.1.0.1; giant weeps until stream forms—F531.5.1.5; giant takes sea captain to Isle of Youth—F361.3.0.1. SEE ALL ENTRIES G100-G199. SEE F531ff. SEE ALSO: BIRD; CANNIBAL; CYCLOPS; OGRE; STRONG; TALL MAN.

GIFT: Gift of figs, thrown at donor, is glad he didn't bring beets—J2563; task, coming both with and without a gift—H1056.

GILLS: Origin fish gills--A2341.4, F911.4.1.

GILYARD: Brer Rabbit poisons Brer Gilyard—

--K1082.0.2; Brer Rabbit sings of stealing Brer Gilyard's sheep--K1066.7; big animals try to steal Brer Gilyard's treasure--K649.9.2.

GINGERBREAD: Gingerbread house lures children—G412.1; gingerbread house--G412.1; gingerbread man--Z33.1.2; gingerbread St. Nicholas—V429.4.

GINGKO: Eldest girl offers to pick gingko nuts for wolf and takes sisters into tree--K2011.0.1.

GINSENG: Man on quest given ginseng for strength—H1385.3E.

GIRAFFE: Color of giraffe—A2411.1.6.8; elephant and giraffe farm with hare, each thinks hare does half work—K364.1; Madame Giraffe promises leopard to bring game, brings lion—Z43.6.5; origin giraffe's neck--A2351.4.4.

GIRL: Escape by pretending to dance so as to be untied—K571; fearless girl needs no husband, grinds goblins in mill at night, screams at sight of mouse—H1419.2; kind and unkind girl, kind rewarded—Q2.1+; girl escapes ogre husband—G561, S62.1; peasant girl puts leaves on water so passing general can only sip slowly and will not become ill—J1111.4.1; dead parents appear in palace and peasant girl is allowed to wed king—E328; clever peasant girl —H561.1, H586, J1111; reindeer turns girl to lamp and they capture moon—A753.1.0.1; girl resuscitates by placing bite of oatmeal mixed with victim's blood in victim's mouth—E43; girl rescued by skillful companion's. To whom does she belong?--H621.2; girl sacrifice slays serpent—B11.11.7.2; girl performs ogre's tasks or advises lad in performance of tasks—G530.2; three girls each claim to be Tipingee--H161.0.1.1; animals must defeat woman's little girl in wrestling to get fire—F617.2.3. SEE ALSO HEROINE; MAID; SISTER; WOMAN; ETC. No attempt is made to list all tales with girls as characters here.

GIUFA: Giufa gives food to clothes--J1561.3; Giufa kills fly on judge's nose--J1193.1.0.1.

GIZZARD: Alligator needs Brer Rabbit's gizzard —K544; magic gizzard causes silver to shower one who has swallowed--D551.1I.

GIZO: Gizo spider coats stomach with wax and crawls over fig pile—K378.1.1.

GLACIER: Old woman on Aletsch Glacier invites souls of those lost on glacier in to warm selves—E354.

GLAIVE: Task, fetch White Glaive of Light from realm of the Big Woman—H1331.1.3Al.

GLASS: Air castle, basket of glassware to be sold—J2061.1.1; girl kept in glass cage—R49.4; glass coffin—F852.1, Z65.1; King Gideon has wife thrown into sea in glass coffin—T210.2; castle and maid in two glass coffins--F852.1.2; glass mountain--F751; task, climbing glass mountain to reach princess--H1385.3Ca; climb glass mountain and rescue princess from Troll --H321F; princess on glass mountain contest--H331.1.1; glass slippers--R221. SEE ALSO CRYSTAL.

GLASSES: Peasant bets merchant he doesn't have what he wants, eyeglasses for ox--K92.4; Bouki buys glasses. They're no good, he still can't read--J1746.2.

GLOATING: Hen disobeys and is caught, cock says "I told you so"--J652.5.

GLOOSKAP: Glooskap cannot subdue baby who replies "Goo" to all threats--L410.8; Glooskap as Green Giant--D1652.1.9.3; Gluskabe puts piece of tobacco in grasshopper's mouth to last forever--A2472.2; Glooskap teaches loon cry--A2426.2.19; Glooskap gives magic snowshoes--D1065.3.1; Glooskap promises dead trees to always revive in spring--A2760.2; Kuloskap gives whale tobacco to smoke, why spouts--A2479.14. SEE ALSO ENTIRE COLLECTION Macmillan, Cyrus. GLOOSKAP'S COUNTRY. Hill, Kay. GLOOSCAP AND HIS MAGIC; BADGER, THE MISCHIEF MAKER; MORE GLOOSKAP STORIES.

GLOVE: Merwyn gives jewelled glove to babe to play with, only babe floating in cradle survives flood--F944.1. SEE ALSO GLAIVE; MITTEN.

GLUSKABE, GLUSKAP: SEE GLOOSKAP.

GLUTTON: Offered three wishes, greedy man asks for house with cellar full of food, more food, chute into cellar--C773.1.3; Clever Gretel eats as cooks--K2137; who is greatest glutton? --W125.6; glutton gets head stuck licking out pot (mortar)--J2131.5.2.1, W125.3.1; glutton interrupted each time he tries to eat something --X12; lazy refuses to help until food is brought out--W111.7ff; Thin Neck grabs biggest piece and chokes to death--W125.7; mother sings that daughter ate "five pies today," changes song to "spun five skeins" when king comes by--D2183B; glutton overeats and cannot get out entrance--K1022.2; men break off more of sky than needed to eat--A625.2.8; wife eats meal while cooking--W125.2. SEE ALSO EATING; GREED.

GNAT: Gnat apologizes for lighting on bull's horns--J953.10; gnat puts elephant to sleep--L315.6.1; gnats overcome lion but are killed by spider--L478; lion harms self slapping at gnat--N333.0.1; gnat on wing shod--F660.1B.

GNOME: Gnome asks for bread, beats lad keeping house--K1931.2C. SEE ALSO DWARF.

GOAT: Goat driven off by ant--Z39.1.0.1; ass frightens goats from cave for lion--K2324.1.1; beard on she goat does not make a male--U112; bee bites goat and drives him home--Z39.1; goat with bells--G610Aa; goat in house of lion calls out boasts and intimidates--

K1711.2; goat butts fat cat off of bridge, eaten victims emerge--Z33.2; two goats on bridge, each refuses to give way--W167.1; bull pursued by lion has no time to fight goat--J371.1; grateful goat brings gold to butcher who spared--B413.1; chain tale, goat driven home--Z39.1.0.2; why goats can't climb trees--A2581.1; goat in fox's house routed by cock--Z39.1; trickster shams death to avoid debt--K341.2.0.1; devil in form of goat--G303.3.3.1.6.1; black goat on wagon turns to devil--C12.5.9; goat and bull argue over who is elder, goat wins because of beard--B841.1.3; fool convinced his goat is another animal--K451.2.1; goat given funeral--X459.3; goatherd neglects own goats in attempt to catch wild goats--J345.1; brother transformed when drinks from animals hoofprints--P253.2.0.1; goat's horn lost in river, given fish, etc., chain--K251.1.7; broken horn will tell tale--J1082.1; goat begins to build a house, tiger finds foundation and adds to it, each claims--K1715.3.2; husband learns to rule wife as goat does--B216Af; goats make jackal (wolf) believe they have eaten many jackals by showing dead jackal's tail--K1715.3; Kantchil has goats eat red flowers feigning bloody mouths--K1715.16; lion turns on goat rescuer--J1172.3; lion and goat make peace on seeing waiting vulture--J218.1; lion hiding in goat's cave answers call--K607.1; goat bluffs lion "Bring me a younger lion"--K1715.2; elephant kills, lion avenges self on goats--U31.1; goat intimidates lion, finding he cannot eat meat they kill him--U131.2; goat sings of ten thousand lions he killed--K1715.17; lying goat says sons didn't feed him--K1151; magic goat provides food--D830.1.1; goat knocked from cliff turns to maid--D334; alleged message-carrying goat sent home--K131.1.3; monkey foresees that goat will disturb cook and be set afire--Z49.23; mother goat sees lamb playing with her son--W165.2.1; goat nurses children--N455.4Ad; alleged speaking hare sold as messenger--K131.1.1; Foni rejects sorcerer's advances, he turns her goats to stone--T75.2.1.3; why goat's tail is short--A2378.2.2.1; goat talks, killed--B210.1.2; task, coming neither on horse nor on foot--H1053.1; thief thinks goat is ogre--K1161.1; supposed goat producing well--K111.5; goat tricked into well--K652; vixen in well invites goat in to bathe, escapes on goat's horns--K652.2; wolf tries to entice goat down from high place--K2061.4; goat sees self in pool and decides he need not fear a wolf--W165.3.

GOAT, BILLY: Three billy goats gruff--K553.2; lad rides to Hell on billy goat on quest--G530.2M; trickster repeatedly substitutes billy goat for nanny goat on way to Helm--J1703.5; goat butts clay pot boy and breaks--Z33.7; Tatterhood rides billy goat--L145.1A.

GOAT, KID: Kid frightens tiger and fox "I ask you to bring ten tigers"--K1715.2.1; wasp routs Carlanco and rescues kids--K311.3B; well trained kid does not open to wolf--K311.3; kid on roof mocks wolf--J974; kid persuades wolf to play for him to dance, gods hear and rescue

--K561.2; wolf and the seven little kids—
K311.3A.

GOAT, MOUNTAIN: Why mountain goat lives on mountain tops—A2433.3.22; origin goat clan totem, goats invite cruel humans to feast and destroy-A1578.1.

GOATSKIN: Goatskin weds princess, lad wearing goatskin--G610Ak; goatskin grows to back of priest imitating devil—K335.0.1.2.1.

GOBBAGES: Thistles are only picked in Moon of Gobbages—K499.3.1.

GOBBORN SEER: W181.2.

GOBLET: Flute sounds from crystal goblet—
E633.1.

GOBLIN: Goblin babies hatch from eggs found on Halloween--F481.0.1.1.2; girl dancing with goblins sends them for articles of clothing to procrastinate until cockcrow--Q2.1.3; green goblin ghosts--F348.5.1; goblin makes grocer's cask talk--F451.6.2.5; hobyahs kidnap little girl--B332; goblin kidnaps three sisters--G561.2C; goblin routed by hidden needle, lobster, etc.—K1161.4; goblin's soul in eggshell—G561.2C; tabu, seeing goblin who aids washer girl—C311.1.5. SEE ALSO DEMON; FAIRIES.

GOD: Man asks God for money, no answer. Says God might as well kill him - an axe falls--J1289.28.1; God teaches bee to make honey—A2813; devil and God divide crops—K171.1; St. John sent by God to stop festival, given seat by drums and stays to dance--D2174.1; Death preferred to God, treats all equally—D1825.3.1; J486.1; God creates dog--A1831.1.1; God pulls donkey's ears long--A2325.3; donkeys seek news of ambassador to God--A2232.8.1; man praising king given duck filled with golden coins, he sells to man praising God—N351; fake god chases lazy man in answer to prayer for help up mountain—W111.9; fake god speaks from basket ordering spirits to release Pupu--E461.1.1; girl to answer all questions "The Gods know" after trading places with sacred horse in temple—C495.1.1; plant patch of melons for self and one for God, steals from God's patch--W211.5; monkey begs God for misery, thinks is honey—J1805.2; man says he is god's son-in-law and asks lodging, taken to mosque--J1261.1.1.1; "No-king-as-great-as-God" trusts in God, ring appears in fish--N211.1B; students believe God will provide—J2215.4.0.2; Allah blamed for letting pumpkin vines produce larger fruit than nut trees—J2571; God curses stones never to grow—A975.1.2; wagers that God is stronger than Devil—N452C; chain, what is strongest - God--L392.0.5; Z42; God takes tails from tadpoles--A2378.2.6.1; tigers object to saying "Papa God first, man next, tiger last"—J2132.6.0.2; misfortune for failing to say "If God wills"--N385.1.

GODS: Tabu, eating Gods' offerings--C57.1.3; gods paid with tallow oxen revenge selves—

K236.1.1. SEE ALL ENTRIES A100-A499 Gods; A500-A599 Demigods and culture heroes. SEE ALSO VARIOUS CREATION ENTRIES FOUND BETWEEN A600 and A2817. SEE ALSO B0-B99 Mythical animals. SEE ALSO BATARU GURU; BRAHMA; CHRIST; DEVIL; IMAGE; KANNONSAMA; KAYAMANON; KRISHNA; KWAN-YIN; RATU LORO KIDUL; SAINTS: SANDE-NYAME; SEA-GOD; SKY-GOD; ZEUS.

GODS, GOD OF THE FOREST: Shows how to make flute—A1461.8.2.

GODS, OLDMAN GOD: Oldman God gives turtle feathers—K1041.1.1.

GODFATHER: Godfather Death--D1825.3.1.1.1; Godfather Death shows candle of princess is nearly out—D1724; godfather gives helpful horse —H1213.1G; trickster pretends to stand godfather, consumes stores--K372.

GODMOTHER: Fairy godmother—R221; human as godmother to fairy child--F372.2.2; godmother steals child, raises—N711.1.

GOGWANA: Lad defeats witch with aid of dogs—B524.1.2G.

GOLD: Alleged gold-dropping animal sold--K111.1; Golden Antlers--K815.15C; golden apples stolen nightly from tree—H1331.1.3; ass dropping gold —B103.1.1; gold smelted by grateful badger for priest—B393.1; lost golden ball to be returned or girl dies—H1411.4.11; gold drawn to black gold bell--D1252.3.1; bird with golden dung—B103.1.5; fairies give coals which turn to gold—F342.1; golden cock causes Tsar's son to be sent to battle--B143.1.5; Prince of Seven Golden Cows—B103.3.2; crane's golden feathers—A2411.2.6.14; four ducks take gold legs from incense burner, must pull up when sleeping—A2479.13; gold dust entrusted turns to sand—J1531.2.0.1; dwarfs must spread all gold in sun one hour or turns bad—F451.3.2.2.1; dwarf's gold, seeming worthless gift turns to gold--F451.5.1.4; goose lays golden eggs--D876; hen lays golden eggs—F54.2.1; bird lays golden eggs or money—B103.2.1; golden feather starts quest for golden bird--H1331.1.3; immortal's finger turns all to gold--W151.13; flour pasted on man turns to gold when falls off—K1917.3H; fool spreads pot of gold in sun to dry—J2461E; kind girl dipped in gold—Q2.1.1C; man replies to ghostly voice "let it fall"--E373.1.1; tabu, letting anything fall into spring, finger and hair touch water, turn golden--G671; quest for three golden hairs of giant—H1273.2; golden hen with golden chicks—H465Ba; Mother Luck will fill beggar's sack with gold but must stop her before sack breaks--J514.7; son opens door freeing golden lynx--G671Ba; Midas touch, all turns to gold--J2072.1; Brer Buzzard abandons Brer Rabbit on top of tree, Brer Rabbit finally remembers where he hid their gold mine—K2347; lad sewed in skin to be carried onto mountain by birds, to throw down treasure—K1861.1A; golden objects traded for nights with husband--H1385.4; princess compromises self to possess golden objects--H465B; gold covered pirate's table at bottom of pool--F945.1; pot of gold turns to demon cow--E427; rice turned to gold--D475.1.6; riding on gold road sign of nobility--H1321.1Aa; sand turns to gold--F342.1.1; grateful snake gives gold piece daily--B103.0.4.1; snakes poured by greedy neighbor turn to gold when fall into good man's house--N182.1; snake revenges self by pouring gold on man's head--K602.3; hag makes three daughters spin gold--H1021.8.1; golden spindle, princess compromises self to possess--H465B; golden spindle, traded for night with husband--H1385.4; squash with baby inside, bath water turns gold as hits child --T555.1.1.1; entrance to woman's room in golden statue (golden lion, golden parrot, etc.)--K1341.1; stone lion vomits gold into buckets--J2415.16; sun king weeps = gold--A736.1.3.1; gold thrown behind deters maid's followers--R221C; trees with silver leaves and golden blossoms from grave--N455.4C; twelve dancing princesses pass golden woods--F1015.1.1. SEE ALSO ALCHEMY; APPLE; AXE; GOOSE.

GOLDEN ANTLERS: K815.15C.

GOLDEN HOOD: K2011.0.1.

GOLDFISH: SEE FISH, GOLDFISH; FISH, CARP.

GOLDILOCKS: N831.1.2.

GOLDSMITH: Goldsmith blamed for chain of events leading to theft--J2233, Z49.11.2; goldsmith ungrateful for rescue from pit--W154.8; tailor and goldsmith enter circle of dancing fairies--F344.1.4.

GOLEM: D1635.

GOLIATH: Devil advises preacher to make story of David and Goliath bigger--X904.4.1.

GONAVE ISLE: Horseman in black chases youth to death over precipice--E422.1.1.3.3;

GONG: Monkey trades objects in chain of events, procures gong and sings--Z47.2; tiger told that ant's nest is gong--K1023.1.

GOO: Why baby says "goo"--A1399.5; Glooskap cannot vanquish baby, just says "goo"--L410.8.1.

GOOD: Association of good and evil--J450ff; what is fattest thing? Good deed--H653.2; "That's bad, no that's good...", chain--Z51ff.

GOOD LUCK: SEE LUCK.

GOOD MAN, BAD MAN: SEE ALL ENTRIES AND CROSS REFERENCES J2415 Foolish imitation of lucky man.

GOOSE: SEE BIRD, GOOSE.

GOPHER: SEE PRAIRIE DOG.

GORILLA: SEE MONKEY, GORILLA.

GOSSIP: All animals confess weaknesses, Brer Rabbit confesses last, says he is a gossip--W141.1; tattling mischief maker beheaded, head laughs, buried coconut grows, still gurgles--A2611.3.1; suspicions sown between friends--K2131.1; gossiping wife's tale discredited--J1151.1.1; why women are prattlers--A1372.1. SEE ALSO RUMOR. .

"GOT YOU": Tall tale teller frightens listener--Z13.1.

GOTHAM: Build hedge to hold cuckoo--J1904.2; argue over driving sheep over bridge--J2062.1. SEE ENTIRE COLLECTION Jagendorf, Moritz. THE MERRY MEN OF GOTHAM.

GOURD: Large gourd turns to boy, small gourds to children--T555.2.1; white cloud from gourd makes enemy banish--D882.1Bbb; old woman pursued by green gourd she cuts--R261.2; hornets trapped in gourd--K714.2.6; smallest brother plants gourds, has rat put brother's rice into his gourds--K1611Da; trickster returns rolling inside gourd--K553.0.3; golden gourd turns to wasp's nets in rich brother's hands--N182.2.

GRAIN: Grain carried out one at a time--Z11.1; bird drops grain, chain--Z41.6; grinding grain, making better of good--H583.2.3.1; supernatural wife leaves, grain is ripened magically--C31.4.2.1. SEE ALSO BARLEY; CORN; SOWING; ETC.

GRAMMAR: Pedagogue asks ferryman if he has ever studied grammar--J1229.4.

GRANA: Ogress Grana eats--D1162.2.2.

GRANDFATHER: Grandfather gives kind girl bracelet--Q2.1.2Da; grandfather vows never to look on granddaughter--R221Z; three golden hairs of grandfather-know-it-all--H1273.2.

GRANDMOTHER: Blind boy throws cruel grandmother into lake, she becomes white whale--A2135.1; the dragon and his grandmother--M211.7.1; whale sends wave to destroy village, only great grandmother saves, rides waves in rocker--B81.2.1. SEE ALSO DEVIL'S GRANDMOTHER.

GRANDPARENTS: Old Verlooka gets little girl, little boy, grandma--K1161.12.

GRAPES: Boys beg for grapes and one boy is given three. "All taste the same"--J1340.3; fox and sour grapes--J871; sent to buy grapes for a friend, he haggles the price down, feels he should get the grapes for doing that work--J1650.1; man coming from vineyard, "Guess what I have in my basket?"--J2712.3. SEE ALSO VINEYARD.

GRASS: Hare escapes in bundle of grass thrown down--K521.10; grass stalk wants to be herb--Z42.4; grass judges in favor of snake, not man--J1172.3.2.4; rooster must clean bill on grass

—Z41.2.3; the wormwood (grass) does not rock the sparrow—Z41.7.

GRASSHOPPER: Ant and lazy grasshopper—J711.1; origin of death from falsified message—A1335.1.0.1ff; grasshopper thought to be devil—J1785.1; grasshopper plague, Great Spirit sends coyote to eat grasshoppers—A2108.1; grasshopper breaks teeth—Z32.6; Gluskap puts piece of tobacco in grasshopper's mouth, to last forever—A2472.2.

GRATEFUL: Grateful animals—B350-B399; grateful dead—E341.1.

GRAVE: Burial in old grave so angel will think he has been dead a long time and pass him by—J2212.2; mother in grave cares for baby until found—E323.1.1; man strikes a dog rummaging in grave—J836; gifts from grave of helpful animal—R221F; goatskin grows to back of priest imitating devil—K335.0.1.2.1; task, guarding father's grave—H331.1.1B; hand from grave reaches for food—H1440D; hare tells lion he's killed alligator and bear and shows 'grave'—K1715.15; boy sticks knife through coattail when dared to stick into grave, thinks is held—N384.2; valet digs up gold leg of lord's wife—E235.4.2.1; dead lover carries sweetheart into grave with him—E215; man takes refuge from robbers in open grave, feigning dead—J2311.3ff; tree on mother's grave gives gifts—R221F; reincarnation in tree from grave—E631; trees with silver leaves and golden blossom from grave—N455.4C; friends vow to invite each other to wedding even if dead—D2011.1.4; winding sheet stolen from grave—E236.1. SEE ALSO CEMETERY; DEAD.

GRAVEDIGGER: Three sisters wed to first three men to pass, one wed to gravedigger—B314E.

GREASE: Grease on coin betrays thief—J1141.1.3.4.2; trickster eats the common food supply and smears grease on dupe's mouth—K401.1.

GREAT HEAD: Great Head as ogre—G361.2.

GREAT SPIRIT: Great Spirit sends eggs to bird's nests—A2431.3.5; swallow as Great Spirit's messenger—A2431.3.5; Great Spirit, Halach-Vinic, punishes quail—A2431.3.10.

GREAT WALL: SEE WALL.

GREBE: SEE BIRD, GREBE.

GREECE: King of Greece's daughter stolen by hero—H1331.1.3Aj; King of Greece's daughter enchanted by King of Darkness—E341.1B; stepmother substitutes own daughter as bride of Prince of Greece—H1385.5Ae.

GREED: Buffalo demands overmuch of lion captive—K553.1.0.1; man wants longer summer day so laborers can work more—W151.11; greedy man, cat, etc. eats all it meets—Z33.2ff, Z33.6.1; greedy person gets head stuck—W151.9; greedy

hunters take more game than need—F451.5.2.9.1; immortal seeks ungreedy man—W151.13; Mother Luck will fill beggar's sack but he must stop her before sack breaks—J514.7; Luno cannot be filled, thrown into sky, becomes moon—A741.4; magic pot, always to leave some in pot—D861Ib; greedy woman pursues man to collect, at dawn he turns to skeleton—E425.1.9; poor brother is given gold by stone lion, must stop before bucket is full—J2415.16; first girl wishes all for self, receives so much gold cannot lift and it falls back into well—Q2.1.6A. SEE ALSO ALL ENTRIES J2415 Foolish imitation. SEE ALSO FAT; GLUTTON; ETC.

GREEN: Green children from other world—F103.1; Green Giant—D1652.1.9.3; girl to be green, boy to be greyhound—B641.1; green goblin ghosts—F348.5.1; what is greenest? May—H646.1; green squash with baby inside—T555.1.1.1.

GREENIES: Land of Greenies—F373.2.

GREETING: Fool told to give greeting uses it in wrong circumstances—J2461.2; fool repeating phrase to himself thought to be giving inappropriate greeting—J2671.2.1; three numskulls quarrel as to whom greeting of stranger was intended—J1712.

GRETEL: Clever Gretel—K2137; Hansel and Gretel—G412.1.

GREYHOUND: SEE DOG, GREYHOUND.

GRIEF: Judgment over true owner of slain elephant, one man weeps all night—J1171.5. SEE ALSO CRYING; TEARS.

GRIFFIN: Griffin will carry, leap on back after battle, disenchanted princess leaps on instead—H1385.4D; quest for three feathers of griffin's tail—H1273.2D; lad to call for magic aid "in the name of the Griffin of the Green Wood"—H1321.1B.

GRINDING STONE: Turtle as grinding stone is thrown away—A2433.3.19.0.1.

GRISELDA: Patient wife—H461.

GROACH: The Groach of the Isle of Lok—G405.1.1.

GROCER: Goblin makes grocer's cask talk—F451.6.2.5.

GROOM: Groom steals horse's corn but grooms well—W152.13.2.

GROUNDHOG: Groundhog teaches dance and song to escape wolves—K606, K606.2; young groundhogs see traces of spring root on mother's teeth, realize spring has come—J1122.3; why groundhog has short tail—A2378.4.9. SEE ALSO PRAIRIE DOG.

GROUND OWL: SEE BIRD, GROUND OWL.

GROVE: Why frog croaks in wet weather, afraid mother's grove by river will wash away—A2426.4.1.2.

GROWTH: Supernatural growth of child—T543.3.2; supernatural growth, boy eats from dish, grows large as dish, etc.—T615.0.1; too tall, eats lard for shortening—X912.1; lie, fast-growing corn-stalk—X1402.3.1; plant grows to sky—F54.2ff. SEE ALSO BEANSTALK.

GRUAGACH: Task, discovering why Gruagach Gaire stopped laughing—H1199.19.

GRUMBLING: Fairy spins for girl, not to grumble when unwinding—F348.0.1.1.

GUADELUPE: Miraculous image of Virgin appears on shawl—V121.1.

GUAM-AM TONG-TU: The Compassionate Protector of Children—T210.1.1.

GUARANI: Guarani man saves Cloud Goddess and Moon Goddess from tiger, given maté—A2691.6.

GUARD: Guard asks why he serves with no one to relieve him—H1273.2N.

GUARDIAN ANGEL: V238; Guardian Angel gives Jack lantern to carry until judgment day, origin Jack O' Lantern—Q565Ah.

GUAVA: Panditji addresses guava tree—J2368.

GUBRICH: Woman obeying dwarfs is given silver pine cones, healing herb—F451.5.1.10.1.

GUDGEON: SEE FISH, GUDGEON.

GUESSING: Guessing contests, princess offered to correct guesser—H511; guessing name of creature—C432.1.3, D2183, E443.3; test, guessing person's thoughts—H524. SEE ALSO NAME.

GUEST: Wife demands tale of each guest—M231.2; servant causes master to chase guest with butcher knife—K2137; storyteller given lodging on condition he will tell tales all night—Z11.4; guest with no story cast out, has adventures—N231ff. SEE ALSO HOSPITALITY; INN.

GUGGIALP: Ghostly boar on Guggialp—H1411.4.1.

GUILLEMOTS: Creation—A1947.1.1.

GUILT: True murderer's blood only antidote for snake bite—B522.1.2; accused man gives over seed which will bear golden pears if planted by man who has never stolen or cheated, no one can be found to plant—H263.1. SEE ALSO CONFESSION; COURT; CRIME; JUDGE; MURDER; TRUTH.

GUINEA: SEE BIRDS, GUINEA.

GUITAR: Hare hits buzzard over head with guitar—A2351.9; hare hits buzzard over head

with guitar and holds wings outstretched to glide back to earth—K1041.3; fairies remove hunchback's hump when ends their song—F344.1.3; ghost chases to return guitar—J1495.4; pseudo-magic resuscitating object sold—K113; man finally sends money to purchase guitar. "Now I see you really mean to play it"—J1382.3.

GULF: Maksil, God of the Gulf, claims victim each year in whirlpool—F420.5.2.2.4.

GULL: SEE BIRD, GULL.

GUN: Gun goes off accidentally, killing much game—X1124.3; gun bent to make spectacular shot—X1122.3; lion flees sound of gun—K2324.2; looking through gun barrel—J2131.4.1; gun given stupid ogre as pipe—K1057. SEE ALSO HUNTING; MARKSMAN.

GUNO AND KOYO: Sixth rice cake is the one that satisfies—J2213.3; dig hole to put dirt from hole being dug—J1934; Guno and Koyo find kris—J1516.1.

GUSLI: Magic gusli, pluck string and sea appears, etc.—D831Bb; wife of captured king plays gusli for enemy king and chooses husband as boon—J1545.4.3.

GUYANA: Origin—A1231.3.

GWARWYN-A-THROT: Fairy leaves when named—F381.1.

GYPSY: Why gypsies have no church—X1863; gypsy lad throws cows over sea, hangs onto tail of last to ride across—X1133.8; gypsy carries off girl from dead band of gypsies—D621.0.2; gypsy fiddle—D1233.0.1; devil turns girl's father into fiddle, mother to bow, brothers to strings—D1233.0.2; gypsy shelters Holy Family—A222.1.1; gypsy woman told Lord is coming to visit turns away three beggars—Q292.1; gypsy fishes old copper pots from pond—W48.2; gypsy and wife carry pots over river by floating them across in giant cauldron—J1689.3; horse in snowstorm eats charcoal, keeps gypsies warm by heat from tail—X1203.1; "Who's going to eat?" Gypsy, "I shall", etc. "Who's going to work?" Gypsy, "Speak up, men!"—W111.7.2. SEE ETHNIC AND GEOGRAPHICAL INDEX.

HABETROT: D2183.1 Jacobs.

HABIT: Monkey and rabbit in habit-breaking contest—K263.1; man learns to stand smell of tannery—U133.

HABITAT: SEE A2430+ Animal characteristics - dwelling and food.

HADDAM: Witches from Haddam and East Haddam fight over rights to kill cattle—G243.1.2.

HADJI: Children's teeth fall out in memory of Hadji—A1316.6.1; spider web over hole saves Hadji—A2221.5.2, A2231.7.1.2, B523.1. SEE ALSO MOHAMMED; MOSLEM.

HAG: Hag-of-the-mist, princess stolen—R111.1.3Aq.

HAIL: Blackbirds (mice) tie coyote in bag so 'hail' won't hurt him—K711.5; hail as spirit medium—F962.5.0.1.

HAIR: As many hairs on your head as in ass's tail—H703.1; kind girl combs head—Q2.1.1B; coyote insists on secret of sapsucker's hairdo, uses pitch—J2449.1; hair cut by fairies never regrows—F344.1.4; as many stars in heaven as hairs on my donkey—H702.2.1; frog challenges tiger to spitting contest, feigns having spit out hair of tiger's tail—K1715.12.2; king overhears girl say will bear son with hair of gold—N455.4A; hair touching tabu. Spring turns to gold—B316A; grandfather vows never to look on granddaughter after daughter dies, never cuts hair—R221Z; jewels fall from old lady's hair as girl combs—Q2.1.1E; magic hairs, rub together and sheep appear—K1931.2E; man steals bathing maiden's hair, scroll with secrets of nature is inside hair—D672H; ogre's hair tied to prevent pursuit—K635.2; quest for three golden hairs of giant (devil)—H1273.2; quest for princess caused by sight of dropped hair—H1213.1; Rapunzel, long hair as ladder into tower—F848.1; task, charcoal made from human hair—H1021.1.4; small animal sends one of his 'hairs' as threat to larger animal, sends quill, feather, etc. to bluff—K1711.1; enemy's hair tied down to prevent pursuit—K635; witch ties up hero's animals with magic hair—R111.1.3Ag, S12.1.0.1Bb; faithful wife cutting hair thought to have murderous intent—T210.1.1; young wife pulls out gray hair, old wife black—J2112.1. SEE ALSO BALDNESS; BEARD.

HAIRPINS: Student kills Naga Queen and has bones made into hairpins—J21B.

HAIRY MAN: Dogs rescue lad from hairy man—B524.1.2H.

HAITI: Origin of donkeys on Haiti—A1882.2; man forbidden to set foot on Haitian soil, fills boots with other soil—J1161.3.2; why there are no tigers in Haiti—A2434.2.5. SEE ALSO ETHNIC AND GEOGRAPHICAL INDEX.

HALACH-VINIC: Great Spirit punishes quail—A2431.3.10.

HALDE HAT: Giant at wedding feast wears hat of invisibility—D1361.14.1.

HALF: Neighbor wears hat half red and half green to provoke quarrel between two who never disagree—K419.5.1.

HALF CHICK: B171.1, Z52.2.

HALLOWEEN: Owls turn back to conjure wives on Halloween—D153.2.1; corpse drops piecemeal down chimney on Halloween eve—H1441.1; lost fiddler heard on Halloween—E425.2.5.1; six eggs found on Halloween hatch baby goblins—F481.0.1.1.2; hare leaps to beekeeper for safety, gypsy advises to tie hare to arm on Hallow's Eve, bees aid and sting witch, hare turns to girl—E501.5.5.1.1; to tie withe around foot of man hung on Halloween—F302.1.6; spin scissors in sieve on Halloween night and see lover—D1323.20; Tamlane rides with elfland queen on Halloween—F324.3.1; girl seeks wisning well on Halloween Eve—Q2.1.6A. FOR OTHER HALLOWEEN TALES SEE: GHOST; GOBLINS; HAUNTED HOUSES; ETC. FOR ENTIRE COLLECTIONS OF HALLOWEEN TALES SEE Harper, Wilhelmina. GHOST AND GOBLINS. Hoke, Helen. WITCHES, WITCHES, WITCHES. Hope-Simpson, Jacynth. A CAVALCADE OF WITCHES. Leach, Maria. THE THING AT THE FOOT OF THE BED. Leodhas, Sorche Nic. GAELIC GHOSTS; GHOSTS GO HAUNTING. Manning-Sanders, Ruth. A BOOK OF GHOSTS AND GOBLINS; A BOOK OF DEVILS AND DEMONS; A BOOK OF WITCHES. Mayne, William. GHOSTS. Sechrist, Elizabeth Hough. HEIGH-HO FOR HALLOWEEN. Spicer, Dorothy Gladys. THIRTEEN GHOSTS.

HAM: Literal numskull drags ham on string—J2461B.

HAMELIN: Pied Piper—D1427.1.

HAMMER; Borrow hammer so won't wear own down by pounding—W153.19; magic hammer causes Issun-Boshi to grow—F535.1.1E; magic hammer causes Devil to stick to it—Q565A; magic hammer, shake and room fills with food—N777.0.3; Smith Liam drops hammer to earth—D672K; threat to throw sledge hammer to moon—K18.2.

HAMMERHEAD: SEE BIRD, HAMMERHEAD.

HAN DYNASTY: K2366.2.

HANANIM: Case between fly and sparrow, why fly rubs hand and sparrow hops—A2441.2.4, A2479.10.

HAND: Cruel brother cuts off hands of sister—B491.1.3; cold hands and feet sign of dead person, numskull believes self dead—J2311.7; drowning tax collector refuses to "give hand"—W153.5.1; fool cannot find right hand in the dark—J1735; ghost hand haunts—E221.1.1; the prince with the golden hand—H1385.1D; hand from the grave reaches for food—H1440D; boy kills giant whale by painting magic symbols, crab, hand, star, kayak on left hand and on kayak—B877.1.3; why man's hand is like lizard's—A1311.1.1; hand and ring prove murdering suitor—S62.1; sale, deceived man allowed to claim hand with settlement of "handful of copper"—J1511.17; King Robert Bruce sends monk to fetch hand of St. Fillan to battlefield—V143.2.2. SEE ALSO LEFT; RIGHT.

HAND-OF-GLORY: Hand of glory points out

treasure and causes sleepers to sleep on—
D1162.2.1.1.

HANDICAPPED: SEE BLIND; CRIPPLED; DEAF;
HUNCHBACKED; LAME.

HANDKERCHIEF: Handkerchief tied to wound of
hero in disguise—R222.1A; handkerchief taken
to hero—H1385.1; suitor forced to learn trade
weaves handkerchief by which queen identifies
him—H335.0.2.2.1.

HANDLESS: Devil has maid's hands cut off—
H1385.3L.

HANDMILL: Handmill that grinds pancakes to
piroges—Z52.4.2.1.

HANDSHAKING: Frog's hands flat from too much
handshaking—A2375.2.9.1.

HANGING: Cobbler about to hang self tells demon
he is making noose to tie up all demons in underworld—G501G; hanged man asks to be taken on
back to fetch drink of water—F302.1.6; trickster feigns hanging to distract owner from goods
—K341.3; innocent executed because he fits
gallows, because guilty cannot be spared, etc.—
J2233.2; grateful dead aid hero who redeems
corpse—E341.1; to tie withe around foot of man
hung on Halloween—F302.1.6; Father's advice,
"If you wish to hang yourself, do so by the
stone which I point out"—J21.15. SEE ALSO
GALLOWS.

HANOMAT: Hanomat spills bag of sand to form
mountains—A963.10; Hanomat snips off top of
Mt. Karong, creates volcanoes—A966.3.

HANSEL AND GRETEL: G412.1.1.

HANUMAN: SEE HANOMAT.

HAPPINESS: Charm for wealth and happiness—
H588.7.2; Chang Kung's happiness secret,
writes "kindness" one hundred times, becomes
Kitchen God—A411.2; ring which makes happy
sad and sad happy—D1076.1; king seeks shirt
of happy man—N135.3; what trade brings greatest happiness? Tilling soil—H1273.2I; unhappy
traveler cheered, man steals knapsack and
leaves it on road ahead—U69.

HAPPY BOZ'LL: Dog cut in half catches both
rabbits—X1215.11.1.

HARDY HARDHEAD: Jack's companion on adventure—F601.2Ad.

HARE: Hare in age debate—B841.1.6; air-castle
to sell hare—J2061.3.2; hare tricks antelope—
K717.2; baboon invites hare to beer in treetop—
J1565.1; hare sets fire to wood on badger's back
—K2345.0.1; hare tricks badger into making mud
boat—J2171.1.3; Brer Rabbit tells Brer B'ar
that Brer Wolf and Brer Fox are chasing him—
K2131.9; hare shaved by skillful barber—
F660.1B; hare returns in barrel rolling—
K553.0.3; bees substituted for hare's children

in baboon's bag—K527.1; hare tricks birds into
cage—K714.2.4.1.1.1; blind, deaf, lame capture
hare—X1791; boy jealous of two adopted boys
becomes hare, halibut, etc.—D100.2; hare tricks
captor into throwing him into briar patch—
K581.2; hare sees leopard grasp horns of hiding
bushbuck thinking them branches, hare tries to
warn both of mistake—B335.6.1; Brer Buzzard
abandons Brer Rabbit on tree top until Rabbit
remembers where he hid their gold—K2347; hare
on buzzard's back aloft, hits over head with
guitar, then holds wings outstretched until
glides to earth—A2351.9, K1041.3; daughter
sent to shoo cabbage eating rabbit, carries her
off—G561.2D; hare to carry money to landlord in
time—J1881.2.2; hare flees fox's cat husband—
K2324; Manstin rabbit turns child into giant
child with long ears and slit lip—B535.0.16;
Brer Rabbit's children open door when Brer
Wolf imitates Brer Rabbit's voice—K311.3F; Brer
Rabbit hides in chimney, spits tobacco juice in
Brer Fox's eyes when looks up—K1161.11; all
animals confess weaknesses—W141.1; woodpecker
steals conjure bag—D1274.1.1; hare raises alarm
that Magasa, cow's owner, is coming and all flee
leaving him cooked cow—K484.4; cow tricked
into running horn into tree—K771; coyote forces
hare to sing song for him—G555.1.3; hare gives
crane red head—A2320.3.2; hare causes crocodile to laugh and escapes from mouth—
K561.1.0.1; hare builds house (cage) for crocodile—K714.2.4.2; hare uses crocodiles as bridge
by counting them—K579.2.2; hare distracts dog
so that crow can escape—K648.1; escape by pretending to dance so as to be untied—K571; hare
feigns dead and is thrown on basket of bananas
—K371.1; hare files down deer's teeth—
A2345.3.1; disguise, Brer Rabbit rolls in honey
and scares others away as Will-er-de-wust—
K335.0.4.7; disguise, Brer Rabbit ties tin plates
and coffee pot on self and attacks as Ole Man
Spewter-Splutter—K335.0.4.8; disguise, hare disguises self in leaves and honey and calls self
"King of the Leaves"—K1991.1; trickster disguises as leprous animal and makes others think
that trickster has put a hex on enemies—K1995;
dog bites, then caresses hare—K2031; hare outruns dog—U242; Brer Rabbit steals dog's shoes,
why dog's chase hares—A2494.4.4; Brer Rabbit
sings in drum, making noise to frighten others
off—K335.0.4.9; hare tricks dupe into changing
place—K842.0.3; Brer Rabbit eats butter and
smears on dupe possum's mouth—K401.1; why
rabbit has long ears—A2325.1.1; hare convinces
elephant that moon is in lake—K1716; hare escapes in bundle of grass thrown down—K521.10;
hare tricks farming partner—K171.1, K364.2;
hare has wildcat feign dead and calls turkey to
celebrate—K751; hare has coon feign dead,
frogs to dig hole to bury—K751.0.2; animal
feigns dead repeatedly and then entices owner
from goods—K341.2.1; feigns dead, Brer Rabbit
tricks sham dead Brer Fox into saying "Wahoo"—
K607.3; Sungura's fiancée refuses lion, elephant,
prefers hare like herself—J416.2; hare steals
fire for man—A1415.0.2.1, A1415.0.2.6; hare
flees from falling tree, thinks end of world, etc.
—Z43.3.1, Z43.3.2; why hare's flesh is sweet
because of eaten honey—A2511.2; rabbit gets

secret of flint, explodes and splits lip--
A2342.1.1; fool calls to hare to follow--J2461K;
Brer Rabbit's lucky rabbit's foot--D882.0.1;
Brer Rabbit ties Brer Fox on false promise--
K713.1.3.1; hare persuades wolf and fox to put
their heads in loops on rope to strangle tiger
and are dragged to death--K713.3; the hare with
many friends--H1558.4; hares find frogs are
more timid than they--J881.1; lad gambles with
hare--E577.2.1.2; let me catch you better game
K553.1, K553.1.0.4; hare learns word to open
gate, forgets--N455.3.2; Brer Rabbit forced to
show Brer Gilyard's treasure--K649.9.2; Brer
Rabbit poisons Brer Gilyard--K1082.0.2; alligator needs Brer Rabbit's gizzard--K544; goat in
hare's house, bee routs--Z39.1; hare tricks
guineas into cage--K714.2.4.1; hare betrays
hidden guests--Z43.6.1; Brer Rabbit wants to
show treasure before being eaten by Hawk--
K551.25.1; hare fetches healing root and restores
slain lad--R111.1.3Al; herding hares--H1112;
rabbit kills man-eating hill from within--F912.2.6;
Brer Rabbit traps Brer Wolf in hollow tree--
K714.3; Sungura eats honey from boy, substitutes stones--K526.3; why hare hops--
A2441.1.11.1; hornets rout animals chasing Brer
Rabbit--K641.5; hare tells coyote hornet's nest
is bell--K1023.1.0.2; Brer Rabbit puts hornet's
nest in fox's bag--K526.4; hare tricks enemy
hiding in house into answering--K607.1; Brer
Rabbit pollutes house so that he is left in pos-
session--K355; old woman hides hare in basket
as wild hunt passes--E501.5.5.1; hunter was
going to give hare to thief anyway--J1395; Sungura saves hunter from lion--K649.13; hare
tricked into leaving food by hyena disguised
as monster--K335.0.4.3; White Hare of Inaba--
K1014.3; hare as judge re-enacts rescue of ungrateful tiger--J1172.3; judge hare puts out
burning sandbank, as logical as horse bearing
calf--J1191.1.1; judge cat eats hare--K815.7;
hare defeats fox in jumping contest--K17.5; hare
knocks out leopard's teeth--K721.2; hare tricks
leopard into holding up cave--K1251; hare sold
as letter-carrier--K131.1.1; hare frightens lion
by showing him own reflection in well--K1715.1;
hare takes lion hunting, stakes out and rolls
boulder on him--K815.19.1; hare as nurse eats
lion cubs--K933, K1066; lion leaves hare to follow stag--J321.3; hare shows lion 'graves' of
alligator and bear he has killed--K1715.15; hare
shows lion (leopard) reflection in well and lion
attacks--K1715.1; hare presumes to demand
rights from lions--J975; why hare's lip is split--
A2342.1; hare claims left liver in cave, underwater queen wants--K544; man is turned to hare
and has fantastic adventures--M231.1Bd; Manabush goes as White Rabbit to steal fire from
Dawn People--A1415.0.2.5; hare falsifies message of man's rebirth--A1335.1.0.1; hare sold
as messenger--K131.1.1; hare in the moon--
A751.2ff; hare scratches moon--A751.5.1; hare
as ambassador of the moon--K1716; Brer Rabbit
tells Brer Fox, B'ar and Wolf that pot of gold
is with moon in pond--J1791.3.3; old man on
moon pounding paddy and throwing chaff to
rabbit--A751.1.6; mother to be killed, hidden--
K311.3.1; animal captor persuaded to talk and
release victim from mouth--K561.1; Nansi ties

rope to leg and tells wife to pull when soup is
done, hare reties to own leg--K171.0.2.2; why
hare's nose twitches--Z49.6.0.7; ocean created
when Brer Rabbit cuts string holding banks of
river together--A924.5; whose family is older,
hare is referred to in Han Dynasty classics--
B841.1.4; hare has cricket dress opossum's
tail for dance--A2317.12.3; hare eats berry
cache and blames ostrich--K251.1.6; hare tricks
otter and badger out of goods--K441.5; hare
tricks otter into water--A2433.2.2.2; hare chews
down path and wins race--K11.9; hare evades
by returning home repeatedly for forgotten
pillow (hoe)--K1839.12.1; Brer Rabbit feigns
being poisoned by meat--K341.2.2.2; Brer Rabbit, poling boat, escapes paddling Brer Fox--
K636.2; hare makes trouble for late possum--
T92.11.2; Rabbit prince weds bird maiden--
H1385.3Fg; hare teaches fox to play on quills--
K1066.4; hedgehog defeats hare in race--K11.1;
turtle defeats hare in race--K11.3; Brer Fox
caught when Brer Rabbit drops rail fence on
neck--K1111.2; hare frees rattlesnake, coyote re-
enacts--J1172.3; hare flees from reflection in
well--K1715.1.0.1; hare saddles dupe and rides
--K1241; Brer Rabbit nails Brer Fox's tail down
while roofing house--K729.1; hare convinces
animal biting leg that it has root in mouth--K543;
seasons change as hare jumps up and down--
D2011.1.3.1; skillful flayer skins running hare--
F660.1Bb; Brer Rabbit sings courting song to
win girl--K1066.8; opossum releases snake, hare
re-enacts--J1172.3; Brer Rabbit taught incriminating song--K1066.7; Hodja serves soup of the
soup of the hare -- J1551.6; hare blames spider
for theft, spider returns to lower world--
K401.2.3.1; Olokun gives food producing spoon
--D861.2.1; hare beats dust from stone--K62.1;
hare seeks strongest, ice, sun, etc.--L392.0.5;
arctic hare steals sun from Ke'let--A721.1.3;
Sungura convinces Toto to tell mother to kill
cock and feed Sungura, rather than kill Sungura
--K511.1; hare buries cow's tail in ground, says
cow sunk--K404.1; why hare has short tail--
A2378.4.1; Anansi tells hare to dip tail in rum
and put into sea, fish bite off--K1021; hare
tricks fox into fishing through ice with tail--
K1021; tailless hare persuades others to cut off
tails--J758.1.3; hare caught by tarbaby--K741;
suitor tasks, herding hares--H1045.0.1; thief
thinks hare is hunter searching for gun--
K1161.2; hare tricks tiger into eating stones,
fishing with tail, getting burnt in brush--
K553.1.0.6, K1021, K1043.2; hare rides elephant's back and bluffs tiger--K1715.2.1; hare
ties tiger for safety in storm--K713.1.1; origin
of rabbit trap--A1458.2; Brer Rabbit trapped in
hollow tree--K629.2.4; hare tricks hyena--
N455.3.1; Brer Rabbit introduces Brer Fox to
"Mr. Trouble"--H1376.11; hare arranges tug of
war between elephant and hippo--K22.1; deceptive tug of war, large animal's tail tied to tree
root--K22.2; hare and monkey have no-scratch-
ing and no-twitching contest--K263.1; Sungura
claims name is 'visitor' and is given food--
K359.2; hare refuses to help dig well, muddies
waters--A2233.1.1; Brer Rabbit rescued from
bucket in well by Brer Fox descending in other
bucket--K651; Brer Rabbit convinces Brer Fox

to attack wildcat since its tracks show no claws --K1039; hare leaps to beekeeper for safety, turns to girl, bees sting witch--E501.5.5.1; tailor imitates witch who jumps into water and turns to hare--G211.2.7.2; witch as hare--G275.12.2; hare loses both wives to Sayno skunk--N2.6.0.1; Brer Rabbit's wife spills boiling water on wolf being pulled up on rope--K1034.1; Brer Wolf imitates Brer Rabbit, is burnt in a log--J2411.6.2; hare tricks wolves into dancing, escapes--K606.2; elephant, giraffe farm with hare, each think hare does half work--K364.1: SEE ALSO COTTONTAIL.

HAROUN-AL-RASHID: Allows Abunawas to kill flies and Abunawas kills one on Haroun-Al-Rashid --J1193.1.0.1.

HARP: Family tradition that ancestor was great harp player--A1578.3; lad beguiles monsters with harp--H1385.1A; bee, harp, mouse, and bumclock dance--H341.2.1; harper drawn away from city about to be drowned--F944.1.2; magic fairy harp misused--F348.7.1.3; woman buys child back from Sidh with golden harp of Wrad-- F321.3.0.2; magic harp stolen--F54.2.1, G610Ac; harp made of breastbone and hair of drowned girl sings of murder--E632.0.1; wife plays harp and sea-maid brings up kidnapped husband-- R111.1.3Cd; tiger told bamboo is king's harp-- K1023.1.3.

HARPSICHORD: Princess hidden in harpsichord-- B314E; entrance to woman's room in golden harpsichord--K1341.1.

HARROW: Task, lying on harrow--F601.2Abb.

HART: SEE DEER.

HARTEBEESTE: Hartebeeste's coat--A2411.1.6.9.

HAT: Anansi hides beans in hat, dances from heat--A2323.1, W125.3.1; bear in hat taken for man by wife, respected--J1762.2.3; fools with hats beside them on bench, put on hats and pull bench to stretch it--J2723; alleged bill-paying hat--K111.2; clay hats two feet wide stop fighting--J1199.5; dupe guards hat while trickster steals goods--K1252; fool carries milk in hat, turns inside out--J2663; giant at wedding feast wears hat of invisibility--D1361.14.1; hats given to Jizo statues--J1873.1; peasant to recognize king, one with hat on--J1289.27; magic listening cap--D1067.2.1; monkeys imitate cap peddler-- B786.1; origin of hats--A1437; man wears hat half red and half green to provoke quarrel-- K419.5.1; hat that sees all--D832.1; hat that shoots from six corners--D831Ab; magic soldier producing hat stolen by host in inn--D861.1G.

HATCHET: Hatchet soup--K112.2; traveler finds hatchet, companion claims half until rightful owner returns--W197.3. SEE ALSO AX.

HATRED: Origin hatred--A1388. SEE ENMITY.

HAUNTED HOUSE: Wife convinces husband castle site is haunted, fake ghost--K2349.2; cats in haunted house say "Wait till Caleb comes"--

J1495.2; person enters dark, dark house, etc.-- Z13.1.4; haunted house given to those who exorcise--Q82.0.1; man frightens away Gafes (evil spirits of dead) and obtains magic medicine bag--A1539.2; SEE ALL H1411ff Fear test: staying in haunted house. SEE ALSO DEMONS; DEVIL; EVIL SPIRITS; GHOSTS; GOBLINS; HALLOWEEN.

HAWILI FALLS: A935.3.

HAWK: SEE BIRD, HAWK.

HAWTHORN: Man in moon with hawthorn bush-- A751.1.5.

HAYSTACK: Bear burnt on haystack--K1013.2; needle, coin, etc. lost in hay--J2461.

HAYWAGON: Fat man can get through city gate if haywagon can pass--J1411.

HAZEL: Hazel staff means of locating King Arthur's sleeping place--D1960.2; hazel twig causes cliff face to open--H1331.1.3Ae.

HAZELNUT CHILD: F535.1.1Db.

HEAD: Tattling mischief maker is beheaded-- A2611.3.1; beheaded head tells servant to fetch king, on return head is silent and servant is beheaded--B210.2.3.1; man's head bitten off, did he ever have one?--J2381; Friar Bacon makes head of brass--D1711.6.5; calf's head in murderer's hand turns to corpse's--Q551.3.3; deer head on stick turns to nightingale on lime tree-- Q2.1.5Ba; Brer Fox and wife convinced sleeping with heads off is the fashion--J2413.4.5; kind girl combs heads--Q2.1.1Ba; girl opens her head and puts her belongings inside--F511.0.4.2; girl's head replaced with sheep's head--L145.1B; great head as ogre--G361.2; man's head lost by accident and companions debate whether he even had a head--J2381; man puts legs on pillow to reward, head on ground--J2351.1.1; pull rope and crack heads of those tied to both ends-- K301B; father stands on head until hen lays another egg--Z39.5.1. SEE ALSO: BEHEAD.

HEADHUNTER: Ruler gets headhunter to agree to take but one head more, sends his own--W28.5.

HEADLESS: Headless horseman challenges to race --E422.1.1.3.1.1; headless woman is at least a good woman as has no tongue--E422.1.1.3.2.

HEALING: Crow caught and forced to bring water from well of healing--R111.1.3An; dwarfs heal boy--F451.5.1.10.2; lad with healing fruits in basket--H346; princess to wed imposter lad slain, hare fetches healing root and restores-- R111.1.3Al; foolish imitation of healing--J2411.1, N452; princess given to man who can heal her-- H346; shepherd refuses to say "to your good health" when king sneezes--H328.9; wax with healing properties--H1440C. SEE ALSO DOCTOR; MEDICINE.

HEARING: Lie, first sees mosquito on cliff mile

away, second man hears it tromping-X938.1; person of remarkable hearing--F660.1C, F601.2; thief stealing bronze bell stuffs ears with cotton fearing din will raise authorities--J2259.1. SEE ALSO DEAF; EAR.

HEART: Magic bird heart, gold under pillow when eaten--R111.1.3AI; death from broken heart--F1041.1.2.2.5; greedy trickster cuts heart from inside of fat giving cow--F929.3; heart of man, deepest thing--H643.1; choice, money or three walnuts given "from the heart"--J229.3.1; lad hides in heart of princess--H321E; iron bands around heart break--D195.1; accused of eating lamb's heart, thief maintains that it had no heart--K402; mole brings girl's heart to lover--A2433.3.20.1; crocodile captures monkey for heart--K544; ogre made to believe hero has cut out heart--G524.0.1.

HEARTH: Hearth abode of unpromising hero--L114.1, R221; origin gods of the hearth--T211.2.1.1. SEE ALSO FIREPLACE.

HEAT: SEE HOT, HEAT.

HEATHER: Secret of heather ale--C429.2.

HEAVEN: Heaven entered to pick up cap, apron--K2371.1.1; yard-long chopsticks in heaven--W47; man says is going to climb to heaven, crowd gathers and tramples field--K474.1; dupe persuaded to be killed in order to go to heaven--K843.1; King Yudhisthera refuses to enter heaven unless dog is admitted too, dog becomes Dharma--A489.5; ascent to heaven holding on to elephant--J2133.5.2; how far to heaven--H682.1.1+; footstool thrown from heaven--F1037.1.1, L435.3; unsuccessful imitation of resuscitation--K213C; trickster pretends to jump back into heaven--J2326.5; numskull lies in grave and believes self in heaven--J2311.6; St. Peter refuses souls won by Padre at cards--Q565Ai; shoemaker tosses apron into heaven and hops in "on own property"--Q565Ae; smith refused entry to heaven--Q565F; smith bored with heaven leaves--Q565Ae; heaven entered by trick--K2371.1+; turtle borrows feathers and flies to heaven--K1041.1.1.1; believing visitor comes from Paradise, woman gives him goods for husband in heaven--J2326. SEE ALL A660 Nature of the upper world; A700-A799 The Heavens. SEE ALSO HELL; PARADISE; SKY.

HEDGE: Cuckoo flies over hedge built to contain her--J1904.2; hedges cut down around vineyards, vineyards destroyed--W181.1.1; why wren lives in hedge--A2433.4.7.

HEDGEHOG: Hedgehog defeats hare in race--K11.1; hedgehog and jackal divide crops--K171.1; marriage to hedgehog prince--B641.5; hedgehog gets fox to throw him out of pit--J1662.4, K652.3; why hedgehog lives underground--A2433.3.24.

HEDLEY COW: E427.

HEEL: SEE FOOT.

HEIR: SEE INHERITANCE.

HEIRLOOM: Origin of family heirloom--A1578.2.

HELL: Hell banknotes, gold given in country of ghosts turns to paper money used at funerals--F129.4.4.1; lad rides to hell on Billy Goat--G530.2M; yardlong chopsticks in hell--W47.1; threat to build church in hell--K1781; musician in hell playing for devils breaks fiddle strings--K606.1.2; man admitted to neither heaven nor hell--Q565; hogboon banished to hell--F381.16; descent to lower world--F81ff; recovered patient asked by doctor for news from hell--J1432; task, to make person say he lies, says person's father is in hell--H342.3; task, carry letter to under-world--F601.2Ac; task, fetch flail from hell--G610Ak; task, fetch master's grandfather from hell--F615.3.1.5. SEE ALSO DEVIL; HEAVEN; LOWER WORLD; UNDERWORLD.

HELM: Trickster repeatedly substitutes billy goat for nanny on way to Helm--J1703.5; tie up moon's reflection in barrel--J1791.2.2; Helmite reverses shoes and returns home--J2014.2; four men carry beadle on rounds so as not to track snow--J2163.3; carry stones back uphill to roll down--J2165; town of fools--J1703. SEE ALSO ALL ENTRIES IN THESE COLLECTIONS: Simon, Solomon. WISE MEN OF HELM. Simon, Solomon. MORE WISE MEN OF HELM.

HELMET: Fostedina wears golden helmet at wedding to hide crown of thorn scars--A1437.1.

HELVA: Never made helva before for never had flour and butter in house at same time--J1250.12.

HEMP SMOKER: Embarrassed hemp smoker and hemp grower feign death and are put into grave--K1869.1.

HEN: SEE CHICKEN.

HENNY PENNY: Z43.3, Z53.

HEN WIFE: Aids ash-maid--R221Db.

HENRY, FAITHFUL HENRY: D195.1.

HENRY MORGAN: Golden altar covered with earth to hide from pirate Henry Morgan--V116.1.

HERB: Woman asked by dwarfs to gather pine cones elsewhere obliges and finds silver cones, is given healing herb--F451.5.1.10.1; grass stalk wants to be herb--Z42.4.

HERCULES: Hercules slays Antaeus, pygmy friends of the dead giant drive Hercules off--F531.6.12.6.0.1; Hercules refuses to greet Plutus--J451.3; statue of Hercules overcoming lion--J1454; ox driver must put shoulder to wagon before Hercules will help--J1034.

HERDING: Suitor tasks: herding hares--H1045.0.1; task, herding mares for three days--H1199.12.4; servant tells king that his "servant" can herd wild animals--G671B. SEE ALSO

SHEPHERD.

HERLA: King Herla--F378.1A.

HERMIT: Devil Aghiutsa turns hermits Chirila and Manaila against each other by pretending to tell each a secret--A1342.1; Holyman Chyavana meditates so well ants build mound over him, he is caught up with fish, etc.--D1960.5; ghost of hermit gives wishing bone--D882.1Ga; ghostly girl asks man to take place of ancient hermit--E379.7; hermit offers one coin earned honestly or one hundred dishonestly--Q3.3; hawk drops mouse into hands of hermit--L392.0.1; hermit turns mouse to cat, dog, etc.--W154.2.1.1; servant attempts to steal money in hermit's staff, serpent engulfs him--K331.6.1. SEE ALSO HOLYMAN; PRIEST.

HEROINE: Godasiyo, the woman chief--A1333.2; clever peasant daughter--H561.1, H582.1.1, H583+, H586, H691.1.1, H1053.2, H1054.1, J1111, J1545.4; heroine Mizilca charges dragon. Sent disguised as Knight to Sultan by father--H1578.1.7; woman outwits dragon ogres--G501C; woman as dragon slayer--B11.11.7+; girl foot-racer of Payuki defeats men of Tukuvi--H1594.3; The Green Sergeant. Princess performs feat as man--K1236.2; kind and unkind girls--Q2.1+; Mastermaid, girl helps hero perform tasks--G530.2; girl offers self as sacrifice to monster snake--B16.5.1.3; maid offers self as sacrifice to sea-serpent, slays--K1853.2.12; Mulan disguises as soldier and leads army in battles--K1837.6.1; girl rescues prince from troll woman--K975.2.1; youngest daughter steals from trolls--G610Ae; wife seeks lost husband (lover)--H1385.4, H1385.5; strong woman must be wrestled--F617.2.1, F617.2.2, F617.2.3.

HERON: SEE BIRD, HERON.

HIBERNATE: Why bears hibernate--A2481.1.

HIBISCUS: Token of identity in race between turtel and lion--K11.1.

HICKATHRIFT: Tom Hickathrift--F628,2.3.1.

HIDES: Dupes kill cows for hides--K941.1; alleged oracular hide sold--K114.1; hide feigned prophetic--K842Bb.

HIDING: What will cranberries do if wolves come? Hide--J641.2; boy hiding from father changes to nut--Z43.5; entrance to woman's room by hiding in statue--K1341.1; suitor test, hiding from princess--H321; thief hidden in cage carried into house--K312; tree hides a kind girl--Q2.1.2Cb.

HIISI: Poor farmer to go to Hiisi--D861.1F.

HILL: Creation of mountains (hills)--A960+; suitor task, running up steel hill--H331.1.1E; task, climbing glass hill--D721.5B, F751, H321F, H331.1.1, H1385.3Ca, H1385.5B; origin hills, earth dropped by giant--F531.6.6.3.1; origin characteristics of hills--A969.11.

HILLEL: Rav Hillel does not admire Roman culture--J652.4.3.

HILLMAN: Hillman borrows pan--F451.5.10.4.1.

HIMALAYAS: Origin of mountains--A955.10.3.

HINA; Goddess in moon with calabash at her side--A751.8.3.1; Hina's rainbow tapa hang over Cave-of-the-Mist near Rainbow Falls--A791.14.

HIPPOPOTAMUS: Hippopotamus's tug of war with elephant--K22.1.

HIRAM: Clever parrot becomes advisor to King--K1346.0.1.

HITANYAKSIPU: Vishnu strikes down Asura king--D1840.1.4.

HITCHHIKER: Ghostly hitchhiker--E332.3.3.1.

HOARD: Companion steals common food supply--K343.3; shrew mouse Umulumba and vole mouse Mgeva compete for kingship, Mgeva hides food--B241.2.5.1; miser's hoard stolen, advised to imagine it is still there--J1061.4. SEE ALSO TREASURE.

HOBYAHS: B332.1.

HODJA: Thankful he wasn't on ass when stolen--J2561; lost ass as reward to finder--J2085.1; ass is not at home, it brays. Believe an ass rather than me?--J1552.1.1; cannot find ass he is sitting on--J2022; pumpkin thought to be ass's egg--J1772.1+; ass's saddle taken in retribution for stolen coat--J1862; buys back worthless cow - persuasive auctioneer--J2087; rides backwards--J2024; persistent beggar invited upstairs for refusal--J1331; daughter beaten before she breaks pitcher--J2175.1.2; thank god camels don't fly--J2564; warmed by sight of candle--K231.14.1; warmed by sight of distant candle, prepares feast over one candle--J1191.7.1+; stolen meat and weighed cat--J1611; Hodja grunts for woodcutter as he works and claims half pay, paid in clink of money--J1172.2.1; Hodja returns to feast in finery after being shunned for poor clothes and gives food to clothes--J1561.3.0.2; witness claims borrowed coat--J1151.2; ten horses counted, nine when mounted--J2031.2; cow was swift when only a calf--J2212.5; cannot find right hand in dark--J1735; believes self dead when frightened by bird--J2311.1.3.2; dead man meets mule drivers in heaven--J2311.6; with cold hands and feet, believes self dead--J2311.7, J2311.7.1; believing self dead allows wolf to eat ass--J2311.7; believes self dead when donkey brays three times--J2311.1; dead man points out the way--J2311.4; falls off tree and believes self dead--J2311.1.6; goes on to doctor to say he isn't needed--J2241; rider holds sack to relieve donkey--J1874.1; man sits on load to take weight off donkey--J1874.3; demands ten coins in dream, on waking will settle for nine--J1473; overzealous visitor couldn't wait to dress--J2517; dupe tricked waiting for trickster--

X905.4.1; center of earth under ass's hoof—H681.3.1; guess what I have and I'll give it to you to make an egg cake--J2712.1; suit for chickens from boiled eggs--J1191.2; "either give me my bag or....I'll have to get another!"—K1771.2.1; ferryman loses one of group, comforts that it is one less to pay for—J2566; pummelled with figs. Thank god they weren't beets—J2563; Hodja loses bet to stay all might without fire because he warmed self by sight of distant candle, he prepares feast for winners over heat of one candle--J1191.7.2; fools identifying pumpkin tied to another's leg--J2013.3; will not accept less than one thousand gold pieces from God, neighbor leaves 999--J1473.1; refused to say if God wills it—J21.52.7.1; how does goose concern me? Carrying it to your home. How does that concern you?--J1353; goose without a leg--K402.1; buried in old grave to deceive angel--J2212.2; hides from robbers in open grave--J2321.3, J2311.3.1; as many hairs in head as in ass's tail— H703.1; wants holidays year round—J2231; digging a hole to throw the dirt from hole in--J1934; horse taught to live without food--J1914; selling half house to buy the other half--J2213.6; shah tricked into saying "Impossible"--X905.1; no clothes needed for judgment day--J1511.7; fool implies king is an ass--J1352.3; students pretend they cannot find own legs. Teacher helps with a switch--J2021.0.1; cannot lend clothes line--J1552.1.3; must carry letter in person as none can read—J2242.2; liar reduces size of lie—X904.3, X904.4; cuts off limb on which he is sitting—J2133.4; hens to walk ahead to market—J1881.2.4; fool changes meal from other's sack into own--J1393; recommends medicine in addition to miracle--J762.2; thank god melons don't grow on trees—J2571; miller, his son and the ass—J1041.2; wants bathroom in minaret to improve singing—J2237; stars made from old moon—J2271.2.2; millstone made from old moon—J2271.2.1.1; lightning made from old moon--J2271.2.1; moon rescued from water—J1791.2; agreement to work for "nothing"--J1521.5.2; working for "nothing" at all"--J2496.1; punishes the ox for last week's misdemeanor—J1861; tally by pebbles in pot, daughter throws in a handful--J2466.2; penny charges awarded, plaintiff strikes judge and awards him the penny—J1193.2; pot has a child and dies--J1531.3; crow steals meat "But I've got the recipe"--J2562; take saplings out to guard them at night—J2224; does not know self from another identically clad--J2012.5; Hodja induced to climb tree, takes shoes along, thwarting thiefs—J1521.1.1; shoots holes in garment, lucky I wasn't in it—J2235; silence wager--J2511; soup of the soup of the hare—J1551.6; as many stars as hairs on ass--H702.2.1; task of surviving on mountain top - give each only half of supplies—H1546; horse swifter than rain—K134.2; those who know teach those who don't —X452; in farmer's clothing Hodja amazes theologist with his knowledge—J31.2; thief blown into garden—J1391.1; thief selling ladders in garden--J1391.2; thief claims to have been transformed into ass--K403.1; thief persuaded to climb down moonbeam--K1054; owner wants to see what thief

can find—J2223; owner helps thief--J1392.1.1; thieves were quarreling over his quilt--J2672; can't lend forty year old vinegar on principle—J1552.1.2; people go in opposite directions each morn so world won't tip over--J2274.1.1. SEE ENTIRE COLLECTIONS Downing, Charles. TALES OF THE HODJA; Kelsey, Alice. ONCE THE HODJA. SEE ALSO MULLAH.

HOE: Magic date tree with golden hoe—R221C; how hoe came to the Ashanti self-hoeing hoe--D1651.15; farmer calls to wife that he has hidden hoe, thief hears—J2356.1.

HOE HANDLE: Hoe handle questions girl—Q2.1.2Eb.

HOG: SEE PIG (HOG).

HOGBOON: Hogboon banished—F381.16.

HOICHI: Blind lute player forced to sing for ghosts--E434.11.

HOLDING: Holding up the roof--K1251+.

HOLE: Contest in pushing hole into tree—K61; digging hole to put the dirt in--J1934; If I have four pennies in my pocket and they fall out, what's left? A hole—J2213.10.

HOLIBURN: Giant taps human friend in play and kills—F531.5.1.5.

HOLIDAYS: Told to prepare food for "The Holidays", wife gives it to two men--K362.1; why can't we have holidays the year round?--J2231. SEE ALSO CHRISTMAS; FESTIVAL; HALLOWEEN.

HOLLAND: Robbers' heads cut off as they enter house, origin carving over doorway--K912. SEE ALSO ETHNIC AND GEOGRAPHIC INDEX.

HOLLOW: Hollow found where thrown bulls landed —A983.1.

HOLLOW TREE: Brer Rabbit trapped in hollow tree—K629.2.4; dupe tricked into entering hollow tree--K714.3; secret whispered into hollow tree--D1316.5.0.2.

HOLLY: Origin of holly—A2612.4.

HOLMOLA: Lobster taken for tailor with shears--J1909.8.3; sickle drowned in Finnish town of fools--J1865. SEE ALSO HELM.

HOLY ISLE: Isle taken from Fin folk--F742.1.

HOLY MAN: Student cares for beggar who is Holy Chang To-nyong in disguise--V226.1; asked to breathe on foot and cure it, holy man recommends usual medicines--J762.2; son gets holyman to turn him to lizard and creeps through crevice to rescue father--D197. SEE ALSO HERMIT; MONK; PRIEST.

HOLY WATER: Leaves and dirt sprinkled with

holy water turn to gold—F342.1.

HOMESICKNESS: Longing in fairyland to visit home—F377, F420.6.1.3.1.

HOMINY: Old woman in moon with hominy pot—A751.8.1.1; terrapin makes hominy spoon of wolf's ear—K1715.3.3.

HONESTY: Hermit offers one coin earned honestly or one hundred dishonestly—Q3.3.

HONEY: King introduces Korean alphabet by writing on leaves with honey so ants will eat out letters—A1484.2.1; air-castle, jar of honey is broken—J2061.1; drop of honey causes chain of accidents—N381; bear dreams eats honey, fox has same dream so eats—K444; drones to make honey, fail—J581.4; disguise, girl smears self with honey and feathers—G561B; disguise, Brer Rabbit rolls in honey and leaves, scares all as Will-er-de-Wust—K355.0.4.7; bouquet of all flowers (honey)—H1377.2; fool sells honey to flies—J1852.1.4; fool carries honey in pocket—J2461D; God teaches bee to make honey—A2813; hare feigns ill, rides lion's back and eats honey—K1241.2; why hare's flesh is sweet, because of honey eaten—A2511.2; dupe tricked into hollow tree by promise of honey—K714.3; honey is honey of all honeys—H659.29; kobalds help with remodeling castle, to receive annual honey feast—F481.1.1; hare stakes lion out to 'catch' honey, rolls rock onto him—K815.19.1; honey eaten by monkey and replaced with mud, queen passes it around and all agree that it is excellent—K144.3.1; acolyte eats honey master says is poison, claims to have been attempting suicide—J2311.2.2; pygmies demand honey, given honey with bees in comb—K1023.0.1; man frees bear, fox re-enacts, broke tabu about showing reward pot of honey—J1172.3; spirit of honey wed to a mortal—C31.9.1; honey tree left standing—J241.2; getting honey from the wasp nest—K1023; man weds sister of the honey bees—C435.1.1.

HONEY BIRD: SEE BIRD, HONEY.

HONEY GATHERERS: Honey gatherers' three sons argue as to who is most important in saving father—H621.4.2.

HONEY GUIDE: SEE BIRD, HONEY GUIDE.

HONOR: Fire, Water and Honor travel together—W45.2.

HOOD: Hood of invisibility—D1361.15.2.

HOOF: Center of earth under hoof of ass—H681.3.1; fox (wolf) tricked into pulling thorn from hoof of horse (ass), reading inscription on it, etc.—K1121.1.

HOOFPRINTS: Brother transformed when drinks from animals hoofprints—P253.2.0.1; water in hoofprint to turn bloody if hero dead—R111.1.3Ag.

HOOKEDY CROOKEDY: Jack, King of Ireland's son hired by Giant of the Hundred Hills—B316C.

HOOP: Bride test, jumping through hoop—B614Ad; why dog's tail curves, playing hoop and pole game—A2378.1.7.1.

HOP-O'-MY-THUMB: K1611C.

HOPI TURTLE: Coyote threatens baby Hopi Turtle—G555.1.1.

HORN, ANIMAL: Broken horn will tell tale—J1082.1; lion persuades bull to have ugly horns cut—J642.1.1; Kalulu hare warns bushbuck and leopard that leopard has grasped bushbuck's horns thinking them branches—B335.6.1; horn tossed in well supposedly turns to whole goat—K111.5; hyena wears fake horns—K1991; magical food giving animal horns—B115.1, B335.2; mice generals wear horns, caught—L332.1; animal with horn of plenty—B115; princess with horns will be restored if eats certain fruit—B216.6; animal tricked into running horns into tree—K771; stag caught by horns in tree—L461; given wish for each horn, neighbor imitates, says ox had four horns—Q1.1B; four wishes for four horns—J2075.5.

HORN, MUSICAL INSTRUMENT: Magic horn causes dancing, dwarf king must twirl on nose—D1415.2.1; horn notes frozen, thaw—X1623.7.2; Onsongo blows horn from thorntree top and Masai leave cattle to investigate strange bird, thus artist steals cattle—K341.5.3; respite until blows on horn—K551.3; pseudo-magic resuscitating objects sold—K113.

HORNBILL: SEE BIRD, HORNBILL.

HORNED WOMEN: Horned women fooled by calling out that their mountain is on fire—F381.8.1.

HORNETS: Hare tells coyote that hornet's nest is bell—K1023.1.0.2; hornet attacks crab's enemy, monkey—K1161.6; hornet's nest traded to dupe as "hum-house"—K1023.1.0.1; fox bumps hornet's nest in hare's 'laughing place'—K1023.5; fox tail is banner of advance, hornet's sting under tail and army retreats—K2323.1; Brer Rabbit puts hornet's nest in fox's bag—K526.4; hornet's nest as magic object, stolen at inn—D861.1F; hornets route animals chasing Brer Rabbit—K641.5; hornets enter spider's gourd—K714.2.6.

HORSE: Horse aids in quest, becomes prince—B316, H1213.1+; quest to devil for four wild bulls, horse aids—H1331.3; Aldar-Kas disguises own horse, enemy kills wrong—K415.0.2; horse lets ass die of overburden—W155.1; ass jealous of horse—L452+; baron turned to horse—Q584.2.1; peasant persuades baron to trade horses for ease of guarding in night, baron cheated—K289.1; horse rings bell to demand justice—B271.3; task, steal horse with bells—G610Ae, K1611Bb; horse painted black on one side and white on other to cause argument about horse's color—K419.5; telling horses apart,

—K1811.6, Q1.1; selfish guest expels host—P332; inhospitality to beggar, woman bears pig-headed child—T551.3.5; guest's storytelling impresses inhospitable man, vows to allow guests in future—M231.3. SEE ALSO GENEROSITY; GUEST; INNKEEPER.

HOT, HEAT: Man blows on soup to cool it, blows on hands to warm them, Satyr shuns—J1801.1; heat endurance contest for property of song—G555.1.3; horse in snowstorm eats charcoal, heat from tail keeps gypsy warm—X1203.1; lie, extraordinary effects of heat—X1632; person melts away from heat—F1041.4.1; remarkable companion with magical cooling power in red-hot room—F601.2; fool eats hot soup, "Run for your life, my belly's on fire"—J2214.1.1; test, drinking boiling water—H221.4.1.

HOT, SPICY: SEE PEPPER.

HOUNDS: Hounds of Hell—E501.18.4.1; three fat ewes for three fine hounds—S12.1.0.1Ba. SEE ALSO DOG.

HOUR: What part of hour is best?—H561.4.1.

HOUSE: Animals build house, rout thief—K1161.2; house burnt by dupe to sell ashes—K941.2; all comers invited to enter until house bursts—J2199.5; bushbuck tricks leopard with whom he has built house, shows leopard skin and leopard flees—K1715.3.2; house burnt down to get rid of cat—J2101; origin of Sangasang Ceremony for dedicating house—A1549.2.1; man builds house in fairy path, constant trouble—F361.4.1; floating house from which fish flow—A2109.2; fool does not recognize own house—J2014; ghostly burning house—E531.1; girl unkind to animals in house where shelters—Q2.1.3C; goat in fox's house routed by cock—Z39.1; goat begins to build a house, tiger finds foundation and adds to it, each thinks is his house—K1715.3.2; hare builds 'house' for crocodile—K714.2.4.2; fool sells half house to get money to buy other half—J2213.6; house greeted by owner and hidden enemy tricked into answering—K607.1; the house that Jack built—Z44; house sold except for peg—K182.3; pig goes to build house with sheep, goose, hare, cock—B296.0.1; house poles, floor, roof argue as to who is most useful—J461.9; Brer Rabbit pollutes house so that he is left in possession—K355; house post used must be returned—K251.2.1; riddle, house has neither eyes nor ears—H583.8; Sumatrans shape roofs like horns of karbau—B264.6; monkeys to build house 'tomorrow'—J2171.2.1; tortoise likes his house, must carry it—A2231.1.4; small trickster in house of larger animal intimidates with loud boasts—K1711.2; the house in the woods—P253.2.0.1F. SEE ALSO HAUNTED HOUSE.

HOUSEKEEPING: dwarf asks food of each of three lads who take their turn at cooking—K1931.2; flowerpot, mudcake, cabbage, etc. keep house—J512.7.2; mouse, bird, sausage keep house—J512.7; mysterious housekeeper unseen by man—N831.1.

HUALACHI: God Pachacamac gives magic sandals to Hualachi, quipa carrier in Cuzco—D1521.1.1.

HUATHIACURI: Huathiacuri is taught language of animals—B216.5.

HUDDEN: Hudden, Dudden and Donald O'Neary—K842A.

HUMILITY: False humility, man wears net on shoulders to remind self of humble origins until is made judge, then discards net—J703.3.

HUMMINGBIRD: SEE BIRD, HUMMINGBIRD.

HUMOR: SEE J1700-J2749 FOOLS. SEE ENTIRE CHAPTER X HUMOR.

HUMPBACKED: SEE HUNCHBACKED.

HUMS: Persian town of fools, man ties pumpkin to leg as identifier—J2013.3.

HUMU-HUMU-NUKU-NUKU-A-PUAA: Origin of fish—A2130.1.

HUN: Origin of Magyars and Huns—A1611.5.5.

HUN-APU: Twins Hun-Apu and Xbalanque vanquish God Vukub Caxix—A515.1.1.4.

HUNCHBACK: Hunchback carries crib for Christ Child—D1622.2.1; helpful humpbacked colt—H1213.1E, H1213.1Ib; fairies remove hump or replace it—F344.1; hunchback girl's tears become holly—A2612.4; old man on moon is hunchback—A751.0.2; hunchback's hump beaten brings rain—A957.1; old woman's hump strikes sky as she sweeps, she strikes sky with broom and it raises—A625.2.3; alleged hunchback cure is stocks—K842.0.2.

HUNG VRONG: King Hung Vrong comes to site of legend and chews limestone, areca and betel together = blood red spittle—A2691.5.

HUNGARY: Origin of Magyars, Huns—A1611.5.5; SEE ALSO ETHNIC AND GEOGRAPHIC INDEX.

HUNGARY: Dreams he will become King of Hungary—L425Aa.

HUNGER: Box full of stones is full, but can still add pail of sand, can still add pail of water, stomach like this—J1341.7.1; widowed father tells children of food they'll eat one day to stifle their hunger—D452.1.6.1.1; boys begging for grapes are given three, all taste the same so don't need more—J1340.3; hike teaches hunger—J1606.2; last cake eaten satisfies—J2213.3; task, come neither hungry nor satiated—H1063. SEE ALSO EATING; FOOD; GREED.

HUNS: Origin of Magyars and Huns—A1611.5.5; St. Genevieve saves Paris from Huns—V229.7.2.

HUNTING: Captive offers to catch better game—K553.1; hunting tales filled with contradictions—Z19.2ff; hunter daydreams and frightens off sleeping deer—J2061.3; hunter dreams female dove saves his life, wakes and it is so—F1068.4; fool dreams goes bear hunting, takes dog to bed —F1068.5.1; female duck stabs breast and kills self before hunter who killed her mate— F1041.1.2.2.5; dwarf causes bad hunter's jaws to freeze together—F451.5.2.6.1; lies, tall tales about hunting—SEE ALL ENTRIES X1100-X1135; hare hears case of lion vs. hunter and wife, has lion hold up cave, hunter escapes—K1251; hunters take more game than need—F451.5.2.9.1; Kasiapsak refuses to kill seals and walrus— W10.3; skillful hunter shoots antelope, runs ahead and skins, etc., before bullet reaches— F660.1.2; hunter was going to give hare to thief anyway—J1395; hunter wants to be shown lion tracks, not lion—W121.1; origin of rabbit trap— A1458.2; trickster reports approaching enemy and partner flees leaving game—K335.0.1; vengeful hunter trees another—R251B; Mana-bozo changes to large wolf with big tail, it is the small wolf who actually is best hunter—J292. SEE ALSO ARROW; GAME; GUN; SHOOT; WILD HUNT.

HURON: Micmac escapes Huron captors on magic snowshoes—D1065.3.1.

HUSBAND: Bear aids hen-pecked man, cuffs wife —J1762.2.3.1; old woman tells buzzard that he reminds her of husband—J1762.10; cock shows man how to rule wife—T252; cockroach chooses husband—Z32.3.1; dead husband returns to break vow—E321.6; Double Arend of Meeden picks up wife's family and puts outside— F624.1.0.1; husband smashes up furniture after fly—N333.0.3; foolish husband ties self to cow on roof—J2132.2; foolish husband lets wine run in cellar—J2176; fox widow chooses fox husband —T211.6; fox's husband feared—K2324; gullible husbands made to believe selves dead— J2311.0.1.1; gullible husband made to believe he has cut off wife's nose—J2315.2; husband shoots horse as lesson to wife—T251.2.3.0.1; husband with knowledge of animal languages learns to rule wife—B216A; widowed Longspur weds another longspur—J416.3; most powerful husband sought—L392.0.1+; taming the shrew— T251.2+; silence wager with husband—J2511ff; husband makes increasingly poor trades— J2081.1; arguing with wife in bed, she brings up first husband and he brings up first wife— J1250.14; husband undertakes wife's work— J2431. SEE ALSO BRIDE; COURTING; MAR-RIAGE; WIFE.

HUSBAND, SUPERNATURAL: Girl married to the devil—G303.12.5.1; tabu, wife of supernatural husband seeing old home—A762.1.

HYDRAX: Why hydrax lacks tail—A2235, A2378.2.5.

HYENA: Hyena carried aloft falls—K1041+; hyena claims bull bore calf—J1191.1.3; hyena forgets phrase and is caught in cave—N455.3.1; hyena claims child born because egg was destroyed— S215.1; hyena kills chief's child and puts in basket as meat—K2151.2; origin of color of hyena—A2411.1.7.1ff; must not look as trickster cooks or dish will spoil, hyena blamed for look-ing—K1084.1.3; coward falls on hyena's back— N392.1.3; dupe trades places with tied up hyena --K842.0.3; father hyena alone eats cow killed with two sons, when he is in need sons do not help father—W197.4; guilty one's stick to grow during night, hyena chops off his stick— J1141.1.4; hyena tricked into cage by guinea fowl—K715.1.1; hyena tricks hare into leaving food by disguising as monster—K335.0.4.3; hare tricks hyena into letting self be saddled and ridden—K1241; hyena wears wax horns—K1991; hyena paints leopard's spots—A2412.1.2; nine hyenas hunt with lion but lion takes largest share of kill—J811.1.2; why hyena limps— A2441.1.4.1; why hyena lives apart— A2433.3.4.2; why hyena lives in rock den— A2433.3.4.1; lynx is hexed by hyena—A781.1.1; hyena drops bone and dives for moon—J1791.3; origin of hyenas—K1041.0.2; animals tell pet peeves—W141.1.1; scorpion asks hyena to hold his tail—K1121.3; hyena believes own tale of more food in next village and follows crowd— X902.1.

HYMN: Fiddler engaged to play on Christmas Eve for Devils plays holy carol—G303.25.17.2.1.

HYMNAL: Magic healing hymnal—T102.1.

HYUKI: Hyuki on moon—A751.7.

ICE: Ice bear carved, causes polar bear to stop— K547.15; fox substitutes berries (ice) for lost eye—E781.1; bear builds house of wood, fox of ice—J741.1; turtle races under ice—K11.1; Raven sings up ice—C752.2.1.1; hare slips on ice, asks who is stronger—L392.0.5; tail caught in ice—K1021. SEE ALSO FREEZE; SNOW; WINTER.

ICE MAN: People can't put out fire in huge pop-lar stump, send for Iceman—F433.2; ice man causes snow, young man brings flowers— A1158.1.

ICE-RUNNER: Man falling through ice becomes ice-runner driving sleigh under ice—E514.

ICICLE: Fox thinks icicle is bone—J1772.15.

IDAHO FALLS: Origin of Idaho Falls—A935.1.

IDENTITY: Bee identifies princess from identical maids—B582.2A, H162, H1213.1F; identical girls wear identical dresses and claim to be same girl—H161.0.1.1; man does not know self— J2010ff. SEE ALL ENTRIES H0-H199.

IDOL: Idol smashed reveals coins inside—V123.2. SEE ALSO IMAGE.

IGLOO: Boy eats cod, seal, etc. Cannot re-enter igloo—X1723.4.

IGNORANCE: Absurd ignorance—J1730–J1749, J1900.

IGNORE: Lad ignores girl in tree and feeds yams to dog and meat to goat. She berates and comes down to show correct way—H343.3.

IGUANA: Black snake tricked iguana into letting him hold iguana's poison box—A2523.2.2.

IJAPA: SEE TORTOISE, IJAPA.

IKAN LELEH: SEE FISH, IKAN LELEH.

IKKYU: Merchant gets Ikkyu to promise to carry home "as he directs", directs not to cross bridge —J1179.2.7; anyone who breaks Sesshu's painted vase to die—J1189.4. SEE ENTIRE COLLECTION Edmonds, I. G. THE POSSIBLE IMPOSSIBLES OF IKKYU THE WISE.

ILLNESS: Visitors of sick stag eat up all provisions—W151.2.1. SEE ALSO DOCTOR; HEALING; MEDICINE; SICKNESS.

ILLNESS, FEIGNED: Life of helpful animal demanded as cure for feigned illness—B335.2; capture by feigning illness—K757; donkey tells ox to feign ill and escape work—K1633.1; quests assigned because of feigned illness—S12.1; sham sick trickster wins race—K11.5; thief shams sickness and steals—K341.2.2.2; thief shams sickness to be taken into house—K325.

ILLUSION: Pear seed grows and bears fruit as men watch—F971.7.1.

ILMARINEN: Gull a transformed maiden—A1945.2; Ilmarinen, smith makes moon and stars—A744.1.

ILSWETRIX: Coyote kills monster Ilswetrix—F912.2.9.

IMAGE: Ass carrying image thinks people bow to him—J953.4. SEE ALSO IDOL; STATUE.

IMAGINARY: Imaginary dog has to be shot—X902.2. SEE ALSO AIR-CASTLES.

IMITATION: Brer Wolf imitates Brer Rabbit and is burnt in log—J2411.6.2; camel tries in vain to dance, imitating monkey—J512.3; crow imitates partridge's walk—J512.6; why ducks pull up one leg when sleeping, imitate ducks who took gold legs from incense burner—A2479.13; father tries to imitate supernatural sons-in-law—J2411.3.1; foolish imitation of lucky man—J2415ff; foolish imitation—J2400–J2449; farm girl stands in sun waiting to grow wings, all girls in China imitate—Q22.1; foolish imitation, love through sight of finger—T11.4.8; imitation of miraculous horseshoeing unsuccessful—J2411.2; why monkey mimics—A2538.1; ogre made to believe hero has cut out heart, cuts out own—G524.0.1; foolish imitation of killing and reviving—H1213.1C, J2411.1, Q565; dupe imitates trickster's thefts and is caught—K1026; unsuccessful imitation of shoe-dropping trick—K341.6.1.

IMMIGRANTS: Bauchan of MacIntosh family refuses to travel to America on boat with MacLeods and MacDonalds—F482.3.1.2.

IMMORTALITY: Pill of immortality—D1346.7.1; Raven leaves world after daring to combat serpent without cloak of immortality—A568.1; crow sent for water of immortality drinks of it—A1335.19.

IMMORTALS: Eight immortals—A501.2; immortals pull nose long—J2415.25; one of Eight Immortals seeks ungreedy man—W151.13.

IMPATIENCE: Impatient farmer pulls on rice to make it taller—J1973.2; turtle carried aloft speaks too soon—J657.2.3, J2357.

IMPOSTER: Imposters abandon hero in lower world—K1931.2; imposter abandons youth in well and takes place—H1213.1F; false bride takes a true bride's place—K1911.1; impostures—K1900–K1999.

IMPRISONMENT: SEE Q433. SEE ALL R0–R85 Captivity. SEE ALSO CAPTIVE; PRISONER.

INCA: Golden sun from Cuzco temple gambled away—V400.1. SEE ALSO COLLECTIONS.

INCENSE BURNER: Four ducks take gold legs from incense burner—A2479.13.

INCRIMINATING: Dupe induced to incriminate self—K1066.

INDECENCY: Princess brought to laughter by indecent show in quarrel with old woman at well—H341.3.1.

INDECISION: Crane courts heron and she refuses, she courts him and he refuses, etc.—W123.2; man invited to two feasts cannot decide which to attend—J2183.1.1ff; Manabush can't decide how to eat moose—W123.5; man lets mangoes rot in indecision over them—J2183.1.4; man can't decide if oven should face east or west, builds on cart—J1041.3; worker set to cutting seed potatoes can't decide which are good and which are bad—W123.3;

INDIA: Wife from India is murdered—E221.1.1.

INDIAN: Horseman refuses ride to Indian, Indian eats lunch and now has lighter burden—J1612.1.1; Makonaima uses white clay from sky to make some Indians white, others black after clay becomes dirty—A1614.6.1; witches from Haddam and East Haddam fight over rights to kill cattle. Indian Devil Chief orders them off—G243.1.2. SEE ALSO ETHNIC AND GEOGRAPHICAL INDEX.

INDIAN PIPE: Origin Indian pipe plant—A2667.

INDIGO: Jackal falls in vat of indigo—J2131.5.6.

INDUSTRY: Lad begins with all seeds that stick to one finger, raises lettuce, etc.—W48.1. SEE

WORK.

INFANTA: Dragon weds Infanta Isabelle of Madrid —R111.1.3Aa; test, guessing skin from which Infanta's tambourine is made—H522.1.1.

INFIDELITY: Mosquito is man still trying to re-claim blood from unfaithful wife—A2034.5.

INGRATITUDE: Guinea hen asks eggs what will do for her when hatched, Fo-Fo replies "Noth-ing"—J267.1.1; Ingratitude—W154; SEE ALSO GRATITUDE.

INHERITANCE: Origin of Ashanti custom of leav-ing inheritance to sister's son—A1423.1.1; goat said to leave money to church—X459.3; secret message on scroll tells of inheritance—J1199.4; old father feigns treasure and is treated well in hopes of inheritance—P236.2; treasure in vine-yard, sons dig and crops flourish—H588.7+; will interpreted so that older brother owns trees, game, must remove these so youngest, who owns land, can mine his gold—L223. SEE ALSO WILL.

INHOSPITALITY: Brother given riches proves inhospitable to angel on succeeding year—Q1.1A. SEE HOSPITALITY.

INJUSTICE: Man criticizes injustice of God wreck-ing ship, he then kills swarm of ants—U21.3; horse treated unjustly rings bell—B271.3. SEE JUSTICE.

INNKEEPER: Lad puts charm under table leg so that all must chant—D1413.17; inn mistress turns men to horses—G263.1.0.2; inn mistress tricked by 'pira pira' game—K341.19.1; innkeep-er steals magic objects—D861.1; girl sets up inn and requires all staying to tell story—H1385.5Af, M231.2.

INNOCENCE: Fishermen mock girl telling to pray to Saint Porthole, she walks over water—D2125.1.0.1; miraculous snow in mid-summer confirms innocence of woman—F962.11.2.

INSANITY: Feigning insanity in court on lawyer's advice, continues to feign insanity when lawyer comes for fee—K1655; wife's tale discredited by making her appear insane—J1151.1.3; husband made to believe he is insane—J2311.0.1.1. SEE ALSO CRAZY; MAD.

INSECTS: Man rescues insects from flood, they aid—W154.8.4.1; origin of insects which bite man—A2034.3.2; insect simulates snoring—K661.3; war between insects and animals—B263.9. SEE ALSO ANT; BEDBUGS;; BEE; BEETLE; BUTTERFLY; CANDLEFLY; CATER-PILLAR; CENTIPEDE; CICADA; CRICKET; DRAGONFLY; DUNG-BEETLE; FIREFLY; FLY; GRASSHOPPER; HORNET; LIGHTNING BUG; LOCUST; MOTH; ETC.

INSULT: Father-in-law's remark construed as in-sult by son-in-law—W198; lad praises king and is beaten, tries insults—J1289.30; insult repeat-ed as harmless remark—K1775.

INSTRUMENTS: Quest for magic instruments—Q2.1.2G. SEE MUSICAL INSTRUMENT.

INTELLIGENCE: Crow drops pebbles into water jar to raise level—J101; farmer to go home for 'intelligence' which tiger came to see—K341.8.1.0.1; which is most important, luck or intelligence—N141ff; magpie feels children are smart enough to fend for selves—J13.1; tasks performed through cleverness or intelligence—H961.1. SEE ALSO WISDOM; WIT.

INTERRUPTION: Mad interrupted each time he tries to eat—X12.

INTESTINES: Spirit of String Figures uses own intestines when runs out of string—F499.4.

INTIMIDATION: Fox brings wolf to help exact taxes of man—K641.2; small creature with loud voice hides in house and frightens all away—K1711.2.

INVINCIBILITY: Crazy Horse chews flint to pow-der and smears self, thus invincible—A526.1.1.1.

INVISIBILITY: Cap of invisibility—D1361.15; cloak of invisibility—D1361.12; hero follows dancing princesses wearing invisible cloak—F1015.1.1; giant at wedding feast wears hat of invisibility—D1361.14.1; lad wearing invisible belt steals in giant's forest—G666.2; children escape in ogre's invisible cloak—K717.4; farmer given magic stone which makes invisible—M211.11; straw coat of invisibility burnt, rolls in ashes and becomes invisible, ashes wash off mouth when drinks—D831.1.

IRELAND: King of Ireland disguised as King of the Tinkers to test bride—H465; King of Ire-land's son hired by giant—B316C; riddle, Ire-land or Scotland first inhabited—R111.1.3Ah.

IRISH: Irish fool wouldn't want pillow of feathers, sleeping on one feather was unbearable—J2213.9; Welshman threatens to knock out all thirty-two of Irishman's teeth, how did he know how many Irishman had?—J1749.3.

IRON: Iron bands around heart break—D195.1; iron bathhouse red-hot—F601.2A; if husband strikes fairy wife with iron she must leave—F420.6.1.5.1; fire hides in iron during flood—A1414.7.2.1; prisoner until iron floats—D1899.1; trustee claims iron scales were eaten by mice—J1531.2; lost princess reaches iron stove with enchanted prince inside—H1385.5D; task, mak-ing man of iron—H1021.12; task, making living man of iron—H1021.14.

IRON HANS (JOHN): Prince loses golden ball in wild man's cage, taken away by wild man—G671.

ISLAND: Island of Cebu created—A955.0.1.1; island of the dead—E481.2.0.1; island of Fin folk taken—F742.1; fools pull island nearer to their town with ropes—J2287.1; invisible island —F742; king to be abandoned on island makes it liveable first—J711.3; origin, Hanomat throws mountain tops—A966.3; origin, Maui fishes up— A955.8; origin, mud dripping from spear of Izanagi, origin Japan—A822.2; origin of island— A955+. SEE ALSO ISLAY; SKYE.

ISLAY: Redstart finds person kind enough to receive fire on Islay—A1414.4.2.

ISSUN-BOSHI: Little One Inch—F535.1.1E.

ITCH: Anansi thrown in itchy cowitch plants— K629.2.3; monkey tries to stop habit of scratching—K263.1.

IVORY: Building ivory palace—H1151.6.2.

IYA: Sucking monster swallows all—F913.5.

IZANAGI: Japan from mud dripping from spear— A822.2; Izanagi descends to bring Izanani back from Land of the Dead—F81.1.0.1

JABIRU STORK: SEE BIRD, STORK--JABIRU.

JABUTI: Jabuti tricks jaguar in race—K11.1; origin of Jabuti's color—A2412.1.8; Jabuti arranges tug between tapir and whale—K22.

JACK: Jack obtaines bee, harp, mouse and bumclock—H341.2.1; Jack and the beanstalk— F54.2.1; Jack the giant killer—G512.0.4; the house that Jack built—Z44; Jack, King of Ireland's son hired by giant—B316C; Jack and Jill —A751.7; Lazy Jack—J2461A; Jack defeats stupid ogre—K1951.1A, G501E; Jack refuses buttermilk to witch—K526B. SEE ALSO ENTIRE COLLECTIONS Chase, Richard, JACK TALES. SEE ENTRIES IN TITLE INDEX BEGINNING "JACK."

JACK-IN-THE-PULPIT: Root eaten by tricked fox —K1023.1.0.1.

JACK-O'-LANTERN: Origin—Q565Ah.

JACKAL: Jackal has barber remove thorn from nose—Z47.4; beeswax on tortoise shell catches jackal—K741; jackal dyed blue—J512.12, J2131.5.6; jackal gnaws bowstring and bow snaps killing jackal—J514.2; rich jackal aids Brahmin father-in-law—D861.1J; jackal asks bulbul bird where he plans to go each day, bulbul bird goes elsewhere—K688.5; jackal's calf claimed born to another's goat (bull)—J1191.1.2; jackal addresses cave and hiding lion (crocodile) responds—K607.1; jackal teaches crocodile babies, eats—K933; jackal tricks hiding crocodile into revealing self—K607.2+; jackal and hedgehog divide crops—K171.1; jackal refuses to help free deer—K642.3+; donkey and jackal in garden, donkey sings and is captured—J2137.6; jackal dropped by eagle—K1041.0.1; jackal and empty drum—J262.1; jackal cheats cohorts out of ele-

phant—K171.0.2; jackal trapped in elephant's hide—K565.2; jackal tricks feigned dead crocodile into betraying self—K607.3; jackal bluffs tiger by calling "shoot him" and setting off firecrackers—K1715.2; fish shared by cutting lengthwise—J1249.3; turtle makes flute of jackal's thighbone—K1775.1; goats make jackal believe they have eaten many of his kind—K1715.3; small trickster in house of larger animal intimidates with loud boasts—K1711.2; why jackal howls at night—A2513.1.2; hare judges against man—J1172.3.2.2; jackal as king of animals— B240.16; jackal imitates ewes call and is let in, eats lambs—K311.3D; jackal turns buffalo and tiger (bull and lion) against each other— K1084.1.1; presumptuous wolf (jackal) annoys lion—J952.1; jackal makes lion suspicious of bull —K2131.2; jackal ordered to take meat to lion's family, takes it to his own—K361.1; monkey frees jackal from snare—J1179.25; mousedeer calls "I told you to bring ten leopards" to jackal bringing leopard—K1715.2; origin of jackal— A1831.3; rabbit feigns dead repeatedly and entices jackal from goods—K341.2.1; jackal puts old shoes on ears and calls self Rajah—J951.6; jackal licking spilt blood is caught between fighting rams—J624.1.1; jackal re-enacts scene and leaves tiger trapped—J1172.3; jackal tells crocodile biting foot that he has root—K543.0.1; turtle tells jackal biting foot that he has root— K543; jackal raises tail as battle flag, bee stings—K2323.1; jackal ties lion to tail of shamdead horse—J2132.5.3; jackal tied to leopard's tail—J2132.5.1; tailless jackal tries in vain to induce other jackals to cut off tails—J758.1; jackal invites tiger into palanquin (trap)—K714.2.4.3; jackal invites tiger—J1565.1.4; turtle persuades jackal to soak him in pond—K553.5; jackal wins bride for master—K1917.3H.

JACKDAW: SEE BIRD, JACKDAW.

JACKETS: Fools attempt to push church to line of jackets—J2328.1.

JADE: Jade turns to hot coal and burns shop down—D2100.2.1; man catches crow and forces to give magic jade which grants wishes—D551.1C; magic jade assures luck, woodpecker carries under wing—D931.0.5.

JAGUAR: Jaguar brags of strength to lightning— C984.5; jaguar's color—A2412.1.8; curassow tells cautionary tale of Kikushie—L471.1; jaguar tricked in race with jabuty—K11.1; why jaguar is strong—A2528.2.

JAM: Lad commits suicide with "poisoned" jam— J2311.2.3.

JAMOJAJA: Jamojaja dies and is turned into Waringen tree—A2681.15.

JAN THE EIGHTH VAN ARKEL: Chins self on beam holding horse between knees—F610.3.7.

JAPAN: Origin of Japan, mud dropped from spear of culture hero—A822.2

JAR: Animals invite all comers to join them in jar, until it ruptures—J2199.5.

JAW: Jaws removable—F557.0.1.

JAY: SEE BIRD, BLUEJAY; BIRD, JAY.

JEALOUSY: Origin of jealousy, wife forces her husband to tell secret which causes him to die, her ashes are scattered = evil, selfishness and jealousy wherever they fall—B216Ac; boy, jealous of two adopted boys, wishes he were a snow-goose, becomes one—D100.2; Silver Tree asks trout in well who is most beautiful queen in world—D582.2; witch asks mirror who is most beautiful queen—Z65.1. SEE ALL ENTRIES W181+ Jealousy. SEE ALL ALL ENTRIES Q2.1.1 Kind and unkind girls. SEE ALSO ENVY.

JEAN SOT: Fool frightens others off—K335.1.1.1; Jean Sotte outriddles king—H952.1.

JELLYFISH: Why jellyfish has no bones—A2367.1.2; jellyfish beaten to pulp for telling monkey that dragon queen wants his liver—K544.1.

JERUSALEM: Pious man polishes marble block until smooth, unable to move it to Jerusalem. Elijah moves—D1641.2.1.1.

JESTER: King orders celebration of Christmas as Holiday of Fools—V92.1; Christ Child smiles at juggler—V92.0.1; princess declares her love for court jester—T55.2; Virgin smiles at juggler—V92.

JESUS: SEE CHRIST.

JEWELS: Jewels fall from old lady's hair as girl combs—Q2.1.1E; king to give princess to one who brings healing jewel from neck of King Pelican—H1321.1Cd; jewel gift vanishes when its secret is revealed—C423.3.1; jewel given by grateful serpent—D882.1B, W154.8; dancing stars wear jewels of teeth and shells—A761.0.1; magic jewels cause ebb and flow of tides—U136.0.1. SEE ALSO DIAMOND; EMERALD; GEMS; JADE; PEARL; ETC.

JEWELS, JEWELRY: Crow steals mecklace, drops in snake's hole—K401.2.2; uncle kills pet bird, tree grows from buried bones which gives blossoms of jewelry—J2415.17; jewelry given by grateful tiger—W154.8. SEE ALSO BRACELET; GEMS; JEWELS; NECKLACE.

JEWISH: Polish landlord asks ragged tenant if he is not cold. "Is your nose cold?" "No." "I'm all nose."—J1309.1. SEE ALSO ETHNIC AND GEOGRAPHIC INDEX. SEE ALSO HELM.

JIANG KIEU: Emerges from painting and encourages students for exams—T111.1.5.1.

JINN: Helpful Jinn aids in search for firebird—H1331.1.3An; magic flute from Jinn—D1415.2.3.4. SEE ALSO GENIE.

JIP: With one-eye Little Jip entices goblin into bag of cherries—K526C.

JIZO: Jizo brought to court as witness—J1141.1.3.4; hats given to Jizo—J1873.1; farmer disguised as scarecrow taken for Jizo statue by monkeys—J2415.23; jizo hides person from oni—N777.0.1; thief to vow innocence on Jizo—J1141.10.1.

JODER: Bishop Joder asks Devil to carry him to Pope and back before cockcrow—K1886.3.1.1.

JOFUKU: Gives paper crane—E80.5.

JOHNNY CAKE: Z33.1.3.

JOKE: Women tell jokes until enemy laughs, can identify him by his short teeth—B301.9.2. SEE ALL J1700-J2729 Fools. SEE ENTIRE CHAPTER X Humor.

JOKWA: Empress Jokwa mends broken pillar supporting heaven—A665.2.0.1.1.

JOOST: Joost (devil) claims Bell of Stavoren—F993.1.1; man sells soul to Joost to build barn—M211.2.

JOSHUA: Steer carries Joshua—A2221.5.1; Joshua says wisdom is kept in plain container—J1319.3.

JOURNEY CAKE: Journey cake rolls away—Z33.1.8.

JOVE: Frog's ask Jove for king—J643.1.

JUAN BOBO: Juan Bobo things pig wants to go to mass—J1849.5; Juan Bobo kills tiger with aid of onion and vine—K1161.6.

JUDGE: Apprentice ruled entitled to keep any objects thrown at him—J1179.17; bell to ring when guilty touches—J1141.10.2; when judges can agree on definition of bread may judge him—H501.5; man falling on another from bridge to have the other fall onto him—J1173; cat as judge of sparrow and hare, eats both—K815.7; cat with three legs burns down warehouse—J1175.1; jackal learns solution of case by overlooking child's game—J123; fine square of cloth, one is of stolen silk—J1141.1.3.4; witness claims coat is borrowed—J1151.2; pot to crow when guilty touches—J1141.10.3; dividing, first divides, second chooses—J1249.2; dog to be rewarded with pat rather than kick—J1179.18; donkey to bray when thief pulls tail—J1141.1.0.1; to cut off defendant's ear, stopped and fined when begins to do so, proof of nature—J1179.26; suit for chickens from boiled eggs—J1191.2; fly as witness, guilty inadvertently admits guilt—J1141.1.3.3; to kill fly wherever sees one, on judges nose—J1193.1; thief has grease from stolen fowl, guilty feels beard—J1141.1.2; Sungura hare hears case of lion vs. hunter and wife—K1251; judge divides horses—J1249.3; horse thief asked which of horse's eyes is blind—J1141.17; man who pulled off horse's tail to

keep horse until grows another—J1173; Ikkyu to
carry money home without crossing river starts
to walk around it—J1179.27; men refuse to pay
fine until reach jail town, then pay up, got ride
for price of fine—J1179.21; to vow innocence on
head of Jizo statue—J1141.10.1; bride fined two
hundred ounces of silver for cat claims she is
owed three thousand ounces for lost ladle—
J1179.24; spectators fined for laughing in court
—J1141.1.3.4.1; witness lies, excellent witness
—J1159; first person to pass gate to be new
judge—H171.8; a penny for a blow—J1193.2;
thief to smell like pickles, guilty sniffs hands—
J1141.1.2.1; boy can have three huge porcelain
dogs if will carry one home alone—J1179.19;
judge re-enacts scene and returns ungrateful
animal to captivity—J1172.3; judge reverses
ruling when discovers he is the defendant—
J1130.1; scroll inheritance interpreted by judge
—J1199.4; judge punishes servant of guilty
woman, knowing they have changed clothes—
J1179.23; suit about the ass's shadow—J1169.7,
J1172.2.3; fine for stealing smell is beating
shadow—J1172.2.2; clink of money for smell of
food—J1172.2; Solomon's judgment, the divided
child—J1171.1; snake's wife to kill prince after
he has borne as many sons as snake has—
J1173.1; guilty man's stick to grow—J1141.1.4;
judge mocks criminals, turns to stork—A1966.1;
judge orders man refusing to pay taxes to open
orphanage, thus becoming tax exempt—J1179.15;
thief to sneak stolen goods back—J1179.20; tree
as witness—J1141.1.3.2; woman to be killed as
soon as vase is paid for—J1173.1.2; wagon to
have borne a colt—J1191.1; agreement to return
'whatever you want', man keeps all money.
Judge rules he must return it since he 'wanted'
that—J1521.5.2; talkative wife's tale discredited
by sausage rain—J1151.1.1+; tiger had to ask
wife's advice before choosing which horse to
take—T252.4.2; wife disguises self as Cadi,
Hasan's case is brought to court and he is recognized—S268B. SEE ALL ENTRIES J1130-
J1249 Cleverness in the law court; J1280+
Repartee with judge. SEE ALSO COURT;
HODJA; MAGISTRATE; MULLAH; OOKA.

JUDGMENT DAY: Burial upside down so as to be
right side up when tossed headlong on Judgment
Day—J2212.2.1; trickster has dupes roast sheep
for him as tomorrow is end of the world anyway
—J1511.7; when will the world end?—H707.2.
SEE ALSO DOOMSDAY.

JUG: Devil trapped in jug—G303.16.3.1.3; man
leaves jug set so that wind hums over mouth—
K1725.11.

JUGGLER: SEE JESTER.

JULY: Man to call wife a liar mispronounces "July"—J1805.1.2.

JUMP: Jumping into the breeches—J2161.1; four
men hold cloth for two to jump—J2133.5.0.1;
jumping contest—K17.5; contest, jumping horse
high enough to kiss princess—H331.1.1F; marvelous jumper—F660.1; boast of jump on Rhodes
—J1477.

JUNIPER: Juniper tree—N271Aa.

JUNKMAN: Magic badger teakettle dances for
junkman—D1171.3.1.

JUNO: Juno refuses peacock lovely voice—W128.4.

JUPITER: Jupiter grants ass's request and ass
ends in tannery—N255.2; Jupiter punishes bee,
sting suicidal—A2232.2; Jupiter turns cat to
maiden—J1908.2; Jupiter offers prize for prettiest child, monkey claims—T681.2; frogs ask
Jupiter for king—J643.1; Jupiter creates man—
A46; Jupiter grants wishes—J2074, J2075. SEE
ALSO ZEUS.

JUSTICE: King observes justice among animals—
J52; cock crows each morning to remind world
that all have right to justice—A2426.2.18.1;
horse rings bell for justice—B271.3. SEE ALSO
COURT; JUDGE; LAW.

JUSTINIAN, EMPEROR: Rules in favor of rescuer
from pit—W154.8.2.

KABONIYAN: Cave with trees bearing agate gems,
property of Kaboniyan spirit—N773.0.1.

KADAWBAWA: Fools cannot count selves—
J2031.0.2.

KAGUYA: Princess Kaguya, moon maiden—
A753.1.3.1.

KA-HA-SI: Two older brothers on sea lion hunt
fail to leap ashore—L114.1.

KAHLBERG: Ghosts of family reward former
tenant—E363.5.2.

KAHOA: Chief Kahoa takes away sun, moon,
stars—A721.1.6.

KAHP-TOO-OO-YOO: Brings rain—D482.1.3.

KAIL: Giant steals cabbages of exiled queen—
G561.1D.

KAKOK: SEE BIRD, KAKOK.

KAKUI: SEE BIRD, KAKUI.

KALULU: SEE HARE.

KAMAJAJA: Wife beseeches Kamajaja and husband
is turned into waringen tree after death—
A2681.15.

KAMAPUAA: Pig man changed to fish—A2130.1;
pig-boy tricks chief—J2461.10.

KAMBARA: Why there are no mosquitoes on Kambara—A2434.2.4.

KAMPEN: Town of fools—J1703.

KANA: Kana steals back sun, moon, stars—A721.1.6.

KANNON: SEE KWAN YIN.

KANNON-SAMA: Helps supplicant, first thing he touches on leaving temple will bring luck—N222.1.

KANTCHIL: Carabao's tail pulled off. Judgment, keep until it grows back—J1173; Kantchil crosses stream on backs of crocodiles—K579.2.1; Kantchil tells crocodile biting his leg that he is biting tree root—K543.0.1; Kantchil tells crocodile biting tree root that he is biting leg—K543.0.2; Kantchil tricks crocodile masking as log into moving upstream—K607.2; Kantchil distracts mowers and saves eggs of ground owl—K644; Kantchil catches Giant Gergassi in sticky pit—K741.2; Giant Gergassi is subdued by Kantchil—K1931.2Za; Kantchil in house of larger animal intimidates—K1711.2; Kantchil advises Karbau to put ungrateful crocodile back under log and leave—J1172.3.0.1; Kantchil bluffs leopard (tiger) calls, "You promised me seven leopards" to jackal—K1715.2; mousedeer tries to break up friendship between hare and parrot—K2131.8; Kantchil escapes from pit on animals' backs or through sneezing and being thrown out—K652.1; Kantchil races snail—K11.1; Kantchil terrifies in disguise as raksha—K335.0.4.4; Kantchil claims soul is in jar (bees)—K1023.1.0.3; deceptive stamping contest—K17.6; enmity between Kantchil and tiger, friendship with elephant—A2493.36; Kantchil tricks tiger into magic bag—K714.2.3.2; tiger allowed to guard 'king's drum' (wasp nest), 'king's food' (rotten leaves), 'king's girdle' or 'turban' (snake), etc.—K1023.1; Kantchil shows tiger man with gun—K553.1.0.5; tiger puts tongue in split bamboo to 'play flute'—K1111.0.1.1; Kantchil ties tiger in bag, tiger floats ashore—N228; tiger made to believe porcupine quill is his enemy's whisker—K1711.1.

KANTELE: Dupe wishing to learn to play the kantele has finger caught in tree cleft—K1111.0.1.

KAPPA: Kappa reclaims severed arm—K782.3.2.

KARA MUSTAFA: Cowardly fool as hero—K1951.1J.

KARAKOUSH: Thief rules—Z49.11.2.

KARANG-BOLONG CLIFFS: SEE CAVE, BIRD'S NEST.

KARBAU: Donkey things Karbau is making row—J132.1. SEE: BUFFALO, CARABAO.

KARI WOODENSKIRT: B335.2D, R221L.

KARL-KATZ: Sets bowling pins for dwarfs—D1960.1.

KAROK: Karok man intercedes with God on Coyote's behalf, why Coyote befriends Karoks—A2235.2.

KASSA KENA GENANINA: Kills terrorizing bird—F615.9.1, K1931.2Zb.

KATE CRACKERNUTS: L145.1B.

KATCHI KATCHI MOUNTAIN: Hare says burning noise is Katchi Katchi Mountain—K2345.0.1.

KAWAI: Listener, a Niihau abucted by batlike spirit—E423.3.12.

KAWITJAKSANA: Magic lance shaft given to Kawitjaksana—A2681.16.

KAYAK: Kayak steals crane's eyes—J2199.1.3; tiny kayak—F451.5.1.6.2; boy kills giant whale by painting magic symbols on hand and on kayak—B877.1.3.

KAYAMANAN: Goddess Kayamanan turned away in beggar guise—A2062.

KAZAN: Cowardly fool as hero—K1951.1.

KEEWAK: Raven makes a clay egg and hatches a goose—K1041.2.

KE'LET: Steal sun—A721.1.3, K1041.0.1.1.

KELP: Captive lured into pit by voice thrown from kelp tube—A2034.3.1, K741.4.

KELPIE: Water kelpie curses water which girl drinks so that she cannot speak—F420.5.2.6.6.1.

KENKI: Why flies swarm around Kenki—A2433.5.2.1; leopard and Kenki wrestle—A2412.1.2.2.

KENNREIRK: SEE BIRD, OWL—KENNEREIK.

KERNEL: Boy size of kernel—F535.1.1Cb; bird drops kernel on head—F615.9.

KETTLE: Kettle turns into badger—D1171.3.1; Woman of Peace (fairy woman) borrows kettle and returns full of bones each evening—F391.4; kettle as plaything of ghosts in haunted house—H1411.4.2; kettle sent home by self—J1881.1.3; alleged self-cooking kettle sold—K112.1.1; witch tricked into kettle—G512.3.2.2. SEE ALSO POT; TEAKETTLE.

KEWALU: Kuku seeks Kewalu in underworld—F81.1.0.3.

KEY: House appears on sixteenth birthday, key unlocks—H1213.1G; boy finds box and key. What's inside?—Z12.2; key in flax reveals laziness—H382.1; old or new key is best?—Z62.1; key stained in forbidden room—G561.1, S62.1; fool warns thief not to take key—J2091.

KEYHOLE: Ghost claims to have entered through keyhole—K717.7.

KHAN: Khan and family caused to dance by magic

cowherd—D1415.2.3.5; one on whom white falcon rests to be be new Khan—H171.2; Maharaja of India sends three golden dolls to Khan of Mongolia—H506.13.

KICKING: College educated son invents self-kicking machine—J1689.2.

KID: SEE GOAT, KID.

KIKUSHIE: Curassow tells jaguar cautionary tale of Kikushie—L471.1.

KILDARE POOKA: F381.3.

KILLER WHALES: Killer whales tow house of fish to shore—A2109.2.

KIM QUI: Golden turtle gives Emperor magic golden nail to build wall between Vietnam and China —A132.15.1; golden turtle gives white flowers to make nose grow—D551.1C.

KIN KIN: Kin Kin bird sings telling King of Forest to repair ravages of animals trying to clear—D1487.3.1.

KINDNESS: Good man, bad man imitates—J2415+; Kindness—W10+; lion tamed through kindness— B848.2.1; secret of happiness, Chang Kung writes "kindness" one hundred times—A411.2; Redstart to give fire to kind person—A1414.4.2. SEE ALL Kind and Unkind Girls—Q2.1+. SEE ALSO UNKINDNESS.

KING: Animal king chosen by contest—B236.0.1; king of animals—B240+ (king of elephants— B241.2.11; king of frogs—J643.1; king of mice— B241.2.5; king of monkeys—B241.2.2); bard makes up derisive song about king—J611.1; how much is king's beard worth?—H712.2; king turned to beggar reforms—L411.1; election of King of Birds—B236.1.1; king shows boatman skill of his advisor—H1574.4.1; sparrows say one of three travelers will be chosen ruler—B217.9; king to be chosen by pigeon lighting on head— H1440D; first person crossing bridge to be chosen king—N683.1; clever dealing with king— J1675.2.1; old woman prays for safety of cruel tyrant for fear a worse will succeed him— J215.2.1; king prefers company of educated man —J146.1; to be King of England if sees Long Compton Church—G263.2.1.2; frogs ask Zeus for king—J643.1; king for a year provides for future—J711.3; hawk persuades doves to elect him their king—K815.8; incognito king saved from robbers—K1812.1.0.1; king oberves justice among animals—J52; minstrel sings "dog is great among dogs, yet serves men," king refuses to extend this to include kings—L435.5; peasant to recognize king, will be one with hat on—J1289.27; peasant and king trick ministers with riddle—H561.6.1, H585.3; lad praises king and is beaten—J1289.30; king asks prime minister candidates what object in stream is, one swims out to fetch it—H1574.4; king overhears girl boast about what she would do as queen— N455.4; two kings on road—W167.1.1; king kills thief, chain—L392.0.6; king persuaded to stand

on head, kiss ass's tail, etc. by trickster— K1288.1; how much is king worth?—H711.1. SEE ALSO KHAN; SHAH; ETC.

KING ARTHUR: St. Cadog to send one hundred cows for each of King Arthur's soldiers slain by Lipessawe—D1711.6.6; King Arthur and men sleep underground—D1960.2.

KING DAVID: Escapes by shamming madness— K523.1; King David saved by helpful fly— B524.2.1.2; spider web over hole saves fugitive —B523.1.

KING HAKON: Lad sees King Hakon, dead six-hundred and fifty years ago—D2138.1.

KING HERLA: King Herla at elfin wedding— F378.1A.

KING LAURIN: Dwarf King Laurin given hospitality on Christmas Eve—F451.1.5.0.2.

KING O'TOOLE: Deceptive land purchase, as much land as goose can fly over without lighting —K185.3.1.

KING SOLOMON: King Solomon's ring—D1076.1; to wed witch, lad stalls until obtains her magic King Solomon's ring—G405.1.2.

KINGFISHER: SEE BIRD, KINGFISHER.

KINSHIP: Origin of Ashanti custom of leaving inheritance to sister's son—A1423.1.

KINTAIL: Witches' cry—G242.7; origin of mountains, five sisters of Kintail—A962.1.3.

KINTARO: Strong boy—F611.3.2.7.

KINURU: SEE BIRD, KINURU.

KISANDER: Anansi and Moos-Moos are caught stealing Kisander's pudding from dokanoo tree— K419.11.

KISS: Kiss turns beast to prince—D735.1; suitor contest, leaping high enough to kiss princess— H331.1.1F; disenchantment by kiss—D735; pure girl to kiss enchanted maid on lips on St. John's Eve and never let go through transformations— D757.1; king must kiss horse's rump—H1045.0.1; trickster induces girl to kiss him—H1045.0.1; trickster asks man's wife for kiss, man calls "Give him what he wants", thinking he asks for tool (pay)—K362.10.

KITCHEN: Origin Gods of the hearth—A411.2, T211.2.1.1.

KITE: Kite flown terrorizes enemies who flee— K2369.15; Maui uses winds from calabash to fly kite—A1124.1.

KITE: SEE BIRD, KITE.

KITTEL-KITTEL CAR: Children flee in ogre's kittel-kittel car—G526.1.

KLING-KLING: SEE BIRD, KLING-KLING.

KNAPSACK: Knapsack lent to balance load--J1874.2.1; devil bet he can't fit into knapsack--K717.2; devil pounded in knapsack--K213; knapsack thrown into heaven and trickster wishes self inside knapsack--K213A.

KNEADING: Cinderlad rows over lake in kneading trough--G610Ac; maid kneads devil in bread trough--K606.1.2.

KNEE: Knee stiff from knocker's hammer--F456.2.2.5.

KNEE-HIGH MAN: Horse and bull advise to grow large so can fight, owl advises staying small so no one will challenge--J291.

KNIFE: Boatman bets he can recover lost knife by marking spot on side of boat--J1922.2.1; three brothers leave knives at crossroads, if rusty in trouble--R111.1.3Af; lad touches fish in frying pan with magic knife and they turn to men--G263.1.0.1.1; witch sends flying knife to pursue--G530.2Bj; dare to stick knife into grave--N384.2; to get two horses with knife (walking sticks)--H586.8.1; daughter gives magic knife which draws horses, tells where to dig gold--G530.2Fb; seal grateful for removal of knife from side--B389.1; fools leave knife in shadow of cloud to mark spot--J1922.2.

KNIGHT: Almond blossoms token of knight--H87.1; knight with cross on armor (St James of Compostella) slays dragon--B641Dd.

KNITTING: Girl given golden chain for industrious knitting but unravels yarn to find way back and loses--F348.7.1.4.1; devil to work for bride, when devil's work vanishes knitted clothes vanish from wearers--D2183E.

KNOB: Gold knob on spindle rolls away--D1472.2.12.

KNOCK: Strange visitor knocks, then enters piece by piece--Z13.1.1; strange being knocks and calls to conjure wives--D183.2.

KNOCKERS: Mine spirits--F456.2.2.5.

KNOT: Untying knot raises wind--D2142.1.2.

KNOW-IT-ALL, DAME: Youth blessed by Dame Know-it-all succeeds in making princess talk but without Luck no one believes him--N141.0.1.

KNOWLEDGE: Demon is torn asunder by Thunderbolt of Knowledge in his stomach--K741.3; hedgehog asks fox to throw him out of pit, tells fox to help self with his seventy-sevenfold understanding--K652.3; Gods teach people all they know--A1404; two merchants robbed, one with knowledge in head makes way to new wealth--J231.2; wise man pours water into bowl with eyes only on top, interpretation, pupil must be ready to accept learning before he can be filled with knowledge--H591.4. SEE ALL J0-J199

Acquisition and possession of knowledge. SEE ALSO CLEVERNESS; INTELLIGENCE; WISDOM; ETC.

KNUCKLEHEAD JOHN: J1874.2.1.

KNURREMURE: Cat is really dwarf whose sweetheart was claimed by Knurre-Murre--B342B.

KOBALDS: Kobalds help with remodeling of castle--F481.1.1; to hatch cobald carry cock's egg under armpit three weeks--F481.0.1.1.1.1.

KOJATA: King's beard is grabbed as drinks, forced to promise "what finds at home"--G530.2Db.

KOLA-NUTS: Youngest son given only Kola-Nuts--B582.2F.

KONAKADET: Raven's beak mistaken for nose of Konakadet--A2335.2.3; Konakadet monster vanquished by Raven--C752.2.1.1.

KORAN: Figs promised for dessert never produced. In Koran reading guest omits word "figs." "You forgot the figs." "No, you did"--W158.1.

KORBES: Cock and hen go to visit Mr. Korbes--K1161.7.

KOREA: King introduces Korean alphabet by writing on leaves with honey--A1484.2.1; Chu Mong, founder of Korea, is born when cloud floats inside mother's dress--A511.1.4.5. SEE ALSO ETHNIC AND GEOGRAPHIC INDEX.

KORRIGAN: Changeling--F321.1.1 Picard.

KOSCHEI: Hero gives water to chained Koschei the Deathless--B314C; frog maid must be sought in land of Koschei the Deathless--K1385.3Ka; Koschei the Deathless holds princess captive--H1331.1.3Ad; hero steals Marya Moryevna from Koschei the Deathless--H1199.12.4B

KOTEI: Emperor Kotei invents boat--A1459.2.1; Emperor Kotei--D1313.17.

KOTSKY, PAN: Cat husband, Pan Kotsky--K2324.

KOYO: Guno and Koyo find kris--J1516.1.

KRAKOW: Stone near Krakow says, "If you turn me over, I shall tell you something"--F809.10.

KRIS: Fight over kris--K2144; Guno and Koyo find kris--J1516.1; origin of the Kris--A1459.1.6.

KRISHNA: Krishna the Avenger worshipped by cowherds--A489.6; weaver cursed by Brahma to lose all gained outsmarts fate by throwing all received to beggars as soon as received--K2371.2.1.

KUAN YIN: SEE KWAN YIN.

KULOSKAP: SEE GLOOSKAP.

KUKALI: Kukali is carried by huge bird—B31.1.3.

KURAI: Old man Kurai—K1951.1M.

KURAT: Evil spirit Kurat creates wolf—A1833.4.

KWAN YIN: Goddess of Mercy—A483.1; quest to Kwan Yin for answers to questions—H1273.2Lb; witch as old lady turns to statue of Kannon—K607.4.1. SEE ALSO KANNON-SAMA.

KWATEE: Kwatee the changer—K606.2.3; Kwatee changes man making tools into animals—A2262.4.

KWAKU TSIN: Escapes to sky and becomes sun—A711.0.1.

KWELANGA: Suitor tasks—G530.2Fc.

LA RAMÉE: Private La Ramée dares to pull king's beard—H359.3.

LABAN: Task, carrying bowl of laban on head while climbing palm—H331.10.1.

LACE: Origin of ñanduti lace, spiderweb—A1465.2.1; pancake nibbled to resemble lace, task, making pillow lace—D2183C; poison lacing for dress—Z65.1; spider wife spins lace for sale—B643.4 Virgin gives mantilla of spider webs—D1623.3.

LADDER: Ladder swallowed by drakestail rescues from well—Z52.1; ladder to moon—A751.0.4, F772.1.2.1; thief climbing rope discovered and rope cut—K1622; thief climbs ladder into garden, claims he is selling ladders—J1391.2; man to keep first thing touched, prize on platform but touches ladder first—K285; father keeps children in treehouse, let down ladder when he chants—K311.3E; wolves (tigers) form ladder by climbing on backs—J2133.6ff.

LADY OF THE MOORS: Leads men astray—E425.1.8.

LAGOS: Fools of Lagos fill one hole by digging another—J1934.

LAIDLEY WORM: Girl enchanted—D732.0.1; hero kills Laidley Beast in loch and rescues princess—R111.1.3Cd.

LAKE: City sinks under lake—F944ff; lake formed by coyote's paw—A920.1.0.1.1; spring from fish basket of fleeing man forms lake of sacred fish—A920.1.18; lake as footprints—A920.1.10.1; geese with feet frozen to lake, fly off with lake—X1606.2.4.1; whirlwind carries lovers to heaven, lake left on spot, origin—T91.6.4.4; lake origin, Ice Man causes while putting out fire—F433.2; beautiful lakeland scene, if only they had not put water in it—J2201.

LAKE, LAKE BOURO: Origin of pawing of great bull—A920.1.2.

LAKE, LAKE MAIDEN: Water-maid refuses hard baked bread, unbaked, lad wins with soft bread—F420.6.1.5.1.

LAKE, LAKE OF BALATON: Jealous queen causes lake—A920.1.17.

LAKE, LAKE SPIRIT: Lake spirit gives three wishes—J2075.

LAKE, LAKE TITICACA: Fox tries to drink Lake Titicaca dry—K526.2.

LAKE, LLYN GLASFRYN: Well spirit overflows forming lake—C41.5.

LAMBTON WORM: B11.12.4.1.1.

LAME: Fairy lames girl who forgets to leave food out for him—F361.14.6; lamed man's hunting partner leaves, returns when he becomes fine hunter again—W175.2; lame boy frees tall boy on condition he carry him along in race—K11.2.1. SEE ALSO CRIPPLED.

LAMIA: Ogress civilly treated aids—H1213.1H.

LAMINAK: To build castle by cockcrow—F420.5.2.13, K1886.3.1.1.

LAMP: Magic lamp produces genie—D871.1; man in heaven cleans lamp so will burn longer—E765.1.1.2; life bound up with lamp, if it goes out person dies—E765.1ff; selling wind (fan) to buy moon (lamp)—H583.4.7; oil lamp thinks it outshines stars—L475; reindeer turns girl to lamp and they capture moon—A753.1.0.1; over-fat boy explodes when touches seal oil lamp—X1723. SEE ALSO LANTERN.

LANAI: King's son is exiled to Lanai for uprooting breadfruit plants—K688.6.

LANCE: Magic lance shaft cut from Waru Wanggi tree—A2681.16. SEE ALSO SPEAR.

LAND: Forbidden to set foot on king's land, fills boots with own soil—K1161.3.1.

LANDLORD: Money sent to landlord by hare—J1881.2.2; wives bet landlord they can make fools of husbands—J2311.0.1.1. SEE ALSO INN-KEEPER.

LANGUAGE: Knowledge of animal language—B216; secrets overheard from animal conversation—N451ff; secret remedy overheard from animal conversation—N452; foolish attempt of second man to overhear secrets from animals—N452B, N452C, N452D; confusion due to misunderstandings—J2496.1; lad learns language of dogs, birds, frogs—B217.9; answer to each question is "I don't understand" which foreigner takes to be a person's name—J1802.1; language of Canadian Geese learned from pets—B165.3; Huathia-curi is taught language of animals by father

Paucca--B216.5; husband with knowledge of animal languages learns to rule wife--B216A; misunderstanding because of lack of knowledge of a different language--J2496.3; nun gives leaf to chew to understand language of animals--D532D; princess to wed one who knows language she does not know--H342.2; origin of Puget Sound languages--A1482.2; sign language mutually misunderstood--H607.1.1ff; snake king gives knowlege of animal languages--B216Aa; three travelers each know one phrase of foreign language--J2496.3.

LANTERN: Dragon-girl turns to baby at lantern festival--T542.2; task, bring fire wrapped in paper = lantern--H506.12, H583.4.7; origin of onion shaped iron lanterns of Strozzi Palace--A1447.3.1; task, lantern that sheds light and learning on whole kingdom fetched--G610Ad; brothers tell king that Pinkel can fetch witch's golden lantern--G610Aa. SEE ALSO LAMP.

LANTERN-BEARER: Mouse warms joints of faithful lantern bearer during long cold night--B437.2.1.

LAO-TZU: Lao-Tzu charms raiding tiger, leaves sleeping goat safely in tiger's den--B431.3.2.

LAPP: Lad weds sun's daughter, leaves when sun strikes, he is not to look back, does and one-third of reindeer herd disappear--C31.3.2.

LARK: SEE BIRD, LARK; BIRD, MEADOWLARK.

LARS: Magic helper Lars appears when prince finds paper in nest of boxes saying "Lars, My Lad"--D882.1Fb.

LASHES: Doorman receives half reward, trickster asks for lashes--K187.1.

LATE: Animal late at distribution of characteristics--A2235. SEE ALSO TARDINESS.

LATEX: Pit lined with sticky latex catches--K741.2.

LATHE: Skulls turned on lathe--H1440A.

LAUGH: Bean laughs until it splits--A2741.1, F1025.1; bubble bursts laughing--F1025.1.1; frog bursts laughing, spider breaks legs--Z32.6; fine for laughing in court--J1141.1.3.4.1; trickster causes crocodile to laugh and escapes from mouth--J561.1.0.1; task, come laughing and crying at same time--H1064; eel's eyes narrow from laughing--A2332.3.2.1; frog in moon laughs and water spills out--A751.3.1.3; hare laughs, cause of split lip--A2211.2; hare's 'laughing place', dupe is stung--K1023.5.1; man laughs causing monkeys to drop him--J2415.23; laughing betrays presence to ogres--C460.1; old woman makes funny faces and oni laugh, spitting out water--J1791.3.2.2; princess brought to laughter by people sticking together--H341.1; princess brought to laughter by foolish actions of hero--H341.3.1; princess made to laugh by bee, harp, mouse and bumclock--

H341.2.1; St. Beatus' cloak ceases to be magic after he commits sin of laughing during Mass--C69.1; girl to bear son and daughter with hair half gold and half silver, sunshine when laughs, rain when cries--N455.4Ab; lad tells tall tale ending with fox reading newspaper which says "Now princess can eat for she has laughed"--H341.5; unkind girl! disobeys and laughs at trees--Q2.1.2Ea; wasp pinches sides in laughing--A2355.1.3; witch sees mouse-bride laugh, thus spell broken--B641B.

LAUGHING JACKASS: SEE BIRD, KINGFISHER.

LAUNDRY: Anansi to hang out laundry so Fire will know which house to burn--K415.0.1.

LAUREL: Magic laurel tree grants wish if cared for--F1015.1.1D.

LAW: Fox says law of peace among animals is passed--J1421.

LAWYER: Lawyer advises client to feign insanity in court. When he demands fee client still feigns insanity--K1655. SEE ALSO COURT; JUDGE; ETC.

LAZY: Buyer returns ass associating with lazy comrades--J451.1; lazy man leans on hoe, turns into baboon--A1863.1; lazy mother's baby stolen by fairies--F321.0.2; those on whom sun shines while in bed will be short lived--W111.10; contest in laziness--W111.1; man too lazy to turn string of doughnuts on his neck around--W111.5.8.2; Duendes keep putting cleaning equipment in hands of lazy wife--Q321.2.3; little man in red comes out of flower and forces gardener to work--Q321.2.1; fool waits for God to provide, nearly starves--J2215.4; man too lazy to dig up pot of gold, wolf to eat foolish man eats him--H1273.2H; ant and lazy grasshopper--J711.1; man feigns death rather than reap wheat--K341.2.0.3; lazy wife given ten helpers, enter her fingers and force to work--Q321.2.2; fish returned to water gives ability to do work magically--B375.1.3; man says he is going to climb to heaven, crowd which gathers tramples field for him--K474.1; lazy refuses to help until food is brought out--W111.7.2; little red hen must do all work--W111.6ff; lazy hunter rubs sole of boots on stone to wear out so looks as if walked far--W111.8; key hidden in flax reveals laziness of fiancée--H382.1; laziest person to carry drum, monkey says he won't carry it--J1141.9.1; man carves monkey to clean up after lazy villagers--A1861.3.1; fake god chases lazy man in answer to prayer for help up mountain--W111.9; on sea lion hunt two elder brothers fail to leap ashore--L114.1; lazy girl to spin remarkable amount--D2183+; lazy man refuses barn full of toast unless someone spreads honey on it--W111.5.10.1.1; lazy girl hides toothpicks in tatami--Q321.3; lazy boy digs up field in search of treasure--H588.7.3; lazy lad wed to princess reforms through hardships--H465F; cat beaten for not working, lazy wife must hold cat--W111.3.2; lazy wife is not fed until she works--T251.2.6. SEE ALL W111ff Laziness.

LEADERS: First Father chases lazy progeny out of house, from those who hide in house descend leaders, those under house servants, etc.--A1650.4.

LEAK: Tiger frightened of 'leak' in house--J2633, N392.1.1.

LEARNING: Man fears only one thing, learning--H1419.1.

LEAVES: Old man Autumn to wipe paint brushes on fox if can paint reflection of a leaf--A2411.1.3.2; tiny God arrives in leaf boat--A541.0.1; dupe persuaded to eat rotten leaves thinking they are 'king's food'--K1023.1.2; leaves remain flat from sky resting on them—A625.2.5; why leaves turn red--A2769.2; riddle, how many leaves on tree?--H705.3; snake shows leaf to heal snakebite—B522.1, W154.8.3.1; Glooskap promises that dead trees will revive in spring, wolf-wind killed all deciduous--A2760.2.

LEGBA: A781.2.1.

LEGS: Boys tease teacher saying they cannot find their own legs, he helps with switch--J2021.0.1; cat with broken leg burns warehouse--J1175.1; crane lets fugitive cross stream on leg--R246; cursed to break his leg in forty days the man breaks it immediately. "That's from someone elses curse. When mine takes effect you'll have to crawl"--M405; why dog lifts leg—A2473.1; origin dog's leg--A2371.1.1; dog breaks fox's leg, man breaks dog's, etc.—J52; coyote tricks giant into cutting off legs—G524.0.2; valet digs up gold leg of lord's wife from grave—E235.4.2.1; trickster claims cooked goose (crane, etc.) had only one leg--K402.1; man puts legs on pillow to reward--J2351.1.1; riddle, what has no legs, then two, then four? Tadpole--H761.2; riddle, Sphinx asks "What goes on four legs in morning, two at noon, three in evening?"—H761; riddle, what runs without legs? Water--H734.1.

LEHUA: Pele destroys Lehua groves of Hiiaka--A285.2.

LEMBU GUMARONG: Calf Lembu Gumarong tries to destroy rice and battle of Gods ensues--A162.9, A2685.6.1.1.

LEMON: Maidens from opened lemons--D721.5.

LENDING: Lending and repaying, progressively worse bargain--Z41.5. SEE ALSO BORROWING; LOAN.

LENORE: Dead love--E215.

LENTEN SEASON: Gamblers refuse to play after midnight on Shrove Tuesday when Lent begins, lad gambles with hare and loses all--E577.2.1.2.

LEOPARD: Bushbuck impersonates evil spirit and forces leopard to stir porridge with paws and tail--K335.0.4.6; hare tricks leopard into holding up cave--K1251; leopard's own children substituted for bushbuck's children in bag--K527.1; origin of color of leopard--A2411.1.1.1+; leopard and rabbit court--T92.11.4; hyena rides leopard courting--K1241.1; leopard tricked into drum--K714.2.5; small trickster in house of larger animal intimidates with loud boasts--K1711.2; goat begins to build house, tiger finds foundation and adds to it, each thinks is his--K1715.3.2; bushbuck tricks leopard with whom he has built house, shows leopard skin--K1715.3.2; duel of leopard and lizard--B264.3.1; leopard asks Tota monkey where he pastures—K688.2; mousedeer bluffs leopard "You promised me seven leopards to eat"--K1715.2; origin of leopard's spots—A2411.1.1.1.1; hare shows leopard reflection in well—K1715.1; leopard plans to eat snail who freed him--J1172.3.0.6; leopard hides in spider's house—K607.1; leopard's spots—A2412.1.2, F617.2.3; leopard tricked by Anansi ties tail to tree--K713.1.11; jackal tied to leopard's tail--J2132.5.1; talking leopard refuses to talk--B210.2.2; hare knocks out leopard's teeth—K721.2; Anansi ties up leopard in 'game'—K713.1.10; leopard, Kenki wrestle--A2412.1.2.2.

LEPCHAS: Lepchas build tower to sky--J2133.6.2.1.

LEPER: Man opens mountain tops letting fire in earth out, leper with flaming arms emerges and burns sky--A625.2.10; trickster disguises as leprous animal--K1995; leprous friend to be cured if bathed in blood of children--S268c; friend lends beauty to leprous friend--D1500.3.1.2; magic healing hymnal heals--T102.1; unkind sister made leprous--Q2.1.1Ba; leprous wife, dog, hawk, rat, and snake rescued--D882.1.

LEPRECHAUN: Marks all bushes to disguise marked treasure--J1922.2.1.

LETTER: Man carries written order for his own execution--H808, K511; altered letter of execution gives princess to hero—K1355; letter of execution changed—K511; ghost laid when letter found—E451.11; ghost returns for hidden letter—E415.1.3; hen takes 'letter' to king--Z52.3; scribe uses large letters writing to deaf man--J2242.2.1; scribe cannot write letter because has bad leg and cannot carry it, no one else could read it--J2242.1+; man carrying letter for swamp maiden given magic purse--D812.15.

LETTUCE: Eating of lettuce (cabbage) turns one to donkey--D551.1; boy starts wealth by raising lettuce, all seeds that stick to one finger—W48.1.

LIAM: Smith Liam drops hammer to earth--D672K.

LICHEN: Origin of lichen--A2689.1.

LIE: Lying traveler praises apes, rewarded—J815.1; who does not tell truth will be hanged. Lie, "I am going to be hanged"--J1180; what is heard at greatest distance? Lie--H659.27; chief deliberately stays away to prove Mamadi a liar—K511.0.1; forcing princess to say "that's a lie"—H342.1; sack full of lies--H1045.0.1; if calls liar to become his slave--H342.4; snake fears hot tar, man says he fears gold--K602.3; son fabricates fantastic false answer, "just like his father"--T615.1.1; task, telling long string of lies--H509.5.3; suitor test, telling one hundred lies--H509.5.2; test, making girl's mother say "that's a lie"--Z51.4; test, telling five lies which closely resemble the truth--H509.5.1. SEE ALL X900-X1899 Humor of lies and exaggerations.

LIFE: Life bound up with candle--E765.1; life extended by chess playing gods--A163.1.1.1; life expectancy, frog, tortoise, fish each tell how long they expect to live--L395; man and animals readjust span of life--A1321; water of life resuscitates two sisters--E82.1, G561C.

LIFTING: Task, lifting mountain--H1149.9.

LIGHT: Light seen from tree leads to adventure --N776; White Cloud of North calls Blue Cloud from South and Yellow Cloud from West to shed light--A1412.4; if ray of light touches lion will turn to dove for seven years--H1385.4D; house goes to boy who fills it completely, fills with light--H1023.2.6; carrying light into windowless house--J2123+; origin of light--A1412.4; told to put out light, puts it outdoors--J2499.9; lad follows girl with two red lights all night, is really Osgaert devil ghost--E421.3.8; light kept by seagull--A1411.3; theft of light--A1411; woman wishes for light. Sun, moon and stars appear--A710. SEE ALSO DAY; LAMP; LANTERN; SUN; SUNLIGHT; ETC.

LIGHTNING: Girl calls to heavens and lightning kills chief, rain puts out fire to boil her--F511.0.4.2; Pele destroy lehua groves of Hiiaka, Goddess of Lightning--A285.2; jaguar brags of strength to lightning--C984.5; lightning made from old moon--J2271.2.1; lightning sparks from millstone ground from old moon--J2271.2.1.1; origin of lightning--A1141; lightning is ram--A1141.8.2; lightning is flashing sword --A1141.2.1; task, split rock and light fire under it, lightning performs--H1385.3M; lightning stick gift of Thunderbird to hero--B16.5.1.4; old woman is adopted by animals and lightning--K1711.2.3.

LIGHTNING BUG: Lightning bug gives light to aid Brer Rabbit--K1082.0.2.

LILY: Daughter demanded because of lily picked --D735.1D; two golden lilies grow, wither if ill or dead--R111.1.3Ak; bat eats forbidden lily, origin chain of unkindness--A1341.4.

LIMB: Told he will fall off limb and die, fool falls (saws limb off) and believes self dead--J2133.1.6, J2133.4.

LIME: Kantchil's lime pit--K652.1. SEE ALSO BETEL.

LIMERICK: First person crossing bridge to be new mayor of Limerick--N683.1.

LIMPET: Shining boy born of tears of lost girls which fell into limpet shells--G275.7.0.1.

LIN: Miss Lin, the Sea Goddess--A421.1.2.

LINDEN TREE: Golden linden tree with golden bird--H1331.1.3Ai.

LINOU: Directs birds from Milky Way--A778.11.

LION: Anansi poisons meat and lion dies--K171.0.2.1; lion decrees ants may live everywhere--A2434.1.4; lion fears arrow, man's message--J32; ass frightens goats from cave for lion to kill--K2324.1.1; fox leads ass to lion's den but is himself eaten--K1632; ass chases lion frightened by cock--J952.2; ass insults dying lion--W121.2.1; lion's skin worn by ass--J951.1; bear has lion reach down throat and pull up bear grease--R111.1.3Am; lion and bear fight over carcass to exhaustion, fox takes--J218.1.1; lion overawed by blind man, shown quill for hair, etc.--K1715.12.1; lion and wild boar make peace rather than slay each for benefit of vulture--J218.1; lion asks judgment of his breath--J811.2.1; buffalo demands overmuch of lion captive--K553.1.0.1; lion and bull made enemies by jackal--K1084.1.2; lion convinces bull to have 'ugly' horns cut off--J642.1.1; bull invited by lion sees preparations to cook bull and flees--J425.2; lion succeeds when bulls separate--J1022; lion sneezes forth cat--A1811.2; lion left in mud by cat--J1172.3.0.5; cattle thief is lion, cowherd flees--J561.2; lion comforted for fear of cock--J881.2; lion believes cock's tailfeather is hair--K1711.1; lioness has only one cub, but a lion--J281.1; hare as nurse eats lion cubs--K933, K1066.3; lion as sham doctor looks at horse's foot--K1121.1; dog flees at lion's roar--J952.3; dogs tear up lion skin--W121.2.4; alliance of lion and dolphin--B267.5; lion drinks and becomes intoxicated and drunken coward rides lion home--N691.1.2.1; lion leaps at dupe and misses, trickster insists dead animal had no brains or would not have returned--K402.3.2; lion promised first thing met at home--H1385.4J; fox ceases to fear lion--U131.1; fox goes hunting without lion, killed--J684.1; fox preceding lion thinks all flee from him--J684.1.1; fox tells lion that cure lies in wrapping self in wolf skin--K961.1.1; lion and Brer Gilyard fight--K1082.0.2; girl lives with lion in cave--B610.2; lion harms self slapping at gnat--N333.0.1; gnats overcome lion--L478; goat sings of ten thousand lions she killed--K1715.17; goat intimidates lions, finding he cannot eat meat they kill him--U131.2; lion and goat make peace on seeing vulture waiting--J218.1; goat bluffs lion by calling to fox "You promised a younger lion"--K1715.2; poor brother given gold by stone lion who vomits gold--J2415.16; entrance to woman's room in golden lion statue--K1341.1; lion rescued from pit grateful--W154.8.1; lion flees sound of gun--K2324.2; hare offers better game to lion--K553.1; monkey loaned blanket by hare, hare has taken it from lion--K1066.6; hare takes lion hunting for honey, rolls rock on lion--K815.19.1; hare tells lion he's killed alligator and bear shows 'graves'--K1715.15; lion leaves hare to follow stag, loses both—J321.3; lion hiding in hare's house discloses presence—K607.1; lion investigates hare's rumor of end of world—Z43.3.1; small trickster in house of larger animal intimidates with loud boasts—K1711.2; hunter wants to see lion tracks, not lion—W121.1; if ray of light touches lion will turn to dove for seven years—H1385.4D; man tells lion to put paw in split log—K1111.0.2; Mantis hides in bag to enter lion's house—K1892.3; mongoose saves ostrich chicks from lion—K649.9.1; lion spares mouse, mouse frees lion—B371.1, B545.2; freed from trap by mouse, lion threatens to eat rescuer—J1172.3; mouse on lion's mane—J411.8; lion bride tramples mouse husband—B363.1; the ogre's heart in the egg—B314F, D532A; lion fears partridge for sound—K2324.2.1; animals pledge peace and each reveals his pet peeve—W141.1.1; lion turns on rescuer—J1172.3; man resuscitates lion which devours him—J563; fool rides lion—K1951.1; trickster makes dupe believe that he is holding up great rock—K1251; roaring contest between elephants and lion—K84.2; shy lion stays away from settlement—A2433.3.16; lion's share—J811.1+; girl sings to charm lions—D735.1B; stag escapes hunter, is eaten by lion—N255.1; statue of man overcoming lion would differ if made by lion—J1454; flood will come when eyes of two stone temple lions turn red—W154.8.4; best not to bring stone lion to life—J563.1; lion suitor allows teeth, claws extracted—J642.1; lion tricked by turtle in swimming match—K11.1; lion tied to tail of sham dead horse—J2132.5.3, K1047; task, bringing milk of lioness—N141.0.6; animal allows himself to be tied so as to avoid being carried off by storm—K713.1.1; deception into being tied in game—K713.1.10; lion tricked into bag by tortoise—K714.2.3.1; tortoise persuades lion captor to rub mud on him—K553.5.1; fox sees tracks going into lion's cave, none coming out—J644.1; lion and turtle swimming match—K11.1; lion hearing echo or seeing reflection in well belies another lion is there—K1715.1; woman removes lion's whisker—B848.2.1; woodpecker removes bone from lion's throat—W154.3; wolf raised by lioness thinks self equal of cubs—J952.1.1; youth who could become an ant, lion, or eagle—R111.1.3Aj.

LIPUNISHKA: F535.1.1Cc.

LISP: Lisping girls have been warned against speaking but forget and are found out—K1984.1.

LISTENER: Remarkable companion—F601.2.

LITERAL FOOL: SEE J2450-J2499.

LITTLE EARTH MEN: Little earth men taught last line of song and spell broken—F344.1.3.

LIU CHU'AN: Origin of God of Good Luck—D2011.1.3.1.

LIVER: Dragon Queen desires monkey's liver—K544.1; hare tells animals that Great Mugassa will be furious if cooked cow's liver is eaten—K484.4; cottontail shoots sun down and pastes thin slices of liver over sun—A727.4C; thief maintains that lamb never had a heart (liver). He has eaten it—K402.3; witch removes victim's liver with stone fingers—G262.2.1.

LIZARD: Lizard asks Ananse to fill hole with yams in return for his cloak of flies—K275.1; catfish wants to marry lizard—J414.3.1; chicken rescued lays eggs and saves life of starving lizard—K641.3; barren woman finds two green plants, turn to lizards, then children—T554.8.2; lizard steals python's drum—K1079.2; lizard thinks five is magic number because of five fingers on children's hands—Z71.3.3; frog to guard Nyame's well refuses water to other animals—A2378.2.3.1; giant lizard killed by coyote—B11.2.1.2.2; lizard turned to gold by saint—E121.4.3; why man's hand is like lizard's—A1311.1.1; why lizard bobs head up and down—A2474.1.1; why lizard is killed by man—A2231.7.1.2; duel of leopard and lizard—B264.3.1; daughter to be given to whoever guesses name—H323; saints have to dance when hear drums, drought ends—D2174.1; lizard rescued from burning bush with shepherd's crook—D882.1Bba; why lizard has rough skin—A2311.9.1; son gets holy man to turn him to lizard and creeps through crevice to rescue father—D197; lizards envy stag—L458; lizard's "Tjik" begins chain—Z49.6.0.6; lizard says tortoise's bundle was "found along road"—J151 ; J1511.14.1; lizard hides from enemies between shield and dives into creek, turns to turtle—A2312.0.3; why lizard says "Tzch"—A2464.4.3.

LIZARD, MOLOCH LIZARD: Why has rough skin—A2311.9.1.

LIZARD, MONITOR LIZARD: Origin of color—A2411.5.8. SEE ALSO CHAMELEON; IGUANA; ETC.

LLANGOSE: Origin Llangose Lake—F944.1.

LLEWELLYN: St. Mary of Trefrew sent in guise of beggar as wizard in Prince Llewellyn's party so that prince has wizard the equal of King John's—D1711.6.4.

LLEWELYN: Llewelyn and his dog—B331.2.

LLWYD: Enchanter's wife as mouse is caught—D117.1.1.

LLYN FYNNON: Maid entices Afanc water monster out of water and sings to sleep—B11.11.7.1.

LLYN GLASFRYN: Well spirit overflows forming lake—C41.5.

LO HANS: Eighteen Lo Hans—A501.3.

LOAF: Elder two brothers bring little water for mother to make loaf since pitcher leaks. Refuse to share small loaf with old lady met—R111.1.3Aq; lad given invisibility belt and taken to Giant's feast, steals loaf of bread—G666.2. SEE ALSO BREAD.

LOAN: Thirty reasons for not loaning one hundred lire. First, I don't have it—J1552.2.1. SEE ALSO BORROWING; LENDING.

LOBSTER: Opium eater spends night in haunted house, lobster demon—N612.3; lobster stomps flounder flat—A2332.4.4; fools drown lobster—J1736.1.1; animal thinks self largest in world—J953.20; lobster taken for tailor with shears—J1909.8.3; lobster in water bucket attacks thief—K1161.4.

LOCK: Mechanic tries to open chest by secret method, never thinks to just lift lid—J253.

LOCUSTS: Man reveals magic song and bison wife turns to locust—C31.3.1; chain of attackers—Z49.15; coyote wants to learn locust's song—G555.1.2; cicada (locust) leaves skin with rock inside, Coyote attacks and breaks teeth on rock—K525.1.4; what is in hand? Locust—N688; locusts carry oats, one at a time—Z11.1; grasshopper plague, Great Spirit sends coyote to eat grasshopperr—A2108.1; Goddess Kayamanon is turned away in beggar guise. She turns rice to locusts—A2062. SEE ALSO CICADA.

LOG: Log carried uphill to roll it down—J2165; log carried sidewise—J1964.0.1; crocodile masking as log obeys suggestion that he move upstream—K607.2; man mistakes dragon for log and sits on it—J1761.8; dwarf caught by beard in cleft—K1111.1; frogs given log as king—J643.1; man tells lion to put paw in split log—K1111.0.2; trying to stretch log—J1964.1; test, pass thread through curved hole in log—H506.4; woman drops log on foot and imagines death of unborn grandson—J2063.2.

LOKE: Thor, Loke and Thiaffe visit Giant's hall—F531.6.15.1.1.

LONDON: As Whittington leaves London the Bells call to "turn again"—N411.1A.

LONDON BRIDGE: Dream of treasure on bridge—N531.1.

LONG COMPTON: King to be King of England if climbs hill and sees Long Compton church—G263.2.1.2.

LONGSPUR: SEE BIRD, LONGSPUR.

LOOKING: Tabu, looking back—C331.

LOON: SEE BIRD, LOON.

LORD: In dream Good Lord told lad to ask Don Alfonso for money, told Don Alfonso not to lend it—J1552.10; fool waits for Lord to provide, nearly starves—J2215.4.0.1; gypsy woman told Lord is coming to visit turns away three beggars—Q292.1.1; lord stuck to Misery's magic chair, grants one hundred years of life—Z111.2.2.1; Padre Ulivo offers hospitality to twelve strangers (disciples)—Q565Ai. SEE ALSO CHRIST.

LORD BAG OF RICE: Reward for slaying Giant

Centipede is never ending bag of rice—Q82.3.

LORIKEET: SEE BIRD, LORIKEET.

LORNE: Asleep in mountain—D1960.2.

LOST: Lost ass, saddle and bridle offered as reward to finder—J2085.1; girl given golden chain for industrious knitting unravels yarn to find way back, lost—F348.7.1.4.1.1; girl to find way around palace without becoming lost, unwinds thread—H389.1; crumb trail eaten by birds, lost persons cannot find way home—R135.

LOTUS: Dog's hind leg is lotus blossom transformed by Buddha—A2371.1.1, A2473.1; girl emerges from lotus at night—N712.2; girl dies, to cover her with lotus blossoms and wait seven times seven days—G530.2Bj.

LOUHI: Antti asks Louhi, Mistress of the Northland, what trade brings greatest happiness—H1273.2I.

LOUISIANA: Louisiana line blown east by big wind—X1611.1.10.1.

LOUP GAROU: Dogs protect kind sisters from Loup Garou—Q2.1.6C; loup garou and demons eat imitator—N452E.

LOUSE: Louse falls into beer brewings—Z32.2.4.1; louse and crow, louse eats all met—Z33.4.1; louse has bruise on hip from drunken brawl—A2412.3.1; flea bites man and louse is killed—J2137.1; flea eats pudding while louse chops wood in 'contest'—K372.2; louse falls in soup—Z32.2.4. SEE ALSO FLEA.

LOUVIE: Tailor sews on haunted alp—D1385.18.1.

LOVE: Trickster assigned tasks by Mammy-Bammy Big-Money for love charm—H961.1; princess requests moon snow, declares ashes of chimney sweep to be this, seen through eyes of love—L393.1; riddle, what is sweetest?—H633; girl loves her father like "salt"—H592.1; varieties of love, as many as hens who love rooster—H1556.1.1; boy wishes every woman to fall in love with him—D856. SEE ALL B600-B699 Marriage of person to animal; T0-T99 Love. SEE ALSO BRIDE; SWEETHEART; WEDDING; WIFE.

LOVER: Lover retrieves lost ball and saves girl—H1411.4.11; bamboo shoots grow from spot of dead lovers, blood flows from shoots—A939.3; lover saves girl by hiding in cave—R161.5; lover returns from dead on horseback for sweetheart—E215; dead lovers, whom cruel maid caused to leap into sea, claim her—F944.6; dead sweetheart follows faithless lover in form of pig—E211.3; death feigned to meet lover—K1837.9, K1862; disguise as man to escape importunate lover—K1236; grateful dwarf gives girl magic seeds to transform her to dog, gives lover seeds to restore her—D141; girl swims to reach flute playing lover—T35.5.1; gypsy finds dead band of gypsies and girl he loves in woods. Carries her off, she lives by night—D621.0.2; horse leads bride to lover's castle—B151.1.1.0.4; mermaid gives ring to put on true love's finger, lad chooses poor lass—B81.13.11; youth turns to parrot to be by side of love—D157.1; lover forces poison intended for girl down old suitor's throat and weds girl—T92.15; maiden rescued from monster lover, she has rescuer beaten and mourns lost monster—G550.1; girl spins scissors in sieve to see man she will wed—D1323.20; returning father thinks shadow is wife's lover—J21.2.1; two girls abandon boy who sleeps all day on rock—D1841.4.3.3; Spinning Maiden Chuc Nu weds Shepherd Ngau Lang, set on opposite shores of Milky Way River—A778.3.1; hardhearted lady sends lover on repeated quests—T93.6; whirlwind takes lovers to heaven, princess and impoverished man—T91.6.4.4; girl wears yellow ribbon around neck all life, untied her head falls off—Z13.4.4.1; judge agrees girl shall belong to man whose yurt she is in at that moment—T92.0.1.1. SEE ALSO PARAMOUR.

LOVER'S LEAP: A968.2ff~

LOWER WORLD: Imposters abandon hero in lower world—K1931.2; descent to lower world—F81.1ff. SEE F80-F109 Underworld. SEE ALSO HELL.

LUCIFER: Lucifer's wedding—G561.1E.

LUCK: Bad luck banished, brother digs it up—N250.4ff; man expects luck to change—J894; youth blessed by Dame-Know-It-All succeeds in making princess talk but without Luck no one believes him—N141.0.1; lucky man succeeds even when selling dates in Cairo—N427; boy finds bag of gold on road early in morning but man who lost it must have been up earlier than he. Is it lucky to get up early?—N129; luck lost due to failure to eat fish from head downward—B175.3; unlucky man sells food stuffed with gold to lucky man—N351; origin God of Good Luck, Liu Chu'an and Bad Luck, Yuan Chao—D2011.1.3.1; which is most important, luck or intelligence—N141; sent by stepmother to gather strawberries in winter, girl comes to house of Mother Luck—Q2.1.4Bb; God of Poverty leaves home which is too poor—N250.5; Bad Luck put into sack—N112.1; poor man with no money but sense offers to multiply money for rich man with money but no sense—J1061.5; king to become lucky when puts on shirt of lucky man—N135.3; Luck depends on which stool Fate sits when one is born—N138; thief named "Luck" thinks self named—N611.1.1; poor man bets rich he can make woodcutter richer than rich man can—N66.1. SEE CHAPTER N. CHANCE AND FATE. SEE ALSO BAD LUCK; FATE; FORTUNE; TROUBLE.

LUDOVINE: Serpent with head of woman—H1385.3Cc.

LUMAWIG: Lumawig causes bamboo to grow, first man and woman emerge—A1271.5.

LUNGALEBE: Beast carries girl off—F511.0.4.2.

LUPA: Cebu created for sun god's son—A955.0.1.1.

LUSIGNAM: Melusine is half serpent on Saturdays—F420.6.1.5.2.

LUST: Fog rolls in leaving only bones of man with impure thoughts—A1533.3.

LUTE: King plays on lute to confuse enemy—K2366.2; four monkeys invent instruments—A1461.0.1; note played over and over, found perfect note—J1060.2; prince is lured through forest in attempt to tame white elephants with his lute playing—K754.2.1; task, making lute of stone—H1021.12.

LUTIN: Lutin is shown 'picture' (mirror) of other guest, flees—J1795.1.1.

LYNX: Giant lynx Pichou—A2411.2.1.22; hero fastens lynx claws to feet to climb glass mountain—H331.1.1C; son opens door freeing golden lynx—G671B; Morning Star's wife, Lynx, is hexed by Hyena—A781.1.1; why lynx has short tail—A2378.4.11; sword of lynx stolen by thunder—A1141.2.1.

MA BA: Sister of the honey bees—C435.1.1.

MA-IX: Origin of maize—A2685.1.1.

MABINOGIAN: Enchanter's wife as mouse—D117.1.1.

MACARONI: Wolf invited to make macaroni by gosling—K891.1.1.3.

MACCODRUM: Clan MacCodrum of the Seals—B651.8.

MACDONALD: Origin of hand print over gate of MacDonald castle—H1412.2.

MACEDONIA: Dragon kills slayer of King Pindus and guards body until Macedonians arrive—B11.6.1.2.

MACINTOSH: Bauchan of the MacIntosh family refuses to travel on boat with MacLeods and MacDonalds—F482.3.1.2.

MACIO SERRA DE LANGUICANO: Gambles away golden sun from Cuzco temple—V400.1.

MACKEREL: SEE FISH, MACKEREL.

MACLEOD: Fairy flag of Dunvegan will save clan MacLeod—F305.1.2.

MAD: SEE ANGER; TEMPER; ETC.

MADNESS: Escape by shamming madness—K523.1. SEE ALSO INSANITY.

MAFUITE: Maui asks fire of Mafuite—A1414.4.1.

MAGI: Bring gifts—N816.1.

MAGIC: Magic bow. Three sons left magic bow, magic deer, magic bird that tells all--F660.1F; magic word to open cave, gate—N455.3.2. SEE ENTIRE CHAPTER D. SEE ALSO NAME OF MAGIC ITEM, i.e. STONE, ETC.

MAGICIAN: Magician's apprentice—D1711.0.1.1; poor couple take in magician, is Elijah—Q1.1D; prepares hell broth, to get Marec the Enchanter's horse to drink--G275.1.2. SEE ALL ENTRIES D1710-D1711.6.6 Magician. SEE ALSO SORCERER.

MAGISTRATE: Magistrate orders three fools sent --H1312.4. SEE ALSO JUDGE.

MAGNUS: SEE SAINT MAGNUS.

MAGPIE: SEE BIRD, MAGPIE.

MAGUEY: Tepoztan abandoned in Maguey plant—A511.2.2.3.

MAGYAR: Origin of Magyars and Huns--A1611.5.5.

MAHADEO: Mahadeo sends cat to man's horse—A2513.2.1.

MAHARAJAH: Maharajah of India sends three golden dolls to Khan of Mongolia--H506.13; poor shoemaker gives last pair of shoes to beggar, Maharajah in disguise—Q45.1.4.

MAHARASHTRA: Origin of fast for sixty-four yoginees by mothers in Maharashtra State on last day of Shravana—A1541.2.2.

MAHON MACMAHON: Boy appears to smith in dream and asks to free from Giant Mahon MacMahon--F321.3.2.

MAID: Maids kill cock to sleep later-- K1636; maid given magic cloth by beggar, makes her lovely and pain leaves—J2415.19; crab tells maid witch's secret name—C432.1.2; maid kneads Devil in bread trough--K606.1.2; Maid Maleen serves as maid in kitchen at lover's castle—K1816.0.2.1; ogre's maid aids hero—G530.2; maid entices Afanc water monster out of water and sings to sleep—B11.11.7.1.

MAIDEN: Men detained by maids six months find two hundred years have passed--D2011.1.5. SEE ALSO GIRL; HEROINE; SERVANT.

MAIKOHA: Maikoha turns self to paper mulberry tree to provide for daughter--A1453.5.

MAILMAN: Anansi to pay snake postman by allowing him to take a bite of Anansi's head—K75.

MAIZE: Coyote dives for maize, really moon—J1791.3; origin—A2685.1.1; why maize is pierced —A2701. SEE ALSO CORN.

MAKAH: Wild dogs at Neah Bay turned into Makah by Kwatee—A1611.1.4.

MAKAIL: God of the Gulf claims one victim each year in whirlpool--F420.5.2.2.4.

MAKE-UP: Origin of painting eyebrows--A1599.5.1.2.

MAKI: Maki in wooden barrel, landlord in earthen vessel—J2171.1.3.0.1.

MAKONAIMA: Makonaima uses white clay from sky to make some Indians white, rests and clay becomes dirty--A1614.6.1.

MALDONADA: Puma cares for abandoned girl--B538.3.2.

MALINTZIN: Girl translates for Spaniards, dies of sadness, wailing still heard from Mt. Tepocatepec--E425.1.11.

MALLET: Father abandons daughter, leaves mallet hanging so will bang against tree—Q2.1.4D; Issun Boshi grows to normal size when struck with magic mallet--F535.1.1E; good brother finds wishing mallet in dream of children—J2415.15.

MAMA OULLO: Culture hero teaches arts and crafts—A541.

MAMMY-BAMMY BIG-MONEY: Feigns dead—K1047; trickster assigned tasks--H961.1.

MAN: Bear in hat taken for man by wife--J1762.2.3; animals bequeath characteristics to man—B592; task, making man of iron--H1021.12; origin of man—SEE ALL A1200-A1299 Creation of man; riddle, man made for woman or woman for man? Which came first men or brutes?—R111.1.3Ah; riddle, how long will man continue to live and die?--H887; man as trickster tells lion to put paw in split log--K1111.0.2; man imitates sounds of Vainamoinen's clothing--A2272.1.4; wolf is shown better game to eat, man with gun--K553.1.0.5. SEE ALSO A1200-A1699 CREATION AND ORDERING OF HUMAN LIFE.

MANABOZHO: Manabozho cannot put toe in mouth as baby does—L410.8; Manabozho tricks ducks into dancing with eyes closed and eats--K826; Manabozho puts earth ball on water and sets mouse on it to spin ball--A812.9; Manabozho tells feet to watch baking duck as he sleeps--J2351.1.2; Manabozho gives grebe red eyes for telling—A2332.5.7; Manabozho paints kingfisher for giving information about Manabozho's nephew killed by giant Lynx Pichou—A2411.2.1.22; Manabozho paints squirrel--A2411.1.4.1; Manabozho kills giant sturgeon, cuts heart from within--F912.2.7; Manabozho cuts giant sturgeon into pieces = fish—A2102; Wabun (west wind) can be harmed only by oldest thing on earth, certain black rock—Z312.3; Manabozho changes self to large wolf with big tail—J292. SEE ALSO COLLECTION Leekley, Thomas. WORLD OF MANABOZO; Reid, Dorothy. TALES OF NANABOZHO.

MANABUSH: Manabush steals fire from Dawn People—A1415.0.2.5; Manabush can't decide how to eat moose--W123.5.

MANAGUA: Image of Santo Domingo de Guzmán taken to Managua each year—V128.0.2.

MANCO CAPAC: Culture hero teaches arts and crafts—A541.

MAN-CROW: Man-Crow killed by Soliday-- A2433.5.3.3.1.

MANDIOCA: SEE MANIOC.

MANGER: Dog in the manger--W156; manger of man who gave savings to others--D1622.2.3. SEE ALSO CRECHE.

MANGO: Healing mango cures princess--H346; mangos rot while man debates which to eat-- J2183.1.4.

MANI: Manioc springs from grave of Mani-- A2685.5.

MANIOC: Origin--A2685.5.

MANITOU: Manitou gives golden feathers to crane —A2411.2.6.14.

MANSTIN: Manstin rabbit turns child into a giant child with long ears and split lip like self —B535.0.16.

MANTICORE: Manticore of North Cerney befriends boy and gives flute, image carved on church-- B27.

MANTILLA: Mantilla spun by spider—A1465.2.1; Virgin gives mantilla of spider webs--D1623.2.

MANTIS: Young Mantis and Young Kwammang-a cut All-Devourer open and true bushes and sheep emerge--A1884.0.2; bee carries Mantis over water at beginning of world, seeds of first human in Mantis—A1291.2; Mantis creates an eland--A1875.2; Mantis steals fire from ostrich— A1415.0.2.2; Mantis hides in bag to enter lion's house--K1892.3; moon is ostrich feather thrown by Mantis--A741.5; why Mantis has flat sides-- A2305.3; Mantis rescues springbok from stomach of elephant--F929.4; Mantis sends Striped Mouse to vanquish Beetle--K688.7.

MANURE: Wife delighted with husband's trade for cow-manure--J2081.1.

MAPUNDU: Beast steals princess--F511.0.4.2.

MARBLE: Pious man polishes marble block until smooth, unable to move it to Jerusalem— D1641.2.1.1.

MARCH: Unkind brother curses March--Q2.1.4Ad; Why March has thirty-one days--A1162, K688.1.

MAREC THE ENCHANTER: Turns giant to stone for stealing sheep--F531.6.12.8.3; witch pre-

pares hell broth to get Marec's horse to drink-- G275.1.2.

MARGERY DAW: Saint Margery Daw—V411.12.

MARGRETTE: Maid marries merman--B82.1.1.

MARICOPAS: Origin of Maricopas--A1610.7.

MARILKA: Marilka is lost, in sorrow river dries up, etc.—Z39.5.2.

MARIMI: Girl weds handsome stranger, really a Marimi--G302.7.1.3.

MARK: Marked culprit marks everyone else and escapes detection--K415; leprechaun marks all bushes to disguise marked treasure--J1922.2.1; marking the place on the boat where knife drops --J1922ff.

MARKO THE RICH: Lad to become son of Marko— H1273.2F.

MARKSMAN: Remarkable companion--F601.2; marksman shoots all five eggs in half with one shot--F660.1; astronomer sees princess, thief steals, marksman kills dragon, etc.—H621.2.4; son practices until can avenge father's death by tiger--F912.2.12.

MARMOT: Escape by persuading captors to dance --K606.2.

MARRAKESH: Sultan buys house for stork with pearl given--B463.4.

MARRIAGE: Marriage to animal—B600-B699; marriage to person in beast form--B641ff; marriage to beast by day and man by night--D735.1, H1385.4; marriage to demon--G302.7.1; marriage to fairy--F300ff; marriage to ghost--E474.2; unsuccessful marriage due to different habits-- J414.3; poor man sends gifts to prince and princess, they wed—T53.7; vain attempts to escape prophesied marriage--M383. SEE ALL T100-T199. SEE ALSO BRIDE; GROOM; WEDDING; ETC.

MARSH: Frogs ask marsh saved, trees cut would cause to dry up--D435.2.2; marsh grass runs off to water's edge in fright—A2701; marsh wren builds in cat-tail tops in marsh--A2431.3.13.

MARTIN: Wait till Martin comes--J1495.2.

MARYA MOREVNA: Hero gives water to chained Koschei the Deathless at Marya Morevna's house —B314C; lad steals Marya Morevna from Koschei with steed--H1199.12.4B.

MARZIPAN: Girl makes a marizpan prince— H1385.5C.

MASAI: Cattle stolen from Masai by clever lad who blows horn in treetop—K341.5.3.

MASI: Fools of Masi dive for sunbeam-- J1791.3.3.1.

MASK: Fox takes mask for face--J1793; boy given spirit mask--A1542.2.2.

MASON: Thief blames mason for building poor house--J2233, Z49.11.2. SEE ALSO BRICKLAYER.

MASS: To be saved if hears mass at churches in Jerusalem, Galicia, and Rome in one night, devil carries--D2121.5.1; Juan Bobo thinks pig wants to go to mass, dresses--J1849.5; St. Beatus' cloak ceases to be magic after he sins by laughing during mass--C69.1.

MASTER: Master of all masters, maid told silly names for objects--X1506.1.

MASTERMAID: Maid of ogre helps hero--G530.2.

MAT: Mat is transformed badger--D421.8; old woman protected by objects which attack intruding ogre--K1161.3. SEE ALSO TATAMI.

MATCH: Fool carries matchbox in horsecart--J2461D.

MATCHMAKER: Poor man sends gifts to prince and princess, they wed--T53.7.

MATE: Origin--A2691.6.

MATENKO: Feigns dead--J2511.1.2.1.

MATH: Customer takes mathematical computations as ever increasing prices--J2035.1; the interrupted calculation, keeps adding in numbers mentioned in conversation--J2035; selling half house--J2213.6; four pennies, one falls out, what's left?--J2213.10; Mullah divides seventeen donkeys in fractions to three buyers--J1249.5. SEE ALSO COUNTING; DIVIDING.

MATTHEW: Outlaw Matthew does penance--V21.7.

MAUI: Maui invents colored birds--A1908; Maui tries to kill Death--A310.1.1; Maui gets secret of fire from Mud Hens--A1415.0.2.4; Maui asks fire of Mafuite in underworld--A1414.4.1; Maui Kiji-Kiji brings fire to Tongo--A1415.5; Maui invents barbed fish-spear--A1457.1.1; Maui invents fish-trap--A1457.5; Maui fishes up island--A955.8; Maui invites kite--A1124.1; Maui kills monster Mo-o--B11.2.1.2.1; Maui pushes sky up--A625.2.5; Maui snares sun--A728.2; Maui follows mother to underworld--H1252.1.1.

MAUNAKEA: Certain slope of Maunakea left to Poliahu--A289.2.

MAY: May is the greenest thing--H646.1.

MAYOR: Mayor and comrade convince dupe pig is dog--K451.2.2; new mayor to be first person crossing bridge--N683.1; as Whittington leaves London the bells call to "turn again," will be mayor--N411.1A.

MAZEL: Shlimazel (bad luck) wins bet--N141.0.6.

MCCOUL, FINN: As babe in cradle--K521.4.1.5.

MEADOWLARK: SEE BIRD, MEADOWLARK.

MEAL: Pot of barley meal to be sold broken--J2061.1.2.1; boy weds girl whose meal sticks to shell--K1816.0.2.2.

MEASURE: Cat borrow's measure for master's money--K1917.3; snake tied to pole to be measured--K713.1.9. SEE ALSO WEIGH.

MEAT: Chunk O' Meat , old man, old woman and little boy find fat meat in hollow log and eat. "Where's my chunk o' meat?"--E235.4.3.1; fool sells meat to dogs--J1752.1.3; owner persuaded that his goods are spoiled--K344; stolen meat handed about, thief who has it can honestly say he wasn't the one who stole it--K475.1; vow to eat no meat until established--W11.14.1. SEE ALSO GAME.

MEATBALL: Meatball allows Saynday to take bite out of her--A2412.1.7.

MECCA: Cholera, Death and Fear visit Mecca--Z111.7; pilgrim on way to Mecca has horse taken by trickster, Kura Hyena--K1241.

MECHANIC: Mechanic works hours trying to open chest by secret method, never thinks to just lift lid--J253.

MEDICINE: Origin of balsam--A2681.14; plant growing from spot where gold eagle is burnt cures princess--A2693.1; origin of medicine--A1438+; doctor's fee reduced with claim that he spilled medicines on priceless rug and ruined--K499.11; medicine shown by serpent or animal--B512; man sees tiger use healing leaf--A751.8.5.2. SEE ALSO DOCTOR; HEALING.

MEDICINE, GOD OF MEDICINE: God of Medicine lets Ngoc Tam restore wife by letting three drops of blood fall on body--A2034.5.

MEDICINE LODGE: Plans given to scarface hero--H1284.1.

MEDICINE PIPE: Thunder gives medicine pipe to be smoked when Thunder returns with rains in spring--A284.5.

MEDIO POLLITO: Half chick--B171.1.2, Z52.2.

MEDITATION: Holyman, Chyavana, meditates so well ants build mound over him--D1960.5. SEE ALSO HERMIT.

MEDOC: SEE MOUNTAIN LION.

MEERSCHAUM: Magic pipe summons St. Nicholas when stroked on Christmas Eve--D1662.4.

MEETING: Animals tell pet peeves--W141.1.1; short tailed animals organize protest meeting--J429.3.

MEIRINGEN: Town of fools--J1922.1, J1973,

J2123, J2133.5.

MELONS: Melons become pale on bottom from being shoved around--A2701; old man and wife drop staff and melon into water, then fall in, turn to frogs, still call for melons--A2426.4.1; man plants patch of melons for self and patch for God, steals from God's patch--W211.5.

MELROSE ABBEY: St. Cuddy--V429.1.

MELT: SEE FAT, ANIMAL FAT.

MELTING: Wife made of spirit of magic calf's fat made to cook, melts--A2146, F1041.4.1.

MELUSINE: Melusine is half serpent on Saturdays --F420.6.1.5.2.

MEMORY: Two men going to sow millet continue three line conversation over three years--H1595.1.1.

MENEHUNES: Menehunes flee leaving nets--F451.3.2.1.3; menehunes put back stones moved onto their land--F271.2.8.1.

MERCILESS ONE: Old woman is adopted by animals and lightning who protect from The Merciless One--K1711.2.3.

MERCURY: Gives axe to woodsman--Q3.1; Mercury finds his statue priced low--L417.

MERCY: Goddess of Mercy, Kwan Yin--A483.1. SEE KANNON; KWAN YIN.

MERISIER: Aids in quest for drum--A1461.10.

MERLIN: Grants wish for child size of thumb--F535.1.1; advises Childe Rowland on means of rescue for Burd Ellen--F324.0.1. SEE ALSO MERVYN.

MERMAID: Girl as duck is captive of mermaid who pulls her back to water on invisible gold chain --Q2.1.5Bbb; mermaid enticed ashore by hero on quest for firebird--H1381.1.3; girl becomes mermaid when fish-lover is killed by family--B654.1; mermaid rescued by fisherman gives reward, penny to drop from wife's mouth with every word--D1454.2.0.1; lad plays magic pipe, dances undersea with mermaid--D1415.2.4.2; mermaid gives ring to put on true love's finger --B81.13.11; mermaid mistreated inundates village in sand--F948.5; mermaid pulls ships under water--H1440D; bite of mermaid's shoulder causes never to age--D1349.2.4; Urashima Taro--F420.6.1.3.1; mermaid takes lad to hear princess play violin by sea--D532B; mermaid weds mortal --B81.2.4; whale restrains mermaid while lad, maid flee--D1154.1; Ichabod the Whaler promises not to harpoon Long John Whale if he'll let mermaid bridle, ride him--B612.3. SEE ALL ENTRIES B81. SEE ALSO F420 Water-spirits.

MERMAN: Merman abducts girl, destroys castle--G561.1H; merman cares for girl thrown overboard--Q2.1.5Bbc; merman offers to exchange baskets of jewels for baskets of fruit daily--B82.6; maid marries merman--B82.1.1. SEE ALL ENTRIES B82.

MERVYN: Mervyn gives jeweled glove to babe, only babe in cradle is saved from flood--F944.1. SEE ALSO MERLIN.

MESSAGE: Fake message carrying animal sold, messenger presents empty envelope at house and joins in feast--J2192.0.1; finding no messenger, fool carries letter to wife himself--J2242.0.1; foolish messenger muddles message--J2671.4.

METSCH RIVER: Why runs white--A939.1.

MEW: Why cats mew when chewing--A2435.2.1.

MIDAS: Golden touch--J2072.1.

MIDGARD: Thor, Loke and Thiaffe contest at Giant's hall, contest includes lifting Midgard--F531.6.15.1.1.

MIDGET: Tiny god teaches industries and crafts--A541.0.1; knee-high man--J291. SEE ALL ENTRIES F535.1 Thumbling.

MIDRIDGE: F361.17.8.

MIDSUMMER EVE: Crop destroyed each midsummer eve--H1331.1.3.

MIDWIFE: Brownie rides for midwife--F482.5.4.1; dwarfs have human midwife--F235.4.1A, F372.1, F451.5.1.4.1; mortal midwife or nurse to fairy child gets fairy ointment in eyes--F235.4.1A.

MIGRATION: Crane's gold color taken away as punishment for migrating--A2411.2.6.14; why Siberian brown owl does not migrate--A2482.4.

MIKADO: Girl kills sea serpent, finds statue of Mikado in cave--K1853.2.1.2.

MILITARY: SEE SIEGE; SOLDIERS; WAR.

MILK: Lad chooses white milk (magic ability to play on alphorn) when given choice by three men on mountain--A1461.9; bath in boiling milk--milk in pot turns color when lad in danger--H1331.1.3Fe; daydreams of profit from milk and spills--J2061.2; dead mother provides milk to babe--E323.1.1; jealous girl rubs bowl of milk left for helpful fairies with gentian root--F384.5; why goat gives milk to people--A2513.4.1; Brer Rabbit tricks cow into running horn into tree, then milks--K771; task, bringing milk of a lioness--N141.0.6; cow holds back half milk for the little people--F348.7.1.2; cows give ponds of milk, men skim cream from boats--X1235.2.2; snake who drank contents of milk bottle has to spit out milk to escape bottle--K1022.0.3; Witch of Pendle drowns and dissolves in stream of milk when cow kicks over her bottomless pail--G274.1.1; worm comes daily to Lambton Hall to be fed milk of nine cows--B11.12.4.1.1.

MILKMAN: Milkman sells half water, half milk.

Monkey throws half money to stream—J1551.9.

MILKY WAY: Milky Way as invisible warrior's bow string—R221G; badger fans self with tengu's magic fan until nose grows to sky, becomes bridge over Milky Way—D1376.1.3.1; pulp of pumpkin forms Milky Way—A641.3. SEE ALL A778+ Origin Milky Way.

MILL: Devil grinds miller's paltry offering in mill at night, carries miller off—Q272.1.2; spending night in haunted mill—H1411.2; fearless girl grinds in haunted mill—H1419.2; mill inheritance to apprentice with finest house—B641D; fugitive slave hides in mill—N255.4; mill grinds witch up —Q2.1.2Cb.

MILL, HANDMILL: Magic mill obeys only master— D1651.3.1; magic mill stolen by host at inn— D861.1; self-grinding mill—D1602.21.

MILLER: Miller, his son, and the ass. Who should ride?—J1041.2; cuckolded miller overhears— J1344.1; numskull caught by miller changing meal from other's sack into own—J1393.

MILLET: Task, planting millet porridge— H1023.1.1; why millet is flat rooted—A2793.8.1.

MILLSTONE: Strong man thinks millstones thrown on him are gravel, wars as hat—F615.3.1.5; lightning is the sparks from a millstone made from an old moon—J2271.2.1; numskull sticks his head in the millstone—J2131.5.4; ogre throws self over the stream by tying millstone to neck—K1611Bb; old woman is protected by objects which attack intruding ogre—K1161.3; millstone is thought to be a spinning wheel— K1718.2.1; millstone dropped on stepmother— N271; keeping warm by dragging millstone= K119.3.

MINANGKABAU: Sumatrans shape roof like horns of Karbau and call land Minangkabau—B264.6.

MINARET: Called down from minaret by beggar, takes him back up to say no—J1331; fool can sing in bathroom, wants bath built on minaret so voice will carry—J2237.

MINE: Genie of the Silver Mine gives lad silver ore seen in dream—F456.4.3; older brothers ordered to remove trees from land so youngest can mine gold—L223. SEE KNOCKERS.

MINERVA: Creates horse—A46.

MINISTER: Minister banishes hogboon—F381.16. SEE ALSO PREACHER; PRIEST; PRIME MINIS-TER.

MINK: Why mink has white down on chest— A2412.1.9; crow pretends to be ghost and Mrs. Mink throws delicacies to him in fear— K335.0.4.5; mink cuts hole in darkness to bring down dawn—A1174.1.1; mink persuades sun to let him carry torch, falls into Milky Way and torch is extinguished = eclipse—A737.9; Kwatee the Changer changes man making tools into animals—A2262.4; mink fails to follow shoreline exactly—A2411.1.2.1.2.1.

MINSTREL: Blind minstrel covers body with scrip-tures as protection from ghosts—E434.11; min-strel takes revenge on shoemaker for botching his songs—J981; minstrel sings "dog is great among dogs, yet he serves men", king refuses to extend this to include kings—L435.5.

MINT: Brer Fox told money is minted when rear wagon wheels overtake front wheels—J2066.7.

MIRACLE: King introduces Korean alphabet by writing on leaves with honey so ants will eat out letters, then claims miracle—A1484.2.1; miracu-lous stone hen—B811.7. SEE ALSO SAINTS.

MIRALI: Mirali proves flies live only where man lives—J1289.32.

MIRROR: Barber says mirror will show spots on face of any who have sinned—D1163.1; enchant-ed cat sees ill father in mirror—H1321.1D; son and daughter with mirror, homely daughter to overcome face with character—J244.1; demon shown mirror and dies—J1795.1.2; genies from magic mirror—D882.1l; man shows ghost its own reflection and frightens it—K1715.1.2; Lutin is shown 'picture' of guest soon to arrive (mirror) —J1795.1.1; skillful companions resuscitate girl, see her in magic mirror—H621.1; image in mirror mistaken for mother or other person—J1795.2; princess's magic mirror reveals hiding places— H321B; quest for rejuvenating mirror— H1321.1Cc; fool stands before mirror with eyes shut to see how looks in sleep—J1936; man takes mirror to bed to see whether he sleeps with his mouth open—J1936.1; mirror tells of Snow White's beauty—Z65.1. SEE ALSO REFLECTION.

MIRYEK: Mole to wed sky, sun, cloud, wind, stone miryek—L392.0.2.

MISCHIEF: What better than a gebetta board to keep a small boy out of trouble?—K251.1.3; "May the Mischief take me if I ever come here again"—C12.2.3.

MISER: Miller gives paltry sum, Devil grinds it in mill—Q272.1.2; miser boards up doors to avoid door tax—J1179.15; miser dreams—W153.17; mi-ser accepts pot with "child"—J1531.3; miser ad-vised to pretend stolen treasure is still there— J1061.4; miser builds wall of flour—W153.16; bread is as good as butter - takes butter. But-ter is as sweet as oil. Oil is clear as water, buys water—J2478. SEE ALL W153ff Miserliness.

MISERY: Misery banished and freed—N250.4; death magically bound to a tree, why misery is in world—Z111.2.1.1; monkey demands 'misery', thinking is syrup—J1805.2.

MISFORTUNE: Misfortune banished and freed— N250.4. SEE ALSO BAD LUCK.

MISSIONARIES: Pirate kills missionaries, ship haunts—E535.3.

MIST: Magic chant, mist behind, light before—R221Bb; man loves Daughter of the Mist—A791.5.1; Daughter of the Mist—F383.4.3.1. SEE ALSO FOG.

MR. MIACCA: Boy caught by Mr. Miacca—G82.1.2.

MISTLETOE: Owl advisor warns to kill oak saplings as bird lime will be made of mistletoe on oaks—J621.1.

MISTRESS: Ignored wife of Caliph camps near him in desert and has affair—K1814.5.

MISUNDERSTANDING: Misunderstanding the names, wife gives hog to Mr. "Present-Need", etc.—K362.1.1. SEE ALSO LANGUAGE.

MITTEN: Girl sent back for father's mitten finds three birds nesting there—Q2.1.5Bba; animals invite all comers to join them in abode until mitten house ruptures—J2199.5.

MOCCASIONS: Dwarfs heal boy, give moccasions that never wear out—F451.5.1.10.2; magic moccasins—H1132.1.5.3.

MOCKING: Tabu, mocking at belief in demons—C17; man scoffs at old ways, wild hunt carries off—E501.18.4.1.

MOCKINGBIRD: SEE BIRD, MOCKINGBIRD.

MOHAMMED: Cats always land on feet, reward for killing snake about to strike sleeping prophet—A2441.1.10.1; spider web over hole saves fugitive Mohammed—A2221.5.2, A2231.7.1, B489.1, B523.1. SEE ALSO: HADJI; MOSLEM.

MOLASSES: Brer Rabbit offers Brer Wolf taste from jug of 'fox's blood' (molasses)—K1715.3.1.

MOLE: Why mole is blind—A2332.6.5; fox, sandpiper, mole, and weasel steal fire from wind-people—A1415.2.3; coyote opens mole's bag of fleas—J2131.2.2; why mole's forepaws are bent backward—A2375.2.7; why mole lives underground—A2433.3.20.1; mole helps dig to upper-world—A1024.1; mole pushes sun back in sky—A727.2; mole wed to sky, sun, cloud, wind, stone miryek—L392.0.2.

MOLES: Stork is tramping down wheat, foolish men from Moles carry one to scare off stork—J2163.4; fools dig hole for dirt from hole—J1934.

MOLLY WHUPPIE: K1611.

MOLOCH LIZARD: Why moloch lizard has rough skin—A2311.9.1.

MOMOTARO: T543.3.2.

MOMUS: Momus driven from Olympus for fault finding—A46.

MONEY: Brahman will accept only money King earns himself—W11.3.1; payment with clink of money—J1172.2+; happy friar becomes unhappier as he receives more money—J1085.1; ghost drops money after calling "I am letting it fall"—E371.1; in country of ghosts gold turns to paper money burned at funerals—F129.4.4.1; man finally given money to purchase guitar, "Now I see you really mean to play it"—J1382.3; judge rules man who was told to "return whatever you want" must return money, since he wants to keep it—J1521.5.2; money hidden in loaf, loaf given away—N351; money sticks to measure revealing wealth—K1454.1; monkey throws half water to stream, payment for watered milk—J1551.9; money in path overlooked—N351.2; if fool found purse with 50,000 rubles he would ask a reward if it belonged to a rich man, would ask none if it belonged to poor man—J2259.2; riddle, use of money. One part "give away" etc.—H585.1.1; throwing away of money into fire does not bother son until rupee he worked to earn is thrown away—J702.3; girl steals old woman's moneybag—Q2.1.2Cb; wagon full of money, hare given ride—K371.1; why everyone looks for "money", man "Money" weds chief's daughter to suitor and absconds with brideprice—A1375.2. SEE ALSO CASH; COUNTING; GOLD; MINT; THIEF; WEALTH.

MONGOOSE: Woman slays faithful mongoose in error—B331.2.1; grateful mongoose gives magic ring—H621.3; mongoose saves ostrich chicks from lion—K649.9.1.

MONK: Cat as monk eats mice worshippers—K815.16.1; cat shows monk how to cure rich man's daughter—B522.1.1; cat causes coffin to rise into air and only monk who befriended her kittens can make it descend—D1641.13.1; monk invited to two feasts, both men pull him in their direction—J2183.1.2.1; fiddler employed to play on Christmas Eve for devils, plays holy carol and captive monk's soul freed—G303.25.17.2.1; White Snake Lady causes flood but monk spreads robe and protects mountain top—B656.2.1; animals judge against monk—J1172.3.2; acolyte eats honey master says is poison—J2311.2.2; monk shaves head of captor, he thinks self to be monk—J2012.1.2; statue of monk points to treasure, but ten fingers point ten different directions—C429.3; Friar tells tale enabling him to loosen belt as gesture after heavy meal—K263.2; man refuses to kill tiger, left holding tiger by tail—X459.2; attack on monk by ungrateful tiger—J1172.3; monk admits waterhorse to church—F420.1.3.3.1. SEE ALSO CAPUCHIN; PRIEST.

MONKEY: Monkey in age debate—B841.1.1; why bananas belong to monkeys—K741.0.1, K741.0.12; monkey as bride—B641C; monkeys construct a bridge across ocean—B846; monkey evens up cakes by eating—K452.1.2; monkeys imitate cap peddler—B786.1; man carves monkeys to clean up after lazy villagers—A1861.3.1; monkey flatters cat into pulling chestnuts from fire—K334.3; monkey foresees chain in which stables are set afire—Z49.23; chameleon accuses monkey of setting fire, shows blackened palms—A2494.16.2.1; boar steals child and lets monkey 'rescue'—K231.1.3.2; Jupiter offers prize to prettiest child, monkey comes to claim prize—T681.2; mistress and master use magic cloth, become monkeys—J2415.19; crab's friends attack intruding monkey—K1161.6; creation of monkey—A1861; monkey tricks crocodile masking as rock into talking—K607.2.1; monkey tricks crocodile into opening mouth—K607.2.3; monkey tells crocodile he left heart at home—K544; why men dance like monkeys—A1542.1.1; dragon king wants monkey's liver—K544.1, K961.1; monkeys kill bird who tells them firefly is not fire—J1064.1, J1761.3; monkey tries to fish and almost drowns—J516; monkeys show edible foods to man—B441.1.0.1; monkey in sheet as ghost—K1682.1; prince takes girl from floating basket, leaves monkey in her place—K1625; girls preening in cave mock old woman, turn to monkeys—A1861.3.1; frog insists black handed monkey wash until hands are white—J1565.1.2; hare (jackal) calls "thanks for the tiger" to monkey bringing tiger—K1715.2.1; monkey hides food in hat—W125.3.1.1; monkey and heron contest in branch sitting—K54; honey eaten by monkey and replaced by mud, queen passes it around—K144.3.1; monkeys to build house tomorrow—J2171.2.1; animal in cave (house) tricked into calling out—K607.1; farmer disguised as scarecrow taken as Jizo and carried off by monkeys—J2415.23; monkey judges against man—J1172.3.2; monkeys dig up Kantchil's soul (bees)—K1023.1.0.3; monkey insists on keeping house for lawyer—D318.1; lazy man with hoe as tail becomes monkey—A1863.1; laziest person to carry drum, monkey says he will not—J1141.9.1; monkey lets all other lentils fall from hand to search for one dropped—J344.1; monkey loaned blanket by hare, hare took it from lion—K1066.6; why apes, monkeys, gorillas, chimpanzees have face, hands and feet like men—A2375.11; scaffold to obtain moon breaks hole in moon and lava covers plain, men turn to gorillas and baboons, children to monkeys—A1861.4; milkman sells half water, half milk and monkey tosses half money into stream—J1551.9; why monkey mimics—A2538.1; monkey asks for misery—J1805.2; monkey companion for Momotaro—T543.3.2; monkeys invent musical instruments—A1461.0.1; monkey dons stolen necklace when tricked into showing off—K1066.1; seven brothers hire monkey nursemaid—B441.0.2; old woman's friends attack monkey—K1161.3; leopard asks Tota monkey where he will pasture next day—K688.2; monkey drops pomegranate seed and asks owner to cut down olive tree so seed can grow—Z41.6.4; Mr. Luck bathes in pool and becomes monkey—D551.1G; monkey becomes prince when girl comforts—D735.1G; monkey beaten by snail in race—K11.1; monkey claims razor for cut tail, chain—Z47.2; monkey saved from pit rewards rescuer—W154.8; monkey attacks rescuer—J1172.3.0.4; monkeys pull up saplings in order to water—J1973.1; monkey and rabbit in no scratching contest—K263.1; shipwrecked monkey rescued by dolphin—J1803.1.1; monkey sneezes in king's presence J2413.6; Anansi eats tiger's food, teaches little monkeys incriminating song—K1066.5; sparrow's nest destroyed by monkey—J1064.2; monkeys think man is statue, he lets self be carried off—

J2415.23; man falls into hole in tree (well), monkey puts tail in hole and man pulls it off—K619.4; tailless monkey persuades others to cut off tails—J758.1.4; enmity between tiger and monkey—A2494.10.4; monkey tied to tiger's tail—J2132.5.1; monkey sees all tracks going into pond and none coming out, drinks through straw—J644.2; monkey beats trail into Guinea Fowl's farm, claims—K453.1; monkey gets top half of tree, it withers—K171.9.1; why monkeys live in trees—A2433.3.19.0.1; monkey pulls wedge from split tree and it shuts on his private parts—K1111; Biri monkey plans to leave Zomo hare in well. Zomo hides in last bale and is hauled out—K306.5; monkey wins bride for master—K1917.3G; girl tosses wooden monkeys behind to detain pursuing monkeys—D672E. SEE ALSO ORANGUTAN.

MONKEY, APE: King of Apes asks visitors how they like his children, truthful visitor punished—J815.1; origin of confusion, ape directs all animals to do disruptive things—A1382.2, Z43.7; boar dreams he is to eat antelope, king rules he may. Ape dreams he is to wed king's daughter—J2326.2.1; apes attacking firefly hit each other—K1082.3.2; why apes, monkeys, gorillas, chimpanzees have face, hands and feet like men—A2375.11; ape caught on tar man—K741.0.11; ape grateful for removal of thorn—B381.4.

MONKEY, BLACK HANDED: Frog makes black handed monkey wash until hands are white—J1565.1.2.

MONKEY, COLUBUS: Origin—A1861.5.

MONKEY, MONKEY GOD: Sun Wu-Kung—B241.2.2.1.

MONKEY, GORILLA: Girl rescued from gorilla's little finger—F913.4.

MONKEY, MONKEY KING: King of the monkeys forms bridge over stream with body to let subjects escape—B241.2.2.2; Monkey King gives characteristics to son—A1861.5; task, fetch gong of Monkey King—G530.2Bj; King of Monkeys rewards liar who praises monkeys—J815.1; Monkey King in forest takes necklace of Demon from forest pool to king. Says anyone bathing there gets a necklace. All eaten—Z49.23.1; Sun Wu-Kung—B241.2.2.1.

MONKEY, TEBE: Origin—A1861.5.

MONSIEUR RAPOTOU: Devil monster—G501 Cooper.

MONSOON: Origin—A1129.2.1.

MONSTER: Hyena disguises self as monster—K335.0.4.3; straw dolls thrown into monster's throat—Q2.1.2Fa; culture hero overcomes monster—A531; maiden rescued from monster lover has rescuer beaten, mourns lost lover—G550.1; sucking monster—F913.5, G332; sun's sons kill monsters—F17.1; Temba cuts off monster's big toe, rescues family—F913.3. SEE CHAPTER G.

OGRES. SEE ALSO GIANT; OGRE; SEA MONSTER.

MONTHS: Twelve months reward kind girl, punish unkind—Q2.1.4. SEE ALSO CALENDAR; MARCH; YEAR.

MONTIERI: Village of fools--J1819.3.1.

MO-O: Giant lizard—B11.2.1.2.1.

MOON: Moon is Anansi who escaped to sky--A711.0.1; Anansi to give moon to son--A740.1; antelope's mother in moon—A751.8.8; Bochica's wife, Chia, becomes moon--A747.1; moon in box --A755.1, A758; offended boy on moon—A751.0.3; boy is disrespectful to moon and is abducted—F53.1; sun and moon brawl--A751.5.2.2; girl with buckets on moon—A751.7+; man on moon with bush--A751.1.4.1, A751.1.5; diving for cheese (moon)--J1791.3; children with yoke and bucket on moon--A751.7; queen to bear children like Sun, Moon, and Star (or with these on forehead)—N455.4; moon is woman's comb hung on sky--A625.2.2.1; moon jumps in cooking pot to kill self, jumps to door sill, roof, tree, sky--A736.1.4.4.1; moon blessed for cool light--L351.2; crab tries to catch moon--B94.1; moon (Chia) is creator himself, Nemequene--A711.1.1; fear moon will burn crops when low in sky--J2271.5; condemned to have coarse cry for addressing moon disrespectfully when sent to awaken--A2426.2.26; moon made by coyote of tule grass--A717.2; coyote steals sun, cuts off pieces for stars and moon--A721.1.5; why coyotes howl at full moon—A717.2, A2427.4.1; cursing vegetable seller flies to moon--A751.1.2.1; Porang on moon shoots souls of dead--A751.0.4; dirt on moon's face--A751.5.2, A751.5.2.3; monster dog in moon--A751.1.10; hare convinces elephant that moon is in lake--J1791.12; K1716; fools try to capture moon in barrel of water--J1791.2.2; frog in moon--A751.3; thistles are only picked in moon of Gobbages—K499.3.1; halfmoon stolen by trickster--K1611G; man pounding chaff with hare--A751.1.6; hare in moon—A755.1.1, A751.2, A751.5.1; Heng O, moon lady--A751.8.7; goddess Hina on moon--A751.8.3.1; hunchback on moon fishes—A751.0.2; hunter shoots arrow in eye of sun and moon, they refuse to rise for three years—A727.3; the moon husband--A762.1Ab; Smith Ilmarine makes moon--A744.1; Princess Kaguya, moon maiden--A752.1.3.1; laughing wife's face on moon--A752.1.4.0.1; why sun and moon live in sky--A736.1.4.4; Luno thrown into sky—A741.4; smoke from Mt. Fuji carries messages of love to moon maiden —A240.1.1; man in moon's origin--A751; mole being carried to moon droped--A2433.3.20.2; moon hangs moss on trees to warm children--A2683.1.1; moon hides food for mother under fingernails--A759.8; mouse seeks moon for spouse--L392.0.1.; Simba Islanders throw mud to dim moon--J2271.6; moon set in sky by Nyame--H621.4.1; lightning, millstone, stars made from old moon--J2271.2.1; origin of light--A1412.4; ostrich feather thrown into sky by Mantis--A741.5; owl in moon--A751.12; helpful woman changed to palm tree by moon--A2681.5; moon's phases--A717.2, A755+, A758.1;

moon torn by sea creatures, god cuts off torn bits and throws into sea = phosphorescence--A2116; moon falls into pit--A754.1.1.1; fool asks where new moon is, looks at pointing finger--J1849.6; man tries to poke moon down--A625.2.7; ruler of moon shows man how to make pottery—A1451.1; powder horn hung on moon--X1851.1; Princess Radha weds Prince Moon--A751.1.9; moon sends message of rebirth to man--A1335.1.0.1; fox tells wolf moon's reflection is cheese--K1021.0.1; duck dives for moon's reflection--J1791.8; fool kills donkey for drinking moon's reflection--J1791.1; raking moon's reflection from pond--J1791.3; riddle, full moon and the thirtieth of the month--H582.1.1; riddle, how big is moon? Four quarters--H691.1.1; sun prince and moon prince kidnapped by water spirits when fail to answer riddle--F420.5.2.2.5; plot to put moon out with salt water--A751.5.8; sand thrown on moon's face—A751.5.2; scaffold to obtain moon, moon breaks--A1861.4, C771.1; moon gives magic shell which draws fish--C322.3; silver is tears of moon--A978.4; how big is moon? Size of penny--H697.1; moon comes for girl on sleigh—A752.1.0.1; smith bored with heaven leaves--Q565Ad; moon snow requested by princess--L393.1; you are the full moon and my sovereign is the new moon--H599.3; pumpkin vine from grateful sparrow grows to moon--A751.1.8; moon child of woman wed to star husband--A762.1Be; moon stolen--A758; moon flees sun--A735.0.1; sun and moon must withstand forest of swords, pond of teeth, etc.--H328.7; sun and moon as man and woman—A736.1; sun and moon as brother and sister--A736.1.2.1; man in moon punished for burning brush on Sunday--A751.1.1; moon flung into sky by Tao—A625.2.11; tarring moon--A751.4; tears on moon--A751.5.6; contest, battle axe thrown to moon--K18.2; bluff, throwing weight into moon--K1746; tower reaches moon--F772.1.2; tower to moon--A751.5.7; tower to moon falls--J2133.6.2; girl with tree on moon--A751.8.5; twin and pets go to heaven and become moon--R111.1.3Ai; which is most useful, sun or moon?--H675; Vela Chow as moon, sun's lover--A736.1.3.1; when mother washes sun and moon, shiny dust falls on earth. Men it falls on become wealthy--N455.4D; woman weaving and cat unraveling on moon--A751.8.1.1; numskull tries to rescue moon from well--J1791.2; selling wind (fan) to buy moon (lamp)—H583.4.7; moon gives yam to man--A1423.1.2; moon goddess gives yerba maté--A2691.6. SEE ALL ENTRIES A740-A759 The Moon.

MOONBEAM: Thief persuaded to climb down moonbeam--K1054.

MOON-CAKE: Boy nibbles moon-cake to make it conform to changes of moon--J1249.4.

MOONFISH: SEE FISH, MOONFISH.

MOONLIGHT: Moonlight to strike thief first--J1149.13.

MOORING PILE: Badger transforms to piling and swims with boat--D612.1.1.

MOORISH RELIGION: Christian prisoner teaches Moors Christianity—D2003; knight with cross on armor slays dragon—B641Dd; lad to endure three nights of beatings to free Moorish girl—H1411.4.3.1; twin brother captured by King of Moors—R111.1.3Aa.

MOORLANDS: Lady of the Moors leads men astray—E425.1.8.

MOOS-MOOS: Anansi and Moos-Moos are caught stealing from Kisander's Dokano pudding tree—K419.11.

MOOSE: Giants killed on horns—G511.2; man weds moose—B651.5.1.

MOOSEBIRD: SEE BIRD, MOOSEBIRD.

MOOWIS: Girl weds man of snow—T117.12.

MORAVIA: Sons and bundle of sticks—J1021.

MORINJI: Temple in Tatebayashi—D1171.3.1.

MORNING: Shoshone learn hymn to the morning from meadowlark—A1461.0.2. SEE ALSO DAWN.

MORNING STAR: Morning star announces coming of day—A712; coyote steals sun from old women, cuts off pieces for moon and morning star—A721.1.5; Morning Star loves Gray Elk—D1898; origin of morning star—A781.1; Scarface as companion of Morning Star—H1284.1; morning star drives spear into earth as strides across sky each morn—A781.1.1; lad weds star of morning—H1385.1C. SEE ALSO VENUS.

MORTAR: Mortar over door falls on intruder—K1161.6; glutton gets head stuck in mortar—J2131.5.2, W125.3.1; magic mortar—D1262; magic mortar won't stop producing—D1651.3.1; mortar found in field taken to king by peasant against daughter's advice. King demands pestle too—H561.1.2; mortar turns rice to gold when pounded—D475.1.6; coin causes rice urn to be self-replenishing—K1161.3.5; stolen magic mortar cannot be stopped and fills sea with salt—A1115.2.1. SEE ALSO GRINDING STONE.

MORYEVNA: SEE MARYA MORYEVNA.

MOSES: Remarkable strong man unable to move when certain feather falls on him—F615.9.

MOSLEM: Hornbill refuses water to Moslems—A2231.7.3; why pork is never eaten by Moslems—A2221.5.3. SEE ALSO ALLAH; HADJI; MOHAMMED; MOSQUE.

MOSQUE: Prayer in tiny mosque more efficacious than prayer in large mosque—J2495.1.1; man asks lodging saying he is God's son-in-law, taken to mosque—J1261.1.1.1; quest for nightingale for mosque—H1331.1.3Ea.

MOSQUITOES: Mosquitoes confer about eating man before big ones come—X1286.1.5.1; God of Medicine lets man restore wife by letting three drops of blood fall, man turns to mosquito, still seeks to get back his blood—A2034.5; firefly carries fire because mosquito tries to bite—Z49.6.0.1; fox prefers sated mosquitoes—J215; mosquito mistaken for ghost—N384.0.2; giant mosquito Moppo shot by coyote's magic arrow shrinks to present size—A2034.4; why there are no mosquitoes on Kambara—A2434.2.4; mosquitoes fly off with kettle—X1286.1.4; king kills mosquito and self with blow of gavel—J2102.3; lie, man sees mosquito on cliff a mile away—X938.1; mosquito loses lying contest to Anansi—X905.1.3; why male mosquito does not buzz or sting—A2426.3.5.1; monster is burned in pit but turns into mosquito—A2034.3.1; origin of mosquitoes in slain monster—A2034.3.2; princess to one who guesses origin of hide—H522.1.1.1; task, stay in room full of mosquitoes without driving them off, tells story and slaps self to illustrate—K263.3; mosquitoes point out room with girls to Tall Tree—W154.8.5.

MOSS: Anansi finds mossy stone which makes one fall unconscious—C498.2.1; moon answers mother's prayer and hangs moss on tree to warm freezing children (origin Spanish moss)—A2683.1.1; origin of red moss on tundra—A2683.1.2.

MOTH: Moth loses lying contest to Anansi—X905.1.3.

MOTHER: Baby camel cries and mother runs to suckle it, judge rules it belongs to owner of this camel—H495.4; advice of mother camel to child proves true—J21.53; motherhood contest, one to fill pot with tears is mother—J1171.1.3; dead mother provides milk for babe—E323.1.1.1; dead mother buried under helpful Juniper Tree—N271; dead mother as helpful animal—B313.1.1; gifts from tree on dead mother's grave—R221B; mother kills son in dove form—D154.1; mother weds dragon, betrays son—S12.1C; mother weds giant and plots to rid self of son—S12.1; Guinea Hen asks eggs what will do for her when hatched—J267.1.1; all mothers to be killed, trickster hides his—K311.3.1, K944; "only one, but a lion!" Lioness thus answers animal who says she has only one child—J281.1; mother seeking food meets twelve months—Q2.1.4Ae; moon answers mother's prayer and hangs moss on trees to warm freezing children—A2683.1; each likes his own children best—T681; poor woman with twelve children drinks rice water left from their meal—P231.3.1; mother sings for three daughters to open door, Philamandré to stay in corner—K311.3K; Solomon's judgment, the divided child—J1171.1; witch as girl gets lad to steal mother's savings—G264.3; twin brothers return home and pour magic liquid on mother's grave, great rock emerges—R111.1.3Ai.

MOTHER-IN-LAW: Mother-in-law believed dead—P262.2; hot soup brings tears. Wife weeps for dead mother, husband because mother didn't take wife with her—J1478.

MOTHER LUCK: Mother Luck fills beggar's sack, must stop her before it breaks—J514.7.

MOTMOT: SEE BIRD, MOTMOT.

MOTZEYOUF: Culture hero teaches sacred rites—A1539.3.

MT. ARAYAT: Hermit judges animals—Z49.6.0.1.

MT. FUJI: Smoke from Mt. Fuji carries emperor's poems to Princess Kaguya in heaven—A240.1.1.

MT. KARANG: Formed by sand spilled by Hanomat —A963.10; top snipped off by Hanomat—A966.1.

MT. MARATI: Stonecrusher is stronger than mountain—Z42.0.2.

MOUNT NAM-NHU: Princess of Mount Nam Nhu appears at Flower Festival in temple garden—F377.0.1.

MT. PATARAIMA: Origin—A1231.3.

MT. PULOSAKI: Formed by sand spilled by Hanomat—A963.10.

MT. RORAIMA: Origin—A1231.3.

MT. SHASTA: Origin—A963.12.

MOUNT TOM: Noises of Devil Chief from Mount Tom—G243.1.2.

MOUNT VERNON, WASHINGTON: Wife of star husband descends via cedar rope on Big Rock Mountain nearby—A762.1Bd.

MOUNTAIN: Creation by flapping of buzzard—A961.1; clapping mountains, clap together at intervals—D1553.1; man on mountain warmed by sight of distant fire—J1191.7.1; princess on glass mountain—H331.1.1; glass mountain—F751; mountains from sand spilled by Hanomat—A963.10; mouse (stonecutter) stronger than mountain—L392ff, Z42.0.2; mountain in labor brings forth mouse—U114; mountains open to magic formula—N455.3; origin of mountains—A852.1, A955, 10.3, A960ff, A969ff; origin of mountains, pieces of rock tossed when great bull smashes rock—A963.11; mountain in Taiwan splits in middle when golden cock killed—B755.2; task, removing mountain in one day—H1331.1.3; task, lifting mountain. Countertask, placing it on my shoulders—H1149.9; task, bring pig as large as mountain—H951.1; mountains are humps on turtle's back—A961; lad sewn in skin to be carried up onto mountain by birds, there to throw down treasure—K1861.1.

MOUNTAIN GOAT: Task, Mountain Goat lends horns so can leap onto head—H335.7.3.

MOUNTAIN LION: Medoc brains badger with cat-tail—K473.2.

MOUSE: Mouse advises girl—Q2.1.2Ea; mouse aids rabbit prince—H1385.3Fg; mouse aids lad —B582.2D; rodents gnaw all straps of sleeping army—B582.2.6; mouse spins for children at Baba Yaga's house—Q2.1.2CeBa; mouse rings bell to lead bear away from girl—Q2.1.3B; bee, harp, mouse and bumclock dance—H341.2.1; belling the cat—J671.1; birds in snare fly to King of Mice who gnaws free—K581.4.1.1; blind man says king holds three mice, the one is pregnant—E279.6.1; boar's ears (wolf's tail) taken for mouse by cat who pounces—K2324.0.1; mouse gnaws enemies' bow strings—K632; mouse teases bull—L315.2; cat as monk with mice worshippers—K815.16.1; mouse tells cat a tale, cat "Even so I eat you"—K561.1.1; association with cat ceases as soon as danger is past—J426; cat feigns dead, mice not deceived—K2061.9; mouse pallbearers eaten by sham dead cat—K827.4.1; mouse persuades cat to wash before eating—K562; mouse let loose to test cat-maiden—J1908.2; chain to sew mouse up—Z41.4.1; mouse and coal go journeying—F1025.1.2; cockroach and her suitors—Z32.3; animals confess sins, larger are absolved—K1024.1; mouse emerges from box and cooks for prince—N831.1; old man rolls down hole into mouse country—N777.0.3; mice trick coyote into bag to escape 'hail'—K711.5; mouse warms man's joints in cold, origin mouse as family crest—B437.2.1; Manabozo puts earth ball on water and sets mouse on it to spin ball—A812.9; enchanter's wife as mouse—D117.1.1; mouse advises Ergosa-Batyr—K1951.1F; mouse helps steal fire—A1415.2.2.2.; prize to carver on whose mouse cat pounces, one carves of fish—K2.1.1; why mouse and flea bother man—A2585.2; mice bite color from tip of fox's tail—A2378.8.1.0.1; frog and mouse tie legs together—J681.1; girl fears nothing, screams at mouse—H1419.2; girls as cat and mouse disenchanted—H1385.3D; mouse advises girl in goblin's clutches—Q2.1.3Ab; mouse tricked by cat as godfather—K372; why mouse's hair is short—A2311.11; helpful mouse makes king think master is wealthy—K1917.3F; hermit turns mouse to cat, dog, etc.—K722, W154.2.1.1; mice generals affect horns and are caught—L332.1; mouse turned to saddle horse for Ashpet—R221K; mouse, bird and sausage keep house—J512.7; iron bar claimed to have been eaten by mice—J1531.2; King of Mice—B241.2.5; mouse climbs to heaven to fetch down light—A1412.6; mouse on lion's mane—J411.8; mouse to wed lion, trampled—B363.1; mouse frees lion and is in turn threatened—J1172.3; mouse frees lion from net—B371.1, B545.2; what is drum made of? Mouse tells. Is louse skin—H522.1.1; mouse forced to retrieve magic object —D882.1; marriage to mouse bride—B641.0.1B; mouse maiden to marry strongest—L392ff; mountain in labor brings forth mouse—U114; mouse leads to cave of outlaw Matthew—V21.7; mouse in corn basket overeats and cannot escape—K1022.1; King of Pigeons is caught in net, mouse gnaws free—K687.2; mouse hides prince in underground nest and gives arrow to prince —H328.10; mouse frees rattlesnake—J1172.3; Saint Cadog and the mouse, mouse brings grain in famine—B437.2.3; mouse escapes fox by singing—K606; all animals confess sins—K1024.1; mouse tail in mouth of sleeping thief causes to cough up stolen object—D882.1; stonecutter makes a crystal ball for mouse to hide in—B437.2.2; cat catches mouse and orders suit of clothes made—Z49.24; boy wins back sun with aid of totem and mouse—A721.3; mouse gnaws snared sun free—A728.1; cat bites off mouse's tail—Z41.4; mouse imitates tailor to make clothes —Z49.3.3; Titty Mouse falls in pot and dies. Tatty Mouse weeps—Z32.2.2; town mouse and country mouse—J211.2; mouse gnaws turtle free —K642.2; mouse helps dig hole to upper world A1024.1; mouse asks wooer how will beat her— Z32.3.2; mouse sees sunrise first, hence Year of the Mouse—K52.3. SEE ALSO RAT.

MOUSE, LONG-NOSED: Beetle throws stick and hits—K688.7.

MOUSE, SHREW: Shrew mouse, Umulumba, and vole mouse, Mgeva, compete for kingship— B241.2.5.1.

MOUSEDEER: SEE KANTCHIL.

MOUTH: Crane removes bone from lion's throat but props mouth open with stick first—K639.1; Brer Rabbit proposes sewing dog's mouth shut— J671.1.1; girl serves seven mouthed prince— Q2.1.1Fa; treasure falls from mouth— D1454.2.0.1; wry-mouthed family—X131.

MOVE: Merchant living between noisy blacksmith and coppersmith pays each to move—N255.8.

MOWING: Mowing contest, ogre given a dull sickle—K42.2.

MUCHIE LAL: Pet fish of Ranee—B644.1.

MUCK, ISLE OF: Bauchan of MacIntosh family travels to America—F482.3.1.2.

MUD: Dupe makes boat of mud, it melts— J2171.1.3; buffalo cakes self with mud and defeats tiger—B264.3; skillful boy taken to court to flick mud pellets into mouth of talkative courtiers—F661.13; ducks dive for earth, mudhen returns dead but with ears full of mud—A812.6; raccoon plasters sleeping wolf's eyes with mud— A2411.2.1.13.1; fool rolls in mud to get 'coat of clay'—J163.2.2; honey eaten by monkey and replaced by mud—K144.3.1; house of mud built by pig—K891.1.1; flowerpot, mud cake, cabbage, flea, feather and needle keep house—J512.7.2; lies about deep mud—X1655.2; duel of leopard and lizard, lizard cakes self with mud—B264.3.1; man made from clay image and vivified— A1241.3; wasp teaches swallow to make nest of mud—A2431.3.5, B362.1; relief from mud pellet by sitting in water—A2491.2.1; mud pony comes alive—D445.1.2; throwing the stone into the cliff, a mud clod is thrown—K18.5; tiger told mud is king's pudding—K1023.1.2. SEE ALSO EARTH; SOIL.

MUDANGS: King has seventh daughter abandoned, becomes Mudang—D2161.5.7.1.

MUDHEN: SEE BIRD, MUDHEN.

MULAN: Girl enters army in father's place— K1837.6.1.

MULBERRY: Mulberry tree favors snake, not man —J1172.3.2.

MULE: Ostler wishes to trade places with archbishop's mule—V119.2.1; mule brags mother was a race horse—J954.1.1; man or runaway mule going "where mule wishes"—J1483.2; thief waves arms at end of field when farmer goes to see, accomplice steals mule—K365.4; wolf reads mule's name on hoof—K1121.0.1.

MULE-DRIVERS: Numskull believes self dead, is beaten by mule drivers—J2311.6.

MULLAH: Thief claims to have been transformed into ass—K403.1; ass's saddle taken in retribution for stolen coat—J1862; persistent beggar invited upstairs for refusal—J1331; borrower finds no corn since he didn't return it last year —J1381; buzzard steals meat "but I've got the recipe"—J2562; warmed by light of distant candle—K231.14.1; stolen meat and weighed cat —J1611; payment with clink of money—J1172.2; welcome to the clothes—J1561.3; his servants could not be the thieves, would not have left the coats—J1179.5; demands ten coins in dream, on waking will settle for nine—J1473; cow was swift when only a calf—J2212.5; cow punished for calf's misdeeds—J1863; believes self dead because of cold hands and feet so allows wolf to eat ass—J2311.7; dead man meets mule driver in heaven—J2311.6; donkey sold for one dinar tied to cat for one hundred dinars—K182.0.1; rider holds sack to relieve donkey—J1874.1; buys donkey for magic nosebag—D1469.1.8; patient ate too many donkeys—J2412.4; three men buy seventeen donkeys. One pays half price, one one-third, one one-ninth. Cannot decide. Mulla adds his donkey making eighteen. Gives first man half = nine, second one-third = six, third one-ninth = two. Rides off on his—J1249.5; biting one's own ear off—J2376, J2376.1; remodeled falcon—J1919.1; pummeled with figs , thank god they weren't turnips—J2563; finder must shout three times in marketplace. Does so at three a.m.—J1161.12; fool's identifying pumpkin tied to another's leg—J2013.3; clever carving of fowl—H601; pays frogs for frightening ass from water—J1851.1.3; test of guilt, pulling donkey's tail—J1141.1.0.1; cannot find right hand in dark—J1735; did the man ever have a head—J2381; horse taught to live without food—J1914; no clothes needed for judgment day —J1511.7; flatters king into buying turban, only he would pay the price—J829.1.1; must carry letter in person as no one can read writing— J2242.1; reduces size of lie—X904.4.1; master must be here as they saw him enter, "I could have gone out the back!"—J1552.1.1.2; stars made from old moon—J2271.2.2; wears net to symbolize humility—J703.3; punishes the ox for last week's misdemeanor—J1861; pot has a child and dies—J1531.3; calls cat in to see if it's raining—W111.2.4; does not recognize own reflection—J1791.7; wife thinks reflection is thief's wife—J1791.7.2; mustn't mention robe— J2512.1; saved from tree with rope—J2434; ass loaded with salt falls in river—J1612; shoots holes in shirt, lucky I wasn't in it—J2235; sign language misunderstood--H607.1.1, J1804.1; soup of the soup of the hare--J1551.6; you are the full moon, my sovereign is the new moon--J599.3; those who know teach those who don't--X452; owner hides from thief, ashamed of poor goods--J1392.1.2; thieves were quarreling over his quilt--J2672; how tower was built, fantastic answers--J2711; calls undertaker as well as doctor--J2516.9; runs to find how far voice will reach from tower--J1941; obstinate wife sought upstream--T255.2; couldn't lift huge stone in youth either--J2214.2. SEE ENTIRE COLLECTIONS Kelsey, Alice. ONCE THE MULLAH, Shah, Idries. THE INCOMPARABLE EXPLOITS OF NASREDDIN MULLA.

MULUNGU: Mulungu has spider spin rope and climbs up to live in sky--A1279.2.

MUNACHAR AND MANACHAR: Z41.10.

MUNCHAUSEN: Munchausen tales--X900.1.

MUNGU: As creator--A2235; Mungu lets Hyena fall--K1041.0.2.

MUNTJAC: SEE DEER.

MURDER: Only brother will help bury murdered man--H1558.1.0.1; dog avenges master's murder--B301.2.1; fool tells of treasure found, kills man, brothers replace body with goat, tale discredited--J1151.1.4; ghost of slain girl appears to murderer--E231.7; murderer revealed--N270ff; servant sent to kill arranges for escape of victim--K512; murder from within body of enemy--F912, K952. SEE ALSO CORPSE.

MUSIC: Origin of music--A1542.2.2. SEE ALSO DANCE; NOTE; SINGING; SONG.

MUSICAL INSTRUMENT: Girl releases instruments from box , cannot return--Q2.1.2; four monkeys invent instruments--A1461.0.1; pigs arranged so as to play tune by pulling pig's tails--J1675.5.1. SEE ALSO BALANGI; FIDDLE; FIFE; FLUTE; GUSLI; HARP; HARPSICHORD; HORN; LUTE; NOTE; PIPE; SINGING; VIOLIN; ETC.

MUSICIAN: Bremen Town musicians--K335.1.4; fiddler on walls plays such melancholy music that enemy becomes homesick and deserts--K2368.6; three musicians enter haunted castle one at a time, unseen hands feed, dwarf beats--K1931.2M; musician strums one note over and over, others searching for perfect note, he has found it--J1060.2; musician saves self from wolf by music--K551.3.1.

MUSKRAT: SEE RAT.

MUSSEL: Mussel releases crow on promise of uncle's kayak and goods--K579.9.1; Ah Po thinks mussels clicking are laughing at him--J2461J.

MUSTARD SEED: Cure for all troubles, burn mustard seed from house with no troubles--

N135.3.2.

MUTSMAG: K1611Bb.

MYSTIC: Mystic threatened with death can't prove powers--J1289.21.

NAGA: Naga keeps girl in cave until fish husband comes for her--B644.1; hairpins made from Naga bones, riddle--J21B; Naga investigates startled animals--Z49.6.0.7; lad kills Naga King and disenchants three daughters--H1321.1E; marriage to Naga--B604.1.1.

NAGASAKI: Rats of Nagasaki--Z11.3.

NAHUAL: Bird as witch--G275.12.3.

NAIL: For want of a nail the horse was lost--Z45; nail soup--K112.2.

NAKED: Naked person made to believe he is clothed--K445; overzealous visitor couldn't wait to dress, goes naked--J2517; task, coming neither naked nor clad--H1054.1.

NAM-NHU: Princess of Mount Nam-Nhu--F377.0.1.

NAMASHEPANI: Fairies--F206.

NAME: Tintinyin learns identity of King of Spirit World, wins contest--B216.4; Skunny-Wundy and fox in name guessing contest--C432.1.3; cuckoo given title of "nightingale"--U119.5.1; grateful dead goes thrice as bird and overhears secret name of princess--E341.1C; dwarf promises mortal much money if he will guess name--D2183; dwarf suitor desists when name is guessed--D2183; fairy maid must stay when name guessed--C31.8; fairy leaves when he is named--F381.1; fool sent for child's name forgets, hears passerby say 'Ridiculous'--J2241.1.1; Silly Matt forgets wife's name and looks for it on ground--J2671.5; man overhears ghosts tell names while sheltering in haunted temple--E443.3.1; guessing name of supernatural creature gives power over him--C432.1; lad with lengthy name refused food, too many of him--J1552.9; man named 'million' sacrificed--H602.3.1; caller writes "Stupid Oaf" on gate, householder goes to see him. "I came as soon as I saw your name on my gate"--J1369.6; 'Ah me', ogre's name uttered--C21; origin of personal names--A1577; secret name overheard eavesdropping--N475; cats seek name of strongest thing in world--L392.0.4; suitor test, learning girl's name--H323+; tabu, prohibition against uttering name--C430; tabu, uttering name of supernatural wife--C435.1.1; animals cannot eat fruit until learn name of tree--J2671.4.1.

NAME, EQUIVOCAL: Escape by assuming equivocal name--K602; answer to each question is "I don't understand" which foreigner takes to be person's name--J1802.1; obtaining goods by use of equivocal name--K359.2ff; peasant tells gatekeeper he is called "me myself," tells Lord he is named "hold me back"--K602.4; cat takes name "Stranger," dog, "Traveler"--A2494.1.5; sausage kept for "The Long Winter"--K362.1; boy who worked for "nothing at all"--J2496.1.

NANANBOUCLOU: Origin of star--A781.2.2.

ÑANDUTI: Paraguayan lace--A1465.2.1.

NAPKIN: Magic date tree cleansed with magic napkin--R221C.   SEE ALSO TABLECLOTH.

NAPLES: Provence and Naples united through marriage--N352.0.1.

NAPOLEON: Shows tailor meaning of fear--J2071.2.

NARWHAL: Origin of narwhal--A2135.1.

NASAN: Giant Nasan has feathered wings made and flies to woo Evening Star--A284.2.1.

NAT: Nat judges against man--J1172.3.2.

NAVEL: Mantis enters through elephant's navel and leaves via trunk--F929.4.

NAVIGANCE: Why waters of Navigance turn white each year--A939.2.

NAXOS: King Naxos introduces squash seeds to populace--J1199.3.

NAZAR: Cowardly hero--K1951.1I.

NECESSITY: 'Necessity' will teach how to fix cart --J103.

NECKEN: Boy tricks necken into wrestling with bear--K11.6. SEE ALSO WATER, WATER SPRITE.

NECKLACE: Bird snatches necklace when hero opens casket--S268B; princess gives half necklace token to dog and cat--R111.1.3Ai; kingfisher wears white necklace--A2321.5; maiden's life depends upon her necklace which must be in possession at all times--E711.4; origin loon's necklace--F952.7.1; monkey dons stolen necklace when tricked into showing off--K1066.1; monkey king in forest takes necklace of demon from forest pool--Z49.23.1; necklaces are exchanged with sleeping ogre's children--K1611; necklace snatched from princess in high window --K331.1.2.2; hero reproduces exactly necklace princess demands--H1931.2.1; necklace dropped into snake's hole by crows--K401.2.2.

NECKTIE: Frozen snake as necktie thaws--X1321.4.11.

NEEDLE: Needle attacks intruder--K1161.3.4; bride test, wed girl whose needle makes no sound as she sews--H383.2.4; needle embroiders room for maid--H1311.2; needles thrown to frogs --J1851.1.5; flees, throws gold needle at pursuing wolf and kills--H1385.6.1; needle carried in hay--J2461C; needle leaps to head of another-- G530.2Bi; flowerpot, mud cake, needle, etc. keep house--J512.7.2; magic needle--D1181.1; cock and hen go nutting, take along needle-- K1161.7.2; serpent pierces skin on needles on floating gourd and dies--R221Di; fools sow needles--J1932.5; needle wrapped in straw-- J2461.1.10; sun sisters stick embroidery needles in your eyes if you look at sun--A736.1.1.1; task, making stove, pan, knife out of needle-- H1022.6.0.1; needle thrown out of window kills thief in treetop--Z11.5; needle as sword for Thumbling--F535.1.1E; tortoise possessed first needle, sews up cracked shell--A2312.1.8; golden needle stuck into Troll's heart to kill-- K1015.1.1B.

NEEDLEWORK: Recognition by unique needlework --H35.3.

NEGRO: SEE RACE, BLACK. SEE ALSO ETHNIC AND GEOGRAPHIC INDEX.

NEPHEW: Origin of Ashanti custom of leaving inheritance to sister's son--A1423.1.1.

NEPTUNE: Creates bull--A46.

NERA: Adventures on Halloween--F302.1.6.

NERO: Old woman prays for safety of cruel tyrant fearing worse successor--J215.2.1.

NEST: How birds learned to build nest--A2431.1; bird to move nest when farmer decides to reap himself--J1031; bird's build first nests-- A2431.3.11; magpie teaches (or is taught) building of nest--A2271.1; riddle, seven tongues in one head, nest in horse's skull--H793; sparrow's nest destroyed by monkey--J1064.2; wasp teaches swallow to make nest of mud--A2431.3.5, B362.1. SEE ALSO BIRD; CAVE, BIRD'S NEST.

NET: Birds in net fly off with net--K581.4.1, K687; deer freed by friends crow, mouse and tortoise--K642.2; small fish escape through net --L331; man wears net on shoulders to remind self of humble origin--J703.3; menehunes flee leaving nets, lad learns how to make-- F451.3.2.1.3; monkey meddles with fishnet, nearly drowned--J516; lion freed from net by mouse--B371.1; origin of net--A1457.3.2; quails (doves) caught in net rise up in body with net and escape--J1024; rat gnaws net--B545.2; man copies spider making web and makes net to catch animals--A1457.3.1; stove wrapped in net to keep from escaping--J1942.1; witch's magic steel net thrown over witch--G263.1.0.1.1. SEE ALSO SNARE.

NETTLES: Boy grasps nettles too lightly--J656.2.

NEW AMSTERDAM: Meerschaum pipe summons St. Nicholas--D1662.4.

NEW YEAR'S EVE (DAY): Cave opens only on New Year's Eve--C761.4; sandal seller trades wares with charcoal seller. On New Year's Eve charcoal turns to gold--F342.1.3; kind ferryman gives ride to ill man on New Year's Eve-- N534.9; origin New Year's customs of red papers and firecrackers--A1541.7; to grab bridle of horse passing on New Year's Day--N250.5; six Jizos bring food to door on New Year's Eve--J1873.1; stones of Plouhinec go to river to drink on New Year's Eve--N511.6.1.

NEW YORK: Why there are pigeons in New York-- A2434.4.1.

NEWCASTLE: Coal is sold in Newcastle--N411.6.

NEWS: Chain of bad news--Z46; bad news delivered so that victim states the tragedy himself-- J1675.2.1.

NEZ PERCÉ: Nez Percé girl weds Blackfoot boy, origin enmity between tribes--A1388.2; origin of Nez Percé--A1610.8.

NGAU LANG: Heavenly shepherd Ngau Lang weds spinning maiden Chuc Nu--A778.3.2.

NICOLA PESCE: Lad holds up pillar supporting Sicily--A842.3.

NIGHT: Fools with shutters closed think it night --J1819.3.1; fool thinks caught night under basket--J1961.2; behind me night, before me day, formula for fleeing--R255; purse in dead Djabbe's stomach contains day and night-- F912.2.8; night in package ripped open by weasel--A1174.1.1. SEE ALSO DARKNESS; DAY; NOCTURNAL.

NIGHT, GREAT NIGHT: Woos maid--B642.6.2.

NIGHTCAP: Nightcaps exchanged with ogre's children--K1611B; monkeys imitate peddler selling nightcaps--B786.1.

NIGHTGOWN: Spriggans enchant nightgown and it prickles thereafter--F351.2.1.

NIGHTHAWK: SEE BIRD, NIGHTHAWK.

NIGHTINGALE: SEE BIRD, NIGHTINGALE.

NILI: Creates earth--A852.1.

NIPU: Makes sky--A852.1.

NIRANTALI: Nirantali lets cat into house-- A2513.2.4; creates horse--A1881.2.

NIX: Nix at millpond abducts man--F420.5.2.2.3. SEE ALSO WATER, WATER SPIRIT.

NOAH: A1021.

NOCTURNAL: Why nocturnal--A2491ff.

NOISE: Man complaining of noise level advised to add more animals to household--Z49.15; donkey thinks Karbau is making row, is really small dog --J132.1.

"NOMAN": Equivocal name given--K602.

NONSENSE: Cumulative nonsense, each repeats the other--Z54.

NORTH: Fox asks bear with seagull in mouth which way wind blows--K561.1.0.5. SEE ALSO WIND, NORTH.

NORTHERN LIGHTS: Piece of light trapped in seal gut and given to former owner and daughter who move to North Pole--A795.1; robin sets fires--A2411.2.1.18.3; Northern Lights as suitor keeps Linou waiting--A778.11. SEE ALSO AURORA BOREALIS.

NOSE: Fools stick noses in mud to count selves-- J2031; dog to be chief of animals as soon as he dries his wet nose at man's fire--A2513.1.4; why dog's nose is wet--A2335.2.6; man steals magic drum, nose pulled long--J2415.22; dwarf long nose--D1376.1.4; why elephant has long nose-- A2335.3.3; fairies give good man short nose, bad long--F344.1; return feast, each insults other's nose--J1565.1.5; Golden Turtle or Buddha gives white flowers to make nose grow-- D551.1C; fly on nose, told to kill fly wherever he sees one--J1193.1; immortals pull nose long-- J2415.25; gullible husband made to believe he has cut off wife's nose--J2315.2; husband believes wife's cut-off nose grew back--K1512; Raven's beak thought to be nose of the Konakadet--A2335.2.3; magic object makes nose long --D1376.1.3; why ox's nose is smooth-- A2221.5.1; Polish landlord asks ragged tenant if he is not cold, "Is your nose cold?" "No." "I'm all nose."--J1309.1; snake pulls nose of unkind man out long--Q2.1.1Ea; troll with nose three ells long to wed maid's lost husband--H1385.4Aa; wish, whatever pulled will be long. Nose pulled --J2071.1.

NOSEBAG: Dupe buys donkey for 'magic' nosebag --D1469.18.

NOSEGAY: Princess to say 'please' to get nosegay --R222.1.

NOTE: Lad tells tale, ends with fox opening note which says "now princess can eat for she has laughed"--H341.5.

NOTE, MUSICAL: Man plays same note over and over, has perfect note--J1060.2; frozen note thaws and plays--X1623.7.2.

NOTHING: Bandit forced to trade 'nothing' for killing club--D831B; equivocal name 'nothing-at-all'--K359.2.3; agrees to work for 'nothing', demands payment--J1521.5.2; boy who worked for 'nothing at all' goes to town and demands 'nothing at all'--J2496.1.

NOTORIETY: Dog thinks clog is distinction, mistakes notoriety for fame--J953.1.

NOTRE DAME: Virgin smiles at tumbler--V92.

NOVA SCOTIA: Whale given tobacco to smoke for ferrying Kuloskap to Nova Scotia--A2479.14.

NOY, MR. Girl to be freed if lover refrains from eating or drinking until all fairy babies are rocked to sleep—F320.4.

NTZI: God—A1811.4.

NU KUA: Goddess creates mankind—A1241.3.

NUGGET: Man takes gold nugget to Khan, wife substitutes rock—J1151.0.1.

NULIAJUK: Orphan girl thrown overboard, origin seals, walrus—A2101.

NUMSKULL: SEE FOOL.

NUN: Nun is transformed badger—D421.8.

NURSE: Cherry tree blossoms every anniversary of nurse's death—E631.6.1.

NUT: "Ay, ay, ay" nuts—H1377.3; cracking nuts taken for bones crackling—D2183.1 Eells; boy with hand full of nuts in pitcher—W151.9.1; boy hiding from father changes to nut—Z43.5; girl rolls nuts to fairy babies—L145.1B; magic fox comes from nut and aids—D1033.2; task, shelling walnuts, tokgabbies aid—R221I. SEE ALSO ALMOND; HAZELNUT; PEANUT; PINE NUT; WALNUT.

NUT SHELL: Dress in nutshell—R221D; nutshells traded for bag of leaves and dung—J1516.

NUT TREE: Nut tree pulled to pieces to get nuts —W154.6; man contends pumpkin vines should not produce larger fruit than nut tree—J2571.

NYAME: SEE SKY GOD.

NZAMBI: God—A2231.10.

OAK: Conifers flaunt green needles in winter's face as promise of spring. Oak joins them— A2765.2; owl advises killing oak saplings since birdlime will be made of mistletoe on oaks— J621.1. SEE TREE, OAK.

OATMEAL: Magic mill floods home with oatmeal— D1651.3.1.

OATS: Oats carried out one at a time—Z11.1.

OBSIDIAN: Ground squirrel carries off acorns, sunflower seeds, obsidian chips, back is strip-ed from sharp obsidian—A721.1.2.

OBSTACLE: Fugitives throw objects behind them which magically become obstacles—D672.

OCEAN: Frog swallows ocean—A751.3.1.3; ocean created when Brer Rabbit cuts string holding banks of river together—A924.5. SEE SEA.

OCHARA: Church of Ochara unearthed—H171.7.

OCTOPUS: Octopus helps build canoe, catches shaken fruit in test—F601.2Ga; Ratu defeats Giant Octopus—B874.9; octopus beats jellyfish and is banned—K544.1 Sakade; why octopus lives alone—A2433.8; octopus forces shark to promise to leave men alone—B477.

ODALA: Girl sings and fruit grows—Q2.1.6D.

ODIN: Vow sworn on Odin Stone—E321.6.

ODYSSEUS: Meet cyclops—K602.0.1.

OEDIPUS: Answers riddles of Sphinx—C822.

OG: Giant Og rides on roof of ark—F531.6.12.8.2.

OGOUN: God of iron—A781.2.1.

OGRE: Ogre's beard caught in split anvil— K1111.1; ogress spits in face and calls, "My body to you, yours to me"—R221N; ogre/ogress turns brothers to birds or holds captive— P253.2E; ogre to build stairway before cockrow— K1886.3.1.1; daughter promised to ogre as bride—D735.1, H1385.4; ogre told he has died, runs home to see if is true—J2311.15; ogre grieves for can never know a family—G586; ogres tricked into fighting each other—K1082; the ogre's heart in the egg—D532; ogre intrud-er killed by hidden needle, stone, etc.— K1161.3; secret of eternal soul learned by de-ception—D532, E710, K956; stealing from ogre to help a friendly king—G610; stupid ogre in-timidated by trickster—G501; youth promised to ogre visits ogre's house—G530.2Be, G530.2Bg, G530.2Bi, G530.2Bk, G530.2Bl, S211, S222, V21.7. SEE ENTIRE CHAPTER G. OGRES. G400-G499 Falling into ogre's power and G500-G599 Ogre defeated.

OGRE, ONI: Oni-Roku builds bridge—C432.1.1; Issun Boshi defeats ogres—F535.1.1E; man hid-ing on Jizo's head crows and gambling oni flee— N777.0.2; Momotaro defeats oni—T543.3.2; old woman cooking for oni steals their rice paddle and flees—J1791.3.2.2, N777.0.1. SEE ALSO GIANT; MONSTER.

"OH AND ALAS": Ogres name uttered, he ap-pears—C21.

OIL: Oily coins betray thieves—J1141.1.3.4.2; oil is clear as water so fool buys water—J2478.

OJJE: Remarkable strong man unable to move feather which falls on him—F615.9.

OKAB: Yusaf promises son to Giant Okab— G530.2Bl.

OL' BOY: SEE DEVIL.

OLD: Old people banished to mountains, hidden old person saves kingdom by wisdom—J151.1; debate over who is oldest—B841.1.1; young claims old bolts food since has no teeth to chew, old claims young eats more because has teeth— J234; aged animal saved by faked rescue—

K231.1.3.3; love through sight of finger, old woman chosen--T11.4.8; old man sends traveler to older, etc.--F571.2; raven child who says will not save parents when they are old is the one saved. He must save his young—J267.1; son carves wooden bowl for father to use in his old age since that is all he gives grandfather—J121.1; son asks father to save sled used to abandon grandfather since he will need it for his father later--J121.3; youth and old age are alike. He couldn't lift this stone in youth either—J2214.2; choice of suffering in youth or old age --J214; old lady tells condemned lad she will free if he weds her, turns to young girl after wedding--T91.4.1.2. SEE ALSO AGE.

OLD MAN: Old Man Above--A963.12; wife makes old man carry her in bag up to dovecote holding bag in teeth--D861.1K. NOTE THAT ALL TALES CONTAINING OLD MEN ARE NOT GIVEN IN REFERENCE HERE.

OLD MAN ABOVE: Makes Mt. Shasta--A963.12.

OLD WOMAN: Old woman is adopted by animals and lightning--K1711.2.3; old woman asks who will spend night, bear answers and eats--Z13.1B; boar makes demands of old lady--K1161.3.4; old woman gives magic box to baker's son--D882.1Ec; old woman returns rolling in drum and escapes ogre--K553.0.3; old woman sees tail under coat of one of fox men--D313.1.2; old woman is pursued by green rolling gourd—R261.2; princess brought to laughter by indecent show in quarrel with old woman at well—H341.3.1; animals rout intruder for old woman--K1161.3; old woman monster sucks in all—F912.2.11; old woman in moon--A751.8.1.1; old woman jeers and falls into pit with animals--K735.0.1; old woman and strange visitor--Z13.1; wolf demands magic coin found by old woman—K1161.3.5. NOTE THAT ALL TALES CONTAINING OLD WOMEN ARE NOT GIVEN IN REFERENCE HERE.

OLIVE: Olive brags of never losing her leaves, heavy snow breaks--J832.1; task, tending olive twig until sprouts--H1129.12.

OLLI: Troll offers own daughter as bride to three brothers--G610Ag.

OLODE: Hunter finds land behind door in tree—C611.1.

OLOKUN: Princess sacrificed to Olokun, God of the Sea--R111.1.2Ai.

OLOJA: Oloja sends eclipse--J1172.3.0.6.

OLUWERI: Girl pulled into pool by goddess Oluweri--A2494.13.10.3.3.

OLWEN: Einion weds fair Olwen, bears Taliessin--F302.1.5.

OMELETTE: Shah charged fantastic price for omelette--U85.

OMEN: Peasant accused of being bad omen for ruler to see, beaten. Peasant, "Who is a bad omen for who?"--J1289.24.

ONEATA: Why there are no shellfish on Oneata--A2434.2.4.

ONI: SEE OGRE, ONI.

ONÍ: Oní born with boots on which grow as he grows—H36.1.2.

ONION: Men see each other as cows, eating onions remedies this--D551.2.5; jackal gets tops of onion crop--K171.1; origin of onion shaped iron lanterns——A1447.3.1; origin custom of planting onions--A1441.5; Pleiades are six wives cast out for eating onions--A773.2.1; onion helper flies into tiger's eye--K1161.6.

ONIROKU: Ogre and carpenter—C432.1.1.

OOKA: SEE ENTIRE COLLECTION Edmonds, I. OOKA THE WISE.

OOLICHANS: Why people share oolichans with raven--A2229.7.

OONA: Oona and Finn McCoul--K521.4.1.5.

OOSTERLITENS: Dream of treasure on bridge—N531.1.1.

OOZI: Elephant driver left dangling in tree—J2133.5.0.1.

OPEN: Secret formula for opening treasure mountain overheard--N455.3.

OPIUM: Drunkard in cemetery poses as ghost, learns of buried treasure. Opium eater imitates --J2415.12; opium eater spends night in haunted house—N612.3.

OPOSSUM: Possum bones thrown into river turn into man—A1263.7.1; why opossum plays dead--A2466.1; escape by shamming death—K522; Hairy Man turns to opossum, trapped—B524.1.2H; hare goes ahead and creates trouble for late arriving possum--T92.11.2; sleeping possum framed for theft by Brer Rabbit who rubs stolen butter on mouth--K401.1; opossum releases Brer Snake from brick, Brer Rabbit re-enacts--J1172.3; why opossum has bare tail—A2317.12; Buh Possum catches Buh Rabbit with tar man--K741.0.3.1.

"OR ELSE": Do this "or else"--K1771.2.

ORANGE: Youngest daughter wishes to wed Great Bear of Orange—D735.1B; healing oranges cure princess--H346; imaginary oranges, father rebukes son for presenting such big ones—W152.18; orange leaf heals princess--N452E; maidens from opened orange--D721.5; fruit causes nose to grow—D551.1; tree to bear quinces if plays sad tune, oranges if lively—D1223.1; orange tree grows when girl sings—Q2.1.6Db.

ORANGUTAN: Kantchil calls "I told you to bring two tigers" to orangutan bringing tiger—K1715.2.1; why tiger eats orangutan—A2494.10.4.

ORDEAL: Guilt or innocence established by ordeal--H220.

ORGAN: Pig organ, pull tails—J1675.5.1.

ORGAN GRINDER: Lures foxes from hole--K815.15.

ORIGINS: Origin Rock Olumo--R111.1.3A. SEE CHAPTER A.

ORIOLE: SEE BIRD, ORIOLE.

ORION: King of Stars discusses Christ Child's birth--V211.1.2.2; origin Orion—A722.1.

ORISHA: Orisha gives hawk permission to take chicks—A2494.13.10.3.2.

ORKNEY: Origin Orkney--R111.1.4A; origin one of Orkney Isles--F742.1; St. Magnus routs army—V229.7.3. SEE ALSO ETHNIC AND GEOGRAPHIC INDEX.

ORPHANS: Shoeless orphan boy sticks bare foot in face of monster—J1782.8.1; orphan gains fortune--N421.1; miser avoiding tax forced to take in orphans, thus no tax--J1179.15.

ORPHEUS: Journey to the land of dead—F81.1.

OSA LAGOON: Origin—R111.3Ai.

OSANYIN: Origin of Tortoise sacrifice to Osanyin—A1545.3.4.

OSGAERT: Osgaert, devil ghost leads lad astray—E421.3.8.

OSTLER: Ostler wishes to trade places with archbishop's mule--U119.2.1.

OSTRICH: SEE BIRD, OSTRICH.

OTTER: Dog, falcon, otter aid lad—R111.1.3Cd; otter given gift of not feeling cold--A2411.2.6.14.1; fish shared cut lengthwise--J1249.6; fox divides fish for otters, keeps middle—K452.1.1; hare tricks otter and badger out of goods--K441.5; why otter lives in water—A2433.2.2.1.

OTTER, LAND OTTER: Drowned son (nephew) as Land Otter—E324.3.

OTTER, SEA OTTER: Girl becomes Sea Otter--T75.2.1.1.

OUTLAW: Outlaw Matthew carries water in mouth to water tree in penance--V21.7. Robin Hood--N884.1. SEE ROBBER; THIEF.

OUTSIDER: Partridge notices that game cocks mistreat even each other—J892.

OVEN: Girl aids oven—Q2.1.2; oven built on cart since can't decide which way should face--J1041.3; aid to woman cleaning oven—Q2.1.2G; ogre deceived by feigned ignorance, hero must be shown how to get into oven—— G526; ogre burnt in own oven—G512.3.2; rat invited into warm room = oven—K251.1.2.

OWEN: Owen answers riddles and becomes heir, taken to fairyland--F373.1.

OWL: SEE BIRD, OWL.

OX: SEE COW, OX.

OYSTER: Oyster catches beak of crane (heron) trying to eat him—J219.1.

PACA: Paca has dull coat. lost race with beetle—A2411.1.7.2, K11.10.

PACHACAMAC: God Pachacamac gives magic sandals to Hualachi--D1521.1.1; granddaughter of Pachacamac gives manioc—A2685.5; Pachacamac as condor gives potato--A2686.4.4.

PACKETS: Student given three packets to open in need--J21C.

PADDLE: Duck dives for copper paddle--F601.2I. SEE ALSO RICE PADDLE.

PADISHAH: Padishah's daughter kidnapped nightly--F1015.1.1C.

PADRE ULIVO: Padre Ulivo offers hospitality to twelve strangers—Q565Ai.

PAGODA: White Snake Lady is imprisoned under pagoda—B656.2.1.

PAINTING: Journey to Land of Cats, gift is picture of dog—J2415.9; painted cat kills rat demon—D435.2.1.1; picture of Christ appears miraculously on painter's easel--V121.0.1; paints cock in five minutes, practiced one year—H504.4; emperor drowns in painted sea storm—D435.2.1.2; rapid painting, ten earthworms painted with fingers--H504.3; painted fish swims off--D435.2.1.3; painter's apprentice scolded for losing fish from basket, paints fish on stairs, taken for real—H504.1.4; painting comes to life—D435.2.1ff; marriage to heavenly maid emerging from painting—T111.1.5; origin of specific painting—A1465.9.1; miraculous image of Virgin Mary appears painted on shawl—V121.1; maid emerges from painting and encourages student—T111.1.5.1; mother-in-law sets fire to chest of paintings but daughter pulls out picture of waterfall and quenches flames--D434.2.1.4. SEE ALSO ARTIST; SCROLL.

PAKALA: Pakala and Tandala--J1516.

PALACE: SEE CASTLE.

PALANQUIN: Jackal invites tiger into palanquin--K714.2.4.3.

PALLBEARERS: Mouse pallbearers eaten by sham dead cat---K827.4.1.

PALM: Tortoise steals food by means of dancing palm tree—K741ff; man weaving palm basket in palm tree daydreams of profits, kicks and falls from tree—J2061.5; palm tree judges against man--J1172.3.2; task, climbing palm with bowl of laban on head--H331.10.1; woman helpful to tribe is changed into palm tree by moon—A2681.5.

PALM SUNDAY: Baby trapped in magically opened treasure cave which opens only on Palm Sunday--B11.6.2.4.

PALM WINE: Palm wine tapper's pots broken on three nights, follows deer to adventure—B216Ac; palm wine tapper gives wine to "whence we come" not to "whence we go", judge advises giving to past—J313; witch gives palm wine to animals and twin and turns to stone--R111.1.3Ai.

PAMPAS: Gaucho doomed to roam pampas forever—E513.

PAMPERO: South Wind Pampero brings rain--A282.2.

PAN: Magic flying pan carries hero after abducted princess--F1015.1.1Bb; hillman borrows saucepan--F451.5.10.4.1; rat bride arrives in frying pan—B641.0.1Bd.

PAN KOTSKY: K2324.

PAN KU: World created by Pan Ku--A610.

PANCAKE: Fleeing pancake rolls away—Z33.1ff; nibbled pancake taken for lace--D2183C; talkative wife discredited with pancake rain tale—J1151.1.1.

PANCHO VILLA: Devil as Pancho Villa's horse--G303.3.3.1.3.

PANDERER: Bird saves girl from panderer by telling her tale—T53.0.2.

PANDITIJI: Panditiji addresses quava trees—J2368.

PANDORA: Pandora's box--C321.

PANTHER: Drunkard rides panther--J1758.5; fox and panther contest beauty—J242.3; hummingbird pecks mud from eyes of panther—A2411.2.1.19.3; panther threatens mouse rescuer--J1172.3.

PANTS: Jumping into the trousers—J2161.1; boy in moon with pants leg missing—A751.0.3; princess loves man so poor has no clothing, one pair of pants between self and father—T91.6.4.4; Sultan's baggy trousers filled with bees—Z52.4. SEE ALSO CLOTHING, TROUSERS.

PAPANTLA: Image of Virgin walks to Papantla each night--V143.2.1.

PAPENBURG BRIDGE: Dream of treasure--N531.1.

PAPER: Paper charm under table leg makes all chant--D1413.17; paper charm under pillow which causes all to sleep--T72.2.1; paper crane to ride to Land of Perpetual Life--E80.5; girl sent in paper dress to fetch strawberries in winter--Q2.1.4B; task, bring wind and fire in paper = fan and lantern--H506.12, H583.4.7.

PAPERBAG: Haunted object is paperbag--H1411.4.2.

PAR BEACH: Fairies' destination--F282.4.

PARADISE: Good brother visits paradise--Q1.1C; student from 'Paradise' is given goods for dead there--J2326.1; thief has gone up to heaven, steals horse while dupe looks up--K341.9. SEE ALSO HEAVEN.

PARADOX: Deaf man hears scream, blind man sees, crippled man runs for help--X1791.1.1.

PARALYZE: Old woman paralyzes would be murderer—D2072.7.

PARAMOUR: Guest reveals where wife has hidden food for paramour--J1344ff; hidden cuckold offers rhymes revealing presence--K1556. SEE ALSO LOVER.

PARCHEESI: Brothers lose all gambling--H1331.1.3Ag.

PARENTS: Cow punished for calf's misdeeds, should have taught calf better--J1863; dead parents appear, living in palace, in order that peasant girl can wed king--E328; lad sells parents for money--H808. SEE ALSO FATHER; MOTHER.

PARIS: St. Genevieve persuades Parisians not to desert city—V229.7.2.

PARROT: SEE BIRD, PARROT.

PARSLEY: Frog is girl Parsley taken by witch—B641A; parsley stolen from witch (Rapunzel)--F848.1.

PARSON: Herdsman disguises as abbot and answers questions—H561.2. SEE ALSO PREACHER; PRIEST; ETC.

PARTNERS: Elephant and giraffe farm with hare. Each think other does half work--K364.1; two hunt or steal together. Trickster reports approaching enemy and partner flees leaving game--K335.0.1. SEE ALSO COMPANIONS.

PARTRIDGE: SEE BIRD, PARTRIDGE.

PARTY: Owl blinded for reading at party--A2491.2.5; owls at party kept past dawn—J2332.1.1. SEE ALSO FEAST.

PARVATI: Parvati turns cat into maiden--B601.12.

PASSOVER: Elijah visits in disguise--Q1.1D.

PASSWORD: Secret formula for opening treasure cave--N455.3.

PAST: Palm wine tapper advised to prize future more than past--J313; travel into past--D2138.1. SEE ALSO FUTURE.

PASTURE: Thief asks trickster where he will pasture next day--K688.1.

PATH: Farm claimed on basis of path to it--K453.1; men feasting magically create path and man follows it home--D2031.0.2.1.

PATIENCE: Patient wife Griselda--H461; way to tame a lion--B848.2.1; displaced bride tells wrongs to stone of patience--K1911.1.4.

PATRICK: Dark Patrick--L223.

PAULA GAMBARA COSTA DE BENEVAGIENNA (LADY PAULA): V412.3.

PAW: Dupe puts paws into cleft of tree--K1111; why mole's paws are turned backward--A727.2;

PEA: Bird drops pea in mill handle, chain ensues--Z41.6.2; monkey lets all peas drop to search for one--J344.1; princess on the pea--H41.1; all of replenishing food never to be eaten--D877.0.2; old lady given hundreds of peas to sow, one grows to sky--Z52.4.2; student with pocketful of peas thought to have pocketful of money and is treated royally--K1952.0.3; trail of peas to find way home--S62.1C.

PEACE: Eternal peace in land hidden through time--F173.2.1; fox tells cock of peace among animals--J1421; animals pledge peace and each reveals his pet peeve--W141.1.1; origin of peace pipe--A1533.1; men quarrel even while smoking peace pipe, Great Spirit turns them to Indian Pipe plants--A2667.

PEACH: Peach blossom land hidden through time--F173.2.1; magic peach--F81.1.0.1; Momotaro born from giant peach--T543.3.2; fruit causes nose to grow--D551.1.

PEACOCK: SEE BIRD, PEACOCK.

PEAHENS: Youngest son catches peahens robbing golden apple tree--H1385.3Ja.

PEANUT: Brer Rabbit cheats in peanut farming--K171.1, K364.2; witch crackling bones pretends is eating peanuts--K311.3H.

PEAR: Self-replenishing pear obtained by climbing on statue of Buddha--D1652.1.7.3; healing pear cures princess--H346; lie, giant pear--X1411.4; fruit causes nose to grow--D551.1; pear seed grows and bears as is watched--F971.7.1; pear seed which will bear golden pears if planted by man with no guilt--H263.1;

quest for pears for ill mother--Q2.1.2Fa.

PEAR TREE: Pear tree carries man about when he wishes could see all kingdom from its top--D1720.1.5; Death magically bound to a tree--Z111.2.1.1; Devil sticks to pear tree--Q565Af; brothers given wish when offer pear to stranger--Q1.1A.

PEARL: Boy caught by clam persuades clam he feels pearl and clam opens--K561.1.0.2; cock prefers single corn to peck of pearls--J1061.1; pearl color of fig will disenchant rosebush--N271B; dragon must spit out pearl--H1273.2M; dragon can't enter heaven until pearl removed from head--H1273.2L; hen loses hawk's pearl necklace, it breaks--A2494.13.10.3.1; crow forced to give magic wish granting jade--D551.1C; magic jewel dropped into sea, Da Trang still searches in form of crab--B216B; magic pearl used by fox in transformation--D313.1.5; snake asks why has not become a spirit, must remove pearl from head--H1273.2J; poor man with no money but sense multiplies money for rich man with no sense, causes mollusks to produce pearls--J1061.5; one hundred bushels of pearls buried on seashore--R221J; princess weeps pearls, recognized by sight of type of pearl which she weeps--H71.8.1.

PEASANT: Peasant outwits baron, persuades to change horses--K289.1; why bear and peasant are enemies--A2494.8.3; bear and peasant divide crops--K171.1; boyar insists peasant work till sun's little brother, the moon, sets also--J1530.0.1; peasant to recognize king, will be the one with the hat on--J1289.27.

PEBBLES: Pebbles strewn to find way home--G412.1.1.

PEDDLER: Peddler hides cuckolded man in basket to overhear--K1556.

PEERIFOOL: D2183D.

PEG: Peg not sold with house--K182.3.

PEIK: Tricky Peik--K110.1.

PEIKO: Stupid ogre--G501D.

PEKING: Water stolen by dragon--B11.7.1.

PEKKA: K110.1.

PELE: Goddess of fire, Pele--A493.1; Pele destroys lehua groves of Hiiaka--A285.2; pig man changed to fish for trying to woo Pele--A2130.1; Goddess of Snow duels with Pele--A289.2.

PELICAN: SEE BIRD, PELICAN.

PENNY: Boy loses penny, given another wails, "If I hadn't lost mine, I'd have two now"--W211.1.1; how big is moon? Size of penny, holds penny up and it covers moon--H697.1; three pennies multiply--D2100.2.1.

PEONY: Poet weds peony maiden—D621.2.2.1.

PEPPER: Pepper given as ointment for burns—K1014; crow cheats sparrow in red pepper eating contest—Z41.2.2.1; hot peppers fed cows so they flee tax collector—K1181.1; crocodile allowed to eat king's peppers, are hot peppers—K1023.1.3; lie, hot peppers grown by planting when mad—X1439.1; test, eating red peppers without grimacing—K263.3; peppers thought to be called "Whee-ai"—H1377.3; pepper put on witch's skin—G229.1.1.

PEPPERCORN: Peppercorn oxen, size of peppercorn—B184.2.2.3.

PEPPI: Peppi and the magic ox—B335.2H.

PEPPINO: Peppino seeks princess abducted—K1931.2G.

PER, LORD PER: K1917.3D.

PERI: Crow Peri aids—H1151.6.2.2; peri kidnaps princess nightly—F1015.1.1C; quest for item from Queen of Peris—N455.4Ad.

PERSIMMON: Sis Cow tricked into running horn into persimmon tree by Brer Rabbit—K771.

PESTLE: Sky poked when pestle moves off—A625.2.2.1ff.

PET PEEVE: Animals pledge peace and each tells pet peeve—W141.1.1.

PHAM: Wife remarries, first husband returns, first burnt by accident, other two commit suicide—T211.2.1.1.

PHEASANT: SEE BIRD, PHEASANT.

PHILIPPINES: Kite flies too near sky and sky drops earth on sea = Philippines—A817.1.

PHILOSOPHER: Philosopher in farmer's clothing working in field is questioned by traveling theologian—J31.1.1; king prefers educated men as company—J146.1; peasant addresses man carrying grapes with high titles hoping to get grapes, man says he is as learned as philosopher so why give donation to his equal—J1289.4.1. SEE ALSO SAGE; WISE MAN; ETC.

PHOENIX: SEE BIRD, PHOENIX.

PHOSPHORESCENCE: Pieces of moon thrown into sea = phosphorescence—A2116.

PHYAIM: Protector of the Buddha—A773.8.

PHYSICIANS OF MYDDFAI: Fairy wife teaches sons art of healing—F420.6.1.5.1.

PHYSICIANS: SEE DOCTORS.

PICARO: SEE BIRD, PICARO.

PICT: Scots try to get secret of brewing heather ale from last two Picts who know secret—C429.2.

PICTURE: Love through sight of picture—S268; quest because of sight of picture—H1213.1G, H1213.1J; wife paints pictures to sell. They are recognized as work of Sultan's daughter by Turks and she is stolen back—E341.1D. SEE ALSO PAINTING.

PIE: Girl must eat of pudding, apple, pie before they will hide her—Q2.1.2CeA; woman's daughter eats five pies. She sings of this—D2183; Toontoony bird to be made into pie—Z49.3.2.

PIECE: Land where everything is cut into pieces—Q589.4.

PIED PIPER: D1427.1.

PIERRE OF PROVENCE: Provence and Naples unite when Pierre weds—N352.0.1.

PIF PAF POULTRIE: Z31.1.

PIG (HOG): Pig's acorns explode in intruder's face—K1161.4; pig from which bacon can be cut repeatedly—G610Ae; child born with pig head—T551.3.5; dead sweetheart follows faithless lover in form of pig—E211.3; pig feigns deaf until pancake comes close—K911.5, Z33.1.7; owner convinced pig is dog—K451.2.2; sow claims her young better than dogs—J243.1; hog eats dynamite and blows up—X1233.2.1; trickster says fears pigs and bees, these are thrown at him—K975.1.2; goblin pig helps girl wash—C311.1.5; hogs root up gold for saint—B562.1.1; haunted object—H1411.4.2; pig goes to build a house—B296.0.1; pig told by judge raven he may have "corn and peas and silken bed"—J2671.4.2; pig man changed to fish—A2130.1; Juan Bobo dresses pig to go to mass—J1849.5; why pork isn't eaten by Moslems—A2221.5.3; pig organ, tails pulled to produce squeals—J1675.5.1; ox envies pigs' diet—J212.2; pig offers ride to fleeing pancake—Z33.1.1; mother feigns ill, needs porker of the sow in the other world—S12.1C; hog butchered, wife gives to "Present Need"—K362.1.1; why pigs root—Z33.1.7; pig in silver wood asks lad to kill witches with silver branches—D136.1; pig shrieks on way to slaughter—J1733; imitation pig squeal applauded, real mocked—J2232; man kills pig, taken by Master of Stone—H1561.1; why hog lives in sty—J2671.4.2; hog sees sunrise first—K52.1; all pigs with curly tails belong to trickster—K171.4; trickster claims pigs were lost in mud, only tails showing—K404.1.1; tall hog, man can't touch if reaches his highest—K196.2; task, bring pig as large as mountain—H951.1; thief thinks pig is smith with tongs—K1161.2; three little pigs—K891.1.1; throwing water on pig, keeps doing all day what begun—J2073.1; pig entices girls to trolls' lair—G561G; pigs' heads pushed in trough, choke—J1903.5; pig's trunk caught in bamboo tube, cut off—A2335.4.1.1; water buffalo envies pig—L457; hog offers to save lad if will wed—K31.1; youngest daughter to wed pig from the north—H1385.4I; girl weds suitor with gold teeth, turns to pig—G303.12.5.12; pig, gives wish for wisdom—B375.1.3; witch in form of hog—G211.1.6; witch turns lad to goose, pig—G263.1.0.3; five little pigs and wolf—K891.1.1.4; one little pig and ten wolves—K891.1.4; old woman and her pig—Z41.

PIG, PIGLET: Fairy takes place of piglet in thief's bag—F482.5.5.0.

PIG, PIGLING: Pigling aids in quest for lost princess—H1385.1G.

PIG, SOW: Wildcat creates dissension between eagle and sow—K2131.1; mother feigns ill, needs porker of the sow in the other world—S12.1C; witch causes sow to stay thin, buys cheap—G265.6.1.2; sow kicks wolf in stream—K1121.2ff.

PIG, WILD: Boy joins wild pig people—B538.3.3.

PIGEON: Pigeon to restore sight to man—K1853.3. SEE BIRD, PIGEON.

PIGKEEPER: Sister to wed pigkeeper—B314E.

PIKE: Little fish leaves deep waters, big pike remains to starve and be caught—L331.1.

PILGRIM: Bernardino saves money for pilgrims to Bethlehem—D1622.2.3; pilgrim's horse stolen by hyena—K1241. SEE ALSO MECCA.

PILING: Badger transforms to piling and swims off with boat—D612.1.1.

PILL: Pill of immortality—D1346.7.1.

PILLAR: Earthquakes when strong man holding up pillar shifts position—A1145.4; Empress Jokwa mends broken pillar supporting heaven—A665.2.0.1.1; lad holds up broken pillar under Sicily—A842.3.

PILLOW: Bedcover is stolen, fool waits for thief to return for the bolster—J2214.3.2; one feather makes a hard pillow, sackful would be unbearable—J2213.9; lion sent to collect, hare goes home for forgotten pillow—K1839.12.1; student sleeping on porcelain pillow finds self in wealthy future—D1812.3.3.2.1.

PILLOWLACE: Girl goes to moon and is given pillow for pillowlace making with gold bobbins—H1385.5Ac; test, making pillow lace—D2183C.

PIMA: Origin of Pima tribe—A1610.7.

PIMMERLY PLUM: Fox waits for fruit to fall—K1035.1.

PIN: Hiding from Fairy Helena, turns to pin in cover of her magic book—H321C; pin stuck in girl's head turns her to dove—K1911Ac; princess pulls three pins from head of white dove and he turns to prince—D765.1.2.1.

PINDUS: Dragon slays killer of King Pindus—B11.6.1.2.

PINE: Pine wants needles of glass—A2723.1; woodcutter mends three broken branches of pine, is showered with gold—D2171.1.0.1.

PINE CONES: Christ hid in pine cone—A2711.3.1; woman asked by dwarfs to gather her pine cones elsewhere obliges and finds silver cones—F451.5.1.10.1.

PINE NUTS: Coyote and crow steal pine nuts from geese, drop in valleys as fly over Shoshoni country—A1425.0.1.2.

PINKEL: G610Aa.

PINT: Pint measure dances on dresser—F473.6.11.

PIPAL: Girl aids broken pipal tree—Q2.1.2Da; pipal tree judges against man—J1172.3.2.

PIPE: Dead man smokes pipe, saves life of lad who holds pipe for him—E555; mother offers ghost pipe to smoke in effort to distract—E425.1.10; gun given stupid ogre as pipe—K1057; lighting magic pipe summons supernatural—D1421.1.2; magic Meerschaum summons St. Nicholas on Christmas Eve—D1662.4; origin of the peace pipe—A1533.1.

PIPE, INDIAN PIPE PLANTS: Origin, men quarreling while smoking peace pipe turned to Indian Pipe plants—A2667.

PIPE, MUSICAL: Magic pipe compels to follow—D1427.1; magic pipe causes dancing—D1415.2ff; pseudo-magic resuscitating objects sold—K113; Conal plays pipes and miserly cobbler's shoes march to home of needy—F823.5.

PIPER, SEE BAGPIPER.

PIRA PIRA GAME: Trickster makes up game—K341.19.1ff.

PIRAEUS: Monkey claiming to be Athenian thinks "Piraeus" is a man—J1803.1.1.

PIRATES: Golden altar covered with earth to hide from pirate Henry Morgan—V116.1; pirates steal bells of abbey, they swell and sink ship—F993.2; pirates raised from dead to dance with princess—F1015.1.1Bc; pirate hoards gold, engulfed in flood—F945.1; pirate kills missionaries, ship haunts him—E535.3.3.

PISCES: Lato, good swimmer as Pisces—K1836.5.

PISGIES: Fairy lames girl who forgets to leave food—F361.14.6.

PISKEY: Piskies spin plates on floor, cause pint measure to dance—F473.6.11. SEE ALSO FAIRIES.

PIT: Hero abandoned in lower world, rope dropped into pit—K1931.2; Ananse digs pit outside door of his home and covers—K735.1.1; hedgehog gets self thrown out of pit—K652.3; Kantchil tricks animals into pit and gets self thrown out—K652.1; lie, man goes for spade to dig self out—X1731.2.1; ogre tricked into latex lined pit --K741.2; animals grateful for rescue from pit— W154.8; old woman jeering falls into pit with animals— K735.

PITCH: Pitch falls on unkind girl—Q2.1.2Aa. SEE ALSO TAR.

PITCHER: Pure girl to kiss enchanted maid and never let go of golden pitcher through transformations. Maid turns to ape, demon, etc.-- D757.1; father beats daughter before she fetches water to prevent her from breaking pitcher— J2175.1.2; inexhaustible pitcher obeys only owner--D1651.4; inexhaustible pitcher--D1652.5.4; task, diving for pitcher, is really reflection of pitcher in tree--J151.1; King Corc's daughter falls into well, water will not stop flowing until her golden pitcher is brought up--F944.7.

PITCHFORK: Shepherd pulls pitchfork from foot of wounded giant—G666.2.

PITY: Wolf pities fox fallen in well. "Save your pity and go fetch a rope"--J2175.2.1; if poor man with pity picks up dead rat will become rich--N222.3. SEE ALSO CHARITY; MERCY.

PLAGUE: Michael Scott plagued by demon because he hid the plague in a bag-- G303.16.19.3.5.

PLANE TREE: Plane tree blamed for not bearing fruit by those in its shade--W154.7.

PLANT: Extraordinary plants--B210.1.1, G263.1.0.2; old man planting tree for future generations—J701.1; plants from grave of dead person or animal--A2611.0.1; plants offer selves as healing medicines--A1438.2; lie, fast growing plant—X1402; barren woman finds two green plants, turn to lizards then children--T554.8.2; origins and characteristics of plants--A2600-A2799; wife of ruin becomes small plant that grows amid ruins—A1389.1; plant grows to sky —F54.2; task, plant coltsfoot plants. Plant upside down—G530.2J. SEE ALSO FLOWER; LEAVES, ROOT, TREES, ETC.

PLANTAINS: Anansi gives one of four plantains to each family member, keeps none for self. They each give back half—J1241.7.

PLATES: one of fairies not invited to christening as there are not enough place settings-- D1960.3; piskies spin plates on floor--F473.6.11.

PLEIADES: Origin of Pleiades—A773ff.

PLOTTING: Clay hats two feet wide stop plotting--J1199.5.

PLOUHINEC: Stones of Plouhinec go to river to drink on New Year's Eve— N511.6.1.

PLOVER: Plover attacks ocean--J1968.0.1.

PLOW: Little Liang's dog plows for him--

J2415.21; plow small enough to be pulled by dog --F451.5.1.6.3; to come home when dog does, beats dog till it runs home—K1411; value of golden plow--J1199.2; magic plow leaves when farmer curses—D1209.3.

PLUCKING: Plucking the fowl--H561.6.1.

PLUDIHEN: Why men of Pludihen wear sheepskin coat and sailcloth kilt on Christmas Eve— V211.1.8.4.

PLUM: Fox waits with open mouth for plum to fall --K1035.1; girl grabbed picking plums and kept in house of plumstone as servant—G530.2L; kind girl straightens plum branches—Q2.1.2Da; dividing the plum pudding—J1562.1.2; plumstone fairies beset girl who hides plumstones in tatami--Q321.3.

PLUTUS: Hercules refuses to greet Plutus— J451.3.

POET: Student poet meets ghost maid—E474.2.1.

POETRY: Barber takes poet's words as accusation and confesses—J21.1.1; princess composes poem which stops flood--D1275.4.1. SEE RHYMES.

POFFERTJIS: First to speak must wash poffertjis pan—J2511.0.3.

POISON: Anansi poisons meat and lion dies-- K171.0.2.1; cat keeps tail curled around cup to keep anyone from poisoning it--A2378.9.7; Brer Rabbit poisons Brer Gilyard—K1982.0.2; lover forces poison intended for girl down old suitor's throat—T92.15; murderer puts poison in another's food, second kills first and then eats food—K1685; boy eats 'poison' preserves— J2311.2.1; Brer Rabbit feigns being poisoned by meat—K341.2.2.2; Raccoon pretends roast geese were poisoned, sells fox remedy—K355.2; rattlesnake given poison--A2523.2.1; relative takes poison intended for another—K1613.3; horse is poisoned, raven eats and dies, robbers eat raven—H802; why black snake is poisonous, tricked iguana into letting him hold poison bag —A2523.2.1; servant eats 'poison', claims is attempting suicide—J2311.2.1.

POLAMAN: Spring from fish basket forms lake of sacred fish--A920.1.18.

POLE: Fool tries to carry broadside through gate —J2171.6.2.

POLENTA: Villagers tire of eating polenta— J1606.2.

POLIAHU: Goddess of snow, Poliahu duels with Pele--A289.2.

POLICEMAN: Fool hired to keep thieves from Chelm--J1703.2.

POLISH: Polish landlord asks ragged tenant if is not cold. Tenant, "Is your nose cold?" "No."

"I'm all nose"--J1309.1. SEE ALSO ETHNIC AND GEOGRAPHIC INDEX.

POLLEN: Girl who obeys mother becomes golden bee, paws carry dough = pollen--A2012.0.1.1.

POLLUTION: Trickster pollutes house so that he is left in possession--K355; farmer throws his slops onto invisible house--F451.4.4.4.

POLYPHEMUS: SEE CYCLOPS.

POMEGRANATE: Pomegranate and apple tree dispute--J466.1; three girls emerge from pomegranates--D721.5C; dragon at well gives three pomegranates with jewels inside--F813.8.3; monkey drops pomegranate seed, asks owner to cut down olive tree so seed can grow--Z41.6.4; donkey brays and seller wonders who is selling these--J1499.1.

PONCHO: Love emerges from under magic poncho when conditions are propitious--D1052.2.

POND: Pond carried in bill--Z52.2. SEE ALSO LAKE; POOL; ETC.

PONTIUS PILATE: Pontius Pilate causes storms when thrown into Tiber and Rhone--A935.2.

PONY: Series of clever unjust decisions--J1173; mud pony comes alive--D445.1.2. SEE ALSO HORSE.

POOKA: Pooka leaves when given clothes--F381.3.

POOL: Devil's Knee (lava hill) exorcised, pool left where knee receded--A934.14; girl pulled into pool by Goddess Oluweri--A2494.12.10.3.3; bathing in pool gives strength--F617.4; pool of wine shown by grateful monkey--D925.0.2.1. SEE ALSO LAKE; POND; ETC.

POOR: Rich merchant is poorer in happiness than poor man--J347.4; poor man sends gifts to prince and princess. They wed--T53.7; rich man foolishly imitates poor--J2415; poor man made rich is miserable--J1085.1.1. SEE ALSO POVERTY; RICH.

POPCORN: Lie, popcorn in fields pops from heat--X1633.1.

POPE: Devil carries man to pope and back--K1886.3.1.1, M211.8.1; lad hears frog say he'll be made Pope--B217.9; Michael Scot to go to Rome to ask Pope when Shrove Tide falls--A1485.1.

PORCELAIN DOGS: Boy may have all three porcelain dogs if carries one home alone--J1179.19.

PORCELAIN PILLOW: Student sleeping on porcelain pillow finds self in wealthy future--D1812.3.3.2.1.

PORCUPINE: Porcupine in age debate--B841.1.2; porcupine kills buffalo from within--K952.1; origin porcupine clan--B538.3.5; why porcupine and dog are enemies--A2494.4.14; porcupine tricks other out of ham, dreams he ate it--K444; giant's soul in egg in porcupine's head--D532; porcupine owns self-hoeing hoe--D1651.15; porcupine suggests hosts leave if can't stand prickles--P332; wed to porcupine prince--B641.5; origin of porcupine's quills--A2311.5.1; girl follows porcupine to sky world--A762.1C; squirrel weds porcupine--J414.3.2; tiger made to believe porcupine's quill is his enemy's whisker--K1711.1; porcupine arranges tug of war between elephant and hippo--K22; porcupine's voice--K2422.15. SEE ALSO QUILL.

PORGY: SEE FISH, PORGY.

PORPOISE: Origin porpoise--A2135.3.1.

PORRIDGE: If porridge pot cold, sign that hero has died--H335.7.1; porridge with butter in middle, clever dividing--J1562.1.1; magic porridge pot will not stop filling--C916.3; ring in porridge pot identifies maid--R221M; man asks for ladder to reach heaven to take porridge up to St. Peter--D1472.2.12; task, planting millet porridge--H1023.1.1; farmer's wife smears house with porridge--Z32.2.3; if porridge spills wife must eat it--C229.7.

PORT-AU-PRINCE: Horseman in black chases youth to death--E422.1.1.3.3.

PORTER: Fool asks porter to carry bag to his house but refuses to tell where he lives--J2092.1; porter drops load 'don't let anyone tell you this isn't broken'--J163.4.2.

PORTRAIT: Love at sight of portrait--S268A. SEE ALSO PICTURE.

PORTUGAL: King of Portugal as beggar husband--H465D. SEE ETHNIC AND GEOGRAPHIC INDEX.

POT: Childless couple create clay pot boy--Z33.7; camel lies down on potter's cargo--J1511.6.1; borrowed pot said to have had a child--J1531.3; earthen and brazen pots in river--J425.1; fox disguised as Buddha tricked into bathing in rice pot--K717.1; blackened pot to crow when guilty man touches--J1141.10.3; gypsy and wife carry pots over river by floating in cauldron--J1689.3; gypsy fishes old copper pots from pond where count has thrown them--W48.2; cooking pot judges in favor of crocodile--J1172.3.2.1; killing pot--G378; porter given advice rather than money throws down load of pots--J1511.6.1; boiling pot on floor thought to be self-cooking--J1813.4; three legged pot sent to walk home--J1881.1.3; pot worn over girl's head until wed--K1815.0.2; wolf tricked down chimney into pot--K891.1.1. SEE ALSO KETTLE; POTTER; POTTERY; WATER JAR; ETC.

POT, MAGIC: Magic pot loses power when cleaned--D877.1.1; magic pot keeps cooking--C916.3; magic pot duplicates anything put in--D1652.5.7.1; inexhaustible pot--D1652.5.7; magic pot obeys only master--D1651.3; Goddess

Durga gives replenishing pot—D861.1G; tabu on magic pot broken—D861.1I; magic thieving pot—D1605.1.

POT OF GOLD: SEE TREASURE.

POTATO: Devil gets tops of potato crop—K171.1; origin of potato—A2686.4.4.

POTTER: Brahman daydreams and breaks pot in potter's shop—J2061.1.2.1; pots dance and sing while potter is gone—D1615.6.1; potter cannot get pole through gate—J2171.6+; potter needs sun—U148.1; task, make pot large enough to wash elephant—H1023.6.2.

POTTERY: Craft of pottery making taught—A753.1.4.0.1, A1451.1.

POTTLE OF BRAINS: J163.2.1.

POULPICAN: Poulpican changeling—F321.1.1.

POVERTY: God of Poverty leaves home. It is too poor—N250.5; quest to learn what poverty is—H1376.10; St. Peter finds people on earth pay attention to Lord only in times of poverty—V229.26.1.2. SEE ALSO POOR.

POWDER HORN: Powder horn hung on moon—X1851.1.

POWIS: SEE BIRD, POWIS.

PRACH: Island of fools in Yugoslavia—J2287.1.

PRAIRIE DOG: Coyote tricks prairie dogs—K826.1. SEE ALSO GROUNDHOG.

PRAISE: Lad praises king and is beaten—J1289.30; elephant praised at court, each animal thinks this is because of quality which is similar to own—W197.1.

PRANK: Schoolboy had no part in prank, only watched and laughed—J1250.13.

PRAYER: Captor persuaded to pray, victim escapes—K562.1; captive prays so loudly help is summoned—K551.1.0.2; man prays for one thousand coins, will not accept less. Joker sends 999—J2473.1; fox disguised as Buddha sticks out tongue when monk prays—K607.4; hens to pray with monk fox, caught—K815.16.2; passenger refuses to pray in storm, safety of ship is responsibility of crew—J2137.9; respite while victim says endless prayer—K555.1.0.1; girl says Christian prayer and wind dashes witch against rocks—G271.1.

PRAYER, LORD'S PRAYER: Respite from death until Lord's Prayer is said—K551.1.0.1.

PREACHER: Devil advises preacher to make story of David and Goliath bigger, sits in front row and shakes head when not big enough—X904.4.1; disguised tyrant listens to sermon attacking self and then reveals identity—J1289.26. SEE ALSO MINISTER; MONK; PRIEST; SERMON; ETC.

PRECOCIOUS: Son three months old full grown—H1385.1.

PREGNANT: Pregnant woman craves Rapunzel leaves—F848.1.

PRESERVES: Boy commits 'suicide' by eating the 'poison' pot of preserves—J2311.2.1.

PRESUMPTION: Gnat apologizes for lighting on bull's horns—J953.10.

PREY: Chain of attackers, each unaware he is about to be attacked—Z49.15; white ant neglects to watch behind self, frog is following, snake is following frog, etc.—Z49.22.

PRICE: Price of object depends on buyer—U85; farmers throw wheat into river to keep prices high—A939.1.

PRIDE: Baron turned to horse reforms—Q584.2.1; traits animals brag of are those for which men kill them—L461.1; camel asks Lord of Heaven for larger feet and hump—A2356.2.13; king turned beggar reforms—L411; proud brought low—J212.3; proud oriole—W116.9. SEE ALSO BRAG.

PRIEST: Anansi is sham holyman—K1961.1.6; grateful badger earns gold for priest—B393.1; priest is transformed badger—D612.1.2; priest buys magic badger-teakettle—D1171.3.1; priest turns dead souls to cattle—E423.1.8.2; trickster's cow leads parson's one hundred to him—K366.1.1; trickster greets curate first in morning—K176.1; priest and devil farm together, devil gets turnip tops—K171.1; parson feeds sermon to dog—X452.2; doubter to say "ahem" when exaggerates too much—X904.4; priest and comrades convince dupe pig is dog—K451.2.2; female duck stabs breast with beak and dies before hunter who killed her mate. Hunter becomes priest—F1041.1.2.2.5; fat can fit through gate if haywagon can—J1411; priest gives magic geta, coin drops at every step—J2415.8; priest takes on hike to teach hunger—J1606.2; paramour priest in chest revealed—J1344.1; parson has no need to preach, those who know may tell those who do not know—X452; parson saws pulpit, predicts it will fall—K1961.1.3; sexton as priest answers king's riddles—H524.1, H561.2; worshippers fall on floor in imitation of priest—J2417.3; priest frightened into treetop by Yamabushi—B857.2. SEE ALSO HADJI; HERMIT; HODJA; MONK; MULLA; PREACHER; SAGE; SERMON.

PRIME MINISTER: Minister observes all, servant little—H1574.4.1; prime minister chosen by test, king asks what is object in stream—H1574.4.

PRINCE: Prince as beggar weds haughty princess—H465; enchanted princes in underground palace—F1015.1.1; girl performs vigil beside sleeping prince—K1911.1.4; NOTE THAT ALL TALES CONTAINING PRINCES ARE NOT INDEXED HERE.

PRINCESS: Imposters abandon hero in lower world, he rescues princesses—K1931.2; animals help hero win princess—B582.2; princesses who dance out slippers nightly—F1015.1.1; magic dwarf brings princess to hero's room nightly—D1421.1.2; princess takes frog into bed, turns to prince—D195.1; princess of Heaven drops ring to earth, mountains raked up in search—A962.5.1; princess brought to laughter by people sticking together—H341.1; princess forced to say "that's a lie"—H342.1; princess loves man so poor father and he share one pair of pants—T91.6.4.4; quest for stolen princess—H1385.1; quest for vanished wife—H1385.3; princess defeated in repartee—H507.1.0.1; girl rescued by skillful companions, to whom does she belong?—F660.1Cc, H621.2; princess will not talk—F954.2.1, H343; task, following princess—E341.1; suitor test—hiding from princess—H321; haughty princess wed to beggar—H465. NOTE THAT NOT ALL TALES CONTAINING PRINCESSES ARE INDEXED HERE.

PRINCESS LEARNED IN LAW: Princess Learned In Law settles case—H621.3.

PRISONER: Prisoner escapes by thread and brought by beetle up tower—R121.4.1.

PROFIT: Quarrel and fight over details of air-castle from imagined profits—J2060.

PROMETHEUS: Punishment of Prometheus—Q501.4.

PROPHECY: Vain attempts to avoid prophecy—N371; man taken to fairyland and given gift of prophecy—F329.1. SEE M200-M399. Prophecies.

PROPHET: Prophet foretelling future is advised his home has been robbed—J1062.3.

PROTEST: Short tailed animals organize protest meeting—J429.3.

PROUD: Why camel looks proud—A1873.2. SEE PRIDE.

PROVENCE: Provence and Naples unite when Pierre weds—N352.0.1.

PRUNING: Prunes fruit-giving vine, it dies—D876.3.

PSALTER: To read psalter over witch's coffin three nights—H1411.4.4.

PTARMIGAN: SEE BIRD, PTARMIGAN.

PTOLEMY: St. George kills dragon and saves daughter of King Ptolemy—R111.1.3F.

PUDDING: Anansi and Moos Moos are caught stealing Kisander's puddings from dookanoo tree—K419.11; flea suggests wood chopping contest, slips back and eats pudding—K372.2; milk pudding, girl must eat before they will hide her—Q2.1.2CeA; plum pudding, each turns bowl with plums on his side—J1562.1.2; tiger told

mud is king's pudding—K1023.1.2; Tom Thumb in pudding—F535.1.1C Grimm.

PUFFIN: SEE BIRD, PUFFIN.

PUGET SOUND: Origin of languages—A1482.2; origin tribes—A1611.1.3.

PUHUY: SEE BIRD PUHUY.

PULPIT: Parson predicts pulpit will fall—K1961.1.3.

PUMA: Puma cares for abandoned girl—B538.3.2.

PUMICE: Brother and sister escape by sea with pumice tied to arms and legs—K635.2; boy walks on water with pumice, giant imitates with rocks—G512.11.1.

PUMP: Pump handle screeches "quit hanging round" when hare is near—A2233.1.1.

PUMPKIN: Pumpkin thought to be ass's egg—J1772.1; carriage from pumpkin—R221; wife prays for child even if is pumpkin, daughter in pumpkin—T555.1.1; escape in huge pumpkin shell—K553.0.3; fool ties pumpkin to leg so as to recognize self—J2013.3; giant pumpkin chases boy, smashed parts form earth, sky, etc.—A641.3; monkey steals magic pumpkins—J2415.21; woman inside pumpkin, it rolls off—X1411.2.1; returns rolling in pumpkin and escapes—D981.11.1, K553.0.3; boy who saves wounded sparrow given magic pumpkin seed—A751.1.8, J2415.13; man thinks pumpkins should grow on trees—J2571.

PUNIA: Punia tricks King of the Sharks—K341.16; Punia in shark's belly—F911.4.2.

PUNISHMENT: Who does not tell truth will be hanged. Lie, "I am going to be hanged"—J1180.

PURITY: Grateful badger must earn money by honest means for gift to pure priest—B393.1; barber says mirror will show spots on face of any who have sinned—D1163.1; pure human unharmed by wild animals—D771.0.2.

PURSE: Purse found in stomach of Djabbe gives day and night—F912.2.8; Dame Fortune offers gift, he chooses full purse—D1192.1; inexhaustible purse—D1451; magic purse—D1192.1; magic purse given by swamp maiden—D812.15; if fool found purse with fifty thousand rubles he would ask a reward only if it belonged to a rich man—J2259.2.

PUSHING: Contest in pushing hole in tree—K61.

PUSS IN BOOTS: K1917.3.

PUSSY WILLOW: Coyote throws eyes into air, they stick in willow tree—A2681.1.1. SEE ALSO WILLOW.

PUZZLE: Absurd puzzle, how was tower built?—J2711.1.

PYGMY: Pygmy friends of dead giant Antaeus drive Hercules off--F531.6.12, 6.0.1; pygmies demand honey, bees put in comb--K1023.0.1; lad respectful to little people rewarded--F451.5.1.6.2ff.

QALUTALIGSSUAG: Shoeless orphan boy pursued by Qalutaligssuag monster--J1782.8.1.

QUADRUPEDS: Tricksters sells "two dozen quadrupeds", delivers rabbits--W165.4.

QUAIL: SEE BIRD, QUAIL.

QUARREL: Numskull refuses to read prayers over dead friend. They had a quarrel and he would not listen--J2500ff; Devil Aghiusta turns hermits against each other--A1342.1.

QUEDELISH: Cedar disks representing clean mind and clean body given to man visiting underwater longhouse--A1546.0.4.

QUEEN: Queen induced to cluck like hen by trickster--K1289; queen-mother orders Dawn, Day and Queen served to her--D1960.3B. SEE ALSO SHEBA. NOTE THAT NOT ALL TALES CONTAINING QUEENS ARE INDEXED HERE.

QUESTION: "What's a silly question?" Circular tale--Z17.2; questions to be asked of ogre--H1273.2. SEE ALSO RIDDLE. SEE ALL H510 Tests in guessing. H540-H899 Riddles.

QUESTS: SEE ALL H900-H1199 TESTS OF PROWESS: TASKS. H1200-H1399 TESTS OF PROWESS: QUESTS.

QUETZAL: SEE BIRD, QUETZAL.

QUICK: Swift acts--F660.1.2. SEE ALSO SWIFT.

QUILL: Magic quill--H1213.1A; playing music on quills--K1066.4; origin of porcupine quills--A2311.5.1ff; tiger made to believe porcupine quill is his enemy's whisker--K1711.1, K1715.12.1; tortoise recovers stolen quills--K752.1. SEE ALSO PORCUPINE.

QUILT: Man investigates night noise wrapped in quilt, thieves steal it. He reports that they were quarreling over the quilt, when they got it, they left--J2672; quilt too short, wife cuts strip off top to sew onto bottom--J1978. SEE ALSO BEDCOVER; COMFORTER.

QUINCES: Tree to bear quinces if plays sad tune--D1223.1.1.

QUIPU: God Pachacamac gives magic sandals to Hualachi, quipu carrier in Cuzco--D1521.1.1.

RABBI: Rabbi Joshua Ben Levi asks for glimpse of paradise--K2371.1.1.1; Rabbi Simon takes eighty men to dance with witches, hold them powerless over heads--G273.8.

RABBIT: SEE HARE.

RACE, CONTEST: Payupki girl defeats all men of Tikuvi--H1594.3. SEE ALL ENTRIES K11 Race won by deception. SEE ALSO RUNNING.

RACES OF MAN: SEE ALL ENTRIES A1614ff Origin of races.

RACES OF MAN, BLACK: Master to wash black slave white--J511.1.1; why the black man works--A1671.1.1. SEE ALSO ETHNIC AND GEOGRAPHIC INDEX, U.S., BLACK.

RACES OF MAN, CAUCASIAN: White man set adrift in boot sole--A1614.9.1; following spear lost in elephant's side, man meets first white man--D1602.6; how white man got hoe--D1651.15; origin of white race according to Pima--A1610.7. SEE ALSO ETHNIC AND GEOGRAPHIC INDEX.

RACCOON: Blind men duped into fighting--K1081.3; color of raccoon--A2411.1.2.6; raccoon feigns dead to catch crayfish--K751; hare has raccoon feign dead, frogs to dig hole to bury Coon--K751.0.2; enmity between raccoon and fox--A2494.9.3; why raccoon lives in trees--A2433.3.23; raccoon tricks fox with magic paw-paw and is tricked with "hum-house" (hornet's nest)--K1023.1.0.1; raccoon pretends roast geese were poisoned--K355.2; raccoon advises possum to put tail in fire--A2317.12.2; Tlacuache nominated to be saint in rainmaking procession--J953.19; day and night divided evenly as stripes on raccoon's tail--A1172.6; raccoon plasters mud over wolf's eyes--A2411.2.1.13.1.

RADEN SAMISAN: Raden Samisan refuses throne and is turned into bird--A2681.15.

RADISH: Man invited for duck soup is given radish broth--J1551.6.1.

RAGS AND TATTERS: Princess to wed one who catches rose--H465D.

RAHU: SEE ECLIPSE.

RAIATEA: Why sharks do not kill people near Raiatea--A2586.

RAIN: Talking bird made to believe it rained--J1151.1.3.1; call cat to see if it is raining--W111.2.4; white fox weds girl, showers during sunshine on wedding day--B601.14.1; guinea fowl runs into hare's cage for protection from fake rain--K714.2.4.1; hornet's enter spider's gourd to shelter from fake rain--K714.2.6; one who beats on hunchback's hump to receive rain--A957.1; miracle must wait until all agree on when want rain--K1785.1; told not to run from God's rain, runs so as not to defile it with feet--J1650.3; Tlacuache nominated to be saint in rainmaking procession--J953.19; rain of sausages, bread, etc. fool made to believe—J1151.1.3; skillful brother flourishes sword so fast keeps dry in rain—F660.1B; trickster keeps clothes dry under saddle and claims horse outran rain—K134.2.

RAIN GOD, RAIN SPIRIT: Rain Spirit in form of bull courts—F433.0.1; Rain God orders dam built—A2431.3.9; dragon as rain spirit—B11.7; dragon rain spirit allows man to drop rain on village—B11.7.0.1; Rain God drops rain when frogs, toads croak—A2426.4.1.2.1ff.

RAINBOW: Birds fly through rainbow—A2411.2.0.1; origin color of hummingbird—A2411.2.1.19; rainbow as shoulder strap of invisible warrior—R221G; Rainbow Boy weds girl whose meal sticks to shell—K1816.0.2.2. SEE ALL ENTRIES A791ff Origin of rainbow.

RAINMAKER: Tree on which Rainmaker sits grows to sky—D482.1.3.

RAINSTORM: Old woman Rainstorm sticks hole in sky, rains when she cries—A1231.2.

RAJA: Doctor-know-all accidentally saves Raja—N688.1; fanged Raja eats blood—D112.2.1.3; minister dupes raja into entering body of dead parrot—K1175; stonecutter wishes to be raja—Z42.0.2.

RAKE: Man surrenders to rake—J2613; raking the moon from pond—J1791.3.

RAKSHASA: Man persecuted by Rakshasa in form of beautiful wench—G369.1.5.

RAM: SEE SHEEP, RAM.

RAMADAN: Man counts days of fast month by throwing a pebble into pot each day—J2466.2; wife causes guest to flee with chicken, husband chases—K2137.1.

RAPATOU: Monsieur Rapatou—G501 Cooper.

RAPU: Yam brought from Rapu—A2794.2.2.

RAPUNZEL: F848.1.

RASPBERRIES: Wild animal sends children home with raspberries—B531.6.

RAT: Ananse in rat kingdom—K735.1; rat makes one bargain too many—K251.1.2; cat on rat infested isle—J2415.1.0.1; association of rat and cat ends as soon as mutual danger is passed—J426; cat in rat infested land sold for fortune—N411.1; rat and young cat are playmates until taught differently—J425.3; origin color of rat—A2411.1.4.3; rat demon killed by artist's paintings of cats—D435.2.1.1; enmity between cat and rat—A2494.1.4; enmity between dog and rat—A2494.4.3.1; why giant rat's tail is two-colored—A2378.9.5.1; kingdom of rats—N777.0.3; rat seeks to marry sun, cloud, etc.—L392.0.2; rat forced to retrieve magic object—D882.1; rat on moon gnaws fishline—A751.0.2;

trickster claims ogre's blow was like rat running past—K525.1; rats jump overboard one at a time—Z11.3; panther threatens rat rescuer—J1172.3; rats charmed from town by piper—D1427.1; if poor man with pity picks up dead rat, he will become rich—N222.3; cat descends from scroll and kills rats—D435.2.1.1.1; why horse, donkey, and ox share with rat—A2493.37; rat eats sky-line—A1811.4; rat eats hair off squid's head—A2317.13; rat assumes student's identity—D315.1.1; weds rat—B641Bd. SEE ALSO MOUSE.

RAT, MUSKRAT: Sent to dive for earth—A812.7.

RAT, SENDJI: Why lacks tail—A2235.

RATA: Birds carve canoe and carry to sea for Rata—B364.4.

RATCATCHER: Maiden marries strongest spouse, is ratcatcher—L392.0.3.

RATTLES: Evil clan turned to rattlesnakes with dancing rattles affixed to tails—A2145.9.1.

RATTLESNAKE: SEE SNAKE, RATTLESNAKE.

RATU: Ratu defeats Giant Clam and Octopus—B874.9.

RATU LORO KIDUL: Offering to goddess of bird's nest caves—C57.1.3.

RAVEN: SEE BIRD, RAVEN.

RAZOR: Hen loses hawk's razor—A2494.13.10.3.1; razor demanded in return for cut off tail—Z47.2.

READING: Ass taught to read—K491.0.1, K551.11; ghost must finish reading holy book before is free—E451.13; Bouki buys glasses. They are no good, still can't read—J1746.2; owl blinded for reading at party—A2491.2.5; wolf reads name on mule's hoof—K1121.0.1.

REAPING: Reaping girl cuts off clothes, does not know self—J2012.2.

RECIPE: Coyote insists recipe for acorn cake must be difficult, given a false one—J2724; a hawk steals fool's meat, but fool still has the recipe—J2562.

RED CAP: Man echoes fairies' cry, "I wish I had my wee red cap" and flies off—F282.4.2; Red Riding Hood—K2011.0.1.

RED ETTIN: Attempts to free princess from Red Ettin—R111.1.3Ah.

RED RIDING HOOD: K2011.

RED SEA: Banishment to Red Sea for fourteen generations—F369.10; maid must cut out eleventh reed on shore of Red Sea and beat caterpillar in order to break spell—H1385.4D.

RED SKY: Red sky in morning—A1128.3.

REDBIRD: SEE BIRD, REDBIRD.

REED: Magic speaking reed betrays secret which was whispered into hole—D1316.5.0.2; reed grows from grave, sings truth—E632.0.4; reed by hut sings of prince in coma within—E362.0.2; reed bends before wind—J832.

REEDBUCK: Tortoise races reedbuck—K11.1.

RE-ENACTMENT: Judge re-enacts scene leaving aggressor trapped—J1172.3.

REFLECTION: Old Man Autumn is to wipe paint brushes on fox if can paint reflection of leaf—A2411.1.3.2; fools see bee's nest reflected and try to carry off well—J1791.9; Clamshell Boy takes witch to sea to see reflection—T554.12.1; coyote dives for reflected chokecherries—J1791.3.5; dog drops meat for reflection—J1791.4; fool sees reflection in well and thinks self drowning—J1791.2.1; elephant fears agitated reflection of moon in water—K1716, K1791.12; weak animal shows strong animal his own reflection and frightens him—K1715, K1715.0.1; fugitive discovered by reflection in water—R351; fugitive discovered by reflection in water by maiden—U136.0.1; fugitive discovered by reflection in water by witch—G276.2; goose dives for star thinking it a fish—J1791.8; konkadet monster dives for reflection—C752.2.1.1; falling in love with reflection in water—K1815.0.2; rescuing moon from well—J1791.2; donkey killed for drinking moon's reflection—J1791.1; moon's reflection captured in barrel of water—J1791.2.2; does not recognize own reflection, thinks it another person—J1791.7+; task, diving for pitcher, is really reflection, pitcher in tree—J151.1; suitor's contest, shooting birds. Pikoi takes aim in calabash of water—H331.4.3; shooting at suns, Prince aims at reflections in pool and five of six suns disappear—A720.1.2; stars reflected thought to be drowning—J1791.2.1; ugly woman sees beautiful woman reflected in water and thinks it is self—J1791.6.1. SEE ALSO MIRROR.

REFORM: Baron turned to horse reforms—Q584.2.1; boy sets dog adrift in canoe but dog later saves his life. Boy reforms—W11.5.13; child reforms and vows never to open door again—K815.15+; Buh Coon says, "You got to begin charity next door. But if you want to reform, it's got to begin at home"—U236.2; king turned to beggar reforms—L411.1.

REGRET: "Sorrow not over what is lost forever", advice of released bird—J21.12.1.

REINCARNATION: SEE ALL ENTRIES E600-E699.

REINDEER: Boy jealous of adopted boys wishes he were a reindeer, becomes one—D100.2; reindeer turns girl to lamp and they capture moon—A753.1.0.1; lad weds sun's daughter, looks back as she leaves and one-third of reindeer herd disappear—C31.3.2.

REJUVENATION: Rejuvenation by throwing ashes of burnt dogs on bones of boiled king—D882.1H; imitation of magic rejuvenation unsuccessful—J2411.1.

RELAY: Coyote organizes relay to steal fire—A1415.2.2.4.

RELIGION: Three rings given, only one is good. Same with three religions—J462.3.1.1. SEE ENTIRE CHAPTER V. RELIGION. SEE ALSO BUDDHA; CHRIST; CHRISTIAN; MOHAMMED; MOSLEM; ETC.

REMEDY: Pulling out eye to stop pain, worked with his tooth—J2412.2; reason for dying man is withering tree in garden—N452.1.2. SEE ALSO DOCTOR; HEALING; MEDICINE.

RENT: Brownies collect rent for impoverished couple—F482.5.4.3; rent sent by hare—J1881.2.2.

REPETITION: Magic repetition, person must keep doing thing begun over and over all day—D1413.17, J2073.1; stories which repeat over and over—Z17.

RESCUE: SEE R100-R199.

RESTAURANT: The bill paying hat—K111.2; suit over chicks that might have hatched from eaten eggs—J1191.2; suit over stolen smell from kitchen—J1172.2.0.1.

RESUSCITATION: Fake resuscitating object sold—K113; girl resuscitated, to whom does she belong?—H621.2; God resuscitates boy—A185.12.1.1; unsuccessful imitation of resuscitation—J2411.1, K213C; man resuscitates a lion—J563.2.

REVENGE: Sparrow's revenge on elephant—L315.6.1.

REVIVAL: Animals confess weaknesses after revival meeting—W141.1.

REVOLT: Jan the Eighth Van Arkel quells revolt by show of extraordinary strength—F610.3.7.

REWARD: SEE CHAPTER Q. REWARDS AND PUNISHMENTS.

REYNARD: SEE FOX.

RHODES: Man boasts of jump on Rhodes—J1477.

RHONE: Devil attempts to flood Rhone Valley—G303.16.12.1.

RHYMES: Fool repeats rhymes at auspicious times, thought wise—N685.1.

RIBBON: Poison ribbon sold to Snow White—Z65.1; girl wears yellow ribbon around neck all life. Untied, her head falls off—Z13.4.4.1.

RICE: Rice left as offering to Gods turns to along-along grass when villagers raid—A2688.2;

Bataru Guru gives rice to man, calf Lembu Gumarong tries to destroy—A162.9; three orphan girls rescue bird, it lays rice and fish for them —J2415.17; angel of grains sent to strip stalk as punishment to men is persuaded to leave bit at top of stalk by birds—A2771.4.1; Bookoo bird calls "Boo Koo" (plant rice) at rice planting season—A2426.2.24; rice from stroking cat's fur—D1472.1.24.5; reward for slaying giant centipede is never ending bag of rice—Q82.3; village named Derma after kind woman who shares rice—A1529.1; Gods poison Dewi Sri and rice grows from grave. Calf Lembu Gumarong tries to destroy—A2685.6.1.1; rice just eaten must be returned—K251.2.1; impatient farmer pulls on rice to make it taller—J1973.2; fish 'steals' rice by causing family to eat more rice when having such a fine meal—J1341.7.1; rice on hair turns to gems—B641E; rice turned to gold when pounded in mortar—D475.1.6; son left bags of 'gold' on condition he buy them. Contains rice—H588.7.1; pursued hero climbs mango tree, restores it with three magic rice grains as witch gouges it with horns—B524.1.2C; old man on moon pounding paddy and throwing chaff to rabbit—A751.1.6; origin of rice—A2685.6; animals route rice thief for old woman—K1161.3.6; Tikgi birds reap and transport to granary by magic—D366.

RICE BALL: All fools smash riceballs into noses—J2417.2; rolling rice ball leads to adventure—N777.

RICEBIRD: SEE BIRD, RICEBIRD.

RICE BOWL: Issun-Boshi uses rice bowl as boat —F535.1.1E.

RICE CAKE: Monkey divides rice cake, eats both —K452.1.2; sixth rice cake satisfies hunger—J2213.3.

RICE FIELDS: Old man on mountain top sees approaching tidal wave, sets fire to rice fields—J1688.

RICE PADDLE: Oni force old woman to cook with magic rice paddle—J1791.3.2.2; magic rice paddle—N777.0.1.

RICE PUDDING: Fools imitate leader who slips and falls with rice pudding—J2417.2.

RICE STICK: Stepmother sends girl to take rice stick to wizard to wash after she drops it—Q2.1.2Eb.

RICH: How to get rid of beggars, have two pillars of cliff carved into statues. This takes all wealth—J1199.1; birds plant garden, magic fruit kills rich—W11.17; rich merchant is poorer in happiness than poor man—J347.4; poor man foolishly imitates rich—J2415; rich man foolishly imitates poor—J2415; dispossessed rich man becomes lizard—A2426.4.3; poor man made rich becomes miserable—J1085.1+; poor man bets rich he can make woodcutter richer than rich man can—N66.1; riddle, what is richest?—H636.1; rich woman accused of crime forces servant to change clothes with her—J1179.23. SEE ALSO POOR.

RIDDLES: The dragon and his grandmother—M211.7.1; guess what I have in my hand and I'll give it to you to make an egg cake with, fool misses—J2712.1; spared old father solves riddle —J151.1; fish provides answers to riddles posed by threatening demon—B375.1.4; riddle, Ireland or Scotland first inhabited?—R111.1.3Ah; student kills Naga, riddle about bones made into hairpins—J21B; sun and moon as man and woman —A736.1; Sun Prince and Moon Prince kidnapped by water spirits when fail to answer riddle—F420.5.2.2.5. SEE ALL ENTRIES H530-H899 Riddles. SEE ALSO NAME; QUESTION.

RIDERS: Girl at witch's house sees riders in white, red and black pass—Q2.1.2CeBb, Z65.3.1.

RIDING: Trickster rides dupe horseback—K1241; lion thought to be a donkey, drunkard rides it—J1758.5; task, coming neither on horse nor on foot—H1053.1. SEE ALSO HORSE.

RIFLE: Rifle stolen—F54.2.1.

RING: Animals recover lost ring—D882.1.1; which animal did most to recover ring?—H621.3; magic amber ring from inside head of calf lights way to flee, opens rock to other world—G530.2Bk; returning crusader drops ring in cup—H94.4.1; fish recovers ring from sea—B582.2; ring in fish—K1355A, N211.1; ring token from princess on glass mountain—H331.1.1B; princess of heaven drops ring to earth, mountains raked up in search for ring—A962.5.1; identification by ring—H94; ring in soup, bread, cake, etc. identifies maid—H94.1, R221D, R221M; ring from finger appearing from lake—B652.1.1; magic ring tells how to win princess—H465; magic ring retrieved by cat and dog—D882.1; magic ring in seashell makes lad invisible—D1361.17.1; ring on dead hand proof of murderer—S62.1; ring sticks to finger and calls to ogre—K603; grateful snake gives magic ring—D882.1B; snake's father gives magic ring—D817.1.2.2; King Solomon's ring—D1076.1; ring and stick game played by buffalo, ring is captured girl—R111.1.13.2; task, recovering lost ring from sea—H1132.1.1; turns self to ring to enter thieves' den—D1711.0.1.1.1; magic wishing ring—D882.1.1B, D882.2, H1385.3.

RIP VAN WINKLE: D1960.1.

RIVER: Countertask to dipping out sea, stop all rivers—H1143; crossing river by counting crocodiles—K579.2; deer challenges rabbit to jump over river, then widens magically—D483.1.1; river depth calculated from ducks or frogs—J1919.2; dogs try to drink river dry—J1791.3.2; river swallowed by drakestail—Z52.1; giant swallows river, tickled until spits out—F531.6.8.3.2.1; giant plans to dam up river—F531.6.6.3.1; gypsy and wife carry pots over river by floating in cauldron—J1689.3; river on fire—X909.4.5; hen carries river in basket—

Z52.3; river judges in favor of snake, not man—N1172.3.2.4; origin of rivers--SEE ALL ENTRIES --A934ff; origin of river by heavenly servant raking earth for lost ring--A962.5.1; rivers accuse sea of making waters salty--W128.3; woodpecker calls back son of Sartak-Pai who is digging river in wrong direction--A2435.4.12; river imitates sound of Vainamoinen's boots—A2272.1.4.

RIVER, NAVIGANCE: Why river turns white each year--A939.2.

RIVER, SNAKE: Origin--A934.16.

RIVER, VAZOUZA: Rushes to sea in spring--A939.4.

RIVER, VISTULA: Dragon drinks dry—B11.11.10.

RIVER, VOLGA: Rushes to sea in spring—A939.4.

ROAD: Giant attacks hero using his road--F628.2.3.1; road judges against man—J1172.3.2; lizard claims tortoise's bundle "found along road", tortoise was dragging it on string--J1511.14.1; "Don't throw stones from not yours to yours", admonition to rich man throwing stones into road—H599.10; task, coming neither by road nor by footpath--H1051.1; task, bring cloth as long as road—H951.1.

ROADRUNNER: SEE BIRD, ROADRUNNER.

ROANEY: X1130.2.2, X1132.2.

ROAR: Roaring contest between elephant and tiger (lion)--K84.2; lion hears echo of roar and attacks--K1715.1.0.2.

ROBBER: Animals climb on one another's backs and cry out, frighten robbers--K335.1.4; robber bridegroom, maid in den of robbers—S62.1C; man steals robber's coat as he robs house--J2092.3; lad as cook for robbers spies out camp --K2357.16; ferryman gives robber ride, ill robber dies--N534.9; robber ghost holds up people --E593.6; robbers' heads cut off one by one as enter--K912; lad has no fear of robbers--H1440B; robbers change letter of execution to read "wed to princess"--K1355; thieves eat poisoned raven, die--H802; old robber frees three sons by telling three stories--R153.3.3; man enchants robbers by toasting them—K1812.1.0.1; Tom Thumb pretends to help robbers--F535.1.1. SEE ALSO THIEF.

ROBE: Told not to mention robe, fool says "We mustn't mention the robe, must we?"--J2512.1; origin of sleeping robes--A1437.4; SEE ALSO CLOAK; COAT.

ROBERT BRUCE, KING: Sends monk to battle with hand of St. Fillian--V143.2.2.

ROBIN: SEE BIRD, ROBIN.

ROBIN HOOD: N884.1.

ROC: Roc carries--H1385.3Fa; Sindbad--B31.1.

ROCK: Rocks clap together at intervals--D1553.1, H1385.3Faa; food giving rock, one tries to pry it open--D876.3; dupe made to believe trickster is holding up rock--K1251; masking as rock--K607.2.1; origin of rocks--A970ff; rolling rock pursues coyote--C91.1; crow sings up stretching rock with two bluebirds on it--D482.4.1; rock as witness--J1141.3.4.3. SEE ALSO STONE.

ROCK, GREAT ROCK OLUMO: Origin—R111.1.3A.

ROCK SQUIRREL: SEE SQUIRREL, ROCK SQUIRREL.

ROCKING: Wormwood (grass) does not want to rock the sparrow—Z41.7.

ROLAND: Girl flees with sweetheart Roland—G530.2Da.

ROLLING: Hare, wolf, bear, fox threaten bun—Z33.1.6; rolling rice ball, pancake, etc. followed leads to adventure--N777.

ROMAN: Rav Hillel does not admire Roman culture --J652.4.3.

ROME: Origin weather vane in Rome—B171.1.2.

ROMULUS AND REMUS: Founded Rome--B535.0.9.1.

ROOF: Called down from roof by beggar, takes him back up on roof to tell no--J1331; cow grazed on roof--J1904.1; shingling the fog--X1651.1; lazy does not need roof when fair, cannot put it on when it rains--J2171.2.1; Brer Rabbit helps Brer Fox roof house, nails down Brer Fox's tail --K729.1; roof removed to let in light--J2123.1.

ROOT: Trickster tells crocodile biting his foot that he is biting a root—K543.0.1; deceptive crop division, trickster gets bottoms of root crops--K171.1; monkeys pull up trees to water roots--J1973.1; willow root put into neighbor's net by mean man turns to helpful dog--K32.1.

ROPE: Imposters abandon hero in lower world, drop rope--K1931.2; hairy man makes all ropes in county disappear--B524.1.2H; fools' disastrous attempt to save man from tree by pulling on rope--J2434; pull rope and crack heads of those tied to rope--K301B; rope maker, Ropo, makes unbreakable ropes--F601.2E; cutting rope to kill ogre--K678; stealing rope with ox on other end--K188; countertask, make rope of sand--H1021.1; task, make rope of ashes—H1021.2.1; thief climbing rope discovered and rope cut--K1622; rope cut and victim dropped--K963.

RORAIMA: Origin Mt. Roraima--A1231.3.

ROOSTER: SEE CHICKEN, ROOSTER.

ROSARY: Rosary thrown around golden duck and ducklings, turn to maid and children--F302.4.2.3.

ROSE: Rose and amaranth contest--J242.1; bread

in apron of charitable woman turns to roses--V412.2; rose tree as perch of reincarnated child bird--N271Ab; full blown rose to be brought in January, embroidered rose brought--E451.12; magic rose to draw itself to princess--B314E; fool loans ox to rosebush--J1853.3; girl changed to rosebush by cruel stepmother--N271B.

ROSE RED: Rose Red and Snow White befriend bear--D113.2.2.

ROSEMARY: Girl pulls rosemary and man asks why she steals his firewood and leads through hole to underground palace--H1385.4G.

ROSEWATER: Rosewater disenchants--H1331.1.3An.

ROWAN: Rowan rods in field dull reaper's blade--K171.1.

ROWING: Three women and old man, each refuses to take a second turn rowing--W167.3.

ROWLAND, CHILDE: F324.0.1.

RUBBER: An image covered with tar captures the intruder--K741.

RUBLE: Forbidden to tell secret unless in Tsar's presence, tells when sees Tsar's face on ruble--H561.6.2.

RUBY: Prince emerges from ruby, weds princess--H1385.4K; magic jewel dropped into sea, Da Trang searches for it in form of sand crab--R216B; tortoise asks greedy man to give back first ruby given on pretext of matching it with a second--K439.7.1.

RUG: Doctor's fee reduced on pretext that he spoiled priceless rug with medicines--K499.11. SEE ALSO CARPET.

RUIN: Origin of ruin--A1389.1.

RUM: Ananse tells hare to dip tail in rum and put into sea, fish bite--K1021.

RUMOR: Wife multiplies secret--J2353. SEE ALSO GOSSIP.

RUMPELSTILTSKIN: D2183.

RUNAWAY: Man on runaway horse says he is going wherever the horse wishes--J1483.2.

RUNNER: Marvelous runner--F601.2, F660.1; runners relay fire--A1415.2.2.4; suitor contest, running up steep hill--H331.1.1E.

RUSHES: Maid in cloak of rushes--R221E.

RUSSIA: Origin of first Russian--A1414.1.1.2; Russian peasant outwits Baron, each to carry the other--K289.1; origin of steam engine, Russian carpenter invents boiler--A1439.5.

RUSTEM: Rustem raised in nest of Simurg--

B535.0.5.1.

RUWA: Temba carried to Kingdom of Ruwa in sky by father's stool--T555.3.

SABRE: Cat's tail taken as sabre--K2323. SEE ALSO SWORD.

SACK: SEE BAG.

SACRIFICE: Daughter casts self into molten metal to allow perfect bell for father--S261.0.2; practice of sacrificing wife with dead husband is abandoned--A1547.1.1; dragon slayer rescues maiden being sacrificed--R111; each family member offers self for others but fails as sacrifice--G530.2BI; own child sacrificed to restore faithful servant (friends)--S268; girl sacrifice slays serpent--B11.11.7.2; sacrifical hen provides magic hen producing mud--D877.3; lamb prefers to be sacrificed--J216.2; sage's advice followed, human sacrifice thrown into tank to stop leak, it is sage--K1673.1; origin of animal sacrifice to Saint Gabre Manfas--A1545.3.0.1; substitute for sacrifice--K1853.2.1.1.

SADDLE: Fool thinks ass has stolen coat and takes ass's saddle in return--J1862; offers ass's saddle and bridle as reward to finder of lost ass--J2085.1; fool as doctor sees saddle and bridle under bed and diagnoses patient's illness as eating too many donkeys--J2412.4; horse lets man saddle him so he can catch stag--K192; saddle of swiftness--B314G; trickster saddles and bridles dupe and rides--K1241ff. SEE ALSO BRIDLE.

SADDLEBAG: Wildcat and bear leap on saddlebag from opposite sides of horse and kill each other--X1114.3.

SADDLECOTH: Man gives old father half saddlecloth to keep warm, child keeps other half, says is for his father when he grows old--J121.

SADNESS: SEE CRYING; GRIEF; TEARS.

SAGE: Sage's advice followed, sacrifice made to stop leaky tank. He is thrown in--K1673.1.

SAIL: Task, making sail from one bundle of linen--H1022.3.

SAILORS: Sailor raises wind by untying knots--D2142.1.2; if Miss Lin appears in storm sailors will reach shore safely--A421.1.2; storytelling round--Z17ff. SEE ALSO SHIP.

SAINT AGATA: J552.5.1.

SAINT ANTHONY: Statue of St. Anthony falls on cow-witch--G263.1.3.1.

SAINT AUGUSTINE. St. Augustine appears on Candlemas and King, celebrating Christmas as Holiday of Fools, repents--V92.1.

SAINT BEATUS: Cloak ceases to be magic after commits sin of laughing during mass—C69.1; laughs at devil in church—G303.24.1.7.0.1.

SAINT BRIDGET: Nurses infant Jesus—V211.1.8.1.

SAINT CADOG: Mouse leads St. Cadog to grain in famine—B437.2.3; to send one hundred cows for each of King Arthur's soldiers slain—D1711.6.6.

SAINT CHRISTOPHER: Grants wishes—J2073.1, Q1.1.

SAINT CUTHBERT (SAINT CUDDY): V429.1.

SAINT DOMINGO: Image of Santo Domingo de Guzman taken to Managua each year—V128.0.2.

SAINT ELIZABETH: V412.3.

SAINT FILLIAN: King Robert Bruce sends monk to fetch hand of Saint Fillian to battlefield—V143.2.2.

SAINT FRANCIS: Tells wolf to kill no more men —B279.1.2; restores fried fish—E121.4.2.

SAINT GENEVIEVE: Tears fall in water and mother's sight restored when washes—V221.12.1; persuades Parisians not to desert city in face of Huns—V229.7.2.

SAINT GEORGE: Kills dragon rescuing King Ptolemy's daughter—R111.1.3Fa.

SAINT JAMES OF COMPOSTELLA: Slays dragon —B641Dd.

SAINT JOHN: Has to dance when hears drums, drought ends—D2174.1.

SAINT JOHN'S EVE: Pure girl to kiss enchanted maid on St. John's Eve—D757.1; meadow cropped on St. John's Eve—H331.1.1.

SAINT KAVIN: Deceptive land purchase, as much as goose can fly over—K185.3.1.

SAINT MAGNUS: Saint Magnus routs Scots from Orkney—V229.7.3.

SAINT MARGERY DAW: V411.12.

SAINT MARTHA: Tames dragon with sign of cross—B11.11.7.

SAINT MARY OF TREFREW: Sent as wizard with Prince's party—D1711.6.4.

SAINT NEOT: Stands in well to say prayers, restores fish to life—V229.27; calls wild animals to help when oxen are stolen—V229.28.

SAINT NICHOLAS: Origin baker's dozen, St. Nicholas' Day—V429.4; called by magic meerschaum pipe—D1662.4; St. Nicholas as Santa Claus—N816; St. Nicholas grants wishes—

J2073.1; Q1.1; wolf cursed by St. Nicholas to go crookshanks—K254.1.

SAINT PATRICK: Saints have to dance when hear drums, drought ends—D2174.1.

SAINT PETER: Lord pounds St. Peter on anvil to rejuvenate, blacksmith imitates—J2411.1.0.1; saints have to dance when hear drums, drought ends—D2174.1; gives magic flute—D1415.2.3.3; gives lad magic objects—D861.1G; man asks troll for ladder to reach heaven and takes porridge up to St. Peter—D1472.2.12; St. Peter finds people call on Lord only in poverty—V229.26.12; unsuccessful imitation of resuscitation—K213C; Lord hangs trombone on St. Peter's back—V229.26.1.2; Padre Ulivo offers hospitality to twelve strangers (disciples)—Q565Ai; St. Peter gives blacksmith wishes—K1811.1, Q565A.

SAINT PETER'S CATHEDRAL: To be saved if hears mass at Church in Jerusalem, Galicia and St. Peter's in Rome in same night—D2121.5.1; weathervane on St. Peter's Cathedral—B171.1.2.

SAINT PORTHOLE: Fisherman mocks girl telling to pray to "Saint Porthole"—D2125.1.0.1.

SAINT SEBASTIAN: Fool gives clothing to statue —J1853.1.0.1.

SAINT STANISLAUS: Give wolf permission to eat human flesh, but only blacksmith—B279.1.1.

SAINT THEDULE: Bishop of Sion carried home by Devil—K1886.3.1.

SAINT VENERE: J552.5.1.

SAINT VITUS: Origin St. Vitus' dance—D1415.2.5.2.

SAINTE-DODO: Fools town, sow needles—J1932.5.

SAINTS: Cobbler's deity puts fingers in mouth in horror at girl eating offering—V128.5; hospitality to saint rewarded—Q1.1; inhospitality to saint punished—Q292.1; patron saint's statue costs more than other saint's—J552.5.1; statues change poses over course of time. Saint "Quien Sabe" and Saint "Que Pasa"—V128.4; saints set Treageagle sweeping sand forever—E459.8; saint gives three wishes—J2075. SEE ALL V220ff. SEE ALSO BUDDHA; GOD; JESUS; KWAN YIN; MARY.

SAKE: Draper swallows a fly in his sake—Z49.14.1.

SAKKA: King of the sky sends kings to woo maid —T11.2.1.1.

SALE: Woman sells ox for five pennies, tied to twelve florin cock—K182. SEE ALSO SELLING.

SALMON: Tinker of Tamlacht turns to salmon in River Erne—Q565Af. SEE FISH, SALMON.

SALT: Ass loaded with salt lies in water to lighten load—J1612; girls eat salty yeast, man who gives water in dreams will wed--H1385.5Ab; man to drown, eats salt so will have thirst--J861.2; girl loves father with "love like salt"--H592.1; Asin god of salt kingdom--A1115.4; self grinding salt mill--D1601.21.1; trickster puts salt in soup, ogre goes for water--K1611B; origin of salt--A978.5; food oversalted--K337; most precious thing--H659.28; bathing in salt water as false remedy for hare--K1014.1; why sea is salt--A1115.2.1; salt bricks fall into sea --A1115.4; Sheba not to take anything Solomon doesn't give her. Fed salty food and takes water--K337.0.1; salt in saltless land sold-- N411.4.1; salt is spice of all spices--H659.29; task, first to bring salt from ocean to wed-- K11.1.1.1; salt fed to nag thief has substituted for fine horse. Nag leads to thief for water-- K366.1.2.1; pours salt down chimney, steals candlestick when troll goes for water--G610Ae; must not look as trickster cooks or dish will be ruined. Leaves out salt and blames hyenas for looking--K1084.1.3; salt put on witch's skin— G229.1.1.

SALTWATER: Saltwater thrown on moon to put out--A751.5.8. SEE ALSO SALT.

SAMEBITO: Man shelters banished Samebito-- B11.6.1.3.

SAMISEN: Spider goblin as priest or maid plays samisen and entraps man--E423.8.1.

SAM'L DANY: Fool doesn't recognize own house and family--J2014.

SAMURAI: Blind lute player forced to sing for samurai ghosts--E434.11; samurai frees self from goblin spider playing samisen—E423.8.1; tiny samurai toothpick imps--Q321.3.

SAN FRANCISCO BAY: A920.1.0.1.1.

SAND: City inundated with sand--F948.5; countertask, thread of sand--H1021.13; countertask, making rope of sand--H1021.1; sand turns to gold--F342.1.1; sack of sand chosen rather than gold--D882.1C; sandbanks formed from grain thrown overboard—N211.1A; saints set Treageagle to sweeping sand forever—E459.8.

SANDALS: Sandal seller trades wares with charcoal seller on New Year's Eve. Charcoal turns to gold--F342.1.3; God Pachacamac gives magic sandals to Hualachi—D1521.1.1.

SANDBANK: Burning sandbank as logical as horse bearing calf—J1191.1.1.

SANGASANG: Origin of Sangasang Ceremony for dedicating house before building--A1548.2.1.

SANSA: Thumb piano played—B210.2.1.

SANTA CLAUS: N816. SEE ALSO SAINT NICHOLAS.

SANTIAGO: Claims as reward wild bulls he raised in youth—H1331.3.

SANTO DOMINGO: Image of Santo Domingo de Guzman taken to Managua each year—V128.0.2.

SAO: Sao bird made to believe it rained-- J1151.1.3.1; why birds only repeat--A2422.12.

SAP: Bad woodcutter is showered with sap-- D2171.1.0.1.

SAPSUCKER: SEE BIRD, SAPSUCKER.

SARDINIA: Fairies of Sardinia give magic date tree--R221C.

SASQUATCH: Origin of Sasquatch--B29.9.1.

SATYR: Man blows on soup to cool, on hands to warm. Satyr flees such a one--J1801.1.

SAUCER: The silver saucer and the transparent apple--E632.0.4.

SAUCEPAN: SEE PAN.

SAUNA: Cock dying of heat in sauna--Z32.1.1.4.

SAUSAGE: Mouse, bird and sausage keep house --J512.7; testimony of foolish lad discredited by making him believe it has rained sausages-- J1151.1.3; three wishes, sausage wished on spouse's nose--J2075.

SAUSAGE TREE: Monkeys plan attack, using fruit of sausage tree—J1172.3.0.4.

SAW: Numskull saws off tree limb on which he sits--J2133.4; the sawed pulpit falls as preacher predicts--K1961.1.3.

SAW-WHET: SEE BIRD, SAW-WHET.

SAWMILL: Lie, sawmill in treetop—X907.1.1.

SAYNDAY: Saynday discovers buffalo and brings --A1878.2; Saynday tricked by sham sick coyote in race--K11.5; Saynday accepts red ant's advice not to revive dead--A2355.1.2.2; Saynday files down teeth of deer--A2345.3.1; meat ball allows Saynday to take bite of her-- A2412.1.7; Saynday makes soup, splashes on Bobcat's fur--A2412.1.7; Saynday puts hand in sky = stars--A779.4; fox plays ball with sun-- A721.1.4; Saynday trapped in closing tree— D1556.3; trickster pretends to ride home for tools, steals horse--K341.8.1; Saynday woos whirlwind—Z115.2.

SCALES: SEE WEIGHT.

SCANTLIE MAB: D2183.1 Jacobs.

SCARECROW: Identifies tiny God arriving in leaf boat--A541.0.1; image covered with tar captures intruder—K741; farmer disguised as scarecrow taken for Jizo statue by monkeys-- J2415.23.

SCARF: Scarf as source of strength—S12.1B.

SCARFACE: Seeks sun to ask removal of scar—H1284.1.

SCHILDA: Town of fools, wrap stove in rabbit net—J1942.1.

SCHILDBURG: Town of fools burns house to kill cat—J2101.

SCHIPPETARO: Kills goblin cats—K1853.2.1.1.

SCHNITZLE: Dwarf King Laurin is given hospitality on Christmas Eve by bossy Schnitzle, Schnotzle and Schnootzle—F451.5.1.5.0.2.

SCHLARAFFENLAND: X1503.

SCHMALTZ: Hen is good as schmaltz—J2478.

SCHOLAR: Scholar displays book as evidence of wisdom—J2238.1; scholar disguised as rustic answers questions of visitor--J31.1.1; pedagogue tells ferryman half his life is lost if has never studied grammar. Ferryman asks pedagogue if he can swim "Then all your life is lost." Boat is sinking--J1229.4; scholar puts his own cloak and scholar's turban on fox, now it will starve to death--J1229.2; scholars resuscitate lion--J563.2; learned professor at one university examines by signs a professor of another university--H607.2.1.

SCHOOL: Old father sent to school—P236.2.

SCIMITAR: Scimitar offered for fantastic price, stretches to five time length in battle--W211.7.

SCIOROVANTE: Girl will wed one with gold head and gold teeth--T72.2.1.

SCISSORS: Lad given magic scissors--D856; spin scissors in sieve and see man to wed—D1323.20; obstinate wife makes scissors motions as she sinks--T255.1.

SCORPION: Scorpion as haunted object--H1411.4.2; scorpion asks hyena to hold his bow (tail)--K1121.3; scorpion cursed for wanting to sting Mohammed--A2231.7.1.4; witch lets brown ant and scorpions bite tongue to change voice—K311.3E.

SCOTLAND: Scots try to get secret of heather ale--C429.2; riddle, Ireland or Scotland first inhabited?--R111.1.3Ah; Scots routed from Orkney--V229.7.3. SEE ALSO ETHNIC AND GEOGRAPHIC INDEX.

SCOTT: Michael Scott plagued by demon because he hid the plague in a bag—G303.16.19.3.5.

SCRAPEFOOT: N831.1.2.

SCRAPS: Bride test, making dress from scraps—H381.1.

SCRATCHING: Agreement not to scratch, con-

test—K263.

SCRIBE: Scribe uses large letters writing to deaf man—J2242.2.1; scribe cannot write letter since has bad leg and cannot carry it—J2242.1.

SCRIPTURES: Blind lute player must sing for ghosts, body covered with scriptures to protect—E434.11. SEE ALSO BIBLE.

SCROLL: Cat descends from scroll and kills rats—D435.2.1.1.1; secret message on scroll tells of inheritance—J1199.4; marriage to heavenly maid who emerges from painting--T111.1.5. SEE ALSO PAINTING.

SCULPIN: Why sculpin has pointed tail—A2378.9.1.2.

SCULPTURE: Manticore of North Cerney befriends boy, his image is carved on church—B27.

SCURVEYHEAD: Lad as king's gardener hides hair under wig—B316A.

SCYTHE: Devil's scythe dulled by iron stakes—K171.1; land of no scythes—N411.1B; magic scythe never to be tempered in fire, melts--F348.7.1.1.

SEA: Foolish criticism of the sea—J1968.0.2; sea creatures tear at moon, pieces cut off become phosphorescence—A2116; how deep is sea?—H681.4.1; attempt to punish the sea—J1968.0.1; rivers accuse sea of making waters salty—W128.3; why sea is salt--A1115.2.1; shipwrecked shepherd distrusts sea--J11; hero's companion swallows sea—F601.2De; big mouth swallows sea and spits onto court—F660.1D; task, dipping ocean dry. Countertask, holding back streams—H1143; task, how much water is in sea? Stop all rivers and I will measure it—H696.1.1; task, dipping out sea with cup—H1143; Thor, Loke, Thiaffe contest with Fire, Sea, Thought, etc.—F531.6.15.1.1; crabs chase waves, war on sea—A2171.2.1; sea says it is calm but wind blows it up—J1891.3; witch adrift in sea, stirs sea with ladle and causes high seas—G275.1.2. SEE ALSO OCEAN; TIDE.

SEA GOD: Farmer cooling feet, has feet caught by Sea God—G561.1Cb; Maksil, God of the Gulf, claims one victim each year in whirlpool—F420.5.2.2.4; rescue of princess sent as sacrifice to Sea God—R111.1.3Ai, R111.1.3D; Sea God turns to needle and leaps into Urho's head—G530.2Bi.

SEA GODDESS: Sedna's finger pieces become Sea Goddess--A2101; Mis Lin, Sea Goddess—A421.1.2.

SEAGULL: SEE BIRD, SEAGULL.

SEA KING: Sea king helps brother find lost fish hook—U136.0.1; girl finds snake, King of the Sea, on blouse and has to promise to wed—

B654.3.

SEA LION: Man wrestles sea lions, abandoned on rocks—F617.4.

SEA MAIDEN: Lad pledged to wed sea maiden—R111.1.3Cd.

SEA MONSTER: Sea monster entices girl down cliff to retrieve dropped buckets--Q2.1.1Cb; brother kills six-headed sea monster and rescues princess--R111.1.3Ai. SEE ALSO SEA SERPENT.

SEA RAVENS: Raven dropped into sea by geese brides breaks into pieces = sea ravens—A2182.6.

SEA SERPENT: Sea monster swallows hero and pot of coals, fire built inside and serpent dies. Teeth = Orkney and Shetland Isles. Tongue cuts passage between Denmark and Sweden. Body = Iceland, still burning—R111.1.4A; lad kills sea serpent and rescues princess--R111.1.3Ea; girl takes place of sacrifice, kills--K1853.2.1.2. SEE ALSO SEA MONSTER.

SEA WEED: Princess wed to Spirit of the Sea, her hair seen drifting in tide = sea weed—B82.1.3.

SEA WITCH: Kauila strikes sea witches kidnapping his father with lightning, splintering them = mackerel--A2121.1.

SEAL: Enemies throw Avunang through seal hole, turns to seal--D100.1; seals from chips old man whittles—A2109.1, H1385.3Ff; seal grateful for removal of knife from side—B389.1; King of Seals as brother-in-law—B314F; seal maiden comes into man's power when he hides her skin--F302.4.2.2; marriage to seal in human form—B651.8, F420.6.1.1.1; seal rescues children of man who saved young— F420.5.1.10.1; Sedna's finger pieces become seals--A2101; why seals flee whales-- A2494.15.1.

SEARCH: Lost object hunted outside. Too dark to hunt in house—J1925.

SEASON: What season is best?--H561.4.1; seasons change as hare jumps up and down-- D2011.1.3.1. SEE ALSO AUTUMN; MONTHS; SPRING; SUMMER; WINTER.

SEAWEED: Origin certain sea weed--A2171.4; SEE ALSO DECEPTION PASS; KELP.

SECRET: Cottontail tricks coyote by claiming to have secret—K551.30; Devil Aghiusta turns hermits against each other by pretending to tell each a secret--A1342.1; dream (prophecy) of future greatness causes punishment when told--L425; elephant in guise of man tries to learn hunter's secret transformations-- D615.0.1; farmer calls to wife that he has hidden hoe, thief overhears--J2356.1; "Can you keep a secret?" "Then so can I." Doesn't tell

--J1482.1; you cannot expect others to act as your own storehouse, don't tell secret—J1087.1; secret whispered into ground betrayed by reed --D1316.5; servant can't tell secret or will turn to stone--S268; turn to stone if tell secret. Whispers into tree to avoid—S268E; secret of strength treacherously discovered--K975; tabu, uttering secret—C420ff; woman tells of treasure. It is stolen--C424.1; man about to tell wife fatal secret overhears cock tell how he rules hens--B216Aa; wife multiplies secret--J2353; man enchanted in wolf form to be freed if lad refrains from telling secret for seven years-- C420.2.1.

SEDNA: A2101.

SEEDS: Seeds acquired from Dawn People by Chipmunk--A1425.0.1.1; cooked seeds planted, as easy to raise grain thus as to hatch chicks from boiled eggs--J1191.2; seed corn eaten— W153.16; boy buys all seeds that stick to one finger--W48.3; man given first seeds--A1425.2; fool takes seed out of ground at night to guard --J2224; fox carried to heaven by condor, falls and bursts, seeds eaten scatter, origin seeds-- A2684; magic treasure producing seed given to kind brother--J2415.13; seed traded by monkey for fruit, seed grows for crab--K1161.6; mustard seed from house with no troubles— N135.3.2; road plowed up in famine, seeds fallen there grow--J151.1; swallow in vain urges other birds to eat seed as fast as is sown --J621.1; task, sowing seeds--H1023.1.2; one tree has all vegetables, felled and seeds scatter —A2686. SEE ALSO BEAN; GRAIN.

SEKKIM: Tower to sky in Sekkim--J2133.6.2.1.

SELF CENTERED: Self centeredness--W197ff.

SELFISHNESS: Origin of selfishness in world-- B216Ac; unkind girl wishes all three wishes for self--Q2.1.6A. SEE ALL Q2.1 Kind and unkind girls.

SELLING: Fool sells butter to stone--J1853.2; to sell cloth for four rubles, fool refuses to take six rubles for it--J2461.7. SEE ALSO PEDDLER; SALE.

SENDJI RAT: SEE RAT, SENDJI.

SENSE: Common sense and luck, which is better? N141; fox with only one basket of wit defeats tiger with many--J1662.1; poor man with no money but sense offers to multiply money for rich man with no sense—J1061.5.

SEOUL: Man dares to cross Seoul during storm and drive three nails in roof of east gate— H1419.1.

SEPPO ILMARINEN: Seppo Ilmarinen forges bird of copper which pecks at Ukko Untamoinen's insides—F912.3.2.

SERGEANT: Pincess disguises as man--K1236.2.

SERMON: Those who know may tell those who don't know—X452; wolf loses interest in sermon --U125. SEE ALSO PREACHER; PRIEST.

SERPENT: Serpent interprets dream-- D1812.3.3.5.2; girl sacrifice slays serpent— B11.11.7.2; serpent pierces skin on floating gourds and dies—R221Di; journey to serpent kingdom—F127.1; serpent lover killed by girl's family—B654.2; serpent with head of woman (Ludovine) asks deliverance—H1385.3Cc; man rescues maid from serpent--W154.8.4.1; marriage to serpent in human form—B656.2; hero kills serpent for Thunderbird—B16.5.1.4; man wounds serpent god, snakes plague--V11.7.1.1. SEE ALSO SEA SERPENT; SNAKE.

SERVANT: Poor servant woman leaves on Christmas Eve, finds fairy cabin—F343.21; maids kill cock to sleep later--K1636; boy eats breakfast, dinner and supper one after the other then sleeps—W111.2.6; faithful servant can be revived if own children killed—S268A; heroine in menial disguise at lover's home—K1816.0.2ff; servant lies in coffin alongside master, accompanies on nightly haunts--E415.1.2.1; Prince of the Seven Golden Cows reveals secret of wealth to servant—B103.3.2; why servant is only servant--H1574.4.1; SEE ALSO MAID; STOVE.

SESAME: Secret formula for opening treasure mountain overheard from robbers—N455.3.

SESSHO: Anyone who breaks Sessho's painted vase to die--J1189.4;

SEVEN: Boastful fly killer "Seven at a blow"— K1951.1.

SEVERN: Course dug by giants--F531.6.6.3.1.

SEWING: Skillful tailor sews bean together after bean has split from laughing--F662.3; bride test, to wed girl whose needle makes no sound as she sews--H383.2.4; fox allows partridge to sew his mouth shut so he can learn to whistle--K713.4; tailor dared to sew in haunted church—H1412.2; Virgin sews own robes—D1623.2.

SEXTON: Sexton as ghost in belltower—H1440. SEE ALSO PRIEST.

SHADOW: Man hires ass , driver claims he didn't hire shadow—J1169.7; peddler buys shade of tree, follows it into house--J1169.7.1; devil to take last one leaving room, gets shadow— G303.19.3; fool thinks shadow is man pursuing— J1790.1; brother seeks sister in Land of Shadows --F81.1.0.4; returning man thinks shadow is wife's lover—J21.2.1; payment for stolen smell with shadow—J1172.2.0.2; payment for shadow with shadow--J1172.2.3; punishment for stolen smell, beating shadow--J1172.2.2; task, coming neither in shadow nor in sun, wears sieve-- H1057.1; wolf thinks self huge from shadow— J953.13.1.

SHAH: Shah charged fantastic price for omelette, not eggs that are rare but the visit of kings--

U85.

SHAM WISE MAN: Sham wise man hides something and is rewarded for finding it--K1956.2. SEE DEATH, FEIGNED; DOCTOR, SHAM; ILLNESS, SHAM.

SHAMAN: Hero weds daughter of shaman— F601.21; hero kills two shamans who come from princess's nostrils at night--J21F; raven's shaman hat broken--A2335.2.3.

SHANGO: God of lighning—A781.2.1.

SHANNON: Ogres Granna falls into River Shannon —D1162.2.2.

SHARING: Anansi gives each of family members whole plantain and keeps none for self. Each share half with him—J1241.7; two brothers divide bed—K171.7.1; fox leaves all work to goose then claims crop--K641.1; sharecropper beats owner in crop division--K171.1; man feigns death rather than share--K341.2.0.2; fish shared by cutting lengthwise--J1249.6; Guno and Koyo find Kris, trouble sharing--J1516.1; lad eats moon-cake to conform to changes of moon-- J1249.4; boy never shares stories with other children--M231.1Bc; task of surviving on mountain top, each given half of supplies—H1546; monkey gets top half of tree--K171.9.1; one partner does work , other takes "Tiredness"-- J1249.7. SEE ALSO DIVIDING.

SHARK: SEE FISH, SHARK.

SHARPSHOOTER: Extraordinary companion— F601.2.

SHASTA, MT.: Origin—A963.12.

SHAVE: Barber shaves hare on run—F660.1B; barber demands wood and ox for shave-- J1511.17.1.

SHEBA: Queen of Sheba proposes riddle for Solomon—H540.2.1; Sheba not to take anything Solomon does not give her. He feeds spicy foods and she takes water--K337.0.1.

SHEEP: Ti Malice steals king's sheep "My Joy", tells Boqui to wear sheepskin and sing "I ate My Joy"—K1066; brother transformed when drinks from sheep's hoofprints--P253.2.0.1; sheep dance and sing--K606; sheep said to have come from lake bottom, dupes dive for sheep-- K842, K1051; sheep jealous of dog--W181.1; told to cast sheep's eyes at girl, does so literally— J2462.2; sheep refuses to pay bushel of corn wolf demands when hart is sent to collect— J625.1; fox consumes nine sheep on pretence of making sheepskin jacket for leopard--K254.1.1; Young Mantis and Young Kwamman-a cut All-Devourer open and true bushes and sheep emerge--A1884.0.2; sheep doesn't understand why pig shrieks--J1733; dupe taught incriminating song about stealing sheep--K1066.7; stag tries to borrow grain from the sheep using wolf as security--J1383; thief distracts shepherd with sounds of ram fighting, shoes left on road, etc. and steals sheep—K341.6; thief entering house thinks sheep is shoemaker with awl—K1161.2; sheep winter inside huge turnip—X1401.1.2; too many turtles, sheep aid by trampling them—K641.4; wolf (fox) in sheepskin—K828.1; sheep terrorize wolf with wolf-head(tail) in sack—K1715.3; wolf proposes abolition of dog guards—K2061.1.1; treaty between sheep and wolves—K191. SEE ALSO WOOL.

SHEEP, EWE: Ewe eats ashes of dead babies and bears lambs with silver wool and golden horns—N455.4.C; jackal imitates ewe's call and is let in, eats two lambs—K311.3D; three fat ewes for three fine hounds—S12.1.0.1Ba.

SHEEP, LAMB: Brother transformed to lamb when drinks from animal's hoofprints—P253.2.0.1; dove tries to carry off lamb like eagle—J2413.3; lamb falls on ice—L392.0.5; jackal imitates ewe's call and is let in, eats two lambs—K311.3D; Lambikin rolls home in drum—K553.0.3; lamb prefers being sacrificed—J216.2; lamb with diamond star in forehead to which all stick—H341.1; wolf accuses lamb downstream of muddying water—U31; lamb tells wolf to wait until he's grown—K553.0.2; sick wolf asks lamb to bring drink—K815.11.

SHEEP, RAM: Escape under ram's belly—K603; wolf captor scared by fiddle playing of ram—K2327; two rams fight till nothing left but tails—X1204.3; ram to fox bringing wolf asks "Only one"—K1715.2; kind girl shears ram—Q2.1.2Ab; jackal licking spilt blood is caught between fighting rams—J624.1.1; magic object stolen by host at inn—D861.1; lightning is ram—A1141.8.2; ram to which all stick—H341.1; ram lends hero strength to leap on head—F601.2I, H335.7.3; fox brings wolf to help exact taxes of ram—K641.2; ram to jump into wolf's belly—K553.3; wolf acts as judge before eating rams—K579.5.1.

SHEET: Task, stealing sheet from bed—K362.2.

SHELL: Shining boy is born of tears which fall into limpet shells—G275.7.0.1; child found on beach returns when hears shell—F329.4.4; child size of shell—F535.1.10Da; magic shell draws fish—C322.3; hero steals giant shell of Kintyel for eagle's—B455.3.2; maid from shell sent as reward for filial piety—N831.1; boy to wed girl whose meal sticks to abalone shell—K1816.0.2.2; magic ring in seashell which makes lad invisible—D1361.17.1; task, shell listens to distant chief—H335.7.3; dropped shell trail shows way home—G275.7.0.1; quest for cast off house of spirit = turtle's shell—H1273.2M. SEE ALSO CLAM; CONCH; OYSTER.

SHELLFISH: Why are there no shellfish on Oneata?—A2434.2.4.

SHENSHU: Guardian of the Gate—A411.1.

SHEPHERD: Shepherds witness defeat of Devil's host at birth of Christ—G303.16.19.10; disguise as herdsman—K1816.6; fox chosen as shepherd for fine voice—K934; fox disguised as shepherd, cannot run in smock—K828.1; shepherd loses sheep and starving enemy chases them, scattered and routed—K2368.7; lizard rescued from burning wood with shepherd's crook—D882.1Bba; March asks where shepherd is taking sheep and rains there—K688.1; wolf as shepherd—K2061.1.

SHERIFF: Coward hired as sheriff—K1951.2.1.1.

SHETLAND: Teeth of sea serpent from Orkney and Shetland Isles—R111.1.4A.

SHIELD: Shield that no spear can pierce—X909.5.1; lizard hides from enemies between shields and dives into creek = turtle—A2312.0.3.

SHILIN: Origin of rock in field near Shilin—A974.0.9.

SHINGLING: Shingling the fog—X1651.1.

SHINNY: Prairie falcon defeats crow in shinny match—K23.

SHLIMAZEL: Shlimazel (bad luck) wins bet—N141.0.6.

SHIP: Bells of abbey stolen, sink ship—F993.2; flying ship that goes on land or sea—F601.2A, H341.1Ab; ship made of special tree will not move until girl touches—F441.2.0.2; ghost ship haunts pirate—E535.3.3; ghost ship, Flying Dutchman—E511.1.2; pretended fool marks place on ship's side where he drops object—J1922.1.1; tall tree becomes a mast for huge ship—X909.4.3; passenger refuses to pray in storm, safety of ship is crew's responsibility—J2137.9; riddle , dead carries the living—R111.1.3Ah.

SHIPPETARO: K1853.2.1.1.

SHIPWRECK: Bat, seagull and thornbush in shipwreck—A2275.5.3; man criticizes Gods for wrecking ship, then kills swarm of ants—U21.3; lad rescues ship by subduing mermaid who is pulling ship down—H1440D; shipwrecked shepherd distrusts sea—J11; sea blames wind for shipwreck—J1891.3.

SHIRT: Man shoots deer through shirt and explains hole by saying he was shot. Was hunting illegally—J2235.1; disenchantment by sewing shirts for enchanted brothers—P253.2; fool shoots shirt full of holes. Lucky I didn't have it on—J2235; fools have shirt with no hole for head, beat it on—J2161.2; happiest couple have only one shirt—J1085.5; dragon gives heroic shirt—K2213.0.1; lie, shirt with seven sleeves for child with seven arms—X909.4.5; luck bringing shirt. King to be lucky when puts on shirt of lucky man, only man who says is lucky has no shirt—N135.3; alleged self-warming shirt—K119.3; shirt spun, woven, sewn in one day as bride task—B641Be.

SHIVA: Prays to Parvati, wife of Shiva. Parvati turns cat to maid—B601.12.

SHIVER: Lad who could not shiver—H1440.

SHOELACE: Shoelace as ghost--E443.3.1.

SHOEMAKER: Shoemaker tosses apron into heaven and hops in—Q565Ag; poor shoemaker gives last pair of shoes to beggar sheltering with him. Beggar is Maharajah--Q45.1.4; cobbler about to hang self tells demon he is making noose to tie up all demons in underworld--G501G; cobbler's diety puts fingers in mouth in horror at girl eating offering--V128.5; fairies make shoes for shoemaker—F346.1; fox as shoemaker has wolf walk through lime wash and receive boots—K254.1; shoemaker braves ghostly boar in alpine chalet--H1411.4.1; life bound up with candle, when candle goes out person dies--E765.1; shoemaker ruins ministrel's songs--J981; Conal plays pipes and miserly shoemaker's shoes march to homes of needy--F823.5; shoemaker given wealth by rich man returns it--J1085.1.1.

SHOES: Bird has suit, shoes, hat made—Z49.3.1; boat taken for giant shoe—K1718.2.1; bubble, straw, and shoe go journeying—F1025.1.1; shoes found danced to pieces each morning—F1015.1.1; daughter throws self into molten metal to cast perfect bell for father. Her shoe alone is saved. Bell tolls Ko-Ai (her name) Hsieh (shoe)—S261.0.2; dead man requests shoes--E412.3.3; man cheats devil by giving his sole instead of soul—K219.5; fool dreams he hurts foot, wears shoes to bed--F1068.5; dog's new shoes stolen by Brer Rabbit--A2494.4.4.1; shoes that fly--D832.1; giant shoes intimidate ogre--K1717; glass shoes--R221; man to wear leather shoes over gold to protect--J1703.1; shoe as haunted object--H1411.4.2; Hodja induced to climb tree, takes shoes along--J1521.1; task, wandering till iron shoes worn out—H1385.4I, H1385.4J, H1385.5; punishment, dancing in red hot iron shoes—Z65.1; shoe lost at ball--R221; magic shoes walk man into lake--D1520.10.2, G561.1C; fool carries new shoes—J2199.4.1; master puts on his mismatched pair of shoes, sends servant back, second pair same as first--J2689.1; shoes pointing direction of journey--J2014.2; unavailing attempt to get rid of shoes--N211.2; task, coming neither barefoot nor shod, soles cut from shoes--H1055; slipper test, identification by fitting--H36.1, R221; slipper test, pulled from prince rescuing princess--R111.1.3Ag; thief drops two shoes on road and steals goods when man goes back for first shoes--K341.6. SEE ALSO BOOTS; GETA; SLIPPER.

SHOES, HORSESHOES: Skillful smith shoes horse on gallop--F660.1B; lad has witch in horse form shod--G211.1.1.2A; wolf to take off shoes of horse before eating--K566.1. SEE ALSO BLACKSMITH.

SHOPPING: Fool told butter is sweet as oil, oil clear as water, buys water--J2478.

SHORTENING: Eats lard for shortening to grow shorter--X912.1.

SHOSHONE: Origin of seeds in Shoshone country —A1425.0.1.2; Shoshone learn music from birds —A1461.0.2.

SHOSHONE FALLS: Origin--A935.1.

SHOT: Man shoots deer through shirt--J2235.1; Devil gives gun that never misses, wife in tar and feathers tricks--K31.1; extraordinary shot —F601.2; fool shoots shirt full of holes. Lucky I wasn't in it--J2235; trickster threatens to shoot one thousand boars at once--K1741.2. SEE ALSO ARROW; GUN.

SHREW: Devil frightened by shrewish woman— T251.1.1ff; taming the shrew--T251.2ff; wager on wife's complacency, obedience--N11, N12. SEE ALSO WIFE.

SHREWSBURY: Plan to drown--F531.6.6.3.1.

SHRIKE: Shrike leads fish merchant on chase while fox eats fish--K341.5.2.1.

SHRIMP: Why shrimp has broken back-- A2356.2.15; origin of sacred red prawns-- A2171.4.

SHROUD: Spun by spider--A1465.2.1.

SHROVETIDE: Saving the food for "Shrovetide"-- K362.1; Michael Scot to go to Rome to ask Pope when Shrove Tide falls--A1485.1.

SHUDDER: Lad who could not shudder--H1440.

SHUTTERS: Fool with shutters closed thinks it night--J1819.3.1.

SIAMESE: Why cat has curl at end of tail— A2378.9.7.

SIBERIAN BROWN OWL: SEE BIRD, OWL--SIBERIAN.

SICILY: Lad holds up pillar supporting Sicily— A842.3; Count Roger refuses offer of Fata Morgana to make him king of Sicily--Q113.3.1; parts of Sicily seen in waters at Reggio in Calabria--Q113.2.1. SEE ALSO ETHNIC AND GEOGRAPHIC INDEX.

SICK: Old Man turns Bad Sickness to Chipmunk —A1859.2; capture by feigning illness--K757; origin of disease and sickness--A1337.0.8; sick wolf gets fox to bring deer to dance for him— J644.1.1. SEE ALSO DOCTOR; HEALING; ILLNESS; MEDICINE.

SICKLE: Sickle drowned--J1865; sickle sold in land without sickles--N411.1B.

SIDH: Woman buys child back from sidh— F321.3.0.2. SEE ALSO FAIRIES.

SIDI-BARABAS: Devil cannot name "cross" in game--G303.16.8.2.

SIEGE: King plays lute to confuse enemy--

K2366.2; enemy caused to give up siege by making it look as if the besieged have gotten reinforcements--K2368.4; dummy's made of straw are fired on by enemy--K2369.14.

SIEVE: To bring water in sieve, home is flooded --D882.1Fc; bird flies from under sieve and makes lad shudder--H1440B; task, coming neither in shadow nor in sun, wears sieve over head --H1057.1; task, carrying water in a sieve— H1023.2; spin scissors in sieve and see man to wed--D1323.20.

SIGAKOK BIRD: SEE BIRDS, SIGAKOK.

SIGIRIS SIMNO: K1951.1L.

SIGN: Conversation by sign language, misunderstood by bystander—J1804.1; man is dying of good signs (sweating, fever, etc.)--J1435; princess declares her love through sign language-- H607.3.1; maid says she lives at the "Sign of the Broken Ladle"—R221Db, R221De; learned professor from one university examines by signs a professor from another university—H607.2.1.

SIGHT: Lie, sees mosquito on mountaintop— X938.1; magic sight by looking through wolf's eyelashes--D1821.3.11. SEE ALSO EYES.

SILENCE: Disenchantment by maintaining silence for year or more--D758.2; crow to be disenchanted if princess will live with him and keep silent no matter what--D758.1; princess defeated in repartee, silenced--H507.1.0.1; wife refuses to talk for fear of stuttering--T255.8; man and wife wager who shall speak first--J2511. SEE ALSO TALK.

SILK: Tree with leaves of silk--J2415.17; origin of silk--A2811; girl has small piece of silk needed for prince's robe--J214.

SILKWORM: Bad brother cuts silkworms of good brother in half, both halves grow—J2415.15; girl's horse lover slain, horsehide wraps around her and she becomes silkworm--B611.3.

SILVER: Silver ball stained in forbidden room-- G561.1 Manning-Sanders; return from dead to demand silver dollars from eyes--E236.5; Genie of Silver Mine gives lad silver--F456.4.3; trees with silver leaves and golden blossoms from grave—N455.4C; twelve dancing princesses pass silver wood--F1015.1.1; pig in silver wood asks lad to kill witch--D136.1. SEE ALSO AXE, SILVER.

SILVERSMITH: Borrows spoon which has baby, watch which dies--J1531.3.

SILVERWARE: Silverware reward from magic egg —Q2.1.2H.

SIM: Clever Sim who would "Squeeze"--K301E.

SIMBA ISLANDERS: Throw mud to dim moon-- J2271.6.

SIMNEL: Origin of simnel cake--A1455.2.1.

SIMURGH: Rustem raised in nest of Simurgh-- B535.0.5.1.

SIN: Children punished for father's sins—P242; animals confess sins--K1024.1; task, tending olive twig until it sprouts leaves, penance for sins—H1129.12.

SINBAD: Sinbad meets Roc--B31.1.

SING: Princess Niassa is kept in bag and made to sing--G422.1.1.3; Banikan sings and children must follow into jungle--D1427.1.1; cat (monkey) sings of chain trade which procured his instrument—Z47.2; because of charm at inn all must sing--D1413.17; animals sing for coats [hyena-- A2411.1.7.1.2], [hartebeeste--A2411.1.6.9], [zebra--A2413.1.1], [leopard--A2411.1.1.1.2]; fox flatters crow into singing and dropping cheese--K334.1; Devil in troubadour contest cannot answer verse "Jesus, Joseph, Mary"— G303.16.8.1; donkey insists on singing while thieving and is caught--J2137.6; dog insists on singing while thieving and is caught--J581.1; girl put into drum and forced to sing--G422.1.1; escape by singing song--K606; fox has wolf fish with tail in ice, sings "Let wolf's tail be frozen fast"—K1021.0.2; girl sings and fruit grows-- Q2.1.6D; geese persuade wolf to sing, escape-- K606.2; coyote tells baby hopi turtle to sing or will eat--G555.1.1; ten cloth merchants captured are ordered to dance, sing in code and capture robbers--K606.0.4; mockingbird's song learned from cardinal's singing instructor--A2426.2.22; prince vows to wed singer of song--B641.0.1Ah; turtle persuades tiger's cook to put his tail in river and will sing more sweetly--K553.5.3; prince hears waterlily singing--H1021.8.1; wolf persuaded to sing--K561.2. SEE ALSO SONG.

SINGED: SEE BURNT.

SION: St. Theodule, Bishop of Sion, carried home by Devil--K1886.3.1.1; fish says one of three companions will be elected president of Sion--B217.9.1.

SIPGNET: Goddess--A1115.4.

SISTER: Sister discovers brother's secret strength, betrays--S12.1.0.1A; sister weds giant, betrays brother--S12.1.0.1; blind boy uses sister as hunting bladder--A2135.1.1; girl abandoned by brother is raised by caravan traders, taken by brother as bride when grown —H12.2.0.1; cruel brother cuts off hands of sister—B491.1.3; cruel sister turns into bird— A1999.6; cruel father forces sisters to jump over hole until brother confesses--S11.3.3.1.1; king, what is your sister doing?--H583.5.1; brother digs in potato patch and pulls buried hair, sister calls of murder--E632.1; third girl sends sisters home in bag carried by ogre-- G561.1; younger sister sees vanished older sister--H1385.6.1; sister seeks brothers transformed to birds--P253.2; girl dreams father and brothers lost in storm, holds brothers in hand, father in teeth--A421.1.2; sister and brother become sun and moon--A736.1.2.1; loaves reproach uncharitable sister--V429.2.

SISTER-IN-LAW: Sister-in-law tries to murder husband's brother--B536.2.

SIT: First man taught to sit--A1392.1.

"SITTINCAWNBIN": Trickster hides in food and eats it--K371.

SITTING: Sitting still contest--K54.

SIZE: Little Bowman has Big Bima, washerman, pose as bowman while he performs deeds--K1951.6; hare and bull advise knee-high man to grow large so can win fights, owl advises staying small so won't have to fight--J291; trickster to be made larger by Mammy Bammy Big Money--H961.1; wolf with small tail is better hunter than large wolf with big tail--J292.

SKELETON: Man feigns being skeleton to consort with spirits--E463.2; skeleton is left hanging in tree. Ghost appears and leads to skeleton--E412.3.0.1; girl abducted by revenant with whom she danced, kept in baobab seven weeks until loses flesh--E462; skeleton of wooer who killed lady comes each night to take her skull--E451.14; origin of Toromiro carvings of Rapa-Nui, chief sees sorcerors asleep with skeleton bodies, dares not tell of this so carves figures--A1465.5.1; a greedy woman pursues man to collect, he turns to skeleton, she dies of fright--E425.1.9.

SKILL: Brothers acquire extraordinary skill--F660.1; recognition by skillful weaving--H35.3.3.

SKILLYWIDDEN: Fairy child--F329.4.1.

SKIN: Disenchantment by hiding skin--D721.2; disenchantment by destroying skin--D721.3, E324.3.1 land-otter; escape by disguise in animal skin--K521.1; animal maiden comes into man's power when he hides her skin--F302.4.2.2; lad sewn in skin to be carried up onto mountain by birds to throw down treasure--K1861.1; tabu, burning skin of animal--C35.3; tabu, returning skin of animal wife--C35.4; task, selling skin and returning with skin and price of it--W181.2.0.1; witch's skin salted--G229.1.1.

SKIN COLOR: Master tries to wash slave white--J511.1.1. SEE ALSO RACE.

SKINKOOTS: Skinkoots steals springtime--A1151.1.

SKINNING: Horse made to jump out of skin--X1132.2.

SKITTLES: Playing skittles with skulls and bones--H1440A.

SKOANKIN HUNTIN': Tale filled with contradictions--Z19.2.1.

SKRATTEL: Bear frightens trolls--K1728.

SKULL: Ananse joins spirits splashing stream dry. They use own skulls to dip water--A2320.1.2; bowling with skulls--H1440A; girl sent home with skull of fire on stick--Q2.1.2CeBb; skull put in window, dog says here comes "Rattle-Rattle", is dead girl--Q2.1.4D; jay, Wiskedjak, gets head caught in bear skull--D1313.4; skulls turned on lathe--H1440A; animals live in skull--J2199.5; sip taken from Raven's skull gives understanding of language of animals--B216.2; riddle, seven tongues in one head, nest in horse's skull--H793; Saynday with head caught in buffalo skull--D1313.4; skeleton of wooer who killed lady comes each night to take her skull--E451.14; talking skull refuses to talk--B210.2.3. SEE OX; SKULL.

SKUNK: Skunks eat beaver--A2433.3.12.1; skunk outwits coyote in race--K826.1; trapped skunk changes places with fox--K842.0.11; skunk caught by gum doll--K741.0.13; hare loses both wives to Sayno, skunk--N2.6.0.1; polecat appointed king of the barnyard--J951.7.

SKUNNY WUNNY: Wins stories from fox--C432.1.3.

SKY: Creation of the sky--A701, A852.1; sky falls on duck's feet--A2375.2.8.1; sky falling alarm--Z43.3.1; Temba carried to Kingdom of Ruwa in sky by father's stool--T555.3; leaves remain flat from sky resting on them--A625.2.5; sky people steal Kunda's wife and cow--H1385.3M; Empress Jokwa mends broken pillar supporting heaven and torn sky--A665.2.0.1.1; plant grows to sky--F54.2; question, how far from earth to sky?--H682.1.1; why sky raises away from earth or is raised--A625.2ff; sky rope--F53ff; tower to sky falls--J2133.6.2.1.

SKY BLUE: Sky blue filly--D1415.2.3.1.

SKY GOD: Nyame sets moon in sky--H621.4.1; Nyame resuscitates boy--A185.12.1.1; Ananse earns stories from Nyame--A1481.2.1; turtle takes leopard in drum to Nyame--K714.2.5; Sky-God takes wife who says will bear child of gold and child of silver = sun and moon--N455.4D; Ananse proposes test of wisdom, bring kingdom to Nyame with one grain of corn--K251.1.0.1.

SKY LINE: Skyline eaten by rat--A1811.4.

SKY WINDOW: SEE WINDOW, SKY.

SKY WOMAN: Sky woman aids boy in sky world--F53.1.1.

SKY WORLD: Hare blames spider for theft, spider returns to lower world, taking web along--K401.2.3.1.

SKYE: Origin mountains near Isle of Skye--A862.1.3.

SLAVE: Aesop tells fellow slaves to take smallest loads, he largest. Is bread for noon meal--J1612.1; slaves learn magic word so can fly back to Africa—D2135.0.3.1; if others call teller a liar, they will become his slaves. Tells tale saying others are already his slaves—H342.3; losers of lying contest to be slaves of winner—X905.1.4; slave bets price of freedom that he will be invited to eat at master's table—K1954.3; slave takes refuge in mill—N255.4; worker cutting seed potatoes cannot decide which are good and which are bad—W123.3; girl leaves prince's side after vigil. Slave claims to have performed vigil—K1911.1.4; master tries to wash slave white—J511.1.1. SEE ALSO ANDROCLES; SERVANT.

SLED: Sleds set facing direction of town, trickster turns—J2014.2; man taking father to woods on sled to abandon him is reminded by son to bring back sled as he'll need it one day to carry his father off—J121.3; magic sled, all who touch stick—H341.1Aa.

SLEEP: Sleeping beauty—D1960.3; boy who sleeps all day abandoned by girls on rock—D1841.4.3.3; paper charm under pillow which causes all to sleep—T72.2.1; devil writes name of those who sleep in church—G303.24.1.7.0.1; quest for water from country of sleep—H1321.1F; Earth under Big Sleep—A1412.4; Brer Fox and wife convinced sleeping with heads off is the fashion—J2413.4.5; fox guarding shop ignores "sleeping" thief—J2243.1; sleeping potion given to maid's husband to prevent her contacting him—H1385.4; king asleep in mountain—D1960.2; fool stands before mirror with eyes shut to see how he looks in his sleep—J1936—man takes mirror to bed to see whether he sleeps with his mouth open—J1936.1; origin of sleep—A1399.2.1.1; origin of saying "Whoever falls asleep on highway loses either his hat or his head"—A1599.17; man peeks in own window to see if he sleepwalks—J1936.2; song induces sleep for one-eye, two-eye, two-eyes, three-eyes—D830.1.1; song induces sleep—F601.2Ga; what is sweetest? Sleep—H633.1; task, guard sleeping man—D754.1, L145.1B; magic sleep for years—D1960.1.

SLEEPING ROBES: Origin of sleeping robes—A1437.4.

SLEIGH: Fox feigns dead and is thrown on sleigh with fish—K371.1. SEE ALSO SLED.

SLIDING: Bear persuaded to slide down rock, wears off tail—K1021.3; raven persuades fox to imitate his sliding game—J2413.10.

SLIPPERS: Cinderella glass slippers—R221; fur slippers under bed are brother's and princess's—G530Gb; task, guessing material of slippers, gigantic pet caterpillar—H522.1.1.1; poison slipper for Snow White—Z65.1Ac; unavailing attempt to get rid of slippers, they return—N211.2; lad grabs golden slipper from foot of swan maiden—B652.1.1. SEE ALSO SHOE.

SLOOGEH DOG: Shadow of dog beaten for stealing smell—J1172.2.2.

SLOP: Slops thrown down dwarf's chimney—F451.4.4.4.

SMALL: Small hero—F535.1.1; animals confess sins, blame fastened on smallest—K1024.1. SEE ALSO SIZE.

SMALLPOX: General Verrette carries misery to heaven—Z111.2.1.

SMART: Trickster to be made smarter by Mammy-Bammy Big-Money—H961.1.

SMELL: Man feigning extraordinary sense of smell becomes ant—A2011.2; fox refuses to judge lion's bad breath—J811.2.1; fox wife leaves when her odor is mentioned—A2330.9, C35.6; guests fed with smell of food—K231.14.2; judge arranges test causing guilty man's hands to smell—J1141.1.2.1; guilty man afraid to touch donkey which will bray when thief touches. His hands do not smell of spearmint rubbed there—J1141.1.0.1; Golden Turtle (Kim Qui) gives flower to smell and nose grows—D551.1C; payment for smell of food with smell of money (clink)—J1172.2.0.1; punishment for smelling food, beating shadow—J1172.2.2; ogre smells an earthly man—R111.1.3Ah; man learns to stan smell of tannery—U133; odor of wine cask—J34.

SMITH: Devil pounded in knapsack—K213; Devil as smith's apprentice rejuvenates boyar's wife—J2411.0.2; boy appears to smith in dream and asks to free from Giant Mahon MacMahon—F321.3.2; Smith Liam drops hammer to earth and Arton catches and retuns—D672K; smith refused entry to hell—Q565A; moon and stars made by smith—A744.1; Ukko Untamoinen and Seppo Ilmarinen to dance on his tongue and swallows. Seppo Ilmarinen forges copper bird which pecks at insides—F912.3.2. SEE ALSO ILMARINEN.

SMOKE: Countertask, smoke carrying pad—H1021.12; who can stay longest in smoky hole, deer children trick bear cubs in revenge—K851.1; thunder gives medicine pipe to be smoked when Thunder returns with rains in spring—A284.5; why Mt. Fuji smokes—A2816.1; why whale spouts, given tobacco to smoke by Kiloskap—A2479.14. SEE ALSO PIPE.

SMOKEHOLE: Boy in moon went up through smokehole—A751.0.3; stolen sun squeezed out smokehole by raven—A721.1.1.

SNAIL: Snail carries house so firefly won't burn—Z49.6.0.1; mysterious housekeeper—N831.1; snail frees leopard, leopard plans to eat snail—J1172.3.0.6; snail beats monkey (mousedeer) in race with aid of relatives—K11.1; task, pass thread through snail shell—H506.4.

SNAKE: Snake puts tail in hole in ark—A2145.2; respite until prince who widowed snake bears as many sons as she has—K551.29; snake curls tail around bowl—J1565.1.3; serpent killed by cat's severed head—B331.0.1; why snake turns belly to sky in death—A2579.1; man dies from bite, thinking it snakebite—F1041.1.11.4; pet snake grows into dragon—D861.1D; snake interprets king's dream—B145.2.1; origin of enmity between serpent and man—A2523.2.1; snake trades voice for earthworm's eyes -A2241.12; snake's father gives magic object—D817.1.2.2; taken to underwater home of snake chiefs, to pull feather from roof of cave—B491.1.1; serpent attacks file —J552.3; snake on fish's back bites--J2137.6.2; snake serves frog king as mount. Eats frogs— J352.2; friendship of snake and frog ends when snake wants to eat--J426.2; frozen snake thaws— X1321.4.11; snakes besiege unkind girl—Q2.1.2Ab, Q2.1.2Ea; clay figure of girl with snake inside-- F582.1.1; snake befriends banished girl with hands cut off—B491.1.3; snakes plague man who wounds serpent god—V11.7.1.1; girl, mother turn to snakes. Enter crack in cave, bring back gold coins in mouths—J2415.20; greedy neighbor pours pot of serpents. Turn to gold on good man's head—N182.1; gold producing serpent— B103.0.4.1; gold producing serpent to be slain-- D876.2; grateful snake gives magic object-- D882.1.B; helpful snake—B491.1; snake husband --H1385.4G; animals judge in favor of snake-- J1172.3.2; snake king shows river between king- doms—K1931.2Vb; snake coils round king—K151.1; underworld kingdom of snakes—F92.7; knowledge of animal languages reward from King of Snakes —B216Aa; servant tastes white snake, under- stands language of animals--B217.1.1; serpent licks ears, animals languages learned--B216; magic object from snake's father--D817.1.2; snake maiden rewards--D882.1C; man who kills snake claims reward in maiden's bed—D195.1.2; marriage to snake—B604.1; marriage to person in snake form—B646.1; meadowlark outwits snake --K567.2; snake tied to stick to be measured— K713.1.9; snake drinks while in milk bottle, has to spit out milk to escape—K1022.0.1; mother res- cues daughter from sleeping snake's belly-- K311.3C; necklace dropped by crow into snake's hole leads men to snake--K401.2.2; snake tricked into noose—K717.2; water snakes nurse girl's son—K1911Aa; snake ogre bluffed—K1741.1, K1741.2.1, K1741.3; trickster defeats giant snake ogre--G501C; opossum releases snake, hare re-enacts--J1172.3; snake rescued from pit, gives jewel, bites king—W154.8; porcupine sug- gests snake leave if can't stand prickles--P332; snake postman to take bite of Anansi's head— K75; snake taken to bed becomes prince— D195.1.1; Brer Snake gives Brer Rabbit poison --K1082.0.2; rainbow is snake—A791.2.1; ser- pent refuses reconciliation--J15; snakes show remedy—B512, B522.1; snake turns on rescuer --J1172.3; snake gives a powder to restore princess he has bitten--B522.1.2; task, bring- ing faggots without rope. Helpful snake coils about them--B491.1.1; snake becomes rope— K1911A; prince emerges from ruby, turns to green serpent—H1385.4K; why snake hasn't be- come spirit yet, due to pearl on head—H1273.2J; tall tale, snakes eat each other up—X1204.2; task, chop leaning palm so won't fall on village. Snakes wrap tails round tree, pull—B582.2F; test, sleeping in room full of snakes--H328.10; test, plow field of snakes barefoot--H328.11; monk sucks poison, tiger ungrateful--J1172.3; tiger thinks snake is belt--J1761.6.0.1, K1023.1.1; toad slays monster snake, rescuing maid--B16.5.1.3; ungrateful snake threatens benefactor--J1172.3.2.3, J1172.3.2.4; ungrate-

ful snake plans to eat rescuer--J1172.3; why snakes are venomous--A2523.2.1; why snake has no voice--A2241.12; snake rids self of wasp-- J2102.2; snakes in water jar injure intruder— K1161.3.2; snake's wife cannot kill prince until princess bears as many sons as she has--J1173.1; snake wraps tail around sumo wrestler's legs and head around tree across river—F617.2.1; girl finds snake king on blouse, must promise to wed—B654.3; girl refuses to wed, is thrown to snakes. Sings and charms--D735.1B; prin- cess weds snake prince—D735.1F; Zeus says snake should have bitten first foot to step on it--J623.1. SEE ALSO NAGA; SERPENT.

SNAKE, ADDER: Lad in tower to avoid death. Adder comes from firewood—E530.1.7.1; cow, tree judge for adder, not man--J1172.3.2; adder turns on rescuer--J1172.3.

SNAKE, ANACONDA: Father tosses hot stone down throat, Anaconda regurgitates daughter-- F912.3.1.1.

SNAKE, BLACKSNAKE: Blacksnake scorched fetching fire—A2411.5.9; blacksnake revenges self. Pours gold on man—K602.3; blacksnake tricks iguana. Iguana lets him hold poison box --A2523.2.2; blacksnake pulls two feathers from tree prison—D1050.2.

SNAKE, BOA: Boa as host coils around bowl— J1565.1.3; dog sheltes with boa who owns fire, tail catches fire, flees--A1415.2.4; girl clothed in water boa skin—R221Ya.

SNAKE, BULLSNAKE: Guest bullsnake fills house with tail--J1565.1.3.1.

SNAKE, COBRA: Camel fails to trick black cobra —K710.1.1; black cobra kills all chickens that stray--K1459.1; hunters pass green grass snake on path. Cobra thinks it safe spot, sleeps there there, killed--J2413.11; man falls into well, ac- cidentally kills cobra—N624.

SNAKE, PYTHON: Doctor agrees to come when children sing to him and carry down to village on shoulders--B491.1.2; lizard steals python's drum--K1079.2; rescued python gives magic gourd—D882.1B; python tied to pole to measure --K713.1.9; python forms rope to sky—H1385.3M; python swallows dog which swallowed cat which swallowed fowl, etc.--Z43.5; Rock Python re- gurgitates hero, lets wed daughter—F914.0.1; man takes Rock Python to river, given lovely wife. Bad man imitates, given shrew--J2415.11; witch in python form destroyed—K1611Db.

SNAKE, RATTLESNAKE: Hare (mouse) frees rattlesnake, coyote re-enacts--J1172.3; evil clan turned to rattlesnakes with dancing rattles fixed to tails--A2145.9.1; where rattlesnake got fangs --A2345.5.1; why rattlesnake's head is flat— A2320.1.0.1; rattlesnake bites off North Star's finger—A774.1; rattlesnake given poison be- cause all step on him. Given rattles so animals can hear--A2523.2.1; man kills rattlesnake. Snakes declare war—B268.7.

SNAKE, SNAKE RIVER: Dams thrown up by Coyote to stop flow of Snake River--A935.1.

SNAKE, SNAKESKIN: Bird's colors from snakeskin--A2411.2.5.1.1.

SNAKE, WATER BOA: Girl wears boa skin--R221Ya.

SNAKE, WHITE SNAKE: White snake lady causes flood. Monk spreads robe, protects mountain top --B656.2.1; animal languages learned from eating white snake--B217.1.1. SEE ALSO NAGA; SERPENT.

SNARE: Birds in snare fly to King of Mice who gnaws them free--K581.4.1.1. SEE NET.

SNEEZE: Keep doing all day what begins, sneezes --J2073.1; lad climbs statue of Buddha to obtain self-replenishing pear. Climbs into nostril. Buddha sneezes--D1652.1.7.3; to clap hands when sneezes. Man being rescued by rope sneezes--J2516.3.2; cock persuades wolf to hold by tail, feathers cause to sneeze--K561.1.0.6; thief to say "the devil take the bride's soul" each time she sneezes--C12.2.2; to die when donkey sneezes three times--J2311.1; if sneezes thrice and no one says "God bless us", dwarf can take bride--F451.5.17; hidden prince sneezes as princess is exorcised. Guards think is demon exiting. Flee--K1996; shepherd refuses to say "to your good health" when king sneezes--H328.9; one who sneezes to be thrown out of pit--K652.1; lad's magic ring causes sneezing, makes princess laugh--H341.4.

SNEEZY SNATCHER: Boy caught by Sneezy Snatcher--G82.1.2.

SNOOKS: Snooks family with wry mouths cannot blow out candles--X131.

SNORING: Insect simulates snoring--K661.3.

SNOW: Beadle carried on rounds so won't track up snow--J2163.3; snow girl as child of old couple--T546.3; man steps into chimney during big snow--X1653.3; horse eats charcoal in snowstorm, keeps gypsies warm by heat from tail-- X1203.1; man stores much fuel. Manages to save self from Snow King's visit--A289.3; girl weds Man of Snow--T117.12; princess requests moon snow--L393.1; shaking Mother Holle's featherbed causes snow to fly to earth--Q2.1.2Aa; Goddess of Snow, Poliahu, duels with Pele--A289.2; Raven creates earth from snow--A618.3; girl sweeps snow from door of dwarf's home. Finds strawberries underneath--Q2.1.4; snow in mid-summer confirms innocence--F962.11.2; snow in summer, lie--X1653.4.2; Woman of the Snow, witch freezes --T115.1; witsduks, snow the wind blows and drifts--A289.4. SEE ALSO WINTER.

SNOWSHOES: Glooscap gives magic snowshoes-- D1065.3.1.

SNOW WHITE: Snow White and Rose Red befriend bear--D113.2.2; Snow White and the Seven Dwarfs--Z65.1.

SNUFFBOX: Cat tricks Devil into snuffbox-- K1917.3J; magic snuffbox--D882.1E; little men in magic snuffbox--D882.1Ea.

SOAP: Boy to buy soap, forgets--J2671.2.1; black crow steals soap--J2211.5.

SOCCER: Demons and drowned father play soccer --E577.1.

SOCIETY: Origin of spirit societies--A1539.2. SEE ENTIRE CHAPTER P.

SOCKS: Jumping into socks--J2161.1.

SOFA: Boy caught by Mr. Miaca, puts out sofa leg instead of own leg--G82.1.2.

SOIL: Megu sends messengers to scrap earth from boots of foreigners leaving Ethiopia, soil most precious thing--P711.10; forbidden to set foot on certain soil, trickster fills boots with another soil--J1161.3.1. SEE ALSO EARTH; MUD.

SOLDIERS: Devil pounded in knapsack by soldier--K213; the dragon and his grandmother hire three soldiers--M211.7.1; girl disguises as soldier--K1837.6.1; army routed bv magic storm --D2142.1.6.1. SEE ALSO WAR.

SOLE: SEE FISH, SOLE.

SOLES: New soul promised demon, king meant boot sole--G530.2Bf; man cheats devil by giving him sole instead of soul--K219.5; giants invulnerable on soles--G511.2; soles cut from shoes, task going neither barefoot nor shod--H1055. SEE ALSO: SHOES.

SOLOMON: Solomon's judgment, divided child-- J1171.1; Solomon as master of magicians-- D1711.1.1; King Solomon favors maize in argument of plants--A270.1; golden plow valueless if doesn't rain in May--J1199.2; Queen of Sheba propounds riddle. Bee shows Solomon which are real flowers--H540.2.1; Sheba not to take anything Solomon doesn't give her. He feeds spicy food, she takes water--K337.0.1.

SOMBRERO: Six men on bench with sombreros, cannot fit. Put on hats, stretch bench. Fit now --J2723; magic sombrero sticks forever to head-- D1067.1.1.

SON: Son seeking herb for dying mother turns to bird--A1999.5; son on gallows bites mother's ear for bad upbringing--Q586; handsome son to make character good too--J244.1; asked to define difficult word, son promptly fabricates a false answer. Delighted father, "Just like his father"-- T615.1.1; king has donkey led in with name of boy's father painted on it. Boy changes sign to read Chu-Kuo-Tze-Yu's Donkey--J1289.29; sons return as doves, one is eaten--D154.1; king's fool sent by advisor with letter saying "execute this man." Advisor's son offers to deliver it for him--K511.0.2; father kills son for eating apple-- S11.3.3.1.1; honey-gatherer's three sons, one hears fall, one follows trail and puts back together--H621.4.2; son prophesied to kill father --N731.2.1; gold dust entrusted turns to sand, friend says son turned to parrot--J1531.2.0.1; father with riddling remark imparts knowledge that sons are dead--H585.2; woodcutter's four sons cannot answer riddles. Turned to stone-- H541.4; three sons seek water of life for father-- H1321.1Aa. SEE ALSO FATHER; MOTHER.

SON-IN-LAW: Father-in-law's remark construed as insult by son-in-law--W198; quiet son-in-law proves deep thinker--P265.2.

SONG: Cock given free passage to Cadiz if can please captain with his coplas--J1653.1; Brer Bar taught crude courting song, Brer Rabbit fine song--K1066.8; coyote wants to learn locust's song--G555.1.2; coyote forces hare to sing for him--G555.1.3; devil learns mother's song, tricks girls--K311.3K; goat singing threatening song bought off with food, jewels--K1767; groundhog sings to escape wolf captors--K606.2.1; gunni-wolf forces little girl to sing--G555.1.4; hunch-back finishes fairies' song, hump removed-- F344.1.3; incriminating song taught--K1066; fox sings incriminating song--K473; bard makes up derisive song about king--J611.1; daughter per-forms tasks with magic song--G530.2Fc; origin of particular song--A1464.2.1; abandoned girl about to wed brother sings of plight. Parent's recognize--H12.0.1; rescue from ogre by sing-ing--G555.1.1ff; song ruined by bootmaker, blacksmith, etc.--J981; song induces sleep-- D830.1.1; swan song--B752.1; turtle makes flute of jackal's thighbone, sings of this--K1775.1; man listens to bird song, years pass--F377.0.2. FOR TALES INCLUDING MUSICAL NOTATIONS SEE Robinson, Adjai. SINGING TALES OF AF-RICA; Serwadda, Moses. SONGS AND STORIES FROM UGANDA; Tracey, Hugh. THE LION ON THE PATH; Wolkstein, Diane. THE MAGIC ORANGE TREE.

SORCERER: Sorcerer orders girl drowned to stop flood. Magistrate drowns sorcerer instead, builds dam with sorcerer's wealth--R111.1.3Db; sorcer-er turns Foni's goat to stone--T75.2.1.3; most precious thing in world=salt--H659.28; sorcerer weds girl--G302.7.1.1. SEE ALSO MAGICIAN.

SORCERER'S APPRENTICE: D1711.0.1.2.

SORIA MORIA CASTLE: Princess rescued-- H1385.3A.

SORROW: 'Sorrow' tricked into making self small enough to fit into hub of cart wheel--K717.3. SEE ALSO CRYING; GRIEF.

SOSONDOWAH: Great Night woos maid as black-bird--B642.6.2.

SOUL: A 'new soul' promised demon, king meant boot sole--G530Bf; man cheats devil, gives sole instead of soul--K219.5; man sells soul to devil-- M211; soul won from devil in card game--E756.2, K1811.6; Kantchil claims soul is in jar (bees)-- K1023.1.0.3; man in moon shoots souls of dead-- A751.0.4; soul becomes star after death--E741.2;

water spirit keeps souls of drowned persons in dishes at home--F420.5.2.3. SEE ALL E700-E799.

SOUND: Fox rubs tail on door making sound "Zui", knocks head on door "Ten", thus calls Zuiten-- K1887.4; origin of echo--A1195.1; payment for smell of food with sound of coin--J1172.2; thun-der, sound of Vainamoinen's boots, river imitates sound of Vainamoinen's cloak, etc.--A2272.1.4.

SOUP: Bat tells bush-bat not to boil self to make soup--A2491.1.0.1; Sayday puts hot stone in bowl, makes soup. It splashes on bobcat's fur. Why bobcat has spots--A2412.1.7; dipping bread in lake full of ducks, eating duck soup--J1250.7; fool eats hot soup--J2214.1.1; hot soup brings tears to wife's eyes--J1478; friends of friends who gave hare came to dinner. Served soup of the soup of the hare--J1551.6; fools throw meal in lake, jump in to taste porridge--J1938; man invited for duck soup given radish broth. Takes friend duck hunting, aims at radish tops-- J1551.6.1; ring token in soup--R221D; man blows on hands to warm, on soup to cool, Satyr flees-- J1801.1; soup stone (nail)--K112.2; man thinks of soup, boy knocks on door begging for some-- J1849.7; turtle sweats, others get idea of turtle soup--A2351.5.1; soup made of wife served to man by badger--G61.3.

SOUTH: Carriage points south--D1313.17; Pam-pero, South Wind, bringer of rain--A282.2.

SOW: SEE PIG.

SOWING: Landlady sows grain in fireplace nightly, transforms guests to horses--G263.1.0.2; riddle, making many out of few. Sowing grain-- H583.2.2. SEE ALSO GRAIN; SEEDS.

SPADE: Espen Cinderlad finds self-chopping axe, spade, walnut--H1115.1.1; lie, man goes for spade to dig self out--X1731.2.1.

SPAIN: King of Spain's golden bird stolen by hero--H1331.1.3Aj. SEE ALSO ETHNIC AND GEOGRAPHIC INDEX.

SPAN: Span high man--D882.1Eb.

SPANIARD: Spaniard tells Indians that donkey speaks Spanish--K1977; origin of Spaniard-- A1614.2.

SPANISH: Three travelers know one phrase each of foreign language--C495.2.2.2.

SPANISH MOSS: Moon answers mother's prayer. Hangs moss on trees to warm freezing children --A2683.1.1.

SPARROW: SEE BIRD, SPARROW.

SPEAK: Princess brought to speak--H343ff.

SPEAKING: Speaking tabu--C400ff; tabu, speak-ing while digging treasure--F348.11. SEE ALSO LANGUAGE; SILENCE; TALKING.

SPEAR: Spear driven through Baobab tree—F636.6; count to ten before spear reaches ground— H331.18; earth dripping form spear of culture hero, origin Japan—A822.2; self-returning spear —D1602.6; spear that can pierce any shield-- X909.5.1.

SPEED: Remarkably swift person--F660.1.2. SEE ALSO SWIFT.

SPENDTHRIFT: Riddle, field already harvested. Belongs to spendthrift who has already spent the money--H586.4.

SPHINX: Oedipus destroys Sphinx--C822; riddle of the Sphinx—H761; Sphinx gives throne to Thothmes--B51.1.

SPIDER: Anansi in age debate—B841.1.2; why spider is bald, Ananse's head rubbed with hot oil—A2317.2.2; why spiders hide in bananas— A2433.5.3.6; spider spinds basket shut while other animals argue—K396; spider floating on leaf inspiration for first boat--A1459.2.1; Anansi passes test of drinking boiling water— H221.4.2; spider falls in brew vat, flea mourns-- Z32.2.3.1; spider as bride--B643.4; Anansi takes all candlefly's egg cache—Q272.5; spider hands box to ant, refuses to take back. Hence ants carry huge loads--A2243.1; why spider lives in ceiling—A2433.5.3.3, A2433.5.3.4; poorly dress- ed spider persuades well dressed companion to exchange clothes--K499.8.1; spider rescued by sun spins clouds--A1133.5; Anansi asks grain of corn to hide him--Z43.5.1; bat, spider, bull court together—T92.11.3; Anansi's signing causes Granny to dance--D2174.2; spider feigns death, comes from 'grave' to rob garden nightly —K341.2; spider shams death thinking dead must be well fed--K341.2.0.4; spider cheats boy of eggs, boy feigns death. Snake returns eggs fearing death--K1867; how debt came to the Ash- anti, Anansi advises--A1378; trickster disguises as leprous animal, says trickster is putting hex on enemies to cause this disease—K1995; feigned knowledge from dream--D1810.8.5; bird taken on back becomes heavier and heavier, turns to Dry Bone Man—G303.3.5.3.1; Anansi gets ele- phant stuck between two trees, says must cut off hind parts to get free--A2362.2; man bound by fairies finds spider web over self in morning-- F361.2.3; fat cut from inside of cow--F929.3; in- appropriate feast repaid--J1565.1.1; spider in- vited to two feasts--J2183.1.3; spider flies with birds to island. They take back feathers, leave— K1041.1.5; spider flies too near sun with arti- ficial feathers--K1041.1; Anansi borrows feathers to fly—K1041.1.3; Gizo spider coats stomach with wax, crawls over crow's fig pile—K378.1.1; fox, sandpiper, mole, weasel steal fire— A1415.2.2.3; spider spins web to star to fetch fire—A1414.7.5; today's catch of fish traded for prospective larger catch tomorrow—J321.1.1; spider spectre in pool is ghost of Empress Otawa —E423.8.3; gnats overcome lion, killed by spi- der—L478; spider goblin as priest (maiden) play- ing samisen entraps--E423.8.1; two spider grand- fathers lower coyote back to earth in web— D482.1.2; spider grandmother aids girl racer--

H1594.3; spider grandmother aids sun's sons— F17.1; why spider walks in grass—A2433.5.3.2; spider transformed for greediness, occupies dark corners—A2433.5.3; Anansi tells hare to dip tail in rum and put into sea. Fish bite—K1021; Anan- si hides food in hat--W125.3.1; Anansi joins spirits splashing stream dry. They use own skulls to dip water. He imitates, cannot put head back on—A2320.1.2; Ananse steals self-hoeing hoe— D1651.15; Anansi traps hornets--K714.2.6; why spider is not killed by men—A2221.5.2; spider web as origin of lace—A1465.2.1; spider slaps his legs laughing and breaks—Z32.6; Anansi tricks leopard into tieing tail to tree—K713.1.11; Anansi ties leopard in game—K713.1.10; Anansi claims mosquito, moth and fly are his to eat, anyone who calls him a liar to be eaten— X905.1.3; spider spins web to sky to fetch light —A1412.6; spider maiden spins marvelous cloth for rescuer—B652.2.1; man-crow is killed by Soliday, spider claims feat and princess— A2433.5.3.3.1; spider spins web over hole and saves hiding Mohammed (Hadji)--A2221.5.2, B523.1; all animals are inside mountain, spider smokes them out--A1714.3.2; man copies spider making web and invents nets to catch animals— A1457.3.1; spider has spun web to keep phan- toms from tree where girl is kept—E461; Ananse drops pig's money in bamboo tube, pig gets trunk caught and must cut off—A2335.4.1.1; Anansi traps all sent to arrest him in pitfall-- K735.1.1; Anansi gives one of four plantains to each family member, they return half each— J1241.7; Anansi finds magic pot, breaks tabu and whips come out—D861.1la; Anansi ties python to pole to 'measure'—K713.1.9; Spider gives Brer Rabbit thread—K1082.0.2; spiders spin ropes to hold rainbow--A791.11; Nyame resuscitates boy to fulfill Anansi's promise— A185.12.1.1; Nansi ties rope to leg and tells wife to pull when soup is done—K171.0.2.2; Anansi and son escape dragon to sky--K671.1; Mulungu has spider spin rope and climbs up to live in the sky—A1279.2; Anansi obtains stories by performing assigned task--A1482.2.1; spider set to making string by creator, swallows string —A2356.2.8.1; Anansi forgets word to stop cutting sword—A2796.1; thieving spider cap- tured by tarbaby--K741; Anansi captures fairy with tarbaby--K741; why spider has thread in back of body—A2356.2.8.1; Anansi eats tiger's food, teaches monkey incriminating song— K1066.5; trickster beats trail into Guinea Fowl's farm, claims farm on evidence of trail--K453.1; spider sells fake horse and arranges tug of war —K22.1; Anansi tricks turtle in dividing match —K16.2; Anansi defeated in race by turtle-- K11.1; Anansi sends turtle to wash repeatedly at feast--K278; spider tries to rescue Two Feathers--D1050.2; Virgin gives mantilla of spider webs--D1623.2; Anansi chooses animals with best voice to talk at court, prince chooses voice for his own--A2423.1.2.2; why spider has small waist--A2355.1.1; man copies spider and devises art of weaving--A1453.2.1; daughter weaving refuses to go to mother when called, turned to spider--A2091.2; hare blames spider for theft, spider returns to lower world taking web along—K401.2.3.1; spider must spin fragile webs—N455.4D; Anansi drops pot of wisdom—A1481.1; Anansi fulfills test of wisdom, brings kingdom to Nyame with one grain of corn —K251.1. SEE ENTIRE COLLECTION Appiah, Peggy. ANANSE THE SPIDER; Arkhurst, Joyce C. THE ADVENTURES OF SPIDER; Sherlock, Philip. ANANSI, THE SPIDER MAN.

SPINDLE: Countertask, making spindle and loom from one stick of wood -- H1022.3; girl to ask she-bear for golden spindle—Q2.1.1Fa; spindle leads prince to maid—H1311.2; girl to prick finger on spindle and die—D1960.3A; girl sent to wash spindle drops it into well—Q2.1.2Aa.

SPINNING: Bride test, spinning—H388.2.1; magic cow spins flax—D830.1.1, Q2.1.1E; three witches (hags) deformed from much spinning—D2183.1; girl spins with doll's help—Q2.1.2CeBb; fairy spins, not to grumble when winding, does so, thread vanishes—F348.0.1.1; daughters spin gold, youngest talks to prince and her thread tarnishes—H1021.8.1; key in flax reveals laziness—H382.1; task, making loom of two splinters—H1022.3.1; millstone thought spinning wheel—K1718.2.1; spider maiden spins clouds—A1133.5; supernatural wife or daughter spins marvelous cloth for rescuer—B652.2; tabu, spinning—C832; mother boasts foolishly, assigned spinning task—H914; task, spinning impossible amount—H1092; task, done by supernatural helper—D2183. SEE ALSO SPINDLE.

SPINNING MAID CHUC NU: Weds shepherd on opposite shore of Milky Way—A778.3.1.

SPINNING WHEEL: Spinning wheel sent home by itself—J1881.1.5.

SPIRIT: Friend in basket speaks as voice of God and orders spirits to release Pupu who has been reclaiming stolen food plants—E461.1.1; spirit of chief killed in battle returns to body and passes through fire surrounding body to re-enter it—E38.2; evil spirit moves signal flag causing death of man—E279.6.1; spirit disguised as friend goes hunting for frogs, says is eating them as fast as can catch them—E434.12; Tintinyin knows language of animals, learns secret identity of king of spirit world—B216.4; king's son is exiled to Lanai for uprooting breadfruit plants, he outwits spirits there and survives—K688.6; spirit monster gives mask and teaches dance—A1542.2.2; lad, rescues princesses from unclean spirit on horse—H1199.12.4A; spirits toss man into air—F153.2; quest for cast off house of spirit, turtle shell —H1273.2M. SEE ALSO GENIE; TREE SPIRIT.

SPIRIT SOCIETIES: Origin of Spirit Societies—A1539.2,

SPIT: Men hang in chain until top man spits on hand—J2133.5; frog challenges tiger to spitting contest and spits out hairs he bit off tiger's tail—K1715.12.2; ghosts fear human spittle—E463.1; ogress spits in face and calls "my body to you, yours to me", takes girl's mother's body

—R221N; philosopher spits in king's beard—J1566.1.

SPLIT: Man tells lion to put paw in split log—K1111.0.2.

SPONGE: Ass loaded with salt lies in river to lighten load, tries again with load of sponges—J1612.

SPOON: Silver spoon said to have had baby—J1531.3; mouse bride (doll bride) arrive drawn in spoon—B641Be; girl follows spoon dropped in river—Q2.1.2H; terrapin makes hominy spoon of wolf's ear—K1715.3.3; soldier lays sword on table ostentatiously, farmer brings in manure shovel to go with big knife—J1225.1; Tatterhood carries wooden spoon—L145.1A; "Pete, go thrash some wheat." "I have a stomach-ache." "Pete, come and eat." "Where's my big spoon?" —W111.7; witch with head under arm entices Buttercup from hiding with silver spoon—K526A; witch Baba Yaga counts spoons and dwarf is enticed from hiding—H1385.3Fe.

SPRAT: SEE FISH, SPRAT.

SPRIGGANS: Spriggans bind man fast—F361.2.3; spriggans enchant nightgown and it prickles—F351.2.1.

SPRING: Arbutus as sign of spring—A1158.1; most beautiful thing—H641.1; chain, louse falls in beer, spring floods—Z32.2.4.1; Lough of Cork from spring from drowned pitcher—F944.7; Dewi Kesumo turned to spring, husband to waringen tree—A2681.15; why spring has gone dry —H1273.2; tabu, letting something fall into spring, dipped finger turns gold—G671; little green man muddies spring—K1611Ba; old man causes snow, young brings flowers—A1158.1; spring of wine—D925.0.2.1, F718.3; spring of youth—D1338.1.1.2. SEE ALSO WELL.

SPRINGBOK: Mantis rescues springbok from stomach of elephant—F929.4.

SPRINGTIME: Glooskap brings summer back to Canada—A1153.1; young groundhogs see traces of spring root on mother's teeth—J1122.3; springtime stolen by Skinkoots—A1151.1; Vazouza and Volga run to sea in spring—A939.4.

SPONGE: Boy throws sponge at suspended cake to soften—K301C.

SPRUCE CONE: Sky woman gives magic spruce cone—F53.1.

SPYING: Tabu, spying on fairies at work—F346.1.

SQUASH: Baby from squash, water turns to gold when bathed—T555.1.1.1; King of Naxos obtains squash seeds, people refuse to eat, he places seeds under guard and all are stolen—J1199.3; man given first seeds of squash—A1425.2.

SQUEEZING: Contest in squeezing water from stone—K62.

SQUID: Rat eats hair off squid's head--A2317.13.

SQUIRREL: Squirrel draws bear up tree, bear falls—Z33.6; why squirrel hops backwards--A2441.1.13; squirrel as judge has scene re-enacted—J1172.3; squirrel in leopard's house intimidates--K1711.2.2; squirrel and leopard build house, each thinks it is his—K1715.3.2; why squirrel lives in trees--A2433.3.9; Manabozho kills giant sturgeon with aid of squirrel —F912.2.7; squirrel mother feeds man on ledge —G211.1.7.1; squirrels get in bag to help crack nuts--K711.7; Manabozo paints squirrel—A2411.1.4.1; squirrel weds porcupine, too prickly--J414.3.2; squirrel tries to free snared sun--A728.0.1; why squirrel's tail turns up—A2378.9.6; thieving squirrel caught by sticky figure--K741.0.8. SEE ALSO FLYING SQUIRREL.

SQUIRREL, RED SQUIRREL: Red Squirrel steals bag but stops at streams to eat nuts, distributing over land--A1425.0.1.2.1.

SQUIRREL, ROCK SQUIRREL: Coyote steals fire from cranes with rock squirrel's aid—A1413.0.2.1.

STAFF: Staff blooms at Christmas in memory of water horse—F420.1.3.3.1.

STAIRS: Ogre to build stairs before cockcrow—K1886.3.1.1.

STAMPING CONTEST: Chameleon wins--K17.1.

STAN BOLOVAN: Stan Bolovan vanquishes dragon with his one hundred children—G501C.

STANISLAUS: Stanislaus hears outlaw Matthew's confession—V21.7.

STAR: When helpful animals are beheaded and then cremated trees spring up from their ashes. These are burnt and twelve new stars appear in heavens—S12.1.0.1A; stars are those captives who escaped to sky with Kwaku Tsin—A711.0.1; woman is to bear two children with golden hair. The boy will have a half moon on his forehead, the girl will have a star—N455.4Ad; stars discuss the birth of the Christ Child--V211.1.2.2; coyote throws stars into the sky—A763.3; deermice chew straps and coyote steals the sun from two old women. Coyote trims off pieces for stars—A721.1.5; dancing stars wearing teeth and shell jewelry leap into sky—A761.0.1; dawn binds Saynday and turns maid into star over forehead—B642.6.2; the deer, the hare and the toad help put stars in sky—B841.1.6; Earth Magician breathes on magic water and it freezes = sun, moon and stars—A614.0.1; fire from piece broken off star—A1414.7.5; star on forehead of kind girl—Q2.1.1C; star on forehead —F545.2.1, N455.4; fugitives rise and become stars—A773.4.1; star husband takes mortal as

wife—A762.1; origin of light--A1412.4; a lad weds star maiden--A762.2, F302.4.2.4; stars are made from old moon--J2271.2.2; the stars are a woman's necklace hung on the sky--A625.2.2.1; origin of stars--A764; youth tries to knock down a star with a bamboo pole--J2275.2; the star princess turns house to lake, guests to frogs--A762.2.2; the stars are pieces of the sun stolen by Raven--A721.1; fool thinks stars that are reflected in water are drowning--J1791.2.1; riddle, as many stars as hairs on ass --H702.2.1; riddle, how many stars in heaven—H702; Saynday puts hand in sky = five stars—A799.4; stars are seeds of calabash—A617.2; stars are seeds of pumpkin—A641.3; girl seeks stars, pursues them, falls out of bed and wakes up—F1068.0.1; poor girl gives lost food and clothing away, stars fall from heaven and turn to silver—V411.10; stars made by smith—A744.1; dead souls become new stars—A1335.17; soul becomes star after death—E741.2; Lippo fails to weave shelter tight enough and starlight strikes wife, she leaves--A1611.5.6; star belt flung into sky by Tao—A625.2.11; twins born with stars on forehead--R111.1.3Ac. SEE ALL A760-A789.

STAR, ALCOR: Chickadee with pot = star Alcor --A771.0.1.

STAR, BIG DIPPER: Origin—A771ff.

STAR, EVENING STAR: Origin of evening star—A781.2.1.

STAR, MILKY WAY: Origin--A778ff.

STAR, MORNING STAR: Children like sun, moon and star of morning—N455.4Ac; morning star announces dawn—A712; origin of morning star —A781.1.

STAR, NORTH: Rattlesnake bites off North Star's finger—A774.1.

STAR, ORION: Origin--A772.1.

STAR, VENUS: Girl La Belle Venus with star on forehead—A781.0.1.

STARGAZER: Stargazer falls into well—J2133.8. SEE ALSO ASTROLOGER; ASTRONOMER.

STARING: Girl is taken up to the moon for staring at the moon. This is considered bad manners—A751.7.1.

STARLING: SEE BIRD, STARLING.

STAROST: Devil sends witch to steal Starost's daughter—G261.2.

STATUTE: How to get rid of beggars, have two pillars of cliff carved into statues. Takes all wealth—J1199.1; statue of old man in cemetery puts hands on heads of carved dogs by side--E521.2.4; wooden image of Christ Child walks in fields--V128.3; fool gives clothing to statue —J1853.1.0.1; statue brought to court as witness--J1141.1.3.4; lad refurbishes neglected statue of Devil, rewarded--G303.22.11.1; stone hen miraculous--B811.7; statue of man overcoming lion displeases lion--J1454; best not to bring statue of lion to life--J563.1; stone temple lions to turn red when flood imminent--W154.8.4; Mercury finds his statue priced low--L417; statue of Mikado thrown into sea causes illness--K1853.2.1.2; statue of monk points to treasure--C429.3; origin of statue of peddler and dog--A1465.9.1; statue of patron saint costs more than other saints--J552.6.1; statues change postures, Saint "Quien Sabe" and Saint "Que Pasa"--V128.4; figure of girl with piece of bread, drop of blood and snake inside, kills stepmother--F582.1.1; origin of Toromiro carvings of Rapa-Nui--A1465.5.1; statue kicks man out of undersea kingdom--F420.6.1.3.2; mole to wed sky, sun, cloud, wind, stone Miryek (statue)--L392.0.2. SEE ALSO BUDDHA; JIZO; SAINTS; VIRGIN.

STAVOREN: Bell of Stavoren not blessed when moved, claimed by Joost--F993.1.1; origin of sandbank outside Stavoren--N211.1.

STEALING: Hare attempts to cure dog of thieving --A2455.6; plants patch of melons for self and patch for God, then steals from God's patch--W211.5; jailed for stealing pears, man gives pear seed to ruler which will bear golden pears if planted by man who has never stolen or cheated, none can plant--H263.1. SEE ALSO ROBBER; THIEF.

STEAM: Origin of steam engine--A1439.5.

STEPMOTHER: Father hangs up boot with hole, if holds water will remarry--Q2.1.4B; Chile plant grows from girl murdered by stepmother--E632.0.5; Cinderella--R221; stepmother cooks and serves child to family--N271; stepmother feigns illness to require sacrifice of helpful animal--B335.2; girl taken to moon, rescued from stepmother--A751.7.1; stepmother stranded on magic orange tree--Q2.1.6Db; snake comes from mouth of figurine and kills stepmother--F582.1.1; Snow White--Z65.1; second wife seals son of first wife in hole to starve--S31.6. SEE ALL Q2.1.2+ (Kind and Unkind Girls). NOTE THAT NOT ALL STEPMOTHER MOTIFS ARE INDEXED HERE.

STICK: Bundle of sticks turns to army--F601.2A; guilty man's stick will grow during night--J1141.1.4; stick horse, fool as tired as if had walked--J1946; house of sticks blown in--K891.1.1; magic object stolen by host at inn--D861.1; man in moon gathering sticks--A751.1.1; strength in bundle of sticks--J1021; sticks thrown at animal becomes tails--A2215.1; test, to find relationships among three sticks. Which comes from top of plant, middle, bottom? --H506.10.

STINGY: Man refuses to share chicken. "It belongs to my wife." "Then why are you eating it?" "She told me to."--J1552.5; father rebukes son for giving imaginary oranges which are too

large, fingers too far apart--W152.18.

STOCKING: "Shall I tell you the story of Johnny McGory and the red stocking?" Catch tale--Z17.3.

STOCKS: Alleged hunchback cure in stocks--K842.0.2.

STOLEN: SEE THIEF.

STOMACH: Why other members must serve belly--A1391, J461.1; 'stomach' bag slit in deceptive eating contest--K81.1; person swallowed, disgorged--F912.3.1, F914.0.1; person swallowed pecks or eats on swallower's insides until disgorged--F912.3ff; victim kills swallower from within--F912ff; magic stomach swallows water, fire, etc., releases as needed--K1161.5, Z52.1, Z52.4; victim rescued from swallower's belly--F913ff; why spider has thin stomach--A2355.1.

STONE: Stone which advises what to do--B216.6; contest, beating dust from stone--K62.1; do not answer when bird speaks or will turn to stone--N455.4Aa; contest, biting the stone--K63; witch in stone boat--K1911Ab; first two brothers fail and are turned to stone--B582.2; countryman thinks city strange, stones tied up (cobblestones)--J1819.4; cockcrow stone must turn round thrice at each cockcrow--F809.5.1; magic stone mocked by coyote pursues--D931.0.6; stones cry out, will turn to stone if turn around at sound--H1331.1.3Fd; dragon tests lads ability to move stone--K1931.2P; fire hides in rocks during flood--A1414.7.2.1; fool sells butter to stone--J1853.2; fools carry stones back uphill to roll them down--J2165; Marec the enchanter turns giant into stone--F531.6.12.8.3; stand on stone in middle of chamber, it sinks into chamber below with two glass coffins--F852.1.2; crow gives God's gifts to stone, stone never to feel old--A2431.3.6.4; why stones do not grow--A975.1.2; horse turned to stone--A974.0.9; lad licks stone daily to satisfy hunger--W154.8.4; Joringel turned to stone--D771.11.1; judge thinks stone in purse is bribe--K1765; stone near Krakow bears legend saying will tell secret if turned over, underneath says "I was so heavy"--F809.10; stone tells legends--A1481.2.2; origin of betel chewing with limestone--A2691.5; stone lion, best not to bring to life--J563.1; stone lions turn red as warning of flood--W154.8.4; magic stone, all who poke fire, stick there--D1413.17; magic stone dropped into river by animals retrieved by dog and cat--D882.1; magic stone replenishes wine--D882.1A; magic stone in cock's head--D882.1.1; magic grinding stone--D1262; girl says would rather marry a stone than suitors, turns to stone--C26.1, T75.2.1.2; playing music on a stone as reasonable as goat bearing calf--J1191.1.2; stone turns to ogre and abducts girl--D931.0.7; origin of stone--A970ff; displaced bride tells wrongs to stones of patience--K1911.1.4; Pele turns Hopoe to stone--A285.2; man kills pig, door in rock opens and he is taken by Master of Stone for seven days--H1561.1; stones of Plouhinec walk to sea to drink--N511.6.1;

turned to stone on quest for bird—H1331.1.3F; rich man throws stones over wall into road, admonished "Don't throw stones from not yours to yours"—H599.10; sea is a stone's throw deep—H681.4.1; turn to stone if tell secret—S268E; stone soup—K112.2; stone splits at girl's request—J214A; contest, squeezing water from stone—K62; stone tried and lashed for stealing—J1141.1.3.4.1; task, making stone lute—H1021.12; task, making stone cape—H1021.13; test, lift stone, witch (Baba Yaga) is in land under stone—R111.1.3Ae; test, lifting stone, third year strong boy heaves it out of the valley—B335.2F; test, throwing the stone into the cliff, mud clod thrown—K17.5; treasure under stone, stone rolls away for short time—N511.6.1; origin walking on hot stones—A1542.3; stones move when whistle is blown—F809.5.2; girl breathes on witch and flock of white doves cover, turning witch to stone—G530.2Bg; witch turns girls to stone—Q2.1.2Cb. SEE ALSO GEM; JEWEL; ROCK.

STONE COATS: Stone coat giants—G511.2.

STONECUTTER: Stonecutter wishes he were Raja—Z42.0.2.

STOOL: Luck depends on what stool fate sits on when one is born—N138; Temba carried to Kingdom of Ruwa in sky by father's stool—T555.3; talking stool—B210.1.1.

STOREHOUSE: Boy told to take what he needs, takes all—J2461.4.1.

STORK: SEE BIRDS, STORK.

STORM: "It was a dark and stormy night", circular tale—Z17.1; storm produced by magic—D2141.2; grateful mermaid warns of storm—F420.5.1.1; emperor drowns in painted storm—D435.2.1.2; animal tied for safety during storm—K713.1.1; storm produced by whistling—D2142.1.6.1.

STORY: Tailor makes coat. Wears out so makes jacket, etc. Just enough left to make a story—Z49.24.1.1.

STORYTELLING: Girl seeking lost lover builds bathhouse and gives free bath to all who tell story—H1385.5Af; after storyteller dies, black bear found in hut grows to ceiling, children climb it to sky, return as old men and tell tales—A1481.3; servant sent to buy a story—N612.4; let us carry each other, i.e. tell stories—H586.3; cat running up and down pillar telling stories—B641Ad; mouse tells cat a tale, cat, "Even so, I eat you"—K561.1.1; circular stories begin over and over again—Z17; dragon eats two brothers for not telling story—X905.1.5; endless tales—Z11ff; execution escaped through storytelling—J1185.2; at fairy ball man sent out for failing to tell tale, has to carry coffin—M231; lad tells tall tale and ends with fox opening paper saying, "Now princess can eat for she has laughed"—H341.5; story told as excuse to make certain gesture—K263; story-

telling of guest impresses inhospitable man—M231.3; wife demands tale of each guest—M231.2; helpful mouse advises hero to always be generous to minstrels—K1951.1F; man in night lodging has no tale to share, cast out. He has fantastic adventures, returns with tale—M231.1; storyteller allowed in house on condition he tell tales all night long—Z11.4; storyteller to lose life if doesn't tell new tale nightly—M231.1Bd; bird saves girl from panderer by telling her tale—T53.0.2; princess brought to speech by tale with question end—F954.2.1, H621.2; storytellers invited to cheer princess, one tells of twelve enchanted bird princes, she goes and breaks enchantment—B647.1.1.1; raven puts bear to sleep with stories, moon stolen—A758.1; reocgnition through storytelling—H11; old robber frees his three sons by relating frightful adventures—R153.3.3; old man sells story to lad which can win princess—Z11.5; boy never shares stories with other children, stories plot to harm him—M231.1Bc; Skunny-Wunny wins stories from fox, leaves for men—C432.1.3; man with no tale sees story spirits—M231.1B; stone tells legends—A1481.2.2; suitor test, telling a story that has never been heard by Tsar—H509.5.2; suitor test, tale lasting dawn to dusk—H359+; stories to be told only in summertime—A779.4; tall tale teller's daughter vanquishes visiting storyteller—J31.0.1; tengu forces kidnapped man to tell stories nightly—J1185.2; test, making king say "enough" to taleteller—H507.2.1; story of cleverest man told, thief tells of thief—J1177.2; long story told to detain troll until sunrise—K1917.3C, K1917.3D; unfinished tale "if the bowl had been stronger my tale had been longer", etc.—Z12ff.

STOVE: Lost princess reaches iron stove with enchanted prince inside—H1385.5D; secrets told to stove—B133.3; task, making stove out of needle—H1022.6.0.1; lad travels to Czar on stove—B375.1.3; numskull ties yarn around stove to keep heat from escaping—J1942.

STRANGE VISITOR: Enters piecemeal—Z13.1.1.

STRANGER: Origin of custom of inviting strangers to share feast—A1598.1; can't tell time of day when asked, is a stranger here himself—J2259.4.

STRAW: Straw magically cools bathhouse—F601.2A; bean (bubble), straw and coal (shoe) go journeying—F1025.1; to take all straw can carry, takes whole stack—F628.2.3.1; straw coat of invisibility—D831.1; straw dolls thrown into monster's throat—Q2.1.2F; straw hats given to Jizo—J1873.1; house of straw blown in—K891.1.1; straw ladder made to escape tower—F848.1; first thing touched to bring luck, is straw—N222.1; milky way is straw—A778.12; strawman covered with sticky substance catches thief—K741; strawman dummies are fired on by enemy, arrows stick and weapons thus replenished—K2369.14; animals are caught on tarred straw ox—Z32.4.1; girl captured by rabbit leaves dummy in place and flees—G561.2D. SEE ALSO SCARECROW.

STRAWBERRY: Bear gets bottoms of strawberry crop—K171.1; girl sent for strawberries in winter, sweeps snow from door of dwarfs—Q2.1.4B; dwarfs capture girl picking strawberries—G561.2Db; origin strawberries, wife fleeing stops to pick strawberries—A2687.3.1.

STREAM: Water from sacred stream revives stone pilgrim—H1331.1.3Fe; stream swallows all —Z32.2.3.1; kind girl unclogs stream—Q2.1.2Da. SEE ALSO RIVER.

STRENGTH: Even strongest man cannot make baby obey—A1399.5; strong man breaks three clubs before finding one strong enough, kills three giants—F615.3.1.4; what is strongest? Earth—H631.3; Strength Giver wrestles with hero to teach strength—F617.4; strong man intimidates master—F615.3.1.5; mouse stronger than wall, wind, mountain, etc—L392ff; secret of strength treacherously discovered—K975; giant raises Thumbling and teaches strength—F615.3.1.3; peasant's wife wrestles strong man —F617.2.2; cat seeks strongest creature as companion, stays with woman—A2513.2.2. SEE ALSO STRONG.

STRETCH: Remarkable man can stretch self—F601.2C; two bluebird brothers abandoned on stretching rock—D482.4.1.

STRING: Spider set to making string by creator, swallows string—A2356.2.8.1.

STRONG: Bear's son defeats Baba Yaga—B635.1.4; strong boy, Kintaro—F611.3.2.7; strong man's labor contract, to give blow at end of year—F613.1.1; Badang the Strong given strength by demon—F610.3.8; Double Arend of Meeden picks up wife's family and puts outside—F624.1.0.1; Jan the Eighth Van Arkel chins self on beam holding horse between knees—F610.3.7; contract, as much money as companion can carry—F601.2Abd, F601.2D; on sea lion hunt two brothers fail to leap shore on sea lion rocks, youngest succeeds—L114.1; Strong Sam refuses to fight for plunder, defeats enemy single handed when attacked—F610.3.6; strong man pushes over previously weakened trees to intimidate opponents—K46.1; hero has full strength when young—F611.3.2ff. SEE ALSO STRENGTH; SUMO.

STROP: Magic strop beats—B335.2B.

STROZZI PALACE: Origin of onion shaped iron lantern of Strozzi Palace in Florence—A1447.3.1.

STUB TOE: Unkind girl chants "stub toe" and kind girl trips—Q2.1.1Da.

STUBBORN: First to speak must shut the door —J2511; three women and old man, each refuses to take a second turn rowing—W167.3; stubborn son does opposite of father's com-

mands—W167.4; stubborn wife sought upstream —T255.2.

STUDENT: Fox's daughter gives student mirror in which he sees her face if studies hard—B651.1.1; student poet meets ghost maiden—E474.2.1; wise man pours water into bowl with eyes only on top of jar, likens to pupil who must be ready to accept learning before can be filled with knowledge—H591.4; teacher helps students find legs with switch—J2021.0.1; student given three packets to open when in need —J21C; Jiang Kieu emerges from painting and encourages students in exam—T111.1.5.1; student sleeping on priest's procelain pillow finds self in wealthy future—D1812.3.3.2.1; student with pockets full of peas thought to have pocketful of money, treated royally—K1952.0.3; rat assumes student's identity—D315.1.1; student flavors rice with smell of food—J1172.2. SEE ALSO SCHOOL; TEACHER.

STUMP: Stump as repository of fire—A1414.7.1; frog throws fire into stump—A1415.2.2.1.1ff; stump in primeval sea —A812.4; alleged self-heating stump—K112.1.2.

STUPID: Ogre (Old Stupid Head) told he has died, runs home to see if is true—J2311.13. SEE ALSO FOOLS.

STURGEON: SEE FISH, STURGEON.

STUTTERING: Wife refuses to talk for fear of stuttering—T255.8.

SUBMARINE: SEE UNDERWATER.

SUBSTITUTION: Substituted object left in bed while victim escapes—K525.1; letter of execution changed, or substitute deliverer given letter—K511.0.2.

SUCKERS: SEE FISH, SUCKERS.

SUCKING: Sucking monster—F913.5, G332; ogre sucks princess out of window and carries off—F660.1Cc; old woman ogre sucks in all—F912.2.11.

SUFI: Sufi mystic and Mulla communicate by signs—H607.1.1.

SUGAR: Sugar put in soup, ogre goes for more water—K1611Bc.

SUGARCANE: Crocodile promises to steal no more—K714.2.4.2; porcupine destroys dog's cane—A2494.4.14.

SUICIDE: Boy commits suicide by eating the 'poison', a pot of pickled walnuts (preserves, etc.)—J2311.2.1.

SUIT: Lord demands suit people will notice—K445.1.

SUITOR: Asin in disguise as bald, ugly stranger woos—T111.1.1.1; rejected suitor feigns earthquake—K1889.7; foolish girl and family daydream of ill which might befall child of potential union, suitor leaves to seek greater fools—J2063; princess offered to correct quesser—H511.1; magically created suitors turned to lilies in morning—G302.7.1.2; widowed Longspur weds another Longspur—J416.2; five daughters waiting in vain for suitors turned to mountains—A962.1.3; suitor sent from relative to relative—Z31.1; princess to man who can out-riddle her—H551; which of two women being courted would he save if both fell into river—H359.5; poorly dressed spider persuades well dressed companion to exchange clothes on courting trip—K499.8.1; girl would rather marry a stone, turns to stone—C26.1; girl rejecting suitor turns to stone (otter)—T75.2.1.1ff; girl's father weds particular girl to first man passing window—H465. SEE ALL ENTRIES H310-H359 Suitor tests. SEE ALSO COURTING; LOVER.

SULPHUR: Dragon fed sheep stuffed with sulphur—B11.11.10.

SULTAN: Crime for which excuse is worse than crime, sneaks into Sultan's room at night and kisses him. Excuse, thought it was the sultan's wife—J1211.4; Sultan prepares to sit on rooster, rooster lets out bees—Z52.4.

SUMATRA: Calf from Sumatra defeats Javanese bull—B264.6.

SUMMER: Glooskap brings summer to Canada—A1153.1; coyote steals summer—A1151.1.1; Fisher helps release summer—A771.0.3; Saynday puts hand in sky = five stars seen only in summertime—A779.4.

SUMO: Sumo wrestler meets girl, mother and grandmother who can out-wrestle him—F617.2.1; sumo wrestler wrestles sixty foot serpent—F617.3.

SUN: Formerly ten suns, Heavenly Archer, Yi, shoots nine down—A720.1.1; sun from armpits of sun-man—A722.5; hunter shoots arrow in eye of sun and moon, they refuse to rise for three years—A727.3; one hitting sun with first arrow to own—A721.3; sun caught in snare, beaver gnaws free—A728.0.1; those on whom sun shines while in bed will be short lived—W111.10; bird refuses to wake sun—Z49.6.0.2; origin of man from drop of sun's blood—A1263.1.3; sun's brother banished for annoying her—A220.1.1; sun cursed for burning rays—L351.2; copper canoe given from Sun—F617.4; boy says sun is nearer that Ch'ang An—H682.1.4.1; sun's child—C322.3; queen to bear children like sun, moon, and star of morning—N455.4Ac; sun refuses to rise, cock tricks up—A739.6.1; Cottontail shoots sun down and pastes liver over—A727.4; coyote shoots arrow chain into sun—B11.2.1.2.2; coyote makes sun of tule grass ball—A717.2; sun will allow man to live forever if his dead daughter can be brought back from the dead—F81.1.0.2; demons vanish when struck by

setting sun—G304.2.5.1; sun eats water, water eats fire, etc.—Z43.6.6; Sun spits in pool and scalds Eetoi to death—A566.3; origin of sun from emu's egg thrown onto wood in sky—A714.3.1; sun fire rekindled each morning—A712; frogs fear increase of sun's power will dry up puddles—J613.1; sun god sends eclipse to aid snail—J1172.3.0.6; sun goddess hides in cave—A220.1.1; greedy rich man tries to hold sun back with pitchfork so workers will work longer—W151.11; hare plays ball and steals sun—A721.1.3; sun and moon must go live in sky when house is flooded—A736.1.4.4; Kahoa steals back sun, moon, and stars of blind aunt—A721.1.6; Sun King weeps = gold—A736.1.3.1; sun is Kwaku Tsin who escaped to sky—A711.0.1; sun's warmth brings first man to life—A1241.3.1; lad digs up light of day—and releases—H1385.1C; origin of light—A1412ff; sun and moon as man and woman—A736.1ff; sun snared for burning boy's mantle—A728.1; sun cuts off pieces of moon—A755.4.0.1; sun and moon fight and sun has red face—A751.5.2.2; moon flees sun—A735.0.1; sun throws sand in moon's face—A751.5.2; mouse gnaws sun free—A728.1; mouse wishes to wed sun—L392; sun prince and moon prince kidnapped by water spirits when fail to answer riddle—F420.5.2.2.5; sun, moon, wind aid in quest—D721.5, H1273.2; sun stolen by raven—A721.1.1, A1411.2; raven breaks off pieces of stolen fire-ball and hurls into sky as flies, hence suns appear at various distances apart during year—A1411.1.1; formerly six suns, Prince aims at reflections in pool and shoots out five—A720.1.2; riddle, what is yellow and shining but not gold?—H762.1; Hou Ye gives golden bird, ancestor of rooster, to wake sun—A751.8.7; sun gives comb to rooster who wears it on head, teeth up—A2321.10.0.2; Scarface seeks sun to ask removal of scar—H1284.1; animal scorched while gnawing sun free—A727.1, A728; sister and brother become sun and moon—A736.1.2.1; sun sisters stick embroidery needles in eyes if look at sun—A736.1.1.1; Sky God takes fourth wife who says will bear child of gold and child of silver = sun and moon—N455.4D; sun's sons seek father—C322.3, F17.1; spider rescued by sun spins clouds—A1133.5; envoy sent to find out why sun stopped shining—H1273.2K; sun, Suá, as creator's son—A711.1.1; sun from sun-man thrown into sky—A714.0.1; sun flung into sky by Tao—A625.2.11; Thumbling attacks sun—Z52.5; troll bursts when sun shines on him—G304.2.5; which is most useful, the sun or the moon?—H675; mother washes sun and moon and shining dust falls on earth. Those on whom it falls become wealthy—N455.4D; sun withstands forest of swords, etc. to wed girl—H328.7; contest of wind and sun—L351; wind, sun and frost quarrel—J1712.1; woman wishes for light. Sun, moon and stars appear—A710.1; sun stolen by witch, trickster puts sugar in soup and steals back—K1611Bc. SEE ALL A710-A739 Creation and Attributes of sun.

SUN BEAM: Sunbeam sprites protect babe whom

they shine on when first born--F499.1.2; sun beam <u>fairies</u> spin for fish--D2183.1; <u>fools</u> dive for sunbeam--J1791.3.3.1.

SUN DANCE: Sun Dance taught to Scarface—H1284.1.

SUN LIGHT: Sunlight carried into windowless house in <u>baskets</u>—J2123; sun's <u>daughter</u> wed to mortal, sun must never strike—C31.3.2; sun gives <u>daughter</u> to woman, sun must never strike—T521.0.1; sunlight causes <u>demons</u> to vanish—D567.1; sunlight fatal to <u>fairies</u>—F383.4.3.1; no sunlight in <u>house</u>? Put house in garden where sunlight is—J2123.3.

SUN MAID: Frog steals eye of sun maid—T53.6.

SUN RISE: <u>Contest</u> in seeing sun first--K52.1; <u>rooster</u> wakes Buzzard in time to catch rising sun and collect debt—A2494.13.10.7; Blue Jay and Ground <u>Squirrel</u> get basket containing dawn and release it--A721.1.2; sun rises in west to win bet for lad—D1223.1.1. SEE ALSO <u>DAWN</u>.

SUN SET: <u>Clamshell</u> boy makes bow of mother's copper <u>bracelet</u>, if he appears at sunset sky is red—T554.12.2; setting sun mistaken for <u>fire</u>--J1806.

SUN WU-KUNG: Monkey God, Sun Wu-Kung—B241.2.2.1.

SUNDAY: Mounted <u>bride</u> dismounts as gate can not be torn down on Sunday--J2171.6.1; task, washing monster children of <u>Mother Sunday</u>—Q2.1.5Aa; wish for a <u>week</u> of Sundays—W111.11.

SUNGURA: Sungura, the hare. SEE COLLECTION Heady, Eleanor. JAMBO SUNGURA.

SUPERNATURAL CHILD: Son of maid and Rain God slays intimidating <u>bear</u>--A2411.2.0.3; origin of <u>culture hero</u>—A511+; <u>miraculous conception</u>--T510+; <u>marriage</u> of person to animal--B600-B699.

SUPERNATURAL WIFE: SEE WIFE, SUPERNATURAL.

SUSPICIONS: Suspicions sown between friends—K2131.1.

SVATOPLUK: King Svatopluk--J1021.

SWABIANS: Seven Swabians attack hare (crayfish)—J2612.

SWAFFHAM: Peddler of Swaffham—A1465.9.1, N531.1.

SWALLOW: Boy eats cod, seal, whale, etc. Explodes--X1723.4; <u>glutton</u> swallows everyone it meets--Z33.2ff; swallowed victim <u>kills</u> from within--K952; victim <u>rescued</u> from swallower's stomach--F912ff; hero's companion swallows <u>sea</u>—F601.2De; Big Mouth drinks <u>sea</u> dry and

spits onto court—F660.1D; trickster get self swallowed by <u>Sea Serpent</u> and kills from within—R111.1.4A. SEE ALSO BIRD, SWALLOW; EAT; MOUTH; STOMACH.

SWAMP: Swamp maiden gives letter to carry—D812.15.

SWAN: SEE BIRD, SWAN.

SWEAT: <u>Charm</u> for wealth and happiness calls for calabash <u>full</u> of sweat—H588.7.4; <u>disease</u> and sickness from sweat of Earth Magician's hands as disappears into earth—A1337.0.8; <u>Mantis</u> subdues Blue Crane by rubbing sweat on her face—A591.1; turtle sweats and gives idea of <u>turtle soup</u>--A2351.5.1.

SWEDEN: Dragon strikes earth with tongue cutting passage between Denmark and Sweden--R111.1.4A. SEE ETHNIC AND GEOGRAPHIC INDEX.

SWEET: What is sweetest?--H633.

SWELLING: Swelling removed by <u>dwarfs</u>—F344.1.2; <u>helpful person</u> swells so pursuer can not pass--F53.1.2.

SWIFT: Skillful <u>brother</u> is extraordinarily swift—F660.1.1; what <u>is</u> swiftest? Thought—H632.1; old <u>woman</u> is so quick she has killed, cooked and <u>eaten</u> horse by time they arrive—F660.1.1. SEE ALSO SPEED.

SWIMMING: Fools swim in <u>dry</u> river bed—J1972.1; <u>ferryman</u> tells pedagogue all life is lost if cannot swim as boat is sinking--J1229.4; girl swims to reach flute-playing <u>lover</u>--T35.5.1; swimming <u>match</u> between turtle and lion—K11.1; turtle <u>holds</u> beaver's tail in swimming <u>match</u>--K11.2; trickster takes pack on swimming <u>match</u> and dupe backs out—K1761.

SWING: Girl swung too high, carried off by <u>buffalo</u>—R111.1.13.2; child on swing in <u>demon girl</u>'s ruse—H1440D.

SWORD: Father makes sword strong for son, third made does not <u>break</u>--R111.1.3Cd; <u>cat's tail</u> taken as sword--K2323; Rabbi asks for glimpse of paradise while alive, holds sword of Angel of <u>Death</u> as assurance he will not be harmed, jumps into heaven--K2371.1.1; sword so heavy hero must take magic <u>drink</u> before lifting—H1385.3; origin of <u>fairy</u> sword--A1459.1.7; lad returned from fairyland forges <u>fairy</u> sword—F321.3.0.1; <u>fairies</u> drive sword through iron door--F361.17.8; soldier lays sword on table ostentatiously, <u>farmer</u> lays manure shovel beside it, big spoon to go with big knife--J1225.1; fool sticks sword in shirt--J2461Aa; <u>lightning</u> is flashing sword--A1141.2.1; magic sword responds only to magic commands--D1651.2.1; <u>magic</u> sword given, if anyone else draws it will die--E711.10.1; Anansi steals <u>magic</u> cutting sword, cannot stop it—A2796.1; <u>needle</u> as sword for thumbling--F535.1.1.12; sword flourished so fast keeps dry in <u>rain</u>—

F660.1B; sword inscribed with "Seven at a blow" —K1951.1; numskull rushes up to first person met and surrenders sword—W211.6; thief drops sheath and sword on road to distract owner from goods—K341.6; white sword of light stolen by hero—H1331.1.3Am; white glaive of light stolen from ogre—K1611Ba. SEE ALSO SAMURAI.

SYCAMORE: Sycamore dies before man wakes— F377.0.2; lightning deposits first fire in sycamore—A1415.0.2.6.

SYMBIOTIC: Crow has right to first new corn, watches fields and eats corn-beetle grubs— A2685.1.0.2.

SYMBOLS: Boy kills giant whale by painting magic symbols on kayak and left hand—B877.1.3.

SYRIA: Martha tames dragon with sign of cross and holy water—B11.11.7; Rogues exchange objects and cheat each other, Syrian and Egyptian—J1516.

SYRUP: Syrup sold to flies—J1852.1.4; man slips and gets syrup on self, goblins think he is candy man and carry off—J2415.22; monkey asks for 'misery', thinking is syrup—J1805.2.

TABLE: Fool sends table to go by self—J2461.1D; magic objects stolen by host at inn—D861.1; gold covered table of pirate at pool bottom— F945.1.

TABLECLOTH: Magic tablecloth loses power when cleaned—D877.1.1; magic tablecloth provides food—D861.1; magic objects stolen by host at inn—D861.1.

TABU: Uncovering dish—H1554.1. SEE ENTIRE CHAPTER C.

TADPOLES: SEE FROG, TADPOLE.

TAIL: Air-castle to sell sleeping fox's tail— J2061.3.1; raising tail as sign of retreat in battle, animal stung—K2323.1; bear's tail caught in ice—A2216.1, K1021; three sisters wed to beasts with tails—G302.7.1.4; quest for tail of Boom Boomy Beast—F611.3.3.3; host curls tail around bowl—J1565.1.3; cow's tail (pig, ox) buried, dupe believes animal sank in mud— K404.1; why deer has short tail—A2378.4.10; why dog wags tail—A2479.12; tail of dog is hoop —A2378.1.7; seller cuts off donkey's dirty tail before sale—J2099.2; creature comes to reclaim eaten tail—E235.4.3.2; tail set afire spreads fire—J2101.1; fishing with tail in water—K1021; fox puts tail out of hole as punishment—J2351.1; boy given ride on fox's tail—K815.15; how frog loses tail—A1415.2.2.1, A2378.2.6.1; goats frighten jackals with jackal tail (wolf)—K1715.3; tail in ground, trickster says animal sunk from sight—K404.1; why hare has short tail— A2378.4.1; calf tail would reach from heaven to earth, if long enough—H682.1.7; lazy man's hoe becomes tail and he turns to baboon (monkey)— A1863.1; man falls into hole in tree, monkey puts tail in hole and man pulls it off—K619.4; wolf to start eating horse from tail—K553.4; horse's tail pulled off. Judgment, keep horse until tail grows back—J1173; animal tied to sham dead horse's tail—K1047; fox duped into believing he can catch horse by tying tail to horse's tail—J2132.5.2; guest's tail fills house— J1565.1.3.1; why hydrax lacks tale—A2235; tailless fox convinces other foxes to fish with tails in ice—K1021.0.3; leopard ties tail to tree, tricked—K713.1.11; Manabozo changes self to large wolf with big tail, finds it was smaller wolf that was best hunter—J292; motmot's tail ruined —A2431.3.9; Oniyeye to bring beast with one hundred fifty-two tails—K751.0.3; why opossum has bare tail—A2317.12.1; the origin of animal's tails—A2378; pigs with curly tails belong to trickster—K171.4; why Senji rat lacks tail— A2235; Brer Rabbit helps Brer Fox roof house, nails Brer Fox's tail down—K729.1; wolf to choose fattest tail of sheep—K579.5.1; short tailed animals organize meeting—J429.3; bear persuaded to slide down rock, wears off tail— K1021.3; tail asked to steer, steers out to sea— K579.2.3; tail from stick thrown at animal's rump—A2215.1; if tail had been longer, tale had been longer—Z12.1.1; tailless hare persuades other hares to cut off tails—J758.1.3; tailless fox tries in vain to get others to cut off tails— J758.1; animal allows himself to be tied to another's tail and is dragged—J2132.5; why tiger can't move tail soundlessly—A2581; other animal's tail tied to tiger's (leopards), killed when tiger flees—J2132.5.1; small hero bluffs tiger, "I thought I told you to bring two tigers", tiger flees dragging animal tied to tail— K1715.2.1; tail buried and dupe attacked by trickster—K1021.1; deceptive tug-of-war, large animal's tail tied to tree root—K22.2; why wagtail wags tail—A2479.1. SEE ALL A2378 Origin of tails.

TAILOR: Tailor ordered to make ever more caps from cloth—W153.18; cat catches mouse and orders a suit of clothes made or will eat—Z49.24; tailor dares to sew in haunted church—H1412.2; tailor makes increasingly smaller items from piece of cloth—Z49.24.1; tailor betrays hidden customers—Z43.6.3; tailor with three dog companions—B524.1.2B; skillful tailor sews eggs back together and chicks hatch with only red seam on necks—H660.1; tailor and goldsmith dance with fairies—F344.1.4; tailor throws footstool from heaven—F1037.1; gallant tailor kills seven flies at a blow—K1951.1; tailor tricks stupid giant—G501 Wiggin; goat carries tailor off on horns to stone hole—F852.1.2; transformation, man to goose, three tailors and white goose—D161.2; lobster taken for tailor with shears—J1909.8.3; Napoleon shows tailor meaning of fear—J2071.2; tailor married to princess betrays trade by asking for needle and thread— H38.2.1; astronomer sees princess, thief steals, marksman kills dragon, tailor repairs boat— H621.2.4; fox pretends to make sheepskin jacket —K254.1.1; tailor makes clothing from scraps for poor brother and sister so they can enter singing contest—W11.18; tailor mends hole in sky—H359.4; tailor promises Allah he will not steal again, turned to tortoise with colors of all clothes stolen—A2312.1.0.2; tailor imitates witch who jumps into water and turns to hare—G211.2.7.2; tailor pretends to measure wolf's tail, harms—J2133.6.1; tailor clothes woman carved by woodcarver—H621. SEE ALSO SEWING.

TAIRA: Blind lute player forced to sing for ghosts of Taira clan—E434.11.

TAIWAN: ruler gets head hunters to agree to take only one head more, sends his own—W28.5; mountain splits when golden cock killed—B755.2; origin of Taiwan—A955.10.3.

TALIESSIN: Einion weds fairy, Olwen, son Taliessin born—F302.1.5.

TALISMAN: Animal gives part of body as talisman for summoning aid—B314.

TALKING: talking animal refuses to talk—B210.2; animal taught to speak—K551.11; talking goat killed, meat talks, skin talks, burnt, ashes talk, shout, "Here are the thieves"—B210.1.2; animal captor persuaded to talk and release victim from mouth—K561.1; choice, loss of speech or loss of beauty—N711.1; skillful boy taken to court to flick mud pellets into mouths of talkative courtiers—F661.13; talking bird discredited—J1151.1.3.1; princess will not talk—F954.2.1, H343; princess cannot be defeated in repartee—H507.1.0.1; talking skull refuses to talk, causes man to be killed—B210.2.3; talking stool—B210.1.1; talkative turtle carried up tree by holding to liana, speaks and falls—A2312.1.3.1; talkative turtle being carried aloft by birds speaks and falls—J2357; talkative wife discredited—J1151.1.3; man with wife carried in bag held between teeth asked question—J2133.5.1; talkative wife given penny for every word spoken, too much—D1454.2; headless woman is good woman, has no tongue—E422.1.1.3.2. SEE ALSO LANGUAGE; SILENCE; SPEAKING.

TALL TALES: Tall tale teller's daughter vanquishes visiting storyteller—J31.0.1; fool believes own tall tales—X902; man claims ox that travels one thousand li in day, etc.—K130.1. SEE ENTIRE CHAPTER X.

TALLOW: Gods paid with oxen of tallow—K236.1.1; tallow drips on shirt revealing that wife is spying on sleeping husband—H1385.4.

TAMARACK: Tamarack failed to drink deep enough of magic oil so loses needles—A2765.2.

TAMARIND: Tamarind tree shows value of thrift—W11.14.1.

TAMBOURINE: Test, guessing nature of certain skin—H522.1.1.

TAMERLANE: Hodja eats leg of goose presented to Tamarlane and claims geese are one-legged—K402.1.

TAMLANE: F324.3.1.

TAN KUN: Culture hero teaches arts and crafts—A541; she bear bears Tan Kun—A511.1.8.4.

TANDALA: Pakala and Tandala, rogues cheat each other—J1516.

TANGALOA: God throws down mountainous islands—A955.8.1.

TANNERY: Jupiter grants requests, ends at tanners—N255.2; man learns to stand smell—U133.

TAO: Tao strikes sky with pestle—A625.2.11.

TAOIST: Taoist priests as magicians—D1711.6.3.

TAPA: Origin of tapa cloth—A1453.5.

TAPIR: Tortoise arranges tug of war between tapir and whale—K22.

TAR: Ogre gilds beard in tar—K1013.1; wife tars and feathers self and goes on all fours, devil cannot identify this animal—K31.1; girl in honey and feathers disguise—G561B; wife tarred and feathered doesn't know self—J2012.2.3; figure covered with tar (tarman) captures intruder—K741; detection by footprints in tar—R221B; tar falls on bad man calling "let it fall", gold falls on good man—E373.1.1; tarring the moon—A751.4, F772.1.2.1; animals are caught on a straw tarred ox—Z32.4.1; gold coins in street picked up by trickster with tar on shoes—K378.1; tar on stairs catches maid's shoes as flees—R221B. SEE ALSO PITCH.

TARANTULA: Origin from trickster Tarantula—A2091.3.

TARBABY: Catches thief—K741.

TARBOOSH: Monkey imitates peddler—B786.1.

TARDINESS: Fairy causes man to arrive too late for wedding—F361.1.2.2. SEE ALSO LATE.

TARTAR: Peasant outwits tartar, is carried—K289.1. SEE ALSO ETHNIC AND GEOGRAPHIC INDEX.

TASKS: SEE ENTIRE SECTION H900-H1199.19. SEE ALSO QUESTS; TESTS.

TATAMI: Tatami is transformed badger—D421.8; toothpicks hidden in mat seek vengeance—Q321.3. SEE ALSO MAT.

TATTERCOATS: R221Z.

TATTERHOOD: L145.1A.

TATTLETALE: Tabu, telling of fairy gifts—F348.5.1; tattling mischief maker is beheaded, head laughs and is buried, coconut tree grows, coconut still gurgles--A2611.3.1. SEE ALSO BETRAYAL.

TAURUS: Daughter of one of Pleiades is Taurus-- A773.2.1.

TAX: Bat refuses to pay taxes as either bird or animal--B261.1.0.3; fraudulent tax collector made to swallow records, clever successor prints records on bread (yufka)--J1289.23; tax collector refuses to "give" hand even when drowning --W153.5.1; miser boards up doors to avoid door tax--J1179.15; hot peppers fed cows so they flee tax collector--K1181.1; fox brings wolf to help exact taxes of ram, ram brings camel--K641.2.

TCAKABESH: Tcakabesh snares sun--A728.0.1.

TCHAPOGUI: Man to return fate to baby Tcha- pogui--N115.

TCHI-NUI: Goddess Tchi-Nui weaves for poor man--T111.1.3.

TEA: Origin of Yerba Maté--A2691.6.

TEACHER: Teacher mounts ass backwards to lead students through village--H599.7; trickster paid to educate an ass--K491.0.1; ten years respite while teaching ass to speak--K551.11; in return for release from captivity, the bird (fox) gives the man three teachings--K604; sage Wang Shen challenges pupils to get him out of cave, one says can get him back into cave if he comes out, comes out to see--J1686; when teacher's donkey dies, students hide behind stable and moan-- J1529.1; employed to educate baby animals, trickster eats them--K933; teacher killed by gazelle, chain--Z42.0.6; boys tease teacher say- ing cannot find thier own legs, he helps them with a switch--J2021.0.1. SEE ALSO SCHOOL; STUDENTS.

TEAKETTLE: SEE KETTLE.

TEARS: Tears cure blindness (Rapunzel)-- F848.1; calabash of girl's tears--C432.1.2.1; St. Genevieve's tears fall in water, mother washes with water and sight is restored--V221.12.1; tears on grave cause rose tree to flower-- N271Ab; tears turn to holly--A2612.4; sister discovers brother's secret strength and betrays, must cry jar full of tears--S12.1.0.1A; jewels from tears--Q2.1.1; tears on moon--A751.5.6; motherhood test, one to fill pot with tears is mother--J1171.1.3; origin of tears--A751.5.6, A1344.1; owl spills pan of bird's tears meant for ritual drowning--A2491.2.2; ownership test, one man cries all night for lost animal--J1171.5; girl fills pitcher with tears, servant fills last two inches and weds awakened prince-- K1911.1.4B; task, bringing one hundred pots of tears--H1021.12, H1021.14.

TEENY TINY: Teeny tiny woman terrorized by voice demanding bone--E235.4.3.

TEETH: Where beaver got his teeth--A728.2.1;

why children's teeth fall out--A1316.6.1; why deer has short teeth--A2345.3.1; dragon's teeth produced as token--R111.1.3Eb; dragon's teeth knocked out = Orkney and Shetland Isles-- R111.1.4A; three ghosts met, each with longer teeth--F544.3.5.1; Welshman threatens to knock out all thirty-two of Irishman's teeth. "How did he know how many teeth I have?"--J1749.3; leopard's teeth knocked out by hare--K721.2; lion suitor allows teeth pulled--J642.1; old com- plains that young eats more as has teeth to chew, young complains that old bolts food as doesn't have to bother chewing--J234; two sons with golden hair and silver teeth--N455.4C; tortoise brushes teeth after eating up food, puts food in bat's mouth, bat blamed--K401.1; wife carried in bag held by teeth--J2133.5.1.

TELEGRAPH: Telegraph thought to work because other end of wire turns when he turns this one --J2289.1.

TELESCOPE: Bamboo tube claimed to be telescope --D831.1; man with telescope sees ill princess-- H355.0.1.

TEMLAHAM: Origin of goat clan emblem-- A1578.1.1.

TEMPER: Knight with temper kills priest--W185.7. SEE ALSO ANGER.

TEMPERANCE: Must stop magic lion vomiting gold before bucket fills--J2415.16.

TEMPEST: SEE STORM.

TEMPLE: Temple is transformed badger--D421.8; cats painted on temple wall kill rat demon-- D435.2.1.1; man visits old temple and is afraid roof will fall in--J1250.5; magic teakettle in temple--D1171.3.1. SEE ALSO CHURCH; MOR- INJI TEMPLE, MOSQUE, ETC.

TEMPLE, TENJOKU TEMPLE: Quest to Tenjoku TEMPLE--H1273.2G.

TEMPLE, TU-VYEN TEMPLE: Origin of temple in Hanoi--T111.1.5.1.

TEMPURA: Student flavors rice with smell of tempura shop--J1172.2.

TENGU: Badger steals fan from tengu children-- D839.3; magic fan makes nose grow longer, bad- ger obtains tengu's magic fan by trickery-- D1376.1.3; tengu tricked out of coat of invisi- bility--D831.1; tengu's nose made to grow long with magic fan, used as clothes pole-- D1376.1.3.2; tengu forces kidnapped man to tell stories nightly--J1185.2; old man joins dance of tengus, they take his wen--F344.1.1.

TENJOKU TEMPLE: Quest to Tenjoku Temple-- H1273.2G.

TEOSINTE: Ma-ix weds Teosinte--A2685.1.1.

TEPOZTAN: Culture hero nurtured by maguey

plant, ants—A511.2.2.3.

TEPOZTECO: Tepozteco criticized for appearing at feast in poor garb, returns in finery and gives food to clothing—J1561.3; Tepozteco's drum heard still—A1195.1.

TEPOZTON: Church bells cannot be raised to tall steeple, Tepozton performs task—V115.5; Tepozton shows cave open only on New Year's Eve—C761.4; Tepozton swallowed by giant cuts hole in stomach and kills—F912.2.10.

TEQUENDAMA FALLS: Origin Tequendama Falls—A935.4.

TERMITE: Termite eats corn, eaten by snake, chain—Z43.6.6; termites gnaw tree to fell lizard—K1079.2.

TEST: SEE ENTIRE CHAPTER H. TESTS. SEE ALSO QUESTS; TASKS.

TEXAS: Why Texas is so big—X1611.1.10.1.

TEXOCOTEPEC MOUNTAIN: Malintzin, translator for the Spaniards, dies of sadness, her wailing can still be heard from Mt. Texocotepec—E425.1.11.

THANKS: Great drum becomes soundless to punish man for breaking his word—C939.13; tabu, thanking fairy—F348.10.

THATCH: Thatch threshed again in famine—J151.1.

THAW: Volga and Vazouza rush to sea in spring thaw—A939.4.

THIEF: Bedcover is stolen, fool waits for thief to return for the bolster—J2214.3.2; thief stealing bronze bell stuffs ears with cotton fearing din will raise authorities—J2259.1; victim berated for leaving door unlocked, not being awake, etc. "Isn't the thief to blame too?"—J2233.3; thief blames mason for poor house—J2233, Z49.11.2; thief claims he was blown into garden—J1391.1; fool hired to keep thieves from Chelm has series of mishaps letting thieves escape—J1703.2; thieves could not have been his servants as they didn't steal the coats, his servants are more thorough—J1179.5; thief thinks self named, "That is the first," etc., thieves eavesdrop outside window of sham wise man and hears him counting—N611.5; animal cry imitated to lure owner from goods—K341.7; sham doctor steals from patient with bad eyes—J1169.1; theft by posing as doctor—K352; thieving contest, first steals eggs from under bird, second meantime steals pants of first—K305.1; king executes thief, in chain sequence—L392.0.6; fool watches thief hoping thief will find something of value so he can take it back from thief—J2223; fool warns thief not to steal, telling where things are—J2091; thief frightens owner from goods—K335; thief steals repeatedly from enemy general, enemy flees in fright—K2369.17; thief and ghost argue over who is to rob man

first, he awakes and flees—J581.3; thief with stolen goods claims he "didn't steal it." Second thief claims he "doesn't have it."—K475.1; thief claims to be from heaven and is given presents to carry back—J2326; farmer calls to wife that he has hidden hoe, thief hears and takes—J2356.1; thief guards pursuer's horse while pursuer follows false trail—K346.1; thief jumps from tree onto pursuer's horse and escapes—K341.4.1.1; man sees thieves breaking into a house but he does not want to get involved—J1392.6; Issy-Ben-Aran pursues thief to present bill of sale for horse so will not be hung as a horse thief—J1392.7; thief who climbed into garden via ladder claims he is selling ladders—J1391.2; magic object acquired by stealing—D838; magic object stolen by neighbor—D861.2; magic object stolen by host at inn—D861.1; master thief—K301; master thief steals ring from finger and sheet from bed—K362.2; thief persuaded to climb down moonbeam, falls—K1054; robbed man pretends to have more money to stash, thief puts back stolen funds in hopes of getting more—K1667.1.1; thief on gallows bites mother's ear for bad upbringing—Q586; thief waves arms at end of field, when farmer goes to see what is wrong, he says. "I can't believe you would plow with only one mule." Confederate has stolen one of the mules meantime—K365.4; salt fed to nag which has been substituted for fine horse, nag leads to owner's stable for water—K366.1.2.1; owner helps thief fill sack—J1392.1; owner hides in cupboard, says is ashamed that there is nothing worthy of thief's attention—J1392.1.2; magic thieving pot—D1605.1; astronomer sees princess, thief steals, marksman kills dragon, tailor repairs boat—H621.2.4; thief released on condition he return stolen goods—J1179.20; thief steals rope with ox on end—K188; children are asked to write essay at school about what they ate last week, thief of hare detected—J1144.3; sham wise man "finds" stolen goods, he has really forced thieves to tell him its whereabouts—K1956.2; servant attempts to steal money in hermit's staff, serpent engulfs him—K331.6.1; thief hears story about crane's motions being told, thinks man is observing him creeping through fields and flees—N612.2; thief robs stubborn couple who refuse to speak—J2511.0.1; worthless object substituted for valuable (magic) while owner sleeps—D861.1, D871.1, K331.3; thief tells tale of clever thief, betrays self—J1177.2; goat talks, killed. Meat thrown in river, skin talks, burnt. Ashes talk, tell thieves to put ashes on lips as disguise, lips shout, "Here are the thieves"—B210.1.2; theft as a task—H1151ff; thief falls on tiger's back and is carried off—N392.1.1; thief caught stealing fruit in tree, claims to be songbird—J1391.9; passerby criticizes victim who has subdued thief and is sitting on him—J2233.4; Ijapa carries wife to steal, he swears he didn't steal, she swears she didn't walk there—K475.1.1; thief tricked into well by boy—K345.2. SEE ALSO ROBBER; STEALING.

THIKINH: Quam-Am Tong-Tu, the Compassionate Protector of Children—T210.1.1.

THIMBLE: Golden thimble collects magic blood of troll's heart--F1015.1.1B; to choose sister from seven statues, puts thimble on each, turns black on all but one--H1385.6.1.

THIRST: Crow drops stones into jar to raise water level--J101; hero's companion Thirsty can drink all--F601.2Ea.

THIRTEENTH: Thirteenth steals from ogress--G610Ab.

THISTLES: Ass prefers thistles to delicacies on his back--J1061.1.1; thistles are only picked in Moon of Gobbages--K499.3.1.

THOMAS THE RHYMER: F329.1.

THONE: Pontius Pilate causes storm when thrown into Thone--A935.2.

THOR: Thor, Loke, and Thiaffe visit giant's hall, contest--F531.6.15.1.1.

THORN: Removing thorn from ape's paw--B381.4; prince falls from tower and blinds self on thorns --F848.1; Devil stuck on magic thornbush--Q565A; thorn removed from elephant's foot--B381.3; magic fiddle causes master to dance in thorns--D1415.2.5.1; thornbush blamed by fox for wounding him--J656.1; moneylender told he'll be paid with fleece caught on thornbush--J2060.2.1; thorn removed from lion's paw--B381; maid to leap into thorns, emerges in fine clothing--R221lb; man in moon with thornbush--A751.1.4; ladder to moon topped with thornbush --F772.1.2.1; thornbush clutches at passerby--A2275.5.3; thorn attacks thief--K1161.5; thornbush marked for treasure--J1922.2.1; wolf to pull thorn from shoe of ass (horse)--K566. SEE ALSO BRAMBLE; BRIAR.

THOTMES: Thotmes given throne by Sphinx--B51.

THOUB-AN: Devil in troubador contest cannot answer verse "Jesus, Joseph, Mary"--G303.16.8.1.

THOUGHTS: Fox with a thousand thoughts is killed, crane with one thought escapes--J1662.2; what is swiftest? Thought--H632.1; test, guessing person's thought--H524ff; Thor, Loke, and Thiaffe visit giant's hall, contest with Sea, Thought, etc.--F531.6.15.1.1.

THREAD: Prisoner escapes by rope tied to thread brought up tower by beetle--R121.4.1; man's life linked to life of thread--E765.3.6; girl to find way around palace without becoming lost, unwinds thread--H389.1; magic thread protects against demons--D1385.18.1; counter-task, making thread of sand--H1021.13; thread which never grows shorter--Z11.5; spider set to making string by creator swallows string--A2356.2.8.1; hag makes three daughters spin gold, youngest breaks tabu by talking to prince and thread tarnishes--H1021.8.1; task, pass thread through curved hole in log (snail shell)--H506.4.

THREAT: Chameleon threatens to eat lion--K641.3; goat singing a threatening song bought off--K1767; sham threats--K1771.2ff. SEE ALSO BLUFF.

THREE KINGS: Magi--N816.1.

THRESHING: Threshing contest--K42.1.

THRIFT: Friends vow to live frugally until established--W11.14; bride test, making dress from worsted flax--H381.1.

THROWING: Deceptive throwing contest--K18ff; bluff, throwing club into moon--K1746; throwing the stone into the cliff, a mud clod is thrown-- K18.5; skillful boy taken to court to flick mud pellets into mouths of talkative courtiers--F661.13; remarkable thrower--F636.6. SEE ALSO TOSS.

THRUSHBEARD: Weds haughty girl--H465A.

THUMB PIANA (SANSA): Played by tortoise--B210.2.1.

THUMBELINA: F535.1.1F.

THUMBLING: Giant raises Thumbling and teaches strength--F615.3.1.3; Thumbling swallows thorn, moss, egg, routs ogre--K1161.5; Thumbling attacks sun--Z52.5; adventures of Thumbling, person size of thumb--F525.1.1.

THUNDER: Man overhears thunder spirits come to temple to borrow thunder cart for attack on his district--A284.4; thunder bears drum--A1141.2.1; thunder is ewe, mother of ram lightning--A1141.8.2; thunder fears man and moves to sky--F434.1; Coyote and others steal fire from thunder--A1415.2.2.2; thunder is giant's fighting--A1142.9.0.1; what is heard at greatest distance, thunder and lie--H659.27; Thunder gives medicine pipe to be smoked--A284.5; thunder caught in tree--A1142.3.1; thunder, sound of Vainamoinen's boots--A2272.1.4.

THUNDER GOD: Man as helper of Thunder God--K1112.2; one brother kills six-headed sea monster with aid of animals and God of Thunder--R111.1.3Ai.

THUNDERBIRD: A284.2ff; Thunderbird gives first fire--A1415.0.2.6; Giant Nasan has feathered wings made and flies to woo Evening Star, is captured by Great Spirit and turned to Thunderbird, voice is thunder, flapping of wings is lightning--A284.2.1; carried to nest of Thunderbird, sleeps for three years--D1960.1.1; hero kills serpent for Thunderbird--B16.5.1.4.

TI MALICE: Ti Malice buys allegedly magic gun --K119.5.

TI PIERRE: Ti Pierre sleeps with four children in demon's house, wears one of their nightcaps --K1611Dd.

TIBER: Pontius Pilate causes storm when thrown

into Tiber—A935.2.

TICK: Tick in chain--Z42.0.6.

TICKBIRD: SEE BIRD, TICKBIRD.

TICKLING: Giant swallows river, tickled until spits it out—F531.6.8.3.2.1; sheet stolen by tickling until rolls over--H1151.3.

TIDAL WAVE: Helpful horse Marth carries lord to saftety before tidal wave--B401.2; old man on mountain sees impending tidal wave, set fire to own rice fields to draw villagers up mountain —J1688.

TIDE: Boy caught by clam persuades clam he feels pearl in it, clam opens—K561.1.0.2; drinking contest, trickster drinks on falling tide— K82.1.1; when crab comes from hole water rushes in = ebb tide--A913.5; gull asks land birds about tide--J2753; jewel of ebb tide and jewel of flood tide--U136.0.1; man sitting on hole in ocean--A813.6; woman thinks tides recede because she dips into water--J1959.3.

TIDINESS: Belt hung from beam instead of put away becomes snake in night--N231.1Ba. SEE ALSO LAZY.

TIED: Fool ties rope to leg and to cow on roof— J2132.2; animals tied together for safety— K713.1.2; animal tied for safety in storm— K713.1.1; animal allows self to be tied to another's tail and is dragged--J2132.5ff.

TIEN DUNG: Princess loves man so poor has only one pair of pants between self and father— T91.6.4.4.

TIGER: Tigers climb on backs to reach man in tree--J2133.6.0.2; tiger put in bag by Kantchil, floats ashore and finds mate--K714.2.3.2, N228; small trickster in house of larger animal intimidates with loud boasts--K1711.2; tiger grateful for removal of bone from throat—B382.1; helpful animal brothers-in-law--B314; buffalo and tiger made enemies by jackal--K1084.1.1; piece of tiger's liver turns into cat--A1811.4; cat doesn't teach tiger all she knows--A2581; group fails to count properly, believes one of group has been eaten by tiger--J2031.0.1; tiger feigning dead-- K607.3; tiger dances to magic drum--D1415.2.7.1; elephant and tiger as enemies--A2494.11.4; tiger repays inappropriate feast--J1565.1.4; escape by pretending debate, fox escapes--K622.1; frog rides on tiger's tail in jumping contest— K11.2; giant tiger killed from within--F912.2.12; tiger claims goat stepped on tail--J1179.22; Kantichil has goats eat red flowers and feign bloody mouths from 'eating tigers'--K1715.16; hare tricks tiger into fishing with tail--K1021; hare tricks tiger into eating stones--K1043.2; hare tricks tiger into getting burnt in brush— K553.1.0.6; goat begins to build house, tiger finds foundation, adds to it. Each claims-- K1715.3.2; tiger dupe hangs out laundry signal and his house is burnt rather than Anansi's-- K415.0.1; animal calls to house, dupe laying in

wait within answers--K607.1; tiger in human form revives tiger skins--A2434.2.5; farmer to go home for 'intelligence' which Tiger came to see--K341.8.1.0.1; tiger killed by Juan Bobo-- K1161.13; unjust animals judge in favor of tiger guarding 'king's food'--K1023.1.2; 'king's girdle' --K1023.1.1; 'king's drum'--K1023.1; Tiger tricked into pit by Kantchil--K652.1; throwing crumbs around to keep the tigers away. Effective, isn't it?--J1250.1; tiger thinks thief falling on back is "Terrible Leak"--N392.1.1, N691.1.2; marriage to person in tiger form—B651.9; task, bringing tiger's milk--N831.1.0.1; tiger cubs give milk--K1911A; enmity between tiger and monkey--A2494.10.4; tiger told mud is king's pudding--K1023.1.2; tiger tricked into palanquin by jackal--K714.2.4.3; tiger rescued from pit gives jewels--W154.8; Kantchil tricks tiger into believing porcupine's quill is his enemy's whisker--K1711.1; puppy teases tiger--L315.2.1; hero in tiger form vanquishes blood drinking Raja--D112.2.1.3; tiger threatens to eat rescuer, scene re-enacted--J1172.3; fox shows tiger reflection in well--K1715.1; fool rides tiger thinking it mule--N691.1.2; hare rides tiger--K1241; tiger thinks man riding him is monster--N392.1,1; roaring contest between elephant and tiger— K84.2; tiger routed by hidden objects--K1161.10; tiger has smith put hot iron down throat so can sing in mother's voice--K311.3G; Sim fastens tiger skin to colt of Yun's mare and mare flees with Yun--K310E; tiger told snake is king's turban or belt--K1023.1.1; tiger to take place of son whom he ate--B431.3.1; frog challenges tiger to spitting contest and spits out hairs of tiger's tail--K1715.12.2; stripes of tiger— A2413.4; monk refuses to kill tiger, left holding tiger by tail--X459.2; tiger has monkey (fox) tied to his tail, flees dragging monkey--J2132.5.1; deception into being tied in game--K713.1.10; tiger allows self tied for safety in storm— K713.1.1; tiger frightened by trickster who calls to fox (jackal) "I asked for ten tigers"-- K1715.2; Kantchil tricks tiger into playing "King's trumpet"--K1111.0.1.1; tiger changes voice to trap little girls--K311.3; Harimau drinks from "Emperor's well"--K735.5.1; tiger's whisker removed by woman--B848.2.1; ghost tiger as witch--K311.3H; man breaks tigress's spell, she becomes woman--B651.9.

TIGHTROPE: Magic badger teakettle walks tightrope--D1171.3.1.

TIKPI TIKPI: SEE BIRD, TIKPI.

TILL ULENSPIEGEL: Teaches ass to read— K491.0.1, K551.11.

TIM: Charm for wealth--H588.7.4.

TIME: Supernatural lapse of time in fairyland— F377; quest to Mother of Time--H1273.2B; land hidden through hundreds of years in peace— F173.2.1; time personified--Z122.0.1; man can't tell time of day, is stranger here himself-- J2259.4; travel into past--D2138.1; years thought days--D2011ff; sleep over many years--D1960.1ff; three years sleep in Thunderbird's nest—

D1960.1.1. SEE ALSO CLOCK.

TINDERBOX: Striking brings supernatural helper--D1421.1.2.

TINKARD: Tinkard to wed Tom Hickathrift's daughter--F628.2.3.1.

TINKER: Tinker exorcises ghost--H1411.1; hillman causes pan to spoil milk equal to price of unpaid tinkering--F451.5.10.4.1; princess weds king of the tinkers--H465C; Tinker of Tamlacht turns to salmon in River Erne--Q565Af; Tinker of Tamlacht--D1825.3.1.1.2.

TINNI PLANT: Anansi steals magic cutting sword, cannot stop it. It turns to Tinni plant, still cuts--A2796.1.

TINY: Teeny tiny woman--E235.4.3.

TIP: At bath man leaves large tip on receiving poor service. Next time receives good service and leaves small tip, "This tip is for last time, the tip last time was for this time"--J1229.3.

TIPINGEE: Three girls each claim to be Tipingee--H161.0.1.1.

TIREDNESS: One partner does work, other lays around and takes the tiredness--J1249.7.

TITTY MOUSE: Titty mouse falls in pot and dies--Z32.2.2.

TLACHTLI: Game among gods--A515.1.1.4.

TLACUACHE: Tlacuache nominated to be saint in rain-making procession--J953.19.

TOAD: Man who offends Great Spirit of Toad must carry Toad on shoulders as penance--B98.1; toad tricks donkey in race--K11.1; wed to toad maid--B641.0.1A; toads fall from mouth of unkind girl--Q2.1Aa; whose family is older, Toad wins--B841.1.4, B841.1.6; Rain God agrees to rain whenever toad croaks--A2426.4.1.2.1; grateful toad woman gives skin gift--R221Di; toad slays monster snake to save maid--B16.5.1.3; why toad has warts on back--A2356.2.1.1.1. SEE ALSO FROG.

TOAD, HORNED TOAD: Why horned toad has flat body--A2305.4.

TOAST: Lazy man refuses barn full of toast unless someone spreads honey on it for him--W111.5.10.1.1.

TOASTING: Man enchants robbers by toasting them--K1812.1.0.1.

TOBACCO: Why grasshopper chews tobacco--A2472.2; Master Tobacco--T102.1; origin of tobacco--A2691.2; tobacco seller misuses magic gift--D2100.2.1; man gives tobacco to spirit world--E474.6.

TOBACCO POUCH: Magic pouch bites imposter--D1050.2.

TOES: Monster's big toe to be cut off and eaten victims emerge--F913.3; shoeless orphan boy frightens monster by sticking big toe in face--J1782.8.1; stepsisters mutilate feet to fit slipper--R221B; person shoots off toes, thinking them ghosts--J1782.8; unkind girl chants "stub toes"--Q2.1.1Da; witch with long, knife-like toenail--G219.3.1.

TOKEN: Token to prove slaying of beast--H105.4.1.

TOKGABBI: Tokgabbis aid mistreated step-daughter in tasks--R221Ib; man convinces Tokgabbi he is a skeleton--K335.1.1.4.

TOM HICKATHRIFT: F628.2.3.1.

TOM THUMB: F535.1.1, F1611C.

TOM TIT TOT: D2183B.

TOMAHAWK: Taken to underwater home of Snake Chiefs, to pull tomahawk from wall--B491.1.1.

TOMB: Man woos maid, finds only tomb on spot of her home. Maid was ghost--E474.2.

TOMBASA: Princess of Tombasa--D551.1Bf.

TOMORROW: Today's catch of fish traded for prospective larger catch tomorrow--J321.1.1.

TOMTE: Lazy wife given ten helpers who enter fingers and force to do work--Q321.2.2.

TONGA: Butterfly challenges crane to fly to Tonga--K25.1.1; Maui Kiji Kiji brings fire to Tonga--A1415.5; cruel King of Tonga--R161.5.

TONGUE: Why animal has no tongue--A2344.2ff; punishment for cutting off bird's tongue--Q285.1.1; quest for best dish in world--H1305.2.1; dog's tongue stretched for tattling--A2344.4.1; fox disguised as Buddha sticks out tongue--K607.4; goblin makes grocer's cask talk--F451.6.2.5; why horsefly has no tongue--A2236.1; riddle, seven tongues in one head, nest of birds in horse's skull--H793; thief named Tongue identified accidentally by fake wise man--N611.1.1; sea serpent tongues as token--R111.1.3Ea; tiger duped into putting tongue between two sticks to play "flute"--K1111.0.1.1.

TONTLAWALD: Enchanted forest--F582.1.1.

TOONTOONY: Bird has thorn in throat--Z41.8.1.

TOOTHPICK: Toothpick imps revenge selves on slovenly girl who hides them in tatami cracks--Q321.3.

TOROMIRO: Origin Toromiro carvings of Rapa-Nui--A1465.5.1.

TORTOISE: SEE TURTLE.

TOSS: Demons toss man into air as game--F153.2. SEE ALSO THROW.

TOTEM: Origin of goat clan totem--A1578.1.1; boy wins back sun with aid of totems and mouse --A721.3.1.

TOURNAMENT: Unknown knight wins three days in different armor--R222.1.

TOWER: Absurd suggestions as to how tower was built--J2711.1; baboons build tower of their bodies to reach dead king to God--F772.1.3; to climb tower and take flute from under pillow, play it and tower will follow--H1213.1H; maid in tower (Rapunzel)--F848.1; prince wants moon, tower built, moon breaks--C771.1; tower to moon--F772.1.2ff; tower to moon falls (sky)--J2133.6.2.

TOWN: Fool fails to recognize own town--J2014.2. SEE ALSO CITY.

TOYS: Two girls follow trail of toys and come to witch's stone hut--G412.0.1.

TRACKS: Animal sees tracks going into den and none coming out--J644.1; hunter wants to see lion tracks, not lion--W121.1; monkey sees tracks going into water and none coming out-- J644.2; Christ as beggar tells to follow silver tracks--Q1.1C; Brer Rabbit convinces Brer Fox to attack wildcat since its tracks show no claws --K1039.1.

TRADE: Brother with best trade to get inheritance--F660.1B; what trade brings greatest happiness? Tilling soil--H1273.2I.

TRADER: Origin Russian traders--A1414.1.1.2.

TRADING: The eaten grain and the cock as damages--K251.1; dupe trades places with imprisoned trickster--K842; foolish bargain, horse for cow, cow for hog, etc.--J2081.1; magic object exchanged for worthless--D871.1; rogues exchange objects and cheat each other--J1516.

TRAIL: Cat covers dung to hide trail--A2495.1; trickster makes trail to farm, claims as his on evidence of trail--K453.1; crumb (grain) trail eaten by birds and lost person cannot find way back--R135.

TRAIN: Dog runs beside train, cools off hot boxes--X1215.7.1; railroad bridge built by devil for one hundred fifty souls if completed by cockcrow--G303.16.19.4.0.1.

TRAINING: Twin parrots, one raised by bandit calls "Kill him", one raised by Brahmin calls "Feed him"--J451.6.

TRAITOR: Host betrays hidden visitors-- Z43.6.1ff; offer to lure others to hunter if released--K553.1.0.2. SEE ALSO BETRAYAL.

TRAMP: Tramp makes nail soup--K112.2.

TRANSFORMATION: Large animal tricked into transforming self to small size--K717, K722. SEE ENTIRE SECTION D0-D699 Transformations. SEE ALSO DISENCHANTMENT.

TRAP: Deceiver falls into own trap--K1601. SEE ALSO PIT; SNARE.

TRAVEL: Animals go a' journeying--B296; unhappy traveler brightened, man steals his knapsack then leaves it on road ahead--U69.

TRAY: Trays stick to girl polishing, becomes turtle--A2147.1.

TREAGEAGLE: Treageagle sweeps sands forever --E459.8.

TREASURE: Animal shows man treasure--B562.1; castle in the sea with treasure--K1861.1C; treasure to be divided three ways, one-third to poor, one-third to church, third for self-- H1440; dream of treasure bought--N531.3; dream of treasure on bridge--N530ff; man given treasure by fairies is too greedy--F348.7.1; fairy shows treasure in return for freedom--F244.2; treasure feigned, old father treated well--P236.2; fool's tale of treasure discredited--J1151.1.4; laid ghost gives treasure--H1440; treasure shown by ghost must be shared with needy--E415.1.2, H1440; Brer Gilyard's treasure--K649.9.2; leprechaun marks all bushes to disguise marked treasure--J1922.2.1; miser advised to pretend stolen treasure was still there--J1061.4; three discover treasure, one brings poison wine, others kill him, then drink--K1685; inscription on treasure pot, "first of seven", etc.--N535.0.1; robber's treasure found by ferryman--N534.9; lad sewn in skin to be carried up onto mountain to treasure-- K1861.1; spirit of treasure rewards fearless bride--Q82.0.1; tabu, speaking while digging treasure--F348.11; victim pretends is putting more money in hiding place, thief puts stolen funds back in hopes of getting even more-- K1667.1.1; treasure in vineyard, spaded by seekers it then flourishes--H588.7; treasure turns to wasps or filth for bad man, gold for good--N182.2. SEE ALSO GOLD.

TREE: Cave with tree bearing agate gems found when deer followed into cave--N773.0.1; tree gives handle for axe, cut down--U162; man abandoned in desert finds axe and arrows in tree --D882.1Ga; blinded trickster finds way by asking names of trees--D1313.4; trees made to blossom by old man--D1571.1; tree carrying contest, deceptive trickster rides--K71; caught in cleft in tree, or between branches--K1111; trees uprooted by coward on runaway horse--K1951.2.1; crow gives god's gifts to tree, to bear fruit without replenishing--A2431.3.6.4; large tree is cut open. Men and women come out--A1263.7.1; trees cut down to gather fruit--J2126.1; Death magically bound to a tree--Z111.2.1.1; hunter finds land behind door in tree--C611.1.1; tree bent into lake to drink--J1973; dupe persuaded to climb tree, falls--K1113.1; man falls from tree and routs enemy--N696.1.1; object falls on robbers from tree--K335.1.1.1; task, gathering fruit shaken from tree—F601.2Ga; girls chased up tree by tiger—K311.3I; tree with silver leaves and golden blossoms from grave, tree caresses father and lashes new wife—N455.4C; tree from mother's grave gives gifts—R221B; holding up the tree—K1251; man falls into hole in tree, monkey puts tail in hole and man pulls it off—K619.4; honey tree left standing—J241.2; animal tricked into running horns into tree—K771; tree judges for snake, not man—J1172.3.2; king finds maid in tree and weds—P253.3B; tree maiden dies when tree is cut—F441.2.3.1.1; Na-Tao trees planted on graves—E221.6; to name three trees first, contest—N51; must learn name of trees before can eat—J2671.4.1; nut tree pulled to pieces to get nuts—W154.6; ogre tries to cut down tree and capture fugitive—R251; magic tree (ogre) grows in an hour, bends for children to climb on and runs off with them—G422.1.1.3; origin of particular tree—A2600.1; Outlaw Matthew carries water in mouth to water tree until it bears—V21.7; only one person can pick from tree—D830.1.1; old man planting tree for future generations—J701.1; princess enchanted in tree form, one thing missing from palace, talking tree—D215.9; quest for tree of golden stars—N455.4; tree to bear quinces if plays sad tune, oranges if lively—D1223.1.1; reed bends, tree does not—J832; tree regrows magically—H1115.1; riddle, sits between heaven and earth (in tree)—H583.3.2; riddle, cutting live trees and planting dead ones—H583.2.6; disastrous attempt to save man from tree by pulling on rope—J2434; why tree does not flourish, gold (serpent) in roots—H1273.2; saplings pulled up in order to judge by length of roots how much water to give—J1973.1; Saynday trapped in closing tree—D1556.3; fool sells hen to tree—J1853.4; tree blamed for not bearing fruit by those in its shade—W154.7; trees make sound of Vainamoinen's sleeves—A2272.1.4; tree spirit to be made into ship will not move until girl touches—F441.2.0.2; man marries spirit of willow tree—F441.2.3.1.1; tree magically stretches upward—D482.1; strongman pushes over trees previously weakened, intimidates opponent—K46.1; tall tale, tree grows from deer, horse, repeoples earth after flood—W154.8.5; reason for withering tree overheard in conversation of animals—N452.1.2; tree as witness—J1141.1.3.2; tree as witness, has man inside—K451.3; Brer Wolf holes Brer Fox up in tree—K522.9.1; woodsman bribed by dwarf to spare tree—J2075; SEE ALSO FRUITS; HOLLOW TREE; LOG; MULBERRY; PALM; PIPAL; SAPLINGS; SAUSAGE.

TREE, APPLE: Apple tree grateful for being shaken—Q2.1.2Cb.

TREE, BEE-GUM: Dupe trapped with leopard in bee-gum—K1023.6.

TREE, BIRCH: Fool gives ox to birch—J1853.3; maid clothes self in birchbark dress—R221G.

TREE, EVERGREEN: Evergreens shelter children fleeing from Wolf-Wind. Glosskap promises that dead trees will always revive in spring,

deciduous were killed by Wolf-Wind—A2760.2; why trees are evergreen—A2765.1.

TREE, FIR: Fir will wish was bramble when woodsman comes—J212.4.

TREE, LAUREL: Laurel grants wishes if tended—F1015.1.1. Lang.

TREE, MAPLE: Why leaves of maple turn red in fall—A2769.2.

TREE, OAK: Conifers flaunt green needles in winter's face as promise of spring, oak joins them—A2765.2; owl advises killing oak saplings since birdlime will be made of mistletoe on oaks—J621.1; reed bends before wind, oak breaks—J832.

TREE, PEAR: Bears fruit as one watches—F791.7.1.

TREE, SYCAMORE: Sycamore judges in favor of snake, not man—J1172.3.2.4.

TREE, TAMARIND: Leaves soon stripped from small tree, wait until grown and will always supply—W11.14.1.

TREE, WILLOW: Man marries spirit of willow tree—F441.2.3.1.1.

TRICHLEGG ALP: Dream of treasure—N531.1.

TRICK: Cat saves self with one trick—J1662ff; wait here and trickster will play trick, rides off and never returns—K341.8.1. SEE ENTIRE CHAPTER K. Deceptions.

TRIPE: Boy to ask someone when his tripe is washed enough, calls in sailors on sea—J2461.2E.

TRIVILLIP: D2183G.

TROLL: Bear frightens troll—K1728; lad plays cards with troll—H1440C; troll hag sits on self-sticking chair—E341.1A; troll's lost child returned, reward—H1213.1J; troll told christening guests include Virgin, etc.—K1736; elder brother tells king Cinderlad can steal from troll—G620Ac; cow Bukola moos and lad finds in cave of trolls—G530.2E; lad flees with troll's daughter—G530.2C; single eye among three trolls—K333.2; troll and farmer raise crops together—K171.1; troll lets first two goats pass—K553.2; troll owner of golden bird, horse, maid—H1331.1.3A; troll kidnaps three sisters—G561G; gold knob on spindle rolls away, man accuses troll Kidmus of taking it—D1472.2.12; golden needle in heart kills troll abductor of dancing princess—F1015.1.1B; twelve princesses scratching twelve troll heads of troll—H1385.1F; little men and birds aid in service to troll—G530.2Gb; king promises son to troll—G530.2Ae; troll sees sun and bursts—G304.2.5; troll hag to wed maid's lost husband—H1385.4; King weds Troll Ingeborg, son Sigurd rescues her—H1385E; troll stones move when whistle blown—F809.5.2; troll wife comes wading in floor—H1385.1E; lad feeds children of troll <u>wife</u>, she gives magic fish hooks—G666.1; girl rescues prince from troll <u>women</u>—K975.2.1.

TROMBONE: Lord hangs trombone on St. Peter's back, guest expect him to play—V229.26.1.1.

TRONG CAO: Origin of gods of the hearth—T211.2.1.1.

TROUBLE: Trouble buried by poor <u>brother</u>, released by rich—N250.4; dupe to see "trouble" in grass, trickster sets grass afire—K1055.2; Trouble tricked into making self <u>small</u>—K717.3; Brer Wolf meets "Mr. <u>Trouble</u>"—H1376.11. SEE ALSO BAD LUCK; MISCHIEF.

TROUBLEMAKER: <u>Brer Rabbit</u> causes trouble between Brer Fox and wife with conflicting tales—K2131.6; <u>cat</u> brings suspicions between eagle and sow—K2131.1; <u>jackal</u> tells tale so as to get buffalo and tiger to <u>kill</u> each other—K1084.1.1.

TROUSER: Tailor sews trousers in <u>haunted</u> church—H1412.2; <u>jumping</u> into the breeches—J2161.1; man exchanges trousers for coat, <u>pays</u> for neither—K233.4.1. SEE ALSO BREECHES; PANTS.

TROUT: SEE FISH, TROUT.

TRUE: Untrue eats up True's provisions, blinds and leaves—N452B.

TRUMPET: Dupe believes <u>bamboo</u> stalks are trumpet, puts tongue between and waits for wind to blow—K1111.0.1.1; town of <u>fools</u> buys trumpet, thinking it puts out fire—J1703.7.

TRUTH: <u>Bird</u> sings truth—N271Aa; advice, never tell a falsehood in <u>court</u>—J21E; <u>dispute</u> among Truth, Falsehood, Fire and Water—K2143; riddle, how far from truth to falsehood?—H685.2; <u>task</u>, sack full of truth—H1045.

TSAP-TSARAP: Cat sold in land with no cats—N411.1E.

TSAR: Peasant to recognize king. Will be one with <u>hat</u> on—J1289.27; to tell secret only in presence of Tsar, tells in presence of Tsar's face on <u>ruble</u>—H561.6.2; <u>quest</u> to Tsar for rent—H1273.2F. SEE ALSO CZAR.

TSAREVNA: Tsarevna as Snow White—Z65.1Ab.

TSIKSIMENA: Quest for Tsiksimena bird—H1331.1.3.

TSIMSHIAN: Restoration of eagle clan of Tsimshian—A1611.1.6.

TUBMAKER: Tubmaker flies to sky—K1112.2.

TUCKONIE: Tuckonie elves sing tree up—D482.1.1.

TUG OF WAR: Trickster arranges tug between two larger animals, each thinks he pulls against

trickster—K22.

TULE: Sun and moon made of tule grass—A717.2.

TULIPS: Fairies care for tulip bed—F339.2.

TUMBLEWEEDS: Eagles fight tumbleweeds—B455.3.2.

TUNA: SEE FISH, TUNA.

TUNIS: Triplets of Tunis—H621.1.1.

TUPÁ: God Tupá—A2560+.

TUPPEN: <u>Little</u> Tuppen—Z43.3; <u>Little</u> Tuppen coughs—Z32.1.1.2.

TURBAN: Man sells turban for <u>fantastic price</u>—J829.1; turban of <u>invisibility</u>—F1015.1.1C; <u>tiger</u> told snake is king's turban—K1023.1.1.

TURKEY: Turkey Brother and Two Feathers—D1050.2; turkey convinces <u>emu</u> to cut off wings—A2377.1; turkey pecks out eyes of <u>giants</u>—G511.2; turkey <u>girl</u> given raiment for dance—R221W; why turkey has two <u>young</u>—A2486.5.

TURKISH: Turks recognize work of Sultan's <u>daughter</u> and rescue—E341.1D; <u>Little Rooster</u> and the Turkish Sultan—Z52.4.

TURNIP: <u>Bear</u> gets tops of turnips—K171.1; pulling up turnip, <u>chain</u>—Z49.9; farmer takes an extraordinary turnip to the king as a present—J2415.1; man takes <u>figs</u> to king instead of turnips and they are thrown at him, "Thank God they weren't turnips"—J2563; man in <u>moon</u> for stealing turnip—A751.1.4.1; <u>sheep</u> live inside huge turnip all winter—X1401.1.2.

TURTLE (TERRAPIN, TORTOISE): Turtle suggests being held captive in older <u>bag</u>, escapes—K581.8; turtle holds <u>beaver's</u> tail and wins swimming match—K11.2; <u>beeswax</u> on tortoise shell catches jackal—K741; tortoise as <u>bride</u> provides bride test gifts—B641.0.1E; lizard claims tortoise's <u>bundle</u> "Found it along road", tortoise was dragging it on a string—J1511.14.1; terrapin to be <u>burnt</u> in grass, hare burns fox instead—K1055.2; at tortoise's suggestion <u>bushbuck</u> impersonates evil spirit and terrifies leopard—K335.0.4.6; <u>California</u> created on the back of six turtles—A815; <u>caraboa</u> kicks turtle and splits hoof—A2376.1.0.1; tortoise wins race <u>climbing</u> down tree, jumps—K15.2; why <u>cockroach</u> is flat, too slow in putting tortoise's shell back together—A2305.2.1; <u>coconut</u> with shell like turtle shell and water like turtle's tears inside—A2611.3.2; turtle persuades tiger's <u>cook</u> to put his tail in river and will sing more sweetly—K553.5.3; origin of <u>death</u> from falsified message—A1335.1; turtle and crow free <u>deer</u>—K642.2; trickster disguises as leprous <u>animal</u> and says trickster is putting a hex on enemies to cause <u>disease</u>—K1995; Anansi tricks land turtle in <u>diving</u> match—K16.2; tortoise being hauled up on rope to dog's mother is dropped—A2319.1.9; <u>drowning</u> punishment for turtle—K581.1; tortoise tricks leopard into drum and takes to Nyame—K714.2.5; tortoise breaks tabu with king's magic food producing drum—D861.1H; earth rebuilt from blood with magic mold carried on back of tortoise—A815.0.1; earth on turtle's back—A815, A1145.2.1; tortoise has no head and feet when called to come work, produces them when called to come eat—W111.7.1; spider and turtle exchange dinner invitations, inappropriate feast repaid—J1565.1.1ff; baboon must cross charred field to wash before tortoise will let him partake of feast—K278; spider sends turtle to wash repeatedly before feast—K278; turtle borrows feathers and goes to heaven—K1041.1.1.1; turtle borrows feathers, falls—K1041.1.1; turtle flies with borrowed feathers—K1041.1.4; turtle makes flute of jackal's thighbone—K1775.1; turtle playing flute and dancing untied by children —K571; turtle begs eagle to teach him to fly—K1041.0.3; flying turtle lets self be carried by eagle and dropped—J657.2; flying turtle speaks and loses his hold on the stick while being carried by birds—J2357; Brer Terrapin falls from shelf onto Brer Fox—K1161.11; fox tricked by terrapin into sitting under tree with mouth open waiting for plums to fall—K1035.1; Ijapa overuses magic fufu tree—D861.1lc; tortoise suggests killing him by covering with grain—K81.7; tree from grave of turtle—F54.2.2; turtle as grinding stone is thrown away—A2433.3.19.0.1; turtle defeats hare in race—K11.1, K11.3; turtle needs hare's liver for queen—K544; heron caught in coral is freed by turtle—B545.3; Ijapa given second horse, if first had lived would now have two—W211.1.1.1; terrapin makes hominy spoon of wolf's ear—K1715.3.3; Brer Rabbit puts hornet's nest in fox's bag, frees terrapin—K526; turtle passes hot water drinking test—H221.4.1; animal calls to house, dupe answers—K607.1; turtle carries house fearing firefly's fire—Z49.6.0.1; turtle calls to house, hidden enemy answers from within—K607.1; turtle as mysterious housekeeper—N831.1.0.1; turtle tells jackal biting foot he has root—K543; turtle judges in favor of snake not man—J1172.3.2.3; tortoise to jump over elephant—K11.1; why there are land and water turtles—A2433.6.1.3; tortoise as barber ties hair of leopard to tree—J1172.3.0.6; tortoise brags of long life, is caught by fisherman—L395; tortoise tricks lion into bag—K714.2.3.1; lizard hides from enemies between shields and dives into creek, turns to turtle—A2312.1.0.3; tortoise in magic dancing palm—K741; tortoise sent to learn tree's name remembers—J2671.4.1; suitor test, learning girl's name—H323; tortoise possesses first needle, sews up cracked shell with thread given by Jungies—A2312.1.8; tortoise paints hyena—A2411.1.7.1.1; tortoise paints giraffe—A2411.1.1.1; tortoise paints zebra—A2413.1; tortoise paints leopard—A2411.1.1.1.1; tortoise stealing food by means of magic dancing palm tree—K741.0.10; animals pledge peace and each reveals his pet peeve—W141.1.1; youngest son, turtle, insists on wedding youngest of three princesses—D672F; rock python regurgitates him and allows to wed daughter—F914.0.1; tortoise receives stolen quills—K752.1; tortoise defeats Anansi in race with relative helpers—K11.1;

tortoise asks greedy man to give him back first ruby. It was given him to be sure second will be perfect match—K439.7.1; origin of tortoise sacrifice to Osanyin—A1545.3.4; turkey steals scalp from tortoise—A2351.8; too many turtles come, sheep called to aid, trample—K641.4; why turtle has shell—A2466.2.1; terrapin teases woman and she throws stone at him and cracks shell—A2312.1.5; tortoise hiding in bundle speaks and frightens bird carrying him. Is dropped and shell cracked—A2312.1.3, J2357.1; terrapin falls from tree spilling pot of wisdom and cracking shell—A2312.1.4; origin of turtle's hard shell—A2312.1.0.1; why turtle's shell is cracked—A2312.1.1; turtle dropped by eagle, hence cracks in his shell—A2312.1.1; quest for cast off house of spirit-turtle's shell—H1273.2M; singing tortoise—B210.2.1; turtle persuades captor to soak him in pond—K533.5; turtle soup, origin turtle soup—A2351.5.1; Ijapa carries wife to steal, he swears he didn't steal, she swears she didn't walk there—K475.1.1; turtle defeats lion in swimming match—K11.1; turtle makes rope tail to repay feast—J1565.1.3; tailor promises Allah will not steal cloth again, turns to tortoise with colors of cloth pieces stolen—A2312.1.0.2; tortoise carried by bird talks and loses hold on stick, falls—A2312.1.3; image covered with tar captures intruder—K741; girl polishing two brass trays refuses to go to mother when called, trays stick to her = turtle—A2147.1; monkey gets top half of tree, it withers—K171.9.1; man turned to tree with fruit like turtle shell—A2681.18; turtle arranges tug-of-war between tapir and whale—K22; deceptive tug-of-war, large animal's tail tied to tree root—K22.2; turtle shoots splinters into turkey's legs—A2371.2.13; grateful turtle carries Urashima Taro to undersea kingdom—F420.6.1.3.1; why turtle walks slowly—A2441.4.5; turtle beaten by man, turtle's war party attacks—A2312.1.7; turtle recruits war party of strange objects—F1025.2; partridge borrows terrapin's whistle and doesn't return—A2426.2.25; turtle drops pot of wisdom—A1481.1; cat teaches turtle all wrestling jujus save one—J1662.0.1.1.

TURTLE, GOLDEN TURTLE: Kim Qui, Golden Turtle, gives white flowers which cause nose to grow and shorten when smelled—D551.1C; Kim Qui, Golden Turtle, gives Emperor An Duong Vyong magic golden nail with which he can build wall to protect Vietnam from China—A132.15.1.

TURTLE, HOPI TURTLE: Coyote tells baby Hopi turtle to sing or will eat—G555.1.1.

TURTLE, SEA-TURTLE: Sea-turtle sent to bring monkey to dragon queen—K544.1.

TUSCALOOSA: Brer Fox caught when Brer Rabbit drops rail fence on neck, to "see the pretty girls from Tuscaloosa"—K1111.4.

TUSKS: Boar sharpens tusks when no enemy around—J674.1.

TU-VYEN: Origin Tu-Vyen temple in Hanoi—T111.1.5.1.

TWIGS: Magic food producing twigs—D1472.1.3.3.

TWILIGHT: Demon thinks thief astride him is "Twilight"--N392.1.2.

TWIN: Twin sons, colts, dogs, trees, from eaten magic fish--R111.1.3A; Sultan's wife and fisherman's wife to share fish, bear sons--S268B; twin parrots, one raised by bandit calls "kill him", one raised by brahman calls "feed him"--J451.6; brother counts to eight and spoils song of devils, hump taken as punishment, given to twin brother who imitates—F344.1.3; twins born with stars on forehead—R111.1.3Ac; twins Hun-Apu and Xbalanque vanquished god Vukub Cakix—A515.1.1.4.

TWIN FALLS: Origin of Twin Falls—A935.1.

TYLWYTH: Lady of the Tylwyth Teg gives ferryman silver coin which replaces self--F342.3.

TYRANT: Ruler, "Am I a tyrant or a learned man?"--J1289.25; repartee with ruler—J1280ff; disguised tyrant listens to sermon attacking himself and then reveals identity--J1289.26. SEE ALSO KING; TSAR.

TZAKOL: Parent of maize—A2685.1.1.

UGLY: Asin in disguise as bald, ugly stranger is seen bathing without disguise--T111.1.1.1; ugly princess moves to land of perpetual darkness--F576.1; girl to be sacrificed to stop dragon causing flood is ruled to ugly to be sacrificed by compassionate magistrate--R111.1.3Db; ugly prince has golden image made of girl, will wed only one as lovely--T11.2.1.1; disfigured man chosen over handsome groom--T55.2; demon shown mirror and dies--J1195.1.2; ugly sister helps pretty one--L145.1.

UKO: God Uko puts daughter Linou in Milky Way --A778.11.

UKKO UNTAMOINEN: Ukko Untamoinen asks Seppo Ilmarin to dance on tongue and swallows— F912.3.2.

ULYSSES: Ulysses and Cyclops--K602.0.1.

UNBORN: Distress over imagined troubles of unborn child—J2063.

UNCLE: Cruel uncle kills sons of brother—S71.2.

UNCLEAN: Princess rescued from Unclean Spirit --H1199.12.4A.

UNDERTAKER: Asked to call doctor, fool calls undertaker as well—J2516.9. SEE ALSO CEMETERY; DEATH; FUNERAL; GRAVE.

UNDERWATER: Submarine castle—F725.3; magic boat of bamboo carries to undersea kingdom-- D454.7.2; marriage to princess from undersea kingdom—T111.1.4; man visiting underwater longhouse given magic Quedelish--A1546.0.4; dupe persuaded sheep were acquired in underwater land--K1051.0.1; lad dives and finds one of three pillars holding up Sicily is almost eaten through--A842.3; Snake Chief--B491.1.1; spider invited to underwater feast--J1565.1.1; Vodoun priest falls underneath water and returns with message from dead wife--E481.10.1; Urashima Taro visits undersea kingdom--F420.6.1.3.1. SEE ALSO DRAGON KING.

UNDERWORLD: Hero trapped in underworld flown back by giant bird—K1931.2P; journey to land of dead to bring back person from the dead—F81; Maui follows mother to underworld--H1252.1.1; Maui asks fire of Mafuite in underworld-- A1414.4.1; rolling riceball leads to underground --N777; man gives tobacco to spirit world--E474.6.

UNICORN: Mother of Confucius steps in unicorn's footprint--A511.1.3.4.

UNITY: Birds rise together in net and escape-- J1024; lion succeeds when bulls separate—J1022; strength in bundle of sticks--J1021. SEE ALSO COOPERATION; DIVISION.

UNKINDNESS: Bat eats forbidden lily, origin of chain of unkindness--A1341.4. SEE ALSO ENMITY; KINDNESS.

UNTRUE: Untrue eats True's provisions, blinds and leaves—N452B. SEE ALSO TRUTH.

UPBRINGING: Twin parrots, one raised by bandits, one by brahmin--J451.6.

UPPER WORLD: Bird carries person to upper world—K1931.2; tree to upper world—F54.2. SEE ALSO HEAVEN; SKY.

URASHIMA TARO: F420.6.1.3.1.

URINE: Urination produces river preventing pursuit—F81.1.0.1.

VALET: Valet digs up gold leg of lord's wife, she calls from grave—E235.4.2.1.

VAMPIRE: E251.1.3; vampire as disguised lover --G561.2A; Sir Buzz competes with vampire in changing contest--D882.1Eb; Raja with fangs drinks blood—D112.2.1.3.

VANAISA: Vanaisa sentences Vanpagan to stick on moon--F722.1.2.1; moon and stars made by smith on order of Vanaisa--A744.1.

VANAPAGAN: Eagle carries to realm of Vanapagan for twelve-toned bell needed in task-- B582.2E; Vanapagan builds ladder to moon— F772.1.2.1; Vanapagan stuck on moon--A751.4.

VANISH: White cloud makes enemy vanish when gourd is unstopped--D882.1Bbb.

SEE ALSO DISAPPEAR.

VANITY: Motmot bird too vain to help build dam —A2431.3.9. SEE ALSO PRIDE.

VASE: Death penalty for broken vase to be carried out after payment of one hundred mon fine at one mon per year—J1173.1.2; lad to be released if find lost vase by noon, finds in lake—F320.2; anyone who breaks Sessho's vase to die—J1189.4.

VASILISSA: Vasilissa the Beautiful—Q2.1.2CeBb; Vasilissa the Wise as frog bride—B641Ad.

VASILY: Vasily the Luckless—H1273.2F.

VAUDAIRE: Devil attempts to flood Rhone Valley, cannot touch churches, causes windstorm, the Vaudaire—G303.16.12.1.

VAVAU: People of isle killed—R161.5.

VAZOUZA: Vazouza flows to sea in spring—A939.4.

VEGETABLE: Lies about huge vegetable—X1401.1; man selling wilted vegetables flies to moon—A751.1.2.1; magic vegetable tree, cut down = origin of vegetables—A1423.0.1.1, A2686. SEE ALSO CABBAGE; CARROT; ETC.

VEIL: Quest for lost veil of lady of seven veils-=-H1213.1C.

VELA CHOW: Sun King kisses moon, Vela Chow, = eclipse—A736.1.3.1.

VENGEANCE: Train of troubles from sparrow's vengeance—N261.

VENICE: Venetian merchant in East Indies gives cat to catless country—F708.1, N411.1; Venetian rescued from pit ungrateful—W154.8.1.

VENUS: Venus turns cat to maiden—J1908.2; girl La Belle Venus with star on forehead sent to live on mountain top—A781.0.1. SEE ALSO MORNING STAR.

VERLOOKA: Old Verlooka gets little girl, little boy, grandma—K1161.12.

VETERINARIAN: Man healing dragon named patron saint of veterinarians—B11.6.1.5, V229.29; mermaid's son becomes veterinarian—F420.6.1.5.1.1.

VIDYE MUBI: At tortoise's suggestion Bushbuck impersonates Vidye Mubi, the Evil Spirit—K335.0.4.6.

VIETNAM: Kim Qui, golden turtle, gives Emperor An Duong magic golden nail with which he can build wall to protect Vietnam from China—A132.15. SEE ALSO ETHNIC AND GEOGRAPHIC INDEX.

VIGIL: Enchanted prince guarded by maid—H1411.4.5; youngest son successful in vigil for devastating monster in orchard—H1471; vigil-ence test, guarding princess—H1473; thumb cut and salt put in to remain awake—H1481; vigil, to guard sleeping man—D754.1, L145.1B; vigil at tomb—H1460.

VIJAYA: Man persecuted by Rakshasa in form of beautiful wench—G369.1.5.

VINE: Dagun Vine is pulled out of shape—A2701; lie, fast growing vine—X1402.1; vine helper trips tiger—K1161.13.

VINEGAR: Mr. Vinegar—J2091.1, K335.1.1.1A; Fools sold vinegar in place of wine—J2099.3.

VINEYARD: Sons to find treasure dig up vineyard, it flourishes—H588.7. SEE ALSO GRAPES.

VIOLETS: Girl sent for violets in winter—Q2.1.4Ac.

VIOLIN: Cat at barbershop has tail cut off, demands razor, etc., ends with violin—Z47.3; princess plays violin by sea and mermaid brings lad up to hear—D532B; lad plays violin as last request, all must dance. Origin St. Vitus dance—D1415.2.5.2.

VIRGIN: Poor girl prays to Virgin for protection from fighting bulls—Q2.1.6B; chili plant grows from grave of murdered girl, they dig up and find her alive, protected by Virgin—E632.0.5; Boqueron volcano destroys San Jorge de Olanche where Spaniards refused gold for Virgin's crown—F969.8; wife sold to Devil prays to Virgin and burns Devil if he touches her—T251.1.1.4; dragon falls when Alyosha Popovich invokes Virgin—B11.4.1.1; Virgin sews own robes—D1623.2; miraculous image of Virgin appears on shawl in which roses are gathered for Virgin—V121.1; Virgin smiles at tumbler—V92.

VIRGIN OF PAPANTLA: Image of Virgin appears beside little tree and man carves image in tree. It walks to Papantla each night—V143.2.1.

VIRGIN OF SURAPA: Two boys find lump under blanket in field, is statue of Virgin—V128.0.2.

VIRILITY: Hawk to restore virility—K1853.3.

VIRTUE: Most precious thing—H1648.3; wild goose is considered bird of five virtues—B259.6.

VISCACHA: Fox claims middle of viscacha's blanket—J1241.6.

VISE: Ogre terrified by woman's legs, thinks are vise—K1755.

VISHNU: Vishnu strikes down Asura King—D1840.1.4; Vishnu threatens ocean—J1968.0.1.

VISITORS: Visitors told master is out say they saw him enter. He pokes head out window and refutes—J1552.1.1.2; strange visitor enters piece by piece—Z13.1.1; trickster claims he is "Visitor" and is fed delicacies—K359.2. SEE ALSO GUEST; HOSPITALITY.

VISTULA: Vistula nearly drunk dry by dragon—
B11.11.10.

VITUS: Origin St. Vitus dance—D1415.2.5.2.

VIXEN: SEE FOX, VIXEN.

VODOUN: Vodoun priest falls beneath water and
returns with message from dead wife—E481.10.1.

VOICE: Most beautiful voice contest—H1596.0.4;
voice changed—F556ff; cock persuaded to crow
with closed eyes—K721; origin cricket's voice—
A2426.3.4, A2241.12; voice disguised to gain access to goods (children)—K311.3; disguised by
changing voice—K1832; why earthworm has no
voice—A2241.12; fox chosen as shepherd for
fine voice—K934; recognition of voice brings
about rescue from ogre—H12.2.0.1; origin peacock's voice—A2423.1.2.1ff; origin snake's
voice—A2241.12; numskull cries from tower then
runs to see how far voice will reach—J1941.
SEE ALSO SILENCE; SINGING; SONG; SPEAK-
ING; TALKING.

VOLCANIC ACTIVITY: Boqueron volcano destroys
San Jorge de Olancho because Spaniards refuse
gold for Virgin's crown—F969.8; Lava Hill,
Devil's Knee, exorcised—A934.14; smoke of Mt.
Fuji—A240.1.1; lad in lion form rescues girl at
volcano—D532D; Hanomat creates volcanoes—
A966.1; volcano put out with long hose made of
bark—J1689.1; man opens mountain tops and
leper with flaming arms emerges and burns sky
—A625.2.10; origin volcanoes—A966ff.

VOLGA: Rushes to sea in spring—A939.4.

VOLKH: Volkh given wishes which work only
when wished for other person—D1720.1.2.

VOMIT: Lion vomits gold into bucket—J2415.16;
first medicine vomited by Goddess—A1438.

VOODOO: Saints have to dance when hear drums,
drought ends—D2174.1.

VOUIVRE: Baby trapped in magically opened
treasure cave—B11.6.2.4.

VOW: Vow sworn on Odin Stone erased by dead
husband—E321.6.

VOWELS: Ass taught to read vowels—K491.0.1.

VUFFLENS: Castle of Vufflens with four towers—
A1435.9.1.

VUKUB CAKIX: Twins Hun-Apu and Xbalanque
vanquish Vukub Cakix—A515.1.1.4.

VULTURE: SEE BIRD, VULTURE.

WABASSI: Wabassi sticks feathers in belt and
tries to fly—K1041.4.

WAGER: Grateful bull draws one hundred carts
for wager for master—B587.3; peasant bets merchant he doesn't have what he needs, eyeglasses
for ox—K92.4; wager to stay all night on mountain without fire—K231.14.1; sun rises in west
to win bet for lad—D1223.1.1; bet on wife's complacency—N11. SEE ALSO GAMBLING.

WAGON: Ox driver must put should to wheel before Hercules will help—J1034. SEE ALSO
WHEELS.

WAGTAIL: SEE BIRD, WAGTAIL.

WAILUKU: Falls on Wailuku River—A791.14.

WAIST: How spider got a thin waist—A2355.1.1;
J2183.1.3.

WAITING: Lad to disenchant girl if waits faithfully—H1385.3Ca. SEE ALSO VIGIL.

WAKE: Parents gone to exchange sorrow, i.e.
gone to wake—H583.4.2.

WAKING: Waking contest won by deception—K51.
SEE ALSO COCKCROW; DAWN; ETC.

WALES: St. Mary of Trefrew sent in guise of
beggar in Prince Llewellyn's party so that
prince has wizard the equal of King John's—
D1711.6.4. SEE ALSO ETHNIC AND GEO-
GRAPHIC INDEX.

WALI DAD: Wali Dad as matchmaker—T53.7.

WALL: Wall of flour—W153.16; sacrifice for Great
Wall of China—H602.3.1; mouse wishes to wed
wall—L392.0.2; wall to protect Vietnam from
China—A132.15.

WALNUT: Ants cross river in walnut shell—
Z11.0.1; Espen Cinderlad finds self-chopping
axe, spade, walnut, water flows from nut—
H1115.1.1; choice, money or three walnuts given
"from the heart"—J229.3.1; Man says pumpkins
should grow on walnut tree—J2572; boy commits suicide by eating "poison" pot of pickled
walnuts—J2311.2.1. SEE ALSO NUT.

WALPE: I to Walpe, You to Walpe—Z54.

WALRUS: Walrus from chips whittled from stick
by old man—A2109.1; Sedna's finger pieces become walrus—A2101.

WANG SHEN: Sage Wang Shen challenges pupils
to get him out of cave—J1686.

WAR: Ruler raises false alarm twice. When enemy
really attacks, soldiers do not respond—
J2199.1.4; bat joins first one side then other—
B261.1; war of birds and quadrupeds—B261;
cat pounces on boar's ear—K2324.0.1; cat's tail
taken as sabre—K2323; war of crows and owls—
B263.3; fox's tail as banner in war of animals
and birds—K2323.1; on hearing of marvelous
garden, enemy king refuses to attack such a
country—D1711.0.1.4; unknown hero wins

battle thrice—R222.1; drop of honey causes chain—N381; mice gnaw straps of sleeping army —B582.2.6, K632; for want of a nail the battle was lost—Z45; war of plants—A2701; turtle's war party—F1025.2. SEE ALL K2350+ Military strategy. SEE ALSO BATTLE; CRAZY HORSE; SAMURAI; SIEGE; SOLDIER.

WARINGEN: Man turned to Waringen tree after death—A2681.15.

WARM: Keeping warm by watching distant flame —K231.14.1; keeping warm by dragging millstone around—K119.3. SEE ALSO FIRE; HOT.

WARMING PANS: Warming pans sold in West Indies—N411.6.

WARTHOG: Baby warthog hides in pot taken to lion's home and overhears plot—K961.1.2; lion turns on warthog rescuer—J1172.3; warthog leads moslems to water—A2221.5.3.

WARU WANGGI: Snake from Brahma becomes Waru Wanggi Tree to rescue hermit—A2681.16.

WASHCLOTH: Girl given magic cloth, wash and become lovely—J2415.19.

WASHING: Blindness cured by washing in tears —F848.1, V221.12.1; why cat eats first and washes later—A2545.2; cat persuaded by mouse to wash before eating—K562; task, washing elephant white—H1023.6.2; goose persuades wolf to wash him first—K553.5.2; magic object loses power if washed—D877.1.1; giant (wolf) agrees to wash piglets before eating—K1121.2.1; task, washing drops of tallow from shirt—H1385.4Aa; task, washing black wool white—A2.1.2Ab; white—Q2.1.2Ab; wash water from sun and moon causes wealth—N455.4D.

WASP: Wasp routs Carlanco and saves kids— K311.3B; wasp swallowed by drakestail and released in court—Z52.1; getting honey from the wasp nest—K1023.0.2; house burnt with wasp's nest—J2102.5; wasp attacks crab's enemy, monkey—K1161.13; why wasp makes poison—A2813; snake rids self of wasp by being run over— J2102.2; wasp teaches sparrow to build nest— A2431.3.5; tiger duped into thinking wasp's nest is drum—K1023.1; in dream wasp tells of treasure—N531.3; treasure turns to wasps for bad man—N182.2; why wasp has small waist— A2355.1.3; wasp in well rescued by swallow— B362.1; town of fools tries to buy wisdom, are given bag of wasps, mouse, etc.—J1703.6.

WASTE: River Metsch turns white from wheat thrown into river—A939.1.

WATCH: Gold watch dies—J1531.3; snake gives magic watch—D882.1Ba Lang.

WATCHING: Trees faithfully keep watch, become evergree—A2765.1; watchman wonders who will carry saddle now horse is gone—J2377. SEE ALSO VIGIL.

WATER: Mr. Luck bathes in pool and becomes monkey, second pool restores—D551.1G; sent for water trickster bluffs threatening to bring whole well—K1741.3; task, drinking boiling water trickster sets in sun to heat up more—H221.4ff; caravan drivers think journey almost over and discard water—J701.3; why cats fear water— A2534.2; family guards two chests, water in one, fire in other—A1414.7.4; water of death substituted for water of life kills ogre—G561.1C; fairy lames girl who forgets to leave food and water out for him—F361.14.6; dispute among Falsehood, Truth, Fire and Water—K2143; sent to fetch water daughter makes series of excuses—Z18.2; oil is clean as water so fool buys water—J2478; nightingale brings water from Fountain of Dew to disenchant princess—B582.2B; glass of all waters (sea water)—H1377.1; hare forbidden drink disguises self in leaves and honey and calls self "King of the Leaves"—K1991.1; water from heaven and water from nether world needed. Sparrow hawk fetches but dies—B582.2D; lady has hero cut into pieces, boiled and revives with water of heaven—H1213.1C; Fire, Water and Honor travel together. If Honor is lost can never be found—W45.2; crow drops stones into jar to raise water level—J101; quest for water of life —H1321.1A, H1331.1.3; mother raven fetches water of life and water of death—H1213.1G; groom to bathe in boiling milk, restored with water of life—H1213.1D; farmer cooling feet has feet caught by Sea God, daughter demanded, quest for water of life—G561.1Cb; water of life and death—E82.1; water of life—E80; all to pour wine (milk) into bowl, all pour water—K231.6.1.1; dragon steals Peking's water supply—B11.7.1; runner to fetch water before princess—F601.2; what runs without legs?—H734.1; cold water down back teaches lad to shiver—H1440A; quest for water from country of sleep—H1321.1F; in time of sour cream shortage, water is called "sour cream" to remedy shortage—J1703.4; drinking water to stretch stomach before eating —J1341.7; task, set magic helper to water plants, cannot stop—D1711.0.1.2; water people flood house of sun and moon—A736.1.4.4; Gone-Down-To-The-Sea walks on water—D1841.4.3.3. SEE ALSO REFLECTION; UNDERWATER.

WATER, DANCING WATER: Quest for dancing water—N455.4.

WATER, WATERBUCKETS: Children with water-buckets on moon—A751.7.

WATER, WATERFALL: Origin of Hawaili Falls— A935; origin of Idaho Falls, American Falls, Twin Falls, Shoshone Falls—A935.1; origin of falls—A935; mother-in-law sets fire to chest of paintings but daughter pulls out picture of waterfall and quenches flames—D435.2.1.4; Pontius Pilate when thrown into Tiber and Thone causes storms, put in small lake and mountain top causes water to run over into larger lake at bottom—A935.2; origin of Tequedama Falls— A935.4.

WATER, WATER HORSE: Girl frees fairy calf when it is stuck in bog. It fights and kills water horse, rescuing her—F420.1.3.4; water horse admitted to church--F420.1.3.3.1; water horse--F420.1.3.3.

WATER, WATER JAR: Baluba monster helps children put waterpots on heads—B531.6; bird calls causing women with waterjars to look up and jars fall and break—K1079.1; girl falls into water jar, boy throws stone breaking jar and saving her--J1687; intruder injured when reaching for water in water jar--K1161.3ff; water buffalo with head stuck in water jar—J2113.

WATER, WATER LILY: Prince hears water lily singing--H1021.8.1.

WATER, WATERMILL: Fools believe they push it over coats—J2328.1.

WATER, WATER POLLUTION: Girl offends fairies by embittering waters of stream with her tears—F324.4; water kelpie curses water girl drinks so she cannot speak. She had dropped comb into the well—F420.5.2.6.6.1; River Metsch runs white with wheat thrown in—A939.1.

WATER, WATER SPIRIT: Water spirit returns a silver axe to the woodchopper in place of the one he has lost—Q3.1; water maid refuses hard baked bread--F420.6.1.5.1; water demon abducts three girls--G561C; water spirit faints away when kept too long from water—F420.4.6.0.1; water spirit as horse—F420.1.3.3; boy tricks necken into wrestling with bear--K11.6A; brother and sister fall down well and water nixie makes them work—D672A; water spirit keeps souls of drowned persons in dishes in his home--F420.5.2.3; sun prince and moon prince kidnapped by water spirits when fail to answer riddle—F420.5.2.2.5. SEE ALL F420 Water spirits. SEE ALSO KELPIE; MERMAID.

WATERBUFFALO: Fools carry waterbuffalo--J1041.2; waterbuffalo judges against man—J1172.3.2; lion succeeds only when bulls separate—J1022. SEE ALSO BUFFALO, CARABAO.

WATERMELON: Watermelon thought to be horse's egg—J1772.1; man glad watermelons do not grow on trees--J2571.

WAVES: Maid given wind, wave and wandering flame to aid--D672K; task, bringing the waves—H1144.2.1; tidal wave warned by burning fields —J1688. SEE ALSO SEA; TIDE.

WAX: Magic healing wax—H1440C; Gizo, spider, coats stomach with wax and crawls over crow's fig pile--K378.1.1. SEE ALSO TAR BABY.

WEAK: Elephant kills, lion avenges self on gnats —U31.1.

WEAKNESS: Animals confess at revival, Brer Rabbit confesses last, he is gossip--W141.1.

WEALTH: Charm for wealth requires calabash of sweat--H588.7.4; wash water from sun and moon falls to earth. Those on whom it falls become

wealthy—N455.4D; Plutus is God of Wealth--J451.3. SEE ALSO POVERTY; RICHES; TREASURE.

WEAPONS: Wild bull sharpens tusks when no enemy is in sight--J674.1. SEE ALSO GUN, SWORD.

WEASEL: Escape by persuading captors to dance —K606.2; color of weasel's coat--A2411.1.2.1.2; weasel rips open pack of darkness--A1174.1; fox, sandpiper, mole and weasel steal fire from windpeople--A1415.2.2.3; weasels have first fire—A1415.0.2.6; grateful weasel gives magic ring—H621.3; weasels catch mice generals--L332.1; weasel leaps down sleeping monster's throat--F912.2.5; weasel gives magic ring--D882.1B; why weasel's tail tip is dark--A2411.1.2.1.1; deceptive tug-of-war--K22.2; weasel woman—G262.6.

WEATHER: If Clamshell Boy appears at sunset sky becomes red and fair weather promised for morrow—T554.12.2; good weather for one is bad for another—U148; Maui forecasts weather with kite—A1124.1; red sky before wind—A1128.3; dragons cause weather in Taiwan Straits—A955.10.3; weather vane is half chick—B171.1.2. SEE ALSO RAIN; SNOW; SUN; WIND.

WEAVING: Weaver cursed by Bramah—K2371.2.1; weaving maid and cowherd lover set in heaven—A778.3.2; Goddess weaves for poor man who sacrificed for father's funeral--T111.1.3; hen can't guess name in year--D2183F; jackal wins bride for poor weaver--K1917.3H; man in the moon is an old woman weaving—A751.8.1.1; recognition by weaving--H35.3.3; daughter weaving turned to spider--A2091.2; man copies spider--A1453.2.1; supernatural wife or daughter (crane maiden, clam maiden, spider maiden, etc.) weaves marvelous cloth--B652.2.

WEB: Spider web over cave saves fugitives—B523.1; spider web as shroud (mantilla)--A1465.2.1. SEE ALSO SPIDER.

WEDDING: Bowl over head until wed—K1815.0.2; mouse let loose at wedding to test cat maiden's nature--J1908.2; wedding of cockroach and rat --Z32.3; all husbands die on wedding night—J21F; fool shopping for feast buys water since oil was 'clear as water'--J2478; wedding of frog and mouse--B284.1.1; inappropriate comment at wedding--J2461.2F; hand and ring produced at wedding to accuse bridegroom of murder--S62.1B; numskull runs after wedding procession to give daughter foolish advice--J2549.2. SEE ALSO BRIDE; MARRIAGE.

WEDDING GOWN: Girl daydreams about wedding dress, suitor leaves--J2063.3; wedding dress from sea bottom required--H1331.1.3C; Virgin sews wedding gown for girl--D1623.2.

WEDGE: Dupe puts paw in split log and wedge is pulled out—K1111.

WEE MEG BARNILEG: Fairies carry away to fairyland--F320.1.

WEE RED CAP: Man echoes fairies' cry, "I wish I had my wee red cap", flies—F282.4.2.

WEE RED MAN: Throws ball of yarn at giant and turns to stone—K1931.2K; wee red man cuts off horse's legs and puts in fire to reshoe—J2411.2.1.

WEE WEE MANNIE: Z39.2.

WEEK DAYS: Fairies remove hunchback's hump when he supplies suitable conclusion to their song by naming days of week—F344.1.3.

WEEPING: Giant weeps in sorrow until a stream forms—F531.5.1.5. SEE ALSO CRYING; GRIEF; SORROW.

WEIGHT: Silver bracelet sold with thread to make weigh more—J2083.7; theft of three pounds of meat blamed on cat. Cat itself weighs only three pounds—J1611; test, weighing the elephant—H506.1; bluff, throwing weight into moon—K1746. SEE ALSO SCALES.

WELL: Imposters abandon hero in lower world, drop rope down well and refuse to lift him out—K1931.2; Brer Rabbit trapped in well bucket is rescued by Brer Fox descending in other bucket—K651; man falls into well and accidentally kills cobra—N624; animal refuses to help dig well—A2233.1.1; bluff, digging up the well—K1741.3; Drakestail lets ladder out of stomach and saves self from well—Z52.1; dupe tricked into well—K735.5; man saved from falling into well by Fortune—N111.4.2; frog demands visit with princess in return for ball fallen into well, turns to prince—D195.1; frog to guard Nyame's well refuses water to other animals. Nyame takes his tail away—A2378.2.3.1; frogs decide well might be a trap in drought—J752.1; trickster feigns goat producing well—K111.5; vixen in well invites goat in to bathe, escapes on goat's horns—K652.2; girl gives flowers from hair to hand from well—Q2.1.5Bbb; kind girl combs head at well—Q2.1.1B; fools dig hole to put dirt from well—J1934; well spirit overflows Lake Lyn Glasfryn—C41.5; cheese (moon) in well—J1791.3; Panditji addresses guava trees, "May I pluck four or five of your fruit?" Answers, "Why not forty or fifty?"—J2368; wolf pities fox fallen in well, save pity and fetch a rope—J2175.2.1; quest to find out why well is dry—H1273.2; fools see bee's nest reflected and try to carry off well—J1791.9; weak animal shows strong animal reflection and frightens him—J1791.7.2; chick attacks reflection in well—J1191.5.3; rooster swallows all water in well—Z52.4; girl sent to wash spindle, drops it into well—Q2.1.2Aa; boy tricks thief into well—K345.2; Harimau, tiger, drinks from "Emperor's well"—K735.5.1; Espen Cinderlad finds magic walnut which provides well of water—H1115.1.1; well of wine—D925.0.2.1, F718.3; Well O' the World's end—B316C, D195.2, H1321.1Ad. SEE ALSO PIT; SPRING.

WELSH: Welshman threatens to knock out all thirty-two of Irishman's teeth—J1749.3. SEE ALSO ETHNIC AND GEOGRAPHIC INDEX.

WENS: Wens removed by fairies—F344.1.2.

WEREWOLF: Brothers turned to werewolves—P253.2F; unfaithful wife hides clothing so wolf husband is unable to return to human form—D113.1.1.1.

WESTERSCHOUWEN: F948.5.

WHALES: Blind boy uses sister as hunting bladder—A2135.1.1; blind boy throws cruel grandmother into water. She becomes white whale with grey hair in brain—A2135.1.2; whale boat—R245; boy eats cod, seal, ooglook, white whale—X1723.4; whale released from use as bridge—H1273.2F; dolphin and whale scorn crab as peacemaker—J411.6; as eagle lad drops whale on beach for villagers—S71.2; boy kills giant whale, which has dog head, by painting magic symbols—B877.1.3; Glooskap carried south by whale—A1153.1; Kagwaii, giant whale, eats boy disguising as halibut, killed from within—F912.2.4; animal thinks self largest in world—J953.20; whale restrains mermaid while lad and maid flee—D1154.1; Ichabod the whaler pledges not to harpoon Long John Whale if he'll let mermaid bridle and ride him—B612.3; pet whale killed by jealous sorceror—B301.9.2; crow makes animals believe beached whale is poison—K344.1.5; raven dwells inside whale, loves whale-spirit maiden—F911.2.1; raven claims to have left whale on beach, eats children's seal when they go to see whale—K341.1.1; Ratu rescues parents from inside Giant Blue Whale—B874.9; contest between whale and sandpiper—B263.10; why whale lives in sea—A2433.7.1; why seals flee whales, Raven has tricked—A2494.15.1; Sedna's finger pieces become whales—A2101; why whale spouts, given tobacco by Kuloskap—A2479.14; tug-of-war between elephant and whale—K22; family rescues girl wed to whale—C26.1.

WHEAT: Bear (devil) gets bottoms of wheat—K171.1; lowliest flower = wheat—B641Ah; why River Metsch runs white, wheat thrown into river to keep prices up—A939.1; girl eating kernel of wheat before going to stepmother's house cannot be harmed—D1033.2.

WHEELBARROW: Magic traveling wheelbarrow—R221Dg.

WHEELER: Anansi discovers "wheeler" in tree, is thrown a mile—C498.2.

WHEELS: "Sorrow" tricked into making self small enough to fit into hub of cart wheel—K717.3; dupe waits for rear wheels to overtake front wheels—J2066.7.

WHIP: Unkind brother curses March, given magic whip which beats him—Q2.1.4Ad; soldiers with magic whip—M211.7.1; magic whip helps build Great Wall of China—D1208.1.

WHIPPING: Father beats daughter before she fetches water to prevent her from breaking pitcher—J2175.1.2; imagined dead fool roused with whip—J2311.12; pupils helped to find legs with switch—J2021.0.1. SEE ALSO BEATING; SWITCH.

WHIPPETY STOURIE: D2183.1.

WHIRLPOOL: Floating house drifts near whirlpool at end of the world—A2109.2; Makail, God of the Gulf, claims one victim each year in whirlpool—F420.5.2.2.4.

WHIRLWIND: Dog protects people from whirlwind—A1024.1; Saynday woos Whirlwind—Z115.2; princesses carried off by whirlwind—K1931.2F. SEE ALSO WIND.

WHISKER: Task, stealing lion's whisker—B848.2.1; tiger made to believe porcupine quill is his enemy's whisker—K1711.1.

WHISPERING: Clay hats two feet wide stop whispering and plotting—J1199.5.

WHISTLE: Whistle no bird can resist sold—K842C; magic whistle calls animals—H341.1Aa, H1045, H1112; magic whistle herds hares—H1112; pseudo-magic resuscitating object sold—K113; stones move when whistle blown—F809.5.2; partridge borrows terrapin's whistle and doesn't return—A2426.2.25.

WHISTLING: Whistling contest, ogre tricked—K84.1; fox allows partridge to sew his mouth shut so he can learn to whistle—K713.4; whistling calls up storm—D2142.1.6.1.

WHITE: White cat—B641D; telling horses apart, black one is two inches taller than white—J2722.

WHITE GLAIVE OF LIGHT: SEE SWORD, WHITE GLAIVE OF LIGHT.

WHITE MAN: SEE RACES OF MAN.

WHITE SNAKES: SEE SNAKE, WHITE SNAKE.

WHITELAND: Three princesses of Whiteland—H1385.3Ba.

WHITTINGTON: Cat in mouse infested land sold for fortune—N411.1.

WHITTLING: Salmon, seals, walrus from chips whittled from stick by old man—A2109.1.

WICKED JOHN: Smith meets Devil—Q565.

WIDERSHINS: Passing changeling widershins around well every Wednesday at dawn—F321.1.4.1.2; return to living form by walking around church in opposite direction of widershins—E44; going widershins round church causes girl to be stolen by fairies—F324.0.1.

WIDOW: Wife agrees to wed Emperor if he will honor her dead husband, after funeral she leaps to death in river—T81.6.1; widow Longspur weds another Longspur—J416.2.

WIFE: False alarm raised to entertain wife—

J2199.1.4; wife carried in bag in teeth—J2133.5.1; bear in hat is taken for man by wife and landlord—J1762.2.3; bear aids hen-pecked man, enters house and cuffs wife—J1762.2.3.1; fool to bring 'pottle of brains', means wise wife—J163.2.1; wife remarries. First husband returns. Is burnt in straw pile by accident, wife throws self on pyre too. Second husband follows—T211.2.1.1; wife disguises self as cadi. She and Husain seek Hasan. Dispute over lost necklace is brought to her court and Hasan is discovered—S268B; wife sells monk's chicken, asked to give piece of chicken, "It belongs to my wife"—J1552.5; clever wife sets countertasks—N951.1; cock shows man how to rule wife—B216A; wage on wife's complacency—N11; on deathbed, husband tells wife to dress up in her finery, maybe the Angel of Death will take her instead of him—X773; wife in feathers and tar tricks Devil—K31.1; wife sold to Devil prays to Virgin and is blessed, burns Devil if he touches her—T251.1.1.3; shrewish wife terrorizes Devil—T251.1.1; dog trades places with master, puts wife in place—J1762.3.2; magic pot duplicates anything put into it including wife—D1652.5.7.1; wife is promised a last request before dying, request that husband die when she does—J1545.4.2; wife eats meal while cooking—W125.2; exiled wife allowed to take dearest possession, takes husband—J1545.4; man fattens wives until can't move—D671A; firetongs stretch ten times length when wife chases him with them—W211.7; frog's two wives invite him to come at same time—J2183.1.2; wife dies and man does not grieve. Donkey dies and he grieves. Friends told him they'd find a better wife but no one made such a promise about the donkey—X771; patient wife, Griselda—H461; wives make gullible husbands believe they are dead, insane, etc.—J2311.0.1.1; wife of captured king plays gusli for enemy king and chooses husband as her boon—J1545.4.3; wives take turns pulling out hair until husband is bald—J2112.2; faithful wife cutting hair thought to have murderous intent, turned out—T210.1.1; wife haunts unfaithful husband—E221.1.1, E221.6; horse shot is lesson to wife—T251.2.3.0.1; mysterious housekeeper—N831.1.0.1; king claims kitten was born of his cat because it goes to his (catnip was rubbed on), wife points out that cat is a male—J1191.1; lazy wife is not fed until she works—T251.2.6; task, calling wife a liar—J1805.1.2; wife obtains lion's whisker, can tame husband in same way—B848.2.1; wife made of magic calf's fat is made to cook and melts—A2146.1; image in mirror mistaken for wife—J1795.2; obstinate wife looked for upstream—T255.2; obstinate wife makes scissors motions as she sinks—T255.1; Pambito hides in house, answers for wife and receives meat handed in by Ol-Ambu—K2131.7; wife's paramour betrayed by hidden guest—J1344; wife and paramour discomfited by hidden cuckold—K1566; if porridge spills wife must eat, she spills much—C229.7; "Come quick your wife has lost her reason!" "Impossible, she never had any"—X772; dead wife reborn as young girl, weds husband again years later—E474.3; who rules the roost—T252.4.2; sea maid takes lad, wife plays harp and sea-maid brings him up—

R111.1.3Cd; forced to tell wife secret, overhears cock tell how he rules wife--B216Aa; wife forces to tell secret and he dies--B216Ac; wife tells husband's secret--H585.1.1; wife discovers secret vulnerability of husband--Z312.4; test of wife's ability to keep secret, the buried sheep's head--J1151.1.1; wife multiplies secret--J2353; taming of the shrew--T251.2; silence wager--J2511; wife refuses to speak for fear of stuttering--T255.8; talkative wife discredited--J1151 J1151.1.1; talkative wife, gift of penny for every word too much--D1454.2.0.1; bet that wife will be unfaithful during absence on pilgrimage--H466.1.1; wife as wager--N2.5; why wife washes dishes--J2511.0.3.1; wish for good wife--Q1.1A; husband wishes sausage on wife's nose--J2075; two identical wives, one is witch----D312.4. SEE ALSO SHREW; WIDOW.

WIFE, SUPERNATURAL: Marriage to animal wife--B600-B699; tabu offending supernatural wife--C31.2ff; maid comes into man's power when he hides her skin--D361.1.1, F302.4.2.2, N831.1; spying on supernatural wife--C35.2; mortal weds water spirit--F420.6.1.3ff.

WIG: Lad hides hair under wig and calls self Scurveyhead--B316A; wig carried off by wind--X52.2.

WILD: Wild man released aids hero--G671.

WILDCAT: Brer Rabbit convinces Brer Fox to attack wildcat since its tracks show no claws--K1039.1; cougar has food and no fire, wildcat fire and no food--A2378.4.15; hare has wildcat feign dead and calls turkey to celebrate--K751.0.1; wildcat flatters heron into singing--K334.1; wildcat and bear both attracted by steak in saddle bag, leap from opposite sides, wildcat leaps down bear's throat--X1114.3; wildcat creates dissension between eagle and sow--K2131.1; wildcat's spots--A2412.1.2.1; wildcat in form of man's wife--D312.4.

WILD HUNT: Wild hunt carries person off--E501.18.4.1; old woman hides hare in basket and wild hunt passes by--E501.5.5.1.

WILIWILI: Kauila turns three sisters to wiliwili trees--A2681.17.

WILL: Will interpreted so that older brothers own trees and game. They must remove these so youngest can mine gold as he owns land--L223. SEE ALSO INHERITANCE.

WILL-O'-THE-WISP: Origin of will-o-the-wisp--Q565; Brer Rabbit rolls in honey and leaves, scares everyone as will-er-de-wust--K335.0.4.7.

WILLOW: Men rise up from under willow trees at beginning of earth--A1236.0.1; girl with tree carried to moon , seen there--A751.8.5; man cutting willows finds silver and gold willows and follows upstream--F424.1; man marries spirit of willow tree--F441.2.3.1.1; willow as witness--J1141.1.3.2.

WILLOW, PUSSY WILLOW: Ejapa, coyote, gets eyes stuck in willow tree = pussy willow--J2423.1.

WIND: North, South, East and West Winds aid maid in search for husband--H1385.4; bag of winds--C322.1; boy traps wind in bag--A1122.5; wind cursed for hot breath--L351.2; fox asks bear with bird in mouth which direction wind blows--K561.1.0.5; task, bring wind trapped in paper = fan--H506.12; flour (feathers) sent by wind--J1881.1.8; wind judges between man and snake--J1172.3.2.4; man leaves jug set so wind hums over mouth--K1725.1.1; wind raised by loosening knots--D2142.1.2; lies about great wind--X1611.1.10.1; wind produced by magic--D2142.1.2; mother curses wind to be hated, moon to wed--A759.8; Shoshone learn their music from the wind--A1461.0.2; origin of particular wind, Chinook--A1129.4; servant hears Spanish wind and wind from France tell how to rescue princess from enchanted castle--S268D; wind gives directions on quest--H1232; riddle, selling wind to buy moon--H583.4.7; Saynday woos wind--Z115.2; sea blames wind for shipwreck--J1891.3; wind stronger than cloud--L392, Z42.0.1; contest of wind and sun--L351; Wind, Sun and Frost quarrel--J1712.1; thief claims he was blown into garden and vegetable uprooted by wind--J1391.1; Wabun, West Wind, can only be harmed by oldest living thing on earth--Z312.3; North Wind blows on moon causing to wane--A717.2; wind trapped by boy must give red sky warning when blows--A1128.3; wind, wave and wandering flame to aid in search for stolen maid--D672K. SEE ALSO WEATHER.

WIND DEMON: Brother rescues sister from wind demon--B314B.

WIND, NORTH: North Wind carries fox to northland--A1832.1.

WIND PEOPLE: Fox, sandpiper, mole and weasel steal fire from wind people and relay home--A1415.2.2.3.

WIND PIPE: To make horse go fast as the wind, blow through goose's windpipe--R111.1.4A.

WIND, WHIRLWIND: Three princesses carried off by whirlwind when allowed outside--K1931.2F; whirlwind carries off princess--H1385.1A.

WINDING SHEET: Stolen from grave--E236.1.

WINDOW: Fools build windowless house--J2123.

WINDOW, SKY-WINDOW: Sky window from digging up plant in upper world--F56.1.

WINE: Death tricked into bung-hole--K213; odor of wine cask--J34; stolen wine inspires dance styles--A1542.1.1; dragon drinks drugged wine--K929.1.1; fool lets wine run in cellar--J2176; lake filled with wine, bird falls asleep--H1213.1H; servant drinks 'poison' wine--J2311.2.1; pool of wine shown by grateful monkey—D925.0.2.1; pool filled with wine intoxicates elephants—H1151.6.1; wish for river of wine—Q1.1A; wine spigot left open—J2176; task, bring as much wine as in sea—H951.1; thief made hole at bottom of wine barrel but wine missing from top—J1319.4; fools sold vinegar—J2099.3; to pour wine into vessel, all pour water—K231.6.1.1; well of wine—F718.3; wine kept in plain container, wisdom like wine—J1319.3; mortal drinking with witches is left behind in wine cellar—G242.7.

WINE JAR: Must have been fine wine to leave behind such a smell—J1319.2.

WINE SELLER: Shown pool of wine by grateful monkey—D925.0.2.1.

WINGS: Why bat has wings—A2377.3; thank god camels have no wings—J2564; fairy comes into man's power when he steals her wings—F302.4.2; farm girl stands in sun waiting to grow wings—Q22.1; wings of bird maiden hidden—H1385.3F; why flying squirrel has no wings—A2377.2; swan maiden finds wings and resumes form—D361.1.1. SEE ALSO FLYING.

WINGS, ARTIFICIAL: Flight on artificial wings—K1041.1.

WINTER: Glooskap drives winter from Canada—A1153.1; Peboan as winter-freezer, Segun causes flowers—A1158.1; dwarf sends in paper dress to fetch strawberries in winter—Q2.1.4B; girl sent for violets in winter meets Twelve Months around fire—Q2.1.4Ac. SEE ALSO ICE; FREEZE; SNOW.

WINTER SPIRIT: Fleeing wife calls on her father, Winter Spirit, at North Pole. He freezes water—D672G.

WISDOM: How can one attain wisdom? "Listen to what those who know tell you."—J1060.3; storyteller dies, black bear found in his hut grows to ceiling. Children climb to sky, return as old men and disperse wisdom—A1481.3; wisdom compared to carrots, best part hidden, etc.—H599.8; fish returned to water gives ability to do work magically, pike saves later and gives second wish, for wisdom—B375.1.3; town of fools tries to buy wisdom, are given bag of wasps, etc.—J1703.6; wisdom of old saves kingdom—J151.1; origin of wisdom—A1481; wisdom kept in plain container—J1319.3; dupe to become wise in sack of wisdom—K842.0.1; test of wisdom—H501ff; Ananse fulfills test of wisdom, brings kingdom with one grain of corn—H501.4; wisdom of one town is stupidity of another—J1041.2; white man can store knowledge through paper and pencil—A1671.1.1.

WISEMAN: Learned professor from one university examines by signs a professor at another university—H607.2.1; three wise men seek Christ Child—N816.1. SEE ALSO PHILOSOPHER.

WISEMAN, SHAM: Sham wise man finds stolen goods, he has forced thieves to tell of its

whereabouts, or has hidden it himself—K1956.2+; sham wise man to guess contents of dish or box, calls out own name, by coincidence this is in the box—N688.

WISH: Absent minded wisher takes princess—D1720.1.5; king has couple sealed in barrel, they wish a ship, etc.—D1720.1.4; wish for ever higher status leads to content with lot—Z42; wishing contest, third wishes for all the others wished for—H507.3.1; twice the wish to the enemy—J2074; fairies grant wishes—F341; fish grants wishes—B375.1; fish's bones grant wishes—R221J; three foolish wishes—J2071ff; four wishes for four horns—J2075.5; boy wishes every woman to fall in love with him—D856; three wishes selflessly used—A2612.4; tabu, unreasonable requests, wishes overstep moderation and is punished—C773.1.2; Volkh given six wishes, they work only when wished for other person—D1720.1.2; wishing well, girl seeks on Halloween Eve—Q2.1.6; article wished on body of wife by husband—J2075; wife says ask for head and hands so can do twice as much work—D1720.1.3.

WISKEDJAK: Origin of lichen, wiskedjak's blood on rocks and willows become lichen—A2689.1.

WIT: Fox with a thousand thoughts is killed, crane with one thought feigns dead and escapes—J1662.2. SEE ALSO INTELLIGENCE.

WITCH: Witch professes to be able to avert anger of gods—J1062.3.1; girl scratches back of witch, covered with broken glass—Q2.1.6B; girl at witch's house sees men on stairs in black, green and red—Z65.3.1; witch flies through air on broomstick—G242.1; witch with head under arm entices Little Buttercup—K526; Jack refuses buttermilk to witch—K526B; witch puts calf's (sheep's) head on girl—L145.1A; witch in form of cat—G211.1.7; witch to eat children in night—K1611; Clamshell Boy makes witch think she can become lovely, takes to sea to show reflection—T554.12.1; witch powerless at cockcrow—G273.3; test, combing witches' hair—R221K; Coyote tries to destroy four witches by burning—A2441.1.15; Coyote breaks witches' dam and releases fish—A1421.0.0.1; witch-cow—G263.1.3.1; Debbo Engal the witch—K1611Db; lad defeats witch with aid of dogs—B524.1.2G; witch pinned to log by ear lobes under pretense of piercing ears—G275.7.0.1; elephant and buffalo hide twelve girls in mouths—G276.3; Esben steals from witch—G610Ah; witch exorcised—G271.2; witch exorcised, burns when magic book is burned—G271.4.1.1; witches steal eyes when allowed to comb lad's hair—G266.2; horned women call out three times, "The mountain of the Fennin women is on fire." Witches rush off—F381.8.1; lad discovers fish in frying pan are witch's former lovers—G405.1.1; man gambles his sons to wed witch's daughter—G530.3Bj; girls work together and push witch into fire—G512.3.2.0.1; witch turns lad into goose, pig—G263.1.0.3; witches from Haddam and East Haddam fight over cattle—G243.1.2; witch as hare is shot—G275.12.2; hare leaps to beekeeper for safety, is girl pursued by witch—E501.5.5.1.1; tailor imitates witch who jumps into water and turns to hare—G211.2.7.2; Ivanko and the witch —R251A; witch defeated by Jack—H1385.3D; witch tricked into kettle, fire lit—G512.3.2.2; witch as old lady turns into statue of Kannon (Kwan Yin)—K607.4.1; witches laugh so hard at sight of frog in pony cart that they are cured—B641.0.1A; witch removes victims' livers with stone finger as they sleep—G262.2.1; Witch of Lok Island turns all lovers into fish— G263.1.0.1.1; witch maid entices lad to rob mother—G264.3.2; Witch of Pendle dissolves and drowns in stream of milk—G274.1.1; mill grinds witch up—Q2.1.2Cb; witch's name revealed by crab—C432.1.2; witch tricked into oven—G412.1.1; witch eats peddler's mackerel and horse—G276.2; pig in silver woods asks lad to kill witches with branch—D136.1; brothers tell king that Pinkel can fetch golden lantern from witch's isle—G610Aa; witch steals back princess abducted by lad with helpful animals—B582.6; to read psalter over witch's coffin three nights—H1411.4.4; witch sees reflection of boy in pond, sends ants up tree to bite boy so that he falls out into net—G530.2N; witch rides man as horse—G211.1.1.2A; mortal rides with witches—G242.7; witch set adrift by enchanter, high seas when she stirs with ladle —G275.1.2; girl in service of witch—Q2.1.2Cb; witch out of skin, her skin is salted—G229.1.1; witches give magic objects to spin , weave and sew by selves—D2183.1 Leodhas; three witches deformed from much spinning—D2183.1; Devil sends witch to steal Starost's daughter— G261.2; witch comes up in stone boat and changes with queen on deck—K1911Ab; witch turns girls to birds, boys to stone—D771.11.1; witch turns twin brothers and animals to stone —R111.1.3; swan maid in power of witch— H1385.3Jb; tiger witch traps girls pretending to be aunt—K311.3H; witch with long knifelike toenail—G219.3.1; witch keeps girl in tower—F848.1; two girls follow trail of ivory toys and come to witch's stone hut—G412.0.1; girl given by Sun is treed by witch, tree magically hardens so witch cannot gnaw— T521.0.1; weasel woman Tsihlihla lures victims up feigning distress—G262.6; wife is witch— G211.1.7.1. SEE ALL G200-G299 Witches. SEE ALSO SEA-WITCH.

WITNESS: Excellent witness, lies marvelously and wins case—J1159; tree as witness— J1141.1.3.2; tree as witness (man inside)— K451.3. SEE ALSO COURT.

WITSDUKS: Snow the wind blows and drifts is called witsduks—A289.4

WOLF: Ass begs wolf to pull thorn out of foot before eating him—K566; ass begs wolf to take off shoes before eating—K566.1; ten wolves climb on backs to reach pig—K891.1.4; wolf carried in bill—Z52.2; blind man recognizes savage nature of young wolf—J33; Brer Rabbit's wife spills boiling water on wolf being pulled up on rope—K1034.1; wolf tricked into chest, boiling water poured in—K891.1.3;

magic bone jumps into Ivan's head, Wolf puts own head near so that bone jumps to his head —G552.1; fox has wolf walk through lime wash and receive boots "light as air"—K254.1; abandoned boy is cared for by wolves, turns to wolf—B539.0.9; boy who cried "wolf"—J2172.1; wolf asks how to make bread—Z49.5.2; wolf helps rescue girl from buffalo, decides to be loner henceforth—R111.1.13.2; Brer Wolf imitates Brer Rabbit, is burnt in log—J2411.6.2; wolf's candy house lures children—G412.1.2; end of chain, wolf eats pig, "God commanded me to eat"—Z43.2; wolf dives for cheese in well—J1791.3, K651; wolf feigns theft of child to restore dog in master's graces—K231.1.3; wolf jumps down chimney—K891.1, K2011; dupe puts hand (paws) into cleft of tree—K1111; wolf demands magic coin which causes rice urn to be self-replenishing—K1161.35; color of wolf —A2411.1.3.4; Brer Rabbit rides Brer Wolf courting—K1241.1; what will cranberries do if wolves come? Hide.—J641.2; crane plucks bone from wolf's mouth—W154.3; Brer Wolf tricked in crop division—K171.1; wolves persuaded to dance, captive escapes—K606.2, K606.2.3; devil creates wolf—A1831.1.1, A1833.4; enmity between dog and wolf— A2494.4.15; wolf flees from master, not dog— J953.5; wolf becomes dog, settles with man— A2513.1.3; wolf proposes abolition of dog guard for sheep—K2061.1.1; wolf prefers liberty and hunger to dog's servitude and plenty— L451.3; hare persuades wolf and fox to put their heads in loops on rope to strangle tiger and are dragged to death—K713.3; drunkard rides wolf—J1758.5; man enchanted in wolf form to be freed if lad refrains from telling secret for seven years—C420.2.1; wolf's eyelashes give magic sight—D1821.3.11; dupe wishing to learn to play fiddle has finger caught in cleft of tree—K1111.0.1; wolf puts flour on his paw to disguise self—K311.3; Brer Wolf holes Brer Fox up in a tree—K522.9.1; Brer Rabbit offers to show wolf bigger game, man with gun—K553.1.0.5; hare learns magic word to open wolf's garden gate—N455.3.2; geese persuade wolf to sing, escape—K606.2; wolf will not hurt pure girl—B771.0.2; girl he left behind by people is cared for by wolves— B539.0.9; wolf tries to entice goat down— K2061.4; wolf tricked by fox as godfather— K372; wolf intruder thinks goose is man with tongs, etc.—K1161.2; wolf poses as grandmother and kills child—K2011; seven wolves catch groundhog, he teaches song and dance and escapes—K606; Gunniwolf forces little girl to sing for him—G555.1.4; hare convinces wolf biting leg that he has stalk in mouth—K543; wolf tricked into hollow tree—K714.3; wolf to start eating horse from rear—K553.4; wolf kicked by horse, approached too near—K1121; hare addresses house and hiding wolf answers —K607.1; wolf blows house in—Z81; wolf calls to house, hiding bear answers—K607.1; wolf and the seven little kids, wolf eats—K311.3A; kid on roof mocks wolf—J974; evil spirit Kurat creates wolf—A1833.4; sick wolf asks lamb to bring him drink—K815.11; wolf accuses lamb downstream of muddying water—U31; wolf must devour lazy, stupid man to cure pain—H1273.2H; wolf objects to lion stealing sheep which he just stole--U21.4; presumptuous wolf (jackal) annoys lion--J952.1; wolf raised by lioness thinks self equal of cubs--J952.1.1; wolf tied to sham dead Mammy Bammy Big Money--K1047; Manabozo changes himself to a large wolf, small wolf proves better hunter--J292; wolf has harmed all so can expect no mercy--H1558.4.1; musician meets wolf in trap but saves self by music—B848.1; wolf waits for nurse to throw away child--J2066.5; wolves nurse hero back to health--B536.2; wolf aids hero in quest for golden bird, horse, maid—H1331.1.3; ram jumps down wolf's throat, knocks him out—K553.3; wolf judges rams and is butted--K579.5.1; Red Riding Hood--K2011; redbird pecks mud from wolf's eyes--A2411.2.1.13.1; wolf rescued would eat rescuer—J1172.3; Romulus and Remus set adrift in basket, cared for by wolf--B535.0.9; Saint Francis tells wolf to kill no more men and they will feed it, begs door to door--B279.1.2; Saint Stanislaw gives wolf permission to eat human flesh, but only blacksmith--B279.1; wolf loses interest in sermon on seeing sheep--U125; wolf thinks self big as shadow--J953.13.1; wolf and sheep treaty--K191; wolf locked up with sheep--J2172.2.2.1; wolf orders sheep to pay bushel of corn to hart--J625.1; wolf raised with sheep to become watchdog, eats--J1908.4; sheep frighten wolf with wolf-head in sack--K1715.3; wolf in sheepskin--K828.1; wolf as shepherd--K2061.1; wolf criticizes shepherds devouring mutton--J1909.5.1; sick wolf gets fox to bring deer to dance for him, kills—J644.1; wolf persuaded to sing--K561.2; wolf as dog's guest sings, is killed—J581.1; wolf kicked in stream by sow--K1121.2; wolf cut open and filled with stones—Q426; Brer Wolf mistakes setting sun for fire--J1806; fox asks wolf to stand on hind legs and see if sun is rising, leaps on wolf's shoulders—K652.0.1; why wolf has short tail--A2378.4.13; wolf's nose, tail pounced on, taken as mouse--K2324; wolf fishes with tail in ice--K1021; tailor 'measures' wolf's tail--J2133.6.1; animal captor persuaded to talk and release victim from mouth—K561.1; tar wolf catches trickster-K741; fox brings wolf to help exact taxes of man, ram brings camel--K641.2; terrapin makes hominy spoon of wolf's ear--K1715.3.3; thief disguises voice and is allowed access to goods (children)--K311.3; wolf swallows entrails and Tom Thumb directs wolf to father's storehouse, raises alarm--F535.1.1B; bear, wolf, fox serve twins--R111.1.3Ai; wolf kills ox and sets fox to guard carcass and catch bird coming to feed, bird forced to go for water from magic well--R111.1.3An; wolf descends in bucket rescuing fox from well--K651; dupe made to believe that trickster becomes a wolf when he yawns three times--K335.0.4.1.

WOLF, WEREWOLF: Magic golden apple beats enemy, obtained from werewolf--D1601.5.3.

WOLF, WOLFSKIN: Fox tells lion that his only cure lies in wrapping himself in the wolf's skin

—K961.1.1.

WOMAN: "Do not take a woman's advice", counsel proved wise--J21.37; task, fetch white glaive of light from realm of Big Woman--H1331.1.3Ai; 'brave' man claims to have woman's name when captured--K514.0.1; cat seeks fearless companion, chooses woman—A2513.2.1; City of Woman--H1385.4B; woman disguised in City Without Woman—T210.2; skillful companions create a woman--H621; man creates woman from leaf of palm, petal of lily, etc., adds parrot's tongue--A1275.11; woman sticks carding combs into Devil's back, her curse--K171.1; disguises as man to escape importunate lover—K1236; disguises as man to escape with lover-K1837.9; why woman's elbows are cold--A1319.15; Goddess Nu-Kua creates mankind—A1241.3.3; man's guile triumphs over woman's, girl proves wrong--J1547; women tell jokes until enemy laughs so can identify by his teeth—B301.9.2; wife's lover provides new wife for wronged husband--K1837.9; man made for woman or woman for man?—R111.1.3Ah; why women are prattlers--A1372.1; to which rescuer does woman belong?--H621.1; Strength Giver teaches, hero wrestles sea lions—F617.4; she-bear eats twenty-one garlic cloves, turns to woman and bears Tan-Kun--A511.1.8.4; teeny-tiny woman and bone--E235.4.3; headless woman is at least a good woman as has no tongue --E422.1.1.3.2; village of woman--B524.1.2G; what does woman want most? Her own way--H775; Sumo wrestler meets girl, mother and grandmother who can out-wrestle him--F617.2.1; peasant's wife wrestles strong man—F617.2.2. SEE ALSO DAUGHTER; GODDESS; HEROINE: OLD WOMAN; WIFE.

WOMAN, WOMAN OF PEACE: Faery woman borrows kettle and returns full of bones each evening--F391.4.

WOOD: Babes abandoned in wood—S143; man gives father wooden bowl , son saves one to use for his father when old--J121; animals steal fire, wood swallows--A1415.2.2.1.2; man in moon, punishment for gathering wood on Sunday--A751.1.1. SEE ALSO FOREST.

WOODBORER: Woodborers gnaw tree so can fall with one blow--H335.7.1.

WOODCARVER: Woodcarver watches men playing Chong-Kak and years pass in moments—D2011.1.3; woodcarver carves woman, others bring to life—H621.

WOODCHOPPING: Flea suggests a woodchopping contest, slips back and eats prize—K372.2.

WOODCOCK: Each likes his own children best--T681.

WOODCUTTER: Woodcutter loses ax in pool and goddess returns golden axe—Q3.1; woodcutter asks tree for handle for axe, then cuts down—U162; barber demands wood and cart as price. Forced to shave both woodcutter and ox—

J1511.17.1; woodcutter hides fairy's robe—F302.4.2.0.3; man claims ox, wood and cart in sale, woodcutter allowed to claim hand, as bargain was for "handful of coppers"—J1511.17; woodcutter mends three broken branches of pine, is showered with gold—D2171.1.0.1.

WOODENSKIRT: Disguise of maid—B335.2, R221L.

WOODGROUSE: SEE BIRD, WOODGROUSE.

WOODMAIDENS: Woodmaidens capture Smolicheck—K815.15C.

WOOL: Gathering wool left in briars by sheep—H583.4.2.1. SEE ALSO SHEEP.

WORD: Words frozen thaw later—X1623.2.1; magic word that can kill—K1084.3.1; magic word opens gate, cave—N455.3.2.

WORK: Work contract, first to lose temper breaks—K172; donkey tells ox to feign ill and escape work—K1633.1; Brahman will accept only money king earns himself—W11.3.1; money thrown into fire, son does not care until money he earned himself is thrown in—J702.3; men exchange jobs because each believes other's work easier—J1516, U136.0.1; fish returned to water gives ability to do work magically—B375.1.3; wife says ask for extra head and hands so can do twice as much work—D1720.1.3; mother advises son to keep working no matter what the employment, second lad's mother advises to work only for his true worth—W48.1; one partner does work, other takes "tiredness"—J1249.7; charm for wealth and happiness needs a calabash of sweat—H588.7.4; why man must work—A625.2.8; man takes over wife's work—J2431. SEE ALSO INDUSTRY.

WORLD: When will the world end?—H707.2; end of the world—J1511.7, J2212.2.1. SEE ALSO EARTH.

WORM: Why worm is blind—A2241.12; chief's daughter feeds pet worm. It becomes a devouring dragon—F911.6.2; worm gnaws foot of king—L392.0.6; worm in lion's ear—A2434.1.4; first worm pecked in half by Maui, origin of man—A955.8.1; Rev Hillel does not admire Roman culture, worm does not admire song of bluebird—J652.4.3; worm tricked into hiding from feigned enemy, burnt—K1917.3E Fillmore.

WORM, EARTHWORM: Ant as matchmaker for earthworm and caterpillar—A2355.1.2.1. SEE ALSO EARTHWORM.

WORM, MEASURING WORM: Two bluebird brothers sleep on stretching rock. Crow sings it up. Measuring worm rescues—D482.4.1.

WREN: SEE BIRD, WREN.

WRESTLING: Boy tricks necken into wrestling with bear—K11.6; wooden Buddha defeats golden Buddha in wrestling match—L311.0.1; cat teaches tortoise all wrestling jujus save one—J1662.0.1.1; wrestling match held to decide which animal could live in palace, cat cannot be thrown—A2433.3.1.2; wrestler throws elephant into other wrestler's house—X941.2.1; little girl defeats animals in wrestling match—F617.2.3; king and nephew wrestle for judgment—H1562.9.1; wrestling match won by deception—K12; wrestler ties pumpkin to leg to recognize self in city—J2013.3; sumo wrestler wrestles sixty foot serpent—F617.3; peasant's wife wrestles strongman—F617.2.2; strong women wrestle men to defeat—F617.2.1.

WRETIN: Wretin Hill—F531.6.6.3.1.

WRITING: God of writing and books is son of White Snake Lady—B656.2.1.

WU FENG: Ruler gets headhunters to agree to take but one head more, sends his own—W28.5.

XBALANQUE: Twins, Hun-Apu and Xbalanque, vanquish god Vukub Cakix—A515.1.1.4.

YAKIMA: Origin of Yakima tribe—A1610.8.

YAM: Foreigners require hostage before letting Ashanti have yams as fear they will become overly strong if fed on yams—A1423.1.1; yam shaped like boy comes to life—T555.3; why yams have eyes—A2794.2.2; why yams live in ground—A2794.2.1; magic yam—D983.2; mother eats boy's yams and gives calabash in place—K251.1.4; origin of yams—A1423.1; yam is shot with poison arrow, why is poison—A2701; Ijapa carries wife to steal. He swears he did not steal, she swears didn't walk there—K475.1.1; angry yams pursue Tiger—D983.2.1.

YAMATO: Prince Yamato Take—Z200.1.

YANKEE DOODLE: Nippy steals fife—K1611G.

YARA: Yara entices man away from village—F302.3.1.5.

YARN: Girl given golden chain for industriousness unravels yarn to find way back—F348.7.1.4.1; student unrolls ball of yarn in fake game and backs out door without paying—K341.19.1.

YAWNS: Dupe believes trickster becomes wolf when yawns three times—K335.0.4.1; sleepy woman counts her yawns, robbers flee—N611.2; witch overheard saying "When I yawn I'm a troll"—K1911Ab.

YEAR: Origin Year of the Mouse—K52.3; years spent in the other world or asleep seem as as days--D2011.

YEAST: Girls to eat salty yeast, man who gives water in dreams to wed--H1385.5Ab.

YELLOW: Girl wears yellow ribbon around her neck all life--Z13.4.4.1.

YELLOWSTONE: Coyote drops basket of fish in water and water runs off forming Snake River--A934.16.

YERBA MATÉ: Origin of tea--A2691.6.

YES-NO-SPIRIT: Samik always equivocates--W123.4.

YMIR: Ymir makes the world from his members--A614.

YOGI: Tells yogi that a fish once saved his life. He was on the verge of starvation--J1250.4; lad on quest for Yogi seen in dream--H1331.1.3Fe.

YOGINEES: Origin of feast for sixty-four yoginees--A1541.2.2.

YOKUT: Origin of Yokut people--A1611.1.5.

YORUBA: Frogs defeat Yorubas in war--B263.11.

YOUTH: Wife drinks too much of fountain, becomes baby--D1338.1.1.2; fountain of youth--D1338.1.1; youth given man by horse--B592; giant takes sea captain to Isle of Youth--F361.3.0.1; quest for the spring of youth--H1321.1Ae; old racehorse still laments vanity of youth--J14; youth and old age alike, could not lift this stone when young either--J2214.2; choice, suffering in youth or old age--J214.

YS: Bells of Ys still heard on Easter Day--F944.6.

YU LU: Shen Shu and Yu Lu, Guardians of the Gate--A411.1.

YUAN CHAO: Origin God of Ill Fortune--D2011.1.3.1.

YUFKA: Fraudulent tax collector made to swallow his records, clever successor prints his on yufka (bread)--J1289.23.

YULE: Robin on way to sing for king on Yule morn--Z55. SEE ALSO CHRISTMAS.

YUM CHAC: Yum Chac commands dam built--A2431.3.9.

YURT: Judge agrees girl belongs to one whose yurt she is in at the moment--T92.0.1.1.

ZEBRA: Origin of stripes--A2413.1.

ZEUS: Calf promised Jupiter if bull found, lion has bull, bull promised if man escapes--J561.2; Zeus creates camel--A1873.1; dog's embassy to Zeus chased out--A2232.8.1; dungbeetle causes Zeus to shake eagle eggs from lap--L315.7; Jupiter assures male goats that beards will not make females male--U112; Zeus says snake should have bitten first foot that stepped on him--J623.1. SEE ALSO JUPITER.

ZEZOLLA: Cinderella variant--R221C Toor.

ZODIAC: Born under the sign of the donkey--J2212.6.1; the zodiac grows up, the kid becomes a goat--J2212.6.

ZOMO: Hare trickster. SEE ENTIRE COLLECTION. Sturton, Hugh. ZOMO THE RABBIT.

ZUITEN: Fox rubs tail on door making sound "Zui", thus calls boy--K1887.4.

4

Ethnic and Geographic Index

USE OF ETHNIC AND GEOGRAPHIC INDEX

This is an index to help locate tales from a given geographical or ethnic area. It is not cross-referenced to the MOTIF, TITLE, and SUBJECT Indexes.

Complete bibliographical information about the titles listed here appears in the BIBLIOGRAPHY. Several collections which were not included in the TITLE and SUBJECT Indexes are included in the ETHNIC AND GEOGRAPHIC INDEX. These added titles are identified in the BIBLIOGRAPHY by a "G" following the entry.

Not all titles listed in the BIBLIOGRAPHY are included in the ETHNIC AND GEOGRAPHIC INDEX. Many juvenile collections make no note of the ethnic or geographic origin of their tales. These collections are not indexed in the ETHNIC AND GEOGRAPHIC INDEX.

Entries are arranged within the following area groupings: AFRICA; ASIA; EUROPE; LATIN AMERICA; THE MIDDLE EAST; NATIVE AMERICAN; NORTH AMERICA; OCEANIA.

Within each area a Geographic Area Index is given first, followed by an Ethnic Group Index. A detailed outline showing all areas and groups indexed is given here. Note that Ethnic and Geographic denominators are listed as they were given in the source, so variations of spelling and terminology occur.

Outline of Ethnic and Geographic Index

Ethnic Groups

LATIN AMERICA

Geographical Areas

Ethnic and Geographic Index

AFRICA

Geographical Areas

AFRICA, GENERAL

Single Tales in Collections and Picture Books:

Belting ELVES 15-21
Jagendorf NOODLEHEAD 85-88
Manning-Sanders BOOK...GHOSTS 103-110
Manning-Sanders BOOK...PRINCES 9-13
Manning-Sanders BOOK...WIZARDS 22-25
Montgomerie MERRY 28-31
Withers WORLD 57-58, 59-66

Collections:

Aardema, Verna. MORE TALES FROM THE
STORY HAT.
Aardema, Verna. TALES FROM THE THIRD
EAR FROM EQUATORIAL AFRICA.
Aardema, Verna. TALES FROM THE STORY
HAT.
Arnott, Kathleen. AFRICAN MYTHS AND
LEGENDS.
Bryan, Ashley. THE OX OF THE WONDERFUL
HORNS AND OTHER AFRICAN FOLKTALES.
Carpenter, Frances. AFRICAN WONDER TALES.
Courlander, Harold. THE KING'S DRUM AND
OTHER AFRICAN STORIES.
Frobenius, Leo and Douglas C. Fox. AFRICAN
GENESIS.
Green, Lila. FOLKTALES AND FAIRY TALES
OF AFRICA.
Guillot, René. GUILLOT'S AFRICAN FOLK-
TALES.
Kaula, Edna. AFRICAN VILLAGE FOLKTALES.
Nunn, Jessie A. AFRICAN FOLK TALES.
Stuart, Forbes. THE MAGIC HORNS.

CENTRAL AFRICA

CONGO

Single Tales in Collections and Picture Books:

Carpenter WONDER...DOGS 95-100
Kirn, Ann. BEESWAX CATCHES A THIEF. pb
Leach HOW 95

Collections:

Burton, William. THE MAGIC DRUM: TALES
FROM CENTRAL AFRICA.
Cobble, Alice. WEMBI, THE SINGER OF
STORIES.
Holladay, Virginia. BANTU TALES.
Savory, Phyllis. CONGO FIRESIDE TALES.

ZAIRE

Single Tales in Collections and Picture Books:

Luzzato LONG 44-49

EAST AFRICA

Single Tales in Collections and Picture Books:

Sheehan FOLK 93-99

Collections:

Arnott, Kathleen. TALES OF TEMBA.
Harmon, Humphrey. TALES TOLD NEAR A
CROCODILE: STORIES FROM NYANZA.
Heady, Eleanor. JAMBO SUNGURA: TALES
FROM EAST AFRICA.
Heady, Eleanor. SAFIRI THE SINGER.
Heady, Eleanor. WHEN THE STONES WERE
SOFT: EAST AFRICAN FIRESIDE TALES.

ETHIOPIA

Single Tales in Collections and Picture Books:

Courlander RIDE 106-111

Collections:

Courlander, Harold and Wolf Leslau. THE
FIRE ON THE MOUNTAIN AND OTHER
ETHIOPIAN STORIES.
Davis, Russell and Brent Ashabranner. THE
LION'S WHISKERS: TALES OF HIGH AFRICA.
Price, Christine. THE RICH MAN AND THE
SINGER.

KENYA

Single Tales in Collections and Picture Books:

Aardema, Verna. BRINGING THE RAIN TO
KAPITI PLAIN. pb
Robinson THREE 17-31

TANZANIA

Single Tales in Collections and Picture Books:

Arnott ANIMAL 31-37
Luzatto LONG 44-49

UGANDA

Collections:

Serwadda, Moses. SONGS AND STORIES FROM UGANDA.

ZANZIBAR

Single Tales in Collections and Picture Books:

Withers I SAW 143-146

NORTH AFRICA

Single Tales in Collections and Picture Books:

Manning-Sanders BOOK...SORCERER'S 122-125

Collections:

Gilstrap, Robert and Irene Estabrook. THE SULTAN'S FOOL AND OTHER NORTH AFRICAN TALES.
Holding, James. THE KING'S CONTEST, AND OTHER NORTH AFRICAN TALES.

ALGERIA

Single Tales in Collections and Picture Books:

Holding KING'S 98-108

EGYPT

Single Tales in Collections and Picture Books:

Carpenter WONDER...DOGS 89-94, 184-185
Courlander RIDE 101-105
Edmonds TRICKSTER 120-128
Holding KING'S 39-47, 58-68
HOW DJADJA-EM-ANKH SAVED THE DAY: A TALE FROM ANCIENT EGYPT. pb

Collections:

Green, Roger Lancelyn. TALES OF ANCIENT EGYPT.
James, T. G. H. MYTHS AND LEGENDS OF ANCIENT EGYPT.
Zagloul, Ahmed and Jane Zagloul. THE BLACK PRINCE AND OTHER EGYPTIAN FOLK TALES.

MOROCCO

Single Tales in Collections and Picture Books:

Berson, Harold. KASSIM'S SHOES. pb
Holding KING'S 18-27, 87-97, 109-116

Collections:

Chimenti, Elisa. TALES AND LEGENDS OF MOROCCO.

TUNISIA

Single Tales in Collections and Picture Books:

Berson, Harold. WHY THE JACKAL WON'T SPEAK TO THE HEDGEHOG. pb

SOUTHERN AFRICA

Single Tales in Collections and Picture Books:

Arnott ANIMAL 104-111
Courlander RIDE 112-115

Collections:

Aardema, Verna. BEHIND THE BACK OF THE MOUNTAIN: BLACK FOLKTALES FROM SOUTHERN AFRICA.
Berger, Terry. BLACK FAIRY TALES.

RHODESIA

Collections:

Tracey, Hugh. THE LION ON THE PATH.

WEST AFRICA

Collections:

Appiah, Peggy. ANANSE THE SPIDER.
Arkhurst, Joyce Cooper. THE ADVENTURES OF SPIDER: WEST AFRICAN FOLK TALES.
Courlander, Harold and George Herzog. THE COW-TAIL SWITCH AND OTHER WEST AFRICAN STORIES.
Courlander, Harold and Albert Kofi Prempeh. THE HAT-SHAKING DANCE AND OTHER TALES FROM THE GOLD COAST.
Dorliae, Peter G. ANIMALS MOURN FOR DA LEOPARD, AND OTHER WEST AFRICAN TALES.
Fuja, Abayomi. FOURTEEN HUNDRED COWRIES AND OTHER WEST AFRICAN TALES.
Guillot, René. GUILLOT'S AFRICAN FOLK TALES.
Haskett, Edythe. SOME GOLD, A LITTLE IVORY: COUNTRY TALES FROM GHANA AND THE IVORY COAST.

LIBERIA

Single Tales in Collections and Picture Books:

Courlander RIDE 116-119

Collections:

Haskett, Edythe. GRAINS OF PEPPER: FOLK TALES FROM LIBERIA.

NIGERIA

Single Tales in Collections and Picture Books:

Bryan BEAT 14-29
Gerson, Mary-Joan. WHY THE SKY IS FAR AWAY. pb
Luzzato LONG 36-43

Collections:

Courlander, Harold and Ezekiel A. Eshugbayi.
OLODE THE HUNTER, AND OTHER TALES
FROM NIGERIA.
Sturton, Hugh. ZOMO THE RABBIT.
Walker, Barbara K. THE DANCING PALM
TREE AND OTHER NIGERIAN FOLK-TALES.
Walker, Barbara K. NIGERIAN FOLK TALES.

SIERRA LEONE

Single Tales in Collections and Picture Books:

Robinson THREE 7-15, 33-47

Collections:

Robinson, Adjai. SINGING TALES OF AFRICA.

SUDAN

Single Tales in Collections and Picture Books:

Manning-Sanders BOOK...SORCERER'S 91-98

UPPER VOLTA

Collections:

Guirma, Frederich. TALES OF MOGHO: AFRI-
CAN STORIES FROM UPPER VOLTA.

Ethnic Groups

ABALUYA

Single Tales in Collections and Picture Books:

Harmon TALES 163-185

ABALUHYA

Single Tales in Collections and Picture Books:

Nunn AFRICAN 68-74

AKAN

Single Tales in Collections and Picture Books:

Arnott AFRICAN 5-12, 64-67

AMHARA

Single Tales in Collections and Picture Books:

Davis LION'S 32-44, 45-53, 53-61, 61-67,
68-69, 70, 72
Kaula AFRICAN 142-145

ASHANTI

Single Tales in Collections and Picture Books:

Aardema, Verna. HALF-A-BALL-OF-KENKI. pb
Aardema MORE 7-11, 22-25
Aardema TALES 51-58
Bryan OX 3-10
Courlander COW-TAIL 25-29, 47-57, 103-106.
107-112, 113-118
Courlander KING'S 28-31, 32-35, 36-40
Kaula AFRICAN 26-31
Leach HOW 45-46, 82-83, 107

McDermott, Gerald. ANANSI THE SPIDER. pb

Collections:

Appiah, Peggy. ANANSE THE SPIDER.
Appiah, Peggy. TALES OF AN ASHANTI
FATHER.
Arkhurst, Joyce. ADVENTURES OF SPIDER.
Courlander, Harold and Alfred Kofi Prempeh.
THE HAT-SHAKING DANCE AND OTHER
TALES FROM THE GOLD COAST.

BAGENDA

Single Tales in Collections and Picture Books:

Arnott AFRICAN 119-123
Kaula AFRICAN 67-70
McDowell 3rd 29-30

BAKONGO

Single Tales in Collections and Picture Books:

Courlander KING'S 58-59, 60-63, 64-66

BALUBA

Single Tales in Collections and Picture Books:

Kaula AFRICAN 72-76

BAMUM

Single Tales in Collections and Picture Books:

Courlander KING'S 56-57

BANTU

Single Tales in Collections and Picture Books:

Aardema BEHIND 42
Arnott AFRICAN 13-15, 108-111, 153-155,
179-185
Arnott ANIMAL 31-37
Domanska, Janina. THE TORTOISE AND THE
TREE. pb
Jagendorf NOODLEHEAD 89-92
Nunn AFRICAN 75-80

Collections:

Arnott, Kathleen. TALES OF TEMBA.
Holladay, Virginia. BANTU TALES.
Savory, Phyllis. LION OUTWITTED BY HARE.

BASUTO

Single Tales in Collections and Picture Books:

Carpenter WONDER...DOGS 101-110

BAVENDA

Single Tales in Collections and Picture Books:

Bryan BEAT 53-69
Kaula AFRICAN 100

BEMBA

Single Tales in Collections and Picture Books:

Single Tales in Collections and Picture Books:

Harmon TALES 29-56

SHANKILLA

Single Tales in Collections and Picture Books:

Davis LION'S 140-143, 143-149

SHOA

Single Tales in Collections and Picture Books:

Courlander FIRE 111-116, 119-120

SOMALI

Single Tales in Collections and Picture Books:

Courlander FIRE 81-88, 103-104, 121-128
Courlander KING'S 78-79
Davis LION'S 7-9, 179-184, 189-191

SONINKE

Single Tales in Collections and Picture Books:

Courlander COW-TAIL 79-86

SUKUMA

Single Tales in Collections and Picture Books:

Kaula AFRICAN 63-64
Withers I SAW 140

SWAHILI

Single Tales in Collections and Picture Books:

Arnott AFRICAN 85-100, 135-139
Kaula AFRICAN 130-132

SWAZI

Single Tales in Collections and Picture Books:

Kaula AFRICAN 94-95

TEMNE

Single Tales in Collections and Picture Books:

Aardema MORE 12-15
Withers I SAW 138

THONGA

Single Tales in Collections and Picture Books:

Aardema BEHIND 49-56

TIGRE

Single Tales in Collections and Picture Books:

Davis LION'S 153-158, 158-160, 162-166

TIV

Single Tales in Collections and Picture Books:

Arnott AFRICAN 74-77

TSHINDAO

Single Tales in Collections and Picture Books:

Aardema BEHIND 19-25, 66-73

TUGEN

Single Tales in Collections and Picture Books:

Nunn AFRICAN 62-67

VAI

Single Tales in Collections and Picture Books:

Withers I SAW 141

WAKAMBA

Single Tales in Collections and Picture Books:

Nunn AFRICAN 26-30

WOLOF

Single Tales in Collections and Picture Books:

Courlander KING'S 19-21

XHOSA

Single Tales in Collections and Picture Books:

Arnott AFRICAN 78-84, 180-184

YAO

Single Tales in Collections and Picture Books:

Leach HOW 39-40, 60-61, 77

YORUBA

Single Tales in Collections and Picture Books:

Arnott AFRICAN 124-132

Collections:

Courlander, Harold OLODE THE HUNTER.
Fuja, Abayomi. FOURTEEN HUNDRED COWRIES.
Gleason, Judith. ORISHA: THE GODS OF
YORUBALAND.

ZULU

Single Tales in Collections and Picture Books:

Aardema BEHIND 3-10, 24, 41, 57-65, 74-80,
195-199
Arnott AFRICAN 68-73
Kaula AFRICAN 89-90

ASIA

Geographical Areas

ASIA, GENERAL

Collections:

Asian Cultural Center for Unesco. FOLK TALES FROM ASIA FOR CHILDREN EVERYWHERE. BOOK ONE.
Asian Cultural Center for Unesco. FOLK TALES FROM ASIA FOR CHILDREN EVERYWHERE. BOOK TWO.
Asian Cultural Center for Unesco. FOLK TALES FROM ASIA FOR CHILDREN EVERYWHERE. BOOK THREE.
Asian Cultural Center for Unesco. FOLK TALES FROM ASIA FOR CHILDREN EVERYWHERE. BOOK FOUR.
Buck, Pearl. FAIRY TALES OF THE ORIENT.
Carpenter, Frances. THE ELEPHANT'S BATH-TUB. WONDER TALES FROM THE FAR EAST.
Courlander, Harold. THE TIGER'S WHISKER AND OTHER TALES AND LEGENDS FROM ASIA AND THE PACIFIC.

AFGHANISTAN

Single Tales in Collections and Picture Books:

Asian FOLK...BOOK THREE 5-10
Bulatkin EURASIAN 80-81
Carpenter ELEPHANT'S 82-90
Courlander RIDE 60

ANNAM

Single Tales in Collections and Picture Books:

Carpenter ELEPHANT'S 166-175
Withers I SAW 120-121

ASSAM

Single Tales in Collections and Picture Books:

Withers I SAW 115-116

BANGLADESH

Single Tales in Collections and Picture Books:

Asian FOLK...BOOK ONE 9-12
Asian FOLK...BOOK FOUR 5-11
SEE ALSO PAKISTAN.

BURMA

Single Tales in Collections and Picture Books:

Asian FOLK...BOOK THREE 11-17
Carpenter ELEPHANT'S 13-21, 114-124
Carpenter WONDER...CATS 52-63
Courlander RIDE 42-45
Courlander TIGER'S 20-23, 24-28, 29-32, 33-34
Leach HOW 105-106

Collections:

Brockett, Eleanor. BURMESE AND THAI FAIRY TALES.
Htin Aung, Maung and Helen G. Trager. A KINGDOM LOST FOR A DROP OF HONEY AND OTHER BURMESE FOLKTALES.
Keeley, H. H. and Christine Price. THE CITY OF THE DAGGER.
Russell, Maurice. TOLD TO BURMESE CHILDREN.

CAMBODIA

Single Tales in Collections and Picture Books:

Asian FOLK...BOOK FOUR 12-16
Carpenter ELEPHANT'S 22-30, 100-107
Edmonds TRICKSTER 86-90
Tooze THREE...TURTLE 24-43

CEYLON SEE SRI LANKA.

CHINA

Single Tales in Collections and Picture Books:

Abisch, Roz. MAI-LING AND THE MIRROR. pb
Arnott ANIMAL 122-128
Baker TALKING 251-255
Bang, Molly. TYE MAY AND THE MAGIC BRUSH. pb
Buck FAIRY 51-53, 154-161, 232-236, 264-268
Carpenter WONDER...DOGS 173-183
Cheng, Hou-Tien. SIX CHINESE BROTHERS. pb
Courlander RIDE 38-41
Courlander TIGER'S 38-39, 40-42, 46-48
Frost LEGENDS 55-63, 69-75
Hardendorff TRICKY 29-32, 41-43, 51-53
Holland, Janice. YOU NEVER CAN TELL. pb
Jagendorf NOODLEHEAD 75-77, 78-83
Leach NOODLES 22
Littledale GHOSTS 83-86
Manning-Sanders BOOK...DRAGONS 20-24
Mui, Y. T. THE MAGIC BRUSH. pb
Ross BURIED 135-138, 139-146
Van Woerkom, Dorothy. THE RAT, THE OX AND THE ZODIAC. pb
Withers I SAW 126-128
Withers WORLD 30-31, 70-72, 73-75
Wolkstein, Diane and Ed Young. WHITE WAVE. pb
Young, Ed. THE ROOSTER's HORNS. pb
Young, Ed. THE TERRIBLE NUNG GUAMA. pb
Ziner, Feenie. CRICKET BOY. pb

Collections:

Alexander, Frances. PEBBLES FROM A BROKEN JAR. FABLES AND HERO STORIES FROM OLD CHINA.
Birch, Cyril. CHINESE MYTHS AND FANTASIES.
Bonnet, Leslie. CHINESE FOLK AND FAIRY TALES.
Carpenter, Frances. TALES OF A CHINESE GRANDMOTHER.
Chang, Isabelle. CHINESE FAIRY TALES.
Chang, Isabelle. TALES FROM OLD CHINA.
Cheou, Kang-Sié. A BUTTERFLY'S DREAM AND OTHER CHINESE TALES.
Dolch, Edward W. and Marguerite P. Dolch. STORIES FROM OLD CHINA
Hume, Lotta Carswell. FAVORITE CHILDREN'S STORIES FROM CHINA AND TIBET.
Kendall, Carol and Yao-wen Li. SWEET AND SOUR: TALES FROM CHINA.
Lin, Adet. THE MILKY WAY AND OTHER CHINESE TALES.
Lum, Peter. FAIRY TALES OF CHINA.
Manton, Jo and Robert Gittings. THE FLYING HORSES: TALES FROM CHINA.

Mar, Shuh Yin Lu. CHINESE TALES OF FOLK-
LORE.
Ritchie, Alice. THE TREASURE OF LI-PO.
Wyndham, Lee. FOLK TALES OF CHINA.
Wyndham, Robert. TALES THE PEOPLE TELL
IN CHINA.
SEE ALSO TAIWAN.

INDIA

Single Tales in Collections and Picture Books:

Arnott ANIMAL 174-178
Asian FOLK...BOOK ONE 13-18, 19-25
Asian FOLK...BOOK FOUR 17-23
Baker GOLDEN 58-79, 80-88
Baker TALKING 236-241, 242-250
Brown, Marcia. THE BLUE JACKAL. pb
Brown, Marcia. ONCE A MOUSE. pb
Buck FAIRY 19-28, 68-80, 168-171
Bulatkin EURASIAN 69-70, 71-84, 111-113
Carpenter ELEPHANT'S 75-81, 108-113, 184-
194
Carpenter WONDER...DOGS 81-88, 154-162,
204-212
Courlander RIDE 46-52
Courlander TIGER'S 52-57, 58-62, 63-71, 72-75
Duff, Maggie. RUM PUM PUM. pb
Edmonds TRICKSTER 5-13
Frost LEGENDS 142-146, 147-153
Galdone, Paul. THE MONKEY AND THE
CROCODILE. pb
Gobhai, Mehlli. THE BLUE JACKAL. pb
Gobhai, Mehlli. USHA, THE MOUSE MAIDEN.
pb
Hardendorff TRICKY 97-99, 109-110
Jagendorf NOODLEHEAD 19-23, 24-29, 30-33,
34-36
Leach HOW 17
Manning-Sanders BOOK...DEVILS 51-55
Manning-Sanders BOOK...MERMAIDS 41-45
Montgomerie MERRY 42-46
Price, Christine. THE VALIANT CHATTEE-
MAKER. Pb
Quigley, Lillian. THE BLIND MEN AND THE
ELEPHANT. pb
Ross BURIED 75-80, 81-88
Sheehan FOLK 100-111
Skurzynski, Gloria. THE MAGIC PUMPKIN. pb
Towle, Faith. THE MAGIC COOKING POT. pb
Withers I SAW 1-2-114
Withers WORLD 1, 2-6, 50, 76-77, 89, 101-103

Collections:

Crouch, Marcus. THE IVORY CITY.
Gaer, Joseph. THE FABLES OF INDIA.
Gray, J. E. B. INDIA'S TALES AND LEGENDS.
Haviland, Virginia. FAVORITE FAIRY TALES
TOLD IN INDIA.
Jacobs, Joseph. INDIAN FOLK AND FAIRY
TALES.
Jatakas. JATAKA TALES.
Jatakas. MORE JATAKA TALES.
Korel, Edward. LISTEN AND I'LL TELL YOU.
MacFarlane, Iris. TALES AND LEGENDS FROM
INDIA.
Reed, Gwendolyn. THE TALKATIVE BEASTS:
MYTHS, FABLES AND POEMS OF INDIA.

Ryder, Arthur. THE PANCHATANTRA.
Spellman, John. THE BEAUTIFUL BLUE JAY,
AND OTHER TALES OF INDIA.
Turnbull, Lucia. FAIRY TALES OF INDIA.
Wyatt, Isabel. THE GOLDEN STAG, AND
OTHER FOLK TALES FROM INDIA.
Wyndham, Lee. FOLK TALES OF INDIA.
SEE ALSO KASHMIR.

INDIA, BENGAL

Single Tales in Collections and Picture Books:

Bang, Betsy. THE OLD WOMAN AND THE RED
PUMPKIN: A BENGALI FOLKTALE. pb
Bang, Betsy. TUNTUNI, THE TAILOR BIRD.
pb

INDONESIA

Single Tales in Collections and Picture Books:

Asian FOLK...BOOK TWO 7-12
Asian FOLK...BOOK THREE 18-22
Carpenter ELEPHANT'S 159-163
Courlander RIDE 28-33
Kimishima, Hisako. PRINCESS OF THE RICE
FIELDS. pb

Collections:

Bro, Marguerite H. HOW THE MOUSE DEER
BECAME KING.
Courlander, Harold. KANTCHIL'S LIME PIT,
AND OTHER STORIES FROM INDONESIA.
De Leeuw, Adèle. INDONESIAN LEGENDS AND
FOLK TALES.

INDONESIA, JAVA

Single Tales in Collections and Picture Books:

Courlander TIGER'S 115-117, 118-121

JAPAN

Single Tales in Collections and Picture Books.

Arnott ANIMAL 184-189
Asian FOLK...BOOK TWO 13-17
Asian FOLK...BOOK THREE 29-34
Bartoli, Jennifer. STORY OF THE GRATEFUL
CRANE. pb
Bryant, Sara Cone. THE BURNING RICE
FIELDS. pb
Buck FAIRY 47-50, 89-91, 91-97, 125-128, 138-
140, 181-183, 218-220, 221-223, 223-224, 251-
256, 281-285, 297-305
Bulatkin EURASIAN 82-84
Carpenter WONDER...DOGS 128-135, 136-144,
195-203
Courlander TIGER'S 83-86, 87-89
Durham, Mae. TOBEI: A JAPANESE FOLKTALE.
pb
Edmonds TRICKSTER 14-20, 61-67, 129-137
Garner CAVALCADE...GOBLINS 36-39, 78-81,
128-132
Harper GHOSTS 205-209
Hodges, Margaret. THE WAVE. pb
Ishii, Momoko. ISSUN BOSHI. pb
Jagendorf NOODLEHEAD 97-99, 100-101

Leach HOW 118-120
Littledale GHOSTS 73-78, 157-164
Manning-Sanders BOOK...DRAGONS 38-42
Manning-Sanders BOOK...DWARFS 104-108
Matsui, Tadashi. ONIROKU AND THE
   CARPENTER. pb
Matsutani, Miyoto. THE CRANE MAIDEN. pb
Matsutain, Miyoto. THE FISHERMAN UNDER
   THE SEA. pb
Matsutani, Miyoto. THE FOX WEDDING. pb
Matsutain, Miyoto. HOW THE WITHERED TREE
   BLOSSOMED. pb
McDermott, Gerald. THE STONE-CUTTER. pb
Rackham FAIRY 84-86, 87-88, 89-91
Ross BURIED 147-160, 161-172, 173-187
Sheehan FOLK 112-118
Spicer 13 GHOSTS 24-35
Stamm, Claus. DUMPLINGS AND DEMONS. pb
Stamm, Claus. THREE STRONG WOMEN. pb
Stamm, Claus. VERY SPECIAL BADGERS. pb
Tabrah, Ruth. MOMOTARO: A PEACH BOY. pb
Titus, Eve. TWO STONECUTTERS. pb
Van Woerkom, Dorothy. SEA FROG, CITY
   FROG. pb
Withers I SAW 128-130
Wolkstein LAZY 11-18
Yashima, Taro. SEASHORE STORY. pb
Yoda, Junichi. ROLLING RICE BALL. pb

Collections:

   Bang, Garrett. MEN FROM THE VILLAGE DEEP
      IN THE MOUNTAINS AND OTHER JAPANESE
      FOLK TALES.
   Carpenter, Frances. PEOPLE FROM THE SKY.
      AINU TALES FROM NORTHERN JAPAN.
   Edmonds, I. G. OOKA THE WISE.
   Edmonds, I. G. THE POSSIBLE, IMPOSSIBLES
      OF IKKYU THE WISE.
   Haviland, Virginia. FAVORITE FAIRY TALES
      TOLD IN JAPAN.
   Hearn, Lafcadio. BOY WHO DREW CATS.
   Hearn, Lafcadio. EARLESS HO-ICHI.
   Hearn, Lafcadio. JAPANESE FAIRY TALES.
   MacAlpine, Helen and William. JAPANESE
      TALES AND LEGENDS.
   Marmur, Mildred. JAPANESE FAIRY TALES.
   Novak, Miroslav. FAIRY TALES FROM JAPAN.
   Ozaki, Yei Theodora. JAPANESE FAIRY BOOK.
   Pratt, Davia and Elsa Kula. MAGIC ANIMALS
      OF JAPAN.
   Sakade, Florence. JAPANESE CHILDREN'S
      STORIES.
   Sakade, Florence. JAPANESE CHILDREN'S
      FAVORITE STORIES.
   Scofield, Elizabeth. A FOX IN ONE BITE, AND
      OTHER TASTY TALES FROM JAPAN.
   Scofield, Elizabeth. HOLD TIGHT, STICK
      TIGHT: A COLLECTION OF JAPANESE FOLK
      TALES.
   Uchida, Yoshiko. THE DANCING KETTLE, AND
      OTHER JAPANESE FOLK TALES.
   Uchida, Yoshiko. THE MAGIC LISTENING CAP:
      MORE FOLK TALES FROM JAPAN.
   Uchida, Yoshiko. THE SEA OF GOLD, AND
      OTHER TALES FROM JAPAN.
   Yasuda, Yuri. OLD TALES OF JAPAN.

JAVA SEE INDONESIA, JAVA.

KASHMIR

Single Tales in Collections and Picture Books:

   Courlander TIGER'S 76-78-79, 80-82
   Manning-Sanders BOOK...PRINCES 125-128
SEE ALSO INDIA.

KOREA

Single Tales in Collections and Picture Books:

   Asian FOLK...BOOK ONE 26-31
   Asian FOLK...BOOK FOUR 24-29
   Courlander TIGER'S 11-15, 16-19
   Edmonds TRICKSTER 138-143
   Leach HOW 115
   Littledale GHOSTS 45-49
   Manning-Sanders BOOK...CHARMS 21-33

Collections:

   Anderson, Paul. THE BOY AND THE BLIND
      STORYTELLER.
   Carpenter, Frances. TALES OF A KOREAN
      GRANDMOTHER.
   Jewett, Eleanor Myers. WHICH WAS WITCH?
      TALES OF GHOSTS AND MAGIC FROM KOREA.
   Kim, So-Un. THE STORYBAG.

LAOS

Single Tales in Collections and Picture Books:

   Asian FOLK...BOOK ONE 32-40
   Asian FOLK...BOOK FOUR 30-33
   Carpenter ELEPHANT'S 176-183
   Courlander TIGER'S 111-114
   Withers I SAW 119
   Wolkstein LAZY 3-43

MALAYA

Single Tales in Collections and Picture Books:

   Carpenter ELEPHANT'S 40-48
   Courlander TIGER'S 237-231

MALAYSIA

Single Tales in Collections and Picture Books:

   Arnott ANIMAL 155-160
   Asian FOLK...BOOK TWO 21-27
   Asian FOLK...BOOK FOUR 34-41
   Leach HOW 27, 31
SEE ALSO SARAWAK.

MONGOLIA SEE EUROPE, *Mongolian.*

NEPAL

Single Tales in Collections and Picture Books:

   Asian FOLK...BOOK TWO 28-33
   Asian FOLK...BOOK FOUR 42-46

Collections:

   Hitchcock, Patricia. THE KING WHO RIDES A
      TIGER, AND OTHER FOLK TALES FROM
      NEPAL.

PAKISTAN

Single Tales in Collections and Picture Books:

Arnott ANIMAL 136-140
Asian FOLK...BOOK TWO 34-39
Asian FOLK...BOOK THREE 35-41
Courlander RIDE 53-59
Edmonds TRICKSTER 104-112

Collections:

Crouch, Marcus. THE IVORY CITY.
Siddiqui, Ashraf and Marilyn Lerch. TOON-
  TOONY PIE AND OTHER TALES FROM
  PAKISTAN.
SEE ALSO BANGLADESH.

PHILIPPINES

Single Tales in Collections and Picture Books:

Asian FOLK...BOOK FOUR 47-53
Carpenter ELEPHANT'S 91-99
Courlander RIDE 25-27

Collections:

Robertson, Dorothy Lewis. FAIRY TALES FROM
  THE PHILIPPINES.
Sechrist, Elizabeth Hough. ONCE IN THE
  FIRST TIMES: FOLK TALES FROM THE
  PHILIPPINES.

PHILIPPINES, LUZON

Single Tales in Collections and Picture Books:

Asian FOLK...BOOK TWO 40-46
Leach HOW 22
Withers I SAW 131-132

SARAWAK

Single Tales in Collections and Picture Books:

Arnott ANIMAL 59-66

SINGAPORE

Single Tales in Collections and Picture Books:

Asian FOLK...BOOK ONE 37-40
Asian FOLK...BOOK THREE 42-47

SRI LANKA

Single Tales in Collections and Picture Books:

Arnott ANIMAL 190-194
Asian FOLK...BOOK TWO 47-55
Asian FOLK...BOOK THREE 48-59
Carpenter ELEPHANT'S 134-140, 141-150
Courlander TIGER'S 49-51
Jagendorf NOODLEHEAD 72-73, 73-74
Tooze THREE...TURTLE 8-21, 46-61

Collections:

Tooze, Ruth. THE WONDERFUL WOODEN
  PEACOCK FLYING MACHINE; AND OTHER
  TALES OF CEYLON.

TAIWAN

Collections:

Cheney, Cora. TALES FROM A TAIWAN
  KITCHEN.

THAILAND

Single Tales in Collections and Picture Books:

Asian FOLK...BOOK ONE 41-46
Asian FOLK...BOOK FOUR 54-59
Carpenter ELEPHANT'S 58-65, 212-219
Carpenter WONDER...DOGS 43-51
Courlander RIDE 34-37
Krueger, Kermit. THE GOLDEN SWANS. pb

Collections:

Brockett, Eleanor. BURMESE AND THAI FAIRY
  TALES.
Feinstein, Alan S. FOLKTALES FROM SIAM.
Krueger, Kermit. THE SERPENT PRINCE:
  FOLKTALES FROM NORTHEASTERN THAI-
  LAND.

TIBET

Single Tales in Collections and Pictures Books:

Carpenter WONDER...DOGS 111-118
Montgomerie MERRY 42
Withers I SAW 123-125
Withers WORLD 79

VIETNAM

Single Tales in Collections and Picture Books:

Asian FOLK...BOOK ONE 47-51
Asian FOLK...BOOK THREE 55-59
Carpenter ELEPHANT'S 151-158
Clark, Ann Nolan. IN THE LAND OF SMALL
  DRAGON. pb
Taylor, Mark. THE FISHERMAN AND THE
  GOBLET. pb
Withers I SAW 122

Collections:

Graham, Gail B. THE BEGGAR IN THE BLAN-
  KET AND OTHER VIETNAMESE TALES.
Robertson, Dorothy Lewis. FAIRY TALES
  FROM VIET NAM.
Schultz, George F. VIETNAMESE LEGENDS.
Sun, Ruth Q. LAND OF SEAGULL AND FOX.
Vo-Dinh. THE TOAD IS THE EMPEROR'S
  UNCLE. ANIMAL TALES FROM VIETNAM.

Ethnic Groups

CH'UAN MIAO

Single Tales in Collections and Picture Books:

Leach HOW 63-64, 92-93

KHMER

Single Tales in Collections and Picture Books:

Asian FOLK...BOOK TWO 18-20

SHAN

Single Tales in Collections and Picture Books:

Courlander TIGER'S 20-23, 24-28
Withers I SAW 120-121

EUROPE

Geographical Areas

ALBANIA
Collections:

Wheeler, Post. ALBANIAN WONDER TALES.

ALSACE   SEE FRANCE.

ARCHANGEL   SEE RUSSIA.

ARMENIA
Single Tales in Collections and Picture Books:

Bulatkin EURASIAN 39-43, 57-63, 90-94
Deutsch MORE 45-54

Collections:

Tashjian, Virginia A. ONCE THERE WAS AND
WAS NOT: ARMENIAN TALES.
Tashjian, Virginia A. THREE APPLES FELL
FROM HEAVEN: ARMENIAN TALES RETOLD.

AUSTRIA
Single Tales in Collections and Picture Books:

Jagendorf NOODLEHEAD 216-221
Manning-Sanders BOOK...SORCERER'S 65-68
Sawyer WAY 71-81

AUSTRIA, TIROL
Single Tales in Collections and Picture Books:

Manning-Sanders BOOK...GHOSTS 27-34
Manning-Sanders BOOK...WIZARDS 40-46
Sawyer WAY 71-81

BELGIUM
Single Tales in Collections and Picture Books:

Courlander RIDE 186-188
Frost LEGENDS 302-307, 309-312, 312-333
Withers I SAW 79-80
SEE ALSO FLANDERS; *Flemish.*

BOHEMIA
Single Tales in Collections and Picture Books:

Manning-Sanders BOOK...WITCHES 115-122
Manning-Sanders BOOK...WIZARDS 26-39

Collections:

Michael, Maurice and Pamela. FAIRY TALES
FROM BOHEMIA.
Quinn, Zdenka and John Paul. THE WATER
SPRITE OF THE GOLDEN TOWN.
SEE ALSO CZECHOSLOVAKIA.

BRITAIN
Single Tales in Collections and Picture Books:

Belting ELVES 41-46
Courlander RIDE 189-193
Garner CAVALCADE...GOBLINS 56-61

Collections:

Williams-Ellis, Amabel. FAIRY TALES FROM
THE BRITISH ISLES.
SEE ALSO ENGLAND; IRELAND; MAN; SCOT-
LAND; WALES.

BRITTANY   SEE FRANCE.

BULGARIA
Collections:

Pridham, Radost. A GIFT FROM THE HEART:
FOLK TALES FROM BULGARIA.

CANTABRIA   SEE SPAIN, CANTABRIA.

CAUCASUS   SEE RUSSIA, CAUCASUS.

CORSICA   SEE FRANCE, CORSICA.

CRIMEA   SEE RUSSIA, CRIMEA.

CZECHOSLOVAKIA
Single Tales in Collections and Picture Tales.

Bulatkin EURASIAN 114-119
Courlander RIDE 128-130
Spicer 13 DEVILS 118-127

Collections:

Fillmore, Parker. THE SHEPHERD'S NOSEGAY:
STORIES FROM FINLAND AND CZECHOSLO-
VAKIA.
Fillmore, Parker. THE SHOEMAKER'S APRON:
A SECOND BOOK OF CZECHOSLOVAK FAIRY
TALES AND FOLK TALES.
Haviland, Virginia. FAVORITE FAIRY TALES
TOLD IN CZECHOSLOVAKIA.
SEE ALSO BOHOMIA.

DENMARK
Single Tales in Collections and Picture Books:

Baker GOLDEN 34-40, 41-45
Baker TALKING 104-112, 113-117
Bason, Lillian. THOSE FOOLISH MOLBOES! pb
Courlander RIDE 166-168
Jagendorf NOODLEHEAD 147-155
Kent, Jack. THE FAT CAT. pb
Manning-Sanders BOOK...DEVILS 9-14, 98-109

Manning-Sanders BOOK...DWARFS 112-124
Manning-Sanders BOOK...MERMAIDS 9-14, 36-40
Manning-Sanders BOOK...OGRES 123-127
Manning-Sanders BOOK...TROLLS 110-122
Manning-Sanders BOOK...WITCHES 46-61,
  104-114
Sheehan FOLK 9-13
Withers WORLD 90-100

Collections:

Hack, Inge. DANISH FAIRY TALES.
Hatch, Mary Cottam. MORE DANISH TALES.
Hatch, Mary Cottam. THIRTEEN DANISH
  TALES.
Haviland, Virginia. FAVORITE FAIRY TALES
  TOLD IN DENMARK.
SEE ALSO JUTLAND; SCANDINAVIA.

DOLOMITES SEE ITALY, DOLOMITES.

ENGLAND

Single Tales in Collections and Picture Books:

Arnott ANIMALS 210-219
Baker TALKING 25-32, 33-39
De Regniers GIANT 3-15, 18-30
Edmonds TRICKSTER 113-119
Frost LEGENDS 1-25
Garner CAVALCADE...GOBLINS 116-125
Harper GHOSTS 222-224, 225-227
Jacobs, Joseph. HEREAFTER THIS. pb
Jacobs, Joseph. TOM TIT TOT. pb
Jagendorf NOODLEHEAD 115-117, 117-118, 119-
  121, 122-124
Leach NOODLES 30-34, 35, 36, 37
Leach THING 17-19
Littledale GHOSTS 35-38, 78-82
Manning-Sanders BOOK...GIANTS 9-17
Manning-Sanders BOOK...GHOSTS 62-67, 74-
  79
Manning-Sanders BOOK...WITCHES 11-17
Rackham FAIRY 1-14
Sawyer WAY 189-200
Sheehan FOLK 1-7
Spicer 13 DEVILS 19-24, 63-70
Spicer 13 GHOSTS 16-23, 73-82
Spicer 13 MONSTERS 32-40, 59-65, 109-115,
  116-127
Withers I SAW 59-71
Withers WORLD 45-46, 47

Collections:

Carrick, Malcolm. THE WISE MEN OF GOTHAM.
Colwell, Eileen. ROUND ABOUT AND LONG
  AGO: TALES FROM THE ENGLISH COUNTIES.
Haviland, Virginia. FAVORITE FAIRY TALES
  TOLD IN ENGLAND.
Jacobs, Joseph. ENGLISH FOLK AND FAIRY
  TALES.
Jacobs, Joseph. MORE ENGLISH FAIRY TALES.
Jagendorf, Moritz A. THE MERRY MEN OF
  GOTHAM.
Reeves, James. ENGLISH FABLES AND FAIRY
  STORIES.
Steel, Flora Anna Webster. ENGLISH FAIRY
  TALES.

Williams-Ellis, Amabel. FAIRY TALES FROM
  THE BRITISH ISLES.
SEE ALSO BRITAIN; MAN.

ENGLAND, CAMBRIDGESHIRE

Single Tales in Collections and Picture Books:

Colwell ROUND 64-67

ENGLAND, CHANNEL ISLANDS - GUERNSEY

Single Tales in Collections and Picture Books:

Spicer 13 MONSTERS 77-82

ENGLAND, CHANNEL ISLANDS - JERSEY

Single Tales in Collections and Picture Books:

Spicer 13 MONSTERS 66-76

ENGLAND, CHESHIRE

Single Tales in Collections and Picture Books:

Colwell ROUND 15-18

ENGLAND, CORNWALL

Single Tales in Collections and Picture Books:

Calhoun, Mary. THE WITCH'S PIG. pb
Colwell ROUND 117-121, 122-124
Manning-Sanders BOOK...CHARM 120-124
Manning-Sanders BOOK...GIANTS 32-35, 44-66

Collections:

Manning-Sanders, Ruth. PETER AND THE
  PISKIES: CORNISH FOLK AND FAIRY TALES.

ENGLAND, CUMBERLAND

Single Tales in Collections and Picture Books:

Colwell ROUND 30-33

ENGLAND, DERBYSHIRE

Single Tales in Collections and Picture Books:

Colwell ROUND 90-94

ENGLAND, DEVONSHIRE

Single Tales in Collections and Picture Books:

Colwell ROUND 114-116

ENGLAND, DURHAM

Single Tales in Collections and Picture Books:

Colwell ROUND 40-42

ENGLAND, GLOUCESTERSHIRE

Single Tales in Collections and Picture Books:

Leach HOW 98

ENGLAND, HEREFORDSHIRE

Single Tales in Collections and Picture Books:

    Colwell ROUND 97–104

ENGLAND, LANCASHIRE

Single Tales in Collections and Picture Books:

    Colwell ROUND 19–22

ENGLAND, LINCOLNSHIRE

Single Tales in Collections and Picture Books:

    Colwell ROUND 57–60
    Garner CAVALCADE...GOBLINS 42–51, 216–221

ENGLAND, NORFOLK

Single Tales in Collections and Picture Books:

    Colwell ROUND 61–63

ENGLAND, NORTHAMPTONSHIRE

Single Tales in Collections and Picture Books:

    Colwell ROUND 82–84
    Garner CAVALCADE...GOBLINS 11–12

ENGLAND, NORTHUMBERLAND

Single Tales in Collections and Picture Books:

    Colwell ROUND 34–39

ENGLAND, NOTTINGHAMSHIRE

Single Tales in Collections and Picture Books:

    Colwell ROUND 85–86, 87–89

ENGLAND, SHROPSHIRE

Single Tales in Collections and Picture Books:

    Colwell ROUND 95–96

ENGLAND, SOMERSET

Single Tales in Collections and Picture Books:

    Colwell ROUND 110–113

ENGLAND, SUFFOLK

Single Tales in Collections and Picture Books:

    Colwell ROUND 68–69, 70–76

ENGLAND, SUSSEX

Single Tales in Collections and Picture Books:

    Colwell ROUND 105–107, 108–109

ENGLAND, WARWICKSHIRE

Single Tales in Collections and Picture Books:

    Colwell ROUND 77–81

ENGLAND, WESTMORLAND

Single Tales in Collections and Picture Books:

    Colwell ROUND 23–26, 27–29

ENGLAND, YORKSHIRE

Single Tales in Collections and Picture Books:

    Colwell ROUND 43–45, 46–50, 51–56
    Jagendorf NOODLEHEAD 119–121
    Spicer 13 DEVILS 19–24

ESTONIA

Single Tales in Collections and Picture Books:

    Deutsch MORE 19–23
    Manning-Sanders BOOK...GHOSTS 14–20, 90–94
    Withers, Carl. PAINTING THE MOON. pb

Collections:

    Maas, Selva. THE MOON PAINTERS AND OTHER ESTONIAN FOLK TALES.

FINLAND

Single Tales in Collections and Picture Books:

    Arnott ANIMAL 112–121
    Deutsch MORE 1–5
    Jagendorf NOODLEHEAD 192–195, 196–201, 202–206
    Manning-Sanders BOOK...DEVILS 30–38
    Spicer 13 DEVILS 33–42

Collections:

    Bosley, Keith. THE DEVIL'A HORSE: TALES FROM THE KALEVALA.
    Bowman, James Cloyd. TALES FROM A FINNISH TUPA.
    Fillmore, Parker. THE SHEPHERD'S NOSEGAY: STORIES FROM FINLAND AND CZECHOSLOVAKIA.

FLANDERS

Single Tales in Collections and Picture Books:

    Manning-Sanders BOOK...WIZARDS 109–117
SEE ALSO BELGIUM; *Flemish.*

FRANCE

Single Tales in Collections and Picture Books:

    Carpenter WONDER...DOGS 25–34, 119–127, 222–234
    Courlander RIDE 173–177
    De Beaumont. BEAUTY (Crowell) pb
    De Regniers GIANT 49–59
    Edmonds TRICKSTER 99–102
    Frost LEGENDS 215–222, 223–229, 230–239
    Hardendorff TRICKY 23–25, 81–85, 93–96, 119–120
    Jagendorf NOODLEHEAD 133–135, 136–141, 142–146
    Manning-Sanders BOOK...GHOSTS 47–54, 101–102, 124–127
    Manning-Sanders BOOK...PRINCESS 97–107
    Perrault, Charles. CINDERELLA (Bradbury) pb

Perrault, Charles. CINDERELLA (Little). pb
Perrault, Charles. CINDERELLA (Scribner's). pb
Perrault, Charles. PUSS IN BOOTS (Harcourt). pb
Perrault, Charles. PUSS IN BOOTS (Scribner's). pb
Perrault, Charles. PUSS IN BOOTS (World). pb
Perrault, Charles. SLEEPING BEAUTY (Knopf). pb
Perrault, Charles. SLEEPING BEAUTY (Viking). pb
Rackham FAIRY 52-65
Ross BURIED 113-120
Scribner, Charles. DEVIL'S BRIDGE. pb
Sheehan FOLK 84-92
Spicer 13 MONSTERS 41-51
Todd, Mary Fidelis. THE JUGGLER OF NOTRE DAME. pb
Wahl, Jan. DRAKESTAIL. pb
Withers I SAW 75-78
Withers WORLD 7-8, 19.

Collections:

Cooper, Lee. FIVE FABLES FROM FRANCE.
De Larue, Paul. FRENCH FAIRY TALES.
Haviland, Virginia. FAVORITE FAIRY TALES TOLD IN FRANCE.
Holman, Felice and Nanine Valen. THE DRAC: FRENCH TALES OF DRAGONS AND DEMONS.
Manning-Sanders, Ruth. JONNIKIN AND THE FLYING BASKET
Perrault, Charles. COMPLETE FAIRY TALES.
Perrault, Charles. FAMOUS FAIRY TALES.
Perrault, Charles. FAVORITE FAIRY TALES TOLD IN FRANCE.
Perrault, Charles. PERRAULT'S FAIRY TALES.
Picard, Barbara Leonie. FRENCH LEGENDS, TALES AND FAIRY STORIES.

FRANCE, ALSACE

Single Tales in Collections and Picture Books:

Manning-Sanders BOOK...DEVILS 87-97

FRANCE, ALSACE-LORRAINE

Single Tales in Collections and Picture Books:

Harper GHOSTS 234-249

FRANCE, BRITTANY

Single Tales in Collections and Picture Books:

Belting ELVES 77-83
Manning-Sanders BOOK...PRINCES 57-65, 108-117
Sawyer LONG 135-150

Collections:

Mason, Elsie. FOLK TALES OF BRITTANY.

FRANCE, CORSICA

Single Tales in Collections and Picture Books:

Manning-Sanders BOOK...GHOSTS 21-24

FRANCE, GASCONY

Single Tales in Collections and Picture Books:

Manning-Sanders BOOK...DEVILS 70-86

GASCONY SEE FRANCE, GASCONY.

GEORGIA SEE RUSSIA, GEORGIA.

GERMANY

Single Tales in Collections and Picture Books:

Edmonds TRICKSTER 45-50
Jagendorf NOODLEHEAD 184-188, 189-191
Manning-Sanders BOOK...DRAGONS 79-85, 114-122
Manning-Sanders BOOK...DWARFS 42-48, 49-52, 78-83, 125-128
Manning-Sanders BOOK...GIANTS 90-97, 107-117
Manning-Sanders BOOK...OGRES 101-109
Manning-Sanders BOOK...MERMAIDS 66-72
Manning-Sanders BOOK...SORCERER'S 33-36
Manning-Sanders BOOK...WITCHES 27-37, 72-82, 83-93
Spicer 13 DEVILS 102-110
Withers I SAW 81-85
Withers WORLD 33, 35-42, 43-44, 48-49, 55-56

Collections:

Picard, Barbara Leonie. GERMAN HERO-SAGAS AND FOLK-TALES.
Preussler, Otfried. THE WISE MEN OF SCHILDA.
SEE ALSO BIBLIOGRAPHY, all entries for Grimm, Jakob Ludwig Karl and Wilhelm Karl Grimm.
SEE ALSO RÜGEN.

GREECE

Single Tales in Collections and Picture Books:

Aliki. THE EGGS. pb
Aliki. THREE GOLD PIECES. pb
Aliki. THE TWELVE MONTHS. pb
Courlander RIDE 120-127
Edmonds TRICKSTER 68-76
Leach NOODLES 17, 20, 25
Manning-Sanders BOOK...DRAGONS 9, 43, 62, 123

Collections:

Haviland, Virginia. FAVORITE FAIRY TALES TOLD IN GREECE.
Manning-Sanders, Ruth. DAMIAN AND THE DRAGON.
Neufield, Rose. BEWARE THE MAN WITHOUT A BEARD.
Wilson, Barbara Kerr. GREEK FAIRY TALES.

GREECE, MACEDONIA

Single Tales in Collections and Picture Books:

Frost LEGENDS 114-119, 120-126
Jagendorf NOODLEHEAD 37-39, 40-41, 43-44
Manning-Sanders BOOK...DRAGONS 76-78

HUNGARY

Single Tales in Collections and Picture Books:

Arnott ANIMAL 129-135
Baker TALKING 191-198, 199-203
Ginsburg, Mirra. TWO GREEDY BEARS. pb
Harper GHOSTS 212-221
Jagendorf NOODLEHEAD 2-7-211, 212-215
Manning-Sanders BOOK...DEVILS 39-50, 56-58, 69-75
Manning-Sanders BOOK...GHOSTS 55-61
Manning-Sanders BOOK...PRINCES 49-56
Manning-Sanders BOOK...WIZARDS 86-94
Severo, Emöke de Papp. THE GOOD-HEARTED YOUNGEST BROTHER. pb

Collections:

Hoffmann, Peggy and Gyuri Bíró. THE MONEY HAT AND OTHER HUNGARIAN FOLKTALES.
Manning-Sanders, Ruth. THE GLASS MAN AND THE GOLDEN BIRD: HUNGARIAN FOLK AND FAIRY TALES.

ICELAND

Single Tales in Collections and Picture Books:

Belting ELVES 84-90
Courlander RIDE 194-197
Jagendorf NOODLEHEAD 161-163
Manning-Sanders BOOK...MERMAIDS 15-24
Manning-Sanders BOOK...OGRES 38-65, 75-79, 91-100
McGovern, Ann. HALF A KINGDOM. pb
Withers WORLD 69

Collections:

Boucher, Alan. MEAD MOONDAUGHTER AND OTHER ICELANDIC TALES.

IRELAND

Single Tales in Collections and Picture Books:

Baker TALKING 48-51, 52-62
Belting ELVES 55-60
Boden, Alice. THE FIELD OF BUTTERCUPS. pb
Carpenter WONDER...DOGS 64-73
De Paola, Thomas. FIN M'COUL. pb
De Regniers GIANT 109-124
Frost LEGENDS 25-33
Garner CAVALCADE...GOBLINS 92-97
Gruenberg FAVORITE 359-363
Harper GHOSTS 150-165
Jacobs, Joseph. CROCK OF GOLD. pb
Jacobs, Joseph. HUDDEN AND DUDDEN AND DONALD O'NEARY. pb
Jacobs, Joseph. MUNACHAR AND MANACHAR. pb
Jagendorf NOODLEHEAD 130-132
Littledale GHOSTS 61-66
Manning-Sanders BOOK...DRAGONS 87-94
Manning-Sanders BOOK...DWARFS 38-41 64-72, 95-103
Manning-Sanders BOOK...GHOSTS 68-73, 80-86, 119-123

Manning-Sanders BOOK...GIANTS 25-31, 79-84, 85-89
Manning-Sanders BOOK...MERMAIDS 59-65, 73-78, 295-300
Manning-Sanders BOOK...SORCERER'S 24-32, 45-55, 56-64
Manning-Sanders BOOK...WITCHES 123-128
O'Faolain, Eileen. CHILDREN OF THE SALMON. pb
Rackham FAIRY 24-51
Sawyer LONG 45-60
Sawyer WAY 111-120, 205-216, 239-247, 259-270, 319-333
Spicer 13 GHOSTS 36-44
Spicer 13 MONSTERS 52-58, 83-92, 101-108
Wetterer, Margaret. THE MERMAID'S CAP. pb

Collections:

Danaher, Kevin. FOLKTALES OF THE IRISH COUNTRYSIDE.
Haviland, Virginia. FAVORITE FAIRY TALES TOLD IN IRELAND.
Jacobs, Joseph. CELTIC FOLK AND FAIRY TALES.
Jacobs, Joseph. MORE CELTIC FAIRY TALES.
MacManus, Seumas. THE BOLD HEROES OF HUNGRY HILL AND OTHER IRISH FOLK TALES.
MacManus, Seumas. DONEGAL FAIRY TALES.
MacManus, Seumas. DONEGAL WONDER BOOK.
MacManus, Seumas. HIBERNIAN NIGHTS.
MacManus, Seumas. IN CHIMNEY CORNERS.
MacManus, Seumas. THE WELL O' THE WORLD'S END.
O'Faolain, Eileen. IRISH SAGAS AND FOLK-TALES.
Picard, Barbara Leonie. CELTIC TALES, LEGENDS OF TALL WARRIORS AND OLD EN-CHANTMENTS.
Pilkington, Frances Meredith. SHAMROCK AND SPEAR: TALES AND LEGENDS FROM IRE-LAND.
Stephens, James. IRISH FAIRY TALES.
Wilson, Barbara Kerr. FAIRY TALES OF IRE-LAND.

ISLE OF MAN   SEE MAN.

ISLE OF RÜGEN SEE RÜGEN.

ITALY

Single Tales in Collections and Picture Books:

Baker GOLDEN 89, 100, 101-110
Baker TALKING 9-17, 18-24
Belting ELVES 11-14, 91-94
Cawley, Lorinda. THE GOOSE AND THE GOLDEN COINS. pb
De Paola, Tomi. STREGA NONA. pb
Hardendorff TRICKY 75-80, 87-91
Jagendorf NOODLEHEAD 164-172, 173-174
Manning-Sanders BOOK...MERMAIDS 25-35
Manning-Sanders BOOK...OGRES 66-74
Manning-Sanders BOOK...PRINCESS 76-83
Manning-Sanders BOOK...SORCERER'S 112-121
Manning-Sanders BOOK...WITCHES 62-71
Manning-Sanders BOOK...WIZARDS 118-127

Rackham FAIRY 66-76
Ross BURIED 103-108, 109-112
Sawyer WAY 219-225
Sheehan FOLK 72-83
Werth, Kurt. THE COBBLER'S DILEMMA. pb
Zemach, Harve. TOO MUCH NOSE. pb

Collections:

Cimino, Maria. THE DISOBEDIENT EELS AND
  OTHER ITALIAN TALES.
Davis, Mary Gould. THE TRUCE OF THE WOLF
  AND OTHER TALES OF OLD ITALY.
Hampden, John. THE HOUSE OF CATS AND
  OTHER STORIES.
Haviland, Virginia. FAVORITE FAIRY TALES
  TOLD IN ITALY.
Jagendorf, Moritz A. THE PRICELESS CATS,
  AND OTHER ITALIAN FOLK STORIES.
Lum, Peter. ITALIAN FAIRY TALES.
Manning-Sanders, Ruth. GIANNI AND THE
  OGRE.
Mincieli, Rose Laura. OLD NEAPOLITAN FAIRY
  TALES.
Toor, Frances. THE GOLDEN CARNATION AND
  OTHER STORIES TOLD IN ITALY.
Vittorini, Domenico. OLD ITALIAN TALES.

ITALY, DOLOMITES

Single Tales in Collections and Picture Books:

Sawyer LONG 121-134

Collections:

Huldschiner, Robert. THE COW THAT SPOKE
  FOR SEPPL AND OTHER ALPINE TALES.

JUTLAND

Single Tales in Collections and Picture Books:

Manning-Sanders BOOK...DWARFS 73-77
Manning-Sanders BOOK...GIANTS 36-43
SEE ALSO DENMARK.

LAPLAND

Single Tales in Collections and Picture Books:

Arnott ANIMAL 79-82
Carpenter WONDER...DOGS 15-24
Stalder, Valerie. EVEN THE DEVIL IS AFRAID
  OF A SHREW. pb

LATVIA

Single Tales in Collections and Picture Books:

Carpenter WONDER...DOGS 35-42, 74-80
Rudolph, Marguerita. THE BRAVE SOLDIER
  AND A DOZEN DEVILS. pb

Collections:

Durham, Mae. TIT FOR TAT, AND OTHER
  LATVIAN FOLK TALES.
Huggins, Edward. BLUE AND GREEN WONDERS
  AND OTHER LATVIAN TALES.

LITHUANIA

Single Tales in Collections and Picture Books:

Deutsch TALES 56-62
Littledale GHOSTS 153-156
Rudolph, Marguerita. I AM YOUR MISFORTUNE.
  pb

LUXEMBOURG

Single Tales in Collections and Picture Books:

Courlander RIDE 169-172

MACEDONIA SEE GREECE.

MAJORCA

Collections:

Mehdevi, Alexander. BUNGLING PEDRO AND
  OTHER MAJORCAN TALES.
SEE ALSO MALLORCA.

MALLORCA

Single Tales in Collections and Picture Books:

Manning-Sanders BOOK...GHOSTS 9-13
SEE ALSO MAJORCA.

MAN

Single Tales in Collections and Picture Books:

Sawyer WAY 35-42
Spicer 13 GHOSTS 112-114

Collections:

Young, Blanche Cowley. HOW THE MANX CAT
  LOST ITS TAIL AND OTHER MANX FOLK
  STORIES.

NETHERLANDS

Single Tales in Collections and Picture Books:

Courlander RIDE 278-285
Frost LEGENDS 177-179, 181-182, 183-185, 186-
  189
Hardendorff TRICKY 33-39, 121-122
Littledale GHOSTS 87-96, 125-134
Ross BURIED 121-126, 127-134
Spicer 13 GHOSTS 7-16, 45-52
Spicer 13 MONSTERS 19-31, 93-100

Collections:

De Leeuw, Adèle. LEGENDS AND FOLK TALES
  OF HOLLAND.
Spicer, Dorothy Gladys. THE OWL'S NEST:
  FOLKTALES FROM FRIESLAND.

NORWAY

Single Tales in Collections and Picture Books:

Asbjørnsen, Peter and Jørgen Moe. THE RUN-
  AWAY PANCAKE. pb
Asbjørnsen, Peter and Jørgen Moe. THE

Courlander RIDE 154-158
Damjan, Mischa. IVAN AND THE WITCH. pb
Daniels, Guy. FOMA THE TERRIBLE. pb
Daniels, Guy. THE PEASANT'S PEA PATCH. pb
Frost LEGENDS 89-98, 99-113
Galdone, Paul. STRANGE SERVANT. pb
Jagendorf NOODLEHEAD 235-240
Jameson, Cynthia. CATOFY THE CLEVER. pb
Jameson, Cynthia. THE CLAY POT BOY. pb
Lang, Andrew. TO YOUR GOOD HEALTH. pb
Littledale GHOSTS 21-25, 97-100
Lowrie, Richard. SOLDIER AND TSAR IN
    THE FOREST. pb
Manning-Sanders BOOK...CHARMS 62-66
Manning-Sanders BOOK...OGRES 9-19
Manning-Sanders BOOK...PRINCESS 40-48
Manning-Sanders BOOK...SORCERER'S 9-23
    69-90
Manning-Sanders BOOK...WITCHES
Manning-Sanders BOOK...WIZARDS 95, 108
McDermott, Beverly. THE CRYSTAL APPLE.
    pb
Montgomerie MERRY 8-13, 32-37, 47-55
Pushkin, Alexander. THE TALE OF THE CZAR
    SALTAN. pb
Pushkin, Alexander. THE TALE OF THE
    GOLDEN COCKEREL. pb
Rackham FAIRY 92-99
Ransome, Arthur. THE FOOL OF THE WORLD
    AND THE FLYING SHIP. pb
Robbins, Ruth. BABOUSHKA AND THE THREE
    KINGS. pb
Ross BURIED 13-18, 19-26, 27-30, 31-34
Sawyer WAY 285-294
Sheehan FOLK 51-60
Spicer 13 DEVILS 43-52, 91-100
Spicer 13 GHOSTS 92-100
Whitney, Thomas. MARKO THE RICH AND
    VASILY THE UNLUCKY. pb
Whitney, Thomas. THE STORY OF PRINCE
    IVAN, THE FIREBIRD AND THE GRAY WOLF.
    pb
Whitney, Thomas. VASILISA THE BEAUTIFUL.
    pb
Withers I SAW 95-99
Withers WORLD 19-22, 23
Zemach, Harve. SALT. pb
Zemach, Harve. THE SPECKLED HEN. pb

Collections:

Almedingen, E. M. RUSSIAN FOLK AND FAIRY
    TALES.
Carey, Bonie. BABA YAGA'S GEESE, AND
    OTHER RUSSIAN STORIES.
Carrick, Valery J. MORE RUSSIAN PICTURE
    TALES.
Carrick, Valery J. STILL MORE RUSSIAN
    PICTURE TALES.
Daniels, Guy. FALCON UNDER THE HAT:
    RUSSIAN MERRY TALES AND FAIRY TALES.
Dolch, Edward W. and Marguerite Dolch.
    STORIES FROM OLD RUSSIA.
THE FIREBIRD AND OTHER RUSSIAN FAIRY
    TALES (Viking).
Ginsburg, Mirra. THE LAZIES: TALES OF THE
    PEOPLES OF RUSSIA.
Ginsburg, Mirra. ONE TRICK TOO MANY: FOX
    STORIES FROM RUSSIA.

Ginsburg, Mirra. THREE ROLLS AND ONE
    DOUGHNUT: FABLES FROM RUSSIA.
Ginsburg, Mirra. THE TWELVE CLEVER
    BROTHERS AND OTHER FOOLS.
Gottschalk, Fruma. THE RUNAWAY SOLDIER
    AND OTHER TALES OF OLD RUSSIA.
Haviland, Virginia. FAVORITE FAIRY TALES
    TOLD IN RUSSIA.
Higonnet-Schnopper, Janet. TALES FROM
    ATOP A RUSSIAN STOVE.
Jameson, Cynthia. TALES FROM THE STEPPES.
Ponsot, Marie. RUSSIAN FAIRY TALES.
Ransome, Arthur. OLD PETER'S RUSSIAN
    TALES.
Riordan, James. TALES FROM CENTRAL RUS-
    SIA. RUSSIAN TALES, VOLUME ONE.
Riordan, James. TALES FROM TARTARY.
    RUSSIAN TALES, VOLUME TWO.
Stevens, H. C. RUSSIAN FOLK TALES.
Titiev, Estelle and Lila Pergment. HOW THE
    MOOLAH WAS TAUGHT A LESSON AND
    OTHER TALES FROM RUSSIA.
Wheeler, Post. RUSSIAN WONDER TALES.
Whitney, Thomas. IN A CERTAIN KINGDOM:
    TWELVE RUSSIAN FAIRY TALES.
Wyndham, Lee. TALES THE PEOPLE TELL IN
    RUSSIA.
Wyndham, Lee. RUSSIAN TALES OF FABULOUS
    BEASTS AND MARVELS.
Yeoman, John. THE APPLE OF YOUTH AND
    OTHER RUSSIAN FOLK STORIES.
SEE ALSO ARMENIA; ESTONIA; LATVIA; LITH-
UANIA; MIDDLE EAST; AZERBAIJAN.

RUSSIA, MINORITY ETHNIC GROUPS

Collections:

Deutsch, Babette and Avrahm Yarmolinsky.
    MORE TALES OF FARAWAY FOLK.
Deutsch, Babette and Avrahm Yarmolinsky.
    TALES OF FARAWAY FOLK.
Ginsburg, Mirra. HOW WILKA WNT TO SEA
    AND OTHER TALES FROM WEST OF THE
    URALS.
Ginsburg, Mirra. THE KAHA BIRD: TALES
    FROM THE STEPPES OF CENTRAL ASIA.
Ginsburg, Mirra. THE MASTER OF THE WINDS
    AND OTHER TALES FROM SIBERIA.
Masey, Mary Lou. STORIES OF THE STEPPES:
    KAZAKH FOLKTALES.
SEE ALSO EUROPE, Ethnic Groups.

RUSSIA, ARCHANGEL

Single Tales in Collections and Picture Books:

Manning-Sanders BOOK...PRINCES 28-29

RUSSIA, CAUCASUS

Single Tales in Collections and Picture Books:

Deutsch TALES 44-51
Ginsburg, Mirra. THE STRONGEST ONE OF
    ALL. pb
Tripp, Wallace. THE TALE OF A PIG. pb

Collections:

Foster, Ruth. THE STONE HORSEMEN: TALES FROM THE CAUCASUS.

RUSSIA, CRIMEA

Single Tales in Collections and Picture Books:

Bulatkin EURASIAN 120-122

RUSSIA, GEORGIA

Single Tales in Collections and Picture Tales:

Carpenter WONDER...DOGS 213-221
Ginsburg, Mirra. FISHERMAN'S SON. pb
Ginsburg, Mirra. GRASSHOPPER TO THE RESCUE. pb
Manning-Sanders BOOK...GIANTS 18-24

Collections:

Papashvily, George. YES AND NO STORIES.

RUSSIA, SIBERIA

Single Tales in Collections and Picture Books:

Arnott ANIMAL 83-86
Deutsch MORE 15-17, 79-84
Deutsch TALES 7-16, 55-56
Manning-Sanders BOOK...GHOSTS 95-100

Collections:

Ginsburg, Mirra. THE MASTER OF THE WINDS AND OTHER TALES FROM SIBERIA.

RUSSIA, UKRAINE

Single Tales in Collections and Picture Books:

Bloch, Marie. IVANKO AND THE DRAGON. pb
Courlander RIDE 137-141
Deutsch MORE 25-29
Deutsch TALES 1-6
Manning-Sanders BOOK...PRINCES 84-96
Tresselt, Alvin. THE MITTEN. pb
Yaroslava. TUSYA AND THE POT OF GOLD. pb

SCANDINAVIA

Single Tales in Collections and Picture Books:

Arnott ANIMAL 141-151
Belting ELVES 70-76
Hardendorff TRICKY 11-22, 71-74, 101-108, 111-118
Ross BURIED 55-64

Collections:

Jones, Gwyn. SCANDINAVIAN LEGENDS AND FOLK-TALES.
Sperry, Margaret. THE HEN THAT SAVED THE WORLD.
Sperry, Margaret. SCANDINAVIAN STORIES.
SEE ALSO DENMARK; FINLAND; NORWAY; SWEDEN.

SCOTLAND

Single Tales in Collections and Picture Books:

Arnott ANIMAL 95-99
Baker GOLDEN 135-147, 148-160
Baker TALKING 63-70, 71-76
Edmonds TRICKSTER 30-35
Frost LEGENDS 13-19
Harper GHOSTS 192-194
Jacobs, Joseph. THE STARS IN THE SKY. pb
Jagendorf NOODLEHEAD 127-129
Leodhas, Sorche Nic. ALWAYS ROOM FOR ONE MORE. pb
Littledale. GHOSTS 139-152
Manning-Sanders BOOK...MERMAIDS 79-85, 108-113
Sewell, Marcia. WEE, WEE MANNIE AND THE BIG, BIG COW. pb
Sheehan FOLK 21-22
Spicer 13 MONSTERS 9-18
Rackham FAIRY 15-27
Withers I SAW 71

Collections:

Haviland, Virginia. FAVORITE FAIRY TALES TOLD IN SCOTLAND.
Leodhas, Sorche Nic. BY LOCH AND BY LIN: TALES FROM SCOTTISH BALLADS.
Leodhas, Sorche Nic. GAELIC GHOSTS.
Leodhas, Sorche Nic. GHOSTS GO HAUNTING.
Leodhas, Sorche Nic. HEATHER AND BROOM: TALES OF THE SCOTTISH HIGHLANDS.
Leodhas, Sorche Nic. SEA-SPELL AND MOOR MAGIC: TALES OF THE WESTERN ISLES.
Leodhas, Sorche Nic. THISTLE AND THYME.
Leodhas, Sorche Nic. TWELVE BLACK CATS.
Sheppard-Jones, Elisabeth. SCOTTISH LEGENDARY TALES.
Wilson, Barbara Ker. SCOTTISH FOLK TALES AND LEGENDS.

SCOTLAND, ORKNEY ISLANDS

Collections:

Cutt, Nancy and W. Towrie. THE HOGBOON OF HELL AND OTHER STRANGE ORKNEY TALES.

SERBIA

Single Tales in Collections and Picture Books:

Garner CAVALCADE...GOBLINS 105-114
Manning-Sanders BOOK...PRINCES 66-75
Rackham FAIRY 100-111
Spicer 13 DEVILS 7-18, 111-117

Collections:

Spicer, Dorothy. LONG AGO IN SERBIA.
SEE ALSO YUGOSLAVIA.

SIBERIA SEE RUSSIA, SIBERIA.

SICILY

Single Tales in Collections and Picture Books:

Manning-Sanders BOOK...CHARMS 85-97
Manning-Sanders BOOK...OGRES 32-37
Manning-Sanders BOOK...PRINCESS 118-129
Manning-Sanders BOOK...WIZARDS 9-21

SLOVENIA

Single Tales in Collections and Picture Books:

Ginsburg, Mirra. HOW THE SUN WAS BROUGHT BACK TO THE SKY. pb

Collections:

Kavcic, Vladimir. THE GOLDEN BIRD: FOLK-TALES FROM SLOVENIA.
SEE ALSO YUGOSLAVIA.

SPAIN

Single Tales in Collections and Picture Books:

Baker TALKING 138-178
Edmonds TRICKSTER 91-98
Hardendorff TRICKY 45-50, 63-70
Manning-Sanders BOOK...GHOSTS 25-29, 87-89
Montgomerie MERRY 24-27
Ross BURIED 35-42, 43-54
Sawyer WAY 21-31, 85-96, 151-170, 229-236, 297-304
Sheehan FOLK 61-71

Collections:

Boggs, Ralph Steele. THREE GOLDEN ORANGES AND OTHER SPANISH TALES.
De La Iglesia, Maria Elena. THE CAT AND THE MOUSE AND OTHER SPANISH TALES.
Eells, Elsie Spicer. TALES OF ENCHANTMENT FROM SPAIN.
Gunterman, Berta. CASTLES IN SPAIN AND OTHER ENCHANTMENTS: SPANISH LEGENDS AND ROMANCES.
Haviland, Virginia. FAVORITE FAIRY TALES TOLD IN SPAIN.
Marks, John. SPANISH FAIRY TALES.
Sawyer, Ruth. PICTURE TALES FROM SPAIN.
SEE ALSO MAJORCA; MALLORCA.

SPAIN, CANTABRIA

Single Tales in Collections and Picture Books:

Sawyer WAY 85-86

SWEDEN

Single Tales in Collections and Picture Books:

Baker GOLDEN 46-53, 54-57
Baker TALKING 77-87, 88-103
Courlander RIDE 163-165
Wither I SAW 89
Zemach, Harve. NAIL SOUP. pb

Collections:

Haviland, Virginia. FAVORITE FAIRY TALES TOLD IN SWEDEN.
Kaplan, Irma. FAIRY TALES FROM SWEDEN.
Löfgren, Ulf. THE BOY WHO ATE MORE THAN THE GIANT AND OTHER SWEDISH FOLK-TALES.
Owen, Ruth Bryan. THE CASTLE IN THE

SILVER WOOD AND OTHER SCANDINAVIAN FAIRY TALES.
SEE ALSO SCANDINAVIA.

SWITZERLAND

Single Tales in Collections and Picture Books:

Jagendorf NOODLEHEAD 229-232

Collections:

Duvoisin, Roger. THE THREE SNEEZES AND OTHER SWISS TALES.
Muller-Güggenbühl, Fritz. SWISS-ALPINE FOLK-TALES.

TIROL   SEE AUSTRIA.

TRANSYLVANIA

Single Tales in Collections and Picture Books:

Manning-Sanders BOOK...DEVILS 15-29
Manning-Sanders BOOK...SORCERER'S 99-111.
SEE ALSO RUMANIA.

UKRAINE   SEE RUSSIA, UKRAINE.

WALES

Single Tales in Collections and Picture Books:

Baker TALKING 40-44, 45-47
Belting ELVES 22-26, 53-54
Frost LEGENDS 19-25
Manning-Sanders BOOK...WIZARDS 78-85
Spicer 13 GHOSTS 53-64, 120-128

Collections:

Jones, Gyn. WELSH LEGENDS AND FOLK-TALES.
Pugh, Ellen. MORE TALES FROM THE WELSH HILLS.
Pugh, Ellen. TALES FROM THE WELSH HILLS.
Sheppard-Jones, Elizabeth. WELSH LEGENDARY TALES.

YUGOSLAVIA

Single Tales in Collections and Picture Books:

Carpenter WONDER...DOGS 235-244, 245-255
Courlander RIDE 131-136
Frost LEGENDS 240-244, 245-249, 250-262
Jagnedorf NOODLEHEAD 241-243
Manning-Sanders BOOK...PRINCES 14-27
Valjavec, Matija and Cene Vipotnik. THE MAGIC RING. pb

Collections:

Ćurcija-Prodanović, Nada. HEROES OF SERBIA. FOLK BALLADS.
Ćurcija-Prodanović, Nada. YUGOSLAVIA FOLK-TALES.
Fillmore, Parker. THE LAUGHING PRINCE: A BOOK OF JUGOSLAV FAIRY TALES AND FOLK TALES.
Kavcic, Vladimir. THE GOLDEN BIRD: FOLK-

TALES FROM SLOVENIA.
Spicer, Dorothy Gladys. LONG AGO IN
    SERBIA.
SEE ALSO SERBIA; SLOVENIA.

Ethnic Groups

ALTAI

Single Tales in Collections and Picture Books:

Deutsch MORE 7-10, 15-17
Deutsch TALES 17-27, 27-35
Ginsburg, Mirra. LITTLE RYSTU. pb
Leach HOW 30

AVAR

Single Tales in Collections and Picture Books:

Titiev HOW 9-26

BURYAT

Single Tales in Collections and Picture Books:

Ginsburg KAHA 13-20

BYELORUSIAN

Single Tales in Collections and Picture Books:

Courlander RIDE 145-153

CARPATHIAN

Single Tales in Collections and Picture Books:

Manning-Sanders BOOK...DEVILS 110-116

CELTS

Collections:

Hodges, Margaret. THE OTHER WORLD:
    MYTHS OF THE CELTS.

CHECHEN

Single Tales in Collections and Picture Books:

Titiev HOW 1-8

CHEREMIS

Single Tales in Collections and Picture Books:

Withers I SAW 100-101

ESKIMO, RUSSIAN

Single Tales in Collections and Picture Books:

Ginsburg, Mirra. THE PROUD MAIDEN,
    TUNGAK, AND THE SUN. pb

FLEMISH

Single Tales in Collections and Picture Books:

Jagendorf NOODLEHEAD 175-179
SEE ALSO BELGIUM; FLANDERS.

GYPSY

Single Tales in Collections and Picture Books:

Arnott ANIMAL 66-70, 166-173
Jagendorf NOODLEHEAD 156-158
Manning-Sanders BOOK...SORCERER'S 37-44
Sawyer LONG 61-68

Collections:

Hampden, John. THE GYPSY FIDDLE, AND
    OTHER TALES TOLD BY GYPSIES.
Jagendorf, Mortiz A. and C. H. Tillhagen.
    THE GYPSIES' FIDDLE.
Manning-Sanders, Ruth. THE RED KING AND
    THE WITCH. GYPSY FOLK AND FAIRY
    TALES.

JEWISH

Single Tales in Collections and Picture Books:

Baker TALKING 218-231, 232-235
De Regnier GIANT 131-134
Gruenberg FAVORITE 357-359
Hirsh, Marilyn. COULD ANYTHING BE WORSE?
    pb
Hirsh, Marilyn. THE RABBI AND THE TWENTY-
    NINE WITCHES. pb
Jagendorf NOODLEHEAD 45-47, 48-52, 52-58,
    59-62
Shulevitz, Uri. THE MAGICIAN. pb
Singer, Isaac. MAZEL AND SHLIMAZEL. pb
Suhl, Yuri. SIMON BOOM GIVES A WEDDING.
    pb
Zemach, Margot. IT COULD ALWAYS BE
    WORSE. pb

Collections:

Barash, Asher. A GOLDEN TREASURY OF
    JEWISH TALES.
Dobbs, Rose. MORE ONCE-UPON-A-TIME
    STORIES.
Ish-Kishor, Judith. TALES FROM THE WISE
    MEN OF ISRAEL.
Ish-Kishor, Sulamith. THE CARPET OF SOLO-
    MON.
Nahmad, H. M. A PORTION IN PARADISE AND
    OTHER JEWISH FOLKTALES.
Serwer, Blanche Luria. LET'S STEAL THE
    MOON.
Simon, Solomon. MORE WISE MEN OF HELM.
Simon, Solomon. THE WISE MEN OF HELM AND
    THEIR MERRY TALES.
Singer, Isaac. WHEN SHLEMIEL WENT TO
    WARSAW.
Singer, Isaac. ZLATEH THE GOAT.
SEE ALSO ISRAEL, MIDDLE EAST.

KALMUK

Single Tales in Collections and Picture Books:

Bulatkin EURASIAN 98-102

KARAKALPAK

Single Tales in Collections and Picture Books:

Deutsch TALES 36-43

KARELIA

Single Tales in Collections and Picture Books:

Deutsch TALES 36-43

KAZAKH

Single Tales in Collections and Picture Books:

Deutsch MORE 55-64, 65-68

Collections:

Masey, Mary Lou. STORIES OF THE STEPPES:
KAZAKH FOLKTALES.

KIRGHIZ

Single Tales in Collections and Picture Books:

Ginsburg KAHA 90-96

LAPP

Single Tales in Collections and Picture Books:

McHale, Ethel. SON OF THUNDER. pb

LETTISH

Single Tales in Collections and Picture Books:

Deutsch TALES 63-68

MONGOLIAN

Single Tales in Collections and Picture Books:

Bulatkin EURASIAN 22-26
Otsuka, Yuzo. SUHO AND THE WHITE HORSE.
pb

NANA

Single Tales in Collections and Picture Books:

Deutsch MORE 39-43
Deutsch TALES 7-16

NENETZ

Single Tales in Collections and Picture Books:

Deutsch MORE 69
Deutsch TALES 7-16

SAMOYED

Single Tales in Collections and Picture Books:

Deutsch MORE 69
Titiev HOW 27-35

SLAV

Single Tales in Collections and Picture Books:

Manning-Sanders BOOK...DRAGONS 103-117
Manning-Sanders BOOK...GIANTS 67-78

TARTAR

Single Tales in Collections and Picture Books:

Bulatkin EURASIAN 85-89, 123-124

TATAR

Single Tales in Collections and Picture Books:

Ginsburg KAHA 53-54

TURKMENIAN

Single Tales in Collections and Picture Books:

Ginsburg KAHA 131-137, 139, 140-141

UDMURT

Single Tales in Collections and Picture Books:

Deutsch MORE 73-78
Ginsburg, Mirra. STRIDING SLIPPERS. pb

UYGUR

Single Tales in Collections and Picture Books:

Ginsburg KAHA 88-89

VOTYAKS SEE *UDMURT*.

YAKUTS

Single Tales in Collections and Picture Books:

Deutsch MORE 79-84

LATIN AMERICA

Geographical Areas

LATIN AMERICA, GENERAL

Collections:

Barlow, Genevieve. LATIN AMERICAN TALES:
FROM THE PAMPAS TO THE PYRAMIDS OF
MEXICO.
Carpenter, Frances. SOUTH AMERICAN
WONDER TALES.
Finger, Charles Joseph. TALES FROM SILVER
LANDS.
Henius, Frank. STORIES FROM THE AMERICAS.
Jagendorf, Moritz A. and Ralph Steele Boggs.
THE KING OF THE MOUNTAIN, A TREASURY
OF LATIN AMERICAN FOLK STORIES.
Newman, Shirlee. FOLK TALES OF LATIN
AMERICA.

ARGENTINA

Single Tales in Collections and Picture Books:

Barlow LATIN 9-17, 18-22, 23-27
Carpenter SOUTH 11-17, 71-82, 160-166
Courlander RIDE 202-205
Jagendorf KING 15-18, 18-23, 23-27
Littledale GHOSTS 39-44
Newman FOLK 73-82, 83-88

BAHAMAS

Single Tales in Collections and Picture Books:

Jagendorf KING 23-30, 31-33
Leach HOW 80-81

BOLIVIA

Single Tales in Collections and Picture Books:

Barlow LATIN 50-56
Courlander RIDE 206-212
Jagendorf KING 43-48
Newman FOLK 39-52

BRAZIL

Single Tales in Collections and Picture Books:

Baker TALKING 179-182, 184-190
Carpenter LATIN 36-42, 64-70, 93-99, 100-107, 108-113, 137-143
Courlander RIDE 198-201
Frost LEGENDS 263-269, 273-277
Newman FOLK 67-71
Sheehan FOLK 127-137
Spicer 13 DEVILS 72-81
Withers I SAW 55

Collections:

Eells, Elsie Spicer. FAIRY TALES FROM BRAZIL.
Eells, Elsie Spicer. TALES FROM THE AMAZON.

CARIBBEAN, GENERAL

Single Tales in Collections and Picture Books:

Bryan, Ashley. THE DANCING GRANNY. pb
McDowell 3rd 72-87
Withers WORLD 32

Collections:

Carter, Dorothy Sharp. GREEDY MARIANI AND OTHER FOLKTALES OF THE ANTILLES.
Sherlock, Philip M. THE IGUANA'S TAIL: CRICK CRACK STORIES.
Sherlock, Philip M. WEST INDIAN FOLK TALES.
Sherlock, Philip M. and Hilary Sherlock. EARS AND TAILS AND COMMON SENSE.

CARIBBEAN, BARBADOS

Single Tales in Collections and Picture Books:

Jagendorf KING 34-49

CARIBBEAN, CUBA

Single Tales in Collections and Picture Books:

Carter GREEDY 23-29, 62-67, 125-131
Courlander RIDE 257-258
Withers I SAW 53-54

CARIBBEAN, DOMINICAN REPUBLIC

Single Tales in Collections and Picture Books:

Carter GREEDY 9-13
Courlander RIDE 265
Jagendorf KING 102-106, 106-110
Newman FOLK 101-105

CARIBBEAN, HAITI

Single Tales in Collections and Picture Books:

Carter GREEDY 14-17, 35-40, 91-98, 99-105
Courlander RIDE 259-264
Jagendorf KING 155-161
Leach HOW 67

Collections:

Courlander, Harold. THE PIECE OF FIRE, AND OTHER HAITIAN TALES.
Courlander, Harold. UNCLE BOQUI OF HAITI.
Johnson, Gyneth. HOW THE DONKEYS CAME TO HAITI AND OTHER TALES.
Thoby-Marcelin, Philippe. THE SINGING TURTLE AND OTHER TALES FROM HAITI.
Wolkstein, Diane. THE MAGIC ORANGE TREE AND OTHER HAITIAN FOLKTALES.

CARIBBEAN, JAMAICA

Single Tales in Collections and Picture Books:

Arnott ANIMAL 87-91
Carter GREEDY 73-78, 79-83, 84-90
Jagendorf KING 171-176

Collections:

Sherlock, Philip M. ANANSI, THE SPIDER MAN: JAMAICAN FOLK TALES.

CARIBBEAN, PUERTO RICO

Single Tales in Collections and Picture Books:

Belpré, Pura. DANCE OF THE ANIMALS. pb
Belpré, Pura. PEREZ AND MARTINA. pb
Carter GREEDY 18-24, 41-45, 106-111, 112-118
Cothran MAGIC 55-59, 60-65, 66-68
Jagendorf KING 242-244, 244-248
Leach THING 63-64
Newman FOLK 95-99
Withers I SAW 99-52
Withers WORLD 67-68

Collections:

Alegría, Ricardo E. THREE WISHES: A COLLECTION OF PUERTO RICAN FOLKTALES.
Belpré, Pura. ONCE IN PUERTO RICO.
Belpré, Pura. THE TIGER AND THE RABBIT AND OTHER TALES.

CARIBBEAN, TRINIDAD

Single Tales in Collections and Picture Books:

Jagendorf KING 249-251

CARIBBEAN, VIRGIN ISLANDS, ST. CROIX

Single Tales in Collections and Picture Books:

Cothran MAGIC 71-72, 73-74

CARIBBEAN, VIRGIN ISLANDS, ST. THOMAS

Single Tales in Collections and Picture Books:

Cothran MAGIC 75-82

CENTRAL AMERICA

Collections:

Bowes, Anne La Bastille. BIRD KINGDOM OF THE MAYAS.
Carter, Dorothy Sharp. THE ENCHANTED ORCHARD AND OTHER FOLKTALES OF CENTRAL AMERICA.
SEE ALSO COSTA RICA; EL SALVADOR; GUATEMALA; NICARAGUA; PANAMA.

CHILE

Single Tales in Collections and Picture Books:

Barlow LATIN 28-37
Carpenter SOUTH 83-92
Courlander RIDE 279-282
Jagendorf KING 65-69, 69-71, 72-78
Newman FOLK 31-37
Withers I SAW 56

COLOMBIA

Single Tales in Collections and Picture Books:

Barlow LATIN 82-88
Courlander RIDE 224-225
Jagendorf KING 79-80, 81-82, 83-88
Newman FOLK 53-60

COSTA RICA

Single Tales in Collections and Picture Books:

Courlander RIDE 238-240
Harper GHOSTS 228-233
Jagendorf KING 89-93

Collections:

Lupe de Osma. THE WITCHES' RIDE.

ECUADOR

Single Tales in Collections and Picture Books:

Barlow LATIN 68-81
Courlander RIDE 217-219
Jagendorf KING 111-113, 113-116

EL SALVADOR

Single Tales in Collections and Picture Books:

Barlow LATIN 119-125
Courlander RIDE 241-242
Jagendorf KING 117-119, 119-121

GUATEMALA

Single Tales in Collections and Picture Books:

Barlow LATIN 126-152

Courlander RIDE 250-252
Garner CAVALCADE...GOBLINS 4-10
Jagendorf KING 122-126, 126-131, 132-135, 135-138
Newman FOLK 107-110

GUIANA

Single Tales in Collections and Picture Books:

Carpenter LATIN 43-49, 165-174, 175-181
Jagendorf KING 139-141, 142-144, 144-148, 148-151, 151-154

HONDURAS

Single Tales in Collections and Picture Books:

Barlow LATIN 113-118
Courlander RIDE 243-249
Jagendorf KING 162-163, 164-167, 167-170

MEXICO

Single Tales in Collections and Picture Books:

Aardema, Verna. THE RIDDLE OF THE DRUM: A TALE FROM TIZÁPAN, MEXICO. pb
Arnott ANIMALS 1-5
Balet, Jan. THE FENCE. pb
Barlow LATIN 138-144
Courlander RIDE 253-256
Edmonds TRICKSTER 77-85
Frost LEGENDS 190-199, 199, 214
Hardendorff TRICKY 55-61
Jagendorf KING 181-186, 187-189, 190-193, 193-198, 198-202, 202-204
Jagendorf NOODLEHEAD 268-270
Kouzel, Daisy. THE CUCKOO'S REWARD. pb
Ross BURIED 89-94
Wolkstein LAZY 19-29

Collections:

Brenner, Anita. THE BOY WHO COULD DO ANYTHING, AND OTHER MEXICAN FOLK TALES.
Campbell, Camilla. STAR MOUNTAIN AND OTHER LEGENDS OF MEXICO.
Jordan, Philip. THE BURRO BENEDICTO.
Piggott, Juliet. MEXICAN FOLK TALES.
Ross, Patricia Fent. IN MEXICO THEY SAY.
Roy, Cal. THE SERPENT AND THE SUN: MYTHS OF THE MEXICAN WORLD.
Storm, Dan. PICTURE TALES FROM MEXICO.
Traven, B. THE CREATION OF THE SUN AND THE MOON.

NICARAGUA

Single Tales in Collections and Picture Books:

Courlander RIDE 234-237
Jagendorf KING 205-208, 208-211, 211-218, 218-221

PANAMA

Single Tales in Collections and Picture Books:

Barlow LATIN 97-103
Courlander RIDE 231-233

Jagendorf KING 222-225

PARAGUAY

Single Tales in Collections and Picture Books:

Barlow LATIN 38-42, 43-49
Courlander RIDE 213-214
Jagendorf KING 229, 229-232

PERU

Single Tales in Collections and Picture Books:

Barlow LATIN 57-61, 62-67
Bierhorst, John. BLACK RAINBOW: LEGENDS
OF THE INCAS AND MYTHS OF ANCIENT
PERU. pb
Courlander RIDE 220-223
Dewey, Ariane. THE THUNDER GOD'S SON. pb

SURINAM

Single Tales in Collections and Picture Books:

Carpenter SOUTH 18-26
Leach THING 20-21, 41-45

URUGUAY

Single Tales in Collections and Picture Books:

Courlander RIDE 215-216
Jagendorf KING 252-256, 256-259

VENEZUELA

Single Tales in Collections and Picture Books:

Arnott ANIMALS 100-103
Barlow LATIN 89-96
Courlander RIDE 226-230
Jagendorf KING 260-264, 265-269, 269-273
Newman FOLK 111-117

Ethnic Groups

ARAUCANIAN

Single Tales in Collections and Picture Books:

Barlow LATIN 28-37
Carpenter SOUTH 151-159

AYMARA

Single Tales in Collections and Picture Books:

Arnott ANIMAL 224-230
Barlow LATIN 50-56
Carpenter LATIN 57-63

CARIB

Single Tales in Collections and Picture Books:

Carpenter SOUTH 18-26
Sherlock WEST 7-12, 13-20, 21-26, 27-33, 34-38, 39-44

CHOCO

Single Tales in Collections and Picture Books:

Carpenter SOUTH 149-150

CUNA

Single Tales in Collections and Picture Books:

Barlow LATIN 97-103

ESMERALDA

Single Tales in Collections and Picture Books:

Barlow LATIN 82-88

GUARANI

Single Tales in Collections and Picture Books:

Barlow LATIN 38-42, 43-49

INCA

Single Tales in Collections and Picture Books:

Arnott ANIMAL 224-230
Barlow LATIN 68-81
Carpenter LATIN 50-56
Carpenter SOUTH 27-35, 115-128, 134-136
Jagendorf KING 233-236, 236-238, 238-241
Newman FOLK 13-18, 19-26

Collections:

Bierhorst, John. BLACK RAINBOW: LEGENDS
OF THE INCAS.

MAYA

Single Tales in Collections and Picture Books:

Barlow LATIN 113-118, 119-125, 134-137
Garner CAVALCADE...GOBLINS 4-10

Collections:

Bowes, Anne La Bastille. BIRD KINGDOM OF
THE MAYAS.

QUECHUA SEE INCA.

QUICHE

Single Tales in Collections and Picture Books:

Barlow LATIN 126-132

TEHUELCHE

Single Tales in Collections and Picture Books:

Barlow LATIN 9-17

TIMOTEAN

Single Tales in Collections and Picture Books:

Barlow LATIN 89-96

WAURRAU

Single Tales in Collections and Picture Books:

Carpenter SOUTH 167-174

MIDDLE EAST

SEE ALSO AFRICA, NORTH AFRICA.

Geographical Areas

MIDDLE EAST, GENERAL

Single Tales in Collections and Picture Books:

Berson, Harold. KASSIM'S SHOES. pb
Van Woerkom, Dorothy O. ABU ALI: THREE
TALES OF THE MIDDLE EAST. pb

Collections:

Nahmad, H. M. THE PEASANT AND THE
DONKEY: TALES OF THE NEAR AND
MIDDLE EAST.
Spicer, Dorothy Gladys. THE KNEELING TREE
AND OTHER FOLKTALES FROM THE MIDDLE
EAST.

ARABIA

Single Tales in Collections and Picture Books:

Arnott ANIMAL 231-240
Buck FAIRY 269-280
Carpenter ELEPHANT'S 49-57
Carpenter WONDER...DOG 145-155
Courlander TIGER'S 90-99
Green, Nancy. ABU KASSIM'S SLIPPERS. pb
Jagendorf NOODLEHEAD 68-71
Manning-Sanders BOOK...DWARFS 53-63
Manning-Sanders BOOK...MERMAIDS 122-168
Manning-Sanders BOOK...WIZARDS 58-77

AZERBAIJAN

Single Tales in Collections and Picture Books:

Bulatkin EURASIAN 106-110

IRAN

Single Tales in Collections and Picture Books:

Arnott ANIMAL 14-22
Asian FOLK...BOOK ONE 19-25
Asian FOLK...BOOK THREE 23-28
Buck   FAIRY 98-124
Bulatkin EURASIAN 64-68, 103-105
Carpenter ELEPHANT'S 31-39
Courlander RIDE 63-65
Edmonds TRICKSTER 51-60
Jagendorf NOODLEHEAD 93-96
Withers WORLD 80-81

Collections:

Brockett, Eleanor. PERSIAN FAIRY TALES.
Kelsey, Alice Geer. ONCE THE MULLAH:
PERSIAN FOLK TALES.
Mehdevi, Anne Sinclair. PERSIAN FOLK AND
FAIRY TALES.
Mittleman, Gertrude. THE BIRD OF THE
GOLDEN FEATHER.
Nahmad, H. M. THE PEASANT AND THE
DONKEY. TALES OF THE NEAR AND FAR
EAST.

SEE ALSO AZERBAIJAN.

IRAQ

Single Tales in Collections and Picture Books:

Carpenter ELEPHANT'S 66-74, 125-134, 195-203
Courlander RIDE 66-76

ISRAEL

Single Tales in Collections and Picture Books:

Courlander RIDE 99-100

LEBANON

Single Tales in Collections and Picture Books:

Courlander RIDE 92-94

Collections:

Skurzynski, Gloria. TWO FOOLS AND A FAKER:
THREE LEBANESE FOLK TALES.

PALESTINE

Single Tales in Collections and Picture Books:

Arnott ANIMAL 6-13

SAUDI ARABIA

Single Tales in Collections and Picture Books:

Courlander RIDE 85-91

SYRIA

Single Tales in Collections and Picture Books:

Courlander RIDE 77-81
Jagendorf NOODLEHEAD 63-67

TURKEY

Single Tales in Collections and Picture Books:

Belting ELVES 61-65
Buck FAIRY 29-34, 81-88, 225-231, 237-250,
257-263, 306-320
Courlander RIDE 82-84
Edmonds TRICKSTER 36-44
Jagendorf NOODLEHEAD 102-104, 105-110
Leach HOW 30
Price, Christine. SIXTY AT A BLOW. pb
Walker, Barbara K. THE COURAGE OF KAZAN.
pb
Walker, Barbara K. THE IFRIT AND THE
MAGIC GIFTS. pb
Walker, Barbara K. JUST SAY HIC! pb
Walker, Barbara K. and Mime Sümer. STAR-
GAZER TO THE SULTAN. pb
Walker, Barbara K. and Ahmet E. Uysal. NEW
PATCHES FOR OLD. pb

Collections:

Downing, Charles. TALES OF THE HODJA.
Ekrem, Selma. TURKISH FAIRY TALES.
Kelsey, Alice Geer. ONCE THE HODJA.
Walker, Barbara K. KOROLULU, THE SINGING

BANDIT.
Walker, Barbara K. ONCE THERE WAS AND
TWICE THERE WASN'T.
Walker, Barabara K. WATERMELONS, WALNUTS
AND THE WISDOM OF ALLAH, AND OTHER
TALES OF THE HOCA.

YEMEN

Single Tales in Collections and Picture Books:

Courlander RIDE 95-98

Ethnic Groups

BERBER

Single Tales in Collections and Picture Books:

Holding KING'S 87-97

TOUAREG

Single Tales in Collections and Picture Books:

Holding KING'S 69-79

NATIVE AMERICANS

Ethnic Groups

NATIVE AMERICAN, GENERAL

Single Tales in Collections and Picture Books:

Arnott ANIMAL 23-30
Belting ELVES 27-34
Field AMERICAN 3-12, 40-54, 62-70, 71-73
Frost LEGEND 161-164
Littledale GHOSTS 111-120
Manning-Sanders BOOK...CHARMS 81-84
Manning-Sanders BOOK...MERMAIDS 54-58
Mobley, Jane. STAR HUSBAND. pb
Toye, William. THE FIRE STEALER. pb

Collections:

Baylor, Byrd. AND IT IS STILL THAT WAY.
Belting, Natalie. THE LONG-TAILED BEAR,
AND OTHER INDIAN LEGENDS.
Brown, Dee. TEPEE TALES OF THE AMERICAN
INDIAN.
Chafetz, Henry. THUNDERBIRD AND OTHER
STORIES.
Cunningham, Caroline. THE TALKING STONE,
BEING EARLY AMERICAN STORIES TOLD
BEFORE THE WHITE MAN'S DAY ON THIS
CONTINENT BY THE INDIANS AND THE
ESKIMOS.
Curtis, Edward. THE GIRL WHO MARRIED A
GHOST AND OTHER TALES FROM THE
NORTH AMERICAN INDIAN.
DeWit, Dorothy. THE TALKING STONE: AN
ANTHOLOGY OF NATIVE AMERICAN TALES
AND LEGENDS.
Harrison, Amelia (Williams). AMERICAN INDIAN
FAIRY TALES.
Haviland, Virginia. NORTH AMERICAN

LEGENDS.
Hooke, Hilda Mary. THUNDER IN THE
MOUNTAINS: LEGENDS OF CANADA.
Hulpach, Vladimir. AMERICAN INDIAN TALES
AND LEGENDS.
Jones, Hettie. COYOTE TALES.
MacMillan, Cyrus. CANADIAN WONDER TALES.
Manning-Sanders, Ruth. RED INDIAN FOLK
AND FAIRY TALES.
Marriott, Alice and Carol K. Rachlin. AMERI-
CAN INDIAN MYTHOLOGY.
Robinson, Gail and Douglas Hill. COYOTE THE
TRICKSTER.
Schoolcraft, Henry Rowe. THE FIRE PLUME:
LEGENDS OF THE AMERICAN INDIANS.

ABENAKI

Collections:

Crompton, Anne. THE WINTER WIFE.

ACOMA

Single Tales in Collections and Picture Books:

Belting LONG 93-94

Collections:

Rushmore, Helen and Wolf Robe Hunt. THE
DANCING HORSES OF ACOMA.

ACHOMAWI

Single Tales in Collections and Picture Books:

Belting LONG 51-53
Fisher CALIFORNIA 60-73

ALGONQUIN

Single Tales in Collections and Picture Books:

Garner CAVALCADE...GOBLINS 52-54, 210-212

Collections:

Bierhorst, John, ed. THE FIRE PLUME:
LEGENDS OF THE AMERICAN INDIANS.

APACHE, JICARILLA

Single Tales in Collections and Picture Books:

Leach HOW 23-24

APACHE, LIPAN

Single Tales in Collections and Picture Books:

Belting LONG 26-28
Leach HOW 62

ASSINIBOIN

Single Tales in Collections and Picture Books:

Belting LONG 23-25

BELLABELLA

Single Tales in Collections and Picture Books:

Belting LONG 60-61

BLACKFOOT

Single Tales in Collections and Picture Books:

Cunningham TALKING 80-86, 87-94
San Souci, Robert. LEGEND OF SCARFACE. pb

Collections:

Grinnell, George Bird. BLACKFOOT LODGE
TALES.

CALIFORNIA

Collections:

Curry, Jane Louise. DOWN FROM THE LONELY
MOUNTAIN. CALIFORNIA INDIAN TALES.
Fisher, Anne B. STORIES CALIFORNIA
INDIANS TOLD.
SEE ALSO Names of Tribes.

CATAWBA

Single Tales in Collections and Picture Books:

Leach HOW 47-48

CHEROKEE

Single Tales in Collections and Picture Books:

Belting LONG 25-26, 29-33, 57-59, 62-66
Cunningham TALKING 41-44
Leach HOW 49-51, 125, 136-137

Collections:

Bell, Corydon. JOHN RATTLING GOURD OF
BIG COVE: A COLLECTION OF CHEROKEE
INDIAN LEGENDS.
Bird, Traveller. THE PATH TO SNOWBIRD
MOUNTAIN: CHEROKEE LEGENDS.
Scheer, George F. CHEROKEE ANIMAL TALES.

CHEYENNE

Single Tales in Collections and Picture Books:

Field AMERICAN 13-31, 55-61

Collections:

Erdoes, Richard. THE SOUND OF FLUTES.

CHIPPEWA

Single Tales in Collections and Picture Books:

Cunningham TALKING 58-59
Leach HOW 96

Collections:

Leekley, Thomas B. THE WORLD OF
MANABOZHO. TALES OF THE CHIPPEWA
INDIANS.

CHUKCHANS SEE YOKUT.

CHUCKCHEE

Single Tales in Collections and Picture Books:

Leach HOW 41-43

COEUR D'ALENE

Single Tales in Collections and Picture Books:

Leach HOW 57

COOS

Collections:

Running, Corinne. WHEN COYOTE WALKED
THE EARTH.

CREE

Single Tales in Collections and Picture Books:

Belting LONG 67-70, 79-84

CREEK

Single Tales in Collections and Picture Books:

Belting LONG 16-25, 46-50, 54-56

CREEK, YUCHI-CREEK

Single Tales in Collections and Picture Books:

Leach HOW 15-16

CROW

Collections:

Erdoes, Richard. THE SOUND OF FLUTES.

ESKIMO

Single Tales in Collections and Picture Books:

Belting ELVES 47-52
Coalson, Glo. THREE STONE WOMAN. pb
Cothran MAGIC 3-7, 13-17, 18-21, 22-24
Cunningham TALKING 19-23
Edmonds TRICKSTER 21-29
Houston, James. KIVIOK'S MAGIC JOURNEY.
  pb
Leach HOW 37-38, 138-139
Leach NOODLES 83
McDermott, Beverly. SEDNA. pb
San Sourci, Robert. SONG OF SEDNA. pb

Collections:

Caswell, Helen. SHADOWS FROM THE SINGING
HOUSE.
Dolch, Edward W. and Marguerite P. STORIES
FROM ALASKA.
Field, Edward. ESKIMO SONGS AND STORIES.
Gilham, Charles. BEYOND THE CLAPPING
MOUNTAINS: ESKIMO STORIES FROM
ALASKA.
Gilham, Charles. MEDICINE MEN OF HOOPER
BAY: MORE TALES FROM THE CLAPPING
MOUNTAINS OF ALASKA.
Maher, Ramona. THE BLIND BOY AND THE

Leach HOW 133-134
Sheehan FOLK 141-148
Toye, William. HOW SUMMER CAME TO
    CANADA. pb

Collections:

Hill, Kay. BADGER, THE MISCHIEF MAKER.
Hill, Kay. GLOOSCAP AND HIS MAGIC.
Hill, Kay. MORE GLOOSCAP STORIES.
Marriott, Alice Lee. WINTER-TELLING STORIES.

MIWOK

Single Tales in Collections and Picture Books:

Fisher CALIFORNIA 89-95

MODOC

Single Tales in Collections and Picture Books:

Cunningham TALKING 16-18

MONO

Single Tales in Collections and Picture Books:

Fisher CALIFORNIA 54-59

NASKAPI

Single Tales in Collections and Picture Books:

Cunningham TALKING 60-65

NAVAJO

Collections:

Hausman, Gerald. SITTING ON THE BLUE-
    EYED BEAR.

NEZ PERCÉ

Single Tales in Collections and Picture Books:

Matson LEGENDS 64-69, 69-75

Collections:

Heady, Eleanor. TALES OF THE NIMIPOO FROM
    THE LAND OF THE NEZ PERCE INDIANS.
Martin, Frances Gardiner McEntee.   NINE
    TALES OF COYOTE.

NISQUALLY

Single Tales in Collections and Picture Books:

Matson LEGENDS 19-24, 24-28, 28-31

NORTHWEST COAST

Single Tales in Collections and Picture Books:

Toye, William. THE MOUNTAIN GOATS OF
    TEMLAHAM. pb

Collections:

Ayre, Robert. SKETCO THE RAVEN.
Clark, Ella. INDIAN LEGENDS OF THE

PACIFIC NORTHWEST.
Dolch, Edward W. and Marguerite P. STORIES
    FROM ALASKA.
Harris, Christie. ONCE UPON A TOTEM.
Martin, Fran. NINE TALES OF RAVEN.
Martin, Fran. RAVEN-WHO-SETS-THINGS-
    RIGHT.
Matson, Emerson N. LEGENDS OF THE GREAT
    CHIEFS.
Matson, Emerson N. LONGHOUSE LEGENDS.
Running, Corinne. WHEN COYOTE WALKED
    THE EARTH.
SEE ALSO Names of Tribes.

OJIBWA

Single Tales in Collections and Picture Books.

Cothran WITH 84-89
Cunningham TALKING 24-29

OJIBWAY

Collections:

Reid, Dorothy M. TALES OF MANABOZHO.

ONONDAGA

Single Tales in Collections and Picture Books:

Cunningham TALKING 37-40

PAIUTE

Single Tales in Collections and Picture Books:

Hodges, Margaret. THE FIRE BRINGER. pb

PAPAGO

Collections:

Baker, Betty. AT THE CENTER OF THE
    WORLD. BASED ON PAPAGO AND PIMA
    MYTHS.

PASSAMAQUODDY

Single Tales in Collections and Picture Books:

Leach HOW 79, 97

PAWNEE

Single Tales in Collections and Picture Books:

Belting LONG 42-45

PENOBSCOT

Single Tales in Collections and Picture Books:

Gruenberg FAVORITE 333-335
Leach HOW 109-110

PIMA

Collections:

Baker, Betty. AT THE CENTER OF THE
    WORLD. BASED ON PAPAGO AND PIMA
    MYTHS.

Single Tales in Collections and Picture Books:

    Harris ONCE 5-30, 61-85
    Toye, William. THE LOON'S NECKLACE. pb

Collections:

    Harris, Christis. ONCE MORE UPON A TOTEM.

WABANAKI SEE MICMAC.

WINTU, SACRAMENTO VALLEY
Single Tales in Collections and Picture Books:

    Belting LONG 34-26
    Cothran WITH 65-66

WISHOSK
Single Tales in Collections and Picture Books:

    Leach HOW 84

WIYOT SEE WISHOSK.

YOKUT, SAN JOAQUIN VALLEY
Single Tales in Collections and Picture Books:

    Cothran WITH 56-64

YOKUT, CHUKCHANS
Single Tales in Collections and Picture Books:

    Belting LONG 39-41
    Fisher STORIES 36-45
    Leach HOW 44

YUCHI-CREEK SEE CREEK-YUCHI

NORTH AMERICA

Geographical Areas

CANADA, GENERAL

Single Tales in Collections and Picture Books:

    Courlander RIDE 272-278
    Frost LEGENDS 278-282, 283-286, 287-294
    Jagendorf NOODLEHEAD 263-267
    Withers I SAW 48

Collections:

    Barbeau, Marius. THE GOLDEN PHOENIX AND
      OTHER FRENCH-CANADIAN FAIRY TALES.
    Carlson, Natalie Savage. SASHES RED AND
      BLUE.
    Carlson, Natalie Savage. THE TALKING CAT
      AND OTHER STORIES OF FRENCH CANADA.

CANADA, FRENCH

Single Tales in Collections and Picture Books:

    Leach NOODLES 17-18

Littledale GHOSTS 101-110

CANADA, NATIVE AMERICAN SEE All Indigenous
  Tribes under NATIVE AMERICANS.

CANADA, NOVA SCOTIA
Single Tales in Collections and Picture Books:

    Leach THING 15-16
    Leach NOODLES 14, 79

CANADA, PRINCE EDWARD ISLE
Single Tales in Collections and Picture Books:

    Leach THING 65-67

UNITED STATES, GENERAL
Single Tales in Collections and Picture Books:

    Bang, Betsy. WILEY AND THE HAIRY MAN. pb
    Barth, Edna. JACK-O-LANTERN. pb
    Courlander RIDE 268-271
    Credle, Ellis. BIG FRAID AND LITTLE FRAID.
     pb
    Field AMERICAN 77-107, 154-156, 295-302
    Frost LEGENDS 174-176
    Galdone, Joanna. THE TAILYPO. pb
    Leach THING
    Withers WORLD 25-27, 28-30, 82-87

Collections:

    Cothran, Jean. WITH A WIG, WITH A WAG.
    Cothran, Jean. THE MAGIC CALABASH.
    Field, Rachel. AMERICAN FOLK AND FAIRY
      TALES.

ALABAMA
Single Tales in Collections and Picture Books:

    Jagendorf FOLK 3-28
    SEE ALSO NORTH AMERICA, *BLACK, ALABAMA.*

APPALACHIA
Single Tales in Collections and Picture Books:

    Chase, Richard. JACK AND THE THREE
      SILLIES. pb
    Chase, Richard. WICKED JOHN AND THE
      DEVIL. pb
    Cothran WITH 26-33

Collections:

    Chase, Richard. GRANDFATHER TALES.
    Chase, Richard. THE JACK TALES
    Credle, Ellis. TALL TALES FROM HIGH HILLS.

ARKANSAS
Single Tales in Collections and Picture Books.

    Jagendorf FOLK 29-66
    SEE ALSO OZARK MOUNTAINS.

ATLANTIC
Collections:

    Jagendorf, Moritz. UPSTATE, DOWNSTATE.

PENNSYLVANIA

Single Tales in Collections and Picture Books:

Carpenter WONDER...DOGS 163-172
Jagendorf UPSTATE 107-228

RHODE ISLAND

Single Tales in Collections and Picture Books:

Jagendorf NEW ENGLAND 219-269

THE SOUTH

Single Tales in Collections and Picture Books:

Harper GHOSTS 195-199

Collections:

Jagendorf, Moritz. FOLK STORIES OF THE SOUTH.

SOUTH CAROLINA

Single Tales in Collections and Picture Books:

Jagendorf FOLK 205-230
SEE ALSO NORTH AMERICA, *BLACK, SOUTH CAROLINA.*

TENNESSEE

Single Tales in Collections and Picture Books:

Jagendorf FOLK 231-268

TEXAS

Single Tales in Collections and Picture Books:

Jagendorf FOLK 269-296

VERMONT

Single Tales in Collections and Picture Books:

Jagendorf NEW ENGLAND 79-116

VIRGINIA

Single Tales in Collections and Picture Books:

Jagendorf FOLK 297-318
SEE ALSO NORTH AMERICA, *BLACK, VIRGINIA.*

Ethnic Groups

BLACK, ALABAMA

Single Tales in Collections and Picture Books:

Bang, Betsy. WILEY AND THE HAIRY MAN. pb

BLACK, NORTH CAROLINA

Single Tales in Collections and Picture Books:

Leach HOW 73-74, 89-90, 113-114

BLACK, SOUTH CAROLINA

Single Tales in Collections and Picture Books:

Leach HOW 65
Withers I SAW 17-47

BLACK, VIRGINIA

Single Tales in Collections and Picture Books:

Leach NOODLES 15-16

BLACK, UNITED STATES

Single Tales in Collections and Picture Books:

Cothran WITH 40-43

Collections:

Courlander, Harold. TERRAPIN'S POT OF SENSE.
Faulkner, William. THE DAYS WHEN THE ANIMALS TALKED: BLACK AMERICAN FOLKTALES AND HOW THEY CAME TO BE.
Harris, Joel Chandler. BRER RABBIT: STORIES FROM UNCLE REMUS.
Harris, Joel Chandler. THE COMPLETE TALES OF UNCLE REMUS.
Harris, Joel Chandler. THE FAVORITE UNCLE REMUS.
Harris, Joel Chandler. NIGHTS WITH UNCLE REMUS: MYTHS AND LEGENDS OF THE OLD PLANTATIONS.
Harris, Joel Chandler. UNCLE REMUS, HIS SONGS AND HIS SAYINGS.
Lester, Julius. BLACK FOLKTALES.
Lester, Julius. THE KNEE-HIGH MAN.
Rees, Ennis. BRER RABBIT AND HIS TRICKS.

DUTCH, NEW YORK

Single Tales in Collections and Picture Books:

Cothran WITH 18-22

FRENCH, LOUISIANA

Single Tales in Collections and Picture Books:

Leach NOODLES 26-27

NATIVE AMERICAN SEE NATIVE AMERICAN section.

OCEANIA

AUSTRALIA

Single Tales in Collections and Picture Books:

Arnott ANIMAL 76-78, 195-201
Courlander RIDE 20-24
Frost LEGENDS 295-297
Leach HOW 18-19

Collections:

Bates, Daisy. TALES TOLD TO KABBARLI: ABORIGINAL LEGENDS.
Bunter, Bill M. J. DJUGURBA: TALES FROM

5

*Key Motifs for
Aarne–Thompson Types 300–1199*

Aarne-Thompson types 300-1199 are described under the key motif numbers given below.

300 The Dragon-slayer. SEE R111.1.3.

301 The Three Stolen Princesses. SEE K1931.2.

301A Quest for a Vanished Princess. SEE K1931.2.

302 The Ogre's (Devil's) Heart in the Egg. SEE D532, K956.

302B Hero with Life Dependent on his Sword. SEE E711.10.

303 The Twins or Blood-brothers. SEE R111.1.3.

306 The Danced-out Shoes. SEE F1015.1.1.

310 The Maiden in the Tower. Rapunzel. SEE F848.1.

311 Rescue by the Sister. SEE G561.1.

312 The Giant Killler and his Dog (Bluebeard). SEE S62.1.

313 The Girl as Helper in the Hero's Flight. SEE G530.2.

313A The Girl as Helper of the Hero on his Flight. The Youth has been promised to the Devil. SEE G530.2B.

313B Above + the Forbidden Box. SEE G530.2K.

313C Above + the Forgotten Fiancee. SEE G530.2A.

313D Magic Flight and Transformation to Bird. SEE G530.2D.

313G Three Brothers Search for Stolen Cow. SEE G530.2S.

313H Flight from the Witch. SEE D672, Q2.1.2CeB.

314 The Youth Transformed to a Horse (Goldener). SEE B316.

314A The Shepherd and the Three Giants. SEE R111.1.3Ba.

315 The Faithless Sister. SEE K2212.0.2, R111.1.3E.

315A The Cannibal Sister. SEE B524.1.2, G312.

316 The Nix of the Mill-pond. SEE F420.5.2.2.

325 The Magician and His Pupil. SEE D1711.0.1.

326 The Youth Who Wanted to Learn What Fear Is. SEE H1440.

327 The Children and the Ogre. SEE G412.1, K1611.

327A Hansel and Gretel. SEE G412.1.

327C The Devil (Witch) Carries the Hero Home in a Sack. SEE K526.

327D The Kiddelkaddelkar. SEE G526.

328 The Boy Steals the Giant's Treasure. SEE F54.2, G501, G512.0.4, G610.

329 Hiding from the Devil. SEE: H321.

330 The Smith Outwits the Devil.

330A The Smith and the Devil (Death). SEE Q565.

330B The Devil in the Knapsack (Bottle, Cask). SEE K213.

330D Bonhomme Misère. SEE Z111.2.

332 Godfather Death. SEE D1825.3.1.

333 The Glutton (Red Riding Hood). SEE Z18.1.

361 Bear-skin. SEE K217.

365 The Dead Bridegroom Carries Off His Bride (Lenore). SEE E215.

400 The Man on a Quest for His Lost Wife. SEE H1385.3.

402 The Mouse (Cat, Frog, etc.) as Bride. SEE B641.

402A Princess Transformed to Toad. SEE D732.

403 The Black and White Bride. SEE K1911.

403A The Wishes. SEE Q2.1.5Bb.

403B SEE Q2.1.4B.

405 Jorinde and Joringel. SEE D771.11.

408 The Three Oranges. SEE D721.5.

410 Sleeping Beauty. SEE D1960.3.

425 The Search for the Lost Husband. SEE H1385.4.

425B The Disenchanted Husband: The Witch's Tasks. SEE H1385.4E.

425C Beauty and the Beast. SEE D735.1.

425D Vanished Husband Learned of by Keeping Inn (Bath-house). SEE N352.

425G False Bride Takes Heroine's Place. SEE K1911.1.4.

425N Bird Husband. SEE H1385.4B.

426 The Two Girls, the Bean and the Dwarf. SEE D113.2.

431 The House in the Wood. SEE Q2.1.3C.

432 The Prince as Bird. SEE H1385.4, H1385.5.

433B King Lindorm. SEE B646.1.

437 The Supplanted Bride (The Needle Prince).
SEE K1911.1.4.

440 The Frog King or Iron Henry. SEE D195.

441 Hans my Hedgehog. SEE B641.5.

450 Little Brother and Little Sister. SEE P253.2.

451 The Maiden Who Seeks Her Brothers. SEE
P253.2.

461 Three Hairs from the Devil's Beard. SEE
H1273.2.

462 The Outcast Queens and the Ogress Queen.
SEE Z215.

465 The Man Persecuted Because of His Beautiful
Wife. SEE N831.1.0.1.

471 The Bridge to the Other World. SEE
H1199.12.3.

471A The Monk and the Bird. SEE D2011.1.

475 The Man as Heater of Hell's Kettle. SEE
K2213.

480 The Spinning-women by the Spring. The
Kind and Unkind Girls. SEE Q2.1.2.

500 The Name of the Helper (Rumpelstilzchen).
SEE D2183.

501 The Three Old Women Helpers. SEE D2183.1.

502 The Wild Man. SEE G671.

503 The Gifts of the Little People. SEE F344.1.

506 The Rescued Princess. SEE E341.1.

507A The Monster's Bride. SEE G512.

510 Cinderella and Cap O' Rushes. SEE R221.

510A Cinderella. SEE R221.

510B The Dress of Gold, of Silver, and of Stars
(Cap O' Rushes). SEE R221.

511 One-Eye, Two-Eyes, Three-Eyes. SEE D830.1.

511A The Little Red Ox. SEE B335.2.

513, 514 The Helpers. SEE F601.2.

513 The Extraordinary Companions. SEE F601.2.

513A Six Go Through the Whole World. SEE
F601.2D.

513B The Land and Water Ship. SEE F601.2A.

513C The Son of the Hunter. SEE H1151.6.1.

516 Faithful John. SEE S268.

517 The Boy Who Learned Many Things. SEE L425.

530 The Princess on the Glass Mountain. SEE
H331.1.1.

531 Ferdinand the True and Ferdinand the False.
SEE H1213.1.

533 The Speaking Horsehead. SEE B133.3.

545 The Cat as Helper. SEE K1917.3; K1952.1.1.

545B Puss in Boots. SEE K1917.3.

546 The Clever Parrot. SEE K1346.

550 Search for the Golden Bird. SEE H1331.1.3.

551 The Sons on a Quest for a Wonderful Remedy
for Their Father. SEE H1331.1C.

552 The Girls Who Married Animals. SEE B314.

552A Three Animals as Brothers-in-law. SEE: B314.

552B The Animal Sons-in-law and Their Magic
Food. SEE J2411.3.

554 The Grateful Animals. SEE B582.2.

555 The Fisher and His Wife. SEE B375.1.

560 The Magic Ring. SEE D882.1.1.

561 Aladdin. SEE D871.1.

562 The Spirit in the Blue Light. SEE D1421.1.2.

563 The Table, the Ass, and the Stick. SEE
D861.1.

565 The Magic Mill. SEE A1115.2, C916.3,
D1651.3.1.

566 The Three Magic Objects and the Wonderful
Fruits (Fortunatus). SEE D551.1.

567 The Magic Bird-heart. SEE D551.1.

569 The Knapsack, the Hat, and the Horn.
SEE D831.

570 The Rabbit-herd. SEE H1045.

571 All Stick Together. SEE H341.1.

575 The Prince's Wings. SEE K1346.

577 The King's Tasks. SEE H1115.1.

580 Beloved of Women. SEE D856.

581 The Magic Object and the Trolls. SEE K333.2.

585 Spindle, Shuttle, and Needle. SEE H1311.2.

590 The Prince and the Arm Bands. SEE S12.1.

590A The Treacherous Wife. SEE K2213.

591 The Thieving Pot. SEE D1605.1.

592 The Dance Among Thorns. SEE D1415.2.5.

593 Fiddevav. SEE D1413.17.

610 The Healing Fruits. SEE H346.

611 The Gifts of the Dwarfs. SEE T102.

612 The Three Snake-leaves. SEE K2213.5.

613 The Two Travelers (Truth and Falsehood).
SEE N452.

621 The Louse-skin. SEE H522.1.1.

650A Strong John. SEE F613.2.

652 The Prince Whose Wishes Always Come True;
The Carnation. SEE D212.1.

653 The Four Skillful Brothers. SEE F660.1,
H621.2.

653A The Rarest Thing in the World. SEE
H355.0.1.

654 The Three Brothers. SEE F660.1.

655A The Strayed Camel and the Clever Deductions. SEE J1661.1.1.

665 The Man Who Flew Like a Bird and Swam Like
a Fish. SEE R532B.

670 The Animal Language. SEE B216.

671 The Three Languages. SEE B217.

673 The White Serpent's Flesh. SEE B217.1.1.

676 Open Sesame. SEE N455.3.

678 The King Transfers His Soul to a Parrot.
SEE K1175.

700 Tom Thumb. SEE F535.1.1.

703 The Artificial Child. SEE T546.3.

704 Princess on the Pea. SEE H41.1.

707 The Three Golden Sons. SEE H1320,
H1331.1.3F, N455.4.

709 Snow-White. SEE Z65.1.

709A The Stork's Daughter. SEE S352.2.

711 The Beautiful and the Ugly Twin.
SEE L145.1.

715 Demi-coq. SEE Z52.1.

720 My Mother Slew Me; My Father Ate Me.
Juniper Tree. SEE N271.

725 The Dream. SEE L425.

726 The Oldest on the Farm. SEE F571.2.

730 The Axe Falls into the Stream. SEE Q3.1.

735 The Rich Man's and the Poor Man's Fortune.
SEE N250.4.

736A The Ring of Polycrates. SEE N211.1.

738 The Battle of Serpents. SEE Q82.3.

750A The Wishes. SEE Q1.1.

750D Three Brothers Each Granted a Wish by an
Angel Visitor. SEE Q1.1A.

751A The Peasant Woman Is Changed into a Woodpecker. SEE A1958.0.1.

753 Christ and the Smith. SEE J2411.1.

757 The King's Haughtiness Punished. SEE L411.

759 God's Justice Vindicated. SEE J225.

761 The Cruel Rich Man as the Devil's Horse.
SEE Q584.2.

763 The Treasure Finders Who Murder One
Another. SEE K1685.

766 The Seven Sleepers (Rip Van Winkle).
SEE D1960.1.

780 The Singing Bone. SEE E632.

782 Midas and the Ass's Ears. SEE D1316.5.

785A The Goose with One Leg. SEE K402.1.

800 The Tailor in Heaven. SEE F1037.1.

812 The Devil's Riddle. SEE M211.7.1.

813 A Careless Word Summons the Devil.
SEE C12.

821A Thief Rescued by the Devil. SEE
G303.22.11.

830C If God Wills. SEE N385.1.

834A The Pot of God and the Pot of Scorpions.
SEE N182.

845 The Old Man and Death. SEE C11.

850 The Birthmarks of the Princess. SEE
D1425.2.6.1.

851 The Princess Who Cannot Solve the Riddle.
SEE H551.

852 The Hero Forces the Princess to Say, "That is a Lie." SEE H342.1.

854 The Hero Catches the Princess with Her Own Words. SEE H507.1.0.1.

858 The Golden Ram. SEE K1341.

858 When the King Sneezes the Shepherd Refuses to Cry "God Bless You!" SEE H328.9.

860 Nuts of "Ay ay ay!" SEE H1377.3.

870 The Princess Confined in the Mound. SEE K1816.0.2.

870A* The Enclosed Girl Follows Her Lover. SEE R49.4.

874* Ariadne-thread Wins the Prince. SEE H389.1.

875 The Clever Peasant Girl. SEE H561.1.

875C The Queen as Gusli-player. SEE J1545.4.

877 The Old Woman Who Was Skinned. La Vecchia Scorticata. SEE T11.4.8.

894 The Ghoulish Schoolmaster and the Stone of Pity. SEE K1911.1.4.

898 Daughter to Be Given to Sun When Twelve. SEE T521.

900 King Thrushbeard. SEE H465.

901 Taming of the Shrew. SEE T251.2.

910 Precepts Bought or Given Prove Correct. SEE J21.

922. The Shepherd Substituting for the Priest Answers the King's Questions. SEE H561.2.

923 Love Like Salt. SEE H592.1.

930 The Prophecy. SEE K1355.

930D Fated Bride's Ring in the Sea. SEE N211.1.

934D Outwitting Fate. SEE K2371.2.

936 The Golden Mountain. SEE K1861.1.

945 Luck and Intelligence. SEE F945.2.1.

953 The Old Robber Relates Three Adventures to Free His Sons. SEE R153.3.3.

955 The Robber Bridegroom. SEE S62.1.

964 Thief (Murderer) Deceived Into Betraying Himself by a Gesture. SEE J1141.1.

967 The Man Saved by a Spider Web. SEE B523.1.

1000 Bargain Not to Become Angry. SEE K172.

1029 The Woman as Cuckoo in the Tree. SEE K1691.

1060-1114 Contest Between Man and Ogre. SEE G501.

1072 Race with Little Son. SEE K11.6.

1074 Race Won by Deception: Relative Helpers. SEE K11.1.

1088 Eating Contest. SEE K81.1.

1115 Attempted Murder with Hatchet. SEE K525.1.

1137 The Ogre Blinded (Polyphemus). SEE K602.

1145-1154 The Ogre Frightened or Overawed. SEE G501.

1149 Children Desire Ogre's Flesh. SEE G501C.

1161 The Bear Trainer and His Bear. SEE K1728.

1164 The Evil Woman Thrown Into the Pit. SEE T251.1.4.

1164D The Demon and the Man Join Forces. SEE C12.4.1, T251.1.1.

6

---

*Bibliography of Collections
and Single Editions Indexed*

NOTE: pb = picture book
P = collection only partially indexed.
N = collection not indexed. However, some tales from this collection are cited because they were included in other collections which are indexed.
G = Included in Ethnic and Geographic Index only.

398.2 Aardema, Verna. BEHIND THE BACK OF THE MOUNTAIN: BLACK FOLKTALES FROM SOUTHERN AFRICA. Illus. Leo and Diane Dillon. New York: Dial, 1973.

j _____. BRINGING THE RAIN TO KAPITI PLAIN: A NANDI TALE. Illus. Beatriz Vidal. New York: Dial, 1981. G, pb

_____. HALF-A-BALL-OF-KENKI: AN ASHANTI TALE. Illus. Diane Stanley Zuromskis. New York: Warne, 1979. pb

398.2 _____. MORE TALES FROM THE STORY Aarm HAT. Illus. Elton Fax. New York: Coward-McCann, 1966.

398.2 _____. THE NA OF WA. Illus. Elton Fax. Aa7n New York; Coward-McCann, 1960. pb

398.2 _____. OTWE. Illus. Elton Fax. New Aa7o York: Coward-McCann, 1960. pb

398.2 _____. THE RIDDLE OF THE DRUM: A TALE FROM TIZAPÁN, MEXICO. Illus. Tony Chen. New York: Four Winds, 1979. pb

398.2 _____. THE SKY-GOD STORIES. Illus. Aa7s Elton Fax. New York: Coward-McCann, 1960.

398.2 _____. TALES FOR THE THIRD EAR FROM EQUATORIAL AFRICA. Illus. Ib Ohlsson. New York: Dutton, 1969.

398.2 _____. TALES FROM THE STORY HAT. Illus. Elton Fax. New York: Coward-McCann, 1960.

398.2 _____. WHO'S IN RABBIT'S HOUSE? A MASAI TALE. Illus. Leo and Diane Dillon. New York: Dial, 1977. pb

398.2 Abisch, Roz. MAI-LING AND THE MIRROR. Illus. Boche Kaplan. Englewood Cliffs, N.J.: Prentice-Hall, 1969. pb

398 Adams, Adrienne. SEE GRIMM - TWELVE DANC-25ta ING PRINCESSES.

d18b Adams, Kathleen and Frances Elizabeth Atchinson. A BOOK OF GIANT STORIES. Illus. Robert W. Lahr. New York: Dodd, Mead, 1926.

398 _____. A BOOK OF PRINCESS STORIES. Adl Illus. Lois Lenski. New York: Dodd, Mead, 1927. P

Aesop. AESOP; FIVE CENTURIES OF ILLUS-

TRATED FABLES. Selected by John J. McKendry. New York: Metropolitan Museum of Art; distributed by New York Graphic Society, Greenwich, Conn., 1964.

j888.6 Ae8o _____. AESOP'S FABLES. Edited and illustrated by Boris Artzybasheff. New York: Viking, 1933.

j888.6 Ae8am _____. AESOP'S FABLES. Translated by V.S. Verson Jones. Illus. Arthur Rackham. New York: Watts, 1968. P

j888.6 Ae8qa _____. AESOP'S FABLES. Illus. Fritz Kredel. New York: Grosset & Dunlap, 1947.

j888.6 Ae8ai _____. AESOP'S FABLES. Selected and adapted by Louis Untermeyer. Illus. A. and M. Provensen. New York: Golden, 1965.

j888.6 Ae8aew _____. AESOP'S FABLES. Retold by Anne Terry White. Illus. Helen Siegl. New York: Random, 1964.

j888.6 Ae8fw _____. FABLES FROM AESOP. Retold by James Reeves. Illus. Maurice Wilson. New York: Walck, 1962.

j888.6 _____. THE FABLES OF AESOP. Selected, told anew and their history traced by Joseph Jacobs. New York: Macmillan, 1950.

_____. THE MILKMAID AND HER PAIL OF MILK. Reteller, Katherine Evans. Illus. Katherine Evans. Chicago: Albert Whitman, 1959. pb

_____. THE MILLER, HIS SON AND THEIR DONKEY. Illus. Roger Duvoisin. New York: McGraw-Hill, 1962. pb

398.2 Alegría, Ricardo E. THREE WISHES: A COLLECTION OF PUERTO RICAN FOLKTALES. Trans. Elizabeth Culbert. Illus. Lorenzo Homar. New York: Harcourt, Brace & World, 1969.

398.2 Alexander, Frances. PEBBLES FROM A BROKEN JAR. FABLES AND HERO STORIES FROM OLD CHINA. Illustrated with papercuts by children. Indianapolis: Bobbs-Merrill, c1963, 1967. P

Aliki. THE EGGS: A GREEK FOLK TALE. Retold and illustrated by Aliki. New York: Pantheon, 1969. pb

_____. THREE GOLD PIECES: A GREEK FOLK TALE. Retold and illustrated by Aliki. New York: Pantheon, 1967. pb

_____. THE TWELVE MONTHS: A GREEK FOLK-TALE. Retold and illustrated by Aliki. New York: Greenwillow, 1978. pb

398.4 Almedingen, E. M. RUSSIAN FOLK AND FAIRY TALES. Illus. Simon Jeruchim. New York: Putnam, c1957, 1963. G

398.2 Ambrus, Victor G. THE LITTLE COCKEREL. New York: Harcourt, Brace & World, 1968. pb

Ambrus, Victor G. THE VALIANT LITTLE TAILOR. Illus. Victor G. Ambrus. Oxford, 1980. pb

Andersen, Hans Christian. THE PRINCESS AND THE PEA. Illus. Paul Galdone. New York: Seabury, 1978. pb

_____. THE WOMAN WITH THE EGGS. Adapted by Jan Wahl. Illus. Ray Cruz. New York: Crown, 1974. pb

Anderson, Paul. THE BOY AND THE BLIND STORYTELLER. Illus. Yong Hwan Kim. New York: W. R. Scott, 1964.

Appiah, Peggy. ANANSE THE SPIDER: TALES FROM AN ASHANTI VILLAGE. Illus. Peggy Wilson. New York: Pantheon, 1966.

_____. TALES OF AN ASHANTI FATHER. Illus. Mora Dickson. Andre Deutsch, 1981. G

Arbuthnot, May Hill. THE ARBUTHNOT ANTHOLOLGY OF CHILDREN'S LITERATURE. Chicago: Scott, Foresman, 1961. P

_____. TIME FOR FAIRY TALES OLD AND NEW. Chicago: Scott, Foresman, 1961. P

_____. TIME FOR OLD MAGIC. Chicago: Scott, Foresman, 1970. P

Arkhurst, Joyce Cooper. THE ADVENTURES OF SPIDER: WEST AFRICAN FOLK TALES. Illus. Jerry Pinkney. Boston: Little, Brown, 1964.

Arnott, Kathleen. AFRICAN MYTHS AND LEGENDS. Illus. Joan Kiddell-Monroe. New York: Walck, c.1962, 1963.

_____. ANIMAL FOLK TALES AROUND THE WORLD. Illus. Bernadette Watts. New York: Walck, c.1970, 1971.

_____. TALES OF TEMBA: TRADITIONAL AFRICAN STORIES. Illus. Tom Feelings. New York: Walck, 1967.

Artzybasheff, Boris. SEVEN SIMEONS: A RUSSIAN TALE. Retold and illustrated by Boris Artzybasheff. New York: Viking, 1937. pb SEE ALSO: Aesop. AESOP'S TALES.

Aruego, Jose and Ariane Aruego. A CROCODILE'S TALE: A PHILIPPINE STORY. Illus. Jose and Ariane Aruego. Scholastic. G

Asbjørnsen, Peter Christen and Jørgen Moe. EAST OF THE SUN AND WEST OF THE MOON. Illus. Hedvig Collin. New York: Macmillan, 1953.

_____. EAST OF THE SUN AND WEST OF THE MOON. Retold by Gudrun Thorne-Thompson. Illus. Gregory Orloff. New York: Row, Peterson, 1946.

_____. EAST OF THE SUN AND WEST OF THE MOON, AND OTHER TALES COLLECTED BY P. C. ASBJØRNSEN AND JØRGEN F. MOE. Illus. Tom Vroman. New York: Macmillan, 1963.

_____. EAST OF THE SUN AND WEST OF THE MOON: OLD TALES FROM THE NORTH. Illus. Kay Nielsen. Garden City, New York: Doubleday, c.1976, 1977.

_____. EAST OF THE SUN AND WEST OF THE MOON: TWENTY-ONE NORWEGIAN FOLKTALES. Edited and illustrated by Ingri and Edgar Parin D'Aulaire. New York: Viking, 1938, c.1969.

_____. NORWEGIAN FOLK TALES. From the collection of Peter Christen Asbjørnsen and Jørgen Moe. Illus. Erik Wereskiold and Theodor Kittleson. New York: Viking, 1960.

_____. THE RUNAWAY PANCAKE. Trans. Joan Tate. Illus. Otto S. Svend. Larousse, 1980. G, pb

_____. THE SQUIRE'S BRIDE: A NORWEGIAN FOLKTALE. Illus. Marcia Sewall. New York: Atheneum, 1975. pb

_____. THE THREE BILLY GOATS GRUFF. Illus. Marcia Brown. New York: Harcourt, Brace & World, 1957. pb

_____. THE THREE BILLY GOATS GRUFF. Illus. Paul Galdone. New York: Seabury, 1973. pb

_____. THE THREE BILLY GOATS GRUFF. Reteller William Stobbs. Illus. William Stobbs. New York: McGraw-Hill, 1968. pb

Ashabranner, Brent. SEE Davis, Russell.

Asian Cultural Center for Unesco. FOLK TALES FROM ASIA FOR CHILDREN EVERYWHERE: BOOK ONE. New York: Weatherhill, 1975.

_____. FOLK TALES FROM ASIA FOR CHILDREN EVERYWHERE: BOOK TWO. New York: Weatherhill, 1975.

_____. FOLK TALES FROM ASIA FOR CHILDREN EVERYWHERE: BOOK THREE. New York: Weatherhill, 1976. P

_____. FOLK TALES FROM ASIA FOR CHILDREN EVERYWHERE: BOOK FOUR. New York: Weatherhill, 1976.

Association for Childhood Education International. TOLD UNDER THE GREEN UMBRELLA. New York: Macmillan, 1930.

Aulaire, Ingri and Edgar Parin D'. SEE D'Aulaire, Edgar Parin and Ingri.

Ayre, Robert. SKETCO THE RAVEN. Illus. Phillip Surrey. Toronto: Macmillan, 1961. G

Babbitt, Ellen C. SEE JATAKAS.

j398
Bag
Baker, Augusta. THE GOLDEN LYNX. Illus. Johannes Troyer. Philadelphia: Lippincott, 1960.

_____. THE TALKING TREE. Illus. Johannes Troyer. Philadelphia: Lippincott, 1955.

j398.2
Baker, Betty. AT THE CENTER OF THE WORLD. Illus. M. Tinkelman, New York: Macmillan, 1973.

_____. PARTNERS. Illus. Emily Arnold McCully. New York: Greenwillow, 1978. pb

j
Balet, Jan. THE FENCE: A MEXICAN TALE. Illus. Jan Balet. New York: Delacorte, 1969. pb

Bandeira Duarte. SEE Duarte.

j398.2
Bang, Betsy. THE OLD WOMAN AND THE RED PUMPKIN: A BENGALI FOLK TALE. Trans. and adapted by Betsy Bang. Illus. Molly Garrett Bang. New York: Macmillan, 1975. pb

j398.2
_____. THE OLD WOMAN AND THE RICE THIEF: APAPTED FROM A BENGALI FOLKTALE. Illus. Molly Garrett Bang. New York: Greenwillow, 1978. pb

j398.2
_____. TUNTUNI, THE TAILOR BIRD. Adapted from a Bengali Folktale by Betsy Bang. Illus. Molly Garrett Bang. New York: Greenwillow, 1978. pb

_____. WILEY AND THE HAIRY MAN. Adapted from an American Folk Tale. New York: Macmillan, 1976. pb

j398.2
Bang, Garrett. MEN FROM THE VILLAGE DEEP IN THE MOUNTAINS AND OTHER JAPANESE FOLK TALES. Trans. and illus. by Garrett Bang. New York: Macmillan, 1973.

j398.2
Bang, Molly. THE GOBLIN'S GIGGLE AND OTHER STORIES. Illus. Molly Bang. New York: Scribner's, 1973. pb

J
_____. TYE MAY AND THE MAGIC BRUSH. Adapted from the Chinese by Molly Bang. Illus. Molly Bang. New York: Greenwillow, 1981. G

Barash, Asher. A GOLDEN TREASURY OF JEWISH TALES. Trans. Murray Roston. New York: Dodd, Mead, 1966. G

Barbeau, Marius. THE GOLDEN PHOENIX AND OTHER FRENCH-CANADIAN FAIRY TALES. Retold by Michael Hornyansky. Illus. Arthur Price. New York: Walck, 1958.

j398.2
B24L
Barlow, Genevieve. LATIN AMERICAN TALES: FROM THE PAMPAS TO THE PYRAMIDS OF MEXICO. Illus. William M. Hutchinson. Chicago: Rand McNally, 1966.

Basile, Giovanni Battista. SEE MINCIELLI, ROSE LAURA.

Bason, Lillian. THOSE FOOLISH MOLBOES! Illus.

Margot Tomes. New York: Coward, McCann & Geoghegan, 1977.

J
Barth, Edna. JACK-O-LANTERN. Illus. Paul Galdone. New York: Seabury, 1974. pb

J 398.2
Bartoli, Jennifer. THE STORY OF THE GRATEFUL CRANE: A JAPANESE FOLKTALE. Illus. under the direction of Kozo Shimizui. Chicago: Albert Whitman, 1977. pb

Bates, Daisy. TALES TOLD TO KABBARLI: ABORIGINAL LEGENDS COLLECTED BY DAISY BATES. Retold by Barbara Ker Wilson. Illus. Harold Thomas. New York: Crown, 1972. G

Baumann, Kurt. THE PIED PIPER OF HAMELIN. illus. Jean Claverie. New York: Methuen, 1978. pb

j398.2
Baylor, Byrd. AND IT IS STILL THAT WAY: LEGENDS TOLD BY ARIZONA INDIAN CHILDREN. New York: Scribner's, 1976.

j398.2
B413
Bell, Corydon. JOHN RATTLING GOURD OF BIG COVE: A COLLECTION OF CHEROKEE INDIAN LEGENDS. New York: Macmillan, 1955. P

j398.2
Belpré, Pura. DANCE OF THE ANIMALS: A PUERTO RICAN FOLK TALE. Illus. Paul Galdone. New York: Warne, 1972. pb

_____. ONCE IN PUERTO RICO. Illus. Christine Price. New York: Warne, 1973. P

j398
B41P
_____. PEREZ AND MARTINA. Illus. Carlos Sanchez. New York: Warne, 1932. pb

j398.2
B41.8
_____. THE TIGER AND THE RABBIT AND OTHER TALES. Illus. Tomie de Paola. Philadelphia: Lippincott, 1965. *1946*

Belting, Natalia M. ELVES AND ELLEFOLK: TALES OF THE LITTLE PEOPLE. Illus. Gordon Laite. New York: Holt, Rinehart & Winston, 1961.

_____. THE LONG-TAILED BEAR AND OTHER INDIAN LEGENDS. Illus. Louis F. Carey. Indianapolis: Bobbs-Merrill, 1961.

Bernstein, Margery and Janet Kobrin. THE FIRST MORNING: AN AFRICAN MYTH. Illus. Enid Warner Romanek. New York: Scribner's, 1972, c.1976. pb

Berry Erick. THE MAGIC BANANA AND OTHER POLYNESIAN TALES. Illus. Nicholas Amorosi. New York: John Day, 1968.

Berson, Harold. HOW THE DEVIL GOT HIS DUE. Adapted and illus. by Harold Berson. New York: Crown, 1972. pb

j398.2
_____. KASSIM'S SHOES. Illus. by Harold Berson. New York: Crown, 1972. pb *1977*

_____. THE THIEF WHO HUGGED A MOONBEAM. Illus. Harold Berson. New York: Seabury, 1972. pb

J398.2

Berson, Harold. WHY THE JACKAL WON'T SPEAK TO THE HEDGEHOG: A TUNISIAN FOLK TALE. Retold and illus. by Harold Berson. New York: Seabury, 1969. pb

Bierhorst, John. BLACK RAINBOW: LEGENDS OF THE INCAS AND MYTHS OF ANCIENT PERU. Edited and trans. by John Bierhorst. Illus. Jane Byers Bierhorst. New York: Farrar, Straus & Giroux, 1976. N

_____. THE FIRE PLUME: LEGENDS OF THE AMERICAN INDIANS. Collected by Henry Rowe Schoolcraft. Illus. Alan E. Cober. New York: Dial, 1969.

_____. THE RING IN THE PRAIRIE. A SHAWNEE LEGEND. Illus. Leo and Diane Dillon. New York: Dial, 1970. pb

Birch, Cyril. CHINESE MYTHS AND FANTASIES. Illus. Joan Kiddell-Monroe. New York: Walck, 1961.

Bird, Traveller (Tsisghwanai). THE PATH TO SNOWBIRD MOUNTAIN: CHEROKEE LEGENDS. New York: Farrar, Straus & Giroux, 1972. G

J398.2 Black, Algernon D. THE WOMAN IN THE WOOD: A TALE FROM OLD RUSSIA. Illus. Evaline Ness. New York: Holt, Rinehart, Winston, 1973. pb

Bleecker, Mary Noel. BIG MUSIC OR TWENTY MERRY TALES TO TELL. Illus. Louis S. Glanzman. New York: Viking, 1946.

Bloch, Marie Halum, translator. IVANKO AND THE DRAGON: AN OLD UKRAINIAN FOLK TALE. From the Original Collection of Ivan Rudchenko. Illus. Yaroslava. New York: Atheneum, 1969. pb

J.398.2 _____. UKRAINAIN FOLK TALES. Trans. from the Original Collections of Ivan Rudchenko and Maria Lukiyanenko. Illus. J. Hnizdovsky. New York: Coward, McCann, 1964.

Boden, Alice. THE FIELD OF BUTTERCUPS. New York: Walck, 1974. pb

J398.2 Boggs, Ralph Steele and Mary Gould Davis. THREE GOLDEN ORANGES AND OTHER SPANISH FOLK TALES. Illus. Emma Brock. New York: McKay, c.1936, c.1964.

SEE ALSO Jagendorf, Moritz. THE KING OF THE MOUNTAIN.

Bollinger, Max. NOAH AND THE RAINBOW: AN ANCIENT STORY. Trans. Clyde Robert Bulla. Illus. Helga Aichinger. New York: Crowell, 1972. pb

J398.2 Bonnet, Leslie. CHINESE FOLK AND FAIRY TALES. Illus. Maurice Brevannes. New York: Putnam, 1958. P

Bontemps, Arna and Jack Conroy. THE FAST SOONER HOUND. Illus. Virginia Lee Burton.

Boston: Houghton Mifflin, 1942. pb

J398 Borski, Lucia Merecka. GOOD SENSE AND GOOD FORTUNE AND OTHER POLISH FOLK TALES. Illus. Erica Gorecka-Egan. New York: McKay, 1970.

J398 Borski, Lucia Merecka and Kate B. Miller. THE JOLLY TAILOR AND OTHER FAIRY TALES. Trans. from the Polish. Illus. Kazimir Klepacki. New York: McKay, 1928, c.1956. P

J398.2 Bosley, Keith. THE DEVIL'S HORSE: TALES FROM THE KALEVALA. New York: Pantheon, 1966. G

J398.2 Boucher, Alan. MEAD MOONDAUGHTER AND OTHER ICELANDIC FOLK TALES. Illus. Karolina Larusdottir. Philadelphia: Chilton, 1967. N

Bowes, Anne LeBastille. BIRD KINGDOM OF THE MAYAS. Illus. Anita Benarde. Princeton, N.J.: Van Nostrand, 1967.

J398.2 Bowman, James Cloyd and Margery Bianco. TALES FROM A FINNISH TUPA. From a translation by Aili Kolehmainen. Illus. Laura Bannon. Chicago: Albert Whitman, 1936, 1964.

Brenner, Barbara. LITTLE ONE INCH. Illus. Fred Brenner. New York: Coward, McCann & Geoghegan, 1977. pb

J398.2 Bro, Margueritte Harmon. HOW THE MOUSE DEER BECAME KING. Illus. Joseph Low. Garden City, N.Y.: Doubleday, 1966.

Brockett, Eleanor. BURMESE AND THAI FAIRY TALES. Illus. Harry and Ilse Toothill. Chicago: Follett, c.1965, 1967.

_____. PERSIAN FAIRY TALES. Illus. Harry Toothill. New York: Follett, 1962. G

J741 Brooke, Leslie. THE GOLDEN GOOSE BOOK. Illus. Leslie Brooke. New York: Warne, 1905. pb

J741 _____. THE STORY OF THE THREE BEARS. Illus. Leslie Brooke. New York: Warne, 1934. pb

J741 _____. THE STORY OF THE THREE LITTLE PIGS AND HISTORY OF TOM THUMB. Illus. Leslie Brooke. New York: Warne, n.d. pb

SEE ALSO Grimm. HOUSE IN THE WOOD.

J398.2 Brown, Dee. TEPEE TALES OF THE AMERICAN INDIAN. Retold for Our Times by Dee Brown. Illus. Louis Mofsie. New York: Holt, Rinehart and Winston, 1979.

Brown, Marcia. BACKBONE OF THE KING: THE STORY OF PAKA'A AND HIS SON KU. New York: Scribner's, 1966. G

J398.2 _____. THE BLUE JACKAL. Told and illus. by Marcia Brown. New York: Scribner's, 1977. pb

J398.2 _____. THE BUN: A TALE FROM RUSSIA.

Illustrated by the author. New York: Harcourt, Brace, Jovanovich, 1972. G, pb

Brown, Marcia. DICK WHITTINGTON AND HIS CAT. Told and cut in linoleum by Marcia Brown. New York: Scribner's, 1950. pb

_____. THE NEIGHBORS. Told and illustrated by Marcia Brown. New York: Scribner's, 1967. pb

_____. ONCE A MOUSE. A fable cut in wood by Marcia Brown. New York: Scribner's, 1961. pb

_____. STONE SOUP: AN OLD TALE. Illus. Marcia Brown. New York: Scribner's, 1947. pb

Bruchac, Joseph. TURKEY BROTHER AND OTHER TALES: IROQUOIS FOLK STORIES. Illus. Kahonhes. Trumansburg, New York: The Crossing Press, 1975.

Bryan, Ashley. THE ADVENTURES OF AKU. Retold and illustrated by Ashley Bryan. New York: Atheneum, 1976.

_____. BEAT THE STORY DRUM, PUM-PUM. Illustrated by the author. New York: Atheneum, 1980. G

_____. THE DANCING GRANNY. Retold and illustrated by Ashley Bryan. New York: Atheneum, 1977. pb

_____. THE OX OF THE WONDERFUL HORNS AND OTHER AFRICAN FOLKTALES. Illustrated by the author. New York: Atheneum, 1971.

Bryant, Sara Cone. THE BURNING RICE FIELDS. Illus. Mamoru Funai. New York: Holt, Rinehart and Winston, 1963. pb

_____. EPAMINONDAS AND HIS AUNTIE. Illus. Inez Hogan. Boston: Houghton Mifflin, 1907. pb

Buck, Pearl S. FAIRY TALES OF THE ORIENT. Illus. Jeanyee Wong. New York: Simon & Schuster, 1965. P

Buffet, Guy and Pam. PUA PUA LENA LENA AND THE MAGIC KIHA-PU. Ed. Ruth Tabrah. Illus. Guy Buffet. New York: Weatherhill (Island Heritage), 1972. G, pb

Bulatkin, I. F. EURASIAN FOLK AND FAIRY TALES. Illus. Howard Simon. New York: Criterion, 1965.

Bunter, Bill M. J. DJUGURBA: TALES FROM THE SPIRIT TIME. Bloomington: Indiana University Press (Australian National University Press), c. 1974, 1976. G

Burton, William Frederick Padwick. THE MAGIC DRUM: TALES FROM CENTRAL AFRICA.

Illus. Ralph Thompson. New York: Criterion, c. 1961, 1962.

Calhoun, Mary. THE WITCH'S PIG: A CORNISH FOLKTALE. Illus. Lady McCrady. New York: Morrow, 1977. pb

Campbell, Camilla. STAR MOUNTAIN AND OTHER LEGENDS OF MEXICO. Illus. Frederic Marvin. New York: McGraw-Hill, 1946. G

Carey, Bonnie. BABA YAGA'S GEESE, AND OTHER RUSSIAN STORIES. Illus. Guy Fleming. Bloomington, Indiana: Indiana University Press, 1973. P

SEE ALSO GRASSHOPPER TO THE RESCUE.

Carle, Eric. ERIC CARLE'S STORYBOOK: SEVEN TALES BY THE BROTHERS GRIMM. Illustrated and retold by Eric Carle. New York: Watts, 1976.

Carlson, Natalie Savage. SASHES RED AND BLUE. Illus. Rita Fave. New York: Harper, 1956. P

_____. THE TALKING CAT, AND OTHER STORIES OF FRENCH CANADA. Illus. Roger Duvoisin. New York: Harper, 1952. P

Carpenter, Frances. AFRICAN WONDER TALES. Illus. Joseph Escourido. Garden City, New York: Doubleday, 1963.

_____. THE ELEPHANT'S BATHTUB. WONDER TALES FROM THE FAR EAST. Illus. Hans Guggenheim. Garden City, New York: Doubleday, 1962.

_____. PEOPLE FROM THE SKY: AINU TALES FROM NORTHERN JAPAN. Illus. Betty Fraser. Garden City, New York: Doubleday, 1972. G

_____. SOUTH AMERICAN WONDER TALES. Illus. Ralph Creasman. Chicago: Follett, 1969.

_____. TALES OF A CHINESE GRAND-MOTHER. Illus. Malthe Hasselriis. Garden City, New York: Doubleday, 1937.

_____. TALES OF A KOREAN GRAND-MOTHER. Illustrated with reproductions from old Korean paintings. Garden City, New York: Doubleday, 1947.

_____. WONDER TALES OF CATS AND DOGS. Illus. Ezra Jack Keats. Garden City, New York: Doubleday, 1955.

_____. WONDER TALES OF SEAS AND SHIPS. Illus. Peter Spier. Garden City, New York: Doubleday, 1959. N

Carrick, Malcolm. THE WISE MEN OF GOTHAM. Illus. Malcolm Carrick. New York: Viking, 1973. G

Carrick, Valery J. MORE RUSSIAN PICTURE TALES. Trans. Nevill Forbes. Illus. Valery J. Carrick. New York: Dover, 1970. G

_____. STILL MORE RUSSIAN PICTURE TALES. Trans. Nevill Forbes. Illus. by Vallery J. Carrick. New York: Dover, 1970.

Carter, Dorothy Sharp. THE ENCHANTED ORCHARD AND OTHER FOLKTALES OF CENTRAL AMERICA. Illus. W. T. Mars. New York: Harcourt, Brace, Jovanovich, 1973.

_____. GREEDY MARIANI AND OTHER FOLKTALES OF THE ANTILLES. Illus. Trina Schart Hyman. New York: Atheneum, 1974.

Caswell, Helen. SHADOWS FROM THE SINGING HOUSE. Illus. Robert Mayokok. Rutland, Vt.: Tuttle, 1968.

Cathon, Laura E. and Thusnelda Schmidt. PERHAPS AND PERCHANCE. TALES OF NATURE. Illus. Anne Marie Jauss. Nashville: Abingdon, 1962. P

j398.2 Cauley, Lorinda Bryan. THE GOOSE AND THE GOLDEN COINS. Illus. Lorinda Bryan Cauley. Harcourt, Brace, Jovanovich, 1981. G, pb

Chafetz, Henry. THUNDERBIRD AND OTHER STORIES. Illus. Ronni Solbert. New York: Pantheon, 1964.

Chang, Isabelle. CHINESE FAIRY TALES. Illus. Shirley Errickson. New York: Schocken, 1965.

j398z.2 _____. TALES FROM OLD CHINA. Illus. Tommy Chen. New York: Random, 1948. 1968

j398.2 Chase, Richard. GRANDFATHER TALES: AMERICAN-ENGLISH FOLK TALES. Illus. Berkeley Williams, Jr. Boston: Houghton Mifflin, 1948.

_____. JACK AND THE THREE SILLIES. Illus. Joshua Tolford. Boston: Houghton Mifflin, 1950. pb

j398.2
C38
_____. THE JACK TALES. Appendix compiled by Herbert Halpert. Illus. Berkeley Williams. Boston: Houghton Mifflin, 1943.

_____. WICKED JOHN AND THE DEVIL. Illus. Joshua Tolford. Boston: Houghton Mifflin, 1951. pb

j821.17
C39cf
Chaucer, Geoffrey. CHANTICLEER AND THE FOX. Adapted and illustrated by Barbara Cooney. New York: Crowell, 1958. pb

Cheney, Cora. TALES FROM A TAIWAN KITCHEN. Illustrated with Chinese paper cuttings by Teng Kung Yun-Chang (Grandma Teng) and others. New York: Dodd, Mead, 1976.

Cheng, Hou-Tien. SIX CHINESE BROTHERS: AN ANCIENT TALE. Illustrated with scissor cuts by Hou-Tien Cheng. New York: Holt, Rinehart

& Winston, 1979. pb

Cheou, Kang-Sié. A BUTTERFLY'S DREAM AND OTHER CHINESE TALES. Illus. Chi Kang. Rutland, Vt.: Tuttle, 1950. G

j Child Study Association of America. CASTLES AND DRAGONS: READ-TO-YOURSELF FAIRY TALES FOR BOYS AND GIRLS. Illus. William Pène du Bois. New York: Crowell, 1958. P

Chimenti, Elisa. TALES AND LEGENDS OF MOROCCO. Trans. Arnon Benamy. Ivan Obolensky, 1965. G

j Chrisman, Arthur Davie. SHEN OF THE SEA: A BOOK FOR CHILDREN. New York: Dutton, 1925. P

j398.2
Cimino, Maria. THE DISOBEDIENT EELS AND OTHER ITALIAN TALES. Illus. Claire Nivola. New York: Pantheon, 1970.

Clark, Ann Nolan. IN THE LAND OF SMALL DRAGON: A VIETNAMESE FOLKTALE. Told by Dang Manh Kha to Ann Nolan Clark. Illus. Tony Chen. New York: Viking, 1979. pb

Clark, Ella E. INDIAN LEGENDS OF THE PACIFIC NORTHWEST. Illus. Robert Bruce Inverarity. Berkeley, California: University of California Press, 1966. G

j398.2
Coalson, Glo. THREE STONE WOMAN. New York: Atheneum, 1971. G, pb

Cobble, Alice D. WEMBI, THE SINGER OF STORIES. Illus. Doris Hallas. St. Louis: Bethany, 1959.

Colum, Padraic. LEGENDS OF HAWAII. Illus. Don Forrer. New Haven: Yale University Press, 1937. P

j _____. THE STONE OF VICTORY AND OTHER TALES. Illus. Judith Gwyn Brown. New York: McGraw-Hill, 1966. P

Colwell, Eileen. THE MAGIC UMBRELLA AND OTHER STORIES FOR TELLING. Illus. Shirley Felts. New York: McKay, 1976.

j398.2
_____. ROUND ABOUT AND LONG AGO: TALES FROM THE ENGLISH COUNTIES. Illus. Anthony Colbert. Boston: Houghton-Mifflin, c.1972, 1974.

j398
_____. A SECOND STORYTELLER'S CHOICE: A SELECTION OF STORIES WITH NOTES ON HOW TO TELL THEM. Illus. Prudence Seward. New York: Walck, 1965.

j808.8
_____. THE YOUNGEST STORYBOOK: A COLLECTION OF STORIES AND RHYMES FOR THE YOUNGEST. Illus. Margery Gill. New York: Watts, c.1967, 1968. P

Compton, Margaret, pseud. SEE HARRISON, AMELIA.

Conger, Lesley. TOPS AND BOTTOMS. Illus. Imero Gobbato. New York: Four Winds, 1970. pb

Cooke, Donald Ewin. SORCERER'S APPRENTICE. Illus. Donald E. Cooke. Philadelphia: Winston, 1947. pb

Coombs, Patricia. THE MAGIC POT. New York: Lothrop, Lee & Shepard, 1977. pb

Cooper, Lee. FIVE FABLES FROM FRANCE. Illus. Charles Keeping. Abelard-Schuman, 1970.

Corrin, Sam & Stephen. MRS. FOX'S WEDDING. Illus. Errol Le Cain. Garden City, N.Y.: Doubleday, 1980. pb

Cothran, Jean. THE MAGIC CALABASH: FOLK TALES FROM AMERICA'S ISLANDS AND ALASKA. Illus. Clifford N. Geary. New York: McKay, 1956.

_____. WITH A WIG, WITH A WAG, AND OTHER AMERICAN FOLK TALES. Illus. Clifford N. Geary. New York: McKay, 1954.

Courlander, Harold. KANTCHIL'S LIME PIT AND OTHER STORIES FROM INDONESIA. Illus. Robert W. Kane. New York: Harcourt, Brace, 1950.

_____. THE KING'S DRUM, AND OTHER AFRICAN STORIES. Illus. Enrico Arno. New York: Harcourt, Brace & World, 1962.

_____. PEOPLE OF THE SHORT BLUE CORN: TALES AND LEGENDS OF THE HOPI INDIANS. Illus. Enrico Arno. New York: Harcourt, Brace Jovanovich, 1970. P

_____. THE PIECE OF FIRE, AND OTHER HAITIAN TALES. Illus. Beth and Joe Krush. New York: Harcourt, 1942, 1964.

_____. RIDE WITH THE SUN: AN ANTHOLOGY OF FOLK TALES AND STORIES FROM THE UNITED NATIONS. For the United Nation's Women's Guild. Illus. Roger Duvoisin. New York: Whittlesey House, 1955.

_____. TERRAPIN'S POT OF SENSE. Illus. Elton Fax. New York: Holt, 1957.

_____. THE TIGER'S WHISKER, AND OTHER TALES AND LEGENDS FROM ASIA AND THE PACIFIC. Illus. Enrico Arno. New York: Harcourt, Brace & World, 1959.

_____. UNCLE BOUQUI OF HAITI. Illus. Lucy Herndon Crockett. New York: Morrow, 1942. P

Courlander, Harold and Ezekiel A. Eshugbayi. OLODE THE HUNTER, AND OTHER TALES FROM NIGERIA. Illus. Enrico Arno. New York: Harcourt, Brace & World, 1968.

Courlander, Harold and George Herzog. THE COW-TAIL SWITCH AND OTHER WEST AFRICAN STORIES. Illus. Madye Lee Chastain. New York: Holt, Rinehart and Winston, 1947.

Courlander, Harold and Wolf Leslau. THE FIRE ON THE MOUNTAIN AND OTHER ETHIOPIAN STORIES. Illus. Robert W. Kane. New York: Holt, 1950.

Courlander, Harold and Albert Kofi Prempeh. THE HAT-SHAKING DANCE, AND OTHER TALES FROM THE GOLD COAST. Illus. Enrico Arno. New York: Harcourt, Brace, 1957.

Craig, M. Jean. THE DONKEY PRINCE. Adapted from Grimm by M. Jean Craig. Illus. Barbara Cooney. Garden City, N.Y.: Doubleday, 1977. pb

Credle, Ellis. BIG FRAID AND LITTLE FRAID. Illus. Ellis Credle. New York: Nelson, 1964. pb

_____. TALL TALES FROM THE HIGH HILLS. Illus. Richard Bennett. New York: Nelson, 1957.

Crompton, Anne Eliot. THE WINTER WIFE: AN ABENAKI FOLKTALE. Illus. Robert Andrew Parker. Boston: Little, Brown, 1975. pb

Crossley-Holland, Kevin, reteller. THE PEDLAR OF SWAFFHAM. Illus. Margaret Gordon. New York: Seabury, 1971. pb

Crouch, Marcus. THE IVORY CITY: AND OTHER STORIES FROM INDIA AND PAKISTAN. Illus. William Stobbs. Pelham, 1981. G

Cunningham, Caroline. THE TALKING STONE. Illus. Richard Floethe. New York: Knopf, 1939.

Curcija-Prodanovic, Nada. HEROES OF SERBIA. FOLK BALLADS. Illus. Dusan Ristic. New York: Walck, 1969. G

_____. YUGOSLAV FOLK-TALES. Illus. Joan Kiddell-Monroe. New York: Walck, 1957, 1960. G

Curley, Daniel. BILLY BEG AND THE BULL. Illus. Frank Bozzo. New York: Crowell, 1978. pb

Curry, Jane Louise. DOWN FROM THE LONELY MOUNTAIN. CALIFORNIA INDIAN TALES. Illus. Enrico Arno. New York: Harcourt, Brace & World, 1965.

Curtis, Edward S. THE GIRL WHO MARRIED A GHOST AND OTHER TALES FROM THE NORTH AMERICAN INDIAN. Collected, and with photographs by Edward S. Curtis. Ed. John Bierhorst. New York: Four Winds, 1978.

Cutt, Nancy and W. Towrie. THE HOGBOON OF HELL AND OTHER STRANGE ORKNEY TALES. Illus. Richard Kennedy. London: André Deutsch, 1979.

Dalgliesh, Alice. THE ENCHANTED BOOK. Illus. Concetta Cacciola. New York: Scribner's, 1947.

Damjan, Mischa. IVAN THE WITCH: A RUSSIAN

TALE. Adapted by Mischa Damjan. Illus. Toma Bogdanovic. New York: McGraw-Hill, 1969. pb

Danaher, Kevin. FOLKTALES OF THE IRISH COUNTRYSIDE. Illus. Harold Berson. New York: David White, 1970.

j398 Daniels, Guy. FALCON UNDER THE HAT: RUSSIAN MERRY TALES AND FAIRY TALES. Illus. Feodor Rojankovsky. New York: Funk & Wagnalls, 1969.

_____. FOMA THE TERRIBLE: A RUSSIAN FOLKTALE. Illus. Imero Gobbato. New York: Delacorte, 1970. pb

j398.2 _____. THE PEASANT'S PEA PATCH: A RUSSIAN FOLKTALE. Illus. Robert Quackenbush. New York: Delacorte, 1971. G, pb

j808.2 Darrell, Margery, editor. ONCE UPON A TIME: THE FAIRY TALE WORLD OF ARTHUR RACKHAM. New York: Viking, 1972.

j398.2 Dasent, George Webbe. THE CAT ON THE DOVREFELL: A CHRISTMAS TALE. Illus. Tomie de Paola. New York: Putnam, 1979. pb

D'Aulaire, Edgar Parin and Ingri. D'AULAIRE'S TROLLS. Illus. Edgar and Ingri D'Aulaire. Garden City, N.Y.: Doubleday, 1972. P

j741 _____. DON'T COUNT YOUR CHICKS. Garden City, N.Y.: Doubleday, 1943. pb

Davis, Mary Gould. A BAKER'S DOZEN, THIRTEEN STORIES TO TELL AND TO READ ALOUD. Illus. Emma Brock. New York: Harcourt, 1930.

_____. THE TRUCE OF THE WOLF AND OTHER TALES OF OLD ITALY. Illus. Jan Van Everen. New York: Harcourt, Brace, 1931. N

SEE ALSO Boggs, Ralph Steele. THREE GOLDEN ORANGES.

Davis, May Gould and Ernest Balintuma Kalibala. WAKAIMA AND THE CLAY MAN AND OTHER AFRICAN FOLKTALES. New York: Longman, Green, 1946. N

j398.2 D297L Davis, Russell and Brent Ashabranner. The LION'S WHISKERS: TALES OF HIGH AFRICA. Illus. James G. Teason. Boston: Little, Brown, 1959.

j398.2 D33W Dayrell, Elphinstone. WHY THE SUN AND THE MOON LIVE IN THE SKY. Illus. Blair Lent. Boston: Houghton Mifflin, 1968. pb

j398.2 D363C De La Iglesia, Marie Elena. THE CAT AND THE MOUSE AND OTHER SPANISH TALES. Illus. Joseph Low. New York: Pantheon, 1966.

De La Mare, Walter. ANIMAL STORIES. New York: Scribner's, c.1939, 1940. P

_____. JACK AND THE BEANSTALK. Illus. Joseph Low. New York: Knopf, c.1927, 1959. pb

De La Mare, Walter. TALES TOLD AGAIN. Illus. Alan Howard. New York: Knopf, 1927, 1959.

De Larue, Paul. FRENCH FAIRY TALES. Illus. Warren Chappell. New York: Knopf, c.1956, c.1968. G

De Leeuw, Adèle. INDONESIAN LEGENDS AND FOLK TALES. Illus. Ronni Solbert. New York: Nelson, 1961.

_____. LEGENDS AND FOLK TALES OF HOLLAND. Illus. Paul Kennedy. New York: Nelson, 1963. P

De Paola, Tomie. THE CLOWN OF GOD: AN OLD STORY. Told and illus. by Tomie de Paola. New York: Harcourt, Brace Jovanovich, 1978. pb

_____. FIN M'COUL: THE GIANT OF KNOCKMANY HILL. Illus. Tomie de Paola. Holiday, 1981. G

_____. STREGA NONA: AN OLD TALE RETOLD AND ILLUSTRATED BY TOMIE DE PAOLA. Englewood Cliffs, N.J.: Prentice-Hall, 1975. pb

j398. D449 De Regniers, Beatrice Schenk. THE GIANT BOOK. Illus. William Lahey Cummings. New York: Atheneum, 1966. P

j398 _____. LITTLE SISTER AND THE MONTH BROTHERS. Pictures by Margot Tomes. New York: Seabury, 1976. pb

Deutsch, Babette and Avrahm Yarmolinsky. MORE TALES OF FARAWAY FOLK. Illus. Janina Domanska. New York: Harper & Row, 1963.

j _____. TALES OF FARAWAY FOLK. Illus. Irene Lorentowicz. New York: Harper, 1952.

Dewey, Ariane. THE THUNDER GOD'S SON: A PERUVIAN FOLKTALE. Illus. Ariane Dewey. New York: Greenwillow, 1981. G, pb

j398.2 De Wit, Dorothy. THE TALKING STONE: AN ANTHOLOGY OF NATIVE AMERICAN TALES AND LEGENDS. New York: Greenwillow, 1979. P

j398 Diamond, Donna. SEE Grimm. THE SEVEN RAVENS.

j398 Dobbs, Rose. MORE ONCE-UPON-A-TIME STORIES. Illus. Flavia Gág. New York: Random, 1961.

j _____. NO ROOM. Illus. Fritz Eichenberg. New York: Coward-McCann, 1944. pb

j372 D65 _____. ONCE UPON A TIME. TWENTY CHEERFUL TALES TO READ AND TELL. Illus. Flavia Gág. New York: Random, 1950. P

Dolch, Edward W. and Marguerite P. Dolch. PUEBLO STORIES. Illus. Robert S. Kerr. Champaign, Ill.: Garrard, 1956. P

_____. STORIES FROM ALASKA. Illus. Carl Heldt. Champaign, Ill.: Garrard, 1961. P

Dolch, Edward W. and Marguerite P. Dolch. STORIES FROM OLD CHINA. Champaign, Ill.: Garrard, 1964.

_____. STORIES FROM OLD RUSSIA. Champaign, Ill.: Garrard, 1962.

j398.2 Domanska, Janina. BEST OF THE BARGAIN. New York: Greenwillow, 1977. pb

j398.2 _____. KING KRAKUS AND THE DRAGON. New York: Greenwillow, 1979. pb G

j _____. LOOK, THERE IS A TURTLE FLYING. Illus. Janina Domanska. New York: Macmillan, 1968. pb

j _____. MARILKA. Illus. Janina Domanska. New York: Macmillan, 1970. pb

_____. THE TORTOISE AND THE TREE: ADAPTED FROM A BANTU FOLKTALE. New York: Greenwillow, 1978. pb

j398.2 _____. THE TURNIP. Illus. Janina Domanska. New York: Macmillan, 1969. pb

j398.2 Dorliae, Peter G. ANIMALS MOURN FOR DA LEOPARD, AND OTHER WEST AFRICAN TALES. Illus. Irein Wangboje. Indianapolis: Bobbs-Merrill, 1970.

j398.2 D75r Downing, Charles. RUSSIAN TALES AND LEGENDS. Illus. Joan Kiddell-Monroe. New York: Walck, 1957.

_____. TALES OF THE HODJA. Illus. William Papas. New York: Walck, 1965.

Duarte, Margarida Estrela Bandeira. THE LEGEND OF THE PALM TREE. Illus. Paulo Werneck. New York: Grosset, 1940. pb

DuBois, William Pène, illustrator. THE THREE LITTLE PIGS. New York: Viking, 1962. pb

DuBois, William Pène and Lee Po. THE HARE AND THE TORTOISE AND THE TORTOISE AND THE HARE: LA LIEBRE Y LA TORTUGA Y LA TORTUGA Y LA LIEBRE. Garden City, N.Y.: Doubleday, 1972. pb

j398.2 Duff, Maggie. RUM PUM PUM: A FOLKTALE FROM INDIA. Pictures by Jose Aruego and Ariane Dewey. New York: Macmillan, 1978. pb

j398.2 D93t Durham, Mae. TIT FOR TAT, AND OTHER LATVIAN FOLK TALES. Retold by Mae Durham from the translation of Skaidrite Rubene-Koo. Notes by Alan Dundes. Illus. Harriet Pincus. New York: Harcourt, Brace & World, 1967.

_____. TOBEI: A JAPANESE FOLKTALE. illus. Mitsu Yashima. Scarsdale, N.Y.: Bradbury, 1974. G

Duvoisin, Roger. THE THREE SNEEZES AND OTHER SWISS TALES. Illus. Roger Duvoisin. New York: Knopf, c.1941, 1957.

j398.2 Ed50 Edmonds, I. G. OOKA THE WISE: TALES OF OLD JAPAN. Illus. Sanae Yamazaki. Indianapolia: Bobbs-Merrill, 1961.

_____. THE POSSIBLE, IMPOSSIBLES OF IKKYU THE WISE. Illus. Robert Byrd. Philadelphia: Macrae Smith, 1971. P

j398.2 Ed5t _____. TRICKSTER TALES. Illus. Sean Morrison. Philadelphia: Lippincott, 1966.

Eells, Elsie Spicer. FAIRY TALES FROM BRAZIL: HOW AND WHY TALES FROM BRAZILIAN FOLKLORE. Illus. Helen M. Barton. New York: Dodd, Mead, c.1917, 1950. N

_____. TALES FROM THE AMAZON. Illus. Florence Choate and Elizabeth Curtis. New York: Dodd, Mead, c.1927, 1958. N

_____. TALES OF ENCHANTMENT FROM SPAIN. Illus. Maud and Miska Petersham. New York: Dodd, Mead, 1950. N

j398.2 Ek7t Ekrem, Selma. TURKISH FAIRY TALES. Illus. Lila Bayrack. New York: Van Nostrand, 1964. P

j Elkin, Benjamin. SIX FOOLISH FISHERMEN. Illus. Katherine Evans. Chicago: Childrens Press, 1957. pb

j _____. WHY THE SUN WAS LATE. Illus. Jerome Snyder. New York: Parent's Magazine Press, 1966. pb

Erdoes, Richard. THE SOUND OF FLUTES AND OTHER INDIAN LEGENDS. Told by Lame Deer, Jenny Leading Cloud, Leonard Crow Dog, and others. Illus. Paul Goble. New York: Pantheon, 1976. G

j398 Evans, C.S. THE SLEEPING BEAUTY. Told by C. S. Evans. Illus. Arthur Rackham. New York: Viking, 1920, 1972. pb

j Evans, Katherine. A BUNDLE OF STICKS. Illus. Katherine Evans. Chicago: Albert Whitman, 1962. pb

j _____. THE MICE THAT ATE IRON. Illus. Katherine Evans. Chicago: Albert Whitman, 1963. pb

Farjeon, Eleanor and William Mayne. A CAVALCADE OF KINGS. Illus. Victor Ambrus. New York: Walck, 1965. P

_____. A CAVALCADE OF QUEENS. Illus. Victor Ambrus. New York: Walck, 1965. P

j398.2 Faulkner, William. THE DAYS WHEN THE ANIMALS TALKED: BLACK AMERICAN FOLKTALES AND HOW THEY CAME TO BE. Illus. Tony Howell. Chicago: Follett, 1977.

Feinstein, Alan S. FOLK TALES FROM SIAM. illus. Pat Pibulsonggram. New York: A. S. Barnes, 1969. G

J Fenner, Phyllis R. ADVENTURE: RARE AND MAGICAL. Illus. Henry C. Pitz. New York: Knopf, 1945.

J _____. GHOSTS, GHOSTS, GHOSTS. Illus. Manning de V. Lee. New York: Watts, 1952. P

_____. GIANTS AND WITCHES, AND A DRAGON OR TWO. Illus. Henry C. Pitz. New York: Knopf, 1943.

J398 F36 _____. PRINCESSES AND PEASANT BOYS: TALES OF ENCHANTMENT. Illus. Henry C. Pitz. New York: Knopf, 1944.

_____. TIME TO LAUGH: FUNNY TALES FROM HERE AND THERE. Illus. Henry C. Pitz. New York: Knopf, 1942. P

Field, Edward. ESKIMO SONGS AND STORIES. Collected by Knud Rasmussen on the fifth Thule Expedition. Selected and Translated by Edward Field. Illus. Kiakshuk and Pudlo. New York: Delacorte Press /S. Lawrence, 1973.

J398 F458 Field, Rachel. AMERICAN FOLK AND FAIRY TALES. Illus. Margaret Freeman. New York: Scribner's, 1929. P

J398 Fillmore, Parker. THE LAUGHING PRINCE: A BOOK OF YUGOSLAV FAIRY TALES AND FOLK TALES. Illus. Jay Van Everen. New York: Harcourt, Brace & World, 1921.

_____. MIGHTY MIKKO: A BOOK OF FINNISH FAIRY TALES AND FOLK TALES. Illus. Jay Van Everen. New York: Harcourt, Brace & World, 1922.

J398 F485 _____. THE SHEPHERD'S NOSEGAY: STORIES FROM FINLAND AND CZECHOSLO-VAKIA. Edited by Katherine Love. Illus. Enrico Arno. New York: Harcourt, Brace & World, 1919, 1958.

J398 F48 _____. THE SHOEMAKER'S APRON: A SEC-OND BOOK OF CZECHOSLOVAK FAIRY TALES AND FOLK TALES. Illus. Jan Matulka. New York: Harcourt, Brace, c.1919, 1920, 1922, c.1958.

J398 F49 Finger, Charles Joseph. TALES FROM SILVER LANDS. Illus. Paul Honore. Garden City, N.Y.: Doubleday, 1924. P

Finlay, Winifred. TATTERCOATS AND OTHER FOLKTALES. Illus. Shirley Hughes. New York: Harvey House, 1976.

J398.2 THE FIREBIRD, AND OTHER RUSSIAN FAIRY TALES. Illus. by Boris Zvorykin. Ed. and with an introduction by Jacqueline Onassis. New York: Viking, 1978. G

J398.2 F51m Firethunder, Billy. MOTHER MEADOWLARK AND BROTHER SNAKE. An Indian Legend by Billy Firethunder. Illus. John Peterson. New York: Holt, Rinehart & Winston, 1963. pb

Fischer, Hans. SEE Grimm. GOOD-FOR-NOTHINGS, TRAVELING MUSICIANS.

Fisher, Anne B. STORIES CALIFORNIA INDIANS TOLD. Illus. Ruth Robbins. Berkeley, Calif.: Parnassus Press, 1957.

Foster, Ruth. THE STONE HORSEMEN. TALES FROM THE CAUCASUS. Illus. Judith Gwyn Brown. Indianapolis: Bobbs-Merrill, 1965. G

J398.2 Fournier, Catharine. THE COCONUT THIEVES. Illus. Janina Domanska. New York: Scribner's, 1964. pb

Frobenius, Leo and Douglas C. Fox. AFRICAN GENESIS. New York: Benjamin Blom, 1937, 1966. N

Front, Sheila. THE THREE SILLIES. Illus. Charles Front. New York: Addison-Wesley, 1974. pb

J398.2 Frost, Frances. LEGENDS OF THE UNITED NA-TIONS. New York: Whittlesey House, 1943. P

J398.2 Fuja, Abayomi. FOURTEEN HUNDRED COWRIES, AND OTHER AFRICAN TALES. Illus. Ademola Olugebefola. New York: Lothrop, Lee & Shepard, 1971.

Gaer, Joseph. THE FABLES OF INDA. Illus. Randy Monk. Boston: Little, Brown, 1955. P

J Gág, Wanda. GONE IS GONE, OR THE STORY OF A MAN WHO WANTED TO DO HOUSEWORK. Re-told and illus. by Wanda Gág. New York: Coward-McCann, 1935. pb

J398 _____. THE SORCERER'S APPRENTICE. New York: Coward-McCann, 1979. pb SEE ALSO Grimm, Jakob Ludwig and Wilhelm Karl. JORINDA AND JORINGEL, MORE TALES FROM GRIMM, SNOW WHITE AND THE SEVEN DWARFS, TALES FROM GRIMM, THREE GAY TALES FROM GRIMM.

J398 Galdone, Paul. CINDERELLA. Illus. Paul Gal-done. New York: McGraw-Hill, 1978. pb

J398 _____. THE GINGERBREAD BOY. Illus. Paul Galdone. New York: Seabury, 1975. pb

_____. HENNY PENNY. Illus. Paul Galdone. New York: Seabury, 1968. pb

_____. THE HOUSE THAT JACK BUILT. Illus. Paul Galdone. New York: McGraw-Hill, 1961. pb

J398.2 _____. THE MONKEY AND THE CROCODILE: A JATAKA TALE FROM INDIA. Illus. Paul Galdone. New York: Seabury, 1969. pb

J _____. OBEDIENT JACK: AN OLD TALE. Illus. Paul Galdone. New York: Watts, 1972. pb

_____. THE OLD WOMAN AND HER PIG.

Illus. Paul Galdone. New York: Whittlesey, 1960. pb

j398 Galdone, Paul. PUSS IN BOOTS. New York: Seabury, 1976. pb

_____. THE SORCERER'S APPRENTICE. Illus. Paul Galdone. New York: Coward, Mc-Cann, 1979. pb

_____. A STRANGE SERVANT: A RUSSIAN FOLKTALE. Trans. Blanche Ross. Illus. Paul Galdone. New York: Knopf, 1977. pb

j398.2 _____. THREE AESOP FOX FABLES. Illus. Paul Galdone. New York: Seabury, 1971.

jER _____. THE THREE BEARS. Illus. Paul Galdone. New York: Seabury, 1972. pb

_____. THE THREE WISHES. Illus. Paul Galdone. New York: McGraw-Hill, 1961. pb

j888.6 _____. THE TOWN MOUSE AND THE COUNTRY MOUSE. Illus. Paul Galdone. New York: McGraw-Hill, 1975. pb
SEE ALSO Asbjørnsen. THREE BILLY GOATS GRUFF; Grimm. LITTLE RED RIDING HOOD, THE TABLE, THE DONKEY AND THE STICK; Jacobs. HEREAFTERTHIS, KING OF THE CATS.

j Galdone, Joanna. THE TAILYPO: A GHOST STORY. Illus. Paul Galdone. New York: Seabury, 1977. pb

j398.2 Garner, Alan. A CAVALCADE OF GOBLINS. Illus. Krystyna Turska. New York: Walck, 1969. P

Garshin, V. M. THE TRAVELING FROG. Trans. Marguerita Rudolph. Illus. Jerry Pinkney. New York: McGraw-Hill, 1945, 1966. pb

j398.2 Gerson, Mary-Joan. WHY THE SKY IS FAR AWAY: A FOLKTALE FROM NIGERIA. Illus. Hope Meryman. New York: Harcourt, Brace Jovanovich, 1974. pb

j917.98 G41 Gilham, Charles E. BEYOND THE CLAPPING MOUNTAINS: ESKIMO STORIES FROM ALASKA. Illus. Chanimun. New York: Macmillan, 1943.

j398.2 _____. MEDICINE MEN OF HOOPER BAY: MORE TALES FROM THE CLAPPING MOUNTAINS OF ALASKA. Illus. Chanimun. New York: Macmillan, 1955. G

Gilstrap, Robert and Irene Estabrook. THE SULTAN'S FOOL AND OTHER NORTH AFRICAN TALES. Illus. Robert Greco. New York: Holt, Rinehart and Winston, 1958.

j398.2 Ginsburg, Mirra. THE FISHERMAN'S SON. Adapted from a Georgian Folktale. Pictures by Tony Chen. New York: Greenwillow, 1979. pb

j398.2 _____. THE FOX AND THE HARE. Illus. Victor Nolden. New York: Crown, 1969. pb

Ginsburg, Mirra. HOW THE SUN WAS BROUGHT BACK TO THE SKY. Adapted from a Slovenian Folk Tale. Illus. Jose Aruego and Ariane Dewey. New York: Macmillan, 1975. pb

j398.2 _____. HOW WILKA WENT TO SEA AND OTHER TALES FROM WEST OF THE URALS. Trans. and edited by Mirra Ginsburg. Illus. Charles Mikolaycak. New York: Crown, 1975. G

j398.2 _____. THE KAHA BIRD: TALES FROM THE STEPPES OF CENTRAL ASIA. Illus. Richard Cuffari. New York: Crown, 1971. N

j398.2 _____. THE LAZIES: TALES OF THE PEOPLE OF RUSSIA. Illus. Marian Parry. New York: Macmillan, 1973.

_____. LITTLE RYSTU: ADAPTED FROM AN ALTAI FOLKTALE. Illus. Tony Chen. New York: Greenwillow, 1978. pb

j398.2 _____. THE MASTER OF THE WINDS AND OTHER TALES FROM SIBERIA. Illus. Enrico Arno. New York: Crown, 1970. G

j398.2 _____. ONE TRICK TOO MANY: FOX STORIES FROM RUSSIA. Illus. Helen Siegl. New York: Dial, 1973.

j398.2 _____. THE PROUD MAIDEN, TUNGAK, AND THE SUN: A RUSSIAN ESKIMO TALE. Illus. Igor Galanin. New York: Macmillan, 1974. G, pb

j398.2 _____. STRIDING SLIPPERS. Illus. Sal Murdocca. New York: Macmillan, 1978. pb

j741 _____. THE STRONGEST ONE OF ALL: BASED ON A CAUCASIAN FOLKTALE. Illus. Jose Aruego and Ariane Dewey. New York: Macmillan, 1978. pb

j398.2 _____. THE THREE ROLLS AND ONE DOUGHNUT: FABLES FROM RUSSIA. Illus. Anita Lobel. New York: Dial, 1970.

_____. THE TWELVE CLEVER BROTHERS AND OTHER FOOLS. FOLKTALES FROM RUSSIA. Collected and adapted by Mirra Ginsburg. Illus. Charles Mikolaycak. New York: Lippincott, 1979.

_____. TWO GREEDY BEARS. ADAPTED FROM A HUNGARIAN FOLKTALE. Illus. Jose Aruego and Ariane Dewey. New York: Macmillan, 1976. pb

Gittins, Anne. TALES FROM THE SOUTH PACIFIC ISLANDS. Illus. Frank Rocca. Jacket design by Tom Kealiinohomoku. Owings Mills, Md.: Stemmer House, 1977.

Gleason, Judith. ORISHA: THE GODS OF YORUBALAND. Art by Aduni Olorisa. New York: Atheneum, 1971. G

j398.2 Gobhai, Mehlli. THE BLUE JACKAL. Illus. Mehlli Gobhai. Englewood Cliffs, N.J.: Prentice-Hall, 1968. pb

J398.2 Gobhai, Mehlli. USHA THE MOUSE-MAIDEN. Illus. Mehlli Gobhai. New York: Hawthorn, 1969. pb

j398.2 Godden, Rumer. THE OLD WOMAN WHO LIVED IN A VINEGAR BOTTLE. Illus. Mairi Hedderwick. New York: Viking, 1970. pb
_1972_

J398.2 Gottschalk, Fruma. THE RUNAWAY SOLDIER AND OTHER TALES OF OLD RUSSIA. Illus. Simon Lissim. New York: Knopf, 1946. G, pb

J398.2 Graham, Gail B. THE BEGGAR IN THE BLANKET AND OTHER VIETNAMESE TALES. Illus. Brigitte Bryan. New York: Dial, 1970.

J398.2 GRASSHOPPER TO THE RESCUE: A GEORGIAN STORY. Trans. from the Russian by Bonnie Carey. Illus. Lady McCrady. New York: Morrow, 1979. G, pb

Gray, J. E. B. INDIAN TALES AND LEGENDS. Illus. J. E. B. Gray. New York: Walck, 1961. G

Green, Lila. FOLKTALES AND FAIRY TALES OF AFRICA. Illus. Jerry Pinkney. Morristown, N.J.: Silver Burdett, 1967.

Green, Margaret. THE BIG BOOK OF ANIMAL FABLES. Illus. Janusz Grabianski. New York: Watts, 1965.

J398.2 Green, Nancy. ABU KASSIM'S SLIPPERS: AN ARABIAN TALE. Retold by Nancy Green. Illus. W. T. Mars. Chicago: Follett, 1963. pb

j398.2 Green, Roger Lancelyn. A CAVALCADE OF DRAGONS. Illus. Krystyna Turska. New York: Walck, 1973. P

J3982 _____. TALES OF ANCIENT EGYPT. Illus. Elaine Raphael. New York: Walck, 1968. G
_1970_

Greene, Ellin. CLEVER COOKS: A CONCOCTION OF STORIES, CHARMS, RECIPES AND RIDDLES. Illus. Trina Schart Hyman. New York: Lothrop, Lee & Shepard, 1973.

J _____. MIDSUMMER MAGIC: A GARLAND OF STORIES, CHARMS AND RECIPES. Illus. Barbara Cooney. New York: Lothrop, Lee & Shepard, 1977. P

Grimm, Jakob Ludwig Karl and Wilhelm Karl Grimm. ABOUT WISE MEN AND SIMPLETONS: TWELVE TALES FROM GRIMM. Trans. Elizabeth Shub. Illus. Nonny Hogrogian. New York: Macmillan, 1971.

J398 _____. THE BEAR AND THE KINGBIRD: A TALE FROM THE BROTHERS GRIMM. Trans. Lore Segal. Illus. Chris Conover. New York: Farrar, Straus and Giroux, 1979. pb

_____. THE BEARSKINNER: A STORY BY THE BROTHERS GRIMM. Illus. Felix Hoffmann. New York: Atheneum, 1978. pb

J398 _____. THE BREMEN TOWN MUSICIANS.

Illus. Paul Galdone. New York: McGraw-Hill, 1968. pb
_1981_

Grimm, Jakob Ludwig Karl and Wilhelm Karl Grimm. THE BREMEN TOWN MUSICIANS. Illus. Ilse Plume. Garden City, N.Y.: Doubleday, 1980. pb
_1981_

_____. THE BROTHERS GRIMM: POPULAR FOLK TALES. Trans. Brian Alderson. Illus. Michael Forman. Garden City, N.Y: Doubleday, 1978.

_____. CINDERELLA. Retold and illus. Nonny Hogrogian. New York: Greenwillow, 1981. pb

_____. CINDERELLA. Illus. Otto S. Svend. Trans. Anne Rogers. New York: Larousse, 1978. pb

_____. THE DONKEY PRINCE. Adapted by M. Jean Craig. Illus. Barbara Cooney. Garden City, N.Y.: Doubleday, 1977. G, pb

_____. THE ELVES AND THE SHOEMAKER. Illus. Katrin Brandt. Chicago: Follett, 1967. pb

_____. THE ELVES AND THE SHOEMAKER. Retold by Frances K. Pavel. Illus. Joyce Hewitt. New York: Holt, Rinehart and Winston, 1961. pb

J398 _____. FAVORITE FAIRY TALES TOLD IN GERMANY. Retold by Virginia Haviland. Illus. Susanne Suba. Boston: Little, Brown, 1959.

_____. THE FISHERMAN AND HIS WIFE. Illus. Katrin Brandt. Chicago: Follett, 1969. pb

_____. THE FISHERMAN AND HIS WIFE. Illus. Madeleine Gekiere. New York: Pantheon, 1957. pb

J398 _____. THE FISHERMAN AND HIS WIFE. Trans. Elizabeth Shub. Illus. Monika Laimgruber. New York: Greenwillow, 1978. pb
_1980_

J398 _____. THE FISHERMAN AND HIS WIFE. Reteller, Margot Zemach. Illus. Margot Zemach. New York: Norton, 1966. pb

J398 _____. THE FOUR CLEVER BROTHERS. Illus. Felix Hoffmann. New York: Harcourt, Brace & World, 1966, 1967. pb

J398 _____. THE FROG PRINCE. Illus. Paul Galdone. New York: McGraw-Hill, 1975. pb

J398 _____. THE GOLDEN GOOSE. Illus. William Stobbs. New York: McGraw-Hill, c. 1966, 1967. pb

_____. THE GOOD-FOR-NOTHINGS. Illus. Hans Fischer. New York: Harcourt, Brace, 1945. pb

J398 C889.8 _____. THE GOOSE GIRL. Illus. Marguerite De Angeli. Garden City, N.Y.: Doubleday, 1964. pb

J398 _____. GRIMM'S FAIRY TALES. Illustrated.

New York: World, 1947.

_____. GRIMM'S FAIRY TALES. Selected and illus. by Elenore Abbott. New York: Scribner's, 1920.

_____. GRIMM'S FAIRY TALES. By the Brothers Grimm, trans. by Mrs. E. V. Lucas, Lucy Crane and Marian Edwardes. Illus. Fritz Kredel. New York: Grosset & Dunlap, 1945.

_____. GRIMM'S FAIRY TALES. Editor Frances Jenkins Olcott. Chicago: Follett, 1968.

J398 _____. GRIMM'S FAIRY TALES. TWENTY STORIES. Illus. Arthur Rackham. New York: Viking, 1973.

J398 _____. HANS IN LUCK. Reteller, David McKee. Illus. David McKee. New York: Abelard-Schuman, 1967. pb

J398 _____. HANS IN LUCK: A STORY BY THE BROTHERS GRIMM with pictures by Felix Hoffmann. New York: Atheneum, 1975. pb

J398 _____. HANSEL AND GRETEL. Trans. Elizabeth D. Crawford. Illus. Lisbeth Zwerger. New York: Morrow, 1979. pb

J398 _____. HANSEL AND GRETEL. Illus. Arnold Lobel. New York: Delacorte, 1971. pb

_____. HANSEL AND GRETEL. Trans. Charles Scribner, Jr. Illus. Adrienne Adams. New York: Scribner's, 1975. pb

J398 _____. THE HOUSE IN THE WOOD, AND OTHER OLD FAIRY STORIES. Illus. L. Leslie Brook. New York: Warne, 1909, 1944. have 1966

J398 _____. HOUSEHOLD STORIES, from the collection of the Bros. Grimm. Translated from the German by Lucy Crane, and done into pictures by Walter Crane. New York: McGraw-Hill, 1886, 1966. have 1963

J398 _____. JORINDA AND JORINGEL. Trans. Wanda Gág. Illus. Margot Tomes. New York: Coward-McCann, 1978. pb

J398. G881 _____. JORINDA AND JORINGEL. Trans. Elizabeth Shub. Illus. Adrienne Adams. New York: Scribner's, 1968. pb

J398 _____. THE JUNIPER TREE AND OTHER TALES FROM GRIMM. 2 vols. Selected by Lore Segal and Maurice Sendak and Randall Jarrell. Trans Lore Segal. Illus. Maurice Sendak. New York: Farrar, Straus, and Giroux, 1973.

_____. KING GRISLEY-BEARD. Trans. Edgar Taylor. Illus. Maurice Sendak. New York: Farrar, Straus & Giroux, 1973. pb

J398 _____. KING THRUSHBEARD. Illus. Felix Hoffmann. New York: Harcourt, Brace & World, 1969, 1970. pb

Grimm, Jakob Ludwig Karl and Wilhelm Karl Grimm. LITTLE RED RIDING HOOD. Illus. Bernadette. New York: Harcourt, Brace & World, 1969. pb

_____. LITTLE RED RIDING HOOD. Illus. Paul Galdone. New York: McGraw-Hill, 1974. pb

J398. LITTLE RED RIDING HOOD. Illus. Harriet Pincus. New York: Harcourt, Brace & World, 1968. pb

_____. THE HEDGEHOG AND THE HARE. Retold by Wendy Watson. Illus. Wendy Watson. New York: Harcourt, Brace & World, 1969. pb

J398 _____. MORE TALES FROM GRIMM. Trans. and illus. Wanda Gág. New York: Coward-McCann, 1947.

_____. MOTHER HOLLY. Illus. Bernadette Watts. New York: Crowell, 1972. G, pb

J398 _____. RAPUNZEL. Illus. Felix Hoffmann. New York: Harcourt, Brace & World, 1949, 1960.

J398 _____. RUMPELSTILTSKIN. Illus. Jaqueline Ayer. New York: Harcourt, Brace & World, 1967. pb

J398 _____. THE SEVEN RAVENS. Illus. Felix Hoffmann. New York: Harcourt, Brace & World, 1962. pb have 1963

_____. THE SEVEN RAVENS: A GRIMM'S FAIRY TALE. Retold and illus. Donna Diamond. New York: Viking, 1979. pb

J398 _____. THE SHOEMAKER AND THE ELVES. Illus. Adrienne Adams. New York: Scribner's, 1960. pb

_____. THE SLEEPING BEAUTY. Illus. Felix Hoffmann. New York: Harcourt, Brace & World, 1959. pb

_____. THE SLEEPING BEAUTY. Retold and illus. Warwick Hutton. New York: Atheneum, 1979. pb

_____. THE SLEEPING BEAUTY. Retold and illus. Trina Schart Hyman. Boston: Little, Brown, 1977. pb

_____. THE SLEEPING BEAUTY. Illus. Lieselotte Schwartz. New York: Scroll, 1967. pb

_____. SNOW WHITE. Freely translated from the German by Paul Heins. Illus. Trina Schart Hyman. Boston: Little, Brown, 1974. pb

J398 _____. SNOW WHITE AND ROSE RED. Illus. Adrienne Adams. New York: Scribner's, 1964. pb

_____. SNOW WHITE AND ROSE RED. Illus. Barbara Cooney. New York: Delacorte, 1965. pb

_____. SNOW WHITE AND THE SEVEN DWARFS. Trans. and illus. Wanda Gág. New York: Coward-McCann, 1938. pb

Grimm, Jakob Ludwig Karl and Wilhelm Karl Grimm. SNOW-WHITE AND THE SEVEN DWARFS: A TALE FROM THE BROTHERS GRIMM. Trans. Randall Jarrell. Illus. Nancy Ekholm Burkert. New York: Farrar, Straus, and Giroux, 1972. pb

_____. THE TABLE, THE DONKEY, AND THE STICK. Retold and Illus. Paul Galdone. New York: McGraw-Hill, 1976. pb

_____. TALES FROM GRIMM. Freely trans. and illus. Wanda Gág. New York: Coward-McCann, 1936.

_____. THORN ROSE. Illus. Errol Le Cain. Scarsdale, N.Y.: Bradbury, 1975. pb

_____. THREE GAY TALES FROM GRIMM. Freely trans. and illus. Wanda Gág. New York: Coward-McCann, 1943.

_____. THE TRAVELING MUSICIANS. Illus. Hans Fischer. New York: Harcourt, Brace & World, 1944. pb

_____. THE TWELVE DANCING PRINCESSES. Illus. Adrienne Adams. New York: Holt, 1966. pb

_____. THE TWELVE DANCING PRINCESSES. Illus. Errol Le Cain. New York: Viking, 1978. pb

_____. THE TWELVE DANCING PRINCESSES. Trans. Elizabeth Shub. Illus. Uri Shulevitz. New York: Scribner's, 1966. pb

_____. THE WOLF AND THE SEVEN LITTLE KIDS. Illus. Felix Hoffmann. New York: Harcourt, Brace & World, 1957. pb

_____. THE WOLF AND THE SEVEN LITTLE KIDS. Trans. Anne Rogers. Illus. Otto S. Svend. New York: Larousse, 1977. pb

_____. SEE ALSO Haviland. FAVORITE FAIRY TALES TOLD IN GERMANY.

Grinnell, George Bird. BLACKFOOT LODGE TALES: THE STORY OF A PRAIRIE PEOPLE. New York: Scribner's, c.1892, c.1920. N

Gross, Michael. THE FABLE OF THE FIG TREE. Illus. Mila Lazarevich. New York: Walck, 1975.

Gruenberg, Sidonie M. FAVORITE STORIES OLD AND NEW. Illus. Kurt Wiese. Garden City, N.Y.: Doubleday, 1942, 1955. P

_____. MORE FAVORITE STORIES OLD AND NEW FOR BOYS AND GIRLS. Illus. Richard Floethe. Garden City, N.Y.: Doubleday, 1948. P

Guillot, René. GUILLOT'S AFRICAN FOLK TALES. Selected and trans Gwen Marsh. Illus. William Papas. New York: Watts, 1965. N

Guirma, Frederich. PRINCESS OF THE FULL MOON. Trans. John Garnett. New York: Macmillan, 1970. pb

Guirma, Frederich. TALES OF MOGHO: AFRICAN STORIES FROM UPPER VOLTA. Illus. Frederich Guirma. New York: Macmillan, 1971.

Gunterman, Berta. CASTLES IN SPAIN, AND OTHER ENCHANTMENTS: SPANISH LEGENDS AND ROMANCES. Illus. Mahlon Blaine. New York: McKay, c.1928, c.1956. P

Hack, Inge. DANISH FAIRY TALES. Illus. Harry and Ilse Toothill. Chicago: Follett, 1964.

Hague, Kathleen and Michael. EAST OF THE SUN AND WEST OF THE MOON. Illus. Michael Hague. New York: Harcourt, Brace Jovanovich, 1980.

_____. THE MAN WHO KEPT HOUSE. Illus. Michael Hague. New York: Harcourt, Brace Jovanovich, 1981. G, pb

Haley, Gail E. A STORY A STORY: AN AFRICAN TALE. Retold and illus. Gail E. Haley. New York: Atheneum, 1970. pb

Halliwell, J. O. THE STORY OF THE THREE LITTLE PIGS. Paul Galdone, reteller. Illus. Paul Galdone. New York: Seabury, 1970. pb

Hampden, John. THE GYPSY FIDDLE, AND OTHER TALES TOLD BY GYPSIES. Illus. Robin Jacques. Introduction by Jan Yoors. New York: World, 1969.

_____. THE HOUSE OF CATS AND OTHER STORIES. Illus. Enrico Arno. New York: Farrar, Straus & Giroux, c.1966, 1967.

Hardendorff, Jeanne B. THE FROG'S SADDLE HORSE, AND OTHER TALES. Illus. Helen Webber. Philadelphia: Lippincott, 1968. P

_____. JUST ONE MORE. Illus. Don Bolognese. Philadelphia: Lippincott, 1969.

_____. THE LITTLE COCK. Illus. Joseph Domjan. Philadelphia: Lippincott, 1969. pb

_____. SLIP! SLOP! GOBBLE! Illus. Emily McCully. Philadelphia: Lippincott, 1970. pb

_____. TRICKY PEIK AND OTHER PICTURE TALES. Illus. Tomie de Paola. Philadelphia: Lippincott, 1967.

Harman, Humphrey. TALES TOLD NEAR A CROCODILE: STORIES FROM NYANZA. Illus. George Ford. New York: Viking, c.1962, 1967.

Harper, Wilhelmina. GHOSTS AND GOBLINS: STORIES FOR HALLOWE'EN AND OTHER TIMES. Illus. Wilfred Jones. New York: Dutton, 1936.

_____. THE GUNNIWOLF. Illus. William Wiesner. New York: Dutton, c.1918, 1967. pb

Harris, Christie. ONCE UPON A TOTEM. Illus. Douglas Tait. New York: Atheneum, 1963. N

Harris, Joel Chandler. BRER RABBIT: STORIES

FROM UNCLE REMUS. Adapted by Margaret Wise Brown, with the A. B. Frost pictures redrawn for reproduction by Victor Dowling. New York: Harper & Row, 1941.

j398 Harris, Joel Chandler. THE COMPLETE TALES OF UNCLE REMUS. Compiled by Richard Chase. Illus. Arthur Burdette Frost. Boston: Houghton Mifflin, 1955.

j398 _____. THE FAVORITE UNCLE REMUS. Illus. A. B. Frost. Selected, arranged and edited by George Van Santvoord and Archibald C. Coolidge. Boston: Houghton Mifflin, 1948.

_____. NIGHTS WITH UNCLE REMUS: MYTHS AND LEGENDS OF THE OLD PLANTATION. Boston and New York: Houghton Mifflin, 1883.

_____. UNCLE REMUS, HIS SONGS AND HIS SAYINGS. Illus. A. B. Frost and E. W. Kemble. New York: Appleton, 1920.

Harris, Rosemary, reteller. BEAUTY AND THE BEAST. Illus. Errol Le Cain. Garden City, N.Y.: Doubleday, 1979. pb

j398.2 Harrison, Amelia (Williams). AMERICAN INDIAN FAIRY TALES. Illus. Lorence F. Bjorklund. New York: Dodd, Mead, 1971. P

j398.2 Haskett, Edythe Rance. GRAINS OF PEPPER: FOLKTALES FROM LIBERIA. Illus. Musu Miatta (author). New York: John Day, 1967. N

j398.2 _____. SOME GOLD, A LITTLE IVORY: COUNTRY TALES FROM GHANA AND THE IVORY COAST. New York: John Day, 1971. G

j398.2 Hatch, Mary Cottam. MORE DANISH TALES. Illus. Edgun. New York: Harcourt, Brace & World, 1949.

j398.2 _____. THIRTEEN DANISH TALES. Illus. Edgun. New York: Harcourt, Brace & World, 1947.

Hausmann, Gerald. SITTING ON THE BLUE-EYED BEAR. Westport, Ct.: Lawrence Hill, 1976. G

Haviland, Virginia. THE FAIRY TALE TREASURY. Illus. Raymond Briggs. Selected by Virginia Haviland. New York: Coward, McCann & Geoghegan, 1972.

j398 _____. FAVORITE FAIRY TALES TOLD IN DENMARK. Illus. Margot Zemach. Boston: Little, Brown, 1971.

j398 _____. FAVORITE FAIRY TALES TOLD IN CZECHOSLOVAKIA. Illus. Trina Schart Hyman. Boston: Little, Brown, 1966.

j398 _____. FAVORITE FAIRY TALES TOLD IN ENGLAND. Retold from Joseph Jacobs by Virginia Haviland. Illus. Bettina. Boston: Little, Brown, 1959.

j398 Haviland, Virginia. FAVORITE FAIRY TALES TOLD IN FRANCE. Retold from Charles Perrault by Virginia Haviland. Illus. Roger Duvoisin. Boston: Little, Brown, 1959.

_____. FAVORITE FAIRY TALES TOLD IN GERMANY. Retold from the Brothers Grimm by Virgina Haviland. Illus. Susanne Suba. Boston: Little, Brown, 1959.

j398 _____. FAVORITE FAIRY TALES TOLD IN GREECE. Illus. Nonny Hogrogian. Boston: Little, Brown, 1970.

j398 _____. FAVORITE FAIRY TALES TOLD IN INDIA. Illus. Blair Lent. Boston: Little, Brown, 1973.

j398 _____. FAVORITE FAIRY TALES TOLD IN IRELAND. Illus. Artur Marokvia. Boston: Little, Brown, 1961.

j398 _____. FAVORITE FAIRY TALES TOLD IN ITALY. Illus. Evaline Ness. Boston: Little, Brown, 1965.

j398 _____. FAVORITE FAIRY TALES TOLD IN JAPAN. Illus. George Suyeoka. Boston: Little, Brown, 1967.

j398 _____. FAVORITE FAIRY TALES TOLD IN NORWAY. Illus. Leonard Weisgard. Boston: Little, Brown, 1961.

j398 _____. FAVORITE FAIRY TALES TOLD IN POLAND. Illus. Felix Hoffmann. Boston: Little, Brown, 1963.

j398 H295fr _____. FAVORITE FAIRY TALES TOLD IN RUSSIA. Illus. Herbert Danska. Boston: Little, Brown, 1961.

j398 H295fs _____. FAVORITE FAIRY TALES TOLD IN SCOTLAND. Illus. Adrienne Adams. Boston: Little, Brown, 1963.

_____. FAVORITE FAIRY TALES TOLD IN SPAIN. Illus. Barbara Cooney. Boston: Little, Brown, 1963.

_____. FAVORITE FAIRY TALES TOLD IN IN SWEDEN. Illus. Ronni Solbert. Boston: Little, Brown, 1966.

_____. NORTH AMERICAN LEGENDS. Illus. Ann Strugnell. New York and Cleveland: Collins, 1979. P

j398.2 H329i Hayes, William D. INDIAN TALES OF THE DESERT PEOPLE. Illus. William D. Hayes. New York: McKay, 1957. G

j398.2 H337j Heady, Eleanor B. JAMBO SUNGURA: TALES FROM EAST AFRICA. Illus. Robert Frankenberg. New York: Norton, 1965.

j398.2 _____. SAFIRI THE SINGER. Illustrated. Chicago: Follett, 1973.

Heady, Eleanor B. SAGE SMOKE: TALES OF THE SHOSHONI-BANNOCK INDIANS. Illus. Arvis Stewart. Chicago: Follett, 1973.

_____. TALES OF THE NIMIPOO: FROM THE LAND OF THE NEZ PERCE INDIANS. Illus. Eric Carle. New York: World, 1970.

_____. WHEN THE STONES WERE SOFT: EAST AFRICAN FIRESIDE TALES. Illus. Tom Feelings. New York: Funk & Wagnalls, 1968.

Hearn, Lafcadio. THE BOY WHO DREW CATS AND OTHER TALES. Illustrated. New York: Macmillan, 1963.

_____. EARLESS HO-ICHI: A CLASSIC JAPANESE TALE OF MYSTERY. Intro. Donald Keene. Illus. Masakazu Kuwata. Tokyo: Kodansha International, 1966.

_____. JAPANESE FAIRY TALES. Illus. Sonia Roetter. New York: Liveright, 1953.

_____. JAPANESE FAIRY TALES. New York: Peter Pauper, 1958.

Helfman, Elizabeth S. THE BUSHMEN AND THEIR STORIES. Illus. Richard Cuffari. New York: Seabury, 1971.

Henius, Frank. STORIES FROM THE AMERICAS. Illus. Leo Politi. New York: Scribner's, 1944. G

Herzog, George. SEE Courlander, Harold. THE COW-TAIL SWITCH.

Hewett, Anita. THE LITTLE WHITE HEN. Illus. William Stobbs. New York: Whittlesey, McGraw-Hill, c.1962, 1963. pb

Higonnet-Schnopper, Janet. TALES FROM ATOP A RUSSIAN STOVE. Illus. Franz Altschuler. Chicago: Albert Whitman, 1973.

Hill, Kay. BADGER, THE MISCHIEF MAKER. Illus. John Hamberger. New York: Dodd, Mead, 1965. P

_____. GLOOSCAP AND HIS MAGIC: LEGENDS OF THE WABANAKI INDIANS. Illus. Robert Frankenberg. New York: Dodd, Mead, 1963. P

_____. MORE GLOOSCAP STORIES: LEGENDS OF THE WABANAKI INDIANS. Illus. John Hamberger. Toronto: Dodd, Mead, 1970. P

Hirsh, Marilyn COULD ANYTHING BE WORSE? A YIDDISH TALE. Retold and Illus. Marilyn Hirsh. New York: Holiday. 1974. pb

_____. THE RABBI AND THE TWENTY-NINE WITCHES: A TALMUDIC LEGEND. Retold and illus. Marilyn Hirsh. New York: Holiday, 1976.

Hitchcock, Patricia. THE KING WHO RIDES A TIGER AND OTHER FOLK TALES FROM NEPAL.

Illus. Lillian Sader. Berkeley, Calif.: Parnassus, 1966.

Hodges, Margaret. THE FIRE BRINGER: A PAIUTE INDIAN LEGEND? Retold Margaret Hodges. Illus. Peter Parnall. Boston: Little, Brown, 1972.

_____. THE OTHER WORLD: MYTHS OF THE CELTS. Illus. Eros Keith. New York: Farrar, Straus and Giroux, 1973. G

_____. THE WAVE. Illus. Blair Lent. Boston: Houghton Mifflin, 1964. pb

Hoffmann, Felix. SEE Grimm. BEARSKINNER; HANS IN LUCK; KING THRUSHBEARD; RAPUNZEL; SLEEPING BEAUTY; WOLF AND THE SEVEN LITTLE KIDS.

Hoffmann, Peggy and Gyuri Bíró. THE MONEY HAT AND OTHER HUNGARIAN FOLK TALES. Illus. Gyuri Bíró. Philadelphia: Westminster, 1969. G

Hogrogian, Nonny. THE CONTEST. Illus. Nonny Hogrogian. New York: Greenwillow, 1976. N, pb

Hoke, Helen. DRAGONS, DRAGONS, DRAGONS. Illus. Carol Barker. New York: Watts, 1972. P

_____. SPOOKS, SPOOKS, SPOOKS. Illus. W. R. Lohse. New York: Watts, 1966.

_____. WITCHES, WITCHES, WITCHES. Illus. W. R. Lohse. New York: Watts, 1958. P

Holding, James. THE KING'S CONTEST AND OTHER NORTH AFRICAN TALES. Illus. Charles Keeping. New York: Abelard-Schuman, 1964.

_____. THE SKY-EATER AND OTHER SOUTH SEA TALES. Illus. Charles Keeping. New York: Abelard-Schuman, 1965.

Holdsworth, William Curtis. THE GINGERBREAD BOY. Illus. William Curtis Holdsworth. New York: Farrar, Straus and Giroux, 1968. pb

_____. THE LITTLE RED HEN. New York: Farrar, Straus and Giroux, 1969. pb

Holladay, Virginia. BANTU TALES. Ed. Louise Crane. Illus. Rocco Negri. New York: Viking, 1970.

Holland, Janice. YOU NEVER CAN TELL. Trans. Arthur W. Hummel from the Huai Nan Tzu. Illus. Janice Holland. New York: Scribner's, 1963. G, pb

Holman, Felice and Nanine Valen. THE DRAC: FRENCH TALES OF DRAGONS AND DEMONS. Illus. Stephen Walker. New York: Scribner's, 1975.

Holme, Bryan, editor. TALES FROM TIMES PAST. New York: Viking, 1977.

Hooke, Hilda Mary. THUNDER IN THE MOUN-
TAINS: LEGENDS OF CANADA. Illus. Clare
Bice. New York: Oxford University Press, 1947.
G

Hope-Simpson, Jacynth. A CAVALCADE OF
WITCHES. Illus. Krystna Turska. New York:
Walck, c.1966, 1967. P

Houston, James. KIVIOK'S MAGIC JOURNEY: AN
ESKIMO LEGEND. New York: Atheneum, 1973.
G, pb

HOW DJADJA-EM-ANKH SAVED THE DAY: A TALE
FROM ANCIENT EGYPT. Trans. from the original hieratic. With illus. and commentary by Lise
Manniche. New York: Crowell, c.1976, 1977. G,
pb

Htin Aung, Maung and Helen G. Trager. A KING-
DOM LOST FOR A DROP OF HONEY AND OTHER
BURMESE FOLKTALES. Illus. Paw Oo Thet.
New York: Parents, 1968.

Huggins, Edward. BLUE AND GREEN WONDERS
AND OTHER LATVIAN TALES. Illus. Owen
Wood. New York: Simon and Schuster, 1971.

Huldschiner, Robert E. THE COW THAT SPOKE
FOR SEPPL AND OTHER ALPINE TALES. Illus.
Carol Wilde. Garden City, N.Y.: Doubleday,
1968. G

Hulpach, Vladimir. AMERICAN INDIAN TALES
AND LEGENDS. Illustrated. Hamlyn, 1965. N

Hume, Lotta Carswell. FAVORITE CHILDREN'S
STORIES FROM CHINA AND TIBET. Illus.
Lo Koon-chiu. Rutland, Vt.: Charles E.
Tuttle, 1962.

Hürlimann, Ruth. THE CAT AND THE MOUSE
WHO SHARED A HOUSE. Retold with pictures
by Ruth Hürlimann. Transl. from the German
by Anthea Bell. New York: Walck, 1973. pb

Hutchison, Veronica S. CANDLE-LIGHT STORIES.
Illus. Lois Lenski. New York: Minton, Balch,
1927.

_____. CHIMNEY CORNER FAIRY TALES.
illus. Lois Lenski. New York: Minton, Balch,
1926.

_____. CHIMNEY CORNER STORIES: TALES
FOR LITTLE CHILDREN. Illus. Lois Lenski.
New York: Minton, Balch, 1925.

_____. FIRESIDE STORIES. Illus. Lois Len-
ski. New York: Minton, Balch, 1927.

Hyman, Trina Schart. SEE Grimm. THE SLEEP-
ING BEAUTY; SNOW WHITE.

Ish-Kishor, Judith. TALES FROM THE WISE MEN
OF ISRAEL. Illus. W. T. Mars. Philadelphia:
Lippincott, 1962. N

Ish-Kishor, Sulamith. THE CARPET OF SOLO-
MON: A HEBREW LEGEND. Illus. Uri Shulevitz.
New York: Pantheon, 1966.

Ishii, Momoko. ISSUN BOSHI, THE INCHLING:
AN OLD TALE OF JAPAN. Trans. Yone Mizuta.
Illus. Fuku Akino. New York: Walker,
c.1965, 1967. pb

Jablow, Alta and Carl Withers. THE MAN IN THE
MOON: SKY TALES FROM MANY LANDS. Illus.
Peggy Wilson. New York: Holt, Rinehart and
Winston, 1969.

Jacobs, Joseph. THE BURIED MOON. Illus.
Susan Jeffers. Englewood Cliffs, N.J.: Bradbury, 1969. pb

_____. CELTIC FOLK AND FAIRY TALES.
Illus. John D. Batten. New York: Putnam, n.d.
P

_____. THE CROCK OF GOLD. Illus. William
Stobbs. Chicago: Follett, 1971. pb

_____. ENGLISH FOLK AND FAIRY TALES.
Illus. John D. Batten. New York: Putnam, n.d.

_____. EUROPEAN FOLK AND FAIRY TALES.
illus. John D. Batten. New York: Putnam,
c.1916, 1967.

_____. THE FABLES OF AESOP. SEE AESOP.

_____. FAVORITE FAIRY TALES TOLD IN
ENGLAND. SEE Haviland, Virginia.

_____. HEREAFTERTHIS. Adapted from a
folktale by Joseph Jacobs. Illus. Paul Galdone.
New York: McGraw-Hill, n.d. pb

_____. HUDDEN AND DUDDEN AND DONALD
O'NEARY. Illus. Doris Burn. New York:
Coward-McCann, 1968. pb

_____. INDIAN FOLK AND FAIRY TALES.
Illus. John D. Batten. New York: Putnam, n.d.

_____. JOHNNY-CAKE. Illus. Emma Brock.
New York: Putnam, 1933. pb

_____. JOHNNY-CAKE. Illus. William Stobbs.
New York: Viking, 1972. pb

_____. KING OF THE CATS. Illus. Paul
Galdone. Boston: Houghton Mifflin, 1980. pb

_____. LAZY JACK. Illus. Barry Wilkinson.
New York: World, 1970. pb

_____. MASTER OF ALL MASTERS. Illus.
Anne Rockwell. New York: Grosset and Dunlap,
1972. pb

_____. MORE CELTIC TALES. Illus. John D.
Batten. New York: Putnam, 1902.

_____. MORE ENGLISH FAIRY TALES. Illus.
John D. Batten. New York: Putnam, n.d.

Jacobs, Joseph. MUNACHAR AND MANACHAR: AN IRISH STORY. Illus. Anne Rockwell. New York: Crowell, 1970. pb

_____. THE STARS IN THE SKY: A SCOTTISH TALE. Illus. Airdrie Amtmann. New York: Farrar, Straus and Giroux, 1979. pb

_____. THE THREE SILLIES. Illus. Margot Zemach. New York: Holt, Rinehart and Winston, 1963. pb

_____. TOM TIT TOT: AN ENGLISH FOLK TALE. Illus. Evaline Ness. New York: Scribner's, 1965. pb

SEE ALSO Aesop. FABLES OF AESOP.

Jagendorf, Moritz A. FOLK STORIES OF THE SOUTH. Illus. Michael Parks. New York: Vanguard, 1972. N

_____. THE GHOST OF PEG-LEG PETER: AND OTHER STORIES OF OLD NEW YORK. Illus. Lino S. Lipinski. New York: Vanguard, n.d. N

_____. THE MERRY MEN OF GOTHAM. Illus. Shane Miller. New York: Vanguard, 1950.

_____. NEW ENGLAND BEAN-POT. Illus. Donald McKay. New York: Vanguard, 1948. N

_____. NOODLEHEAD STORIES FROM AROUND THE WORLD. Illus. Shane Miller. New York: Vanguard, 1957.

_____. THE PRICELESS CATS AND OTHER ITALIAN FOLK STORIES. Illus. Gioia Fiamenghi. New York: Vanguard, 1956.

_____. SAND IN THE BAG, AND OTHER FOLK STORIES OF OHIO, INDIANA AND ILLINOIS. Illus. John Moment. New York: Vanguard, 1952. N

_____. UPSTATE, DOWNSTATE. FOLK STORIES OF THE MIDDLE ATLANTIC STATES. Illus. Howard Simon. New York: Vanguard, 1949. N

Jagendorf, Moritz A. and Ralph Steele Boggs. THE KING OF THE MOUNTAIN: A TREASURY OF LATIN AMERICAN FOLK STORIES. Illus. Carybé. New York: Vanguard, 1960.

Jagendorf, Moritz A. and C. H. Tillhagen. THE GYPSIES' FIDDLE AND OTHER GYPSY TALES. Illus. Hans Helweg. New York: Vanguard, 1956.

James, T. G. H. MYTHS AND LEGENDS OF ANCIENT EGYPT. Illus. Brian Melling. New York: Grosset and Dunlap, 1971. G

Jameson, Cynthia. CATOFY THE CLEVER: ADAPTED FROM A RUSSIAN FOLKTALE. Illus. Wallace Tripp. New York: Coward, McCann and Geoghegan, 1972. pb

Jameson, Cynthia. THE CLAY POT BOY. Adapted from a Russian Tale. Illus. Arnold Lobel. New York: Coward, McCann and Geoghegan, 1973. pb

_____. TALES FROM THE STEPPES. Illus. Christopher J. Spollen. New York: Coward, McCann and Geoghegan, 1975.

Jatakas. JATAKA TALES. Retold by Ellen C. Babbitt. Illus. Ellsworth Young. New York: Appleton-Century-Crofts, 1912, 1940.

_____. MORE JATAKA TALES. Retold by Ellen C. Babbitt. Illus. Ellsworth Young. New York: Appleton-Century-Crofts, c.1922, c.1950. P

Jewett, Eleanore Myers. WHICH WAS WITCH? TALES OF GHOSTS AND MAGIC FROM KOREA. Illus. Taro Yashima. New York: Viking, c.1953, 1950.

Johnson, Gyneth. HOW DONKEYS CAME TO HAITI AND OTHER TALES. Illus. Angelo di Benedetto. New York: Devon-Adair, 1949.

Jones, Gwyn. SCANDINAVIAN LEGENDS AND FOLK-TALES. Illus. Joan Kiddell-Monroe. New York: Oxford University Press, 1956.

_____. WELSH LEGENDS AND FOLK-TALES. Illus. Joan Kiddell-Monroe. New York: Walck, 1955. G

Jones, Hettie. COYOTE TALES. Illus. Louis Mofsie. New York: Holt, Rinehart and Winston, 1974.

_____. LONGHOUSE WINTER: IROQUOIS TRANSFORMATION TALES. Illus. Nicholas Gaetano. New York: Holt, Rinehart and Winston, 1972.

Jordan, Philip. THE BURRO BENEDICTO: AND OTHER FOLKTALES AND LEGENDS OF MEXICO. New York: Coward-McCann, 1960. G

Kaplan, Irma. FAIRY TALES FROM SWEDEN. Illus. Carol Calder. Chicago: Follett, 1967.

Karasz, Ilonka, illustrator. THE TWELVE DAYS OF CHRISTMAS. New York: Harper, 1949. pb

Kaula, Edna Mason. AFRICAN VILLAGE FOLKTALES. Illus. Edna Mason Kaula. New York: World, 1968.

Kavčič, Vladimir. THE GOLDEN BIRD: FOLKTALES FROM SLOVENIA. Illus. Mae Gerhard. Transl. Jan Dekker and Helen Lenček. New York: World, 1969.

Keeley, H. H. and Christine Price. THE CITY OF THE DAGGER AND OTHER TALES FROM BURMA. Illus. Christine Price. New York: Warne, 1971. P.

Kelsey, Alice Geer. ONCE THE HODJA.

Illus. Frank Dobias. New York: McKay, 1943.

Kelsey, Alice Geer. ONCE THE MULLAH: PERSIAN FOLK TALES. Illus. Kurt Werth. New York: McKay, 1954.

Kendall, Carol and Yao-wen Li. SWEET AND SOUR: TALES FROM CHINA. Illus. Shirley Felts. New York: Seabury, c.1978, 1979.

Kent, Jack. THE FAT CAT: A DANISH FOLKTALE. Illus. Jack Kent. New York: Parents, 1971. pb

_____. MORE FABLES OF AESOP. Illus. Jack Kent. New York: Parents, 1974.

Kijima, Hajime. LITTLE WHITE HEN. Illus. Setsuko Hane. New York: Harcourt, Brace & World, 1967, 1969. pb

Kim, So-Un. THE STORY BAG: A COLLECTION OF KOREAN FOLK TALES. Trans. Setsu Hagashi. Illus. Kim Eui-hwan. Rutland, Vt.: Tuttle, 1955.

Kimishima, Hisako. THE PRINCESS OF THE RICE FIELDS: AN INDONESIAN FOLK TALE. Illus. Sumiko Mizushi. New York: Walker/Weatherhill, 1970. pb

Kirn, Ann. BEESWAX CATCHES A THIEF: FROM A CONGO FOLKTALE. Illus. Ann Kirn. New York: Norton, 1968. pb

_____. NINE IN A LINE: FROM AN OLD, OLD FOLKTALE. Illus. Ann Kirn. Arabic by Leila Leonard. New York: Norton, 1966. pb

_____. THE PEACOCK AND THE CROW. Illus. Ann Kirn. New York: Four Winds, 1969. pb

Korel, Edward. LISTEN AND I'LL TELL YOU. Illus. Quentin Blake. Philadelphia: Lippincott, c.1962, 1964.

Kouzel, Daisy, adaptor and translator. THE CUCKOO's REWARD / EL PREMIA DEL CUCO: A FOLK TALE FROM MEXICO IN SPANISH AND ENGLISH. Illus. Earl Thollander. New York: Doubleday, 1977. pb

Krueger, Kermit. THE GOLDEN SWANS: A PICTURE STORY FROM THAILAND. Illus. Ed Young. New York: World, 1969. G

_____. THE SERPENT PRINCE: FOLKTALES FROM NORTHEASTERN THAILAND. Illus. Yoko Mitsuhashi. New York: World, 1969. P

La Fontaine, Jean de. THE HARE AND THE TORTOISE. Illus. Brian Wildsmith. New York: Watts, c.1966, 1967. pb

_____. THE LION AND THE RAT. Illus. Brian Wildsmith. New York: Watts, 1963. pb

_____. THE MILLER, THE BOY AND THE DONKEY. Illus. Brian Wildsmith. New York:

Watts, 1969. pb

La Fontaine, Jean de. THE NORTH WIND AND THE SUN. Illus. Brian Wildsmith. New York: Watts, 1964. pb

_____. THE RICH MAN AND THE SHOEMAKER. Illus. Brian Wildsmith. New York: Watts, 1965. pb

Lang, Andrew. THE BLUE FAIRY BOOK. Illus. H. J. Ford and J. P. Jacomb Hood. New York: Longmans, Green, 1929. P

_____. THE CRIMSON FAIRY BOOK. Illus. H. J. Ford. New York: Longmans, Green, 1903. N

_____. FIFTY FAVORITE FAIRY TALES. Chosen from the color fairy books of Andrew Lang by Kathleen Lines. Illus. Margery Gill. New York: Watts, c.1963, 1964. P

_____. THE GREEN FAIRY BOOK. Illus. Dorothy Lake Gregory. Forword by Mary Gould Davis. New York: Longmans, Green, 1948. P

_____. THE GREY FAIRY BOOK. New York: Dover, 1967. N

_____. THE OLIVE FAIRY BOOK. Illus. H. J. Ford. New York: Longmans, Green, 1907.

_____. THE ORANGE FAIRY BOOK. Illus. Christine Price. Foreword by Mary Gould Davis. New York: McKay, 1949. N

_____. THE PINK FAIRY BOOK. New York: Dover, 1967. N

_____. THE RED FAIRY BOOK. Illus. H. J. Ford and Lancelot Speed. New York: Longmans, Green, 1929.

_____. THE ROSE FAIRY BOOK. Illus. Vera Bock. New York: McKay, 1948. P

_____. TO YOUR GOOD HEALTH: A RUSSIAN FOLK TALE. Illus. Mehlli Gobhai. New York: Holiday, 1973. pb

_____. THE VIOLET FAIRY BOOK. Illus. H. J. Ford. New York: Longmans, Green, 1901.

_____. THE YELLOW FAIRY BOOK. Illus. Jennie Harbour. New York: McKay, 1927.

Langstaff, John. FROG WENT A'COURTIN'. illus. Feodor Rojankovsky. New York: Harcourt, Brace & World, 1955. pb

Leach, Maria. HOW THE PEOPLE SANG THE MOUNTAINS UP: HOW AND WHY STORIES. Illus. Glen Rounds. New York: Viking, 1967.

_____. THE LION WHO SNEEZED: FOLKTALES AND MYTHS OF THE CAT. Illus. Helen Siegl. New York: Crowell, 1977.

_____. THE LUCK BOOK. Illus. Kurt Werth

Cleveland: World, 1964.

Leach, Maria. NOODLES, NITWITS AND NUM-SKULLS. Illus. Kurt Werth. Cleveland: World, 1961.

————. THE THING AT THE FOOT OF THE BED AND OTHER SCARY TALES. Illus. Kurt Werth. Cleveland: World, 1959.

Le Cain, Errol. THE WHITE CAT. Retold and Illus. Errol Le Cain. New York: Bradbury, 1973. pb

Leekley, Thomas B. THE WORLD OF MANABOZ-HO. TALES OF THE CHIPPEWA INDIANS. Illus. Yeffe Kimball. New York: Vanguard, 1965.

Leeuw. SEE DE LEEUW.

Lefevre, Felicite. THE COCK, THE MOUSE AND THE LITTLE RED HEN. Illus. Tony Sarg. Philadelphia: Macrae-Smith, n.d. pb

Leodhas, Sorche Nic. ALWAYS ROOM FOR ONE MORE. Illus. Nonny Hogrogian. New York: Holt, Rinehart & Winston, 1965. pb

————. BY LOCH AND BY LIN: TALES FROM SCOTTISH BALLADS. Illus. Vera Bock. New York: Holt, Rinehart & Winston, 1969. N

————. GAELIC GHOSTS. Illus. Nonny Hogrogian. New York: Holt, Rinehart & Winston, 1963.

————. GHOSTS GO HAUNTING. Illus. Nonny Hogrogian. New York: Holt, Rinehart & Winston, 1965.

————. HEATHER AND BROOM: TALES OF THE SCOTTISH HIGHLANDS. Illus. Consuelo Joerns. New York: Holt, Rinehart & Winston, 1960.

————. SEA-SPELL AND MOOR MAGIC: TALES OF THE WESTERN ISLES. Illus. Vera Bock. New York: Holt, Rinehart & Winston, 1968. P

————. THISTLE AND THYME: TALES AND LEGENDS FROM SCOTLAND. New York: Holt, Rinehart & Winston, 1962.

————. TWELVE GREAT BLACK CATS: AND OTHER EERIE SCOTTISH TALES. Illus. Vera Bock. New York: Dutton, 1971.

Lester, Julius. BLACK FOLKTALES. Illus. Tom Feelings. New York: Richard W. Baron, 1969. P

————. THE KNEE-HIGH MAN. Illus. Ralph Pinto. New York: Dial, 1972.

Lexau, Joan M. CROCODILE AND HEN. Illus. Joan Sandin. New York: Harper, 1969. pb

————. IT ALL BEGAN WITH A DRIP, DRIP, DRIP... Illus. Joan Sandin. New York :

McCall, 1970. pb

Lin, Adet. THE MILKY WAY AND OTHER CHIN-ESE FOLK TALES. Illus. Enrico Arno. New York: Harcourt, Brace & World, 1961.

Lines, Kathleen. DICK WHITTINGTON. Illus. Edward Ardizzone. New York: Walck, 1970. pb

Littledale, Freya. GHOSTS AND SPIRITS OF MANY LANDS. Illus. Stefan Martin. Garden City, N.Y.: Doubleday, 1970.

Löfgren, Ulf. THE BOY WHO ATE MORE THAN THE GIANT AND OTHER SWEDISH FOLKTALES. Trans. from the Swedish by Sheila LaFarge. New York and Cleveland: William Collins and World Publishing Company in cooperation with the U.S. Committee for UNICEF, 1978.

Lowe, Patricia Tracy. THE LITTLE HORSE OF SEVEN COLORS AND OTHER PORTUGUESE FOLK TALES. From translations from the Portuguese by Anne Marie Jauss. New York: World, 1970.

Lowrie, Richard, translator. SOLDIER AND TSAR IN THE FOREST. Illus. Uri Shulevitz. New York: Farrar, Straus and Giroux, 1972. pb

Lu Mar, Shuh Yin. SEE MAR, SHUH YIN LU.

Lubin, Leonard B. THE WHITE CAT by Madame d'Aulnoy. Adapted and illus. Leonard B. Lubin. Boston: Little, Brown, 1978.

Lum, Peter. FAIRY TALES OF CHINA. Illus. G. W. Miller. New York: Dutton, 1959.

————. ITALIAN FAIRY TALES. Illus. Harry and Ilse Toothill. Chicago: Follett, 1963.

Lunn, Janet: THE TWELVE DANCING PRINCESS-ES: A FAIRY STORY RETOLD. Illus. Lazlo Gal. New York: Methuen, 1970. pb

Lupe de Osma. THE WITCHES' RIDE AND OTHER TALES FROM COSTA RICA. New York: Morrow, 1957. N

Lurie, Alison. CLEVER GRETCHEN AND OTHER FORGOTTEN FOLKTALES. Illus. Margot Tomes. New York: Crowell, 1980.

Luzzatto, Paola Caboara. LONG AGO WHEN THE EARTH WAS FLAT: THREE TALES FROM AFRICA. Illus. Aimone Sambury. Designed by Bruno Munari. New York: Collins, 1980. pb

Maas, Selva. THE MOON PAINTERS AND OTHER ESTONIAN FOLK TALES. Illus. Lazlo Gal. New York: Viking, 1971.

MacFarlane, Iris. TALES AND LEGENDS FROM INDIA. Illus. Eric Thomas. New York: Watts, 1965. G

MacManus, Seumas. THE BOLD HEROES OF HUNGRY HILL AND OTHER IRISH FOLK TALES.

Illus. Jay Chollick. New York: Farrar, 1951. P

MacManus, Seumas. DONEGAL FAIRY STORIES. Illus. Frank Verbeck. New York: Dover, 1900, 1968. N

_____. DONEGAL FAIRY TALES. Garden City, N.Y.: Doubleday, 1937. N

_____. DONEGAL WONDER BOOK. New York: Frederick A. Stokes, 1926. N

_____. HIBERNIAN NIGHTS. Intro. Padraic Colum. Illus. Paul Kennedy. New York: Macmillan, 1963. P

_____. IN CHIMNEY CORNERS: MERRY TALES OF IRISH FOLK LORE. Garden City, N.Y.: Doubleday, 1937. N

_____. THE WELL O' THE WORLD'S END AND OTHER FOLK TALES. Illus. Richard Bennett. New York: Macmillan, 1939.

MacMillan, Cyrus. CANADIAN FAIRY TALES. New York: Dodd, 1922. G

_____. CANADIAN WONDER TALES. New York: Dodd, 1918. N

_____. GLOOSKAP'S COUNTRY AND OTHER INDIAN TALES. Illus. John A. Hall. New York: Oxford University Press, 1956. N

Maestro, Giulio. THE TORTOISE'S TUG OF WAR. Illus. Giulio Maestro. Scarsdale, N.Y.: Bradbury, 1971. pb

Maher, Ramona. THE BLIND BOY AND THE LOON, AND OTHER ESKIMO MYTHS. Illustrated. New York: Day, 1969.

Maitland, Anthony. IDLE JACK. Retold and illus. Anthony Maitland. New York: Farrar, Straus and Giroux, c.1977, 1979. pb

Manning-Sanders, Ruth. A BOOK OF CHARMS AND CHANGELINGS. Illus. Robin Jacques. New York: Dutton, c.1971, 1972. P

_____. A BOOK OF DEVILS AND DEMONS. Illus. Robin Jacques. New York: Dutton, 1970.

_____. A BOOK OF DRAGONS. Illus. Robin Jacques. New York: Dutton, c.1964, 1965.

_____. A BOOK OF DWARFS. Illus. Robin Jacques. New York: Dutton, c.1963, 1964.

_____. A BOOK OF GHOSTS AND GOBLINS. Illus. Robin Jacques. New York: Dutton, c.1968, 1969.

_____. A BOOK OF GIANTS. Illus. Robin Jacques. New York: Dutton, c.1962, 1963.

_____. A BOOK OF MAGICAL BEASTS.

Illus. Raymond Briggs. Camden, N.J.: Nelson, c.1965, 1970.

Manning-Sanders, Ruth. A BOOK OF MERMAIDS. Illus. Robin Jacques. New York: Dutton, c.1967, 1968.

_____. A BOOK OF OGRES AND TROLLS. Illus. Robin Jacques. New York: Dutton, c.1972, 1973.

_____. A BOOK OF PRINCES AND PRINCESSES. Illus. Robin Jacques. New York: Dutton, 1969.

_____. A BOOK OF SORCERERS AND SPELLS. Illus. Robin Jacques. New York: Dutton, c.1973, 1974.

_____. A BOOK OF WITCHES. Illus. Robin Jacques. New York: Dutton, c.1965, 1966.

_____. A BOOK OF WIZARDS. Illus. Robin Jacques. New York: Dutton, c.1966, 1967.

_____. A CHOICE OF MAGIC. Illus. Robin Jacques. New York: Dutton, 1970.

_____. DAMIAN AND THE DRAGON. MODERN GREEK FOLK-TALES. Illus. William Papas. New York: Roy, 1965.

_____. GIANNI AND THE OGRE. Illus. William Stobbs. New York: Dutton, c.1970, 1971.

_____. THE GLASS MAN AND THE GOLDEN BIRD: HUNGARIAN FOLK AND FAIRY TALES. Illus. Victor G. Ambrus. New York: Roy, 1968.

_____. JONNIKIN AND THE FLYING BASKET: FRENCH FOLK AND FAIRY TALES. Illus. Victor G. Ambrus. New York: Dutton, 1969. N

_____. PETER AND THE PISKIES. CORNISH FOLK AND FAIRY TALES. Illus. Raymond Briggs. New York: Roy, 1958. P

_____. RED INDIAN FOLK AND FAIRY TALES. Illus. C. Walter Hodges. New York: Roy, c.1960, 1962. N

_____. THE RED KING AND THE WITCH. GYPSY FOLK AND FAIRY TALES. Illus. Victor G. Ambrus. New York: Roy, 1964.

_____. TORTOISE TALES. Illus. Donald Chaffin. Nashville, Tenn.: Nelson, c.1972, 1974.

Manton, J. and Robert Gittings. THE FLYING HORSES: TALES FROM CHINA. Illus. Derek Collard. New York: Holt, Rinehart & Winston, 1977.

Mar, Shuh Yin Lu. CHINESE TALES OF FOLKLORE. Illus. Howard Simon. New York: Criterion, c.1964.

Marks, John. SPANISH FAIRY TALES. Illus.

Roberta Moynihan. New York: Knopf, 1958. G

Marmur, Mildred. JAPANESE FAIRY TALES. Illus. Benvenuti. New York: Golden, 1960. G

Marriott, Alice Lee. WINTER-TELLING STORIES. Illus. Richard Cuffari. New York: Crowell, c.1947, 1969.

Marriott, Alice and Carol K. Rachlin. AMERICAN INDIAN MYTHOLOGY. New York: Crowell, 1968. G

Martignoni, Margaret E., editor. THE ILLUS-TRATED TREASURY OF CHILDREN'S LITERA-TURE. Compiled with the original illustrations under the direction of P. Edward Ernest. New York: Grosset and Dunlap, 1955. P

Martin, Frances Gardiner McEntee. NINE TALES OF COYOTE. Illus. Dorothy McEntee. New York: Harper, 1950. P

Martin, Fran. NINE TALES OF RAVEN. Illus. Dorothy McEntee. New York: Harper, 1951.

_____. RAVEN-WHO-SET-THINGS-RIGHT. INDIAN TALES OF THE NORTHWEST COAST. Illus. Dorothy McEntee. New York: Harper & Row, 1975.

Masey, Mary Lou. STORIES OF THE STEPPES: KAZAKH FOLKTALES. Illus. Helen Basilevsky. New York: McKay, 1968.

Masson, Elsie. FOLK TALES OF BRITTANY. Ed. by Amena Pendleton. Philadelphia: Macrae-Smith, 1929. N

Matson, Emerson N. LEGENDS OF THE GREAT CHIEFS. Illustrated. Nashville: Nelson, 1972.

_____. LONGHOUSE LEGENDS. Illus. Lorence Bjorklund. Camden, N.J: Nelson, 1968. P

Matsui, Tadashi. ONIROKU AND THE CARPENTER. Trans. Masako Matsuno. Illus. Suekichi Akaba. Englewood Cliffs, N.J.: Prentice-Hall, 1968. pb

Matsutani, Miyoko. THE CRANE MAIDEN. . Illus. Chihiro Iwasaki. New York: Parent's, 1968. pb

_____. THE FISHERMAN UNDER THE SEA. Illus. Chihiro Iwasaki. New York: Parent's, 1969.

_____. THE FOX WEDDING. Illus. Yasuo Segawa. Trans. Masako Matsuno. Chicago: Encyclopaedia Britannica,1963. G, pb

_____. HOW THE WITHERED TREES BLOS-SOMED. Illus. Yasuo Segawa. Philadelphia: Lippincott, 1969. pb

Mayer, Marianne. BEAUTY AND THE BEAST. Illus. Mercer Mayer. New York: Four Winds, 1978. pb

Mayne, William. GHOSTS: AN ANTHOLOGY. New York: Nelson, 1971. P

Mayne, William. WILLIAM MAYNE'S BOOK OF GIANTS. Illus. Raymond Briggs. New York: Dutton, 1969. P

McAlpine, Helen and William. JAPANESE TALES AND LEGENDS. Illus. Joan Kiddell-Monroe. New York: Walck, 1958.

McDermott, Beverly Brodsky. THE CRYSTAL APPLE: A RUSSIAN TALE. New York: Viking, 1974. G, pb

_____. SEDNA: AN ESKIMO MYTH. Adapted and illustrated by Beverly Brodsky McDermott. New York: Viking, 1975. pb

McDermott, Gerald. ANANSI THE SPIDER: A TALE FROM THE ASHANTI. New York: Holt, Rinehart & Winston, 1972. pb

_____. THE STONE-CUTTER: A JAPANESE FOLKTALE. New York: Viking, 1975. pb

McDowell, Robert E. and Edward Lavitt. THIRD WORLD VOICES FOR CHILDREN. Illus. Barbara Kohn Isaac. New York: Odakai, 1971. P

McGovern, Ann. HALF A KINGDOM: AN ICE-LANDIC FOLKTALE. Illus. Nola Langner. New York: Warne, 1977. pb

_____. HEE HAW. Illus. Eric von Schmidt. Boston: Houghton Mifflin, 1969. pb

_____. TOO MUCH NOISE. Illus. Simms Taback. Boston: Houghton Mifflin, 1967. pb

McHale, Ethel Kharasch. SON OF THUNDER: AN OLD LAPP TALE RETOLD. Illus. Ruth Bornstein. Chicago: Children's Press, 1974. G, pb

McKee, David. THE MAN WHO WAS GOING TO MIND THE HOUSE: A NORWEGIAN FOLK TALE. Illus. David McKee. New York: Abelard-Schuman, 1972. pb

McKinley, Robin. BEAUTY: A RETELLING OF THE STORY OF BEAUTY AND THE BEAST. New York: Harper, 1978.

McNeil, James. THE DOUBLE KNIGHTS. MORE TALES FROM ROUND THE WORLD. Illus. Theo Dimson. New York: Walck, 1964.

Mehdevi, Anne Sinclair. PERSIAN FOLK AND FAIRY TALES. Illus. Paul E. Kennedy. New York: Knopf, 1970.

Melzack, Ronald. THE DAY TUK BECAME A HUNTER, AND OTHER ESKIMO STORIES. Illus. Carol Jones. New York: Dodd, Mead, 1967.

_____. RAVEN, CREATOR OF THE WORLD. Illus. Laszlo Gal. Boston: Little, Brown, 1970.

Merriam, Eve, reteller. EPAMINONDAS. Illus. Trina Schart Hyman. Chicago: Follett, 1968. pb

Michael, Maurice and Pamela. FAIRY TALES

FROM BOHEMIA. Illus. John Lathey. Chicago: Follett, c.1966, 1968. G

Michael, Maurice and Pamela. PORTUGUESE FAIRY TALES. Illus. Harry and Ilse Toothill. Chicago: Follett, 1965. P

Minard, Rosemary. WOMENFOLK AND FAIRY TALES. Illus. Suzanne Klein. Boston: Houghton Mifflin, 1975.

Mincieli, Rose Laura. OLD NEAPOLITAN FAIRY TALES. Selected and retold from II Penta-merone. Illus. Beni Montresor. New York: Knopf, 1963.

Mittlemann, Gertrude. THE BIRD OF THE GOLD-EN FEATHER AND OTHER ARABIC FOLKTALES. Illus. Gertrude Mittlemann. New York: Roy, 1969.

Mobley, Jane. THE STAR HUSBAND. Illus. Anna Vojtech. Garden City, N.Y.: Doubleday, 1979. pb

Mohan, Beverly. PUNIA AND THE KING OF THE SHARKS, A HAWAIIAN TALE. Illus. Don Bolognese. Chicago: Follett, 1964. pb

Montgomerie, Norah. THE MERRY LITTLE FOX, AND OTHER ANIMAL STORIES. Illus. Norah Montgomerie. New York: Abelard-Schuman, 1964.

_____. TWENTY-FIVE FABLES. Illus. Norah Montgomerie. New York: Abelard-Schuman, 1961.

Mui, Shan. SEVEN MAGIC ORDERS. Illus. Y. T. Mui. Ed. Ruth Tabrah. New York: Weather-hill, 1972. pb

Mui, Y. T. THE MAGIC BRUSH. Adapted from the original folktale by Robert B. Goodman and Robert A. Spicer. Ed. Ruth Tabrah. Illus. Y. T. Mui. Honolulu, Hawaii: Island Heritage. pb 1974.

Müller-Guggenbühl, Fritz. SWISS-ALPINE FOLK TALES. Trans. Katherine Potts. Illus. Joan Kiddell-Monroe. New York: Walck, 1958. P

Nahmad, H. M. THE PEASANT AND THE DON-KEY: TALES OF THE NEAR AND MIDDLE EAST. Illus. William Papas. New York: Walck, 1968. G

_____. A PORTION IN PARADISE, AND OTHER JEWISH FOLKTALES. New York: Norton, 1970. G

Ness, Evaline. LONG, BROAD, AND QUICKEYE. New York: Scribner's, 1969. pb

_____. MR. MIACCA: AN ENGLISH FOLK TALE. Illus. Evaline Ness. New York: Holt, Rinehart & Winston, 1967. pb

SEE ALSO Jacobs. TOM TIT TOT.

Neufield, Rose. BEWARE THE MAN WITHOUT A BEARD AND OTHER GREEK FOLKTALES. Illus. Marjorie Auerback. New York: Knopf, 1969.

Newell, Edythe W. THE RESCUE OF THE SUN AND OTHER TALES FROM THE FAR NORTH. Illus. Franz Altschuler. Chicago: Albert Whitman, 1970.

Newman, Shirlee. FOLK TALES OF LATIN-AMERICA. Indianapolis: Bobbs-Merrill, 1962.

Nickless, Will. THE BOOK OF FABLES. Illus-trated. New York; Warne, 1963.

Novak, Miroslav. FAIRY TALES FROM JAPAN. Illus. Jaroslav Serýeh. New York: Hamlyn, 1970.

Nunn, Jessie A. AFRICAN FOLK TALES. Illus. Ernest Crichlow. New York: Funk and Wag-nalls, 1969.

O'Faolain, Eileen. CHILDREN OF THE SALMON AND OTHER IRISH FOLK TALES. Illus. Trina Hyman. Boston: Little, Brown, 1965. G

_____. IRISH SAGAS AND FOLK-TALES. Illus. Joan Kiddell-Monroe. New York: Walck, 1954. G

Olcott, Frances Jenkins. WONDER TALES FROM FAIRY ISLES, ENGLAND, CORNWALL, WALES, SCOTLAND, MAN AND IRELAND. Illus. Con-stance Whittmore. New York: Longmans, 1929. N

Opie, Iona and Peter Opie. THE CLASSIC FAIRY TALES. Illus. New York: Oxford University Press, 1974.

Otsuka, Yuzo. SUHO AND THE WHITE HORSE: A LEGEND OF MONGOLIA. Illus. Suekichi Akaba. Trans. Yasuko Hirawa. Indianapolis: Bobbs-Merrill, 1969. pb

Owen, Ruth Bryan. THE CASTLE IN THE SILVER WOOD AND OTHER SCANDINAVIAN FAIRY TALES. Illus. Marc Simont. New York: Dodd, 1939.

Ozaki, Yei Theodora. THE JAPANESE FAIRY BOOK. Illus. Kakuzo Fujiyama. New York: Dover, 1967.

Palazzo, Tony, reteller. THE LITTLE RED HEN. Illus. Tony Palazzo. Garden City, N.Y.: Doubleday, 1958. pb

Palmer, Robin. DRAGONS, UNICORNS, AND OTHER MAGICAL BEASTS: A DICTIONARY OF FABULOUS CREATURES WITH OLD TALES AND VERSES ABOUT THEM. Illus. Don Bolognese. New York: Walck, 1966. P

_____. FAIRY ELVES. Illustrated. New York: Walck, 1964. P

Papashvily, George. YES AND NO STORIES: A

BOOK OF GEORGIAN FOLK TALES. Illus. Simon Lissim. New York: Harper, 1946. N

Parker, Arthur Caswell. SKUNNY WUNDY: SENECA INDIAN TALES. Illus. George Armstrong. Chicago: Albert Whitman, c.1926, c.1970.

Parker, Katherine Langloh. AUSTRALIAN LEGENDARY TALES. Selected and edited by H. Drake-Brockman. Illus. Elizabeth Durack. New York: Viking, 1966. N

Pearce, Philippa. BEAUTY AND THE BEAST. Illus. Alan Barrett. New York: Crowell, 1972. pb

Pellowski, Anne. THE NINE CRYING DOLLS: A STORY FROM POLAND. Illus. Charles Mikolaycak. New York: Philomel, 1980. G, pb

Penny, Grace Jackson. TALES OF THE CHEYENNES. New York: Houghton, 1953. G

Perrault, Charles. CINDERELLA. Adapted from Perrault's CENDRILLON of 1697 by John Fowles. Illus. Sheilah Beckett. Boston: Little, Brown, 1974. pb

_____. CINDERELLA OR THE LITTLE GLASS SLIPPER. Illus. Marcia Brown. New York: Scribner's, 1954. pb

_____. CINDERELLA OR THE LITTLE GLASS SLIPPER. Illus. Errol Le Cain. Scarsdale, N.Y.: Bradbury, 1972. pb

_____. FAMOUS FAIRY TALES. Illus. Charles Mozley. Trans. Sarah Chokla Gross. New York: Watts, 1969. P

_____. FAVORITE FAIRY TALES TOLD IN FRANCE. SEE Haviland, Virgina.

_____. THE LITTLE RED RIDING HOOD. Illus. William Stobbs. New York: Walck, 1972. pb

_____. PERRAULT'S COMPLETE FAIRY TALES. Trans. A. E. Johnson and others. Illus. W. Heath Robinson. New York: Dodd, Mead, 1961. P

_____. PERRAULT'S FAIRY TALES. Trans. A. E. Johnson. Illus. Gustave Doré. New York: Dover, 1969. P

_____. PUSS IN BOOTS. Illus. Marcia Brown. New York: Scribner's, 1952. pb

_____. PUSS IN BOOTS. Illus. Hans Fischer. New York: Harcourt, Brace & World, c.1957, c.1959.

_____. PUSS IN BOOTS. Illus. Barry Wilkinson. New York: World, 1969.

_____. THE SLEEPING BEAUTY. Warren Chappell, reteller. Illus. Warren Chappell. New York: Knopf, 1961.

_____. SLEEPING BEAUTY. Illus. Arthur Rackham. New York: Viking, 1972.

Picard, Barbara Leonie. CELTIC TALES, LEGENDS OF TALL WARRIORS AND OLD ENCHANTMENTS. Illus. John G. Galsworthy. New York: Criterion, 1964.

_____. FRENCH LEGENDS, TALES AND FAIRY STORIES. Illus. Joan Kiddell-Monroe. New York: Walck, 1958.

_____. GERMAN HERO-SAGAS AND FOLKTALES. Illus. Joan Kiddell-Monroe. New York: 1958. G

Piggott, Juliet. MEXICAN FOLK TALES. Illus. Joan Spencer. New York: Crane Russack, c.1933, 1936. G

Pilkington, Francis Meredith. SHAMROCK AND SPEAR: TALES AND LEGENDS FROM IRELAND. Illus. Leo and Diane Dillon. New York: Holt, Rinehart & Winston, 1966. P

Ponsot, Marie. RUSSIAN FAIRY TALES. Illus. Benvenuti. New York: Golden, 1960.

Pratt, Davis and Elsa Kula. MAGIC ANIMALS OF JAPAN. Berkeley, Calif.: Parnassus, 1967.

Preussler, Otfried. THE WISE MEN OF SCHILDA. Trans. Anthea Bell. Illus. Fr. J. Tripp. New York: Abelard-Schuman, 1962. G

Price, Christine. THE RICH MAN AND THE SINGER. FOLK TALES FROM ETHIOPIA. Told by Mesfin Habte-Mariam. Edited and illus. Christine Price. New York: Dutton, 1971. G

_____. SIXTY AT A BLOW: A TALL TALE FROM TURKEY. Illus. Christine Price. New York: Dutton, 1968. pb

_____. THE VALIANT CHATTEE-MAKER: A FOLKTALE OF INDIA. New York: Warne, 1965. pb

Pridham, Radost. A GIFT FROM THE HEART: FOLK TALES FROM BULGARIA. Illus. Pauline Baynes. Cleveland: World, 1967.

Provensen, Alice and Martin. THE PROVENSEN BOOK OF FAIRY TALES. New York: Random House, 1971. P

Pugh, Ellen. MORE TALES FROM THE WELSH HILLS. Illus. Joan Sandin. New York: Dodd, Mead, 1971.

_____. TALES FROM THE WELSH HILLS. Illus. Joan Sandin. New York: Dodd, Mead, 1968.

Pushkin, Alexander. THE TALE OF CZAR SALTAN: OR, THE PRINCE AND THE SWAN PRINCESS. Retold by Patricia Tracy Lowe. Illus. I. Bilibin. New York: Crowell, 1975. G, pb

_____. THE TALE OF THE GOLDEN COCKEREL. Retold by Patricia Tracy Lowe. Illus. I. Bilibin. New York: Crowell, 1975. G, pb

Pyle, Howard. TWILIGHT LAND. New York: Harper, n.d. N

_____. THE WONDER CLOCK: OR FOUR AND TWENTY MARVELOUS TALES, BEING ONE FOR EACH HOUR OF THE DAY. Illus. Howard Pyle. Embellished with verses by Katharine Pyle. New York: Harper, 1887, 1915. P

Quigley, Lillian. THE BLIND MEN AND THE ELEPHANT: AN OLD TALE FROM THE LAND OF INDIA. Illus. Janice Holland. New York: Scribner's, 1959. pb

Quinn, Zdenka and John Paul. THE WATER SPRITE OF THE GOLDEN TOWN: FOLK TALES OF BOHEMIA. Illus. Deborah Ray. Philadelphia: Macrae Smith, 1971. G

Rackham, Arthur. ARTHUR RACKHAM FAIRY BOOK. Illus. Arthur Rackham. Philadelphia: Lippincott, n.d.

_____. FAIRY TALES FROM MANY LANDS. Illus. Arthur Rackham. New York: Viking, 1974. P

SEE ALSO Aesop. AESOP'S FABLES; Darrell, Margery.

Ransome, Arthur. THE FOOL OF THE WORLD AND THE FLYING SHIP. Illus. Uri Shulevitz. New York: Farrar, Straus & Giroux, 1968. pb

_____. OLD PETER'S RUSSIAN TALES. Illus. Dmitri Mitrokhin. New York: Nelson, 1916.

Reed, Gwendolyn. THE TALKATIVE BEASTS: MYTHS, FABLES AND POEMS OF INDIA. Photographs by Stella Snead. New York: Lothrop, Lee & Shepard, 1969.

Rees, Ennis. BRER RABBIT AND HIS TRICKS. Illus. Edward Gorey. New York: Young Scott, 1967. G.

Reeves, James. ENGLISH FABLES AND FAIRY STORIES. Illus. Joan Kiddell-Monroe. New York: Walck, 1954.

SEE ALSO Aesop. FABLES FROM AESOP.

Regniers. SEE De Regniers.

Reid, Barbara and Ewa Reid. THE COBBLER'S REWARD. Illus. Charles Mikolaycak. New York: Macmillan, 1978. pb

Reid, Dorothy M. TALES OF NANABOZHO. Illus. Donald Grant. New York: Walck, 1963. G

Rice, Eve. ONCE IN A WOOD: TEN TALES FROM AESOP. Adapted and illus. Eve Rice. New York: Greenwillow, 1979.

Richardson, Frederick. GREAT CHILDREN'S STORIES. Illus. Frederick Richardson.

Northbrook, Ill.: Hubbard, 1972.

Rickert, Edith. THE BOJABI TREE. Illus. Gleb Botkin. Garden City, N.Y.: Doubleday, 1923. pb

Riordan, James. TALES FROM CENTRAL RUSSIA. RUSSIAN TALES. VOLUME ONE. Illus. Krystyna Turska. Harmondsworth, Middlesex: Kestrel Books, 1976.

_____. TALES FROM TARTARY. RUSSIAN TALES. VOLUME TWO. Illus. Anthony Colbert. New York: Viking, 1979.

Ritchie, Alice. THE TREASURE OF LI-PO. Illus. T. Ritchie. New York: Harcourt, Brace, 1949.

Robbins, Ruth. BABOUSHKA AND THE THREE KINGS. Illus. Nicolas Sidjakov. Berkeley, Calif.: Parnassus, 1960. pb

Robertson, Dorothy Lewis. FAIRY TALES FROM VIET NAM. Illus. W. T. Mars. New York: Dodd, 1968.

_____. FAIRY TALES FROM THE PHILIPPINES. Illus. Howard M. Burns. New York: Dodd, 1971.

Robinson, Adjai. SINGING TALES OF AFRICA. Illus. Christine Price. New York: Scribner's, 1974.

_____. THREE AFRICAN TALES. Illus. Carole Byard. New York: Putnam, 1979.

Robinson, Gail and Douglas Hill. COYOTE THE TRICKSTER. LEGENDS OF THE NORTH AMERICAN INDIANS. Illus. Graham McCallum. New York: Crane Russak, c.1975, 1976.

Roche, A. K. THE CLEVER TURTLE. Adapted from an African Folktale. Illus. A. K. Roche. Englewood Cliffs, N.J.: Prentice-Hall, 1969. pb

Rockwell, Anne. THE OLD WOMAN AND HER PIG AND TEN OTHER STORIES. Told and illus. Anne Rockwell. New York: Crowell, 1979. pb

_____. THE STOLEN NECKLACE. Illus. Anne Rockwell. New York: World, 1968. pb

_____. THE THREE BEARS AND FIFTEEN OTHER STORIES. Illus. Anne Rockwell. New York: Crowell, 1975. pb

_____. TUHURAHURA AND THE WHALE. Illus. Anne Rockwell. New York: Parent's, 1971. G, pb

_____. WHEN THE DRUM SANG: AN AFRICAN FOLKTALE. Illus. Anne Rockwell. New York: Parent's, 1970. pb

SEE ALSO Jacobs, Joseph. MASTER OF ALL MASTERS.

Rose, Anne. AKIMBA AND THE MAGIC COW: A FOLKTALE FROM AFRICA. Woodcuts by Hope

Meryman. New York: Four Winds, 1976. pb

Ross, Eulalie Steinmetz. THE BLUE ROSE: A COLLECTION OF STORIES FOR GIRLS. Illus. Enrico Arno. New York: Harcourt, Brace and World, 1966.

_____. THE BURIED TREASURE AND OTHER PICTURE TALES. Illus. Josef Cellini. Philadelphia: Lippincott, 1958.

_____. THE LOST HALF-HOUR. Illus. Enrico Arno. New York: Harcourt, Brace and World, 1963.

Ross, Patricia Fent. IN MEXICO THEY SAY. Illus. Henry C. Pitz. New York: Knopf, 1942. P

Rostron, Richard. SORCERER'S APPRENTICE. Illus. Frank Lieberman. New York: Morrow, 1941.

Roy, Cal. THE SERPENT AND THE SUN: MYTHS OF THE MEXICAN WORLD. Illus. Cal Roy. New York: Farrar, Straus and Giroux, 1972. G

Rudolph, Marguerita. THE BRAVE SOLDIER AND A DOZEN DEVILS. Illus. Imero Gobbato. New York: Seabury, 1970. pb

_____. I AM YOUR MISFORTUNE. Illus. Imero Gobbato. New York: Seabury, 1968. pb

_____. THE MAGIC EGG AND OTHER FOLK STORIES OF RUMANIA. IIllus. Wallace Tripp. Boston: Little, Brown, 1971.

Running, Corinne. WHEN COYOTE WALKED THE EARTH: INDIAN TALES OF THE PACIFIC NORTHWEST. Illus. Richard Bennett. New York: Holt, 1949. N

Rushmore, Helen and Wolf Robe Hunt. THE DANCING HORSES OF ACOMA AND OTHER ACOMA INDIAN STORIES. Illus. Wolf Robe Hunt. Cleveland: World, 1963. N

Russell, Maurice. TOLD TO BURMESE CHILDREN. Illus. Monica Walker. New York: Roy, 1957. G

Ryder, Arthur. THE PANCHATANTRA. Chicago: University of Chicago, 1956. P

Sakade, Florence. JAPANESE CHILDREN'S STORIES. Illus. Yoshio Hayashi. Rutland, Vt.: Tuttle, c.1952, Rev. 1959.

_____. JAPANESE CHILDREN'S FAVORITE STORIES. Illus. Yoshisuke Kurosaki. Rutland, Vt.: Tuttle, 1958.

San Souci, Robert. THE LEGEND OF SCARFACE: A BLACKFEET INDIAN TALE. Illus. Daniel San Souci. Garden City, N.Y.: Doubleday, 1978. pb

_____. SONG OF SEDNA. Illus. Robert San Souci. Garden City, N.Y.: Doubleday, 1981. G

Savory, Phyllis. CONGO FIRESIDE TALES. Illus. Joshua Tolford. New York: Hastings House, 1962.

_____. LION OUTWITTED BY HARE AND OTHER AFRICAN TALES. Illus. Franz Altschuler. Chicago: Albert Whitman, 1971. G

Sawyer, Ruth. JOURNEY CAKE HO! Illus. Robert McCloskey. New York: Viking, 1956. pb

_____. THE LONG CHRISTMAS. Illus. Valenti Angelo. New York: Viking, 1941.

_____. PICTURE TALES FROM SAPIN. Illus. Carlos Sanchez. New York: Lippincott, 1936.

_____. THIS WAY TO CHRISTMAS. Illustrated. New York: Harper, 1916.

_____. THE WAY OF THE STORYTELLER. New York: Viking, 1962.

Saxe, John Godfrey. THE BLIND MEN AND THE ELEPHANT. Illus. Paul Galdone. New York: McGraw-Hill, 1963. pb

Schatz, Letta. EXTRAORDINARY TUG-OF-WAR. Illus. John Burningham. New York: Follett, 1968. pb

Scheer, George P. CHEROKEE ANIMAL TALES. Illus. Robert Frankenberg. New York: Holiday, 1968.

Schiller, Barbara. THE WHITE RAT'S TALE. Illus. Adrienne Adams. New York: Holt, Rinehart & Winston, 1967. pb

Schimmel, Nancy. JUST ENOUGH TO MAKE A STORY: A SOURCEBOOK FOR STORYTELLING. Berkeley: Sister's Choice Press, 1978. N

Schoolcraft, Henry Rowe. SEE Bierhorst, John.

Schultz, George F. VIETNAMESE LEGENDS. Adapted from the Vietnamese by George F. Schultz. Rutland, Vt.: Tuttle, 1965. N

Scofield, Elizabeth. A FOX IN ONE BITE, AND OTHER TASTY TALES FROM JAPAN. Illus. K. Wakana. Palo Alto, Calif.: Kodansha, 1965.

_____. HOLD TIGHT, STICK TIGHT: A COLLECTION OF JAPANESE FOLK TALES. Illus. K. Wakana. Palo Alto, Calif.: Kodansha, 1966.

Scribner, Charles Jr. THE DEVIL'S BRIDGE. Illus. Evaline Ness. New York: Scribner's, 1978. pb

Sechrist, Elizabeth Hough. HEIGH-HO FOR HALLOWEEN. Illus Guy Fry. Philadelphia: Macrae Smith, 1948. P

_____. ONCE IN THE FIRST TIMES: FOLK TALES FROM THE PHILIPPINES. Illus. John Sheppard. Philadelphia: Macrae Smith, 1969.

Seed, Jenny. THE BUSHMAN'S DREAM: AFRI-CAN TALES OF THE CREATION. Illus. Bernard Brett. Scarsdale, N.Y: Bradbury, 1974. G

Seredy, Kate. THE GOOD MASTER. Illus. Kate Seredy. New York: Viking, 1935. N

Serraillier, Ian. THE BISHOP AND THE DEVIL. Illus. Simon Stern. New York: Warne, 1971. pb

Serwadda, W. Moses. SONGS AND STORIES FROM UGANDA. Transcribed and edited by Hewitt Pantaleoni. Illus. Leo and Diane Dillon. New York: Crowell, 1974. P

Serwer, Blanche Luria. LET'S STEAL THE MOON: JEWISH TALES, ANCIENT AND RECENT. Illus. Trina Schart Hyman. Boston: Little, Brown, 1970.

Seuling, Barbara. THE TEENY-TINY WOMAN: AN OLD ENGLISH GHOST TALE. New York: Viking, 1976. pb

Severo, Emöke de Papp, translator. THE GOOD-HEARTED YOUNGEST BROTHER: AN HUN-GARIAN FOLKTALE. Illus. Diane Goode. Scarsdale, N.Y.: Bradbury, 1981.

Sewell, Marcia, illustrator. THE WEE, WEE MAN-NIE AND THE BIG BIG COO: A SCOTTISH FOLKTALE. Boston: Little, Brown, 1977. pb

Shah, Idries. THE INCOMPARABLE EXPLOITS OF NASREDDIN MULLA. Illustrated. New York: Dutton.

Shedlock, Marie. THE ART OF THE STORY-TELLER. New York: Dover, c.1951, 1952.

Sheehan, Ethna. FOLK AND FAIRY TALES FROM AROUND THE WORLD. Illus. Mircea Vasilu. New York: Dodd, 1970.

Sheppard-Jones, Elisabeth. SCOTTISH LEG-ENDARY TALES. Illus. Paul Hogarth. Edinburgh: Nelson, 1962.

————. WELSH LEGENDARY TALES. Illus. Paul Hogarth. Edinburgh: Nelson, 1959.

Sherlock, Philip M. ANANSI THE SPIDER MAN: JAMAICAN FOLK TALES. Illus. Marcia Brown. New York: Crowell, 1954.

————. THE IGUANA'S TAIL: CRICK CRACK STORIES FROM THE CARIBBEAN. Illus. Gioia Fiammenghi. New York Crowell, 1969.

————. WEST INDIAN FOLK-TALES. Illus. Joan Kiddell-Monroe. New York: Walck, 1966.

Sherlock, Philip M. and Hilary Sherlock. EARS AND TAILS AND COMMON SENSE: MORE STORIES FROM THE CARIBBEAN. Illus. Aliki Brandenberg. New York: Crowell, 1974. G

Showalter, Jean B. THE DONKEY RIDE. Illus.

Tomi Ungerer. Garden City, N.Y.: Doubleday, 1967. pb

Shub, Elizabeth. SEE Grimm. ABOUT WISE MEN; FISHERMAN AND HIS WIFE; JORINDA AND JOR-INGEL; TWELVE DANCING PRINCESSES.

Shulevitz, Uri. THE MAGICIAN. An adaptation from the Yiddish of I. L. Peretz. New York: Macmillan, 1973. pb

Siddiqui, Ashraf and Marilyn Lerch. TOON-TOONY PIE AND OTHER TALES FROM PAKIS-TAN. Illus. Jan Fairservis. Cleveland: World, 1961.

Simon, Solomon. MORE WISE MEN OF HELM. Illus. New York: Behrman House, 1965.

————. THE WISE MEN OF HELM AND THEIR MERRY TALES. Illus. Lillian Fischel. New York: Behrman House, 1945.

Singer, Isaac Bashevis. MAZEL AND SHLIMAZEL: OR THE MILK OF A LIONESS. Illus. Margot Zemach. New York: Farrar, Straus and Giroux, 1967. pb

————. WHEN SHLEMIEL WENT TO WARSAW, AND OTHER STORIES. Illus. Margot Zemach. Trans. by the author and Elizabeth Shub. New York: Farrar, Straus and Giroux, 1968. P

————. WHY NOAH CHOSE THE DOVE. Illus. Eric Carle. Trans. Elizabeth Shub. New York: Farrar, Straus and Giroux, 1973. pb

————. ZLATEH THE GOAT, AND OTHER STORIES. Illus. Maurice Sendak. Trans. from the Yiddish by the author and Elizabeth Shub. New York: Harper & Row, 1966. P

Skurzynski, Gloria. THE MAGIC PUMPKIN. Illus. Rocco Negri. New York: Four Winds, 1971. pb

————. TWO FOOLS AND A FAKER: THREE LEBANESE FOLK TALES. Illus. William Papas. New York: Lothrop, Lee and Shepard, 1977.

Sleator, William. THE ANGRY MOON. Illus. Blair Lent. Boston: Little, Brown, 1970. pb

Sleigh, Barbara. NORTH OF NOWHERE: STORIES AND LEGENDS FROM MANY LANDS. Illus. Victor Ambrus. New York: Coward-McCann, 1964.

Spellman, John. THE BEAUTIFUL BLUE JAY AND OTHER TALES OF INDIA. Illus. Jerry Pinkney. Boston: Little, Brown, 1967.

Sperry, Margaret. THE HEN THAT SAVED THE WORLD. Illus. Per Beckman. New York: Day, 1952.

————. SCANDINAVIAN STORIES. Illus. Jenny Williams. New York: Watts, 1971.

Spicer, Dorothy Gladys. THE KNEELING TREE,

AND OTHER FOLKTALES FROM THE MIDDLE EAST. New York: Coward-McCann, 1971. G

Spicer, Dorothy Gladys. LONG AGO IN SERBIA. Illus. Linda Ominsky. Philadelphia: Westminster, 1968.

_____. THE OWL'S NEST: FOLKTALES FROM FRIESLAND. Illus. Alice Wadowski-Bak. New York: Coward-McCann, 1963.

_____. 13 DEVILS. Illus. Sofia. New York: Coward-McCann, 1967.

_____. 13 GHOSTS. Illus. Sofia. New York: Coward-McCann, 1966.

_____. 13 GOBLINS. Illus. Sofia. New York: Coward-McCann, 1969. P

_____. 13 MONSTERS. Illustrated. New York: Coward-McCann, 1964.

Squire, Roger. WIZARDS AND WAMPUM: LEGENDS OF THE IROQUOIS. Illus. Charles Keeping. New York: Abelard-Schuman, 1972.

Stalder, Valerie. EVEN THE DEVIL IS AFRAID OF A SHREW: A FOLKTALE OF LAPLAND. Adapted by Ray Broekel. Illus. Richard Brown. Reading, Mass.: Addison-Wesley, 1972. pb

Stamm, Claus, reteller. THE DUMPLINGS AND THE DEMONS. Illus. Kazue Mizumura. New York: Viking, 1964. pb

_____. THREE STRONG WOMEN: A TALL TALE FROM JAPAN. Illus. Kazue Mizumura. New York: Viking, 1962.

_____. THE VERY SPECIAL BADGERS: A TALE OF MAGIC FROM JAPAN. Illus. Kazue Mizumura. New York: Viking, 1960. pb

Steel, Flora Annie Webster. ENGLISH FAIRY TALES. Illus. Arthur Rackham. New York: Macmillan, 1918.

_____. THE TIGER, THE BRAHMAN, AND THE JACKAL. From the TALES OF THE PUNJAB by Flora Annie Steel. Illus. Mamoru Funai. New York: Holt, Rinehart and Winston, 1963. pb

Stephens, James. IRISH FAIRY TALES. Illus. Arthur Rackham. New York: Macmillan, c.1920, c.1948.

Stevens, H. C. RUSSIAN FOLK TALES. Illus. Alexander Lindberg. London: Paul Hamlyn, 1967. G

Stobbs, William, reteller. HENNY PENNY. Illus. William Stobbs. Chicago: Follett, 1970. pb

_____. JACK AND THE BEANSTALK. Illus. William Stobbs. New York: Delacorte, 1966. pb

_____. LITTLE RED RIDING HOOD. Illus.

William Stobbs. New York: Walck, 1972. pb

Stobbs, William. THE STORY OF THE THREE BEARS. Illus. William Stobbs. New York: Whittlesey House, McGraw-Hill, 1965. pb

SEE ALSO Grimm. GOLDEN GOOSE; Jacobs. JOHNNY CAKE.

Storm, Dan. PICTURE TALES FROM MEXICO. Illus. Mark Storm. Philadelphia: Lippincott, 1941. G

Strindberg, Gert. NORWEGIAN FAIRY TALES. Illus. Gert Strindberg. Chicago: Follett, 1968. G

Stuart, Forbes. THE MAGIC HORNS: FOLK TALES FROM AFRICA. Illus. Charles Keeping. Reading, Mass.: Addison-Wesley, 1974.

Sturton, Hugh. ZOMO THE RABBIT. Illus. Peter Warner. New York: Atheneum, 1966.

Suhl, Yuri. SIMON BOOM GIVES A WEDDING. Illus. Margot Zemach. New York: Four Winds, 1972. pb

Sun, Ruth Q. LAND OF SEAGULL AND FOX: FOLK TALES OF VIETNAM. Illus. Ho Thanh Duc. Rutland, Vt.: Tuttle, c.1966, 1967. P

Tabrah, Ruth, editor. MOMOTARO: PEACH BOY. Illus. George Suyeoka. New York: Weatherhill (Island Heritage), 1972. pb

TALL BOOK OF NURSERY TALES. Illus. Feodor Rojankovsky. New York: Harper, 1944. P

Tarrant, Margaret. FAIRY TALES. New York: Crowell, 1978.

Tashjian, Virginia A. JUBA THIS AND JUBA THAT: STORY HOUR STRETCHES FOR LARGE OR SMALL GROUPS. Illus. Victoria de Larrea. Boston: Little, Brown, 1969.

_____. ONCE THERE WAS AND WAS NOT: ARMENIAN TALES. RETOLD. Based on stories by H. Toumanian. Illus. Nonny Hogrogian. Boston: Little, Brown, 1966.

_____. THREE APPLES FELL FROM HEAVEN: ARMENIAN TALES RETOLD. Illus. Nonny Hogrogian. Boston: Little, Brown, 1971.

_____. WITH A DEEP SEA SMILE: STORY HOUR STRETCHES FOR LARGE OR SMALL GROUPS. Illus. Rosemary Wells. Boston: Little, Brown, 1974.

Taylor, Mark. THE FISHERMAN AND THE GOBLET. Illus. Taro Yashima. San Carlos, Calif.: Golden Gate Junior Books, 1971. pb

Thoby-Marcelin, Philippe and Pierre Marcelin. THE SINGING TURTLE AND OTHER TALES FROM HAITI. Illus. George Ford. Trans. Eva Thoby-Marcelin. New York: Farrar, Straus and Giroux, 1971.

Thompson, Vivian Laubach. HAWAIIAN LEGENDS OF TRICKSTERS AND RIDDLERS. Illus. Sylvie Selig. New York: Holiday, 1969.

_____. HAWAIIAN MYTHS OF EARTH, SEA AND SKY. Illus. Leonard Weisgard. New York: Holiday, 1966.

_____. HAWAIIAN TALES OF HEROES AND CHAMPIONS. Illus. Herbert Kawainui Kane. New York: Holiday, 1966. G

Titiev, Estelle and Lila Pergment. HOW THE MOOLAH WAS TAUGHT A LESSON AND OTHER TALES FROM RUSSIA. Trans. and adapted by Estelle Titiev and Lila Pargment. Illus. Ray Cruz. New York: Dial, 1976.

Titus, Eve. TWO STONECUTTERS. Illus. Yoko Mitsuhashi. Garden City, N.Y.: Doubleday, 1967. pb

Todd, Mary Fidelis. THE JUGGLER OF NOTRE DAME: AN OLD FRENCH TALE. Illus. Mary Fidelis Todd. New York: Whittlesey, 1954.

Tolstoy, Alexei. THE GREAT BIG ENORMOUS TURNIP. Illus. Helen Oxenbury. New York: Watts, 1968. pb

Toor, Frances. THE GOLDEN CARNATION, AND OTHER STORIES TOLD IN ITALY. Illus. Anne Marie Jauss. New York: Lothrop, 1960.

Tooze, Ruth. THREE TALES OF MONKEY. ANCIENT FOLK TALES FROM THE FAR EAST. Illus. Rosalie Petrash Schmidt. New York: Day, 1967.

_____. THREE TALES OF TURTLE. ANCIENT FOLK TALES FROM THE FAR EAST. Illus. Rosalie Petrash Schmidt. New York: Day, 1968.

_____. THE WONDERFUL WOODEN PEACOCK FLYING MACHINE AND OTHER TALES OF CEYLON. Illus. Rosalie Petrash Schmidt. New York: Day, 1969.

Towle, Faith M. THE MAGIC COOKING POT. Illus. Faith Towle. Boston: Houghton Mifflin, 1975. pb

Toye, William. THE FIRE STEALER. Illus. Elizabeth Cleaver. New York: Oxford University Press, c.1979, 1980. pb

_____. HOW SUMMER CAME TO CANADA. Illus. Elizabeth Cleaver. New York: Walck, 1969. pb

_____. THE LOON'S NECKLACE. Illus. Elizabeth Cleaver. New York: Oxford University Press, 1977. pb

_____. THE MOUNTAIN GOATS OF TEMLAHAM. Illus. Elizabeth Cleaver. New York: Walck, 1969. pb

Tracey, Hugh. THE LION ON THE PATH AND OTHER AFRICAN STORIES. Illus. Eric Byrd.

Music transcribed by Andrew Tracey. New York: Praeger, c.1967, 1968. N

Traven, B. THE CREATION OF THE SUN AND THE MOON. Illus. Alberto Beltrán. New York: Hill and Wang, 1968. G

Tresselt, Alvin. THE MITTEN: AN OLD UKRAINIAN FOLKTALE. Illus. Yaroslava. Adapted from the version by E. Rachev. New York: Lothrop, Lee & Shepard, 1964. pb

Tripp, Wallace. THE TALE OF A PIG: A CAUCASIAN FOLKTALE. Illus. Wallace Tripp. New York: McGraw Hill, 1968. G, pb

Turnbull, Lucia. FAIRY TALES OF INDIA. Illus. Hazel Cook. New York: Criterion, 1959.

Turska, Krystyna. THE WOODCUTTER'S DUCK. New York: Macmillan, 1972. pb

Uchida, Yoshiko. THE DANCING KETTLE, AND OTHER JAPANESE FOLK TALES. Illus. Richard C. Jones. New York: Harcourt, Brace, 1949.

_____. THE MAGIC LISTENING CAP: MORE FOLK TALES FROM JAPAN. Illus. Yoshiko Uchida. New York: Harcourt, Brace, 1955.

_____. THE SEA OF GOLD, AND OTHER TALES FROM JAPAN. Illus. Marianne Yamaguchi. New York: Scribner's, 1965.

Undset, Sigrid. TRUE AND UNTRUE AND OTHER NORSE TALES. Illus. Frederick C. Chapman. New York: Knopf, 1945.

United Nations Women's Guild. SEE Courlander, Harold.

Untermeyer, Louis. SEE Aesop. AESOP'S FABLES.

Ure, Jean. RUMANIAN FOLK TALES. Illus. Charles Mozley. New York: Watts, c.1960, 1961.

Valjavec, Matija and Cene Vipotnik. THE MAGIC RING: A PICTURE STORY FROM YUGOSLAVIA. Illus. Marlenka Stupica. Cleveland: World, 1957. G, pb

Van Woerkom, Dorothy O. ABU ALI: THREE TALES OF THE MIDDLE EAST. Illus. Harold Berson. New York: Macmillan, 1976.

_____. ALEXANDRA THE ROCK-EATER: AN OLD RUMANIAN TALE RETOLD. Illus. Rosekrans Hoffman. New York: Knopf, 1978. pb

_____. MEAT PIES AND SAUSAGES: THREE TALES OF FOX AND WOLF. Illus. Joseph Low. New York: Greenwillow, 1976.

_____. THE RAT, THE OX AND THE ZODIAC. A CHINESE LEGEND. Illus. Errol Le Cain. New York: Crown, 1976. G, pb

_____. SEA FROG, CITY FROG. Adapted from a Japanese Folk Tale by Dorothy O. Van

Woerkom. Illus. Jose Aruego and Ariane Dewey. New York: Macmillan, 1975. pb

Varga, Judy. THE MARE'S EGG. Illus. Judy Varga. New York: Morrow, 1972. pb

Vittorini, Domenico. OLD ITALIAN TALES. Illus. Katheryn L. Fligg. New York: McKay, 1958.

Vo-Dinh. THE TOAD IS THE EMPEROR'S UNCLE. ANIMAL FOLKTALES FROM VIET-NAM. Illus. Vo-Dinh. Garden City, N.Y.: Doubleday, 1970.

Wahl, Jan. DRAKESTAIL. Adapted from a French Folktale by Jan Wahl. Illus. Byron Barton. New York: Greenwillow, 1978. pb

Walker, Barbara K. THE COURAGE OF KAZAN. Illus. James and Ruth McCrea. New York: Crowell, 1970.

_____. THE DANCING PALM TREE AND OTHER NIGERIAN FOLKTALES. Illus. Helen Siegl. New York: Parent's, 1968.

_____. THE IFRIT AND THE MAGIC GIFTS. Illus. Ati Forberg. Chicago: Follett, 1972. G, pb

_____. JUST SAY HIC! Illus. Don Bolognese. Chicago: FOLLETT, 1965. pb

_____. ONCE THERE WAS AND TWICE THERE WASN'T. Illus. Gordon Kibbee. Chicago: Follett, 1968.

_____. WATERMELONS, WALNUTS, AND THE WISDOM OF ALLAH, AND OTHER TALES OF THE HOCA. Illus. Harold Berson. New York: Parent's, 1967.

Walker, Barbara K. and Mime Sumer. STARGAZER TO THE SULTAN. Illus. Joseph Low. New York: Parent's, 1967. pb

Walker, Barbara K. and Ahmet E. Uysal. NEW PATCHES FOR OLD: A TURKISH FOLKTALE. Illus. Harold Berson. New York: Parent's, 1974. G, pb

Walker, Barbara K. and Warren S. Walker. NIGERIAN FOLK TALES. As told by Olawale Idewu and Omotayo Adu. Illus. Margaret Barbour. New Brunswick, N.J.: Rutgers, 1961. N

Weil, Lisl. SORCERER'S APPRENTICE. Illus. Lisl Weil. Boston: Little, Brown, 1962. pb

Weiss, Harvey. THE SOONER HOUND: A TALE FROM AMERICAN FOLKLORE. Illus. Harvey Weiss. New York: Putnam, c.1959, 1960. pb

Werth, Kurt. THE COBBLER'S DILEMMA: AN ITALIAN FOLKTALE. Illus. Kurt Werth. New York: McGraw-Hill, 1967. G, pb

_____. KING THRUSHBEARD. Illus. Kurt Werth. New York: Viking, 1968. pb

Werth, Kurt. LAZY JACK. New York: Viking, 1970. pb

_____. THE MONKEY, THE LION AND THE SNAKE. New York: Viking, 1967. pb

_____. THE VALIANT TAILOR. Illus. Kurt Werth. New York: Viking, 1965. pb

Wetterer, Margaret K. THE MERMAID'S CAPE. Illus. Elsie Primavera. New York: Atheneum, 1981. G

Wheeler, Post. ALBANIAN WONDER TALES. Illus. Maud and Miska Petersham. Garden City, N.Y.: Doubleday, 1936.

_____. HAWAIIAN WONDER TALES. Illus. Jack Matthew. New York: Beechhurst Press, 1953.

_____. RUSSIAN WONDER TALES. Illus. Bilibin. New York: Beechhurst Press, c.1912, c.1946. G

White, Anne Terry. See Aesop. AESOP'S FABLES.

Whitney, Thomas. IN A CERTAIN KINGDOM: TWELVE RUSSIAN FAIRY TALES. Illus. Dieter Lange. New York: Macmillan, 1972.

_____. MARKO THE RICH AND VASILY THE UNLUCKY. Illus. Igor Galanin. New York: Macmillan, 1974. N, pb

_____. THE STORY OF PRINCE IVAN, THE FIREBIRD, AND THE GRAY WOLF. Illus. Nonny Hogrogian. New York: Scribner's, 1968. pb

_____. VASILISA THE BEAUTIFUL. Trans. from the Russian by Thomas P. Whitney. Illus. Nonny Hogrogian. New York: Macmillan, 1970. pb

Wickes, Frances Gillespy. HAPPY HOLIDAYS. Illus. Gertrude Kay. New York: Rand, 1921. N

Wiesner, William, reteller. HAPPY-GO-LUCKY. Illus. William Wiesner. New York: Seabury, 1970. pb

_____. TURNABOUT. A Norwegian Tale retold and illus. by William Wiesner. New York: Seabury, 1972. pb

Wiggin, Kate Douglas. TALES OF LAUGHTER: A THIRD FAIRY BOOK. Garden City, N.Y.: Doubleday, 1954.

Wiggin, Kate Douglas and Nora Archibald Smith. THE FAIRY RING. Rev. Ethna Sheehan. Illus. Warren Chappell. Garden City, N.Y.: Doubleday, 1967. P

_____. TALES OF WONDER: A FOURTH FAIRY BOOK. Garden City, N.Y.: Doubleday, 1936.

Wildsmith, Brian. THE MILLER, THE BOY AND THE DONKEY. New York: Watts, 1969. pb

_____. THE TWELVE DAYS OF CHRISTMAS. New York: Watts, 1972. pb

Wilkinson, Barry. THE DIVERTING ADVENTURES OF TOM THUMB. New York: Harcourt, Brace & World, c.1967, 1969. pb

Williams, Jay. THE SURPRISING THINGS MAUI DID. Illus. Charles Mikolaycak. New York: Four Winds, 1979.

Williams-Ellis, Amabel. FAIRY TALES FROM THE BRITISH ISLES. Illus. Pauline Diane Baynes. New York: Warne, c.1960, 1964.

_____. ROUND THE WORLD FAIRY TALES. Illus. William Stobbs. New York: Warne, 1963. P

Wilson, Barbara Ker. FAIRY TALES OF IRELAND. Illus. G. W. Miller. New York: Dutton, 1959.

_____. GREEK FAIRY TALES. Illus. Harry Toothill. Chicago: Follett, c.1966, 1968.

_____. SCOTTISH FOLK-TALES AND LEGENDS. Illus. Joan Kiddell-Monroe. New York: Oxford University Press, 1954. P

Winter, Jeanette. THE CHRISTMAS VISITORS: A NORWEGIAN FOLKTALE. New York: Pantheon, 1968. G, pb

Withers, Carl. I SAW A ROCKET WALK A MILE: NONSENSE TALES, CHANTS, AND SONGS OF MANY LANDS. Illus. John E. Johnson. New York: Holt, 1965.

_____. THE MAN IN THE MOON. SEE Alta Jablow.

_____. PAINTING THE MOON: A FOLKTALE FROM ESTONIA. Illus. Adrienne Adams. New York: Dutton, 1970. pb

_____. A WORLD OF NONSENSE: STRANGE AND HUMOROUS TALES FROM MANY LANDS. Illus. John E. Johnson. New York: Holt, Rinehart & Winston, 1968.

Wojiechowska, Maia. WINTER TALES FROM POLAND. Illus. Lazlo Kubinyi. Garden City, N.Y.: Doubleday, 1973. P

Wolkstein, Diane. LAZY STORIES. Illus. James Marshall. New York: Seabury, 1976.

_____. THE MAGIC ORANGE TREE AND OTHER HAITIAN FOLKTALES. Illus. Elsa Henriquez. New York: Knopf, 1978.

Wolkstein, Diane and Ed Young. WHITE WAVE: A CHINESE TALE. New York: Crowell, 1979. pb

Wright, Freire and Michael Foreman. SEVEN IN ONE BLOW. New York: Random, 1981. pb

Wyatt, Isabel. THE GOLDEN STAG, AND OTHER FOLK TALES FROM INDIA. Illus. Anne Marie Jauss. New York: McKay, 1962.

Wyndham, Lee. FOLK TALES OF CHINA. Illus. Jeanne Chall. Indianapolis: Bobbs-Merrill, 1963.

_____. FOLK TALES OF INDIA. Illustrated. Indianapolis: Bobbs-Merrill, 1962.

_____. RUSSIAN TALES OF FABULOUS BEASTS AND MARVELS. Illus. Charles Mikolaycak. New York: Parent's, 1968, 1969.

_____. TALES PEOPLE TELL IN RUSSIA. Illus. Andrew Natal. New York: Messner, 1970.

Wyndham, Robert. TALES PEOPLE TELL IN CHINA. Illus. Jay Yang. New York: Messner, 1971.

Yaroslava. TUSYA AND THE POT OF GOLD: FROM AN OLD UKRAINIAN FOLKTALE. Illus. Yaroslava. New York: Atheneum, 1971. pb

Yashima, Taro. SEASHORE STORY. New York: Viking, 1967. pb

Yasuda, Yuri. OLD TALES OF JAPAN. Illus. Yoshinobu Sakakura and Eiichi Matsui. Rutland, Vt.: Tuttle, 1956. G

Yellow Robe, Rosebud. TONWEYA AND THE EAGLES AND OTHER LAKOTA INDIAN TALES. Illus. Jerry Pinkney. New York: Dial, 1979.

Yeoman, John. THE APPLE OF YOUTH AND OTHER RUSSIAN FOLK STORIES. Illus. Barbara Swiderska. New York: Watts, 1967. G

Yoda, Junichi. THE ROLLING RICE BALL. Illus. Saburo Watanabe. Trans. Alvin Tresselt. New York: Parent's, 1968. pb

Young, Blanche Cowley. HOW THE MANX CAT LOST ITS TAIL, AND OTHER MANX FOLK STORIES. Illus. Nora S. Unwin. New York: McKay, 1959.

Young, Ed. THE TERRIBLE NUNG GUAMA: A CHINESE FOLKTALE. From the retelling of Leslie Bonnet. Illus. Ed Young. New York: Collins & World, 1978. pb

Young, Ed with Hilary Beckett. THE ROOSTER'S HORNS. Illus. Ed Young. New York: Collins & World, 1978. pb

Zagloul, Ahmed and Zane Zagloul. THE BLACK PRINCE AND OTHER EGYPTIAN FOLK TALES. Illus. Beverly Armstrong. Garden City, N.Y.: Doubleday, 1971. G

Zajdler, Zoë. POLISH FAIRY TALES. Illus. Hazel Cook. Chicago: Follett, 1959.

Zemach, Harve. DUFFY AND THE DEVIL. Illus. Margot Zemach. New York: Farrar, Straus, and Giroux, 1973. pb

Zemach, Harve. NAIL SOUP: A SWEDISH FOLK-TALE. Illus. Margot Zemach. Chicago: Follett, 1964. pb

_____. SALT. A Russian tale adapted by Harve Zemach from a literal translation by Benjamin Zemach, of the Russian of Alexei Afanasev. Illus. Margot Zemach. New York: Follett, 1965. pb

_____. THE SPECKLED HEN: A RUSSIAN NURSERY RHYME. Illus. Margot Zemach. New York: Holt, Rinehart & Winston, 1966. pb

_____. TOO MUCH NOSE: AN ITALIAN TALE. Illus. Margot Zemach. New York: Holt, Rinehart & Winston, 1967. pb

Zemach, Margot. IT COULD ALWAYS BE WORSE. A Yiddish folk tale retold and with pictures by Margot Zemach. New York: Farrar, Straus and Giroux, 1976. pb

_____. THE THREE SILLIES. Illus. Margot Zemach. New York: Holt, Rinehart and Winston, 1963. pb

Ziner, Feenie. CRICKET BOY: A CHINESE TALE. Retold by Feenie Ziner. Illus. Ed Young. Garden City, N.Y.: Doubleday, 1977. pb